CW01524194

Civil Fraud

Law, Practice & Procedure

First Edition

Civil Fraud

Law, Practice & Procedure

First Edition

General Editors

Thomas Grant QC BA (Bristol)
Dip Law, Barrister, Maitland Chambers

David Mumford QC MA (Oxon)
Dip Law, Barrister, Maitland Chambers

SWEET & MAXWELL

Published in 2018 by Thomson Reuters, trading as Sweet & Maxwell. Registered in England & Wales, Company No.1679046. Registered Office and address for service: 5 Canada Square, Canary Wharf, London, E14 5AQ.

For further information on our products and services, visit *www.sweetandmaxwell.co.uk*

Typeset by Letterpart Limited, Caterham on the Hill, Surrey, CR3 5XL.

Printed and bound by CPI Group (UK) Ltd, Croydon, CR0 4YY.

No natural forests were destroyed to make this product: only farmed timber was used and re-planted.

A CIP catalogue record of this book is available from the British Library.

ISBN: 978-0-414-03944-5

Thomson Reuters, the Thomson Reuters Logo and Sweet & Maxwell ® are trademarks of Thomson Reuters.

Crown copyright material is reproduced with the permission of the Controller of HMSO and the Queen's Printer for Scotland.

Authors and Contributors

General Editors

Thomas Grant QC BA (Bristol)
Dip Law, Barrister, Maitland Chambers
David Mumford QC MA (Oxon)
Dip Law, Barrister, Maitland Chambers

Contributors

Andrew Ayres QC MA (Oxon)
Dip Law, Barrister, Maitland Chambers
Louise Hutton MA (Oxon)
Barrister, Essex Court Chambers
Benjamin John MChem (Oxon)
Dip Law, Barrister, Maitland Chambers
James Kinman MA (Cantab)
Dip Law, Barrister, Maitland Chambers
Thomas Munby MA (Oxon) FCIArb
Dip Law, Barrister, Maitland Chambers
Watson Pringle MA (Oxon)
Barrister, Maitland Chambers
His Honour Judge Jonathan Russen QC
(Univ. Coll. of Wales, Aberystwyth); LLM (Cantab)
Circuit Commercial and TCC Judge, Bristol Business and Property Courts
James Sheehan MA (Cantab)
Dip Law, Barrister, Essex Court Chambers
Anthony Trace QC MA (Cantab)
Barrister and Mediator, 4 Pump Court
Caley Wright MA (Oxon)
Dip Law, Barrister, Maitland Chambers

Acknowledgements

This book has been a long time in the gestation and we would like to record our thanks to a number of people who helped it along the path to seeing the light of day. These include Siward Atkins, Laurie Brock, George Hayman QC, Richard Morgan QC and Matthew Smith. We are also grateful to our former colleague Lord Justice Newey for writing the foreword. Finally we pay tribute to our contributors, and their industry and good humour in the face of constant harassment from their editors. We would particularly like to thank James Sheehan, who was instrumental to the project's genesis, and whose enthusiasm and diligence throughout have been invaluable.

Throughout this book we have used the male pronoun for ease of exposition. Whenever the words "he", "his" or "him" appear, they should be taken to encompass the feminine and the neuter cognates.

We have endeavoured to state the law as at 31 July 2018, although certain later decisions have been referenced where time allowed.

Thomas Grant QC and David Mumford QC
Maitland Chambers, Lincoln's Inn, London

Foreword

The last book by Tom Grant that I read was "Jeremy Hutchinson's Case Histories". Described by a Guardian columnist as "gripping", it became, deservedly, a Sunday Times bestseller. It also helped to inspire the son of some friends of mine to read law at university.

It can confidently be predicted that the present volume will not achieve as many sales (the market for legal treatises being, inexplicably, smaller!), but it is no less good. As its title indicates, its subject is civil fraud. Such allegations loom large in the work of the Business and Property Courts. Sometimes a fraud could have happened in any age, on other occasions it may have been facilitated by modern technology. I have dealt with more than one case, for example, in which a payment has been diverted from its proper destination by means of hacking into an email account.

The word "fraud" can obviously be used to refer to fraudulent misrepresentation, but there are many are other species of fraud claims. Some are tortious, but a claimant may also invoke principles of equity, property and unjust enrichment, as well as statutory provisions such as s.423 of the Insolvency Act 1986 (dealing with transactions defrauding creditors). Fraud may be relied on, too, in a procedural context (for instance, to seek to impeach a judgment).

This work addresses both the substantive law and related points of procedure and practice. Tom Grant and David Mumford are highly capable practising barristers familiar with fraud claims. With the assistance of a very able team of contributors, they bring to bear not only their practical experience but impressively comprehensive research. The book thus provides both a detailed account of the law and authorities and also helpful comments on practical matters such as how to handle witness evidence. Unlike some practitioners, moreover, the authors have been prepared to comment critically on the state of the law and to make suggestions as to how it should develop in the future.

I strongly recommend the book.

Guy Newey
Royal Courts of Justice, Strand, London WC2A 2LL

To Hester and Jane

TABLE OF CONTENTS

2. CONSPIRACY

SECTION B
Equitable Claims

9. ESTABLISHING A TRUST

10. BREACH OF TRUST

12. KNOWING RECEIPT

13. DISHONEST ASSISTANCE

SECTION C
Other Claims

14. UNJUST ENRICHMENT

15. UNDUE INFLUENCE AND DURESS

SECTION D
Liability For or Through Others

20. JOINT LIABILITY IN TORT

SECTION E
Relief and Bars To It

21. DAMAGES

22. EQUITABLE REMEDIES: RESCISSION, ACCOUNT OF PROFITS, COMPENSATION & FORFEITURE

24. ILLEGALITY

SECTION F
Interim Remedies

26. THE COURT'S POWERS TO GRANT INTERIM RELIEF

27. THE WITHOUT NOTICE APPLICATION

28. FREEZING AND PROPRIETARY INJUNCTIONS

29. DISCLOSURE ORDERS

30. SEARCH ORDERS

32. THE RETURN DATE

SECTION G
Trial, Judgments And Enforcement

34. PROVING A CLAIM IN FRAUD: EVIDENCE AND OTHER TRIAL ISSUES

36. OTHER SANCTIONS FOR PROCEDURAL DEFAULT

37. ENFORCEMENT OF JUDGMENTS

SECTION H
Cases with an International Element

40. CONFLICT OF LAWS

TABLE OF CASES

xlix

TABLE OF STATUTES

TABLE OF STATUTORY INSTRUMENTS

CHAPTER I

CIVIL FRAUD: INTRODUCTION

A. THE MEANING OF FRAUD

The word fraud in English civil law is protean. Over at least three centuries **I1–001** judges and commentators have observed that it is elusive of any hard and fast definition. So Lord Hardwicke, writing in 1759 three years after he had stepped down as Lord Chancellor, commented, in an often—quoted sentence, that "Fraud is infinite, and were a Court of Equity once to lay down rules, how far they would go, and no further, in extending their relief against it, or to define strictly the species or evidence of it, the jurisdiction would be cramped and perpetually eluded by new schemes which the fertility of man's invention would contrive."[1]

Almost 150 years later Sir James Fitzjames Stephen, in his *A History of the Criminal Law of England*,[2] wrote the following[3]: "Fraud—There has always been a great reluctance amongst lawyers to attempt to define fraud, and this is not unnatural when we consider the number of different kinds of conduct to which the word is applied in connection with different branches of law, and especially in connection with the equitable branch of it. I shall not attempt to construct a definition which will meet every case which might be suggested, but there is little danger in saying that whenever the words 'fraud' or 'intent to defraud' or 'fraudulently' occur in the definition of a crime two elements at least are essential to the commission of the crime: namely, first, deceit or an intention to deceive or in some cases mere secrecy; and, secondly, either actual injury or possible injury or an intent to expose some person either to actual injury or to a risk of possible injury by means of that deceit or secrecy."

In the event the criminal law, as partially codified in the Fraud Act 2006, has itself taken a more expansive view of the concept of fraud. Sections 2 to 4 of that Act now provide that the offence of fraud encompasses not only "fraud by false representation" but also "fraud by failing to disclose information" and "fraud by abuse of position." It will be seen that whereas the tort of deceit is an analogue to the first conception of fraud in this list, the second and third are considerably outside it. In particular, section 4 created the offence of fraud by abuse of position, the elements of which are as follows: "(1) A person is in breach of this section if he—(a) occupies a position in which he is expected to safeguard, or not to act against, the financial interests of another person, (b) dishonestly abuses that

---

[1] Quoted in *Cavell USA Inc v Seaton Insurance Company* [2009] EWCA Civ 1363; [2009] 2 C.L.C. 991, at [15], per Longmore LJ. The passage derives from a letter to Lord Kames. Longmore LJ wrongly ascribes to Lord Hardwicke the word "continue" in place of "contrive."

[2] Sir J.F. Stephen, *A History of the Criminal Law of England*, (London: Macmillan, 1883), Vol. 2.

[3] Stephen, *A History of the Criminal Law of England* (1883), p.121.

position, and (c) intends, by means of the abuse of that position— (i) to make a gain for himself or another, or (ii) to cause loss to another or to expose another to a risk of loss." Hence, to take an example proposed by the Law Commission[4]: "If an employee embezzles her employer's money, both lawyers and non-lawyers would agree that her conduct can properly be described as fraud even if she makes no representation (for example, by falsifying the accounts)." Similarly the company director who misappropriates company assets would be perceived by civil lawyers to have perpetrated a fraud, regardless of the absence of a false representation.

So, a few years after Sir James Fitzjames Stephen's observations, Lord MacNaghten said in *Reddaway v Banham*,[5] in somewhat over-elaborate language: "Fraud is infinite in variety: sometimes it is audacious and unblushing; sometimes it pays a sort of homage to virtue, and then it is modest and retiring; it would be honesty itself if it could only afford it. But fraud is fraud all the same; and it is the fraud, not the manner of it, which calls for the interposition of the Court."[6] This dictum was stated in a passing-off case where "the whole gist of the action was that the defendants were endeavouring to palm off their goods as the goods of the plaintiffs by selling them under a designation which would enable purchasers from them in this country to deceive customers abroad. That is, as it seems to me, a charge of dishonesty…"[7] So Reddaway was not a claim in deceit, but the sentiment contained in Lord MacNaghten's speech points the way to a concept of fraud which is not related to a specific cause of action but to a type of behaviour which prompts the law to respond both in terms of formulating forms of action and fashioning remedial responses.

Yet terminological difficulties have persisted. In *Derry v Peek*,[8] the locus classicus of the modern cause of action in deceit, that cause of action was said to involve "actual fraud", equated with an "intention to deceive." Of course deceit is the claim most associated with the concept of fraud. If we move forward into the twentieth century we find that Buckley J was willing to hold, in *In re London and Globe Finance Corporation Ltd*,[9] that "To defraud is to deprive by deceit." 60 years later in *Barclays Bank v Cole*[10] the Court of Appeal interpreted the phrase "a charge of fraud", contained in s.6(1)(a) of the Administration of Justice (Miscellaneous Provisions) Act 1933 (for the purpose of establishing a right to jury trial in civil proceedings), as having a meaning confined to a claim in deceit. Diplock LJ cited the 3rd edition of *Bullen & Leake* and said "'fraud' in civil actions at common law, whether as a cause of action or as a defence, has meant an intentional representation (or, in some cases, concealment) of fact made by one party with the intention of inducing another party to act on it which does induce the other party to act on it to his detriment."

---

[4] Law Commission, *Fraud* (HMSO, 2002), Law Com. No.276, Cm.5560, at para.7.20.
[5] *Reddaway v Banham* [1896] A.C. 199.
[6] *Reddaway v Banham* [1896] A.C. 199 at 220.
[7] *Reddaway v Banham* [1896] A.C. 199 at 219.
[8] *Derry v Peek* (1889) 14 App Cas 337.
[9] *In re London and Globe Finance Corporation Ltd* [1903] 1 Ch. 728, at 732.
[10] *Barclays Bank v Cole* [1967] 2 QB 738.

Nonetheless, less than a decade later the House of Lords, sitting in the criminal appeal in *Scott v Commissioner of Police for the Metropolis*,[11] declined to interpret the common law offence of conspiracy of defraud in such a way as to require the intended means to constitute the civil tort of deceit. Viscount Dilhorne held that "conduct to be fraudulent need not be deceitful....to 'defraud' ordinarily means, in my opinion, to deprive a person dishonestly of something which is his or of something to which he is or would or might but for the perpetration of the fraud be entitled."[12] Similarly, Lord Diplock, notwithstanding his earlier statement as Diplock LJ, said that "the intended means by which the purpose [of the conspiracy to defraud] is to be achieved must be dishonest. They need not constitute the civil tort of deceit. Dishonesty of any kind is enough."[13]

But more recently, in *Kensington International Ltd v Republic of Congo*,[14] Moore-Bick LJ took the view that the expression "any other offence involving any form of fraudulent conduct or purpose", which appears in section 13 of the Fraud Act 2006 (partially abrogating the privilege against self-incrimination), was to be understood as being concerned with deception – albeit in a somewhat wider sense than understood by the civil law of deceit:

> "the essence of fraud is deception of one kind or another coupled with injury or an intention to expose another to a risk of injury by means of that deception...Both misrepresentation and the wrongful withholding of information, when knowing and deliberate, amount to calculated deception and even abuse of position of the kind falling within section 4 can be described as deception of a kind since the wrongdoer deliberately deceives the person whose interests he is bound to safeguard by allowing him to believe in his trustworthiness while actively falsifying that belief. Although I find it difficult to see how fraud of any kind properly so called can be committed without dishonesty, dishonesty is not the critical distinguishing mark of fraud. These considerations lead me to the conclusion that in order for an offence to involve some form of fraudulent conduct or purpose it must involve an element of deception in the sense mentioned earlier."[15]

Sometimes the courts have been obliged to attempt a definition of fraud in the civil context. In *Cavell USA, Inc v Seaton Insurance Company*[16] the parties had agreed to settle claims which A might have against B except "in the case of fraud" on the part of B. The question arose whether a subsequent claim in "dishonest abuse of fiduciary position" sought to be asserted by A against B had thereby been compromised. On this narrow issue a large question was engaged. The judge at first instance held that "fraud" meant a claim in deceit alone and therefore the new claim was within the reach of the compromise. The Court of Appeal disagreed, although it declined to embark upon any form of definition of the word fraud. In particular Longmore LJ contented himself with saying[17]:

---

[11] *Scott v Commissioner of Police for the Metropolis* [1975] A.C. 819.

[12] *Scott v Commissioner of Police for the Metropolis* [1975] A.C. 819, at 836.

[13] *Scott v Commissioner of Police for the Metropolis* [1975] A.C. 819, at 840.

[14] *Kensington International Ltd v Republic of Congo* [2007] EWCA Civ 1128; [2008] 1 W.L.R. 1144.

[15] *Kensington International Ltd v Republic of Congo* [2007] EWCA Civ 1128; [2008] 1 W.L.R. 1144, at [59].

[16] *Cavell USA, Inc v Seaton Insurance Company* [2009] EWCA Civ 1363; [2009] 2 C.L.C. 991.

[17] *Cavell USA, Inc v Seaton Insurance Company* [2009] EWCA Civ 1363; [2009] 2 C.L.C. 991, at [19].

"in the commercial context of this case the concept of 'fraud' is wider than the concept of the tort of deceit where a fraudulent misrepresentation (or equivalent) is required. I do not consider, therefore, that the second paragraph of the judge's order can stand and I would set it aside and substitute a declaration that the exception "in [the] case of fraud" …is not confined to claims in deceit but extends to at least some cases of dishonest abuse of fiduciary position. I would be prepared to add in this judgment (but not as part of the declaration) that the defendant is not to be held to have acted dishonestly unless he was doing something that ordinary people would regard as dishonest and he knew that ordinary people would so regard it."

These last words must now be read in the light of the decision of the Supreme Court in *Ivey v Genting Casinos (UK) Ltd*,[18] which we discuss below.

The word "fraud" also appears in other contexts in the civil law. For instance, s.32 of the Limitation Act 1980 prescribes a special limitation period for, amongst others, claims based on "fraud." As we consider in Ch.25, "fraud" in s.32 is not by any means co-terminous with the tort of deceit, though it requires that the cause of action is founded on some form of dishonesty.

The concept of fraud has a long and complex history in the court's equitable jurisdiction. Equity developed the twin notions of constructive or equitable fraud and actual fraud. The former extended to conduct which involved no form of dishonesty. So in *Nocton v Ashburton*[19] Lord Haldane said that "in Chancery the term 'fraud' thus came to be used to describe what fell short of deceit, but imported breach of a duty to which equity had attached its sanction." Later in *Hart v O'Connor*[20] Lord Brightman defined constructive fraud as "conduct which falls below the standard demanded by equity, traditionally considered under its more common manifestations of undue influence, unconscionable bargains and frauds on a power. Fraud in this equitable context does not mean, or is not confined to, deceit: 'it means an unconscientious use of the power arising out of the circumstances and conditions of the contracting parties.'"[21] So in *Vatcher v Paull*[22] Lord Parker commented that the concept of a "fraud on a power" did not necessarily "connote any conduct on the part of the appointor amounting to fraud in the common law meaning of the term." It will be seen that this conception of fraud is so wide that it comes close to emptying it of any content.[23]

In *Armitage v Nurse*[24] a trustee's exemption clause was stated not to extend to liability for damage "caused by his own actual fraud." Millett LJ explained that the concept of "actual fraud" was not used to describe the tort of deceit. Instead it connoted dishonesty, which was explained as "at the minimum an intention on the part of the trustee to pursue a particular course of action, either knowing that it is contrary to the interests of the beneficiaries or being recklessly indifferent whether it is contrary to their interests or not…It is the duty of a trustee to manage the trust property and deal with it in the interests of the beneficiaries. If he acts in a way which he does not honestly believe is in their interests then he is

---

[18] *Ivey v Genting Casinos (UK) Ltd* [2017] UKSC 67; [2017] 3 W.L.R. 1212.
[19] *Nocton v Ashburton* [1914] A.C. 932, at 954.
[20] *Hart v O'Connor* [1985] A.C. 1000, at 1024.
[21] The quotation derives from *Earl of Aylesford v Morris* (1873) LR 8 Ch. App. 484, at 491, per Lord Selbourne LC.
[22] *Vatcher v Paull* [1915] A.C. 372, at 378.
[23] See generally, J. McGhee (ed) *Snell's Equity*, 33rd edn (London: Sweet & Maxwell, 2014), Ch.8.
[24] *Armitage v Nurse* [1998] Ch. 241.

acting dishonestly. It does not matter whether he stands or thinks he stands to gain personally from his actions. A trustee who acts with the intention of benefiting persons who are not the objects of the trust is not the less dishonest because he does not intend to benefit himself".

This brings us to the concept of "dishonesty." This has troubled the courts in the civil sphere, particularly when seeking to establish the basis for liability as an assister in a breach of trust. As is well known the concept of dishonesty was recently the subject of an extended review in *Ivey v Genting Casinos (UK) Ltd.*[25] Lord Hughes JSC stated (following the decision of the Privy Council in *Clowes International Ltd v Eurotrust International Ltd*)[26]:

> "...When dishonesty is in question the fact-finding tribunal must first ascertain (subjectively) the actual state of the individual's knowledge or belief as to the facts. The reasonableness or otherwise of his belief is a matter of evidence (often in practice determinative) going to whether he held the belief, but it is not an additional requirement that his belief must be reasonable; the question is whether it is genuinely held. When once his actual state of mind as to knowledge or belief as to facts is established, the question whether his conduct was honest or dishonest is to be determined by the fact-finder by applying the (objective) standards of ordinary decent people. There is no requirement that the defendant must appreciate that what he has done is, by those standards, dishonest." [27]

Whilst this accords with what was coming to be understood as the orthodox view of dishonesty in the context of dishonest assistance claims, it was a significant decision in the criminal context; as is notorious, it involved overruling the decision of the Court of Appeal in *R v Ghosh*,[28] which had decided that dishonesty required that the defendant actually appreciate that his conduct was dishonest, by reference to the standards of "ordinary honest" people.

However, what is also clear is that there is no single concept of dishonesty applicable to the broad range of causes of action which we consider in this book. For example, the mens rea for knowing receipt is different from that required in dishonest assistance; and a claim in deceit will require proof of a specific mental state not required for establishing restitutionary liability.

From this survey we can conclude, first, that the English law concept of fraud is much wider that the tort of deceit; secondly, that there is no free-standing cause of action in fraud; and thirdly, that the word's meaning is not fixed—'fraud' is a portmanteau expression with different meanings in different contexts. It is descriptive of a range of types of act or omission which the law characterises as to a greater or lesser degree unconscionable.

In keeping with its origins, English law does not proceed by an overarching conception of fraud. It moves incrementally and by hammering out principle on the anvil of fact. There is no unitary "law of fraud"; instead, as we conceive it, it is an expression which encompasses a widely disparate series of causes of action, substantive remedies and procedural mechanisms, which together constitute the law's response to what may be broadly described as dishonest or unconscionable behaviour.

---

[25] *Ivey v Genting Casinos (UK) Ltd* [2017] UKSC 67; [2017] 3 W.L.R. 1212.

[26] *Clowes International Ltd v Eurotrust International Ltd* [2005] UKPC 37; [2006] 1 W.L.R. 1476.

[27] *Clowes International Ltd v Eurotrust International Ltd* [2005] UKPC 37; [2006] 1 W.L.R. 1476, at [74].

[28] *R v Ghosh* [1982] Q.B. 1053.

B. THE MODERN CONCEPT OF FRAUD LITIGATION

I1–002   In practice, whatever the terminological difficulties encountered by the courts, the concept of fraud litigation is now embedded in modern legal practice. Solicitors' firms have "fraud" departments; solicitors and barristers characterise themselves as "fraud" specialists. What lawyers generally mean when they use the word "fraud" in this way is a broad range of commercial or quasi-commercial activity, which involves the infliction of economic harm on a claimant in order to obtain a commensurate and illegitimate gain, via conduct which is intentional and which is usually dishonest by reference to the varying conceptions of dishonesty that the law has formulated, or at least unconscionable. This category of behaviours is very wide indeed; the basic common factors are intentionality rather carelessness and some degree of mens rea. The law of fraud, unlike the law of breach of contract, is not based on strict liability.

A review of the law reports and the online legal platforms demonstrates that litigation in relation to this area is burgeoning. It also reveals how much international fraud work comes before the English courts. Vast litigation behemoths, like the proceedings in *Ablyazov*, *Pugachev* and *Arkhangelsky*, have kept very substantial numbers of English lawyers and judges busy for many years. These are just the most notable examples of a growing trend for international litigants to use the English courts as the platform from which to seek remedies for frauds perpetrated outside of England. The popularity of the English courts with international litigants in the fraud arena is we think a reflection not only of the efficiency and quality of English judges (and lawyers), but also of the sophistication of English legal principles, remedies and procedures and the flexibility with which they can be deployed in response to fraudulent behaviour. The *Ablyazov* litigation alone, with which many of the authors of this book have been involved at varying times, has to date generated in excess of 35 reported decisions and provides a striking contemporary demonstration of this sophistication and flexibility, particularly in the number and range of different legal doctrines that were engaged by what was at its most basic level a series of alleged acts of corporate misappropriation.

C. THE REACH OF THIS BOOK

I1–003   In this book we have adopted a purposive approach to the concept of fraud. As we have said, in our view the law of fraud is best understood as a disparate series of principles and remedies, both interim and final, procedural and substantive, which respond to a broad type of activity in order to either prevent or reverse it. Unlike, say, a book on the law of agency, a book on fraud should not aspire to any form of crystalline intellectual uniformity. It can, we think, only exist successfully on a practical level, albeit one which reviews with rigour the complex substantive law which forms the bedrock of the subject. The first questions which a victim of fraud will typically ask his lawyers are as follows: Who should I sue? In which court? Utilising which causes of action? What immediate steps should I take? How can I recover or remedy my loss? These are acutely real-world questions and this book endeavours to provide a framework with which to answer them.

In Sections A to C we have sought to identify and analyse the causes of action which will typically be utilised in fraud cases. These claims have no jurisprudential unity. Rather they are a suite of causes of action and doctrines – spanning the common law, equity and statute – which experience shows can be deployed whether separately or in tandem as a response to fraudulent activity. Thus we consider not only the tortious claim in deceit, but also the torts of conspiracy, inducing a breach of contract, unlawful interference, intimidation, malicious falsehood and conversion, as well as bribery, which exists both as a sui generis tortious cause of action and an equitable wrong. We then consider claims in equity that arise where there is a pre-existing relationship between the parties which is capable of being abused by the fraudulent defalcations or profiting of a party in whom trust is reposed: those for breach of trust and breach of fiduciary duty, as well as the accessory liability claims parasitic upon them of knowing receipt and dishonest assistance. Finally, we consider three other groups of causes of action of likely relevance to a fraud claim which are not conveniently categorised as either tortious or equitable: unjust enrichment, undue influence and duress, and claims under statute (specifically, transaction avoidance claims under s.423 of the Insolvency Act 1986 (commonly described as involving "fraud" on creditors) and claims relating to misleading the securities markets under the Financial Services and Markets Act 2000).

In Section D we consider legal concepts which involve rules of ascription of liability for wrongs committed by one party to another. In circumstances where frauds are often perpetrated by collective action or through corporate avatars, familiarity with these rules is vital in order to ensure that the correct defendants are before the courts and the basis of liability for the acts of others is properly identified.

In Section E we discuss the substantive remedies available to a claimant who brings a claim in fraud, both pecuniary and non-pecuniary – including, importantly, the making of equitable proprietary claims to assets which are said to represent the proceeds of a fraud in the hands of fraudsters and other defendants. We also consider the law of illegality and limitation so far as it applies to fraud claims.

Section F involves an extended discussion of interim remedies: freezing and search orders; passport orders; receivership orders; and the suite of asset disclosure orders which are available together with various other interim orders typically encountered in fraud claims. The speed with which, over the last 40 years or so, the courts have developed a judge-made procedural law to respond to fraudulent behaviour has been breath-taking. Any book on fraud requires to place this law at its heart. This is because in practice activity which may be described as fraudulent generally requires an immediate response both in terms of preventing dissipation of assets and/or in terms of identification of assets which have been misappropriated. The vast amount of fraud litigation is conducted at an interim stage: for every hundred freezing orders obtained at the early stages of proceedings (or even before proceeding have been issued) there is probably only case which goes to trial. Most fraud claims are in practice won or lost at the interim stage. This book is intended to be intensely practical and so we have not only provided what we hope is a comprehensive analysis of the law relevant to interim remedies in fraud litigation, but also, at Chs 27 and 32, a discussion of practice and procedure on without notice applications and at return dates.

Section G is intended to continue the practical thrust of the book. At Ch.34 we discuss the practicalities of fraud trials and how a claimant sets about proving a claim in fraud. Chapter 35 involves an extended discussion of the law of contempt. This is because experience shows that defendants to fraud claims frequently breach court orders and the contempt jurisdiction will often need to be resorted to. Comittal applications play a large part in fraud litigation. But breach of court orders can also have other consequences within the litigation which claimants need to be aware of and so at Ch.36 we review sanctions available to courts for procedural default. As we show in that chapter there are also mechanisms at the disposal of courts to bring claims to an end (or to delimit participation in litigation) in the event of a failure by parties – typically defendants – to abide by court orders. At Ch.37 we look beyond the obtaining of judgment and examine practical issues which arise when seeking to enforce judgments. Finally, at Ch.38 we have attempted what we believe is the first systematic extended analysis in a textbook of the jurisdiction to set aside a judgment for fraud.

Finally, Section H considers the key principles likely to be engaged in fraud claims with an international element, which in practice will be many. Chapter 39 focuses upon the rules governing when the English courts will have (and will exercise) jurisdiction to try a fraud claim with an international element; and Ch.40 examines the most salient principles by which the English court will determine which country's laws apply to such a claim.

Thomas Grant QC
David Mumford QC
Maitland Chambers
August 2018

SECTION A

COMMON LAW CLAIMS

CHAPTER 1

DECEIT

A. INTRODUCTION

(1) The Foundations of the Tort

The tort of deceit (sometimes known as fraudulent misrepresentation)[1] is the actionable wrong most closely identified with the civil law concept of fraud. It is also an area in which "law and morality are inextricably interwoven."[2] Indeed it has been said that "the very notion of deceit with its overtones of wickedness is drawn from the moral world."[3] In essence the tort provides a basis for a person who has been lied to or otherwise deliberately misled to seek redress for harm he has suffered as a consequence.

1–001

The tort itself is reasonably straightforward in its description (though less so in its practical operation). It gives rise to what might be described as a free-standing, autonomous cause of action, which is not dependent on any pre-existing legal relationship between the parties, whether contractual, equitable, or statutory, and is not based on any assumption of responsibility such as to give rise to a common law duty of care. Thus it does not matter for the purposes of establishing a claim in deceit whether the defendant stands in a fiduciary or like relation to the claimant, or whether there can be said to be any sort of proximity between them; indeed, the claim can be made out even when the claimant is wholly unknown to the defendant.[4]

1–002

In order for a claimant to succeed in the tort of deceit he must establish that[5]:

1–003

(1) The defendant made a representation which was false.[6]
(2) The defendant knew that the representation was made and that it was untrue, or was reckless as to its truth or falsity.
(3) The defendant intended that the representation would induce the claimant to act or refrain from acting.

---

[1] See e.g. *Eco3 Capital Ltd v Ludsin Overseas Ltd* [2013] EWCA Civ 413, at [80], per Jackson LJ.
[2] *Smith New Court Securities Ltd v Citibank N.A.* [1997] A.C. 254, at 280, per Lord Steyn.
[3] O.W. Holmes, *The Common Law* (Cambridge: Harvard University Press, 2009), p.106.
[4] See para.1–107 below.
[5] Derived from the leading cases of *Derry v Peek* (1889) 14 App. Cas. 337; *Angus v Clifford* [1891] 2 Ch. 449; *Armstrong v Strain* [1951] 1 T.L.R. 856; and *AIC Ltd v ITS Testing Services (UK) Ltd (The Kriti Palm)* [2006] EWCA Civ 1601; [2007] 1 All E.R. (Comm) 667.
[6] Although of course a defendant may be vicariously liable for the false representations of others: see Section F below.

(4) The claimant was in fact induced by the representation to act or refrain from acting.

(5) The claimant thereby suffered loss.[7]

Each of the first four elements of the cause of action is considered separately in detail below; damages are considered in Ch.22.

1–004 The tort of deceit is only complete once the representee has acted to his detriment by reason of the representation: as in the tort of negligence, damage is the "gist" of the tort.[8]

1–005 A claim in deceit is to be distinguished from other claims arising out of misrepresentations or misstatements:

(1) A claim for negligent misstatement, as developed in the case law since the decision of the House of Lords in *Hedley Byrne & Co Ltd v Heller & Partners Ltd*,[9] requires the circumstances to warrant the imposition of a duty of care on the representor. Whether there is a duty of care owed by the representor to the representee is irrelevant in a claim for deceit; the ambit of the tort is instead circumscribed by the requirements to demonstrate knowledge of (or recklessness as to) falsity and intended reliance by the representee.

(2) A claim under s.2(1) of the Misrepresentation Act 1967 presupposes that the representation has induced entry into a contract between representor and representee; but once this is established, a claim in damages will lie without having to establish fraud, if the representation would have given rise to a claim in damages had it been made fraudulently (unless the representor can prove that he had reasonable grounds to believe and did believe the representation to be true).[10] A claim in deceit, in contrast, will lie whether or not a contract has resulted from the misrepresentation, and, if a contract has resulted, whether or not the representor is a party to it.

(3) There are also statutory provisions governing liability for statements published in connection with listed securities, including (but not limited to) ones made dishonestly. These provide an important overlay upon the common law claim in deceit in connection with such statements and are considered separately in this book, in Ch.17.

---

[7] The statement of the elements of the tort in *Eco 3 Capital Ltd v Ludsin Overseas Ltd* [2013] EWCA Civ 413, per Jackson LJ at [77], has recently proved popular with first instance judges: see e.g. *Khakshouri v Jimenez* [2017] EWHC 3392 (QB), per Green J at [17]; and *London Executive Aviation Ltd v The Royal Bank of Scotland Plc* [2018] EWHC 74 (Ch), per Rose J at [255].

[8] *Smith v Chadwick* (1884) 9 App Cas 187, per Lord Blackburn at 195, citing *Pasley v Freeman* (1789) 2 Sm L C 66, at 73, 86 (8th ed); *Briess v Woolley* [1954] A.C. 333; *Hayward v Zurich Insurance Co Plc* [2016] UKSC 48; [2017] A.C. 142, at [62], per Lord Clarke ("The vice of the defendant's conduct consists in dishonestly making a false representation with the intention of influencing the representee to act on it to its detriment. If it does not cause the representee to do so, the mischief against which the tort provides protection will not have occurred").

[9] *Hedley Byrne & Co Ltd v Heller & Partners Ltd* [1964] A.C. 465.

[10] Though of course it is perfectly possible for a fraudulent misrepresentation to have induced entry into a contract, in which case the claimant may have claims both under the Misrepresentation Act 1967 and in the tort of deceit.

In short, in deceit the law provides an avenue for redress when the five elements **1–006** of the cause of action summarised above are made out, not because of any existing or resulting factual or legal nexus between the parties, but on the essentially moral basis that people cannot be allowed to tell lies with impunity.

The tort of deceit should also be distinguished from the "right" which the victim **1–007** of a misrepresentation has to rescind any contract which he has thereby been induced to enter. Rescission is in principle (and subject to certain conditions) available whenever a contract has been induced by a misrepresentation, whether the representation was made fraudulently, negligently or innocently. Rescission, and the restitutionary and proprietary rights to recover money or property transferred under a contract which can flow from it, are important weapons in the fraud litigator's armoury, and they are considered elsewhere in this work.[11] Insofar as different principles may apply when establishing deceit for the purposes of rescission from those which apply when establishing it for the purposes of a claim in damages, that is addressed in this chapter, at para.1–119.

(2) The Decision to Allege Fraud

An allegation of fraud is a serious and potentially very harmful one, most **1–008** obviously in reputational terms. Allegations of fraud, once made, and whether or not they have been adjudicated upon, can irreversibly damage a defendant. The potential for such harm is even more acute in the internet age. Such allegations can also impose substantial strain on a defendant seeking to defend himself. The law of defamation is unlikely to provide any redress for unfounded allegations which form part of the judicial process, which is protected by absolute privilege for these purposes. Conscious of these matters, the law erects various safeguards against the improper pleading of claims in deceit, and in fraud-based claims generally, as well as other protections for a defendant to a claim in fraud.

Professional Obligations. First, stringent professional obligations govern **1–009** lawyers who advance such allegations. There are two aspects to this: the first is that a claim in deceit can only properly be advanced if there is reasonably credible material to support the allegation.[12] This can mean that a lawyer is obliged to refuse to plead or allege fraud even when so instructed by his client. The decision to plead or allege fraud in the absence of proper instructions and

---

[11] See also Chs 23 (Personal Equitable Remedies) and 15 (Unjust Enrichment).

[12] In relation to solicitors, Ch.5 of the SRA Code of Conduct 2011 relates to a solicitor's duties to the court. One of the "indicative behaviours" which may tend to show a failure to comply with such duties is IB(5.8) which refers to "suggesting that any person is guilty of a crime, fraud, or misconduct unless such allegations: (a) go to a matter in issue which is material to your own client's case; and (b) appear to be supported by reasonable grounds". In relation to barristers, r.C9.2.c of the Code of Conduct provides: "you must not draft any statement of case, witness statement, affidavit or other document containing ... any allegation of fraud, unless you have clear instructions to allege fraud and you have reasonably credible material which establishes an arguable case of fraud." Note that the material on which reliance is placed for these purposes need not be admissible in court proceedings: *Medcalf v Mardell* [2002] UKHL 27; [2003] 1 A.C. 120 (where the material in question was privileged).

reasonable grounds for so doing can lead to regulatory action against the lawyer. It can also expose him to the possibility of a wasted costs order.[13]

1–010 Needless to say, as against this a legal representative has a countervailing obligation to promote and protect his client's interests to the best of his ability. These potential conflicting duties may engage difficult questions of judgment. As Lord Steyn commented in *Medcalf v Mardell*[14]:

> "This particular professional duty sometimes poses difficult problems for practitioners. Making allegations of dishonesty without adequate grounds for doing so may be improper conduct. Not making an allegation of dishonesty where it is proper to make such allegations may amount to dereliction of duty. The barrister must promote and protect fearlessly and by all proper and lawful means his lay client's interests ... Often the decision will depend on circumstantial evidence. It may sometimes be finely balanced. What the decision should be may be a difficult matter of judgment on which reasonable minds may differ."[15]

1–011 The second aspect is that any allegation of fraud must be made clearly, unequivocally and with sufficient particularity so that the defendant understands the case he is required to meet.[16] As we note below, the representation which is said to have been made fraudulently will need to be identified with precision (something that is particularly important where the representation is said to be implicit or derived from conduct). As to the mental element of the tort, these requirements do not necessarily mean that the word "fraud" or "dishonesty" has to be used, since the facts alleged may be consistent only with an allegation of fraud; but if those facts are also consistent with innocence, then the pleader must make it plain that fraud is alleged. It bears note that the common formula "the Defendant knew or ought to have known" is not sufficient for these purposes, since it is treated as being a composite allegation of constructive knowledge rather than an allegation of actual knowledge with an allegation of constructive knowledge in the alternative.[17]

---

[13] Pursuant to s.51 of the Senior Courts Act 1981 and CPR r.46.8.

[14] *Medcalf v Mardell* [2002] UKHL 27; [2003] 1 A.C. 120, at [35], per Lord Steyn.

[15] Hence it will be a comparatively rare event that a lawyer is exposed to a wasted costs order for improperly pleading or alleging fraud.

[16] The courts have long emphasised these requirements: see, e.g., *Smith v Kay* (1859) 7 HLC 750 (HL); 11 E.R. 299; *Davy v Garrett* (1878) 7 Ch. D. 473, at 489, per Thesiger LJ; *Bradford Third Equitable Building Society v Borders* [1941] 2 All E.R. 205, at 207; *Belmont Finance Corp Ltd v Williams Furniture Ltd* [1979] Ch. 250, at 268, per Buckley LJ; *Armitage v Nurse* [1998] Ch. 241, at 256–257, per Millett LJ; *Three Rivers DC v Bank of England (No.3)* [2001] UKHL 16; [2001] 3 All E.R. 513, at [184]–[185], per Lord Steyn; *First Subsea Ltd v Baltec Ltd* [2017] EWCA Civ 186; [2018] Ch. 25, at [65]–[67], per Patten LJ. See also CPR PD 16, para.8.2(1) and the Admiralty and Commercial Courts Guide at C1.2, which provides that "full and specific details should be given of any allegation of fraud, dishonesty, malice or illegality" and that "where an inference of fraud or dishonesty is alleged, the facts on the basis of which the inference is alleged must be fully set out"; and the Chancery Guide at 2.8(1) to like effect.

[17] *Armitage v Nurse* [1998] Ch. 241, at 257B, per Millett LJ. See the recent decision of HH Judge Keyser QC in *Autogas (Europe) Ltd v Ochocki* [2018] EWHC 2345 (Ch), at [15], a case concerning dishonest assistance, which confirms that unless fraud is expressly pleaded, the primary facts must be consistent only with dishonesty for a finding of fraud.

Standard of Proof.   Secondly, although an allegation of deceit only needs to be   **1–012**
proven to the normal civil standard, that is the balance of probabilities,[18] it has
often been suggested that the evidential burden on the claimant is in practice
heightened, on the basis that "the more serious the allegation the less likely it is
that the event occurred and, hence, the stronger should be the evidence before the
court concludes that the allegation is established on the balance of probability."[19]
However, this observation needs to be treated with caution: the standard of proof
does not vary with the gravity of the misconduct alleged, nor is it correct as a
proposition of law that a more serious allegation requires more cogent evidence
to prove it.[20] Rather, the court should have regard to the inherent probabilities. As
a matter of common sense, and as a very broad generalisation, it is inherently less
likely that a defendant will be dishonest than that he will be incompetent; but all
depends on the particular circumstances, and the question is always, ultimately,
whether on the evidence before the court the allegation of deceit has been
established to the usual civil standard.[21]

Summary Judgment and Appeals.   Thirdly, it is rare (though not unprec-   **1–013**
edented) for summary judgment to be granted in fraud cases. In one such case,
where the evidence passed the very high threshold test for summary judgment to
be granted in a case of fraud, the then President of the Queen's Bench Division[22]
remarked as follows[23]:

> "I do not underestimate the importance of a finding adverse to the integrity to one of the
> parties. In itself, the risk of such a finding may provide a compelling reason for allowing a
> case to proceed to full oral hearing, notwithstanding the apparent strength of the claim on

---

[18] *Hornal v Neuberger Products* [1957] 1 Q.B. 247.

[19] *Re H (Minors)* [1996] A.C. 563, at 586–587, per Lord Nicholls; *AIC Ltd v ITS Trading Services
(UK) Ltd* [2006] EWCA Civ 1601; [2007] 1 All E.R. (Comm) 667, per Rix LJ at [259]; *In Re B* [2005]
UKHL 35; [2009] 1 A.C. 11, per Lady Hale at [70]; *Dadourian Group International Inc v Simms*
[2009] 1 Lloyd's Rep. 601, per Arden LJ at [32]; *Foodco UK LLP v Henry Boot Developments Ltd*
[2010] EWHC 358 (Ch), per Lewison J at [3]; *JSC BTA Bank v Mukhtar Ablyazov* [2013] EWHC 510,
per Teare J at [76].
[20] *Re B* [2008] UKHL 35; [2009] 1 A.C. 11, per Lord Hoffmann at [13]–[15]; *Re S-B* [2005] UKSC
17; [2010] 1 A.C. 678, per Lady Hale at [11]–[13]; *Re J* [2013] UKSC 9; [2013] 1 A.C. 680, per Lady
Hale at [35].
[21] See *Otkritie International Investment Management Ltd v Urumov* [2014] EWHC 191 (Comm), per
Eder J at [85]–[89]; *Kazakhstan Kagazy Plc v Zhunus* [2017] EWHC 3374 (Comm), per Picken J, at
[155]–[159].
[22] Sir Igor Judge.
[23] *Wrexham Association Football Club Ltd (In Administration) v Crucialmove Ltd* [2006] EWCA Civ
237; [2007] B.C.C. 139, at [57]–[58]. Another example is *Cheshire BS v Dunlop Hayward* [2008]
EWHC 51 where summary judgment was entered against a surveying company in respect of the
deceit of one of its employees for dishonestly overvaluing properties being offered for security for
lending purposes. That was a case where the defendant made "no admission" in relation to the
allegation of fraudulent misrepresentation. See also *Allied Fort Insurance Services Ltd v Creation
Consumer Finance Ltd* [2015] EWCA Civ 841, per Etherton LJ, where the Court of Appeal declined
to grant summary judgment, commenting, at [82], that "the length of the written evidence deployed by
the parties both on the application for, and the discharge of, the freezing order and relied upon by both
sides on the hearing of the summary judgment application, as well as the length of the hearing
challenging the freezing order, should immediately have sent a warning signal to the deputy Judge."
The court went on, at [94], to refer to "the dangers of evaluating disputed evidence in a complex case
on a summary judgment application."

paper, and the confident expectation, based on the papers, that the defendant lacks any real prospect of success. Experience teaches us that on occasion apparently overwhelming cases of fraud and dishonesty somehow inexplicably disintegrate. In short, oral testimony may show that some such cases are only tissue paper strong. As Lord Steyn observed in *Medcalf v Weatherill*,[24] when considering wasted costs orders:

'The law reports are replete with cases which were thought to be hopeless before investigation but were decided the other way after the court allowed the matter to be tried.'

And that is why I commented in *Fashion Gossip Ltd v Esprit Telecoms UK Ltd*,[25] that I was:

'troubled about entering summary judgment in a case in which the success of the claimant's case involves, as this one does, establishing allegations of dishonesty and fraud, which are strongly denied, and which cannot be conclusively proved by, for example, a conviction before a criminal court. This collective judicial experience does not always, or inevitably, provide a compelling reason for requiring a seemingly unanswerable case to proceed to trial, nor for that matter require the judge considering the summary judgment application to reject the conclusion that there is no real prospect of a successful defence of the claim if he is satisfied that there is none on the evidence before him. That is not what the Rules provide,[26] and if that had been intended,[27] express provision would have been made. It is however a factor constantly to be borne in mind, if and when, as here, the reason for concluding summary judgment is appropriate is consequent on a disputed finding, adverse to the integrity of the unsuccessful party.'"

1–014   For essentially similar reasons, once a claim in deceit has proceeded to trial and been rejected on the evidence, an appellate court will be very slow to intervene and upset the first instance judge's conclusions. Doubts, even grave ones, as to the correctness of the judge's findings will not suffice; the appellate court must be "convinced that he is wrong".[28]

1–015   **Jury Trial.**   Fourthly, this is one of the few remaining areas of civil litigation in which the defendant may on principle demand trial by jury, at least if the matter is proceeding in either the County Court[29] or the Queen's Bench Division of the High Court.[30]

1–016   **Costs Sanctions.**   Fifthly, if serious allegations of deceit are unsuccessfully pursued and are shown to have been unfounded, then the claimant will find himself in danger of being met with judicial disapproval, which may find

---

[24] Otherwise known as *Medcalf v Mardell* [2002] UKHL 27; [2003] 1 A.C. 120, at [42], per Lord Steyn.
[25] Unreported 27 July 2000.
[26] See generally CPR r.24.2.
[27] The CPR expressly provides that admiralty claims in rem and possession claims cannot be disposed of by way of summary judgment: CPR r.24.3(2).
[28] *Gross v Lewis Hillman Ltd* [1970] Ch. 445.
[29] County Courts Act 1984 s.66(3)(a).
[30] Senior Courts Act 1981 s.69(1): "Where, on the application of any party to an action to be tried in the Queen's Bench Division, the court is satisfied that there is in issue—(a) a charge of fraud against that party ... the action shall be tried with a jury, unless the court is of opinion that the trial requires any prolonged examination of documents or accounts or any scientific or local investigation which cannot conveniently be made with a jury." See *Stafford Winfield Cook & Partners v Winfield* [1981] 1 W.L.R. 458 for the position which arises when the proceedings have been issued in the Chancery Division.

expression in costs being awarded on the indemnity basis.[31] This will also be the case where a deceit case is discontinued.[32] Such orders are in part reflective of the fact that a defendant has no choice but to come to court to defend such allegations, and the unpleasant and distressing experience which the defendant will have endured as the target of the allegations over the inevitably lengthy period over which a case runs its course.[33] As noted earlier, in serious cases, it may be that the claimant's lawyers will find themselves held liable for some or all of the costs of the defendant, pursuant to the wasted costs jurisdiction.

Avoidance of Insurance Policies.　Sixthly, when suing an insured defendant it should be borne in mind that policies of indemnity insurance will usually exclude cover for claims arising from the insured's own dishonesty or fraud. Framing a claim in deceit may therefore leave a claimant reliant on the defendant's own resources for recovery.　　1–017

(3)　Advantages of Pleading Fraud

On the other hand, if a fraud is proved, the claimant enjoys various special advantages, which distinguish his position from that of the claimant who founds his claim on causes of action which do not involve proof of intentional dishonesty.　　1–018

No Defence of Contributory Negligence.　However careless or negligent the claimant himself may have been, for instance in entering into the transaction said to have been induced by the relevant deceit, no defence of contributory negligence will avail the wrongdoer so as to reduce his damages liability.[34] By contrast, if the relevant misrepresentation was only negligently made then the defendant is entitled to set up a defence of contributory negligence if the facts warrant it.　　1–019

---

[31] See for instance the well-known judgment of Tomlinson J in *Three Rivers District Council v Bank of England* [2006] EWHC 816 (Comm); [2006] 5 Costs L.R. 714.

[32] *Clutterbuck v HSBC Plc* [2015] EWHC 3233 (Ch).

[33] See for instance the last paragraph of Popplewell J's Judgment in *Madoff Securities International Ltd v Raven* [2013] EWHC 3147.

[34] See for instance *Alliance & Leicester Building Society v Edgestop Ltd* [1993] 1 W.L.R. 1462; *Corporación Nacional del Cobre de Chile v Sogemin Metals Ltd* [1997] 1 W.L.R. 1396; *Standard Chartered Bank v Pakistan National Shipping Corp (Nos 2 and 4)* [2003] 1 A.C. 959. The law on the non-availability of the defence of contributory negligence in intentional torts was comprehensively reviewed in the Court of Appeal decision of *Co-operative Group (CWS) Ltd v Pritchard* [2011] EWCA 329; [2012] Q.B. 320. Note, however, that where the party claiming in deceit was itself under specific duty to detect that very deceit (such as an auditor), the proper analysis may be that the cause of its loss is not the deceit but its own failure to detect it: *Barings Plc v Coopers & Lybrand* [2003] EWHC 1319 (Ch); [2003] P.N.L.R. 34, at [727]–[729], per Evans-Lombe J. This reasoning was adopted in *Singularis* where a bank liable in negligence under the *Quincecare* doctrine (see *Barclays Bank Plc v Quincecare Ltd* [1992] 4 All E.R. 363) for permitting a transfer of funds by a company was unable to set up the deceit of its director, even if that deceit could be attributed to the company, as a defence: see, at [73]–[80], per Steyn J. We discuss this further in Ch.22.

1–020   **Limitation.**   Further, the claimant is able to take advantage of s.32(1)(a) of the
Limitation Act 1980, which provides that, in claims based upon the "fraud of the
defendant" (which of course includes claims in deceit)[35] time does not start
running for limitation purposes until he knew of the fraud or could with
reasonable diligence have discovered it.[36]

1–021   **Damages.**   Moreover, in cases where an intentional wrong has been
established, such as deceit, the courts are prepared to show a degree of flexibility
as regards causation and damages which favour the claimant.[37] The general rule
in a claim for deceit is that any actual damage which flows directly from the
fraudulent inducement can be the subject of recovery, meaning: (a) that the
claimant is not necessarily required to give credit for the value of an asset
acquired as a result of the deceit as at the date of its acquisition (it may be
appropriate only to bring into account the actual proceeds realised on a later sale);
(b) the claimant can recover consequential losses (such as expenses incurred by
reason of having acquired an asset or entered into a transaction, or profits
foregone on an alternative acquisition or transaction); and (c) the claimant can
recover losses which would be too remote in a contractual or negligence based
case (that is, not reasonably foreseeable or within the reasonable contemplation
of the parties).[38] Damages are also not capped with reference to what the position
would have been had the deceitful representation been true.[39] Further, a claimant
in a deceit claim can, in an appropriate case, recover aggravated and exemplary
damages.[40] We consider the question of damages below at Ch.21.

1–022   **Exclusion Clauses.**   The law, on public policy grounds, will not permit a party
to a contract to exclude or limit liability for his own fraud and a provision that

---

[35] This might be thought obvious, but the contrary was argued—and rejected—in *Regent Leisuretime
Ltd v NatWest Finance Ltd* [2003] EWCA Civ 391, at [100], per Jonathan Parker LJ.
[36] *Paragon Finance Plc v Thakerar & Co* [1999] 1 All E.R. 400, at 418, per Millett LJ; *Biggs v
Sotnicks (A Firm)* [2002] Lloyd's Rep. P.N. 331. We discuss this further in Ch.26.
[37] Allowing more generous recovery for torts involving dishonesty or intentional wrongdoing serves
the legitimate purpose of deterrence, and as between the fraudster and the innocent party moral
considerations militate in favour of requiring the former to bear the risk of unforeseen events: *Smith
New Court Securities Ltd v Citibank N.A.* [1997] A.C. 254, at 280A–280C, per Lord Steyn.
[38] *Doyle v Olby* [1969] 2 Q.B. 158, at 167–168, per Winn LJ (approving the dictum of Lord Adkin in
Clark v Urquhart [1930] A.C. 28, at 67–68, per Lord Atkin); *Smith New Court Securities Ltd v
Citibank N.A.* [1997] A.C. 254, at 264–265, per Lord Browne-Wilkinson. A claimant in a deceit claim
will, however, be unable to recover losses attributable to his own failure to take steps reasonably
available to him to extricate himself from a transaction which he has been deceived into entering,
once the fraud has been discovered (i.e. he is still subject to the "duty" to mitigate his losses): *Downs
v Chappell* [1997] 1 W.L.R. 426; *Smith New Court Securities Ltd v Citibank N.A.* [1997] A.C. 254, at
266G, per Lord Browne-Wilkinson. He also will not be able to recover for losses which, whilst
connected to the deceit in a "but for" sense, nevertheless in substance flow from a separate
intervening cause.
[39] In which respect *Downs v Chappell* [1997] 1 W.L.R. 426, at 443, per Hobhouse LJ, was wrongly
decided: *Smith New Court Securities Ltd v Citibank N.A.* [1997] A.C. 254, at 283, per Lord Steyn.
[40] *Archer v Brown* [1985] Q.B. 401 (aggravated damages to compensate for injured feelings resulting
from deceit); *Rookes v Barnard* [1964] A.C. 1129, at 1223, per Lord Devlin, and *Kuddus v Chief
Constable of Leicestershire* [2001] UKHL 29; [2002] 2 A.C. 122 (exemplary damages available in
principle where defendant's conduct calculated to make a profit which exceeds the amount of
compensation).

purports to do so (which could include a clause that stipulates that no representations are being made or that no reliance is being placed on any representations made) will not be enforced.[41] It is therefore now standard for exclusion clauses to have express carve-outs for fraud; and even absent an express carve-out, an exclusion clause in general terms would probably be construed as not being intended to cover fraud.[42] A claim in deceit, if established, will thus enable a claimant to avoid any contractual limitations on the defendant's liability.[43]

It would, however, appear that the public policy bar to the enforcement of contracts excluding liability for fraud does not extend to provisions excluding liability for the fraud of a third party (such as an agent or employee) for which the defendant might otherwise be liable, at least where the third party is not an alter ego of the defendant and the defendant is not itself aware of or complicit in the fraud.[44] Very clear wording would, however, generally be required for the Court to conclude as a matter of construction that this is what was intended.[45]   **1–023**

Illegality Defence.   In cases where the fraud alleged against the defendant might also be attributed to the claimant (for example, where the claimant is a company and the defendant is a former director of it), issues can arise as to whether the claim should be barred by application of the ex turpi causa principle. Recent authority on how attribution works for these purposes has considerably reduced the scope for difficulty for a claimant on this front; but the point nevertheless merits mention. It is considered in detail in Chs 19 and 24.   **1–024**

Interim Remedies.   Prior to trial, if the claimant is able to advance a reasonably cogent case of fraud, this may well permit him to obtain powerful forms of interim relief, most notably freezing and/or search orders, together with disclosure orders, which are intended to ensure that enforcement of any eventual   **1–025**

---

[41] *S Pearson & Son Ltd v Dublin Corp* [1907] A.C. 351, at 356, per Lord Halsbury; *HIH Casualty & General Insurance Ltd v Chase Manhattan Bank* [2003] UKHL 6; [2003] 2 Lloyd's Rep. 61, at [16] and [76], per Lords Bingham and Hoffman; *Bonhams 1973 Ltd v Cavazzoni* [2014] EWHC 682 (QB), at [10]–[12], per Cooke J; *Property Alliance Group Ltd v Royal Bank of Scotland Plc* [2016] EWHC 3342 (Ch), at [226] and [231], per Asplin J.

[42] See *Government of Zanzibar v British Aerospace Ltd* [2000] 1 W.L.R. 2333, at 2346, per Raymond Jack QC, and *Six Continents Hotels Inc v Event Hotels GmbH* [2006] EWHC 2317 (QB), at [53], per Gloster J; but note the different view of Jacob J in *Thomas Witter Ltd v T.B.P. Industries Ltd* [1996] 2 All E.R. 573, at 598, per Jacob J.

[43] Public policy considerations do not always point in favour of the claimant in a fraud claim and there are circumstances in which liability for fraud is precluded on policy grounds. One noteworthy example is witness immunity: there can be no liability in deceit for statements made in the course of giving evidence in court proceedings, however dishonestly; see *Sprecher Grier Halberstam LLP v Walsh* [2008] EWCA Civ 1324. As the case makes clear, the immunity extends to statements made outside Court in the course of preparing evidence, and statements made by solicitors in correspondence on instructions from the witness (on which the witness could have been cross-examined): at [50]–[52], per Ward LJ.

[44] *HIH Casualty & General Insurance Ltd v Chase Manhattan Bank* [2003] UKHL 6; [2003] 2 Lloyd's Rep. 61, at [122], per Lord Scott.

[45] *HIH Casualty & General Insurance Ltd v Chase Manhattan Bank* [2003] 2 Lloyd's Rep. 61, at [16], per Lord Bingham. Other controls on the enforcement of exclusion clauses, such as s.3 of the Misrepresentation Act 1967, would also have to be considered.

judgment will not be thwarted by assets being dissipated or otherwise diminished whilst proceedings remain at the interim stage.[46] Cogent allegations of fraud, particularly when coupled with the use of a network of offshore companies in connection with the alleged fraud, may of themselves provide powerful support for a case of a real risk of dissipation such as to justify a freezing order.[47] That said, it is always necessary for the Court to scrutinise any allegation of fraud carefully to see whether the dishonesty in question does indeed justify a conclusion that assets are likely to be dissipated.[48]

1–026   **Rescission and Proprietary Remedies.**   As is considered further below, one remedy for a claim in deceit which may be available is rescission of the contract, gift or other transaction induced by the fraud. When property is transferred or money paid pursuant to such a transaction, beneficial title passes to the recipient unless and until the transaction is rescinded; but if it is rescinded, beneficial title is revested in the transferor/payer by means of a constructive (or possibly resulting) trust, apparently with retrospective effect—at least to the extent that the transferor/payer can use the equitable rules of tracing to trace his revested beneficial ownership and then assert a proprietary claim to the property, money or proceeds in the hands of the original recipient or a further recipient who is not a bona fide purchaser for value without notice of the fraud.[49]

1–027   **Execution.**   Post-trial, the fact that the defendant has been proven to be a fraudster is likely to facilitate considerably the claimant's task of investigating, securing and executing the judgment which has been obtained against assets held by the defendant. It may also give rise to allegations of contempt of court and the associated threat of committal to prison.[50]

(4)   Conclusion

1–028   Proceedings in which allegations of fraud are advanced can therefore properly be described as "high stakes" litigation. If the relevant evidential thresholds are crossed then the claimant may, depending on the relevant stage of the proceedings, be given access to a wide range of procedural tools and substantive rights which will assist in pursing the wrongdoer. On the other hand, if allegations are advanced without a proper foundation then the consequences for the claimant (and possibly his legal representatives) may be serious.

1–029   It is all too easy to state these principles in the abstract. Experience shows, however, that in real life the fraud claimant (or putative claimant) and his legal advisers are often placed in a difficult position because of the paucity of information available to them. Those who tell lies in order to gain an advantage

---

[46] For a discussion of such interim remedies, see Chs 26–33.

[47] *VTB Capital Plc v Nutritek International Corp* [2012] EWCA Civ 808; [2012] 2 Lloyd's Rep. 313, at [174] and [178], per Lloyd LJ.

[48] See *National Bank Trust v Yurov* [2016] EWHC 1913 (Comm) at [70], per Males J.

[49] *Lonrho v Fayed (No.2)* [1992] 1 W.L.R. 1, at 12, per Millett J; see further Ch.10, para.10–007, and Ch.23, paras 23–047—23–048, and the cases referred to there.

[50] See Chs 35 (Contempt) and 37 (Enforcement of Judgments).

or cause harm to others do not tend to be forthcoming about the true nature of their intentions and activities. A person who considers that he has suffered harm as a result of being misled is therefore in danger of reaching incorrect conclusions or drawing false inferences on the basis of a limited understanding of the factual position. In some cases, a claimant may conclude that there has been a fraud when in fact there is an entirely innocent explanation for what has happened. In other instances, the claimant is correct that a fraud has been perpetrated against him, but may then proceed by making allegations against a party who turns out not to have been involved, or to have played only an innocent part in the events which unfolded. As further information and documentary disclosure emerges during the course of proceedings it is incumbent on the claimant and his advisers carefully to reassess the merits of the allegations which have been advanced, and to test them against the evolving evidential backdrop, which often looks very different from the one which appeared at the pre-action stage.

B. The Misrepresentation

(1) Introduction

At the core of any claim in deceit is the representation in question. Its falsity, and the honesty of the person who made the representation, cannot begin to be considered until the representation on which the claim in deceit is to be founded has been identified. In the case of a written document, the task of identification of the representation is usually a simple one, although it may be said that, given the context, an implied representation can be construed out of the written words. In the case of an oral representation, the identification may be a more difficult process, involving disputed testimony from representee and representor.[51] Difficult questions can also arise where, as the law recognises is in certain circumstances possible, a representation is alleged to arise out of the conduct of the representor or indeed his silence.

1–030

Accordingly, when formulating and pleading a case in fraud it is vital accurately and clearly to identify the representation which it is said has caused the claimant loss. It is not every case that will permit this to be done simply by reference to a document that is clear in its terms. Even an express representation (especially one made orally)[52] will require interpretation against the context in which it was made; and where the representation is said to be implicit or to have arisen from conduct, care will be needed to identify with precision what the content of the

1–031

---

[51] This paragraph is drawn from the judgment of Rix LJ in *AIC Ltd v ITS Testing Services (UK) Ltd* [2016] EWCA Civ 1601; [2007] 1 All E.R. (Comm) 607, at [252]. The judgment is perhaps the leading modern analysis of the law of deceit.

[52] *AIC Ltd v ITS Testing Services (UK) Ltd* [2016] EWCA Civ 1601; [2007] 1 All E.R. (Comm) 607, at [252], per Rix LJ: "although it is of course possible to be more or less deliberate about one's speech, nevertheless the natural ebb and flow of conversation as part of an essentially interactive process means that it differs significantly from a written document. It does not necessarily have a single writer's logic, it is not composed, and it cannot be read as a whole before its communication ... evidence of contemporary views of what the parties to the relevant conversation understood themselves to be saying or hearing may be of special importance."

representation was and how it is said to have arisen. As was stated in *Cassa di Risparmio della Reppublica di San Marino SpA v Barclays Bank Ltd*[53]:

> "In order to determine whether any and if so what representation was made by a statement requires (1) construing the statement in the context in which it was made, and (2) interpreting the statement objectively according to the impact it might be expected to have on a reasonable representee in the position and with the known characteristics of the actual representee."

1–032 Moreover, the task can be yet more complex and delicate when formulating a claim in deceit, because, as will be seen below (and in contradistinction to other forms of misrepresentation), the claimant must show that he understood the representation in the way that the defendant intended it to be understood.

(2) Falsity and Half-truth

1–033 In order to be actionable the representation must of course be false. But the necessary element of falsity may be established even if the representation is not on its face false. The task is to identify what the representor intended the representee to understand by the representation. So if a representation is made which is literally true, but the representor intended the representee to understand the representation in the opposite, or some different, sense, for instance by the adoption of an ironical tone, or a raised eyebrow (or some similar device), and the representee in fact interpreted the representation in that opposite or different sense, then the representor may be liable in deceit if the representation is false in that different sense.[54] (Of course if the representee fails to appreciate the representor's irony and interprets the representation in its literal meaning then, notwithstanding the attempt to deceive, the claim will not be made out.)

1–034 Similarly, if a true fact is represented, but the representor intentionally omits other information which is material to, and substantially alters the intended import of, the facts represented, then he may equally be liable in deceit. As it was observed in a leading case:

> "It is a trite observation that every document as against its author must be read in the sense which it was intended to convey. And everybody knows that sometimes half a truth is no better than a downright falsehood."[55]

---

[53] *Cassa di Risparmio della Reppublica di San Marino SpA v Barclays Bank Ltd* [2011] EWHC 484 (Comm); [2011] 1 C.L.C. 701, at [215], per Hamblen J. See also *Raiffeisen Zentralbank Osterreich AG v The Royal Bank of Scotland Plc* [2010] EWHC 1392 (Comm); [2011] 1 Lloyd's Rep. 123, at [81], per Christopher Clarke J; *Kyle Bay Ltd v Underwriters Subscribing under Policy No. 01957/08/01* [2007] EWCA Civ 57; [2007] 1 C.L.C. 164, at [30]–[33], per Neuberger LJ.

[54] "If a person makes a representation of that which is true, if he intends that the party to whom the representation is made should not believe it to be true, that is a false representation": *Moens v Heyworth* (1842) 10 M&W 147, at 158, per Parke B.

[55] *Gluckstein v Barnes* [1900] A.C. 240, at 250–251, per Lord Macnaghten. Quoted with approval by the House of Lords in *HIH Casualty and General Insurance Ltd v Chase Manhattan Bank* [2003] UKHL 6; [2003] 1 All E.R. (Comm) 349, at [71], per Lord Hoffman, referring to "that form of nondisclosure which makes a positive statement misleading—the half truth which, without disclosure of the other half, is, as Lord Macnaghten said.... 'no better than a downright falsehood'." In *Smith*

Thus, in that case, a statement in a company prospectus that a property to be sold to the company for £180,000 had been purchased for £140,000, whilst being true "in the letter", was, when taken together with the undisclosed fact that the vendors had made a profit of £20,000 on certain charges on the property, misleading and fraudulently so: the statement was intended to convey that the vendors' profit on the resale to the company would be only £40,000, when in reality it would be £60,000.[56]

To establish a misrepresentation it is necessary to show that what was said (expressly or by implication) was *materially* false. A representation that is substantially correct, even if not entirely correct, is not a misrepresentation. The question is whether the difference between what was represented and the truth would have been likely to induce a reasonable person in the position of the claimant to act in the way that has given rise to the claim.[57]

1–035

The question of the falsity (in this sense) or otherwise of the representation must be determined at the date when it is acted upon.[58]

1–036

(3)   Representation of Fact

It is a cardinal principle of the law of deceit that to found liability the representation must be one of existing fact.[59] However, as we shall see below, the limitations on the action in deceit suggested by this pre-requisite are in the main illusory and representations which on the face of it are not of existing fact can often nonetheless be actionable. The law has over time shown an increasing flexibility in its interpretation of representations; and its general tendency has been to expand the ambit of actionability.

1–037

New Court Securities Ltd v Citibank N.A. [1997] A.C. 254, at 274, Lord Steyn said that it has "rightly been said that a cocktail of truth, falsity and evasion is a more powerful instrument of deception than undiluted falsehood. It is also difficult to detect."

[56] But see *Thorp v Abbotts* [2015] EWHC 2142 (Ch), in which a claim for fraudulent misrepresentation against vendors of a property failed: although the vendors had failed to disclose the fact that they were aware of and had had communications about planning applications for nearby developments, they had nevertheless answered the questions in their property information form about communications affecting the property, and discussions with neighbours affecting the property, accurately in the negative. On their proper construction, those questions did not encompass the planning applications or the communications about them, so this was not a case where something withheld falsified the intended import of something explicitly said.

[57] *Avon Insurance v Swire Fraser* [2000] 1 All E.R. (Comm) 573, at [17], per Rix J; *Raiffeisen Zentralbank Osterreich AG v The Royal Bank of Scotland Plc*, above, at [149].

[58] *Briess v Woolley* [1954] A.C. 333. See generally below at para.1–067 "Continuing Representations".

[59] It has been suggested by J. Cartwright in *Misrepresentation, Mistake and Non-Disclosure*, 3rd edn (London: Sweet & Maxwell, 2012), para.5.08, that this delimitation on the action in deceit should be abandoned. But it would require the Supreme Court to over-rule the many authorities which insist upon this element of the cause of action.

(4) Representations of Opinion and States of Mind

1–038   It follows that, technically, a representation of opinion is not in itself actionable. However this proposition is now so narrowly interpreted as to be almost meaningless as a curtailment on the claim in deceit. As stated in *Clerk & Lindsell on Torts*:

> "A statement of opinion is invariably regarded as incorporating an assertion that the maker does actually hold that opinion; hence the expression of an opinion not honestly entertained and intended to be acted upon amounts to fraud."[60]

For instance, where a valuer puts forward his professional opinion as to the true value of property in circumstances where he does not actually hold the opinion that the property is worth the amount ascribed, then he will be potentially liable in deceit.[61]

1–039   Similarly, a statement of belief is a representation of fact as to the representor's state of mind.[62] If a vendor of a horse represents that he does not believe that the horse is suffering from any diseases when, to his knowledge, the horse is indeed suffering disease, then the mere fact that the representation is couched in terms of belief will not avail the representor. Indeed, a statement of belief must connote at least some basis for the belief, in the sense that one could not honestly believe to be true that which one in fact has not the least idea about; but that is not (without more) the same as representing that one's belief is objectively justified.

1–040   That said, an express representation of opinion or belief may also be interpreted as carrying with it implied representations[63] as to the grounds for holding that opinion or belief. So, for example, in *William Sindall Plc v Cambridgeshire CC*[64] it was held that a representation made in answer to pre-contract enquiries by a vendor that there were no defects in title "so far as the vendor is aware" was not merely a representation that the vendor had no actual knowledge of any defects, but also an implied representation that it had made such investigations as could reasonably be expected of it to ascertain whether any existed. If to its knowledge it had not made such investigations, it could in principle have been liable in deceit (even if the express representation as to its lack of actual awareness of defects was true).[65]

1–041   The basis for this further implication seems to be the fact that the representor is better equipped with information or the means of getting it than the representee, and is in a position where his belief could reasonably be expected to be justified (being, for example, a professional, or having retained professionals, in the

---

[60] M.A. Jones, A.M. Dugdale and M. Simpson (eds), *Clerk & Lindsell on Torts*, 21st edn (London: Sweet & Maxwell, 2014), para.18–13. The classic authority for this proposition is *Brown v Raphael* [1958] Ch. 636. "[T]he existence of an opinion in the person stating it is a question of fact": *Bisset v Wilkinson* [1927] A.C. 177, at 182, per Lord Merrivale.

[61] See for instance *Nationwide BS v Dunlop Haywards* [2007] EWHC 1374 (Comm).

[62] See the words of Bowen LJ in *Edgington v Fitzmaurice* (1885) 29 Ch. D. 459, at 483, quoted in fn.71 below.

[63] In relation to implied representations, see para.1–059 below.

[64] *William Sindall Plc v Cambridgeshire CC* [1994] 1 W.L.R. 1016.

[65] *Economides v Commercial Assurance* [1998] Q.B. 587, at 598, per Simon Brown LJ.

relevant field). So, in the case of a statement of opinion, where the facts which inform the relevant opinion are not equally well known to both sides, such a statement by the one who knows the facts best may carry with it an implication that he is aware of facts which reasonably justify it, or bona fide believes himself to have reasonable grounds for holding it. The authorities which support this proposition (*Smith v Land and House Property Corp*[66] and *Brown v Raphael*)[67] both relate to non-fraudulent misrepresentations and care must be taken in applying them to deceit cases. This is because the task of identifying the representation in such cases, and imposing liability in respect of it, is an objective one, whereas, in deceit, if the maker of the representation is not aware (however unreasonably) that he is making the implied representation alleged to be false, then he cannot be liable.[68]

It is also (and conversely) the case that what at first blush appears to be a statement of fact may in fact amount to no more than a statement of opinion or a contention. For example, lawyers advancing their client's cause will often make unqualified positive averments about aspects of the case to the other side; but these are not usually actionable representations. Similarly, a statement by a loss adjuster to the insured's loss assessor as to the effect of the policy, in the context of the negotiation of the settlement of a claim under an insurance policy, was held just to be a contention, when the representee was a professional who had (or was reasonably believed to have) independent access to the terms of the policy.[69] So too, a statement which in isolation appears to be an outright statement of fact may be qualified by other statements which accompany it and which would indicate to

1–042

---

[66] *Smith v Land and House Property Corp* (1884) 28 Ch. D. 7, at 15, per Bowen LJ: "But if the facts are not equally well known to both sides, then a statement of opinion by the one who knows the facts best involves very often a statement of a material fact, for he impliedly states that he knows facts which justify his opinion."

[67] *Brown v Raphael* [1958] Ch. 636 (statement by solicitors for vendor of a reversion that annuitant was believed to have no estate for duty purposes). See particularly at 643, at per Lord Evershed MR: "What would be the effect of this language upon the mind of a possible purchaser? Clearly, I should have thought, it would flow from the language used and would be intended to be understood by a reader of the particulars that persons who knew the significance of this matter and who were experienced and competent to look into it were expressing a belief founded upon substantial and reasonable grounds.". Modern examples of the application of this principle are *Barings Plc v Coopers & Lybrand* [2002] EWHC 461 (Ch); [2002] P.N.L.R. 823, at [48]–[52], per Evans-Lombe J; and *AIC Ltd v ITS Testing Services Ltd* [2006] EWCA Civ 1601, at [255], per Rix LJ; but cf. *Economides v Commercial Assurance*, above, at 606, per Gibson LJ (further implied representation not found where assured layperson stated belief as to value of contents for insurance purposes).

[68] See *Cassa di Risparmio della Repubblica di San Marino SpA v Barclays Bank Ltd* [2011] EWHC 484 (Comm); [2011] 1 C.L.C. 701, at [221], per Hamblen J: "In a deceit case it is also necessary that a representor should understand that he is making the implied representation and that it had the misleading sense alleged. A person cannot make a fraudulent statement unless he is aware that he is making that statement." See further para.1-085 below.

[69] *Kyle Bay Ltd v Underwriters Subscribing under Policy No.019057/08/01* [2007] EWCA Civ 57, at [33]–[35]. Another reason why such statements are often not actionable is that they are not intended to be relied upon as such: see further para.1–061 below.

a reasonable person that what was being said was only a statement of belief whose factual accuracy and completeness had not been verified and could not be relied upon.[70]

(5) Representations of Intention/as to the Future

(i) Introduction

1–043   Because of the law's insistence on the requirement of a representation of present fact as a precondition to any liability in deceit, statements of intention or as to the future will only be potentially actionable as (false) representations concerning the representor's current state of mind or knowledge.[71] The mere fact that the intended event does not in fact occur will not in itself create liability, unless the representation has contractual effect.[72]

(ii) Statements of intention

1–044   Yet the law does not shrink from inferring from a statement of intention a representation of present fact.[73] So, if a person represents to another that, in the

---

[70] See *Raiffeisen Zentralbank Osterreich AG*, above, at [86], per Christopher Clarke J, cited by Hamblen J in *Cassa di Risparmio della Repubblica di San Marino SpA v Barclays Bank Ltd*, above, at [222]. The question will arise as to whether a provision to that effect is in substance an exclusion clause (in which case it would not be effective to exclude liability for fraud) or whether it goes to the logically prior question of whether a representation is made at all. That is a question of substance and not form, and will depend on all the facts: *Raiffeisen*, at [310]–[312], per Christopher Clarke J.

[71] In the time-honoured, and often-cited, words of Bowen LJ in *Edgington v Fitzmaurice* (1885) 29 Ch. D. 459, at 483: "There must be a misstatement of an existing fact: but the state of a man's mind is as much a fact as the state of his digestion. It is true that it is very difficult to prove what the state of a man's mind at a particular time is, but if it can be ascertained it is as much a fact as anything else. A misrepresentation as to the state of a man's mind is, therefore, a misstatement of fact." The facts in *Edgington* provide a paradigm example of liability in deceit being imposed in respect of representations of intention.

[72] See *Hagen v ICI Chemicals & Polymers Ltd* [2001] EWHC 548 (QB); [2002] Lloyd's Rep. PN 288, at [131], per Elias J: "By definition the claimant is always complaining in circumstances where the intention has not been carried into effect. It is only because of that fact that the claimant can allege that the representation made was false. The difficulty facing many, if not most, claimants, is that their real complaint is that the intention was not carried out. But absent some contractual undertaking to do so, there never was a representation that it would be." The point is succinctly made in K.R. Handley, *Spencer Bower, Turner and Handley: Actionable Misrepresentation*, 4th edn (London: LNUK, 2000), para.17: "What the representee is generally found to complain of is the failure to carry out the intention, which shows that what really induced him to alter his position was his belief that the intention would be carried out. In other words, he relied upon the statement as if it were a promise, not as a representation. His belief that the representor had a present intention to act according to his statement would not have influenced him unless he had also believed that the intention would be carried out." See also *Tudor Grange Holdings Ltd v Citibank NA* [1992] Ch. 53, at 67 where Browne-Wilkinson V-C said: "A representation as to future conduct has no effect unless it constitutes a contract."

[73] So it was said in *Wales v Wadham* [1977] 2 All E.R. 125, per Tudor Price J at 136, that a statement of intention is only false if the person making the statement does not honestly hold the intention being expressed at the time. Of course the fact that the intention is not fulfilled is not, in itself, proof that it did not exist when the representation was made: *Beattie v Lord Ebury* (1872) 7 Ch. App. 777, at 804, per Mellish LJ. Moreover there is a distinction between a statement of present intention to act in a

event of receipt of a sum of money from the representee, he will use that money for a particular purpose, this constitutes a representation of present intention and so a statement of fact.[74] Hence if the representor does not actually harbour that intention at the time of making the representation, or if he knows that he will not be able to put the stated intention into effect, then the representor may be liable in deceit because he has made a false representation as to his present state of mind.[75] (Moreover, such a misrepresentation will almost always be fraudulent, since it is the representor's own true intentions or knowledge that falsifies the representation.)[76]

By extension of this reasoning it has been held that a director, who executes a contract on behalf of a company by which the company promises payment at some future date, knowing that the company will in fact not be able to make the payment, can be personally liable in deceit: by so doing the director impliedly represents that the company has the capacity to meet its obligations under the contract, knowing that representation to be false.[77] This may be particularly significant where the company is insolvent, such that any claim in breach of contract is of limited value. At first blush this seems surprising. That by entering the contract the company impliedly represents that it has the present intention, and capacity, to perform its obligations can be understood; but that the director who does no more than sign the contract on the company's behalf makes a similar representation, personally, as to what the company intends and is able to do would seem to make a significant inroad into the principles of separate corporate personality and limited liability.[78] It may be wondered why, if this is correct, there is not in every case of a contract entered into by a company also, in principle at least, a potential personal liability on the part of the director or other

1–045

---

certain manner, and a promise to do so: *British Airways Board v Taylor* [1976] 1 W.L.R. 13, at 17 where Lord Wilberforce said: "the distinction in law between a promise as to future action, which may be broken or kept, and a statement as to existing fact, which may be true or false, is clear enough. There may be inherent in a promise an implied statement as to a fact, and where this is really the case, the court can attach appropriate consequences to any falsity in, or recklessness in the making of, that statement. Everyone is familiar with the proposition that a statement of intention may itself be a statement of fact and so capable of being true or false."

[74] "That which is in form a promise may be in another aspect a representation": Jones, Dugdale and Simpson, *Clerk & Lindsell on Torts* (2014), para.18-12, quoting Lord Herschell in *Clydesdale Bank Ltd v Paton* [1896] A.C. 381, at 394, per Lord Herschell.

[75] In *East v Maurer* [1991] 1 W.L.R. 461 where a hairdresser was found liable in deceit where he had represented to the purchaser of a salon that he would not be working in the vicinity of the salon after the sale; whereas in fact he intended so to do. Recent examples are *Al Khudairi v Abbey Brokers Ltd* [2010] EWHC 1486 (Ch); [2010] P.N.L.R. 32 (a case involving the claimant establishing liability in deceit where a claim in contract was of limited value because of the contracting party's insolvency); and *Watts v Watts* [2014] W.T.L.R. 1781.

[76] *Abbar v Saudi Economic & Development Co (SEDCO) Real Estate Ltd* [2013] EWHC 1414 (Ch), at [197], per David Richards J.

[77] *Contex Drouzbha Ltd v Wiseman* [2007] EWCA Civ 1201.

[78] It is acknowledged that *Standard Chartered Bank v Pakistan National Shipping Corp* [2002] UKHL 43; [2003] 1 A.C. 959 makes it clear that an agent of a company who makes a dishonest representation cannot escape liability on the basis that he was only doing so on behalf of the company; but there the agent (a director) had plainly made a representation. The question under consideration here is whether a director who does no more than sign his company's contract on its behalf can be said to be making a representation at all.

agent through whom the company acted.[79] Nevertheless, the proposition has Court of Appeal support,[80] albeit on the proviso that any case of implied representation will necessarily turn on its facts.

1–046 Claims founded on representations of intention are nonetheless fraught with difficulty. First, proof of the historical state of a person's mind will likely be difficult to establish. The mere fact that the represented intention has not in the event been carried into effect is not a sure guide as to the representor's state of mind when the representation was initially made. Circumstances may have changed; the representor may have changed his mind, and, absent a contractual obligation, the law allows him to do so with impunity. Secondly, even if a false representation as to the representor's state of mind can be made out, it will still be necessary to establish that it was upon this representation as to intent, and not just upon the promise of future fulfilment of it, that the representee relied and was intended to rely.[81] Where the intended reliance is in fact only upon the promise, then, unless the representation has been fortified by incorporation into a contract, the law of tort cannot assist.

(iii)   Representations about future events

1–047 A representation as to the occurrence of a future event will equally generally be interpreted as a representation of existing fact. So, if a person represents that something will happen on a given day (or at some time, however ill-defined) in the future he is making a representation that (a) he honestly believes that the event will occur[82] and (b) depending on the circumstances, that he has reasonable grounds for believing that that is the case.

If the event relates to something within the representor's control then there will be generally implied a representation that the representor intends to do that which he says he will do or procure the happening of a particular event, i.e. a representation as to present intention.[83] These are all statements of fact, which will be actionable if such belief and the reasonable grounds which might support it are absent, or if the intention is absent.

(iv)   Negotiations and sales talk

1–048 An important caveat should be noted. It is a daily occurrence that where parties are engaged in negotiating a contract they adopt negotiating positions which do

---

[79] Of course, it is only where the company is foreseeably going to be unable to fulfill its promise at the time of entering the contract (because, for example, it is insolvent) and the director knows this to be so, or is dishonestly reckless as to the true position, that liability in deceit on his part would arise. This will naturally limit the scope for separate personal liability.

[80] *Contex Drouzbha Ltd v Wiseman* [2007] EWCA Civ 1201. The point on appeal was strictly concerned with the application of Lord Tenterden's Act to the claim (see below, at para.1–073); but the decision below as to the implied representation was endorsed, at [24], per Waller LJ.

[81] See the passage from Handley, *Spencer Bower, Turner and Handley: Actionable Misrepresentation* (2000), mentioned in fn.72 above.

[82] *FoodCo UK LLP v Henry Boot Developments Ltd* [2010] EWHC 358 (Ch), per Lewison J at [198].

[83] *FoodCo UK LLP v Henry Boot Developments Ltd* [2010] EWHC 358 (Ch), per Lewison J at [193]–[197].

not necessarily represent their final position. The law has traditionally adopted a realistic view on representations made in such circumstances and judges have been unwilling to impose liability in situations where dissembling is a fact of life (such that both parties can reasonably be expected to be aware of and engaged in it).[84] However, where the line should be drawn in imposing liability is not always clear.[85]

The law similarly takes a realistic view over what used to be described as "puffs" but in more modern parlance is referred to as "sales talk".[86] Statements, typically by vendors, which are put in such general terms may be incapable of constituting actionable representations: they cannot reasonably be understood as containing statements of fact upon which the counterparty should rely. Again, the line between non-actionable sales talk and representations about the characteristics of the property or goods to be sold may be a difficult one to draw.[87]   1–049

(6) Representations of Law

The old distinction between representations of opinion and those of fact created doubt as to whether a representation as to the law was in itself actionable. In practice it is doubtful that this distinction materially hindered the prosecution of claims in deceit. A representation as to the law will be likely to be interpreted as containing within it an implied representation that the representor in fact believed, and had reasonable grounds for believing, that the law was as stated. Now that the distinction between mistakes of law and mistakes of fact has been discredited in the law of restitution,[88] and common mistakes of law are capable of vitiating a contract,[89] it can be confidently stated that a statement of law is now actionable within the law of deceit if the representor's state of mind can be brought within the established categories, without the necessity of relying upon an implied representation.[90]   1–050

---

[84] *Vernon v Keys* (1810) 12 East 632; (1812) 4 Taunt 488.

[85] Thus in *Haygarth v Wearing* (1872) L.R. 12 Eq 320 a statement about the value of an estate inherited by a vendor, which was made by a purchaser to induce the vendor to sell, was not merely an assessment given as part of a negotiation, but an answer to a specific question made by a party who was in an unequal position of knowledge and genuinely sought guidance. Cf. *Armstrong v Strain* [1951] 1 T.L.R. 856.

[86] Although not necessarily representations as to intention or the future, these are conveniently mentioned here, there being an obvious similarity with the law's approach to statements made in the course of negotiations.

[87] See *Kingspan Environmental Ltd v Borealis A/S* [2012] EWHC 1147 (Comm), at [420]. Old cases include *Dimmock v Hallett* [1866] L.R. 2 Ch. App. 21 and *Johnson v Smart* (1860) 2 Giff 151, at 156, per Sir John Stuart V-C.

[88] *Kleinwort Benson Ltd v Lincoln City Council* [1999] 2 A.C. 349.

[89] *Brennan v Bolt Burdon* [2004] EWCA Civ 1017; [2005] Q.B. 303.

[90] The leading decision is *Pankhania v Hackney LBC* [2002] EWHC 2441 (Ch), which conducted a thorough review of the earlier authorities. *Pankhania* was followed in *Mears Ltd v Shoreline Housing Partnership Ltd* [2015] EWHC 1396 (TCC). See also Cartwright, *Misrepresentation, Mistake and Non-Disclosure* (2012), para.7–1, where the view is expressed that the courts "have now abandoned the formal distinction between misrepresentations of law and misrepresentations of fact".

(7) Silence

1–051 As a general rule silence by itself cannot found a claim in deceit, however morally wrong the party who chooses not to speak may be thought to be.[91] The vendor of a house who knows it is suffering from subsidence is not liable to the purchaser, notwithstanding that the vendor knows that the purchaser is ignorant of that fact and would be unlikely to purchase were he aware of it: *caveat emptor*.[92] However it has been said that in practice the line between misrepresentation and non-disclosure is often imperceptible[93] and there are a number of exceptions to this rule which go a long way to reducing its apparent width. Moreover, the court may find the existence of a representation by conduct even where no words are used.

(i) Duty to speak

1–052 It has long been the law that where a person has a duty of disclosure to the claimant and dishonestly fails to discharge that duty, then he may be liable in deceit.

> "[W]here there is a duty or an obligation to speak, and a man in breach of that duty or obligation holds his tongue and does not speak, and does not say the thing he was bound to say, if that was done with the intention of inducing the other party to act upon the belief that the reason why he did not speak was because he had nothing to say, I should be inclined myself to hold that that was fraud also."[94]

---

[91] See *Peek v Gurney* [1873] L.R. 6 HL 377, at 403, per Lord Cairns: "Mere non-disclosure of material facts would in my opinion form no ground for an action in the nature of an action for misrepresentation. There must, in my opinion, be some active misstatement of fact, or at all events, such a partial and fragmentary statement of fact, as that the withholding of that which is not stated makes that which is stated absolutely false." See also *Bradford Third Equitable Benefit Building Society v Borders* [1941] 2 All E.R. 205, at 211, per Lord Maugham; *J D Wetherspoon Ltd v Van den Berg & Co Ltd* [2007] EWHC 1044 (Ch); [2007] P.N.L.R. 28, at [17], per Lewison J.

[92] Though see *Wood v Balfour* [2011] NSWCA 382, an Australian decision which seems to state the opposite: this is not the law in England, although see below under "Representation by Conduct". The law in England remains as stated by Lord Campbell LC in *Walters v Morgan* (1861) 3 De G F&J 718, at 723–724: "There being no fiduciary relation between vendor and purchaser in the negotiation, the purchaser is not bound to disclose any fact exclusively within his knowledge which might reasonably be expected to influence the price of the subject to be sold. Simple reticence does not amount to legal fraud, however it may be viewed by moralists. But a single word, or (I may add) a nod or a wink, or a shake of the head, or a smile from the purchaser intended to induce the vendor to believe the existence of a non-existing fact, which might influence the price of the subject to be sold, would be sufficient ground for a Court of Equity to refuse a decree for a specific performance of the agreement." Although these dicta were stated in the context of a claim for specific performance they are of equal application to a claim in deceit. The passage quoted shows how fine the line is between non-actionable silence and actionable misrepresentation.

[93] *Pan Atlantic Insurance Co Ltd v Pine Top Insurance Co Ltd* [1995] 1 A.C. 501, at 549, per Lord Mustill.

[94] *Brownlie v Campbell* (1880) 5 App Cas. 925, at 950, per Lord Blackburn. Quoted with approval by Lord Hoffmann in *HIH Casualty & General Insurance Ltd v Chase Manhattan Bank*, above, at [72].

The existence of such a duty must be founded upon some prior fiduciary, or quasi-fiduciary, relationship[95]: the mere fact of the dishonesty does not create the duty of disclosure.[96] So in *Conlon v Simms*[97] it was held that a person who was negotiating with others the entry into a prospective partnership was under such a duty and so his failure to disclose certain facts concerning his prior dishonest behaviour was itself a deceit giving rise to liability in damages on the basis that had the claimants known of the prior behaviour they would not have concluded the partnership contract.[98] "Non-disclosure where there is a duty to disclose is tantamount to an implied representation that there is nothing relevant to disclose."[99] Similarly, in *J D Wetherspoon Ltd v Van den Berg & Co Ltd*[100] the court held that an action in deceit could in principle lie where a fiduciary had an obligation to disclose certain facts to his principal and dishonestly failed to do so.[101]

A duty to speak will also arise where (irrespective of the nature of the relationship **1–053** between representor and representee) a representation has been made which was true, or honestly believed to be true, at the time when made, but which the representor subsequently discovers to be false before it is acted upon. If the representation is treated as being a continuing one (as it usually will be), the representor will be under a duty to correct it and will be liable in deceit if he consciously refrains from doing so.[102]

(ii) Representation by conduct

An actionable representation may be held to have been made even though it **1–054** involved no words, written or spoken. By his conduct a defendant may be held to have represented a fact to the claimant, for doing which he may be liable in deceit if the other elements of the tort can be proven.

---

[95] Although contracts for insurance impose a duty of disclosure upon the prospective assured, a dishonest breach of that duty does not appear to ground a claim in deceit: see *Banque Keyser Ullmann SA v Skandia (UK) Insurance Co Ltd* [1990] 1 Q.B. 665.

[96] It has been suggested that where a person knowingly makes or circulates dangerous chattels he may be liable in deceit: *Hamble Fisheries Ltd v L Gardner & Sons Ltd* [1999] 2 Lloyd's Rep. 1, at 9, per Tuckey LJ. This proposition is doubted in Jones, Dugdale and Simpson, *Clerk & Lindsell on Torts* (2014), para.18–17.

[97] [2006] EWCA (Civ) 1749; [2008] 1 W.L.R. 484, at [127]–[130], per Jonathan Parker LJ, upholding (in this respect) the decision of Lawrence Collins J, at [2006] EWHC 401 (Ch); [2006] 2 All E.R. 1024, at [193]–[202], a judgment which repays close reading. The decisions are founded upon the House of Lords' judgment in *Bell v Lever Brothers Ltd* [1932] A.C. 161, at 227, per Lord Atkin. In particular the Court of Appeal in *Conlon* confirmed, at [130], that "where the breach of the duty of disclosure is fraudulent, a party to whom the duty is owed who suffers loss by reason of the breach may recover damages for that loss in the tort of deceit."

[98] If the non-disclosure is not dishonest then the only remedy will be rescission of the contract which was entered into.

[99] *J D Wetherspoon Ltd v Van den Berg & Co Ltd* [2006] EWCA Civ 1749; [2008] 1 W.L.R. 484, at [130], per Jonathan Parker LJ.

[100] [2007] EWHC 1044 (Ch); [2007] P.N.L.R. 28.

[101] See also *JSC BTA Bank v Ablyazov* [2013] EWHC 510 (Comm) for another example: at [170], per Teare J.

[102] See para.1–067 below.

1–055   A simple example is *Gordon v Selico*,[103] where the defendant was found liable in deceit where he had deliberately covered up active patches of dry rot in a flat which was for sale: the concealment was held to be a knowingly false representation that the flat did not suffer from dry rot. Another simple example is where a party orders goods or services (such as a meal in a restaurant): generally, he will thereby be taken to represent that he intends and is able to pay for them.[104] Similarly, a person who uses a credit card is generally understood to represent by doing so that he has authority to use the card to pay for goods.[105] And where a company pledged a necklace which it did not own as security for a loan, it was held to have represented by its conduct that it did own the necklace.[106]

1–056   In more complex factual scenarios representations may likewise be deduced from the defendant's conduct. So in *Lindsay v O'Loughnane*[107] the defendant foreign exchange dealer was held, by its conduct in accepting the claimant's order, to have represented that his company was trading properly and legitimately in the sense that the business was not insolvent and that funds paid by the claimant would be held on trust in accordance with the Terms and Conditions until paid out to purchase foreign exchange on behalf of the claimant. Another example is *Spice Girls Ltd v Aprilia World Service BV*,[108] in which the approving by a pop group of certain promotional material featuring all five of the then members, the participation by all of them in photoshoots and the provision of a draft agreement referring to the group as "currently comprising" the five of them were all held, in the overall context of the negotiation of a sponsorship agreement for the future use of such materials, to involve a repeated representation that they did not know, and had no reasonable ground to believe, that any member intended to leave the group during the term of the intended agreement.[109]

1–057   Finally, in a recent case concerning the alleged manipulation of LIBOR interest rates in connection with certain swap transactions, the Court of Appeal held (overruling the first instance judge on this point) that in the context of lengthy discussions between a bank and a customer regarding, and through its conduct in

---

[103] *Gordon v Selico* (1986) 18 H.L.R. 219.

[104] *DPP v Ray* [1974] A.C. 370. See also *In Re Shackleton* (1875) L.R. 10 Ch. App. 446 and *In Re Eastgate* [1905] 1 K.B. 465, in which it was held that a buyer, who took delivery of goods from a seller, represented that he was able and willing to pay for them. All three of these cases were referred to with apparent approval by the Court of Appeal in its recent decision in *Property Alliance Group Ltd v The Royal Bank of Scotland* [2018] EWCA Civ 355 (at [126], per Etherton LJ), considered further below. However, compare the decision in *Contex Drouzhba v Wiseman*, above, where the representation that the company had the capacity to make payment was expressly said to have derived *not* simply from the presentation of the signed contract for the goods concerned, but from an express term as to payment contained in the contract itself.

[105] *R v Lambie* [1982] A.C. 449.

[106] *Advanced Industrial Technology v Bond Street Jewellers* Ltd [2006] EWCA Civ 923. Similarly in *Richardson v Silvester* (1873) L.R. IX Q.B. 34 an advertisement placed in the press offering a farm house to let, when the advertiser had no authority to let it, was held to give rise to an action in deceit founded on the implied representation that he did have authority.

[107] *Lindsay v O'Loughnane* [2010] EWHC 529; [2012] BCC 153. The case also involved implied representations based on email communications; but these were said to confirm representations already to be derived from the representor's conduct in accepting the orders.

[108] *Spice Girls Ltd v Aprilia World Service BV* [2002] EWCA Civ 15; [2002] E.M.L.R. 27.

[109] See [54]–[63], per Sir Andrew Morritt V-C.

proposing, swap transactions which were referenced to a LIBOR rate, the bank had made a representation that it was not manipulating and did not intend to manipulate that LIBOR rate.[110]

However in cases of representation by conduct, there may be greater difficulty in identifying the fact represented, and the required dishonest intention to mislead by representing that fact, than in cases of representations by written or spoken words.

1–058

(iii)   Implied representations

Closely related to representations by conduct are implied representations.[111] As has been seen above, a statement which might not otherwise be actionable because it concerns a matter of opinion or future events can amount to an actionable representation on the basis that implicit in it, but unstated, is an assertion of present fact (be it as to the representor's state of mind, as to the grounds for his stated opinion or belief, or as to his willingness to carry out his stated intention). Similarly, we have already noted that an express statement which is on its face literally true may nevertheless involve a misrepresentation because of relevant matters which the representor omits to mention.[112] In such a case there is implicit in what is said a representation as to the matters omitted (or perhaps an implicit representation that no relevant matters have been omitted), which is false.

1–059

The law will thus not shrink from imposing liability where a representor is silent on something *if* there can be implied, from what he has said, a representation which is false. Whether or not an implied representation has been made will inevitably involve a fact sensitive question. "Context is everything".[113] It is difficult, and perhaps dangerous, to attempt to formulate a clear statement of the principle and the relevant proposition is best understood by reference to decided examples, which provide ample evidence of the realism and flexibility of the law in this area:

1–060

---

[110] *Property Alliance Group*, above. This decision appears to have been based at least in part on the notion that a party to a transaction such as the swap transactions in that case needs to be certain of its counterparty's honesty at the time the contract is made (see [125] and [141], per Etherton LJ). It may be questioned whether such reasoning elides the distinction between a representation claim and one based upon a duty to speak (see para.1–052 above). Certainly, if the decision was intended to indicate, or were read as indicating, that a counterparty to any transaction (or even any financial transaction such as a swap) makes a representation as to its honesty at the time the transaction is entered into, its consequences would, it is suggested, be far-reaching.

[111] The two are often elided and the principles by which representations are derived from conduct and by way of implication from what is said are similar; but distinguishing between them can be important, at least where the representation is as to the credit of a third party and Lord Tenterden's Act (which requires such a representation to be in writing and signed) comes into play, as was the case in *Lindsay v O'Loughnane*.

[112] The principle has an old vintage: in *Oakes v Turquand* (1867) L.R. 2 HL 325, Lord Chelmsford said, at 342–343: " ... it is said that everything that is stated in the prospectus is literally true, and so it is; but the objection to it is, not that it does not state the truth as far as it goes, but that it conceals most material facts with which the public ought to have been made acquainted, the very concealment of which gives to the truth which is told the character of falsehood."

[113] *AIC Ltd v ITS Testing Services Ltd* [2006] EWCA Civ 1601, above, at [252], per Rix LJ.

(1)   So where the owner of an antique business represented to a potential purchaser that the business "enjoyed an impeccable reputation", while that representation was true, it nevertheless arguably carried with it an implied representation that there were no facts known to the owner which rendered that reputation liable to be destroyed, which representation was said to be false because it was alleged that the owners had been engaging in a systematic fraud.[114]

(2)   Where a shop assistant informed a customer that the terms printed on a receipt which she was asked to sign exempted the shop from liability for certain specified sorts of damage to her property, but failed to mention that it also exempted liability for other damage, there was an implicit misrepresentation (albeit innocent) that the exemption did not extend beyond the matters identified, which prevented the shop from relying on it.[115]

(3)   Where a director of a company signed a contract on behalf of the company which contained a promise to pay for goods to be ordered in the future he was taken to have impliedly represented that the company had the financial capacity to pay for the goods to be ordered thereafter.[116]

(4)   Similarly, where a director sent an email and trade note confirming that a foreign exchange trade had been executed in accordance with the claimant's instruction, he was held to have impliedly represented that the company of which he was a director was carrying on its foreign exchange trading properly and legitimately.[117]

(5)   Where a solicitor represented that he knew of no restrictive covenants affecting certain land he impliedly represented that he had investigated the deeds.[118]

(6)   Where (in addition to and in the context of the conduct identified in the preceding section) a pop group sent a fax stating that they were "committed" to various promotional activities which were the subject of a proposed sponsorship contract, they thereby impliedly represented that they did not know, and had no reasonable ground to believe, that any member intended to leave the group during the term of the intended contract.[119]

(7)   Where a director of a company presented the accounts to a prospective purchaser without informing it that the business was being run in a

---

[114] *Mellor v Patridge* [2013] EWCA (Civ) 477. The point was argued on an attempted strike out of the Particulars of Claim. Lewison LJ commented, at [17]: "a representation which is literally true may nevertheless be a misrepresentation if relevant facts are concealed."

[115] *Curtis v Chemical Cleaning and Dyeing Co* [1951] 1 K.B. 805.

[116] *Contex Drouzhba v Wiseman*, above. As noted above, the implications of this decision are far-reaching. As also noted above, the Court of Appeal was clear that this was a case of an implied representation (implied from the terms of the company's contract) rather than a representation simply by conduct (the presentation of the signed contract), which was important because it meant that the requirements of Lord Tenterden's Act were met (see below, at para.1–073).

[117] *Lindsay v O'Loughnane*, above.

[118] *Nottingham Patent Brick & Tile Co v Butler* (1866) 16 Q.B.D. 778.

[119] *Spice Girls Ltd v Aprilia World Service BV*, above, at [27]–[29] and [57], per Sir Andrew Morritt V-C. In this respect the case was one of an implied representation: what was expressed was an assurance as to the future; but it implicitly contained a representation that the group did not presently know or have reason to believe that something would happen in the future that would be inconsistent with fulfilling the stated commitment (i.e. which might falsify the express assurance).

fundamentally dishonest way, which materially contributed to the profit-ability of the company, he was found to have made an implied (and false) representation that the profits had been made by lawful trading.[120]

(8) Where a bank, which had originally arranged a CDO transaction with Party A through an adviser, invited Party B to "intermediate" in the transaction (such that the bank contracted with Party B and Party B in turn contracted with Party A), the bank impliedly represented to Party B that it believed Party A's director and the adviser to be honest and did not have significant doubts as to their honesty, and that it did not know that the transaction opportunity which it was presenting to Party B was tainted by the bribery of Party A's director—essentially because no reputable or honest bank would have proposed such a transaction to another bank if it had not had such belief, or had had such doubts or knowledge.[121]

It has been said that in determining whether, and if so in what terms, an implied **1–061** representation has been made, the Court has to consider what a reasonable person would have inferred was being implicitly represented by the representor's words and conduct in their context.[122] This was said in the context of a claim under s.2(1) of the Misrepresentation Act 1967 and it is suggested that care needs to be taken when applying it in the context of a deceit claim. It may be right that when determining whether an implied representation has been made it will be necessary (or at least helpful) to ask whether a reasonable person in the position of the representee would have understood the implication. But it must not be forgotten that for an implied representation to give rise to liability in deceit, the *representor* would need to have appreciated the implication,[123] because of the requirement (considered in the next section) that he should know that he was making a representation and that it was untrue.[124]

---

[120] *Briess v Woolley* [1954] A.C. 333.

[121] *UBS AG v Kommunale Wasserwerke Leipzig GmbH* [2014] EWHC 3615 (Comm). In that case there was the additional factor that the bank had told Party B that its credit lines with Party A were full and that it had done due diligence on Party A. This was considered by Asplin J at first instance in *Property Alliance Group v The Royal Bank of Scotland* as having been significant to the judge's (Males J) reasoning and as therefore distinguishing *UBS* from a case where (as in *Property Alliance Group* itself) nothing express had been said by the bank and the alleged representations were said to arise from the mere presentation of the relevant swap transactions, albeit in their factual context (see [2016] EWHC 3342 (Ch), at [406]). However, the Court of Appeal disagreed, concluding that the additional factors above had not been not decisive in Males J's mind in the *UBS* case, and that the two cases were comparable in that both involved transactions which had been preceded by lengthy discussions (see [2018] EWCA Civ 355, at [133]).

[122] *IFE Fund SA v Goldman Sachs International* [2007] 1 Lloyd's Rep. 264, per Toulson J at [50]; and *Cassa di Risparmio della Repubblica di San Marino SpA v Barclays Bank Ltd* [2011] EWHC 484 (Comm), per Hamblen J at [215c]. See also *MCI WorldCom International Inc v Primus Telecommunications Inc* [2004] EWCA Civ 957, per Mance LJ at [30]: the question is to be "judged objectively according to the impact that whatever is said may be expected to have on a reasonable representee in the position and with the known characteristics of the actual representee;" but note the qualification: "The position in the case of a fraudulent representation may of course be different."

[123] Although note the obiter comments of the Court of Appeal in *Property Alliance Group*, above, at [158], considered further below.

[124] See para.1–085 below.

1–062   It has also been said that a "helpful test" in determining whether a representation should be implied is whether the representee would naturally assume that the true state of facts did not exist and that, had it existed, he would have been informed.[125] In the recent *Property Alliance Group* case[126] this test was considered and approved by the Court of Appeal, although with the express caveat that the test:

> "is not to water down the requirement that there must be clear words or conduct of the representor from which the relevant representation can be implied".[127]

It is suggested that this caveat is important and that assumption alone ought not to be enough (whether in the context of establishing that a representation was made at all or in the context of inducement, considered, at para.1–112 below).[128]

1–063   Care should be taken in pleading the implied representation(s). The more elaborate and widely drawn they are the less likely it will be held that such representations were made or that they were understood and relied upon by the representee.[129]

1–064   The implication of a representation as to the reliability or completeness of facts stated can be prevented by appropriate language qualifying the basis upon which those facts are put forward. So, for example, in *IFE Fund SA v Goldman Sachs International*[130] a Syndicate Information Memorandum inviting participation in a loan syndicate stated that the information in it had been derived from many sources and had not been verified independently, and that no responsibility for its accuracy was accepted. That was held to be effective to prevent the implication of

---

[125] *Geest Plc v Fyffes Plc* [1999] 1 All E.R. (Comm) 672, per Colman J at 683.

[126] Above, at [128]–[132].

[127] So, in that case, the Court of Appeal referred (at [133]) to lengthy discussions between the parties prior to the conclusion of the relevant swap transactions as having been significant in giving rise to the representations by the bank regarding the LIBOR rate referenced in those transactions (although it is noted that those prior discussions, as described in the relevant paragraphs of the first instance judgment, concerned the proposed swap transactions in general rather than the LIBOR rate specifically).

[128] On the distinction between an assumption made by the representee on the one hand and an understanding by the representee that he was being (implicitly) told something (via the representor's words or conduct) on the other, see *Raiffeisen*, above, at [113]–[121] and [127]–[128], per Christpoher Clarke J.

[129] Although the Courts have recently shown a somewhat surprising willingness to recast or simplify pleaded (allegedly fraudulent) representations on occasion: see e.g. *UBS AG v Kommunale* [2014] EWHC 3615 (Comm), at [747], per Males J; and *Property Alliance Group*, above, at [122]. Cf. the judicial comments in *The Kriti Palm*, above, at [404], per Buxton LJ, *Lindsay v O'Loughnane*, above, at [105], per Flaux J and *Foster v Action Aviation* [2013] EWHC 2439 (Comm), at [99], per Hamblen J.

[130] *IFE Fund SA v Goldman Sachs International* [2006] EWHC 2887 (Comm); [2007] 1 Lloyd's Rep. 264, upheld on appeal, at [2007] EWCA Civ 811; [2007] 2 Lloyd's Rep. 449. Since on its proper analysis such a provision went to the question of whether there was a representation at all, reliance on it was not precluded by s.3 of the Misrepresentation Act 1967 (as to which, see also *William Sindall Plc v Cambridgeshire CC* [1994] 1 W.L.R. 1016, per Hoffmann LJ at 1034). It is suggested that there is equally no public policy objection to relying on such language as bearing evidentially on the question of whether an implied representation was made (and whether it was intended to be relied upon).

representations (as alleged by the claimant) that the defendant was not aware of facts which showed that the statements made in the memorandum might be incorrect.

(8) Representations and Contractual Warranties

At its heart, whether express or implicit, an actionable representation involves the communication of information—the making of a statement of fact (understanding 'fact' for these purposes as set out above). For that reason, a warranty contained in a contract, even though it may concern a question of current or past fact, is not, without more, something on which a claim for misrepresentation (including deceit) can be based: it is a promise that something is the case, intended to give rise to a claim for breach of contract if it turns out that it is not the case, rather than a means by which information is imparted; and the act of concluding the contract is a communication only of the warrantor's assent to the terms of the warranty and his intent to be bound by it.[131]

1–065

A contractual warranty might, nevertheless, found a claim in deceit if, for example, the terms of the contract make it clear that the parties intended that it should operate as a representation as well as a warranty[132]; and where a warrantor can in all the circumstances be taken also to be expressing an opinion on the matter warranted, then there may well be the usual implied representation as to the grounds for that opinion.[133] The pre-contractual communication by one party to another of language that is intended to be included in a warranty might also, depending on the particular facts of the case, form the basis of an actionable representation in the terms of the draft warranty[134]; but for these purposes merely providing or offering to sign (or indeed signing) an execution copy of the contract containing the warranty is unlikely to suffice, since that involves only the communication of a willingness to give the intended warranty, not a separate statement of fact in the terms of the warranty.[135]

1–066

(9) Continuing Representations

It is well established that, where a representation of present fact is made (i.e. a representation capable of founding a claim in deceit), then, at least where it is made in the context of a contractual negotiation, or something akin to a contractual negotiation, it will generally be treated by the law as a continuing representation until it is acted upon to the representee's detriment (generally by

1–067

---

[131] *Sycamore Bidco Ltd v Breslin* [2012] EWHC 3443 (Ch), per Mann J at [200]–[211], declining to follow the earlier decision of Arnold J to the contrary in *Invertec Ltd v De Mol Holding BV* [2009] EWHC 2471 (Ch). See also *Idemitsu Kosan Co Ltd v Sumitomo Corp* [2016] EWHC 1909 (Comm), considering both decisions and preferring that in *Sycamore*.

[132] See *Bikam OOD, Central Investment Group SA v Adria Cable S.a.r.l.* [2012] EWHC 621 (Comm).

[133] *Avrora Fine Arts Investment Ltd v Christie, Manson & Woods Ltd* [2012] EWHC 2198 (Ch); [2012] P.N.L.R. 35, at [132]–[134], per Newey J.

[134] *Eurovideo Bildprogramm Gmbh v Pulse Entertainment Ltd* [2002] EWCA Civ 1235.

[135] *Idemitsu*, above, at [28]–[31], per Andrew Baker QC.

the entry into the contract) and a cause of action arises.[136] If there follows an interval of time before it is acted upon, the representation is deemed to be repeated throughout the interval until it is acted upon, unless the representor withdraws or modifies it, or its falsity otherwise becomes known to the representee.[137]

1–068   The significance of this principle was demonstrated in *Briess v Woolley*. The director of a company had been negotiating the potential sale of the shares in the company without the knowledge of the shareholders, and had made various fraudulent misrepresentations to a prospective purchaser. He then informed the shareholders of the interest of the prospective purchaser and they appointed him their agent to continue the negotiations. It was held that the shareholders were liable for the director's prior deceit, not because they had ratified it but because it was a continuing one and so was deemed to be made during the period of his agency.[138]

1–069   The converse can also be true: where a representation is made to (rather than by) an agent prior to commencement of his agency, and negotiations towards a contract continue once he has become an agent, the representation will be deemed to be repeated to him in that new capacity, thereby giving the principal (who may not have existed at the time of the original representation) a claim in respect of a contract entered into by it in reliance on the representation.[139]

1–070   But the continuing representation principle has other ramifications. If a representation, which was true when made, subsequently becomes false to the representor's knowledge, then the representor is bound to correct it and, if he fails to do so, he may be liable in deceit[140] but only if he has made a conscious

---

[136] So, if a representation is made for the purpose of an intended transaction it will be treated as continuing until the transaction is completed or abandoned or the representation ceases to be operative on the mind of the representee: *With v O'Flanagan* [1936] Ch. 575, at 585, per Lord Wright MR.

[137] *Briess v Woolley* [1954] A.C. 333, at 354, per Lord Turner, and 358, per Lord Cohen. The origin of this principle appears to be *Smith v Kay* (1859) 7 HLC 750, at 769, per Lord Cranworth.

[138] Per Lord Reid at 349: "The misrepresentations were continuing representations intended to induce the other party to make the contract, and when that party made the contract to his detriment, a cause of action arose, and in my opinion it arose against both the agent and the principal. The agent continued to be fraudulent after he was appointed. It was his duty, having made false representations, to correct them before the other party acted on them to his detriment, but he continued to conceal the true facts." See also per Lord Tucker at 353: "The tort of fraudulent misrepresentation is not complete when the representation is made. It becomes complete when the misrepresentation—not having been corrected in the meantime—is acted upon by the representee. Damage giving rise to a claim for damages may not follow or may not result until a later date, but once the misrepresentation is acted upon by the representee the tortious act is complete provided that the representation is false at that date."

[139] *Cramaso LLP v Ogilvie-Grant* [2014] UKSC 9; [2014] A.C. 1093.

[140] See *With v O'Flanagan* [1936] Ch. 575, at 586, per Romer LJ: "If A with a view to inducing B to enter into a contract makes a representation as to a material fact, then if at a later date and before the contract is actually entered into, owing to a change of circumstances, the representation then made would to the knowledge of A be untrue and B subsequently enters into the contract in ignorance of that change of circumstances and relying upon that representation, A cannot hold B to the bargain. There is ample authority for that statement and, indeed, I doubt myself whether any authority is necessary, it being, it seems to me, so obviously consistent with the plainest principles of equity." This was a misrepresentation case. See also *Brownlie v Campbell* (1880) 5 App Cas 925, at 950, per Lord Blackburn; and *Cramasco LLP v Ogilvie-Grant* [2014] UKSC 9; [2014] A.C. 1093. In such cases liability in deceit will depend upon an intentional decision to stay silent. See *Slough Estates Plc v*

decision not to disclose the change of facts to the representee: he must both know of the change and of its significance for the statement he has previously made.[141] Similarly where the representor believes the representation to be true when it is made but subsequently discovers that in fact the representation, when made, was false.

By contrast, because the falsity or otherwise of the representation is only relevant at the time that it is acted upon, it has been said that if a false representation becomes true before it is acted upon then it is not actionable.[142] It is suggested that this proposition is open to question. The fact that a person has made a fraudulent misrepresentation may itself be highly material to the representee's decision to proceed. It has been said that a representor who has practised deceit has a continuing duty to correct his prior falsehood.[143] Even if the untruth has subsequently been remedied the representee may not have wished to proceed because of the representor's dishonesty.

1–071

(10)   Representations made by Third Parties

Where a false statement is made by a third person and passed by the defendant on to the claimant representee, the defendant may adopt and approve the statement and so make it his own. In such a case there is no difficulty with treating the defendant as a representor.[144] Equally, the defendant, without adopting the statement, may nevertheless by passing it on implicitly make separate representations of his own, for example as to his belief in its accuracy and as to his not having any reason to believe that it might be false.[145] But it is also possible that the third person's statement is passed on simply as such, that is as material as to which the defendant has no knowledge or belief of his own, in which case no representation would be made by the defendant—provided, that is, that it is passed on fairly and accurately, and without, for example, omitting a material part that changes the import of what is passed on (in which case a fresh misrepresentation may be made).[146]

1–072

Welwyn-Hatfield DC [1996] 2 P.L.R. 50 and *Fitzroy-Robinson Ltd v Mentmore Towers Ltd* [2009] EWHC 1552 (TCC); [2009] B.L.R. 505. In the latter case architects had represented that a certain employee would be involved throughout the duration of a proposed project for the client. Subsequently, but before the contract was entered into, the employee resigned, which meant that he would only be involved in a small segment of the project. The architects intentionally failed to correct the representation, which had become untrue as a result of the resignation. They were held liable in deceit.

[141] *FoodCo UK LLP v Henry Boot Developments Ltd* [2010] EWHC 358 (Ch), at [213]–[215], per Lewison J.

[142] *Briess v Woolley* [1954] A.C. 333, at 354, per Lord Turner.

[143] *Briess v Woolley* [1954] A.C. 333, at 349, per Lord Reid.

[144] See e.g. *Bradford Third Equitable Benefit Building Society v Borders* [1941] 2 All E.R. 205 (HL), per Lord Maugham at 211 and Lord Wright at 220.

[145] The *IFE Fund SA* case, above, was an example of this (since the statements contained in the relevant memorandum did not originate with the defendant bank), albeit the implied representations contended for were rejected on the facts.

[146] *FoodCo UK LLP*, above, at [218], per Lewison J.

(11)   Representations as to Credit of Third Persons

1–073   A potential trap for the unwary claimant in a deceit claim is s.6 of the Statute of Frauds Amendment Act 1828 (generally known as Lord Tenterden's Act). This provides as follows:

> "No action shall be brought whereby to charge any person upon or by reason of any representation or assurance made or given concerning or relating to the character, conduct, credit, ability, trade, or dealings of any other person, to the intent or purpose that such other person may obtain credit, money, or goods upon, unless such representation or assurance be made in writing, signed by the party to be charged therewith."

1–074   Representations within the ambit of the section are thus only actionable if made in writing and signed by the defendant.

1–075   The section only applies to representations made fraudulently (despite its apparently broad terms).[147] It has obvious scope for relieving an otherwise undeserving fraudster of liability, and so the Courts have interpreted it narrowly. In particular, it has been emphasised that the mischief at which the section is directed, and in light of which it should be construed, is ensuring that the relevant representation is proved by evidence; it is not concerned with excusing fraudulent conduct.[148]

1–076   To be caught by the section the representation must be one made to the intent or purpose that another person may obtain money or goods upon credit.[149] A deceit practised in order that a payment obligation should be deferred or not enforced (for example, by dishonestly representing that the third party will soon be in a position to pay) does not therefore engage the protection afforded by the section.[150] The representation must also be as to "character, conduct, credit, ability, trade or dealings" of the would-be debtor, so far as relevant to the obtaining of credit; that is, it must concern the creditworthiness of the would-be debtor—his ability to satisfy his pecuniary obligations.[151]

1–077   A representation will satisfy the requirement of being "made in writing" if it can be implied from a document, just as much as if it is expressed in it; but not, it would appear, if it can be inferred only from conduct.[152]

---

[147] It may also apply to claims under s.2(1) of the Misrepresentation Act 1967, given that a defendant is only liable under that provision if he "would be liable to damage in respect thereof had the misrepresentation been made fraudulently": *UBAF Ltd v European American Banking Corp* [1984] Q.B. 713.

[148] *Contex Drouzhba Ltd v Wiseman*, above, at [16], per Waller LJ. The purpose of enacting the section was to stop claimants evading the provision of the Statute of Frauds, which prevented enforcement of a guarantee that was not in writing, by suing the would-be surety for fraudulent misrepresentation as to the debtor's credit instead: *Banbury v Bank of Montreal* [1918] A.C. 626, at 639, per Lord Finlay.

[149] As drafted the section is ungrammatical; but this is how it should be read: *Roder UK Ltd v Titan Marquees Ltd* [2011] EWCA Civ 1126; [2012] Q.B. 752, at [16], per Longmore LJ.

[150] *Roder UK Ltd v Titan Marquees Ltd*, above.

[151] See e.g. *Diamond v Bank of London & Montreal* [1979] Q.B. 333.

[152] *Contex Drouzhba Ltd v Wiseman*, above, at [10]–[12], per Waller LJ; *Lindsay v O'Loughnane*, above, at [107]–[108], per Flaux J.

The requirement for signed writing is satisfied if the representation is contained **1–078** in an email, provided (it would appear) that the email contains an electronic signature or is signed by typing the name of the sender after words such as "regards". The mere fact that the sender is identified by the email address from which the email is sent would not suffice for these purposes.[153] A representation is signed by a company (which is a "person" for the purposes of the section)[154] if it is signed by its duly authorised agent acting within the scope of his authority, since it is only by an agent that a company can sign at all[155]; but because a partnership does not have separate corporate personality, partners (like other individuals) will generally be entitled to the protection of the section unless they themselves have signed.[156] Where a representation is contained in a document (such as a contract) signed by a director on behalf of his company, if the circumstances are such that the director would otherwise be liable personally for deceit by making the relevant representation, his signature satisfies the requirements of the Act for the purposes of a claim in deceit against him personally, even though it was placed on the document as agent for the company.[157]

C.   KNOWLEDGE OR RECKLESSNESS

(1)   The Test

The next question is what state of mind must be shown on the part of the maker **1–079** of the representation in order to found liability in deceit. The classic statement of the law remains that of Lord Herschell in *Derry v Peek*,[158] which continues to be cited or referred to in the modern cases as representing the law:

> "First, in order to sustain an action in deceit, there must be proof of fraud and nothing short of that will suffice. Secondly, fraud is proved when it is shown that a false representation has been made (1) knowingly, (2) without belief in its truth, or (3) recklessly, careless whether it be true or false."[159]

The fundamental necessity of establishing this form of dishonesty cannot be **1–080** overstated: "the fraud proved must be actual fraud, a mens rea, an intention to deceive."[160] However negligent a person may be in making the statement, he

---

[153] *Pereira Fernandes v Mehta* [2006] EWHC 813 (Ch); [2006] 1 W.L.R. 1543; *Lindsay v O'Loughnane*, above, at [95], per Flaux J.
[154] *Hirst v West Riding Union Banking Co Ltd* [1901] 2 K.B. 560.
[155] *UBAF Ltd v European American Banking Corp*, above.
[156] *Williams v Mason* (1873) 28 LT 232; *Swift v Jewsbury and Goddard* L.R. 9 Q.B. 301.
[157] *Contex Drouzhba Ltd v Wiseman*, above, at [15]–[16], per Waller LJ.
[158] *Derry v Peek* (1889) 14 App Cas 337, at 374, per Lord Herschell.
[159] Lord Herschell continued as follows, at 374: "Although I have treated the second and third as distinct cases, I think the third is but an instance of the second, for one who makes a statement under such circumstances can have no real belief in the truth of what he states. To prevent a false statement being fraudulent, there must, I think, always be an honest belief in its truth. And this probably covers the whole ground, for one who knowingly alleges that which is false, has obviously no such honest belief ..."
[160] *Nocton v Lord Ashburton* [1914] A.C. 932, at 963, per Lord Dunedin.

cannot be liable in fraud if his belief is honest.[161] Mere carelessness or incompetence is not enough. In *Armstrong v Strain*[162] Devlin J explained the knowledge necessary to found a claim in deceit within Lord Herschell's category (1):

> "A man may be said to know a fact when once he has been told it and pigeon-holed it somewhere in his brain where it is more or less accessible in case of need. In another sense of the word a man knows a fact only when he is fully conscious of it. For an action of deceit there must be knowledge in the narrower sense; and conscious knowledge of falsity must always amount to wickedness and dishonesty. When Judges say, therefore, that wickedness and dishonesty must be present, they are not requiring a new ingredient for the tort of deceit so much as describing the sort of knowledge which is necessary."

So, where the representor represents a fact in circumstances where he at one stage knew information which falsified that fact, if he has forgotten that information when he makes the representation he cannot be liable in deceit.

1–081 As to category (3), recklessness is treated as a species of dishonest knowledge. In both cases there is an absence of belief in truth. It is for that reason that there is "proof of fraud" in the cases of both knowledge and recklessness. Although Lord Herschell uses the word "careless" in the passage from *Derry v Peek* quoted above, that is not to be equated with negligence: it refers to the representor not caring one way or the other whether the representation is false.[163]

1–082 It follows that if, however unreasonably, the defendant believes that the representation he is making is true, then he cannot be liable in deceit. The test of dishonesty is in this sense wholly subjective,[164] although of course as a matter of evidence the more unreasonable the defendant's stated belief the less likely it will be that the court will accept his evidence.

1–083 Complex questions arise concerning aggregation of knowledge and vicarious liability in relation to scenarios where liability is sought to be imposed upon principals for misrepresentations made by their agents. We consider those below in Section F.

---

[161] For example see *Niru Battery Manufacturing Co v Milestone Trading Ltd* [2003] EWCA Civ 1446; [2004] Q.B. 985. See also the observation of Rix LJ in *The Kriti Palm*, above, at [256] that: "As for the element of dishonesty, the leading cases are replete with statements of its vital importance and of warnings against watering down this ingredient into something akin to negligence, however gross."

[162] *Armstrong v Strain* [1951] 1 T.L.R. 856, at 871, per Devlin J.

[163] A point made by the Court of Appeal in *Angus v Clifford* [1891] 2 Ch. 449, at 471, per Bowen LJ: "Not caring, in that context, did not mean not taking care, it meant indifference to the truth, the moral obliquity of which consists in a wilful disregard of the importance of truth, and unless you keep it clear that that is the true meaning of the term, you are constantly in danger of confusing the evidence from which the inference of dishonesty in the mind is to be drawn—evidence which consists in a great many cases of gross want of caution—with the inference of fraud, or of dishonesty itself, which has to be drawn after you have weighed all the evidence."

[164] Subjective in that it depends upon what the defendant believed and not the reasonableness of that belief; it is of course not subjective in the sense of depending on the Defendant's own view as to what is or is not dishonest: *Ivey v Genting Casinos UK Ltd* [2017] UKSC 67; [2017] 3 W.L.R. 1212.

(2) Awareness of Representation

In a claim in deceit the requirement of dishonest knowledge, in the sense considered above, means that the representor should be aware that he is making the relevant representation, as well as that it is false in the relevant sense (as to which, see the following section). A person cannot make a fraudulent statement unless he is aware that he is making that statement,[165] or, as it was put in one case, "One cannot know that a representation is untrue unless one knows of the representation and knows that it is to be made or is being made".[166] The dishonest state of mind required for deceit is not simply knowledge of facts in the abstract, but knowledge with reference to the making of a representation.

1–084

So, in the case of an implied representation, even if the representee understands from an express representation that a further implied representation is being made and even if the court concludes that any reasonable person in the position of the representee would also have understood the representation that way, it would seem that if the representor did not himself understand that he was making the implied representation, then he cannot be liable in deceit.[167]

1–085

However, some doubt has recently been cast on this last point by the obiter comments of the Court of Appeal in *Property Alliance Group*.[168] As noted above, in that case the Court found that the defendant bank had, in the context of discussing and proposing swap transactions referenced to a LIBOR rate, made an implied representation that it was not manipulating and did not intend to manipulate that LIBOR rate. Although the Court of Appeal left open the question of whether that representation (which it found was not false) had been made fraudulently, it nonetheless commented that[169]:

1–086

"If we had concluded that the implied representation was false it would be necessary to decide how the normal rule, that, for a finding of fraud, the representor must have intended to make a representation he knew to be false (see *Akerhielm v De Mare* [1959] A.C. 789, at 804, per Lord Jenkins, *Gross v Lewis Hillman Ltd* [1970] Ch. 445, per Cross LJ and *Raiffeisen v RBS* [2011] 1 Lloyd's Rep. 123, at 338–340, per Christopher Clarke J) can apply to an implied representation when the implication is not present to the representor's mind.[170]. It may be the

---

[165] *Cassa di Risparmio della Repubblica di San Marino SpA v Barclays Bank Ltd* [2011] EWHC 484 (Comm); [2011] 1 C.L.C. 701, at [221], per Hamben J, citing *Goose v Wilson Sandford & Co* [2001] Lloyd's Rep. PN 189, at [41], per Morritt LJ.

[166] *Anglo-Scottish Beet Sugar Corp Ltd v Spalding Urban District Council* [1937] 2 K.B. 607, at 626, per Atkinson J.

[167] *Gross v Hillman Ltd* [1970] 1 Ch. 445; *Barton v County NatWest* [1999] Lloyd's Rep. Bank 408, at [32], per Morritt LJ; *Goose v Wilson Sandford & Co* above. It was suggested by Christopher Clarke J in the *Raiffeisen* case, above, at [222] that if a representor intended that what he said would be relied on, he must be taken to have intended that the representee should rely on the objective meaning of what he said, including any other representation implicit in it—even if he did not appreciate what the Court later holds to be the implications of what he said. This is no doubt true in the case of an innocent or statutory misrepresentation claim; but its application in a deceit claim must be doubtful, given the authorities just cited.

[168] Above.

[169] At [158].

[170] In that case the evidence from the bank's witnesses was that it had never occurred to them that when entering into the relevant swap transactions, the bank was making any representations about the LIBOR rate. That evidence was not challenged in cross-examination, which led to the rejection at first

case that an implied representation of this kind can never (or quite rarely) be fraudulent; on the other hand recent decisions about dishonesty, such as *Barlow Clowes International Ltd v Eurotrust International Ltd* [2005] UKPC 37; [2006] 1 W.L.R. 1476 and *Ivey v Genting Casinos UK Ltd* [2017] UKSC 67; [2017] 3 W.L.R. 1212, may be relevant. It is unnecessary for us to resolve that question in this case."

1–087   The above passage, while obiter, is notable in seemingly hinting at the possibility of a different rule in the case of implied, as opposed to express, representations, and, moreover, one which does not require the implication of the representation to have been "present to the representor's mind" in order for fraud to be established.[171] Such a distinction between the requirements for fraud in the case of express representations and on the other hand implied representations does not appear from prior authority (indeed two of the cases cited by the Court of Appeal as embodying the "normal rule" were cases involving implied representations) and would, it is suggested, be unsatisfactory. It may well be that it will often be difficult to establish fraud in the case of an implied representation (or a representation by conduct), but it will not be impossible[172] (and may even be relatively straightforward in certain well recognised categories of implied representation arising from express statements)[173]; and it should not be possible unless it is established that the representor was aware of the relevant implication.

---

instance of the claimant's case in fraud (see [2016] EWHC 3342 (Ch), at [485]), per Asplin J. On appeal, the claimant contended that (but the Court did not formally decide whether) it was sufficient that it had been put to the bank's witnesses (and they had accepted) that they had known that the bank was entering into LIBOR-referenced swap transactions with counterparties and that those counterparties would assume the LIBOR rate was not being manipulated.

[171] The view taken in this work is that the defendant's awareness of the representation (whether express or implicit) may be seen as either part of, or a separate requirement from, the requirement that the defendant must have intended to make a false representation on which the claimant would rely. The necessary intention is addressed in further detail below, but it is suggested that a party cannot have intended to make a false representation, or for the claimant to rely on that representation, if that party was not aware he was making that representation at all. It is noted that in some statements of the elements of the tort (such as that in *Eco 3 v Ludsin*, above, at [77]), per Jackson LJ, the requirement that the defendant knows that the representation was made (as well as that it was false and that of intention to induce) is not separately spelled out.

[172] An example of a case where a fraudulent representation was found to have been made by conduct is *Lindsay v O'Loughnane*, above, although it is observed that in that case there was no express analysis of whether the defendant knew the particular representation found to have been made by conduct was being *made* (as well as that it was false; see e.g. [108], per Flaux J). The same is true of *UBS AG v Kommunale*, above, where the requisite "intention to deceive" was found against the bank's employee without specific consideration being given to whether that employee knew that the bank was making the implied representations found to have been made by the Court (see e.g. [767]–[769], per Males J).

[173] For example, it would seem very difficult indeed for a party making an express statement of opinion or belief to resist the inference that he was aware that he was also making an implicit statement that he actually held that opinion or belief, or (where the party was a professional) that he had reasonable grounds for holding that opinion or belief (see *Goose v Wilson Sandford & Co*, above, at [38]–[41]).

(3)   Ambiguity and Subjective Meaning

The same analysis applies in respect of a representation which conveys meaning **1–088**
X (which is false) to the representee, but which the representor understands to
have meaning Y (which is not false). The representor must have understood not
only that he was making the representation but also that the representation had
the misleading sense alleged.[174] Thus, in order to establish liability in deceit, it is
necessary "to show that the representor intended his statement to be understood
by the representee in the sense in which it was false."[175]

As such, a representor is not liable if he genuinely understood the representation **1–089**
to have a meaning which was true (even if the representee understood it to have a
different meaning which was false). This proposition holds good however
unreasonable the representor's understanding may have been and however
reasonable it may have been for the representee to understand the representation
differently; and thus even in the case of a representation which cannot properly be
described as ambiguous (as to which, see below), in the sense that it has a clear
objective meaning, a representor who honestly understood the representation in
some different and true sense will not be liable in deceit.[176]

The representee must also show that he relied upon the representation in the sense **1–090**
in which it was in fact false.[177] Hence if the representee did not himself
understand the representation in the (false) sense intended by the representor then
there can be no liability, because there is no deception.[178]

These are rather nebulous concepts (although they derive from a simple premise, **1–091**
viz that at its core deceit involves deliberate misleading) and can be best
understood by example. The classic analysis is contained in the Privy Council's
decision in *Akerhielm v de Mare*.[179] There the defendant had represented (by
what was described as "representation (c)") in a circular seeking subscribers for
shares in a company that "one third of the share capital had already been
subscribed in Denmark." In fact some of the shares had been allotted to persons
resident in Kenya for services rendered in Denmark in connection with the
formation of the company. The judge held that, although it was objectively
untrue, the defendant representors honestly believed the truth of the statement in
the sense in which they understood it (that is, as including subscriptions for
services rendered in Denmark, and not just subscriptions by persons resident
there). But the Court of Appeal took a different view. In the Privy Council, Lord
Jenkins said, in what has become a classic statement of the law[180]:

---

[174] *Cassa di Risparmio della Repubblica di San Marino SpA v Barclays Bank Ltd*, above, at [221], per Hamblen J.

[175] *Goose v Wilson Sandford & Co*, above, at [41], per Morritt LJ, cited by Hamblen J in *Cassa di Risparmio della Repubblica di San Marino SpA v Barclays Bank Ltd*, above, at [221].

[176] Of course, as noted later, the unreasonableness of the representor's professed understanding will bear on how credible it is that he genuinely had it; and an unreasonable understanding, if honest, could still give rise to liability for negligent misstatement and/or statutory misrepresentation.

[177] *Smith v Chadwick* (1884) 9 App Cas. 187.

[178] *Arkwright v Newbold* (1881) 17 Ch. D. 301, at 324, per Cotton LJ.

[179] *Akerhielm v de Mare* [1959] A.C. 789.

[180] Which continues to be cited on a regular basis.

"...the Court of Appeal construed the language of representation (c) as they thought it should be construed according to the ordinary meaning of the words used, and having done so went on to hold that on the facts known to the defendants it was impossible that either of them could ever have believed the representation, as so construed, to be true. Their Lordships regard this as a wrong method of approach. The question is not whether the defendant in any given case honestly believed the representation to be true in the sense assigned to it by the court on an objective consideration of its truth or falsity, but whether he honestly believed the representation to be true in the sense in which he understood it albeit erroneously when it was made."[181]

1–092　　As noted above, this is an analysis of general application. A defendant cannot be held liable in deceit solely by reference to the objective meaning of the representation, or to its meaning as understood by the claimant. However, it is not a general licence to a defendant to rely upon his own idiosyncrasy to evade liability. The courts acknowledge that the meaning placed by the defendant on the representation made may be so far removed from the sense in which it would be understood by any reasonable person as to make it impossible to hold that the defendant honestly understood the representation to bear the meaning claimed by him and honestly believed it in that sense to be true.[182]

1–093　　As a result, in practice this analysis is likely to be of relevance primarily in the case of representations which are ambiguous and so capable of being interpreted in different ways. The fact that the representation is ambiguous does not preclude liability (the suggestion that a representation must be "unequivocal" to found a claim is thus misleading)[183]; but, in such a case, the requirement that the representor understood it to be false and intended the representee to rely upon its false meaning[184] (or, at least, that the representor deliberately used the ambiguity in the representation for the purpose of deceiving the representee)[185] will likely be of greater significance.

1–094　　The approach advocated in *Akerhielm v de Mare* has since been followed consistently by English courts.[186] A recent example is *Foster v Action Aviation*

---

[181] At 805. The Privy Council relied upon *Derry v Peek* (1889) 14 App. Cas. 337; *Angus v Clifford* [1891] 2 Ch. 449 and *Lees v Tod* (1882) 9 Rettie 807, at 854. It follows that Lord Halsbury's dictum in *Arnison v Smith* (1889) 41 Ch. D. 348, at 368 ("A deliberate statement was made and the defendants cannot be heard to say that they did not know the popular meaning of the words they used") is no longer good law, a point recognised in *Foster v Action Aviation Ltd* [2014] EWCA Civ 1368, at [32], per Longmore LJ.

[182] *Akerhielm v de Mare*, above, at 805, per Lord Jenkins. It is for a similar reason that, as noted above, it is suggested (as regards awareness of the representation) that a defendant ought not to be held liable in deceit simply by virtue of having been aware of the facts which the Court has held gave rise to the representation unless the defendant was himself aware that the representation was being made. Again, however, there may be cases in which a defendant's contention that he was not so aware is so implausible that it will be rejected by the Court, and the necessary fraudulent knowledge therefore found to be established.

[183] *The Kriti Palm*, above, at [253], per Rix LJ. If there was a fraud and a statement was intended to mislead, its ambiguity would not be a defence: *Low v Bouverie* [1891] 3 Ch. 82, at 113, per Kay LJ.

[184] *Bank of Tokyo-Mitsubishi UFJ, Ltd v Baskan Gida Sanayi VE Pazarlama A.S.* [2009] EWHC 1276 (Ch), at [1002], per Briggs J, citing *Angus v Clifford* [1891] 2 Ch. 449, at 466, per Lindley LJ.

[185] *The Kriti Palm*, above, at [253], per Rix LJ.

[186] See e.g. *Goose v Sandford*, above. An example of its application is *Gross v Hillman Ltd* [1970] Ch. 445, at 459, per Cross LJ. "Finally, I come to the representation that the company was a 'going concern,' which was made if one reads the two letters together, as I think one should. If James

Ltd,[187] in which the director of a vendor company represented to the prospective purchaser of an aircraft that it had never had an accident. In fact the aircraft had sustained an event, but which the director did not consider to be an accident. The result was that the claim in deceit against the director was dismissed because, on his subjective understanding of the word "accident", he had not known that he was telling a falsehood; on the other hand the claim in negligent misstatement against the company was upheld, because, on an objective construction, the event was properly to be interpreted as an accident and so the representation was, objectively, false.[188]

(4) Motive Irrelevant

Once the necessary state of mind has been established the motive of the defendant is an irrelevant enquiry. The representor's intentions in deceiving the representee may be innocuous. He may harbour no ill-feeling towards the representee and need not be actuated by any desire to benefit from the representee's deception.[189] Indeed he may wish actually to benefit the representee. On the other hand the existence of a motive is likely to be evidentially important in establishing a claim in deceit.[190] Most deceits are perpetrated with a view to generate direct commercial advantage.

1–095

> "By and large dishonest people are dishonest for a reason. They tend not be dishonest wilfully or just for fun. Establishing a motive for deceit or conspiracy, is not a legal requirement, but if a motive cannot be detected or plausibly suggested then wrongful intention (to tell a deliberate lie in order to deceive) is less likely."[191]

The question of motive is bound up with the element of the tort of deceit constituted by the defendant's intention, to which we now turn.

---

intended the letters to convey the impression that the company was a going concern, or was willing that a recipient should get that impression, clearly he was guilty of fraud, because he knew very well that it was not a going concern. But although that is, in my view, the impression that the letters read together would naturally create, James cannot be held guilty of fraud unless he intended or was willing that they should be read in that way. That appears clearly from *Angus v Clifford* [1891] 2 Ch. 449 and from the Privy Council decision of *Akerhielm v De Mare* [1959] A.C. 789, 805, 806."

[187] *Foster v Action Aviation Ltd* [2014] EWCA Civ 1368.

[188] Another example of the application of the principle is *Bonham-Carter v SITU Ventures Ltd* [2012] EWHC 3598 (Ch).

[189] *Derry v Peek*, above, at 365 and 374, per Lord Herschell; *Standard Chartered Bank v Pakistan National Shipping Corp (No.2)* [1999] EWCA Civ 3028; [2000] 1 Lloyd's Rep. 218, at 224, per Evans-Lombe J.

[190] See *Barings Plc v Coopers & Lybrand* [2002] EWHC 461 (Ch), at [62], per Evans-Lombe J: "Nevertheless, in trying to decide whether a person made a statement which he must have known to be false (or which satisfied the other tests set out above), it must be relevant to consider why he should have done so. A man is more likely knowingly to make a false statement if he has some reason for doing so."

[191] *Mortgage Agency Services Number One Ltd v Cripps Harries LLP* [2016] EWHC 2483 (Ch) per Mann J at [88]; followed in *Group Seven Ltd v Nasir* [2017] EWHC 2466 (Ch), per Morgan J, at [440]. In the *Mortgage Agency* case the allegedly dishonest representors stood to gain nothing from the alleged fraud; this was relevant in weighing the likelihood of their having an intention to deceive.

D. THE DEFENDANT'S INTENTION

(1) Introduction

1–096 The claimant representee must further prove that the defendant representor intended that he should act upon the false representation.[192] It has been said that it is of the essence of the claim in deceit that the defendant intended to deceive and a deception requires an intention that the representee should be induced to act on the basis of a false apprehension of the true position.[193] It will generally be impossible to adduce evidence directly bearing on this element of the cause of action, but the court will not be slow to infer such an intention if dishonesty, in the sense identified above, is proven.[194] However, care should be taken with the concept of "intention to deceive". It was recently confirmed by the Court of Appeal in *Eco 3 Capital Ltd v Ludsin Overseas Ltd*[195] that such an intention is not a freestanding or separate element of the tort of deceit: it is merely a compendious way of describing the two mental elements of the tort: i.e knowledge of falsity (as analysed above in Section C) and an intention that the claimant should rely upon the misrepresentation (as analysed in this Section).[196]

1–097 Indeed, where the representor makes a fraudulent misrepresentation, capable of founding a claim in deceit, there is, it appears, a rebuttable presumption that he intends the representee to rely upon it.[197] Where the representation is directly addressed by the claimant to the defendant then no doubt the application of this

---

[192] *Bradford Third Equitable Benefit Building Society v Borders* [1941] 2 All E.R. 205, at 211, per Lord Maugham.

[193] As a general proposition this is true; but note that there can be cases in which inducement is established even if the representee does not believe the representation to be true (and so is not under a misapprehension): see 1–132—1–133 below. For the same reason, some care needs to be taken when using the language of "reliance" upon the representation.

[194] But see *Standard Chartered Bank v Pakistan National Shipping Corp (No.2)* [1999] EWCA Civ 3028; [2000] 1 Lloyd's Rep. 218, at [27], per Evans LJ: "It is not necessary that the maker of the statement was 'dishonest' as that word in used in the criminal law. The relevant intention is that the false statement shall be acted upon by a person to whom it is addressed. If the false statement was made knowingly and that intention is proved, then the basis for liability for the tort of deceit is established. That conduct and state of mind was described as 'dishonest' in *Derry v Peek* and may also be called 'fraudulent'; but that is not necessarily using those words in their criminal sense."

[195] *Eco 3 Capital Ltd v Ludsin Overseas Ltd* [2013] EWCA Civ 413, at [78], per Jackson LJ.

[196] So it was said in *OMV Petrom SA v Glencore International AG* [2015] EWHC 666 (Comm), at [125], per Flaux J, that "it is no answer for the defendant to say: 'I did not intend to deceive', if the defendant knows that the representation is false and intends that the claimant should rely upon it." Similarly the fact that the defendant had no general "desire to defraud", or believed his conduct was justified, is irrelevant to his potential liability in deceit: *Brown Jenkinson & Co Ltd v Percy Dalton (London) Ltd* [1957] 2 Q.B. 621. Determining liability in deceit is not to be equated with some broad ethical enquiry into the defendant's conduct.

[197] *Goose v Wilson Sandford & Co*, above, at [47], per Morritt LJ: "If a fraudulent misrepresentation is found to have been made it will give rise to a rebuttable presumption of fact that the representor intended the representee to act in reliance on it. There is obvious sense in such a presumption for if the representor did not intend the representee to act on the faith of his statement why did he lie." *Pan Atlantic Insurance Co Ltd v Pine Top Insurance Co Ltd* [1995] 1 A.C. 501, at 542A, per Lord Mustill and *Barton v County NatWest Ltd* [1999] Ll.L.R.(Banking) 408, at 421, per Morritt LJ were cited in support of this proposition. It was followed in *Dadourian v Simms* [2006] EWHC 2973 (Ch); [2006] ArbLR 18, at [542], per Warren J.

presumption will present few difficulties; but where, as happens, the claimant is not the direct addressee of the representation, then the applicability (and logic) of this presumption is more doubtful. Hence it has been said that intention is usually a live issue only where it is said that the representation was not addressed to the claimant or to a class of persons of whom the claimant was one, or that it was not intended to be acted on for the purposes of the transaction into which the claimant entered (e.g. if the representation was in a prospectus and he purchased in the open market) or any transaction.[198]

Nonetheless, establishing this element of the cause of action is not always a formality. It serves a similar purpose to the pre-requisite of the existence of a duty of care in the law of negligence because it limits the actionability of a dishonest representation to those who are, broadly speaking, within its purview. **1–098**

The classic example of the case where, although a false representation was undoubtedly made, no claim in deceit was made out because of the absence of the required intent, is *Tackey v McBain*.[199] There the manager of an oil company falsely informed the chairman of the Shanghai Stock Exchange and various brokers that no information had been received concerning an oil find, whereas in fact a major find had been reported to him some days previously. That information, had it been known to the market, would have increased the share price of the company. The claimant sold his shares in the company at a consequent undervalue. The claim in deceit was nonetheless dismissed; the director wished by his falsehood to protect the company's confidential information rather than to mislead the claimant. Still less did he intend that the claimant should be induced by his falsehood into selling his shares. **1–099**

(2)   The Requisite Intention

(i)   The test

The requisite intention is proven not only where it is established that the defendant positively intends the claimant to act upon the misrepresentation, but also where he appreciates that it is likely that the claimant will so act. In the criminal law, the relevant mens rea in murder is established not only if there is a positive intention to kill or cause serious bodily harm, but also if the defendant appreciates that that result was a virtual certainty (barring some unforeseen intervention) as a result of the defendant's actions.[200] It was held in *Shinhan Bank Ltd v Sea Containers Ltd*[201] that a similar test of intention applies in the law of deceit, although it is suggested that the test should be modified such that the **1–100**

---

[198] *Raiffeisen Zentralbank Osterreich AG* [2010] EWHC 1392 (Comm); [2011] 1 Lloyd's Rep 123, at [226], per Christopher Clarke J.
[199] *Tackey v McBain* [1912] A.C. 186. Whilst the facts of this case vividly exemplify the relevant legal proposition, regrettably the reasoning of the judgment of the Privy Council is exiguous.
[200] *R v Nedrick* [1986] 1 W.L.R. 1025; *R v Woolin* [1999] 1 A.C. 82.
[201] [2000] 2 Lloyd's Rep. 406.

representor need only appreciate that it is likely that the claimant will act in reliance upon the representation, not that it is certain, or virtually certain, that he will so do.[202]

(ii)   What must the representor intend?

1–101   In order to found liability, must the representor intend (in the sense identified above) the representee to act in the specific way he in fact does? In other words must the requisite intention be narrower than simply a general intention that the representee should be deceived? In *Bradford Third Equitable Benefit Building Society v Borders*[203] it was said that the representor must have intended that the representation "should be acted on by the plaintiff... in the manner which resulted in damage to him". That dictum might suggest a narrower test of intention; but it seems contrary to the underpinnings of the law of deceit that a person guilty of a fraudulent misrepresentation should be able to evade liability by asserting that he intended the representee to act in specific manner X, rather than manner Y. It has since been clarified by the Court of Appeal in *Goose v Wilson Sandford & Co* that, at least in cases where a representation is made to the claimant, the representor need not intend that the claimant undertake the specific act which gives rise to the loss claimed in the action. "The more normal formulation is that the representor should intend to deceive the representee, with intent, that is to say, that it shall be acted upon by him."[204] This formulation has since been taken to represent the law.[205]

1–102   Nonetheless, although the law has yet to fully grapple with the issue, there must be limits on such a principle. Take the famous example enunciated by Lord Cairns in *Peek v Gurney*[206]:

> "I put the case of a person having built a house and desiring to sell it. He comes to me and wishes me to purchase it; he describes it as a highly advantageous purchase, and makes statements of fact to me with regard to the house which are untrue and are misrepresentations; but I decline to purchase, and our overtures come to an end. He subsequently sells it to some other person, upon what terms I know not. That other person completes the purchase, and that other person, desiring to raise money on mortgage, applies to me to lend him money. I lend him money upon a mortgage of the house. The facts stated to me originally turn out to be untrue, and are so material as that the house, not being as represented, becomes comparatively worthless. I then apply to the original vendor, remind him of what he told me, and complain to him that my money lent upon mortgage has been lost, and I commence an action against him for damages to recover my loss. I ask, could such an action be maintained? I know of no authority for it, and I am of opinion that an action of that kind would not lie."

---

[202] There is some suggestion that in a case of deceit it suffices that the circumstances were such that the representor "must have supposed" that inducement was likely: *Cullen v Thomson* (1862) 6 L.T. 870, at 874, per Lord Wensleydale; but it is not clear whether that means "ought to have supposed" (an objective test) or "did, it should be inferred, suppose" (a subjective one). It is suggested that the latter is more consistent with the cases considered in this section.

[203] *Bradford Third Equitable Benefit Building Society v Borders* [1941] 2 All E.R. 205, at 211, per Lord Maugham.

[204] *Goose v Wilson Sandford & Co*, above, at [48], per Morritt LJ.

[205] See *e.g. Mead v Babington* [2007] EWCA Civ 518, at [16], per Longmore LJ: "It was not the specific action of the claimant which had to be intended; it was only necessary that there should be an intention that the representation should be acted on."

[206] *Peek v Gurney* (1873) L.R. 6 HL 377, at 411–412, per Lord Cairns.

It is suggested that the law would not answer this question differently now. Thus while it is not necessary to establish that the representor intended that the representee should act in the specific way that he in fact did act in reliance on the representation, liability will not arise where the manner of the representee's reliance is wholly unforeseeable.[207]

1–103

(iii)   Representations to third parties passed on to the claimant

Where, however, the representation is made not to the claimant directly, but to a third party to be communicated to the claimant,[208] then it appears that the broader test of intent considered above has no application and the claimant must show a more specific intention on the part of the representor as regards the manner in which the claimant (as the ultimate representee) should act upon the representation.[209]

1–104

(3)   Representation Directed at the Claimant or a Class to which he Belongs

A representation need not be made directly by the defendant to the claimant for it to be actionable. It is clear that if a representor makes a false representation to X, intending or expecting that it will be passed to, and acted upon, by Y, then the representor may be liable to Y in deceit[210]; so too where the representor knows that a false representation to X has been passed on to Y and allows it to go uncorrected before contracting with Y.[211]

1–105

---

[207] Something along these lines appears to be suggested by Longmore LJ's rider in *Mead v Babington*, above, at [16], per Longmere LJ: "No doubt that will be subject to the rules on remoteness of damage." Consideration would need to be given to how such a limitation fits with the general principle that damages for deceit are not subject to the limitations that might otherwise apply in a tortious or contractual claim as to foreseeability and remoteness (see paras 21–035—21–042).

[208] As to which, see the following sub-section.

[209] *Goose v Wilson Sandford & Co*, above, at [49], per Morritt LJ. In *Peek v Gurney*, above, at 413, per Lord Cairns, the following dictum of Page-Wood VC in *Barry v Croskey* (1861) J&H 1, 23, was approved: "every man must be held responsible for the consequences of a false representation made by him to another, upon which a third person acts, and so acting, is injured or damnified, provided it appear that such false representation was made with the intent that it should be acted upon by such third person in the manner that occasions the injury or loss ... But to bring it within the principle, the injury, I apprehend, must be the immediate and not the remote consequence of the representation thus made. To render a man responsible for the consequences of a false representation made by him to another upon which a third person acts, and so acting is injured or damnified, it must appear that such false representation was made with the direct intent that it should be acted upon by such third person in the manner that occasions the injury or loss."

[210] See e.g. *Swift v Winterbotham* (1873) L.R. 8 Q.B. 244. Modern examples of liability being imposed in such circumstances are *Standard Chartered Bank v Pakistan National Shipping Corp (No 2)* [1998] 1 Lloyd's Rep. 684 and *OMV Petrom SA v Glencore International AG* [2015] EWHC 666 (Comm).

[211] *Pilmore v Hood* 132 E.R. 1042; (1838) 5 Bing. N.C. 97: the representee contracted with the fraudulent representor for the purchase of a public house but before completion passed on the contract to the plaintiff with the representor's consent. It was averred that the representor had notice that the representee had communicated the representation to the plaintiff prior to completion and took no steps

1–106   However, the courts have been concerned to ensure that, once made, a fraudulent misrepresentation is not actionable by whomsoever, however removed from the original purview of the representor, should come to rely upon it; and the requirement that the representor should intend that the claimant rely on his representation provides the necessary limiting consideration. So where a fraudulent misrepresentation was made by the defendant to X in relation to the financial strength of the tenant of freehold premises owned by the defendant, in reliance on which X contracted to purchase the premises, the plaintiff, who had, also in reliance on the misrepresentation, agreed with X to acquire the benefit of the contract, could not maintain an action in deceit against the defendant. Once the contract between X and the defendant was executed the representation was held to be "spent".[212] Similarly, plaintiffs who bought shares in the market in reliance on the terms of a fraudulent prospectus issued by the defendant promoters of a company could not succeed in their claim in deceit against the defendants, since the purpose of issuing a prospectus was to induce people to apply for shares, not to induce them to buy in the market shares already issued. The function of the prospectus was exhausted with the allotment, and the plaintiffs could not show that they came within the class of persons at which it was directed.[213]

1–107   Nonetheless, in order to be liable, the representor need not intend that the particular claimant who in fact subsequently relies upon the representation to his detriment should rely upon the representation; indeed there may be liability in deceit to a person whose existence the defendant representor is entirely unaware of. The representor need only intend, in the extended sense identified above, that a particular class of persons should rely upon the representation, provided that the claimant is within that class.[214] Such a class may be very large indeed—indeed it may comprise the public generally: so in *Richardson v Silvester*[215] the defendant placed an advertisement in a newspaper offering a farm for letting (whereas in fact he had no right to let the farm) and the claimant had, in reliance on the truth

---

to retract it. In those circumstances the plaintiff was held to have a cause of action notwithstanding that the representation had not been made to him and that the vendor had not authorised its transmission to him.

[212] *Gross v Hillman Ltd* [1970] Ch. 445, at 461 and 463, per Cross LJ. This case needs to treated carefully as founded upon a very specific fact-situation. Cross LJ himself entered a caveat, at 461, that if the defendant had repeated the misrepresentations to the claimant, or if it had known that X was proposing to assign the contract to the claimant and repeat to her the misrepresentations made by the defendant to it, then she would likely have had a claim. In that event the case would have been on all fours with *Pilmore v Hood*, above. For a discussion of both cases see *Clef Acquitaine SARL v Laporte Materials (Barrow) Ltd* [2001] Q.B. 488.

[213] *Peek v Gurney*, above, particularly per Lord Cairns at 411–413. Note that the result in the case would now be affected by s.90 of the Financial Services and Markets Act 2000, as to which see para.16–048 below; and even at common law the facts may be such that it can be concluded that statements made in documents like a prospectus were directed at purchasers in the secondary market: see *Taberna Europe CDO II Plc v Selskabet AF1.September 2008* [2015] EWHC 871 (Comm), at [115]–[118], per Eder J; though see the judgment of the Court of Appeal, at [2016] EWCA Civ 1262; [2017] 2 W.L.R. 803.

[214] *Bradford Third Equitable Benefit Building Society v Borders* [1941] 2 All E.R. 205, at 211, per Lord Maugham.

[215] *Richardson v Silvester* (1873) L.R. 9 Q.B. 34; reliance was placed upon Quain J's judgment, quoted above at fn.218 in *Swift v Winterbotham*, below.

of the advertisement, expended money in inspecting and valuing the property. Even though the defendant had no prior knowledge of the claimant or any other connection with him, he was potentially liable in deceit.[216]

Thus, to summarise the position: in addition to the case where a false representation is dishonestly made directly by the defendant to the claimant or his agent[217] (in which case the intent to induce the claimant to act on it can probably be presumed), a representation can also be actionable in a claim for deceit if it is made (a) to a third party, provided that the defendant intended or expected that it should be passed on to and relied upon by the claimant or his agent (which would include a case where he knew that it had been passed on), and (b) if it is directed at a class of persons to which the claimant belongs.[218]

1–108

(4)   Intention that Representation be Understood in Sense in which False

The representor must have intended his statement to be understood by the representee in the sense in which it was false, or was willing that he should do so.[219] This is just another way of stating the requirement that, to be liable in deceit, the representor must subjectively have appreciated that he was making a false representation and it has been discussed above in Section C.

1–109

(5)   Circumstances which Negative Defendant's Intention

It is necessary for the statement relied on to have the character of a statement upon which the representee was intended, and entitled, to rely.[220] In some cases, for example, the statement in question may have been accompanied by other statements by way of qualification or explanation which would indicate to a reasonable person that the putative representor was not assuming a responsibility for the accuracy or completeness of the statement or was saying that no reliance can be placed upon it. So, the defendant may qualify what might otherwise have been an outright statement of fact by saying that it is only a statement of belief,

1–110

---

[216] Numerous cases have grappled with the question whether the claimant was within the class of persons the defendant intended should act upon the representation: see for instance *Peek v Gurney*, above; *Gross v Hillman Ltd*, above.

[217] As noted below (para.1–124), a misrepresentation to an agent can be actionable in a claim by the principal for deceit if relied upon by the agent, even if the representation was not passed on to, and not separately acted on by, the principal.

[218] See *Swift v Winterbotham* (1873) L.R. 8 Q.B. 244, per Quain J at 253: "in order to enable a person injured by a false representation to sue for damages, it is not necessary that the representation should be made to the plaintiff directly; it is sufficient if the representation is made to a third person to be communicated to the plaintiff, or to be communicated to a class of persons of whom the plaintiff is one, or even if it is made to the public generally with a view to its being acted on, and the plaintiff as one of the public acts on it and suffers damage thereby."

[219] *Goose v Wilson Sandford & Co* [2001] 1 Lloyd's Rep. P.N. 189, at [41] and [42], per Morritt LJ, citing *Akerhielm v De Mare* [1959] A.C. 789.

[220] Indeed, this is often analysed as an aspect of the question of whether a statement is a representation at all; and the points noted here therefore overlap substantially with those made in section B above.

that it may not be accurate, that he has not verified its accuracy or completeness, or that it is not to be relied on. In such a case the necessary intention to found a claim in deceit might be negatived.[221]

1–111 It has already been observed that statements made in the course of negotiations and sales "puffs" or contentions are generally not actionable as fraudulent misrepresentations, because they do not have the necessary character of representations of fact.[222] Another way of analysing the same point is that they are generally not intended to be (and would not reasonably be understood to be intended to be) relied upon as statements of fact.

E. INDUCEMENT OF CLAIMANT

(1) Introduction

1–112 The burden is upon the claimant to establish that he was induced[223] to act by the relevant misrepresentation and (in a claim for damages in deceit) thereby sustained loss. This is a question of fact,[224] although, as explained below, the law rebuttably presumes inducement in certain circumstances, which are likely to be applicable in any case where other elements of the tort (and in particular dishonesty and an intention to induce) are made out.

(2) The Test of Inducement

1–113 In order to establish this element of the tort of deceit the claimant must show that the defendant's representation caused or contributed to him acting, or refraining from acting, in such a way that resulted in the loss which he claims in the action. There are a number of aspects of this seemingly simple proposition which require separate treatment.

(i) Representation need not be sole cause

1–114 In reality companies or individuals rarely take a particular step or embark upon a course of conduct as a result of a single external factor or inducement.[225] The law

---

[221] *Raiffeisen*, above, at [86], per Christopher Clarke J; and fn.69 above.

[222] See para.1–049 above.

[223] In what follows we refer interchangeably to the concepts of "inducement" and "reliance". We take the view that, at least so far as presently relevant, they are essentially the same thing, albeit viewed from different perspectives: the representor induces, the representee relies; but both involve essentially the same inquiry as to the causal connection between the representation and the way that the representee acts or refrains from acting.

[224] *Dadourian Group International Inc v Simms* [2009] EWCA Civ 169; [2009] 1 Lloyd's Rep. 601, at [99]–[101], per Arden LJ.

[225] See *JEB Fasteners v Marks Bloom & Co (A Firm)* [1983] 1 All E.R. 583, at 589, per Donaldson LJ.

recognises this and does not require the representation to be the sole cause of the reliance alleged, or even that it be the decisive cause.[226]

This is so even where the claimant is actuated in part by a mistake of his own making, and would not have acted but for that mistake. So in the leading case of *Edgington v Fitzmaurice*[227] the claimant invested money in debentures issued by a company formed to run a provision market in Regent Street. Five months later the company was wound up and he lost nearly all his money. He sued the directors who had issued the prospectus, alleging that they had fraudulently or recklessly represented that the debenture issue was to raise money for the expansion of the company's business ("develop the arrangements ... for the direct supply of cheap fish from the coast") when in fact it was to pay off pressing liabilities. The judge found the allegation proved and that the representation played a part in inducing the plaintiff to take the debentures. But another reason for his taking the debentures was that he thought, without any reasonable grounds, that the debentures were secured upon the company's land. Cotton LJ said[228] that this did not matter:

> "It is true that if he had not supposed he would have a charge he would not have taken the debentures; but if he also relied on the misstatement in the prospectus, his loss nonetheless resulted from that misstatement. It is not necessary to shew that the misstatement was the sole cause of his acting as he did. If he acted on that misstatement, though he was also influenced by an erroneous supposition, the defendants will still be liable."

As it was put by Lord Hoffmann in *Standard Chartered Bank Plc v Pakistan National Shipping*[229]:   **1–115**

> "...if a fraudulent representation is relied upon, in the sense that the claimant would not have parted with his money if he had known it was false, it does not matter that he also held some other negligent or irrational belief about another matter and, but for that belief, would not have parted with his money either. The law simply ignores the other reasons why he paid."

(ii)   Nature of the causal contribution required

To the above extent the law on inducement is clear. What is less clear is the level   **1–116**
of causal contribution that the misrepresentation needs to have made to the representee's decision, short of being the decisive cause, for a claim to lie.

On the one hand it has been said (with approval at Court of Appeal level) that the   **1–117**
misrepresentation must make a "real and substantial contribution" to the conduct alleged to constitute reliance,[230] and that (which appears to be the same thing) the

---

[226] *Edgington v Fitzmaurice* (1885) 29 Ch. D. 459; *Standard Charted Bank Plc v Pakistan National Shipping* [2002] UKHL 43; [2003] 1 A.C. 959, at [15], per Lord Hoffman; *Dadourian Group International Inc v Simms* [2009] EWCA Civ 169; [2009] 1 Lloyd's Rep. 601, at [99] and [101], per Arden LJ; *Raiffeisen Zentralbank Osterreich AG v Royal Bank of Scotland Plc* [2010] EWHC 1392 (Comm); [2011] 1 Lloyd's Rep. 123, per Christopher Clarke J, at [153].

[227] *Edgington v Fitzmaurice* (1885) 29 Ch. D. 459.

[228] *Edgington v Fitzmaurice* (1885) 29 Ch. D. 459, at 481.

[229] *Standard Charted Bank Plc v Pakistan National Shipping* [2002] UKHL 43; [2003] 1 A.C. 959, at [15].

[230] *Dadourian Group International Inc v Simms* [2009] EWCA Civ 169; [2009] 1 Lloyd's Rep. 601, at [99] and [101], per Arden LJ.

misrepresentation must have been an effective cause of that conduct in the "but for" sense.[231] In this context it has been said that this means that the claimant must establish that, unless the representation made to him, he would not have transacted at all, or would not have done so on the same terms; [232]; and that, short of this, the fact that the representation might have provided the claimant with comfort or encouragement in the course of action he subsequently embarks upon is insufficient.[233]

1–118   Against this, there is a body of authority which suggests that, in the case of a fraudulent misrepresentation (as opposed to a negligent or innocent one), all that is required is that the misrepresentation should have been "actively present to the mind of" the claimant when the contract (or other relevant act of reliance) was made,[234] or, to put it another way, that he *might* have acted differently had the misrepresentation not been made.[235] There are also a number of cases stressing the inappropriateness of engaging in counterfactual enquiries as to how the claimant would otherwise have acted, in circumstances where he has been lied to,

---

[231] See e.g. *Leni Gas & Oil Investments Ltd v Malta Oil Pty Ltd* [2014] EWHC 893 (Comm), at [16]–[19], per Males J, applying to a deceit claim the analysis of inducement in *Raiffeisen*, at [180]: "If [the claimant] would have entered into the relevant contract even if the representation had not been made, he has no valid complaint". In *Leni Gas & Oil Investments Ltd* it was said that "The relevant enquiry is whether the claimant would have entered into the contract if the representation had not been made at all and not whether it would have done so if a different representation (i.e. the truth) had been made to it". See also *Nash v Calthorpe* [1905] 2 Ch. 237 (claim in relation to a prospectus under s.38 of the Companies Act 1867).

[232] *Raiffeisen*, at [171], per Christopher Clarke J: "The authorities show that inducement is, in essence, a question of causation and that the misrepresentation must be an effective cause of the representee entering into the contract in the 'but for' sense. 'But for' causation means that unless the alleged cause (X) had come about the alleged result (Y) would not have occurred. In the present context that means showing that, unless the representee had had the representation made to him, he would not have contracted (or would not have done so on the same terms). If such causation is necessary in respect of a single misrepresentation, it must also be necessary in relation to an individual representation which is one of several."

[233] *Raiffeisen*, at [153], per Christoper Clarke J. See also *JEB Fasteners v Marks Bloom & Co (A Firm)* [1983] 1 All E.R. 583.

[234] *Edgington v Fitzmaurice* (1885) 29 Ch. D. 459, per Bowen LJ at 483; *Ross River Ltd v Cambridge City Football Club Ltd* [2007] EWHC 2115 (Ch), per Briggs J at [202] ("In cases of fraudulent misrepresentation a more rigorous rule is applied, sometimes described as being by way of deterrence…It is not enough for the representor to show that the representee would, even if the representation had not been made, still have entered the contract. It is sufficient for the representee to show that the misrepresentation was "actively present to his mind.") and [241]. See also *Barton v Armstrong* [1976] A.C. 104 (no inducement if a representation did not "affect his judgment"); and *Pan Atlantic Insurance v Pine Top Insurance* [1995] 1 A.C. 501, per Lord Goff at 517 (inducement established if "influence on [his] judgment").

[235] In *Raiffeisen* itself Christopher Clarke J recognised that this more limited requirement may well apply in a fraud case, but distinguished for these purposes the claim before him (which was based on a non-fraudulent misrepresentation): "I do not, however, regard that authority as compelling the conclusion that in a case where the representation is not shown to be fraudulent it is unnecessary to establish 'but for' causation" (at [198]). But it is not clear whether a distinction between a fraudulent and non-fraudulent misrepresentation in terms of the test for inducement is a legitimate one, given s.2(1) of the Misrepresentation Act 1967 and *Royscot Trust Ltd v Rogerson* [1991] 2 Q.B. 297.

or of weighing the relative importance of contributing causes.[236] As the Hon RK Handley has put it, writing extra-judicially:

> "The representor must have decided to make the misrepresentation because he or she judged that the truth or silence would not, or might not, serve their purposes or serve them so well. In doing so they fashioned an evidentiary weapon against themselves, and the court should not subject the victim to 'what if' inquiries which the representor was not prepared to risk at the time."[237]

Reconciling these differing approaches is by no means straightforward. It does at least appear reasonably clear that where *rescission* is sought for a fraudulent misrepresentation the law does not require it to be established that, but for the misrepresentation, the contract or other transaction would not have been entered into[238]; and that is consistent with the approach taken to rescission on other vitiating grounds. The question is whether the inducement requirement is more onerous for a claimant in a case where damages are sought (that is, where the claim is in the tort of deceit). Our tentative suggestion is that it is not: it would be more coherent, and more consistent with the older authorities, to hold that the inducement test is the same whether a fraudulent misrepresentation is relied on to found a right to rescind or a damages claim. Where concepts such as "but for" and effective causation properly come into play in the latter claim is, we would suggest, when assessing what if any loss has resulted. **1–119**

On any view, the misrepresentation must at least have operated on the mind of the representee (that is, had some appreciable effect on his decision or affected his judgment). As has been emphasised in a number of authorities, it is therefore a necessary pre-requisite for a claim in deceit (as part of what is required to show inducement)[239] that the claimant understood the representation to have been made: **1–120**

---

[236] See e.g. *Reynell v Sprye* 42 E.R. 710, at 728–729, per Cranworth LJ; *Smith v Kay* (1859) 7 HLC 750, at 759, per Lord Chelmsford ("Can it be permitted to a party who has practised a deception with a view to a particular end which has been attained by it, to speculate on what might have been the result if there had been a full communication of the facts?"); *Barton v Armstrong* [1976] A.C. 104, per Lord Cross at 118–119 (a case of rescission for duress, but which was reasoned by analogy to a case of fraudulent misrepresentation: "If it were established that Barton did not allow the representation to affect his judgment then he could not make it a ground for relief ... If on the other hand Barton relied on the misrepresentation Armstrong could not have defeated his claim to relief by showing that there were other more weighty causes which contributed to his decision ... for in this field the court does not allow an examination into the relative importance of contributing causes ..."); *Downs v Chappell* [1997] 1 W.L.R. 426, at 433, per Hobhouse LJ (a deceit case, where it was said that "The judge was wrong to ask how they [the representees] would have acted if they had been told the truth. They were never told the truth. They were told lies in order to induce them to enter into the contract.").

[237] *Causation in Misrepresentation*, 2015 L.Q.R. 277, at 284.

[238] See e.g. *UCB Corporate Services Ltd v Williams* [2002] EWCA Civ 555, at [85]–[90]; and D. O'Sullivan, S. Elliott and R. Zakrzewski, *The Law of Rescission*, 2nd edn (Oxford: OUP, 2015), para.4.104. *Reynell v Sprye* 42 E.R. 710; *Smith v Kay* (1859) 7 HLC 750 and *Barton v Armstrong* [1976] A.C. 104, referred to above, were also rescission cases. See also *BV Nederlandse Industrie Van Eiprodukten v Rembrandt Enterprises Inc* [2018] EWHC 1857 (Comm), at [99], per Teare J.

[239] Although in *Raiffeisen*, above, it was addressed as a separate, free-standing requirement; see [80(b)] and [113]–[121], per Christopher Clarke LJ.

"...a claimant must show that it understood that the representation alleged was being made to it. Without such an understanding, there can be no question of any reliance on the representation."[240]

This is a particularly important consideration in the case of implied representations, since it means that the representee must at least establish that he understood a representation to have been made in the sense contended for; otherwise it is difficult to see how any case of inducement could be made out.[241]

1–121 Further, for the purposes of the inquiry into inducement in this limited sense, it does appear to be legitimate to take into account evidence by the claimant to the effect that he would have acted differently had he known the *truth*:

"as has been frequently emphasised, analysis of misrepresentation, particularly in relation to materiality and inducement, requires a comparison to be carried out between the statement actually made, and the truth, rather than between the statement made and silence, i.e. no statement ..."[242]

However, that is not because such a counterfactual test is a necessary component of inducement; it is rather because if in fact the claimant would have acted in the same way even had he known the truth, it would be very difficult to argue that the representation influenced him at all.[243] But the converse is not true: even if it were to be established that the representee would have acted differently had he been told the truth, that would still leave open the possibility that he gave no

[240] *Leni Gas & Oil v Malta Oil*, above, at [15], per Males J. See also *Raiffeisen*, above, at [80(b)] and [87], per Christopher Clarke LJ; *Cassa di Risparmio della Repubblica di San Marino SpA v Barclays Bank Ltd*, above, at [224], per Hamblen J; *Brown v Innovatorone* [2012] EWHC 1321 (Comm), at [904]; *Foster v Action Aviation*, above, at [101] (in which Hamblen J noted the distinction between a case of misrepresentation and one of non-disclosure in this context).

[241] This was the reason for the rejection of the inducement element of the claimant's case at first instance in *Property Alliance Group Ltd v Royal Bank of Scotland Plc* [2016] EWHC 3342 (Ch), where Asplin J found (at [417]–[419]) that although the claimant's witnesses had assumed that the LIBOR rate in the relevant swap transactions would be set in a straightforward and proper manner, they had not understood the alleged representations about the LIBOR rate to have been made to them by the bank at the time the transactions were entered into. On appeal, the claimant conceded its lack of "active" understanding of the alleged representations but contended that a subconscious assumption (or a form of "passive" reliance) was sufficient in the case of implied representations. The Court of Appeal did not decide that issue, but it is suggested that (at least on the present state of the law) Asplin J's decision was correct and that assumption (as opposed to understanding) is insufficient. On this distinction in an inducement context, see in particular *Raiffeisen*, above, at [113]–[121] and [127]–[128], per Christopher Clarke J.

[242] *Ross River Ltd v Cambridge City Football Club Ltd* [2007] EWHC 2115 (Ch), at [243], per Briggs J. See also *Standard Chartered Bank v Pakistan National Shipping*, above, at [15], per Lord Hoffman (the passage quoted in [110] above); *Parabola Investments Ltd v Browallia Cal Ltd* [2009] EWHC 901 (Comm), at [105], per Flaux J; and *Hayward v Zurich Insurance Co Plc* [2016] UKSC 48; [2017] A.C. 142, at [36], per Lord Clarke.

[243] *Dadourian Group International Inc v Simms*, above, at [107], per Arden LJ.

thought to the alleged representation at the time or did not understand it to have been made,[244] which, as we have said, would be inconsistent with inducement in any sense.[245]

(iii) Reliance may take the form of inaction

In the vast majority of cases the claimant's case will be that he relied upon the relevant representation by taking a positive step, typically by entering into a contract under which he has sold or purchased property at an under—or overvalue. However actionable reliance may take the form of inaction, that is a conscious decision, induced by the misrepresentation, not to take a step which, if taken, would have avoided the loss claimed in the action.[246] Examples of such a claim in the decided cases are rare.[247] Similarly persistence in an existing course of conduct may constitute reliance sufficient to ground a claim in damages, on the basis that absent the fraudulent misrepresentation, or had the claimant known the truth, he would not have persisted in that course of action.[248]

1–122

(iv) Inducement through non-human agency

Whether the claimant is a company or an individual the causal link between representation and the action which gives rise to the loss will almost invariably be mediated in the mind of a human actor. Nonetheless this is not an essential precondition. It suffices if the inducement has occurred mechanically: for instance, if the claimant's computer systems are programmed to deal with orders placed with the claimant in a particular way (such as by giving a discount to the price) depending on the information provided by the prospective purchaser, and if the prospective purchaser deliberately provides false information with a view to obtaining the discount, without which the discount would not be available, then a claim in deceit should lie.[249]

1–123

---

[244] *Raiffeisen*, above, at [187], per Christopher Clarke J. For that reason it is suggested that the statement by Flaux J in *Parabola Investments Ltd v Browallia Cal Ltd*, above, at [106], that evidence from a claimant that he would have acted differently had he known the truth would "in itself" suffice to show inducement, goes too far.

[245] There may also be cases where the very fact of making the representation causes a factor which the representee would not otherwise have thought about to become important to him. In such a case, the relevant question may be whether the representee would have inquired further if told that the representation was not correct: see *Raiffeisen*, above, at [191], per Christopher Clarke J.

[246] See *Barton v County NatWest Ltd* [1999] Lloyd's Rep. Banking 408, per Morritt LJ at [55]: "…it is not essential that its effect should be to induce some positive action. The abstention from something bearing on the material interests of the plaintiff is enough."

[247] Though see *McBride v Christie's Australia Pty Ltd* [2014] NSWSC 1729.

[248] *Australian Steel & Mining Corp Pty Ltd v Corben* [1974] 2 N.S.W.L.R. 202; *Parabola Investments Ltd v Browallia Cal Ltd* [2009] EWHC 901 (Comm), at [106]–[107], per Flaux J.

[249] See *Renault UK Ltd v Fleetpro Technical Services* [2007] EWHC 2541; [2008] Bus L.R. D17, at [122], per Richard Seymour QC: "I see no objection in principle to holding that a fraudulent misrepresentation can be made to a machine acting on behalf of the claimant, rather than to an individual, if the machine is set up to process certain information in a particular way in which it would not process information about the material transaction if the correct information were given."

(v)   Inducement of agent

1–124   Furthermore, it is clear that where an agent acting on behalf of the principal has relied on the fraudulent misrepresentation by committing the principal in a particular way, and the principal has thereby suffered loss, the principal can recover in deceit even if the relevant representation was not actually passed to him.[250]

(vi)   Inducement by an ambiguous representation

1–125   As we have noted above (section C), to have a claim in deceit a representee must establish that he acted upon the representation in the sense in which it was false, that also being the sense in which the representor intended that he should act upon it.[251]

(vii)   Reasonableness of reliance and materiality

1–126   If the other elements of the tort are established, then the law will not inquire into the reasonableness or otherwise of the representee in relying upon the representor's fraudulent misrepresentation: a fraudster who dishonestly makes a representation with the intent that it should be acted upon cannot be heard to say that reliance upon it was unreasonable or unforeseeable.[252] Nonetheless the more objectively unreasonable or unforeseeable the representee's alleged reliance, the less likely it may be that (a) the representor harboured the necessary intention analysed in Section D above and (b) the representee actually was induced by the representation.

1–127   For similar reasons, the representor cannot evade liability by pointing to the representee's negligence in failing to establish the truth or his gullibility or folly in giving credence to the representation.[253]

1–128   It has been suggested that it is a necessary element of the tort of deceit that the misrepresentation should have been "material", in the sense of being such as was

---

[250] *OMV Petrom SA v Glencore International AG* [2015] EWHC 666 (Comm), at [139], per Flaux J. The judge cited H. Beale (ed), *Chitty on Contracts*, 31st edn (London: Sweet & Maxwell, 2012), para.6–031: "If a person asks an agent to find some property for him, and the agent, relying on the fraudulent inducements of the vendor, recommends the vendor's property, the buyer will be entitled to relief for misrepresentation even though the agent did not actually pass on the fraudulent statements."

[251] See para.1–109.

[252] *Smith v Kay* (1859) 7 H.L.C. 750.

[253] The authorities in support of these propositions are legion. Lord Cranworth in *Reynell v Sprye* (1852) 1 De G.M. & G 660, at 710 remarked that "[n]o man can complain that another had too implicitly relied on the truth of what he has himself stated." In *Nocton v Ashburton* [1914] A.C. 932, at 962 Lord Dunedin stated "No one is entitled to make a statement which on the face of it conveys a false impression and then excuse himself on the ground that the person to whom he made it had available the means of correction". In *Strover v Harrington* [1988] Ch. 390, at 410 Sir Nicolas Browne-Wilkinson V-C stated "... if it is once shown that a misrepresentation has been made, it is no answer for the representor to say that the representee has been negligent and could have found out the true facts if he had acted otherwise ...". See also *Redgrave v Hurd* (1881) 20 Ch. D. 1 and *Commissioner for New Towns v Cooper (Great Britain)* [1995] Ch 259.

likely to induce the representee to act on it.[254] We think the better view is that this is not a separate requirement, but simply something that bears on the question of whether there was in fact inducement in the sense considered above[255] (including in particular whether the presumption of inducement, which is mentioned below,[256] is raised).

(viii)   Knowledge of truth

Nonetheless if the defendant actually knows, or subsequently learns, the true position then inducement will not usually be made out. As it was put in a recent case,

    1–129

> "the essence of the tort of deceit is that the claimant was deceived, and if he knows that what he is being told is a lie, he is not deceived".[257]

The relevant date is the moment when reliance is actually placed on the representation by the claimant so as to cause loss or to irreversibly set the claimant on a course which will cause loss (typically the entry into a contract with the representor or some third party). Where a misrepresentation does not have a continuing effect, for example because it is withdrawn or lapses, or because the other party discovers the true state of affairs before the contract is concluded, it cannot induce the other party to enter into the contract and therefore cannot affect its validity or give rise to a remedy in damages for any loss resulting from its conclusion.[258] If the representor seeks to assert withdrawal of the representation then the court will look carefully as to whether its withdrawal or modification was sufficiently clear and unambiguous.[259]

    1–130

---

[254] E.g. in *Downs v Chappell*, above, per Hobhouse LJ at 433.

[255] See *Pan Atlantic Insurance v Pine Top Insurance* [1995] 1 A.C. 501, per Lord Mustill at 533; and *Barings Plc v Coopers & Lybrand* [2002] EWHC 461; [2002] P.N.L.R. 39, at [117], per Evans-Lombe J.

[256] At para.1–134.

[257] *Holyoake v Candy* [2017] EWHC 3397 (Ch), per Nugee J at [388].

[258] *Cramaso LLP v Ogilvie-Grant* [2014] A.C. 1093.

[259] See for instance *Arnison v Smith* (1889) 41 Ch. D. 348. In that case the claimants took debenture stock in a company in reliance upon statements in a prospectus issued by the directors that £200,000 of share capital had been subscribed, when it had in fact only been allotted in full paid-up shares to the contractor. After allotment, the directors sent to the allottees along with their share certificate a circular, which amid statements about other matters, stated the truth as to the matter misrepresented, but did not admit the misrepresentation, nor inform the allottees that they could retire and have their money returned. Lord Halsbury said at 370: "I will observe that assuming a fraud to have been committed it obviously lies on those who rely on a subsequent explanation to show that such explanation was quite clear. If the directors had repented of what they had done, and had been desirous of making reparation, they would have called the attention of the Plaintiffs to the fact that there was a serious error in the prospectus." This case was relied upon in the recent case of *Mortgage Express v Countrywide Surveyors Ltd* [2016] EWHC 224 (Ch) where the defendant had produced numerous fraudulent valuations. Before the claimant had relied upon them in making loans to the owners of the properties the subject of the valuations the defendant wrote stating that the valuations "may" have been overstated and requesting the "opportunity to review our advice before any further lending decisions are made", but did not clearly state that it suspected the valuer who had produced the valuations was guilty of fraud. The claimant succeeded. See also *Abu Dhabi Investment Co v H Clarkson* [2008] EWCA Civ 699.

1–131   The above principle does not apply to the knowledge of agents, which will not be imputed to the principal to defeat a claim in deceit, except where the agent's purported reliance itself founds the claim.[260]

1–132   Nevertheless, a fraudulent misrepresentation can (at least in an unusual case) induce a representee to act even in circumstances where the representee does not believe the representation to true. Inducement is a question of fact which goes to the issue of causation and, whilst belief in the truth of the representation is likely in most cases to be highly relevant to the question, such belief is not separately a necessary ingredient of the tort. As we have seen, what is required is that the representation should influence the mind of the claimant in the sense of impacting on the course he decides to take; but that need not be (although it usually will be) because he credits the representation as being true.

1–133   So, where a claimant in a personal injury claim made fraudulent statements as to the extent of his injuries, the fact that the insurers who settled the claim did not believe those statements to be true (and indeed were strongly of the view that they were likely to be false) did not prevent them from claiming to set aside a compromise agreement entered into with the claimant by reason of his deceit: their decision to settle was still influenced and so induced by the relevant representations, because they believed that (whatever their own views) those representations might be believed by a judge.[261] Indeed, this reasoning would tend to suggest that, in a suitable case, inducement could be established even if a representee knew (and not just suspected) a representation to be untrue.[262]

(3)   Presumption of Inducement

1–134   Where the defendant has made a fraudulent misrepresentation which he intended the claimant to act upon (in the sense analysed above in Section D), then, if the representation is of such a nature that it would be likely to play a part in the decision of a reasonable person to enter into a transaction then the law presumes

---

[260] See the classic decision of *Wells v Smith* [1914] 3 K.B. 722, at 725–726, per Scrutton J: "I am not aware of any case, and counsel did not refer me to one, where, when a man has made a statement untrue to his knowledge to induce another, whom he does not believe to know its untruth, to act upon it, and that other has acted upon it in ignorance and to his damage, the maker of the false representation has been allowed to protect himself by proving that an agent of the other knew of the untruth." (This principle was considered in the non-fraud case of *Strover v Harrington* [1988] 1 Ch. 390; it may be that in cases under the Misrepresentation Act 1967 a less rigorous rule pertains). Where the claimant is an individual this rule may be easy to apply; but where the claimant is a company, which can only have knowledge at all for the purpose of receiving the fraudulent misrepresentation and acting upon it via human agency, the analysis may be more difficult. What if the deceit is communicated to director A but the truth is subsequently learnt by director B?
[261] *Hayward v Zurich Insurance Co Plc* [2016] UKSC 48; [2017] A.C. 142. As explained by Nugee J in *Holyoake v Candy* [2017] EWHC 3397 (Ch), this was a case "where A lies to B and B is induced to act in a particular way because of the risk that A might tell the same lie to C and the effect that that might have on C". He went on to express the view that it was difficult to see how it could apply to a case where there was no "C" involved: at [393]. In the *Zurich* case "C" was of course the Court.
[262] [2016] UKSC 48; [2017] A.C. 142, at [44]–[45].

(rebuttably) that the claimant did in fact rely upon the representation.[263] In such a case the evidential burden will be shifted onto the representor to show, if he can, that in fact the representee was not influenced by the representation in the sense discussed above.[264] It has been suggested that in a fraud case the presumption of inducement is very difficult indeed to rebut.[265]

(4)   Inducement and Causation of Loss

Although no doubt closely related, and although it has repeatedly been said that **1–135** inducement is a question of causation, it is important to have in mind that inducement and the causation of loss are two different things: inducement is concerned with whether the representation led the claimant to act or refrain from acting (for example by entering into a transaction), causation is concerned with whether the losses for which the claimant seeks compensation flow directly from the tort.[266] Even if when looking at the inducement question it is not appropriate to engage in counterfactual "but for" enquiries, clearly such enquiries may well be appropriate and necessary when establishing whether and if so in what amount the claimant has suffered a compensatable loss. Questions of causation in this sense are considered elsewhere in this work.[267]

---

[263] *Pan Atlantic Insurance Co Ltd v Pine Top Insurance Ltd* [1995] 1 A.C. 501, at 542A, per Lord Mustill; *Barton v County NatWest Ltd* [1999] Lloyd's Rep. Banking 408, per Morritt LJ at [54]–[58]; *Dadourian Group International Inc v Simms* [2009] EWCA Civ 169, [2009] 1 Lloyd's Rep. 601, at [99] and [100]; *Ross River Ltd v Cambridge City Football Club Ltd* [2008] 1 All E.R. 1004, per Briggs J at [241].

[264] See *Dadourian Group International Inc v Simms*, above, at [99], per Arden LJ: "the presumption of inducement is rebutted by the representor showing that the misrepresentation did not play a real and substantial part in the representee's decision to enter into the transaction; the representor does not have to go so far as to show that the misrepresentation played no part at all ... the issue is to be decided by the court on a balance of probabilities on the whole of the evidence before it ...". But see paras 1–117—1–121 above for doubt as to whether that correctly describes the test of inducement in a fraudulent misrepresentation. In *Barton v County NatWest Ltd*, above, at [61], per Morritt LJ it was said that the rejection by the trial judge of the representees' evidence that they would have acted differently but for the representation still left the presumption in operation, unless it could affirmatively be established by the representor that the representation was not an inducement.

[265] *Hayward v Zurich Insurance Co Plc* [2016] UKSC 48; [2017] A.C. 142, at [37], per Lord Clarke, referring to *Sharland v Sharland* [2016] A.C. 871, per Lady Hale DPSC at [32]: "As was held in *Smith v Kay* (1859) 7 HL Cas 750, a party who has practised deception with a view to a particular end, which has been attained by it, cannot be allowed to deny its materiality." See also H. Beale (ed), *Chitty on Contracts*, 32nd edn (London: Sweet & Maxwell, 2017), para.7–040: "the inference [of inducement] is particularly strong where the misrepresentation was fraudulent". This principle appears to be confirmed in *BV Nederlandse Industrie Van Eiprodukten v Rembrandt Enterprises Inc* [2018] EWHC 1857 (Comm), at [104], per Teare J.

[266] See *Downs v Chappell* [1997] 1 W.L.R. 426, at 433E–433H, per Lord Hobhouse LJ; *UCB Corporate Services Ltd v Williams* [2002] EWCA Civ 555, at [89], per Jonathan Parker LJ; *Barings Plc v Coopers & Lybrand*, above, at [126]–[131], per Evans-Lombe J.

[267] See Ch.22.

F. THE LIABILITY OF PRINCIPALS AND AGENTS IN DECEIT

1–136   It is necessary to consider how the law of agency interacts with the law of deceit. There are three questions which call for examination: first (and most straightforwardly) whether an employee or agent can be personally liable in the tort of deceit when acting in his capacity as such; secondly, in what circumstances an employer or principal will be vicariously liable (even though personally innocent) for the deceit of his employee or agent; and thirdly, how the law grapples with the requirement of dishonest knowledge and an intent to deceive (as analysed elsewhere in this chapter) in an agency situation.

(1)   Liability of the Employee/Agent

1–137   Where an employee or agent makes a fraudulent misrepresentation in the course of his employment or on behalf of his principal, then it is clear that he may be personally liable, alongside his employer or principal. This is the case even where the fraudulent misrepresentation is made by a director on behalf of a company. This proposition may seem self-evident but it was rejected by the Court of Appeal in *Standard Chartered Bank v Pakistan National Shipping Corp*,[268] in which it was decided that where a person makes a fraudulent representation in his capacity as a director of a company then the company alone is liable. It required a further appeal to the House of Lords for the law to be correctly stated.[269] The agent is primarily liable; he has committed a tort irrespective of his capacity. His principal's liability is vicarious or secondary to that primary liability. The significance of this principle is that it allows a claimant to establish personal liability against an individual even where that individual is acting in his capacity as director of a company. Unlike in cases of negligent misstatements made in that capacity, the claimant's remedy is not confined to a claim against what may well be a company without assets.[270]

1–138   Nonetheless, it is open to question whether this principle applies to more junior employees. Where such a junior employee is instructed by a more senior member of staff to provide information to a third party, doubts have been raised as to whether the more junior employee could incur a personal liability as a "representor" in his own right.[271] It is respectfully suggested that these doubts are misplaced: the concern in that case appears to have been with whether it would be just to hold a junior employee liable on the basis that he lacked an honest belief in the truth of the information he was providing, since he may have been entirely reliant on and subservient to the person on whose instructions he acted. But the answer to that concern lies, it is suggested, in approaching with care the mental element of the tort (in the situation postulated, the junior employee may well not have been acting with a dishonest state of mind), rather than arbitrarily drawing the line for personal liability at a certain level of seniority. If, in this example, the

---

[268] *Standard Chartered Bank v Pakistan National Shipping Corp* [2000] EWCA Civ 230; [2001] Q.B. 167.
[269] *Standard Chartered Bank v Pakistan National Shipping Corp (Nos 2 and 4)* [2003] 1 A.C. 959.
[270] Compare *Williams v Natural Life Foods Ltd* [1998] 1 W.L.R. 830.
[271] *GE Commercial Finance Ltd v Gee* [2005] EWHC 2056 (QB); [2006] 1 Lloyd's Rep. 337.

junior employee had provided the information knowing full well that it was false, why, it may be asked, should his juniority be any answer to a claim that he is personally liable for deceit (along, no doubt, with the person on whose instructions he was acting)? Any perceived unfairness could be righted by the law of contribution in allocating responsibility as between the various people liable.

(2) Liability of the Employer/Principal

(i) The test: actual/apparent authority

Just as with any other tort, an employer may be vicariously liable for the deceit of his employee (or other agent), irrespective of the employer's own personal culpability, or lack of it. However the general principles of vicarious liability, as expounded in cases such as *Lister v Helsey Hall Ltd*[272] and *Dubai Aluminium Co Ltd v Salaam*,[273] are not directly applicable to claims in deceit. Because the tort of deceit is a tort involving reliance by the claimant upon the truth of a representation made by a person, the employer is not liable for his employee's representation unless made within his actual or ostensible authority. "[T]he essence of the employer's liability is reliance by the injured party on actual or ostensible authority."[274] Thus, at least in the (usual) case where the deceit is practised in connection with the entry into a contract or other transaction,[275] the usual test applicable to vicarious liability for torts—that is whether the tort was committed by the employee in the "course of employment"—is displaced in favour of an authority test that would more commonly be seen in a contract case.[276]

1–139

---

[272] *Lister v Helsey Hall Ltd* [2002] 1 A.C. 215.

[273] *Dubai Aluminium Co Ltd v Salaam* [2002] UKHL 48; [2003] 2 A.C. 366. These principles were recently affirmed and extended by the Supreme Court in *Mohamud v WM Morrison Supermarkets Plc* [2016] UKSC 11; [2016] A.C. 677 and *Cox v Ministry of Justice* [2016] UKSC 10; [2016] A.C. 660.

[274] *Armagas Ltd v Mundogas SA: The Ocean Frost* [1986] A.C. 717, at 782. The relevant authorities are *Uxbridge Permanent Benefit Building Society v Pickard* [1939] 2 K.B. 248 and *Lloyd v Grace, Smith & Co* [1910] A.C. 716. The Court of Appeal in *So v HSBC Bank Plc* [2009] EWCA Civ 296; [2009] 1 C.L.C. 503 declined to apply the reasoning in *Armagas* to claims in negligent mistatement, holding that the normal course of employment test applied. This reasoning may be inconsistent with the Privy Council decision of *Kooragang Investments Pty Ltd v Richardson & Wrench Ltd* and is doubted in P.G. Watts (ed), *Bowstead and Reynolds on Agency*, 21st edn (London: Sweet & Maxwell, 2017), para.8–180, albeit the Court of Appeal doubted the same proposition in an earlier edition of *Bowstead*.

[275] One reading of *The Ocean Frost* is that it relates solely to cases of representations as to the employee's authority to bind his principal. Hence in that case the dishonest employee had falsely represented to the claimant that he had authority to contract on his employer's behalf. It was held that the contract was not binding on the defendant employer because it had not been made within the scope of the employee's actual or ostensible authority; there is some obvious merit in a rule which prevents imposition of a liability denied in contract via the law of tort. Whether the broader reasoning in *The Ocean Frost* is compatible with the modern law of vicarious liability, which has been in a state of constant recent development, will have to await further consideration by the Supreme Court. One might detect an element of doubt as to the foundation of *The Ocean Frost* in Morgan J's judgment in *Group Seven Ltd v Nasir* [2017] EWHC 2466 (Ch) at [549].

[276] In *Barings Plc (In Liquidation) v Coopers & Lybrand* [2003] EWHC 1319 (Ch); [2003] P.N.L.R. 639 it was held at [700], per Evans-Lombe J, that the authority-based test was only applicable to

1–140   Moreover, there is support for the proposition that this applies to agents even if they are not employees and so may not fall within the vicarious liability rules for tort,[277] at least in cases where they represent their principals in connection with a transaction.[278] Thus it has been held that liability may be imposed on a vendor of land for the deceits of his estate agent and (in another case) of his solicitor, neither of whom could be described as servants or employees.[279]

1–141   Liability will be imposed on this basis regardless of whether the statement was made for the benefit of the employee or agent (or a third party), and not that of the employer or principal.[280] So, the fact that the employer or principal is as much an intended victim of the fraud as the third party who seeks to hold the employer or principal liable will not affect his potential liability.[281]

1–142   Because the foundation of the principal's vicarious liability is the claimant's reliance on his agent's ostensible (or actual) authority, if the claimant knows that the agent does not in fact have authority to make the deceitful representation, the principal cannot be liable.[282]

---

deceit in the "contractual context" and that, outside that context, the usual course of employment test applied, relying on *Credit Lyonnais Nederland NV v Export Credits Guarantee Department* [2000] 1 A.C. 486; but it is not clear that that point was in issue in *Credit Lyonnais* and this may be reading too much into the use of the expression "course of employment" in that case. Nonetheless, the decision in *Barings*, which supports the narrow reading of *The Ocean Frost* as proposed in the previous footnote, has much to recommend it. The ambit of *The Ocean Frost* outside deceit claims was discussed, but not decided, in *Frederick v Positive Solutions (Financial Services) Ltd* [2018] EWCA Civ 431, at [77], per Flaux LJ.

[277] However it should be recognised that the recent Supreme Court cases appear to propose a unified theory of vicarious liability, which is not dependent on the legal characterisation of the relationship between the primary wrongdoer and the person on whom it is sought to impose vicarious liability.

[278] *Colonial Mutual Life Assurance Society Ltd v Producers and Citizens Cooperative Co of Australia Ltd* (1931) 46 C.L.R. 41, per Dixon J (a defamation case).

[279] See Watts (ed), *Bowstead and Reynolds on Agency* (2017), para.8–182, and the cases cited there. In both *Kwei Tek Chao v British Traders and Shippers Ltd* [1954] 2 Q.B. 459 and *Bradford Third Benefit Building Society v Borders* [1941] 2 All E.R. it appears to have been considered that there could be vicarious liability for the deceit of an agent who was not a servant, if the authority test was satisfied, albeit it was negatived on the facts. For a recent case of vicarious liability being imposed for deceit see *Khakshouri v Jimenez* [2017] EWHC 3392 (QB). The judge, Green J, there stated this approach in relation to deceit cases (at [123]): "The basis on which a principal becomes responsible for the statements of an agent (who is neither an employee or partner stricto sensu) is, as P.G. Watts (ed), *Bowstead and Reynolds on Agency*, 20th edn (London: Sweet & Maxwell, 2014), observes at para.8–182, "*somewhat Ltd*" and is confined to cases where: "… the function entrusted is that of representing the person who requests his performance in a transaction with others, so that the very service to be performed consists in standing in his place and assuming to act in his right and not in an independent capacity.": cf *Colonial Mutual Life Assurance Society Ltd v Producers and Citizens Cooperative Co of Australia Ltd* (1931) 46 CLR. 41, per Dixon J at 48–49; *Kwei Tek Chao v British Traders* [1954] 2 Q.B. 459, at 470, per Devlin J; *The Litsion Pride* [1985] 1 Lloyd's Rep. 437, at 513–514, per Hirst J.

[280] See e.g. *Uxbridge Permanent Benefit Building Society v Pickard*, above (solicitor liable for fraud of his managing clerk inducing plaintiffs to lend money on the faith of false title documents, notwithstanding that the fraud was not perpetrated for the benefit of the solicitor).

[281] But see *Kwei Tek Chao v British Traders and Shippers Ltd*, above, rejecting the attribution of knowledge on the part of agents of a deceit to their principals, because the principals were the intended victims of the deceit.

[282] *J.J. Coughlan Ltd v Ruparelia* [2003] EWCA Civ 1057, at [31], per Dyson LJ.

Under normal principles, a principal can additionally be liable for his agent's **1–143** deceit if he has specifically instigated, authorised or ratified the act; but such liability is probably better analysed as being primary rather than vicarious,[283] the principal thereby making himself a joint tortfeasor with his agent (as indeed any third party could).

However, to found vicarious liability against the employer (or principal), *all* of **1–144** the acts which are said to constitute the tort of deceit must be ones which fall within the scope of the employer's vicarious liability (that is, within the course of employment, or, more accurately, within the scope of the employee's actual or ostensible authority). This principle was applied in *Credit Lyonnais Nederland NV v Export Credits Guarantee Department*.[284] In that case the employee of the defendant had acted as an accessory to a fraudster (by authorising certain guarantees), so as to give rise to a personal liability on his part as a joint tortfeasor with the fraudster. However, not all the acts necessary to give rise to liability for the tort of deceit (whether committed by him or by the fraudster with whom he was jointly liable) were ones within the course of his employment, and so the defendant was not vicariously liable:

> "The conduct for which the servant is responsible must constitute an actionable tort and to make the employer responsible for that tort the conduct necessary to establish the employee's liability must have occurred within the course of the employment."[285]

That said, this is only true of the acts necessary to constitute the tort; and, as we **1–145** have already seen, the tort does not require that all of the acts of communicating the representation to the representee have to have been committed by the tortfeasor. So, the fact that the fraudulent agent passes information to the claimant through another agent (or indeed through the principal) who is innocent would not detract from the principal's vicarious liability, since the use of an innocent conduit to communicate the misrepresentation would not detract from the agent's own liability.[286]

---

[283] Indeed, arguably the liability considered above based on the scope of the agent's actual or apparent authority is also primary (as it is in contract) rather than vicarious.

[284] *Credit Lyonnais Nederland NV v Export Credits Guarantee Department* [2000] 1 A.C. 486. The decision was given a wide application in *Frederick v Positive Solutions (Financial Services) Ltd* [2018] EWCA Civ 431, at [74], per Flaux LJ, a case relating to vicarious liability in the financial services field.

[285] At 495, per Lord Woolf. As to the use of the expression "within the course of employment", see fn.276 above.

[286] This is the true import of the decisions in *S Pearson & Son Ltd v Dublin Corp* [1907] A.C. 351 (communication through innocent principal); and *London County Freehold and Leasehold Properties Ltd v Berkeley Property and Investment Co Ltd* [1936] 2 All E.R. 1039 (communication through another, innocent agent), both as subsequently analysed in *Anglo-Scottish Beet Sugar Corp Ltd v Spalding Urban District Council* [1937] 2 K.B. 607.

(ii) Partners

1–146   A partnership will be liable for the deceit of a partner if the representation made is within "the ordinary course of the business of the firm" for the purposes of s.10 of the Partnership Act 1890.[287] The relevant wrongful conduct must be:

> "so closely connected with acts the partner … was authorised to do that, for the purpose of the liability of the firm … to third parties, the wrongful conduct may fairly and properly be regarded as done by the partner while acting in the ordinary course of the firm's business".[288]

For these purposes it is necessary not just to consider the class or category into which the relevant acts fall, and whether that is within the ordinary business of the firm, but also the nature and characteristics of the particular acts and the substance of the transaction to which they pertain. The motive or purpose of the relevant partner is, however, irrelevant.[289]

(3)   Agency and the Required Dishonest State of Mind

1–147   Given the need for subjective dishonesty in order to establish the tort of deceit, particular problems arise where the representation has been made by an agent. The governing principle (which may sound obvious, but which has been obscured in a number of earlier cases) is that a for a principal to be liable in deceit there must be fraud—that is, dishonest knowledge and an intent to deceive in the sense that has been considered elsewhere in this chapter—either on his part or on the part of someone for whose acts he is responsible. In the case of a company (which can only have guilty knowledge through the knowledge of its agents), this means that a company cannot be liable in deceit unless some agent has a fraudulent state of mind with reference to the representation in issue.[290]

1–148   Thus if an agent makes a representation innocently (such that there can be no question of vicarious liability for a deceit by him), the fact that the principal is aware of facts which render the representation false will not suffice to make him liable.[291] It would have to be shown that the principal intended the claimant to be misled (or at least was indifferent as to whether he would be), for example by expressly authorising the innocent agent to make the misrepresentation, or deliberately providing the agent with false information or withholding from him true information with a view to the claimant then being misled. So, in the leading case of *Armstrong v Strain*, estate agents innocently told a purchaser that a property was sound when the owner knew it not to be; but, since the owner was

---

[287] *Dubai Aluminium v Salaam*, above (a case concerned with dishonest assistance, rather than deceit, but which nevertheless contains a helpful analysis of the scope of s.10). This was applied to the tort of deceit in *J.J. Coughlan Ltd v Ruparella*, above.

[288] *Dubai Aluminium*, above, per Lord Nicholls at [23].

[289] *J.J. Coughlan Ltd v Ruparella*, above, at [26], [27] and [30], per Dyson LJ.

[290] *Anglo-Scottish Beet Sugar Corp Ltd v Spalding UDC* [1937] 2 K.B. 607, at 625–627, per Atkinson J.

[291] The converse is also true: if the principal innocently made a representation, but an agent happened to know facts that rendered it false, there would be no liability on the part of the principal (*Anglo-Scottish Beet Sugar Corp Ltd v Spalding*, above).

not aware that the representation was being made and had not specifically authorised it (even though the agents had a general authority to make representations on his behalf), he was not liable.[292] The fact that the owner would have been liable in deceit if he had made the representation himself was not to the point.

As has already been noted, the fact that a representation may be made through an innocent agent does not affect the question of liability on the part of a principal who authorised the agent to make it, or who consciously permitted the agent to remain ignorant of the true position with a view to the claimant being misled: in such a case the principal has a primary liability in deceit and the innocent agent is just the conduit for the making of the representation. The same is also true, it would seem, if it is another agent who has the guilty state of mind and who authorises the misrepresentation or consciously refrains from preventing it: in that case, the second agent has a primary liability in deceit; and if he acted within the scope of his actual or apparent authority, the principal, even if himself wholly innocent, could be vicariously liable for that.[293]

1–149

[292] See per Devlin J at first instance (*Armstrong v Strain* [1951] 1 T.L.R. 856, at 872): "You cannot add an innocent state of mind to an innocent state of mind and get as a result a dishonest state of mind." This analysis was approved in the Court of Appeal, at [1952] 1 K.B. 232.
[293] See *UBS AG v Kommunale Wasserwerke Leipzig GmbH* [2014] EWHC 3615 (Comm), at [757]–[759], per Males J. An example of this is *Standard Chartered Bank v Pakistan National Shipping* [2000] 1 Lloyd's Rep. 218, at [30], per Lord Hoffman, where one employee of the defendant bank authorised, or knowingly allowed, the sending by another employee of a letter to an issuing bank that the former employee, but not the latter, knew was false. A further example is where an estate agent produces sales particulars which (through an innocent mistake) wrongly overstate the size of the land being sold; the vendor is sent the particulars in draft and sees the mistake. He does nothing and the sales particulars are sent out. The vendor would be liable in deceit if a purchaser purchased in reliance on the representation.

CHAPTER 2

CONSPIRACY

A.   INTRODUCTION

(1)   The Practical Relevance of Conspiracy in Fraud Cases

A fraud-based claim against more than one defendant will very often include a   **2–001**
claim in conspiracy. Dishonesty is not a necessary element of a conspiracy claim
as such,[1] and conversely many claimants bringing fraud-based claims against
multiple defendants have no need to rely on the tort. Instead they might bring
claims against joint tortfeasors, or pursue secondary defendants on other bases,
such as accessories in an equitable claim, liable for dishonest assistance or
knowing receipt.

However, from a claimant's perspective a claim in conspiracy can be a useful   **2–002**
way of proceeding against multiple defendants in two principal and overlapping
types of case: first, where there are identifiable civil wrongs or crimes committed
by one or more defendants but where for whatever reason (e.g. potential inability
to meet a judgment, or difficulty in establishing a basis for jurisdiction) there is a
practical benefit in pursuing other defendants in addition; and secondly, where a
claimant wishes to pursue a particular party in circumstances where the evidence
establishing the basis for a direct claim against that party is limited, but there is
evidence suggesting that the party concerned was nevertheless involved with
others in a concerted attempt to harm the claimant. In this second type of
situation, it will often be possible to identify unlawful acts carried out by one or
more defendants. A conspiracy claim can allow a claimant to impose liability for
damage caused by those acts beyond their immediate perpetrators.

A conspiracy claim may even go further than that, allowing a claimant to recover   **2–003**
damages for harm caused by acts carried out pursuant to a combination between
several people, when—absent the combination—the acts would not be
actionable. Other than in certain situations where the unlawful means identified
are a crime,[2] or breach of statutory duty,[3] this is the domain of a lawful means
conspiracy claim. Whilst such claims are sometimes pleaded together with claims
for unlawful means conspiracy, they very rarely succeed,[4] because of the need to

---

[1] Although in practice the two generally go hand-in-hand: see paras 2–139—2–140 below.
[2] See paras 2–051—2–055 below.
[3] See paras 2–062—2–067 below.
[4] A relatively recent example of a successful claim in lawful means conspiracy is *Apax Global Payment & Technologies Ltd v Morina* [2011] EWHC 2983 (Ch); [2011] 108 (27) L.S.G. 22 albeit the judgment contains no analysis of the predominant purpose test. Earlier examples of successful claims

show that the defendants' predominant purpose was to injure the claimant—rather than, for example, to further their own private interests. Defendants in fraud cases invariably do act primarily to benefit themselves.

2–004   Other procedural advantages of a conspiracy claim over alternative claims against the same defendants are considered at the end of this chapter.[5]

(2)   The Essentials of the Tort

2–005   The essence of a conspiracy claim is a combination between two or more persons to harm another. There are two types. One is an unlawful means conspiracy, its generally accepted label. The other has been given many different labels: e.g. lawful means conspiracy; conspiracy to injure; unlawful purpose conspiracy; unlawful object conspiracy. Lawful means conspiracy is the label used in this book: that is the principal label adopted in the most recent House of Lords and Supreme Court decisions,[6] and it illustrates most clearly the key distinction between that and the other type of conspiracy recognised by the law.

2–006   It remains unclear whether the two types of conspiracy are properly to be classified as subspecies of the same tort or as separate torts. For practical purposes it is unlikely to matter.[7]

2–007   The ingredients of a claim in unlawful means conspiracy can be summarised as follows:

(1)   A combination or agreement between a given defendant and one or more others;
(2)   An intention to injure the claimant;
(3)   Unlawful acts carried out pursuant to the combination or agreement as a means of injuring the claimant;
(4)   Causing loss suffered by the claimant.[8]

---

for lawful means conspiracy, in the field of trade disputes, include *Quinn v Leathem* [1901] A.C. 495 and *Huntley v Thornton* [1957] 1 W.L.R. 321. Lord Neuberger suggested in *Revenue & Customs Commissioners v Total Network SL* [2008] UKHL 19; [2008] 1 A.C. 1174, at [228] that, whilst HMRC brought no lawful means conspiracy claim in that case, had they done so it might have succeeded.

[5] See para.2–150 below.

[6] *OBG Ltd v Allan* [2007] UKHL 21; [2008] 1 A.C. 1, per Lord Hoffmann at [15] (who also used (at [20]) the label "malicious *Quinn v Leathem* conspiracy"); *Revenue & Customs Commissioners v Total Network SL* [2008] UKHL 19; [2008] 1 A.C. 1174, per Lord Hope at [38] and [41], per Lord Scott at [56], per Lord Walker at [66] and [73] (also using the label "unlawful object" conspiracy), and per Lord Neuberger at [216] and [222] (also using the label "conspiracy to injure"); *JSC BTA Bank v Khrapunov* [2018] UKSC 19; [2018] 2 W.L.R. 1125.

[7] *Kuwait Oil Tanker v Al Bader* [2000] 2 All E.R. (Comm) 271, at [108]. In *JSC BTA Bank v Khrapunov* [2018] UKSC 19; [2018] 2 W.L.R. 1125, conspiracy was described as a single tort with two forms: see [8]–[9]. For discussion of how the question of classification might affect the future development of the tort, see H. Carty, *An Analysis of the Economic Torts*, 2nd edn (Oxford: OUP, 2010), pp.150–152.

[8] *Kuwait Oil Tanker v Al Bader* [2000] 2 All E.R. (Comm) 271, at [108]; *Constantin Medien AG v Ecclestone* [2014] EWHC 387 (Ch), at [321].

The ingredients of a claim in lawful means conspiracy can be summarised as follows:

2–008

(1)   A combination or agreement between the defendant and one or more others;
(2)   A predominant purpose to injure the claimant;
(3)   Acts carried out pursuant to the combination or agreement;
(4)   Causing loss suffered by the claimant.[9]

There are thus two crucial differences between the two types of conspiracy: first, as to whether the acts carried out pursuant to the conspiracy must be unlawful; secondly, as to the degree of intentionality required. The first of these differences has led to lawful means conspiracy being described as a *"highly anomalous"* cause of action, in that it founds liability for what would be a lawful act if done by one person alone, because instead that act was done pursuant to an agreement with others.[10]

2–009

There are important differences between a tortious conspiracy and a criminal conspiracy. The crime of conspiracy is committed as soon as there is an agreement to carry out acts which constitute a criminal offence: it is not necessary for matters to proceed beyond the agreement to the actual commission of the offence.[11] In a civil conspiracy, by contrast, damage is the gist of the cause of action. An agreement in itself is not actionable (though, theoretically, its existence may found the basis for a quia timet injunction): to found liability in damages the agreement must be put into effect through unlawful acts which cause the claimant damage.[12] It is not, however, necessary that every unlawful act be done by every conspirator.[13]

2–010

B.   CONSIDERATIONS COMMON TO BOTH TYPES OF CONSPIRACY

(1)   The Combination

The first element of the tort of conspiracy, common to both species of the tort, is the combination or agreement.

2–011

"Agreement" in this context is to be understood loosely. As the Court of Appeal explained in the *Kuwait Oil Tanker* case, which remains perhaps the leading modern case on the law of unlawful means conspiracy:

2–012

---

[9] *Kuwait Oil Tanker v Al Bader* [2000] 2 All E.R. (Comm) 271, at [108].
[10] See *Lonrho Ltd v Shell Petroleum Co Ltd (No.2)* [1982] A.C. 173, at 188–189; *Lonrho Plc v Fayed* [1992] 1 A.C. 448, per Lord Bridge at 463; *Revenue and Customs Commissioners v Total Network SL* [2008] UKHL 19; [2008] 1 A.C. 1174, at [39], [56], [66]–[67], [118] and [221].
[11] *Mulcahy v The Queen* (1868) L.R. 3 H.L 306, at 317; *Phillips v News Group Newspapers Ltd* [2012] UKSC 28; [2013] 1 A.C. 1, at [43].
[12] *Crofter Hand Woven Harris Tweed Co Ltd v Veitch* [1942] A.C. 435, at 439–440; *Kuwait Oil Tanker v Al Bader* [2000] 2 All E.R. (Comm) 271, at [110], citing *Lonrho Ltd v Shell Petroleum Co Ltd (No.2)* [1982] A.C. 173, per Lord Diplock at 188.
[13] *Kuwait Oil Tanker* [2000] 2 All E.R. (Comm) 271, at [110]. See para.2–118 below.

"[I]t is not necessary to show that there is anything in the nature of an express agreement, whether formal or informal. It is sufficient if two or more persons combine with a common intention, or, in other words, that they deliberately combine, albeit tacitly, to achieve a common end".[14]

2–013   In *Belmont Finance Corp v Williams Furniture Ltd (No.2)*,[15] Buckley LJ said that "the word 'agreement' in this context does not mean an agreement in any contractual sense but a combination and common intention to do the act which is the object of the alleged conspiracy." Other labels used in the cases include "bargain", "compact",[16] and "arrangement".[17]

2–014   In practice it is usually impossible to establish a specific agreement by direct evidence.[18] Instead it is generally both necessary and sufficient for a claimant to piece together evidence of what each defendant did and knew at the various stages of the alleged conspiracy, from which a combination can be inferred.[19] In principle a combination can exist even where the conspirators have never even met or corresponded, and do not know each other's names.[20] But the parties to the alleged conspiracy must be shown to have been sufficiently aware of the relevant circumstances and have a sufficiently similar objective before it can be inferred that they were acting in combination at the time of the acts complained of.[21]

2–015   If, where a conspiracy is alleged, the explanations given by defendants for their conduct are rejected as inherently improbable or internally inconsistent, it is legitimate for the Court to infer a conspiracy both from the fact that it is the most probable alternative explanation for the defendants' conduct and from the fact that an untrue explanation has been given, subject to the need for awareness that lies are not always told to cover up guilt.[22]

2–016   There is a close overlap between the tests for liability as a co-conspirator and liability as a joint tortfeasor. This is most relevant in claims in unlawful means conspiracy, where there may be a decision to be made as to whether to frame the claim against particular defendants in either or both of these ways. The factors bearing on the bases on which to frame a claim in conspiracy and/or joint tortfeasorship are considered in paras 2–149—2–151 below.

---

[14] *Kuwait Oil Tanker* [2000] 2 All E.R. (Comm) 271, at [111].

[15] *Belmont Finance Corp v Williams Furniture Ltd (No.2)* [1980] 1 All E.R. 393, at 404.

[16] *Crofter Hand Woven Harris Tweed Co v Veitch* [1942] A.C. 435, at 439 and 461 respectively.

[17] *Revenue & Customs Commissioners v Total Network SL* [2008] UKHL 19, 1 A.C. 1174, per Lord Neuberger at [213].

[18] One of the leading cases, *Kuwait Oil Tanker v Al Bader* [2000] 2 All E.R. (Comm) 271, provides a rare example. See also *Kuwait Oil Tanker*, at [111], citing O'Connor LJ in the criminal case of *R v Siracusa* (1990) 90 Cr.App.R. 340, at 349: "the origins of all conspiracies are concealed and it is usually quite impossible to establish when or where the initial agreement was made, or when or where other conspirators were recruited. The very existence of the agreement can only be inferred from overt acts. Participation in a conspiracy is infinitely variable: it can be active or passive."

[19] In this respect there is an obvious overlap between various elements of the tort, namely combination, acts carried out and the intention behind those acts.

[20] *HMRC v Sunico* [2013] EWHC 941 (Ch), per Proudman J at [77].

[21] See paras 2–120—2–126 below.

[22] *Do-Buy 925 Ltd v National Westminster Bank Plc* [2010] EWHC 2862 (QB), per Andrew Popplewell QC at [52]; *Stevenson v Singh* [2012] EWHC 2880 (QB), per HHJ Richard Seymour QC at [18].

(2) Conspiring with a Company

Like other claims in the civil fraud context, conspiracy claims frequently involve corporate defendants, from active trading companies to special purpose vehicles. A particular company may be an obvious defendant to a claim in conspiracy, for example because of its involvement in particular acts carried out pursuant to the conspiracy, or because pursuing the company as a defendant would assist a claimant in establishing jurisdiction in England against other defendants or in enforcing any eventual judgment in its favour—for example, if the fruits of the conspiracy have been channelled into a corporate vehicle, as frequently happens in fraud cases. **2–017**

However, companies can only act through individuals, and can only be said to have relevant knowledge or intention via the human agents whose knowledge or intention is properly to be attributed to them. Where two companies each act in combination through separate individuals, there should be no difficulty in establishing, in an appropriate case, that the companies are liable as co-conspirators.[23] However the law goes further and, in principle, the concept of separate corporate personality means that, for example[24]: **2–018**

(1) A director can conspire with a company of which he is a director[25];
(2) A shareholder can conspire with a company in which he owns shares;
(3) A parent company can combine with its subsidiary[26]; and
(4) Two subsidiaries can conspire with each other.

The position is more difficult where an individual is said to have combined in his personal capacity with himself as the embodiment of, or as agent for, a company which he controls. The answer given by the criminal law to this conundrum is that a combination between a one-man company and its sole controller is a legal impossibility, because it is (impossibly) artificial to describe the company as a separate "person" or "mind" if the human controller is the only person who acts on its behalf.[27] This issue has practical importance for the reasons set out above, and particularly given that the mastermind of a fraud will not uncommonly use companies controlled by him to carry out a fraud or as a repository or conduit for the proceeds. **2–019**

A number of recent cases have considered the equivalent question in the civil context, but unfortunately have not produced a clear answer: **2–020**

---

[23] Depending on the application of ordinary principles of corporate attribution, which are discussed separately in Ch.19 of this book.

[24] *Digicel (St Lucia) Ltd v Cable & Wireless Plc* [2010] EWHC 774 (Ch), per Morgan J at Annex I [61] and [77].

[25] See, to the same effect, *Concept Oil Services Ltd v En-Gin Group LLP* [2013] EWHC 1897 (Comm), per Flaux J at [53], a case (argued on one side only) involving two individual and several corporate conspirators; and *Holyoake v Candy* [2017] EWHC 3397 (Ch) per Nugee J at [442].

[26] However, it will not normally be enough merely to show that the parent company knew or suspected that an unlawful act was being committed by its subsidiary and did nothing to stop it; still less so in the case of two subsidiaries under common ownership. See *Digicel*, at Annex I, [77].

[27] *R v McDonnell* [1966] 1 Q.B. 233, at 245C–245E.

(1)   In *Fiona Trust & Holding Corp v Privalov*,[28] Andrew Smith J noted that it was unclear whether a company could be liable in civil conspiracy with its sole controller but did not determine the point.

(2)   In *AAH Pharmaceuticals Ltd v Birdi*,[29] Coulson J declined to grant summary judgment on a conspiracy claim against an individual defendant and the companies he controlled on the basis that the availability of such a claim as a matter of law was in doubt.[30] He considered that it would be *"unattractive"* for the position to be radically different in civil conspiracy from that in criminal conspiracy. It seems the allegation in *Birdi* was that only one individual, Mr Birdi, was involved in the conspiracy.

(3)   In *Barclay Pharmaceuticals Ltd v Waypharm LLP*,[31] Gloster J held, without argument, that a company and its sole controller were liable in conspiracy. She did so in reliance on an Irish case, *Taylor v Smyth*,[32] in which an individual was held liable in conspiracy with a company of which he was the sole controller. In the latter case it was also suggested that two or more companies controlled by the same individual could be liable in conspiracy. However the reasoning in *Taylor v Smyth* is not altogether satisfactory.[33]

(4)   In *Twentieth Century Fox Film Corp v Harris*,[34] Barling J held that there was no reason in principle or in authority why a defendant could not conspire with a company which was his *alter ego*, and found such a conspiracy to exist on the facts of that case. He relied for that conclusion on Morgan J's decision in *Digicel*, though the latter case was not concerned with, and did not separately address, the position of sole controllers.[35]

(5)   In *Reuse Collections Ltd v Sendall*,[36] HHJ Stephen Davies considered it to be clear that a company can conspire with its directors, other than in the

---

[28]   *Fiona Trust & Holding Corp v Privalov* [2010] EWHC 3199 (Comm), at [1521].

[29]   *AAH Pharmaceuticals Ltd v Birdi* [2011] EWHC 1625 (QB), at [31].

[30]   The judge referred to the Irish case *Taylor v Smith* [1991] 1 IR 142, considered further below.

[31]   *Barclay Pharmaceuticals Ltd v Waypharm LLP* [2012] EWHC 306 (Comm), at [227]–[229].

[32]   *Taylor v Smyth* [1991] 1 IR 142.

[33]   A policy justification was given for the decision, namely that it would be invidious that the assets of a limited company should not be liable to answer for conspiracy where its assets had been augmented as a result of an alleged conspiracy (at 165). But in such circumstances there may be other claims available against the company (e.g. knowing receipt). And this policy justification would not exist where the company had obtained no benefit, yet it is hard to see how this would affect its liability since benefit to the defendant is not an element of the cause of action. It was also said (at 166) that there was no reason in principle why the mere fact that one individual controls a limited company should give immunity to both from liability. With respect, this seems to look at the matter the wrong way round. The real question must be: on what basis can a company be said to conspire with its sole controller? It could not be said that, every time an individual acts to the detriment of another, he is taken to have done so pursuant to a combination between himself and every company of which he is in fact the sole controller. There must, it is suggested, at least be some factual basis for concluding that the sole controller in fact conspired on behalf of (or as) the company as well as on his own behalf. But *Taylor v Smyth* offers no guidance on the question. Finally, the Court in *Taylor v Smyth* placed reliance on *Belmont Finance (No.1) v Williams Furniture* [1979] Ch. 250; but the issue of conspiring with a sole controller did not arise and was not considered in *Belmont*.

[34]   *Twentieth Century Fox Film Corp v Harris* [2014] EWHC 1568 (Ch), at [150].

[35]   See e.g. *Digicel (St Lucia) Ltd v Cable & Wireless Plc* [2010] EWHC 774 (Ch), at [205]–[213] where the judge considered the common factual issues arising in relation to the conspiracy allegations; and [557].

[36]   *Reuse Collections Ltd v Sendall* [2014] EWHC 3852 (QB); [2015] I.R.L.R. 226, at [171].

case of criminal conspiracy involving a pure "one man" company. He found such a conspiracy to exist; though since the defendant company also had a second director acting on its behalf in the conspiracy, the status of this case as authority for the proposition that a company can conspire with its sole controller is questionable.

(6) In *Muduroglu v Reddish LLP*,[37] HHJ Keyser QC referred to *Taylor v Smyth* and *Barclays Pharmaceuticals v Waypharm*. He held (obiter) that it "may well be" that a company could conspire with its sole controller; but "it is quite a different thing to say that any unlawful action of an individual who stands to benefit via a corporate entity that he controls, or any unlawful action of a corporate entity performed by the person who controls it, is a conspiracy."[38]

On the basis of these cases, it seems that a sole controller can in principle conspire with his company. However, until the matter is considered at appellate level, there will remain room for doubt as to the correctness of the proposition.[39] In particular, if the criminal law requires two individual "minds" before a conspiracy can exist, it is not obvious why that requirement should be absent in the civil law.[40] Nor is it clear what sort of evidence will be required before such a conspiracy will be established on the facts of a particular case. It is suggested that there must at least need to be some positive evidence showing that the sole controller in fact acted both on behalf of the company and on his own behalf in the particular circumstances, and a basis for attributing the controller's knowledge to the company, before such a conspiracy will be established.

2–021

Morgan J suggested in *Digicel*[41] that a director or shareholder who does no more than carry out his constitutional role as such within the company will not ordinarily be liable with the company in conspiracy (seemingly notwithstanding that person's culpability and knowledge of the relevant facts). Again, however, it is not wholly clear what the content of this limitation, borrowed from the field of joint torts,[42] will be in this context. In particular, it may be difficult in a given case to argue that a director or shareholder who has the necessary intention to injure a claimant is nevertheless simply carrying out his constitutional role within the company. Directors can be liable for a conspiracy entered into before a board meeting to induce the board to cause the company to breach a contract it has entered into.[43] Indeed framing a claim in this way may help avoid the

2–022

---

[37] *Muduroglu v Reddish LLP* [2015] EWHC 1044 (Ch).

[38] *Muduroglu v Reddish LLP* [2015] EWHC 1044 (Ch), at [156].

[39] A company conspiring with its sole director has been described as "a difficult notion": P.G. Watts (ed), *Bowstead and Reynolds on Agency*, 21st edn (London: Sweet & Maxwell, 2017), para.9–119.

[40] Though note that criminal and civil law give different answers to the question of whether a husband and wife can conspire together (see fn.222 below).

[41] *Digicel (St Lucia) Ltd v Cable & Wireless Plc* [2010] EWHC 774 (Ch), at Annex 1 [78], referring to *MCA Records Inc v Charly Records Ltd* [2001] EWCA Civ 1441; [2003] 1 B.C.L.C. 93, a decision on joint tortfeasors.

[42] See Ch.20.

[43] *De Jetley, Marks v Greenwood* [1936] 1 All E.R. 863, at 872–873 provides some support for this proposition.

consequences of the company's insolvency and inability to meet a damages award in favour of the innocent party to the contract.

2–023 Where the facts would justify the lifting of the corporate veil (on principles recently and authoritatively set out by the Supreme Court),[44] that allows the claimant to treat a company and its controller "as one". It is suggested that this should nevertheless not prevent that same claimant from treating the company and its controller as separate entities so as to found a claim against them in conspiracy. The rule exists to protect claimants from defendants who set up corporate structures in order to avoid their legal obligations. It is to be used only for the purpose of depriving companies within those structures and their controllers of that illegitimate advantage.[45] It is difficult to see any principled basis for its application *in favour of* such companies or their controllers.

2–024 Where the conspiracy alleged is an unlawful means conspiracy and the unlawful means are constituted by a freestanding tort, in addition to (or instead of) a conspiracy claim against the company and its controller, the claimant may pursue a claim against the controller and the company personally on the basis that they are joint tortfeasors.[46] In a similar case where the unlawful means alleged are a breach of contract by the company, a claim may lie against the controller for inducing the breach of contract.[47]

(3) Employees and Agents

2–025 Complex conspiracies in particular can involve the principal actors requiring, or at least making use of, minor players to carry out acts in furtherance of the conspiracy. These minor players may be employees or agents of the principal actors. If such employees or agents, independently of their status as such, share their principals' intentions and play a full part in the conspiracy, there should be no difficulty in principle with their being liable as co-conspirators. What is less clear is whether any lesser state of mind will suffice to create liability on the part of an employee or agent who follows the instructions of his or her conspirator principal.

2–026 In *Crofter Hand Woven Harris Tweed Co Ltd v Veitch*[48] an injunction was sought against two individual trade union representatives, one the superior of the other. The House of Lords upheld the refusal of the injunction on the basis that the defendants' predominant purpose was the legitimate protection of their own lawful interests. It had also been argued that the subordinate, Mr Mackenzie,

---

[44] *Petrodel Resources Ltd v Prest* [2013] UKSC 34; [2013] 2 A.C. 415 and *VTB Capital Plc v Nutritek International Corp* [2013] UKSC 5; [2013] 2 A.C. 337: see Ch.18.

[45] *Petrodel v Prest*, above, per Lord Sumption JSC at [35].

[46] For a summary of the relevant principles involving directors and companies as joint tortfeasors, see *MCA Records Inc v Charly Records Ltd* [2001] EWCA Civ 1441; [2003] 1 B.C.L.C. 93, at [49]–[52]; and *Twentieth Century Fox Film Corp v Harris* [2014] EWHC 1568 (Ch), at [135]–[137]. See also Ch.20.

[47] See Ch.3.

[48] *Crofter Hand Woven Harris Tweed Co Ltd v Veitch* [1942] A.C. 435.

should not be regarded as having combined with his superior, Mr Veitch, on the basis that Mr Mackenzie was simply following Mr Veitch's instructions. As to this, Viscount Simon LC said[49] that:

> "Even if Mackenzie could be regarded as only obeying orders received from his superior, the combination would still exist if he appreciated what he was about."

Conversely Lord Wright said[50] that the fact that a defendant uses employees or agents to carry out his business would not per se make the latter co-conspirators.

The analysis of Viscount Simon LC was followed by Widgery J in *Morgan v Fry*,[51] where it was held that the fact that a transport union official was following instructions from his superior afforded him no defence to a claim against him in intimidation, where he had played a sufficiently active role to make him liable as a joint tortfeasor. However, the same analysis has also been criticised in other commentary.[52]   **2–027**

It accordingly remains unclear from these cases what exactly is required to establish liability against an employee or agent who is following instructions in carrying out acts which form part of a conspiracy. It is, not least, unclear what Viscount Simon LC meant by the phrase "if he appreciated what he was about"; and it is also to be observed that the decisions referred to above pre-date the modern analysis of the tort of conspiracy and its constituent elements. It is suggested that, if an employee or agent can be shown to have combined with his employer or principal, and to have the necessary intention (according to the type of conspiracy alleged), it will not be a defence for the employee or agent to show that he was in any event required by an instruction to act as he did. But it is also thought that, unless each element of the tort can be established separately against the employee or agent, he will not be liable.   **2–028**

In addition it may happen that an employee or agent, who at an initial stage simply follows his instructions without thereby becoming a conspirator, subsequently develops into a conspirator through greater knowledge and complicity in the actions of his employer or principal. In such a case it will be important to analyse (and to plead precisely) the stage at which the employee or agent became a conspirator.[53] This is not least because this may have an impact on the acts and losses for which he can be held responsible: see paras 2–123 and 2–127—2–128 below.   **2–029**

---

[49] *Crofter*, above, at 441.

[50] *Crofter*, above, at 468.

[51] *Morgan v Fry* [1968] 1 Q.B. 521, at 548. The decision of Widgery J was reversed in part by the Court of Appeal [1968] 2 Q.B. 710 but not on this point.

[52] See M. Jones (ed), *Clerk & Lindsell on Torts*, 22nd edn (London: Sweet & Maxwell, 2017), para.24–96. The criticism is based on inconsistency with cases in other legal contexts (procuring breach of contract, negligent misstatement, vicarious liability). However, searching for such consistency may not be useful in light of the many differences between these legal contexts.

[53] The importance of this type of close analysis is demonstrated by the judgment of the Court of Appeal in *Credit Lyonnais Bank Nederland NV v Export Credit Guarantee Department* [1998] 1 Lloyd's Rep. 19, per Hobhouse LJ.

2–030   The above analysis considers the situation in which an employee or agent can be made liable in conspiracy together with his employer or principal. This is to be distinguished from the reverse scenario, in which it is sought to make an employer or principal liable for his employee or agent's acts on the basis of vicarious liability. In such a case, the basic principle is that the employer or principal will be liable to a third party for acts carried out by the employee or agent in the course of his employment (or in the course of the agency relationship).[54] Whilst this test may be satisfied where the principal is also a conspirator, in such a case the principal will be primarily liable. It is inherently unlikely that this test will be satisfied in the employment context in relation to acts carried out pursuant to a conspiracy; it goes without saying that the roles and responsibilities of an employee will not ordinarily extend to involvement in an unlawful conspiracy. Consistently with this it has been said that an employer could only be made vicariously liable for an employee's actions as an unlawful conspirator in an exceptional case.[55]

(4)   Acts Carried Out

2–031   It is necessary for the claimant to prove each unlawful act relied on as causative of loss as a freestanding wrong, and that such act was carried out pursuant to the alleged conspiracy.[56] But a party's participation in a conspiracy can be active or passive, for example if a majority shareholder and director consents to the use of his company for the purposes of a conspiracy[57]; such use might consist of drug smuggling being carried out in the company's name[58] or of fictitious invoices being issued by the company. It is of the essence of the law of conspiracy that a defendant may be a party to a combination (and so liable in conspiracy) but not himself carry out any of the unlawful acts carried out pursuant to that combination.[59] It is not even necessary that each conspirator should be aware of

---

[54] See, for example, *Credit Lyonnais Bank Nederland NV v Export Credit Guarantee Department* [2000] 1 A.C. 486, per Hobhouse LJ at 494.

[55] *Credit Lyonnais Bank Nederland NV v Export Credit Guarantee Department* [1998] 1 Lloyd's Rep. 19, at 41, per Hobhouse LJ, giving the trade union context as one such possible exception.

[56] *Kuwait Oil Tanker v Al Bader* [2000] 2 All E.R. (Comm) 271, at [132].

[57] *Kuwait Oil Tanker v Al Bader* [2000] 2 All E.R. (Comm) 271, at [111], citing *R v Siracusa* (1990) 90 Cr.App.R. 340, at 349.

[58] *R v Siracusa* (1990) 90 Cr.App.R. 340, at 349.

[59] *Brown v Bennett* [1999] B.C.C. 91, at 100, per Rattee J; *Digicel (St Lucia) Ltd v Cable & Wireless Plc* [2010] EWHC 774 (Ch), at Annex I [76], per Morgan J; *Barclay Pharmaceuticals Ltd v Waypharm LLP* [2012] EWHC 306 (Comm), at [222], per Gloster J. In *CIBC Mellon Trust Co v Stolzenberg* [2004] EWCA Civ 827 Arden LJ had said in passing (at [135]) that whether each conspirator had to have committed an overt act pursuant to the conspiracy was an open question. Whilst it may be in a given case that the only way of establishing the involvement of a particular conspirator is by pointing to acts carried out by him, there is no basis in principle for this being a requirement. The absence of any requirement for any positive act (or omission) by a given defendant marks a crucial distinction between the tort of conspiracy on the one hand, and the related torts of causing loss by unlawful means and inducing breach of contract on the other: *Barclay Pharmaceuticals Ltd v Waypharm LLP* at [222] and [230].

each act carried out pursuant to the conspiracy; what matters is whether the conspiratorial act "fell within the overall scope of [the conspirators'] common design".[60]

Whilst many of the cases refer to "overt acts",[61] the word "overt" is not thought to have any special meaning in this context beyond connoting an act carried out pursuant to the conspiracy and which can be established by evidence. The phrase is sometimes used in the older cases to mark a distinction from the prior agreement pursuant to which the act is carried out.[62] In addition, at least in an unlawful means conspiracy there is no reason in principle why a defendant's participation in the conspiracy cannot be established from his omission, i.e. by a failure to stop wrongful acts being carried out pursuant to a conspiracy.[63]

2–032

So, in the Singaporean case of The "Dolphina",[64] a defendant (Universal) was held liable in conspiracy where it knew that cargo had been delivered and that a bill of lading should accordingly have been returned to it, and also knew that the bill of lading was instead being falsely represented by another defendant (KOSB) as valid in order to secure a payment to which KOSB was not entitled. Universal could have prevented this by demanding the return of the bill of lading from KOSB, but failed to do so, which could only be explained on the basis that Universal was party to the conspiracy. It is however suggested that liability will not arise by omission unless the party concerned is in a position of authority over others or is otherwise able (legally or in practice) to stop those others from carrying out wrongful acts, such that his failure to stop them from doing so can properly be said to amount to (at least) tacit approval of what they are doing.[65] Silence or subsequent cover up will not make a party liable as a conspirator after he leaves a conspiracy in the absence of evidence that he played a part in or took a benefit from later acts pursuant to the conspiracy.[66]

2–033

(5) Damage

The principles governing proof of damage and recovery of damages are the same for both types of conspiracy. Those principles are examined at paras 2–134—2–137 below.

2–034

---

[60] Kuwait Oil Tanker v Al Bader [2000] 2 All E.R. (Comm) 271, at [133].

[61] See e.g. Quinn v Leathem [1901] A.C. 495, at 529; Crofter Hand Woven Harris Tweed Company Ltd v Veitch [1942] A.C. 435, at 439, 468; Belmont Finance Corp Ltd v Williams Furniture Ltd [1979] Ch. 250, at 263; Midland Bank Trust Co Ltd v Green (No.3) [1979] Ch. 496, at 503, 524; Kuwait Oil Tanker Co SAK v Al Bader [2000] 2 All E.R. (Comm) 271, at [110]–[111]; Revenue and Customs Commissioners v Total Network SL [2007] EWCA Civ 39; [2008] 1 A.C. 1174, at [47], [63].

[62] See e.g. Quinn v Leathem [1901] A.C. 495, at 530, per Lord Brampton.

[63] Kuwait Oil Tanker v Al Bader [2000] 2 All E.R. (Comm) 271, at [111]; Attorney General of Zambia v Meer Care & Desai (A Firm) [2007] EWHC 952 (Ch), at [317] (decision reversed on appeal on a different point); The "Dolphina" [2011] SGHC 273; [2012] 1 Lloyd's Rep. 304 (High Court of Singapore), at [269].

[64] The "Dolphina" [2012] 1 Lloyd's Rep. 304 (High Court of Singapore), at [267]–[278].

[65] See, to this effect, Digicel (St Lucia) Ltd v Cable & Wireless Plc [2010] EWHC 774 (Ch) per Morgan J at Annex I [74], referring to Kuwait Oil Tanker, at [111].

[66] Kuwait Oil Tanker v Al Bader [2000] 2 All E.R. (Comm) 271, at [154].

(6) Single or Multiple Conspiracies

2–035 A series of acts may be carried out pursuant to a single conspiracy. Alternatively those acts may be carried out pursuant to separate conspiracies. There may be an overarching conspiracy and sub-conspiracies, with varying parties to each. It is possible, for example, to have an umbrella conspiracy between A, B and C, pursuant to which they enter into specific schemes with D and E respectively, but without D or E becoming parties to (and so liable in respect of) the wider conspiracy.[67]

2–036 In some cases, the issue will be a dry analytical one with no practical consequences (for example, if the same group of defendants had the same involvement in all the same acts carried out over a period). In other cases, though, a finding that there were separate conspiracies may allow some defendants to escape or limit their liability if they are not held to have been party to a single over-arching conspiracy. An example of this is *AG of Zambia*,[68] in which Peter Smith J held some defendants liable pursuant to an overarching conspiracy, and others pursuant to specific conspiracies in relation to specific misappropriations of funds.[69]

2–037 The point is also capable of having practical importance in the context of how the claimant's claim is pleaded. In *AG of Zambia*, only one overarching conspiracy had been pleaded. This was not held to preclude a lesser finding of liability based on sub-conspiracies, but it appears the defendants did not contend that it should have done.[70] And there are examples going the other way: see e.g. *Colliers CRE Plc v Pandya*,[71] in which HHJ Seymour QC held that the claimant's decision to limit its pleading to a single conspiracy precluded a finding that a particular corporate defendant was party to it, since it was not party to the initial agreement. A claimant who wishes to preserve the possibility of presenting its claim according to these alternative analyses would be well advised to ensure the alternatives are each pleaded. In addition, whether there is one overarching conspiracy or multiple conspiracies can in principle be relevant to the court's jurisdiction over different defendants.[72]

---

[67] *Latmar Holdings Corp v Media Focus Ltd* [2013] EWCA Civ 4; [2013] I.L.Pr. 19 (CA), at [25].

[68] *Attorney General of Zambia v Meer Care & Desai (A Firm)* [2007] EWHC 952. The decision of Peter Smith J was partially reversed by two decisions of the Court of Appeal, but the principle as expressed in this paragraph of the main text is not affected by those decisions.

[69] For another recent example of consideration being given to alternative analyses see *Twentieth Century Fox Film Corp v Harris* [2014] EWHC 1568 (Ch), per Barling J especially at [151].

[70] *AG of Zambia v Meer Care & Desai* [2007] EWHC 952 (Ch), at [202].

[71] *Colliers CRE Plc v Pandya* [2009] EWHC 211 (QB), at [108]. The correctness of this result is, however, open to question on the basis that, even if there were only one conspiracy, the corporate defendant could have been found to have joined it at a later date, without the need to plead a second conspiracy to which it was party. See fn.252 below.

[72] See *Latmar Holdings Corp v Media Focus Ltd* [2013] EWCA Civ 4; [2013] I.L.Pr 19. (CA) (especially at [38]–[46]), considering (and rejecting) the submission that separate conspiracies were alleged against different defendants and the different claims were not so closely connected that they had to be heard together to avoid the risk of inconsistent judgments.

C. UNLAWFUL MEANS CONSPIRACY

(1) Combination

This is considered at paras 2–011—2–016 above.

2–038

(2) Intention

To be liable in unlawful means conspiracy, a defendant must intend to cause 2–039
damage to the claimant. It is not necessary for that to be the defendant's
predominant purpose (unlike in lawful means conspiracy). Whilst it had at one
time been thought that the more exacting test of "predominant purpose" applied
to both types of conspiracy,[73] this was a misconception corrected by the House of
Lords in *Lonrho Plc v Fayed*.[74] All that is needed for unlawful means conspiracy
is an intention to injure.[75] In reality almost all conspiracies are undertaken with a
view to illicit gain on the part of the conspirators at the expense of the victim. As
we explain below, where gain to the conspirators is necessarily at the expense of
loss to the victim then the requisite intention to injure is shown.

In *OBG Ltd v Allan*,[76] the House of Lords considered the level of intentionality 2–040
required to establish liability in the related economic torts of inducing a breach of
contract and unlawful interference. Whilst the many subtle differences between
the various economic torts mean it cannot be assumed that the same principles
will apply to ingredients common to different causes of action, it now appears
settled that the test of intention as formulated in *OBG Ltd v Allan* applies also to
unlawful means conspiracy.[77]

As Lord Hoffmann stated in *OBG Ltd v Allan*, it is necessary to distinguish 2–041
between ends, means and consequences. If harm to the claimant is the end sought
by the defendants (because, say, of some animus harboured by the defendants
against the victim of the conspiracy), the requisite intention is made out. The
same is true if harm to the claimant is the means by which the defendants seek to
secure some other end (e.g. benefit to themselves), even if the defendants would
rather have secured that end without causing harm to the claimant. On the other
hand, if harm is neither an end nor a means, but merely a foreseeable
consequence, the requisite intention is not made out.[78] An example may be

---

[73] This was how the Court of Appeal in *Metall und Rohstoff AG v Donaldson Lufkin & Jenrette Inc*
[1990] 1 Q.B. 391 interpreted the House of Lords' decision in *Lonrho Ltd v Shell Petroleum Co (No.2)*
[1982] A.C. 173.
[74] *Lonrho Plc v Fayed* [1992] 1 A.C. 448, at 463–468.
[75] *Lonrho Plc v Fayed* [1992] 1 A.C. 448, at 468; *Kuwait Oil Tanker v Al Bader* [2000] 2 All E.R.
(Comm) 271, at [118].
[76] *OBG Ltd v Allan* [2007] UKHL 21; [2008] 1 A.C. 1.
[77] See *Meretz Investments NV v ACP Ltd* [2007] EWCA Civ 1303; [2008] Ch. 244, at [146]; *Bank of
Tokyo-Mitsubishi UFJ Ltd v Başkan Gida Sanayi Ve Pazarlama AS* [2009] EWHC 1276 (Ch), per
Briggs J at [826]–[833]; *Digicel (St Lucia) Ltd v Cable & Wireless Plc* [2010] EWHC 774 (Ch), per
Morgan J at Annex I [84].
[78] *OBG Ltd v Allan* [2007] UKHL 21; [2008] 1 A.C. 1, per Lord Hoffmann at [42]–[43], [62]; per
Lord Nicholls at [164]–[166].

borrowed from the tort of inducing breach of contract to illustrate this. In *Millar v Bassey*,[79] the singer Shirley Bassey broke her recording contract with her record label, with the consequence that the label in turn broke its contract with its session musicians. But this consequence was no more than that; it was neither the end sought by Ms Bassey nor a means to her end of extricating herself from her contract. In those circumstances *Millar v Bassey* was overruled in *OBG Ltd v Allan*, Lord Hoffmann saying that the Court of Appeal had been wrong to allow Mr Millar's case to proceed.[80]

2–042 However, where loss to the claimant is the obverse side of the coin to gain to the defendants, i.e. the two are inseparably linked, the requisite intention is made out.[81] However, if a claimant relies on the "obverse side of the coin" analysis in order to infer an intention to injure on the part of the defendants, the "inseparable link" between the defendants' primary intention and damage to the claimant must nevertheless be established. It is not enough, for example, that conspirators intend to benefit themselves at the expense of a class of persons of which the claimant was one.[82] On the other hand, it has been said that recklessness as to whether the claimant would be harmed should in principle be sufficient to found liability.[83]

2–043 In the *Kuwait Oil Tanker* case[84] it was said that, if an act is done deliberately and with knowledge of its consequences, the person doing the act cannot sensibly say that they did not intend those consequences. This must now be read in the light of the principles authoritatively set out in *OBG Ltd v Allan*. In fact the *Kuwait Oil Tanker* case is probably best understood as an example of the "obverse side of the coin" analysis in its application.[85]

2–044 The necessary intention must of course be proved, but not necessarily by direct evidence. It can be inferred from the acts themselves.[86]

2–045 In *OBG Ltd v Allan* Lord Hoffmann disapproved of the approach taken by the Court of Appeal in that case to the interplay between the scope of "unlawful means" and the test of intention in the unlawful interference tort, concluding that the Court of Appeal had adopted an unduly wide approach to what constituted unlawful means and an unduly narrow approach to intention, "insisting upon a highly specific intention, which 'targets' the plaintiff".[87] Whilst (as explained

---

[79] *Millar v Bassey* [1994] E.M.L.R. 44.

[80] *OBG Ltd v Allan* [2007] UKHL 21; [2008] 1 A.C. 1, at [43].

[81] *OBG Ltd v Allan* [2007] UKHL 21; [2008] 1 A.C. 1, per Lord Nicholls at [167].

[82] *WH Newson Holding Ltd v IMI Plc* [2013] EWCA Civ 1377; [2014] 1 All E.R. 1132, at [38]–[41]. The Court of Appeal found that loss to the claimant was not an inevitable consequence of the defendants' actions. *Newson* was referred to with approval in *Emerald Supplies Ltd v British Airways Plc* [2015] EWCA Civ 1024; [2016] Bus.L.R. 145, at [152].

[83] *Bank Gesellschaft Berlin International SA v Zihnali* [2001] All E.R. (D) 192 (Jul), per Colman J, (16 July 2001), at [31]. It is perhaps debatable whether this remains the position after *OBG Ltd v Allan*.

[84] *Kuwait Oil Tanker v Al Bader* [2000] 2 All E.R. (Comm) 271, at [121], quoting with approval from *Bourgoin SA v Minister of Agriculture, Fisheries and Food* [1986] Q.B. 716, at 777.

[85] See *Kuwait Oil Tanker v Al Bader* [2000] 2 All E.R. (Comm) 271, at [121]; and *Bank of Tokyo-Mitsubishi UFJ Ltd v Başkan Gida Sanayi Ve Pazarlama AS* [2009] EWHC 1276 (Ch) per Briggs J at [830]–[832].

[86] *Kuwait Oil Tanker v Al Bader* [2000] 2 All E.R. (Comm) 271, at [120].

[87] *OBG Ltd v Allan* [2007] UKHL 21; [2008] 1 A.C. 1, at [60] and [135].

above) subsequent cases have treated *OBG Ltd v Allan* as authoritative on the mental elements of an unlawful means conspiracy claim, the House of Lords in the later decision in *Total Network* reintroduced the concept of action "targeted" at or "directed" against the claimant.[88]

This concept, of unlawful means directed against the claimant, is best categorised as a limiting factor in the scope of what unlawful means can give rise to liability in conspiracy. It is accordingly considered in that context below (see paras 2–085—2–086). However, to answer the question of whether a defendant's conduct is directed against the claimant also involves analysis of that defendant's intention. In cases of unlawful means conspiracy, therefore, intention needs to be considered at two stages of the analysis: first, in considering whether there is the necessary intention to cause loss; but secondly and additionally, in considering whether relevant unlawful means have been used.

2–046

(3)   Unlawful Means or Acts

(i)   Introduction

The tort being examined here is commonly known as "unlawful means conspiracy". Each of the words in the phrase "unlawful means" encapsulates a separate concept. The first concerns the unlawfulness of the act (or means), and requires consideration of which types of unlawful act are, as a matter of law, capable of founding liability. The second concept concerns the question of whether an unlawful act is, in fact, the "means" by which injury is inflicted on the claimant pursuant to the conspiracy.[89] It is clear from the House of Lords' decision in *Total Network* that these are two separate concepts. Consistently with this binary categorisation, in *JSC BTA Bank v Khrapunov* the Supreme Court considered that the real test for what constitutes unlawful means in the tort of conspiracy is whether there is a just cause or excuse for combining to use unlawful means, which depends in turn on:

2–047

(i)   the nature of the unlawfulness, and
(ii)   its relationship with the resultant damage to the claimant.[90]

This section is concerned with the first of these concepts, and will use the label "unlawful act". The second can be reformulated as requiring consideration of whether the unlawful act is the means by which damage is inflicted on the claimant, or alternatively whether the unlawful act is targeted against the claimant. This second concept is considered in paras 2–081—2–091 below.

2–048

---

[88] *Revenue & Customs Commissioners v Total Network SL* [2008] UKHL 19; [2008] 1 A.C. 1174, at [43], [99] and [124].

[89] Morgan J drew this distinction in *Digicel (St Lucia) Ltd v Cable & Wireless Plc* [2010] EWHC 774 (Ch) at Annex I, in particular, at [3].

[90] *JSC BTA Bank v Khrapunov* [2018] 2 W.L.R. 1125, at [11].

2-049   In *OBG Ltd v Allan* the House of Lords considered what qualified as an unlawful act as far as the separate tort of unlawful interference[91] was concerned, deciding in particular that the unlawful act had to be independently actionable.[92] It had been thought by many commentators that the same principle should apply to unlawful means conspiracies. That would have had the advantage of aiding a coherent and consistent approach across related economic torts.[93] However, in *Total Network* the House of Lords declined to apply the approach taken in *OBG Ltd v Allan* to unlawful means conspiracies. *Total Network* decided that (at least some) crimes can qualify as "unlawful acts" for the purpose of the tort of unlawful means conspiracy, even if they are not independently actionable.[94] Accordingly, the category of relevant "unlawful acts" is wider in unlawful means conspiracy than it is in the tort of unlawful interference.[95]

2-050   The wider effect of *Total Network*, however, has generally fallen to be considered on a case-by-case basis. Although the Supreme Court in *Khrapunov* (where the wrong in question was criminal contempt of court) invited focus on the nature of the unlawful act, its analysis was focused on crimes and expressly left open the question of what other unlawful acts could found a claim in conspiracy, which was said to give rise to "more complex problems".[96] Thus no clear statement of principle has yet emerged which might enable a free-standing analysis of whether a given act will count as an "unlawful act". Those situations which have arisen in the cases are examined below. Given the distinction which emerged from *OBG Ltd v Allan* and *Total Network*, care must be taken before seeking to apply decisions on one tort to claims involving another.

(ii)   Crimes

2-051   It is clear from the House of Lords' decision in *Total Network* that crimes are capable of constituting "unlawful acts" for the purpose of unlawful means conspiracies. Lord Walker said in that case[97]:

> "I derive a general assumption, too obvious to need discussion, that criminal conduct engaged in by conspirators as a means of inflicting harm on the claimant is actionable as the tort of conspiracy, whether or not that conduct, on the part of a single individual, would be actionable as some other tort."

2-052   Lords Scott, Hope and Mance made statements to broadly similar effect.[98] There are, however, differences of expression between the judgments in the case which made it difficult to extract a single consistent principle as to which crimes will

---

[91] See Ch.4.

[92] Unless loss was the only missing element of the cause of action.

[93] See e.g. *Mbasogo v Logo Ltd* [2005] EWHC 2034 (QB), at [59] (on appeal this issue was not addressed [2006] EWCA Civ 1370; [2007] Q.B. 846). See to the same effect Jones (ed), *Clerk & Lindsell on Torts* (2017), para.24–101.

[94] In doing so they overruled Court of Appeal authority to the contrary: *Powell v Boladz* [1998] Lloyd's Rep. Med 116.

[95] *Total Network* [2008] 1 A.C. 1174, at [100], [123], [224].

[96] *JSC BTA Bank v Khrapunov* [2018] UKSC 19; [2018] 2 W.L.R. 1125, at [11] and [15].

[97] *Total Network* [2008] UKHL 19; [2008] 1 A.C. 1174, at [94].

[98] *Total Network* [2008] UKHL 19; [2008] 1 A.C. 1174, at [45], [56], [119]–[120].

constitute relevant unlawful acts, and in what circumstances.[99] However, Lords Walker[100] and Hope[101] indicated that no distinction should be drawn between common law and statutory offences,[102] and—as has subsequently been noted[103]—it is difficult to find support in *Total Network* for the drawing of any distinction between more or less serious crimes, still less any principled method for applying such a distinction in practice.

It was subsequently suggested at first instance that all crimes may qualify as unlawful acts for the purposes of the tort of unlawful means conspiracy.[104] The decision of the Supreme Court in *Khrapunov* provides strong support for this conclusion, treating common law and statutory offences as falling within a single relevant category of failures to comply with the criminal law.[105] (The question of whether a crime is unlawful *means* is, of course, a different question; see paras 2–084—2–091 below.)   **2–053**

Prior to the decision in *Khrapunov*, in *UPL Europe Ltd v AgChemAccess Ltd*[106] Proudman J held that the ambit of unlawful means conspiracy should not be extended to include a breach of regulatory legislation, albeit criminal in nature, where the governmental authority charged with enforcement has said that no prosecution lies. The correctness of that decision may now be open to question. The facts in *UPL* were unusual. Moreover, the basis for the statement by the relevant authority (the Health and Safety Executive) was that criminal proceedings would be an abuse of process. Accordingly the better analysis in such circumstances may be, not that no civil claim lies as a matter of law, but that its pursuit would similarly be an abuse of process.   **2–054**

Total Network and *Khrapunov* concerned offences under the English common law.[107] The same principles do not necessarily apply to offences under foreign   **2–055**

---

[99] See, for example, the qualifications expressed by Lord Mance, at [119]–[120] and by Lord Neuberger, at [221] and [224].

[100] *Total Network* [2008] UKHL 19; [2008] 1 A.C. 1174, at [95].

[101] *Total Network* [2008] UKHL 19; [2008] 1 A.C. 1174, at [45].

[102] In *Belmont Finance Corp v Williams Furniture Ltd (No.2)* [1980] 1 All E.R. 393, a claim succeeded in unlawful means conspiracy on the basis of a breach of s.54 of the Companies Act 1948 (which made it an offence punishable by fine for a company to give financial assistance for the purchase of its own shares). Although the directors in Belmont were also found to be in breach of their duties to the company of which they were directors (see 405f-g), this does not appear to have been a ground for deciding that there was an unlawful means conspiracy, which was founded on the breach of s.54 alone (see 400f). In *Holyoake v Candy* [2017] EWHC 3397 (Ch), at [446], Nugee J accepted that blackmail, an offence under s.21 of the Theft Act 1968, may be relied on as unlawful means (but the allegation of blackmail failed on the facts).

[103] *Digicel (St Lucia) Ltd v Cable & Wireless Plc* [2010] EWHC 774 (Ch), at Annex I [49].

[104] *Digicel (St Lucia) Ltd v Cable & Wireless Plc* [2010] EWHC 774 (Ch), at Annex I [53]–[54].

[105] *JSC BTA Bank v Khrapunov* [2018] UKSC 19; [2018] 2 W.L.R. 1125, at [15], where breaches of the criminal law were considered as a whole, and distinguished from various types of "non-criminal acts".

[106] *UPL Europe Ltd v AgChemAccess Ltd* [2017] EWHC 1880 (Ch), at [143].

[107] Albeit the Court of Appeal in *Khrapunov* considered that they were dealing with civil contempt, in contrast to the Supreme Court which treated the unlawful means alleged as criminal contempt: compare [2017] EWCA Civ 40; [2017] Q.B. 853, at [48] with [2018] UKSC 19; [2018] 2 W.L.R. 1125, at [16]. See further at para.2–068 below.

laws, but which are not recognised as crimes by the English law. This issue is addressed at paras 2–072—2–076 below.

(iii)   Civil wrongs actionable by the claimant

2–056   **Tort.**   Early authority indicates in general terms that a conspiracy to commit a tort would be actionable as what is now understood as an unlawful means conspiracy.[108] Examples from cases prior to *Total Network* include torts such as intimidation through threats to breach a contract,[109] inducing breach of contract,[110] unlawful interference with business,[111] and deceit.[112] Where the conspiracy is to commit a tort, the conspiracy does not merge in the tort. In other words, the claimant is not precluded from alleging both the conspiracy and the tort, though it will frequently be the case that the defendants to the tort claim will be a smaller group than the defendants to the conspiracy claim.[113]

2–057   **Breach of Contract.**   In *Rookes v Barnard*[114] the question of whether a breach of contract could qualify as a relevant unlawful act was left open. After *Total Network*, Morgan J in the *Digicel* case discussed the issue but declined to decide it, though expressing doubt as to the appropriateness of recognising liability for a conspiracy to breach a contract existing alongside liability for inducing breach of contract.[115] However, more recent cases have consistently held that a breach of contract can amount to an unlawful act for the purposes of unlawful means conspiracy.[116] That includes breach of an employee's implied duties of good faith and fidelity.[117]

2–058   **Breach of (Civil) Statutory Duty.**   As explained below,[118] there is continued controversy as to whether a breach of statutory duty must be separately

---

[108] *Sorrell v Smith* [1925] A.C. 700, at 730.

[109] *Rookes v Barnard* [1964] A.C. 1129; *Messenger Group Newspapers Ltd v National Graphical Association* [1984] I.R.L.R. 397, at [53]–[54].

[110] *Mogul Steamship Co Ltd v McGregor, Gow & Co* [1892] A.C. 25, at 37; *Messenger Group Newspapers Ltd v National Graphical Association* [1984] I.C.R. 345, at [53]–[54]. It was said in *De Jetley Marks v Greenwood* [1936] 1 All E.R. 863, at 872 that, in a case of unlawful means conspiracy involving inducement of a breach of contract, the breach is a necessary element of the cause of action. This is supported by *OBG Ltd v Allan* [2007] UKHL 21; [2008] 1 A.C. 1, per Lord Hoffmann at [44]. Dicta suggesting otherwise in earlier cases (*Torquay Hotel Co Ltd v Cousins* [1969] 2 Ch.106, at 138; *Merkur Island Shipping Corp v Laughton* [1983] 2 A.C. 570, at 607–608) are no longer good law. They were also disapproved in *OBG* by Lord Nicholls (at [181]–[190]) and Lord Walker (at [264]).

[111] *Messenger Group Newspapers Ltd v National Graphical Association* [1984] I.R.L.R. 397, at [53]–[54].

[112] *Crofter Hand Woven Harris Tweed Co Ltd v Veitch* [1942] A.C. 435, at 462.

[113] *Kuwait Oil Tanker v Al Bader* [2000] 2 All E.R. (Comm) 271, at [122]–[132].

[114] *Rookes v Barnard* [1964] A.C. 1129, at 1209–1210, per Lord Devlin.

[115] *Digicel (St Lucia) Ltd v Cable & Wireless Plc* [2010] EWHC 774 (Ch), at Annex I [63]–[68].

[116] *Aerostar Maintenance International Ltd v Wilson* [2010] EWHC 2032 (Ch), at [170]–[172] (although Morgan J repeated the concerns as to dual liability which he had expressed in *Digicel*); *Fiona Trust & Holding Corp v Privalov* [2010] EWHC 3199 (Comm), at [69]; *Novoship (UK) Ltd v Mikhaylyuk* [2012] EWHC 3586 (Comm), at [103] (overturned in part on appeal but not on this point: [2014] EWCA Civ 908; [2015] Q.B. 499).

[117] *Reuse Collections Ltd v Sendall* [2014] EWHC 3852 (QB); [2015] I.R.L.R. 226, at [173].

[118] Paragraphs 2–062—2–064 below.

actionable by the claimant in order to be the unlawful act founding the basis of a conspiracy claim. The problem is that a breach of statutory duty is not necessarily actionable by a private litigant harmed by the breach (there is substantial jurisprudence on this question). This may be what Lords Sumption and Lloyd-Jones had in mind when they observed in *JSC BTA Bank v Khrapunov* that the relevance of a breach of civil statutory duty may depend on the purpose of the relevant provision, which may or may not be consistent with its deployment as an element in the tort of conspiracy.[119] The cases discussing the problem necessarily proceed, however, on the footing that a breach of statutory duty *will* qualify as a relevant unlawful act if it *is* separately actionable by the claimant. Indeed a privately actionable breach of statutory duty is analogous to a tort, and it is difficult to see why the latter should sustain a claim in conspiracy but the former should not. The breach of a directly applicable provision of EU law ought to engage the same principles as the breach of a domestic statute.[120]

A transaction defrauding creditors caught by s.423 of the Insolvency Act 1986 can in principle count as a relevant unlawful act.[121]   **2–059**

Breach of Fiduciary Duty.   Recent authority indicates that a breach of fiduciary duty will qualify as a relevant unlawful act.[122]   **2–060**

Breach of Confidence.   Breach of confidence has been relied on successfully where it also amounts to a breach of contract.[123] In *Douglas v Hello! Ltd (No.6)*[124] the Court of Appeal held (obiter) that a breach of confidence independent of contract could amount to unlawful means for the purpose of the tort of unlawful interference. The House of Lords[125] allowed the appeal without the majority considering this point in terms.[126] Lord Hoffmann's view that acts against a third party would only count as "*unlawful means*" for the unlawful interference tort if they affected the third party's freedom to deal with the   **2–061**

---

[119] *JSC BTA Bank v Khrapunov* [2018] UKSC 19; [2018] 2 W.L.R. 1125, at [15].

[120] This is also the view of the authors of Jones (ed), *Clerk & Lindsell on Torts* (2017), para.24–105.

[121] *Concept Oil Services Ltd v En-Gin Group LLP* [2013] EWHC 1897 (Comm), per Flaux J at [50], who did not actually decide the point. There is some support for the possibility of a transaction susceptible to being set aside under s.423 of the Insolvency Act 1986 being sufficient unlawful means in *Gerald Metals SA v Timis* [2017] EWHC 1375 (Comm), at [14].

[122] *Aerostar Maintenance International Ltd v Wilson* [2010] EWHC 2032 (Ch), at [170]–[172]; *Fiona Trust & Holding Corp v Privalov* [2010] EWHC 3199 (Comm), at [69]; *Novoship (UK) Ltd v Mikhaylyuk* [2012] EWHC 3586 (Comm), at [103], citing views to that effect expressed by Thomas J without deciding the point in *Sphere Drake Insurance v Euro International Underwriting* [2003] Lloyd's Rep. IR 525, at [85]–[88].

[123] *Indata Equipment Supplies Ltd v ACL Ltd* [1998] F.S.R. 260 (obiter); *Croesus Financial Services Ltd v Bradshaw* [2013] EWHC 3685 (QB), at [114]–[120].

[124] *Douglas v Hello! Ltd (No.6)* [2005] EWCA Civ 595; [2006] Q.B. 125, at [229]–[235].

[125] *OBG Ltd v Allan* [2007] UKHL 21; [2008] 1 A.C. 1.

[126] It was argued in the House of Lords that breach of confidence was not capable of constituting unlawful means for the purpose of the tort of unlawful interference: see [2007] UKHL 21; [2008] 1 A.C. 1, at 16A-B. Lord Nicholls would have rejected this argument (see [162]). In *National Westminster Bank Plc v Bonas* [2003] EWHC 1821 (Ch) a claim for unlawful interference, the "unlawful means" alleged being breach of confidence, the claim failed for lack of causation; it does not appear to have been argued that breach of confidence was incapable of amounting to "unlawful means" (see [155]).

claimant[127] prevented breach of confidence from satisfying the test in that case. But this limiting factor has not taken hold in the jurisprudence concerning unlawful means conspiracy.[128] It is suggested that any breach of confidence should be capable to constituting an unlawful act for the purposes of grounding a claim in unlawful means conspiracy.

(iv) Civil wrongs not actionable by the claimant

2–062   Here the position is more complicated. Before *Total Network*, it had been considered that an unlawful act had to be separately actionable at the suit of the claimant in order to found liability in unlawful means conspiracy. The Court of Appeal in *Total Network* considered themselves bound to follow the decision to that effect in *Powell v Boladz*.[129]

2–063   In *Total Network* the House of Lords overruled *Powell v Boladz* in holding that (at least some) criminal acts which were not also separately actionable by the claimant could nevertheless qualify as unlawful acts for the purposes of conspiracy. However, that left a complete lack of clarity as to whether civil wrongs not actionable by the claimant remained outside the scope of relevant unlawful acts. As Morgan J said in the *Digicel* case,[130] the overruling of *Powell v Boladz*

> "does not necessarily mean that it is now the law that all crimes and all breaches of contract are unlawful acts for the purposes of this tort."

2–064   In *Digicel* itself, Morgan J concluded that non-actionable breaches of a non-criminal statute could not constitute "unlawful acts" for the purposes of unlawful means conspiracy. The judge expressed concern about the need to proceed incrementally, and the potentially wide effect of extending (as he saw it) the law in this way. He expressed a specific concern that, in light of the fact that companies within the same group can conspire with each other,[131] "it would not be difficult to turn non-actionable breaches of a statute into an actionable conspiracy in many cases where one has the involvement of more than one company in a group of companies".[132]

2–065   Similarly, Hamblen J held in *Brown v InnovatorOne Plc*[133] that a breach of statutory duty could not found an unlawful means conspiracy unless the relevant statutory obligation was, on its proper construction, imposed for the benefit of a particular class (though he did not address the question of whether the class needed to include the claimant). *Lonrho Ltd v Shell Petroleum Co Ltd (No.2)*[134]

---

[127] *OBG Ltd v Allan* [2007] UKHL 21; [2008] 1 A.C. 1, at [51] and [129].
[128] The Court of Appeal in *Douglas v Hello! Ltd (No.6)*, above, went one step further, deciding that the duty of confidence did not need to be one owed to the claimant (see [234]). On the status of civil wrongs not actionable by the claimant after *Total Network*, see paras 2–062—2–067 below.
[129] *Powell v Boladz* [1998] Lloyd's Rep. Med 116.
[130] *Digicel (St Lucia) Ltd v Cable & Wireless Plc* [2010] EWHC 774 (Ch), at Annex I [25].
[131] See paras 2–017—2–024 above.
[132] *Digicel (St Lucia) Ltd v Cable & Wireless Plc* [2010] EWHC 774 (Ch), at [55]–[62].
[133] *Brown v InnovatorOne Plc* [2012] EWHC 1321 (Comm), at [527].
[134] *Lonrho Ltd v Shell Petroleum Co Ltd (No.2)* [1982] A.C. 173.

was cited as authority for this proposition. (However, it is thought that such a reading of the *Lonrho* case cannot survive the decision of the House of Lords in *Total Network*, who considered that the real point decided in *Lonrho* was simply that an intention to injure was a necessary ingredient in the cause of action for conspiracy.)[135] And in *Chang v Mishcon de Reya*[136] HHJ Hodge QC held that neither non-actionable breaches of a non-criminal statute, nor breaches of professional conduct rules, were "unlawful acts" for the purpose of unlawful means conspiracy.

In *Fiona Trust*,[137] Andrew Smith J said that **2–066**

> "the law does not require that the unlawful means should themselves be actionable at the suit of the claimant: the means might be a criminal action, a breach of contract, a director's fiduciary duty to a company[138] or fraud."

Notably, apart from the crime example, all of these examples are of conduct which, in principle, would be actionable by a third party. Consistently with this, it has subsequently been held that non-criminal acts against a third party would only count as relevant unlawful acts if actionable by that third party.[139]

It is therefore suggested that, provided that an actionable civil wrong has been **2–067** committed by one or more conspirators, there will be an unlawful act capable of founding a claim in unlawful means conspiracy, even if that act is not actionable at the suit of the claimant. Indeed, any more restrictive conclusion would risk making the scope of unlawful acts narrower in the tort of conspiracy than it is in the tort of unlawful interference, whereas it was held in *Total Network* that the opposite is the case.[140]

---

[135] *Revenue & Customs Commissioners v Total Network SL* [2008] UKHL 19; [2008] 1 A.C. 1174. See per Lord Hope at [38]; per Lord Walker at [79], [82], [87] and [103]; and per Lord Mance at [116]. Lord Walker did, however, suggest, at [96] that the sorts of considerations which govern whether a breach of statutory duty is actionable privately might overlap or occasionally coincide with the issue of unlawful means in the tort of conspiracy.

[136] *Chang v Mishcon de Reya* [2015] EWHC 164 (Ch), at [49]–[50].

[137] *Fiona Trust & Holding Corp v Privalov* [2010] EWHC 3199 (Comm), at [69].

[138] There is authority prior to *Total Network* which offers some support for this: in *Prudential Assurance Co Ltd v Newman Industries Ltd (No.2)* [1981] Ch. 257 Vinelott J held at first instance that the defendant directors were liable to a shareholder for a conspiracy to commit breaches of fiduciary duty owed to a company by the defendants as directors. The Court of Appeal ([1982]. Ch 204) allowed the appeal on the basis that the shareholders' claim was barred by the rule against reflective loss. The question of whether the unlawful means had to be separately actionable by the claimant does not seem to have been argued.

[139] *Thames Valley Housing Association Ltd v Elegant (Guernsey) Ltd* [2011] EWHC 1288 (Ch); [2011] N.P.C. 54, at [103], citing *OBG Ltd v Allan* [2007] UKHL 21; [2008] 1 A.C. 1. Although *OBG* was an unlawful interference case, it is suggested that this particular principle can be carried over into the tort of conspiracy.

[140] See para.2–049 above.

(v) Other wrongs

2–068   **Contempt of Court.** In *Acrow Automation v Rex Chainbelt Inc*[141] the Court of Appeal held that criminal contempt of court qualified as an unlawful act for the purposes of what is now understood to be the unlawful interference tort. The Supreme Court confirmed the correctness of this proposition in *JSC BTA Bank v Khrapunov*[142] (albeit no reference is made in the judgments to the *Acrow Automation* case itself). The Court of Appeal, also in the *Khrapunov* case, held that civil contempt (in the form of disobedience to a court order) similarly qualifies as an unlawful act[143] for the purposes of conspiracy.

2–069   This confirmation that both civil and criminal contempt of court qualify as relevant unlawful acts is a development of some practical importance in the fraud context. As noted in *Phoenix Group Foundation v Cochrane*,[144] the complicity of a third party in a breach of a court order may open up the possibility of a claim in conspiracy against that third party and so the further possibility of obtaining a freezing injunction against him as a cause of action defendant. Among other things this may allow a claimant to overcome the difficulties in establishing jurisdiction over a defendant against whom no substantive cause of action is asserted, for the sole purpose of seeking a freezing order.[145] Indeed this appears to have been part of the rationale behind the claim in *Khrapunov*.

2–070   In *Khrapunov*, the Supreme Court rejected the contention that to recognise criminal contempt of court as capable of giving rise to a civil claim in conspiracy would be contrary to public policy.[146] However, this is subject to an exception (recognised in *Khrapunov* itself) where the contempt consists in the giving of false evidence in court. In such a case the claimant would be precluded from bringing an action based on the rule of public policy preventing witnesses from being sued in respect of evidence given by them in judicial proceedings.[147]

---

[141] [1971] 1 W.L.R. 1676, per Lord Denning at 1682–1683, in the context of criminal contempt as accessory to the breach of a court order. In *Khrapunov* Sales LJ described the *Acrow* case as supporting the argument that civil contempt qualified as unlawful means (see [2017] EWCA Civ 40; [2017] Q.B. 853, at [49]), though this is uncertain.

[142] *JSC BTA Bank v Khrapunov* [2018] UKSC 19; [2018] 2 W.L.R. 1125.

[143] [2017] EWCA Civ 40; [2017] Q.B. 853. It is not clear from the respective judgments why the Court of Appeal addressed their analysis to civil contempt ([2017] Q.B. 853, at [48] in particular), whereas the Supreme Court stated ([2018] 2 W.L.R. 1125, at [16]) that the unlawful means alleged was criminal contempt. It may be that the Court of Appeal was addressing the position from the perspective of Mr Ablyazov as party to the court order, whereas the Supreme Court was considering Mr Khrapunov's position as a third party, not directly bound by the order but liable in criminal contempt if he assisted a breach of it.

[144] *Phoenix Group Foundation v Cochrane* [2017] EWHC 418 (Comm), at [20] and [24], per Popplewell J.

[145] See the discussion of the *Chabra* jurisdiction, at paras 28–157—28–196.

[146] *JSC BTA Bank v Khrapunov* [2018] UKSC 19; [2018] 2 W.L.R. 1125, at [17]–[23].

[147] *JSC BTA Bank v Khrapunov* [2018] UKSC 19; [2018] 2 W.L.R. 1125, at [23]. See also *Hargreaves v Bretherton* [1959] 1 Q.B. 45; *Marrinan v Vibart* [1963] 1 Q.B. 528 and *Irish Response Ltd v Direct Beauty Products* [2011] EWHC 37 (QB). However, if the giving of false evidence is not a necessary allegation in the claim but is merely an incidental part of a wider conspiracy, the witness immunity rule does not apply: *Surzur Overseas Ltd v Koros* [1999] 2 Lloyd's Rep. 611; [1999] C.L.C. 801, at 811–812.

Conduct Not Amounting to an Unlawful Act.   A false statement which is not   **2–071**
in itself actionable is not a relevant unlawful act.[148] Similarly, putting together
false documentation to cover up previous actions, not in themselves tortious, will
not be an unlawful act such that a conspiracy to carry out those actions becomes
tortious.[149] The better view seems to be that an arrangement which the court
would not enforce on public policy grounds (e.g. a contract in restraint of trade) is
not, for that reason alone, an unlawful act for these purposes.[150]

(vi)   Acts unlawful under foreign laws

The question of whether offences under foreign laws are capable of constituting   **2–072**
unlawful acts for the purposes of an English unlawful means conspiracy has
received comparatively little attention by the courts and in commentary. Given
the international nature of many modern conspiracies, however, sooner or later it
will be necessary for the question to be properly grappled with at the judicial
level. Where acts said to be unlawful under foreign laws are concerned, there are
a number of additional and complicating factors which need to be considered.

The first question to be considered in such a case will be whether English law   **2–073**
applies to the conspiracy claim in the first place. In general the English Court
currently determines the applicable law in accordance with the Rome II
Regulation, in particular art.4.[151] Whilst the primary rule in art.4(1) points to the
law of the place where the damage occurs, a proliferation of unlawful acts abroad
may mean that the conspiracy is manifestly more closely connected with another
country such that the claim as a whole is in fact governed by a foreign law.[152]

If the law applicable to the conspiracy claim as a whole is English law, logically   **2–074**
the next question is whether conflicts of laws principles then allow reliance on
acts unlawful under foreign law as part of an English law conspiracy claim. It is
thought that there is no reason in principle why not[153]; it is not uncommon for
claims under English law to require reference to a foreign system of law for some
specific purpose.[154] There is, however, little authority on the point.

---

[148] *Stocznia Gdanska SA v Latvian Shipping Co* [2001] 1 Lloyd's Rep. 537, at [304].

[149] *Fiona Trust & Holding Corp v Privalov* [2010] EWHC 3199 (Comm), at [69].

[150] *Mogul Steamship Co Ltd v McGregor, Gow & Co* [1892] A.C. 25, at 39, 45–46, 51, 57, 58; *Davies v Thomas* [1920] 2 Ch. 189, at 202–203; *Eastham v Newcastle United FC* [1964] Ch. 413, per Wilberforce J at 453. Though some doubt was cast on this principle in *Daily Mirror Newspapers Ltd v Gardner* [1968] 2 Q.B. 762, that decision has itself been questioned: see *Revenue & Cusoms Commissioners v Total Network SL* [2008] UKHL 19; [2008] 1 A.C. 1174, per Lord Walker at [91] and [93].

[151] Regulation (EC) No. 864/2007, applicable in relation to the period from January 2009 onwards (see art.32).

[152] Article 4(3).

[153] This is also the view of the authors of Lord Collins of Mapesbury and J. Harris (eds), *Dicey, Morris and Collins on the Conflict of Laws*, 15th edn (London: Sweet & Maxwell, 2017), Fourth supplement, para.34–069.

[154] For a recent example, see *Erste Group AG v JSC "VMZ Red October"* [2015] EWCA 379; [2015] 1 C.C.C. 706, which involved a preliminary dispute as to the applicable law of a conspiracy claim. The Court (at [148(iv)]) pointed out that (as was common ground), even if the conspiracy claim was governed by English law, Russian law would still govern the relationships between the various defendants (i.e. questions such as attribution of knowledge and intention).

2–075   Assuming there is no conflicts problem, that does not necessarily mean that (simply as a matter of English domestic law) foreign unlawful acts can be relied on to found an unlawful means conspiracy. Several decisions have contemplated that they can or indeed proceeded on that basis, but without this particular point being argued.[155] The decision in *Irish Response Ltd v Direct Beauty Products*[156] arguably lends some support to the opposite view, but it was not interpreted in *Emerald Supplies Ltd v British Airways Plc*[157] as having decided the point, and in the latter case Peter Smith J also declined to do so as a preliminary issue.

2–076   Where the foreign unlawful act relied on is a breach of a foreign penal or public law, an English law conspiracy claim founded on such an unlawful act may well be open to the objection that its adjudication is prevented by the rule against direct or indirect enforcement of a foreign penal or other public law.[158]

(4)   The Defendant Need Not Know that the Acts Carried out were Unlawful

2–077   It has been explained above[159] that it is not necessary to show knowledge on the part of a given defendant of all the acts carried out pursuant to the conspiracy in order to fix that defendant with liability. However, to be party to an unlawful means conspiracy, a defendant must have sufficient knowledge that unlawful acts are being carried out so as to implicate him in liability for those unlawful acts. The question is whether it is sufficient for the defendant to know simply that acts are being carried out and for those acts to be held to have been unlawful, or whether the defendant must also know that the acts are unlawful. Whilst this question has not been given a consistent answer in the decided cases, on the current state of the authorities it seems that such knowledge is not necessary, i.e. lack of knowledge that the relevant conduct is unlawful is no defence.

2–078   In *British Industrial Plastics Ltd v Ferguson*,[160] a conspiracy claim failed against a company approached by the claimant's former employee to exploit a secret process, on the basis that the company did not know that its involvement would cause the former employee to breach his contract with the claimant. An apparently divergent decision was later reached in *Belmont Finance Corp v*

---

[155] See *Kuwait Oil Tanker v Al Bader* [2000] 2 All E.R. (Comm) 271, at [131] (a decision concerned with double actionability, now abolished); *Mahonia Ltd v JP Morgan Chase Bank (No.2)* [2004] EWHC 1938 (Comm), at [253] and [364]; *A-G of Zambia v Meer Care & Desai* [2007] EWHC 952 (Ch); *Digicel (St Lucia) Ltd v Cable & Wireless Plc* [2010] EWHC 774 (Ch), at [22]–[23]; [220]–[221] and Annex I [10]; *Lebara Mobile Ltd v Lycamobile UK Ltd* [2015] EWHC 3318 (Ch), at [37]–[38] (in that case it was common ground that foreign unlawful acts could found a claim in unlawful means conspiracy).
[156] *Irish Response Ltd v Direct Beauty Products* [2011] EWHC 37 (QB), at [136] and [153].
[157] *Emerald Supplies Ltd v British Airways Plc* [2014] EWHC 3514 (Ch), at [91]–[102]. The decision was appealed but not on this point: [2015] EWCA Civ 1024; [2016] Bus L.R. 145, at [127].
[158] See Collins, Harris (eds), *Dicey, Morris & Collins on the Conflict of Laws* (2017), r.3, para.5R–019 and following.
[159] Paragraph 2–031.
[160] *British Industrial Plastics Ltd v Ferguson* [1938] 4 All E.R. 504 (CA); [1940] 1 All E.R. 479 (HL).

Williams Furniture Ltd (No.2)[161] (in which the *Ferguson* case was not cited). Buckley LJ held in *Belmont Finance* that:

> "If all the facts which make the transaction unlawful were known to the parties, as I think they were, ignorance of the law will not excuse them."

The issue resurfaced in the Court of Appeal in *Meretz Investment NV v ACP Ltd*.[162] Arden LJ held (at [124]–[127]) that, since the defendants in that case believed they had a lawful right to act as they did, they did not have the necessary intention to induce a breach of contract.[163] She did so in reliance on an earlier decision of her own in which *Belmont Finance* had not been cited.[164] Toulson LJ agreed with Arden LJ and, though he thought it unnecessary to decide the point, would have extended the principle to the unlawful means conspiracy claim (at [174]).

2-079

These (probable) obiter dicta in *Meretz v ACP* were followed by Briggs J in *Bank of Tokyo-Mitsubishi UFJ Ltd v Başkan Gida Sanayi Ve Pazarlama AS*[165] and Morgan J in the *Digicel* case.[166] Morgan J noted the conflict between the authorities on the point, and also observed that, if there were a defence of "honest belief" in this context, since no such general defence exists to a claim against joint tortfeasors, this would make it easier for a claimant to succeed in the latter type of claim than in a claim in unlawful means conspiracy. He left open[167] the question of who bears the burden of proof on the availability or otherwise of the defence of honest belief.

2-080

Shortly after *Digicel* was decided, David Richards J said in *Revenue & Customs Commissioners v Begum*[168] that it was difficult to see why ignorance that the relevant acts are criminal offences should provide a defence to a civil claim in conspiracy, and noted that *Belmont Finance* had decided that it did not. He did not decide the point himself, however. He also suggested (at [48]) that the defendant's knowledge of unlawfulness was not an element of the cause of action which had to be pleaded.

2-081

Subsequent first instance judges who have considered this controversy have felt bound to follow *Belmont Finance* over *Meretz*.[169] Accordingly, unless and until

2-082

---

[161] *Belmont Finance Corp v Williams Furniture Ltd (No.2)* [1980] 1 All E.R. 393, at 404–405.

[162] *Meretz Investment NV v ACP Ltd* [2007] EWCA Civ 1303; [2008] Ch. 244.

[163] This may fairly be said to confuse lack of intention with justification. If a party intends to induce a breach of contract, a belief on his part that he is entitled to do so may give rise to a defence of justification, but it is less obvious that it should be taken to affect his intention.

[164] *Mainstream Properties Ltd v Young* [2005] EWCA Civ 861; [2005] I.R.L.R. 964, upheld by the House of Lords in *OBG Ltd v Allan* [2007] UKHL 21; [2008] 1 A.C. 1.

[165] *Bank of Tokyo-Mitsubishi UFJ Ltd v Başkan Gida Sanayi Ve Pazarlama AS* [2009] EWHC 1276 (Ch), at [836]–[837].

[166] *Digicel (St Lucia) Ltd v Cable & Wireless Plc* [2010] EWHC 774 (Ch) at Annex I [94]–[118].

[167] *Digicel* [2010] EWHC 774 (Ch), at Annex I [119].

[168] *Revenue & Customs Commissioners v Begum* [2010] EWHC 1799 (Ch); [2011] B.P.I.R. 59, at [50].

[169] *First Subsea Ltd v Balltec Ltd* [2014] EWHC 866 (Ch) at [150]–[157], per Norris J (not affected on appeal [2017] EWCA Civ 186; [2018] Ch. 25); *Capital for Enterprise Fund LP v Bibby Financial Services Ltd* [2015] EWHC 2593 (Ch), at [11]–[13], per HHJ Pelling QC (In *Swain v Swains Plc* [2015] EWHC 660 (Ch), at [135] the same judge had expressed the same conclusion, but without

these decisions are overruled at appellate level, it is thought that the law must be taken to be as set out in *Belmont Finance*: ignorance of the law is no defence to a claim in unlawful means conspiracy; all that it is necessary to show is knowledge of the facts that gave the relevant unlawful acts their quality of unlawfulness.

2–083   However, the line between (a) knowledge of facts giving rise to unlawfulness; and (b) knowledge of unlawfulness itself may not always be easy to draw.

In *Clydesdale Bank Plc v Stoke Place Hotel Ltd*,[170] a defendant was held not liable in a conspiracy to extract unauthorised loans from the claimant until the point at which he learned that his co-conspirator, a bank representative, did not have authority to approve the loans. This result can be accommodated within the above distinction, so long as the question of the representative's authority is understood as a factual question (there was a £3 million limit on the borrowing which the representative could sanction).[171] But in other cases authority may be a mixed question of fact and law, making the distinction a more difficult one to draw.

(5)   Unlawful Acts as "Unlawful Means"

2–084   It was explained above (para.2–047) that, in *JSC BTA Bank v Khrapunov*, the Supreme Court considered the ambit of "unlawful means" to be delineated by two concepts: first, the nature of the unlawfulness; and secondly, the relationship of the unlawfulness with the resultant damage to the claimant. The first concept was considered in paras 2–047—2–076 above. This section is concerned with the second concept, which in turn has two aspects to it: intention and causation.

(i)   Intention

2–085   The Supreme Court in *Khrapunov*[172] explained the concept of the relationship between the unlawfulness and the damage caused to the claimant by reference to the judgments of Lords Walker, Mance and Hope in *Total Network*. In the latter case Lord Walker held that "unlawful means" included criminal conduct, "provided that it is indeed the means ... of intentionally inflicting harm."[173] Lord Mance agreed,[174] referring to the commission of an offence "intentionally targeted at" the claimant in that case. He cited the example of a pizza delivery

---

reference to *Meretz*). In *Lebara Mobile Ltd v Lycamobile UK Ltd* [2015] EWHC 3318 (Ch), at [51], Nicholas Lavender QC noted the controversy without deciding the point. By contrast, in *UPL Europe Ltd v AgChemAccess Ltd* [2017] EWHC 1880 (Ch), at [150], Proudman J expressed the obiter view that she would have followed the decision of Morgan J in *Digicel*; but it appears that neither *Swain v Swains* nor *Capital for Enterprise Fund v Bibby* was cited to her. Similarly, in *FM Capital Partners Ltd v Marino* [2018] EWHC 1768 (Comm), at [95], Cockerill J referred to the analysis in *Meretz* as an accurate statement of the law, but it appears that neither *Belmont Finance* nor the more recent cases referred to at the beginning of this footnote were cited to her.
[170] *Clydesdale Bank Plc v Stoke Place Hotel Ltd* [2017] EWHC 181 (Ch).
[171] See [15].
[172] *JSC BTA Bank v Khrapunov* [2018] UKSC 19; [2018] 2 W.L.R. 1125, at [11]–[15].
[173] *Revenue & Customs Commissioners v Total Network SL* [2008] UKHL 19; [2008] 1 A.C. 1174 at [95].
[174] See [116] and [119] in particular.

business which conspired with its directors to obtain more custom to the detriment of its competitors by breaking speed limits and jumping red lights. In such a scenario the unlawful means are not targeted at the competitors but might be described as incidental or collateral to the damage caused to them.[175]

This marks another important distinction between unlawful means conspiracy and unlawful interference. In the context of the latter tort, in *OBG Ltd v Allan* Lord Hoffmann deprecated the decision of the Court of Appeal which, he considered, had struck the wrong balance in seeking to delimit liability for unlawful interference, adopting too wide a definition of "unlawful means" and seeking to bring the scope of liability back into balance by "insisting upon a highly specific intention, which 'targets' the plaintiff."[176] Following *Total Network* and *Khrapunov*, the concept of targeting the claimant is now firmly established as part of the tort of unlawful means conspiracy.

2–086

(ii) Causation

In *Khrapunov*, the Supreme Court treated the language of unlawful acts "targeted at" or "directed against" the claimant as effectively synonymous with Lord Walker's requirement in *Total Network* that the unlawful act must in truth be the means by which intentional damage is inflicted on the claimant. There is a large degree of overlap between the two. However, the language used by Lord Walker in *Total Network* is thought to express more than just a particular aspect of the element of intention; it also expresses a requirement of causation.

2–087

It has always been clear that—as for claims in tort generally—a claimant alleging an unlawful means conspiracy must show damage caused by the conspiracy.[177] However, as a result of the seminal cases decided in the first decade of the 21st century, it has become clear[178] that a claimant must go further than showing that (a) one or more defendants acted unlawfully as part of a conspiracy with an intention to harm the claimant and that (b) acts carried out pursuant to the conspiracy in fact caused damage to the claimant.

2–088

Instead a claimant must show that the unlawful acts carried out pursuant to the conspiracy themselves caused the damage—and were the means of doing so.

In first instance cases after *Total Network*, the House of Lords' decision in that case has been interpreted as demonstrating that the two words in the phrase "unlawful means" denote two separate requirements. The first is that one or more unlawful acts were committed pursuant to the conspiracy (considered in paras 2–047—2–076 above). The second is that the unlawful acts must be the means by which harm is inflicted on the claimant—or, put another way, that the loss

2–089

---

[175] *Digicel (St Lucia) Ltd v Cable & Wireless Plc* [2010] EWHC 774 (Ch), at Annex 1 [71].

[176] *OBG Ltd v Allan* [2007] UKHL 21; [2008] 1 A.C. 1, at [60].

[177] *Crofter Hand Woven Harris Tweed Co Ltd v Veitch* [1942] A.C. 435, at 440; *Midland Bank Trust Co Ltd v Green (No.3)* [1979] Ch. 496, at 522–524; *Kuwait Oil Tanker Co SAK v Al Bader* [2000] 2 All E.R. (Comm) 271, at [108].

[178] The question of whether unlawful acts, carried out incidentally in the course of implementing an otherwise lawful plan, would give rise to liability for unlawful means conspiracy was raised, but not answered, in *British Midland Tool Ltd v Midland International Tooling Ltd* [2003] EWHC 466 (Ch), [2003] 2 B.C.L.C. 523, at [79].

suffered by the claimant was caused by those unlawful acts.[179] Loss caused by other acts carried out further to the conspiracy, but not in themselves unlawful, will not be capable of founding a claim for damages. So for example in *Adams v Atlas International Property Services Ltd*,[180] property agents had persuaded the claimant purchasers to part with the first instalment of the purchase price. Whilst this was alleged to be part of an overall conspiracy between the agents and others, it did not involve any unlawful acts (which only came later). Accordingly the first instalment was held not to be recoverable pursuant to the conspiracy.

2–090   Notwithstanding these exacting requirements as to causation, however, it is inappropriate for the court to become involved in attempts to assess the precise causative significance of a particular defendant's involvement in the conspiracy.[181] Once it is shown that a defendant has joined a conspiracy, then he will be liable for all loss sustained by a claimant by unlawful acts carried out pursuant to the conspiracy, notwithstanding his greater or lesser role in the conspiracy relative to those of other co-conspirators. The issues arising where different defendants have differing levels of involvement are considered at paras 2–111—2–133 below.

2–091   Causation may also arise as an issue at a logically prior stage in the analysis of the cause of action. In the context of unlawful interference, it has been held that it is necessary to show that the defendant's intention to injure the claimant was a cause of his unlawful conduct, so that if (a) the defendant would have carried out the same unlawful conduct without such intention, and (b) that intention alone would not have led him to act as he did, the defendant is not liable despite the fact that he intended to injure the claimant and carried out unlawful acts which did so.[182]

It does not necessarily follow, however, that this requirement would also apply in the context of unlawful means conspiracy—not least because applying such a causation requirement in this context would in practice be likely to be much more difficult in a multi-party conspiracy, where (by definition) more than one

---

[179] See *Bank of Tokyo-Mitsubishi UFJ Ltd v Başkan Gida Sanayi Ve Pazarlama AS* [2009] EWHC 1276 (Ch), at [835] and [837]; *HMRC v Begum* [2010] EWHC 1799 (Ch); [2011] B.P.I.R. 59, at [85]; *Digicel (St Lucia) Ltd v Cable & Wireless Plc* [2010] EWHC 774 (Ch), at Annex I [2]–[3], [49]; see also *Adams v Atlas International Property Services Ltd* [2016] EWHC 3120 (QB), at [219]. In *Bank of Tokyo-Mitsubishi*, at [837], Briggs J went further and said that the defendant must have known that the unlawful part of the conduct carried out pursuant to the conspiracy would cause harm to the claimant, though the question of what knowledge is required on the part of a defendant must now be assessed in light of the authorities referred to in paras 2–077—2–083 above.

[180] *Adams v Atlas International Property Services Ltd* [2016] EWHC 3120 (QB).

[181] *Grupo Torras SA v Al-Sabah* [2001] C.L.C. 221 (CA), at [119] (approving the decision at first instance). *Grupo Torras* was cited with approval in *Casio Computer Co Ltd v Sayo (No.3)* [2001] EWCA Civ 661; [2001] I.L.Pr. 43, at [53] (in the context of dishonest assistance) and in *Otkritie International Investment Management Ltd v Urumov* [2014] EWHC 191 (Comm), at [79].

[182] *OBG Ltd v Allan* [2007] UKHL 21; [2008] 1 A.C. 1, per Lord Nicholls at [166], citing the judgment of Cooke CJ in *Van Camp Chocolates Ltd v Aulsebrooks Ltd* [1984] 1 N.Z.L.R. 354, at 360: "If the defendant would have used the unlawful means in question without that intent and if that intent alone would not have led him to act as he did, the mere existence of the purely collateral and extraneous malicious motive should not make all the difference."

defendant must share an intention to injure the claimant, but not every defendant has to carry out an unlawful act in order to be liable.[183]

D.   LAWFUL MEANS CONSPIRACY

(1)   Introduction

The tort of lawful means conspiracy allows defendants to be made liable for acts which, if they had been carried out by one of them alone, would not be wrongful. The mischief is said to arise out of the fact that the acts are carried out pursuant to a combination between defendants. The justification for this has principally been expressed to be that "a combination may make oppressive or dangerous that which if it proceeded only from a single person would be otherwise".[184] This may have made some sense in cases of employers facing concerted industrial action by disgruntled employees, albeit the justification was highly contentious and was seen by many as being a means by which trade union activity was suppressed. But by the 1980s this rationale was already being described as out of touch with the economic and commercial realities of the time.[185] The tort is now firmly embedded in the jurisprudence. But its anomalous nature is such that a lawful means conspiracy claim will only succeed in the most exceptional case.

2–092

(2)   Combination

This is considered at paras 2–011—2–016 above.

2–093

(3)   Predominant Purpose to Injure

(i)   The true test

As has been seen, as regards the mental element of the tort, cases concerning unlawful means conspiracy use the language of *intention*. In lawful means conspiracies, on the other hand, the cases talk of the defendants' *purpose*. In *Crofter Hand Woven Harris Tweed v Veitch*,[186] Viscount Simon LC considered it better, when analysing lawful means conspiracy claims, to avoid words like "motive" and "intention", and instead to ask what was the "purpose" or "object" of a combination.

2–094

---

[183] See paras 2–114—2–119 below.

[184] *Mogul Steamship Co Ltd v McGregor, Gow & Co* (1889) 23 Q.B.D. 598, at 616; see, to the same effect, *Quinn v Leathem* [1901] A.C. 495, at 538: "Numbers may annoy and coerce where one may not."

[185] *Lonrho Ltd v Shell Petroleum Co Ltd* [1982] A.C. 173, per Lord Diplock at 189.

[186] Above, at 444–445. Viscount Maugham expressed the view (at 452) that "real purpose" and "true motive" meant the same thing but that "motive" and "intention" were different. Lord Wright considered that "object" was the most appropriate word (see 469).

2–095   The *Crofter* case also saw the adoption of the phrase "predominant purpose" as an integral element of the tort. As to this, Viscount Simon LC said (emphasis added)[187]:

> "Next, it is to be borne in mind that there may be cases where the combination has more than one 'object' or 'purpose.' The combiners may feel that they are killing two birds with one stone, and, even though their main purpose may be to protect their own legitimate interests notwithstanding that this involves damage to the plaintiffs, they may also find a further inducement to do what they are doing by feeling that it serves the plaintiffs right. The analysis of human impulses soon leads us into the quagmire of mixed motives, and even if we avoid the word 'motive,' there may be more than a single 'purpose' or 'object.' *It is enough to say that if there is more than one purpose actuating a combination, liability must depend on ascertaining the predominant purpose.* If that predominant purpose is to damage another person and damage results, that is tortious conspiracy. If the predominant purpose is the lawful protection or promotion of any lawful interest of the combiners (no illegal means being employed), it is not a tortious conspiracy, even though it causes damage to another person."

2–096   Notwithstanding this apparently clear formulation of the test, several statements in some of the early cases focused not so much (or not only) on what the defendants' predominant purpose was, but (or also) on whether that purpose was legitimate in the eyes of the law.[188] These early statements are capable of providing some support in principle for the suggestion that, whilst a predominant purpose to injure would be *sufficient* to found liability, it might not be *necessary* in all cases, if the defendants' purpose were nevertheless illegitimate and as long as *an* intention to harm the claimant could be proved. Similarly, in *JSC BTA Bank v Khrapunov*,[189] Lords Sumption and Lloyd-Jones considered that, rather than saying a conspiracy would be tortious if it used unlawful means or had injury to the claimant as its predominant purpose, a more useful concept was "the absence of just cause or excuse".

2–097   Against that, most of the statements in the earlier cases on lawful means conspiracy are probably to be read as using the concept of legitimacy simply as a label for conduct which does not give rise to liability because the requisite predominant purpose to injure the claimant is absent, rather than as a test for liability as such. A bare test of legitimacy would be extremely difficult to define or apply in practice, and, in the absence of objective principles to govern its application, would be likely to give rise to varying results across different cases

---

[187] *Crofter Hand Woven Harris Tweed v Veitch* [1942] A.C. 435, at 445. Viscount Maugham described (at 452) the investigation as one concerning the *"real or predominant purpose of the combination"*. Lord Porter contemplated (at 490) that there might be a *"predominant purpose"* test but did not reach a conclusion on the point.

[188] *Mogul Steamship Co Ltd v McGregor, Gow & Co* [1892] A.C. 25, per Lord Watson at 42; per Lord Field at 54, 57; per Lord Hannen at 58; *Allen v Flood* [1898] A.C. 1, per Lord Shand at 168–169; *Quinn v Leathem* [1901] A.C. 495, per Lord Shand at 512, 514; per Lord Brampton at 520; *Ware v De Freville* [1921] 3 K.B. 40, per Bankes LJ at 60–61; per Scrutton LJ at 71; *Sorrell v Smith* [1925] A.C. 700, at 749 (though Lord Dunedin preferred to avoid the word "legitimate", which in his view begged the question (see 717)); *Crofter*, per Viscount Simon LC at 445–446; per Viscount Maugham at 451, 453; per Lord Thankerton at 460; per Lord Wright at 462–463, 469–472, 478–480.

[189] *JSC BTA Bank v Khrapunov* [2018] UKSC 19; [2018] 2 W.L.R. 1125, at [10].

with similar facts. It would also risk leading to an expansion of the circumstances giving rise to liability in conspiracy, a prospect about which judicial concern has previously been expressed.[190]

In any event, there is little basis for concluding that a test of legitimacy has taken root in subsequent cases. Notwithstanding their appeal in *Khrapunov* to an overall touchstone of absence of just cause or excuse, Lords Sumption and Lloyd-Jones went on to explain[191] how that concept underpinned the established requirements for unlawful means and lawful means conspiracies in turn, without any indication that they were advocating a departure from or relaxation of those requirements (which, on the contrary, they had earlier restated).[192] It is true that lawful means conspiracies are rare, and there are many cases which refer to the test of predominant purpose without having to decide whether or not that is the correct test. In addition the courts continue to grapple with the precise scope of the economic torts, and decisions such as *Total Network* illustrate that further judicial reworking of the principles in future cannot be ruled out. Nevertheless, the test of predominant purpose has been restated on so many occasions in the appellate courts[193] that the likelihood of the test for liability in lawful means conspiracy being altered or expanded must be taken to be remote.

2–098

Just as the existence of a combination often has to be inferred from evidence of acts carried out, so a predominant purpose to injure the claimant may only be possible to establish as a matter of inference. In *Jarman & Platt Ltd v I Barget Ltd*,[194] the Court of Appeal gave the following guidance on the application of the test:

2–099

"If the predominant purpose or object which the persons combining together have in view is the promotion of their own interests, no action will lie. If they are shown to have no real or substantial interests to pursue, it will be much easier to infer that their true purpose was to inflict harm on the other party. Similarly, if it is shown that they had malevolent or vindictive feelings towards the plaintiff, it will be easier to infer that their predominant purpose was to injure."

The presence of some intention to harm the claimant (e.g. as punishment for his actions) is not sufficient.[195] Pursuit of a long-term legitimate object may be sufficient to avoid liability even if the short term result is damage to the claimant.[196] On the other hand, whilst the test of intention is a subjective test (in that the Court does not assess for itself whether the means used to further that

2–100

---

[190] See *Lonrho v Shell Petroleum Ltd (No.2)* [1982] A.C. 173, per Lord Diplock at 189F.

[191] *JSC BTA Bank v Khrapunov* [2018] UKSC 19; [2018] 2 W.L.R. 1125, at [10].

[192] *JSC BTA Bank v Khrapunov* [2018] UKSC 19, at [8].

[193] In addition to *Khrapunov*, see, for example, *Lonrho Ltd v Shell Petroleum Co Ltd (No.2)* [1982] A.C. 173, per Lord Diplock at 189D; *Lonrho Plc v Fayed* [1992] 1 A.C. 448, per Lord Bridge at 465H; *Lonrho Plc v Fayed (No. 5)* [1993] 1 W.L.R. 1489, at 1492H-1493A, 1500G, 1506H; *Kuwait Oil Tanker Co SAK v Al Bader* [2000] 2 All E.R. (Comm) 271, per Nourse LJ at [107]; *Revenue & Customs Commissioners v Total Network SL* [2008] UKHL 19; [2008] 1 A.C. 1174, per Lord Hope at [41]; and (in essentially the same terms), per Lord Scott at [56] and Lord Neuberger at [221]. Lord Neuberger spoke of "legitimate" conduct, at [229] but it is difficult to read him as proposing a new formulation of the test.

[194] *Jarman & Platt Ltd v I Barget Ltd* [1977] F.S.R. 260, at 278.

[195] *Eastham v Newcastle United FC* [1964] Ch. 413, at 453–454.

[196] *Crofter Hand Woven Harris Tweed Co v Veitch* [1942] A.C. 435, at 469, per Lord Wright.

purpose are reasonable),[197] if the damage inflicted on a claimant is disproportionate to the benefit to themselves sought or obtained by the alleged conspirators, this may indicate that their true or predominant purpose is to injure the claimant.[198]

2–101   It has been seen above (at para.2–042 that, in unlawful means conspiracies, an intention to injure the claimant can be inferred where such injury is the "obverse side of the coin" of benefit to the defendants. In *Total Network*,[199] Lord Neuberger suggested that the same analysis applied to lawful means conspiracies. He indicated that HMRC's better route to liability might have been lawful means conspiracy, and that it could have established that the defendants' predominant purpose was injury to HMRC on the basis that this was the obverse side of the coin from gain to themselves. This analysis was followed by David Richards J in *HMRC v Begum*,[200] who said that:

> "where persons conspire to obtain money by cheating or fraud, the necessary injury to the person cheated or defrauded is inseparable from the obtaining of the money. The conspirators cannot say that their predominant purpose was not to injure the victim but was to obtain money. They are the obverse of each other and necessarily both contribute the predominant purpose of the conspirators."

2–102   However, if the obverse side of the coin analysis were to be applied to all lawful means conspiracies, the practical effect would be to render the tort of unlawful means conspiracy obsolete, as Lord Neuberger acknowledged in *Total Network*.[201] That would in turn widen the scope of the tort of conspiracy in general. There is also a greater conceptual difficulty in applying such an analysis in order to decide which of the defendants' purposes is predominant, since it might be thought that there can only be one answer to that question.[202] In the context of unlawful means conspiracy, there is no such difficulty with *an* intention to harm existing alongside an intention to benefit oneself. Moreover, to say that such analysis applies to the scenarios suggested by David Richards J in *HMRC v Begum* (obtaining money by cheating or fraud, or burglary) may be to do no more than to say that, in such cases, harm to the claimant is the means by which the defendant enriches himself. If so then this test is no different from the test of intention formulated by Lord Hoffmann in *OBG Ltd v Allan* and applicable to unlawful means conspiracies.

2–103   There are a number of older cases of high authority which proceeded on the basis that the obverse side of the coin analysis does not apply to lawful means

---

[197] *Crofter Hand Woven Harris Tweed Co v Veitch* [1942] A.C. 435, at 469.
[198] *Crofter Hand Woven Harris Tweed Co v Veitch* [1942] A.C. 435, per Viscount Simon LC at 447.
[199] *Revenue & Customs Commissioners v Total Network SL* [2008] UKHL 19; [2008] 1 A.C. 1174, at [228].
[200] *HMRC v Begum* [2010] EWHC 1799 (Ch); [2011] B.P.I.R. 59, at [60] (an application to amend particulars of claim). Whilst David Richards J noted that unlawful means were alleged, it is clear that his quoted comments were directed at lawful means conspiracy.
[201] Above, at [228].
[202] One commentator has suggested that the purpose of the defendants in *Total Network* was "obviously" to further their own interests by obtaining money: Carty, *An Analysis of the Economic Torts* (2010), p.144.

conspiracies, and which would or might have been decided differently if it did.[203] And the issue seems now to have been laid to rest by the Court of Appeal in *JSC BTA Bank v Khrapunov*,[204] in which Sales LJ rejected the "idea floated by" Lord Neuberger in *Total Network* as being of any general application, noting its logical difficulties as well as its inconsistency with other authority, and reaffirming the requirement of proving a predominant purpose to injure, otherwise than as the obverse of benefiting oneself.

Without the obverse side of the coin analysis being available in this context, it may well be that lawful means conspiracy is reserved for those cases where it can truly be said that the defendants acted principally, not out of desire to benefit themselves, but out of a vindictive desire to harm the claimant. This leaves very little room for the application of the tort. Indeed its only place may be where the claimant can show that the defendants acted with "disinterested malevolence"[205] towards him (a concept found in US law). **2–104**

In the *Crofter* case, Viscount Maugham expressed the view[206] that action taken out of dislike of the religious views or the politics or the race or the colour of the claimant, or "a mere demonstration of power by busybodies", would give rise to liability in conspiracy. Although he appeared to do so in order to illustrate his disapproval of the "predominant purpose" test, it is suggested that in fact a combination to harm a claimant for religious, political or racial reasons is nonetheless a combination to harm a claimant if that is its predominant purpose. Action to demonstrate power is perhaps more difficult, such that whether or not such action would give rise to liability would turn on a close examination of the facts. **2–105**

Application of the "predominant purpose" test is also difficult in the case of the mercenary, the defendant paid to carry out acts pursuant to someone else's conspiracy. On the one hand, a mercenary may act solely or predominantly for his own financial gain. On the other hand, the mercenary can only earn his fee by carrying out acts which he may know are intended by others to cause harm. Is he liable? The question was considered in the *Crofter* case. Lord Wright noted the difficulty[207] but thought it unnecessary to attempt to resolve it. Other passages in the judges' speeches support the proposition that a mercenary would be found to have the necessary intention to harm.[208] However, if the obverse side of the coin analysis is not applicable to lawful means conspiracies, it is likely to be very **2–106**

---

[203] See, for example, *Mogul Steamship Co Ltd v McGregor, Gow & Co* (1889) 23 Q.B.D. 598 (CA), at 614; *Hadmor Productions Ltd v Hamilton* [1983] 1 A.C. 191, at 228; *Crofter Hand Woven Harris Tweed Co v Veitch* [1942] A.C. 435, at 493–494; *Yukong Line Ltd v Rendsburg* [1998] 1 W.L.R. 294, at 311B.

[204] *JSC BTA Bank v Khrapunov* [2017] EWCA Civ 40; [2017] Q.B. 853, at [11].

[205] See e.g. *Nann v Rainist* (1931) 255 NY 307, at 319, per Cardozo J; *Swarna v Al-Awadi* (2010) 622 F.3d 123.

[206] *Crofter Hand Woven Harris Tweed Co v Veitch* [1942] A.C. 435, at 451.

[207] Above, at 479–480.

[208] Above, per Viscount Maugham at 451; per Viscount Simon LC at 445–446; per Lord Thankerton at 460; per Lord Porter at 491, 495.

difficult to show that even a mercenary's predominant purpose was anything other than to bring about his own financial gain.[209]

(ii)   The test applied in practice in previous cases

2–107   The earlier cases in which lawful means conspiracy claims failed to provide an illustration of how difficult it is in practice to establish the requisite predominant purpose. For example:

(1)   In *Mogul Steamship Co Ltd v McGregor, Gow & Co*[210] defendants were held not liable where they combined to appropriate for themselves the trade of their competitors and so drive them out of business.

(2)   In *Ware & De Freville Ltd v Motor Trade Association*[211] defendants were held not liable for blacklisting a supplier who had advertised a car for sale at a price higher than that fixed by the association. It was said that it was "no part of the duty of the Court to inquire whether the action of the defendants … was either selfish or unreasonable", or if they used coercion and threats.

(3)   In *Crofter*,[212] a concerted embargo imposed on the transport of materials to (and products from) trade rivals was lawful even though it "might well destroy their business altogether without offering any locus poenitentiæ".[213] Lord Thankerton said[214] that, even if a defendant was "stupid or wrongheaded, or acted without making proper inquiries", that would not of itself show a predominant purpose to injure (in fact it may do the opposite).

2–108   The few successful cases further illustrate the narrowness of the tort of lawful means conspiracy. For example:

(1)   In *Quinn v Leathem*,[215] the claim succeeded where the jury found that the defendants' purpose in "blacklisting" the claimant was "to injure the plaintiff in his trade as distinguished from the intention of legitimately advancing their own interests".[216]

(2)   In *Giblan v National Amalgamated Labourers Union*,[217] union representatives were found liable in conspiracy where their object was to prevent the claimant from obtaining employment; it was no defence that they did this in order to secure the payment of a debt due from him to the union.

---

[209] For the view that a mercenary would be held liable, see Carty, *An Analysis of the Economic Torts* (2010), p.142.

[210] *Mogul Steamship Co Ltd v McGregor, Gow & Co* [1892] A.C. 25. As it was put by Lord Morris at 49: "It is not illegal for a trader to aim at driving a competitor out of trade, provided the motive be his own gain by appropriation of the trade, and the means he uses be lawful weapons". The case may not be decided the same way today in light of modern competition law; but the principle remains valid.

[211] *Ware & De Freville Ltd v Motor Trade Association* [1921] 3 K.B. 40, at 61–62.

[212] *Crofter Hand Woven Harris Tweed Co v Veitch* [1942] A.C. 435.

[213] Above, per Viscount Simon LC at 441.

[214] Above, at 459.

[215] *Quinn v Leathem* [1901] A.C. 495.

[216] Above, at 514.

[217] *Giblan v National Amalgamated Labourers Union* [1903] 2 K.B. 600.

(3)   In *Huntley v Thornton*,[218] defendant union representatives were liable in conspiracy when, in procuring the dismissal of the claimant from employment, they were not thinking of the interests of the union but "only of their own ruffled dignity" and the vindication of their authority.[219]

(iii)   *Justification in lawful means conspiracy*

There is some authority that there exists a defence of justification in lawful means conspiracy cases.[220] However, such authority mostly dates from the period before the tort of conspiracy had fully developed into the forms it takes today, and the dicta in question overlap to some extent with dicta suggesting a focus on the legitimacy of the defendants' conduct rather than a straightforward test of "predominant purpose". It would accordingly be dangerous to assume that a separate defence of justification survives, if indeed it ever existed. It is difficult to find any analysis in the cases of circumstances which might give rise to a defence of justification in the face of a finding that the defendants' predominant purpose was to injure the claimant. It might be thought equally difficult to find support for such an outcome as a matter of principle. **2–109**

In light of all these points, it is suggested that the better view is that there is no separate defence of justification, but that whether concerted action is "justified" is simply the obverse of whether its predominant purpose is to injure the claimant.[221] This was supported by the way the matter was analysed by the Supreme Court in *JSC BTA Bank v Khrapunov*,[222] namely that a defendant liable in lawful means conspiracy cannot show a just cause or excuse for his conduct where his predominant purpose was to injure the claimant. **2–110**

E.   THE DIFFERENT POSITION OF EACH DEFENDANT

(1) Introduction

A conspiracy claim will almost always be brought against more than one defendant, and will very often seek to recover the claimant's overall loss from each such defendant. However, ordinarily the various parties to a conspiracy will have had varying degrees of involvement and have carried out different acts at different times. These variations merit careful consideration, because of the practical impact they have on questions such as which conspirators should be joined as defendants, whether they are liable, and if so to what extent. **2–111**

---

[218] *Huntley v Thornton* [1957] 1 W.L.R. 321.

[219] *Huntley v Thornton* [1957] 1 W.L.R. 321, at 341.

[220] *Giblan v National Amalgamated Labourers' Union* [1903] 2 K.B. 600, at 617–619, followed in *Crofter Hand Woven Harris Tweed Co v Veitch* [1942] A.C. 435, at 475–476; *Huntley v Thornton* [1957] 1 W.L.R. 321, at 340; *Rookes v Barnard (No.1)* [1964] A.C. 1129, per Lord Devlin at 1215–1216; *Lonrho Ltd v Shell Petroleum Co Ltd (No.2)* [1981] Com L.R 74, per Eveleigh LJ at [75]; *Revenue & Customs Commissioners v Total Network SL* [2008] UKHL 19; [2008] 1 A.C. 1174, per Lord Neuberger at [229].

[221] *Sorrell v Smith* [1925] A.C. 700, at 712. See also paras 2–101—2–104 above.

[222] [2018] UKSC 19; [2018] 2 W.L.R. 1125, at [10].

(2) Joinder of Defendants

2–112 It is not necessary to join every party to an alleged conspiracy as a defendant. As Oliver J explained in *Midland Bank Trust Co Ltd v Green (No.3)*,[223]

> "the gist of the action here was not the act of conspiring but the damage suffered as a result and hence it became possible to sue one conspirator alone without joining the others."

Indeed, it may be impossible in practice to join a particular party to the conspiracy as a defendant: for example, a corporate conspirator may have been dissolved (and it may be pointless to seek to restore it), or it may be impossible to establish jurisdiction over a particular defendant. In many other cases certain participants in a conspiracy are not worth suing or the precise identity of all the conspirators is incapable of being established. An extreme example is provided by *Credit Lyonnais Bank Nederland NV v Export Credits Guarantee Department*,[224] in which none of the primary conspirators were sued; instead, the claim was brought against the employer of one conspirator on the basis of vicarious liability.

2–113 Whether to join a party as defendant to a conspiracy claim will obviously depend partly on practical considerations such as those identified in the previous paragraph. Where there is an identifiable conspiracy, the strength of a claim against any given defendant will depend primarily on two factors: whether it can be said that they were party to the conspiracy in the first place; and, if so, to what extent they can be held liable to the claimant for damage suffered as a result. These interrelated factors are examined in the sections which follow.

(3) Different Conduct

2–114 Examination of a defendant's conduct will first of all be relevant for the purposes of ascertaining whether or not they were party to a conspiracy with others. As has already been noted,[225] it will very rarely be possible to find direct evidence of a specific agreement in conspiracy cases: conspirators rarely commit their plans to writing. Instead, a combination is ordinarily inferred from, among other things, the acts carried out by the parties to it. As it was put in *Bird v O'Neal*,[226] a defendant's liability can be examined by:

> "looking to see what part, if any, each [defendant] had played in connection with each specific incident … and then considering whether such part necessarily compelled the inference that the particular [defendant] was party to a conspiracy to use unlawful means".

---

[223] *Midland Bank Trust Co Ltd v Green (No.3)* [1979] Ch. 496, at 522. This case also decided that a husband and wife can combine together in a civil conspiracy.
[224] *Credit Lyonnais Bank Nederland NV v Export Credits Guarantee Department* [2000] 1 A.C. 486. The claim ultimately failed on the basis that vicarious liability could not be established on the facts.
[225] See para.2–014 above.
[226] *Bird v O'Neal* [1960] A.C. 907, at 920–921.

Mere facilitation or assistance in another's tort is not enough on its own to make **2–115** a person liable in conspiracy. Even "knowing assistance" is not enough[227]; although a defendant who knowingly assists another to carry out acts to harm the claimant must get quite close to the line beyond which he will be considered a conspirator. It was said in *First Subsea Ltd v Balltec Ltd*[228] to be essential that an alleged co-conspirator joined in the implementation of the plan; acting unlawfully is not enough in itself, since the unlawful act may have been a purely incidental one of no causative potency in the context of the implementation of the overall plan.

The mere fact that one company or individual has financial and voting control **2–116** over another company does not give rise to an inference that the first company or individual was a party to concerted action carried out by the second company.[229] If a parent company merely looks on with approval at acts carried out by its subsidiary, that does not give rise to liability as a joint tortfeasor.[230] Neither, it is suggested, would it give rise to liability as a conspirator.

Conspiracies, by their very nature, often involve the channelling of funds to **2–117** ultimate recipients through intermediaries in such a way as to disguise the purpose of the payments, their ultimate recipient, or both. Payments may also be made by conspirators to "third party" recipients on commercial terms, perhaps in order to disguise the purpose of the payments or as part of a process of money laundering. A claimant may wish to know whether such intermediaries or recipients can be held liable in conspiracy, particularly if there are good practical reasons for suing them rather than (or in addition to) other defendants. The question arose in *CIBC Mellon Trust Co v Stolzenberg*.[231] There, Etherton J rejected the defendants' contention that a party who receives funds, knowing them to be the product of fraud, can never be liable in conspiracy if the terms on which he obtains the money and purposes for which he uses it are legitimate and commercial. The judge also rejected the claimant's rival contention that anyone who receives money, knowing it to be stolen, is necessarily a conspirator. As the judge held, liability must ultimately depend on the facts of any given case. In *Colliers CRE Plc v Pandya*,[232] HHJ Seymour QC held that a defendant who was only involved in an alleged conspiracy on a one-off basis (as the conduit for misappropriation of money on a single occasion) could not be said to be party to the conspiracy and liable for its consequences.

---

[227] *Credit Lyonnais Bank Nederland NV v Export Credit Guarantee Department* [1998] 1 Lloyd's Rep. 19, at 46, cited with approval in *Fish & Fish Ltd v Sea Shepherd UK* [2015] UKSC 10; [2015] A.C. 1229 by Lord Sumption (in a dissenting judgment), at [42] and by Lord Neuberger JSC, at [58].
[228] *First Subsea Ltd v Balltec Ltd* [2014] EWHC 866 (Ch), per Norris J at [162]; (not affected on appeal [2017] EWCA Civ 186; [2018] Ch. 25).
[229] *Unilever Plc v Chefaro Proprietaries Ltd* [1994] F.S.R. 135. at 141–142 (a joint tortfeasor case).
[230] *Sandman v Panasonic UK Ltd* [1998] F.S.R. 651, at [663–664] citing *The Mead Corp v Riverwood International Corp* [1997] F.S.R. 484, per Laddie J at 490. The line between merely looking on with approval and becoming implicated by a failure to act (see paras 2–031—2–033 above) may be a fine one.
[231] *CIBC Mellon Trust Co v Stolzenberg* [2003] EWHC 13 (Ch), at [67]–[74]. The defendants were refused permission to appeal this aspect of the decision: [2004] EWCA Civ 827, at [136]–[137] and [183]–[185] in particular.
[232] *Colliers CRE Plc v Pandya* [2009] EWHC 211 (QB), at [104].

2–118 The evidentiary focus in conspiracy cases on what each alleged conspirator actually did—whilst inevitable because of the almost universal need to prove the existence of a combination by inference, e.g. from conduct—should not be understood as importing a requirement that any particular defendant must have carried out any particular act pursuant to the conspiracy before he will be held liable. A defendant who played a key role in the acts which caused the claimant harm will find it more difficult to deny that he was a party to the conspiracy. But, in principle, status as a conspirator can be established by other means—for example, by (exceptionally) the existence of an express agreement, or by inference from a particular defendant's knowledge and approval of what others were doing, if such an inference is justified on the facts.

2–119 Once the existence of a conspiracy is proved:

(1) It is not necessary for each defendant to be shown to have taken part in each act carried out pursuant to the conspiracy. What must be shown is that each act was carried out pursuant to the agreement or combination to which each defendant was a party.[233] Indeed, at least in an unlawful means conspiracy, it may be that only certain defendants would be capable of committing the operative wrongful acts (such as breaching a contract or committing a breach of fiduciary duty). It has already been noted that a defendant can in principle be liable in conspiracy even if he does not personally carry out any act pursuant to it.[234]

(2) The actions of any one conspirator in furtherance of its objects will be attributed to all conspirators.[235] It has also been said in the context of civil conspiracy that the acts and admissions of one conspirator are admissible against co-conspirators.[236] These are essentially two ways of putting the same point: evidence of acts carried out in furtherance of a conspiracy is *admissible* against all conspirators because it is relevant to the case against them all; it is *relevant* because such acts are attributed to all those who are proved to be parties to the conspiracy.

---

[233] *Kuwait Oil Tanker v Al Bader* [2000] 2 All E.R. (Comm) 271, at [133]. See also *Michaels v Taylor Woodrow Developments Ltd* [2001] Ch. 493, per Laddie J at 516: "it is possible to sue for wrongful means conspiracy in cases where only some but not all of the conspirators would be liable individually for the wrongful act."

[234] See para.2–031 above. See also *AA v Southwark LBC* [2014] EWHC 500 (QB), at [252]: "It is not necessary for each conspirator to join in all the actions giving rise to the unlawful conspiracy. What must be shown is that each conspirator joined in the execution of the conspiracy to a significant extent."

[235] *DC Thomson & Co Ltd v Deakin* [1952] Ch. 646, at 674.

[236] *Derby & Co Ltd v Weldon (No.5)* [1989] 1 W.L.R. 1244, at 1254F–1254G. This broadly reflects the position in respect of criminal conspiracies: see *R. v Gray (Philip Ronald)* [2007] EWCA Crim 2658, at [27]–[30].

(4)   Different Knowledge or Intention

The different tests of intention or purpose in unlawful means conspiracy and lawful means conspiracy have been examined above.[237] In *Huntley v Thornton*,[238] Harman J spoke of the need for each defendant to *"entertain the same object"*. Later cases have adopted similar language.[239] In some cases the absence of a shared object or intention may mean that there is no conspiracy at all because there is no combination. In others, where the nefarious object was shared by some defendants but not all of them, it may mean that only the defendants who had the necessary intention would be liable.[240] Ultimately, it is only by application of the relevant test to a particular defendant that the question of whether that defendant has the necessary intention to be liable as a conspirator can be answered. As Proudman J said in *HMRC v Sunico A/S*,[241] "What must be common amongst the conspirators is an intention to harm the claimant".[242]

2–120

Provided the test of intention can be met in relation to a given defendant, it is not necessary to show that each conspirator had *exactly* the same aim in mind.[243] For example, defendants may have had a sufficient identity of object even if they sought to obtain different advantages by that object.[244] The question ultimately remains whether a particular defendant, having regard to his knowledge, utterances and actions, was sufficiently a party to the combination.[245] This is inevitably a somewhat vague test, the application of which will depend heavily on the facts of the particular case.

2–121

The overlap between intention and knowledge in the field of conspiracy is significant. This is not least because evidence of what a defendant knew is

2–122

---

[237] See paras 2–039—2–046 and 2–094—2–108 respectively

[238] *Huntley v Thornton* [1957] 1 W.L.R. 321, at 343. In that case, two defendants who were not told all the facts that made the conspirators' actions unjustified, and who were found not to have a *"predominant motive"* to injure the claimant, were not liable in conspiracy with their co-defendants.

[239] See, for example, *Kuwait Oil Tanker Co SAK v Al Bader* [2000] 2 All E.R. (Comm) 271, at [111]; *Hemsley v Graham* [2013] EWHC 2232 (Ch), at [417]; *First Subsea Ltd v Balltec Ltd* [2014] EWHC 866 (Ch), at [162].

[240] It was suggested in the Australian case of *McKernan v Fraser* (1931) 46 CLR 343, at [411], that there could only be one agreement, so that unless all parties to the combination shared the necessary intention to injure the claimant, even those parties who did have that intention would not be liable. It is thought that this goes too far. In such a case, whether the defendants who *did* have the necessary intention are liable may instead turn on the question of whether their intentions and actions can be shown to have caused the claimant's loss.

[241] *HMRC v Sunico A/S* [2013] EWHC 941 (Ch), at [79].

[242] It was suggested in *Pratt v British Medical Association* [1919] 1 K.B. 244, at 279 that, where a combination is proved, the intentions of one or more combiners can be attributed to the others. This was disapproved in the Australian case of *McKernan v Fraser* (1931) 46 CLR 343, at 407–408 and no such principle appears to have taken root in English law either.

[243] *Crofter Hand Woven Harris Tweed Co v Veitch* [1942] A.C. 435, per Lord Wright at 479. Although if a defendant has his own separate aim this may tend to indicate that he did not participate in the conspiracy at all, at least if he did not share the knowledge of the other defendants: see Jones (ed), *Clerk & Lindsell on Torts* (2017), para.24–97.

[244] *Crofter Hand Woven Harris Tweed Co v Veitch* [1942] A.C. 435, per Lord Wright at 479.

[245] *First Subsea Ltd v Balltec Ltd* [2014] EWHC 866 (Ch), at [162].

(together with evidence of what he did) often the material from which the court draws an inference as to that defendant's intention. As Etherton LJ said in *Baldwin v Berryland Books*[246]:

> "in this area of the law, knowledge and intention are intimately connected. Intention to injure, and indeed acting in concert, cannot be inferred in the absence of the requisite knowledge."

Accordingly, an analysis of the level of knowledge of each particular defendant will generally be necessary, in order to ascertain any differences and their effect on the liability of each defendant as a conspirator.

2–123　　In a case where only one of the alleged conspirators knows the facts which render unlawful the conduct carried out pursuant to a common design, this is likely to mean in practice that there is no actionable conspiracy, at least until more than one party has the requisite knowledge. For example, in *Clydesdale Bank Plc v Stoke Place Hotel Ltd*,[247] a bank representative, acting without authority, had caused the bank to make a number of loan facilities to companies controlled by the second defendant. Nugee J found that the second defendant did not know that the representative was acting without authority until after a number of facilities had already been granted. Accordingly he was only liable in conspiracy in respect of the period after he learned of the lack of authority.[248]

2–124　　It is clear that a particular defendant need not know all the details of a conspiracy in order to be liable for all of its consequences. If, for example, there is an overall scheme to steal from the conspirators' employer by any available means, it is not necessary for each conspirator to be fully aware of the circumstances of each theft (e.g. the date it is to be carried out and the precise mechanism to be employed) in order for him to be liable for its consequences.[249] However, a certain level of knowledge is necessary before the requisite intention can be inferred. It was suggested in two recent first instance cases (decided by the same judge) that, in order to be liable in unlawful means conspiracy, a given defendant must at least be aware of the means intended to be used and that such means were unlawful, and agree to the use of those means.[250] As far as knowledge of unlawfulness is concerned, this seems inconsistent with the prevailing view as described in paras 2–077—2–083 above. It may be that an agreement to the use of the relevant means is necessary, but there would seem to be no reason in principle why such agreement could not be inferred in light of a defendant's knowledge, in the same way that other elements of the tort are frequently established by inference.

---

[246] *Baldwin v Berryland Books* [2010] EWCA Civ 1440, at [48].

[247] *Clydesdale Bank Plc v Stoke Place Hotel Ltd* [2017] EWHC 181 (Ch), at [161] in particular.

[248] See para.2–083 above for discussion of this decision in the context of whether knowledge of unlawfulness is necessary.

[249] *Kuwait Oil Tanker Co SAK v Al Bader* [2000] 2 All E.R. (Comm) 271, at [133]. See also *The "Dolphina"* [2012] 1 Lloyd's Rep. 304 (High Court of Singapore), at [282]: "A conspirator need not know all the details of the plot as long as he is aware of the common objective and what his role in bringing it about involves."

[250] *TCP Europe Ltd v Perry* [2012] EWHC 1940 (QB), at [36]; *Stevenson v Singh* [2012] EWHC 2880 (QB), at [18], per HHJ Seymour QC.

These issues are likely to be most acute in relation to subsidiary participants in a conspiracy, who may have been engaged on a "need-to-know" basis. In *Bank of Tokyo-Mitsubishi UFJ Ltd v Başkan Gida Sanayi Ve Pazarlama AS*,[251] Briggs J examined the question of knowledge in this context. He found support in earlier authority for the proposition that

2–125

> "where a bit-player in a multifaceted fraud knows only of one aspect of the fraud, and is ignorant of the others, he may not be liable for anything more than the loss properly attributable to that part of the fraud of which he is aware".

Application of this principle to the facts was left to further inquiry.

The above analysis is concerned with the necessary extent of a defendant's knowledge. As to its quality, Nelsonian or blind-eye knowledge may be sufficient, at least if it can be shown that the reason the particular defendant abstained from inquiry was that the state of affairs he did not wish to confirm by such inquiry was one which he believed was likely to exist (rather than simply suspecting that was the case).[252]

2–126

(5) Involvement at Different Times

It is not necessary for all parties to a conspiracy to have joined the conspiracy at the same time in order for them to be liable. However, two important points must be noted in relation to the timing of a given defendant's involvement in a conspiracy. First, a defendant will have no liability for specific losses incurred or caused before he became a party to the conspiracy,[253] or (it would logically follow) for acts which have already occurred and which may give rise to loss in the future. To take an example: a valuer is suborned to participate in a mortgage fraud scheme where properties are purchased at inflated prices (backed by fraudulently high valuations) in order to extract lending from banks at higher levels than would otherwise be made available. The valuer joins the scheme after ten such properties have already been purchased. At this stage it is not clear what the extent of the bank's losses might be in respect of the ten loans already advanced. The fraudulent borrower may succeed in repaying the lending. In the

2–127

---

[251] *Bank of Tokyo-Mitsubishi UFJ Ltd v Başkan Gida Sanayi Ve Pazarlama AS* [2009] EWHC 1276 (Ch), at [842] onwards, in particular [846], and at [948]–[952].

[252] *Bank of Tokyo-Mitsubishi UFJ Ltd v Başkan Gida Sanayi Ve Pazarlama AS* [2009] EWHC 1276 (Ch), at [840]; *HMRC v Sunico A/S* [2013] EWHC 941 (Ch), at [87].

[253] *Kuwait Oil Tanker Co SAK v Al Bader* (Moore-Bick J, unreported, 17 December 1998); *Erste Group Bank AG v JSC "VMZ Red October"* [2013] EWHC 2926 (Comm); [2014] B.P.I.R. 81, at [103] (overturned on appeal [2015] EWCA Civ 379; [2015] I.C.L.C. 706, but not on this point). It was suggested in in *Colliers CRE Plc v Pandya* [2009] EWHC 211 (QB), at [105], that, if a conspirator joined halfway through a conspiracy, the mechanism for doing so must be the making of a fresh conspiracy, since otherwise the conspirator would be liable for the operation of the conspiracy prior to joining it. It is thought that this mechanistic analysis is unnecessary, and that a conspirator can in principle join a pre-existing conspiracy, subject to the limitation identified by Moore-Bick J in *Kuwait Oil Tanker*. This is not to say that the facts of any given case might not support the analysis of a fresh conspiracy, in which case practitioners acting for the claimant should consider whether the claim should be pleaded on that basis.

event of a default and a shortfall being sustained the valuer will only be liable for the later loans made after he joined the scheme.

2–128   Secondly, the facts of a given case may show that a defendant's involvement in a conspiracy was limited to a particular period, such that he cannot be made liable for losses attributable to the period after his involvement in the conspiracy ceased.[254] Whether this is so will ultimately depend on the facts, in particular an examination of the scope of the combination to which he is a party. Since a defendant can be liable in conspiracy even if he does not carry out some or all of the acts pursuant to the conspiracy himself, it follows that a defendant who once actively participated in a conspiracy would not *necessarily* cease to be liable simply by ceasing actively to participate, if losses incurred by subsequent acts carried out by others were nevertheless within the scope of the initial conspiracy to which the defendant was a party. In the *Kuwait Oil Tanker* case, the judge's finding that a particular defendant, Captain Stafford, was liable even after he left the scene of the conspiracy was overturned on appeal, but on the basis that the agreement on which the conspiracy was founded could not be said to have extended to the subsequent period.[255] The question whether "withdrawal" from a conspiracy was possible on principles analogous to withdrawal from a criminal joint enterprise was noted but not examined. It is likely to be more difficult to identify when a given defendant left a conspiracy than to identify when he joined it.

(6)   Contribution and Apportionment Between Defendants

2–129   Subject to the principles outlined above, the starting point is that the defendants to a successful conspiracy claim will be jointly and severally liable to the claimant in respect of the damage caused by the conspiracy. The key exception to this principle is that—as illustrated above—a defendant will not be liable for damage caused before he joined the conspiracy and may equally not be liable for damage caused after he left the conspiracy (if that can be shown to have happened).

2–130   One defendant to a conspiracy who has been compelled to satisfy the claimant's judgment may wish to seek a contribution from his co-defendants who may bear equal responsibility for the claimant's loss. And co-defendants to a conspiracy claim commonly have varying degrees of involvement, culpability and responsibility for the acts carried out. The "mastermind" of a conspiracy may not have carried out any unlawful acts himself, but without his influence the wrongdoing may never have occurred. Conversely, a given defendant may have been suborned into committing unlawful acts causing damage to the claimant, but because of pressure placed on him by someone in a position of influence. In circumstances such as these, questions of contribution and apportionment between defendants are likely to arise.

---

[254] This was found by the Court of Appeal to be the case for one of the defendants in *Kuwait Oil Tanker Co SAK v Al Bader* [2000] 2 All E.R. (Comm) 271 (see [143]–[155]).
[255] *Kuwait Oil Tanker Co SAK v Al Bader* [2000] 2 All E.R. (Comm) 271, at [148].

Under s.1(1) of the Civil Liability (Contribution) Act 1978, any person liable in **2–131** respect of any damage suffered by another person may recover contribution from any other person liable in respect of the same damage (whether jointly with him or otherwise). It is clear that this extends to liability in tort[256] and it has obvious potential application to a conspiracy claim. In particular co-conspirators will generally be liable in respect of the "same damage", with the caveat explained above in relation to damage caused prior to or after a given defendant's involvement in the conspiracy.

It was once considered that a defendant could not claim contribution in respect of **2–132** liability for an act carried out by him which either was manifestly unlawful or was known by him to be so.[257] If this were true, it would have a significant effect on the availability of contribution in conspiracy cases. However, Ferris J held in *K v P*[258] that this (effectively the ex turpi causa principle) did not apply to claims under the 1978 Act, since Parliament had clearly intended contribution to be available regardless of the basis of the liability of the contribution claimant. *K v P* has since been referred to with express or apparent approval in a number of subsequent decisions[259] and is considered to represent the law.[260] Indeed there is no obstacle in principle (e.g. on the basis of the "clean hands" doctrine) to a defendant accused of fraud seeking a freezing injunction in support of his contribution claim against a co-defendant.[261]

Under s.2(1) of the 1978 Act, contribution is to be assessed at an amount which **2–133** the court considers to be just and equitable having regard to the extent of that person's responsibility for the damage in question. The court accordingly has a large degree of discretion in the award of contribution. A detailed exposition of the principles by reference to which that discretion falls to be exercised is beyond the scope of this book. A number of points of particular potential relevance to conspiracy claims may nonetheless be outlined:

(1) In principle the apportionment of liability can be anything from 0 per cent[262] to 100 per cent[263] as between any given defendants.

(2) The terms of s.2(1) direct the court primarily to the causative responsibility of the defendant in question, which is likely to be the most important factor in the exercise of apportionment. But the wide terms of the sub-section

---

[256] Civil Liability (Contribution) Act 1978 s.6(1).

[257] *Burrows v Rhodes* [1899] 1 Q.B. 816, at 828.

[258] *K v P* [1993] Ch. 140.

[259] See e.g. *Friends' Provident Life Office v Hillier Parker May & Rowden* [1997] Q.B. 85, at 103; *Niru Battery Manufacturing Co v Milestone Trading Ltd (No.2)* [2004] EWCA Civ 487; [2004] 1 C.L.C. 882, at [42]; *Dubai Aluminium Co Ltd v Salaam* [2002] UKHL 48; [2003] 2 A.C. 366, at [53]–[54]; *Great North Eastern Railway Ltd v Hart* [2003] EWHC 2450 (QB), at [84]; *Dawson v Bell* [2016] EWCA Civ 96; [2016] 2 B.C.L.C. 59, at [50].

[260] The suggestion in *African Strategic Investment (Holdings) Ltd v Main* [2011] EWHC 2223 (Ch), at [26] that illegality was a bar to a contribution claim is accordingly not to be followed.

[261] *Kazakhstan Kagazy Plc v Zhunus* [2016] EWCA Civ 1036; [2017] 1 W.L.R. 1360, at [28]–[30].

[262] See for example *Dawson v Bell* [2016] EWCA Civ 96; [2016] 2 B.C.L.C. 59, in which a claim for contribution failed where the contribution claimant had misappropriated funds for his own benefit and his claim against the contribution defendant was based on the contention that she had owed a duty to stop his wrongdoing.

[263] See for example *Dubai Aluminium Co Ltd v Salaam* [2002] UKHL 48; [2003] 2 A.C. 366.

equally enable the court to take account of factors which are not strictly causative, such as wider wrongdoing or culpability in relation to the subject-matter of the claim.[264] In an unlawful means conspiracy, this could for example include the fact that a particular defendant was guilty of widespread deceit on the claimant, even if it was in the event some other wrong (e.g. a breach of contract) which caused most of the claimant's loss.

(3)   This focus on causative impact may mean that a more serious fault having less causative impact may represent an equivalent responsibility to a less serious fault having greater causative impact. So in *Downs v Chappell*,[265] accountants who negligently verified fraudulent statements made by the seller of a bookshop business regarding its profitability were equally liable with the seller where their verification of the figures, whilst less culpable than the seller's fraud, played a greater role in inducing the purchaser to buy the business.

(4)   As well as fault and causative impact, any benefit obtained by a given defendant is important. This has obvious potential relevance to a conspiracy claim, in which there may be many participants in a conspiracy but some may retain the lion's share of the proceeds of the fraud and others may have received no benefit at all. In *Dubai Aluminium Co Ltd v Salaam*,[266] this led to two conspirators being liable to make a 100 per cent contribution to a solicitors' firm which was vicariously liable for the actions of one of its partners, who had dishonestly assisted in the fraud but received no benefit. If one conspirator received proceeds from the fraud but subsequently paid them away, this may mean he is to be treated as not having received the proceeds in the first place; it all depends on the facts (and in particular the circumstances of the onward payment).[267]

(5)   Where a defendant is found to have been party to a conspiracy but only to have played a minor role, this will impact on the degree to which he should bear liability. An illustration of this is provided by *Schott Kem Ltd v Bentley*,[268] in which one defendant who was considered to have played a subordinate role in an alleged conspiracy was ordered (on appeal) to make a much smaller interim payment than the major wrongdoers.

(6)   As explained above, it is not necessary to join every conspirator to the claim. The situation may thus arise in which a defendant found liable to the claimant (i.e. the "contribution claimant") seeks a contribution against another defendant or against a third party (i.e. the "contribution defendant"), but in circumstances where the mastermind behind the conspiracy is not a defendant to either the claimant's claim or the contribution claim.[269] In those circumstances the contribution defendant

---

[264] *Re-Source America International Ltd v Platt Site Services Ltd* [2004] EWCA Civ 665, 95 Con. L.R. 1, at [51].

[265] *Downs v Chappell* [1997] 1 W.L.R. 426, at 445.

[266] *Dubai Aluminium Co Ltd v Salaam* [2003] 2 A.C. 366.

[267] *Charter Plc v City Index Ltd* [2007] EWCA Civ 1382; [2008] Ch. 313, at [59], per Carnwath LJ.

[268] *Schott Kem Ltd v Bentley* [1991] 1 Q.B. 61. The case did not concern s.2(1) of the 1978 Act but the principles are analogous.

[269] Perhaps because he is insolvent or jurisdiction cannot be established against him (e.g. because he has proved impossible to serve).

may argue that his liability to contribute must be assessed by reference to the fact that the mastermind bore primary responsibility for the damage, so that (for example) even if the contribution claimant and contribution defendant bore equal responsibility as between them, the contribution defendant's liability to the contribution claimant should be assessed at less than 50 per cent. It is not clear what would happen in this situation. Under the predecessor to the 1978 Act it was held inappropriate for the court to take into account the potential liability of a party not before the court.[270] However, it has more recently been suggested that it may be appropriate in some circumstances to do so, and thus—pursuing the illustration—to reduce the contribution defendant's liability to the contribution claimant because the mastermind bore primary responsibility. It is thought that the ability to take into account the responsibility of strangers to the litigation is consistent with the wording of s.2(1) and must in principle be open to the court.

(7)   There is no inconsistency in principle between a defendant denying the alleged fraud (and thus liability to the claimant) on the one hand, and seeking contribution from another defendant on the other hand on the alternative basis that he was involved in the fraud. This is commonplace, but remains true even if the claimant settles against the contribution defendant so that the contribution notice is served at a time when no party's primary case is that he was involved in a fraud.[271]

F.   DAMAGES

It is often said that damages are "at large" in a conspiracy claim.[272] This **2–134** expression has the potential to mislead. It is best understood as meaning that, once a claimant has discharged the burden of showing that he suffered loss as a result of the conspiracy, the Court is not limited to awarding those damages which are strictly proven.[273] In coming to a view as to the level of damages which a defendant ought to pay, the court will consider all the circumstances of the case, including the conduct of a defendant and the nature of his wrongdoing[274]; the exact factors going to precise assessment are not to be "*weigh[ed] in golden scales*".[275] The claimant is not limited to damage which can be precisely measured and specifically proved, but is entitled more generally to damage representing the court's best assessment of financial loss in fact suffered and proved.[276] As was explained in *Capital for Enterprise Fund LP v Bibby Financial Services Ltd*,[277] this principle involves a recognition that, in a conspiracy case, it may be difficult for a claimant to prove strictly what pecuniary loss has been caused by the conspiracy.

---

[270] *Maxfield v Llewellyn* [1961] 1 W.L.R. 1119.

[271] *Kazakhstan Kagazy Plc v Zhunus* [2016] EWCA Civ 1036; [2017] 1 W.L.R. 1360.

[272] See e.g. *Pratt v British Medical Association* [1919] 1 K.B. 244, at 281–282.

[273] *Noble Resources SA v Gross* [2009] EWHC 1435 (Comm), per Gloster J at [223].

[274] *Noble Resources SA v Gross*, at [223].

[275] *Huntley v Thornton* [1957] 1 W.L.R. 321, at 350.

[276] *Lonrho Plc v Fayed (No.5)* [1993] 1 W.L.R. 1489, at 1509B.

[277] *Capital for Enterprise Fund LP v Bibby Financial Services Ltd* [2015] EWHC 2593 (Ch), at [14].

2–135   The concept of damages being "at large" does not, however, mean that the Court is possessed of some general discretion to make awards of (or akin to) general damages. It is necessary to show that actual damage has been suffered by the acts carried out pursuant to the conspiracy.[278] The damage claimed must be pecuniary and it must be pleaded with sufficient particularity; there must be some nexus between the act causing the loss and the damage for which compensation is claimed.[279] The concept of damages at large cannot be used, for example, to recover secret profits made by the defendants.[280]

2–136   The following are examples of heads of damages which have been held to be recoverable as damages for conspiracy:

(1)   Costs of management time expended in investigating and tackling a conspiracy, provided that (a) the fact and extent of the diversion of employee time is properly established, and (b) the diversion caused significant disruption to the claimant's business.[281] In such a case the cost of the management time may be regarded as a proxy for the loss suffered by the business.[282]

(2)   Loss of profits, including specific losses consequential in a drop in orders for a claimant's products or services (albeit such losses might in a general sense be said to result from damage to reputation, as to which see below).[283]

(3)   Loss of a business and closure costs.[284]

(4)   A loss of "goodwill" in the sense of an asset of measurable value.[285]

2–137   Conversely, the following have been held not to be recoverable as heads of damages for conspiracy:

(1)   Injury to feelings or reputation outside the specific context referred to above.[286]

---

[278] *Crofter Hand Woven Harris Tweed Co v Veitch* [1942] A.C. 435, at 440; *Lonrho Ltd v Shell Petroleum Co Ltd (No.2)* [1982] A.C. 173, at 188; *Kuwait Oil Tanker Co SAK v Al Bader* [2000] 2 All E.R. (Comm) 271, at [108]. It is suggested in Jones (ed), *Clerk & Lindsell on Torts* (2017), para.24–93 that the tort arises when damage is "caused or threatened" by the combination. It is respectfully thought that the mere threat of damage would not be sufficient to give rise to a cause of action if no damage is actually suffered; though that is not to say that, in an appropriate case, an injunction could not be sought on a quia timet basis to restrain an act which, if carried out, would cause damage for which a defendant would be liable in conspiracy.

[279] *Lonrho Plc v Fayed (No.5)* [1993] 1 W.L.R. 1489, at 1505B–E.

[280] *Airbus Operations Ltd v Withey* [2014] EWHC 1126 (QB), at [471]–[475], per HJ Havelock-Allan QC.

[281] *Aerospace Publishing Ltd v Thames Water Utilities Ltd* [2007] EWCA Civ 3; [2007] Bus. L.R. 726, at [86].

[282] *Lancaster City Council v Thomas Newall Ltd* [2013] EWCA Civ 802; [2013] J.P.C. 1531, at [22].

[283] *Lonrho Plc v Fayed (No.5)* [1993] 1 W.L.R. 1489 (CA), at 1494–1497, 1504–1505, 1509.

[284] *British Midland Tool Ltd v Midland International Tooling Ltd* [2003] EWHC 466 (Ch); [2003] 2 B.C.L.C. 523, at [188] and [200] in particular.

[285] *British Midland Tool Ltd v Midland International Tooling Ltd*, above, at [188] and [200].

[286] *Lonrho Plc v Fayed (No.5)* [1993] 1 W.L.R. 1489, per Dillon LJ at 1496C; *Colman v Scott* [2007] EWHC 142 (QB), at [50]. Though in *Joyce v Sengupta* [1993] 1 W.L.R. 337 a Court of Appeal constituted differently from that in *Lonrho (No.5)* had held that damages for injury to feelings could

(2) General damages for personal injury.[287]

(3) Other damages which reflect an entitlement to compensation on a basis which does not reflect actual financial loss suffered by the claimant—for example, damages on the basis of the "user principle", or damages awarded in lieu of an injunction, such awards often being referred to as "*Wrotham Park*" damages.[288]

G. PRACTICAL AND PLEADING POINTS

(1) Burden and Standard of Proof

The claimant bears the burden of pleading and proving all elements of the cause of action in conspiracy.[289] An allegation of conspiracy is a serious one. Accordingly, the standard of proof (though it remains the balance of probability) is a high one, commensurate with the seriousness of the allegation. A conspiracy claim must be clearly pleaded and clearly proved with convincing evidence.[290]

2–138

(2) Dishonesty

Dishonesty is not, strictly speaking, an element of the cause of action in conspiracy (of either type).[291] A conspiracy claim can, in principle, succeed without a finding of dishonesty. In *Belmont Finance Corp v Williams Furniture Ltd (No.2)*,[292] for example, a finding of unlawful means conspiracy was upheld by the Court of Appeal in circumstances where there was no finding of dishonesty.

2–139

However, for practical purposes most conspiracy claims involve an allegation of dishonesty, even if no fraud as such is alleged.[293] It is difficult to see how defendants who are held liable in lawful means conspiracy, and thus are found to

2–140

---

be recovered in conspiracy. For a criticism of *Lonrho (No.5)* on this point, see J. Edelman (ed), *McGregor on Damages*, 20th edn (London: Sweet & Maxwell, 2017), paras 48–024—48–025. If such losses cannot be claimed, then this is one procedural disadvantage of bringing a conspiracy claim as distinct, for example, from a claim in defamation or malicious falsehood.

[287] *Lonrho Plc v Fayed (No.5)* [1993] 1 W.L.R. 1489, per Stuart-Smith LJ at 1501E.

[288] *Pell Frischmann Engineering Ltd v Bow Valley Iran Ltd* [2009] UKPC 45; [2011] 1 W.L.R. 2370, at [60]; *Marathon Asset Management LLP v Seddon* [2017] EWHC 300 (Comm); [2017] I.C.R. 791, at [220]–[221], per Leggatt J.

[289] *Crofter Hand Woven Harris Tweed Co v Veitch* [1942] A.C. 435, at 459, 471–472; *JT Stratford & Son Ltd v Lindley* [1965] A.C. 269 (CA), at 298. Compare the position on the question of whether a defence of justification exists to a claim for inducing a breach of contract: see paras 3–066—3–076 and *JT Stratford*, at 338. If, contrary to the view expressed in paras 2–109—2–110 above, there is a defence of justification, it is thought that the defendants bear the burden of proof on this issue: *Crofter Hand Woven Harris Tweed Co v Veitch* [1942] A.C. 435, per Lord Porter at 494–495.

[290] *Jarman & Platt Ltd v I Barget Ltd* [1977] F.S.R. 260, at 267–268.

[291] *Sybron Corp v Barclays Bank Plc* [1985] Ch. 299, at 312 and 323–324; *ED&F Man Sugar Ltd v T&L Sugars Ltd* [2016] EWHC 272 (Comm) per Leggatt J at [33].

[292] *Belmont Finance Corp v Williams Furniture Ltd (No.2)* [1980] 1 All E.R. 393; see 405–406 in particular.

[293] See, for example, *R+V Versicherung AG v Risk Insurance & Reinsurance Solutions SA (No.1)* [2004] EWHC 2682 (Comm); [2006] Lloyd's Rep. I.R. 253, at [107]–[111].

have acted with the predominant purpose of injuring the claimant, could nevertheless be said to have acted without dishonesty. In *HMRC v Sunico A/S*,[294] Warren J expressed the view that involvement in an unlawful means conspiracy was wholly inconsistent with an absence of fraud or dishonesty (such that an allegation of such involvement satisfied the requirement that an allegation of fraud must be expressly pleaded, even if the words "fraud" or "dishonesty" were not used). It is respectfully thought that this is likely to be true in most cases of unlawful means conspiracy, subject perhaps to issues as to the nature of the unlawful means used and the knowledge of those means held by any given defendant; though the *Belmont Finance* case provides an apparent exception.[295]

(3)   Pleading Considerations

2–141   It is accordingly clear from the cases addressed above that, for practical purposes, an allegation of conspiracy engages the same professional issues as to what allegations can properly be made and how they must be pleaded as any other claim in which dishonesty is an element of the cause of action.[296]

2–142   This has the potential to cause particular difficulty in a lawful means conspiracy case. As has already been stated above, claimants in conspiracy cases are generally hard pushed to find direct evidence of the defendants' intentions. Instead an intention to injure the claimant will generally be pleaded (at least prior to disclosure) by way of inference. However, whilst (in unlawful means conspiracy cases) it may be proper to plead an inference that the defendants had the necessary intention to injure in circumstances where damage to the claimant was the inevitable consequence of the defendants' actions, a proper basis for an allegation (necessary in lawful means conspiracy cases) that defendants acted with the predominant purpose of injuring the claimant will generally be less easy to find. Care should be taken that such an allegation is not made unless there is sufficient material to support it. If the allegation is pleaded, it should be made clear that a predominant intention to injure is alleged.

2–143   As Laddie J warned in *Douglas v Hello! Ltd (No.2)*[297]:

---

[294] *HMRC v Sunico A/S* [2012] EWHC 4156 (Ch), at [7]. See, to the same effect, comments of Neuberger J in *Somerfield Corp Ltd v Lorch Schilling (UK) Ltd*, unreported, 23 May 2000.

[295] See paras 2–077—2–083 above on the question of whether knowledge of unlawfulness must be shown in unlawful means conspiracy claims.

[296] See in particular *Jarman & Platt Ltd v I Barget Ltd* (fn.289 above). The applicable requirements where fraud allegations are pleaded were recently reviewed by Flaux J in *JSC Bank of Moscow v Kekhman* [2015] EWHC 3073 (Comm), at [15]–[23]. See also paras 1–008—1–011 above in the context of deceit.

[297] *Douglas v Hello! Ltd (No.2)* [2002] EWHC 2560 (Ch), per Laddie J at [32]. His decision was overturned on appeal but there was no appeal on this point: [2003] EWCA Civ 139; [2003] E.M.L.R. 28, at [31]. It has also been said that, particularly in a lawful means conspiracy case, it is vital to plead the defendants' alleged motive for causing injury to the claimant: *Elite Property Holdings Ltd v Barclays Bank Plc* [2017] EWHC 2030 (QB) per HHJ Waksman QC, at [97]. Strictly speaking it is thought unnecessary to plead motive, which is not an element of the cause of action, but there may well be cases in which pleading the defendants' alleged motive will lend the claim a greater coherence and credibility.

"An allegation of conspiracy to injure is a strong one. It should only be pleaded when there is some credible material to support it. If it is to be asserted, it should be pleaded clearly and explicitly ... The unsupported assertion that the defendants intended to cause the claimants damage, that is to say financial loss, is simply not an allegation of a predominant intention to injure."

In any event, it will often not be necessary to plead a lawful means conspiracy where the facts support a claim for unlawful means conspiracy. What is more, in such cases it may be a waste of time and cost to pursue an allegation that defendants acted with the predominant purpose of injuring the claimant, given that the requisite intention in unlawful means cases can in practice be straightforward to establish in light of the "obverse side of the coin" principle.[298]   **2–144**

Moreover, the following statement of Millett LJ is highly pertinent in this context (particularly in the context of proving the relevant knowledge of a given defendant):   **2–145**

"It is well established that fraud must be distinctly alleged and as distinctly proved, and that if the facts pleaded are consistent with innocence it is not open to the court to find fraud. An allegation that the defendant 'knew or ought to have known' is not a clear and unequivocal allegation of actual knowledge and will not support a finding of fraud even if the court is satisfied that there was actual knowledge. An allegation that the defendant had actual knowledge of the existence of a fraud perpetrated by others and failed to disclose the fact to the victim is consistent with an inadvertent failure to make disclosure and is not a charge of fraud. It will not support a finding of fraud even if the court is satisfied that the failure to disclose was deliberate and dishonest. Where it is expressly alleged that such failure was negligent and in breach of a contractual obligation of disclosure, but not that it was deliberate and dishonest, there is no room for treating it as an allegation of fraud."

(4)   Other Procedural and Professional Considerations

Bearing in mind the difficulties which claimants can have in putting forward a cogent case in conspiracy at the pleadings stage, it can be tempting for a defendant (or those acting for him) faced with a claim which is thinly pleaded to seek to strike out the claim in its early stages, in an attempt to avoid the time, costs and litigation risk inherent in fighting a conspiracy claim—and perhaps to avoid giving the claimant an opportunity to bolster his case by amendment or further particularisation after disclosure.   **2–146**

Such attempts can be ill-fated. It is crucial to have in mind the difference between a pleading which discloses no reasonable grounds for bringing the claim (which is accordingly liable to be struck out) and a pleading which, although not fully particularised, nevertheless discloses a cause of action if the facts pleaded can be established. There has been wide judicial recognition of the difficulties of pleading a fully particularised claim in conspiracy at the outset of proceedings, bearing in mind that matters such as the defendants' knowledge or intentions are peculiarly within the defendant's knowledge and (if the claim is justified) likely to have been concealed from the claimant.[299]   **2–147**

---

[298] See para.2–042 above.

[299] For some recent examples, see *AstraZeneca UK Ltd v Albemarle* [2010] EWHC 1028 (Comm); [2011] 1 All E.R. (Comm) 510, at [78] in particular (jurisdiction challenge based on the alleged

2–148   A conspiracy claim will, by its very nature, probably involve multiple parties. This inevitably increases complexity and can slow down the process of determination of the claim. Where legal advisors are approached to act on behalf of more than one defendant to a single conspiracy claim, it goes without saying that care needs to be taken at the outset and on an ongoing basis as to whether there are actual or potential conflicts between defendants that would preclude joint representation. In some cases joint representation may even give the impression of supporting the very combination which the defendants deny. The possibility of a contribution claim between defendants will often make it inappropriate for them to be jointly represented.

2–149   Practitioners acting for a claimant contemplating the pursuit of an unlawful means conspiracy claim will often have to consider whether free-standing claims should also be brought in respect of the unlawful means themselves (e.g. breach of contract, breach of fiduciary duty, deceit, etc.). Of course, the unlawful means may not be independently actionable, at least as against all defendants.[300] The interplay between free-standing claims and claims in conspiracy has given rise to a number of issues worthy of consideration. In the tort context, it was previously suggested that a conspiracy to commit a tort "merged" in the tort, such that the conspiracy allegation added nothing.[301] This suggestion was rejected by the Court of Appeal in *Kuwait Oil Tanker v Al Bader*.[302] Accordingly, it is now clear that both claims can, in principle, be pursued alongside each other.[303]

2–150   It has been noted that a plea of conspiracy can offer the claimant procedural advantages which he may not enjoy from the pursuit of other claims.[304] Whilst specific examples of such advantages are not easy to find in the cases, the following points are worth bearing in mind from a practitioner's perspective:

(1)   Where it can be shown that a wrongful act has been carried out and that damage has been caused to the claimant, a conspiracy claim offers the claimant a potential evidential advantage if there are difficulties in showing which participant in the conspiracy carried out the wrongful act, or in showing precisely how the damage was caused.[305]

(2)   It may be that bringing a conspiracy claim would make it easier for the claimant to obtain aggravated damages than a simple joint tortfeasance claim.[306]

---

absence of a serious issue to be tried); *Dar Al Arkan Real Estate Development Co v Al-Refai* [2013] EWHC 1630 (Comm) (strike-out/summary judgment); *Emerald Supplies Ltd v British Airways Plc* [2014] EWHC 3514 (Ch), at [13] and [39]–[50] in particular (strike-out/summary judgment).

[300]   See paras 2–051—2–054 and 2–062—2–070 above.

[301]   *Ward v Lewis* [1955] 1 W.L.R. 9.

[302]   *Kuwait Oil Tanker v Al Bader* [2000] 2 All E.R. (Comm) 271, at [122]–[132].

[303]   Compare the view expressed by the authors of (Jones (ed)), *Clerk & Lindsell on Torts* (2017), para.24–08, that, where there is a claim against two defendants as joint tortfeasors, the claimant should not add unnecessary charges of conspiracy.

[304]   *Metall und Rohstoff v Donaldson, Lufkin & Jenrette Inc* [1990] 1 Q.B. 391, at 466H.

[305]   J. Eekelaar, "The Conspiracy Tangle" (1990) 106 L.Q.R. 223, at 224.

[306]   *Sorrell v Smith* [1925] A.C. 700, at 713; *Michaels v Taylor Woodrow Developments Ltd* [2001] Ch. 493, at 516.

(3) There are, however, limits to the advantages that can be obtained by pleading conspiracy. For example in *Hesperides Hotels v Aegean Hotels*[307] the claimant was not permitted, by pleading a conspiracy, to circumvent the rule of private international law preventing the English court from adjudicating on an allegation of trespass to foreign land.[308]

(4) A claimant who pursues a conspiracy claim also sets himself hurdles which may not arise in free-standing claims, such as a claim against joint tortfeasors. An obvious example is the effective requirement to plead and prove dishonesty, considered in paras 2–139—2–140 above. More generally, whilst an intention to harm of one kind or another is an essential element in all conspiracy claims, to be liable as a joint tortfeasor it is not necessary that a defendant should intend to harm the claimant.[309]

Whether or not a conspiracy claim is pursued alongside associated claims (e.g. direct claims for wrongful acts which are also relied on as "unlawful means" in a conspiracy claim) might also have an impact on questions of applicable law, jurisdiction and appropriate forum. In *VTB Capital Plc v Nutritek*,[310] for example, Lord Mance and Lord Neuberger each expressed the view that, whilst the claimant's deceit claim was governed by English law, the same was not necessarily true of a claim in conspiracy to commit that deceit. To adopt the language of the Rome II Regulation,[311] the damage may not occur in the same place for each claim. Similarly, as far as jurisdiction is concerned, how a claim is characterised might, for example, affect the answer to the question of where the "harmful event occurred"[312] or where damage was sustained.[313]

2–151

---

[307] *Hesperides Hotels v Aegean Hotels* [1979] A.C. 508.

[308] It appears that trespass would have formed the basis of an unlawful means conspiracy (see 535–536); since the trespass could effectively not be made out, neither could the conspiracy. See also paras 2–072—2–076 above in relation to the rule against enforcement of a foreign public or penal law.

[309] *Fish & Fish Ltd v Sea Shepherd UK* [2015] UKSC 10; [2015] A.C. 1229, per Lord Neuberger JSC at [60].

[310] *VTB Capital Plc v Nutritek* [2013] UKSC 5; [2013] 2 A.C. 337, per Lord Mance JSC at [7] and per Lord Neuberger JSC at [100].

[311] Regulation (EU) 864/2007 art.4(1).

[312] Article 7(2) of the recast Brussels Regulation (EU) 1215/2012.

[313] CPR Practice Direction 6B, para.3.1(9).

CHAPTER 3

INDUCING BREACH OF CONTRACT

A. INTRODUCTION

(1) The Origin and Development of the Tort

The tort of inducing breach of contract is based on the general principle that a **3–001** person who procures another to commit a wrong incurs liability as an accessory.[1] Liability for inducing breach of contract is therefore a form of secondary liability.[2] The origins of the tort lie in the seminal decision in *Lumley v Gye*.[3] Lumley, a theatre owner, entered into a contract with the singer Johanna Wagner for her to perform at Lumley's theatre. The defendant, Gye, induced Wagner to break her engagement with Lumley in order that she could sing at Gye's own theatre. Gye was held liable in tort for inducing Wagner's breach of contract.

In the 150 years following the decision in *Lumley v Gye*, the tort of inducing **3–002** breach of contract underwent a somewhat uneasy development. Only fairly recently have the principles of the tort and its proper place among the economic torts been authoritatively restated, by the House of Lords in *OBG Ltd v Allan*.[4] Lord Hoffmann's speech in particular contains a masterly account of the history of the tort of inducing breach of contract, and of its development alongside and (erroneously) in tandem with the tort of unlawful interference, a tort considered below at Ch.4. In light of the decision in *OBG*, the detail of the historical twists and turns taken by these two torts is unlikely to be of much relevance to the fraud practitioner. Any consideration of the case law in this area prior to *OBG* nevertheless requires an understanding that a "unified theory" formerly held traction, which considered unlawful interference to be a sub-species, or indirect form, of the tort of inducing breach of contract[5]; and that such a theory was rejected in *OBG*. Whilst many principles from earlier cases still hold good, those authorities now require to be treated with caution.

---

[1] *OBG Ltd v Allan* [2007] UKHL 21; [2008] 1 A.C. 1, per Lord Hoffmann at [3].

[2] *OBG Ltd v Allan* [2007] UKHL 21; [2008] 1 A.C. 1, per Lord Nicholls at [172]; per Lord Brown at [320]. This distinguishes inducing breach of contract from unlawful interference (sometimes called causing loss by unlawful means), which is a tort of primary liability: see para.4–007.

[3] *Lumley v Gye* (1853) 2 E&B 216.

[4] *OBG Ltd v Allan* [2007] UKHL 21; [2008] 1 A.C. 1.

[5] In particular since *DC Thomson & Co Ltd v Deakin* [1952] Ch. 646.

(2) Practical Applications in the Fraud Context

3–003   Like other economic torts such as unlawful means conspiracy, the chief practical relevance of the tort of inducing breach of contract in a fraud case is its potential to cast the net of liability beyond the immediate wrongdoer in any given situation. A defendant's fraud may involve the misappropriation of the claimant's funds via the suborning of its employee or director. Or a contracting party may be persuaded into a defendant's scheme by the lure of some benefit to himself, but with the inevitable consequence that, as part of the scheme, he breaches his contract with the claimant. In such cases, whilst there may be a straightforward contractual claim against the employee, director or other contracting party, in practice there may be greater difficulties in enforcing any judgment against such a party (e.g. because he is an individual of limited means, or is insolvent) than against other participants in the fraud. On the right facts, the tort of inducing breach of contract may provide a means of fixing those other participants with liability and recovering against them.

(3) The Overlap Between Inducing Breach of Contract and Unlawful Interference

3–004   The torts of inducing breach of contract and unlawful interference are related in several respects. It is not difficult to conceive of circumstances in which a defendant would be liable in both torts. For example, if A:

(1)   Makes a false representation to B which causes him to breach his contract with C;
(2)   Threatens to assault B unless he repudiates his contract with C[6];
(3)   Pressurises B into taking steps which result in a breach of B's contract with C in circumstances amounting to the of harassment of B; or
(4)   Physically detains B so that he is unable to fulfil his contractual obligations to C[7];

then, in each case, A is liable to C both for inducing B's breach of contract, and for unlawful interference. Indeed, in any situation in which B is induced to breach his contract with C by the use of unlawful means employed by A, there is the potential for liability in both torts. In addition, the torts can in principle work cumulatively. If B is C's employee, and is persuaded by A to give false information (in breach of his employment contract) to D as part of A's scheme to harm D, then A is liable to D for unlawful interference, the requisite "unlawful means" being A's commission of the tort of inducing B's breach of contract with C.

---

[6] An example postulated by Lord Hoffmann in *OBG Ltd v Allan* [2007] UKHL 21; [2008] 1 A.C. 1, at [21].
[7] An example postulated by Sir Raymond Evershed MR in *DC Thomson & Co Ltd v Deakin* [1952] Ch. 646, at 678.

However, there are important differences between the two torts. In *OBG Ltd v* **3–005**
Allan,[8] Lord Hoffmann identified four key differences:

(1)   Unlawful interference is a tort of primary liability; that is to say, it exists
      independently of any other wrong committed by a third party against the
      claimant. Inducing breach of contract, by contrast, is a tort of secondary
      liability. It cannot exist independently of a primary wrong, usually in the
      form of a breach of contract, committed by a third party against the
      claimant.[9]

(2)   Whereas unlawful interference requires the use of means which are
      unlawful in themselves, liability for inducing breach of contract requires
      only "the degree of participation in the breach of contract which satisfies
      the general requirements of accessory liability for the wrongful act of
      another person". Those requirements are considered in detail in this
      chapter.

(3)   Unlike the inducement tort, liability for unlawful interference does not
      depend on the existence of a prior contractual relationship. In *OBG* itself,[10]
      Lord Hoffmann used the famous example of an 18th Century case[11] in
      which a ship's master deprived a rival of trade by firing a cannon to drive
      away a canoe approaching the rival from the shore seeking to do business.
      There was no contract between the respective occupants of the canoe and
      the rival ship, but that would not have prevented liability from arising in
      unlawful interference.

(4)   Both torts are torts of intention, but the result which must have been
      intended is different for each: for unlawful interference, damage to the
      claimant must be intended. For the inducement tort, on the other hand,
      intention to cause a breach of contract is both necessary and sufficient to
      found liability. Intention is considered in more detail in paras 3–048—3–
      065 below.

(4)   The Tort does not Provide a Remedy for the Party Induced to Breach His Contract

It is important to note that the tort does not create a cause of action in favour of **3–006**
the contracting party whose breach is induced by the defendant, even if that party
also suffers loss as a result. In *Boulting v Association of Cinematograph
Television and Allied Technicians*,[12] the defendant trade union sought to compel
the claimant directors to join a trade union. The directors sought an injunction to
prevent such conduct, in part on the basis that it threatened to put them in breach
of their duty of loyalty to the company of which they were directors. The Court of
Appeal dismissed the action. On this particular point, Upjohn LJ said that:

---

[8]   *OBG Ltd v Allan* [2007] UKHL 21; [2008] 1 A.C. 1, at [8].
[9]   The inducement of certain other wrongs is also actionable: see paras 3–023—3–024.
[10] *OBG Ltd v Allan* [2007] UKHL 21; [2008] 1 A.C. 1, at [6], [8].
[11] *Tarleton v M'Gawley* (1794) Peake 270.
[12] *Boulting v Association of Cinematograph Television and Allied Technicians* [1963] 2 Q.B. 606.

"If A procures B to break his contract with C, C can complain because A commits a well-established tort against C. But B has no right at law to restrain A from attempting to suborn him from his duty to C. He must resist A's efforts by strength of will."[13]

B. BREACH OF CONTRACT

3–007   A breach of contract is "of the essence" of this tort: "If there is no primary liability, there can be no accessory liability".[14] So, it is now clear that there is no liability in this tort for "interference" with contractual relations in the absence of a breach. Lord Hoffmann so held in *OBG Ltd v Allan*,[15] disapproving statements in earlier cases to the effect that a breach was not necessary, and that merely hindering a contracting party's performance would be sufficient. It is not per se tortious to prevent one party from contracting with another.[16] Similarly, action which merely makes another's contractual rights less valuable is not actionable. So in *RCA Corp v Pollard*,[17] the Court of Appeal struck out a claim by a recording company against bootleggers for inducing a breach of the recording company's exclusive contract with Elvis Presley. The bootleggers' illegal sales of Elvis recordings had made the recording company's rights under its contract less valuable, but they had not induced any breach of that contract.[18] Inducing conduct by a third party falling short of a breach of contract may, however, give rise to liability in the tort of unlawful interference (see Ch.4 below).

3–008   In order for liability to arise, the breach induced must also be of an enforceable contract. A void contract cannot, of course, be breached. A voidable contract, on the other hand—unless and until it is set aside—subsists and is capable of being breached by both parties, including the party who may be entitled to have the contract set aside. However, there can be no liability for inducing a party to a voidable contract lawfully to rescind that contract with the claimant; the contracting party commits no wrong and thus there can be no secondary liability on the part of the defendant. This principle was upheld in *Proform Sports Management Ltd v Proactive Sports Management Ltd*,[19] where a representation contract with the footballer Wayne Rooney was held to be voidable by him on the grounds of his (then) minority. This reflects the underlying principle that the

---

[13] *Boulting* [1963] 2 Q.B. 606, at 639–640.

[14] *OBG Ltd v Allan* [2007] UKHL 21; [2008] 1 A.C. 1, per Lord Hoffmann at [8]. As explained below, it is possible in principle to obtain a *quia timet* injunction preventing the inducement of a breach of a contract not yet entered into at the time of the order, as happened for example in *JT Stratford & Son Ltd v Lindley* [1965] A.C. 269 and *Torquay Hotel Co Ltd v Cousins* [1969] 2 Ch. 106, but the wrong restrained by such an injunction remains the inducement of a breach of contract (rather than, say, preventing a contract from being made in the first place). If and when the claimant then enters into the anticipated contract, the defendant will be prevented by the injunction from inducing a breach of it.

[15] *OBG Ltd v Allan* [2007] UKHL 21; [2008] 1 A.C. 1, at [44].

[16] *Allen v Flood* [1898] A.C. 1, per Lord Herschell at 120–121; *Midland Cold Storage Ltd v Steer* [1972] Ch. 630, at 645. It is different, of course, if unlawful means are used such as to give rise to liability for unlawful interference, as for example in *Tarleton v M'Gawley* (see para.3–005 above).

[17] *RCA Corp v Pollard* [1983] Ch. 135.

[18] *RCA Corp v Pollard* [1983] Ch.135, per Slade LJ at 157.

[19] *Proform Sports Management Ltd v Proactive Sports Management Ltd* [2007] 1 All E.R. 542, at [27]–[33].

inducement tort is one of secondary liability: since the contract could not be enforced against the third party footballer, it would be illogical to enable its indirect enforcement against the alleged inducer. However, in the *Proform* case HHJ Hodge QC extended the principle to reach the conclusion that it was not tortious to induce the breach of a voidable contract. As a conclusion of general principle, it is thought that this goes too far. The party entitled to avoid a voidable contract is also entitled to affirm it. If he does so, he will be liable for any breach of contract he committed whilst the contract was voidable. Likewise a third party who induces such a breach ought, it is suggested, to be liable in tort if the contract is then affirmed.[20]

Conversely, any breach of an enforceable contract induced by the defendant will in principle suffice to give rise to the necessary secondary liability, if the claimant thereby suffers loss. A defendant cannot escape liability, for example, on the basis that the breach was only temporary—such as conduct to induce "suspension" of orders for a newspaper, which the claimants succeeded in preventing by injunction in *Daily Mirror Newspapers Ltd v Gardner*.[21] In such a case the temporary nature of the breach would go only to the quantum of the claimant's loss.

3–009

The situation may arise in which the defendant interferes in the operation of a contract between the claimant and the contracting party such that circumstances arise in which the contracting party has a right to terminate the contract, and does so on inducement from the defendant. On the face of it, the defendant could not be liable for inducing breach of contract: if the contracting party's termination was lawful there was no breach. However, the position may not be so simple, at least if the defendant acted unlawfully in bringing about the circumstances allowing termination. In *Emerald Construction Co Ltd v Lowthian*,[22] the defendant union representatives called a strike which prevented the claimant from progressing with building works as required by the contract. Lord Denning held[23] (on an interim basis) that, even if this entitled the other contracting party to terminate the contract, it did not allow the defendants to escape liability since in doing so they would be relying on their own wrongful act. This may be explicable as an expression of the principle of public policy preventing a party from relying on his own wrong (so that the termination would in effect be regarded as a breach), or as a reference to liability arising instead in unlawful interference. But otherwise it would be inconsistent with the rule, re-affirmed in *OBG Ltd v Allan*, that there can be no liability for inducement without breach.

3–010

There is no reason in principle why an injunction could not be sought in an appropriate case to restrain (on a quia timet basis) action to induce a breach of contract, before there has actually been any breach. Thus an injunction was

3–011

---

[20] There is also old authority to the effect that the voidability of a contract is no defence to a claim in tort against the inducer: *Keane v Boycott* (1795) 2 Blackstone (H.) 511, at 515. It is suggested that this remains good law. For a contrary view see M. Jones (ed), *Clerk & Lindsell on Torts*, 22nd edn (London: Sweet & Maxwell, 2017), para.24–21.

[21] *Daily Mirror Newspapers Ltd v Gardner* [1968] 2 Q.B. 762.

[22] *Emerald Construction Co Ltd v Lowthian* [1966] 1 W.L.R. 691.

[23] *Emerald Construction Co Ltd v Lowthian* [1966] 1 W.L.R. 691, at 701.

granted by the Court of Appeal in *Emerald Construction Co Ltd v Lowthian*[24] where officers of a trade union pursued industrial action with a view to bringing about the wrongful termination of a contract for the supply of labour by the claimant subcontractor to the main contractor. The contract remained in place but the industrial action threatened to bring about its wrongful termination. An injunction was granted to prevent that state of affairs from materialising. And in *Torquay Hotel Co Ltd v Cousins*,[25] the Court of Appeal upheld the grant of an injunction against defendants who had made it clear that they would block supplies of oil to the claimant hotel company, in circumstances where this threatened to bring about the breach of a future contract not yet entered into between the hotel and the supplier at the time of the injunction.

C. OTHER WRONGS

(1) Introduction

3–012   There is a wealth of authority to suggest that the principles governing the tort of inducing breach of contract are applicable mutatis mutandis to the inducement of at least certain other wrongs by a third party. In *Lumley v Gye*[26] itself, Erle J described the tort in this way:

> "It is clear that the procurement of the violation of a right is a cause of action in all instances where the violation is an actionable wrong, as in violations of a right to property, whether real or personal, or to personal security: he who procures the wrong is a joint wrong-doer, and may be sued, either alone or jointly with the agent, in the appropriate action for the wrong complained of."

3–013   In the leading case of *Quinn v Leathem*,[27] Lord McNaghten considered that *Lumley v Gye* was correctly decided

> "on the ground that a violation of legal right committed knowingly is a cause of action, and that it is a violation of legal right to interfere with contractual relations recognised by law if there be no sufficient justification for the interference."

As has been subsequently noted,[28] the first half of this statement expresses the principle in terms of general applicability, beyond the ambit of breaches of contract.

3–014   However, the question of the extent to which *Lumley v Gye* principles can be applied to the inducement of other actionable wrongs has not received the sort of comprehensive restatement given by the House of Lords in *OBG Ltd v Allan* to the principles governing inducement of a breach of contract. Of the two leading speeches in that case, Lord Hoffmann (although referring with apparent

---

[24] *Emerald Construction Co Ltd v Lowthian* [1966] 1 W.L.R. 691.
[25] *Torquay Hotel Co Ltd v Cousins* [1969] 2 Ch. 106, in particular at 140D–140F, 141D–141E, 143F and 146D–146F.
[26] *Lumley v Gye* (1853) 2 E&B 216, at 232.
[27] *Quinn v Leathem* [1901] A.C. 495, at 510.
[28] *F v Wirral MBC* [1991] Fam.69, per Ralph Gibson LJ at 108F.

approval[29] to the broad expression of the principle in *Lumley v Gye* itself) did not in terms address inducement of other wrongs. Lord Nicholls expressly left open the question of how far the tort applies to "inducing a breach of other actionable obligations such as statutory duties or equitable or fiduciary obligations".[30] Accordingly, the answer to the question must be found elsewhere, principally by examining earlier authority. Those areas most likely to be relevant for the civil fraud practitioner are examined below.

(2)   Breach of Statutory Duty

A number of cases support the proposition that the *Lumley v Gye* principle extends to inducing a breach of statutory duty. The most prominent example is *Associated British Ports v TGWU*.[31] There Butler-Sloss LJ described a general tort, of which inducing a breach of statutory duty was an example, of "interference with rights" or "direct invasion of legal rights".[32] The value of this case as authority for such a broad statement is, however, reduced by two principal factors: first, the existence of a tort of inducing breach of statutory duty was common ground between the parties[33]; secondly (like many of the older cases in this area of the law), the case was decided on an application for an interim injunction, requiring only a "serious issue to be tried" to be shown (by reference to *American Cyanamid* principles). What can nonetheless be taken from the *TGWU* case is that, for the claimant to be able to sue in this form of secondary liability, the breach of statutory duty must be directly actionable at the suit of the claimant.[34] More recently, in *Wilson v Housing Corp*,[35] Dyson J recognised the tort of inducing a breach of statutory duty, but held that the duty in question had to be one which was actionable in the courts: so that, in that case, an employee's statutory right not to be unfairly dismissed, which could only be asserted in an employment tribunal, did not qualify as a right on which liability in this tort could be founded.

3–015

(3)   Equitable Obligations

The extent to which inducing a breach of equitable obligations gives rise to liability in the *Lumley v Gye* tort is uncertain. The position is complicated by the existence of a separate set of principles (with its own jurisprudence) governing accessory liability in equitable claims, such as knowing receipt and dishonest assistance. Those principles are considered separately in Chs 12 and 13.

3–016

---

[29] *OBG Ltd v Allan* [2007] UKHL 21; [2008] 1 A.C. 1, at [3] and [13] in particular. See, to the same effect, per Lord Brown at [320].

[30] *OBG Ltd v Allan* [2007] UKHL 21; [2008] 1 A.C. 1, at [189].

[31] *Associated British Ports v TGWU* [1989] 1 W.L.R. 939.

[32] At 959B.

[33] As recorded by Neill LJ at 951H.

[34] See per Neill LJ at 952B–952E, per Butler-Sloss LJ at 959H–960A, per Stuart-Smith LJ at 964F–965B. The decision of the Court of Appeal was reversed by the House of Lords on other grounds [1989] 1 W.L.R. 939. By contrast, in the tort of unlawful interference, the breach need only be actionable by the third party: see paras 4–012—4–014.

[35] *Wilson v Housing Corp* [1998] I.C.R. 151.

3-017 In *Prudential Assurance Co v Lorenz*,[36] the claimant insurance company sought to prevent industrial action by the defendant union, who had ordered collecting agents to bank all moneys collected on the claimant's behalf but to withhold payment from it, as well as withholding information about the amounts collected. Although the agents were in contractual relationships with the claimant, the union was protected by statute from liability for the tort of inducing breach of contract. Accordingly, the claimant framed the wrong alleged as an interference with the agents' equitable obligations to account to the claimant. Plowman J held the claimants to have made out a prima facie case (under the principles pre-dating *American Cyanamid* which required more than just a serious triable issue to be shown) sufficient to entitle them to an interim injunction. Two of the three judges in *Associated British Ports v TGWU* referred to Plowman J's decision with apparent approval.[37]

3-018 Another equitable obligation, namely the duty of a fiduciary to avoid conflicts of interest, was considered by the Court of Appeal in *Boulting v Association of Cinematograph Television and Allied Technicians*.[38] The case did not turn on whether procuring a breach of this duty would be a tort, but two of the judges in the Court of Appeal considered that it would[39]; by reference in particular to *Bents Brewery Co Ltd v Hogan*.[40] In the *Bents Brewery* case, the claimant breweries sought a declaration that the defendant union official was not entitled to answers to a questionnaire addressed by him to the claimants' employees, on the grounds that to seek such answers was to induce the breach by the employees of their duty of confidence to their employer. The court granted the declaration, holding[41] that it did not matter whether such duty arose as a matter of contract, as a fiduciary duty or by virtue of the employee's status as such.

3-019 These cases provide some support for the proposition that an equitable obligation is akin to a contractual obligation for the purposes of the *Lumley v Gye* tort. However, the courts have refused to recognise a tort of inducing a breach of trust, on the basis that "The principles of the law of trusts, in particular those expounded by Lord Selborne LC in *Barnes v Addy*[42] are quite sufficient to deal with those persons who incite a breach of trust or wrongfully meddle with trust assets or interfere with the relationship of trustee and beneficiary".[43] On the same basis, Norris J held more recently that there is no general tort of inducing a breach of fiduciary duty.[44] He considered that the statement of principle in *Lumley v Gye* did not extend beyond the inducement of a breach of an obligation enforceable at common law; whilst accepting:

---

[36] *Prudential Assurance Co v Lorenz* (1971) 11 K.I.R. 78.
[37] *Associated British Ports v TGWU* [1989] 1 W.L.R. 939, per Butler-Sloss LJ at 959C–959D and per Stuart-Smith LJ at 964C.
[38] *Boulting v Association of Cinematograph Television and Allied Technicians* [1963] 2 Q.B. 606.
[39] Lord Denning MR at 627 and Diplock LJ at 648–649.
[40] *Bents Brewery Co Ltd v Hogan* [1945] 2 All E.R. 570.
[41] At 576F–576H.
[42] *Barnes v Addy* (1873–1874) L.R. 9 Ch. App. 244.
[43] *Metall und Rohstoff AG v Donaldson Lufkin & Jenrette Inc* [1990] 1 Q.B. 391, at 481G.
[44] *First Subsea Ltd v Balltec Ltd* [2014] EWHC 866 (Ch), at [351]–[353].

"that there are cases[45] where there is a contractual obligation and an identical fiduciary obligation (e.g. to account) in which the inducement tort has been held to apply to both obligations",

Norris J nevertheless held that those cases "do not provide a sufficient foundation for the proposition that there is a general tort of inducing breach of fiduciary duty".

It is not easy to reconcile the above authorities. Norris J's apparent attempt to limit the scope of the principle in *Lumley v Gye* to concurrent contractual and equitable obligations is at odds with *Prudential Assurance Co v Lorenz* in particular (where the only possible basis for liability was for inducement of a breach of the equitable obligation). The proper scope of the tort in the context of equitable obligations accordingly remains an open question.

3–020

(4)   No Tort of Inducing a Tort

There is no separate tort of inducing a tort by another. Instead, in such a case the inducer and induced party will be liable as joint tortfeasors.[46] However, the basis for liability in such a claim is the same as the basis for liability under the *Lumley v Gye* tort.[47] The point is thus one of form, dictating how the case should be pleaded and argued, rather than one of substance.

3–021

(5)   Obligations Under a Judgment or Order

On the current state of the authorities, it is at least arguable that liability under *Lumley v Gye* can arise for inducing the breach of obligations under a judgment or order. In *Marex Financial Ltd v Sevilleja Garcia*,[48] the claimant had obtained money judgments against a number of corporate defendants. Subsequently, the individual who controlled the companies (Mr Sevilleja) was alleged to have dishonestly taken steps, after the judgment was handed down, to strip the companies of their assets, rendering them unable to meet their obligations to pay under the judgments. Knowles J dismissed a jurisdiction challenge by Mr Sevilleja founded on the contention that the claim disclosed no cause of action, concluding that the claimant had at least a good arguable case. The judge reasoned that non-payment of a judgment debt was an actionable wrong,[49] and that accordingly the procurement of that wrong could give rise to liability as an

3–022

---

[45] Presumably those cited above, though none was expressly referred to in the judgment.

[46] *Smith v Pywell, The Times*, 29 April 1959, per Diplock J; *CBS Songs Ltd v Amstrad Consumer Electronics Plc* [1988] A.C. 1013, per Lord Templeman at 1058; *Fish & Fish Ltd v Sea Shepherd UK* [2015] UKSC 10; [2015] A.C. 1229, per Lord Toulson at [19]. On joint torts generally, see Ch.20 below.

[47] *OBG Ltd v Allan* [2008] 1 A.C. 1, per Lord Hoffmann at [36].

[48] *Marex Financial Ltd v Sevilleja Garcia* [2017] EWHC 918 (Comm); [2017] 4 W.L.R. 105. The decision of Knowles J was overturned on appeal [2018] EWCA Civ 1468, but not on this issue.

[49] In reliance on earlier authority including *Rubin v Eurofinance SA* [2012] UKSC 46; [2013] 1 A.C. 236, at [9]; some of this earlier authority referred to the juridical basis for the liability being in implied contract.

accessory.[50] If correct (for reasons discussed below there are other aspects of the decision which are open to doubt), this may be a significant decision in the fraud context: it will be a common occurrence, in the absence of a freezing order, that a fraudster will seek to prevent a company complying with a judgment obtained against it by extracting its assets so as to make it judgment proof. The significance of the decision is diminished, however, by the decision of the Court of Appeal, which allowed Mr Sevilleja's appeal on the basis that the claimant's claim was barred by the rule against reflective loss.[51]

3–023   The violation of rights under an existing judgment must be contrasted, however, with a claimant's inchoate right to seek a judgment which he has not yet obtained. The latter right is not protected by the *Lumley v Gye* tort. In *Law Debenture Trust Corp v Ural Caspian Oil Corp Ltd*,[52] there had been a series of share transfers from one defendant to another. The first transfer was from L to H, in breach of a contract with the claimant, and was procured by H (in circumstances which it was common ground gave rise to liability under *Lumley v Gye*). The second transfer was from H to C. The claimant sought to claim against C for interfering with the claimant's rights to an order against H to re-transfer the shares to L. The Court of Appeal held that there was no cause of action: until there was an order against H, there was no obligation which H could have breached so as to make C liable as an accessory.[53]

3–024   Of course, in a case where the claimant's claim is brought to enforce a pre-existing contract with a company, and prior to judgment the defendant takes steps to strip the company of its assets, then the claimant may have a claim under *Lumley v Gye* for inducing breach of the pre-existing contract—subject to the question of whether asset-stripping amounts to "inducement" (considered in para.3–030 below), the application of the rule against recovery of reflective loss to claims by creditors, and potentially to issues of causation: in particular the defendant may be able to show, in a case where the company's original breach of contract pre-dated the asset-stripping, that the claimant's loss was suffered upon breach and prior to the asset-stripping. This will be a fact-sensitive question.

D.   INDUCEMENT

(1)   The Definition of Inducement

3–025   The tort discussed in this chapter has been given various different labels in the jurisprudence. The most common are "inducement" and "procurement" of a breach of contract, and for practical purposes these two labels are probably

---

[50] The judge also held that there was nothing in a further argument that Mr Sevilleja had merely prevented the companies' performance of their obligations. This aspect of his decision is perhaps open to doubt: see para.3–030 below.

[51] *Marex Financial Ltd v Sevilleja Garcia* [2018] EWCA Civ 1468.

[52] *Law Debenture Trust Corp v Ural Caspian Oil Corp Ltd* [1995] Ch. 152.

[53] *Law Debenture Trust Corp v Ural Caspian Oil Corp Ltd* [1995] Ch. 152, per Sir Thomas Bingham MR at 166B–166D, and per Beldam LJ at 170F–170G in particular.

synonymous.[54] The term "inducement" is used in this book, as best expressing the interrelation between the conduct of the defendant and its effect on the conduct of the contract breaker. In *Meretz Investments NV v ACP Ltd*[55] Arden LJ said that the tort is committed when a person, with the requisite knowledge and intention (discussed below), "procures or persuades" another person to breach his contract with the claimant. As Toulson LJ pointed out in the same case,[56] it is necessary to show that the defendant's conduct "operated on the will of the contracting party". In *OBG Ltd v Allan*,[57] Lord Hoffmann talked of "the defendant's acts of encouragement, threat, persuasion and so forth". It is clear from these passages that, to be actionable, an inducement need not amount to the suborning of the will of the contracting party; persuasion (in the sense explained in *Meretz*) is enough. The term "interference", found in a number of the older cases, is best avoided since it is reminiscent of the rejected "unified theory" referred to in para.3–002 above.

(2) The Inducement Can Take Any Form

Very often the necessary element of inducement will be found in communications between the defendant and the contract breaker. For example, A may offer to purchase property from B at a price higher than that which B has already agreed to sell the property to C; or A may threaten to stop ordering products from his supplier, B, if B continues to honour his contract to supply C, a competitor of A, with a particular product.

3–026

However, actionable inducement may take more subtle forms. The communications might take place through an intermediary: it does not matter whether any communication between the defendant and the contracting party is direct or indirect. Whilst once thought relevant, that distinction has been erased by *OBG Ltd v Allan*.[58] Inducement can also be implicit. Even silence can in principle give rise to inducement, as recognised in *Lonmar Global Risks Ltd v West*.[59] There, it was alleged that the defendant had induced former employees of the claimant to solicit its clients and employees, in breach of their contracts of employment. The claim failed on the facts. But the judge thought that, if the evidence had shown that the former employees had required, and sought, the defendant's approval before taking action in breach of contract, then it might have been possible to imply inducement from the defendant's silence in response to the employees' request.

3–027

---

[54] In *OBG Ltd v Allan* [2007] UKHL 21; [2008] 1 A.C. 1 both Lord Hoffmann and Lord Nicholls used both terms interchangeably.

[55] *Meretz Investments NV v ACP Ltd* [2007] EWCA Civ 1303; [2008] Ch. 244, at [86]. This echoes the language used by Lord Nicholls in *OBG Ltd v Allan* [2007] UKHL 21; [2008] 1 A.C. 1, at [191].

[56] *Meretz Investments NV v ACP Ltd* [2007] EWCA Civ 1303; [2008] Ch. 244, at [177].

[57] *OBG Ltd v Allan* [2007] UKHL 21; [2008] 1 A.C. 1, at [36].

[58] *OBG Ltd v Allan* [2007] UKHL 21; [2008] 1 A.C. 1, in particular per Lord Hoffmann at [34]–[38].

[59] *Lonmar Global Risks Ltd v West* [2010] EWHC 2878 (QB), [2011] I.R.L.R. 138, per Hickinbottom J at [220].

(3) Mere Prevention of Performance is not Enough

3–028   It had previously been thought that, if A merely prevented B from performing his obligations under a contract with C, A could be liable to C in the *Lumley v Gye* tort. So, in *GWK Ltd v Dunlop Rubber Co Ltd*,[60] the defendant, Dunlop, was found liable to ARM in this tort when its employees removed ARM's tyres from cars made by GWK the night before a motor show, and substituted Dunlop tyres. This put GWK in breach of its contractual obligation to ARM to display ARM's tyres on its cars at motor shows. But Dunlop had done nothing to "operate on the will of GWK"; its conduct simply prevented GWK from fulfilling its contractual obligations. Following *OBG Ltd v Allan*,[61] Dunlop's liability in that case is properly to be understood as arising in unlawful interference, not in inducement. Where there is no element of persuasion or inducement, and the defendant's conduct simply prevents a third party from performing its contractual obligations to the claimant, there is no liability under *Lumley v Gye*.

3–029   This principle is neatly illustrated by the decision of the Court of Appeal in *Meretz Investments NV v ACP Ltd*.[62] The case concerned a complex contractual arrangement governing the development of a number of penthouse flats. As part of the arrangement, the defendant leaseholder (ACP) was to undertake the development and had granted a leaseback option to the claimant (C2), exercisable in the event that ACP failed to meet the contractual timetable for the development. Separately, the second defendant (FP) had provided finance to ACP for the project, and had taken a charge over the leasehold containing a power of sale. When the project failed, FP exercised its power of sale. This made it impossible for ACP to fulfil its obligation to grant a leaseback to C2. C2's claim against FP for inducing breach of contract failed. As Arden LJ held,[63] this was not a case of inducement but prevention; FP's actions left ACP with no choice about whether to perform its contract.[64]

3–030   By contrast, in *Marex Financial Ltd v Sevilleja*[65] Knowles J held that the claimant had at least a good arguable case that a defendant alleged to have stripped a number of corporate defendants of their assets, rendering them unable to pay money judgments obtained against them by the claimant, did not merely prevent compliance with the money judgment but procured their breach. Whilst the judgment sets out only a summary of the facts alleged, it is not altogether easy to see how such conduct would amount to "inducement" in the relevant sense (and in particular how it "operated on the will" of the companies, in circumstances where the defendant was their controller and beneficial owner).

---

[60] *GWK Ltd v Dunlop Rubber Co Ltd* (1926) 42 T.L.R. 376. The claimants were GWK and ARM; GWK's own claim was for trespass to goods.

[61] *OBG Ltd v Allan* [2007] UKHL 21; [2008] 1 A.C. 1, at [24], [47] and [177]–[178].

[62] *Meretz Investments NV v ACP Ltd* [2007] EWCA Civ 1303; [2008] Ch. 244.

[63] At [137]–[138].

[64] See also *DC Thomson & Co Ltd v Deakin* [1952] Ch. 646, per Jenkins LJ at 693: "acts of a third party lawful in themselves do not constitute an actionable interference with contractual rights merely because they bring about a breach of contract, even if they were done with the object and intention of bringing about such breach".

[65] *Marex Financial Ltd v Sevilleja Garcia* [2017] EWHC 918 (Comm); [2017] 4 W.L.R. 105, at [24]–[26], overturned on appeal [2018] EWCA Civ 1468 but not on this point.

It seems that the contracting party's absence of choice can prevent a finding of inducement even where that party seeks the defendant's consent to carry out acts in performance of the former's contract with the claimant, and the defendant refuses. In *RBS v McCarthy*,[66] a former partner in a firm of solicitors sought to defend a claim by the bank for repayment of a loan facility provided to finance his capital contribution, on the basis that the bank had procured the firm to breach its contract to refund the contribution on the partner's retirement. The bank had written to the firm (of which it was also a creditor) demanding that no repayments of partners' capital should be made without its consent. Picken J held that this did not amount to an inducement. Even had the bank been asked for, and refused, such consent, that would at most be a case of prevention, not inducement.[67]

3–031

(4) Advice to be Distinguished from Inducement

A contracting party who decides to breach a contract will often reach that decision in light of information or advice communicated to him by a third party. It may be in such a case that the third party's communication of the information or advice induced the breach, in a general sense. For example: A has contracted to sell a property to B for £1,000,000, but is then told by C that there has been a rapid rise in the market since the contract was executed, and accordingly A sells to D at a higher price, thereby breaching his contract with B. If all that C was doing was passing on information, he would not be liable. But the circumstances may show that C passed on the information precisely to induce A to breach his contract with B (if, say, C and D were related and had special reasons of their own for wanting to acquire the property). If so, C would be liable. It is therefore necessary to distinguish between the provision of advice or information which leads to a breach of contract, and conduct which actually induces a breach of contract (in the sense explained above). The line between these two types of conduct is fundamental to whether liability arises, but the cases illustrate the difficulties in knowing where to draw it in any given case.

3–032

In *South Wales Miners Federation v Glamorgan Coal Co Ltd*,[68] the defendant mining federation had passed resolutions and given directions to coal miners (who were members of the federation) to stop work with a view to keeping up the price of coal and, therefore, the members' wages. Whilst it would have been within the federation's legitimate remit to give advice to its members, it went beyond that remit and was held liable. This case is a good illustration of the fact that "advice which is intended to have persuasive effects is not distinguishable from inducement".[69] More recently but in a similar context, in *Govia Thameslink Railway Ltd v The Associated Society of Locomotive Engineers and Firemen*[70] a reminder issued by the railway union to its members that there was no agreement

3–033

---

[66] *RBS v McCarthy* [2015] EWHC 3626 (QB).

[67] At [84]–[85]; in fact the defendant's case to that effect had been abandoned prior to judgment.

[68] *South Wales Miners Federation v Glamorgan Coal Co Ltd* [1905] A.C. 239, at 249 and 254 in particular.

[69] *Camden Nominees Ltd v Slack* [1940] Ch. 352, at 366.

[70] *Govia Thameslink Railway Ltd v The Associated Society of Locomotive Engineers and Firemen* [2016] EWHC 985 (QB), at [48]–[56].

in place between the union and the train company for drivers to operate particular trains was held arguably to amount to an inducement to drivers to disobey instructions from the train company to do so.

3–034 Cases going the other way include *The Camellia*,[71] where the defendant union official had passed on information to other union officers relating to negotiations in a dispute over wages and conditions. In doing so he was held (on appeal) not to have induced any breach by the union members of their employment contracts, even if it was his desire that the members would refuse to obey their employer's instructions if necessary: the decision on that question was one for the union itself. Similarly, in *Cutsforth v Mansfield Inns Ltd*,[72] the defendant brewery company required its tied houses to procure amusement machines only from certain nominated suppliers which did not include the claimants. Some houses had previously hired machines from the claimants, under contracts terminable on notice. The defendant informed the houses that, if they maintained the claimants' machines on their premises, they would be in breach of their contracts with the defendant, but left it to them to decide whether to give proper notice to terminate their contracts with the claimants. In those circumstances the defendant had not induced any breach of contract by the houses: again the decision was left to the contracting party. And in *Middlebrook Mushrooms v TGWU*,[73] a leaflet campaign aimed at encouraging shoppers to boycott a particular supplier of mushrooms was held not to have induced shop owners to breach their contracts with the supplier. Hoffmann LJ said[74] that the defendant had merely communicated the fact that its leaflet campaign would continue for as long as the shop owners continued to place orders with that supplier.

3–035 Even a request by a parent company made to its (properly managed) subsidiary to take action resulting in a breach of contract might not necessarily be an actionable inducement. In *Stocznia Gdanska SA v Latvian Shipping Co*,[75] the claimant conceded that, ordinarily, consideration of the request by an independent board of the subsidiary would prevent liability for inducement from arising. Thomas J concluded on the facts that such a request would not be treated as an instruction but would instead be "considered by the subsidiary which then made its own independent decision". It may be questioned whether the decision of Thomas J would now be followed. The fact that the contracting party made its own decision does not necessarily mean that there was no persuasion or encouragement by the alleged inducer, or that the latter's conduct did not "operate on the will" of the contracting party. Moreover, in many cases, a request by an alleged inducer ought in principle to be sufficient to prevent the contracting party's decision from properly being considered "independent".

---

[71] *Camellia Tanker SA v International Transport Workers Federation* [1976] 2 Lloyd's Rep. 546; [1976] I.C.R. 274.
[72] *Cutsforth v Mansfield Inns Ltd* [1986] 1 W.L.R. 558.
[73] *Middlebrook Mushrooms v TGWU* [1993] I.C.R. 612.
[74] At 626.
[75] *Stocznia Gdanska SA v Latvian Shipping Co* [2001] 1 Lloyd's Rep. 537, at [227] and [236] in particular. This conclusion was not disturbed by the Court of Appeal [2002] 2 All E.R. (Comm) 768, at [107]–[108].

One can draw from these cases that, in drawing a distinction between persuasion **3–036** or inducement on the one hand, and the communication of advice, suggestion or information on the other, a close examination of the facts will be necessary, with the emphasis on two questions: first, whether the defendant's communication is properly to be viewed as inducing (i.e. in this context, causing) the breach of contract or whether the contracting party made its own independent decision, unaffected by the defendant's conduct (the resolution of this question being heavily fact-dependent); and secondly whether the defendant intended a breach (the test of intention is considered in Section F below). Only if both these conditions are satisfied will the defendant be liable.

(5) Dealings "Inconsistent With" the Contract May Give Rise to Liability

Prior to *OBG Ltd v Allan*,[76] defendants had been found liable for entering into **3–037** arrangements inconsistent with a third party's contract with the claimant. In *British Motor Trade Association v Salvadori*,[77] for example, members of the claimant association sold cars and extracted covenants not to re-sell them within 12 months (as a form of price control). The defendant dealers were liable for inducing breach of contract where they bought cars from the customers within that period. In *DC Thomson & Co Ltd v Deakin*, Jenkins LJ, in listing the categories of conduct which in his view would give rise to liability, said that[78]:

> "[T]he contract breaker may himself be a willing party to the breach, without any persuasion by the third party, and there seems to be no doubt that if a third party, with knowledge of a contract between the contract breaker and another, has dealings with the contract breaker which the third party knows to be inconsistent with the contract, he has committed an actionable interference."

The unified theory of "interference" espoused by the Court of Appeal in the *DC* **3–038** *Thomson* case was rejected in *OBG Ltd v Allan*,[79] leaving some doubt as to the continued correctness of Jenkins LJ's proposition. Its terms fit uneasily with the conclusion of Toulson LJ in *Meretz Investments NV v ACP Ltd*[80] that liability would only arise if the defendant's conduct operated on the will of the contracting party. However, in *Lictor Anstalt v Mir Steel UK Ltd*,[81] David Richards J held that nothing in *OBG Ltd v Allan* had cast doubt on the correctness of the proposition from *DC Thomson* set out above. He held it to be arguable that a defendant who entered into a contract to purchase steel from a company in administration, in breach of the company's contract with its own supplier, was liable for inducing breach of contract.

---

[76] *OBG Ltd v Allan* [2007] UKHL 21; [2008] 1 A.C. 1.
[77] *British Motor Trade Association v Salvadori* [1949] Ch. 556.
[78] *DC Thomson & Co Ltd v Deakin* [1952] 1 Ch. 646, at 694.
[79] *OBG Ltd v Allan* [2007] UKHL 21; [2008] 1 A.C. 1.
[80] *Meretz Investments NV v ACP Ltd* [2007] EWCA Civ 1303; [2008] Ch. 244, at [177].
[81] *Lictor Anstalt v Mir Steel UK Ltd* [2011] EWHC 3310 (Ch); [2012] 1 All E.R. (Comm) 592, at [49]–[52].

3–039 The correctness of this analysis is open to doubt in light of *Meretz v ACP*, not apparently cited in *Lictor Anstalt*. Whilst many cases of inconsistent dealing will involve conduct operating on the will of the contracting party, many others will not. If a company (A) enters into an exclusivity agreement with a supplier (B) but later approaches B's rival (C), and C then agrees to supply rival products to A, it is hard to characterise C as having induced A's breach of its contract with B, even if C knows of the exclusivity arrangement. This is further illustrated by a recent Scottish case, *Calor Gas Ltd v Express Fuels (Scotland) Ltd*.[82] There it was said that *OBG Ltd v Allan*[83] had re-affirmed the requirement of inducement. In that case, dealers of gas cylinders who had accepted the return by customers of empty gas cylinders when those customers had contracted to return them to the claimant were held not to have induced the customers' breach of contract, but at most to have provided an opportunity for them to do so. Although this was a case of "inconsistent dealing", liability was not made out.

E. COMPANIES AND AGENTS

(1) The Rule in Said v Butt

3–040 The question of inducement requires special examination in the context of companies and agents. Companies in particular can only act through individual agents. In a sense, everything a company does is induced (or, more accurately, procured) by its agent(s), including action taken in breach of contract. The law has long recognised, however, that it would be wrong to impose tortious liability on every agent who brings about a breach of his principal's contract with a third party. The first clear exposition of the principle is found in *Said v Butt*.[84] The plaintiff was refused entry to a theatre of which the defendant was the chairman and managing director, who was held not liable for procuring a breach by the theatre of its contract with the plaintiff[85]: it was held that a servant who causes a breach of his master's contract is the "alter ego" of his master, whose "acts are in law the acts of his employer". Accordingly an agent acting bona fide[86] within the scope of his authority who procures the breach of his principal's contract is not liable in tort for doing so.[87] It is suggested that the central justification for the rule is that the principal cannot be liable in tort for inducing a breach of his own

---

[82] *Calor Gas Ltd v Express Fuels (Scotland) Ltd* 2008 S.L.T. 123, at [45]–[48].

[83] *OBG Ltd v Allan* [2007] UKHL 21; [2008] 1 A.C. 1.

[84] *Said v Butt* [1920] 3 K.B. 497.

[85] In fact there was held to be no valid contract, so the decision on inducement was obiter.

[86] In *Reeves v Sprecher* [2007] EWHC 117 (Ch); [2008] B.C.C. 49, at [32] Lewison J declined to decide whether the good faith requirement applied only to the question of whether the employee was acting within the scope of his employment, or more generally. It is thought that the requirement is a general one, in light of the way the point was considered in *Said v Butt* [1920] 3 K.B. 497 itself (at 504).

[87] The statement now found in Jones (ed), *Clerk & Lindsell on Torts* (2017), para.24–36 that, if a director has ordered or procured the breach by the company, then he may be liable in tort given that he possesses the requisite knowledge and intention, was held by Gloster J in *Crystalens Ltd v White*, unreported, 7 July 2006, at [10]–[15] not to provide any support for deviation from the principle in *Said v Butt*.

contract.[88] The converse of the rule is, of course, that an agent who trespasses outside the scope of his authority is at risk of liability.[89]

Agency is one of two bases on which a company acts through its director. The **3–041** second (separate) basis is where the director is the "directing mind and will" of the company. If the central justification for the rule in *Said v Butt* is as set out in the previous paragraph, then it ought to apply with equal force to this second basis. In *Stocznia Gdanska SA v Latvian Shipping Co*,[90] Thomas J considered that there might be "considerable force" in this argument, though it did not arise on his findings. He also rejected (obiter) the contention that a shadow director would have the benefit of the rule in *Said v Butt*; a shadow director is not part of the ordinary governance of a company and does not act as its agent.[91]

The allegation that the director or employee was acting other than bona fide and **3–042** within the scope of his authority is one which must be specifically pleaded and proved by the claimant. Thus in *Holding Oil Finance Inc v Marc Rich & Co AG*[92] the claimants' case was struck out where they had failed to plead the necessary allegation against the defendant directors.

It is important to note that the above principles are specific to the tort considered **3–043** in this chapter and, in particular, the question of whether an agent can have a secondary tortious liability for his principal's wrong. In other contexts, such as in a claim in deceit, the fact that an agent is acting within the scope of his principal's authority will not be a defence to personal liability.[93]

(2) Shareholders May Claim the Protection of the Principle

The rule in *Said v Butt* extends to decisions of shareholders, taken in their **3–044** capacity as such, to cause the company to breach a contract. This is true whether the shareholders act formally (in a properly constituted meeting) or informally; in either case, the acts of the shareholders are, in that context, the acts of the company itself.[94] The concept of fixing shareholders or parent companies with liability for a company's breach of contract cuts squarely across the principle of separate corporate personality, and attempts to impose such liability are in practice likely to be difficult. In the *Stocznia Gdanska Shipping* case, the company was left unable to make contractual payments because its parent company decided not to put it in funds. Thomas J held that the refusal of a parent

---

[88] *Welsh Development Agency v Export Finance Co Ltd* [1992] B.C.C. 270, per Dillon LJ at 289.

[89] *DC Thomson & Co Ltd v Deakin* [1952] Ch. 646, per Evershed MR at 681.

[90] *Stocznia Gdanska SA v Latvian Shipping Co* [2001] 1 Lloyd's Rep. 537, at [246]. The points arising from this case relevant to the discussion in this chapter were unaffected on appeal [2002] 2 All E.R. (Comm) 768.

[91] *Stocznia Gdanska SA v Latvian Shipping Co* [2001] 1 Lloyd's Rep. 537, at [251].

[92] *Holding Oil Finance Inc v Marc Rich & Co AG* [1996] C.L.Y. 1085. In *Lifestyle Equities CV v Santa Monica Polo Club Ltd* [2017] EWHC 3313 (Ch); [2018] F.S.R. 15, at [162]–[165] the claim failed where no allegation of conspiracy or dishonesty had been pleaded against the director, let alone proved.

[93] See para.1–137.

[94] In *Stocznia Gdanska SA v Latvian Shipping Co* [2001] 1 Lloyd's Rep. 537 Thomas J accepted this was a proper analysis of the law, but it was unnecessary to apply it on the facts: see [244].

to fund a subsidiary, where it is under no obligation to do so, is not an actionable inducement, even if the inevitable result is to place the subsidiary in breach of contract because of inadequacy of funds.[95] A fortiori, if all that happens is that a company fails to make a payment which its ultimate beneficial owner (in accordance with whose instructions the company would act) knows to be due, the principle of limited liability will prevent any claim for inducing breach of contract against the owner.[96]

(3) Receivers and Administrators

3–045   Where a receiver or administrator is appointed in respect of a company's affairs, there is an inherent tension between the rights and duties of the office-holder—who may need to terminate contracts entered into by the company in order to achieve the objectives of their appointment—and the rights of contracting parties. In general this tension has been resolved in the cases in which it has arisen by the application of the rule in *Said v Butt*.

3–046   As far as receivers are concerned, in *Telemetrix Plc v Modern Engineers of Bristol (Holdings) Plc*[97] Peter Gibson J accepted that a receiver and manager was not quite a "pure agent" of the sort examined in *Said v Butt* but nevertheless did not appear to consider that there would be a cause of action against such a receiver for inducing a breach of the company's contract.[98] In *Welsh Development Agency v Export Finance Co Ltd*[99] a company (Parrot), which manufactured floppy disks, entered into a contract with a finance company (Exfinco) to export the disks. The contract required payments received by Parrot from buyers of the goods to be paid into a collection account. Receivers were appointed by a third party creditor over Parrot's property. The receivers called on buyers of the goods to make payment to them rather than into the collection account. Although in doing so they were procuring a breach of Parrot's contract with Exfinco, a majority of the Court of Appeal held them not liable as they were acting bona fide within the scope of their authority.[100]

3–047   There is no reason why the principles applied to administrators should be any different. Indeed they were applied by David Richards J in *Lictor Anstalt v Mir Steel UK Ltd*.[101] That decision, and later decisions in the same case, also

---

[95] *Stocznia Gdanska SA v Latvian Shipping Co* [2001] 1 Lloyd's Rep. 537, at [252].
[96] *Moran Yacht & Ship Inc v Pisares* [2014] EWHC 1098 (Comm) [2014] 2 Lloyd's Rep. 88, per Males J at [115].
[97] *Telemetrix Plc v Modern Engineers of Bristol (Holdings) Plc* (1985) 1 B.C.C. 99417.
[98] The position may be different in respect of a court-appointed receiver who is not an agent of the contracting party: see *Telemetrix* (1985) 1 B.C.C. 99417, at 99420 and *Re Botibol* [1947] 1 All E.R. 26.
[99] *Welsh Development Agency v Export Finance Co Ltd* [1992] B.C.C. 270.
[100] Though Dillon LJ accepted and applied the principle in *Said v Butt* with "grave reservations": [1992] B.C.C. 270, at 289; and Staughton LJ thought it "anomalous" (at 305).
[101] *Lictor Anstalt v Mir Steel UK Ltd* [2011] EWHC 3310 (Ch); [2012] 2 All E.R. (Comm) 592, in particular at [38], [54] and [68].

addressed the question of when administrators who cause a company's breach of contract could be entitled to rely on the defence of justification. This issue is addressed in para.3–072 below.

F. INTENTION AND KNOWLEDGE

(1) An Intention to Induce a Breach of Contract is Necessary and Sufficient

It is settled law that, in order to be liable for the tort of inducement, the result which the defendant must intend is a breach of contract. This is both necessary and sufficient, as Lord Hoffmann explained in *OBG Ltd v Allan*[102]:

> "Necessary, because this is essential for liability as accessory to the breach. Sufficient, because the fact that the defendant did not intend to cause damage, or even thought that the breach of contract would make the claimant better off, is irrelevant."

This principle is graphically illustrated by the decision in *South Wales Miners' Federation v Glamorgan Coal Co Ltd*.[103] Members of a miners' federation were held liable for loss caused by their having induced miners to breach their employment contracts with the claimant (by calling a strike) even though their intention was to restrict coal production, raise prices and thereby benefit both the miners and their employer (the claimant). Of course if, in such a scenario, the defendants' intention to benefit the claimant is realised, the claimant may suffer no loss, in which case (and for that reason) the claimant will have no claim. But the law provides that, if the claimant does suffer a loss, he can make the defendant liable for the foreseeable consequences of his intentional conduct.

(2) Intention Defined

The test of intention for inducing breach of contract[104] was defined in the House of Lords' decision in *OBG Ltd v Allan*.[105] As Lord Hoffmann explained, it is necessary to distinguish between ends, means and consequences. If the breach of contract is the end sought by the defendant, the requisite intention is clearly made out. The same is true if the breach of contract is the means by which the defendant seeks to secure some other end (e.g. to obtain some advantage for himself), even if he would rather have secured that end without the claimant's contract being breached. On the other hand, if the breach of contract is neither an end nor a means, but merely a foreseeable consequence, the requisite intention is not made out.

3–048

3–049

3–050

---

[102] *OBG Ltd v Allan* [2007] UKHL 21; [2008] 1 A.C. 1, at [8].

[103] *South Wales Miners' Federation v Glamorgan Coal Co Ltd* [1905] A.C. 239.

[104] The definition of intention is the same in inducing breach of contract, unlawful interference and unlawful means conspiracy (though the required intended result in the latter two torts is not a breach of contract but damage to the claimant).

[105] *OBG Ltd v Allan* [2007] UKHL 21; [2008] 1 A.C. 1, per Lord Hoffmann at [42]–[43], [62], per Lord Nicholls at [164]–[166].

3–051	A case of the breach of contract being an end in itself, whilst not difficult to envisage in principle, would require a purity of malevolence unlikely to be encountered in practice: a defendant is much more likely to intend a breach of contract as a means to an end, namely to obtain some other advantage for himself. The practitioner's focus is more likely to be on the difference between a means to an end and a mere foreseeable consequence. An example of the first situation is the Canadian case of *Jones v Fabbi*.[106] The defendant dairy was held to have induced a breach of a contract between the claimant transporter and third party milk producers by telling the producers that it would be taking over the transport of milk to its dairy, causing the producers to repudiate their contracts with the claimant.

3–052	On the other side of the line is *Millar v Bassey*.[107] The singer Shirley Bassey breached her contract with a recording company to record an album, with the foreseeable consequence that the company would in turn breach its contract with her backing musicians. But that latter breach was neither a means to an end nor an end in itself. It was simply a consequence of her decision not to perform her obligation to the company. She was accordingly not liable for inducing the company's breaches of contract. Similarly, in *RBS v McCarthy*, considered above,[108] whilst Picken J considered that it may have been a foreseeable consequence of the bank's demand that the firm would breach its obligations to repay partners' capital, that fell short of establishing the requisite intention.[109] However, since intention is to be judged objectively,[110] the greater the foreseeability that a breach of contract will result from a defendant's actions, the harder it will be for him to argue that he did not intend that result (either as an end in itself or, more likely, as a means to an end).

(3)   Knowledge of the Contract (and that it will be Breached) is Necessary

3–053	As Lord Nicholls put it in *OBG Ltd v Allan*,[111] "Intentional interference presupposes knowledge of the contract". Intention and knowledge, whilst theoretically separate concepts, are in practice closely bound up with each other. A defendant's degree of knowledge is likely to be highly material to any examination of his intention: the less a defendant knows about a contracting party's obligations to the claimant, the harder it will be to prove that the defendant intended a breach of those obligations (and vice versa).

---

[106] *Jones v Fabbi* (1973) 28 D.L.R. (3d) 224. Laskin J held at 231–232 that: "This is not a case where the defendants merely caused a breach of contract, although knowing of its existence, in pursuit of a different object of their own, but one where there was an intentional and knowing procurement of the breach through pressure on the contracting producers in pursuance of the same object as that realized by [the claimant] in consummating his contracts with the producers."

[107] *Millar v Bassey* [1994] E.M.L.R. 44.

[108] See para.3–031.

[109] *RBS v McCarthy* [2015] EWHC 3236 (QB), at [103].

[110] *Greig v Insole* [1978] 1 W.L.R. 302, per Slade J at 337H–338B.

[111] *OBG Ltd v Allan* [2007] UKHL 21; [2008] 1 A.C. 1, at [192].

"Knowledge of the contract" in this context means knowledge that there is a contract, as well as sufficient knowledge of its terms for the defendant to know that the conduct he is inducing will be a breach of it. As Lord Hoffmann said in *OBG Ltd v Allan*[112]:

> "To be liable for inducing breach of contract, you must know that you are inducing a breach of contract. It is not enough that you know that you are procuring an act which, as a matter of law or construction of the contract, is a breach. You must actually realize that it will have this effect. Nor does it matter that you ought reasonably to have done so."

3–054

Accordingly, a stranger to a contract who induces a breach of it by offering an inconsistent deal to one contracting party, thereby persuading that party to default on his contractual obligations, is not liable if he does so without knowing anything about the existence of the contract.[113] However,

> "it is no answer to a claim based on wrongfully inducing a breach of contract, to assert that the defendants did not know with exactitude all the terms of the contract. The relevant question is whether they had sufficient knowledge of the terms to know that they were inducing a breach of contract".[114]

3–055

So, in the example of the rival supplier given in para.3–039 above, the rival supplier (C) may know that B has a contract to supply products to A, but the contract may contain provisions as to exclusivity of which C is unaware, such that C does not know he is inducing a breach of contract. And in a case involving the solicitation of a company director or employee by a competitor, the competitor may know (or be taken to know, on the basis examined below) that the director or employee has a contractual relationship with the former employer, but not know enough about the relevant post-termination provisions to be liable for inducing breach of contract. Where a claimant suspects future action by a third party to induce a breach by the counterparty to a contract, taking steps to put the third party on notice of the contract and of its terms may increase the prospect of deterring the inducement in the first place, or otherwise making the third party liable if the deterrence fails.

(4)   Knowledge can be Inferred or Imputed

In most cases, in the fraud context at least, adducing direct evidence that the defendant had knowledge of a contract's terms is likely to be difficult. Few defendants will actually have sight of a written contract before taking steps to induce a breach of it. Many claimants will be unable to adduce any direct evidence of what the defendant said, did or knew. Where the essential obligations under a contract would be obvious to an outsider whether he saw it or not, however, the courts have shown a preparedness to infer the necessary knowledge on the part of the defendant.

3–056

---

[112] *OBG Ltd v Allan* [2007] UKHL 21; [2008] 1 A.C. 1, at [39].

[113] *OBG Ltd v Allan* [2007] UKHL 21; [2008] 1 A.C. 1, per Lord Nicholls at [191].

[114] *JT Stratford & Son Ltd v Lindley* [1965] A.C. 269, per Lord Pearce at 332D–332E.

3–057   *Merkur Island Shipping Corp v Laughton*[115] concerned the blacking of a ship by a trade union, as a result of which tugmen refused to allow the ship to berth or to leave port, causing a breach of a time charter to which the ship was subject. The union argued that the evidence fell short of showing that it knew of the time charter. O'Connor LJ dismissed the submission[116] on the basis (among other things) that the union officials were sufficiently experienced that they must have known the ship charterers would have had contractual obligations to leave port and proceed to the ship's destination.[117] In *JT Stratford & Son Ltd v Lindley*,[118] Lord Reid rejected a submission that the defendant union officers were not sufficiently aware of the terms of the claimant's barge hire contracts to know that their actions would procure a breach. The officers knew that the barges were always brought back promptly on completion of the job for which they were hired and it could therefore be inferred—from the fact that it was obvious—that the officers knew this was because the hirers were contractually obliged to do so. The decisions in *Merkur Island Shipping* and *JT Stratford* both carry the caveat that they were interim injunction cases (with the standard of proof reduced accordingly) but illustrate that there is room for inference in a proper case.

3–058   Knowledge can also be imputed in an appropriate case, e.g. through an agent. In *Meretz Investments NV v ACP Ltd*, at first instance,[119] Lewison J considered the general rule that, where an agent employed in a transaction acquires knowledge of a fact on his principal's behalf and is under a duty to communicate the fact to the principal, knowledge of the fact will be imputed to the principal. Applying that general rule, the judge held[120] that although one defendant, Mr Tamimi, had no personal grasp of the detail of the contracts in question, his solicitor's knowledge was imputed to him. He also held, however, that *intention* could not be imputed from one natural person to another in the context of inducing breach of contract.[121] In this sense inducement of a breach of contract is, like deceit, a tort of pure subjective intention.

---

[115] *Merkur Island Shipping Corp v Laughton* [1983] 2 A.C. 570.

[116] At 582D–582E. Sir John Donaldson similarly thought the union must be "deemed to have known" of a contract of carriage of one form or another: see 591E. It is likely that he meant the relevant knowledge could be inferred.

[117] The decision was overruled by the House of Lords in *OBG Ltd v Allan* [2007] UKHL 21; [2008] 1 A.C. 1 insofar as it recognised liability in tort for interference with a contract without procuring its breach, but the principle quoted remains good law. A similar example is *Associated Newspapers Group v Wade* [1979] 1 W.L.R. 697, where Lawton LJ held (at 717) that an official of a printing union, which had instructed its members not to use material provided by certain advertisers, must have known that this would interfere with newspapers' contracts with those advertisers.

[118] *JT Stratford & Son Ltd v Lindley* [1965] A.C. 269, at 323F–324B. See to similar effect per Viscount Radcliffe at 328B–328G and per Lord Pearce at 332G (describing the obligation breached as a "simple commonplace obligation").

[119] *Meretz Investments NV v ACP Ltd* [2006] EWHC 74 (Ch); [2007] Ch. 197, at [324]–[325].

[120] *Meretz Investments NV v ACP Ltd* [2006] EWHC 74 (Ch) [2007] Ch. 197, at [386].

[121] At [366].

(5) Recklessness is Sufficient

In certain circumstances, the requisite knowledge (either of the terms of the contract or the fact that it will be breached) can also be proved on the basis of recklessness. The classic statement of the law in this area is that of Lord Denning MR in *Emerald Construction Co Ltd v Lowthian*[122]:

3–059

> "Even if they did not know the actual terms of the contract, but had the means of knowledge—which they deliberately disregarded—that would be enough. Like the man who turns a blind eye. So here, if the officers [of the union] deliberately sought to get this contract terminated, heedless of its terms, regardless whether it was terminated by breach or not, they would do wrong. For it is unlawful for a third person to procure a breach of contract knowingly, or recklessly, indifferent whether it is a breach or not."

In the *Emerald Construction* case the defendant union officers had called on a building contractor to terminate a subcontract by a given deadline. They knew of the contract but not its terms; but since (arguably) their demand was made unequivocally and without any enquiry as to whether the contract could lawfully be terminated within that deadline, the claimant was granted an interim injunction in support of its claim for inducing breach of contract. To similar effect is *Greig v Insole*.[123] Members of an international cricket association announced a ban on any players who had entered into contracts with an Australian promoter, in order to induce them to withdraw from those contracts. Some such players could lawfully withdraw whilst others could not. Since the ban was indiscriminate in its expressed scope, the defendants' contention that in fact they only intended to persuade those players who could lawfully withdraw was rejected. In effect they were indifferent to whether or not there would be a breach of contract.[124] The principle can also extend to recklessness as to whether there was a contract at all. In *Torquay Hotel Co Ltd v Cousins*[125] Winn LJ considered that the blocking of fuel deliveries to the claimant hotel, "without regard to whether, and without investigating whether" there was a contract in place for such deliveries, would suffice for liability.

3–060

---

[122] *Emerald Construction Co Ltd v Lowthian* [1966] 1 W.L.R. 691, at 700–701. This passage from the *Emerald Construction* case was approved by Lord Hoffmann in *OBG Ltd v Allan* [2007] UKHL 21; [2008] 1 A.C. 1, at [41]. Arden LJ's conclusion in *Mainstream Properties Ltd v Young* [2005] EWCA Civ 861; [2005] I.R.L.R. 964, at [79] that "the tort of interference with contractual rights is not satisfied by showing that the defendant was reckless as to whether his conduct interfered with the claimant's contractual rights or not" is therefore thought not to represent the law. *Mainstream* went to the House of Lords and was decided alongside *OBG Ltd v Allan*.

[123] *Greig v Insole* [1978] 1 W.L.R. 302, at 338C and 344C–344G in particular. For a more recent example in the trade union context, see *Govia Thameslink Railway Ltd v Associated Society of Locomotive Engineers and Firemen* [2016] EWHC 1320 (QB); [2016] I.R.L.R. 686, at [51]–[60].

[124] See also *BGC Brokers LP v Tullet Prebon Plc* [2010] EWHC 484 (QB); [2010] I.R.L.R. 648, at [151] and [177]–[179], where Jack J held that a recruiting employer was liable for inducing breach of contract where it encouraged the claimant's employees to leave and offered indemnities to them, and intended them to leave whether or not they had good grounds for claiming constructive dismissal.

[125] *Torquay Hotel Co Ltd v Cousins* [1969] 2 Ch. 106, at 146. Lord Denning MR talked (at 138) of turning a blind eye, referring to the *Emerald Construction* case. In *Meretz v ACP* [2007] EWCA Civ 1303; [2008] Ch. 244, at [114], Arden LJ held that blind-eye knowledge of the contract would suffice, in reliance on *OBG Ltd v Allan*, at [41] and [192].

3–061   Nevertheless, a finding of recklessness requires some degree of knowledge or suspicion of the existence of a contract and its relevant terms, such that there was a *deliberate*[126] or *conscious*[127] decision not to enquire. A simple failure to enquire, without more, will not give rise to liability. Sufficient knowledge or suspicion appears to have been considered to be present in the *Torquay Hotel* case, where Winn LJ said that "even a single delivery of goods bought is made in performance of a contract for sale and delivery",[128] such that the existence of a contract must have been sufficiently obvious. The potential overlap here between inferred knowledge and recklessness is clear. But, critically, the stranger who "unknowingly and unintentionally" induces a breach of contract is not liable, even if he is careless or negligent.[129] In *Unique Pub Properties Ltd v Beer Barrels & Minerals (Wales) Ltd*,[130] the claimant brewery landlord brought proceedings against the defendant beer supplier for (what was then, prior to the decision in *OBG Ltd v Allan*, termed) interference with the claimant's contract with a tied public house, by supplying beer in breach of the tie. The defendant was alleged to have known of the tie because the public house appeared on a list historically provided to the defendant by the claimant which contained the relevant information. The Court of Appeal overturned the judge's finding that the defendant was reckless and should thus be treated as having the requisite knowledge. Chadwick LJ said that the case was "not a blind eye case; where the defendant has chosen not to search for what he knows is there to be found."

3–062   In addition, it is thought that liability on the basis of the above principles does not extend to recklessness as to what the contracting party might actually do as a result of the conduct said to be amount to inducement (as opposed to whether that would amount to a breach of contract). In *DC Thomson & Co v Deakin*[131] Jenkins LJ considered that inducement to general conduct such as stopping supplies to a particular customer, or refusing to handle a trader's goods, would not be an inducement to interfere with contractual rights where such action might be taken unlawfully but could equally be taken lawfully. Moreover, liability based on recklessness as to the contracting party's conduct itself would risk undermining the requirement in *OBG Ltd v Allan*[132] that the breach of contract must be more than a foreseeable consequence.

---

[126] See the passage from the *Emerald Construction* case cited above.

[127] *OBG Ltd v Allan* [2007] UKHL 21; [2008] 1 A.C. 1, per Lord Hoffmann at [41].

[128] *Torquay Hotel Co Ltd v Cousins* [1969] 2 Ch. 106, at 146.

[129] *OBG Ltd v Allan*, per Lord Nicholls at [191].

[130] *Unique Pub Properties Ltd v Beer Barrels & Minerals (Wales) Ltd* [2004] EWCA Civ 586; [2005] 1 All E.R. (Comm) 181; see [36] in particular. Chadwick LJ also held that knowledge was not to be equated with means of knowledge—so that it was not enough that information as to the relevant contract had been previously provided to the defendant if that information was not in the mind of the defendant's relevant employees at the time of the acts complained of. Again, the parallel with the necessary mental element in the law of deceit is striking.

[131] *DC Thomson & Co v Deakin* [1952] Ch. 646, at 697–698.

[132] *OBG Ltd v Allan* [2007] UKHL 21; [2008] 1 A.C. 1, at [43] and [62], per Lord Hoffmann.

(6) No Liability Where the Defendant Honestly but Mistakenly Believes that there will be No Breach of Contract

The previous paragraphs considered the situation where a defendant knows or suspects that the conduct it is inducing will be a breach of contract. That situation is to be distinguished from the position where the defendant honestly but mistakenly believes that there will be no breach. In the latter scenario, the defendant is not liable, however wrong-headed or unreasonable his belief might be.

3–063

So in *British Industrial Plastics Ltd v Ferguson*,[133] the defendant was not liable for inducing breach of contract where, as the result of a wrong-headed understanding of patents, he believed that the contracting party had a right to act as he did. Both appellate courts upheld the decision of the judge which "vindicated the honesty of [the defendant] at the expense of his intelligence."[134] And in *Mainstream Properties Ltd v Young*,[135] a defendant who financed the acquisition of development land by a joint venture in circumstances which gave rise to breaches of contractual and fiduciary duty owed to the claimant by the other parties to the joint venture was not liable for inducing those breaches; he had made enquires about a potential conflict of interest and had been assured, incorrectly, that none existed. These cases illustrate that—in this context— ignorance of the law is a defence. This is in contrast to the position in unlawful means conspiracy and unlawful interference.[136]

3–064

The facts in *Mainstream Properties Ltd v Young* were considered by Arden LJ in *Meretz Investments NV v ACP Ltd* to be directly comparable to the facts in *Meretz* itself.[137] Arden LJ concluded that, in exercising a power of sale of a leasehold, the defendant mortgagee (FP) did not intend to induce a breach by the leaseholder (ACP) of a leaseback obligation owed to the claimant, and the same was true of the defendant purchaser (Mr Tamimi). FP and Mr Tamimi considered that they were entitled to act as they did because the claimant had consented to FP's charge having priority. Insofar as this meant that they believed that the exercise of the power of sale would not cause any breach of the leaseback obligation at all, Arden LJ's analysis is consistent with principle. But she appears to have gone further in holding that, in circumstances where FP and Mr Tamimi "considered that they were entitled to cause ACP to breach its obligation" to grant the leaseback, it was "sufficient to avoid liability for inducing breach of contract that FP and Mr Tamimi believed that they were entitled to act as they did." So expressed, Arden LJ's analysis is thought to go beyond the proper scope of the relevant principle, since it involves the defendants escaping liability on the basis, not of a belief that they were not inducing a breach of contract, but a belief that

3–065

---

[133] *British Industrial Plastics Ltd v Ferguson* [1938] 4 All ER 504 (CA); [1940] 1 All E.R. 479 (HL).
[134] [1938] 4 All E.R. 504, per MacKinnon LJ at 513.
[135] One of the three cases reported in the House of Lords as *OBG Ltd v Allan* [2007] UKHL 21; [2008] 1 A.C. 1: see [66]–[69].
[136] See paras 2–077—2–083 and paras 4–032—4–033 respectively.
[137] *Meretz Investments NV v ACP Ltd* [2007] EWCA Civ 1303; [2008] Ch. 244, at [122]–[127]. See para.3–029 above for an explanation of the facts.

they had a superior right entitling them to do so. This appears to confuse intention with the defence of justification,[138] considered in the next section below.

G. JUSTIFICATION

(1) Introduction

3–066 Early in the development of the tort of inducing breach of contract in a fraud case, the law recognised a defence of justification. As Lord McNaghten put it in *Quinn v Leathem*,[139] "it is a violation of legal right to interfere with contractual relations recognised by law if there be no sufficient justification for the interference." Shortly afterwards it was said in *South Wales Miners Federation v Glamorgan Coal Co*[140] that:

> "it would be extremely difficult, even if it were possible, to give a complete and satisfactory definition of what is 'sufficient justification', and most attempts to do so would probably be mischievous".

To some extent this statement holds good over a century later, and perhaps the most notable thing to have emerged from subsequent cases is the rarity of the circumstances in which the defence is available. Nevertheless some broad principles can be drawn from the authorities.

(2) Justification Must be Based on the Defendant's "Equal or Superior Right"

3–067 In the *South Wales Miners Federation* case,[141] a defence of justification was put forward on the basis that there was a common interest between the defendant federation and its worker members to keep up the price of coal, and the federation was under a duty to advise its members (even if the advice was to breach their contracts). The defence was rejected. Whilst avoiding any definition of justification (as explained above), Romer LJ also said[142] that, in considering whether the defence lies,

> "regard might be had to the nature of the contract broken; the position of the parties to the contract; the grounds for the breach; the means employed to procure the breach; the relation of the person procuring the breach to the person who breaks the contract; and I think also to the object of the person in procuring the breach."

---

[138] Arden LJ did not consider justification in detail given her findings on intention but expressed the brief obiter view, at [142] that a justification defence would have succeeded. Toulson LJ agreed, at [179].

[139] *Quinn v Leathem* [1901] A.C. 495, at 510.

[140] *South Wales Miners Federation v Glamorgan Coal Co* [1903] 2 K.B. 545, per Romer LJ at 573–574.

[141] *South Wales Miners Federation v Glamorgan Coal Co* [1903] 2 K.B. 545 (CA); [1905] A.C. 239. For an explanation of the facts, see para.3–033 above.

[142] At 574.

Subsequently, the defendant committee members in *Brimelow v Casson*[143] successfully raised the defence in a claim by the claimant theatre manager for inducing chorus girls to breach their contracts with him. In circumstances where the girls were paid so little that they were, so it was said, "resorting to immorality", Russell J held that the defendants had a moral duty to take all necessary steps to secure a living wage for the chorus girls. This has rightly been described as an "extreme case", and there is no subsequent reported case upholding a defence of justification based on moral duty. Certainly, this sort of scenario is unlikely to arise in a fraud case.

3–068

Instead, the law has crystallised into a recognition of the defence where a defendant induces a breach of contract to protect an "equal or superior right" of his own. The leading case is *Edwin Hill & Partners v First National Finance Corp Plc*.[144] There, the defendant bankers had provided finance to a property developer for a particular project. When the development faltered on the collapse of the property market, the bankers (instead of calling in the loan as they were entitled to do) agreed to finance the completion of the development on condition that the developer replaced his architect. As a result the developer breached his contract with the architect, who sued the bankers for inducement. The bankers' actions were held by the Court of Appeal to be justified. It was common ground that they would have been entitled to call in the loan altogether to protect their contractual rights. The fact that they reached an accommodation with their borrower, the developer, which protected those rights in a different way, did not change the result. Much more recently the existence of a defence of a justification based on an equal or superior right was recognised, expressly without elaboration, by Lord Nicholls in *OBG Ltd v Allan*.[145]

3–069

(3) What Counts as an "Equal or Superior Right"?

In the *Edwin Hill* case, Stuart-Smith LJ gave the following guidance as to what constitutes an equal or superior right[146]:

3–070

"Justification for interference with the plaintiff's contractual right based upon an equal or superior right in the defendant must clearly be a legal right. Such right may derive from property, real or personal, or from contractual rights. Property rights may simply involve the use and enjoyment of land or personal property. To give an example put in argument by Sir Nicolas Browne-Wilkinson V-C, if X carries on building operations on his land, they may to the knowledge of X interfere with a contract between A and B to carry out recording work on adjoining land occupied by A. But unless X's activity amounts to a nuisance, he is justified in doing what he did.[147] Alternatively, the law may grant legal remedies to the owner of property

---

[143] *Brimelow v Casson* [1924] 1 Ch. 302.

[144] *Edwin Hill & Partners v First National Finance Corp Plc* [1989] 1 W.L.R. 225.

[145] *OBG Ltd v Allan* [2007] UKHL 21; [2008] 1 A.C. 1, at [193].

[146] *Edwin Hill & Partners v First National Finance Corp Plc* [1989] 1 W.L.R. 225, at 233. Rose J at first instance had held that it was not necessary for the defendant to have subjectively considered that he had a right justifying his conduct; it was enough that he in fact had that right. That conclusion does not appear to have been challenged on appeal.

[147] It is unlikely that, on the current state of the law, such a scenario would give rise to liability for inducing breach of contract in the first place, since there is no inducement; rather, this would more likely be a prevention case: see paras 3–028—3–031.

to act in defence or protection of his property; if in the exercise of these remedies he interferes with a contract between A and B of which he knows, he will be justified. If, instead of exercising those remedies, he reaches an accommodation with A, which has a similar effect of interfering with A's contract with B, he is still justified notwithstanding that the accommodation may be to the commercial advantage of himself or A or both. The position is the same if the defendant's right is to a contractual as opposed to a property right, provided it is equal or superior to the plaintiff's rights."

3–071   To recognise that a defendant may be justified in inducing a breach of contract in order to protect a superior *proprietary* right of his own gives rise to no particular conceptual difficulty. In *Edwin Hill* itself, the defendant had such a right as a secured lender. Similarly, in *Meretz Investments NV v ACP Ltd*,[148] the right which Arden LJ considered (obiter) would have given the defendants a defence of justification was a mortgagee's power of sale, which in the overall contractual framework had priority over the claimant's right to a leaseback. A further example of a secured lender's right was considered in *RBS v McCarthy*, considered above.[149] There, Picken J held (obiter) that the bank was justified in its conduct, including restricting the circumstances in which the firm could comply with its contractual obligations to repay partners' capital, because in doing so it was relying on its contractual rights; those rights were superior to the partner's rights because they were secured lenders, whereas the partner only had an unsecured right against the firm to repayment of his capital contribution.[150]

3–072   Conversely, in *Pritchard v Briggs*[151] the defence of justification failed where it arose out of a merely personal right which was subordinate to the claimant's prior proprietary right. And similarly in *Lictor Anstalt v Mir Steel UK Ltd*,[152] it was held (obiter) that the defence would not have been available to administrators whose statutory rights and duties were inferior to the claimant's prior proprietary rights over property held by the company, but which the administrators had sold to a third party.[153] Asplin J also held that, even if available to the administrators, the defence would not be available to the purchasers who induced the breach of contract, who did not enjoy the same rights and duties as the administrators.

3–073   It is more difficult, however, to define the circumstances in which one *personal* contractual right will be considered "equal or superior" to another. One such circumstance may exist where the contract breached is inconsistent with a prior contract of which the defendant has the benefit. As Buckley LJ said in *Smithies v National Association of Operative Plasterers*,[154]

---

[148] *Meretz Investments NV v ACP Ltd* [2007] EWCA Civ 1303; [2008] Ch. 244.

[149] *RBS v McCarthy* [2015] EWHC 3626 (QB). See paras 3–031 and 3–052.

[150] *RBS v McCarthy* [2015] EWHC 3236 (Ch), at [112]–[114].

[151] *Pritchard v Briggs* [1980] Ch. 338, at 415–417.

[152] *Lictor Anstalt v Mir Steel UK Ltd* [2014] EWHC 3316 (Ch), at [265]–[281].

[153] Asplin J nevertheless appeared to recognise a general principle that an administrator would have a defence of justification if he acted reasonably to satisfy himself that the continued performance of the contract (i) would impede his achievement of the objectives of the administration (ii) was not in the interests of the company's creditors as a body, and (possibly) if (iii) the breach was carried out in a manner consistent with the administrator's general duties. It is thought that, in such circumstances, an administrator would be highly likely to be able to rely on the rule in *Said v Butt* (see para.3–040 above) and so would have no need to plead justification.

[154] *Smithies v National Association of Operative Pla* [1909] 1 K.B. 310, at 337.

"[n]o doubt there are circumstances in which A is entitled to induce B to break a contract entered into by B with C. Thus, for instance, if the contract between B and C is one which B could not make consistently with his preceding contractual obligations towards A, A may not only induce him to break it, but may invoke the assistance of a Court of Justice to make him break it."

However, this principle, whilst recognised in later cases, does not appear ever to have been applied so as to uphold a justification defence. It has also been observed[155] that the example given by Buckley LJ[156] to illustrate his point would in fact have involved a defendant having a superior proprietary right.

On the other hand it is clear that the following do not amount to justification: **3–074**

(1)   absence of malice or intention to injure the claimant;
(2)   the commercial or other best interests of the inducer or the contract breaker[157];
(3)   the fact that the claimant is in breach of some independent contract with the defendant (i.e. in contrast to the example of linked contracts from *Smithies*, above[158]); or
(4)   the fact that the contract of which a breach was induced was entered into in breach of some obligation owed by the contract breaker to a third party.[159]

The law of Australia imposes a requirement that, in order to be justified, conduct   **3–075** which induces a breach of contract must be no more than reasonably necessary to protect the defendant's own rights.[160] This proportionality requirement has not been expressly adopted in England and Wales, but the *Edwin Hill* case provides some indirect support for it. There, whilst the bankers' conduct in inducing their borrower to induce its contract with its architects was held justified to protect their rights as lender, Nourse LJ considered that the defence might not have been available if the objective of the new arrangement had been to give the bankers a profit over and above that which they were entitled to under the previous arrangement.[161]

---

[155] *ZHU v Treasurer of New South Wales* [2004] HCA 56; (2004) 211 ALR 159, at [144].
[156] "If B having agreed to sell a property to A subsequently agrees to sell it to C, A of course may restrain B by injunction from carrying out B's contract with C."
[157] In *Timeplan Education Group Ltd v NUT* [1997] I.R.L.R. 457 a defence of justification was unsuccessfully raised on the basis that the contract breached, which was for the publication of an advertisement for supply teachers, was contrary to the statutory code for the employment of teachers because it would have led to the undercutting of prescribed rates of pay.
[158] For propositions (1) to (3), see *Edwin Hill & Partners v First National Finance Corp Plc* [1989] 1 W.L.R. 225, per Stuart-Smith LJ at 230.
[159] *Greig v Insole* [1978] 1 W.L.R. 302, at 341–342.
[160] See *ZHU v Treasurer of New South Wales* [2004] HCA 56, (2004) 211 ALR 159, at [161]–[162].
[161] *Edwin Hill & Partners v First National Finance Corp Plc* [1989] 1 W.L.R. 225, at 235.

(4) Who Bears the Burden of Proof?

3–076   Since justification is normally referred to in the authorities as a defence, it would be logical to expect the burden to be on the defendant to plead and prove it. However the cases are not clear on the point. In *Edwin Hill*,[162] the judge at first instance had held that the onus of proof was on the defendants, and that conclusion was not challenged on appeal. By contrast, in *Timeplan Education Group Ltd v National Union of Teachers*,[163] Peter Gibson LJ said that, once the defendant had raised the defence, it was for the claimant to rebut it. Most recently in *Meretz Investments NV v ACP Ltd*,[164] Lewison J said that it did not matter (on the facts of that case) whether the absence of justification was part of the gist of the tort (i.e. an ingredient in the cause of action) or whether justification was a defence. On the basis of the *Edwin Hill* and *Timeplan Education Group* cases, it is thought that it is for the defendant to plead justification (rather than for the claimant to anticipate the defence by expressly pleading absence of justification in the particulars of claim), and in turn the better view, it is suggested, is that the burden of proof is also on the defendant.

H.   DAMAGES

(1) Damages "At Large"

3–077   As in claims for conspiracy, it has been said that damages for inducing breach of contract are "at large".[165] However, this expression has the potential to mislead. Lord Esher MR said in *Exchange Telegraph Co v Gregory*,[166] an early case on inducing breach of contract:

> "Though I think there must be some damage to support an action for the infringement of the plaintiffs' common law right, it is enough to shew that the act complained of was done in such a way as to be likely to damage the plaintiff, though proof of specific damage be not given."

It is also possible to find historic examples of damages for economic torts being assessed in an apparently very broad manner, such as in *Pratt v British Medical Association*,[167] where McCardie J awarded the three claimants differing levels of damages without any express assessment of their actual loss, but taking into account "the deliberate and relentless vigour" with which the defendants pursued their actions against them, and the long period during which the claimants "suffered humiliation and menace". In *Rookes v Barnard*,[168] Lord Devlin described the principle as follows:

---

[162] *Edwin Hill & Partners v First National Finance Corp Plc* [1989] 1 W.L.R. 225; see 228C.
[163] *Timeplan Education Group Ltd v National Union of Teachers* [1997] I.R.L.R. 457, at [21].
[164] *Meretz Investments NV v ACP Ltd* [2006] EWHC 74 (Ch); [2007] Ch. 197, at [379].
[165] See e.g. *DC Thomson & Co Ltd v Deakin* [1952] Ch. 646, at 680.
[166] *Exchange Telegraph Co v Gregory* [1896] 1 Q.B. 147, at 153.
[167] *Pratt v British Medical Association* [1919] 1 K.B. 244, at 281–282. Another example of assessment on a broad basis is *Goldsoll v Goldman* [1914] 2 Ch. 603, at 616.
[168] *Rookes v Barnard* [1964] A.C. 1129, at 1221.

"It must be remembered that in many cases of tort damages are at large, that is to say, the award is not limited to the pecuniary loss that can be specifically proved. In the present case, for example, and leaving aside any question of exemplary or aggravated damages, the appellant's damages would not necessarily be confined to those which he would obtain in an action for wrongful dismissal. He can invite the jury to look at all the circumstances, the inconveniences caused to him by the change of job and the unhappiness maybe by a change of livelihood. In such a case as this, it is quite proper without any departure from the compensatory principle to award a round sum based on the pecuniary loss proved."

However, there is no more modern reported example of damages being assessed so broadly for inducing breach of contract. It was said recently in *Airbus Operations Ltd v Withey*[169] that:

> "the rule that damages are 'at large'" simply means that the cause of action can succeed without proof of any particular damage, provided some loss was inevitable".

The rule could assist a claimant in particular in the early stages of proceedings (e.g. a reverse summary judgment or strike-out application) where there is no direct evidence of specific loss being suffered, or even at trial where an inquiry as to damages is sought.[170] But it does not allow a claimant to obtain a final award of damages where he cannot show that any loss was suffered. Thus an acknowledgement by the claimant in *Airbus Operations Ltd v Withey* that it had suffered no pecuniary loss was fatal to its claim in inducing breach of contract.

(2) Particular Principles Governing the Assessment of Damages

Generally speaking damages fall to be assessed on ordinary principles of causation and remoteness applicable to claims in tort, though the fact that inducing breach of contract is a tort of intention will tend to influence and broaden the scope of the loss in respect of which the claimant may recover. In *Quinn v Leathem*,[171] the defendants boycotted the claimant's meat supply business, causing him to lose orders from a valuable customer. As to the claimant's loss, Lord Lindley said:

> "This violation of duty by the defendants resulted in damage to the plaintiff – not remote, but immediate and intended. The intention to injure the plaintiff negatives all excuses and disposes of any question of remoteness of damage."[172]

Whilst a claimant will often be seeking to recover in respect of the same loss against both the contracting party and the inducer, the application of contractual principles to the first claim and tortious principles to the second means that the measure of damages may well be different in respect of each defendant. For a full examination of the principles governing the measure of damages in tort, the

3–078

3–079

3–080

---

[169] *Airbus Operations Ltd v Withey* [2014] EWHC 1126 (QB), per HHJ Havelock-Allan QC at [473], relying on the decision of Norris J in *National Grid Electricity Transmission Plc v McKenzie* [2009] EWHC 1817 (Ch), at [109].
[170] As happened in *British Motor Trade Association v Salvadori* [1949] Ch. 556, where the argument that the claimants had not proved loss was rejected, and an inquiry was ordered.
[171] *Quinn v Leathem* [1901] A.C. 495.
[172] *Quinn v Leathem* [1901] A.C. 495, at 537.

reader is referred to specialist works on the subject.[173] The key cases nevertheless provide some illustrations of the applicable principles. In *Lumley v Gye*,[174] Crompton J suggested (without deciding) that damages for inducing breach of contract "might be calculated on a very different principle from the amount of the debt which might be the only sum recoverable on the contract." He postulated the example of a defendant who begs his rival's banker or other debtor not to pay a debt owing to the rival, and thereby "ruins or greatly prejudices" him, and indicated that the rival (i.e. the claimant) in such a case might recover more than the amount of the debt owed to him if necessary to compensate him for his loss. In the same case Erle J[175] contemplated a number of situations in which the liability of the inducer may be greater than that of the contracting party:

(1) Where the remedy under the contract was inadequate because the measure of damages was restricted in some way. A subsequent example of this is *Torquay Hotel Co Ltd v Cousins*,[176] in which the contracting party was relieved of liability to pay damages for its breach of contract by reason of a force majeure clause, but the claimant was nevertheless entitled to claim damages against the inducer for the loss caused. Similarly, where the contract breaker may be able to rely upon a limitation of liability clause, that will not avail the inducer. It is, however, important to note that in the *Torquay Hotel* case, the primary obligation of the contracting party to perform the contract remained. As has been said above, where that is not the case (e.g. if the contract is void), the claimant will be unable to recover against either the contracting party or the inducer.[177]

(2) In a case of non-payment of debt where the damage may be bankruptcy to the creditor but the measure of damages against the debtor is interest only.

(3) In the case of non-delivery of goods, which may lead to the forfeiture of payment under a contract to complete work within a time, but where the contractual measure of damages may be limited to the difference between the contract price and the market value of the goods at the time of breach.

3–081 The possibility of liability arising where the inducer has wrongfully brought about circumstances entitling the contracting party to terminate his contract with the claimant has been examined at para.3–010 above. In such a situation the inducer would be liable but the third party would not. Conversely, the liability of the inducer may conceivably be lesser than the liability of the contracting party, by virtue of the different rules as to remoteness applicable in contract and in tort. If, for example, A enters into a contract with B for the supply of a product by B for an unusual and highly profitable venture of A's of which B is aware, then in a claim for breach of contract by A against B, under the second limb of *Hadley v Baxendale*[178] damages for the loss of the venture would be recoverable. But if B's

---

[173] J. Edelman (ed), *McGregor on Damages*, 20th edn (London: Sweet & Maxwell, 2017), para.48–004 and following in particular; and Jones (ed), *Clerk & Lindsell on Torts* (2017).

[174] *Lumley v Gye* (1853) 2 E&B 216, at 229–230.

[175] At 234.

[176] *Torquay Hotel Co Ltd v Cousins* [1969] 2 Ch. 106.

[177] *Joe Lee Ltd v Dalmeny* [1927] 1 Ch. 300, where the contract was void as a gaming contract.

[178] *Hadley v Baxendale* (1854) 9 Ex. 341.

breach was induced by C, who knew nothing of the particular venture, he may be able to escape liability in damages for its loss on the basis that it was not reasonably foreseeable.

CHAPTER 4

UNLAWFUL INTERFERENCE

A. INTRODUCTION

(1) The Essence of the Tort

The essence of this tort is wrongful interference by the defendant with the actions   **4–001**
of a third party, with the intention and effect of causing loss to the claimant. At
the end of the 19th century, in the seminal case of *Allen v Flood*,[1] Lord Watson
explained that there were two grounds on which a person who procures the act of
another can be made legally responsible for its consequences. The first was
inducing breach of contract. The second was that, where the act induced was
within the right of the immediate actor (i.e. the third party) but damaged the
claimant, the inducer could be liable "if he can be shewn to have procured his
object by the use of illegal means directed against [the claimant]." Whilst the tort
of unlawful interference has undergone much development (and its examination
has engendered much confusion) in the 100 or so years since *Allen v Flood* was
decided, Lord Watson's formulation still captures much of the essence of the tort.

In the same way as for the other economic torts,[2] dishonesty is not an essential   **4–002**
element of the cause of action. In that sense the tort may be thought not to require
detailed discussion in a practitioner's text on fraud. However, fraudulent conduct
and liability for economic torts such as unlawful interference often go hand in
hand. To give an example, in a straightforward fraud case a defendant may be
liable in deceit to claimant A. However if the defendant's fraudulent
misrepresentations were not made to claimant B but nonetheless were made with
the intention and result of causing him loss, then claimant B would also be able to
claim against the defendant on the basis of unlawful interference. Perhaps the
most famous example of a claim in unlawful interference founded on a deceit is
Lonrho Plc v Al-Fayed (No.1),[3] where it was alleged by the claimant that the
defendant had intentionally caused it loss by making fraudulent statements to the
directors of the company which owned Harrods, which had induced the directors
to accept his bid for Harrods in preference to that of the claimant. It was held that
an action would lie in unlawful interference if those facts were proved.

---

[1] *Allen v Flood* [1898] A.C. 1, per Lord Watson at 96. See also 97–98 and 106.
[2] The label "economic torts" is here used to cover lawful means conspiracy, unlawful means
conspiracy, inducing breach of contract, unlawful interference and intimidation. However, in
conspiracy cases dishonesty in practice tends to be alleged against the defendants: see para.2–140.
[3] *Lonrho Plc v Al-Fayed (No.1)* [1990] 2 Q.B. 479.

4–003   In this way, unlawful interference, like the other economic torts, can be a useful tool against defendants who act in ways that may be calculated to avoid incurring direct liability towards those who suffer loss. Whereas the torts of conspiracy and inducing breach of contract serve in a sense to broaden the ambit of potential defendants, unlawful interference can also broaden the ambit of potential claimants, giving a right of redress to parties beyond the immediate victim of a defendant's wrongful act.[4]

4–004   The tort of unlawful interference may equally broaden the ambit of potential defendants: for example, a claimant who has the benefit of a contract with defendant A which is broken as a result of unlawful action taken by defendant B against defendant A (e.g. a false representation or intimidatory threat) may be able to sue defendant A for breach of contract and defendant B for unlawful interference (as well as for inducing breach of contract). It will be seen from this example that there is considerable potential overlap between unlawful interference and inducing breach of contract. The key similarities and differences between the two torts are considered in Ch.3 on inducing breach of contract.

4–005   The principles governing the related torts of inducing breach of contract and unlawful interference (and their differences) were authoritatively restated in 2007 by the House of Lords in *OBG Ltd v Allan*,[5] overruling and explaining a number of earlier cases. Accordingly the detailed history of the tort of unlawful interference (like that of inducing breach of contract) is likely to be of limited relevance to the civil fraud practitioner today. Many older cases remain valuable as authority on particular sets of facts, but every case decided prior to 2007 must now be read through the prism of the decision in *OBG* and the principles articulated in that decision.

(2)   Terminology

4–006   Like other economic torts, unlawful interference has been the subject of varying terminology in the cases and in academic writing. In *OBG Ltd v Allan*,[6] Lord Hoffmann referred to the tort as "causing loss by unlawful means". Lord Nicholls gave the tort the long title "interference with a trade or business by unlawful means"[7] and the short title "unlawful interference".[8] Whilst these variations in terminology reflect differing views as to the proper characterisation of the tort, at

---

[4] The indirect victim has a claim because, as Lord Lindley said in *Quinn v Leathem* [1901] A.C. 495, at 535, "the wrong done to others reaches him".

[5] *OBG Ltd v Allan* [2007] UKHL 21; [2008] 1 A.C. 1.

[6] *OBG Ltd v Allan* [2007] UKHL 21; [2008] 1 A.C. 1, in particular per Lord Hoffmann at [6] and per Lord Nicholls at [141].

[7] Although there is no reason of principle why the tort need be confined to situations involving a trade or business, in practice most claims of any substance will involve such a situation, not least given the requirement that the defendant should interfere with the actions of a third party in which the claimant has an economic interest.

[8] In *Meretz Investments NV v ACP Ltd* [2007] EWCA Civ 1303; [2008] Ch. 244, at [115], Arden LJ adopted Lord Hoffmann's formulation in *OBG* but in the same paragraph referred to "the unlawful interference tort". There are many further examples of both formulations being used in subsequent cases, and no judicial consensus appears to have emerged as to terminology.

least since *OBG* the various labels all describe the same tort.[9] The practitioner's essential task is to understand its constituent elements and the circumstances in which liability will arise. An examination of the differing terminology is not necessary for such an understanding. This book uses the term "unlawful interference", which succinctly summarises the essence of the tort.

(3)   A Three-Party Tort

Given the essence of the tort as described above, the tort of unlawful interference has been described, accurately, as a "three-party tort".[10] In his authoritative restatement of the tort in *OBG Ltd v Allan*,[11] Lord Hoffmann acknowledged a similar species of liability in two-party cases, which he described as the tort of intimidation, which we address in the next chapter. Whilst he saw intimidation as a variant of the broader tort examined in this chapter,[12] he expressly confined his analysis to the three-party situation.[13] Subsequent cases have treated the three-party situation as giving rise to a distinct tort,[14] and the same course is adopted in this chapter. Despite being a "three-party tort", however, unlawful interference is a tort of primary liability; that is to say, it exists independently of any other wrong committed by a third party against the claimant.[15]

4–007

B.   INGREDIENTS OF THE TORT

In *OBG* Lord Hoffmann described the essence of the tort as

4–008

> "(a) a wrongful interference with the actions of a third party in which the claimant has an economic interest and (b) an intention thereby to cause loss to the claimant".[16]

This has echoes of the way it was put in *Quinn v Leathem*[17] by Lord Lindley, who explained that liability will arise where the:

> "interference is wrongful and is intended to damage a third person, and he is damaged in fact—in other words, if he is wrongfully and intentionally struck at through others, and is thereby damnified".

---

[9] In *Revenue & Customs Commissioners v Total Network SL* [2008] UKHL 19; [2008] 1 A.C. 1174, at [216] Lord Neuberger appeared to refer to two separate torts of unlawful interference and causing loss by unlawful means. However, it is considered that these are in reality two different labels for the same tort (and nothing in Lord Neuberger's reasoning in fact suggests otherwise).

[10] *Revenue & Customs Commissioners v Total Network SL* [2008] UKHL 19; [2008] 1 A.C. 1174, at [124], per Lord Mance.

[11] *OBG Ltd v Allan* [2007] UKHL 21; [2008] 1 A.C. 1, at [61].

[12] *OBG Ltd v Allan* [2007] UKHL 21; [2008] 1 A.C. 1, at [7]. Similarly, in *Emerald Supplies Ltd v British Airways Plc* [2015] EWCA Civ 1024; [2016] Bus. L.R. 145, at [127], the Court of Appeal referred to an "exceptional" two-party case where the claimant is intimidated into a course of action which causes him damage.

[13] *OBG Ltd v Allan* [2007] UKHL 21; [2008] 1 A.C. 1, at [61].

[14] *Emerald Supplies* [2015] EWCA Civ 1024; [2016] Bus. L.R. 145, at [127]; *Holyoake v Candy* [2017] EWHC 3397 (Ch), per Nugee J at [434].

[15] *OBG Ltd v Allan* [2007] UKHL 21; [2008] 1 A.C. 1, at [8].

[16] *OBG Ltd v Allan* [2007] UKHL 21; [2008] 1 A.C. 1, at [47].

[17] *Quinn v Leathem* [1901] A.C. 495, at 535.

4–009 The ingredients of the tort of unlawful interference can accordingly be summarised as follows[18]:

(1)   Unlawful acts used against, and independently actionable by, a third party;
(2)   Interference with the actions of the third party in which the claimant has an economic interest;
(3)   Intention to cause loss to the claimant by the use of unlawful means;
(4)   Loss in fact caused to the claimant.

We consider each of these ingredients below.

C.   UNLAWFUL ACTS

(1)   Introduction

4–010 The carrying out of unlawful acts is the touchstone of liability in this tort. It was held by a majority in the leading case of *Allen v Flood*[19] that it was not unlawful deliberately to harm a third party, even maliciously, provided that no unlawful means are used. This is a characteristic shared with the tort of unlawful means conspiracy. Unlawful interference therefore differs from inducing breach of contract (where liability consists essentially in the deliberate procurement of a wrong by the third party) and lawful means conspiracy (where liability consists in concerted action with the predominant purpose of harming the claimant). In *Allen v Flood* itself[20] Lord Watson put the principle in terms that

> "a person who by illegal means, that is means which in themselves are in the nature of civil wrongs, procures the lawful act of another, which act is calculated to injure, and does injure, a third party [i.e. the claimant], commits a wrong for which he may be made answerable".

This aptly describes the scope of unlawful means.

4–011 The phrase "unlawful acts" is used here in distinction to the phrase "unlawful means" because of the importance of bearing in mind two separate concepts inherent in the phrase "unlawful means". The first concerns the unlawfulness of the act(s), which requires consideration of which types of unlawful act are, as a matter of law, capable of founding liability in unlawful interference. The second concerns the question of whether an unlawful act is, in fact, the "means" by which the defendant inflicts harm on the claimant via the third party. This distinction is important to unlawful means conspiracy claims[21]; the importance of distinguishing the two also in the present context is illustrated by the passage quoted above from *Allen v Flood*.

---

[18] *OBG Ltd v Allan* [2007] UKHL 21; [2008] 1 A.C. 1, per Lord Hoffmann at [47] and [51].
[19] *Allen v Flood* [1898] A.C. 1.
[20] *Allen v Flood* [1898] A.C. 1, at 97–98.
[21] See para.2–047.

(2)   The Unlawful Act Must be Actionable by the Third Party

Prior to the decision in *OBG Ltd v Allan*, there was considerable doubt (and inconsistency in the case law) as to what precisely was capable of amounting to an unlawful act for the purposes of the unlawful interference tort. There was also disagreement between the judges in *OBG* itself on this question. Lord Nicholls would have held that "all acts a defendant is not permitted to do, whether by the civil or the criminal law" could qualify, which would have included "common law torts, statutory torts, crimes, breaches of contract, breaches of trust and equitable obligations, breaches of confidence, and so on."[22] Lord Hoffmann, on the other hand, held that the following limitation should apply to the concept of unlawful means:

4–012

> "In my opinion, and subject to one qualification, acts against a third party count as unlawful means only if they are actionable by that third party. The qualification is that they will also be unlawful means if the only reason why they are not actionable is because the third party has suffered no loss."[23]

Lord Hoffmann's was the majority view.[24] Accordingly, it is now settled that only actionable wrongs against a third party will suffice to give rise to liability in unlawful interference. Crimes, breaches of statutory duty which are not actionable by the third party and other non-actionable wrongs[25] thus do not provide a basis for liability. This marks a divergence of approach across the economic torts: for example, less than a year after *OBG Ltd v Allan* was decided, the House of Lords held in *Total Network*[26] that crimes were in principle capable of amounting to unlawful means in the context of unlawful means conspiracy; and the Supreme Court has more recently held that contempt of court qualifies as unlawful means in that context.[27]

4–013

The proviso to the requirement of actionability, as explained by Lord Hoffmann, is that acts against a third party will count as relevant unlawful acts if they are not actionable only because the third party suffers no loss (damage being an essential element for liability in most torts). So, for example, if A fraudulently misrepresents to B that C (A's rival) is selling defective products in the market, and B acts on that misrepresentation by deciding to stop buying from C but instead to buy from A at the same price, then (assuming the products are otherwise of equal quality) B suffers no loss, and thus will have no claim in deceit against A. But, provided that all the other elements of liability are established, A's deceit practised on B will be sufficient to give C a cause of action

4–014

---

[22] *OBG Ltd v Allan* [2007] UKHL 21; [2008] 1 A.C. 1, at [150]–[162], in particular the first and last of those paragraphs.

[23] *OBG Ltd v Allan* [2007] UKHL 21; [2008] 1 A.C. 1, at [49].

[24] *OBG Ltd v Allan* [2007] UKHL 21; [2008] 1 A.C. 1, per Lady Hale at [302] and per Lord Brown at [320]. Lord Walker did not directly address this particular point.

[25] It is uncertain whether contempt of court qualifies: see paras 4–028—4–030 below.

[26] *Revenue & Customs Commissioners v Total Network SL* [2008] UKHL 19; [2008] 1 A.C. 1174.

[27] *JSC BTA Bank v Khrapunov* [2018] UKSC 19; [2018] 2 W.L.R. 1125. For consideration of the *Total Network* and *Khrapunov* decisions in the context of unlawful means conspiracy, see Ch.2, in particular paras 2–051—2–055 and 2–068—2–070.

against A in unlawful interference. Lord Hoffmann in *OBG v Allan*[28] gave a similar example of intimidatory threats made against a third party to which the third party submits, causing the claimant to suffer loss rather than the third party. And in the old case of *Tarleton v M'Gawley*,[29] the master of a ship anchored off the coast of West Africa was held liable for firing a cannon to drive away a canoe which was approaching a rival ship for trade, deterring future customers. There, it was irrelevant whether the potential customers themselves suffered loss.

(3)   What Wrongs Qualify as Unlawful Acts?

4–015   Since the decision in *OBG Ltd v Allan*, the courts have offered limited further guidance on what counts as an unlawful act in the tort of unlawful interference. However it seems in principle that *any* act actionable by the third party will be sufficient. The limiting factor of actionability gives coherence to the tort and prevents it from extending beyond rational limits. Within those limits, however, it is difficult in principle to see why any further constraints should be imposed on the concept of unlawfulness. In the following paragraphs we give examples of the sorts of acts which have been recognised in previous cases as capable of giving rise to liability. As has already been stated, care must be taken in relying on cases decided prior to *OBG Ltd v Allan*.

(i)   Torts

4–016   A tort committed against a third party is an archetypal unlawful act for the purposes of unlawful interference, at least in a fraud case. Torts likely to be of most relevance in this area are examined below.

4–017   **Deceit.**   In *Lonrho Plc v Al-Fayed (No.1)*,[30] the defendants were accused of having made false statements to the directors of Harrods in order to induce them to accept the defendants' bid to acquire the business and not to refer the bid to the competition authorities. In doing so, it was alleged, they thereby prevented the claimants from acquiring the business. The Court of Appeal upheld the claim as sufficiently arguable to go to trial. An earlier example is provided by *National Phonograph Co Ltd v Edison Bell Consolidated Phonograph Co Ltd*,[31] in which the defendants, one of whom was on the claimant's blacklist, were liable in unlawful interference where they had obtained the claimant's goods by concealing their true identities from a third party through whom the claimant sold its goods.

---

[28] *OBG Ltd v Allan* [2007] UKHL 21; [2008] 1 A.C. 1, at [49].

[29] *Tarleton v M'Gawley* (1794) Peake 270.

[30] *Lonrho Plc v Al-Fayed (No.1)* [1990] 2 Q.B. 479, referred to with approval by Lord Hoffmann in *OBG Ltd v Allan* [2007] UKHL 21; [2008] 1 A.C. 1, at [50]. An appeal to the House of Lords in the *Lonrho* case was dismissed: see [1992] 1 A.C. 448.

[31] *National Phonograph Co Ltd v Edison Bell Consolidated Phonograph Co Ltd* [1908] 1 Ch. 335, referred to with approval by Lord Hoffmann in *OBG Ltd v Allan* [2007] UKHL 21, [2008] 1 A.C. 1 at [49].

Inducing Breach of Contract. In *OBG Ltd v Allan*, Lord Hoffmann stated in terms that "To induce a breach of contract is unlawful means when the breach is used to cause loss to a third party".[32] This is also illustrated by earlier cases.[33] It is considered that inducement of other wrongs, insofar as such inducement gives rise to liability for the *Lumley v Gye* tort,[34] will also be capable of constituting the unlawful act for the purposes of the tort of unlawful interference.

4–018

Intimidation. This is illustrated by the leading case of *Rookes v Barnard*.[35] Rookes was an employee of the British Overseas Airways Corp (BOAC). He resigned from the defendant union, following which the other union members who were employees of BOAC threatened to withdraw their services (i.e. in breach of their employment contracts) if Rookes was not removed from his position. The House of Lords held that the defendants' threats to breach their employment contracts amounted to the tort of intimidation against BOAC, which in turn constituted unlawful means making them liable to Rookes for unlawful interference.

4–019

Other Torts. The above is not a complete list. Any tort actionable by the third party should in principle be capable of forming the necessary unlawful act. For example, torts such as assault[36] and trespass to goods[37] or land,[38] although less likely to come across the desk of a civil fraud practitioner, will qualify.

4–020

(ii)   Breach of contract

It is clear that a breach of contract is capable of amounting to an unlawful act for the purposes of the tort of unlawful interference.[39] Indeed, this follows axiomatically once it is realised that inducing breach of contract and intimidation by a threat to breach a contract can qualify: it would be absurd to make a

4–021

---

[32] *OBG Ltd v Allan* [2007] UKHL 21; [2008] 1 A.C. 1, at [32].

[33] See for example *JT Stratford & Son Ltd v Lindley* [1965] A.C. 269, per Lord Reid at 324C and 325B; per Viscount Radcliffe at 328G; *Hadmor Productions v Hamilton* [1981] 3 W.L.R. 139, at 150G, per Lord Denning MR; cf the decision of the House of Lords in the same case which did not cast doubt on this: [1983] 1 A.C. 191, at 224–225, per Lord Diplock.

[34] The question of how far the inducement of wrongs other than a breach of contract gives rise to liability in the *Lumley v Gye* tort is considered at paras 3–012—3–024.

[35] *Rookes v Barnard* [1964] A.C. 1129. See in particular Lord Reid at 1167–1169; Lord Evershed at 1182–1183, Lord Hodson at 1201, Lord Devlin at 1207 and Lord Pearson at 1235. Although *Rookes v Barnard* was (also) a conspiracy case, their Lordships considered that if any of the defendants had acted alone they would still have been liable (see Lord Reid at 1171, Lord Evershed at 1188–1189, Lord Hodson at 1202, Lord Devlin at 1211–1212 and Lord Pearson at 1235). The decision was cited with approval by Lord Hoffmann in *OBG Ltd v Allan* [2007] UKHL 21; [2008] 1 A.C. 1, at [47].

[36] *Rookes v Barnard* [1964] A.C. 1129, at 1188, per Lord Evershed.

[37] *GWK Ltd v Dunlop Rubber Co Ltd* (1926) 42 T.L.R. 376.

[38] *OBG Ltd v Allan* [2007] UKHL 21; [2008] 1 A.C. 1, at [261], per Lord Nicholls. In OBG's case specifically, it was not in dispute that the receivers were liable in trespass, and it was not suggested that this was incapable of forming the necessary unlawful act.

[39] Despite concerns expressed in some quarters that this represents an inroad into the doctrine of privity of contact: for discussion of these concerns, see M. Jones (ed), *Clerk & Lindsell on Torts*, 22nd edn (London: Sweet & Maxwell, 2017), para.24–90.

defendant liable for threatening to do an act but not for doing it.[40] The availability of a claim in unlawful interference based on a breach of contract was confirmed by both Lord Hoffmann and Lord Nicholls in *OBG Ltd v Allan*.[41] There is of course no need for the breach of contract to be one enforceable by the claimant[42] (who could otherwise simply sue the defendant on the contract itself).

(iii) *Breach of statutory duty*

4–022   There is a substantial body of jurisprudence addressing the circumstances in which a breach of statutory duty is privately actionable, an issue which is beyond the scope of this book. As can be seen from the discussion of breach of statutory duty as an unlawful act in the tort of conspiracy,[43] in that context there is continuing controversy as to whether a breach of statutory duty needs to fulfil the actionability requirement to qualify. In a claim for unlawful interference, the answer is thought to be clear, at least as a matter of principle: given the overriding requirement of actionability by the third party, a non-actionable breach of statutory duty will not qualify. However, as long as the actionability requirement is met, there should be no reason why a breach of statutory duty could not be used to found a claim in unlawful interference. Indeed, leaving actionability aside, there is no principled basis for a more restrictive approach in the context of unlawful interference than in the context of unlawful means conspiracy or inducing breach of contract.[44]

4–023   In addition, the recognition of liability in unlawful interference based on a breach of statutory duty would be consistent with the treatment given to earlier cases on this issue in *OBG Ltd v Allan*.[45] In each of those cases, the claimant sought to found a claim in unlawful interference on the defendant's breach of statutory duty. The key bar to liability in each case was (on Lord Hoffmann's analysis) the fact that there was no interference with the third party's dealings with the claimant. Lord Hoffmann did not suggest, however, that an actionable breach of statutory duty could not qualify as an unlawful act in this context.[46]

---

[40] *Rookes v Barnard* [1964] A.C. 1129, at [1168].

[41] *OBG Ltd v Allan* [2007] UKHL 21; [2008] 1 A.C. 1, at [48], per Lord Hoffmann and [151] (Lord Nicholls, describing how even the most narrow view of what constituted unlawful means would include torts and breaches of contract). See, to the same effect, *Digicel (St Lucia) Ltd v Cable & Wireless Plc* [2010] EWHC 774 (Ch) at Annex 1 [66]: "A breach of contract constitutes unlawful means for the purpose of the tort considered in [*OBG Ltd v Allan*]".

[42] *Associated British Ports v TGWU* [1989] 1 W.L.R. 939, at 965, per Stuart-Smith LJ.

[43] See para.2–058.

[44] In the latter context there are a number of cases supporting the proposition that inducing a breach of statutory duty gives rise to secondary liability: see para.3–015.

[45] *OBG Ltd v Allan* [2007] UKHL 21; [2008] 1 A.C. 1. See in particular Lord Hoffmann's discussion of *RCA Corp v Pollard* [1983] Ch. 135; *Isaac Oren v Red Box Toy Factory Ltd* [1999] F.S.R. 785 and *Lonrho Ltd v Shell Petroleum Co Ltd (No.2)* [1982] A.C. 173 in *OBG*, at [52], [54] and [55] respectively.

[46] Lord Hoffmann went on to say at [57] that "it is not for the courts to create a cause of action out of a regulatory or criminal statute which Parliament did not intend to be actionable in private law." Seemingly, if Parliament did intend the statute (or rather a breach of it) to be actionable, then a cause of action in unlawful interference should be available, notwithstanding that the immediate right of action is vested in the third party.

(iv)   Breach of fiduciary duty

There is as yet no specific guidance in the cases following *OBG Ltd v Allan*   **4–024**
concerning whether a breach of fiduciary duty can qualify in this context. As far
as earlier cases are concerned, in *Green v Skandia Life Assurance Co Ltd*[47]
Christopher Nugee QC (as he then was) seems to have considered that a breach of
fiduciary duty was capable in principle of constituting an unlawful act for the
purposes of unlawful interference. The claim failed on the basis that the conduct
alleged to have amounted to the breach was not aimed or targeted at the
claimant.[48] Likewise in *Et Plus SA v Welter*[49] Gross J appeared to consider that a
breach of fiduciary duty could in principle found a claim in unlawful
interference.[50]

With the somewhat tentative support offered by these cases, it is considered that   **4–025**
breach of fiduciary duty qualifies in principle. Recent authority on unlawful
means conspiracy suggests that a breach of fiduciary duty qualifies in that
context.[51] There is no good reason in principle why the position should be any
different in the sphere of unlawful interference. This therefore marks a distinction
with the *Lumley v Gye* tort, where the courts have so far refused to recognise a
common law tort of inducing a breach of fiduciary duty,[52] but where different
considerations apply in light of the separate body of principles governing
accessory liability in equity. Since unlawful interference, like conspiracy, is a tort
of primary liability, those considerations cannot be said to apply in the same way
here.

(v)   Breach of confidence

There is perhaps stronger support in the authorities for breach of confidence as a   **4–026**
qualifying unlawful act in this tort. In *Indata Equipment Supplies Ltd v ACL
Ltd*,[53] a majority of the Court of Appeal[54] held, obiter, that a breach of confidence
committed by the representative of a finance house in disclosing the claimant
broker's profit margins to the broker's client, coupled with what was
enigmatically described as the representative's "ruthless conduct", provided the

---

[47] *Green v Skandia Life Assurance Co Ltd* [2006] EWHC 1626 (Ch), at [74]–[77].

[48] A formulation which would not now stand following *OBG Ltd v Allan* [2007] UKHL 21; [2008] 1 A.C. 1.

[49] *Et Plus SA v Welter* [2005] EWHC 2115 (Comm); [2006] 1 Lloyd's Rep. 251, at [85].

[50] See also *Indata Equipment Supplies Ltd v ACL Ltd* [1996] C.L.C. 957, in which a claim succeeded in unlawful interference on the basis of a breach of fiduciary duty owed by the defendant to the claimant himself. On appeal [1998] F.S.R. 248 it was held that there was no such duty, but the claim was upheld on the basis of a breach of confidence: see para.4–026 below.

[51] *Aerostar Maintenance International Ltd v Wilson* [2010] EWHC 2032 (Ch), at [170]–[172]; *Fiona Trust & Holding Corp v Privalov* [2010] EWHC 3199 (Comm), at [69]; *Novoship (UK) Ltd v Mikhaylyuk* [2012] EWHC 3586 (Comm), at [103], citing views to that effect expressed by Thomas J without deciding the point in *Sphere Drake Insurance v Euro International Underwriting* [2003] Lloyd's Rep. I.R. 525, at [85]–[88].

[52] See *First Subsea Ltd v Balltec Ltd* [2014] EWHC 866 (Ch), at [351]–[353], considered at para.3–019.

[53] *Indata Equipment Supplies Ltd v ACL Ltd* [1998] F.S.R. 248.

[54] *Indata* [1998] F.S.R. 248, at 260, per Otton LJ, and at 262–263, per Owen J.

requisite unlawful act for a claim in unlawful interference.[55] Some further support may be gleaned from the *Douglas v Hello!* case decided as one of the appeals in *OBG Ltd v Allan*. At first instance, Tugendhat J dismissed the unlawful interference claim on the basis that there was no intention to injure, but would have upheld breach of confidence as unlawful means.[56] The Court of Appeal took a similar approach.[57] In the House of Lords, Lord Hoffmann considered that the defendant did have the necessary intention, but that the claim failed because there had been no interference with the dealings between the claimant (*OK!*) and the third party (the Douglases).[58] No criticism was made, however, of the conclusion of either of the courts below that breach of confidence was a relevant unlawful act.

(vi) Crimes

4–027   It is now clear from the majority decision in *OBG Ltd v Allan* that crimes will not qualify as unlawful acts for the purposes of this tort. That is not to say, however, that a claim in unlawful interference should not be considered where there is evidence that a crime has been committed. Frequently, conduct amounting to a crime will also amount to a common law tort actionable either by the claimant himself or by a third party, potentially opening the door to a claim in unlawful interference; or to a breach of statutory duty actionable on the same basis and with the same potential consequences.

(vii) Contempt of court

4–028   It has recently been confirmed by the Supreme Court in *JSC BTA Bank v Khrapunov*[59] that contempt of court is capable of constituting an unlawful act for the purposes of unlawful means conspiracy.[60] It is far less certain, however, whether the same is true in the context of unlawful interference. In *Acrow (Automation) Ltd v Rex Chainbelt Inc*,[61] Lord Denning MR had held that it was. However, this was long prior to the decision in *OBG Ltd v Allan* and was on the basis of the broader formulation of unlawful means adopted by Lord Nicholls in that case but rejected by the majority. It is now clear that, to qualify as unlawful in this context, conduct needs to satisfy the twin requirements set out by Lord Hoffmann in *OBG Ltd v Allan* and addressed in this chapter, namely that the conduct:

---

[55] It is an oddity of the case that the duty of confidence was owed by the defendant to the claimant himself, and thus *Indata* did not concern the three-party situation addressed by Lord Hoffmann in *OBG Ltd v Allan* and which is the focus of this chapter. But this is not thought to affect the reasoning on this point.

[56] [2003] EWHC 786 (Ch); [2003] E.M.L.R. 31, at [249]. He would also have upheld a breach of the Data Protection Act 1998 as unlawful means.

[57] [2005] EWCA Civ 595; [2006] Q.B. 125, at [233].

[58] *OBG Ltd v Allan* [2007] UKHL 21; [2008] 1 A.C. 1, at [129].

[59] *JSC BTA Bank v Khrapunov* [2018] UKSC 19; [2018] 2 W.L.R. 1125.

[60] See the more detailed discussion in Ch.2, at paras.2–068—2–070.

[61] *Acrow (Automation) Ltd v Rex Chainbelt Inc* [1971] 1 W.L.R. 1676, at 1682–1683.

(1)   is actionable by the third party and
(2)   affects the third party's freedom to deal with the claimant.[62]

On the first of these points, is a contempt of court "actionable" at the suit of the   **4–029**
wronged party? This is potentially a complicated question which the cases have
not addressed directly, but the answer is probably no. In the *Khrapunov* case itself
the Court of Appeal re-affirmed the principle that breach of a court order does not
itself constitute a cause of action in private law sounding in damages.[63] The
Supreme Court considered that issue irrelevant to the case before it and so did not
decide it.[64] Notwithstanding that the civil contempt jurisdiction may be said to
exist in part (or even primarily) for the protection of the beneficiary of a court
order or undertaking to secure compliance by the respondent,[65] and that a breach
of such an order or undertaking undoubtedly gives the beneficiary a right to bring
proceedings for contempt,[66] it is thought that this is insufficient to make the
contempt of court "actionable" in the sense contemplated by Lord Hoffmann in
OBG.[67] Criminal contempt of court is even less likely to be within this principle,
since in the punishment of such wrongs the emphasis is more firmly upon the
protection of the public interest. In contrast to the civil contempt jurisdiction,
committal proceedings for criminal contempt require the permission of the
court.[68] This makes it even more difficult for conduct amounting to a criminal
contempt to be considered "actionable by" a party to litigation affected by such
conduct.

If it were possible to characterise a contempt of court (whether civil or criminal)   **4–030**
as "actionable" at the suit of a third party private litigant, it would remain
necessary to satisfy the further requirement that the contempt affected the third
party's freedom to deal with the claimant (see further at paras 4–035—4–038
below). This is conceivable in principle: a respondent to a court order may for
example refuse to deliver up goods pursuant to a court order, making it
impossible for the beneficiary of the order to deliver those goods to the claimant.
Or a witness may give false evidence in judicial proceedings which misleads the
other party to those proceedings into taking action which damages the claimant.

---

[62] The *Acrow* case was cited in argument in *OBG Ltd v Allan* but not addressed directly in any of the judgments.

[63] *JSC BTA Bank v Khrapunov* [2017] EWCA Civ 40; [2017] Q.B. 853, at [26]–[34], relying on the decision of the House of Lords in *Customs and Excise Commissioners v Barclays Bank Plc* [2006] UKHL 28; [2007] 1 A.C. 181. This excludes the possible special category of wilful disobedience to a subpoena: see *Khrapunov* (CA), at [32]–[33].

[64] [2018] UKSC 19; [2018] 2 W.L.R. 1125, at [17]. Lords Sumption and Lloyd-Jones JJSC did, however, go on to refer to some of the authorities for and against the existence of such a cause of action, at [18]–[23].

[65] See *A-G v Times Newspapers* [1974] A.C. 273, at 307H–308A, per Lord Diplock.

[66] Cf Beatson LJ in *Dar Al Arkan v Al Refai* [2015] EWCA Civ 715; [2015] 1 W.L.R. 135, who, at [58], referred to a director's involvement in a company's breach of a court order as giving rise to a "cause of action" entitling the beneficiary of the order to bring proceedings for contempt.

[67] Lord Hoffmann also referred, in the context of statutory obligations, to the need for conduct to be "actionable in private law": see *OBG Ltd v Allan* [2007] UKHL 21; [2008] 1 A.C. 1, at [57].

[68] See generally the discussion of contempt in Ch.35.

However, this limiting principle undoubtedly narrows the potential scope for contempt of court to fulfil the role of unlawful act in a claim for unlawful interference.

(4)   Conduct Actionable Under Foreign Law

4–031   The question of whether conduct which is actionable only under a foreign system of law can qualify as unlawful in the particular context of unlawful interference is not one which has received any real attention in the cases. The issue is considered more fully in the context of unlawful means conspiracy,[69] and the same considerations are thought to apply in the present context. In summary:

(1)   Where the claim is based on conduct which is illegal abroad, the first question to consider is whether an English law claim in unlawful interference is available at all; or whether instead, as a matter of English conflicts of law principles, the cause of action as a whole is one arising under the foreign legal system.

(2)   If the application of conflicts principles identifies a cause of action in unlawful interference in English law, in principle there should be no reason why acts unlawful under a foreign law cannot qualify as an unlawful act; but there is little authority on the point in the conspiracy context and still less guidance in the context of unlawful interference.

(3)   Where the foreign law in question is penal or public, then—assuming that the conduct complained of would be actionable by the relevant third party at all—an unlawful interference claim founded on such conduct may well run up against the rule against direct or indirect enforcement of such laws by the English courts.

(5)   Must the Defendant Know that what He is Doing is Unlawful?

4–032   It has also been suggested in the context of unlawful means conspiracy that ignorance of the law may amount to a defence, albeit the preponderance of recent authority is against the recognition of such a defence.[70] The recent cases do not specifically consider the defence in the context of unlawful interference, save for a brief conclusion in one of them that there was a serious issue to be tried on the question for the purposes of an interim injunction.[71]

4–033   On this issue at least, it is difficult to see any principled justification for a difference of approach between unlawful interference and unlawful means conspiracy. The position is however different from that which obtains in relation

---

[69] See paras 2–072—2–076.

[70] In particular see *First Subsea Ltd v Balltec Ltd* [2014] EWHC 866 (Ch), at [150]–[157], per Norris J (not affected on appeal [2017] EWCA Civ 186; [2018] Ch. 25); *Swain v Swains Plc* [2015] EWHC 660 (Ch), at [135], per HHJ Pelling QC; *Capital for Enterprise Fund LP v Bibby Financial Services Ltd* [2015] EWHC 2593 (Ch), at [11]–[13] (also HHJ Pelling QC). The issue is discussed more fully at paras 2–077—2–083 in the context of unlawful means conspiracy.

[71] *Lebara Mobile Ltd v Lycamobile UK Ltd* [2015] EWHC 3318 (Ch), at [51].

to the tort of inducing breach of contract, where ignorance of the law can provide a defence.[72] This makes sense: if a defendant does not know (e.g. because of his ignorance of the law) that the conduct he induces amounts to a breach of contract, then it is hard to say that he intends to bring about that result. By contrast, a defendant can commit an unlawful act and intend to cause damage to the claimant without any need to show knowledge of the unlawfulness.

D.   INTERFERENCE

The "interference" required to found a cause of action is an interference in some way with the dealings between the third party, who is directly wronged, and the claimant, who is thereby indirectly harmed. Many of the leading cases prior to *OBG Ltd v Allan* described liability as arising for interference with contractual relations.[73] However, whilst the loss suffered by a claimant will very often be connected in some way with a contract (e.g. a loss of benefits under an existing contract with the third party, or of the opportunity to contract with the third party in the first place), this is not necessary. It is sufficient that the (intended) consequence of the wrongful act is damage in any form; for example, to the claimant's economic expectations.[74] The law is indifferent to the nature of the interest which is damaged.[75] As a result, as long as the claimant can identify damage of some kind arising from the defendant's interference (which will invariably be economic loss), the precise way in which that damage arises is not important.

4–034

Potentially more difficult, both in principle and in practice, is the requirement set out by Lord Hoffmann in *OBG Ltd v Allan* that the defendant's unlawful act must affect the freedom of the third party to deal with the claimant.[76] One obvious situation which may arise in the fraud context, is that of the third party who suffers loss as a result of the defendant's wrongful action against it, which in turn deprives the third party of the financial resources with which to do business with the claimant or to comply with its contractual or other obligations to the claimant.[77] In *Marex Financial Ltd v Garcia*,[78] the director was alleged to have stripped a company of assets, in breach of his fiduciary duty, rendering the

4–035

---

[72] See para.3–064.

[73] Though some of these cases were addressing the tort which would now be understood as inducing breach of contract, rather than unlawful interference.

[74] *OBG Ltd v Allan* [2007] UKHL 21; [2008] 1 A.C. 1, per Lord Hoffmann at [8].

[75] *OBG Ltd v Allan* [2007] UKHL 21; [2008] 1 A.C. 1, per Lord Hoffmann at [32].

[76] *OBG Ltd v Allan* [2007] UKHL 21; [2008] 1 A.C. 1, at [51]. See also Lady Hale's formulation, at [306]: "striking through a third party who might otherwise be doing business with your target". A contention that the "freedom to deal" requirement was not a necessary element of the cause of action was dismissed by Roth J in *Secretary of State for Health v Servier Laboratories Ltd* [2017] EWHC 2006; [2017] 5 C.M.L.R. 17, on the basis that *OBG* had clearly established such a requirement.

[77] For further examples see *McLeod v Rooney* 2010 S.L.T. 499, at [19]; and the claim pursued (but dismissed on appeal on jurisdictional grounds) in *Erste Group Bank AG v JSC "VMZ Red October"* [2013] EWHC 2926 (Comm); [2014] B.P.I.R. 81 (Comm Ct); [2015] EWCA Civ 379; [2015] 1 C.L.C. 706 (CA), namely that the defendants had stripped a borrower of its assets rendering it unable to make loan repayments to the claimant creditor. In those circumstances the claimant had pleaded claims against the defendants in unlawful interference (as well as inducing breach of contract and lawful and unlawful means conspiracy).

company unable to comply with a judgment in the claimant's favour. Knowles J held that "a very point" of asset-stripping in this context was to take away from the company its freedom to meet its obligation to the claimant.

4–036   Two examples discussed in *OBG* in which the "freedom to deal" requirement was not met are *RCA Corp v Pollard*[79] and *Isaac Oren v Red Box Toy Factory Ltd*.[80] In *RCA Corp v Pollard*, the claimant had an exclusive right from Elvis Presley's estate to exploit his records. The defendant sold bootleg Elvis records. But whilst this conduct would have been actionable by the estate (as a breach of statutory duty) and had the effect of reducing the value of the claimant's exploitation rights, it had no effect on the freedom of the Elvis estate to perform its contract with the claimant. Similarly, in *Isaac Oren*, the exclusive licensee of a registered design for a child's play mattress had no claim against the defendant who manufactured an infringing product, because the infringement did not affect the rights between the licensor and licensee. And likewise in *Douglas v Hello! Ltd (No.3)*,[81] *OK!* magazine's claim against its rival *Hello!* failed because the actions of the rival's photographer in infiltrating a celebrity wedding to take pictures which the rival then published had not affected the freedom of the third party (the wedding couple) to deal with *OK!*. All that had happened was that the rival's actions made the rights given to *OK!* by the wedding couple less profitable.[82]

4–037   The cases addressed in the previous paragraph all concerned existing contractual rights.[83] There is however no reason why the same principle cannot apply in relation to prospective contracts. A colourful early example is *Tarleton v M'Gawley*,[84] in which customers were prevented from trading with the claimant when the defendant drove a canoe away from the claimant's ship by cannon fire. But in the case of a prospective contract it remains necessary to show that the third party's freedom has truly been interfered with. In *Future Investments SA v FIFA*,[85] the claimant, Future, claimed the exclusive rights to certain video footage, and alleged that FIFA was liable in unlawful interference by falsely warranting to a third party, IMG, that it had the right to grant IMG a licence to such footage. This was said to interfere with IMG's freedom to contract with Future for such a licence because IMG was thereby wrongly reassured that it did not need to do so. Floyd J struck out the claim: IMG either needed a licence from Future or it did not, and nothing FIFA was alleged to have done affected the position. Unlike in *Tarleton*'s case, the relations between IMG and Future were untouched.

[78] *Marex Financial Ltd v Garcia* [2017] EWHC 918 (Comm); [2017] 4 W.L.R. 105; see in particular [29]–[36]. The decision was overturned on appeal on the basis that the claim was barred by the rule against recovery of reflective loss: see [2018] EWCA Civ 1468.
[79] *RCA Corp v Pollard* [1983] Ch. 135.
[80] *Isaac Oren v Red Box Toy Factory Ltd* [1999] F.S.R. 785.
[81] One of the three appeals reported as *OBG Ltd v Allan* [2007] UKHL 21; [2008] 1 A.C. 1.
[82] *OBG Ltd v Allan* [2007] UKHL 21; [2008] 1 A.C. 1, at [129].
[83] For a further example see the Scottish case of *McLeod v Rooney* 2010 S.L.T. 499, in which it was held that unlawful action taken against a company did not affect the latter's freedom to deal with its shareholders; rather it simply made the shares less valuable.
[84] *Tarleton v M'Gawley* (1794) Peake 270.
[85] *Future Investments SA v FIFA* [2010] EWHC 1019 (Ch); [2010] I.L. Pr. 34.

The issue was addressed fleetingly by the Court of Appeal in its recent decision in **4–038** *Emerald Supplies Ltd v British Airways*.[86] The claimant freight shippers brought an unlawful interference claim based on alleged breaches of competition law. The only relevant effect of the anti-competitive practices was to increase the price at which freight services could be acquired by the claimants from freight forwarders. The Court expressed itself "very doubtful" as to whether this interfered with the freedom of freight forwarders to deal with the claimants, even if it affected the way in which the freedom could be exercised. The line between an interference with the third party's freedom on the one hand, and with the way in which it can be exercised on the other, might be considered a thin one; but the need to "enquire with precision"[87] into the question of whether interference in its true sense has taken place makes it inevitable that liability may turn on such matters.

E. INTENTION

A claimant in unlawful interference must show that the defendant intended to **4–039** cause him loss. However, until the decision of the House of Lords in *OBG Ltd v Allan*, the question of what level of intention was required was uncertain. In 1989 the Court of Appeal had held that a predominant purpose to injure the claimant was not necessary.[88] But even by the time of the decision of the Court of Appeal in *Douglas v Hello! Ltd (No.3)*,[89] uncertainty remained, only to be resolved by the judgments given in the House of Lords.

As Lord Hoffmann stated in *OBG*, it is necessary to distinguish between ends, **4–040** means and consequences. If harm to the claimant is the end sought by the defendants (because, say, of some animus harboured by the defendant against him), the requisite intention is made out. The same is true if harm to the claimant is the means by which the defendant seeks to secure some other end (e.g. benefit to himself), even if the defendant would rather have secured that end without causing harm to the claimant. On the other hand, if harm is neither an end nor a means, but merely a foreseeable consequence, the requisite intention is not made out.[90] Lord Hoffmann disapproved of the approach taken by the Court of Appeal in *Douglas v Hello!* to the interplay between the scope of "unlawful means" and the test of intention in unlawful interference, concluding that the Court of Appeal

---

[86] *Emerald Supplies Ltd v British Airways* [2015] EWCA Civ 1024; [2016] Bus. L.R. 145, at [128]–[129].

[87] *Future Investments SA v FIFA* [2010] EWHC 1019 (Ch); [2010] I.L. Pr. 34, at [25], per Floyd J.

[88] *Lonrho Plc v Al-Fayed (No.1)* [1990] 2 Q.B. 479, per Dillon LJ at 488G–489A, per Ralph Gibson LJ at 492A–492B, per Woolf LJ at 494B–494D.

[89] *Douglas v Hello! Ltd (No.3)* [2005] EWCA Civ 595; [2006] Q.B. 125; see the menu of possible options at [159] and the conclusion at [223] that the object or purpose of the defendant must be to inflict harm either as an end in itself or a means to an end; and the further conclusion at [224] that it was also necessary to show "targeted or directed harm".

[90] *OBG Ltd v Allan* [2007] UKHL 21; [2008] 1 A.C. 1, per Lord Hoffmann at [42]–[43], [62]; per Lord Nicholls at [164]–[166]. Whilst much of what Woolf LJ said on the subject of intention in *Lonrho Plc v Al-Fayed (No.1)* [1990] 2 Q.B. 479 continues to represent the law, his suggestion (at 494D) that a defendant's knowledge of the "probable consequences" of his actions to the claimant would suffice for the purposes of intention does not.

had adopted an unduly wide approach to what constituted unlawful means and an unduly narrow approach to intention, "insisting upon a highly specific intention, which 'targets' the plaintiff".[91]

4–041   Where loss to the claimant is the obverse side of the coin to gain to the defendants, i.e. the two are inseparably linked, the requisite intention is made out.[92] However, if a claimant relies on the "obverse side of the coin" analysis in order to infer an intention to injure on the part of the defendant, the "inseparable link" between the defendant's primary intention and damage to the claimant must nevertheless be established. In addition, it seems that the defendant's intention to harm the claimant must be a contributing cause of his actions. In other words, if the defendant would have acted as he did in any event, and his nefarious intention was purely collateral and extraneous, he will not be liable. So in the New Zealand case of *Van Camp Chocolates Ltd v Aulsebrooks Ltd*,[93] the defendant produced food bars using the claimant's confidential processes. The judge found that the defendant's intention was simply to make a profit for himself, and it was conceded that any intention to harm the claimant was not a causative element of the defendant's conduct. In those circumstances the defendant was held not liable in unlawful interference. However, a defendant who knows that sales of his competing product will impact on sales of the claimant's product and intends that result may be thought to come very close to falling foul of the "obverse side of the coin" analysis, particularly if there is a finite market for the product. A defendant found to have used unlawful means and to have intended to harm the claimant may also find it difficult to persuade a trial judge that his intention was merely incidental.

4–042   It will be seen from the above analysis that the test of intention is the same as that in unlawful means conspiracy.[94] In the latter context it has been said that it is not enough that conspirators intend to benefit themselves at the expense of a class of persons of which the claimant was one.[95] So in *Emerald Supplies Ltd v British Airways Plc*[96] the claim in unlawful interference against the defendant airline, BA, was struck out on the basis that, even if BA knew that, by charging higher

---

[91] *OBG Ltd v Allan* [2007] UKHL 21; [2008] 1 A.C. 1, at [60] and [135]. Earlier formulations of the intention requirement (see e.g. *Lonrho Plc v Al-Fayed (No.1)* [1990] 2 Q.B. 479, at 489, per Dillon LJ, "in some sense directed against the plaintiff or intended to harm the plaintiff") must be read in light of *OBG Ltd v Allan*.

[92] *OBG Ltd v Allan* [2007] UKHL 21; [2008] 1 A.C. 1, per Lord Nicholls at [167].

[93] *Van Camp Chocolates Ltd v Aulsebrooks Ltd* [1984] N.Z.L.R. 354, approved by Lord Nicholls in *OBG Ltd v Allan*, above, at [166]. Although Lord Hoffmann did not refer to *Van Camp*, there is no reason to read any divergence of view into their analysis of intention: see *Emerald Supplies Ltd v British Airways Plc* [2015] EWCA Civ 1024; [2016] Bus. L.R. 145, at [140].

[94] See *Meretz Investments NV v ACP Ltd* [2007] EWCA Civ 1303; [2008] Ch. 244, at [146]; *Bank of Tokyo-Mitsubishi UFJ Ltd v Başkan Gida Sanayi Ve Pazarlama AS* [2009] EWHC 1276 (Ch), per Briggs J at [833]; *Constantin Medien AG v Ecclestone* [2014] EWHC 387 (Ch), at [333], per Newey J. For discussion of intention in unlawful means conspiracy see paras 2–039—2–046.

[95] *WH Newson Holding Ltd v IMI Plc* [2014] Bus. L.R. 156, at [38]–[41]. The Court of Appeal found that loss to the claimant was not an inevitable consequence of the defendants' actions. *Newson* was referred to with approval in *Emerald Supplies Ltd v British Airways Plc* [2015] EWCA Civ 1024; [2016] Bus. L.R. 145, at [152].

[96] *Emerald Supplies Ltd v British Airways Plc* [2015] EWCA Civ 1024; [2016] Bus. L.R. 145; see [168]–[169] in particular.

prices, it would profit at someone else's expense, it had no idea where the loss would ultimately fall down a customer chain. In those circumstances it was not possible for the claimant shippers to prove that BA intended to cause them loss as the "obverse side of the coin" from its own gain.

On the other hand, it has been said that recklessness as to whether the claimant would be harmed should in principle be sufficient to found liability.[97] The same principles apply as in the conspiracy context. The necessary intention must of course be proved, but not necessarily by direct evidence. In an appropriate case it can be inferred from the acts themselves.[98]

4–043

F.   JUSTIFICATION

It is possible to find suggestions in academic writing and in cases pre-dating *OBG Ltd v Allan*[99] that a defence of justification is available to a claim in unlawful interference.[100] There is considerable difficulty in placing reliance on earlier cases, however, which adopted the "unified theory" which considered inducing breach of contract and unlawful interference as sub-species of the same tort, a theory roundly rejected by the House of Lords in *OBG*. There was no discussion in *OBG* of the possibility of justification as an available defence in this context.[101]

4–044

The availability of a defence of justification is, in any event, difficult to justify in the context of unlawful interference, in which liability depends on the use of unlawful means and an intention to cause damage to the claimant. How, it might be thought, could such action be justified in law?[102] There is here an important difference between the torts of inducing breach of contract and unlawful interference. In the former context (see paras 3–060—3–076), where a specific intention to cause loss to the claimant is not required for liability to arise and nor is the independent use of unlawful means, the defence of justification is available and can be supported on the basis that there are circumstances in which an intention to bring about someone else's breach of contract might be excused (for instance in reliance on a superior right). The same cannot be said of unlawful interference. Equally, were justification an available defence, the need for unlawful means actionable by the third party (save where damage is the only missing ingredient in the cause of action) would have the anomalous result that it would be available against the claimant but not against the third party, such that

4–045

---

[97] *Bank Gesellschaft Berlin International SA v Zihnali* [2001] All E.R. (D) 192 (Jul), per Colman J, (16 July 2001), at [31]. It is perhaps debatable whether this remains the position after *OBG Ltd v Allan*.

[98] *Kuwait Oil Tanker v Al Bader* [2000] 2 All E.R. (Comm) 271, at [120].

[99] *OBG Ltd v Allan* [2007] UKHL 21; [2008] 1 A.C. 1.

[100] See for example the comments of Lord Denning MR in *Morgan v Fry* [1968] 2 Q.B. 710, at 729F–792G; *Cory Lighterage v TGWU* [1973] 1 W.L.R. 792, at 817C–817D; and see H. Carty, *An Analysis of the Economic Torts*, 2nd edn (Oxford: OUP, 2010), pp.100–101, expressing the view that, if the defence exists, it must be "very residual".

[101] Lord Nicholls did refer to the defence in the context of inducing breach of contract: see [2008] 1 A.C. 1, at [193].

[102] As Lord Lindley put it in *Quinn v Leathem* [1901] A.C. 495, at 537: "The intention to injure the plaintiff negatives all excuses".

the court might be called upon to hold that the same conduct both (a) was justified and (b) amounted to an actionable civil wrong.

G. DAMAGE

4-046   Unlawful interference is a tort concerned with economic loss. As Lord Hoffmann put it in *OBG Ltd v Allan*,[103] "it is sufficient that the intended consequence of the wrongful act is damage in any form; for example, to the claimant's economic expectations."[104] As has been seen above,[105] the tort is also concerned with interference with the actions of a third party in which the claimant has an economic interest. Unlawful interference is thus set apart from many other torts in that the recovery of economic loss is not the exception but the rule. Indeed Lord Hoffmann's label for the tort of "causing loss by unlawful means" must be taken to refer to economic loss.

4-047   Accordingly, whilst it is clear that economic loss is recoverable, it must be doubted whether the tort allows recovery of other heads of damage, such as (for example) damage to property or injury to feelings. Little guidance is offered by the cases. In a case of fraud the claimant will usually only be seeking to recover in respect of economic loss, but this uncertainty as to the availability of wider recovery of damages must be borne in mind where it is relevant. With that caveat, however, there is thought to be no reason in principle why damages in unlawful interference should not be "at large", in the same way as for inducing breach of contract and conspiracy.[106] Accordingly the issues surrounding the principle of damages at large as explained elsewhere in the context of those torts will be relevant here too.

4-048   Just as, in a conspiracy case, it is necessary to establish causation, i.e. the damages sought must be referable to the act causing the pecuniary loss which constitutes the tort,[107] so too in unlawful interference. The relevant damage for the purposes of the unlawful interference tort is the damage which is caused by the interference with the third party's freedom of action. Damage which is suffered by the claimant which is not the consequence of interference with the third party's freedom of action is not within the purview of the tort.[108] The loss suffered by the claimants in *RCA v Pollard* and *Isaac Oren v Red Box Toy Factory Ltd*[109] failed to meet this test, being simply a decline in value of contractual rights which were not interfered with. Whilst both cases can be

---

[103] *OBG Ltd v Allan* [2007] UKHL 21; [2008] 1 A.C. 1, at [8].
[104] Lord Nicholls put it as follows, at [153]: "The law seeks to provide a remedy for intentional economic harm caused by unacceptable means".
[105] At para.4–008
[106] See para.3–077 for inducing breach of contract and paras 2–134—2–135 for conspiracy. Lord Devlin discussed the concept of damages at large in *Rookes v Barnard* [1964] A.C. 1129, on one view an unlawful interference case, at 1221 and 1128–1130. Support for the proposition in the text can also be found in *The Bodo Community v The Shell Petroleum Development Co of Nigeria Ltd* [2014] EWHC 1973 (TCC), at [130].
[107] *Lonrho Plc v Fayed (No.5)* [1993] 1 W.L.R. 1489, at 1505B–1505E.
[108] *Future Investments SA v FIFA* [2010] EWHC 1019 (Ch); [2010] I.L. Pr. 34, at [25], per Floyd J.
[109] See para.4–036 above.

understood simply as cases where the element of interference was lacking, they nevertheless illustrate that loss is not recoverable unless it can be properly linked (as a matter of causation) with any interference which the claimant is able to prove on the facts of a given case.

Since the whole focus of the tort is on economic loss, and damages are at large, **4–049** any economic loss ought in principle to be recoverable, subject of course to satisfaction of the usual requirements of causation and remoteness. As with inducing breach of contract and conspiracy, the fact that unlawful interference is a tort of intention will tend to influence and broaden the scope of the loss in respect of which the claimant may recover. As Lord Lindley held in *Quinn v Leathem*[110] (now best understood as a lawful means conspiracy case),

> "this violation of duty by the defendants resulted in damage to the plaintiff – not remote, but immediate and intended. The intention to injure the plaintiff negatives all excuses and disposes of any question of remoteness of damage."

The following are examples of the sorts of loss which would in principle be **4–050** recoverable in an unlawful interference claim[111]:

(1)   Loss of profits, including specific losses consequential on a drop in orders for a claimant's products or services.
(2)   Costs of management time expended in investigating and tackling the defendant's actions.
(3)   Loss of a business and closure costs.
(4)   A loss of "goodwill" in the sense of an asset of measurable value.

---

[110] *Quinn v Leathem* [1901] A.C. 495, at 537. The differing tests of intention in lawful means conspiracy and unlawful interference are not thought to undermine the basic applicability of this principle in the present context.
[111] These are similar to the examples postulated in the context of conspiracy claims, at para.2–136. In many fraud cases involving multiple defendants, both causes of action will be pursued together.

CHAPTER 5

INTIMIDATION

A. INTRODUCTION

(1) Nature of the Tort

The tort of intimidation deserves treatment in a book on civil fraud as an intentional civil wrong which can sometimes be used by fraudsters to achieve their ends. The tort, at least in its "two-party" form, has not been the subject of significant judicial analysis, although it seems that over the last 10 years or so it has grown in popularity amongst litigants.[1]

5–001

The cases speak of two categories of intimidation:

5–002

(1) Two-party intimidation, in which A threatens B in such a way that causes B loss.[2]
(2) Three-party intimidation, which encompasses the scenario where A threatens B in such a way as to cause B to act so as to cause loss to C.[3]

Three-party intimidation is, after *OBG Ltd v Allan*,[4] now comprehended within the unlawful interference tort (discussed in Ch.4), whereby the "unlawful means" are constituted by intimidation of B by A. The classic example of this is *Rookes v Barnard*[5] in which the defendant union officials were held liable for threatening to withdraw the services of union employees if the employer did not remove the

5–003

---

[1] For instance there were claims in intimidation brought in the high-profile cases of *Berezovsky v Abramovich* [2010] EWHC 647 (Comm); and *Holyoake v Candy* [2017] EWHC 3397 (Ch).

[2] Two party intimidation is a rare tort: in *Berezovsky v Abramovich* [2010] EWHC 647 (Comm) it was agreed between the parties that there were by that stage only two reported cases on two-party intimidation—*Godwin v Uzoigwe* [1993] Fam. Law 65 and *News Group Newspapers Ltd v SOGAT (No.2)* [1987] I.C.R. 181. A third example is provided by *Kolmar Group AG v Traxpo Enterprises Pvt Ltd* [2011] 1 All E.R. (Comm) 46, which was decided between the close of argument and handing down of judgment in *Berezovsky*.

[3] See in particular per Lord Devlin in *Rookes v Barnard* [1964] A.C. 1129, at 1205, quoting from J.W. Salmond and R.F.V. Heuston, *Salmond on the Law of Torts*, 13th edn (London: Sweet & Maxwell, 1961), where this categorisation was employed. Salmond had defined two-party intimidation as follows: "Although there seems to be no authority on the point, it cannot be doubted that it is an actionable wrong intentionally to compel a person, by means of a threat of an illegal act, to do some act whereby loss accrues to him: for example, an action will doubtless lie at the suit of a trader who has been compelled to discontinue his business by means of threats of personal violence made against him by the defendant with that intention ..."

[4] *OBG Ltd v Allan* [2008] 1 A.C. 1.

[5] *Rookes v Barnard* [1964] A.C. 1129.

claimant (a fellow employee) from his position. The employer proceeded to suspend and then dismiss the claimant employee, giving him a cause of action against the union officials in (three-party) intimidation. This analysis, which characterises the intimidation of B as unlawful means actionable by B, necessarily presupposes the existence of intimidation as a freestanding tort actionable directly in a two-party scenario. And the same conduct may in principle give rise to liability in both torts. If for example A threatens B that, unless he breaches his contract with C, A will assault B, and B succumbs to the threat, breaching his contract with C and causing loss to both B and C, then A is liable to B in intimidation and to C in unlawful interference (assuming the necessary intention to cause loss).[6]

5–004 However, despite the conceptual overlap between them, two-party intimidation and unlawful interference are logically separate, not least because, as Lord Hoffmann noted in *OBG Ltd v Allan*,[7] unlawful interference does not require threats. In contrast, a coercive threat is the touchstone of liability in two-party intimidation. In his discussion in *OBG*, Lord Hoffmann expressly carved out two-party intimidation on the basis that it "raised altogether different issues".[8] Similarly this chapter is focused on two-party intimidation. The principles discussed below are nevertheless necessary to an understanding of unlawful interference when it takes the form of three-party intimidation, the elements of threat and coercion needing to be present as regards the third party.

5–005 Without the same modern restatement from which related torts such as inducing breach of contract, unlawful interference and unlawful means conspiracy have benefited,[9] the practitioner is left with what limited assistance can be derived from the very few reported cases on two-party intimidation,[10] together with such principles as can legitimately be imported from the three-party context (as well as from the doctrine of economic duress, referred to below). In a way which reflects the uneasy jurisprudential development of the economic torts since the late nineteenth century, older cases often elided two- and three-party intimidation by referring to types of unlawful means which are "directed" not only against the claimant but also against a third party.[11]

5–006 Intimidation is also a wrong which is allied to the doctrine of duress, analysed below at Ch.15. Duress is not a tort (although there is some rather loose language in some of the cases which suggests otherwise),[12] but is instead part of the law of unjust enrichment and also provides a basis for avoidance of a contract or other

---

[6] In this scenario A would also be liable to C for inducing B's breach of contract.

[7] *OBG Ltd v Allan* [2007] UKHL 21; [2008] 1 A.C. 1, at [7].

[8] *OBG Ltd v Allan*, above, at [61].

[9] *OBG Ltd v Allan*, above, in respect of inducing breach of contract and unlawful interference; *Revenue & Customs Commissioners v Total Network* [2008] UKHL 19; [2008] 1 A.C. 1174 in particular in respect of unlawful means conspiracy.

[10] Steyn LJ noted in *Godwin v Uzoigwe* [1993] Fam. Law 65 that "there is very little guidance in the decided cases on the requirements of this tort". The position has not changed materially since.

[11] See e.g. *Mogul Steamship Co Ltd v McGregor, Gow & Co* (1889) 23 Q.B.D. 598, per Bowen LJ at 614–615.

[12] For example, in *Alec Lobb (Garages) Ltd v Total Oil (Great Britain) Ltd* [1985] 1 W.L.R. 173, at 177 and in *Huyton SA v Peter Cremer GmbH & Co* [1999] 1 Lloyd's Rep. 620, at 638 the court

transaction. It will often be the case that the doctrine of duress, which appears to be based on wider foundations than the tort of intimidation (as to which see below), provides a sufficient basis for the claimant to obtain adequate redress. Indeed in some cases a claim in intimidation will be capable of being asserted as an alternative to a claim in duress and the two claims will succeed or fail together.[13] Nonetheless the two concepts are separate:

> "The use of economic duress is not a tort in itself, though the particular form that some economic duress takes may amount to a tort. The remedy to which economic duress gives rise is not an action for damages but an action for restitution of property or money extracted under such duress and the avoidance of any contract that is induced by it. In some cases the economic duress may amount to a tort, in which case the restitutionary remedy for money had and received is merely an alternative remedy to an action for damages in tort. The two are however distinct."[14]

Hence, where the claimant has suffered loss which is wider than the transmission of benefits to the defendant pursuant to a contract said to be procured by duress, then the claimant will have to resort to the tort of intimidation.

(2) Elements

The classic definition of the tort of intimidation was given by Lord Denning MR in *Morgan v Fry*[15]: **5–007**

> "there must be a threat by one person to use unlawful means (such as violence or a tort or a breach of contract) so as to compel another to obey his wishes; and the person so threatened must comply with the demand rather than risk the threat being carried into execution. In such circumstances the person damnified by the compliance can sue for intimidation."

Morgan v Fry was a case of three-party intimidation, but the definition applies equally to two-party intimidation.[16] The elements of the tort of (two-party) intimidation may be summarised as follows: **5–008**

---

referred to the "tort of economic duress". See generally the discussion in N. Enonchong, *Duress, Undue Influence and Unconscionable Dealing*, 2nd edn (London: Sweet & Maxwell, 2012), paras 28–089—28–091.

[13] *Universe Tankships of Monrovia Inc v ITF* [1983] 1 A.C. 366, at 383–387. In *Kolmar Group AG v Traxpo Enterprises Pvt Ltd* [2011] 1 All E.R. (Comm) 46 the two claims succeeded in parallel.

[14] *Progress Bulk Carriers Ltd v Tube City IMS LLC* [2012] EWHC 273 (Comm); [2012] 2 All E.R. (Comm) 855, per Cooke J at [25]. See also, to similar effect, *Universe Tankships of Monrovia Inc v ITF* [1983] 1 A.C. 366, per Lord Diplock at 384 (Lord Scarman, who was in the minority, suggested that duress was itself actionable as a tort: see at 400); per Lord Goff, in *Dimskal Shipping Co SA v ITF* [1992] 2 A.C. 152, at 169: "it is not to be forgotten that conduct does not have to be tortious to constitute duress for the purpose of English law; this is so even at common law…"; *Investec Bank (Channel Islands) Ltd v The Retail Group Plc* [2009] EWHC 476 (Ch), per Sales J at [122]; *Al Nehayan v Kent* [2018] EWHC 333 (Comm), per Leggatt LJ at [222]–[224].

[15] *Morgan v Fry* [1968] 2 Q.B. 710, at 724C.

[16] It was cited with approval by Longmore LJ in *Berezovsky v Abramovich* [2011] EWCA Civ 153; [2011] 1 W.L.R. 2290, a two-party intimidation case.

(1) A threatens B with the commission of an illegal act, whether by himself or by a third party, unless B takes some step or refrains from taking some step or course of action.

(2) A intends that B should act upon the threat in the sense of being coerced into taking, or refraining from taking, the particular step or course of action; and also intends to cause loss to B.

(3) The threat in fact coerces B into taking a step, or refraining from taking a step.

(4) As a result B suffers loss or damage.[17]

5–009 So far as the three-party tort is concerned, it is considered that the elements in (1) to (3) above apply in the same way, subject to the variation that A's intention will be to cause loss to C (the victim and claimant) rather than (or as well as) to B (the party threatened). Similarly as far as the element in (4) is concerned, it is C who will suffer damage rather than (or as well as) B.

B. THE THREAT

(1) Introduction

5–010 A "threat" will be actionable if it involves the intimation by the defendant of an intention (whether on his part or that of a third party) to commit an unlawful act against the claimant unless the claimant does that which is demanded of him by the defendant. A well-known recent example is *Berezovsky v Abramovich*, in which the claimant alleged that the defendant had threatened that he would procure the Russian state unlawfully to expropriate the claimant's property unless the claimant agreed to sell him assets at an undervalue.[18]

(2) Threat to be Distinguished from Warning

5–011 It seems that an actionable threat is to be distinguished from a non-actionable warning. Lord Herschell said in *Allen v Flood*[19] that the "law cannot regard the act differently because you choose to call it a threat or coercion instead of an intimation or warning", and it is obviously correct that whether conduct is actionable cannot depend simply on whatever word may be used to describe it, either at the time or afterwards.

---

[17] See the analysis in *Berezovsky v Abramovich* [2011] EWCA Civ 153; [2011] 1 W.L.R. 2290, at [5].
[18] The claim was dismissed after a much-publicised trial: see [2012] EWHC 2463 (Comm). The claim failed on the facts, but Gloster J also expressed the (provisional and obiter) view that the intimidation claim would in any event have been governed by Russian law: see [960]–[964]. The judgment accordingly contains no analysis of the English law principles governing the tort of intimidation.
[19] *Allen v Flood* [1898] A.C. 1, at 129.

However, a distinction of substance between threats and warnings was recognised **5–012** in two early twentieth century decisions of the Court of Appeal.[20] In both of these cases the essential facts were that the claimant employee was told by the defendant union members that, if the claimant did not join the defendants' union, the other employees would refuse to work for the employer. In both cases the statements made were held to be mere warnings, not amounting to threats. It is also fair to point out that in both cases the defendants had threatened to leave the employer's service after giving due notice, which they were entitled to do, and this appears to have influenced the court's analysis. Nevertheless it is clear that the law essentially differentiates between that which is intended to be interpreted coercively (and acted on accordingly) and that which is intended to be interpreted merely as the provision of information as to future events. In *JT Stratford & Sons v Lindley (No.1)*,[21] Lord Denning MR illustrated the distinction by saying that, to be actionable, the threat must be coupled with a demand

> "capable of being expressed in the form, 'I will hit you unless you do what I ask,' or 'if you do what I forbid you to do.' A bare threat without a demand does not to my mind amount to the tort of intimidation. If a man says to another, 'I am going to hit you when I get you alone,' it is undoubtedly a threat: and an injunction can be obtained to restrain him from carrying out his threat. But the threat itself does not give rise to a claim for damages. It is only when he delivers the blow that it is actionable: and then as an assault, not as intimidation."

There is thus significant overlap between (a) threat and (b) intention to coerce as **5–013** key elements of the tort. The touchstone of a threat, as opposed to any other kind of utterance, is improper coercion.[22] It consists in the defendant indicating that the claimant must take a particular step "or else" the defendant will carry out his threatened unlawful act. So for example, in *Associated Newspapers Group Ltd v Wade*,[23] a union wrote letters to a number of companies which advertised in a local newspaper with which the union was in dispute, telling them that, unless they stopped advertising in the newspaper, their advertisements in other newspapers would be "blacked" (i.e. not printed) by the union's members. As Lord Denning MR put it,[24] the advertisers "are told they must damage the [newspaper] employers or else they will suffer damage themselves".

In this area, context is everything. Hence a threat may be implied rather than **5–014** expressed and may be discerned from the context.[25] The implication may also be derived from conduct rather than words. If, for example, the claimant is assaulted following a particular step taken by him, say, to meet a business associate with a view to discussing a profitable future venture, this may carry the implication that,

---

[20] *Gaskell v Lancashire and Cheshire Miners' Federation* (1912) 28 T.L.R. 518, CA; *Santen v Busnach* (1913) 29 T.L.R. 214, CA. See also, drawing the same distinction, *Conway v Wade* [1909] A.C. 506, per Lord Loreburn LC at 510.

[21] *JT Stratford & Sons v Lindley (No.1)* [1965] A.C. 269, at 284.

[22] *Rookes v Barnard* [1964] A.C. 1129, at 1209, per Lord Devlin.

[23] *Associated Newspapers Group Ltd v Wade* [1979] 1 W.L.R. 697.

[24] At 714 (Lord Denning MR concurred in the continuation of an injunction but dissented in his reasoning).

[25] See e.g. the example given in *Berezovsky v Abramovich* [2011] EWCA Civ 153; [2011] 1 W.L.R. 2290, at [81]: "If you want to stay healthy, get out of London" would probably be construed as a threat if uttered by a Mafia mobster whereas it could hardly be so construed if said to a patient by his doctor."

if the claimant meets his associate again, he will be assaulted again.[26] In contrast, idle banter or empty abuse will not constitute a threat, essentially because it is not to be taken seriously and so is not coercive.[27]

(3) Unlawful Acts

5–015   There is substantial uncertainty as to the types of unlawful act which, when threatened by a defendant, may give rise to liability in intimidation. The uncertainty arises from the uneasy development of the economic torts since the late 19th century and the absence of any authoritative restatement of the law in the two-party intimidation context. This issue affects not just two-party intimidation but also three-party intimidation, which—forming part of the tort of unlawful interference—requires the threat to be actionable by the third party (save for the need to prove loss) in order to make the defendant liable to the claimant.

(i)   Acts which would be actionable by the claimant

5–016   It is clear that torts and breaches of contract against the claimant are within the ambit of threatened unlawful acts in intimidation.[28] These are the classic examples of threats which might be made against a claimant to coerce him into acting to his detriment and to the defendant's benefit. A modern example of intimidation by threatened breach of contract is *Kolmar Group AG v Traxpo Enterprises Pvt Ltd*.[29] The claimant agreed to buy a quantity of methanol from the defendant, to be shipped from a port in India. Before the methanol had been loaded onto the ship the defendant threatened to refuse to deliver it unless the claimant paid an increased price. Christopher Clarke J held that the claimant was entitled to recover the increased price in the tort of intimidation,[30] as well as in restitution for economic duress.

5–017   The bringing of vexatious proceedings is capable of giving rise to a cause of action, in the tort of abuse of process.[31] On that basis, a threat to bring such proceedings would amount to an unlawful act for the purposes of an intimidation claim.[32] However, whilst all proceedings brought as an abuse of the court's process are liable to be struck out, not all such proceedings will amount to the tort of abuse of process. The distinction is important, if the conduct threatened must

---

[26] An example along these lines was given in *Rookes v Barnard* [1964] A.C. 1129, per Lord Evershed at 1188; per Lord Devlin at 1208–1209.

[27] See *News Group Newspapers Ltd v SOGAT (No.2)* [1987] I.C.R. 181, at 204: "If a threat is little more than idle abuse and is not to be taken seriously, then it would not be sufficient to found an action for intimidation."

[28] See generally *Rookes v Barnard* [1964] A.C. 1129 in which the House of Lords overturned the decision of the Court of Appeal that threatened breaches of contract were not included within the tort.

[29] *Kolmar Group AG v Traxpo Enterprises Pvt Ltd* [2010] 1 All E.R. (Comm) 46.

[30] *Kolmar Group AG v Traxpo Enterprises Pvt Ltd*, above, at [119]–[121].

[31] See the discussion of the principles by Nugee J in *Holyoake v Candy* [2017] EWHC 3397 (Ch), at [413]–[431].

[32] *Global Asset Capital Inc v Aabar Block SARL* [2016] EWHC 298 (Comm), per Walker J at [181]–[182]; *Holyoake v Candy*, above, at [412].

be actionable by the claimant in order to give rise to liability for the threat itself. The decision in *Global Asset Capital Inc v Aabar Block SARL* appears to have proceeded on the basis that only threatened conduct which would give rise to a cause of action in tort will suffice.[33] On the basis of the principles discussed in the next section below, this is considered to be the correct view.

It is not necessary for the threatened unlawful act to be one actually to be carried out by the party who threatens the claimant, so long as the threat is understood by the claimant in such a way as to indicate that the defendant has the power to cause the unlawful act to be carried out.[34] Thus in *Berezovsky v Abramovich*, the deletion by amendment of an allegation that Mr Abramovich was liable as a joint tortfeasor with the Russian president Vladimir Putin (in circumstances where the threat was of expropriation by order of the president) was held not to be fatal to Mr Berezovsky's cause of action. It was not necessary to plead any actual relationship between Mr Abramovich and Mr Putin, only a threat by the former to work with the latter to expropriate Mr Berezovsky's assets. It is nevertheless considered that, in such a scenario, the carrying out of the threat would have to involve the threatening party in an unlawful act, though this would almost invariably be the case where that party caused the unlawful act of another.[35] Longmore LJ in the Court of Appeal held that a threat of unlawful action by a third party would usually carry with it the implication that the defendant would do what he could to ensure that such unlawful action occurred.[36] **5–018**

(ii)   Acts which would not be actionable by the claimant

What is less clear is whether acts which would not themselves be actionable by the claimant give rise to a cause of action if threatened as part of an intimidatory course of conduct. On the one hand, there is support in the authorities for the proposition that any act which is unlawful, whether viewed through the eyes of the criminal or civil law, can give rise to liability in intimidation. In *Rookes v Barnard*,[37] the House of Lords treated it as axiomatic that a threat of a crime would suffice. Although *Rookes v Barnard* was a case of three-party intimidation, it was clearly the view of at least Lord Evershed[38] that the same principles applied to two-party intimidation. In the most recent case directly to consider the principles of the tort of intimidation, *Berezovsky v Abramovich*, it was common ground that criminal acts were within the purview of the tort.[39] **5–019**

---

[33] *Global Asset Capital Inc v Aabar Block SARL* [2016] EWHC 298 (Comm), at [193].

[34] *Berezovsky v Abramovich* [2010] EWHC 647 (Comm), at [163]–[164], citing Lord Devlin in *Rookes v Barnard* [1964] A.C. 1129, at 1211, holding that the tort of intimidation could not be committed "unless the intimidator has or is believed by the party threatened to have the coercive power which is the essence of the tort".

[35] For example, as an accessory to a criminal offence, for inducing breach of contract, or as a joint tortfeasor.

[36] [2011] 1 W.L.R. 2290, at [82]; Stanley Burnton and Laws LJJ agreed.

[37] *Rookes v Barnard* [1964] A.C. 1129, in particular per Lord Evershed at 1182, 1188, per Lord Devlin at 1206. The other members of the House also talked in general terms of a distinction between lawful and unlawful acts.

[38] *Rookes v Barnard* [1964] A.C. 1129, at 1182–1183.

[39] *Berezovsky v Abramovich* [2010] EWHC 647 (Comm), at [187].

5–020   On the other hand, there are several reasons of principle why, at least in two-party intimidation cases, the ambit of threatened unlawful acts should be limited to those acts which would, if carried out, be actionable by the claimant. For example:

(1)   If unlawful acts extend as far as crimes and other unlawful acts which would not be actionable in private law by the claimant (for example, acts actionable only by a third party), the tort of intimidation allows a claimant to claim damages for loss suffered as a result of a threat by the defendant to carry out an act which, if the defendant had simply carried it out without threatening to do so, would give the claimant no cause of action. In principle this is anomalous, unless it is considered that the tortious nature of such conduct consists in the combination of the threat (with its associated demand) and the unlawfulness (in whatever sense) of the threatened conduct.[40]

(2)   Whilst complete coherence across the economic torts will be impossible unless the law is re-written, to limit unlawful acts to those which would be actionable by the claimant would give at least some consistency to the principles governing two- and three-party intimidation. As explained above, three-party intimidation is now subsumed within the tort of unlawful interference, following *OBG Ltd v Allan*,[41] in which it was held that, to qualify as unlawful means for the tort of unlawful interference, conduct must be actionable by the third party through whom the defendant injures the claimant.[42]

(3)   On the other hand, the need (in a three-party case) for the conduct to be actionable by the third party might be said to be a separate issue from the question of what type of threat would be actionable by the third party, so that consistency of this sort is not required. In other words, to hold that non-actionable conduct is, when threatened, actionable as intimidation, is simply to say that, if threatened against a third party, such conduct would therefore satisfy the requirement of actionability by the third party to allow recovery by the indirect victim in unlawful interference.

(4)   It might also be said that actionability is in principle irrelevant: the premise of the tort of intimidation is that the claimant does something (or avoids doing something) which causes him loss in order to avoid the defendant carrying out his threatened unlawful act in the first place. It is this that gives the claimant a cause of action, rather than the unlawful act (which will ex hypothesi not be committed if the defendant's threat achieves its purpose).

5–021   If non-actionable criminal conduct is within the tort of intimidation, then this opens up the possibility of liability to the claimant for threatening civil wrongs against a third party. Although this might be said to involve an unjustifiable

---

[40] As in the analogous crime of blackmail: see paras 5–027—5–029 below.
[41] *OBG Ltd v Allan* [2007] UKHL 21; [2008] 1 A.C. 1. As also explained above, Lord Hoffmann expressly excluded cases of two-party intimidation from his consideration: see [61].
[42] At [49].

extension of liability, a claim for unlawful means conspiracy can be founded on civil wrongs which are only actionable by third parties,[43] and accordingly it cannot be said that there is no basis in principle for such an extension.

These questions are not easily answered, and their resolution will have to await judicial consideration. In practice, however, most threats against a claimant will involve conduct actionable by him, not least because a wrong threatened against the claimant himself is much more likely to have coercive effect than a wrong threatened against a third party.[44] And threatened conduct which amounts to a crime (such as violence in particular) will very often amount to a tort civilly actionable by the claimant as well.

5–022

(iii)   Lawful acts

Conversely, to threaten to do that which you have a right to do cannot constitute the tort of intimidation. As Lord Reid said in *Rookes v Barnard*:

5–023

> "there is a chasm between doing what you have a legal right to do and doing what you have no legal right to do, and there seems to me to be the same chasm between threatening to do what you have a legal right to do and threatening to do what you have no legal right to do."[45]

(iv)   "Illegitimate" acts

In *Berezovsky v Abramovich* the parties agreed, purely for the purpose of an interlocutory appeal,[46] that the threatened action did not need to be technically unlawful, if it could be categorised as "illegitimate". The court did not rule on this issue but assumed for the purpose of the determination of the appeal that it was correct. The concept of "illegitimate" acts is drawn from the law of duress, where, as discussed below at Ch.15 it has been held that the pressure brought to bear on the claimant need not be unlawful for it to constitute duress, provided that it is "illegitimate".[47]

5–024

---

[43] See paras 2–062—2–067.

[44] Though the example of a threat of physical violence against members of the claimants' family, which is by no means unheard of in the context of international commercial disputes, provides a possible exception.

[45] *Rookes v Barnard*, above, at 1168–1169. And see also per Lord Devlin at 1207: "The essence of the offence is coercion. It cannot be said that every form of coercion is wrong. A dividing line must be drawn and the natural line runs between what is lawful and unlawful as against the party threatened." See also *Sorrell v Smith* [1925] A.C. 700, at 730 per Lord Dunedin: "Expressing the matter in my own words, I would say that a threat is a pre-intimation of proposed action of some sort. That action must be either per se a legal action or an illegal, i.e., a tortious action. If the threat used to effect some purpose is of the first kind, it gives no ground for legal proceeding; if of the second, it falls within the description of illegal means, and the right to sue of the person injured is established."

[46] *Berezovsky v Abramovich* [2011] EWCA Civ 153; [2011] 1 W.L.R. 2290, at [5].

[47] See generally *CTN Cash & Carry Ltd v Gallaher Ltd* [1994] 4 All E.R. 714, at 718–719 where it was held that the courts are willing to apply a standard of impropriety rather than technical unlawfulness; so that the critical inquiry will be not whether the conduct is lawful but whether it is morally or socially unacceptable. Examples include *Thorne v Motor Trade Association* [1937] A.C. 797, at 806–807 and *Mutual Finance Ltd v John Wetton & Sons Ltd* [1937] 2 K.B. 389.

5–025   However, at first instance, the issue was a live one between the parties. It was argued by the claimant that in two-party intimidation, as opposed to three-party intimidation, "illegitimate" conduct was sufficient to found the tort. This was defined as a threat of:

> "conduct not amounting to a criminal act, tort, breach of contract or of fiduciary duty which causes and is intended to cause the claimant to act in such a way that he suffers loss or damages."

The judge, Sir Anthony Colman, held[48]:

> "Whether a threat of conduct towards a claimant which is neither a crime, nor a tort, nor a breach of contract or of fiduciary duty is capable of founding a claim in tort, even if made for the purpose of damaging the claimant, with the effect that he is induced to act in such a way that he suffers loss, is, in my view, extremely doubtful. No decision of the English courts has gone that far and it is, in my view, very improbable that the law will develop in that way. For that would render substantial areas of trade competition vulnerable to potential tortious liability. However, if outside the field of legitimate competition, such threats were made exclusively in order to inflict loss on the claimant, it may be that the courts will provide a remedy going beyond restitution and going as far as damages."

5–026   This was a decision on an amendment application, and the point was judged sufficiently arguable to be pleaded and determined at trial. Although some uncertainty arises as a result of the decisions in *Berezovsky v Abramovich*, it is suggested that the ambit of the tort of intimidation was circumscribed in *Rookes v Barnard* and that it is clear from that decision that the threatened act has to be in itself unlawful (with the question mark identified above as to whether criminal unlawfulness is sufficient).[49] In addition, in the context of duress the question is whether C's will was coerced because of pressure which the court must evaluate as legitimate or illegitimate; there is no other benchmark for liability. In intimidation on the other hand, the court simply has to decide whether or not the defendant was entitled to do what he threatened to do. Since there is no recognised cause of action for the taking of "illegitimate" action against the claimant (and it is almost impossible to see how the parameters of such a cause of action could be set), it is thought that there is no justification for recognising a threat of "illegitimate" action as giving rise to a cause of action.

---

[48] *Berezovsky v Abramovich* [2010] EWHC 647 (Comm), at [190].

[49] It was so held at first instance in *Dawson v Bell*, appended to the Court of Appeal judgment [2016] EWCA Civ 96; [2016] B.C.L.C. 59, at Annex A [125], quoting Atkin LJ in *Ware and De Freville Ltd v Motor Trade Association* [1921] 3 K.B. 40, at 87: "an intimation that a man is going to do what he lawfully may do is not a threat." M. Jones (ed), *Clerk & Lindsell on Torts*, 22nd edn (London: Sweet & Maxwell, 2017), para.24–63 disputes that "illegitimate" acts can found a claim in intimidation. The point was pursued on appeal in *Dawson v Bell*, above, but did not need to be decided since the appeal failed on other grounds.

(v)   Blackmail

There is substantial possible overlap in principle between criminal liability in **5–027** blackmail and civil liability in intimidation, at least where the "menaces"[50] used involve a threat of a civil wrong against the claimant himself.

A more difficult question is whether conduct amounting to the offence of blackmail is sufficient to satisfy the "unlawful act" element of the tort, even where the conduct threatened is in itself lawful. In other words, is there an exception to the requirement that the conduct threatened must be unlawful, where the threat itself is unlawful? In *Al Nehayan v Kent*,[51] Leggatt LJ (sitting in the High Court) held that the answer is yes. Reasoning that

> "where a victim of blackmail succumbs to the blackmailer's demand and thereby suffers loss, it would be a serious defect in the common law if it did not afford a civil remedy in damages",

the judge went on to hold that blackmail was covered by the tort of intimidation on the basis that "the tort encompasses actual unlawful conduct by one person to another, as well as threatened unlawful conduct".[52]

Strictly speaking, this part of the decision in *Al Nehayan* is obiter, since Leggatt **5–028** LJ had in any event found threats of violence to have been made, coercing the claimant into action which caused him loss. It remains to be seen whether his reasoning will gain traction. There are certain difficulties with it, even recognising the desirability in principle of the extension in the law which Leggatt LJ articulated. First, there is no prior reported case recognising the existence of blackmail as a tort; and in an unreported decision in 1997, the Court of Appeal held (albeit without analysis of principle or authority) that no such tort existed.[53] To recognise blackmail as giving rise to liability in the tort of intimidation where actual coercion and loss are proven would cut across that decision.

Secondly, there is no doubt that the decision in *Al Nehayan* creates an inroad into **5–029** the principle that a defendant can only be liable in intimidation if the conduct he threatens is unlawful. Even leaving aside the issues outlined above in relation to the ambit of unlawful acts, a recognition of concurrent liability would allow the imposition of liability in tort for threatening a lawful act[54] (such as a threat by the defendant to expose the claimant's extra-marital affair to his wife unless the

---

[50] Section 21(1) of the Theft Act 1968 provides that the crime of blackmail is committed where an unwarranted demand with menaces is made by the defendant with a view to gain for himself or another or with intent to cause loss to another.

[51] *Al Nehayan v Kent* [2018] EWHC 333 (Comm), at [227]–[231].

[52] The judge relied on a passage in the judgment of Steyn LJ in *Godwin v Uzoigwe* [1993] Fam. Law 65 to the effect that both assaults and threats of assault fell to be regarded, in the circumstances of that case, as subsumed under the tort of intimidation.

[53] *Sanray Export Services Ltd v National Westminster Bank Plc*, unreported, 26 June 1997 CA, Lexis Citation 3746. The appellant was unrepresented and the respondent did not appear.

[54] See *Thorne v Motor Trade Association* [1937] A.C. 797, at 806–807, per Lord Atkin: "The ordinary blackmailer normally threatens to do what he has a perfect right to do – namely, communicate some compromising conduct to a person whose knowledge is likely to affect the person threatened. Often indeed he has not only the right but also the duty to make the disclosure, as of a felony, to the competent authorities. What he has to justify is not the threat, but the demand of money. The gravamen of the charge is the demand without reasonable or probable cause: and I cannot think

claimant pays him money). But this would require the law to straddle the "chasm" between threatening to do what you have a legal right to do and threatening to do what you have no legal right to do, which in *Rookes v Barnard*[55] Lord Reid considered (like many judges before him) to form the bright line which determines civil liability in any given case. It is considered doubtful whether the fact that blackmail is a crime is enough in itself to put the defendant who threatens a lawful act on the wrong side of the line. To say this makes all the difference would be to conflate the different legal underpinnings of the crime and the tort: the crime is committed on the making of the threat, whereas the cause of action in intimidation depends also on the threat being effective and the claimant suffering loss as a result.[56] Recognising blackmail as a narrowly-confined exception to the usual principle might reduce these anomalies, but it would not eliminate them.

(vi)   Must the defendant know that the conduct he threatens is wrongful?

5–030   In the context of economic duress, a threat made in good faith will not be considered "illegitimate" so as to give rise to liability. So, in *CTN Cash and Carry Ltd v Gallaher Ltd*[57] the defendants wrongly believed that title in certain goods had passed to the claimant making it liable to pay for them, and proceeded to threaten withdrawal of the claimant's credit facility unless payment was made. The defendants' good faith (among other things) prevented them from being liable in economic duress.[58] It has since been suggested on the basis of the decision in *CTN* that, where a threat is made in good faith, there can be no liability in tort for intimidation.[59] If this is correct, it may involve recognition of a defence to liability where the defendant wrongly believes that the conduct he threatens is lawful. Similar issues have been debated in the decisions on other economic torts.[60] By analogy with the reasoning which prevails in the context of unlawful means conspiracy and unlawful interference, it is suggested that ignorance of the law in this sense should not amount to a defence.

---

that the mere fact that the threat is to do something a person is entitled to do either causes the threat not to be a 'menace' within the Act or in itself provides a reasonable or probable cause for the demand."

[55] [1964] A.C. 1129, at 1168–1169.

[56] An analogous distinction may be drawn between criminal and civil conspiracies: see para.2–140.

[57] *CTN Cash and Carry Ltd v Gallaher Ltd* [1994] 4 All E.R. 714, at 718 and 719.

[58] In addition, the defendants' withdrawal of their credit facilities was lawful.

[59] *Berezovsky v Abramovich* [2010] EWHC 647 (Comm), at [189].

[60] See paras 2–077—2–083 (conspiracy), 3–063—3–065 (inducing breach of contract) and 4–032—2–033 (unlawful interference).

C.   INTENTION

(1)   Intention to Coerce

Intimidation is a tort of intentionality. Hence it must be proved that the defendant **5–031**
intended by his words that the claimant be coerced into taking a step or desisting
from taking a step which he would otherwise not have taken (or would have
taken, as the case may be). This aspect of intention is inherent within the notion
of coercion. As Lord Denning MR put it in *JT Stratford & Son v Lindley*,[61] the
threat

> "must be intended to coerce a person into doing something that he is unwilling to do or not
> doing something that he wishes to do."

More recently the need for an intention to coerce was recognised by the Court of
Appeal in *Berezovsky v Abramovich*.[62] As to the degree of intention required, it is
considered that the analysis in Ch.4 on unlawful interference is equally applicable
to the question of intention to coerce in the tort of intimidation.[63]

(2)   Intention to Cause Loss

It also seems that an intention to injure (in the sense of causing loss to) the **5–032**
claimant is necessary. This aspect of the requirement of intention was not
specifically mentioned in the summary of the elements of the tort in *Berezovsky v
Abramovich*.[64] However, in each of the three prior reported cases of two-party
intimidation, an intention to cause loss to the claimant was cited as a necessary
element of the cause of action.[65] This does not mean that the defendant needs to
be actuated by any spite or malice towards the claimant; merely that there was an
intention to cause loss which—again—it is considered carries the same meaning
as in the context of unlawful interference; the principles are considered, at paras
4–039—4–043. In the three-party tort, of course, those principles apply directly.

D.   ACTUAL COERCION

The threat must, as a matter of causation, actually coerce the claimant into **5–033**
complying with the threat. If the claimant resists the threat or takes the step which
founds the claim for reasons other than the coercive effect of the threat then he is
not coerced in the relevant way. We deal with the concept of coercion in the
context of a consideration of the law of duress, at Ch.15 below. It is not thought

---

[61] *JT Stratford & Son Ltd v Lindley* [1965] A.C. 269, at 283G–284A.

[62] *Berezovsky v Abramovich* [2010] EWCA Civ 153; [2011] 1 W.L.R. 2290, at [5], referring to the
parties' agreement on this point with approval.

[63] See paras 4–039—4–043.

[64] *Berezovsky v Abramovich* [2010] EWCA Civ 153; [2011] 1 W.L.R. 2290, at [5].

[65] *News Group Newspapers Ltd v SOGAT (No.2)* [1987] I.C.R. 181, at 204; *Godwin v Uzoigwe*
[1993] Fam. Law 65, per Stuart-Smith LJ and Steyn LJ; *Kolmar Group AG v Traxpo Enterprises Pvt
Ltd* [2011] 1 All E.R. (Comm) 46, at [119]. See, to the same effect, *Dawson v Bell*, appended at [2016]
EWCA Civ 96; [2016] 2 B.C.L.C. 59, Annex A at [125], per HHJ Havelock-Allan QC.

that the law differs in relation to the tort of intimidation and the two were assumed to be the same by the Court of Appeal in *Dawson v Bell*.[66] In the specific context of intimidation, it has been suggested that the threat must be the "effective cause" of the action taken by the claimant to his detriment.[67] Where the threat is one of violence, however, Leggatt LJ (sitting in the High Court) has held that the test for causation is the same as in the law of duress by threat of violence. In this particular context it is sufficient for the threat to have been "a" cause of the claimant's action, even if the claimant might well have acted in the same way without the threat.[68]

5–034　　As with most other torts damage is the gist of the action and so the tort of intimidation is not complete unless the person threatened succumbs to the threat and damage is suffered. Nonetheless, in keeping with the law on quia timet injunctions, injunctive relief can be granted to restrain the threatened unlawful act.[69]

E. DAMAGE

5–035　　There is no reported decision on the principles applicable to the assessment of damages in two-party intimidation cases. It is considered, however, that the principles governing the award of damages for unlawful interference will generally apply: see paras 4–046—4–050. The decision of the Court of Appeal in *Godwin v Uzoigwe*[70] suggests that aggravated and exemplary damages may be awarded in an appropriate case. Whilst of limited practical relevance to the fraud practitioner, the same case shows that awards in the nature of general damages for pain, suffering, distress and humiliation are in principle available for intimidation, which thus expands the cause of action for intimidation beyond the immediate confines of the economic torts.

---

[66] *Dawson v Bell* [2016] EWCA Civ 96; [2016] 2 B.C.L.C. 59, at [32]: "neither a defence to a contractual claim nor a claim in tort can succeed unless it is shown that the will of the 'victim' has been coerced. The practical effect of the pressure must be compulsion or the absence of choice."

[67] *Holyoake v Candy* [2017] EWHC 3397 (Ch), at [411].

[68] *Al Nehayan v Kent* [2018] EWHC 333 (Comm), at [232]–[233], referring back to the judge's earlier conclusions on duress, at [190]. There was, however, no argument on the point.

[69] *News Group Newspapers Ltd v SOGAT (No.2)*, above, at 205.

[70] *Godwin v Uzoigwe* [1993] Fam. Law 65. Although the amount awarded by the trial judge was varied on appeal, no doubt was cast on his conclusion that aggravated and exemplary damages are available.

CHAPTER 6

MALICIOUS FALSEHOOD

A. INTRODUCTION

(1) History and Context

The law of malicious falsehood is complex in its historical origins and accordingly idiosyncratic in its ambit.[1] The tort (or set of overlapping torts) has, over the centuries, been known by various titles,[2] but the judicial search for a guiding principle has led to the now universal adoption of the title of malicious falsehood. It is in essence one of the economic torts, whose principal use has historically been—and remains—to protect businesses from false disparagement by trade competitors or rivals. Accordingly it is not classically a tort which has a central place in the civil law of fraud. A recent, and typical, example of the use of malicious falsehood is the case of *Ajinomoto Sweeteners Europe v Asda Stores Ltd*,[3] where the defendant marked on a range of its health food products the words "no hidden nasties; no artificial colours or flavours and no aspartame". The manufacturers of aspartame, a sugar substitute and lawful food additive, concerned that the defendant's packaging would harm the market for its product, claimed for malicious falsehood, asserting that the defendants had falsely stated that its product was harmful or unhealthy. However, whilst the tort of malicious falsehood is most usually deployed in litigation between businesses, it has been successfully asserted by individual claimants in relation to personal matters.[4]

6–001

Nonetheless malicious falsehood deserves some treatment in a book on civil fraud: one ingredient of the tort is malice which, as we will see, involves proof of a similar mental state to that in the tort of deceit, and the tort is designed to protect against deception. Much of the legal intricacy of the law of malicious falsehood relates to the extent to which the relevant statement must identify the

6–002

---

[1] An account of the historical development of the tort is to be found in H. Carty, *An Analysis of the Economic Torts*, 2nd edn (Oxford: OUP, 2010), p.200 and following.

[2] Such as slander of title, slander of goods, trade libel and injurious falsehood: see *Joyce v Sengupta* [1993] 1 W.L.R. 337, at 341.

[3] For an account of the proceedings, which appear to have been compromised prior to trial, see: *Ajinomoto Sweeteners Europe v Asda Stores Ltd* [2009] EWHC 1717 (QB); [2010] Q.B. 204.

[4] Famously in *Kaye v Robertson* [1991] F.S.R. 62 where a television actor was recuperating in hospital from an accident and was interviewed by a newspaper reporter who had managed to enter his private hospital room without permission. The claimant was in no fit state to consent to the interview. It was held that publishing a story which suggested that the claimant had consented to the interview would be an arguable malicious falsehood. Damages for malicious falsehood were awarded in *Khodaparast v Shad* [2000] 1 W.L.R. 618, where the defendant had distributed mocked up photographs purporting to show the claimant advertising sexual services in a magazine.

claimant or his property and how far self-promotion must verge into specific false disparagement of another to become actionable. These issues are not considered in depth here.[5] This chapter is designed to give an overview of the tort in the context of fraud claims.

(2) Summary of the Tort

6–003 The tort of malicious falsehood has been the subject of a process of rationalisation over the last century or so. The late 19th century decision of the Court of Appeal in *Ratcliffe v Evans*[6] is generally held to mark the birth of the modern law, as summarised in the classic dictum of Bowen LJ:

> "That an action will lie for written or oral falsehoods, not actionable per se nor even defamatory, where they are maliciously published, where they are calculated in the ordinary course of things to produce, and where they do produce, actual damage, is established law. Such an action is not one of libel or of slander, but an action on the case for damage wilfully and intentionally done without just occasion or excuse, analogous to an action for slander of title."

More recently it has been said that the object of the cause of action is to provide a person with a remedy for a false statement made maliciously which has caused him damage.[7]

(3) Connection with the Law of Defamation and Deceit

6–004 The same facts may give rise to causes of action in defamation and malicious falsehood, and indeed both claims are sometimes pleaded in the same proceedings.[8] Both torts involve the publication of untruths concerning the claimant. But they protect different interests. The tort of defamation protects a person's reputation and so, in order for the publication to be actionable it must disparage the reputation of the claimant in the eyes of "right-thinking people".[9] By contrast malicious falsehood protects economic interests. Accordingly a falsehood published about the claimant may be in no sense defamatory (a well-known case being where the defendant asserted that the claimant's business had closed down)[10] yet still be actionable if damage is caused. On the other hand, subject to well-established defences, defamation is a tort of strict liability, whereas the tort of malicious falsehood, as its name makes clear, requires proof

---

[5] See the analysis in H. Carty, *An Analysis of the Economic Torts* (2010), pp.206–210.

[6] [1892] 2 Q.B. 524, at 527.

[7] *Joyce v Sengupta* [1993] 1 W.L.R. 337.

[8] A recent example is *Dar Al Arkan v Al Refai* [2012] EWHC 3539 (Comm).

[9] A recent statement of the law is to be found in *Modi v Clarke* [2011] EWCA Civ 937, citing the famous dictum of Greer LJ in *Tolley v Fry* [1930] 1 K.B. 467, at 479: "Words are not defamatory, however much they may damage a man in the eyes of a section of the community unless they also amount to disparagement of his reputation in the eyes of right thinking men generally. To write or say of a man something that would disparage him in the eyes of a particular section of the community but will not affect his reputation in the eyes of the average right thinking man is not actionable within the law of defamation."

[10] *Joyce v Motor Services Ltd* [1948] Ch. 252.

of malice. Further, whereas in defamation claims the burden is placed upon the defendant to prove the truth of the matters published, no such assistance is extended to the claimant suing in malicious falsehood. The burden of proving both malice on the part of the defendant and the falsity of the statement said to have been published is squarely placed on the claimant.[11] It should be noted that the suggestion made in *Khodaparast v Shad*[12] that malicious falsehood is a branch of the law of defamation is historically inaccurate. The tort has an entirely separate juridical foundation.

The central difference between the torts of deceit and malicious falsehood lies in the fact that the former involves the deception of the claimant by the defendant and the taking of action consequent upon the deception which causes loss to the claimant; whereas the latter tort involves deception by the defendant of third parties, which in turn causes loss to the claimant.   **6–005**

B. ELEMENTS OF THE TORT

The tort of malicious falsehood may be broken down into a number of elements: **6–006**

(1) The publication by the defendant of words, whether orally or in writing (or communication by conduct);
(2) That those words (or the communication) are about the claimant or chattels produced by him or property belonging to him;
(3) The falsity of those words (or of the meaning conveyed by conduct);
(4) That the defendant published the words (or make the communication) maliciously;
(5) That the words were calculated to cause pecuniary damage or in fact have caused pecuniary damage.[13]

We consider each element in turn below.

(1) Publication

Publication is a well-known concept in the law of defamation and the applicable principles are the same in the context of malicious falsehood. The falsehood must be made to at least one third party (i.e. publication solely to the claimant will be   **6–007**

---

[11] It has also been established that the "single meaning" rule in defamation, whereby the words published are accorded their "natural and ordinary meaning" (*Slim v Daily Telegraph* [1968] 2 Q.B. 157) does not apply in malicious falsehood claims: see *Ajinomoto Sweeteners Europe SAS v Asda Stores Ltd* [2010] EWCA Civ 609; [2011] Q.B. 497 and *Cruddas v Calvert* [2013] EWCA Civ 748; [2014] E.M.L.R. 5, at [30], per Tugendhat J.

[12] *Khodaparast v Shad* [2000] 1 W.L.R. 618, at [42].

[13] See the statement of the elements of the tort in *Kaye v Robertson* [1991] F.S.R. 62, at 67 (with added numbering): "The essentials of this tort are that the defendant has [1] published about the plaintiff [2] words which are false, [3] that they were published maliciously, and [4] that special damage has followed as the direct and natural result of their publication. As to special damage, the effect of Section 3(1) of the Defamation Act 1952 is that it is sufficient if the words published in writing are calculated to cause pecuniary damage to the plaintiff."

insufficient). In the trade cases, often the publication complained of is in the form of advertising, packaging or prospectuses having wide circulation; i.e. there is publication in effect to the world.

6–008 As in the law of deceit a malicious falsehood may be made orally or in writing, and may be made by implication as well as expressly. A statement of opinion or value judgment is not actionable as a falsehood except on the basis that the defendant claims to hold an opinion which he does not in fact hold.[14] It is theoretically possible for a malicious falsehood to be made by conduct, though that is likely to be a rare case.

6–009 A defendant may be responsible for a publication not actually made by himself. For instance if the defendant publishes the falsehood to X without causing any loss to the claimant and X then re-publishes it to further persons, causing loss to the claimant, the defendant may be liable for the republication. The law has established a reasonable foreseeability test for establishing liability for such republications.[15]

(2) Relating to the Claimant

6–010 The words must relate to the claimant or to his goods, property or economic interests. The claimant himself need not be expressed mentioned, nor even his goods. Whether the publication sufficiently references the claimant will be a fact-sensitive question.[16] No complete statement of principle is possible. However the courts have taken an expansive view of the issue and have consistently held that specific reference to the claimant is unnecessary.[17]

---

[14] *Euromoney Institutional Investor Plc v Aviation New Ltd* [2013] EWHC 1505 (QB), at [102], per Tugendhat J. The judge continued, at [103] by drawing a parallel with the law of deceit: "The statement that a person holds an opinion is for the purposes of the law of misrepresentation and fraud treated as a statement of fact about that person's state of mind. There is no reason why it should be treated differently for the purposes of the law of malicious falsehood."

[15] See generally *McManus v Beckham* [2002] EWCA Civ 939; [2002] 1 W.L.R. 2982, at [34] and [43] (a case in slander: Victoria Beckham entered the claimant's celebrity memento shop asserting to the shoppers present that purported signatures of her husband were fakes; the allegations were reported to newspapers who published articles about the incident, resulting in an alleged downturn of business for the claimant's shop. It was held that the defendant was potentially liable for the loss sustained by the newspaper articles).

[16] Though extravagant, and knowingly false praise of his own products will not be actionable, as insufficiently connected to the claimant: *Schulke & Mayr UK Ltd v Alkapharm UK Ltd* [1999] F.S.R. 165, at 166.

[17] See generally *Marathon Mutual Ltd v Waters* [2009] EWHC 1931 (QB): [2010] E.M.L.R. 3, at [9c], per Judge Moloney QC: "the law must require that there be some reference, direct or indirect, in the words complained of to the claimant or to his business, property or other economic interests, though it is not necessary to go further and establish identification of the claimant in the minds of the publishees." See further *Riding v Smith* (1875-6) LR 1 Ex. D. 91 (a case in which the words accused the claimant's wife of adultery, but he was permitted to bring a claim for business losses occasioned by people shunning his draper's shop as a result, notwithstanding that the falsehood was not directed to him); *Serville v Constance* [1954] 1 All E.R. 662 and *Customglass v Salthouse* [1976] 1 N.Z.L.R. 36.

(3) Falsity

The claimant must prove that the words published were false. There is no presumption of falsity in favour of the claimant in this regard. The truth of the words published, however malicious the defendant's motives, will be an absolute defence to liability (although it may be, at least in principle, that the claimant would be able to succeed in another tort notwithstanding the truth of the words, such as conspiracy to injure).[18] Although the origins of the tort lie in notions of disparagement or denigration (whether of the claimant's goods or title to property), there is no such delimitation now. The falsehood need not in any sense be defamatory. Hence a false statement that the claimant was employed by the defendant, in itself wholly innocuous, was actionable as a malicious falsehood.[19]

6–011

However, when deciding whether the published words were false the court must consider the reasonably available meanings (if there are more than one), decide if a substantial number of persons would reasonably have understood the words to have such a meaning and then decide, in respect of a meaning which is in fact false and damaging, whether the author was actuated by malice (we consider this question below). In this regard the law of malicious falsehood is actually less constrained than the law of defamation, which, as is notorious, operates a "single meaning" rule.[20]

6–012

The courts have guarded against the use of malicious falsehood claims to arbitrate on comparative advertising complained of by the claimant. Assertions that one person's products or services are better than someone else's will be given wide latitude by the courts, who are reluctant to hold such statements actionable.[21]

6–013

---

[18] However, for policy reasons the law is fairly set against the idea of an actionable "conspiracy to tell the truth". Dillon LJ said in *Lonrho v Al Fayed (No. 5)* [1993] 1 W.L.R. 1489, at 1496, "it would in my judgment be lamentable if a plaintiff could recover damages against defendants who had combined to tell the truth about the plaintiff and so had destroyed his unwarranted reputation". See further Ch.4.

[19] *Balden v Shorter* [1933] Ch. 427.

[20] See *Cruddas v Calvert* [2013] EWCA Civ 748; [2014] E.M.L.R. 5, at [30]–[32]. At [32] Longmore LJ said: "It might appear that there is a tension, even an incompatibility, between the proposition that a particular meaning is plainly wrong and the proposition that it is nevertheless a possible meaning. The reason why it is not necessarily so lies in the difference between libel and malicious falsehood. In malicious falsehood every reasonably available meaning, damaging or not, has to be considered. In libel, the artifice of a putative single meaning requires the court to find an approximate centre-point in the range of possible meanings. If, instead, a court of first instance selects as the single meaning for libel purposes one of the peripheral meanings in the range relevant to malicious falsehood, an appellate court may very well be satisfied that it has erred, because the single meaning has, generally speaking, to be the (or a) dominant one."

[21] *White v Mellin* [1895] A.C. 154, at 165, where Lord Herschell deprecated the idea that "the Courts of law would be turned into a machinery for advertising rival productions by obtaining a judicial determination of which of the two was better"; and, more recently, see *Vodafone Group Plc v Orange Personal Communications Services Ltd* [1997] F.S.R. 34. The law on this area, which falls outside the ambit of this work, is analysed in detail in H. Carty, *An Analysis of the Economic Torts* (2010), pp.207–210.

(4) Malice

6–014   The claimant must prove that the defendant was actuated by malice. This is the central kernel of the action. Malice is tantamount to an accusation of fraud or dishonesty and therefore must be pleaded with precision. The courts are vigilant against formulaic assertions of malice.[22] Equally, they are vigilant to prevent any dilution of the hurdle required to be surmounted by a claimant in proving malice. Courts have been influenced by the protection accorded to free speech by art.10 of the European Convention on Human Rights to accord wide latitude to robust or partial assertions by defendants, especially in the fields of commerce and politics.[23] Malice may be established in two separate ways.

6–015   First, if the defendant knows that the statements published are false or is reckless as to their truth or falsity, then the required mental state will be established.[24] In this first sense malice approximates to the relevant mental state required to be proved in the law of deceit. Provided the defendant believed the truth of the statement, the fact that he did not have reasonable grounds for such belief will not matter.[25] On the other hand the absence of any desire on the part of the defendant to injure the claimant will not prevent liability arising if the defendant can be shown to have published the false words with the mental state set out above.

6–016   There is a second meaning of malice, which Hazel Carty describes as "motive malice"[26], i.e. an intention to harm the claimant (as opposed to an intention to promote the interests of the defendant). Such an intention may be founded upon

---

[22] On pleading malice see *Niche Products Ltd v MacDermid Offshore Solutions LLC* [2013] EWHC 3540 (IPEC), per Birss J at [55], and *Thompson v James* [2003] EWHC 515 (QB), per Tugendhat J at [16].

[23] See for instance *Quinton v Pierce* [2009] EWHC 912 (QB); [2009] F.S.R. 17 (an unsuccessful claim brought by a losing candidate against the victorious candidate in a local election over the contents of an electioneering leaflet).

[24] See *Wilts United Dairies v Robinson* [1957] RPC 220, at 237. However recklessness, in the sense of indifference to the truth, is not to be equated with carelessness, impulsiveness or irrationality in arriving at a positive belief that it is true. In his classic speech in *Horrocks v Lowe* [1975] A.C. 139, Lord Diplock said, at 149: "The freedom of speech protected by the law of qualified privilege may be availed of by all sorts and conditions of men. In affording to them immunity from suit if they have acted in good faith in compliance with a legal or moral duty or in protection of a legitimate interest the law must take them as it finds them. In ordinary life it is rare indeed for people to form their beliefs by a process of logical deduction from facts ascertained by a rigorous search for all available evidence and a judicious assessment of its probative value. In greater or in less degree according to their temperaments, their training, their intelligence, they are swayed by prejudice, rely on intuition instead of reasoning, leap to conclusions on inadequate evidence and fail to recognise the cogency of material which might cast doubt on the validity of the conclusions they reach. But despite the imperfection of the mental process by which the belief is arrived at it may still be 'honest,' that is, a positive belief that the conclusions they have reached are true. The law demands no more." Although this was said in the context of malice in a libel action, to defeat a plea of qualified privilege, the analysis is equally applicable to malicious falsehood actions.

[25] *Khader v Aziz* [2009] EWHC (QB), at [31]–[32]. As in the law of deceit, if a defendant believes that the words he is publishing bear one meaning, in which he has an honest belief, it would not necessarily be sufficient to establish malice on his part if the court were to find that his words bore a different meaning, in the truth of which he had no belief: see *Loveless v Earl* [1999] E.M.L.R. 530 and *Cruddas v Calvert* [2015] EWCA Civ 171, at [114].

[26] Op cit, p.212.

ill-will or spite against the claimant; or some other improper motive.[27] This will be sufficient to found the tort of malicious falsehood even if the defendant actually believes the facts alleged against the claimant to be true. So Stable J in *Wilts United Dairies v Robinson*[28] stated:

> "If you publish a statement which turns out to be false but which you honestly believe to be true, but you publish that statement, not for the purpose of protecting your own interest and achieving some advantage to yourself but for the purpose of doing him harm and it transpires, contrary to your belief, that the statement you believed to be true has turned out to be false, notwithstanding the bona fides of your belief because the object that you had in mind was to injure him and not to advantage yourself, you would be liable for injurious falsehood".[29]

In trade cases it will be in general very difficult to establish malice in this second meaning for the obvious reason that rival businesses are far more likely to be actuated by a desire to promote their own interests rather than injuring that of their competitor.[30] There is no concept of transferred malice. If the defendant is actuated by malice (i.e. an intention to injure) against X, that is not sufficient to found a claim in malicious falsehood by Y.[31]

6–017

(5) Damage

(i)   "Calculated to harm"

Finally it seems that the claimant must show that the false statement was "calculated to harm" the claimant. We say "it seems" because the authorities do not speak with one voice on the subject. It is sometimes said that proof of actual consequential economic loss is sufficient, or, where s.3 of the Defamation Act 1952 applies (as to which see below), the claimant can establish the tort by showing that the words were calculated to cause him pecuniary loss even in the absence of proof of actual loss.[32] On the other hand it has been stated that it is a separate and distinct element of the tort that the words are calculated to produce economic harm or injury.[33] We consider the meaning of this concept below. One also finds in the cases the suggestion that the loss in respect of which damages are

6–018

---

[27] See *Spring v Guardian Assurance* [1983] 2 All E.R. 273 in the Court of Appeal (the decision of the House of Lords did not touch on this point), where it was held that there was no distinction between the meaning of the word "malice" in malicious falsehood and defamation.

[28] *Wilts United Dairies v Robinson* [1957] RPC 220, at 237. See also *Halsey v Brotherhood* (1881) 19 Ch. D. 386, at 388.

[29] i.e. what is now described as malicious falsehood.

[30] "A plea of malice is a plea of dishonesty. In cases such as this, where the parties are competitors in business, a plea of malice in the form of intention to injure is difficult to sustain. Rival businesses intend to promote their own interests. The fact that to some extent business is a zero sum game means that promoting one business may result in harming another": *Euromoney Institutional Investor Plc v Aviation New Ltd* [2013] EWHC 1505 (QB), at [109], per Tugendhat J. See also per Collins MR in *Dunlop v Maison Talbot* (1904) 20 T.L.R. 579, at 581: "it [is] not malice if the object of the interference was to push his own business ... to make the act malicious it must be done with the direct object of injuring that other person's business".

[31] *Cruddas v Calvert* [2013] EWHC 1096 (QB), at [16]–[18].

[32] See for instance *Cruddas v Calvert* [2013] EWHC 1096 (QB), at [18].

[33] See for instance *Wilts United Dairies v Robinson* [1957] RPC 220, at 237; and *Kaye v Robertson* [1991] F.S.R. 62, at 67.

sought must be shown to be the direct or natural result of the false words. It is not clear whether this is some added hurdle; properly analysed it is suggested that it is a different formulation of the "calculated to harm" test.

(ii)   Need for proof of special damage?

6–019   At common law proof of special damage caused by the false words is required to complete the cause of action.[34]

> "Unless the plaintiff has in fact suffered loss which can be and is specified, he has no cause of action. The fact that the defendant has acted maliciously cannot supply the want of special damage, nor can a superfluity of malice eke out a case wanting in special damage."[35]

The law's insistence on special damage no doubt reflected a concern to prevent malicious prosecution being used as a proxy action to vindicate reputation (i.e. to trespass into the law of defamation) and to confine it to its origins as an action protecting economic interests.[36]

6–020   It might very well be difficult for the claimant to produce actual evidence of specific harm caused by the false words published by the defendant. As a result Parliament intervened to mitigate the rigour of the common law rule, in the form of s.3(1) of the Defamation Act 1952, which provides as follows:

> "In an action for slander of title, slander of goods or other malicious falsehood, it shall not be necessary to allege or prove special damage:
> (a)   if the words upon which the action is founded are calculated to cause pecuniary damage to the plaintiff and are published in writing or any other permanent for; or
> (b)   if the said words are calculated to cause pecuniary damage to the plaintiff in respect of any office, profession, calling, trade or business held or carried on by him at the time of the publication. "

6–021   On its face the phrase "calculated to cause pecuniary damage" is an elusive concept. (As we have seen this concept also has significance under the common law as, probably, a necessary element of the cause of action in malicious falsehood.) In fact it means no more than more likely than not to cause pecuniary damage.[37] Notwithstanding the use of the word "calculated", which in ordinary parlance suggests some element of subjective intention, the question thrown up

---

[34] The meaning of "special damage" was discussed in *Ratcliffe v Evans*, above.

[35] Lord Robertson emphasised this in *Royal Baking Powder Co v Wright Crossley & Co* (1900) 18 RPC 95, at 103.

[36] Although, as we have seen, the claim in malicious falsehood has to some extent managed to escape this restriction.

[37] See *Cruddas v Calvert* [2013] EWHC 2298 (QB), at [195]; *Tesla Motors v BBC* [2013] EWCA Civ 152, at [27]; *International Business Machines Corp v Web-Sphere Ltd* [2004] EWHC 529 (Ch); [2004] F.S.R. 39, at [74]. In the latter case, Lewison J followed *Ferguson v Associated Newspapers Ltd* (3 December 2001) where Gray J had held that, in the light of art.10 of the European Convention on Human Rights, which requires any restriction on the right of freedom of expression to be strictly justified as necessary in a democratic society, the word "calculated" should be interpreted as meaning "likely" or "probable", in an objective sense, rather than something which might well happen or was a possibility. Whether or not the words were "calculated" to cause the claimant pecuniary loss is a matter to be judged, not by reference to what might subsequently have happened, but rather as at the time of publication.

by the phrase is to be answered purely objectively.[38] Hence conduct is only calculated to cause damage within the meaning of s.3(1) of the Defamation Act 1952 if damage is, in the ordinary course of events, viewed objectively, likely to be caused by the conduct of which complaint is made.[39] When relying upon s.3 the claimant need not specify the amount of pecuniary loss which it is said the falsehoods were calculated to cause; nonetheless he must particularise the nature of the loss and the mechanism by which it is likely to be sustained.

Irrespective of whether the claimant is able to rely upon s.3, he must show a causal link between the false words published and loss sustained by him. This may be very difficult, especially where the actionable words are intermingled with other words which are not actionable and which have a similar tendency (e.g. commending the defendant's product relative to that of the claimant).[40] **6–022**

A claimant who relies upon s.3, because he is unable to prove any specific compensatable pecuniary loss, is not as a result restricted to nominal damages. The court is nonetheless entitled to award substantial damages, taking account of all the evidence available. **6–023**

If special damage can be shown, or the case can be brought within s.3 of the 1952 Act, damages may additionally be awarded for the claimant's anxiety, distress and injury to feelings (but not for injury to reputation, which is the sole preserve of the action in defamation). Aggravated damages may be awarded.[41] **6–024**

---

[38] Hence, rather oddly, in the *IBM* case, above, the claim in malicious falsehood was dismissed, because, although it was held that the defendant had intended to harm the claimant, the words published were not likely to cause harm: at [84].

[39] *Fage UK Ltd v Chobani UK Ltd* [2013] EWHC 630 (Ch), at [151].

[40] See the facts in *Niche Products Ltd v MacDermid Offshore Solutions LLC* [2013] EWHC 3540 (IPEC) in particular, at [49]–[54].

[41] See generally *Khodaparast v Shad* [2000] 1 W.L.R. 618, at [34] and following.

CHAPTER 7

BRIBERY

A. INTRODUCTION

(1) The Concept of Bribery

The concept of bribery has multiple applications in English law. The giving or **7–001**
receiving (or attempted giving or receiving) of a bribe can of course found
criminal liability both at common law and under statute.[1] In the civil context, a
bribe can be used as a basis for rescinding a contract or other transaction; it may
in some circumstances render a contract void; it can found a cause of action
sounding in damages or entitling the claimant to an account of profits; and
moneys or other value paid over as a bribe can be the subject of a proprietary or
restitutionary claim at the instance of the principal.[2]

English law takes a broad and stringent view of what constitutes a bribe for the **7–002**
purpose of civil claims and of the civil remedial consequences of a bribe.[3] This
derives from the traditional protectiveness which the law has shown towards
those who place trust and confidence in others to act for or on behalf of them in
connection with their relations with third parties. The starting point is that the
principal is entitled to be confident that his agent will act wholly in his interests
and that the agent's duty and interest will not be placed in actual or potential
conflict.[4] The payment or offer of a bribe tends to create such a conflict. It
deprives the principal, without his knowledge or informed consent, of the
disinterested advice which he is entitled to expect from his agent, free from the
potentially corrupting influence of an interest of his own. The law of bribery has
evolved over time, as an aspect of the law of agency and fiduciaries, so as to
serve the central purpose of ensuring that the agent's duty to his principal is not
corrupted.

The way that a bribe can corrupt an agent is perhaps best exemplified by the facts **7–003**
of one of the leading cases in the law of bribery, the Privy Council's decision in

---

[1] This chapter does not consider the very complex criminal law of bribery. See generally F. Horlick,
Lissack and Horlick on Bribery, 2nd edn (London: LNUK, 2014).
[2] Indeed, it would seem that the principal can sue the putative briber to recover monies promised but
not in fact paid as a bribe, at least where he adopts the transaction: see para.7–058.
[3] *Fiona Trust v Privalov* [2010] EWHC 3199 (Comm), at [70].
[4] *Daraydan Holdings Ltd v Solland International Ltd* [2005] EWHC 622 (Ch); [2005] Ch. 119, at
[52], per Lawrence Collins J: "An agent should not put himself in a position where his duty and
interest may conflict, and if bribes are taken by an agent, the principal is deprived of the disinterested
advice of the agent, to which the principal is entitled. Any surreptitious dealing between one principal
to a transaction and the agent of the other is a fraud on the other principal."

Mahesan v Malaysia Government Officers' Co-Operative Housing Society Ltd.[5] Land was for sale at $456,000. The land was attractive to the claimant principal. The defendant director and employee of the claimant connived with a third party (T) that T should purchase it and then sell it to the claimant for $944,000. T paid the sum of $122,000, being a proportion of the profit made on the turning of the property, to the defendant by way of bribe. The claimant was thereby deprived of the opportunity to purchase the land at the lower price. The defendant had been corrupted by the third party so that he breached his fiduciary duty to his principal by failing to inform it that the land was for sale at the lower price and instead procuring that the claimant purchase it for a higher price from his confederate. The case provides a good example of why English law has traditionally taken a rigorous approach to cases of bribery.

7–004   Indeed, according to James LJ, speaking in *Parker v McKenna*,[6] the prevention of bribery is vital "for the safety of mankind." Lord Templeman was hardly less forthright more than a century later when, in *Attorney General of Hong Kong v Reid*,[7] he referred to bribery as "an evil practice which threatens the foundations of any civilised society." In an age where virtually all business is conducted via some form of agency, whether that be a broker, director, employee etc., and so where the principal is dependent to a greater or lesser extent on the integrity of another, these statements have lost none of their relevance.[8] As we shall see, the rigour of the law applies not only to obvious cases of subornment, such as occurred in *Mahesan*, but also to cases where on the face of it there is no moral defalcation by the agent at all.

---

[5] *Mahesan v Malaysia Government Officers' Co-Operative Housing Society Ltd* [1979] A.C. 374.

[6] *Parker v McKenna* (1874) L.R. 10 Ch. App. 96, at 122–124. Similar sentiments were expressed 14 years later in the leading case of *Boston Deep Sea Fishing & Ice Co v Ansell* (1888) 39 Ch. D. 339, at 362, per Bowen LJ: "This is an age, I may say, when a large portion of the commercial world makes its livelihood by earning, and by earning honestly, agency commission on sales or other transactions, but it is also a time when a large portion of those who move within the ambit of the commercial world, earn, I am afraid, commission dishonestly by taking commissions not merely from their masters, but from the other parties with whom their master is negotiating, and with whom they are dealing on behalf of their master, and taking such commissions without the knowledge of their master or principal. There never, therefore, was a time in the history of our law when it was more essential that Courts of Justice should draw with precision and firmness the line of demarcation which prevails between commissions which may be honestly received and kept, and commissions taken behind the master's back, and in fraud of the master." For a modern statement of the continued relevance and importance of these principles, see *Imageview Management Ltd v Jack* [2009] EWCA Civ 63; [2009] 2 All E.R. 666, per Mummery LJ at [65].

[7] *Attorney General of Hong Kong v Reid* [1994] 1 A.C. 324, at 330.

[8] See most recently *FHR European Ventures LLP v Cedar Capital Partners LLC* [2014] UKSC 45; [2015] 1 A.C. 520, at [42], per Lord Neuberger: "Secret commissions are also objectionable as they inevitably tend to undermine trust in the commercial world. That has always been true, but concern about bribery and corruption generally has never been greater than it is now—see for instance, internationally, the OECD Convention on Combating Bribery of Foreign Public Officials in International Business Transactions 1999 and the United Nations Convention against Corruption 2003, and, nationally, the Bribery Acts 2010 and 2012. Accordingly, one would expect the law to be particularly stringent in relation to a claim against an agent who has received a bribe or secret commission."

Judicial pronouncements on the danger and evils of bribery are echoed outside of **7–005**
the courts. The Lord Chancellor and Secretary of State for Justice, Jack Straw,
when introducing the Bribery Bill in Parliament in 2009, stated that:

> "Bribery eats away at the heart of both business and public life and has no place in British
> commerce. It blights free and fair competition and adds to the cost of doing business. It is
> particularly harmful to trade and development in the fragile economies of the developing
> world."

The Bill was based on the Law Commission Report (LC. No. 313) *Reforming
Bribery* which opened as follows[9]:

> "The damage and inefficiency caused by corruption, in either financial or social terms, should
> not be underestimated. The effective combating of corrupt practices requires an effective law
> of bribery."[10]

The Report refers to the World Bank's estimate, itself dating back to 2004, that
more than US$ 1 trillion is paid in bribes annually.[11] That figure is likely to have
increased substantially since.

(2)   Fiduciary Basis of the Law of Bribery

Although it has been described as a wrong which "is sui generis and defies **7–006**
classification",[12] the law of bribery is, in its fundamentals, a manifestation of the
law of agency and fiduciary duties. Underlying it are three central equitable
principles: first, that an agent owes a fiduciary duty to his principal, because he is
someone who has undertaken to act for or on behalf of that principal in a
particular matter in circumstances which give rise to a relationship of trust and
confidence; secondly, as a result, an agent must not make a profit out of his trust
and must not place himself in a position where his duty and his interest may
conflict; thirdly, a fiduciary who acts for two principals with potentially
conflicting interests without the informed consent of both is in breach of the
fiduciary obligation of undivided loyalty—he puts himself in a position where his
duty to one principal may conflict with his duty to the other.[13] This is not to say
that the briber must necessarily stand in any particular relation with the bribed
agent. The litmus test is whether the payment creates a real risk of conflict
between the agent's fiduciary duty of loyalty to his principal and his own
personal interest or his perceived sense of duty to a third party.[14]

---

[9] Part 1 para.1.1.

[10] The resultant Bribery Act 2010 does not alter the civil law but extended the criminal law of bribery
significantly.

[11] World Bank, "The Costs of Corruption" (8 April 2004). These passages were quoted by Hamblen J
in *Nayyar v Denton Wilde Sapte* [2009] EWHC 3218 (QB); [2010] P.N.L.R. 15.

[12] *Mahesan v Malaysia Government Officers' Co-Operative Housing Society Ltd*, above, at 383.

[13] See generally *FHR European Ventures LLP v Cedar Capital Partners LLC* [2014] UKSC 45;
[2015] 1 A.C. 520, at [5]; *Bristol and West BS v Mothew* [1998] Ch. 1, at 18; and *Phipps v Boardman*
[1967] 2 A.C. 46, at 123. On these "core" fiduciary proscriptions more generally, see Ch.11.

[14] *Fiona Trust v Privalov* [2010] EWHC 3199 (Comm), at [73]; *Novoship (UK) Ltd v Mikhaylyuk*
[2012] EWHC 3586 (Comm), at [106].

7–007   We consider in Ch.11 the circumstances in which a relationship of fiduciary agency arises. Suffice it to say here that the law of bribery takes a broad approach to who constitutes an agent: it is not limited to those who have the authority to alter the legal relations of their principals, but extends to others (including those sometimes described as mere "canvassing agents") who are put in a position to influence or affect the principal's dealings with third parties.[15] In one leading case it was said that in this context "fiduciary relationship" is used "in a very loose, or at all events a comprehensive sense:"

> "… for the present purpose a 'fiduciary relation' exists (a) whenever the plaintiff entrusts to the defendant property, including intangible property as, for instance, confidential information, and relies on the defendant to deal with such property for the benefit of the plaintiff or for purposes authorised by him, and not otherwise … and (b) whenever the plaintiff entrusts to the defendant a job to be performed, for instance, the negotiation of a contract on his behalf or for his benefit, and relies on the defendant to procure for the plaintiff the best terms available."[16]

7–008   Nevertheless, the elasticity of the concept of a fiduciary agent in the bribery context should not be taken too far: the court should still engage in a careful analysis of the particular facts of the relationship between the principal and his putatively bribed agent (including, importantly, the terms of any relevant contract) to test whether, and if so in what respects, the policy and principle of the law of bribery is engaged.[17]

(3)   Definition of Bribery

7–009   The classic modern definition of a bribe is to be found in *Industries & General Mortgage Co Ltd v Lewis*,[18] where it was stated that a bribe was paid where:

> "(i) the person making the payment makes it to the agent of another person with whom he is dealing; (ii)…he makes it to that person knowing that that person is acting as the agent of the other person with whom he is dealing; and (iii)… he fails to disclose to the other person with whom he is dealing that he has made that payment to the person whom he knows to be the other person's agent."

7–010   This definition has subsequently been cited in a substantial number of first instance decisions.[19] A shorter encapsulation of it was provided in the later case

---

[15] In *Novoship (UK) Ltd v Mikhayluk* [2012] EWHC 3586 (Comm), Christopher Clarke J said, at [108]: "The recipient of the bribe (or the person at whose order the bribe is paid) must be someone with a role in the decision-making process in relation to the transaction in question e.g. as agent, or otherwise someone who is in a position to influence or affect the decision taken by the principal."

[16] *Reading v The King* [1949] 2 K.B. 232 (CA), per Asquith LJ at 236; confirmed in *Reading v The King* [1951] A.C. 507, per Lord Porter at 516.

[17] *Conway v Eze* [2018] EWHC 29 (Ch), at [96]–[115]. In that case it was held, per Judge Keyser QC, that a "property acquisition agent", who introduced a property deal to a purchaser (after the purchase price had been agreed in principle) and then facilitated the parties in reaching an exchange of contracts and had a limited authority to instruct solicitors to that end was not an agent in the sense required to engage the law of bribery.

[18] *Industries & General Mortgage Co Ltd v Lewis* [1949] 2 All E.R. 573, at 575, per Slade J.

[19] See e.g.: *Taylor v Walker* [1958] 1 Lloyd's Rep. 490, at 509–512; *Armagas v Mundogas* [1985] 1 Lloyd's Rep. 1, at 18; *Petrotrade Inc v Smith* [2000] 1 Lloyd's Rep. 486, at [16]; *Davis v Giladi*, unreported, 10 July 2000, at 20; *Boc Ltd v Youngman LLP* [2003] EWHC 776 (QB), at [34]; *Tesco*

of *Anangel Atlas Compania Naviera SA v Ishikawajima-Harima Heavy Industries Co Ltd*[20]: a bribe "consists of a promise or payment of commission or other inducement, which is given by a third party to an agent as such, and which is secret from his principal."

Two points about these definitions should be noted at the outset. First, they are in an important sense wider than the ordinary (and indeed criminal) concept of bribery, in that a bribe may be deemed paid even where the third party (C) is retaining the relevant agent (A) as his *own* agent, in circumstances where A is also acting as agent of another with whom he is dealing (B) and the payment by C to A gives rise to a risk of conflict with A's duties to B; and even if C does not intend by making the payment to suborn A in the performance of his duties to B.[21] In such a case the term "secret commission" has been said to be the more appropriate one[22]; but the payment (or promise of it) is nevertheless a bribe for the civil law purposes considered in this chapter.[23] What makes it so is the risk of conflict and the fact that the payment is kept secret from B. As a result the statement in *A-G for Hong Kong v Reid*[24] that a "bribe is a gift accepted by a fiduciary as an inducement to him to betray his trust" is stated too narrowly. The most recent judicial attempt at a definition, and, it is suggested, the most helpful and accurate, is to be found in the first instance judgment of Christopher Clarke J in *Novoship (UK) Ltd v Mikhaylyuk*[25]:

7–011

Stores v Pook [2003] EWHC 823, at [38]–[40]; *Nayyar v Denton* [2009] EWHC 3218, at [85]; *Fiona Trust v Privalov* [2010] EWHC 3199 (Comm), at [70]; *SoS for Justice v Topland* [2011] EWHC 983, at [56]; *Bank of Ireland v Jaffery* [2012] EWHC 1377, at [295] and [388]; *Novoship v Mikhaylyuk* [2012] EWHC 3586, at [104]; *Conway v Eze* [2018] EWHC 29 (Ch), at [127]. The latter case contains a thorough analysis of how Slade J's definition is consistent with prior Court of Appeal authority in *Panama and South Pacific Telegraph Co v India Rubber, Gutta Percha, and Telegraph Works Co* (1875) L.R. 10 Ch. App. 515; *Shipway v Broadwood* [1899] 1 Q.B. 369; *Hovenden and Sons v Millhoff* (1900) 83 L.T. 41 and *Re a Debtor* [1927] 2 Ch 367.

[20] *Anangel Atlas Compania Naviera SA v Ishikawajima-Harima Heavy Industries Co Ltd* [1990] 1 Lloyd's L.R. 166, at 169, per Leggatt J.

[21] As for example was the position in *FHR European Ventures LLP v Mankarious* [2011] EWHC 2308 (Ch); [2012] 2 B.C.L.C. 39 (Simon J), where the agent was retained by a vendor to sell a hotel and was also retained by the purchaser; the purchaser nevertheless recovered the commission which the agent received from the vendor.

[22] See P.G. Watts (ed), *Bowstead and Reynolds on Agency*, 21st edn (London: Sweet & Maxwell, 2017), para.6–085.

[23] Because an intent to suborn or corrupt another's agent by the payment is not a necessary element of a bribe as the civil law understands it: see para.7–016 and following below. Secret commissions and bribes are for these purposes the same: see e.g. *Hurstanger Ltd v Wilson* [2007] EWCA Civ 299; [2007] 1 W.L.R. 2351, at [38], per Tuckey LJ: "the payment or receipt of a secret commission is considered to be a form of bribe and is treated in the authorities as a special category of fraud in which it is unnecessary to prove motive, inducement or loss up to the amount of the bribe." See also *Airbus Operations Ltd v Withey* [2014] EWHC 1126 (QB), per HHJ Havelock-Allan QC, at [88]; *Conway v Eze* [2018] EWHC 29 (Ch), at [117]; and Watts (ed), *Bowstead and Reynolds on Agency* (2017), at [8–222].

[24] *A-G for Hong Kong v Reid* [1994] 1 A.C. 324, at 330.

[25] *Novoship (UK) Ltd v Mikhaylyuk* [2012] EWHC 3586 (Comm), at [106].

"The essential character of a bribe is, thus, that it is a secret payment or inducement that gives rise to a realistic prospect of a conflict between the agent's personal interest and that of his principal."[26]

7–012   Secondly, although paradigmatically payment of a bribe will be made or offered in the context of a proposed contractual dealing between the payer of the bribe and the agent's principal, there is no requirement that there should be such a dealing, let alone that it should lead to a concluded contract. In fact, there have been occasions where the law has attached legal consequences to bribes which do not meet any such requirement. So in *Reading v Attorney General*[27] the claimant was a sergeant in the British forces stationed in Cairo and was paid money by smugglers to assist in the illicit transportation of spirits whereby he accompanied the lorries in uniform so as to avoid their inspection by the relevant authorities. The claimant's behaviour was a plain breach of his duties to his employer. The Crown was held entitled to seize the proceeds of such activity notwithstanding that it had not entered into any arrangement with the payer of the bribes. The bribes paid to Reading did not fall within the definition set out in *Industries & General Mortgage Co Ltd v Lewis* quoted above. Similarly in *Attorney General of Hong Kong v Reid*[28] the defendant was a lawyer employed by the Government of Hong Kong as a senior prosecutor who had taken sums of money from prospective criminal defendants in return for obstructing their prosecutions. Again the claimant was entitled to recover these sums as bribes received by Reid. A further recent example in the commercial context is *Petrotrade Inc v Smith*,[29] in which the claimant oil traders chartered vessels on terms which allowed them to nominate port agents. The claimant's employee (S) appointed the defendant (A) in return for the payment to S of a commission, so allowing A to make substantial profits. A never had any form of dealing with the claimant and this was raised by it as an objection to the claim. The judge dismissed this objection:

"Neither common sense nor authority supports the proposition that the payment must induce a contract between the principal of the recipient of the payment and the donor. The secret payment is just as corrupt in the absence of an agreement (though often enough the payment will be intended to achieve such a purpose). In its ordinary meaning, the word bribe includes any reward given with a view to perverting the judgment or conduct of the recipient."[30]

---

[26] Cf. s.176 of the Companies Act 2006, which now provides that "(1) A director of a company must not accept a benefit from a third party conferred by reason of–(a) being a director; or (b) his doing (or not doing) anything as a director." Section 176(4) provides that "This duty is not infringed if the acceptance of the benefit cannot reasonably be regarded as likely to give rise to a conflict of interest."

[27] *Reading v Attorney General* [1950] A.C. 507.

[28] *Attorney General of Hong Kong v Reid* [1994] A.C. 324.

[29] *Petrotrade Inc v Smith* [2000] 1 Lloyd's Rep. 486.

[30] At 490, per David Steel J. See also *Re South London Fish Market Co* (1888) 39 Ch. D. 324. The concluding words in the passage quoted ("with a view to perverting the judgment or conduct of the recipient") are not a *necessary* element of the legal concept of a bribe, as outlined in the preceding paragraph and expanded upon in para.7–016 and following below.

B. THE INCIDENTS OF THE CLAIM IN BRIBERY

(1) A Freestanding Tort

In the past, cases where a bribe has been paid have tended to be shoehorned into other causes of action (typically deceit) and, clearly, the existence of a bribe may give rise to multiple bases of conventional liability on the part of the agent and the payer of the bribe. Although there has been some confusion about its status as a freestanding tort or equitable wrong, it can now be stated with confidence that bribery is a cause of action[31] in itself which can found a claim in damages and other relief, as well as a claim in restitution. This cause of action has often been referred to as "fraud",[32] but it is suggested that such a label is both unhelpful, in that it suggests that it is an aspect of the law of deceit, and misleading, in that it suggests that dishonesty is an element of the cause of action. The liability in bribery is distinct from any liability in deceit which the agent (or the third party) may come under for misleading the principal, e.g. for wrongly informing the principal that there are no other suitable counterparties in respect of the proposed contract or that the price being offered is the best price available. Further, as discussed below, liability for having paid a bribe is not dependent on proof of dishonesty. It is preferable to dispense with the term "fraud" and speak simply of a claim in bribery.

7–013

However, the earlier authorities have tended to avoid analysing bribery as a cause of action because in general bribery is legally relevant as a ground for rescission of a contract or a basis for obtaining recovery (from the third party or the agent) of the sum said to constitute a bribe. It is rare that a principal will seek damages, or their equitable equivalent, in their standard tortious compensatory sense. This is because, whereas what needs to be proved to found a ground of rescission or restitution has been stated in very narrow terms, if a claim for damages is made then concepts of causation, otherwise irrelevant, become material. We consider the cause of action in bribery further below.

7–014

Although the corruption of the agent is at the heart of the concept of bribery as commonly understood, the law sets a low threshold for the purpose of establishing whether a bribe has been paid, and so whether the elements of the cause of action have been made out (because, as with many aspects of fiduciary law, it is the *risk* of corruption that is legally significant). It is therefore necessary to analyse what precisely needs to be proven, and what does not need to be proven, in order to establish a bribe. The claimant in an action for bribery will

7–015

---

[31] It is said in M.A. Jones, A.M. Dugdale and M. Simpson (eds), *Clerk & Lindsell on Torts*, 22nd edn (London: Sweet & Maxwell, 2017), para.18–055, that the giving of a bribe can lead to the imposition of "tortious liability" both on the part of the agent and the briber.

[32] See for instance *Panama and South Pacific Telegraph Co v India Rubber, Gutta Percha and Telegraph Works Co* (1875) L.R. 10 Ch. App. 515, at 526, per James LJ: "any surreptitious dealing between one principal and the agent of the other principal is a fraud on such other principal, cognizable in this court"; and *Petrotrade Inc v Smith* [2000] 1 Lloyd's Rep. 486, at 490, per David Steel J: "[T]he claim based on bribery is not a species of deceit but a special form of fraud where there is no representation made to the principal of the agent let alone reliance."

typically be the principal whose agent has accepted or been offered a bribe. The defendants will typically be the agent and/or the payer of the bribe (the briber).

(2) No Need to Prove Dishonesty, Intent to Corrupt or Actual Corruption

7–016 Although, as we have seen, many of the cases refer to bribery as a form of fraud, in fact, in order to make good its claim there is no necessity for the principal to show dishonesty or corruption on the part of the briber or the agent. The practical effect of this is that the principal need not establish that either party knew that what it was doing was either contrary to the law or morally culpable; nor is it necessary to show that either party acted with a corrupt intent, let alone that the agent was in fact corrupted. It is sometimes said that corruption and fraud are presumed.[33]

7–017 So Chitty LJ said in *Shipway v Broadwood*[34]:

> "Directly it is established that money was paid or promised to the agent of the other party, it is quite unnecessary to go further and see what effect that had on the mind of the person to whom it was paid or to be paid…. I wish to state again emphatically that in such a case as this it is an immaterial inquiry to what extent the bribe or the offer of it influenced the person to whom it was given or offered. A contrary doctrine would be most dangerous, for it would be almost impossible to ascertain what had been the effect of the bribe; and, further, the real evil is not the payment of money, but the secrecy attending it."

Hence, in *Shipway* the defendant had agreed to purchase a pair of horses from the claimant provided that they were passed sound by a veterinary surgeon retained by him to examine them. The vet having certified the horses as sound, the defendant sent a cheque for the price to the claimant. It turned out that the vet had been offered a sum of money by the claimant in the event that the horses were sold. The claimant's claim on the defendant's cheque was dismissed, despite the lack of any evidence concerning the vet's mental state (or indeed that of the claimant). It was sufficient that the claimant, knowing of the vet's position, had placed the vet in a position in which his duty conflicted with his interest without the defendant's knowledge or consent. Chitty LJ's dictum, quoted above, has since been cited with approval on numerous occasions.[35]

---

[33] "A man who is the agent of A. in a transaction between A. and B., and who also acts secretly for B. in the same transaction, is presumed to act corruptly. Common law authorities require the Court to hold that that is a corrupt practice and, in my opinion, the Court ought to presume fraud in such circumstances": *In Re a Debtor* [1927] 2 Ch. 367, at 376, per Scrutton LJ. But this presumption is not just confined to cases where the agent is also acting for B in some agency capacity.

[34] *Shipway v Broadwood* [1899] 1 Q.B. 369, at 373.

[35] See for instance *Logicrose v Southend United Football Club* [1988] 1 W.L.R. 1256, at 1260H, per Millett J ("It is immaterial whether the agent's mind has been affected or whether the principal has suffered any loss as a result"); and *Hurstanger Ltd v Wilson* [2007] 1 W.L.R. 2351, at [39]. In *Boston Deep Sea Fishing v Ansell* (1888) 39 Ch. D. 339, where the managing director of a company had received a surreptitious commission Fry LJ said, at 368: "We were invited to consider the state of mind of Mr. Ansell; whether he thought it wrong; in other words we are invited to take as the standard for our decision the alleged conscience of a fraudulent servant. I decline to accept any such rule as one on which the Court is to decide such questions." See also *Conway v Eze* [2018] EWHC 29 (Ch), at [130].

Similarly, and as is apparent from the decision in *Shipway*, no inquiry is necessary into the subjective mental state of the maker of the payment—the briber. All that need be proved is that the payer of the alleged bribe knew that the recipient was the agent of the principal and of the agent's personal interest:

    7–018

> "It is clear that a promise or offer of a sum of money was made by the plaintiff, the seller of the horses, and was accepted by Pinkett, the agent of the defendant, and that the plaintiff was aware of the position in which Pinkett stood in relation to the buyer. Under these circumstances it is not necessary to embark on the inquiries suggested by counsel for the plaintiff."[36]

The principal need not go on to show that the payer knew, or even suspected, that the payment was to be kept secret from the principal[37]; rather, it will be for the briber or agent, whose conduct is being impugned, positively to show that the principal knew of and consented to the payment (as to which see further below).[38]

    7–019

Further, it is irrebuttably presumed that the person paying the sum alleged to be a bribe intended that the agent would be influenced by it so as to act favourably to the payer, and that the agent was in fact induced to act in favour of the briber in relation to the relevant transaction.[39] Proof of a corrupt motive or intent is therefore unnecessary[40]; and it matters not that, notwithstanding the bribe, the agent acted, or sought to act, in the principal's best interests.[41]

    7–020

Thus in another Court of Appeal decision, *In Re a Debtor*,[42] the principal employed a broker to negotiate a loan he wished to obtain with a money-lender who, unknown to the principal, paid a "commission", constituting a percentage of the amount loaned, to the agent. It was held that the payment of such commission

    7–021

---

[36] Per Chitty LJ, at 372.

[37] See para.7–035 and the cases there cited.

[38] At para.7–043.

[39] See *Hovenden & Sons v Millhoff* (1900) 83 L.T. 41, where the law was stated as follows, per Romer LJ at 851: "If a bribe be once established to the court's satisfaction, then certain rules apply. Among them the following are now established, and, in my opinion, rightly established, in the interests of morality with the view to discouraging the practice of bribery. First, the court will not inquire into the donor's motive in giving the bribe, nor allow evidence to be gone into as to the motive. Secondly, the court will presume in favour of the principal and as against the briber and the agent bribed, that the agent was influenced by the bribe; and this presumption is irrebuttable. Thirdly, if the agent be a confidential buyer of goods for his principal from the briber, the court will assume as against the briber that the true price of the goods as between him and the purchaser must be taken to be less than the price paid to, or charged by, the vendor by, at any rate, the amount or value of the bribe. If the purchaser alleges loss or damage beyond this, he must prove it. As to the above assumption, we need not determine now whether it could in any case be rebutted. As at present advised, I think that, in the interests of morality, the assumption should be held an irrebuttable one; but we need not finally decide this, because in the present case there is nothing to rebut the presumption."

[40] The fact that Romer LJ had earlier in *Hovenden & Sons v Millhoff* defined a bribe as a gift made "with the view of inducing the agent to act in favour of the donor" is, given his observations quoted in the preceding footnote, not to be understood as imposing a requirement to establish intent to induce: see *Industries & General Mortgage Co, Ltd v Lewis*, above, per Slade J at 577B–577C; *Taylor v Walker* [1958] 1 Lloyd's Rep. 490, at 509–512; *Tesco Stores Ltd v Pook* [2003] EWHC 823 (Ch), per Peter Smith J, at [38]–[45]; and *Conway v Eze* [2018] EWHC 29 (Ch), at [127].

[41] *Daraydan Holdings Ltd v Solland International Ltd* [2005] Ch. 119, at [53]; *Fiona Trust v Privalov* [2010] EWHC 3199 (Comm), at [72].

[42] *In Re a Debtor* [1927] 2 Ch. 367.

rendered the contract of loan voidable at the instance of the principal for bribery, notwithstanding the absence of any suggestion of dishonesty or corruption. The Court of Appeal held that the questions whether the commission was intended to induce the broker to act against the interests of the principal or in fact induced the agent so to act were irrelevant[43]:

> "It would therefore appear that, if money were paid by the lender to the borrower's agent without the consent of the borrower ... that is sufficient. [Counsel for the lender] has suggested that there is nothing to show that the commission paid by the lender to [the broker] was not paid as a matter of generosity, or that it altered to the debtor's disadvantage, the terms of the loan, or induced [the broker] to act against the interests of his principal, the debtor, and that such a commission was not fraudulent unless paid with the object of inducing [the broker] to act in the interest of the lender only; but it seems to me, following *Shipway v Broadwood*, that if a sum is offered by the money-lender to the borrower's agent, it can only be accepted with the knowledge and assent of the borrower."

7–022   A more modern, and vivid, application of the same principle can be found in *Ross River v Cambridge City Football Club*,[44] where a company negotiating for the purchase of overage rights from the defendant football club made certain payments to a director of the football club. The payments were made in order to save the director from financial embarrassment at being unable to fund his daughter's forthcoming wedding, and not with any intent to procure favourable influence in the negotiations (nor was it found that they in fact did so). Nevertheless, the resulting overage sale agreement was rescinded for bribery, because of the propensity of payments to undermine the director's loyalty, coupled with its non-disclosure to the club. It was legally irrelevant that the briber was unaware of the potential conflict and had no consciously improper motive or intent[45]:

> "Despite its emotive label, it has never been an essential part of the cause of action in bribery to prove that the payer or the agent had a consciously improper motive or intent. Bribery is established wherever the payment brings about the requisite conflict of interest which is not disclosed to, or consented to, by the principal. It follows that in a case of non-disclosure, bribery may be established even where both the payer and the agent were unaware that they were doing anything wrong."

(3) Inducement/Causation

7–023   Intimately related to the question of dishonesty is the issue of inducement. As is clear from the authorities cited in the preceding section, at least where the remedy sought is rescission, or an account or restitution of the bribe, it is legally irrelevant whether the bribe or promise of payment has induced the agent to act differently, or, therefore, whether the bribe has caused the principal a loss. For these purposes, the law sets its face against speculative inquiries into whether the principal would have behaved differently had it known of the payment said to constitute a bribe, or how, if at all, the agent has been affected by the payment or

---

[43] *In Re a Debtor* [1927] 2 Ch. 367, at 373, per Scrutton LJ.
[44] *Ross River v Cambridge City Football Club* [2007] EWHC 2115 (Ch).
[45] *Ross River v Cambridge City Football Club*, above, at [218], per Briggs J.

promise of it: "It is immaterial whether the agent's mind has been affected or whether the principal has suffered any loss as a result."[46]

Where, however, the principal is seeking a compensatory remedy, then it is suggested that questions of inducement and causation become highly pertinent. We discuss this issue further below.

7–024

(4)   Offer of Bribe Sufficient

It is not necessary for the principal to establish that a bribe was actually paid in advance of the transaction in question. It is sufficient that a bribe has been offered.[47] This makes sense: the mischief which the law of bribery is designed to prevent is the risk of corruption of the agent and the offering of an inducement may equally have a corrupting effect just as the actual payment of that inducement might. Hence in *Shipway v Broadwood*[48] the fact that there was no evidence that the certifying vet had actually received the offered payment prior to making the certification which caused the defendant to receive the horses was immaterial to the outcome. Similarly, in *Conway v Eze*[49] the promise of a commission to the other party's "property agent" upon completion of the sale of a house would have amounted to a bribe (had the necessary agency relationship existed), notwithstanding that it was never paid.

7–025

The bribe need not be monetary. It has, for example, been held that an offer of employment can be sufficient to constitute a bribe.[50]

7–026

(5)   Identity of Recipient of Bribe

For obvious reasons, the sophisticated agent will often insist that any bribe is paid not to him personally but to another entity, typically a company incorporated at his instigation. It is well-established that the fact that the bribe is not paid to the agent directly is itself irrelevant to the legal consequences that flow from the payment or offer of a bribe. All that is necessary is that the payment has been made at the direction of the agent.[51]

7–027

---

[46] *Logicrose Ltd v Southend United FC* [1988] 1 W.L.R. 1256, at 1260, per Millett J. As explained in *Conway v Eze* [2018] EWHC 29 (Ch), at [130], the reference in *Logicrose* to the deprivation of the agent's disinterested advice is a reference to the agent having a potentially conflicting personal interest; it is not a reference to the agent's advice in fact being compromised by the bribe.

[47] See e.g. *Novoship (UK) Ltd v Mikhaylyuk* [2012] EWHC 3586, at [106], per Christopher Clarke J: "A bribe encompasses not just a payment of money but the conferring of any advantage or benefit, and may be an actual benefit or merely the promise of a benefit held out by the payer or an expectation of one."

[48] *Shipway v Broadwood* [1899] 1 Q.B. 369.

[49] *Conway v Eze* [2018] EWHC 29 (Ch).

[50] *Amalgamated Industries Ltd v Johnson & Firth Brown*, *The Times*, 15 April 1981.

[51] *Novoship (UK) Ltd v Mikhayluk* [2012] EWHC 3586, at [107].

7–028   That said, as we note below, if it were to be established that the putative briber honestly believed that a payment promised or made at the direction of the other party's agent was for the benefit of the other party himself, there would be no bribe.

(6) Irrelevant who Instigated the Bribe

7–029   Although bribery is often analysed in terms of the corruption of the agent by the third party dealing with the agent's principal, the question as to who was the original instigator of the bribe is legally irrelevant.[52] In fact the cases show that it is often the agent who, placed in a position where he can influence the principal's choice of contracting party, or whether and if so on what terms to contract, insists upon the bribe as the price of ensuring that the briber, who may well be an unwilling participant, obtains the contract.[53]

(7) Capacity in which the Payment was Received

7–030   The payment (or other benefit) said to constitute the bribe must be paid to (or at the direction of) the agent "as such": i.e. it must be received by the agent in circumstances that make him accountable for it to his principal. The test laid down in *Bowstead & Reynolds on Agency* and cited with approval by the Court of Appeal in *Imageview Ltd v Jack* is as follows:

> "Clearly not everything acquired in the course of the agency relationship can be made the subject of account to the principal ... It can be said that the test is to ask whether acquisitions on the agent's own account would be inconsistent with his undertaking to act for his principal. It will be inconsistent where the benefit is acquired within the scope of the activities which the agent has undertaken to pursue on his principal's behalf or where the agent uses his position or connection with the principal to obtain a benefit; or obtains one while holding himself out to another party as representing the principal."[54]

7–031   However the payment will be treated as a bribe whether or not it is expressly paid for supposed influence, or for services actually performed for the third party, "or on any other ground at all."[55]

---

[52] *Logicrose Ltd v Southend United FC* [1988] 1 W.L.R. 1256, at 1261: "It is, of course, immaterial whether the initiative for the agent's taking an interest of his own came from the agent himself or from the other party to the transaction."

[53] See e.g. *Taylor v Walker* [1958] 1 Lloyd's Rep. 490 (insurance intermediary insisted to insurer that he would only recommend a settlement proposal to the insured client if a fee was paid).

[54] *Imageview Ltd v Jack* [2009] EWCA Civ 63; [2009] Bus L.R. 1034, at [31], per Jacob LJ.

[55] *Boston Deep Sea Fishing v Ansell* (1888) 39 Ch. D. 339, at 363. See also *Keogh v Dalgety & Co Ltd* (1916) 22 C.L.R. 402, at 418: it does not make "any difference whether the surreptitious profit was gained as a pure gift or for services rendered or for any other reason".

The principle extends to sub-agents employed by the agent, notwithstanding the absence of any privity of contract between the principal and the bribed sub-agent, such that a principal will be able to maintain a claim in restitution against the sub-agent in respect of the bribe.[56]

7–032

(8) Knowledge of the Payer of the Bribe which Must be Proved

The principal seeking a remedy as against the third party briber must establish that the third party knew that the recipient (or offeree) of the payment was the agent of the principal and that the payment was not going to be passed on to his principal.[57] Knowledge here means actual knowledge or wilful blindness as to the true position.[58] But even if the relevant knowledge concerning the existence of the agency or the agent's personal interest is acquired after the payment has been made, the contract may be rescinded where the third party has subsequently contracted with the principal.[59]

7–033

The permutations by which a bribe can be dressed up are infinite and there will be occasions when the agent demands a payment which is described as, for instance, an "application fee". If that fee is in fact to be retained by the agent but the third party believes that it is part of the overall consideration payable, then the agent's principal cannot impugn the transaction or otherwise claim against the third party. There may be no covert relationship between the third party and the agent at all; indeed the third party's connection or means of communication with the principal may be solely through the agent. In such a case the third party may make a payment which he believes is for the benefit of the principal but which is in fact diverted by the agent to himself. In such a case, if the principal is to obtain any form of relief against the third party, then he must establish that the third party had actual knowledge of (or was wilfully blind to) the fact that the payment was not for the benefit of the principal.

7–034

But where the third party makes or promises a payment to an agent behind the principal's back, knowing that the agent is not disclosing their dealings to his principal, he takes the risk that the payment is for the agent's personal benefit even if he does not know it to be so.[60] Conversely, where the third party makes a payment which he knows to be for the personal benefit of the principal's agent, and does not disclose it to the principal, he cannot afterwards assert that he

7–035

---

[56] See *Daraydan Holdings Ltd v Solland International Ltd* [2004] EWHC 622 (Ch); [2005] Ch. 119, at [52], citing *Powell & Thomas v Evan Jones & Co* [1905] 1 K.B. 11, at 18. *Powell* was disapproved by the Supreme Court in *FHR European Ventures LLP v Mankarious* [2014] UKSC 45; [2015] 1 A.C. 250 on a different point.

[57] Hence in *Fyffes Group Ltd v Templeman* [2000] 2 Lloyd's Rep. 643 there was a substantial dispute as to whether the alleged briber had thought that the sum alleged to constitute a bribe was in fact for the benefit of the principal or whether it was for the benefit of the agent. Had it been the former then the defendant would not have been liable in bribery.

[58] *Logicrose Ltd v Southend United FC* [1988] 1 W.L.R. 1256, at 1261: "In particular, constructive notice will not do. Parties to negotiations do not owe each other a duty to act reasonably, but only to act honestly. In the present context, the principal's right is a right to rescind for fraud, not negligence."

[59] *Grant v Gold Exploration and Development Syndicate Ltd* [1900] 1 Q.B. 233.

[60] *Logicrose Ltd v Southend United FC* [1988] 1 W.L.R. 1256, at 1262.

believed that the agent would disclose the payment to his principal.[61] Indeed, transactions have been set aside for bribery even where the third party was given positive assurances by the agent that he would disclose the payment to his principal.[62]

7–036 We consider below the level of knowledge required by the principal of the payment to cleanse the payment made to the agent of any legal consequences.

(9) Connection with the Relevant Transaction

7–037 The principal's complaint will generally relate to a particular transaction which it asserts was procured because of, or was otherwise influenced by, the bribe. However, it is not necessary for the principal to show that the alleged bribe was given in connection with any particular transaction or series of transactions. The briber may have made payments to the agent so as to influence him generally in favour of the payer, e.g. in connection with the granting of future contracts.[63] As we have seen above, the payment will be sufficiently connected with the relevant transaction if it creates a "realistic prospect of a conflict between the agent's personal interest and that of his principal."[64] This will be a fact-sensitive enquiry.

(10) The Size of the Payment

7–038 The law recognises that some gifts or benefits are too small to create even a real possibility of a conflict of interest and so too small to be treated as a bribe. So in *The Parkdale*[65] Gorell Barnes J described payments received by the master of a vessel from consignees as

> "a little present, not in any sense antagonistic to his owners, but simply because the consignee thought that he had discharged the cargo so well that he was entitled to a small sum."

It is a question of fact depending on the circumstances of each case where the line is to be drawn between "a little present" and a bribe, and so unsurprisingly there

---

[61] *Shipway v Broadwood* [1899] 1 Q.B. 369, at 373 ("It was the plaintiff's duty to inform the defendant of the promise made to Pinkett if he wished to escape the consequences of having made it"); *Grant v Gold Exploration and Development Syndicate Ltd* [1900] 1 Q.B. 233, at 249–250; *Logicrose v Southend United Football Club* [1988] 1 W.L.R. 1256, at 1262 ("Where, therefore, knowing that the agent has an interest of his own he does not himself disclose it to the other party, then in the words of Collins LJ, at 249: "he must at least accept the risk of the agent's not doing so."). No doubt is cast upon the dicta of Millett J in *Logicrose* by the Court of Appeal's decision in *UBS v Kommunale Wasserwerke Leipzig GmbH* [2017] EWCA Civ 1567: see the analysis in *Conway v Eze* [2018] EWHC 29 (Ch), at [133]–[138].

[62] See e.g. *Taylor v Walker* [1958] 1 Lloyd's Rep. 490.

[63] *Daraydan Holdings Ltd v Solland International Ltd* [2005] Ch. 119, at [53]. For an example see *Smith v Sorby* (1875) 3 Q.B.D. 552n. In *Fiona Trust v Privalov* [2010] EWHC 3199 (Comm) Andrew Smith J said that the effect of a bribe will in such circumstances be to taint all future transactions "between the principal and the person making [the bribe] in which the agent acts for the principal or in which he is in a position to influence the principal's decisions, so long as the potential conflict of interest remains a real possibility": at [73(i)].

[64] *Novoship (UK) Ltd v Mikhaylyuk* [2012] EWHC 3586 (Comm), at [106].

[65] *The Parkdale* [1897] P. 53, at 58–59.

is little guidance about this in the authorities. The test applied by Andrew Smith J in *Fiona Trust v Privalov*[66] was whether the payment was sufficiently large to create a "real possibility" of a conflict between interest and duty, not whether such a conflict is actually created.[67] It will be seen that this test is in all essentials the same as the one propounded by Christopher Clarke J in *Novoship (UK) Ltd v Mikhaylyuk.*[68]

(11)   Vicarious Liability

Where a third party directly bribes a principal's agent, that third party's liability is clear. But the factual position may be less simple: the bribe may have been agreed or paid to the principal's agent by the third party's agent. In such a case it is established that the third party may be liable in damages or restitution, and any contract which it has entered into directly with the principal will be liable to be rescinded, if the third party's agent has paid or agreed to pay the bribe in the course of his agency, applying general principles of vicarious liability.[69] The third party's liability will arise irrespective of whether it authorised the bribe or whether it knew or even should have known about it. However, whether the bribe was paid within the scope of the agent's agency relationship with the third party can be a complex inquiry.[70]

7–039

It is clear that the entity which has paid or agreed to pay the bribe is unable to avoid liability by showing that the person(s) responsible acted outside of their actual or ostensible authority.[71] In this regard the law draws a distinction between vicarious liability in relation to the tort of deceit and in relation to the tort of bribery. In *Armagas Ltd v Mundogas SA*,[72] a case in deceit, the House of Lords

7–040

---

[66] Citing *Imageview Management v Jack* [2009] 1 Lloyd's Rep. 436, at [6], per Jacob LJ.

[67] *Fiona Trust v Privalov* [2010] EWHC 3199 (Comm), at [73(ii)].

[68] *Novoship (UK) Ltd v Mikhaylyuk* [2012] EWHC 3586 (Comm), at [106]. See para.7–011 above.

[69] See the decision of the Court of Appeal in *Armagas Ltd v Mundogas SA (The Ocean Frost)* [1986] 1 A.C. 717, at 743, relying on a decision of the Supreme Court of Canada, *Barry v Stoney Point Canning Co* (1917) 55 SCR 51. Similarly an innocent partner will be liable if his partner bribes the principal's agent in the course of carrying out the business of the firm: "It is too well established by the authorities to be now disputed that a principal may be liable for the fraud or other illegal act committed by his agent within the general scope of the authority given to him, and even the fact that the act of the agent is criminal does not necessarily take it out of the scope of his authority. If the act done by the agent is within the general scope of the authority given to him, it matters not for the present purpose that it was directly contrary to the instructions of his principal, or even that it may have been an offence against society itself." *Hamlyn v John Houston & Co* [1903] 1 K.B. 81, at 85. For a more recent example of a third party being affected by a bribe paid by its agent see *Petrotrade Inc v Smith* [2000] Lloyd's Rep. 486.

[70] See for instance the first instance decision in *UBS AG v Kommunale Wasserwerke Leipzig GMBH* [2014] 3615 (Comm), at [591] and following; but note that on appeal ([2017] EWCA Civ 1567) the premise that there was an agency relationship at all was held to be wrong.

[71] Which is unlikely to be difficult: "Indeed it is not easy to envisage an agent having actual, let alone ostensible, authority to proffer bribes"; per Steel J in *Petrotrade*, above. For an example where the bribe was specifically authorised by the principal see *Panama and South Pacific Telegraph Co v India Rubber, Gutta Percha and Telegraph Works Co* (1875) L.R. 10 Ch. App. 515.

[72] *Armagas Ltd v Mundogas SA* [1986] A.C. 717.

had declined to apply a dictum in *Navarro v Moregrand Ltd*[73] in support of the proposition that the absence of authority is not decisive in showing that conduct is not within the course of employment (or agency). Lord Keith explained that the

> "dictum ... may have some validity in relation to torts other than those concerned with fraudulent misrepresentation, but in my opinion it has no application to torts of the latter kind, where the essence of the employer's liability is reliance by the injured party on actual or ostensible authority".[74]

We have seen that the tort of bribery is distinct from the tort of deceit and is not founded on any form of misrepresentation or reliance. The liability of a principal for bribes paid or offered by his agents will therefore be established by reference to the question whether the conduct complained of was within the scope of their agency or employment.[75]

7–041 In *Armagas Ltd v Mundogas SA* Goff LJ left open the question of whether a contract, which has been procured by the bribery of the principal's agent by a person who was *not* the agent of the third party who later entered into the contract with the principal, was liable to be rescinded at the instance of the principal.[76] As a general rule, in such a case the conscience of the counterparty against whom rescission is sought would need to have to be affected by the bribe for rescission to lie against them. Absent a relationship of agency/vicarious liability, this would generally have to be on the basis that the counterparty had actual knowledge of the bribe; but in *UBS AG v Kommunale Wasserwerke Leipzig GMBH* the Court of Appeal held that the counterparty's conscience could also be sufficiently affected in such a case where it was party to a corrupt arrangement with the briber and dishonestly assisted the briber in abusing its fiduciary duties to the other principal, even if it did not know of the bribe itself.[77]

(12)   Informed Consent and Disclosure

7–042 As we have seen the true mischief of a bribe is the fact that it is secret from the principal. "The real evil is not the payment of money, but the secrecy attending it."[78] Accordingly there can be no bribe, as legally understood, and no attendant liability, if, prior to the relevant transaction, disclosure of the payment, or the arrangement which might or will lead to the payment, is made to the principal. But, as we have noted, the third party cannot, by way of defence, afterwards assert that he believed that the agent would disclose the payment (which he

---

[73] *Navarro v Moregrand Ltd* [1951] 2 T.L.R. 674, at 680. See also *Lloyd v Grace, Smith & Co* [1912] A.C. 716.
[74] At 782.
[75] See *Petrotrade Inc v Smith* [2000] 1 Lloyd's Rep. 486.
[76] *Armagas Ltd v Mundogas SA* [1986] 1 A.C. 717, at 745. This was doubted in *Donegal International Ltd v Zambia* [2007] EWHC 197 (Comm), at [496], and in the first instance decision in *UBS AG v Kommunale Wasserwerke Leipzig GMBH* [2014] 3615 (Comm), at [584].
[77] *UBS AG v Kommunale Wasserwerke Leipzig GMBH* [2017] EWCA Civ 1567, at [113].
[78] Per Chitty LJ in the leading case of *Shipway v Broadwood* [1899] 1 Q.B. 369, at 373.

knows is for the agent's benefit) to the principal himself. In such a case the third party must bear the risk of the agent's not disclosing the fact of the payment to his principal.[79]

However, to cleanse the agent, and the third party payer of the payment of what is said to be a bribe, of any potential liability there must be "full disclosure" of the facts such that the principal can give "informed consent" to the proposed payment or arrangement.[80] There is a rich jurisprudence which has developed around the question whether proper disclosure has been made to the principal in respect of the bribe or secret commission (or indeed any secret profit which is made by the agent). The following principles may be extracted[81]: **7–043**

(1)   An agent may not put himself in a position where, or enter into a transaction in which, his personal interest, or his duty to another principal may conflict with his duty to his principal unless his principal, with full knowledge of all the material circumstances, and of the nature and extent of the agent's interests, consents.[82]

(2)   It is for the agent (or third party briber) to prove that full disclosure has been given to its principal.[83]

(3)   What constitutes full disclosure will depend on the facts of each case given that the requirement is for the principal's informed consent to his agent acting with a potential conflict of interest.[84]

(4)   But it is not sufficient for the agent merely to disclose that he has an interest in the transaction or to make such statements as would put the principal on enquiry.[85]

(5)   The materiality of what must be disclosed is to be assessed on the basis of whether it might have affected the principal's decision and not whether it would have done so. It is an irrelevant inquiry to ask whether, had the principal been provided with sufficient disclosure, it would have given permission for the payment or proceeded with the transaction.

(6)   The issue sometimes arises whether the principal must be informed of the precise amount of the payment said to constitute a bribe or secret commission. Again the answer depends on the particular facts of the case. Where there is a trade custom that the agent will be paid by the other party to the transaction, and where the amount of the payment is standard and ascertainable, then precise knowledge may not be required (at least where the principal is on notice of the trade custom). But where the principal is

---

[79] See paras 7–033 and following above and the cases there cited.

[80] *Dunne v English* (1874) L.R. 18 Eq 524, at 533.

[81] See also Ch.11.

[82] *Hindmarsh v Brigham & Cowan Ltd* (1943) Ll L Rep. 141, at 151; *FHR European Ventures LLP v Mankarious* [2011] EWHC 2308 (Ch); [2012] 2 B.C.L.C. 39, at [75].

[83] *Hurstanger Ltd v Wilson* [2007] EWCA Civ 299; [2007] 1 W.L.R. 2351, at [35].

[84] *Hurstanger Ltd v Wilson* [2007] EWCA Civ 299; [2007] 1 W.L.R. 2351, at [35].

[85] *Hurstanger Ltd v Wilson* [2007] EWCA Civ 299; [2007] 1 W.L.R. 2351, at [35].

vulnerable or unsophisticated, or where the payment received by his agent is out of the ordinary, then full disclosure of the payment and its amount will be required.[86]

(7)   Where the agent has more than one principal then the disclosure must be made to each, unless one principal is expressly or implicitly authorised by the other(s) to receive disclosure on behalf of the other(s).[87]

(13)   Bribery and Ex Turpi Causa[88]

7–044   A claimant who has paid a bribe or attempted to pay a bribe is likely to find that any claim founded on the bribe is defeated by the defence of ex turpi causa. So, in *Nayyar v Denton Wilde Sapte*,[89] the claimant brought proceedings against the defendant solicitors in negligence, where the alleged loss was constituted by sums paid out by the claimant in an attempt to obtain a lucrative contract. Those sums were held to be properly categorised as attempted bribes. The judge held[90]:

> "As appears from Lord Mansfield's statement of policy in *Holman v Johnson*,[91] the principle of *ex turpi causa* can extend to immoral as well as illegal acts and may apply to improper conduct evincing serious moral turpitude. Bribery involves serious moral turpitude. The moral turpitude involved on the part of the briber is much the same in the case of an attempted bribe as it is in the case of an actual bribe. That that involves sufficient turpitude to bring in to play the principle of *ex turpi causa* is borne out by the approach of the criminal law."

The claim was accordingly dismissed.

7–045   It follows that where the third party agrees to pay the principal's agent a sum of money which is properly categorised as a bribe, then the agent will be unable to enforce the contract: a contract *to* bribe is unenforceable.[92] However, the contract between principals procured by the payment or promise of a bribe is not unenforceable on ex turpi causa grounds simply by reason of it having been procured by a bribe.[93] If the contract is to be unenforceable, it must either be because the bribed agent's principal has elected to rescind it or (if the agent concluded the contract) the contract is void for want of authority.[94]

---

[86] *Hurstanger Ltd v Wilson* [2007] EWCA Civ 299; [2007] 1 W.L.R. 2351, at [36]. *FHR European Ventures LLP v Mankarious* [2011] EWHC 2308 (Ch); [2012] 2 B.C.L.C. 39, at [81]–[82], in which the earlier authorities are considered.

[87] *FHR European Ventures LLP v Mankarious* [2011] EWHC 2308 (Ch); [2012] 2 B.C.L.C. 39, at [83]–[84]. As to disclosure where the principal is a company see *Ross River Ltd v Cambridge City FC Ltd* [2007] EWHC 2115 (Ch); [2008] 1 All E.R. 1004, at [206] and following.

[88] See generally Ch.24, on Illegality.

[89] *Nayyar v Denton Wilde Sapte* [2009] EWHC 3218 (QB); [2010] P.N.L.R. 15.

[90] At [92], per Hamblen J.

[91] *Holman v Johnson* (1775) 1 Cowp 341.

[92] As accepted in *Honeywell International Middle East Ltd v Meydan Group LLC* [2014] EWHC 1344 (TCC); [2014] Lloyd's Rep. 133, at [185].

[93] *Honeywell International Middle East Ltd v Meydan Group LLC* [2014] EWHC 1344 (TCC); [2014] Lloyd's Rep. 133, at [185].

[94] See Section C below.

C.   REMEDIES

(1)   Introduction

Where a bribe is held to have been made or promised there are various potential remedies available to the principal, both against the agent and the third party briber.

7–046

(2)   Void Contract

It is a trite principle of the law of agency that, where an agent enters into a contract purportedly on behalf of his principal and the counterparty to that contract is aware that the agent has exceeded his authority, then the contract is void (as opposed to voidable) as against the principal, unless the principal chooses to ratify it.[95] This principle may be applicable in a bribery case where the agent who has been bribed has himself executed the subsequent contract, at least where by reason of the bribe the agent has acted dishonestly or in conscious disloyalty to his principal (as will commonly be the case).[96] In circumstances where the counterparty to the contract is the payer of the bribe, it is unlikely (although not inconceivable) that he will be able to rely on the ostensible authority of the agent to save the contract, because he will almost certainly be taken to be on notice of the facts and matters depriving the agent of actual authority.[97]

7–047

(3)   Rescission[98]

(i)   General principles

Any contract entered into after the giving or offering of a bribe is, in principle, avoidable at the instance of the principal, whether or not the agent's mind has been affected by the bribe.[99] It is in the context of the law of rescission that the

7–048

---

[95] *Heinl v Jyske Bank (Gibraltar) Ltd* [1999] Lloyd's Rep. Bank 511 (CA), at 521, at 533.

[96] See Watts (ed), *Bowstead and Reynolds on Agency* (2017), art.23 (para.3–010): "Authority to act as agent includes only authority to act honestly in pursuit of the interests of the principal." The view that a bribe can therefore render a contract concluded by an agent void is supported by D. O'Sullivan, S. Elliott and R. Zakrzewski, *The Law of Rescission*, 2nd edn (Oxford: OUP, 2015), paras 1.85–1.87 and in a dictum of the Court of Appeal in *Fiona Trust v Privalov* [2007] EWCA Civ 20; [2007] Bus L.R. 686, at 699C–699E.

[97] See, by analogy, *Wrexham Association Football Club Ltd v Crucialmove Ltd* [2006] EWCA Civ 237. We consider that the principles in that case are not concerned solely with the authority of directors of companies, but extend to agents generally.

[98] For the principles generally applicable to rescission, see Ch.22.

[99] *Panama & South Pacific Telegraph Co v India Rubber, Gutta Percha, and Telegraph Co* (1875) 9 Ch. App. 515, per James LJ at 526: "I take it to be clear that any surreptitious dealing between one principal and the agent of the other is a fraud on such other principal, cognizable in this Court. That I take to be a clear proposition, and I take it, according to my view, to be equally clear that the defrauded principal, if he comes in time, is entitled, at his option to have the contract rescinded."; *Logicrose Ltd v Southend United FC* [1988] 1 W.L.R. 1256, at 1260F: "It is well established that a

law of bribery operates in its fullest rigour. This is because the principal may rescind the contract regardless of whether the contract is financially disadvantageous to it or not. This has been justified on the basis that the principal, having been (presumptively) deprived by the other party to the contract to the transaction of the disinterested advice of his agent, is entitled to a further opportunity, with full knowledge of the factual position, to consider whether it is in his interests to affirm the contract or not.[100] Of course the principal may decide that, notwithstanding the bribe, it wishes to preserve the contract in being for commercial reasons. Whether or not to do so is a matter for the principal, although if the contract has been performed and the parties have changed their positions in a way which is incapable of being unravelled, then rescission may be unavailable (and may in any event be of no avail to the principal).

7–049 The right to rescind is additional to, and independent of, the principal's right to recover the amount of the bribe, considered below.[101] So where a principal had brought proceedings for rescission of the contract against the briber and proceedings for the recovery of the bribe against the agent, the fact that the principal had compromised his claim against the briber on terms that the contract induced by the bribe remained in place, that did not affect the principal's pecuniary claim against the agent.[102] Conversely, the fact that the bribe has been subsequently passed by the agent to his principal (or the principal has obtained judgment against the agent in the amount of the bribe) does not affect the principal's right to rescind.[103]

7–050 All the usual bars to rescission recognised by the law generally seem to be equally applicable to a contract procured by a bribe. So rescission is only possible if, and must be on terms that, there is restitito in integrum of the pre-transaction position of both parties[104]; but the obligation on the part of the rescinding party to give counter-restitution does not extend to the bribe itself, if that sum has been obtained by the principal from the agent.[105] Further the right may be lost if, with full knowledge of the facts, the principal chooses to affirm the contract.[106] However it was suggested in *Logicrose v Southend United F.C.*[107] that, even

---

principal who discovers that his agent in a transaction has obtained or arranged to obtain a bribe or secret commission from the other party to the transaction is entitled, in addition to other remedies which may be open to him, to elect to rescind the transaction ab initio."

[100] *Logicrose Ltd v Southend United FC* [1988] 1 W.L.R. 1256, at 1261A.

[101] *Mahesan v Malaysia Government Officers' Co-Operative Housing Society Ltd* [1979] A.C. 374, at 380.

[102] *Bagnall v Carlton* (1877) 6 Ch.D. 371.

[103] *Grant v Gold Exploration and Development Syndicate Ltd* [1900] 1 Q.B. 233, at 251; *Logicrose Ltd v Southend United FC* [1988] 1 W.L.R. 1256, at 1262–1263.

[104] *Panama & South Pacific Telegraph Co v India Rubber, Gutta Percha, and Telegraph Co* (1875) 9 Ch. App. 515, at 527, 532–533.

[105] *Logicrose Ltd v Southend United FC* [1988] 1 W.L.R 1256, at 1263–1264.

[106] See *Bartram & Sons v Lloyds* (1904) 90 L.T. 357.

[107] *Logicrose v Southend United F.C.* [1988] 1 W.L.R. 1256, at 1260.

where it is "too late" for the principal to rescind the contract ab initio, he may "bring it to an end for the future." The precise ambit of this dictum has yet to be explored.[108]

(ii) Rescission as of right

Rescission operates both at common law and in equity. At common law the wronged party has an absolute right to rescind,[109] provided that there are no bars to rescission, which is not dependent on judicial intervention. By contrast, in equity rescission is an equitable remedy which (save perhaps in cases of fraud)[110] depends on the exercise of discretion by the court rather than the unfettered entitlement of the wronged party.[111] The reason for these different jurisdictions is because the law and equity recognise different bases for rescission: grounds for rescission recognised by the common law are fraudulent misrepresentation, duress and, it appears, bribery.[112]

7–051

(iii) A "half-way house"

In *Hurstanger Ltd v Wilson*[113] a lender had disclosed to the borrower that it might make a payment by way of commission to the broker who acted as the borrower's agent in obtaining the loan, but did not disclose the amount of the payment or that it had in fact been paid. The Court of Appeal held that there was insufficient

7–052

---

[108] In *Tigris International NV v China Southern Airlines Co Ltd* [2014] EWCA Civ 1649, at [143], Christopher Clarke LJ suggested as follows: "At law bribery, whether at or after contract, amounts to a repudiatory breach by the bribing party which, on discovery, his counterparty may accept as bringing the contract to an end. Whether that is because bribery is a stand-alone ground for termination, or the obligation to restrain from it an incident or an implied term of every contract is debatable and, for present purposes, does not matter."

[109] *Conway v Eze* [2018] EWHC 29 (Ch), at [143]–[156].

[110] See Ch.22, and the discussion in O'Sullivan, Elliott and Zakrzewski, *The Law of Rescission* (2015), paras 11.56–11.108.

[111] *Johnson v EBS Pensioner Trustees Ltd* [2002] EWCA Civ 164; [2002] Lloyd's Rep. PN 309, per Dyson LJ at [78] and [79]: "In relation to rescission, in my view the judge was right to say (paragraph 46) that, whatever the position in relation to a claim to rescind based on misrepresentation, the right to rescission on grounds of undue influence, abuse of confidence or breach of fiduciary duty depends on the exercise of the discretion by the court to intervene in the enforcement of legal rights.... When exercising its equitable jurisdiction, the court considers what fairness requires not only when addressing the question of the precise form of relief, but also when considering whether the remedy should be granted at all."

[112] See O'Sullivan, Elliott and Zakrzewski, *The Law of Rescission* (2015), para.8.53; *Snell's Equity*, para.15–011; Watts (ed), *Bowstead and Reynolds on Agency* (2017), para.8–222. But see the confusion introduced by *Hurstanger Ltd v Wilson* [2007] EWCA Civ 299; [2007] 1 W.L.R. 2351, at [46], where Tuckey LJ speaks of the "equitable remedy of rescission" being deployed "in aid of the common law". This is a misunderstanding of the role of the court. As explained in Ch.22, the role of the court in cases of common law rescission is to pronounce upon the efficacy of the wronged party's purported exercise of its election and give effect to its consequences by awarding judgment on claims and cross-claims for restitution of benefits that have previously passed under the contract. There is no scope for the exercise of judicial discretion in deciding whether to rescind or what the consequences should be.

[113] *Hurstanger Ltd v Wilson* [2007] EWCA Civ 299; [2007] 1 W.L.R. 2351.

disclosure for there to be informed consent by the borrower to the payment, but that, equally, it could not be said that the payment was "secret". Tuckey LJ asked[114]:

> "Is there a half-way house between the situation where there has been sufficient disclosure to negate secrecy, but nevertheless the principal's informed consent has not been obtained? Logically I can see no objection to this. Where there has only been partial or inadequate disclosure but it is sufficient to negate secrecy, it would be unfair to visit the agent and any third party involved with a finding of fraud and the other consequences to which I have referred,[115] or, conversely to acquit them altogether for their involvement in what would still be a breach of fiduciary duty unless informed consent had been obtained."

7–053   In the circumstances the Court of Appeal held that the borrower was not entitled to "deploy the full armoury of remedies which would have been available if this had been a true secret commission case"[116] and that the borrower was deprived of his common law right of rescission for bribery; rather he had to rely upon the more flexible equitable remedy. The borrower's remedy was confined to equitable compensation in the amount of the secret commission paid to the borrower's agent. This analysis is heterodox: the law traditionally deems a payment made by a third party to the agent of the principal to be a bribe unless full disclosure of it has been provided. Nonetheless the decision was interpreted without questioning its accuracy by Briggs J in *Ross River Ross River Ltd v Cambridge City FC Ltd*[117] as follows:

> "If [the principal] knew of the payment, but did not give his informed consent, the court may award rescission as a discretionary remedy, if it is just and proportionate to do so."[118]

(iv)   Existence of bribe as a defence?

7–054   There are some suggestions in the authorities that a principal being proceeded against on a contract may set up the fact that the contract was induced by a bribe as a defence to the action, without having rescinded the contract (or seeking its rescission) and without the contract being void on the principles considered above. Thus in *Shipway v Broadwood*, discussed above, it was held that, where the defendant had given a cheque for the horses which he had then stopped, and where the claimant vendor had then sued on the cheque, the fact of the offer of an inducement to the vet whose certificate was a condition subsequent to the contract was sufficient to "vacate the certificate and the sale which depended on

---

[114] *Hurstanger* [2007] EWCA Civ 299; [2007] 1 W.L.R. 2351, at [39].

[115] A reference to [38], where Tuckey LJ had analysed the law as follows: "Obviously if there has been no disclosure the agent will have received a secret commission. This is a blatant breach of his fiduciary duty but additionally the payment or receipt of a secret commission is considered to be a form of bribe and is treated in the authorities as a special category of fraud in which it is unnecessary to prove motive, inducement or loss up to the amount of the bribe."

[116] *Hurstanger* [2007] EWCA Civ 299; [2007] 1 W.L.R. 2351, at [46].

[117] *Ross River Ross River Ltd v Cambridge City FC Ltd* [2007] EWHC 2115 (Ch); [2008] 1 All E.R. 1004, at [203].

[118] The proposition that there is an equitable discretion to refuse rescission where it would be unfair or disproportionate was also endorsed by the Court of Appeal in *UBS AG (London Branch) v Kommunale Wasserweke Leipzig GmbH* [2017] EWCA Civ 1567, at [157].

that certificate." Similarly, in *Alexander v Webber*[119] the claimant repudiated a contract to purchase a car and sued for the return of the deposit. He was held to have repudiated the contract wrongfully; but it was discovered during the action that his chauffeur had taken a secret commission from the vendor, and this was held to "justify the repudiation on account of the fraud".[120]

However, it is doubtful that such a separate principle exists. The decision in *Shipway* can better be explained on the basis that, on the proper construction of the contract of sale, a certificate procured by a bribe did not constitute a valid certificate and so the condition on which liability for the price depended had not been satisfied. Further, both it and *Alexander v Webber* were cases in which the innocent party had already disaffirmed the contract, albeit not at the time in knowledge of the bribe. The orthodox view is that a contract procured by the bribe is (unless it was unauthorised) voidable and that it remains in force unless and until rescinded.

7–055

(4) Proprietary Liability in Respect of the Bribe

All bribes are a form of secret profit made by a fiduciary.[121] Of course a fiduciary is strictly accountable to his principal for any secret profit made by him.[122] On that basis if an agent receives, without the principal's informed consent, a payment or other benefit which the law deems to be a bribe, then the agent holds the bribe, and the property from time to time representing the bribe, on constructive trust for the principal and the principal is entitled to recover it from the agent by way of proprietary claim.[123] The effect of this is that where, say, a cash bribe is invested in property and the value of the property appreciates, then the principal has a proprietary claim to trace into the property (or a proportionate part of it in the event that part of the purchase price was funded by non-tainted funds).[124] Of course if property acquired with the bribe subsequently depreciates in value that fact cannot be deployed by the agent to reduce his personal, as opposed to proprietary, liability: the amount of the bribe itself constitutes an irreducible minimum liability which will be owed to the principal as a "debtor in equity", as it has sometimes been described.

7–056

---

[119] *Alexander v Webber* [1922] 1 K.B. 642.

[120] *Alexander v Webber* [1922] 1 K.B 642, at 645, per Bray J.

[121] *Armagas Ltd v Mundogas SA, The Ocean Frost* [1985] 1 Lloyd's Rep. 1, at 19, per Staughton J.

[122] The law was stated in *Regal (Hastings) Ltd v Gulliver (Note)* [1967] 2 A.C. 134, at 144–145; see further Ch.11.

[123] "By the early years of the 19th century it had become an established principle of equity that an agent who received any secret advantage for himself from the other party to a transaction in which the agent was acting for his principal was bound to account for it to his principal: *Fawcett v Whitehouse* (1829) 1 Russ. & M. 132. The remedy was equitable, obtainable in the Court of Chancery": *Mahesan v Malaysia Government Officers' Co-Operative Housing Society Ltd* [1979] A.C. 374, at 380, per Lord Diplock.

[124] "As soon as the bribe was received it should have been paid or transferred instanter to the person who suffered from the breach of duty. Equity considers as done that which ought to have been done. As soon as the bribe was received, whether in cash or in kind, the false fiduciary held the bribe on a constructive trust for the person injured": *A-G v Reid*, above, at 331, per Lord Templeman.

7–057   This simple analysis has only been definitively stated as constituting the law very recently, after many decades of legal dispute extending back at least to the 1860s. It had been on occasion suggested that the principal only had a personal remedy, rather than a proprietary remedy, against his agent in respect of the bribe.[125] This is an important distinction, where the agent is insolvent or where the bribe, or its product, has been passed to a third party (so that, if the claim is proprietary the principal can claim to trace and follow it). It also affects the limitation period applicable to any claim. The question was finally resolved by a 7-member Supreme Court in *FHR European Ventures LLP v Cedar Capital Partners LLC* [126] where it was held that a bribe or secret commission received by an agent was held by the agent on constructive trust for his principal, additionally to the agent's personal obligation to account or pay equitable compensation to the principal in the amount of the bribe (as to which see below).[127]

(5)   Restitutionary Liability

7–058   Regardless of the proprietary liability of the agent in respect of the bribe, both the agent and the payer of the bribe[128] are jointly and severally liable in restitution[129] for the amount of the bribe, whether paid or, it seems, only promised.[130] This liability is sometimes described as a liability for money had and received[131] or an

---

[125] See e.g. *Tyrrell v Bank of London* (1862) 10 HL Cas 26 and *Lister & Co v Stubbs* (1890) 45 Ch. D. 1. In the latter case it had been held, at 15, per Lindley LJ, that the relationship between bribed agent and principal was "that of debtor and creditor; it is not that of trustee and cestui que trust." The views expressed in this decision by a strong Court of Appeal had great influence for many decades.

[126] *FHR European Ventures LLP v Cedar Capital Partners LLC* [2014] UKSC 45; [2015] 1 A.C. 520.

[127] The case is notable as witnessing one of the more remarkable judicial volte faces of modern times. Lord Neuberger delivered the judgment of the Court in *FHR* and disapproved his own decision, while sitting in the Court of Appeal, in *Versailles v Sinclair* [2012] Ch. 453. Given that the decision in *FHR* provides a definitive analysis, it is thought unnecessary to rehearse the law's tergiversations on the issue and the numerous authorities and academic commentaries which preceded it, though Lord Millett's two articles on Bribes and Secret Commissions, at [1993] Rest L.R. 7 and [2012] CLJ 583 repay reading.

[128] The restitutionary liability of the briber in the amount of the bribe was controversial until it was established in *Grant v Gold Exploration and Development Syndicate Ltd* [1900] Q.B. 233 and *Hovenden and Sons v Millhoff* (1900) 83 L.T. 41. The liability of the briber in the amount of the bribe is conceptually odd, given that it involves the briber having to pay the bribe a second time, but it is probably now too late to question it: *Mahesan v Malaysia Government Officers' Co-Operative Housing Society Ltd* [1979] A.C. 374, at 383. See further the analysis in *The Ocean Frost* [1986] 1 A.C. 717, at 743–744 and in *Logicrose*, at 1263.

[129] Early authorities refer to the cause of action being a claim for money had and received; this has now been subsumed by the law of restitution.

[130] See *Whaley Bridge Calico Printing Co v Green and Smith* (1879) 5 Q.B.D. 109, per Bowen J at 113: "the principal, under circumstances such as these, is entitled to stand in the agent's shoes and compel a payment of money directly to himself". The ratio of the case appears to be that the principal can treat the contract to pay the bribe as made on behalf of himself and so sue on it; but it is suggested that this is better analysed now as a restitutionary claim.

[131] So Bowen LJ said in *Boston Deep Sea Fishing and Ice Co v Ansell* (1888) 39 Ch. D. 339, at 367–368. "... the law implies a use, that is to say, there is an implied contract, if you put it as a legal proposition – there is an equitable right, if you treat it as a matter of equity – as between the principal and agent that the agent should pay it over, which renders the agent liable to be sued for money had and received, and there is an equitable right in the master to receive it, and to take it out of the hands of the agent, which gives the principal a right to relief in equity."

equitable liability to account by way of payment of equitable compensation in the amount of the bribe.[132] The legal basis for this liability, whilst undoubted, has been put in the cases in various ways, and it is doubtful whether any useful purpose is served by analysis of the jurisprudential justifications for it.

The agent's liability exists irrespective of whether or not the principal purports to rescind the contract.[133] However it would appear that if the principal rescinds the contract then it is unable to then proceed against the third party briber in respect of the amount of the bribe.[134] Similarly, it is suggested that if a third party pays a bribe to the agent but no contract or other arrangement with the principal results, the principal's sole claim will be against the agent. **7–059**

Further, the liability, being restitutionary rather than compensatory, exists regardless of whether or not the principal has sustained any loss as a result of the agent's conduct or the entry into the underlying transaction.[135] Although it may obtain judgment in the amount of the bribe against both the agent and the briber, clearly the principal cannot recover more than the sum total of the bribe. **7–060**

(6) Liability in Damages/Equitable Compensation

(i) Introduction

We have seen that bribery is now recognised as a free-standing tort, although the traditional remedies of rescission and restitution (or a proprietary remedy in respect) of the amount of the bribe do not require analysis of the law of bribery in tortious terms. However the principal may wish to go further and claim damages from the agent and briber in a sum greater than the amount of the bribe. **7–061**

Where the principal has entered into a contract with the third party briber in circumstances where the third party has paid or promised a bribe to the principal's agent then the principal has a potential tortious claim in damages against both the third party and the agent. The precise elements of the cause of action have not been the subject of a definitive statement but it is suggested that the ingredients of such a liability are as follows: **7–062**

---

[132] See e.g. *FHR v Cedar Capital*, above, at [7].

[133] See *Logicrose*, at 1262–1263.

[134] *Logicrose*, at 1263: "As against the other party to the transaction, he is entitled to treat the benefit obtained by or promised to the agent as part of the consideration which should have been received by the principal (if he is a vendor) or as excess consideration provided by the principal (if he is a purchaser). In either case, *if he elects to affirm the transaction*, he is entitled to recover the amount of the benefit from the other party as money had and received to his use, but must give credit for anything already recovered from the agent." (Emphasis added). This passage provides a rationalisation for the briber's restitutionary liability: it is presumed by the law that the amount of the bribe is a sum the briber would otherwise have been willing to pay the principal (or relieve the principal from in terms of price reduction). *Whaley Bridge Calico Printing Co v Green and Smith*, above, similarly suggests that suing the briber for payment of a bribe that has not been paid goes hand in hand with accepting the underlying transaction: see 112.

[135] *Reading v Attorney-General* [1949] 2 K.B. 232 (CA); [1951] A.C. 507 (HL). In earlier cases the courts have spoken in terms of an irrebuttable presumption that the principal has suffered loss in the amount of the bribe (see for instance *Hovenden & Sons v Millhof* (1900) 83 L.T. 41), but the position is now so clear that there is no necessity to resort to such presumptions.

(1) The third party should have made a payment or bestowed some other benefit upon the agent knowing of the agent's personal interest and that he is the agent of the principal with whom the third party is proposing to contract.

(2) That payment or benefit has been kept secret by both the third party and the agent in the sense identified above.

(3) It has caused the principal to enter into a contract with the third party briber or otherwise to act to his detriment.

(4) The principal has thereby suffered loss. How loss is to be measured is discussed below.

7–063 The claim in bribery is a joint tort of briber and agent for which either or both may be sued. It will be seen that the tort of bribery is similar to the equitable wrong of dishonest assistance in a breach of fiduciary duty: however a critical distinction is that the tort of bribery is not dependent on proof of dishonesty and although the word "dishonesty" has been given a wide, objective meaning for the purpose of the law of dishonest assistance,[136] there are many cases where a bribe has been held to have been made where the briber is not tainted by dishonesty in any form.[137] The measure of damages/equitable compensation is the same.[138]

(ii) Principles for assessment of damages

7–064 Although, as discussed earlier, the principal need establish no loss caused by the receipt of the bribe in order to found a claim for recovery of the bribe or an entitlement to rescind the contract, by contrast if the principal is to obtain damages in excess of the amount of the bribe then he must prove his actual loss sustained in consequence of his entering into the transaction in respect of which the bribe was given.[139] In such a case the court will proceed by reference to the fundamental principle of damages, namely that the object of the law is to put the injured party in the same position as it would have been in but for the wrong.[140]

7–065 There is very little analysis in the authorities as to the correct approach to the assessment of damages. In *Fyffes Group Ltd v Templeman*[141] the parties agreed that the court should postulate an agent who is a hypothetical "honest and prudent negotiator owing undivided loyalty" to his principal, who presumably would have done his best to negotiate on behalf of his principal the best terms reasonably available, and then to compare the terms of the contract in fact negotiated with the terms which, on the balance of probabilities, would have been negotiated by that hypothetical agent. The judge (Toulson J) recorded that he had questioned whether this was the right approach, without finally ruling on the

---

[136] See generally Ch.13 on dishonest assistance.

[137] See above, para.7–016 and following.

[138] *Fyffes Group Ltd v Templeman* [2000] 2 Lloyd's Rep. 643, at 660.

[139] *Mahesan v Malaysia Government Officers' Co-Operative Housing Society Ltd* [1979] A.C. 374, at 383.

[140] *Fyffes Group Ltd v Templeman* [2000] 2 Lloyd's Rep. 643, citing *Duke of Westminster v Swinton* [1948] K.B. 524, at 534.

[141] *Fyffes Group Ltd v Templeman* [2000] 2 Lloyd's Rep. 643.

question one way or the other[142]: presumably the judge had in mind that a different, and possibly more appropriate, analysis involved asking what terms the actual agent would, on the balance of probabilities, have negotiated, assuming he had not been corrupted by the bribe. On this basis if the agent was, even absent the corrupting effect of the bribe, generally supine and a poor negotiator then he and the briber could take advantage of that fact to reduce their potential damages liability. In reality it seems unlikely that a court would be attracted by such contentions. The agent will inevitably owe a duty of care to his principal and the court should assess damages on the assumption that he discharged that duty. That assumption involves assuming an "honest and prudent negotiator owing undivided loyalty." In truth it seems unlikely that, bar special circumstances, a court would arrive at a different conclusion if it were to postulate, as its comparator, the hypothetical honest and prudent agent or the uncorrupted actual agent.

What the principal must prove is loss actually caused by the bribe. This may involve showing that absent the bribe, and on the balance of probabilities, the principal would either not have contracted with the third party at all (usually because it would have contracted with a different counterparty on better terms to those agreed with the third party),[143] or would have contracted with the third party on different, and better terms. This inquiry of course involves an investigation as to whether the third party or some other counterparty would have agreed to those better terms. Although there is no room for presumptions when it comes to assessing tortious damages (other than the in reality redundant presumption that the loss is at least in the amount of the bribe[144]) the size of the bribe is likely to be a relatively sure guide to the loss sustained: for example if the bribe is, say, 2 per cent of the price payable by the principal under the contract, the court may well take the view that, absent the bribe, the third party would have been willing to contract for the contracted price less 2 per cent.[145]   **7–066**

Given that bribery is an intentional tort, the defence of contributory negligence is not available.[146] It is probable that the test of remoteness is the same as that which applies in claims in deceit.[147]   **7–067**

(iii)   Loss of a chance?

In *Fyffes Group Ltd v Templeman* the claimant advanced an alternative analysis in respect of its claim for losses sustained by the making of the bribes. It contended that even if, in relation to any of the many contracts which it entered into with the   **7–068**

---

[142] The judge concluded that he did not need to adjudicate on the correctness of this approach where the parties had jointly agreed that damages should be assessed on this basis.

[143] Although it is perfectly conceivable that the corrupt agent has, as a result of the bribe, caused the principal to enter into a contract which, had it known the truth, it would not have entered into at all.

[144] Which, in the context of the tortious claim has no significance given that the law now recognises the principal's entitlement to claim the amount of the bribe from both agent and third party briber as a restitutionary claim.

[145] See for instance *Salford Corp v Lever* [1891] 1 Q.B. 168.

[146] *Corporacion Nacional del Cobre del Chile v Sogemin Metals* [1997] 1 W.L.R. 1396.

[147] As to which, see Ch.21.

third party briber, it was unable to show on the balance of probabilities that an honest and prudent negotiator would have negotiated a more favourable agreement, nonetheless it was entitled to damages reflecting the value of the lost chance that it would have done so. This analysis was, correctly, rejected. If the claimant failed to establish as a matter of probability that it had overpaid (or undercharged) the third party briber in any particular respect it had failed to establish causation of a head of loss. As the judge held:

"The reason for recognising a loss of a chance in certain circumstances as a head of loss is not to provide a fall back for a claimant who fails to provide his primary case, but because there are circumstances in which deprivation of a chance is the essence of the wrong."[148]

(7)   Account of Profits

7–069   The primary liability of a fiduciary who has obtained a secret benefit in breach of his duty of fidelity to his principal is to disgorge that benefit to his principal. Such a remedy is a form of account of profits. As we have seen it was finally resolved by the Supreme Court in *FHR European Ventures LLP v Cedar Capital Partners LLC*[149] that the bribed agent holds the bribe and any property representing the bribe on trust for his principal and so the law of bribery was brought into line with the general law of secret profits.

7–070   The more involved question of whether an account of profits was available against the third party briber was first grappled with in *Fyffes Group Ltd v Templeman*. Of course the briber is in a different position to the bribed agent. He is not a fiduciary of the wronged principal and owes him no positive duties. Nonetheless, after a lengthy review of the authorities relating to the position of a recipient of confidential information and of fiduciaries who have diverted opportunities away from their principal, the judge held that the briber of an agent, notwithstanding the absence of any personal obligations to the principal, may be required to account to the principal for benefits obtained from the corruption of the agent: "The law should not assist a party to retain the profits of such a vice."[150] However the judge emphasised that an account of profits was a discretionary remedy and it has subsequently been held that it may be refused where it is disproportionate to the particular form and extent of the wrongdoing.[151] However the remedy of an account of profits is only available

---

[148]   At 668, per Toulson J.

[149]   Above.

[150]   Toulson J relied upon a passage from the decision of Gibbs J in *Consul Development Pty Ltd v DPC Estates Pty Ltd* (1975) 132 C.L.R. 373, at 397, which has proved influential in English law: "If the maintenance of a very high standard of conduct on the part of fiduciaries is the purpose of the rule it would seem equally necessary to deter other persons from knowingly assisting those in a fiduciary position to violate their duties. If, on the other hand, the rule is to be explained simply because it would be contrary to equitable principles to allow a person to retain a benefit that he had gained from a breach of his fiduciary duty, it would appear equally inequitable that one who knowingly took part in the breach should retain a benefit that resulted therefrom. I therefore conclude, on principle, that a person who knowingly participates in a breach of fiduciary duty is liable to account to the person to whom the duty was owed for any benefit he has received as a result of such participation."

[151]   *Novoship (UK) Ltd v Nikitin* [2014] EWCA Civ 908; [2015] 1 Q.B. 499, at [119] (which endorsed the availability of the remedy in principle). The judge in *Fyffes* actually declined to grant the remedy

where the briber is liable in dishonest assistance in a breach of fiduciary duty, rather than simply in the tort of bribery.[152] As we have seen the elements of the former wrong are more stringent than the latter tort.

(8)   Election between Remedies

The principal may claim against the agent and the payer of the bribe both in respect of the bribe itself and for damage for any loss flowing from the entry into the contract or transaction which has been induced by the bribe. Indeed, as we have seen, the principal may additionally bring a claim for an account of profits. However these are alternative rather than cumulative remedies and the principal must, prior to entry of judgment, elect between them. Prior to 1979 the law had been obscure on this question,[153] but the matter was resolved by the Privy Council in *Mahesan v Malaysia Government Officers' Co-Operative Housing Society Ltd*.[154] The facts are stated above at para.7–003. The claimant principal claimed against the agent (the briber having absconded) for both the amount of the bribe and, in addition, the loss sustained by it as a result of the agent's conduct. It was decided, applying the earlier House of Lords decision in *United Australia Ltd v Barclays Bank Ltd*[155] that the principal could not obtain judgment for both remedies, but was obliged to elect between them, though such election was not irrevocable until judgment was recovered on one cause of action or the other. Of course the decision how to elect is likely to be dependent on whether the actual loss sustained by entry into the contract in respect of which the bribe was given was less or greater than the amount of the bribe.

7–071

---

of account of profits because he found that in that case it was highly likely that had the agent not been dishonest the claimant would still have contracted with the third party briber, albeit on more favourable terms. Insofar as the briber made an ordinary profit element, it was not caused by the bribe but was profit for the provision of services for which there would have been a contract in any event. On the remedy of an account of profits and the causation requirement in a case where it is sought against a third party briber/dishonest assister, see further Ch.22.

[152] Toulson J's analysis was approved subsequently in a number of first instance authorities: see *Ultraframe (UK) Ltd v Fielding* [2005] EWHC 1638 (Ch), at [1658]–[1659], per Lewison J; *Tajik Aluminium Plant v Ermatov* [2006] EWHC 7 (Ch), at [23], per Blackburne J; *OJSC Oil Co Yugraneft v Abramovich* [2008] EWHC 2613 (Comm), at [377] and [392], per Christopher Clarke J; *Fiona Trust and Holding Corp v Privalov* [2010] EWHC 3199 (Comm), at [66], per Andrew Smith J and *Otkritie International Investment Management Ltd v Urumov* [2014] EWHC 191 (Comm), at [79], per Eder J. The Court of Appeal in *Novoship (UK) Ltd v Nikitin* [2014] EWCA Civ 908; [2015] 1 Q.B. 499 reviewed these authorities and approved them.

[153] Two early cases had suggested that the principal could recover both the amount of the bribe and any loss sustained by the principal: *Salford Corp v Lever* [1891] 1 Q.B. 168 and *Hovenden and Sons v Millhoff* (1900) 83 L.T. 41.

[154] *Mahesan v Malaysia Government Officers' Co-Operative Housing Society Ltd* [1979] A.C. 374. See also *Hurstanger v Wilson* [2007] EWCA Civ 299; [2007] 1 W.L.R. 2351, at [38], per Tuckey LJ; *Novoship (UK) Ltd v Mikhaylyuk* [2012] EWHC 3586 (Comm) (reversed on appeal but not on this point), at [111], per Christopher Clarke J.

[155] *United Australia Ltd v Barclays Bank Ltd* [1941] A.C. 1. In that case the principle was confirmed that where the same facts give rise in law to two causes of action against a single defendant, one for money had and received and the other for damages in tort, the claimant must elect between the remedies.

7–072 It is perfectly proper for the claimant to seek a determination from the court of the sums which would be due in respect its various remedies. This is because the claimant will not know, prior to then, which remedy it will be to its advantage to elect for. Having received the court's judgment on these questions it can then make its election prior to the making of the final order.

7–073 *Mahesan* was a case where the claim was brought against the agent alone. What it decided was that the principal cannot obtain judgment against the agent for the amount of the bribe *and* the amount of its loss caused by the bribe.[156] By contrast, where both agent and briber are proceeded against, the fact that the principal compromises its claim against the briber on terms of payment of a sum of money does not affect its claim against the agent for the sum of the bribe.[157]

(9)   Forfeiture of Remuneration[158]

7–074 It is a trite principle of the law of agency that where an agent has acted dishonestly then he will forfeit his right to fees paid or payable by the principal.[159] That principle applies where the agent has received a bribe from a third party which is directly related to performance of the duties in respect of which the fees are payable. It follows that where the principal has paid the agent such fees then he may additionally claim to recover them, in addition to any claim in respect of the bribe (or, where the fees have not been paid, set up the bribe as a defence to the agent's claim). Although the principle was stated in robust terms by the Court of Appeal in *Rhodes v Macalister*[160] and restated with similar robustness very recently in *Imageview Management Ltd v Jack*[161] it is suggested that the courts should be astute to ensure that the forfeiture does not extend beyond the purview of the transaction induced by the bribe and that where

---

[156] The suggestion to the contrary in *Fiona Trust & Holding Corp v Skarga* [2013] EWCA Civ 275, per Longmore LJ at [1], seems merely an infelicity of expression.

[157] *Bagnall v Carlton* (1877) 6 Ch.D. 371.

[158] On this generally, see Ch.22, section E.

[159] See *Snell's Equity*, op cit, para.7–062; and Ch.22, section E.

[160] *Rhodes v Macalister* (1923) 29 Com. Cas. 19, per Scrutton LJ at 27: "The law I take to be this: that an agent must not take remuneration from the other side without both disclosure to and consent from his principal. If he does take such remuneration he acts so adversely to this employer that he forfeits all remuneration from the employer, although the employer takes the benefit and has not suffered a loss by it." See also *Andrews v Ramsay* [1903] 2 K.B. 635; *Hippisley v Knee Bros.* [1905] 1 K.B. 1.

[161] *Imageview Management Ltd v Jack* [2009] EWCA Civ 63; [2009] Bus L.R. 1034, at [50], per Jacob LJ: "The policy reason runs as follows. We are here concerned not with merely damages such as those for a tort or breach of contract but with what the remedy should be when the agent has betrayed the trust reposed in him—notions of equity and conscience are brought into play. Necessarily such a betrayal may not come to light. If all the agent has to pay if and when he is found out are damages the temptation to betray the trust reposed in him is all the greater. So the strict rule is there as a real deterrent to betrayal. As Scrutton LJ said in *Rhodes's* case 29 Com Cas 19, at 28: "The more that principle is enforced, the better for the honesty of commercial transactions".

the acceptance of the bribe was not attended by any absence of good faith on the part of the agent, the remedy of forfeiture will not be appropriate.[162]

---

[162] Compare the result in *Keppel v Wheeler* [1927] 1 K.B. 577 and see the recent comments of Vos J in *Governor and Co of the Bank of Ireland v Jaffery* [2012] EWHC 1377 (Ch), at [371] and Newey J in *Avrahami v Biran* [2013] EWHC 1776 (Ch), at [343].

CHAPTER 8

CONVERSION

A.   INTRODUCTION

The tort of conversion protects claimants' rights to possess corporeal personal property.[1] If B interferes with A's use and possession of his goods, then the tort of conversion provides A with a means of seeking redress for losses and (in appropriate cases) the recovery of the goods in question.

8–001

Frauds frequently involve the transfer of goods from one person to another. In each such case, it is worth considering whether the tort of conversion is engaged. Three particular situations in which this is likely to be the case are as follows:

8–002

(1)   First, the effect of the fraud is such that possession of goods has passed from A to B under a completely void (as opposed to voidable) transaction. This may (but not necessarily will) be the case in instances of identity fraud (see e.g. *Shogun Finance v Hudson*).[2] In such cases, B will typically not have received any right to exclude A from possession of the goods at all, and will be liable to A for conversion much as he would have been if he had simply stolen the goods in question.

(2)   Second, the effect of the fraud is such that possession of the goods has passed from A to B under a voidable transaction, and that transaction is, in fact, avoided. An example would be where A sells to B a valuable painting at an undervalue because B, a crooked art dealer, has fraudulently represented to him that what was in fact painted by Constable is a fake. From the point of avoidance (but not earlier), B will typically no longer have any right to exclude A from possession of the painting, and may be liable to A for conversion if he refuses to return it.[3]

(3)   Third, as a consequence of B's wrongdoing, A's goods have been transmitted to a third party, C. This might be because B has resold goods received from A before B's fraud was discovered (as occurred in *Shogun*), or because B has purported to transact with C on behalf of A without authority to do so (see e.g. *Farquharson Brothers & Co v C. King & Co*).[4] In such cases, the question of whether A is able to sue C in conversion will

---

[1] I.e. tangible things, other than land. For brevity, we use the term "goods".

[2] *Shogun Finance v Hudson* [2004] 1 A.C. 919.

[3] See D. O'Sullivan, S. Elliott and R. Zakrzewski, *The Law of Rescission*, 2nd edn (Oxford: OUP, 2015), paras 14.14–14.17.

[4] *Farquharson Brothers & Co v C. King & Co* [1902] A.C. 325—albeit in that case the fraudulent agent concealed the identity of the true owner of the timber altogether.

depend upon whether the transaction between B and C conferred upon C a superior right to possess the goods than that enjoyed by A. This is a complex area of law. The default rule is that B cannot transmit greater rights to goods than B himself possesses.[5] However, this rule is subject to extensive qualification by both common law and statute. A useful—but far from exhaustive—introduction to this topic can be found in Ch.7 of *Benjamin's Sale of Goods*.[6]

B.   THE ELEMENTS OF THE TORT

8–003   The elements of the tort of conversion have been variously defined.[7] While the precise formulation of the elements may vary, their key features can now be stated with some confidence, at least pending Parliamentary intervention or a revision of this area of the law by the Supreme Court:

(1)   There must be (or have been) corporeal personal property.

(2)   At the time of the conduct complained of, the claimant must have possessed the goods or had an immediate right to possess the goods which was superior to any enjoyed by the defendant.

(3)   The conduct in question must have been (a) (subject to one exception) deliberate; (b) inconsistent with the claimant's rights in respect of those goods; and (c) so extensive as to exclude the claimant from the possession and use of the goods in question. Patently, the simple theft of goods will fulfil these requirements.

These elements form the structure for much of the remainder of this chapter.

8–004   The pleader should also be mindful of para.7.2 of CPR PD 16 (claimants seeking the return of goods to state the value of those goods) and CPR r.19.5A(1) (claimants to plead the name and address of every non-party known to have an interest in the goods in question).

---

[5] Or, as it is still sometimes put, *nemo dat quod non habet.*

[6] M. Bridge (ed), *Benjamin's Sale of Goods*, 10th edn (London: Sweet & Maxwell, 2017). In cases concerning actual or purported agents, reference should also be made to P.G. Watts (ed), *Bowstead and Reynolds on Agency*, 21st edn (London: Sweet & Maxwell, 2017), articles 83 to 89. Cases involving corporate agents or transfers of goods across jurisdictional boundaries will require reference to specialist works on such subjects.

[7] See, in particular, *Kuwait Airways Corp v Iraq Airways Co (Nos 4 and 5)* [2002] 2 A.C. 883, at [119]; *Bunnings Group Ltd v CHEP Australia Ltd* [2011] NSWCA 342, at [124] and The Eighteenth Report of the Law Reform Committee (Conversion and Detinue) 1971 Cmnd 4774, at 38 (although note that this last document described the tort of conversion before its enlargement by s.2 of the Torts (Interference with Goods) Act 1977).

(1)   The Current or Prior Existence of Corporeal Personal Property

The tort of conversion is—at least at present—exclusively concerned with corporeal personal property. Generally speaking, these goods will exist at the time at which the conversion complained of occurs, however this is not necessarily the case. If a bailee fails to deliver bailed goods upon demand at the expiration of the bailment, the failure to deliver the goods would itself constitute a conversion, even if they had been destroyed or lost at some prior point in time.[8]

8–005

(i)   The position in relation to land

Land cannot be the subject of a conversion (*Mackintosh v Trotter*).[9] However items which were formerly part of land until severed and removed may be. An example of such a case is *Creative Foundation v Dreamland Leisure Ltd*, in which tenants of a building were liable for the conversion of the Banksy mural entitled "Art Buff", which they had detached from a wall.[10]

8–006

(ii)   The position in relation to intangible property and electronic data

The question of whether intangible property can be the subject matter of a conversion was answered in the negative by the House of Lords in *OBG v Allan*.[11] It follows that software and other electronic data (as opposed to physical computer hardware) cannot be the subject matter of a conversion either—see the Court of Appeal decisions in *Your Response Ltd v Datateam Business Media Ltd*[12] and *Environment Agency v Churngold Recycling Ltd*,[13] in which the question was expressed to have been put "beyond doubt", at least at the level of the Court of Appeal.

8–007

(iii)   The position in relation to money

Whether money can be the subject of conversion is sometimes the subject of confusion. Specific physical banknotes or coins are personal property and are capable of conversion. Thus, if B steals a £10 note from A's wallet, or finds a £10

8–008

---

[8] This form of conversion would, prior to the coming into force of s.2 of the Torts (Interference with Goods) Act 1977, have been termed detinue.

[9] *Mackintosh v Trotter* (1838) 3 Meeson and Welsby 184.

[10] *Creative Foundation v Dreamland Leisure Ltd* [2015] EWHC 2556 (Ch); [2016] Ch. 253.

[11] See *OBG v Allan* [2007] UKHL 21; [2008] 1 A.C. 1, at [95]–[100], [105], [106], [271], [321] and [322]. This 3 to 2 decision has its critics, and it is possible that it might be revisited in the future. It is perhaps worth noting that, in the recent Queensland case of *Aklia Holdings Pty Ltd v The Carter Group Pty Ltd* [2017] QSC 75, an application to strike out a claim for the conversion of intangible rights was unsuccessful. One should also be aware of the potential application of the proprietary restitutionary claim, distinct from a claim for delivery up of converted goods which was recognised in respect of intangible goods in *Armstrong DLW GmbH v Winnington Networks Ltd* [2012] EWHC 10 (Ch); [2013] Ch. 156, at [84]–[94].

[12] *Your Response Ltd v Datateam Business Media Ltd* [2014] EWCA Civ 281; [2015] Q.B. 41, at [27].

[13] *Environment Agency v Churngold Recycling Ltd* [2014] EWCA Civ 909, at [16].

note which has fallen from A's pocket and uses it for his own purposes, B may be liable for conversion.[14] Where banknotes and coins differ from other goods is that the *nemo dat quod non habet* rule does not apply to them. If they are paid over in good faith and for consideration (and thereby pass into currency), the recipient will always become entitled to possess those notes and coins to the exclusion of anyone else.[15] There would be no question of that recipient being sued for conversion of the notes and coins (although the person who paid them over might be).

8–009   Cases of fraud in which it is necessary to plead conversion of physical banknotes or coins are likely to be relatively few and far between. In circumstances in which A has been tricked out of money by B, A's rights are likely to be adequately—and more naturally—vindicated by the tort of deceit, the law of unjust enrichment, and his various rights in equity. Nevertheless, there may be rare instances in which a claim in conversion is a necessary or appropriate course to take.

(iv)   The position in relation to negotiable instruments and other documents

8–010   A cheque can, provided that the drawer has sufficient funds to his credit, be converted.[16] Similarly, physical documents which evidence or guarantee an obligation to pay, such as bearer bonds, share certificates, insurance policies or guarantees may be converted.[17] Title deeds, historically, could be converted.[18] In practice, these latter categories are likely to become of decreasing relevance in future years as the use of physical documents in financial and property transactions decreases.

(2)   Possession or an immediate right to possess the goods superior to any enjoyed by the defendant

8–011   The claimant must have, at the time of the conversion complained of, either possession of the goods converted or an immediate right to possess the goods which is superior to any enjoyed by the defendant. Ownership of the goods in question is neither necessary nor sufficient.[19] One should note the following points.

(i)   Possession

8–012   What "possession" means in the law of tortious interference with goods is a complex (and woefully neglected) subject. What follows is (necessarily) the

---

[14] *Hall v Dean* (1599) Cro. Eliz. 841 and *Burn v Morris* (1834) 2 Cr. & M. 579.
[15] On the significance of coins or banknotes passing into currency—see C. Proctor, *Mann on the Legal Aspect of Money*, 7th edn (Oxford: OUP, 2012), paras 1.72–1.79.
[16] *Morison v London County and Westminster Bank Ltd* [1914] 3 K.B. 356, at 379.
[17] *MCC Proceeds Inc v Lehman Bros (International) Europe* [1998] 4 All E.R. 675, at [696] and [699].
[18] *Plant v Cotterill* (1860) 5 H. & N. 430.
[19] *Bute (Marquess) v Barclays Bank LD* [1955] 1 Q.B. 202, at 211.

briefest of outlines of the relevant law. In any case in which there is any doubt as to whether a claimant had possession of goods in the relevant sense, one should consult the leading textbooks on the subject.[20]

The meaning of possession in this context is almost, but not quite, the same as what a layman would call possession. The elements of legal possession have been summarised thus:

8–013

> "A thing taken by a person of his own motion and for himself, and subject in his hands, or under his control, to the uses of which it is capable, is in that person's possession."[21]

Possession can be broken into two elements.

First, the possessor must have acquired factual possession of the asset. This can be acquired in any number of ways, and can be done by the possessor personally, or via agents or employees.[22] Often, a possessor will have obtained factual possession following the delivery of the asset to him by a previous possessor. The key is to receive or establish exclusive control of the asset (or, which is to say the same thing in different words, that one is in a position to exclude unauthorised interference with the asset).[23] In *The Tubantia*, the claimants took possession of a Dutch steamship, sunk by the German Imperial Navy in 1916, by attaching buoys over the ship, cutting through its hull, and sending divers within to retrieve its cargo. It was found that factual possession over the sunken ship had been acquired by the claimants because, with the buoys in place, it would have been impossible for others to take control of the sunken ship save by force.

8–014

The second element is "the manifest intent of sole and exclusive dominion."[24] The possessor must intend to control the asset, at a time at which it is in his factual possession, for his own purposes, and that intention must have an outward manifestation. Thus (to adapt an example used by A.P. Bell),[25] a well-behaved guest at a dinner party would not legally possess the host's silver cutlery. Although the guest may be physically using the cutlery, he would not intend to exclude the guest's control over the cutlery. Even if the thought crossed the guest's mind to steal the cutlery, legal possession would not actually be usurped until the guest manifested that intention by slipping the cutlery into his pocket. For modern discussions of intention to possess (or *animus possidendi* as it is still sometimes known) see *Parker v British Airways Board* and *Waverley BC v Fletcher*.[26]

8–015

---

[20] See, in particular, F. Pollock, *Pollock and Wright on Possession in the Common Law* (Oxford: Clarendon Press, 1888) (still the leading textbook on the subject) and the useful summaries in A.P. Bell, *Modern Law of Personal Property in England and Ireland* (London: Butterworths, 1989), pp.33–61 and Bridge et al, *The Law of Personal Property*, (London: Sweet & Maxwell, 2013), paras 2–001—2–060.

[21] *The Tubantia (No.2)* [1924] P. 78, at 89, per Sir Henry Duke P.

[22] See M.A. Jones, A.M. Dugdale and M. Simpson (eds), *Clerk & Lindsell on Torts*, 22nd edn (London: Sweet & Maxwell, 2016), para.17–56.

[23] *Waverley BC v Fletcher* [1996] Q.B. 334, at 339.

[24] Pollock, *Pollock and Wright on Possession in the Common Law* (1888), pp.20–21.

[25] See Bell, *Modern Law of Personal Property in England and Ireland* (1989), p.61.

[26] *Parker v British Airways Board* and *Waverley BC v Fletcher* [1982] Q.B. 1004 and [1996] Q.B. 334 respectively.

8–016   Two further things should be noted regarding legal possession.[27] First, it is exclusive. While a chattel might have many owners, it can have no more than one possessor at any one time. Second, so long as goods exist, their possessor continues to enjoy the legal possession of goods until that legal possession (and not mere custody) is either intentionally abandoned by the possessor, intentionally delivered by the possessor to a third party, or intentionally seized by a third party. Thus, if A leaves his bike unchained outside a library while he goes inside, the bike remains in his legal possession even though it is not in his physical custody or control. That possession continues until B steals the bike, bringing A's possession to an end.

(ii)   Immediate right to possess

8–017   Even if A does not legally possess the goods which were converted, he may sue in conversion if he had an immediate right of possession at the time of the conversion. Bailment at will is an example: if A lends B his lawnmower, on the understanding that B will return the lawnmower on demand, A has transferred legal possession, but retains an immediate right of possession. By contrast, if B hires A's caravan for the fixed term of one year, A will not have an immediate right to possession of the caravan until the fixed term expires.

8–018   One should note that there is a degree of controversy as to whether a merely contractual right to possess the property in question is sufficient to found an action in conversion, or whether some form of right in rem is required. It now appears to be the better view that a contractual right to immediate possession suffices.[28] However, one should note the view expressed in *Clerk & Lindsell on Torts*.[29]

(iii)   Possession, and rights to possess, are what is important, not ownership as such

8–019   The distinction between rights to possess and ownership is less esoteric than it may appear. Imagine B gets cranberry juice on his bedsheets, takes them to the drycleaners to be cleaned and does not pay his bill. Pending payment, the drycleaners are entitled to retain physical possession of the sheets. B remains the owner of the sheets, but he neither possesses them nor has the immediate right to do so; the drycleaners do. The drycleaners are therefore entitled to exclude B from possession of the sheets without committing a conversion. Furthermore, if B broke into the drycleaners and took the sheets, B would be liable for converting the sheets, notwithstanding that the sheets are his own property.[30]

---

[27] See further Pollock, *Pollock and Wright on Possession in the Common Law* (1888), pp.20–25.

[28] See the obiter discussion in *Iran v The Bakarat Galleries Ltd* [2007] EWCA Civ 1374; [2009] Q.B. 22, at [30]–[31]. See also S. Green, J. Randall, *The Tort of Conversion* (London: Hart Publishing, 2009), p.95 onwards.

[29] Jones, Dugdale and Simpson (eds), *Clerk & Lindsell on Torts* (2016), para.17–61.

[30] See e.g. *Brierly v Kendall* (1852) 17 Q.B. 937 in which the bailee of certain goods successfully sued his bailors in trespass and conversion.

Even if a third party, C, broke into the drycleaners and stole B's sheets, B would not have a claim in conversion against him, because B's right to possess the sheets is in abeyance pending payment to the drycleaners; it is not immediate.[31] **8–020**

However, the law of tort is not without assistance for B where wrongs are done to his goods while they are out of his possession; the law now recognises a tort of reversionary injury.[32] Depending on the precise facts, the loss, damage or destruction of his goods may also give rise to liability for breach of contract or duty of care. **8–021**

(iv) It is necessary to have a better right to the goods than the defendant, not the best right in the world

Related to the fact that the tort of conversion protects rights of possession rather than ownership is the fact that it operates within a sphere of relative, rather than absolute, rights. **8–022**

This is illustrated by the famous case of *Armory v Delamirie*.[33] A sweeper's boy found a jewel and took it to a goldsmith for valuation. The goldsmith removed some stones from the jewel and kept them for himself. The boy was able to successfully sue the goldsmith in conversion. Notwithstanding the fact that the boy had no right to the jewel when he found it, he acquired legal possession when he did find it, and that possession conferred rights upon him which were enforceable against anyone who did not have a better right to possession than he did (his action against the goldsmith would have failed if, for example, the goldsmith had been the individual who had misplaced the jewel). **8–023**

Costello v Chief Constable of Derbyshire is a similar, albeit more striking, case.[34] It concerned a stolen car. The Court of Appeal found that the (presumed) thief was entitled to sue the police for keeping the car from him when their statutory authority to do so expired. Again, this was because Costello's possession of the car, even though apparently founded on theft, was enforceable against anyone with an inferior right to the car. (Again, Costello's action would have failed if he had stolen the car in question from the Derbyshire police force.) **8–024**

(3) Conduct which is (A) Deliberate; (B) Inconsistent with the Claimant's Rights and (C) so Extensive as to Exclude the Claimant from the Possession and use of the Goods in Question

(i) Deliberate conduct

The act whereby the defendant deprives the claimant of his possessory rights must be deliberate in the sense that the defendant intended to do the act in **8–025**

---

[31] *Gordon v Harper* (1796) 7 Term Reports 9.
[32] See further Jones, Dugdale and Simpson (eds), *Clerk & Lindsell on Torts* (2016), paras 17–148—17–149.
[33] *Armory v Delamirie* (1721) 1 Stra. 505.
[34] *Costello v Chief Constable of Derbyshire* [2001] EWCA Civ 381; [2001] 1 W.L.R. 1437.

question and thereby intended to assert possessory rights over the goods converted. It is not, however, necessary to show any intention on the part of the defendant towards the claimant.[35]

8–026　By way of an example: if B finds A's cat wandering the streets, takes it home and adopts it, that is a conversion. B has deliberately asserted possessory rights over the cat. The questions of whether or not B knew, suspected, or should have known or suspected, that the cat formerly belonged to anyone else are irrelevant. His act would still be a conversion of A's property even if B genuinely and reasonably believed that the cat had lived in the wild its entire life. By contrast, if A's cat enters B's house via an open window, B has not converted A's cat, as B has not deliberately asserted possessory rights over the cat; the cat found its way into B's custody without B's knowledge or intent.

8–027　The one exception to the requirement for deliberate conduct is the case in which a bailee fails to return goods to his bailor because the goods were lost, destroyed or otherwise rendered inaccessible as a consequence of the bailee's breach of duty. This would formerly give rise to an action in detinue (as well as, possibly, negligence and breach of bailment). Following the enactment of s.2 of the Torts (Interference with Goods) Act 1977, this fact pattern now gives rise to an action in conversion.

(ii)　Inconsistent with the claimant's rights

8–028　The act complained of must be inconsistent with the claimant's rights. Obviously, the claimant cannot complain of conduct in relation to his property which he has authorised (explicitly or impliedly), or which is authorised by law (such as seizure of property under writs/warrants of control).

(iii)　So extensive as to exclude the claimant from the possession and use of the goods in question

8–029　Conduct which does not amount to a deprivation of the claimant's possession and use of the goods in question will not be a conversion, although it may be a trespass. If B steals A's computer, that is a conversion. If he merely uses it without permission, that is a trespass, but not a conversion.[36]

8–030　Whether the defendant's conduct amounted to a deprivation of the claimant's possessory title is a matter of fact and degree, dependent on all the circumstances of the case, and the degree of deprivation required for conversion depends on context. Ultimately, whether a particular act amounts to a conversion is a matter for the evaluation of the court.

---

[35] *Marfani & Co Ltd v Midland Bank Ltd* [1968] 1 W.L.R. 956, at 970–971.

[36] See too Professor Tettenborn's description of the difference as that between moving a bottle of wine (trespass) and drinking the bottle (conversion), Jones, Dugdale and Simpson (eds), *Clerk & Lindsell on Torts* (2016), para.17–02.

The types of conduct which may amount to conversion are potentially infinite in variety. Professor Tettenborn has suggested the following broad categories, further discussion of which can be found in *Clerk & Lindsell on Torts*[37]:   **8–031**

(1) when goods are wrongfully taken or received by someone not entitled to do so;
(2) when goods are wrongfully parted with;
(3) when goods are lost by a bailee in breach of his duty to the bailor and, as a consequence, not delivered to the bailor upon demand at the termination of the bailment;
(4) when goods are wrongfully sold, even without delivery, so as to pass good title to the buyer;
(5) when goods are wrongfully retained[38];
(6) when goods are wrongfully misused or destroyed; and
(7) when the defendant, without physically interfering with the goods, wrongfully denies access to them to the claimant.

The fine line which can exist between conversion and trespass is demonstrated by the two cases of *Fouldes v Willoughby*[39] and *Hiort v Bott*.[40]   **8–032**

In *Fouldes*, the proprietor of a ferry removed a passenger's horses from the ferry with the intention of inducing the passenger to disembark. The passenger refused and the ferry continued its journey, leaving the horses on the quayside. The defendant could not, given the circumstances of the removal of the horses, be said to have sought to assert any kind of possessory right over the horses, and so was not liable in conversion. The proprietor's conduct inherently recognised, and relied upon, the fact that the horses belonged to the passenger.   **8–033**

Conversely in *Hiort*, the defendant had received a consignment of barley by mistake. He informed a third-party broker of the mistake and, in order that the broker could return the barley to the seller, indorsed the delivery order in favour of the broker. Instead of returning the barley, the broker absconded with it. The seller successfully sued the defendant in conversion, on the basis that, by indorsing the delivery order in favour of the broker, the defendant had (with the best of motives) exercised rights of possession over the barley which were inconsistent with (and exclusive of) those of the seller.   **8–034**

C.   REMEDIES

At common law, the relief in respect of a conversion is damages. However, the remedial powers of the Court are now extended by s.3 of the Torts (Interference with Goods) Act 1977, which provides: **8–035**

---

[37] Jones, Dugdale and Simpson (eds), *Clerk & Lindsell on Torts* (2016), paras 17–07—17–34.
[38] *Mainline Private Hire Ltd v Nolan* [2011] EWCA Civ 189.
[39] *Fouldes v Willoughby* (1841) 8 M & W 540; 151 E.R. 1153.
[40] *Hiort v Bott* (1874) L.R. 9 Ex 86.

"(1)   In proceedings for wrongful interference against a person who is in possession or in control of the goods relief may be given in accordance with this section, so far as appropriate.

(2)   The relief is—

    (a)   an order for delivery of the goods, and for payment of any consequential damages, or

    (b)   an order for delivery of the goods, but giving the defendant the alternative of paying damages by reference to the value of the goods, together in either alternative with payment of any consequential damages, or

    (c)   damages.

(3)   Subject to rules of court—

    (a)   relief shall be given under only one of paragraphs (a), (b) and (c) of subsection (2),

    (b)   relief under paragraph (a) of subsection (2) is at the discretion of the court, and the claimant may choose between the others. "

8–036   Orders for delivery up under s.2(a) will not generally be granted where damages would be an adequate remedy.[41]

8–037   The measure of any damages awarded is, in principle, the same as that for any other tort. The object is to put the claimant in the same position as he would have been but for the defendant's wrongdoing. In circumstances in which the claimant is permanently deprived of the goods in question, he will typically receive the market value of the goods at the time of the conversion (even if it is proved that but for the conversion, someone else would have stolen the goods in question).[42] The court will generally consider the market value to be the price that would have been obtained on disposal rather than replacement value, but there is a degree of flexibility as to the approach to be taken.[43]

If the claimant can show additional loss arising from the conversion (such as a loss of the opportunity to benefit from an increase in the goods' value after the conversion, loss of use, loss of profits, etc), then that loss will be similarly recoverable, albeit defendants who were not aware of their own wrongdoing will be protected by the usual rules of remoteness.[44]

---

[41] *Blue Sky One Ltd v Blue Airways LLC* [2009] EWHC 3314 (Comm), at [309]–[316].

[42] *Kuwait Airways Corp v Iraqi Airways Co (Nos 4 and 5)* [2002] 2 A.C. 883, at [82] and [129].

[43] Jones, Dugdale and Simpson (eds), *Clerk & Lindsell on Torts* (2016), para.17–98.

[44] See further Jones, Dugdale and Simpson (eds), *Clerk & Lindsell on Torts* (2016), paras 17–106—17–114.

SECTION B

EQUITABLE CLAIMS

CHAPTER 9

ESTABLISHING A TRUST

A.   INTRODUCTION

(1)   Scope of this Chapter and its Importance

This chapter is concerned with the question of whether property held by a person   **9–001**
or group of persons, typically the defendant in legal proceedings (who we shall
refer to in this chapter as "B") is (or was) held on trust for another person or
group of persons, who will usually be the claimant (and who we shall refer to in
this chapter as "A"). Establishing that property is or was so held will commonly
be a matter of importance where party A is the claimant in a fraud claim (and,
conversely, resisting a claim put in that way will usually be of importance to a
defendant). One of the principal reasons is that, where property is or has been
held on trust, the claimant may be able to assert a claim for its return, or the
return of property acquired with it or profits derived from it, on a proprietary
basis. Such proprietary claims hold great tactical advantages for claimants for a
number of reasons, including that:

(1)   they avoid the need for the claimant to participate in a distribution of the
      defendant's estate pari passu with other unsecured creditors when a
      defendant is insolvent;
(2)   they can enable the claimant to take the benefit of an increase in value of
      the relevant property;
(3)   they expand the range of potential defendants, by opening up claims against
      subsequent recipients of the property; and
(4)   in a number of respects, there is a wider range of, or more generous
      approach to, interim relief for a claimant with a proprietary claim.

There are, however, many other purposes for which it is necessary to identify   **9–002**
whether property is or was held on trust. For example, the identification of
property as trust property may be the first element of a personal claim by party A
(as claimant) against party B (as defendant) for breach of trust; it may be the first
element of a personal claim by party A (as claimant) against a third party
defendant for dishonest assistance in a breach of trust or knowing receipt of the
proceeds of a breach of trust; or it may be a necessary step for a third party
claimant to enforce a judgment obtained against party A (as defendant) by some
form of execution against property held by B on trust for A.

(2) Structure of this Chapter

9–003   This chapter will address the following topics:

(1)   Some fundamentals of trust law (in section B) including:
  (i)   The nature of a trust;
  (ii)   The fundamental requirement for ascertainable and distinct property; and
  (iii) The conventional classification of trusts by method of creation;
(2)   Express trusts (in section C);
(3)   Resulting trusts (in section D);
(4)   Constructive trusts (in section E);
(5)   Statutory trusts (in section F).

9–004   The questions of how one identifies the property which is amenable to a trust-based proprietary claim and how one pursues such a claim are addressed in Ch.24. Personal claims for breach of trust are addressed in Ch.23, dishonest assistance in a breach of trust is addressed in Ch.14 and unconscionable receipt of the proceeds of a breach of trust is addressed in Ch.13. The relevance of trusts in the enforcement context is addressed in Ch.40.

B. SOME FUNDAMENTALS OF TRUST LAW

(1) Nature of a Trust

9–005   A full analysis of the juridical nature of the trust in English law is beyond the scope of this work. In essence, a trust describes a situation in which "B" is the owner of property as a matter of common law, but the Court will compel B (and, in some circumstances, third parties) to proceed on the basis that B is obliged as a matter of equity to hold that property on certain terms for the benefit of "A"; with the result that, while B may be described as the "legal" owner of the property, A is regarded as the "equitable" or "beneficial" owner.[1]

9–006   In this situation, B is described as the "trustee", and A as the "beneficiary", of a trust. Importantly for practical purposes, in the case of most types of property, it is B who will appear in any applicable formal record of ownership (the title register at the Land Registry in the case of registered land, the share register in the case of company shares, the bank's mandate in the case of a bank account and so forth), while the interest of A will not be recorded and may be difficult to ascertain. However, although in the classic situation the trustee of a trust holds legal title to the trust property, it is now equally possible in principle for a trust to exist of equitable or other property vested in the trustee.

---

[1] There is academic controversy as to whether the interest created under a trust is properly to be regarded as "proprietary": see the helpful summary by Lord Mance JSC in *Akers v Samba* [2017] UKSC 6; [2017] A.C. 424, at [15]–[16]. The conventional view is that it is.

(2) Fundamental Requirement for Ascertainable and Distinct Property Subject to the Trust

All trusts concern the ownership of property. Therefore, there can be no trust without some property subject to the trust which is, at least in principle, distinct and ascertainable. That requirement is both fundamental and obvious. But some of its implications, as will appear from Section C below, are not. The property need not necessarily be in England for an English law trust to exist in relation to it, although additional conflicts of laws questions (which fall outside the scope of this chapter) will of course arise when it is not. **9–007**

(3) Conventional Categorisation of Trusts by Method of Creation

Trusts are conventionally divided into four categories, by reference to the way in which they come into existence, namely: express trusts, resulting trusts, constructive trusts and statutory trusts. Each category is addressed further below in the next section. But it is helpful to begin with a brief explanation of the nature of each category, so that the terminology may be understood. While the boundaries and conceptual basis of the categorisation are subject to academic debate, it is conventionally understood as follows. **9–008**

(1) *Express trusts.* An express trust is a trust created deliberately by operation of the *actual intention* of the person creating the trust. The person creating the trust (known as the settlor) may declare that he holds certain property upon trust. Alternatively, he may cause property to be transferred to third party trustees (either while alive or under the terms of his will) on terms that it be held on a specific trust. As is addressed further below, although the nature of the beneficiary's proprietary interest in an express trust is the same as that in any other type of trust, there are important differences between express and other types of trust (both in relation to the restrictions which apply to the creation of the trust and in relation to the obligations of the trustee).

(2) *Resulting trusts.* A resulting trust describes a situation where a transferee of property, or a recipient of property acquired with funds which have been provided by another, is found to hold all or part of the interest in that property on trust for the transferor/funder by operation of law either (1) because the transferor/funder has parted with the property gratuitously and is therefore presumed not to have intended to part with beneficial ownership, unless there is some material to establish that he did so intend, or (2) because the transferor has given the property to the transferee to be held on an express trust, but without accounting for all of the beneficial interest in the property. It is conventionally said that in both types of resulting trusts the law operates to recognise a *presumed intention* of the

settlor,[2] although there do appear to be cases in which a resulting trust arises in response to evidence demonstrating an actual intention to retain beneficial ownership.

(3) *Constructive Trusts.* A constructive trust arises by operation of law because equity deems property received or held in certain circumstances to be held on trust, without reference to intention. It is important to appreciate that, in English law as it currently stands (unlike in some other leading common law jurisdictions), all constructive trusts are "institutional" rather than "remedial".[3] In other words, they arise by the application of fixed legal rules to given factual circumstances; although the Court may declare that a constructive trust exists in the circumstances, the Court does not create the trust. As we will see the constructive trust plays a very significant role in civil fraud litigation.

(4) *Statutory trusts.* A statutory trust arises by operation of one of the many statutes which create trusts. A complete survey of such trusts is beyond the scope of this work. It is important to appreciate that, although a statutory trust is likely to share many of the characteristics of trusts which arise under the general law, its existence and characteristics will ultimately be a matter of construction of the statute in question: it is not always to be assumed that, when Parliament uses the word "trust", it intends to import all of the rules of conventional trust law.[4]

C. EXPRESS TRUSTS

(1) Practical Context: The Express Trust in Fraud Cases

9–009   This section addresses the principles which determine whether or not an express trust has been created. Often, when an express trust is involved in fraud litigation, the trust forms part of the state of affairs which existed before the alleged fraud occurred, and its existence is uncontroversial; the controversies in such a case will typically arise because it is alleged that the trustees have engaged in a fraud in relation to the trust fund, or have themselves been defrauded by third parties. There are, nevertheless, fraud cases in which there will be significant cause for controversy as to whether an express trust has been created at all. To give some examples:

---

[2] See L. Tucker, N. Le Poidevin and J. Brightwell, *Lewin on Trusts*, 19th edn (London: Sweet & Maxwell, 2014), para.7–002; J. McGhee, *Snell's Equity*, 33rd edn (London: Sweet & Maxwell, 2014), para.21–018.

[3] It is unclear to what extent there remains an open possibility, at least at Supreme Court level, of English law developing along the same lines: See *Westdeutsche Landesbank Girozentrale v Islington LBC* [1996] A.C. 669, at 716, per Lord Browne-Wilkinson; *London Allied Holdings Ltd v Lee* [2007] EWHC 2061 (Ch), at [259]–[264], per Etherton J; *Thorner v Major* [2009] UKHL 18; [2009] 1 W.L.R. 776, at [20], per Lord Scott of Foscote; *Sinclair Investments (UK) Ltd v Versailles Trade Finance Ltd* [2010] EWHC 1614 (Ch), at [23], per Lewison J and in the Court of Appeal [2010] EWCA Civ 347; [2012] Ch. 453, at [37] (although those decisions must now be read subject to the decision of the Supreme Court in *FHR* cited below); *Clarke v Meadus* [2010] EWHC 3117 (Ch), at [83], per Warren J; *CrossCo No.4 Unlimited v Jolan Ltd* [2011] EWCA Civ 1619, at [84]; and *FHR European Ventures LLP v Cedar Capital Partners LLC* [2014] UKSC 45; [2015] 1 A.C. 250, at [47].

[4] See para.9–090 below.

(1) In cases where a defendant of doubtful integrity has acted as a broker or agent or promoter of investments on an insufficiently formalised basis, it may be crucial to know whether he received property as express trustee for the claimant (giving instant access to a suite of claims, rights and remedies considered elsewhere in this work, including proprietary tracing claims, interim remedies such as proprietary freezing orders and *Bankers Trust* orders, claims for breach of trust on a strict liability basis, trust-based accessory claims against third parties and so forth) or whether it was intended that he should receive all of the property in question beneficially and owe solely personal obligations to the claimant (in which case the claimant must rely upon other claims, which may be less straightforward to establish and/or give less powerful relief).

(2) Likewise, questions as to express trusts arise frequently in cases where assets have been dealt with in an informal manner between friends, relatives or close business associates; and one party now alleges that the other is failing to honour the terms on which particular property was entrusted to them.

(3) A further common example arises in cases where a claimant suspects that a defendant is seeking to conceal assets by alleging that he holds property on trust for third parties, or alleging that third party trustees hold property on trust for beneficiaries other than him.

(2) Overview of Requirements for the Creation of an Express Trust

An express trust is easily created. Subject to the requirements addressed below, an express trust will be created when: **9–010**

(1) An absolute legal and beneficial owner of property declares that henceforth he holds it on a given trust;

(2) A beneficial owner of property which is held for his benefit by third party nominees or trustees directs those third parties that henceforth they should hold it on a given alternative trust;

(3) An owner of property transfers it (or takes sufficient steps to transfer it) to third party trustees together with a declaration that they should hold it on a given trust;

(4) A non-owner having a power of disposition over property (by way of power of appointment or a power of advancement under an existing trust) makes a valid exercise of that power to declare that the property should be held on a given trust; or

(5) Probate is granted of a will containing a declaration of trust in relation to property which the testator was entitled to dispose of by will.[5]

---

[5] In the case of trusts created by some other methods (for example the trust which arises upon the entry into of a specifically enforceable contract), there might be scope for dispute whether they are better considered express as opposed to resulting or constructive trusts.

9–011 Whichever of those methods of creating a trust is in issue, some requirements must be met. It is traditionally said that "three certainties" are required for the creation of an express trust:

(1) certainty of words as to the intention to create a trust;
(2) certainty as to the intended subject matter of the trust; and
(3) certainty as to the persons or objects intended to be benefitted.[6]

The requirements for the creation of an express trust are not limited to those "three certainties", but the principal requirements can conveniently be categorised by reference to them as:

(1) requirements relating to the declaration of trust;
(2) requirements relating to the subject matter of the trust; and
(3) requirements relating to the objects or beneficiaries of the trust.[7]

9–012 Of course, an express trust which is validly created by reference to those trust law requirements may nevertheless be void or capable of being set aside by reference to other doctrines of general application: lack of personal or corporate capacity of the settlor, misrepresentation, mistake, undue influence, s.173 Law of Property Act 1925, various provisions of the Insolvency Act 1986 and so forth. Many of those doctrines are considered elsewhere in this work.

(3) Requirements 1: The Declaration of Trust—Certainty of Words/Intention, Necessary Formalities, Bona Fides and Sham Trusts, Illegality of the Trust etc

9–013 **Certainty of Words/Intention.** It is necessary for the words and/or conduct of the alleged settlor to show an intention to create a relationship with the essential characteristics of a trust: namely a relationship in which the holders of specific property will be subject to enforceable obligations to hold that property for the benefit of others. The use of the word "trust" will obviously be a very strong indication of such an intention, although it is not determinative in all cases.[8] Equally, so long as the requisite intention appears from the alleged settlor's other conduct, it does not matter that the word "trust" is not used[9]; or that no words are

---

[6] *Knight v Knight* (1840) 3 Beav 148, at 173, per Lord Langdale.

[7] Underlying these requirements is what was described by Millett LJ in *Armitage v Nurse* [1998] Ch. 241, at 253G–253H as the "irreducible core" of a trust: "there is an irreducible core of obligations owed by trustees to the beneficiaries and enforceable by them which is fundamental to the concept of a trust. If the beneficiaries have no rights enforceable against the trustees there are no trusts."

[8] See the discussion of sham trusts below. See also the discussion of the protean meaning of the word "trust" in *Tito v Waddell (No.2)* [1977] Ch. 106, at 211 and following, per Megarry VC. Contrast the conventional approach taken in the conveyancing context in *Bath and North East Somerset Council v Attorney General* [2002] EWHC 1623 (Ch).

[9] See, for example, *Re Hanbury, Cominskey v Bowring-Hanbury* [1905] A.C. 84 (bequest under a will made, on a true construction, on trust although the word "trust" was not used) *Re Burley, Alexander v Burley* [1910] 1 Ch. 215 (another will case); *Re Young* [1951] Ch. 344 (another will case); *Re Kayford Ltd* [1975] 1 W.L.R. 279 (company acting on advice of accountant to pay money received from

used at all[10]; or indeed that the alleged settlor is not familiar with the legal concept of a trust,[11] or (seemingly) had no subjective intention to create a trust.[12] But if the requisite intention does not appear from the alleged settlor's words and conduct properly construed,[13] then no express trust will arise. The relevant words and/or conduct to which the test is to be applied are those alleged to create the trust; subsequent statements as to the settlor's subjective intention are inadmissible.[14] Applying that test in particular cases: no express trust will arise if the alleged settlor's words are merely "precatory" so as to seek to impose a moral or social obligation but no legally enforceable obligation[15]; no express trust will arise, subject to the exceptions discussed at paragraph 9–032 below, if the alleged settlor's words show an intention to make an absolute gift rather than hold the property on trust and he then fails to take sufficient steps to transfer the property by way of gift[16]; no express trust will arise merely by virtue of a company setting monies aside into a separate bank account or investment portfolio in connection with a particular transaction if the remaining circumstances do not reveal the requisite intention that the monies be held on trust.[17] But the requirement for certainty of intention may interact to this extent with the requirement of certainty of subject matter (considered at para.9–028 below): in cases where there is scope for doubt as to the existence of the relevant intention, a failure to make provision

---

customers whose orders it could not honour into a separate "customers trust deposit account", but using for that purpose an account in its own name which was only formally designated *"Customers' Trust Deposit Account"* several months later); *Paul v Constance* [1977] 1 W.L.R. 527 (repeated oral statements that "The money is as much yours as it is mine" in relation to a bank account held by one member of an unmarried couple and used to deposit their joint bingo winnings); *Wallbank v Price* [2007] EWHC 3001 (Ch) [2008] 2 F.L.R. 501, at [50] (homemade document signed by joint-owner of a house stating inter alia that "I revoke any rights in the disposal of the above property. The only exception to this is that my Daughters ... should receive my half share of the property on its disposal or at the discretion of my husband ..."); *Shah v Shah* [2010] EWHC 313 (Ch), at [44] (letters stating inter alia that "I am as from today holding 4000 shares in the above company for you subject to you being responsible for all tax consequences and liabilities arising from this declaration and letter" accompanied by signed stock transfer forms).

[10] *Dhingra v Dhingra*, 20 July 1999 CA, (1999-2000) I.T.E.L.R. 262, per Lindsay J.

[11] *Paul v Constance*, above.

[12] *RP Medplant Ltd v Pensions Regulator* [2017] UKUT 385 (TCC), at [21], applying to express declarations of trust the principles set out by the House of Lords in the Quistclose trust context in *Twinsectra Ltd v Yardley* [2002] 2 A.C. 164.

[13] Note that the process of construction of a unilateral written instrument may not mirror that for a contract: see, for example, *Public Trustee v Harrison* [2018] EWHC 166 (Ch) on the limited scope for factual matrix evidence.

[14] *Wilkinson and Ors v North and another* [2018] EWCA Civ 161; [2018] 4 W.L.R. 41, at [53], per David Richards LJ.

[15] This has been the general trend of the authorities in the context of wills since *Lambe v Eames* (1871) 6 Ch. App. 597. See *Re Adams and the Kensington Vestry* (1884) 27 Ch. D. 394; *Re Hamilton* [1895] 2 Ch. 370; *Hill v Hill* [1897] 1 Q.B. 483 and many other cases cited in the specialists works on wills. The will cases cited in fn.9 above where the opposite conclusion was reached, and other similar cases, constitute exceptions to the general trend and all appear to turn upon specific features of the wills in question.

[16] See the cases cited, at para.9–031 below.

[17] *Re Multi-Guarantee Co Ltd (No.3)* [1987] B.C.L.C. 257; *Re TXU Europe Group Plc (in Administration)* [2003] EWHC 3105 (Ch). But see further the discussion of *Quistclose* trusts below, at paras 9–047—9–051.

for specific trust property to be segregated will be a powerful indication that there was in fact no intention to create a trust.

9–014   **Formalities.**   As appears from the preceding paragraph, the general rule is that no formalities of any sort are required for the creation of an express trust. But that general rule is subject to two statutory exceptions now contained in s.53 Law of Property Act 1925,[18] as follows:

(1)   The first exception applies to the creation of trusts in respect of interests in land. By s.53(1)(b)

> "a declaration of trust respecting any land or any interest therein must be manifested and proved by some writing signed by some person who is able to declare such trust or by his will".

Importantly, the declaration of trust need not actually be *made* in writing. A declaration of trust made orally (or, it would seem, to be inferred from conduct) will satisfy the sub-section so long as it is *evidenced* in writing or by will at the time the matter comes before the Court[19]; and, once so evidenced, the declaration will be given effect as from the time it was originally made.[20] This represents a significant exception to the general principle that an interest in land can only be created or disposed of by writing.[21] However, in order to satisfy s.53(1)(b) it is necessary for the writing to evidence not only the *existence* but also the precise *nature* or *terms* of the trust.[22] Moreover, it is necessary for the writing to be signed by "some person who is able to declare such trust", which will not be the legal owner of the property in a case where the property is already said to be held on trust.[23] There is no provision for signature by an agent.[24] It has been said that the English court should always apply s.53(1)(b) to land outside the jurisdiction, on the basis that it should be regarded (for conflicts of laws

---

[18] These provisions were not new in 1925. See, among their antecedents, ss.7 to 9 of the Statute of Frauds 1677.

[19] *Forster v Hale* (1798) 3 Ves Jun 696 (affirmed 5 Ves Jun 308), *Randall v Morgan* (1806) 12 Ves Jun 74; *Morton v Tewart* (1842) 2 Y & CCC 67; *Childers v Childers* (1857) 1 De G & I 482; *Rochefoucauld v Boustead* [1897] 1 Ch. 196, at 206; *Re Holland* [1902] 2 Ch. 360. Indeed, it would seem possible in principle for a Statement of Case signed by the relevant party to satisfy the requirements of s.53(1)(b): see (by analogy) *Hampton v Spencer* (1693) 2 Vern 288; *Cottington v Fletcher* (1740) 2 Atk 155; and see *Nab v Nab* (1717) 10 Mod 404.

[20] *Gardner v Rowe* (1828) 5 Russ 258.

[21] Section 53(1)(a) Law of Property Act 1925. See also the stricter requirements for a contract for the disposition of an interest in land under s.2 of the Law of Property (Miscellaneous Provisions) Act 1989.

[22] *Forster v Hale*, at 707; *Morton v Tewart*, at 80; *Smith v Matthews* (1861) 19 Beav 330; 3 De G F & J 139; *Rochefoucauld v Boustead*, at 205–206. It is thought that the incorporation of such terms by reference to another document will suffice.

[23] *Tierney v Wood* (1854) 19 Beav 300; *Kronkheim v Johnson* (1877) 7 Ch. D. 60; *Dye v Dye* (1884) 13 Q.B.D. 147.

[24] Unlike in s.53(1)(c) discussed in the following sub-paragraph.

purposes) as a procedural rule governed by the lex fori[25]; but that reasoning appears doubtful and the better view may be that s.53(1)(b) should be applied only where English law would be the governing law of the alleged trust.[26]

(2) The second exception applies to dispositions of pre-existing equitable interests. By s.53(1)(c):

> "a disposition of an equitable interest or trust subsisting at the time of the disposition, must be in writing signed by the person disposing of the same, or by his agent thereunto lawfully authorised in writing or by will".

Unlike s.53(1)(b), this sub-section extends to all species of property and is not limited to trusts of interests in land. But it is limited to dispositions of *pre-existing* equitable interests; and has no application to the creation of a new trust by someone who is (up until that point) the absolute legal and beneficial owner of the property in question. What constitutes a *disposition* within the meaning of the sub-section has proven, except in obvious cases, a difficult and subtle question.[27] Where the sub-section does apply, the disposition of the equitable interest must actually be made (not simply evidenced) in signed writing or by will. Unlike s.53(1)(b), it is a substantive rather than evidential requirement. However, for the purposes of this sub-section, "signed writing" can be signed on behalf of the person making the disposition provided that the agent is himself authorised in writing. And it appears that the "signed writing" need not set out in full the terms on which the equitable interest is to be held, but can refer to trusts which have previously been declared orally.[28]

But, importantly, both of those statutory exceptions apply only to express trusts. By s.53(2), it is provided that s.53 "does not affect the creation or operation of resulting, implied or constructive trusts". In several situations a failed express trust can take effect as a resulting or constructive trust, so that the requirements of s.53 will be avoided. Three such situations merit mention here.[29] First, a trust

9–015

---

[25] *Rochefoucauld v Boustead*, at 207, relying by analogy upon the decision in *Leroux v Brown* (1852) 12 CB 801 in relation to s.4 Statute of Frauds 1677 (relating to oral contracts for the disposition of an interest in land).

[26] As to the position at common law, see the reasoning in *Maddison v Alderson* (1883) 8 App Cas 467; *Morris v Baron & Co* [1918] A.C. 1; and *G & H Montage GmbH v Irvani* [1990] 1 W.L.R. 667, at 684 and 690–691. But that position may well now be superseded by art.8 of the Hague Trusts Convention, given effect in English law by the Recognition of Trusts Act 1987 (as to which see the terms of art.4 and art.8, and also Lord Collins of Mapesbury and J. Harris (eds), *Dicey, Morris & Collins on the Conflict of Laws*, 15th edn (London: Sweet & Maxwell, 2012), paras 7–031 and 29–038).

[27] Reference may be made to the specialist works on this rather technical subject, and to some of the leading cases: *Grey v Inland Revenue Commissioners* [1960] A.C. 1; *Drakeford v Cotton* [2012] EWHC 1414 (Ch); *Vandervell v Inland Revenue Commissioners* [1967] 2 A.C. 291; *Re Vandervell Trusts (No.2)* [1974] Ch. 269; and *Re Danish Bacon Co Ltd Staff Pension Fund Trusts* [1971] 1 W.L.R. 248.

[28] *Re Tyler* [1967] 1 W.L.R. 1269.

[29] Fuller reference may be made to the treatment of resulting and constructive trusts at sections D and E below. For instance, it appears that s.53(2) is the mechanism by which secret trusts and half-secret trusts escape the effects of s.53(1).

declared in exchange for value will prima facie be capable of specific performance and will accordingly give rise to a constructive trust.[30] Second, a failed attempt to declare an express trust may give rise to a common intention constructive trust.[31] Third and perhaps most strikingly, by virtue of the principle that the Court will not permit a statute to be used as an engine of fraud,[32] a person to whom land is conveyed in the knowledge that they are to take it as trustee cannot rely upon s.53 to keep the land for himself,[33] and nor can volunteers or creditors claiming under him[34]; but in such a case it is an unresolved question whether he will hold the land upon the intended express trust or rather upon a resulting trust for the person who transferred the land to him.[35]

9–016 Finally in relation to formalities, it is important to appreciate that s.53 addresses formality requirements for the creation of a valid trust as a matter of trust law. Of course, depending upon the nature of the intended settlor, other formalities may be required by the laws governing the general validly of the purported acts of a settlor of that nature. Thus (for example): where the intended settlor is a corporation, formalities required by its constitution or otherwise by the law of companies may need to be complied with; where the intended settlor is a deceased person and the trust is purportedly declared by will, the will must comply with the requirements of the Wills Act 1837; and where the intended settlor is purporting to exercise a power of appointment or other power, formalities may be required for the valid exercise of that power.

9–017 **Bona Fides/Sham Trusts.** The principles relating to "shams"[36] apply to purported declarations of express trusts as they do to other transactions or

---

[30] See also *Oughtred v Inland Revenue Commissioners* [1960] A.C. 206, per Lord Radcliffe at 227, per Lord Cohen at 230, per Lord Denning at 233, and per Lord Jenkins at 239; *Neville v Wilson* [1997] Ch. 144, at 155–158; *Singh v Anand* [2007] EWHC 3346 (Ch). See also academic discussion, at [1996] CLJ 436 (R. Nolan) and [1996] Conv. 368 (M.P Thompson).

[31] See paras 9–078—9–080 below. See also *Samad v Thompson* [2008] EWHC 2809 (Ch); [2008] NPC 125.

[32] See para.9–097 below.

[33] See *Lincoln v Wright* (1859) 4 De G & J 16, at 22, *Haigh v Kaye* (1872) 7 Ch. App. 469; *Re Duke of Marlborough* [1894] 2 Ch. 133; *Rochefoucauld v Boustead* [1897] 1 Ch. 196, at 206; *Bannister v Bannister* [1948] 2 All E.R. 133; *Hodgson v Marks* [1971] Ch. 892.

[34] See in particular *Lincoln v Wright*, above, and *Re Duke of Marlborough*, above.

[35] There is extensive academic debate. See for example [1984] CLJ 306, at 334 (Youdan); [1987] Conv 246 (Feltham); 1988 Conv 267 (Youdan); M.L. Ascher, A.W. Scott and W.F. Fratcher, *Scott & Ascher on Trusts*, 5th edn (Aspen Publishers, 2017), Vol.1, para.6.11; P.B.H. Birks and F.D. Rose (eds), *Restitution and Equity* (London: Mansfield Press/LLP, 2000), Vol.1, Ch.4 (Swadling); C. Mitchell, D.J. Hayton and P. Matthews, *Underhill & Hayton: Law of Trusts and Trustees*, 18th edn (London: LNUK, 2010), paras 2.12 and 12.70–12.72; A.J. Oakley, *Constructive Trusts*, 3rd edn (London: Sweet & Maxwell, 1997), pp.55–56.

[36] The legal meaning of the word sham was stated in *Snook v London and West Riding Investments Ltd* [1967] 2 Q.B. 786, at 802: "it is … necessary to consider what, if any, legal concept is involved in use of the this popular and pejorative word. I apprehend that, if it has any meaning in law, it means acts done or documents executed by the parties to the 'sham' which are intended by them to give to third parties or the court the appearance of creating between the parties legal rights and obligations different from the actual legal rights and obligations (if any) which the parties intend to create. But one thing, I think, is clear in legal principle, morality and the authorities (see *Yorkshire Railway Wagon Co v Maclure* (1882) 21 Ch.D. 309 and *Stoneleigh Finance Ltd v Phillips* [1965] 2 Q.B. 537), that for acts or documents to be a 'sham', with whatever legal consequences follow from this, all the

documents[37]; and are, for obvious reasons, often invoked in the fraud context in relation to purported express trusts. The success of a fraud will often depend not merely on its execution but upon the subsequent secretion of the funds so as to render them, so far as possible, immune to attempts by the victim to either locate or recover them. Hence, in one common fact pattern, the fraudster may settle assets into a trust for, say, the ostensible benefit of his wider family, when in fact the intention all along is that he should retain control of the assets; or, with slightly more sophistication, he may place assets in the hands of an associate, who is ostensibly to hold those assets on an express trust for third parties, while in fact holding them as bare nominee for the fraudster. Indeed the fraudster may take such steps in advance of his fraudulent activity, against the risk of subsequent proceedings against him by the victim. In such cases the victim of the fraud is likely to wish to impeach the trust; one way of doing so is via invocation of the doctrine of sham.[38] There are other avenues which the claimant can follow under the Insolvency Act. We consider claims under s.423 in Ch.16 above. Indeed the fraudster may wish to create a genuine trust in order to protect the assets. That may prevent invocation of the sham doctrine, but will not necessarily render the trust immune from a claim under s.423.

The cases sometimes use the term "sham trust", but it has been pointed out that **9–018** this is a misnomer. As was said in a leading New Zealand case:

> "The two situations (valid trust and sham trust) do not fall into combination. The finding that the purported trust is void as a sham does not amount to an invalidation of a trust. It is not the trust as such which is a sham. There is no trust to be a sham. It is the trust documentation that is the sham."[39]

Nonetheless in this chapter we use the term as a convenient shorthand.

The test for whether a purported express trust (which on the face of it purports to **9–019** constitute or create a valid trust relationship) is a "sham" turns upon the *intent* of the parties. A finding of "sham" will be made in relation to a purported declaration of trust if it can be shown that the relevant parties to the transaction both:

(1) intended, in practice, not to give effect to the terms of the purported trust; and also

---

parties thereto must have a common intention that the acts or documents are not to create the legal rights and obligations which they give the appearance of creating." *Snook* was not a trust case but is directly applicable.

[37] The interrelation between the doctrine of "sham" and the doctrine of "piercing the corporate veil" has been much elucidated, but remains less than fully clear, following the restatement of the latter doctrine by the Supreme Court in *Petrodel Resources Ltd v Prest* [2013] UKSC 34; [2013] 2 A.C. 415. The doctrine of "piercing the corporate veil" is discussed in Ch.18.

[38] A recent example is *JSC Mezhdunarodniy Promyshlenniy Bank v Pugachev* [2017] EWHC 2426 (Ch). In that case the claimant had obtained a substantial judgment against P. Prior to the proceedings P had settled property into discretionary trusts of which his partner and their children were amongst the beneficiaries. C sought an order requiring the assets of the trust to be paid to it on the basis that P held the beneficial interest in all the assets because the trusts were shams.

[39] *Official Assignee v Wilson* [2008] 3 N.Z.L.R. 45, at [48]–[49]. The point was endorsed by the judge in *JSC Mezhdunarodniy Promyshlenniy Bank v Pugachev* [2017] EWHC 2426 (Ch), at [145]–[146].

(2)   intended to use the purported declaration to give a false impression to third parties.[40]

Both limbs of that test must be satisfied.[41] The test of intention for these purposes is subjective.[42] In this sense a sham trust is generally, indeed it may be thought necessarily, a creature of a dishonest mental state.[43] But it is important to distinguish intention as to the true effect of the transaction (which is relevant) from the motives for entering into it (which are not); a trust which is genuinely intended to be operated in accordance with its terms is not rendered a "sham" by the fact that the settlor had a nefarious motive or ulterior purpose for creating the trust.[44] Nor is such a trust rendered a "sham" if the terms of the trust reserve wide-ranging rights to the settlor[45] or if it is anticipated that the trustees will tend in practice to act as the settlor would wish them to act, so long as this is consistent with the operation of the trust according to its terms.[46] The relevant terms of the trust for these purposes are chiefly those which relate to the ownership and application of the trust property in the future; it seems that misleading recitals alone will not generally be enough to make a document a sham.[47]

9–020   Crucially, the "shamming intent" (as opposed to any motive)[48] must be shared by the purported settlor and any purported trustees or other necessary parties to the transaction (which does not include the identified beneficiaries of the purported trust),[49] although it appears that a party who signs a document recklessly (without caring what it says) may be held to share sufficiently in the "shamming intent"

---

[40] *Snook v London and West Riding Investments Ltd* [1967] 2 Q.B. 786, at 802, per Diplock LJ, *WT Ramsay Ltd v Inland Revenue Commissioners* [1982] A.C. 300, at 323, per Lord Wilberforce and at 337, per Lord Fraser of Tullybelton, *Hitch v Stone* [2001] EWCA Civ 63; [2001] STC 214, at [62]–[70], per Arden LJ.

[41] *Hitch v Stone*, above. There has been a recent attempt to import a related but separate doctrine of the "illusory trust" into English law, founded on the Bermudan authority of *Re AQ Revocable Trust* [2010] 13 I.T.E.L.R. 260; see *JSC Mezhdunarodniy Promyshlenniy Bank v Pugachev* [2017] EWHC 2426 (Ch), at [155]–[159] and [167]–[169].

[42] *Hitch v Stone*, at [66].

[43] *National Westminster Bank Plc v Jones* [2001] B.C.L.C. 98, at [59], per Neuberger J. But see the caveat registered by Birss J in *JSC Mezhdunarodniy Promyshlenniy Bank v Pugachev* [2017] EWHC 2426 (Ch), at [152].

[44] *Chase Manhattan Equities Ltd v Goodman* [1991] B.C.L.C. 897, at 921, per Knox J (a case relating to a deed of gift, to which similar principles apply); *Miles v Bull* [1969] 1 Q.B. 258, at 264, per Megarry J.

[45] Of course, this may have the effect that the trust does not achieve whatever taxation or asset-protection purpose the settlor hopes it will achieve; but it will not render the trust a "sham".

[46] See, for example, *Hill v Spread Trustee* [2005] EWHC 336 (Ch); [2005] B.P.I.R. 842 (affd. on other points, at [2006] EWCA Civ 542; [2007] 1 W.L.R. 2404).

[47] *Slocom v Tatik* [2014] EWCA Civ 831, at [60]–[61], per Briggs LJ: "In my view the judge's distinction between recitals which paint a false picture of the history, and operative parts which are alleged falsely to describe the parties' obligations going forward is, in general at least, both principled and correct. An agreement is not a sham merely because it makes reference to a sham agreement in its recitals, or merely because it deliberately misdescribes history."

[48] See *Chase Manhattan* and *Miles v Bull*, cited above.

[49] *Snook v London and West Riding Investments Ltd*, at 802; *Hitch v Stone*, at [69]; *Re Esteem Settlement* [2003] J.L.R. 188; *Shalson v Russo* [2003] EWHC 1637 (Ch); [2005] Ch. 281, at [190], per Rimer J, *A v A* [2007] EWHC 99 (Fam); [2009] W.T.L.R. 1, at [34], per Munby J. If the trustees did not share the "shamming intent" then obviously, in practical terms, the "sham" would not work. See

for these purposes.[50] Where the trustee is a professional person an allegation of shamming intent is a serious matter and making good such an allegation will accordingly be difficult.[51] Evidence that the trustees may have done something later which was contrary to the terms of the trust deed may support a finding of sham, although it may merely show that they have acted in breach of trust. Where the trustees are corporate entities then the relevant intention is that of the natural person(s) who manage and control the relevant actions of the company, i.e the directing mind(s) in respect of the relevant act or omission.[52] A finding of sham may be assisted by a consideration of the character and motivations of the settlor at the time of the creation of the trust.

The *point in time* by reference to which the parties' intent must be tested is generally the point at which the relevant document or arrangement is entered into, although it seems that there may potentially (in rare circumstances) be exceptions to that rule. Two categories of cases require to be considered: **9–021**

(1) In the first, there is no sufficient "shamming intent" at the moment when a declaration of trust is made. In such a case, assuming all other requirements for the creation of an express trust are satisfied, a valid express trust is created. Accordingly, a subsequent failure to operate the trust in accordance with its terms should give rise to no question of "sham". Rather, the question will be whether the failure amounts to a breach of trust or a proper variation/termination of the trust under the so-called rule in *Saunders v Vautier* (which entitles all of the beneficiaries of a trust, provided they are fully ascertained and have capacity and agree, jointly to direct the application of the trust property regardless of the express terms of the trust).[53] But a situation could be envisaged in which a beneficiary or group of beneficiaries entitled to vary or determine the trust under the rule in *Saunders v Vautier* entered into an arrangement with the trustees to do so while maintaining a fiction that the terms of the original express trust continued to apply. In such a situation, it might be said that a genuine trust had become a "sham".[54]

(2) In the converse situation, a sufficient "shamming intent" exists at the moment when the purported declaration of trust is made. In that case, there is only ever a "sham" trust (with the potential consequences considered

---

also *MacKinnon v Regent Trust Co Ltd* [2005] JCA 066; [2005] W.T.L.R. 1367. Hence in *Shalson*, because the claimant asserting the sham trust had conceded that the professional trustees had acted honestly, no finding of sham could be made.

[50] *A v A*, at [50]–[52], seeking to reconcile prima facie contradictory statements in *Midland Bank Plc v Wyatt* [1995] 1 F.L.R. 696, at 699; *Minwalla v Minwalla* [2004] EWHC 2823 (Fam) [2005] 1 F.L.R. 771, at [54]–[55]; *Re Esteem Settlement*, above, and *CI Law Trustees Ltd v Minwalla* [2005] JRC 099; [2006] W.T.L.R. 807.

[51] Such a finding was made in *JSC Mezhdunarodniy Promyshlenniy Bank v Pugachev* [2017] EWHC 2426 (Ch), at [152].

[52] *El Ajou v Dollar Land Holdings* [1994] BCC 143, at 150–151; followed by Birss J in *JSC Mezhdunarodniy Promyshlenniy Bank v Pugachev* [2017] EWHC 2426 (Ch), at [154].

[53] *Saunders v Vautier* (1841) 4 Beav 115. See treatments of the rule in the specialist works on trusts.

[54] *Shalson v Russo*, at [190]; *A v A*, at [42]–[44]. If a genuine trust came into existence and the parties subsequently ceased to give effect to it, then it will prima facie be a case of breach of trust rather than sham.

further below). But it has been said that a sham trust can in principle become genuine if honest trustees are subsequently appointed and begin to operate the trust according to its terms.[55]

9–022 The *scope* of the "sham" may vary from case to case. In the classic case, the parties enter into the entire declaration of trust as a "sham"; their true intention is for the beneficial ownership of the relevant assets to remain with the settlor or be transferred somewhere else entirely. However, it is possible in some cases for a transaction or a document to be divisible between a part which is a "sham" and a part which is intended to have genuine effect.[56] (The fact that the doctrine of sham may apply to only part of a transaction does not detract from the essentially binary nature of the doctrine: the relevant transaction, or part of a transaction, is either a "sham" or it is not.)[57]

9–023 The *burden of proof* lies upon the party making the allegation of "sham", and it may be a difficult burden to discharge as there is a strong and natural presumption against holding a provision or a document to be a "sham".[58] The difficulty is, in practice, especially great where it must be shown that professional trustees were party to it. The evidence relied upon may include inter alia any relevant discussions between the parties before the alleged "sham" trust was purportedly created and also their subsequent conduct (although, for obvious reasons, it is difficult to prove a sham from subsequent conduct alone).[59]

9–024 The *consequences* of a finding of sham are not yet fully worked out in the authorities. It has often been said that a "sham" is simply void; but it is not entirely clear what is meant by this. In practice, it seems that the consequences of a finding of "sham" differ depending upon who wishes to rely upon the "sham", so that:

(1) the "shammers" will not be able to rely on it as representing the true position as to the rights and obligations they have created and the court can ignore it in determining what those rights are (so that if, say, a judgment creditor of the settlor successfully impeaches the trust as a sham, then the trustees will be held to hold the settled assets on constructive or resulting trust for the settlor, with the result that the assets are amenable to execution), but

(2) as against an innocent third party (e.g. a beneficiary under the purported trust or the creditor of such a beneficiary), it cannot lie in the mouths of the "shammers" to assert to the disadvantage of that innocent party that the transaction is a sham and of no effect.[60]

---

[55] *A v A*, at [45]–[49].

[56] *AG Securities v Vaughan* [1990] 1 A.C. 417; *National Westminster Bank v Jones*, at [45] and [59], per Neuberger J, *Hitch v Stone*, at [85].

[57] *A v A*, at [58].

[58] *National Westminster Bank v Jones* [2001] 1 B.C.L.C. 98, at [59], per Neuberger J (affirmed on other points, at [2001] EWCA Civ 1541; [2002] 1 B.C.L.C. 55); *A v A*, at [53]–[54].

[59] See *Hitch v Stone*, above, at [65] and [68].

[60] See for example *Carman v Yates* [2004] EWHC 3448 (Ch), at [219].

As a matter of analysis, it *may* be that this situation can be explained on the basis that, although the "sham" transaction is entirely void, the "shammers" have become subject to estoppels by reason of their conduct. But the correct juridical analysis remains unclear; and it may be that the correct analysis will not become clear until the Courts consider in detail the effect of a sham as between two innocent parties.

Illegality and Trusts Contrary to Public Policy. It is necessary to distinguish two situations. In the first, the terms of the trust themselves are unlawful or contrary to public policy. Classic instances of this first situation include terms discouraging entry into the armed forces or into public office, terms encouraging the commission of offences, conditions in restraint of marriage, clauses purporting to oust the jurisdiction of the court to enforce the trust, clauses purporting to make the beneficiary's interest inalienable on bankruptcy, clauses purporting to restrict the use of the trust property to some pointless use, terms breaching the rules on perpetuities and accumulations and so forth.[61] In such cases, depending upon the context and the terms of the trust in question, either the whole trust or the offending term may be held to be void. **9–025**

In the second situation (perhaps more likely to be encountered in the fraud context), the trust is inoffensive on its face but may have been created for an improper purpose (perhaps to conceal wrongfully acquired assets, or simply to conceal assets so as to permit the beneficiary to misrepresent his financial position to third parties such as creditors or revenue authorities). Such impropriety may (of course) give rise to criminal or similar consequences; and may expose the property to the risk of confiscation or civil claims by the relevant authorities or by the "victims". But does the improper purpose in itself negate the trustee's legal title to the trust property, remove the beneficiary's equitable ownership of that property or (insofar as this is conceptually distinct) render the trust unenforceable? If the impropriety arises pursuant to a specific statute, the terms of the statue may of course point to one or more of those consequences. But in the absence of specific statutory provision, the position at common law is in a state of development. **9–026**

In *Patel v Mirza*,[62] the Supreme Court has recently re-examined the general principles which underlie the common law defence of "illegality" (or "ex turpi causa"). Following *Mirza*, some things are now clear. An illegal purpose underlying the transfer of property does not prevent the property from passing. Equally, the reasoning of the House of Lords in *Tinsley v Milligan*[63] is not to be followed; and accordingly the test for whether a claim is to be barred for illegality is *not* whether the claimant is required to "rely upon" the illegality in order to plead its claim. Instead, the court is to decide whether a claim is barred for illegality in a manner which respects the rationale of the doctrine: namely that in some cases the court will deny an otherwise valid claim because it would be contrary to the public interest to enforce a claim if to do so would be harmful to **9–027**

---

[61] See the helpful review in Ch.5 of Tucker, Le Poidevin and Brightwell, *Lewin on Trusts* (2014).

[62] *Patel v Mirza* [2016] UKSC 42; [2017] A.C. 467.

[63] *Tinsley v Milligan* [1994] 1 A.C. 340.

the integrity of the legal system or, possibly, to certain (still ill-defined) aspects of public morality. But this does not mean that the Court is free to adopt an undisciplined approach. In each case, what is required of the Court is a principled and transparent assessment of the relevant considerations, with particular focus on:

(i) the underlying purpose of the prohibition which has been transgressed,
(ii) any other relevant public policy on which denying the claim might have an impact, and
(iii) whether denial of the claim would be a proportionate response to the illegality bearing in mind that punishment is a matter for the courts.

How this new approach is to operate in practice, and what its implications are for the creation of trusts, remain to be worked through in future cases.

(4) Requirements 2: The Trust Property—Certainty of Subject Matter, the Need to Constitute the Trust, Trusts of Future Property etc

9–028 **Certainty of Subject Matter.** Trusts concern the ownership of property. Accordingly, for a trust to be created, there must be identifiable trust property and that property must be identified with sufficient certainty. One could not simply declare a trust of "£100" (unless, of course, the context made it possible to ascertain, as a matter of construction, that a specific fund was being referred to). Likewise, where a wine merchant holds many similar bottles of wine, a purported trust of a lesser number of bottles is invalid unless the specific bottles in question are set aside or identified in some way.[64] However, the Court has upheld a declaration of trust in relation to 50 out of a total of 950 shares held by the settlor in a company, on the basis that there could be no difference between the individual shares.[65] On that basis, there seems no reason why there could not be a declaration of trust in respect of a specific amount of money in an account containing a larger total; but both the amount and the account in question would itself need to be identified with sufficient certainty.[66] It has been held possible to create a trust over constantly changing assets (or over a share therein); and the Court has even been prepared to countenance a trust of an undivided share in a trading business, while recognising the formidable practical difficulties that

---

[64] *Re London Wine Co (Shippers)* [1986] PCC 121. See *Re Goldcorp Exchange Ltd* [1995] 1 A.C. 74 and *Westdeutsche Landesbank Girocentrale v Islington LBC* [1996] A.C. 669, at 705.
[65] *Hunter v Moss* [1994] 1 W.L.R. 452; *Re Harvard Securities* [1998] BCC 567; *Shah v Shah* [2010] EWHC 313 (Ch) (affirmed [2010] EWCA Civ 1408).
[66] See *Re Lehman Brothers International (Europe)* [2010] EWCA Civ 917; [2011] Bus L.R. 277, at [171], [235] and [243] (the point in question was not before the Supreme Court on the appeal, at [2012] UKSC 6). See also *Wright v National Westminster Bank Plc* [2014] EWHC 3158 (Ch), at [23]–[24].

would create.[67] Unsurprisingly, the requirement of certainty of subject matter can give rise to subtle arguments as to the true construction of the declaration of trust.[68]

If there is insufficient certainty of subject matter at the moment of the trust's purported creation, then the consequence is seemingly that no trust arises: there are no assets for the trust to bite on. This must, however, be distinguished from the situation where a valid trust has been created, and the trust assets are dealt with in such a way that their identity becomes confused; in that situation, one must look to the tracing rules addressed in Ch.24.

9–029

Trusts of Future Property. It is obvious that, where a trust is purportedly created over future property (i.e. property not yet owned by the settlor), the trust cannot take effect at the time of creation: at that time there is no property for the trust to bite upon. But is such a trust invalid altogether, or does it take effect if and when the property is subsequently acquired? The general rule is the same as that for purported equitable assignments of future property: if the trust was created gratuitously then it is simply invalid[69]; but if it was created for consideration then, on the principle that equity treats as done that which ought to be done, the trust will take effect when the property is acquired, subject to the usual rules as to priorities.[70] It is important for these purposes, however, to distinguish between future property in the true sense and existing property the fruits of which will only accrue in the future. In the case of the latter category, of course, no difficulty arises; but the distinction may be an elusive one.[71]

9–030

Need to Constitute the Trust. As trusts relate to the ownership of property, a trust cannot take effect unless and until trust property is vested in the intended trustees. Where the settlor declares himself a trustee of part of his property no issue of this sort arises; the property in question is already vested in him, so that the trust is "constituted" as soon as it is declared. Likewise, there should in general be no difficulty where a settlor directs trustees or nominees who already hold property on his behalf (or subject to a power of disposition which he is entitled to exercise) to hold that property upon new trusts. However, in the common situation where the settlor intends to transfer property (or cause property to be transferred) to third parties who will take on trust, it is possible for a situation to arise in which all other steps necessary for the creation of the trust have been taken but there is a failure to effect a transfer to the intended trustees of

9–031

---

[67] *Wilkinson v North*, above, at [19]–[24] building on the decision in *Re Lehman Brothers*, above.

[68] See the specialist texts for a fuller account of the many decisions on various different facts. But two examples may give a flavour: in *Palmer v Simmonds* (1854) 2 Drew 221 a trust under a will of "the bulk of" the residuary estate failed for uncertainty; in *Re Golay Will Trust* [1965] 1 W.L.R. 969 a legacy of "a reasonable income" was held to be valid on the basis that by those words the testator had intended an objectively reasonable amount which could be determined by the Court.

[69] See *Meek v Kettlewell* (1842) 1 Hare 464; *Re Ellenborough* [1903] 1 Ch. 697; *Re Brooks Settlement Trusts* [1939] Ch. 993.

[70] See *Tailby v Official Receiver* (1888) 13 All Cas 523; *Re Lind* [1915] Ch. 345; *Horwood v Millar's Timber and Trading Co Ltd* [1917] 1 K.B. 305; *Re Gillott's Settlement* [1934] Ch. 97; *Re Burton's Settlements* [1955] Ch. 82.

[71] Reference should be made to specialist texts on trust law.

title to the trust property. Such a situation is commonly referred to as an "incompletely constituted trust", but that name can mislead. The general rule is that until some property is vested in the trustees, the trust does not take effect at all: the intended trust property remains the property of the intended settlor and the intended trustees do not begin to owe duties as trustees. In general, the intended settlor will not be treated as having constituted himself trustee of the property in his own hands pending the failed transfer, because declaring oneself a trustee of property is a fundamentally different sort of transaction from transferring the entirety of one's interest in property to a separate trustee.[72]

9–032   But that general rule is subject to significant exceptions. Perhaps most importantly, where there is a contractual obligation to transfer property to be held on trust which is supported by consideration and specifically enforceable, the property may become subject to a constructive trust in the hands of the intended transferor/settlor.[73] Even where the intended beneficiary has given no consideration, there are three doctrines of controversial extent and uncertain application under which the intended transferor/settlor may in some circumstances be held to have constituted himself as a trustee: first, where he has taken all the formal steps which lie exclusively within his power to make the transfer to the intended trustees[74]; second, where he has acted in such a way as to make it inequitable for him to resile from the transfer[75]; and third, where the circumstances permit his actions to be construed as a declaration of trust in his own hands rather than a failed transfer.[76]

(5)   Requirements 3: The Beneficial Interests—Certainty of Objects, the Need for Human or Charitable Objects, Perpetuities and Accumulations etc

9–033   **Certainty of Objects.**   For a valid express trust to be created, the declaration of trust must make sufficiently certain who are the beneficiaries of the trust. The requisite degree of certainty depends upon whether the intended trust is a fixed trust (i.e. a trust in which the relevant trust fund is directed simply to be held for specified persons or a specified class of persons with the result that each person is entitled to a fixed proportion of the relevant fund) or a discretionary trust (i.e. a trust in which the relevant fund is directed to be held for persons selected on a discretionary basis by trustees or other third parties out of a specified class of potential beneficiaries). In the case of a fixed trust, the terms of the declaration of trust must make it possible in principle at the time when the trust is declared to

---

[72] *Milroy v Lord* (1862) 4 De G.F.& J 264; *Richards v Delbridge* (1874) L.R. 18 Eq 11; *Jones v Lock* (1865) 1 Ch. App. 25; *Antrobus v Smith* (1806) 12 Ves Jr 39; *Pappadakis v Pappadakis* [2000] W.T.L.R. 719; *Curtis v Pulbrook* [2011] EWHC 167 (Ch); [2011] 1 B.C.L.C. 638.

[73] See para.9–088 below.

[74] See *Re Rose* [1949] Ch. 78; *Re Rose* [1952] Ch. 499; *Mascall v Mascall* (1985) 50 P & CR 119; *Pennington v Waine* [2002] EWCA Civ 227; [2002] 1 W.L.R. 1075; *Re Dalmar Properties Ltd, Zeital v Kaye* [2010] EWCA Civ 159; [2010] 2 B.C.L.C. 1; *Curtis v Pulbrook* [2011] EWHC 167 (Ch); [2011] 1 B.C.L.C. 638.

[75] See *Pennington v Waine* [2002] EWCA Civ 227; [2002] 1 W.L.R. 1075.

[76] See *Re Ralli's Will Trust* [1964] Ch. 288; *T Choithram International SA v Pagarani* [2001] 1 W.L.R. 1.

ascertain who each of the beneficiaries is and what proportion of the fund each beneficiary takes; and in the case where the fund is directed to be held in equal shares for a particular class of persons, this means that it must be possible in principle at the time of the declaration to draw up a complete list of the intended beneficiaries.[77] In the case of a discretionary trust, the test is less demanding: the terms of the declaration of trust must make it possible in principle at the time when the trust is declared to say whether or not any particular individual is a member of the class of potential beneficiaries,[78] even if it is not possible in principle to draw a complete list.[79] It appears that even where the test for certainty of object as stated above is met, it may be possible for an express trust to fail on the related ground of "administrative unworkability", where the definition of beneficiaries is so hopelessly wide as not to form anything like a class, but the extent of the principle remains unclear.[80]

It is important to appreciate that a failure of certainty of object (unlike failure of the other "certainties" considered above) does not necessarily undermine the trust relationship between the putative trustee and the putative trust assets, but simply the intended terms of the trust. Accordingly, a failure of certainty of object will not cause the putative trustee to take the beneficial interest in the putative trust **9–034**

---

[77] *Re Gulbenkian Settlement Trust, Whishaw v Stephens* [1970] A.C. 508, at 523 and following, per Lord Upjohn, *OT Computers Ltd (in Administration) v First National Tricity Finance Ltd* [2003] EWHC 1010 (Ch), at [21]; see also *Re LPA Umbrella Trust, Pensions Regulator v A Admin Ltd* [2014] EWHC 1378 (Ch) where the uncertainty related to the method of computation of the entitlement of beneficiaries. Provided it is possible in principle to establish the extent of each beneficial interest, an evidential difficulty in establishing what has become of a particular beneficiary will not invalidate the trust; it will simply present the trustees with an administrative difficulty in distributing that beneficiary's share.

[78] A full analysis of the discretionary trust is outside the remit of this book. However the rights of beneficiary under such a trust were described by Lewison LJ in *JAC Mezhdunarodniy Promyshlenniy Bank v Pugachev* [2015] EWCA Civ 139; [2016] 1 W.L.R. 160, as follows, at [13] and [15]: "A beneficiary under a discretionary trust has a right to be considered as a potential recipient of benefit by the trustees. That is an interest which equity will protect. The trustees must apply some objective criterion in deciding whether or not to exercise their discretion in favour of a particular beneficiary; so that each beneficiary has more than a mere hope. But that right is not a proprietary interest in the assets held by the trustees, although it can be described as an interest of sorts: *Gartside v IRC* [1968] A.C. 553, 617–618. In some areas of the law, such as matrimonial finance, legislation is drawn widely enough to enable the court to take into account the likelihood that trustees will exercise their discretion in favour of a particular beneficiary in deciding what provision to make for a former spouse on divorce: *Whaley v Whaley* [2011] EWCA Civ 611. But even then the trust assets are not owned by the beneficiary spouse.... On the face of it assets held by the trustees of a discretionary trust would not be amenable to execution if judgment is entered against one of the class of potential beneficiaries at the suit of a third party. The trustees might in such circumstances decide to confer a benefit on the beneficiary to save him from bankruptcy; but that would be a matter for them. If they did exercise their discretion in favour of a particular beneficiary the amount of the benefit would thereupon cease to be a trust asset and would become the asset of the beneficiary. It would then truly be his asset."

[79] *Re Baden Deed Trust (No.1), McPhail v Doulton* [1971] A.C. 424; *Re Baden's Deed Trusts (No.2)* [1973] Ch. 9; *Re Hay's Settlement Trust* [1982] 1 W.L.R. 202; *Re Barlow's Will Trust* [1979] 1 W.L.R. 278; *Public Trustee v Butler* [2012] EWHC 858 (Ch). We consider discretionary trust further at Ch.37, in the context of a judgment creditor seeking to enforce his judgment where assets are held subject to a discretionary trust.

[80] See the references collected in Tucker, Le Poidevin and Brightwell, *Lewin on Trusts* (2014), para.4–041.

assets; instead, he will hold them in accordance with the beneficial interest next in priority or (if none) upon a resulting trust for the settlor.[81]

9–035   **Need for Beneficiaries or Charitable Purpose.**   The general rule is that a trust will only be valid if it is either a trust for beneficiaries (who could in principle enforce it) or a trust for a charitable purpose (in which case the Crown acting through the Attorney General can enforce it).[82] A trust for an abstract purpose which is not recognised by the law as charitable will, in general, be void and unenforceable.[83] Judicial and professional ingenuity have identified a number of apparent exceptions or limitations to that general rule, most of which are unlikely to be of relevance in the fraud context: reference should be made to specialist trust law works. Perhaps most relevantly for present purposes, the rule does not prevent a trustee in certain circumstances from holding property for beneficiaries subject to a *power* to apply the property for a stated purpose. That is the situation which arises in so called *Quistclose* trusts, described further at paras 9–047—9–951 below in the context of resulting trusts. In any situation where property appears to have been entrusted to someone who might be characterised as a trustee for a specific purpose, careful consideration should be given to the possibility that a *Quistclose*-type trust has arisen.

9–036   **Perpetuities and Accumulations.**   A trust under which the beneficial interests do not vest immediately in specific beneficiaries will also need to satisfy the rules as to perpetuities and accumulations in order to be valid. That is a technical and potentially complex issue in respect of which reference should be made to the specialist works on trust law.[84]

D.   RESULTING TRUSTS

(1)   The Two Types of Resulting Trust

9–037   As set out briefly at para.9–008 above and explained in more detail below, a resulting trust is conventionally said to exist where a transferee of property (or the recipient of property acquired with funds transferred by another) is found to hold all or part of the interest in that property on trust for the transferor by operation of law either:

---

[81] See below at paras 9–044—9–046.

[82] The law of charities is beyond the scope of this work. Reference should be made to the specialist works, in particular W. Henderson and J. Fowles, *Tudor on Charities*, 10th edn (London: Sweet & Maxwell, 2015) and H. Picarda, *The Law and Practice Relating to Charities* (London: Bloomsbury Professional, 2014).

[83] See for example *Bowman v Secular Society* [1971] A.C. 406, at 411, per Lord Parker, *Re Astor's Settlement Trusts* [1952] Ch. 534; *Leahy v Attorney General for New South Wales* [1959] A.C. 457, at 478, per Lord Simonds.

[84] See, for instance, the treatment in Ch.5 of Tucker, Le Poidevin and Brightwell, *Lewin on Trusts* (2014).

(1)   because the transferor has parted with the property gratuitously and is therefore presumed not to have intended to part with beneficial ownership unless there is some material to establish that he did; or

(2)   because the transferor has given the property to the transferee to hold on an express trust but without accounting for all of the beneficial interest in the property.

It is convenient to consider each of those two types of resulting trust separately. As will be seen, in many cases of alleged fraud it will be possible for a claimant to allege one—or both—types of resulting trust; and such allegations may carry real tactical advantages.   **9–038**

(2)   Type 1: Unexplained Transfers and Purchases in the Name of Another

The first type of resulting trust was described as follows by Lord Browne-Wilkinson in *Westdeutsche Landesbank v Islington LBC*[85]:   **9–039**

> "where A makes a voluntary payment to B or pays (wholly or in part) for the purchase of property which is vested in B alone or in the joint names of A and B, there is a presumption that A did not intend to make a gift to B: the money or property is held on trust for A (if he is the sole provider of the money) or in the case of a joint purchase by A and B in shares proportionate to their contributions. It is important to stress that this is only a presumption, which presumption is easily rebutted either by the counter-presumption of advancement or by direct evidence of A's intention to make an outright transfer."

As appears from that statement, the gratuitous transfer to another or gratuitous payment for the purchase of property in the name of another gives rise to a presumption of resulting trust, which can be rebutted in either of two ways: **9–040**

(1)   First and most importantly, the party seeking to rebut the presumption may adduce a positive case supported by evidence to establish that the property was in fact transferred with the intention that the transferee would take as beneficial owner. For these purposes, it appears that what is principally relevant is the transferor's intention (or lack of intention) that the transferee would take beneficial ownership; so that, for example, a resulting trust can still arise in favour of a transferor who intended to part with beneficial ownership by transferring property to a trustee to hold for third party beneficiaries where such trusts prove to be invalid.[86] But there is support for the view that the intentions of both parties, rather than simply of the transferor, must be established.[87]

---

[85] *Westdeutsche Landesbank v Islington LBC* [1996] A.C. 669, at 708.

[86] *Re Vandervell (No.2)* [1974] Ch. 269. See the conflicting formulations per Lord Browne-Wilkinson in *Westdeutsche*, above, at 708–709 (to the effect that the resulting trust responds to the transferor's intention to create a trust) and per Lord Millet in *Air Jamaica v Charlton* [1999] 1 W.L.R. 1399, at 1412 (to the effect that what is relevant is the lack of intention to transfer beneficial ownership to the transferee).

[87] See McGhee, *Snell's Equity* (2014), para.25–011 and *National Crime Agency v Gui Hui Dong* [2017] EWHC 3116 (Ch), at 38.

(2) Secondly, in some circumstances where a family relationship between the parties involves an obligation on the part of the transferor to support or provide for the transferee, the presumption may be rebutted by the counter-presumption known as "the presumption of advancement". Provision has been made for the complete abolition of the presumption of advancement by s.199 Equality Act 2010, but that section is still awaiting a date to be appointed for its coming into force. In relation to transfers effected before that section is ultimately brought into force (if it ever is), it will still be necessary to consider whether the presumption of advancement applies. Traditionally the presumption of advancement applies in three specific situations: transfers from husband to wife; transfers from father to child; and transfers from a person in loco parentis.[88] But there is considerable support in the authorities for the application of the presumption of advancement in other specific situations (eg. transfers between spouses other than from husband to wife and by mothers to children) or more generally in any situation where a transfer is made from a person who might be expected to provide for the transferee.[89] As in the case of the presumption of resulting trust to which it forms an exception, the presumption of advancement is capable of being rebutted by evidence of the actual intentions.

9–041 The authorities over the last 50 years are littered with statements to the effect that both the presumption of resulting trust and the presumption of advancement are weak and easily rebutted; and that they will apply in practice only as rules "of last resort" in rare cases where there is no evidence of the transferor's intentions.[90] Such statements perhaps underestimate the tactical significance which the presumption of resulting trust may carry, perhaps especially in fraud litigation. In particular:

(1) Until recently, the presumption of resulting trust (or, as the case may be, counter-presumption of advancement) could prove determinative in favour of one party where the other was unable to rebut the relevant presumption without relying upon the own impropriety to explain the intentions of the transferor. But now that the reasoning in *Tinsley v Milligan* has been departed from by the Supreme Court in *Patel v Mirza*,[91] it seems likely that this consideration will no longer apply;

(2) It remains the case that it is perhaps most often in fraud litigation (where contempt applications abound and serious failures of documentary

---

[88] See the references gathered in Tucker, Le Poidevin and Brightwell, *Lewin on Trusts* (2014), paras 9–025—9–034.

[89] *Re Cameron (Decd)* [1999] Ch. 368; *Laskar v Laskar* [2008] EWCA Civ 347; [2008] 1 W.L.R. 2695; *Close Invoice Finance v Abaowa* [2010] EWHC 1920 (QB); *Musson v Bonner* [2010] W.T.L.R. 1369.

[90] See for example *Vandervell v IRC* [1967] 2 A.C. 291, at 312; *Pettitt v Pettitt* [1970] A.C. 777, at 814, per Lord Upjohn, *McGrath v Wallis* [1995] 2 FRL 114; *Lavelle v Lavelle* [2004] 2 FCR 418, at [13]–[14]; *Kyriakides v Pippas* [2004] 2 FCR 434, at [74]–[76]; *Stack v Dowden* [2007] UKHL 17; [2007] 2 A.C. 432, at [101]; *Laskar v Laskar* [2008] EWCA Civ 347; [2008] 1 W.L.R. 2695, at [20], per Lord Neuberger MR, *M v M* [2013] EWHC 2534 (Fam).

[91] See 9–027 above.

disclosure are common) that parties are debarred from defending claims (as to which see Chs 35 and 36 below), with the result that the incidence of any presumption may again be crucial;

(3) Even where the party seeking to rebut the presumption is not wholly prevented from doing so, it may be restricted in the evidence upon which it can rely by the so called rule in *Shepherd v Cartwright*.[92] That "rule" provides that acts and declarations subsequent to the relevant transaction can be relied upon against the person who made them, but not in that person's favour. There is currently a division in the authorities as to whether that "rule" should be treated simply as a guide to the weight to be given to evidence,[93] or as a fully-fledged rule prohibiting the admission of evidence[94];

(4) Simply from a tactical point of view, especially in the early stages of some fraud claims, when the factual picture may still be obscure to the claimant but interlocutory warfare may be intense, it may be of assistance to the claimant to be able (subject, of course, to his obligation to put forward a truthful case and to his duties of full and frank disclosure on any ex parte application) to rely upon a claim which throws upon the defendant the burden of putting forward a factual case; and

(5) In the situation where a successful claimant seeks to establish that property apparently owned by a separate company, not subject to a judgment in favour of that claimant, is in fact held on trust for the defendant judgment debtor (and the defendant is, as is often the case, unforthcoming in relation to the underlying arrangements), it may be easier for the claimant to invoke the presumption of resulting trust than to invoke the difficult doctrine of piercing the corporate veil or to seek to apply the machinery of conventional enforcement against whatever property remains in the name of the defendant (perhaps shareholdings or some other interest in an international corporate/trust structure which is far removed from the underlying asset).[95] But this will, of course, depend upon the circumstances. In *Prest v Petrodel Resources Ltd*[96] Lord Sumption said:

> "Whether assets legally vested in a company are beneficially owned by its controller is a highly fact-specific issue. It is not possible to give general guidance going beyond the ordinary principles and presumptions of equity, especially those relating to gifts and resulting trusts."

---

[92] *Shepherd v Cartwright* [1955] A.C. 431.
[93] *Lavelle v Lavelle*, above, at [17]–[19], *M v M*, above, at 184–188; *National Crime Agency v Gui Hui Dong*, above, at 38; [2017] EWHC 3116 (Ch).
[94] *Antoni v Antoni* [2007] UKPC 10 (and contrast the cases cited in the preceding footnote).
[95] See for example *JSC BTA Bank v Solodchenko* [2015] EWHC 3680 (Comm); *NRC Holding Ltd v Danilitskiy* [2017] EWHC 1431 (Ch). The latter case is a classic example of the practical utility of the resulting trust in the execution phase of a fraud case. The judgment debtor (D), had been sued for fraudulent conduct. A judgment of $5million was obtained which went unsatisfied. A property in London was located, owned by a BVI company. The ultimate beneficial owner of the company had been D, who provided the purchase monies for the property. There was no evidence that D had advanced the monies by way of loan or capital subscription Thereafter the beneficial interest in the company passed to D's daughter. It was held that the property was held by the company on resulting trust for D.
[96] *Prest v Petrodel Resources Ltd* [2013] 2 A.C. 415, at [52].

9–042   Although this type of resulting trust is generally said to be founded on a presumed intention, it appears that it can also be found to exist on the basis of positive evidence of intention.[97] There appears, therefore, to be scope for the use of this type of resulting trust as a "route through" a situation in which a finding of express trust is blocked by some failure of formality or other failure which does not apply to resulting trusts.[98]

9–043   Nevertheless, despite the broad terms in which the presumption of resulting trust is expressed in the authorities (as in the passage of *Westdeutsche* set out above), it is important to appreciate that there are limits to the situations in which the presumption will arise. In particular:

(1)   There is some doubt whether the presumption of resulting trust still applies to gratuitous transfers of land (as opposed to purchases of land in the name of another) in light of s.60(3) Law of Property Act 1925, which provides that

> "In a voluntary conveyance, a resulting trust for the grantor shall not be implied merely by reason that the property is not expressed to be conveyed for the use or benefit of the grantee".

The wording of that section might appear on its face to abolish the presumption of resulting trust upon gratuitous conveyances; but there are significant arguments that its intention was no more than to avoid the creation of technical difficulties in the drafting of conveyances as part of the 1925 property law reforms In *Lohia v Lohia*, Nicholas Strauss QC (sitting as a Deputy High Court Judge) held that s.60(3) did have the effect of abolishing the presumption where it applied, but the point was expressly left open in the Court of Appeal[99]; and Chief Master Marsh has since reached the opposite conclusion in another case.[100] In any event, however, even if the presumption of resulting trust does not arise in such situations, it appears that a resulting trust can still be established by positive evidence of the transferor's intention (or lack of intention).[101]

(2)   In the case of a gratuitous payment of money (where the presumption of advancement does not apply), it appears that there is a presumption of a

---

[97] *Hodgson v Marks* [1971] Ch. 891; *Tribe v Tribe* [1996] Ch. 107; *Lohia v Lohia* [2001] W.T.L.R. 101; *Lavelle v Lavelle* [2004] 2 FCR 418, at [13]–[14]; *Ali v Khan* [2002] EWCA Civ 974; *M v M* [2013] EWHC 2534 (Fam), at [171]–[173]; *JSC BTA Bank v Solodchenko* [2015] EWHC 3680 (Comm); *NRC Holding Ltd v Danilitskiy* [2017] EWHC 1431 (Ch). See also *Chen v Ng* [2017] UKPC 27 for an arguable case of resulting trust founded upon positive evidence as to the parties' intention in the face of a suite of formal documents executed by the parties (although without binding effect) recording that the relevant transfer was to occur by way of sale.

[98] See *Hodgson v Marks*, above, where, even if s.53(1)(b) Law of Property Act 1925 would have blocked the creation of an informal express trust for the benefit of the transferor of land, an equivalent resulting trust would give effect to the transferor's intention under s.53(2).

[99] *Lohia v Lohia* [2001] W.T.L.R. 101 and, on appeal, at [2001] EWCA Civ 1691.

[100] *National Crime Agency v Gui Hui Dong* [2017] EWHC 3116 (Ch).

[101] *Ali v Marks*; *M v M* (both cited above).

debt to repay.[102] But it is not clear whether (and, if so, why) this should preclude a finding of resulting trust being made.

(3)   In the case of property purchased in the name of a company which is wholly owned by the party funding the purchase, it has been said by distinguished equity judges that there is little scope for the application of the presumption and that the natural inference is that the company is to be the beneficial owner (on the logic, it would appear, that the use of the company would otherwise serve little purpose).[103] But other eminent judges have more recently expressed the contrary view (at least in the case of matrimonial homes)[104]; and there have been attempts to explain or minimise the former decisions.[105] It might be concluded that the line of cases on this topic well illustrate the tendency of the "presumption" as to intention (as expressed in the traditional formulation of the principle underlying this variety of resulting trust) to become an inference as to intention on the basis of the available evidence.

(4)   In the case of jointly owned property (especially, although not exclusively, family homes), the presumption of resulting trust now plays a relatively small and contested part among a network of other doctrines, in particular common intention constructive trust.[106]

(3)   Type 2: Transfers which Fail to Dispose of the Whole Beneficial Interest

The second type of resulting trust was described by Lord Browne-Wilkinson in *Westdeutsche* as follows: "Where A transfers property to B on express trust, but the trusts declared do not exhaust the whole beneficial interest".   **9–044**

In order for such a resulting trust to arise, it must first be shown on a true construction of the relevant documents and circumstances that the transferor intended to transfer the property to the transferee to hold on trust. Obviously no trust will arise if the transferee was in fact intended to take the property beneficially, whether as an outright gift, as a payment giving rise to merely contractual obligations, or otherwise.[107] Secondly, it must be shown that the intended trust fails to exhaust the beneficial interest in the property: this will often depend upon technical questions of trust law, but examples of such   **9–045**

---

[102] *Seldon v Davidson* [1968] 1 W.L.R. 1083; *Markham v Karnsten* [2007] EWHC 1509 (Ch); *Chapman v Jaume* [2012] EWCA Civ 476.

[103] See *Stockholm Finance Ltd v Garden Holdings Inc*, unreported, 26 October 1995, at 10–11, per Robert Walker J and *Nightingale Mayfair Ltd v Prakash Mehta* [2000] W.T.L.R. 901, per Blackburne J.

[104] See *Prest v Petrodel Resources Ltd* [2013] UKSC 34; [2013] 2 A.C. 415, at [52], per Lord Sumption JSC, applied in *JSC BTA Bank v Solodchenko* [2015] EWHC 3680 (Comm) per Phillips J.

[105] *NRC Holding Ltd v Danilitskiy* [2017] EWHC 1431 (Ch).

[106] See more generally the specialist works on trust and property law in relation to the ever-evolving law upon equitable ownership in the domestic context.

[107] For example, as a gift with further obligations grafted onto it so as to engage the so-called rule in *Lassence v Tierney* or rule in *Hancock v Watson*. See (for a convenient explanation of that rule) in Tucker, Le Poidevin and Brightwell, *Lewin on Trusts* (2014), para.8–022.

situations would include[108] where (in each case without any subsequent interest under the trust being accelerated to fill the gap) the declared trust proves to be invalid for lack of certainty of objects, for failure to comply with s.53 Law of Property Act 1925 or for breaching the rules against perpetuities; or where an intended beneficiary disclaims their interest without any provision having been made for that eventuality; or where the declared trust simply overlooks part of the beneficial interest in the property transferred (perhaps by conferring a life interest on an individual and failing to provide for what should happen after their death). It does not need to be shown that the transferor would have intended the beneficial ownership to revert to himself on resulting trust, and indeed resulting trusts can arise where this is highly inconvenient to the transferor[109]; but, if it can be established that the transferor has positively disclaimed any beneficial interest in the property, the beneficial interest will pass by way of bona vacantia to the Crown rather than on resulting trust to the transferor.[110]

9–046   As will be apparent from the preceding description, resulting trusts of this second type arise most often when a problem has occurred in the intended creation of an express trust. In the fraud context, however, this second type of resulting trust is perhaps more likely to be encountered in the special instance known as the "*Quistclose*" trust, to which the following section relates.

(4)   A special Case of Type 2: "Quistclose" Trusts

9–047   The *Quistclose* trust takes its name from *Barclays Bank v Quistclose Investments Ltd*[111] and was given its current form by the authoritative analysis of the House of Lords in *Twinsectra v Yardley*.[112] In essence, it describes a situation in which property is transferred or money paid by A to B to be used only for a specific purpose, with the legal result that the property/money is held by B on resulting trust for A subject to a power for B to apply it for the stated purpose. Although such a situation might look superficially like a "purpose" trust, it is not. The beneficial interest remains vested in A throughout, unless and until there is a valid exercise of the power. Accordingly, the *Quistclose* trust is classified as a special instance of the second type of resulting trust.[113] Such a trust is most often invoked by the payer in order to attempt to save a payment from falling into the payee's general estate in the event of its insolvency; although, in the fraud context, it may equally provide a route to all of the forensic benefits of trust claims which are identified at the beginning of this chapter.

---

[108] See, for a few well known examples, *Vandervell v IRC* [1967] 2 A.C. 291; *Re Vandervell Trusts (No.3)* [1974] Ch. 269; *Air Jamaica v Charlton* [1999] 1 W.L.R. 1399.

[109] See the *Vandervell* cases cited above.

[110] See *Westdeutsche*, above, at 708.

[111] *Barclays Bank v Quistclose Investments Ltd* [1970] A.C. 567.

[112] *Twinsectra v Yardley* [2002] 2 A.C. 164, per Lords Hoffmann and Millett. See also the recent helpful summaries in *Bieber v Teathers* [2012] EWHC 160 (Ch); [2012] 2 B.C.L.C. 585, per Norris J (accepted on appeal with slight modification, at [2012] EWCA Civ 1466) and in *Challinor v Juliet Bellis & Co* [2015] EWCA Civ 59, per Briggs LJ.

[113] *Westdeutsche*, above, at 708.

In order to establish that a *Quistclose* trust has arisen, it is necessary to establish **9–048** that there was an intention on the part of the transferor to create a trust. Unlike the first type of resulting trust (considered above), such an intention must be proved without reliance upon a presumption.[114] But this does not mean necessarily that the transferor must expressly have had in mind the idea of a trust; in this context an intention to create a trust means an intention to enter into arrangements which, viewed objectively, have the effect in law of creating a trust.[115] As to this:

(1)   The key feature which the intended arrangements must have in order to give rise to a *Quistclose* trust is that the property/money transferred is not to be at the free disposal of the transferee but to be used only for a specified purpose. This must be an intention that there should be a binding restriction upon the transferee's ability to use the specific property or fund of money; a mere expectation that the property/money will be used in a certain way is not sufficient.[116]

(2)   To this end, it is normally required that the property/money should have been intended to be held separately by the transferee, and a willingness on the part of the transferor for that property/money to be mixed with other property/money in the hands of the transferee will normally be fatal to an allegation of *Quistclose* trust.[117]

(3)   What is not yet entirely clear from the authorities is the extent to which it is necessary to show, in addition to the intention that the property should not be at the free disposal of the transferee, a positive intention that ownership should remain with the transferor unless and until the intended purpose is achieved. In its recent decision in *Bieber v Teathers*,[118] it was held that

> "it is ... necessary to be satisfied not merely that the money when paid was not at the free disposal of the payee but that, objectively examined, the contractual or other arrangements properly construed were intended to provide for the preservation of the payor's rights and the control of the use of the money through the medium of a trust. Critically, this involves the court being satisfied that the intention of the parties was that the monies transferred by [A] should not become the absolute property of [B] (subject only to contractual restraint on their disposal) but should continue to belong beneficially to [A] unless and until the conditions attached to their release were complied with".

Such an additional requirement is, however, hard to spell out of the line of authority culminating in the formulation of principles endorsed by the Court of Appeal more recently in *Challinor v Juliet Bellis* (albeit apparently without citation of the decision of the Court of Appeal in *Bieber*).[119]

---

[114] *Challinor v Juliet Bellis & Co* [2015] EWCA Civ 59, at [57], per Briggs LJ.

[115] *Twinsectra*, above, at [75]; *Challinor*, above, at [56].

[116] *Twinsectra*, above, at [75]; *Shalson v Russo*, at [2003] EWHC 1637 (Ch), at [128]–[130]; *Bieber v Teathers*, above, at [17].

[117] *Patel v Mirza* [2014] EWCA Civ 1047, at [18]. But see *Cooper v PRG Powerhouse Ltd* [2008] EWHC 498 (Ch); [2008] 2 All E.R. (Comm) 964.

[118] Above, at [15]; per Patten LJ, with whom Sullivan and Arden LJJ agreed.

[119] Above, at [53]–[65].

9–049 The relevant intention is to be ascertained objectively from the transferor's words and conduct (and his subjective intentions are irrelevant).[120] In any given case, the question whether a *Quistclose* trust has arisen will require a close focus upon the words of the transferor or (particularly in a case where the transferor has made the transfer in response to an invitation, request or undertaking) the transferee.[121]

9–050 Once a *Quistclose* trust has come into existence, the beneficial ownership of the property or money remains with the transferor unless and until that property/money is applied in valid exercise of the trustee's power to give effect to the intended purpose. In order for that power to be valid, it must satisfy a requirement of certainty; the court must be able to say whether a given application of the money or property does or does not fall within the terms of the power.[122] If the power is in fact not valid or cannot be validly exercised, then the money or property will be held on an unqualified resulting trust for the transferor.[123]

9–051 For obvious reasons, the doctrine of *Quistclose* trusts is of frequent application in the context of alleged frauds; in particular in cases where A has transferred money or property to B, which then appears to have been misapplied (for example any case involving an apparently fraudulent investment scheme). In such a case, a claim based upon a *Quistclose* trust (or a similar express trust) and a claim based upon misrepresentation[124] represent the two most obvious alternative—and complementary—ways of formulating a claim which may lead to proprietary or tracing remedies. The *Quistclose* trust (or similar express trust) claim will turn upon A being able to demonstrate that the original transaction gave rise to a trust and that the subsequent application of the money/property by B has not been in accordance with its terms; whereas the misrepresentation claim will turn upon A being able to demonstrate (among the other necessary elements) the untruth of representations made at the time of the transaction giving rise to an extant right to rescind. Which is the more apt and fruitful claim for A to advance will of course depend upon the facts of the particular case. But where the terms of the original transaction are such as to permit a case to be made that it gave rise to a *Quistclose* trust, a claim on that basis may have real advantages over a misrepresentation claim as a route to recovery, including:

(1) the absence of any need to engage with difficult factual questions as to representations, falsehood, dishonesty, inducement and the other matters considered in Ch.1 above,

---

[120] *Twinsectra*, above, at [71]; *Bieber*, above, at 21; *Challinor*, above, at [58]–[61].

[121] See inter alia *Re Nanwa Goldmines Ltd* [1955] 1 W.L.R. 1080; *Quistclose*, itself, above; *Re Eastern Capital Futures* [1989] B.C.L.C. 371; *Re Goldcorp Exchange*, above; *Twinsectra*, above; *Beiber v Teathers*, above; *Brown v InnovatorOne* [2012] EWHC 1321 (Comm); *Eleftheriou v Costi* [2013] EWHC 2168 (Ch); *Gabriel v Little* [2013] EWCA Civ 1513, at [40]–[46]; *Challinor, Gore v Mishcon de Reya* [2015] EWHC 164 (Ch); *LSC Finance v Abensons Law Ltd* [2015] EWHC 1163 (Ch) and *Re MK Airlines Ltd (in Liquidation)* [2018] EWHC 540 (Ch) for examples of such an exercise of construction being conducted.

[122] *Twinsectra*, above, at [16] and [101].

[123] *Twinsectra*, above, at [101].

[124] See the fuller analysis of such claims, at paras 9–058—9–063.

(2)   the absence of a risk that a right to rescind will have been lost by reason of the sort of matters considered in Ch.23 below,

(3)   the absence of a need to engage with the law considered in the same chapter as to the status of A's interest in the relevant money/property pending rescission for misrepresentation, and

(4)   the lack of a need to elect to rescind, if there are other elements of the transaction of which A might wish to keep the benefit.

E.   CONSTRUCTIVE TRUSTS

(1)   The Nature of Constructive Trusts

As it was explained by Millett LJ in *Paragon Finance Plc v DB Thakerar & Co*[125]:   **9–052**

> "a constructive trust arises by operation of law whenever the circumstances are such that it would be unconscionable for the owner of property (usually but not necessarily the legal estate) to assert his own beneficial interest in the property and deny the beneficial interest of another".

But that is perhaps best regarded as a description of the juridical nature of the constructive trust rather than a definition, let alone a universal test. Indeed, it has been said rightly that:

> "English law provides no clear and all-embracing definition of a constructive trust. Its boundaries have been left perhaps deliberately vague so as not to restrict the court in technicalities in deciding what the justice of a particular case might demand".[126]

Accordingly, the identification by the court of the circumstances in which a constructive trust arises has proceeded (and continues to proceed) incrementally on a case by case basis. As matters now stand, there are numerous established categories of circumstances in which it has been held that a constructive trust will arise. There is no reason to believe that those categories are closed; but the court can be expected to take a cautious approach in extending them further. As explained by Millett LJ in the passage cited above, the common factor is that, by contrast with express trusts, the constructive trust does not arise by the consent and intention of the parties, but is imposed by operation of law for the purpose of reversing or preventing unconscionable behaviour or the unconscionable assertion of title to property. It follows, as we will see, that the constructive trust is, in the context of fraud litigation, a vitally important legal concept.

The remainder of this section will examine the established categories of   **9–053**
constructive trusts, arranged (for the purposes of this work) into four broad groups as follows:

(1)   Constructive trusts arising from impugnable transfers/payments (without a prior fiduciary relationship);

---

[125] *Paragon Finance Plc v DB Thakerar & Co* [1999] 1 All E.R. 400, at 409.
[126] *Carl Zeiss Stiftung v Herbert Smith & Co (No.2)* [1969] 2 Ch. 276, at 300, per Edmund-Davies LJ.

(2)   Constructive trusts arising from a prior fiduciary relationship;

(3)   Constructive trusts arising from a prior agreement or understanding; and

(4)   Other constructive trusts less directly relevant to the fraud context.

9–054   Before doing so, however, it is worth emphasising four important general points concerning constructive trusts.

9–055   **(1) Not a Discretionary Remedy.**   First, as set out at para.9–008 above, in English law as it currently stands (unlike the law of some other common law jurisdictions) all constructive trusts are "institutional" rather than "remedial". In other words, they arise by the application of fixed legal rules to given factual circumstances; although the Court may declare that a constructive trust exists in the circumstances, the Court does not create the trust. It is, accordingly, an error to think of a constructive trust as a "remedy", let alone a discretionary remedy.

(2) Certainty of Subject Matter and of Object.   Secondly, a constructive trust, although differing in obvious respects from an express trust, remains a relationship whereby property held by one legal owner is owned beneficially by another. Accordingly, for a valid constructive trust to arise, sufficient certainty both of the subject matter and of the beneficial object(s) of the trust is presumably required (see para.9–028 above).[127] The requirement for those certainties is an aspect of the proprietary nature of a trust. Naturally, however, the question of certainty of intention does not arise in the case of a constructive trust.

(3) Limited Duties of Trustee.   Thirdly, as the trustee of a constructive trust has not assumed their trusteeship voluntarily, it cannot be assumed that they will per se owe fiduciary duties; or, indeed, any duties other than the duty to hold the trust property on a bare trust for the benefit of the beneficiary and return it on request.[128] Of course, fiduciary or other further duties may be owed in any given case in light of the particular relationship between the parties; but this will not, it seems, be by virtue of the constructive trusteeship itself.

(4) Confusions of Terminology.   It is important to be aware of a widespread inconsistency in the use of the terminology of "constructive trust" and "constructive trustees". In addition to their more proper use in describing a proprietary constructive trust of the sort described in this section, those phrases have often been used (and still are used from time to time) to describe the personal liability of defendants to equitable claims in dishonest assistance and knowing receipt, which are examined in Chs 12 and 15. When used in that way, the phrases "constructive trust" and "constructive trustees" do not in any way imply that any property has in fact come to be held on trust or that the relevant individual has in fact become a trustee; they are instead a "mere formula of equitable relief", used because the historical rationale of the equitable claims in dishonest assistance and knowing receipt was that the defendant should be

---

[127] See *Re Goldcorp*, above; *Tackaberry v Hollis* [2007] EWHC 2663 (Ch); [2008] W.T.L.R. 279, at 85.5.

[128] See *Lonrho Plc v Fayed* (No.2) [1992] 1 W.L.R. 1, at 12, and the cases cited in fn.4 to Ch.10.

"accountable as constructive trustee", meaning that he should be personally accountable as if he had been a trustee.[129] In addition to that confusion, it is important to be aware that the trustee of a resulting trust is often (and equally confusingly) referred to as a "constructive trustee".

(2) Constructive Trusts Arising from Impugnable Transfers/payments (without Prior Fiduciary Relationship)

Those constructive trusts which can arise, without the existence of any prior fiduciary relationship, from an impugnable transfer or payment—for example one procured by fraud, or caused by mistake, or pursuant to a transaction capable of rescission on other grounds, or tainted by lack of authority—are obviously of considerable importance in the fraud context. Unfortunately, they also represent an area of analytical confusion in English law. In what is perhaps the most common factual scenario (a transfer or payment pursuant to a transaction which is capable of being rescinded because it has been induced by fraudulent misrepresentation), the position now appears to be relatively well-settled. But there is controversy as to when a constructive trust will arise in a number of related scenarios, leaving the correct analysis of these constructive trusts uncertain and (accordingly) the future development of the law hard to predict.

9–056

The latest decision of the Supreme Court in this area, *Re D & D Wines International Ltd*, seems effectively to circumscribe the circumstances in which such constructive trusts *might* arguably arise, while leaving open for future argument questions as to the exact circumstances in which they do. As Lord Sumption put it[130]:

9–057

"The exact circumstances in which a restitutionary proprietary claim may exist is a controversial question which has given rise to a considerable body of judicial comment and academic literature. For present purposes it is enough to point out that where money is paid with the intention of transferring the entire beneficial interest to the payee, the least that must be shown in order to establish a constructive trust is (i) that that intention was vitiated, for example because the money was paid as a result of a fundamental mistake[131] or pursuant to the contract having been rescinded,[132] or (ii) that irrespective of the intentions of the payer, in the eyes of equity the money has come into the wrong hands, as where it represents the fruits of a

---

[129] See *Selangor United Rubber Estates Ltd v Cradock (No.3)* [1981] 1 W.L.R. 1555, at 1582, per Ungoed-Thomas J, *Paragon Finance v DB Thakerar* above at 409, per Millett LJ, *Central Bank of Nigeria v Williams* [2014] UKSC 10; [2014] A.C. 1189, at [7]–[11], per Lord Sumption JSC and [57]–[67], per Lord Neuberger PSC. But see C. Mitchell, P. Mitchell and S. Watterson, *Goff & Jones: The Law of Unjust Enrichment*, 9th edn (London: Sweet & Maxwell, 2016), paras 38–19—38–23 for a robust defence of the traditional terminology.

[130] *Re D & D Wines International Ltd* [2016] UKSC 47; [2016] 1 W.L.R. 3179, at [39]. The other members of the court agreed.

[131] See paras 9–064—9–066 below for the contentious subject of constructive trusts arising by reason of mistake.

[132] See para.9–058 below for constructive trusts arising upon rescission following a fraudulent misrepresentation (a relatively well-settled subject) and para.9–063 below for constructive trusts arising upon rescission for other reasons (a more uncertain subject).

fraud, theft[133] or breach of trust or fiduciary duty against a third party.[134] One or other of these is a necessary condition, although it may not be a sufficient one."

A consideration of specific categories follows.

9–058   **Transactions Capable of Being Rescinded for Fraudulent Misrepresentation.** A strong line of authority now establishes that, when property is transferred or money paid pursuant to a contract, gift or other transaction induced by fraudulent misrepresentation, beneficial title passes to the recipient unless and until the transaction is rescinded. We consider the law of rescission at Ch.22 below. If the transaction is rescinded, however, beneficial title to property which remains traceable is revested in the transferor/payer by means of a constructive (or possibly resulting)[135] trust. That revesting (like the rescission which gives rise to it) appears to have a retrospective effect, to the extent that the transferor/payer can use the rules of tracing (see Ch.24) to trace his beneficial ownership through substitutions of property which occurred after the original transfer but prior to the rescission, and claim such traceable proceeds in the hands of the original recipient or a further recipient who is not a bona fide purchaser for value without notice of the fraud.[136] But that limited retrospective effect does not apparently go so far as to enable the transferor to pursue personal claims in breach of trust (or the allied claims in dishonest assistance or knowing receipt) in respect of dispositions which occurred prior to rescission at a time when the recipient was not yet a constructive trustee.[137] Pending rescission, the right of the transferor/payer has been described as a "mere equity", being the right (which of course may be lost in the ways analysed in Chs 22 and 23) to set aside the transaction.[138] The better view appears to be that the revesting occurs immediately upon the making of the election to rescind, without the need to wait for the order of the

---

[133] See para.9–060—9–062 below for the contentious subject of constructive trusts arising by reason of fraud or theft.

[134] Constructive trusts arising by reason of breach of pre-existing fiduciary duty or breach of trust are addressed in the following sub-section, at paras 9–068—9–076 below.

[135] The authorities differ in their characterisation of the trust as resulting or constructive. See *National Crime Agency v Robb* [2014] EWHC 4384; (Ch) [2015] Ch. 520, at [49].

[136] *Lonrho v Fayed (No.2)* [1992] 1 W.L.R. 1, at 12; *El Ajou v Dollar Land Holdings Plc* [1993] 3 All E.R. 717, at 734 (reversed on other grounds [1994] 2 All E.R. 685); *Halifax Building Society v Thomas* [1996] Ch. 217; *Bristol & West Building Society v Mothew* [1998] Ch. 1, at 22–23; *Box v Barclays Bank Plc* [1998] Lloyd's Rep. Bank 185; *Shalson v Russo* [2003] EWHC 1637 (Ch); [2005] Ch. 281, at [106]–[120]; *Papamichael v National Westminster Bank Plc* [2003] EWHC 164 (Comm); [2003] 1 Lloyd's Rep. 341; *London Allied Holdings v Lee* [2007] EWHC 2061 (Ch), at [275]–[280]; *Independent Trustee Services Ltd v GP Noble Trustees Ltd* [2013] Ch. 91 (CA), at [52]–[53]; *National Crime Agency v Robb* [2014] EWHC 4384 (Ch); [2015] Ch. 520, at [40]–[46]; *Re Crown Holdings (London) Ltd and Crown Currency Exchange Ltd* [2015] EWHC 1876 (Ch), at [25] and following.

[137] *Lonrho v Fayed and Papamichael* (both cited above). On the other hand if A pays money to B induced by B's fraud and B subsequently, prior to rescission, becomes bankrupt, it appears that A is still entitled to rescind the transaction and assert a proprietary claim to the money paid over, so long as it is still identifiable.

[138] *Twinsectra v Yardley* [1999] Lloyd's Rep. Bank 439, at 461 (CA), per Potter LJ who explained that the equity "binds volunteers and those taking with notice of the equity, but not purchasers for value without notice". So if A sells property to B induced by B's fraudulent misrepresentations, and B subsequently sells to C, who is ignorant of B's fraud, then C takes a good title even if A subsequently rescinds the contract.

court[139] (which would be consistent with the fact that, in the case of fraud, unlike some other grounds for rescission, rescission occurs at common law and probably also in equity as a "self help" remedy immediately upon the rescinding party giving notice or in some circumstances even without notice).[140] In such a case the function of the court is to adjudicate upon the validity of the prior purported act of rescission and to make, so far as necessary, coercive orders carrying into effect the legal consequences of that act.

What is far from clear, however, is how the line of authorities addressing the rather specific category of trust just described (i.e. the trust which arises when a transaction is rescinded for fraudulent misrepresentation) "fits" between two *potential* categories of constructive trust of rather wider application, which are addressed next below: a constructive trust arising simply from fraud or theft; and a constructive trust arising upon rescission of a transaction on any other grounds.

9–059

Property/Money Stolen or Obtained by Fraud. In a much-cited passage in *Westdeutsche*, Lord Browne-Wilkinson dealt with the hypothetical example of a stolen bag of coins. After explaining the argument raised before him (which turned upon the more favourable tracing process which would be available to the victim of the theft if it were possible to trace the proceeds of the coins in equity on the basis of a trust interest, rather than being confined to tracing at common law), he concluded:

9–060

> "I agree that the stolen moneys are traceable in equity. But the proprietary interest which equity is enforcing in such circumstances arises under a constructive, not a resulting, trust. Although it is difficult to find clear authority for the proposition, when property is obtained by fraud equity imposes a constructive trust on the fraudulent recipient: the property is recoverable and traceable in equity. Thus, an infant who obtained property by fraud is bound in equity to restore it: *Stocks v Wilson* [1913] 2 KB 235, 244; *R Leslie Ltd v Sheill* [1914] 3 KB 607. Moneys stolen from a bank account can be traced in equity: *Bankers Trust Co v Shapira* [1980] 1 W.L.R. 1274, at 1282C–128E: see also *McCormick v Grogan* (1869) LR 4 HL 82, 97."[141]

There is an obvious difficulty in reconciling that dictum of Lord Browne-Wilkinson in *Westdeutsche* with the line of authorities as to transactions induced by fraudulent misrepresentation which is addressed at para.9–058 above[142]; and it has been the subject of judicial and academic criticism both for its breadth and for its arguably over-expansive reading of the previous authorities which Lord Browne-Wilkinson cites.[143] Nevertheless, a number of decisions have recognised or applied this dictum apparently without consideration of that difficulty.[144] Other

9–061

---

[139] *Lonrho*, at 11–12; *Shalson v Russo*, at [120] and following, *Independent Trustee Services v GP Noble*, at [53]; *National Crime Agency v Robb*, at [47] (all cited above).

[140] See (at common law) *Car and Universal Finance Co Ltd v Caldwell* [1965] 1 Q.B. 525 and (in equity) *Reese River Mining Co v Smith* (1869) L.R. 4 LH 64, at 73.

[141] *Westdeutsche*, above, at 716.

[142] See *Halifax Building Society v Thomas* [1996] Ch. 217; *Box v Barclays Bank* [1998] All E.R. (D) 108; *Shalson v Russo*, above.

[143] *Shalson v Russo*, above, at [110]. See *London Allied*, above, at [266]–[267], per Etherton J, leaving the position open. See also the discussion in Ch.23 below.

[144] *Commerzbank Aktiensgesellschaft v IMB Morgan Plc* [2004] EWHC 2771 (Ch), at [36], per Lawrence Collins J (payments made by victims of "advanced fee fraud" on the pretext that the making

decisions have sought to solve the problem by drawing a distinction between a situation in which property is simply taken without consent (where a constructive trust is said to arise immediately on a *Westdeutsche* basis) and a situation where property is transferred pursuant to a fraudulently procured consent (where beneficial title passes unless and until the transaction embodying the consent— whether that transaction is contractual or a gift—is rescinded in accordance with the authorities cited in the preceding section).[145] Such a distinction has some intuitive appeal. But the difficulty of maintaining the distinction in practice is well illustrated by two decisions of the Court of Appeal in which the fact that the relevant transfer/payment took place pursuant to purported contractual arrangements was held not to prevent an immediate constructive trust from arising without the need for rescission: *Collings v Lee* (in which the contractual arrangements were held not to be a bar because the claimants "did not intend to transfer the property to the first defendant [i.e. their own fiduciary agent who had taken the transfer secretly under an assumed name] and they did not intend to transfer for no consideration [i.e. without the agent actually making the payments which he had said that the supposed third party purchaser was to make]")[146]; and *Halley v Law Society* (in which the relevant contractual arrangements were held to be void as mere "instruments of fraud", effectively bogus transactions which were no more than "device to extract money").[147]

9–062 A separate (and more specific) difficulty arises in the case of Lord Browne-Wilkinson's example of a stolen bag of coins, and generally in the case of stolen chattels (or other similar categories of assets). The traditional view is that a thief will not acquire even legal (let alone beneficial) title to a stolen chattel.[148] But, it was asked by Rimer J in *Shalson v Russo*, if the thief does not acquire even legal

---

of such payments was necessary to enable transactions which would result in reimbursement of larger sums); *Bank of Ireland v Pexxnet Ltd* [2010] EWHC 1872 (Comm), at [55]–[57], per Jonathan Hirst QC (money paid pursuant to forged cheques).

[145] *Collings v Lee* [2001] 2 All E.R. 332 in the Court of Appeal (see below); *Halley v Law Society* [2003] EWCA Civ 97; [2003] W.T.L.R. 845, at [42]–[56] (see below); *Papamichael*, at [232]–[245], per Judge Chambers QC (money coming pursuant to a fraud into the hands of a third party and then of the fraudster without any "supervening barrier such as a contract" to the existence of a constructive trust); *Armstrong DLW GmbH v Winnington Networks Ltd* [2012] EWHC 10 (Ch); [2013] Ch. 156, at [127]–[129] and [273]–[277], per Stephen Morris QC (transfer of European Union carbon allowances from an electronic account by a third party using electronic details procured by a phishing fraud); *Re Crown Holdings*, at [34(a)], per Mr M Rosen QC distinguishing Lord Browne-Wilkinson's dictum in *Westdeutsche* on the grounds that it does not "refer to a situation where the result of the fraud is to induce a party to enter into a contract".

[146] *Collings v Lee*, above. It is unclear to what extent the decision should be considered as turning upon the fiduciary status of the transferee, upon the false identity of the transferee as a fundamental flaw in the contract and/or upon the overall "bogus" nature of the arrangement.

[147] *Halley v Law Society* [2003] EWCA Civ 97; [2003] W.T.L.R. 845, at [42]–[56]. See the criticism of that decision and *Collings*, at C. Mitchell, P. Mitchell and Watterson, *Goff & Jones: The Law of Unjust Enrichment*, 8th edn, (London: Sweet & Maxwell, 2011), para.40–24. See also the treatment of *Halley* in *Re Crown Holdings*, above, at [34(b)], per Mr M Rosen QC, where he said that that decision is "not (to my mind) to be categorised as one of fraudulent misrepresentation and rescission but rather as if the contracts were void ab initio, or closer to non-contractual restitution". See also *Billingdon v Davies* [2016] EWHC 2629 (Ch), where *Shalson* was distinguished on the grounds that the contract was itself an "instrument of fraud".

[148] And hence an action in conversion will lie: see M.A. Jones, A.M. Dugdale and M. Simpson (eds), *Clerk & Lindsell on Torts*, 21st edn (London: Sweet & Maxwell, 2014), para.17–37.

title, how can any form of trust arise?[149] The point is of practical significance because the equitable tracing and other remedies available to a beneficial owner of trust property are, in various respects, superior to the common law remedies for the recovery of property. In principle, the same difficulty might be argued to arise in the case of a fraudulently induced transfer of chattels in respect of which legal title will revest upon rescission.[150] This difficulty has not yet been answered definitively by the court. But the solution, as suggested by some commentators,[151] may lie in the relativity of title at common law; in that mere possession of the chattel *does* confer upon a thief title to that chattel as against anyone who does not have a superior right to it,[152] and there is no reason why that limited possessory title could not be held on constructive trust for the victim.

Transactions Capable of Being Rescinded/Avoided on Grounds Other than Fraudulent Misrepresentation. Perhaps surprisingly, there is uncertainty as to how far the principles set out at para.9–058 above, which apply where a transaction is rescinded on grounds of fraudulent misrepresentation, also apply where a transaction is rescinded on other grounds. Species of rescission, on grounds other than fraudulent misrepresentation, in respect of which there is authority for holding that a similar trust arises include: undue influence,[153] the sort of mistake which merits the setting aside of a gratuitous disposition under the principles set out in *Pitt v Holt*,[154] and non-fraudulent misrepresentation.[155] But it is unclear whether those instances can be generalised into a universal rule, and indeed whether they are beyond argument in themselves.[156] Indeed, as the authorities considered in the preceding two sections demonstrate, there is doctrinal uncertainty as to whether the well-established trust arising upon rescission of a fraudulently induced transaction arises by virtue of the fraud, by virtue of the rescission, or both.[157]
    9–063

Mistake, Void Transactions, Failure of Consideration and "Unconscionable Receipt." There is some authority (see below) for the proposition that a constructive (or possibly resulting) trust may arise in cases where money is paid,
    9–064

---

[149] See *Shalson v Russo*, above, at [110]. See also G. Virgo, *The Principles of Equity and Trusts* (Oxford: OUP), pp.298–299 and C. Mitchell, P. Mitchell and Watterson, *Goff & Jones: The Law of Unjust Enrichment* (2016), para.8–68.

[150] See *Car & Universal Finance v Caldwell* [1965] 1 Q.B. 525 for the principles in relation to goods.

[151] See D. Fox, *Property Rights in Money* (Oxford: OUP, 2008) [4.103]–[4.106].

[152] *Costello v Chief Constable of Derbyshire* [2001] EWHCA Civ 381; [2001] 1 W.L.R. 1437, which does not appear to have been cited in *Shalson v Russo*.

[153] *Allcard v Skinner* (1887) 36 Ch. D. 145; *Pearce v Beverley* [2013] EWHC 2627 (Ch). On undue influence generally see Ch.15.

[154] *Pitt v Holt* [2013] UKSC 26; [2013] 2 A.C. 108, *Bainbridge v Bainbridge* [2016] EWHC 898 (Ch) per Master Matthews.

[155] *Bristol & West v Mothew* [1998] 1 Ch. 1, at 22–23. See also *Twinsectra v Yardley* [1999] Lloyd's Rep. Bank 438, at 461–462 (CA).

[156] See, for example, *Re Goldcorp Exchange* [1995] 1 A.C. 74, at 102–103, per Lord Mustill.

[157] A full rehearsal of the arguments is beyond the scope of this work. But it is fair to say that the law could be accused with some justice of inconsistency if rescission of a voidable contract were held to give rise to a resulting or constructive trust in all cases, where the House of Lords has held in *Westdeutsche* that no such trust arises as standard in the case of a contract which is wholly void, as set out below in para.9–064.

or property transferred, by mistake. But it remains uncertain whether that proposition will be held to be well-founded; and, if so, what its rationale, and its true extent, will be held to be (given that, as set out immediately below, there are now decisions of the House of Lords and of the Supreme Court which confine closely on two sides its possible extent).

(1)   On the one hand, in *Westdeutsche*, the House of Lords held that no trust arises as a general rule when a payment is made pursuant to a contract which is void (whether on grounds of ultra vires, as in that case, or of mistake or otherwise).[158] But crucially for present purposes, in doing so, did not expressly overrule *Chase Manhattan Bank NA v Israel British Bank (London) Ltd*,[159] an earlier decision of Goulding J which had recognised a resulting trust of money paid by mistake duplicating a previous payment, with Lord Browne-Wilkinson saying that

> "although I do not accept the reasoning of Goulding J, [the case] may well have been rightly decided. The defendant bank knew of the mistake made by the paying bank within two days of the receipt of the monies... The judge treated this fact as irrelevant ... but in my judgment it may well provide a proper foundation for the decision. Although the mere receipt of the moneys, in ignorance of the mistake, gives rise to no trust, the retention of the moneys after the recipient bank learned of the mistake may well have given rise to a constructive trust...".[160]

That reasoning has been the subject of academic criticism,[161] but has been applied in several first-instance decisions (albeit with little consensus as to the principles giving rise to the trust),[162] while being expressly left open in others.[163]

---

[158] Per Lord Goff of Chieveley at 689C–690G, per Lord Browne-Wilkinson at 705–716, per Lord Slynn of Hadley at 718, per Lord Woolf at 720–721, and per Lord Lloyd of Berwick at 738.

[159] *Chase Manhattan Bank NA v Israel British Bank (London) Ltd* [1981] Ch. 105.

[160] At 715, per Lord Browne-Wilkinson. Lord Goff made no comment on the correctness of the decision in *Chase Manhattan*.

[161] See Swadling "Property and Conscience" (1998) 12(4) Trust Law International 228; Lord Millett "Restitution and Constructive Trusts" (1998) 114 L.Q.R. 399, at 412–413.

[162] *Papamichael*, above, at [221]–[231], per Judge Chambers QC (where the view was taken that a constructive trust could arise whenever the recipient acquired actual knowledge of the mistake, even if after the making of the payment, so long as there remained identifiable proceeds); *Commerzbank*, above, at [36], per Lawrence Collins J (where the key factor was said to be that it was the recipient which had requested double payment); *Farepak Food & Gifts Ltd* [2006] EWHC 3272 (Ch) [2008] BCC 22, at [37]–[44], per Mann J (money received into a savings scheme after, unknown to the payers, it had been decided to cease trading for reasons of insolvency); *Re Crown Holdings*, above, at [53]–[62], per Mr M Rosen QC (where the reasoning builds in part upon the decision of the Court of Appeal in *Re D & D Wines International*, now reversed by the Supreme Court as set out below); *Bainbridge v Bainbridge* [2016] EWHC 898 (Ch) per Master Matthews (where the relevant transfer into trust had been set aside on grounds of mistake following *Pitt v Holt* [2013] 2 A.C. 108 and the proprietary consequences were treated as equivalent to those in a case of rescission on grounds of fraudulent misrepresentation).

[163] See *London Allied*, above, at [268]–[272], per Etherton J leaving the position open and *Fitzalan-Howard v Hibbert* [2009] EWHC 2855 (QB) [2010] P.N.L.R. 11, at [49]–[50], per Tomlinson J (observing that the position remains unclear and speculating that the relevant time need not be the moment of knowledge but might be the time at which the recipient should have acted to return the property).

(2) On the other hand, however, in *Re D & D Wines* ,[164] the Supreme Court has comprehensively rejected the proposition that a constructive trust will arise in favour of the transferor/payer on the grounds of unconscionable receipt by a transferee/payee who knows at the point of receipt that there will inevitably be a total failure of consideration for the transfer/payment. That heretical proposition had received the support of a short line of authority which reached its high points in the decisions of Bingham J in *Neste Oy v Lloyds Bank Plc* and Nicholas Warren QC in *Re Japan Leasing (Europe) Plc*,[165] both expressly overruled by the Supreme Court in *Re D & D Wines*. In reaching that decision, Lord Sumption[166] deprecated generalised references to "good conscience" or "fairness" as tests for the creation of a constructive trust, saying:

> "Bingham J's point of departure in *Neste Oy* was that the recipient of the money may be liable to account for it as a constructive trustee if he cannot in good conscience assert his own beneficial interest in the money against some other person of whose rights he is aware. As a general proposition this is plainly right. But it is not a sufficient statement of the test, because it begs the question what good conscience requires. Property rights are fixed and ascertainable rights. Whether they exist in a given case depends on settled principles, even in equity. Good conscience therefore involves more than a judgment of the relative moral merits of the parties. For that reason it seems to me, with respect, that Bingham J's observation in *Neste Oy* that any reasonable and honest director would have returned [the relevant payment] upon its receipt begs the essential question whether he should have returned it. It cannot be a sufficient answer to that question to say that it would be 'contrary to any ordinary notion of fairness' for the general creditors to benefit by the payment. Reasoning of this kind might be relevant to the existence of a remedial constructive trust, but not an institutional one."[167]

While overruling the *Neste Oy* line of authorities and apparently disapproving the sweeping "unconscionable receipt" test which underlay them, the Supreme Court was careful (as appears from the passage set out at para.9–057 above) not to trespass on the question of when an impeachable transaction will in fact give rise to a constructive trust within the broad parameters which they set. In particular, their Lordships expressly left open the question of mistake, with Lord Sumption saying: **9–065**

> "Mistake was not argued in *Neste Oy*. Bingham J had refused to allow the shipowners to rely on it because they took the point too late. But it has subsequently been suggested that since the shipowners presumably paid the money in the belief that PSL was in a position to disburse it to the service-providers, mistake would have been a better basis for the decision: *In re Farepak Food and Gifts Ltd* [2008] B.C.L.C. 22, at [39]–[40], per Mann J. Whether that is correct is not a question which arises on this appeal".

What remains unclear therefore is whether there is scope for constructive/ resulting trusts to arise in situations of mistaken payments and transfers, if such   **9–066**

---

[164] Above.

[165] Respectively, [1983] 2 Lloyd's Rep. 658 and [1999] B.P.I.R. 911. See also *Friends Provident Life Office v Hillier Parker May & Rowden* [1997] Q.B. 85 and *Re Goldcorp Exchange*, above, at 104 for earlier apparent support for those authorities. See *Box v Barclays*, above, at 200 and *Shalson v Russo*, above, at 320 for earlier criticism.

[166] With whom the rest of the Court agreed.

[167] At [28].

trusts are not created either purely by the fact of a transaction being void (per *Westdeutsche*) or purely by the apparent unconscionability of a payment/transfer being received or retained (per *Re D & D Wines*). A line of first instance authorities (all pre *Re D & D Wines*) suggest that there is, as set out above. But if so, it is far from clear what is the underlying rationale for such trusts, what is the applicable test of mistake and (in answering those two questions) how the creation of such trusts is to be kept within reasonable bounds.

9–067   **Transactions Ineffective for Lack of Authority.**   A transaction purportedly entered into by an agent (including, for example, a company director) without actual or apparent authority will be ineffective (and, in that sense, void).[168] Accordingly, at least where the transaction involves the transfer of property formerly held on trust or owned outright by a company, it has been held that equitable title will not pass, with the result that the recipient will hold the property on constructive trust unless the principal elects to ratify the transaction (or equitable title is otherwise lost).[169] The rationale for distinguishing such cases from the sorts of void transactions considered in *Westdeutsche* is not easy to follow or to apply.

(3)   Constructive Trusts Arising from Fiduciary Relationships

9–068   There are categories of constructive trust which can arise from the existence of a fiduciary relationship (or the breach of the duties inherent in such a relationship); and they are often of relevance in fraud cases. There is no single generally accepted taxonomy. But, for present purposes, they can conveniently be analysed by reference to two broad categories, which should (of course) be considered in the context of the principles underlying the relevant breaches of duty as set out in Ch.11.

9–069   **Constructive Trust of Benefits Received by a Fiduciary in Breach of Fiduciary Duty.**   The law upon this topic has been much simplified by the landmark decision of the Supreme Court in *FHR European Ventures LLP v Cedar Capital Partners LLC*.[170] In that case, the Supreme Court appears to have endorsed a unitary rule under which all benefits received by a fiduciary in breach of fiduciary duty are held on constructive trust for the principal/beneficiary of the fiduciary duty, subject, naturally, to:

(1)   the right of the claimant to elect between his in personam and proprietary claims; and
(2)   the jurisdiction to grant the fiduciary an equitable allowance for his expenses or in respect of his skill and effort, as considered in Ch.22.

---

[168] *Criterion Properties Plc v Stratford UK Properties LLC* [2004] 1 W.L.R. 1846 (HL).

[169] *Heinl v Jyske Bank (Gibraltar) Ltd* [1999] Lloyd's Rep. Bank 511 (CA), at 521; *Clark v Cutland* [2004] 1 W.L.R. 738 (CA) See Ch.12, in relation to the analytical and practical difficulties which arise in the common fact pattern where the agent is a fiduciary and the unauthorised transaction also a breach of fiduciary duty.

[170] *FHR European Ventures LLP v Cedar Capital Partners LLC* [2014] UKSC 45; [2015] A.C. 250.

That unitary rule reflects the "no profit" rule considered in Ch.11, giving effect to **9–070** the principle that a fiduciary cannot be heard to say that any benefit acquired in the course of performing their duties was acquired for his benefit rather than the benefit of his principal/beneficiary.

Specific items of property coming to the fiduciary's attention qua fiduciary but **9–071** acquired purportedly for his own benefit are the classic subject matter of the rule.[171] It is plain that the rather more amorphous category of diverted "business opportunities", of the sort considered in Ch.11, at para.11–101, also falls within the rule, although it appears that the trust in such a case applies to the benefits arising from the opportunity (as an opportunity is not itself an item of property), giving rise to potential issues of causation in identifying the extent of the relevant benefits.[172] It is now settled by *FHR* (following many years of academic and judicial controversy) that the rule also extends to bribes and secret commissions, of the sort considered at Ch.7, which ex hypothesi could never have been acquired by the fiduciary for the benefit of his principal/beneficiary.[173]

Given the strict application of the "no profit" rule once it is found that a fiduciary **9–072** duty applies (and the sweeping presumptions made in cases of alleged bribery as set out in Ch.7) it is hard to overstate the potential benefit of the rule for fraud claimants. But, although stating the principle in general terms, *FHR* and the line of authority on which it builds[174] are principally concerned with situations in which the fiduciary receives benefits from a third party. They do not necessarily answer the related questions which arise when the property has been acquired from the principal/beneficiary of the fiduciary duty, in circumstances which involve a breach of that duty; those questions are addressed next.

---

[171] Among a very extensive case law, see cases such as *Keech v Sandford* (1726) Sel Cas Ch 61; *Phipps v Boardman* above, *Don King Productions Inc v Warren* [2000] Ch. 291, at 340 or, at another factual extreme, *Cobbetts LLP v Hodge* [2009] EWHC 786 (Ch) [2010] 1 B.C.L.C. 30.

[172] See the House of Lords' celebrated decision in *Phipps v Boardman*, above, *Murad v Al Saraj* [2005] EWCA Civ 959 [2005] W.T.L.R. 1573, the Court of Appeal's decision in *FHR European Ventures LLP v Mankarious* [2013] EWCA Civ 17; [2014] Ch. 1, per Lewison LJ at [57]–[58], and *Global Energy Horizons v Gray* [2015] EWHC 2232 (Ch), at [128], per Asplin J. Compare *Gamatronic (UK) Ltd v Hamilton* [2016] EWHC 2225 (QB); [2017] BCC 670, a case in which the requisite causal connection could not be made out.

[173] The contrary line of authority (represented in decisions such as *Tyrell v Bank of London* (1862 10 HL Cas 26, *Metropolitan Bank v Hieron* (1880) 5 Ex D 319; *Lister & Co v Stubbs* (1890) 45 Ch. D. 1 and *Sinclair v Versailles* [2011] EWCA Civ 347; [2012] Ch. 453) has been departed from and overruled.

[174] In a very long chain of authorities, some of the main links are: *Keech v Sandford*, above, *Sugden v Crossland* (1856) 3 Sm & G 192; *Bowes v City of Toronto* (1858) 11 Moo PC 463; *Bagnall v Carlton* (1877) 6 Ch. D. 371; *Re Caerphilly Colliery Co* (1877) 5 CH. D. 336; *Nant-y-glo and Blaina Ironworks Co v Grave* (1878) 12 Ch. D. 738; *Cook v Deeks* [1916] 1 A.C. 554; *Williams v Barton* [1927] 2 Ch. 9; *Boardman v Phipps* [1964] 1 W.L.R. 993; [1967] 2 A.C. 46, Attorney General for Hong Kong v Reid [1994] 1 A.C. 324; *Fyffes Group v Templeman* [2000] 2 Lloyd's Rep. 643; *Bhullar v Bhullar* [2003] EWCA Civ 424; [2003] 2 B.C.L.C. 241; *Daraydan Holdings Ltd v Solland International Ltd* [2004] EWHC 622 (Ch); [2005] Ch 119.

9–073   **Constructive Trust of Property Received from the Principal/Beneficiary of the Fiduciary Duty in a Transaction Tainted by Breach of Fiduciary Duty.** There are numerous cases in which a fiduciary, who had received property from the principal/beneficiary pursuant to a breach of fiduciary duty, has been found to hold such property on constructive trust for the principal; and, equally, in which a third party who has received property from the principal/beneficiary pursuant to a fiduciary's breach of duty (other than a bona fide purchaser for value of the legal estate without notice) has been found to receive it on constructive trust.

9–074   Where the receipt of property is a straightforward defalcation without colour of right, there is little difficulty; and, when considering the position of the trustee, it is perhaps unimportant whether the constructive trust arises as a continuation of the fiduciary's original trustee-like duties,[175] as a result of the lack of authority to make the transfer,[176] as a result of the breach of fiduciary duty itself, by application of the principle in *FHR European Ventures LLP* or simply as a result of the fraud (as it might be in the non-fiduciary situation addressed above).[177]

9–075   Likewise, where the property is received pursuant to a purported transaction which is rendered void by breach of fiduciary duty, then (assuming the recipient has acquired any legal title at all) there is relatively little conceptual difficulty in finding that the recipient receives the property on constructive trust. But, as addressed in Ch.11, it may not be clear whether the effect of the breach of duty is to render the transaction void rather than voidable; and, if void, whether void in law or merely in equity. Where the transaction is void in equity (as, it seems, may be the case when a dispositive power is exercised in bad faith or for improper purposes, at least by a company director,[178] and (possibly) where a fiduciary is guilty of self-dealing),[179] the legal transfer will be effective to transfer beneficial title and will therefore result in the property being held on trust. Where the transaction is void in law (as, for example, in the case of some dispositive acts of company directors undertaken without proper authority under the company's constitution)[180] then there may be scope for dispute as to the extent to whether the fiduciary acquires any legal title at all; but, insofar as he does, it will be held on constructive trust.[181]

9–076   On the other hand, if the transaction is merely voidable for breach of fiduciary duty (which appears still to be the case in respect of breaches of the fair-dealing rule,[182] and has been said to be the general principle applicable to breaches of fiduciary duty),[183] it is hard to see why a constructive trust should arise unless and until the principal/beneficiary elects to avoid the transaction. In *Guinness Plc v Saunders*, Lord Goff rejected the notion that a constructive trust could arise in

---

[175] See, for example, *JJ Harrison (Properties) Ltd v Harrison* [2001] EWCA Civ 1467; [2002] BCC 729, at [29], per Chadwick LJ.

[176] *Clark v Cutland* [2003] EWCA Civ 810; [2004] 1 W.L.R. 783.

[177] See paras 9–060—9–061.

[178] See Ch.11.

[179] See Ch.11.

[180] See cases such as *Clark v Cutland*, above, *Guinness v Saunders* below.

[181] Compare the well-known example of the stolen "bag of coins" considered above, at para.9–062.

[182] See e.g. *Johnson v EBS Pensioner Trustees Ltd* [2002] Lloyd's Rep. PN 309 (CA).

[183] *Abacus Trust Co (Isle of Man) v Barr* [2003] Ch. 409, per Lightman J at 421.

respect of sums paid under a contract voidable for breach of fiduciary duty, unless the contract has actually been rescinded (with any attendant restitutio ad integrum).[184] The logic of that view is compelling, although:

(1)   as we have said, the border between breaches of fiduciary duty giving rise respectively to void or voidable transactions is not a clear-cut one; and
(2)   the question has been raised by at least one commentator whether the Supreme Court's apparent endorsement of a unitary rule in *FHR European Ventures LLP* has altered, or dispensed with, the need for rescission to give rise to a constructive trust in relation to all transactions in which it is the trustee—rather than a third party—who receives a benefit in breach of fiduciary duty.[185]

(4)   Constructive Trusts Arising from a Prior Agreement or Understanding

There are three recognised categories of constructive trusts which arise to give   9–077
effect to an express or implied agreement or understanding as to the ownership of property, which is insufficiently formalised to take effect at common law but from which it would be unconscionable for the legal owner of the property to resile. It is helpful to make three preliminary points before turning to those categories in more detail:

(1)   These three categories are sometimes of relevance in a fraud case, and so an overview is given here. But it is important to appreciate that they represent an area of law which is in a perpetual state of development (as they form an important part of the law concerning ownership of the family home, which has been revisited regularly by the highest courts for at least the last 50 years); and a full treatment is not attempted. Moreover, these categories of constructive trust have a close relationship (the nature of which remains highly contentious)[186] with the doctrine of proprietary estoppel, which is beyond the scope of this book.
(2)   In the case of each category the vast majority (or all) of the authorities are concerned with real property. Although it is not easy to see a principled basis for a distinction, the lopsided nature of the authority leaves it unclear to what extent these categories of constructive trust are applicable to other types of property.
(3)   There is enduring controversy as to the extent to which these categories of constructive trust should operate at all outside the domestic context.

Common Intention Constructive Trust.   In the case of property used as a   9–078
family home, a constructive trust can arise where:

---

[184] *Guinness Plc v Saunders* [1990] 2 A.C. 663, at 698.
[185] See Conaglen [2014] CLJ 490.
[186] See *Thorner v Major* [2009] UKHL 18; [2009] 1 W.L.R. 776; *Crossco No.4 v Jolan* [2011] EWCA Civ 1619.

(1)   the relevant parties (most often romantic partners) have a "common intention" that they will each have an interest in the property which does not correspond to the legal ownership of the property; and

(2)   one party relies on that common intention to his or her detriment.

9–079   To summarise the current position[187]: where there is a valid and effective trust deed or other formal document entered into by the parties defining the beneficial ownership of the property (which is not impeachable under some other legal doctrine), then that document will determine the beneficial ownership *at the time when the document is entered into*[188], although it is apparently still possible for the beneficial ownership subsequently to be varied by a common intention constructive trust founded on later conduct. Where there is no trust deed or other document determining the beneficial ownership, the legal ownership of the property (i.e. whether in the sole name of one party or in the names of both parties as joint tenants) will provide the starting point as to the parties' assumed intentions as to ownership; and the party seeking to establish a contrary "common intention" will bear the burden of doing so. The relevant "intention" for these purposes is the intention which each party reasonably understood the other to have. Such "intention" may be either express or inferred from the parties' conduct (although it generally may not be imputed—in the sense of the Court attributing to the parties a "common intention" which they did not in fact have [189].) It appears that, as the "common intention" of the parties may change over time during the period of ownership of the property, so the constructive trust can change to give effect to that changing intention.

9–080   The principles governing "common intention constructive trusts" of the sort described above have been developed overwhelmingly in cases relating to ownership of a family home. There are some eminent judicial statements providing support for the view that they reflect policy considerations which are only applicable in such cases and should accordingly be confined to them.[190] It is possible that the law will develop in that direction. But the present position is unclear. There are cases in which a common intention constructive trust has been held to arise in relation to investment property (usually in a family business context)[191]; and the Court of Appeal has held that the so-called "*Pallant v*

---

[187] Among a vast range of authority, the principal peaks are perhaps: *Pettit v Pettitt* [1970] A.C. 777; *Gissing v Gissing* [1971] A.C. 886; *Lloyd's Bank v Rosset* [1991] 1 A.C. 107; *Stack v Dowden* [2007] UKHL 17; [2007] 2 A.C. 432; *Abbott v Abbott* [2007] UKPC 53; *Jones v Kernott* [2011] UKSC 53; [2012] 1 A.C. 776; *Barnes v Phillips* [2015] EWCA Civ 1056.

[188] The Privy Council (by a majority) recently affirmed that proposition in relation to personal property in *Whitlock v Moree* [2017] UKPC 44 (account opening documents determinative as to beneficial ownership of accounts).

[189] Save in a situation where the Court has found an express or common intention that the parties should share the ownership of the property in a way which does not correspond to the legal ownership, but lacks evidence to make findings as to what proportions were intended. In such a case the Court is permitted to "impute" an intention based upon what appears fair having regard to the whole course of dealing in relation to the property.

[190] See *CrossCo v Jolan*, above, at [85], per Etherton LJ (dissenting) and the citations gathered there.

[191] See *Agarwala v Agarwala* [2013] EWCA Civ 1763; *Bhushan v Chand* [2015] EWHC 1298 (Ch); *Sandhu v Sandhu* [2016] EWCA Civ 1050; *Matchmove Ltd v Dowding* [2016] EWCA Civ 1233 (a case of former friends).

Morgan equity" (considered in the following section) is to be considered as a species of common intention constructive trust, despite the fact that it has historically arisen in a commercial context (although that must now be considered doubtful in light of the subsequent decisions considered below).[192] But if common intention constructive trusts are capable of arising outside the domestic context, this does not (of course) necessarily mean that the principles worked out within that context (particularly those worked out in the recent House of Lords and Supreme Court decisions which dominate this area) will necessarily apply in their full and unmodified form.

The Pallant v Morgan Equity. The so called "*Pallant v Morgan* equity"[193] is **9–081** the name commonly given to a constructive trust which arises where:

(1) A has acquired property in furtherance of an arrangement or understanding with B that B should obtain an interest in the property,
(2) A has obtained an advantage, or B has suffered a detriment, by B's compliance with his side of the arrangement or understanding, and
(3) the circumstances render it inequitable for A to retain the property for himself in a manner inconsistent with their arrangement.

Crucially, the *Pallant v Morgan* constructive trust can arise despite the fact that the parties have not reached the point of entering into (or even thinking that they are entering into) a binding contract; a belief that there would be such a contract in due course is sufficient if the other requirements for the constructive trust are met. However, the rationale of the constructive trust and the applicable test remain contentious. The leading authority is still generally said to be *Banner Homes Group Plc v Luff Developments Ltd*,[194] in which (after cautioning against attempts to impose exhaustive classifications upon the possible applications of underlying equitable principle) Chadwick LJ identified five propositions, which can be summarised as follows:

(1) A *Pallant v Morgan* equity may arise where the arrangement or understanding on which it is based precedes the acquisition of the relevant property by one party to that arrangement.
(2) It is unnecessary that the arrangement or understanding should be contractually enforceable. Indeed, if there is an agreement which is enforceable as a contract, there is unlikely to be any need to invoke the *Pallant v Morgan* equity.
(3) It is necessary that the pre-acquisition arrangement or understanding should contemplate that one party ("the acquiring party") will take steps to acquire the relevant property; and that, if he does so, the other party ("the non-acquiring party") will obtain some interest in that property. Further, it is necessary that, whatever private reservations the acquiring party may

---

[192] See *CrossCo* (again), at [129], per Arden LJ with whom MacFarlane LJ agreed. But that must now be read in the light of *Generator Developments Ltd v Lidl UK GmbH* (below).
[193] After *Pallant v Morgan* [1953] Ch. 43.
[194] *Banner Homes Group Plc v Luff Developments Ltd* [2000] Ch. 372 (CA), at [397].

have, he has not informed the non-acquiring party before the acquisition[195] that he no longer intends to honour the arrangement or understanding.

(4) It is necessary that, in reliance on the arrangement or understanding, the non-acquiring party should do (or omit to do) something which confers an advantage on the acquiring party in relation to the acquisition of the property, or is detrimental to the ability of the non-acquiring party to acquire the property on equal terms (it need not be *both* advantageous to one and detrimental to the other—either suffices). In many cases the advantage/detriment will be found in the agreement of the non-acquiring party to keep out of the market, although that is not a necessary feature.

(5) What is essential is that the circumstances make it inequitable for the acquiring party to retain the property for himself in a manner inconsistent with the arrangement or understanding on which the non-acquiring party has acted.

9–082 Subsequent decisions of courts at all levels have (at least nominally) followed, applied or approved *Banner Homes*.[196] But the terms in which they have done so make it necessary to treat the wide statement of principles by Chadwick LJ in that case with some caution. The academic reception of *Banner Homes* has also been mixed. The topic is plainly ripe for reconsideration by the Supreme Court.[197] A full analysis is not attempted here. But some key authorities are briefly addressed.

9–083 In *Cobbe v Yeomans Row Management Ltd*,[198] Lord Scott accepted the correctness of the *Pallant v Morgan* line of authority culminating in *Banner Homes*. But he characterised the *Pallant v Morgan* constructive trust more narrowly as one arising "out of joint ventures relating to property" as follows:

"If two or more persons agree to embark on a joint venture which involves the acquisition of an identified piece of land and a subsequent exploitation of, or dealing with, the land for the purposes of the joint venture, and one of the joint venturers, with the agreement of the others who believe him to be acting for their joint purposes, makes the acquisition in his own name but subsequently seeks to retain the land for his own benefit, the court will regard him as holding the land on trust for the joint venturers. This would be either an implied trust or a constructive trust arising from the circumstances and if, as would be likely from the facts as described, the joint venturers have not agreed and cannot agree about what is to be done with

---

[195] Or, perhaps more accurately, before it is too late for the parties to be restored to a position of no advantage/no detriment.

[196] *London & Regional Investments Ltd v TBI* [2002] EWCA Civ 355 (in which the fact that all the negotiations were expressly stated to be "without prejudice" was fatal to the constructive trust claim; *Kilcarne Holdings Ltd v Targetfollow (Birmingham) Ltd* EWCA Civ 1355; *Cobbe v Yeomans Row Management Ltd* [2008] UKHL 55; [2008] 1 W.L.R. 1752, at [30]–[37]; *Baynes Clarke v Corless* [2010] EWCA Civ 338; *Crossco No.4 Ltd v Jolan Ltd* [2011] EWCA Civ 1619; *Kearns Brothers Ltd v Hova Developments Ltd* [2012] EWHC 2968 (Ch); *Credit & Mercantile Plc v Kaymuu* [2014] EWHC 1746 (Ch) (revised in part [2015] EWCA Civ 655); *Generator Developments LLP v LIDL (UK)* GmbH [2016] EWHC 816 (Ch); *Farrar v Miller* [2018] EWCA Civ 172; *Generator Developments Ltd v Lidl UK GmbH* [2018] EWCA Civ 396.

[197] See for example B. McFarlane "Constructive trusts on receipt of property sub condition" (2004) L.Q.R. 667 and S. Gardner "Reliance-Based Constructive Trusts" in C. Mitchell (ed), *Constructive and Resulting Trusts* (London: Hart Publishing, 2010).

[198] *Cobbe v Yeomans Row Management Ltd* [2008] UKHL 55; [2008] 1 W.L.R. 1752, at [30]–[37].

the land, the land would have to be resold and, after discharging the expenses of its purchase and any other necessary expense of the abortive joint venture, the net proceeds of sale divided equally between the joint venturers."

In that case, the House of Lords decided that no *Pallant v Morgan* constructive trust could arise firstly because the property had been owned by the defendant before the claimant arrived on the scene, but secondly on the basis that:

    9–084

"the agreement ... was known by both to be unenforceable, that an unenforceable promise to perform a legally unenforceable agreement—which is what an agreement binding in honour comes to—can give no greater advantage than the unenforceable agreement, that [the claimant's] expectations of an enforceable contract ... was inherently speculative and contingent on [the defendant's] decisions regarding the incomplete agreement and that [the claimant] never expected to acquire an interest in the property otherwise than under a legally enforceable contract".

The first of those reasons is a direct application of Chadwick LJ's first proposition in *Banner v Luff*; but the second is not easy to reconcile with the *Pallant v Morgan* principle as explained in *Banner v Luff*. Moreover, Lord Scott in *Cobbe* went on to say that:

"a claim for the imposition of a constructive trust in order to provide a remedy for a disappointed expectation engendered by a representation made in the context of incomplete contractual negotiations is, in my opinion, misconceived and cannot be sustained by reliance on unconscionable behaviour on the part of the representor."[199]

Otherwise, his Lordship reasoned, many claims in deceit based upon the making of such representations would give rise, not merely to conventional damages to compensate the victim for their losses, but also to an unprincipled proprietary claim to grant them their lost expectations.

In *Crossco No.4 Ltd v Jolan Ltd*, Etherton C[200] (dissenting on this point) expressed the view that, building on Lord Scott's analysis in *Cobbe*, the *Pallant v Morgan* equity should be regarded as an application of the principles relating to the acquisition of property in breach of fiduciary duty, with the previous authorities explained on the basis that in each case the party acquiring the legal title had made itself a fiduciary for the non-acquiring party by some form of joint venture arrangement. He rejected an argument that the *Pallant v Morgan* equity was to be considered as a variety of common intention constructive trust, rejected the analogy drawn by Chadwick LJ between the *Pallant v Morgan* equity and proprietary estoppel[201] and (by implication) rejected the reliance/detriment/advantage analysis set out by Chadwick LJ in *Banner Homes*. But the majority in the Court of Appeal (McFarlane and Arden LJJ)[202] considered themselves bound by *Banner Homes* to regard the *Pallant v Morgan* equity as a species of common intention constructive trust, and to accept the reasoning of Chadwick LJ in that

    9–085

---

[199] At [38].

[200] Above, at [74]–[96].

[201] Pointing out (at [89]) that in *Stack v Dowden*, above, at [37] Lord Walker had rowed back from the analogy between proprietary estoppel and common intention constructive trusts which he had drawn in *Yaxley v Gotts* and on which Chadwick LJ had relied in *Banner Homes*.

[202] Above, at [117]–[123] and [125]–[133].

case. However, in doing so, they expressed themselves attracted to Etherton C's analysis, leaving open the possibility that the Supreme Court might adopt it in due course[203]; and also raised the separate possibility that the Supreme Court might in future decide that the *Pallant v Morgan* equity (together with other forms of common intention constructive trust) should be confined to non-commercial/family situations.[204]

9–086   In *Farrar v Miller*, the Court of Appeal applied *Banner Homes* and *Cobbe* to find that a *Pallant v Morgan* trust was arguable in a commercial context on the basis of an alleged oral joint venture agreement of dubious enforceability.[205]

In *Generator Developments Ltd v Lidl UK GmbH*, the Court of Appeal was attracted by the analysis of Etherton C in *Crossco* but considered itself bound loyally to follow the decision of the majority as to the juridical nature of the trust. However, in relation to the application of the trust, they went further, holding that the relevant principles "operate quite differently in a commercial context from the way in which they operate in a domestic context", with the result that (as in the case of a proprietary estoppel following the decision in *Cobbe*) they have no application "in a commercial case like this one where each party knows that they are not legally bound". They considered the position to be, effectively, a fortiori where the words "subject to contract" had been used by the parties.[206]

In short, the authorities are now hard to reconcile and the principles hard to identify with any confidence; and real doubts must remain until the whole area has been reconsidered at a higher level.[207]

9–087   **Constructive Trust to Prevent use of a Statute as an Instrument of Fraud/Undertaking to Respect an Unprotected Interest in Land.**   There is a third category of constructive trust which may arise to give effect to a prior agreement or understanding. It is founded on the principle that a person may not unconscionably rely upon the absolute character of a conveyance to defeat a beneficial interest which, according to the true bargain between the parties, was to belong to another; in such circumstances the person who takes the conveyance (usually the purchaser of land), although his title takes priority under the rules of conveyancing and land registration, may be found to hold that title on constructive trust in whole or part for the benefit of the party whose inadequately formalised or registered rights he agreed to respect. This is said to be an application of the principle that a constructive trust can arise to prevent a statute being used as an instrument of fraud.[208] Stated in those terms, this category of constructive trust would appear to have very wide potential application, and (indeed) it is not obvious why the underlying principle should be confined to

---

[203] Per McFarlane LJ at [121]–[122], and per Arden LJ at [133].

[204] Per Arden LJ at [129].

[205] *Farrar v Miller* [2018] EWCA Civ 172.

[206] *Crossco No.4 Ltd v Jolan Ltd* [2011] EWCA Civ 1619, at [34]–[34] and [78]–[79], per Lewison LJ.

[207] In the Court of Appeal in *Kaymuu*, above, at [61]–[62], per Sales LJ (with whom Tomlinson and Longmore LJJ agreed) recognised the *Pallant v Morgan* equity as an area of difficulty and expressly reserved his view upon the appeal on that issue, in circumstances where it did not need to be decided.

[208] *Rochefoucauld v Boustead* [1897] 1 Ch. 196, *Bannister v Bannister* [1948] 2 All E.R. 133.

cases involving the purchase of land. As the authorities currently stand,[209] however, this category of constructive trust appears to arise in cases where a transfer of land might allow the transferee to take free of another party's interests, and to be confined to situations in which the transferee has undertaken a new obligation not otherwise existing to give effect to the relevant interests. Accordingly, it is fair to say that this category of constructive trust appears less often in fraud litigation than might be supposed from the language used to describe it.

(5) Other Categories of Constructive Trust Less Directly Relevant in Fraud Context

There are numerous other categories of constructive trust which are not addressed in any detail in this work, as they are less commonly encountered in the fraud context (and in respect of which reference should be made to the specialist works) including:

9–088

(1)   The constructive trust (if it is correctly categorised as constructive) which arises in respect of a specifically enforceable transaction pending completion on the grounds that equity looks upon as done that which ought to be done;

(2)   The constructive trusts which sometimes to arises to save an "imperfect gift"[210];

(3)   The constructive trust which arises to give effect to a "secret trust";

(4)   The constructive trust which arises under the doctrine of "mutual wills"; and

(5)   The constructive trust which arises to prevent a killer from benefiting financially from an unlawful killing.

F.   STATUTORY TRUSTS

Numerous statutory regimes create "trusts". A complete survey is far beyond the scope of this work. A selection of examples illustrating the diversity of the field might include s.137B Financial Services and Markets Act 2000 (which, together with the rules adopted pursuant thereto by the financial services regulators, creates statutory trusts of client moneys held by regulated entities); Sch.1, Pt II, para.6 of the Solicitors Act 1974 (creating a trust of solicitors' client money vested in the law society following an intervention); and s.46–47 Administration of Estates Act 1925 (creating the statutory trust of the estates of those who die intestate).

9–089

---

[209] *Lyus v Prowsa Developments Ltd* [1982] 1 W.L.R. 1044; *Ashburn Anstalt v Arnold* [1989] Ch. 1; *Lloyd v Dugdale* [2001] EWCA Civ 1754; [2002] W.T.L.R. 863, at [50]–[52], *Chaudhary v Yavuz* [2011] EWCA Civ 1314; [2013] Ch. 249; *Groveholt v Hughes* [2012] EWHC 3351 (Ch); [2013] 1 P & CR 20.
[210] Mentioned briefly, at para.9–032 above.

9–090 The nature and effect of any statutory "trust" is always ultimately a question of construction of the statute in question. By the use of the word "trust", Parliament may have intended to create a situation in which all of the conventional rules of trust law will apply; but equally it may not.[211]

---

[211] See *Re Lehman Brothers International (Europe)* [2012] UKSC 6; [2012] Bus L.R. 667, per Lord Clarke at [121], per Lord Dyson at [145], and per Lord Collins at 189 and 196 in relation to the statutory trust created pursuant to s.139(1) Financial Services and Markets Act 2000 by Ch.7 of the Client Assets Sourcebook within the Financial Services Authority Handbook (now replaced by the equivalent trust arising under the new s.137B(1) of that Act pursuant to the same part of the Financial Conduct Authority Handbook). But see also the contrasting approach of Lord Walker, dissenting, at [84].

CHAPTER 10

BREACH OF TRUST

A.   SCOPE OF THIS CHAPTER

This chapter addresses personal claims against trustees for breach of trust. **10–001**
Proprietary claims to recover the trust property or its traceable proceeds are
addressed in Ch.23. Personal claims against third parties for participation in the
breach of trust and unconscionable receipt of its proceeds are addressed in Chs 13
and 12 respectively.

As Millett LJ said in *Armitage v Nurse*:   **10–002**

> "Breaches of trust are of many different kinds. A breach of trust may be deliberate or
> inadvertent; it may consist of an actual misappropriation or misapplication of trust property or
> merely of an investment or other dealing which is outside the trustees' powers; it may consist
> of a failure to carry out a positive obligation of the trustees or merely of a want of skill and
> care on their part in the management of trust property; it may be injurious to the interests of
> the beneficiaries or actually to their benefit."[1]

Among that diversity of possible breaches of trust, this chapter will address only **10–003**
those breaches which involve the trustees acting (whether when gathering in,
investing or applying trust property) outside the authority or contrary to the strict
duties given to them by the terms of the relevant trust and by the general law of
trusts. This chapter will not address either:

(1)   Breach of the trustees' fiduciary duties of loyalty, which are equivalent to
       those owed by other categories of fiduciary and are considered in Ch.11; or
(2)   Breach of their duty to exercise skill and care in the use of their powers or
       the execution of their duties,[2] which may also be referred to without
       inaccuracy as a "breach of trust" but engages rather different principles and
       falls outside the scope of a book concerned with fraud.

A personal claim for a breach of trust (either generally or in the narrower sense **10–004**
with which we are concerned here) is not per se a fraud claim; indeed, as set out
below, liability may in principle be strict without any need to demonstrate fault at
all, and even where the breach is deliberate it may be committed in good faith in

---

[1] *Armitage v Nurse* [1998] Ch. 241, at 250.
[2] Now placed, in part, on a statutory basis under the Trustee Act 2000.

the belief that it will assist the trustees.[3] However, for these very reasons, it can represent an important route of claim for a claimant in many cases of alleged fraud, either:

10–005   (1)   For the purposes of establishing liability against an alleged fraudster who is a trustee, as it is often more straightforward to establish liability, or it may be possible to quantify loss on a more favourable basis, in breach of trust than it would be in the familiar causes of action which would lie against a non-trustee;

(2)   For the purposes of providing the foundation for potential proprietary claims and claims against third parties, as mentioned above; or

(3)   For the purposes of establishing liability against an innocent trustee who has parted with trust money (for example a solicitor who has paid funds to the alleged fraudster which should have been held for the claimant in its client account) and who may afford a better prospect of recovery than the alleged fraudster.

B.   ESTABLISHING A BREACH OF TRUST

(1)   Suitable Trust to Found Liability in Breach of Trust

10–006   The principles to be applied in establishing the existence and contents of a trust are addressed in Ch.9. Not every trust, however, imposes the same obligations upon the trustee. This chapter will address the personal liability which may be incurred by the trustee of an express trust for a breach of his obligations in relation to the trust property. But the same obligations may not be owed by the trustee of a resulting or constructive trust, depending upon the circumstances in which the relevant resulting or constructive trust arises. For example, an innocent recipient of the traceable proceeds of trust money, although he may be considered a constructive trustee in the sense that he is subject to a proprietary claim for so long as the assets remain in his hands, probably owes few obligations (if any) other than the duty to return the assets when he becomes aware of his position.[4]

(2)   Locus Standi to Sue for Breach of Trust

10–007   The trustees of a trust are proper claimants to bring a claim for breach of trust. Even if the claimant trustees may themselves have been guilty of breach of trust in parting with the trust property, the defendant trustee (or former trustee) cannot

---

[3] *Armitage v Nurse*, above, at 250.

[4] See *Lonrho v Fayed (No.2)* [1992] 1 W.L.R. 1, at 12, per Millett LJ, and writing extra-judicially (1998) 114 L.Q.R. 3999, at 405 and following; *Allied Carpets Group Plc v Nethercott* [2001] BCC 81, per Colman J; *Allan v Rea Brothers Trustees Ltd* [2002] EWCA Civ 85; [2002] Pens L.R. 169, at [52]–[55], per Robert Walker LJ; *Clark v Cutland* [2003] EWCA Civ 810; [2004] 1 W.L.R. 783, at [30], per Arden LJ; *Nabb Brothers Ltd v Lloyds Bank International (Guernsey) Ltd* [2005] EWHC 405 (Ch), at [69], per Lawrence Collins J. See also *Westdeutsche*, above, at 705–706, per Lord Browne-Wilkinson, expressing the view that, for this reason, the constructive trust cannot arise at all until the constructive trustee has notice of the matters giving rise to the trust.

rely upon that to afford a defence[5] (although the court may, in such a situation, wish to be given comfort that the beneficiaries have been given notice of the position when considering how, in its discretion, to formulate relief).

Any beneficiary of the relevant trust also has locus standi to pursue a claim against the trustees (or former trustees) for breach of trust, so long as the breach affects their interests under the trust.[6] Where the trust is anything other than a bare trust for the benefit of a single beneficiary, care will be needed in tailoring the relief sought so as to ensure that it properly reflects the limited interests of each beneficiary.[7] For that reason, even where the claim is brought by a beneficiary, the relief granted will usually require payment to be made by the defaulting trustees into the trust fund in the hands of its current trustees,[8] unless the trust (or relevant part of the trust) is no longer subsisting, in which case the relief will consist of an order to pay equitable compensation to the beneficiaries who have become absolutely entitled.[9]   **10–008**

(3)   The Breach of Trust

A trustee commits a breach of trust (in the sense with which we are now concerned—see para.10–003 above) when he deals with the trust assets in a manner which exceeds the equitable authority conferred on him (or fails to take steps required by the strict duties imposed on him) by the terms of the relevant trust and of the general law. Such breaches may be hugely varied in nature, and could not be set out comprehensively without a survey of the substantive law of trusts (together with the provisions commonly encountered in instruments creating trusts). The most commonly encountered in a fraud context are active payments away of trust money in an unauthorised manner, although there may be circumstances in which passive failures to gather in trust assets or failures to invest them in the required manner will be relevant.   **10–009**

In the case of all such breaches (unlike the sort of "breach of trust" which arises where the trustee takes an authorised or required step but does so in a careless manner—see para.10–003 above), liability is strict, subject to the defences identified in Section C below. The juridical nature of the liability has been for some time, and remains, the subject of academic and judicial controversy across   **10–010**

---

[5] *Dalriada Trustees Ltd v Woodward* [2012] EWHC 21626 (Ch), at [37]. See also *Bracken Partners v Gutteridge* [2003] EWCA Civ 1875 and *Montrose Investments Ltd v Orion Nominees Ltd* [2004] EWCA Civ 1032; [2004] W.T.L.R. 1133.

[6] See L. Tucker, N. Le Poidevin and J. Brightwell, *Lewin on Trusts*, 19th edn (London: Sweet & Maxwell, 2012), para.39–071 and following for a more detailed consideration of the position of those with various sorts of (more or less remote) interests under a trust.

[7] *Patel v Brent LBC (No.2)* [2003] EWHC 3081 (Ch); [2004] W.T.L.R. 577, at [32].

[8] Where the defaulting trustees remain in post, the relief sought may include orders for the replacement of those trustees. Reference should be made to the specialist works for the relevant principles, as proof of a breach of trust is neither necessary nor sufficient to warrant removal.

[9] *Target Holdings v Redfern* [1996] A.C. 421, at 434–436, per Lord Browne-Wilkinson; *AIB v Mark Redler & Co* [2014] UKSC 58; [2015] A.C. 1503; *Brudenell-Bruce v Moore* [2014] EWHC 3679 (Ch); [2015] W.T.L.R. 373, at [245]–[250], per Newey J.

the common law world.[10] In England, following the decisions of the House of Lords in *Target Holdings Ltd v Redferns* and of the Supreme Court in *AIB Group (UK) Plc v Mark Redler & Co Solicitors*,[11] it appears to be established that the liability is fundamentally compensatory in nature, consisting of an obligation to compensate the beneficiaries for loss to the trust fund which would not have been suffered but for the breach, with that obligation being mediated either through the procedural route of an account or that of a claim for equitable compensation[12]: see further Chapter 22. There remains a significant school of thought, however, which regards the traditional machinery of an account as informing the substantive nature of the trustee's liability, such that in a situation where the trustees have paid away trust assets, unless the trustee can demonstrate that the payment was authorised under the terms of the trust and of the general law, he will be liable to reconstitute the fund to the full current value of the assets, without any need either to demonstrate breach of trust or (crucially) to demonstrate "but for" causation between the breach of trust and the loss actually suffered. For some in this school of thought, the English courts have simply gone astray in *Target* and *AIB*; but for others there remains a hope of confining the reasoning of those cases so that it applies only (as an exception to what they would regard as the general rule) in a situation where the trust is no longer subsisting at the time of claim,[13] or only within a particular factual context.[14]

10–011   As mentioned above, the claim for breach of trust has three key tactical uses in the fraud context:

(1)   as a "shortcut" to liability and a favourable quantification of loss against an alleged fraudster who can be shown to be a trustee;

(2)   as a stepping-stone to proprietary claims or personal claims against third parties; and

(3)   as a route to visit the loss suffered by the trust estate upon non-fraudulent trustees (perhaps the innocent dupes of the fraudster) who may afford a better prospect of recovery.

10–012   In recent times, one of the most important applications in the fraud context of the strict liability for breach of trust has been of the third kind: namely, claims by purchasers of property or by lenders (1) against their own solicitors, in circumstances where those solicitors have paid away the purchase or loan monies outside the terms of the trust governing the basis on which the monies are being held by the solicitors (which terms are to be found, expressly or impliedly, in their retainer and instructions)—or (2) against the purported vendor's solicitors in

---

[10] In *AIB v Mark Redler*, above, the Supreme Court was referred to over 900 pages of academic writing, together with a wealth of English and Commonwealth authority.

[11] Above. The Court of Appeal had little difficulty in applying those authorities in *Re Ahmed* [2018] EWCA Civ 519.

[12] See Tucker, Le Poidevin and Brightwell, *Lewin on Trusts* (2012), paras 39–010—39–015, Televantos [2015] Conv 348, Turner [2015] CLJ 188.

[13] See, for example, C. Mitchell, D.J. Hayton and P. Matthews, *Underhill & Hayton Law of Trusts and Trustees*, 19th edn (London: LNUK, 2016), paras 87.01–87.30.

[14] See the recent claim of the Court of Appeal in *Interactive Technology Corp v Ferster* [2008] EWCA Civ 1594; and contrast *Re Ahmed*, above.

circumstances where those solicitors have paid the money away outside the terms of a trust allegedly created by their undertaking to hold the funds to the order of the purchaser's solicitors.[15]

While the same principles will apply to all express trusts, these solicitor cases **10–013** illustrate the power of the rule that liability for breach of trust is strict—in that a wholly innocent, and indeed defrauded, trustee may become liable. But they also illustrate the importance of focusing closely upon the circumstances in which a payment is or is not permitted by the terms of the relevant trust. In other contexts it has been held (on the one hand) that a trustee who is robbed of the trust fund is not liable unless he has taken insufficient care[16] and (on the other hand) that a trustee who has paid out money against fraudulent documents is liable.[17] But the recent solicitor cases make vivid that the position is likely to depend ultimately upon the terms of the trust, which may turn upon difficult questions of construction or implication.[18] The importance of focusing upon the terms of the particular trust when determining whether a breach of trust has occurred (subject of course to the requirements of the general law) is echoed by the emphasis placed in *Target* and *AIB* upon the specific nature of the obligations and the (commercial or non-commercial) relationship between the parties when considering the measure of loss flowing from the breach.[19]

(4) Fraudulent Breach of Trust

Although, as we have seen, the liability of trustees for breach of trust is usually **10–014** strict, nonetheless the law recognises the concept of the "fraudulent breach of trust", recently explained as follows:

> "For a breach of trust to be fraudulent it is not enough to show that it was deliberate.[20] There must also be an absence of honesty or good faith. This can include being reckless as to the consequences of the action complained of."[21]

---

[15] For the recent high points of the relevant case law, see *Lloyds TSB Bank Plc v Markandan & Uddin* [2012] EWCA Civ 65; *Nationwide Building Society v Davisons* [2012] EWCA Civ 1626; *Santander v RA legal Solicitors* [2014] EWCA Civ 183; *Purrunsing v A'Court* [2016] EWHC 789 (Ch); *Dreamvar (UK) Ltd v Mishcon De Reya* [2016] EWHC 3316 (Ch), at [82]–[95] and on appeal [2018] EWCA Civ 1082, at [83]–[97]. In the context of claims against the purported vendor's solicitors in relation to the trust allegedly arising from an undertaking to hold money to the order of the purchaser's solicitors, see *P&P Property Ltd v Owen White & Cailtin LLP*, above, [2016] Bus L.R. 1337; *Purrunsing v A'Court*, above; *Dreamvar*, above, at [101] and following; and the combined judgment of the Court of Appeal in the *P&P* and *Dreamvar* cases, [2018] EWCA Civ 1082.

[16] See for example, *Jones v Lewis* (1751) 2 Ves Sen 240, at 241.

[17] *Eaves v Hickman* (1861) 30 Beav 136.

[18] For example, in the conveyancing context, the solicitor cases cited above have turned in part upon debates (a), in the context of lender claims, as to the construction of the phrase "must hold the loan on trust until completion" in the Council of Mortgage Lenders Handbook, (b), in the context of purchaser claims, as to whether a term can be implied into a retainer authorising the payment of funds only upon a genuine completion and (c), in the context of claims against the purported vendor's solicitors on a trust allegedly arising from the undertaking to hold money to order, upon the construction of the Law Society Code for Completion by Post.

[19] See *AIB*, above, at [170]–[171], per Lord Toulson JSC and [137], per Lord Reed JSC.

[20] A trustee may deliberately exceed his powers in good faith and in the belief, which does not fall below the normally acceptable standards of honest conduct, that he is acting in the interests of the

This concept is highly relevant in the context of limitation (considered in detail in Ch.25), as s.21(1)(a) of the Limitation Act 1980 excepts from limitation:

"an action by a beneficiary under a trust, being an action ... in respect of any fraud or fraudulent breach of trust to which the trustee was a party or privy."

But whether or not the breach is fraudulent is also likely to be relevant in various other contexts:

(1)   In deciding whether a trustee is entitled to avail himself of s.61 of the Trustee Act 1925 (addressed at paras 10–019—10–023 below);
(2)   In the context of awarding contribution between wrongdoers under the Civil Liability (Contribution) Act 1978 (addressed at para.10–030 below); and
(3)   When considering whether a trustee is entitled to take advantage of a trustee exclusion clause in respect of breaches of trust alleged against him (addressed at para.10-024 below).

10–015   As with the rules of pleading deceit, which we have considered in Ch.1, a plea of fraudulent breach of trust must be distinctly alleged and proved.

---

beneficiaries. In so doing he is not committing a fraud. In *Fattal v Walbrook Trustees (Jersey) Ltd* [2010] EWHC 2767 (Ch); [2012] Bus L.R. D7 Lewison J said, at [81] that "what is required to show dishonesty in the case of a professional trustee is: i) A deliberate breach of trust; ii) Committed by a professional trustee: a) Who knows that the deliberate breach is contrary to the interests of the beneficiaries; or b) Who is recklessly indifferent whether the deliberate breach is contrary to their interests or not; or c) Whose belief that the deliberate breach is not contrary to the interests of the beneficiaries is so unreasonable that, by any objective standard, no reasonable professional trustee could have thought that what he did or agreed to do was for the benefit of the beneficiaries."

[21] *First Subsea Ltd v Balltec Ltd* [2017] EWCA Civ 186; [2017] W.L.R. (D) 232, at [64], per Patten LJ. In *Armitage v Nurse* [1998] Ch. 241 the term "actual fraud" when applied to trustees was held, at 251, to connote "at the minimum an intention on the part of the trustee to pursue a particular course of action, either knowing that it is contrary to the interests of the beneficiaries or being recklessly indifferent whether it is contrary to their interests or not. It is the duty of a trustee to manage the trust property and deal with it in the interests of the beneficiaries. If he acts in a way which he does not honestly believe is in their interests then he is acting dishonestly. It does not matter whether he stands or thinks he stands to gain personally from his actions. A trustee who acts with the intention of benefiting persons who are not the objects of the trust is not the less dishonest because he does not intend to benefit himself."

C. DEFENCES

(1) Concurrence, Release, Ratification and Acquiescence

There may be no liability in respect of a breach of trust to the extent that the relevant beneficiary (having legal capacity) has concurred in the breach at the time when it occurred. The test was stated authoritatively by Wilberforce J in *Re Pauling's Settlement Trusts (No.1)*[22] as follows:

> "... the court has to consider all the circumstances in which the concurrence of the cestui que trust was given with a view to seeing whether it is fair and equitable that, having given his concurrence, he should afterwards turn round and sue the trustees; ... subject to this, it is not necessary that he should know that what he is concurring in is a breach of trust, provided that he fully understands what he is concurring in, and that it is not necessary that he should himself have directly benefited by the breach of trust".

As the test was subsequently glossed by Harman LJ in *Holder v Holder*,[23]

> "there is therefore no hard and fast rule that ignorance of a legal right is a bar, but the whole of the circumstances must be looked at to see whether it is just that the complaining beneficiary should succeed against the trustee".

In the fraud context, however, the key dispute will often be whether the beneficiary did indeed "fully understand what he was concurring in", or whether the defendant's deception had the effect that any alleged concurrence was given on a false basis.

10–016

After a breach of trust has been committed, the defaulting trustee may cease to be liable if the relevant beneficiary expressly releases the liability or ratifies the transaction. Conduct short of an express release or ratification may amount to acquiescence sufficient to bring an end to the trustee's liability. It appears that the test set out by Wilberforce J for concurrence at the time of the breach applies also to subsequent acquiescence.[24] The general principles relevant to acquiescence are addressed further in the context of limitation of actions in Ch.25.

10–017

Crucially, concurrence, release, ratification or acquiescence by one beneficiary will affect the entitlement of that beneficiary alone. The rights of other beneficiaries will not be affected. How this is to be reflected in a claim for breach of a subsisting trust, where the remedy will generally take the form of an order to reconstitute the trust fund rather than to pay equitable compensation direct to beneficiaries, may require some ingenuity in the formulation of relief.[25]

10–018

---

[22] *Re Pauling's Settlement Trusts (No.1)* [1962] 1 W.L.R. 86, at 108, per Wilberforce J (decision partially upheld by the Court of Appeal without consideration of this point, at [1964] CA 303, at 339), approved by the Court of Appeal in *Holder v Holder* [1964] Ch. 353, at 394, per Harman LJ, 299, per Danckwerts LJ and 406, per Sachs LJ.

[23] As above.

[24] *Holder v Holder*, above.

[25] See for example *Brudenell-Bruce v Moore*, above, at [249].

(2)   Relief from Liability under Section 61 Trustee Act 1925

10–019   By s.61 Trustee Act 1925, the court has power to relieve a trustee either wholly or partly from personal liability for a breach of trust if it appears that he:

> "has acted honestly and reasonably, and ought fairly to be excused for the breach of trust and for omitting to obtain the directions of the court in the matter in which he committed such breach".

The application of the section involves a two-stage analysis.[26]

10–020   At the first stage, the trustee bears the burden[27] of proving that he acted "honestly and reasonably". For this purpose:

(1)   The trustee need not demonstrate that his conduct was perfect or complied with best practice in every respect[28]; but it seems that negligent conduct will not qualify as "reasonable" for these purposes.[29] Indeed, it has been said that the standard is a high one, consistent with equity's high expectations of a trustee discharging fiduciary obligations.[30]

(2)   Equally, the trustee need prove only that his conduct was reasonable insofar as it was "causally connected" with the loss for which relief is sought.[31] The exact degree of causal connection which is required for conduct to be considered relevant is not clearly defined, but it appears to be something less than "but-for" causation, with the result that the trustee who has acted unreasonably will not necessarily qualify for relief by virtue of the fact that the loss would have occurred in any event.[32]

(3)   Related to the last point, it has been said that the trustee's conduct is not to be looked at by reference to each separate complaint, but in the round.[33]

10–021   At the second stage, the court must exercise its discretion to decide whether the trustee ought fairly to be excused for the breach, having regard to the effect of the grant of relief not only on the trustee but also on the beneficiaries.[34] Accordingly, it seems that relief may more readily be granted where the claimant is, for

---

[26] *Santander UK v RA Legal Solicitors* [2014] EWCA Civ 183; [2014] P.N.L.R. 20, at [19]–[34]. See also the helpful recent summary of principles in *P & P Property Ltd v Owen White and Catlin LLP* [2016] EWHC 2276 (Ch), at [252], per Robin Dicker QC; applied in *Dreamvar (UK) Ltd v Mishcon de Reya* [2016] EWHC 3316 (Ch), at [181], per David Railton QC and on appeal [2018] EWCA Civ 1082, at [103]–[111].

[27] *Santander*, at [20].

[28] *Davisons (Solicitors) v Nationwide Building Society* [2012] EWCA Civ 1626; [2013] P.N.L.R. 20.

[29] *Santander*, at [30]–[32], where an analogy with the provision for relieving company directors from liability under s.727 Companies Act 2006 was disapproved.

[30] *Lloyds TSB v Markandam & Uddin* [2012] EWCA Civ 65; [2012] 2 All E.R. 884, at [60]–[61]; *Santander*, above, at [109]; *Purrunsing v A'Court & Co (A Firm)* [2016] EWHC (Ch); [2016] P.N.L.R. 26, at [38].

[31] *Davidsons*, above.

[32] *Santander*, above, at [25]–[29].

[33] *Santander*, above, at [97]; *Purrunsing*, above, at [38].

[34] *Santander*, above, at [33] citing *Marsden v Regan* [1954] 1 W.L.R. 423 and *Bartlett v Barclays Trust Co (No.1)* [1980] Ch. 515; *Daniel v Tee* [2016] EWHC 1538 (Ch), at [186].

example, an institutional lender which may be insured (or effectively self-insured) than where the claimant is an individual who has lost their personal savings.[35] Equally, it is well established that a paid trustee will be held to a higher standard of knowledge and diligence than an unpaid trustee.[36]

However, it is right to observe that the recent authorities on the application of s.61, which are reflected in the analysis above, have mostly concerned its application to solicitors acting as trustees of client money in conveyancing transactions. It remains possible that an analysis of the older authorities would allow arguments to be mounted for a somewhat different approach in other contexts. **10–022**

Finally, it will be apparent from the discussion above that it may be highly relevant for a claimant to contend and prove that a breach of trust was fraudulent (in the sense discussed above) or at least negligent, in order to prevent the trustee from seeking to take advantage of the relieving jurisdiction created by s.61 of the Trustee Act 1925. **10–023**

(3)   Exemption Clauses

While not a defence arising as a matter of general law, it is important to appreciate that express trusts set out in writing in a formal instrument commonly contain wide exemption clauses, exempting the trustees from liability for breaches of duty.[37] Such clauses, although they are to be construed strictly, will be given effect so long as they do not exclude liability for loss resulting from the trustee's own fraud (in the sense of conduct falling below the objective standard of an ordinary honest trustee).[38] A clause which exceeds its permitted bounds may nevertheless be read down and given effect in a more limited form.[39] In the leading decision of *Armitage v Nurse* the relevant clause excluded liability for any loss or damage to the fund or the income thereof at any time or from any cause unless it was caused by the trustee's "own actual fraud." It was held that the concept of "actual fraud"[40] was to be contrasted with "equitable fraud" or **10–024**

---

[35] *Re Windsor Steam Coal Co* (1901) Ltd; [1929] 1 Ch. 151, at 164. *Santander*, above, at [33].

[36] *Lloyds Bank v Sutton* [1952] 2 All E.R. 1054, per Harman J; *Re Pauling's Settlement Trust (No.1)* [1964] Ch. 303; *Bartlett v Barclays Bank Trust Co Ltd*, above; *Santander*, above, at [30]; *Purrunsing*, above, at [45].

[37] *Bartlett v Barclays Bank Trust Co Ltd* [1980] Ch. 536.

[38] Among the substantial body of authority in relation to trustee exclusion clauses, see in particular: *Armitage v Nurse* [1998] Ch. 241; *Walker v Stones* [2001] Q.B. 902; *Spread Trustee Co Ltd v Hutcheson* [2011] UKPC 13; [2012] A.C. 194; and *Barnsley v Noble* [2016] EWCA Civ 799; [2017] Ch. 191.

[39] *Midland Bank Trustee (Jersey) Ltd v Federated Pension Services Ltd* [1996] Pens L.R. 179, at [146]–[147].

[40] See also the analysis of the Court of Appeal in *Walker v Stones* [2001] QC 902 of the phrase "wilful fraud or dishonesty", also in a trustee exemption clause. The court in that case may be said to have modified the test adumbrated in *Armitage v Nurse*. At 939 Sir Christopher Slade said: "At least in the case of a solicitor-trustee, a qualification must in my opinion be necessary to take account of the case where the trustee's so-called 'honest belief', though actually held, is so unreasonable that, by any objective standard, no reasonable solicitor-trustee could have thought that what he did or agreed to do was for the benefit of the beneficiaries. I limit this proposition to the case of a solicitor-trustee, first, because on the facts before us we are concerned only with solicitor-trustees and, secondly, because I

"constructive fraud". The former concept requires dishonesty (although not in the sense of deceit, because there may be no intention to deceive a third party)[41]; gross or culpable negligence is not enough. The latter concept does not import the requirement of dishonesty. It evolved in the Court of Chancery to mean something much wider and far removed from the modern concept of fraud.[42]

(4) Contributory Negligence

10–025 As the law currently stands, it appears to be the case that there is no defence of contributory negligence to a claim for breach of trust,[43] although there may be cases in which a beneficiary's failure to mitigate the consequences of the breach become so egregious that the loss can no longer be regarded as having been caused by the breach.[44] See the analysis of quantification more generally in Ch.22.

10–026 The position may be otherwise where the relevant "breach of trust" is a breach of the trustee's duty to exercise skill and care; but such claims are beyond the scope of this work.

---

accept that the test of honesty may vary from case to case, depending on, among other things, the role and calling of the trustee." See further the analysis of dishonesty in the context of accessory liability in Ch.13.

[41] The word "fraud" may be found in similar documents. So in *Halliwells LLP (In Administration) v Austin* [2012] EWHC 1194 (Ch) a partner in a law firm had retired from the partnership and the retirement deed had provided for cross-releases of claims excluding "any claim for fraud." It was held that the word fraud was to be construed in a sense which required dishonesty to be present so that it could apply to a dishonest abuse of fiduciary position. However it did not extend to "equitable fraud."

[42] See *Nocton v Lord Ashburton* [1914] A.C. 932, at 965, per Viscount Haldane LC: "But when fraud is referred to in the wider sense in which the books are full of the expression, used in Chancery in describing cases which were within its exclusive jurisdiction, it is a mistake to suppose that an actual intention to cheat must always be proved. A man may misconceive the extent of the obligation which a Court of Equity imposes on him. His fault is that he has violated, however innocently because of his ignorance, an obligation which he must be taken by the Court to have known, and his conduct has in that sense always been called fraudulent, even in such a case as a technical fraud on a power. It was thus that the expression "constructive fraud" came into existence. The trustee who purchases the trust estate, the solicitor who makes a bargain with his client that cannot stand, have all for several centuries run the risk of the word fraudulent being applied to them. What it really means in this connection is, not moral fraud in the ordinary sense, but breach of the sort of obligation which is enforced by a Court that from the beginning regarded itself as a Court of conscience."

[43] *Lloyds TSB v Markandam & Uddin* [2010] EWHC 2517 (Ch); [2011] P.N.L.R. 6, at [38]–[43] (affirmed [2012] EWCA Civ 65; [2012] 2 All E.R. 884). Compare the related authorities in relation to breaches of fiduciary duty: *Nationwide v Balmer Radmore* [1999] P.N.L.R. 606, at 676; *Day v Cook* [2002] B.C.L.C. 1, at [47]; *De Beer v Naraar & Co* [2002] EWHC 688 (Ch), at [92]. A different approach has been taken in some Commonwealth jurisdictions, at least in the context of claims for equitable compensation: see *Day v Mead* [1987] 2 N.Z.L.R. 443; *Canson Enterprises Ltd v Broughton & Co* (1991) 85 D.L.R. 129, but contrast *Pilmer v Duke Group Ltd* (2001) 207 C.L.R. 165, at [85]–[86].

[44] See *Corporacion Nacional Del Cobre De Chile v Sogemin Metals* [1997] 1 W.L.R. 1396, at 1403, per Carnwath J and *AIB Group (UK) Plc v Mark Redler & Co Solicitors*, above, at [86]–[87], per Lord Reed JSC, both citing with approval passages from *Canson v Boughton*, above. Causation in the context of claims to equitable compensation is considered more generally in Ch.22.

(5)   Limitation of Actions

The rules as to limitation which apply to claims for breach of trust under s.21   **10–027**
Limitation Act 1980 are somewhat elaborate, and are addressed at Ch.25.

D.   LIABILITY FOR OTHERS

(1)   Liability for the Acts of Co-Trustees

As a general rule, a trustee is liable only for his own breach of trust. He acquires   **10–028**
no liability ex officio for breaches committed by his fellow trustees.[45] In practice,
however, the duty of trustees to act jointly, coupled with the trustees' duties to
protect the trust assets, has the result that the circumstances in which trustee A
fails to prevent a breach of trust by trustee B will often entail a direct breach by
trustee A.[46] Where two or more trustees cause the same damage by their
respective breaches, they are jointly and severally liable, subject to any right to
contribution as between them.[47]

(2)   Liability for the Acts of Agents etc

Under Pt IV Trustee Act 2000, trustees are given express powers: **10–029**

(1)   to delegate certain of their functions to agents; and
(2)   to place assets with nominees or custodians.

Where those powers are exercised, the trustees are placed by s.22 of the Act
under express statutory duties to review the conduct of the relevant appointees.
But they are also exempted by s.23 for liability for any act or default of the agent,
nominee or custodian, unless they have failed to comply with the duty of skill and
care imposed by the other provisions of the Act.

---

[45] *Townley v Sherborne* (1633) Bridg. 35; and see the learned consideration of the old authorities in
Tucker, Le Poidevin and Brightwell, *Lewin on Trusts* (2012), paras 39–094—39–097; and Mitchell,
Hayton and Matthews, *Underhill & Hayton Law of Trusts and Trustees* (2016), paras 96.1–96.9, now
more relevant again following the repeal of s.30(1) Trustee Act 1925. For the potential liability of a
solicitors' firm for the breaches of trust by a partner within that firm acting qua trustee of a trust under
s.10 of the Partnership Act see *Walker v Stones* [2001] Q.B. 902.
[46] See, for some old examples, *Brice v Stokes* (1805) 11 Ves Jun 319, at 327, per Lord Eldon; *Booth
v Booth* (1838) 1 Beav 125, per Lord Langdale MR; *Re Flower* (1884) 27 Ch. D. 592, at 597, per Kay
J (subject now to the statutory regime for delegation).
[47] See *Ashurst v Mason* (1875) L.R. 20 Eq 225, at 233; *Re Duckwari* [1999] Ch. 253, at 262.

E.   POSITION BETWEEN THOSE RESPONSIBLE

(1)   Contribution

10–030   Where several persons are liable in respect of a breach of trust (whether trustees or third parties), there may be a statutory power to order contribution under the Civil Liability (Contribution) Act 1978. The relevant principles are not confined to cases of breach of trust (or, indeed, cases of alleged fraud) and their detailed consideration lies beyond the ambit of this book. Applying those principles, where one of the liable trustees (T1) wrongfully obtained property belonging to the beneficiary, then in any claim for contribution by another liable trustee (T2) who did not obtain such property, the apportionment exercise should take account of that fact, which might lead to the conclusion that T1 should make contribution to T2 up to the extent of 100 per cent.[48] A similar analysis will apply where the party seeking contribution is liable in dishonest assistance in a breach of trust: if such a person has settled his liability to the claimant and pursues the primary wrongdoer for contribution, then the fact that the assister received none of the proceeds of the breach, whereas the primary wrongdoer did, will weigh heavily in the apportionment of contribution as between these parties. On the other hand, if the party seeking contribution is liable in knowing receipt, that does not act as an absolute bar to his claim in contribution from others who were merely potentially liable to the original claimant in negligence or some other non-receipt based liability.[49]

10–031   Where the 1978 Act does not apply, there is an inherent equitable jurisdiction to order contribution.[50] It has been held that the court will not apportion contributions so as to penalise those who have taken a more active part in the breach of trust, because it does not wish to discourage trustees from actively

---

[48] See *Dubai Aluminium v Salaam* [1999] 1 Lloyd's Rep. 415, at 475, per Rix J, and on appeal in the House of Lords [2003] 2 A.C. 366, at 383–384, per Lord Nicholls. "The object of contribution proceedings under the Contribution Act is to ensure that each party responsible for the damage makes an appropriate contribution to the cost of compensating the plaintiff, regardless of where that cost has fallen in the first instance. The burden of liability is being redistributed. But, of necessity, the extent to which it is just and equitable to redistribute this financial burden cannot be decided without seeing where the burden already lies. The court needs to have regard to the known or likely financial consequences of orders already made and to the likely financial consequences of any contribution order the court may make."

[49] *City Index Ltd v Gawler* [2007] EWCA Civ 1382; [2008] Ch 313.

[50] *Bacon v Camphausen* (1888) L.T. 851; *Ramskill v Edwards* (1885) 31 Ch. D. 100. There are cases in which it has been said that the transaction may be so tainted with fraud that the court should hold itself aloof: see *Tarleton v Hornby* (1833) 1 Y & C 333 and *A.G v Wilson* (1840) Cr & Ph 1. But it is unclear how that principle would be reconciled with the modern approach to illegality following the decision of the Supreme Court in *Patel v Mirza* [2016] UKSC 42 [2017] A.C. 217.

undertaking their duties[51]; but, naturally, a different approach is likely to be taken where there has been dishonesty on the part of some trustees but not others.[52]

(2)   Impounding of Beneficial Interests

A beneficiary implicated in a breach of trust may have his beneficial interest "impounded" either: **10–032**

(1)   For the benefit of other beneficiaries, under the court's equitable jurisdiction, so that he is unable to benefit from the trust until his default has been remedied[53];

(2)   In a suitable case, pursuant either to the court's inherent equitable jurisdiction or to the express statutory power under s.62 Trustee Act 1925, so as to indemnify a trustee who has become liable in respect of a breach committed at the beneficiary's instigation or request, or even with his consent, provided the relevant beneficiary was aware of the facts amounting to the breach.[54]

These powers apply equally where the beneficiary in question is also a co-trustee.[55]   **10–033**

F.   REMEDIES

The principal remedies likely to be relevant in a personal claim for breach of trust in the sense considered in this chapter are the taking of an account, with associated orders for the payment of any balance found to be due, and equitable compensation. We consider these in Ch.22.   **10–034**

The remedy of impounding beneficial interests, which is available against a trustee who is also a beneficiary, has been addressed above.

In addition, by way of exception to the usual rule under the Debtors Act, a trustee who fails to pay any sum in his possession or under his control as ordered

---

[51] *Bahin v Hughes* (1886) 31 Ch. D. 390, at 398, per Fry LJ ("In my judgment the Courts ought to be very jealous of raising any such implied liability as is insisted on, because if such existed it would act as an opiate upon the conscience of the trustees; so that instead of the cestui que trust having the benefit of several acting trustees, each trustee would be looking to the other or others for a right of indemnity and so neglect the performance of his duties"); but compare Cotton LJ in more moderate terms at 394–396 and Bowen LJ agreeing with the result only reluctantly at 397.

[52] The impact of the receipt of a direct or indirect benefit by some trustees from the breach may be a subtle matter: see Tucker, Le Poidevin and Brightwell, *Lewin on Trusts* (2012), para.39–089; and Mitchell, Hayton and Matthews, *Underhill & Hayton Law of Trusts and Trustees* (2016), para.97.13.

[53] *Re Dacre* [1916] 1 Ch. 344; *Selangour United Rubber Estates Ltd v Craddock (No.4)* [1969] 1 W.L.R. 1773.

[54] *Raby v Ridehalgh* (1855) 7 De G.M & G 104; *Ricketts v Ricketts* (1891) 64 L.T. 263; *Re Somerset* [1894] 1 Ch. 265; *Bolton v Curre* [1895] 1 Ch. 544; *Chillingworth v Chambers* [1896] 1 Ch. 685; *Fletcher v Collis* [1905] 2 Ch. 34; *Re Pauling's Settlement Trusts (No.2)* [1963] Ch. 576.

[55] *Raby v Ridehalgh*, above; *Chillingworth v Chambers*, above.

by a court of equity may be imprisoned for no more than a year, under a procedure analogous to that for contempt of Court.[56]

CHAPTER 11

FIDUCIARY DUTIES

A. INTRODUCTION

(1) Relevance in the Civil Fraud Context

Proof of the tortious, restitutionary and statutory claims discussed earlier in this **11–001** book generally does not require the demonstration of a pre-existing connection between the parties: as a very broad generalisation, it is the circumstances of the particular wrongful dealing (or circumstances vitiating consent) that give rise to the remedy. In contrast, this chapter (like some of the others in this section of the book) is concerned with claims arising from antecedent relationships between the wrongdoer and wronged party that impose constraints on how the wrongdoer can deal with the wronged party, with his property or with third parties in transactions that have a sufficient connection to that relationship. In chapters 9 and 10 we consider such constraints as they arise out of the relationship between trustee and trust. This chapter is concerned with fiduciary duties, which are among the duties owed by a trustee as such, but which are also (paradigmatically) owed by a director to his company, an agent to his principal, a partner to his fellow partners and a solicitor to his client. Importantly, they also arise, in different ways, in a number of other sorts of relationship which are likely to be of relevance to a civil fraud claim, as we consider below.

There are a number of reasons why it might be important to frame a fraud claim **11–002** with reference to a breach of fiduciary duty:

(1) First, and most obviously, fiduciary duties provide the basis for a cause of action that is flexible in its application to a wide range of factual circumstances and likely readily to be made out in a fraud context: if someone who owes fiduciary duties to another practises a fraud on that other, then, quite apart from any liability which may arise in tort or otherwise, it will almost certainly amount to a breach of the core fiduciary obligation of loyalty. A claim will lie by virtue of that breach, irrespective of whether the fact pattern of the case is such as to give rise to a cause of action in deceit or one of the other claims considered elsewhere in this book.

(2) Secondly, establishing a breach of fiduciary duty on the part of the defendant fraudster gives rise to a range of equitable remedies against him which may not otherwise be available. These include not just compensatory remedies that are similar in scope and application to common law damages;

but also accounts and enquiries, and obligations to disgorge profits: it is a peculiarity of fiduciary law that the claimant can obtain remedies which put him in the position in which he would have been had the fiduciary done the act under challenge for his (the claimant's) benefit, rather than had it not been done at all.

(3) Thirdly, benefits obtained in breach of fiduciary duty, including (it is now established) bribes and secret commissions,[1] will be held on constructive trust for the principal, giving him the ability to recover them in priority to other creditors in the event of the fiduciary's insolvency, as well as rights to take the benefit of any appreciation in value, and to trace or follow them into the hands of third parties and into substitute assets.

(4) Fourthly, a breach of fiduciary duty may enable a transaction entered into by reason of the breach to be set aside, or indeed may (subject to usual agency principles) render it void for want of authority.

(5) Fifthly, a breach of fiduciary duty will in principle open up equitable accessory liability claims against third parties, most notably those who have dishonestly assisted in the breach and those who have unconscionably received money or assets transferred by reason of the breach.[2]

(6) Sixthly, a breach of fiduciary duty owed with respect to property which belongs beneficially to a claimant will enable the claimant to follow the property, once misappropriated in the fraud, and to trace its value by using the more flexible principles of equity, and thereby make it possible to assert proprietary claims to the original assets or to those acquired with or substituted for them.[3]

11–003 The practical reality is that many fraud cases have at their heart the abuse of fiduciary relationships: a company director may divert a business opportunity to another vehicle in which he is interested rather than bringing it to fruition on his company's behalf; a partner charged with managing a joint venture may account to his partners for only part of the profit made on a joint venture transaction and pocket the rest; an agent negotiating a deal on his principal's behalf may be promised a secret commission by his principal's counterparty; a solicitor may use monies in his client account to support a business in which he is interested without informing his clients. In such cases, a claim for breach of fiduciary duty, or one against a third party predicated on a breach of fiduciary duty, is a powerful weapon in the fraud litigator's armoury.[4]

---

[1] See Ch.7 for claims with respect to bribes and secret commissions generally; and see paras 9–069—9–072 for the constructive trust that can arise with respect to profits obtained in breach of fiduciary duty.

[2] These are considered in Chs 13 and 12 respectively.

[3] Such claims are considered in Ch.23.

[4] Which is of course not to say that they are the only claims available: in these examples claims for breach of contract, conspiracy, deceit, the tort of bribery and breach of trust may (variously) also lie. The point is rather that a claim for, or based on, a breach of fiduciary duty may have advantages in any particular case that these other claims do not.

(2) Scope of this Chapter

In the first section of this chapter we consider in what circumstances fiduciary **11–004**
duties are owed, with particular focus upon cases outside the paradigm
relationships mentioned above, and how fiduciary duties can co-exist with, and
be moulded by, contractual relationships. We then mention some other general
aspects of fiduciary duties (whether a fiduciary's duty of care is itself a fiduciary
duty, the concept of a dishonest breach of fiduciary duty and the duration of
fiduciary duties). The next section addresses the "core" proscriptive fiduciary
obligations (or inhibitions), being those against conflicts of interest and the
making of a profit out of the relationship; it also considers the application of these
duties to a common civil fraud fact pattern—the diversion of business
opportunities—and the modified forms of the duties applicable to company
directors under the Companies Act 2006, as well as the defence of fully-informed
consent. We then, in the final section, consider the duty of "good faith"; whether
there is a fiduciary duty of disclosure; various other constraints on the exercise of
powers that are commonly described as being "fiduciary"; and the bases on
which directors may be liable for the misapplication of company property.

The question of when the relationship of trustee and beneficiary arises (including **11–005**
under a resulting or constructive trust) merits its own separate treatment, which is
given in Ch.9; and the claims which may lie against a trustee for breach of his
non-fiduciary duties (such as with respect to the gathering in, investment and
application of trust property) are considered in Ch.10. The personal equitable
remedies available against a fiduciary or a dishonest assistant are considered in
Ch.22; and proprietary equitable remedies are dealt with in Ch.23.[5]

B. WHEN FIDUCIARY DUTIES ARE OWED

(1) Fiduciary Relationships and Fiduciary Duties

Whilst the term "fiduciary" is commonly used as a way of characterising a **11–006**
position which one person, A, occupies with respect to another, B, or the
relationship between A and B, it is better understood as describing certain duties
which A may owe to B, those duties having a particular character and attracting
particular legal consequences. As observed by Dr P.D. Finn in his seminal book
on the subject, a fiduciary "is not subject to fiduciary obligations because he is a
fiduciary; it is because he is subject to them that he is a fiduciary".[6]

There are nevertheless certain established categories of legal relationship which **11–007**
can usefully be described as being "inherently fiduciary",[7] because there is a
strong presumption[8] that these relationships involve one party owing fiduciary
duties to another and because the imposition of fiduciary duties in other cases

---

[5] Since a constructive trust is not, strictly speaking, a remedy, its establishment in cases of breach of
fiduciary duty is (as we have already noted) considered in Ch.9.

[6] P.D. Finn, *Fiduciary Obligations* (Law Book Company, 1977), p.2.

[7] *Chirnside v Fay* [2006] NZSC 68, at [73].

[8] *Lac Minerals Ltd v International Corona Resources Ltd* (1989) 61 D.L.R. (4th) 14, at [28].

often draws upon analogies with them. As we have noted above, these "settled categories" include: trustee and beneficiary (an express trustee has been said to be the paradigm example of someone who owes duties of a fiduciary nature); agent and principal[9]; partner and fellow partner in a legal partnership; solicitor and client; and director and company.[10]

11–008 However, fiduciary duties will be found to be owed outside these settled categories of relationship where the facts and circumstances of the relationship justify their imposition. We consider in the following section some of the principles that might assist in identifying when fiduciary duties will be owed outside the settled categories and in paras 11–032–11–057 we consider some examples of other relationships which have, at least on the facts of particular cases, been held to give rise to such duties. The enquiry is, however, highly fact-sensitive:

> "the facts and circumstances of each case must be carefully examined to see whether a fiduciary relationship exists in relation to the matter of which complaint is made".[11]

In the commercial fraud context, one particularly important consideration will be the terms of any contract or similar arrangement by which the parties have chosen to allocate and define the scope of their respective responsibilities. We consider this at paras 11–018—11–031 below.

11–009 Moreover, it must be emphasised that:

(1) The identification of a relationship that presumptively involves, or of circumstances that justify the imposition of, fiduciary duties is only part of the enquiry. There remains the question which duties of a fiduciary character are owed, what the content of those duties is and to what aspects of the relationship they pertain.[12] The "fiduciary" duties owed by a company director, for example, are not the same in all respects as those owed by a trustee, and those which are imposed outside the settled categories may be different again, particularly where they arise out of a contractual or like relationship, to which (it has been repeatedly said) any superimposed fiduciary duty will need to accommodate itself.[13]

(2) This aspect of the enquiry is rendered more difficult by the fact that there is considerable uncertainty as to what is and is not truly a "fiduciary" duty

---

[9] "Agent" is an imprecise term. An agent in the strict sense of someone who has the agreed authority to affect his principal's relations with third parties will certainly owe fiduciary duties. Whether those who act on behalf of or represent a principal in some respects, but lack the authority to affect their legal relations with other parties, owe fiduciary duties will depend on the particular facts. See further paras 11–053—11–056 below.

[10] The duties owed by directors have now been partially codified in the Companies Act 2006, ss.170–177. These are considered below paras 11–122—11–136.

[11] *In Plus Group Ltd v Pyke* [2002] 2 B.C.L.C. 201, per Brooke LJ at [75]. Cf. *Re Coomber* [1911] 1 Ch. 723, per Fletcher Mouton LJ at 728–729: "There is no class of case in which one ought more carefully to bear in mind the facts of the case, when one reads the judgment of the Court on those facts, than cases which relate to fiduciary and confidential relations and the action of the Court with regard to them".

[12] *Wilkinson v West Coast Capital* [2007] B.C.C. 717.

[13] *Henderson v Merrett Syndicates* [1995] 2 A.C. 145, per Lord Browne-Wilkinson at 206.

(although much light has been shed on this by the seminal analysis of Millett LJ in *Bristol & West Building Society v Mothew*),[14] and the cases do not use the term consistently. What is clear is that not all of the duties owed by a person who occupies a fiduciary position viz-a-viz another will be fiduciary duties at all; and not all of those which can appropriately be described as being fiduciary will be so in the same sense, or attract the same remedial consequences.[15]

This is, therefore, an area of the law in which the practitioner must proceed with real caution. We have sought to structure this chapter in a way that, it is hoped, will assist in identifying when fiduciaries duties will be owed and what the content of those duties will be; but the taxonomy we have applied to the subject (which owes much to other commentators) is by no means uncontroversial. Ultimately, as Lord Upjohn cautioned in *Phipps v Boardman*[16]:   **11–010**

> "...[r]ules of equity have to be applied in such a great diversity of circumstances that they can be stated only in the most general terms and applied with particular attention to the exact circumstances of each case."

(2) What Gives Rise to Fiduciary Duties?

Whilst there has been no definitive analysis in the English cases of the circumstances in which fiduciary duties will be owed (indeed it is unlikely that there could be such an analysis), a useful guiding principle, for which there is judicial support, is that they are owed where one person has undertaken (expressly or by implication) to act for or on behalf of another in circumstances which give rise to a relationship of trust and confidence.[17] Put another way (and at some risk of circularity), they are duties that are owed where the circumstances give rise to a legitimate expectation that one person will not use his position in a way that is adverse to the interests of another.[18] The paradigm such circumstance is where one person assumes to act in relation to the property or (generally financial) affairs of another[19]: thus a trustee is appointed to hold property which belongs beneficially to the beneficiaries; an agent agrees to act on behalf of a principal and assumes a power to alter his legal position; and a director takes an office in which he is responsible for managing the business and controlling the assets of a company.   **11–011**

However, fiduciary obligations are not owed simply by dint of there being an existing relationship of trust and confidence (since there are relationships that have that feature which are not usually fiduciary in character, such as the relationship between employer and employee); nor is it sufficient to identify a legitimate expectation that the fiduciary will not act adversely to the interests of   **11–012**

---

[14] *Bristol & West Building Society v Mothew* [1998] Ch. 1.
[15] See Section E below.
[16] *Phipps v Boardman* [1967] 2 A.C. 46.
[17] *Bristol & West Building Society v Mothew* [1998] Ch. 1, at 18; *FHR European Ventures LLP v Cedar Capital Partners LLC* [2014] UKSC 45, at [5].
[18] *Arklow Investments Ltd v Maclean* [2000] 1 W.L.R. 594, at 598.
[19] *White v Jones* [1995] 2 A.C. 207, per Lord Browne-Wilkinson at 271.

the other party (that too may be a feature of many non-fiduciary relationships; and, as will be seen below, fiduciary duties are not simply concerned with avoiding harm to the principal). What is peculiar to a fiduciary relationship is that a fiduciary is expected to subordinate his or her interests to those of the principal and not (without the principal's freely given and fully-informed consent) benefit from the relationship.[20] The essential characteristic of the core obligation owed by a fiduciary to his principal is self-denying loyalty; and for that obligation and the fiduciary duties associated with it to be owed, the fiduciary must have undertaken to perform a function, or assumed a responsibility, for another that gives rise to a reasonable expectation that he will act in that way.

11–013 This point was captured by Gloster J when rejecting the submission that the relationship between an investment advisor and client was fiduciary, by dint of the reliance and trust that the latter placed in the former[21]:

> "But the mere fact that one party to a commercial relationship 'trusts' the other does not predicate a fiduciary relationship. The word 'trust', like the word 'advice' has a variety of meanings. In a broad sense, trust is an important element in many commercial dealings. As Steyn J (as he then was) pointed out in *Barclays Bank Plc v Quincecare Ltd* [168]: '... trust, not distrust, is also the basis of a bank's dealings with its customers ...' Springwell no doubt 'trusted' Chase to conduct itself in a commercially appropriate manner. But I do not consider that Springwell had any legitimate expectation that, in its commercial dealings with Springwell, Chase would subordinate its interests to those of Springwell."

11–014 The guiding principles have perhaps best been encapsulated in a single formula by Finn J, in the Australian case of *Grimaldi v Chameleon Mining NL (No.2)*[22]:

> "a person will be in a fiduciary relationship with another when and insofar as that person has undertaken to perform such a function for, or has assumed such a responsibility to, another as would thereby reasonably entitle that other to expect that he or she will act in that other's interest[23] to the exclusion of his or her own or a third party's interest."

11–015 In ascertaining when such a reasonable expectation will arise, outside the settled categories of relationship, the following have been identified (non-exhaustively) as circumstances which point towards, but do not determine, that conclusion[24]:

> "... the existence of a relation of confidence ...; inequality of bargaining power ...; an undertaking by one party to perform a task or fulfil a duty in the interests of another party ...; the scope for one party to unilaterally exercise a discretion or power which may affect the rights or interests of another ...; and a dependency or vulnerability on the part of one party that causes that party to rely on another ..."

11–016 In a similar vein the Law Commission has recently expressed the view that

---

[20] Fiduciaries will generally agree to act for their principal on the basis that they are remunerated under a contract which defines the terms of that remuneration. Because it is done with the principal's consent, benefiting in this way is perfectly consistent with their fiduciary obligations.

[21] *JP Morgan Chase Bank v Springwell Navigation Corp* [2008] EWHC 1186 (Comm), at [574] (not doubted on appeal, at [2010] EWCA Civ 1221).

[22] *Grimaldi v Chameleon Mining NL (No.2)* [2012] FCAFC 6, at [177].

[23] Or, in the case of partners, their joint interests.

[24] *Breen v Williams* (1996) 186 C.L.R. 71, per Gaudron and McHugh JJ, at [24].

"the key test is whether there is a legitimate expectation that one party will act in another's interest. However, discretion, power to act and vulnerability are indicators of such an expectation."[25]

Unsurprisingly, the question of whether the circumstances justify the imposition of fiduciary obligations on one party to a relationship falls to be answered objectively: it does not depend on that party appreciating that he was undertaking to act for another in a way that gave rise to a relationship of trust and confidence and a core obligation of self-denying loyalty, nor does it depend upon the other party consciously having the expectation that he would so act. Moreover, often the fiduciary obligations will arise not because of some specific assumption of responsibility (in the sense known to the law of negligence), but rather because the fiduciary undertakes a particular role or function with respect to the affairs of another that implies such an assumption.[26]

11–017

(3) Fiduciary Duties in the Commercial and Contractual Context

It has been observed that fiduciary obligations should not usually be found to have been assumed by parties to a "purely commercial relationship", outside the settled categories (directors and agents, for example, plainly do owe such obligations despite usually operating in a commercial context). It is certainly right that if the proper conclusion to draw from the terms and circumstances of the relationship is that each party could reasonably be expected not to have to subordinate his own interests to those of the other party, then necessarily the fully-fledged fiduciary obligation of self-denying loyalty will not be owed. But that is not to say that fiduciary obligations cannot be owed in a commercial context, outside the settled categories, if the particular circumstances and terms of the relationship justify that conclusion, and a number of cases have so held. That will often be so where the commercial arrangements between the parties are such that a substantial measure of control over the property or interests of one party is given to the other. Examples of such cases are considered in paras 11–032—11–057 below.

11–018

The other, related point to note about fiduciary duties in the commercial context is that parties operating in that context will usually seek to define the scope and terms of their relationship by way of contract. The interests of commercial certainty militate against the superimposition of equitable duties on those which have expressly been agreed, and any fiduciary obligations must accommodate themselves to and not be inconsistent with the contractual relationship.

11–019

These points were well summed up by Sales J in *F&C Alternative Investments (Holdings) Ltd v Barthelemy*[27]:

11–020

---

[25] *Fiduciary Duties of Investment Intermediaries*, Law Com No.350, para.3.24.
[26] *Vivendi SA v Richards* [2013] EWHC 3006 (Ch); [2013] BCC 771, at [139]: someone who takes on the role of a trustee or director cannot be heard to say that he did not thereby intend to assume fiduciary duties.
[27] *F&C Alternative Investments (Holdings) Ltd v Barthelemy* [2012] Ch. 613, at [223].

"Fiduciary obligations may arise in a wide range of business relationships, where a substantial degree of control over the property or affairs of one person is given to another person. Very often, of course, a contract may lie at the heart of such a business relationship, and then a question arises about the way in which fiduciary obligations may be imposed alongside the obligations spelled out in the contract. In making their contract, the parties will have bargained for a distribution of risk and for the main standards of conduct to be applied between them. In commercial contexts care has to be taken in identifying any fiduciary obligations which may arise that the court does not distort the bargain made by the parties: see the observation of Lord Neuberger of Abbotsbury writing extra-judicially in *"The Stuffing of Minerva's Owl? Taxonomy and Taxidermy in Equity"* [2009] CLJ 537, 543 and *Vercoe v Rutland Fund Management Ltd* [2010] EWHC 424 (Ch), at [351]–[352]. The touchstone is to ask what obligations of a fiduciary character may reasonably be expected to apply in the particular context, where the contract between the parties will usually provide the major part of the contextual framework in which that question arises."

11–021 The classic statement of the principle is that of Mason J in *Hospital Products v United States Surgical Corp*[28]:

"That contractual and fiduciary relationships may co-exist between the same parties has never been doubted. Indeed, the existence of a basic contractual relationship has in many situations provided a foundation for the erection of a fiduciary relationship. In these situations it is the contractual foundation which is all important because it is the contract which regulates the basic rights and liabilities of the parties. The fiduciary relationship, if it is to exist at all, must accommodate itself to the terms of the contract so that it is consistent with, and conforms to them. The fiduciary relationship cannot be superimposed upon the contract in such a way as to alter the operation which the contract was intended to have according to its true construction."[29]

11–022 Wider duties than are spelled out in the contract will not lightly be imposed, particularly where the contract is negotiated at arms' length between parties with comparable bargaining power and where there are detailed express provisions as to the governance of the relationship and matters in which fiduciary duties might otherwise intervene, such as resolving conflicts of interest, accounting for profits and disclosure.[30] Fiduciary duties should not be superimposed on contractual (or indeed tortious) duties simply to plug perceived gaps in the relationship or improve the range of relief available to the claimant.[31]

11–023 Similarly, even where it is appropriate to find fiduciary obligations supervening on contractual ones, given the sensitivity of what the content of those obligations are to the contractual context, the correct approach is not to start with a fixed idea of what a particular fiduciary duty is and then ask whether there can be implied a basis for cutting it down, but rather to ask what precise fiduciary obligation(s) could reasonably be expected to apply in the particular context created by the contractual agreement existing between the parties.[32]

---

[28] *Hospital Products v United States Surgical Corp* (1984) 156 C.L.R. 41, at 97.
[29] See also *Henderson v Merrett Syndicates Ltd* [1995] 2 A.C. 145, per Lord Browne-Wilkinson at 206; and *Hilton v Barker Booth & Eastwood* [2005] 1 W.L.R. 567, per Lord Walker at [30]: fiduciary obligations "may have to be moulded and informed by the terms of the contractual relationship".
[30] *Ross River Ltd v Cambridge City Council* [2008] 1 All E.R. 1004, at [197].
[31] *Breen v Williams* (1996) 186 C.L.R. 71, per McHugh JJ at [33].
[32] *F&C Alternative Investments (Holdings) Ltd v Barthelemy (No.2)* [2012] Ch. 613, at [249].

That said, fiduciary obligations are of a different character from those which   **11–024**
derive from any contract between the parties.[33] Whilst their source may be the
voluntary assumption by one party of a role with respect to another, they are not
implied terms of the agreement between the parties (or the equivalent of such
terms), but rather are best understood as controls imposed in equity by dint of the
vulnerability of one party to the intervention by another in his affairs in the
discharge of that role. Fiduciary duties will not be overlaid where they would be
inconsistent with or would fundamentally alter the bargain between the parties,
and the process of ascertaining whether fiduciary duties are owed against a
contractual background has, it may be accepted, some similarities with the
process of deciding whether terms fall to be implied into the contract[34]; but
fiduciary duties can, in an appropriate case, operate in a way that adds to the
obligations which have been expressly assumed, and they do more than simply
spell out what the parties' agreement is to be understood to be.

There is no reason in principle why parties in a contractual relationship (at least   **11–025**
outside the established categories of inherently fiduciary relationship) cannot
expressly stipulate that their relationship is not fiduciary in character; and it is
thought that the Court will usually give effect to such a provision, provided that it
does not amount to a "rewriting of history" by a party taking advantage of a
dominant position over a vulnerable counterparty.[35]

Further, even within the established categories, the scope and content of the   **11–026**
fiduciary duties which are presumed to be owed can be modified and attenuated
by the agreement of those to whom they are owed. In the case of the relationship
between director and company, Articles of Association may define the director's
duties in specified situations and provide for a narrower duty than might
ordinarily apply, or exclude the application of a particular duty in those situations
altogether: for example, the standard form Articles of Association in Table A of
the Companies Act 1948 and 1985 relaxed the self-dealing rule for directors (as
to which see paras 11–086—11–088 below), provided that disclosure of the
nature and extent of the director's interest was made to the Board.[36] An
agreement made between all of the shareholders and the company itself and
which is stated to take precedence over the Articles of Association is also capable
of modifying the duties which would otherwise rest on a director.[37] Moreover,
"agreement" in this context is not limited to contracts in the strict sense: what is
permissible within the bounds of a fiduciary's duties will be affected by
considerations such as the terms of any contract of engagement, the scope and
nature of the business in which his principal is engaged, his role within that
business and any understandings between the parties (which may fall short of

---

[33] *Re Goldcorp Exchange Ltd* [1995] 1 A.C. 74, at 98.
[34] *F&C Alternative Investments (Holdings) Ltd v Barthelemy (No.2)* [2012] Ch. 613, per Sales J at
[225].
[35] *Thomas v Barclays Bank Plc* [2014] EWHC 2882 (QB), at [90].
[36] Regulation 84 in the 1948 Act Table A and regs 85 and 86 in the 1985 Act Table A. For
observations about the effect of similarly worded articles see *Movitex v Bulfield* [1988] B.C.L.C. 104
and *Gwembe Valley Development Company Ltd v Koshy* [2004] 1 B.C.L.C. 131, at [47]–[54]. As to
the position under the Companies Act 2006, see paras 11–126—11–130 below.
[37] *Wilkinson v West Coast Capital* [2007] B.C.C. 717.

having contractual force and may be manifested only in a course of dealings) as to the other activities in which he might properly engage.[38]

11–027 In a number of cases concerning joint ventures it has been held that the fact that it was agreed or (objectively) intended that the person found to owe fiduciary duties should have his own interest in the joint venture entailed that the strict rule against conflicts of interest or profits from the fiduciary position was relaxed: where the role of the fiduciary is to serve the joint interests of the parties, rather than exclusively the interests of his counterparty, these duties must necessarily assume a less stringent form. Thus in *Ross River Ltd v Waverly Commercial Ltd*[39] the duty on the defendant fiduciary who controlled the receipt and application of joint venture revenues was not the full "no profit" duty, but rather took the modified form of a duty not to "do anything in relation to the handling of the joint venture revenues which favoured itself to the disadvantage of [the claimants]" and in particular not to pay any sum other than such as was properly required for the purposes of the joint venture or to which the claimants had agreed.[40]

11–028 Similarly, a director nominated by a shareholder under the terms of a joint venture or shareholders agreement may be entitled to take into account the interests of the nominating shareholder without breaching his fiduciary duty to the company of which he is director, provided that he exercises independent judgment and still acts in what he genuinely considers to be the company's best interests.[41] Where he is also a director of or otherwise interested in the nominating shareholder, the fact that a dual role is inherent in the contractual arrangements between the parties is likely to mean that he is not in breach of fiduciary duty simply by dint of the fact his duties to the company might conflict with his duties to or interests in the nominating shareholder: the potential conflict is taken to have been authorised[42]; and in one case it was held that, even in the case of an actual conflict, the fact that the agreement between the parties envisaged representatives of both venturers being on the board (such that conflicts were mediated through the governance structures of the joint venture) meant that the fiduciary obligations of each director to the venture vehicle required only that they "strive to maintain a fair balance" between the separate interests of the venturers "bundled up collectively" in the venture vehicle.[43]

11–029 That said, where there is express agreement (such as in the Articles of Association) providing for the relaxation of the fiduciary obligations on directors of a company, it will not be possible to imply further relaxations of the fiduciary duties simply by reason of the fact that the company was in the nature of a joint

---

[38] See *New Zealand Netherlands Society "oranje" Inc v Laurentius Cornelis Kuys* [1973] 1 W.L.R. 1126 (PC).

[39] *Ross River Ltd v Waverly Commercial Ltd* [2013] EWCA Civ 910.

[40] *Ross River Ltd v Waverly Commercial Ltd* [2013] EWCA Civ 910, at [41] and [93].

[41] *Boulting v Association of Cinematograph* [1963] 2 Q.B. 606, at 626–627; *Hawkes v Cuddy* [2009] 2 B.C.L.C. 427, at [33].

[42] *Richmond Pharmacology Ltd v Chester Overseas Ltd* [2014] EWHC 2692 (Ch), at [73]; see also *Fattal v Walbrook*, above, at [126]–[127] (no breach of fiduciary duty in trustees also acting as trustees of other trusts when the beneficiaries were party to a joint venture agreement to which the trustees were also party in their capacity as trustees of both trusts).

[43] *F&C Alternative Investments (Holdings) Ltd v Barthelemy (No.2)* [2012] Ch. 613, at [236]–[239].

venture.[44] It is also doubtful whether it is possible by agreement or assent to release a director entirely from his basic general duty to act in the best interests of the company of which he is a director.[45]

To take another well-known example: where a sales agent (such as an estate agent or broker) operates a general agency business and acts for a number of vendors, it will be an implied term of the retainer (and an equivalent delimitation in the fiduciary duties owed) that the agent can act for other vendors whose interests may compete, and that he can keep confidential information that he has received from other vendors[46]:

  "In a case where a principal instructs as selling agent for his property or goods a person who to his knowledge acts and intends to act for other principals selling property or goods of the same description, the terms to be implied into such agency contract must differ from those to be implied where an agent is not carrying on such general agency business. In the case of estate agents, it is their business to act for numerous principals: where properties are of a similar description, there will be a conflict of interest between the principals each of whom will be concerned to attract potential purchasers to their property rather than that of another. Yet, despite this conflict of interest, estate agents must be free to act for several competing principals otherwise they will be unable to perform their function. Yet it is normally said that it is a breach of an agent's duty to act for competing principals. In the course of acting for each of their principals, estate agents will acquire information confidential to that principal. It cannot be sensibly suggested that an estate agent is contractually bound to disclose to any one of his principals information which is confidential to another of his principals. The position as to confidentiality is even clearer in the case of stockbrokers who cannot be contractually bound to disclose to their private clients inside information disclosed to the brokers in confidence by a company for which they also act. Accordingly in such cases there must be an implied term of the contract with such an agent that he is entitled to act for other principals selling competing properties and to keep confidential the information obtained from each of his principals. Similar considerations apply to the fiduciary duties of agents."[47]

The position was summarised in the following terms by Lord Browne-Wilkinson in *Henderson v Merrett Syndicates Ltd*[48]:

  "The phrase 'fiduciary duties' is a dangerous one, giving rise to a mistaken assumption that all fiduciaries owe the same duties in all circumstances. That is not the case. Although, so far as I am aware, every fiduciary is under a duty not to make a profit from his position (unless such profit is authorised), the fiduciary duties owed, for example, by an express trustee are not the same as those owed by an agent. Moreover, and more relevantly, the extent and nature of the fiduciary duties owed in any particular case fall to be determined by reference to any underlying contractual relationship between the parties. Thus, in the case of an agent employed under a contract, the scope of his fiduciary duties is determined by the terms of the underlying contract...The existence of a contract does not exclude the co-existence of

11–030

11–031

---

[44] *Gwembe Valley Development Company Ltd v Koshy* [2004] 1 B.C.L.C. 131, at [55]-[56].

[45] *Re Southern Counties Fresh Foods Ltd* [2008] EWHC 2810 (Ch), at [67] and [69]. Such an agreement would probably now infringe s.232 of the Companies Act 2006.

[46] *Kelly v Cooper* [1993] A.C. 205; see also *Diamond Sofa Co Ltd v Rossetti Marketing Ltd* [2012] EWCA Civ 1021, at [23]. But note the limits of this principle, which probably turns on the particular market practices of estate agents. In *Hilton v Barker Booth & Eastwood* [2005] 1 W.L.R. 567 (a case concerning a solicitor acting for two clients with conflicting interests) it was observed that where "a solicitor is unwise enough to undertake irreconcilable duties it is his own fault, and he cannot use his discomfiture as a reason why his duty to either client should be taken to have been modified" (per Lord Walker at [46]).

[47] *Kelly v Cooper* [1993] A.C. 205, at 214.

[48] *Henderson v Merrett Syndicates Ltd* [1995] 2 A.C. 145, at 206A–206D.

[317]

concurrent fiduciary duties (indeed, the contract may well be their source); but the contract can and does modify the extent and nature of the general duty that would otherwise arise."

(4) Fiduciary Duties Arising Outside the Settled Categories of Relationship

11–032 The following are examples of relationships or situations of potential relevance to a civil fraud claim, not involving the established categories of fiduciary relationship identified above, in which the question of whether fiduciary obligations were owed has been considered. It must be emphasised again that it is only part of the enquiry to ask whether fiduciary duties are owed at all; there is always also the question of what the content of such duties is.

(i) Directors to Shareholders/Other Third Parties

11–033 Directors stand in a fiduciary relationship to their company because they are appointed to manage its affairs and are vested with powers to control its property and otherwise affect its interests[49]; they are the human agents who must necessarily represent and bind the company in its dealings with third parties (the company being an artificial person which can only act through human agents).[50] The fiduciary duties which they owe by reason of that relationship are owed to the company and not to its shareholders.[51] This simply reflects the principle that a company has a corporate personality separate from its members; but it is also supported by policy considerations, such as the desirability of not undermining the collective nature of the shareholders' association in the company, not exposing directors to a multiplicity of suits, including from dissenting minority shareholders, and not generating potential conflicts between the duties owed by directors to the company and those owed to particular shareholders.[52] The Companies Act 2006 is now explicit that the statutory general duties of directors (which replace the common law rules and equitable principles on which they are based) are owed to the company.[53]

11–034 It is, nevertheless, possible for fiduciary duties to be owed directly by directors to shareholders alongside the (now statutory) duties owed by directors to the company. Such duties will arise not from the relationship between the directors and the company, but from the existence of a separate and special factual relationship between the directors and shareholders in the particular case.[54] That may be because the directors have held themselves out as agents for the shareholders in connection with a transaction concerning their shares,[55] or have

---

[49] *Bairstow v Queens Moat Houses Plc* [2001] 2 B.C.L.C. 531, at 548; *Customer Systems Plc v Ranson* [2012] EWCA Civ 841, at [20] and [24].
[50] By the Companies Act 2006 s.154 a private company is required to have at least one director and a public company at least two.
[51] *Percival v Wright* [1902] 2 Ch. 421; *Multinational Gas and Petrochemical Co Ltd v Multinational Gas and Petrochemical Services Ltd* [1983] Ch. 258, per Dillon LJ at 288.
[52] See *Sharp v Blank* [2015] EWHC 3220 (Ch), per Nugee J at [9(3)].
[53] Section 170(1) of the Companies Act 2006.
[54] *Peskin v Anderson* [2001] BCC 874, at [33]–[34].
[55] *Allen v Hyatt* (1914) 30 T.L.R. 444.

made material representations to them or supplied them with specific information and advice on which they have relied, particularly in circumstances (such as of a family relationship) where trust and confidence is placed in them or where they stand to benefit from the transaction in question.[56] But what is required is a particular dealing or communication directly between directors and shareholders, or a close personal relationship, and (in almost all cases) some transaction in which the directors and shareholders are involved. The mere fact that the directors are in possession, in their capacity as such, of information that would be of possible value to the shareholders is not sufficient,[57] nor is the fact that they have the power to affect the shareholders' interests (since that will almost always be the case).[58]

It is right to acknowledge that where directors, with their greater knowledge of the company's affairs, undertake to provide information and advice to shareholders on how to vote in a general meeting of the company, they come under an equitable duty to provide sufficient information to enable the shareholders to make an informed decision, and not to conceal relevant information or mislead. But that falls short of the fiduciary duties associated with single-minded loyalty; it stems instead from the requirements of common fairness when inviting shareholders to participate in a meeting.[59]   **11–035**

A nominee director (one nominated for appointment to the Board by a shareholder, usually under the terms of a shareholders agreement) does not, at least without more, owe fiduciary duties to the nominating shareholder.[60]   **11–036**

Directors will also not ordinarily owe fiduciary duties to creditors[61] of the company (even in circumstances where the company is in financial difficulties such that the directors are obliged to have regard to the interests of creditors), or to others who are indirectly interested in its success.[62]   **11–037**

A director of a company will similarly not normally owe fiduciary obligations to third parties who deal with the company, even where the company owes fiduciary obligations to them: the company and its management are, of course, distinct. However, in special circumstances such obligations can arise: for example, in a joint venture relationship where there was a pre-existing relationship of trust and confidence with the director personally before he took office as such, or where the director personally assumed control of the joint venture's affairs and was paid a fee that was deducted from the profits available for distribution.[63]   **11–038**

---

[56] *Coleman v Myers* [1977] 2 N.Z.L.R. 225.

[57] *Peskin v Anderson* [2001] BCC 874, at [57]–[59].

[58] *Sharp v Blank* [2015] EWHC 3220 (Ch), at [12].

[59] *Sharp v Blank* [2015] EWHC 3220 (Ch), at [15]–[21] (the sufficient information duty was conceded in that case: [5]–[6]).

[60] *Hawkes v Cuddy* [2009] 2 B.C.L.C. 427.

[61] *Yukong Line Ltd v Rendsberg Investments Corporate (No.2)* [1998] 1 W.L.R. 294.

[62] Such as the beneficiaries of a trust of which the company is trustee: *Gregson v HAE Trustees Ltd* [2008] 2 B.C.L.C. 542.

[63] See *Ross River Ltd v Waverly Commercial Ltd* [2012] EWHC 81 (Ch), per Morgan J at [261]–[262], upheld on appeal [2013] EWCA Civ 910.

(ii)   Shareholders to each other

11–039   Shareholders in a company do not generally owe fiduciary duties to each other or to their company as such: their shares are their own property and they are entitled to exercise the rights attached to them (such as of voting at general meetings of the company) in their own private interests.[64] This is subject to the principle that shareholders representing a majority in general meeting must not use their rights to alter the company's constitution in a manner that is oppressive to the minority: they must exercise those rights in good faith in the interests of the company as a whole[65]; but that is better characterised as being an equitable limitation on their power to pass resolutions of the company than as a fiduciary duty which they owe to their fellow shareholders.

(iii)   Other relationships involving companies (de facto directors, shadow directors and third party advisers)

11–040   A de facto director is someone who assumes to act as a director and who is held out by the company as a director, although he has not been validly appointed as such.[66] He will owe fiduciary duties to his company in just the same way as a de jure director does.[67] The position of a shadow director—a person in accordance with whose directions or instructions the directors of a company are accustomed to act, but who is not held out as a director[68]—has proved more controversial. In *Ultraframe (UK) Ltd v Fielding*[69] Lewison J decided that a shadow director, who does not directly deal with or claim the right to deal directly with the company's assets, would usually not owe fiduciary duties; but that was doubted (it is respectfully suggested, for convincing reasons) by Newey J in *Vivendi SA v Richards*,[70] who preferred the view that, typically, a shadow director will owe such duties, at least in relation to the instructions which he gives to the de jure directors. The Companies Act 2006 now provides that the general duties specified in ss.171–177 of that Act "apply to a shadow director of a company where and to the extent that they are capable of so applying".

11–041   A third party, such as a solicitor or investment banker, who undertakes to act for or advise a company client, may also owe fiduciary obligations towards a shareholder or director from whom it takes instructions and who is known to "stand behind" the company. Fiduciary duties may arise out of, but they are not necessarily co-terminous with, the contractual retainer. However, it would be unusual for such duties to be owed to the individual as well as the company which is the client, and will require it to be shown, on the particular facts, that the

---

[64] *Re Astec (BSR) Plc* [1999] BCC 59, at 83; but contrast the position of shareholders in a (small) charitable company: *Lehtimaki v The Children's Investment Fund Foundation (UK)* [2018] EWCA Civ 1605.

[65] *Re Charterhouse Capital Ltd* [2015] BCC 574, at [90] and [108].

[66] See *Re Kaytech International Plc* [1999] 2 B.C.L.C. 351.

[67] *Re Canadian Land Reclaiming and Colonizing Co* (1880) L.R. 14 Ch. D. 660; *Ultraframe (UK) Ltd v Fielding* [2005] EWHC 1638 (Ch), at [1257].

[68] Companies Act 2006, s.251.

[69] *Ultraframe (UK) Ltd v Fielding* [2005] EWHC 1638 (Ch), at [1289]–[1290].

[70] *Vivendi SA v Richards* [2013] EWHC 3006 (Ch); [2013] BCC 771, at [142]–[143].

adviser has undertaken to advise, or assumed a responsibility with respect to the affairs of, the individual personally as well as to the company.[71]

(iv)   Joint venturers

A "joint venture" is not a legal term of art and to describe something as such does not imply any particular legal relationship or entail any particular legal consequences.[72] Instead,

> "each relationship which is described as a joint venture has to be examined on its own facts and terms to see whether it does carry any obligations of a fiduciary nature".[73]

11–042

Where a joint venture amounts to a partnership under the Partnership Act 1890 then fiduciary duties will be owed between the venturers on that basis; similarly, where on the proper analysis one joint venturer acts as agent for another, he will owe fiduciary duties to that other in that capacity. But, absent such relationships, it would require "particular and special features" for commercial co-venturers to owe obligations of a truly fiduciary character to each other.[74] Whether they do so will depend, ultimately, on "examination of the detail of what they have agreed and done".[75] The existence of express contractual stipulation—as to matters such as the resolution of potential conflicts of interest (for example by providing for decisions to be voted upon by representatives of the venturers), disclosure and the promotion of the success of the venture in good faith or with reasonable commercial endeavours—will usually eliminate or substantially curtail the scope for superimposing fiduciary obligations, since they would either be inconsistent with the parties' express agreement or superfluous.[76] A contractual right to carry on competitive business will likewise limit the scope of any fiduciary obligations that might otherwise be owed.[77] Conversely, where parties embark together on a venture and have yet to settle the precise terms of their relationship, the scope for fiduciary obligations arising out of the trust and confidence on which their relationship is necessarily based at that stage may be greater.[78]

11–043

In *Murad v Al Saraj*[79] it was held that a joint venture to acquire a hotel did give rise to fiduciary obligations owed by the defendant director to the claimant, who was an indirect joint owner with the defendant of the joint venture company. This was because the relationship was one of trust and confidence, the defendant assumed a number of responsibilities in connection with the affairs of the joint

11–044

---

[71] Contrast *Johnson v Gore Wood* [1998] EWCA Civ 1763 (the Court of Appeal decision), where it was held arguable that such duties were owed, with *Diamantides v JP Morgan Chase Bank* [2005] EWCA Civ 1612, where a claim to similar effect was struck out.

[72] *John Alexander's Clubs Pty Ltd v White City Tennis Club Ltd* [2010] HCA 19, at [44].

[73] *Ross River Ltd v Waverly Commercial Ltd* [2013] EWCA Civ 910, at [34].

[74] *Crossco No.4 Unlimited v Jolan Ltd* [2011] EWCA Civ 1619, at [88].

[75] *John Alexander's Clubs Pty Ltd v White City Tennis Club Ltd* [2010] HCA 19, at [44].

[76] See e.g. *Fattal v Walbrook Trustees* [2010] EWHC 2767 (Ch), at [114]; *F&C Alternative Investments (Holdings) Ltd v Barthelemy (No.2)* [2012] Ch. 613, at [205] (iv) and [214].

[77] *Global Container Lines Ltd v Bonyad Shipping Co (No.1)* [1998] 1 Lloyd's Rep. 528.

[78] *United Dominions Corp v Brian Pty* (1985) 157 C.L.R. 1.

[79] *Murad v Al Saraj* [2004] EWHC 1235 (Ch). The finding that fiduciary duties were owed was not challenged on appeal.

venture (in some respects acting as agent for the claimant), and the claimant lacked relevant experience or knowledge and instead entrusted the defendant with a wide measure of discretion to act in ways that affected his interests. This gave rise to a direct duty to account for unauthorised profits made by the defendant, even though the parties had agreed to carry on their venture through the medium of a company to which the defendant owed duties as a director and in which the claimant was indirectly interested as the owner of a company which in turn owned shares.

11–045   In *Ross River Ltd v Waverly Commercial Ltd*[80] a joint venture agreement between the claimants and the defendant company concerning the development of a site gave rise to unexpressed fiduciary duties on the part of the defendant company to act in good faith in relation to the conduct of the joint venture and payment of money to the claimants, and not to do anything in relation to the handling of joint venture revenues which favoured itself to the disadvantage of the claimants. This was because the defendant was charged under the agreement with handling disposals, incurring expenditure and receiving sale proceeds, and accounting for the net profit. The defendant had complete control over such matters, and the claimants had no shares in it and no representatives on the board of the defendant in order to be able to influence its management, such that a high degree of trust was reposed by the claimants in the defendant. Further, the duties in question were consistent with the express provisions of the joint venture agreement. These duties represented a modified form of the usual no conflict and no profit duties, reflecting the fact that the contractual arrangements between the parties were such that the defendant fiduciary had its own interests in the venture to which it was entitled to have regard.[81]

11–046   Such duties were also held to be owed personally by the individual who stood behind the corporate defendant and joint venture party, notwithstanding that he was a director of the latter and owed it duties as such. He personally controlled the joint venture project and had been involved in pursuing it before the incorporation of the defendant company, and he was paid a fee for his efforts personally, which was deductible in the calculation of the net profits to which the joint venturers were entitled.[82]

11–047   In contrast, in *Pennyfeathers Ltd v Pennyfeathers Property Company Ltd*[83] the individual participants in a development project who signed a shareholders agreement were held not to owe each other fiduciary duties, including because it was envisaged that all of them would participate as equals in carrying the project forward (such that trust was not reposed in one or more with a greater control over the venture's affairs than the others) and their written agreement contained both "entire agreement" and "no partnership" clauses.[84]

---

[80] *Ross River Ltd v Waverly Commercial Ltd* [2012] EWHC 81 (Ch).
[81] As explained on appeal: *Ross River Ltd v Waverly Commercial Ltd* [2013] EWCA Civ 910, at [90].
[82] At [43]–[44], [63].
[83] *Pennyfeathers Ltd v Pennyfeathers Property Company Ltd* [2013] EWHC 3530 (Ch).
[84] See also, more recently, *Baturina v Chistyakov* [2017] EWHC 1049 (Comm), per Carr J at [183]–[184], where it was held that the joint venture was an arms-length commercial agreement between parties with at least comparable bargaining power.

(v)   LLPs (limited liability partnerships)

An LLP is not a partnership; it is a new form of corporate person (s.1(1)(2) of the **11–048**
Limited Liability Partnerships Act 2000) and, save as expressly preserved by that
Act, the general law of partnership does not apply to it.[85] The Limited Liability
Partnerships Act 2000 envisages that the governance of the LLP and the
relationship between its members will be governed by the agreement between the
parties which establishes the LLP.[86] Accordingly, it cannot be said that the
members of an LLP owe fiduciary duties to each other simply by virtue of their
being associated in that way, by analogy to partners. Instead, the question of
whether they owe such duties will depend on the circumstances, including in
particular the terms of the agreement between them. Where under their agreement
the members do not constitute themselves agents for each other or assume
responsibility for the management of each other's affairs, it is unlikely that the
members will themselves owe fiduciary obligations towards each other in that
capacity.[87]

Similarly, in circumstances where the members do not assume responsibility for **11–049**
the management of the property or affairs of the LLP itself, and where a board or
management committee is appointed to do so instead, the members of an LLP
will not generally owe fiduciary duties to the LLP. However, by s.6(1) of the
Limited Liability Partnerships Act 2000 members are agents of the LLP, and there
is nothing in the Act to indicate that they should not owe the usual fiduciary
duties of an agent towards his principal so far as concerns their role as agents.

Those appointed to manage the affairs of an LLP (as members of its board or **11–050**
management committee) will owe personal fiduciary duties to the LLP by
analogy to the position of directors of a company.[88] The fact that they may also be
representatives of one of the members of the LLP is not inconsistent with this,
although, in accordance with the principles outlined earlier, it may entail a
relaxation of the strict no conflict duty that might otherwise arise from such a
dual employment. Their primary duty will, nevertheless, be to act in good faith in
the best interests of the LLP (albeit they will be entitled to take into account the
interests of the nominating member where not inconsistent with that); and that
tends to indicate that they do not owe separate fiduciary obligations as agents of
the nominating member.[89]

(vi)   Employees to employers

An employee does not, merely be reason of his role as an employee, assume **11–051**
fiduciary obligations towards his employer.[90] The employer/employee relationship is at heart contractual and the question of whether and if so what fiduciary

---

[85] Limited Liability Partnerships Act 2000 s.1(5).
[86] Limited Liability Partnerships Act 2000 s.5(1).
[87] *F&C Alternative Investments (Holdings) Ltd v Barthelemy (No.2)* [2012] Ch. 613, at [213].
[88] *F&C Alternative Investments (Holdings) Ltd v Barthelemy (No.2)* [2012] Ch. 613, at [205(i)].
[89] *F&C Alternative Investments (Holdings) Ltd v Barthelemy (No.2)* [2012] Ch. 613, at [205(i)].
[90] *Customer Systems Plc v Ranson* [2012] EWCA Civ 841.

duties are owed by an employee will depend heavily upon the terms of the contract of employment and the role undertaken by the employee pursuant to it:

"...the essence of the employment relationship is not typically fiduciary at all. Its purpose is not to place the employee in a position where he is obliged to pursue his employer's interests at the expense of his own. The relationship is a contractual one and the powers imposed on the employee are conferred by the employer himself. The employee's freedom of action is regulated by the contract, the scope of his powers is determined by the terms (express or implied) of the contract, and as a consequence the employer can exercise (or at least he can place himself in a position where he has the opportunity to exercise) considerable control over the employee's decision making powers. This is not to say that fiduciary duties cannot arise out of the employment relationship itself. But they arise not as a result of the mere fact that there is an employment relationship. Rather they result from the fact that within a particular contractual relationship there are specific contractual obligations which the employee has undertaken which have placed him in a situation where equity imposes these rigorous duties in addition to the contractual obligations. Where this occurs, the scope of the fiduciary obligations both arises out of, and is circumscribed by, the contractual terms; it is circumscribed because equity cannot alter the terms of the contract validly undertaken."[91]

11–052   An employee will, however, usually owe an implied (if not express) obligation of good faith and fidelity.[92] This differs from the fiduciary duty of loyalty in that: (a) it is a contractual duty and so owes its existence to the express or implied agreement of the parties to the relationship; and (b) it would not ordinarily be understood to require the single-minded and exclusive loyalty that would characterise a fully-fledged fiduciary relationship: the difference is between, on the one hand, being required faithfully (that is, with a view to the employer's interests) to carry out the job which one has agreed to do and, on the other, being required in all matters falling within the scope of the relationship wholly to subordinate one's own interests to those of one's principal.[93]

(vii)   Brokers/introducing agents and their clients

11–053   We have noted above that it will be a fact-sensitive question whether those who are not agents in the strict sense of having the agreed authority to affect their principal's legal relations with third parties will nevertheless owe fiduciary obligations. Brokers and introducing agents, who effect introductions on behalf of, and sometimes advise, their clients, but who (usually) leave the clients to enter into binding agreements with third parties, are a case in point.

11–054   A number of cases have considered the position of credit brokers who introduce lenders to borrowers, the issue of whether they are fiduciaries usually arising because the brokers act for the borrowers but take a commission which is paid by the lenders. In *Commercial First Business Ltd v Pickup, Vernon*,[94] the suggestion that a broker who obtained loan proposals for experienced property investors owed those investors fiduciary obligations which precluded the taking of a partly-disclosed commission from the lenders was rejected: the brokers did no more than provide the borrowers with an application form and quotation for the

---

[91] *University of Nottingham v Fischel* [2000] I.C.R. 1462, per Elias J at 1491.
[92] *Wessex Dairies Ltd v Smith* [1935] 2 K.B. 80.
[93] *Customer Systems v Ranson* [2012] EWCA Civ 841, at [41]–[43].
[94] *Commercial First Business Ltd v Pickup, Vernon* [2017] CTLC 1.

loan (the borrowers having responded to the broker's advertisement and provided information as to their loan requirements) and submitted the completed form to the lenders. In contrast, in *Hurstanger Ltd v Wilson* (a significant case, because it introduced the concept of a commission being "half-secret"), the Court of Appeal had regarded it as "obvious" that a broker in a not dissimilar position owed fiduciary obligations to the borrower.[95] The point was conceded rather than argued; but the conclusion was endorsed by the Court of Appeal in *McWilliam v Norton Finance (UK) Ltd*,[96] Tomlinson LJ observing in that case that it was not a critical feature in favour of the finding of a fiduciary relationship that the broker should offer advice or a recommendation[97]: the reliance relevant to a finding that fiduciary duties were owed was not the same as that relevant to a finding of a duty of care; what mattered was instead the vulnerability of the client to the broker's disloyalty.[98]

It may seem that what distinguished *Hurstanger* and *McWilliam* on the one hand from cases such as *Pickup* on the other is therefore the level of sophistication of the borrower client. But doubt is cast on that by the recent decision of Teare J in *Medsted Associates Ltd v Canaccord Genuity Wealth (International) Ltd*,[99] where it was held that a broker who introduced wealthy and experienced investor clients (interested in trading contracts for difference) to a financial services institution, in return for a share of the commission charged by the institution to the clients, owed fiduciary obligations which required the broker to disclose to the clients how the commissions were split. Relevant to that determination appears to have been that the broker was implicitly making a recommendation to the clients to trade with the relevant institution, and that the clients, even though more financially sophisticated, were still "vulnerable to any disloyalty ... and reliant on its good faith".[100]   **11–055**

The better view is therefore probably that what matters is the extent to which the broker's role is more than merely ministerial, and he is acting or advising in a way that is capable of materially altering the principal's position (even if that falls short of committing him to a binding contract), such that the principal is reliant on him acting loyally and in good faith. So, for example, where an introducing agent negotiated the terms of the sale of a hotel on behalf of the purchasing joint venture, and advised the venture in connection therewith, there was said to be "no doubt" that it owed fiduciary duties, even though the purchase agreement was concluded between vendor and purchaser directly.[101]   **11–056**

---

[95] *Hurstanger Ltd v Wilson* [2007] 1 W.L.R. 2351, at [33].

[96] *McWilliam v Norton Finance (UK) Ltd* [2015] EWCA Civ 186.

[97] Although there was an implicit, limited recommendation made in *McWilliam* that the terms offered by the lender were the most competitive to which the broker had access: see [44].

[98] See [45]–[46].

[99] *Medsted Associates Ltd v Canaccord Genuity Wealth (International) Ltd* [2017] EWHC 1815 (Comm).

[100] See [93]–[94].

[101] *FHR European Ventures LLP v Mankarious* [2011] EWHC 2308 (Ch), at [99] (the first instance decision, which was not doubted on this point on appeal).

(viii)   John v James: Contracts for the exploitation of rights

11–057   In *John v James*,[102] contractual arrangements under which copyrights were assigned by an artist (Elton John) to a publisher absolutely, but with the intention that they should be exploited for the joint benefit of the publisher and the artist, gave rise to fiduciary duties on the part of the publisher to exploit the copyrights only in a way that it honestly believed was for the joint benefit of the parties and not to make any unauthorised profit from them for its own separate account. Even though there was no trust of the copyrights, nevertheless the publisher was given complete control over how they were to be exploited for the economic benefit of both parties, and so the artist placed trust and confidence in the publisher as to how it discharged its exploitation function.

C.   SOME OTHER GENERAL POINTS ON FIDUCIARY DUTIES

(1)   Equitable Duty of Care (Generally) not Fiduciary

11–058   It is probably now well-established that the duty to exercise skill and care, which will commonly be owed by persons described as fiduciaries towards their principals and which may be equitable in origin, is nevertheless not a fiduciary duty:

> "A servant who loyally does his incompetent best for his master is not unfaithful and is not guilty of a breach of fiduciary duty."[103]

11–059   Thus a solicitor who carelessly investigates a title or drafts a lease may be liable to pay damages for breach of his professional duty, but he is not in breach of fiduciary duty.[104] Similarly, the statutory duty of care that a director owes a company under s.174 of the Companies Act 2006 is expressly carved out as not being fiduciary in character by s.178 of the Act.[105] That reflects the position as it was at common law before the Act.[106]

11–060   Breach of the duty of skill and care will therefore not render void or voidable a transaction entered into by or at the instigation of his fiduciary, nor will it give rise to the restitutionary, restorative or proprietary remedies available for breach of a fiduciary duty properly so-called: it will sound in an award of damages or equitable compensation for the claimant's loss.[107]

---

[102] *John v James* [1991] F.S.R. 397.

[103] *Permanent Building Society v Wheeler* (1994) 14 ACSR 109, at 157–158; *Bristol & West Building Society v Mothew* [1998] Ch. 1, at 18.

[104] *Hilton v Barker Booth & Eastwood* [2005] UKHL 8, at [29].

[105] "The duties in those sections (with the exception of section 174 (duty to exercise reasonable care, skill and diligence)) are, accordingly, enforceable in the same way as any other fiduciary duty owed to a company by its directors."

[106] *Colin Gwyer & Associates Ltd v London Wharf (Limehouse) Ltd* [2003] 2 B.C.L.C. 153, at [83], per Leslie Kosmin QC; *Extrasure Travel Insurance Ltd v Scattergood* [2003] 1 B.C.L.C. 598, at [87]–[90], per Jonathan Crow QC.

[107] For these purposes common law damages and equitable compensation will be indistinguishable: *Bristol & West Building Society v Mothew* [1998] Ch. 1, at 17G–17H.

That said, whilst the above propositions can be applied with some confidence in most factual scenarios, there will be cases where the distinction between a duty of care and a fiduciary duty is not so clear. Thus, for example, a trustee who fails properly to identify, and to exercise proper care and diligence in obtaining information and advice on, the considerations relevant to the exercise of a discretion will be in breach of duty, and the decision will be voidable on that basis. Consistently with that being the relief available, the Supreme Court has (post-*Mothew*) described this as amounting to a breach of fiduciary duty.[108]

11–061

(2) Dishonest Breaches of Fiduciary Duty

A breach of fiduciary duty can be characterised as dishonest if the fiduciary deliberately acts (or fails to act), either knowing that the course of action in question is contrary to the interests of his principal or being recklessly indifferent as to whether it is contrary to its interests. Put another way, a fiduciary dishonestly breaches his duty if he acts deliberately and without honest belief that he is acting in the interests of her principal.[109] In *Armitage v Nurse* Millett LJ explained that dishonesty on the part of a trustee:

11–062

> "connotes at the minimum an intention on the part of the trustee to pursue a particular course of action, either knowing that it is contrary to the interests of the beneficiaries or being recklessly indifferent whether it is contrary to their interests or not. It is the duty of a trustee to manage the trust property and deal with it in the interests of the beneficiaries. If he acts in a way which he does not honestly believe is in their interests then he is acting dishonestly. It does not matter whether he stands or thinks he stands to gain personally from his actions. A trustee who acts with the intention of benefitting persons who are not the objects of the trust is not the less dishonest because he does not intend to benefit himself."[110]

In *Fattal v Walbrook Trustees (Jersey) Ltd*,[111] Lewison J suggested that the required lack of honest belief that a proposed course was in the interests of the beneficiary or principal would, at least in the context of a professional trustee or fiduciary, include having a belief which was so unreasonable that, by any objective standard, no reasonable professional trustee could have thought that what he did or agreed to do was for the benefit of the beneficiaries.

11–063

The breach of trust or fiduciary duty must also be deliberate, in the sense that the act or omission constituting the breach is deliberate; a conscious intention that the act or omission should amount to a breach is not required.[112]

11–064

---

[108] *Pitt v Holt* [2013] 2 A.C. 108, at [73].

[109] *Gwembe Valley Development Co Ltd v Koshy* [2004] 1 B.C.L.C. 131, at [131], applying *Armitage v Nurse* [1998] Ch 241.

[110] *Armitage v Nurse* [1998] Ch. 241, at 251E–251F.

[111] *Fattal v Walbrook Trustees (Jersey) Ltd* [2010] EWHC 2767 (Ch), at [79]–[81]. See also *Walker v Stones* [2001] Q.B. 902, at 939C and 941D (solicitor-trustee's honest perception of interests of beneficiaries could be so unreasonable as to amount to dishonesty for the purposes of the exception to an exemption clause).

[112] *Nationwide Building Society v Balmer Radmore (A Firm)* [1999] P.N.L.R. 606, at 638; *Madoff Securities International Ltd (In Liquidation) v Raven* [2013] EWHC 3147 (Comm), at [326]. As we have seen above, carelessness can give rise to a breach of a duty of care, whether owed in equity or at common law, but will not constitute a breach of fiduciary duty.

11–065 Since it is not necessary to establish dishonesty in order to establish a breach of fiduciary duty (see Section D below), the principal significance of being able to establish dishonesty in the above sense will be that the claimant can invoke s.21 of the Limitation Act 1980 to avoid the primary limitation period that would otherwise apply.[113] The proven dishonesty of a fiduciary may also have other effects, including (for example): that he cannot rely upon a trustee exoneration clause; and that he cannot make use of the Court's powers to relieve company directors or trustees of liability under s.1157 Companies Act 2006 and s.61 Trustee Act 2000 respectively.

(3) The Duration of Fiduciary Duties

11–066 Fiduciary duties only subsist as long as the fiduciary holds the office or position that gives rise to them:

> "We do not recognize the concept of a fiduciary obligation which continues notwithstanding the determination of the particular relationship which gives rise to it."[114]

Once the fiduciary relationship has ended, the potential for conflict between interest and duty (or disloyalty) which underlies the Court's equitable jurisdiction to intervene is no longer there.[115]

11–067 By way of significant exception to this principle, where a fiduciary has resigned office in order to exploit for his own benefit an opportunity, information or property that belongs or ought to be made available to his principal, the exploitation (but not the resignation itself) will amount to a breach of fiduciary duty, notwithstanding that the fiduciary office has terminated.[116]

11–068 Where the fiduciary office continues, fiduciary duties continue to be owed even if the fiduciary's power to act has been circumscribed. Thus a director continues to owe the core duty of loyalty to his company, and continues to be prevented from making an unauthorised profit by reason of his position as such or from the company's property, notwithstanding that an administrative receiver has been appointed.[117] Such an appointment may limit the opportunities to breach that duty, but the duty remains.

11–069 That said, where, exceptionally, a director has, although still formally in office, been excluded entirely from exercising his functions as such by his fellow director(s), there can no longer be a basis for a conflict between his duty to his company and his interest in or duties to a competing company. This was held to be so where, on unusual facts:

> "The Defendant's role as a director of the claimants was throughout the relevant period entirely nominal, not in the sense in which a non-executive director's position might (probably

---

[113] On this and other aspects of limitation, see Ch.25.
[114] *A-G v Blake* [1998] Ch. 439, at 453–454.
[115] *Prince Jefri Bolkiah v KPMG* [1999] 2 A.C. 222, per Lord Millett at 235.
[116] See further para.11–115 below.
[117] *Ultraframe (UK) Ltd v Fielding* [2005] EWHC 1638 (Ch), at [1329].

wrongly) be called nominal but in the concrete sense that he was entirely excluded from all decision-making and all participation in the claimant company's affairs. For all the influence he had, he might as well have resigned."[118]

D.   THE CORE DUTIES

(1)   Overview

As has been noted, the question of which duties are properly characterised as "fiduciary" and what it means to describe them as such is not without difficulty. In *Bristol & West v Mothew* Millett LJ held that only those duties which are "peculiar to fiduciaries and the breach of which attracts legal consequences differing from those consequent upon the breach of other duties"[119] can properly be described as fiduciary duties; but even the seminal analysis in that case admits of some doubt as to what falls within that class. Moreover, there are other duties which almost certainly do not meet this test, but which are nevertheless sometimes described in the authorities as being "fiduciary", including equitable duties owed by fiduciaries in the exercise of their powers, but which do not spring from their core obligation of self-denying loyalty.   **11–070**

This part of this chapter focuses upon the duties that are uncontroversially fiduciary in the strict *Mothew* sense: these are the core proscriptive duties to avoid conflicts of interest and not to profit from the fiduciary office. These are considered both as they arise under the general law and in the modified form that they take under the Companies Act 2006. We also consider their application in the particular context of the diversion of commercial opportunities, a commonly occurring fact pattern in commercial fraud cases.   **11–071**

The following part of this chapter looks at other obligations that have commonly been associated with fiduciaries and sometimes described as being "fiduciary", albeit they do not share many of the distinguishing features of the no conflict and no profit duties. These are: **11–072**

(1)   The good faith/best interests duty, as paradigmatically owed by company directors;
(2)   The equitable constraints that apply to the exercise of powers by fiduciaries (and their analogues in the statutory duties owed by company directors); and
(3)   The trustee-like duties owed with respect to the application of property controlled in a fiduciary capacity.

However, even this tentative division risks giving a false impression that there are clearly-defined duties and that the question is only whether they are properly characterised as being fiduciary or not. In truth, at least outside the paradigm settled cases, the content of the duties is itself flexible and fact sensitive. As it was put by Sales J: **11–073**

---

[118] *In Plus Group Ltd v Pyke* [2002] 2 B.C.L.C. 201, at [90].
[119] *Bristol & West v Mothew* [1998] Ch. 1, at 16C.

"In some contexts, for instance in the paradigm cases described by Lord Browne-Wilkinson, the content of the fiduciary obligations which arise will be reasonably standard and well known, having been worked out in the cases over decades if not centuries. Where a person agrees to be appointed as a company director in ordinary circumstances, for example, the fiduciary obligations which are attached to that role are known, at least in general terms. However, there has always been scope for fiduciary duties to be found to arise in a range of other contexts which have important similarities to the paradigm cases, but also significant differences. In those contexts, it is necessary to examine with some care what is the precise content of the particular fiduciary obligations arising in the specific circumstances of the individual case."[120]

(2) The "Core" Proscriptive Duties: Introduction

11–074　The starting point is the essential fiduciary obligation of loyalty and the subordination of self-interest: *"the principal is entitled to the single-minded loyalty of his fiduciary"*.[121] This finds expression in two core duties or "equitable disabilities",[122] which are "facets" of that underlying obligation.[123] These are:

(1)　The duty not to place oneself in (or allow oneself to remain in) a position in which one's duty conflicts or may conflict with one's personal interests: the "no conflict" duty; and

(2)　The duty not to make an unauthorised profit from one's position as a fiduciary, or from property controlled or information obtained in a fiduciary capacity: the "no profit" duty.

11–075　These are uncontroversially and quintessentially fiduciary duties: they are peculiar to fiduciaries, and they serve the same underlying, prophylactic purpose of ensuring that the fiduciary does not allow his performance of his primary obligations to his principal to be influenced by considerations of self-interest.[124] Both duties are also proscriptive: they do not tell the fiduciary what he should do for his principal; they tell him what he should avoid doing, in order that there is no sensible risk of him acting other than in the best interests of his principal and in accordance with his other (non-fiduciary) duties.[125]

11–076　The no conflict and no profit duties were described in the following terms in a leading Australian case,[126] which has since been cited with approval in a number of English cases[127]:

---

[120] *F&C Alternative Investments Ltd v Barthelemy* [2012] Ch. 613, at [222].

[121] *Bristol & West Building Society v Mothew*, above, at 18.

[122] The characterisation of them as equitable disabilities rather than rules is from *Tito v Waddell* [1977] 1 Ch. 107, per Sir Robert Megarry VC at 248–251. However that is not consistent with Millett LJ's exposition in *Mothew* and was rejected as a valid distinction, at least for the purposes of s.21 of the Limitation Act 1980, in *Gwembe Valley Development Co Ltd v Koshy* [2004] 1 B.C.L.C. 131, at [108].

[123] *Bristol & West v Mothew* [1998] Ch. 1, at 18.

[124] See M. Conaglen, "The Nature and Function of Fiduciary Loyalty" (2005) 121 L.Q.R. 452–480.

[125] *Breen v Williams* (1996) 186 C.L.R. 71; *A-G v Blake* [1998] Ch. 439, at 454.

[126] *Chan (Kak Loui) v Zacharia* 154 C.L.R. 178, at 198–199.

[127] *Don King Productions Inc v Warren* [2000] Ch. 291, at 340H; *Ultraframe (UK) Ltd v Fielding* [2005] EWHC 1638 (Ch), at [1305].

> "The first is that which appropriates for the benefit of the person to whom the fiduciary duty is owed any benefit or gain obtained or received by the fiduciary in circumstances where there existed a conflict of personal interest and fiduciary duty or a significant possibility of such conflict: the objective is to preclude the fiduciary from being swayed by considerations of personal interest. The second is that which requires the fiduciary to account for any benefit or gain obtained or received by reason of or by use of his fiduciary position or of opportunity or knowledge resulting from it: the objective is to preclude the fiduciary from actually misusing his position for his personal advantage."

If the fiduciary breaches these proscriptive duties by allowing other interests (even potentially) to intrude, he is treated as if he had acted for his principal.[128] As a result, these duties attract peculiar remedial consequences: they give rise to equitable remedies that are "primarily restitutionary or restorative rather than compensatory",[129] including in particular rescission (the right at the principal's election to set the relevant transaction aside), the obligation to account for and disgorge unauthorised profit, and proprietary remedies based on constructive trust.[130]
 11–077

The "no conflict" duty extends not just to situations of conflict between the fiduciary's duty to his principal and his personal interest, but also between his duty to his principal and his duty to a third party. In this part of this chapter we consider the duty to avoid a conflict between duty and duty separately from that to avoid a conflict between duty and interest[131]; but they are just different aspects of the same rule.
 11–078

The "no profit" duty was said by Lord Upjohn in *Boardman v Phipps* to be "part of the wider rule that a trustee must not place himself in a position where his duty and his interest may conflict"[132]; but it is generally considered now to operate as a distinct rule.[133] The rationale for the prohibition on a fiduciary profiting from his position may well be that it will commonly put him in a position of conflict between interest and duty; but it appears that the rule can be engaged even absent such a conflict (or the possibility of it), such as where a director of a company has
 11–079

---

[128] Sir Peter Millett, *Equity's Place in the Law of Commerce* (1998) 14 L.Q.R. 214.

[129] *Bristol & West Building Society v Mothew* [1998] Ch. 1, at 18.

[130] See Ch.22 and (for constructive trusts) Ch.9. It would now appear that a dishonest assistance claim can lie against third parties where the underlying claim is that the fiduciary is accountable for profits made in breach of the no conflict or no profit duties; a claim in knowing receipt, in contrast, presupposes some misapplication of "trust" property: see *Novoship (UK) Ltd v Mikhaylyuk* [2015] Q.B. 499, at [90]–[93] (resolving the doubt on the point identified in *Gencor ACP Ltd v Dalby* [2000] 2 B.C.L.C. 734, at [86]–[87]; although note that for these purposes "trust" property can include property with respect to which fiduciary obligations are owed, even if not under a trust properly so-called, and property held on constructive trust).

[131] The Law Commission's 1992 Consultation Paper *Fiduciary Duties and Regulatory Rules* (No.124) treated the duty to avoid a conflict between duty and duty as a third core fiduciary obligation, which it described as the duty of "undivided loyalty". The Law Commission identified a fourth core proscriptive duty, being not to misuse confidential information; but whilst that duty is equitable in origin, it is not fiduciary in the sense with which this chapter is principally concerned (see *Arklow Investments Ltd v Maclean* [2000] 1 W.L.R. 594, at 600).

[132] *Boardman v Phipps* [1967] 2 A.C. 46, at 123.

[133] See e.g. *In Plus Group Ltd v Pyke* [2002] 2 B.C.L.C. 201, at 220; *Ultraframe (UK) Ltd v Fielding* [2005] EWHC 1638 (Ch), at [1305], [1306] and [1318].

resigned office but takes advantage post resignation of a commercial opportunity which came to his attention while he was acting as a director.[134]

11–080 In the case of company directors, the no conflict and no profit duties have been modified in a number of certain important respects by the Companies Act 2006. The relevant statutory provisions are considered below at paras 11–122—11–136.

(3) The Obligation to Avoid Conflicts Between Duty and Interest

11–081 **The Nature of the Obligation.** A fiduciary is obliged not to place himself in (or, if he has come into it inadvertently, allow himself to remain in)[135] a position where his duty to his or her principal conflicts or may conflict with his or her own personal interest:

> "…it is a rule of universal application that no one having [fiduciary] duties to discharge shall be allowed to enter into engagements in which he has or can have a personal interest conflicting or which possibly may conflict with the interest of those whom he is bound to protect."[136]

11–082 This is a "prophylactic" duty, which is concerned with the risk that a fiduciary may be tempted to act contrary to the interests of his principal in breach of other obligations owed to him.

11–083 The duty is engaged not just in cases of actual conflict, but in any case where a reasonable person would regard there as being "a real sensible possibility of conflict".[137] A risk of conflict which is conceivable, but not a significant or real possibility, should not suffice. Nor (obviously) can the duty be engaged where the fiduciary owes no other duty to the principal with respect to a particular dealing with which his self-interest in that dealing could conflict.[138]

11–084 Because the duty is concerned with deterrence, in establishing a breach:

(1) It is not necessary to demonstrate that the fiduciary has in fact breached some other duty owed to the principal by reason of his self-interest;
(2) It is irrelevant that the dealing in question was fair to, or has benefited, the principal[139];
(3) It is also irrelevant that the fiduciary's potentially conflicting interest is not one that the principal could himself have exploited;
(4) It is not necessary to demonstrate that the fiduciary acted in bad faith, let alone dishonestly.

---

[134] See para.11–115 below and *Ultraframe (UK) Ltd v Fielding* [2005] EWHC 1638 (Ch), at [1309].
[135] *In Plus Group Ltd v Pyke* [2002] 2 B.C.L.C. 201, at [86].
[136] *Aberdeen Railway Co v Blaikie Brothers* [1843-60] All E.R. Rep. 249, per Lord Cranworth LC at 252.
[137] *Boardman v Phipps*, above, per Lord Upjohn at 124C.
[138] Hence it not applying to the director who has been entirely excluded from management, such that his duty to the company had "been reduced to vanishing point": *In Plus Group Ltd v Pyke* [2002] 2 B.C.L.C. 201; see para.11–069.
[139] "So strictly is this principle adhered to that no question is allowed to be raised as to the fairness or unfairness of a contract so entered into" *Aberdeen Railway Co v Blaikie Brothers*, above, at 252.

Thus the duty can be breached even in circumstances where the fiduciary has acted in perfectly good faith for the intended and actual benefit of his principal.[140]

Interests which are capable of giving rise to conflicts need not be ones which the fiduciary has directly or personally: they could, for example, be held through a company in which the fiduciary is a shareholder or a partnership of which the fiduciary is a member. In one more recent case it has been suggested (in the context of company directors) that the rule extends to an interest held by any person whose relationship with the fiduciary is such as to create a "real risk of conflict between duty and personal loyalties".[141]

11–085

Self-Dealing and Fair-Dealing. In the context of transactions entered into by trustees and other fiduciaries the duty to avoid a conflict has developed into two sub-rules, known as the rules against "self-dealing" and "fair-dealing".[142] The self-dealing rule is engaged where a fiduciary purchases property that is held on trust or that he or she controls in a fiduciary capacity, such that the fiduciary is effectively on both sides of the transaction[143]; and it entitles the beneficiary to avoid the sale as of right, irrespective of how fair or advantageous to the beneficiary it was. This includes where the fiduciary acts on the purchasing side of the transaction in a representative capacity (such as qua director of the purchasing company). The fair-dealing rule is engaged where a trustee purchases the beneficial interest of a beneficiary, or a fiduciary purchases property with respect to which he or she owes fiduciary obligations from the principal, or otherwise enters into a transaction with the principal which falls within the fiduciary relationship. In that case the beneficiary or principal can have the transaction set aside not as of right, but if the fiduciary (on whom the burden lies) fails to show that he or she took no advantage of his or her position, that full disclosure was made and the transaction was fair and honest.

11–086

In both cases the transaction will not be avoided if entered into with the fully-informed consent of the principal. It may well be that these are not in reality different rules, but simply different applications of the same underlying rule against conflicts to different factual contexts. What is objectionable in both cases is that there is at least a risk of conflict between the fiduciary's duty and his or her interest in the transaction. In both cases the principal ought to be able to have the transaction set aside as of right, subject only to having given their fully informed consent and irrespective of its fairness. The reason why the "fair-dealing" rule has developed what appears to be a more relaxed approach (in allowing the fiduciary to uphold the transaction on the footing that it was fair and honest) is probably not that this is a separate defence, but that in a fair-dealing situation the principal will be party to the transaction and so necessarily will have consented to it. The

11–087

---

[140] *Boardman v Phipps*, above, being a striking example: the solicitor to the trust who took advantage of information obtained in that capacity to bid for further shares in a company in which the trust held shares was accountable for the profit that he made, even though he acted entirely in good faith with a view to improving the value of the trust's shareholding, and that in fact happened.

[141] *Newgate Stud Co v Penfold* [2008] 1 B.C.L.C. 46.

[142] Summarised in *Tito v Waddell (No.2)* [1977] Ch. 106, at 241.

[143] It should be noted that a contract between a fiduciary and him or herself may also be void at common law if it involves a contract to which there is only one party.

fairness and honestly of the dealing will therefore bear evidentially on the question of whether that consent was fully-informed.[144] Conversely, if it could be demonstrated that a principal had provided his or her fully-informed consent to a transaction with the fiduciary that was not fair (in the sense that there was an unequal exchange), that should still provide a defence.[145]

11–088   However, against the elision of the rules is the proposition (which is itself controversial) that they have different remedial consequences: whilst infringement of the fair-dealing rule renders a transaction voidable at the instance of the principal/beneficiary rather than void,[146] there is support for the view that self-dealing goes to the authority of the fiduciary and so renders a transaction void.[147]

(4)   The Obligation to Avoid Conflicts Between Duty and Duty

11–089   A fiduciary is also bound not to place him or herself in (or remain in) a position in which his duty to his principal might conflict with his duty to a third party. That is so irrespective of whether the fiduciary has a personal interest in the dealing in question, since there is still a temptation (albeit possibly a lesser one) to act other than in the best interests of the first principal.[148] This principle may preclude the fiduciary from entering into a particular transaction; but it equally may preclude him from accepting dual employment in the first place.

11–090   As with the duty to avoid a conflict of duty and interest (of which the duty to avoid conflicts between duty and duty is the cognate), it is the potential for conflict that gives rise to the breach[149]; and the informed consent, given with full knowledge of the facts material to the decision to retain the fiduciary despite the potential conflict,[150] is a defence.[151]

11–091   It should be noted that consent to the potential conflict in acting for two principals does not absolve the fiduciary from his duty to act in good faith in the interests of each of his principals.[152] The consent is an answer to the allegation that the very fact of accepting dual employment placed the fiduciary in breach,

---

[144] See J. McGhee, *Snell's Equity*, 33rd edn (London: Sweet & Maxwell, 2014), para.7–022 and the cases cited there.

[145] See, e.g., *Ex p. James* (1803) 8 Ves. 337, at 353: the question is not "whether the price was fair between the trustees and cestui que trust at the time, but, whether a person, who had a confidential situation previously to the purchase, had at the time of the purchase shaken off that character by the consent of the cestui que trust, freely given, after full information."

[146] See e.g. *Johnson v EBS Pensioner Trustees Ltd* [2002] Lloyd's Rep. PN 309 (CA). In *Abacus Trust Co (Isle of Man) v Barr* [2003] Ch. 409, Lightman J expressed the view that breaches of fiduciary duty generally render a transaction voidable (at 421).

[147] *JJ Harrison (Properties) Ltd v Harrison* [2002] 1 B.C.L.C. 162 (CA) and D. O'Sullivan, S. Elliott and R. Zakrzewski, *The Law of Rescission*, 2nd edn (Oxford: OUP, 2015), paras 1.72–1.76; but there are authorities that suggest the contrary: see e.g. *Re Sherman* [1954] Ch. 653; *Holder v Holder* [1968] Ch. 353, at 398, and *Tito v Waddell (No.2)* [1977] Ch. 106, at 241A.

[148] *Ex p. Bennett* (1805) 10 Ves. 381, at 399 (32 E.R. 893, at 899).

[149] *Bristol & West Building Society v Mothew* [1998] Ch. 1, at 18.

[150] *Bristol & West Building Society v Mothew* [1998] Ch. 1, at 19.

[151] *Clark Boyce v Mouat* [1994] 1 A.C. 428, at 435; and see further paras 11–137—11–142 below.

[152] *Bristol & West Building Society v Mothew* [1998] Ch. 1, at 19.

because of the potential for conflict; but it is not an answer to the fiduciary preferring the interests of one principal over the other with respect to a given dealing, or allowing the performance of his obligations towards one principal to be influenced by his relationship with the other. However, breach in such circumstances (being a breach of the duty of good faith) probably requires either dishonesty,[153] or the intentional or conscious favouring of the interests of one of the other (which may be short of dishonesty), rather than doing so incompetently or by unconscious omission.[154] A breach of the latter sort, unrelated to the fact of dual employment, might be a breach of an equitable duty of care, but not of a fiduciary duty.

Further, consent to the dual employment of the fiduciary will not be a defence if **11–092** the fiduciary finds himself in a situation of *actual* conflict between his duties to two principals with respect to a particular transaction.[155] Thus, for example, a solicitor who acts for two parties to a transaction with the consent of both will still be in breach of fiduciary duty if he finds himself in possession of information which his duty to one principal requires him to disclose to that principal, but his duty to the other principal requires him not to.[156] In that circumstance, the fiduciary would be obliged to cease to act.[157] The strictness of this principle may, however, be relaxed where the circumstances of the fiduciary's engagement are such that it could not reasonably be envisaged that he should be disqualified from acting by reason of the conflict, provided that he continues in good faith to advance his principal's interests whilst taking account of the other party to whom he owes duties.[158]

There is old authority for the proposition that there is nothing inherently **11–093** objectionable in a company director becoming engaged, personally or as the director of another company, in a competing business, provided that he does not breach any express restrictive agreement or misuse any confidential information belonging to the first company.[159] However, despite subsequent approval in the House of Lords,[160] the proposition seems to be out of step with the modern law of fiduciary duties as explained in *Bristol & West v Mothew* and a number of more recent cases have doubted it or treated it as "limited".[161] The case may now best be explained as turning on its unusual facts (the director in question appears never to have acted as such in relation to the plaintiff company or attended any

---

[153] As in *Nationwide Building Society v Thimbleby & Co* [1999] P.N.L.R. 733.

[154] *Bristol & West Building Society v Mothew* [1998] Ch. 1, at 19, 21; *Nationwide Building Society v Richard Grosse & Co* [1999] Lloyd's Rep. P.N. 348, at 356.

[155] *Commonwealth Bank of Australia v Smith* 102 A.L.R. 453.

[156] *Moody v Cox and Hatt* [1917] 2 Ch. 71; *Hilton v Barker Booth & Eastwood* [2005] 1 W.L.R. 567.

[157] *Bristol & West Building Society v Mothew* [1998] Ch. 1, at 19.

[158] *Edge v Pensions Ombudsman* [1998] Ch. 512, per Sir Richard Scott VC at 538F–541F; *F&C Alternative Investments (Holdings) Ltd v Barthelemy (No.2)* [2012] Ch. 613, at [228]–[230].

[159] *London & Mashonaland Exploration Co Ltd v New Mashonaland Exploration Co Ltd* [1891] WN 165.

[160] *Bell v Lever Bros Ltd* [1932] A.C. 161, at 193–196.

[161] See particularly *In Plus Group Ltd v Pyke* [2002] 2 B.C.L.C. 201, per Sedley LJ at [79]–[88] (although the other members of the Court of Appeal declined to resolve the controversy: see [75] and [93]). See also *Scottish Co-operative Whoelsale Society Ltd v Meyer* [1959] A.C. 324, per Lord Denning at 368; *Coleman Taymar Ltd v Oakes* [2001] 2 B.C.L.C. 749; *British Midland Tool Ltd v Midland International Tooling Ltd* [2003] 2 B.C.L.C. 523.

board meetings). It is also to be noted that there is now an express prohibition on unauthorised conflicts between duty and duty in the case of directors of companies in the Companies Act 2006: s.175(7).

(5)   The Obligation Not to Profit from the Fiduciary Position

11–094   It is a breach of fiduciary duty to make an unauthorised profit from property that is subject to the fiduciary relationship, or otherwise in the course of the fiduciary relationship or by reason of one's position as a fiduciary. The rule is "that no agent in the course of his agency, in the matter of his agency, can be allowed to make any profit without the knowledge and consent of his principal" and it must be applied "inexorably",[162] being an "inflexible rule of a court of equity".[163]

11–095   It is the fact of profit being made, and the resulting temptation to act other than in the best interests of the principal, that gives rise to the breach; accordingly:

(1)   It is irrelevant that the fiduciary acted honestly, in good faith, openly and in what he thought were the best interests of the principal[164];

(2)   It is also irrelevant whether the principal could have obtained the profit for himself[165];

(3)   The principal does not need to establish that he has suffered a loss.[166] The Court "is not entitled ... to receive evidence, or suggestion, or argument as to whether the principal did or did not suffer any injury in fact by reason of the dealing of the agent".[167]

11–096   This was encapsulated by Lord Russell of Killowen in *Regal (Hastings) Ltd v Gulliver*, as follows[168]:

> "The rule of equity which insists on those, who by use of a fiduciary position make a profit, being liable to account for that profit, in no way depends on fraud, or absence of bona fides; or on such questions or considerations as whether the profit would or should otherwise have gone to the plaintiff, or whether the profiteer was under a duty to obtain the source of the profit for the plaintiff, or whether he took a risk or acted as he did for the benefit of the plaintiff, or whether the plaintiff has in fact been damaged or benefited by his action. The liability arises from the mere fact of a profit having, in the stated circumstances, been made."

---

[162] *Parker v MacKenna* (1874) 10 Ch.App 96, per James LJ at 124.

[163] *Bray v Ford* [1896] A.C. 44, HL, 51–2.

[164] *Regal (Hastings) Ltd v Gulliver* [1967] 2 A.C. 134, at 153; *Murad v Al-Saraj* [2005] EWCA Civ 959, at [83] and [121]–[122] *Wrexham Associated Football Club Ltd v Crucialmove Ltd* [2006] EWCA Civ 237, at [51].

[165] Thus in *Keech v Sandford* (1726) Sel Cas Ch 61; 25 E.R. 223 the trustee was not able to secure a renewal of the lease (which was held on trust) on behalf of the infant beneficiary, and so he acquired it himself, intending to pass it on to the beneficiary subsequently. Nevertheless, "the trustee is the only person of all mankind who might not have the lease", per Lord King LC, at 223.

[166] *Regal (Hastings) Ltd v Gulliver* [1967] 2 A.C. 134, at 154.

[167] *Parker v MacKenna*, above, at 124.

[168] *Regal (Hastings) Ltd v Gulliver* [1967] 2 A.C. 134, at 144–145.

However, because it is the risk of the fiduciary being influenced to act other than in accordance with his or her duties that underlies the rule, it is thought that it is not engaged where the fiduciary profits involuntarily.[169] **11–097**

The precise ambit of the rule is not clear. It is plainly engaged where the fiduciary takes personal advantage of property held in a fiduciary capacity: thus a solicitor who earned interest on money held for the benefit of his clients was liable to account to the clients for it.[170] Similarly, a trustee of a lease could not renew the lease for his own benefit,[171] the renewed lease being treated as a continuation of the old one and the transaction thus amounting to the trustee benefiting personally from the trust property. The rule also applies (on Court of Appeal authority) to the purchase of the reversion, even though this is not in the same way part of the trust property, because it may still involve profiting from the trust estate or the position of trustee.[172] The same is true of a contract entered into by a partnership that is then renewed in the name of one partner alone[173]; and likewise a contract entered into by a company which is then taken over by its directors.[174] **11–098**

Use of the fiduciary's position to profit in other ways (short of the exploitation of property belonging to the principal) will also infringe the rule: a trustee who procured the employment of his firm to value the trust securities breached the rule,[175] as did a trustee who used the trust shares to vote himself in as a director of the company, for which he was remunerated,[176] and a director who received a bonus for procuring the supply by a company in which he was interested as a shareholder of ice to a company of which he was director.[177] **11–099**

Receipt of a bribe or secret commission will also involve a breach of the rule, since it involves an unauthorised profit obtained by reason from the fiduciary's position as such. The topic of bribes is considered in more detail in Ch.7. It suffices to note here that, in addition to the other bases on which the fiduciary may be liable and the bribe may be recovered, the fiduciary will owe an obligation to account for it by reason of the breach of the no profit rule (and, in all likelihood, also the rule against conflict between duty and interest).[178] On that basis of liability, the honest intentions of the fiduciary and of the payer of the bribe are irrelevant.[179] **11–100**

---

[169] *Re Northcote's Will Trusts* [1949] 1 All E.R. 442, at 443.

[170] *Brown v Inland Revenue Commissioners* [1965] A.C. 244.

[171] *Keech v Sandford*, above; see also *Re Biss* [1903] 2 Ch. 40, at 61.

[172] *Protheroe v Protheroe* [1968] 1 W.L.R. 519; but not so where the acquisition of the reversion came about as a result of some other interest or right and not because of the fiduciary's position as such: *Ward v Brunt* [2000] W.T.L.R. 731, at 749.

[173] *Lindsley v Woodfull* [2004] 2 B.C.L.C. 131.

[174] *Quarter Master UK Ltd v Pyke* [2005] 1 B.C.L.C. 245. We consider in the next subsection the liability of directors for the exploitation of "maturing" business opportunities more generally.

[175] *Williams v Barton* [1927] 2 Ch. 9.

[176] *Re Macadam* [1946] Ch. 73.

[177] *Boston Deep Sea Fishing & Ice Co v Ansell* (1888) 39 Ch.D. 339, at 355.

[178] *FHR European Ventures LLP v Cedar Capital Partners LLC* [2014] UKSC 45; [2015] A.C. 250.

[179] *Boston Deep Sea Fishing & Ice Co v Ansell* (1888) 39 Ch.D. 339, at 369; *Ross River Ltd v Cambridge City Football Club Ltd* [2007] EWHC 2115 (Ch), at [218].

(6)   The Core Duties Applied: The Diversion of Commercial Opportunities

11–101   The application of the above rules in the context of the exploitation of commercial opportunities that were or may have been of interest to the principal is of particular relevance to commercial fraud. Commonly this arises with directors who divert for their own benefit or that of a company in which they are interested a "maturing business opportunity", which either was being pursued by, or ought properly to have been disclosed to, the company to which they owe their duties as directors. In that context, reference must now be made to the duties set out in the Companies Act 2006 (as to which, see paras 11–122—11–136 below); but the underlying principles derived from the cases remain relevant to understanding and applying the statutory duties, and, in any event, the principles apply to fiduciaries more generally.

11–102   Clearly a fiduciary who has been charged with acquiring property or negotiating the acquisition of property on behalf of his principal (be it a company or otherwise) will breach his fiduciary duty if he acquires it for himself: in such a case the fiduciary will hold the property on trust for the principal and be amenable to an order requiring him or her to transfer it in specie (albeit he may be entitled to an allowance as against the principal for his outlay in acquiring the property).[180]

11–103   But fiduciary duties will also preclude a director, agent or other fiduciary from exploiting for his own benefit property or the benefit of a contract in circumstances where he was not specifically charged by the principal with obtaining it. The clearest such cases are those where the opportunity in question was something which the fiduciary's principal was itself contemplating pursuing. In the leading case of *Regal (Hastings) Ltd v Gulliver*[181] a company was proposing to subscribe for shares in a subsidiary that would then be used to acquire and dispose of certain cinemas, and the directors of the company instead subscribed for the shares themselves. They did so in good faith, and because the company was unable to finance the whole subscription itself; but they were nevertheless liable to account for profits made on a disposal of their shares. The basis for liability was that the directors took for themselves the very property which the company was proposing to (but in the event was unable to) acquire.

11–104   In *Industrial Development Consultants Ltd v Cooley*[182] the defendant director was appointed by the claimant construction company because of his contacts with certain gas boards, and he entered into correspondence with one particular board with a view to the company being engaged to design and construct some new depots. That proposition in the event came to nothing; but a little over a year later a new executive of the gas board in question approached the defendant director privately and informed him that the board was again looking to engage someone to design and construct new depots, that the work was urgent and that a certain capital sum would be involved. The defendant secured his release from the

---

[180] See paras 9–069—9–072.
[181] *Regal (Hastings) Ltd v Gulliver* [1967] 2 A.C. 134.
[182] *Industrial Development Consultants Ltd v Cooley* [1972] 1 W.L.R. 443, at 451G.

claimant company and obtained the relevant contracts personally. It was held that he was liable to account to the claimant for the profits made under the contracts obtained. Although the information about the potential contracts came to his attention in the course of a meeting which he purportedly attended in a "private" capacity, it was nevertheless information which "came to him while he was managing director and…was of concern to the [claimant] and was relevant for the [claimant] to know", such that it was his duty to pass it on.[183] What seems to have made the opportunity one which it was his duty to pass on to his company was that the contracts were in substance for the same design and construction work as the company (through the defendant) had unsuccessfully tendered for the year before. The fact that the claimant could not be shown as a matter of causation to have lost out on the contracts was irrelevant.

Similarly, liability for the diversion of corporate opportunities arose in *CMS Dolphin Ltd v Simonet*[184] because the defendant director appropriated to a new company in which he was separately interested the benefit of existing advertising contracts with clients of the claimant company and the maturing opportunity to enter into new advertising contracts with those clients. There was found to be a continuum between the work which the new company undertook for those clients and that which had been undertaken by the claimant, such that the former effectively "stepped into the shoes" of the latter; and to the extent that there were not already contracts in place for that work with the claimant, the preparatory work for the new contracts taken by the defendant's vehicle had been done by the claimant. Further, the defendant was held to have taken advantage of confidential information about the clients, their projects and their contracts, which belonged to the claimant company and which went beyond the defendant's own "fund of know-how".[185]   **11–105**

Canadian Aero Service Ltd v O'Malley[186] involved a similar sort of corporate opportunity to that which was the subject of the *CMS Dolphin* case: there the defendant directors secured for their own benefit a contract with the Canadian Government for mapping and aerial photography services, for which the claimant company had been negotiating and in the preparations for which the defendant directors had been intimately involved. Other cases along these lines include *Lindsley v Woodfull*,[187] which concerned the entry by one partner into a contract for which that partner had been negotiating on behalf of the partnership, and *Quarter Master UK Ltd v Pyke*,[188] in which two directors and their company took over and continued for their own benefit a contract which had previously been performed by their company for the benefit of another company.   **11–106**

The rule can also be engaged where the relevant opportunity is neither an existing contract with the principal nor one which the principal was pursuing. Thus in   **11–107**

---

[183] *Industrial Development Consultants Ltd v Cooley* [1972] 1 W.L.R. 443, at 451G.
[184] *CMS Dolphin Ltd v Simonet* [2001] 1 B.C.L.C. 704.
[185] *CMS Dolphin* [2001] 1 B.C.L.C. 704, at [129]–[130].
[186] *Canadian Aero Service Ltd v O'Malley* (1973) 40 D.L.R. (3d) 371.
[187] *Lindsley v Woodfull* [2004] 2 B.C.L.C. 131.
[188] *Quarter Master UK Ltd v Pyke* [2005] 1 B.C.L.C. 245.

Cook v Deeks[189] three directors were held liable to account for profits derived from a railway construction contract entered into through their own separate corporate vehicle, despite that not being a contract for which the company to which they owed their duties was negotiating. The new contract nevertheless constituted "business which should properly belong to the company they represent".[190] The basis for this appears to have been: (a) the contract was for the construction of a railway line and the company had been formed for the purpose of undertaking railway construction work; (b) the new contract was with a particular client, for whom the company had previously constructed numerous other railway lines under similar contracts, and it in that sense represented a continuation of the business of the company with that client; (c) the defaulting directors appear to have negotiated for the new contract in part on the footing that the company would take it; and (d) they caused the company to accelerate its work on an existing contract with the client in order to improve their prospects of winning the new contract. There was therefore a substantial connection between the new contract and the existing business of the company.

11–108   *Bhullar v Bhullar*[191] was similarly a case in which the opportunity in question—to acquire an investment property—could not properly be described as an opportunity of the claimant company, in that it was not one which the company had itself been pursuing. But the acquisition of the property by the defendant directors (through another company) was said to breach their fiduciary duties because "it would have been 'worthwhile' for the company to have acquired the property".[192] So stated, the reasoning in the case would appear to broaden considerably the scope for fixing liability in the exploitation of a corporate opportunity. However, while the reasons why it would have been "worthwhile" for the company to acquire the property were not elaborated upon, it is clear that it was not the mere fact that profitable use of the opportunity might have been made by the company that gave rise to liability. There were the additional features that the company was in the business of buying commercial property, and held one other investment property already; that the acquisition property was adjacent to that investment property; and, moreover, that the acquisition property was used in part by tenants of the company's existing investment property. There was, accordingly, an obvious connection, and potential synergy, between the company's existing portfolio and the property acquired by the defaulting directors.

11–109   Similarly, *Crown Dilmun v Sutton*[193] concerned a company which engaged in property development activity, and the subject of complaint was an opportunity to participate in a new development of which the company was unaware and which it had not been actively pursuing. Nevertheless the diversion of that opportunity to a company in which the defendant director was interested was a breach of fiduciary duty giving rise to a liability to account, because: (a) the property deal was "of the type" that the company engaged in; (b) it was with a counterparty

---

[189] *Cook v Deeks* [1916] A.C. 554.
[190] *Cook v Deeks* [1916] A.C. 554, at 563.
[191] *Bhullar v Bhullar* [2003] 2 B.C.L.C. 241.
[192] *Bhullar v Bhullar* [2003] 2 B.C.L.C. 241, at [41].
[193] *Crown Dilmun v Sutton* [2004] 1 B.C.L.C. 468.

with whom the company had a successful existing relationship; and (c) the opportunity had been offered by that counterparty in confidence to the director because of (amongst other things) that existing corporate relationship.[194]

The "line of business" approach to the conflict question can also be seen in the Scottish case of *Commonwealth Oil and Gas Co Ltd v Baxter*,[195] where a director pursued through another company an offshore oil project in Azerbaijan. The claimant company was not itself engaged in or pursuing offshore projects, but it was engaged in the oil business in the region and was pursuing further oil opportunities in Azerbaijan. The defendant director's attempt to distinguish between the claimant's onshore line of business and the offshore nature of this opportunity was therefore rejected; in the circumstances:

11–110

> "a reasonable person would have thought that there was a real sensible possibility that the opportunity ... would have been commercially attractive to [the claimant]".[196]

It bears emphasis, however, that it is not a requirement for a breach of fiduciary duty to be established that the commercial opportunity should be one in the same "line of business" as that of the principal, just as it is not a requirement that the opportunity should be one which the principal was actively pursuing; other circumstances may justify the application of the rules considered in this chapter. An example is *O'Donnell v Shanahan*,[197] where the Court of Appeal (reversing the Deputy Judge on the very point) held that directors of a company which carried on business in the provision of business advice and assistance were liable for exploiting an opportunity to acquire an investment property, notwithstanding that: (a) investing in property was outside the scope of the company's existing business; and the directors had been allowed to pursue other property investment activities on their own account without complaint. The reason was that the company, despite operating in quite a different "line of business", had been acting as effectively an estate agent on behalf of the vendor of the property in question and, in that context and acting on the company's behalf, the defendant directors had acquired knowledge about the availability of the property when the intended sale fell through, its value and its potential for development. The liability therefore arose from their use of valuable information which quite clearly came to them in their capacity as directors of the company and which, absent fully informed consent, they were obliged to deploy for the company's benefit rather than their own.

11–111

It is difficult and probably artificial to seek to draw out a single unifying theme in these and other business opportunity cases. There are dicta to the effect that the basis of the fiduciary's liability is that the opportunity itself constitutes an intangible asset which belongs in equity to the principal[198]; but it is respectfully suggested that it is difficult to characterise an opportunity as being something in

11–112

---

[194] *Crown Dilmun v Sutton* [2004] 1 B.C.L.C. 468, at [56].

[195] *Commonwealth Oil and Gas Co Ltd v Baxter* [2009] CSIH 75.

[196] *Commonwealth Oil and Gas Co Ltd v Baxter* [2009] CSIH 75, at [81].

[197] *O'Donnell v Shanahan* [2009] BCC 822.

[198] *Brown v Bennett* [1999] BCC 525; *CMS Dolphin Ltd v Simonet* [2001] 1 B.C.L.C. 704, at [96]; *Woodfull v Lindsley* [2004] 2 B.C.L.C. 131, at 139, 140.

which there can be proprietary interests, properly so-called.[199] The better view, at least in cases where the fiduciary remains in office, is probably simply that liability arises because the circumstances of the case are such that the exploitation of the opportunity by the principal gives rise to a sensible possibility of conflict. As it was expressed by Jonathan Parker LJ in *Bhullar v Bhullar*[200]:

> "In a case such as the present, where a fiduciary has exploited a commercial opportunity for his own benefit, the relevant question, in my judgment, is not whether the party to whom the duty is owed (the company, in the instant case) had some kind of beneficial interest in the opportunity: in my judgment that would be too formalistic and restrictive an approach. Rather, the question is simply whether the fiduciary's exploitation of the opportunity is such as to attract the application of the rule [against conflicts between interest and duty]."

11–113 At the risk of unduly circumscribing the application of an equitable principle whose flexibility is of the essence, it is suggested that the exploitation of a commercial opportunity will "attract the application of the rule" in circumstances where:

(1) the opportunity was something which the principal was itself pursuing;

(2) the opportunity, albeit not something that the principal was pursuing, nevertheless came to the attention of the fiduciary by reason of or in the course of his fiduciary office; or

(3) the existence of the opportunity was information which would have been "relevant for the company to know"[201] or "of concern"[202] to the principal, because of some sensible connection between that information and the business of the principal.

Plainly the second and third points are closely related, since it may often be the connection between the opportunity and the affairs of the principal that leads to the conclusion the information was acquired in the course of the fiduciary's role as such: thus Lord Macmillan encapsulated the test as being:

> "that what the directors did was so related to the affairs of the company that it can properly be said to have been done in the course of their management and in utilisation of their opportunities and special knowledge as directors"[203].

---

[199] See the observations of Lewison LJ in the Court of Appeal in *FHR European Ventures LLP v Mankarious* [2013] 3 W.L.R. 466, at [57].

[200] *Bhullar v Bhullar* [2003] 2 B.C.L.C. 241, at [28].

[201] *Bhullar v Bhullar* [2003] 2 B.C.L.C. 241, at [41].

[202] *Industrial Development Consultants Ltd v Cooley* [1972] 1 W.L.R. 443, at 451G.

[203] *Regal (Hastings) Ltd v Gulliver* [1967] 2 A.C. 134, at 153. For that reason it did not avail the Defendants in *Industrial Development Consultants Ltd v Cooley* [1972] 1 W.L.R. 443 or *Bhullar v Bhullar* [2003] 2 B.C.L.C. 241 to say that the information came to them in a private capacity: at the material times they had only one relevant capacity, that of directors of the claimant companies. See *Cooley*, at 451G; and *Bhullar*, at [41]. See also the factors identified in *Foster Bryant Surveying Ltd v Bryant* [2007] Bus LR 1565, at [8(8)].

But in no case is it necessary to demonstrate that the opportunity could or in fact would have been exploited by the principal.[204]

There may also be a separate (but overlapping) basis for liability if in exploiting the opportunity the fiduciary makes use of confidential information or property belonging to the principal, beyond the "stock-in-trade" of knowledge and business connections that he or she has acquired as a director and is free to use after ceasing to be.[205] But it is not necessary, to establish liability for breach of the no conflict or no profit rule, to demonstrate that confidential information or special knowledge acquired by the director as such has been misused.[206]

11–114

As we have already noted, ordinarily fiduciary obligations last only so long as the fiduciary holds the position that gives rise to them[207]; but in the context of the exploitation of corporate opportunities an anti-avoidance principle has developed to the effect that a director or other fiduciary who resigns office in order to exploit an opportunity which is being pursued by, or ought to be disclosed to, his principal is still treated as being in breach of fiduciary duty.[208] The question (at common law) was whether the resignation "can fairly be said to have been prompted or influenced by a wish to acquire for himself the opportunity".[209] In this respect, at least, the duty appears to be capable of being breached even though the possibility of conflict between interest and duty has been removed. Since the power of resignation is not itself fiduciary in character (a director can resign in accordance with the company's constitution even if doing so will damage the company's interests),[210] the basis of liability in the post-resignation cases may best be understood as being that the exploitation of the information or opportunity which the fiduciary acquired before resignation, and in the course of or by reason of his fiduciary position, infringes the no profit rule.[211] As noted in

11–115

---

[204] In *Industrial Development Consultants Ltd v Cooley* [1972] 1 W.L.R. 443 it was found that there was at most a 10% chance of the company securing the contract in question for itself, and an award of damages would only have compensated it for the loss of that chance; nevertheless, the director was fully accountable for the profit made.

[205] As in *CMS Dolphin Ltd v Simonet* [2001] 1 B.C.L.C. 704; see [129]–[130].

[206] *Canadian Aero Service Ltd v O'Malley* (1973) 40 D.L.R. (3d) 371, at 388, 390.

[207] *A-G v Blake* [1998] Ch. 439, at 453.

[208] *Industrial Development Consultants Ltd v Cooley* [1972] 1 W.L.R. 443; *Canadian Aero Service Ltd v O'Malley* (1973) 40 D.L.R. (3d) 371; *CMS Dolphin Ltd v Simonet* [2001] 1 B.C.L.C. 704; see also now s.170(2) of the Companies Act 2006. Contrast *Island Export Finance Ltd v Umunna* [1986] B.C.L.C. 460, where it was found that the resignation was not prompted by a desire to exploit the opportunity.

[209] *Canadian Aero Service Ltd v O'Malley* (1973) 40 D.L.R (3d) 371, at 382; see also *CMS Dolphin Ltd v Simonet* [2001] 1 B.C.L.C. 704, at [2], and *Foster Bryant Surveying Ltd v Bryant* [2007] Bus LR 1565, at [8(7)]. In the former case it appears to be suggested that post-resignation liability might arise in the alternative ("or") if "it was his position with the company rather than a fresh initiative that led him to the opportunity"; but for the reasons given by Lawrence Collins J in *CMS Dolphin*, at [91], it is thought that the "or" in the relevant passage in the judgment in *Canadian Aero* should be an "and". Note that Lewison J appears to have thought otherwise in *Ultraframe (UK) Ltd v Fielding* [2005] EWHC 1638 (Ch), at [1339]; and the position under s.170(2)(a) of the Companies Act 2006 appears to be that it is no longer necessary to show that the resignation was influenced by the wish to exploit the opportunity.

[210] *CMS Dolphin Ltd v Simonet* [2001] 1 B.C.L.C. 704, at [87].

[211] See *Quarter Master UK Ltd v Pyke* [2005] 1 B.C.L.C. 245, per Paul Morgan QC, at 264.

the following section, in the case of directors subject to the Companies Act 2006, this is now the subject of express statutory provision.

11–116 It is to be noted that, short of this (and absent the exploitation of property belonging to the principal), it is not a breach of fiduciary duty for a director or partner who resigns from his position to compete with his former principal.

(7) Profit Made By/Opportunity Diverted to a Company or Partnership

11–117 A fiduciary can be personally accountable for profit not made personally and directly, but by a company which he controls or in which he has a substantial interest.[212] Otherwise, of course, the fiduciary could side-step the rule by the utilisation of a corporate entity to acquire the opportunity diverted. Certainly profit made by a company (or any third party) may on the proper analysis be held as nominee or trustee for the fiduciary, in which case it is the fiduciary's profit. On more extreme facts, it may be possible to pierce the corporate veil and treat the company as being the alter ego of the fiduciary under the "evasion" principle[213]; although cases which appear to have been decided on that basis in the past may now, following the Supreme Court's rationalisation of the law on piercing of the corporate veil in *Prest v Petrodel Resources Ltd*, be better explained as cases where the company was the fiduciary's nominee or trustee.[214] A fiduciary will also be accountable where profits are received by a company and he receives the benefit of them indirectly by, for example, the consequent increase in the value of his shareholding.[215]

11–118 In all such cases the fiduciary is in fact accounting for his own profit. What is more controversial is whether the fiduciary can be accountable for profit made by a company (or indeed any other third person) with which he has some association absent such circumstances. In *CMS Dolphin Ltd v Simonet* Lawrence Collins J was prepared to find that the defaulting director was accountable for profits made by the company to which the relevant commercial opportunities had ultimately been diverted on the broader basis that the company was "formed … to take unlawful advantage of the business opportunities" and had "jointly participated in the breach of trust".[216] This was expressly not on the basis that the company was the director's alter ego. That decision has since proved controversial and in *Ultraframe (UK) Ltd v Fielding* it was held that the fact that a fiduciary had a substantial interest in a company which received the relevant profit did not (in

---

[212] E.g. *Ross River Ltd v Waverly Commercial Ltd* [2012] EWHC 81 (Ch), per Morgan J at [263], upheld on appeal [2013] EWCA Civ 910.

[213] This was the stated basis on which receipt of a profit by a company was treated as receipt by the fiduciary in *Trustor AB v Smallbone (No. 2)* [2001] 1 W.L.R. 1177 and in *Gencor ACP Ltd v Dalby* [2000] 2 B.C.L.C. 734. Piercing the corporate veil is considered in Ch.18.

[214] See Lord Sumption JSC's analysis of *Gencor ACP Ltd v Dalby* in *Prest v Petrodel Resources Ltd* [2013] 2 A.C. 415, at [31].

[215] *Gwembe Valley Development Co Ltd v Koshy* [2004] 1 B.C.L.C. 131, at [137]; *Aerostar Maintenance International Ltd v Wilson* [2010] EWHC 2032 (Ch), at [201]–[207].

[216] [2001] 1 B.C.L.C. 704, at [103].

itself) make the fiduciary personally accountable.[217] In so doing, Lewison J followed *Regal (Hastings) Ltd v Gulliver*,[218] in which the defendant director was held not liable to account for the profits made by two companies which exploited the relevant opportunity (by subscribing for shares), despite his having an interest in those companies, on the basis that it was not established at trial that he had in fact profited through that interest.

The decision in *CMS Dolphin v Simonet* that the director was personally accountable may nevertheless be right; but it is respectfully suggested that this is not because of a joint accounting liability between the director and the company in which he was interested, but rather because the director had in fact originally profited from the relevant opportunity directly (in a partnership, as to which see the following paragraph) and had subsequently transferred the diverted business to the company. Clearly that further transaction could not affect the fiduciary's original liability for receipt of the entire profit.[219] (Of course, the company in such a case might, depending on the facts, be separately liable for dishonest assistance in the fiduciary's breach of duty and/or in knowing receipt, as discussed below.) **11-119**

Where a fiduciary is a partner in a partnership and the profit in respect of the diverted opportunity is shared with his partners, clearly the fiduciary should be accountable for (at least) his own share of that profit. But there would appear to be a principle that in such a case the fiduciary should be accountable for the *whole* of the profit made by the partnership from the relevant dealing and not just his partnership share (and irrespective of whether the other partners are also liable).[220] This may be rationalised on the basis that the fact that the fiduciary has chosen to share the profit made by reason of the breach (and that would have otherwise have been received by him entirely) with his partners should not affect his liability. The same has been held to apply where the profit is diverted to a joint venture, rather than a partnership in the legal sense.[221] **11-120**

The company or partnership to which the profit is diverted or by which an opportunity is exploited may also have a liability to account. It has been said that this is because they are jointly liable with the fiduciary for the latter's breach of trust or fiduciary duty[222]; but it is suggested that the sounder basis for third party liability would be either (in the case of the partners) vicarious liability for acts of their fellow partner or (in either case) knowing receipt and/or dishonest assistance **11-121**

---

[217] *Ultraframe (UK) Ltd v Fielding* [2005] EWHC 1638 (Ch), at [1575]–[1576]. A number of subsequent decisions have expressed sympathy with Lewson J's criticism of the reasoning in *CMS Dolphin Ltd v Simonet* [2001] 1 B.C.L.C. 704: see e.g. *Fiona Trust Holding Corp v Privalov* [2007] EWHC 1217 (Comm), at [29]; *National Grid Electricity Transmission Plc v McKenzie Harbour Management Resources Ltd* [2009] EWHC 1817 (Ch), at [117]; and *Novoship (UK) Ltd v Mikhaylyuk* [2012] EWHC 3586 (Comm), at [99]–[100].

[218] *Regal (Hastings) Ltd v Gulliver* [1967] 2 A.C. 134.

[219] See at [131].

[220] *Imperial Mercantile Credit Association v Coleman* (1873) L.R. 6 HL 189; *CMS Dolphin Ltd v Simonet* [2001] 1 B.C.L.C. 704, at [99].

[221] *National Grid Electricity Transmission Plc v McKenzie Harbour Management Resources Ltd* [2009] EWHC 1817 (Ch), at [118].

[222] *CMS Dolphin Ltd v Simonet* [2001] 1 B.C.L.C. 704, at [103].

in the underlying breach (as to which, see Chs 12 and 13).[223] Joint participation in a breach of trust or fiduciary duty is not a cause of action known to English law.[224] It may also be that the facts could justify making an order for relief against the company on the footing that the principal has an independent right against the fiduciary and the company has been interposed to defeat that right or frustrate its enforcement: the so-called "evasion principle", which involves piercing the corporate veil in the true sense.[225]

(8) The No Conflict and No Profit Duties as they Appear in the Companies Act 2006

11–122 The no conflict and no profit duties as they apply to directors are now contained (principally) in ss.175–177 of the Companies Act 2006. It is provided in s.170 of the Act that:

(1) The duties set out in these sections (and otherwise in ss.171–177) are "based on certain common law rules and equitable principles as they apply in relation to directors and have effect in place of those rules and principles as regards the duties owed to a company by a director"; and

(2) They are to be "interpreted and applied in the same way as common law rules or equitable principles, and regard shall be had to the corresponding common law rules and equitable principles in interpreting and applying" them.

11–123 The first proposition means that, except in those cases where it appears from the Act that a common law duty is preserved, claimants will now need to plead and prove breaches of the duties as set out in the Act rather than the common law rules or equitable principles from which they are derived. The one place where the statue explicitly preserves a non-statutory duty (or aspect of a duty) is s.172(3), pertaining to the duty to consider or act in the interests of creditors of the company (see paras 11–160—11–165 below). It may be that common law duties and equitable rules which are not reflected at all in the statutory general duties are also preserved.

11–124 The second proposition means: (a) that existing case law on the common law rules and the equitable duties applicable to directors will remain relevant to the interpretation and application of the stautory duties [226] (b) the Courts will be able to take into account continuing developments in "corresponding" common law and equitable rules and principles in the interpretation and application of the

---

[223] This appears to have been the basis for the company's liability in *Cook v Deeks* [1916] A.C. 554, at 565.

[224] See *Ultraframe (UK) Ltd v Fielding* [2005] EWHC 1638 (Ch), at [1574].

[225] See *Prest v Petrodel Resources Ltd* [2013] 2 A.C. 415, at [28]. This appears to have been the basis on which the company was found liable as a constructive trustee in *Pennyfeathers Ltd v Pennyfeathers Property Co Ltd* [2013] EWHC 3530 (Ch), at [118].

[226] It has been said that the Companies Act duties "extract and express the essence of the rules and principles which they have replaced": *Towers v Premier Waste Management Ltd* [2011] EWCA Civ 923.

statutory duties. The "corresponding" rules and principles are presumably intended to be the rules and principles of trusts and agency, from which or by analogy with which the duties of directors have developed. What this fails to recognise, however, is that there are some respects in which the statutory duties clearly differ from the rules and principles which they replace—the no conflict and no profit duties being a good example.

These duties find expression in the Act in three sets of rules: **11–125**

(1)   First, rules governing transactions between the director and company, which are in effect all concerned with "self-dealing" (the director being on both sides of the transaction). These are to be found in s.175(3), s.177 and s.182 of the Act, and in Ch.4 of Pt 10 of the Act;

(2)   Secondly, a prohibition on the personal exploitation of company property, information and opportunities, found in s.175(1) and (2) of the Act; and

(3)   Thirdly, a prohibition on receipt of benefits from third parties in exchange for the exercise of directorial powers: s.176 of the Act.

(i)   Self-dealing

The most striking difference between the rules for dealing with conflicts of interest under the Act and under the general law is that, in the case of transactions or arrangements with the company (self-dealing transactions), the Act generally requires only that the director's interest should be disclosed. In contrast, under the general law (as has been seen above) fiduciaries are not obliged to make such disclosure; rather, they are obliged to refrain from acting at all, and disclosure coupled with informed consent provides a basis on which they can legitimately do so. **11–126**

By s.175(3) of the Act, the duty provided for in s.175(1) to avoid a situation in which the director has, or can have, a direct or indirect interest that conflicts, or possibly may conflict, with the interests of the company is disapplied in relation to transactions or arrangements with the company. Instead, a director who is in any way, directly or indirectly, interested in a proposed transaction or arrangement with the company must declare the nature and extent of that interest to the other directors before the transaction or arrangement is entered into (ss.177(1) and (4)). The declaration can be made at a meeting of directors, or by a notice as provided for in ss.184 and 185 of the Act. A declaration is not required where the director is not (and ought not reasonably to be) aware of the interest or of the transaction or arrangement (s.177(5)), or if the interest could not reasonably be regarded as likely to give rise to a conflict or the other directors are already aware of it (s.177(6)).[227] **11–127**

Provided that these declaration requirements are met, the relevant transaction or arrangement is not liable to be set aside by virtue of any common law rule or equitable principle requiring the consent or approval of the members of the company, subject to contrary provision in any enactment or in the company's **11–128**

---

[227] The subsection also has a carve-out for conflicts arising out of the terms of the director's service contract.

constitution.[228] Failure to make the required declaration will, on ordinary principles, make the transaction voidable at the election of the company (subject to third party rights): the consequences of breach of the duties set out in ss.171–177 of the Act are the same as would apply if the corresponding common law rule or equitable principle applied, and in all but the case of the statutory duty of care in s.174, are enforceable "in the same way as any other fiduciary duty owed to a company by its directors".[229] For further consideration of remedies, see Ch.22.

11–129   There is a separate statutory rule (in s.182 of the Act) requiring a declaration of the nature and extent of a director's direct or indirect interest in a transaction or arrangement that has already been entered into by the company, which must (rather than may) be done either at a meeting of directors, or by a notice as provided for in ss.184 and 185 of the Act. Because this is not one of the general duties covered by s.178 of the Act, the only consequence of breach of this is the criminal sanction provided for by s.183 of the Act.

11–130   Sections 177 and 182 are not, however, a complete code governing self-dealing transactions; in fact, many such transactions are likely to fall within the more exacting provisions of Ch.4 (and 4A) of Pt 10 of the Act, which govern (in summary) substantial property transactions, loans and like transactions, and particular aspects of directors' service contracts/remuneration. For transactions within the scope of these provisions, approval (at shareholder level) is generally required; and the consequences of non-compliance, including as to the validity of the transaction and the liability of the director, are spelled out. A detailed analysis of these provisions is beyond the scope of this work.

(ii)   Exploitation of property etc.

11–131   The governing rule in s.175(1) is that a director

> "must avoid a situation in which he has, or can have, a direct or indirect interest that conflicts, or possibly may conflict, with the interests of the company".

As under the general law, a conflict of interest is taken to include a conflict of interest and duty and a conflict of duties (s.175(7)). Given the carving out of self-dealing transactions considered above, the principal (but not exclusive) application of this prohibition is to the exploitation of company property, information or opportunities, as is recognised by s.175(2).

11–132   The duty under s.175(1) is not infringed if either the situation "cannot reasonably be regarded as likely to give rise to a conflict of interest" or the matter has been authorised by the directors, in the latter case discounting the interested directors for the purposes of determining quorum and votes (s.176(6)).

---

[228] Section 180. Where the articles do stipulate that approval is required, a failure to obtain it will render the transaction voidable: *Hely-Hutchinson v Brayhead Ltd* [1968] 1 Q.B. 549. In contrast, where the complaint is that the transaction has been entered into by the wrong body of the company (a committee of the board rather than the full board), the transaction is void for want of the required power to act in the first place: *Guinness Plc v Saunders* [1990] 2 A.C. 663.

[229] Section 178.

There are three points of note about these provisions and their relationship to the general law considered in previous sections: **11–133**

(1) First, the rule against the exploitation of company property, information and opportunities is now rationalised solely with reference to the overarching duty to avoid a conflict of interest; insofar as the rule against profiting from one's fiduciary office ever provided a separate source of inhibition (which, on the modern approach seen in cases such as *Bhullar v Bhullar* (considered above) is probably doubtful[230]), it does not any longer;

(2) Secondly, disclosure to and authorisation by the director's disinterested fellow directors will suffice to avoid a breach. Under the general law, there were certainly circumstances in which it was considered that only authorisation by the company's shareholders would suffice for these purposes;

(3) Thirdly, for there to be a breach the situation must be one that could reasonably be regarded as likely to give rise to a conflict. On its face, this appears to be a higher threshold than the *Phipps v Boardman* test of a real sensible possibility of conflict. It remains to be seen whether the Courts will discern a real difference here.

As under the general law, it is immaterial whether the company could take advantage of the property, information or opportunity: s.175(2). **11–134**

(iii) Benefits from third parties

Under s.176 a director is prohibited from accepting a benefit from a third party conferred by reason of his being a director or his doing or not doing anything as director, unless the acceptance of the benefit cannot reasonably be regarded as likely to give rise to a conflict of interest (which, again, includes a conflict of interest and duty and a conflict of duties). This duty would of course be infringed by the director's receipt of a bribe or secret commission. **11–135**

(iv) Duration of the duties

By s.170(2) a person who ceases to be a director continues to be subject to: (a) the duty in s.175 as regards the exploitation of any property, information or opportunity of which he became aware at a time when he was a director; and (b) the duty in s.176 as regards things done or omitted by him before he ceased to be a director. The first of these provisions gives statutory force to the principle, considered, at para.11–115 above, that when it comes to the exploitation of commercial opportunities in breach of fiduciary duty, a director will remain subject to liability following termination of the relationship which gives rise to the duty. Indeed, it arguably extends the principle, since the only requirement is that the property, information or opportunity should have come to his attention while he was a director, and not that his resignation should have been influenced by a desire to exploit it. **11–136**

---

[230] See 11–112.

(9) Defences: Fully Informed Consent of the Principal

11–137 Since the essence of a fiduciary duty is loyalty and the subordination of the fiduciary's interests to those of his principal, it is possible for the principal to relax the obligation by consent, either generally, or with respect to the particular dealing that might otherwise put the fiduciary in breach.

11–138 The attenuation of strict fiduciary duties where the possibility of conflict or profit is inherent in the contractual or like arrangements from which the fiduciary relationship arises has been considered above.[231]

11–139 Outside such circumstances, for consent to provide a defence to a claim that a fiduciary obligation has been breached it must be fully informed, following full and frank disclosure by the fiduciary of both the fact and the nature of his potentially conflicting interest. It is not enough for the fiduciary to disclose simply that he has an interest,[232] or to make statements that put the principal on inquiry.[233] Thus for a director to avoid having to account for a profit that he stands to make personally from his position, he must disclose not just the nature of his interest, but also the source and scale of the profit in question.[234] Likewise, a broker who earns a commission must usually disclose not just the fact of the commission, but its amount, to avoid being accountable.[235] That said, there is support in the authorities for the proposition that where there is a customary usage of charging commission to the counterparty in a particular market, and the amount of the commission is standard and ascertainable on enquiry, a claimant who is deemed to be on notice of the market practice and who failed to make enquiry as to the amount will be fixed with knowledge, and thus consent.[236] Ultimately, whether there has been sufficient disclosure will depend on the facts of each case, given that the requirement is for the principal's informed consent to his fiduciary acting with a potential conflict of interest.[237]

11–140 Where there is a deficiency in disclosure, it is not sufficient for the fiduciary to demonstrate that the principal would still have consented, had full information been provided.[238] The test for the materiality of what was not disclosed is

---

[231] See paras 11–018–11–031.

[232] See *Hurstanger Ltd v Wilson* [2007] 1 W.L.R. 2351, at [35], and the first instance decision in *FHR European Ventures LLP v Mankarious* [2011] EWHC 2308 (Ch), at [78] (reversed on other grounds in the Supreme Court).

[233] *Novoship (UK) Ltd v Mikhaylyuk* [2012] EWHC 3586 (Comm), at [83], affirmed on this point at [2014] EWCA Civ 908.

[234] *Gwembe Valley Development Company Ltd v Koshy* [2004] 1 B.C.L.C. 131, at [65].

[235] *Hurstanger v Wilson* [2007] 1 W.L.R. 2351, at [44]; *McWilliam v Norton Finance (UK) Ltd* [2015] EWCA Civ 186, at [51]; *Medsted Associates Ltd v Canaccord Genuity Wealth (International) Ltd* [2017] EWHC 1815 (Comm), at [97].

[236] *Great Western Insurance Company v Cunliffe* (1874) 9 Ch. App 525, at 539; *Hindmarsh v Brigham & Cowan Ltd* [1943] 76 Ll L.R. 141, at 152r; *FHR European Ventures LLP v Mankarious* [2011] EWHC 2308 (Ch), at [82].

[237] *Hurstanger v Wilson* [2007] 1 W.L.R. 2351, at [35].

[238] *Murad v Al-Saraj* [2005] EWCA Civ 959.

whether it might have affected the principal's decision, not whether it would have done.[239] Nor is the sufficiency of disclosure sensitive to the level of risk of conflict of interest.[240]

However, consent need not precede the breach (a principal can consent so as to absolve his fiduciary of liability after the event), and in appropriate circumstances it can be inferred or implied. Thus, for example, where directors of one company were at the request of that company appointed directors of another company and given qualification shares in the latter company by the former company so that they could hold that second office, their remuneration as directors of the second company was not something for which they were accountable: it was a fair inference from the circumstances that the first company had agreed to them receiving it.[241]   **11–141**

In the case of a director, the general law required that disclosure was made to and consent given by the shareholders, in some cases unanimously,[242] although common form Articles of Association provided that disclosure to the Board would suffice where the transaction was with the company. The position under the 2006 Act has been considered in the preceding section.   **11–142**

(10)   Relief from Liability

Certain categories of fiduciary can invoke the jurisdiction of the Court to exclude or limit their liability. In particular: **11–143**

(1)   Section 1157 of the Companies Act 2006 empowers the Court to relieve an officer of a company from liability, in whole or in part, where

> "it appears to the court hearing the case that the officer or person...acted honestly and reasonably, and that having regard to all the circumstances of the case (including those connected with his appointment) he ought fairly to be excused".

(2)   Section 61 of the Trustee Act 1925 confers a similar power on the Court in relation to the personal liability of a trustee for breach of trust.

A detailed consideration of the first of these provisions is outside the scope of this work. The second is considered in Ch.10, at paras 10–019—10–023. As is clear from their terms, they will not avail a fiduciary who has dishonestly breached his duties.   **11–144**

---

[239] *Andrews v Ramsay & Co* [1903] 2 K.B. 635, at 637–638.
[240] *McWilliam v Norton Finance (UK) Ltd*, above, at [55].
[241] *Re Dover Coalfield Extension Ltd* [1907] 2 Ch. 76, as explained in *Re Macadam* [1946] Ch. 73, at 82.
[242] *Cook v Deeks* [1916] 1 A.C. 554.

E. OTHER DUTIES AND CONSTRAINTS ASSOCIATED WITH FIDUCIARIES

(1) The Good Faith/Best Interests Duty: Introduction

11–145   When identifying the facets of the core fiduciary obligation of loyalty in *Bristol & West v Mothew* Millett LJ identified, along with the no conflict and no profit duties, a duty "to act in good faith". Whether this is really a separate fiduciary duty and, if it is, what it requires and when it is owed are the subject of some controversy.

11–146   There are broadly three different (but overlapping) senses in which a duty of good faith might be said to be owed by one person (A) who stands in a fiduciary relation to another (B). These are:

(1)   First, A may be said to owe a duty to act in good faith in the best interests of B. This is a prescriptive duty which requires the fiduciary to serve the best interests of his principal, and the role that the concept of good faith plays is that compliance with the duty is tested subjectively rather than objectively: that is, the duty is to act in what the fiduciary honestly and genuinely considers to be the best interests of the principal, even if it may not in fact be. This duty is certainly owed by directors to their companies and there is support for the view that it is owed by others who occupy similar fiduciary offices in which they are entrusted with a broad discretion to manage the affairs of another. At least at one point in *Bristol & West v Mothew* Millett LJ appears to have been using the expression the "duty of good faith" in this sense.[243] Understood in this way, the duty requires conscious wrongdoing, or at least an absence of genuine and honest (or possibly rational) belief that what is being done is in the interests of the principal, to be breached.

(2)   Secondly, A may be said to be required to exercise particular powers that are conferred on him in good faith. In this sense, the content of the requirement will be sensitive to the facts; but, at a minimum, it connotes the absence of bad faith—that is, that A should act honestly, genuinely and responsibly; and sometimes the expression also captures the idea of acting for a proper purpose (although this is more often thought of as being a separate equitable limitation on the exercise of powers). All fiduciaries can be said to be obliged to act in good faith in this sense[244]; but it is not a requirement that is peculiar to fiduciaries: it applies to others who exercise powers or discretions in a non-fiduciary capacity, such as mortgagees in the exercise of their power of sale,[245] shareholders in the exercise of their power (by majority vote) to amend the company's constitution[246] and lenders in the exercise of their power to alter the terms of a loan

---

[243] See [1998] Ch. 1, at 19D.

[244] *Armitage v Nurse* [1998] Ch. 241; *Bristol & West Building Society v Mothew* [1998] Ch. 1; *Item Software (UK) Ltd v Fassihi* [2004] EWCA Civ 1244; [2005] 2 B.C.L.C. 91.

[245] *Yorkshire Bank v Hall* [1999] 1 W.L.R. 1713.

[246] *Allen v Gold Reefs of West Africa* [1900] 1 Ch. 656.

syndication.[247] A duty of good faith can also arise as a matter of express or implied contractual stipulation between parties to an arms-length agreement, in which context it has been said to require honesty, observation of reasonable commercial standards of fair dealing and faithfulness to the agreed common purpose of the contract, but not the subordination of self-interest.[248]

(3) Thirdly, the "duty of good faith" may simply be a shorthand way of encapsulating other fiduciary obligations and requirements, including for example the requirement of full disclosure when entering into a transaction with the principal. In this sense the duty connotes fairness and openness in the fiduciary's dealings with his principal; but this probably does not add materially to the core no conflict and no profit duties mentioned in the preceding section; nor (if understood in this way) does it require conscious wrongdoing to be breached.[249]

So far as the first sense is concerned, the bulk of English authority appears to support the existence of such a duty at least in relation to particular sorts of office-holding fiduciaries (as set out below); but the position is not clear cut. There is controversy as to whether it is a separate duty owed by fiduciaries (at least beyond the established category of company directors) at all and, if it is, whether and in what sense it can be described as being a fiduciary duty. For example, the Law Commission has recently expressed the view the duty owed by a trustee to act honestly in the best interests of the beneficiaries is not a separate fiduciary duty, but simply a shorthand for a number of different non-fiduciary obligations owed in the administration of the trust.[250] The view has also been expressed[251] that, whilst the obligation of good faith in this first sense provides the rationale for the no conflict and no profit rules, it is only through those rules that it has been developed as a source of fiduciary liability and only they are fiduciary duties properly so-called.[252] In Australia, it has similarly been held that, beyond the duties to account and restore property which arise as a result of breach of the core proscriptive no conflict and no profit duties,

11–147

---

[247] *Redwood Master Fund Ltd v TD Bank Europe Ltd* [2002] EWHC 2703 (Ch); [2006] 1 B.C.L.C. 149.

[248] See e.g. *Berkeley Community Villages Ltd v Pullen* [2007] EWHC 1330, at [86]–[97]; *Macqurie International Health Clinic Pty Ltd v Sydney South West Area Health Service* [2010] NSWCA 268, at [146]–[148].

[249] *Sharp v Blank* [2015] EWHC 3220 (Ch), per Nugee J at [23(1)]. Sales J similarly appears to have regarded the "duty of good faith" as a way of encapsulating other fiduciary duties (including, in his view, a best interests duty): *F&C Alternative Investments (Holdings) Ltd v Barthelemy* [2012] Ch. 613, at [227(iv)].

[250] Law Commission, *Fiduciary Duties of Investment Intermediaries*, (HMSO, 2014) Law Com No.350, paras 3.41–3.43.

[251] See, for example, L. Ho, "Good Faith and Fiduciary Duty in English Law" (2010) 4 *Journal of Equity*, 29.

[252] It is right that a lack of good faith is neither a necessary nor sufficient condition for establishing breach of the no conflict and no profit duties; but that, it would be said, is because they are prophylactic rules designed to ensure that the fiduciary is not tempted to act other than in good faith in the best interests of his principal.

"the law of this country does not…impose positive legal duties on the fiduciary to act in the best interests of the person to whom the duty is owed".[253]

11–148 That said, there is certainly support for the view that particular sorts of fiduciary who occupy offices similar to those of a company director owe such a duty—that is, fiduciary office holders who are entrusted with powers of management for the benefit of another, but who are not under the immediate control and supervision of that other.[254] Examples would include partners of partnerships who occupy a managerial role, agents who are afforded a discretion as to how to act by their instructions or as part of their relationship, and the operators and managers of joint ventures.

11–149 Even in such cases, not all agree that the duty is properly characterised as being fiduciary, precisely because it can be prescriptive, in requiring the person subject to it to act in a particular way rather than merely to avoid certain situations and dealings that are potentially inconsistent with loyalty to the principal.[255] However, the prevailing view in the English cases appears to be that, where it is owed, it is a fiduciary duty, at least for the purposes of understanding how it is to be enforced and its remedial consequences[256]; and a leading Australian case, having considered the point with reference to the duties of directors, has reached the view that it is.[257]

11–150 This section therefore focuses upon the duty to act in good faith in the best interests of the principal, as paradigmatically owed by directors to their companies. One particular topic which has arisen in the context of the duty as it is owed by directors, but which is potentially of broader significance for fiduciaries who have involved themselves in commercial fraud, is whether there is a positive fiduciary duty of disclosure, including a duty to disclose one's own wrongdoing. This is considered at paras 11–166—11–171 below.

11–151 The distinction between the senses identified above should not be overstated, however. It can be said that a directors' duty to act in good faith in the best interests of his company is simply an instance of, or at least derives from, the more general requirement that those vested with powers to affect the interests of others should exercise them in good faith and for a proper purpose, the difference

---

[253] *Breen v Williams* (1996) 186 C.L.R. 71, per Gaudron and McHugh JJ, at 113. The case concerned the fiduciary duties alleged to be owed by a doctor to her patient. See also *P&V Industries Pty Ltd v Porto* [2006] VSC 131, at [23].

[254] See G.M.D. Bean, *Fiduciary Obligations and Joint Ventures* (Oxford: Clarendon Press, 1995), at pp.165–167, cited with approval in *Ross River Ltd v Waverly Commercial Ltd* [2013] EWCA Civ 910, at [51]–[52].

[255] P. Finn, "Fiduciary Law and the Modern Commercial World", Ch.1 in E. McKendrick (ed.), *Commercial Aspects of Trusts and Fiduciary Relationships* (Oxford: Clarendon Press, 1992); M. Conaglen, "The Nature and Function of Fiduciary Loyalty" (2005) 121 L.Q.R. 452, 454–460.

[256] E.g. *Item Software (UK) Ltd v Fassihi* [2005] 2 B.C.L.C. 91, at [41]; *Sinclair Trade Finance v Versailles* [2012] Ch. 453, at [35]–[36]. In *Madoff Securities International Ltd (In Liquidation) v Raven* [2013] EWHC 3147 (Comm) the duty was described as "*a fiduciary duty because it is a duty of loyalty*" [188]; see also *Ultraframe (UK) Ltd v Fielding* [2005] EWHC 1638 (Ch), at [1295]. The duty as it now appears in the Companies Act 2006 (s.172) is characterised as being fiduciary: see s.178.

[257] *Westpac Banking Corp v The Bell Group Ltd (In Liquidation.) (No.3)* [2012] WASCA 157.

simply being that in the case of a director the power is a general one of management which will (often) otherwise be unconstrained by the terms of the directors' engagement by the company.

(2) The Director's Best Interests Duty: Nature of the Duty

Company directors have long been held to owe a duty to act bona fide in the best interests of their company:

11–152

> "a corporate body can only act by agents, and it is of course the duty of those agents so to act as best to promote the interests of the corporation whose affairs they are conducting".[258]

The characterisation of the duty as one of "good faith" is important, however: as noted above, it underscores that acting in the best interests of the principal is not a separate and objective aspect of the duty. Rather, the duty is

11–153

> "to exercise their discretion bona fide in what they consider—not what a court may consider—is in the interests of the [principal]."[259]

This is reflected now in the wording of s.172 of the Companies Act 2006, which frames the duty as one to act "in the way [the director] considers, in good faith, would be most likely to promote the success of the company".[260] The following passage from the judgment of Jonathan Parker J in *Regentcrest Plc v Cohen* has frequently been cited with approval[261]:

> "The question is not whether, viewed objectively by the court, the particular act or omission which is challenged was in fact in the interests of the company; still less is the question whether the court, had it been in the position of the director at the relevant time, might have acted differently. Rather, the question is whether the director honestly believed that his act or omission was in the interests of the company. The issue is as to the director's state of mind. No doubt, where it is clear that the act or omission under challenge resulted in substantial detriment to the company, the director will have a harder task persuading the court that he honestly believed it to be in the company's interest; but that does not detract from the subjective nature of the test."

Thus it has been said in another case that "crass incompetence might give rise to a claim for breach of a duty of care, or for breach of contract, but not for a breach of fiduciary duty".[262]

11–154

This may be subject to two qualifications in the company law context: first, where a company is insolvent or in financial difficulty such that the interests of creditors intrude (as to which, see paras 11–160—11–165 below), those interests

11–155

---

[258] *Aberdeen Railway Company v Blaikie Brothers* [1843-60] All E.R. Rep. 249, at 252. cf. *Stears v the South Essex Gaslight and Coke Company* (1860) 9 CB (NS) 180, at 201: a director's duty is to "look exclusively to the interests of the company".

[259] *Re Smith and Fawcett Ltd* [1942] Ch. 304; cf. *Item Software (UK) Ltd v Fassihi* [2005] 2 B.C.L.C. 91, at [41].

[260] Which has been held to "come to the same thing" as the common law formulation of the duty: *Re Southern Counties Fresh Foods Ltd* [2008] EWHC 2810 (Ch), at [52].

[261] *Regentcrest Plc v Cohen* [2001] BCC 494, at [120].

[262] *Extrasure Travel Insurance Ltd v Scattergood* [2003] 1 B.C.L.C. 598, at [89].

have been said to be "paramount", which suggests that the Court will trespass into the substance of how the directors exercise their discretion (paramountcy suggesting not just that the interests of creditors have to be considered in good faith, but that they have to be accorded precedence).[263] Secondly, where a director fails to consider whether an act is in the best interests of the company, the Court will not find him in breach ipso facto, if an honest and intelligent person in the position of a director of the company concerned could, in the circumstances, have reasonably believed that the act was for the benefit of the company.[264]

11–156   There is also some support in the authorities for there being limits beyond which even the honest belief of the fiduciary as to the best interests of his principal will not be an answer to a claim for breach of this duty: it has thus been suggested that the belief must at least be a rational one, such that

> "a breach will have occurred if it is established that the relevant exercise of the power is one which could not be considered by any reasonable director to be in the interests of the company".[265]

The point was put in stark terms by Bowen LJ in *Hutton v West Cork Rly Co*[266]:

> "Bona fides cannot be the sole test, otherwise you might have a lunatic conducting the affairs of the company, and paying away its money with both hands in a manner perfectly bona fide yet perfectly irrational."

11–157   It is suggested that this view should be treated with caution. It is obvious that the unreasonableness of a director's professed view as to the best interests of the company will bear (as a matter of evidence) on whether the Court believes his assertion that he held it at the time[267]; but if, despite its unreasonableness, the Court concludes that the view was honestly held, then the conclusion should be, consistently with the nature of the duty, that there is no breach.

(3)   The Director's Best Interests Duty: Void or Voidable?

11–158   The view has been expressed in several cases that a transaction entered into by a director on behalf of his company in breach of the duty to act in good faith in the best interests of the company is not just voidable in equity but void. This is on the

---

[263] *Re HLC Environmental Projects Ltd* [2014] BCC 337. It is respectfully suggested that this view is questionable: whilst the imminence of insolvency might affect whose interests have in good faith to be considered, it is not obvious why they should require more than that they be considered in good faith.

[264] *Charterbridge Corp Ltd v Lloyds Bank Ltd* [1970] Ch. 62, at 74E–74F.

[265] *Re Southern Counties Fresh Foods Ltd* [2008] EWHC 2810 (Ch), at [53].

[266] *Hutton v West Cork Rly Co* (1883) 23 Ch. D. 654, at 671.

[267] *Extrasure Travel Insurance Ltd v Scattergood* [2003] 1 B.C.L.C. 598, at [90]: "The fact that his alleged belief was unreasonable may provide evidence that it was not in fact honestly held at the time: but if, having considered all the evidence, it appears that the director did honestly believe that he was acting in the best interests of the company, then he is not in breach of his fiduciary duty merely because that belief appears to the trial judge to be unreasonable, or because his actions happen, in the event, to cause injury to the company."

basis that the director lacks actual authority to act other than in the best interests of his principal (and this has been said to be true of any agent).[268]

This appears to represent a departure from old authority,[269] which had been to the effect that there was an important distinction between exceeding one's authority (which would render a transaction void) and abusing it (which would render it voidable). That distinction has now been explained on the basis that in the latter case the director or agent will lack actual authority, but may nevertheless have apparent authority.[270]

11–159

(4) The Director's Best Interests Duty in the Context of Potential Insolvency

The duty to act in what the director in good faith considers to be the best interests of the company has long been understood to be subject to a duty to consider, or possibly to act in, the interests of the company's creditors in circumstances where the company is insolvent or in financial difficulties. Section 172 of the Companies Act 2006 acknowledges this, without spelling out the content of this qualifying duty or when it arises, by providing that the overarching duty in that section:

11–160

> "has effect subject to any enactment or rule of law requiring directors, in certain circumstances, to consider or act in the interests of creditors of the company".[271]

The rationale for this extension of the interests which the director must consider beyond those of his immediate principal has been said to be the prospective entitlement of the company's creditors to deal, through the mechanism of a liquidation, with the company's assets[272]; but it has been said to be engaged in circumstances short of actual insolvency (let alone liquidation). The "trigger point" for the duty has been variously said to be:

11–161

---

[268] *Re Capitol Films Ltd* [2010] EWHC 2240 (Ch); *GHLM Trading Ltd v Maroo* [2012] 2 B.C.L.C. 369, at [170]–[171]. See also *Belmont Finance Corp Ltd v Williams Furniture Ltd (No.2)* [1980] 1 All E.R. 393. This may be the explanation for the finding in *JJ Harrison (Properties) Ltd v Harrison* [2001] EWCA Civ 1467; [2002] BCC 729 that a director who acquired land from his company without full disclosure and then profited from its onward sale held the land as constructive trustee "from the first" (i.e. without the transaction having first to be rescinded).

[269] *Macmillan Inc v Bishopsgate Trust (No.3)* [1995] 1 W.L.R. 978, per Millet J at 984.

[270] *Hopkins v TL Dallas Group Ltd* [2005] 1 B.C.L.C. 543, per Lightman J at [88]–[89]. Assuming that this apparent shift in judicial attitudes is well-founded, it remains unclear how far transactions will be held to be void in equity (rather than voidable) either (i) when the transaction tainted by the fiduciary's bad faith is not brought about by a direct exercise of the fiduciary's own powers or (ii) when the fiduciary in question is not a company director.

[271] The reference to an "enactment" must contemplate the statutory duty of care imposed on directors by s.214 of the Insolvency Act 1986 when there is no reasonable prospect of the company avoiding insolvent liquidation.

[272] *Kinsela v Russell Kinsela Pty Ltd* (1986) 4 N.S.W.L.R. 722, per Street CJ at 730, approved by the English Court of Appeal in *West Mercia Safetywear Ltd (In Liquidation) v Dodd* [1988] B.C.L.C. 250, at 252–253, per Dillon LJ.

(1)   where the company is "doubtfully solvent"[273];

(2)   where the company is in a "very dangerous financial position" or "parlous financial state"[274];

(3)   where the company is "on the verge of insolvency and it is the creditors' money that is at risk"[275]; and

(4)   where there is "a real and not remote risk that [creditors] will be prejudiced by the dealing in question".[276]

11–162   In *Re HLC Environmental Projects Ltd*, the judge expressed the view that there was no real difference between these formulations and he synthesised the relevant underlying principle as being[277]:

> "that directors are not free to take action that puts at real (as opposed to remote) risk the creditors' prospects of being paid, without first having considered their interests rather than those of the company and its shareholders".

11–163   However, the language of "risk" of prejudice to creditors obscures the fact that insolvency must (at least) be *imminent* for the directors to be required to consider (or prioritise) the interests of creditors. Although the duty was not the subject of specific consideration in the Supreme Court case of *Jetivia SA v Bilta (UK) Ltd (In Liquidation)*,[278] it is noteworthy that their Lordships encapsulated the test not in terms of risk to creditors, but rather as being when the company was "insolvent or bordering on insolvency",[279] or "actually or prospectively insolvent".[280] In *BAT Industries Plc v Sequana S.A.* the question arose as to whether the duty was engaged where the relevant liabilities were of a long-term and uncertain nature, where the company had provided for those liabilities in its accounts, but there was inherent uncertainty as to whether that provision would prove sufficient, and where the directors were contemplating paying a dividend which (it was alleged) would prejudice the creditors' prospects of being paid should it turn out not to be. It was held that this did not suffice to engage any duty to consider or act in the creditors' interests[281]:

> "It cannot be right that whenever a company has on its balance sheet a provision in respect of a long term liability which might turn out to be larger than the provision made, the creditors' interests duty applies for the whole period during which there is a risk that there will be insufficient assets to meet that liability. That would result in directors having to take account of creditors' rather than shareholders' interests when running a business over an extended period. This would be a significant inroad into the normal application of directors' duties. To

---

273 *Brady v Brady* (1987) 3 BCC 535, per Nourse LJ at [40h–I].

274 *Facia Footwear v Hinchcliffe* [1998] 1 B.C.L.C. 218, per Sir Richard Scott V-C at 228.

275 *Colin Gwyer & Associates Ltd v London Wharf (Limehouse) Ltd* [2003] 2 B.C.L.C. 153, per Leslie Kosmin QC at [74]; cf. *"near insolvent"* in *Nicholson v Permakraft (NZ) Ltd* [1985] 1 N.Z.L.R. 242, at 249.

276 *Kalls Enterprises Pty Ltd v Baloglow* [2007] NSWCA 191, per Giles JA at [162], cited with approval by Newey J in *Vivendi SA v Richards* [2013] EWHC 3006 (Ch), at [150].

277 *Re HLC Environmental Projects Ltd* [2014] BCC 337, at [89], per John Randall QC.

278 *Jetivia SA v Bilta (UK) Ltd (In Liquidation)* [2015] BCC 343.

279 *Jetivia SA v Bilta (UK) Ltd (In Liquidation)* [2015] BCC 343, per Lord Toulson and Lord Hodge at [123].

280 *Jetivia SA v Bilta (UK) Ltd (In Liquidation)* [2015] BCC 343, per Lord Sumption at [104].

281 *BAT Industries Plc v Sequana S.A.* [2016] EWHC 1686 (Ch), per Rose J at [479].

hold that the creditors' interests duty arises in a situation where the directors make proper provision for a liability in the company's accounts but where there is a real risk that that provision will turn out to be inadequate would be a significant lowering of the threshold as currently described and applied in the cases to which I have referred. I can see no justification in principle for such a change."

Where the interests of creditors do intrude as objects of the director's fiduciary consideration, there are dicta to the effect that they must be treated as "paramount" and so (it might be thought) take priority over the interests of shareholders (and other stakeholders).[282] However, whilst that might be justified in circumstances where insolvency has occurred or is about to occur, it is more difficult to justify if the risk of insolvency is more remote than that; and other dicta suggest a more flexible test of having "regard to" the interests of creditors.[283]   **11–164**

The duty remains one owed to the company; it is not actionable at the suit of creditors, who, if they wish to obtain redress for a breach, must do so through the appointment of a liquidator who can sue in right of the company.   **11–165**

(5)   A Fiduciary Duty of Disclosure?

The question of whether a fiduciary is obliged to disclose his own wrongdoing to his principal has an obvious relevance to fraud claims. Whilst it might be said that the dishonest fiduciary who acts in fraud of his principal is hardly going to volunteer that fact to his principal because he is under a duty to do so, a duty of disclosure over and above the duty breached by the underlying wrongdoing may give rise to relief that would not otherwise be available. For example, in *Item Software (UK) Ltd v Fassihi*,[284] the fact that the fiduciary had sought unsuccessfully (but nevertheless in breach of fiduciary duty) to divert an intended contract with his principal to himself had not itself been causative of any loss, because the contract was lost by reason of the uncompromising negotiating stance that the principal took; but it was found that had the fiduciary disclosed his attempted diversion, the principal would have taken a different stance in negotiating with the third party and the contract would have been secured.   **11–166**

In that case, the duty owed by directors of companies to act in what they in good faith consider to be the best interests of his company was described by the Court of Appeal as being "dynamic and capable of application in cases where it has not previously been applied but the principle or rationale of the rule applies".[285] Arden LJ approved American academic commentary to the effect that there was a   **11–167**

---

[282] *Colin Gwyer & Associates Ltd v London Wharf (Limehouse) Ltd* [2003] 2 B.C.L.C. 153, at [74]; *Re HLC Environmental Projects Ltd* [2014] BCC 337, at [92].

[283] *GHLM Trading Ltd v Maroo* [2012] 2 B.C.L.C. 369, at [168]; see also *Facia Footwear Ltd v Hinchcliffe* [1998] 1 B.C.L.C. 218, at 228, approving a passage from *Kinsela* in which Street CJ said that "the plainer it is that it is the creditors' money that is at risk, the lower may be the risk to which the directors, regardless of the unanimous support of all the shareholders, can justifiably expose the company". The paramountcy approach was expressly rejected in the subsequent Australian case of *The Bell Group Ltd v Westpac Banking Corp (No.9)* [2008] WASC 239, at [4436].

[284] *Item Software (UK) Ltd v Fassihi* [2005] 2 B.C.L.C. 91.

[285] *Item Software (UK) Ltd v Fassihi* [2005] 2 B.C.L.C. 91, at [41].

general fiduciary duty of loyalty in the corporate context, of which the established particular equitable rules were simply an "explication" and which remained a "residual concept that can include factual situations that no one has foreseen and categorised".[286] On that basis, the duty was said to require a director positively to disclose his own misconduct, when there was "no basis on which [he] could reasonably have come to the conclusion that it was not in the interests of [the company] to know" of it.[287]

11–168 On this analysis, the duty of disclosure is not a separate fiduciary obligation, but an application of the director's duty now set out in s.172 of the Companies Act 2006. The reference to reasonableness might therefore be thought anomalous, since the duty is judged by subjective good faith rather than objective reasonableness; but, plainly, on the facts of that case (involving dishonest attempts to divert a company contract) the decision not to disclose was not taken in good faith either.

11–169 Because the touchstone of the obligation is what the director in good faith believes is in the best interests of the company, the duty can require disclosure of matters beyond the director's own wrongdoing, including the wrongdoing of others and other matters (such as information about an intended transaction of which the director is aware and which would be detrimental to the company's interests[288] or an attempt by a competitor to poach members of the company's workforce)[289]; and it can, in an appropriate case, require that the disclosure be made not to the board, but to the shareholders.[290]

11–170 A fiduciary will also have disclosure "obligations" in the following senses:

(1) First, as part of his duty to account for dealings with the principal's property, or, in the partnership context, for "all things affecting the partnership".[291] This duty has also been held to be owed by directors, by analogy to trustees.[292] It is a primary duty owed by the fiduciary, and not just a remedy for another wrong;

(2) Secondly, as part of the remedy of accounting for profits made in breach of the no conflict or no profit duties: see Ch.22;

(3) Thirdly, as a precondition for obtaining the fully-informed consent of the principal to a situation or dealing that would otherwise involve a breach of the no conflict or no profit duties: see paras 11–137—11–142 above. This is not a duty owed by the fiduciary, but a requirement for establishing the defence of consent (although in *Gwembe Valley Development Company Ltd*

---

[286] *Item Software (UK) Ltd v Fassihi* [2005] 2 B.C.L.C. 91, at [42]–[43].

[287] *Item Software (UK) Ltd v Fassihi* [2005] 2 B.C.L.C. 91, at [44].

[288] *Re Coroin Ltd* [2012] EWHC 2343 (Ch), at [550].

[289] *British Midland Tool Ltd v Midland International Tooling Ltd* [2003] 2 B.C.L.C. 241, per Hart J at [27].

[290] *GHLM Trading Ltd v Maroo* [2012] 2 B.C.L.C. 369, at [192]–[200] (finding that the analogy applies at least where the director has received company property).

[291] Partnership Act 1890, s.28.

[292] *GHLM Trading Ltd v Maroo* [2012] 2 B.C.L.C. 369, at [148]–[149]. A director will also have statutory obligations with respect to the keeping of proper accounting records: ss.386–389 of the Companies Act 2006.

v Koshy it appears to have been considered that the fiduciary dealing rules generated a positive obligation of disclosure, breach of which could give rise to a claim in equitable compensation)[293];

(4) Fourthly (and by way of statutory modification of the position under (3) above), under s.177 of the Companies Act 2006: see para.11–127 above.

In this context, it should of course be recalled that the need for disclosure of relevant matters can arise in practice as a result of claims to which the fiduciary may be subject without any disclosure (or, indeed, evidence) of such matters. The duty on a fiduciary entrusted with property for the benefit of another to account for the use to which that property is put means that there is in effect a reversal of the burden of proof where it is established that such property has come into the hands of the fiduciary or his dealings with it are otherwise challenged: it is for him to show that the transaction in question was proper, rather than for the principal to show that it was improper.[294]

11–171

(6) Other Equitable Limitations upon the Exercise of Powers

There are equitable limitations on the manner in which those who are vested with powers to control the property or affairs of others must exercise such powers, which have developed particularly in the context of traditional trusts. These include that such powers must be exercised:

11–172

(1) in good faith, which in this context is to say honestly and genuinely (as has been considered above);
(2) taking into account relevant considerations and disregarding irrelevant ones; and
(3) for the purpose for which the powers were conferred.

Whilst trustees are, paradigmatically, subject to such principles, similar principles have developed with respect to the powers vested in directors of companies; and they now find expression (in modified form) in the duties owed by directors under the Companies Act 2006 to act for a proper purpose (s.171) and to exercise independent judgement (s.173).[295]

11–173

The equitable requirements that powers be exercised in good faith and for a proper purpose delineate the scope of the power and a failure to observe them will result (usually) in an exercise of the power being void in equity, rather than voidable—that is, whilst it may take effect at law, it will not be effective to alter

11–174

---

[293] *Gwembe Valley Development Company Ltd v Koshy* [2003] EWCA Civ 1048, at [146].
[294] *Ross River Ltd v Waverly Commercial Ltd* [2013] EWCA Civ 910, at [94].
[295] Note also that similar sorts of constraints can be imposed on the exercise of a contractual discretion or reaching of a contractual decision by the implication of a term: see e.g. *Braganza v BP Shipping Ltd* [2015] 1 W.L.R. 1661; *BHL v Leumi ABL Ltd* [2017] 2 Lloyd's Rep. 237.

the beneficial interest in any property transferred pursuant to it.[296] In contrast, a failure to take into account relevant considerations probably renders the exercise of the power voidable.[297]

11–175 So far as the requirement to take into account only relevant considerations, this is certainly a constraint upon the proper exercise by trustees of their powers.[298] It has also been said to apply to other fiduciary donees of discretionary powers,[299] although in the commercial context it is probably unrealistic to judge fiduciaries who are required to make business judgments by reference to the particular considerations that they did and did not take into account (provided that their judgment is reached in good faith).[300] The duty does not require a positive mistake[301] in order for it to be breached—ignorance or inattention may suffice—but it does require fault on the part of the fiduciary (a failure to take into account a relevant consideration because erroneous professional advice was given on it would not suffice).[302] A failure to comply with this duty renders the exercise of the power voidable at the discretion of the Court.

11–176 Those who have powers vested in them in a fiduciary capacity[303] are also required to exercise those powers for a proper purpose:

> "[T]he donee, the appointor under the power, shall, at the time of the exercise of that power, and for any purpose for which it is used, act with good faith and sincerity, and with an entire and single view to the real purpose and object of the power, and not for the purpose of accomplishing or carrying into effect any bye or sinister object (I mean sinister in the sense of its being beyond the purpose and intent of the power) which he may desire to effect in the exercise of the power."[304]

11–177 A failure to observe these constraints is described in the traditional trust context as a "fraud on the power", although the fraud is an equitable fraud and does not (necessarily) connote dishonesty. The paradigm case is the exercise of a power of appointment under a trust for the purpose of benefiting the donee of the power or a third party who was not the object of the power; but the exercise of other powers (such as of investment) will also be set aside as a "fraud" (in this sense) where it is not for the purpose for which the power was given.[305]

---

[296] See e.g. *Cloutte v Storey* [1911] 1 Ch. 18, CA (fraud on an equitable power) and Nolan, *Controlling Fiduciary Power* [2009] CLJ 68(2), 293–323.

[297] *Abacus Trust Co (Isle of Man) v Barr* [2003] Ch. 409; *Hunter v Senate Support Services Ltd* [2005] 1 B.C.L.C. 175, at [178]

[298] The principles governing this duty, which was formerly known as the principle in *Re Hastings-Bass*, have been authoritatively set out by the Supreme Court in *Pitt v Holt* [2013] 2 A.C. 108.

[299] Such as a Mental Health Act receiver (*Pitt v Holt* [2013] 2 A.C. 108, at [57], [97]) and a director (*Hunter v Senate Support Services Ltd* [2005] 1 B.C.L.C. 175, at [165]–[180].)

[300] See the observation of Nourse LJ in *Re Edennote Ltd* [1996] 2 B.C.L.C. 389, at 394.

[301] Mistake provides a separate basis for setting aside the exercise of a power in equity, which is not dependent on any breach of fiduciary duty: *Pitt v Holt* [2013] 2 A.C. 108.

[302] *Pitt v Holt* [2013] 2 A.C. 108, at [41].

[303] In the trust context, this means the donees of "limited" and "fiduciary" powers, but not "beneficial" powers (i.e. ones which the fiduciary is entitled to exercise for his own benefit).

[304] *Duke of Portland v Lady Topham* (1864) 11 H.L.C. 32, per Lord Westbury L.C. at 54.

[305] *Cowan v Scargill* [1985] Ch. 270, at 288; *Hayim v Citibank N.A.* [1987] A.C. 730, at 746 (PC); *Edge v Pensions Ombudsman* [1998] Ch. 512, at 535 (on appeal, at [2000] Ch. 602, CA).

In a similar way, and of more relevance in the commercial fraud context, a company director owes what has been described as a fiduciary duty to exercise the powers conferred on him by the constitution of the company in accordance with the constitution and for the purposes for which they were conferred. This duty is now set out in s.171 of the Companies Act 2006.[306] It is distinct from the fiduciary duties of loyalty, and it can be breached even if the director honestly believes himself to be acting in his company's best interests and without knowledge that the purpose for which he was acting was collateral.[307]

11–178

Thus, in the recent case of *Eclairs Group Ltd v JKX Oil & Gas Plc*,[308] directors, who exercised a power to impose restrictions on voting on shares in good faith and with a view to maximising the chances of certain resolutions being passed at an AGM in a manner which they thought was in the best interests of the company, were nevertheless in breach of s.171 of the Companies Act 2006, because the purpose for which the power to impose restrictions was conferred was limited to ensuring compliance with information requests that had been made of the relevant shareholders and protecting the company from the consequences of non-compliance. It was not a proper purpose to use the shareholders' non-compliance with the information requests as a pretext to seek to influence the outcome of a general meeting.

11–179

That said, there will be circumstances in which the question of whether a power has been exercised for a proper purpose will depend upon questions of commercial judgment, as to which the Court will always respect, rather than seek to second-guess, the honest views of the directors.[309]

11–180

In determining whether a power has been exercised for a proper purpose the court will apply a four stage test, which is to identify:

11–181

(1)   the power whose exercise is in question;
(2)   the proper purpose for which such power was conferred;
(3)   the substantial purpose for which the power was exercised in the instant case; and
(4)   whether that purpose was proper.[310]

---

[306] It was previously often said that directors who participated in the commission of acts that were ultra vires their company were in breach of their fiduciary duties to the company: see e.g. *Peskin v Anderson* [2001] BCC 874, at [39].

[307] *Hogg v Cramphorn Ltd* [1967] 1 Ch. 254, 266G-269A; *Extrasure Travel Insurance Ltd v Scattergood* [2003] 1 B.C.L.C. 598, at [92].

[308] *Eclairs Group Ltd v JKX Oil & Gas Plc* [2016] BCC 79.

[309] "There is no appeal on merits from management decisions to courts of law": *Howard Smith Ltd v Ampol Petroleum Ltd* [1974] A.C. 821, at 832E. This is why in *Ultraframe (UK) Ltd v Fielding* [2005] EWHC 1638 (Ch), at [1643], Lewison J found that the bona fide belief of the directors that the transaction in question was necessary to ensure continuing supplies to the company was an answer to the improper purpose allegation. That he had in mind the objective nature of the proper purposes test is clear from [1293].

[310] *Howard Smith Ltd v Ampol Petroleum Ltd* [1974] A.C. 821, 835F-H; *Extrasure Travel Insurance Ltd v Scattergood* [2003] 1 B.C.L.C. 598, at [92].

11–182 The law was summarised in the following terms by the Court of Appeal of Western Australia[311]:

> "The *Ampol* decision is important for a number of reasons. Firstly, it unequivocally turned on whether a fiduciary power vested in directors was exercised for a proper purpose, not whether it was exercised bona fide for the benefit of the company. Secondly, it rejected the proposition that the answer depends on whether the directors in exercising the power honestly believed they were advancing the company's interests. Thirdly, it shows that the purpose for which a power is conferred is not governed only by the proper construction of the article conferring the power: 'a wider investigation may have to be made'. Fourthly, the proper exercise of a particular fiduciary power confided to directors is not governed by any absolute rule e.g. that the power to issue new shares can only be exercised to raise capital for the company, but by all the relevant circumstances of the case, including whether a particular exercise of power is intra vires the article conferring the power, the nature of the company and its business, the commercial setting in which the exercise of the power occurred, the motivations of the directors for the exercise of power and whether the exercise of the power involved a decision on matters of management and if so, the extent to which the court should defer to the business judgment of the directors."

(7) A Director's Trustee-Like Duty not to Misapply Company Property?

11–183 It has already been noted that directors, as the human agents of a company, owe fiduciary duties in part because they are vested with powers to control its property.[312] As such, they have also been said to be quasi-trustees of the company's assets under their control. The classic statement of the law is that of Lindley LJ in *Re Lands Allotments Co*[313]:

> "Although directors are not properly speaking trustees, yet they have always been considered and treated as trustees of money which comes to their hands or which is actually under their control; and ever since joint stock companies were invented directors have been held liable to make good moneys which they have misapplied upon the same footing as if they were trustees …"[314]

11–184 As such, in addition to their proscriptive fiduciary duties properly so-called, directors have been said to owe a trustee-like duty not to misapply the company's property:

> "the powers to dispose of the company's property, conferred upon the directors by the articles of association, must be exercised by the directors for the purposes, and in the interests of, the company".[315]

Directors who dispose of a company's property in breach of such limitations upon their powers are treated as having committed a breach of trust, meaning that:

---

[311] *Westpac Banking Corp v The Bell Group Ltd (In Liquidation) (No.3)* [2012] WASCA 157, at [2023].

[312] See para.11–033 above.

[313] *Re Lands Allotments Co* [1894] 1 Ch. 616, at 631.

[314] See also *Cook v Deeks* [1916] A.C. 555, at 564; *Re Duckwari Plc (No.2)* [1998] 2 B.C.L.C. 315, at 321; *Belmont Finance Corp Ltd v Williams Furniture (No.2)* [1980] 1 All E.R. 393, at 405C–405E; *Sinclair Investments (UK) Ltd v Versailles Trade Finance Ltd* [2011] 2 B.C.L.C. 501, at [34].

[315] *JJ Harrison v Harrison* [2002] B.C.L.C. 162, per Chadwick LJ at [25].

(1)   they hold such property (if they receive it themselves) on trust for the company[316];

(2)   they come under a personal liability to pay equitable compensation restoring the value of what has been misapplied, if it cannot be returned in specie[317]; and

(3)   third parties who assist in or receive property as a result of the breach are exposed to liability in equity.[318]

However, care must be exercised in analysing the source of the relevant limitation **11–185** (that is, in what sense it can be said that there has been a *mis*application of the company's property) and the nature of the director's liability for exceeding it. Under the scheme of the Companies Act 2006 there are a number of ways in which a misapplication of company property by directors might give rise to liability on the part of the director:

(1)   First, a director may apply property in a manner not permitted by the company's constitution, which would now be analysed as a breach of s.171(a) of the Companies Act 2006[319];

(2)   Secondly, a director may apply property in a manner that is permitted by the company's constitution, but not for a proper purpose—in breach, that is, of the duty in s.171(b) of the Companies Act 2006;

(3)   Thirdly, the director may apply property in a manner that contravenes some other limitation derived from the common law or statute. An example of this is the payment or transfer of the company's assets to its shareholders otherwise than by way of distribution of its available profits (which would contravene the common law rule in *Trevor v Whitworth*[320] and Pt 23 of the Companies Act 2006);

(4)   Fourthly, a director may apply property other than in what he considers in good faith would be most likely to promote the success of the company—in breach of s.172 of the 2006 Act;

(5)   Fifthly, a director may take advantage of the company's property (or information and opportunities) so as to make a personal profit, in breach of s.175(1)&(2) of the 2006 Act.

---

[316] *JJ Harrison v Harrison* [2002] B.C.L.C. 162, per Chadwick LJ at [25], although the basis on which the further trust arises is not entirely clear. It appears to be that the transaction is ineffective in equity and so the property is impressed with a trust at the point when it comes into the director's hands. See further paras 9–073—9–076.

[317] See Ch.22 Section D.

[318] On the dishonest assistance or knowing receipt bases, considered in Chs 12 and 13.

[319] See *Brady v Brady* (1987) 3 BCC 535, per Nourse LJ at 550: "In its broadest terms the principle is that a company cannot give away its assets. So stated, it is subject to the qualification that in the realm of theory a memorandum of association may authorise a company to give away all its assets to whomsoever it pleases, including its shareholders. But in the real world of trading companies—charitable or political donations, pensions to widows of ex-employees and the like apart—it is obvious that such a power would never be taken. The principle is only a facet of the wider rule, the corollary of limited liability, that the integrity of a company's assets, except to the extent allowed by its constitution, must be preserved for the benefit of all those who are interested in them, most pertinently its creditors." (not disapproved on appeal to the House of Lords).

[320] *Trevor v Whitworth* (1887) 12 App Cas 409.

11–186   Obviously a given fact pattern can involve breaches of more than one of these duties and rules.

11–187   The breach of trust analogy is perhaps most apt in the case of breaches of the first three sorts of limitation, in that (subject to the point noted in the following paragraph) liability is determined objectively with reference to limitations upon the director's powers to dispose of the company's property (and so is in that sense strict); in the fourth case, as we have seen, liability is assessed subjectively, and the fifth, as we have also seen, is an application of the director's proscriptive fiduciary obligations.

11–188   In the third case, the law providing for the relevant limitation may also specify the nature of the director's liability for the misapplication; but where it does not, there is scope for argument as to whether the director's liability is truly strict (in the way that it would be for a breach of trust) or requires some mental element—such as knowledge that the payment was improper, or of the facts that make it so, or alternatively constructive knowledge. In the particular context of a director's personal liability for the payment of an unlawful dividend, there are two conflicting lines of old authority on the question, albeit recent obiter observations in the Court of Appeal and Supreme Court are to the effect that the strict view is to be preferred.[321]

11–189   Just as a trustee who knowingly permits a co-trustee to commit a breach of trust will himself be in breach of trust,[322] so too it has been said that a director will be in breach of fiduciary duty (and not merely in breach of the statutory duty of care) if, with knowledge of a fellow director's misapplication of company property or other improper dealing, he stands by and takes no steps to prevent it—the inference being that he has authorised it.[323] This is so even if his knowledge is only of a practice of dealing in a certain way and not of the particular transactions carried out by the other director pursuant to it.[324]

---

[321] *Revenue and Customs Commissioners v Holland, In Re Paycheck Services 3 Ltd* [2010] 1 W.L.R. 2793, per Lord Hope at [45]–[47] (Supreme Court); and ([2010] Bus L.R. 259), per Rimer LJ at [81]–[84] (Court of Appeal). For the contrary view see e.g. *Re Kingston Cotton Mill (No.2)* [1896] 1 Ch. D. 331, at 346, and *Bairstow v Queens Moat House* [2000] BCC 1025, at 1033.

[322] See para.10–028.

[323] See e.g. *Walker v Stones* [2001] Q.B. 902, at 921D–921E.

[324] *Neville v Krikorian* [2006] EWCA Civ 943, at [49]–[51]; and *Lexi Holdings Ltd v Luqman (No.1)* [2007] EWHC 2652 (Ch), at [201]–[205].

CHAPTER 12

KNOWING RECEIPT

A. INTRODUCTION

(1) The Nature of the Claim and its Elements

English law recognises two claims that may lie in equity against a third party who comes to be mixed up in a breach of trust or fiduciary duty:

12–001

(1) "knowing receipt" (or, as it is also known, "unconscionable receipt") of trust property or its traceable proceeds; and
(2) "dishonest assistance" in a breach of trust or fiduciary duty.[1]

This chapter is concerned with the first of these claims; the second is the subject of Ch.13. Although the claims are distinct (and, after a certain amount of categorical confusion in the early cases, their separate elements have been more clearly identified over the last 30 years or so), nonetheless it is common to see such claims pleaded together against the same defendant. The defendant who receives trust property may well have also assisted the primary wrongdoer in the original breach of trust or fiduciary duty.

12–002

The essential requirements of a claim in knowing receipt can be derived from two Court of Appeal judgments, *El Ajou v Dollar Land Holdings Plc* and *Bank of Credit and Commerce International (Overseas) Ltd v Akindele*.[2] A claimant must show:

12–003

(1) Receipt of the claimant's assets (or their traceable proceeds) by the defendant;
(2) Such receipt arising from a breach of fiduciary duty or trust owed to the claimant by a third party; and
(3) Knowledge on the part of the defendant that the assets he received are traceable to a breach of fiduciary duty or trust, sufficient to make it unconscionable for him to retain the benefit of the receipt.

---

[1] These bases of liability derive from Lord Selborne's famous statement of principle in *Barnes v Addy* (1874) LR9 Ch. App. 244, at 251–252, albeit his short articulation of the claims has subsequently been refined and elaborated upon, in terms of the conditions that must be satisfied for liability to arise.
[2] Respectively: *El Ajou v Dollar Land Holdings Plc* [1994] 2 All E.R. 685, at 700 and *Bank of Credit and Commerce International (Overseas) Ltd v Akindele* [2001] Ch. 437, at 455. These two cases were treated as the leading authorities in *City Index Ltd v Gawler* [2007] EWCA Civ 1382; [2008] Ch. 513, at [7].

12-004 Each of these elements is considered in detail in this chapter. Importantly, it is not necessary for a claimant to show dishonesty on the part of the defendant as a condition for imposing liability on him, although it will often be the case that the knowing recipient will have been dishonest. Nonetheless, the liability is not strict and remains "fault-based".[3]

12-005 If each of these elements is proved, then the defendant is said to be "personally liable to account as a constructive trustee".[4] This statement must be treated with some care. It does not mean that, if a claimant can establish a claim in knowing receipt against a defendant, the defendant is—strictly speaking—a trustee (constructive or otherwise). Rather, it means that the defendant will be subject to certain personal liabilities *as if* he were a trustee. These personal liabilities are distinct from any proprietary rights which the claimant may have to any assets which the defendant may have in his hands (which are considered in detail in Ch.23).

12-006 In practical terms, these personal liabilities provide the claimant with a choice.[5] He can claim from the defendant either:

(a) the value of the assets received, together with any profits derived therefrom; or

(b) the loss which the claimant suffered as a consequence of the misappropriation of the assets in issue.[6]

Typically, a claimant would seek the former in cases in which the value of his assets has increased or they have been used profitably, and the latter where his assets have been dissipated in an unprofitable manner.

12-007 If the claimant elects to recover the value of the asset received, there is an unresolved question as to the date at which the value of the asset is calculated: i.e. whether it is the date of judgment, or the date on which the defendant received the asset. This question will, most likely, arise in cases in which the asset in question has risen in value after the defendant has disposed of it (and therefore the defendant has not profited from the post-disposal increase in value). The issues involved are complex and, should the issue arise in practice, practitioners

---

[3] There has been a good deal of academic encouragement to restate the law and found liability on a non-fault, restitutionary basis, subject to the usual defences to unjust enrichment claims: see for instance (writing extra-judicially) Lord Nicholls in "Knowing Receipt: The Need for a New Landmark", in W. Cornish (ed), *Restitution: Parts, Present and Future* (London: Hart Publishing, 1998), pp.231 and following. These efforts have not succeeded: see *BCCI v Akindele*, above, at 455–456 and *City Index Ltd v Gawler* [2007] EWCA Civ 1382, [2008] Ch. 513, at [7]. However, see the discussion regarding whether, separate from the law of knowing receipt, a breach of trust or fiduciary duty can be an "unjust factor" for the purposes of the law of unjust enrichment (at para.14–077, below).

[4] See e.g. *Williams v Central Bank of Nigeria* [2014] UKSC 10; [2014] A.C. 1189, at [19].

[5] In rare cases, other remedies might be available, see further C. Mitchell, P. Mitchell and S. Watterson, *Goff & Jones: The Law of Unjust Enrichment*, 9th edn (London: Sweet & Maxwell, 2016), para.8–199.

[6] See e.g. *City Index Ltd v Gawler* [2007] EWCA Civ 1382; [2008] Ch. 513, at [64].

should consult the commentary identified in the footnote below.[7] It is tentatively suggested that, at least so long as liability in knowing receipt is regarded by the courts as rooted within the law of unconscionability as opposed to the law of unjust enrichment, it should be possible to claim the value of the assets as at the date of judgment.[8]

If the claimant elects to recover the loss caused by the misappropriation of the **12–008** assets, the question arises as to how that loss is to be quantified. In the ordinary course, the answer will be simple: it will be the value of the misappropriated assets which the defendant has received. However, difficult issues can arise. The Hong Kong case of *Thanakharn Kasikorn Thai Chamkat (Mahachon) v Akai Holdings Ltd* provides an example.[9] The director of a company, purportedly acting on behalf of that company, pledged shares in a subsidiary to a bank in order to secure loans to that company. The company failed to repay the loans, and the bank sold the shares in the subsidiary to recover the debt. The company subsequently claimed that the director lacked authority to enter into the transaction on its behalf, and asserted that the bank was liable in knowing receipt in respect of the shares. One issue which arose was the quantum of the claim. The shares reduced in value from the date at which the director pledged them (and the alleged claim in knowing receipt arose), to the date at which the bank sold them, and had become worthless by the date of judgment. The company claimed that it was entitled to recover the value of the shares as at the date at which they were originally pledged to the bank. The Court of Final Appeal—the judgment of which was given by Lord Neuberger—disagreed. The claimant's entitlement to equitable compensation was limited to losses which *"on a common sense view of causation were caused by the breach"*.[10] The Court held that the appropriate quantum was the value for which the bank had sold the shares in circumstances in which:

(a)   it was open to the company to seek to recover the shares from the bank up until the bank sold the shares; and

(b)   it was apparent that, if the company had recovered the shares earlier, it would have held the shares until their value was extinguished.[11]

---

[7] See the differing views expressed in C. Mitchell, P. Mitchell and Watterson, *Goff & Jones: The Law of Unjust Enrichment* (2016), paras 8–202 and 8–203; G. Virgo, *Principles of the Law of Restitution*, 3rd edn (Oxford, OUP, 2015), p.651; J. McGhee, *Snell's Equity*, 33rd edn (London: Sweet & Maxwell, 2017), para.30–71; L. Tucker, N. Le Poidevin and J. Brightwell, *Lewin on Trusts*, 19th edn (London: Sweet & Maxwell, 2012), para.42–032 and C. Mitchell and Watterson "Remedies for Knowing Receipt" in Mitchell (ed), *Constructive and Resulting Trusts* (London: Hart Publishing, 2010), pp.128–131.

[8] For an introduction to this debate, see C. Mitchell, P. Mitchell and Watterson, *Goff & Jones: The Law of Unjust Enrichment* (2016), paras 8–127—8–141, and 8–196—8–203; McGhee, *Snell's Equity* (2017), paras 30–073 and 30–074; and Virgo, *Principles of the Law of Restitution* (2015), pp.652–655.

[9] *Thanakharn Kasikorn Thai Chamkat (Mahachon) v Akai Holdings Ltd (In Liquidation)* [2010] HKCU 2362; [2010] HKCFA 63.

[10] See at [152]. It is unclear whether Lord Neuberger regarded *"the breach"* in this context as the director's unauthorised share pledge, or the bank's refusal to return the shares when asked to do so.

[11] See, at [148]–[155].

12–009   While the Court was not prepared to allow the bank to retain the benefit of shares which it had knowingly received in breach of fiduciary duty, nor was it prepared to allow the company to obtain a windfall benefit which it would never have obtained but for the director's transgressions.

(2)   Relevance in Fraud Claims

12–010   It will be obvious from the discussion above that a claim in knowing receipt is commonly brought in fraud claims, many of which have at their root the misappropriation of trust assets or assets which are in some way managed in a fiduciary capacity. It is typical for those assets to be passed on by the primary wrongdoers to third parties with a view to their secretion and dispersal. Through the deployment of the equitable rules of tracing, which we consider in Ch.23 below, and which permit the claimant to follow the proceeds of the fraud through potentially multiple successive recipients, the claim in knowing receipt can extend the net of potential defendants very widely indeed. Defendants to such claims are often active conspirators with the primary wrongdoers, but, as we shall see, need not be.

(3)   Locus Standi

12–011   A claim in knowing receipt will usually be brought by the beneficiary/principal of a defaulting trustee or other fiduciary (and the text below is written on that assumption). However, that is not necessarily the case. There is authority to the effect that a trustee can himself bring claims on behalf of his beneficiaries for knowing receipt, even in circumstances in which it was his breach which led to the misappropriation of the assets.[12] In certain circumstances, a knowing recipient might even bring a claim against another knowing recipient on behalf of the underlying beneficiary.[13]

(4)   Associated Claims

12–012   No introduction to knowing receipt can fail to point out that there may be a number of different claims which cover the same facts or overlap in relation to the same broad set of facts. Expansive pleading may be appropriate in some cases. Besides liability for dishonest assistance (for behaviour falling short of, or different from, actual receipt), a claimant might assert:

(a)   equitable proprietary claims based upon the relevant property or its traceable proceeds being still identifiable in the defendant's hands by reference to the principles set out in *Foskett v McKeown*[14] (see Ch.23);

(b)   liability under general principles of unjust enrichment (see Ch.14); or

---

[12] See *Pulvers v Chan* [2007] EWHC 2406 (Ch), [2008] P.N.L.R. 9, at [380].

[13] *Smalley v Bracken Partners Ltd* [2003] EWCA Civ 1875, at [12]–[17].

[14] *Foskett v McKeown* [2001] 1 A.C. 102. See *Armstrong DLW GmbH v Winnington Networks Ltd* [2012] EWHC 10 (Ch); [2013] Ch. 156, where both claims were run together.

(c)   (to the extent that it is distinct) liability under the so-called personal *Diplock* claim against "volunteer" recipients of monies paid in breach of trust.[15]

In certain circumstances, a claimant may be able to rely upon statutory receipt-based claims, such as those provided by the Insolvency Act 1986.

B.   RECEIPT OF THE CLAIMANT'S ASSETS

(1)   The Claimant's Assets or their Traceable Proceeds

An asset is the claimant's in this context if he has a subsisting equitable proprietary interest in it. This will include assets which the claimant owns outright, assets which are held on trust on his behalf and (probably) assets over which the claimant has a charge or mortgage.[16] It will also include the traceable proceeds of such assets. Practitioners should note that, following the Supreme Court's decision in *FHR European Ventures LLP v Cedar Capital Partners LLC*,[17] bribes, secret commissions, and (potentially) any other profit earned by a fiduciary in breach of his fiduciary duties will be held on trust for his beneficiary and, therefore, transfer of such profits to third parties may well constitute a transfer of the claimant's property for the purposes of engaging the law in knowing receipt.[18]   **12–013**

Assets for these purposes include land, money, chattels and (at least some) statutory rights.[19] They do not include contractual rights under executory contracts,[20] nor (probably) most forms of information.[21]   **12–014**

It should be noted that if assets are transferred to the defendant under an ostensibly binding contract between the claimant and the defendant, they are no longer (from the point of transfer) the claimant's assets, and no action in knowing   **12–015**

---

[15] See *Re Diplock* [1948] 465, where the defendant is in principle liable even if the property can no longer be specifically identified, and where guilty knowledge is not a requirement. This type of claim is of use principally in the administration of estates, for an underpaid beneficiary who has first exhausted his remedy against the personal representatives to be able to make a claim directly against an overpaid beneficiary on a strict liability basis. It is somewhat anomalous but still relevant.

[16] See *El-Ajou v Dollar Land Holdings Plc (No.2)* [1995] 2 All E.R. 213, at 219 and *Buhr v Barclays Bank Plc* [2001] EWCA Civ 1223, at [45]–[50]. Note, however, Tucker, Le Poidevin and Brightwell, *Lewin on Trusts* (2012), para.42–041.

[17] *FHR European Ventures LLP v Cedar Capital Partners LLC* [2014] UKSC 45; [2015] A.C. 250.

[18] See *FHR European Ventures LLP v Cedar Capital Partners LLC* [2016] EWHC 359 (Ch), at [58]–[78].

[19] *Armstrong DLW GmbH v Winnington Networks Ltd* [2012] EWHC 10 (Ch); [2013] Ch. 156, at [61].

[20] *Criterion Properties Ltd v Stratford UK Properties Ltd* [2004] UKHL 28; [2004] 1 W.L.R. 1846, at [27]: "The creation by the contract of contractual rights does not constitute a 'receipt' of assets in the sense that a 'knowing receipt' involves a receipt of assets."

[21] See *Farah Constructions Pty Ltd v Say-Dee Pty Ltd* [2007] HCA 22, at [118]–[121]. Although, note the High Court of Australia stated that trade secrets might form property for these purposes. See also (although in a different context) *OBG Ltd v Allen* [2007] UKHL 21; [2008] 1 A.C. 1, at [275]. Also note obiter suggestions that information might form property for these purposes in *Satnam Investments Ltd v Dunlop Heywood* [1999] 3 All E.R. 652, at 671.

receipt will lie, even if the contract was entered into in an obvious breach of fiduciary duty, of which the defendant knew. So long as the contract subsists, the defendant is entitled to rely upon his contract with the claimant to justify his receipt of the assets. In order to pursue an action in knowing receipt in such circumstances it is necessary, first, to set aside the contract (which it will frequently be possible to do, though the claimant will lose the benefit thereof).[22]

12–016 It is often said that the property in question must have been, prior to the point of receipt, held on trust for the claimant.[23] However, this is potentially misleading, and such statements tend to be followed by an assertion that "trust" in this context is given a broad meaning, which includes property held by "quasi-trustees".[24] Hence a director of a company has traditionally been treated as a form of trustee[25] so as to permit a claim in knowing receipt brought by the company against the recipient of company funds which have been transferred by the director in breach of his fiduciary duty. It is simpler, and more accurate, to say that the claim can arise wherever:

(a) the claimant has a proprietary interest in transferred assets, whether or not the claimant's title is equitable only; and

(b) those assets are transferred in breach of a fiduciary duty (which includes a breach of trust) owed to him.[26]

---

[22] *Criterion Properties Plc v Stratford UK Properties LLC* [2004] UKHL 28; [2004] 1 W.L.R. 1846, at [4]: "If . . . the agreement is found to be valid and is therefore not set aside, questions of 'knowing receipt' by [the defendant] do not arise. So far as [the defendant] is concerned there can be no question of [the company]'s assets having been misapplied. [The defendant] acquired the assets from [the company], the legal and beneficial owner of the assets, under a valid agreement made between him and [the company]". Note that Lord Nicholls' analysis in that paragraph of the consequences if the contract is set aside are discordant with the view of the law stated in *BCCI v Akindele*, above, and should be treated with care. The principle set out in the text was applied in *Madoff Securities International Ltd v Raven* [2013] EWHC 3147 (Comm) so as to defeat the claim.

[23] See e.g. *Armstrong DLW GmbH v Winnington Networks Ltd* [2012] EWHC 10 (Ch); [2013] Ch. 156, at [125]–[129]; and *Novoship (UK) Ltd v Mikhaylyuk* [2014] EWCA Civ 908; [2015] Q.B. 499, at [89]: "in order to found liability for knowing receipt there must be trust property."

[24] See e.g. Tucker, Le Poidevin and Brightwell, *Lewin on Trusts* (2012), para.42–034.

[25] See e.g. *Selangor Rubber v Cradock (No.3)* [1968] 1 W.L.R. 1555, at 1574.

[26] The Privy Council explicitly recognised that claims in knowing receipt arise in such circumstances in the absence of any trust in *Arthur v Attorney General of the Turks and Caicos Islands* [2012] UKPC 30, at [31], where Sir Terence Etherton put the point clearly: "A defendant incurs an equitable liability for knowing receipt when he or she acts unconscionably by receiving and retaining trust property with the knowledge that it was transferred in breach of trust. Liability for knowing receipt can also be incurred when property is transferred in breach of a fiduciary duty other than a breach of trust. An obvious example would be the transfer of a company's property in breach of the directors' fiduciary duties, a director not being a trustee of the company's assets. That is also the basis of the claim in the present case since it is not alleged that the Property was held by or for the Crown on trust, but rather that the Minister acted in breach of fiduciary duty to the Crown in authorising the transfer to the appellant." This analysis draws from the statement of principle laid down by Millett J in *Agip (Africa) Ltd v Jackson* [1990] Ch. 265, at 290. Note that the Courts are prepared to treat grantors of security interests as owing limited fiduciary duties to the beneficiaries of that security for the purposes of tracing and, it is suggested, will do for the purposes of knowing receipt; see *Buhr v Barclays Bank Plc* [2001] EWCA Civ 1223, at [45]–[50].

Applying this analysis will require the claimant to establish that the person who has procured the transfer is a trustee or fiduciary viz-a-viz that claimant.[27] That may sometimes involve analytical difficulty: see the discussion on fiduciaries at Ch.11 above. Couching the requirement in these terms explains why a claim in knowing receipt arises in circumstances in which a company's agent misappropriates or diverts corporate assets,[28] without resorting to a fiction that the company is the beneficiary of a trust,[29] or to ill-defined terms such as "quasi-trustee". It will be apparent that this relaxation of the criteria for the imposition of liability has significant consequences for the utility of this cause of action in fraud claims. Moreover, it allows the use of equitable tracing rules (examined in Ch.23) to be deployed even where there is no trust in the strict sense.

(2) "Receipt"

The defendant must have received the relevant assets, or their traceable proceeds, and received them for "his own use and benefit",[30] rather than on behalf of another.[31] In the simplest case, receipt into a bank account held by the defendant will constitute (absent special circumstances) such beneficial receipt.[32] It is sometimes said that receipt in a "ministerial capacity" is insufficient. The distinction is founded on the analysis that a person who receives property merely as an agent has no interest of any kind in it himself and must simply account to his principal for it.[33] Receipt by him is therefore treated as equivalent of receipt by the principal (notwithstanding that the agent does not subsequently pass on the asset to the principal: receipt by the agent will at that moment be treated as receipt by the principal irrespective of later events). Take this example: A holds a painting on trust for B. In breach of his trust, he sells it to C. C sends his employee, D, to collect it. Provided that it is unconscionable (as to which, see below) for C to retain the benefit of the painting, he is liable in knowing receipt at the point at which D collects the painting. D is not liable in knowing receipt, regardless of his knowledge, because he is not receiving the painting for himself, but as the agent of another. That position would change if D took the painting for himself. **12–017**

The above notwithstanding, the agent of a knowing recipient is not immune to liability. In the example above, B may have a cause of action against D for **12–018**

---

[27] We consider whether a thief falls into that category below, at para.12–031.

[28] As in *Agip (Africa) Ltd v Jackson* [1990] Ch. 265, at 290.

[29] Though it is clear that all forms of trusteeship, whether it is express, resulting or constructive, will suffice: see for instance *Twinsectra v Yardley* [2002] UKHL 12; [2002] 2 A.C. 164.

[30] The term used by Millett J in *Agip (Africa) Ltd v Jackson* [1990] Ch. 265, at [292].

[31] *Uzinterimpex JSC v Standard Bank Plc* [2008] EWCA Civ 819; [2008] Bus L.R. 1762, at [38] and [39]. In that case, the issue was whether a bank which receives monies which have been paid in breach of fiduciary duty on behalf of its customer can plead mere ministerial receipt in answer to a claim for knowing receipt.

[32] *The Law Society of England and Wales v Habitable Concepts Ltd* [2010] EWHC 1449 (Ch), at [14].

[33] Hence in *El Ajou v Dollar Land Holdings Plc* [1993] 3 All E.R. 717 it was noted that receipt qua trustee would mean that the recipient was not liable because it did not receive the money beneficially.

dishonest assistance, or, to the extent that it is distinguishable from dishonest assistance, for dealing with the painting inconsistently with B's rights therein.[34]

12–019 Moreover, the precise boundaries of the concept of receipt by a defendant "for his own use and benefit" are necessarily unclear. The receipt does not have to be beneficial receipt whereby title ostensibly passes to the defendant. Control or some other interest in the assets short of ownership may be sufficient, and in this sense not all parties describing themselves as "agents" will necessarily have an absolute defence.[35]

12–020 There have been attempts to broaden the categories of cases in which a defendant is deemed to have received the claimant's assets or their traceable proceeds to include circumstances in which the defendant has received a causally-connected enrichment flowing from a transfer of the claimant's assets. For example, in *OJSC Oil Co Yugraneft v Abramovich*,[36] an argument was run that a vendor of shares could be liable in knowing receipt because the value of his company was swollen by misappropriated assets. This argument failed. The vendor had not received the misappropriated assets, or their proceeds, himself.[37]

12–021 Receipt of money by banks for the credit to a customer's account gives rise to difficult questions. The orthodox view is that, when a bank receives money for credit to a customer's account, it receives the money in a ministerial capacity, save to the extent that the money is used to clear a bank's overdraft, in which case it receives the money beneficially.[38] However, this view is open to criticism.[39] Generally speaking, when a bank receives money for crediting to a customer's account, the bank becomes liable in debt to that customer in the amount of the payment, but is entitled to deal with the money as it sees fit. It is therefore not clear why the bank should escape liability on the basis that it has received the money in a ministerial capacity; it has not. The fact that the receipt of the money created a corresponding liability in debt to the customer should not make any difference in circumstances in which the bank possesses sufficient knowledge to be liable in knowing receipt. Other defendants who give value for trust property knowing that it is being transferred in breach of trust are liable in knowing receipt; banks should not be any different. A revision to the orthodox view is

---

[34] See McGhee, *Snell's Equity* (2017), paras 30–069 and 30–075—30–076. Some judges have described the latter form of liability as a distinct sub-category of knowing receipt as opposed to a third form of liability which can be placed alongside dishonest assistance and knowing receipt—see Millett J in *Agip (Africa) Ltd v Jackson* [1990] Ch. 265, at 291–292.

[35] See the complex facts of *Uzinterimpex JSC v Standard Bank Plc* [2008] EWCA Civ 819; [2008] Bus L.R. 1762, where it was held that "In my view, whether the Bank received funds paid into the Transaction Account as a trustee or simply as agent for the Syndicate, it received them in a capacity which gave it a sufficient interest to render it liable as a constructive trustee if it had the required degree of knowledge" at [40]–[42]. See also the analysis of Scott LJ in *Polly Peck International v Nadir (No.2)* [1992] 4 All E.R. 769, 777 in relation to receipt by a bank.

[36] *OJSC Oil Co Yugraneft v Abramovich* [2008] EWHC 2613 (Comm).

[37] *OJSC Oil Co Yugraneft v Abramovich* [2008] EWHC 2613, at [365]: "The mere fact that a defendant has benefited from a breach of trust does not give rise to claims in knowing receipt or restitution." See further C. Mitchell, P. Mitchell and Watterson, *Goff & Jones: The Law of Unjust Enrichment* (2016), para.8–201.

[38] *Agip (Africa) Ltd v Jackson* [1990] Ch. 265, at 292. See also McGhee, *Snell's Equity* (2017), para.30–069.

[39] See Virgo, *Principles of the Law of Restitution* (2015), pp.647–648.

possible: in *Uzinterimpex JSC v Standard Bank Plc*, Moore-Bick LJ (speaking obiter) described these criticisms as having "a great deal of force".[40]

(3) Receipt by Companies as Receipt by Director/Guiding Mind

If the receipt is by a company (for instance into a bank account held in its name), can that receipt be treated as also by the controlling mind of the company who has, say, procured the receipt? In *Trustor AB v Smallbone (No.2)*[41] the claimant brought proceedings against S for knowing receipt. Money had been paid from the claimant to a company which S controlled and which had no independent business or directors other than that which S procured it to do. The court held that for the purposes of establishing liability in knowing receipt, the receipt by the company could be treated as receipt by S on the basis that it was appropriate to "pierce the corporate veil."[42] This case has subsequently been considered by the Supreme Court in *Prest v Prest*[43] and explained not by reference to the veil-piercing concept (the application of which was said to be "illegitimate"), but simply on the more conventional basis that the company was treated as the nominee or agent of S. In the light of the decision in *Prest*, it is unlikely that resort can in future be had to the veil-piercing concept in order to establish liability in knowing receipt. The focus will be on the capacity in which the company receives the asset and whether it does so as agent for another. What *Prest* establishes is that existing legal concepts are generally able to accommodate scenarios such as that which arose in *Trustor* to achieve a just result.[44]

12–022

It is worth noting in passing an argument run in *VTB Capital Plc v Nutritek International Corp* before the Court of Appeal.[45] There, it was contended that it was possible to find the director of a company liable in knowing receipt on the basis of a receipt by the company, without either showing that the company had received it as agent for the director or piercing the corporate veil.[46] The argument was based upon the judgment of Lawrence Collins J in *CMS Dolphin Ltd v*

12–023

---

[40] *Uzinterimpex JSC v Standard Bank Plc* [2008] EWCA Civ 819, at [40].

[41] *Trustor AB v Smallbone (No.2)* [2001] EWHC 703; [2001] 1 W.L.R. 1177.

[42] See, at [23], per Morritt V-C: "In my judgment the court is entitled to 'pierce the corporate veil' and recognise the receipt of the company as that of the individual(s) in control of it if the company was used as a device or façade to conceal the true facts thereby avoiding or concealing any liability of those individual(s)." In *The Law Society of England and Wales v Habitable Concepts Ltd & Anor* [2010] EWHC 1449 (Ch), a solicitor's firm paid out mortgage advances to H Ltd in breach of trust. H Ltd's sole shareholder and director was O. In a claim for knowing receipt against H Ltd and O brought by the Law Society, standing in the shoes of the firm, the claim against H Ltd succeeded where H Ltd had no plausible explanation for the receipt of the funds. The claim in knowing receipt against O failed because, according to the judge, he could not be sure that receipt by H Ltd was a "deceptive mask to hide receipt by" O. However, the claim in dishonest assistance succeeded.

[43] *Prest v Prest* [2013] 2 A.C. 415, at [32]–[33], per Lord Sumption. See further Ch.18.

[44] In the earlier case of *Cowan de Groot Properties v Eagle Trust Plc* [1992] 4 All E.R. 700 Knox J had correctly held that where a company had received assets the parent of that company was not liable in knowing receipt by reason of its relationship with the subsidiary. He refused to apply the veil-lifting doctrine.

[45] *VTB Capital Plc v Nutritek International Corp* [2012] EWCA Civ 808; [2012] 2 Lloyd's Rep. 313.

[46] See, at [74].

Simonet, a case involving a director who was found liable for diverting corporate business and opportunities to a separate company in which he was interested.[47] In that case, both the director and his company were found jointly liable because they had *"jointly participated in the breach of the trust"*.[48] In *VTB*, the Court of Appeal declined to express a view on whether liability in knowing receipt could similarly arise on a joint and several basis between a director and his corporate alter ego (and the issue did not arise before the Supreme Court in that case). Pending a ruling by the appellate Courts, the point is still arguable, although this aspect of the reasoning in *CMS* is doubtful and has been disapproved at first instance.[49]

12–024   Even where a director/shareholder cannot be fixed with liability in knowing receipt, it will often be the case that an alternative claim in dishonest assistance, which is not a receipt-based liability, will succeed, although it will be borne in mind that the mens rea which must be proved against the knowing assister is different from that of the knowing recipient (see generally Ch.13).

(4) Successive Recipients

12–025   Provided that they remain identifiable in accordance with equitable tracing rules (which are considered below at Ch.23), a recipient of assets may be liable in knowing receipt even if they have passed through multiple hands before reaching the defendant.

C.   ARISING FROM A BREACH OF FIDUCIARY DUTY OWED TO THE CLAIMANT

(1) The Requirement

12–026   The nature of fiduciary duties is considered in Ch.11.

12–027   In order for an action in knowing receipt to arise, the initial transfer of the asset out of the trust or fiduciary relationship in which it should have been held must be a direct result of a breach of fiduciary duty[50] (which includes a breach of trust). It is suggested that the first transfer must either:

(a)   be a breach in and of itself; or
(b)   be effected by a fiduciary while he is, and because he is, in breach of his fiduciary duties.

---

[47] *CMS Dolphin Ltd v Simonet* [2002] B.C.C. 600, at [98]–[105]. See also *Airbus Operations Ltd v Withey* [2014] EWHC 1126 (QB) (a case on secret commissions), at [453]–[461].
[48] *CMS Dolphin Ltd v Simonet* [2002] B.C.C. 600, at [103].
[49] *Ultraframe (UK) Ltd v Fielding* [2005] EWHC 1638 (Ch), at [1561]–[1576]; and *National Grid Electricity Transmission Plc v McKenzie* [2009] EWHC 1817 (Ch), at [114]. See further Ch.11.
[50] Which is not to be confused with a breach of duty by a fiduciary. A fiduciary may commit a breach of duty which is not a breach of fiduciary duty: see generally *Bristol & West BS v Mothew* [1998] 1 Ch. 1, at 16–17.

There is no need to show that the breach was a dishonest one.[51] After the first transfer, each subsequent recipient will be liable provided that they have the requisite knowledge and provided the relevant asset remains traceable.

The leading case, *Brown v Bennett*,[52] illustrates the point. A company, Pinecord Ltd, entered into insolvency proceedings. A new company, "Oasis", purchased Pinecord's former business from the administrative receiver. Oasis was owned and managed by Pinecord's former directors. It was alleged by minority shareholders in Pinecord that the company only went into insolvency proceedings because of deliberate mismanagement of the company by the directors, aimed at increasing their share of the Pinecord business.   **12–028**

The minority shareholders sued Oasis in knowing receipt (having taken an assignment of Pinecord's rights for that purpose). Their case was that the business received by Oasis was transferred as a result of the former directors' earlier breaches of fiduciary duty, and that the directors' knowledge of that fact should be attributed to Oasis.   **12–029**

The claim failed. Whether or not the former directors had breached their fiduciary duties owed to Pinecord before the onset of the administrative receivership, the transfer of the business by the administrative receiver to Oasis was not itself a breach of fiduciary duty or effected as a consequence of the administrative receiver's breach of duty. Accordingly, no liability for knowing receipt could arise from it.[53] What the claimants should have done, if the facts warranted such a claim, was bring proceedings (via the assignment from Pinecord) against the directors personally for breach of fiduciary duty.   **12–030**

(2)   Stolen Assets

Particular considerations arise at the intersection of the law of theft and of knowing receipt. Imagine A steals assets from B, and gives them to C. C knows the assets were stolen from B. Does B have a claim against C in knowing receipt?   **12–031**

There is certainly support in the authorities for the proposition that B does, on the basis that the thief (A) held whatever interest he acquired in the stolen assets on a form of trust for the person with legal title to the assets (B); and, therefore, that the transmission of the assets to C amounted to a breach of trust which would give rise to liability in knowing receipt on C's part.[54]   **12–032**

The notion that A might in these circumstances owe fiduciary duties to B is, however, controversial. A has, after all, not undertaken to act on behalf of B, or to   **12–033**

---

[51] *Agip (Africa) Ltd v Jackson* [1990] Ch. 265, at 292.
[52] *Brown v Bennett* [1999] B.C.C. 525.
[53] *Brown v Bennett* [1999] B.C.C. 525, at 530–531.
[54] See *Westdeutsche Landesbank Girozentrale v Islington London BC* [1996] A.C. 669, at 716; *Twinsectra Ltd v Yardley* [1999] Lloyd's Rep. Bank. 438, at [99] (reversed on appeal, but not on this point), and *Armstrong DLW GmbH v Winnington Networks Ltd* [2012] EWHC 10 (Ch), [2013] Ch. 156, at [125]–[129].

subordinate his interests to B. Their dealings (i.e. the theft) have been wholly adversarial, and therefore fundamentally opposed to a fiduciary relationship. The question is considered further in Ch.9.

D. KNOWLEDGE/UNCONSCIONABILITY

(1) The Knowledge Requirement

12–034   Over the last few decades, debate has occurred over what mental state is required to be established in order to found liability in knowing receipt. The very description of this liability makes it clear that some degree of knowledge is required. The question is what? Positions have been adopted which range from, on the one hand, treating liability as tantamount to strict to, on the other, treating it as requiring nothing less than dishonesty on the part of the recipient. In the end some form of middle ground position has been adopted which draws a clear distinction between the mental element required for dishonest assistance and that required in knowing receipt, the latter being of a lower order of culpability than the former.

12–035   The starting point is simple: liability in knowing receipt is dependent upon the defendant "knowing" in the relevant sense that the assets which he has received are traceable to a breach of trust or of fiduciary duty[55] i.e. the defendant need only "know" that the assets were held on trust (or subject to fiduciary duties) and of the circumstances which made the transfer a breach of that trust (or duty). It is not necessary for the defendant to have been aware of any intention to harm or perpetrate a fraud the claimant.[56]

12–036   However, much turns on what constitutes "knowledge" for these purposes.

12–037   The leading case on this subject is now *Bank of Credit and Commerce International (Overseas) Ltd v Akindele*.[57]

12–038   At first instance, Carnwath J held that the recipient must have a level of knowledge of the underlying breach of fiduciary duty such as to fall into one of the first three so-called "Baden Categories" of knowledge which had been formulated by Peter Gibson J in the earlier decision of *Baden Delvaux v Société Générale pour Favoriser le Développement du Commerce et de l'Industrie en France SA*.[58] The full list of categories is as follows:

(i)   actual knowledge;
(ii)   wilfully shutting one's eyes to the obvious;

---

[55] Returning to Hoffmann LJ's formulation in *El Ajou v Dollar Land Holdings Plc* [1994] 2 All E.R. 685, at 700g: " ... the plaintiff must show ... knowledge on the part of the defendant that the assets he received are traceable to a breach of fiduciary duty."

[56] See *Eagle Trust Plc v S.B.C. Securities Ltd* [1993] 1 W.L.R. 484, at 497, and *Belmont Finance Corp v Williams Furniture Ltd (No.2)* [1980] 1 All E.R. 393, at 412.

[57] *Bank of Credit and Commerce International (Overseas) Ltd v Akindele* [2001] Ch. 437.

[58] *Baden Delvaux v Société Générale pour Favoriser le Développement du Commerce et de l'Industrie en France SA* [1993] 1 W.L.R. 509, at 575–576. This was a case of dishonest assistance.

(iii)   wilfully and recklessly failing to make such inquiries as an honest and reasonable man would make;

(iv)   knowledge of circumstances which would indicate the facts to an honest and reasonable man;

(v)   knowledge of circumstances which will put an honest and reasonable man on inquiry.[59]

Traditionally, types (1) to (3) have been regarded as forms of "actual knowledge" or notice and types (4) and (5) have been regarded as forms of "constructive knowledge" or notice. The effect of Carnwath J's holding was that actual dishonesty on the part of the recipient was necessary.

The Court of Appeal both rejected Carnwath J's conclusion that dishonesty was a necessary element of a claim in knowing receipt and disapproved his reliance on the *Baden* categories. In the words of Nourse LJ (giving the leading judgment):   **12–039**

> "What then, in the context of knowing receipt, is the purpose to be served by a categorisation of knowledge? It can only be to enable the court to determine whether, in the words of Buckley LJ in *Belmont Finance Corp Ltd v Williams Furniture Ltd (No.2)* [1980] 1 All E.R. 393, at 405, the recipient can 'conscientiously retain [the] funds against the company' or, in the words of Sir Robert Megarry V-C in *re Montagu's Settlement Trusts* [1987] Ch. 264 , 273, '[the recipient's] conscience is sufficiently affected for it to be right to bind him by the obligations of a constructive trustee'. But, if that is the purpose, there is no need for categorisation. All that is necessary is that the recipient's state of knowledge should be such as to make it unconscionable for him to retain the benefit of the receipt.
>
> For these reasons I have come to the view that, just as there is now a single test of dishonesty for knowing assistance, so ought there to be a single test of knowledge for knowing receipt. The recipient's state of knowledge must be such as to make it unconscionable for him to retain the benefit of the receipt…"[60]

The obvious problem with this test is that, given unconscionability is a legal conclusion, it begs the question. It amounts to saying that, in order to be liable in knowing receipt, a recipient must have the state of knowledge which would be necessary to make him liable in knowing receipt.   **12–040**

In simple cases, the difficulties in Nourse LJ's formulation do not arise. Imagine A controls a company which is hopelessly insolvent. To keep the company's assets out of the hands of the Revenue, he transfers its assets for no consideration to his close associate, C. He tells C what he is doing, and why he is doing it. C's retention of the benefit of those assets in those circumstances would plainly be unconscionable, because he is knowingly the beneficiary of A's overt breach of duty.[61]   **12–041**

---

[59] See [1999] B.C.C. 669, at 677.

[60] *Bank of Credit and Commerce International (Overseas) Ltd v Akindele* [2001] Ch. 437, at 455. It is ironic that in the very case that had decided that there was a single test for liability in dishonest assistance, Lord Nicholls had deprecated adoption of a test of unconscionability, on the basis that its meaning was unclear: see *Royal Brunei Airlines v Tan* [1995] 2 A.C. 378, at 392. There have, nevertheless, been numerous later cases in which *Akindele* has been applied: see for instance *Ali v Al-Basri* [2004] EWHC 2608 (QB); *Dyson Technology Ltd v Curtis* [2010] EWHC 3289 (Ch); and *Templeton Insurance Ltd v Brunswick* [2012] EWHC 1522 (Ch).

[61] This was the case in *Relfo v Varsani* [2012] EWHC 2168 (Ch), although note the comments made on *Akindele*, at [78] and [79].

12–042 However, in less straightforward cases, Nourse LJ's test becomes rather more difficult to apply. Just what state of mind makes a receipt unconscionable? In *Armstrong DLW GmbH v Winnington Networks Ltd*, counsel for both sides and the judge found themselves obliged to revert to the Baden categories:

> "… Both parties agreed that it was thus helpful (and indeed necessary) to consider which types of Baden 'knowledge' would render receipt of trust property 'unconscionable' and then each made arguments in line with their arguments on the issue of 'notice' for the bona fide purchaser defence, suggesting that the tests for knowledge and for notice overlap considerably. I agree. …
>
> In my judgment, the position, in a commercial context, can be summarised as follows: (1) Baden types (1) to (3) knowledge on the part of a defendant render receipt of trust property 'unconscionable'. It is not necessary to show that the defendant realised that the transaction was 'obviously' or 'probably' in breach of trust or fraudulent; the possibility of impropriety or the claimant's interest is sufficient. (2) Further Baden types (4) and (5) knowledge also render receipt 'unconscionable' but only if, on the facts actually known to this defendant, a reasonable person would either have appreciated that the transfer was probably in breach of trust or would have made inquiries or sought advice which would have revealed the probability of the breach of trust."[62]

12–043 It remains to be seen what the appellate courts will make of this renewed reliance upon the very Baden Categories which Nourse LJ appeared to disavow in the context of knowing receipt claims. However, one can see that this approach has the virtue of offering a structured means to analyse such claims while allowing for considerable flexibility in application. It is also (it is submitted) apt to produce results which are largely consistent with the authorities.[63]

12–044 In any event, it now seems clear that something short of actual knowledge of the breach of the fiduciary duty will be enough to affix the defendant with liability in knowing receipt,[64] but precisely what is required will vary according to the

---

[62] *Armstrong DLW GmbH v Winnington Networks Ltd* [2012] EWHC 10 (Ch); [2013] Ch. 156, at [131]–[132]. This analysis was followed by Morgan J in *Group Seven Ltd v Nasir* [2017] EWHC 2466 (Ch), at [478]. In *Bank of Tokyo-Mitsubishi UFJ, Ltd v Baskan Gida Sanayi VE Pazarlama A.S.* [2009] EWHC 1276 (Ch), Briggs J said that "Knowledge for that purpose [i.e. imposing liability in knowing receipt] is to be distinguished from mere notice, and requires at least 'a clear suspicion'", referring to *Uzinterimpex JSC v Standard Bank Plc* [2008] EWCA Civ 819, per Moore-Bick LJ, at [44].

[63] One exception to this is the judgment of the Court of Appeal in *Criterion Properties Plc v Stratford UK Properties LLC* [2002] EWCA Civ 1783; [2003] 1 W.L.R. 2108. In *Armstrong*, it was suggested that a defendant who actually knows that he has received an asset in breach of trust will invariably be held to be an unconscionable recipient. However, in *Criterion*, at [38], the Court of Appeal appeared to hold that, depending on the circumstances, a person could have actual knowledge that the person with whom he was dealing was acting in breach of his fiduciary duties, and still not be acting unconscionably. The House of Lords in the same case criticised the Court of Appeal for muddling the law of agency and the law of knowing receipt (see [2004] UKHL 28; [2004] 1 W.L.R. 1846) and, in light of that criticism, the Court of Appeal's judgment is of uncertain weight.

[64] See, however, Virgo, *Principles of the Law of Restitution* (2015), pp.650–651, and also *Latchworth Ltd v Dryer* [2016] EWHC 3424 (Ch), at [106]: "The question that remains concerns the level of guilty knowledge that must be demonstrated if a claim of this sort is to succeed. In order to succeed in a claim of this sort, the claimant must prove receipt by the defendant with either actual knowledge of the relevant facts or that he wilfully shut his eyes to the obvious or wilfully and recklessly failed to make such enquiries as an honest and reasonable man would make in the circumstances. Mr Tilly's case is that the payments were made on the instructions of Mr Barzani and that he thought they came from another (Swiss) account controlled by Mr Barzani." (per HHJ Pelling QC). In *Papamichael v National Westminster Bank Plc* [2003] 1 Lloyd's Rep. 341, HHJ Chambers QC observed at 375 that

precise circumstances of the case. The question has been phrased as an enquiry into whether, taking account of the context in which the defendant is acting, he has acted in bad faith,[65] or, in commercial contexts, whether or not the defendant has acted in a commercially unacceptable manner.[66] This is thought to be the same test as that to determine whether the defendant would have a change of position defence in the law of unjust enrichment.[67]

The interrelationship between the "unconscionable" state of knowledge in knowing receipt claims and "notice" in proprietary claims is unclear. Lord Sumption has stated obiter that the two concepts are precisely the same,[68] while leading commentators perceive a distinction between the two concepts (albeit they do so on the basis of case law which may have been overtaken by *Akindele*).[69] **12–045**

(2)   The Relevant Time

The time at which the defendant must have the relevant knowledge depends upon whether the defendant received the claimant's assets for value without notice of the claimant's interest in the property. **12–046**

If a defendant received the claimant's assets for value without notice and, subsequently, acquired the knowledge which would have made retention of the assets unconscionable, then no action will lie against him in knowing receipt.[70] **12–047**

On the other hand, if a defendant is a volunteer, and acquires knowledge which would make continuing retention of the claimant's assets unconscionable at a time at which those assets or their traceable proceeds still rest in his hands, then the defendant may become liable in knowing receipt from that point forward.[71] **12–048**

Akindele "makes it clear that dishonesty is not necessary to a finding of knowing receipt. It is also pretty clear that the type of knowledge that is required is actual rather than constructive knowledge."
[65] *Arthur v The Attorney General of the Turks & Caicos Islands* [2012] UKPC 30, at [40].
[66] *Armstrong DLW GmbH v Winnington Networks Ltd* [2012] EWHC 10 (Ch); [2013] Ch. 156, at [122] and [123].
[67] *Armstrong DLW GmbH v Winnington Networks Ltd* [2012] EWHC 10 (Ch); [2013] Ch. 156, at [122], Virgo, *Principles of the Law of Restitution* (2015), p.650.
[68] *Papadimitriou v Crédit Agricole Corp and Investment Bank* [2015] UKPC 13; [2015] 1 W.L.R. 4265, at [33].
[69] See Tucker, Le Poidevin and Brightwell, *Lewin on Trusts* (2012), para.42–064; and McGhee, *Snell's Equity*, (2017), para.20–074.
[70] See L. Tucker, N. Le Poidevin and J. Brightwell, *Lewin on Trusts*, 18th edn (London: Sweet & Maxwell, 2007), para.42–083.
[71] *In Re Diplock* [1948] Ch. 465, at 477 (although note this simply reflects a concession by Counsel for the recipients in that case); *Agip (Africa) Ltd v Jackson* [1990] 1 Ch. 265, at 291G: "The first [of the two main classes of case] is concerned with the person who receives for his own benefit trust property transferred to him in breach of trust. He is liable as a constructive trustee if he received it with notice, actual or constructive, that it was trust property and that the transfer to him was a breach of trust; or if he received it without such notice but subsequently discovered the facts. In either case he is liable to account for the property, in the first case as from the time he received the property, and in the second as from the time he acquired notice." See also *Heperu Pty Ltd v Belle* [2009] NSWCA 252; (2009) 258 A.L.R. 727, at [159]–[164].

12–049 If, contrary to Lord Sumption's views referred to above, there is a difference between "notice" of the claimant's interests and a state of knowledge which makes retention of the claimant's assets "unconscionable", then there is a third possibility: the defendant may receive the claimant's assets for value, and with notice of the claimant's interest, but without sufficient knowledge at the time of the transfer to make retention of those assets unconscionable at the time of the initial receipt. If the defendant subsequently acquires the state of knowledge which makes retention of the claimant's assets "unconscionable" then, in the view of leading commentators, the defendant will become liable for knowing receipt in respect of the remnants of the assets or their traceable proceeds which remain in the defendant's hands at that point.[72]

(3) Attribution of Knowledge

12–050 Where the defendant to a knowing receipt claim is a company then, since a company can only know something through its officers, the issue may arise whether the knowledge of a director or other person can be imputed to the company. In *El Ajou v Dollar Land Holdings Plc* [73] the claim at first instance failed because, although all the other constituent elements of the liability in knowing receipt had been made out, it was found that the relevant director's knowledge could not be imputed to the defendant company. On appeal, the Court of Appeal reversed the judge below and set out the two bases for attribution of knowledge to a company:

(1) the "directing mind and will" doctrine; and
(2) imputation of knowledge via agency principles.

We consider the law of attribution below at Ch.19. Given that knowledge is the core ingredient of liability in knowing receipt, it is likely that attribution questions will arise frequently in such claims when brought against companies.[74]

E. REMEDIES

12–051 As we have seen above, the defendant's liability may be either personal or proprietary. The proprietary remedies available to the claimant will be those considered in Ch.23, by which the claimant's ownership of the asset or its substitute is vindicated. The personal accountability of the knowing recipient is that of a constructive trustee, and so includes both a liability to pay equitable compensation and (it would appear) account for profits. These remedies are considered in Ch.22.

---

[72] Tucker, Le Poidevin and Brightwell, *Lewin on Trusts* (2007), para.42–083.
[73] *El Ajou v Dollar Land Holdings Plc* [1994] B.C.C. 143.
[74] See for instance *Courtwood Holdings S.A. v Woodley Properties Ltd* [2016] EWHC 1168 (Ch).

The nature of the remedies available was summarised in these terms by the Privy **12–052** Council in *Arthur v The Attorney General of the Turks & Caicos Islands (Turks and Caicos Islands)*[75]:

> "When considering relief for the consequences of knowing receipt it is necessary to distinguish between proprietary and personal remedies. The beneficiaries or innocent trustees will pursue a proprietary claim by following the trust property wrongly transferred or tracing its inherent value into something substituted for it: *Foskett v McKeown* [2001] 1 A.C. 102, at 127–129 (Lord Millett). The claim for personal liability is for the recipient to account as a constructive trustee and will usually only be necessary where following or tracing is not possible because, for example, the property has been acquired by a *bona fide* purchaser for value without notice or has been dissipated and is otherwise no longer identifiable. As Sir Robert Megarry V-C said in *Re Montagu's Settlement Trusts* [1987] 1 Ch. 264, at 285: 'The equitable doctrine of tracing and the imposition of a constructive trust by reason of the knowing receipt of trust property are governed by different rules and must be kept distinct. Tracing is primarily a means of determining the rights of property, whereas the imposition of a constructive trust creates personal obligations that go beyond mere property rights."

---

[75] *Arthur v The Attorney General of the Turks & Caicos Islands (Turks and Caicos Islands)* [2012] UKPC 30.

CHAPTER 13

DISHONEST ASSISTANCE

A. INTRODUCTION

(1) The Nature of the Claim and its Elements

As noted in the previous chapter, English law recognises two claims that may lie **13–001**
in equity against a third party who comes to be mixed up in a breach of trust or
fiduciary duty:

(1) "knowing receipt" of trust property or its traceable proceeds; and
(2) "dishonest assistance" in a breach of trust or fiduciary duty.[1]

This chapter is concerned with the second of these claims. Despite the seemingly **13–002**
recondite nature of this ground of liability, dishonest assistance is in practice a
significant cause of action for the fraud litigator. As long ago as 1874 this basis of
liability was referred to as participation in fraudulent conduct.[2] One hundred
years later the liability was stated to be concerned with the "furtherance of
fraud."[3] In well-known cases it has enabled liability to be established against
accountants who had assisted in the misapplication of property by laundering the
money through bank accounts controlled by them[4]; a director for procuring a
breach of trust by a company which acted as agent for the claimant, whereby the
company expended client monies for its own purposes[5]; an offshore financial
services provider which set up and administered companies for its clients, which
companies received monies stolen by a director from the claimant company[6]; and
a solicitor who drafted sham agreements, which gave the appearance of
legitimacy to onward payments of the proceeds of a fraud.[7] These exemplify
paradigm forms of behaviour in fraud claims.

In the leading modern case of *Royal Brunei Airlines Sdn Bhd v Tan*,[8] the claim **13–003**
was described as being:

---

[1] Derived from Lord Selborne's famous statement of principle in *Barnes v Addy* (1874) LR9 Ch. App.
244, at 251–252, albeit his short articulation of the claims has subsequently been refined and
elaborated upon, in terms of the conditions that must be satisfied for liability to arise.
[2] *Barnes v Addy* (1874) LR9 Ch. App. 244, at 251.
[3] *Agip (Africa) Ltd v Jackson* [1990] Ch. 265, at 293.
[4] *Agip (Africa) Ltd v Jackson*, above.
[5] *Royal Brunei Airlines Sdn Bhd v Tan* [1995] A.C. 378.
[6] *Barlow Clowes International Ltd v Eurotrust International Ltd* [2006] 1 W.L.R. 1476.
[7] *Dubai Aluminium Co Ltd v Salaam* [2003] 2 A.C. 366.
[8] *Royal Brunei Airlines Sdn Bhd v Tan* [1995] A.C. 378.

"a liability in equity to make good resulting loss [which] attaches to a person who dishonestly procures or assists in a breach of trust or fiduciary obligation".

This encapsulates the elements of the cause of action, which are:

(1) A breach of trust or fiduciary duty;
(2) Procurement of or assistance in that breach by the defendant;
(3) Dishonesty on the part of the defendant.

13–004 Each of these elements is considered in turn in this chapter. The liability of a dishonest assister has been said to be "secondary", in that it only arises where there has been a breach of trust or fiduciary duty by another.[9]

13–005 The claim is fault-based, rather than receipt-based or restitutionary: the claimant is seeking redress for a wrong.[10] It follows that, as we will see, the mental state that must be established is different from that of the knowing recipient, whose liability we consider in Ch.12. Moreover, the dishonest assister's liability does not arise out of any pre-existing trust or fiduciary relationship between him and the claimant (even if his liability is sometimes, unhelpfully, described as involving an accountability to the claimant as a constructive trustee).[11] He is more accurately described as being "accountable in equity"; he never claims to assume the position of trustee—nor need the claimant assert as much—and his liability can arise without ever having received or handled trust property.[12]

13–006 It follows that the remedies available for dishonest assistance are personal[13]: principally, equitable compensation for loss caused by the breach which has been assisted; but also, it is now established, an account of any profits obtained by reason of the assistance.[14] These remedies are considered in Ch.22. As explained there and as mentioned further below, whilst in principle the compensatory remedy against the dishonest assister ought to be coextensive with that against the defaulting trustee or fiduciary (to whose breach he is an accessory), where one is concerned with requiring the assister to disgorge a profit, it would appear that common law principles of causation will be applied by analogy, and there is a discretion to refuse relief, whereas the fiduciary's accountability is stricter.[15]

---

[9] *Royal Brunei Airlines Sdn Bhd v Tan*, above, per Lord Nicholls at 382E.

[10] *Twinsectra v Yardley* [2002] 2 A.C. 164, per Lord Millett at 194.

[11] E.g. see Lord Browne-Wilkinson's speech in *Westdeutsche Landesbank Girozentrale v Islington LBC* [1996] A.C. 669, at 705. In *Bank of Scotland Plc v A Ltd* [2001] 1 W.L.R. Lord Woolf said of liability in dishonest assistance, at [26]: "This potential accountability in equity is sometimes referred to as a liability as a constructive trustee, but that expression is ambiguous and may be misleading." Similar views were expressed by Lord Millett in *Dubai Aluminium Co Ltd v Salaam* [2003] 2 A.C. 366, at [141].

[12] *Paragon Finance Plc v D B Thakerar & Co* [1999] 1 All E.R. 400, at 409; *Dubai Aluminium Co Ltd v Salaam* [2003] 2 A.C. 366, per Lord Millett at [141].

[13] *Sinclair Investment Holdings SA v Versailles Trade Finance Ltd* [2007] EWHC 915 (Ch); [2007] 2 All E.R. (Comm) 993, per Rimer J at [109]–[135]. It also follows that a dishonest assister can avail himself of limitation defences that a true trustee could not: *Williams v Central Bank of Nigeria* [2014] A.C. 1189. See further para.25–014.

[14] *Novoship (UK) Limted v Mikhaylyuk* [2015] Q.B. 499, at [66]–[93].

[15] *Novoship*, above, at [109]–[115]; and, at [119], applying the discretion to withhold relief identified in non-fiduciary accounting cases in *A-G v Blake* [2001] 1 A.C. 268.

Liability in dishonest assistance can attach even when the defendant acts as an agent of the trustee whose breach gives rise to the primary liability.[16] Thus dishonest assistance is a means by which a director of a company can (in effect) be rendered personally liable for the default of the company, where the company is a trustee or fiduciary and in breach of its duties as such.[17] Indeed, this mechanism for imposing personal liability on directors for wrongful actions which they have procured via companies is one of the most important practical applications of the dishonest assistance basis of liability. In this way equity, just as the common law in the tort of deceit,[18] has been able to evade the corporate veil without needing to pierce it.

13–007

A dishonest assistance claim can be brought by a beneficiary, principal or company, to whom the relevant underlying trust or fiduciary obligations are owed. In the case of a trust, the trustee himself can sue, even if his breach is the source of the alleged accessory liability[19]; but, more commonly, the claim will be brought by a successor trustee.

13–008

(2)   Significance in Fraud Litigation

As we have seen, many fraud claims are founded on a breach of trust or fiduciary duty by a primary wrongdoer, commonly involving the misappropriation of assets belonging beneficially to the claimant. Such wrongdoers are often part of a larger combination of participants in the wrongdoing. A typical example will be the misappropriation of funds belonging to a claimant, which are then channelled far and wide through and with the assistance of a cohort of parties all complicit to a greater or lesser degree in the execution of the fraud and the concealment of its proceeds. Similarly to the tort of conspiracy, the claim in dishonest assistance allows the claimant to cast the net of liability widely, encompassing defendants who have not actually received any of the claimant's assets and who do not stand in a direct trust or fiduciary relationship with the claimant; and, moreover, defendants who are often more likely to have "deeper pockets" for the purposes of recovery than the principal wrongdoer.

13–009

As Lord Nicholls said in *Royal Brunei*[20]:

13–010

"The proper role of equity in commercial transactions is a topical question. Increasingly plaintiffs have recourse to equity for an effective remedy when the person in default, typically a company, is insolvent. Plaintiffs seek to obtain relief from others who were involved in the transaction, such as directors of the company, or its bankers, or its legal or other advisers. They

---

[16] *Attorney-General v Corp of Leicester* (1844) 7 Beav. 176, per Lord Langdale MR, at [179].

[17] As happened in *Royal Brunei Airlines Sdn Bhd v Tan*, above.

[18] As discussed in Ch.1, a director who makes a deceitful representation in the name of the company cannot avoid personal liability by asserting that the representation was made by him only as agent of the company: see para.1–137.

[19] *Montrose Investments Ltd v Orion Nominees Ltd* [2004] EWCA (Civ) 1032. It is easy to envisage circumstances where a dishonest stranger to the trust has (say) knowingly misled the trustee into committing an innocent breach of trust. In such a case both the beneficiary and the trustee would have a claim against the accessory and the beneficiary will also have a claim against the trustee.

[20] Above, at 381–382.

seek to fasten fiduciary obligations directly onto the company's officers or agents or advisers, or to have them held personally liable for assisting the company in breaches of trust or fiduciary obligations."

13–011 Indeed one often finds claims in unlawful means conspiracy and other economic torts being pleaded alongside claims in dishonest assistance, arising out of the same essential facts.[21] Similarly, dishonest assistance will commonly be available as a basis for liability on the part of a briber of the claimant's agent, in addition to claims for relief on the basis of the bribe.[22] Nevertheless, a claim in dishonest assistance in such situations does not merely frank the liability that would otherwise arise in tort; rather, it is a powerful additional weapon in the fraud litigator's armoury, including because:

(1) It enables a claimant to recover not just loss caused by the underlying wrong, but also profits made by the assister;

(2) It can lie against those whose involvement in the underlying wrong post-dated it (such as those who assist in the laundering of the proceeds of a fraud, even if not complicit in it before that); and it does not require one to establish a combination to which the primary wrongdoer and assister were both party;

(3) It enables recovery of the losses flowing from the underlying wrong, even if the assistance did not itself cause those losses; and

(4) It is available even where the primary wrongdoer cannot be proven himself to have acted dishonestly.

B. BREACH OF TRUST OR FIDUCIARY DUTY

(1) The Underlying Relationship

13–012 The equitable claim in dishonest assistance lies only where there is a trust or fiduciary relationship, the breach of which gives rise to the primary liability. A trust relationship in the formal sense of one whereby property is vested in one person to be held by him on trust for another is the paradigm, but by no means only, example. Quasi-trust relationships, such as those between a director and a company and between certain sorts of agents and their principals, in which a fiduciary has possession and/or control of property which belongs (legally and beneficially) to another, will also suffice.[23] So too, it would now appear, will fiduciary relationships which do not bear that analogy to trust ones[24]; but the duty which is breached, and which gives rise to the primary liability, must in such a

---

[21] An example in the context of a bank fraud is *Heinl v Jyske Bank (Gibraltar) Ltd* [1999] Lloyd's Rep. Bank 511. In *Brown v Bennett* [1999] BCC 525 it was accepted (and the concession was regarded as being correct by the Court of Appeal) that the equitable claim in dishonest assistance and the tortious claim in conspiracy stood or fell together.

[22] As for example in *Novoship (UK) Ltd v Mikhaylyuk* [2015] Q.B. 499.

[23] *Selangor United Rubber Estates Ltd v Cradock (No.3)* [1968] 1 W.L.R. 1555, at 1574–1577; *Belmont Finance Corp Ltd v Williams Furniture Ltd (No.2)* [1980] 1 All E.R. 393; *Agip (Africa) Ltd v Jackson* [1990] Ch. 265; [1991] Ch. 547 (CA); *Cowan de Groot Properties Ltd v Eagle Trust Plc* [1992] 4 All E.R. 700.

[24] See the following sub-section.

case nevertheless be a fiduciary one, as distinct from a duty (such as an equitable duty of care) which happens to be owed by a fiduciary.[25]

Conversely, a relationship which does not involve fully-fledged fiduciary obligations, but which does involve informal trusteeship, will also suffice: so, liability in dishonest assistance can arise wherever the primary wrongdoer is in possession or control of property belonging to another, which he can only deal with for the benefit of or as authorised by that other[26]—including a constructive trustee (in the first sense identified in *Paragon Finance*), a resulting trustee or a bare trustee.[27]

13–013

(2) Breach Need not Involve Misapplication of Property

After some uncertainty, it is now established that it is not necessary to found liability in dishonest assistance for the underlying breach of duty to have involved a misapplication of trust (or quasi-trust) property[28]: thus in *Novoship (UK) Ltd v Mikhaylyuk*,[29] a dishonest assistance claim could lie where the primary liability was that of a manager and director of the claimant company whose breach of fiduciary duty involved the negotiation and entry into charters of the claimant's vessels (for which he had received bribes) that did not involve any disposition of the company's property. This is in contrast to liability in knowing receipt, where, by definition, there must have been receipt of trust property or its traceable proceeds.[30]

13–014

It would seem to follow from this that it is not necessary (although it is sufficient) for the underlying relationship to be one that involves the fiduciary having possession or control over his principal's property.

13–015

(3) Breach Need not be Dishonest

It is now established that there is no requirement that the breach of trust or fiduciary duty should itself be dishonest.[31] As we have noted above, this is significant because liability on the part of an accessory will often arise in circumstances where he has misled or otherwise induced a trustee or fiduciary

13–016

---

[25] As to which, see *Bristol and West Building Society v Mothew* [1998] Ch. 1 and paras 11–058—11–061. It seems that liability may arise for dishonest assistance in a breach of confidence: see *Thomas v Pearce* [2000] F.S.R. 718.

[26] *Baden v Societe General pour Favoriser du Developpement du Commerce et de l'Industrie en France SA* (1983) [1993] 1 W.L.R. 509, at 573E–573F.

[27] See the observations of Mance J in *Grupo Torras SA v Al-Sabah* [1999] C.L.C. 1469, at 1664. This seems to have been assumed in *Bank Terjerat v Hong Kong Banking Corp (CI) Ltd* [1995] 1 Lloyd's Rep. 239.

[28] *J D Wetherspoon Plc v Van de Berg & Co Ltd* [2009] EWHC 639 (Ch), cited with approval in *Novoship (UK) Limted v Mikhaylyuk* [2015] Q.B. 499, at [91]–[93]. For the contrary view, which has now been overtaken, see *Satnam Investments Ltd v Dunlop Heywood & Co Ltd* [1999] 3 All E.R. 652.

[29] Above.

[30] *Satnam Investments Ltd v Dunlop Heywood & Co Ltd* [1999] 3 All E.R. 652, per Nourse LJ at 671, as considered in *Goose v Wilson Sandford & Co* [2001] Lloyd's Rep. PN 189, per Morritt LJ at [88].

[31] *Royal Brunei Airlines Sdn Bhd v Tan* [1995] A.C. 378.

into a breach for which they may not be morally culpable, or at least culpable to the level required to be shown to make out a case of dishonesty. Previously it had been understood that dishonesty on the part of the trustee or fiduciary was a requirement where the claim was for assistance in the breach, but not where it was for procurement of it. That distinction has now gone and cases which predate the decision in *Royal Brunei* should therefore be treated with caution on this aspect. The focus is now in all cases on the state of mind of the accessory; if he is dishonest in the sense discussed below, the dishonesty or otherwise of the principal wrongdoer is irrelevant. This makes sense: the liability of the dishonest accessory should not depend on the state of mind of the primary wrongdoer and to link the two questions creates anomalies which could allow liability to be avoided based on matters which are likely to be extraneous to the culpability of the accessory.[32]

(4)   Where no Liability for the Primary Breach

13–017   There must be a breach of trust or fiduciary duty for liability in dishonest assistance to arise: that follows from the fact that it is a form of accessory liability. However it does not follow that the trustee or fiduciary whose breach is the springboard for the claim should himself be liable: if the trustee or fiduciary has the benefit of an enforceable exemption clause which excuses him from liability (as distinct from a clause that prevents there being a breach in the first place), then, provided that there is a breach, the dishonest assister could be liable even though the trustee or fiduciary is not. The same is probably true where a director has (in principle) the primary liability but is relieved of liability under s.1157 of the Companies Act 2006 or where the trustee's liability is relieved under s.61 of the Trustee Act 1925.

C.   ASSISTANCE/PROCUREMENT

(1)   What Amounts to Actionable Assistance

13–018   Whether a defendant has assisted in a breach of trust or fiduciary duty is quintessentially a question of fact and the categories of assistance are not closed: what is required, or at least sufficient, for the ingredient of assistance is simply conduct (or an omission) which in fact assists the fiduciary to commit the act which constitutes the breach of trust or fiduciary duty.[33] It is not necessary that the assistance should play any part in the mental state of the trustee or fiduciary, still less that it should assist the mental state in a way which is necessary to render the act a breach of trust or fiduciary duty.[34]

---

[32] As discussed in *Royal Brunei Airlines Sdn Bhd v Tan* [1995] A.C. 378, at 384–385.

[33] *Madoff Securities International Ltd v Raven* [2013] EWHC 3147 (Comm), per Popplewell J at [351].

[34] *Madoff Securities International Ltd v Raven* [2013] EWHC 3147 (Comm), per Popplewell J at [351].

Conduct can amount to assistance even if the breach would possibly still have occurred (or the proceeds of the breach still have been dissipated) without it.[35] Hence it is an irrelevant and illegitimate inquiry to consider what would have happened absent the defendant's acts or omissions which are said to constitute assistance. Nonetheless, to constitute assistance the conduct complained of must have some causative effect.[36] So where directors in (alleged) breach of their fiduciary duties caused a company to enter into administrative receivership, with a view to the sale of its business to another vehicle, the company which acquired the business from the receivers was held not liable: the directors' breaches and the resultant damage were complete before the acquiring company came on the scene, and its acts in acquiring the business could not therefore amount to assistance in them.[37]

13–019

In the well-known case of *Brink's Ltd v Abu-Saleh (No.3)*,[38] the defendant wife accompanied her husband abroad on money laundering trips, thereby giving the trips an air of legitimacy (and so, it could be said, facilitating the fraud); but she was held not liable, because her assistance was not "of a nature sufficient to make her an accessory". It is right to note that this conclusion appears to have been influenced by the fact that her presence on the trips was not *intended* by her to be as cover for her husband, but in her capacity as his wife; had it been otherwise, the result might well have been different. What is "sufficient" for these purposes is inevitably difficult to state in the abstract; but one academic commentator has suggested that all that is required is that the dishonest assister's actions or omissions "have at least made the commission of the breach easier than it would otherwise have been".[39]

13–020

Examples of assistance in the cases include:

13–021

(1)   Causing (as director of a company) monies held by the company as trustee to be used for the company's own business purposes[40];
(2)   Authorising onward payments of monies derived from trust monies to accounts of companies controlled by those involved in the fraud[41];
(3)   Drafting (as a solicitor) sham agreements in purported pursuance of which unauthorised payments were made and then divided between the parties to a fraud[42];

---

[35] C. Mitchell, D.J. Hayton and P. Matthews, *Underhill & Hayton Law of Trusts and Trustees*, 19th edn (London: LNUK, 2016), para.98.53; *Balfron Trustees Ltd v Peterson* [2001] I.R.L.R. 758, per Laddie J at [21].

[36] *Brown v Bennett* [1999] BCC 525, per Morritt LJ at 533.

[37] *Brown v Bennett* [1999] BCC 525, per Morritt LJ at 533.

[38] *Brink's Ltd v Abu-Saleh (No.3)* [1996] C.L.C. 133, at 148–149.

[39] Elliot and Mitchell, *Remedies for Dishonest Assistance* (2004) 67(1) M.L.R. 16–47, which would need to be read subject to the point noted below that it is not just assistance in the original commission of the breach that is actionable.

[40] *Royal Brunei Airlines Sdn Bhd v Tan* [1995] A.C. 378.

[41] *Barlow Clowes International Ltd v Eurotrust International Ltd* [2006] 1 W.L.R. 1476.

[42] *Dubai Aluminium Co Ltd v Salaam* [2003] 2 A.C. 366.

(4) Providing research (which was alleged to be valueless), submitting invoices for it and making arrangements to receive payments, all as a false pretext for the making of company payments in (alleged) breach of directors' duties[43];

(5) Negotiating as agent towards the conclusion of contracts with the defaulting fiduciary's principal.[44]

(2) Assistance After the Original Breach

13–022　It is important to note that the assistance need not precede or be directly contemporaneous with the original breach of trust or duty: as Lord Millett observed in *Twinsectra v Yardley*,[45] the liability:

> "extends to everyone who consciously assists in the continuing diversion of the money. Most of the cases have been concerned, not with assisting in the original breach, but in covering it up afterwards by helping to launder the money."

Thus, as has already been noted, the facilitation of the onward payment of monies misapplied in breach of trust or fiduciary duty is a classic example of actionable assistance; so would concealment of the original misapplication be.[46]

13–023　The justification for this approach is that (in a money laundering case) the breach of trust is not regarded as having been completely implemented until the proceeds have been put beyond the reach of the beneficiaries. Where the breach is complete in this sense, subsequent acts of the defendant cannot assist its commission.[47]

(3) Procurement

13–024　Liability will also attach to a defendant who induces or procures, rather than assists in, a breach of trust or fiduciary duty. Thus in one leading case a parent who induced trustees to make a distribution of trust property to his illegitimate children by producing a forged marriage certificate was held liable to make good the resulting loss to the trust fund.[48] Equally, where the director of a company causes that company to act in breach of trust or fiduciary duty, then he can be said to have procured the breach and will be liable accordingly.[49]

---

[43] *Madoff Securities International Ltd v Raven* [2013] EWHC 3147 (Comm).

[44] *Novoship (UK) Limted v Mikhaylyuk* [2015] Q.B. 499, at [55] (the defaulting fiduciary being in breach of duty by conducting such negotiations on behalf of the principal without disclosing that he was sharing secret commissions with the other side's agent).

[45] Above, at 194.

[46] See *Agip (Africa) Ltd v Jackson* [1990] Ch. 265; *Grupo Torras SA v Al-Sabah* [1999] C.L.C. 1469; *Heinl v Jyske Bank (Gibraltar) Ltd* [1999] Lloyd's Rep. Bank 511; and *Independent Trustee Service Ltd v GP Noble Trustees Ltd* [2010] EWHC 1653 (Ch), at [242]–[244].

[47] *Ultraframe (UK) Ltd v Fielding* [2005] EWHC 1638 (Ch), per Lewison J at [1509]–[1510]. This was one of the bases on which Mr Soler escaped liability in *Grupo Torras*, above, at 1668.

[48] *Eaves v Hickson* (1861) 30 Beav. 136. This case was cited in *Royal Brunei Airlines Sdn Bhd v Tam* [1995] A.C. 378, with approval, at 385.

[49] *Royal Brunei*, above.

(4) Causation

The liability of a dishonest assister is not limited to losses (or indeed profits) that can be said to result directly from their assistance; instead, the relevant causal connection is between the loss or profit claimed and the breach of trust or fiduciary duty which has been dishonestly assisted.[50] This would appear to be so even if (in line with the principles identified above) the assistance postdates the breach. As in a claim in conspiracy, it is inappropriate to engage in attempts to assess the precise causative significance of the assistance in relation to the breach.[51]

13–025

It follows that (as has been noted above)[52] it is no answer to a claim in dishonest assistance to say that the defaulting trustee or fiduciary would have brought about the loss claimed even without the assistance.

13–026

However, care must be taken to identify the breach or breaches of trust or fiduciary duty in which there has been assistance. What may be characterised as a single dishonest scheme may nevertheless involve a number of distinct breaches, and the loss recoverable from the dishonest assister is only that which may be said to have resulted from the particular breach or breaches in which he assisted.[53] So where payments are abstracted from the claimant and channelled through a number of different routes to different ultimate recipients as part of a single "scheme", it may be open to a defendant who is implicated only in the onward diversion of one of the payments but not others to contend that the relevant breach of trust in which he assisted is only that by which that particular payment was made and concealed, and so the loss which he must bear (even when analysed with reference to the underlying breach of trust and not the assistance in it) is limited to that particular payment.[54]

13–027

It has been observed in a recent case that the liability of the assistant is "for such loss as the party in breach of fiduciary duty would be liable",[55] and that it therefore falls to be assessed (as in a claim for equitable compensation against the

13–028

---

[50] *Grupo Torras SA v Al-Sabah* [2001] C.L.C. 221 (CA), at [119]. See also *Casio Computer Co Ltd v Sayo* [2001] IL Pr 694, at [16] (it is loss "caused by the breach of fiduciary duty [which is] recoverable from the accessory"); and *Madoff Securities International Ltd v Raven* [2013] EWHC 3147 (Comm), per Popplewell J at [340] ("It is not necessary to show that the assistance itself is causative of any loss"). Although the Court of Appeal in *Novoship (UK) Limted v Mikhaylyuk* [2015] Q.B. 499, referred (when considering the remedy of an account of profits) to the question of what had happened "as a result of [the] dishonest assistance" (at [114]), it seems clear from the rest of that paragraph and from the fact that *Grupo Torras* and *Casio Computer* were cited (at [103]) that it was not intended to cast doubt upon these propositions.
[51] *Grupo Torras SA v Al-Sabah* [2001] C.L.C. 221 (CA), at [119].
[52] Paragraph 13–019.
[53] See *Grupo Torras SA v Al-Sabah* [1999] C.L.C. 1469, per Mance J at 1666.
[54] But to different effect see the decision of Peter Smith J in *Independent Trustee Service Ltd v GP Noble Trustees Ltd* [2010] EWHC 1653 (Ch), where one of the defendants (Mr Starkey) was implicated in the creation of bonds designed to help put out of reach funds paid away in breach of trust from a pension trust. There were two "waves" of such payments, and Mr Starkey was held liable for the losses arising from both, even though he only became involved after the first wave of payments had been made.
[55] *Madoff Securities International Ltd v Raven* [2013] EWHC 3147 (Comm), per Popplewell J at [340].

defaulting trustee or fiduciary himself) taking account of events post-dating the original breach up to the date of trial, with the full benefit of hindsight.[56] Those observations fit with the accessory nature of the liability. However, as we have noted at the start of this chapter, the Court of Appeal has also held that, because the dishonest assister is not in an antecedent fiduciary relationship with the claimant, common law concepts of causation and remoteness should be applied by analogy and not the stricter rules applicable to trustees and fiduciaries.[57] The two approaches may be reconciled on the basis that the latter case was concerned with the assister's accountability for profits, and the former cases with his liability to compensate losses, although the Court of Appeal's reasoning is cast in broader terms.

13–029   In fact, the dishonest assister's liability could end up being larger than that of the defaulting trustee or fiduciary, where the former is dishonest and the latter is not, given the equitable jurisdiction to award compound interest. Of course, if the breach of trust is innocent and the trustee has the benefit of an exemption clause, or obtains relief under the Trustee Act, then the trustee may have no pecuniary liability at all, in contrast to the accessory.

(5)   Contributory Negligence

13–030   As in a claim in deceit, it is no answer to a claim in dishonest assistance to say that the claimant had the opportunity to discover the wrongdoing and unreasonably failed to do so.[58]

13–031   However, a claimant's acts or omissions, particularly in circumstances where he is aware of or on notice of the fraud but fails to take reasonable steps to prevent a loss, may be so egregious as to break the chain of causation, making him the "author of his own loss".[59]

D.   DISHONESTY

(1)   The Legal Test

13–032   The touchstone of liability for dishonest assistance is dishonesty. Although there is a long history of judicial attempts to define this concept, which have yielded over the years a number of decisions at first instance and in the Court of Appeal which are difficult to reconcile, the current position is relatively settled. The law

---

[56] *Central Bank of Ecuador v Conticorp SA* [2015] UKPC 11, per Lord Mance at [170], referring to *AIB Group (UK) Plc v Mark Redler & Co Solicitors* [2015] A.C. 1503.

[57] *Novoship (UK) Limted v Mikhaylyuk*, above, at [107]; for the principles applicable to trustees and fiduciaries, see paras 22–120—21–123.

[58] *Corporacion Nacional Del Cobre De Chile v Sogemin Metals Ltd* [1997] 1 W.L.R. 1396; and see generally paras 21–088—21–094, which consider the defence of contributory negligence in the context of intentional wrongs generally.

[59] See the analysis of equitable compensation by McLachlin J in the Canadian Supreme Court decision *Canson Enterprises Ltd v Boughton & Co* (1991) 85 D.L.R. (4th) 129, at 161–162. McLachlin J's judgment was cited with approval in both *Target Holdings Ltd v Redferns* [1996] A.C. 421 and *AIB Group (UK) Plc v Mark Redler & Co Solicitors* [2015] A.C. 1503.

can, in essence, be found in two Privy Council decisions and one House of Lords decision which are discussed in this section.

For these purposes, dishonesty means simply not acting as an honest person would in the circumstances.[60] Dishonesty may consist in knowledge that a transaction is one in which one cannot honestly participate (such as the misappropriation of money belonging to others), or, importantly, in suspicion to that effect coupled with a conscious decision not to make inquiries which might result in knowledge.[61] An honest person does not "deliberately close his eyes and ears, or deliberately not ask questions, lest he learn something he would rather not know, and then proceed regardless".[62]

13–033

Dishonesty is concerned with subjective states of mind, in the sense that it falls to be assessed with reference to what the defendant actually knew (rather than what he ought to have known) and it requires advertent rather than inadvertent conduct.[63] Imprudence is not dishonesty. Since the state of a person's mind can never directly be known, dishonesty can only be established by drawing inferences from other facts[64]; but that is not to say that the *standard* of what constitutes dishonesty, given the defendant's subjective knowledge and intentions, is itself subjective. It is not: in judging whether the defendant's conduct in light of his subjective mental state is dishonest, the Court applies an objective standard—that is, what by "ordinary standards" is dishonest.[65] The fact that the defendant has an idiosyncratic personal moral code cannot absolve him of liability if his conduct is by normal standards dishonest: hence in *Barlow Clowes International Ltd v Eurotrust International Ltd*[66] the judge at first instance held that one of the defendants had:

13–034

"an exaggerated notion of dutiful service to clients, which produced a warped moral approach that it was not improper to treat carrying out clients' instructions as being all important. Mr Henwood may well have thought this to be an honest attitude, but, if so, he was wrong."

The Privy Council upheld this finding.

In *Twinsectra Ltd v Yardley*, Lord Hutton (which whom the majority agreed) appeared to suggest that there is an additional subjective component to the test of dishonesty—that:

13–035

---

[60] *Royal Brunei Airlines Sdn Bhd v Tan* [1995] A.C. 378, per Lord Nicholls at 389C.

[61] *Manifest Shipping Co Ltd v Uni-Polaris Insurance Co Ltd* [2003] 1 A.C. 469.

[62] *Royal Brunei Airlines Sdn Bhd v Tan*, above, per Lord Nicholls at 389F–389G.

[63] *Royal Brunei Airlines Sdn Bhd v Tan*, above, per Lord Nicholls at 389D.

[64] *Barlow Clowes International Ltd v Eurotrust International Ltd* [2006] 1 W.L.R. 1476, at [26]: "Since there is no window into another mind, the only way to form a view on these matters is to draw inferences from what [the Defendant] knew, said and did, both then and later, including what he said in evidence."

[65] *Barlow Clowes International Ltd v Eurotrust International Ltd* [2006] 1 W.L.R. 1476, at [10]. "Ordinary standards" means just that; the fact that there may be a body of opinion which takes a different view is irrelevant: *Starglade Properties Ltd v Nash* [2010] EWCA Civ 1314, per Morritt C at [32].

[66] Above, at [12].

"for liability as an accessory to arise the defendant must himself appreciate that what he was doing was dishonest by the standards of honest and reasonable men".[67]

On the face of it, that requirement would involve an impossibly refined inquiry into the mental processes of the defendant. It would also absolve the psychopath of liability. But Lord Hutton's observations have subsequently been "explained" by Lord Hoffmann (giving the advice of the Privy Council in *Barlow Clowes Ltd v Eurotrust Ltd*) as meaning only that the defendant's knowledge of the transaction has to be such as to render his participation contrary to normally acceptable standards of honest conduct, and not to require that the defendant should have reflected upon what those normally acceptable standards are.[68] The law therefore remains as stated in *Royal Brunei*: in essence, the court assesses the defendant's conduct by reference: (a) first to the facts he actually knew (rather than the facts he ought to have been aware of); and then (b) to the ordinary standards of honesty (rather than by reference to his own private value system). This is not to say that the well-advised claimant will not seek to establish at trial that the defendant was subjectively dishonest in the sense identified by Lord Hutton. Liability will clearly be made out if the defendant is shown to have been conscious of his own wrongdoing.

13–036 Whilst the doctrine of precedent might arguably require that the unvarnished *Twinsectra* test be favoured until it is reconsidered by the Supreme Court, the better view is almost certainly that Lord Hoffmann's subsequent gloss on it in *Barlow Clowes* is to be preferred[69]; and this can probably be reconciled with the doctrine of precedent on the footing that the point was not necessary to the decision in *Twinsectra*,[70] and the Privy Council in *Barlow Clowes* expressed itself to be explaining, rather than departing from, what the House of Lords had previously said.[71] Recently the Supreme Court in *Ivey v Genting Casinos (UK)*

---

[67] *Twinsectra Ltd v Yardley* [2002] 2 A.C. 164, at [35]–[36]; see also per Lord Hoffmann at [20].

[68] *Barlow Clowes International Ltd v Eurotrust International Ltd* [2006] 1 W.L.R. 1476, at [15]–[16].

[69] As it has been in a number of subsequent cases, including: *Abou-Rahmah v Abacha* [2006] EWCA Civ 1492, per Arden LJ at [68]–[69] (although note the reservations of the other members of the Court of Appeal on the issue); *Aerostar Maintenance International Ltd v Wilson* [2010] EWHC 2032 (Ch), per Morgan J at [183]–[184]; *Starglade Properties Ltd v Nash* [2010] EWCA Civ 1314; [2011] 1 Lloyd's Rep. F.C. 102; *Vivendi SA v Richards* [2013] EWHC 3006 (Ch), per Newey J at [182]–[183]; *Madoff Securities International Ltd v Raven* [2013] EWHC 3147 (Comm), per Popplewell J at [353]; *Singularis Holdings Ltd v Daiwa Capital Markets Europe Ltd* [2017] EWHC 257 (Ch), per Rose J at [143]–[145]. In *Group Seven Ltd v Nasir* [2017] EWHC 2466 (Ch) Morgan J held that he was bound by the Court of Appeal decision in *Starglade* to proceed on the basis that *Barlow Clowes* correctly stated the law.

[70] The solicitor, Mr Leach, was not dishonest because, although he knew the terms of the third party undertaking to which the relevant monies were subject, and so knew the facts which (as it was found) made it a breach of trust to pay the money away to the client, he genuinely thought that the money, once in his client account, was held for the client's account only. That was misguided, but not (even objectively) dishonest, and the Judge was able to make that finding without explicitly making any finding about the solicitor's subjective appreciation of the honesty or otherwise of what he was doing. There is no need to resort to Lord Hutton's surmise (at [42]) that the judge had implicitly applied a combined objective/subjective test.

[71] See for example *Singluaris Holdings Ltd v Daiwa Capital Markets Europe Ltd*, above, where Rose J directed herself that the test for dishonesty was that set out in *Twinsectra*, but as explained in *Barlow Clowes*: [143]–[145] (not challenged on appeal: [2018] EWCA Civ 84; [2018] 1 W.L.R. 2777). Arden LJ took the same approach in *Abou-ramah v Abacha*, above, at [68].

Ltd (t/a Crockfords)[72] expressed the view, albeit obiter, that the test established in *Barlow Clowes* represents the English law.

(2) Knowledge of the Underlying Trust or Fiduciary Relationship

A question which often comes up is what knowledge about, or suspicion as to, the underlying trust or fiduciary relationship is required for the assistance to be dishonest. In *Brinks Ltd v Abu-Saleh (No.3)*,[73] Rimer J expressed the view that a person cannot be liable for dishonest assistance in a breach of trust unless he knows of the existence of the trust or at least the facts giving rise to it. This view was rejected by the Privy Council in *Barlow Clowes*, where it was held that (in the case of assistance in the misappropriation of monies held on trust for investors) knowledge or a suspicion that the person with primary liability was not entitled to use the funds in question as their own (coupled, in the case of a suspicion, with a conscious decision not to inquire further) sufficed: it is not necessary to show that the particular nature of the inhibition on dealing, or the facts giving rise to it, was known.[74] Put more generally, it is sufficient if the assister knows or suspects (without further enquiry) that the transaction is not one in which he can honestly participate.[75] As observed by Millett J in *Agip (Africa) Ltd v Jackson*[76]:

> "it is no answer for a man charged with having knowingly assisted in a fraudulent and dishonest scheme to say that it was 'only' a breach of exchange control or 'only' a case of tax evasion. It is not necessary that he should have been aware of the precise nature of the fraud or even of the identity of its victim. A man who consciously assists others by making arrangements which he knows are calculated to conceal what is happening from a third party, takes the risk that they are part of a fraud practised on that party."

In *Twinsectra*, the same judge (then Lord Millett) expressed the view that:

> "It is sufficient that [the Defendant] knows that the money is not at the free disposal of the principal. In some circumstances it may not even be necessary that his knowledge should extend this far. It may be sufficient that he knows that he is assisting in a dishonest scheme".[77]

Similarly, ignorance as to the unlawfulness of a transaction will not be a defence: thus a director of an insolvent company, who, knowing it to be insolvent, caused the company to pay away its funds to certain creditors in order to frustrate the

13–037

13–038

13–039

---

[72] *Ivey v Genting Casinos (UK) Ltd (t/a Crockfords)* [2017] UKSC 67; [2018] A.C. 391, at [62].

[73] In *Brinks Ltd v Abu-Saleh (No.3)* [1996] C.L.C. 133, at 151. Mance J expressed support for this view in *Grupo Torras SA v Al Sabah* [1999] C.L.C. 1469.

[74] At [28]. Similarly in *Ultraframe (UK) Ltd v Fielding* [2005] EWHC 1638 (Ch), Lewison J held that the assistant must know that the person he is assisting is not entitled to do what he is doing and, although he need not know all the details of the whole design, he must in broad terms know what the design is (see, at [1504]–[1506]).

[75] *Abou-Rahmah v Abacha* [2007] 1 All E.R. Com 827, per Rix LJ at [39]; *Madoff Securities International Ltd v Raven* [2013] EWHC 3147 (Comm), per Popplewell J at [351].

[76] *Agip (Africa) Ltd v Jackson* [1990] Ch. 265, at 295, cited with approval by Rix LJ in *Abou-Rahmah v Abacha*, above, at [38].

[77] *Twinsectra Ltd v Yardley* [2002] 2 A.C. 164, at [135], which, although it was in a dissenting speech, was referred to with approval by Lord Hoffmann in *Barlow Clowes*, above, at [28].

claim of a person for whom the company had agreed to hold funds on trust, acted dishonestly, even if he did not know that doing so contravened the rules against preferences.[78]

13–040 It is also not necessary, in order to establish the requisite mental state, to show that the defendant intended that the victim should be defrauded. It is (usually) dishonest, by ordinary standards, to assist in a transaction whereby money belonging to another is applied in a way that one knows is not authorised, even if ones hopes that in due course the money will be repaid.[79] Fraud includes taking a risk to the prejudice of another's rights, when that risk is known to be one which there is no right to take, even if one hopes the risk will pay off.[80] Hence a finding of dishonesty does not require a finding that the defendant has been actuated by selfish motives or a desire to further his interests (or those of the defaulting trustee or fiduciary) to the detriment of the claimant. In this sense it is not necessarily oxymoronic to speak of dishonest assistance which is well-intentioned. But nonetheless the dishonesty must have been directed "towards the [claimant]" in relation to property held or potentially held on trust; findings of generic dishonesty are not enough.[81]

(3) Doubts, Suspicions and Recklessness

13–041 When something short of actual knowledge on the defendant's part that a dealing is unauthorised is shown, the question will be whether the defendant entertained doubts or a suspicion such that it was dishonest, by ordinary standards, consciously to refrain from further inquiry before proceeding. There may be more than one course that an honest person would take when faced with such doubts (such as refusing to proceed, making further inquiries, giving advice, etc.) and in assessing the defendant's response the court will take account of all of the relevant circumstances as known to them (including the nature and importance of the transaction, the practicability of proceeding otherwise, the degree of doubt entertained and the seriousness of the consequences for the potential victims). The Court will also take account of the defendant's own attributes, such as his

---

[78] *Starglade Properties Ltd v Nash* [2010] EWCA Civ 1314; [2011] 1 Lloyd's Rep. F.C. 102.

[79] *Royal Brunei Airlines Sdn Bhd v Tan*, above, per Lord Nicholls at 393A–393D. But note the concept of a "judicious" breach of trust, which, although deliberate (i.e. done knowing it is not authorised), is not dishonest when done in good faith and in the honest belief that it is for the benefit of the beneficiaries: see *Armitage v Nurse* [1998] Ch. 241, per Millett LJ at 250–251; and *Walker v Stones* [2001] Q.B. 902, particularly the qualification to this at 939C and 941D (solicitor-trustee's honest perception of interests of beneficiaries could nevertheless be so unreasonable as to amount to dishonesty for the purposes of the exception to an exemption clause).

[80] *Baden v Societe Generale pour Favoriser le Developpement du Commerce et de I'Industrie en France S.A. (Note)* [1993] 1 W.L.R. 509, per Peter Gibson J at 574.

[81] *Grupo Torras SA v Al-Sabah* [1999] C.L.C. 1469, at 1665–1666, per Mance J; although the reference to property held on trust should probably now be understood more broadly, in light of the developments noted in paras 13–012—13–015 above.

experience, intelligence and reasons for acting.[82] This is a preferable approach to trying to fit the defendant's degree of suspicion into some preconceived category of culpable knowledge.[83]

Two important points should be made about suspicions in this context: first, a suspicion for these purposes must be "firmly grounded and targeted on specific facts"; a vague feeling of unease (which might also be called a suspicion) would not suffice.[84] Secondly, what makes the state of mind dishonest is the deliberate decision, having a suspicion in that sense, to avoid confirming that the facts in whose existence the defendant has good reason to believe.[85]

13–042

In a commercial context, dishonesty has for these purposes been equated with, or closely allied to, what is commercially unacceptable. Thus in *Abou-Ramah v Abacha*[86] the Court of Appeal upheld the conclusion of the judge that it was not dishonest for a bank to receive and pay on proceeds of a fraud, despite the relevant bank officer having a general suspicion that the persons directing the payments "might be, in the course of their business, from time to time assisting corrupt politicians to launder money". The officer was found not to have any knowledge or suspicion concerning the particular transactions in issue which was such as to render it commercially unacceptable to implement the instructions the bank had received, particularly given the commercial setting in which banks are required to act on proper instructions, the fact that local regulatory requirements were observed and the fact that cash transactions were commonplace in the relevant jurisdiction.[87]

13–043

It should also be noted that dishonesty in this area of the law is not to be equated with recklessness: acting in reckless disregard of another's possible rights is certainly strong evidence of dishonesty; but it is not the same thing, particularly

13–044

---

[82] Establishing a motive is not a legal requirement, but if a motive cannot plausibly be suggested, then a wrongful intention is less likely: per Mann J in *Mortgage Agency Services Number One Ltd v Cripps Harries LLP* [2016] EWHC 2483 (Ch), at [88], cited by Rose J in *Singularis Holdings Ltd* [2017] EWHC 257 (Ch), at [158].

[83] *Royal Brunei Airlines Sdn Bhd v Tan* [1995] A.C. 378, per Lord Nicholls at 390F–391B and 392G.

[84] See *Manifest Shipping Co v Uni-Polaris Insurance Co* [2003] 1 A.C. 469, per Lord Scott at [116], which was relied on in the context of a dishonest assistance claim by Morgan J in *Group Seven Ltd v Nasir* [2017] EWHC 2466 (Ch), at [445]–[447].

[85] *Manifest Shipping Co v Uni-Polaris Insurance Co* [2003] 1 A.C. 469, per Lord Scott at [116]. So in *Barlow Clowes* Lord Hoffmann endorsed the view that Mr Henwood would be dishonest if he "had solid grounds for suspicion which he consciously ignored that the disposal in which [he] participated involved dealings with misappropriated trust funds": [2006] 1 W.L.R. 1476, at [19]–[20]; and in *Att. Gen. of Zambia v Meer Care & Desai* [2008] EWCA Civ 1007 Lloyd LJ held that "...if Mr Meer had a clear suspicion that this was the case and he deliberately decided not to enquire in order to avoid having confirmation that it was so, that is properly characterised as dishonesty, of the kind often called blind-eye, or Nelsonian". It is not enough to show that a reasonable person would draw the inference that there was a probability that the funds were misappropriated, if the defendant did not in fact draw that inference or consciously shut his eyes to grounds for suspicion: *Heinl v Jyske Bank* [1999] Lloyd's LR Banking 511.

[86] *Abou-Ramah v Abacha* [2006] EWCA Civ 1492.

[87] See particularly per Arden LJ at [72]; but note the serious doubts expressed by Rix LJ (without dissenting).

because (as noted above) an evaluation of circumstances such as the experience and intelligence of the defendant, and his reasons for acting, may point to a different conclusion.[88]

(4) Standard of Proof

13–045 As in other areas of the law, a finding of dishonesty is to be made on the balance of probabilities. Previous suggestions in the cases that the serious nature of the allegation will require stronger evidence before the Court reaches that conclusion applying that standard, dishonesty being inherently less likely than negligence,[89] are to be treated with caution: whilst the Court must of course take into account inherent probabilities and improbabilities, there is no necessary connection between seriousness and probability.[90]

E. VICARIOUS LIABILITY

(1) Dubai Aluminium

13–046 The leading case on vicarious liability for dishonest assistance is *Dubai Aluminium Co Ltd v Salaam*.[91] Whilst the case was concerned with the vicarious liability of partners for acts of their fellow partners under s.10 of the Partnership Act 1890, it was observed that this provision assimilated the vicarious liability of partners with that of employers and was drafted deliberately widely, so that the law applicable to partners could keep step with the general law.[92]

13–047 The following propositions were confirmed in or can be derived from the case:

(1) There can be vicarious liability for dishonest assistance: nothing in s.10 of the 1890 Act or the general law limits vicarious liability to tortious wrongdoing.[93]

(2) It is not necessarily an answer to the imposition of vicarious liability (and is unlikely on its own to be an answer) that the partner or employee acted dishonestly and for his own benefit[94]; nor that the particular act constituting the assistance was not authorised (e.g. a solicitor drafting a sham agreement to conceal an unauthorised payment), it being sufficient that he is

---

[88] *Clydesdale Bank Plc v Workman* [2016] EWCA Civ 73, per Lewison LJ at [48]–[52].

[89] See e.g. *Chang v Mischon de Reya* [2015] EWHC 164 (Ch), at [8], citing *Re H (Minors) (Sexual Abuse: Standard of Proof)* [1996] A.C. 563, per Lord Nicholls at 586D–586F.

[90] See *Otkritie International Investments Management Ltd v Urumov* [2014] EWHC 191 (Comm), at [84]–[91]; *Group Seven Ltd v Nasir* [2017] EWHC 2466 (Ch), at [49]–[50]; and *JSC BM Bank v Kekhman* [2018] EWHC 791 (Comm), at [46]–[66].

[91] *Dubai Aluminium Co Ltd v Salaam* [2003] 2 A.C. 366.

[92] Per Lord Millett at [106]–[108].

[93] *Dubai Aluminium*, above, per Lord Nicholls at [10]–[12]; per Lord Millett at [103]–[111].

[94] *Lloyd v Grace Smith & Co* [1912] A.C. 716, cited in *Dubai Aluminium*, above, by Lord Millett at [121].

authorised to do acts of the kind in question (e.g. drafting agreements).[95] That said, the Court could conclude that, on an overall evaluation of the facts, in acting dishonestly, for his own benefit or the benefit of a co-conspirator rather than his employer or firm, the person primarily liable departed so far from the ordinary course of business that he was acting on a frolic of his own (such that no vicarious liability would arise).[96]

(3)   Where one is concerned with dishonest, and not merely negligent, conduct, there must be intense focus on the connection between what the employee or partner is employed or authorised to do and the relevant wrongdoing.[97] The question is ultimately whether the dishonest assistance is so closely connected with acts which the partner or employee was authorised to do that, for the purpose of the liability of the firm or the employer to third parties, the dishonest assistance may fairly and properly be regarded as done while acting in the ordinary course of the firm's business or the employee's employment.[98]

(4)   For there to be vicarious liability for dishonest assistance, all of the features of the wrong which are *necessary* to make the employee (or partner) liable must have occurred in the course of employment; but it does not matter that there may be other acts which could also give rise to a liability in dishonest assistance which were carried out outside the scope of employment.[99]

The "close connection" test was further considered by the Supreme Court in **13–048** *Mohamud v Wm Morrison Supermarkets Plc*.[100] Lord Toulson summarised the correct approach in the following terms:

> "In the simplest terms, the court has to consider two matters. The first question is what functions or 'field of activities' have been entrusted by the employer to the employee, or, in everyday language, what was the nature of his job. As has been emphasised in several cases, this question must be addressed broadly …
>
> Secondly, the court must decide whether there was sufficient connection between the position in which he was employed and his wrongful conduct to make it right for the employer to be held liable under the principle of social justice which goes back to Holt CJ. To try to measure the closeness of connection, as it were, on a scale of 1 to 10, would be a forlorn exercise and, what is more, it would miss the point. The cases in which the necessary connection has been found for Holt CJ's principle to be applied are cases in which the employee used or misused the position entrusted to him in a way which injured the third party."

---

[95] *Navarro v Moregrand Ltd* [1951] 2 T.L.R. 674, cited in *Dubai Aluminium*, above, by Lord Millett at [122].

[96] *Dubai Aluminium*, above, per Lord Nicholls at [33] (citing *Kooragang Investments Pty Ltd v Richardson & Wrench Ltd* [1982] A.C. 462); and per Lord Millett at [128]–[130].

[97] *Dubai Aluminium*, above, per Lord Millett at [129], drawing upon (inter alia) the observations of Lord Steyn about vicarious liability for intentional wrongdoing in *Lister v Hesley Hall Ltd* [2002] 1 A.C. 215, at 224.

[98] *Dubai Aluminium*, above, per Lord Nicholls at [23].

[99] *Credit Lyonnais Bank Nederland NV v Export Credits Guarantee Department* [2000] 1 A.C. 486, as interpreted and applied in the context of the vicarious liability of partners for dishonest assistance in *Dubai Aluminium*, above, per Lord Nicholls at [39] and Lord Millett at [114]–[115].

[100] *Mohamud v Wm Morrison Supermarkets Plc* [2016] A.C. 677, at [44]–[45]. This was not a dishonest assistance case; but its principles were said to be applicable to dishonest assistance in *Group Seven Ltd v Nasir* [2017] EWHC 2466 (Ch).

F.   NEGLIGENCE LIABILITY

13–049   A claim in dishonest assistance is concerned with fixing with liability a third party who interferes in the proper administration of a trust (as that concept is broadly interpreted) dishonestly. The liability attaches because of his dishonesty and irrespective of the innocence or otherwise of the trustee who is primarily liable. But what of the situation where the trustee (or other fiduciary) is acting dishonestly and the third party assists (or fails to intervene) in circumstances where, although not himself dishonest, he is dealing with the trustee and ought reasonably to have detected the underlying fraud?

13–050   There is no general claim in negligence available to victims of a fraudulent breach of trust or fiduciary duty against third parties who deal negligently, but not dishonestly, with their defaulting principal:

> "as a general proposition ... beneficiaries cannot reasonably expect that all the world dealing with their trustees should owe them a duty to take care lest the trustees are behaving dishonestly."[101]

Whether such a liability in negligence exists will therefore depend on establishing, on usual principles, circumstances justifying the imposition of a duty of care, or the existence of a similar duty in contract.

13–051   One common situation where such a liability may arise is where bankers to the victims of a fraud facilitate the diversion of the misappropriated funds by a fraudulent trustee or fiduciary, by (for example) acting on an instruction to make a payment. In *Barclays Bank Plc v Quincecare Ltd* it was held that a bank owed an implied contractual duty of care (and a coextensive duty in tort) to its customer to exercise reasonable skill and care in and about executing the customer's orders.[102] As an aspect of this duty,

> "a banker must refrain from executing an order if and for as long as the bank is 'put on inquiry' in the sense that he has reasonable grounds (although not necessarily proof) for believing that the order is an attempt to misappropriate funds".

The standard applicable is that of the ordinary prudent banker. The limited time and information that banks will often have when deciding whether to act on instructions, the fact that they will owe contractual obligations generally to honour instructions and the fact that they are entitled to assume, absent information to suggest otherwise, that their customers are trustworthy are among the reasons why breaches of this duty are not easy to establish.[103]

---

[101] *Royal Brunei Airlines Sdn Bhd v Tan* [1995] A.C. 378, per Lord Nicholls at 392C.

[102] *Barclays Bank Plc v Quincecare Ltd* [1992] 4 All E.R. 363. The decision (of Steyn J) was cited with approval by the Court of Appeal in *Lipkin Gorman v Karpnale Ltd* [1987] 1 W.L.R. 987.

[103] For a case (thought to be the only one) in which the duty was found to have been breached, see *Singularis Holdings Ltd v Daiwa Capital Markets Europe Ltd* [2017] EWHC 257 (Ch), upheld on appeal at [2018] EWCA Civ 84; [2018] 1 W.L.R. 277. The Court of Appeal explained that the duty is to protect the funds held in the customer's account from fraudulent disposition, in circumstances that put the bank on inquiry. It was therefore nothing to the point that the customer was insolvent, such that only its creditors would benefit from the bringing of the claim: see [81]–[90].

It is also worth noting that it may not always be necessary to establish a duty owed by the assister directly to the beneficiary: the assister may owe a contractual or tortious duty of care to the trustee, which may (in special circumstances) be enforced derivatively by the beneficiary on the basis that the contract or claim forms part of the trust property.[104]

13–052

G. REMEDIES

The principal remedies available for dishonest assistance are personal, not proprietary[105]:

13–053

(1)   Equitable compensation for losses resulting from the breach induced or assisted; and

(2)   An account of profits (if any) made by the dishonest assister.[106]

The limiting principles of causation are considered earlier in this chapter.[107] Other principles applicable to these remedies are considered in Ch.22.

13–054

Dishonest assistance is also a basis on which rescission can be ordered: where party A to a contract with party B dishonestly assists B's agent (C) to breach his fiduciary obligations to B in bringing about or advising on the contract, C's breach of fiduciary duty provides a ground for rescinding the contract and, because of his dishonest assistance in that breach, A's conscience is affected such that (subject to other bars) he cannot resist rescission.[108]

13–055

---

[104] See L. Tucker, N. Le Poidevin and J. Brightwell, *Lewin on Trusts*, 19th edn (London: Sweet & Maxwell, 2012) at 43–006—43–016. For consideration of whether the duties owed by directors of a trustee company to that company can be enforced directly by the beneficiaries of the trust see *Gregson v HAE Trustees Ltd* [2008] EWHC 1006 (Ch).

[105] Dishonest assistance does not give rise to proprietary rights by way of constructive trust: *Sinclair Investment Holdings S.A. v Versailles Trade Finance Ltd* [2007] EWHC 915 (Ch); [2007] 2 All E.R. (Comm) 993, at [109]–[135].

[106] This was established by the Court of Appeal in *Novoship (UK) Limted v Mikhaylyuk* [2015] Q.B. 499, at [93]. See further paras 22–089—22–093.

[107] Paragraphs 13–025—13–029.

[108] *UBS AG (London Branch) v Kommunale Wasserweke Leipzig GmbH* [2017] EWCA Civ 1567. As to this, and rescission more generally, see Ch.22, Section B.

SECTION C

OTHER CLAIMS

CHAPTER 14

UNJUST ENRICHMENT

A. INTRODUCTION

(1) What is Unjust Enrichment?

"Unjust enrichment" is probably[1] best described as an umbrella term which encompasses a number of different causes of action that have certain thematic similarities, in much the same way as tort is.[2] However, it serves a wholly different purpose. The purpose of the law of tort is the compensation of (or restitution of value to) claimants for the legal wrongs of defendants—wrongdoing is its essence. By contrast, wrongdoing (legal or equitable) is neither necessary nor sufficient to engage the law of unjust enrichment. Rather, the law of unjust enrichment is concerned with the circumstances in which a defendant is enriched at the expense of a claimant. If those circumstances are such that it is unjust for the defendant to retain that enrichment, then the law of unjust enrichment will—subject to defences—provide for its return to the claimant.

14–001

"Unjust" in this context is a term of art. It does not mean "unjust" in the colloquial sense of an ethically undesirable outcome, and it does not invite or allow the judge to exercise discretion according to his own sense of fairness. An

14–002

---

[1] This qualification deserves some explanation. As English law presently stands, "unjust enrichment" is an umbrella term which encompasses causes of action arising from a number of "unjust factors" (i.e. distinct circumstances in which a Court will deem an enrichment unjust). Other jurisdictions—notably Scotland, Canada and Germany—regard unjust enrichment as a unitary cause of action which arises whenever a defendant is enriched at the expense of the claimant without any legally recognised explanation or basis for that enrichment (e.g. the giving of a gift, the performance of a contract, or the payment of a judgment debt). In P. Birks, *Unjust Enrichment*, 2nd edn (Oxford: OUP, 2005), pp.108–117, Professor Birks powerfully argued that this "absence of basis" analysis had been adopted by the English Courts, and that the "unjust factors" should be regarded as causing an "absence of basis", rather than giving rise to liability themselves. While Professor Birks's views received some measure of tentative endorsement from Lord Walker in *Deutsche Morgan Grenfell Plc v Inland Revenue Commissioners* [2006] UKHL 49; [2007] 1 A.C. 558, at [155]–[158], judges in the House of Lords and the Supreme Court have since repeatedly stated that English law does not recognise any liability arising from an "absence of basis" in isolation. See e.g. Lord Sumption in *Patel v Mirza* [2016] UKSC 42; [2017] A.C. 467, at [246].
[2] See e.g. *Lampson (Australia) Pty Ltd v Fortescue Metals Group Ltd (No. 3)* [2014] WASC 162, at [50]–[51].

enrichment is unjust for these purposes[3] if it arises either from a recognised "unjust factor", or from a justified extension of one.[4]

14–003 A number of the unjust factors which may arise in the context of a fraud claim are considered below. They are united by the fact that they arise in circumstances in which a transferor's consent to the enrichment of the transferee was either impaired, qualified or absent, and it is this absence of effective consent on the part of the transferor which causes the enrichment to be unjust.[5]

14–004 A restitutionary claim may also lie in the fraud context where money is paid or property transferred under a contract or other transaction which is illegal or entered into for an unlawful purpose. This is considered separately, along with the illegality doctrine more generally, in Ch.24.[6]

(2) The Advantages of a Claim in Unjust Enrichment

14–005 The great strength of the law of unjust enrichment—and the reason why it merits serious attention by the fraud practitioner—is that it can enable the victim of an alleged fraud "to get his money back" from parties who are either wholly innocent, or against whom the claimant cannot prove (or does not wish to allege) wrongdoing. In some circumstances, this will be the only route to any recovery at all.

14–006 The seminal House of Lords decision in *Lipkin Gorman v Karpnale Ltd*[7] provides an illustration of such a situation. Norman Cass was a partner in the solicitors' firm Lipkin Gorman. He stole some £223,000[8] from Lipkin Gorman's client account and gambled it at the Playboy Club. Sometimes he won; largely he lost; the result was that the Club retained a net £154,965 of the money Cass had stolen. Cass subsequently fled to Israel, was extradited to the UK, and sentenced to three years' imprisonment for theft.

14–007 The law of tort could not assist Lipkin Gorman. Cass had undeniably committed tortious wrongs against Lipkin Gorman, but had no money with which to compensate Lipkin Gorman for those wrongs. The Playboy Club had been enriched by Lipkin Gorman's money, but had committed no wrong which would entitle the latter to compensation.

---

[3] And subject to the possibility that English law will adopt an "absence of basis" approach—see fn.1 above.

[4] I.e. the list of "unjust factors" is open to growth and to evolution. See *Gibb v Maidstone and Tunbridge Wells NHS Trust* [2010] EWCA Civ 678; [2010] I.R.L.R. 786, at [26]–[27].

[5] As noted below, the treatment of unjust factors by this book is far from comprehensive. Some unjust factors cannot (or cannot naturally) be regarded as relating to the transferee's consent. See the two-fold categorization of unjust factors between those relating to consent and those relating to policy adopted by Professor A. Burrows in *A Restatement of the English Law of Unjust Enrichment* (Oxford: OUP, 2012), p.30 and Professor Birks in *Unjust Enrichment* (2005), pp.105–106, and the three-fold division between claimant orientated grounds of restitution, defendant orientated grounds of restitution and policy-orientated grounds of restitution proposed by Professor G. Virgo in *Principles of the Law of Restitution*, 3rd edn (Oxford, OUP, 2015), pp.121–125.

[6] See paras 24–062—24–072 below.

[7] *Lipkin Gorman v Karpnale Ltd* [1991] 2 A.C. 548.

[8] Or, more precisely, he stole £323,222.14 but repaid £100,313.16.

However, the law of unjust enrichment did provide a remedy—the Playboy Club **14–008** had been enriched at Lipkin Gorman's expense, and that enrichment was unjust because Lipkin Gorman did not consent to it (in that, while Cass had authority to make withdrawals from the client account, he had no authority to make such withdrawals in order to feed his gambling habit). Accordingly, the Playboy Club was ordered to pay Lipkin Gorman the £154,965 by which it had been enriched at the latter's expense.[9]

(3) The Difficulties of a Claim in Unjust Enrichment

The recognition of a general doctrine of unjust enrichment in English law is a **14–009** very recent development in the history of the law, having occurred over the last forty years or so.[10] The problem with employing such a juvenescent concept is that there is still a high degree of uncertainty regarding its scope and effect. This is—in part—a consequence of the fact that while recognition of "the doctrine of unjust enrichment" is recent, many of the liabilities imposed by the law of unjust enrichment are ancient. Both the courts of common law and equity have imposed restitutionary remedies (i.e. remedies which respond to a defendant's gain, rather than the claimant's loss) for centuries under legal labels such as quasi-contract, money had and received, accounts etc. The law of unjust enrichment has grown out of the work of academics and jurists attempting to identify, categorise and describe the disparate situations in which the law will impose these remedies. Unfortunately, in many areas, there is not as yet a clear consensus on which of those situations form part of the law of unjust enrichment; which belong exclusively to an independent area of law; and which give rise to independent but parallel restitutionary remedies under both the law of unjust enrichment and an independent area of law.

Lipkin Gorman is, itself, illustrative of this difficulty. Despite the seemingly **14–010** unambiguous language used by Lord Goff ("I accept that the solicitors' claim in the present case is founded upon the unjust enrichment of the club"),[11] there is controversy as to whether the case demonstrates an application of the law of unjust enrichment at all, with some commentators regarding it as a case in which Lipkin Gorman vindicated property rights in money paid to the Playboy Club independently of the law of unjust enrichment.[12]

---

[9] Although changes to gambling legislation mean that the Playboy Club may well have a defence were the same facts to arise today. The Playboy Club sought to argue that it had changed its position on receipt of the money by entering into gambling contracts with Mr Cass. That defence failed because those contracts were void by s.18 of the Gaming Act 1845. The effect of ss.334 and 335 of the Gambling Act 2005 is that those contracts may well have been valid if entered into today. However, the broad principles established by the decision are not undermined.

[10] Compare the statement of Lord Diplock in *Orakpo v Manson Investments Ltd* [1978] A.C. 95, at 104C–104D, to the statements of Lords Clarke, Kerr and Wilson in *Menelaou v Bank of Cyprus UK Ltd* [2015] UKSC 66; [2016] A.C. 176, at [49] and [141].

[11] *Lipkin Gorman v Karpnale Ltd* [1991] 2 A.C. 548, at 578C.

[12] See, e.g. Virgo, *Principles of the Law of Restitution* (2015), pp.13–14 and 48–50. This view was judicially endorsed by Mr Stephen Morris QC in *Armstrong DLW GmbH v Winnington Networks Ltd*

14–011   While the law of unjust enrichment continues to settle, the pragmatic response of practitioners should—it is suggested—be to adopt a belt-and-braces approach in pleading. If a claim can be conceptualised either as an invocation of the law of unjust enrichment or as engaging some other legal principle, the safest course may be to plead the claim in the language of both areas of law, so as to protect the client's position against shifts in the boundaries of what is thought to be unjust enrichment.

(4)   Pleading a Claim in Unjust Enrichment

14–012   The practice of pleading claims in unjust enrichment is still in its comparative infancy, and even leading precedent books suggest that claims in unjust enrichment should be pleaded using the language of the ancient forms of action (i.e. actions for money had and received; actions for money paid; *quantum valebat*; and quantum meruit). The use of such language has been judicially criticised as concealing as much as it reveals about the cause of action.[13]

14–013   While such language might be retained as a matter of prudence, it is important not to let its use hide the need—as prescribed by CPR 16.4—to set out the facts upon which the claimant relies to complete a cause of action in unjust enrichment. Specifically, the claimant must plead the facts which show that:

(1)   the defendant has been enriched;
(2)   the enrichment was at the expense of the claimant; and
(3)   the enrichment was unjust, in the sense that it arose from a recognised unjust factor or the justified extension of one.[14]

14–014   Discussion of these three elements will form the structure of much of the rest of this chapter, which will then turn to consider the remedies available to the successful claimant and, finally, the various defences a defendant might seek to employ.

(5)   Unjust Enrichment in Fraud Claims

14–015   As noted above, the law of unjust enrichment (at least as far as it is considered by this book) can be engaged by circumstances in which the claimant provides an enrichment to the defendant, but either does not consent to that transfer or does consent, but in a manner which is impaired or qualified. These circumstances will often arise in fraud claims, as the purpose and effect of a given fraud is often to procure a consent which would not otherwise be given. It is because claims in

---

[2012] EWHC 10 (Ch); [2013] Ch. 156, at [84] and [95]. However, see C. Mitchell, P. Mitchell and S. Watterson, *Goff & Jones: The Law of Unjust Enrichment*, 9th edn (London: Sweet & Maxwell, 2016), paras 6–65 and 8–21—8–26.

[13] See e.g. the comments of Lord Neuberger in *Benedetti v Sawiris* [2013] UKSC 50; [2014] A.C. 938, at [178].

[14] *Banque Financière de la Cité v Parc (Battersea) Ltd* [1999] 1 A.C. 221, at 227B–227F and *Uren v First National Home Finance Ltd* [2005] EWHC 2529 (Ch), at [16]–[18].

unjust enrichment will frequently arise within the context of a fraud, and because of the advantages which a claim in unjust enrichment confers upon the claimant, that the subject merits consideration by any fraud practitioner faced with the task of framing his client's case.

B.   THE ENRICHMENT OF THE DEFENDANT

(1)   General Principles: Objective Value and Subjective Devaluation

In many cases, the issue of whether or not—and the amount by which—the defendant has been enriched will scarcely need to be considered at all. In *Lipkin Gorman*, for example, there was little doubt that the Playboy Club had been enriched by Cass's gambling, and that the relevant enrichment was the difference between the total amount of money wagered by Cass and the amount which he had won on such wagers. However, not every case will be so simple. The issue can be broken down into two questions, which are to be answered as at the time (or times) of enrichment[15]:

14–016

(1)   Can the claimant show that, objectively speaking, the defendant has received a benefit which has or could be given a monetary value (the enquiry into "objective value")?

(2)   Can the defendant show that—by reason of his own idiosyncratic preferences or the use he made of the benefit[16]—he ascribes (or would have ascribed, if given the choice) a lesser or nil value to that benefit (an enquiry into what has been termed "subjective devaluation")?[17]

The result of the above is that the Courts will treat the value of any enrichment received by the defendant as either its objective value or a reduced amount based on the subjective preferences or actions of the defendant. An argument has been made that a third possibility should exist—that the value of the enrichment could be an *increased* amount based on the subjective preferences of the defendant

14–017

---

[15] *Benedetti v Sawiris* [2013] UKSC 50; [2014] A.C. 938, at [14].

[16] Mitchell, Mitchell and Watterson, *Goff & Jones: The Law of Unjust Enrichment* (2016) are of the firm view that the actual use made of the benefit by the defendant should not determine the extent of the defendant's enrichment (see paras 5–05—5–29). Nevertheless, the Court of Appeal have on two occasions stated that it is legitimate to calculate the value of a benefit to a defendant by reference to the use which that defendant made of the enrichment in question—see *Littlewoods Ltd v Revenue and Customs Commissioners* [2015] EWCA Civ 515; [2016] Ch. 373, at [148]–[187]; and *The Test Claimants in the Franked Investment Income Group Litigation v The Commissioners of Her Majesty's Revenue and Customs* [2016] EWCA Civ 1180, at [264]–[266].

[17] See the comments of Lord Clarke in *Benedetti v Sawiris* [2013] UKSC 50; [2014] A.C. 938, at [18] and [26]; and of Etherton LJ (as he then was) in *Harrison v Madejski* [2014] EWCA Civ 361, at [54]–[57].

(so-called "subjective overvaluation" or "subjective revaluation"). These arguments were rejected (albeit with some equivocation) by the Supreme Court in *Benedetti v Sawiris*.[18]

(2) Circumstances in which Subjective Devaluation will not be Available to the Defendant

14–018 The purpose of the principle of subjective devaluation is to protect the ability of people within this jurisdiction to make idiosyncratic decisions as to what they wish to spend their money on, rather than having such decisions foisted on them by the courts.[19] Suppose a well-meaning but unethical grandparent used fraudulent misrepresentations to deceive a celebrity into attending their grandchild's birthday party. Such appearances have a market value and many people would pay that value to secure them. However, the grandchild might personally detest the celebrity in question, and would not wish to have them attend their birthday party at any price. In those circumstances, the law will not regard the grandchild as enriched because—from his perspective—he has received nothing of value. Assuming his ignorance of his grandparent's wrong, to require him to make a restitutionary payment to the celebrity would be to override his right to dispose of his wealth as he chooses.

14–019 However, in certain circumstances, the defendant's ability to run arguments based on subjective devaluation may be fettered or removed altogether. In *Benedetti*, at [25], Lord Clarke identified two broad categories of case in which subjective devaluation would not be available to the defendant:

(1) Cases of incontrovertible benefit; and
(2) Cases in which the defendant requested or freely accepted the benefit conferred.

Cases of incontrovertible benefit probably include the following:

14–020 **(1) The Benefit Conferred is Money.**   Money is a measure of enrichment. In the words of Goff J (as he then was): "Money has the peculiar character of a universal medium of exchange. By its receipt, the recipient is inevitably benefited".[20] It would be extremely difficult—if not impossible—for a defendant successfully to argue that a subjective devaluation should be applied to the face value of the money received.

14–021 **(2) The Benefit Conferred Saves the Defendant Inevitable Expense.**   If the claimant pays for expenses which would otherwise have been inevitably incurred by the defendant then the net effect is identical to the claimant simply giving the

---

[18] *Benedetti v Sawiris* [2013] UKSC 50; [2014] A.C. 938. See, in particular, the judgments of Lord Clarke at [29]–[34], and Lord Neuberger at [193]–[200]. Note Lord Neuberger's suggestion that—in certain circumstances—a defendant might be estopped from relying upon the objective value of its enrichment, and be forced to litigate on the basis that it was enriched by some greater value.
[19] *Benedetti v Sawiris*, at [18].
[20] *BP Exploration Co (Libya) Ltd v Hunt (No.2)* [1979] 1 W.L.R. 783, at 799.

defendant money. So long as the expense truly was inevitable, then it is unlikely that there will be any question of the defendant's autonomy being abridged. "Inevitable" in this context can bear one of two potential meanings:

(i) The first is "legally compellable", into which category would fall debts (including judgment debts) and statutory liabilities.[21]
(ii) The second potential meaning is "factually necessary". Thus, a defendant will be enriched if the claimant pays for things which otherwise the defendant would, realistically speaking, have otherwise had to have paid for—even if a court could not have compelled him to do so. [22]

(3) The Defendant Receives a Benefit by the Claimant's Mistake, is Able to Return it, and Refuses to do so.   If the defendant refuses to give the benefit back, it does not lie in his mouth to say that he does not regard the benefit as having its objective value. This is demonstrated by the two cases of *McDonald v Coys of Kensington*[23] and *Harrison v Madejski*.[24] Both cases concerned the sale of cars which were, by mistake, transferred together with the right to use prestige number plates. Both recipients refused to return the right to use the numberplate. In *McDonald*, the recipient sought to argue that he had not been enriched at all by the right to use the numberplate. This was rejected by the Court of Appeal on the basis that the fact that the recipient had refused to return the right to the numberplate rather suggested that he did regard it as valuable. In *Harrison*, the recipient acknowledged that he had been enriched, but sought to argue that he had been enriched by less than the objective value of the right to use the numberplate. The objective value of the numberplate in question was £50,000, but the recipient was able to show by communications preceding the transfer that he regarded it as worth no more than £30,000. On appeal, there was an argument as to whether the

14–022

---

[21] The old case of *Exall v Partridge* (1799) 8 TR 308 provides an illustration of such a case. Mr Partridge and two other defendants rented business premises from a Mr Welch. The two other defendants assigned their interest in the lease to Mr Partridge, who carried on a business as a coach maker from the premises. Mr Exall, knowing that the two other defendants had assigned their interest in the lease to Mr Partridge, left his carriage with Mr Partridge for repairs. Unfortunately, Mr Partridge was in arrear on his rent, and Mr Exall's carriage was distrained by Mr Welch for those arrears. Mr Exall was forced to pay Mr Welch those arrears to recover his carriage, and was able to sue all three defendants to recover that money. This was because, notwithstanding the assignment of the lease, all three defendants remained liable to Mr Welch for the arrears and Mr Exall had benefitted all three of them by settling that debt. (Of course, the same facts may give rise to a different outcome following the enactment of the Landlord and Tenant (Covenants) Act 1995).

[22] *Craven-Ellis v Canons Ltd* [1936] 2 K.B. 403 is frequently cited as an example of such a situation. In that case the claimant worked as the managing director of the defendant development company. The contract under which he provided his services (and which provided for his reimbursement) was void. The Court of Appeal held that the company had to pay for the services which it had received from the claimant on the basis that "if [the services] had not been performed by the plaintiff, [the company] would have had to get some other agent to carry [them] out", at 412, per Greer LJ.

[23] *McDonald v Coys of Kensington* [2004] EWCA Civ 47; [2004] 1 W.L.R. 2775. Reported as *Cressman v Coys of Kensington*.

[24] *Harrison v Madejski* [2014] EWCA Civ 361.

recipient should be treated as enriched by £30,000 or £50,000. The Court of Appeal held that he should be treated as enriched by £50,000.[25]

14–023 **(4) The Objective Value of the Benefit is Realised.** It does not infringe a defendant's autonomy for the courts to recognise monetary benefits which he has actually received, even if they were received as a consequence of the receipt of goods or services which the defendant would not have selected for himself. Imagine a defendant receives a sculpture. The market values the sculpture at £50,000. The defendant hates the sculpture, and regards it as worthless. If he nevertheless successfully sells the sculpture for £50,000, he will be regarded as enriched by £50,000. Similarly, imagine someone owns a painting which they wish to sell. If someone mistakenly provided restoration work (objectively worth £5,000), which resulted in an increase of a painting's realised value from £50,000 to £60,000, the owner of the painting could not say that he had not been enriched by £5,000's worth of services, notwithstanding that he would not, given the choice, have employed the restorer. An example of such a case is *Greenwood v Bennett*.[26]

14–024 **(5) The Objective Value of the Benefit is Realisable.** Where the benefit is realisable, but has not yet been realised, the tension between recognising an enrichment and protecting the defendant's autonomy becomes more acute. Take the example above, in which £5,000 of restoration work is mistakenly performed upon a painting worth £50,000, increasing its value to £60,000. So long as the defendant always wanted to sell—and has sold—the painting, his autonomy is not infringed; he would have sold the painting in any event, and is not financially worse off by reason of having compensated the restorer for his services. The position is rather different if he has a deep attachment to the painting and would not wish to sell the painting under any circumstances. The fact of the restoration work may—in an abstract sense—have increased his wealth by £10,000, but an order by the court to pay the restorer £5,000 of that increase would nevertheless have the effect of compelling the defendant to hold £5,000 of his wealth in the painting (and subject to the risks of depreciation in the art market) rather than in cash. Notwithstanding these problems, the view of Mance LJ (as he then was) in *McDonald* is that a defendant should be regarded as enriched if he has received a readily realisable benefit, even if that benefit has not been realised.[27]

---

[25] See [53]–[59] in the judgment of Etherton C (as he then was), giving the only reasoned judgment of the Court. Professor Virgo's view is that the defendant should have been entitled to a subjective devaluation on the facts of the case—see Virgo, *The Principles of the Law of Restitution* (2015), pp.71–72.

[26] *Greenwood v Bennett* [1973] Q.B. 195. This case concerned a Jaguar in need of repairs. The workman employed to do the repairs used the Jaguar, crashed it, stole it, and sold it to an innocent recipient for £75. The innocent recipient spent £226 fixing the car. The Jaguar was recovered by the owner and sold for £450. The innocent recipient was entitled to recover the £226 spent repairing the Jaguar from the owner because the owner was enriched by that amount.

[27] See *McDonald*, at [33]–[36]. This is an approach which appeared to be approved of by the Court of Appeal in *Harrison* (see [57]–[58]), but it has received academic criticism from some quarters: see Professors J. Edelman and E. Bant, *Unjust Enrichment*, 2nd edn (London: Hart Publishing, 2016), pp.72–74; and Virgo, *The Principles of the Law of Restitution* (2015), pp.84–85.

As to cases in which the defendant requested or freely accepted the benefit conferred:　　　**14–025**

(1)　The Benefit has been Provided to the Defendant at His Request.　If a　　**14–026** defendant requests or demands that a claimant provide a benefit to him, understands that the claimant will expect to be paid, and the relevant benefit is in fact provided, a contract will usually arise, and the claimant will be able to rely upon his contractual rights without reference to the law of unjust enrichment. However, rare cases do arise in which a request has been made, a corresponding benefit has been supplied, but no contract governed that supply. In such circumstances, the defendant's decision to request the relevant goods or services will likely preclude any attempt to rely on subjective devaluation. However, if possible, the level of the remuneration may be fixed taking into account the parties' expectations: In *Vedatech Corp v Crystal Decisions (UK) Ltd*,[28] the parties anticipated that the claimant would be paid on a commission basis and the defendant's enrichment was valued on that basis.[29] By contrast, in *Amin v Amin*,[30] the parties only anticipated that the claimant would be paid if and to the extent that the defendant could afford to pay her; this formed the basis of valuing the defendant's enrichment.[31]

(2)　The Benefit was Freely Accepted by the Defendant.　"Free acceptance"　　**14–027** describes those cases in which a defendant did not expressly request the provision of a benefit, but nevertheless can be deemed to have chosen it. It will arise in circumstances in which two criteria are met:

(a)　the defendant did not take a reasonable opportunity open to him to reject the proffered benefit[32]; and
(b)　the defendant knew that the claimant expected to be remunerated for the benefit.[33]

Again, in such circumstances the defendant cannot be heard to say that his autonomy has been infringed by being made to pay for the benefit conferred.[34]

---

[28] *Vedatech Corp v Crystal Decisions (UK) Ltd* [2002] EWHC 818 (Ch).

[29] See *Vedatech Corp v Crystal Decisions (UK) Ltd* [2002] EWHC 818 (Ch), at [82].

[30] *Amin v Amin* [2009] EWHC 3356 (Ch) and [2010] EWHC 528 (Ch).

[31] See *Amin v Amin* [2010] EWHC 528 (Ch), at [11].

[32] *Chief Constable of the Greater Manchester Police v Wigan AFC Ltd* [2008] EWCA Civ 1449; [2009] 1 W.L.R. 1580, at [47].

[33] *Chief Constable of the Greater Manchester Police v Wigan AFC Ltd* [2008] EWCA Civ 1449; [2009] 1 W.L.R. 1580, at [38], and *The Queen (on the application of) Rowe v Vale of White Horse DC* [2003] EWHC 388 (Admin); [2003] 1 Lloyd's Rep. 418, at [14] (although note that in *Rowe* analysis of whether free acceptance had been established arose in the context of discussion as to whether or not Mr Rowe's unwitting enjoyment of sewage services without charge was unjust, rather than whether or not Mr Rowe had been benefitted—which he plainly had).

[34] Note also that there are suggestions in case law that any enrichment which is freely accepted at the claimant's expense will be unjust—see e.g. *Rowe* and *Dry Bulk Handy Holding Inc v Fayette International Holdings Ltd* [2012] EWHC 2107 (Comm), at [81]–[82]. Allowing "free acceptance" to constitute an unjust factor is controversial, but there is a growing body of English authority which

(3) Money

14–028 The transfer of money to a defendant enriches the defendant in two senses. The first and most obvious sense is that the recipient has more money than he once did, and he can exchange that additional money for goods and services of equal value (so-called "exchange" or "face" value). Secondly, the fact of that receipt enables the recipient to make profitable investments or earn interest, which it would not otherwise have been open to him to make or to earn, and/or to avoid borrowing money, which it would have cost him interest to borrow (so-called "use" or "time" value). The value of the defendant's enrichment will be the "exchange" or "face" value in circumstances in which the money received by the defendant was his "to keep".[35] Whether a defendant will be liable for the time value of money in circumstances in which the enrichment complained of is the temporary use of money is now in doubt following the judgment of the Supreme Court in *Prudential Assurance Co Ltd v Revenue and Customs Commissioners* [2018] UKSC 39; [2018] 3 W.L.R. 652, at [68]–[73], [77]–[79] and [123].[36]

14–029 The receipt of money confers an objective benefit on any recipient equal to its face value. Nevertheless, issues may arise in relation to the proper quantification of the receipt by which the recipient is benefited. If the recipient is paid money in circumstances in which he has paid over an equal sum, or is subject, at the point of receipt, to a binding obligation to repay that money or to pay that money onwards, he may—in truth—have received nil face value.[37] Similarly, it appears that a recipient will not be deemed to be enriched by the receipt of money to the extent that he holds that money on trust for others.[38]

14–030 The time value of money, if still recoverable—by contrast to its face value—will be powerfully influenced by the specific characteristics of the defendant, and it may well be open to subjective devaluation.

14–031 As to the objective value of the time value of money, this is taken to be the compounded interest rate at which a commercial loan would be made to the defendant. This takes into account the particular characteristics of the defendant

---

appears to support doing so. See further Mitchell, Mitchell and Watterson, *Goff & Jones: The Law of Unjust Enrichment* (2016), paras 17–01——17–18 and Edelman and Bant, *Unjust Enrichment* (2016), pp.323–328.

[35] Following the Supreme Court decision in *Prudential Assurance Co Ltd v Revenue and Customs Commissioners* [2018] UKSC 39; [2018] 3 W.L.R. 652, at [68]–[73], [79] and [123].

[36] An example might be where a payment in respect of a debt is mistakenly made before the date for repayment.

[37] *Jeremy D Stone Consultants Ltd v National Westminster Bank Plc* [2013] EWHC 208 (Ch), at [240]–[243]. Note, however, that where a recipient is subject to an obligation to pay money forward by way of a loan or to settle some pre-existing liability, and the money received enables him to meet that obligation, the recipient may well still be deemed to have received the face value of that money—see e.g. *Goss v Chilcott* [1996] A.C. 788, at [796]–[800].

[38] *Challinor v Bellis* [2015] EWCA Civ 59, [2015] 2 P. & C.R. DG3, at [113], although note the criticism of Professor Virgo in Virgo, *The Principles of the Law of Restitution* (2015), p.73.

in question. So, for example, the objective time value of money to the British Government will be lower than that of money to struggling commercial businesses.[39]

Subjective devaluation of this objective time value will be open to the defendant if it is able to show that—given the choice—it would not have paid the prevailing commercial rates to enjoy the use of the money which it had received. For example, a prosperous defendant with no borrowings, no investment appetite and sufficient income to meet his outgoings may well be capable of borrowing at 4% but would never choose to do so, as he would not have a use for the money so borrowed.

14–032

There has been some uncertainty over the extent to which evidence of the defendant's actual use of the money received is relevant to the issue of subjective devaluation. Following the decision of the Court of Appeal in *Littlewoods Retail Ltd v HMRC*,[40] the position appears to be that such evidence is not only admissible, but necessary. The Court held that the opportunity to use the money transferred could "only sensibly be valued in the light of knowledge of the use the defendant had made of the opportunity".[41]

14–033

(4) Real Property and Chattels

Like money, land and some chattels can be conceived of as having both exchange values and use values. For example, a car has both a retail and rental value. However, this will not be true of all chattels, at all times and in all quantities—one would not rent a pint of beer. However, it will generally not be appropriate to claim both the exchange and the use value of a land or chattel transferred. This is because the exchange value itself takes into account the use value of the asset—one can say that someone is enriched because they have been given a car, or that they are enriched because they do not have to pay to rent a car, but one would not ordinarily say that the two enrichments are cumulative; owning a car in itself obviates the need to rent one. However, if one is claiming specific restitution of a particular car, one might also seek the use value of that

14–034

---

[39] *Sempra Metals Ltd v IRC* [2007] UKHL 34; [2008] 1 A.C. 561, at [49] and [128]. Note that Professor Burrows in *A Restatement of the Law of Unjust Enrichment* (2012) regards the taking into account of the credit strength of the defendant as a part of the enquiry into subjective devaluation (pp.157–158). The judgment of the Court of Appeal in *The Test Claimants in the Franked Investment Income Group Litigation v The Commissioners of Her Majesty's Revenue and Customs* [2016] EWCA Civ 1180, at [258] suggests that the credit strength of the defendant is taken into account at the objective stage. However, see now the Supreme Court decision in *Prudential Assurance Co Ltd v Revenue and Customs Commissioners* [2018] UKSC 39; [2018] 3 W.L.R. 652, at [68]–[73], [77], [79] and [123].

[40] *Littlewoods Retail Ltd v HMRC* [2015] EWCA Civ 515; [2016] Ch. 373 (reversed on different grounds).

[41] *Littlewoods Retail Ltd v HMRC* [2015] EWCA Civ 515; [2016] Ch. 373, at [186]. See, however, Mitchell, Mitchell and Watterson, *Goff & Jones: The Law of Unjust Enrichment* (2016), paras 5–22—5–23.

car during the period in which it was in the defendant's possession.[42] Depending on the value of the car at the point of transfer, the rate of its depreciation in value, and prices in the rental market, such a course might produce a claim either more or less valuable than a claim for the exchange value.

14–035   By analogy with claims in unjust enrichment for money or services, the objective exchange value of property is likely to be the price at which the defendant could have obtained the relevant property in the market. This might then be subjectively devalued on the basis of the principles set out above. If a defendant already has a fridge-full of fish, he might legitimately say that he does not consider himself enriched by a mistaken delivery of further fish to his door—particularly if there is only a limited market for second hand and gradually warming fish in his community.

14–036   As to the objective use value of property, this will generally be the rate at which the defendant could have rented the land or chattel in question—a question which will take into account any agreement as to price reached between the parties.[43] Again, subjective devaluation may be open to the defendant and it appears—following the Court of Appeal's judgment in *Littlewoods Ltd v Revenue and Customs Commissioners*[44]—that the defendant can seek to subjectively devalue his benefit by reference to the actual use which he made of the property.[45]

14–037   Analysing enrichment in the context of stolen property requires particular care. Stolen property clearly has a use value; provided one has the keys and avoids the police, a stolen car can be driven just as well as one legally owned. The question of whether stolen property has an exchange value in the law of unjust enrichment has not been definitively settled—but the judgment of the Court of Appeal in *Costello v Chief Constable of Derbyshire Constabulary*[46] suggests that it should be answered in the affirmative. In *Costello*, the police seized a car which was "obviously stolen". Following the expiry of the police's statutory authority to hold the car, Mr Costello (from whom it was seized) sued the police for its unlawful detention in the tort of conversion. Somewhat surprisingly, he was successful. The Court of Appeal held that the mere possession of property conferred upon the possessor rights to that property which are legally enforceable against anyone who did not have a superior claim to that property. The true owner of the stolen car had a better claim to it than Mr Costello, but the police did not

---

[42] See further Dr A. Lodder, *Enrichment in the Law of Unjust Enrichment and Restitution* (London: Hart Publishing, 2012), pp.96–97. However, see now the Supreme Court decision in *Prudential Assurance Co Ltd v Revenue and Customs Commissioners* [2018] UKSC 39; [2018] 3 W.L.R. 652, at [68]–[73], [77], [79] and [123].

[43] See *Lewisham LBC v Masterton* (1999) 80 P & CR 117, at 123–124.

[44] *Littlewoods Ltd v Revenue and Customs Commissioners* [2015] EWCA Civ 515; [2016] Ch. 373, at [148]–[187].

[45] A proposition which had previously been rejected in *Lewisham LBC v Masterson* (1999) 80 P & CR 117, at 123–124. As noted above, *Goff & Jones* regards the Court of Appeal as having taken a wrong turning in this respect and appears to regard the *Littlewoods* decision as applicable only to cases concerned with monetary enrichment—see Mitchell, Mitchell and Watterson, *Goff & Jones: The Law of Unjust Enrichment* (2016), para.5–34. It is not clear that the Court of Appeal regarded their decision as so confined.

[46] *Costello v Chief Constable of Derbyshire Constabulary* [2001] EWCA Civ 381; [2001] 1 W.L.R. 1437.

and, accordingly, could not withhold it from him absent statutory authority. One would expect that this right could have an exchange value in the law of unjust enrichment.

(5) Choses in Action

Just as a defendant can be enriched by the physical receipt of money or property, he can be enriched by receipt of intangible rights. If our unethical grandparent procured a bank transfer to his grandchild by means of fraudulent representations, the grandchild has received a chose in action against the bank for the transferred sum, and is enriched thereby. **14–038**

Again, just as physical money or property can have exchange values and use values, so too can choses in action. **14–039**

(6) Services

The question of whether or not a defendant has been enriched by receipt of a service is particularly difficult for two reasons. First, services are by their nature ephemeral; once provided, they have no continuing existence which can be identified and valued. Secondly, the provision of a service will often be worth more to the recipient than the market value of the service itself. For example, in the example given above, restoration work increased a painting's value from £50,000 to £60,000, yet the market value of the work was only £5,000. **14–040**

The approach of the English Courts has been, in general, to regard the recipients of services as being enriched by the service's market value, rather than the value of that service to the recipient.[47] If the service in question would ordinarily be remunerated by means of a commission in money or in kind, the amount of the commission foregone by the claimant might be used to quantify the defendant's enrichment.[48] **14–041**

(7) The Discharge of Obligations

Just as money, property and services can constitute enrichment, the discharge of obligations to pay or provide the same may also constitute enrichment. If a fraudster tricks the claimant into paying £100 into the fraudster's innocent child's bank account, and the child's bank account is overdrawn, the child is enriched by the clearing of that debt just as much as they would have been if they had received the £100 in cash.[49] **14–042**

---

[47] See e.g. *Yeoman's Row Management Ltd v Cobbe* [2008] UKHL 55; [2008] 1 W.L.R. 1752, at [40]–[41], although note the different approach taken in the context of the Law Reform (Frustrated Contracts) Act 1943 in *B.P. Exploration Co (Libya) Ltd v Hunt (No.2)* [1979] 1 W.L.R. 783.

[48] See *Benedetti*, at [147].

[49] *Exall v Partridge* (1799) 8 TR 308, referred to in the first footnote to para.14–021 above, is an example of this.

C.   ENRICHMENT AT THE EXPENSE OF THE CLAIMANT

(1)   A Direct Transmission of a Benefit from Claimant to Defendant

14–043   The question of what constitutes an enrichment "at the expense of the claimant" is an important one. Particularly in the context of fraud or other unlawfulness, there will often be circumstances in which a potential defendant appears to be the indirect beneficiary of a wrongdoer's illegality, and yet will not obviously have received any benefit directly from the wronged party. It is therefore necessary to know the circumstances in which a sufficient connection will exist between any money lost by the wronged party and any gain enjoyed by the beneficiary.

14–044   This aspect of the law of unjust enrichment was for a long time somewhat obscure, but it has now received focused and welcome attention from the Supreme Court in *Investment Trust Companies v Revenue and Customs Commissioners.*[50]

14–045   In overview, the case concerned a number of investment funds which received supplies of services from investment managers. Pursuant to the service contracts between the funds and the investment managers, the managers were remunerated by the payment of fees plus VAT "if applicable". VAT was thought to be applicable under UK law, and was accordingly paid by the funds to the managers, who subsequently provided for such sums in their VAT returns to HMRC. However, it subsequently emerged that the charging of VAT was contrary to EU law, and that all of the payments in respect of the VAT levied on the service charges were made under a mistake of law.

14–046   The funds sued HMRC for the return of the money paid over by mistake. There was little doubt that HMRC had been enriched by the payment of the VAT, and that that enrichment was "unjust" in that it arose from a mistake. However, what was not clear was whether HMRC had been enriched "at the expense of" the funds. After all, the funds had not paid any VAT to HMRC. They had paid the VAT to the managers.

14–047   Lord Reed, giving the judgment of the Supreme Court, made the following initial observations:

14–048   First, claims in unjust enrichment are claims of right, not an exercise in judicial discretion:

> "A claim based on unjust enrichment does not create a judicial licence to meet the perceived requirements of fairness on a case-by-case basis: legal rights arising from unjust enrichment should be determined by rules of law which are ascertainable and consistently applied."[51]

14–049   Secondly, the adoption of unjust enrichment in modern law as a unifying principle underlying a number of different types of claim does not provide the

---

[50] *Investment Trust Companies v Revenue and Customs Commissioners* [2017] UKSC 29; [2018] A.C. 275; see in particular [32]–[72].
[51] *Investment Trust Companies v Revenue and Customs Commissioners* [2017] UKSC 29; [2018] A.C. 275, at [39].

Courts with a *tabula rasa* entitling them to disregard or distinguish authorities which pre-date *Lipkin Gorman*. The doctrine of precedent continues to apply.[52]

Thirdly, the four questions posed in a claim in unjust enrichment: **14–050**

(1)   Has the defendant been enriched?
(2)   Was the enrichment at the claimant's expense?
(3)   Was the enrichment unjust?
(4)   Are there any defences available to the defendant?

are not to be considered as though they are the words of a statute. Rather, they are broad headings which identify the essential elements of such a claim.

> "If they are not separately considered and answered, there is a risk that courts will resort to an unstructured approach driven by perceptions of fairness, with consequent uncertainty and unpredictability."[53]

His Lordship went on to observe that the requirement that an enrichment be "at **14–051** the expense of the claimant" reflects and describes the nature and purpose of claims in unjust enrichment, which is to "correct normatively defective transfers of value".

It followed, in the Court's judgment, that transfers of value had generally to be **14–052** made directly from the claimant to the defendant in order to engage the law of unjust enrichment. The purpose of the law of unjust enrichment being to reverse a defective transfer, rather than provide more general compensation to the claimant, one had to identify a particular transfer to reverse.[54] It followed that the funds were not able to sue HMRC for the VAT which they had paid the managers, because there was no transfer by which the funds had provided anything to HMRC which the law of unjust enrichment could reverse.

This position is simple to state; however, one must be alive to certain nuances **14–053** which may not be immediately apparent.

First, there may be direct transfers of benefit in three party cases which are **14–054** not—on the face of things—obvious. If our unethical grandparent induces a charity for the relief of childhood illness to pay money to his grandchild on the basis of fraudulent representations that his grandchild has cancer, there is no question that the grandchild has been enriched at the expense of the charity. However, if the charity had paid the money to a creditor of the grandchild in discharge of the grandchild's debt, that would also constitute a direct enrichment of the grandchild by the charity, as the discharge of the grandchild's debt is itself an enrichment. Similarly, if a claimant's agent confers services on a defendant on behalf of the claimant, or if money or property in which a claimant has a

---

[52] *Investment Trust Companies v Revenue and Customs Commissioners* [2017] UKSC 29; [2018] A.C. 275, at [40].

[53] *Investment Trust Companies v Revenue and Customs Commissioners* [2017] UKSC 29; [2018] A.C. 275, at [41].

[54] *Investment Trust Companies v Revenue and Customs Commissioners* [2017] UKSC 29; [2018] A.C. 275, at [60].

proprietary interest is transferred to a defendant, the claimant can be said to have directly enriched the defendant, notwithstanding the interposition of a third party.[55]

14-055 Secondly, not every direct transfer of value from a claimant to a defendant will be at the claimant's expense. An exception arises in the case of so-called incidental benefits. An example often given is a case in which the claimant heats his flat and, in doing so, warms the flat above. The person living in the flat above cannot be regarded as enriched at the claimant's expense, because that person is merely receiving an incidental and foreseeable benefit from the comfort which the claimant is choosing to confer upon himself.[56] *Swynson Ltd v Lowick Rose LLP*[57] is, at least on one view, an example of a case in which the enrichment of the defendant did not give rise to a claim in unjust enrichment because the impugned enrichment was incidental to an intended enrichment. The facts of the case were these:

(1) S Ltd, the first claimant, lent money to E Ltd in order to enable E to acquire M Ltd.

(2) In doing so, S was acting in reliance on a report prepared by the defendant, L LLP. This report was negligently prepared and, had it been properly prepared, S would not have made the above loan.

(3) In the event, revenue from M was insufficient to enable E to repay S, and E defaulted on the loans.

(4) At a later date, for tax reasons, the second claimant, H (the owner of S who had subsequently become the majority owner of E) lent money to E to enable it to repay its debt to S, which it did so.

(5) S and H then sued L for negligence. Liability was established in favour of S, but L argued that S had suffered no loss, because its loans had—in the event—been repaid.

(6) Importantly for present purposes, one of the points which H and S sought to run in the alternative to their primary damages claim was a claim in unjust enrichment. At least before the Supreme Court, it was articulated on the following basis: L's release from liability to S was an enrichment, which it enjoyed at the expense of H, and that enrichment was unjust because it arose as a consequence of H's mistaken belief that the refinancing of S's loans to E would not affect L's liability.

---

[55] *Investment Trust Companies v Revenue and Customs Commissioners* [2017] UKSC 29; [2018] A.C. 275, at [46]–[51]; and *Argyle UAE Ltd v Par-La-Ville Hotel and Residencies Ltd* [2018] EWCA Civ 1762, at [49]. See also Mitchell, Mitchell and Watterson, *Goff & Jones: The Law of Unjust Enrichment* (2016), paras 6–49—6–70 and the cases cited there. One should note also the academic disagreement (summarised in those passages) over whether receipt of money or property in which the claimant has a proprietary claim gives rise to a claim in unjust enrichment at all and, if it does, whether it arises because the defendant has been directly enriched by the claimant, or because of some other analysis.

[56] See *Investment Trust Companies*, at [52]–[58]. As recognised by Lord Reed, cases of incidental benefit will typically also lack any unjust factor. See also the comments of Lord Mance in *Swynson Ltd v Lowick Rose LLP* [2017] UKSC 32; [2018] A.C. 313, at [68]: "… the questions whether a benefit was obtained 'at the expense of' the claimant and whether it would be 'unjust' for the defendant to retain it are likely to be difficult to separate."

[57] *Swynson Ltd v Lowick Rose LLP* [2017] UKSC 32; [2018] A.C. 313.

The Supreme Court held that no such claim in unjust enrichment arose. Even if L could be regarded as "enriched", their lordships were not prepared to accept that this was unjust, or that this could properly be regarded as "at the expense of" H. The transaction which H had intended to enter into was a loan transaction with E, for tax purposes. That transaction was effected as intended and its purposes were achieved. The fact that there was also an unintended enrichment of L did not mean that L could be said to have benefited "at the expense of H" for the purposes of the law of unjust enrichment; it was merely incidental.[58] **14–056**

Thirdly, while the Supreme Court in *Investment Trust Companies* rejected reference to "the economic reality" of any given situation as too unstructured, they accepted that it was legitimate to regard a sequence of coordinated transactions as, in effect, one transaction transmitting a benefit directly from the claimant to the defendant.[59] *Menelaou v Bank of Cyprus UK Ltd*[60] was described as such a case. It is likely that *Relfo Ltd (In Liquidation) v Varsani*[61] (in which reference was made to the "economic reality" of a series of transactions) might also be regarded as such a case. **14–057**

An open question arising from the Supreme Court's decision is how one distinguishes between: **14–058**

(a)   cases in which one might say that the "economic reality" is that a benefit has been transferred from the claimant to a defendant, but no claim in unjust enrichment arises (such as in *Investment Trust Companies* itself); and

(b)   cases in which there are a series of coordinated transactions which can legitimately be treated as a single transaction giving rise to a claim in unjust enrichment (such as in *Menelaou*).

On the facts of *Investment Trust Companies*, it was held that the payment of the VAT from the funds to the managers and the payment from the managers to HMRC could not be regarded as a single transaction because:

"there is no question of the transactions being a sham or involving an artificial step, or of their comprising a single scheme. The first transfer did not even bring about the second transfer as a matter of causation ... the fact that, as a matter of economic reality, the lead claimants bore the cost of the undue tax paid by the managers to the commissioners does not in itself entitle them to restitution from the commissioners."[62]

---

[58] See the judgments of Lord Mance, at [87]–[88] (although note his comment, at [68]) and Lord Neuberger (with whom Lord Clarke agreed), at [115]. Note that Lord Sumption, with whom Lords Neuberger, Clarke and Hodge all agreed, was prepared to assume that L was enriched at the expense of H, albeit he recognised that this was "an odd assumption to make on the facts of this case" (see [20]).

[59] See *Investment Trust Companies v Revenue and Customs Commissioners* [2017] UKSC 29; [2018] A.C. 275, at [59]–[66]. See also *Argyle UAE Ltd v Par-La-Ville Hotel and Residencies Ltd* [2018] EWCA Civ 1762, at [50].

[60] *Menelaou v Bank of Cyprus UK Ltd* [2015] UKSC 66; [2016] A.C. 176.

[61] *Relfo Ltd (In Liquidation) v Varsani* [2014] EWCA Civ 360; [2015] 1 B.C.L.C. 14.

[62] See *Investment Trust Companies v Revenue and Customs Commissioners* [2017] UKSC 29; [2018] A.C. 275, at [72], per Lord Reed.

This suggests that questions of causation, and whether or not two transactions form part of a single transaction, will be important in distinguishing between the two types of case.

14–059   Finally, one should note that the Court left the door open to further development of the law regarding what constituted enrichment at the expense of the claimant:

> "It has often been suggested that there is a general rule, possibly subject to exceptions, that the claimant must have directly provided a benefit to the defendant. The situations discussed in the two preceding paragraphs [i.e. transactions through the intermediation of an agent or the repayment of a debt owed by the defendant to a third party] can be reconciled with such a rule, if it is understood as encompassing a number of situations which, for the purposes of the rule, the law treats as equivalent to a direct transfer, in the sense that there is no substantive or real difference. So understood, the suggested rule is helpful. It may nevertheless require refinement to accommodate other apparent exceptions, and it would be unwise at this stage of the law's development to exclude the possibility of genuine exceptions, or to rule out other possible approaches."[63]

(2)   The Relationship Between the Claimant's Loss and the Defendant's Gain

14–060   The defendant's gain operates as a cap on the amount which the claimant can recover from him in the law of unjust enrichment, irrespective of whether the claimant has actually lost a greater amount. If the claimant, who can only borrow at seven per cent. p.a., mistakenly transfers money to a defendant who can borrow at one per cent. p.a., the time value of the money lost by the claimant will be greater than the time value of the money obtained by the defendant. However, the claimant will only be able to recover the time value of the money obtained by the defendant. The reason for this lies in the function of the law of unjust enrichment—it is a strict liability to provide restitution of enrichment which the law deems it unjust for the defendant to retain. If defendants were to be required to go further, and to compensate the claimant for losses which have not enriched them, this would generate injustice; blameless defendants would be liable for losses which were not their fault, and which—often—the defendant in question would have been powerless to foresee or to prevent.[64]

14–061   Whether or not the claimant's loss should operate as a cap on its recovery is more controversial.[65] If a defendant who can only borrow at seven per cent. p.a. receives a mistaken payment from a claimant who can borrow at one per cent. p.a., it is not obviously the case that the claimant should be entitled to recover from the defendant on the basis of the defendant's higher time value for the money—particularly given that the Supreme Court has rejected the notion of subjective overvaluation.[66] Nevertheless, the approach the English courts have

---

[63] *Investment Trust Companies v Revenue and Customs Commissioners* [2017] UKSC 29; [2018] A.C. 275, at [50], per Lord Reed.
[64] See, e.g. *Test Claimants in the FII Group Litigation v HMRC* [2010] EWCA Civ 103, at [179].
[65] See Virgo, *The Principles of the Law of Restitution* (2015), pp.116–117.
[66] See para.14–017 above.

taken appears to be that the claimant's loss does not cap its potential recovery from a defendant in the law of unjust enrichment.[67]

D. UNJUST FACTORS

(1) The Importance of Justifying Grounds, or the "Presence of Basis Bar"

The following is fundamental to the law of unjust enrichment, but frequently overlooked by practitioners: an enrichment is, generally speaking, neither unjust, nor recoverable in the law of unjust enrichment, if it was conferred on the defendant in satisfaction of a valid and subsisting legal right (such as a contractual or statutory right, or a judgment)—in other words, where there is a basis for the enrichment. Whether there are any exceptions to this general rule is debatable, and—to the extent that exceptions exist—they operate within a very narrow compass.[68] As it was put in *Kleinwort Benson v Lincoln CC*,[69] "the payee cannot be said to have been unjustly enriched if he was entitled to receive the sum paid to him."[70]   **14–062**

However, if the relevant contractual right, judgment or (in theory) statutory obligation is or becomes inoperative, then the law of unjust enrichment will be free to operate, as the legal right which was satisfied by the enrichment will have fallen away.   **14–063**

By way of example, suppose A buys an original painting from a gallery for £1,000,000. The gallery owner knows, but A does not, that a large quantity of copies of the same painting are about to be released onto the market, which is likely to cause the value of the painting itself to collapse, and that is in fact what happens. The gallery owner has clearly been enriched at A's expense, and one might say—in colloquial terms—that that enrichment was unjust. However, unless A can find some way to vitiate the contract of sale (for example, on the basis of some misrepresentation as to the gallery owner's knowledge), the law of unjust enrichment will not be engaged; the gallery owner is entitled to the £1,000,000 because A contractually agreed to give it to him on a condition which was satisfied.   **14–064**

A contract may bar the application of the law of unjust enrichment even if it is not between the claimant and the defendant. The leading English case in this area is *Costello v MacDonald, Dickens & Macklin (a Firm)*.[71] The facts were simple but   **14–065**

---

[67] See *Sempra*, at [30]–[31], [66] and [126]–[129]; *Littlewoods Retail Ltd v HMRC* [2010] EWHC 1071 (Ch), at [145]–[147]; and *Amin v Amin* [2010] EWHC 528 (Ch), at [4].

[68] See Burrows, *A Restatement of the English Law of Unjust Enrichment* (2012), pp.33–35; and Virgo, *The Principles of the Law of Restitution* (2015), pp.139–141.

[69] *Kleinwort Benson v Lincoln CC* [1999] 2 A.C. 349, at 408B, per Lord Hope.

[70] See also the Privy Council in *DD Growth Premium 2X Fund v RMF Market Neutral Strategies (Master) Ltd* [2017] UKPC 36, at [62]: "It is fundamental that a payment cannot amount to enrichment if it was made for full consideration; and that it cannot be unjust to receive or retain it if it was made in satisfaction of a legal right."

[71] *Costello v MacDonald, Dickens & Macklin (a Firm)* [2011] EWCA Civ 930; [2012] Q.B. 244.

instructive: Mr and Mrs Costello wanted to develop certain land in Bournemouth owned by them personally. They approached a firm of builders to do so, and made clear to the builders that they would be hired through Oakwood Residential Ltd, a company which was solely owned and managed by the Costellos. The builders performed some of the work pursuant to their contract with Oakwood before the parties fell out. The builders then sued Oakwood and the Costellos for the value of their work, the Costellos being said to be liable on the basis that they had been unjustly enriched by that work: their land had received the benefit of the building work and its value had been enhanced thereby.

14–066 While the builders were successful at first instance, the judgment against the Costellos was overturned on appeal. As Etherton LJ put it[72]:

> "I am clear ... that the unjust enrichment claim against Mr and Mrs Costello must fail because it would undermine the contractual arrangements between the parties, that is to say, the contract between the claimants and Oakwood and the absence of any contract between the claimants and Mr and Mrs Costello. The general rule should be to uphold contractual arrangements by which parties have defined and allocated and, to that extent, restricted their mutual obligations, and, in so doing, have similarly allocated and circumscribed the consequences of non-performance. That general rule reflects a sound legal policy which acknowledges the parties' autonomy to configure the legal relations between them and provides certainty, and so limits disputes and litigation."

(2) Introduction to the Unjust Factors

14–067 We set out below a number of unjust factors which are presently thought to give rise to a claim in unjust enrichment and may arise in the context of a fraud claim.

14–068 Two things should be noted at the outset. First: this list is not comprehensive. This is for two reasons:

(a) as noted above,[73] the list of unjust factors is not settled; and
(b) some unjust factors are recognised in situations which are unlikely to arise in the context of a fraud. Examples include situations in which public authorities have unlawfully obtained enrichment, or a claimant has intervened in the affairs of another out of necessity (as in cases of maritime salvage). Both examples have accumulated a body of authority which do not require explication in the context of a book on civil fraud.

14–069 The second point to note is that entire books are dedicated to each of the legal concepts encountered below; their summary treatment in this chapter must be treated as what it is—a sketch of some of the relevant principles.

---

[72] *Costello* [2011] EWCA Civ 930; [2012] Q.B. 244, at [23].
[73] At para.14–002.

(3)   Mistake

It will often be the case that a fraudster dishonestly induces a payment or other transfer of value by his victim to a third party. One can, of course, sue the rogue for his deceit. If the third party is a party to the fraud, one might also sue them in tort or equity on any number of potential bases, which are explored further in other chapters in this book. However, if the third party is innocent (or one cannot prove that he was complicit in the fraud), then one might sue in unjust enrichment, on the basis that the enrichment was unjust because it was mistaken—i.e. the fraud caused the victim to believe something to be true which was untrue.   **14–070**

The question of whether a mistake will found a remedy in the law of unjust enrichment is best answered by reference to the three-fold enquiry set out by Lord Hope in *Kleinwort Benson Ltd v Lincoln City Council*: "(1) Was there a mistake? (2) Did the mistake cause the payment? And (3) did the payee have a right to receive the sum which was paid to him?"[74]   **14–071**

As to the first question, "*mistake*" in this context has a particular meaning, which is often overlooked. It is this: an incorrect belief in the existence of a fact or law, relating to the transaction in question.[75] Crucially, it does not extend to mere ignorance (although it will extend to mistakes arising out of ignorance)[76] or to mispredictions, whether or not those mispredictions are induced by another person. While the Supreme Court has recognised that the distinction between mistakes, ignorance and mispredictions can get blurred,[77] it is an important one, as is demonstrated by the case of *Dextra Bank & Trust Co Ltd v Bank of Jamaica*.[78]   **14–072**

In *Dextra*, three fraudsters approached Dextra Bank and asked it to lend money to the Bank of Jamaica. Dextra Bank proceeded to give them a cheque for the requested sum, and told them that they could give it to the Bank of Jamaica in exchange for a promissory note for repayment of the amount lent. Instead, the fraudsters gave the cheque to the Bank of Jamaica in exchange for cash, which they kept for their own benefit.   **14–073**

Dextra Bank attempted to recover the sum which the Bank of Jamaica had drawn under the cheque on the basis that the cheque had been handed over under a mistake—the alleged mistake being that Dextra Bank believed it was providing the cheque as a loan to the Bank of Jamaica. The Privy Council rejected that argument on the footing that what had caused Dextra Bank to hand the cheque to the fraudsters was not a belief that—at the moment of handing over the cheque—a loan had been made. Rather, Dextra Bank had handed the cheque to   **14–074**

---

[74] *Kleinwort Benson Ltd v Lincoln City Council* [1999] 2 A.C. 349, at 407H.

[75] A mistake as to the indirect consequences of a transaction will not suffice. The quality of the mistake must generally be such that it constitutes a defect in the transaction, or means that the claimant's expectation of some feature of the transaction for which he has bargained is absent (see *Swynson Ltd v Lowick Rose LLP* [2017] UKSC 32; [2018] A.C. 313, at [34], [87]–[89] and [119]).

[76] *Pitt v Holt* [2013] UKSC 26; [2013] 2 A.C. 108, at [108].

[77] *Pitt v Holt* [2013] UKSC 26; [2013] 2 A.C. 108, at [104].

[78] *Dextra Bank & Trust Co Ltd v Bank of Jamaica* [2002] 1 All E.R. (Comm) 193.

the fraudsters on the basis of a misprediction that the fraudsters would do as they were told, and only pass the cheque to the Bank of Jamaica once confirmation of the loan was given by way of a promissory note.

14–075 As to the second question (whether or not the mistake caused the enrichment complained of), it appears that this will be determined on a "but for" basis, unless the mistake was caused by a fraud by the defendant or of which the defendant had notice at the time of the enrichment, in which case a lower threshold may apply.[79]

14–076 As to the third question (whether or not the defendant has a right to the enrichment in question), this refers back to the "presence of basis bar" considered above. For example:

(1) If a mistake caused the claimant to make a payment to the defendant pursuant to a contract, the claimant will only be able to recover that payment in the law of unjust enrichment if that mistake (or some other factor) entitles the claimant to set the contract in question aside. Whether or not the contract can be set aside must be answered by reference to the law of contract, rather than the law of unjust enrichment.

(2) If a mistake caused the claimant to make a payment to the defendant, intending the payment to be a gift, then the circumstances must be such that the claimant is entitled to resile from that donative intention. Examples might be where the mistake is caused by a misrepresentation made by (or known to) the defendant[80] or where the mistake is of such seriousness that it would be unconscionable for the defendant to be allowed to retain the enrichment.[81]

(4) Lack of Consent, Lack of Authority and (Possibly) Breach of Fiduciary Duty

14–077 A mistake can render enrichment unjust because the transferor's consent to the enrichment was given on a false basis. Cases in which there is no consent at all, therefore, provide an even stronger basis for imposing a restitutionary liability on the recipient.[82] This can explain why, when Mr Holiday accidentally dropped a £500 note on the floor of Tattersall's betting and auction house, and Mr Sigil found it and kept it, Mr Sigil was obliged to pay £500 to Mr Holiday.[83]

14–078 Similarly, if a fraudster takes money belonging to the claimant, and—without authority to do so—gives it to a third party, this can impose a restitutionary

---

[79] See Burrows, *A Restatement of the Law of Unjust Enrichment* (2012), pp.64–65.

[80] See, e.g. *Deutsche Morgan Grenfell Group Plc v Inland Revenue Commissioners* [2006] UKHL 49; [2007] 1 A.C. 558, at [87].

[81] *Pitt v Holt* [2013] UKSC 26; [2013] 2 A.C. 108, at [125]–[128].

[82] Although, again, one should note the suggestions that this liability arises predominantly or exclusively in the law of property, see e.g. the judgment of Mr Stephen Morris QC in *Armstrong DLW GmbH v Winnington Networks Ltd* [2012] EWHC 10 (Ch); [2013] Ch. 156, at [95] and Virgo, *The Principles of the Law of Restitution* (2015), pp.152–153.

[83] *Holiday v Sigil* (1826) 2 C. & P. 176.

liability on the third party—as was the case in *Relfo*, *Lipkin Gorman* and the similar case of *Re Hampton Capital Ltd*.[84]

One question raised by the cases, but not yet definitively answered, concerns transfers in breach of fiduciary duty. If A owes fiduciary duties to B, and—in breach of those duties—pays B's money or transfers B's property to C, it is not clear whether C can be subject to strict liability in unjust enrichment, or only fault-based liability in knowing receipt. There has been some judicial reluctance to recognise such a strict liability claim in such circumstances.[85] Nevertheless, there is good reason to think that the law is developing in this direction:

    14–079

(1)   In *Clegg v Pache*[86] the recipient of a series of payments by a company procured by a director in breach of his fiduciary duties was found liable (subject to a change of position defence) to give restitution, notwithstanding that she was unaware of the breach of fiduciary duty.[87]

(2)   It is arguable that *Relfo* recognised a claim in unjust enrichment arising from breach of fiduciary duty. Mr Varsani was held to be liable in the law of unjust enrichment for money which he had received (albeit indirectly) from Relfo Ltd. The unjust factors relied upon were both that the director of Relfo Ltd had procured the transfer in breach of his fiduciary duty to the company and that he had transferred the money without authority to do so.[88]

(3)   Jersey recognised such a claim in *Re Esteem Settlement*.[89]

(4)   There is powerful support for such a move from commentators and from the obiter and extra-judicial writings of judges.[90]

(5) Individual Incapacity

Fraudsters and other wrongdoers not uncommonly target the aged or the mentally disabled, encouraging them to transfer their property or money either to the fraudster himself, or to someone connected to the fraudster. In such situations, the law of unjust enrichment may provide a remedy.[91]

    14–080

---

[84] *Relfo Ltd v Varsani* [2014] EWCA Civ 360; *Lipkin Gorman v Karpnale Ltd* [1991] 2 A.C. 548; and *Hampton Capital Ltd* [2015] EWHC 1905 (Ch).

[85] See, for example, the judgment of Nourse LJ in *Bank of Credit and Commerce International (Overseas) Ltd v Akindele* [2001] Ch. 437, at 456D–456E.

[86] *Clegg v Pache* [2017] EWCA Civ 256.

[87] *Clegg v Pache* [2017] EWCA Civ 256, at [82]–[91]. Note that the Court of Appeal appears to have regarded this as a form of the restitutionary liability recognised in *Re Diplock* [1948] Ch. 465.

[88] See the judgment of Sales J [2012] EWHC 2168 (Ch), at [88].

[89] *Re Esteem Settlement* [2002] J.L.R. 53, at [157].

[90] See e.g. Burrows, *A Restatement of the Law of Unjust Enrichment* (2012), at 96–98; Lord Millett's speech in *Dubai Aluminium Co Ltd v Salaam* [2002] UKHL 48; [2003] 2 A.C. 366, at [87]; and Mitchell, Mitchell and Watterson, *Goff & Jones: The Law of Unjust Enrichment* (2016), paras 8–119—8–141, and the works cited therein.

[91] The law of unjust enrichment might also be engaged in transactions involving minors, or corporations acting outside of their powers. However, the former is unlikely to arise in the context of fraud, and the latter will only arise in extremely narrow circumstances following the statutory abridgment of the ultra vires doctrine—currently set out in s.39 of the Companies Act 2006.

14–081   In order to found a claim for unjust enrichment arising out of individual incapacity there must—obviously—have been a lack of capacity at the time at which the relevant enrichment occurred. Whether or not there was a lack of capacity is a question to be answered primarily by reference to common law, although regard should also be had to ss.2 and 3 of the Mental Capacity Act 2005.[92]

14–082   Where someone who is alleged to have lacked capacity has made a gift or entered into a contract, then the crucial question, as posed by in *Re Beaney*,[93] is whether or not the person making the gift or entering the contract "was capable of understanding the effect of the deed when its general purport has been fully explained to him".[94] The degree of understanding of which the person transferring the relevant value must be capable varies depending on the transaction in question. It is not hard to understand the effect of placing £5 on the collection plate; it is rather harder to understand the effect of signing a TR1 transferring one's house to one's community support worker. Consequently, a higher capacity for understanding must be demonstrated in the context of the more momentous transaction.[95] However, the question is whether the person entering into the transaction would have been able to understand what he was doing if it was explained to him, rather than whether or not he did in fact understand what he was doing.[96] If he was able to understand the transaction, but did not, it may be that a different unjust factor was present (such as mistake).

14–083   If the enrichment complained of was a bare gift, then the position appears to be that the person who made the gift can sue in unjust enrichment whether or not the recipient was aware (or should have been aware) that the donor lacked the capacity to understand what they were doing. The lack of capacity appears to be, in and of itself, sufficient to prevent the transfer from being a gift.[97]

14–084   The position is somewhat different in relation to contracts. Contracts may only be avoided on the grounds of incapacity arising from a lack of ability to understand the transaction in question if the counterparty was either aware of the lack of capacity (see *Imperial Loan Co v Stone*)[98] or, possibly, if the counterparty ought to have known of the lack of capacity (see *Dunhill v Burgin (Nos 1 and 2)*).[99]

---

[92] See the detailed discussion of the interplay between the common law and statutory tests for capacity set out by Stephen Morris QC in *Re Smith* [2014] EWHC 3926 (Ch); [2015] 4 All E.R. 329, at [37]–[66].

[93] *In Re Beaney* [1978] 1 W.L.R. 770.

[94] *In Re Beaney* [1978] 1 W.L.R. at 773A–773B, per Mr Martin Nourse QC.

[95] See *In Re Beaney* [1978] 1 W.L.R. at 774F.

[96] See *Re Smith* [2014] EWHC 3926 (Ch); [2015] 4 All E.R. 329, at [27].

[97] See, e.g. *Simpson v Simpson* [1992] 1 F.L.R. 601, at 616H–617A.

[98] *Imperial Loan Co v Stone* [1892] 1 Q.B. 599.

[99] *Dunhill v Burgin (Nos 1 and 2)* [2014] UKSC 18; [2014] 1 W.L.R. 933, at [1]. Although note the comments in H. Beale, *Chitty on Contracts*, 32nd edn (London: Sweet & Maxwell, 2015), paras 9–078—9–088.

(6)   Total Failure of Consideration/Basis/Condition

This unjust factor is a simple concept shrouded by opaque language. It is **14–085** commonly the case that a person will transfer value to another person on a certain basis or (which is to express the same concept in different language) subject to a condition. If that basis fails, or the condition is not satisfied, the law of unjust enrichment will impose a restitutionary liability on the transferee. As Lord Toulson put it in *Barnes v Eastenders Cash & Carry Plc*[100]:

> "Failure of basis, or failure of consideration as it has been generally called, does not necessarily require failure of a promised counter-performance; it may consist of the failure of a state of affairs on which the agreement was premised."

A succinct summary of the meaning of failure of consideration was given by Professor Birks in his *An Introduction to the Law of Restitution* (Oxford: OUP, 1989), p.223 (cited with approval by the Court of Appeal in *Sharma v Simposh Ltd* [2013] Ch. 23, at [24]):

> "Failure of the consideration for a payment ... means that the state of affairs contemplated as the basis or reason for the payment has failed to materialise or, if it did exist, has failed to sustain itself".

The underlying rationale is that the transferor's consent to the transfer of the **14–086** value in question is qualified by the basis on which the transfer is made, whether that basis is the anticipated counter-performance of the transferee, or some state of affairs or other thing. If the counter-performance is not provided, or the state of affairs does not arise or continue, then it cannot be said that the transferor truly consented to transfer the value in question.[101]

Two examples elucidate the concept: **14–087**

(1)   In *Patel v Mirza*[102] (discussed in detail in Ch.24) Mr Mirza told Mr Patel over a Friday night poker game that he would have advance notice of an announcement by the Chancellor of the Exchequer, which would alter the price of shares in the Royal Bank of Scotland. It was agreed that Mr Patel would give Mr Mirza money, and Mr Mirza would use his inside information to profit from the anticipated share price movements, sharing the proceeds with Mr Patel. Mr Patel then gave Mr Mirza £620,000, but the anticipated inside information never materialised and the trading never occurred. Mr Patel was able to recover his £620,000 from Mr Mirza because the basis of the transfer had failed.

(2)   In *Re Ames Settlement*,[103] Mr Louis Ames covenanted to settle £10,000 on a trust for the benefit of his son, Mr John Ames, and his son's fiancée, Miss Chrystabel Hamilton, on the condition that they should marry within one year of the covenant. The marriage was solemnised in 1908, and the money

---

[100] *Barnes v Eastenders Cash & Carry Plc* [2014] UKSC 26; [2015] A.C. 1, at [106]–[107].
[101] See Robert Walker LJ in *Gribbon v Lutton* [2001] EWCA Civ 1956; [2002] Q.B. 902, at [60].
[102] *Patel v Mirza* [2016] UKSC 42; [2017] A.C. 467.
[103] *Re Ames Settlement* [1946] Ch. 217.

paid over as covenanted. However, in 1926, the marriage was declared void on the basis that John Ames had been unable to consummate it. The consequence was that the personal representatives of Louis Ames became entitled to the return of the money.

14–088 It is important to note two important constraints upon claims in unjust enrichment founded upon a failure of basis.

14–089 First, for the reasons discussed above, if the enrichment was transferred pursuant to a contractual obligation, that contractual obligation—and any other contractual obligation which would prevent the recovery of the enrichment—must have ceased to be operative. Further, if the enrichment was transferred pursuant to an arrangement which falls short of an enforceable contract, then there may,[104] in certain circumstances, be a distinct requirement that the arrangement must be incapable of being carried out. If the other party is still willing and able to perform his side of the bargain, the basis of the enrichment will not have failed, provided that there is no other condition to the transfer which remains unsatisfied.[105]

14–090 Secondly, there is—probably[106]—a requirement that the basis of the enrichment has failed "totally" (or, again to express the same concept in different words, there must have been "a total failure of consideration"). This requires a careful analysis of the basis on which the transferor is enriching the transferee; or, in the words of Lord Goff in *Stocznia Gdanska SA v Latvian Shipping Co*[107]:

> "I start from the position that failure of consideration does not depend upon the question whether the promisee has or has not received anything under the contract... Indeed, if that were so, in cases in which the promisor undertakes to do work or render services which confer no direct benefit on the promisee, for example where he undertakes to paint the promisee's daughter's house, no consideration would ever be furnished for the promisee's payment. In truth, the test is not whether the promisee has received a specific benefit, but rather whether the promisor has performed any part of the contractual duties in respect of which the payment is due."

---

[104] But there may not. See Mitchell, Mitchell and Watterson, *Goff & Jones: The Law of Unjust Enrichment* (2016), para.13–31.

[105] Compare *Thomas v Brown* (1876) 1 Q.B.D. 714 and *Chillingworth v Esche* [1924] 1 Ch. 97. *Thomas* concerned a contract for the sale of land which was unenforceable by reason of non-compliance with the Statute of Frauds. The claimant paid money by way of deposit under the supposed contract, and then decided not to proceed to sale. He was unable to recover the deposit. In *Chillingworth*, the claimant paid over a deposit "subject to contract" for the purchase of a nursery and other land. He then decided not to enter into the contract in question. The Court of Appeal held that he was entitled to return of the money. Professor Virgo reconciles these cases by explaining *Thomas* as a case in which the basis for the transfer of the deposit was performance by the defendant. The defendant was ready, willing and able to perform; therefore the basis of the transfer had not failed. By contrast, he regards *Chillingworth* was a case in which the basis of the transfer of the deposit was a contract which did not come into existence. The basis of the transfer had therefore failed (see Virgo, *The Principles of Restitution* (2015), p.316).

[106] While this appears to be the state of the law at present, there are powerful criticisms made of it, and some indications in recent decisions that this requirement may have fallen, or will fall, away (see further Mitchell, Mitchell and Watterson, *Goff & Jones: The Law of Unjust Enrichment* (2016), paras 12–16—12–32).

[107] *Stocznia Gdanska SA v Latvian Shipping Co* [1998] 1 W.L.R. 574, at 588C–588D.

If in fact any part of the basis on which the transfer was made has survived, then there will (again, probably) be no claim in unjust enrichment. So, in *Stocznia Gdanska*, the fact that a shipyard had begun work on building ships meant that there could be no claim by the employer on the basis of a total failure of consideration, notwithstanding the employer did not receive the ships, or any benefit under the contract. Similarly, in *Patel*, had Mr Mirza received the inside information which he said he was going to receive, and used it to bet on the movement of RBS share prices, and lost all of Mr Patel's money in doing so, Mr Patel would have no claim in unjust enrichment for failure of basis.

14–091

The bald statement that there must be a "total" failure of basis is, however, subject to a certain amount of qualification, in three areas in particular:

14–092

(1) Legal Rights to Return Benefits Received. A purchaser might pay for goods which are in fact delivered. If the purchaser then exercises a legal right to reject the goods in question, it will still lie in the purchaser's power to recover the price which they paid for the goods.[108]

14–093

(2) Incidental or Collateral Benefits. Imagine A books a flight from London to New York. The plane takes off, A consumes an inflight meal, and watches an inflight film. Somewhere over Ireland, the plane is forced to turn back to London as a consequence of negligent maintenance of the plane by A's carrier.[109] Assuming the absence of specific statutory or contractual provisions which may provide for such scenarios, it would be no answer to a claim in unjust enrichment by A for his carrier to point to the meal and movie which he enjoyed and to assert that he had received some of the benefit which he had contracted for. This is because "the essential bargain contracted for was transportation to [New York]".[110] The food and the movie were nothing more than collateral, or incidental, benefits.

14–094

(3) Apportionable or Severable Benefits. If A pays B £30 for 30 widgets at £1 each, and B only delivers A 15 widgets, one might argue that A is entitled to recover £15 from B on the basis that there has been a total failure of basis (or consideration) in respect of 15 of the pounds which he paid B.[111] The Courts have, in certain cases, accepted such arguments. For example:

14–095

(i)   In the case of *Goss v Chilcott*,[112] a lender advanced a loan to the defendant company, who paid interest on that loan to the lender. However, the defendant's contractual liability to repay the loan was invalidated, and the lender was forced to claim repayment in the law of unjust enrichment. The fact that the lender had received interest payments was held not to bar a

---

[108] See, e.g. *Rogers v Parish (Scarborough) Ltd* [1987] Q.B. 933.

[109] Broadly the same example was used by Stadlen J in *Giedo van der Garde BV v Force India Formula One Team Ltd* [2010] EWHC 2373 (QB), at [289]–[290].

[110] *Giedo van der Garde BV v Force India Formula One Team Ltd* [2010] EWHC 2373 (QB), at [290], per Stadlen J.

[111] A modified version of the example given at Virgo, *Principles of the Law of Restitution* (2015), p.326.

[112] *Goss v Chilcott* [1996] A.C. 788.

claim for return of the capital sum on the grounds of failure of basis. This was because the obligation to pay interest was held to be consideration for the use of the capital sum—separate from the obligation to repay the capital sum—in respect of which there had been a total failure of consideration. Further, Lord Goff stated obiter that—even if part of the capital sum had been repaid—he would have been prepared to hold that there had been a total failure of consideration in respect of the unpaid sum.[113]

(ii)   Similarly, in *D.O. Ferguson & Associates v Sohl*,[114] a builder did work adjudicated to be worth £22,065.75 and received £26,738.75 for it. The Court of Appeal dismissed an appeal against the judge's decision that the £4,673 differential should be repaid to the employer, with both Hirst LJ and Nourse LJ stating that there had been a total failure of consideration in relation to that money.

By contrast, Stadlen J found that no apportionment was possible in *Giedo van der Garde BV v Force India Formula One Team Ltd*.[115] In that case, Mr van der Garde—an aspiring racing driver—had paid USD 3,000,000 to the defendant in exchange for being permitted to drive a Formula One car in testing for 6,000 km, together with a number of other benefits, such as the chance to race as a reserve driver. In the event, Mr van der Garde was only permitted or offered 2,270 km of testing. The reason why apportionment was not possible was the presence of the other benefits. Mr van der Garde had paid USD 3,000,000 for a package of rights, some of which were completely different from others, and—in the absence of any agreement between the parties as to how the price was allocated to the different types of rights purchased—Stadlen J felt unable to apportion value between them as a judicial act. Had the contract been one simply for kilometers of testing, then Stadlen J would have felt able to say that there had been a total failure of consideration with respect to roughly two thirds (i.e. 4,730/6000) of the purchase price.[116] The consequence was that Mr van der Garde's claim in unjust enrichment for failure of basis failed.

(7)   Relief of the Liabilities of Another Under the Legal Compulsion of a Third Party

14–096   If two defendants are liable to the same claimant, and the payment by one defendant results in a pro tanto release of the second defendant's liability, that second defendant is enriched at the first defendant's expense. That enrichment will be unjust in either of two circumstances (a) justice required that the defendants share in the liability, but the first defendant has paid more than his share; or (b) justice required that the second defendant should pay the entirety of the liability.

---

[113] *Goss v Chilcott* [1996] A.C. 788, at 797E–798F.

[114] *D.O. Ferguson & Associates v Sohl* (1992) 62 B.L.R. 95.

[115] *Giedo van der Garde BV v Force India Formula One Team Ltd* [2010] EWHC 2373 (QB).

[116] *Giedo van der Garde BV v Force India Formula One Team Ltd* [2010] EWHC 2373 (QB), at [366], [367], [373] and [374].

One should also be aware that this is an area in which the first defendant may have statutory recourse against the second defendant pursuant to the Civil Liability (Contribution) Act 1978.

An example of this unjust factor operating in the context of a fraud is *Niru* **14–097** *Battery Manufacturing Co v Milestone Trading Ltd (No.2)*.[117] The facts of the case are relatively complex, but in short summary:

(1) M agreed to sell lead to N. Payment would be made upon presentation of certain documents confirming that M was shipping the lead.

(2) M had no material assets. Therefore, in order to acquire the lead which it was selling to N, M borrowed money from C. C secured its lending by taking possession of the lead.

(3) The result was an impasse, M could not repay C so as to take possession of the lead and ship it to N without money from N, but N would not pay M until M was shipping the lead.

(4) The solution M hit upon was to commit a fraud. Fraudulent documents were presented to N to the effect that the lead was in the possession of M's freighters.

(5) Among those documents was a certificate issued by S. This certificate was issued as a consequence of S's negligence.

(6) Payment from N was delayed, during which time C sold the lead.

(7) Following the sale, N paid C for the lead, in reliance upon the fraudulent documentation and negligently-issued certificate from S. C then paid that money to M's group.

(8) N obtained a judgment against each of C and S.[118] C was held liable to N on the basis that it had received payment under a mistake of fact and that no change of position defence applied. S was held liable for negligence on the basis that, but for its certificate, payment would not have been made to C.

(9) N then proceeded to enforce judgment against S, and S paid in full.

S was able to recover the full amount of the judgment from C, the reason being **14–098** that: (a) S had extinguished C's liability to N; (b) this constituted an enrichment of C at the expense of S; and (c) given S had been compelled to enrich C, the enrichment (as between C and S) was unjust.[119]

While, on the facts of *Niru*, it was held that S should be able to recover the **14–099** entirety of the judgment from C on the basis that, if C had not paid the money out to M then neither C nor S need have suffered any loss, the judgment of the Court of Appeal in *Charter Plc v City Index Ltd*[120] makes clear that there is no

---

[117] *Niru Battery Manufacturing Co v Milestone Trading Ltd (No.2)* [2003] EWHC 1032 (Comm) and [2004] EWCA Civ 487; [2004] 2 All E.R. (Comm) 289.

[118] See *Niru Battery Manufacturing Co v Milestone Trading Ltd (No.1)* [2002] EWHC 1425 (Comm); [2002] 2 All E.R. (Comm) 705, and [2003] EWCA Civ 1446; [2004] Q.B. 985.

[119] See [64], [72], [80] and [90] of the judgment of the Court of Appeal.

[120] *Charter Plc v City Index Ltd* [2007] EWCA Civ 1382; [2008] Ch. 313.

automatic presumption that one form of liability (i.e. the restitutionary liability of C or the tortious liability of S) will attract a larger share of liability than another.[121]

14–100 It should be noted that while this unjust factor will generally involve the claimant being the subject of threatened or actual legal proceedings, this is not necessarily the case.[122]

(8) Duress, Undue Influence and Unconscionable Bargains

14–101 Each of these is recognised as an unjust factor. They are addressed separately in the following chapter.

E. DEFENCES

(1) Introduction

14–102 We consider below two defences which arise specifically in the context of unjust enrichment claims. However, these should not be treated as an exhaustive list of the defences to such claims. This is for two reasons. First, a great many of the more general defences which English law affords a defendant (limitation, equitable set-off, estoppel, illegality, etc.) may also be available. Secondly, given the still developing nature of the law of unjust enrichment, it is quite possible that defences which have not yet been explicitly recognised by the English courts (such as a potential defence of "passing on" in circumstances in which a claimant recoups the transferred enrichment from a third party)[123] may yet be introduced into English law.

---

[121] See Carnwath LJ, at [59]: "There is no automatic presumption that one form of liability attracts a larger share than the other (even in a case where one party has been fraudulent: *Downs v Chappell* [1997] 1 W.L.R. 426). It all depends on the facts, which can only be assessed at trial." *Charter Plc* was a case in which the treasury manager of a multinational group of companies paid corporate monies to the defendant in order to fund his personal betting transactions. The companies sued the defendant, and the defendant made Pt 20 claims against the claimants' auditors and directors seeking contribution or indemnity under the Civil Liability (Contribution) Act 1978, on the basis that they caused the unauthorised transactions to go undetected. Summary judgment was entered for the Pt 20 defendants at first instance, but set aside on appeal. There was no automatic presumption that the defendant (as a conscious wrongdoer) should bear liability to the exclusion of the negligent defendants and auditors.

[122] Hence the case of *Exall v Partridge* (1799) 8 TR 308, referred to in fn.21 above, is an example of a claimant paying the defendant's liability to a third party under legal compulsion, but in the absence of proceedings (the compulsion in that case being Mr Welch's enforcement of his rights of distraint against Mr Exall's carriage).

[123] See further Mitchell, Mitchell and Watterson, *Goff & Jones: The Law of Unjust Enrichment* (2016), Ch.32.

(2) Change of Position

A defendant to a claim in unjust enrichment will generally[124] have a defence to that claim to the extent that:

14–103

(1)   the defendant's position has changed, such that repaying the enrichment would leave him worse off than he would have been if he had never received the enrichment at all;
(2)   the change of position was caused by (or in anticipation of) the enrichment; and
(3)   it would, in light of the change of position, be inequitable to require the defendant to make a restitution of the enrichment.

The policy behind this defence is simple. Take the example given earlier in this chapter: a grandparent, by means of a fraud practiced upon a bank, induces the payment of £100 to his innocent grandchild's account. Notwithstanding the fact that the grandchild is wholly ignorant of the fraud, the law of unjust enrichment will require the grandchild to repay the £100 to the bank. One can see the justice in this result—the grandchild should never have had the money, and is obliged to return it.

14–104

The justice of the case is different in circumstances in which the grandchild spends the £100 which he receives as a consequence of his grandparent's fraud in non-routine expenditure. Suppose the grandchild is surprised by the amount of money which he has left in his account at the end of the month, and—as a consequence—pays £100 to charity. To require the grandchild to pay back the £100 received in these circumstances would create an injustice, as the grandchild would be left with £100 less than he would have had if the grandparent had not practised his deceit. The innocent grandchild would be left compensating the bank for the tort of his grandfather. The change of position defence operates to prevent this injustice from arising.

14–105

We examine below the three elements of the defence.

14–106

(i)   Change of position

The change of position defence is primarily concerned with "disenrichment",[125] i.e. one looks to see whether the enrichment has caused the defendant's position to change such that, in pecuniary terms, he has divested himself of all or part of the enrichment. Obvious means by which a defendant might have "disenriched" himself might be the giving of gifts, gambling or the purchase and consumption of consumables.

14–107

---

[124] It is worth noting that in limited circumstances—which are unlikely to arise in a fraud context—the defence may not be available, such as where money is paid over to public authorities which are acting ultra vires (see e.g. *Ipswich Town Football Club Co Ltd v Chief Constable of Suffolk* [2017] EWHC 375 (QB), at [79]).

[125] See e.g. *Test Claimants in the FII Group Litigation v Revenue and Customs Commissioners* [2014] EWHC 4302 (Ch), at [354].

14–108 However, it is important to note that the

> "mere fact that the defendant has spent the money, in whole or in part, does not of itself render it inequitable that he should be called upon to repay, because the expenditure might in any event have been incurred by him in the ordinary course of things".[126]

Professor Birks gives the example of the weekly shop or the credit card bill[127]—if the grandchild spent the £100 he received as a consequence of his grandparent's fraud on exactly the same food as he buys every week, or on paying his existing debts as and when they fell due—then the grandchild would not have changed his position. This is because, if one forced him to pay back the £100 which he received from the bank, he would be left in exactly the same position as he would have been in if he had not received the £100 in the first place.

14–109 One should also note that payment of money is not the only mode by which a person can change their position.[128] Case law suggests that the provision of goods,[129] or services,[130] or decisions to give up a job, start a family or even consent to divorce on certain terms may all potentially qualify.[131]

(ii) Causation

14–110 In order for a change of position defence to arise, it is necessary for the defendant to establish, on the balance of probabilities, that "but for" the relevant enrichment, he would not have changed his position.[132] So long as the "but for" test is satisfied, a change of position made in anticipation of the enrichment, as well as one made as a result of the receipt of it, will qualify.[133]

14–111 While the change of position must be causally related to the enrichment, it appears that it does not need to be made in reliance upon the enrichment.[134] The importance of this distinction is best illustrated by example. Suppose, by means of a fraud, A procures a payment by B into C's account. A then takes that money out of C's account. C is at all times unaware that payments have been made to or from his account. In this example, C has been enriched, and then disenriched as a consequence of that enrichment (assuming that A would not have taken money out of C's account in any event). However, he has not taken any step in reliance on the enrichment, because he was unaware of it. It appears that English law will, nevertheless, permit C a change of position defence.[135] Further, just as a change of position made by a defendant in anticipation of the enrichment will qualify

---

[126] Per Lord Goff in *Lipkin Gorman* at 580F–580G.

[127] Mitchell, Mitchell and Watterson, *Goff & Jones: The Law of Unjust Enrichment* (2016), p.211.

[128] *Commerzbank AG v Gareth Price-Jones* [2003] EWCA Civ 1663, at [39] and [65]–[72].

[129] *Pearce v Lloyds TSB Bank Plc* [2001] EWCA Civ 1907.

[130] *Mahme Trust Reg v Tayeb* [2002] EWHC 1543 (Ch); [2003] W.T.L.R. 21.

[131] See *Commerzbank AG v Gareth Price-Jones* [2003] EWCA Civ 1663, at [39] and [69].

[132] See *The Test Claimants in the Franked Investment Income Group Litigation v The Commissioners of Her Majesty's Revenue and Customs* [2016] EWCA Civ 1180, at [310]; and *Scottish Equitable Plc v Derby* [2001] EWCA Civ 369; [2001] 3 All E.R. 818, at [31].

[133] *Commerzbank AG v Gareth Price-Jones* [2003] EWCA Civ 1663, at [38].

[134] *T & L Sugars Ltd v Tate & Lyle Industries Ltd* [2015] EWHC 2696 (Comm), at [135]–[137].

[135] See further Mitchell, Mitchell and Watterson, *Goff & Jones: The Law of Unjust Enrichment* (2016), paras 27–34—27–35.

him for the defence, there is no obvious reason in principle why a change of position imposed upon him by a third party because the third party (and not the defendant) anticipates the enrichment should not also qualify him for the defence.

(iii)   Inequity

The general position is that, where a defendant has changed his position because of an enrichment, it would be inequitable to require him to make restitution of the enrichment to the claimant.   **14–112**

However, this will not always be the case. In *Lipkin Gorman* Lord Goff identified two circumstances in which it would not be[136]: "(a) if the defendant changed his position in bad faith; and (b) if the defendant is a wrongdoer."   **14–113**

The paradigm example of a bad faith change of position defence is where the defendant deliberately pays away the enrichment in the knowledge that it was paid to him by mistake.[137] Further, a defendant who deliberately pays away an enrichment in the knowledge that an enrichment *might* have been paid to him by mistake would also appear to be disqualified from relying on the defence.[138] "Bad faith" in this context has been described as equating to "commercially unacceptable conduct".[139]   **14–114**

It appears that, in theory, a defendant who changes his position on the basis of an enrichment which he foolishly or negligently—but honestly—believes that he is entitled to will not be barred from relying on a change of position defence.[140] However, it is worth bearing in mind that the Courts are likely to approach evidence that a defendant did not recognise the obvious with a healthy skepticism.[141]   **14–115**

The law on when "wrongdoing"—as distinct from bad faith—will bar reliance upon the change of position defence is unclear. Broadly three strands of thought can be identified: **14–116**

(1)   If the Change of Position Involved Illegal Conduct, One is Not Entitled to Rely Upon it.   This was the view taken by Laddie J in *Barros Mattos Junior v General Securities & Finance Ltd* [142] and seemingly conceded to be correct in *O'Neil v Gale*.[143] In the former case, fraudsters caused a bank to pay US dollars to middlemen, who converted the dollars into Nigerian naira before paying them to third parties. On a summary judgment application, it was accepted that the   **14–117**

---

[136] See *Lipkin Gorman*, at 580.

[137] See *Lipkin Gorman*, at 580.

[138] *Hampton Capital Ltd v Elite Performance Cars Ltd* [2015] EWHC 1905 (Ch); [2016] 1 B.C.L.C. 374, at [72].

[139] See *Abou-Rahmah v Abacha* [2006] EWCA Civ 1492, at [52] and [99].

[140] *Armstrong DLW GmbH v Winnington Networks Ltd* [2012] EWHC 10 (Ch); [2013] Ch. 156, at [110]; and *Abou-Rahmah v Abacha* [2006] EWCA Civ 1492, at [62], [83], [84], [95] and [99]–[102].

[141] As Nugee J did in *Webber v Department for Education* [2014] EWHC 4240 (Ch), at [52]–[57] and Proudman J *Barclays Bank Plc v Kalamohan* [2010] EWHC 1383 (Ch)—see [70], [71] and [75].

[142] *Barros Mattos Junior v General Securities & Finance Ltd* [2004] EWHC 1188 (Ch); [2005] 1 W.L.R. 247, at [42]–[44].

[143] *O'Neil v Gale* [2013] EWCA Civ 1554, at [26]–[27].

middlemen were innocent of the fraud. They were, nevertheless, barred from any reliance on a change of position defence because, by exchanging the dollars for naira, they had breached Nigerian currency controls. This absolutist approach is almost certainly inapplicable following the decision of the Supreme Court in *Patel v Mirza*[144] (discussed further in the Ch.24 on Illegality).

14–118　**(2)　Wrongdoing Does Not Disqualify a Defendant to an Unjust Enrichment Claim from a Change of Position Defence to that Claim.**　Henderson J's view in *Test Claimants in the FII Group Litigation v Revenue and Customs Commissioners*[145] is that when Lord Goff said that a change of position defence would not be available to a wrongdoer, what he meant was that a change of position defence would not enable someone accused of a wrong (e.g. a tortfeasor, contract breaker or equitable wrongdoer) to avoid liability for that wrong. He was not saying that someone facing a claim in unjust enrichment would disqualify themselves from a change of position defence by committing a wrong. This view is endorsed by Professor Burrows in *A Restatement of the English Law of Unjust Enrichment* (2012).[146]

14–119　**(3)　A Wrongdoer will not be Allowed to Rely Upon a Change of Position Defence if to Allow such a Defence would Undermine an Overriding Policy or Principle of the Law.**　There will be certain circumstances in which allowing a change of position defence to a defendant would weaken (or "stultify") protections which the law has been designed to offer. The fact that it has now been accepted that the danger of "stultification" explains why a change of position defence is not available in certain contexts,[147] and that *Patel v Mirza* analysed the illegality defence in terms of stultification, suggests that this is the way in which Courts will approach the interrelationship between wrongdoing and the defence of change of position in the future. The facts of *O'Neil v Gale*[148] give a possible example of how this might work in the context of a fraud. *O'Neil* concerned a Ponzi scheme run by Mr Gale contrary to the provisions of the Financial Services and Markets Act 2000. Mr Gale co-opted his wife, Mrs Gale, who allowed him to use her bank accounts to channel money into and out of the scheme. At first instance it was found that Mrs Gale had not acted in bad faith, but that she had committed a crime and as a result—following *Barros Mattos Junior*—she could not rely upon a change of position defence. On appeal, the Court of Appeal expressly did not comment upon the proposition that illegality would necessarily bar Mrs Gale from a change of position defence,[149] but Vos LJ did remark[150]:

---

[144] *Patel v Mirza* [2017] A.C. 467.

[145] *Test Claimants in the FII Group Litigation v Revenue and Customs Commissioners* [2008] EWHC 2893 (Ch), at [320], [337]–[342]. One should be aware of the qualification of some of these comments in *The Test Claimants in the FII Group Litigation v The Commissioners for Her Majesty's Revenue and Customs* [2014] EWHC 4302 (Ch), at [309]–[315].

[146] Burrows, *A Restatement of the Law of Unjust Enrichment* (2012), p.121.

[147] See Henderson J in *The Test Claimants in the FII Group Litigation v The Commissioners for Her Majesty's Revenue and Customs* [2014] EWHC 4302 (Ch), at [309]–[315].

[148] *O'Neil v Gale* [2013] EWCA Civ 1554.

[149] *O'Neil v Gale* [2013] EWCA Civ 1554, see [26]–[27].

[150] *O'Neil v Gale* [2013] EWCA Civ 1554, at [28].

"it would be strange if the recipient of invested monies could successfully oppose an innocent investor's restitutionary claim by relying on the very payments that resulted in the losses (namely the subsequent bets and the payment of dividends) that were themselves unlawful under legislation designed to protect just such investors."

—in other words, allowing Mrs Gale to escape liability on the basis of her change of position would stultify the legislative intention behind the provisions of the 2000 Act.

(3) Ministerial Receipt

If an agent receives an enrichment on behalf of his principal and, consequently, passes that enrichment on to his principal, then he will generally have a defence of change of position (subject to the considerations set out above) against any claim in unjust enrichment.   **14–120**

However, it is possible that the agent will have a defence to any claim in unjust enrichment even before he passes the enrichment to his principal. This is on the basis that the enrichment is in truth the principal's, even while it is in the agent's hands; the agent has not really been enriched.   **14–121**

It is not yet clear whether this is the law of England. This issue recently arose in *Marsfield Automotive INC v Kamal Siddiqi*[151] in a summary judgment application. In that case the claimant intended to enter into a contract with another company, and paid a deposit to the company's director. Following the collapse of the relationship, the claimant sued the director in unjust enrichment for the return of the deposit. The defendant director still held some of the money, but ran a defence that he only ever received the payment as agent for the company. Teare J held that that defence stood a real prospect of success, and declined to order the defendant to pay money into Court in order to defend the claim.[152]   **14–122**

F. REMEDIES

(1) Personal Restitutionary Awards

The "standard response"[153] which is sought from and awarded by Courts in an unjust enrichment claim is a personal restitutionary award. This is a monetary award, which will be equal in value to the defendant's enrichment (measured on the principles set out above), insofar as it was at the claimant's expense and has not been cut down by any change of position on the part of the defendant, or any other defence which is deployed.   **14–123**

---

[151] *Marsfield Automotive INC v Kamal Siddiqi* [2017] EWHC 187 (Comm).
[152] *Marsfield Automotive INC v Kamal Siddiqi*, see [30]–[37].
[153] Per Lord Neuberger in *Menelaou v Bank of Cyprus UK Ltd* [2015] UKSC 66; [2016] A.C. 176, at [81].

(2) Proprietary Remedies

14–124   The question of whether and, if so, when a claim in unjust enrichment will entitle a claimant to a proprietary remedy is controversial and uncertain. The crux of the problem is as identified in the introduction to this chapter: unjust enrichment is a recent categorisation of pre-existing legal remedies, and there is no academic or judicial consensus as to precisely which of those pre-existing legal remedies belong in the "unjust enrichment" category. The words of Lord Goff are as true now as they were 20 years ago[154]:

> "Ever since the law of restitution began, about the middle of this century, to be studied in depth, the role of equitable proprietary claims in the law of restitution has been found to be a matter of great difficulty. The legitimate ambition of restitution lawyers has been to establish a coherent law of restitution, founded upon the principle of unjust enrichment; and since certain equitable institutions, notably the constructive trust and the resulting trust, have been perceived to have the function of reversing unjust enrichment, they have sought to embrace those institutions within the law of restitution, if necessary moulding them to make them fit for that purpose. Equity lawyers, on the other hand, have displayed anxiety that in this process the equitable principles underlying these institutions may become illegitimately distorted; and though equity lawyers in this country are nowadays much more sympathetic than they have been in the past towards the need to develop a coherent law of restitution, and to identify the proper role of the trust within that rubric of the law, they remain concerned that the trust concept should not be distorted, and also that the practical consequences of its imposition should be fully appreciated."[155]

14–125   Notwithstanding this uncertainty, it is possible to make a number of tentative observations:

(1)   The law of property and the law of unjust enrichment are conceptually distinct. (See *Menelaou v Bank of Cyprus UK Ltd*).[156]

(2)   However, one set of facts will often give rise to both a proprietary claim and a claim in unjust enrichment. (See e.g. *Relfo Ltd (In Liquidation) v Varsani*,[157] and *Keown v Nahoor*).[158]

(3)   It follows that the pragmatic response to this uncertainty is likely to be, so far as is possible and sensible, to adopt a belt and braces approach to pleading, asserting claims both in the language of unjust enrichment and that of vindicating property rights.

(4)   It appears to be established that proprietary security rights may arise in the law of unjust enrichment in at least two circumstances[159]:

    (i)   The first is where A discharges B's secured liability. To the extent that an unjust enrichment arises as a result, the claimant may be entitled to

---

[154] See e.g. Lord Sumption in *D&D Wines International Ltd (In Liquidation)* [2016] UKSC 47; [2016] 1 W.L.R. 3179, at [30].

[155] *Westdeutsche Landesbank Girozentrale v Islington LBC* [1996] A.C. 669, at 685.

[156] *Menelaou v Bank of Cyprus UK Ltd* [2015] UKSC 66; [2016] A.C. 176, at [37]–[38].

[157] *Relfo Ltd (In Liquidation) v Varsani* [2014] EWCA Civ 360; [2015] 1 B.C.L.C. 14.

[158] *Keown v Nahoor* [2015] EWHC 3418 (Ch).

[159] These are both examples of situations in which equitable subrogation has been used to reverse unjust enrichment. Lord Sumption has warned that the principles applicable in this area of restitution cannot be uncritically applied to others. See *Lowick Rose LLP (In Liquidation) v Swynson Ltd* [2018] A.C. 313, at [30].

the benefit of the security relating to the discharged liability (as in *Banque Financière de la Cité v Parc (Battersea) Ltd*).[160]

(ii) The second is where A releases security over B's asset in circumstances in which that release unjustly enriches B. In such circumstances, A may be entitled to a substitute security interest so as to reverse the unjust enrichment (as in *Menelaou v Bank of Cyprus UK Ltd*).[161]

(5) By contrast, it also appears to be established that proprietary rights will not arise in circumstances in which money is paid on a basis which subsequently fails—the resulting claim in unjust enrichment has been described by Lord Sumption in *D&D Wines International Ltd (In Liquidation)* as "simply a process of contractual readjustment, giving rise like the contract itself to purely personal obligations."[162]

The circumstances in which a claimant may be able to assert an interest under a resulting or constructive trust are considered in Ch.9; and the means by which such a claim, and other equitable proprietary claims, can be advanced (including the rules of tracing and following) are considered in Ch.23.

14–126

---

[160] *Banque Financière de la Cité v Parc (Battersea) Ltd* [1999] 1 A.C. 221.

[161] Above.

[162] *D&D Wines International Ltd (In Liquidation)* [2016] UKSC 47; [2016] 1 W.L.R. 3179, at [30].

CHAPTER 15

UNDUE INFLUENCE AND DURESS

A. INTRODUCTION

(1) The Practical Relevance of these Claims

As this book seeks to demonstrate, what may be described broadly as **15–001** "fraudulent" conduct can take a number of forms. Whilst the paradigm manifestation of such conduct is found in the tort of deceit, deception is but one way to manipulate the will of another person in order to obtain an illegitimate advantage. A fraudster may equally subvert another's will to further his illicit ends by the exercise of pressure or coercion which does not involve the telling of untruths, but which the law nevertheless regards as illegitimate. This chapter considers two key legal concepts which are concerned with providing redress in such circumstances: undue influence and duress. Indeed, it is not unusual to find that a claim alleging deceit will also include allegations of undue influence or duress against the same defendant or related defendants, all such claims being at heart directed at conduct by which the consent of one party to a transaction or gift is improperly procured.[1]

The boundaries of undue influence and duress are necessarily unclear, because **15–002** they cover a multitude of different factual situations. Human experience shows that coercion or pressure by one person upon another can take different forms: on the one hand, it may involve a direct or implicit threat between parties at arm's length; on the other, it may involve a gradual acquisition of emotional or psychological hegemony by one person over another with whom he is in a relationship of proximity, whether that be familial, spiritual, professional or sexual. And between these two poles, there are infinite gradations. People are of course subject to daily pressures where influence is brought to bear in relation to the making of contracts, the gifting of money or assets, or in taking steps which may be to their apparent disadvantage. Those pressures can be emotional, psychological or financial. Some people can be specifically vulnerable to pressure because of their physical or mental characteristics, or their general life

---

[1] A recent example is *Holyoake v Candy* [2017] EWHC 3397 (Ch). Indeed, see per Lord Cross in *Barton v Armstrong* [1976] A.C. 104, at 118: "At common law the only remedy available to the man defrauded was an action for deceit but equity in the same period in which it was building up the doctrine of 'undue influence' came to entertain proceedings to set aside dispositions which had been obtained by fraud: see Holdsworth, *A History of English Law*, vol. v (1924), pp. 328–329. There is an obvious analogy between setting aside a disposition for duress or undue influence and setting it aside for deceit. In each case—to quote the words of Holmes J. in *Fairbanks v Snow* (1887) 13 N.E. 596, 598— 'the party has been subjected to an improper motive for action.'"

circumstances; alternatively, they can be vulnerable because of the occurrence of a particular situation, even a transitory one. It has been the task of the law to attempt to create a coherent set of principles which differentiates between ordinary influence and illegitimate pressure.

15–003　So, where some transaction or gift is sought to be impugned because it was procured by some form of pressure or coercion, the question for the court is always similar: whether the pressure or coercion was or was not legitimate in the circumstances of the particular case. If not, and providing any applicable rules as to causation are fulfilled, the court may step in and provide a remedy, generally by setting the transaction or gift aside and trying to restore the status quo ante.

15–004　In what might be called purely commercial situations, claims for undue influence or duress are less common than in personal or family situations, for the simple reason that it is expected that commercial parties of full capacity are able to stand up for themselves. Commercial life would soon falter if claims based on actionable pressure were too readily allowed. Nonetheless "economic duress" is now a recognised form of claim, providing an important legal safety valve where conduct falls outside what is considered to be legally acceptable, albeit that the incidents of its successful deployment are relatively rare.

(2)　The Difference Between the Two Types of Claim

15–005　Duress is a creature of the common law and undue influence is a creature of equity. Nevertheless, many of the factual circumstances which in practice arise allow for both types of claim, and also for a third type of claim (which is also considered, briefly, in this chapter) called "unconscionable dealing".[2] Because, however, of the practical way in which the claim for undue influence can be applied, in particular where the burden can in certain circumstances be placed on the defendant to prove that the influence exercised was not undue (as we discuss below), undue influence has become a much more prevalent claim deployed in fraud cases, and tends to be at the forefront of many claimants' arguments, particularly where there is a more "human" element to the alleged misconduct.

15–006　The touchstone of undue influence is that there is a relationship of trust and confidence, and that that relationship is somehow abused. Relief is available in equity on the basis of injustice to the claimant, to save them from being victimised by others through the reversal of the unconscionable conduct. As Lindley LJ said in *Allcard v Skinner*,[3] it is something which is not capable of being confined within any clear legal definition:

> "the equitable doctrine of undue influence has grown out of and been developed by the necessity of grappling with insidious forms of spiritual tyranny and with the infinite varieties of fraud ... As no Court has ever attempted to define fraud so no Court has ever attempted to define undue influence, which includes one of its many varieties. The undue influence which Courts of Equity endeavour to defeat is the undue influence of one person over another; not the influence of enthusiasm on the enthusiast who is carried away by it ..."

---

[2] See generally N. Enonchong, *Duress, Undue Influence and Unconscionable Dealing*, 2nd edn (London: Sweet & Maxwell, 2012).
[3] *Allcard v Skinner* (1887) 35 Ch. D. 145, at 183, a case involving the influence of religious advisers.

Undue influence assumes that the intention of the claimant in relation to a   **15–007**
particular transaction is real but seeks to examine how that intention was
procured.[4] The cornerstone of common law duress, however, is that there is no
real independent resolution to take a particular step or embark on a particular
course of action on the part of the person subject to the duress, which vitiates in
law the relevant consent to act.

(3)   Statutory Claims

There are also statutory claims, which allow for redress in circumstances of   **15–008**
unfair or unconscionable dealing, usually in favour of individuals or consumers.
These include claims under the Consumer Rights Act 2015, the Financial
Services and Markets Act regime, and trading standards and the criminal law.
Such claims lie outside the scope of this book.

B.   UNDUE INFLUENCE

(1)   Introduction

The English law of undue influence has a long history dating back to at least the   **15–009**
beginning of the nineteenth century. However, the law was comprehensively
analysed and restated by the House of Lords in the landmark decision of *Royal
Bank of Scotland Plc v Etridge (No.2)*.[5] Although it typically applies in domestic
situations it is sometimes deployed in commercial cases[6]: a striking recent
example is *The Libyan Investment Authority v Goldman Sachs International*[7] in
which it was alleged that employees of Goldman Sachs had exerted undue
influence over members of the Libyan Investment Authority so as to procure the
Authority to enter into trading transactions.

Undue influence is a ground of relief developed by the courts so that the   **15–010**
influence of one person over another is not abused. It is treated in equity as a
species of fraud.[8] If the intention to enter into a transaction is procured by what
the law considers to be unacceptable means, then the courts will not permit the
transaction to stand. The means used are treated as an exercise of improper—i.e.
"undue"—influence, and so unacceptable, whenever the consent so procured
ought not fairly to be treated as the expression of a person's free will.[9] If undue
influence is proved, it allows the court to intervene to set aside the transaction
procured by the undue influence as against the undue influencer. There are two

---

[4] *Huguenin v Baseley* (1807) 14 Ves. 273, 300 per Lord Eldon.
[5] *Royal Bank of Scotland Plc v Etridge (No.2)* [2001] UKHL 44; [2002] 2 A.C. 773 ("*Etridge*").
[6] A classic example being *Lloyds Bank v Bundy* [1975] Q.B. 326, concerning the relationship
between banker and customer.
[7] *The Libyan Investment Authority v Goldman Sachs International* [2016] EWHC 2530 (Ch).
[8] *Dunbar Bank Plc v Nadeem* [1998] 3 All E.R. 876, 883; *CIBC Mortgages Plc v Pitt* [1994] 1 A.C.
200, 209.
[9] *Etridge*, at [7].

evidential ways of establishing undue influence by one person, or set of persons, over another: these have been given the labels actual and presumed undue influence.

15–011 Actual undue influence and presumed undue influence have in the past sometimes been treated as two different species. In reality, they are emanations of the same composite doctrine, with the former requiring direct proof of the abuse of the relationship in question, often by particularised pressure or coercion, and the latter operating on the basis of shifting the evidential burden to the defendant to prove that the relationship in question was not abused in relation to any given transaction or series of transactions.[10] With respect to actual undue influence and its difference from presumed undue influence, Lindley LJ said in the leading case of *Allcard v Skinner*[11]:

> "First, there are the cases in which there has been some unfair and improper conduct, some coercion from outside, some overreaching, some form of cheating, and generally, though not always, some personal advantage obtained by a donee placed in some close and confidential relation to the donor …
>
> The second group consists of cases in which the position of the donor to the donee has been such that it has been the duty of the donee to advise the donor, or even to manage his property for him. In such cases the Court throws upon the donee the burden of proving that he has not abused his position, and of proving that the gift[12] made to him has not been brought about by any undue influence on his part. In this class of cases it has been considered necessary to shew that the donor had independent advice, and was removed from the influence of the donee when the gift to him was made."

(2) Actual Undue Influence

15–012 The first way of establishing undue influence is by proving *actual* undue influence. This means that the complainant proves that the transaction in issue was actually procured by overt and identified acts of improper pressure or coercion. This is sometimes known in earlier cases as "Class 1" undue influence. As to this:

(1) The court must usually (though see below) find that the complainant's free will has been impaired by overt acts of pressure or persuasion, which "overcome the will without convincing the reason". In considering this question, the court will pay attention to the personalities and position of the parties. Particular vulnerability in the complainant, for example because of age or mental or physical illness, will be relevant, as will the forcefulness

---

[10] *Royal Bank of Scotland Plc v Etridge (No.2)* [2001] UKHL 44; [2002] 2 A.C. 773. See, for a case at the other end of the factual spectrum, *Libyan Investment Authority v Goldman Sachs International* [2016] EWHC 2530 (Ch).

[11] *Allcard v Skinner* (1887) 35 Ch. D. 145, at 181–182. See also Cotton LJ at 170–171.

[12] Of course transactions amenable to the undue influence jurisdiction extend beyond gifts. *Allcard v Skinner* was a gift case, but the principles enunciated are of general application.

of the alleged influencer. But a claim in actual undue influence is not dependent on a prior relationship between the parties, whether or not of trust and confidence.[13]

(2)   Such pressure or persuasion may be by illegitimate action or threats (such as a threat of violence or to institute criminal proceedings),[14] or by bullying or importunity.[15] So, in one case a wife executed a charge over the matrimonial home in support of a loan to her husband's business because her will to resist had been worn down by the use of wounding and insulting language and allegations of disloyalty and an overriding fear that her marriage was in jeopardy if she did not sign. The judge described this conduct as "moral blackmail."[16]

(3)   Actual undue influence may also exist in a more indirect way, where either (1) there has been deliberate misrepresentation[17], or even concealment, in relation to a proposed transaction in the course of a relationship in which the defendant owes a duty of candour to the complainant[18]; or (2) in cases where the complainant's free will has been impaired as a result of a relationship where the defendant had actual domination over the mind of the complainant, so that the complainant will simply do what the defendant asks. Domination of this kind may be due to a fear of the perceived consequences of refusing to do what the defendant requests; and it may justify a finding of actual undue influence even where there is no specific threat or pressure in relation to the impugned transaction. One way of posing the relevant question is to ask: "has the mind of the complainant become a mere channel through which the wishes of the defendant flow?" Often a relationship of domination arises where the defendant has subjected the complainant (typically a wife) to violence or bullying, but it may also arise as a result of the cultural or religious background of the parties.[19]

---

[13] *Holyoake v Candy* [2017] EWHC 3397 (Ch), per Nugee J at [405]; *Libyan Investment Authority v Goldman Sachs* [2016] EWHC 2530 (Ch), per Rose J at [136]–[137].

[14] *Daniel v Drew* [2005] EWCA Civ 507, at [40]. See also at [36]: "The donor may be led but she must not be driven and her will must be the offspring of her own volition, not a record of someone else's." In *Yedina v Yedin* [2017] EWHC 3319 (Ch) it was held, unsurprisingly, that the alleged conduct of a wife who "cried, scolded and reproached" her husband was not sufficient for an actual undue influence claim: see at [276], per Mann J.

[15] *BCCI v Aboody* [1990] 1 Q.B. 923.

[16] *Bank of Scotland v Bennett* [1999] 1 F.L.R. 1115.

[17] The courts are pretty flexible about shoehorning misrepresentation cases into undue influence cases: see *Annulment Funding Co Ltd v Cowey* [2010] EWCA Civ 711.

[18] In *Hewitt v First Plus Financial Group Plc* [2010] EWCA Civ 312, the husband failed to inform the wife that he had started an affair with another woman; in ignorance of that matter, she agreed to a remortgage over the matrimonial home which freed up significant sums to repay the husband's debts. It was held that her consent to the remortgage had been procured by actual undue influence. She had not made a freely informed choice given her ignorance of the affair. Hence, undue influence does not depend, as a necessary pre-requisite, upon a conclusion that the victim made no decision of her own, or that her will and intention was completely overborne. No doubt there are many examples where that is shown; but a conscious exercise of will may nonetheless be vitiated by undue influence. Note, however, that there is no general duty of disclosure, breach of which will constitute undue influence: *RBS v Chandra* [2010] EWHC 105 (Ch), at [130].

[19] For instance in *Barclays Bank Plc v Coleman* [2002] 2 A.C. 773 the husband and wife were Hassidic Jews, and obedience and subservience to a husband's wishes was culturally expected. This allowed a holding of actual undue influence: see at [130].

(4) Further, in all cases, the conduct on the part of the defendant which constitutes the undue influence must be unconscionable (though certain cases have rather watered this requirement down). In one case, the court referred to the "unconscientious use of power."[20] This involves a consideration of whether the defendant took unfair advantage of the weakness of the complainant.

15-013 The key practical point in relation to actual undue influence is that the burden of proof remains on the claimant to prove the illegitimate conduct. For this reason, and because of the potential evidential difficulties of proving bullying or similar conduct, which is often, if not covert or surreptitious, then not independently witnessed, these claims are less common or put less at the forefront of a claimant's case. The practitioner should however be astute to consider whether appropriate inferences can be drawn as to fraudulent or improper conduct which must have taken place as between claimant and defendant. This involves some measure of thoughtful reconstruction; but if there is no explanation other than that illegitimate pressure was applied to procure some outcome which was not the true voluntary act of the claimant, or that is overwhelmingly the most likely explanation, then actual undue influence will be a viable and proper claim to assert. Where the actual undue influence alleged consists of threats, menaces or coercion, as will often by the case in commercial scenarios, then the overlap with the law of duress will be almost complete and a claim in undue influence will be likely to add nothing beyond the duress claim.[21]

(3) Presumed Undue Influence

15-014 The second way of proving undue influence is by establishing *presumed* undue influence. In that scenario, the complainant must establish two things:

(1) *First*, the existence of a pre-existing relationship of trust and confidence between the complainant and the defendant such that the defendant was able to acquire and exert influence over the complainant. This relationship is usually in relation to the financial affairs of the complainant, but it need not be.[22] The necessary type of relationship is not restricted to the usual categories of confidential or fiduciary relationships,[23] but can arise out of the particular factual circumstances of any individual situation. It is important to scrutinise the facts carefully to see whether there is a

---

[20] *Hart v O'Connor* [1985] 1 A.C. 1000, at 1024. The courts recognise that persuasion and attempts to influence are perfectly ordinary aspects of daily life: "The objective is to ensure that the influence of one person over another is not abused. In everyday life people constantly seek to influence the decisions of others. They seek to persuade those with whom they are dealing to enter into transactions, whether great or small." (*Etridge*, at [6]).

[21] *Holyoake v Candy* [2017] EWHC 3397 (Ch) at [407]. It was suggested by the claimant in that case that one practical difference was that, in contrast to a claim in duress, it was not necessary to establish that the claimant would not have entered the impugned transaction but for the undue influence, citing *UCB Corporate Services Ltd v Williams* [2002] EWCA Civ 555.

[22] See *Etridge*, at [14]; *Thompson v Foy* [2010] 1 P&CR 16, at [100].

[23] *Tate v Williamson* (1866) L.R. 2 Ch. App. 55.

relationship of this nature in any particular case.[24] But not every confidential relationship will justify an inference of the existence of influence sufficient to satisfy the requirement for the presumption of influence to arise. We elaborate on this issue a little further below.

(2) *Secondly*, that the transaction in issue must be one which "calls for explanation". We also consider this issue further below.[25]

If those two elements are established then, absent more, undue influence will be presumed, even in the absence of any proof that the complainant was *actually* victimised or exploited by the defendant. However, the presumption is rebuttable by the alleged influencer (or any interested third party, who might be said to be affected by the undue influence, such as a bank), if he can prove that in fact the transaction in question occurred as a result of the exercise of full and informed volition of the complainant.[26]

15–015

How can that presumption be rebutted? This was recently explained as follows, in *Smith v Cooper*[27]:

15–016

> "If that is shown, as Lord Nicholls said, the presumption of undue influence applies, that is to say, the court will presume that the transaction was procured by undue influence exercised by one party over the other, in other words by the abuse by the one of the position of influence that he has over the other. In such a case it is then up to the one party to prove that the transaction was not procured by an abuse of his position of influence but was rather the free exercise of the will of the other party as a result of full, free and informed thought. Lord Nicholls' phrase 'in the absence of satisfactory explanation' in paragraph 14 of *Etridge* refers to the dominant party satisfying this burden of showing that the transaction was not procured by undue influence. Full understanding of the transaction is of course necessary but by no means sufficient, because the problem is lack of independence, not lack of understanding. As was said by Buxton LJ in *Turkey v Awadh* [2005] EWCA Civ 382, at paragraph 15: 'He would normally discharge that burden – as, for instance, now at least occurs in husband and wife cases – by showing that the Defendant entered into the matter with his will fully unconstrained, usually with the benefit of independent legal advice.'"

Thus the nature of the evidential presumption means that it will be for the defendant to show independent action on the part of the claimant, with a full appreciation of what was occurring. This will usually involve establishing some reasonable explanation for the transaction or gift with reference to ordinary motives or the relationship with the defendant. The fact that the alleged influencer can show he did not act wrongfully in the sense that he did not intend to cheat the complainant is not determinative.[28]

15–017

---

[24] *Turkey v Awadh* [2005] EWCA Civ 382, where the relationship arose from the very transaction itself.

[25] It is important to note that this is different from the question of whether a bank is put "on inquiry" (as to which, see para.15–025 below).

[26] Lord Nicholls put it as follows in *Etridge* (No.2) at [14]: "On proof of these two matters the stage is set for the court to infer that, in the absence of a satisfactory explanation, the transaction can only have been procured by undue influence. In other words, proof of these two facts is prima facie evidence that the defendant abused the influence he acquired in the parties' relationship. He preferred his own interests. He did not behave fairly to the other. So the evidential burden then shifts to him. It is for him to produce evidence to counter the inference which otherwise should be drawn."

[27] *Smith v Cooper* [2010] EWCA Civ 722, at [61].

[28] *Niersmans v Pesticcio* [2004] EWCA Civ 372.

15–018   The taking of independent advice by the complainant is often powerful evidence that the transaction involved the free exercise of his will; but it will not necessarily be sufficient to rebut the presumption—the quality and scope of that advice and the source of it will be relevant factors. The position was analysed in *Hackett v CPS* as follows[29]:

"a)   Where independent advice is given 'it must be given with knowledge of all relevant circumstances and must be such as a competent and honest advisor would have given if acting solely in the interests of the donor' (per Lord Hailsham LC in *Inche Noriah v Shalik Allie Bin Omar* [1929] A.C. 127, at 135–136);

b)   It is unlikely that this requirement will be satisfied if the person allegedly receiving the advice is together with the person who is regarded as exerting the alleged undue influence. 'Lord Browne-Wilkinson stressed the need for the wife to be seen and communicated with separately from her husband. This was clearly appropriate since, if the purpose is to satisfy oneself that the wife is acting freely in knowledge of the true facts, an interview in the presence of the husband is unlikely to achieve this objective if she has been improperly influenced by him. Lord Browne-Wilkinson concluded that the requirement of a personal interview did not impose such an additional administrative burden as to make the bank's position unworkable'. (per Lord Hobhouse in *Etridge* [113]);

c)   It is important that the independent person gives advice so that the recipient of that advice is able to reach a decision knowing the nature and the consequence of what they are being asked to do. 'All that is necessary is that some independent person, free from any taint of the relationship, or of the consideration of interest which would affect the act, should put clearly before the person what are the nature and the consequences of the act. It is for adult persons of competent mind to decide whether they will do an act, and I do not think that independent and competent advice means independent and competent approval. It simply means that the advice shall be removed entirely from the suspected atmosphere; and that from the clear language of an independent mind, they should know precisely what they are doing.' per Fletcher Moulton LJ In *Re Comber, Coomber v Coomber* [1911] 1 CH 723, at 730 approved by Lord Nicholls in *Etridge*, at [60];

d)   'Advice will not be independent if the solicitor is acting for both the claimant and the defendant' (*Smith v Cooper* [71]);

e)   If the advice is inadequate, it may not rebut the presumption see *Inche Noriah* (supra) where the solicitor was not fully aware of the circumstances surrounding the transaction. "

15–019   It is necessary to expand on the two matters mentioned above. In relation to the *first* factor, a relationship of trust and confidence can itself be established in one of two ways:

(1)   *First*, there are certain relationships where the court presumes irrebuttably that one person acquired influence (but not necessarily undue influence) over the other. These include parent and child, solicitor and client, medical advisor and patient, spiritual leader and follower.[30] This is sometimes known, in the earlier cases, as a class 2A case. This class does not include the relationship of husband and wife. Nor is it irrebuttably presumed that a child has influence over a parent.

---

[29] *Hackett v CPS* [2011] EWHC 1170 (Admin) at [73].
[30] See *Etridge*, at [18]: "In these cases the law presumes, irrebuttably, that one party had influence over the other. The complainant need not prove he actually reposed trust and confidence in the other party. It is sufficient for him to prove the existence of the type of relationship".

(2) *Secondly*, by positive proof (the burden being on the complainant) of an actual relationship of trust and confidence whereby the defendant has acquired influence over the complainant. This is sometimes known as a class 2B case. A recent example where this was proved, in a relationship between an elderly and deaf mother and her son, was the case of *Hackett v CPS*.[31]

As to the *second* factor, a transaction "calls for explanation" if the transaction is such as to constitute an advantage of such a nature to the defendant (or disadvantage to the claimant) that it is not explicable on the basis of ordinary human behaviour. So, for example, where the transaction involves a sizeable proportion of the person's net asset value or leaves that person without any significant means of support into the future, a cogent explanation will be required. What must be shown is the transaction is:

15–020

> "one that cannot be reasonably accounted for on the ground of friendship, relationship, charity, or other ordinary motives on which ordinary people act."[32]

These words, deriving from a famous 19th century case, remain the classic test.[33] It is not necessary to prove that the defendant acted in a reprehensible way[34]; rather, the complainant must prove "that the transaction is not readily explicable by the relationship of the parties".[35] Even if a transaction calls for explanation, if a satisfactory explanation is available then this second factor will not be shown.[36]

To take a well-known example, *Allcard v Skinner*[37]: there, the claimant became a sister within a protestant sisterhood, under which she was bound by rules of poverty, chastity and absolute obedience to the lady superior. As a result, having inherited substantial property, the claimant gave the very large part of that property to the lady superior of the order to hold on trust for the general purposes of the sisterhood. It was held that given the size of the gift and the nature of the relationship between the claimant and the defendant a presumption of undue influence arose. But if the claimant had given moderate Christmas presents to the lady superior, or the sisterhood, then the transaction would not have called for explanation.[38] A more modern example is *Abbey National Bank Plc v Stringer*,[39] where it was held that a mother's charging of her house to support lending to her son (and his two business associates) for a new business, about which she knew

15–021

---

[31] *Hackett v CPS* [2011] EWHC 1170 (Admin).

[32] *Allcard v Skinner* (1887) 36 Ch. D. 145, at 185.

[33] See *Smith v Cooper* [2010] EWCA Civ 722, at [60].

[34] *Pesticcio v Huet* [2004] EWCA Civ 372, at [20]; and *Hammond v Osborn* [2002] EWCA Civ 885; [2002] W.T.L.R. 1125.

[35] *Etridge*, at [21]. In *Bank of Montreal v Stuart* [1911] A.C. 120, 137 Lord Macnaghten used the phrase "immoderate and irrational" to describe this concept.

[36] See *Turkey v Awadh* [2005] 2 P. & C.R. 29: "If on the evidence the transaction cannot so be explained — that is to say, the transaction calls for an explanation *and that explanation is not forthcoming*—the burden then shifts to the claimant to show that in fact, and despite the terms and nature of the agreement, he did not in truth abuse the position that he held." (at [15]).

[37] *Allcard v Skinner* (1887) 36 Ch. D. 145.

[38] See *Etridge*, at [156].

[39] *Abbey National Bank Plc v Stringer* [2006] EWCA 338; [2006] EWCA 338.

nothing and from which she would obtain no benefit, was not "explicable according to the ordinary motives of mankind." And the gift by an elderly mother of her major asset, a house, to her son equally called for explanation.[40]

(4) Causation

15–022   There must be causation, in the sense that the undue influence must have been a significant reason or contributing factor for the transaction in question.[41] But the court does not impose any further causation hurdle. It has never been part of the law of undue influence that the court must enquire whether, but for the relevant abuse of trust, the impugned transaction would not have been entered into. The right to set aside the transaction arises not because, on a "but for" causation analysis, it would otherwise not have occurred, but because of the equitable wrong constituted by the abuse of confidence which was part of the process by which the victim's consent to it was obtained.[42]

(5) Remedies

15–023   Once the relevant elements are established, and assuming the defendant has been unable to rebut any applicable relevant presumptions, the victim of undue influence is entitled to have the transaction set aside, subject to certain equitable impediments.[43] The usual bars to rescission will in principle apply. The transaction is voidable by the claimant (not void) and so can be affirmed, but that affirmation also needs to be free from undue influence in order to be effective. Estoppel by representation or convention, delay and acquiescence can also amount to defences. A transaction may be set aside even where there has been performance and even though full restitution is not possible.

15–024   Where no restitution is possible, the court can instead award equitable compensation reflecting the value of what the complainant has given up under the transaction.[44]

(6) Rescission Against Third Parties on Notice

(i)   Introduction

15–025   Generally, a third party to the undue influence cannot be affected by it unless:

---

[40] *Hackett v CPS*, above.
[41] *Hewett v First Plus Financial Group* [2010] EWCA Civ 312, at [84].
[42] *Hewett v First Plus Financial Group Plc* [2010] EWCA Civ 312.
[43] For rescission more generally, see Ch.22.
[44] *Mahoney v Purnell* [1996] 3 All E.R. 61.

(1)   he had actual notice of it (requiring knowledge of the relevant conduct by the influencer)[45];

(2)   the influencer was acting as the third party's agent[46]; or

(3)   (it would appear) the third party was a volunteer.[47]

However, in certain situations the courts have relieved a party of the burden of a transaction as against a third party where it was induced by undue influence of which the third party ought to have been, but was not actually, aware. Typically (but not exclusively), such situations involve a husband and wife, or a parent and child, executing a charge in favour of a bank over property jointly owned by them to secure lending to one of them (or their company). In such a case, the spouse or parent is standing as guarantor and executing a charge over their own property to secure that guarantee. A substantial jurisprudence has developed to the effect that, in such situations, the third party creditor may be held to be on notice of any undue influence exerted by the debtor on the surety, merely by being "put on inquiry" as to the possibility of it and failing to take steps to satisfy itself that the transaction is not tainted.

15–026

A full analysis of that jurisprudence is beyond the scope of this book and what follows is a summary of the relevant law; but, broadly, there are two questions:

15–027

(1)   Has the lender been put on inquiry as to the possibility of undue influence in relation to the execution of the guarantee and charge?

(2)   If so, has the lender taken sufficient steps to prevent it having notice of any undue influence?

When is a bank put on inquiry? The wider principle has been stated in *Enonchong on Duress, Unconscionable Dealing and Undue Influence*[48] as follows:

15–028

> "A creditor is put on enquiry if he is aware of two factors:
> (i)   that the relationship between the surety and the debtor is one which indicates that the debtor is likely to have influence over the surety…; and
> (ii)   the transaction is on its face not to the financial advantage of the surety. "

The threshold for putting the bank on inquiry is not placed very high:

15–029

(1)   The case where a wife becomes surety for her husband's debts is, in this context, a straightforward one: the bank is put on inquiry. The same analysis applies where a husband stands surety for his wife's debts and in the case of unmarried couples, whether heterosexual or homosexual, and whether or not cohabiting.[49]

---

[45] *Etridge*, at [40], citing *Cobbett v Brock* (1855) 20 Beav 524, 528, 531, per Sir John Romilly MR, *Kempson v Ashbee* (1874) LR 10 Ch. App. 15, 21, per James LJ, and *Bainbrigge v Browne* 18 Ch. D. 188, 197, per Fry J.

[46] *O'Brien*, at 195.

[47] See e.g. *Huguenin v Baseley* (1807) 14 Ves 273.

[48] Enonchong, *Duress, Undue Influence and Unconscionable Dealing*, (2012), para.24–001.

[49] *Etridge*, at [44]–[47].

(2) On the other side of the line is the case where money is being advanced, or has been advanced, to husband and wife jointly. That of course is not a guarantee liability at all, unless the bank is privy to facts which demonstrate that in reality the loan is not in substance a joint loan.[50]

(3) In the case where the wife becomes surety for the debts of a company whose shares are held by her and her husband the bank is put on inquiry, even when the wife is a director or secretary of the company.[51] In *Mahon v FBN Bank (UK) Ltd*[52] it was suggested that where the wife's interest or involvement in the company was substantive rather than titular, if she is an active participant in managing the company's affairs and is rewarded by remuneration for work and/or by way of dividends etc., the loan may well be equated with a joint loan; but the position will be different if the financial arrangements are negotiated with the bank by the husband and the wife plays no part but is asked to stand as surety for the company debts. So in *Mahon* the fact that the wife who stood as surety was the nominal 100 per cent owner of the shares was not sufficient to prevent the bank being on inquiry.

15–030 The relationships between surety and debtor which are such as to put the bank on inquiry (subject to the transaction not being on its face to the financial advantage of the surety) are not limited to emotional or sexual ones: they extend to other relationships where one party can easily acquire influence over another. Hence in *Etridge* the general rule was propounded that the creditor is put on inquiry where the relationship between the surety and debtor is "non-commercial."[53] An early example of such a relationship outside the emotional and sexual sphere being held to be sufficient to put the bank on inquiry was *Credit Lyonnaise Bank Nederland NV v Burch*,[54] which concerned an employer and junior employee. The bank was held to have known the facts from which the existence of a relationship of trust and confidence could be inferred.

15–031 However, the categorisation of a relationship as "commercial" or "non-commercial" is an inherently difficult exercise.[55] Further, even if it can be established that the relationship between the debtor and surety falls the right side of the line for relief to lie, if the creditor is not aware of the non-commercial character of the relationship at the time of the transaction, then the creditor is not put on inquiry. So in a Hong Kong case, *Li Sau Ying v Bank of China*,[56] Lord Scott said[57]:

> "In *Etridge* Lord Nicholls said that a bank would be 'put on inquiry' not only in a case where a wife was becoming a surety for her husband, or his company, but in every case in which the

---

[50] *Etridge*, at [48].

[51] *Etridge*, at [49].

[52] *Mahon v FBN Bank (UK) Ltd* [2011] EWHC 1432 (Ch).

[53] *Etridge*, at [86].

[54] *Credit Lyonnaise Bank Nederland NV v Burch* [1997] 1 All E.R. 144.

[55] See the discussion in Enonchong, *Duress, Undue Influence and Unconscionable Dealing* (2012), para.24–010.

[56] *Li Sau Ying v Bank of China* [2005] 1 HKLRD 106.

[57] Formerly a member of the House of Lords, and part of the Court which decided *Etridge*.

relationship between the surety/mortgagor and the principal debtor was 'non-commercial' (see paras 49 and 87). It must be borne in mind, however, that the relationship between the surety and the principal debtor must be looked at with the eyes of the bank. The bank would generally, but not always, know whether the surety was the wife of the principal debtor, its customer. Some wives, however, do not take their husbands' surnames and the concept of a 'non-commercial' relationship is inherently imprecise. It is certainly not necessary for a proposed mortgagee to make inquiries about the relationship between its principal debtor and the proposed surety/mortgagor before deciding on the steps it should take to satisfy itself that the surety understands the transaction he or she is entering into. Nothing Lord Nicholls said in *Etridge* suggests the contrary. And for a bank/mortgagee to make inquiries of that character would in most cases be an unwarrantable impertinence."[58]

However, although the creditor is not required to make inquiries about the nature of the relationship between the surety and the principal debtor, if the bank turns a blind eye to circumstances which would have given it actual knowledge of the non-commercial relationship of the parties, it is likely that it will be held to have had constructive notice of the relationship and therefore would be put on inquiry. **15–032**

If the bank is put on inquiry, what then must it do to avoid having constructive notice of any impropriety? In *Etridge* new standards were laid down (at least in relation to cases where the complainant is a wife)[59] for transactions postdating the judgment. The steps to be taken are as follows. **15–033**

(1) The furthest a bank can be expected to go is to take reasonable steps to satisfy itself that the guarantor has had brought home to him, in a meaningful way, the practical implications of the proposed transaction.[60]

(2) Therefore it must communicate directly with the guarantor, informing him that for its own protection it will require written confirmation from a solicitor, acting for him, to the effect that the solicitor has fully explained to him the nature of the documents and the practical implications they will have for him.[61]

(3) The guarantor should be told that the purpose of this requirement is that thereafter he should not be able to dispute he is legally bound by the documents once he has signed them. He should be asked to nominate a solicitor whom he is willing to instruct to advise him, separately from the debtor, and act for him in giving the necessary confirmation to the bank. He should be told that, if he wishes, the solicitor may be the same solicitor as is acting for the debtor in the transaction. If a solicitor is already acting for the debtor, he should be asked whether he would prefer that a different solicitor should act for him regarding the bank's requirement for confirmation from a solicitor.

(4) The bank should not proceed with the transaction until it has received an appropriate response directly from the guarantor.

(5) Although the bank is not obliged to meet and advise the guarantor directly, nonetheless representatives of the bank are likely to have a much better picture of the debtor's financial affairs than the solicitor and so, if the bank

---

[58] At [41].

[59] At [50].

[60] At [54].

[61] See generally at [79].

is not willing to undertake the task of explanation itself (for fear that the guarantor may later make allegations concerning the adequacy of the advice etc.), the bank must provide the solicitor who is to advise the guarantor with the financial information he needs for this purpose.

(6) Accordingly, if a bank is to rely on confirmation from a solicitor for its protection, the bank must send to the solicitor the necessary financial information to allow the solicitor to provide informed advice. What is required must depend on the facts of the case. Ordinarily, this will include information on the purpose for which the proposed new facility has been requested, the current amount of the debtor's indebtedness, the amount of the current overdraft facility, and the amount and terms of any new facility.

(7) If the bank's request for security arose from a written application by the debtor for a facility, a copy of the application should be sent to the solicitor. The bank will, of course, need first to obtain the consent of its customer to this circulation of confidential information. If this consent is not forthcoming the transaction will not be able to proceed.[62]

(8) However, it was recognised that, exceptionally, there may be a case where the bank believes or suspects that the guarantor had been misled by the debtor or was not entering into the transaction of his own free will. If such a case occurs the bank must inform the guarantor's solicitors of the facts giving rise to its belief or suspicion.

(9) The content of the advice to be given by the solicitor is analysed in *Etridge*.[63] However, the bank cannot know what advice has been given in any given case, because the contents of the meeting will be privileged and the precise nature of the advice is a matter for the solicitor, acting in the best interests of the client guarantor. Deficiencies in the advice actually given may expose the solicitor to a damages claim, but will not (ordinarily) be attributable to the bank.[64]

(10) Having taken the steps above the bank is entitled to proceed in reliance upon a certificate from the solicitor, acting for the guarantor, that he has advised the guarantor appropriately.

(11) The solicitor need not act solely for the guarantor (though, if he is acting for the debtor too, the solicitor must consider whether there is any conflict); however, the meeting should take place between solicitor and guarantor alone.[65]

C. DURESS

(1) Introduction

15–034 The legal concept of duress embraces the situation where a person takes a step—for instance the payment of money, or the entry into a contract—which is procured by the exercise of pressure or threats, such that the will of the

---

[62] See at [79].
[63] At [64]–[68].
[64] At [75]–[78].
[65] At [69]–[74].

complainant, although not destroyed, is illegitimately coerced, so that it cannot be said that he took the relevant step voluntarily.[66] The rationale of this area of law has been described as that the complainant's

"apparent consent was induced by pressure exercised upon him by that other party which the law does not regard as legitimate, with the consequence that the consent is treated in law as revocable unless approbated either expressly or by implication after the illegitimate pressure has ceased to operate on his mind."[67]

The key ingredient is compulsion which vitiates consent.

"The classic case of duress is ... the victim's intentional submission arising from the realisation that there is no other practical choice open to him."[68]

Hence the fact that the decision to enter into the transaction sought to be impugned for duress involved an exercise of rational and independent judgment or was taken with the benefit of legal advice does not preclude a finding of duress.[69]

One must look to see whether the transaction in issue has been procured by threats or pressure which are illegitimate, and which caused the victim to have no practical choice but to do as he did. The courts recognise that in many commercial transactions there will be pressure borne out of the fact that one party has a stronger bargaining position than the other. Taking advantage of such a position is permissible. The critical question is to distinguish between that which is legitimate and that which is illegitimate.[70]   **15–035**

It is now clearly established that duress may take a number of forms: it may involve duress through threats to the person or relating to his property, or duress   **15–036**

---

[66] Recent academic commentary has emphasised that the concept of involuntariness must be treated expansively. In many cases, the complainant who is subject to duress has made an informed and rational decision to take a step, which, in the circumstances presented, represents the lesser of two evils. This does not mean that the decision cannot be reversed subsequently as induced by duress: see generally C. Mitchell, P. Mitchell and S. Watterson, *Goff & Jones: The Law of Unjust Enrichment*, 9th edition (London: Sweet & Maxwell, 2016), para.10–08. Nonetheless, the courts still talk in terms of coercion. See for instance *Dawson v Bell* [2016] EWCA Civ 96, where a strong Court of Appeal said of economic duress, at [32]: "neither a defence to a contractual claim nor a claim in tort [in intimidation] can succeed unless it is shown that the will of the 'victim' has been coerced. The practical effect of the pressure must be compulsion or the absence of choice."
[67] *Universe Tankships Inc of Monrovia v ITWF* [1983] 1 A.C. 366, at 384.
[68] *Universe Tankships Inc of Monrovia v ITWF* [1983] 1 A.C. 366, at 400.
[69] *Al Nehayan v Kent* [2018] EWHC 333 (Comm) at [189].
[70] See per Lord Wilberforce and Lord Simon of Glaisdale in *Barton v Armstrong* [1976] A.C. 104, 121: "for in life, including the life of commerce and finance, many acts are done under pressure, sometimes overwhelming pressure, so that one can say that the actor had no choice but to act. Absence of choice in this sense does not negate consent in law: for this the pressure must be one of a kind which the law does not regard as legitimate. Thus, out of the various means by which consent may be obtained—advice, persuasion, influence, inducement, representation, commercial pressure—the law has come to select some which it will not accept as a reason for voluntary action: fraud, abuse of relation of confidence, undue influence, duress or coercion. In this the law, under the influence of equity, has developed from the old common law conception of duress—threat to life and limb—and it has arrived at the modern generalisation expressed by Holmes J—'subjected to an improper motive for action': *Fairbanks v Snow*, 13 NE Reporter 596, 598."

through economic pressure. The law developed initially from cases involving threats of physical harm to life or limb[71] and later to property. More recently it has been applied more generally to commercial situations where the threat or pressure brought to bear involves potential economic harm; in this arena, one talks of "economic duress".

(2)   The Legal Consequences of Duress

15–037   The doctrine of duress analysed in this chapter is to be distinguished from the tort of intimidation (which we have discussed above at Ch.5. The exercise of duress (in whatever form) to induce another person to part with money, or to enter into a contract, or to take any other step is not a tort per se (unless the facts amount to the tort of intimation).[72] Duress is a basis for avoiding the relevant transaction (and hence avoiding any executory obligations)[73] and, so far as necessary, obtaining restitution of any monies paid or property transferred as a result of the duress.[74] In this sense, duress is a part of the wider law of unjust enrichment. Hence duress may be pleaded as a defence to a claim on a contract or as a form of cause of action seeking recovery of property and/or declaratory relief; the complainant may be either defendant or claimant. But a contract induced by duress (by contrast with the doctrine of non est factum) is not void ab initio; it is voidable and so the usual bars to rescission are potentially applicable. So:

> "an agreement obtained through duress is invalid in the sense that the party subject to the duress has the right to withdraw from the agreement, though that right may be lost if that party later affirms the agreement or waives the right to withdraw from it."[75]

See generally Ch.22.

---

[71] See e.g. *Skeate v Beale* (1841) 11 Ad. & El. 983. "Duress to the person is where a threat of physical violence is directed against the claimant or a close relation or associate of the claimant": see per Nugee J in *Holyoake v Candy* [2017] EWHC 3397 (Ch), at [397], in which this form of duress was unsuccessfully asserted. The complainant succeeded in proving duress by threats to the person in *Al Nehayan v Kent* [2018] EWHC 333 (Comm), at [216].

[72] See for instance *Dimskal Shipping v ITWF* [1992] A.C. 152, at 163. Both claims can be advanced simultaneously. See also *Progress Bulk Carriers Ltd v Tube City IMS LLC* [2012] EWHC 273 (Comm); [2012] 1 C.L.C. 365, at [25]. In *Al Nehayan v Kent* [2018] EWHC 333 (Comm), at [224] Leggatt LJ concluded that conduct amounting to duress is not ipso facto a tort. He quoted from Sales J in *Investec Bank (Channel Islands) Ltd v The Retail Group Plc* [2009] EWHC 476 (Ch), at [122]: "The primary object of a plea of economic duress in relation to a contract is to avoid the contract, which is a legal consequence significantly different from establishing a cause of action in damages. So far as a cause of action in damages is to be made out, I can see no proper basis in principle why it should be on any basis other than a pleading of facts and matters sufficient to establish a cause of action for the tort of intimidation." In *Holyoake v Candy* [2017] EWHC 3397 (Ch), Nugee J suggested at [403] that in "practical terms, most if not all cases of duress will also amount to the tort of intimidation".

[73] See *Dimskal Shipping Co Ltd v I.T.W.F.* [1992] 2 A.C. 152, at 171, per Lord Lowry: "English law says generally that a contract induced by coercion (whether tortious or not) can be avoided at the instance of the party coerced."

[74] See generally *Universe Tankships of Monrovia v ITWF*, above, at 385.

[75] *Borrelli v Ting* [2010] UKPC 21; [2010] Bus LR 1718, at [35]. An example of a case where the complainant was held to have affirmed a contract which would have otherwise have been voidable for duress is *North Ocean Shipping Co Ltd v Hyundai Construction Co Ltd* [1979] Q.B. 705.

(3) Economic Duress

Until the later part of the twentieth century, the concept of duress was confined to   **15–038**
situations where threats were made to the person or goods of the complainant. In
the 1970s, the courts extended the concept to the commercial sphere where a
party to contractual negotiations or in the wider context of a business relationship
applies pressure to another.[76] The concept of economic duress is far more elusive
than that of threats to the person or property and has generated substantial
jurisprudence where the task of the courts has been to identify the boundaries
between the normal and legitimate exploitation of superior bargaining power and
the use of illegitimate pressure. But the courts have consistently emphasised that
rather than resorting to simple formulae, it is necessary to focus on the facts of
the individual cases and ask whether it amounts to duress.

(4) Elements of Duress

Nonetheless, in broad terms, one can identify three fundamental elements in the   **15–039**
wrong of duress:

(1) illegitimate pressure brought to bear on the complainant;
(2) whose practical effect is that there is compulsion on, a lack of practical
     choice for, the complainant, which;
(3) is a significant cause inducing him to act as he did.[77]

We will consider these three elements below primarily as they are to be
interpreted in claims for "economic duress", which is, in the context of this book,
the most significant manifestation of the law of duress.

(i) Illegitimate pressure

There is no bright line test that can be applied to the facts of any given case in   **15–040**
order to establish whether pressure or threats exerted upon a complainant are
sufficient to found a claim in actionable duress. The illegitimacy of the threat or
pressure must be examined for two issues: the nature of the pressure and the
nature of the demand which the pressure is applied to support.[78] The law of

---

[76] See in particular the decisions of Kerr J in *Occidental Worldwide Investment Corp v Skibs AIS Avanti (The Siboen and The Sibotre)* [1976] 1 Lloyd's Rep. 293; of Mocatta J in *North Ocean Shipping Co Ltd v Hyundai Construction Co Ltd* [1979] Q.B. 705, and of the Privy Council in *Pao On v Lau Yiu Long* [1980] A.C. 614.

[77] See the statement of principle of Dyson J in *Carillion Construction Ltd v Felix (UK) Ltd* [2001] B.L.R. 1, at [24], which has been adopted by judges on a number of occasions since: see e.g. *Adam Opel GmbH v Mitras Automotive (UK) Ltd* [2007] EWHC 3481 (QB); and *Progress Bulk Carriers Ltd v Tube City IMS LLC* [2012] EWHC 273 (Comm); [2012] 1 C.L.C. 365; *Marsden v Barclays Bank* [2016] EWHC 1601 (QB); and *Times Travel (UK) Ltd Nottingham Travel (UK) Ltd v Pakistan International Airlines Corp* [2017] EWHC 1367 (Ch).

[78] *R v Her Majesty's Attorney-General for England and Wales* [2003] UKPC 22, at [16]. There, the nature of the demand made upon the complainant, viz, to sign a confidentiality agreement preventing him from revealing his activities as a member of the SAS, was patently relevant to the legitimacy or

duress is an area where the court necessarily has to engage in fact-sensitive and extra-legal value judgments concerning a person's conduct.[79] Hence in the specific circumstances of a case a party may be in breach of contract but not exercising illegitimate pressure. So, in one case the conduct of an alleged wrongdoer was described as "reasonable behaviour by a contractor acting bona fide in a very difficult situation", notwithstanding that he was acting in breach of contract.[80]

15–041   Nonetheless the threat of unlawful action, such as a breach of contract,[81] or a breach of statutory duty or tort[82] or to bring unfounded legal action for an ulterior and improper purpose[83], or what would amount to a crime, is generally considered to be illegitimate. Actual violence to the person or threats of violence or imprisonment are obviously illegitimate. Wrongful threats to seize or detain the complainant's goods, or to damage property, are also illegitimate.[84] Yet pressure can still—albeit in rare cases—be treated as illegitimate so as to constitute duress even where the threat is of action which in itself would be lawful, especially when it is coupled with a demand for payment.[85]

---

otherwise of the pressure. By contrast, a demand for money to which the alleged wrongdoer has no legitimate entitlement on any view may well render the pressure coupled with the demand illegitimate. The need to examine both the pressure and the demand it accompanies is acute in cases of alleged blackmail. A relevant question will often be: does the demand go substantially beyond what is normal or legitimate in commercial arrangements? (see *Marsden v Barclays Bank* [2016] EWHC 1601 (QB), at [35]).

[79] "[T]he decision on the fundamental question whether the pressure has crossed the line from that which must be accepted in normal robust commercial bargaining involves at least some element of value judgment": *Adam Opel GmbH v Mitras Automotive (UK) Ltd* [2008] EWHC 3205 (QB), at [26].

[80] *DSND Subsea Ltd (formerly DSND Oceantech Ltd) v Petroleum Geo Services ASA* [2000] B.L.R. 530, at [134].

[81] See per Lord Scarman in *Universe Tankships*, above, at 401: "The law regards the threat of unlawful action as illegitimate, whatever the demand." This is not however an immutable rule.

[82] For instance, a threat of harassment or a threat to reveal confidential information, which might constitute the tort of misuse of private information or breach of confidence.

[83] *Grainger v Hill* (1838) 4 Bing (NC) 212; *Gulf Azov Shipping Co Ltd v Idisi* [2001] 2 Lloyd's Rep. 727.

[84] *North Ocean Shipping Co Ltd v Hyundai Construction Co Ltd* [1979] Q.B. 705; *Dimskal Shipping Co Ltd v I.T.W.F* [1992] 2 A.C. 152.

[85] See generally *CTN Cash & Carry Ltd v Gallaher Ltd* [1994] 4 All E.R. 714, at 718–719 where it was held that the courts are willing to apply a standard of impropriety rather than technical unlawfulness; so that the critical inquiry will be not whether the conduct is lawful but whether it is morally or socially unacceptable. Examples include *Thorne v Motor Trade Association* [1937] A.C. 797, at 806–807 and *Mutual Finance Ltd v John Wetton & Sons Ltd* [1937] 2 K.B. 389. However, it will be relatively rare for "lawful act duress" to be established, although blackmail is one instance where it may well be. As Lord Atkin said in *Thorne*, at 806: "The ordinary blackmailer normally threatens to do what he has a perfect right to do—namely, communicate some compromising conduct to a person whose knowledge is likely to affect the person threatened. Often indeed he has not only the right but also the duty to make the disclosure, as of a felony, to the competent authorities. What he has to justify is not the threat, but the demand of money." It has been suggested that since *CTN* was decided there has been not one reported case in which lawful act duress has been established in a commercial context: *Holyoake v Candy* [2017] EWHC 3397 (Ch), at [399]. *However Times Travel (UK) Ltd v Pakistan International Airlines Corp* [2017] EWHC 1367 (Ch); and *Borrelli v Ting* [2010] UKPC 21; [2010] Bus L.R. 1718 are such examples. In the latter case, the Privy Council set aside a settlement agreement as having been obtained through duress consisting of "unconscionable conduct". Under the agreement the liquidators of a company had agreed not to sue the defendant (a shareholder accused of misappropriating assets of the company) in return for his agreement to

Other factors which are, or may be, relevant to the legitimacy or otherwise of the pressure applied to the complainant have been said to include the following[86]:

15–042

(1)   The existence or otherwise of a prior relationship between the parties[87];
(2)   The fact that the person allegedly exerting the pressure had previously committed an unlawful act, such as a breach of contract[88];

---

withdraw his opposition to a scheme of arrangement which was needed to raise funds for the liquidation. There was a background of unlawful conduct as the defendant had previously used forgery and provided false evidence in opposing the scheme. But neither the demand to which the liquidators agreed (to drop claims against him) nor the accompanying threat (to vote against the scheme) was unlawful. In *Holyoake*, by contrast, the judge held that "for a creditor with an acknowledged debt to insist on part-payment of the debt as a price for granting an extension in respect of the balance does not seem to me to be capable of being characterised as illegitimate pressure." Similarly he said at [236], that he could not see "that it can amount to economic duress for a creditor who believes that he has an accrued cause of action against a debtor to threaten to bring proceedings, even if the result is likely to be disastrous for the debtor, and even if the creditor spells out in strong language why it will be disastrous." For a full discussion of "lawful act duress" see *Al Nehayan v Kent* [2018] EWHC 333 (Comm), at [179] and following, in which Leggatt LJ appears to contemplate a wider incidence of such duress than previously thought. See at [187]: "Whereas the distinction between lawful and unlawful behaviour may be critical in determining whether the defendant's conduct is actionable in tort, I see no reason why it should be decisive of whether the defendant can retain money or other benefits demanded from a claimant in a situation of extreme vulnerability. For this purpose it is appropriate to take account of the legitimacy of the demand and to judge the propriety of the defendant's conduct by reference not simply to what is lawful but to basic minimum standards of acceptable behaviour. To the complaint that this makes the law uncertain, I would give two replies. First, as the authorities have emphasised, the standard of unconscionability is a high one and it is only in cases where the demand made and means used to reinforce it are completely indefensible that the courts will intervene. Second, no apology is needed for intervening in such cases, as the enforcement of basic norms of commerce and of fair and honest dealing is an essential function of a system of commercial law." See also "Lawful Act Duress" (2018) 134 L.Q.R. 5.

[86] See *Carillion Construction Ltd v Felix (UK) Ltd* [2001] B.L.R. 1 and *DSND Subsea Ltd (formerly DSND Oceantech Ltd) v Petroleum Geo Services ASA* [2000] B.L.R. 530. *Carillion* provides a good example of economic duress. The defendant sub-contractor threatened to suspend delivery of certain materials needed in relation to the construction of an office block unless the claimant contractor agreed a final account which was considerably in excess of its true entitlement. The claimant was obliged to agree the account because suspension of delivery of the materials would have had very serious impact on its own position viz à viz the employer. In *Adam Opel GmbH v Mitras Automotive (UK) Ltd* [2008] EWHC 3205 (QB) the judge, David Donaldson QC, having quoted from *Carillion* commented at [26]: "There is plainly scope for overlap between the three ingredients of pressure, illegitimacy, and causative effect. The list of matters to be considered in assessing legitimacy is not exhaustive, and the weight to be attached to each of them will depend on the facts of the individual case."

[87] See for instance *CTN Cash & Carry Ltd v Gallaher Ltd* [1994] 4 All E.R. 714, at 717–718. Economic duress will be far less likely to be held to exist in arm's length commercial dealings between two trading companies who are not in an existing contractual relationship. This is because no person can be compelled to contract with another and a person, even if he is in a monopoly position, is entitled to contract on such terms as he likes.

[88] *Borrelli v Ting* [2010] UKPC 21; [2010] Bus L.R. 1718; *Progress Bulk Carriers Ltd v Tube City IMS LLC* [2012] EWHC 273 (Comm); [2012] 1 C.L.C. 365, at [36]. In the latter case, the fact that the alleged wrongdoer had committed a prior repudiatory breach of contract was of great significance to the holding that its subsequent conduct constituted economic duress. Hence a "threat" not to contract with another except on the basis of some benefit being conferred by the complainant will very rarely constitute actionable duress: a good example being the Australian case of *Smith v William Charlick Ltd* (1924) 34 C.L.R. 38.

(3)   Whether the person allegedly exerting the pressure has acted in good or bad faith.[89] So it will be relevant to the question whether the pressure is illegitimate that the alleged wrongdoer genuinely thought that the position he was adopting was a reasonable one, even if, on analysis, he had no legal right to adopt it or his position proves on analysis to be wrong[90];

(4)   Whether the victim had any realistic practical alternative but to submit to the pressure[91];

(5)   Whether the victim protested at the time;

(6)   Whether he affirmed and sought to rely on the contract.[92]

(ii)   Compulsion

15–043   The second element of actionable duress is that the illegitimate pressure must have the practical effect that there is compulsion of, or a lack of practical choice for, the complainant. It will be immediately seen that, as regards this element, there is a substantial overlap with both the first and the third elements of actionable duress. What the second element serves to emphasise is that pressure can only constitute actionable duress if it leaves the complainant with no realistic or practical alternative but to comply with the requirements of the wrongdoer. Otherwise the objective element of coercion is not present.[93] This involves an

---

[89] *CTN Cash & Carry Ltd v Gallaher Ltd* [1994] 4 All E.R. 714 where the defendant genuinely believed that they were entitled to a sum of money from the claimant and threatened to withhold credit facilities unless the sum was paid. A claim in duress failed; the genuineness of the defendant's belief was relevant. In this sense the enquiry is not simply directed at the position of the complainant, for whom the genuineness or otherwise of the alleged wrongdoer's belief is likely to be neither here nor there. An early example where bad faith was relevant is *D&C Builders v Rees* [1966] 2 Q.B. 617 where the defendant owed a sum of money to the claimant but exploited the claimant's urgent need for money by offering less than what was due in final settlement against a threat to otherwise pay nothing. The defendant was cynically exploiting the claimant's weakness. The claimant was entitled to recover the balance and was not held to its agreement to accept the lesser sum in full and final settlement. By contrast see *Williams v Roffey Bros & Nicholls (Contractors) Ltd* [1991] 1 Q.B. 1: where a party to a contract stated that he would be unable to finish the job without additional payment (for instance because he has underpriced the job, or because of a change in the prevailing economic climate, or because the contractor is in financial difficulties) that may amount to an intimation of a breach of contract, without that necessarily constituting actionable duress.

[90] See for instance the facts in *DSND Subsea Ltd v Petroleum Geo-Services ASA* [2000] B.L.R. 530.

[91] This factor is best analysed in the context of the second element of duress, discussed below.

[92] Although this is one of the list of potentially relevant factors set out by Dyson J in the *Carillion* case, it is suggested that in fact this is best considered as an entirely separate concept which is relevant only to the question whether the complainant has lost his right to avoid through subsequent affirmation.

[93] As Lord Scarman put it in *Universe Tankships of Monrovia*, above, at 400: "There must be pressure, the practical effect of which is compulsion or the absence of choice." To similar effect, see *B&S Contracts and Design Ltd v Victor Green Publications Ltd* [1984] I.C.R. 419, at 426 and *Hennessy v Craigmyle & Co Ltd* [1986] I.C.R. 461, at 468. Enonchong disputes (in *Duress, Undue Influence and Unconscionable Dealing* (2012), para.4–024) and following the existence of this second element of duress as a freestanding requirement; but it is submitted that the weight of authority is against that view and that in any event this element serves an important purpose in ensuring a minimum level of objective coercion in order to keep the ambit of economic duress within acceptable limits. However, it does appear to be correct that where the duress is to the person or goods then the law does not ask the additional question whether there was a practical alternative, or at least readily finds that there was no reasonably practical alternative: see for instance *Antonio v Antonio* [2008]

objective assessment of the nature of the pressure brought to bear in the particular circumstances in which the complainant finds himself. The question will often resolve itself into whether the complainant had a ready legal remedy; and the courts generally take a realistic view on this. Often the cost, delay and uncertainty of outcome attendant upon legal proceedings will mean that the alternative of legal redress is not realistically available to the complainant,[94] because the commercial difficulty in which he finds himself is time-sensitive. Further, time-sensitivity will often preclude the ability of the complainant to seek an alternative supplier where the alleged wrongdoer is threatening to withhold supply. Indeed in general it is the very existence of time-sensitivity that provides the wrongdoer with the platform from which to subject the complainant to illegitimate pressure. Hence the classic case of economic duress is where a person has agreed to provide a time-sensitive service (or goods) and then threatens to withhold that service (or delivery of those goods) unless additional non-contractual payments are made.[95]

(iii) Causation

The illegitimate pressure must coerce the complainant; otherwise, it is not legally relevant. Hence a key element of the doctrine of duress is a causal connection between the pressure exerted by the defendant on the mind of the complainant and the transaction which is sought to be avoided by the later proceedings. In simple terms, there must be "coercion of the will so as to vitiate consent"[96] The concept of vitiation of consent necessarily carries with it the requirement of a causal link.   **15–044**

However, to understand the nature of the causation element of duress, one must understand the meaning of the word "vitiation" as it is used in the authorities. Duress vitiates consent in the eyes of the law not because it destroys the understanding,[97] but because it presents the complainant with no practical alternative but to submit to the pressure being applied.[98] The will is deflected.[99]   **15–045**

EWHC 1199 (QB) (duress to the person); and *The Alev* [1989] 1 Lloyd's Rep. 138 (duress of goods).

[94] See e.g. the facts of *Adam Opel GmbH v Mitras Automotive (UK) Ltd* [2007] EWHC 3481; and contrast the outcome in *Pao On v Lau Yiu Long*, above, where it was held that a realistic alternative legal remedy was available, which precluded (above) a holding of economic duress.

[95] For instance the *B&S Contracts* case, where the claimant had contracted with the defendant to build exhibition stands for a trade show starting on a particular day. When the claimant made it clear, 11 days before the trade show was due to open, that it would cancel the contract unless further payments were made, the defendant had no realistic alternative; in the time available, it could not go to an alternative supplier.

[96] *Pao On v Lau Yiu Long* [1980] A.C. 614, at 635. The concept of vitiation of consent is now more usually expressed as "deflection" of consent.

[97] See *D.P.P. v Lynch* [1975] A.C. 653, at 680, per Lord Wilberforce (a criminal case): "the victim completes the act and knows that he is doing so; but the addition of the element of duress prevents the law from treating what he has done as a crime. One may note—and the comparison is satisfactory—that an analogous result is achieved in a civil law context: duress does not destroy the will, for example, to enter into a contract, but prevents the law from accepting what has happened as a contract valid in law."

[98] See *Universe Tankships*, above, at 384, per Lord Diplock and at 400, per Lord Scarman.

[99] *D.P.P. v Lynch* [1975] A.C. 653, at 695, per Lord Simon: "Similarly with duress in the English law of contract. Duress again deflects, without destroying, the will of one of the contracting parties. There

In this sense the concept of vitiation of consent requires a qualitative judgment on the nature of the pressure applied (as to which see element (ii) above), but also an inquiry into its effect on the mind of the complainant.

15–046   The question of the nature of the causal link which needs to be shown was addressed directly in *Barton v Armstrong*,[100] a particularly vivid case. The defendant was held to have threatened the claimant with death on numerous occasions unless he signed certain deeds. The defendant's case was that he would have signed them even absent the threats. The Privy Council held that all that needed to be established was that the pressure applied was *a* reason, not *the reason*, nor the *predominant* reason why the complainant acted as he did; and that the complainant will be entitled to succeed even though he might well have entered the relevant contracts even if the threats had not been uttered.[101]

15–047   However, in subsequent cases, the reasoning of the majority in *Barton v Armstrong*, which cannot be described as sophisticated, has been confined to direct threats of violence to the person. So in *Dimskal Shipping v ITWF*,[102] without addressing the issue in terms, Lord Goff talked of the illegitimate pressure having to constitute a "significant cause inducing the plaintiff to enter into the relevant contract". And the question was directly confronted in *Huyton SA v Peter Cremer GmbH*,[103] where Mance J held that in the field of economic duress a simple "but for" test was appropriate.[104] Although his reasoning has been criticised,[105] it is suggested that *Huyton* was correctly decided on this point and that, at least in economic duress cases, where the law must be careful to delimit the ambit of the doctrine, the court should require the claimant to surmount the normal common law causation hurdle.[106] Similarly, although in *Barton* there was some suggestion of the evidential burden shifting to the alleged wrongdoer, at least in economic duress cases the burden of proof should be upon the complainant.

---

is still an intention on his part to contract in the apparently consensual terms; but there is *coactus volui* on his side. The contrast is with non est factum. The contract procured by duress is therefore not void: it is voidable—at the discretion of the party subject to duress."

[100] Above.

[101] See at 119.

[102] *Dimskal Shipping v ITWF* [1992] 2 A.C. 152, at 165.

[103] *Huyton SA v Peter Cremer GmbH* [1999] C.L.C. 230, at 250.

[104] "The minimum basic test of subjective causation in economic duress ought, it appears to me, to be a 'but for' test. The illegitimate pressure must have been such as actually caused the making of the agreement, in the sense that it would not otherwise have been made either at all or, at least, in the terms in which it was made. In that sense, the pressure must have been decisive or clinching."

[105] See Enonchong, *Duress, Undue Influence and Unconscionable Dealing* (2012), at pp.67–68.

[106] Christopher Clarke J agreed that a "but for" causation test was appropriate in *Kolmar Group AG v Traxpo Enterprises PVT Ltd* [2010] EWHC 113 (Comm); [2010] 1 C.L.C. 256, at [92]; as did Warren J in *Times Travel (UK) Ltd Nottingham Travel (UK) Ltd v Pakistan International Airlines Corp* [2017] EWHC 1367 (Ch), at [253]: "In other words, but for the duress, the victim would not have entered into the contract. It is not necessary to show that the threat was the overwhelming or predominant cause of the relevant conduct by the victim." It is not the case that there is a further requirement of economic duress that the claimant had no reasonable alternative to giving in to the illegitimate pressure. Rather, the absence of reasonable alternative is very strong evidence going to whether the claimant was induced by the threat or other illegitimate pressure to enter into the contract: *Al Nehayan v Kent* [2018] EWHC 333 (Comm), at [191].

(5) Evidential Factors

In an influential passage in his judgment in *Pao On*,[107] Lord Scarman laid down   **15–048**
a number of factors which were relevant to determining the question of whether
there had been actionable duress:

> "In determining whether there was a coercion of will such that there was no true consent, it is
> material to inquire whether the person alleged to have been coerced did or did not protest[108];
> whether, at the time he was allegedly coerced into making the contract, he did or did not have
> an alternative course open to him such as an adequate legal remedy[109]; whether he was
> independently advised; and whether after entering the contract he took steps to avoid it. All
> these matters are, as was recognised in *Maskell v Horner* [1915] 3 K.B. 106, relevant in
> determining whether he acted voluntarily or not."

(6) Other Forms of Duress

There are other forms of duress, which have accumulated around them over the   **15–049**
centuries a very substantial body of authority. These include payments made to
obtain the performance of a public duty, where the public official is bound to
confer the benefit either without payment or for a sum greater than the
complainant is in law obliged to pay,[110] and the improper threat of legal
proceedings against the complainant or a third party connected to the
complainant.[111] Both subjects are beyond the scope of this book.

D. UNCONSCIONABLE DEALING

(1) Introduction

A disadvantageous transaction entered into by a vulnerable (or, as the old cases   **15–050**
would have it, "poor and ignorant") person[112] can be set aside under a doctrine
tracing its origins to the protection of expectant heirs from sales of their interests

---

[107] Above, at 635.

[108] The fact that the complainant did not raise a protest at the time the pressure was exerted and he
complied with the demand is an obvious forensic point available to the alleged wrongdoer to rebut the
assertion of duress (see for example *XS Racing & Event Marketing Ltd v Sunseeker Europe AG* [2005]
EWHC 3023 (QB)); but it is not a requirement for relief (see e.g. *T D Keegan v Palmer* [1961] 2
Lloyd's Rep. 449). Conversely, the existence of a contemporaneous protest may be of substantial
probative value to the complainant (see e.g. *Maskell v Horner* [1915] 3 K.B. 106, at p.124), although
it is by no means determinative. The complainant's protest may of course be a considered step made
with a view to keeping his options open at a later date.

[109] It will be seen that the question of whether the complainant had an alternative course open to him
is relevant at various stages of the inquiry.

[110] See generally Mitchell, Mitchell and Watterson, *Goff & Jones: The Law of Unjust Enrichment*
(2016), para.10–41 and following.

[111] See generally Mitchell, Mitchell and Watterson, *Goff & Jones: The Law of Unjust Enrichment*
(2016), para.10–20 and following.

[112] See also J. McGhee, *Snell's Equity*, 32nd edn (London: Sweet & Maxwell, 2010), para.8–036 and
following.

at an undervalue.[113] The boundaries of this doctrine are not fully clear, but where the terms are exorbitant or extravagant and the party aggrieved was at a disadvantage known to the other party, then unconscionability may be a ground for setting aside the transaction. It applies to gifts as much as to contracts and other transactions.[114]

(2) Elements of the Claim

15–051   There is no general jurisdiction to set aside transactions which are considered unfair, or which involve an inequality of bargaining power.[115] The bargain or gift must be oppressive in overall terms, the party aggrieved must be suffering from some sort of significant bargaining weakness and the other party must have acted unconscionably or reprehensibly taken advantage of the party aggrieved. The absence of legal advice for the disadvantaged party is not an essential element.[116] Provided the basic elements of the claim are met, the burden shifts to the other party to show that the transaction was not objectionable—that is, that it was fair and reasonable.

15–052   Thus there are (it is considered) three key elements of the claim[117]:

(1)   The claimant is suffering from a particular kind of vulnerability or special disadvantage.
(2)   The terms of the transaction are oppressive to the claimant.
(3)   The defendant knowingly took advantage of the claimant's vulnerability, in a way that amounts to impropriety.

15–053   **Special Disadvantage.**   The vulnerability can take the form of illiteracy or poor education, age or poverty[118]; also illness, weakness of mind, intoxication or necessity. The phrase "poor and ignorant" is nowadays understood to mean from a low socio-economic income group or less well educated.[119] Vulnerability must be assessed in light of the context of the transaction sought to be impugned and not generally.[120] The law is not designed to protect the claimant against his disadvantage in a general sense; instead, there must be some relational

---

[113] *Fry v Lane* (1888) 40 Ch. D. 312, at 320. See also *Backhouse v Backhouse* [1978] 1 W.L.R. 243; *Boustany v Piggott* UKPC 17; (1995) 69 P. & C.R. 298 PC, *Crédit Lyonnais Bank Nederland NV v Burch* [1997] 1 All E.R. 144 and *Portman Building Society v Dusangh* [2000] 2 All E.R. (Comm) 221.

[114] *Evans v Lloyds* [2013] EWHC 1725 (Ch) (contrast with *Langton v Langton* [1995] 2 F.L.R. 890).

[115] *Boustany v Piggott* UKPC 17; (1995) 69 P. & C.R. 298 PC, at [303].

[116] Although, as noted below, it will often be difficult to show that one party knowingly took advantage of the weakness of the other if the other was (to the first party's knowledge) legally represented and advised.

[117] *Irvani v Irvani* [2000] 1 Lloyd's Rep. 412; *Portman Building Society v Dusangh* [2000] 2 All E.R. (Comm) 221; *Mitchell v James* [2001] All E.R. (D) 116 and *Strydom v Vendside Ltd* [2009] EWHC 2130 (QB).

[118] For poverty, see *Proof v Hines* (1735) Cas T Talbot 111.

[119] *Cresswell v Potter* [1978] 1 W.L.R. 255.

[120] A principle which has echoes in the law relating to lack of capacity. See also *Chagos Islanders v Attorney General* [2003] EWHC 2222 (QB).

disadvantage between the parties too.[121] Further, the disadvantage must be something capable of being classified as "serious".[122] It must be recognised that the court is not merely protecting against the consequences of an inequality of bargaining power.

Oppression. The oppressiveness of the terms must be such as to "shock the conscience of the court".[123] Imprudence or acting for the benefit of a spouse is not enough. Inadequacy of consideration, to this limited extent, is an important factor to take into account, but it is not determinative.[124] Claims may well succeed on the basis of undue influence where they will not succeed on the basis of unconscionable dealing.[125]   **15–054**

Unconscionability. Some form of moral culpability or impropriety is also necessary.[126] This must include some knowing exploitation of the situation or circumstances. The issue of knowledge is important, because one cannot act unconscionably if one is not aware of the special disadvantage.[127] It is impossible to define all the circumstances which might fall within this requirement: findings of deceit, duress or threats or undue influence will usually be sufficient, but situations of haste and surprise (when combined with the element of knowledge) can also amount to impropriety. Impropriety can be proved by actual evidence and also by raising a presumption, either from the terms of the transaction itself for from the clear inequality of the parties.   **15–055**

Where a weaker party is represented and advised by a lawyer, that will normally be enough to counter any unconscionability: a stronger party is normally entitled to assume that the involvement of a solicitor is enough to redress any imbalance between them.[128]   **15–056**

(3)   Remedies

The principal remedy, as for undue influence and duress, is to have the contract, transaction or gift set aside. It remains unclear whether equitable compensation is available, but there appears to be no reason why not, especially where some other factor bars the setting aside of the transaction and restoration of the status quo ante. The remedial objective is to achieve practical justice and so monetary   **15–057**

---

[121] With respect to alleged ignorance, the state of knowledge must be relevant to the transaction at hand: *Norwich Union Life Assurance Society v Qureshi* [1999] Lloyd's Rep. IR 263; affirmed [1999] 2 All E.R. 707.

[122] *Jones v Morgan* [2001] EWC Civ 9950, at [40].

[123] *Alec Lobb (Garages) Ltd v Total Oil Great Britain Ltd* [1983] 1 W.L.R. 87, at 94–95, per Peter Millett QC, affirmed on appeal ([1985] 1 W.L.R. 173).

[124] *How v Weldon* (1754) 2 Ves Sen 516.

[125] *Humphreys v Humphreys* [2004] EWHC 2201 (Ch).

[126] *Jones v Morgan* [2001] EWC Civ 995, reversing the decision of the judge and holding that the transaction was not unconscionable, because the defendant was not aware of a mistake belief by the claimant as to the effect of the transaction. cf. also *Minder Music Ltd v Sharples* [2015] EWHC 1454 (IPEC), at [34]–[35].

[127] *Hart v O'Connor* [1985] 1 A.C. 1000.

[128] *Jones v Morgan* [2001] EWC Civ 995.

adjustments can be made, for example, to ensure that a subsequent loss in the value of property acquired is shared between the parties.[129] It is suggested that a third party receiving a benefit under the tainted transaction will not be subject to the setting aside of the transaction unless he is on notice as to the unconscionable dealing, or the party who has behaved unconsciably is his agent, or he is a volunteer.[130]

---

[129] *Cheese v Thomas* [1994] 1 W.L.R. 129 (CA).
[130] By analogy to the position with undue influence; see para.15-025 above.

[470]

CHAPTER 16

STATUTORY CLAIMS

A.   INTRODUCTION

(1)   Statute and the Common Law Concept of Fraud

In English civil law fraud is fundamentally a common law concept: as we have   **16–001**
seen in the preceding chapters, through an accumulation of decided cases various
private law causes of action have come to be recognised, whereby a particular set
of facts involving conduct that can be characterised as fraudulent can give rise to
a liability on the part of a wrongdoer to compensate a victim for harm suffered (or
disgorge enrichment received) as a result. Legal taxonomy applied to the decided
cases operates to categorise the relevant wrongdoing and identify the elements
that need to be established for a claim. The same is true of the equitable bases of
liability addressed in Chapters 9 to 13 of the book, although the trigger for these
will usually arise out of the abuse of some pre-existing relationship between the
parties concerned (or at least some of them), which the Courts have come to
recognise as giving rise to obligations or constraints on how one party to the
relationship can act towards the other and with respect to property under his
control.

There are, however, a limited number of instances where Parliament has   **16–002**
legislated, in the civil context, against types of activity which might commonly
involve fraudulent conduct. With the important exception, which is addressed in
this chapter, of s.423 of the Insolvency Act 1986, the legislation generally does so
in the context of investor or consumer protection. These are areas in which the
opportunity to make dishonestly false representations capable of causing loss to a
wide range of persons is obvious; but the law of deceit (with its requirement for
intended inducement of the representee) and the other economic torts considered
in this work (which generally require wrongdoing directed at a particular victim)
are not always apt to provide a remedy. At the risk of generalising, such statutory
provisions are aimed at establishing liability on the part of a defendant whose
wrongdoing may be perpetrated at a time when he has no particular victim in
mind. This is also true in the case of s.423, which operates, albeit in a different
context, to confer a private cause of action upon a single victim (so labelled), but
where the relief which the court may grant rests upon the notion of "class
recovery" for all who may have suffered as a result of the wrongdoing, whether
or not they were known to the defendant at the time of the impugned transaction.

In all such cases where Parliament has anticipated the particular type of   **16–003**
potentially fraudulent activity it is, of course, the legislation rather than

established case law which primarily operates to define the parameters of liability, albeit the statutory wording will often be the subject of detailed analysis in the cases. As the purpose of these statutes is on the whole to supplement the common law, the parameters of liability differ from, and are in some important respects wider than, whatever may be the most closely analogous common law cause of action. For example, a prospectus for shares can be misleading in a way that is actionable under statute without those responsible for it being guilty of deceit in the tortious sense, and the improper purpose which triggers the claim to impugn a transaction under s.423 need not by any means be the only purpose that motivates that transaction and need not involve any "misappropriation" of property, other than the defendant's own.

(2)   The Statutory Provisions Considered in this Chapter

16–004   This chapter is concerned with three statutory claims which are thought to be of greatest potential relevance to the civil fraud practitioner, and which (unusually) give rise to private law claims at the suit of the victim of the relevant wrongdoing. These are:

(1)   Claims for relief with respect to transactions defrauding creditors, under s.423 of the Insolvency Act 1986;
(2)   Claims for compensation for false or misleading listing particulars or prospectuses, under s.90 of the Financial Services and Markets Act 2000 ("FSMA"); and
(3)   Claims against issuers (or proposed issuers) of securities for untrue or misleading statements in published information or announcements made in connection with those securities, under s.90A of FSMA.

16–005   These statutory provisions are not all natural bedfellows but they require to be analysed in this book. The first because the deliberate placing of assets outside the reach of potential claimants is, in a real sense, a fraud on those claimants, and a claim under s.423 may well be needed where the victim of a fraud has not managed at an earlier stage to restrain the defendant from entering into such a transaction by a freezing injunction. The second and third because any claimant contemplating a claim in deceit arising out of the marketing of securities clearly needs to be aware of the claims (in some respects broader) that may be available under FSMA.

(3)   Other Statutory Provisions

16–006   There are a number of other statutory provisions of which the fraud practitioner should be aware, because of their potential relevance to a fraud claim, but which are not appropriate subjects for this book, either because they are not by their terms or in their underlying rationale directed at conduct which is necessarily fraudulent or because they do not give rise to private law rights of action for the victim of the conduct in question.

For example, in the context of insolvency, ss.127 and 284 of the Insolvency Act 1986 operate to invalidate dispositions of property made by a company or individual after the presentation of a winding up petition (or any earlier resolution to wind up or application for an administration order) or bankruptcy petition respectively. It is quite possible that, where the relevant disposition is made knowing that insolvency proceedings have been commenced (as will often be the case), it will have been made "fraudulently", in the sense of an attempt to cheat one or more creditors by putting assets beyond their reach. But the invalidation for which the statute provides certainly does not rest upon the need to establish "fraud" and the rationale for the invalidation simply lies in the principle of pari passu distribution of assets amongst the insolvent's unsecured creditors. The provisions of the Insolvency Act for challenging preferences[1] and transactions at an undervalue[2] rest upon that same principle: whilst transactions caught by such provisions might, on the facts of a given case, properly be characterised as fraudulent, that will not necessarily be so. The proper place for an analysis of these various provisions is therefore a work on insolvency, not civil fraud.

16–007

Similarly, a transaction by which a director (or shadow director) or some person connected with him fraudulently acquires property from his company might also constitute a breach of the statutory provisions governing "substantial property transactions" between a company and such persons. These are to be found in ss.190–196 of the Companies Act 2006. Section 190 prohibits such transactions unless the arrangement has been approved by a resolution of the company's members. If such approval is not obtained, then s.195 operates to render the transaction voidable. However, the fact that the statute might, on the facts of the particular case, provide a further ground for challenging such an arrangement does not mean that the provisions are properly characterised as being concerned with fraud; they are instead an aspect of the regulation of dealings between a company and its directors. The reader is therefore referred to the specialist works on company law for a detailed consideration of these provisions, including such matters as the particular exceptions to the prohibition (ss.192–194), the constraints upon the avoidance of any infringing arrangement (s.195(2)) and the ability of members to affirm it within a reasonable time so that it is no longer voidable (s.196).

16–008

There are then cases where Parliament can be said to have legislated against "fraudulent" conduct, but the absence of any available cause of action for an individual victim of that conduct is another reason not to address it in this chapter. Perhaps the most obvious examples of such provisions are those of the Insolvency Act 1986 which operate to impose liability on those who have been guilty of "fraudulent trading". The relevant sections impose liability, subject to the court's discretion in relation to the grant of any relief, on those who are knowingly party to the carrying on of a company's business "with intent to defraud creditors of the company or creditors of any other person, or for any

16–009

---

[1] See ss.239 and 340 of the Insolvency Act 1986, which relate to corporate and individual insolvencies respectively.

[2] See ss.238 and 339 of the Insolvency Act 1986, which relate to corporate and individual insolvencies respectively.

fraudulent purpose".[3] However, the important qualification is that the company in question must either be in the course of being wound up or be in administration[4]; and the application for a declaration that the person concerned is liable to make a contribution to the company's assets must be made by the liquidator or the administrator (as the case may be). In no sense, therefore, do these sections give rise to a private cause of action for the direct recovery of loss suffered individually as a result of fraud.[5] If an individual claimant is to pursue a claim in respect of conduct which might also constitute fraudulent trading under the 1986 Act (whether against the company or those who are its directing mind and will) then a private cause of action such as deceit must be identified.[6]

16–010   Another example of fraudulent (or potentially fraudulent) activity leading to liability otherwise than in favour of a private claimant is provided by the behaviour which constitutes market abuse under the provisions of FSMA This includes making misleading statements or concealing information to the detriment of investors and has been said to create a "civil offence" alongside the criminal offence of insider trading. However, it does not follow from the fact that the Financial Conduct Authority has power to seek injunctive relief or a restitution order on behalf of those who have suffered loss as a result of market abuse that any private cause of action exists in respect of it.[7]

B.   TRANSACTIONS DEFRAUDING CREDITORS

(1)   Introduction

16–011   Sections 423–425 of the Insolvency Act 1986 make provision for challenging what are commonly described (including in the heading to s.423) as "transactions defrauding creditors". It is, however, important to note both that the application of these provisions is not confined to the insolvency context[8] and that the language in the body of the sections themselves does not use that phrase. The

---

[3] See s.213 (liquidation) and s.246ZA (administration) of the Insolvency Act 1986. For the less onerous provisions concerned with "wrongful trading" (on the part of directors and shadow directors) see ss.214 and 246ZB.

[4] The equivalent criminal offence created by s.993 of the Companies Act 2006 (or s.9 of the Fraud Act 2006 in relation to businesses not within s.993) is expressly not so circumscribed.

[5] Unlike earlier statutory provisions in the 1948 and 1985 Acts, which (subject to the court being alive to the risk of potential double jeopardy in the event of a later or further claim by the liquidator) also permitted applications by creditors or contributories: see, e.g., *In re Cooper Chemicals Ltd* [1978] 1 Ch. 262, 268G.

[6] For such claims in deceit, see, e.g., *Standard Chartered Bank v Pakistan National Shipping Corp* [2002] UKHL 43; [2003] 1 A.C. 959 and *Lindsay v O'Loughnane* [2010] EWHC 529 (QB), at [86]–[104]. On these cases and more generally in relation to deceit, see Ch.1.

[7] *Hall v Cable & Wireless* [2009] EWHC 1793 (Comm); [2010] 1 B.C.L.C. 95, at [23] referring to a restitution order available under s.383 of FSMA.

[8] In *Inland Revenue Commissioners v Hashmi* [2002] EWCA Civ 981; [2002] 2 B.C.L.C. 489, at [22], Arden LJ noted that: "Section 423 plays an important role in insolvency law. It can moreover apply even though the debtor is not in a formal insolvency. The counter-consideration is that, unlike transactions at an undervalue and preferences, which may be avoided only in a formal insolvency, under s 423 the stricter requirements of s 423(3) [relating to the transferor's purpose] must be satisfied."

provisions have antecedents that date back centuries[9] and the fact that their focus is upon the nature of the transaction rather than the solvency or otherwise of the transferor is highlighted by the fact that the immediate statutory predecessor was found in s.172 of the Law of Property Act 1925 ("fraudulent conveyances"), rather than in insolvency legislation. The insolvency of the transferor is relevant only in determining that any s.423 claim must in such a case be brought either by the office holder or, with the court's permission only, by a victim.

In *Fortress Value Recovery Fund I LLC v Blue Skye Special Opportunities Fund LP*[10] Flaux J pithily expressed the ingredients of a claim under the section as follows: **16–012**

> "There are thus four requirements for relief to be granted:
> (1)   a debtor[11];
> (2)   who enters into a transaction;
> (3)   at an undervalue;
> (4)   with the purpose of putting assets beyond the reach of or prejudicing the interests of a person with an actual or potential claim. "

Many if not most claims under s.423 are concerned with a transaction under which a person has transferred property (whether real property or movables) with a view to frustrating recovery by an existing creditor or prejudicing the interests of someone who is either already making or who might in the future make a hostile claim.[12] The wording of the section is deliberately wide in order to protect existing or potential creditors against assets being moved away from the transferor or "debtor"[13] and out of their reach, and it should be understood as embracing all manner of transactions that result, by reason of their being gratuitous or for a value which is not substantially reciprocated by the transferee, in a depletion of the transferor's assets.[14] The transferor may be an individual, or company or other entity. **16–013**

The section clearly has potential extra-territorial effect, so that ss.423–435 can in principle be applied so as to order the reversal of a transaction between foreign **16–014**

---

[9] In *Inland Revenue Commissioners v Hashmi* [2002] EWCA Civ 981; [2002] 2 B.C.L.C. 489, at [21], Arden LJ noted a textbook reference to there having been "a provision on these lines since 1571, and that ultimately its ancestry could be traced back to the Paulian action of Roman law."

[10] *Fortress Value Recovery Fund I LLC v Blue Skye Special Opportunities Fund LP* [2013] EWHC 14 (Comm), [104].

[11] It is not necessary that the transferor of property is a debtor at the time of the transaction itself, whether of the claimant or of anyone else: see paras 16–024—16–025 below.

[12] The first in a non-exhaustive list of potential remedies on a successful s.423 claim is identified in s.425(1)(a) as an order requiring any property transferred as part of the transaction to be vested in any person, either absolutely or for the benefit of all the persons on whose behalf the claim is treated as made. Section 436 of the Act defines property so as to include "money, goods, things in action, land and every description of property wherever situated." Section 423(3)—see para.16–024 below— refers to "assets" rather than "property" in connection with the first limb of the statutory purpose.

[13] Section 423(5) states that, for the purposes of the two later sections prescribing who may apply for relief and the nature of the relief that may be granted, the person who entered into the impugned transaction is referred to as "the debtor"; but, as we note below, the claimant need not be in an established debtor/creditor relationship with this person.

[14] *BTI 2014 LLC v Sequana S.A.* [2016] EWHC 1686 (Ch), at[500], per Rose J.

parties and in relation to foreign property.[15] However, the Court will not exercise its discretion under these provisions unless a sufficient connection with England and Wales is shown; and, in addition, the court's discretion under s.425 in relation to the grant of relief may require it to have regard to any foreign legal or insolvency proceedings which may affect the assets in issue.[16] Despite previous authority to different effect, the Court of Appeal has recently decided that a claimant who wishes to obtain permission to serve a s.423 claim out of the jurisdiction can rely on the gateway relating to claims "under an enactment" (now CPR PD6B, para.3.1(20)).[17]

(2)   Time within which Claim to be Brought

16–015   There are no express time limits stated in s.423 for claims brought under the section. For limitation purposes, the identity of the claimant (whether an office holder or an individual victim claiming on behalf of all other such victims) has been described as "an ingredient of the cause of action" so that, as the opening words of s.424(1)(a)) indicate, there can be no claim by an office holder before the relevant event of insolvency.[18] This means that a claim to challenge a transaction which might be statute barred if brought by a victim[19] (even though he could be one of the more recent victims of it) might not be barred if brought by

---

[15] In *Jyske Bank (Gibraltar) Ltd v Spjeldnaes* [1992] 2 B.C.L.C. 101, 122–124, the claim under s.423 was made in respect of an assignment between two Irish companies of a contract made and to be performed in Ireland and governing the disposition of Irish land. Evans-Lombe J was persuaded to exercise jurisdiction in circumstances where the relevant defendants were two of many defendants to "the main action" which had been tried by him (and that was one of the reasons underpinning the judge's observations that they could be served abroad without the court's permission then being required under the relevant rules) and there had been no application to stay the proceedings on forum non conveniens grounds. See also *Re Krug International (UK) Ltd* [2008] EWHC 2256 (Ch), where permission to serve the s.423 proceedings upon a US company was given on the basis that it was a proper party to proceedings which also involved misfeasance claims against the directors of the English company in liquidation.

[16] *Re Paramount Airways (No.2)* [1993] Ch. 223, at 239–240; *Fortress Value Recovery Fund I LLC v Blue Skye Special Opportunities Fund LP (A Firm)* [2013] EWHC 14 (Comm), at [113]–[114]; and *Erste Group Bank AG v JSC "VMZ Red October"* [2015] EWCA Civ 379; [2015] 1 C.L.C. 706, at [120]–[125].

[17] *Orexim Trading Ltd v Mahavir Port and Terminal Prive Ltd* [2018] EWCA Civ 1660. The first instance decision of Flaux J to different effect in *Erste Group Bank AG v JSC "VMZ Red October"* [2013] EWHC 2926, at [150], was said in *Orexim Trading* to have been wrongly decided. *In re Harrods (Buenos Aires) Ltd (No.2)* [1992] Ch. 72, at 116; *In re Banco Nacional de Cuba* [2001] 1 W.L.R. 2039, at [17]–[19].

[18] *Hill v Spread Trustee Ltd* [2006] EWCA Civ 542; [2007] 1 W.L.R. 2404, at [148]–[150], per Sir Martin Nourse (with whom Waller LJ agreed on this aspect but Arden LJ did not). Even though the facts giving rise to a claim under the s.423 may be actionable as a tort, s.423 does not constitute some form of "statutory" tort: *Erste Group Bank AG v JSC "VMZ Red October"* [2013] EWHC 2926 (Comm), at [95], per Flaux J (who, on an application for service out of the jurisdiction, was analysing the section from the perspective of private international law principles rather than the limitation angle. His decision was overturned on appeal [2015] EWCA Civ 379; [2015] 1 C.L.C. 706, but not on this point).

[19] It should be noted, however, that the status of "victim", for the purposes of the accrual of a cause of action, may date not from the transaction in question but from *later* events giving rise to a claim which is "capable of being prejudiced" within the meaning of s.423(5): see *Giles v Rhind (No.2)* [2008] EWCA Civ 118; [2009] Ch. 191, at [56], where Arden LJ found it unnecessary to decide

the office holder of the insolvent estate (in which all victims—older and more recent—may have an interest). Whether the start date of the limitation period is the date of the transaction or the insolvency event, the relevant period will either be 12 years if the claim is be analysed as an action on a speciality to set aside the transaction (s.8(1) of the Limitation Act 1980) or 6 years if analysed as an action for a sum of money recoverable by virtue of s.423 (s.9(1) of the 1980 Act).[20] To work out which period is applicable the Court will "look to see what is actually claimed".[21] Should limitation be a potential issue it will therefore be necessary to look at the substance of the relief sought. Where the transaction sought to be set aside is a simple payment of a sum of money, the Court is likely to apply a 6-year limitation period.[22] On the other hand a claim to set aside a transfer of property (e.g. shares or real property) and simply re-vest the property in the defendant is more likely to attract a 12-year limitation period.

In *JSC BTA Bank v Ablyazov*[23] Mr Laurence Rabinowitz QC held that, looking at the substance and essential nature of the claim, a claim under s.423 for the return of a fund to the bank account from which its transfer had been made was one for the recovery of money within the meaning of s.9(1) of the Limitation Act and accordingly the six-year limitation period would have applied instead of the 12-year period provided for by s.8(1). However, the Deputy Judge would have concluded (in the event of liability under s.423 having been established when he found otherwise) that the claimant benefited from the extended limitation period provided for by s.32 of the Act. If liability had been established, the second defendant transferee would, for the purposes of s.32, have been claiming an entitlement to the fund "through, under or by the act of" the fraudulent first defendant.[24]   **16–016**

In *Abylazov* the provisions of s.32 of the 1980 Act were considered against the background of allegations that there was fraud or deliberate concealment on the part of the transferor in relation to the transfer of monies. In *Giles v Rhind (No.2)*[25] there was no allegation that steps had in fact been taken deliberately to conceal the transaction which was sought to be impugned under s.423; the issue was instead whether the claimant could rely upon the provisions of s.32(2) of the Limitation Act which deemed there to be deliberate concealment where the transaction involved "the deliberate commission of a breach of duty" which was "unlikely to be discovered for some time". The relevant deed (conferring upon the transferee wife an 80 per cent beneficial interest in the matrimonial home) had not been registered at the Land Registry and the claimant could not   **16–017**

whether the judge was right in his conclusion on the point. See also the language of s.423(3) in relation to "statutory purpose" (operating to defeat potential future claims): see para.16–007 below.
[20] See also *Re Yates (A Bankrupt)* [2005] B.P.I.R. 476, at [183], per Charles J.
[21] *Hill v Spread Trustee Ltd* [2006] EWCA Civ 542; [2007] 1 W.L.R. 2404, at [115].
[22] *Re Priory Garage (Walthamstow) Ltd* [2001] B.P.I.R. 144, per John Randall QC at 160F–160G. See ss.8(2) and 9(1) of the Limitation Act 1980.
[23] *JSC BTA Bank v Ablyazov* [2016] EWHC 3071 (Comm), at [155]. The Deputy Judge's observations, at [159]–[179] were obiter in the light of his finding that the claim under s.423 failed; and his conclusion on s.9(1) of the Limitation Act 1980 was not challenged on appeal ([2018] EWCA Civ 1176).
[24] On this the Deputy Judge was upheld on appeal: [2018] EWCA Civ 1176.
[25] *Giles v Rhind (No.2)* [2008] EWCA Civ 118; [2009] Ch. 191, at [36]–[55].

reasonably have discovered its existence before the defendants told him about it; but it was disputed that a claim under s.423 was a claim for a breach of duty. The Court of Appeal upheld the decision of the David Richards J in concluding that it was: the expression "breach of duty" in s.32(2) was not limited to breach of a contractual, tortious or fiduciary duty, but also included legal wrongdoing relied upon in support of a claim under s.423.

(3)　The Requirement of a Transaction at an Undervalue

16–018　As already noted, the section is designed to catch transactions which are gifts or which have a gratuitous element, thereby depleting the assets of the debtor available to meet claims against him. Despite the express reference to a "gift" and the fact that one limb of the defined offending purpose on the part of the transferor refers to him "putting assets beyond the reach of" current or future creditors, the section is not by its terms limited to transactions that involve a transfer of money or property as such (and so could extend, for example, to the execution of a charge or the giving of a guarantee). Instead, what engages the section is that the transaction is either for no consideration, or that the consideration moving from the person entering into the transaction is significantly greater than that provided in return.

16–019　The concept of undervalue is captured by s.423(1) as follows:

> "This section relates to transactions entered into at an undervalue; and a person enters into such a transaction with another person if—
> (a)　he makes a gift to the other person or he otherwise enters into a transaction with the other on terms that provide for him to receive no consideration;
> (b)　he enters into a transaction with the other in consideration of marriage or the formation of a civil partnership; or
> (c)　he enters into a transaction with the other for a consideration the value of which, in money or money's worth, is significantly less than the value, in money or money's worth, of the consideration provided by himself. "

16–020　As in contract law, the concept of consideration is broad enough to include forbearance from suing.[26] Where there is *some* consideration for the transaction (such that limb (a) cannot be relied upon), the need to establish that the transaction is one in which there is a significant discrepancy between the consideration provided and that received (measured in money or money's worth) means that it may be more difficult to challenge transactions which do not involve an outright transfer of money or property, such as those involving the creation of security. In *Re MC Bacon Ltd*[27] (a case concerning s.238 of the Insolvency Act 1986, which has the same undervalue requirement) Millet J held that the mere creation of security over assets does not deplete or diminish the value of the chargor's assets; it simply means that the value is appropriated to the

---

[26] For valuable consideration in the form of a wife's forbearance from presenting a divorce petition and seeking a property adjustment order in respect of the property that was later the subject matter of an unsuccessful s.423 claim, see *Papanicola v Fagan* [2008] EWHC 3348 (Ch); [2009] B.P.I.R. 320, at [29]–[30] (citing *Haines v Hill* [2007] EWCA Civ 1284 on the same issue under s.339 of the Act).
[27] *Re MC Bacon Ltd* (1990) BCC 78, 92E. See also *Re Mistral Finance Ltd* (2001) BCC 27, at [37]–[38]; and *National Bank of Kuwait v Menzies* [1994] BCC 119 (CA).

benefit of the chargee rather than any unsecured creditors of the chargor. But if this is to be understood as suggesting that the grant of security can as a matter of law *never* constitute a transaction falling within s.423(1)(c), that is doubtful (since what that subsection refers to is a transaction in which consideration is given, not a transaction by which assets are depleted; and the grant of security can amount to the giving of consideration).[28] The case may better be understood as turning on the fact that it was not possible meaningfully to compare, in money or money's worth, the value of the granting of the security against the consideration received in return (forbearance from pursuing a previously unsecured debt or the making of further advances under the security). If there had been no consideration received in return at all, or that purported to be given had been illusory, then the analysis would presumably be different, as s.423(1)(a) would be engaged.

The declaration of a dividend by a company has been held at first instance to be capable of being caught by s.423, even though, ultimately, the basis of its payment (and receipt) is a pre-existing legal relationship between company and shareholder formed at a time when there will generally have been no question of the improper purpose (addressed below) being present. In *BTI 2014 LLC v Sequana S.A.*[29] Rose J held that the decision to pay the dividend and the choice as to its value is not the consequence of that relationship, because it is discretionary not only in its amount but also in whether it is paid at all. She went on to observe:

16–021

> "It is not difficult to see that a blanket exclusion of dividend payments from the scope of section 423 will quickly reduce the efficacy of the provision given the many instances where the directors and shareholders of a company are the same or linked individuals."

However, whilst a transaction need not be a contract, it is normally understood as involving some element of dealing between two parties (particularly because the section refers to the transaction being "entered into"). Thus in *Re Hampton Capital Ltd*[30] (again a case under s.238) it was held that the transfer of money from a company's bank account into the account of a third party, at the behest of a director who was thereby misappropriating the company's assets, was not a transaction at an undervalue, because the third party payee had no involvement in the payment. The Deputy Judge (George Bompas QC) observed:

16–022

> "I cannot accept that the mere transmission of money, the mere making of a payment, without any form of dealing between the paying company and the payee, can constitute the entering into of a transaction by the company with the payee (at any rate where the transaction is not a 'gift'). What is required, on the language of section 238(4), is the entering into of a transaction between two parties. Without straining the language of the section, this must require some

---

[28] *Hill v Spread Trustee Ltd* [2006] EWCA Civ 542; [2007] 1 W.L.R. 2404, at [93].

[29] *BTI 2014 LLC v Sequana S.A.* [2016] EWHC 1686 (Ch), at [500]–[501] (the point is to be considered in a pending appeal). The judge found that the statutory purpose under s.423(3) was established in relation to one dividend but not another. For the consequential relief granted in this case, see [2017] EWHC 211 (Ch) discussed at para.16–043 below.

[30] *Re Hampton Capital Ltd* [2015] EWHC 1905 (Ch). See also *Re Taylor Sinclair Ltd* [2001] 2 B.C.L.C. 176, at para.20: "...as I read the section it does envisage that, apart perhaps from the case of a mere gift which is expressly included within sections 238 and 436, a transaction will be something which involves at least some element of dealing between the parties to the transaction."

engagement, or at least communication, between the two parties and not merely a disposition of money which results in one party's money landing up in the bank account of the other without anything said or done by that other."

16–023   The fact that the impugned transaction does not in and of itself achieve the statutory purpose (as to which, see below) without some further step being taken or other event happening does not mean that the transaction cannot be caught by the section. So, in *Hill v Spread Trustee Co Ltd* the transaction sought to be set aside was a settlement, which was alleged to have been entered into with the purpose of deceiving the revenue. The submission that s.423 could not apply, because the deceit could only be carried into effect by a (separate) misstatement of the value of the settled land to the revenue, was rejected.[31]

(4)   The Improper Purpose Requirement

16–024   It is not enough to show simply that the effect of the transaction is a significant reduction in the net value of that person's estate: the shorthand description of the section as being concerned with transactions "defrauding creditors" reveals that, crucially, an element of improper purpose is required.

The transferor (i.e. the "debtor" as defined in s.423(5)) needs to be motivated by one of the two alternative purposes identified in the section. Section 423(3) states:

"In the case of a person entering into such a transaction, an order shall only be made if the court is satisfied that it was entered into by him for the purpose—
(a)   of putting assets beyond the reach of a person who is making, or may at some time make, a claim against him, or
(b)   of otherwise prejudicing the interests of such a person in relation to the claim which he is making or may make. "

16–025   It will immediately be apparent that either of the purposes set out in s.423(3) is one that might well be operating upon the mind of someone who has been guilty of some prior fraud (or other actionable wrongdoing) and who is being, or fears he might be, held to account for it.[32] The language of the subsection resonates with the underlying purpose behind a freezing injunction (compare "the enforcement principle" discussed in Ch.28) and, as we have noted, the statutory claim may avail a victim of such wrongdoing who was not able to act quickly enough, or did not previously know enough about the defendant's intentions, to obtain such interim relief. Seen from the perspective of s.423, it might be said that a primary purpose of obtaining a freezing order against the proposed transferor is to obviate the need (and the attendant risk and uncertainty) of having to pursue later s.423 proceedings. That is not to suggest, however, that where the

---

[31]   *Hill v Spread Trustee Co Ltd* [2007] 1 W.L.R. 2404 (at [102]).
[32]   See, for example, *4 Eng v Harper* [2009] EWHC 2633 (Ch), at [22], where the transferor knew he was at risk of substantial claims if the previous payment of bribes was discovered, and *Hall v Elia* [2015] EWHC 3199 (Ch), at [144]–[150], where, shortly before his bankruptcy, the bankrupt had purported to assign to his mother his equity in a flat which (as was agreed between the office-holder applicants of trustee in bankruptcy and liquidator) had recently been purchased using monies belonging to the company.

transaction has taken place but is later challenged under s.423, the court is powerless to grant a freezing injunction against the transferee.[33]

However, the need to establish the relevant purpose means that a claim under s.423 cannot rest simply upon the transaction having had the *consequence* of in fact prejudicing the interests of such a victim. The decision in *Inland Revenue Commissioners v Hashmi*[34] shows that consequences are different from purposes. That said, prejudice to actual or potential creditors is a necessary ingredient of both limbs of the statutory purpose. In *BTI 2014 LLC v Sequana S.A.*[35] Rose J said:

16–026

> "If a person or a company has plenty of assets left with which to meet the claim, then however many additional assets are gifted to people, he or it cannot have the s 423 purpose. This must be inherent in the wording of section 423(3)(a), and is confirmed by the second limb which refers to action 'otherwise prejudicing the interests of' the claimant, implying that the transaction in the first limb must prejudice those interests too."

If the statutory purpose exists, then the fact that the transaction was entered into without any dishonest intent, or even with the benefit of legal advice to support it, will not save it from a successful challenge. In *Arbuthnot Leasing International Ltd v Havelet Leasing Ltd (No.2)*[36] the business and assets of a company (including leasing agreements that had been financed by the claimant) were transferred to another company in the same group with a view to saving the business and persuading banks to recommence funding. Yet that did not prevent a finding that assets had been deliberately put out of reach of the claimant (to be replaced by an obligation upon the transferee to account for payments under the leasing agreement quarterly in arrears).

16–027

In *Inland Revenue Commissioners v Hashmi*[37] the Court of Appeal confirmed that the statutory purpose under s.423(3) need not be the dominant purpose; but it must be a real, substantial purpose behind the transaction. If the relevant purpose forms only a trivial part of the motive behind it, or can be described as a by-product of a transaction entered into for some other reason, the claim under s.423 will fail.[38] However, a claim may be sustained if the statutory purpose co-exists alongside another substantial reason behind the transaction.

16–028

---

[33] See *Aiglon Ltd v Gau Shan Ltd* [1993] 1 Lloyd's Rep. 164; [1993] B.C.L.C. 1321, 1329, where Hirst J granted a freezing order against the transferee "both on general principles and having regard to the terms of s. 423(2)(b)".

[34] *Inland Revenue Commissioners v Hashmi* [2002] EWCA Civ 981; [2002] 2 B.C.L.C. 489, at [23], and see para.16–034 below.

[35] *BTI 2014 LLC v Sequana S.A.* [2016] EWHC 1686 (Ch), at [517].

[36] *Arbuthnot Leasing International Ltd v Havelet Leasing Ltd (No.2)* [1996] BCC 636, where Scott J remarked that the words "intention" and "motive" might be used interchangeably with that of "purpose".

[37] *Inland Revenue Commissioners v Hashmi* [2002] EWCA Civ 981; [2002] 2 B.C.L.C. 489, at [25], [32], [39]. See also *Kubiangha v Ekpenyong* [2002] EWHC 1567 (Ch); [2002] 2 B.C.L.C. 597, at [12].

[38] In *Papanicola v Fagan* [2008] EWHC 3348 (Ch); [2009] B.P.I.R. 320, at [31]–[34] the wife's threat to bring divorce proceedings and seek ancillary relief was not only fatal to the allegation of undervalue but also undermined the existence of the statutory purpose.

16–029 In *JSC BTA Bank v Ablyazov*[39] the Deputy Judge considered the guidance in *IRC v Hashmi* and expressed the test in relation to the statutory purpose as requiring it to be shown that the transferor was "substantially motivated" by the statutory purpose. He went on to observe that, although a conclusion that the transaction is one that the debtor might well have entered into in any event will not, as a matter of principle, preclude a finding that there was such substantial motivation, the court must in those circumstances be alert not to make such a finding too readily. In the Court of Appeal Leggatt LJ expressed the view that the description of the relevant purpose as "substantial" was not necessary to the decision in *Hashmi* and that it risked causing confusion. The question is simply whether the transaction was entered into by the debtor for the prohibited purpose.[40]

16–030 In *Ablyazov* the Deputy Judge dismissed the s.423 claim on the facts. The gratuitous transfer of £1.1m from an account in the joint names of father and son into an account in the son's sole name was to enable the son to obtain an investment visa in place of his student visa. Although by the date of the transfer the father had been knowingly involved in the dishonest embezzlement of funds from the claimant bank on a massive scale, and the father would have been aware that he would face claims by the bank to make him accountable and to recover assets, the process to obtain the visa had been set in train over a year before. It was also relevant that the amount involved represented approximately 0.03 per cent of the total value of Mr Ablyazov's fraud (so that it was almost de minimis from his perspective) and that the ultimate source of the £1.1m was a BVI company, whose retention of the monies (rather than their transfer into a Swiss and then London bank account) might be said to have been a more effective way of keeping them out of the reach of creditors.[41]

16–031 On the language of the section, the mental state of the *transferee* is irrelevant to whether or not liability is triggered by the statutory purpose.[42] However (as explained in para.16–046 below), the degree of culpability on the part of the transferee may be highly material to the exercise of the court's discretion in relation to the appropriate relief to be granted.

(5) The "Victim"

16–032 Prejudice (actual or potential) from the transaction also serves to delimit who can bring a claim in respect of it. The expression "victim" in s.423(5) is defined with reference to such prejudice, and so is not confined to creditors (whether present or contingent). In *Clydesdale Financial Services v Smailes*[43] David Richards J said:

> "Section 423(5) defines a victim of a transaction as a person 'who is, or is capable of being, prejudiced by it'. In choosing the term 'victim' and this definition, it is I think clear that it was

---

[39] *JSC BTA Bank v Ablyazov* [2016] EWHC 3071 (Comm), at [128]–[142].
[40] [2018] EWCA Civ 1176, at [14].
[41] Upheld on appeal at [2018] EWCA Civ 1176.
[42] *JSC BTA Bank v Ablyazov*, [2016] EWHC 3071 (Comm), at [11].
[43] *Clydesdale Financial Services v Smailes* [2009] EWHC 3190 (Ch); [2010] B.P.I.R. 77; [2010] Lloyd's Rep. IR 577, [73].

intended to be a wider category than simply creditors. The words used are ordinary English words with no technical meaning and the correct approach in any given case is to ask whether, on the facts of the case, the Claimant is a person who is, or is capable of being, prejudiced by the transaction."

Whilst, therefore, many claims under s.423 to unravel an impugned transaction will be brought by judgment creditors of the transferor/debtor, and will in substance be an exercise in seeking to recover under an unsatisfied judgment previously obtained against the debtor,[44] the class of claimant is much wider than that of unsatisfied judgment creditors. In particular, a claimant victim need not have been a creditor of the debtor at the time of the transaction, nor need his claim against the debtor yet have been established at the time he brings the s.423 claim (there may be claims where the debtor and the other party to transaction will, as defendants, be seeking to challenge the claimant's standing as a victim)[45]; and the source of the prejudice that constitutes him a victim need not even be a direct claim or other right against the debtor.[46]   **16–033**

Moreover, the statutory purpose need not be directed at the victim who brings the claim, or at any particular victim. If the debtor has acted with a view to prejudicing the interests of *a person* who is making or might make a claim against him, then it does not matter that the eventual claimant under s.423 is a different victim.[47] Indeed, it is not necessary that the debtor should have any creditors at all at the time of the transaction for a claim to lie; s.423 catches transactions designed to protect the debtor against future but unknown creditors, so long as the statutory purpose is made out.[48] Furthermore, although it seems unlikely that the court would risk acting in vain by granting relief in later proceedings in the absence of an established victim, it should be noted that the term "victim" does not find expression in the subsections which actually trigger the court's jurisdiction to make an order reversing the transaction. In *Hill v Spread Trustee Ltd*[49] Arden LJ observed: **16–034**

"It is correct that normally the court would consider that it was not proportionate to hear an application unless it could be shown at that date that there was a person who could benefit by a positive finding under s 423. But there are bound to be cases where that cannot be shown, perhaps because the person who seems to have been prejudiced has to establish his claim in foreign proceedings, or because there are creditors whose claims have not yet matured into present debts. Here the Revenue has grounds for saying that they were deceived as to Mr Nurkowski's means and as to his ability to raise loans from the settlement. There is as it seems

---

[44] See, for example, *Ali v Bashir* [2014] EWHC 3853 (Ch), at [12]–[13] and [36], where the claimant's entitlement to recover costs from the debtor meant there was no dispute that he was a victim.

[45] In *Pinewood Joinery v Starelm Properties Ltd* [1994] 2 B.C.L.C. 412, 418, the court rejected the argument that the applicants could not be victims when they had yet to establish themselves to be judgment creditors, but nevertheless found that they were incapable of being prejudiced by the transaction when the value of the transferred property was greatly exceeded by the value of the bank's security over it.

[46] *Clydesdale Financial Services v Smailes*, above, was a case where the victim was "indirectly" prejudiced, being an insurer of the creditor with the claim against the debtor.

[47] *4 Eng v Harper* [2009] EWHC 2633 (Ch), at [22], per Sales J and *Fortress Value Recovery Fund I LLC v Blue Skye Special Opportunities Fund LP* [2013] EWHC (Comm), at [111].

[48] *Midland Bank Plc v Wyatt* [1997] 1 B.C.L.C. 242, at 253.

[49] *Hill v Spread Trustee Ltd* [2006] EWCA Civ 542; [2007] 1 W.L.R. 2404, at [136].

to me a deliberate avoidance of the term "victim" in s 423(1) and (3), which set out the conditions which have to be satisfied before the court can make an order under s 425. On the contrary, all that has to be shown is that the person is making or may at some time make a claim (see s 423(3)(a) and (b))."

16–035   Importantly, to qualify as a "victim" under the section the claimant must be a victim both of the improper statutory purpose *and* of the undervalue:

"the undervalue is not merely a piece of background which happens to exist but which does not contribute to the injustice; it is at the heart of the injustice, or prejudice".[50]

So in a case where the putative victim would have suffered prejudice from the impugned transaction even had it taken place at full value, it could not claim under the section.[51]

(6)   The Claim and the Relief

16–036   As we have noted, s.424 of the Insolvency Act 1986 identifies those who may apply for relief under s.423. If the debtor has been made bankrupt or been wound up, then the claim may be brought, as appropriate, by the official receiver, trustee in bankruptcy, liquidator or administrator, or (with the permission of the court)[52] by a victim of the transaction. In all other cases, a victim of the transaction may bring a claim without the need for the court's permission. As we have seen, a "victim" of the transaction is defined broadly by s.423(5) as "a person who is, or is capable of being, prejudiced by it."

16–037   Whether the application is made by an office-holder of an insolvent estate or by an individual victim, s.424(2) provides that the application is to be treated as made on behalf of every victim of the transaction. Just as a freezing injunction does not secure any priority over the frozen assets for a claimant who suspected something akin to the s.423 purpose at a stage when he was able to pre-empt the feared transaction, so too a private (non-office holder) claimant under s.423 must share the fruits of any success with any other victims of any transaction which is later sought to be undone, provided those victims are identified.

16–038   The claimant's need to establish the statutory purpose under s.423(3) (see paras 16–024–16–029 above) is such that that the "debtor" will invariably be named as a defendant to the claim and the relief sought will usually begin with a declaration that the transaction in question was one within the scope of the section. However, although the debtor can be presumed to have interests allied to the other party to the transaction, in resisting such declaration—and relief consequential to it—it is the other party who is the true defendant to the claim. Prima facie, the other party to the impugned transaction, as the recipient of the

---

[50] *Westbrook Dolphin Square Ltd v Friends Life Ltd* [2014] EWHC 2433 (Ch); [2015] 1 W.L.R. 1713, per Mann J at [405]–[406].

[51] Above. See also *Vasdev v Bellnorth Ltd (In Liquidation)* [2017] EWHC 1395 (Ch).

[52] For an example of such permission being granted to a creditor of company in liquidation (and where there had been no proceedings brought by the liquidator despite there being matters surrounding the transaction which required investigation) see *Re Ayela Holdings Ltd* [1993] B.C.L.C. 256.

benefit under it, will be expected to disgorge that benefit. In a claim brought by an office holder, the absence of any direct financial interest on the part of the debtor in the grant or refusal of such consequential relief will be obvious from the fact that his property (including any attendant chose in action arising under s.423) will have vested for the benefit of the insolvent estate.[53] For all types of claim, including one brought by an individual victim, the absence of an interest on the part of the debtor which is equivalent to that of the other party to the transaction is also clear from the language of s.423(2).

Section 423(2) provides as follows: **16–039**

> "Where a person has entered into such a transaction, the court may, if satisfied under the next subsection, make such order as it thinks fit for—
> (a)   restoring the position to what it would have been if the transaction had not been entered into, and
> (b)   protecting the interests of persons who are victims of the transaction. "

It is clear that limbs (a) and (b) of s.423(2) are to be read conjunctively: the   **16–040**
purpose of any relief granted should be *both* the restorative one of restoring the position to what it would have been but for the transaction *and* the protective one of protecting the interests of victims. The reference to the court making "such order as it thinks fit" for these purposes is, however, subject to the provisions of s.425(2) (see para.16–045 below), which provide that any order shall not prejudice any interest acquired (otherwise than from the debtor) in good faith, for value and without notice of the relevant circumstances. Accordingly, the power under s.423(2) "is a power to restore and protect as far as is practicable".[54]

Section 425(1) lists various types of relief that may be granted. The potential   **16–041**
relief includes the vesting of any property transferred (or any proceeds from its sale) in the applicant, the disgorgement of any benefits received under the transaction and the release or discharge of any security that may have been given under the transaction. The list is a non-exhaustive one and is not intended to limit the broad scope of s.423(2). In *Re Krug International (UK) Ltd*[55] HH Judge Purle QC noted that s.423(2) "gives the court great flexibility in fashioning an appropriate remedy". The court was there prepared to recognise that if the transfer of stock back to the defendant in return for the restoration of a cancelled debt was not practicable, the section was wide enough to permit an order that the defendant to pay compensation after giving credit for the true value of the stock. If the debtor/transferor were to transfer real property worth, say £1million, for only £500,000, this reasoning would support an order requiring the other party to restore the difference between the value of the property and the consideration paid, rather than seeking to unravel the transaction (which might in any event be problematic).

---

[53] Compare *Heath v Tang* [1993] 1 W.L.R. 1421.
[54] *Chohan v Saggar* [1994] 1 B.C.L.C. 706, at 713A, per Nourse LJ. At first instance ([1992] BCC 750) Evans Lombe J had observed that it would only be in an exceptional case where it would not be appropriate to grant any remedy on the basis that an order would be otiose in the sense of being incapable of conferring any benefit for victims.
[55] *Re Krug International (UK) Ltd* [2008] EWHC 2256 (Ch); [2008] B.P.I.R. 1512, at [37].

16–042   In *4 Eng v Harper*[56] Sales J described the nature of the relief provided for by s.425 as follows:

> "A claim under s 423 is a claim for some appropriate form of restorative remedy, to restore property to the transferor for the benefit of creditors, who may then seek to execute against that property in respect of obligations owed by the transferor to them. In an appropriate case, an order might be made to require the transferee to pay sums or transfer property direct to the creditors, if the position in relation to execution is clear and any further costs associated with execution ought to be avoided. But often the appropriate order will be for the transferee to pay sums or transfer property back to the transferor, leaving the distribution of those sums or property as between the creditors of the transferor to be governed by the general law. This may be particularly important if the transferor is bankrupt or in liquidation (or about to become bankrupt or go into liquidation) and has a range of creditors not all of whom are before the court on the application made under s 423."

16–043   This passage in *4 Eng v Harper* together with the Court of Appeal's observations in *Chohan v Saggar* about the objective of s.423 were cited with approval by Rose J in *BTI 2014 LLC v Sequana S.A.*[57] The judge noted that the principle to be derived from that case law is that the overriding purpose of s.423 is to recover assets for the victims so as to protect their interests. Notwithstanding that s.423(2)(a) directs attention to what the position would have been if the transaction had not been entered into, she rejected the submission that the impossibility of unravelling all the matters that had occurred since the payment of the impugned dividend was a reason to refuse to grant any relief on the ground of change of circumstances. She also rejected the submission that relief should be limited with reference to the liability which the debtor company had contractually assumed towards the claimant victim under a compromise agreement entered into after the impugned transaction (a dividend). The victim had claimed a right of indemnity from the debtor company with respect to certain environmental clean-up costs, which right was disputed and had not been established at the time of the dividend. After the dividend (and after the s.423 proceedings had commenced), separate proceedings in which that right of indemnity was in issue were compromised by an agreement between the debtor company and various putative victims, who were directly or indirectly liable for the clean-up costs, which provided for a more limited obligation on the part of the debtor to indemnify the claimant. The defendant recipient of the dividend argued that its liability to return the dividend should be capped with reference to this new, more limited, indemnity obligation, which was the limit of the relevant prejudice that the victims of the transaction could have suffered; but the Judge concluded that the dividend should be repaid to the full extent that the claimant victims were out of pocket in meeting clean-up costs. The compromise did not determine the full extent of the relevant prejudice when it was itself "influenced" by the payment of the dividend.

---

[56] *4 Eng v Harper* [2009] EWHC 2633 (Ch); [2010] B.P.I.R. 746, at [9].
[57] *BTI 2014 LLC v Sequana S.A.* [2017] EWHC 211 (Ch), at [23]–[24]: the judgment following the "Consequentials Hearing". For "the Main Judgment" see [2016] EWHC 1686 (Ch) referred to at paras 16–021—16–026 above.

The decision[58] suggests that the court will take a broad and flexible approach to identifying the prejudice to victims of the transaction that needs to be addressed by its award of relief. Mrs Justice Rose said[59]: **16–044**

> "I do not read Sales J's judgment in *4Eng* as indicating that the remedy under section 423 cannot go further than the value of any obligations of the transferor to the victims at the time when the court comes to consider the imposition of the remedy. Such a principle would risk creating an unfairness to the victims where, as here, a substantial period of time has elapsed between the date of the impugned transaction and the date when the remedy is devised and where the relationship between the various parties has changed in ways which have, at the least, been influenced by the fact that the impugned transaction took place. The 4Eng judgment was not intended to limit the exercise of the court's discretion in the way suggested. Such a conclusion would be inconsistent with the passages in that judgment and in the other case law referring to the need for the relief to be carefully tailored to the justice of the particular case and to the absence of any 'hard and fast rules' that might impede a just result. A focus on the specific debt owed at any particular time by the transferor to the victim is also inconsistent with the comment of Arden LJ in *Hill v Spread Trustee* [2006] EWCA Civ 542 ('Hill v Spread Trustee'). Arden LJ noted in paragraph 101 that the definition of 'victim' in section 423(5): ' ...is not restricted to creditors with present or actual debts: whether a person is a victim turns on actual or potential prejudice suffered. The definition of 'victim' is employed in relation to the criteria for relief in subs (2). It is not used in subs (3), which defines the necessary purpose.'"

As noted above, the court's ability to grant relief is qualified by s.425(2), which, despite what is otherwise the general width of the jurisdiction, operates to prevent it making an order which would operate to prejudice the interests of, or impose any payment obligation upon, any third party who was not a party to the transaction with the debtor and who, in effect, is "equity's darling", through having acted in good faith, for value and without notice of the relevant circumstances giving rise to the claim.[60] As the transferee (taking directly from the debtor and a party to the transaction with him) clearly cannot claim the status of a bona fide purchaser *for sufficient value*, given that the element of undervalue will already have been established, the ignorance or otherwise on the part of the transferee of the purpose behind the transaction cannot be material to whether or not a transaction falls within s.423 so as to be susceptible to reversal or the grant of other relief under s.425. **16–045**

However, *4 Eng v Harper*[61] shows that the innocence or otherwise of the transferee may well be relevant to the scope of any relief which is granted under s.425. The transferee may, at one end of the scale, be in the position of an unwitting volunteer who may have changed his position in relation to the asset transferred or, at the other, be in the position of a knowing recipient who is prepared to further the attempt to cheat the debtor's creditors. However, if the transferee is somewhere in the middle of the scale and (whilst not having been guilty of any dishonesty) has knowingly participated in the transaction, then the **16–046**

---

[58] Which, it should be noted, is subject to appeal on this point, as well as on the question of whether the dividend was a transaction at an undervalue at all.

[59] *BTI 2014 LLC v Sequana S.A*, at [39].

[60] See, for example, the formulation of the relief in *Arbuthnot Leasing International Ltd v Havelet Leasing Ltd* (No. 2) [1990] BCC 636, 645G and *Chohan v Saggar* [1994] 1 B.C.L.C. 706, 715D-G (protecting, respectively, the interests of creditors of the transferee who had become such after the date of the transfer and the legal chargee of the transferee who had advanced monies under its charge).

[61] *4 Eng v Harper*, at [13]–[14].

interests of the victims should prevail in all but the exceptional case.[62] In *4 Eng* itself, the court found that the wife to whom the husband had transferred the property was not aware of the original purpose behind the transfer, but that she had later lied about its beneficial ownership so as to dissuade the creditor from enforcing against the husband's share. She was ordered not only to transfer the legal title back into their joint names but also to make a money payment to reflect the fall in the property's value after her act of deceit.

16–047 In *Rubin v Dweck*[63] Registrar Jones cited what he described as the obiter dicta in *4 Eng v Harper* in observing that:

> "account should be taken (amongst other matters) of the mental state of the transferee and the degree of their involvement in the fraudulent scheme of the debtor/transferor".

In relation to the change of position defence, the Registrar said:

> "In exceptional cases the court can exercise its discretion by withholding relief even though the requirements of the section are otherwise satisfied, for example in cases when it is appropriate to take into account a change of position defence by a recipient acting in good faith (see *Re Ramrattan (In Bankruptcy)* [2010] EWHC 1033 (Ch), 1059 and *Trustee in Bankruptcy of Claridge v Claridge and anor.* [2011] EWHC 2047 (Ch); [2011] B.P.I.R. 1529)."

C. FALSE OR MISLEADING LISTING PARTICULARS OR PROSPECTUSES

(1) Introduction

16–048 Section 90 of FSMA now contains the law relating to liability for untrue or misleading statements in listing particulars or prospectuses for shares and other securities. It is the latest in a line of statutory provisions which have widened the basis for recovery with respect to such statements relative to that available under a common law action for deceit.[64] The decision of Lightman J in *Possfund Custodian Trustee Ltd v Diamond*[65] contains a useful summary of this statutory overlay and its evolution since the decision in the well-known case of *Derry v Peek*[66] and other late nineteenth century authorities.

16–049 The introductory provisions of s.90 are as follows:

> "(1)   Any person responsible for listing particulars is liable to pay compensation to a person who has –
>
> (a)   acquired securities to which the particulars apply; and
> (b)   suffered loss in respect of them as a result of –
> (i)   any untrue or misleading statement in the particulars; or
> (ii)   the omission from the particulars of any matter required to be included by section 80 or 81.
> (2)   Subsection (1) above is subject to exemptions provided by Schedule 10. "

---

[62] *BTI 2014 LLC v Sequana S.A.* [2017] EWHC 211 (Ch), at [25].
[63] *Rubin v Dweck* [2012] B.P.I.R. 854, at [13]. See also *BTI 2014 LLC v Sequana S.A.* [2017] EWHC 211 (Ch), at [25].
[64] For the limitations which apply to a claim at common law in deceit, see Ch.1.
[65] *Possfund Custodian Trustee Ltd v Diamond* [1996] 2 All E.R. 774, 781f–783g.
[66] *Derry v Peek* (1889) 14 App Cas 337.

If the listing particulars are required to include information about the absence of a **16–050** particular matter then the absence of such information is to be treated as a statement that there is no such matter: s.90(3).

Listing particulars apply of course to listed securities. The provisions outlined **16–051** above also apply with modifications to any prospectus for "transferable securities", which are not listed on the London Stock Exchange but which are offered to the public or admitted to an EU regulated market.[67] Such transferable securities include units in an open-ended collective investment scheme and specified classes of non-equity transferable securities. However, a person is not to be subject to a liability on the basis of a summary in the prospectus[68] unless that summary, when read with the rest of the prospectus, is misleading, inaccurate or inconsistent (or it fails to provide key information specified elsewhere in the statute).[69] Liability in relation to key investor information produced in relation to a collective investment scheme (or a sub-fund of one) is addressed by its own section.[70]

(2) Potential Defendants

The potential liability under s.90 (and s.90ZA) is directed at "any person **16–052** responsible" for the listing particulars (or prospectus). The FCA's Prospectus Rules[71] identify the following as those responsible for equity issues:

(1) the issuer;
(2) if the issuer is a corporate body:
    (i) each person who is a director of the issuer when the prospectus is published;
    (ii) each person who has authorised himself to be named, and is named, in the prospectus as a director or as having agreed to become a director either immediately or at a future time; and
    (iii) each person who is a senior executive of any external management company of the issuer;
(3) each person who accepts, and is stated in the prospectus as accepting, responsibility for the prospectus;
(4) the offeror, if this is not the issuer and, if the offeror is a company, each person who is a director when the prospectus is published;

---

[67] Section 90(11)-(12). Section 102A of FSMA defines the "securities" *governed by listing particulars* by reference to any which have been or may be admitted to the official list but so as to exclude those "transferable securities" covered by a prospectus (s.102A(3)).

[68] A prospectus must have a summary unless the transferable securities in question are ones in relation to which the prospectus rules provide that one is not required: s.87A(5). The requirements of a summary and, from 1 July 2012, the inclusion of key information within them are the result of the Prospectus Directive 2003/71/EC (amended by 2010/73/EU) and regulations made in compliance with them.

[69] Section 90(12).

[70] Section 90ZA.

[71] See r.5.5.3, which also applies to warrants or options to subscribe for equities and transferable securities having similar characteristics. The Prospectus Rules are made under s.84(4) of FSMA. See r.5.5.4 for those responsible for other kinds of transferable securities.

(5) the person requesting admission, if this is not the issuer; and if that person is a company, each person who is a director when the prospectus is published; and

(6) each person not falling within any of the previous paragraphs who has authorised the contents of the prospectus.

16–053 It is clear from s.90(8) of FMSA, and probably also from the last category of person identified in the Prospectus Rules, that a "promoter" of a company may fall within the class of persons potentially liable under s.90; but (as s.90(8) provides) the liability of a person[72] by reason of being a promoter or otherwise in respect of any failure to disclose does not extend to anything that he would not be required to disclose in listing particulars if he were responsible for them, or anything which he is entitled to omit by virtue of s.82. The expression "promoter" is not statutorily defined; but it probably captures all the activities described by Bowen J in *Whaley Bridge Calico Printing Co v Green* as follows[73]:

> "The term promoter is a term not of law, but of business, usefully summing up in a single word a number of business operations familiar to the commercial world by which a company is generally brought into existence. In every case the relief granted must depend on the establishment of such relations between the promoter and the birth, formation and floating of the company as render it contrary to good faith that the promoter should derive a secret profit from the promotion."

(3) Elements of Liability

16–054 Compensation under s.90 is payable in circumstances where a person has acquired securities to which the listing particulars or prospectus applies and has suffered loss as a result of any untrue or misleading statement, or omission, within the document.[74] This is the latest in a series of successive statutory provisions which recognised and codified a prospectus-based liability of a type familiar to the common law, but (as demonstrated by the outcome in *Derry v Peek*[75]) only on the narrower basis of deceit. In a book on civil fraud it is sensible

---

[72] Which includes any other person being entitled to be granted any civil remedy or to rescind or repudiate an agreement: s.90(9). Compare *Erlanger v New Sombrero Phosphate Co* (1878) 3 App Cas 1218. In the absence of fraud on the part of the promoter, rescission of any agreement entered into by the company during the course of its promotion will be refused where the parties cannot be restored to their original position: *Lagunas Nitrate Co v Lagunas Syndicate* [1899] 2 Ch. 392, at 433–434 (where, on the facts, the cause of the loss was not attributable to a misleading prospectus).

[73] *Whaley Bridge Calico Printing Co v Green* (1879) 5 Q.B.D. 109, 111. A claim by the company for recovery of the promoter's secret profit. The fiduciary relationship between a promoter and the company was established in *Erlanger v New Sombrero Phosphate Co* (1878) 3 App Cas 1218, at 1236, per Lord Cairns.

[74] However, for claims based upon any summary in a prospectus the burden is greater as (unless key information is missing) the test is whether the summary "when read with the rest of the prospectus" is misleading, inaccurate or inconsistent: s.90(12). For the requirements of such a summary, when read with the rest of the prospectus, see s.87A(6).

[75] *Derry v Peek* (1889) 14 App Cas 337. It was the directors' honest but incorrect belief that the company did have the right to use steam power instead of horses which led to them escaping liability for a statement to that effect in the prospectus by reference to Lord Herschell's authoritative exposition (at 374) of the ingredients of deceit. This type of outcome was swiftly reversed by the Directors Liability Act 1890 (more recent statutory predecessors of s.90 being s.67 of the Companies

to point out (as indeed Lord Herschell did in *Derry v Peek* in relation to the common law claim)[76] that "it matters not that there was no intention to cheat or injure the person to whom the statement was made."

The important point of departure from the common law claim is of course that the **16–055** statutory liability under s.90 does not depend upon the dishonest state of mind required for a claim in deceit.[77] Instead, liability depends simply upon whether an untrue or misleading statement, or omission, within the purview of the section has been made and whether a person who has acquired securities has suffered loss as a result. That liability is then subject to the exemptions provided for in Sch.10 of FSMA,[78] which rest essentially upon the person who might otherwise be liable satisfying the court that he had a reasonable belief (having made such enquiries as were reasonable) that the statement was not untrue or misleading, or that the omission was proper, and that such belief continued until either the matter was corrected or the securities were acquired.[79] There is also an exemption from liability in the case of those who may be very loosely described as "knowing investors".

It is clear from s.90(1) that the liability may arise not only out of a positive **16–056** statement which is untrue or misleading, but also from the omission of any matter that is required to be included within listing particulars or "key information" required to be included in a prospectus.[80] FSMA specifies by other sections the matters to be included within these documents (in addition to any specifically required by listing rules or by the Financial Conduct Authority): for the listing particulars and supplementary listing particulars the relevant sections in FSMA are ss.80 and 81,[81] and for prospectuses it is s.87A. The focus in these parallel provisions is upon the provision of information which would reasonably be required by an investor for the purpose of making an informed assessment of the issuer and of the rights attaching to its securities (s.80(1)), or to enable the investor to understand the securities to which the prospectus relates and to decide whether to consider the offer further (ss.87(9) and (10)). As the specified key information for inclusion within any prospectus makes clear, the information is directed to the investor being able to make an informed assessment of the essential characteristics of and risks associated with the issuer and with the investment in the securities.

Act 1985 and s.150 of the Financial Services Act 1986). Compare now the stricter conditions for an exemption from liability under paras 1 and 2 of Sch.10 to FSMA: see the following paragraph.

[76] *Derry v Peek*, at 374.

[77] As noted in Section D below, the wider potential liability on the part of the issuer for any omission from "published information" under s.90A requires dishonesty: paras. 3(3) and (5) of Sch.10A.

[78] Subsections 90(2) and (5).

[79] Paragraphs 1 and 3 of Sch.10. There is also an exemption based upon reasonable reliance upon statements made by experts (paras 2 and 4) and official statements (para.5).

[80] Reflecting this and by way of shorthand in the context of the various exemptions from liability, para.1 of Sch.10 to FSMA provides that a "statement" includes not only an untrue or misleading one but also the omission of any matter required to be included.

[81] Section 90(4)-(5) addresses separately the liability that may arise if there is a "significant change" affecting any matter (caught by s.80, listing rules or FCA rules) between the preparation of the listing particulars and commencement of dealing in the securities. And there is a discrete defence based upon a reasonable belief that the change or new matter was not such as to call for supplementary listing particulars: para.7 of Sch.10.

16–057   There is an argument that the failure to comply with the provisions of ss.80–81 or 87A could also support a case for the Financial Conduct Authority seeking a restitution order under s.382 of FSMA, in respect of profit accrued or loss suffered, against any person who has knowingly contravened a "relevant requirement". However, in circumstances where listing rules are excluded from those rules which, when breached, may give rise to a breach of statutory duty claim under s.138D of FSMA, it is clear that there is no private cause of action available to an individual investor in respect of such a failure, otherwise than under s.90.[82]

16–058   The provisions of s.90 in relation to compensation do not affect any liability which may be incurred apart from the section.[83]

(4) Potential Claimants

16–059   The liability under s.90 arises in favour of any person who acquired relevant securities and suffered loss in respect of them as a result of any untrue or misleading statement, relevant omission or failure to comply with s.81: ss.90(1) and (4).

16–060   Eligibility to claim compensation under the section does not rest upon the common law concepts of inducement and reliance, which is consistent with the statutory liability being imposed in the interests of investor protection. Instead, Sch.10 puts the onus on the defendant to satisfy the court that the claimant acquired the securities with knowledge of the relevant misstatement, omission or failure if he is to escape liability.[84] However, it is plainly not sufficient for the subscriber to show that the investment has been disadvantageous, or is otherwise regretted; a causal link to the wrongdoing must be established by showing that the loss has been suffered "as a result of" it. If the securities are worth less as a result of anything untrue, misleading or omitted, the claimant need not be the original purchaser of them: there being no requirement to establish inducement or reliance, the section is wide enough to permit a claim by a later buyer of the securities on the market; but, given the causation requirement, such a claim is probably only likely to succeed if the statutory breach emerges while the securities are in his ownership.[85] The greater the distance in time between the

---

[82] Section 138D(5)(a) of FSMA and see *Hall v Cable & Wireless* [2009] EWHC 1793 (Comm); [2010] 1 B.C.L.C. 95, [12]–[22]. Obviously there may be cases where the contravention of a requirement which *is* actionable by a "private person" under what is now s.138D of FSMA is one that involves fraudulent conduct. However, in circumstances where no particular mental state on the part of the wrongdoer is required for any such breach of statutory duty claim, s.138D is not given separate treatment in this chapter.

[83] Section 90(6). Perhaps the most obvious one is a claim for rescission on the basis of misrepresentation or damages for deceit: compare *Re Leeds & Hanley Theatres Of Varieties Ltd* [1902] 2 Ch. 809, 814 (a case of a fraudulent prospectus).

[84] See para.6 of Sch.10. Its terms are such that it perhaps most obviously applies to those subscribers who are somehow involved in the wrongdoing.

[85] In *Possfund Custodian Trustee Ltd v Diamond* [1996] 2 All E.R. 774, 783, Lightman J made the obiter observation that under the predecessor provision in s.150 of the Financial Services Act 1986 "protection was afforded to all purchasers of listed securities (whether placees or after-market

offending publication and the after-market purchase, the greater the likely difficult in establishing that it (as opposed to other more general market or risk factors) was the cause of the loss.

For the purposes of testing eligibility to claim, the "acquisition" of securities expressly includes contracting to acquire them or any interest in them: s.90(7). This would extend to agreeing to acquire the security under a contract for the allotment of shares and also to the purchase of a derivative in the security, such as a call or put option, a subscription right or stock purchase warrant[86]; but not to the purchase of a right whose value is merely fixed or partly fixed by reference to the value of the security.

16–061

(5) Compensation

The compensation payable under ss.90(1) and (4) is referable to the "loss in respect of [the securities] as a result of" the untrue or misleading statement, omission or failure to comply with s.81. This language clearly suggests a tortious (reliance-based) measure of damages rather than a contractual (expectation-based) one—that is, the statute does not appear to envisage compensation for any loss of bargain that might exist regardless of the mis-selling.

16–062

However, there remains a potential question as to whether the compensation should be measured as if the defendant were liable to pay damages for deceit, or instead by reference only to the element of overpayment for the securities (or interest in them) which is attributable to the inaccurate or defective listing particulars or prospectus. Damages for deceit may include all losses which the claimant has directly incurred as a result of being induced to acquire the securities on the basis of it, whether or not foreseeable and assessed with the benefit of hindsight, and can, in appropriate circumstances, extend beyond the element of overvaluation attributable to the deceit assessed as at the date of purchase.[87] Although the phrase "suffered loss ... as a result of" might be said to be ambiguous in this regard, it is suggested that the better view is that it is only the element of overpayment—the mispricing—that is recoverable, particularly because the language of the section is suggestive of a direct causal link between the misstatement or omission and the loss, and because liability does not depend upon establishing fraud or intended inducement of the claimant.

16–063

---

purchasers)". Teare J (again obiter) "assumed likewise" in relation to s.90 in *Hall v Cable & Wireless* [2009] EWHC 1793 (Comm); [2010] 1 B.C.L.C. 95, [20].

[86] As noted in fn.41 above, the FCA's Prospectus Rules apply also to warrants and options to subscribe for equities and similar transferable securities.

[87] *Smith New Court Securities v Scrimgeour Vickers (Asset Management) Ltd* [1997] A.C. 254, 266–267, per Lord Browne-Wilkinson. See generally Ch.22.

D.   THE LIABILITY OF ISSUERS

16–064   Separate from but closely allied to any liability under s.90 of FSMA—addressed in Section C above—is the potential liability of an issuer of securities which have been admitted to trading (on a UK securities market or of a UK company traded on an overseas exchange).

16–065   Section 90A and Sch.10A of FSMA make provision for this liability, which exists alongside potential liability for breach of contract, under the Misrepresentation Act 1967 or for negligent misstatement.[88]

16–066   An issuer of securities may be liable under these provisions for an untrue or misleading statement, or the omission of any matter required to be included, within information published and announcements made by it in connection with those securities. The expression "published information" is given an extensive statutory definition, which includes information provided through a recognised information service for the market in question.[89] For these purposes, the term "issuer" also covers those who propose to issue securities.[90] However, such is the close alliance with s.90, this liability in relation to "published information" cannot duplicate or widen any liability which has arisen under s.90 because the information is contained in listing particulars or a prospectus.[91]

16–067   The language of s.90A is similar to that of s.90(1) in providing for liability to pay compensation to a person who has suffered loss as a result of a misleading statement or omission in published information (or, under s.90A, a delay in publishing information). But an important distinction is that s.90A requires the omission or delay to be *dishonest*: the issuer will be liable in respect of an untrue or misleading statement in such published information only if there is an element of deceit on the part of someone with managerial responsibility (that is, where such a person knew the statement to be untrue or misleading or was reckless as to whether it was untrue or misleading); and liability in respect of any omission from published information, or a delay in providing it, will not arise unless a person discharging managerial responsibilities within the issuer knew the omission to be a dishonest concealment of a material fact or acted dishonestly in delaying the publication (as the case may be).[92] For these purposes "dishonesty" has both an objective and subjective element: a person's conduct is dishonest

---

[88] These other forms of liability (as well as liability under s.90, liability under rules made by virtue of s.954 of the Companies Act 2006, liability to a civil penalty and criminal liability) are preserved by para.7(3) of Sch.10A. Otherwise, para.7(1) provides that the issuer is not subject to any liability (which includes being subject to rescission or repudiation of an agreement) other than that provided for by paras 3 and 5 in respect of statements, omissions or delays in publication which are covered by Sch.10A.

[89] Schedule 10A, para.2.

[90] Section 102A(6).

[91] Schedule 10A, para.4: if the issuer is liable under s.90 in respect of the particular statement or omission, then it cannot be liable under Sch.10A, para.3.

[92] Schedule 10A, paras 3(2) and (3) and 5(2).

only if it is regarded as dishonest by persons who regularly trade on the securities market in question and the person was aware or must be taken to have been aware that it was so regarded.[93]

In further contrast to a claim under s.90, the claimant is required to show that he **16–068** actually and reasonably relied upon the statement or omission in acquiring, continuing to hold or disposing of the securities.[94] In both respects, the basis of liability on the part of the issuer is much closer to the common law liability in deceit under *Derry v Peek*.[95]

---

[93] Schedule 10A, para.6.
[94] Schedule 10A, para.3(4).
[95] Compare the observations about the nature of the liability under s.90 (including exemptions from it) in paras 16–054—16–058 above. It follows from the stricter test for liability under s.90A, including the need for the claimant to establish reliance, that the "knowing investor" exemption does not feature in Sch.10A.

SECTION D

LIABILITY FOR OR THROUGH OTHERS

CHAPTER 17

AN INTRODUCTION TO THE KEY CONCEPTS

A. INTRODUCTION

It is in the nature of frauds that those who perpetrate them often seek to disguise **17–001** or conceal their involvement and to secrete the proceeds. One of the ways in which it is common for fraudsters to achieve these aims is to act through, or with the assistance of, others; those others are sometimes human, but often corporate entities or special purpose vehicles and often incorporated in jurisdictions in which it is difficult to glean information about the corporate structure, how it is operated, by whom and for whose benefit. It is, accordingly, particularly important for the fraud litigator: (i) to have at his fingertips the principles which the law has developed to deal with these tactics, namely principles designed to hold one legal entity responsible for the conduct or state of mind of another and to "see through" complex and obscure corporate or asset-holding structures; and (ii) to be clear-eyed about distinguishing what the law is doing under each of the different principles and to what types of factual situation they do and do not apply.

This section of the book explores the most important of these principles from a **17–002** fraud litigation perspective: (a) piercing the corporate veil; (b) attribution; and (c) joint liability in tort.

Vicarious liability, which is also relevant in this context, is addressed separately **17–003** in the chapters concerned with particular causes of action.[1]

Critical distinctions between these principles, and when they apply, are discussed **17–004** and explained in the relevant chapters; but by way of introduction it is helpful to give an overview of the basic ideas at work, how they differ and why.

B. THE KEY PRINCIPLES DISTINGUISHED

(1) Attribution

Attribution is the legal principle by which the actions or state of mind of one legal **17–005** person, B, are actually attributed to—laid at the door of—another, A, and treated as the actions or state of mind of A himself.[2] The result is that A is not merely

---

[1] See Chs 7 and 13.

[2] It has recently been authoritatively considered and rationalised by the Supreme Court in *Bilta (UK) Ltd (In Liquidation) v Nazir (No.2)* [2015] UKSC 23; [2016] A.C. 1.

liable or responsible for any wrong committed by B, but is treated in law as actually having committed, himself, any wrong which the actions and/or state of mind attributed would entail. That may well be a wrong which B himself has not committed.[3]

(2)   Vicarious Liability

17–006   As we discuss further in Ch.19, attribution is to be critically distinguished from vicarious liability, which is when A will be held *liable* for the completed wrong of another, B. It does not require that A has done anything wrong at all; and it does not require any *attribution* of wrong-doing, actions or states of mind of B to A: it is, instead, a form of strict liability without fault and it arises by operation of a series of rules which determine when (as a matter of policy, in essence) it is right that A should be held liable (or legally responsible) for B's wrong.[4] It is most commonly encountered, at least in the fraud context, as an incident of the law of agency: a company (or individual principal) is liable for the wrongs of its agent committed within the scope of the agency.[5]

(3)   Piercing the Corporate Veil

17–007   The concept of piercing the corporate veil articulates and defines the very limited circumstances in which English law will disregard the separate legal personality of a company[6] (as famously expounded in *Salomon v A Salomon and Co Ltd*[7]) so as to identify that company, its rights, liabilities or assets, with its shareholder(s), their rights, liabilities or assets, for particular purposes.[8] It applies *only*

> "when a person is under an existing legal obligation or liability or subject to an existing legal restriction which he deliberately evades or whose enforcement he deliberately frustrates by interposing a company under his control".[9]

---

[3] Because, for example, although he has the requisite state of mind—which is then attributed to A—B has not performed the act required for a particular wrong to have been committed by B himself. E.g. (in the case of deceit) B may have knowledge that fact X is wrong; but has not himself made a representation to a third party that fact X is correct—that has only been done by A. If B's knowledge of falsity can be attributed to A, then A will have committed the tort of deceit; but B will not have done.

[4] See, in relation to the distinction between attribution and vicarious liability, e.g. Bilta *(UK) Ltd (In Liquidation) v Nazir (No.2)* [2015] UKSC 23; [2016] A.C. 1, per Lord Sumption at [70].

[5] Equally, attribution is to be distinguished from the law in relation to ostensible authority in the law of contract, another facet of the law of agency, by which a principal may be held to be contractually bound to a third party via the acts of his agent.

[6] This principle is, in effect, what we mean by "the corporate veil".

[7] *Salomon v A Salomon and Co Ltd* [1897] A.C. 22.

[8] The doctrine of piercing the corporate veil has recently been clarified and explained by the Supreme Court in *Prest v Petrodel Resources Ltd* [2013] UKSC 34; [2013] 2 A.C. 415.

[9] *Prest* [2013] UKSC 34; [2013] 2 A.C. 415, at [35].

It is, in essence, a principle arising out of the public policy that a party ought not to be able to gain the benefit of a legal principle or privilege (in this case the benefit of the *Salomon* principle and the privilege of trading with limited liability) by, or for, dishonest purposes.

It is vital to appreciate that this is an entirely separate concept from both attribution and vicarious liability: piercing the corporate veil does not involve attributing any action, state of mind or conduct of the shareholder/controller to the company; nor is the company being held liable on a strict no-fault basis for a wrong committed by the shareholder/controller. **17–008**

Equally, as we discuss in detail in Ch.18 it is essential to distinguish veil piercing from both: **17–009**

(1) legitimate use of corporate structures (including in a way which seeks to limit the liability of shareholders for the conduct of the affairs of a company), which is the bedrock of, and essential for, the commercial life of the world, and
(2) a range of situations in which the commission of frauds using or involving company structures is addressed by the courts using other legal principles which do not involve disregarding, but instead respecting, the corporate veil.

This latter range of situations includes not only the principles relating to attribution, vicarious liability and ostensible authority, but also situations in which the court finds that a company or a corporate structure is part of a device or façade concealing the true position as to the beneficial ownership of assets or the rights and liabilities of the company and its owner; or that an asset is held, or actions were undertaken, by a company on behalf of its owner (whether as trustee or nominee or agent). It also includes cases where a shareholder/controller is jointly liable for a wrong with the company he owns/controls. That is but one example of the principles of joint tortfeasorship, our third and final specific chapter in this section. **17–010**

(4) Joint Liability in Tort

A person—be he a shareholder, director, employee or agent of a company—may be jointly liable in tort for a wrong he has committed either as the company's agent or acting jointly with the company. For example, an individual who makes a fraudulent misrepresentation in his capacity as director of a company is jointly liable in deceit with the company,[10] and cannot hide behind the façade of separate corporate personality to evade liability (saying that, because of the capacity in which he made the representation, it is the company and not him which is liable). That is because he himself has made a fraudulent misrepresentation, not because of any application of the veil-piercing doctrine. **17–011**

---

[10] Assuming the conditions are present for the company to be liable for fraudulent misrepresentation, which may involve an application of the principles of attribution.

17–012   But, of course, the principle of joint tortfeasorship goes wider than that—to encompass not only torts committed by officers or employees of companies jointly with those companies, but torts committed by any entities, natural or legal, whose only association may be the joint commission of a wrong.

17–013   As we consider in detail in Ch.20, the most complex situations arise in circumstances in which it is desired to hold a person, A, liable on a joint tortfeasorship basis with a primary tortfeasor, B, whom A has "merely" assisted in the commission of the tort. In this context the law has developed a test pursuant to which A will be liable for the tort jointly with B, if he has assisted in the commission of the tort pursuant to a "common design" that the acts constituting or giving rise to the tort be carried out. The essential feature of this type of liability is that B is not being held liable independently for the *assistance* he has given: he is liable *for the tortious act of A*, because, by reason of the assistance, the law treats him as party to it.

17–014   Again, as is apparent, this is to be contrasted with the principles at play in both the attribution and vicarious liability contexts; and indeed with the principles which operate in other accessory liability situations—e.g. liability for dishonest assistance in a breach of trust or duty and knowing receipt, considered in Chs 12 and 13 above. In those situations, the assistant or recipient *is* being held independently liable for the assistance given, or receipt, in the context of their own dishonesty or knowledge respectively.

CHAPTER 18

PIERCING THE CORPORATE VEIL

A. INTRODUCTION

(1) What is "Piercing the Corporate Veil"?

The fundamental basis of English company law is the principle of separate legal personality authoritatively articulated in *Salomon v A Salomon and Co Ltd*[1] at the end of the 19th century: a company is a separate juridical person from its shareholders; it has rights and liabilities of its own which are distinct from those of its shareholders; and its property is its own, and not that of its shareholders.[2] This principle is of universal application to companies: in particular, there is no exception for so-called "one-man" companies (where the company has a sole shareholder and director)[3]; nor does it matter if any other shareholders are merely nominees of one individual who is in effective control.[4] It is the separate legal personality of a company, as distinct from that of its shareholders, that constitutes the "veil of incorporation".

18–001

The concept of piercing[5] the corporate veil articulates and defines the very limited circumstances in which English law will, notwithstanding the *Salomon* principle, disregard the separate legal personality of a company so as to identify the company, its rights, liabilities or assets, with its shareholder(s), their rights,

18–002

---

[1] *Salomon v A Salomon and Co Ltd* [1897] A.C. 22.

[2] Lord Templeman, writing extra-judicially, described the *Salomon* principle as the "unyielding rock" on which company law is constructed: see *Forty Years On* (1990) 11 Co Law 10. It has been re-affirmed countless times since, most recently in *Prest v Petrodel Resources Ltd* [2013] UKSC 34; [2013] 2 A.C. 415, now the leading case on veil-piercing.

[3] *Macaura v Northern Assurance Co Ltd* [1925] A.C. 619, especially at 626–627; *Prest*, at [8].

[4] See *Salomon*, above, at 45, per Lord Herschell.

[5] Various terminology is used in the case law and commentaries, not all of it consistent and some of it positively confused and confusing. In particular, in many authorities "piercing" and "lifting" the corporate veil are used interchangeably to mean the same thing; but in others "piercing" and "lifting" are used to mean different things (see, for example, the distinction drawn in *Atlas Maritime Co SA v Avalon Maritime Ltd (No.1)* [1991] 4 All E.R. 769, at 779G); and see also *VTB Capital Plc v Nutritek International Corp* [2013] UKSC 5; [2013] 2 A.C. 337, at [118]. In this work, we use the term piercing the corporate veil in the same sense as it is used by the Supreme Court in *Prest* to mean disregarding the presence of the veil—the separate legal personality of the company—to identify the company with its shareholder/controller for a particular purpose. That is the only proper meaning of the term. When considering case law (and commentary), the practitioner must be careful to identify in what sense the court used whatever terminology was adopted. We avoid the use of the word "lifting"; similarly, "peeping behind" the corporate veil, which is also sometimes found in the commentaries.

liabilities or assets, for particular purposes. As it was put by the Court of Appeal in *VTB Capital Plc v Nutritek International Corp*[6]:

> "in cases in which that is done, the authorities show that it will or may lead to the granting of remedies against the company which, veil piercing apart, might appear in principle to be available only against those controlling it; and, equally, against the controllers when they might appear in principle to be available only against the company."[7]

18–003 The very limited circumstances in which the doctrine operates—as recently explained by the Supreme Court in *Prest v Petrodel Resources Ltd*[8]—are considered and explained in section C below.[9] But the doctrine represents something unusual, in that it is one of a few examples where the law permits the abrogation of an otherwise absolute principle in order to avoid someone gaining the benefit of that principle by, or for, dishonest purposes. In this case, it operates to deprive a shareholder/controller or his company of the benefit he would obtain by the operation of the *Salomon* principle, when that benefit has been obtained dishonestly in an attempt to evade the shareholder/controller's proper obligations or liabilities.[10] It is effectively borne of a public policy imperative.[11]

(2) Relevance to Fraud Claims

18–004 The relevance of the doctrine of piercing the corporate veil to fraud litigation is obvious. It is a common incident of fraud that the fraudster will seek, in both the commission of the fraud and in dealing with (and holding) the proceeds of it, to interpose between the fraud and/or its proceeds, on the one hand, and himself, on the other hand, corporate structures which both disguise his involvement and seek to "proof" him from personal liability. Piercing the corporate veil is one of the tools by which the court seeks to deal with such conduct so as to ensure that the victims of fraud do not go without redress. The principles articulated below are therefore an important part of the armoury of the fraud litigator.

---

[6] *VTB Capital Plc v Nutritek International Corp* [2012] EWCA Civ 808; [2012] 2 B.C.L.C. 437.

[7] *VTB Capital*, at [47].

[8] *Prest v Petrodel Resources Ltd* [2013] UKSC 34; [2013] 2 A.C. 415.

[9] From uncertain origins—probably in the case of *Gilford Motor Co Ltd v Horne* [1933] Ch. 935 (considered further in detail below)—via an almost casual, and certainly obiter, remark of Lord Keith of Kinkel in *Woolfson v Strathclyde Regional Council* 1978 SC (HL) 90 (at 96) which has proved influential, the doctrine has had a chequered history, bedevilled by confusions of terminology and, at times, uncertainty as to its very existence. The Supreme Court's decision in *Prest* brings much needed clarity. Accordingly, save insofar as considering certain examples serves to illuminate the test as now articulated in *Prest* (which we do below), it is neither necessary nor helpful to examine the evolving path of the case law.

[10] See *Prest*, at [18].

[11] See *Prest*, at [18] and [35].

B. PIERCING THE CORPORATE VEIL DISTINGUISHED FROM OTHER PRINCIPLES

As explained in Ch.17, it is absolutely critical to a proper understanding of the doctrine, and to the identification by practitioners of situations arising in their cases in which it is and is not appropriate to seek to pierce the corporate veil, to distinguish veil piercing from both:

18–005

(1) Legitimate use of corporate structures (including in a way which seeks to limit the liability of shareholders for the conduct of the affairs of a company), and

(2) A range of situations in which the commission of frauds using or involving company structures is addressed by the courts using other legal principles which do not involve disregarding, but instead respecting, the corporate veil.

(1) The Legitimate use of Corporate Structures

It is the very essence of incorporation that the shareholder/controller of a company limits his liability in relation to the *future* conduct of the company's affairs: in normal circumstances, his liability is limited to the value of his investment in the company, represented by his shares. That is as true of the "one-man" company as it is of public companies. There is nothing wrong with

18–006

that[12]—indeed, it represents the foundation of much of the commercial life of the world.[13] As it was put by Lord Neuberger, delivering the advice of the Privy Council in *Persad v Singh*,[14]

> "one of the reasons that an individual, either on their own or together with others, will take advantage of limited liability is to avoid personal liability if things go wrong".[15]

He continued:

> "if such a factor justified piercing the veil of incorporation, it would make something of a mockery of limited liability both in principle and in practice".[16]

18–007   Equally inherent in the concept of incorporation is the legitimate use of group structures (of companies) specifically designed to minimise liability—or the risk of it—in relation to any particular future activity of the group. That includes, as is common, tax liabilities; but also arrangements of corporate structures which seek to insulate the ultimate beneficial owners of the group and/or other member companies in the group from legal liability that may arise from the *future* conduct of business and to isolate such liability in e.g. a special purpose vehicle, which will often be under-capitalised and asset poor.[17]

---

[12] Because of this (legitimate) advantage of trading through an incorporated entity, incorporation is viewed by the law as "a privilege", not to be abused (there are mechanisms—over and above the doctrine of piercing the corporate veil—by which that privilege can be withdrawn or withheld to a greater or lesser extent: see, for example, the regime for disqualification of directors (which effectively deprives the one-man of a one-man company from trading with the privilege of incorporation if he has shown himself unfit to do so) and s.7(2) of the Companies Act 2006 (which provides that a company may not be formed for an unlawful purpose)). That privilege also has an obverse: just as the shareholder's personal liability for the conduct of the affairs of the company is limited, so is his ability to seek legal redress for wrongs done to the company which diminish the value of his investment: the so-called reflective loss principle, adumbrated in *Johnson v Gore Wood & Co* [2002] 2 A.C. 1, provides that only the company may sue for losses caused to the company (that itself flows from the *Salomon* principle: the separate legal personality of the company means that the wrong done to the company results in a cause of action vested in the company, and only the company).

[13] The general position was articulated by Lord Hoffmann in his speech in *Standard Chartered Bank Plc v Pakistan National Shipping Corp* [2003] 1 A.C. 959, at [36]: "The incorporation of companies is vitally important for commerce since it allows transactions to be entered into and carried out, property to be held and actions to be raised by, or against, a body which continues in existence despite changes in the individuals who conduct or invest in the business. The company is a separate entity, distinct from the directors, employees and shareholders. The law has rightly insisted that the distinction should be duly observed: *Lee v Lee's Air Farming Ltd* [1961] A.C. 12. In particular the company does not act as the agent of the directors and, in general, they do not incur personal liability for the acts of the company or its employees: *Rainham Chemical Works Ltd v Belvedere Fish Guano Co Ltd* [1921] 2 A.C. 465, at 488, per Lord Parmoor." See also, in the context of deciding whether the director/shareholder of a one-man company assumed a duty of care to a third party when operating via the company, the rigorous articulation of the principle in *Williams v Natural Life Foods Ltd* [1998] 1 W.L.R. 830.

[14] *Persad v Singh* [2017] UKPC 32.

[15] *Persad v Singh* [2017] UKPC 32, at [20].

[16] *Persad v Singh* [2017] UKPC 32, at [20].

[17] As expressly endorsed by the Court of Appeal in, for example, *Adams v Cape Industries Plc* [1990] Ch. 433, in which the court said, at 544: "we do not accept as a matter of law that the court is entitled to lift the corporate veil as against a defendant company which is the member of a corporate group

The emphasis on the word "future" in the preceding paragraphs is important, particularly when it comes to the distinction with veil piercing: it encapsulates the attitude which the law takes to corporate structures which seek to minimise or isolate *possible future*, but not *actual present*, legal liabilities. As is explained in more detail below, the law will not condone the use of incorporation as a way of evading existing legal liabilities; but causing future legal liabilities to be incurred by a particular corporate entity for purposes of limiting or isolating liability in that entity is the common currency of international commerce and tax planning.[18] **18–008**

An understanding of the legitimate use of company structures, and the policy imperative of encouraging business enterprise which lies behind it, is essential to enable the practitioner to identify what conduct in a particular fact pattern is and is not objectionable—and, particularly, what, if any, conduct (even if otherwise objectionable) represents an abuse of the *Salomon* principle of separate legal personality such as to engage the veil-piercing doctrine. **18–009**

(2)   Other Principles not Involving Piercing the Corporate Veil

There are a range of situations in which the law addresses the incidence and distribution of liability between a company and its shareholders/controllers— including particularly in the fraud context—which do not involve (and in which there is no question of) piercing the corporate veil. Again, it is vital for the practitioner to be clear-eyed as to the circumstances in which those other principles operate, so as to be able accurately to identify when it is truly appropriate to pierce the corporate veil. That task has been made more difficult due to confusions of language in the case law, the use of language more appropriate to one legal principle in relation to another and, until recently explained by the Supreme Court in *Prest*, misapprehension and mischaracterisation as to whether particular cases have involved veil piercing at all. **18–010**

Nevertheless, as now appears with clarity, the following do not involve—and must be distinguished from—piercing the corporate veil: **18–011**

(1)   Situations in which the court will not be duped by the involvement of a corporate entity (and will "look around" the veil, as it were, but not disregard it) in order to identify the true legal position which a company

---

merely because the corporate structure has been used so as to ensure that the legal liability (if any) in respect of particular future activities of the group (and correspondingly the risk of enforcement of that liability) will fall on another member of the group rather than the defendant company. Whether or not this is desirable, the right to use a corporate structure in this manner is inherent in our corporate law. [It was] urged on us that the purpose of the operation [in this instant case] was in substance that Cape would have the practical benefit of the group's asbestos trade in the United States of America without the risks of tortious liability. This may be so. However, in our judgment, Cape was in law entitled to organise the group's affairs in that manner and ... to expect that the court would apply the principle of Salomon in the ordinary way."

[18] Further, it is worth underlining that the mere fact that a company was, for example, set up in order to hold properties in a tax efficient manner, has fee-paid professional directors and is not a trading entity does not, *of itself*, justify the suggestion that the structure is objectionable, still less that the company's veil can be pierced: see, for example, *Ben Hashem v Al Shayif* [2008] EWHC 2380 (Fam), at [86] and [149].

structure conceals: such as where the court finds that a company or a corporate structure is part of a device or façade[19] concealing the true position as to the beneficial ownership of assets or the rights and liabilities of the company and its owner; or that an asset is held, or actions were undertaken, by a company on behalf of its owner (whether as trustee or nominee or agent). These are the sorts of situation which are most easily confused with veil-piercing; and as such, they are considered in more detail below in section C;

(2) Cases where a shareholder/controller is jointly liable with the company he owns/controls for a wrong he has committed either as the company's agent or acting jointly with the company, such as might be the case when he has made fraudulent representations inducing a third party to contract with his company[20];

(3) Situations in which the court exercises its personal jurisdiction over an owner/controller of a company, usually in equity, to require the owner/controller to procure the company to do or refrain from doing something[21];

(4) The attribution to the company of actions, knowledge or states of mind of a director, employee or other agent of a company[22];

(5) Situations governed by the law of vicarious liability, by which (inter alia) companies are held liable (or legally responsible) for the completed wrongs of its directors, employers or other agents; and

(6) Situations governed by the law relating to ostensible authority, by which a company may be held to be contractually bound to a third party via the acts of his agents.

18–012 With that introduction, we turn to: (i) consider the circumstances in which the court will in fact pierce the corporate veil and (ii) distinguish those circumstances more clearly from those in which the court merely looks to see—legally—the true position a corporate structure conceals. It will be convenient to adopt the nomenclature used by Lord Sumption in *Prest*: the second category—(ii) in the preceding sentence—Lord Sumption calls the "concealment principle". The situations in which it is permissible to pierce the corporate veil—(i) above—are, by contrast, described by reference to the "evasion principle".

---

[19] The word "sham", which is used in some of the cases, is best avoided here: in this context "sham", of course, means a device or façade concealing the true position, not a company which is not "really" or "validly" a company. Nevertheless, it is liable to confuse: see *VTB v Nutriek* in the Court of Appeal—[2012] EWCA Civ 808, at [68].

[20] See *Prest*, at [16]. As discussed in Ch.1 above, it was held in *Standard Chartered Bank Plc v Pakistan National Shipping Corp* [2003] 1 A.C. 959 that an individual who makes a fraudulent misrepresentation in his capacity as director of a company is jointly liable in deceit with the company: see [39]–[41]. He cannot hide behind the façade of separate corporate personality; but that is because he himself has made a fraudulent misrepresentation, not because of any application of the veil-piercing doctrine.

[21] See *Prest*, at [16].

[22] See *Bilta (UK) Ltd (In Liquidation) v Nazir (No.2)* [2015] UKSC 23; [2016] A.C. 1, at [65] (and per contra Lady Hale's apparent solecism in this regard in *Prest*, at [95]). We consider the principles of attribution in Ch.19.

C. PIERCING THE CORPORATE VEIL: THE PRINCIPLE AND ITS ELABORATION

(1) The Basic Principle: The "Evasion Principle"

The only articulated circumstance in which it is permissible under English law to pierce the veil or incorporation was set out by the Supreme Court in *Prest* in these terms: veil piercing is a limited principle which applies

> "when a person is under an existing legal obligation or liability or subject to an existing legal restriction which he deliberately evades or whose enforcement he deliberately frustrates by interposing a company under his control".[23]

18–013

In such circumstances, the court may pierce the corporate veil for the purpose, and only for the purpose, of depriving the company or its controller of the advantage that it would otherwise have obtained by (abuse of) the company's separate legal personality.[24] Further, the court will only pierce the corporate veil if no other route to appropriate relief is available: i.e. if application of more orthodox principles[25] solves the problem before the court, then there is no need to pierce the corporate veil—indeed, it would be wrong to do so, because there is in such a situation no need to invoke public policy to abrogate the otherwise sacrosanct *Salomon* principle to avoid it being taken advantage of dishonestly.[26] This is important because well-known cases in which the doctrine has in fact been applied[27] are situations where, it appears, an alternative route to relief is likely to have been available to the court. Accordingly, although it is not in doubt that the doctrine exists,[28] there is some doubt as to whether any case has come before the English court in which it has been appropriate, on the facts, to pierce the corporate veil. In almost all cases there is an alternative analysis—applying other relevant principles—which would lead to an appropriate result.[29]

18–014

Although there is room for argument as to whether a majority of the Supreme Court in *Prest* coalesced around Lord Sumption's exegesis of the law as encapsulated above, it is probably right (subject to one important caveat) that a

18–015

---

[23] *Prest*, at [35].

[24] In that regard, the Supreme court echoed previous dicta of Munby J in *Ben Hashem v Al Shayif* [2008] EWHC 2380 (Fam), at [164], and Warren J in *Dadourian Group International Inc v Simms* [2006] EWHC 2973 (Ch), at [682].

[25] Such as relevant principles of the law of agency, or nomineeship, or the law of trusts, etc.

[26] *Prest*, at [35], echoing Munby J in *Ben Hashem*.

[27] Such as *Gilford Motor Co Ltd v Horne* [1933] Ch. 935 and (perhaps less clearly) *Jones v Lipman* [1962] 1 W.L.R. 832.

[28] Although Lord Walker doubted its existence in *Prest* (at [106], saying that in his view it was "not a doctrine at all, in the sense of a coherent principle or rule of law", but was a label "to describe the disparate occasions on which some rule of law produces apparent exceptions to the principle of the separate juristic personality of a body corporate reaffirmed ... in *Salomon*"), all the other members of the Court recognised that it did.

[29] As Lord Sumption observed in *Prest*, at [35], the principle "is properly described as a limited one, because in almost every case where the test is satisfied, the facts will in practice disclose a legal relationship between the company and its controller which will make it unnecessary to pierce the corporate veil".

bare majority endorsed Lord Sumption's approach (Lords Neuberger,[30] Mance,[31] and Clarke).[32] The caveat relates to whether the evasion principle is the *only* circumstance in which the veil piercing doctrine can operate in English law. Lord Sumption—and possibly Lord Neuberger[33]—suggested that it was. But Lords Mance and Clarke specifically declined so to hold: they did not wish definitively to close the class of circumstances in which it might be permissible to pierce the corporate veil; but they did underline that any new category of case would be rare, very hard to establish and would probably turn on novel circumstances.[34]

(2)   The Critical Distinction: Evasion vs. Concealment

(i)   Introduction

18–016   As we have already identified, the important point for the practitioner is to distinguish between situations in which it is necessary to pierce the corporate veil and situations which, on analysis, do not require it. Notwithstanding the labels that may have been used in the somewhat confused case law, Lord Sumption was of the view that the cases could in fact be rationalised by reference to the two principles which we have already referred to: the concealment principle and the evasion principle. It is worth for convenience quoting Lord Sumption's summary of the distinction between them:

> "The concealment principle is legally banal and does not involve piercing the corporate veil at all. It is that the interposition of a company or perhaps several companies so as to conceal the identity of the real actors will not deter the courts from identifying them, assuming that their identity is legally relevant. In these cases the court is not disregarding the 'facade', but only looking behind it to discover the facts which the corporate structure is concealing. The evasion principle is different. It is that the court may disregard the corporate veil if there is a legal right against the person in control of it which exists independently of the company's involvement, and a company is interposed so that the separate legal personality of the company will defeat the right or frustrate its enforcement."[35]

18–017   Thus, the distinction between concealment and evasion is the crucial touchstone by which to distinguish situations in which it will be appropriate to pierce the corporate veil; but it is also when the concealment principle is or might be in play that the practitioner will find it most difficult—but therefore most critical—to analyse the factual situation accurately. Lord Sumption conducted an analysis of the somewhat confused case law, identifying which cases where it has popularly been thought the veil has been pierced[36] in fact involved an application of the evasion principle and which only an application of the concealment principle.[37] That analysis, which repays reading in full, is illuminating as to the difference

---

[30] *Prest*, at [60]–[62] and [81].

[31] *Prest*, at [97]–[98].

[32] *Prest*, at [103].

[33] It is not entirely clear from his judgment.

[34] See *Prest*, at [100]–[102] (Lord Mance; the possible example Lord Mance raises as [101] does not strike us as likely to be a good one) and [103] (Lord Clarke).

[35] See *Prest*, at [28].

[36] Including by the Judges who made the relevant decisions!

[37] See *Prest*, at [29]–[34].

between the concealment principle and the evasion principle; and also provides useful examples for the practitioner of situations in which each might be encountered. The key points are extracted below.

(ii) Cases where there is veil piercing: examples of the evasion principle

Gilford Motor Co Ltd v Horne.[38]   Mr Horne had a contractual obligation to the Gilford Motor Co, of which he had been managing director, not to engage in any competing business in a certain area for a certain period after the end of his employment "either solely or jointly with or as agent for any other person, firm or company." He left Gilford and carried on a competing business in the area, initially in his own name. He then formed a company, JM Horne & Co Ltd, named after his wife, in which she and a business associate were shareholders. The Judge found that in reality the company was being used as "the channel through which" Mr Horne was carrying on his business; and that it had been set up in this way to enable the business to be carried on under his own control but without incurring liability for breach of the covenant. The Court of Appeal granted an injunction restraining continued conduct of the business against both Mr Horne and the company.

18–018

As explained by Lord Sumption[39]:

18–019

(1)   As against Mr Horne, the injunction was granted on the concealment principle. Lord Hanworth MR[40] said that the company was a "mere cloak or sham"[41] because the business was really being carried on by Mr Horne. Because the restrictive covenant prevented Mr Horne from competing with his former employers whether as principal or as agent for another, it did not matter whether the business belonged to him or to JM Horne & Co Ltd, provided that he was carrying it on. The only relevance of the interposition of the company was to maintain the pretence that it was being carried on by others.

(2)   As against the company, the court applied the evasion principle,[42] based on the conclusion that the company had been set up as it was to enable the business to be carried on under Horne's own control, but without incurring liability for breach of the covenant: i.e. to evade the *existing* obligation Mr Horne owed to his former employers. Lawrence LJ said that the defendant company was

---

[38] *Gilford Motor Co Ltd v Horne* [1933] Ch. 935.

[39] *Prest*, at [29].

[40] In *Gilford*, at 961–962.

[41] In the sense of being a "device or façade" – see fn. 19 above.

[42] Lord Sumption says that this is clear from the judgments of Lawrence and Romer LJJ, at 965 and 969 in *Gilford*. Lord Neuberger is plainly doubtful as to whether the court in *Gilford* thought that was what they were doing (see *Prest*, at [70]), but agrees (*Prest*, at [69]) that the decision can "fairly be said to have rested on the doctrine if one takes the language of the judgments at face value". The Court of Appeal in *VTB v Nutritek* also considered that this was an example of the application of the doctrine of veil piercing (see [2012] EWCA Civ 808, at [63]).

> "a mere channel used by the defendant Horne for the purpose of enabling him, for his own benefit, to obtain the advantage of the customers of [Gilford], and that therefore the defendant company ought to be restrained as well as the defendant Horne"

i.e. the veil was pierced, and the defendant company was treated as if it too had the same obligation as Mr Horne (such that it was directly enjoined from carrying on the business), in order to ensure that Mr Horne was deprived of the benefit which he might otherwise have derived from the separate legal personality of the company.

(3)   Having said that, Lord Sumption observed that the court in *Gilford*

> "might have justified the injunction against the company on the ground that Mr Horne's knowledge was to be imputed to the company so as to make the latter's conduct unconscionable or tortious, thereby justifying the grant of an equitable remedy against it".[43]

In other words, on Lord Sumption's analysis as set out in *Prest*, there was an alternative route to grant relevant relief against the company, and so the veil ought not to have been pierced (and would not be on the same facts today).

18–020   **Jones v Lipman.**[44]   Mr Lipman entered into a sale agreement in respect of a property with Jones. Before completion, Lipman transferred it to an off-the-shelf company wholly owned and controlled by him, called Alamed Ltd, "solely for the purpose of defeating [Jones'] rights to specific performance." The judge decreed specific performance against both Mr Lipman and Alamed Ltd. As Lord Sumption explains[45]:

(1)   As against Mr Lipman, relief was granted by application of the concealment principle. Because Mr Lipman owned and controlled Alamed Ltd, he was in a position specifically to perform his obligation to the claimant by exercising his powers of control over the company. This did not involve piercing the corporate veil, but only identifying Mr Lipman as the man in control of the company. Russell J held that Alamed was "a device and a sham, a mask which [Mr Lipman] holds before his face in an attempt to avoid recognition by the eye of equity."[46]

(2)   But as against Alamed Ltd itself, the decision was an application of the evasion principle.[47] It is inherent in the decision that the judge considered that, in the circumstances, Alamed should be treated as having the same obligation to convey the property to the claimant as Mr Lipman had, even though it was not party to the contract of sale. The interposition of the company was a deliberate attempt by Mr Lipman to evade his *existing* obligation of specific performance.

---

[43] *Prest*, at [29].

[44] *Jones v Lipman* [1962] 1 W.L.R. 832.

[45] *Prest*, at [30].

[46] *Jones v Lipman*, at 36. This formulation captures the essence of the concealment principle.

[47] The court in *Jones v Lipman* justified its decision on this aspect by express reference to the *Gilford* case.

(3) Lord Sumption did not comment on whether any other route to relief might have been available, but it is very possible that it was.[48] So, again, although the court did decide to pierce the corporate veil in *Jones v Lipman*, it might not do so on the same facts today, applying the *Prest* test.[49]

(iii) Cases where there is no veil piercing[50]: examples of the concealment principle.

Gencor ACP Ltd v Dalby.[51] In this case, Gencor ACP made a large number of claims against a former director, Mr Dalby, for misappropriating its funds and other assets. The claims included one for an account of a secret profit (derived from a diverted business opportunity) which Mr Dalby procured to be paid by a third party to a BVI company under his control called Burnstead, rather than to himself directly. Rimer J held[52] that Burnstead was "in substance little other than Mr Dalby's offshore bank account held in a nominee name", and "simply ... the alter ego through which Mr Dalby enjoyed the profit which he earned in breach of his fiduciary duty to ACP." He ordered an account against both Mr Dalby and Burnstead, holding that if it was necessary to pierce the corporate veil to achieve that result, it was appropriate to do so.

Lord Sumption did not think it was necessary to do so:

> "[Rimer J's] findings about Mr Dalby's relationship with the company and his analysis of the legal consequences show that both Mr Dalby and Burnstead were independently liable to account to ACP, even on the footing that they were distinct legal persons. If, as the judge held, Burnstead was Mr Dalby's nominee for the purpose of receiving and holding the secret profit, it followed that Burnstead had no right to the money as against Mr Dalby, who had in law received it through Burnstead and could properly be required to account for it to ACP. Burnstead itself was liable to account to ACP because, as the judge went on to point out, Mr Dalby's knowledge of the prior equitable interest of ACP was to be imputed to it. As Rimer J observed, 'the introduction into the story of such a creature company is ... insufficient to prevent equity's eye from identifying it with Mr Dalby.' This is in reality the concealment principle. The correct analysis of the situation was that the court refused to be deterred by the legal personality of the company from finding the true facts about its legal relationship with Mr Dalby. It held that the nature of their dealings gave rise to ordinary equitable claims against both. The result would have been exactly the same if Burnstead, instead of being a company, had been a natural person, say Mr Dalby's uncle, about whose separate existence there could be no doubt."[53]

The evasion principle was not engaged in this case because, for the particular purpose in respect of which it might have been sought to pierce the corporate veil (i.e. the claim to an account of the secret profit received) the director, Mr Dalby, was not seeking to evade the relevant existing liability (i.e. to account for the secret profit) by the interposition of the company. He had no liability to account unless and until it was established that receipt by Burnstead "counted" as receipt

18–021

18–022

18–023

---

[48] See, for example, the observations of Lord Neuberger in this regard, at [73] in *Prest*.

[49] Although, once again, that does not mean that the Court would not be granting effective relief against Mr Lipman and, as necessary, Alamed—it would just be granting it by a different route.

[50] Even though it was thought that there was.

[51] *Gencor ACP Ltd v Dalby* [2000] EWHC 1560 (Ch); [2000] 2 B.C.L.C. 734.

[52] *Gencor ACP Ltd v Dalby*, at [26].

[53] *Prest,,* at [31].

by him. Thus, as Lord Sumption put it, "Mr Dalby was liable only if the true facts were that the company had received the money as [his] agent or nominee."[54]

18–024 **Trustor AB v Smallbone (No.2).**[55] The judgment of Sir Andrew Morritt V-C in this case articulated, until *Prest*, the generally accepted test for piercing the corporate veil: the veil could be pierced if the company was used as a "device or facade to conceal the true facts thereby avoiding or concealing any liability of those individual(s)".[56] In *Prest*, Lord Sumption described this formulation as a "confusion of concepts"[57]—it elides the "quite different concepts" of conceal-ment and evasion. Again, Lord Sumption considered that this case did not involve veil piercing at all.

18–025 Mr Smallbone, the former managing director of Trustor, had improperly procured large amounts of Trustor's money to be paid out of its account to a Gibraltarian company called Introcom Ltd, which was owned and controlled by Mr Smallbone (via a Liechtenstein trust). The question was whether Mr Smallbone himself was liable to account as a constructive trustee on the footing of knowing receipt—in circumstances in which the money had in fact been received by Introcom. Of the conclusion that Introcom's corporate veil should be pierced to hold Mr Smallbone liable, Lord Sumption said:

> "As I read [Sir Andrew Morritt's] reasons for giving judgment against Mr Smallbone, at paras 24–25, he [held him liable] on the concealment principle. It had been found at the earlier stage of the litigation that Introcom was 'simply a vehicle Mr Smallbone used for receiving money from Trustor', and that the company was a 'device or facade' for concealing that fact. On that footing, the company received the money on Mr Smallbone's behalf. This conclusion did not involve piercing the corporate veil, and did not depend on any finding of impropriety. It was simply an application of the principle summarised by the Vice-Chancellor at para 19 of his judgment, that receipt by a company will count as receipt by the shareholder if the company received it as his agent or nominee, but not if it received it in its own right. To decide that question, it was necessary to establish the facts which demonstrated the true legal relationship between Mr Smallbone and Introcom. Mr Smallbone's ownership and control of Introcom was only one of those facts, not in itself conclusive. Other factors included the circumstances and the source of the receipt, and the nature of the company's other transactions if any."[58]

18–026 Just as in *Gencor ACP*, the evasion principle was not, and could not have been, engaged in *Trustor v Smallbone*: Introcom was not incorporated or inserted to evade an existing liability of Mr Smallbone's in knowing receipt. But, critically, in both cases the owner/shareholder (Mr Dalby and Mr Smallbone respectively) did not escape liability. What Lord Sumption's judgment in *Prest* demonstrates is that existing legal principles will generally lead to the "right" result without the need to rely upon veil piercing in its strict sense.

---

[54] *Prest*, at [33].
[55] *Trustor AB v Smallbone (No.2)* [2001] 1 W.L.R. 1177.
[56] *Trustor AB v Smallbone (No.2)* [2001] 1 W.L.R. 1177, at [23].
[57] *Prest*, at [32].
[58] *Prest*, at [32].

(iv) The essential features of the doctrine as they emerge from Prest

The examples explored above, and the analysis of Lord Sumption in *Prest*, underline the vital importance of careful analysis of the factual situation when determining whether or not it is appropriate to pierce the corporate veil.

18–027

In particular, it is essential to keep firmly in mind the particular purpose for which it is desired to pierce the corporate veil and the very nature of what piercing the veil does: it *identifies* the company with the shareholder/controller *for a particular purpose*; that purpose must necessarily relate to an *existing* liability or obligation of the shareholder/controller, with which liability or obligation the company is sought to be identified. Only then is the veil being pierced to prevent a relevant abuse of corporate legal personality. So, for example, in *Jones v Lipman* the doctrine identified the company, Alamed Ltd, with its owner/controller Mr Lipman for the purpose of the existing liability to convey the property to the original purchaser, Jones; such that the company itself was treated as having the *same* obligation as Lipman to convey the property.

18–028

Generic wrong-doing or notions of evasion will not suffice:

18–029

(1) The fact that an owner/shareholder may be liable for a number of wrongs does not matter, if there is not a particular wrong in respect of which corporate legal personality is being abused. Thus, in *Trustor v Smallbone*, Mr Smallbone may well have been liable for any number of wrongs against Trustor, including most obviously large-scale breaches of fiduciary duty. But most of those wrongs were not wrongs in which Introcom was involved at all; and the wrong in which Introcom was involved did not give rise to a pre-existing liability or obligation on Mr Smallbone in respect of which it was desired to identify the company with Mr Smallbone.

(2) Equally, the fact that a corporate structure is set up with the aim of locating or isolating an obligation in a particular entity is not itself an abuse of the concept of separate corporate legal personality. As Lord Sumption put it in *Prest*:

> "it is not an abuse [of corporate legal personality] to cause a legal liability to be incurred by the company in the first place. It is not an abuse [of legal corporate personality] to rely upon the fact (if it is a fact) that a liability is not the controller's because it is the company's. On the contrary, that is what incorporation is all about."[59]

Thus, whilst it may be that a corporate structure set up to receive the proceeds of a fraud will not protect those proceeds, or those companies, from legal liability to disgorge them on ordinary principles,[60] the use of such a structure to receive funds is not an abuse of the legal concept of separate legal personality, and does not justify piercing the corporate veil to identify the shareholder/controller with the company in relation to receipt based liability of the shareholder/controller.

18–030

Thus, the essential requirements of the doctrine of piercing the corporate veil may be summarised as follows:

18–031

---

[59] *Prest*, at [34].
[60] Which was the case in both *Trustor v Smallbone* and *Gencor ACP*.

(1) The doctrine is only engaged when it is necessary to do so to prevent the abuse of the concept of separate corporate legal personality.

(2) Subject to the (limited) possibility of it being applied to novel and rare situations not yet encountered by the courts, it applies only when the shareholder/controller has an *existing* liability or obligation which he seeks to evade by the interposition of a company.

(3) Then the veil is pierced so as to identify the shareholder/controller with the company for the purpose, and only for the purpose, of that liability or obligation.

(4) There is no abuse of the concept of separate corporate legal personality (and thus no call to pierce the corporate veil) in arranging affairs such that a particular liability is incurred by a particular corporate entity in the first place.

(5) If, as will very often be the case, relevant relief can be given on conventional principles without invoking the doctrine of veil-piercing, the doctrine is not engaged and the veil should not be pierced.

(6) Whether a company was incorporated or interposed in order to evade an existing liability of the shareholder/controller will depend upon all the facts, including points such as the timing of incorporation or interposition, the context in which it was incorporated/interposed, what else the company did, if anything, and the opacity or otherwise of its structure and governance.

(3) Other Examples of the Principles in Practice: The Decision in Prest and VTB v Nutritek

18–032 *Prest* itself was a case originating from the Family Division concerning the availability of assets for distribution between a divorcing couple in proceedings for ancillary relief. As is not uncommon, it threw up questions of whether assets held by companies owned and controlled by the husband were assets which ought to be taken into account when calculating financial provision for the wife under Pt II of the Matrimonial Causes Act 1973. The assets in question were seven properties situated in the UK which were owned by various off-shore companies in the Petrodel Group, of which Mr Prest was the sole owner and controller (by various means). The properties were held in the corporate structure for purposes of "wealth protection and the avoidance of tax"[61]; and in at least some cases had been held in that way long before the divorce proceedings. Applying Lord Sumption's test to the circumstances, there was "no evidence that [Mr Prest] was seeking to avoid any obligation which is relevant in these [ancillary relief] proceedings"[62]; and accordingly, "it follows that the piercing of the corporate veil cannot be justified in this case by reference to any general principle of law".[63]

18–033 However, anxious to ensure that the properties were brought within the ambit of the ancillary relief proceedings, Lord Sumption went on to perform some

---

[61] See *Prest*, at [36].

[62] *Prest*, at [36].

[63] *Prest*, at [36].

analytical gymnastics with the facts of the case to conclude that the properties were in fact held by the companies on resulting trust for Mr Prest—and, accordingly, on conventional principles, his beneficial interest in them could be brought into account on the financial settlement in the divorce. The gymnastics involved making a series of adverse inferences against Mr Prest and the companies arising out of their failure to engage in the litigation properly and to comply with their disclosure obligations, which were necessary if the Supreme Court were to conclude the litigation without having to send it back to the Family Division for further fact-finding. That was a highly unusual approach in the circumstances of this case; but Lord Sumption concluded his analysis with this more general observation[64]:

> "Whether assets legally vested in a company are beneficially owned by its controller is a highly fact-specific issue. It is not possible to give general guidance going beyond the ordinary principles and presumptions of equity, especially those relating to gifts and resulting trusts. But I venture to suggest, however tentatively, that in the case of the matrimonial home, the facts are quite likely to justify the inference that the property was held on trust for a spouse who owned and controlled the company. In many, perhaps most cases, the occupation of the company's property as the matrimonial home of its controller will not be easily justified in the company's interest, especially if it is gratuitous. The intention will normally be that the spouse in control of the company intends to retain a degree of control over the matrimonial home which is not consistent with the company's beneficial ownership. Of course, structures can be devised which give a different impression, and some of them will be entirely genuine. But where, say, the terms of acquisition and occupation of the matrimonial home are arranged between the husband in his personal capacity and the husband in his capacity as the sole effective agent of the company (or someone else acting at his direction), judges exercising family jurisdiction are entitled to be sceptical about whether the terms of occupation are really what they are said to be, or are simply a sham to conceal the reality of the husband's beneficial ownership."

The judgment in *Prest* is a good example of: (i) how a defendant may act improperly in any number of ways in how he manages and structures his affairs,[65] but without including in that impropriety abuse of the concept of separate legal personality of a company (which is what is necessary to engage the doctrine of veil piercing); and (ii) how the more mundane principles of English law (relating, for example, to nomineeship/beneficial ownership) are able to provide a solution to the impropriety in appropriate circumstances. The ramifications of Lord Sumption's approach to the application of those more mundane principles are considered briefly, in the context of fraud litigation, in the next section. **18–034**

In *VTB v Nutritek*,[66] the claimant was induced to lend a large sum to an SPV borrower by means of (alleged) misrepresentations (including as to the identity of the controllers of the SPV). VTB sought to pierce the corporate veil so as to render those who were in fact behind the SPV borrower jointly and severally liable on the SPV borrower's contract of loan and, in particular, on the (English) jurisdiction clause. That contention failed: as explained by Lord Sumption in *Prest*, "the fundamental objection to the argument was that the principle was being invoked so as to create a new liability that would not otherwise exist."[67] In **18–035**

---

[64] *Prest*, at [52].

[65] See, e.g., *Prest*, at [36].

[66] *VTB v Nutritek* [2013] UKSC 5; [2013] 2 A.C. 337.

[67] *Prest*, at [34].

other words, there was no existing liability of the owner/controller of the SPV borrower with which it was sought to identify the company; there was no abuse of the separate legal personality of the company in having the SPV enter into the contract of loan, and in relying on the fact that the obligation was the SPV's and not that of the owner/controllers.[68]

D. THE FUTURE POST-PREST IN THE FRAUD CONTEXT

(1) An Increasing Willingness to Apply the Concealment Principle?

18–036   *Prest* was, of course, a family case[69]; but the issue—the availability of assets held by a company for distribution to a litigant with a claim against the owner/controller of that company—is one which arises all the time in fraud litigation, both at the stage of deciding what freezing or other injunctive relief may be appropriate and at the enforcement stage.[70] The Supreme Court's decision on the facts in *Prest*—and in particular the views of Lord Sumption, at [52] quoted above—may suggest a greater willingness than previously to find, in appropriate circumstances, that assets held by a company are in fact held as trustee for, or nominee of, the shareholder/controller (or indeed some other person). Perhaps understandably, following *Salomon* there was a marked reluctance to make such findings, for fear, no doubt, of undermining the *Salomon* principle that a company's assets are its own and not that of its shareholders. But, over a hundred years later, when the *Salomon* principle is in no doubt, it seems far-fetched to suggest that the principle will be undermined by making findings (on appropriate fact patterns) that the beneficial interest in property does in fact remain with the owner/controller who has transferred the property to a company.

18–037   Thus, with the nudge from *Prest*, the courts may be more willing to make robust assessments of the true disposition of legal and beneficial interests in assets. Accordingly, litigants who hold assets in complex corporate structures, and especially fraudsters, may find the courts subjecting them to more rigorous scrutiny in the future. That may cause some disruption to the operation of

---

[68] See also *Antonio Gramsci Shipping Corp v Aivars Lembergs* [2013] EWCA Civ 730; [2013] 4 All E.R. 157, in which the Court of Appeal reached the same conclusion, on a similar point, post-*Prest*.

[69] As many of the future cases in this area will also be: see, e.g., *M v M* [2013] EWHC 2534 (Fam); *MA v SK* [2015] EWHC 887 (Fam); and *Johnson v Takieddine* [2016] EWHC 1895 (Fam). Another area in which the application of the *Prest* principles is being tested is in confiscation proceedings—an area with direct analogies to the enforcement stage of fraud litigation: see, e.g., *R v Sale* [2013] EWCA Crim 1306; [2014] 1 W.L.R. 663; *R v McDowell: R v Singh* [2015] EWCA Crim 173; [2015] 2 Cr App R (S) 14; *R v Boyle Transport (Northern Ireland) Ltd* [2016] EWCA Crim 19; [2016] 4 W.L.R. 63; *R v Powell* [2016] EWCA Crim 1043; [2016] Lloyd's Rep FC 546.

[70] Under the so-called "*Chabra*" jurisdiction the Court can grant freezing order relief against C in support of a substantive claim by A against B, where C holds assets which (arguably) beneficially belong to B or which would otherwise be available to A by way of execution of a judgment against B (e.g. by attachment of a debt owed to B). That does not involve veil-piercing, properly understood (indeed C need not be a company at all). See, e.g., *Parbulk II AS v PT Humpuss Intermoda Transportasi TBK* [2011] EWHC 3143 (Comm) and, more generally, Chs 28 (at the interim stage) and 37 (at the enforcement stage).

international tax planning devices, but only in limited cases where (as the court would no doubt say) the tax advantage sought was not legitimate if it depended upon fooling the tax authorities that assets were held beneficially by a company when the beneficial title in fact remained with the shareholder/controller.

Equally, fraudsters who set up corporate structures to hold assets *after* litigation has commenced with the aim of frustrating eventual enforcement may find themselves vulnerable (at least in theory) to veil-piercing. **18–038**

Both points are demonstrated by two post-*Prest* cases in the fraud context. Each of those cases arises out of the long-running *Ablyazov* litigation: *JSC BTA Bank v Zharimbetov*[71] and *JSC BTA Bank v Solodchenko*.[72] **18–039**

The *Ablyazov* litigation concerned massive frauds perpetrated on a Kazakh bank by its former managing director and a number of his associates. It is fair to say that the circumstances of the *Ablyazov* litigation, and the perceived intransigence and contumelious contempt of the defendants for the English court, has led to very robust decision making by the Judges of the Commercial Court and Court of Appeal. The (numerous) precedents set by the *Ablyazov* cases need to be treated with some care: in less extreme circumstances, the court may not be prepared to make some of the more adventurous orders made against the defendants in that litigation. That notwithstanding, the two decisions mentioned above are worthy of note: **18–040**

(1) In *BTA v Zharimbetov*, the issue was whether a property in which Mr and Mrs Zharimbetov had lived, but which was held by a company, was beneficially owned by Mr Zharimbetov, who was one of the defendants. Cooke J considered what Lord Sumption said at [52], in *Prest*, and concluded that, in light of the fact that the property had been occupied as a matrimonial home and its purchase had been funded directly by Mr Zharimbetov (not by way of loan to the company), the property was indeed beneficially owned by Mr Zharimbetov and was held by the company on resulting trust for him.[73]

(2) In *BTA v Solodchenko*, the issue was whether two further properties in the UK held by BVI companies were beneficially owned by Mr Zharimbetov. Against the background of the *BTA v Zharimbetov* case, Phillips J

    (i) inferred that the properties were purchased using funds provided by Mr Zharimbetov (although there was no evidence before him as to exactly how they were purchased)[74];

    (ii) held that, even though the properties were not matrimonial homes, the properties were held by the companies on resulting trust for Mr Zharimbetov[75]; and

    (iii) held that, if it were necessary to go further (which it was not), it would have been appropriate to pierce the corporate veil of the

---

[71] Unreported, 14 July 2014.

[72] *JSC BTA Bank v Solodchenko* [2015] EWHC 3680 (Comm).

[73] See *BTA v Solodchenko*, at [6].

[74] See *BTA v Solodchenko*, at [8].

[75] *BTA v Solodchenko*, at [8].

companies to identify Mr Zharimbetov with the companies in respect of the ownership of the properties—because the properties were purchased via the corporate structure at a time when freezing relief had already been obtained against Mr Zharimbetov and deliberately to evade and frustrate the enforcement of Mr Zharimbetov's legal liabilities to the bank.[76]

(2)   Veil-Piercing and Third Party Rights

18–041   The other main issue to mention for the future concerns the impact on the content and operation of the veil-piercing doctrine on third party rights. This issue was not addressed in any detail in *Prest*. The question is whether the fact that piercing the veil will have an adverse impact on rights legitimately acquired by a third party forms any part of the decision as to whether the veil should be pierced.

18–042   Lord Sumption touched on this point in his judgment when considering the position of a third party bank in *Jones v Lipman*, considered above. In that case, the purchase price paid by Alamed Ltd to Lipman was part funded by borrowing from a bank. Lord Sumption observed that the evasion principle was applied

> "notwithstanding that as a result of the transaction, the company's main creditor, namely the bank, was prejudiced by its loss of what appears from the report to have been its [i.e. the company's] sole asset apart from a possible personal claim against Mr Lipman which he may or may not have been in a position to meet. This may be thought hard on the bank, but it is no harder than a finding that the company was not the beneficial owner at all. The bank could have protected itself by taking a charge or registering the contract of sale."[77]

18–043   Although the direction the law may take in this connection is not certain, it is suggested that Lord Sumption's approach is likely to be followed: where the requirements required to engage the veil-piercing doctrine are met, the impact on third parties will not prevent the operation of the doctrine. That said, (i) cases where the veil-piercing doctrine is actually invoked will remain very rare; and (ii) it is likely that the position of third parties will be capable of amelioration (or will have been capable of protection by the third party) in many cases.[78]

---

[76] *BTA v Solodchenko*, at [8] and [9].
[77] See *Prest*, at [30].
[78] Nevertheless, because the operation of the doctrine is grounded in a public policy imperative, it is not inconceivable that in a very unusual case, public policy considerations relating to the position of a particular third party might be required to be weighed in the balance. The Supreme Court has recently espoused such an approach to other policy based areas, such as the illegality principle: *Patel v Mirza* [2016] UKSC 42; [2017] A.C. 467.

CHAPTER 19

ATTRIBUTION

A. INTRODUCTION

(1) What is "Attribution"?

There are many contexts in which the law seeks, in one way or another, to hold one legal entity responsible for the conduct or state of mind of another. It is vital to distinguish what the law is doing in these different situations.

19–001

The most important distinction is that between the law of vicarious liability and the law of attribution.

19–002

As we have already outlined in Ch.17, the law of vicarious liability is about identifying when one party will be held *liable* for the completed wrong of another. It does not require that the vicariously liable party has done anything wrong at all—let alone the wrong for which he is to be held liable. It is a form of strict liability without fault and it arises by operation of a series of rules which determine when (as a matter of policy, in essence) it is right that A should be held liable (or legally responsible) for B's wrong. Most particularly, it does not require any *attribution* of wrong-doing, actions or states of mind of B to A.

19–003

Attribution, by contrast, is about when the actions or state of mind of one legal person are to be actually attributed to—laid at the door of—another, and treated as the actions or state of mind of that other person. The result is that A is not merely liable or responsible for any wrong committed by B, but is treated in law as actually having committed, itself, any wrong which the actions and/or state of mind attributed would entail. That may well be a wrong which B himself has not committed—in this sense, attribution addresses situations where the rules of vicarious liability do not provide a complete answer or are not apt to cover the situation.[1]

19–004

---

[1] See, in relation to the distinction between attribution and vicarious liability, e.g. *Bilta (UK) Ltd (in liquidation) v Nazir (No.2)* [2015] UKSC 23; [2016] A.C. 1, per Lord Sumption at [70]. In *UBS AG (London Branch) v Kommunale Wasserwerke Liepzig GmbH* [2017] EWCA Civ 1567, the majority of the Court of Appeal admitted to some discomfort in coming to a conclusion that, in the context of one of the relevant claims, a director's knowledge was not to be attributed to the company, when the company had, in relation to another of the claims, conceded that it was vicariously liable for the same director's fraudulent statements. Lord Briggs of Westbourne and Hamblen LJ considered themselves bound by the concession, but also said "it may be that the law as to vicarious liability and attribution run in different channels, or that the full implications of the Supreme Court's decision in the *Bilta* case have yet to filter through into the ordinary law of tort" (at [185]). The source of the "discomfort" may be because either the concession on vicarious liability or the decision on attribution was wrong

19–005   A frequently-encountered example, in the fraud context, is the question of whether a company is liable for knowing receipt. In order to be liable, a company which has received relevant funds must have the requisite guilty knowledge, as analysed in Ch.12. The company can only have that state of mind if the knowledge of a relevant human agent is to be legally attributed to it: patently, a company cannot know a fact other than through its human avatars. The law of attribution addresses the circumstances in which the law will impute the knowledge of a human agent to the company in circumstances such as this. If there is a human agent with the requisite knowledge, whose knowledge can be attributed to the company, then, provided the other elements of knowing receipt are made out, the company will be liable to account as a constructive trustee on the footing of knowing receipt; but the agent will not—he has the knowledge, but has not himself received anything.

19–006   This chapter addresses the law of attribution; vicarious liability is considered elsewhere, as it arises in the context of individual causes of action addressed in this work. Similarly, this chapter does not deal with ostensible authority in the law of contract: on that topic, reference should be made to the standard works on contract law.

19–007   Finally, as already underlined in Ch.17, it is important to distinguish attribution of conduct or states of mind to a company from the concept of piercing the corporate veil (which we consider in detail in Ch.18). The two are entirely separate concepts: as Lord Sumption explained in *Bilta (UK) Ltd (in liquidation) v Nazir (No.2)*[2] "it cannot be emphasised too strongly that neither in the civil nor in the criminal context does [attribution] involve piercing the corporate veil. It is simply a recognition of the fact that the law treats a company as thinking through agents, just as it acts through them."[3]

(2)   Relevance to Fraud Claims

19–008   The question of attribution arises in any case in which it is desired to plead a fraud claim against a company, or other type of principal, but where it is necessary to rely, in establishing the case, on the conduct or state of mind of someone else which must be attributed or imputed to the company/principal. Bearing in mind that many causes of action in typical fraud litigation contain "mental elements", such as a requirement of dishonesty or knowledge or a having a particular purpose, fraud claims are replete with situations where an attribution question will arise. Obvious examples include cases where a company (or other principal) is alleged: (i) to have made a fraudulent misrepresentation, (ii) to be liable to account as a constructive trustee on the footing of knowing receipt, (iii) to be liable to account as a constructive trustee on the footing of dishonest

---

(Gloster LJ, in the minority, reached a different conclusion on attribution), or may potentially lie in the fact that the law on vicarious liability in circumstances such as those at issue in the *UBS v KWL* case requires further development, or it may be that the feeling of "discomfort" is misplaced; but it is certainly the case that the law as to vicarious liability and attribution run in different channels.

[2] *Bilta (UK) Ltd (in liquidation) v Nazir (No.2)* [2015] UKSC 23; [2016] A.C. 1.

[3] *Bilta* [2015] UKSC 23, at [65].

assistance in a breach of trust or fiduciary duty, or (iv) to be liable for conspiracy. Difficult questions of attribution also arise in fraud claims less directly—for example, whose consent will suffice in order to establish fully informed consent to a breach of fiduciary duty? Whose illegal act counts as the company's illegal act for the purpose of a defence based on the illegality principle (ex turpi causa)?

In many cases, the answer is straightforward and, even though there is technically an attribution question underlying the analysis, the parties and courts do not consider it overtly. But in some cases the question becomes much more complex. Consider, for example, a case where an agent of the company has made a false representation in a contract without knowing it to be untrue, but there is another employee or agent who does know it to be untrue.[4] Are both statement and knowledge to be, from their separate agents, attributed to the company so as to render it liable in the tort of deceit? If a company sues a director for fraudulent diversion of company funds, is the director's knowledge of his fraud, or the fraud itself, to be attributed to the company so as to give him a defence of fully informed consent or an ex turpi causa defence?[5]   **19–009**

Some of these more complex attribution questions, and especially that relating to the so called "fraud exception" or "*Hampshire Land*" principle,[6] have generated considerable difficulty in the case law over a number of years. That case law has been typified by contradictory decisions from which it had been near impossible to isolate a coherent framework for the law in this area. However, two recent cases—*Moulin Global Eyecare Trading Ltd (in liquidation) v The Commissioner of Inland Revenue* in Hong Kong Court of Final Appeal[7] and *Bilta (UK) Ltd (in liquidation) v Nazir (No.2)* in the English Court of Appeal[8] and Supreme Court[9]—have clarified the law in this area considerably.   **19–010**

(3) The Scope and Focus of this Chapter

We have addressed attribution points in other sections of this work where they are relevant to the exposition of the law on other topics. The purpose of this chapter is to consider, relatively briefly and from a practical perspective, the more general scheme of the law on attribution. That is to enable the practitioner to identify and apply reliably the correct legal framework to attribution questions that arise in fraud litigation that do not necessarily fit neatly into the scenarios considered elsewhere in the text. We will do that with particular reference to the issues that most often arise in the context of fraud litigation. In general, we approach the exposition of the principles and practice from the perspective of attribution in a company context—that is both for ease and because it is the context in which, for obvious reasons, attribution questions most commonly arise in fraud litigation.   **19–011**

---

[4] E.g. *MAN Nutzfahrzeuge AG v Freightliner Ltd* [2005] EWHC 2347 (Comm).

[5] E.g. *Bilta (UK) Ltd (in liquidation) v Nazir (No.2)* [2015] UKSC 23; [2016] A.C. 1.

[6] Springing from the case of *In re Hampshire Land Co* [1896] 2 Ch. 743: this is discussed in detail in section C below.

[7] *Moulin Global Eyecare Trading Ltd (in liquidation) v The Commissioner of Inland Revenue* [2014] HKFCA 22.

[8] *Bilta (UK) Ltd (in liquidation) v Nazir (No. 2)* [2013] EWCA Civ 968; [2014] Ch. 52.

[9] *Bilta (UK) Ltd (in liquidation) v Nazir (No. 2)* [2015] UKSC 23; [2016] A.C. 1.

However, the principles applicable to attribution in a broader agent-principal context are covered within that review—as they are centrally relevant to attribution in a company context too.

B. THE "RULES" OF ATTRIBUTION

(1) The Basic Principle

19–012 The key question, in every case, is simply this: whose act, knowledge or state of mind is *for the relevant purpose* to count as the act, knowledge or state of mind of the company (or other principal)? Very often that question can be answered by orthodox application of the principles (i) of corporate attribution (to be found largely in the constitution of the relevant company) and/or (ii) of the general law of agency. But sometimes the law must fashion a special rule of attribution, bearing in mind the legal context (and the content of, and policy behind, the legal rule in respect of which the attribution question arises) and the relevant factual circumstances.

(2) The Leading Case: Meridian Global

19–013 As has been reiterated in *Moulin*,[10] and *Bilta*,[11] the leading modern authority in relation to how companies "act"—i.e. how the acts, omissions, states of mind and knowledge of individual (or groups of) human actors are to be attributed to a company—is *Meridian Global Funds Management Asia Ltd v The Securities Commission*.[12] In that case Lord Hoffmann delivered the advice of the Privy Council in a masterly exposition of the relevant principles. There is force in the proposition that much of the confusion and difficulty in this area of law in recent years has been caused by practitioners and the courts failing to pay sufficient regard to it.

19–014 The crucial passages in this case[13] bear quoting in full. Lord Hoffmann explained, first, the need for rules of attribution in the company context:

> "Any proposition about a company necessarily involves a reference to a set of rules. A company exists because there is a rule (usually in statute) which says that a *persona ficta* shall be deemed to exist and to have certain of the powers, rights and duties of a natural person. But there would be little sense in deeming such a *persona ficta* to exist unless there were also rules to tell one what acts were to count as acts of the company. It is therefore a necessary part of corporate personality that there should be rules by which acts are attributed to the company. These may be called 'the rules of attribution'."

He underlined the importance of what might be thought an obvious point:

> "Any statement about what a company has or has not done, or can or cannot do, is necessarily a reference to the rules of attribution (primary and general) as they apply to that company.

---

[10] *Moulin Global Eyecare*, per Lord Walker at [77].
[11] *Bitta*, per Lord Sumption at [67].
[12] *Meridian Global Funds Management Asia Ltd v The Securities Commission* [1995] 2 A.C. 500.
[13] *Meridian Global*, at 506A–507F.

Judges sometimes say that a company "as such" cannot do anything; it must act by servants or agents. This may seem an unexceptionable, even banal remark. And of course the meaning is usually perfectly clear. But a reference to a company 'as such' might suggest that there is something out there called the company of which one can meaningfully say that it can or cannot do something. There is in fact no such thing as the company as such, no *ding an sich*,[14] only the applicable rules. To say that a company cannot do something means only that there is no one whose doing of that act would, under the applicable rules of attribution, count as an act of the company."

Lord Hoffmann continued to explain the content of the "rules of attribution": **19–015**

"The company's primary rules of attribution will generally be found in its constitution, typically the articles of association, and will say things such as 'for the purpose of appointing members of the board, a majority vote of the shareholders shall be a decision of the company'.... There are also primary rules of attribution which are not expressly stated in the articles but implied by company law such as 'the unanimous decision of all the shareholders in a solvent company about anything which the company under its memorandum of association has power to do shall be the decision of the company:' see *Multinational Gas and Petrochemical Co v Multinational Gas and Petrochemical Services Ltd* [1983] Ch. 259.

These primary rules of attribution are obviously not enough to enable a company to go out in the world and do business. Not every act on behalf of a company can be expected to be the subject of a resolution of the board or a unanimous decision of the shareholders. The company therefore builds on the primary rules of attribution by using general rules of attribution which are equally available to natural persons, namely, the principles of agency. It will appoint servants and agents whose acts, by a combination of the general principles of agency and the company's primary rules of attribution, count as acts of the company. And having done so, it will also make itself subject to the general rules by which liability for the acts of others can be attributed to natural persons, such as estoppel or ostensible authority in contract and vicarious liability in tort.

.....

The company's primary rules of attribution together with the general principles of agency, vicarious liability and so forth are usually sufficient to enable one to determine its rights and obligations. In exceptional cases, however, they will not provide an answer. This will be the case when a rule of law, either expressly or by implication, excludes attribution on the basis of the general principles of agency or vicarious liability. For example, a rule may be stated in language primarily applicable to a natural person and require some act or state of mind on the part of that person 'himself', as opposed to his servants or agents. This is generally true of rules of the criminal law, which ordinarily impose liability only for the *actus reus* and *mens rea* of the defendant himself. How is such a rule to be applied to a company?

One possibility is that the court may come to the conclusion that the rule was not intended to apply to companies at all; for example, a law which created an offence for which the only penalty was community service. Another possibility is that the court might interpret the law as meaning that it could apply to a company only on the basis of its primary rules of attribution, i.e. if the act giving rise to liability was specifically authorised by a resolution of the board or a unanimous agreement of the shareholders. But there will be many cases in which neither of these solutions is satisfactory; in which the court considers that the law was intended to apply to companies and that, although it excludes ordinary vicarious liability, insistence on the primary rules of attribution would in practice defeat that intention. In such a case, the court must fashion a special rule of attribution for the particular substantive rule. This is always a matter of interpretation: given that it was intended to apply to a company, how was it intended to apply? Whose act (or knowledge, or state of mind) was for this purpose intended to count as the act etc of the company. One finds the answer to this question by applying the usual canons of interpretation, taking into account the language of the rule (if it is a statute) and its content and policy."

---

[14] "Thing-in-itself": the phrase comes from a celebrated passage in Kant's *Critique of Pure Reason* (1781).

19–016 By these principles, he offered clarification of the phrase "directing mind and will", which originated in the speech of Viscount Haldane LC in *Lennard's Carrying Co Ltd v Asiatic Petroleum Ltd*.[15] Save in the very simplest of companies, there will not be one "directing mind and will" for all purposes and in all contexts. Rather, there will be different directing minds for different spheres of the company's activity in different circumstances. When a question of attribution arises, the search is for the mind relevant to the particular context: whose mind counts as the mind of the company for the relevant purpose?[16]

19–017 In *Bilta*, the Supreme Court endorsed and reaffirmed the approach in *Meridian Global*.[17]

(2) Understanding Meridian Global

19–018 It is essential to understand clearly what Lord Hoffmann meant in his judgment in *Meridian Global*—for on that turns the whole law of attribution and the reliable application of it by practitioners and the courts. It helps to illuminate Lord Hoffmann's exegesis: (i) to see how Lord Hoffmann applied the principle to the decision on the facts of *Meridian Global* itself and (ii) to consider and contrast two earlier decisions of the House of Lords on attribution, *Tesco Supermarkets Ltd v Nattrass*[18] and *In re Supply of Ready Mixed Concrete (No.2)*[19], as Lord Hoffmann himself did in order to demonstrate that the rule of attribution is a matter of interpretation or construction of the relevant substantive legal rule.

(i)   The decision on the facts of Meridian Global

19–019 The issue in *Meridian Global* was whether the company, Meridian, was in breach of s.20 of the New Zealand Securities Amendment Act 1988, which imposed a duty on the company to give notice that it had become a substantial security holder in a public issuer "as soon as the [company] knows, or ought to know, that [it] is a substantial security holder in the public issuer." An employee of Meridian called Koo did a deal—for corrupt purposes—pursuant to which Meridian became a substantial security holder in a public issuer; he did not give notice in accordance with s.20 because he did not want Meridian to find out that he had done the deal at all.

---

[15] *Lennard's Carrying Co Ltd v Asiatic Petroleum Ltd* [1915] A.C. 705, 713, which the Privy Council considered had been misunderstood to some extent: see *Meridian Global*, at 506A.
[16] See also, e.g., *MAN Nutzfahrzeuge AG v Freightliner Ltd* [2005] EWHC 2347 (Comm), per Moore-Bick LJ at [156] and [149]; *El Ajou v Dollar Land Holdings Ltd* [1994] 2 All E.R. 685, per Rose LJ at p 699h, and Hoffmann LJ at p.706e.
[17] See *Bilta*, per Lord Sumption at [67], per Lord Mance at [39]–[41], per Lords Toulson and Hodge at [190]–[191], and per Lord Neuberger, with Lords Clarke and Carnwath, at [9]).
[18] *Tesco Supermarkets Ltd v Nattrass* [1972] A.C. 153.
[19] *In re Supply of Ready Mixed Concrete (No.2)* [1994] 3 W.L.R. 1249.

The Privy Council held that, nevertheless, Koo's knowledge of the deal counted as Meridian's knowledge—i.e. it was attributed to Meridian—for the purposes of the knowledge requirement under s.20. Lord Hoffmann's analysis was as follows[20]:

19–020

> "Once it is appreciated that the question is one of construction rather than metaphysics, the answer in this case seems to their Lordships to be...straightforward. The policy of section 20 of the Securities Amendment Act 1988 is to compel, in fast-moving markets, the immediate disclosure of the identity of persons who become substantial security holders in public issuers. Notice must be given as soon as that person knows that he has become a substantial security holder. In the case of a corporate security holder, what rule should be implied as to the person whose knowledge for this purpose is to count as the knowledge of the company? Surely the person who, with the authority of the company, acquired the relevant interest. Otherwise the policy of the Act would be defeated. Companies would be able to allow employees to acquire interests on their behalf which made them substantial security holders but would not have to report them until the board or someone else in senior management got to know about it. This would put a premium on the board paying as little attention as possible to what its investment managers were doing... The fact that Koo did the deal for a corrupt purpose and did not give such notice because he did not want his employers to find out cannot in their Lordships' view affect the attribution of knowledge and the consequent duty to notify.
>
> It was therefore not necessary in this case to inquire into whether Koo could have been described in some more general sense as the 'directing mind and will' of the company."

Lord Hoffmann concluded by saying that

19–021

> "their Lordships would wish to guard themselves against being understood to mean that whenever a servant of a company has authority to do an act on its behalf, knowledge of that act will for all purposes be attributed to the company. It is a question of construction in each case as to whether the particular rule requires that the knowledge that an act has been done, or the state of mind with which it was done, should be attributed to the company...Each [case] is an example of an attribution rule for a particular purpose, tailored as it always must be to the terms and policies of the substantive rule."

(ii)   Tesco v Nattrass & In re Supply of Ready Mixed Concrete

In *Meridian Global*, Lord Hoffmann compared and contrasted these two previous decisions of the House of Lords to demonstrate the principles he was clarifying and how they were to be applied.

19–022

In *Tesco v Nattrass*, Tesco was prosecuted under the Trade Descriptions Act 1968 for displaying a notice that goods were "being offered at a price less than that at which they were in fact being offered...". Due to a store manager negligently failing to notice that he had run out of specially marked low-price packets, a Tesco supermarket advertised that it was selling packets of washing powder at a reduced price, but a customer who asked for one was told he would have to pay the normal price. Section 24(1) provided a defence for a shop owner who could prove that the commission of the offence was caused by "another person" and that "he took all reasonable precautions and exercised all due diligence to avoid the commission of such an offence by himself or any person under his control". Tesco was able to show that it owned hundreds of shops and that the board had instituted systems of supervision and training which amounted, on its part, to taking reasonable precautions and exercising all due diligence to avoid the

19–023

---

[20] *Meridian Global*, at 511C–512B.

commission of such offences in its shops. The question was: whose precautions counted as those of the company? If it was the board, then the defence was made out. If they had to include those of the negligent store manager, then it failed.

19–024 The House of Lords held that the precautions taken by the board were sufficient for the purposes of s.24(1) to count as precautions taken by the company and that the manager's negligence was not attributable to the company. It did so by examining the purpose of s.24(1) in providing a defence to what would otherwise have been an absolute offence: it was intended to give effect to "a policy of consumer protection which does have a rational and moral justification."[21] This led to the conclusion that the acts and defaults of the manager were not intended to be attributed to the company:

> "It may be a reasonable step for an employer to instruct a superior servant to supervise the activities of inferior servants whose physical acts may in the absence of supervision result in that being done which it is sought to prevent. This is not to delegate the employer's duty to exercise all due diligence; it is to perform it. To treat the duty of an employer to exercise due diligence as unperformed unless due diligence was also exercised by all his servants to whom he had reasonably given all proper instructions and upon whom he could reasonably rely to carry them out, would be to render the defence of due diligence nugatory and so thwart the clear intention of Parliament in providing it."[22]

19–025 In *Ready Mixed Concrete*, by contrast, a restrictive arrangement in breach of an undertaking by a company to the Restrictive Practices Court was made by executives of the company acting within the scope of their employment. The board knew nothing of the arrangement; it had in fact given instructions to the company's employees that they were not to make such arrangements. The House of Lords held that for the purposes of deciding whether the company was in contempt, the act and state of mind of an employee who entered into an arrangement in the course of his employment should be attributed to the company. This attribution rule was derived from construing the undertaking against the background of the Restrictive Trade Practices Act 1976: such undertakings by corporations would be worth little if the company could avoid liability for what its employees had actually done on the ground that the board did not know about it. As Lord Templeman said, an uncritical transposition of the *Tesco v Nattrass* construction:

> "... would allow a company to enjoy the benefit of restrictions outlawed by Parliament and the benefit of arrangements prohibited by the courts provided that the restrictions were accepted and implemented and the arrangements were negotiated by one or more employees who had been forbidden to do so by some superior employees identified in argument as a member of the 'higher management' of the company or by one or more directors of the company identified in argument as 'the guiding will' of the company."[23]

---

[21] *Tesco v Nattrass*, per Lord Diplock at 194–195.
[22] *Tesco v Nattrass*, per Lord Diplock at 203.
[23] *Ready Mixed Concrete*, at 1254–1255.

(3)   The General Rules of Attribution in the Law of Agency

(i)   Introduction

As we have explained, in *Meridian Global* Lord Hoffmann identifies three **19–026** sources of "rules of attribution" in a company context:

(1)   the primary rules of attribution;
(2)   the rules of attribution in the law of agency; and
(3)   special rules of attribution.

The primary rules of attribution, to be found in the company's constitution, are matters of company law: for a general survey, the reader is referred to standard works on company law. The rules of attribution in the law of agency are considered in this section.

(ii)   Scope and relevance of the rules

The rules of attribution in the general law of agency are important not just in the **19–027** company context, but more broadly—they apply whenever a question of attribution arises between an agent and his principal, whether that principal is human or corporate.

The key attribution question which arises in respect of agents[24], especially in a **19–028** fraud context, is usually whether knowledge (or a state of mind) held by an agent can be attributed to the principal. The "attribution" of physical actions in this context is usually relatively straightforward and is largely governed by the law on the actual and ostensible authority of agents; although the distinction is not always clearly maintained, mostly because it is not important in many situations.

(iii)   The rules

The key rules of attribution in respect of knowledge/state of mind can be **19–029** summarised as follows[25]:

(1)   The law may impute to a principal knowledge relating to the subject matter of the agency which the agent acquires while acting within the scope of his authority.[26] This is by far the most important rule, both generally and in the

---

[24] As opposed to questions of vicarious liability for wrongs committed by an agent.

[25] A more detailed treatment may be found in specialist works on the law of agency.

[26] See, for example (from a long list of cases), *El Ajou v Dollar Land Holdings Plc* [1994] 2 All E.R. 685, per Hoffmann LJ at 703C–703E ("there are cases in which the agent has actual or ostensible authority to receive communications, whether informative (such as the state of health of an insured: *Blackley v National Mutual Life Association* [1972] N.Z.L.R. 1038) or performative (such as a notice to quit: *Tanham v Nicholson* (1872) L.R. 5 HL 561) on behalf of the principal. In such cases, communication to the agent is communication to the principal"); *Real Estate Opportunities Ltd v Aberdeen Asset Managers* [2007] EWCA Civ 197, per Arden LJ at [49] ("The ordinary rules of attribution are well-known. In general, an employer is deemed to have notice of anything of which any of his employees obtains knowledge in the course of his employment. Likewise a company is in

context of fraud litigation. The key word is "may": as we consider further below, there are circumstances in which—by reason of the need for a special rule of attribution in the relevant circumstances—the law will not impute knowledge to the principal even though it related to the subject matter of the agency and was acquired within the scope of the agent's authority.

(2) Where an agent is authorised to enter into a transaction in which his own knowledge is material, knowledge which he acquired outside the scope of his authority may also be imputed to the principal.[27] The example given in *El Ajou v Dollar Land Holdings Plc*[28] is of an insurance policy, which may be avoided on account of the broker's failure to disclose material facts within his knowledge, even though he did not obtain that knowledge in his capacity as agent for the insured.[29]

(3) Where the principal has a duty to investigate and make disclosure, he may have imputed to him not only facts which he knows but also material facts of which he might expect to have been told by his agents.[30] The rationale is that if the principal has a duty to investigate or to make disclosure, and he employs an agent to discharge such a duty, the knowledge of the agent will be imputed to him.

(4) The Interaction Between the Three Sources of "Rules of Attribution" Identified in Meridian Global

19–030 A question arises from Lord Hoffmann's exposition of the relevant principles in *Meridian Global* as to how the three sources of rules—primary rules of attribution, agency law principles and special rules of attribution —interact with one another. Is it the case that attribution by any of the three routes will suffice? Or is the position more nuanced than that, depending on the legal and factual context?

19–031 There are some cases where the way in which the parties presented their arguments, and the methodology adopted by the courts, support the ideas that (i) a special rule of attribution can supply an additional answer or alternative analysis to the question of whose knowledge and conduct counts as that of a company, even where the other principles of attribution also provide an answer;

---

general deemed to have notice of anything of which any of its directors obtains knowledge in the course of his duties"); *UBS AG (London Branch) v Kommunale Wasserwerke Leipzig GmbH* [2014] EWHC 3615 (Comm), per Males J at [762]–[766].

[27] *El Ajou v Dollar Land Holdings Plc* [1994] 2 All E.R. 685, at 702C–702D.

[28] *El Ajou v Dollar Land Holdings Plc* [1994] 2 All E.R. 685.

[29] In *El Ajou* Hoffmann LJ continued: "As Lord Macnaghten said in *Blackburn Low & Co v Vigors* (1887) 12 App Cas 531, at 542–543: 'But that is not because the knowledge of the agent is to be imputed to the principal but because the agent of the assured is bound as the principal is bound to communicate to the underwriters all material facts within his knowledge'."

[30] *El Ajou*, at 702J.

and (ii) that in such situations attribution by one *or* other route will suffice.[31] Those cases are, probably, best explained by the fact that, in the circumstances, it did not matter which route to attribution was taken; so there was no need to address the question posed above. In cases where it does matter, the case law demonstrates that even in situations where the primary rules of attribution and/or the law of agency provide *an* answer, the court may decide that a special rule of attribution provides the most appropriate answer in the particular factual and legal context at hand. Accordingly, even where there would be attribution under the primary rules of attribution, or where there would be attribution under the agency principles, it is open to the court to determine that, in fact, the relevant rule of attribution should be a special rule and that, under that special rule, knowledge should not be attributed: see, for example, *Meridian Global* itself[32]; *Tesco v Nattrass*; *Re Bank of Credit and Commerce International SA (No.15), Morris v Bank of India*[33]; *MAN Nutzfahrzeuge AG v Freightliner Ltd*[34]; *Lebon v Aqua Salt Co Ltd*[35]; and a large number of the cases in which a special rule of attribution is fashioned in the context of the illegality principle (the ex turpi causa defence).[36]

(5) Examples of the Rules of Attribution in Fraud Claims

The range of situations in which attribution questions might arise in general, or even just in fraud claims, is of course vast. It would be neither practical nor useful for this work to seek to canvas every situation in which attribution questions arise or to survey the entirety of the vast body of case law.

19–032

---

[31] See, e.g., *El Ajou, Arab Bank Plc v Zurich Insurance Co* [1999] 1 Lloyd's Rep. 262; *Mahonia Ltd v JP Morgan Chase Bank and West LB AG* [2004] EWHC 1938 (Comm); *Jafari-Fini v Skillglass Ltd* [2007] EWCA Civ 261 and *The Dolphina* [2012] 1 Lloyd's Rep. 304 (in the High Court of Singapore).

[32] The Privy Council underlined that they should not be understood as meaning that "whenever a servant of a company has authority to do an act on its behalf, knowledge of that act will for all purposes be attributed to the company." Rather, they made clear that, "it is a question of construction in each case as to whether the particular rule requires that the knowledge that an act has been done, or the state of mind with which it was done, should be attributed to the company".

[33] *Re Bank of Credit and Commerce International SA (No.15), Morris v Bank of India* [2005] EWCA Civ 693; [2005] 2 B.C.L.C. 328. As Patten J put it (specifically quoted and approved in this regard by the Court of Appeal, at [96]): "...the primary rules of attribution, based on factors such as the scope of the agent's authority, may require to be modified either restrictively or liberally in order to accommodate the [purpose of the substantive rule] which imposes the liability".

[34] *MAN Nutzfahrzeuge AG v Freightliner Ltd* [2005] EWHC 2347 (Comm).

[35] *Lebon v Aqua Salt Co Ltd* [2009] UKPC 2, [2009] 1 B.C.L.C. 549.

[36] See, for example, *Bilta*, at [202]–[203], per Lords Toulson and Hodge, and, at [40], per Lord Mance; and examples from the case law on this and similar topics: *Belmont Finance Corp Ltd v Williams Furniture Ltd* [1979] Ch. 250 ("*Belmont No.1*"), where a special rule of attribution was fashioned under which there was no attribution when there would have been attribution under the relevant agency principles; *Belmont Finance Corp Ltd v Williams Furniture Ltd (No.2)* [1980] 1 All E.R. 393 ("*Belmont No.2*"), where a special rule of attribution was fashioned under which there was no attribution when there would have been attribution under the primary rules of attribution (the relevant actions had been sanctioned by resolution of the board); *Attorney General's Reference (No.2 of 1982)* [1984] 1 Q.B. 624; *Gluckstein v Barnes* [1900] A.C. 240.

19–033   Nevertheless, it will be of assistance to the busy practitioner to consider briefly some examples in which questions of attribution have arisen in fraud claims, in order to understand how the court approaches the task of applying the rules articulated above to common situations encountered in fraud litigation.

19–034   In *El Ajou v Dollar Land Holdings Ltd*,[37] the issue was whether knowledge of the origin of funds received for investment by Dollar Land could be imputed to it so as to found a liability to account as a constructive trustee on the footing of knowing receipt. That knowledge was held by a Mr Ferdman, who was a non-executive director of Dollar Land, although he had acquired that knowledge in his capacity as a director of another company. Ferdman had made arrangements (acting without the authority of a resolution by Dollar Land's board) by which Dollar Land acquired an interest in assets in which others had invested funds that they had earlier obtained by fraud. A Mr Stern generally managed Dollar Land. The claimant argued that Ferdman's knowledge should be attributed to Dollar Land for the purposes of the knowing receipt claim, either because Ferdman was the directing mind and will of the company in relation to the receipt of the funds (i.e. a special rule of attribution), or because he acted as the company's agent in the transaction (i.e. attribution via the law of agency).[38]

19–035   The Court of Appeal held, applying the principles which Lord Hoffmann would later explain in *Meridian Global*, that—via a special rule of attribution—it was necessary to identify the natural person who has management and control in relation to the particular act or omission in question. Accordingly, the company was fixed with the knowledge of Ferdman because he had acted as its directing mind and will *for the particular purpose* of arranging its receipt of the tainted funds (although not otherwise). The alternative case based on the law of agency failed: (i) Ferdman had not acquired the relevant knowledge in his capacity as agent for Dollar Land (but in his capacity as agent for another company)—so the first principle set out in para.19–029 above did not apply; and (ii) in the context of the relevant claim, there was no duty on Dollar Land to enquire as to the source of the funds it had received—so the third principle set out in para.19–029 above was not engaged either.

19–036   In *Royal Brunei Airlines Sdn Bhd v Tan*,[39] the Privy Council was concerned with the knowledge required to incur liability as a constructive trustee on the footing of dishonest assistance in a (dishonest) breach of trust. The defendant dishonest assistant was a Mr Tan, who was the "one-man" in a one-man company, BLT, which was the defaulting trustee. The case contains a modern illustration of the attribution of knowledge to a company on the basis that its agent was its directing mind and will for all relevant purposes (albeit one which was not necessary to resolve the actual issue before the Court). Lord Nicholls, delivering the advice of the Board, observed that, since Mr Tan had known the relevant facts, he was

---

[37] *El Ajou v Dollar Land Holdings Ltd* [1994] 2 All E.R. 685.
[38] On the facts of *El Ajou*, these were (rightly) treated as alternatives; but see section (4) above in relation to the interaction between the different routes to attribution in any particular case.
[39] *Royal Brunei Airlines Sdn Bhd v Tan* [1995] 2 A.C. 378.

therefore liable in dishonest assistance. He added that (had it been relevant)[40] BLT's breach of trust itself was also dishonest:

"by the same token, and for good measure, BLT also acted dishonestly. Mr Tan was the company and his state of mind is to be imputed to the company".[41]

MAN Nutzfahrzeuge AG v Freightliner Ltd[42] was a case concerning fraudulent misrepresentations. A company called Western Star sold another company, ERF, to the claimant, MAN. A Mr Ellis, the financial controller of ERF, persistently falsified its accounts. Ellis was "involved on [Western Star's] behalf" in the negotiation of the sale agreement for the purpose of talking to ERF's accounts and finances. In the sale agreement, Western Star made a number of representations to MAN regarding ERF's accounts. Owing to Ellis's manipulation of the accounts, those representations were false; but in order to succeed in a misrepresentation claim pursuant to a relevant clause in the sale agreement, MAN had to show that such representations were given fraudulently. MAN contended that Ellis's knowledge of his own manipulation of ERF's accounts and the falsity of the financial statements based on them was to be attributed to Western Star such that the representations in the sale agreement were to be treated as having been made by Western Star fraudulently.

19–037

Applying the *Meridian Global* analysis, Moore-Bick LJ identified the substantive legal rule for which a rule of attribution had to be found: he held that the essence of fraudulent misrepresentation is the making of a statement that is known to be untrue intending that the person to whom it is made will rely on it, such that "liability therefore depends on the conjunction of a false statement and a dishonest state of mind". Once it is established that a false statement has been made by someone who is authorised to speak on the company's behalf, the starting point in deciding whether the company acted dishonestly

19–038

"must be to enquire into the state of mind of the person who made the statement. However, if that person was unaware that the statement was false, it may be necessary to enquire into the state of mind of other persons who directed him to make it or who allowed it to be made."[43]

Moore-Bick LJ considered that entry into an entire contract such as the relevant sale agreement represents

"a single indivisible act of will, despite the fact that the contract itself may contain many different provisions. All representations in the contract were made at the same time by the same legal person at the direction of the same natural person or persons".

He held that

"in these circumstances although several persons may together be regarded as representing the company's controlling mind and will for the purpose of entering into the contract (for

---

[40] Which, of course, it was not because the breach of trust itself does not need to be dishonest to establish that a dishonest assistant should be liable as a constructive trustee.
[41] *Royal Brunei Airlines v Tan*, at 392–393.
[42] *MAN Nutzfahrzeuge AG v Freightliner Ltd* [2005] EWHC 2347 (Comm).
[43] *MAN Nutzfahrzeuge*, at [156].

example, the various members of the board of directors), it is not possible, in my view, for different persons to represent its controlling mind and will in respect of different parts of that contract."[44]

As Ellis had had no part in deciding whether Western Star should make or sign up to the representations in the contract—he had not been among those directors who decided whether or not Western Star should enter into the contract and on what terms—his state of mind in relation to the representations was not relevant (and could not be attributed to the company): it was the state of mind of those who made the statements in the contract that was relevant.[45] None of those people knew what Ellis had been doing, so MAN failed to establish the necessary fraudulent representations.[46]

19–039   *Re Bank of Credit and Commerce International SA (No.15), Morris v Bank of India*[47] arose out of the fraudulent activities and massive insolvency of BCCI. BCCI had placed deposits with Bank of India on unusual terms that were in fact part of a dishonest plan contrived by BCCI's central treasury department to conceal heavy losses which it had incurred. Upon the subsequent collapse of BCCI, the liquidators brought proceedings against Bank of India under s.213 of the Insolvency Act on the ground that it had been knowingly party to the carrying on of business by BCCI with intent to defraud. The judge found that one Mr Samant, the general manager of Bank of India's London branch, had deliberately turned a blind eye to the fraudulent scheme and so had the requisite knowledge. The question was whether, for the purposes of the case under s.213, Mr Samant's knowledge should be attributed to Bank of India.

19–040   The Court of Appeal[48] held that Samant's knowledge should be attributed to Bank of India. The court formulated a special rule of attribution in light of the legal context—and the policy behind s.213—and the factual circumstances. On the former, they summarised their conclusions as follows[49]:

---

[44] *MAN Nutzfahrzeuge*, at [158].

[45] In passing the Judge addressed the concern that there will often be more than one natural person who *does* represent the company for the purpose of a complex transaction (in this case, it was a number of directors of Western Star) and that the state of knowledge of those people may be different. He said that "the knowledge of all those who can be regarded as representing the company will be attributed to it in relation to each part of the contract. In the present case, I am prepared to assume that [each of the relevant] directors of the company all counted as Western Star for the purposes of the [sale agreement] and that the knowledge of each of them is to be regarded as the knowledge of Western Star for the purposes of each of the representations made in it."

[46] The reader should be aware that there is also a line of agency cases in relation to the liability of a principal in the tort of deceit (see especially *Armstrong v Strain* [1952] 1 K.B. 232 and *Anglo-Scottish Beet Sugar Corp Ltd v Spalding UDC* [1937] 2 K.B. 607, discussed in P.G. Watts (ed), *Bowstead and Reynolds on Agency*, 20th edn (London: Sweet & Maxwell, 2014) at 8–185). They do not all involve a question of attribution, as opposed to issues of vicarious liability or direct liability without any need for attribution (and—in particular—do not always maintain an analytical distinction between attribution on the one hand and vicarious liability on the other). Nevertheless, they tend to support the notion that it is necessary to find a human mind with a dishonest intention before dishonesty can be imputed to a principal.

[47] *Re Bank of Credit and Commerce International SA (No.15), Morris v Bank of India* [2005] EWCA Civ 693; [2005] 2 B.C.L.C. 328.

[48] Mummery LJ, Neuberger LJ and Munby J.

[49] *Morris v Bank of India*, at [129]–[130].

"First, the proper approach to the question of attribution in this case turns on the construction and purpose of section 213 . . . Thirdly, the wording of, and policy behind, section 213 indicate that it would be inappropriate, in the case of a company, to limit attribution for its purposes to the board, or those specifically authorised by a resolution of the board. To limit it in such a way would be to ignore reality, and risk emasculating the effect of the provision. In other words, 'insistence on the primary rules of attribution would in practice defeat [the legislative] intention', to quote from Lord Hoffmann in *Meridian*. Fourthly, it would be wrong, on the other hand, to attribute to a company the knowledge of any agent irrespective of the particular facts. To do so would risk obvious injustice to a company which had acted not only in good faith, but with scrupulous care; that would not accord with the purpose of section 213. Fifthly, it therefore must to some extent depend on the facts of each particular case whether an agent's knowledge should be attributed to the company for the purposes of section 213, where the circumstances are such that there would be no attribution on the application of the primary rules. We are of the view that it must typically depend on factors such as these. The agent's importance or seniority in the hierarchy of the company: the more senior he is, the easier it is to attribute. His significance and freedom to act in the context of the particular transaction: the more it is 'his' transaction, and the more he is effectively left to get on with it by the board, the easier it is to attribute. The degree to which the board is informed, and the extent to which it can be said that it was, in the broadest sense, put on inquiry: the greater the grounds for suspicion or even concern or questioning, the easier it is to attribute, if questions were not raised or answers were too easily accepted by the board."

Applying those conclusions to the facts of the case, the Court of Appeal—affirming Patten J at first instance—assessed the various factual elements as follows[50]:

19–041

"The determination of the person possessing the relevant knowledge for the purposes of ascertaining liability under section 213 is not simply a matter of identifying the person who authorised the transaction in accordance with the system of authorisation operated by the company in question. The scheme of delegation of authority might, as in this case, provide only an incomplete picture of what was done. It may not be sufficient for the purposes of determining whether the company should be treated as possessing the requisite knowledge. In most companies of any size there will be a chain of command and delegation of authority and it is likely that the transactions with the fraudulent company will be dealt with at a level in the company below that of the board. It would in practice defeat the effectiveness of the section if liability were limited to those cases in which the board of directors was actually a direct privy to the fraud of the company with whom the transactions were entered into. The question is who had authority in BoI to deal with BCCI in respect of the relevant transactions. That requires a consideration of all the circumstances surrounding the transaction..... Mr. Samant was a senior manager. The board of BoI relied on his judgment in relation to the transactions. He was given a 'blanket permission' to deal with BCCI by negotiating the terms of the transactions with borrowers nominated by BCCI, to make recommendations to the board and to give effect to advance approval of Head Office to enter into the transactions. He was allowed by the board to supervise the relevant transactions with BCCI and ultimately to decide to proceed with them on terms negotiated by him. To use Lord Hoffmann's words in *Meridian*, Mr. Samant was the person in BoI who had 'authority to deal' with BCCI. He was in substance the relevant decision maker for BoI in respect of the relevant transactions which made BoI a party to the fraudulent trading of BCCI. As Mr. Samant had a large measure of responsibility within BoI for the transactions with BCCI, the policy of section 213, justice and good sense combine to justify the treatment of Mr. Samant's knowledge as the corporate knowledge of BoI so as to make it responsible for contributing to the assets of BCCI in the winding up. It is true that the Judge found that the members of the board of BOI personally had no knowledge of the fraud, but they were content to leave the conduct and completion of the negotiations in the hands of Mr. Samant."

---

[50] *Morris v Bank of India*, at [96], [112] and [126].

19–042   The Court of Appeal in *Morris v Bank of India* also rejected a defence based on the "*Hampshire Land* principle"—the so-called "fraud exception" to attribution in certain circumstances—to which we now turn.

C.   HAMPSHIRE LAND AND THE "FRAUD EXCEPTION"

(1)   Introduction and Origin

19–043   The so-called "fraud exception" to the "normal" rules on attribution relates to (very fact sensitive and context-specific) circumstances in which it would be contrary to common sense and justice to impute the act, knowledge or state of mind of an agent or employee (often, but not necessarily, fraudulent) to his company or principal. The paradigm example, but not the only one, is where the company (or principal) is suing the agent for breach of his duty to the company and the agent seeks to attribute his own knowledge of his own breach of duty in order to found a defence of informed consent or ex turpi causa.

19–044   The phrase "fraud exception" is a misnomer, in that the true principle is neither an exception to other rules on attribution, nor is not confined to fraud:

(1)   Rather than being an exception to the "other" rules of attribution, which have been considered above, it is simply part of those rules: more particularly, it is a form of special rule of attribution which is fashioned by the courts to deal with certain legal and factual contexts: see *Bilta*,[51] where all seven Justices agreed on this point.[52]

(2)   In appropriate circumstances, the principle will be engaged when the actions or state of mind of the relevant agent, which are sought to be attributed to the company or principal, are not fraudulent. The circumstances could be infinitely varied, but it is certainly the case that it comprehends cases where the agent has breached his duty without fraud or dishonesty.[53] Nevertheless, the point is most commonly encountered in the context of fraud or dishonesty.

In *Bilta*, Lord Neuberger suggested that the phrase "fraud exception" be abandoned.[54] We agree that would help bring clarity to the nomenclature and would assist practitioners and the courts in applying the true principles accurately.

---

[51] See *Bilta*, per Lord Neuberger, with Lords Clarke and Carnwath at [9], per Lord Mance at [37]–[44], per Lord Sumption at [92], and per Lords Toulson and Hodge at [181] .

[52] That is not to say that there are not scenarios, or groups of scenarios, where it is easiest conceptually to analyse the situation by applying the general rules of attribution and then applying, in appropriate circumstances, an exception in respect of cases involving an attempt to attribute knowledge of an agent's breach of duty to the company/principal. But it is merely a tool of analysis—see Lord Sumption in *Bilta*, at [92].

[53] See, e.g., *Bilta*, per Lord Sumption at [71], Lord Neuberger at [9], and Lords Toulson and Hodge at [181].

[54] See *Bilta*, at [9].

The origin of the doctrine lies in the case of *In re Hampshire Land Co*,[55] in which **19–045** there was in fact no allegation of fraud. The Hampshire Land Company had borrowed money from a building society. The borrowing required the authority of the shareholders in general meeting, but their authority was vitiated by defects in the notice by which the meeting was called. The issue was whether the building society was affected by notice of the irregularity so as to be prevented from relying on the internal management rule (that people transacting with companies are entitled to assume that internal company rules are complied with, even if they are not).[56] The contention was that the building society was on notice because its secretary was also the secretary of the borrower, and in the latter capacity he knew the facts. In the course of his judgment on the actual issue in the case, Vaughan-Williams J observed[57]:

> "If [the secretary] had been guilty of a fraud, [his] personal knowledge…of the fraud that he had committed on the company would not have been knowledge of the society of the facts constituting that fraud; because common sense at once leads one to the conclusion that it would be impossible to infer that the duty either of giving or receiving notice will be fulfilled where the common agent is himself guilty of fraud."

That dictum was approved in the House of Lords in *Houghton & Co v Nothard, Lowe & Wills*[58], where the issue was whether a company was bound by an arrangement adverse to the company's interest which had been made by two of its directors for their own benefit and was never approved by the board. It was contended that the knowledge of the two directors could be attributed to the company so as to found a case of acquiescence. Viscount Dunedin said[59] that

> "It may be assumed that the knowledge of directors is in ordinary circumstances the knowledge of the company…But what if the knowledge of the director is the knowledge of a director who is himself *particeps criminis*, that is, if the knowledge of an infringement of the right of the company is only brought home to the man who himself was the artificer of such infringement? Common sense suggests the answer, but authority is not wanting."

He then cited the dictum of Vaughan Williams J. Lord Sumner said[60] it would be

> "contrary to justice and common sense to treat the knowledge of such persons as that of their company, as if one were to assume that they would make a clean breast of their delinquency."

From those perfectly respectable beginnings, confusion has reigned for a number **19–046** of years due to uncertainty as to both (i) the content—and underpinning analysis—of the principle and (ii) its application in various different types of case. Fortunately, following the recent decisions in *Moulin* and *Bilta*, a long review of the unhappy case law[61] is no longer necessary.[62]

---

[55] *In re Hampshire Land Co* [1896] 2 Ch 743.

[56] See *Royal British Bank v Turquand* (1856) 6 E&B 327.

[57] *In re Hampshire Land Co* [1896] 2 Ch. 743, at 749.

[58] *Houghton & Co v Nothard, Lowe & Wills* [1928] A.C. 1.

[59] *Houghton & Co v Nothard, Lowe & Wills* [1928] A.C. 1, at 14.

[60] *Houghton & Co v Nothard, Lowe & Wills* [1928] A.C. 1, at 19.

[61] Which includes the controversial, and highly problematic, decision of the House of Lords in *Moore Stephens v Stone & Rolls Ltd (in liquidation)* [2009] UKHL 39; [2009] 1 A.C. 1391, whose ratio still defies clear identification. Save as authority for what it actually decided (that, in the circumstances of

(2) The Correct Approach: Moulin and Bilta

19–047   As Lord Sumption observed in *Bilta*,[63] much of the difficulty has been caused by the twin problems of:

(i)   practitioners and the courts focussing on only *one* part of the legal and factual context in which the attribution question arises, viz. the nature of the company's (or principal's) relationship with the relevant agent, to reach a conclusion on the attribution question and

(ii)   then applying the results universally, insensitive to alterations in legal and other factual context.

19–048   The correct approach is, as with any other question of attribution, to consider the totality of the legal and factual context in order to answer the question whether it is appropriate in the circumstances of the case for the act, knowledge or state of mind of the relevant employee or agent to be attributed to the company or principal for the purposes of the particular claim or allegation at hand.

19–049   Once that is understood, the cases on the *Hampshire Land* principle fall—broadly—into three categories. Using the terminology adopted by the Court of Appeal in *Bilta*[64] and Lord Walker in *Moulin*, we will call the first two categories liability cases and redress cases; the third category comprises cases which do not fit comfortably into either the liability or redress categories, most usually involving the company suing a third party (such as an auditor or an insurer) for what amounts to an indemnity against losses suffered by reason of the defaulting director/employee's conduct. These cases tend to turn on a number of factors idiosyncratic to themselves.

19–050   As will be apparent, the crucial distinction between liability and redress cases is the legal context in which the attribution question arises.[65]

(i) Liability cases

19–051   Liability cases are those in which a company (or other principal) is being sued by a third party in a claim arising from the misconduct of a director, employee or other agent of the company. An obvious example is the simple case in which the

---

that case, attribution was appropriate to bar (via the illegality principle) a claim by Stone & Rolls, a one man company, against its auditors for failing to uncover a fraud which was the only purpose for which the company existed and all it ever did), and certain uncontroversial propositions of law which are now clearly articulated in the *Bilta* decision itself, it can thankfully now be laid to rest.

[62] Nevertheless, both Lord Walker's judgment in *Moulin* and the judgments of Lord Sumption and Lords Toulson and Hodge in *Bilta* provide an illuminating discussion (and, to some extent, rationalisation) of the cases and the different legal and factual contexts in which the attribution question can arise.

[63] *Bilta*, at [86].

[64] *Bilta* [2013] EWCA Civ 968; [2014] Ch. 52, at [34]–[35].

[65] Although it is not always easy to categorise a case as a liability or redress case: see the split decision in the Court of Appeal on the proper characterisation of the situation in *UBS v KWL* [2017] EWCA Civ 1567, at [146]–[152], per Lord Briggs of Westbourne and Hamblen LJ, and, at [355]–[368], per Gloster LJ.

director or employee has caused a fraud to be perpetrated by his company on the third party. In these cases, frequently, no question of attribution properly so called will arise—because the company will be vicariously liable for completed wrongs committed by its directors or other agents. But in the cases where attribution is relevant—because the company itself must have a particular state of mind or level of knowledge (such as in dishonest assistance or knowing receipt cases)—the rule of attribution will, subject to all the relevant facts and circumstances as discussed above, usually lead to imputation of the relevant conduct or state of mind to the company *for the purpose of the claim by the third party*. That is so even though the company may in some sense be a "victim" of the fraudulent director or employee, in that it too will suffer losses arising from the director's conduct.

Examples of liability cases include: *El Ajou*,[66] *Meridian Global, McNicholas Construction Ltd v Custom and Excise Commissioners*[67] and *Bank of India v Morris*.[68]

19–052

(ii) Redress cases

In redress cases a company (or other principal) is seeking to make its own delinquent director or employee, or an accomplice of such a person (such as a dishonest assistant, knowing recipient, co-conspirator etc.), accountable for the loss that the company itself has suffered as a result of the director's breach of duty. That is the situation in which the rules of attribution will prevent the company being imputed with the director's or employee's act, knowledge or state of mind, because it would be absurd and unjust to permit such a director or employee to use his own serious breach of duty to his corporate employer or principal as a defence. It matters not whether the breach of duty was perpetrated with the intention of causing direct loss to the company—as in a direct abstraction of its assets—or whether it was perpetrated as part of a larger scheme for a different purpose directed at others.[69] That is because the objection is to the reliance by the directors etc. on their own breach of duty for the purpose of defeating a claim against them for breach of that very duty.

19–053

Accordingly, the result is the same even in a case where the director's wrong-doing necessarily involved the company itself committing a criminal contravention of the law[70] and in the case of a "one-man" company.[71] The

19–054

---

[66] *El Ajou* [1994] 2 All E.R. 685.
[67] *McNicholas Construction Ltd v Custom and Excise Commissioners* [2000] STC 553.
[68] *Bank of India v Morris* [2005] EWCA Civ 693; [2005] 2 B.C.L.C. 328.
[69] *Bilta* in the Court of Appeal, [2013] EWCA Civ 968; [2014] Ch. 52, at [35].
[70] See *Belmont No.1*, where the directors' scheme necessarily involved a criminal contravention by the company of the Companies Act.
[71] See *Bilta*, at [90]. It is important to understand this point in relation to "one-man" companies: the fact that a company may be "one-man" is relevant in the third category of cases—relating to claims by the company against third parties—but it is not relevant in this second category relating to claims against the defaulting agent or his accomplices. In this context a "one-man" company means—at least usually—a company with a sole shareholder and director; although there are cases in which the concept has been extended to include companies where, although there are other directors, they are essentially ciphers for the "one man": see, for example, *Berg, Sons & Co Ltd v Mervyn Hampton*

accomplices of a fraudulent agent cannot be in any better position than the agent himself: their ancillary liability arises because of their participation in the agent's breach of duty.[72]

19-055　Examples of redress cases include: *Gluckstein v Barnes*,[73] *Belmont No.1*,[74] *Beach Petroleum NL v Johnson*[75] and *Bilta* itself.

(iii)　Other cases

19-056　The remaining types of cases—which are relatively few in number—arise in situations where, usually because of the particular legal context, the redress/ liability model is not apposite. The particular factual and legal context in these cases requires a different rule of attribution to be fashioned.

19-057　The usual legal context for cases of this type is this: the company or principal brings a claim against a third party (who is neither the defaulting director or employee, nor an accomplice) seeking recovery of losses arising out of the defaulting director/agent's conduct, which the third party was under a duty to prevent or detect or otherwise to indemnify the company/principal against. Examples include: cases against auditors, who ought to have detected the fraud of the director/agent at an earlier stage and prevented the losses to the company; cases against insurers providing insurance cover against the risk of internal fraud; and cases against bankers owing a duty of care under *Barclays Bank Plc v Quincecare Ltd*[76] to refuse to implement a valid instruction to pay money out of a customer's account in view of obvious signs that the payments were for the benefit of the director and not the creditors of the company. The attribution issue usually arises if the third party insurer, auditor or bank seeks to raise the illegality principle as a defence to the claim: it is asserted that the fraud of the director/employee is to be attributed to the claimant company/principal such that it is relying on its own wrong to found its claim.[77]

Adams [1993] B.C.L.C. 1045; *Royal Brunei v Tan* and the discussion in *Stone & Rolls*, at 1492C to E, in which Lord Walker says he would include cases where there are two or more individual directors and shareholders acting closely in concert, such as the directors in *Attorney General's Reference (No.2 of 1982)* [1984] 1 Q.B. 624 or Mr Chappell and Mr Palmer in *Brink's-Mat Ltd v Noye* [1991] 1 Bank L.R. 68. In *Singularis Holdings Ltd (in official liquidation) v Daiwa Capital Markets Europe Ltd* [2018] EWCA Civ 84, at [53], the Court of Appeal defined the term more broadly as "a company in which, whether there was one or more than one controller, there were no innocent directors or shareholders" (purportedly taken from what the majority in *Bilta* agreed: see [80] of Lord Sumption's judgment and [26] of Lord Neuberger's judgment). Notwithstanding that attempted definition in *Singularis*, the question cannot be regarded as closed and it is probably still correct to say that "[t]he precise definition of a one-man company is still to be worked out...": *Lexi Holdings (UK) Ltd v DTZ Debenham Tie Leugn Ltd* [2010] EWHC 2290 (Ch), at [17], per Briggs J.

[72] *Moulin*, at [104] and [106(7)]; and *Bilta*, at [90].

[73] *Gluckstein v Barnes* [1900] A.C. 240.

[74] *Belmont No.1* [1979] Ch. 250.

[75] *Beach Petroleum NL v Johnson* (1993) 43 FCR 1.

[76] *Barclays Bank Plc v Quincecare Ltd* [1992] 4 All E.R. 363.

[77] We have considered the illegality principle in Ch.24. The law has recently developed significantly in relation to the content and application of the illegality principle: *Patel v Mirza* [2016] UKSC 42; [2017] A.C. 467. There may accordingly be changes to the way in which it has been applied in illegality cases which raise questions of attribution. But the basic landscape in which the attribution

The position in respect of claims against auditors is not entirely clear, partly due to the confusion which still surrounds the decision in *Stone & Rolls*, which was an auditors case, and partly because there are other decisions going either way. Ultimately, the position will depend on the exact legal and factual context, which includes the proper scope of an auditor's duty in a situation such as this (that is a question which remains open following *Stone & Rolls*).[78]   **19–058**

As Lord Walker observed in *Moulin*,[79] in a number of cases against auditors for failure to detect internal fraud, the illegality defence has not worked—because knowledge of the fraud has not been attributed to the claimant company: on the facts of those cases, detecting and preventing internal fraud by a director or employee was the very thing which the auditor had contractually undertaken to do and it would accordingly make no sense to attribute the internal fraud to the company in that legal context.[80] But there are auditor cases in which knowledge of the guilty director/agent has been attributed to the company such as to make good the auditors' illegality defence and bar the claim against them: see *Berg, Sons & Co Ltd v Mervyn Hampton Adams*[81] and *Stone & Rolls* itself. Those are both cases in which the companies in question were "one-man" companies, where there was no manifestation of the company (at director or shareholder level) which could have been misled or let down by the auditors' failure to identify that the company was being used by the "one man" for fraudulent purposes.   **19–059**

Lord Walker called such "one-man" cases "extreme" in *Moulin*[82]; but in *Bilta* Lord Sumption said this of auditors cases[83]:   **19–060**

> "In the first place, the defendant in that case, although presumably in breach of his own distinct duty, is not seeking to attribute his own wrong or state of mind to the company or to rely on his breach of duty to avoid liability. Secondly, as between the company and the outside world, there is no principled reason not to identify it with its directing mind in the ordinary way. For a person, whether natural or corporate, who is culpable of fraud to say to an innocent but negligent outsider that he should have stopped him in his dishonest enterprise is as clear a case for the application of the illegality defence as one could have. *Stone & Rolls* was a case of just this kind. Leaving aside the admittedly important question of the scope of an auditor's duty, if the illegality defence had not applied in that case, it could only have been because:
> (i)   the company was treated in point of law as a mindless automaton, or
> (ii)   the defence could never apply to companies even in circumstances where it would have applied to natural persons.
> Neither proposition is consistent with established principle".

That dictum of Lord Sumption appears to be of general application—not limited to "one-man" cases, and not necessarily limited to auditor cases. Nevertheless, no

---

question sits will remain the same: via attribution of a fraudulent agent's conduct, defendants will continue to seek to defend claims made by companies/principals on the basis that those claims rely on the claimant's fraud and thereby engage the illegality principle as it is post-*Patel*.

[78] See, for example, per Lord Sumption in *Bilta*, at [81].

[79] *Moulin*, at [106(9)].

[80] See, e.g., *MAN Nutzfahrzeuge AG v Freightliner Ltd* [2005] EWHC 2347 (Comm); and *Moulin*, at [106(9)].

[81] *Berg, Sons & Co Ltd v Mervyn Hampton Adams* [1993] B.C.L.C. 1045.

[82] *Moulin*, at [106(9)].

[83] *Bilta*, at [91].

other Justice specifically endorsed this view (even in the one-man context),[84] and attempts to suggest that it represents the law, outside the auditor context and even in the "one-man" company case, have already been rejected at first instance and in the Court of Appeal.[85] Ultimately, the position will depend on the exact legal and factual context—including what exactly the auditor undertook to do and what the scope of his duty is as a matter of law—although it is suggested that a major factor in determining the outcome may continue to be the distinction between "true" "one-man" companies and other principals.

19–061 Insurance cases will turn on the terms of the policy under consideration.[86] In cases in which a company has obtained insurance cover against the risk of internal fraud by directors, employees or agents, it is likely that—in light of the content and policy of the substantive legal rule under consideration—the director's fraud will not be attributed to the company: to do so would render nugatory the contract of insurance itself, as internal fraud by a director/agent was the very thing against which the company sought to protect itself and against which the insurance company undertook to protect the company: see *Arab Bank Plc v Zurich Insurance Co*,[87] *Morris v Bank of India*[88] and *Moulin*.[89]

19–062 A recent case involving the *Quincecare* duty of care was *Singularis Holdings Ltd (in official liquidation) v Daiwa Capital Markets Europe Ltd*.[90] Singularis' sole shareholder and previously dominant director, Mr Al Sanea, had fraudulently funnelled Singularis' funds to other companies he owned through the defendant stockbroker. The liquidators of Singularis sued the defendant stockbrokers, inter alia for breach of their *Quincecare* duty. The defendant asserted that the claim was barred by illegality, on the basis that Mr Al Sanea's conduct should be attributed to Singularis such that it was relying on its wrong in bringing the claim.

19–063 Following the general context-based approach mandated by *Bilta* and *Meridian*, and rejecting a submission, based on Lord Sumption's dictum in *Bilta* discussed above[91], that in any proceedings where a company is suing a third party for breach of a duty owed to it by that third party, the fraudulent conduct of a director must be attributed to the company if it is a one-man company, Rose J held that it would denude the *Quincecare* duty of any value in cases where it is most needed

---

[84] Indeed, other relevant Justices made it quite clear that they regarded attribution to be appropriate (and therefore the illegality defence to be available) in only *some* situations in which there were no innocent shareholders or directors: see e.g. *Bilta*, at [26] and the discussion of this issue in *Singularis Holdings Ltd (in official liquidation) v Daiwa Capital Markets Europe Ltd* [2018] EWCA Civ 84, especially, at [46] and [56]–[59].

[85] See *Singularis Holdings Ltd (in official liquidation) v Daiwa Capital Markets Europe Ltd* [2017] EWHC 257 (Ch) and [2018] EWCA Civ 84, discussed further below. Apart from anything else, matters are complicated by a lack of clarity over what is meant by a "one-man" company in any event.

[86] *PCW Syndicates v PCW Reinsurers* [1996] 1 W.L.R. 1136 and *Group Josi Re v Walbrook Insurance Co Ltd* [1996] 1 W.L.R. 1152 were concerned with corporate knowledge in the context of the statutory obligations of an assured under ss.18 and 19 of the Marine Insurance Act 1906.

[87] *Arab Bank Plc v Zurich Insurance Co* [1999] 1 Lloyd's L.R. 262, at 283.

[88] *Morris v Bank of India*, at [122]–[124].

[89] *Moulin*, at [94] and [106(8)].

[90] *Singularis Holdings Ltd (in official liquidation) v Daiwa Capital Markets Europe Ltd* [2017] EWHC 257 (Ch).

[91] *Bilta*, at [91].

if Al Sanea's fraud, or knowledge of his fraud, were to be attributed to Singularis in the context of their claim against the defendant under that duty. As she observed:

> "The duty is only relevant in a situation where the instructions to pay out the money are given by the person who has been entrusted by the company as a signatory on the bank account. If there were no properly authorised instruction to transfer the money, the company would not need to rely on the *Quincecare* duty. The existence of the duty is therefore predicated on the assumption that the person whose fraud is suspected is a trusted employee or officer. So the duty when it arises is a duty to save the company from the fraudulent conduct of that trusted person."[92]

She also held that, in any event, Singularis was not a "one-man" company in the relevant sense.[93]

The Court of Appeal dismissed an appeal from Rose J on this point: **19–064**

(1) holding that the concept of a "one-man" company was not particularly helpful and that the key question was always an assessment of the overall factual and legal context of the alleged attribution ("I do not think the evaluation of the facts is much assisted by trying first to decide whether the company in question fits within the parameters of various competing definitions of the term 'one-man company'")[94];

(2) in any event rejecting the contention that Singularis was a "one-man" company in the relevant sense[95]; and

(3) endorsing the crucial relevance (at least in the factual context Rose J had found) of the nature of the legal duty and alleged breach of it as expressed by the judge in [184] of her judgment, quoted above.[96]

There are other—more isolated—examples of cases which do not fit the **19–065**
redress/liability model: they are best viewed as turning on the particular statutory context in which the attribution issue arises. Examples include *Moulin* itself, which turned on the construction of the relevant section of the Hong Kong Inland Revenue Ordinance[97]; and *Safeway Stores Ltd v Twigger*,[98] which turned on the legislative scheme set out in s.2 of the Competition Act 1998.

---

[92] *Singularis Holdings Ltd (in official liquidation) v Daiwa Capital Markets Europe Ltd*, at [184].

[93] *Singularis Holdings Ltd (in official liquidation) v Daiwa Capital Markets Europe Ltd*, at [188]–[189].

[94] *Singularis Holdings Ltd (in official liquidation) v Daiwa Capital Markets Europe Ltd* [2018] EWCA Civ 84, at [59].

[95] *Singularis Holdings Ltd (in official liquidation) v Daiwa Capital Markets Europe Ltd*, at [53]–[54] (and [55]).

[96] *Singularis Holdings Ltd (in official liquidation) v Daiwa Capital Markets Europe Ltd*, at [56]–[57].

[97] See *Moulin*, at [134]–[135].

[98] *Safeway Stores Ltd v Twigger* [2010] EWCA Civ 1472; [2011] 2 All E.R. 841.

CHAPTER 20

JOINT LIABILITY IN TORT

A.   INTRODUCTION

(1)   Joint and Several Tortfeasors

We have considered in Ch.2 the law relating to unlawful means conspiracy, which **20–001** allows liability to be imposed on multiple parties by reason of their having combined together. There is a related but separate principle—joint tortfeasorship—which allows liability to be imposed in tort upon multiple parties in respect of a single tort, even if one or more of those parties did not directly commit the tort in question. The concept of joint tortfeasorship is significant in the law of civil fraud, because it will often be the case that multiple parties are in some way implicated in a fraudulent endeavour and the claimant will wish to understand the available bases for seeking to impose liability upon those parties. A claimant should not be beguiled by the torts of joint or accessory liability considered elsewhere in this book into ignoring the possibility of a claim on the basis of joint torfeasorship.

Joint tortfeasors are to be distinguished from several tortfeasors, who **20–002** independently cause damage to the same claimant, but whose liability is distinct and whose conduct gives rise to separate causes of action, even if giving rise to the same or overlapping loss. We say no more of this latter concept in this chapter, which will rarely arise in fraud claims.[1] The distinction between joint and several tortfeasors was formerly of some significance because of the common law rule that there could only be one cause of action in respect of one tort, so that judgment against one tortfeasor would release any claims against the other tortfeasor. This rule was partially mitigated by s.3 of Civil Liability (Contribution) Act 1978, which provides that:

> "Judgment recovered against any person liable in respect of any debt or damage shall not be a bar to an action, or to the continuance of an action, against any other person who is (apart from any such bar) jointly liable with him in respect of the same debt or damage."

In the light of s.3 of the 1978 Act the law has been stated as follows:

---

[1] See generally M.A. Jones, A.M. Dugdale and M. Simpson (eds), *Clerk & Lindsell on Torts*, 21st edn (London: Sweet & Maxwell, 2016), para.4–02. An example of several torts is to be found in the facts of *The Koursk* [1924] P. 140. Several tortfeasorship often arises in road traffic collisions involving multiple parties.

"Judgment recovered against any person liable in respect of any debt or damage is not a bar to an action, or to the continuance of an action, against any other person who is (apart from any such bar) jointly liable with him in respect of the same debt or damage. However, a satisfied judgment (except in the case of a foreign judgment) is a bar to a claim against other tortfeasors, whether joint or several, who are liable for the same damage."[2]

These principles carry with them a number of complex questions concerning the discharge of liability of joint tortfeasors, which are outside the remit of this book.[3]

(2) Types of Joint Tortfeasorship

20–003   There are four principal forms of joint tortfeasorship[4]:

(1)   Where the tortfeasors participate equally in the act giving rise to the tort. For example, two or more people jointly sign and publish a defamatory document or a prospectus containing fraudulent misrepresentations.
(2)   Where a person induces, incites or procures another to commit a tort.[5]
(3)   Where one person assists another to commit a tort.
(4)   Where a principal or employer is vicariously liable for the acts or omissions of an agent or employee. In such a case both the principal/employer and the agent/employee are jointly liable for the same tort.

20–004   It will be obvious that, as regards the first to third categories, liability as joint tortfeasors will often be an alternative basis of liability to liability for unlawful means conspiracy. That does not render the tort of conspiracy redundant, however, since, as we have seen, conspiracy can be founded on unlawful means other than torts.[6]

20–005   As regards the first category of case, no more need be said. As regards the second, again the law is relatively straightforward, having been fully analysed in *MCA Records Inc v Charly Records Ltd*.[7] An important point made in that case

---

[2] *Halsbury's Laws of England*, 5th edn (London: LNUK, 2015) Vol.97, para.449, quoted with approval in *Vanden Recycling Ltd v Bevin Tumulty Bolton Brothers Ltd* [2015] EWHC 3616 (QB).
[3] See Jones, Dugdale and Simpson (eds), *Clerk & Lindsell on Torts* (2016), para.4–07 and following.
[4] See the analysis in *Sea Shepherd UK v Fish & Fish Ltd* [2015] UKSC 10; [2015] A.C. 1229 (henceforth "*Sea Shepherd UK*"), at [19], per Lord Toulson. *Sea Shepherd UK* is now the leading decision on joint tortfeasorship, especially in relation to the third category analysed in the main text.
[5] *CBS Songs Ltd v Amstrad Consumer Electronics Plc* [1988] A.C. 1013, 1058, per Lord Templeman. A recent example of a failed attempt to impose liability on a defendant for having procured a tort is *National Guild of Removers and Storers Ltd v Milner (t/a Intransit Removals and Storage)* [2014] EWHC 670 (IPEC); [2014] F.S.R. 38. In *Smith v Pywell and Spicer, The Times*, 28 April 1959, Diplock J held that "There was no separate tort of procuring a third person to commit a tort, but the procurer was a joint tortfeasor with the person who actually committed it."
[6] It is said in Jones, Dugdale and Simpson (eds), *Clerk & Lindsell on Torts* (2016), para.24–97: "It would appear that the question whether a person is a party to a combination constituting a conspiracy is essentially the same as whether he is liable as a joint tortfeasor in procuring a wrong, by reason of a common design."
[7] *MCA Records Inc v Charly Records Ltd* [2001] EWCA Civ 1441; [2002] F.S.R. 26.

and elsewhere[8] is that a director (or other officer or controlling shareholder) of a company may be jointly liable in tort with the company of which he is director if he intends, procures and shares a common design that the company commit the act which is tortious. The relevant principles in this regard[9] were summarised by Chadwick LJ as follows:

(1) First, a director will not be treated as liable with the company as a joint tortfeasor if he does no more than carry out his constitutional role in the governance of the company (that is to say, by voting at board meetings). That is required to give proper recognition to the identity of the company as a separate legal person. Similarly, a controlling shareholder will not be liable as a joint tortfeasor if he does no more than exercise his power of control through the constitutional organs of the company (for example by voting at general meetings and by exercising the powers to appoint directors). If all that a director is doing is carrying out the duties entrusted to him as such by the company under its constitution, the circumstances in which it would be right to hold him liable as a joint tortfeasor with the company would be rare indeed.

(2) Secondly, there is no reason why a person who happens to be a director or controlling shareholder of a company should not be liable with the company as a joint tortfeasor, if he is not exercising control through the constitutional organs of the company and the circumstances are such that he would be so liable if he were not a director or controlling shareholder. In other words, if, in relation to the wrongful acts which are the subject of complaint, the liability of the individual as a joint tortfeasor with the company arises from his participation or involvement in ways which go beyond the exercise of constitutional control, then there is no reason why the individual should escape liability because he could have procured those same acts through the exercise of constitutional control.

As regards the fourth category of joint liability, we have dealt with the principles of vicarious liability as they apply to a claim in fraud in Ch.1 above.[10]   **20–006**

It is the third category of cases, which is necessarily the most difficult to circumscribe, that has generated the most litigation. The cases in relation to this third category generally analyse joint tortfeasorship by reference to the "primary tortfeasor", i.e. the person who committed the relevant tortious act, and by then considering the role played by the alleged joint tortfeasor in perpetrating the tort.   **20–007**

---

[8] See *Rainham Chemical Works Ltd (In liquidation) v Belvedere Fish Guano Co Ltd* [1921] 2 A.C. 465; *Performing Right Society Ltd v Ciryl Theatrical Syndicate Ltd* [1924] 1 K.B. 1; *C Evans Sons Ltd v Spritebrand Ltd* [1985] 1 W.L.R. 317.

[9] These principles also apply to joint tortfeasorship of the assistance kind: for a recent example, see *Victoria Plum Ltd (t/a Victoria Plumb) v Victorian Plumbing Ltd* [2016] EWHC 291 (director of a company carrying out his responsibilities as such held not to be sufficiently implicated in the company's tort to be jointly liable).

[10] See Section F.

B.   JOINT TORTFEASORSHIP THROUGH ASSISTANCE

20–008   For a defendant to be liable to a claimant as a joint tortfeasor under the third category of case discussed above three conditions must be satisfied:

(1)   First, the defendant must have assisted the commission of an act by the primary tortfeasor;

(2)   Secondly, the assistance must have been pursuant to a common design on the part of the defendant and the primary tortfeasor that the act be committed;

(3)   Thirdly, the act must constitute a tort as against the claimant.[11]

20–009   The latter two of these indicia[12] are no doubt equally applicable to the first and second categories discussed above; but in those categories their application rarely presents difficulties (for example, inducing or procuring a tort will necessarily involve a common intent with the primary tortfeasor to commit the acts which are tortious). It is in the situation where the defendant has been a relatively minor participant in the primary tortfeasor's plan—that is, where he facilitates, rather than actively participates in or procures the tortious acts—that complexities can arise.

20–010   We consider below in further detail each of these conditions. However, the courts have frequently warned against an overly refined or prescriptive exposition of each of these three conditions. This is for two reasons which have been articulated in the authorities: first, because joint tortfeasorship is so fact sensitive; secondly, because it needs to be kept within realistic bounds.

20–011   This form of liability is said to be

> "...not for the assistance. He is liable for the tortious act of the primary actor, because by reason of the assistance the law treats him as party to it: *Credit Lyonnais Bank Nederland NV v Export Credits Guarantee Department* [2000] 1 A.C. 486, at 495–500. This does not, however, mean that the accessory must have joined in doing the very act constituting the tort. Liability as a joint tortfeasor is more commonly an accessory liability."[13]

---

[11] This was established in the seminal decision in *The Koursk* [1924] P. 140, at 151, 156, and 159; and see *Sea Shepherd UK*, above, per Lord Neuberger at [55].

[12] Crisply encapsulated in the following sentence from an earlier edition of *Clerk & Lindsell* which was quoted by all the members of the Court of Appeal in *The Koursk* and said by Lord Toulson, in *Sea Shepherd UK*, at [22], to remain good law: "Persons are said to be joint tortfeasors when their respective shares in the commission of the tort are done in furtherance of a common design."

[13] *Sea Shepherd UK*, at [38], per Lord Sumption; and see further *Amstrad Consumer Electronics Plc v British Phonographic Industry Ltd* [1986] F.S.R. 159. As regards questions relating to the vicarious liability of an employer of the joint tortfeasor whose assistance is not in itself unlawful, see generally *Credit Lyonnais Bank Nederland NV v Export Credits Guarantee Department* [2000] 1 A.C. 486, considered in Ch.1, Section F, above.

(1) Assistance

The assistance provided to the primary tortfeasor must be substantial, in the sense of not being de minimis or trivial.[14] On the other hand the claimant need not show that the tort would not have been committed absent the assistance. The defendant's own liability is not decided by reference to a but-for test. The proper way to reflect the defendant's relative minor role (if such it is) compared to that of the primary tortfeasor is by apportioning liability inter se through the court's jurisdiction to order contribution.[15] Of course such an award has no bearing on the claimant's ability to recover damages. As between the joint tortfeasors and the claimant each of them is liable for 100 per cent of the loss awarded.[16]

20–012

(2) Common Design

Clearly mere assistance, or "facilitation", can never be sufficient. That would impose potential liability indiscriminately widely and potentially impose an unjust burden upon the morally innocent. Moreover, even "knowing" assistance does not suffice[17]: that is, a person who facilitates the commission of the tort is not liable merely because he knows of the primary tortfeasor's intention.[18] Instead, the key condition which serves as a limiting factor is the requirement that the primary and alleged joint tortfeasor are party to a common design[19] that the acts constituting or giving rise to the tort be carried out. As Lord Sumption out it in *Sea Shepherd UK*[20]:

20–013

> "What the authorities, taken as a whole, demonstrate is that the additional element which is required to establish liability, over and above mere knowledge that an otherwise lawful act will

---

[14] *Sea Shepherd UK*, at [57], per Lord Neuberger.

[15] *Sea Shepherd UK*, at [49], per Lord Sumption.

[16] See per Jordan CJ in *Dougherty v Chandler* (1946) 46 SR (NSW) 370, at 375: "If a number of persons jointly participate in the commission of a tort, each is responsible, jointly with the others, and also severally, for the whole amount of the damage caused by the tort, irrespective of his participation."

[17] Per Hobhouse LJ in the Court of Appeal in *Credit Lyonnais Bank Nederland NV v Export Credits Guarantee Department* [1998] 1 Lloyd's Rep. 19, at 46.

[18] *Sea Shepherd UK*, at [39], per Lord Sumption. Hence the person who sells equipment to the primary tortfeasor knowing that the purchaser is likely to use that equipment to infringe copyrights is not liable: see e.g. *Dunlop Pneumatic Tyre Co Ltd v David Moseley & Sons Ltd* [1904] 1 Ch. 164; and *CBS Songs Ltd v Amstrad Consumer Electronics Plc* [1988] A.C. 1013.

[19] Other synonymous phrases have been deployed: e.g. "concerted action"; "agreed on common action": see *Unilever v Gillette* [1989] RPC 583, at 609, per Mustill LJ, where he stated in a very frequently quoted passage that the test was "… whether … (a) there was a common design between [the primary and secondary parties] to do acts which … amounted to infringements, and (b) [the secondary party] has acted in furtherance of that design. I use the words common design because they are readily to hand but there are other expressions in the cases, such as 'concerted action' or 'agreed on common action' which will serve just as well. The words are not to be construed as if they formed part of a statute. They all convey the same idea. This idea does not, as it seems to me, call for any finding that the secondary party has explicitly mapped out a plan with the primary offender. Their tacit agreement will be sufficient. Nor, as it seems to me, is there any need for a common design to infringe. It is enough if the parties combine to secure the doing of acts which in the event prove to be infringements."

[20] *Sea Shepherd UK*, at [44].

assist the tort, is a shared intention that it should do so. The required limitation on the scope of liability is achieved by the combination of active co-operation and commonality of intention."

20–014 The alleged joint tortfeasor

"must share with the other party, or parties, to the design, each of the features of the design which make it wrongful. If, and only if, all those features are shared, the fact that some parties to the common design did only some of the relevant acts, while others did only some other relevant acts, will not stop them all from being jointly liable."[21]

What this means in the context of an intentional tort is that the defendant must have the same mens rea as is required to impose liability on the primary tortfeasor. So, for example, the person who helps write the prospectus which contains the fraudulent misrepresentations on the instruction of the primary tortfeasor cannot be liable in deceit as a joint tortfeasor if he believes the facts set out to be true or if he does not intend that the relevant statements be relied upon.

20–015 The concept of common design can sometimes be difficult to pin down.[22] Must the acts in respect of which there is a common design be the very acts which the primary tortfeasor in the event perpetrates? Where the common design is to pursue a range of activities (such as campaigning against a particular form of conduct, e.g. fox-hunting or whaling), where the activities might, but will not necessarily, involve a tortious element, it appears that a common design with respect to the activities generally is sufficient.[23] If two parties co-operate in a common design to commit a tort in a certain eventuality, and that eventuality occurs and the tort is committed, it is irrelevant that they both appreciated and perhaps even hoped that it would not occur, even if they do not know that the action which constitutes the tort is in fact unlawful.[24]

20–016 The common design will usually be one founded on express communication between the relevant parties. However it can be inferred; and "tacit agreement" may be sufficient.[25]

---

[21] *Vestergaard Frandsen A/S v Bestnet Europe Ltd* [2013] 1 W.L.R. 1556, at [34], per Lord Neuberger.

[22] In *Sabaf v Meneghetti* [2002] EWCA Civ 976; [2003] RPC 14, at [59], Peter Gibson LJ put the concept in the following way: "The underlying concept for joint tortfeasance must be that the joint tortfeasor has been so involved in the commission of the tort as to make himself liable for the tort. Unless he has made the infringing act his own, he has not himself committed the tort. That notion seems to us what underlies all the decisions to which we were referred. If there is a common design or concerted action or otherwise a combination to secure the doing of the infringing acts, then each of the combiners has made the act his own and will be liable." Similarly, in *Twentieth Century Fox Film Corp v Newzbin Ltd* [2010] EWHC 608 (Ch), Kitchin J said, at [108], that "...mere (even knowing) assistance or facilitation of the primary infringement is not enough. The joint tortfeasor must have so involved himself in the tort as to make it his own." In *Sea Shepherd UK* Lord Neuberger commented, at [58] that the concept of making the infringing act "his own" was ultimately circular.

[23] *Sea Shepherd UK*, at [27], per Lord Toulson.

[24] *Sea Shepherd UK*, at [48], per Lord Sumption.

[25] *Sea Shepherd UK*, at [59], per Lord Neuberger.

(3)   Tort has to be Committed

In one sense this is an obvious ingredient. But it establishes the boundaries of   **20–017**
what the claimant needs to establish. It is unnecessary to show that the defendant
appreciated or intended that the act which he assisted pursuant to a common
design constituted or gave rise to a tort: it is the act itself which must have been
the subject of the common design, not its wrongfulness.[26]

(4)   Examples

It assists understanding of the concept of joint tortfeasorship to describe some   **20–018**
examples:

(1)   In *Monsanto v Tilly*[27] a group carried out direct action in protesting against
GM crops by pulling up the plants. The group's media liaison officer, while
not actually pulling up plants himself,

> "reconnoitred the site the day before. He met the press at a prearranged rendezvous and led
> them to the site for the purpose of photographing and reporting the uprooting activities. He
> was present while the others uprooted the plants and he explained the purpose and
> significance of their acts to the media".[28]

He was held to have no arguable defence to a claim that he was a joint
tortfeasor.
(2)   In *Credit Lyonnais v ECGD*[29] an employee of the ECGD guaranteed bills of
exchange issued in relation to fictitious export transactions. This was done
in concert with a third party who used them to deceive the claimant bank.
The employee of the ECGD did not himself deceive the bank, but it was
held in the Court of Appeal (and was common ground in the House of
Lords)[30] that he was a joint tortfeasor because he joined in the common
design.
(3)   In *Shah v Gale*[31] the defendant was held liable as a joint tortfeasor in
assault where she had pointed out to an assailant the address of the claimant
who was then murdered by the assailant.

(5)   Claims in Deceit

So far as relevant to this book, the principles of joint tortfeasorship considered in   **20–019**
this chapter are most likely to be of significance in claims in deceit (since
conspiracy, unlawful interference and inducement of a breach of contract are
already torts of joint or accessory liability). In such a case each of the defendants

---

[26] See the dictum of Mustill LJ in *Unilever v Gillette* [1989] RPC 583, at 609, quoted above at fn.19.
[27] *Monsanto v Tilly* [2000] Env L.R. 313.
[28] *Monsanto v Tilly*, at [46].
[29] *Credit Lyonnais v ECGD* [1998] 1 Lloyd's Rep. 19, at 46, in the Court of Appeal.
[30] *Credit Lyonnais v ECGD* [2000] 1 A.C. 486.
[31] *Shah v Gale* [2005] EWHC 1087 (QB).

must have the relevant mental state which we have analysed in Ch.1, though, of course, each need not actually take all the steps which constitute the tort.

20–020 So, for example, in *Dadourian Group International Inc v Simms*[32] it was held that Mr Simms was liable for the deceit of his co-defendant, Jack, to the effect that Jack was not involved in the relevant transaction except as an intermediary, even though Mr Simms did not himself make the relevant misrepresentation.[33] This was because:

(a) Mr Simms intended, procured and shared a common design to mislead the claimants into thinking that Jack was not involved, and Mr Simms (at the very least) must have known that Jack was presenting himself as only being involved as an intermediary[34];

(b) Mr Simms knew that Jack was in fact involved in the transaction;

(c) Mr Simms intended that the claimants would act on the false impression that Jack was not involved; and

(d) the claimants relied on the relevant misrepresentation.

20–021 As we have seen, in deceit claims the target is often the directors of a company which has assumed contractual obligations and has not discharged them before becoming insolvent.[35] The claimant may well wish to try to ascribe liability in deceit to more than one of the directors by reference to joint tortfeasorship principles. Such an attempt failed in *Inter Export LLC v Townley*.[36] It will be evident from the analysis above that the mere fact that a person is a director of or shareholder in the primary tortfeasor does not, without more, make him liable as a joint tortfeasor.[37]

---

[32] *Dadourian Group International Inc v Simms* [2006] EWHC 2973 (Ch); [2006] ArbLR 18 and on appeal, at [2009] EWCA Civ 169; [2009] 1 Lloyd's Rep. 601.

[33] As Arden LJ observed, at [84]: "It is sufficient for a person to be liable as a joint tortfeasor if another commits a wrongful act pursuant to a common design between the two of them that such act be committed. It is not necessary for that person also to have committed a wrongful act."

[34] It is noteworthy that the Judge (Warren J) held that Mr Simms would also be liable on the basis that he had adopted Jack's misrepresentation: at [575(c)]; although another defendant, Helga, was also held liable on the basis of joint tortfeasorship but expressly not on the basis that she adopted the misrepresentation: [579].

[35] E.g. *Standard Chartered Bank v Pakistan National Shipping Corp* [2003] 1 A.C. 959.

[36] *Inter Export LLC v Townley* [2017] EWHC 530 (Ch).

[37] See at [4] above.

SECTION E

RELIEF AND BARS TO IT

CHAPTER 21

DAMAGES

A. INTRODUCTION

In this chapter we consider the general principles relating to the award of **21–001**
damages in tort, with particular reference to the area which, in any claim in fraud,
is likely to figure most prominently, namely the award of damages in an action
for deceit.

In the individual chapters on the various other common law causes of action, **21–002**
which can be broadly described as fraud-based, we have considered specific
aspects of the law of damages so far as they relate to those causes of action.[1] It is
appropriate to consider damages in deceit separately and at more length, since, in
addition to the centrality of the tort in the fraud arena:

(a) many of the principles developed in the deceit cases are of broader
    application to torts of intentional wrongdoing such as are considered
    elsewhere in this work; and
(b) there are important analogies between the approach to assessing damages in
    deceit and the approach to assessing equitable compensation for breaches
    of trust and fiduciary duty.[2]

B. GENERAL PRINCIPLES

(1) The Fundamental Principle

The purpose of an award of damages to a claimant who has been the victim of a **21–003**
tortious wrong is to place him in the position he would have been in absent the
wrong. The foundational authority remains the speech of Lord Blackburn in
Livingstone v Rawyards Coal Co,[3] which continues to be quoted with approval[4]:

---

[1] See: Conspiracy (Ch.2, Section F); Inducing a Breach of Contract (Ch.3, Section H); Unlawful
Interference (Ch.4, Section G); Intimidation (Ch.5, Section E); Malicious Falsehood (Ch.6, Section
B(5)); Bribery (Ch.7, Section C(6)); Conversion (Ch.8, Section C).
[2] Considered in Ch.22.
[3] *Livingstone v Rawyards Coal Co* (1880) 5 App Cas 25, at 39. This whole passage was quoted with
approval by Lord Browne-Wilkinson in *Smith New Court Securities Ltd v Scrimgeour Vickers Ltd*
[1997] A.C. 254, at 262–263.
[4] As recently as the decision in *Bacciottini v Gotelee and Goldsmith (A Firm)* [2016] EWCA Civ 170;
[2016] 4 W.L.R. 98, where Davis LJ referred, at [56], to "the core principle set out in *Livingstone v
Rawyards Coal Co* (1880) 5 App Cas 25" as determining the outcome of the case. This was a
professional negligence case.

"I do not think there is any difference of opinion as to its being a general rule that, where any injury is to be compensated by damages, in settling the sum of money to be given for reparation of damages you should as nearly as possible get at that sum of money which will put the party who has been injured, or who has suffered, in the same position as he would have been in if he had not sustained the wrong for which he is now getting his compensation or reparation. That must be qualified by a great many things which may arise – such, for instance, as by the consideration whether the damage has been maliciously done, or, whether it has been done with full knowledge that the person doing it was doing wrong. There could be no doubt that there you would say that everything would be taken into view that would go most against the wilful wrongdoer – many things which you would properly allow in favour of an innocent mistaken trespasser would be disallowed as against a wilful and intentional trespasser on the ground that he must not qualify his own wrong, and various things of that sort."

(2)   The Tortious and the Contractual Measure

21–004   It is trite that the law of damages in tort protects against a different interest from the law of damages in contract. Whereas the purpose of an award of damages in tort is to restore the claimant's position to what it would have been absent the wrong, the law of contract seeks to place the claimant in the position in which he would have been in had the defendant fulfilled his contractual obligations. In the context of a fraudulent misrepresentation, the difference is more simply stated as an award which puts the claimant in the position he would have been in had the representation not been made at all and an award which puts him in the position he would have been in had it been true (i.e. had the facts asserted by the defendant been correct).[5] Of course, a false representation may become incorporated into a later contract induced by it and so be actionable both as a deceit and a breach of contract.[6]

21–005   The difference may be exemplified by a simple scenario[7]: A purchases a painting from B for £1 million. B provides a contractual warranty (whether or not fraudulent)[8] that it is painted by Picasso. C has previously fraudulently advised A that the painting was indeed painted by Picasso; and, absent such advice, A would not have proceeded. In fact the painting was painted by another artist and is only worth £400,000. But had the painting indeed been painted by Picasso it would have been worth £2 million. As a matter of general principle, A's measure of damage against B would be £1.6 million (i.e. the difference between the value of the asset obtained and the value of the asset as it was warranted to be) and as against C would be £600,000 (i.e. the difference between the outlay of £1 million

---

[5] See *McConnell v Wright* [1903] 1 Ch. 546 and *Doyle v Olby (Ironmongers) Ltd* [1969] 2 Q.B. 158.

[6] For instance Mr Andrew Baker QC, sitting as a Deputy High Court Judge, held in *Idemitsu Kosan Co Ltd v Sumitomo Corp* [2016] EWHC 1909 (Comm), at [24], that: "It seems to me right in principle that language found in the communication of a negotiating position, or in draft wording for a contract, or in an entire draft contract, passing between the parties during the negotiation of a contract, might amount to or form the content of a pre-contractual representation capable of being actionable under the [Misrepresentation] 1967 Act. That possibility was recognised by the Court of Appeal in *Eurovideo Bildprogramm Gmbh v Pulse Entertainment Ltd* [2002] EWCA Civ 1235, to which Peter Gibson LJ referred in *Leofelis v Lonsdale*, above, at [141], where he emphasised that all would depend on the particular facts of any given case." Similar reasoning applies to a pre-contractual representation which is made dishonestly.

[7] Loosely based on one postulated by Pennycuick VC in *Ford v White* [1964] 1 W.L.R. 885. See also *Karim v Wemyss* [2016] EWCA Civ 27, at [25].

[8] For the purposes of awarding damages in contract it does not matter.

and the value of the asset obtained). In this scenario, damages in contract place A in a counter-factual world in which the contractual promise was true; damages in tort place A in a different counter-factual world in which the contract was never made because he would not have been induced by the fraud. It will be seen that even though damages in tort assume the transaction causing the loss has not been entered into, nonetheless the claimant must give credit for the value of the asset which would (at least in many cases) not otherwise have been acquired.

The example above provides A with a higher recovery in contract than in tort. But that need not always be the case. The underlying bargain may be a bad one (even if the painting had been by Picasso, it might have only been worth £800,000, which would reduce the damages for breach of contract to £400,000). Further, as we shall see, the law of remoteness in deceit is more favourable than in contract to the claimant. **21–006**

Although the different measures are easily stated and distinguished, the earlier authorities are nonetheless replete with category errors[9] and it remains vital to have the principles set out above clearly in mind. **21–007**

(3) Speculative Damages Awards

In many claims founded in fraud, the claimant seeks damages based on an attempted reconstruction of what would (or might) have happened absent the wrong. Such claims are necessarily counter-factual; they involve the attempted recreation, via a pecuniary award, of an alternative world in which the wrong did not occur. In such cases, the courts have warned against the application of a strict balance of probabilities test, which, whilst appropriate to the establishment of certain past asserted losses (e.g. claims that certain expenses in investigating the fraud were incurred), has no place in awards of damages seeking to compensate for wider claimed losses of profits: **21–008**

> "Some claims for consequential loss are capable of being established with precision (for example, expenses incurred prior to the date of trial). Other forms of consequential loss are not capable of similarly precise calculation because they involve the attempted measurement of things which would or might have happened (or might not have happened) but for the defendant's wrongful conduct, as distinct from things which have happened. In such a situation the law does not require a claimant to perform the impossible, nor does it apply the balance of probability test to the measurement of the loss."[10]

Rather, the court estimates the loss sustained by the claimant by making the best attempt it can to evaluate the chances, great or small (unless those chances amount to no more than remote speculation), taking all significant factors into account.[11] The court will adopt a broad brush in such circumstances, where

---

[9] See for example the first instance judgment appealed from in *Doyle v Olby (Ironmongers) Ltd* [1969] 2 Q.B. 158.

[10] *Parabola Investments Ltd v Browallia Cal Ltd* [2009] EWHC 901 (Comm) and [2010] EWCA Civ 486; [2011] Q.B. 477, at [22]. *Parabola* has been cited many times since and is perhaps the leading modern case on damages for deceit.

[11] *Parabola Investments Ltd v Browallia Cal Ltd* [2009] EWHC 901 (Comm) and [2010] EWCA Civ 486; [2011] Q.B. 477, at [23]. See *Davis v Taylor* [1974] A.C. 207, at 212 (Lord Reid); and *Gregg v*

appropriate discounting the damages award by an overall single percentage to reflect the possibility (which may involve a consideration of multiple contingencies) that the asserted profits would not have been made.[12]

C. THE POSITION IN DECEIT CLAIMS: THE BASIC MEASURE

(1) Introduction

21–009
The law has traditionally taken a generous approach to the award of damages to a claimant who has been the victim of a fraudulent misrepresentation. It is not difficult to see why: whereas in awarding damages to compensate for a defendant's negligence or breach of contract, the law is concerned to place appropriate delimitations on the scale of recovery, for example by excluding losses which were not reasonably foreseeable or within the contemplation of the contracting parties, it is subject to fewer constraints when assessing damages for a defendant's intentional dishonesty. As we have seen in Ch.1 above, the underlying principles of the law of deceit are founded at least in part on moral opprobrium against the intentional wrongdoer. A similar instinct actuates the assessment of damages in deceit.[13] The law strives, as best as it can, to make the claimant who has sustained loss whole again, to restore him as completely as possible to the position in which he would have been absent the wrong; and, given the intentionality of the tort, it makes the defendant bear the risk of consequences of his tort that may not have been foreseen or contemplated at the time. The principle may be easily stated, but nonetheless there are a number of provisos to it, which we explore below.

Scott [2005] 2 A.C. 176, at [17] (Lord Nicholls) and [67]–[69] (Lord Hoffmann). In *Fiona Trust & Holding Corp v Privalov* [2016] EWHC 2163 (Comm), where the defendants were seeking to enforce the claimant's cross-undertaking in damages after the discharge of a freezing order, and alleged that, absent that order they would have made considerable profits, a similar approach was applied. Males J said, at [58]: "What the defendants need to prove is that on the balance of probabilities they would have sought to invest in a way that had a real as distinct from fanciful chance of making a profit. If so, it will be necessary to make the best possible assessment of the profit which the defendants would have made, taking account of the uncertainties inherent in this exercise. In a case such as this where there are a number of such uncertainties, what needs to be assessed is the 'overall chance' of the defendants making the profits in question."

[12] See for instance *Tom Hoskins Plc v EMW Law (a firm)* [2010] EWHC 479 (Ch), at [133]–[135].

[13] See *Smith New Court Securities Ltd v Scrimgeour Vickers Ltd* [1997] A.C. 254, per Lord Steyn at 279. "The exclusion of heads of loss in the law of negligence, which reflects considerations of legal policy, does not necessarily avail the intentional wrongdoer. Such a policy of imposing more stringent remedies on an intentional wrongdoer serves two purposes. First it serves a deterrent purpose in discouraging fraud ... in the battle against fraud civil remedies can play a useful and beneficial role. Secondly, as between the fraudster and the innocent party, moral considerations militate in favour of requiring the fraudster to bear the risk of misfortunes directly caused by his fraud."

(2)　The Overriding Compensatory Rule

The law of damages for deceit is dominated by two leading decisions: that of the Court of Appeal in *Doyle v Olby (Ironmongers) Ltd*[14] and of the House of Lords in *Smith New Court Securities v Scrimgeour Vickers Ltd*,[15] in which the House of Lords (Lords Browne-Wilkinson and Steyn giving the leading speeches) built upon the principles laid down in the earlier case.　　**21–010**

The starting point is Lord Steyn's emphatic statement of principle in *Smith New Court*:　　**21–011**

> "There is in truth only one legal measure of assessing damages in an action for deceit: the plaintiff is entitled to recover as damages a sum representing the financial loss flowing directly from his alteration of position under the inducement of the fraudulent representations of the defendants."[16]

What this means in practice is that the claimant is entitled to recover all loss directly caused by the transaction into which the claimant has been induced to enter, and all consequential loss, subject only to certain limiting principles discussed below. "The aim is to put the plaintiff into the position he would have been in if no false representation had been made."[17] Although in the nineteenth century, it was suggested that there were special rules relating to the purchase of shares induced by fraud, the law has now moved to a single rule.[18]

> "The legal measure is to compare the position of the plaintiff as it was before the fraudulent statement was made to him with his position as it became as a result of his reliance on the fraudulent statement."

It follows that the concept of remoteness in the law of deceit is different from that which is applied in the law of negligence (or indeed contract): loss is not to be treated as too remote merely because it was not reasonably foreseeable by or in the contemplation of the representor.[19] A loss is too remote only if it is not in the　　**21–012**

---

[14] *Doyle v Olby (Ironmongers) Ltd* [1969] 2 Q.B. 158.

[15] *Smith New Court Securities v Scrimgeour Vickers Ltd* [1997] A.C. 254.

[16] *Smith New Court Securities v Scrimgeour Vickers Ltd* [1997] A.C. 254, at 284.

[17] *Smith New Court Securities v Scrimgeour Vickers Ltd* [1997] A.C. 254, at 281.

[18] *Clark v Urquhart* [1930] A.C. 28, at 67–68, per Lord Atkin: "I find it difficult to suppose that there is any difference in the measure of damages in an action of deceit depending upon the nature of the transaction into which the plaintiff is fraudulently induced to enter. Whether he buys shares or buys sugar, whether he subscribes for shares, or agrees to enter into a partnership, or in any other way alters his position to his detriment, in principle, the measure of damages should be the same, and whether estimated by a jury or a judge. I should have thought it would be based on the actual damage directly flowing from the fraudulent inducement." It was confirmed by Lord Steyn in *Smith New Court* that there is one rule of damages relevant to any transaction: see at 284. For a consideration of the earlier share purchase cases, see J. Edelman, J. Varuhas and S. Colton (eds), *McGregor on Damages*, 19th edn (London: Sweet & Maxwell, 2014), para.47–009 and following.

[19] The rules of remoteness in contract and negligence may be summarised as follows: A defendant in breach of contract is liable only for damages of a kind that were or should have been within its contemplation at the time the contract was entered into, in the sense that there was a serious possibility of their occurrence or that they were not unlikely to occur. In tort, at least in the tort of

eyes of the law directly caused by a defendant's deceit. The classic statement of the law is in Lord Denning's judgment in *Doyle v Olby*[20]:

> "In contract, the damages are limited to what may reasonably be supposed to have been in the contemplation of the parties. In fraud, they are not so limited. The defendant is bound to make reparation for all the actual damages directly flowing from the fraudulent inducement. The person who has been defrauded is entitled to say: 'I would not have entered into this bargain at all but for your representation. Owing to your fraud, I have not only lost all the money I paid you, but, what is more, I have been put to a large amount of extra expense as well and suffered this or that extra damages.' All such damages can be recovered: and it does not lie in the mouth of the fraudulent person to say that they could not reasonably have been foreseen."[21]

21–013   What this means is explored in the sections that follow, with particular reference to the typical fraud case, in which the claimant is induced to enter into a transaction by the defendant's wrong—generally the purchase of an asset, whether it be real property, a business or a shareholding.

(3)   The Primary Measure: Price Paid Less Value Received

21–014   In such cases, the primary measure of the claimant's loss is the difference between the full price paid by him less credit for the benefits which he has received as a result of the transaction.[22] So the claimant who is dishonestly misled by the defendant about the attribution of a painting purchases it for £50,000 when in fact it is only worth £25,000 at that time[23]; the measure of damages will, in principle, be £25,000, together, in general, with interest to compensate the loss of use of the £25,000 overpaid.

(4)   Date for Assessment

(i)   Introduction

21–015   In applying this primary measure, the difficulty is likely to arise not in determining the price paid pursuant to the impugned transaction, but in valuing the benefit received as a result of it, for which the claimant must give credit. The starting point is that, generally, it will be appropriate to determine the true value

---

negligence, the test is expressed differently and a defendant is liable for any type of damage which is the reasonably foreseeable consequence of its wrongdoing. See *Wellesley Partners LLP v Withers LLP* [2015] EWCA Civ 1146; [2016] 2 W.L.R. 1351.

[20] Quoted with approval by Lord Steyn in *Smith New Court*, at 281.

[21] *Doyle v Olby* [1969] 2 Q.B. 158, at 167. The position was recently restated in *UBS AG (London Branch) v Kommunale Wasserwerke Leipzig GmbH* [2017] EWCA Civ 1567 as follows, at [186]: "The deceiver is liable, on the tortious basis of analysis, for all the loss directly caused to the representee by the fraudulent misrepresentation, without limits derived from the law as to foreseeability or scope of duty."

[22] See the third of Lord Browne-Wilkinson's propositions in *Smith New Court*, at 267. As his sixth proposition recognises, the claimant is also entitled to recover consequential losses. As to these, see the following section of this chapter.

[23] See e.g. *Ford v White* [1964] 1 W.L.R. 885, per Pennycuick VC.

of the benefit received as at the date it was acquired.[24] This is simply an application of what has been described as "the general rule" that damages for tort or breach of contract are assessed at the date of the breach.[25] As a result, absent other factors such as are considered below, subsequent market falls in the value of the asset, or other matters which cause it to depreciate, will not be taken into account in the assessment of damages.[26]

However   **21–016**

> "this rule also should not be mechanistically applied in circumstances where assessment at another date may more accurately reflect the overriding compensatory rule."[27]

In reality, the date of transaction rule will readily be displaced in a deceit claim and cases decided in the 19th century which suggest a rigid rule in the award of damages for deceit (at least in share purchase cases) no longer represent the law.[28] In the sub-sections below we consider aspects of the date of transaction rule and the circumstances in which it can be departed from.

Before doing so, it is important to note that the date at which value is assessed   **21–017**
does not necessarily delimit the information with reference to which value is assessed: there are certainly cases in which the courts have, in carrying out the valuation task as at a given date, taken account of information which casts light on the value as at that date, but which was not in fact available at that date.[29] Obviously, a claimant should not be prejudiced by the fact that full information about the value of the asset was not available to him at the time by reason of the defendant's fraud. However, it would seem that, at least in a deceit case, where a claimant has been defrauded into acquiring an asset, and the market value of that asset at the date of acquisition would normally have priced into it the risk of

---

[24] Per Lord Browne-Wilkinson at 266: "In many cases, even in deceit, it will be appropriate to value the asset acquired as at the transaction date if that truly reflects the value of what the plaintiff has obtained. Thus, if the asset acquired is a readily marketable asset and there is no special feature (such as a continuing misrepresentation or the purchaser being locked into a business that he has acquired) the transaction date rule may well produce a fair result. The plaintiff has acquired the asset and what he does with it thereafter is entirely up to him, freed from any continuing adverse impact of the defendant's wrongful act." See to similar effect Lord Steyn, at 284: "It is right that the normal method of calculating the loss caused by the deceit is the price paid less the real value of the subject-matter of the sale. To the extent that this method is adopted, the selection of a date of valuation is necessary. And generally the date of the transaction would be a practical and just date to adopt."

[25] See Bingham LJ in *County Personnel (Employment Agency) Ltd v Alan R Pulver & Co* [1987] 1 W.L.R. 916, at 925–926.

[26] See, classically, *Waddell v Blockey* (1879) 4 Q.B.D. 678.

[27] Per Bingham LJ in *County Personnel (Employment Agency) Ltd v Alan R Pulver & Co*, above.

[28] See e.g. *Waddell v Blockey* (1879) 4 Q.B.D. 678; *Peek v Derry* (1887) 37 Ch.D. 541; *McConnell v Wright* [1903] 1 Ch. 546. These cases were disapproved in *Smith New Court* in so far as they purported to lay down an inflexible rule as to measure of damages.

[29] In *Peek v Derry* (1887) 37 Ch. D. 541, at 592, Cotton LJ held that "[a]lthough the value of the shares is not to be ascertained at the subsequent period so as to take into account for the benefit of the Plaintiff events subsequent which depreciated their value, yet those events, if they shew that the company was originally, with the capital which it had got, a company which was worthless, may, in my opinion, be taken into account as evidence of what was the value of the shares immediately after they were allotted to the Plaintiff." (The House of Lords did not consider this point). See further *Bwllfa Merthyr Dare Steam Collieries (1981) Ltd v Pontypridd Waterworks Co* [1903] A.C. 426 and *Phillips v Brewin Dolphin Bell Lawrie* [2001] 1 W.L.R. 143.

subsequent adverse events, the court will not allow a defendant to rely upon the fact of those events not having materialised to say that the "real" value of what was acquired was greater. That would involve an illegitimate use of hindsight to derive a value of the asset at the transaction date which even a purchaser on the market who had not been deceived would not have paid.[30]

(ii)   Smith New Court Securities

21–018   The classic analysis of the circumstances in which the date of transaction rule can be disapplied is the leading case of *Smith New Court Securities v Scrimgeour Vickers*.[31] The facts, which are stark, deserve recitation. In July 1989, the claimants acquired shares in a well-known defence contractor, Ferranti, in reliance on fraudulent representations made by a representative of the defendant. The price paid was 82¼p per share. On the open market, they would at that time have fetched 78p per share. The claimants bought the shares as a market-making risk with a view to holding them on their books for a comparatively long period. In September 1989, the board of Ferranti discovered that it had been the victim of a major fraud by a former director ("the Guerin fraud"), which was entirely unrelated to the defendant's own fraud but which pre-dated the claimants' purchase, and in November it published revised audited accounts showing the effect of the fraud. The shares slumped. Between November 1989 and April 1990 the claimants sold their shares in small parcels at prices between 49p and 30p per share. The Court of Appeal held that damages were to be assessed at the date of the acquisition of the shares by reference to the difference between the price paid and the price which the shares would then have attracted on the open market (that market at the time being unaware of the Guerin fraud). However, reversing the Court of Appeal, the House of Lords held that the claimants were entitled to recover the difference between the amount which they paid to purchase the shares and the various amounts for which they were resold. In doing so they disapproved a number of earlier cases which had suggested that damages in fraud should be assessed at the date of the transaction. Lord Steyn held that although the date of transaction rule was "prima face the right date", that rule would readily yield to a different date for assessment in order to fulfil what he described as the "overriding compensatory rule".

> "In an action for deceit the price paid less the valuation at the transaction date is simply a method of measuring loss which will satisfactorily solve many cases. It is not a substitute for the single legal measure: it is an application of it."[32]

---

[30] See *OMV Petrom SA v Glencore International AG* [2016] EWCA Civ 778, at [62], [83] and [84]. The case also considered the (closely related) question of whether it was appropriate to displace the date of transaction rule, as to which see para.21–019 below. See also *McConnell v Wright* [1903] 1 Ch. 546 (in valuing shares acquired as a result of a fraudulent prospectus no account was to be taken of the fact that the company had, by the date of trial, acquired the property that it was falsely represented it had at the date of the prospectus). Note that the position on the use of hindsight in valuation of a contractual claim may well be different: see, e.g. *Ageas (UK) Ltd v Kwik Fit (GB) Ltd* [2014] EWHC 2178 (QB).

[31] *Smith New Court Securities v Scrimgeour Vickers* [1997] A.C. 254.

[32] *Smith New Court Securities v Scrimgeour Vickers* [1997] A.C. 254, at 284.

(iii) When another date for assessment will be appropriate

It is impossible to set out a full compendium of circumstances where the court will award damages referential to a date different from that provided for by the date of transaction rule (or referential to the sale price achieved by the claimant in later ridding himself of the asset). Lord Browne-Wilkinson, whilst expressly disavowing any attempt to state the position comprehensively, suggested that the general rule should normally not apply where either:

21–019

> "(a) the misrepresentation has continued to operate after the date of the acquisition of the asset so as to induce the plaintiff to retain the asset or (b) the circumstances of the case are such that the plaintiff is, by reason of the fraud, locked into the property."[33]

Lord Browne-Wilkinson's first category of case is perhaps more straightforward: where the claimant retains the asset under the continuing influence of the fraud, then, obviously, it would be unjust to limit him only to losses sustained or assessed as at the date of the acquisition. Assuming that there is a ready market for the asset, and that there are no other considerations pointing towards a different conclusion, it would normally be appropriate to award damages assessed instead at the date when the claimant discovered the fraud and either did, or could reasonably have been expected to, offload it. If, on the other hand, the claimant with full knowledge of the fraud decides to retain the asset, then he can be taken to have adopted the transaction and his loss would, generally, fall to be assessed at the transaction date.[34]

21–020

As to cases where the claimant is "locked into" the transaction, a different date for assessment will typically be appropriate in the following circumstances:

21–021

(1) Where the claimant has entered into the transaction on a long-term basis, and so has arranged his affairs on the footing that it will be retained. In *Smith New Court* itself, the date for assessment of the true value of the shares acquired was deferred in part because the shares had been acquired at above market price with a view to holding them as a market-making risk. This will also arise where, for instance, the asset acquired is a business and the claimant has invested time and capital in it, or foregone other business opportunities. The claimant may, quite reasonably, feel constrained to persist in trying to trade out of business difficulties even once the fraud is discovered. In such a case, it would be unreal to assess damages by reference to the value of the business at the date of purchase (or even at the date of discovery of the fraud).[35] This occurred in *Doyle v Olby*

---

[33] *Smith New Court Securities v Scrimgeour Vickers* [1997] A.C. 254, at 267.
[34] *Standard Chartered Bank v Pakistan National Shipping (No.3)* [1999] 1 Lloyd's Rep. 747. The claimant's free decision to adopt the transaction means he cannot claim losses attributable to subsequent falls in the value of the asset; but, equally, the defendant cannot claim greater credit if the value of the asset subsequently rises—both are consequences of the claimant's decision rather than the defendant's fraud: see *Great Future International Ltd v Sealand Housing Corp* [2002] EWHC 2454 (Ch) (considered further below).
[35] There is certainly no rule that losses sustained after discovery of the fraud cannot be claimed. See per Flaux J in *Parabola Investments Ltd v Browallia CAL Ltd* [2009] EWHC 901 (Comm); [2009] 2

(Ironmongers) Ltd.[36] The claimant was induced by the defendant's fraudulent misrepresentations to acquire an ironmongery business. He also acquired the lease from which the business was to be operated. As it was put, the claimant "had burnt his boats and had to carry on with the business as best he could."[37] Damages were awarded representing the totality of the claimant's outlay (which included not only the initial purchase price but also his ongoing losses), less the price he was able to sell the business for some years later.[38]

(2) The claimant may also be "locked in" to the transaction because there is no available market in which to off-load it upon discovery of the fraud.[39] Where a claimant has been fraudulently induced to acquire property and does not wish to retain it, if it is not readily marketable, then it would be wrong to take the date of the transaction or indeed the date of discovery of the fraud as the date for assessing the value of the property.

(3) Where the claimant has incurred consequential losses flowing from the deceit then (at least so far as concerns those losses) it will be inappropriate to award damages as if the loss had been sustained at the moment of acquisition. We consider this further at Section E below.

(4) Where the market value of the asset acquired is itself a false one, because it is affected by the same fraud which has induced the purchase. In such a case, as we have already noted above, it would obviously undercompensate the claimant to assess the market value of the asset acquired at a point when that value is itself distorted by the fraud. The claimant can recover losses attributable to the later drop in price that results from the market correcting itself when the truth emerges.[40]

21–022   The defendant's fraud may also result in a claimant being locked out of an alternative transaction in which he would otherwise have deployed his money. A recent case provides a vivid instance of the disapplication of the so-called date of

---

All E.R. (Comm) 589, at [177]: "A number of the cases recognise that where the adverse effects of a fraudulent misrepresentation continue after the fraud has been discovered, then in principle the claimant can recover as damages the losses he suffers as a consequence of those adverse effects for so long as they remain operative, whether loss of profits or additional expenses or other losses."

[36] *Doyle v Olby (Ironmongers) Ltd*, above.

[37] *Doyle v Olby (Ironmongers) Ltd*, at 165.

[38] The limits of this approach are demonstrated by the facts in the case of *Invertec Ltd v De Mol Holding BV* [2009] EWHC 2471 (Ch). In that case, the claimant had been induced by the defendant's deceit to purchase the issued shareholding in a company. The shares were in fact worthless. Subsequent to the purchase, and after it had discovered all the facts relied upon as giving rise to the later claim in deceit, it made (further) loans to the company to try to keep it afloat and to preserve its investment. In the subsequent proceedings, the claimant claimed both the purchase price and the loans it had made. The judge awarded the claimant damages referential to the purchase price but declined to compensate it in respect of the loans made after discovery of the fraud. In particular, he did not accept the claimant's contention that it was "locked into" the transaction: in fact, it had two alternatives—either to rescind the transaction or to put the company into administration or liquidation. The decision to keep the company trading through loans supporting it was a commercial decision. It was not a reasonable attempt at mitigation, but a commercial gamble. See generally, at [381]–[386].

[39] *Standard Chartered Bank v Pakistan National Shipping (No.3)* [1999] 1 Lloyd's Rep. 747; *Cassa Di Risparmio Della Repubblica Di San Marino Spa v Barclays Bank Ltd* [2011] EWHC 484 (Comm).

[40] *Broome v Speak* [1903] 1 Ch. 856 (affirmed [1904] A.C. 342).

transaction rule in such a scenario. In *Khakshouri v Jimenez*[41] the claimant had lent money to a football club induced by the deceit of the defendants. In doing so, he had withdrawn that money from a potentially profitable investment. The loan was repaid. However, absent the deceit, the claimant would not have withdrawn the money from the prior investment. That investment some years later delivered a substantial return for the investors which the claimant, as a result of the defendant's deceit, missed out on. The defendants argued that the proper time for assessing damages was when the claimant was repaid the loan, since he was at that time freed from the transaction he was deceitfully induced to enter. The court rejected that argument on the basis that the claimant could not at that time have re-acquired his interest in the investment, which was a few months after it was made. Damages were calculated by reference to the lost profits sustained by the claimant which he would have obtained from the investment on its maturity (a number of years later and as it happened about a month before the trial).

(iv)   Inherent defect and subsequent events

The facts of *Smith New Court* were vivid because the deception of the defendants was only directly responsible (at least in one sense) for a relatively small proportion of the overall loss sustained by the claimant; it was the unrelated "Guerin fraud" which was, on one view, the primary cause of its loss and absent that fraud the value of the shares acquired would have been almost the same as the price paid by the claimant. Accordingly, the facts of the case threw up in acute form the question of who should bear the risk of external events which substantially increase a claimant's loss. In confronting that issue, the House of Lords drew a distinction between two situations: first, where the asset is, at the time of the purchase, already subject to an inherent (and possibly unknown) defect, albeit one wholly unrelated to the fraud; and secondly where, subsequent to the purchase, the asset is subject to an event which depreciates or destroys its value. This distinction had been drawn in the famous example posed by Cockburn LJ in the old case of *Twycross v Grant*[42]:   **21–023**

> "If a man buys a horse, as a racehorse, on the false representation that it has won some great race, while in reality it is a horse of very inferior speed, and he pays ten or twenty times as much as the horse is worth, and after the buyer has got the animal home it dies of some latent disease inherent in its system at the time he bought it, he may claim the entire price he gave; the horse was by reason of the latent mischief worthless when he bought; but if it catches some disease and dies, the buyer cannot claim the entire value of the horse, which he is no longer in a condition to restore, but only the difference between the price he gave and the real value at the time he bought."

The distinction drawn in *Twycross*'s case was endorsed as correct and of general application, and applied, in *Smith New Court*: the shares which were purchased were, at the time of the purchase, "pregnant with disaster" and "doomed to collapse" because of the then undiscovered Guerin fraud, which meant that the market value at the time was a false one, albeit not one created by the defendant's   **21–024**

---

[41] *Khakshouri v Jimenez* [2017] EWHC 3392 (QB).
[42] *Twycross v Grant* (1877) 2 C.P.D. 469, at 544–545. A similar point had been made by Cotton LJ in *Peek v Derry* (1897) 37 Ch. D. 541, at 592.

fraud. The claimant was entitled to recover the totality of its loss.[43] But had it been the case that the Guerin fraud was perpetrated *after* the acquisition of the shares, then such loss in the value of the shares as was ascribable to that extraneous event would not have been recoverable and it seems that the House of Lords would have confined the claimant's damages to what was established by the application of the date of transaction rule. This distinction may in some cases be easy to apply. For instance, where real property is purchased by a claimant induced by the defendant's deceit, then, if the property is subsequently burnt down (say by a random electrical fault), or suffers a substantial fall in value as a result of a general market decline, the claimant's damages will in general not be expanded by the loss consequent on those later events. But, especially in the case of shareholdings, the distinction is not always so easily demarcated. A subsequent decline in the value of shares acquired by the claimant may be ascribable to multiple causes, some present at the date of the acquisition, others subsequent. It seems that the courts are in such cases likely to err in favour of a more generous measure.

(v) Asset subsequently increasing in value/risks not materialising

21-025　What of the case where the asset acquired as a result of the fraudulent misrepresentation subsequently rises in value? In such a case it could be said that the claimant has, at the date of the transaction, sustained an immediate money loss by overpaying for an asset and that the subsequent rise in value does not undo that loss. On the other hand, Cotton LJ said in *Peek v Derry*[44] of the claimant: "Of course if he sells and does not sell unreasonably, whatever he gets he must bring into account". It might be wondered why, if a claimant is obliged to give credit for a gain on the asset acquired which has been realised by the date of trial, he should not also be obliged to give credit for an unrealised one (assuming, of course, that it can be established on the evidence available).

21-026　The cases which have considered this issue in the context of claims in deceit appear to lean in favour of not giving defendants the benefit of subsequent increases in the value of an asset acquired by reason of their fraud. Thus in *McConnell v Wright*[45] the claimants were entitled to recover, as damages for misrepresentations in a company prospectus that the company had already acquired a valuable property, the difference between the price paid and the value of the shares acquired at the date of their allotment (taking into account that the property had not in fact been acquired at that date), and no credit fell to be given

---

[43] See for example *Halston Holdings SA v Simons* [2005] EWHC 30 (QB). There, the judge commented, at [93] that "If the company is likened to a horse, it was a horse that was ill on [the date of completion]". Another example of the application of the principle can be found in the context of a bank's attempts to offload a cargo of bitumen which it had acquired as a result of being deceived by falsified bills of lading, in *Standard Chartered Bank v Pakistan National Shipping (No.3)* [1999] 1 Lloyd's Rep. 747.

[44] Above at 593.

[45] *McConnell v Wright* [1903] 1 Ch. 546 (which we have already mentioned above in connection with the question of the use of hindsight).

for the fact that the company did subsequently acquire the property in question.[46] In *Butler-Creagh v Hersham*[47] the claimant purchased a country house induced by the defendants' fraudulent misrepresentations and was awarded damages referable to the purchase price paid less the value of the property at the date of the contract, even though by the time of completion (which was some 15 months later) the value of the property had risen.[48] And in *Great Future International Ltd v Sealand Housing Corp*,[49] the defendants failed to persuade the court to defer the date for assessment of the value of shares acquired by the claimants as a result of their fraud to the date of the inquiry after trial, by which point the shares had increased in value, that increase being thanks largely to the claimants' own efforts and expenditure in salvaging their investment in the teeth of continued concealment and obstruction by the defendants.

The decisions in *McConnell* and *Great Future International*, at least, accord with the principles set out above: where there is an available market for the asset purchased and the claimant makes a free decision to adopt the transaction and retain the asset rather than sell it, subsequent market fluctuations (if not ascribable to some inherent defect specific to the asset acquired) are for the claimant's account and not the defendant's—whether they be upwards or downwards. But that is not to say that there are not cases where, applying the ordinary principles of causation and mitigation (which apply as much in a fraud claim as in any other claim in tort, as to which see below), it could be said that a subsequent rise in the value of an asset acquired as a result of a fraud falls to be brought into account as something which has (or reasonably ought to have) avoided or reduced the claimant's loss.[50]

21–027

---

[46] See per Romer LJ at 557: "The question has to be tried by looking at what was the true value of the shares, of course, at the date of allotment. To shew what was the value of the shares later on, after the company had got these 200,000 Globe shares, is not to the point, nor indeed is it relevant to inquire…". This was, however, decided at a time when the transaction date rule was applied more rigidly.

[47] *Butler-Creagh v Hersham* [2011] EWHC 2525 (QB).

[48] See [103], citing *Smith New Court*, at 266 and 284. This might be thought to be a questionable decision (particularly given that the claimant only parted with the bulk of the purchase money at completion).

[49] *Great Future International Ltd v Sealand Housing Corp* [2002] EWHC 2454 (Ch).

[50] Compare the position taken in negligence cases: in *Hussey v Eels* [1990] 2 Q.B. 227, the question was identified as being "did the negligence which caused the damage also cause the profit", not just in the "but for" sense, but in the sense that the profit was part of a "continuous transaction" of which the tort was the inception (see also *Needler Financial Services Ltd v Taber* [2002] 3 All E.R. 501, per Sir Andrew Morritt VC at 511–12). In *Hussey*, the claimant acquired property in reliance on a negligent survey which was worth less than the sum paid. He subsequently obtained planning permission and was able to sell the property for more than he paid for it. It was held that the subsequent rise in value could not be brought into account by the defendant, because the decision to unlock the development value of the land was a separate decision, taken some years later, for the claimant's own benefit; but this was described as an exceptional case by Peter Gibson LJ in *Gardner v Marsh & Parsons (A Firm)* [1997] 1 W.L.R. 489. In the case of *Bacciottini v Gotelee and Goldsmith (A Firm)* [2016] EWCA Civ 170; [2016] 4 W.L.R. 98, the claimant acquired property which was subject to a planning restriction which depreciated its value by £100,000, but was only awarded £250, being the cost of the planning application which had successfully lifted the restriction and so cured the property of the defect. For analysis of when subsequent benefits fall to be taken into account in assessing damages for breach of contract, see *Fulton Shipping Inc of Panama v Globalia Business Travel SAU* [2017] UKSC 43; [2017] 1 W.L.R. 2581.

21–028 Another situation in which the defendant may wish to rely on subsequent events is where some measure of risk of adverse events is priced into the true value of the asset at the transaction date, but by the date of trial it is known that those risks have not materialised. Can the defendant insist that the value of the credit that the claimant should give should be assessed at the later date, when the notional cost of those risks can be eliminated from the claimant's loss? This question arose in the case of *OMV Petrom SA v Glencore International AG*,[51] a case in which the claimant was deceived by the defendant into purchasing oil of an inferior quality to what was represented. In assessing the true value of the oil acquired at the date of its acquisition, the court took the CIF price and then discounted it to reflect the contingencies and risks for which a buyer of the oil would have allowed, the blends in question not being recognised grades and there being uncertainty as to their performance. By the date of trial it was known that the oil had in fact performed and had not given rise to any issues with reduced yield or damage to plant. The defendant contended that credit for the full CIF price should therefore be given; but the Court of Appeal (upholding the Judge) rejected that contention: as at the date of transaction, those contingencies would be priced in; and, moreover, this was not a case where it was necessary to depart from that as the date of assessment in order to do justice to the wronged party. To depart from that date and factor in the fact that the risks associated with the purchase (which were fraudulently concealed) had not materialised would mean that the defrauded purchaser paid more than the cargo was worth at the point when it was defrauded into buying it, and thus that the fraudster was paid more for the cargo than it could have recovered if it had been honest. The loss was the overpayment of the price and it crystallised at that date; subsequent benefits to the purchaser from risks not materialising would always have been for its account.[52]

21–029 This decision is noteworthy because the Court of Appeal appears to have regarded Lord Browne-Wilkinson's observations in *Smith New Court* on the flexibility of the date of assessment as operating in favour of the claimant but not the defendant, taking as its starting point that when damage is done maliciously or with full knowledge that the person doing it was doing wrong, "you would say everything would be taken into view that would go most against the wilful wrongdoer".[53]

21–030 If it is sought to reduce a claimant's loss by reliance on events post-dating the transaction, then the burden will be on the defendant to plead and prove those events and the reduction flowing from them.[54]

---

[51] *OMV Petrom SA v Glencore International AG* [2016] EWCA Civ 778.
[52] *OMV Petrom SA v Glencore International AG*, at [39], [40], [61]. For essentially similar reasons, it was also inappropriate to value the claim with reference to the anticipated comparative yield of the oil, rather than its market price: [75]–[80].
[53] Per Lord Blackburn in *Livingston v Raywards Coal Co* [1880] 5 App Cas 25, at 39, cited at [39].
[54] *The World Beauty* [1970] P. 144, at 154F–154G and 158D.

(5) No Cap with Reference to the Position had the Representation Been True

In a claim in deceit (in contradistinction to one in negligence) it is not appropriate to limit the measure of damages flowing from the relevant transaction with reference to the position as it would have been had the deceitful representation been *true*. This, the so-called "*SAAMCO* cap", which limits the claimant to recovering the losses attributable to the *falsity* of the relevant statement,[55] is not relevant or helpful in a case in deceit, where the claimant is entitled to recover all losses attributable to having entered into the induced transaction, and the relevant counterfactual is therefore the position as it would have been had the representation not been made.[56]

21–031

(6) Sale of Assets

Of course, a deceit may induce the sale of an asset just as it can induce the purchase of an asset. Hence in *Platt v Platt*[57] the defendant's fraudulent misrepresentation induced the claimants to part with shares in a company. The Court of Appeal proceeded on the basis that the measure of damage was to be determined by reference to the value of the shares at the date of the transfer rather than some later date. No consideration was given to the circumstances, if any, which might make it appropriate to value the asset transferred at some later date. But it remains an open, and undecided, question whether there may be circumstances where the measure of damages should be referable to some later date, at which time the value of the asset has increased. Of course, the defendant's deception may have been designed to obtain an asset which the defendant suspected would appreciate in value. In such a case, not only would it be galling to a claimant to witness the asset appreciating in the defendant's hands and his damages remedy confined to a historical valuation, but it would be, it is suggested, principled to award damages referable to a date later than the date of transaction.[58]

21–032

The issue of how to assess the value of the asset sold as a result of fraud was addressed in *Smith Kline & French v Long*.[59] There, the claimant had been induced to sell goods to a company by the fraudulent misrepresentations of the defendant managing director that the goods were to be sold in a particular territory. The company, having received the goods, failed to pay for certain shipments and became insolvent. The claimant sued for damages referable to the

21–033

---

[55] *South Australia Asset Management Corp v York Montague Ltd* [1997] A.C. 191; *BPE Solicitors v Hughes-Holland* [2017] UKSC 21.

[56] *Smith New Court*, above, per Lord Browne-Wilkinson at 267D–267E and per Lord Steyn at 283C–283G, disapproving a dictum of Hobhouse LJ in *Downs v Chappell* [1997] 1 W.L.R. 426; *Yam Seng Pte Ltd v International Trade Corp Ltd* [2013] EWHC 111 (QB), at [207].

[57] *Platt v Platt* [2001] B.C.L.C. 698.

[58] Compare the decision in *4 Eng Ltd v Harper* [2008] EWHC 915 (Ch); [2009] Ch. 91, where the judge awarded damages to the claimant for its lost opportunity to purchase an alternative company referable to its likely value at the date of trial. The defendant's objection that the claimant would have had to purchase the alternative asset at its full value and therefore had lost nothing was rejected.

[59] *Smith Kline & French v Long* [1989] 1 W.L.R. 1.

price for the unpaid shipments on the basis that, absent the fraud, it would not have sold the goods to the company but would have had the goods in their hands which they could have sold to a third party at the same price. Although the fraud was proved, the judge dismissed the action on the grounds that no loss had been established. It had been conceded by the claimant that the particular batch cost in effect nothing to produce (presumably because all the costs were effectively fixed overheads) and that it could produce as much of the product to meet all demand. The judge held that the true measure of damage should be referable to the cost of production on the basis that would be the cost of replacing the lost goods. Since the cost of production was effectively nil, no loss had been sustained by the fraud. This heretical analysis of the law of damages was put right in the Court of Appeal, which affirmed that the proper starting point was the market value of the property the sale of which had been induced by the fraud. The court did not inquire into its replacement cost. The court proceeded by analogy with its approach in a claim in conversion.[60] This is because the assessment of damages is an objective exercise; the law cannot take cognisance of the subjective question of the capacity of the claimant to produce a replacement article.

21–034 It follows that in any case where the claimant has been induced to part with property by the defendant's fraud, the starting point is the market value of the asset so parted with, subject to any recoveries made.[61] As mentioned above, there may be circumstances where the market value is taken at a later date.

D. FURTHER LIMITING PRINCIPLES

21–035 Notwithstanding the law's predisposition to compensating the victim of a fraud as fully as it can, there are obviously some limits imposed on recovery. In *Smith New Court*, Lord Steyn identified[62] three such limiting principles which, even in a case of deceit, serve to keep wrongdoers' liability within what he described as "practical and sensible"[63] limits: causation, remoteness and the "duty" to mitigate loss.

(1) Causation

21–036 The first limiting principle is that the loss must have been caused by the deceit. This is apparently to be determined by reference to a "pragmatic test whether the condition in question was a substantial factor in producing the result" or by reference to an approach which poses the question whether "in common sense terms there is a sufficient causal connection."[64] The important point is that

---

[60] See the statement of the law by Lord Wright MR in *Ash v Dickie* [1936] Ch. 655, at 663: "in estimating damages for conversion the question is not what it has cost to produce the article, but what the article is worth."

[61] As Slade LJ said, at 11: "If it is clear that the [claimants] could have sold the [goods] in question for £X, but in the event they have only received £Y, then … £X-£Y is the measure of their loss."

[62] *Smith New Court*, at 284–285.

[63] *Smith New Court*, at 284.

[64] *Smith New Court*, at 285.

passing the hurdle of the "but for" test is not in itself sufficient.[65] It will be immediately seen that these dicta hardly provide clear analytical tools with which to set out an intellectually coherent test of causation in the law of fraud. Nonetheless, it is unlikely that any better apparatus will (or indeed can) emerge. The factual scenarios which the law has to grapple with are too multifarious for an easily applicable universal test of precisely what is required, beyond causation in the "but for" sense, to be feasible. There are nevertheless examples in the decided cases which provide guidance as to how the courts approach the causation question.

One example of a claim where there was an insufficient causal connection **21–037** between the deceit and part of the loss claimed was *Invertec Ltd v De Mol Holding BV*,[66] where the judge refused damages in relation to loans made by the claimant to the company, the shares in which it had purchased, induced by the defendant's fraud. The loans were made after discovery of the fraud and were "a commercial gamble" by the claimant. Similarly, in *Downs v Chappell*,[67] the claimant purchased a business induced by the defendant's fraud; subsequently, an offer was made by a third party to acquire the business for £76,000; the claimant declined that offer and it was said that by the time of the trial the business was only worth £60,000. The extra £16,000 was not awarded by way of damages. Hobhouse LJ's reasons are worth quoting in full as giving an insight into judicial approaches to the limits of damages awards:

> "[The claimants] have argued that they did not act unreasonably in rejecting the offers of £76,000 in March 1990. Even accepting that they acted reasonably, the fact remains that it was their choice, freely made, and they cannot hold the defendants responsible if the choice has turned out to have been commercially unwise. They were no longer acting under the influence of the defendants' representations. The causative effect of the defendants' faults was exhausted; the plaintiffs' right to claim damages from them in respect of those faults had likewise crystallised. It is a matter of causation."[68]

A third example can be found in *Dadourian Group International Inc v Simms*, **21–038** where it was held that the costs incurred by the claimant in certain litigation and arbitration not only satisfied the "but for" test of causation by the relevant deceitful representations, but were also sufficiently causally linked to the representations to be recoverable: they were costs of just the sort of dispute that it had been envisaged might arise with the involvement of certain individuals in the

---

[65] See also *Kuwait Airways v Iraqi Airways (Nos 4 and 5)* [2002] 2 W.L.R. 1353, at [71], where Lord Nicholls explained that there is a two-stage approach to causation: the court will first apply a but-for test and then go on to make a value judgment. As to this second stage, his Lordship observed: "In most cases, how far the responsibility of the defendant ought fairly to extend evokes an immediate intuitive response. This is informed common sense by another name. Usually there is no difficulty in selecting, from the sequence of events leading to the plaintiff's loss, the happening which should be regarded as the cause of the loss for the purpose of allocating responsibility. In other cases, when the outcome of the second enquiry is not obvious, it is of crucial importance to identify the purpose of the relevant cause of action and the nature and scope of the defendant's obligation in the particular circumstances. What was the ambit of the defendant's duty? In respect of what risks or damage does the law seek to afford protection by means of the particular tort?"
[66] *Invertec Ltd v De Mol Holding BV* [2009] EWHC 2471 (Ch).
[67] *Downs v Chappell* [1997] 1 W.L.R. 426.
[68] *Downs v Chappell*, at 437.

business and it was for that reason that their involvement had been dishonestly concealed by the defendants from the claimant. However, recovery did not extend to the costs of an unsuccessful application that had been made by the claimant in one of the proceedings, which it was held was made for the claimant's own benefit and was unnecessary:

> "The application did not, in my view, result from the misrepresentation; it resulted from an independent decision of DGI to take a tactical step in a commercial battle with Charlton which had nothing to do with the misrepresentation."[69]

21–039 It will be seen from these examples that the courts, even in a case in fraud, are anxious to place some limits on the ambit of recovery. The fraudulent misrepresentor is not to be treated as an insurer of all losses flowing from the decision to enter into the transaction which was induced by the deceit. Entry into the transaction said to be induced by the defendant's fraud may well set the claimant on a path which leads to further decisions and further expenditures over a very protracted period of time. It does not follow that all such payments can simply be placed at the door of the original misrepresentor: at some point, which is necessarily hard to pin down in the abstract, the causative potency of the fraud wanes and the law treats the supervening decision of the claimant as the "true" cause of the loss.[70]

21–040 Another somewhat different example of the same underlying principle is provided by *Barings Plc v Coopers & Lybrand*.[71] In that case, the defendant auditor brought a counterclaim in deceit alleging that dishonest representations for which the claimant bank was vicariously liable had induced the defendant to sign its audit opinion, thereby exposing it to loss arising out of the claim in negligence against it. The Judge (Evans-Lombe J) held that, whilst the deceit did cause the defendant's loss in the "but for" sense, it was not the legally effective cause; rather, its loss was caused by its own breach of its contractual duties to the claimant in failing to detect the deceit. The auditor was under a pre-existing duty to guard against being misled by just such false statements by the claimant's employees and it would make a "nonsense" of that duty if the very act which ought to have been prevented by it were held to be the cause of its exposure to

---

[69] *Dadourian Group International Inc v Simms* [2006] EWHC 2973, per Warren J at [761], not reversed on appeal, at [2009] EWCA Civ 169.

[70] See e.g. the *cri de coeur* of Eady J in *Butler-Creagh v Hersham* [2011] EWHC 2525 (QB), where the claimant sought damages for very substantial consequential losses arising after its acquisition of a very large country house, at [113]: "One cannot simply spend money in a situation of this kind and express it as a loss flowing from the actionable misrepresentations. It is said that the money has been spent with nothing to show for it. It needs, however, to be demonstrated that it was necessary or reasonable to spend the money to mitigate loss or to preserve the relevant asset. It is surely appropriate to demonstrate that the claimant in question has had to spend the money, not merely as a matter of choice, but as a result of being placed wrongfully in a particular predicament as a result of the misrepresentation(s) comprising the cause of action." In that case, the claimant chose to retain the house it had acquired and the court refused to allow damages referable to the "cost of running and staffing the estate indefinitely"—that was simply a consequence of the claimant's decision to stay: [126].

[71] *Barings Plc v Coopers & Lybrand* [2003] EWHC 1319 (Ch); [2003] P.N.L.R. 34, at [721] and following.

suit (thereby defeating the claim). This was, in effect, a value judgment that one of two competing causes of the same loss trumped the other.[72]

(2) Remoteness

The second limiting principle is remoteness. Lord Steyn's judgment in *Smith New Court* is less than helpful in illuminating the remoteness concept as it applies in the law of deceit. Essentially, losses will not be too remote if they directly flow[73] from the transaction induced by the defendant. The word "direct" is not further elaborated. How this differs from the causation principle analysed above is not readily apparent (although Lord Steyn was clear that there is a conceptual distinction between establishing a "sufficient causal link" on the one hand and that the "entire loss suffered ... is a direct consequence of the fraudulently induced transaction" on the other). In reality, the significant point which emerges from the judgments in *Doyle v Olby* and *Smith New Court* is that the more restrictive remoteness tests in negligence (of reasonable foreseeability)[74] and contract (of what was within the contemplation of the parties) are not applicable to claims in deceit. The result in *Smith New Court*, which yielded a damages award which was far in excess of the immediate effects of the defendant's deceit, provides a vivid illustration of this.

21–041

Some authorities elide the concept of remoteness with that of the next limiting feature, the principle of mitigation. So, Winn LJ in *Doyle v Olby*[75] said that damage will be too remote

21–042

> "not necessarily because it was not contemplated by the representor but in any case where the person deceived has not himself behaved with reasonable prudence, reasonable common sense or can in any true sense be said to have been the author of his own misfortune."

(3) "Duty" to Mitigate Loss

Finally, there is the so-called duty to mitigate loss.[76] The claimant is not entitled to damages in respect of loss which he could reasonably have avoided. The general law of mitigation of loss is applicable equally to deceit claims as any

21–043

---

[72] As noted below, this defence succeeded notwithstanding the principle that contributory negligence is not available as a defence to an intentional tort claim, such as in deceit.

[73] The phrasing comes from Lord Atkin's speech in *Clark v Urquhart* [1930] A.C. 28, at 68. See also the dicta of Dixon J in *Potts v Miller* (1940) 64 C.L.R. 282, at 298–299, and in *Toteff v Antonas* (1952) 87 C.L.R. 647, at 650.

[74] See *Overseas Tankship (U.K.) Ltd v Morts Dock & Engineering Co Ltd (The Wagon Mound)* [1961] A.C. 388.

[75] *Doyle v Olby* [1969] 2 Q.B. 158, at 168.

[76] See generally *Banco de Portugal v Waterlow & Sons Ltd* [1932] A.C. 452 and *Koch Marine Inc v D'Amica Societa di Navigazione ARL ('The Elena D'Amico')* [1980] 1 Lloyd's Rep. 75. Of course, the characterisation of this principle as a "duty" is misleading. The rule is better seen as an aspect of the fundamental principle of causation that a claimant can only recover in respect of damage caused by the defendant's wrong. The rule is not that there is a duty on the claimant to mitigate, but that he cannot recover for a loss avoidable by reasonable action on his part, because if he could reasonably have avoided it, it would (generally) not be regarded as caused by the wrongdoer. A full analysis of

other type of claim.[77] Hence the principles emerging from *Doyle v Olby (Ironmongers) Ltd*[78] (as endorsed in *Smith New Court Securities*), strict though they are, still require the claimant to mitigate his loss once he becomes aware of the fraud. So long as he is not aware of the fraud, it is unlikely that any question of a duty to mitigate could arise.[79] But once the fraud has been discovered, if the claimant is not locked into the asset and the fraud has ceased to operate on his mind, a failure to take reasonable steps, e.g. to sell the property, might constitute a failure to mitigate his loss requiring him to bring the value of the property into account as at the date when he discovered the fraud or shortly thereafter.[80] The burden is on the defendant to establish not only that the claimant acted unreasonably, but that if he had acted reasonably his loss would have been reduced.[81]

21–044 The test applicable was neatly encapsulated by Leggatt J in *Thai Airways International Public Co Ltd v KI Holdings Co Ltd* as follows[82]:

> "The basic test which the doctrine of mitigation involves is whether the claimant has acted reasonably in response to the defendant's wrong. Insofar as the claimant has acted reasonably,

---

the law of mitigation of loss is beyond the ambit of this work; see generally Edelman, Varuhas and Colton (eds), *McGregor on Damages* (2014), at Ch.9.

[77] It was held by Toulson J in *Standard Chartered Bank v Pakistan National Shipping (No.3)* [1999] 1 Lloyd's 747 that there was one single test of reasonableness applicable irrespective of the cause of action; in this respect, the law did not treat claimants in fraud claims more tenderly or favourably than claimants pursuing claims for negligence or breach of contract (contrast the obiter dicta of McLachlin J on the same question in *Canson Enterprises Ltd v Boughton & Co* (1991) 85 D.L.R. (4th) 129, at 161–162). Nonetheless, Toulson J pointed out that in assessing the reasonableness of the behaviour of a claimant placed in a position of embarrassment by a defendant's wrong, the standard applied by the courts is not exacting.

[78] *Doyle v Olby (Ironmongers) Ltd* [1969] 2 Q.B. 158.

[79] See *Smith New Court*, above, per Lord Browne-Wilkinson, at 267: "the plaintiff must take all reasonable steps to mitigate his loss once he has discovered the fraud."

[80] For example, in *Dadourian Group International Inc v Simms* [2006] EWHC 2973 (Ch); [2006] ArbLR 18, the court held the claimants, on the facts, to be in breach of this so-called duty, at [754].

[81] *Roper v Johnson* (1873) L.R. 8 CP 167, confirmed by the House of Lords in *Garnac Grain Co v Faure & Fairclough* [1968] A.C. 1130, at 1140. In *Standard Chartered Bank v Pakistan National Shipping (Assessment of Damages)* [2001] EWCA Civ 55; [2001] 1 All E.R. (Comm) 822, the Court of Appeal, dismissing the defendant's appeal from the judgment of Toulson J, laid down a useful analysis of the typical mitigation scenario in a fraud case, at [39]: "Where as a result of the fraud of the defendant the claimant has been induced to pay out monies which he would not otherwise have expended in respect of goods which he would not otherwise have acquired, and where the value of the goods in his hands is not susceptible of assessment by reference to the price paid for similar goods in an available market then, if (in pursuance of the general requirement to mitigate his loss) the claimant seeks out a purchaser and effects a sale of the goods for which he gives credit to the defendant for the value received, the loss sustained as a result of any shortfall between the price received and the monies he originally paid out is prima facie the measure of the claimant's damage, being loss directly flowing from the original transaction. If an issue is raised by the defendant that the price received was diminished by reason of the claimant's failure to take reasonable steps in negotiating the sale, or by effecting an alternative sale at a higher price, so that the loss suffered (or part of it) is attributable to such failure rather than to the original fraud, then the burden of that issue lies upon the defendant. That being so, it is part of that burden not merely to show that the plaintiff failed in some respect to act reasonably, but that his failure did in fact lead to a diminution in the price he could have obtained had reasonable steps been taken."

[82] *Thai Airways International Public Co Ltd v KI Holdings Co Ltd* as follows [2015] EWHC 1250 (Comm), at [33].

costs and benefits accruing to the claimant are included in the calculation of damages. Insofar as the claimant has not acted reasonably, the claimant's damages are assessed as if it had."

Much will, obviously, depend on what the court regards, in the circumstances, as being reasonable. It has been said in this connection that judges are "reluctant to impose excessive demands on claimants"; and so the court will not, for instance, require a claimant to "risk capital in a speculative venture."[83] As it was put by Leggatt J in the *Thai Airways* case:

21–045

> "The standard of 'reasonableness' is ... applied with some tenderness towards the claimant having regard to the fact that the claimant's predicament has been caused by the defendant's wrongdoing ... Thus, the claimant is not expected to take steps which would involve unreasonable expense, risk or inconvenience ... In addition, the burden of proof is on the defendant to show that there was a course of action which it was reasonable to expect the claimant to adopt that would have avoided all or an identifiable part of the claimant's loss ... Furthermore, there is often a range of responses available to the claimant which will be regarded as reasonable ...".[84]

It will be seen that many of the cases on causation could just as easily be analysed in terms of a failure to mitigate loss. Nonetheless, the principles are distinct: for instance, the failure of the claimants in *Downs v Chappell* to accept the offer for the business they had purchased induced by the defendant's deceit might not be properly characterised as unreasonable, but it still constituted the moment when the causative impact of the fraud was held to have been exhausted. Questions of mitigation are ones of fact, not law.[85]

21–046

E.   LOSSES OTHER THAN PURCHASE (OR SALE) PRICE

As we have seen, most of the cases relate to scenarios where the claimant has, induced by the defendant's fraud, purchased (or sold) an asset. In such a case, the primary claim will be for the money lost as a result of incurring that expenditure: in broad terms, the purchase price paid less the value of the asset acquired (whether taken at the date of transaction or some other date).

21–047

However, after early doubts,[86] the law has now clearly recognised that, in principle, other losses (including so-called consequential losses) incurred by the claimant are recoverable.[87] Of course, the claim may not be a purchase (or sale) case at all. A field where fraud is particularly prevalent is mortgage lending; in such a case, the lender induced to advance money in reliance on fraudulent misrepresentations will be, in principle, entitled to claim as damages the money

21–048

---

[83] *Jewelowski v Propp* [1944] K.B. 510; quoted by Green J in *Khakshouri v Jimenez* [2017] EWHC 3392 (QB), at [185].

[84] *Thai Airways International Public Co Ltd v KI Holdings Co Ltd* [2015] EWHC 1250 (Comm), at [38].

[85] *Payzu v Saunders* [1919] 2 K.B. 581, at 588 and 589 and *The Solholt* [1983] 1 Lloyd's Rep. 605, at 608.

[86] In *McDonnell v Wright* [1903] 1 Ch. 546, Collins MR asserted, in a share purchase case, that the highest the claimant could put his claim was by reference to the purchase price paid (at 554). This statement was stated to be too rigid by Lord Denning MR in *Doyle v Olby*, above, at 166.

[87] See e.g. *Smith New Court Securities*, above, at 282.

lent, and interest thereon, less recoveries made, whether through payments received during the currency of the loan or via the enforcement of the security.[88]

21–049 Alternatively, the case may involve the parting with money (otherwise than by way of purchase),[89] the incurring of wasted expenditure,[90] or the failure to obtain more favourable rights under a contract.[91] There are an infinite number of scenarios in which the claimant may be induced to take a step (or to desist from taking a step) by deceit, where the loss he may thereby suffer will be capable of being the subject of a damages award. In such cases the old, but highly influential, dictum of Lord Atkin in *Clark v Urquhart* prevails: the measure of damage should be constituted by the "actual damage directly flowing from the fraudulent inducement."

21–050 In the sub-sections below, we consider various heads of damages, other than the purchase price, which the courts have allowed claimants in commercial claims in deceit.[92]

(1) Expenses Incurred in the Transaction

21–051 Where a claimant has entered into a transaction induced by fraud then he is in principle entitled not only to the capital outlay, less any residual value in the asset acquired (as to which see above), but also to expenses incurred in making the acquisition which he would not otherwise have made. For instance, the acquisition of shares or land will generally carry with it professional costs and stamp duty. These costs will in principle be recoverable.[93]

(2) Subsequent Costs

21–052 A claimant acquires the shares in a company or a business induced by the defendant's fraud. That claimant makes payments post-completion to support its acquisition. In principle, such costs are recoverable. So in *East v Maurer*,[94] the claimants had purchased the defendant's hair-dressing business induced by his fraudulent misrepresentation that he did not intend to keep working as a hair-dresser in the area. In fact, he continued working at another local salon he had retained and, in the face of this unexpected competition, the claimants

---

[88] For a detailed exposition of damages in lender claims see H. Tomlinson and T. Grant, *Lender Claims* (London: Sweet & Maxwell, 2010).

[89] See e.g. *Standard Chartered Bank v Pakistan National Shipping* [1998] 1 Lloyd's Rep. 684.

[90] See e.g. *Richardson v Silvester* (1873) L.R. 9 Q.B., where, induced by a fraudulently false statement that the defendant was entitled to let a farm, the claimant incurred wasted expenditure in inspecting and valuing the farm. He was held entitled to recover that expenditure by way of damages.

[91] *Clef Aquitaine SARL v Laporte Materials (Barrow) Ltd* [2001] Q.B. 488.

[92] The current edition of *McGregor* provides a wide compendium of examples of consequential losses allowed by the courts in fraud claims across a variety of fields: see para.47–028 and following. These are typically wasted expenditures incurred or losses sustained flowing from steps taken induced by the deceit. Damages have also been awarded for pain and suffering, physical inconvenience and discomfort and mental distress: see the cases gathered by *McGregor*, at para.47–041 and following.

[93] See e.g. *4 Eng Ltd v Harper* [2008] EWHC 915 (Ch); [2009] Ch. 91, at [21].

[94] *East v Maurer* [1991] 1 W.L.R. 461.

expended significant moneys in advertising their business and enhancing it, in order to keep it trading and make the business profitable, while making attempts to sell it. A sale was eventually achieved, some years after the purchase, but at a significant loss on the capital cost. The costs incurred, and the costs of sale of the business, were allowed.[95] Similarly in *Invertec Ltd v de Mol Holdings BV*,[96] the judge allowed the claimant the loss constituted by loans made by it to the company acquired as a result of the defendant's fraud, which were advanced prior to discovery of the true facts. As stated above, the courts are careful not to turn the defendant into an insurer of all the claimant's ongoing losses. Hence, in the *Invertec* case, further loans made by the claimant to the company after discovery of all the facts were disallowed.

Of course, the incurring of expenses may lead to benefits accruing. In such circumstances, corresponding credit would have to be given.[97]   **21–053**

Damages have been awarded where the fraud exposed the claimant to litigation with a third party, such damages being referable to the costs incurred in defending the litigation.[98]   **21–054**

(3) Interest on Loans Taken out to Fund Purchase

Induced by the deceit, the claimant may have borrowed the money used to purchase an asset or make a loan. In such a case, the claimant will inevitably incur interest costs to the lender. In principle, such costs may be claimed from the defendant.[99]   **21–055**

(4) Management Time/Investigation Costs

A major fraud will inevitably be responded to by a corporate claimant by the incurring of management time investigating the facts. The claimant may possibly even resort to the retainer of external investigators. Lost management time is   **21–056**

---

[95] As they were in *Doyle v Olby*, above.

[96] *Invertec Ltd v de Mol Holdings BV* [2009] EWHC 2471 (Ch).

[97] *Spence v Crawford* [1939] 3 All E.R. 271, 288–289. The basic principle is encapsulated in Dixon J's celebrated judgment in *Toteff v Antonas* (1952) 87 C.L.R. 647, at 651: "The measure of damages in an action of deceit consists in the loss or expenditure incurred by the plaintiff in consequence of the inducement on which he relied diminished by the corresponding advantage in money or moneys worth obtained by him on the other side."

[98] *Dadourian Group International Inc v Simms* [2009] EWCA Civ 169; [2009] 1 Lloyds's Rep. 601, at [109]–[148].

[99] There are many examples of this: see e.g. *Archer v Brown* [1985] Q.B. 401, where the claimant had borrowed funds from a bank in order to fund the purchase of shares induced by the fraud. An award of damages was (correctly) made with reference to the interest liability incurred to the bank. The judge referred to the fact that the defendant was aware that the claimant was going to have to resort to bank borrowing to fund the acquisition and so the principle established by the famous case *The Liesbosch* [1933] A.C. 449 (in which, broadly, it was held that a claimant's unforeseen impecuniosity could not increase damages) was not applicable. But, as stated, foreseeability as a test is irrelevant to recovery of damages in deceit; the judge did not need to consider it.

capable of being compensated in damages.[100] Further, investigation expenses actually incurred in favour of a third party are recoverable.[101]

(5)   Lost Profits on Alternative Transaction

21–057   So far, we have largely focused on damages compensating the claimant for his capital loss and other outlays. But experience shows that a claimant's losses may well be considerably wider than simply the loss of a sum of money laid out on a transaction induced by the defendant's fraud and ancillary expenditures. The transaction will often be one where the claimant then commits himself to an ongoing course of conduct which prevents him from making the profits he hoped to make. For instance, a claimant may purchase a business induced by fraudulent misrepresentations. The claimant then seeks to operate the business, into which he is effectively locked. The business is loss-making. The claimant's losses in such a case extend far beyond the capital sum expended and further costs incurred in seeking to keep the business afloat; the claimant had hoped to purchase an asset which would create a profit. Instead, he has purchased an asset which has in fact lost him money.

21–058   One must of course be careful to distinguish between contract and tort damages. Unless he has the benefit of a warranty on which he can sue, the claimant cannot put himself in the position he would have been in had the asset he purchased had the characteristics he hoped it would have. The claimant's case will instead generally be that, had he not been induced by the fraudulent misrepresentation he would not have purchased the relevant asset, but would rather have purchased some alternative asset which would have generated profits for him.

21–059   In such a case, the law recognises that, to be properly compensated, an award of damages with reference to the claimant's lost opportunity to make a profit via an alternative transaction may be appropriate:

> "an award based on the hypothetical profitable business in which the plaintiff would have engaged but for deceit is permissible: it is classic consequential loss."[102]

21–060   So, in *East v Maurer*[103] the claimants were induced to buy a hairdressing salon from the defendants by false representations. After trading unsuccessfully and then discovering that they had been the victims of fraud, the claimants had difficulty in selling the business and eventually did so at a substantial loss. They claimed not only their capital loss, but also loss of profits during the period that

---

[100] See for instance *National Building Society v Dunlop Haywards* [2009] EWHC 254 (Comm); [2010] 1 W.L.R. 258, at [15]–[18] (applying *R+V Versicherung AG v Risk Insurance and Reinsurance Solutions SA* [2006] EWHC 42 (Comm), at [77]). In that case, the damages extended to time spent investigating whether other frauds had been committed.

[101] See e.g. *4 Eng v Harper* [2008] EWHC 915 (Ch); [2009] Ch. 91, at [27]–[40]. In that case, the claimant company had purchased the shares in a company owned by the defendants. The claimant entered into an agreement with its main individual shareholders/directors to pay them £100 an hour in carrying out the investigations. The overall claim for in excess of £600,000 was allowed.

[102] *Smith New Court*, at 282.

[103] *East v Maurer* [1991] 1 W.L.R. 461.

they owned the business. The Court of Appeal held that, while they were not entitled to loss of the profits in relation to the business itself which they might reasonably have expected to make if the defendants' representations had been true (since the action was for deceit and not for breach of a contractual warranty), they were entitled to an award of loss of profits relating to the hypothetical business in which they would have engaged but for the fraud of the defendants. It was not necessary to identify some particular purchase they would have made (in the usual course of events this would be very difficult, although not impossible); the court must do the best it can on the material available.

In *Clef Acquitaine SARL v Laporte Materials (Barrow) Ltd*[104] the Court of Appeal held that a claimant could recover lost profits on a hypothetical alternative transaction even where the transaction entered into by reason of the defendant's deceit was itself profitable: because it was established that, but for the deceit, the claimants would have negotiated more favourable contractual rights for themselves than they in fact did, and those more favourable rights would have resulted in greater profits, and the lost additional profits could be recovered as damages. **21–061**

Another more recent example is *Khakshouri v Jimenez*,[105] which has been considered above in connection with the question of the date of assessment of loss, in which it was held that that a claimant who had lent money induced by the defendants' deceit was entitled to be compensated for the profit which he would have made on an investment from which he had withdrawn funds in order to make the loan. **21–062**

Losses on a hypothetical alternative transaction will of course only be recoverable where the claimant can show that the circumstances are such that the fraud has deprived him of the alternative opportunity. If, for example, the claimant had sufficient funds to complete the fraudulently induced transaction and the hypothetical alternative, the fraud will not have caused such a loss. **21–063**

(6) Loss of Income and Prospect of Capital Appreciation

The claimant may go still further and assert that the alternative transaction would have yielded not only profits greater than those (if any) in fact obtained, but also capital appreciation over time in the business or shares acquired. Certain dicta in earlier cases had suggested that the claimant might be confined to a claim for one or another[106]; but it has now been established that, as a matter of principle, both elements of loss are recoverable, as cumulative and not alternative heads of damage. What is interesting here is that the courts have accepted that the loss of the right to acquire an alternative asset *at market value* (such that there is, strictly **21–064**

---

[104] *Clef Acquitaine SARL v Laporte Materials (Barrow) Ltd* [2001] Q.B. 488.
[105] *Khakshouri v Jimenez* [2017] EWHC 3392 (QB).
[106] *East v Maurer*, at 468, per Mustill LJ citing *Cullinane v British "Rema" Manufacturing Co Ltd* [1954] 1 Q.B. 292. In fact, on analysis, *Cullinane* is authority for no such proposition; rather it decides the (obvious point) that a claim for loss of profit cannot be coupled with a claim for capital loss (being expenditure in installing plant which had been warranted to have particular characteristics).

speaking, no loss as at the date of acquisition) could nonetheless yield a substantive damages award based on future appreciation in value.

21–065 So in *4 Eng Ltd v Harper*[107] the claimants were induced by fraudulent misrepresentations to buy the share capital in a company which provided engineering services. Far from being profitable, the previous owners of the company (and the defendants) had been systematically bribing the employees of its principal customer to make payments to it on inflated or bogus invoices, and it was potentially liable in damages to that customer for a large amount as well at risk of losing its principal source of business. In due course, the defendants were sent to prison for fraud and the company went into liquidation. The judge found that but for the defendants' fraud the claimants would have been able and willing to make an offer for the purchase of an identified different company, and that there was a high likelihood that they would have succeeded in doing so. He awarded (very substantial) damages which included an assessment of the claimants' loss of likely income from the asset and capital appreciation from the alternative acquisition at the date of trial. The analysis of the judge traverses a number of issues and is worth detailed consideration.

21–066 One of the arguments advanced by the defendants was that the date for assessment of the loss should not have been later than the date on which the company (the shares in which were purchased by reason of the defendants' fraud) went into administration, because by then the claimants were freed from the consequences of the defendants' deceit. The judge said[108] that he could follow that submission if on that date the claimants had recovered substantial funds which they could then invest in an alternative acquisition. However, because the company was insolvent and the claimants recovered nothing, they were no more then able to make an alternative acquisition than they had been before it went into administration. The consequences of the defendants' deceit did not stop but continued until trial. In those circumstances, the choice of the date when the company went into administration would be arbitrary and unconnected with the claimants' loss.

21–067 The court decided that the proper way to approach the assessment of the damages referable to the lost alternative acquisition was to apply the approach set out in *Allied Maples v Simmons & Simmons*.[109] This involved conducting, in the counter-factual world which the assessment of damages requires, a four-stage inquiry:

(1) Whether, on the balance of probabilities, the claimant would have been able and willing to made the acquisition; if not, the inquiry ended there; but if so the inquiry continued to the next stage.

(2) Assessing, in percentage terms, the chance that the owners of the alternative company would have been willing to sell to the claimant on acceptable terms.

---

107 *4 Eng Ltd v Harper*, above.
108 *4 Eng Ltd v Harper*, at [55].
109 *Allied Maples v Simmons & Simmons* [1995] 1 W.L.R. 1602.

(3)   Next, the court assessed the profit which the claimant would have derived from the alternative acquisition and the capital value it would have had as at the date of the trial (taking account of the commercial contingencies of lower profits in relation to the alternative acquisition given that the company would be, *ex hypothesi*, under new ownership).[110]

(4)   Finally, the figures arrived at under step (3) were then subjected to the percentage arrived at under step (2).

The inquiry conducted by the judge in *4 Eng* provides a vivid illustration not only of the potentially far-reaching consequences of a fraud in the business sphere (in that case it entirely changed the course of the claimant company's commercial existence, and that of its individual directors and shareholders, for many years), but also of the exacting way the law will respond to such consequences. In that case, the capital award of £550,000 (i.e. the consideration paid out for the worthless shareholding) was overtopped dramatically by the award relating to ancillary and consequential losses (which ran to over £8,000,000).[111]   **21–068**

(7)   Loss of Investment Opportunity

A variant on the claim for lost profits was considered in *Parabola Investments Ltd v Browallia Cal Ltd*.[112] There, the claimant was induced by fraudulent misrepresentations made by a brokerage to embark on a course of trading which involved substantial losses. The claimant not only claimed the capital sum lost (which was uncontentious) but also sought damages to reflect the loss of investment opportunity during the period when its funds were deployed in the loss-making course of conduct. In essence, the claimant contended that, absent the fraud to which it was subject, it would have invested the capital sums in alternative profit-making ventures. Hence an award of interest would be insufficient. The claim was broken into two periods: stage 1, being the period when the claimant was trading via the defendant (a period of less than a year), and stage 2, being the period from the end of stage 1 to the time of trial. As to stage 2, the claimant asserted that the frauds of the defendant had forever depleted the fund which would have otherwise been available to the claimant to trade with. The judge had found, on the balance of probabilities, that had it had the full fund available to it the claimant would have made overall profits, albeit   **21–069**

---

[110] This claim had to give credit for the cost of acquisition of the alternative company.

[111] A similar inquiry was conducted in the later case of *Fiona Trust & Holding Corp v Privalov* [2016] EWHC 2163 (Comm). This was an inquiry under a cross-undertaking in damages; but it involved an analogous exercise. The judge encapsulated the court's task as follows, at [55]: "The true position is that in principle damages can be awarded for loss of profits even if a claimant might have made a loss. The approach which the court will adopt is to ask whether the claimant has proved to a sufficient standard (which may be the balance of probabilities, or sometimes merely that there was a real and substantial chance as in loss of a chance cases) that its trading would have been profitable. If so, the court will make the best assessment of the damages that it can, applying if necessary a discount to reflect whatever uncertainty exists, while recognising that a party seeking to show what might have happened is not required to perform an impossible task with unrealistic precision."

[112] *Parabola Investments Ltd v Browallia Cal Ltd* [2009] EWHC 901 (Comm); and [2010] EWCA Civ 486; [2011] Q.B. 47.

individual trades would have been loss-making: he was able to make that finding based on the average profits made by the claimant in its investment activity both before and after the fraudulent period. He awarded damages for both stage 1 and stage 2, notwithstanding that the claimant was unable to identify specific trades it would have entered into during each of those stages.

21–070   What was noteworthy about the final disposition was that the claimant's capital loss was just over £3 million, whereas the damages which it was awarded by way of loss of investment opportunity amounted to over £15 million. Accordingly, the case raised in a very acute form the issue of the recoverability of damages, in the alternative to an award of interest, for the lost opportunity to turn money, which the claimant has been deprived of by the wrong of the defendant, to advantage, both before and after discovery of the fraud.

21–071   In its decision,[113] the Court of Appeal considered the principles relating to the award of damages. The following principles were identified:

(1)   In quantifying hypothetical losses, having found on the balance of probabilities that the claimant would have sought to engage in profit-making activity (i.e. stage (1) of the inquiry conducted in *4 Eng*) the court does not apply a balance of probability test but rather estimates the loss by making the best attempt it can to evaluate the chances, great or small (unless those chances amount to no more than remote speculation), taking all significant factors into account. This equates to stages (2) and (3) of the inquiry conducted in *4 Eng* discussed above.[114]

(2)   The claimant did not need to be able to identify a specific alternative transaction which would necessarily have been profitable.[115] The court was entitled to proceed on the basis of the evidence available to it. It might be appropriate to reflect the necessarily imprecise task, and to reflect various contingencies, by a process of discounting.

(3)   There was no logical reason to curtail damages to the period of the fraud or the period prior to its discovery.[116] There was no reason to refuse damages for loss of use of moneys as a result of the defendant's wrong for the whole period to trial.[117]

21–072   The court did raise one potential defence which might have been available to limit the defendant's liability. It was suggested that where a claim is made for loss of use of money on an alternative investment after the discovery of the fraud, a fair measurement of the loss might in some cases be the cost of replenishing the depleted fund, i.e. the cost of borrowing the necessary amounts to make the investment, rather than the loss of profits from use of the fund (which is likely to

---

[113] The judgment of Toulson LJ is rightly celebrated.

[114] See *4 Eng*, at [22]–[24].

[115] See, *4 Eng*, at [44] and [47]. Indeed, the claimant had been unable to do so in *East v Maurer* [1991] I W.L.R. 461. And see also *Esso Petroleum Ltd v Mardon* [1976] 1 Q.B. 801.

[116] David Richards J had reached a similar view in the rather different circumstances of *4 Eng*.

[117] See, *4 Eng*, at [41]–[45] and [47]. Compare the decision of the Australian High Court in *Hungerfords v Walker* (1989) 171 C.L.R. 125, concerning damages for loss of use of money, which the Court of Appeal in *Parabola* held represented the common law, at [44].

be a much larger sum), if the possibility of replenishment was reasonably open to the claimant. In *Parabola*, the point had not been investigated; but it is suggested that it is right in principle, it representing no more than an application of the basic principles of causation considered above. It is a potentially significant delimiting principle.

(8)   Where the Alternative Transaction would also have been Loss-Making

We have seen above that a claimant can recover losses with reference to the profits or other gains that would have been made on a hypothetical alternative transaction which he would have entered into, but for the fraud. But what if the alternative transaction would (like the actual transaction) also have resulted in a loss, and it is therefore the defendant who seeks to rely on it, in reduction of the claim? Take the example of a house purchase: The claimant is in principle willing to purchase it for £1 million. The vendor then fraudulently informs him that the property has the benefit of a right of way. The claimant is thereby induced to increase his offer to £1.05 million. The true value of the property in fact is only £700,000. In such a case is the claimant's measure of damage £50,000 (because, but for the misrepresentation, the claimant would have been prepared to purchase the house for £1 million) or £350,000 (because that is the loss that flows "directly" from his having entered into the transaction at all)?

21–073

In *Smith New Court*, Lord Steyn said[118]:

21–074

> "In my view the orthodox and settled rule that the plaintiff is entitled to all losses directly flowing from the transaction caused by the deceit does not require a revision. In other words, it is not necessary in an action for deceit for the judge, after he had ascertained the loss directly flowing from the victim having entered into the transaction, to embark on a hypothetical reconstruction of what the parties would have agreed had the deceit not occurred. The rule in deceit is justified by the grounds already discussed."

However, the point there being addressed was the observation made by Hobhouse LJ in *Downs v Chappell* that the court should cross-check its assessment of the loss with reference to the position as it would have been had the representation been *true*. The point under consideration now is different, in that it (correctly) looks to the position as it would have been had the representation not been made at all.

There is certainly support in the cases for the view that, in a case of deceit, it is inappropriate to speculate as to whether the claimant would in any event have suffered a loss, but for the misrepresentation: it is the policy of the law to transfer the whole risk of the transaction onto the fraudulent defendant and such an enquiry is therefore simply precluded. As it was put by Hobhouse LJ in *Downs v Chappell*[119]:

21–075

---

[118] *Smith New Court*, at 283F–283G.
[119] *Downs v Chappell* [1997] 1 W.L.R. 426, at 441.

"In general, it is irrelevant to inquire what the representee would have done if some different representation had been made to him or what other transactions he might have entered into if he had not entered into the transaction in question. Such matters are irrelevant speculations."[120]

21–076 However, the very fact that in the cases we have considered above (*East v Maurer*, *Clef Acquitaine* and *4 Eng Ltd*) the court was prepared to consider profitable hypothetical alternative transactions in increasing the claimant's damages suggests that this dictum is doubtful: if, in assessing the loss flowing from the deceit, the court can properly speculate on alternative transactions that would have been more profitable to the claimant, why can it not also speculate on alternative transactions that would have been less profitable? There is no difference in principle between loss-making and profit-making transactions for these purposes. If there is an argument for distinguishing them, it must be that (as we have already seen above in other contexts) the policy of the law leans in favour of the claimant, where the tort is an intentional one, such that he in effect has a one-way bet. An alternative view, which commended itself to Leggatt J in *Yam Seng Pte Ltd v International Trade Corp Ltd*,[121] is that the court can and should speculate in both such cases; but that where it is the defendant who is trying to pray in aid the alternative transaction in reduction of the claimant's claim, the burden is on him to demonstrate both that such an alternative transaction would have been entered into and the amount of loss that would have resulted. Unlike a claimant, the defendant will not be assisted by the court making reasonable assumptions in this regard.[122]

(9) Aggravated and Exemplary Damages

21–077 Awards of damages are, of course, intended principally to compensate for loss, whether it be pecuniary or non-pecuniary. Non-pecuniary loss can include mental distress arising from the circumstances in which a tort was committed, such as justified feelings of outrage at the defendant's conduct; and the law recognises that damages for this type of loss can in an appropriate case be awarded. Such damages are sometimes called "aggravated" damages. In contrast, "exemplary" (or "punitive") damages are not compensatory at all; they are additional to a compensatory award and are intended to punish and deter.[123]

21–078 Aggravated damages are available in a claim in deceit on the same basis as they are in contract: in *Archer v Brown*[124] the defendant deceived the claimant into purchasing shares in a company and signing a service agreement with it, when in

---

[120] This dictum was applied in *Slough Estates Plc v Welwyn Hatfield District Council* [1996] 2 P.L.R. 50; and the decision in *Naughton v O'Callaghan* [1990] 3 All E.R. 191 is to similar effect. See also *Dadourian Group International v Simms* [2009] EWCA Civ 169, at [107], where Arden LJ observed that, subject to showing clearly the absence of any inducement, any speculation as to what the representee would or might have done if he had known the truth is immaterial.

[121] *Yam Seng Pte Ltd v International Trade Corp Ltd* [2013] EWHC 111 (QB), at [217].

[122] And so, in that case, whilst Leggatt J was firmly in favour of the view that a reduction in the claimant's damages could in principle be made on this basis, he declined to do so on the evidence before him.

[123] *Kuddus v Chief Constable of Leicestershire* [2002] 2 A.C. 122, per Lord Nicholls at [50]–[51].

[124] *Archer v Brown* [1985] Q.B. 401.

fact the defendant owned no shares in the company to sell, leading to the claimant becoming heavily indebted, losing his employment and suffering considerable distress. He was awarded £500 for injury to his feelings.

As to exemplary damages, the relevant question is whether the defendant's conduct is such as to warrant a punitive award; the cause of action sued on is no longer regarded as a limiting condition.[125] So far as relevant to a private law claim, such as in deceit, exemplary damages will in principle be available where the defendant's conduct was calculated to make a profit which exceeds the compensation likely to be payable.[126] Such an award was recently made in a claim in deceit by an insurer against a number of defendants involved in the making of fraudulent insurance claims in relation to road traffic accidents.[127] Exemplary damages have also been awarded in a case where a bare trustee of real property (which had by error been registered in the defendant's name) misappropriated the property from its beneficial owner.[128] Among considerations relevant to the assessment of an award of exemplary damages are the need for moderation (since the award is punitive and yet is made without the safeguards afforded to a defendant in criminal proceedings), the conduct of the parties and (unusually, since it would not be relevant to a compensatory award) their means.[129] The fact that a defendant has already been punished by the criminal courts is a reason why an award of exemplary damages might be refused.[130]

21–079

F.   CONTRIBUTORY NEGLIGENCE

(1)   Introduction

Where a claimant is partly to blame for the loss which he suffers, the defendant can, in certain circumstances, rely on the defence of contributory negligence. The apportionment of blame between claimant and defendant can lead to a reduction in the damages recoverable by the claimant. The jurisdiction to make such a deduction derives from the Law Reform (Contributory Negligence) Act 1945.[131]

21–080

The principle underlying the law of contributory negligence is that where the defendant can show that the claimant's loss was caused or contributed to by its own act or omission at the time of, or before, the completion of the event which gives rise to the loss,[132] which act or omission involved a failure on the part of the claimant to use reasonable care to look after its own interests, the defendant may

21–081

---

[125] *Kuddus*, above.
[126] *Rookes v Barnard* [1964] A.C. 1129, at 1226. The availability of exemplary damages in such a case in a deceit claim was recognised in *Kuddus*.
[127] *Direct Line Goup Plc v Akramzadeh*, unreported, 15 June 2016, per Flaux J.
[128] *Ramzan v Brookwide Ltd* [2011] EWCA Civ 985.
[129] *Rookes v Barnard*, above, at 1227–1228.
[130] E.g. *Archer v Brown*, above.
[131] For a full consideration of the law of contributory negligence, see Tomlinson and Grant, *Lender Claims* (2010), at Ch.8.
[132] An act or omission on the part of the claimant after the event which gives rise to the loss will be categorised as a failure to mitigate loss, or possibly a new event which breaks the chain of causation, rather than as contributory negligence.

be entitled to a reduction of the damages which would otherwise have been awarded against him. However, contributory negligence can arise not just when the claimant contributes to the *event* which caused the loss but also when it contributes to, or exacerbates, the *damage* thereby caused. This is shown by the paradigm example of contributory negligence: a car passenger fails to wear a seat belt; the claimant passenger who sues his driver may not have contributed to the accident, but if the passenger did not wear a seat belt he may have contributed to the gravity of his own injuries. The defendant can therefore raise a defence of contributory negligence.[133]

(2)   The Statutory Jurisdiction

21–082   Until 1945 contributory negligence was a common law doctrine. If a defendant could prove that the claimant by his own carelessness had caused or contributed to the damage in respect of which he was claiming damages then that was a complete defence. The abrogation of that complete defence, and the creation of an alternative jurisdiction to make a deduction from damages by reason of a claimant's contributory negligence, derives from s.1(1) of the Law Reform (Contributory Negligence) Act 1945 ("the 1945 Act") which provides, in part:

> "Where any person suffers damage as the result partly of his own fault and partly of the fault of any other person or persons,[134] a claim in respect of that damage shall not be defeated by reason of the fault of the person suffering the damage, but the damages recoverable in respect thereof shall be reduced to such extent as the Court thinks just and equitable having regard to the claimant's share in the responsibility for the damage ..."

21–083   This sub-section may be broken down into three parts. The third part (starting with the words "but the damages recoverable ...") deals with the effect of a finding of contributory negligence. The second part (starting with the words "a claim in respect of that damage ...") simply serves to reverse the old common law rule, mentioned above, that the effect of a finding of contributory negligence on the part of the claimant was that the defendant would succeed entirely; and the primary purpose of the 1945 Act was to mitigate this harsh rule. The part of the sub-section relevant to the question of when the defendant can raise the defence of contributory negligence is therefore the first.

21–084   It follows from the statutory definition that contributory negligence can be relied upon as a defence where a claimant suffers damage partly as a result of his own

---

[133] See *Froom v Butcher* [1976] Q.B. 286 (CA).
[134] This wording would make the finding of 100% contributory negligence illogical: see *Pitts v Hunt* [1991] 1 Q.B. 24 (CA), at 50, per Beldam LJ. In *Reeves v Commissioner of Police of the Metropolis* [2000] 1 A.C. 360 (HL), at 372 Lord Hoffmann said that a 100% contributory negligence reduction would give no weight at all to the policy of the law in imposing a duty of care on the defendant and would be tantamount to denying the duty of care itself. See further *Anderson v Newham College of Further Education* [2002] EWCA Civ 505; [2003] I.C.R. 212, at [19]; and *Brumder v Motornet Service and Repairs Ltd* [2013] EWCA Civ 195; [2013] 1 W.L.R. 2783, at [4]. It has also been held that very small percentages of apportionment, under 10%, ought not to be made: *Johnson v Tennant Bros* Unreported November 19, 1954, referred to in *Capps v Miller* [1989] 1 W.L.R. 839 (CA). But see *IG Index Ltd v Aryeh Ehrentreu* [2015] EWHC 3390 (QB), where Supperstone J would have been prepared to make a finding of 95% contributory negligence.

fault and partly as a result of fault on the part of the defendant. It is, therefore, necessary to consider the meaning of "fault" in order to establish whether the partial defence of contributory negligence can apply. For the purpose of s.1, "fault" is defined by s.4 of the 1945 Act as:

> "negligence, breach of statutory duty or other act or omission which gives rise to a liability in tort or would, apart from this Act, give rise to the defence of contributory negligence".

It is important to note that s.1(1) of the 1945 Act refers to the "fault" of both the claimant and the defendant. In *Standard Chartered Bank v Pakistan National Shipping Corp*[135] Lord Hoffmann said that:

21–085

> "the definition of 'fault' is divided into two limbs, one of which is applicable to defendants and the other to claimants. In the case of a defendant, fault means 'negligence, breach of statutory duty or other act or omission' which gives rise to a liability in tort. In the case of a claimant, it means 'negligence, breach of statutory duty or other act or omission' which gives rise (at common law) to a defence of contributory negligence."

The result is that conduct by a claimant cannot be "fault" within the meaning of the 1945 Act unless it would have given rise to a defence of contributory negligence at common law. It will be recalled that prior to the passing of the 1945 Act, the defence of contributory negligence was a doctrine developed by the common law which operated by way of complete, rather than partial, defence. The basis of Lord Hoffmann's distinction was as follows:

21–086

> "this appears to me in accordance with the purpose of the Act, which was to relieve plaintiffs whose actions would previously have failed and not to reduce the damages which previously would have been awarded against defendants. Section 1(1) makes this clear when it says that 'a claim in respect of that damage shall not be defeated by reason of the fault of the person suffering the damage, but [instead] the damages recoverable in respect thereof shall be reduced . . .' "[136]

There are two important points relating to claimant fault. First, the fault of the claimant does not require, notwithstanding the wording of s.4, the breach of any duty owed by the claimant to the defendant. This was established in *Davies v Swan Motor Co (Swansea) Ltd.*[137] Secondly, and notwithstanding the title of the 1945 Act, it is now clear that claimant fault for the purposes of s.1 of the 1945 Act embraces both careless and intentional acts or omissions. In *Reeves v Metropolitan Police Commissioner*[138] the police were held to be in breach of a duty of care owed to a prisoner in their custody to take reasonable steps to prevent the prisoner's suicide. It was held that the prisoner's suicide was not a supervening event which broke the chain of causation but the police were able to rely on the defence of contributory negligence and the prisoner was held to be 50% contributorily negligent for his own death. In this respect, it was held that

21–087

---

[135] *Standard Chartered Bank v Pakistan National Shipping Corp* [2002] UKHL 43; [2003] 1 A.C. 959, at [11].

[136] *Standard Chartered Bank v Pakistan National Shipping Corp* [2002] UKHL 43, at [12].

[137] *Davies v Swan Motor Co (Swansea) Ltd* [1949] 2 K.B. 291 (CA), at 308–309, per Bucknill LJ: "it is not necessary to show that the negligence constituted a breach of duty to the defendant. It is sufficient to show lack of reasonable care by the plaintiff for his own safety."

[138] *Reeves v Metropolitan Police Commissioner* [2000] 1 A.C. 360 (HL).

the definition of "fault" in s.4 of the 1945 Act could include intentional acts, as well as negligence on the part of the claimant.[139]

(3) Intentional Wrongdoing

21-088 However, in relation to defendant fault the position concerning intentional wrongdoing is quite different. This difference stems from the contrasting function that 'fault' plays in relation to claimants and defendants under s.1 of the 1945 Act. In relation to claimants, "fault" ordinarily refers to a failure to take reasonable steps to protect the claimant's own interests, which (in part) causes his loss. Ordinarily, such conduct will simply be careless: but if the claimant intentionally takes a step which has the consequence of inflicting loss upon himself, then this will a fortiori trigger the defence. By contrast, in relation to defendants, "fault" plays a limiting function by identifying those causes of action (and only those) in respect of which the defence can be invoked.

21-089 It is well established that where a defendant is sued in negligence or breach of statutory duty he may plead contributory negligence as a defence.[140] In *Gran Gelato Ltd v Richcliff (Group) Ltd*,[141] Sir Donald Nicholls VC held that in principle a defence of contributory negligence would be available in a claim for damages under s.2(1) of the Misrepresentation Act 1967, insofar as the claim under s.2(1) of the 1967 Act was concurrent with a claim in negligence at common law. (Where there is no such concurrent claim—e.g. because the misrepresentor owes no duty of care—it seems to follow that contributory negligence will not apply to the claim under s.2(1).) The Vice-Chancellor rejected the defence, on the facts. Both at common law and under the 1967 Act, the essential feature of the claim was that the claimant relied on the misrepresentation, as the defendant had intended: it would therefore take a "very special case" before carelessness by the representee would make it just and equitable, under the 1945 Act, for damages to be reduced. More recently in *Taberna Europe CDO II Plc v Selskabet*[142] Eder J reached similar conclusions. While Eder J followed *Gran Gelato* in holding that contributory negligence was in principle available to a claim under s.2(1), he doubted to what extent it could be reconciled with the so-called rule in *Redgrave v Hurd* that "it lies ill in a defendant's mouth" to complain of contributory negligence when they intended the claimant to rely on the representation. The facts fell short of a "very special case" in which it would

---

[139] See per Lord Hoffmann at 369: "the 'defence of contributory negligence' at common law was based upon the view that a plaintiff whose failure to take care for his own safety was a cause of his injury could not sue. One would therefore have thought that the defence applied a fortiori to a plaintiff who intended to injure himself."

[140] For examples of the defence of contributory negligence in actions for breach of statutory duty under FSMA see *Spreadex Ltd v Sekhon* [2008] EWHC 1136 (Ch); [2009] 1 B.C.L.C. 102, at [166]–[184]; and *Bank Leumi (UK) Plc v Wachner* [2011] EWHC 656 (Comm); [2011] 1 C.L.C. 454, at [322]–[324].

[141] *Gran Gelato Ltd v Richcliff (Group) Ltd* [1992] Ch. 560 (ChD).

[142] *Taberna Europe CDO II Plc v Selskabet* [2015] EWHC 871 (Comm).

be just and equitable to reduce damages under the 1945 Act.[143] It follows from these authorities that, although in principle available as a defence to a claim under s.2(1) of the 1967 Act, it seems likely that in most cases it will not provide any material assistance for defendants in practice.

However, s.1 of the 1945 Act does not extend to intentional torts because at common law contributory negligence was no defence to a claim founded on an intentional tort.[144] Such claims include, most importantly, torts or other wrongs based on dishonest conduct, such as when the claimant's claim is in deceit[145] or dishonest assistance in a breach of trust.[146] The principle is that it would not be just for a fraudulent defendant's liability in damages to be reduced on the grounds that the victim has acted carelessly in respect of the relevant transaction.[147] Nonetheless, the inability to raise the defence extends to intentional torts even if dishonesty is not an element. This means that where a claimant succeeds in proving such a tort against a defendant, the defendant cannot successfully raise a defence of contributory negligence, no matter how careless the claimant may have been.

21–090

This does not mean that contributory negligence is irrelevant in fraud litigation. A claimant may itself find that its damages claim is reduced because of its own fraud. A recent example is *Singularis Holdings Ltd v Daiwa Capital Markets Europe Ltd*[148] in which the claimant company brought proceedings against the defendant bank for breach of the so-called *Quincecare* duty, by making payments from the claimant's account at the direction of one of the company's directors and sole shareholder without proper inquiry. It was common ground that the shareholder director was acting fraudulently. Although that fraud could not be attributed to the claimant company (for reasons discussed in Ch.19) nonetheless its damages were reduced by 25% for contributory negligence,[149] for its vicarious liability for the deceit of the director and the failure of the other directors of the company to contact the bank or control the fraudulent director.

21–091

---

[143] *Taberna Europe CDO II Plc v Selskabet* [2015] EWHC 871 (Comm), at [111] and [180]–[181]. The Court of Appeal agreed with this reasoning: see, at [2016] EWCA 1262; [2017] Q.B. 633, at [50]–[52].

[144] See *Quinn v Leathem* [1902] A.C. 495 (HL), at 537, per Lord Lindley. The law on the non-availability of the defence of contributory negligence in intentional torts was comprehensively reviewed in the Court of Appeal decision of *Co-operative Group (CWS) Ltd v Pritchard* [2011] EWCA 329; [2012] Q.B. 320.

[145] See *Alliance & Leicester Building Society v Edgestop* [1993] 1 W.L.R. 1462 (ChD). In that case the argument that the innocent employer, vicariously liable for the actions of a fraudulent employee, should be entitled to plead contributory negligence was rejected. *Edgestop* was followed in *Nationwide Building Society v Thimbleby* [1999] Lloyd's Rep. P.N. 359 (ChD).

[146] *Corporacion Nacional del Cobre de Chile v Sogemin Metals Ltd* [1997] 1 W.L.R. 1396 (ChD).

[147] *Standard Chartered Bank v Pakistan National Shipping Corp (Nos 2 and 4)* [2002] UKHL 43; [2003] 1 A.C. 959, at [16], per Lord Hoffmann: "It would not seem just that a fraudulent defendant's liability should be reduced on the grounds that, for whatever reason, the victim should not have made the payment which the defendant successfully induced him to make."

[148] *Singularis Holdings Ltd v Daiwa Capital Markets Europe Ltd* [2018] EWCA Civ 84. Another example is *Barings Plc v Coopers & Lybrand* [2003] P.N.L.R. 34, where a negligence claim against an auditor was reduced by over 50% to reflect the claimant's failure to manage its fraudulent employee and his unauthorised trading which had given rise to the loss.

[149] The Court of Appeal refused to interfere with the judge's assessment.

21-092   It is now clear that the defence of contributory negligence, or some equitable equivalent, cannot be invoked in a claim for breach of trust or breach of fiduciary duty. The question arose for decision in *Nationwide Building Society v Balmer Radmore*.[150] It was argued on behalf of the defendant solicitors that where the claimant's claim was for equitable compensation for losses resulting from a breach of fiduciary duty, its compensation was liable to be reduced for its contributory negligence. The basis of the argument was that equity was flexible enough to accommodate such a deduction, especially where what had happened was not a misapplication of assets in breach of trust,[151] but simply a breach of fiduciary duty which arose in respect of part of a commercial transaction where the fiduciary had not acted wrongly solely for his own benefit. The defendant did not argue that the 1945 Act applied to equitable claims but that the Act constituted "guidance" and that there was general merit in judge-made law acting in parallel with statute.

21-093   This contention was rejected by Blackburne J in deciding not to follow the approach of the New Zealand Court of Appeal in *Day v Mead*[152] or the Supreme Court of Canada in *Canson Enterprises Ltd v Broughton & Co*[153] he reasoned that English law regards breach of a fiduciary duty more stringently than the law in New Zealand and Canada, in that a greater degree of deliberate intention needs to be shown on behalf of the defendant for it to be established[154] (in *Day v Mead* the trial judge found that the defendant solicitor had "acted quite innocently"). That being so, English law had never treated contributory negligence as a defence to a deliberate tort and equity had always been concerned "to keep persons in a fiduciary capacity up to their duty".[155] On that basis Blackburne J said:

---

[150]   *Nationwide Building Society v Balmer Radmore* [1999] P.N.L.R. 606 (ChD); see also *Nationwide Building Society v Goodwin Harte* [1999] Lloyd's Rep. P.N. 338 (ChD); and *Nationwide Building Society v Thimbleby* [1999] Lloyd's Rep. P.N. 359 (ChD). For more recent and more general discussion of the underlying differences between common law and equitable principles of compensation, see Ch.22 and the Supreme Court decision in *AIB Group (UK) Plc v Mark Redler & Co Solicitors* [2014] UKSC 58; [2014] 3 W.L.R. 1367.

[151]   It is clear that no deduction for contributory negligence, or some equitable equivalent, is available for a claim for breach of trust involving a misapplication or misappropriation of trust assets. For example at first instance in *Lloyds TSB Bank Plv v Markandan & Uddin (A Firm)* [2010] EWHC 2517 (Ch); [2011] P.N.L.R. 6, Roger Wyand QC (sitting as a Deputy Judge of the High Court) rejected an argument that the defendant solicitors could rely on contributory negligence in circumstances where they had acted in breach of trust by paying away mortgage monies without receiving either the documents required to register title or an undertaking. He reasoned as follows, at [42]: "It is clear that the Court of Appeal in *Vesta v Butcher* outlined the limited categories where a defence under the Law Reform Act could be relied on in contractual cases. There is nothing in that decision which can be relied upon to extend the principle to cases of breach of trust. Section 61 of the Trustee Act gives limited relief to trustees where the trustees have acted reasonably and honestly. It could have provided for the conduct of the beneficiary to be taken into account as the defendant here wishes. It did not and it is not for the court to extend the law in a way that was not done by the legislature." There was no appeal on this point: [2012] EWCA Civ 65; [2012] 2 All E.R. 884. See also *Davisons Solicitors (A Firm) v Nationwide Building Society* [2012] EWCA Civ 1626; [2013] P.N.L.R. 188, at [58].

[152]   *Day v Mead* [1987] 2 N.Z.L.R. 443 (New Zealand Court of Appeal).

[153]   *Canson Enterprises Ltd v Broughton & Co* (1991) 85 D.L.R. 4th 129 (Supreme Court of Canada).

[154]   As to which see *Bristol & West Building Society v Mothew* [1998] Ch. 1 (CA).

[155]   *Nocton v Lord Ashburton* [1914] A.C. 932 (HL) at 963, per Lord Dunedin.

"I therefore take the view that where, in order to establish a breach of fiduciary duty, it is necessary to find that the fiduciary was consciously disloyal to the person to whom his duty was owed, the fiduciary is disabled from asserting that the other contributed, by his own want of care for his own interests, to the loss which he suffered flowing from the breach. To do otherwise, as Gummow J. pointed out in his article in 'Equity, Fiduciaries and Trusts', risks subverting the fundamental principle of undivided and unremitting loyalty which is at the core of the fiduciary's obligations."

The fact that a defence of contributory fault is not available in a claim for an intentional tort such as deceit does not mean that a defendant cannot run similar points under the rubric of defences of lack of inducement or causation. Thus, as we have already noted, where a claimant in a deceit claim is itself under specific duty owed to the defendant to take care with respect to the fraud giving rise to the claim (such as an auditor owing contractual duties of care in the detection of the fraud), the proper analysis may be that the legally effective cause of the claimant's loss is not the deceit but its own breach of duty.[156] Because, unlike contributory fault, such a defence bars the claim entirely, it is likely to be only on strong or unusual facts that it will be made out (and, of course, not every case of contributory negligence involves the claimant owing a duty of care to the defendant with respect to their wrong).

21–094

---

[156] *Barings Plc v Coopers & Lybrand* [2003] EWHC 1319 (Ch); [2003] P.N.L.R. 34. See also *Murphy v Culhane* [1977] Q.B. 94 (CA) (a case concerning liability for an assault), as explained in *Nationwide Building Society v Thimbleby* [1999] Lloyd's Rep. P.N. 359 (ChD).

CHAPTER 22

EQUITABLE REMEDIES: RESCISSION, ACCOUNT OF PROFITS, COMPENSATION & FORFEITURE

A. INTRODUCTION

(1) The Remedies Considered in this Chapter

In Ch.21 above we considered the principles on which the court proceeds when assessing damages in fraud-based claims (principally in the tort of deceit). However an award of damages is of course not the only remedy which is potentially available in such claims; and there are other causes of action, which we have considered in previous chapters, for which damages of the sort awarded in a deceit claim are not the most appropriate remedial response to the wrongdoing. In Ch.23 below we consider equitable proprietary remedies (that is, remedies which vindicate a claim that property belongs beneficially to the claimant, under the principles considered in Ch.9). In this chapter we consider the principal forms of non-proprietary relief which are likely to be relevant in a fraud claim and which are (at least in part) equitable in origin. These are: **22–001**

(1)   Rescission[1];
(2)   Accounting for profit;
(3)   Equitable compensation; and
(4)   The forfeiture of fees and remuneration.

Before turning to these, we also consider, briefly, the "remedy" of an account, which, as we note in the following sub-section, is not strictly speaking a remedy at all, but a process by which the dealings by a trustee or fiduciary with the funds or property under his control are examined with a view to identifying and quantifying (among other things) the appropriate relief for any breaches of duty. **22–002**

There are three other potentially relevant equitable remedies which deserve mention: (a) injunction, (b) pecific performance; and (c) rectification.[2] The latter two are outside the scope of a work focused on fraud. Injunctions are obvious highly relevant to claims in fraud, but principally in the context of the interim **22–003**

---

[1] It should immediately be emphasised that, as noted below, rescission is in fact a common law remedy as well as an equitable one. We address both, and the important differences between them, in this chapter. Moreover, rescission may give rise to proprietary consequences: see paras 22–060—22–066.

[2] Declarations are sometimes said to be equitable remedies, but they are probably better regarded as being a creature of statute; and they are in any event of limited relevance in the fraud context.

relief available before or at an early stage of proceedings, and later in aid of the enforcement of judgments (as opposed to as the substantive relief sought for the claimed wrong), and so the remedy is considered in those contexts.[3]

(2) Personal vs Proprietary Relief

22–004   The remedies which are the subject of this chapter are personal rather than proprietary, in that they operate against the person of the defendant wrongdoer, irrespective of whether or not he retains property that may have been the subject of the claim. Rescission is in this regard is somewhat different, since, whilst it is not a proprietary remedy as such, it can operate against parties other than the wrongdoer and can often form the basis for the granting of proprietary relief, in circumstances where its consequence is the re-vesting of property or the beneficial interest in it in the claimant.

22–005   Personal remedies depend for their efficacy (in the usual case) upon the defendant having resources with which to meet them. Proprietary remedies, in contrast, operate against the property in question (including the traceable proceeds of it), irrespective of into whose hands it has come,[4] albeit a claim to a proprietary remedy can be resisted if the person holding the property or its proceeds is a bona fide purchaser for value without notice. Whereas personal claims rank alongside those of other unsecured creditors in the event of the defendant's insolvency, proprietary claims afford priority, since they take the relevant property or part of it out of the defendant's insolvent estate.

22–006   As we have said, proprietary claims and the particular forms of relief by which they might be vindicated are considered in Ch.23. The interrelationship of proprietary and personal equitable relief can give rise to confusion, particularly where a defendant is said to be "accountable for profits" or "accountable as a constructive trustee". It bears emphasis that an account of profits is a *personal* remedy, by which the defendant is required to identify and pay over a sum of money representing the value of the profits made by him in breach of some duty owed to the claimant (or as an accessory to a breach of duty). That defendant may well also hold assets representing the profits on trust for the claimant, such that the claimant has a proprietary claim to them; but, whilst that may ultimately achieve the same result, it is conceptually a different thing, and the claimant has a right to elect between the two remedies.[5]

22–007   Similarly, when judges refer to the liability of a dishonest assister in a breach of trust or fiduciary duty (considered in Ch.13) to account "as a constructive trustee" they are generally referring to a purely personal liability.[6] The liability of a knowing recipient of property disposed of in breach of trust or fiduciary duty

---

[3] See Chs 28, 30 and 37.

[4] And irrespective of whether the recipient has been unjustly enriched: *Foskett v McKeown* [2001] 1 A.C. 102, per Lord Millett at 129.

[5] As confirmed in *FHR European Ventures LLP v Cedar Capital Holdings* LLC [2015] A.C. 250, per Lord Neuberger JSC at [7].

[6] *Royal Brunei Airlines Sdn Bdh v Tan* [1995] 2 A.C. 378, per Lord Nicholls at 387; *Ultraframe (UK) Ltd v Fielding* [2005] EWHC 1638 (Ch), per Lewison J at [1517].

(considered in Ch.12), is also personal, albeit if he retains the trust property or its traceable proceeds he may additionally be exposed to a proprietary claim.[7]

(3)   Accounting as a "Remedy"

Another potential source of confusion is the terminology of "accounting" in the context of claims against trustees and other fiduciaries. For present purposes, there are two relevant senses in which the Court might order an account: an account of funds and an account of profits.[8]   **22–008**

(i)   Accounting for funds

The first is an order for an account of funds, which is what is generally meant when the Courts refer to "taking an account". This is not, strictly speaking, a remedy at all, but rather a process by which a trustee or other fiduciary who has custody of property for his principal is required to justify his dealings with that property.[9] The account will identify whether and if so in what amount there is a deficiency (be it because there has been some dealing with the principal's property that should not have happened, or, conversely, because the trustee or fiduciary has failed to get in some property that he should have), in order that relief may then be ordered against the trustee or fiduciary to restore the fund to what it should have been.[10] In this respect, there is an analogy between accounting and tracing[11]: both are techniques for establishing the factual premises on which relief can be granted.   **22–009**

Another reason why an account in this sense is not strictly a remedy is that it does not depend upon there having been a wrong.[12] The right[13] to an account follows from the existence of the relevant relationship and its availability is not dependent on the establishment of a breach of duty: trustees and fiduciaries who hold assets in a custodial capacity (such as executors, agents controlling their principal's property and receivers) are accounting parties.[14] An order for an   **22–010**

---

[7] *Ultraframe (UK) Ltd v Fielding*, above, per Lewison J at [1486].

[8] See J. McGhee, *Snell's Equity*, 33rd edn (London: Sweet & Maxwell, 2014), para.20–005. For an example of the value of an account in a fraud claim, see *Murad v Al-Saraj* [2004] EWHC 1235 (Ch), considered further at para.22–020 below.

[9] *Ultraframe (UK) Ltd v Fielding & Ors*, above, per Lewison J at [1513].

[10] *Libertarian Investments Ltd v Hall* [2014] 1 H.K.C. 368 (CFA), per Lord Millett NPJ at [168].

[11] As noted by Lewison J in *Ultraframe (UK) Ltd v Fielding*, above, at [1514]: "it is essentially a preliminary to the making of further orders".

[12] *Libertarian Investments v Hall*, above, per Lord Millett NPJ at [167].

[13] Although the obligation to account is part of the irreducible minimum of a trustee's duties (and so in that sense the beneficiary has a right to an account), the Court retains a discretion not to order an account, albeit the circumstances in which it will not will be limited: *Henchley v Thompson* [2017] EWHC 225 (Ch).

[14] *Attorney General v Cocke* [1988] Ch. 414, per Harman J at 420. It is important to keep it in mind that the obligation to account is not peculiarly fiduciary, however: an agent or manager who is not in any sense a trustee for his principal and who is entitled to mix funds received for his principal's account with his own may well nevertheless owe a contractual duty to account (albeit if the agent is not holding funds for the principal the nature of the account may be much more limited). Identifying the source of the obligation to account will be important for limitation purposes. See the

account will also lie against a bare trustee (even though he may not owe fiduciary obligations of undivided loyalty at all)[15] and a knowing recipient of trust property[16]; but strictly speaking it will not lie against a company director by dint of his position as such, unless he receives company property personally.[17]

22–011 The technicalities of taking an account are outside the scope of this work[18]; but some understanding of the process and the concepts involved is important, because they underpin much of the law on the personal monetary relief available against a defaulting trustee or fiduciary.

22–012 In very broad summary there are two forms of account of funds: a common account and an account on the footing of wilful default.

22–013 A *common account* is concerned with the property which the trustee or other fiduciary has actually received in his accounting capacity and what has become of it. The accounting party is "charged" with any property received in that capacity (including its fruits and substitutes, such as where a fund is invested in an asset); and against that is set (in "discharge" of the accounting party's responsibility for what he has received) any payments made to the beneficiary or principal, any administrative outlays and other "just allowances",[19] and anything lost without fault of the accounting party. Where the accounting party has engaged in an unauthorised transaction, such as a misapplication of trust property for his own benefit, the beneficiary can "falsify" that dealing, such that the discharge is removed from the account and the accounting party remains charged with the value of the property misapplied, as if it had remained in the fund. For these purposes the property is valued objectively, as at the date of the taking of the account and so with the full benefit of hindsight.[20] But if the unauthorised transaction has resulted in receipt of a substitute asset that has increased in value, the beneficiary may instead elect to ratify it, so that the transaction is allowed, but the asset received under it becomes a charge on the account in his favour.

22–014 When an account is taken on the footing of *wilful default* the accounting party is charged not just with what he has actually received, but also with what he should have received but for his default (that is, "surcharged"). "Wilful default" in this context means not doing what the accounting party was under a duty to do, or doing what he was under a duty not to do.[21] The "willful" connotes that the act or omission was not unintentional[22]; but it does not necessarily have to have

---

reconsideration of *Nelson v Rye* [1996] 1 W.L.R. 1378 in *Paragon v DB Thakerar* [1999] 1 All E.R. 400 and *Coulthard v Disco Mix Club Ltd* [2000] 1 W.L.R. 707.

[15] *Cheong Soh Chin v Eng Chiet Shoong* [2015] SGHC 173, at [38].

[16] *Arthur v AG of Turks & Caicos Islands* [2012] UKPC 30, at [37].

[17] *GHLM Trading Ltd v Maroo* [2012] EWHC 61 (Ch), per Newey J at [148]. Note that a director, whether he receives company property or not, has a responsibility under ss.386–389 of the Companies Act 2006 to ensure that the company keeps proper accounting records.

[18] For the procedure, see CPR Practice Direction 40A; and for a commentary on it and precedents, see *Atkin's Court Forms, Accounts Vol. 1*.

[19] As to which, see further paras 22–098—22–101 below.

[20] *Libertarian Investments Ltd v Hall*, above, per Lord Millett NPJ at [168].

[21] *Re Owens* (1882) 47 L.T. 61 (CA).

[22] *Re Young and Harston's Contract* (1885) 31 Ch. D. 168 (CA), per Bowen LJ at 174–175.

involved conscious wrongdoing and can, for example, include negligence.[23] Once sufficient wilful default is proved to raise a prima facie inference that there are other instances as yet undiscovered, the Court can (in its discretion) award the claimant a "roving inquiry as to what, but for his fraud or negligence, the defendant should have received"[24]; but the Court can decline to do so where it would be oppressive and more commonly the relief will be confined to the particular instances of default proven.[25]

An accounting party can resist having to account where there is a settled account **22–015** (that is an account which has been agreed, expressly or implicitly, as being correct), unless there are grounds for re-opening it entirely (because of fraud or misrepresentation, or a significant number of errors) or objecting to particular items on the grounds of error, the burden in either case being on the party challenging the settled account.

Once an account is taken (on either of the above bases), orders can be made to **22–016** give the beneficiary redress with respect to any deficiency identified between the amount which has been found to be chargeable to the defendant and the amount of the allowed discharges. This may involve the accounting party being required to make good the deficit by returning property in specie to the fund under his control or the grant of a proprietary remedy over an asset improperly acquired in a transaction which the beneficiary has elected not to falsify. In default of specific restitution, the accounting party will be required to pay the balance shown as being due from his own pocket. This is often described as "equitable compensation"; but as can be seen from the above summary, where the trustee is required to make good a deficit in the fund arising from a transaction that has been disallowed the remedy is more restorative than compensatory, and the language of compensation is perhaps more apt where the monetary remedy is providing redress for the trustee's default in receiving something that he should have received had he acted in accordance with his duties.[26]

Equitable compensation generally, and the particular question of whether these **22–017** distinctions remain meaningful in light of the important Supreme Court decision in *AIB Group (UK) Plc v Mark Redler & Co Solicitors*,[27] is considered in section D below. What is important to note at this stage is that, because the payment of compensation is relief consequent upon the taking of an account, there is no inconsistency between seeking an order for an account and seeking an order for compensation, nor need a claimant elect between the two: one is simply a precursor to the other.[28]

That said, it should also be noted that it is equally not *necessary* for there to be an **22–018** account for there to be an order for equitable compensation: in an appropriate case, a claimant can simply invite the Court to assess the amount of compensation

---

[23] *Coulthard v Disco Mix Club Ltd* [2000] 1 W.L.R. 707, per Jules Sher QC at 733–734.
[24] Ibid.
[25] *Re Stevens* [1897] 1 Ch. 422, at 433.
[26] A point made by Lord Millett NPJ in *Libertarian Investments v Hall*, above, at [168] and [171].
[27] *AIB Group (UK) Plc v Mark Redler & Co Solicitors* [2015] A.C. 1503.
[28] *Libertarian Investments v Hall*, above, at [97]–[99] (Ribeiro PJ) and [166]–[172] (Lord Millett NPJ).

due from the trustee or fiduciary without the formal process of taking an account; and the Court always retains a discretion to decline to order an account, where it would serve no useful purpose to do so. As a matter of practical reality this will often be true where a compensatory or restorative remedy is sought in a fraud case: the default is usually capable of clear identification and a specific remedy can be obtained.

22–019   Finally, the obligation which rests on a trustee or other custodial fiduciary to account for his dealings with property under his control has a litigation significance beyond the formal relief of the taking of an account: it means that, in effect, the burden rests on him to establish the justification for his dealings with his principal's or beneficiary's assets, rather than it being for the person to whom the fiduciary obligations are owed to prove that the dealings were improper.[29] This effective reversal of the burden of proof has been applied to directors (even though, as noted above, they are not generally accounting parties), where it is established that they have received company property or where they have a loan account with the company which has been correctly debited, the burden being on them to justify any credit entries in their favour.[30]

(ii)   Account of profits

22–020   Accounting in the sense considered above should not be confused with the remedy of an account of profits. As has been said, this is generally understood to mean a personal order for the identification and payment of money representing profits which have been made in breach of fiduciary duty or in violation of certain other rights. In the context of a fraud claim, the remedy of an account in this sense is a powerful part of the court's remedial machinery, where the gist of the relief sought is the disgorgement of profits dishonestly made and it is difficult to fashion a remedy in damages that achieves that (for example, because it depends on proving the loss of profits that would have been made in some speculative counterfactual world). So in *Murad v Al-Saraj*[31] Etherton J said that the remedy of account was:

> "a particularly appropriate remedy in the case of deliberate and dishonest conduct designed to achieve a commercial advantage for the fiduciary over those to whom he owes his fiduciary duty."

22–021   An account of profits has some similarities to an account of funds, in that the relief involves the defendant identifying what profit has been made (and an account of profits can of course form part of an account of funds, where a custodial fiduciary is charged with profit made from the property under his control); but it differs in that: (a) it does not depend upon the defendant having funds under his control in a fiduciary capacity; (b) its focus is only upon profit which the defendant has made by reason of the breach in question; and (c) it is

---

[29] *Ross River Ltd v Waverly Commercial Ltd* [2013] EWCA Civ 910 (CA), at [94].
[30] *GHLM Trading Ltd v Maroo*, above, per Newey J at [149]. See also *Re Snelling House Ltd (In Liq.)* [2012] EWHC 440 (Ch), at [40], suggesting that the evidential burden is on the directors to justify payments out of the company's assets even when they are not the recipients.
[31] *Murad v Al-Saraj* [2004] EWHC 1235 (Ch), at [340].

often understood to include not just the identification, but also the payment over, of the profit (although, strictly speaking, the order for payment is probably consequential upon the account; confusingly, that aspect of the relief is also sometimes referred to as "equitable compensation").[32]

The remedy of an account of profits is considered further in section C below. **22–022**

(4) "Clean Hands"

It is a well-known maxim of equity that "he who comes into equity must come   **22–023**
with clean hands". A claimant who seeks an equitable remedy from the Court can
thus be denied it on the basis of his own misconduct or impropriety.

However, the maxim is of limited scope. It is reserved for: **22–024**

> "exceptional cases where those seeking to invoke it have put themselves beyond the pale by reason of serious immoral and deliberate misconduct such that the overall result of equitable intervention would not be an exercise but a denial of equity".[33]

To be engaged, the misconduct or impropriety in question must have "an immediate and necessary relation to the equity sued for".[34]

This is generally understood to mean that, to be denied relief on this basis, the   **22–025**
claimant must, by claiming the relief, be seeking to "derive advantage from his
dishonest conduct in so direct a manner that it is considered to be unjust to grant
him relief"[35]—in other words, there must be a close connection between the
remedy sought and the misconduct in question. Examples include misleading the
Court in the course of litigation directed at securing the relief.[36]

The application of the maxim is of course discretionary; and Courts have recently   **22–026**
declined to apply it where the claimant's misconduct was minor compared to the
seriousness of the defendant's alleged wrongdoing[37] and where the party
invoking the maxim was itself guilty of misconduct.[38] It is noted that the
disproportionality of preventing Miss Milligan from enforcing her equitable
interest in the property and the resulting unjust enrichment of Miss Tinsley were

---

[32] As for example in *FHR European ventures LLP v Mankarious* [2015] A.C. 250, per Lord Neuberger JSC at [6].

[33] *CF Partners (UK) LLP v Barclays Bank Plc* [2014] EWHC 3049 (Ch), per Hildyard J at [1133].

[34] *Dering v Earl of Winchelsea* (1787) 1 Cox Eq Cas 318, per Lord Chief Baron Eyre at 319; *Grobbelaar v News Group Newspapers* [2002] UKHL 40; [2002] 1 W.L.R. 3024, at 3075; *Royal Bank of Scotland Plc v Highland Financial Partners LP* [2013] EWCA Civ 328, at [159]; *Day v Tiuta International* [2014] EWCA Civ 1246, at [65]–[67].

[35] *Royal Bank of Scotland Plc v Highland Financial Partners LP* [2013] EWCA Civ 328, per Aikens LJ at [159] quoting from I.C.F. Spry, *The Principles of Equitable Remedies*, 8th Edn (Lawbook Company, 2010).

[36] *Fiona Trust & Holding Corp v Privalov* [2008] EWHC 1748 (Comm).

[37] *CF Partners (UK) LLP v Barclays Bank Plc* [2014] EWHC 3049 (Ch), per Hilyward J at [1133].

[38] *UBS AG (London Branch) v Kommunale Wasserweke Leipzig GmbH* [2014] EWHC 3615 (Comm), per Males J at [701]; upheld on appeal at [2017] EWCA Civ 1567, at [170]–[177].

suggested by Lord Toulson to be proper reasons for not denying the claim in *Tinsley v Milligan*,[39] despite the rejection of the underlying reasoning in that case in *Patel v Mirza*.[40]

22–027 Accordingly, the "clean hands" maxim does not operate as a blanket bar to one party to a fraud seeking contribution from another party to the fraud. Instead, the scheme of the Civil Liability (Contribution) Act 1978 contemplates that the Court should adjudicate upon a just and equitable distribution of the burden of liability between wrongdoers, even if the wrongdoing is intentional.[41] Nor does the maxim necessarily prevent one alleged fraudster from obtaining a freezing order against another to preserve assets pending determination of such a contribution claim.[42]

(5) Limitation, Laches and Acquiescence

22–028 The application of the defences of (a) limitation under the Limitation Act 1980, (b) laches and (c) acquiescence to claims for equitable remedies is considered in Ch.26.

B. RESCISSION

(1) Introduction: Rescission and Other Concepts Distinguished

22–029 Rescission, in the sense with which this chapter is concerned, is a remedy available both at common law and in equity, by which a contract or other transaction is set aside, retrospectively, on grounds which vitiate the intention of the contracting party or disponor to enter into it. Once rescinded, the contract or transaction is treated as never having come into existence. As will be apparent even from that brief description, rescission is a vitally important remedy potentially available to the victim of fraudulent conduct, in that it achieves the undoing of the effects of the wrongdoing in a far more direct and complete way than (say) a remedy in damages would.

---

[39] *Tinsley v Milligan* [1994] 1 A.C. 340.
[40] *Patel v Mirza* [2016] UKSC 42; [2016] 3 W.L.R. 366, at [112]. On this important decision, and the common law defence of illegality more generally, see Ch.24.
[41] *Dubai Aluminium Co Ltd v Salaam* [2003] 2 A.C. 366, at [60], per Lord Nicholls: "The Contribution Act casts upon the court the task of adjudicating upon a just and equitable distribution of the burden of liability between all manner of wrongdoers. In the present case equality of burden among thieves can hardly be thought an exceptional approach." In *Kazakhstan Kagazy Plc v Zhunus* [2016] EWCA Civ 1036; [2017] 1 W.L.R. 1360 a defendant against whom a claim in fraudulent misappropriation of assets was asserted sought to issue a contribution claim against a co-defendant. The fact that the defendant denied the fraud (and hence that his primary case was that the co-defendant was likewise innocent) did not prevent permission being granted for the bringing of contribution proceedings. It is of course common for contribution proceedings to be founded on an alternative case to the defendant's primary defence. Nor did it matter that the co-defendant had settled the claimant's proceedings which had been brought directly against him. The general law of contribution, which is complex, is outside the scope of this work.
[42] *Kazakhstan Kagazy Plc v Zhunus*, above.

The nature of the remedy can perhaps best be understood by comparing and **22–030** contrasting it with other circumstances in which rights (or apparent rights) under contracts and transactions can be extinguished[43]:

(1) A transaction or contract which is susceptible to rescission is voidable rather than void. Rescission depends upon the election of the party entitled to rescind and, until avoided, the transaction will be effective to create rights and obligations and pass title to property. For that reason, it will generally need to be possible to restore both parties to the position in which they were before it was entered for rescission to be available[44]; but, once rescinded, all rights and obligations under the transaction are extinguished, with retrospective effect, as if the transaction had never occurred.[45] Conversely, the party entitled to rescind may elect to keep the contract in being, notwithstanding his right to rescind, and so confine himself to a claim in damages or otherwise to enforce the contract.

(2) In contradistinction, no rights or obligations can be created in the first place by a contract or transaction which is void ab initio.[46] Its lack of legal effect does not depend upon the election of the innocent party or upon any action of the Court, albeit that the conclusion that the transaction is void may be disputed and only declared by an order of the Court. A contract or transaction may be void in this sense because (for example) of mutual mistake[47] or the parties being at cross-purposes, on the basis of non est factum, or because it was beyond the powers of one of the parties.[48]

(3) A contract or transaction can also be void (or, to avoid confusion with the preceding case, "ineffective") where it was entered into by an agent without actual or apparent authority,[49] or by a trustee, director or other fiduciary with a power to dispose of their principal's property but without due authorisation.[50] Such a transaction is similarly ineffective to create rights or

---

[43] For a fuller survey of this topic, see D. O'Sullivan, S. Elliott and R. Zakrzewski, *The Law of Rescission*, 2nd Edn (Oxford: OUP, 2014), Ch.1.

[44] See paras 22–054—22–059 below.

[45] Contractual rights and obligations which are treated as arising under a separate and severable agreement will survive rescission: the classic example is an arbitration clause, as now reflected in s.7 of the Arbitration Act 1996.

[46] But it does not necessarily follow that title to property transferred under the transaction will not pass: for example, title to money paid pursuant to a void contract will generally pass (e.g. *Westdeutsche Landesbank Girozentrale v Islington LBC* [1996] A.C. 669, per Lord Goff at 689–690), so too will title to registered land transferred pursuant to a void contract (because the registration in the name of the transferee is conclusive as to title: s.58(1) of the Land Registration Act 2002); but title to chattels which passes on delivery may not pass, if the intention to transfer is vitiated.

[47] *Great Peace Shipping Ltd v Tsavliris Salvage (International) Ltd* [2002] EWCA Civ 1407; [2003] Q.B. 679.

[48] Although this will be of little relevance in the company context now, given s.39 of the Companies Act 2006.

[49] *Criterion Properties Plc v Stratford UK Properties LLC* [2004] 1 W.L.R. 1846 (HL).

[50] See for example: *Independent Trustee Services Ltd v GP Noble Trustees* [2012] EWCA Civ 195; [2013] Ch. 91 (CA) (trustee); *Guiness Plc v Saunders* [1990] 2 A.C. 663 and *Clark v Cutland* [2003] EWCA Civ 810; [2004] 1 W.L.R. 783 (CA) (unauthorised payments to company directors). As noted below (para.22–032), transactions entered into by fiduciaries such as directors in misuse of their powers or in breach of their duties of loyalty would also seem to be void/ineffective, rather than merely voidable.

obligations; and in the case of a transfer of trust or company property will not defeat the beneficial interest that the beneficiary or company previously had.[51] But it differs from the preceding case because the principal or beneficiary can ratify it, which will result in the transaction taking effect as if it had been authorised all along. Ineffective transactions are in a sense the converse of voidable ones: in both the principal or beneficiary has a right to elect as to whether the transaction should stand, but a voidable transaction takes effect unless an election is made to avoid it (which is the rescission with which this chapter is concerned), whereas ineffective transaction does not take effect unless an election is made to ratify it.

(4) In further contradistinction, a contact which is terminated for repudiatory breach or renunciation (by the acceptance of the innocent party) is not voidable or void in any of the above senses. Although some cases have used the language of "rescinding" the contract in these circumstances,[52] that is apt to confuse, as the legal process involved is entirely different from rescission in its proper sense: the parties to the contract are discharged from the performance of their primary obligations which have yet to accrue; but rights which have already accrued (and secondary obligations, such as to pay damages) remain enforceable. In general, "rescission" (improperly so-called) in this sense is concerned with defects in the performance of the contract, rather than in its formation: i.e. it (usually) relates to events occurring after the contract has been formed. When a contract is terminated in this sense the contract itself is not impeached; it is simply brought to an end as regards future performance. Termination for breach is not part of the law of fraud.

22–031　It bears emphasis that the same or similar fact patterns could generate quite different outcomes in the above terms. Thus it has been said that an agent who enters into a contract on behalf of his principal, but does so with conscious disloyalty (for example, having been suborned by a bribe), exceeds his authority to bind his principal.[53] If the counterparty with whom the agent entered into a transaction purportedly on behalf of his principal was aware or on notice of the circumstances vitiating the agent's authority, such that he could not rely on the agent's apparent authority, it would follow (from the principles summarised above) that the contract would be void or ineffective, subject only to the principal subsequently ratifying it. But it might also be said that the agent has (to the knowledge of the other party) acted in breach of his fiduciary duties not to place

---

[51] *Heinl v Jyske Bank (Gibraltar) Ltd* [1999] Lloyd's Rep. Bank 511 (CA), at 521; *Clark v Cutland*, above. A recipient of property under the transfer will therefore hold the property as constructive trustee, unless he gives value and lacks notice. On constructive trusts arising out of void or ineffective transactions, see further paras 9–056—9–067.

[52] For example, *Johnson v Agnew* [1980] A.C. 367, at 383A; *Hurst v Bryk* [2002] 1 A.C. 185, at 193–194, per Lord Millett.

[53] See P.G. Watts (ed), *Bowstead and Reynolds on Agency*, 21st edn (London: Sweet & Maxwell, 2018), art.23 and the comment on it (paras 3–010—3–011.

himself in a situation of conflict or profit from his position. That would generally be understood to give the principal a right to rescind (that is, the contract would be voidable rather than void).[54]

Moreover, different consequences would appear to flow depending on what sort of "fiduciary" duty is in play: whereas infringement of the core fiduciary proscriptions against conflicts and profits will generally render a transaction merely voidable,[55] certain breaches may be treated as involving an exceeding of authority, which, if the transaction is made by the fiduciary, would render it void/ineffective in equity (subject to the other party being able to rely on apparent authority). Examples are breaches of the best interests duty[56] and of the duty to exercise a power for a proper purpose,[57] and (possibly) self-dealing.[58] The remedy of rescission is thus (it is at least arguable) not relevant in these cases. The question of whether breaches of fiduciary (and like) duties render transactions void or voidable is a vexed one, however, and a claimant would usually be well advised to plead his case and proceed on the basis that either outcome is arguable.

22–032

(2) Law and Equity

Rescission is a remedy which exists both at common law and in equity. The principal distinction between them is that rescission at common law is a self-help remedy which takes effect upon the communication of the election of the party entitled; rescission in equity is, on the prevailing view (and subject to possible exceptions noted below), a form of relief granted by the court.[59]

22–033

As will be seen in the following section, whether rescission is available at law or in equity will depend on the ground for invoking it. In practical terms, in most cases a claimant will plead that a contract or transaction has been rescinded at law (in which case, the relief he will seek from the court will only be a declaration to

22–034

---

[54] *Panama and South Pacific Telegraph Co v India Rubber, Gutta Percha, and Telegraph Works Co* (1875) L.R. 10 Ch.App. 515; *Logicrose Ltd v Southend United Football Club* [1988] 1 W.L.R. 1256.
[55] See e.g. *Johnson v EBS Pensioner Trustees Ltd* [2002] Lloyd's Rep. PN 309 (CA); and the secret commission cases referred to in the preceding footnote. In *Abacus Trust Co (Isle of Man) v Barr* [2003] Ch. 409, at 421, Lightman J said that the "ordinary principles of equity" were that a decision challenged on the ground of breach of fiduciary duty was voidable and not void.
[56] *Re Capitol Films Ltd* [2010] EWHC 2240 (Ch); *GHLM Trading Ltd v Maroo* [2012] EWHC 61 (Ch), per Newey J at [170]–[171]. See further paras 11–158—11–159.
[57] *Rolled Steel Ltd v British Steel Corp.* [1986] Ch. 246, per Slade LJ at 295F and 297E-F.
[58] This would explain the view that a trust arose immediately, without the need for rescission, in *JJ Harrison (Properties) Ltd v Harrison* [2002] 1 B.C.L.C. 162 (CA) (director purchasing land from company without full disclosure). Self-dealing was said to be an exception to the principle that breaches of fiduciary duty generally render a transaction voidable in *Abacus Trust Co (Isle of Man) v Barr* [2003] Ch. 409, per Lightman J at 421; and the view that it renders a transaction void is endorsed in O'Sullivan, Elliott and Zakrzewski, *The Law of Rescission* (2014), paras 1.72–1.76. But for authorities that suggest a self-dealing transaction is merely voidable, see e.g. *Re Sherman* [1954] Ch. 653; *Holder v Holder* [1968] Ch. 353, at 398, and *Tito v Waddell (No.2)* [1977] Ch. 106, at 241A.
[59] See further paras 22–038—22–041 below.

that effect, together with other consequential relief to achieve restoration of the pre-transaction position) and will seek rescission by the court in equity in the alternative.

22–035 The remedies are nevertheless distinct, not just in terms of the grounds for invoking them, but also as to:

(1) *The time at which rescission takes effect*: at law rescission occurs at the date the innocent party's election is communicated, and so (for example) the contract will from that point be extinguished; in equity, on the prevailing view, rescission only takes effect upon the Court's order. This can be particularly significant where property rights arising in consequence of the rescission are concerned;

(2) *The barring of the remedy*: as further explained below
   (a) the common law does not permit rescission in certain circumstances where equity does (being essentially situations in which common law rules do not allow for restitution or counter-restitution of benefits conferred under the transaction); and
   (b) rescission in equity can (apparently) be refused on certain discretionary grounds not known to the common law;

(3) *The consequences of the rescission*: very broadly, at common law the rescinding party has, immediately upon rescinding, a purely personal claim to recover money he has paid and legal title to any property he has transferred re-vests automatically (subject to certain important exceptions); in equity, both personal and (at least in the case of fraud) equitable proprietary claims to money paid will lie, but legal title to property will not re-vest automatically, albeit (at least in the case of fraud) an equitable proprietary claim will lie.

(3) Grounds

22–036 Rescission will in principle be available as a remedy for:

(1) Fraudulent misrepresentation (at common law and in equity)[60];
(2) Non-fraudulent misrepresentation (in equity only)[61];
(3) Non-disclosure (at common law), in the case of contracts of insurance[62] or suretyship[63];

---

[60] See Ch.1. As noted there (see para.1–119), the test of inducement for rescission for fraud is more relaxed than that applicable to a damages claim for misrepresentation—albeit where the misrepresentation is fraudulent and the damages claim is therefore in the tort of deceit, the position is less clear. For a more recent case of recission for fraudulent misrepresentation where the Court applied a lower threshold test of inducement (whether but for the deceit the innocent party 'might' not have entered into the contract), see *BV Nederlandse Industrie Van Eiprodukten v Rembrandt Enterprises Inc* [2018] EWHC 1857 (Comm).

[61] *Redgrave v Hurd* (1881) 20 Ch. D. 1 (CA).

[62] For example, *Drake Insurance Plc v Provident Insurance Plc* [2004] Q.B. 601 (CA).

[63] *North Shore Ventures Ltd v Anstead Holdings Inc* [2012] Ch. 31 (CA), at [7]–[31], where it was held that the duty of disclosure owed by the creditor to the guarantor is more limited than that in the case of insurance contracts.

(4)   In the case of gratuitous dispositions (but not contracts), unilateral mistake that is sufficiently grave that it would be unconscionable to hold the mistaken party to the transaction (in equity only)[64];

(5)   Breach of the proscriptive fiduciary rules concerned with conflicts and profits (in equity only)[65];

(6)   Bribery (at common law and in equity)[66];

(7)   Undue influence and unconscionable bargains (in equity only), and duress (at common law and in equity).[67]

(8)   Mental incapacity (at common law and in equity).[68]

It will be seen that rescission is available in a number of fraud-based claims. The policy of the law is not hard to discern: where a transaction has been procured by fraud, whether in the narrow sense of deception, or in the wider sense of dishonest or unconscionable conduct or the abuse of a position of trust, the innocent party should have the option of deciding again whether to be bound by it.   **22–037**

(4)   Exercise of the Right to Rescind

Because a transaction remains valid and effective until rescinded, the wronged party's election to rescind must be communicated to the counterparty plainly and openly,[69] unless the counterparty deliberately puts it out of the wronged party's power to communicate with him.[70] The communication can be by conduct, where it involves the unequivocal assertion of rights which are inconsistent with the contract or transaction continuing (such as demanding repayment of money paid under the contract or retaking possession of goods transferred under it).[71] The service of proceedings can amount to effective communication for these purposes,[72] even if the rescission of the transaction is only implicit in the claim made.[73]   **22–038**

---

[64] *Pitt v Holt* [2013] 2 A.C. 108; *Kennedy v Kennedy* [2014] EWHC 4129, per Terence Etherton C, at [36].

[65] See Ch.11. As noted above, self-dealing may actually involve an exceeding of authority and so render the transaction ineffective without the need for rescission.

[66] See Ch.7. For the proposition that rescission is available at common law for bribery, and that the equitable remedy does not displace the common law one, see *Conway v Eze* [2018] EWHC 29 (Ch), at [145]–[156].

[67] See Ch.15.

[68] It will be seen that a number of grounds are recognised both at common law and in equity. The significance of this is that the court can intervene and make an order for rescission in equity where the common law right that might otherwise exist is unavailable, for example because restitution or counter-restitution cannot be made without a court order.

[69] *Reese River Silver Mining Co v Smith* (1869) L.R. 4 HL 64, at 74, per Lord Hatherley LC; *Car & Universal Finance Co Ltd v Caldwell* [1965] 1 Q.B. 525, at 554, per Upjohn LJ.

[70] *Car & Universal Finance*, above, at 555, per Upjohn LJ.

[71] E.g. *Re Eastgate* [1905] 1 K.B. 465.

[72] *Clough v London and North Western Railway* (1871) L.R. 7 Ex. 26. This decision supports the proposition that one can also communicate an election to rescind by pleading it in a defence.

[73] *Shalson v Russo* [2003] EWHC 1637 (Ch); [2005] Ch. 281, at [120], per Rimer J, citing *Banque Belge pour l'Etranger v Hambrouck* [1921] 1 K.B. 321, at 332, per Atkin LJ.

22–039   When determining whether there has been a sufficiently clear communication of the innocent party's election to rescind, the Court is concerned with an objective assessment of what passed between the parties (much as it is when determining whether a contract has been formed), and it is entitled to take into account the whole series of communications and surrounding conduct, which may render equivocal a communication which, if taken in isolation, would appear clear.[74]

22–040   As we have already noted, in the case of common law (as opposed to equitable) rescission, the communication of the innocent party's election is effective to bring about rescission without the need for any Court order.[75] This is subject to the point, noted in para.22–055 below, that unilateral rescission will not be possible in cases where the common law does not allow for the automatic re-vesting in title to any property that has been transferred or a restitutionary claim to it, or does not allow for the return in kind of an intangible benefit received. Where rescission at common law is possible, the role of the Court is thus limited to confirming (by declaration) that rescission has been effected and making any necessary orders consequential upon it (by judgment on any claims or cross-claims for restitution).

22–041   In equity the position is less clear on the authorities; but the better view is probably that an order of the Court is required to effect rescission, save (possibly) in cases of fraud.[76] Rescission in equity therefore does not take effect, generally, until the Court has ordered it. The Court has a discretion as to whether to order rescission, although that discretion is to be exercised in accordance with settled principles, which generally entitle the claimant to rescission provided that the "bars" to it (considered below) are not made out.[77]

(5)   Rescission Where Wrongdoing is not by a Party to the Transaction

22–042   Where a contract is entered into not with the wrongdoer himself, but with another party, rescission as against the counterparty by reason of a wrong done by that third party will generally not be available unless either:

(1)   the wrongdoer was acting as the counterparty's agent, within the scope of his actual or apparent authority[78]; or

---

[74] *Drake Insurance Plc v Provident Insurance Plc* [2004] Q.B. 601 (CA), at [100]–[103].

[75] *Abram Steamship Co Ltd (In Liquidation) v Westville Shipping Co Ltd (In Liquidation)* [1923] A.C. 773, at 781, per Lord Atkinson. In certain cases the rescinding party may also need to tender back what he has received under the transaction for rescission at law to be effective: see O'Sullivan, Elliott and Zakrzewski, *The Law of Rescission*, (2014), paras 11.46 and 14.52–14.6.

[76] See the consideration of this issue in O'Sullivan, Elliott and Zakrzewski, *The Law of Rescission* (2014), paras 11.56–11.108.

[77] *Lagunas Nitrate Co v Lagunas Syndicate* [1899] 2 Ch. 392 (CA), at 456; McGhee, *Snell's Equity* (2014), para.15–012; O'Sullivan, Elliott and Zakrzewski, *The Law of Rescission* (2014), paras 12.22–12.24.

[78] *Armagas Ltd v Mundogas SA (The Ocean Frost)* [1985] 1 Lloyd's Rep. 1, at 18–19 (where the wrongdoing was a fraudulent misrepresentation).

(2) the counterparty had knowledge of the wrongdoing such that his conscience is affected by it.[79]

There would appear to be no such limitations where what is sought to be rescinded is a gratuitous transaction (such as a gift): although the donee may not be implicated in or aware of the wrongdoing, the fact that he gave no consideration for the transaction means that it remains susceptible to rescission.[80]   **22–043**

There are also special rules applicable to suretyship transactions between a surety and creditor who are not in a commercial relationship: where the consent of the surety is vitiated by wrongdoing (usually undue influence or deceit) on the part of the debtor, the creditor will be fixed with notice of that, such that the transaction can be set aside, unless it has taken certain steps to reduce the risk that there has been any wrongdoing.[81] In that type of case, the conscience of the counterparty is affected by a form of constructive notice, which it must take steps to displace.   **22–044**

Otherwise, unless the wrongdoing of the third party falls to be attributed to the counterparty on agency principles, the counterparty must generally have actual, and not merely constructive, knowledge of it.[82]   **22–045**

Where the relevant wrongdoing consists in the deprivation of a fiduciary's disinterested advice by the payment or promise of a bribe or secret commission, the requirement of actual knowledge on the part of the counterparty is attenuated by presumptions that favour the principal. If the counterparty is the one paying or promising the bribe or commission, it suffices that he does so knowing that the recipient is the other party's agent, and that he (the counterparty) does not disclose the payment to the other principal.[83] Knowledge that the fiduciary has in fact wronged his principal (by not disclosing that he has a potentially conflicting personal interest) is not required: where the counterparty is aware that the fiduciary is deriving a personal benefit and does not himself disclose it to the principal, the knowledge of the fiduciary's non-disclosure is effectively inferred; and, conversely, where the counterparty is aware that the fiduciary is dealing behind his principal's back, knowledge that the fiduciary has a potentially conflicting personal interest is inferred.[84] Both situations involve surreptitious   **22–046**

---

[79] *Logicrose Ltd v Southend United F.C.* [1988] 1 W.L.R. 1256, per Millett J at 1261FG; *UBS AG (London Branch) v Kommunale Wasserweke Leipzig GmbH* [2017] EWCA Civ 1567, at [110].

[80] See for example *Bullock v Lloyds Bank Ltd* [1955] Ch. 317 (a case of undue influence upon a settlor, of which the trustee bank was unaware); and *Pitt v Holt* [2013] 2 A.C. 108 (which confirms the equitable jurisdiction to set aside gratuitous dispositions for unilateral mistake unknown to the other party). The law is thus more generous in granting rescission of gratuitous dispositions in at least two respects: first, as identified here, there is no requirement for the other party to the disposition to have knowledge of the vitiating circumstances; secondly, as identified above, a unilateral mistake of sufficient gravity can constitute a vitiating circumstance (when it could not for a contract).

[81] *Royal Bank of Scotland Plc v Etridge* (No.2) [2001] UKHL 44; [2002] 2 A.C. 773, at [37]–[43]. See further Ch.15.

[82] *Logicrose Ltd v Southend United F.C.* [1988] 1 W.L.R. 1256, per Millett J at 1261FG.

[83] *Panama & South Pacific Telegraph Co v India Rubber, etc., Co* (1875) L.R. 10 Ch. App. 515; *Armagas Ltd v Mundogas S.A. (The Ocean Frost)* [1986] A.C. 717, per Robert Goff LJ at 742H–743A (not commented upon on appeal to the House of Lords); *Logicrose Ltd v Southend United F.C.* [1988] 1 W.L.R. 1256, per Millett J at 1261FG.

[84] *Logicrose Ltd v Southend United F.C.*, above, at 1262A-C.

dealing between the counterparty and the fiduciary, which puts the counterparty at risk that the fiduciary is acting in such a way as to give the principal a right to rescind.

22–047 In *UBS AG (London Branch) v Kommunale Wasserweke Leipzig GmbH* the Court of Appeal (by majority) extrapolated from this analysis to derive a broader principle, applicable in cases where the party against whom rescission is sought is neither the payer of the bribe, nor actually aware of it or responsible for it under agency principles:

> "Where a party to an intended transaction deals with the other party's agent secretly and behind his back, and dishonestly assists that agent to abuse his fiduciary duties to the other party so as to bring that transaction about, then the first party's conscience may be affected not merely by the particular form of abuse by the agent of which it actually knew, but also by any other abuse which the agent chose to employ to bring about the transaction with the first party."[85]

22–048 In that case one party to a swap agreement (UBS) had entered into an arrangement with the fiduciary agent (VP) of the other party (KWL), whereby VP would advise its clients to enter into swap transactions regardless of their clients' best interests. This arrangement was held to be dishonest and corrupt. In fact, VP procured that KWL entered into the swap in question by payment of a bribe to a decision maker in KWL. UBS did not know of the bribe itself, nor was the bribe to be treated as having been made by its own agent (since VP was the agent of KWL, not UBS); but this did not prevent UBS's conscience being affected such that the swap could be rescinded against it. In effect, the Court of Appeal held that rescission could lie against UBS because it was guilty of dishonest assistance in VP's breach of fiduciary duty to its principal, even though it was unaware of the particular form that the breach took.[86]

(6) Affirmation and Acquiescence

22–049 The "right" to rescind a transaction will be lost if the wronged party affirms it; and an election to affirm is final.[87] But there can be no affirmation for these purposes without full knowledge of the facts that give rise to, and the existence of, the right[88]; and the party said to be affirming must be free from the relevant

---

[85] *UBS AG (London Branch) v Kommunale Wasserweke Leipzig GmbH* [2017] EWCA Civ 1567, at [113].

[86] In *Armagas Ltd v Mundogas SA*, above, at p.745C, Robert Goff LJ had suggested (without deciding) that there is some separate and general equitable principle that prevents the enforcement of a contract procured by bribery even by a counterparty who is innocent (even vicariously) and unaware of the bribery. This suggestion had been doubted in *Donegal International Ltd v Zambia* [2007] EWHC 197 (Comm), per Andrew Smith J at [496], and at first instance in *UBS AG (London Branch) v Kommunale Wasserweke Leipzig GmbH* [2014] EWHC 3615 (Comm), per Males J at [584]. The Court of Appeal's decision in *UBS* is to the effect that there is some broader general principle in play; but it still depends on the conscience of the counterparty being affected, if not by actual knowledge then by dishonesty.

[87] *Peyman v Lanjani* [1985] Ch. 457.

[88] *Bartram and Sons v Lloyd* (1904) 90 L.T. 357; *Peyman v Lanjani*, above.

vitiating factor (so, for example, any undue influence must have come to an end,[89] and the victim of a deceit must know the true facts).[90]

Affirmation can be established by any words or conduct which unequivocally manifest an intention to affirm[91] (even if, subjectively, the party in question did not in fact intend to affirm[92]). An unqualified demand for payment due under a voidable contract is an example of such conduct.[93] There is no need to demonstrate reliance on the manifested intention: it is the communication of the choice to affirm that makes the election binding, not any form of estoppel which may be generated by it.[94]

22–050

In the case of a bribe or secret commission, the principal does not affirm, so as to lose the right to rescind, merely by recovering and retaining the bribe or commission from his agent: the bribe or commission represents money to which the principal is entitled, whether or not he adopts the transaction, and so no affirmation can be inferred from his accepting it.[95] Conversely, the principal's decision to affirm the underlying transaction does not entail authorisation or ratification of a separate agreement under which the agent is to receive a secret commission.[96] Hence it is no contradiction for the principal to affirm the contract procured by the bribe and thereafter seek recovery of the bribe from his agent.

22–051

Affirmation is to be distinguished from the bar to rescission resulting from acquiescence. In contrast to affirmation, acquiescence:

22–052

(1)   does not, it would appear, require it to be demonstrated that the innocent party was aware of the right to rescind[97]; but

(2)   does require it to be inequitable, in all the circumstances, for the innocent party to exercise his right to rescind.[98]

Closely related to acquiescence is the bar to rescission resulting from laches, which is considered, along with the question of when the Limitation Act 1980 is applied by analogy, in Ch.25.[99]

22–053

---

[89] *Savery v King* (1856) 5 HLC 627.
[90] *Clough v London and North Western Railway* (1871) L.R. 7 Ex. 26.
[91] *Car & Universal Finance v Caldwell* [1965] 1 Q.B. 525, at 550, per Sellers LJ.
[92] *Kammins Ballrooms Co Ltd v Zenith Investments (Torquay) Ltd* [1971] A.C. 850, at 883.
[93] *Ultraframe (UK) Ltd v Fielding* [2005] EWHC 1638 (Ch), at [1449].
[94] *Ultraframe (UK) Ltd v Fielding*, above, at [1442].
[95] *Logicrose Ltd v Southend United F.C.* [1988] 1 W.L.R. 1256, per Millett J at 1263C.
[96] *Hughes v Hughes* [1972] EGD 145; *Accidia Foundation v Simon C Dickinson Ltd* [2010] EWHC 3058 (Ch).
[97] *Goldsworthy v Brickell* [1987] Ch. 378, per Nourse LJ at 412, and per Parker LJ at 416.
[98] *Habib Bank Ltd v Nasira Tufail* [2006] EWCA Civ 374, at [20]. This case also suggests that acquiescence, although an equitable defence, can apply so as to bar rescission at common law.
[99] See paras 25–028—25–033.

(7) **Restitutio in Integrum**

22–054   Whether at law or in equity, for rescission to occur it must be possible to restore the parties to the contract or other transaction to their original positions,[100] so far as concerns rights and obligations arising under it.[101] This is both the object of the remedy and also, where it is not possible, a bar to it.[102]

22–055   This requirement is generally understood to be applied more strictly at common law than in equity. At law, where rescission operates upon the communication by the party entitled of their intention to rescind, the circumstances must be such that the parties can be immediately and fully restored to their prior positions without the need for the intervention of the court. This causes no difficulty in the case of a contract that is purely executory, since the parties can simply be discharged from their obligations. Where the contract has been partly performed, or the transaction is otherwise one under which benefits have passed, rescission at common law will only be possible where the common law allows for title to re-vest automatically or recognises a claim to their recovery (or, in the case of the claimant providing counter-restitution, he returns or tenders what he has received). The common law allows the re-vesting of title to chattels by the unilateral act of the party entitled to rescission,[103] and a common law restitutionary claim to money paid will lie,[104] so these cases cause no difficulty; but rescission at common law of a contract pursuant to which a party has transferred land or shares (or other choses in action) is not possible, because the re-vesting of title will require steps—such as the rectification of a register—

---

[100] *Erlanger v New Sombrero Phosphate Co* (1878) 3 App. Cas. 1218; *Newbigging v Adam* (1886) 34 Ch. D. 582 (CA).

[101] *UBS AG (London Branch) v Kommunale Wasserweke Leipzig GmbH* [2017] EWCA Civ 1567, at [223]–[225]. This is an important qualification: the point of rescission is not to restore the parties to their pre-transaction position more generally, and so the fact that a party has incurred losses to third parties in reliance on the validity of the transaction is not a reason why rescission should be unavailable.

[102] Restitutio in integrum is to be mutual: there should be "a giving back and a taking back on both sides" (*Newbigging v Adam* (1886) 34 Ch. D. 582 (CA), at 595). However, strictly speaking, where the question is whether the impossibility of restitutio in integrum bars relief, it is the position of the defendant that matters. If the claimant wants to rescind on terms that ensure full restitution for the defendant but leave the claimant with less than he previously had, that is a matter for him and does not preclude rescission: *Spence v Crawford* [1939] 3 All E.R. 271.

[103] See para.22–060 below. Where the common law does recognise title re-vesting, the innocent party can probably rescind even if the asset has been sold on by the defendant to a third party, because his proprietary interest can fasten instead on any asset acquired in exchange (if it too is one for which title can pass automatically at law) or he can assert a restitutionary claim to the proceeds of sale representing what was in law, following rescission, his asset.

[104] *Clough v London and North Western Railway* (1871) L.R. 7 Ex. 26, at 37.

which cannot be undertaken unilaterally.[105] The same would appear to be true of contracts for services which have been performed.[106]

In equity these difficulties do not arise. That is both because:

22–056

(1) The requirement that there be restitutio in integrum is, in equity, more relaxed: equity will allow rescission where "substantial", rather than exact, restitution can be achieved, and the court approaches the matter with a measure of discretion and view to achieving a practically just result[107]; and

(2) The court is not hamstrung by the common law rules as to the automatic re-vesting of title and recovery of benefits transferred; it is the court, rather than the innocent party, that effects rescission, and it has other tools available to it to adjust the positions of the parties to what they were before—such as orders for the return of assets, the execution of transfers and the rectification of registers, and/or for the payment of compensation and taking of an account.

Thus, for example, deterioration in an asset transferred into the hands of the innocent party under a contract that falls to be rescinded would preclude rescission at common law (because simply returning the asset would not be sufficient to effect restitution), but it will generally not be a bar in equity (because a compensating financial adjustment could be ordered).[108] The court can also make its order for rescission conditional upon the innocent party providing counter-restitution of any benefits received (so the question of whether a legally

22–057

---

[105] *Feret v Hill* 139 E.R. 400; (1854) 15 C.B. 207 (unregistered land); s.58 of the Land Registration Act 2002 (registered land); *Civil Service Co-operative Society v Blyth* (1914) 17 C.L.R. 601, at 613 (shares). In the case of a contract for the transfer shares induced by fraud, if it is the rescinding (innocent) party who has received them, it would appear that unilateral rescission at law is possible if steps are taken to return the shares.
[106] Because the services cannot unilaterally be returned, and the common law does not appear to recognise a restitutionary claim for their value. See the consideration of this in O'Sullivan, Elliott and Zakrzewski, *The Law of Rescission* (2014), paras 14.41–14.44.
[107] *Erlanger v The New Sombrero Phosphate Co*, above, at 1278; *Cheese v Thomas* [1994] 1 W.L.R. 129 (CA), at 136–137 (where it was said that "justice requires that each party should be returned as near to his original position as is now possible").
[108] An example of how the court goes about this process (in a case where a car was sold to the innocent party who drove it for a period ignorant of his right to rescind) is *Salt v Stratstone Specialist Ltd (t/a Stratstone Cadillac Newcastle)* [2015] EWCA Civ 745. At [22] and [30] Longmore LJ said: "But neither depreciation not intermittent enjoyment should, in my view, be regarded as reasons for saying restitution is impossible. It has always been the case that a court of equity, contemplating rescission, could order an account and/or an inquiry to determine the terms on which restitution should be made...Rescission is prima facie available if 'practical justice' can be done." A rescinding purchaser will usually only be required to compensate the vendor for deterioration in the asset that results from his (the purchaser's) own fault: *Lagunas Nitrate Company v Lagunas Syndicate* [1899] 2 Ch. 392 (CA), at 456–457. The fact that the asset has depreciated in value owing to changes in the market would generally not be regarded as preventing substantial restitutio in integrum in equity (unless the claimant had delayed unreasonably after learning of his right to rescind): *Armstrong v Jackson* [1917] K.B. 822.

enforceable right to counter-restitution exists does not arise).[109] And at least in cases of rescission in equity for fraud (and quite possibly in other cases), equity will recognise the re-vesting of an equitable title, irrespective of the difficulties that may be attendant on transferring legal title.[110] Rescission can occur even if an asset transferred to the defendant has been transferred on by him to a third party, because the defendant can be ordered to account for the proceeds of sale[111] and a proprietary claim to any substitute asset in the defendant's hands can be made.

22–058   In cases where the asset transferred has been sold on or lost by the *rescinding* party, rescission at law would be impossible; but equity will in some cases permit substitutive counter-restitution, such that rescission can still lie. Thus where the asset in question is fungible (such as shares), it would appear that rescission can be awarded in equity because an equivalent asset can be returned or acquired[112]; and in equity restitution of the value of services received can be given in money (by an equitable allowance).[113]

22–059   The innocent party is not required to give counter-restitution if it is because of the defendant's own wrongdoing that he cannot be fully restored to his previous position,[114] or the benefit is one which the defendant was bound to confer in any event.[115] An innocent party is also probably not required to compensate a fraudulent purchaser of an asset for improvements made to the asset before rescission, since (having knowledge of his own deceit) the purchaser is on notice of the defect in his title.[116] A bribe or secret commission is not to be treated as a benefit obtained under the transaction to be rescinded, even if the principal has

---

[109] So the order for rescission can be made conditional upon the re-conveyance of land, the re-transfer of shares or the re-delivery of chattels received by the rescinding party. Where restitution and counter-restitution both require the payment of money, this can be achieved by an account and netting off one against the other.

[110] See paras 22–061—22–066 below.

[111] *New Sombrero Phosphate Co v Erlanger* (1877) 5 Ch. D. 73, at 125–126; *Lagunas Nitrate Co v Lagunas Syndicate* [1899] 2 Ch. 392, at 434, per Lindley MR.

[112] *Smith New Court Securities Ltd v Citibank* [1997] A.C. 254, per Lord Browne-Wilkinson at 262 (obiter, because the rescission claim had been abandoned). The position with non-fungible assets (that is, assets which have individual characteristics) is unclear.

[113] *O'Sullivan v Management Agency and Music Ltd* [1985] 1 Q.B. 428 (CA); *Guiness Plc v Saunders* [1990] 2 A.C. 693, at 698.

[114] *Rees v De Bernardy* [1896] 2 Ch. 437, 446 (defendant used undue influence to procure an agreement that he would provide the claimants with information about certain property belonging to them in return for receiving half of it; the fact that the information provided could not be returned was not a reason to refuse rescission—the communication of the information was part of the fraud).

[115] *Hulton v Hulton* [1917] 1 K.B. 813 (CA) (wife rescinding a separation deed procured by the fraud of her husband not required to return the annuity paid by the husband under the deed, as he would have been obliged to pay that by way of maintenance in any event). In *BV Nederlandse Industrie Van Eiprodukten v Rembrandt Enterprises Inc* [2018] EWHC 1857 (Comm) the difficulty of ordering counter-restitution was avoided by holding that rescission of a varied supply contract had the effect of restoring the original contract. Since product would have been supplied to the rescinding party under the original contract in any event, there was no need for it to return it upon rescission and all that was required was the return by the wrongdoer of the additional profit made under the varied contract.

[116] *Kennedy v Browne* (1796) 3 Ridg PC 462.

recovered the amount of the bribe or commission from his agent, and so it does not have to be returned or credited to the counterparty upon rescission.[117]

(8)   Rescission and Title to Money and Property

We have noted that a contract or other transaction which is merely voidable rather than void is effective to pass title to property prior to it being rescinded. The question then arises: what is the effect upon title to property that has passed prior to rescission taking place, once it does?

22–060

Where rescission takes place at common law upon the communication of the innocent party's election, its effect will be to cause legal title in any chattel that has passed under the contract or transaction rescinded to re-vest.[118] As has been noted, this is not the case (and so self-help rescission at common law is not possible) where the vesting and transfer of title depends upon steps such as the rectification of a register, as will be true of land and shares. As to money paid under the contract or transaction, rescission at common law gives rise to a personal restitutionary claim for repayment, but (it appears) no common law proprietary claim.

A re-vesting of title will also take place upon rescission in equity, certainly in the case of rescission for fraud[119] and, quite possibly, in other cases too.[120] Since the rescission is equitable, it is the beneficial, rather than legal, title which re-vests. The party holding legal title to the property will then be treated as having held it on a bare trust for the other, the other being able call for the transfer of legal title; the legal title, in contrast, will only be re-vested pursuant to an order of the court.

22–061

Rimer J summarised the position in equity thus, in *Shalson v Russo*,[121] a case concerning rescission of contracts of loan which had been procured by fraudulent misrepresentations:

22–062

> "Rescission is an act of the parties which, when validly effected, entitles the party rescinding to be put in the position he would have been in if no contract had been entered into in the first place. It involves a giving and taking back on both sides. If it is necessary to have recourse to

---

[117] *Logicrose Ltd v Southend United F.C.* [1988] 1 W.L.R. 1256, per Millett J at 1263G-1264D.

[118] *Load v Green* (1846) 15 M. & W. 216; 153 E.R. 828; *Car & Universal Finance Co Ltd v Caldwell* [1965] 1 Q.B. 525. These are cases of rescission for fraud, but it is considered that the same should be true of rescission at common law on other grounds (such as duress).

[119] *Lonrho v Fayed (No.2)* [1992] 1 W.L.R. 1, at 12; *El Ajou v Dollar Land Holdings Plc* [1993] 3 All E.R. 717, at 734 (reversed on other grounds [1994] 2 All E.R. 685); *Halifax Building Society v Thomas* [1996] Ch 217; *Bristol & West Building Society v Mothew* [1998] Ch. 1, at 22–23; *Box v Barclays Bank Plc* [1998] Lloyd's Rep. Bank 185; *Shalson v Russo* [2003] EWHC 1637 (Ch); [2005] Ch. 281, at [106]–[120]; *Papamichael v National Westminster Bank Plc* [2003] EWHC 164 (Comm); [2003] 1 Lloyd's Rep. 341; *London Allied Holdings v Lee* [2007] EWHC 2061 (Ch), at [275]–[280]; *Independent Trustee Services Ltd v GP Noble Trustees Ltd* [2013] Ch. 91 (CA), at [52]–[53]; *National Crime Agency v Robb* [2014] EWHC 4384 (Ch); [2015] Ch. 520, at [40]–[46]; *Re Crown Holdings (London) Ltd and Crown Currency Exchange Ltd* [2015] EWHC 1876 (Ch), at [25] and following.

[120] There is support for equitable rescission giving rise to the re-vesting of a beneficial interest in the case of undue influence (*Allcard v Skinner* (1887) 36 Ch. D. 145; *Pearce v Beverley* [2013] EWHC 2627 (Ch)), unilateral mistake of the *Pitt v Holt* kind (*Bainbridge v Bainbridge* [2016] EWHC 898 (Ch)), and non-fraudulent misrepresentation (*Bristol & West v Mothew* [1998] 1 Ch. 1, at 22–23).

[121] *Shalson v Russo* [2005] Ch. 281, at [122].

an action in order to implement the rescission, the Court will make such orders as are necessary to put both contracting parties into the position they were in before the contract was made. There is, however, also a line of authority supporting the proposition that, upon rescission of a contract for fraudulent misrepresentation, the beneficial title which passed to the representor under the contract re-vests in the representee. The representee then enjoys a sufficient proprietary title to enable him to trace, follow and recover what, by virtue of such re-vesting, can be regarded as having always been in equity his own property. This may be an essential means of achieving a proper restoration of the original position if the representor has in the meantime parted with the property and is ostensibly a man of straw unable to satisfy the Court's orders for restoration of the original position."

22–063   Rescission can thus be the foundation of an equitable proprietary claim. Moreover, the re-vesting of beneficial title is (like the rescission itself) treated as operating retrospectively, such that the property transferred under the impugned transaction "can be regarded as having always been in equity his own property".[122] This is treated as having given the claimant a sufficient equitable interest to be able to take advantage of the more favourable rules of equitable tracing and following, and thereby recover property that has been transferred away before the court could intervene.[123] It would appear, however, that the beneficial interest that is treated as having existed by reason of the rescission is not sufficient to subject the holder of legal title to duties as a trustee or fiduciary, or to give rise to claims against third parties for knowing receipt or dishonest assistance.[124]

22–064   Prior to rescission, the party entitled to rescind in equity is said to have a "mere equity", which can only be asserted against (or in such a way as to affect) a third party who is not a bona fide purchaser for value without notice, but which does not constitute the holder of title to any property transferred under the transaction a trustee or fiduciary for the other.[125] The timing of rescission may thus be critical to the availability to the innocent party of proprietary remedies. This equity can, in the case of registered land, be protected by registration or actual occupation.[126] It has been held that the equitable right to rescind a transaction with a company will be lost upon the company going into liquidation, if not exercised before that.[127]

---

[122] See the passage just quoted. Apparently the retrospective beneficial title is treated as having arisen from the outset—i.e. from the impugned transfer (see *Twinsectra Ltd v Yardley* [1999] Lloyd's Rep. Bank 438 (CA), at 461–462 (not reconsidered on this point on appeal to the House of Lords: [2002] 2 A.C. 164)). Presumably when rescission occurs upon the innocent party's election (rather than by court order)—as in equity is probably only the case where the claim is for fraud—the re-vesting occurs then and there is a genuine, rather than fictional, beneficial interest from that point.

[123] See the analysis of Millett J in *El Ajou v Dollar Land Holdings Plc* [1993] 3 All E.R. 717, at 734. As to equitable proprietary claims and the equitable rules of tracing, see Ch.23.

[124] *Lonrho v Fayed (No.2)* [1992] 1 W.L.R. 1; *Bristol & West v Mothew* [1998] 1 Ch. 1, at 23, and *Papamichael v National Westminster Bank Plc* [2003] EWHC 164 (Comm); [2003] 1 Lloyd's Rep. 341.

[125] *Lonrho v Fayed (No.2)*, above, at 11–12. The greater vulnerability of this mere equity to third party rights may be the explanation for the decision in *Re Goldcorp Exchange Ltd* [1995] 1 A.C. 74; see *Shalson v Russo*, above, at [126]: "until rescission, the property is vested in the representor; and if it is disposed of to a good faith purchaser, the purchaser will obtain a title which will be unimpeachable after any rescission."

[126] Land Registration Act 2002, s.116.

[127] *Re Crown Holdings (London) Ltd (In Liquidation)* [2015] EWHC 1876 (Ch).

A vivid illustration of the kinds of issues that arise is found in *Halifax Building Society v Thomas*.[128] There a lender lent money to a borrower on the security of property which was purchased with the loan monies (as a so-called "100 per cent mortgage"). The loan was induced by fraud. After default the lender took possession and sold the property. By this stage the property had increased in value. In the normal course of events the mortgagee would return to the borrower the surplus funds after redemption of its mortgage. The lender sought to assert a clam to that surplus. The claim failed because the lender had affirmed the contract of loan and its related security by taking possession and selling pursuant to its mortgage rights (after it learnt of the fraud). The case demonstrates the nature of the election which the victim of a fraud is put to when it has entered into a fraudulently-induced contract. Does it affirm the contract, and safeguard any security rights which arise under it? Or does it rescind it and thereby forego that security? What the claimant cannot do is both. If the lender had elected to rescind the contract of loan (and hence the related mortgage) it may well have been entitled to recover the totality of the sale proceeds as held on constructive trust for it, being the product of the claimant's money.[129]

22–065

Finally, we note that in the case of fraud it may be contended, based on Lord Browne-Wilkinson's famous dictum about the stolen bag of coins in *Westdeutsche*, that money or other property transferred as a result of the fraud is, automatically (that is, without any rescission) and from the outset, held by the fraudster on constructive trust.[130] We consider this argument in Ch.9.[131] Suffice it to say here that there are some persuasive objections to this analysis (which was, notably, rejected in terms by Rimer J in *Shalson v Russo*),[132] and until it receives more definitive endorsement by the higher courts, the safer course is for a claimant to work on the basis that he must first rescind the transaction under which the money or property passed before he can regain beneficial title to it.

22–066

(9) Rescission "Unfair and Disproportionate"

In *Hurstanger Ltd v Wilson*[133] a lender made a payment to a borrower's broker, thereby putting the broker in a position of conflict of which the lender was on notice (indeed, which it had procured). The lender had, however, disclosed to the borrower in advance that it might make the payment, but not the amount or that it

22–067

---

[128] *Halifax Building Society v Thomas* [1996] Ch. 217.

[129] Similarly in *Chief Constable of Leicestershire v M.* [1989] 1 W.L.R. 20, Hoffman J said, at 21: "None of the lenders have made any claim by way of constructive trust or otherwise to the profits made on the houses bought with their money. They have preferred to affirm the advances and enforce their rights under the mortgages." This fact situation is very common in secured lending scenarios.

[130] *Westdeutsche Landesbank Girozentrale v Islington LBC* [1996] A.C. 669, at 716: "when property is obtained by fraud equity imposes a constructive trust on the fraudulent recipient: the property is recoverable and traceable in equity."

[131] See paras 9–060—9–062.

[132] At [108]–[118], concluding at [119]: "In my view, the position immediately after the making by Mr Mimran of each of his loans to Westland was that the money advanced became Westland's property both legally and beneficially: that is what Mr Mimran intended should happen and that is what did happen.".

[133] *Hurstanger Ltd v Wilson* [2007] 1 W.L.R. 2351.

had in fact been made. This was held not to amount to sufficient disclosure for the borrower to give fully informed consent, so relief in equity was available to the borrower (in this case, equitable compensation from the lender in the amount of the payment). However, the Court of Appeal held that the disclosure made was sufficient to negate secrecy, and it therefore had a discretion to refuse to rescind the loan and associated charge on the grounds that the remedy would be "unfair and disproportionate". Had the commission amounted to a fully secret commission or bribe, rescission would have been available at law and there would have been no such discretion.[134]

22–068   *Hurstanger* was an unusual case (a "half-way house")[135]—since there was no bribe, and no finding that the lender had acted in any way unconscionably, it is not clear why rescission was available at all. The reliance placed by the Court of Appeal upon the decision of the same court in *Johnson v EBS Pensioner Trustees Ltd*[136] is also questionable, since that decision is arguably better explained as a case where rescission was refused because there was no counter-restitution. Nevertheless, the proposition that, where rescission is in equity rather than at law, there is a discretion to refuse it on the grounds that it would be unfair or disproportionate was endorsed by the Court of Appeal in *UBS AG (London Branch) v Kommunale Wasserweke Leipzig GmbH*,[137] albeit in that case the discretion was not exercised against rescission: there was no unfairness or disproportionality when the counterparty to the transaction to be rescinded was dishonestly implicated in the abuse by fiduciary on the other side of his position, even if it would suffer significant losses as a result.[138]

22–069   There is also now a statutory discretion to decline to order rescission of a contract for non-fraudulent misrepresentation and award damages in lieu, where rescission would otherwise be available[139]; but this has no application in a case of fraud.

---

[134] See *Conways v Eze* [2018] EWHC 29 (Ch), at [145]–[156]. Tuckey LJ averted to the possibility that the discretion would not arise in a bribery case in *Hurstanger*, at [46], but in terms of the "equitable remedy of rescission" being deployed in such a situation "in aid of the common law". It is suggested that this involves a misunderstanding of the role of the court in a case where rescission is available at law. As we have seen, in cases of common law rescission the role of the court is to pronounce upon the efficacy of the wronged party's exercise of its election, not to order rescission itself.

[135] Per Tuckey LJ, at [45].

[136] *Johnson v EBS Pensioner Trustees Ltd* [2002] EWCA Civ 164; [2002] Lloyd's Rep. PN 309, a case involving a breach of the fair-dealing rule. See per Dyson LJ at [78] and [79]: "In relation to rescission, in my view the judge was right to say (paragraph 46) that, whatever the position in relation to a claim to rescind based on misrepresentation, the right to rescission on grounds of undue influence, abuse of confidence or breach of fiduciary duty depends on the exercise of the discretion by the court to intervene in the enforcement of legal rights.... When exercising its equitable jurisdiction, the court considers what fairness requires not only when addressing the question of the precise form of relief, but also when considering whether the remedy should be granted at all."

[137] *UBS AG (London Branch) v Kommunale Wasserweke Leipzig GmbH* [2017] EWCA Civ 1567, at [157].

[138] *UBS AG (London Branch) v Kommunale Wasserweke Leipzig GmbH* [2017] EWCA Civ 1567, at [165]–[169].

[139] Section 2(2) of the Misrepresentation Act 1967.

(10)   Intervention of Third Party Rights

It is often also said that the fact that the rights of innocent third parties without **22–070** notice of the circumstances giving rise to the right to rescind have intervened operates as a bar to rescission[140]; but it is doubtful whether this is correct. If A sells an asset to B under a contract which is susceptible to rescission and B sells the asset on to C (who is a purchaser for value without notice) before A elects to rescind, it can readily be seen that A's right to claim against C will be defeated[141]; but it is not obvious why that should preclude rescission as between A and B (if it is otherwise available, on the principles considered above). Instead, justice can be achieved between the three parties involved by allowing C to retain the asset and having B pay over a sum representing the proceeds of sale to A instead[142] (or, if they remain identifiable in his hands, allowing A to trace into them).[143]

Thus in one recent case, where a transfer of land by the claimants to trustees was **22–071** susceptible to rescission, but the land had been sold on to third parties who were good faith purchasers and the proceeds of that sale had been applied to acquire new land, rescission of the original transfers was still allowed, the claimants then having a claim to beneficial ownership of the new land.[144]

Third party rights may, however, preclude rescission where they are prejudiced in **22–072** other ways: so, for example, if C was party to a multi-lateral contract with A and B, but was not implicated in B's wrongdoing, A could not rescind the contract.[145] Similarly, in *Crystal Palace FC v Dowie* rescission of an agreement to terminate a football club manager's employment (which had been induced by his deceit) was refused where the manager had in the intervening period become contractually committed to managing another club: it would not be possible to revive the manager's employment with the claimant club consistently with him observing his obligations as an employee of the new club.[146]

(11)   No Partial Rescission

Rescission is concerned with putting the parties to the impugned transaction back **22–073** in the position in which they were before the transaction was entered, rather than achieving something akin to compensation for the wrong that induced it. English law therefore takes the view that (at least in the case of a contract)[147] partial

---

[140] See *White v Garden* (1851) 10 CB 919.

[141] Which is what *White v Garden* actually decided.

[142] *New Sombrero Phosphate Co v Erlanger* (1877) 5 Ch. D. 73, at 125–126; *Lagunas Nitrate Co v Lagunas Syndicate* [1899] 2 Ch. 392, at 434, per Lindley MR.

[143] *El Ajou v Dollar Land Holdings Plc* [1993] 3 All E.R. 717, at 735; *Shalson v Russo* [2005] Ch. 281, per Rimer J at [122] and [127].

[144] *Bainbridge v Bainbridge* [2016] EWHC 898 (Ch).

[145] *Moody v Condor Insurance Ltd* [2006] 1 W.L.R. 1847.

[146] *Crystal Palace FC v Dowie* [2007] I.R.L.R. 682.

[147] The approach is more relaxed in the case of transactions in which consideration does not move both ways: *Willis v Barron* [1902] A.C. 271; *Kennedy v Kennedy* [2014] EWHC 4129 (Ch); [2015] W.T.L.R. 837, at [46], per Etherton C at [46] ("I see no reason, however, why that limitation should apply to a self-contained and severable part of a non-contractual voluntary transaction"); *Bainbridge v*

rescission cannot be allowed, even if, but for the wrong in question, the transaction would have been entered into on other terms.[148] If the contract or transaction is (on ordinary contractual principles) severable, then there is no objection to rescission of a severable part without rescission of the rest.[149]

C.   ACCOUNT OF PROFITS

(1)   Introduction and Bases

22–074   As we have noted above, an account of profits is a personal remedy by which a wrongdoer (usually, but not exclusively, a fiduciary) is required to identify and disgorge profits or other benefits made in breach of some obligation or violation of some right. It differs from equitable compensation in the sense considered in this chapter in that it is concerned with the gain made by the wrongdoer rather than the loss suffered by the claimant; and it also differs from damages awarded on a "user" basis, since, whilst these in a sense involve the defendant disgorging a gain, they are assessed with reference to hypothetical price at which the claimant would have permitted his rights to be infringed, rather than the profits which the defendant has in fact made by the infringement.[150]

22–075   So far as relevant to this work, an account of profits will in principle be available as relief against:

(1)   a fiduciary who has made a profit within the scope of his duty without the fully informed consent of his principal[151];
(2)   a third party found to have dishonestly assisted in a breach of trust or fiduciary duty[152]; and
(3)   (it would appear) a knowing recipient of trust property.[153]

22–076   As identified below,[154] the applicable principles are somewhat different in the second and third cases from those applicable in the first.

Bainbridge, above (where there were different transfers of land into trust, from different transferors, as part of the same transaction: rescission of each transfer could be considered separately).

[148] *Myddleton v Lord Kenyon* (1794) 2 Ves. 391, at 408; *The Sheffield Nickel and Silver Plating Co Ltd v Unwin* (1877) 2 Q.B.D. 214 (CA), at 223; *TSB Bank Plc v Camfield* [1995] 1 W.L.R. 430, at 437. A different view has been reached in Australia: *Vadasz v Pioneer Concrete (SA) Pty Ltd* (1995) 184 C.L.R. 102; and in New Zealand: *Scales Trading Ltd v Far Eastern Shipping Co Public Ltd* [1999] 3 N.Z.L.R. 26.

[149] See e.g. *Drake Insurance Plc v Provident Insurance Plc* [2004] Q.B. 601 (CA), at [103]: "It is not possible to rescind a contract in part, just as it is not possible to accept a repudiation, another act of election, in part (unless a contract is divisible)."

[150] For an example of an award of damages on a "user" basis and consideration of the distinctions between that and an account of profits, see *Experience Hendrix LLC v PPX Enterprises Inc* [2003] 1 All E.R. (Comm) 830.

[151] See *Boston Deep Sea Fishing v Ansell* (1888) 39 Ch. D. 339; and, more generally, Ch.11.

[152] The claim is considered in Ch.13.

[153] The claim is considered in Ch.12.

[154] See the following sub-section.

An account of profits will also be available, in principle, in claims for (a) breach   **22–077**
of confidence; (b) infringement of intellectual property rights; and (c)
exceptionally, breach of contract.[155] These lie outside the scope of this work and
are not considered further.

(2)   The Relationship Between Profit and Breach: As Against the Fiduciary

In *Ultraframe (UK) Ltd v Fielding*, a case involving the alleged misappropriation   **22–078**
of businesses owned by the claimant companies by a shadow director, Lewison J
identified the following "governing principles" applicable to the central case of
an account of profits against a defaulting fiduciary[156]:

    "i)   The fundamental rule is that a fiduciary must not make an unauthorized profit out of his fiduciary position;

    ii)   The fashioning of an account should not be allowed to operate as the unjust enrichment of the claimant;

    iii)   The profits for which an account is ordered must bear a reasonable relationship to the breach of duty proved;

    iv)   It is important to establish exactly what has been acquired;

    v)   Subject to that, the fashioning of the account depends on the facts. In some cases it will be appropriate to order an account limited in time; or limited to profits derived from particular assets or particular customers; or to order an account of all the profits of a business subject to all just allowances for the fiduciary's skill, labour and assumption of business risk. In some cases it may be appropriate to order the making of a payment representing the capital value of the advantage in question, either in place of or in addition to an account of profits. "

The profit for which an account is ordered must thus be attributable to the breach   **22–079**
of duty, or (perhaps more accurately) fall within the scope of the duty.[157] As to
what is within the scope of the duty, benefits acquired within the scope of the
activities which the fiduciary has undertaken to pursue on his principal's behalf,
or by use of his position or connection with the principal, or which give rise to a
risk of conflict with his duties to the principal, should be the subject of the
account.[158]

---

[155] *Attorney General v Blake* [2001] 1 A.C. 268. Also, the vendor of property under a specifically
enforceable contract of sale who sells, in breach of contract, to a third party at a profit will be liable to
account to the purchaser for that profit; but that is on the basis that the specifically enforceable
contract of sale creates a trust of the property in favour of the purchaser: *Lake v Bayliss* [1974] 1
W.L.R. 1073.

[156] [2005] EWHC 1638, at [1588].

[157] *Phipps v Boardman* [1967] 2 A.C. 46, at 127, per Lord Upjohn; *CMS Dolphin Ltd v Simonet*
[2001] 2 B.C.L.C. 704, per Laurence Collins J at 732 (the profits should be "properly attributable to"
the breach); *Murad v Al-Saraj* [2005] EWCA Civ 959; [2005] W.T.L.R. 1573, at [62], citing the
Australian case of *Warman International Ltd v Dwyer* [1994–1995] 182 C.L.R. 541, at 559. So, for
example, in *Giddings v Giddings* (1826) 3 Russ 241, where a lease was renewed, the beneficiaries
were only entitled to claim that part of the renewed lease comprising land held within the original
lease, and not new land which had come to be added.

[158] See paras 11–094—11–100.

22–080   It does not matter whether the benefits are acquired directly or indirectly.[159]

22–081   The burden will be on the fiduciary to show that a profit which he has made is not one for which he should account, reflecting the deterrent nature of the fiduciary's liability.[160] But the remedy is not meant to be penal[161] and, as indicated by the quotation above from the *Ultraframe* judgment, it is sufficiently flexible that it can be fashioned to fit the justice of the particular case and avoid unjustly enriching the claimant. Exactitude is not required.

22–082   However, it is important to bear in mind that a fiduciary is subject to a pre-existing duty (or inhibition) which springs from his duty of undivided loyalty; and that duty prevents him from retaining any profit made by taking advantage of the position in which his principal has placed him, unless the principal has given his fully informed consent. Absent such consent, the duty of loyalty requires that the profit is treated as having been made for the principal's benefit, irrespective of whether he could or would himself have made it. The remedy of an account of profit is therefore more in the nature of enforcement of the duty of loyalty, than redress for its breach. For that reason, it is does not really make sense to consider the scope of the account separately from the scope of the fiduciary inhibition which underlies it: one reflects the other. As it was put in the leading case of *Parker v McKenna*[162]:

> "Now, the rule of this Court, as I understand it, as to agents, is not a technical or arbitrary rule. It is a rule founded upon the highest and truest principles of morality. No man can in this Court, acting as agent, be allowed to put himself in a position in which his interest and his duty will be in conflict. The Court will not inquire, and is not in a position to ascertain, whether the bank has lost or not lost by the acts of its directors. All that the Court has to do is examine whether a profit has been made by an agent, without the knowledge of his principal, in the course and execution of his agency, and the Court finds, in my opinion, that these agents in the course of their agency have made a profit, and for that profit they must, in my opinion, account to their principal."

22–083   As a result, common law concepts of causation and remoteness have no application.[163] A fiduciary can therefore have to account for a profit within the scope of his duty even if that profit would have been made had the fiduciary done as he should have (and obtained the principal's consent): speculation as to what would have happened had disclosure been made or had the breach not occurred is

---

[159] Such as through the increase of the value of the fiduciary's shares in a company that has received the profit: *Gwembe Valley Development Co Ltd & Anor v Koshy* [2004] B.C.L.C. 131, at [137]–[138] (on this, see the principles summarised in sub-section (6) below); or by profiting from some other property purchased with the proceeds of sale of misapplied trust property: *Murad v Al-Saraj*, above, at [85].

[160] *Manley v Sartori* [1927] Ch. 157; *Warman International Ltd v Dwyer*, above. There is an analogy to the rules applicable to trustees who mingle their own funds with trust funds: *Murad v Al Saraj*, above, at [77]–[79]; and *Global Energy Horizons Corp v Gray* [2015] EWHC 2232 (Ch), per Asplin J at [136].

[161] Albeit the strictness of the liability to account and the placing of the burden on the fiduciary to show that a profit does not fall within the scope of his duty serves an important deterrent function. See e.g. *Warman International Ltd v Dwyer*, above, at 558; *Murad v Al-Saraj*, above, at [74] and [77].

[162] *Parker v McKenna* (1874) L.R. 10 Ch. App. 96, per Lord Cairns LC at 118.

[163] *United Pan-Europe Communications NV v Deutsche Bank AG* [2000] 2 B.C.L.C. 461, per Morritt LJ at [47]; *Murad v Al-Saraj*, above, per Arden LJ at [57] and per Jonathan Parker LJ at [112]; *Global Energy Horizons Corp v Gray* [2015] EWHC 2232 (Ch), per Asplin J at [137].

irrelevant, since the account is not concerned with compensating the principal for what has been lost as a result of the breach.[164]

That principle is strikingly illustrated by *Murad v Al-Saraj*,[165] where one joint venturer in dishonest breach of his fiduciary duty to the others failed to disclose that his contribution to the venture was being made by way of set-off against amounts due or purportedly due to him from the vendor of the joint venture property (including a secret commission). The Court of Appeal rejected the submission that the profit for which he had to account should be limited so as to exclude profit which he would still have been allowed by the claimants to make from the venture had he made full disclosure to them (it having been found by the judge that the venture would still have proceeded, albeit with the claimants insisting on a higher profit share): only actual consent obviates the liability to account and the fact that consent would have been forthcoming if sought to part or all of the profit is irrelevant.[166]

22–084

The requirement that the profit for which the fiduciary is accountable should be attributable to his breach can cause particular difficulty where the fiduciary has diverted his beneficiary or principal's property, or a corporate opportunity, and exploited it profitably as part of a business in which he is himself engaged. As Lord Brougham observed in *Docker v Somes*,[167] if a trustee misappropriates trust money and uses it to purchase silk, which is then worked into a fine fabric, the work exceeding the material many times over in value, then "no reasonable person would ever dream of charging a trustee whose skill thus bestowed had so enormously augmented the value of the capital, as if he had only obtained from it a profit".[168] Conversely, where the business from which the profit is made is substantially the same as that belonging to the principal or beneficiary, the correct approach is more likely to be for the account to extend to all of the profits of the business, subject to an allowance for any expenditure incurred by the fiduciary and the contribution of his skill.[169] Of course, cases will often fall somewhere between these extremes; and the Court will have to fashion the account so as to achieve broad justice on the particular facts.

22–085

---

[164] *Brickenden v London Loan and Savings Co* [1934] 3 D.L.R. 465, per Lord Thankerton at 469; *Gwembe Valley Development Co Ltd & Anor v Koshy*, above, per Mummery LJ at [144]–[145]. This also reflects the difficulty of assessing the counterfactual when the facts are likely to be exclusively within the knowledge of the fiduciary, and the policy consideration of deterrence: see *Murad v Al-Saraj*, above, per Jonathan Parker LJ at [107]. Equitable compensation is in this respect different, since questions of what would have happened but for the breach are relevant: see paras 22–106—22–113.

[165] Above.

[166] See [71], per Arden LJ. For a recent example of a case where the required "reasonable relationship" between the profit and the breach was not made out, see *Gamatronic (UK) Ltd v Hamilton* [2016] EWHC 2225 (QB); [2017] BCC 670.

[167] *Docker v Somes* 2 MY&K 656.

[168] Compare, in the context of the diversion of corporate opportunities, *CMS Dolphin Ltd v Simonet* [2001] 2 B.C.L.C. 704, where the account was limited to the profits derived from the particular contracts diverted from the claimant company (including profits under other contracts that might not have been won without the opportunity or cash-flow benefit which flowed from the contracts diverted), and did not extend to the profits of the new business more generally.

[169] As was held in *Re Jarvis* [1958] 1 W.L.R. 815, where the executrix had essentially revived the testator's business.

22–086 Thus, for example, in the Australian case of *Warman International Ltd v Dwyer*,[170] the general manager of a company which carried on an agency distribution business for a manufacturer took up an opportunity (which had been declined by the company) to go into a joint venture with the manufacturer. The joint venture business was sufficiently similar to that of the company's for an account of the profits of the business generally to be appropriate; but the manufacturer also had a stake in and contributed to the joint venture. The High Court decided that the account should be limited to the first 2 years of operation of the joint venture business, reflecting, on a rough and ready basis, the point beyond which the profits made were likely no longer to be attributable to the breach, but instead to the effort and resources put in by the defendant and the manufacturer.[171]

(3) Interest

22–087 In some cases, however, the exercise of tracing and apportioning the profit attributable to the breach may be too difficult and the Court will, pragmatically, award interest on the sum wrongfully employed instead of an account of profit.[172] So, for example, in *Vyse v Foster*,[173] where an account was sought of the profit attributable to a deceased partner's share that had been left in a business, the Court of Appeal, being unable satisfactorily to determine what share of the profits made by the business the claimants were entitled to (it not being safe to assume that it was simply the same as the share of capital), instead awarded interest on the capital sum to reflect the benefit of its use in the business.

22–088 In cases where a trustee or other fiduciary has wrongfully profited from the use of his beneficiary's or principal's property, the practice has become established of awarding interest on a compound basis in equity. This is intended (at least in part) to reflect the fact that profits made in a business will often be redeployed as working capital and so generate further profits.[174] But the practice is not limited to the misuse of trust property in the course of a business; it extends to any case where a trustee or fiduciary has wrongfully profited, or may be presumed to have wrongfully profited, from having the use of his beneficiary's or principal's money (including claims that are personal as well as proprietary).[175] Indeed, there is

---

[170] Above.

[171] Cf. *Lindsley v Woodfull* [2004] 2 B.C.L.C. 201, where the account was limited to profits earned down to the date on which a partner's retirement took effect, together with a payment of the capital value of the business advantage as a going concern as at that date.

[172] *Burdick v Garrick*, L.R. 5 Ch.App. 233, per Lord Hatherly LC at 241; *Docker v Somes*, above, at 673.

[173] *Vyse v Foster* (1872) 9 Ch. App. 309.

[174] *Wallersteiner v Moir (No.2)* [1975] Q.B. 373, per Buckley LJ at 397.

[175] *Westdeutsche Landesbank Girozentrale v Islington LBC* [1996] A.C. 669, per Lord Goff at 693F and per Lord Browne-Wilkinson at 702DE; *Kuwait Oil Tanker Company SAK v Al Bader*, unreported, 17 December 1998, at p.159.

authority for awarding compound interest in *addition* to an account of profit,[176] which can probably only be justified if there is no element of double-counting or penalty.

(4) Account as Against Dishonest Assister/Knowing Recipient

After some debate in the authorities it is now clear that an account of profits will lie against a defendant who has dishonestly assisted in a breach of trust or fiduciary duty, even if he has not received any trust property: this follows from the premise that the dishonest assister is liable to account as if he were a trustee for the claimant.[177] It would appear that, for essentially the same reason, the same is true of a defendant who has knowingly received property disposed of in breach of trust or fiduciary duty.[178]   **22–089**

However, in two important respects the remedy is more limited when awarded against the dishonest assister than when awarded against the defaulting fiduciary: **22–090**

(1)   First, the requirement of a causal nexus between the profit and misconduct is stricter;
(2)   Secondly, the Court has a discretion to refuse to order an account, including because it would be disproportionate.

As to the first, because the dishonest assister does not owe a pre-existing obligation of loyalty, the considerations identified in the preceding section do not apply: the remedy is not simply enforcing a pre-existing duty and is instead in the nature of redress for an equitable wrong. Common law rules of causation, remoteness and measure of damages are therefore to be applied by analogy.[179]   **22–091**

---

[176] As happened in *Accidia Foundation v Simon C Dickinson Ltd* [2010] EWHC 3058 (Ch), at [97], although the rationale for compounding interest and awarding an account was not discussed.

[177] *Novoship (UK) Ltd v Mikhaylyuk* [2015] Q.B. 499. The proposition had been doubted by Rimer J in *Sinclair Investment Holdings SA v Versailles Trade Finance Ltd* [2007] 2 All E.R. (Comm) 993, at [129]–[134]; but a number of first instance cases had supported it, including *Fyffes Group Ltd v Templeman* [2000] 2 Lloyd's Rep. 643, per Toulson J; *Ultraframe (UK) Ltd v Fielding* [2005] EWHC 1638, at [1589]–[1594], per Lewison J; *Tajik Aluminium Plant v Ermatov (No.3)* [2006] EWHC 7 (Ch), at [23], per Blackburne J; *OJSC Oil Co Yugraneft v Abramovich* [2008] EWHC 2613 (Comm), at [377] and [392], per Christopher Clarke J; *Fiona Trust & Holding Corp v Privalov* [2010] EWHC 3199, at [66], per Andrew Smith J; and *Otkritie International Investment Management Ltd v Urumov* [2014] EWHC 191 (Comm), at [79], per Eder J.

[178] "The person who fraudulently receives or possesses himself of trust property is converted by this court into a trustee...[which] denotes that the parties entitled beneficially have the same rights and remedies against him as they would be entitled to against an express trustee": *Rolfe v Gregory* (1865) 4 De GJ & S 576, at 578 and 579, per Lord Westbury LC. This was cited in support of the availability of an account of profits in *Novoship (UK) Ltd v Mikhaylyuk* [2015] Q.B. 499, at [80], albeit the case was concerned with the remedy for dishonest assistance rather than knowing receipt. As noted in *Novoship* (at [82]), this would appear to be the basis for the order for an account of profits made against the company which received the benefit of the diverted contract in *Cook v Deeks* [1916] 1 A.C. 554.

[179] *Novoship (UK) Ltd v Mikhaylyuk*, above, at [105]–[107]. The Court of Appeal expressly distinguished the position from that in cases relating to a fiduciary's liability to account, where, as we have considered above, questions of causation and what would have happened but for the breach are irrelevant.

Thus, where an individual who owned a charterer dishonestly assisted an agent for a shipowner (who had received and shared out bribes) by negotiating for the entry into charters from the shipowner, he was not liable to account for profit which was made by reason of an unexpected change in the market. What was obtained by reason of the breach which he had dishonestly assisted was only the use of the vessels at the market rate, which was merely the occasion for, and not the effective cause of, his profit.[180]

22–092   The dishonest assister is also not, for like reasons, liable to account for profit which he has not himself made but which has rather been made by the defaulting fiduciary, unless and to the extent that the fiduciary's profit represents a loss to the principal (in which case it would fall within the dishonest assister's liability to compensate the principal for loss resulting from the underlying breach).[181]

22–093   As to the second difference, again because the account is not simply enforcing a pre-existing duty, the account is not automatic against a third party who would otherwise be liable in equity and the Court has a discretion to refuse to order it. One reason to do so would be where it would be disproportionate in relation to the particular form and extent of the wrongdoing.[182]

(5)   Date of Valuation of Profit

22–094   It has already been noted that the principal has a right to elect between vindicating a proprietary claim to any asset representing the profit wrongfully obtained by the fiduciary, and requiring the fiduciary personally to account for its value.[183] One important factor in making that election will be the date at which the value of the profit is ascertained for the latter purposes, in circumstances where it is represented by an asset that has diminished in value since the breach.

22–095   The overriding consideration is that the Court is concerned to do justice in the circumstances of the case before it and the remedy of an account is sufficiently flexible to allow the profit to be valued at an earlier date to that end.[184] So in one case, where a defaulting fiduciary had obtained shares in breach of duty and those shares had at one stage been worth £80 (their highest intermediate value after being acquired by the fiduciary), but were at the date of judgment worth only 20s, the fiduciary was required to pay the full £80 and could not insist on satisfying his liability by simply handing over the shares.[185]

---

[180] *Novoship (UK) Ltd v Mikhaylyuk*, at [114]–[115]. Cf. *Fyffes Group Ltd v Templeman* [2000] 2 Lloyd's Rep. 643, where an account of profits against an assister was refused, because it was highly probable that the claimant would have entered into a service agreement with the third party even if the relevant fiduciary had not been dishonest.

[181] *Ultraframe (UK) Ltd v Fielding*, [2005] EWHC 1638, at [1600].

[182] *Satnam Investments Ltd v Dunlop Heywood* [1999] 3 All E.R. 652, at 672B–672C; *Novoship (UK) Ltd v Mikhaylyuk*, above, at [119].

[183] *FHR European Ventures LLP v Cedar Capital Holdings LLC* [2015] A.C. 250, per Lord Neuberger at [7].

[184] *Global Energy Horizons Corp v Gray* [2015] EWHC 2232 (Ch), at [143].

[185] *Nant-y-glo and Blaina Ironworks Company v Grave* (1878) 12 Ch. D. 738a, per Bacon VC at 747.

In *JJ Harrison (Properties) Ltd v Harrison*[186] Chadwick LJ questioned the **22–096** relevance of this authority to a case in which a director had acquired land from his company without full disclosure, and held that the profit made should only be accounted for at the date of its resale and not the date of its highest intermediate value. The stated reason for this (that *Nant-y-glo* was not a claim against a person who was in a pre-existing trust relationship to the property) appears doubtful as a point of distinction.[187] The better view may simply be that the selection of the date of actual sale better fitted the justice of the case (including because it involved land).

(6)   Profit Made by or Through a Third Party

We have considered the issues which arise where a fiduciary makes a profit by or **22–097** through a third party when looking at the fiduciary duties owed and the circumstances in which they are breached (the making of the unauthorised profit being the essence of the breach and not just an aspect of the relief to which it gives rise).[188] But since those issues are also relevant to the fashioning of the remedy by which the fiduciary is required to account, the principles are summarised again here:

(1)   First, the better view is probably that a fiduciary is not accountable for a profit made by a company in which he has an interest simply by reason of that interest;

(2)   The fiduciary will be accountable for a profit made personally as a result of such interest (through dividends or an increase in the value of his shares); he will also be accountable where he receives the profit and then transfers it to the company;

(3)   The fiduciary may also be accountable for profit made by the company itself, if there are grounds for piercing the corporate veil (under the "evasion principle");

(4)   The company's liability to account for the profit (where it is not itself in a fiduciary relationship with the claimant) will depend upon it being a knowing recipient of the profit, or dishonestly assisting in the fiduciary's breach. This is probably a sounder basis for imposing liability to account on the company than treating it as having some sort of joint liability with the fiduciary;

(5)   If the profits are made by a partnership of which the fiduciary is a partner, the fiduciary and his fellow partners will be jointly and severally liable to account for the whole profit (and not just the fiduciary's share of it).

---

[186] *JJ Harrison (Properties) Ltd v Harrison* [2002] 1 B.C.L.C. 162 (CA), at [51]–[52].
[187] And it is not clear that Lord Browne-Wilkinson was drawing this distinction when referring to the case in *Target Holdings Ltd v Redferns* [1996] A.C. 420, at 440D–440E; he was just distinguishing a claim for equitable compensation for breach of trust from a claim for an account of profits.
[188] At paras 11–117—11–121.

(7) Deductions and Allowances

22–098   When an account of profits is taken the Court can allow the deduction of expenses incurred by the accounting party in achieving the unauthorised profit or grant an equitable allowance in respect of the skill and effort in obtaining the profit.[189] This is closely allied to, and may sometimes be confused with, the question of whether the profit for which the fiduciary is being asked to account is attributable to, or within the scope of, his duty; but conceptually the identification of the profit within the ambit of the account and the deduction of allowances from it are distinct.[190]

22–099   So far as concerns expenses incurred in achieving the profit, the deduction should simply be part of the ascertainment of the profit and ought to be made as a matter of course.[191]

22–100   An allowance for skill and effort is, however, properly discretionary and is, moreover, to be regarded as unusual. In *Imageview Management Ltd v Jack*[192] the Court of Appeal emphasised that:

(1)   if an allowance is to be made, it must be because it would be inequitable for the beneficiaries to take the profit from the fiduciary without paying for the skill and effort[193];

(2)   the power to grant such an allowance to fiduciaries is to be exercised sparingly out of concern not to encourage fiduciaries to act in breach of fiduciary duty[194];

(3)   such an allowance is unlikely[195] to be allowed where the fiduciary has been involved in dishonesty or surreptitious dealing; and

---

[189] *Re Jarvis* [1958] 1 W.L.R. 815, at 820; *Phipps v Boardman* [1964] 1 W.L.R. 993, at 1018 (approved [1965] C 992, at 1020–1021; and [1967] 2 A.C. 46, at 104, 112); *O'Sullivan v Management Agency and Music Ltd* [1985] Q.B. 428; *Badfinger Music v Evans* [2001] W.T.L.R. 1; *Murad v Al Saraj* [2005] EWCA Civ 959. There is some doubt as to whether the jurisdiction can be exercised by the court to award an allowance for skill and effort to a director, where the power to award the director remuneration is reserved to the board of the company or its shareholders: *Guinness Plc v Saunders* [1990] 2 A.C. 663 (HL), at 694 and 701G.

[190] Hence the different approaches considered in *Re Jarvis* [1958] 1 W.L.R. 815. In *Ultraframe (UK) Ltd v Fielding* [2005] EWHC 1638 (Ch) it was doubted by Lewison J whether the jurisdiction could apply where the profit consists of part of the original trust property, as opposed to property received from a third party (see [1542]–[1545]); but that doubt does not yet appear to have been taken up elsewhere and is difficult to reconcile with the general jurisdiction to award a trustee remuneration.

[191] A. Stafford & S. Ritchie, *Fiduciary Duties: Directors and Employees*, 2nd edn (London: LNUK, 2015), para.9.106. Thus, to take a simple example, a defaulting fiduciary who is obliged to account for the profit made on the sale of land should be charged with the amount received on the sale, but entitled to bring to the credit of the account a proportionate part of what he paid for the land and the costs of works which enhanced its value: *JJ Harrison (Properties) Ltd v Harrison* [2002] 1 B.C.L.C. 162 (CA), at [50].

[192] *Imageview Management Ltd v Jack* [2009] Bus L.R. 1034 (CA), at [56], quoting with approval from McGhee, *Snell's Equity*, 31st edn (London: Sweet & Maxwell, 2005), para.7–131.

[193] As it was put by Wilberforce J in the first instance decision in *Boardman v Phipps* [1964] 1 W.L.R. 993, at 1018.

[194] Cf. *Guinness Plc v Saunders* [1990] 1 A.C. 663 (HL), at 701F.

[195] Although it is not impossible, and it will ultimately depend on the justice of the particular case: *O'Sullivan v Management Agency Ltd* [1985] 1 Q.B. 428, per Fox LJ at 468A–468B. As has been said

(4)   the burden is on the fiduciary to convince the court that an accounting of his or her entire profits was inappropriate in the circumstances.

In that case a football agent had negotiated a contract between a player and a **22–101**
club. The player agreed to pay 10 per cent of his salary to the agent. Secretly, the agent agreed with the club that it would pay him a sum of money in return for the agent obtaining a work permit for the player. It was held that the agent was liable to disgorge this sum to the player as a secret profit made in breach of duty. Notwithstanding that the work done by the agent in obtaining the work permit accorded a benefit to the player, no deduction was made to reflect this.

D.   EQUITABLE COMPENSATION

(1)   Introduction

The origins of equitable compensation lie in the jurisdiction of the Courts of   **22–102**
Equity to compel a defaulting trustee to restore to the trust fund any deficit revealed by the taking of an account, using his own funds where specific restitution was not possible. As has been said in the Introduction to this chapter above, an unauthorised or unjustified transaction with trust property (i.e. a breach of the trustee's custodial duty to preserve the trust property except as permitted by the terms of the trust) would be falsified in the account, resulting in an obligation either to restore the misapplied asset in specie or to pay a monetary amount of equivalent value to the trust estate.[196] This compensation was in straight substitution for the return of the asset and came to be referred to as "substitutive" (or "restitutive") compensation,[197] and in assessing its amount there was no counterfactual enquiry into what the condition of the trust estate would have been but for the impugned transaction. In contrast, where a trustee was guilty of default in his managerial duties, the account was surcharged with what would have been received but for the default, and the resulting monetary award had more in common with damages for the loss caused (sometimes referred to as "reparative" compensation). The jurisdiction to award compensation in equity outside the particular context of trusts, in a case where a fiduciary was guilty of an "equitable fraud" which had caused loss to his principal, was then recognised in *Nocton v Lord Ashburton*.[198]

The decision of the House of Lords in *Target Holdings Ltd v Redferns*[199]   **22–103**
appeared to erode some of these distinctions, in that it established that equitable compensation, whether classified as substitutive or reparative, was ultimately

---

above, the jurisdiction to order an account of profits is not a penal one; but clearly the level of culpability of the trustee will be a key consideration in determining whether an allowance should be made and, if so, in what amount.
[196] *Target Holdings v Redferns* [1996] 1 A.C. 421, at 434, per Lord Browne-Wilkinson.
[197] See e.g. Edelman J's exposition in *Agricultural Land Management Ltd v Jackson (No.2)* [2014] WASC 102.
[198] *Nocton v Lord Ashburton* [1914] A.C. 932, at 952, per Viscount Haldane LC.
[199] *Target Holdings Ltd v Redferns* [1996] A.C. 421.

always concerned with making good the loss that could be said to have been caused by the relevant breach of trust[200]:

> "Equitable compensation for breach of trust is designed to achieve exactly what the word compensation suggests: to make good a loss in fact suffered by the beneficiaries and which, using hindsight and common sense, can be seen to have been caused by the breach."

22–104 Whilst this proved a controversial decision in some quarters, precisely because it appeared to elide the different forms of monetary award that could result from the taking of an account, it was reconsidered and endorsed by the Supreme Court almost 20 years later in the case of *AIB Group (UK) Plc v Mark Redler & Co Solicitors*.[201] It is probably safe to assume that the principles stated in *Target* are now settled law, albeit there remains some debate amongst commentators as to their precise scope and, as we note below,[202] *AIB Group* has subsequently been distinguished.[203]

22–105 In what follows we consider first the decision in *AIB Group*; then the question of how it might apply outside the context of trusts and how the principles of causation it endorsed apply to breaches of different sorts of fiduciary duties. For these purposes it is helpful to have in mind the three-fold classification of such breaches deployed by Tipping J in the New Zealand case of *Bank of New Zealand v New Zealand Guardian Trust Co Ltd*[204]: breaches leading directly to damage to or loss of trust property (or what is analogous to trust property); breaches of the core fiduciary obligations of fidelity; and breaches involving a lack of skill and care. Put very broadly, in all three cases it is probably now clear that some minimum test of causation applies; but whereas in the first two cases equity works with hindsight and without regard to questions of foreseeability, in the third case the analogy with common law damages for negligence is much closer.[205]

(2)   The Decision in AIB Group and the Causation Requirement

22–106 The basic causal connection between breach and loss required in a claim for equitable compensation for a breach of trust, according to *Target Holdings Ltd v Redferns*, is that the loss would not have occurred but for the breach.[206]

---

[200] *Target Holdings Ltd v Redferns* [1996] A.C. 421, at 439.

[201] *AIB Group (UK) Plc v Mark Redler & Co Solicitors* [2015] A.C. 1503.

[202] At para.22–113.

[203] The Court of Appeal has also endorsed the continued use of "substitutive" and "reparative" equitable compensation, in *Interactive Technology Corp Ltd v Ferster* [2018] EWCA Civ 1594.

[204] *Bank of New Zealand v New Zealand Guardian Trust Co Ltd* [1999] 1 N.Z.L.R. 664, cited by Lord Toulson in *AIB Group*, at [59]–[60].

[205] Distinguishing between different sorts of claim for equitable compensation against fiduciaries will also be important for limitation purposes: a claim with respect to trust property improperly paid away is sufficiently akin to a claim for a liquidated sum to be treated as "a debt or other liquidated pecuniary claim" for the purposes of s.29(5) of the Limitation Act 1980, whereas a claim for breach of a fiduciary's duty of skill and care is not: *Creggy v Barnett* [2016] EWCA Civ 1004.

[206] *Target Holdings Ltd v Redferns* [1996] 1 A.C. 421, at 434, per Lord Browne-Wilkinson.

The significance of this causation requirement is starkly demonstrated by the **22–107** facts of the *AIB Group* case: AIB agreed to lend £3.3 million to the borrowers on the basis that the borrowers' current indebtedness to another bank secured on their property (comprising a loan of £1.2 million and another loan of £300,000) was paid off and AIB obtained a first legal charge. The £3.3 million was paid by AIB to its solicitors, the defendants, on terms that it would be held on trust for AIB with authority to release it only in exchange for the first legal charge. AIB's solicitors mistakenly released the money having paid off only the first of the existing loans, leaving a little over £300,000 outstanding under the second existing loan, which remained secured by a charge ranking ahead of AIB's. The borrower later defaulted and the security proved insufficient; and of what was realised out of a sale, the prior lender took £300,000 ahead of AIB.

AIB contended that, as trustees who had misapplied the fund in their hands, the **22–108** obligation of the solicitors was to restore the full amount of the fund (i.e. the whole loan of £3.3 million), with credit only for anything that had subsequently been recovered: on the taking of an account, the whole payment out would be disallowed and would become a debit due from the solicitors and that (less anything in fact recovered) was the proper measure of their restorative obligation. The solicitors contended that, whilst the amount lent less the amount recovered might represent the loss resulting from the (as it turned out) unwise lending transaction as a whole, the loss resulting from their *breach* was only the difference between the extent of the security which AIB should have had and that which it in fact had—approximately £300,000. Over and above that, the loss sustained by the lenders resulted from a drop in the value of the security subsequent to the loan and would have been incurred even had the solicitors properly performed their duties.

The Supreme Court unanimously favoured the view that the basic purpose of an **22–109** award of equitable compensation, even if characterised as being restorative, is to put the beneficiary in the same position as if the breach had not occurred; and that it does not require restoration to the trust of sums that would have been lost even had the trustee applied the fund in accordance with their duties. Thus the solicitors' liability was limited to the extent to which AIB's security was less than it would have been had they complied with their instructions and ensured that the prior secured lending had been paid off in full. This was the only loss which, on a "common sense view" and with the benefit of hindsight, could be said to have been caused by their breach.

This conclusion was premised on an analysis of the "basic equitable principles" **22–110** of compensation and a rejection of any fundamental distinction between substitutive and reparative awards emerging from a notional account: "monetary compensation, whether classified as restitutive or reparative, is intended to make good a loss".[207] It would therefore appear that in *all* cases of equitable compensation the question of causation of loss will arise and relief will only be

---

[207] *AIB Group (UK) Plc v Mark Redler & Co Solicitors* [2015] A.C. 1503, per Lord Toulson at [73].

awarded for those losses which would not have occurred but for the breach, and which "on a common sense view of causation" flow from it.[208]

22–111 Nevertheless, whilst on the facts of *AIB Group* this meant that the award of equitable compensation coincided with what would have been awarded as damages for breach of contract or negligence,[209] this will not necessarily always be so. In approaching the question of causation the nature of the duty breached and the context in which it is owed (including in particular the scope and purpose of the relevant trust) will remain important.[210] That is precisely because the causation requirement invites an investigation of what would have happened had the duty been observed.[211] In *Target* and *AIB Group* what mattered was that the trust was part of the machinery for the performance of a contract, in connection with a transaction that had completed; and so the equitable compensatory remedy was limited so as to exclude losses that would have been suffered even had the trust obligations, viewed in their contractual context, been performed.[212]

22–112 In contrast, in the case of a traditional trust (requiring stewardship of property over a number of years for a range of potential beneficiaries), a breach in the nature of the misapplication of trust property may still most appropriately be remedied by an order for full restoration to the trust of what was misapplied, simply because that is likely to be the only way to put the beneficiaries in the position in which they would have been had the breach not occurred.[213] So too in the case of a trust in the context of a commercial transaction that was yet to complete,[214] or where the contractual scheme requires ongoing custody of the funds.

22–113 Thus in the more recent case of *Main v Giambrone & Law*[215] the Court of Appeal held that solicitors who were responsible for holding deposits for the purchase of properties until the property developers provided guarantees meeting certain requirements, but who paid those deposits away without guarantees being provided, were liable to pay equitable compensation in the full amount of the deposits (the purchasers never acquired units in the development, because the development was seized by authorities investigating money laundering allegations). The solicitors' duty was to act as custodians of the deposit monies indefinitely, in contrast to both *Target* and *AIB Group*, where the relevant duty on the solicitors was to take steps to secure a charge or the removal of a prior charge.

---

[208] As Lord Reed made clear in *AIB Group*, when analysing the speech of Lord Browne-Wilkinson in *Target*, the "basic" equitable principle, applicable equally in the context of an accounting for funds held under a traditional trust, was that the beneficiaries were entitled to have restored only what they had been deprived of as a result of the breach: [105]–[108].

[209] Per Lord Toulson, at [76].

[210] Per Lord Toulson, at [70]–[71].

[211] Per Lord Reed, at [93].

[212] Per Lord Toulson, at [71].

[213] Per Lord Toulson, at [67].

[214] As noted by Lord Browne-Wilkinson in *Target Holdings Ltd v Redferns*, above: "I have no doubt that, until the underlying commercial transaction has completed, the solicitor can be required to restore to the client account moneys wrongfully paid away" (at 436).

[215] *Main v Giambrone & Law* [2017] EWCA Civ 1193.

Framing the duty in that different way of course produced a different answer to the question of what would have happened but for the breach.[216]

(3) Application to Other Fiduciaries

How the principles underpinning equitable compensation identified in *Target* and *AIB* should translate to other fiduciaries outside the trust context remains to be seen; but in our view their impact is potentially significant, where what is in issue is the remedy for the misapplication[217] of or direct loss to a fund or property under the stewardship of the fiduciary, and it calls for a re-evaluation of a number of earlier authorities, particularly on the personal liability of directors who have misapplied company assets.   **22–114**

In a number of cases in the company context it had been held that directors who cause company funds to be misapplied have a strict liability to restore the amount paid away without reference to the causation question of what would have happened but for their breach. So, for example: **22–115**

(1) Directors who cause the company to pay dividends in contravention of the rules against the distribution of capital at common law and under the Companies Acts have been held to be liable to restore the full amount of the dividend, without reference to whether and if so in what amount a dividend could lawfully have been paid.[218]

(2) The statutory liability of a director to indemnify his company for loss resulting from an arrangement entered into with the company without shareholder approval in contravention of what used to be s.320 of the Companies Act 1985[219] has been held to extend to the full amount paid away under the arrangement less only what was subsequently realised, thereby making the directors bear losses resulting from subsequent falls in the market value of the asset acquired.[220]

(3) In *Gwembe Valley Development Company Ltd v Koshy* it was observed by the Court of Appeal, more generally, that where a director caused a company's property to be applied without authority, for a purpose which

---

[216] Like Target before it, *AIB Group* has proved a controversial decision. The conclusion that the solicitors should only be liable to the extent that AIB's security was less than it otherwise would have been seems intuitively right; but another route to the conclusion which was ventilated in the case and which would fit squarely within the traditional account-based approach to substitutive compensation would be to treat the payment away of the funds in their client account as being a misapplication only to the extent of the £300,000 that should have been paid to the prior lender rather than to the borrowers. That analysis had been favoured by the first instance judge but then rejected in the Court of Appeal, and it was not pressed further in the Supreme Court; but Lord Reed appears to have endorsed it, obiter: see [140].

[217] For what is meant by "misapplication" in the context of a company and its directors, see the useful definition cited by Nourse LJ in *Re Duckwari Plc* [1998] Ch. 253, at 262D; see also paras 11–183—11–188 of this work.

[218] For example, *Bairstow v Queens Moat Houses Plc* [2001] 2 B.C.L.C. 531, per Robert Walker LJ at [49]–[54]; *Re Loquitur* [2003] STC 1394, per Etherton J at [135]–[137]; and *In Re Paycheck Services 3 Ltd* [2010] 1 W.L.R. 2793, per Lord Hope at [46]–[49].

[219] Now s.190 of the Companies Act 2006.

[220] *Re Duckwari Plc* [1998] Ch. 253.

was not in the interests of the company, equitable compensation was available and the measure of it was simply the value of the property that had been misapplied.[221]

22–116 In *Madoff Securities International Ltd v Raven*,[222] Popplewell J (in obiter observations) synthesised the principles derived from these and other cases as being that in a claim against directors for the misapplication of company property in breach of their fiduciary duties, a distinction fell to be drawn between positive acts of misapplication, for which the remedy was the same as that for a breach of trust and required the restitution of the misapplied property or its equivalent value without reference to the question of what would have happened but for the breach; and omissions, for which the claimant would be entitled to compensation, but only to the extent that he could establish that, but for the omission, the loss would not have occurred.[223] This corresponded to the distinction between different adjustments to the fiduciary's account considered in para.22–102 above.

22–117 These cases all drew upon the analogy between misapplication by a director of company property and breach by a trustee of his trust; but if it is right, following *AIB Group*, that the liability of a trustee to pay compensation in equity for a payment away of trust property in breach of trust cannot extend to losses that would have occurred even but for their breach, then can it be right that the liability of a director for a "positive" misapplication of company property is as strict and blind to questions of causation as the above cases would appear to suggest?

22–118 It has been suggested that the better analysis is now as follows:

(1) Where the director or other fiduciary has himself received the principal's misapplied property, the remedy is restorative in the fullest sense; but that is because the property represents a profit in the fiduciary's hands made by reason of his position, which will be held on constructive trust and for which (if it is no longer in his hands) he will be accountable under the principles considered in section C above.

(2) Outside those circumstances, the director's or other fiduciary's liability to compensate in equity is a liability to compensate for the loss which the principal can prove to have been caused in a "but for" sense by the relevant breach.[224]

22–119 If the cases mentioned above which have held that a director's liability is to compensate in the full restorative measure are now to be followed, it must be on the basis that the nature and context of the duty breached (the duty being one of

---

[221] *Gwembe Valley Development Company Ltd v Koshy* [2003] EWCA Civ 1038, per Mummery LJ (with the concurrence of the rest of the Court) at [142].

[222] *Madoff Securities International Ltd v Raven* [2013] EWHC 3147 (Comm), at [292]–[293].

[223] See also *Bishopsgate Investment Management Ltd v Maxwell* [1993] BCC 120, per Hoffman LJ at 140 (rejecting the submission that the breach was in fact properly characterised as an omission); *Lexi Holdings Plc v Luqman (No.2)*, per Briggs J at [28].

[224] This is the view of the editors of P. Davies and S. Worthington, *Gower: Principles of Modern Company Law*, 10th edn (London: Sweet & Maxwell, 2016), at 16–112.

ongoing stewardship of a fund and the breach consisting in the payment)[225] requires a different answer to the "but for" causation question to that which is given where the trust is part of the machinery for the performance of a contract, as in *AIB Group*. As noted above, this accords with the recognition in *AIB Group* that, whilst the causation question is always important, it is sensitive to the nature and context of the duty.

(4)   Hindsight, Foreseeability and Remoteness

Whilst it would therefore now appear that some causal connection between breach and loss must always be shown for an award of equitable compensation, compensation in equity for breach of trust or fiduciary duty is in important respects more generous than that at common law by way of damages. The fact that the outcome in *AIB Group* coincided with what have been awarded in damages at common law should not obscure the important distinctions between the two remedies. In particular, in the case of equitable compensation, when identifying and quantifying the loss caused by the breach the Court is not concerned with what was reasonably foreseeable at the time of the breach or whether the loss was too remote. So a trustee or fiduciary is liable for all loss that flows directly and on a common sense basis from the breach, provided it would not have been incurred but for the breach, even if there is some other more immediate cause of the loss (such as the failure or dishonesty of a third party which the breach has permitted),[226] and even if it was unexpected.[227]

22–120

Moreover, and relatedly, the assessment of what loss flows from the breach is made as at the date of judgment, "with the full benefit of hindsight".[228] In putting the principal in the position in which he would have been but for the breach, therefore, the Court can (for example) take into account an increase in the value of an asset which has been misapplied, or which in breach of duty the fiduciary has failed to acquire for his benefit, since the date of the breach, as well as evidence coming to light since the breach of the price at which an asset could have been realised,[229] even if those matters could not reasonably have been foreseen.

22–121

In this respect claims for breach of trust and of fiduciary duty have more in common with claims in deceit that claims in contract or negligence. The justification for this approach is that the underpinning of the fiduciary relationship is trust, rather then self-interest, and a breach of trust or fiduciary duty is a wrong in itself, not one judged with reference to its foreseeable

22–122

---

[225] See *Bishopsgate Investment Management Ltd v Maxwell*, above, at 140G.

[226] *Caffrey v Darby* (1801) 6 Ves 488; but not so where the third party's intervention was not itself caused or permitted by the fiduciary's breach: *Canson Enterprises Ltd v Boughton & Co* [1991] 3 SCR 534. The distinction was endorsed by Lord Reed in *AIB Group*, at [135].

[227] *Target Holdings Ltd v Redferns* [1996] 1 A.C. 421, at 434, per Lord Browne-Wilkinson.

[228] *Canson Enterprises Ltd v Boughton & Co* [1991] 3 SCR 534, at 556; *Target Holdings Ltd v Redferns*, above, at 439.

[229] As happened in *Libertarian Investments v Hall*, above.

consequences.[230] Another consideration is the difficulty that is often attendant on detecting breaches where the conduct of a principal's affairs or stewardship of his property is entrusted to another.[231]

22–123 It follows also that it will generally not be an answer to a claim for equitable compensation for breaches of the above sort to say that the claimant (in whose best interests the trustee or fiduciary is expected to act) has failed reasonably to mitigate his loss, unless his failure to mitigate is so egregious that it can be said that he is the author of his own misfortune.[232]

(5) Equitable Compensation and the "Core" Fiduciary Dealing Rules

22–124 Outside the cases of misapplication of, or direct loss to, trust or company property which have been considered above, it would seem to be reasonably well-established that where a fiduciary dishonestly or deliberately fails to disclose a personal and potentially conflicting interest in a transaction to which his principal is party, the remedy of equitable compensation is available.[233] What is more controversial (although in the context of a work on fraud, less relevant) is whether equitable compensation is available where the fiduciary has infringed the rules against conflicts and profits without any want of good faith on his part.[234]

22–125 Either way, it is clear that for relief by way of equitable compensation (rather than rescission or an account of profits) to lie for breach of the fiduciary dealing rules, the principal must show that the breach has caused it a loss. For these purposes, the relevant question is what would have happened had the material facts (namely the existence of the potentially conflicting interest) been disclosed.[235] Where the probabilities are that the principal would have acted the same way even had full disclosure been made, no claim for equitable compensation will lie. Of course, that consideration is not a reason for denying relief by way of rescission or an account of profits.

22–126 One such case was *Canson Enterprises Ltd v Boughton & Co*,[236] a Canadian case in which McLachlin J gave a judgment (agreeing in the result but in a minority on the reasoning) which was cited with approval by both Lord Browne-Wilkinson in *Target Holdings* and Lord Reed in *AIB Group*. There developers of land sued

---

[230] *Canson Enterprises Ltd v Boughton & Co* [1991] 3 SCR 534, at 552–553, cited in *AIB Group* by Lord Reed JSC, at [86].

[231] *Libertarian Investments v Hall* [2014] 1 H.K.C. 368 (CFA), per Ribeiro PJ at [80].

[232] *Canson Enterprises Ltd v Boughton & Co*, above, at 554, quoted with approval in *Corporacion Nacional Del Cobre de Chile v Sogemin Metals Ltd* [1997] 1 W.L.R. 1396, at 1403, and in *AIB Group*, per Lord Reed at [87] (who commented that this might be regarded as simply following from the requirement of a direct causal connection to the breach).

[233] *Gwembe Valley Development Company v Koshy* [2003] EWCA Civ 1038, at [142]–[143].

[234] For a consideration of this question, see M. Conaglen, "Equitable Compensation for Breach of the Fiduciary Dealing Rules", 2003 L.Q.R. 246. The Court of Appeal decision in *Swindle v Harrison* [1997] 4 All E.R. 704 would appear to support the availability of the remedy in these circumstances too.

[235] *Gwembe Valley Development Company v Koshy* [2003] EWCA Civ.1038, at [144]–[147].

[236] *Canson Enterprises Ltd v Boughton & Co* (1991) 85 D.L.R. (4th) 129.

their lawyers who acted on the purchase of the land for failing to disclose a material fact of which the lawyers were aware, namely that a third party was making a secret profit from the purchase. They sought to recover losses incurred on the development, on the basis that they would not have proceeded with the purchase had the secret profit been disclosed. McLachlin J held that, whilst equitable compensation was not simply an equitable analogue of tortious or contractual damages and was in important respects governed by different principles (including the use of hindsight and the irrelevance of foreseeability), it was nevertheless limited to loss flowing on a common sense view from the fiduciary's acts in relation to the interest he undertook to protect.[237] McLachlin J therefore agreed that relief was precluded on the facts of the case; but it was by application of these equitable principles rather than those applicable to a damages claim at common law.

(6) Equitable Duty of Care: Common Law Principles Apply

The exception to the above principles would appear to be a claim for breach of the equitable duty of skill and care, where the prevailing view (albeit one which has been doubted in some academic writing) is that compensation is awarded on principles analogous to those in contract and tort.[238] That is because "the fiduciary relationship…merely provides a setting for a duty which is indistinguishable from a common law duty of care".[239]   **22–127**

The same should be true of breaches of the corresponding statutory duties of care owed by trustees and directors.

(7) Difficulties in Assessment

It is always open in a case of breach of trust or fiduciary duty for the Court to direct the formal taking of an account in order to establish the factual material necessary to quantify the loss which the defendant is to compensate. However, in cases where the difficulties in assessment result from the defendant's own failure properly to account for his stewardship of the trust or his principal's property and to provide disclosure, an account may well prove a costly and ultimately unproductive diversion. In such circumstances the Court can instead adopt a robust approach, resolving doubtful questions against the party whose actions have made an accurate determination of quantum problematic and placing the evidential burden on that party to establish that (where there is evidence that loss has been caused by the breach) that loss would have been suffered in any event.[240] The fiduciary's own falsehoods can be treated as being true, if that   **22–128**

---

[237] Ibid., p.160.
[238] *Bristol and West Building Society v Mothew* [1998] Ch. 1, per Millett LJ at 16.
[239] *Libertarian Investments v Hall* [2014] 1 H.K.C. 868 (CFA), at [77].
[240] *Houghton v Immer* [1997] 44 N.S.W.L.R. 46.

favours the principal; and, as when determining the profits for which a fiduciary is accountable, the Court will strive to do "rough and ready" justice without requiring any degree of precision.[241]

22–129   So in *Libertarian Investments v Hall*,[242] the defendant was entrusted with funds paid into a trust account for the sole purpose of purchasing certain shares to be held beneficially for the claimant. The defendant misled the claimant into believing that the funds had been used for that purpose when in fact they had been misappropriated for the defendant's own purposes. The claimant sought equitable compensation in an amount representing what it contended it would have received had the funds been correctly applied in purchasing the shares and had the shares then been realised. It was held that merely ordering the defendant to restore the monies extracted from the trust account would not adequately reflect the loss suffered: the claimant was entitled to compensation on the footing of wilful default. While the exercise of assessing that compensation would inevitably be hypothetical, and while the evidence before the court as to what (if any) shares had in fact been acquired, and at what price and when they could have been realised, was far from satisfactory, the techniques mentioned above enabled the court to reach a figure without having to go through the process of an account. The court could treat the defendant as having acquired all of the shares he should have acquired (and so treat his lie to that effect as true) and as having sold a portion on pursuant to a particular offer of which there was evidence; and, as to the balance, it could compensate the claimant at their market price at the date of judgment. This approach effectively put the burden on the defendant to prove that profit in some smaller amount would have been achieved, and so visited on him the consequences of there being gaps in the evidence before the court.[243]

(8)   Interest

22–130   We have already referred to the equitable jurisdiction to award compound interest, where available as an alternative to an account of profits made by a defaulting fiduciary. Where equitable compensation is awarded with reference to the amounts which (with the benefit of hindsight) it is found that the trust or principal would have had but for the breach, it would usually be double-counting and punitive for the award of compensation to carry interest on a compound basis.[244]

---

[241] *Libertarian Investments v Hall* [2014] 1 H.K.C. 386 (CFA) , per Lord Millett NPJ at [174].
[242] *Libertarian Investments v Hall*, above.
[243] *Libertarian Investments v Hall*, above, at [123]–[139].
[244] *Libertarian Investments v Hall*, above, at [141]–[142].

(9) Equitable Compensation and Dishonest Assistance/Knowing Receipt

We have noted above that when an account of profits is sought against a dishonest assister, the Court will apply common law concepts of causation and remoteness when considering the necessary causal connection between the breach assisted and the profit. The same is true when a claimant seeks equitable compensation from the dishonest assister for losses caused by the underlying breach.[245] But it is important to bear in mind that the relevant causal connection for these purposes is between the breach of trust or fiduciary duty in which assistance is given and the loss, and not between the assistance itself and the loss.[246]

22–131

Where equitable compensation is sought against a knowing recipient of assets transferred in breach of trust or fiduciary duty, questions of causation and remoteness may be less likely to arise, since in the usual case the measure of the loss will simply be the value of the misappropriated assets which the defendant received (net of any recoveries). Difficult issues can arise where the assets have depreciated in value before judgment: thus in the Hong Kong case of *Thanakharn Kasikorn Thai Chamkat (Mahachon) v Akai Holdings Ltd*[247] the defendant recipient of shares pledged in breach of fiduciary duty was held not to be liable to compensate the claimant for the full value of the shares as at the date when they were originally pledged, but rather for the lower value obtained when they were subsequently sold. Equitable compensation was limited to losses which "*on a common sense view of causation were caused by the breach*",[248] and the initial fall in value did not meet this requirement, since it had been open to the claimant to seek to recover the shares before their sale and it was apparent that, if the claimant had recovered the shares earlier, it would have retained them.[249]

22–132

E. FORFEITURE OF REMUNERATION

(1) Introduction

It is axiomatic that an agent or other fiduciary cannot serve two masters, allow his own interests to conflict (or risk conflicting) with those of his principal, or profit from his position, without the fully informed consent of his principal. Where an agent does, he can forfeit his right to remuneration or commission. This is a principle of long-standing, but it was considered and reaffirmed by the Court of Appeal in *Imageview Management Ltd v Jack*.[250]

22–133

---

[245] *Novoship (UK) Limted v Mikhaylyuk* [2015] Q.B. 499, at [107].

[246] *Grupo Torras SA v Al-Sabah* [2001] C.L.C. 221, at [119]; *Casio Computer Co Ltd v Sayo* [2001] I.L.Pr. 694, at [16]. See further paras 13–025—13–029.

[247] *Thanakharn Kasikorn Thai Chamkat (Mahachon) v Akai Holdings Ltd (In Liquidation)* [2010] HKCU 2362; [2010] HKCFA 63. See further paras 12–007—12–009.

[248] *Thanakharn Kasikorn Thai Chamkat (Mahachon) v Akai Holdings Ltd*, above, at [152].

[249] *Thanakharn Kasikorn Thai Chamkat (Mahachon) v Akai Holdings Ltd*, above, at [148]–[155].

[250] *Imageview Management Ltd v Jack* [20009] EWCA Civ 63; [2009] Bus L.R. 1034.

(2)   The Basis for and Scope of the Remedy

22–134   The basis for the relief is that the principal is entitled to expect disinterested loyalty from his agent and the agent's remuneration is only to be earned through good faith performance of his duties for the principal's benefit: "A principal is entitled to have an honest agent, and it is only the honest agent who is entitled to commission".[251] The remedy serves the same policy purpose of deterrence that we have seen underlies other aspects of relief against fiduciaries.[252] It thus applies even where the principal has benefited from the agent's services; and there is no inconsistency between awarding the principal both damages and a refund of any commission paid (or denying recovery of a commission ostensibly payable), since one compensates the principal for his loss and the other simply reflects the fact that the agent has no entitlement to the commission.[253]

22–135   The principle will certainly be engaged where an agent has acted dishonestly, or has received a bribe or secret commission from a third party.[254] It would also appear to be applicable where there have been other breaches of the core fiduciary obligations of loyalty, even if they do not involve moral turpitude, at least where there is some connection between the unfaithfulness and the duty for the discharge of which the commission is payable.[255] But it has been said not to apply where the breach is one of "harmless collaterality" (that is, which "does not go to the whole contract") or is simply an honest breach of contract, not involving a conflict of interest.[256] The relief is also discretionary and can be refused where it would be disproportionate and inequitable.[257] And where the transactions in which the fiduciary is engaged are severable, forfeiture may be limited to the fees payable in connection with the transaction in which the fiduciary breached his duty.[258]

---

[251] *Andrews v Ramsay* [1903] 2 K.B. 635, per Lord Alverstone CJ at 636. In that case an estate agent engaged by a vendor of property to find a purchaser received a commission of £50 out of the price with the vendor's consent; but he also took an undisclosed commission of £20 from the purchaser. When that second commission was discovered, the agent paid it over to his principal; but that did not prevent him then being successfully sued by the principal for the return of the £50. See also *Stevens v Premium Real Estate Ltd* [2009] 2 N.Z.L.R. 384, at [90].

[252] *Imageview Management Ltd v Jack*, above, at [50].

[253] *Stevens v Premium Real Estate Ltd* [2009] 2 N.Z.L.R. 384.

[254] *Rhodes v Macalister* (1923) 29 Com. Cas. 19; *Imageview Management Ltd v Jack*, above.

[255] *Hippisley v Knee Bros.* [1905] 1 K.B. 1. See also *Imageview Management Ltd v Jack*, above, at [44]: "Once a conflict of interest is shown…the right to remuneration goes."

[256] *Keppel v Wheeler* [1925] 1 K.B. 577 (estate agents who, in good faith and genuinely but wrongly believing that their duty to their principal was at an end, failed to pass on a better offer for the principal's property); *Imageview Management Ltd v Jack*, above, at [44].

[257] As was the case in *Bank of Ireland v Jaffery* [2012] EWHC 1377 (Ch), in which an employee's breaches of fiduciary duty were held to be reasonably isolated incidents in the context of what was otherwise years of hard work and good service, such that forfeiture of his salary and bonuses would be disproportionate. Contrast *Avrahami v Biran* [2013] EWHC 1776 (Ch), where the misfeasance of the defaulting fiduciary in a joint venture was so pervasive that his right to fees was forfeited, even though the relationship was a long-term one.

[258] See *FHR European Ventures LLP v Makarious* [2011] EWHC 2308 (Ch): a secret commission received by an agent on one hotel project did not defeat his entitlement to fees from his principal in respect of other hotel projects.

Forfeiture is also available with respect to the profit share of a partner, where it in **22–136** substance represents a form of remuneration for services.[259] The fact that it may be payable under the terms of a partnership agreement which makes no reference to forfeiture is not to the point, since it is inherent in the principle that it can override contractual entitlements (although the principle can probably be excluded by express agreement).

---

[259] *Hosking v Marathon Asset Management LLP* [2017] Ch. 157.

CHAPTER 23

EQUITABLE PROPRIETARY CLAIMS

A. INTRODUCTION

In Ch.9 we addressed the question of how an equitable proprietary interest in property held on trust (be it express, resulting or constructive) can be established. In this chapter we address the question of how one goes about vindicating such an interest (and also other interests which are for these purposes treated analogously, even though not strictly arising under trusts) by means of an equitable proprietary claim. In particular, we focus on two questions:

23–001

(1) First, how one identifies the specific property that is subject to the trust (or otherwise amenable to an equitable proprietary claim); and
(2) Secondly, how one pursues, and defends, an equitable proprietary claim.

These questions arise frequently in fraud litigation. As we have seen elsewhere in this book the dishonest or dishonestly procured transfer of assets held on trust, or in circumstances giving rise to a trust, is a very common factual backdrop to many claims brought before the English courts. In such claims the fact of the fraud is often obvious and the real difficulty lies in the claimant's attempts to seek recovery of those assets, or their substitutes, from either the primary wrongdoer or third parties, be they accomplices or innocent recipients of the proceeds of the misappropriation.

23–002

Being able to make an equitable proprietary claim will be a matter of considerable importance to a claimant in a fraud claim (and resisting one will correspondingly be of importance to a defendant), for a number of reasons. For example:

23–003

(1) If party B is insolvent, then party A (assuming the proprietary claim is made out) will prima facie still be entitled to recover the relevant property and will not see its entitlements reduced pari passu in line with unsecured creditors;
(2) If the relevant property has risen in value, then party A (again, assuming the proprietary claim is made out) will prima facie be able to take the benefit of that increase;
(3) A proprietary claim may be carried (by means of the tracing rules) through to subsequent recipients of the relevant property, widening the field of potential defendants;

(4) The Court applies a less onerous test for the grant of an interim injunction to prevent the dissipation of alleged trust property than it does for the grant of non-proprietary freezing injunction granted in support of purely personal claims (see Ch.28);

(5) An interim injunction granted to prevent the dissipation of alleged trust property will generally be subject to stricter terms in respect of the payment of legal and living expenses from the injuncted property than a freezing injunction granted in support of purely personal claims (see, again, Ch.28); and

(6) In some other interim procedural contexts, it seems that the Court will also be readier to give assistance to a claimant seeking to recover alleged trust property than a claimant pursuing a purely personal claim, as (for example) in the context of the *Bankers Trust* jurisdiction to order the production of information by third parties (see Ch.29).

23–004 This chapter is structured as follows:

(1) Section B considers whether specific property is (or was) subject to the relevant trust, or otherwise amenable to an equitable proprietary claim, by reference to the law of:
    (i) the rules of "following and tracing"; and
    (ii) priorities of equitable interests;

(2) Section C considers how an equitable proprietary claim is to be pursued, examining:
    (i) the nature of the claim;
    (ii) available defences; and
    (iii) remedies.

B. WHAT PROPERTY IS SUBJECT TO THE CLAIM?

(1) Introduction

23–005 Once it is established that a trust (or relevantly similar relationship) exists in respect of specific property, a question may arise as to whether the beneficiary (or quasi-beneficiary) is in fact able to assert his beneficial ownership of other property (or, in some circumstances, the same property) against the original trustee or a third party: in a fraud case the property may well have been passed to a third party, or used in part or in whole to acquire another asset. Approaching that question from both sides:

(1) The rules of *following and tracing* (paras 23–006—23–023 below) may in some circumstances allow the beneficiary to identify property in the hands of the original trustee or a third party as identical or analytically equivalent to the original trust property (and therefore subject to his claim to beneficial ownership); and

(2) Conversely, the rules of *priorities and loss of beneficial interest* (paras 23–025—23–033 below) may lead in some circumstances to a beneficiary's

claim to a beneficial interest in trust property (whether the original trust property or its traceable proceeds) being defeated by the claim of the legal owner or a third party with a rival interest in the property.

(2)   Following and Tracing

(i)   Nature of following and tracing

Although sometimes spoken of in those terms, "following and tracing" are not claims or remedies. They are artificial rules of evidence which allow property to be identified with other property as a matter of legal (or equitable) analysis.[1] Accordingly, the process of following or tracing may be a necessary step to establishing various different claims, whether proprietary (e.g. a claim for the return of the followed/traced property, or a claim to an equitable lien, or to subrogation) or personal (e.g. a personal claim for breach of trust, or for knowing receipt arising from a dealing with the followed/traced property).

23–006

"*Following*" refers to the process by which the same asset is identified as it is transferred from one person to another. So, to take a simple example, if D1 misappropriates a car which he holds on trust for C and then passes it to D2, C can follow the car into D2's hands and obtain a remedy against D2 requiring the return of the car. "*Tracing*" refers to the process by which a new asset is identified as a substitute for an original asset, so that the party with a claim to the original asset is entitled either to "*follow*" that original asset or to "*trace*" the value of the original asset into the substitute.[2] For obvious reasons, it is "tracing" which is generally the more practically significant and contentious of the two.

23–007

The orthodox view is that separate rules of "*following and tracing*" have evolved at equity and at common law (where they might, for example, support a common law proprietary claim for delivery up of goods or a common law personal claim for money had and received). The common law rules are less generous, in particular in that they do not permit money to be traced once it has become mixed with other money (so that, for example, misappropriated money cannot be traced once paid into a bank account with an existing positive balance or used to pay part only of the purchase price of an asset alongside money from a separate source).[3] That orthodoxy has been subject to criticism at the highest levels (with the view being expressed that following and tracing should be treated as a single analytical process, with the distinction between common law and equity relevant only to the claim in support of which that process is invoked)[4]; but it does not

23–008

---

[1] *Boscawen v Bajwa* [1996] 1 W.L.R. 328, at 334; *Foskett v McKeown* [2001] 1 A.C. 102, at 127–128, in which Lord Millett gave the classic description of tracing: "Tracing is thus neither a claim nor a remedy. It is merely the process by which a claimant demonstrates what has happened to his property, identifies its proceeds and the persons who have handled or received them, and justifies his claim that the proceeds can properly be regarded as representing his property."

[2] As it was simply put by Arden LJ in *Relfo Ltd v Varsani* [2014] EWCA Civ 360; [2015] 1 B.C.L.C. 14, at [1]: "Tracing is the process used to determine what has happened to a person's property".

[3] *Lipkin Gorman v Karpnale* [1991] 2 A.C. 548; *Trustee of the Property of FC Jones & Sons v Jones* [1997] Ch. 159.

[4] *Foskett v McKeown* [2001] 1 A.C. 102, at 113, per Lord Steyn, and at 128–129, per Lord Millett.

appear to have been overturned. In any event, as we are concerned in this chapter with trust property (and its analogues), we will not be concerned with the common law rules. But (as the following section illustrates) it is necessary to keep in mind that an equitable—as opposed to a common law—entitlement is required to access the rules of following and tracing in the form here described.

(ii)   Equitable title to follow or trace in equity

23–009   The traditional rule is that, in order to invoke the equitable (as opposed to the common law) rules of following and tracing, the claimant must have a distinct equitable title to the original property.[5] A claimant whose claim is based simply upon having been the absolute legal and beneficial owner of the original asset does not have a distinct equitable title[6] and, accordingly, is confined to the rules of tracing at common law.

23–010   That rule has an obvious potential to lead to unjust or perverse results: the full legal and beneficial owner of property, whose title would ordinarily be considered "better" than that of a mere beneficial owner, is confined to the common law rules of following and tracing, which are generally considered to be "worse". Like the distinction between common law and equitable tracing rules more generally, it has been criticised at the highest levels,[7] but does not appear (at least yet) to have been overturned.

23–011   It is perhaps for this reason that the court has been relatively generous in determining what constitutes a sufficient "distinct equitable title" for these purposes. A claimant who was a beneficiary under a pre-existing trust (or held any other form of purely equitable interest in the property) will plainly qualify. But so too will a claimant who had the benefit of a fiduciary relationship in relation to the original property before it was misapplied (for example a company which finds its assets misapplied by its directors)[8]; or the victim of a fraudulent misrepresentation with a right to rescind where that victim has been induced to transfer property by the deceit (at least in respect of further transfers of the property undertaken by the transferee following the rescission).[9] More generally, the concern to find a sufficient "distinct equitable title" to trace in equity may be seen to underlie many of the categories of constructive trusts arising on impugnable transactions which are considered in Ch.9. The practical reality is that the vast majority of claimants in fraud claims will be able to invoke the equitable rules of following and tracing by resort to the expansive approach to their field of application which has been adopted by the courts.

---

[5] *Re Diplock* [1948] Ch. 465, at 520 to 521.
[6] *Vandervell v IRC* [1967] 2 A.C. 291, at 311 and 317; *Westdeutsche Landesbank Girozentrale v Islington LBC* [1996] A.C. 669, at 706, per Lord Browne Wilkinson.
[7] At *Bristol & West Building Society v Mothew* [1998] Ch. 1, at 23, per Millett LJ, *Foskett v McKeown* [2001] 1 A.C. 102, at 113, per Lord Steyn, and at 128–129, per Lord Millett.
[8] *Re Diplock* [1948] Ch. 465, at 530. See *Agip (Africa) Ltd v Jackson* [1990] Ch. 265, at 290; [1991] Ch. 547, at 566.
[9] *El Ajou v Dollar Land* [1993] 3 All E.R. 717, at 734; and see generally the treatment of the constructive trust arising on such rescission in Ch.9. See also Ch.22.

(iii) Need for the property still to be subject to the trust or equitable interest

The property must still be subject to the trust or other equitable interest to be capable of being followed or traced. Hence, if property is paid away in a manner consistent with the terms of the trust or other interest subject to which it is held, then naturally the beneficiaries cease to have any entitlement to it (see para.23–026 below).   **23–012**

Equally, if a recipient of the property acquires a right in it which has priority over that of the party seeking to follow or trace (see B(3) below), then it will not be possible to follow or trace any further (although in some cases it may be more accurate to speak of the party who is seeking to trace having lost priority than having lost their interest in the property altogether).   **23–013**

(iv) Identification of property by following and tracing

In order to follow or to trace, it is necessary to show that the asset which is the "target" of the exercise is either (when simply following) the same as the original property or (when tracing) the product of a series of transactions at each stage of which it can be considered a substitute for the value of the original property. It may be possible, where there is insufficient direct evidence of the relevant transactions, to show this by inference from the evidence which is available. So in *Relfo Ltd v Varsani* a dishonest director wrongfully caused a payment to be made from the claimant company to company X. Shortly thereafter a payment in virtually the same amount was made by company Y to the defendant. The Court was willing to infer that the monies had somehow passed from company X to Y so that the claimant could show that the monies received by the defendant represented the traceable proceeds of the original misappropriation.[10] Equally, the party seeking to trace may receive assistance from certain assumptions which arise in relation to payments out of mixed funds (see para.23–018 below) or from the developing jurisprudence as to what may constitute a relevant "substitution" for these purposes (see para.23–020 below). But tracing remains a matter of property rights, rather than of discretion[11]; it requires the "target" asset to be properly treated as having derived from the original asset by the application of the relevant rules (with the benefit of any available inferences and assumptions) and it does not result in the imposition of a general charge over un-related assets of a wrongdoer (or relevant third party).[12]   **23–014**

Clean Swaps. When the original property is swapped directly for another asset, the right either to follow the original asset or to trace into the new asset is straightforward. Thus, to illustrate the position by way of two examples: **23–015**

(1) Where the original property (or its traceable proceeds) consists of physical cash and is paid into a bank account with a zero balance, the physical cash:

---

[10] *Relfo Ltd v Varsani* [2014] EWCA Civ 360, at [56]–[59], per Arden LJ.
[11] *Re Montagu's Settlement Trust* [1987] Ch. 264, at 285B per Megarry J.
[12] *Director of Serious Fraud Office v Lexi Holdings*, above, at [49]–[50].

(a) could in theory be followed into the hands of the bank, although in practice it will cease to be identifiable and, in any event, the rules of priority addressed below will almost always allow the bank to take free as a bona fide purchaser for value of the legal estate without notice (because it has received the money in return for a debt obligation represented by the account balance) or (b) can, more practically, be traced into the asset represented by the new balance of the account (which is, strictly speaking, a chose in action against the bank belonging to the account holder); or

(2) Where the original property (or its traceable proceeds) consists of the balance of a bank account in the name of A and a transfer is made to an account in the name of B with a zero balance in order to pay the whole of the purchase price of some form of property acquired in the name of A (or of a third party C), then the asset represented by the balance of A's account may (a) be traced into the asset represented by the balance of B's account, although B may well be able to take free as a bona fide purchaser for value of the legal estate without notice, or (b) be traced into the real or personal property which has been purchased in the name of A or C.

23–016   **Mixtures.**   The position becomes more complex where property (whether the original property or its traceable proceeds) is swapped for only part of a new asset, with the remainder of the consideration coming from elsewhere, so that a "mixture" occurs. Most commonly this will occur where trust property (or its traceable proceeds) takes the form of money and is paid into a bank account which contains, or comes to contain, money from other sources. It also frequently occurs where trust property (or traceable proceeds) is used to contribute part of the purchase price of a new asset. In both such cases, it is now relatively well established that the general principles set out in the following paragraphs will apply.[13]

23–017   The position will differ depending upon on whether the mixture is with property belonging to another innocent contributor or to a "wrongdoer", a category which includes (for these purposes) not only the original defaulting trustee/fiduciary but also (i) someone who has acquired the relevant property with "notice" (see para.23–029 below) and (ii) someone who has innocently but gratuitously received the relevant property from a wrongdoer, because such a person derives title from the original wrongdoer and can be in no better position than he.[14]

23–018   Where property (either representing the original property or its traceable proceeds) has been mixed with the wrongdoer's own property, a set of presumptions are made with the purpose (insofar as possible) of preserving the value of the original property at the expense of the wrongdoer. The presumptions operate as follows:

---

[13] In the rarer situation where there is a physical mixture of tangible trust property with other tangible property (for example two sets of fungibles placed in the same container or two sets of raw materials combined in manufacturing a finished product) the position is unclear: it may well be that similar principles would apply, but it may be that equity would in some instances follow the common law rules applicable to such mixtures. See the general discussion in L. Tucker, N. Le Poidevin and J. Brightwell, *Lewin on Trusts*, 19th edn (London: Sweet & Maxwell, 2017), paras 41–092—41–095.

[14] *Foskett v McKeown*, above; *Clark v Cutland* [2003] EWCA Civ 810; [2004] 1 W.L.R. 783.

(1)   The mixed property is presumed to belong to the claimant owner of the original property to the extent that the wrongdoer cannot prove that it is his own.[15] Where there have been no subsequent withdrawals or losses from the mixture, this may be done easily enough by looking at the proportions in which contributions were made.

(2)   Where property is withdrawn from the mixture and dissipated, it is presumed that the withdrawal was derived from the wrongdoer's share (because he cannot be heard to say that he has chosen to dissipate the innocent party's money rather than his own).[16] In applying that presumption, the innocent party is entitled to the benefit of hindsight.

(3)   Conversely where a withdrawal is successfully invested while the residue is dissipated, it is presumed that the innocent party's money can be traced into the withdrawal.[17] Again, the innocent party is entitled to the benefit of hindsight. The presumption only operates, however, where the residue is dissipated; where the wrongdoer has retained in a bank account an amount equal to the original trust fund, the tracing party is seemingly not permitted to trace into withdrawals which have resulted in profitable investments unless it can be shown that they must have been made using trust money.[18]

(4)   It is important, however, to understand that those assumptions do not detract from the need for the property into which it is sought to trace to be capable of being properly characterised as the product of a substitution of the original property. As has been said, tracing is a matter of property rights, not of discretion[19]; it does not result in the imposition of a general charge over the wrongdoer's un-related property[20]; and there is no general presumption that subsequent credits by a wrongdoer into a mixed account from his own money are to be treated as "topping-up" the depleted fund.[21] The extent to which it is possible in some circumstances to trace "*backwards*" or through an overdraft (which is, in a sense, obviously a liability rather than an asset) is addressed further at para.23–020 below.

Where the money subject to the equitable claim is mixed with the money of another innocent claimant (and the equities are equal, i.e. neither claimant being treated as a wrongdoer under the principles set out above, or having a worse position under the priority rules considered below), then: **23–019**

---

[15] *El Ajou v Dollar Land* [1993] 3 All E.R. 717, at 735–736; *Re Tilley's Will Trust* [1967] 1 Ch. 1179, at 1183; *Brinks Ltd v Abu-Saleh* [1995] 1 W.L.R. 1478; *Indian Oil Shipping Ltd v Greenstone Shipping SA* [1988] Q.B. 345; *Foskett v McKeown*, above, at 132–133; *Glencore International AG v Metro Trading International Inc* [2001] 2 All E.R. (Comm) 103; *OJSC Oil Co Yugraneft v Abramovich* [2008] EWHC 2613 (Comm), at [349]; *Sinclair Investments (UK) Ltd v Versailles Trade Finance Group* [2011] EWCA Civ 347; [2012] Ch. 543, at [138] (unaffected on this point by the adverse treatment of other parts of that authority by the Supreme Court in *FHR European Ventures v Cedar Capital LLC* [2014] UKSC 45).

[16] *Re Hallett* (1879) 13 Ch. D. 696, at 726 and following.

[17] *Re Oatway* [1903] 2 Ch. 356.

[18] *Turner v Jacobs* [2006] EWHC 1317 (Ch); [2008] W.T.L.R. 307, at [102].

[19] *Re Montagu's Settlement Trust* [1987] Ch. 264, at 285B per Megarry J.

[20] *Director of Serious Fraud Office v Lexi Holdings* [2009] Q.B. 379, at [49]–[50].

[21] *Roscoe v Winder* [1915] 1 Ch. 62; *Bishopsgate v Homan* [1995] 1 All E.R. 347.

(1) None of the contributories are in principle liable to have their interests subordinated to those of any other.[22]

(2) Where the mixture is of money in a bank account, the presumption known as the "rule in *Clayton's Case*" has traditionally been applied to allocate the contents of the account on the basis that each withdrawal from the account is to be treated as having derived from the funds which have been in the account for longest, without paying regard to whether that withdrawal resulted in a dissipation or a successful investment. That rule is sometimes summarised by the phrase "first in, first out". It will be obvious that an application of that rule may have extremely arbitrary consequences and may (in the case where there has been a lot of activity on the relevant account) be extremely complex to apply.

(3) Accordingly, the trend of recent authority has been to treat the rule in *Clayton's case*[23] as a presumption which may be easily displaced either (i) if it is contrary to the actual or presumed intentions of the various innocent parties who have contributed to the fund or (ii) simply if it would be unjust or impractical to apply.[24]

Where the rule in *Clayton's case* is displaced, the court may instead treat the mixed fund as subject to a "rolling charge" in favour of each innocent contributor so that each withdrawal is attributed to each contributor to the fund pro rata to the proportion of the fund properly attributed to them as at the point of the withdrawal (an approach which has been described as fairest in principle but impractical to apply in many cases) or simply treat all withdrawals as borne rateably by all contributors to the account during the relevant period without any adjustment for the order of contributions/withdrawals (a rough and ready approach which is perhaps hard to support as a matter of principle but has the merit of simplicity).

23–020 **"Backward Tracing", The Lowest Intermediate Balance and Overdrafts.** Given that tracing is an analytical process of identification of property with other property for which it has been substituted (rather than a matter of discretionary justice or the imposition of some sort of general ambulatory charge over the assets of a wrongdoer),[25] it has long been a controversial question whether it is possible in any circumstances to trace into an asset which (even applying the various presumptions set out above) cannot have been contributed to directly from the original property or its traceable proceeds. Traditionally, the better view appeared to be that it was not, with the result that: (i) it was not possible to trace *backwards* into an asset which had been acquired before the traceable property was received, (ii) a tracing party seeking to trace through a bank account was confined to the *lowest intermediate balance* of the account between the date on

---

[22] *Foskett v McKeown*, at 132.

[23] *Clayton's case* (1816) 1 Mer 572.

[24] *Barlow Clowes v Vaughan* [1992] 4 All E.R. 22, at 32, 35, 39 and 46; *El Ajou v Dollar Land Holdings* [1995] 2 All E.R. 213, at 219, 222; *Russell-Cooke v Prentis* [2002] EWHC 2227 (Ch) [2003] 2 All E.R. 478, at [55]; *Commerzbank Aktiengesellschaft v IMB Morgan* [2004] EWHC 2771 (Ch), at [46]–[50]; and *Re Ahmed & Co* [2006] EWHC 480 (Ch), at [131]–[138].

[25] See above.

which his funds were credited to an account and the date on which the account-holder topped up the account which his own funds, and (iii) it was impossible to trace through an overdrawn bank account.[26]

But while that traditional view may still accurately state the general rule, recent authority has made clear that there are substantial exceptions. The Court of Appeal has held in *Relfo Ltd v Varsani*[27] that *backward* tracing is possible where in all the circumstances it is possible to infer that there has in fact been a substitution of the value of the traceable property into the previously acquired asset, as in that case where the person using his own funds to acquire that asset "acted on the basis that he would receive reimbursement of the monies he transferred out of the trust funds".[28] Equally, the Privy Council has held in *Brazil v Durant International Corp*[29] that *backward* tracing and tracing through an overdrawn account (and, presumably also therefore, tracing in an amount higher than the *lowest intermediate balance*) may be permitted where the claimant can:

"establish a co-ordination between the depletion of the trust fund and the acquisition of the asset which is the subject of the tracing claim, looking at the whole transaction such as to warrant the court attributing the value of the interest acquired to the misuse of the trust fund."

As to how that test is to be applied in practice, Lord Toulson (giving his opinion of the board) said that: This is likely to depend on inference from the proved fact, particularly since in many cases the testimony of the trustee, if available, will be of little value

Contributions and Improvements to Pre-acquired Assets.   A situation may arise where trust or similarly held property (or its traceable proceeds) is (mis-)applied to maintain, improve or contribute to an asset which was acquired before the use of that property was in mind (and therefore seemingly outside the sort of situation envisaged in *Relfo* or in *Durant*). The ability to trace in such a   **23–021**

---

[26] *Roscoe v Winder* [1915] 1 Ch. 62; *El Ajou v Dollar Land* [1993] 3 All E.R. 717, at 735–736; *Bishopsgate Investment v Homan* [1995] 1 All E.R. 347; *Re Goldcorp Exchange* [1995] 1 A.C. 74 (PC), *Foskett v McKeown* [1998] Ch. 265 (obiter per Hobhouse and Millett LJJ, with Scott VC expressing the contrary view).

[27] Relfo Ltd v Varsani [2014] EWCA Civ 360; [2015] 1 B.C.L.C. 14.

[28] So for instance it sometimes happens that a bank is directed by Y to make payment to X. The Bank makes the payment before it receives the monies from Y (which are the trust monies which the claimant is seeking to trace to X). There is no analytical difficulty here. Monies held on trust can be traced into other assets even if those other assets are passed on before the trust monies are paid to the person transferring them. See e.g. *Agip (Africa) Ltd v Jackson* [1990] 1 Ch. 265, 286, at 289–290. Similarly if D1 directs D2 to make payment to D3 of monies to be paid to D2 by D1, and D2 makes the payment in advance of receipt but on the basis that he is confident of reimbursement by D1, then C will be able to trace the asset into D3's hands. So it was said in *Relfo*, at [63]: "The decision in *Agip* demonstrates that in order to trace money into substitutes it is not necessary that the payments should occur in any particular order, let alone chronological order. As Mr Shaw submits, a person may agree to provide a substitute for a sum of money even before he receives that sum of money. In those circumstances the receipt would postdate the provision of the substitute. What the court has to do is establish whether the likelihood is that monies could have been paid at any relevant point in the chain in exchange for such a promise. I see no reason in logic or principle why this particular way of proving a substitution should be limited to payments to or by correspondent banks."

[29] *Brazil v Durant International Corp* [2015] UKPC 35; [2016] A.C. 297.

case may depend upon the nature of the asset and the nature of the contribution made with the trust funds. Much remains still to be established, but:

(1) In the case of life insurance policies, it is established that traceable trust property used to make periodic premium payments may be traced into the policy supported by such payments and then into the proceeds of the policy when it pays out.[30]

(2) In the case of mortgage payments (whether capital or interest) the position is unclear. Where the entire mortgage is discharged using traceable property, a subrogation claim my lie (see below). But where only certain payments are made, it is unclear whether the tracing party may trace such payments into the value of the mortgaged property.

(3) In the case of money spent on alterations or improvements to land and chattels, the position is again unclear. There is authority in Jersey to the effect that misappropriated trust property (or its proceeds) spent on improvements to land already owned by an innocent donee of the trust property should be capable of being traced into the resulting increase in value of the land.[31] There does not appear to be English authority to the same effect. Indeed, in one case of trust money paid wrongly to innocent recipients under the mistaken belief they were entitled to it as beneficiaries, it has been held that tracing into the land was impossible.[32] Other authorities yield conflicting dicta:

  (a) to the effect that the court could "treat the land as charged with the payment to the plaintiff of a sum representing the amount by which the value of the defendant's land has been enhanced by the use of the plaintiff's money",[33]

  (b) to the effect that (at least in the case where the land is owned by an innocent donee of the trust property) "money expended ... gives rise, at the most, to a proprietary lien to recover the monies so expended [and] in certain cases the rules of tracing in such a case may give rise to no proprietary interest at all if to give such interest would be unfair",[34] or

  (c) to the effect that "if a trustee used trust money to maintain or improve his house, the beneficiaries would ... be entitled to a charge on the house to recover their money [but] unless it appeared that the improvements had increased the value of the house there would be no basis for a claim to a pro rata share of the house and no reason for the imposition of a constructive trust".[35]

---

[30] *Foskett v McKeown*, above.

[31] *Re Eastern Settlement* [2002] J.L.R. 53, at [215]–[217].

[32] *Re Diplock*, above, at 545–548. See also *Shalson v Russo*, above, at [153]–[157] where it was held impossible to trace the proceeds of misappropriated trust property into a yacht belonging to a third party which had been partly constructed using that property, on the grounds that the defaulting fiduciary who had so applied the property would himself have been unable to assert any such interest as against the third party. *Sed quaere*.

[33] *Boscawen v Bajwa*, above, at 335, per Millett LJ.

[34] *Foskett v McKeown*, above, at 109, per Lord Browne-Wilkinson (citing *Re Diplock*, above).

[35] *Foskett v McKeown* [1998] Ch. 256, at 282, per Scott VC in the Court of Appeal, approved by Lord Steyn in the House of Lords (above) at 113–114.

(v) Bars to following or tracing

Where property is in principle capable of being followed or traced pursuant to the **23–022**
rules set out above, the ability to do so (or at least the ability to found any claim
upon the ability to do so) may in practice be barred:

(1)   Where the point is reached at which property (whether the original property
being "followed", or its substitute being "traced") is simply dissipated and
can no longer be identified at all. As addressed above, tracing is an
analytical process of identifying assets with other assets as a matter of
property law; or
(2)   Where the recipient of the property or its traceable proceeds takes priority
over the original beneficial owner under the priority rules addressed below
(for example as a bona fide purchaser for value of the legal estate without
notice).

"*Change of position*" is sometimes spoken of as a potential bar to following or **23–023**
tracing. The applicability of "change of position" in the following/tracing context
is highly contentious. As a matter of strict principle, it is probably better
considered as a potential defence to the substantive proprietary claim which may
follow a tracing exercise, rather than as a "bar" to the analytical process of
tracing. Accordingly it is addressed in this chapter at para.23–049 below.

(vi) Creation of fresh constructive trust as an alternative to following/tracing

In practical terms, it may be important to recall that in some circumstances the **23–024**
application of the rules set out in Ch.9 as to the creation of constructive trusts
may result in a new constructive trust being created (in particular under the "no
profit" rules) which is more favourable to the claimant than any remedy which
may be available upon tracing pre-existing trust property.[36]

(3) Loss of Beneficial Interest and Priorities

The fact that the beneficiaries under a trust are (subject to the terms of the trust **23–025**
and the rules of trust law) the equitable owners of the property or of its traceable
proceeds as against the trustee, does not necessarily mean that they are the
owners as against everyone with a claim on the property. The position is a fortiori
in the case of non-trust equitable interests. As in the case of legal interests in
property, there may be several competing equitable interests in property; and
there are rules to determine which takes priority.

---

[36] See Tucker, Le Poidevin and Brightwell, *Lewin on Trusts* (2017), paras 41–052—41–054.

(i) Proper dispositions

23–026 Naturally, if the trustee or other holder of property which is subject to equitable interests disposes of the property (whether by way of a sale to a third party or a distribution to a particular beneficiary) in a way which is proper within the terms of the trust or permissible under the terms governing the other equitable interest, then the beneficiaries will have no further right to that property.

(ii) Priority as between equitable interests

23–027 As between competing equitable interests, the rule is that *"where the equities are equal the first in time prevails"*.[37] The fact that the person acquiring the later equitable interest had no notice of the earlier interest, or gave value for his interest, is not per se enough to give him priority, although it may be relevant to an allegation that the equities are not *"equal"*.

(iii) The bona fide purchaser for value of the legal estate without notice

23–028 An equitable interest in property will be defeated by the transfer of the property to a bona fide purchaser for value of the legal estate without notice (a category of person sometimes referred to as "equity's darling").[38] Once such a transfer has taken place, any other person deriving title from that purchaser will be protected even if they would not themselves qualify under the rule (e.g. because they have notice of the trust), with the important exception of the original defaulting trustee or fiduciary.[39]

23–029 In order to take advantage of the rule, and to take free of the prior equitable interest, it must be demonstrated that the purchaser satisfied every element of the definition. For this purpose:

(1) It bears emphasis that the purchaser must have purchased "the legal estate" before he acquires notice of the prior claim. If he has purchased a merely equitable right, then the rule as to competing equitable interests will apply. The general rule is, however, subject to two significant exceptions. First, a purchaser who has had the legal title to the purchased property transferred into the name of a nominee or trustee to hold on bare trust for him (rather than having the purchased property transferred into his own name) is treated as a purchaser of the legal estate under the so called "better right to the legal estate" principle.[40] Second, a purchaser who does not have the legal estate at the relevant time may subsequently put himself into the

---

[37] *Macmillan Inc v Bishopsgate Investment Management (No.3)* [1995] 1 W.L.R. 978, at 999.

[38] *Macmillan v Bishopsgate (No.3)* above at 1000.

[39] See *Re Stapleford Colliery Co* (1880) 14 Ch. D. 432, at 445; *West London Commercial Bank v Reliance Buildings Society* (1885) 29 Ch. D. 954.

[40] *Macmillan v Bishopsgate (No.3)*, at 1001–1002. See *Thorndike v Hunt* (1859) De G & J 563; *Assaf v Fuwa* [1955] A.C. 215 and *McCarthy & Stone Ltd v Julian S Hodge & Co Ltd* [1971] 1 W.L.R. 1547 for more difficult cases.

position of a purchaser of the legal estate for these purposes if he gets in the legal estate, so long as he does so without any breach of trust of which he has notice; but the precise ambit of this second exception is difficult.[41]

(2) In relation to the requirement for a "purchaser for value", it is important to appreciate both:

    (a) that the "value" must be an executed consideration rather than an unfulfilled promise,[42] and

    (b) that although the "value" must be more than nominal, it need not be adequate.[43] Perhaps surprisingly, the satisfaction of an existing debt has been held to suffice in some older cases.[44]

(3) In relation to the requirement that the purchaser take "without notice" of the equitable interest, notice may consist of:

    (a) Actual notice, not necessarily including knowledge of equitable claims which are so doubtful that they can only be established by a decision of the Court[45] and not including knowledge derived from another trusteeship[46];

    (b) Constructive notice, where the purchaser "knows of certain facts which put him on inquiry as to the possible existence of the rights of [the holder of the prior equitable right] and he fails to make such inquiry or take such other steps as are reasonable to verify whether such earlier right does or does not exist"[47]; or

    (c) Imputed notice, where the purchaser's agent had actual or constructive notice which can be attributed to him.[48]

(4) In relation to the requirement of bona fides, it is said that this is necessary even where the absence of notice is proved,[49] although it is not immediately obvious in what circumstances the requirement would not be satisfied where there was no notice of the prior equitable interest.

---

[41] See discussion, for instance, in Tucker, Le Poidevin and Brightwell, *Lewin on Trusts* (2017), at 41–135 and following.

[42] *Taylor Barnard Ltd v Tozer* [1984] 1 E.G.L.R. 21.

[43] *Nurdin & Peacock v D B Ramsden* [1999] 1 E.G.L.R. 119. In *Grupo Torres v Al Sabah* [1999] C.L.C. 1469, at 1674 a company receiving money from its controller by way of an interest free loan was held not to have given value.

[44] *Thorndike v Hunt* (1859) 3 De G & J 563; *Taylor v Blakelock* (1886) 32 Ch. D. 560.

[45] *Carl Seiss Stiftung v Herbert Smith & Co* [1969] 2 Ch. 276; *Eagle Trust*, above, at 498–500; *Sinclair v Versailles*, above, at [102]–[108].

[46] Section 28 Trustee Act 1925.

[47] *Barclays Bank v O'Brien* [1994] 1 A.C. 180, at 195–196, per Lord Browne-Wilkinson, as applied in *Bishopsgate v Homan*, above, at 1000. In the application of that test, a body of technical rules apply in relation to transactions in land (see Tucker, Le Poidevin and Brightwell, *Lewin on Trusts* (2017), paras.41–127 and following). In relation to other transactions, the test is applied by asking what a reasonable person in the recipient's position would have understood or done, taking into account their past experience, any expert advice available and any routine procedures followed in transactions of the type in question: *Sinclair Investments v Versailles* [2011] EWCA Civ 347; [2012] Ch. 453, at [97]–[109]; *Credit Agricole Corp and Investment Bank v Papadimitrou* [2015] UKPC 13; [2015] 1 W.L.R. 4265. Until put on enquiry, he is entitled to assume that he is dealing with honest people: *Bishopsgate v Homan*, above, at 1014.

[48] See Ch.19 for a fuller discussion of the relevant rules of attribution.

[49] *Midland Bank Trust Co v Green* [1981] A.C. 513, at 528.

23–030 Where the transaction amounting to a bona fide purchase for value of the legal estate without notice is liable for some reason to be set aside, the defence continues to be available until the transaction is actually set aside.[50]

(iv) Overreaching

23–031 Under s.2 Law of Property Act 1925 (and related provisions in the Settled Land Act 1925), the interest of beneficiaries under a trust of land may, in the event of a sale by the trustees which complies with the statutory requirements, be transferred to the proceeds of sale in the hands of the trustees so that a purchaser in good faith for valuable consideration will take the property free of the trust regardless of whether or not he had notice. This process is known as "overreaching". The statutory requirements are detailed and reference should be made to specialist works in relation to land law. Importantly, the power to overreach may in general only be exercised by trustees of land if they consist of at least two individual trustees or a single trust corporation.[51] In various important respects (including the application of the section to dispositions in breach of trust, and also the meaning of "good faith" for these purposes), the effect of the rule remains unclear.

(v) Registration

23–032 The rules set out above are in some cases varied where a statutory system of registration has been overlaid (usually with a view to the protection of purchasers and, accordingly, a relaxation of the rules as to notice). The most prominent, although far from the only, examples are probably the Land Registration Act 2002 (in the case of interests in registered land) and the Companies Act 2006 (in the case of charges created by companies). Where the alleged trust property is of a kind which is subject to a statutory registration regime, reference must be made to that regime and the relevant specialist works.

(vi) Foreign law priority rules in respect of foreign situated property

23–033 It has been held that the fact that property has passed through the hands of several parties in civil law jurisdictions where the trust concept was not recognised did not prevent an English law tracing claim being pursued against a defendant who received the ultimate proceeds in England.[52] However, it has also been held (and approved at the highest level) that, where the property subject to the trust or other equitable interest is situated in a foreign jurisdiction, a transfer to a third party which has overriding effect under the law of that jurisdiction (even if it would not do so in English law) will be recognised in England as barring a claim against the

---

[50] *Independent Trustee Services Ltd v GP Noble Trustees Ltd*, above, at [114].

[51] Section 27 Law of Property Act 1925 and Sch.3, para.4(8). The position is different in the case of an overreaching transaction carried out by a tenant for life of settled land, a mortgagee or pursuant to a court order.

[52] *El Ajou v Dollar Land Holdings* [1993] BCC 698, at 715, per Millett J (reversed on other points at [1994] BCC 143).

transferee; and that this is so whether or not the relevant foreign law recognises the concept of a trust at all.[53] Naturally, whether or not it remains possible to pursue a tracing claim against the recipient, the original transferor may remain liable in respect of breach of trust if such a claim is open under the law governing the trust. A wider consideration of the conflict of laws rules which apply in the context of trusts and of tracing is beyond the scope of this chapter.

C. Pursuing Equitable Proprietary Claims

Where property is held on trust in accordance with the principles set out in Ch.9, or to be treated as if it were for these purposes (such as in the case of a company director or the holder of property conferred under a contract rescinded for fraud), one potential consequence is the pursuit of a proprietary claim by the beneficiary (or beneficiaries) against that property in the hands of the person holding it. The remainder of this chapter is concerned with such claims, examining in turn:

23–034

(1)   The nature of the proprietary claim;
(2)   Available defences; and
(3)   Remedies.

However, it should be remembered that, as discussed above, the pursuit of such a proprietary claim is only one possible consequence of an analysis which points to property arguably being held (or having been held) on trust. Other possibilities where the beneficiary of the trust is the potential claimant include personal claims for breach of trust (see Ch.10), knowing receipt of trust property (see Ch.12) or dishonest assistance in a breach of trust (see Ch.13). In other circumstances, where it is a defendant who is the arguable beneficiary of a trust of property legally owned by a third party, the consequence may be the taking of steps to enable a money judgment obtained (or hoped to be obtained) by the claimant to be enforced by way of execution against that property; for example by an application for a charging order or other form of execution after judgment, or by a freezing order before judgment.[54]

23–035

(1)   The Nature of the Proprietary Claim

(i)   What is required for the claimant to make out a proprietary claim?

The requirement for an equitable proprietary claim is simply that the claimant can demonstrate (in accordance with the principles set out in Ch.9 and in the preceding parts of this chapter) beneficial rights to the relevant property as against the defendant who currently holds it. In this sense it is not a fault-based

23–036

---

[53] *Macmillan Inc v Bishopsgate Investment Trust (No.3)* [1996] 1 W.L.R. 387, and *Akers v Samba* [2017] UKSC 7; [2017] A.C. 424, at [18] to [34], per Lord Mance, and at [84]–[86].
[54] While the law of execution is not wholly within the scope of this work, aspects of such a situation are addressed in Ch.37.

liability (save to the extent that an initial breach of trust must be proved).[55] So, if a claimant can demonstrate such rights, then the burden falls upon the defendant to establish a contrary right which takes priority or to establish some other defence. It is important to appreciate that the question is as to the relative rights of the claimant, the defendant and any other party to the proceedings before the court. If the defendant cannot show that his rights have at least equal priority to those of the claimant under the principles addressed above, then those rights will not assist him (however meritorious they appear when looked at in isolation)[56]; equally, the defendant will derive no defence from the fact that the claimant holds those rights on trust for some third party not before the Court.[57] Conversely, if the defendant can show that he has rights which take priority over those of the claimant, then the inherent merit of the claimant's claim does not avail him.

23–037   Once it is shown that the claimant can establish a right over the property and the defendant cannot establish the priority of his own rights or some other defence, then the claimant will be entitled to expect the court to exercise its discretionary equitable jurisdiction against the defendant so as to vindicate those rights. But, as there may be wide variation both in the nature of a beneficial interest under a trust and in the extent of the trust interest in any given asset, so the nature of the rights established by the claimant will vary from case to case along with the nature of the vindication which the claimant may expect of the court.

(ii)   Who may bring a proprietary claim?

23–038   The trustees of a trust are proper claimants to bring a proprietary claim against a defaulting trustee or a third party who has obtained trust property. Even if the claimant trustees may themselves have been guilty of breach of trust in parting with the trust property, the defendant cannot rely upon that to afford a defence[58] (although the court may, in such a situation, wish to be given comfort that the beneficiaries have been given notice of the position when considering how in its discretion to formulate relief).

23–039   The standing of the beneficiaries of the relevant trust (or the person treated as being in an equivalent position) to pursue an equitable proprietary claim appears to turn upon the characterisation of the claim, and may give rise to some practical difficulties, as follows:

(1)   On the one hand, it is well established that affected beneficiaries have locus standi to pursue personal claims against a trustee for breach of trust, albeit

---

[55] Nor is the claim in any sense restitutionary or founded on the defendant's unjust enrichment. The claimant's claim is to vindicate property rights: *Foskett v McKeown*, at 129.

[56] *Re Diplock* [1948] Ch. 465, at 530, 536–537; *Foskett v McKeown*, above.

[57] See below. In practice, it may mean that the Court in some cases will wish notice to be given to the third party.

[58] *Dalriada Trustees Ltd v Woodward* [2012] EWHC 21626 (Ch), at [37]. See also *Bracken Partners v Gutteridge* [2003] EWCA Civ 1875 and *Montrose Investments Ltd v Orion Nominees Ltd* [2004] EWCA Civ 1032; [2004] W.T.L.R. 1133.

that (unless the trust is no longer subsisting) the remedy will usually take the form of payment into the trust rather than to the beneficiaries directly.[59]

(2)   On the other hand, it is well established that beneficiaries lack standing to pursue a contractual or tortious claim on behalf of the trust and that such claims can only be pursued in the name of the trustees, except in the special circumstances which will justify a beneficiary to bring a derivative claim for the benefit of the trust, joining the trustees as additional defendants.[60]

(3)   Whether a proprietary claim to recover trust property (in particular a claim to recover such property from a third party) falls within the first or second of those principles may be a subtle question.[61]

(iii)   Who are the necessary defendants to an equitable proprietary claim?

The essential defendants to a proprietary claim are the person or persons who currently hold the relevant property: they are the people against whom the court will be asked to use its powers so as to vindicate the claimants' rights. **23–040**

It will usually be prudent to join also as defendants any others who are known to assert any interest in the relevant property, so that they too can be bound by the outcome of the claim as a matter of res judicata and the risk of further litigation can be avoided. Indeed, it may be necessary to join such a party if their interest (or purported interest) is currently protected in a way which will need to be addressed in order for effective relief to be granted to the claimant; to take just one example, where the claimant seeks to recover as trust property land in England & Wales to which title is now registered in the name of a "wrongdoer" with a charge registered against it in favour of another party, it may be necessary to join both the registered proprietor and the chargee in order to obtain effective relief. **23–041**

In addition, where the relevant property is in the hands of a someone other than the original defaulting trustee and is sought to be recovered on a following/tracing basis, it is usually prudent to join in one set of proceedings both the original defaulting trustee (against whom there are likely also to be other personal claims) and the current holder of the relevant property. In principle, either could be sued alone. But if the current property-holder is sued without the original defaulter being joined, it may (in many cases) be difficult forensically to establish the original "wrongdoing" insofar as that is necessary to set up the right to follow/trace. Conversely, if the defaulter is sued without joining a proprietary claim against the current holders of the property, it will be necessary in any **23–042**

---

[59] See para.10–008.

[60] See generally *Hayim v Citibank* [1987] A.C. 730; *Roberts v Gill* [2008] EWCA Civ 803; [2009] 1 W.L.R. 531, and on appeal, at [2010] UKSC 22; [2011] 1 A.C. 240; *Abouraya v Sigmund* [2014] EWHC 277 (Ch); [2015] BCC 503; *Popely v Popely* [2018] EWHC 276 (Ch).

[61] See, thus, *McEneaney v Stevens*, unreported, 2 May 2017 (Mr Edward Murray sitting as a Deputy Judge of the High Court), in which—albeit without citation of the breach of trust cases—the beneficial owner of shares held on bare trust for him was found to lack standing to pursue in his own name a claim to recover the shares from third party defendants who were alleged fraudulently to have transferred the shares to themselves.

subsequent proceedings advancing the proprietary claim against them to repeat the process of proving the original "wrongdoing", as they will not be bound by the determinations reached in the first set of proceedings. The latter consideration often presents claimants with a practical dilemma in pursuing fraud proceedings, as potential proprietary following/tracing claims against third parties only become known over the course of the proceedings against the principal defaulter as a result of interim orders for the provision of information or as a result of disclosure – leaving the claimant with a choice between delaying the proceedings with applications for joinder and amendment so as to add such claims, or pursuing the proceedings to trial against the principal defaulter as quickly as possible, with the risk of having effectively to repeat that trial should it subsequently be decided to pursue the proprietary claims against the newly discovered third parties.

23–043   Moreover, in considering which defendants should be joined, it is necessary to take into account the expectations now placed by the court upon claimants that they will seek to resolve disputes efficiently with all relevant parties before the court, and the potential sanctions in abuse of process if matters are sought to be determined piecemeal by successive claims without that approach having been approved by the court.[62]

(iv)   What proprietary interest may the claimant assert?

23–044   Where the property subject to the proprietary claim is the original trust property still completely intact in the hands of the defendant, then the claimant will assert simply his beneficial ownership and seek relief aimed at the recovery of that property (or, if he has a lesser beneficial interest, aimed at appropriately vindicating that interest). The orders which the Court may make are considered further at item (3) of the list at para.23–045 below.

23–045   Where the property subject to the claim represents the followable or traceable proceeds of the original trust property, the position becomes somewhat more complex:

(1)   The beneficiary (or group of beneficiaries) who has followed or traced the trust property into the hands of a "wrongdoer" (see above) is, in general, entitled to elect between either:

    (a)   asserting continuing beneficial ownership (either of the whole asset where it all represents the followable or traceable proceeds of the original trust property or of a proportionate share where the original trust property, or its proceeds provided only part of the purchase price),[63] or

---

[62] *Aldi Stores Ltd v WSP Group PLC* [2007] EWCA Civ 1260; [2008] 1 W.L.R. 748; *Stuart v Goldberg* [2008] EWCA Civ 2; [2008] 1 W.L.R. 823; *Gladman Commercial Properties v Fisher Hargreaves Proctor* [2013] EWCA Civ 1466; *Generics (UK) Ltd (t/a Mylan) v Warner-Lambert Co LLC* [2016] EWCA Civ 1006; *Clutterbuck v Cleghorn* [2017] EWCA Civ 137.

[63] Hence Lord Millett said in *Foskett v McKeown*, above, at 130: "if a trustee buys property partly with his own money and partly with trust money, the beneficiary should have the option of taking a proportionate part of the new property or a lien upon it, as may be most for his advantage." The

(b) claiming an equitable lien over those assets as security for the trustee's personal liability to pay compensation for the breach of trust (so as to take the benefit of the asset as security but retain the personal claim for the balance).[64]

Obviously the first option is generally chosen where there has been an overall increase in value, and the second where there is a shortfall. Where the beneficiary elects to assert beneficial ownership of the property, then that ownership will naturally extend to any income or interest attributable to the property.[65] The most celebrated example of the application of these principles is the House of Lords decision in *Foskett v McKeown*. In that case a defaulting trustee mis-applied some £20,000 of trust funds (which had been originally paid in relation to a property development scheme) towards the payment of premiums on a life insurance policy he had taken out. The trustee committed suicide and £1 million was paid under the policy. The dispute was whether the defendants, to whom the £1 million had been paid, were liable to disgorge the amount of the funds misapplied (via the imposition of a lien in favour of the claimants) or a proportionate part of the £1 million, to the extent to which the monies had contributed to its investment value (which was £400,000). The House of Lords held that the claimants were entitled, at their option, to claim the latter.

(2) If the beneficiary (or group of beneficiaries) has followed or traced the trust property not into the hands of a "wrongdoer", but rather into a mixture to which he is now one of several innocent contributors, then there is no question of that beneficiary electing to claim a lien over the mixture as against the other innocent contributors[66]; his only proprietary claim is to beneficial ownership of the portion of the mixture established under the principles described at para.23–019 above.

(3) Where property can be followed or traced into the hands of a person who then uses it not to acquire an asset but rather to pay off a mortgage or other secured borrowing, it may or may not be possible to trace into the asset against which the borrowing was secured by means of the sort of "backward tracing" considered at para.23–020 above. Alternatively, the following/tracing party may be able to invoke the equitable remedy of subrogation, asking the Court to create a new equitable security right for his

---

suggestion which had been made in *re Hallett's Estate* (1880) 13 Ch. D. 696, at 709, that in such a case the beneficiary was entitled only to a lien over the new asset acquired partially by the trust money, was disapproved and the rule was stated as follows, at 131: "Where a trustee wrongfully uses trust money to provide part of the cost of acquiring an asset, the beneficiary is entitled at his option either to claim a proportionate share of the asset or to enforce a lien upon it to secure his personal claim against the trustee for the amount of the misapplied money. It does not matter whether the trustee mixed the trust money with his own in a single fund before using it to acquire the asset, or made separate payments (whether simultaneously or sequentially) out of the differently owned funds to acquire a single asset."

[64] *Foskett v McKeown*, above, at 130–131. Where a lien is chosen, it remains obscure whether interest falling due on the personal liability to repay is added to the security: see *Re Hallett*, above, at 226 and following; and *Foskett v McKeown*, at 277–278.

[65] *Re Diplock* [1948] Ch. 465, at 517, 557.

[66] *Foskett v McKeown*, above, at 132.

benefit over that asset (mirroring the terms of the discharged security) so as to reverse the recipient's unjust enrichment.[67]

(2) Defences

23–046   As has been seen above, the requirements to establish a good title to a beneficial trust interest in an item of property may be complex. A failure to demonstrate such requirements may cause a claim to fail in numerous ways. But the following section is concerned with defences (in the true sense) which a defendant may raise even where the requirements to establish the claimant's interest have been made out.

(i)   Bona fide purchaser and other competing claims

23–047   The defendant may have a defence if he can show that he (or someone through whom he acquired title to the property) acquired it as a bona fide purchaser for value of the legal estate without notice. The requirements of this defence have been considered at paras 23–028—23–030 above. This is a true defence, with the burden being upon the defendant to establish each of its elements including (which is a matter of potential tactical significance) the giving of value and the lack of notice.[68]

23–048   The same will be true of any other competing title which the defendant sets up for his own benefit in reliance on the rules as to priorities (see paras 23–025—23–033 above).

(ii)   A defence of "change of position" or "windfall"

23–049   The defence of "change of position" is a general defence to personal restitutionary claims seeking the reversal of unjust enrichment.[69] There is controversy as to whether such a defence is available in the case of a proprietary claim to recover trust property or (perhaps more plausibly) its traceable proceeds, bound up with controversy as to the extent to which such proprietary claims are to be regarded as founded upon unjust enrichment rather than simply the vindication of property rights.[70] Whatever the merits of the academic debate, the

---

[67] *Boscawen v Bajwa* [1996] 1 W.L.R. 328; *Banque Financiere de la Cite v Parc (Battersea) Ltd* [1999] 1 A.C. 221; *Cheltenham & Gloucester v Appleyard* [2004] EWCA Civ 291; *Menelaou v Bank of Cyprus Plc* [2015] UKSC 66; [2016] A.C. 176. For a fuller account of the law of subrogation, see (for example) Ch.39 of C. Mitchell, P. Mitchell and Watterson, *Goff & Jones: The Law of Unjust Enrichment* (2016) and C. Mitchell's *The Law of Subrogation* (Oxford: Clarendon Press, 1994). The recent reconsideration of that law by the Supreme Court in *Menelaou* may have reduced the need to rely upon a strict process of following/tracing in order to invoke the remedy.
[68] *GL Baker Ltd v Medway Building and Supplies Ltd* [1958] 1 W.L.R. 1216; *Re Nisbet and Potts Contract* [1906] 1 CH 386; *Barclays Bank Plc v Boulter* [1998] 1 W.L.R. 1, at 8–9; [1999] 1 W.L.R. 1919, at 1924–1925 (but see *Shears v Wells* [1936] 1 All E.R. 832).
[69] *Lipkin Gorman v Karpnale* [1992] A.C. 548. See more generally Ch.27 of C. Mitchell, P. Mitchell and Watterson, *Goff & Jones: The Law of Unjust Enrichment* (2016).
[70] See the academic controversy raging in Birks (2001) 54 CLP 231; Burrows (2001) 117 L.Q.R. 412; Smith (2000) 116 L.Q.R. 412; G. Virgo, *Principles of the Law of Restitution*, 2nd edn (Oxford: OUP,

decision of the House of Lords in *Foskett v McKeown* certainly stands as authority for the straightforward proposition that the claim to recover either trust assets or their traceable proceeds is to be regarded as a claim to vindicate property rights rather than one founded on unjust enrichment. It is perhaps less clear whether that decision goes so far as to rule out the possibility of a change of position defence.[71] Moreover, it is unclear how far that decision could be applied to other varieties of claim which may utilise the tracing process but are founded essentially on unjust enrichment, such as the claim in subrogation addressed above.

(iii) "Unclean hands" and the "ex turpi causa"/illegality doctrine

An equitable proprietary claim, like any equitable claim, is capable of being refused relief by the application of the maxim that "he who comes to equity must come with clean hands".[72] The scope of the defence is limited in that the misconduct of the claimant which is relied upon by the defendant must have an immediate and necessary relation to the equity sued for.[73] Equally, the defence (as it has recently been put):

> "does not ... enforce manners, or require apology; it is reserved for exceptional cases where those seeking to invoke [equity] have put themselves beyond the pale by reason of serious immoral or deliberate conduct such that the overall result of equitable intervention would not be an exercise but a denial of equity".[74]

23–050

See the further treatment of this topic in Ch.23 in the context of personal equitable remedies.

There are other cases in which equitable proprietary claims are treated as subject to the denial of relief on grounds of public policy by application of the common law "ex turpi causa"/illegality doctrine.[75] It remains unclear to what extent, in the context of an equitable claim, the equitable "unclean hands" principle and the common law "ex turpi causa"/illegality doctrine are truly to be considered as

23–051

2006), p.569 and following; C. Mitchell, P. Mitchell and Watterson, *Goff & Jones: The Law of Unjust Enrichment* (2016), para.27–55; Tucker, Le Poidevin and Brightwell, *Lewin on Trusts* (2017), paras 41–056—41–059; C. Mitchell, D.J. Hayton and P. Matthews, *Underhill & Hayton Law of Trusts and Trustees*, 19th edn (London: LNUK, 2016), paras 90.6–90.9, and G. Thomas and A. Hudson, *The Law of Trusts* (Oxford: OUP), para.33.93 and following.

[71] Lord Millett at 129 would certainly appear to do so. See also *Campden Hill Ltd v Chakrani* [2005] EWHC 911 (Ch), at [84]–[90]; and *Armstrong DLW GmbH v Winnington Networks Ltd* [2012] EWHC 10 (Ch); [2013] Ch. 156, at [103], in each of which the position was treated as unclear.

[72] Examples include *Murphy v Rayner* [2011] EWHC 1 (Ch), at [351] (a proprietary estoppel claim rather than a trust claim).

[73] *Dering v Earl of Winchelsea* (1787) 1 Cox Eq Cas 318, at 319; *Grobbelaar v News Group Newspapers* [2002] UKHL 40; [2002] 1 W.L.R. 3024, at 3075; *Royal Bank of Scotland Plc v Highland Financial Partners LP* [2013] EWCA Civ 328, at [159]; *Day v Tiuta International* [2014] EWCA Civ 1246, at [65]–[67].

[74] *CF Partners (UK) LLP v Barclays Bank Plc* [2014] 3049 (Ch), per Hildyard J at [1133].

[75] See, for example, *Tinsley v Milligan* [1994] 1 A.C. 340 (which included citation of a wealth of previous authority); and *Davies v O'Kelly* [2014] EWCA Civ 1606; [2015] 1 W.L.R. 2725, although the version of the doctrine applied in those cases has now been overruled by the Supreme Court in *Mirza v Patel*, above. See also Ch.24.

separate or turning upon separate principles. And the area is plainly ripe for revision as the Courts work through the consequences of the fundamental reconsideration of the "ex turpi causa"/illegality doctrine by the Supreme Court in *Patel v Mirza*.[76]

(iv) Limitation, laches and acquiescence

23–052   The Limitation Act 1980 is capable of applying, directly or by analogy, to certain equitable proprietary claims. So too are the equitable defences of laches (in cases where delay by the claimant makes it inequitable for the claim not to be pursued) and acquiescence. This is addressed in Ch.25 below.

(v) Credit to the defendant trustee for his contributions to the property

23–053   **Expenses.**   A trustee may in some circumstances have a right to an indemnity from, or a lien over, trust property for repayment of expenditure which he has incurred. Such a right may arise in different ways:

(1)   A trustee has a right (which has long been given statutory force and now appears in s.31(1) Trustee Act 2000) to reimbursement from the trust fund for expenses properly incurred by him when acting on behalf of the trust, although there is authority (pre-dating the 2000 Act but postdating its predecessor acts) that a trustee in default is not entitled to exercise that right until he has made good the default.[77] The requirement that expenses be incurred *"properly on behalf of the trust"* together with the prohibition (if it applies) on exercise of the right until the trustee has made good any default may be expected to limit the application of that general statutory right in the fraud context. But there will be cases in which it has application.

(2)   There is authority for a right to a lien for expenses (at least up to the value of the improvements effected thereby) incurred by a constructive trustee in improving property which he is found to hold on constructive trust on the basis that it was acquired by making use of a fiduciary position under the principles explained in Ch.11. The basis for that lien is said to be the equitable maxim that he who seeks equity (in this case the beneficiary seeking to recover the property held on constructive trust) must do equity.[78] The extent to which the analysis in those cases can be applied as a general principle to all cases of claims to recover trust property where the trustee is unable to rely upon s.31(1) Trustee Act 2000 is uncertain.

23–054   **Remuneration/Allowance for Skill and Labour.**   A trustee might have a contractual right to remuneration from the beneficiaries, a trustee of an express trust may be permitted remuneration by the trust instrument and certain limited

---

[76] Above.

[77] *Re Johnson* (1880) 15 Ch. D. 548; *Smith v Dale* (1881) 18 Ch. D. 516, at 518; *Re Knott* (1887) 56 LJCh 318. See Tucker, Le Poidevin and Brightwell, *Lewin on Trusts* (2017), Ch.21, section 2 for a detailed commentary on the right to indemnity.

[78] *Rowley v Ginniver* [1897] 2 Ch. 503; and see the analysis of the older cases in Tucker, Le Poidevin and Brightwell, *Lewin on Trusts* (2017), para.20–025.

classes of trustees have a statutory right to remuneration.[79] Reference should be made to the usual specialist works in respect of such rights. Where none of those rights apply, a trustee may still be allowed to take remuneration out of the trust fund by the Court:

(1)   The Court has an inherent jurisdiction, used only in rare circumstances, to allow remuneration for a trustee either prospectively or retrospectively for proper work done, in order to secure the good administration of the trust fund[80]; and

(2)   Under a separate line of authority, when the court requires a trustee[81] to account for a profit obtained in breach of fiduciary duty (a situation which may also give rise to a proprietary constructive trust claim against the property obtained under the principles explained at paras 23–073—23–076), it has jurisdiction to award the fiduciary out of that profit an allowance for the application of his skill and labour in obtaining it.[82] The basis of the jurisdiction is to avoid the inequity of the beneficiary taking the benefit of the skill and labour without paying for it. It has been said that the jurisdiction will be exercised only in exceptional circumstances and not where it would have the effect of encouraging a trustee to put himself in a position of conflict.[83] See further on this Ch.22.

Equitable Accounting.   Where the trustee is also a beneficial co-owner of the property with the claimant (or claimants), expenditure upon the property (and other benefits put into, or taken out of, the property) may also be credited to the trustee (or, indeed, to the claimant) in the division of any proceeds of sale pursuant to an "equitable accounting" directed by the court.[84]   **23–055**

(3)   Remedies

(i)   Declarations

The first head of relief sought in an equitable proprietary claim is usually a declaration (or set of declarations) making clear the beneficial ownership of the relevant property. The jurisdiction to grant a declaration is discretionary, taking into account justice to the parties, whether the declaration will serve a useful   **23–056**

---

[79] See in particular Pt V Trustee Act 2000.

[80] *Re Duke of Norfolk's Settlement* [1982] Ch. 61; *Re Berkeley Applegate (Investment Consultants) Ltd (No 2)* (1988) 4 BCC 279, and many other authorities. See the fuller analysis in Tucker, Le Poidevin and Brightwell, *Lewin on Trusts* (2017), paras 20–240—20–246.

[81] In English law, there is doubt whether the jurisdiction may be exercised for the benefit of a company director: *Guinness Plc v Saunders* [1990] 2 A.C. 663 (HL), at 694 and 701G.

[82] *Re Jarvis* [1958] 1 W.L.R. 815, at 820; *Phipps v Boardman* [1964] 1 W.L.R. 993, at 1018 (approved [1965] C 992, at 1020–1021 and [1967] 2 A.C. 46, at 104, 112); *O'Sullivan v Management Agency and Music Ltd* [1985] Q.B. 428; *Guinness Plc v Saunders* [1990] 2 A.C. 663; *Badfinger Music v Evans* [2001] W.T.L.R. 1.

[83] *Guinness Plc v Saunders*, above, at 701F.

[84] See (briefly) Ch.22 and the summary of the relevant law in Tucker, Le Poidevin and Brightwell, *Lewin on Trusts* (2017), para.9–079 and following.

purpose and any other special considerations.[85] At the conclusion of an equitable proprietary claim, the Court will usually be prepared to grant a declaration encapsulating the findings it has made as to beneficial ownership. Special circumstances where the Court might refuse to grant a declaration (despite the claimant prima facie "winning" the point to which the declaration relates) could include: a situation where the court was being invited to make the declaration by consent without evidence[86]; a situation where potentially affected parties are not before the court, such that a declaration has the capacity to cause mischief if it was (wrongly) understood as being determinative of the position as against those parties; where the declaration seeks to pre-empt criminal proceedings; or a situation where the question is purely hypothetical.[87]

23–057 Although a declaration can be sought in the absence of any other relief,[88] in the context of an equitable proprietary claim it will usually be accompanied by claims for a suite of further relief intended to restore the trust property to its proper owners. Where further relief is sought, the declaration itself is not strictly necessary and it might fairly be said that its utility is somewhat limited. It is binding only upon the parties before the Court[89]; and it does nothing by itself to cause or mandate the return of the trust property. But the declaration does serve some practical functions even where other relief is sought, which explain its popularity as a first head of relief in proprietary claims, in particular in that:

(1) it provides a clear statement of the ownership position which can be of great help in demonstrating the result of the litigation to third parties;

(2) the clear statement of the ownership position can also be of great help in maintaining the focus of the proceedings through the enforcement phase if, as is often the case, there is a need for further post judgment proceedings to secure the just return or disposal of the property; and

(3) when a claim is first pleaded the claimant may be somewhat uncertain as to what form of relief, apart from the declaration, he will ultimately want when judgment is reached.

23–058 In relation to the practical relief which may be sought and granted to give effect to the claimant's beneficial entitlement, the position will differ depending upon whether the claimant has established complete beneficial entitlement to the relevant property; or beneficial co-ownership of the property (where the co-owners are not all fellow claimants with whom he is ad idem); or a right to an equitable lien or charge over the property.

---

[85] See *Nokia Corp v Interdigital Technology Corp* [2006] EWCA Civ 1618 for a review of the relevant consideration.

[86] *Wallersteiner v Moir* [1974] 1 W.L.R. 991.

[87] See more generally J. Woolf, *Zamir and Woolf: The Declaratory Judgment*, 4th edn (London: Sweet & Maxwell, 2011).

[88] CPR r.40.20.

[89] *Financial Services Authority v Rourke* [2002] CP Rep 14.

(ii) *Consequential relief where the claimant(s) is (or are) entitled to the whole of the property*

Where the claimant has established a complete and unqualified beneficial entitlement to the whole of the relevant property, he is entitled to call for that property to be conveyed into his name or that of his nominee; and a group of claimants who between them have all of the beneficial entitlements in the relevant property are entitled to do likewise.[90] In general, therefore, in the fraud context the final relief which will be sought to enforce such a proprietary claim (leaving to one side any related personal claims) will be relief aimed simply at bringing about that transfer. The Court also has powers to remove trustees and to appoint new trustees which might be invoked even in some cases where the claimants between them have the complete beneficial interest, if the claimants wish to preserve intact a pre-existing trust structure—coupled, obviously, with powers to ensure that the trust property is put into the hands of the newly appointed trustees.[91]

23–059

Injunctions and their Enforcement.   The central tool at the Court's disposal to ensure that trust property is put into the right hands is the grant of a final injunction,[92] ordering the party (or parties) currently holding the property to do whatever is necessary to transfer that property to the claimant or the claimant's nominee, with the necessary steps naturally depending upon the nature of the property in question. The primacy of the injunction reflects the equitable maxim that, although of course it is often (as in the case of a trust) concerned with beneficial ownership, "equity acts in personam".

23–060

Where such an injunction is made but not obeyed, the court's powers include the following:

23–061

(1) Committal and Sequestration.   The traditional means available to a court of equity to persuade a party to comply with an injunction is the jurisdiction to punish that party, its directors (if it is a company) or others abetting its disobedience by committal to prison or sequestration of assets. That jurisdiction is considered in detail in Ch.33. Naturally, its efficacy depends upon the relevant physical person either being in (or wishing to be able to come into) the territorial jurisdiction of the court or having assets in (or wishing to be able to bring assets into) that jurisdiction.

23–062

(2) Appointment of Other Persons to Execute Documents under Section 39 Senior Courts Act 1981.   Under s.39(1),

23–063

> "Where the High Court or family court has given or made any judgment or order directing a person to execute any conveyance, contract or other document, or to indorse any negotiable instrument, then if that person:

---

[90] The so called rule in *Saunders v Vautier* (1841) 4 Beav 115. See the fuller treatment in Tucker, Le Poidevin and Brightwell, *Lewin on Trusts* (2017), Ch.24.

[91] Reference should be made to the specialist works on trust law.

[92] Section 37(1) Senior Courts Act 1981. There is an interesting theoretical question as to the extent to which the court retains (and, if so, should exercise) an inherent jurisdiction outside that statute.

(a)   neglects or refuses to comply with the judgment or order; or

(b)   cannot after reasonable enquiry be found, that court may, on such terms and conditions, if any, as may be just, order that the conveyance, contract or other document shall be executed, or that the negotiable instrument may be indorsed, by such person as the court may nominate for the purpose."

Under s.39(2), a document so executed or indorsed

"shall operate, and be for all purposes available, as if it had been executed or indorsed by the person originally directed to execute or indorse it".

The person authorised by such an order to execute or indorse the document in question is usually a Judge, Master or other officer of the Court; and there are obvious practical advantages in having appointed such a signatory (rather than, say, the claimant or his solicitor) when it becomes necessary to persuade third parties to act on the document. As the wording of the section suggests, there is no limit to the classes of document in relation to which such an order can be made or the purposes for which a document executed in accordance with those powers might be used.[93] It has been said that an appointment order should not be made in anticipation of a failure to comply with the original order to execute, unless the party subject to that order has already shown by his conduct that he refuses or will refuse to comply.[94] There are cases in which an appointment order has been made on terms that it take effect only if the original order is not complied with by a specified time may be acceptable,[95] although it may be that such a course was only justified because there were grounds to anticipate non-compliance with the original order.

23–064   **Vesting Orders (and Authority to Convey) under Trustee Act 1925.**   The Trustee Act 1925 contains powers for the court to make vesting orders, including in relation to land[96] or in relation to "any stock or thing in action".[97] Those powers are exercisable in a variety of situations including (relevantly for present purposes): where a new trustee has been appointed by the court or pursuant to a statutory or express power out of court[98]; where a trustee neglects or refuses to transfer the relevant property according to the direction of the person absolutely entitled for a period of 28 days after written request is made[99]; where a trustee fails to comply with certain types of court order in relation to the trust property[100]; and, most generally, where property of the relevant sort is vested in a trustee "whether by way of mortgage or otherwise" and the court considers it to

---

[93] *Astro Exito Navegacion v Soutland Enterprise Co Ltd* [1983] A.C. 787.

[94] *Savage v Norton* [1908] 1 Ch. 290.

[95] See *Astro Exito*, above; and *Bank of Scotland v Waugh* [2014] EWHC 2835 (Ch).

[96] Section 44. Note that in relation to registered land, a vesting order may need to be accompanied by additional relief under the Land Registration Act 2002 to give effect to the requisite alterations of the register. The relevant law in relation to land registration is outside the scope of this work.

[97] Section 51; where "stock" is defined by s.68(14) as including "fully paid up shares, and so far as relates to vesting orders made by the court under this Act, … any fund annuity or security transferable in books kept by any company or society, or by instrument of transfer either alone or accompanied by other formalities, and any share or interest therein".

[98] Section 44(i) and s.51(1)(i).

[99] Section 44(vi) and s.51(1)(ii)(d).

[100] Section 47, s.48 and s.51(1)(ii)(e).

be expedient.[101] The power to make vesting orders under the Trustee Act 1925 extends in principle to property in any part of Her Majesty's dominions except Scotland,[102] although it may be doubted in modern times whether the power would be exercised in relation to property outside England and Wales, at least in the absence of very special circumstances. Any person entitled to a beneficial interest in the trust property has locus to apply for such an order,[103] and a successful claimant upon a proprietary trust claim will accordingly have standing to do so provided one of the conditions specified in the statute is made out. As an alternative to the making of a vesting order, the Act gives the court the power in most cases where a vesting order might have been made to appoint a person to execute the relevant documents to bring about the same effect[104]; and the choice of which form of order to make may be influenced by considerations of expedience. Very often there will be a more convenient route to enforcement of a proprietary trust claim, but an order under the Trustee Act 1925 is (in the right case) a powerful and convenient weapon in the court's arsenal.[105]

Appointment of a Receiver.   The Court has a general power under s.37(1)   **23–065**
Senior Courts Act 1981 and Pt 69 CPR to appoint receivers. The use of that power is considered in detail in Ch.33. As we have discussed in that chapter, the power can be used after judgment in aid of enforcement, most usually by appointing a receiver "by way of equitable execution" over assets of the defendant to ensure that those assets are used to pay a money judgment.[106] But in principle a receiver could also be appointed to undertake the recovery of trust property for delivery up to the claimant or his nominee, where the nature of the property (or of the persons holding it) makes the use of injunctions and other specifically targeted orders impractical. Obviously, such an order would (in general) be a last resort for a claimant given the additional cost of the receivership.

Accounts and Inquiries.   The court has power to order accounts and inquiries   **23–066**
to be taken by the court following judgment. They are perhaps most commonly used to establish the extent of monetary liability between the parties. But in the context of an equitable proprietary claim where the fate of the trust property or its proceeds has not been fully established by the time of judgment, the court may order that there be post-judgment accounts or inquiries as a mechanism by which the relevant defendants can be required to disclose such information and the court can make any necessary further determinations, before further orders are made for the transfer of property so located.

---

[101] Section 44(vii) and s.51(1)(v).

[102] Section 56.

[103] Section 58.

[104] Section 50 and s.51(2).

[105] For a fuller consideration of vesting orders under the 1925 Act, see Ch.18 of Tucker, Le Poidevin and Brightwell, *Lewin on Trusts* (2017).

[106] See *Masri v Consolidated Contractors International Co SAL* [2008] EWCA Civ 303; [2009] Q.B. 450; *Tasarruf Mevduati Sigorta Fonu v Merrill Lynch Bank & Trust Co (Cayman) Ltd* [2011] UKPC 17; [2012] 1 W.L.R. 1721 and *Taurus Petroleum Ltd v State Oil Marketing Co of the Ministry of Oil, Iraq* [2015] EWCA Civ 835 for leading recent authorities on the appointment of receivers by way of equitable execution.

(iii)   Consequential relief where the claimant is a co-owner

23–067   Where the claimant has established only a partial beneficial interest in the relevant property, the court will grant a declaration (as set out above) to record the existence and extent of that interest. But how (and indeed whether) that interest is to be protected and/or realised (and, if realised, how the proceeds of sale are to be distributed or, if not realised, how it is to be used pending realisation) may give rise to further issues between the claimant and the other beneficial owners of the property as to their respective rights, and as to the proper exercise of the court's statutory and inherent powers over trusts.

23–068   Reference should accordingly be made to the specialist works on trust law. But, as a general matter, it is fair to say that, where the partial interests in the property are those of the beneficiary and of the defaulting trustee (or other wrongdoer), the court will exercise its discretion in a way which will facilitate prompt repayment of the beneficiaries.[107]

(iv)   Relief where only a lien is sought

23–069   Where the claimant has established a proprietary interest by way of equitable lien rather than by way of beneficial interest (i.e. an equitable security right rather than an ownership right), the court will (as in the circumstances described above) grant declarations to record that right.

23–070   The claimant's rights to take steps to protect and/or realise that interest will be those of an equitable lien or rather than of a beneficiary under a trust. Reference should therefore be made to the specialist works in relation to mortgages, liens and other security.

(v)   Related non-proprietary claims

23–071   As we have already noted, in practice, an equitable proprietary claim is most often accompanied by personal claims for money judgments, either against the same defendant or other defendants, in breach of trust (Ch.10), breach of fiduciary duty (Ch.11), knowing receipt (Ch.12) or dishonest assistance (Ch.13), in addition to any other common law causes of action.

---

[107] *Foskett v McKeown*, above, at 135G–135H.

CHAPTER 24

ILLEGALITY

A. INTRODUCTION

(1) Origin

The law relating to the so-called illegality defence—ex turpi causa—springs from a dictum of Lord Mansfield, quoted in almost all of the many cases on this subject, in the 18th century case of *Holman v Johnson*.[1] As expressed by him, it is a principle of public policy which denies a wrong-doer access to the courts:

> "The objection, that a contract is immoral or illegal as between plaintiff and defendant, sounds at all times very ill in the mouth of the defendant. It is not for his sake, however, that the objection is ever allowed; but it is founded in general principles of policy, which the defendant has the advantage of, contrary to the real justice as between him and the plaintiff, by accident, if I may so say. The principle of public policy is this; *ex dolo malo non oritur actio*[2]. No court will lend its aid to a man who founds his cause of action upon an immoral or an illegal act. If, from the plaintiff's own stating or otherwise, the cause of action appears to arise ex turpi causa, or the transgression of a positive law of this country, there the court says he has no right to be assisted. It is upon that ground the court goes; not for the sake of the defendant, but because they will not lend their aid to such a plaintiff. So if the plaintiff and defendant were to change sides, and the defendant was to bring his action against the plaintiff, the latter would then have the advantage of it; for where both are equally in fault, *potior est conditio defendentis*[3]."[4]

(2) The 250 Years following Holman v Johnson

The development of the law from that point is a sad tale of the problems that ensue when latin maxims are applied without sufficient critical thinking; dicta relating to public policy from a past age are applied without modification in a vastly different modern world; and the courts develop a distaste for the results of such application, which they are unwilling to confront head-on, but which lead them to distort the law and create exceptions to it on no principled basis other than the desire to achieve a particular result in the instant case.

24–001

24–002

---

[1] *Holman v Johnson* (1775) 1 Cowp. 341; 98 E.R. 1120.
[2] "Ex turpi causa non oritur actio" roughly translates as: "from a dishonorable cause an action does not arise".
[3] "In pari delicto potior est conditio defendentis" roughly translates as: "in equal fault better is the condition of the defendant".
[4] *Holman v Johnson* (1775) 1 Cowp. 341, at 343.

24–003   Thus, until July 2016, the law on the role and impact of relevant illegality on a claim has been "a mess",[5] both conceptually and in terms of its application in practice.[6] The confusion was heightened in recent years by different compositions of the Supreme Court espousing different conceptual frameworks for the law in *Hounga v Allen*[7] and *Les Laboratoires Servier v Apotex Inc.*[8] The division between members of the Supreme Court as to the correct approach was finally stated openly in *Bilta (UK) Ltd v Nazir (No.2)*[9]: at that point, Lord Neuberger said[10] that a seven or nine member court should address the proper approach to the illegality principle as soon as possible.

24–004   That opportunity arose, and the mess has—with two important caveats[11]—now been tidied up by the Supreme Court's judgment, in *Patel v Mirza*.[12]

(3)   The Position Post-Patel: Summary

24–005   The legal position, as articulated by the majority in *Patel*, can be summarised as follows[13]:

(1)   The essential rationale of the illegality doctrine is that it would be contrary to the public interest to enforce a claim if to do so would be harmful to the integrity of the legal system.

(2)   In assessing whether the public interest would be harmed in that way, it is necessary:

    a)   to consider the underlying purpose of the prohibition which has been transgressed by the illegality and whether that purpose will be enhanced by denial of the claim,

    b)   to consider any other relevant public policy on which the denial of the claim may have an impact, including any public policy which might point the other way, and

    c)   to consider whether denial of the claim would be a proportionate response to the illegality, bearing in mind that punishment is a matter for the criminal courts or other bodies entrusted with regulation and control of conduct in specific spheres.

(3)   Within that framework, various factors may be relevant, but it would be a mistake to suggest that the court is free to decide a case in an undisciplined way.

---

[5] See e.g. Lord Sumption in *Patel v Mirza* [2016] UKSC 42; [2017] A.C. 467, at [265].

[6] The case law and commentaries are replete with such criticism. The law has been described as "an intricate set of tangled rules that are difficult to ascertain and that the courts sometimes break" (Law Commission Report No.320, para.3.5); and as "almost impossible to ascertain or articulate principled rules" (*Patel v Mirza* [2014] EWCA Civ 1047; [2015] 1 Ch. 271, at [49]).

[7] *Hounga v Allen* [2014] UKSC 47; [2014] 1 W.L.R. 2889.

[8] *Les Laboratoires Servier v Apotex Inc* [2014] UKSC 55; [2015] A.C. 430.

[9] *Bilta (UK) Ltd v Nazir (No.2)* [2015] UKSC 23; [2016] A.C. 1.

[10] *Bilta*, at [15].

[11] See section C.(5) below.

[12] *Patel v Mirza* [2016] UKSC 42; [2017] A.C. 467.

[13] See Lord Toulson, writing for the majority, in *Patel*, at [120].

"The public interest is best served by a principled and transparent assessment of the considerations identified, rather by than the application of a formal approach capable of producing results which may appear arbitrary, unjust or disproportionate."[14]

The two important caveats—considered in more detail in section C.(5) below—are, first, the extent to which *Patel* is binding on lower courts considering cases in which illegality issues arise; and, secondly, the extent to which there remains uncertainty in how, in any particular set of circumstances, the courts will apply the guidelines set out in *Patel*.   **24–006**

(4) Relevance to Fraud Claims

The illegality principle may be engaged in any type of case and by reference to a vast range of possible "illegality". It is neither practical, nor the function of this book, to summarise or survey all of the potential applications,[15] some of which are far removed from the core subject of this work.   **24–007**

Nevertheless, it is not uncommon for fraudulent conduct of one sort or another to involve, or tip into, "illegality" or "immorality" in the relevant sense,[16] for obvious reasons. Accordingly, this chapter explains the general principles to be applied as they now stand post-*Patel*. It then goes on to consider three main types of situation in which the illegality principle often arises in the context of fraud claims: **24–008**

(1)   claims to enforce, or seek damages for breach in respect of, an illegal contract, a contract entered into for an illegal purpose or a contract which is intended to be or which has been performed illegally;

(2)   claims to recover money paid pursuant to an illegal contract or for an illegal purpose; and

(3)   claims by companies (or other principals) against fraudulent agents.

In general, this chapter does not address in detail the role of illegality insofar as it affects the parties' substantive rights under the law of contract—such as contracts directly prohibited by law, which are void. That topic is more appropriately covered in the standard works on contract law. The present treatment is to do with when the illegality principle will constitute a supervening, essentially public policy, bar to an otherwise good claim.   **24–009**

(5) A Defence?

Illegality is often referred to as a defence. That is both because of the way in which Lord Mansfield framed the principle in *Holman v Johnson* and because, for obvious reasons, it is often raised by a defendant and for his own benefit. But   **24–010**

---

[14] *Patel*, at [120].

[15] Indeed, as Lord Neuberger observed in *Patel* that it would be "little short of foolhardy" to seek to give specific guidance in relation to specific factual scenarios, "bearing in mind the enormous number of different crimes and different factual circumstances which could arise": see at [177].

[16] See section B as to the meaning of these terms in the context of the illegality principle.

it is not a defence, as such: it is a doctrine which looks, in fact, at the claimant's conduct and, in the light of that conduct, may bar an otherwise good claim on the basis of public policy.[17]

24–011   Illegality is accordingly a point which the court can, and in an appropriate case should, take of its own motion: *Patel* itself is an example of a case in which that happened. Of course, it applies as much to a counterclaim as to a claim; and, indeed, to the factual and legal premises which a defendant must establish to advance a substantive defence.[18] We will, accordingly, call it the "illegality principle".

B.   WHAT COUNTS AS AN "ILLEGAL OR IMMORAL" ACT?

(1)   The General Principle

24–012   The question of what counts as an "illegal or immoral" act for the purposes of the illegality principle has now been definitively addressed by the Supreme Court in *Les Laboratoires Servier v Apotex Inc*.[19]

24–013   The illegality principle is concerned with claims founded on acts which are contrary to the public law of the state and engage the public interest. As Lord Sumption explains, that is because

> "the illegality defence, where it arises, arises in the public interest, irrespective of the interests or rights of the parties. It is because the public has its own interest in conduct giving rise to the illegality defence that the judge may be bound to take the point of his own motion, contrary to the ordinary principle in adversarial litigation."[20]

(2)   Criminal and Quasi-Criminal Acts

24–014   The paradigm case of an act which is contrary to the public law of the state and engages the public interest is one which is a criminal offence.

24–015   But also included are what were described in *Les Laboratoires Servier v Apotex Inc* as "quasi-criminal" acts—because they engage the public interest in the same way as criminal acts do. Without necessarily seeking to provide an exhaustive list, the Supreme Court identified three categories of "quasi-criminal" acts: (i) cases of dishonesty or corruption, which, as the Supreme Court observed, have

---

[17] See e.g. *Les Laboratoires Servier v Apotex Inc*, above, in which Lord Sumption put it in this way, at [23]: "...although described as a defence, it is in reality a rule of judicial abstention. It means that rather than regulating the consequences of an illegal act (for example by restoring the parties to the status quo ante, in the same way as upon the rescission of a contract) the courts withhold judicial remedies, leaving the loss to lie where it falls... The ex turpi causa principle precludes the judge from performing his ordinary adjudicative function in a case where that would lend the authority of the state to the enforcement of an illegal transaction or to the determination of the legal consequences of an illegal act."

[18] See, e.g., *Barros Mattos Junior v General Securities* [2004] EWHC 1188 (Ch); [2005] 1 W.L.R. 247, at [28].

[19] *Les Laboratoires Servier v Apotex Inc*, per Lord Sumption at [23]–[29].

[20] *Les Laboratoires Servier v Apotex Inc*, at [23].

always been regarded as engaging the public interest even in the context of purely civil disputes; (ii) cases involving the infringement of statutory rules enacted for the protection of the public interest and attracting civil sanctions of a penal character[21]; and (iii) some anomalous categories of misconduct, such as prostitution, which without themselves being criminal are contrary to public policy and involve criminal liability on the part of secondary parties.

The most significant of those categories from the perspective of the fraud practitioner is, of course, the first: cases of dishonesty and corruption. Examples that might commonly be encountered in fraud litigation are: **24–016**

(1)   Cases involving the payment of bribes when that does not amount to a criminal offence in English law: for example, *Nayyar v Denton Wilde Sapte*[22]; *Marlwood v Kozeny*.[23]

(2)   Cases involving the use of deceit: for example, *ParkingEye Ltd v Somerfield Stores Ltd*[24]; *Brown Jenkinson & Co Ltd v Percy Dalton (London) Ltd*.[25]

(3)   Cases involving the perpetration of a fraud on the Government or where the purpose was to defeat the proper claims of the Commissioners of Inland Revenue: for example, *Miller v Karlinski*[26]; *Napier v National Business Agency*[27]; *Beauvale Furnishings Ltd v Chapman*.[28]

In addition, the illegality principle is—ipso facto—engaged in the case of contracts prohibited by law. But those are something of a special case because such contracts can give rise to no enforceable rights; and, unlike in the majority of illegality cases, the illegality principle can be analysed as part of the substantive law governing the parties' rights. **24–017**

Conversely, acts which are not within the category of "illegal or immoral acts" include those which are merely tortious (other than those in which dishonesty is a critical element), breaches of contract, or statutory or other civil wrongs. Such acts, as Lord Sumption put it, "offend against interests which are essentially private, not public".[29] Thus, for example, in *Donegal v Zambia*[30] Andrew Smith J **24–018**

---

[21] See e.g. the competition law considered in *Safeway Stores Ltd v Twigger* [2010] EWHC 11 (Comm); [2010] 3 All E.R. 577; and [2010] EWCA Civ 1472; [2011] 2 All E.R. 841.

[22] *Nayyar v Denton Wilde Sapte* [2009] EWHC 3218 (QB) per Hamblen J at [118].

[23] *Marlwood v Kozeny* [2006] EWHC 872 (Comm) per Jonathan Hirst QC, at [133].

[24] *ParkingEye Ltd v Somerfield Stores Ltd* [2012] EWCA Civ 1338; [2013] Q.B. 840.

[25] *Brown Jenkinson & Co Ltd v Percy Dalton (London) Ltd* [1957] 2 Q.B. 621: deliberate deceit, even in the absence of moral turpitude, is sufficient.

[26] *Miller v Karlinski* (1945) 62 T.L.R. 85.

[27] *Napier v National Business Agency* [1951] 2 All E.R. 264.

[28] *Beauvale Furnishings Ltd v Chapman* [2000] All E.R. (D) 2038.

[29] There are, however, cases which hold that a contract which has as its aim the deliberate commission of a tort is illegal, even though no criminality or fraud properly so called is involved: see, for example, *Apthorp v Nevill* (1907) 23 T.L.R. 575, where a printer could not recover the cost of printing matter which he knew to be libellous. It is indeed hard to see how a court could order specific performance of such a contract; although the question of damages for past breach, or recovery of the contractual price might be more complicated. Quite how those cases fit into Lord Sumption's analysis in *Apotex* is not clear: he did consider a line of libel cases which might be viewed as exceptions to his general statement (see at [26]); but he did not come to any very clear conclusion about them, and he

held that he would not have regarded as an illegal or immoral act an allegation, had it been made out, that the claimant had unlawfully interfered with contractual relations between relevant parties.

(3)   Conduct Illegal under Foreign Law

24–019   A question which arises in the context of international fraud cases is whether conduct which is contrary to the law of another relevant country is sufficient to engage the illegality principle.

24–020   There are a series of cases relating to the enforceability in England of contracts which are illegal under applicable foreign law, illegal under English law but legal under their applicable foreign law or which involve performance in a foreign country under whose law that performance would be illegal. Those cases do not always maintain clearly the distinction between the operation of the illegality principle with which we are here concerned and the questions of what are the parties' substantive rights under the law applicable to their contractual relations. They are, it is suggested, best analysed in the context of discussion of the parties substantive legal rights under applicable law and the reader is referred to works on the law on contract in this regard.

24–021   Nevertheless, it is right to observe that the illegality principle is a question of English public policy to be applied by the English courts. So, insofar as it can be said that enforcement of a contract with such international elements would engage the interests of the (British) state in the sense described by the Supreme Court in *Apotex*, then the illegality principle will, in appropriate circumstances, bar a relevant claim brought in England. An obvious possible example in the fraud context might be cases which involved the public interest in fighting international corruption (as reflected in the UK's international obligations and/or cooperation in the fighting of corruption); *Marlwood v Kozeny*[31] is an example. In this international context, the UK public interest will include comity between

---

did not mention the *Apthorp* case. These cases "on the borderline" may be ones ripe for further consideration, or re-consideration, in the light of the new *Patel* "range of factors" approach.

[30] *Donegal v Zambia* [2007] EWHC 197 (Comm); [2007] 1 Lloyd's Rep. 397, at [489].

[31] *Marlwood v Kozeny* [2006] EWHC 872 (Comm) per Jonathan Hirst QC, at [133] ("whilst…Mr Kozeny [the claimant] committed no criminal offence in English law, it is abundantly clear that in civil law this corruption would be regarded as immoral and contrary to public policy"). In *Lemenda Trading Co Ltd v Africa Middle East Petroleum Co* [1988] Q.B. 448, Phillips J held that a contract to use personal influence on a foreign official, particularly where it was not apparent to the official that the person using his influence was charging for doing so, was contrary to English public policy if the same public policy applied in the country of performance. The contract in that case was to use influence on a Qatari minister in circumstances where it was essential that the minister should be unaware of the influencer's pecuniary interest. The Court held the contract to be unenforceable. Hence, as was held in *Kozeny*, at [134], it follows, a fortiori, that a contract to bribe a foreign official would be void as contrary to English public policy. It matters not that at the time it did not constitute a criminal offence in this jurisdiction. See also *Barros Mattos Junior v General Securities* [2004] EWHC 1188 (Ch); [2005] 1 W.L.R. 247, where illegality under foreign law was enough to engage the illegality principle.

nations, weighing against the English courts entertaining a claim if that would condone or ignore illegal acts under the law of a foreign friendly state.[32]

(4)   Post-Patel

Although the question of whether a criminal or quasi-criminal act will, in the circumstances of any particular case, engage the illegality principle is now to be determined by reference to the "trio of considerations" and the "range of factors approach" set out in *Patel*—such that not all claims founded on criminal or quasi-criminal acts will now automatically engage the illegality principle—there is no reason that *Apotex* should not remain largely good law in determining what sort of acts are capable *in principle*, subject to the application of the *Patel* approach, of engaging the illegality defence.

24–022

Lord Sumption's consideration in *Apotex*[33] of acts which, although criminal or quasi-criminal, might exceptionally not constitute turpitude for the purposes of the illegality defence may now, in principle, be otiose: the *Patel* approach will incorporate consideration of the particular nature of the criminal or quasi-criminal act concerned. Nevertheless, it seems inconceivable that there will in practice be any change in the recognised exception to the category of criminal acts engaging the illegality principle for "cases of strict liability, generally arising under statute, where the claimant was not privy to the facts making his act unlawful", which Lord Sumption records in *Apotex* by reference to Lord Phillips speech in *Stone & Rolls Ltd v Moore Stephens (A Firm)*.[34] Equally the observation of Lord Rodger in *Gray v Thames Trains Ltd*[35] that some offences might be too trivial to engage the defence is likely to have increased potency in the post-*Patel* era.

24–023

C.   THE ILLEGALITY PRINCIPLE

(1)   Introduction

It is no part of the function of this work to explore the twists and turns of the development of the law in any particular area. Rather, the purpose is to provide a concise and practical statement of relevant legal principles and their application in fraud cases, so as to assist the busy practitioner conducting litigation. Nevertheless, in this area, it is important for the practitioner to understand the basic state of the law prior to the *Patel* decision for two connected reasons. First, to some extent the new law is defined and expressed in *Patel* in opposition to the stance taken by the old law, and by reference to the controversial decisions of the Supreme Court which immediately preceded *Patel*; thus, it helps to understand

24–024

---

[32] Unless those laws were themselves repugnant to English public policy, as might be the case if they represented a breach of fundamental human rights—see, for example, *Kuwait Airways Corp v Iraqi Airways Co (Nos 4 and 5)* [2002] UKHL 19; [2002] 2 A.C. 883.
[33] *Les Laboratoires Servier v Apotex Inc*, at [29].
[34] *Stone & Rolls Ltd v Moore Stephens (A Firm)* [2009] UKHL 39; [2009] 1 A.C. 1391, at [24], [27].
[35] *Gray v Thames Trains Ltd* [2009] UKHL 33; [2009] 3 W.L.R. 167, at [83].

the old law when considering the new law and how it is to be applied. Secondly, although the reasoning in many of the old cases will now be suspect—or simply wrong—the sort of considerations discussed and their application to the facts of the old cases will remain useful guidance in identifying the considerations which will be relevant on the new "range of factors" test; isolating those aspects from the now discredited reasoning of the old cases requires the practitioner to have a proper understanding of that which he is seeking to excise.

24–025 Accordingly, we address in brief below the old law as set out in *Tinsley v Milligan*[36] (the so-called "reliance principle") and the trio of Supreme Court decisions which brought the controversy over the illegality principle to a head, before we address in more detail the decision in *Patel* itself.

(2) The Old Law: Tinsley v Milligan and the Reliance Principle

24–026 The well known facts of *Tinsley* are these: Ms Tinsley and Ms Milligan were tenants in common of a house, but it was put in Ms Tinsley's sole name to facilitate a social security fraud. In the end, Ms Milligan confessed the fraud and she and the Department of Social Security came to an accommodation in that regard. But the couple having fallen out, Ms Tinsley—relying on the fact that the house was in her sole name—brought a claim for possession against Ms Milligan. The latter defended, seeking to enforce her equitable right to half the house.

24–027 In the Court of Appeal,[37] the majority applied the so called "public conscience" test which had been developed over the years preceding the *Tinsley* case: in all the circumstances, would it shock the ordinary citizen to allow the claim? The answer was no: both parties were liable to criminal sanctions, but there was no justification for imposing a disproportionate extra penalty on one party. But the House of Lords unanimously disapproved the public conscience test, holding that it amounted to an undesirable judicial discretion.[38] It upheld (by a 3-2 majority) Lord Mansfield's starkly expressed principle, that an action founded on illegality must be rejected, in these terms[39]: a claimant

> "is entitled to recover [in this case title to property] if he is not forced to plead or rely on the illegality, even if it emerges that the title on which he relied was acquired in the course of carrying through an illegal transaction".

This is what has become known as the "reliance principle".

24–028 In the result, by reason of a pair of presumptions, the House held that Ms Milligan did not need to plead, prove or rely on the illegal nature of the transaction she had entered into to establish her equitable title. That was because a resulting trust in her favour was presumed out of her contributions to the purchase price and the common understanding that the parties were to be joint owners; and she did not need to rebut any countervailing presumption of

---

[36] *Tinsley v Milligan* [1994] 1 A.C. 340.
[37] *Tinsley v Milligan* [1992] Ch. 310.
[38] *Tinsley v Milligan* [1994] 1 A.C. 340, at 358E–358F.
[39] *Tinsley v Milligan*, per Lord Goff at 376E–376F.

advancement which might have arisen if Ms Tinsley and Ms Milligan had stood differently in relation to each other—for example if they had been mother and daughter. But that very circumstance arose in the subsequent case of *Collier v Collier*[40]: this was a case of father against daughter, such that the presumption of advancement operated to treat the relevant transfer as a gift from father to daughter. The father had to rely on the illegal nature of the transaction to rebut that presumption and as a result his claim was barred. The House of Lords in *Tinsley* openly recognised the arguably anomalous results that might arise from their test. But they accepted that anomaly holding that the effect of illegality was not substantive but *procedural*[41]—somewhat surprisingly for a doctrine said to be grounded by Lord Mansfield himself in public policy.

The reasoning in the *Tinsley* case has been much criticised over the decades since it was decided, including in a number of reports and recommendations from the Law Commission. The Law Commission's final position on the way in which the common law should develop, away from the reliance principle towards a more flexible policy based approach, is strikingly similar to the law as now stipulated by *Patel*. **24–029**

(3) Transition and Controversy: ParkingEye, Hounga, Apotex and Bilta

The more flexible approach advocated by the Law Commission gained support from the Court of Appeal in both *Apotex*[42] (as to which see further below) and the *ParkingEye* case.[43] **24–030**

The latter case concerned the repudiation by the defendant of a contract under which the claimant provided it with an automatic control system for its supermarkets' car parks. The defendant met the claim with a plea of illegality based on false representations in some of the demand letters sent by ParkingEye to customers who had not paid for their parking, which had been agreed in pro forma terms at the time the contract was entered into. The sending of these letters constituted a minor part of the performance of an otherwise lawful contract. The judge at first instance held that sending the letters amounted to the tort of deceit, but found that no criminal offence had been committed and that the letters had not been devised or sent dishonestly (in the limited sense that there had been no deliberate intent to obtain payment of sums which were not due by the making of false statements, contrary to the Theft Act 1968 or the Fraud Act 2006). The Court of Appeal upheld the claim to damages for the repudiation and declined to find that the illegality barred the claim. Sir Robin Jacob, with whom Laws LJ agreed, espoused a flexible principle involving weighing the extent of the illegality against the severity of the consequences of barring the claim, saying it would be "*disproportionate*" for ParkingEye to be left without a remedy for loss of income that would have been wholly lawful. There was "*insufficient* **24–031**

---

[40] *Collier v Collier* [2002] B.P.I.R. 1057.
[41] *Tinsley v Milligan* [1994] A.C. 340, at 374E per Lord Browne-Wilkinson.
[42] *Les Laboratoires Servier v Apotex Inc* [2012] EWCA Civ 593; [2013] Bus L.R. 80.
[43] *ParkingEye Ltd v Somerfield Stores Ltd* [2012] EWCA Civ 1338; [2013] Q.B. 840.

justification" for it.[44] In a judgment which pre-figured his judgment in *Patel*, Toulson LJ expressed essentially the same principle, holding that whether the claim should be barred should depend on the scope of the illegality, its seriousness and how central it was to the contract. Taking these into account, would disallowing the claim be a just and proportionate response?[45]

24-032 In *Hounga v Allen*,[46] the claimant was an immigrant who had obtained entry into the UK by fraud and had illegally worked as a servant for the defendant. The defendant had instigated, and was fully complicit in, the illegality. The defendant treated the claimant essentially as a slave, did not pay her any wages and, in the end, with abuse and some violence, threw her out of the house.

24-033 The claimant's claims for unpaid salary and unfair dismissal were dismissed by the employment tribunal, on the ground that they were based on the illegal contract of employment; that decision was upheld by the Employment Appeal Tribunal and there was no further appeal.[47] There remained a claim in the tort of racially discriminatory dismissal from her employment, contrary to s.4 of the Race Relations Act, based on the fact that Ms Hounga had been dismissed because of her vulnerability consequent upon her precarious immigration status and on the abusive manner of her dismissal. The Employment Appeal Tribunal allowed this claim, but was reversed by the Court of Appeal, on the basis that the claim was tainted by the illegal nature of her employment, which, so the court held, would be condoned if the court upheld the claim.

24-034 The Supreme Court reversed that decision, even though Ms Hounga's claim was at least in some sense founded on the illegal contract of employment. Lord Wilson, for the majority, rejected the idea that the case could be resolved by reference to the reliance test and expressed the principles at play as follows[48]:

> "The defence of illegality rests on the foundation of public policy. 'The principle of public policy is this …' said Lord Mansfield by way of preface to his classic exposition of the defence in *Holman v Johnson* (1775) 1 Cowp 341, 343. 'Rules which rest on the foundation of public policy, not being rules which belong to the fixed or customary law, are capable, on proper occasion, of expansion or modification': *Maxim Nordenfelt Guns and Ammunition Co v Nordenfelt* [1893] 1 Ch. 630, 661 (Bowen LJ). So it is necessary, first, to ask 'What is the aspect of public policy which founds the defence?' and, second, to ask 'But is there another aspect of public policy to which the application of the defence would run counter?'"

24-035 Answering those two questions, Lord Wilson addressed, first, the policy consideration of preserving the integrity of the legal system and not allowing persons to profit from their illegal conduct. He concluded that an award of compensation for injury to Ms Hounga's feelings was not a form of profit from her employment; it did not permit evasion of a penalty prescribed by the criminal law; and it did not compromise the integrity of the legal system. Conversely, he

---

[44] *ParkingEye*, at [38]–[39].

[45] *ParkingEye*, at [64]–[79].

[46] *Hounga v Allen* [2014] UKSC 47; [2014] 1 W.L.R. 1889.

[47] Although it is to be noted that Lord Toulson plainly thought that it would—or at least might—not offend the illegality principle (as cast by him in *Patel*) for her to have been paid for her work on a quantum meruit: see *Patel*, at [74].

[48] *Hounga*, at [42].

said that application of the defence could encourage those in the situation of Mrs Allen to believe that they could discriminate against people like Ms Hounga with impunity; and that could thereby compromise the integrity of the legal system. Turning to the second question, of countervailing public policy issues, the Supreme Court held that the Court of Appeal's decision ran strikingly counter to the public policy against people trafficking and in favour of the protection of its victims. Weighing the policy considerations, the Supreme Court concluded that insofar as any public policy existed in favour of applying the illegality defence, it should give way to the countervailing public policy to which its application would be an affront; the Court held that Ms Hounga was entitled to claim damages for racially discriminatory dismissal.

Effectively going the other way, was the Supreme Court decision in *Les Laboratories Servier v Apotex Inc.*[49] In that case, the Court of Appeal had applied a similarly flexible principle[50]; but the majority in the Supreme Court sharply disagreed, albeit obiter. The case in fact turned on whether there was any relevant "illegality"—applying the law as summarised above, the Supreme Court held unanimously that there had been no conduct engaging the illegality principle, the conduct alleged being the merely tortious act of infringing the claimant's patent. But the majority went on to address how the illegality principle, if it had been engaged, should have been applied. The majority, led by Lord Sumption, held that the Court of Appeal's decision could not possibly be justified by the considerations put forward by that court,[51] describing the wide range of considerations taken into account by the Court of Appeal as amounting to no more than "largely subjective judgments about how badly Apotex had behaved and how much it mattered". They reaffirmed the rule-based approach to the doctrine of illegality, as expressed in the reliance principle from *Tinsley*. The *Hounga* decision was not mentioned by the majority. The minority, including Lord Toulson, approved the Court of Appeal's approach, observing that it was in line with *Hounga*. **24–036**

Although the issue did not need to be resolved in the case, *Bilta (UK) Ltd v Nazir (No.2)*[52] affirmed the sharp division of opinion between members of the Supreme Court in relation to the proper approach to the illegality principle. That division was between, on the one hand, a strictly rule-based approach and, on the other hand, a more flexible approach by which the court would look at the policies underlying the doctrine and decide whether they militated in favour of the application of the principle in any particular case, taking into account a range of potentially relevant factors. **24–037**

---

[49] *Les Laboratories Servier v Apotex* [2014] UKSC 55; [2015] A.C. 430.
[50] *Les Laboratories Servier v Apotex* [2012] EWCA Civ 593; [2013] Bus. L.R. 80, at [73] where it was expressed by Etherton LJ in these terms: "The court is able to take into account a wide range of considerations in order to ensure that the defence only applies where it is a just and proportionate response to the illegality involved in the light of the policy considerations underlying it."
[51] *Les Laboratories Servier v Apotex Inc*, at [21].
[52] *Bilta (UK) Ltd v Nazir (No.2)* [2015] UKSC 23; [2016] A.C. 1.

(4)   The New Law: Patel v Mirza

(i)   The facts of Patel

24–038   Mr Patel transferred sums totalling £620,000 to Mr Mirza for the purpose of betting on the price of RBS shares, using advance insider information which Mr Mirza expected to obtain from RBS contacts regarding an anticipated government announcement. No such government announcement was made, and so the intended betting did not take place. Nevertheless, Mr Mirza failed to repay the £620,000 to Mr Patel. Mr Patel claimed for the recovery of the sums which he had paid, on various bases, but most relevantly for present purposes on the ground of unjust enrichment. The agreement between Mr Patel and Mr Mirza amounted to a conspiracy to commit an offence of insider dealing under s.52 of the Criminal Justice Act 1993. In order to establish his claim to the return of his money, it was necessary for Mr Patel to explain and establish the (illegal) nature of the agreement.

24–039   Applying the "reliance principle" stated in *Tinsley v Milligan*,[53] the first instance judge, who raised the illegality principle of his own motion, held that Mr Patel's claim to recover the sum paid was unenforceable because he had to rely on his own illegality to establish it (unless he could bring himself within the exception to the doctrine known as *locus poenitentiae*—but he could not do so because he had not voluntarily withdrawn from the illegal scheme). In the Court of Appeal, the majority agreed with the judge on the reliance issue, but disagreed with him on the application of the *locus poenitentiae* exception. They held that it was enough for the claim to succeed that the scheme had not been executed. Gloster LJ, in the minority, reached the same result but essentially rejected the application of the reliance principle and took an approach which was similar to that taken by the Court of Appeal in *ParkingEye* and *Apotex*, and, in the end, by the majority of the Supreme Court in *Patel*.

(ii)   The reasoning and decision in Patel

24–040   When the case came before the Supreme Court it raised fairly and squarely the question of whether the reliance principle established in *Tinsley* was correct and, if not, what was the right conceptual framework for the illegality principle. Accordingly, the Supreme Court sat as a bench of nine Justices in order to conclude the controversy in this area of the law. By a majority of five—or possibly six[54] – of the Court, they did so (subject to the caveats mentioned in section A above and considered in section C(5) below), rejecting the reliance principle and disapproving the reasoning of *Tinsley v Milligan*. The minority also disapproved the reasoning in *Tinsley*, but did not reject the reliance principle: they said the reliance principle had not been properly applied in *Tinsley* and *Collier*.

---

[53] *Tinsley v Milligan* [1994] 1 A.C. 340.
[54] If Lord Neuberger is included.

Lord Toulson wrote for the majority. The important points in the judgment and reasoning can be summarised as follows: **24-041**

(1)   There are two broad, and linked, policy reasons for the illegality principle at common law: (i) that a person should not be allowed to profit from his own wrongdoing; and (ii) that the law should be coherent and not self-defeating, condoning illegality by giving with the left hand what it takes with the right hand (meaning that the civil law—especially in its approach to illegality in civil claims—and the criminal law must be consistent).

(2)   He then proceeded to identify the "trio of considerations" referred to above by reference to which the Court should, in any particular case, seek to decide whether the policy reasons behind the illegality principle are engaged. They are best stated by Lord Toulson himself:

> " ... [O]ne cannot judge whether allowing a claim which is in some way tainted by illegality would be contrary to the public interest, because it would be harmful to the integrity of the legal system, without a) considering the underlying purpose of the prohibition which has been transgressed, b) considering conversely any other relevant public policies which may be rendered ineffective or less effective by denial of the claim, and c) keeping in mind the possibility of overkill unless the law is applied with a due sense of proportionality. We are, after all, in the area of public policy."

(3)   The emphasis is on the overall public interest in the denial of the relief claimed—rather than the question of whether the contract or transaction should be regarded as tainted by illegality. The former is the true question; the latter only relevant to it.[55]

(4)   In relation to the third of the trio of considerations, proportionality, various factors may be relevant. Lord Toulson did not attempt to lay down a prescriptive or definitive list because of the infinite possible variety of cases; but he particularly mentioned, as potentially relevant, factors such as (a) the seriousness of the conduct, (b) its centrality to the contract, (c) whether it was intentional and (d) whether there was marked disparity in the parties' respective culpability. Additional points which have been highlighted by commentators, and quoted in the judgment, include: (e) how serious denial of enforcement would be for the party seeking enforcement, (f) whether barring the claim will further the purpose of the rule which has been infringed, (g) whether denying enforcement will act as a deterrent, (h) whether barring the claim will ensure that the party seeking enforcement does not profit from the conduct and (i) whether denying relief will avoid inconsistency in the law and help maintain the integrity of the legal system.

(5)   Lord Toulson, accordingly, approved *Hounga* as a decision in which it had been necessary to balance countervailing public interest considerations; and *ParkingEye* as a case in which denial of the claim would have been disproportionate.[56]

---

[55] *Patel*, at [104]–[106] and [109].

[56] Crisply summarising the key points as follows: "The claimant did not set out to break the law. If it had realised that the letters which it was proposing to send were legally objectionable, the text would have been changed. The illegality did not affect the main performance of the contract. Denial of the

(6)   Finally, he disapproved the reliance principle and held that *Tinsley* should
        no longer be followed.

24–042   The result of the application of that new approach to the facts of Mr Patel's
          restitution claim was that he succeeded.[57] On examination of the policy
          underlying the statutory provisions about insider dealing, there was no logical
          basis why considerations of public policy should require Mr Patel to forfeit the
          £620,000 which he paid into Mr Mirza's account, and which was never used for
          the purpose for which it was paid. Such a result would not be a just and
          proportionate response to the illegality. Importantly, Mr Patel was seeking to
          unwind the illegal arrangement, not to profit from it.

        (iii)   Further important points to be drawn from Patel for the future

24–043   **Degrees of Fault.**   The previous—conflicting—law on whether there could be
          "degrees of illegality" and to what extent that was relevant need no longer
          concern practitioners: the Supreme Court has made it clear—in *Patel* itself and
          by its approval of the *ParkingEye* decision—that the seriousness of the illegality,
          and the involvement, knowledge and culpability of the claimant (and indeed the
          defendant) may be relevant factors in determining whether the illegality principle
          is engaged.

24–044   **The "In Pari Delicto" Exceptions.**   Relatedly, there have long been exceptions
          to the application of the illegality principle (even under the reliance principle): (i)
          where the illegality of the claimant is brought about by the fraud of the defendant,
          or by undue influence or duress (such that his participation in the illegality is to
          be treated as involuntary); and (ii) where the law that has been broken was
          specifically enacted to protect the class of people to which the claimant belongs
          (such that the invocation of the illegality principle is impliedly excluded by the
          statutory scheme said to have been contravened). These have been described as
          situations in which the claimant and defendant are not *"in pari delicto"*.[58]
          Although these will no longer be analysed as strict exceptions to the
          principle—rather, in line with the *Patel* approach, these situations are to be
          considered in the round like any other—it seems highly unlikely that any case
          which would previously have fitted within the exception will be resolved any
          differently by application of the *Patel* test.

24–045   **Avoidance of Windfalls.**   When a claim is barred by illegality, a defendant
          will—in many if not most cases—gain a windfall. Although that is—to some

---

claim would have given the defendant a very substantial unjust reward. Respect for the integrity of the
justice system is not enhanced if it appears to produce results which are arbitrary, unjust or
disproportionate".

[57] *Patel*, at [115].

[58] Meaning, as noted above (fn.3), "in equal fault" (although the latin phrase has a precise legal
meaning: it is not about a subjective analysis of the relative blameworthiness of the parties; but
whether the parties are *legally* on the same footing—hence the exceptions, which reflect differences in
the parties legal status in respect of the claim and the alleged illegality: see Lord Sumption's judgment
in *Patel*, at [241]–[244]).

extent—an inevitable consequence of a principle of judicial abstention in the public interest,[59] the approach post-*Patel* permits a more nuanced balance of factors. One which is stressed at several points in *Patel* is the undesirability of depriving a claimant wrongdoer of the fruits of his illegality only to give it, equally unmeritoriously, to an equally guilty defendant wrongdoer.[60] This is one aspect of the balancing of different public interests which may be in play—one of them being the public interest in doing justice between the parties and resolving their private law disputes.

The Relevance of Criminal Law.   The majority in the Supreme Court   **24–046**
expanded upon the role of the criminal law. Prior to *Patel*, the emphasis was very frequently on the importance of the criminal law only in relation to the offence giving rise to the illegality. Civil courts were given on occasion to moralising and censoriousness.[61] In *Patel*, the Supreme Court redressed the balance in this connection. Lord Toulson, for the majority, emphasised that part of the harmony of the law is the division of responsibility between the criminal and civil courts, and that punishment was not generally the function of the civil courts. Civil courts should not undermine the effectiveness of the criminal law, but nor should they impose what would in substance be an additional penalty which may be disproportionate to the nature and seriousness of the wrongdoing.[62]

Since very many civil cases involving illegality issues arise from a breach of the   **24–047**
criminal law[63] or from a breach of other rules enacted for the protection of the public in an increasingly regulated world, Lord Toulson's point gives rise to a need to reappraise the way civil courts address the illegality principle. Henceforth, it will be necessary to consider, first, whether it would undermine the criminal law to allow the claim; and then, secondly, (and even if it would or might undermine the criminal law to some extent to allow the claim) whether it would be disproportionate to disallow it, bearing in mind the division between the criminal and civil law and the fact that it is for the criminal courts—and regulators—to punish or correct criminal behaviour and breaches of regulatory rules.

No doubt because each case will turn on its own facts, *Patel* does not explore this   **24–048**
angle in any detail. But in this context, it is important to note that it is open to a court to refer a case to the DPP or the CPS, or to an appropriate regulator: the latter course was in fact taken by the first instance Judge in *Patel*. That should result in the appropriate body considering whether it is in the public interest to bring criminal or disciplinary proceedings resulting in an appropriate penalty, leaving (in an appropriate case) the parties' private rights inter se to be adjudicated in the normal way by the civil courts. Further, there are also

---

[59] And was a point which Lord Mansfield, in his famous dictum in *Holman v Johnson*, seemed to view with equanimity; or at least as a necessary consequence of the application of the illegality principle.
[60] See, in particular, *Patel*, at [118], [167], [208], [254]. See also *ParkingEye*, at [45] and—from longer ago—*St John Shipping Corp v Joseph Rank Ltd* [1957] 1 Q.B. 267, at 288.
[61] See e.g. Lord Mance's observation on this phenomenon at *Patel*, [202].
[62] *Patel*, at [108].
[63] *Les Laboratoires Servier v Apotex Inc*, at [23]–[28].

indications in the judgments in *Patel* that a court might be able in some cases to satisfy the public interest in upholding the criminal law (or other regulatory principles) by inviting the relevant enforcement authority to make an application under the Proceeds of Crime Act.[64]

24–049 **The "Dignity" of the Court.** In a number of the old cases, something is made of the "dignity of the court"—the idea that court should not be required to "sully its hands" to adjudicate on matters which touch illegal conduct. That is regarded by a number of the Justices in *Patel* as an insufficient basis for the Court to withhold adjudication and "not a reputable foundation for the law of illegality."[65] It seems likely that such reasoning will play no further part in the law of illegality.[66]

(5) The Caveats

24–050 We now return to the two main caveats to the proposition that the decision in *Patel* has resolved the conceptual and practical difficulties in this area of the law.

(i) To what extent is the Patel approach binding?

24–051 This might seem a surprising question to pose so soon after the Supreme Court has so plainly sought to re-state the law in relation to the illegality principle, sitting as a panel of nine specifically in order to resolve the 250 year controversy as to the proper approach to this difficult area of law. But it is necessitated by the first instance decision in *Henderson v Dorset Healthcare Trust*.[67] That case does not relate directly to fraud litigation, but the potential problem it reveals as to the applicability of the *Patel* test to cases involving illegality is of general application.

24–052 In *Henderson*, the claimant had stabbed her mother to death when suffering from mental illness, and pleaded guilty to manslaughter on the ground of diminished responsibility. Her mental functioning and self-control were profoundly and substantially, but not wholly, impaired; she had no significant personal

---

[64] Or possibly even by some other form of payment for the public good, as suggested in the Australian case of *Nelson v Nelson* (1995) 184 C.L.R. 538.

[65] Per Lord Sumption, at [258]. Lord Mance referred disparagingly to what he called "early 20th century moralising" (at [202]).

[66] Nevertheless, it should be noted that Lord Toulson made a tentative suggestion that there might be examples of such heinous crimes that no claim connected to such a crime could be adjudicated by the courts. The example he considered was a claim to recover money paid to a contract killer. To this extent there remained a vestige of the idea that there might be conduct with which the Court ought not to sully its hands. But it is not really consistent with the thrust of the rest of Lord Toulson's judgment; and Lords Neuberger and Sumption disagreed. On the *Patel* approach, there is no reason to withhold the remedy sought—the criminal law will, and should be left to, deal appropriately with the crime or crimes committed in this situation. As between the killer and contractor, the least objectionable result is that the money paid should be returned whence it should always have remained. That relief does not condone or further any of the illegal behaviour concerned. But in any event, the gravity of the crime would be but one of the considerations to be taken account of in the *Patel* range of factors approach—it is not right any longer to speak of a rule and exceptions.

[67] *Henderson v Dorset Healthcare Trust* [2016] EWHC (QB) 3275.

responsibility. The event was caused by the defendant Healthcare Trust's negligence in failing to respond to her mental collapse.

In the relevant part of the case—which was in fact obiter—Jay J held that there was binding authority, *Clunis v Camden and Islington Health Authority*[68] in the Court of Appeal, which could not be distinguished from the facts of the *Henderson* case and which precluded recovery of several heads of the damages claimed, for example damages for loss of liberty, on the ground of public policy. He rejected a submission that, while the decision in *Clunis* was not expressly disapproved or overruled in *Patel*, it was inconsistent with the flexible approach laid down in *Patel* and could not survive that decision. He held that the doctrine of precedent required a court to apply the explicit reasoning of a higher court on the facts before it; it did not permit a court to draw logical inferences from statements of general application, in order to justify departing from other binding authority. Accordingly, he held that, before he could depart from *Clunis*, he had to be satisfied that the application of the *Patel* approach to the facts of *Clunis would* or *must* have yielded a different result—that they *might* do was not good enough. In doing so he gave what he described as "full weight" to the dictum of Lord Halsbury in *Quinn v Leathem*.[69] Jay J held that, as he could not be satisfied that the result would or must be different under the *Patel* approach, and as *Clunis* was indistinguishable on the facts, *Clunis* had to be followed.

24–053

It is difficult to imagine that the majority in *Patel* would view this decision with anything other than frustration and dismay; the same is true of practitioners. The present work is not the place to conduct an examination of the doctrine of precedent and the principle of stare decisis in the modern legal world. But Jay J's decision in *Henderson* must surely be open to question. In circumstances where the new "range of factors" approach is part of the ratio of *Patel*,[70] can it really be right that the *Quinn v Leathem* approach requires courts to ignore statements of general principle which have been expressly made, and expressly made *about the law in general*, in order to resolve an acknowledged uncertainty in the legal position? And is it right that it was necessary for Jay J to be able to say that the application of the *Patel* approach to the facts of *Clunis would* or *must* have yielded a different result before he could hold that *Clunis* could not stand with *Patel*? At least in a context like that of the illegality principle (where the outcome of a case will be the result of the application of a multi-factorial approach which varies from case to case) there must be an argument that as the legal framework changes, each new case must be considered afresh without reference to the old

24–054

---

[68] *Clunis v Camden and Islington Health Authority* [1998] Q.B. 978.

[69] *Quinn v Leathem* [1901] A.C. 495: "... every judgment must be read as applicable to the particular facts proved, or assumed to be proved, since the generality of the expressions which may be found there are not intended to be expositions of the whole law, but governed and qualified by the particular facts of the case in which such expressions are to be found. The other is that a case is only an authority for what it actually decides. I entirely deny that it can be quoted for a proposition that may seem to follow logically from it" (at 506).

[70] Although it is true that Lords Sumption and Mance questioned how far it was necessary to go in deciding the case before the Supreme Court, the majority reached their decision by reference to the new approach set out by Lord Toulson.

case law.[71] The doctrine of precedent and stare decisis are about the application of the law as revealed in previous cases to a set of facts: if the facts are the same and the law is the same, the judge must follow the conclusion reached by the higher court on a previous occasion; but if the facts are the same, but the law is different, then the judge should apply the new law to the facts and reach his own view on the result. In any event, even if Jay J is correct in *Henderson*, it cannot be long before the Supreme Court corrects the position to achieve the result it obviously intended to achieve.

(ii)   Does the Patel approach amount to an arbitrary discretion?

24-055   The second caveat to the proposition that *Patel* clarifies the conceptual and practical operation of the illegality principle is the complaint—made by Lord Sumption in his dissent and by others—that the range of factors approach represents a return to the "public conscience" test rejected by the House of Lords in *Tinsley* and gives the Court what amounts to an open discretion as to whether or not to grant relief in any particular case.

24-056   While Lord Toulson, Lord Neuberger and others have valiantly sought to defend the *Patel* approach as not being akin to the public conscience test and/or a discretion, but as instead being a framework for a principled and transparent assessment of the considerations identified,[72] we consider that it is difficult in *practice* to draw much of a distinction between the public conscience test or an open discretion, on the one hand, and the range of factors (assessing whether the illegality bar is in the public interest) approach in *Patel* on the other.[73]

24-057   Some have argued, and with some force,[74] that it is not (or ought not to be) a "discretion" "in law"—i.e. it is not the case that a decision of a first instance judge should only be disturbed if it is one no reasonable tribunal could have reached. If that were right, an appellate tribunal would be able to substitute its own assessment—as a matter of law—as to whether the illegality principle should be engaged in any particular case; and that would largely answer any objection that any discretionary element in practice could become arbitrary. However, in *Singularis Holdings Ltd (in official liquidation) v Daiwa Capital Markets Europe Ltd*,[75] the Court of Appeal has held that an appellate court should only interfere in a trial judge's decision on the application of the *Patel* test "where the judge made an error of principle or reached a conclusion wholly outside the range of reasonable possibilities"[76]. The point was not contested (it was the test put forward by both parties in that case) and the issue may, accordingly, be

---

[71] In due course, a new body of case law, applying the new approach, will build up. Of course, the doctrines of precedent and stare decisis will apply to that.

[72] See, for example, *Patel*, at [113], [120] and [175].

[73] See, for example, *Gujra v Roath* [2018] EWHC 854 (QB), at [30], where the judge endorsed the idea that "judicial instinct" in relation to whether the public would be "surprised (affronted even)" if a claim were to succeed was a good barometer for applying the *Patel* test.

[74] See, for example, Nicholas Strauss QC's article "The Diminishing Power of the Defendant: Illegality after *Patel v Mirza*" [2016] R.L.R. 145, at 156.

[75] *Singularis Holdings Ltd (in official liquidation) v Daiwa Capital Markets Europe Ltd* [2018] EWCA Civ 84.

[76] *Singularis*, at [64].

re-considered in the future. But, for an evaluative exercise which includes at its heart issues of public policy, it might be thought to be a surprising result.

The related point—that the *Patel* approach leaves it hard to predict what the **24–058** outcome of the evaluation might be in any particular case—holds rather less water in light of the fact that the law is replete with instances where that is exactly what judges have to do.[77] As in any such legal arena, a body of law will build up to aid and guide litigants, practitioners and the courts; and, as summarised below, it is already possible to identify broad propositions as to how the courts are likely to approach the task set by the *Patel* approach.

(6) The General Impact of Patel

In practical terms, the *Patel* decision is plainly intended to confine further the **24–059** applicability of the illegality principle to only those situations in which it is genuinely needed in order to protect the public interests identified by the Supreme Court as central to its purpose. As with any significant shift in the law, it will take time to bed down; but, once it has done so, it appears that it will, to a limited extent, have the narrowing effect it was intended to achieve:

(1) In cases where the court is asked to grant a remedy which gives effect to the relevant illegality,[78] the illegality principle is likely to operate to bar the claim much as it did before. However, there will be cases—where the illegality is "minor" or peripheral to the transaction or its performance or incidental to its purpose—in which the illegality principle may no longer be a bar, where the inflexible reliance principle would have denied the claim.

(2) The *Patel* approach will, in general, mean that claims for recovery of money or property transferred under or pursuant to an illegal arrangement or for an illegal purpose will no longer be barred, whereas previously they would have been.

(3) And in most other cases, it seems likely that the illegality "defence" will be rejected—because, where the court is not asked to give effect to the illegality, allowing the claim is unlikely to undermine the integrity of the law and the balance of public policy considerations will not support the application of the illegality principle.

We consider the position post-*Patel* in cases commonly encountered in fraud **24–060** litigation in Section D below.

---

[77] For example, as Strauss observes in "The Diminishing Power of the Defendant: Illegality after *Patel v Mirza*" [2016] R.L.R. 145, that is the approach taken in deciding whether or not there is a duty of care in a negligence case.

[78] Such as claims to enforce illegal contracts, or for damages for their repudiation.

D.   THE POSITION POST-PATEL: COMMON CASES RELEVANT TO FRAUD LITIGATION

(1)   Introduction

24–061   Although it is impossible to survey the whole range of circumstances in which the Patel illegality principle may be encountered, even in the field of fraud litigation, it is helpful to the practitioner to consider the significant points in relation to three common situations arising in fraud cases. They are, first, claims to recover money paid pursuant to an illegal contract or for an illegal purpose; secondly, claims to enforce, or seek damages for breach in respect of, an illegal contract, a contract entered into for an illegal purpose, or a contract which is intended to be or which has been performed illegally; and, thirdly, claims by companies (or other principals) against fraudulent agents.

(2)   Claims to Recover Sums Paid under or Pursuant to Illegal Transactions

(i)   The general position

24–062   This is the direct subject matter of the Patel decision and the basic law on this is now clear: in general a claim to recover money paid, or property transferred, under an illegal transaction or transaction entered into for an unlawful purpose will not be barred by the illegality principle. A claimant seeking to recover such money or property transferred, in an action for unjust enrichment (on the ground of failure of basis), is asking the court to undo the illegal transaction, not to enforce it. As the majority formulated it in the Patel case:

> "A claimant, such as Mr Patel, who satisfies the ordinary requirements of a claim for unjust enrichment, should not be debarred from enforcing his claim by reason only of the fact that the money which he seeks to recover was paid for an unlawful purpose."[79]

Accordingly, both the search for convenient presumptions to avoid an unpalatable result, and the intricacies of the locus poenitentiae, can be consigned to legal history.

24–063   This provides a clear answer to the question that might arise in many claims in fraud litigation, where a party to a fraud seeks the recovery of money or other property transferred under a transaction made illegal by the fraud or the fraudulent purpose for which it was entered into. Examples in the context of fraud litigation are legion: Patel itself was an arrangement in relation to insider trading; further examples include transactions entered into to deceive counterparties as part of a broader illegal scheme or otherwise[80]; arrangements entered into with

---

[79] Patel, at [121].
[80] An example which would be decided differently under the new approach in Patel is Berg v Sadler and Moore [1937] 2 K.B. 158. In that case the plaintiff, who was formerly a member of a tobacco association but had been placed on its stop-list for breach of its rules and was therefore unable to obtain supplies of cigarettes from any of its members, procured another member of the association to

the purpose of defrauding or deceiving creditors or investors by accounting fraud, or otherwise; transactions designed to disguise or hide the ownership of assets for a fraudulent purpose, of which *Tinsley* was a homely example; corrupt arrangements aimed at procuring an illegitimate benefit, such as a classic bribery case: as early as the 18th century, Lord Mansfield himself held in *Walker v Chapman*[81] that a bribe paid to the defendant to secure a job for the plaintiff in the Government service could be recovered in circumstances where the job was not in fact obtained.

A number of further issues in cases of this type present themselves, and they are considered briefly below.   **24–064**

(ii)   Exceptional cases

The Supreme Court was not setting down a fixed rule in relation to claims to recover money; rather, it was summarising what it would expect to be the result in most such cases, because—absent some very unusual feature—it is hard to see how unwinding the objectionable transaction could fall foul of the proper policy behind the illegality principle. Thus, under the majority's range of factors approach, it is wrong to talk[82] in any particular context of a rule and exceptions. There is only the approach to be applied to the facts of any particular case.   **24–065**

As to what any unusual feature might be, there is little help in *Patel*. As we have already mentioned, there is a tentative suggestion that the involvement of a truly heinous crime—such as a contract to murder someone[83]—might lead the Court to bar even a restitution claim.[84] As we have said, it is hard to see, on the *Patel* approach, why that should be so[85]; but, in any event, the gravity of the crime would be just one factor in the "range of factors" approach.   **24–066**

(iii)   Where the illegal transaction has been partly or fully performed

Patel was a relatively simple example of a case in which the illegal transaction had not been performed. No insider information turned out to be available and so nothing had been done with the money which Mr Patel had paid over to Mr Mirza and no trading had been carried out. Thus, no issue was raised as to whether   **24–067**

---

order from the defendant a supply of cigarettes which the plaintiff required. They deceived the defendant, as part of an illegal scheme to get round the stop-list prohibition. The defendants were paid for the cigarettes using the plaintiff's money, but, having doubts as to the bona fides of the transaction, the defendant refused either to deliver the cigarettes or return the purchase-money. The plaintiff sued to recover the money, but failed because of the illegality principle—just as Mr Patel did at first instance in *Patel*. But on the *Patel* approach set out by the Supreme Court, the plaintiff's action in *Berg* would now be unlikely to be barred by the illegality principle.

[81] *Walker v Chapman* (1773) Lofft 342.
[82] As Lord Neuberger in fact does.
[83] Or drug trafficking—per Lord Toulson, at [116].
[84] Lord Toulson referred to *Tappenden v Randall* (1801) 2 Bos. & Paul. 467, at 471, in which Heath J said that there might be a case "too grossly immoral for the court to enter into any discussion of it".
[85] Both Lord Neuberger and Lord Sumption said that in such a case the money ought to be recoverable whether or not the defendant had given consideration by committing the crime: see *Patel* [136] and [254].

restitution is still possible when there has been performance, or some performance. Further, that question was not addressed in the majority judgments; but both Lord Neuberger and Lord Sumption were of the view that, in general, so long as restitutio in integrum were still possible[86]—an ordinary requirement of a claim in unjust enrichment—then it ought not in general to matter whether there had been part, or even total, performance of the contract.[87]

24–068   Additionally, it is worth noting that any argument run by a defendant to a restitution claim that good consideration has been given by the performance of the illegal act will fail: that is because the failure of basis needed to ground the restitution claim is not the absence of consideration in the contractual sense, but arises because the contract is illegal and therefore unenforceable[88].

(iv)   The change of position defence in restitution claims arising from illegal transactions

24–069   As we have discussed in Ch.14 above, on unjust enrichment, there is a defence to a claim in unjust enrichment based on bona fide change of position. Two aspects are important in the context of restitution claims arising out of illegal transactions. The first is the bona fides of the change of position; the second arises if the change of position itself involves illegality (as might often be the situation in cases of this type). It is important to keep those two separate, for they relate conceptually to different things.[89] The first—bona fides—relates to the defendant's understanding of the facts entitling the claimant to the return of the money; at least as a general proposition, it is only if the defendant changes his position innocent of the claimant's rights to recovery that he can plead that it would be unjust for him to have to repay the full amount.[90] The second raises a separate application of the illegality principle itself —in order to set up his change of position defence, the defendant must rely on his own illegal dealings.[91]

---

[86] If necessary by means of counter-restitution. In this context, restitutio in integrum probably means the courts doing what is "practically just", making appropriate adjustments to achieve substantial restitution, even if precise restoration of the original position is no longer possible—i.e. applying the principle adopted in contract cases: see *Erlanger v New Sombrero Phosphate Co* (1878) 3 App Cases 1218, at 1278; *O'Sullivan v Management Agency and Music Ltd* [1985] Q.B. 458, at 466.

[87] *Patel*, per Lord Sumption at [253], per Lord Neuberger at [167]–[168]; and Lord Clarke and Lord Mance agreed at [220] and [197]–[198].

[88] See, e.g., per Lord Sumption in *Patel*, at [249].

[89] See, e.g., *Barros Mattos Junior v General Securities* [2004] EWHC 1188 (Ch); [2005] 1 W.L.R. 247, at [22] and [23], interpreting Lord Goff's original formulation in *Lipkin Gorman v Karpnale Ltd* [1991] 2 A.C. 548, at 580. The *Barros* case arose out of a large fraud perpetrated on a Brazilian bank by a group of individuals in Nigeria. A sum of money was fraudulently transferred to the defendants, who changed it into Nigerian currency and distributed it to the order of the individual fraudsters. Those representing the bank sought restitution of the sums transferred from the defendants, who said that they believed the sums they obtained were honestly held by the fraudsters and that, in changing and transferring the money to their order, they had bona fide changed their position. However, the foreign exchange transactions pursuant to which the money was converted into Nigerian currency and distributed were illegal under Nigerian law.

[90] *Barros*, at [23].

[91] *Barros*, at [25].

In relation to illegality: in theory the court might separately apply the *Patel* **24–070** approach to the conceptually distinct illegality scenario arising on the change of position defence (having already applied it to the restitution claim itself). If the illegality arising in relation to the change of position defence is different from that relevant to the restitution claim, the court might take this two stage approach. But in situations where the illegality relevant to the change of position defence is the same as that relevant to the restitution claim itself, it seems likely that the court would conduct one "range of factors" approach to the situation as a whole. Such an approach would pay proper attention to the desirability of maintaining a flexible approach to the illegality principle which underpins the majority judgment in the *Patel* case. Making an overall evaluation will allow the court to ensure that the resolution of the case respects the policy aims underlying the illegality principle and any other relevant public interests in play.

As to the outcome of that overall evaluation: in general, if the change of position **24–071** arises from the same illegality as tainted the original transaction, it might be thought an odd result if illegality were not to bar the restitution claim but did bar a change of position defence. That said, the only member of the Supreme Court even to touch upon this issue in *Patel*, Lord Neuberger, said that the court might well be justified in refusing a claim for repayment where the contract has not been performed, but only "if the defendant has spent the money and *was unaware of the facts giving rise to the illegality at the time he spent it*"[92] (our emphasis).

It is suggested that the courts may also need to adopt a more flexible approach to **24–072** the bona fides issue in situations such as this. Imagine, for example, that in *Patel* Mr Mirza had obtained some inside information, but its application in trading in fact led to a loss of, say, £50,000. Mr Mirza has, in such circumstances, arguably changed his position but (i) he has done it by performing the illegal contract, via insider trading, and (ii) he has done it in in the knowledge of the facts which ground Mr Patel's right to recover the £620,000 he originally paid over to Mr Mirza.

The latter point would—on a traditional application of the good faith requirement—preclude Mr Mirza from running a change of position defence in respect of the £50,000 loss. It may be thought that that is the right result. But the good faith requirement is a reflection of the fact that a change of position defence ought only to succeed where a defendant can say it is not just for him to have to repay the full amount by which he has been prima facie unjustly enriched; it is, in general, only if the change of position has come about bona fide that he will be able to sustain such a submission. However, in this situation, Mr Patel and Mr Mirza are equally culpable in relation to the illegal insider trading; Mr Patel has provided all the money with which the speculation would be conducted and Mr Mirza has done that which the parties agreed should be done with that money. If the result is a loss of £50,000, there is at least an argument that it would accord with both the policies underlying the illegality doctrine and the justice between the parties, that Mr Mirza should have a defence to Mr Patel's claim in restitution to the extent of the £50,000. Mr Patel can hardly complain if the illegal trading for which he provided money has produced a loss; indeed one might argue that

---

[92] *Patel*, at [182].

permitting him to recover the full sum he initially provided would permit him to benefit from his illegality. Conversely, allowing the defence would not permit Mr Mirza to profit from his illegality. Ultimately, these are questions with which the Court will have to grapple when appropriate cases come before it.

(3) Claims to Enforce, or for Damages for Breach of, Illegal Contracts etc.

(i) Categories of contract affected by illegality

24-073   Leaving aside contracts or transactions which are specifically prohibited by statute,[93] contracts may be affected by illegality in a number of different ways. They traditionally fall into four broad categories[94]:

(1) Contracts which are illegal as to formation: contracts which cannot be performed in accordance with their terms without the commission of an illegal act.[95]

(2) Contracts which are illegal as to performance: contracts which both (or one) of the parties intend to perform in an illegal manner.[96]

(3) Contracts which are entered into for an illegal purpose: otherwise unobjectionable contracts which were entered into for an illegal purpose.

(4) Contracts not falling into any of the categories above, but which are in fact performed, carried out or used in an illegal manner or for an illegal purpose.

24-074   Under the old law on the illegality principle, none of these categories of contract was enforceable[97]; and, in general, an action, for breach or otherwise, founded on such a contract was barred (although it is fair to say that the law was not always consistently applied to the fourth category; and in all categories one can find old cases where the reliance principle does not appear to have been applied).

---

[93] As to which there is no room for debate, as they are void.

[94] For a fuller discussion, the reader is referred to the standard works on the law of contract.

[95] *Patel* itself is an example of this in the fraud context. So, too, from longer ago was *Scott v Brown, Doering, McNab & Co* [1892] 2 Q.B. 724: that involved an agreement by two parties to deceive the public by making it look as though the market was prepared to pay a premium for shares when it was not.

[96] For the illegality as to performance rule to apply there is no requirement that the illegal performance be intended from the time the contract is entered into; the formation of the intention after the execution of the contract can bring the rule into play: see *ParkingEye*, at [33].

[97] These contracts were held to be "unenforceable" rather than "void" where void means "that the agreement was never made", because "property can pass under an illegal contract" and the court in certain circumstances will "enforce a contract which contains an element of illegality": see *Paros Plc v Wordlink Group Plc* [2012] EWHC 394 (Comm), at [80].

(ii)   The position post-Patel

It remains to be seen, but it is doubtful whether the practical result will change very significantly under the new *Patel* "range of factors" approach, particularly as regards the first three categories. However:

24–075

(1)   It is correct to underline that the conceptual framework has changed. So, for example, the enquiry no longer begins and ends with the proposition that the court cannot enforce an illegal contract, even in the most serious cases of illegality as to formation (where the contract cannot be performed without committing an illegal act). Instead, the approach laid down by *Patel* requires the court to take into account the full range of factors, even though the public interest in the consistency of the law and preventing a wrong-doer from profiting from his wrong is very likely to be the dominant factor in any claim to enforce such a contract.

(2)   In cases where the illegality is "less serious" and/or is not centrally relevant to the relief claimed and/or can be dealt with by other means (such as referral to other supervisory authorities etc.), the courts may find more room to manoeuvre than hitherto.

An example is the *ParkingEye* case, but even there it is important to note that the case had relatively unusual facts: the contract could be performed without any illegality (the form of the deceitful letters to be sent by ParkingEye to customers were not agreed *as part of the contract*; they were approved "collaterally"); the Judge found that there was no fixed intention to perform the contract illegally (even though the form of the letters had been approved prior to the contract's formation); and the contract was entered into for a perfectly legal purpose. Accordingly, the contract only fell into the fourth category above. And the action was for damages for repudiatory breach: in that context, it was possible to compensate ParkingEye for the loss of the lawful benefit of the contract which had been wrongly repudiated without in any way condoning the tangential illegality and whilst making certain that no element of the damages compensated ParkingEye for revenue it would have received by performing the contract in an illegal manner.[98] The fact that, in some limited respects, the contract had historically been performed in an illegal manner did not matter.

24–076

Another example in the fraud context might be the case of *Napier v National Business*.[99] This case involved an otherwise lawful employment agreement which was structured by the parties to evade the payment of income tax: the parties agreed that the plaintiff should be paid £13 a week salary and £6 a week for "expenses"; but the latter was simply disguised salary. Having been sacked, Napier sued for wrongful dismissal. The issue related to his period of notice and he claimed for pay and "expenses" in the total sum of £19 per week for the period which he contended was his proper notice period. It was held, under the law as it then was, that the contract as a whole was unenforceable—and that the claim for

24–077

---

[98] A discount was made, during the complex exercise of assessing damages, to take account of this point: see *ParkingEye*, at [24]–[25].
[99] *Napier v National Business* [1951] 2 All E.R. 264.

£13 per week salary properly so called was not severable. The claim was barred *in toto*. This is a case in which the result might be different under the *Patel* approach: it seems likely that at least the claim for salary as defined in the contract (for £13 per week) could succeed without trespassing on the policy objectives of the illegality principle. But, further, on the *Patel* approach the court could allow the whole claim (for £19 a week), while dealing with the illegality simply by reporting it to the tax authorities. HMRC is the authority whose job it is to enforce tax law and it has ample powers to prosecute or to impose penalties proportionate to the offence, as it considers appropriate in the public interest. Allowing the claim while leaving it to HMRC to deal with the tax fraud would not involve giving effect to the illegal agreement to evade tax, and it would respect the integrity of the law and the division of responsibility between different parts of the State's machinery for law enforcement. It would not be justifiable for the court to impose an additional penalty on the employee by disallowing his claim, which would simultaneously have the undesirable effect of rewarding the equally blameworthy employer.

24–078 The *ParkingEye* case also highlights the crucial importance of the cause of action to the question of whether illegality should bar the claim: as Lord Toulson identified, the key focus for the court is on whether granting the relief claimed would be consistent with public policy; not an abstracted consideration of how "tainted" the transaction may be. Accordingly:

(1)   It is almost inconceivable that the court could order specific performance of a contract illegal as to formation or entered into for an illegal purpose (at least if that purpose is still pursued): it would involve the court ordering to be done that which it is illegal to do; and the balance of policy considerations must, absent some truly extraordinary circumstance, always come down against such a course.[100] The same is probably true of contracts illegal as to performance, at least if the mode of intended performance either cannot be, or has not been, altered. But where an illegal purpose or mode of performance is abandoned for some reason, what remains—if a lawful contract in and of itself, and depending on the other circumstances— might be enforceable on the *Patel* approach.

(2)   The same reasoning would, in general, preclude actions for money due for performance of such contracts, or otherwise already due under such contracts. Such claims are, in effect, enforcement of the terms of an illegal contract. Consider, for example, if the contract in *Patel* had been performed and the insider trading had generated a profit—could Mr Patel have sued for an account of those profits in addition to restitution of the original £620,000? Applying the *Patel* approach, it is suggested that the answer is no: the proper course would be to deny the claim to the account of profits on the basis of the illegality principle and address the windfall to Mr Mirza by appropriate reporting to the relevant authorities who could decide whether to prosecute and/or initiate proceedings for confiscation under the

---

[100] That is certainly the view taken by Lord Neuberger in *Patel*, at [159] and [160]: "For the court to make an order for specific performance in such cases would seem to infringe the principle of consistency" in the law.

Proceeds of Crime Act. Similarly, a claim for payment of an agreed bribe following performance by the bribed agent would fail on the *Patel* approach, as it would have previously.

(3)   Only in cases where the illegality is more minor—and incidental to an otherwise legal contract—might the *Patel* approach permit enforcement of a contractual obligation to pay. Lord Neuberger, in *Patel*, gives an imaginary example of an "extreme case" where

> "an employer employed a builder to carry out construction work which they both knew would inevitably require the builder to park illegally—say on a double red line. If the defendant refused to carry out the work, the contract could not be enforced prospectively by the employer. However, if the builder carried out the work, the employer would not be able to avoid liability to pay in full: the fact that the defendant could not perform his obligations under the contract without committing a relatively technical and incidental crime would not deprive him of the right to payment in full for such performance."[101]

Such an approach is not without its problems, even on the *Patel* "trio of considerations" basis (although it could be justified on the "proportionate response" basis, especially if accompanied by reporting to the relevant parking authorities); an alternative solution in such a case might well be to deny the contractual claim to payment on the basis of the illegality principle, but to permit a quantum meruit for the lawful work done.

(4)   Damages for repudiatory breach of illegal contracts raise similar difficulties to those encountered in actions for specific performance: as Lord Neuberger put it in *Patel*, conceptually, such damages are a substitute for prospective performance; but performance is not something the court can award in relation to contracts such as this. It seems inconsistent with the court's function to penalise a defendant in damages for not doing something illegal or to compensate a claimant for not having a benefit which would have required either or both of the parties to do something illegal. *ParkingEye* was a case in which damages for repudiatory breach were given: but the contract was not itself illegal—in any of the first three categories identified above—and the damages could be awarded without in any way enforcing or condoning the illegal manner in which the contract had previously been (but did not need to be) performed.

(5)   Whether actions for damages for non-repudiatory breach of illegal contracts succeed will depend, it is suggested, on the detailed circumstances, including in particular the severity of the illegality and the particular breach alleged. For example, breach of a contract term requiring the defendant to do something which is not unlawful (or for an unlawful purpose) will not engage the public policy justifications for the illegality principle to the same extent as breaches more directly connected to illegality might. The post-*Patel* position in relation to the *Napier* case might be viewed as an example here.

---

[101] *Patel*, at [178].

(iii) Illegal schemes involving a number of contracts

24–079   Under the old law, if the parties' unlawful conduct was part of a scheme involving a number of contracts, it was not necessary to establish that each contract was unlawful as each would be unenforceable by virtue of being part of the unlawful scheme: *Beijing Jianlong Heavy Industry Group v Golden Ocean Group Ltd*.[102] Again, post-*Patel* the position will depend upon the particular circumstances; but there may be situations in which a more discriminating approach is necessary.

(4)   Claims by Companies (or Other Principals) Against Fraudulent Agents

24–080   This species of claim arises when a principal—typically a company in the hands of a liquidator or other new management—sues to recover monies or other assets fraudulently diverted by previous directors or employees. Defendants can include not only the defaulting agents, but others alleged to be in some way responsible for the fraud or for a failure to prevent it, such as accountants and bankers who it is said owed a duty of care which, had it not been breached, would have prevented the fraud. The illegality issue arises because defendants argue that the wrong-doing of the defaulting agent should be attributed to the principal such that the principal is relying on his own illegality in bringing his action.

24–081   As in the case of *Bilta* itself, which resolved long controversial issues as to the law of attribution in this context, these situations are more appropriately considered as turning on the principles of attribution. That topic is considered in detail in Ch.19.

24–082   That is the approach taken by Rose J in *Singularis Holdings Ltd (in official liquidation) v Daiwa Capital Markets Europe Ltd*,[103] confirmed on appeal,[104] a case of this type decided since *Patel v Mirza*. But, in case that approach should prove to be wrong, the Judge also considered how the new *Patel* test would apply to the factual scenario at hand. Singularis' sole shareholder and previously dominant director, Mr Al Sanea, had fraudulently funnelled Singularis' funds to other companies he owned through the defendant stockbroker. The liquidators of Singularis sued the defendant stockbrokers, inter alia for breach of their duty of care under *Barclays Bank Plc v Quincecare Ltd*[105] to refuse to implement a valid instruction to pay money out of the customer's account in view of obvious signs that the payments were for the benefit of the director and not the creditors of the company. The defendant asserted that the claim was barred by illegality (on the basis that Mr Al Sanea's conduct should be attributed to Singularis such that it was relying on its wrong in bringing the claim). It relied on two illegal acts: Mr

---

[102]   *Beijing Jianlong Heavy Industry Group v Golden Ocean Group Ltd* [2013] EWHC 1603 (Comm), at [27].

[103]   *Singularis Holdings Ltd (in official liquidation) v Daiwa Capital Markets Europe Ltd* [2017] EWHC 257 (Ch).

[104]   *Singularis Holdings Ltd (in official liquidation) v Daiwa Capital Markets Europe Ltd* [2018] EWCA Civ 84.

[105]   *Barclays Bank Plc v Quincecare Ltd* [1992] 4 All E.R. 363. See Ch.13.

Al Sanea's deceit in procuring distributions of funds by the defendant, and his breach of fiduciary duty owed to Singularis. In applying the *Patel* test:

(1) Rose J considered the purpose of the prohibitions at play and concluded that neither would be furthered by barring the claim: the prohibition on breach of fiduciary duty was to protect Singularis from this very type of behaviour; and the balance of protections as between banker and customer represented by the *Quincecare* duty would be disrupted in a way which would not enhance the integrity of the law if this type of illegality were to a bar a claim in which—ex hypothesi—the duty on the stockbroker was engaged and had been breached. She held that neither allowing nor denying the claim was likely to affect the conduct of dishonest directors like Mr Al Sanea.

(2) The Judge held that denial of the claim would have a material impact on the growing reliance on banks and other financial institutions to play an important part in reducing and uncovering financial crime and money laundering: if a regulated entity can escape from the consequences of failing to identify and prevent financial crime by casting on the customer the illegal conduct of its mandated employee, that policy would be undermined.

(3) Finally, Rose J considered that denial of the claim would be an unfair and disproportionate response to the wrongdoing on the part of Singularis, especially as in this case it was possible to make a deduction to reflect Singularis' contributory negligence (which would be a more appropriate adjustment than the rather blunt instrument of the illegality defence).

CHAPTER 25

LIMITATION

A. INTRODUCTION

In preceding parts of this book we have considered a range of causes of action—tortious, statutory and equitable—of likely relevance to a claim in fraud. This chapter considers the different statutory limitation periods, and their equitable analogues, applicable to these causes of action, as well as the concepts of delay and acquiescence, which can provide a defence to a claim in equity where a limitation period does not apply. We also consider specific limitation issues which frequently arise in claims founded on fraud.

25–001

There are many generic limitation questions which can arise in fraud claims, as much as in other civil claims. These include matters such as the extension of the limitation period by acknowledgment and part-payment; the inter-relation between limitation periods and the law of set-off; and procedural questions such as the pleading of new causes of action by amendment or the joinder of new parties outside the relevant limitation period. These issues are not discussed here.[1] What follows is necessarily only an overview of what is in itself a complex subject; and its focus is on those aspects of limitation that are of particular relevance to claims in fraud.

25–002

Whenever a defendant pleads a limitation defence it will be for the claimant to show that the claim is not statute-barred.[2] The burden will be on him to show that he has brought his action within the time period prescribed by the relevant section of the Limitation Act 1980 or otherwise.[3]

25–003

---

[1] A full discussion of such matters may be found in A. McGee, *Limitation Periods*, 7th edn (London: Sweet & Maxwell, 2014).

[2] *London Congregational Union Inc v Harriss & Harriss* [1988] 1 All E.R. 15.

[3] One should note that an action is generally deemed to be brought on the day on which the claim form as issued is received by the Court Office, not the date of issue—see Practice Direction 7A, para.5.1.

B. PRIMARY LIMITATION PERIODS

(1) Claims in Tort Generally

25–004 In the chapters above we have considered numerous common law causes of action, including deceit, conspiracy, inducement of a breach of contract and malicious falsehood. These are all, of course, claims in tort. Accordingly s.2 of the Limitation Act 1980 ("the 1980 Act") is prima facie applicable to all of them.[4] By that section:

> "an action shall not be brought after the expiration of six years from the date on which the cause of action accrued."

25–005 In almost all claims in tort damage is the "gist" of the action[5]: the tort is only complete, and so the cause of action only accrues, when legally recognised damage has been sustained by the claimant. There is a substantial body of authority on that question.[6] However it is vital to bear in mind that s.32(1) of the 1980 Act, considered below, is applicable to any claim "based upon the fraud of the defendant." As discussed below the phrase "based on fraud" has been accorded a narrow meaning and so not all claims which might be thought to fall within the purview of this book will be regulated by s.32 (although s.32 also extends to claims where there has been deliberate concealment by the defendant). In any event, s.32 applies "in the case of any action for which a period of limitation is prescribed by this Act" and its effect is to postpone the commencement of running of that limitation period (rather than to substitute a different period); hence in all cases potentially falling within s.32 it will be necessary first to ascertain what period of limitation is prescribed by the 1980 Act.[7]

(2) Conversion/Theft

25–006 Section 2 of the 1980 Act applies to claims in conversion; but s.3 makes further provision for claims in conversion where there has been a subsequent conversion, and also provides for the consequences of the expiry of the limitation period. In essence:

(1)   the further conversion does not restart time running (time continues to run from the date of the original conversion); and

---

[4] Apart from malicious falsehood, to which (in common with libel) special limitation rules apply: see ss.4A and 32A of the Limitation Act 1980.

[5] The main exceptions are libel and certain types of slander, false imprisonment and trespass to land when the claim is brought by the person in possession of that land. None of these torts are considered in this book.

[6] See generally McGee, *Limitation Periods* (2014), at Ch.5.

[7] Section 14A prescribes an alternative limitation period for actions for "damages for negligence". We do not consider this in this book.

(2) if possession of the chattel has not been recovered by expiry of the limitation period, then the claimant's title to the chattel which has been converted is extinguished.

Section 4 prescribes a separate limitation regime relating to the theft of chattels.[8] In broad summary, although the section is complex and unelucidated by judicial analysis, where chattels are stolen, then time does not run in favour of the thief; but where the claimant's title to the chattels is extinguished by expiry of the limitation period applicable to a claim in conversion, he cannot bring a claim in respect of a theft of the chattels, unless the theft preceded the conversion.

(3)   Claims in Contract

There is, of course, a different statutory provision for claims in contract. By s.5 of the 1980 Act it is provided that: **25–007**

> "An action founded on simple contract shall not be brought after the expiration of six years from the date on which the cause of action accrued".

The crucial difference between the limitation period applicable to a breach of contract and the limitation period in tort is that in contract the cause of action accrues (and hence time starts running) on the occurrence of the breach of contract (irrespective whether any loss flows from breach), whereas in tort the cause of action accrues only when damage recognised by the law is suffered. That might be a later date than the relevant act or omission complained of. This is because, as we have seen, in general in the law of tort damage is the "gist" of the cause of action.   **25–008**

(4)   Claims under Statute

In Ch.16 above we considered claims under s.423 of the Insolvency Act 1986. By s.8(1) of the 1980 Act: **25–009**

> "An action upon a specialty shall not be brought after the expiration of twelve years from the date on which the cause of action accrued".

An "action upon a specialty" includes a claim under a statute. However, by s.8(2) this does not apply where any shorter period of limitation is prescribed by the Act. Section 9(1) is such a provision. It provides:

> "An action to recover any sum recoverable by virtue of any enactment shall not be brought after the expiration of six years from the date on which the cause of action accrued."

In the context of claims under s.423 of the Insolvency Act 1986 it has been held that the question of whether s.8(1) or s.9(1) applies turns on the substance of the

---

[8] Theft includes obtaining chattels by blackmail or by fraud within the definition of the Fraud Act 2006: s.4(5).

relief sought: the Court will "look to see what is actually claimed".[9] Where the transaction sought to be set aside is a simple payment of a sum of money, such that in substance what is being sought is an order for repayment, the Court is likely to apply a six-year limitation period under s.9(1)[10]; but where the claim is to set aside a transfer of property and re-vest the property in the transferor, it is more likely to attract a 12-year limitation period. Note also that, in the case of claims by office holders, time only starts to run on the making of the bankruptcy or winding up order.[11]

(5) Claims for Breach of Trust or the Recovery of Trust Property and Claims against Fiduciaries

25–010   Section 21 of the 1980 Act makes provision for the limitation periods which apply in respect of actions for breach of trust, and for the recovery of trust property. It is a provision which is more complex than it appears; albeit the recent decisions of the Supreme Court in *Williams v Central Bank of Nigeria*[12] and *Burnden Holdings (UK) Ltd v Fielding*,[13] and of the Court of Appeal in *First Subsea Ltd v Balltec Ltd*[14], have substantially clarified its operation.

25–011   The starting point is that any "action by a beneficiary to recover trust property or in respect of any breach of trust" is subject to a six–year limitation period from the date of accrual of the cause of action (s.21(3)).[15] This wording captures:

(1)   claims for breach of trust; and

(2)   accessorial claims in equity arising out of a breach of trust (i.e. dishonest assistance and knowing receipt).[16]

25–012   Breaches of fiduciary duty (properly so called—i.e. the obligation of single-minded loyalty and similar)[17] will also generally fall within s.21(3).[18] However, the Court may instead apply limitation periods applicable to contract and tort to claims for compensation for breach of fiduciary duty in circumstances in which such claims are merely another means of re-formulating, and seeking

---

[9] *Hill v Spread Trustee Ltd* [2006] EWCA Civ 542; [2007] 1 W.L.R. 2404, at [115]. See also *Re Yates (A Bankrupt)* [2005] B.P.I.R. 476, at [183], per Charles J.

[10] *Re Priory Garage (Walthamstow) Ltd* [2001] B.P.I.R. 144, at 160F–160G, per John Randall QC, sitting as a Deputy High Court Judge. See also the (obiter) observations of Laurence Rabinowitz QC, sitting as a Deputy High Court Judge in *JSC Bank v (1) Mukhtar Ablyazov (2) Madiyar Ablyazov* [2016] EWHC 3071 (Comm), at [155].

[11] *Hill v Spread Trustee Ltd*, above, at [150].

[12] *Williams v Central Bank of Nigeria* [2014] UKSC 10; [2014] A.C. 1189.

[13] *Burnden Holdings (UK) Ltd v Fielding* [2018] UKSC 14; [2018] 2 W.L.R. 885.

[14] *First Subsea Ltd v Balltec Ltd* [2017] EWCA Civ 186.

[15] Which provides in part: "an action by a beneficiary to recover trust property or in respect of any breach of trust, not being an action for which a period of limitation is prescribed by any other provision of this Act, shall not be brought after the expiration of six years from the date on which the right of action accrued."

[16] See e.g. *Williams v Central Bank of Nigeria*, above, at [97].

[17] See *Bristol & West Building Society v Mothew* [1998] Ch. 1, at 16–20.

[18] See *Gwembe Valley Development Company Ltd v Thomas Koshy* [2003] EWCA Civ 1048, at [84]–[112].

compensation on the same basis as, claims which have been or could have been couched in terms of breach of contract or tort.[19]

The six-year limitation period set out in s.21(3) is subject to a carve-out, set out in s.21(1):

  25–013

"No period of limitation prescribed by this Act shall apply to an action by a beneficiary under a trust, being an action—

 (a) in respect of any fraud or fraudulent breach of trust to which the trustee was a party or privy; or

 (b) to recover from the trustee trust property or the proceeds of trust property in the possession of the trustee, or previously received by the trustee and converted to his use."

The effect of this provision is that, if a beneficiary under a trust brings an action against a trustee of that trust either (a) in respect of a fraud or fraudulent breach of trust; or (b) to recover from the trustee property or the proceeds of trust property, then no limitation period under the 1980 Act will apply. While it was once thought that no limitation period under the 1980 Act applied in respect of claims against third parties who were accessories to fraudulent breaches of trust,[20] it is now clear post-*Williams* that s.21(1) only disapplies the 1980 Act limitation periods in respect of claims *against trustees*, and will not disapply statutory limitation periods in respect of claims against dishonest assistants and knowing recipients caught up in fraudulent breaches of trust. This might at first blush seem a strange conclusion, when (as noted above) an action "in respect of any breach of trust" in s.21(3) is broad enough to encompass claims against accessories and recipients, and a similar expression appears in s.21(1)(a); but the Supreme Court has determined that the words "to which the trustee was a party or privy" in the latter provision give it a narrower ambit. Section 21(1)(b), which will often be engaged by claims in fraud in addition to s.21(1)(a), was considered by the Supreme Court in *Burnden Holdings (UK) Ltd v Fielding*.[21] The Supreme Court there held that a fiduciary who transfers a trust asset to a company controlled by him is within s.21(1)(b), notwithstanding that he never personally "received" the trust property.

  25–014

In seeking to rely upon s.21(1) of the 1980 Act, it is also important to bear in mind three complications, which we discuss below.

  25–015

First. One must be aware that the 1980 Act uses the terms "trust" and "trustee" in a narrow and specialised sense. Specifically, it is referring to express trustees, persons who have assumed the duties of a trustee (or analogous duties, such as those of a company director)[22] by a lawful transaction which was independent of

  25–016

---

[19] See *Cia de Seguros Imperio v Heath (REBX) Ltd* [2001] 1 W.L.R. 112, at 121–123, and *Gwembe Valley Development Company Ltd*, above, at [95] and [111].

[20] See, for example, *Gwembe Valley Development Company Ltd v Thomas Koshy* [2003] EWCA Civ 1048, at [120].

[21] *Burnden Holdings (UK) Ltd v Fielding* [2018] UKSC 14; [2018] 2 W.L.R. 885.

[22] Regarding the position of company directors, see L. Tucker, N. Le Poidevin and J. Brightwell, *Lewin on Trusts*, 19th edn (London: Sweet & Maxwell, 2017), para.44–072; *First Subsea Ltd v Balltec Ltd* [2017] EWCA Civ 186, at [50] and [58]; and *Burnden Holdings (UK) Ltd v Fielding* [2018] UKSC 14; [2018] 2 W.L.R. 885, at [11].

and preceded the relevant breach of the trust. The terms of s.21(1) will, however, exclude claims against certain types of what would commonly be termed constructive trustees by practitioners.

25–017   The dividing line between the types of constructive trustee who fall within the terms of s.21(1) and those who do not fall within the terms of s.21(1) is set out by Millett LJ in *Paragon Finance Plc v DB Thakerar & Co*,[23] who described the expression "constructive trustee" referring to two different types of case:

> "The first covers those cases already mentioned, where the defendant, though not expressly appointed as trustee, has assumed the duties of a trustee by a lawful transaction which was independent of and preceded the breach of trust and is not impeached by the plaintiff. The second covers those cases where the trust obligation arises as a direct consequence of the unlawful transaction which is impeached by the plaintiff."

25–018   The disapplication of 1980 Act limitation periods only applies to the first of these two categories of case. Millett LJ went on to explain the differences between the two of them. In the first class of case the constructive trustee "really is a trustee." He does not receive the trust property in his own right. He receives it by a transaction by which both parties intend to create a trust from the outset and which is not impugned by the claimant.[24]

25–019   In the second class of case, on the other hand, although the label of constructive trustee is often used to describe the defendant, he in fact never is a trustee. He never assumed the duties of a trustee; but, because of his implication in a fraud, he is held liable to account. He is liable to account as if he were a trustee in respect of property, which he has received adversely to the claimant by an unlawful transaction impugned by the claimant. The constructive trust is the response of equity for dealing with the consequences of fraud. It is different from the response of equity to the consequences of a breach of a pre-existing trust

---

[23] *Paragon Finance Plc v DB Thakerar & Co* [1999] 1 All E.R. 400 (CA), at 414. In *Paragon Finance* the claimant lenders had brought a claim in negligence against solicitors who had become involved in a mortgage fraud. More than six years after the events in question the claimants sought permission to make amendments to introduce new causes of action alleging fraudulent breaches of trust and intentional breaches of fiduciary duty in respect of which they submitted no period of limitation applied. The claimants relied on s.21(1)(a) of the 1980 Act. The application was dismissed. The Court of Appeal initially held that because the amendments sought to make a new allegation of intentional wrongdoing where previously no intentional wrongdoing had been alleged they constituted the introduction of a new cause of action which did not involve substantially the same facts as a claim based on allegations of negligence. Accordingly the question was what was the applicable limitation period to the new causes of action sought to be introduced. It was held that s.21(1)(a) had no application to claims of this type. Similarly, a claim for dishonest assistance where there was no pre-existing trust relationship on the part of the defendants was subject to a primary limitation period of six years. See also *Cattley v Pollard* [2006] EWHC 3130 (Ch); [2007] Ch. 353.

[24] "His possession of the property is coloured from the first by the trust and confidence by means of which he obtained it, and his subsequent appropriation of the property to his own use is a breach of that trust…the circumstances in which he obtained control make it unconscionable for him thereafter to assert a beneficial interest in the property." (*Paragon Finance Plc v DB Thakerar & Co* [1999] 1 All E.R. 400 (CA), at 409B–409D).

obligation. It is used to prevent the legal owner of property, which he has received in his own right, from asserting a beneficial interest in it.[25]

Second. Some trustees can be simultaneously trustees of the first class and trustees of the second class. This is important when one wishes to rely upon s.21(1)(b), which will only apply if the specific trust property which the claimant is seeking to recover is trust property held in the trustee's capacity as a trustee of the first class. For example, in *Gwembe*, a director did not properly declare profits which he made out of contracts entered into by his company with a third party. Such profits were earned in breach of his fiduciary duties, but not by means of him exploiting his pre-existing responsibility for the company's property. As a consequence, s.21(1)(b) was held not to apply on the facts of that case.[26] By contrast, in *JJ Harrison (Properties) Ltd v Harrison*[27] a director transferred his company's property to himself without proper authorisation to do so; he was held to be a constructive trustee of the first class (and, therefore, a claim against him was within s.21(1)(b)).

25–020

The position is different in cases in which one is seeking to rely upon s.21(1)(a). Section 21(1)(a) will apply in any case in which one is suing a trustee of the first class in respect of his fraud or a fraud which he has been a party to. It is not necessary to consider whether the fraud relates to property which he holds as a trustee of the first or second class. Thus s.21(1)(a) will apply to a claim against a company director for dishonest breach of fiduciary duty (because he is treated as a trustee under a pre-existing relationship) even though the breach does not involve the misappropriation of company property.[28]

25–021

Third. The final point to make in relation to the application of s.21(1) of the 1980 Act is that the fraud in question must amount to dishonesty and, in the absence of deliberate concealment, which we consider further below, a claim arising from an honest breach of trust is statute-barred after six years from the date of the breach.[29]

25–022

---

[25] These paragraphs are drawn from the analysis in *Gwembe Valley Development v Koshy* [2003] EWCA Civ 1048; [2004] 1 B.C.L.C. 131, at [86] and following. See *Cattley v Pollard* [2006] EWHC 3130 (Ch); [2007] Ch. 353 and *Williams v Central Bank of Nigeria* [2014] UKSC 10; [2014] A.C. 1189.

[26] Note, however, that it was argued in *Burnden*, above, that where a fiduciary receives a benefit which is, or results from, his breach of duty, it should be held by him on trust for his principal in accordance with *FHR European Ventures LLP v Cedar Capital Partners LLC* [2014] UKSC 45; [2015] A.C. 250 and therefore within the scope of s.21(1)(b). The Supreme Court chose not to address this argument, although it appears likely that it will arise when it hears the appeal in *First Subsea Ltd v Balltec Ltd* [2017] EWCA Civ 186.

[27] *JJ Harrison (Properties) Ltd v Harrison* [2001] EWCA Civ 1467; [2002] B.C.C. 729.

[28] *First Subsea Ltd v Balltec Ltd* [2017] EWCA Civ 186, at [29]–[63].

[29] *Armitage v Nurse* [1998] Ch. 241 (CA), at 263D–263E and 264A–264C, per Millett LJ. In that case Millett LJ had earlier, at 260, explained that the phrase "actual fraud" in a trustee exemption clause "connotes at the minimum an intention on the part of the trustee to pursue a particular course of action, either knowing that it is contrary to the interests of the beneficiaries or being recklessly indifferent whether it is contrary to their interests or not." Note that here dishonesty does not equate to misleading, as in the tort of deceit; it embraces a wider concept.

(6) Claims for Equitable Remedies and Section 36 of the 1980 Act

25–023 Section 36 of the 1980 Act provides that the limitation periods prescribed for claims in tort and contract (amongst certain specified others) do not apply to claims for equitable relief, save to the extent that the Courts apply statutory limitation periods to such claims by analogy. It is important to note that, while the section disapplies some limitation periods under the 1980 Act, it does not disapply all of them. For example, the time limits prescribed in respect of actions relating to trusts and land in ss.15–21 of the 1980 Act apply to claims for equitable remedies which fall within their scope.

25–024 The issues which this section requires one to consider can—in certain circumstances—be extremely complex, and no effort to explore the full range of difficulties which might arise is made here. However, it is suggested that one means of navigating oneself through the questions which arise in the context of equitable remedies and limitation is to ask oneself three questions:

(1)   Is there a claim for an equitable remedy?
(2)   If the answer to question (1) is yes, will the Court apply a limitation period under the 1980 Act by analogy?
(3)   Whether the answer to question (2) is yes or no, is the claim barred by laches or acquiescence?[30]

(i)   Is the claim for an equitable remedy?

25–025 In order for the practitioner to establish whether he need concern himself with s.36 at all, he must establish whether the claim being made is for an equitable remedy.

25–026 In some cases, the remedies sought are unambiguously equitable remedies. This category includes injunctions (including orders for specific performance) and rectification.

25–027 Other remedies may require more careful thought. For example, rescission is available at both common law and equity, but in different circumstances in each of the two jurisdictions.[31] Legal set off takes effect by way of an action (and is therefore subject to limitation considerations), but equitable set off operates by way of defence (and therefore falls outside the 1980 Act).[32] Equity will impose a duty to account on any trustee falling within Millett LJ's first category[33] and may require an account of profits stemming from equitable wrongdoing. However

---

[30] The position taken here, that the defence of laches (by which is meant something more than mere delay) can apply to a claim for an equitable remedy even if the claim is within a statutory time bar, is not uncontroversial, but is consistent with the (obiter) view taken by the Court of Appeal in *P&O Nedlloyd BV v Arab Metals Co* [2006] EWCA Civ 1717; [2007] 1 W.L.R. 2288, at [61]. See Tucker, Le Poidevin and Brightwell, *Lewin on Trusts* (2017), para.44–048 and the cases cited there for the contrary view.

[31] See Ch.23.

[32] Subject to the provisions of s.36(2) of the 1980 Act—see *Filross Securities Ltd v Midgeley* (1999) 31 H.L.R. 465.

[33] See *Henchley v Thompson* [2017] EWHC 225 (Ch).

duties to account may also arise as a matter of contract,[34] or (possibly) in the law of tort.[35] Similarly, to the extent that monetary compensation is being claimed, it may be necessary to give some thought to whether it is being claimed as common law damages, or equitable compensation, or both.

(ii) Will the court apply a limitation period under the 1980 Act by analogy?

Section 36(1) of the 1980 Act provides that specified limitation periods shall not apply to claims for equitable relief   **25–028**

> "except in so far as any such time limit may be applied by the court by analogy in like manner as the corresponding time limit under any enactment repealed by the Limitation Act 1939 was applied before 1st July 1940."

The broad effect of this obscure section is as follows: if a claim is made for   **25–029** equitable relief which is "correspondent to the remedy at law", then the Courts will generally apply the same limitation period to the claim for equitable relief as would be applicable to the correspondent legal remedy.[36] For example, equitable compensation arising from the breach of a contractual or non-contractual duty is correspondent to common law damages for breach of contract or tort, and will therefore tend to be subject to a six-year limitation period.[37] This is the case whether or not the equitable liability arises in parallel with a common law liability[38] or in isolation from any common law liability.[39]

As for claims which do not have a "correspondent remedy at law":   **25–030**

(1) Claims for injunctions and orders for specific performance do not have a correspondent remedy at law.[40] Accordingly, the limitation periods specified in s.36(1) of the 1980 Act do not apply to them. It has been argued persuasively that the same reasoning applies with equal force to claims for rectification.[41]

(2) The position in respect of claims for rescission is somewhat more uncertain. Some academic commentators regard legal rescission as falling

---

[34] As in *Coulthard v Disco Mix Club Ltd* [2000] 1 W.L.R. 707.
[35] See M. Jones (ed), *Clerk & Lindsell on Torts*, 22nd edn (London: Sweet & Maxwell, 2017), para.28–149.
[36] See *P&O Nedlloyd BV v Arab Metals Co* [2006] EWCA Civ 1717; [2007] 1 W.L.R. 2288, at [34]–[54]. Particular complications can arise in the context of the Latent Damage Act 1986. Any reader considering the interaction of ss.14A, 14B and 36 of the 1980 Act should refer to McGee, *Limitation Periods* (2014), para.1.056.
[37] *Coulthard v Disco Club Mix Ltd* [1999] 2 All E.R. 457 and *Cia de Seguros Imperio v Heath (REBX) Ltd* [2001] 1 W.L.R. 112.
[38] As in the *Seguros* case, above.
[39] As in *Raja v Lloyds TSB Bank Plc* [2001] EWCA Civ 210, at [31] and [32].
[40] See *P&O Nedlloyd BV*, at [52].
[41] D. Hodge, *Rectification: The Modern Law and Practice Governing Claims for Rectification for Mistake*, 2nd edn (London: Sweet & Maxwell, 2015), para.6–12.

outside the scope of the 1980 Act altogether,[42] so one might reasonably expect that the statutory limitation periods listed in s.36(1) would not apply to equitable rescission either. There is modern authority which would support that view. So in *Property Alliance Group Ltd v Royal Bank of Scotland Plc*[43] Asplin J stated that claims for rescission were not subject to limitation periods.[44] However, one should be aware that this is in tension with earlier cases, notably *Molloy v Mutual Reserve Life Insurance Company*,[45] in which it was held that a six-year limitation period would apply by analogy to claims for rescission from the point at which the claimant was aware of the right to rescind.[46] Some of these cases (including *Molloy*) were cited before Asplin J and—although she does not say so in terms in her judgment—one might infer that she regarded the older authority as superseded by the Court of Appeal's decision in *P&O Nedlloyd BV*.

(iii)   Is the claim barred by laches or acquiescence?

25–031   A claim for an equitable remedy may be defeated by either acquiescence or laches. These are two separate concepts which will frequently, but not necessarily or invariably, overlap. Broadly stated, the difference is this: acquiescence is engaged by the action (or, on occasion, inaction)[47] of the claimant, and laches is engaged by delay.

25–032   Acquiescence arises in circumstances in which the would-be claimant has conducted himself in such a manner that, in all the circumstances,[48] it would be unconscionable for him to assert his rights to the equitable remedy in question.[49] By way of example, in *Holder v Holder*,[50] the executor of a will took a conveyance of land out of the deceased's estate. The transaction was in breach of the executor's fiduciary duties, and voidable at the election of the beneficiaries. However, the beneficiary who sought to set aside the conveyance had—with full knowledge of the facts of the transaction (though not knowing that he was legally

---

[42] See D. O'Sullivan, S. Elliott and R. Zakrzewski, *The Law of Rescission*, 2nd edn (Oxford: OUP, 2015), para.24.26.

[43] *Property Alliance Group Ltd v Royal Bank of Scotland Plc* [2016] EWHC 3342 (Ch).

[44] *Property Alliance Group Ltd v Royal Bank of Scotland Plc*, see at [257] and [258].

[45] *Molloy v Mutual Reserve Life Insurance Company* 94 LT 756.

[46] *Molloy v Mutual Reserve Life Insurance Company*, see 830–831.

[47] It is often said that "quiescence is not acquiescence" (following submissions by Mr Kekewich before Lord Chelmsford in *Lamare v Dixon* (1873) L.R. 6 H.L. 414, at 422). However, this is too simplistic. If a would-be claimant sees someone infringing their rights, and does nothing about it for a prolonged period of time, that may communicate acquiescence as powerfully as express consent (see e.g. *Gafford v Graham* (1999) 77 P. & C.R. 73, at 81).

[48] The degree to which the would-be claimant was aware of the relevant facts at the time of the conduct said to amount to an acquiescence is a factor, but not the sole or determining factor, in determining whether the defence has arisen—see Tucker, Le Poidevin and Brightwell, *Lewin on Trusts* (2017), para.39–123.

[49] See J. McGhee, *Snell's Equity*, 33rd edn (London: Sweet & Maxwell, 2014), para.18–041, and the cases cited there.

[50] *Holder v Holder* [1968] Ch. 353.

entitled to set it aside)—taken his share of the sale price. The consequence was that he was deemed to have acquiesced in the breach of duty, and was barred from seeking rescission.

Laches arises in circumstances in which the combination of the claimant's delay **25–033** in enforcing his rights, the actions of the parties during that delay, and the matters which have come to pass during that delay, are such that it would be unconscionable to allow the claimant to seek the equitable remedy in question.[51] It was once thought (at least by some) that mere delay, or "gross laches" might engage the defence, but that is now doubted.[52] Rather, the effect of the delay must be such that "it would be practically unjust to give a remedy".[53] This may be as a consequence of some sort of detrimental reliance by the defendant upon circumstances as they appeared during the delay,[54] or for prosaic and practical reasons, such as the loss of evidence over the years, or the death of witnesses.[55]

C. POSTPONEMENT OF RUNNING OF TIME

(1) Introduction

By s.32 of the 1980 Act provision is made for the postponement of the running of **25–034** time for limitation purposes in cases of fraud, concealment and mistake. Much of s.32 is of universal application but, as we shall see, the section has particular relevance in fraud claims.

Section 32(1) of the 1980 Act provides that: **25–035**

> "where in the case of any action for which a period of limitation is prescribed by this Act either:
> (a)   the action is based upon the fraud of the defendant; or
> (b)   any fact relevant to the plaintiff's right of action has been deliberately concealed from him by the defendant; or
> (c)   the action is for relief from the consequences of a mistake;
> the period of limitation shall not begin to run until the plaintiff has discovered the fraud, concealment or mistake (as the case may be) or could with reasonable diligence have discovered it."[56]

Section 32(2) provides that, for the purposes of this provision: **25–036**

> "deliberate commission of a breach of duty in circumstances in which it is unlikely to be discovered for some time amounts to deliberate concealment of the facts involved in that breach of duty".

---

[51] See *Lindsay Petroleum Co v Hurd* (1873-1874) L.R. 5 PC 221, at 239, 240.
[52] See Tucker, Le Poidevin and Brightwell, *Lewin on Trusts* (2017), para.39–113; McGhee, *Snell's Equity* (2014), para.5–011.
[53] Per Rimer J in *Kuppusami v Kuppusami* [2002] EWHC 2758, at [74], quoting Lord Chelmsford in *Lamare*.
[54] See *Fisher v Brooker* [2009] UKHL 41, at [64].
[55] *Bourne v Swan & Edgar Ltd* [1903] 1 Ch. 211, at 219, 220; *Reimers v Druce* (1857) 23 Beavan 145, at 157 and 158.
[56] Section 32(1) continues as follows: "References in this subsection to the defendant include references to the defendant's agent and to any person through whom the defendant claims and his agent."

25-037   It will be seen that s.32(1) describes three scenarios in which the commencement of the limitation period otherwise prescribed by the Act is postponed to a later date. A number of concepts utilised in s.32(1) deserve separate attention.

25-038   Where a defendant pleads a limitation defence then it will be for the claimant to plead and prove whichever limb of s.32 he relies upon in order to defeat the defence and the date when he discovered the relevant facts (whether as set out under sub-paras (a), (b) and/or (c)) or could with reasonable diligence have discovered them.

(2) Fraud

25-039   In order to bring himself within s.32(1)(a) the claimant has to show that his cause of action is "based upon the fraud" of the defendant. This phrase has been interpreted restrictively as meaning that "fraud" must be an essential element of the claimant's claim. So in *Beaman v ARTS Ltd*,[57] where the claimant brought proceedings in conversion, she could not rely upon the relevant wording to delay the commencement of the running of time because the tort of conversion is not dependent on proof of fraud, even though the claimant there alleged that the defendant's behaviour when committing the tort was dishonest. It follows that an action is only "based upon the fraud of the defendant" if it is, for example, a claim for damages for deceit or rescission based on fraudulent misrepresentation, or if dishonesty of some sort is an element to the cause of action.[58] There have been various subsequent decisions considering whether a particular claim is "based upon the fraud of the defendant."[59]

(3) Deliberate Concealment

(i) Concealment

25-040   Where any fact relevant to the claimant's right of action has been deliberately concealed from him by the defendant, the commencement of the running of the period of limitation will be postponed until the concealment is discovered or could with reasonable diligence be discovered. "Any fact relevant to the cause of action" means a fact essential to pleading the cause of action.[60] The words refer

---

[57] *Beaman v ARTS Ltd* [1949] 1 K.B. 550 (CA).

[58] See *Beaman v ARTS Ltd* [1949] 1 K.B. 550 (CA). For cases in which dishonesty, as opposed to fraudulent misrepresentation, has been held to engage s.32(1)(a), see e.g. *Attorney General of Zambia v Meer Care & Desai (a firm)* [2007] EWHC 952 (Ch), at [376]–[386] (fraudulent conspiracy and dishonest assistance), and *JD Wetherspoon PLC v Van de Berg & Co Ltd* [2009] EWHC 639 (Ch), at [620] and following (deliberate breaches of fiduciary duty and dishonest assistance).

[59] See for instance *Regent Leisuretime Ltd v NatWest Finance Ltd* [2003] EWCA Civ 391; [2003] B.C.C. 587 (unsurprisingly held, at [99], that a claim for "fraudulent misrepresentation is a claim based on the defendant's fraud"). See also *Phillips-Higgins v Harper* [1954] 1 Q.B. 550 and *Chagos Islanders v A-G* [2003] EWHC 2222, at [615] and following.

[60] *AIC Ltd v ITS Testing Services (UK) Ltd* [2006] EWCA Civ 1601; [2007] 1 Lloyd's Rep. 555, at [322].

to any fact (as opposed to all facts) which the claimant has to prove to establish a prima facie case, as opposed to evidence which might strengthen that case.[61]

Something is "concealed" if it is "hidden from view".[62] However, it appears that s.32(1)(b) applies if the defendant either "takes active steps to conceal his own breach of duty after he has become aware of it"[63] or, in some cases, withholds relevant information with the intention of concealing the facts in question.[64] Hence deliberate concealment may be shown where the defendant has omitted to do something; it does not require the actual taking of an active step. But concealment must be the intended result[65] (and proving such intention may well be difficult for the claimant to accomplish)[66] and, in the case of intentional concealment by omission to speak (as opposed to by taking active steps), that will only constitute deliberate concealment for the purposes of the sub-section where the defendant "knew himself to be under a duty to disclose."[67]

25–041

So, in *Williams v Fanshaw Porter & Hazelhurst*,[68] the fact that a litigation solicitor had not revealed to the claimant that he had (as was later accepted) negligently consented to an order dismissing a claim brought by the claimant against a third party was a "concealment" for the purposes of s.32(1)(b). It was not necessary to demonstrate that the reason for the failure to report was to prevent a negligence claim being brought. The fact of the dismissal was a fact relevant to the claimant's cause of action against the solicitor; the solicitor had made a conscious decision not to tell her of it. In this sense motive is irrelevant, as opposed to intention. Moreover the defendant need not know that the fact being concealed was "relevant to the cause of action."[69]

25–042

---

[61] [2006] EWCA Civ 1601; [2007] 1 Lloyd's Rep. 555, at [323], per Rix L.J ("Facts which improve prospects of success are not, it seems to me, facts relevant to his right of action"); see also *C v Mirror Group Newspapers* [1997] 1 W.L.R. 131 (CA); *Williams v Lishman, Sidwell, Campbell & Price Ltd* [2010] EWCA Civ 418; [2010] P.N.L.R. 25, at [38], per Rix LJ. The position was recently restated in *Arcadia Group Brands Ltd v Visa Inc* [2015] EWCA Civ 883 as follows: "(1) a 'fact relevant to the plaintiff's right of action' within s.32(1)(b) is a fact without which the cause of action is incomplete; (2) facts which merely improve prospects of success are not facts relevant to the claimant's right of action; (3) facts bearing on a matter which is not a necessary ingredient of the cause of action but which may provide a defence are not facts relevant to the claimant's right of action."

[62] *Giles v Rhind* [2008] EWCA Civ 118; [2008] 3 All E.R. 697.

[63] *Cave v Robinson Jarvis and Rolf (A Firm)* [2002] UKHL 18; [2003] 1 A.C. 384, at [25], per Lord Millett, with whom Lords Mackay and Hobhouse concurred.

[64] *Cave v Robinson Jarvis and Rolf (A Firm)* [2002] UKHL 18, at [60], per Lord Scott (with whom Lords Slynn, Mackay and Hobhouse agreed).

[65] "[T]he defendant must have considered whether to inform the claimant of the fact and decided not to": *Williams v Fanshaw Porter & Hazelhurst* [2004] EWCA Civ 157; [2004] 1 W.L.R. 3185, at [14], per Park J.

[66] *Cave v Robinson Jarvis and Rolf (A Firm)*, above, at [60]: "The standard of proof would be the usual balance of probabilities standard and inferences could of course be drawn from suitable primary facts but, nonetheless, proof of intention, particularly where an omission rather than a positive act is relied on, is often difficult."

[67] *AIC Ltd v ITS Testing Services (UK) Ltd* [2006] EWCA Civ 1601; [2007] 1 Lloyd's Rep. 555, at [321].

[68] *Williams v Fanshaw Porter & Hazelhurst* [2004] EWCA Civ 157; [2004] 1 W.L.R. 3185.

[69] *Williams v Fanshaw Porter & Hazelhurst*, above, at [14], per Park J. Mance LJ left the question open: see at [37].

25–043 In the usual course of events if the defendant is not aware of his error he cannot be said to have deliberately concealed anything; but as the facts in *Williams v Fanshaw Porter & Hazelhurst* show, that does not always follow.

25–044 Section 32(1)(b) postpones the running of time, regardless of whether the concealment in question was contemporaneous with or subsequent to the breach of duty or the accrual of the cause of action.[70] What this means is that time can start running in the normal way from the date of accrual of the cause of action but if, at some time thereafter, the defendant takes a step (or omits to take a step) which constitutes a deliberate concealment from the defendant of a relevant fact then the running of time re-commences from the date of discovery (or constructive discovery) of that concealment. The claimant will thus obtain the benefit of a fresh six-year period of limitation from the date of discovery (or constructive discovery) of the later concealment.

25–045 However, if the claimant is aware of all the relevant facts before the alleged concealment, s.32(1)(b) cannot be relied upon by the claimant.[71]

(ii)   Section 32(2)

25–046 Section 32(2) provides a statutory gloss to s.32(1)(b) by providing that deliberate commission of a breach of duty[72] in circumstances where it[73] is unlikely to be discovered for some time[74] amounts to deliberate concealment of the facts involved in that breach of duty. The word "deliberate" here refers not to the nature of the act or omission simpliciter but requires knowledge on the part of the defendant that his act or failure to act gives rise to a legal wrong. Hence if the defendant intends to do (or refrain from doing) something the fact that that action or inaction constitutes a breach of duty does not make it a deliberate commission of a breach of duty for the purposes of s.32(2) if the defendant is unaware that he

---

[70] *Sheldon v RHM Outhwaite (Underwriting Agencies) Ltd* [1996] A.C. 102 (HL) (disapproving statements by Megarry VC in *Tito v Waddell (No.2)* [1977] Ch. 106, to the effect that, once time begins to run, it runs continuously and a subsequent concealment will not start it running afresh). This decision, which was by a bare majority in the House of Lords, has been much criticised.

[71] *Ezekiel v Lehrer* [2002] EWCA Civ 16; [2002] Lloyd's Rep. P.N. 260, at [32]. There the claimant knew a fact and then apparently forgot it. It was understandably held that he could not rely on s.32(1)(b). See also *Sheldon v Outhwaite* [1996] 1 A.C. 102, where Lord Browne-Wilkinson said, at 144A: "For myself I do not find it absurd that the effect of section 32(1) is to afford to the plaintiff a full six-year period of limitation from the date of discovery of the concealment. In such a case, the plaintiff must have been ignorant of the relevant facts during the period preceding the concealment: if he knew of them, no subsequent act of the defendant can have concealed them from him."

[72] This phrase is to be given a wide meaning so that it approximates to any civilly justiciable legal wrongdoing, and so it includes claims under s.423 of the Insolvency Act 1986: see the lengthy discussion in *Giles v Rhind* [2008] EWCA Civ 118; [2008] 3 All E.R. 697, at [36] and following.

[73] That is the breach of duty, not the facts giving rise to the breach of duty.

[74] It has been held that "some time" may, for these purposes, be a very short period (for example a period of a few days): *Burnden Holdings (UK) Ltd (in liquidation) v Fielding* [2016] EWCA Civ 557, at [54]. See also *Brown v Bird & Lovibond* [2002] EWHC 719 (QB), per Robert Moxon-Browne QC sitting as Deputy High Court Judge. The Supreme Court in *Burnden*, above, at [25] and [26] declined to resolve a point raised by the appellant as to whether the Court of Appeal had been wrong to view s.32 as directed to the time when the wrong might first reasonably have been discovered (as opposed to whether the breach was such that, in the circumstances, it would objectively be regarded as likely to avoid detection "for some time").

has committed a breach of duty.[75] Intentional wrongdoing is therefore required to be proved by the claimant if s.32(2) is to be relied upon.

As an alternative, the claimant may be able to rely on the doctrine of estoppel, in order to avoid the harsh consequences of the operation of the limitation period.[76]   **25–047**

(4)   Mistake

Where a claim is for relief from the consequences of a mistake, the period of limitation does not begin to run until the claimant has discovered the mistake or could with reasonable diligence have discovered it.[77] This only applies if the mistake in question was an essential element of the cause of action, such as claims for the recovery of money paid under a mistake or where a contract is alleged to be void for mistake.[78]   **25–048**

(5)   Discovery of the Fraud/Concealment/Mistake

(i)   Discovery

By s.32(1) time starts running from the date of the claimant's discovery of the fraud, concealment or mistake, as the case may be, or from the date when he could with reasonable diligence have discovered it, if that latter date is earlier.   **25–049**

As regards claims in deceit in *Barnstaple Boat Co Ltd v Jones*[79] the Court held that the phrase "the plaintiff has discovered the fraud" in s.32(1) refers to knowledge of the precise deceit which the claimant alleges had been perpetrated on him. It follows that knowledge of a fraud in a more general sense is not enough to start the limitation period running under s.32(1), although it may lead to the conclusion that the claimant could with reaonable diligence have discovered that precise deceit earlier (as to which see the next section).   **25–050**

---

[75] *Cave v Robinson Jarvis and Rolf (A Firm)* [2002] UKHL 18; [2003] 1 A.C. 384 (over-ruling the extraordinary decisions in *Brocklesby v Armitage & Guest (Note)* [2002] 1 W.L.R. 598 and *Liverpool Roman Catholic Archdiocese Trustees Inc v Goldberg* [2001] 1 All E.R. 182). See also *Mortgage Express v Abensons Solicitors* [2012] EWHC 1000 (Ch); [2012] 27 E.G. 90 and *Grace v Black Horse Ltd* [2014] EWCA Civ 1413; [2015] 3 All E.R. 223.

[76] See *Kaliszewska v John Clague & Partners* (1984) 5 Con. L.R. 62 (QBD) (defendant architect falsely represented to claimant that cracks in building designed by him were insignificant, with the result that limitation period had expired before claimant discovered truth; defendant estopped from relying on limitation period).

[77] See also *Fea v Roberts* [2005] EWHC 2186 (Ch) (executors paid defendant under the mistaken belief that he was the true beneficiary; no reason for them to revisit that assumption before they in fact discovered the truth when the correct beneficiary turned up); *Davies v Sharples* [2006] EWHC 362 (Ch); [2006] W.T.L.R. 839 (no reason to question the word of professional accountants who had dealt with administration of estate trusts).

[78] *Phillips-Higgins v Harper* [1954] 1 Q.B. 411 (CA), approved in *Test Claimants in the Franked Investment Income Group Litigation v Commissioners of Inland Revenue* [2012] UKSC 19; [2012] 2 A.C. 337, at [62] after a very lengthy analysis. See also *Deutsche Morgan Grenfell v IRC* [2006] UKHL 49; [2007] 1 A.C. 558, at [146]–[147], per Lord Walker.

[79] *Barnstaple Boat Co Ltd v Jones* [2007] EWCA Civ 727; [2008] 1 All E.R. 1124, at [34].

Knowledge on the part of the claimant's agent will not be ascribed to the claimant for the purpose of determining the date of discovery.[80]

(ii)   Reasonable diligence

25–051   The final question, which is common to each of the scenarios prescribed by ss.32(1)(a) to (c), is the meaning of "reasonable diligence". In order to postpone the commencement of the running of time to a date later than that otherwise prescribed by the 1980 Act the burden is upon the claimant to show that he did not discover, nor could he have discovered with reasonable diligence, the fraud, concealment or mistake until that later date. It will be for the claimant to plead and prove that later date.

25–052   In *Paragon Finance Plc v DB Thakerar & Co*[81] the Court of Appeal held that the relevant question was:

> "not whether the plaintiffs *should* have discovered the fraud sooner, but whether they with reasonable diligence *could* have done so. The burden of proof is upon them. They must establish that they *could not* have discovered the fraud without exceptional measures which they could not reasonably have been expected to take. In this context the length of the applicable period of limitation is irrelevant…the test was how a person carrying on business of the relevant kind would act if he had adequate but not unlimited staff and resources and were motivated by a reasonable but not excessive sense of urgency". [emphasis in original]

25–053   The rigorous approach disclosed by this passage, which has been much quoted in later cases, should not be taken to constitute a general statement of the legal position. In *Paragon*, which was a claim which arose out of a mortgage fraud, there were numerous pointers which suggested that the claimant might have been the victim of such a fraud. But if there has been no "trigger for an investigation" then the period of reasonable diligence does not begin and it does not make sense to speak of a "reasonable degree of urgency" being required.[82] And in the later decision in *Barnstaple Boat Co Ltd v Jones*,[83] which was a claim in deceit, one detects a more lenient approach to the question of reasonable diligence. In reality the concept of reasonable diligence is vitally dependent on the context.[84]

25–054   In order to establish that a person might with reasonable diligence have discovered a fraud, deliberate concealment or mistake at a particular time, it is not, it seems, sufficient to show that he might have discovered the fraud (etc.) by

---

[80] *Allison v Horner* [2014] EWCA Civ 117, at [15] (a case in deceit).

[81] *Paragon Finance Plc v DB Thakerar & Co* [1999] 1 All E.R. 400 (CA), at 418B–418D.

[82] *JD Wetherspoon v Van de Berg & Co Ltd* [2007] EWHC 1044 (Ch); [2007] P.N.L.R. 28, at [42].

[83] *Barnstaple Boat Co Ltd v Jones* [2007] EWCA Civ 727; [2008] 1 All E.R. 1124.

[84] For example in *Peco Arts Inc v Hazlitt Gallery Ltd* [1983] 1 W.L.R. 1315 (QBD) a work of art believed to be by Ingres (and sold by the defendant on that basis) was subsequently discovered to be a reproduction; "reasonable diligence" did not mean the doing of everything possible nor necessarily the use of any means at the claimant's disposal nor even necessarily the doing of anything at all, but simply the doing of that which the ordinarily prudent buyer and possessor of a valuable work of art would do having regard to all the circumstances. In *Collins v Brebner* [2000] Lloyd's Rep. PN 587 the Court of Appeal held that where the defendant (solicitor) was falsely asserting to the claimant the relevant position, the claimant could not be said to have been able with reasonable diligence to have discovered the true position.

pursuing an inquiry in some collateral matter. Rather, it must be shown that there has been something to put him on inquiry in respect of the matter itself and that, if inquiry had been made, it would have led to the discovery of the real facts. If, however, a considerable interval of time has elapsed between the alleged fraud, concealment or mistake and its discovery, that of itself may be a reason for inferring that it might with reasonable diligence have been discovered much earlier.

SECTION F

INTERIM REMEDIES

CHAPTER 26

THE COURT'S POWERS TO GRANT INTERIM RELIEF

A. INTRODUCTION

(1) The Subject Matter of this Chapter

The practical significance of the court's jurisdiction to grant interim relief in support of claims based upon alleged fraud cannot be overstated. Where a defendant is accused of fraudulent activity giving rise to a claim, there will in most cases probably be good reason to suspect that evasive and dishonest conduct will continue during the life of the claim, with a view to frustrating or undermining the value and enforceability of any eventual judgment. Further, there will commonly be good reason to suspect that the defendant will have already taken steps, or will take steps, to hinder discovery of the fraud, its extent and its consequences. Were the court powerless to act unless and until the claimant had established his case at trial, many a meritorious fraud claim might fail; and many a judgment, if obtained at all, would prove nugatory. For these reasons, the court is equipped with the jurisdiction to grant a wide range of interim remedies.

26–001

In the civil fraud context, the most obvious and potent of such remedies are the freezing injunction and the search order (which are analysed in depth in Chs 30 and 32, respectively); but there are other, less commonly encountered, forms of interim relief that may be appropriate in the particular circumstances of the case.[1] Fraud cases are also obvious potential candidates for relief against third parties under the *Norwich Pharmacal* and *Bankers Trust* jurisdictions, addressed below in Ch.29, and some may justify consideration of quia timet relief even before the cause of action has crystallised. Further, in the modern commercial context, a fraud practitioner will want to be familiar with the powers which the English court has to grant such interim relief not just in support of proceedings before it, but also in support of arbitrations and proceedings being conducted abroad.

26–002

As we explain further below, "jurisdiction" in the strict sense means the court's *power* to grant relief in any given case. The only technically correct meaning of the statement that the court "lacks jurisdiction" to grant relief is that it has no power to do so, no matter in what form the application comes before it and no matter what are its merits. The combined general width of the various jurisdictional platforms considered in this chapter is such that a dispute over jurisdiction in this strict sense will rarely arise in an application for interim relief;

26–003

---

[1] See the forms of relief identified in CPR r.25.1(1): para.26–039 below.

instead, the focus tends to be upon one or both of: (a) the established principles governing the exercise of the court's jurisdiction; and (b) the discretion which the court has as to whether or not, and if so on what terms, to exercise its jurisdiction. Neither of these is a matter of jurisdiction, properly so-called (although the first is often confused with it).[2]

26–004 However, even though the jurisdiction of the High Court to grant interim relief is commonly expressed by statute and in the cases in the widest terms, it is sensible for those advising the applicant for such relief, or the respondent to an application, first to give some thought to analysing the jurisdictional basis for that application. That is both because cases will still arise where jurisdiction in its strict sense may be in issue (because, for example, relief is sought in novel circumstances, to which it is not yet clear that the court's powers extend)[3]; but also because the source of the court's jurisdiction may also identify its limits and inform the manner in which it is properly to be exercised. So, for example, the principal source of jurisdiction with which the fraud practitioner is likely to be concerned when seeking or being faced with injunctive and ancillary relief— s.37(1) of the Senior Courts Act 1981—identifies that such orders are to be made only when "just and convenient". Another important example is where the applicant is relying upon the court's jurisdiction (under s.25 of the Civil Jurisdiction and Judgments Act 1982, addressed below) to grant relief in support of foreign proceedings: there the statute both provides for the court to have the power to act (which it would not otherwise have) *and* stipulates that it may decline to exercise that power where the fact that it would not otherwise have it makes it "inexpedient" to grant relief.

26–005 In what follows in this chapter, we first consider (in Section B) the jurisdictional bases for relief which are likely to be relevant in a fraud claim being brought before the English Courts. These are, in summary[4]:

(1) *Section 37 of the Senior Courts Act 1981*, which is now the principal basis of the English High Court's jurisdiction to grant interim (or final) injunctive relief or to appoint an interim receiver;

(2) *Section 7 of the Civil Procedure Act 1997*, which provides the High Court's power to grant a search order;

(3) *The Court's equitable jurisdiction*, which is relevant to interim proprietary relief, the *Norwich Pharmacal* jurisdiction, disclosure under (inter alia) the so-called *Bankers Trust* jurisdiction, and quia timet relief;

---

[2] As both the first instance judge and the Court of Appeal wrongly did in the leading case of *Fourie v Le Roux* [2007] 1 W.L.R. 320, at [25], per Lord Scott.

[3] For a recent example, see *Abela v Fakih* [2017] EWHC 269 (Ch); [2018] 1 W.L.R. 89, where the court had to decide whether it had jurisdiction under s.7 of the Civil Procedure Act 1997 to make a search order against a third party, who was not a defendant against whom substantive final relief was sought, following judgment against the defendant. It was held that it did. On this decision, see further Ch.30, para.30–008.

[4] We consider the various procedural bases on which orders for disclosure may be made separately, in Ch.29.

(4)   *The provisions of CPR 25.1*, which are not strictly speaking a source of jurisdiction, but which helpfully identify many of the sorts of interim relief which are available in the exercise of the court's jurisdiction;

(5)   Certain *other statutory provisions*, which, whilst being outside the scope of this book, the fraud practitioner may wish to have in mind when considering options for interim relief; these are the provisions for interim orders within Pt XXV of the Financial Services and Markets Act 2000 and under Pt 2 of the Proceeds of Crime Act 2002.

We then go on to consider: **26–006**

(1)   In Section C, the Court's powers to grant interim relief in support of substantive proceedings pending before a foreign court, under *s.25 of the Civil Jurisdiction and Judgments Act 1982*; and

(2)   In Section D, the Court's powers to grant interim relief in support of actual or proposed arbitration proceedings, under *s.44 of the Arbitration Act 1996*.

(2)   Jurisdiction, Proper Exercise of it and Discretion Contrasted

As we mentioned at the outset of this chapter, it is important when considering   **26–007**
questions of jurisdiction to be clear what is meant by that term. Three separate
and successive questions need to be distinguished:

(1)   The question of whether the court has the power to grant relief;

(2)   The question of whether it is proper to exercise that power in principle, applying the settled principles established in the case law and rules of court;

(3)   The question of whether, in a particular case where the power exists and it would otherwise be proper to exercise it, the court should in the exercise of its discretion do so.

Only the first is, in the strict sense, a question of jurisdiction, which is the subject   **26–008**
of this chapter. In the chapters that follow we consider the settled principles
governing the grant of the most frequently encountered types of interim relief in
the context of civil fraud—particularly freezing injunctions, proprietary injunctions and search orders—and the way in which the court has exercised its
discretion in particular cases.

Separately from all of the above is then the question, which will only arise in a   **26–009**
case with an international aspect, of the court's *territorial* jurisdiction. That is,
essentially, whether in a case where the court has the power to grant relief, it is
able to exercise that power over a respondent who is outside its (territorial)
jurisdiction. The importance of distinguishing these two senses in which the
question of "jurisdiction" can arise was made clear by Lord Mustill in *Mercedes*

Benz AG v Leiduck,[5] in the context of an application for freezing (*Mareva*) relief against a respondent based outside the country, against whom no claim for substantive relief was before the court:

> "It is important at the outset to distinguish two questions. The first is concerned with territorial jurisdiction. The foreigner is outside the jurisdiction. The claim against him has no connection with the home territory. No action against him in respect of that claim is brought, or properly could be brought, before the local court. But he has assets within the territory. Assume for this purpose that *Mareva* proceedings could have been commenced by writ or other originating process, and assume also that such relief could properly be given…Does the statutory enlargement of its territorial jurisdiction created by Ord. 11, r.1(1)[6] entitle the court to permit the service of a writ or other originating process claiming such relief on the foreigner out of the jurisdiction, thus compelling him to choose between suffering a judgment in default or appearing before a court which has no other jurisdiction over him to argue that his assets should not be detained?
>
> "The second question is concerned with a different kind of jurisdiction; or, more accurately, a power. Assume for this purpose that the foreign defendant is someone who can be brought before the English court to answer a claim for a *Mareva* injunction, either because he is present here or because…Ord. 11, r.1(1)(b) is wide enough to cover all kinds of injunction. Assume also that the matters in dispute have no connection with the English court, and that the plaintiff neither can, nor as in the present case intends to, bring them before that court. Does the court have power to restrain the free disposition of the defendant's assets in England and Wales, to await the conclusion of proceedings brought against that person in a foreign jurisdiction?"

26–010   Jurisdiction in the territorial sense is the subject matter of Ch.39.

26–011   The distinctions between questions of:

    (a)   jurisdiction (in either sense),
    (b)   the principles on which the court acts, and
    (c)   its discretion to act

were helpfully highlighted by the House of Lords in *Fourie v Le Roux*.[7] In that case the court had discharged a freezing injunction which had been granted without notice against certain individuals who were in England, and who were alleged to have removed assets from South Africa to England, but against whom the applicant had not yet brought any substantive claim or even undertaken to do so. Because the individuals were in the jurisdiction, and had been properly served with the order and the application for it (once it had been granted without notice), the court had *jurisdiction*—both territorially and substantively—to grant an injunction against them. However, in circumstances where the applicant had only indicated an intention to formulate a claim to be brought in South Africa, and had not yet brought any claim or undertaken to do so, it had not been *proper* to exercise that jurisdiction. Moreover, this was not a question of a review of the exercise of the court's discretion; it was a question of the application of the settled principles on which the court would act.

---

[5] *Mercedes Benz AG v Leiduck* [1996] 1 A.C. 284, at 297G–298C.

[6] Now CPR PD 6B, para.3.1.

[7] *Fourie v Le Roux* [2007] 1 W.L.R. 320. See also the discussion in *Kensington International Ltd v Republic of Congo* [2007] EWCA Civ 1128; [2008] 1 W.L.R. 1144, at [18].

As Lord Scott put it[8]:   **26–012**

> "The issue is, in my opinion, not whether Park J [the judge at first instance who had granted the initial without notice order] had jurisdiction, in the strict sense, to make the freezing order but whether it was proper, in the circumstances as they stood at the time he made the order, for him to make it. This question does not in the least involve a review of the area of discretion available to any judge who is asked to grant injunctive relief. It involves an examination of the restrictions and limitations which have been placed by a combination of judicial precedent and rules of court on the circumstances in which the injunctive relief in question can properly be granted. The various matters taken into account by the deputy judge and Sir Andrew Morritt V-C respectively in holding that Park J had no jurisdiction to make the freezing order were really, in my respectful opinion, their reasons for concluding that, in the circumstances as they stood when the matter was before him, it had not been proper for Park J to have made the order."

The decision requires a reconsideration of the well-known earlier case of *The*   **26–013**
Siskina.[9] In that case the claimant had no substantive claim, actual or proposed, against the Panamanian ship-owning company (which was being sued by the same claimant in proceedings in Cyprus) which could be brought before the English court in order to support an injunction intended to restrain the dissipation of a fund of insurance proceeds located here; and, absent such a claim, it was held by the House of Lords that there was no basis for permitting service of proceedings on the defendant, which was out of the jurisdiction. It is important to distinguish two different aspects of Lord Diplock's much-cited speech in the case, and to be clear in what sense it is correct to describe the case as deciding that there was no "jurisdiction" to grant the injunction:

(1)   First, Lord Diplock observed that the jurisdiction under s.37(1) of the Senior Courts Act 1981 (as it now is) to grant an injunction

> "presupposes the existence of an action, actual or potential, claiming substantive relief which the High Court has jurisdiction to grant and to which the interlocutory orders referred to are but ancillary".[10]

He went on[11]:

> "A right to obtain an interlocutory injunction is not a cause of action. It cannot stand on its own. It is dependent upon there being a pre-existing cause of action against the defendant arising out of an invasion, actual or threatened by him, of a legal or equitable right of the plaintiff for the enforcement of which the defendant is amenable to the jurisdiction of the court. The right to obtain an interlocutory injunction is merely ancillary and incidental to the pre-existing cause of action. It is granted to preserve the status quo pending the ascertainment by the court of the rights of the parties and the grant to the plaintiff of the relief to which his cause of action entitles him, which may or may not include a final injunction."

---

[8] At [25].
[9] *Siskina (Owners of cargo lately laden on board) v Distos Compania Naviera SA (The Siskina)* [1979] A.C. 210.
[10] *The Siskina*, above, at 254.
[11] *The Siskina*, above, at 256.

This is the so-called "*Siskina* requirement": the Court will not grant an injunction under s.37(1) in a vacuum, but only in support of a cause of action for substantive relief.

(2)   Secondly, Lord Diplock considered the rule which permitted the service of process on the defendant abroad and came to the view that, on its proper construction, it did not extend to claims for interlocutory injunctions.[12]

26–014   Properly understood in light of the analysis in *Fourie v Le Roux*, only the second point concerned the *jurisdiction* of the court to grant relief (its territorial jurisdiction, in fact)[13]; the first point is better understood as identifying a principle on which the court determines whether it is *proper* to exercise its substantive jurisdiction. Consistently with that, the *Siskina* requirement is one that has evolved in subsequent jurisprudence.[14]

(3)   Human Rights Considerations

26–015   An applicant for interim relief must, in an appropriate case, be alive to the risk of invoking the court's jurisdiction where to do so might run up against a right protected by the European Convention on Human Rights and the Charter of Fundamental Rights of the European Union.

26–016   The grant of an interim remedy may well raise for consideration the potential infringement of Convention rights: most obviously the right to enjoyment of one's possessions (art.1 of the First Protocol) and the right to respect for private

---

[12] The "long-arm" jurisdiction of the court under what was then RSC Ord 11, r.1 (1)(i) and is now CPR PD 6B para.3.1(2): "A claim is made for an injunction ordering the defendant to do or refrain from doing an act within the jurisdiction". Compare CPR PD 6B para.3.1(11): "The whole subject matter of a claim relates to property within the jurisdiction." In the *Siskina* the claimant in the Cypriot proceedings had only a claim to damages in those proceedings and no basis for a proprietary claim upon the fund in England.

[13] Of course, statute has now reversed the result in the *Siskina* on this point: see s.25 of the Civil Jurisdiction and Judgments Act 1982, which we consider below, and CPR PD 6B para.3.1(5), the jurisdictional "gateway" which permits service of proceedings abroad when an injunction is sought under that statute.

[14] So, for example, in *Channel Tunnel Group v Balfour Beatty Construction Ltd* [1993] A.C. 334 it was determined that, whilst an interlocutory injunction had to be incidental to and dependent on the enforcement of a substantive right and could not exist in isolation, it need not be ancillary to a claim for relief to be granted by an English Court. In *TSB Private Bank International SA v Chabra* [1992] 1 W.L.R. 231 it was established that a freezing injunction could be made against a third party against whom no cause of action was asserted at all, if there was reason to suppose that they held assets for or under the control of the defendant against whom a cause of action was asserted (see Ch.28, paras 28–157—28–196). More recently, in *Kazakhstan Kagazy v Zhunus* [2017] 1 W.L.R. 1360, at [23]–[27], the Court of Appeal confirmed that the *Siskina* requirement did not mean that a freezing injunction was unavailable in cases where contribution proceedings have been brought: the court held that it was sufficient that the defendant had the right to commence proceedings claiming the substantive relief even if, strictly speaking, the cause of action was contingent and had yet to accrue; a freezing order was available to prevent such proceedings being frustrated.

and family life (art.8 of the Convention).[15] For example, the grant of *Norwich Pharmacal* relief may raise an issue as to whether the relief is proportionate in the context of art.8 or art.10 (and the public interest in maintaining the confidentiality of journalistic sources).[16]

In most cases any interference with the respondent's activities or property is likely to be justified by reference to the necessity of protecting the applicant's rights. The provision within any search order of the requirement for attendance by a supervising solicitor and the proviso permitting payment of living or legal expenses within any freezing injunction is a reflection of the need to protect the respondent's own rights and property. Article 6(1) of the Convention is generally thought not to be engaged at an interlocutory stage of proceedings, because the grant of an interim injunction does not involve the substantive determination of rights.[17] However, in *Micallef v Malta*[18] the Grand Chamber said that the nature of the interim measure, its objects and purposes, as well as its effects on the right in question, must be scrutinised to see whether art.6 applies. In that case, art.6 was engaged by the proceedings for an interim injunction because the purpose of the injunction, relating to the use of a neighbour's property, was to determine, albeit for a limited period, the same right as the one being contested in the main proceedings and the injunction was immediately enforceable.

26–017

B.   THE JURISDICTIONAL PLATFORMS RELEVANT TO PROCEEDINGS BEFORE THE ENGLISH COURTS

For purely domestic cases, an application for interim relief against the respondent in litigation (who may be the claimant, the defendant, or a third party) will be underpinned by either a statutory provision or the court's equitable jurisdiction. The relevant statutory and equitable bases of jurisdiction are considered below, together with the provisions of Pt 25 of the CPR in which they find expression as particular forms of relief.

26–018

(1)   Section 37 of the Senior Courts Act 1981

Section 37 of the Senior Courts Act 1981 ("the SCA") confirms the jurisdiction of the High Court to grant an injunction or to appoint a receiver, in each case either on an interim or final basis. The section is also now the source of the court's powers to make asset disclosure orders and other orders ancillary to a

26–019

---

[15] *Niemitz v Germany* (1993) 16 E.H.R.R 97, where the European Court of Human Rights held that a search of a lawyer's offices engaged art.8 but was justified on the basis of preventing crime and protecting the rights of others. The court held that no separate issue arose under art.1 of the First Protocol.

[16] See *Ashworth Hospital Authority v MGN Ltd* [2002] UKHL 29; [2002] 1 W.L.R. 2033, at [60]–[62]; *Golden Eye (International) Ltd v Telephonica UK Ltd* [2012] EWCA Civ 1740, at [15]–[19]; and *The Rugby Football Union v Consolidated Information Ltd* [2012] UKSC 55, at [17]–[18], [44]–[45] and para.29–078—29–080 below.

[17] *Ringeisen v Austria* (1971) 1 E.H.R.R. 466, at [94].

[18] *Micallef v Malta* (2010) 50 E.H.R.R. 37, at [85]–[87].

freezing injunction,[19] such as (for example) orders preventing a respondent from leaving the jurisdiction. Reflecting as it does previous statutory provisions which date back to the first Judicature Act 1873, s.37 confers upon the High Court the power to grant such relief which the courts of equity enjoyed before 1873.[20]

26–020 The section provides as follows:

> "(1) The High Court may by order (whether interlocutory or final) grant an injunction or appoint a receiver in all cases where it appears to the court to be just and convenient to do so.
>
> (2) Any such order may be made either conditionally or on such terms and conditions as the court thinks just.
>
> (3) The power of the High Court under subsection (1) to grant an interlocutory injunction restraining a party to any proceedings from removing from the jurisdiction of the High Court, or otherwise dealing with, assets located within that jurisdiction shall be exercisable in cases where that party is, as well as where he is not, domiciled, resident or present within that jurisdiction."[21]

26–021 The jurisdiction is cast in very wide terms: the only proviso to it is that it should appear to the court to be "just and convenient" to grant the relief.[22]

26–022 This does not, however, mean that the power to grant an injunction or appoint a receiver is without any limitation. In *Masri v Consolidated Contractors International (UK) Ltd (No. 2)*[23] Lawrence Collins LJ referred to the incremental changes in practice (since the passing of the Judicature Act 1873) in the shape of new forms of interim remedy—such as the domestic *Mareva* injunction, ancillary orders for disclosure, worldwide *Mareva* relief and anti-suit injunctions—which reflected the application of old principles to new situations. Those principles circumscribe the proper exercise of the jurisdiction. He observed:

> "That does not mean that section 37(1) of the [Senior Courts Act 1981] is to be taken as conferring an unfettered power. As Lord Brandon of Oakbrook said in *South Carolina Insurance Co v Assurantie Maatschappij 'De Zeven Provincien' NV* [1987] A.C. 24, at 40: 'although the terms of section 37(1) of the Act of 1981 and its predecessors are very wide, the

---

[19] See *Mercantile Group A.G. v Aiyela* [1994] Q.B. 366, at 374C, per Hoffmann LJ; and *JSC BTA Bank v Ablyazov* [2011] EWHC 2664 (Comm).

[20] *Fourie v Le Roux* [2007] UKHL 1; [2007] 1 W.L.R. 320, at [25], per Lord Scott (referring to s.19(2)(b) of the SCA 1981).

[21] The section continues by providing that the court's power to appoint a receiver by way of equitable execution over any interest in land shall operate in addition to any charging order and any power to appoint a receiver in support of such an order.

[22] See Jessell MR in *Beddow v Beddow* (1878) 9 Ch. D. 89, at 93: "That being so, it appears to me that the only limit to my power of granting an injunction is whether I can properly do so. For that is what it amounts to. In my opinion, having regard to these two Acts of Parliament [i.e. the Supreme Court of Judicature Act 1873 and the Common Law Procedure Act 1854], I have unlimited power to grant an injunction in any case where it would be right or just to do so: and what is right or just must be decided, not by the caprice of the Judge, but according to sufficient legal reasons or on settled legal principles."

[23] *Masri v Consolidated Contractors International (UK) Ltd (No.2)* [2008] EWCA Civ 303; [2009] Q.B. 450, at [175], [177]. This was cited in *Tasarruf Mevduati Sigorta Fonu v Merrill Lynch Bank and Trust Co (Cayman) Ltd* [2012] 1 W.L.R. 1721, at [57], per Lord Collins (Privy Council) in the context of the relief discussed in para.33–025 below. See also *South Carolina Insurance Co v Assurantie Maatschappij 'De Zeven Provincien' NV* [1987] A.C. 24, at 40, per Lord Brandon of Oakbrook.

power conferred by them has been circumscribed by judicial authority dating back many years.' This point has often been reaffirmed by the House of Lords (and by the Privy Council) in relation to injunctions".[24]

As Lawrence Collins LJ went on to explain in *Masri (No.2)*, one such overarching principle is that which we have considered above—the so-called *Siskina* requirement, that an injunction should only be granted in aid of a substantive and enforceable equitable or legal right. As to this requirement, in *Fourie v Le Roux*[25] Lord Scott said:

> "I would agree that, without the issue of substantive proceedings or an undertaking to do so, the propriety of the grant of an interlocutory injunction would be difficult to defend. An interlocutory injunction, like any other interim order, is intended to be of temporary duration, dependent on the institution and progress of some proceedings for substantive relief."

There is thus a general requirement (subject to the court's power to grant quia timet relief)[26] that an underlying cause of action should have (on the claimant's case) come into existence to support the exercise of the court's jurisdiction to grant interim injunctive relief[27]; but it is important to emphasise again that this is not because the court otherwise lacks the *power* to act under s.37, but rather because case law has established this as a settled principle limiting when the power can properly be exercised. As we have noted above, the principle is thus one that can be, and has been, developed by subsequent decisions.[28]

(2) Section 7 of the Civil Procedure Act 1997

Since the coming into force of s.7 of the Civil Procedure Act 1997, the court's power to grant a "search order" rests (at least in part) upon a statutory basis, whereas previously an applicant for an order (previously known as an *Anton Piller* order) authorising the search for and seizure of materials, documents or articles in possession of the respondent founded his application on the equitable jurisdiction of the court to grant such orders, which had been held to exist in the well-known case of that name.[29] While there is room for debate as to whether the

26–023

26–024

26–025

---

[24] The following cases were cited: *Gouriet v Union of Post Office Workers* [1978] A.C. 435, at 500–501, 516; *Siskina (Owners of cargo lately laden on board) v Distos Cia Naviera SA* [1979] A.C. 210, at 256; *Bremer Vulkan v South India Shipping* [1981] A.C. 909, at 979; *British Airways Board v Laker Airways Ltd* [1985] A.C. 58, at 80–81; *P v Liverpool Daily Post and Echo Newspapers Plc* [1991] 2 A.C. 370, at 420–421; *Channel Tunnel Group v Balfour Beatty Construction Ltd* [1993] A.C. 334, at 341, 360–361; and *Mercedes Benz AG v Leiduck* [1996] A.C. 284, at 298 (Privy Council).

[25] *Fourie v Le Roux* [2007] UKHL 1; [2007] 1 W.L.R. 320, at [32], per Lord Scott.

[26] Which is founded on the claimant's reasonable apprehension that absent the order the defendant would act in a way which infringed the claimant's rights and so created a cause of action: see para.26–036 below.

[27] As it was put by Lord Mustill in *Mercedes-Benz AG v Leiduck* [1996] 1 A.C. 284, at 297B and 301G, interim orders "cannot simply be made in the air", and what is required is an underlying claim before the court for "relief founded on a right asserted by the plaintiff in the action or matter, and enforced through the medium of a judgment by the court in that action or matter".

[28] See fn.14 above.

[29] *Anton Piller KG v Manufacturing Processes Ltd* [1976] Ch. 55.

jurisdiction is now exclusively statutory, the better view seems to be that it is confirmed (rather than conferred) by the Act, it having previously existed independently of it.[30]

26–026 Section 7 provides as follows:

"(1) The court may make an order under this section for the purpose of securing, in the case of any existing or proposed proceedings in the court—
   (a) the preservation of evidence which is or may be relevant, or
   (b) the preservation of property which is or may be the subject-matter of the proceedings or as to which any question arises or may arise in the proceedings.
(2) A person who is, or appears to the court likely to be, a party to proceedings in the court may make an application for such an order.
(3) Such an order may direct any person to permit any person described in the order, or secure that any person so described is permitted—
   (a) to enter premises in England and Wales, and
   (b) while on the premises, to take in accordance with the terms of the order any of the following steps.
(4) Those steps are—
   (a) to carry out a search for or inspection of anything described in the order, and
   (b) to make or obtain a copy, photograph, sample or other record of anything so described.
(5) The order may also direct the person concerned—
   (a) to provide any person described in the order, or secure that any person so described is provided, with any information or article described in the order, and
   (b) to allow any person described in the order, or secure that any person so described is allowed, to retain for safe keeping anything described in the order, and
(6) An order under this section is to have effect subject to such conditions as are specified in the order.
(7) This section does not affect any right of a person to refuse to do anything on the ground that to do so might tend to expose him or his spouse or civil partner to proceedings for an offence or for the recovery of a penalty.
(8) In this section—"court" means the High Court, and "premises" includes any vehicle; and an order under this section may describe anything generally, whether by reference to a class or otherwise."

26–027 We consider the principles applicable to the grant of search orders under this jurisdiction in Ch.30.

(3) Equitable Jurisdiction

26–028 The fact that under s.37 of the SCA the High Court now exercises the jurisdiction to grant interim injunctive relief, which before 1873 had been vested in the Chancery courts (see para.26–019 above), immediately raises the question as to whether any sensible purpose is served by attempting to distinguish the court's equitable jurisdiction when, as a matter of procedure, it is submerged within the

---

[30] See, for example, Dockray and Reece Thomas, (1998) 17 CJQ 272: s.7 "provides an indisputable statutory basis for making orders of the Anton Piller type. However, the Act does not expressly take away such powers as the High Court may previously have possessed". See also Lord Collins of Mapesbury, J. Harris (eds), *Dicey, Morris & Collins on the Conflict of Laws*, 15th edn (London: Sweet & Maxwell, 2012), paras 8–006 and 8–017, comparing the treatment of the statutory jurisdiction for freezing orders provided by s.37 of the Senior Courts Act 1981.

power conferred by that section. Every branch of the High Court has all the jurisdiction of the former Court of Chancery (and other courts) to grant injunctive relief.

In fact, since 1873 to the present day, the courts have consistently talked of their **26–029** equitable jurisdiction as a freestanding basis for exercising judicial powers. The equitable jurisdiction can now be best understood as a series of principles developed in the Court of Chancery and now exercisable by the High Court in whatever manifestation it sits. In the civil fraud context, the two most clearly relevant aspects of the court's equitable jurisdiction are:

(i)   its approach to the grant of interim relief in support of proprietary claims; and

(ii)   the exercise of the so-called *Bankers Trust* jurisdiction to secure disclosure in support of tracing claims.

Of less immediately obvious relevance but still worthy of mention is

(iii)   the court's ability to grant equitable quia timet relief.

(i)   Proprietary claims

In cases where a proprietary claim is brought in the English court, the court's **26–030** power to grant interim relief rests upon the equitable jurisdiction which the statutory predecessors of s.37 of the SCA both confirmed and extended beyond the courts of equity. In such cases, where the court restrains dealings with particular property over which a claim is made, it might do so by reference to the specific power to make orders for the "detention, custody or preservation of relevant property" within the meaning of CPR 25.1(c)(i)[31] or on the basis that it is granting a form of freezing injunction which reflects an underlying proprietary (as opposed to personal) claim.[32]

In an unreported—but often cited—decision of the Court of Appeal in 1978, **26–031** Templeman LJ said[33]:

> "A court of equity has never hesitated to use the strongest powers to protect and preserve a trust fund in interlocutory proceedings on the basis that, if the trust fund disappears by the time the action comes to trial, equity will have been invoked in vain".

---

[31] Under CPR 25.1(c)(i) the court may make an interim order for the detention, custody or preservation of "relevant property". "Relevant property" is defined as "property (including land) which is the subject of a claim or as to which any question may arise on a claim": CPR 25.1(2).

[32] A distinction was apparently drawn by HH Judge Hodge QC in *Wood v Baker* [2015] EWHC 2536 (Ch), at [28], where there was some doubt as to whether a cause of action, to support a freezing injunction, had yet accrued in favour of the applicant trustees in bankruptcy. We would suggest that the equitable jurisdiction to grant relief in preservation of trust property in fact underpins the CPR provision.

[33] *Mediterranea Raffineria Siciliana Petroli SpA v Mabanaft GmbH*, unreported, 1 December 1978 CA, Court of Appeal transcript 816, and cited by, amongst others, Goff J in *A v C* [1981] 1 Q.B. 956, at 958–959, Neuberger J in *Murphy v Murphy* [1999] 1 W.L.R. 282, at 289G–290B, and Newey J in *Royal Westminster Investments v Varm*, above, at [55].

This judicial willingness to protect property to which the claimant lays claim is reflected in the later observations of Staughton LJ in *Republic of Haiti v Duvalier*[34]:

> "It may be that the powers of the court are wider, and certainly discretion is more readily exercised, if a plaintiff's claim is what is called a tracing claim. For my part, I think that the true distinction lies between a proprietary claim on the one hand, and a claim which seeks only a money judgment on the other. A proprietary claim is one by which the plaintiff seeks the return of chattels or land which are his property, or claims that a specified debt is owed by a third party to him and not to the defendant. Thus far there is no difficulty. A plaintiff who seeks to enforce a claim of that kind will more readily be afforded interim remedies, in order to preserve the asset which he is seeking to recover, than one who merely seeks a judgment for debt or damages."

26–032 Of course, the principal advantage which a claim in rem enjoys over a mere right in personam is that it enables the claimant, for so long as he can follow his property or trace its proceeds into the hands of others, to hold persons other than the fraudster accountable for its return. To that extent, and unlike an unsecured money claim, the value of the proprietary claim does not fluctuate with the fortunes of the fraudster (who, by his nature, tends to have more creditors than debtors and not to be good for all of his own debts); and, correspondingly, the court's jurisdiction will extend to the grant of interim injunctive relief (and indeed other relief, such as by way of disclosure) against third parties.

26–033 The differences between the court's approach to the grant of a proprietary injunction and its approach in relation to freezing injunctions in support of personal claims are addressed in Ch.28 below.

(ii) Bankers Trust orders

26–034 The availability of the so-called *Bankers Trust* order—granted in an appropriate case to obtain disclosure of assets that are sought to be traced by the claimant—is a product of the court's willingness to grant interim proprietary-based relief: the dictum of Templeman LJ in *Mediterranea Raffineria Siciliana Petroli SpA v Mabanaft GmbH* quoted above[35] underpins the jurisdiction and was relied upon by Robert Goff J in *A v C*,[36] where one of the first such orders was made.

26–035 The principles on which *Bankers Trust* orders can be obtained are addressed in Ch.29.

(iii) Quia timet relief

26–036 Quia timet[37] relief is founded upon the claimant's fear of a future infringement of some right he enjoys. The threat of such an infringement, which has not yet occurred, means that, in the usual case, his cause of action is only contingent and has not yet accrued. Nevertheless the court has a well-recognised power to

---

[34] *Republic of Haiti v Duvalier* [1990] 1 Q.B. 202, at 213–214.
[35] See para.26–031.
[36] *A v C* [1981] Q.B. 956.
[37] "Because he fears".

intervene to enjoin the threatened behaviour. The absence of an accrued cause of action means that relief cannot be justified at common law, but equity recognises the quia timet action for relief which is designed to protect the claimant against future apprehended loss.

By way of example, quia timet relief may be justified where the claimant is entitled to be indemnified against a loss or claim and there is clear evidence to show that the person subject to the obligation to indemnify proposes to ignore that obligation. This type of contingent cause of action is likely to rest upon a contractual right of indemnity (or some other relationship carrying an express or implied right to an indemnity) and may therefore be of less obvious relevance in a book on civil fraud.[38] Nevertheless, there may be fraud cases where the claimant fears the defendant's likely misapplication of funds or assets, in respect of which the claimant enjoys some contingent right but which are not yet payable or transferable to him, on grounds which justify quia timet relief aimed at preserving them. Even in the absence of a claim of a proprietary nature over such assets, quia timet relief may be justified by reference to the conduct of the defendant when the absence of an accrued cause of action means that no freezing injunction can be granted on conventional grounds. If a freezing injunction is to be sought on quia timet grounds, the applicant will need to show (at the very least) that there is reasonably good evidence that the loss which he fears, and which is presently contingent, will be suffered by him.[39] Such a contingent claim in the fraud context might justify an order restraining the respondent from making distributions out of an estate or fund in a way which would prejudice the applicant's right, when the loss is suffered by him, to be indemnified out of it.[40] **26-037**

(4)   CPR 25.1

Part 25.1 of the CPR sets out an extensive but non-exhaustive list of the types of interim remedy the High Court may grant, and so provides an obvious starting point for any prospective applicant who is looking to identify what sorts of relief might be available under the various jurisdictions which are mentioned in this chapter. **26-038**

CPR 25.1(1) provides as follows[41]: **26-039**

---

[38] Because an allegation of fraud generally predicates existing loss and, therefore, an accrued cause of action based upon the alleged wrongdoing.

[39] See *Rowland v Gulfpac Ltd (No.1)* [1999] Lloyd's Rep. Bank. 86 where Rix J held that he had jurisdiction to grant a freezing order quia timet to support an indemnity claim by X against Y (where Y had an obligation to indemnify X against a liability to a third party), even though the common law claim for an indemnity was not then complete. His decision was more recently followed by Burton J in *Starlight Shipping Co v Allianz Marine & Aviation Versicherungs AG (The "Alexandros T")* [2011] EWHC 3381 (Comm); [2012] 1 Lloyd's Rep. 162. In *Zurich Insurance PLC UK Branch v International Energy Group Ltd (Rev 2)* [2015] UKSC 33; [2016] A.C. 509 Lord Mance referred to these cases with apparent approval, at [87].

[40] See *In re Anderson-Berry* [1928] Ch. 290 where the motion to restrain distributions from the estate was resolved by the defendant taking out an insurance policy against the liability to which the claimant sureties were subject.

[41] Omitting (p), which relates to intellectual property rights.

"(1)   The court may grant the following interim remedies –
  (a)   an interim injunction;
  (b)   an interim declaration;
  (c)   an order –
      (i)   for the detention, custody or preservation of relevant property;
      (ii)   for the inspection of relevant property;
      (iii)   for the taking of a sample of relevant property;
      (iv)   for the carrying out of an experiment on or with relevant property;
      (v)   for the sale of relevant property which is of a perishable nature or which for any other good reason it is desirable to sell quickly; and
      (vi)   for the payment of income from relevant property until a claim is decided;
  (d)   an order authorising a person to enter any land or building in the possession of a party to the proceedings for the purposes of carrying out an order under sub-paragraph (c);
  (e)   an order under section 4 of the Torts (Interference with Goods) Act 1977 to deliver up goods;
  (f)   an order (referred to as a 'freezing injunction') –
      (i)   restraining a party from removing from the jurisdiction assets located there; or
      (ii)   restraining a party from dealing with any assets whether located within the jurisdiction or not;
  (g)   an order directing a party to provide information about the location of relevant property or assets or to provide information about relevant property or assets which are or may be the subject of an application for a freezing injunction;
  (h)   an order (referred to as a 'search order') under section 7 of the Civil Procedure Act 1997 (order requiring a party to admit another party to premises for the purpose of preserving evidence etc.);
  (i)   an order under section 33 of the Supreme Court Act 1981 or section 52 of the County Courts Act 1984 (order for disclosure of documents or inspection of property before a claim has been made);
  (j)   an order under section 34 of the Supreme Court Act 1981 or section 53 of the County Courts Act 1984 (order in certain proceedings for disclosure of documents or inspection of property against a non-party);
  (k)   an order (referred to as an order for interim payment) under rule 25.6 for payment by a defendant on account of any damages, debt or other sum (except costs) which the court may hold the defendant liable to pay;
  (l)   an order for a specified fund to be paid into court or otherwise secured, where there is a dispute over a party's right to the fund;
  (m)   an order permitting a party seeking to recover personal property to pay money into court pending the outcome of the proceedings and directing that, if he does so, the property shall be given up to him;
  (n)   an order directing a party to prepare and file accounts relating to the dispute;
  (o)   an order directing any account to be taken or inquiry to be made by the court . . ."

26–040   Although the expression "interim remedy" is invariably used to describe a form of relief which is granted in support of a claim, pending trial of that claim, CPR r.25.2(1) makes it clear that an order for an interim remedy may not only be granted "before proceedings are started" but also "after judgment has been given."

26–041   It is important to note that CPR 25.1 is (at least in most cases)[42] not itself the source of the court's jurisdiction to grant the forms of relief listed in it; nor does

---

[42] As can be seen, certain provisions of CPR 25.1 expressly identify another source of the relevant jurisdiction. With others, although no such other jurisdiction is identified, it is clear that the power does not derive from CPR 25.1 itself: the grant of an interim injunction being an obvious example. With some of the provisions of the rule, the position is less clear: for example, as we have noted

the listing in CPR 25.1 of numerous types of interim remedy which the court may grant operate to limit the court's jurisdiction to grant other forms of relief pending trial. CPR 25.1(3) states as follows:

> "The fact that a particular kind of interim remedy is not listed in paragraph (1) does not affect any power that the court may have to grant that remedy."

CPR 25.1(1) does not therefore define or circumscribe the court's powers under the jurisdictions mentioned above.

We consider: personal and proprietary freezing orders (CPR 25.1(1)(f) and (c)(i)) **26–042** in Ch.28; interim orders for disclosure (CPR 25.1(1)(g)) in Ch.29; and search orders (CPR 25.1(1)(h)) in Ch.30. Beyond those obvious examples, a case founded upon allegations of fraud may well prompt consideration of other sorts of interim relief referred to in CPR 25.1(1), such as:

(1) An injunction in a form other than the standard form of freezing injunction: CPR 25.1(1)(a) and (c). Such interim injunctive relief will necessarily be in a bespoke form that is said by the applicant to meet the justice and convenience of the case. For example, it might (so far as the alleged facts permit) involve an order restraining the respondent from exercising purported rights over security where the validity of the security (or the bona fides of the respondent in seeking to rely upon it) is impugned[43]; an injunction restraining the respondent from dissipating or dealing with a shareholding in any corporate entity which is said to have received the proceeds of fraud or dissipating or dealing with the business or assets of such an entity[44]; an injunction preventing disposal of an asset where it is said that the respondent has contracted not to dispose of it or where it is said that the respondent is under an obligation not to dispose of it except at a proper price and is threatening to dispose of it at what is asserted to be an undervalue[45]; or, in a case of continuing alleged wrongdoing, an injunction restraining the respondent from further acts of the kind which are said to have already given rise to a cause of action against him.

---

above, it appears to have been suggested by HH Judge Hodge QC in *Wood v Baker* [2015] EWHC 2536 (Ch), at [28], that sub-rule (1)(c)(i) (order for the detention, custody or preservation of relevant property) confers a jurisdiction separate to the equitable jurisdiction to make proprietary injunctions.

[43] Compare *Todaysure Matthews Ltd v Marketing Ways Services Ltd* [2015] EWHC 64 (Comm), at [5], where the applicant had sought an injunction that the respondent should withdraw a demand made upon a performance guarantee and be restrained from making any further demand (and had also sought a worldwide freezing injunction in the event that the bank honoured the guarantee). However, the unavailability of injunctive relief against an issuing bank under such a guarantee or bond or letter of credit, where the bank is not itself aware that the demand is fraudulent, is clear: see *Alternative Power Solution Ltd v Central Electricity Board* [2014] UKPC 31, at [34]–[35].

[44] See *Wood v Baker* [2015] EWHC 2536 (Ch), at [28], where, as we have noted above, HH Judge Hodge QC analysed the relief not as a proprietary freezing injunction, but as relief seeking the "preservation of relevant property" (CPR 25.1(1)(c)(i)) where the applicant trustees in bankruptcy had a good arguable case for piercing the corporate veil by reference to "the evasion principle" recognised by the Supreme Court in *Prest v Petrodel Resources Ltd* [2013] UKSC 34; [2013] 2 A.C. 415, at [28]–[35].

[45] Examples given in *Holyoake v Candy* [2016] EWHC 970 (Ch); [2016] 3 W.L.R. 357, at [8(3)], per Nugee J.

(2)   As another variant, a "notification" injunction, requiring the respondent to notify the applicant before dealing with any assets of significant value. In *Holyoake v Candy*[46] the court recognised the jurisdiction to make an order requiring such prior notification so that the applicant might have the opportunity to seek a freezing injunction if notified of a proposed transaction which was regarded as being damaging to his position. At first instance Nugee J said that in practice the grant of a notification injunction would require the applicant either to assert some substantive right to prevent the disposal of the asset or (more usually) provide some credible evidence of threatened dissipation of a kind that would justify a freezing injunction. Although *potentially* less invasive than a freezing injunction, in a normal case a claimant has no right prior to judgment to know what the defendant's assets are or what he proposes to do with them, so the merits of the claim must be established to the same threshold test of a "good arguable case" rather than the lower *American Cyanamid* standard of a serious issue to be tried. The Court of Appeal in *Holyoake*[47] allowed an appeal against the notification injunction (without questioning the jurisdiction to grant it) on the basis that solid evidence was required to establish the risk that a future judgment would not be met because of unjustifiable dissipation by the respondent and such evidence was lacking. The court recognised that the position might be different if the proposed notification related to a specific property, but otherwise said that a notification injunction expressed in wide terms was in effect a modified version of a conventional freezing injunction and therefore the threshold test for granting it was the same, subject only to the fact that a notification injunction was less invasive and therefore arguments by a respondent founded on the "justice and convenience" of the situation might be less persuasive.

(3)   An order for a specified fund to be paid into court, or otherwise secured, where there is a dispute over a party's right to the fund: CPR 25.1(1)(l). The language of the rule makes it clear that there must be some claim upon the fund in question and that the provision cannot be relied upon to create "security" for a claim which is unsecured (the mere fact that the claim is liquidated or indeed not credibly disputed would not suffice).[48] The court must of course be persuaded of the existence or likely existence of the fund.[49]

---

[46]   *Holyoake v Candy*, above, at [8] and [51]; [2017] EWCA Civ 92, at [17].

[47]   *Holyoake v Candy* [2017] EWCA Civ 92, at [34]–[48].

[48]   *Myers v Design Inc (International) Ltd* [2003] EWHC 103 (Ch); [2003] 1 All E.R. 1168, where Lightman J set aside an order made ex parte under CPR 25.1(1)(l) where the true analysis of the applicant's claim was that of an unsecured loan creditor (giving rise to a chose in action but no claim over an identifiable fund). Compare *Sports Network Ltd v Calzaghe* [2008] EWHC 2566 (QB), where the defendant boxer had applied for an order that 80, per cent of the profit collected from a fight by his promoter should be paid into an account of the parties' solicitors, and the judge observed that the relief might have been granted under this provision on the basis that it involved the preservation of what were said to be trust monies.

[49]   Compare *Vitol v Morley* [2015] EWHC 613 (QB) where the applicant sought an order that a sum be paid into court where there were concerns about the enforceability of a worldwide freezing order already obtained by it in relation to any monies which were located in an overseas bank account. Teare J (whose judgment did not expressly refer CPR 25.1(1)(l) when observing that in principle the

CPR 25.1(4) provides that the court "may grant an interim remedy whether or not **26–043**
there has been a claim for a final remedy of that kind". This means that a remedy
can be granted in support of a claim for substantive relief even though the interim
remedy in question is not mentioned in the claim form; but not that the interim
remedy can be granted in a vacuum, unconnected with any claim to enforce a
legal or equitable right.[50]

(5) Miscellaneous Statutory Provisions

In addition to the jurisdictional platforms summarised above, there are a number **26–044**
of specific statutory provisions which may be relevant to a case where a fraud has
been perpetrated and the suspected proceeds are sought to be frozen. A detailed
analysis of these provisions is beyond the scope of this book and they are
mentioned only with a view to alerting the reader to the risk that their potential
application and impact may be overlooked.

Such specific statutory provisions include those within Pt XXV of the Financial **26–045**
Services and Markets Act 2000 ("FSMA") and those forming part of the
confiscation regime under Pt 2 of the Proceeds of Crime Act 2002 ("POCA").

FSMA.   Section 380(3) of FSMA provides that the Financial Conduct **26–046**
Authority or the Secretary of State may apply to the court for an asset-freezing
injunction where a person has contravened a "relevant requirement" or has been
knowingly concerned in such a contravention.[51] A "relevant requirement" is one
imposed by or under FSMA or by or under any other Act whose contravention
constitutes an offence which the Financial Conduct Authority has power to
prosecute under FSMA. In circumstances where many financial scams are likely
to involve a transgression of FSMA or one or more of the numerous rules (so
designated) in the extensive FCA Handbook—including perhaps breach of the
"general prohibition" under s.19 of FSMA of carrying on a regulated activity
without being authorised—this provision should not be overlooked.[52] If it can be
persuaded to invoke it, the right of the regulator to apply for such interim relief
may be of some significance to an individual victim of such a scam, if the value
of his own claim is sufficiently modest to make an application for his "own"
interim relief disproportionately expensive.

In an appropriate case it may be that the jurisdiction to grant interim relief under **26–047**
FSMA needs to be invoked alongside the court's more general jurisdiction. In
Financial Services Authority v Fitt[53] Lewison J granted a freezing injunction

---

court has jurisdiction or power to make such an order) declined to make such a mandatory order in
circumstances where the respondent had not had a proper opportunity to respond to the serious
allegations against him and where making an order would expose him to penalties for contempt if the
sum did not in fact exist.

[50] See *Royal Westminster Investments v Varma* [2012] EWHC 3439 (Ch), at [42], per Newey J.

[51] Section 380 also contains provision for both prohibitory and mandatory relief to be granted with a
view to restraining further or remedying the contravention.

[52] Contrast the personal claim which is open to any particular victim of a false or misleading
prospectus, or listing particulars, under s.90 of FSMA: see Ch.16 above.

[53] *Financial Services Authority v Fitt* [2004] EWHC 1669 (Ch).

relying both upon s.380(3) of FSMA and s.37 of the SCA 1981. The FSA (as it was) had applied for a freezing injunction not only over the respondent's assets and bank accounts but also bank accounts in the names of investors who had entrusted money to him and over which he held a power of attorney. The judge recognised that this went beyond the scope of s.380, which enables the court to make an order freezing "assets of his", but concluded that

> "until such time as the matters can properly be investigated the court does have power under section 37 of the 1981 Act to make an order freezing the bank accounts of investors over which Mr Fitt has control in order to prevent Mr Fitt from stripping the proceeds of those bank accounts."[54]

26–048   **POCA.**   Under s.41 of POCA the Crown Court[55] has power to make a restraint order (in anticipation of a confiscation order being made after conviction) in circumstances where a criminal investigation or prosecution has been started and there is reasonable cause to believe that the alleged offender has benefitted from his criminal conduct (within the meaning of s.76(4) of the Act).

26–049   In *R v O'Brien*[56] (where the Supreme Court held that a breach of such an order amounted to a civil rather than criminal contempt) Lord Toulson set out the court's jurisdiction under s.41:

> "A restraint order under section 41 of POCA is an interim remedy. Its aim is to prevent the disposal of realisable assets during a criminal investigation or criminal proceedings. Under section 41(7) the court may make such order as it believes is appropriate for the purpose of ensuring that the restraint order is effective. This may include, for example, an order requiring disclosure of assets by the person against whom the restraint order is made. A restraint order may also be reinforced by the appointment of a receiver under section 48 and the court may order any person who has possession of realisable property to which the restraint order applies to give possession of it to the receiver."

26–050   The focus of a restraint order is upon "realisable property", which is defined by s.83 of POCA as any free property (itself defined in s.82 of POCA) of the defendant or any free property held by a recipient of a "tainted gift" (as defined by s.77).

26–051   The reference to "free property" should be borne in mind by those victims of a fraud who consider they may have a proprietary claim upon assets held by the defendant. There may be occasions when the interests of the Crown under a restraint order (or confiscation order) are pitched against those of a claimant who has a proprietary claim running parallel to the criminal prosecution. In *Director of the SFO v Lexi Holdings Plc*[57] the court was persuaded to vary a restraint order, made against M under s.41 of POCA 2002, on the application of a third party, Lexi. Lexi was entitled to assert an equitable charge over monies held by M in two bank accounts and in respect of which M had, from the moment of their

---

[54] *Financial Services Authority v Fitt*, above, at [4].
[55] The application may be made on a without notice basis to a judge in chambers by the prosecutor or an accredited financial regulator, who may appeal to the Court of Appeal if an order is not granted.
[56] *R v O'Brien* [2014] UKSC 23; [2014] A.C. 1246, at [35].
[57] *Director of the SFO v Lexi Holdings Plc* [2008] EWCA Civ 1443; [2009] Q.B. 376, at [41], per Keene LJ giving the judgment of the court.

receipt, become a constructive trustee. In observing that injustice would flow from a refusal of the variation, the court said that it did not seem just that the

> "amount of assets…which are potentially available to (unsecured) victims of the alleged criminal conduct would appear to have been increased by assets which in part originated from Lexi itself and in circumstances where it originally had a proprietary claim to that money in the hands of M".

C. JURISDICTION IN SUPPORT OF FOREIGN PROCEEDINGS

Many, if not the majority, of alleged frauds that come before the English courts involve an international aspect. In some cases the international element will be stronger than the domestic one for the purposes of dictating where the substantive claim should be brought. For the purpose of the present overview of the court's jurisdiction to grant interim relief, it is therefore necessary to address that part of it which enables the English court to grant such relief in aid of foreign proceedings. This jurisdiction forms a key part of the court's role in either stopping or providing redress for international fraud.

26–052

It has already been noted in Section A above that the actual decision of the House of Lords in *The Siskina*[58] has been superseded by statute: s.25 of the Civil Jurisdiction and Judgments Act 1982 ("the CJJA") now enables the English court to grant interim relief in support of substantive proceedings in a foreign court where there is no substantive claim pending in England.

26–053

The Court's ability to grant such relief is subject to the statutory restraint (expressed in qualified discretionary terms) that it may refuse such relief if the absence of any other jurisdictional connection to the proceedings, aside from that arising under the section itself, makes it "inexpedient" to grant it (s.25(2)). Decisions under s.25 over the last two decades have established that the "inexpediency" check is the second of two hurdles that the court erects when deciding whether or not to exercise its jurisdiction under the section. The principles governing the exercise of the jurisdiction under s.25 of the CJJA are discussed in subs.(3) below.

26–054

(1) The Scope of Section 25 of the CJJA 1982

Initially, the English court's jurisdiction under s.25 to grant ancillary interim relief in support of foreign proceedings existed only in cases where those substantive proceedings were pending in a Brussels or Lugano contracting state and the subject matter of the proceedings was within the scope of the Brussels or Lugano Conventions. Since 1997, however, by virtue of the Civil Jurisdiction and Judgments Act 1982 (Interim Relief) Order 1997,[59] the court has had power to

26–055

---

[58] *Siskina (Owners of cargo lately laden on board) v Distos Compania Naviera SA (The Siskina)* [1979] A.C. 210. See para.26–014 and fn.13 above.
[59] SI 1997/302.

grant relief in respect of foreign proceedings wherever they are, or are to be, commenced, and irrespective of whether their subject matter is within the scope of those Conventions.

26–056 Section 25 of the CJJA, as amended, now provides as follows:

"Interim relief in England and Wales and Northern Ireland in the absence of substantive proceedings.

25. – (1) The High Court in England and Wales or Northern Ireland shall have power to grant interim relief where—

    (a)   proceedings have been or are to be commenced in a Brussels Contracting State or a State bound by the Lugano Convention or a 2005 Hague Convention State or a Regulation State or a Maintenance Regulation State other than the United Kingdom or in a part of the United Kingdom other than that in which the High Court in question exercises jurisdiction; and

    (b)   they are or will be proceedings whose subject-matter is either within the scope of the Regulation as determined by Article 1 of the Regulation,[60] within the scope of the Maintenance Regulation as determined by Article 1 of that Regulation, within the scope of the Lugano Convention as determined by Article 1 of the Lugano Convention or within the scope of the 2005 Hague Convention as determined by Articles 1 and 2 of the 2005 Hague Convention (whether or not the Regulation, the Maintenance Regulation, the Lugano Convention or the 2005 Hague Convention has effect in relation to the proceedings).

  (2)   On an application for any interim relief under subsection (1) the court may refuse to grant that relief if, in the opinion of the court, the fact that the court has no jurisdiction apart from this section in relation to the subject-matter of the proceedings in question makes it inexpedient for the court to grant it.

  (3)   Her Majesty may by Order in Council extend the power to grant interim relief inferred by sub-section (1) so as to make it exercisable in relation to proceedings of any of the following descriptions, namely:

    (a)   proceedings commenced, or to be commenced otherwise than in a Brussels or a State bound by the Lugano Convention or Regulation State or Maintenance Regulation State;

    (b)   proceedings whose subject-matter is not within the scope of the Regulation as determined by Article 1 of the Regulation, the Maintenance Regulation as determined by Article 1 of that Regulation or the Lugano Convention as determined by Article 1 of the Lugano Convention.[61]

  ....

  (7)   In this section "interim relief", in relation to the High Court in England and Wales or Northern Ireland, means interim relief of any kind which that court has power to grant in proceedings relation to matters within its jurisdiction, other than—a warrant for the arrest of property; or provision for obtaining evidence."

---

[60] The reference to "the Regulation" means the recast Judgments Regulation—Regulation (EU) No. 1215/2012 of the European Parliament and of the Council of December 12, 2012 on Jurisdiction and the Recognition and Enforcement of Judgments in Civil and Commercial Matters (Recast)—which came into force in the UK on 10 January 2015. Article 1 provides that the Regulation shall apply in "civil and commercial matters whatever the nature of the court or tribunal."

[61] The original reference in s.25(3)(c) to "arbitration proceedings" was repealed by the Arbitration Act 1996 with effect from 31 January 1997. The reason for the repeal was that s.44 of the 1996 Act made separate provision for the grant of interim relief in support of arbitrations (including, by reason of s.2(3), where the seat of the arbitration was outside England and Wales or if there was no seat). As to the jurisdiction under s.44, see Section D below.

The Civil Jurisdiction and Judgments Act 1982 (Interim Relief) Order 1997,[62] as amended, now provides:

26–057

> "2. The High Court in England and Wales or Northern Ireland shall have power to grant interim relief under section 25(1) of the Civil Jurisdiction and Judgments Act 1982 in relation to proceedings of the following descriptions, namely –
> (a) proceedings commenced or to be commenced otherwise than in a Brussels Contracting State, a state bound by the Lugano Convention, a 2005 Hague Convention State or a Regulation State;
> (b) proceedings whose subject-matter is not within the scope of the Regulation as determined by Article 1 of the Regulation."

As noted earlier, the effect of the Order, which in its original form came into effect on 1 April 1997, is to extend this ancillary jurisdiction to grant interim relief in relation to proceedings which are not taking place within a relevant Convention state and also in relation to proceedings within another member state which are outside the scope of the Regulation.[63]

26–058

So far as Convention countries are concerned, the basic principle underlying s.25 is that the courts of each member State should be willing to assist the courts of another relevant member by providing such interim relief as would be available if the assisting court were seised of the substantive proceedings. This has been said to provide a harmonisation of jurisdiction, if not of remedies.[64] In relation to non-Convention countries, the jurisdiction is not one that can be said to be expressly supported by any policy of mutual assistance of the kind reflected in the treaty obligations of Convention states. Nevertheless, it has been said that the approach of the English court should not be materially different when Parliament must have intended it to be exercised by reference to principles of judicial comity which apply in respect of the courts of other countries.[65] Even in these cases there can be said to be an element of harmonisation of jurisdiction, and this is illustrated by the court's consideration of the "expediency" of the proposed relief when exercising its discretion whether or not to grant it: see para.26–071 below.

26–059

The structure of s.25 and the way in which the section has been widened to cover any foreign proceedings, and not just those proceeding in a state within the European Union, means that the English court should in principle generally be willing to grant appropriate interim relief in support of substantive proceedings taking place in another jurisdiction and should not be deterred from doing so by the fact its role is only an ancillary one, unless the circumstances of the particular case make the grant of such relief inexpedient.[66]

26–060

---

[62] SI 1997/302, as amended by the Civil Jurisdiction and Judgments Regulation 2009 (SI 2009/3131), with effect from 1 January 2010, and by the Civil Jurisdiction and Judgments (Hague Convention on Choice of Court Agreements 2005) Regulations 2015 (SI 2015/1644), with effect from 1 October 2015.

[63] See fn.60 above for the meaning of "the Regulation", and its scope.

[64] *Republic of Haiti v Duvalier* [1990] 1 Q.B. 202, per Staughton LJ at 212. See also *Crédit Suisse Fides Trust S.A. v Cuoghi* [1998] Q.B. 818, per Millett LJ at 827E.

[65] *Refco Inc v Eastern Trading Co* [1999] 1 Lloyd's Rep. 159, per Morritt LJ at 172, and per Millett LJ at 174–175; and *Motorola Credit Corp v Uzan (No.2)* [2004] 1 W.L.R. 113, at [65] and [114], per Potter LJ giving the judgment of the court.

[66] *Crédit Suisse Fides Trust S.A. v Cuoghi*, above, at 826B, per Millett LJ.

(2)   The Need for Foreign Substantive Proceedings

26–061   The foreign proceedings to which s.25(1) is referring are proceedings "on the substance of the matter" between the parties.[67] This means that the foreign proceedings must involve the relevant overseas court dealing with the substantive dispute between the parties; and it is not sufficient that they themselves concern only the grant of interim relief in support of proceedings in a third country.

26–062   Arbitral proceedings are not "proceedings" (and so are outside the scope of the Regulation for the purposes of art.2(b) of the 1997 Order). Section 25 cannot therefore be invoked for the purposes of securing relief which is ancillary to foreign arbitration proceedings.[68]

26–063   The court is prepared to avoid analysing the concept of foreign "substantive proceedings" too narrowly so as to ensure that the purpose of international judicial co-operation is served.[69] In *Kensington International Ltd v Republic of the Congo*[70] the Court of Appeal recognised that the English court could, on an application against third parties involved in oil trades with the defendant, grant injunctive relief and require disclosure in support of Swiss proceedings which had been brought to enforce English judgments against the defendant (and in which an interim attachment order had been made by the Geneva court).

26–064   However, the proceedings under s.25 must be capable of being analysed as being ancillary to the foreign substantive proceedings in the sense of being in aid of, or related to, those proceedings. In *ETI Euro Telecom International NV v Republic of Bolivia*,[71] freezing orders which had been obtained under s.25 were set aside, because proceedings brought in the Southern District of New York (and described as being an action for an order of attachment in aid of arbitration) were directed solely at assets located in New York, whereas the proceedings under s.25 were directed at assets in England.

26–065   Further, the English proceedings must be capable of being properly categorised as ones for *interim* relief in support of the foreign substantive claim. In *AB Bank Ltd v Abu Dhabi Commercial Bank*[72] the claimant brought a claim seeking *Norwich Pharmacal* relief against an overseas respondent, who was alleged to have been

---

[67] *ETI Euro Telecom International NV v Republic of Bolivia* [2008] EWCA Civ 880; [2009] 1 W.L.R. 665, at [70] where Lawrence Collins LJ referred to the legislative purpose of s.25 and to the language of what is now art.35 of the recast Judgments Regulation (see fn.60 above). The section can extend to the grant of interim relief by the English court in aid of enforcement of a foreign judgment: *Indosuez International Finance BV v National Reserve Bank* [2002] EWHC 774 (Comm), at [17], per Morison J.

[68] *ETI Euro Telecom International NV v Republic of Bolivia*, above, at [92]. However, note that the arbitration proceedings in that case were constituted pursuant to the sui generis Convention on the Settlement of Investment Disputes of 18 March 1965. In non-ICSID foreign arbitrations, parties may wish to consider whether the Court has jurisdiction to grant injunctions pursuant to s.44 of the Arbitration Act 1996, considered in Section D below.

[69] *ETI Euro Telecom International NV v Republic of Bolivia*, at [76].

[70] *Kensington International Ltd v Republic of the Congo* [2007] EWCA Civ 1128; [2008] 1 W.L.R. 1144.

[71] *ETI Euro Telecom International NV v Republic of Bolivia*, above.

[72] *AB Bank Ltd v Abu Dhabi Commercial Bank* [2016] EWHC 2082 (Comm); [2017] 1 W.L.R. 810, at [6]–[16].

mixed up in a fraud but who was not a party to the relevant substantive foreign proceedings. The claimant had relied upon the jurisdictional gateway under CPR 6, PD 6B, para.3.1(5) (which refers in turn to s.25 of the CJJA) to obtain permission to serve the claim out of the jurisdiction.[73] The court held that, as between the claimant and the present respondent, the relief sought in a *Norwich Pharmacal* claim was not interim but final in nature; there would be no further proceedings between them which would justify describing that remedy as "interim". The permission to serve the *Norwich Pharmacal* claim was accordingly set aside.

(3) The Approach of the Court

The jurisdiction of the English court is primarily territorial, being ordinarily dependent upon the presence of either persons or assets within the jurisdiction. Interim protective measures granted by the court, when the respondent neither resides nor has relevant assets located within the jurisdiction of the foreign court seised of the substantive proceedings, cannot be regarded as exorbitant if the person either resides in England and Wales (for the purposes of any in personam relief) or has assets located here (for the purposes of any order directed against those assets). There is no reason in principle why the court should not (by an order which operates against the respondent personally) restrain a person before it from disposing of assets located either here or abroad and, subject to restrictions in relation to enforcement outside of the jurisdiction and in relation to parties not subject to its jurisdiction, such orders are routinely made in cases involving international fraud.[74]

26–066

In such cases, this generally means that the respondent resides or is domiciled here. Even if the respondent is not resident within the jurisdiction the presence of assets within the jurisdiction will often mean that it is appropriate for the English court to grant protective measures by way of a freezing order against those assets.[75] The grant of relief against someone not resident within the jurisdiction on the basis that he has been made amenable to the court's powers under s.25 CJJA simply by being served with proceedings, when he has no relevant connection with the jurisdiction and no assets here, would be regarded as exorbitant and going beyond the underlying policy of the section and of art.31 of the Judgments Regulation. It would rarely if ever be appropriate or expedient for the court to assume jurisdiction under s.25 where the defendant has no such connection with England and Wales and the court has no sanction over him to enforce the order.

26–067

---

[73] "A claim is made for an interim remedy under s.25(1) of the Civil Jurisdiction and Judgments Act 1982."

[74] By contrast, "It will rarely be appropriate to exercise jurisdiction to grant a freezing order where a defendant has no assets here and owes no allegiance to the English court by the existence of *in personam* jurisdiction over him, whether by way of domicile or residence or for some other reason. Protective measures should normally be left to the courts where the assets are to be found or where the defendant resides or is for some other reason subject to *in personam* jurisdiction": see *ICICI Bank UK Plc v Diminco NV* [2014] EWHC 3124 (Comm); [2014] 2 C.L.C. 647, at [27(1)], per Popplewell J.

[75] *ICICI Bank UK Plc v Diminco NV* [2014] EWHC 3124 (Comm); [2014] 2 C.L.C. 647, at [27(2)], per Popplewell J.

26–068   In cases where the English court is exercising the subsidiary role contemplated by s.25 CJJA, the jurisdiction is an ancillary or supportive one. Accordingly, in determining whether it is appropriate to grant relief under s.25, the court adopts a two-stage approach.

26–069   **First stage.**   First, the court considers whether the facts would warrant the relief sought if the substantive proceedings were brought in England. This means that an applicant for relief under s.25 will first have to address the requirements for particular forms of interim relief discussed in the following chapters. In the case of a freezing injunction, for example, the applicant will need to overcome the test which requires him to show that it is likely that, in the foreign substantive proceedings, he will recover damages (or some other pecuniary relief) for a certain or approximate sum and that there are reasons to believe that the respondent has assets to meet such a judgment, in whole or in part, but steps may be taken in relation to them which mean that they may no longer be available when judgment is given.[76] Consistent with proceeding at this first stage as if the court was itself the primary court seised of the substantive proceedings, the judge is required to conduct a separate exercise of judgment on these evidential matters rather than simply accept any decision or indication upon them by the foreign court.[77]

26–070   In considering whether or not the relief would be appropriate in domestic proceedings, the court considers its own powers to grant interim relief (as if the proceedings were indeed taking place here) and it is not inhibited by the absence of any equivalent power in the foreign court to grant such relief: see s.25(7). However, the absence or existence of an equivalent power in the relevant foreign jurisdiction (and the likelihood or not of any such power being exercised by it) may be very relevant at the second stage of the court's approach, when it considers the issue of expediency.

26–071   **Second stage.**   If the court concludes that interim relief would be appropriate if the substantive claim were a domestic one, the court then considers (as required by the provisions of s.25(2)) whether it is "expedient" to grant it; or, more precisely, it asks itself whether the fact that the substantive proceedings are taking place outside the jurisdiction (such that the court has no jurisdiction over the subject matter of the proceedings) makes it inexpedient to grant the type of relief sought.

26–072   It has been said that the court's ancillary jurisdiction must be exercised with caution, so as to ensure that the English court does not tread on the toes of the foreign court.[78] The English court has, as we have seen, a very broad jurisdiction to grant interim relief, which has been developed through judicial precedent into

---

[76] In *Refco Inc v Eastern Trading Co* [1999] 1 Lloyd's Rep. 159 the Court of Appeal concluded that the applicant failed at this first stage of establishing that there was a real risk of dissipation of assets that would have justified relief if the proceedings had been taking place in England.

[77] *Motorola Credit Corp v Uzan (No.2)* [2004] 1 W.L.R. 113, at [102], per Potter LJ giving the judgment of the court.

[78] *Crédit Suisse Fides Trust S.A. v Cuoghi* [1998] Q.B. 818, at 832A, per Lord Bingham of Cornhill CJ.

a range of different types of order, which the court will, in an appropriate case, willingly deploy to ensure that claims in fraud are not frustrated. It also boasts judges with considerable experience in fraud cases. There is therefore a temptation on the part of claimants to resort to the English court, under its ancillary jurisdiction, as a sort of "international policeman". The court must therefore be astute to check in any given case whether it should indeed act.

In *Motorola Credit Corp v Uzan (No.2)*[79] Potter LJ (giving the judgment of the court) recognised the popularity of English interim remedies with claimants in certain foreign proceedings and summarised the earlier authorities on the issue of "inexpediency" as follows:

> "As the authorities show, there are five particular considerations which the court should bear in mind, when considering the question whether it is inexpedient to make an order. First, whether the making of the order will interfere with the management of the case in the primary court e.g. where the order is inconsistent with an order in the primary court or overlaps with it. That consideration does not arise in the present case. Second, whether it is the policy in the primary jurisdiction not itself to make worldwide freezing/disclosure orders.[80] Third, whether there is a danger that the orders made will give rise to disharmony or confusion and/or risk of conflicting inconsistent or overlapping orders in other jurisdictions, in particular the courts of the state where the person enjoined resides or where the assets affected are located. If so, then respect for the territorial jurisdiction of that state should discourage the English court from using its unusually wide powers against a foreign defendant. Fourth, whether at the time the order is sought there is likely to be a potential conflict as to jurisdiction rendering it inappropriate and inexpedient to make a worldwide order. Fifth, whether, in a case where jurisdiction is resisted and disobedience to be expected, the court will be making an order which it cannot enforce."

In that case, the relevant defendants to proceedings in the Southern District of New York were not within the jurisdiction of the English court and had no connection with England. The Court of Appeal, deciding the matter with particular reliance upon the third and fifth considerations identified by it, discharged worldwide freezing injunctions against those defendants when their connection with this country was "tenuous or non-existent", it was clear that there would be no effective sanction available in the event of their non-compliance with it and the Turkish court (being the court of their domicile) had issued anti-suit injunctions against the claimant in relation to both the New York proceedings and the English proceedings.[81]

In *Refco Inc v Eastern Trading Co*[82] the members of the Court of Appeal were divided as to whether or not it would have been expedient to grant a freezing injunction in aid of proceedings in Chicago had the court not already concluded (at the first stage of the analysis) that the claimant had failed to establish a real risk of asset dissipation. Millett LJ (in the minority) said that judicial comity sometimes required restraint and that the English court should be very slow to

26–073

26–074

26–075

---

[79] *Motorola Credit Corp v Uzan (No.2)*, above, at [114]–[115].
[80] Or indeed whatever other type of order the claimant is seeking from the English court.
[81] See *Belletti v Morici* [2009] EWHC 2316 (Comm); [2010] 1 All E.R. 412, at [58], where Flaux J concluded that the related considerations of an absence of any connection between the parents and the jurisdiction and the impracticality of enforcing the *Chabra* injunction against them made it inexpedient to make the order.
[82] *Refco Inc v Eastern Trading Co* [1999] 1 Lloyd's Rep. 159.

grant relief of a kind which the foreign court had jurisdiction to grant but (by reason of it applying a more exacting test than a risk of dissipation, which the evidence before it would not satisfy) would decline to grant.[83]

26–076　　In *Royal Westminster Investments v Varma*[84] Newey J concluded that it would not have been appropriate to grant an injunction, aimed at preventing the expenditure of company monies on legal proceedings in the BVI in which the company was a defendant, had the substantive proceedings been in England rather than the BVI. The judge referred to the first matter identified for consideration in the *Motorola* case and concluded that there would be a real risk that acceding to the application would obstruct or hamper the management of the BVI litigation, since the making of the proposed order might inhibit the ability of the BVI court to give directions as to the role the company should play in the proceedings.

26–077　　There may also be questions of proportionality to be addressed in the context of the exercise of the court's discretion. In *Ras Al Khaimah Investment Authority v Bestfort Developments LLP*[85] the application under s.25 failed under both limbs of the two-stage test. In relation to the exercise of discretion, the court was not satisfied of the existence of substantial assets in Latvia (if any assets at all) for the purpose of granting relief—freezing injunctions, receiverships and a request for the grant of powers of attorney to render the receiverships effective – which would carry the risk of swallowing up the value of those assets in legal and other fees incurred in its enforcement. In *AB Bank Ltd v Abu Dhabi Commercial Bank*[86] the court decided that an application for *Norwich Pharmacal* relief in support of English proceedings did not fall within the scope of s.25 (as we have noted above), but went on to express the view that it would have exercised its discretion against making an order when the requested disclosure by the defendant bank would have risked it being in breach of the UAE Penal Code.

26–078　　As for the risk identified in *Motorola Credit Corp v Uzan (No.2)*[87] that the s.25 relief might overlap with that granted by the foreign court, it has been held that the fact that the foreign court which is seised of the substantive proceedings has itself ordered a worldwide freezing injunction does not prevent the English court from granting a freezing order, at least in relation to English assets and/or against defendants resident and domiciled within the jurisdiction; but cogent reasons will be required before such overlapping relief is granted.[88] In *GFH Capital Ltd v Haigh*[89] the claimants sought a freezing order which mirrored the terms of an order already made in proceedings in Dubai, subject to the proposed order being limited to English assets and not requiring disclosure of assets. Despite the overlap, Males J granted the relief on the basis that there were two cogent reasons

---

[83] However, as Neuberger J observed in *Ryan v Friction Dynamics Ltd* [2001] CP Reports 75, the majority view in *Refco* shows that it may nonetheless be appropriate to grant interim relief under s.25 even where the foreign court has refused similar relief.

[84] *Royal Westminster Investments v Varma* [2012] EWHC 3439 (Ch), at [61].

[85] *Ras Al Khaimah Investment Authority v Bestfort Developments LLP* [2015] EWHC 3383 (Ch), at [46].

[86] *AB Bank Ltd v Abu Dhabi Commercial Bank* [2016] EWHC 2082 (Comm).

[87] See paras 26–073—26–074 above.

[88] *Ryan v Friction Dynamics Ltd* [2001] CP Reports 75, per Neuberger J.

[89] *GFH Capital Ltd v Haigh* [2014] EWHC 3157 (Comm), at [11]–[22], per Males J.

for doing so. Having noted that the Dubai order contemplated and gave permission for an application to be made to the English court, the judge concluded that the claimants' ability to give notice of the English freezing injunction to the relevant bank (which was not prevented from acting on the defendant's instructions under the Dubai order) and the delay in the provision of information under the foreign order were reasons justifying the grant of relief. These two factors meant that "a freezing order here would confer some extra justifiable and valuable benefit to the claimants".

D. JURISDICTION IN SUPPORT OF ARBITRAL PROCEEDINGS

Alleged frauds often arise in the context of a relationship which is itself governed by an arbitration clause. Depending on the scope of, and parties to, that clause, the victim of a fraud may find himself obliged to pursue any legal remedy through arbitration proceedings rather than the English courts, or those of any other jurisdiction. In such circumstances, the prospective applicant for, or respondent to an application for, interim relief from the Court should give thought to the statutory basis for such relief: s.44 of the Arbitration Act ("AA") 1996.[90]   **26–079**

(1)   The Scope of Section 44 of the AA 1996

Section 44 describes the Court's jurisdiction to make interim injunctions between parties to an arbitration agreement where an arbitration relating to the subject matter of the injunction is on foot or is close to being commenced. In such circumstances, the Court will only exercise any broader power which it may have under s.37 of the SCA sensitively, and with due regard to the scheme and terms of the AA.[91]   **26–080**

Section 44 of the AA provides as follows: **26–081**

> "Court powers exercisable in support of arbitral proceedings:
> (1)   Unless otherwise agreed by the parties, the court has for the purposes of and in relation to arbitral proceedings the same power of making orders about the matters listed below as it has for the purposes of and in relation to legal proceedings.

---

[90] Parties to an arbitration also have a right to use the Court procedures available in legal proceedings to secure a witness's attendance before the arbitral tribunal to give oral evidence or to produce evidence. See s.43 of the Arbitration Act 1996.

[91] *AES Ust-Kamenogorsk Hydropower Plant LLP v Ust-Kamenogorsk Hydropower Plant JSC* [2013] UKSC 35, [2013] 1 W.L.R. 1889, at [60], per Lord Mance. It will generally be inappropriate for the Court to exercise a power broader than that provided for by s.44 of the 1996 Act in circumstances in which an arbitration is on foot or proposed. See, for example, *HC Trading Malta Ltd v Tradeland Commodities SL* [2016] EWHC 1279; [2016] 1 W.L.R. 3120, in which HHJ Waksman QC (sitting in the High Court) set aside a claim form seeking a declaration that an arbitration agreement existed between A and B in circumstances in which A proposed to bring arbitration proceedings. On the other hand, where there is no arbitration on foot or in prospect, the Court's jurisdiction to grant injunctions between the parties is unaffected by s.44 of the Arbitration Act 1996; see *AES Ust-Kamenogorsk Hydropower Plant LLP*, at [43], per Lord Mance. In that case, a party to an arbitration agreement wished to enjoin proceedings in Kazakhstan as a breach of that agreement without commencing an arbitration itself. It was held that the Court had jurisdiction to grant such an order, and that the jurisdiction to do so was found in s.37 of the SCA rather than s.44 of the AA.

    (2)   Those matters are—

        (a)   the taking of the evidence of witnesses;

        (b)   the preservation of evidence;

        (c)   making orders relating to property which is the subject of the proceedings or as to which any question arises in the proceedings—

            (i)   for the inspection, photographing, preservation, custody or detention of the property, or

            (ii)   ordering that samples be taken from, or any observation be made of or experiment conducted upon, the property;

        and for that purpose authorising any person to enter any premises in the possession or control of a party to the arbitration;

        (d)   the sale of any goods the subject of the proceedings;

        (e)   the granting of an interim injunction or the appointment of a receiver.

    (3)   If the case is one of urgency, the court may, on the application of a party or proposed party to the arbitral proceedings, make such orders as it thinks necessary for the purpose of preserving evidence or assets.

    (4)   If the case is not one of urgency, the court shall act only on the application of a party to the arbitral proceedings (upon notice to the other parties and to the tribunal) made with the permission of the tribunal or the agreement in writing of the other parties.

    (5)   In any case the court shall act only if or to the extent that the arbitral tribunal, and any arbitral or other institution or person vested by the parties with power in that regard, has no power or is unable for the time being to act effectively.

    (6)   If the court so orders, an order made by it under this section shall cease to have effect in whole or in part on the order of the tribunal or of any such arbitral or other institution or person having power to act in relation to the subject-matter of the order.

    (7)   The leave of the court is required for any appeal from a decision of the court under this section."

26–082   The jurisdiction of the Court to award interim injunctions in support of actual or proposed arbitral proceedings is, accordingly, subject to three restrictions evident from the face of s.44 itself:

    (1)   The Court has no power under s.44 to grant interim injunctions (or other interim relief) relating to actual or contemplated arbitral proceedings if the parties to the arbitration agreement have agreed that it should not (s.44(1)).

    (2)   The Court may only act pursuant to s.44 if or to the extent that the arbitral tribunal has no power or is unable for the time being to act effectively (s.44(5)).

    (3)   The Court has no power under s.44 to make interim injunctions relating to actual or contemplated arbitral proceedings unless either:

        (a)   the arbitral tribunal or the other parties give their permission in writing; or

        (b)   the case is one of urgency (ss.44(3), (4)). In the latter case, the power may only be exercised where necessary for the purpose of preserving evidence or assets.[92]

26–083   Further, s.2(3) of the AA provides that, while the Court has jurisdiction to exercise its powers under s.44 in respect of arbitrations whose seat is not (or is not likely to be) in England Wales or Northern Ireland, it may refuse to exercise

---

[92] Doubt as to whether subs.(3) was intended to limit the breadth of the Court's powers in (1) and (2) were resolved in the affirmative in *Cetelem SA v Roust Holdings Ltd* [2005] EWCA Civ 618; [2005] 1 W.L.R. 3555, at [38], per Clarke LJ.

that jurisdiction if the fact that the arbitral seat is not (or is not likely to be) in those areas would make it inappropriate to do so.

Finally, there are conflicting authorities as to whether the jurisdiction conferred by s.44 is restricted to making injunctions against persons who are parties to the relevant arbitration agreement. The most recent cases to consider the issue are *Cruz City 1 Mauritius Holdings v Unitech Ltd* and *Dtek Trading SA v Moroz*.[93] In each case the Court held that there was no jurisdiction under s.44 to make an order against a person who was not a party to the arbitration agreement (albeit the comments in *Cruz* on this point were only obiter). However, the state of the authorities[94] means that this issue probably cannot be considered settled until it has been reviewed by the Court of Appeal. **26–084**

(2) Circumstances in which the Arbitral Tribunal has no Power or is Unable to Act Effectively for the Time Being under Subsection 44(5)

The most obvious cases of a situation in which an arbitral tribunal has no power or is unable to act for the time being effectively are where: (a) the arbitral tribunal has not yet been constituted[95]; and (b) the arbitral tribunal has been constituted, but under the rules governing the arbitration in question, it lacks the power to grant the interim relief sought.[96] **26–085**

However, s.44(5) is not limited to these two circumstances, and other situations can and do arise in which the Court will regard the arbitral tribunal as having no power or as being unable to act for the time being effectively. Examples include: **26–086**

(1) *Pacific Maritime Asia Ltd v Holystone Overseas Ltd*, which concerned an order for the detention of a vessel within the jurisdiction. It was successfully argued that an arbitral tribunal's order that the vessel be detained would not be sufficiently effective. Harbour authorities, once made aware of an order of the Court, would be very unlikely to allow the vessel to leave. However, if presented with an arbitrator's order, they may well have felt less comfortable in refusing to allow the vessel to leave (and, indeed, may not have been lawfully able to do so).[97]

---

[93] *Cruz City 1 Mauritius Holdings v Unitech Ltd and Dtek Trading SA v Moroz* [2014] EWHC 3704 (Comm); [2015] 1 All E.R. (Comm) 305 and [2017] EWHC 94 (Comm); [2017] Bus L.R. 628 respectively.

[94] Set out in *Dtek*, at [12]–[36].

[95] See e.g. *Permasteelisa Japan KK v Bouyguesstroi* [2007] EWHC 3508 (QB), at [42], per Ramsey J. See also *Euroil Ltd v Cameroon Offshore Petroleum Sarl* [2014] EWHC 12 (Comm), at [11], per Males J. Although note that some arbitration centres provide—if needed—emergency arbitrators. It has been suggested that the availability of such emergency arbitrators should weigh on the Court's decision as to whether or not the requirements of s.44(5) are satisfied. See D. Sutton, J. Gill and M. Gearing, *Russell on Arbitration*, 24th edn (London: Sweet & Maxwell, 2015), para.7–195.

[96] See e.g. *Barnwell Enterprises Ltd v ECP Africa FII Investments LLC* [2013] EWHC 2517 (Comm), at [40]–[41], per Hamblen J.

[97] *Pacific Maritime Asia Ltd v Holystone Overseas Ltd* [2007] EWHC 2319 (Comm); [2008] 1 Lloyd's Rep. 371, at [76]–[82], per Christopher Clarke J.

(2) *Hiscox Underwriting Ltd v Dickson Manchester & Co Ltd*, in which an arbitrator had been appointed on the day of the hearing of the application before the Court and, as such, was insufficiently familiar with the matter to be expected to make an immediate order.[98]

(3) *Sheffield United Football Club Ltd v West Ham United Football Club Plc*, in which Sheffield sought an interim order restraining West Ham from pursuing an appeal from an arbitral award to the Court of Arbitration for Sport (the "CAS"). Sheffield argued that the CAS had no jurisdiction to hear the appeal, West Ham contended that it did. Sheffield could have referred the matter to the arbitrator, but if the arbitrator ruled that the CAS could not hear the appeal, West Ham would have simply appealed that decision to the CAS as well. Accordingly, the tribunal's ruling would not have been effective.[99]

(3) Urgent Applications Necessary to Preserve Evidence or Assets under Subsection 44(3)

26–087 For relief to be granted under s.44(3), the application must cross 3 hurdles. It must be: (a) urgent; (b) necessary; and (c) aimed at preserving evidence or assets.

26–088 Whether or not urgency exists in any given case will be extremely fact sensitive. However, if an arbitral tribunal would be able to provide relief, or authorise reference to the Court under subs.44(4), before the Court itself could come to a decision, then it is unlikely that the requisite degree of urgency would exist.[100] Conversely, the mere fact that an application could have been made earlier does not necessarily mean that it is not urgent.[101]

26–089 The requirement for necessity is conceptually distinct from urgency. Although in practice the two often blend together, this is not necessarily the case. See, for example, *Company 1 v Company 2*, in which HHJ Saffman (sitting in the High Court) held that an application for relief under s.44(3) was urgent, but was not necessary because the applicant had failed to adduce sufficient evidence that the respondent was likely to destroy evidence or dissipate assets.[102]

26–090 The question of whether any given application is being made to preserve evidence or assets should be given careful consideration, albeit in practice the bar set by this requirement is not a high one and the courts interpret this concept flexibly.

26–091 The Courts have tended to give a wide meaning of the word "assets". The point is well illustrated by *Cetelem SA v Roust Holdings Ltd*.[103] A and B entered into a share purchase agreement in respect of shares in a Russian Bank. The agreement

---

[98] *Hiscox Underwriting Ltd v Dickson Manchester & Co Ltd* [2004] EWHC 479 (Comm); [2004] 1 All E.R. (Comm) 753, at [33], per Cooke J.

[99] *Sheffield United Football Club Ltd v West Ham United Football Club Plc* [2008] EWHC 2855 (Comm), at [31]–[36], per Teare J.

[100] *Jacobs E&C Ltd v Laker Vent Engineering Ltd* [2014] EWHC 4818, at [39]–[40], per Ramsey J.

[101] *Company 1 v Company 2* [2017] EWHC 2319 (QB), at [68], per HHJ Saffman.

[102] *Company 1 v Company 2*, above, at [58]–[78].

[103] *Cetelem SA v Roust Holdings Ltd* [2005] EWCA Civ 618; [2005] 1 W.L.R. 3555.

was subject to an arbitration clause and was conditional, among other things, upon approval being received from the Russian Central Bank before 31 January 2005. The deadline for any application for such approval was 10 December 2004. A successfully applied for an injunction under s.44(3) compelling B to submit the relevant application to the Russian Central Bank, on the basis that "assets" included contractual rights, and the injunction was necessary to preserve A's contractual rights to buy the shares.[104]

However, there remains some doubt as to precisely where the outer bounds of the meaning of the word "assets" should be drawn. In *Permasteelia Japan KK v Bouyguesstroi*, Ramsey J suggested that the right to refer a question to an arbitral panel for interim determination might itself be an "asset" within the meaning of s.44(3).[105] In the view of some commentators, this would be going too far, as it would mean that a s.44(3) application could be made in respect of any matter which might be referred to the arbitral tribunal in due course, and would render the word "asset" essentially meaningless.[106] **26–092**

By contrast, in *Zim Integrated Shipping Services Ltd v European Container KS* and *Euroil Ltd v Cameroon Offshore Petroleum SARL*, Males J expressed doubt as to whether any jurisdiction can arise under s.44(3) to preserve contractual rights between the parties in circumstances in which the existence of those rights is disputed, and suggested that the Court will more readily exercise its powers under that section in circumstances in which the applicant seeks to preserve assets which might be the subject of a freezing order.[107] **26–093**

Zim was itself considered by HHJ Waksman QC (sitting in the High Court) in *GigSky APS v Vodafone Roaming Services*, in which case he held that disputed contractual rights between parties to an arbitration agreement could constitute assets for the purposes of s.44(3).[108] **26–094**

(4) When is it Inappropriate to Grant Relief in Respect of Foreign Arbitrations under Section 2(3)?

The natural court for the granting of interim injunctive relief is the court of the country of the seat of the arbitration, especially where the curial law is that of the same country.[109] Accordingly, although the wording of s.2(3) might suggest that it is for the respondent to demonstrate why it is inappropriate for the court to assist a foreign arbitration, it is in fact for the applicant to demonstrate appropriateness. In doing so, the court will generally adopt a similar approach, and adopt "at least **26–095**

---

[104] *Cetelem SA v Roust Holdings Ltd*, above, at [57]–[71], per Clarke LJ.
[105] *Permasteelia Japan KK v Bouyguesstroi* [2007] EWHC 3508 (QB), at [43], per Ramsey J.
[106] See Sutton, Gill and Gearing, *Russell on Arbitration* (2015), para.7–194.
[107] *Zim Integrated Shipping Services Ltd v European Container KS* [2013] EWHC 3581 (Comm), at [34]; and *Euroil Ltd v Cameroon Offshore Petroleum SARL*, at [18]–[19].
[108] *GigSky APS v Vodafone Roaming Services* [2015] EWHC 4047 (Comm), at [44]–[55].
[109] *Econet Wireless Ltd v Vee Networks Ltd* [2006] EWHC 1568, at [19], per Morison J.

the same degree of caution", as it would in relation to applications in support of foreign litigation (considered above at paras 26–071—26–078).[110]

26–096 Where a party to a pending arbitration has already initiated interim relief proceedings in support of that arbitration before the courts of another jurisdiction, all parties are likely to require cogent reasons for seeking their own interim relief in England, as opposed to that other jurisdiction or the seat of the arbitration.[111]

---

[110] *Mobil Cerro Negro Ltd v Petroleos de Venezuela S.A.* [2008] EWHC 532; [2008] 1 Lloyd's Rep. 684, at [120]–[135], per Walker J.

[111] See *Company 1 v Company 2* [2017] EWHC 2319 (QB), in which A had sought and obtained interim relief against B in the BVI in support of a pending Swiss arbitration. B sought its own interim relief in England while the BVI proceedings were ongoing. The absence of a good reason for B seeking its relief in England rather than the BVI weighed against the grant of relief (see [88]).

CHAPTER 27

THE WITHOUT NOTICE APPLICATION

A. THE BASIS FOR APPLYING WITHOUT NOTICE

The most common forms of interim relief in a fraud claim will be freezing orders (whether or not they have a proprietary element) and search orders. Applications for such relief will almost invariably (although there are important exceptions) be made ex parte, or, in modern parlance, without notice. In this chapter we analyse the various procedural considerations which will arise on any such application.

27–001

(1) Deciding to Apply Without Notice

(i) Proper reasons for applying

A decision to apply to the Court on a without notice basis ought never to be taken lightly. Applicants for interim relief should be aware that proceeding in the absence of the respondent is an exceptional step, no matter how often it may be done in the case of certain classes of interim relief, where the concern is that giving notice to the respondent may well result in him taking steps which pre-empt and prejudice the intended relief.

27–002

Any applicant proposing to proceed in this way must bear in mind the following often-cited observations of Hoffmann J in *Re First Express Ltd*[1]:

27–003

> "It is a basic principle of justice that an order should not be made against a party without giving him an opportunity to be heard. The only exception is when two conditions are satisfied. First, that giving him such an opportunity appears likely to cause injustice to the applicant, by reason either of the delay involved or the action which it appears likely that the respondent or others would take before the order can be made. Secondly, when the court is satisfied that any damage which the respondent may suffer through having to comply with the order is compensatable under the cross-undertaking or that the risk of uncompensatable loss is clearly outweighed by the risk of injustice to the applicant if the order is not made. There is, I think, a tendency among applicants to think that a calculation of the balance of advantage and disadvantage in accordance with the second condition is sufficient to justify an *ex parte* order. In my view, this attitude should be discouraged. One does not reach any balancing of advantage and disadvantage unless the first condition has been satisfied. The principle *audi alterem partem* does not yield to a mere utilitarian calculation. It can be displaced only by invoking the overriding principle of justice which enables the court to act at once when it appears likely that otherwise injustice will be caused."

---

[1] *Re First Express Ltd* [1992] B.C.L.C. 824, at 828.

27–004   In *National Commercial Bank Jamaica Ltd v Olint Corp Ltd (Practice Note)*[2] the same judge, now as Lord Hoffmann sitting in the Privy Council, returned to these questions, in the context of a consideration of provisions of the Jamaica Civil Procedure Rules which are equivalent to those contained in PD 23A and PD 25A of the CPR. He stated:

> "Although the matter is in the end one for the discretion of the judge, *audi alterem partem* is a salutary and important principle. Their Lordships therefore consider that a judge should not entertain an application of which no notice has been given unless either giving notice would enable the defendant to take steps to defeat the purpose of the injunction (as in the case of a Mareva or Anton Piller order) or there has been literally no time to give notice before the injunction is required to prevent the threatened wrongful act. These two alternative conditions are reflected in rule 17.4(4) of the Civil Procedure Rules 2002. Their Lordships would expect cases in the latter category to be rare, because even in cases in which there was no time to give the period of notice required by the rules, there will usually be no reason why the applicant should not have given shorter notice or even made a telephone call. Any notice is better than none."

27–005   It will be evident from these passages that there are only two factual scenarios which justify a litigant proceeding without notice:

(1)   First, where giving notice would potentially defeat or prejudice the purpose of the application. It is usually this first scenario which justifies proceeding without notice to obtain a freezing order (because giving notice might hasten the very events the order is designed to prevent), although the particular facts may involve a combination of this and the second scenario described below.

(2)   Secondly, where the delay involved in giving notice to the potential respondent will defeat the purpose of the application. Such a scenario will usually involve an attempt to prevent a step which is to be taken imminently and which the applicant wishes to prevent by injunction. However, even in such a situation the Court will generally expect *some* form of notice to be given, even if it is short notice, unless it is satisfied that there was as a matter of practical reality no opportunity at all to give notice.

27–006   These principles, which we consider in further detail below, are reflected in the relevant provisions of the CPR, which we also consider below.

(ii)   Secrecy

27–007   It will be evident that the essential requirement of an application made without any notice at all (where the giving of at least some notice is otherwise practicable) is that of secrecy—in the sense of avoiding the respondent being forewarned of the application in a way that might cause him to take steps which might well pre-empt and prejudice the efficacy of the proposed relief. As we have seen, it is an elementary tenet of English law that save in an emergency a court should hear both sides before giving a ruling and (apart from those instances

---

[2] *National Commercial Bank Jamaica Ltd v Olint Corp Ltd (Practice Note)* [2009] UKPC 16; [2009] 1 W.L.R. 1405, at [13].

where a without notice procedure is specifically authorised by statute), if that is to be departed from, it must be on the basis of a well-founded belief that the giving of notice would lead to irretrievable prejudice being caused to the applicant.[3]

(iii)   Urgency

By itself the need for urgency is unlikely to justify a without notice application, because there is almost always the option of giving short notice, even if informally, to the respondent; and some notice is better than none at all.[4]   **27–008**

As explained below, exceptional urgency (as opposed to secrecy) is identified by the CPR as one of the circumstances which may justify the application being made without notice to the respondent.[5] Doing so is of course a derogation from the principle of *audi alteram partem* and the expectation of the court where urgency alone (in the absence of the other circumstances identified in those provisions) justifies applying without notice is that there is, as we have seen from the quotation above, "literally no time to give notice before the injunction is required to prevent the threatened wrongful act."[6]   **27–009**

(iv)   Applying before commencement of proceedings

Most applications for interim relief, even when made without notice, will be made after the commencement of proceedings. This will almost always be the case for any application which is on notice to the respondent (it will be a rare case where the circumstances are such that the applicant is able to give the respondent notice but has not had sufficient time to issue proceedings before he applies). Nonetheless, the existence of an issued claim form is not an absolute precondition to seeking interim relief, and in urgent without notice applications for freezing orders or search orders the court will not expect the claim form to have been issued, although it will generally insist upon an undertaking from the applicant to issue a claim form as soon as reasonably practicable.[7]   **27–010**

---

[3] *FZ v SZ* [2011] 1 F.L.R. 64, at [32], per Mostyn J.

[4] Paragraph 16.2 of the Chancery Guide states that "generally it is wrong to make an application without giving prior notice to the respondent" and, even in an urgent case (unless the giving of notice might frustrate the order), "the applicant should give the respondent informally as much notice of the application as is possible". The Guide also makes provision (at para.16.28) in relation to the conduct of hearings of applications of which proper notice has not been given but at which the respondent appears and states that "the judge may, in an appropriate case, make an order which will have effect until trial or further order as if proper notice had been given."

[5] See CPR Pt 23.4(2) and CPR PD 23A, para.3.

[6] *National Commercial Bank Jamaica Ltd v Olint Corp Ltd (Practice Note)* [2009] UKPC 16; [2009] 1 W.L.R. 1405, at [13]. As noted there, in most cases there will be other factors aside from simple urgency (most notably the need for secrecy and furthering the overriding objective through the efficacy of the requested relief) which justify proceeding without notice.

[7] Because of the principle, considered in Ch.26, that interim relief should not be granted in a vacuum, but in support of a claim for substantive relief.

(v)   The additional burden

27–011   An applicant considering making an application without notice will further want to give considerattion not only to whether he can demonstrate that such circumstances obtain; but also to the fact that, if he is to apply without notice (or even on short notice), there will be a heavy burden on him to ensure that full and frank disclosure is made to the Court. We consider this burden in Section D below.

(2)   An Exceptional Remedy

27–012   To grant an interim remedy in the form of an injunction without notice to the person affected by the injunction (and who would thus ordinarily be the respondent to the application) is therefore "to grant an exceptional remedy."[8] In *FZ v SZ*[9] Mostyn J, referring to his experience as a judge in the Family Division, said that that principle was often turned on its head by

> "a sort of lazy, laissez-faire practice or syndrome [having] grown up which says that provided the return date is soon, and provided that the court is satisfied that no material prejudice will be caused to the respondent, then there is no harm in making the order *ex parte*."

In *O'Farrell v O'Farrell*[10] Tugendhat J referred to this observation and commented:

> "I too have been shocked at the volume of spurious ex-parte applications that are made in the Queen's Bench Division. The number of occasions on which CPR Part 25.2 and CPR 15.3(1) and (3) and PD25A para 4(3) are flouted is a matter of real concern. In these days of mobile phones and emails it is almost always possible to give at least informal notice of an application. And it is equally almost always possible for the Judge hearing such an application to communicate with the intended defendant or respondent, either in a three way telephone call, or by a series of calls, or exchanges of e-mail. Judges do this routinely, including when on out of hours duty. Cases where no notice is required for reasons given in PD 25A para 4.3(3) are very rare indeed."

27–013   The applicant should therefore test rigorously his own case for proceeding without notice, and if the conclusion is that he can properly apply for the relief sought without notice then he should set out his reasoning in full in the affidavit drafted in support. Moreover the mere fact that an applicant is applying for a freezing order does not ipso facto provide a justification for applying without notice.[11] If the freezing order is directed at a particular asset (whether or not the

---

[8] *Moat Housing Group-South Ltd v Harris* [2006] Q.B. 606, at [71] (CA); and *ND v KP* [2011] EWHC 457 (Fam), at [10], per Mostyn J.

[9] *FZ v SZ* [2011] 1 F.L.R. 64, at [32], referred to again by the same judge in *ND v KP*, above.

[10] *O'Farrell v O'Farrell* [2012] EWHC 123 (QB), at [66].

[11] See for instance *Thane v Tomlinson* [2003] EWCA Civ 1272. It is fair to say that in the majority of cases applying without notice will be justified if the application is for freezing relief (because, usually, the apprehended risk of dissipation that justifies the freezing order is also a basis for believing that the giving of notice will cause irretrievable prejudice): see *Legal Services Commission v Lonsdales Solicitors* [2012] EWHC 3311 (QB); and *Gorbunova v Berezovsky (aka Platon Elenin)* [2013] EWHC 76 (Ch).

applicant makes a proprietary claim to that asset) then the character of that asset may mean that there is no real need to apply without notice, either because of its non-liquidity (e.g. a piece of real property) or because, as in *O'Farrell v O'Farrell*, the relevant asset is only to come into the respondent's hands at a date in the future.

For instance, in *Ian Franses (Liquidator of Arab News Network Ltd) v Al Assad*[12] the applicant had made a without notice application for a freezing injunction over the proceeds of a recent sale of a property, by telephone on a Friday evening (the judge having been provided only with draft orders and a chronology by email during the course of that hearing). The applicant's evidence served later in purported compliance with an undertaking contained within the without notice order had not explained why the application had been made without notice. Henderson J said that proceeding in this way reflected "a serious error of judgment" in circumstances where the applicant's solicitors had been put on notice of the property's sale at the beginning of that week and the proceeds of sale were held by a well-known firm of solicitors (who might have been contacted with a view to providing an undertaking against their disposal until the application had been heard). The judge said that the application ought to have been made on notice (if necessary on short notice) during the following week. When it became apparent from the respondent's evidence that there was no proper basis for maintaining the freezing injunction over the sale proceeds the applicant had to pay the respondent's costs on the indemnity basis.[13]

27–014

In *CEF Holdings Ltd v Mundey*[14] the court emphasised that without notice applications should only be granted in very limited circumstances (observing that the more intrusive the relief sought the more compelling the reasons must be for departing from the general requirement to give notice) and further stated that, in every without notice application for an injunction sought without any (or any proper) notice, it is prudent to include a statement supported by facts explaining fully and honestly why proper notice could not have been given: a "bland statement that the defendant might do something if warned is unlikely to satisfy this requirement without some particulars in support."

27–015

A potential question arises as to whether an applicant who proceeds to make a without notice application, without proper regard to these judicial observations, is likely to suffer the discharge of the order obtained in such circumstances by reason of having proceeded on that basis. We suggest that the answer will very probably turn upon whether or not there has, as a consequence, been a breach of

27–016

---

[12] *Ian Franses (Liquidator of Arab News Network Ltd) v Al Assad* [2007] EWHC 2442 (Ch); [2007] B.P.I.R. 1233, at [70]–[74], [85].
[13] See also *Wood v Gorbunova* [2013] EWHC 1935 (Ch) where receivers appointed by the court were ordered to pay the costs of certain respondents, and were also disallowed some of their own costs in respect of which they would ordinarily have been indemnified, for acting unreasonably in applying (on short notice only to other named respondents) for relief that included mandatory provisions against third parties who had not yet been joined to the proceedings. The judge had directed that notice of the application should be given to them (see para.27–027 in relation to the provisions of CPR 23 on this point) and found that those respondents had since behaved properly by indicating a willingness to cooperate with the receivers subject to appropriate constraints.
[14] *CEF Holdings Ltd v Mundey* [2012] EWHC 1524 (QB), at [248]–[251], per Silber J.

the duty of full and frank disclosure (addressed in Section D below) in that the lack of proper care over the decision as to how the application was to be made may well be symptomatic of (and have contributed to or precipitated) a situation in which the court makes an order without knowing of all matters that are relevant to the application. It should be noted that the CPR require the applicant to justify the decision to proceed without notice so that, on application to discharge the resulting order, the focus is likely to be upon material misstatements or omissions in the evidence containing that purported justification. As already noted, in *Ian Franses v Al Assad* there was, exceptionally, no evidence before the judge at the time of the without notice telephone hearing and the question of notice was not raised as a separate point during the course of that hearing. In those circumstances the "serious error of judgment" in proceeding without notice was regarded as being symptomatic of the wider point that, as a result, the court proceeded in ignorance of latent deficiencies in the merits of the application.[15]

B. PRACTICALITIES OF APPLYING WITHOUT NOTICE

(1)   The Civil Procedure Rules

27–017   The relevant provisions of the CPR reflect the law as stated above. They anticipate the need for justification in seeking an interim remedy without giving notice to the respondent by stating that any applicant doing so "must state the reasons why notice has not been given".[16] CPR PD 25A, governing applications for interim injunctions (including search orders and freezing injunctions), also recognises that an application for injunctive relief may be made without notice by providing likewise.[17] As with interim applications generally, an essential need for secrecy is identified as a proper reason (amongst others) for not even notifying the respondent of the application informally.[18]

27–018   In relation to the procedure governing any without notice application, para.4.3 of CPR PD 25A provides as follows, in respect of applications made after issue of the claim form:

> "(1)   the application notice, evidence in support and a draft order (as in 2.4 above) should be filed with the court two hours before the hearing wherever possible,
> (2)   if an application is made before the application notice has been issued, a draft order (as in 2.4 above) should be provided at the hearing, and the application notice and evidence in support must be filed with the court on the same or next working day or as ordered by the court, and
> (3)   except in cases where secrecy is essential, the applicant should take steps to notify the respondent informally of the application."[19]

---

[15] *Ian Franses (Liquidator of Arab News Network Ltd) v Al Assad* [2007] EWHC 2442 (Ch); [2007] B.P.I.R. 1233, at [70]–[74]. For another illustration of an unjustified decision to apply for a freezing injunction without notice being linked to material non-disclosure (justifying its discharge) see *Frenkel v Lyampert* [2017] EWHC 3121 (Ch), at [116].
[16] CPR r.25.3(3).
[17] CPR PD 25A, para.3.4.
[18] PD 25A, para.4.3(3).
[19] To similar effect see CPR PD 23A, para.4.2.

Paragraph 4.4 contains further provisions where the application is made before the issue of a claim form:

27–019

> "(1)   In addition to the provisions set out at 4.3 above, unless the court orders otherwise, either the applicant must undertake to the court to issue a claim form immediately or the court will give directions for the commencement of the claim,
> (2)   where possible the claim form should be served with the order for the injunction,
> (3)   an order made before the issue of a claim form should state in the title after the names of the applicant and respondent 'the Claimant and Defendant in an Intended Action'."

Any application made without notice must be accompanied by evidence explaining the circumstances which justify applying without notice.[20] This specific requirement is often overlooked. Evidence in support of most applications for a freezing injunction or a search order, where relief is to be granted before the respondent has an opportunity to be heard on the return date, must make out a case for saying that any prior notification of the application to the respondent would be self-defeating and jeopardise the overriding objective of dealing with cases "justly."[21] For those two particular forms of relief, the justification will inevitably be bound up with the evidence as to the risk which the respondent is said to present to the preservation of assets or evidence (see, respectively, Chs 30 and 32), but it should be separately addressed. As noted in para.27–013, there will be cases where the initial application for a freezing injunction ought properly to be made on notice to the respondent. There are a number of examples in the reported cases of freezing orders being obtained on notice.

27–020

In a case of extreme urgency an application may be dealt with by telephone.[22] Such a procedure is only really likely to be necessary where the application has unavoidably to be made outside court hours.[23]

27–021

(2)   Private Hearings

The general rule is that any hearing is to be in public.[24] Any hearing held in private by its very nature derogates from the principle of open justice. For that reason CPR 39.2 specifies the particular circumstances in which a hearing may be held in private; though even if such a ground applies it does not follow that the court will direct a private hearing (or that any part of the hearing should be held

27–022

---

[20] CPR 25.3(3).
[21] CPR Pts 1.1 and 1.2 and, specifically, Pt 23.4(2) anticipating the provisions of CPR 25.3 and CPR PD 25A referred to above. See further *CEF Holdings Ltd v Mundey* [2012] EWHC 1524 (QB) referred to in para.27–013 below.
[22] CPR PD 25A para.4.2.
[23] See generally CPR PD 25A, para.4.5 about the procedure for telephone hearings. Duty Judges are available to hear applications after court hours and during weekends in both the Chancery and Queen's Bench Divisions.
[24] CPR 39.2(1).

in private). The court must also be persuaded that the derogation from the open justice principle is strictly necessary to secure the proper administration of justice.[25]

27–023   Practice Direction 39A provides that the decision whether to hold a hearing in public or in private must be made by judge conducting the hearing having regard to any representations which may have been made on the point. In *Global Torch Ltd v Apex Global Management Ltd*[26] Morgan J referred to the relevant Practice Guidance in emphasising that any derogation from the principle of open justice should, where justified, be no more than strictly necessary in the interests of the proper administration of justice. In that case the judge refused to direct that a hearing for interim relief should be held in private in order to avoid the public airing of allegations which were said, amongst other things, to be likely to have an adverse effect upon the reputation of the ruling family of Saudi Arabia and affect the health of an elder prince of that family.

27–024   In a civil fraud case, the more obvious grounds for seeking a private hearing, as specified in CPR 39.2(3), are the following:

(1)   Publicity would defeat the object of the hearing (ground (a)). This ground might apply where the object of the hearing is to obtain relief from the court without tipping off the respondent who, if informed of what was happening, could defeat the object of the hearing by taking action to render the court's order ineffective. Hence, as discussed below, many without notice applications for a freezing or search order will be heard in private.

(2)   It involves confidential information (including information relating to personal financial matters) and publicity would damage that confidentiality (ground (c)).

(3)   It is a hearing of an application made without notice and it would be unjust to any respondent for there to be a public hearing (ground (e)).

(4)   The court considers this to be necessary, in the interests of justice (ground (g)). Although the court has no power to create further exceptions to the open justice principle by a process of analogy "save possibly in the most compelling circumstances", this paragraph is

> "deliberately in general terms to allow a court to take account of what might potentially be a wide range of material considerations in the many different types of case which might arise".[27]

27–025   A without notice application for a freezing injunction or search order will generally begin with an application for the hearing to proceed in private (on the basis that one or more of the above-mentioned grounds is engaged); but it should always be remembered that the need for secrecy, which (sometimes along with a

---

[25] *Scott v Scott* [1913] A.C. 417, at 437. Lord Haldane's reference to the need for the administration of justice being public yielding to the "yet more fundamental principle of securing that justice is done is reflected in ground (g) of 39.2 and the qualifications to the right to a 'public hearing' (and public pronouncement of the judgment) in provisions of article 6 of the Convention on Human Rights."
[26] *Global Torch Ltd v Apex Global Management Ltd* [2013] EWHC 223 (Ch), at [44]–[62], referring to Practice Guidance (Interim Non-Disclosure Orders) [2012] 1 W.L.R. 1003, paras 9–15.
[27] *Global Torch*, at [66].

degree of urgency) is usually said to justify the application being made without notice, is not exactly the same thing as a suggested requirement for privacy. However, even if there is no obvious risk of attendance at court of someone who might "tip off" the respondent before he is notified of any order made, it must be remembered that the listing by names in the Court List of any application which is not to be heard in private, when such listing is available on-line, itself creates a risk that the intended purpose of the relief might be thwarted.

Any applicant seeking a private hearing should have well in mind the following observations by Morgan J in *Global Torch*: **27–026**

> "Derogations from open justice can be justified in exceptional circumstances where the derogation is strictly necessary to secure the proper administration of justice. The burden lies on the party seeking the derogation to satisfy the court that it is necessary. This requires there to be clear and cogent evidence of the alleged necessity. The question for the court whether to allow a derogation from the open justice principle is not a matter of discretion. It is a matter of principle which requires it to be shown that the derogation is indeed necessary.
>
> There is no general exception to the open justice principle simply because privacy or confidentiality is in issue. A hearing should only be in private where the court is satisfied that nothing short of the exclusion of the public would suffice to allow justice to be done, that is, exclusions must be no more than the minimum strictly necessary to ensure justice is done. The holding of a hearing in private is a particularly serious derogation from open justice. It involves a more significant interference with the open justice principle than does an order conferring anonymity on a party or imposing reporting restrictions.
>
> The fact that a hearing in open court may be painful, humiliating and a deterrent either to a party or to a witness is not normally a proper basis for departing from the open justice principle. The interest protected by the open justice principle is the public interest in the administration of justice rather than the private welfare of those involved in court proceedings."[28]

(3) Documents

When making an application without notice ideally (and if time permits) the applicant should have prepared the following documents and lodged them with the court, where possible two hours before the hearing[29]: **27–027**

(1) The application notice, identifying the relief sought, whether issued or not issued.[30]

(2) The claim form, even if not issued, identifying the brief details of the claim and the substantive relief sought in the proceedings.[31]

(3) The Particulars of Claim, if the applicant's legal team has had time to prepare them. If possible it is wise to have the Particulars prepared, because they will provide the court with a clear statement of the nature of the claim.

---

[28] *Global Torch* [2013] EWHC 223 (Ch) at [49]–[52].

[29] CPR PD 25A, para.4.3(1).

[30] As regards the procedural requirements relating to application notices see further CPR 23.3, 23.6; CPR PD 23A para.2; and CPR Pt 22 (need for verification by statement of truth). Often there will be insufficient time to issue the application notice and the applicant will have to give an undertaking to do so.

[31] Again, it may be that there is insufficient time to issue the claim form; that will have to be subject of an undertaking.

Further, a properly prepared Particulars of Claim may also go some way to persuading the court that there is a good arguable case.[32]

(4) The draft order. This is obviously a vital document and care must be taken over the terms of the order sought.[33] The standard forms of freezing injunction and search order are explained in detail in Chs 28 and 30 respectively. As explained below, it is the duty of the applicant's counsel at the without notice stage (finding its basis in the duty of full and frank disclosure) to bring to the attention of the court any departure from the standard form in the terms of the particular relief sought.

(5) The evidence in support of the application. This must be by way of affidavit if a freezing order or search order is sought.[34] The evidence must address, amongst other things:

(i) the reason why the application is being made without notice;

(ii) the reason for any delay in making the application;

(iii) if applicable, why the applicant requests that the hearing be in private;

(iv) all points which should be brought to the court's attention in discharge of the duty of fair presentation;

(v) the elements required to be established for the grant of the interim relief sought and why they are made out;

(vi) the cross-undertaking in damages and, if the facts permit this, why the cross-undertaking should be limited in amount or why applicant should not be obliged to fortify that cross-undertaking (see below).

(6) A skeleton argument setting out the background facts; identifying the relief sought; the reasons why that relief should be granted; and any matters to be brought to the court's attention pursuant to the duty of fair presentation.

(4) The Hearing

27–028   At the hearing the first step will often be an application for the hearing to be in private (as to which see above). It will sometimes be the case that the Court, having read the documents lodged with it in advance, indicates that it is prepared to make the order sought. The applicant's advocate should nonetheless be astute to ensure that he has discharged the duty of fair presentation, which we discuss below. That may require detaining the court. The advocate should not be

---

[32] Hence it has been said that on an application for a freezing order: "When assessing whether there is a good arguable case the Court should be especially mindful of the particular scrutiny applied by the courts to serious allegations of fraud and the courts' approach generally to considering serious allegations including those of fraud: see *Owens Bank v Etoile Commercial* [1995] 1 W.L.R. 44, at 51B–51C; and *Re H* [1996] A.C. 563, at 586D–586H. *Ludsin Overseas Ltd v Eco3 Capital Ltd* [2012] EWHC 1980 (Ch), at [51]." *Elektromotive Group v Pan* [2012] EWHC 2742 (QB), at [33(b)], per Eder J.

[33] CPR PD 25A, para.2.4 provides that: "Whenever possible a draft of the order sought should be filed with the application notice and a disk containing the draft should also be available to the court in a format compatible with the word processing software used by the court. This will enable the court officer to arrange for any amendments to be incorporated and for the speedy preparation and sealing of the order." This provision is obviously now somewhat out of date; and an email now suffices.

[34] CPR PD 25A, para.3.1. If there is insufficient time to swear an affidavit an undertaking will have to be given.

distracted from discharging this duty by any judicial willingness to proceed straight to a consideration of the terms of the order.

A very full note of the hearing should be made. This is because it will be incumbent upon the applicant to serve, with all the other documentation, a note of the hearing, so that the respondent can see clearly what submissions were made and what material the judge was directed to, and what interjections and judgment have been made by the judge.[35] The standard form of freezing order contains an undertaking given on the part of the applicant to provide an affidavit confirming what was said by counsel. **27–029**

(5)   After the Hearing

The order once made must be served as soon as practicable unless the court orders otherwise.[36] In the case of a search order, the order (accompanied by the evidence in support and any documents capable of being copied) must be served personally by the supervising solicitor, during working hours, unless the court otherwise orders.[37] The elementary requirement for service of the order reflects the respondent's entitlement to know at the earliest opportunity (particularly in relation to any forthcoming return date) what the order prohibits him from doing and requires of him. Service of the order (within the time for complying with any positive act such as giving disclosure of assets) is also normally a key step from the applicant's perspective in ensuring that any disobedience of it may potentially be enforced by a subsequent committal application.[38] **27–030**

In some cases, where more than one party is to be served with or notified of the order, it may be appropriate to consider whether service should be effected in a particular sequence. Such a decision will be motivated not only by concerns about the efficacy of the sanction of committal (against a party who is likely to breach the order if tipped off about its terms before he has been personally served **27–031**

---

[35] See *Interoute Telecommunications (UK) Ltd v Fashion Gossip Ltd* [2002] EWHC 2972 (Ch), Times, 10 November 1999; and *Thane Investments Ltd v Tomlinson* [2002] EWHC 2972 (Ch), at [18]–[19]. In the latter case Neuberger J said "I think a respondent is entitled to know as of right, without having to ask, what happened at the hearing in his absence" (but refused to discharge the injunction in circumstances where no such note had been provided). See also the Admiralty and Commercial Courts Guide (para.F2.5).

[36] CPR PD 25A, 5.1 provides that: "Any order for an injunction, unless the court orders otherwise, must contain:....(2) if made without notice to any other party, an undertaking by the applicant to the court to serve on the respondent the application notice, evidence in support and any order made as soon as practicable."

[37] CPR PD 25A, 7.4(1). The Practice Direction further provides that confidential exhibits need not be served but they must be made available for inspection by the respondent in the presence of the applicant's solicitors while the order is carried out (with provision for their retention thereafter by the respondent's solicitors on certain undertakings aimed at avoiding unrestricted access to them by the respondent).

[38] CPR 81.5. The requirement of personal service may be dispensed with in accordance with CPR 81.8 where the court is satisfied that the respondent has had notice of the order by being present when it was made or by being notified of its terms by email, telephone or otherwise. See *Bunge S.A. v Huaya Maritime Corp* [2017] EWHC 90 (Comm), at [26]–[27], where the court dispensed with the requirement of personal service in the light of the respondent's knowledge of the terms of the asset disclosure order made against the company of which he had actual control.

with it) but also the reality of the position, in that the applicant will want the order to be effective despite what may well be the worst intentions of some of those who are intended to be bound by it (whether or not personally served). Thus, for example, an applicant may wish to seek the court's approval of an order which expressly contemplates that the terms of the freezing injunction are notified to the respondent's bank before it is personally served upon the respondent. As a matter of drafting, such a proposal would be reflected by the use of "and no later than" wording as a qualification to the "as soon as practicable" language of the Practice Direction. However, a more principled approach might involve the inclusion within the terms of the order itself a so-called "gagging" (or non-disclosure) provision to the effect that no person served with the order shall notify any other party to the proceedings of its terms, or of the existence of the proceedings, until a specified date (perhaps most obviously the return date).[39] We discuss gagging provisions in Ch.31.

(6)   Undertakings Given to the Court

27–032   Whenever an order is obtained on a without notice the applicant will be required (as the price of the order) to give a suite of undertakings, the precise ambit of which will depend on the factual circumstances then pertaining. So, any order sought on a without notice basis will almost certainly be made on terms which require the applicant to give an undertaking to issue and serve the claim form upon the respondent as soon as reasonably practicable (if either of those steps has not already been taken) and, at the same time, to serve the respondent with copies of the affidavits and exhibits containing the evidence relied upon in support of the application, any other documents provided to the court at the hearing, and an application notice for continuation of the order. If the evidence was presented to the court only in the form of a draft (because of time constraints), then the applicant will be required to cause the witness statement or affidavit (as it must be in support of any freezing injunction or search order) to be made, filed and served.

27–033   In addition (and reflecting the duty of full and frank disclosure addressed below), the court will also require the applicant to undertake to cause an affidavit to be sworn and filed which confirms the substance of any evidential matters relied upon by the Applicant's counsel or advocate which were not set out in evidence. This will be a separate requirement from the obligation to produce a note of the without notice hearing (which is not something the respondent needs to request first), which we have considered above. The purpose of such a note is to inform the respondent of the manner in which the hearing proceeded, including the identification (as opposed to encapsulation) of any evidence relied upon.

27–034   The various undertakings discussed above are included within the standard form of freezing injunction. We consider below, in a separate section, perhaps the most significant undertaking which any without notice (or indeed with notice) applicant must give: the cross-undertaking in damages.

---

[39] Compare the "gagging" provision in para.20 of the standard form of search order which contains an exception for the purposes of obtaining legal advice.

More generally, the provisions of CPR Pt 23.9 (addressing without notice **27–035**
applications generally) provide that, subject to any order to the contrary, the
application notice and evidence in support must be served, together with the order
made, both upon any person against whom the order was made and any person
against whom the order was sought. Further, r.23.9(3) provides that any order
made without notice must contain a statement of the right to make an application
to set aside or vary the order under r.23.10.

C. THE CROSS-UNDERTAKING IN DAMAGES

(1) The Nature of and Basis for the Cross-Undertaking

An applicant for relief of an injunctive nature—including freezing and search **27–036**
orders—must generally be prepared to provide what is described as "a
cross-undertaking in damages" to cover the risk to the respondent (or indeed third
parties, as we discuss below) that the order is later shown to have been wrongly
made, or made in support of a claim that fails, and to have caused loss.[40] This
undertaking is given by the applicant to the court, rather than to the respondent
(or any third party).[41] It is a serious step and, as recent cases have demonstrated,
can lead to very substantial liabilities being subsequently imposed upon the
applicant in circumstances where the undertaking has been enforced.[42] The
requirement to give such an undertaking should be considered carefully before
applying for any form of injunction, including a freezing order; it may lead to the
applicant taking the view that the risks of liability accruing under it are too great.
Given that the without notice applicant will almost invariably be required to
provide such a cross-undertaking as the price of the without notice order sought,
we discuss the cross-undertaking here; although the principles considered apply
equally where interim relief is sought on an inter partes basis.

A cross-undertaking in damages must be given voluntarily; it cannot be ordered.[43] **27–037**
But if an applicant declines to give one, the Court will generally decline to grant
the relief he seeks[44]: the cross-undertaking is "the price for interfering with the

---

[40] Requiring such an undertaking is the long-established practice of the Court when granting
injunctive relief: see *Graham v Campbell* (1878) 7 Ch. D. 490, at 484 and *Tucker v New Brunswick
Trading Company of London* (1890) 44 Ch. D. 249, at 253. The legal background to the requirement
that an applicant for interim injunctive relief provided a cross-undertaking in damages was set out in
the leading decision of *SmithKline Beecham Plc v Apotex Europe Ltd* [2006] 1 W.L.R. 872; [2007]
Ch. 71, at [23]–[25]: "The practice of requiring a cross-undertaking from a plaintiff who sought an
interlocutory (now called 'interim') injunction developed in the 19th century. The reason was that the
court at the interlocutory stage did not know who the ultimate winner would be. So if an injunction
was granted but the case ultimately failed, the person enjoined would have a remedy."
[41] *F. Hoffmann La Roche & Co A.G. v Sec. of State for Trade and Industry* [1975] A.C. 295, at 361,
per Lord Diplock.
[42] For a striking recent example, see *SFC Tankers Ltd (formerly known as Fiona Trust & Holding
Corp) v Privalov* [2017] EWCA Civ 1877, where compensation under the cross-undertaking of more
than $70 million was awarded.
[43] See *A-G v Albany Hotel Co* [1896] 2 Ch. 696, at 699: "Of course such an undertaking must be
voluntary: the Court cannot compel a person to give an undertaking."
[44] See *SmithKline Beecham Plc v Apotex Europe Ltd* [2005] EWHC 1655 (Ch); [2006] 1 W.L.R. 872,
at [38]; and on appeal [2006] 1 W.L.R. 872; [2007] Ch. 71, at [24]: "The court in effect says to the

defendant's freedom before he has been found liable for anything."[45] However, it follows from the fact that the grant or refusal of relief is a discretionary matter that, in an appropriate case, it is within the discretion of the court either to dispense entirely with, or to cap the potential liability under, the cross-undertaking which ordinarily forms part of the "package" of any such relief: see the discussion below.

27–038 Where an order for an interim injunction is silent one way or the other, it will generally be implicit that the applicant has undertaken to compensate the respondent for any loss resulting if the Court so determines (the cross-undertaking is, as has been said in a number of cases, "taken for granted").[46] That said, it is obviously far preferable that the fact and terms of the undertaking are recorded on the face of the order.

27–039 In *JSC Mezhdunarodniy Promyshlenniy Bank v Pugachev* an unlimited cross-undertaking in damages for his protection was described as the "default position".[47] Consistently with this, para.5.1 of CPR PD 25A provides that

> "Any order for an injunction, unless the court orders otherwise, must contain: (1) subject to paragraph 5.3 [which is of no relevance in fraud-related claims], an undertaking by the applicant to the court to pay any damages which the respondent sustains which the court considers the applicant should pay."

The standard form of cross-undertaking (as it is addressed to the respondent to the order) reads as follows:

---

plaintiff (now 'claimant') seeking an interim injunction: 'I will not grant you an interim injunction unless you give the cross-undertaking...It follows that the court cannot impose a cross-undertaking on a claimant against his will—it is the 'price' he must 'pay' for the grant of the injunction.' One reason is that, without a cross-undertaking to compensate the respondent, the risk that the respondent will suffer irremediable harm from the grant of relief will almost always outweigh the risk that the applicant will suffer such harm without it. See *SmithKline Beecham Plc v Apotex Europe Ltd* [2006] 1 W.L.R. 872; [2007] Ch. 71, at [26]: "The fact that an ultimately unsuccessful claimant will have to compensate the defendant for having 'wrongly' stopped his proposed activity is a major factor in assessing the balance of risk."

[45] *JSC Mezhdunarodniy Promyshlenniy Bank v Pugachev* [2015] EWCA Civ 139; [2016] 1 W.L.R. 160, at [68]. See *SCF Tankers (formerly known as Fiona Trust Holding Corp) v Privalov* [2017] EWCA Civ 1877, at [49] for the "pragmatic justice" to be applied at this interim stage. In *Financial Services Authority v Sinaloa Gold Plc* [2013] UKSC 11; [2013] 2 W.L.R. 613 Lord Mance said, at [30]: "In private litigation, a claimant acts in its own interests and has a choice whether to commit its assets and energies to doing so. If it seeks interim relief which may, if unjustified, cause loss or expense to the defendant, it is usually fair to require the claimant to be ready to accept responsibility for the loss or expense. Particularly in the commercial context in which freezing orders commonly originate, a claimant should be prepared to back its own interests with its own assets against the event that it obtains unjustifiably an injunction which harms another's interests."

[46] See the cases referred to by Lewison J in the first instance decision in *Smithkline Beecham Plc v Apotex Europe Ltd* [2005] EWHC 1655 (Ch); [2006] 1 W.L.R. 872, at [26]–[32]. In cases where the respondent obviates the need for an injunction (or a continuation of an injunction obtained without notice) by giving an undertaking in response to the applicant's application for an order, there is an implied undertaking in damages by the party applying for the injunction in favour of the other: see para.5.28 of the Chancery Guide. However, most well advised respondents would stipulate for an express cross-undertaking in such circumstances.

[47] *JSC Mezhdunarodniy Promyshlenniy Bank v Pugachev* [2015] EWCA Civ 139; [2016] 1 W.L.R. 160, at [68].

"If the court later finds that this order has caused loss to the Respondent, and decides that the Respondent should be compensated for that loss, the Applicant will comply with any order the court may make."

In *Pugachev* Lewison LJ explained[48] that it is the requirement of fairness rather than likelihood of loss which underpins the need for a cross-undertaking. At the interim injunction stage no firm decisions upon the merits of the claim have been made and the court cannot be seen to prefer the interests of one litigant over another. Further, at the stage of the without notice application for injunctive relief, the respondent will necessarily not have had the opportunity to give any evidence about loss (or indeed anything else) that the injunction might occasion. Even at the inter partes stage, when the court comes to consider whether to extend the injunction, it is not necessary for the defendant to establish a likelihood of the order causing loss, or loss in a given amount, in order to be entitled to a cross-undertaking unlimited in amount.[49]

27–040

Although commonly described for convenience as a cross-undertaking "in damages", the modern form of cross-undertaking rightly describes it as "compensation for loss".[50] This is consistent with the trigger for any claim upon the cross-undertaking not being confined to the situation where the injunction, of which it formed an integral part, is shown to have been "wrongly granted" (in a way that might have supported a successful appeal made soon after the grant of the original injunction). Rather, the cross-undertaking exists for those cases where the court later decides, with the benefit of hindsight and after full investigation of the facts, that the claimant was not deserving of the relief because, for instance, the underlying claim has been dismissed.[51] Hence, where a

27–041

---

[48] *JSC Mezhdunarodniy Promyshlenniy Bank v Pugachev*, at [77].

[49] *Sinclair Investment Holdings SA v Cushnie* [2004] EWHC 218 (Ch), at [25], per Mann J. Mann J's approach was endorsed in *Pugachev*, at [75]–[78], Lewison LJ commenting that it was not in his experience usual for defendants to set out the prospective loss that they might suffer as a reason for requiring the cross-undertaking.

[50] *SmithKline Beecham Plc v Apotex Europe Ltd* [2006] 1 W.L.R. 872; [2007] Ch. 71, at [25]: "A party who is granted an interim injunction but who ultimately loses the full trial is not regarded as a wrongdoer because he got an interim injunction. Sometimes, for convenience and want of a better term, the expression 'wrongful injunction' is used, but in truth there is nothing wrongful about it. The decision whether or not to grant it is made on the basis of a necessarily incomplete picture. The decision depends on all the circumstances of the case, generally whether or not damages to an ultimately victorious claimant would be an adequate remedy, whether the claimant can show a serious issue to be tried and so on."

[51] See *Yukong Line Ltd v Rendsberg Investments Corp* [2000] EWCA Civ 358; [2001] Lloyd's Rep. 113, [32]–[33] for the meaning of "wrongly granted" (in preference to "improperly obtained") to cover the situation where there may have been no improper conduct by the applicant but "where the court makes an order which is subsequently demonstrated or conceded to have been too wide in its scope or unjustified or inappropriate on the facts". Potter LJ said that if it is established that the injunction was wrongly granted, with or without fault on the applicant's behalf, the court "will ordinarily order an inquiry as to damages in any case where it appears that loss *may* have been caused as a result." It is on this basis that any third party affected by the order and for whose benefit a cross-undertaking may have been given (as to which see below), but who is not a party to the claim, may seek to enforce it. In *Financial Services Authority v Sinaloa Gold Plc* [2013] UKSC 11; [2013] 2 W.L.R. 678, at [18] the Supreme Court observed that "an inquiry into damages will ordinarily be ordered where a freezing injunction is shown to have been wrongly granted, even though the claimant was not at fault", but went on to say that it may be appropriate to await the final outcome of the trial before deciding whether to enforce the cross-undertaking: "it does not follow from the defendant's

freezing order is discharged at the return date the respondent will usually be entitled to an immediate inquiry into damages; but where the freezing order is not discharged but the claimant later fails at trial the respondent will also be entitled, in general (though not always), to an inquiry, even though the order was properly granted at the time it was made on the evidence then available to the court. A better way of putting it, therefore, is that the cross-undertaking is given to cover the possibility that the grant of relief proves to have been inappropriate.[52] Even in such a case the court retains a discretion not to enforce the cross-undertaking if the circumstances make it inequitable to do so.[53] If, however, it is enforced the measure of damages is not discretionary but to be determined upon an inquiry and assessed on the contractual basis, as if the applicant had promised not to prevent the respondent from doing that which the order did in fact restrain.[54]

(2) Discretion to Waive or Limit the Cross-Undertaking

27–042 As the Court of Appeal in *Pugachev* also observed, the acceptance of a more limited cross-undertaking forms part of the judge's discretion to grant relief and there are certain categories of case where the court may either not require the applicant to provide any cross-undertaking at all or at least not require an unlimited one. A limited undertaking will have a cap on the potential liability of the applicant under it in the event that it is ordered that it be enforced. As Lewison LJ summarised the position:

> "This price is not exacted when the applicant is a law enforcement agency simply enforcing the law in the public interest.[55] But that is not this case. There is also another possible exception

success on liability that he did not in fact remove (or seek to remove) assets from the reach of the claimant, justifying an interim freezing order." However, the protection of innocent third parties under an undertaking given in their favour will usually be unqualified by such considerations: see at [19] and [34].

52 *Financial Services Authority v Sinaloa Gold Plc*, above, at [29].

53 See *Société Générale v Sanayi* [2017] EWHC 667 (Comm), at [74]-[76], per Popplewell J. In *Fiona Trust & Holding Corp v Privalov* [2016] EWHC (Comm), at [47], [139], Males J rejected the claimant's argument that relief should be refused on the ground of the defendant's alleged fraud in obtaining an earlier order to enforce the cross-undertaking. The judge said that, even if there had been relevant misconduct amounting to "unclean hands" on the defendant's part, it would have to be considered against the claimant's own misconduct in suppressing material facts when applying for the order.

54 *Hoffman-La Roche & Co AG v Secretary of State for Trade and Industry* [1975] A.C. 295, 361; *Cheltenham and Gloucester Building Society v Ricketts* [1993] 1 W.L.R. 1545, at 1551–1552; and *Harley Street Capital Ltd v Tchigirinski* [2005] EWHC 2471 (Ch), at [19]–[22]. In *SmithKline Beecham Plc v Apotex Europe Ltd* [2007] Ch. 71, at [83]–[84], Jacob LJ observed that this brings into play *Hadley v Baxendale* principles of reasonable foreseeability (derived either from general knowledge of the circumstances or knowledge of the particular circumstances of "the injunctee") and that, in some cases, the notional contract basis may be too narrow. For the assessment of the opportunity lost to Apotex, see the later decision at [2008] EWHC 2347 (Ch); [2009] F.S.R. 3. We consider questions relating to the enforcement of the cross-undertaking in Ch.31.

55 See *Financial Services Authority v Sinaloa Gold Plc* [2013] UKSC 11; [2013] 2 W.L.R. 678, at [33] and [43] where the Supreme Court held that an authority such as the FSA (as was) acting in pursuance of a public duty should not ordinarily be required to give a cross-undertaking in damages in support of a freezing injunction. This is the "starting point" for both the without notice and on notice stages of the application, though any respondent or third party fearing adverse loss might apply for an

where the applicant has no personal interest in the litigation and is bringing the action on behalf of others. One example is where litigation is being brought by liquidators on behalf of an insolvent company where there are no large creditors who can be expected to indemnify them and where it has proved impossible to obtain insurance against unlimited liability on the cross undertaking: *Re DPR Futures Ltd* [1989] 1 W.L.R. 778. In that case an order froze assets of £2.3 million and the applicants who were liquidators were permitted to cap their liability under the cross-undertaking at £2 million. An order to similar effect was made by Laddie J in *RBG Resources Ltd v Rastogi* [2002] B.P.I.R. 1028. That was a case in which Laddie J considered that there was 'an extremely strong case' against the principal defendants; and that if he did not accept the limited undertaking 'the freezing orders will have to go': [51] and [52]."

Those observations reveal that where the applicant seeks to avoid personal   **27–043** exposure under an unlimited cross-undertaking by reference to a lack of available resources or assets to meet it in full (and lacks the personal financial interest in the proceedings of the kind ordinarily seen by the court as justification for such exposure) the court will still be anxious to test whether those who stand behind the litigation, and who do stand to benefit indirectly from it, have the resources to back such an undertaking.[56] If, however, the true picture is revealed to be one where the claimant with no personal interest is at risk of being personally exposed then any decision to dispense with, or to cap the cross-undertaking, is a discretionary one to be made within the overall assessment of the balance of convenience. The apparent strength of the underlying claim may prove to be decisive if the only alternative for the court is to refuse relief because an unlimited undertaking cannot be offered. The court will also be concerned to establish whether the particular nature of the cause of action (assuming it is made out at trial) explains the circumstances in which the applicant currently lacks the resources to back an unlimited undertaking.[57]

---

order that any continuation of the injunction should be conditional upon one being given on terms that the court considered to be "fair". This would require some explanation in evidence of the loss feared. The English court is likely to adopt the same starting point for the benefit of overseas regulators obtaining injunctive relief here: see *United States Securities & Exchange Commission v Manterfield* [2009] EWCA Civ 27; [2010] 1 W.L.R. 27, where the Court of Appeal upheld the judge's decision not to require the SEC to give a cross-undertaking in damages on the grant of a worldwide freezing injunction obtained in support of US proceedings directed at an allegedly fraudulent investment scheme.

[56] See *Wood v Baker* [2015] EWHC 2536 (Ch) where, at the without notice stage, HH Judge Hodge QC accepted a cross-undertaking in damages by a trustee in bankruptcy which was limited to the value of the unpledged assets in the bankrupt's estate (though he was not prepared to exclude the costs, expenses and disbursements of the bankruptcy pending the return date). In *Pugachev* Lewison LJ went on to refer to the decisions in *Hone v Abbey Forwarding Ltd (In Liquidation)* [2014] EWCA Civ 711 and *Abbey Forwarding Ltd (In Liquidation) v HM Revenue & Customs* [2015] EWHC 225 (Ch) as illustrating that the mere fact that litigation is being brought by a liquidator of an insolvent company does not compel the conclusion that the cross-undertaking *must* be capped, as there may be a major creditor who is prepared to provide financial backing for it. In that case the Court of Appeal refused to interfere with the judge's ruling that the cross-undertaking should be unlimited, given the existence of substantial creditors sitting behind the claimant liquidator: contrast the approach in the *DPR Futures* case and *Bloomsbury International Ltd v Holyoake* [2010] EWHC 1150 (Ch), discussed below. It is right to point out that in many cases judges are prepared to accept a limited cross-undertaking from liquidators; but it is not an invariable practice.

[57] In *RBG Resources Ltd v Rastogi* [2002] B.P.I.R. 1028, at [47] Laddie J said "the whole basis upon which the defendants here claim they will be exposed to no compensation under the cross-undertaking in damages is that there has been the massive fraud which the provisional liquidators allege. The circumstances in which a cross-undertaking in damages could not be fulfilled is a circumstance in

(3)   Fortifying the Cross-Undertaking

27–044   On the other hand, there may be situations where a cross-undertaking is not only required (whether in a limited or unlimited amount), but the court goes further and insists upon its being reinforced by some form of security.[58] This will often be the case where the respondent can show that the applicant's financial standing and resources are such that, when compared with what the respondent estimates to be the likely loss caused by the grant of the injunction,[59] there is a risk that such loss will remain uncompensated (because the respondent will be unable to effectively enforce the cross-undertaking). In such cases, some reinforcement of the cross-undertaking might be justified in the form of a guarantee, bond, payment into an escrow account held by the applicant's solicitor (or into court) or similar security for the respondent's potential claim under it.[60] Ordinarily, such issues arise at the inter partes stage when the respondent is heard, and can put in evidence on the question, but in some cases the judge will raise the question of fortification of the court's own initiative at the without notice hearing.[61] Hence, as we have mentioned earlier in this chapter, the applicant for a without notice order should address the issue of the cross-undertaking and the possibility that the court may require it to be fortified at that stage.

27–045   The standard form of freezing injunction contemplates that the court may require the applicant to reinforce his cross-undertaking in damages by providing a guarantee issued by an English bank up to a specified sum.[62] The relevant form of undertaking, which is by no means mandatory, reads as follows:

---

which the fraud has taken place." See also *Independent Trustee Services Ltd v GP Noble Trustees Ltd* [2009] EWHC 161 (Ch), at [33], where Lewison J took account of the strength of the claimant's proprietary claim and noted that any successful defence of it by the defendant would involve the scenario of the claimant being able (on the language of a cross-undertaking fixed by reference to "the assets from time to time of the underlying pension funds") to set off its liability on the undertaking against a genuine secured loan.

[58] The decision in *Bloomsbury International Ltd v Holyoake* [2010] EWHC 1150 (Ch), at [29]–[30], (where the applicant was a company in administration with limited available assets) shows that where there are parties of financial substance behind the applicant (in that case the creditors were banks) such fortification may be justified in the interest of adopting a course which is "least likely to lead to an injustice". Compare the cases mentioned in fn.56 above. In *Bloomsbury* Floyd J said that it is incumbent upon the applicant to produce evidence in support of any suggestion of difficulty in the way of providing such security.

[59] See below and, further, Ch.31, in relation to the need for the respondent to establish a good arguable case that such loss has been suffered or is likely and the estimation of such loss.

[60] In *Brainbox Digital Ltd v Backboard Media GmbH* [2017] EWHC 2465 (QB); [2018] 1 W.L.R. 1149 the court (John Howell QC) held that the court "may require, as a condition for granting or continuing an injunction, that the cross-undertaking given by the applicant is fortified by the provision by someone other than the applicant of an unlimited, or a limited, undertaking, or by the making of some other form of limited provision, to meet any loss that the injunction may cause.... Any fortification required is not necessarily limited in amount. The court has a wide discretion as to the conditions on which it may grant or continue an injunction. Discretions of that kind should not be fettered by rigid judge-made rules."

[61] A recent example being *Brainbox Digital Ltd v Backboard Media GmbH* [2017] EWHC 2465 (QB); [2018] 1 W.L.R. 1149, at [9].

[62] In principle, other forms of security might be considered appropriate in the circumstances, such as a payment into a joint account of the applicant's and respondent's solicitors to be held in escrow or the grant of a charge over property or a pledge of assets. However, the party applying for fortification

"The Applicant will –
(a)   on or before [date] cause a written guarantee in the sum of £ to be issued from a bank with a place of business within England or Wales, in respect of any order the court may make pursuant to paragraph (1) above; and
(b)   immediately upon issue of the guarantee, cause a copy of it to be served on the Respondent."

The Commercial Court Guide[63] addresses the fortification of the undertaking in damages in the following terms: **27–046**

"(a)   Where the applicant for an interim remedy is not able to show sufficient assets within the jurisdiction of the Court to provide substance to the undertakings given, particularly the undertaking in damages, he may be required to reinforce his undertakings by providing security.
(b)   Security will be ordered in such form as the judge decides is appropriate but may, for example, take the form of a payment into court, a bond issued by an insurance company or a first demand guarantee or standby credit issued by a first-class bank.
(c)   In an appropriate case the judge may order a payment to be made to the applicant's solicitors to be held by them as officers of the court pending further order. Sometimes the undertaking of a parent company may be acceptable."

The language of the Commercial Court Guide is such as to put the initial onus upon the applicant to establish the sufficiency of assets within the jurisdiction[64] if he is to avoid the risk of being ordered to fortify the cross-undertaking. The standard practice in any court is to require the evidence in support of any interim relief, where a cross-undertaking is required, to explain the true value of that undertaking. This is usually done by reference to the value of the applicant's unencumbered assets and, in the case of a corporate applicant, most conveniently by reference to its latest accounts.[65]   **27–047**

The Guide is silent in relation to the burden of proof where (usually in advance of the return date) a respondent complains about the absence (or inadequacy) of any fortification on the basis that the applicant's financial resources appear to be inadequate for the purposes of covering the loss which it is feared will be caused by the grant of relief. If the respondent contends that applicant's evidence as to available assets has not adequately covered off the risk of loss, to its true level,   **27–048**

---

may well argue that any form of security which is likely to result in the process of realisation being less straightforward than a claim upon a bank guarantee (or monies held by solicitors in escrow) is inadequate.

[63] Paragraph F15.4.

[64] It might be wondered why the assets need to be in the jurisdiction, in circumstances where assets available in other jurisdictions (such as in the EU) might be equally readily amendable to execution. As it was put by Dillon LJ in *Tasarov v Nassif*, unreported, 29 June 1994, "The essential question is whether there are assets readily available to satisfy any liability under the cross-undertaking" (although in that case the point did not arise). Compare the position with respect to security for costs, where residence outside the jurisdiction is not sufficient to establish the condition in CPR 25.13(2)(a) unless the claimant is also not resident in a Brussels Contracting State, a State bound by the Lugano Convention, a State bound by the 2005 Hague Convention or a Regulation State, as defined in s.1(3) of the Civil Jurisdiction and Judgments Act 1982.

[65] Although what will concern the Court is whether the assets are readily amendable to execution, which the accounts alone may not reveal.

then it seems clear that it is for the respondent to establish the exposure that would justify the case for fortification.[66]

27–049   It will be apparent that any application to fortify the cross-undertaking engages two separate issues: first the question of what losses the respondent might suffer as a result of the interim injunction made against him; and secondly whether the applicant has sufficient readily-available assets to meet that risk of loss. These are separate issues, because if the respondent cannot establish a sufficient risk of loss then there should be no question of fortification and so need to proceed to the second question.[67] The mere fact that the applicant has no assets within the jurisdiction and, say, there would be difficulties enforcing abroad, does not of itself justify an order for fortification.

27–050   In *Energy Venture Partners Ltd v Malabu Oil & Gas Ltd*[68] the Court of Appeal considered for the first time the principles which should govern any application by the respondent for a direction that the cross-undertaking should be reinforced and addressed the first of the two issues identified above.

27–051   A series of propositions may be extracted from *Malabu*[69] and the many first instance decisions considered by it[70]:

(1)   It is not necessary for the respondent to establish the likelihood of loss on the balance of probabilities.

(2)   This is because a "resort to symmetry" required that, given that the applicant claimant had obtained the freezing injunction by reference to a good arguable case test, it was only appropriate that if the defendant could show that he too had a good arguable case that he would suffer loss in consequence of the order then equally he should be protected in respect of that risk of loss.

(3)   Hence the correct principles were those set out in *Jirehouse Capital v Beller*[71]:

---

[66] *Sinclair Investment Holdings v Cushnie* [2004] EWHC 218 (Ch), at [25]; *Harley Street Capital Ltd v Tchigirinski* [2005] EWHC 2471 (Ch), at [18].

[67] *Tarasov v Nassif*, unreported, 29 June 1994 CA, referred to in *Pugachev*, above, at [89]–[90]; and see also *Harley Street Capital v Tchigirinski* [2005] EWHC 2471 (Ch), at [25].

[68] *Energy Venture Partners Ltd v Malabu Oil & Gas Ltd* [2014] EWCA Civ 1295, at [52]–[58]. Tomlinson LJ noted that there was, as a matter of strict legal analysis, an element of doubt over the "symmetry" reasoning, but he observed that in many cases a freezing injunction does have the practical if not theoretical effect of giving the claimant security for his claim.

[69] *Malabu* was a case where a specific sum of money had been frozen and had been brought into court in lieu of a continuation of the freezing order. It was held that in such a case the normal measure of likely loss for the purpose of fortification was the time value of the money which the respondent had been prevented by the freezing order from utilizing as it saw fit, which was usually represented by the usual cost of borrowing an equivalent sum, regardless of what the respondent would have actually done.

[70] Being *Sinclair Investment Holdings v Cushnie* [2004] EWHC 218 (Ch); *Harley Street Capital v Tchigirinski* [2005] EWHC 2471 (Ch); *Jirehouse Capital v Beller* [2008] EWHC 725 (Ch); *Bloomsbury International Ltd v Holyoake* [2010] EWHC 1150 (Ch); and *Fortress Value Recovery Fund v Blue Skye Special Opportunities* [2012] EWHC 1486 (Comm). These propositions must obviously be considered in the light of the court's approach to any later enforcement of the cross-undertaking by the Respondent, as discussed in Ch.31 below.

[71] *Jirehouse Capital v Beller* [2008] EWHC 725 (Ch), at [26].

"Broadly speaking, they require an intelligent estimate to be made of the likely amount of any loss which may be suffered by the applicant for fortification (here the defendants) by reason of the making of an interim order. They require the court to ascertain whether there is a sufficient level of risk of loss to require fortification. They require that the loss has been or is likely to be caused by the granting of the injunction."

In the interlocutory context, showing a sufficient level of risk of loss to require fortification is synonymous with showing a good arguable case to that effect.

(4) Hence the court should not engage in a detailed, scientific, analysis of the potential losses which the respondent might sustain.

(5) Where the freezing order was widely cast (rather than directed to specific assets) it will be easier to infer a risk of loss from the existence of the freezing order.

(6) The answer which is sometimes made by applicants resisting fortification, that the respondent can seek consent to a particular dealing or obtain the permission of the court, is generally an unreal one; such applications are difficult to mount and will take time to come on.

(7) As to the test of causation (in relation to the anticipated claim under the cross-undertaking) it was sufficient for the court to be satisfied that the making of the order is or was a cause without which the relevant loss would not be suffered. The quantum of the anticipated claim was a matter for an intelligent estimate by the defendant.

(8) It was incumbent upon defendants before launching an application to assess coolly and objectively what the loss was likely to be.[72]

Although the approach detailed above is a liberal one,[73] in practice the courts **27–052** have revealed themselves to be suspicious of extravagant contentions by respondents of the risk of loss attendant on the freezing order. There is an element of rigour in practice which is perhaps not sufficiently reflected in the statements of principle. It is notable that in the main contested applications for fortification fail, largely because the losses claimed are very speculative. Hence a respondent seeking fortification, or an increase in it, should be astute in his evidence to:

(a) identify the risk of loss with as much precision as possible,

(b) produce solid evidence which enables the court to conclude that relevant loss[74] is likely to be suffered as a result of the freezing order (as opposed to the litigation generally) and

(c) make an intelligent assessment of its likely magnitude.

---

[72] There is a tendency for applications to seek to put in exaggerated estimates of loss flowing from the injunctive relief which, on analysis, prove to be illusory. This can damage the credibility of the respondent and undermine the claim for fortification overall.

[73] See *Astrozeneca Abukrka v Novo Mesto* [2015] EWCA Civ 484, at [16] on the need for a "liberal but fair assessment of loss" at the later stage of enforcement. And see the approach taken by the judge in *Brainbox Digital Ltd v Backboard Media GmbH* [2017] EWHC 2465 (QB); [2018] 1 W.L.R. 1149 to the evidence put in by the defendant, on an application for fortification, concerning its likely losses, at [41]–[44].

[74] In *Harley Street Capital Ltd v Tchigirinski* [2005] EWHC 2471 (Ch), [19]–[22], in addressing the causation issue, the Deputy Judge (Michael Briggs QC) identified "loss caused by the preventative or, as the case may be, coercive effect of the injunction that is recoverable under the cross-undertaking."

For instance, in *JSC Mezhdunarodniy Promyshlenniy Bank v Pugachev*[75] the judge had required fortification of the cross-undertaking in the sum of $25million on the basis that it was realistic to suppose the freezing injunction could cause significant damage to the defendant's suggested business interests. However, the Court of Appeal overturned her decision on the ground that it lacked evidential foundation. Lewison LJ said it was not difficult to imagine a respondent to a freezing injunction producing evidence of him making deals or engaging in business ventures over a sustained period prior to the grant of the freezing injunction which would stifle them. However, in the present case

> "a single failed real estate venture in the best part of a four year period is, in my judgment, too slender a foundation upon which to build a picture of an established pattern of business activity from which it can be inferred (without more evidence) that the freezing order will cause loss."

(4)   Cross-Undertakings for the Benefit of Third Parties

27–053   CPR PD 25A requires the court to consider whether the applicant's cross-undertaking in damages should also extend to any person other than the respondent who may suffer loss as a consequence of the injunction: para.5.2 provides that

> "when the court makes an order for an injunction, it should consider whether to require an undertaking by the applicant to pay any damages sustained by a person other than the respondent, including another party to the proceedings or any other person who may suffer loss as a consequence of the order."[76]

27–054   Such an undertaking for the benefit of third parties now forms part of the standard form of freezing injunction.[77] Indeed, the origins of the undertaking in damages for the benefit of third parties can be traced to the development of freezing injunctions; and it probably still cannot be said that they are routinely required in

---

[75] *JSC Mezhdunarodniy Promyshlenniy Bank v Pugachev*, above, at [87]–[99]. The court left it open to the defendant to apply for fortification in the future in the event of a future business opportunity arising and not being capable of being exploited with the agreement of the claimant or the permission of the court.

[76] Without an extension of the cross-undertaking to such "other persons" the undertaking may only avail those who are parties to the proceedings or who become such while the undertaking is in force: see *Berkeley Administration Inc v McClelland* [1996] I.L.P. r.772 and *SmithKline Beecham Plc v Apotex Europe Ltd* [2005] EWHC 1655 (Ch); [2006] 1 W.L.R. 872, at [49]. See further fn.78 below.

[77] See Ch.28 below. Paragraph 7 of the standard form provides: "The applicant will pay the reasonable costs of anyone other than the Respondent which have been incurred as a result of this order including the costs of finding out whether that person holds any of the Respondent's assets and if the court later finds that this order has caused such person loss, and decides that such person should be compensated for that loss, the Applicant will comply with any order the court may make". As Jacob LJ noted in *SmithKline Beecham Plc v Apotex Europe Ltd* [2006] 1 W.L.R. 872; [2007] Ch. 71, at [28], "the practice in freezing order cases of requiring from the plaintiff an express undertaking to indemnify any third party affected by the order against all expenses reasonably incurred in complying with the order and all liabilities flowing from such compliance was endorsed by this court in *Z v A-Z* [1982] 1 Q.B. 558".

cases other than freezing injunctions and search orders.[78] Nevertheless, the court has jurisdiction to require the extension of the cross-undertaking to third parties, outside that context, where it is just and convenient to do so.[79]

This addresses a point which previously had been addressed much less clearly in an earlier practice direction, such that the ability of third parties, who had suffered loss as a result of an injunction later shown to have been wrongly granted, was in practice dependent upon the ad hoc exercise of judicial discretion to extend the cross-undertaking in their favour (sometimes requiring the intervention of the third party).[80]   **27–055**

In *Harley Street Capital Ltd v Tchigirinski*[81] the Deputy Judge (Mr Michael Briggs QC) observed: **27–056**

> "There must be many cases in which other innocent parties suffer loss from an injunction which should not have been granted, for example, the intending buyer of property where the seller has been restrained from selling may suffer loss during the currency of the injunction if the property is in a rising market."

In the case of a freezing injunction, if the court considers it appropriate to include within the scope of the order assets which are ostensibly held by the respondent on trust for others but which are said by the applicant to in fact belong to the respondent then   **27–057**

---

[78] See *SmithKline Beecham Plc v Apotex Europe Ltd* [2005] EWHC 1655 (Ch); [2006] 1 W.L.R. 872, at [50]–[57] where, for the purposes of addressing an argument that the applicant was to be taken to have impliedly offered such an undertaking in an injunction granted in a patent infringement action, at first instance Lewison J concluded that as at 2002 they were not routinely required, outside those contexts. This case is a lesson in the difficulties that arise if an interim injunction which is later discharged cause loss to third parties to the litigation, but where the undertaking is directed only at the defendants themselves. In that case third parties had suffered considerable losses as a result of an injunction later discharged but the undertaking was only directed at the defendants in the case; it was held that the third parties could not make any recovery from the claimants. Any third party likely to be affected adversely by an interim injunction during its pendency should intervene to ensure that the undertaking expressly extends to losses it may incur, alternatively its discharge: see *Miller Brewing Co v Mersey Docks & Harbour Co* [2004] F.S.R. 5, at [45]. In *Financial Services Authority v Sinaloa Gold Plc* [2013] UKSC 11; [2013] 2 W.L.R. 678, at [17], the Supreme Court summarised the development of undertakings in damages in favour of third persons. Undertakings to meet the specific costs and expenses (as opposed to general loss) of any third party affected by the order are more usual and involve different considerations: at [35].

[79] *Allied Irish Bank v Ashford Hotels Ltd* [1997] 3 ALL E.R. 309.

[80] *Smithkline Beecham Plc v Apotex Europe Ltd* [2007] Ch. 71, at [28]–[31], where Jacob LJ said (in a case where the standard form had not been used) that the Rules Committee would do well to look again at the practice direction. At first instance, Lewison J concluded that, as at 2002, cross-undertakings for loss suffered by third parties were not routinely required outside the context of a freezing injunction or search order: [2006] 1 W.L.R. 872, at [50]–[57]. In that case companies who had intended to market a product (in respect of which the defendant had been restrained by an injunction granted in support of a patent infringement claim) could not, by being joined to the proceedings after the court had dismissed the claim, recover their losses on the cross-undertaking (where that cross-undertaking did not extend to third parties), or in restitution.

[81] *Harley Street Capital Ltd v Tchigirinski* [2005] EWHC 2471 (Ch), at [15].

"it will usually be appropriate for the cross-undertaking to be extended in terms to cover the purported beneficiary for any loss which is caused by the injunction which is subsequently varied or discharged in respect of the trust assets".[82]

(5)   Enforcing the Cross-Undertaking

27–058   We consider the important topic of applications by respondents for compensation under the cross-undertaking and the principles for the assessment of loss caused by wrongly granted injunctions at Ch.31 below.

D.   THE DUTY OF FULL AND FRANK DISCLOSURE

(1)   Introduction

27–059   When applying for interim relief without notice to the respondent the applicant's duty is to make full and frank disclosure to the court. This is in order to ensure fairness in circumstances where the respondent is not before the court to put his case. The benchmark is one of materiality. The applicant must place before the court all matters which are or might be relevant to the application, whether of fact or law (or procedure), including any matters which are or may be adverse to the application. The width of the duty is such that the phrase "full and frank disclosure" is not wholly apt. It is perhaps better described as a duty of fair presentation.

(2)   When the Duty Arises

27–060   It is important to note that the duty of full and frank disclosure is one that applies not only to applications made without notice, but also to those which are made on short (or inadequate) notice to the respondent. This is because the provision in the CPR which stipulates that at least 3 days' notice should be given of any "with notice" application for relief reflects the *minimum* period allowed, with a view to ensuring the respondent is given a proper opportunity to marshal his evidence and legal submissions and deploy them before the court. If less than that minimum period of notice is given by the applicant, then the respondents to the application cannot be expected to be properly prepared and to be able to put before the court all the relevant legal and factual information. In such circumstances, the obligation of full and frank disclosure continues, but subject to the qualification that if the respondent who has been given inadequate notice appears and then deals with *all* the factual and legal issues, then the applicant for the interim relief

---

[82] *JSC BTA Bank v Solodchenko* [2010] EWCA Civ 1436; [2011] 1 W.L.R. 888, at [49(2)], per Patten LJ. Citing *Yukong Line Ltd v Rendsberg Investments Corp* [2000] EWCA Civ 358; [2001] Lloyd's Rep. 113, Patten LJ observed (at [45]) that, without such an extension of its terms, the ability of the respondent trustee to obtain compensation on the beneficiary's behalf would rest upon the court deciding that the injunction had been "wrongly granted" in the sense described in that earlier authority: see fn.51 above.

is discharged from his own obligation to address those issues. In *CEF Holdings Ltd v Mundey*[83] Silber J summarised the position as follows:

"So the position is that the duty of the applicant who makes an application with less than the prescribed period of notice to give full and frank disclosure continues even when the opposing party is represented on short notice, but significantly he is absolved from this duty, but then only in respect of those legal and factual matters to which that other person has drawn the Court's attention. I stress that he is not discharged from his duty to give full and frank disclosure in respect of any other matters."

(3) Incidents of the Duty

This duty is one owed to the court itself and exists to ensure the integrity of the judicial process and to protect the interests of those who might be affected by any order made.[84] It is neatly encapsulated in the Chancery Guide (para.16.6)[85]:   **27–061**

"On all applications made in the absence of the respondent the applicant and their legal representatives owe a duty to the court to disclose all matters relevant to the application. This includes matters of fact or law which are or may be adverse to the applicant. If made orally, the disclosure must be confirmed by witness statement or affidavit. The applicant or their legal representatives must specifically direct the court to passages in the evidence which disclose matters adverse to the application. This duty also applies to litigants in person. If there is a failure to comply with this duty and an order is made, the court may subsequently set aside the order on this ground alone."

In speaking of without notice applications for injunctive relief, Mummery LJ stated in *Memory Corp Plc v Sidhu (No.2)*[86]:   **27–062**

"It cannot be emphasised too strongly that at an urgent without notice hearing for a freezing order, as well as for a search order or any other form of interim injunction, there is a high duty to make full, fair and accurate disclosure of material information to the court and to draw the court's attention to significant factual, legal and procedural aspects of the case. It is the particular duty of the advocate to see that the correct legal procedures and forms are used; that a written skeleton and a properly drafted order are prepared by him personally and lodged with the court before the oral hearing; and that at the hearing the court's attention is drawn by him to unusual features of the evidence adduced, to the applicable law and to the formalities and procedures to be observed."

---

[83] *CEF Holdings Ltd v Mundey* [2012] EWHC 1524 (QB), at [181]–[183].

[84] In *Memory Corp Plc v Sidhu (No.2)* [2000] 1 W.L.R. 1443, 1455E, Robert Walker LJ referred to "the advocate's individual duty to the court, and the collective duty to the court, on a without notice application, of the plaintiff and his team of legal advisers are duties which often overlap". In *CEF Holdings Ltd v Mundey*, above, at [175], Silber J described "the golden rule" of full and frank disclosure, reflecting the fact that the judge does not have the benefit of submissions on factual and legal issues from the party sought to be restrained, as one of the most basic principles of English law.

[85] See a similar provision in the Queen's Bench Guide (para.7.11.5), the Commercial Court Guide (para.F2.5) and the Circuit Commercial Court Guide paras 1.7 and 8.4. The latter also provides that a note of the hearing of any without notice application, the evidence and skeleton argument in support of it and any order made must be served as soon as possible thereafter.

[86] *Memory Corp Plc v Sidhu (No.2)*, above, at 1459H–1460B. See also the observations of Lord Scott in *Fourie v Le Roux* [2007] 1 W.L.R. 320, at 333H–334B about the "strict rules relating to full disclosure" on a without notice application for injunctive relief being a recognition of the nature of the remedy and its potential for causing injustice to the defendant.

27–063   The ability of the respondent to a without notice application to police compliance with the applicant's obligations of full and frank disclosure is strengthened by the undertakings which the applicant must give to make and file an affidavit confirming any factual matters which were not the subject of sworn evidence but which were stated to the court on the application (or previously set out only in a draft); and the requirement to provide the respondent with a note of the hearing: see para.27–028 above.

27–064   In applications for interim injunctions, the obligation of full and frank disclosure carries with it the risk that a failure to observe it might well lead to the discharge of the injunction, even if the injunction might still have been granted had the material fact been drawn to the attention of the court at the without notice hearing. This sanction, even in cases where the grant and continuation of injunctive relief would otherwise be just and convenient, serves both to deprive the applicant of the remedy wrongly obtained (as a matter of process) and to deter others from proceeding in a way which overlooks the obligation. The principles which govern the question whether a without notice order should be set aside following a breach of the duty to give full and frank disclosure are addressed in Ch.32 below.[87]

27–065   CPR PD 25A makes provision in relation to applications for injunctive relief (in terms which are not specific to without notice applications) for the evidence to extend to "all material facts of which the court should be made aware".[88] However, the duty of full and frank disclosure is wider than this—extending as it does to matters of law or other material matters which may not emerge from the evidence—and is one established by authority.

27–066   In *Siporex Trade SA v Comdel Commodites*[89] Bingham J observed that the duty extends to disclosure of "all facts which reasonably could or would be taken into account by the Judge in deciding whether to grant the application". Such material facts extend beyond those which are actually known to the applicant and include

---

[87] For a recent summary of the principles and the consequences of material non-disclosure in the form of the general rule that the without notice order should be discharged and not renewed (subject to a discretion to be sparingly exercised), see *Metropolitan Housing Trust Ltd v Taylor* [2015] EWHC 2897 (Ch), at [36], per Warren J. The classic statement of principle which is the foundation stone of the modern law are the dicta of Warrington LJ in *Rex v Kensington Income Tax Commissioners, Ex parte de Polignac (Princess)* [1917] 1 K.B. 486, 509, "It is perfectly well settled that a person who makes an ex parte application to the court—that is to say, in the absence of the person who will be affected by that which the court is asked to do—is under an obligation to the court to make the fullest possible disclosure of all material facts within his knowledge, and if he does not make that fullest possible disclosure, then he cannot obtain any advantage from C the proceedings, and he will be deprived of any advantage he may have already obtained by means of the order which has thus wrongly been obtained by him. That is perfectly plain and requires no authority to justify it." In *Metropolitan Housing Trust Ltd v Taylor*, there had been an absence of full and frank disclosure on an application for a freezing injunction. Warren J warned against "compartmentalising" the components which bear upon the exercise of the court's discretion, in such circumstances, to discharge the order but to renew it. The judge observed that, while it may of itself justify its discharge without renewal, any non-disclosure is "also relevant as a factor in relation to the fourth requirement for the grant of a freezing order, namely that the court must be satisfied that it is just and convenient in all the circumstances of the case to grant relief." (see [37] and [384]).

[88] PD 25A, para.3.3.

[89] *Siporex Trade SA v Comdel Commodites* [1986] 2 Lloyd's Rep. 428, at 437.

matters which he would have known if he had made proper inquiries.[90] The leading case of *Brink's Mat Ltd v Elcombe* makes it clear that the materiality of any particular matter is to be decided by the court and not by the assessment of the applicant or his legal advisers; and that duty can be breached by non-disclosure which is "innocent", in the sense that the matter in question was not actually known to the applicant or its relevance to the application was not perceived.[91] For this reason, it is a distraction to inquire too closely into what knowledge should be attributed to a corporate applicant for the purposes of full and fair disclosure. The real question is not about what knowledge is "attributed" to a company, by reference to those who may be said to be its directing mind and will on the matters in question, but whether or not as applicant that company has fulfilled its duty to make a full and frank disclosure of all material facts.[92]

On the test summarised in *Siporex*, the materiality of any particular fact may go either to the strength of the applicant's substantive claim or to the case for him being granted the particular interim relief sought, or both. In *Irish Response Ltd v Direct Beauty Products Ltd*[93] the applicant admitted a breach of its duty to present fairly the without notice application for a freezing injunction, by failing to show the judge correspondence between the applicant's solicitors and the defendant written two years before. That correspondence not only showed that the defendant had been put squarely on notice of a claim, without a risk of dissipation of assets having materialised in the intervening period, but also (in terms of the defendant's response at the time) cast doubt upon the facts upon which the claim relied. **27–067**

The material "facts" may also extend to the intentions which the applicant has in relation to the ongoing litigation in which the application is made. In *Todaysure Matthews Ltd v Marketing Ways Services Ltd*[94] an issue arose (in the context of the defendant's challenge to the terms of a consent order made in the light of an injunction made on the claimant's without notice application) as to whether the **27–068**

---

[90] *Brink's Mat Ltd v Elcombe* [1988] 1 W.L.R. 1350, at 1356G–1357F, per Ralph Gibson LJ.

[91] A recent statement of the principles is to be found in *Alliance Bank JSC v Zhunus* [2015] EWHC 714 (Comm), at [66], per Cooke J: "(1) The duty on the applicant in such circumstances goes beyond merely identifying points of defence which might be taken against him, important though that is. (2) The applicant has to show the utmost good faith, identifying the crucial points for and against the application and not rely on general statements and the mere exhibiting of numerous documents. (3) The applicant has to investigate the nature of the claim asserted and the facts relied on before applying, and has to identify any likely defences. He has to disclose all facts which reasonably could or would be taken into account by the Court. The duty is not restricted to matters of fact but extends to matters of law. (4) The applicant also has a duty to investigate the facts and fairly to present the evidence. (5) There is a high duty to draw the Court's attention to significant factual, legal and procedural aspects of the case. (6) Full disclosure has to be linked with fair presentation. The judge has to have complete confidence in the thoroughness and the objectivity of those presenting the case for the applicant. (7) It is the undoubted duty of counsel to draw to the judge's attention weaknesses in his case and to make sure the judge understands what might be said on the other side even if the judge says he has read the papers." This statement was quoted with approval in *St Vincent European General Partner Ltd v Robinson* [2017] EWHC 3267 (Comm).

[92] *Dar Al Arkan Real Estate v Al Refai* [2012] EWHC 3539 (Comm), at [96], per Andrew Smith J.

[93] *Irish Response Ltd v Direct Beauty Products Ltd* [2011] EWHC 37 (QB), at [100]–[106], per HHJ Richard Seymour QC.

[94] *Todaysure Matthews Ltd v Marketing Ways Services Ltd* [2015] EWHC 64 (Comm), at [20].

claimant should have disclosed its intention to seek a temporary restraining order in the United States (which it did obtain the day after the grant of the English injunction). The claimant argued that the intention to apply for the American injunction was not material when that injunction did not remove the basis (one of alleged fraud) on which the English order had been made and was ancillary and supportive of the first order rather than being an alternative to it. Teare J disagreed, saying that this adopted too narrow a view of materiality which focused upon whether or not the intention to seek the American injunction removed the basis of the claim for the English injunction. He stated:

> "Where a person who applies ex parte for an injunction intends to use the grant of the injunction to support an application for an injunction from another court in a foreign jurisdiction such intention is a matter which 'reasonably could or would be taken into account by the Judge in deciding whether to grant the application'.[95] That is because the intention affects or may affect the consequences of granting the injunction. Any judge of this court when asked to grant an injunction ex parte wishes to know the likely consequences of acceding to the application and making the requested order. If the judge is not informed of the applicant's intention to use the order in support of another application abroad the judge will have an inadequate or incomplete appreciation of the likely consequences of making the requested order. In my judgment the fact that the judge may still make the requested order having been told of the applicant's intention does not make the intention immaterial. The judge would expect to be told what the applicant intends to do with the injunction so that he or she can consider whether it remains appropriate to grant the injunction."[96]

27–069   A failure to disclose an issue or principle of law may also lead to a breach of the duty to give full and frank disclosure (as the relevant provision within the Chancery Guide mentioned above makes clear). The duty to address material issues of law is an inevitable consequence of the need to investigate the nature of the cause of action asserted in support of the relief sought and the likely defences to it.[97] In *Memory Corp Plc v Sidhu (No.2)*[98] Robert Walker LJ observed:

> "I see some force in some of these criticisms, if and so far as the judge intended to draw any fundamental distinction between the litigant's duty of full disclosure of material facts, and the advocate's duty to assist the court by reference to (or correct summary of) relevant authorities, statutory provisions and practice directions. In the context of what should be disclosed to the court on a without notice application, the distinction between fact and law is not clear-cut. Many of the authorities already cited refer almost interchangeably to nondisclosure of 'material facts' or 'relevant matters'. Little weight can be attached to these slight variations in language. But some statements of the principle of full disclosure extend to what the court is told about matters of law."

27–070   *Memory Corp* was a case where counsel for the applicant had put before the judge on the without notice application a draft search order which significantly departed from the standard form of search order which was then to be found in "The White Book" (Sir Geoffrey Vos (editor-in-chief), *Civil Procedure*, 2018 edn (London: Sweet & Maxwell, 2018)), without drawing attention to the departures. This was held to be a serious breach of the duty. It was emphasised that where the proposed form of order differs from the standard form in any material way then

---

[95] A quotation from *Siporex Trade SA v Comdel Commodities* [1986] 2 Lloyd's Rep. 428, at 437.
[96] *Todaysure Matthews Ltd v Marketing Ways Services Ltd*, at [20].
[97] *Siporex Trade SA v Comdel Commodities*, above.
[98] *Memory Corp Plc v Sidhu (No.2)* [2000] 1 W.L.R. 1443, at 1454C–1454D.

counsel must specifically identify and justify the proposed departure. The judge below had held, wrongly, that there was a distinction between the duty of disclosure of facts and the duty of counsel to assist the court. The importance of the Court of Appeal's decision lies, in part, in its formulation of a general principle which did not distinguish between the duty of the applicant to disclose material fact and that of the lawyer to disclose relevant matters of law or procedure; and that breach of either duty could attract the same sanction.

So, in *Dar Al Arkan Real Estate v Al Refai*[99] the applicant on a without notice application for injunctive relief preventing the disclosure of confidential information and documents was in breach of the duty of full and frank disclosure in not referring the judge to a provision of the Human Rights Act 1998 which imposed a more demanding test for imposing a restraint upon publication than the one presented by the applicant.   **27–071**

The duty is not discharged by the presence of documents buried within exhibits to the affidavit which might touch upon the point. The duty is a positive one of actively bringing to the court's attention any issue which is relevant to the application. Hence if, on an application for a freezing order, there has been substantial prior correspondence between the parties concerning the underlying claim, showing engagement in it by the prospective defendant and the articulation of rational defences, then the duty will not be discharged simply by exhibiting that correspondence. The applicant "must identify the crucial points for and against the application, and not rely upon the mere exhibiting of numerous documents."[100]   **27–072**

The existence of without prejudice correspondence between the parties, passing prior to the application, can sometimes pose a problem for the applicant on the without notice application if an inference is sought to be drawn which runs counter to that correspondence. In *Linsen International v Humpuss Sea Transport*[101] Christopher Clarke J made the point that, although it is generally not open to one party to disclose without prejudice materials and to do so might be unfair to the other party, the court must not be misled by sweeping statements (perhaps most obviously as to the suggested evasiveness of the respondent) that the without prejudice correspondence might put in doubt.   **27–073**

In *The Giovanna*[102] Rix J found that, where the defendant had made a without prejudice offer to provide security, the without notice application could not properly be made without referring to the without prejudice correspondence. The offer of full security that had been made within it ran counter to the suggestion, which the court presumed was one intended to be given, that the respondent had abandoned its responsibilities and was seeking to evade its liabilities. The judge said: **27–074**

> "It may be that the correspondence itself could not have been unilaterally presented to the Court by the plaintiffs, but I do not accept that a Mareva injunction can be sought ex parte

---

[99] *Dar Al Arkan Real Estate v Al Refai* [2012] EWHC 3539 (Comm), at [132]–[147].
[100] *Siporex Trade SA v Comdel Commodites*, above, at 437.
[101] *Linsen International v Humpuss Sea Transport* [2010] EWHC 303 (Comm).
[102] *The Giovanna* [2002] 2 Lloyd's Rep. 673.

without at least some mention being made of the existence of an offer of security, an offer which was still current at the time when the plaintiffs went to Court. Such an offer, even though there may be strings attached, runs directly contrary to a Mareva applicant's implicit invocation of the Court's assistance in confronting a real risk of dissipation. It seems to me that the situation is somewhat analogous to one where there is an application to strike out an action for want of prosecution: the fact and even the content of without prejudice negotiations can be disclosed for the purpose of explaining the passage of time and the conduct of the parties in the context of an allegation of inordinate and inexcusable delay: see *Family Housing Association (Manchester) Ltd v Michael Hyde & Partners* [1993] 1 W.L.R. 354."

27–075   It is suggested that in many cases the safe course for the applicant, where there has been some without prejudice correspondence or meetings which have a potentially adverse impact upon the grounds for interim relief, is to refer to the existence of the correspondence but not necessarily the contents of it.[103] The fundamental purpose behind the duty of full and fair disclosure is that the court should not be misled by the applicant's omission of matters (factual or legal) which the respondent might have been expected to bring to the court's attention at the hearing of the application had he had proper notice of it. One might expect a respondent, anxious to demonstrate a degree of good faith or prior engagement with the applicant in response to the claim which might run counter to any particular suggestion of threat or risk which underpins the application, to refer to the existence of any without prejudice overtures.[104] However, it will not always be a breach of the duty for the applicant to fail to do so. In *Linsen International v Humpuss Sea Transport*[105] the applicant was not in breach of the duty in failing to refer to the fact or content of a without prejudice meeting. No agreement had been reached at it nor had any offer capable of acceptance been made. The judge said that the defendants had made a deliberate choice for the meeting not to be open "no doubt with the intention that its content should not be put before a court" and neither the fact nor the content of the meeting cast any real light on whether they would seek to remove their assets from the grasp of the applicant.

27–076   Whether or not the content (and not just the existence) of without prejudice correspondence or negotiations may or should also be put in evidence is a separate question. The answer appears to depend upon whether or not it contains any adverse admission upon an issue that will be before the trial judge. Plainly the applicant should not be permitted to put in evidence admissions of liability by the other party on such issues; and, accordingly, the duty of full and frank disclosure cannot require the applicant to do so. But it would seem that the same is equally true of admissions by the applicant made in without prejudice correspondence. So, in *Somatra v Sinclair Roche and Temperley*,[106] the Court of Appeal held that the applicant was not under a duty to refer to the without

---

[103] The public policy underlying the without prejudice rule is not undermined where the relevant correspondence is not being used as evidence of admissions: *Family Trust Housing Association (Manchester) v Michael Hyde & Partners* [1993] 1 W.L.R. 354 (which concerned the relevance of without prejudice correspondence on an application to strike out for want of prosecution).

[104] See *Pearson Education Ltd v Prentice Hall India* [2005] EWHC 636 (QB) where the court held that an affidavit in support of a without notice application was misleading (in not referring to the fact of a without prejudice response) in giving the impression that no response had been received to the claimant's letter.

[105] Fn.101 above, at [56]–[57].

[106] *Somatra v Sinclair Roche and Temperley* [2000] 1 W.L.R. 2453, at [16].

prejudice correspondence when it (arguably) constituted evidence of admissions by it upon issues for trial. But, once the applicant had done so at the without notice hearing, in a way that was potentially misleading (in seeking to explain the apparent admissions away), the applicant could not resist the respondent relying upon the full content of the relevant communications on an application to discharge or vary the injunction, or indeed at trial.[107] The court held that a party should not be entitled to use without prejudice material on the merits of the case in one context, but then assert a right to prevent his opponent from relying on the same communications on the merits at the trial.

In broad summary, therefore, it might be said that the making of a without notice application is one of those instances where a party may be not only entitled but obliged to refer to without prejudice communications (because the very fact they have taken place may militate against the grant of the interim relief sought); but only where to do so arguably supports the respondent's case, and (it appears) not to the extent of revealing admissions made on the underlying merits of the claim. If an applicant does go further and relies on such admissions at the without notice stage, then he must of course do so fairly and he cannot shut the respondent out from relying on the same communications in support of its case on the merits at trial.   **27–077**

E. FIXING THE RETURN DATE

Paragraph 5.1 of CPR PD 25A states that, unless the court otherwise orders, an order for an injunction made without notice to any other party must contain "a return date for a further hearing at which the other party can be present". This is in contrast to para.5.4, which provides that an injunction made in the presence of all parties to be bound by it, or of which they have had notice, may state that it is effective until trial or further order in the meantime.   **27–078**

The service upon the respondent of an application notice seeking the continuation of the relief granted without notice after an inter partes hearing on the return date will invariably be the subject matter of an undertaking by the applicant given as the price of that relief: see para.27–036 above.   **27–079**

Although the initial order will generally also expressly make provision for the respondent to have permission to make an application for the discharge or variation of the order sooner than the return date, should there be circumstances of urgency justifying such a step, the court must nevertheless decide upon an appropriate return date for the inter partes hearing for inclusion within the order. A balance has to be struck between the prejudice to the respondent in being subject to an order made in his absence which may be susceptible to a valid challenge, and the initial duration of which will be of obvious importance to him, and the prejudice to him if a return date is fixed for a date too soon for the respondent to be able to realistically muster his evidence and arguments against its continuation.   **27–080**

---

[107] The right to use the communications on the return date was conceded, at [18], but the concession was right; as to the right to use the communications at trial, see [22]–[30].

27–081   The Chancery Guide provides that when a judge grants an injunction without notice "it will normally be granted for a limited period only—usually not more than 7 days."[108] The Queen's Bench Guide states that the an injunction "will normally be for a limited period with a return date 1 to 2 weeks ahead", while the Commercial Court Guide refers in more general terms to CPR PD 25A in saying that the return day will usually be a Friday when the Commercial Court hears such applications. The notes to the standard Commercial Court form of freezing injunction state that the return date will usually be 14 days after the grant of the injunction, particularly where parties are outside the jurisdiction.

27–082   In many cases the time estimate for the length of the return date will be such that the inter partes hearing of the application is not effective on the specified return date. In the Chancery Division an "Interim Application by Order" is one that will require an oral hearing of more than two hours (including pre-reading and the giving of judgment) and in the Commercial Court a "heavy application" is one which will require an oral hearing of more than half a day (the time estimate for which, unlike one for an "ordinary application" in that court of half a day or less, should not make allowance for the giving of judgment and consequential matters).[109] For such cases the court guides make provision for a postponement of the return date, by consent without a hearing on the return date and with whatever timetable for further evidence may have been agreed, to a date on which the parties will be able to deal with the substantive issues raised by the application.[110] Experience shows that, at least in heavy cases, the return date fixed at the without notice hearing is very rarely effective as a properly and fully contested hearing. Most such return dates, if they are not compromised in advance, are treated as directions hearings towards a second, fully effective, return date, for which the time estimate may run to days not hours.

27–083   Chapter 32 below addresses the types of issue that often arise at the hearing on the first return date.

---

[108] See para.16.27 of the Chancery Guide which appears under the heading "Freezing Injunctions and Search Orders" but which refers to injunctive relief generally. See also para.7.12.3 of the Queen's Bench Guide and para.15.8 of the Commercial Court Guide and applied by para.9.5 of the Circuit Commercial Court Guide.

[109] See paras 16.15 of the Chancery Guide and Part F of the Admiralty and Commercial Courts Guide.

[110] Relief granted without notice and continued on this basis, under protest by the respondent and without prejudice to his position at the effective return date, avoids the potential pitfalls for a respondent who instead offers an undertaking in lieu of the injunctive relief "until further order" (but who does not expressly stipulate that he is at liberty to apply to be released from it regardless of whether or not there has since been a material change of circumstances or the subsequent discovery of facts which could not reasonably have been ascertained when it was given): see *Emailgen Systems Corp v Exclaimer Ltd* [2013] EWHC 167 (Comm); [2013] 1 W.L.R. 2132, at [19]–[31] where Teare J considered *Chanel Ltd v F.W. Woolworth & Co Ltd* [1981] 1 W.L.R. 485, at 492–493, and other authorities.

CHAPTER 28

FREEZING AND PROPRIETARY INJUNCTIONS

A. OVERVIEW

(1) Introduction

In any case involving alleged fraudulent conduct by a defendant, a claimant will   **28–001**
be concerned to ensure that steps are not taken by the defendant before judgment
that will deprive any judgment in favour of the claimant of meaningful effect, be
it by putting out of reach or diminishing the value of assets against which a
judgment might otherwise be enforced, or, where a proprietary claim is made,
dealing with the very property that is the subject of the claim. Freezing and
proprietary injunctions represent powerful and flexible tools, which the Court can
deploy in order to minimise the risk that any later judgment will be rendered
nugatory by an unscrupulous defendant. Whilst the purely proprietary injunction
has much older antecedents (lying in the old equitable jurisdiction to restrain
improper dealings with trust property), the freezing injunction is a relatively
recent innovation. But after 40 or so years of constant development, the
jurisprudence underlying the modern freezing injunction represents an extraordi-
narily sophisticated and far-reaching body of judge-made law: starting from a
relatively narrow initial conception of the jurisdiction involving the restraint of
foreign defendants from removing assets from the jurisdiction, the courts have
now arrogated to themselves a power to make freezing orders with respect to
assets wherever they may be situated in the world, against defendants whether or
not they are within the jurisdiction, and indeed against third parties against whom
no claim is asserted at all.

A freezing injunction of any sort represents a very real intrusion into the affairs of   **28–002**
a defendant against whom nothing has (yet) been proved. But where given in
support of a purely personal claim it is a particularly draconian form of relief, in
that it restrains a defendant from dealings with assets which are (ex hypothesi)
beneficially his own, in circumstances where there is no allegation in the
underlying claim that the apprehended dealings would infringe some right of the
claimant.[1] The freezing injunction has therefore been aptly described as one of

---

[1] See e.g. *Mercedes Benz A.G. v Leiduck* [1996] A.C. 284, per Lord Mustill at 303E–303F: "With a
Mareva injunction the right to the injunction and the ultimate right to damages or whatever else is
claimed in the action are wholly disconnected. The threatened infringement of the plaintiff's rights
which a *quia timet* injunction forestalls is a wrongful act, although not one which constitutes an
immediate cause of action for substantive relief. By contrast, the threatened dispersal of assets is not

the law's "nuclear weapons."[2] Nonetheless, although the making of such orders will always involve a degree of caution on the part of the court, and the court will be astute to ensure they are not used as instruments of oppression, they are now routinely made in cases of domestic and international fraud. In reality, freezing orders are no longer exceptional in any meaningful sense.

(2) The Purpose of a Non-Proprietary Freezing Injunction: The "Enforcement Principle"

28–003   In *JSC BTA Bank v Ablyazov*,[3] in the Court of Appeal, Beatson LJ addressed the first (and most important) of the three principles which are in play when the court is considering the making of a freezing injunction—"the enforcement principle"—as follows:

> "The first and primary principle is that the purpose of a freezing order is to stop the injuncted defendant dissipating or disposing of property which could be the subject of enforcement if the claimant goes on to win the case it has brought, and not to give the claimant security for his claim: *Z Ltd v A-Z* [1982] QB 558, per Lord Denning MR and Kerr LJ at 571 and 585; *Derby & Co Ltd v Weldon (Nos 3 & 4)* [1990] 1 Ch. 65, per Lord Donaldson MR at 76; *Federal Bank of the Middle East Ltd v Hadkinson* [2000] 1 W.L.R. 1695, per Mummery LJ at 1709G–1079H, and per Nourse LJ at 1714–1715; *JSC BTA Bank v Solodchenko* [2010] EWCA Civ 1436; [2011] 1 W.L.R. 888, per Patten, Aikens and Longmore LJJ at [32], [49], [51] and [52]. Lord Mustill's speech in *Mercedes Benz AG v Leiduck* [1996] A.C. 285 is, despite the difference of context, also instructive. He stated (at 297) that the jurisdiction to make freezing orders, then known as *Mareva* injunctions 'should be exercised with great circumspection', and (at 299) that 'the *Mareva* injunction does not enforce anything, but merely prepares the ground for a possible execution by different means in the future'. The most recent statements by this court are in *Solodchenko's* case. Patten LJ stated (at [32]) that 'the purpose of a freezing order is to prevent the dissipation by a defendant of assets which would otherwise be available to satisfy a judgment in favour of the claimant'. Later in his judgment, when setting out a number of points for the guidance of judges dealing with applications for orders in the new Commercial Court form, he stated (at [49(1)]) that nothing in the judgment was 'intended to cast any doubt upon the established principles which underlie the grant of all freezing orders'. His formulation at this stage was, if anything, narrower. It was that 'the *only* purpose of such an injunction is to prevent the dissipation of assets which would otherwise be available to meet a judgment' (emphasis added)."

28–004   This survey of the authorities emphasises perhaps the most significant legal incident of a conventional freezing order: it operates as an in personam restraint, which prevents the named respondent(s) from dealing with assets; but it has no

---

a wrongful act even against the background of a pending suit in England, for subject to any special rules relating to insolvency, a person can do what he likes with his own...".

[2] *Bank Mellat v Nikpour* [1985] F.S.R. 87, 92, per Donaldson LJ. The impact of a freezing injunction is all the greater now that it has been accepted (at Supreme Court level) that a claim in damages for unlawful means conspiracy can in principle lie against those who connive in the breach of such an order: *JSC BTA Bank v Khrapunov* [2018] UKSC 19.

[3] *JSC BTA Bank v Ablyazov* [2013] EWCA Civ 928; [2014] 1 W.L.R. 1414, at [34]. The second and third principles are those of "flexibility" and "strict construction". This nomenclature was adopted by Lord Clarke in the Supreme Court, who agreed with counsel that the flexibility principle could have no relevance to the proper construction of an order already made; but who cited with apparent approval Beatson LJ's summary of the "enforcement principle": [2015] UKSC 64; [2015] 1 W.L.R. 4754, at [13]–[20]. See para.28–116 below for the decision of the Supreme Court as to the meaning of "assets" in the standard Commercial Court form of freezing order.

impact upon the legal or beneficial ownership of those assets, nor does it operate as a form of attachment or confer any form of security interest or priority on the applicant.[4] The classic statement of this principle in the freezing order context is that of Lord Bingham in *Fourie v Le Roux*[5]:

> "*Mareva* (or freezing) injunctions were from the beginning, and continue to be, granted for an important but limited purpose: to prevent a defendant dissipating his assets with the intention or effect of frustrating enforcement of a prospective judgment. They are not a proprietary remedy. They are not granted to give a claimant security for his claim, although they may have that effect. They are not an end in themselves. They are a supplementary remedy, granted to protect the efficacy of court proceedings, domestic or foreign: see Steven Gee, *Commercial Injunctions*, 5th edn (2004), pp.77–83."

(3) Practical Questions

Consideration of the enforcement principle identified in *JSC BTA Bank v Ablyazov* prompts a number of practical questions. Particularly in the context of a fraud claim, an applicant for a freezing order is usually seeking to anticipate and prevent the type of transaction which, if implemented, might be susceptible to later challenge on the ground that its purpose was to defeat the claims of creditors.[6] This very often (but not invariably) means that speed and initial secrecy are essential elements of the application. As noted in Ch.27, applications for freezing injunctions, alongside those for search orders, provide a classic illustration of the kind of circumstance in which it is appropriate to apply without notice to the respondent. However, as also noted in that chapter, such applications carry with them the heavy burden[7] imposed by the so-called duty of full and frank disclosure (also now described as the duty of fair presentation).

28–005

The applicant must therefore usually be prepared to act with real speed and appropriate stealth if he is to prevent the risk of the respondent acting to the prejudice of his claim. Undue delay or advance notice of what is coming may enable the respondent (if he is indeed a fraudster) to take the very steps which the intended order is aimed at preventing. Yet undue haste in making the application,

28–006

---

[4] In *Gangway Ltd v Caledonian Park Investments (Jersey) Ltd* [2001] 2 Lloyd's Rep. 715, at [14] Colman J stated that the underlying purpose of the jurisdiction is not to provide a claimant with security for its claim or priority over other creditors but to restrain a defendant from evading justice by disposing of assets otherwise than in the ordinary course of business so as to make itself judgment proof with the result that any judgment or award in favour of the claimant goes unsatisfied. Nor does a freezing order affect any genuine security or interest held by a third party: see *Taylor v Van Dutch Marine Holding Ltd* [2017] EWHC 636 (Ch); [2017] 1 W.L.R. 2571, at [10]–[17]. See also *Flightline Ltd v Edwards* [2003] EWCA Civ 63; [2003] 1 W.L.R. 1200, at [47]–[51], per Jonathan Parker LJ, and *Technocrats International Inc v Fredic Ltd (No.3)* [2004] EWHC 2674 (QB), per Jack J at [14]–[17]. Of course, the analysis may be different if a defendant proffers some form of bond or guarantee under a bespoke arrangement which is designed to ward off the possibility of an injunction being granted in the first place: see *Polly Peck International Plc v Nadir (No.2)* [1992] 2 Lloyd's Rep. 238, per Lord Donaldson MR at 249.

[5] *Fourie v Le Roux* [2007] 1 W.L.R. 320, at [2].

[6] See s.423 of the Insolvency Act 1986 addressed in Ch.16.

[7] The burden continues after the grant of the injunction and even after notice has been given to the respondent and an inter-partes hearing taken place. Any change of circumstances which affects the discretion exercised by the court in granting the injunction should be reported to the Court; *Speedier Logistics v Aardvark Digital* [2012] EWHC 2776 (Comm), at [23]–[25].

without proper care and adherence to the duty of full and frank disclosure, may give the respondent (even if he is a fraudster) grounds for a later challenge to any order which might have been made. Obtaining and policing a freezing injunction represents a serious commitment on behalf of the applicant in terms of both time and cost. The procedural requirements for the grant and continuation of a freezing injunction alone are onerous and call for strict compliance. The decision to pursue a freezing injunction is therefore not one that should be taken lightly.

28–007 The enforcement principle also serves to remind the applicant that, at the early stage of the litigation, when such applications are most frequently made, the substantive claim has yet to be established at a trial and may not even have been fully articulated in a pleaded case. In applying for and obtaining a freezing injunction, a claimant is exposing himself to, potentially, significant liability. Unlike the situation where the applicant is challenging the genuineness of a particular transaction after it has been made (or even a specific transaction which has not yet been made but which it is alleged would be wrongful if made), a freezing injunction granted to restrain dealings by the respondent with his assets may catch transactions which ought not to be prevented (or at least not prevented prior to any judgment). The uncertainty inherent in any assessment of the merits of the applicant's claim, at this early stage of proceedings, and the potential for the order to hinder genuine transactions and to disrupt the respondent's business and personal life, justify the requirement that the applicant should give a cross-undertaking in damages (often fortified with security) as the price for obtaining relief.

28–008 These general considerations give rise to the following basic questions, at least, when thought is being given as to whether or not to seek a freezing injunction in support of a claim based on fraud:

(1)   What is the perceived strength of the cause of action? No allegation of fraud should be made lightly; but the potential exposure on the cross-undertaking in damages is such that the applicant for a freezing injunction ought to consider the scenario that, whilst he may be able to establish at the interim stage a good arguable case (which justifies it being granted), he may not succeed at trial. As explained in paras 28–013—28–023 below, the test of a "good arguable case" for the grant of a freezing injunction is a bare minimum threshold and, necessarily at this interim and usually very early stage of the proceedings, it falls well short of that required to make good the claim at trial. If, despite the recognised exceptions for permitted expenditure, the order has operated in the meantime to disrupt the defendant's business or other affairs, then the making of it may ultimately prove to be costly to the claimant.

(2)   Are there likely to be assets on which the freezing injunction can bite? Although a freezing order (in its non-proprietary form) can extend to the defendant's assets generally (usually up to a maximum value) and particular assets need not be identified, the court will not act in vain and the applicant will (consistently with the enforcement principle) need to satisfy it that there are assets against which a judgment could eventually be enforced. If, for example, there has been a significant lapse of time since

the accrual (or discovery) of the cause of action, it may be that the respondent's assets have become depleted, whether by wilful acts of dissipation or through a lifestyle unwittingly funded by the claimant, and that the injunction would be sought after the proverbial horse has bolted. Conversely, the claimant needs to be careful about casting the net too wide. Whilst it is tempting to maximise the chances of catching an asset against which a judgment might eventually be enforced, the more widely the order is drafted in this respect, the more difficult it will be to persuade a court that such a level of intrusion into the affairs of the defendant and those believed (quite possibly wrongly) to hold assets for him is justified, and the greater the claimant's exposure on his cross-undertaking will be.

(3) Even if there is good reason to suppose that the defendant presently retains assets against which a judgment might be enforced, what is the nature of those assets and what are prospects of the freezing injunction (operating as it does in personam) being observed with respect to them by the defendant or, equally importantly, third parties to whom notice of the order may be given? Not all such assets will conveniently take the form of a credit balance with a reputable bank or financial institution which will readily recognise and observe the restraints of an English injunction. The policing and enforcement of a freezing injunction can prove a costly distraction from the main litigation event, and the prospect of embarking upon contempt proceedings against those who have later shown themselves to be prepared to breach the injunction (at yet further legal expense over and above that incurred on the underlying claim) may not hold much allure for a claimant whose primary interest lies in securing financial redress.

(4) Who are the targets for relief? It is a common feature of civil fraud litigation that the assets against which the claimant may in due course wish to enforce any judgment are held through corporate and trust structures, often located offshore. If the claimant can show that there is a good reason to suppose that trustees, companies and other similar vehicles are holding assets for the benefit of the defendant, or are otherwise accountable to him, the court may well be willing to injunct them too.[8] But multiplying the number of respondents to the freezing order application will inevitably increase substantially the cost and distraction involved in the application and the interlocutory skirmishes which almost always follow it, as well as the claimant's exposure under the cross-undertaking in damages. It will also (which is not an insignificant point) result in the instruction of a number of separate sets of legal representatives on the other side of the court from the claimant, each keen to demonstrate their independence from the main respondent but all ultimately aligned in a common cause to make the claimant's litigation effort more difficult.

---

[8] As noted by Robert Walker J in *International Credit and Investment Co (Overseas) Ltd v Adham* [1998] BCC 134, at 136, "it has become increasingly clear, as the English High Court regrettably has to deal more and more often with major international fraud, that the court will, on appropriate occasions, take drastic action and will not allow its orders to be evaded by the manipulation of shadowy offshore trusts and companies formed in jurisdictions where secrecy is highly prized and official regulation is at a low level". On the *"Chabra"* jurisdiction to grant relief against third parties holding assets through such structures, see Section E below from para.28–157.

(4)   The Scope of this Chapter

28–009   In this chapter we focus principally upon freezing injunctions properly so-called (being orders which restrain the defendant from dealing with assets over which no proprietary claim is made, on the basis of an asserted risk that he will otherwise dissipate them). We also address, more briefly, proprietary injunctions (which restrain the defendant from dealing with specific property to which a proprietary claim is made). Both are often described as "freezing injunctions", but, as we identify below, there are important differences in their scope and the principles applicable to their grant, which the fraud litigator should keep well in mind when approaching any application for interim relief of this sort.

28–010   The structure of this chapter is as follows:

    (1)   In Section B we consider the requirements for the grant of a conventional freezing order, being:
        (a)   a good arguable case on the merits;
        (b)   a real risk of dissipation;
        (c)   the existence of assets which would be caught by the order;
        (d)   that it is just and convenient to grant the relief sought.
    (2)   In Section C we consider some international aspects of freezing orders, in particular
        (a)   the worldwide freezing order and the special considerations applicable to its grant; and
        (b)   applications under s.25 of the Civil Jurisdiction and Judgments Act 1982 for a freezing order in aid of proceedings abroad.
    (3)   In Section D we consider a number of aspects of how freezing orders operate, focusing upon the standard forms for such orders contained in the CPR and in the Admiralty and Commercial Court Guide. Particular attention is given to the vexed question of what constitutes the respondent's assets within the terms of such orders.
    (4)   In Section E we consider the jurisdiction to grant freezing orders against third parties against whom no cause of action is asserted, but who hold assets for, or are accountable to, the defendant—the so-called "*Chabra*" jurisdiction.
    (5)   In Section F we consider proprietary injunctions.

B.   REQUIREMENTS FOR A FREEZING INJUNCTION

(1)   Introduction

28–011   Over the years since the freezing order (under its original moniker of the *Mareva* injunction) was devised in the 1970s, there have been multiple decisions developing and refining the elements which must be established to persuade the court that it is proper to make such an order. The law has now largely stabilised and it has been established that the applicant must surmount four hurdles in order to obtain a freezing order from the court. These may be summarised as follows. The applicant must show that:

(1) He has a "good arguable case" in respect of the underlying merits of the claim.
(2) There is a "real risk of dissipation" of assets belonging to the respondent.
(3) There are assets held by or on behalf of the respondent either within the jurisdiction or, if a worldwide freezing order is sought (as to which see below), outside England and Wales.
(4) It is in all the circumstances "just and convenient" to grant the order.

We consider each of these elements in detail below. However we should flag immediately that these elements are not separate hurdles to be considered isolated from each other; for example, the strength of the claim (particularly if it is one in fraud) is likely to bear upon the court's assessment of the risk of dissipation, and the stronger the underlying claim or the greater the risk of dissipation, the more likely it is that the court will be to take the view that it is "just and convenient" to grant the order. Ultimately the court is faced with a discretionary question as to where the greater risk of injustice lies in granting what is on any view likely to be an invasive and disruptive order.   **28–012**

(2) Good Arguable Case

Any applicant for a freezing injunction must show that he has a good arguable claim against the defendant, which is justiciable in the courts of England and Wales (or abroad, if reliance is being placed on s.25 of the CJJA 1982). As has been discussed in greater detail in Ch.26, a freezing order, as with any other injunction, cannot be granted in a vacuum, but must be ancillary to an accrued cause of action which is being, or about to be,[9] pursued in the English or Welsh courts.   **28–013**

---

[9] This is the so-called "*Siskina* requirement": see Ch.26, para.26–013. In cases of extreme urgency an injunction can be granted in advance of the issuing of a claim form (see para.28–019 below; and Ch.27, at para.27–010. But unlike quia timet injunctions, a freezing order cannot be granted prior to the accrual of a cause of action. This requirement of an accrued cause of action has been applied in various cases: see *Steamship Mutual v Thakur Shipping Co Ltd* [1986] 2 Lloyds's Rep. 439 and *Veracruz Transportation Inc v VC Shipping Co Inc* [1992] 1 Lloyd's Rep. 353. However it is a rule which creates a real risk of injustice, for example, if A has a right to a monetary sum from B which falls due in the (near) future and is concerned that B is taking steps to divest itself of assets so as to make himself judgment-proof. Accordingly various creative inroads have been made into the principles to meet such potential injustice: see e.g. *Rowland v Gulfpac Ltd (No.1)* [1999] Lloyd's Rep. Bank 86, a case where the claimant had a right of indemnity against the defendant which had not yet crystallised, but Rix J held that he could grant relief on a quia timet basis to preserve the fund against which the indemnity could be asserted. His decision was more recently followed by Burton J in *Starlight Shipping Co v Allianz Marine & Aviation Versicherungs AG (The "Alexandros T")* [2011] EWHC 3381 (Comm); [2012] 1 Lloyd's Rep. 162, at [37]–[38]); and in *Zurich Insurance PLC UK Branch v International Energy Group Ltd* [2015] UKSC 33; [2016] A.C. 509 Lord Mance referred to these cases with apparent approval, at [87]. See also *Re Q's Estate* [1999] 1 Lloyd's Rep. 931; *Papamichael v National Westminster Bank Plc (No.1)* [2002] 1 Lloyd's Rep. 332 and *HM Revenue*

28–014 In *Derby & Co Ltd v Weldon*[10] Parker LJ said:

> "In my view the difference between an application for an ordinary injunction and a *Mareva* lies only in this, that in the former case the plaintiff need only establish that there is a serious question to be tried, whereas in the latter the test is said to be whether the plaintiff shows a good arguable case."

28–015 The "good arguable case" test derives from the influential and often-cited decision in *The Niedersachsen*[11] where Mustill J (at first instance, without any later substantive qualification on appeal)[12] said that the claimant must have "a case of a certain strength" and that this involves him showing that it is one which is "more than barely capable of serious argument and yet not necessarily one which the judge believes to have a better than fifty per cent chance of success." As was noted by Flaux J in *Linsen International Ltd v Humpuss Sea Transport Pte Ltd*,[13] this is the test which has since been habitually applied in freezing injunction cases.

28–016 It has been observed that there is either no difference or only an imperceptible one between satisfying this test, expressed this way, and establishing a "serious issue to be tried" for the purpose of successfully resisting a strike out application.[14] It is suggested that this is not entirely correct. When it comes to comparing other types of injunctive relief, which are subject to the familiar *American Cyanamid* hurdle of establishing a serious issue to be tried, it is generally understood that establishing a "good arguable case" puts a greater onus upon the applicant.[15] On the other hand, it is probably putting the test of "good arguable case" too high if it is thought to require the claimant to show that he has "much the better of the argument" (as that concept has come to be interpreted in

---

and *Customs Commissioners v Ali* [2011] EWHC 880 (Ch). In *Kazakhstan Kagazy v Zhunus* [2016] EWCA Civ 1036; [2017] 1 W.L.R. 1360, at [23]–[27] the Court of Appeal confirmed that the *Siskina* requirement did not mean that a freezing injunction was unavailable in support of a contribution claim, even though strictly speaking the cause of action was contingent and had yet to accrue: it was sufficient that the defendant had the right to commence proceedings claiming the substantive relief.

[10] *Derby & Co Ltd v Weldon (No.1)* [1990] Ch. 48, at 57H. The judge went on to say that the observations of Lord Diplock in *American Cyanamid*, that this should not involve an attempt to resolve conflicts of fact or to decide difficult questions of law, applied equally to the test of "good arguable case".

[11] *Ninemia Maritime Corp v Trave Schiffahrtsgesellschaft GmbH ("The Niedersachsen")* [1983] 1 W.L.R. 1412; [1983] 2 Lloyds Rep. 600. The judge laid down some useful statements of general principle, at 604–605: "The plaintiff must do more than make a bare assertion of facts which would give the court jurisdiction. (2) The question whether the plaintiff has shown a prima facie case is not an appropriate test, at least where the respondent has adduced evidence in opposition. (3) The Court cannot, and should not attempt to try the issues at the interlocutory stage ….." Mustill J derived the test from the judgment of Lord Denning MR in *Rasu Maritima S.A. v Perusahaan Pertambangan Minyak Dan Gas Bumi Negara (Government of the Republic of Indonesia intervening) (Pertamina)* [1978] Q.B. 644, at 661G.

[12] The Niedersachsen [1983] 1 W.L.R. 1412.

[13] *Linsen International Ltd v Humpuss Sea Transport Pte Ltd* [2011] EWHC 2339 (Comm); [2011] 2 Lloyd's Rep. 663, at [5].

[14] *Madoff Securities International Ltd v Raven* [2011] EWHC 3102 (Comm), at [145], per Flaux J. To similar effect see *Fiona Trust Holding Co v Privalov* [2007] EWHC 1217 (Comm), at [18], per David Steel J.

[15] *Sukhoruchkin v Van Bekestein* [2013] EWHC 1993 (Ch), at [7], per Morgan J and [2014] EWCA Civ 399.

the context of applications to serve out of the jurisdiction).[16] In *PJSC Tatneft v Bogolyubov*[17] Picken J accepted it was not appropriate to apply that higher test to an application for a freezing injunction, where "it is perfectly possible and logical to conclude that both sides have a good arguable case on the material presently available."[18]

In *Metropolitan Housing Trust Ltd v Taylor*[19] Warren J observed that the test was more stringent than that of a "serious question to be tried" applicable to other forms of injunctive relief (including proprietary injunctions), but that the test is not rigid and well-defined, and much is left to the judgment of the court. In support of the relative flexibility of the test when applied to different issues in the case, in *Holyoake v Candy*[20] Nugee J observed that, where the issue is one of construing a document or one of law, the court may well be able at the interlocutory stage to form a view as to which party appears to have the better of the argument, or indeed much the better of it, but that on purely factual questions it is sufficient to establish a case which meets the traditional *Ninemia* test. Even in examining issues such as the construction of a document, determining which party has the better or much the better of the argument may be unsatisfactory or even impossible at the hearing of an ex-parte freezing injunction, which is quite frequently carried out without any or proper pleadings and (necessarily) with only the claimant appearing.

28–017

For the purpose of satisfying the threshold of a good arguable case it is necessary to look both at the claimant's case and, of course, at the merits of any defence raised against it. However, this is not meant to encourage an attempt, at this interlocutory stage, to resolve or provisionally decide contentious factual issues or legal issues of any complexity. Hence it has been said that

28–018

> "It is very important that applications to discharge freezing applications do not turn into mini-trials; parties are often tempted to anticipate the real trial on these applications but that temptation must be firmly resisted."[21]

This principle is perhaps of even greater application in a fraud context. Where serious allegations have been made against the defendant, it would generally be even less desirable for judges to make determinations on the merits at an interlocutory stage; and, indeed, when assessing whether there is a good arguable case it has been said that the court should be "especially mindful of the particular scrutiny applied by the courts to serious allegations of fraud".[22]

---

[16] *Kazkhstan Kagazy Plc v Arip* [2014] EWCA Civ 381, at [25] and [63]–[68]. Longmore LJ could see no reason to apply the test applicable to service out of the jurisdiction to an application for a freezing injunction where the respondent is properly before the court.

[17] *PJSC Tatneft v Bogolyubov* [2016] EWHC 2816, at [110].

[18] In *Finurba Corp Finance Ltd v Sipp SA* [2011] EWCA Civ 465, Lord Neuberger MR made a plea, at [31] for the adoption of a "robust and realistic" approach in fraud cases, but it is not clear that that adds anything to the approach laid down in the authorities discussed in the main text. See also *Antonio Gramsci Shipping Corp v Aivars Lembergs* [2013] EWCA Civ 730; [2013] I.L.Pr .36.

[19] *Metropolitan Housing Trust Ltd v Taylor* [2015] EWHC 2897 (Ch), at [21].

[20] *Holyoake v Candy* [2016] EWHC 970 (Ch); [2016] 3 W.L.R. 357, at [13]–[15].

[21] See *Kazakhstan Kagazy v Arip* [2014] EWCA Civ 381, at [23]; and *Derby & Co Ltd v Weldon (No.1)* [1990] Ch. 48, at 57–58.

[22] *Elektromotive Group Ltd v Pan* [2012] EWHC 2742 (QB), at [33(b)], per Eder J.

28–019   So, in *Sukhoruchkin v Van Bekestein*[23] the Court of Appeal overturned the judge's decision to dismiss an application for a proprietary injunction and worldwide freezing relief. The judge had decided that a detailed analysis of the claim revealed there to be no good arguable case, because the corporate structure adopted by the litigants in their joint venture, including a Cayman Islands investment advisory company, was such that the claimants' claim to recover losses was clearly barred by the "no reflective loss" principle. The Court of Appeal held that it was wrong in principle to decide this issue at the interlocutory stage and thereby conclude that, for the purposes of assessing the existence of a serious issue to be tried in the context of the proprietary claim,[24] the claim was no more than borderline. There were a number of factors which gave rise to doubts over the judge's conclusion that, if the claimants made good their allegations of breach of fiduciary duty by the defendants as co-venturers resulting in a loss of dividends from the Cayman company, then (as a matter of Cayman Islands law) that company would have a direct claim against them for breaches of duty owed by them as shadow directors. The Chancellor stated[25]:

> "The general principle is now well established that, on an application for an interim injunction, the court should not attempt to resolve critical disputed questions of fact or difficult points of law on which the claim of either party may ultimately depend, particularly where the point of law turns on fine questions of fact which are in dispute or are presently obscure: *Derby v Weldon* [1990] Ch. 48, 58F-G, 63G-H."

28–020   In *Sukhoruchkin* the judge had gone too far in attempting to resolve matters best left for trial. In the absence of such an error in principle, however, the general approach of the appeal court is to respect the instincts of experienced commercial and chancery judges on the question of whether or not there is a good arguable case on what presently appear to be the facts.[26]

28–021   This approach to the assessment of the merits of the claim is consistent with the approach of the court on applications to discharge injunctions on the basis of non-disclosure at the without notice hearing, when the contention being advanced is that the applicant has failed to disclose facts which are material to the defence of the claim, when those facts are themselves in issue. It has been said that in complex cases, where facts which are not so plain as to be readily and summarily established, it is not appropriate for the judge to make findings (even on a provisional basis) which are more properly reserved for trial. In such cases, the court should not lose sight of the wood for the trees.[27]

---

[23] *Sukhoruchkin v Van Bekestein* [2014] EWCA Civ 399.
[24] See para.28–204 below.
[25] *Sukhoruchkin v Van Bekestein*, at [32].
[26] *Lakatamia Shipping Company Ltd v Nobu Su Ltd* [2012] EWCA Civ 1195, at [27], per Longmore LJ, and *Kazakhstan Kagazy Plc v Maksat Askaruly Arip* [2014] EWCA Civ 381, at [62], per Elias LJ.
[27] *Kazakhstan Kagazy Plc v Maksat Askaruly Arip* [2014] EWCA Civ 381, at [36]. However, there may be cases where the court is required to conduct a "critical examination of the raw material", to determine whether the claim has a real prospect of success, because the respondent not only contests the basis of the injunction but challenges the merits of the claim for the purposes of a strike out or reverse summary judgment application, or in the context of a jurisdictional challenge: compare *PJSC Tatneft v Bogolyubov*, where the court observed that the need for such critical analysis is no different where the factual dispute relates to the content of foreign law.

Although the test to be surmounted is whether the applicant has shown a "good arguable case", this is the bare minimum. As we will see, the decision whether or not to grant a freezing order depends on a number of other factors, to which the strength of the applicant's case (over and above whether it meets the threshold test) may be relevant; but it is a fair to say in summary that the stronger the case can be shown to be, the more willing the court is likely to be to grant a freezing order. Hence it was famously said that a

    28–022

> "'good arguable case' is no doubt the minimum which the plaintiff must show in order to cross what the judge rightly described as the 'threshold' for the exercise of the jurisdiction. But at the end of the day the court must consider the evidence as a whole in deciding whether or not to exercise this statutory jurisdiction."[28]

As a matter of practice, therefore, the applicant would be well-advised to articulate in his evidence as clear and trenchant a case as possible (consistent, of course, with his duty of fair presentation if applying without notice), while resisting the temptation (even if time allows, which will be unlikely) to deploy all his evidence at this stage.

    28–023

(3)   Real Risk of Dissipation

(i)   Generally

When the *Mareva* jurisdiction was first established in 1975[29] its aim was to prevent a defendant (and specifically, at that stage in the development of the jurisdiction, a foreign one) from *removing his assets from the jurisdiction* so as to defeat any ultimate judgment against him; however, in 1982 the risk of prejudicial dealing with assets, so as to trigger the exercise of the jurisdiction, was widened beyond the concept of asset removal to one of *dissipation* of assets.[30]

    28–024

Hence, under the modern law, any applicant for a freezing injunction must show that there is a real risk that any judgment which might be obtained in his favour at trial will remain unsatisfied if injunctive relief is refused, because of the unjustified dissipation of assets in the interim.[31] However, it is not necessary to show that a judgment would be completely defeated: it is enough to show that the enforcement of any judgment would be more difficult.[32] The exercise here is an

    28–025

---

[28] *Ninemia Maritime Corp v Trave Schiffahrtsgesellschaft GmbH ("The Niedersachsen")* [1983] 2 Lloyd's Rep. 600; [1983] 1 W.L.R. 1412, at 1417.

[29] The first case was *Nippon-Yusen-Kaisha v Karageorgis* [1975] 1 W.L.R. 1093. The second— *Mareva Compania Naviera SA v International Bulk Carriers Ltd* [1975] 2 Lloyd's Rep. 509—provided the name by which freezing injunctions were known until 1999, when the Civil Procedure Rules 1998 came into effect.

[30] *Ninemia Maritime Corp v Trave Schiffahrtsgesellschaft GmbH ("The Niedersachsen")* [1983] 2 Lloyds Rep. 600; [1983] 1 W.L.R. 1412. See the summary of developments in the *Mareva* jurisdiction by Millett LJ in *Credit Suisse Fides Trust S.A. v Cuoghi* [1998] Q.B. 818, at 824D–824H.

[31] *The Niedersachsen* [1983] 2 Lloyds Rep. 600; [1983] 1 W.L.R. 1412, at 1419–1420, and *Ketchum v Group Public Relations Holdings Ltd* [1997] 1 W.L.R. 4, at 13A–13B.

[32] *Congentra AG v Sixteen Thirteen Marine* [2008] EWHC 1615 (Comm), at [49]; and *Metropolitan Housing Trust Ltd v Taylor* [2015] EWHC 2897 (Ch), at [28].

evaluative one, seeking to infer the likelihood of a future event or set of events (and whether it/they are sufficiently likely to warrant the intervention of the court) by reference to the alleged past and current conduct and circumstances of the defendant. At this stage of the proceedings it is not unusual for a claimant to be unable to prove that dissipation either has happened or will happen, and nor does he have to prove that. Rather he must prove that there are objective facts from which a sufficient risk of it can be inferred.[33]

28–026 The application of this test reveals that (as noted at the outset of this chapter) a freezing injunction is not to be used as the basis for obtaining "security" for a claim where none presently exists.[34] Nor should one be granted where there is no credible evidence to suggest that the defendant's present ability (or inability) to meet it is likely to deteriorate materially before judgment is obtained. What the applicant for a freezing injunction must focus upon is demonstrating the need to guard against the ultimate risk of an unsatisfied judgment *by reason* of a likely dissipation or secretion of assets.[35] This is the "enforcement principle", to which we have already referred, which should underpin the making of any freezing injunction.[36]

28–027 In *The Niedersachsen*[37] Kerr LJ said:

> "In our view the test is whether on the assumption that the plaintiffs have shown at least a 'good arguable case', the Court concludes on the whole of the evidence before it, that the refusal of a Mareva injunction would involve a real risk that a judgment or award on favour of the plaintiffs would remain unsatisfied."

28–028 This dictum remains relevant and was quoted as sound law in one of the most recent decisions examining in depth this element of the freezing order jurisdiction, *PJSC Tatneft v Bogolyubov*.[38] Nonetheless, it is not to be taken as an exhaustive statement of the relevant hurdle: in particular, what it does not emphasise is that the risk against which the court will protect is not lawful and ordinary expenditure. If a defendant is expending money in such a way that his asset position is likely to be materially reduced by the time of a putative judgment in favour of the applicant that will not itself justify a freezing order. The jurisdiction does not seek to interfere with a defendant's freedom in respect of his financial affairs merely to preserve an asset base against which to enforce a judgment. Rather, it protects against the risk of dissipation or secretion which would not be in the ordinary course of business or the ordinary running of a defendant's domestic affairs.[39] The key question is whether the dealing against

---

[33] *Holyoake v Candy* [2016] EWHC 970 (Ch); [2016] 3 W.L.R. 357, at [20].

[34] See *Gangway Ltd v Caledonian Park Investments (Jersey) Ltd* [2001] 2 Lloyd's Rep. 715, quoted at fn.4 above.

[35] See the observations of HH Judge Waksman QC in *Cherney v Neuman* [2009] EWHC 1743 (Ch), at [71].

[36] See *JSC BTA Bank v Ablyazov* [2015] UKSC 64; [2015] 1 W.L.R. 4754, at [13] and [20], per Lord Clarke.

[37] *The Niedersachsen* [1983] 1 W.L.R. 1412; [1983] 2 Lloyd's Rep. 600, at 617.

[38] *PJSC Tatneft v Bogolyubov* [2016] EWHC 2816 (Comm). In Picken J's judgment a number of the significant dicta from the various cases on this element are conveniently quoted.

[39] "A debtor is not obliged to keep his assets intact to meet a possible claim by a claimant and can continue to spend them in the ordinary course of business or on his ordinary living expenses, but he is

which the claimant seeks to be protected is "justifiable",[40] judging the matter broadly, as opposed to by reference to the legality of the feared dealing. Hence the test is perhaps best stated as follows: "There must be a real risk, judged objectively, that a future judgment would not be met because of unjustifiable dissipation of assets".[41]

What is often described as the risk of "dissipation" extends to the risk of assets being hidden or secreted away making enforcement impossible or more difficult.[42] Evidence of actual dishonesty on the part of the defendant is not essential and there is no need to show an actual intention to dissipate assets with the specific object of putting assets beyond the reach of the claimant.[43] However, some risk of dealing with assets outside the ordinary or usual course of business (or lifestyle) will have to be shown.[44]

28–029

---

not at liberty to dissipate them so as to render a judgment unenforceable, or indeed to dissipate them if that would be the effect. In such a case the Court will grant a freezing injunction in accordance with what is by now a very well established jurisprudence": *Holyoake v Candy* [2016] EWHC 970 (Ch); [2016] 3 W.L.R. 357, per Nugee J at [8(5)]. See also the wide formulation given to permissible transactions as being those made "in the [ordinary] course of life" by Lloyd LJ in *Normid Housing Association Ltd v Ralphs* [1989] 1 Lloyd's Rep. 274, at 275.

[40] For a dealing which was justifiable see *Mobil Cerro Negro Ltd v Petroleos de Venezuela SA* [2008] EWHC 532 (Comm), where it was held that a business reorganisation or change in the nature of business carried on does not by itself imply a risk of dissipation.

[41] *Candy v Holyoake* [2017] EWCA Civ 92, at [34]. An influential formulation of the relevant test, which rightly emphasises the need for unjustified dissipation rather than expenditure in the ordinary course, is that of Flaux J in *Congentra AG v Sixteen Thirteen Marine SA ("The Nicholas M")* [2008] EWHC 1615 (Comm); [2008] 2 Lloyd's Rep. 602, at [49]; "(i) there is a real risk that a judgment or award will go unsatisfied, in the sense of a real risk that, unless restrained by injunction, the defendant will dissipate or dispose of his assets other than in the ordinary course of business: *The Niedersachsen* [1983] 2 Lloyd's Rep. 600, per Mustill J as interpreted by Christopher Clarke J in *TTMI v ASM Shipping* [2005] EWHC 2666 (Comm); [2006] 1 Lloyd's Rep. 401, at 406 (paragraphs [24]–[27]) or (ii) that unless the defendant is restrained by injunction, assets are likely to be dealt with in such a way as to make enforcement of any award or judgment more difficult, unless those dealings can be justified for normal and proper business purposes: *Stronghold Insurance v Overseas Union* [1996] LRLR 13, at 18–19, per Potter J and *Motorola Credit Corp v Uzan (No.2)* [2004] 1 W.L.R. 113, at 153 (paragraphs [142]–[146]) where the Court of Appeal was applying the same principle in the context of disclosure of assets by the defendant."

[42] *Derby & Co Ltd v Weldon (No.1)* [1990] Ch. 48, at 57D–57E, per Parker LJ.

[43] See *TTMI Ltd of England v ASM Shipping Ltd of India* [2005] EWHC 2666 (Comm); [2006] 1 Lloyd's Rep. 401, per Christopher Clarke J, at [25]. Hence in *Stronghold Insurance Co Ltd v Overseas Union Insurance* [1996] L.R.L.R. 13; [1995] C.L.C. 1268, Potter J upheld the grant of a freezing injunction against a substantial Singaporean company carrying on an insurance business in that country and wanting to transfer assets from London where it had no continuing business. This was an example of a situation well-described by the Court of Appeal of *Ontario Chitel v Rothbart* [1982] 39 O.R. (2d) 513, at 532–533: "The applicant must persuade the court by his material that the defendant is removing or there is a real risk that he is about to remove his assets from the jurisdiction to avoid the possibility of judgment, or that the defendant is otherwise dissipating or disposing of is assets, *in a manner clearly distinct from his usual or ordinary course of business or living*, so as to render the possibility of future tracing of the assets remote, if not impossible in fact or in law".

[44] See the discussion in *Campbell v Campbell* [2017] EWHC 2747 (Ch), at [26]. The judge noted the various ways that courts had attempted to express the point: "in a manner clearly distinct from [the respondent's] usual or ordinary course of business or living" (*Third Chandris Shipping Corp v Unimarine* [1979] Q.B. 645, at 669, per Lord Denning MR), or "other than in the ordinary course of business" (*Laemthong International Lines Co Ltd v ARTIS* [2004] EWHC 2226 (Comm); [2004] 2 All E.R. (Comm) 797, per Coleman J at [54]), or "unjustifiable" (*Ketchum International v Group Public*

28–030 This risk of dissipation needs to be established by "solid evidence."[45] General expressions of fear that assets will be dissipated will carry very little, if any, weight; the court needs to be able to base any inference of the relevant risk upon objective facts.[46] The standard of proof in relation to establish the risk of dissipation has been said to be "relatively high."[47] In *JSC Mezhdunarodniy Promyshlenniy Bank v Pugachev*[48] Mann J made the following observation upon the nature of the evidence required on this aspect:

> "What one has to do is to acknowledge the seriousness of the consequences of a freezing order, and the invasion of liberty that it involves (especially bearing in mind it is usually sought in a without notice application) and to reflect that in requiring proof to an appropriately high standard. Orders are not to be lightly sought and will not be granted on flimsy evidence. The requirement to demonstrate a risk of dissipation is a lot more than formal."

(ii)   Specific factors relevant to assessing a real risk of dissipation

28–031 The principles discussed above are necessarily cast in general terms.[49] They are easy to state but often difficult to apply given the inexact nature of the enquiry involved, both as to the level of the risk to be established and the nature of the conduct which is apprehended. In an attempt to create firmer guidance on the correct application of the test the courts have discussed various factors which will inform the enquiry. At the most obvious level, evidence of actual dissipation will provide sound basis for the grant of a freezing injunction[50]; but in most cases, the evidence of risk of dissipation will be based on inference or inherent probability.

28–032 **Delay on Part of Applicant.**   Where there has been delay on the part of the applicant in seeking a freezing injunction, then, without more, that ought not generally be taken by the court to mean that there is no risk of dissipation. Courts recognise that in a complex case significant time may well be required to investigate the claim. Even if the delay might properly be interpreted as reflecting

---

Relations Holdings [1997] 1 W.L.R. 4, per Stuart Smith LJ at 10; *Congentra v Sixteen Thirteen Marine SA (The "Nicholas M")* [2008] EWHC 1615 (Comm); [2008] 2 Lloyd's Rep. 602, at [49]). It is for this reason that the standard forms of freezing injunction permit expenditure in the ordinary course of business or in payment of ordinary living expenses.

[45] *Thane v Tomlinson* [2003] EWCA Civ 1272, at [21], per Peter Gibson LJ.

[46] *Holyoake v Candy* [2016] EWHC 970 (Ch); [2016] 3 W.L.R. 357, at [19], per Nugee J, citing *O'Regan v Iambic Productions Ltd* (1989) 139 N.L.J. 1378. And see further the decision of the Court of Appeal in *Holyoake v Candy* [2017] EWCA Civ 92; [2017] 3 W.L.R. 1131, emphasising the need (in the case of a "notification" injunction as in the case of a conventional freezing order) for the application to show "a real risk, supported by solid evidence, that a future judgment would not be met because of unjustifiable dissipation" (at [39]). The latter decision establishes that a notification injunction (which in effect prevents dealings with assets other than on the giving of prior notice to the applicant) is not so different to a conventional freezing order as to merit some different, less onerous test of risk of dissipation.

[47] *Leamthong v Artis* [2004] EWHC 2266 (Comm); [2005] 1 Lloyds Rep. 100, at [61], per Colman J.

[48] *JSC Mezhdunarodniy Promyshlenniy Bank v Pugachev* [2014] EWHC 4336 (Ch), at [221].

[49] See the summary of factors to consider in *State Bank of India v Mallya* [2018] EWHC 1084 (Comm); [2018] 1 W.L.R. 3865, at [105]; and *Fundo Soberano de Angola v Dos Santos* [2018] EWHC 2199 (Comm), at [86].

[50] *Dinglis Properties Ltd v Dinglis Management Ltd* [2016] EWHC 818 (Ch); [2016] 4 W.L.R. 72.

the applicant's own assessment of the degree of risk, then it is still only a factor to be weighed in the balance in deciding whether or not to grant the injunction.[51]

However, if a significant period of time has elapsed between a dispute emerging and the application, without any evidence of dissipation (in the sense identified above), that might provide evidence negativing the apprehended risk.[52] Hence in *Holyoake v Candy* it was held by the Court of Appeal that the applicant's delay was   **28–033**

> "a powerful factor militating against any conclusion of a real risk of dissipation. If there had been a real risk of the appellants unjustifiably dissipating their assets, it would have materialised by the time of the application."[53]

Where the delay has given the defendant the opportunity to dissipate substantial assets prior to the application, that should of course not inhibit the court from acting to try to protect that which remains. As it was vividly put by Cooke J in *Antonio Gramsci Shipping Corp v Recoletos Ltd*[54]:   **28–034**

> "In my judgment it is no answer for a defendant to come to the court to say that his horse may have bolted before the gate is shut and then to put that forward as a reason for not shutting the gate. That would be to pray in aid his own efforts to make himself judgment proof – if that, indeed, is what has occurred – and to avoid the effect of any court order which the court might make. If he can show that there is no risk of dissipation on other grounds, that is one thing. If he can show that the claimants do not consider that there is such a risk by virtue of the delay in seeking the order, that again is a relevant factor. However, if the court is satisfied about those matters in favour of the claimant, there is no reason why the court should not shut the gate, however late the application, in the hope, if not the expectation, that some horses may still be in the field or, at the worst, a miniature pony."

Further, even if the feared secretion has occurred, that does not render a freezing order otiose, given the disclosure orders which will almost invariably be made at the same time.[55]

In and of itself, therefore, delay in the making of the application ought not as a matter of principle to preclude the grant of a freezing injunction, and some recent   **28–035**

---

[51] *Madoff Securities International Ltd v Raven* [2011] EWHC 3102 (Comm), at [156], per Flaux J, followed in *Enercon GmBH v Enercon (India) Ltd* [2012] EWHC 689 (Comm); [2012] 1 Lloyd's Rep. 519, at [77]–[78], per Eder J and *PJSC Tatneft v Bogolyubov* [2016] EWHC 2816 (Comm), at [115], per Picken J.

[52] A recent example is *Anglo Financial SA v Goldberg* [2014] EWHC 3192 (Ch), at [53]–[54] in particular. Though see *Antonio Gramsci Shipping Corp v Recoletos Ltd* [2011] EWHC 2242 (QB), per Cooke J at [28]: "It could be said that, in every case where there is a letter before action, the defendant is alerted to the possibility of a claim and the need for dissipation of assets if the defendant is minded so to do in order to make himself judgment-proof. However, time and again the courts have granted freezing orders on commencement of proceedings following exchanges of correspondence where the merits of the claim have been fully debated and the defendant thereby undoubtedly alerted."

[53] *Holyoake v Candy* [2017] EWCA Civ 92, at [62]. In that case, the first intimation of the claim was in May 2014; a detailed letter of claim with draft particulars of claim was sent in December 2014; a revised claim was issued in August 2015 and the applicants repeatedly threatened to seek a freezing order from September 2015 onwards, but the application for an initial notification was not made until February 2016, resulting in a hearing in April 2016.

[54] *Antonio Gramsci Shipping Corp v Recoletos Ltd* [2011] EWHC 2242 (QB), at [29].

[55] As recognised by David Steel J in *Fiona Trust v Privalov* [2007] EWHC 1217 (Comm), at [69]–[71].

decisions suggest that the Courts are more willing than previously thought to grant freezing injunctions notwithstanding substantial delay before the commencement of proceedings[56]; it is instead just one factor that bears on the court's evaluation of the risk of dissipation, and the exercise of its discretion more generally.

28–036   **The Nature of the Underlying Claim.**   In some cases, the nature of the allegations made against the defendant, or the defendant's reaction to the claim, may suffice to establish the risk. In particular, where the claim is founded on the defendant's alleged dishonesty, as will very often be the case in a fraud claim, it may well be possible to infer a risk of dissipation from the nature of the allegations themselves (assuming there to be a good arguable case that they are correct), on the basis that a person who is willing to engage in dishonest conduct is more likely to be one who will take illegitimate steps to put his assets beyond the reach of the claimant.

28–037   There has been some controversy concerning the inferences that can properly be drawn from the nature of the underlying claim. In the well-known case of *Thane Investments v Tomlinson*[57] Peter Gibson LJ observed:

> "Neuberger J said that the matters relied on for the good and [sic] arguable case applied in demonstrating that there was a real danger of the defendants dissipating their assets to defeat the judgment. I regret that I do not see that the judgment does support a conclusion that in the particular circumstances of Mr. Tomlinson and Reyall there was a real risk of assets being dissipated. Mr. Blackett-Ord submitted that it has now become the practice for parties to bring ex parte applications seeking a freezing order by pointing to some dishonesty, and that, he says, is sufficient to enable this court to make a freezing order. I have to say that, if that has become the practice, then the practice should be reconsidered. It is appropriate in each case for the court to scrutinise with care whether what is alleged to have been the dishonesty of the person against whom the order is sought in itself justifies the inference that that person has assets which he is likely to dissipate unless restricted."

28–038   These dicta have been subsequently relied upon by defendants as establishing that dishonesty per se cannot found a real risk of dissipation. However care must be taken with Peter Gibson LJ's judgment: it was given ex tempore in circumstances where the defendant was unrepresented and earlier Court of Appeal decisions which suggest a more nuanced approach were not cited.[58]

---

[56] *Ras Al Khaimah Investment Authority v Bestfort Development LLP* [2017] EWCA Civ 1014; [2018] 1 W.L.R. 1099. See also *Great Station Properties S.A. v UMS Holding Ltd* [2017] EWHC 3330 (Comm) per Teare J at [11] where a delay of 18 months after an arbitral award did not prevent the grant of a freezing injunction. Cf. *St Vincent European General Partner v Bruce Robinson* [2017] EWHC 3267 (Comm) where the evidence relied upon was found to be so out of date as to render it insufficient to establish a current risk of dissipation.

[57] *Thane Investments v Tomlinson* [2003] EWCA Civ 1272, at [28]. See also *Irish Response Ltd v Direct Beauty Products Ltd* [2011] EWHC 37 (QB), at [29]; *Madoff Securities International Ltd v Raven* [2011] EWHC 3102 (Comm), at [163]–[167]; and *Metropolitan Housing Trust Ltd v Taylor* [2015] EWHC 2897 (Ch), at [29].

[58] I.e. *Norwich Union v Eden*, unreported, 25 January 1996; and *Gruppo Torras SA v Al Sabah* 1997 WL 1105536 (21 March 1997), both of which are quoted from in *Tatneft* [2016] EWHC 2816, at [114] and suggest an approach whereby allegations of fraudulent conduct in the underlying claim can themselves found the inference of risk of dissipation.

The recent cases have re-adopted that more nuanced approach. In *VTB Capital* **28–039**
Plc v Nutritek International Corp[59] the Court of Appeal stated[60]:

> "We agree with Peter Gibson LJ that the court should be careful in its treatment of evidence of
> dishonesty. However, where (as here) the dishonesty alleged is at the heart of the claim against
> the defendant, the court may well find itself able to draw the inference that the making out, to
> the necessary standard, of that case against the defendant also establishes sufficiently the risk
> of dissipation of assets."

Having reminded itself of the need to scrutinise the allegations of dishonesty with **28–040**
care for the purpose of testing the inference of risk of dissipation, the Court
concluded:

> "On that basis, it seems to us that it would have been right for the judge to take into account a
> finding of a good arguable case that Mr Malofeev had been engaged in a major fraud, and that
> he operated a complex web of companies in a number of jurisdictions, which enabled him to
> commit the fraud and would make it difficult for any judgment to be enforced. We would
> regard such factors as capable of providing powerful support for the case of a risk of
> dissipation."[61]

In *Metropolitan Housing Trust Ltd v Taylor*[62] Warren J said that where alleged **28–041**
dishonesty is relied on as part of the claimant's case in support of a risk of
dissipation, it is important to consider whether a good arguable case of actual
dishonesty is established in relation to the conduct relied on. If a good arguable
case of dishonesty is not established, the alleged conduct is not relevant to the
court's assessment of the risk. If the case of dishonesty on the part of the
respondent is established to that standard then the approach in *VTB v Nutritek*
requires the court to scrutinise the evidence to see whether the dishonesty in
question does justify a conclusion that assets are likely to be dissipated.[63]

The position in relation to fraud claims can perhaps be put as simply as: in a fraud **28–042**
claim, where allegations of dishonesty are central to the claim itself, it may well
be that making out the claim to the required standard for a freezing injunction
provides the court, on proper examination, with the necessary inference of risk of
dissipation. However it cannot be said that merely because a fraud claim is
brought or because a claim includes allegations of fraud, even when such
allegations reach the standard of good arguable case, that a real risk of dissipation
has been established. Instead, as it was put in a recent Singaporean decision[64]:

---

[59] *VTB Capital Plc v Nutritek International Corp* [2012] EWCA Civ 808; [2012] 2 Lloyd's Rep. 313,
at [177]–[178].
[60] Citing with approval the decision of Flaux J in *Madoff Securities International Ltd v Raven* [2011]
EWHC 3102 (Comm), who had surveyed the law in detail and had concluded that the decision of
Patten J in *Jarvis Field Press v Chelton* [2003] EWHC 2674 (Ch), at [10], represented the correct
approach: "That is not, therefore, a judgment to the effect that a finding of dishonesty (or, in this case,
an allegation of dishonesty) is insufficient to found the necessary inference. It is merely a welcome
reminder that in order to draw that inference it is necessary to have regard to the particular allegations
of dishonesty and to consider them with some care."
[61] Of course, evidence of dishonesty is not essential to the exercise of the jurisdiction: *AH Baldwin
and Sons Ltd v Al Thani* [2012] EWHC 3156 (QB), per Haddon-Cave J, at [31(3)].
[62] *Metropolitan Housing Trust Ltd v Taylor* [2015] EWHC 2897 (Ch), at [369].
[63] *National Bank Trust v Yurov* [2016] EWHC 1913 (Comm), at [69]–[70], per Males J.
[64] *Bouvier v Accent Delight International Ltd* [2015] SGCA 45, at [94], per Sundaresh Menon CJ.

"in each case, it is incumbent on the court to examine the precise nature of the dishonesty that is alleged and the strength of the evidence relied on in support of the allegation…An allegation of dishonesty does not in itself form a substitute for an examination of the degree of risk of dissipation unless that allegation is of a nature or characteristic that sufficiently bears upon the risk of dissipation."

28–043   **Conduct of the Defendant.**   Apart from the nature of the underlying claim against the defendant, if it can be shown that the defendant has behaved in an underhand or discreditable way, whether or not that conduct is part of the cause of action alleged, that is likely to be relevant to the question of whether a real risk of dissipation is established.[65] It will likewise be relevant if the defendant has been evasive in his response to any intimation of the claim or investigations by regulators etc.[66] If, after the making of an ex parte freezing order the defendant has provided an inadequate affidavit of means, that is likely to be relevant to the question of whether to continue the order.

28–044   **The Nature of the Defendant's Assets and How they are Held.**   In general the more liquid or movable the defendant's assets, the greater the risk of their dissipation: funds in a bank account are much easier to move out of reach of a claimant enforcing a judgment than (for example) real property. Similarly, if a defendant's assets are held via opaque off-shore trust or company structures then that will support the inference of risk. There are many cases where the use of and familiarity with a network of offshore companies has been regarded as a factor tending to support the existence of a risk of dissipation, albeit that the weight to be given to such a factor has to be assessed in all the circumstances of each individual case.[67] Such structures are increasingly common in fraud cases of an international nature litigated in the English courts. That the use of such structures may now be widespread and employed for legitimate reasons does not negate or nullify the fact that they may also be used to facilitate the secretion of assets. The presence of such structures may therefore give rise to the inference that there is a real risk of dissipation.

28–045   **The Length of Time the Defendant has been in Business, its Nature and Financial Standing.**   This speaks for itself. A long established and financially sound company is probably less likely to dissipate its assets than a newly formed one, perhaps with modest share capital. An adverse inference might also be drawn against a corporate defendant incorporated in a jurisdiction where the

---

[65] *AH Baldwin and Sons Ltd v Al Thani* [2012] EWHC 3156 (QB), at [31(4)]. See also *Great Station Properties S.A. v UMS Holding Ltd* [2017] EWHC 3330 (Comm) where conduct including manipulating corporate structures to deprive others of sums to which they were entitled and giving false information to regulatory authorities was sufficient to establish a risk of dissipation.

[66] See e.g. *Madoff Securities International Ltd v Raven* [2011] EWHC 3102 (Comm), at [168]–[169]. The defendant's full engagement with the claim counted against the inference of a risk in *Irish Response v Direct Beauty Products Ltd* [2011] EWHC 37 (QB), at [82].

[67] As the Court of Appeal said in *VTB Capital Plc v Nutritek International Corp* [2012] EWCA Civ 808; [2012] 2 Lloyd's Rep. 313, at [174] and [178]. See *JSC Mezhdunarodniy Promyshlenniy Bank v Pugachev* [2014] EWHC 4336 (Ch), at [226]–[227]; *Elektromotive Group Ltd v Pan* [2012] EWHC 2742 (QB), at [84(b)]; *A.H. Baldwin & Sons Ltd v Al-Thani* [2012] EWHC 3156 (QB), at [49]; *Holyoake v Candy* [2016] EWHC 970 (Ch), at [27]; and *National Bank Trust v Yurov* [2016] EWHC 1913 (Comm), at [72]–[76].

accounting requirements are such that its financial position is opaque; as is frequently the case in fraud cases. However, the applicant must be aware that even a single-asset offshore company may be part of a substantial group whose interests in maintaining a good financial reputation are such that the company is likely to honour its debts.[68] The opposite inference could be drawn where it can be shown the parent company has previously been content to see others in its group default on their obligations or suffer insolvency.

The Defendant's Connections with England or Wales. The individual defendant who is firmly established in the jurisdiction, with family and/or business connections, is in general less likely to dissipate his assets (particularly in the sense of moving them out of the jurisdiction) than the defendant with only a fleeting connection with it. A company incorporated abroad, or even an English one controlled by an overseas parent, may present more risks.[69] However, both for corporate and individual defendants, a countervailing factor will be whether or not the enforcement of an English judgment (without undue difficulty or delay) is available in the relevant overseas territory. The transfer of assets overseas by an apparently financially solid defendant may justify the grant of an injunction if the later process of enforcement overseas would prove difficult and involve extra cost and delay.[70]   **28–046**

The Defendant's Credit Record. Clearly a history of default or failure to discharge debts on time will be relevant. However, the relevant inquiry is whether there is a current risk of dissipation; past events may be evidentially relevant, but only if they serve to demonstrate a current risk of dissipation of the assets now held.[71]   **28–047**

Strength of Claim. As we have seen, the stronger the claimant's claim (when that itself is based on allegedly fraudulent behaviour) the more likely a risk of dissipation will be shown. But it is also true that where the claimant has a claim (even if not one based on fraud) which is so strong as to be virtually incapable of being defended, that will be a powerful factor in favour of the grant of relief.[72] We have mentioned earlier how courts are not inclined to conduct "mini-trials" concerning the strength of the claimant's claim so the claimant will need to think carefully to what extent it can press this point. It will, however, be perfectly legitimate (for example) to point to failures by the defendant to answer the case against him, or inconsistencies in any answer given.   **28–048**

---

[68] *The Niedersachsen* [1983] 2 Lloyd's Rep. 600; [1983] 1 W.L.R. 1412.

[69] *Third Chandris Shipping Corp v Unimarine* [1979] Q.B. 645, at 672 and *IOT Engineering Projects Ltd v Dangote Fertilizer Ltd* [2014] EWCA Civ 1348.

[70] *Mobil Cerro Negro Ltd v Petroleos de Venezuela SA* [2008] EWHC 532 (Comm), at [38], per Walker J.

[71] *National Bank Trust v Yurov* [2016] EWHC 1913 (Comm), at [70].

[72] *AH Baldwin and Sons Ltd v Al Thani* [2012] EWHC 3156 (QB), at [31(7)]. This will of course also bear on whether it is "just and convenient" to grant relief, as to which see paras 28–055—28–060 below.

28–049   **Voluntary Disclosure of Assets.**   In some cases a failure by the defendant to make a voluntary disclosure of assets prior to the application may be held against that defendant in assessing the risk of dissipation.[73] Such non-disclosure may also undermine the defendant's assertions that there has been no dissipation in the face of the intimation of a claim, because the court will have no material against which to test those assertions.[74]

28–050   Each of the factors mentioned above were identified by Peter Pain J in *O'Reagan v Iambic Productions Ltd*[75] as factors above which the Court at the without notice hearing should have information about. They are also matters which the defendant seeking to resist a freezing order should think very carefully about addressing in his evidence in response.

(4)   Existence of Assets

28–051   A court will not act in vain. Hence a further hurdle the applicant must surmount is that he must show, to an appropriate standard of proof, that there are or may be assets owned by the respondent which would be caught by the proposed freezing order and which would be available to satisfy a future judgment. Hence, in order to guard against the risk of the court being asked to make an order which proves to be futile, any applicant for a freezing injunction needs to bear well in mind the obvious point that the respondent must be shown to have (or arguably have) assets, either within the jurisdiction or somewhere in the world (if a worldwide freezing order is being sought), and that those assets may effectively be frozen. Moreover, it is inherent in the requirement to show that there is a risk of dissipation of assets that the cases in which freezing injunctions are granted are cases in which there is evidence that the defendant has some assets to dissipate.

28–052   In *A v C*,[76] at an early stage in the development of the jurisdiction, Robert Goff J stated that in order to establish his right to relief, the applicant had at least to give "grounds for believing" that the respondent has assets which will be caught by the order. In *Ras Al Khaimah Investment Authority v Bestfort Developments LLP*[77] the Court of Appeal re-considered this aspect of the test for obtaining a freezing order in the light of the subsequent substantial developments to the jurisdiction over the decades. Longmore LJ noted that the test for showing that the respondent has assets which will in fact be caught by the order was somewhat less clear than the tests applicable to the good arguable case and risk of dissipation hurdles. The court concluded that an applicant was not required to go as far as establish that it was "likely" that assets existed; but that, on the other hand, it would not be enough merely to show that the respondent was an apparently wealthy person who must have assets somewhere. The right test in relation to the existence of assets to be frozen was said to be either a "good

---

[73] *Madoff Securities International Ltd v Raven* [2011] EWHC 3102 (Comm), at [170]–[172].
[74] *Jarvis Field Press v Chelton* [2003] EWHC 2674 (Ch), at [13]–[14].
[75] *O'Reagan v Iambic Productions Ltd* (1989) 139 N.L.J. 1378, at 1379.
[76] *A v C* [1981] Q.B. 956.
[77] *Ras Al Khaimah Investment Authority v Bestfort Development LLP* [2017] EWCA Civ 1014; [2018] 1 W.L.R. 1099, at [39].

arguable case" or (as Longmore LJ preferred) "grounds for belief" that they exist. It was noted that this was not an "excessive burden" to bear. Certainly it is apparent that the claimant need not identify specific assets which are to be frozen,[78] although if he knows of any he should (not least because it is in his interests to) identify them in the evidence and in the draft order.

Even if the existence of assets is established, the court may decline to grant an order on grounds of proportionality; if the defendant owns only limited assets then there is a danger that the costs of policing the order will outweigh its utility.[79]   **28–053**

A respondent who has been made bankrupt or is subject to a corporate insolvency procedure may still be the subject of a freezing injunction, notwithstanding that, prima facie, all the respondent's assets will have transferred to its insolvent estate. Such an order may serve a number of purposes, including preserving assets for the creditors generally, preserving assets not forming part of the insolvent estate, such as assets held on trust for the applicant, or ensuring that an applicant's resources, which may be greater than the office holder's, might be brought to bear in ensuring the proper application of the insolvent party's assets. Of particular relevance in the fraud context, liabilities which would survive the respondent's discharge from bankruptcy may form the basis for a post-bankruptcy freezing injunction.[80]   **28–054**

(5) Just and Convenient

Once a good arguable case on the merits of the claim has been shown, it has been demonstrated that there is a real risk of any judgment on it going unsatisfied if no relief is granted, and the applicant has shown the existence of assets which can be the subject of the proposed relief, the court will finally go on to consider whether it is "just and convenient" to grant a freezing injunction. It should be emphasised that satisfying the Court that it is "just and convenient" to grant relief (an expression which derives from s.37 of the Senior Courts Act 1981) is by no means a rubber stamp exercise.   **28–055**

The concept of what is "just and convenient" informs not only the decision as to whether or not to grant a freezing injunction in the first place, but also the terms of any injunction which is granted and any departure from the standard terms which may be sanctioned by the court. In *Holyoake v Candy*, Gloster LJ said[81]:   **28–056**

---

[78] *Revenue and Customs Commissioners v Cozens* [2011] EWHC 2782 (Ch); [2012] STC 420, per Floyd J at [41]: "The evidence of the existence of assets need not be specific: indeed it may in some cases be unreasonable to expect a party seeking such an injunction to have evidence of precisely what assets his adversary in litigation has. But there must be some material from which it is reasonable to infer or deduce that there are assets on which the injunction will bite. Otherwise the court will run the risk of acting in vain."

[79] *Ras Al Khaimah Investment Authority v Bestfort Development LLP* [2017] EWCA Civ 1014; [2018] 1 W.L.R. 1099, at [40].

[80] *Eco Quest Plc v GFI Consultants Ltd* [2014] EWHC 4329 (QB).

[81] *Holyoake v Candy* [2017] EWCA Civ 92; [2017] 3 W.L.R. 1131, at [45].

"The conclusion that all variants of freezing order must satisfy the same threshold in relation to risk of dissipation should not be taken to suggest that parties need only contemplate the most onerous form of a freezing order, under what would be a misapprehension that the intrusiveness of relief is immaterial. On the contrary, the intrusiveness of relief will be a highly relevant factor when considering the overall justice and convenience of granting the proposed injunction. Hence, even if there is solid evidence of a real risk of unjustifiable dissipation, an applicant should consider what form of relief a court is likely to accept as just and convenient in all the circumstances, including the scope of exceptions to the prohibition on dispositions."

28-057 This passage is a valuable reminder that the applicant should actively consider whether to seek a fully-fledged freezing order, or some lesser form of relief (in that case the applicant had sought a so-called notification injunction, whereby the respondent was obliged to give prior notice of any proposed dealing to allow the applicant to return to court to seek to enjoin that dealing.) The less intrusive the relief, the more readily the Court is likely to be persuaded that its grant is "just and convenient".

28-058 The classic statement of the law is perhaps that of Kerr LJ in *The Niedersachsen*[82]:

"The ultimate test for the exercise of the jurisdiction is whether, in all the circumstances, the case is one in which it appears to the court 'to be just and convenient' to grant the injunction: see section 37 of the Supreme Court Act 1981 which we have already set out. Thus, the conduct of the plaintiffs may be material, and the rights of any third parties who may be affected by the grant of an injunction may often also have to be borne in mind: see *Galaxia Maritime SA v Mineralimportexport* [1982] 1 W.L.R. 539. Further, it must always be remembered that if, or to the extent that, the grant of a Mareva injunction inflicts hardship on the defendants, their legitimate interests must prevail over those of the plaintiffs, who seek to obtain security for a claim which may appear to be well-founded but which still remains to be established at the trial. There is no need to repeat here what was said in that connection in *Z Ltd v. A-Z* and *AA-LL* [1982] QB 558, 585, 586. If the plaintiffs are in a position to contend that their claim is not open to doubt, then they must satisfy the requirements of an application for summary judgment under RSC Ord. 14. But if they apply for a Mareva injunction on the ground that they have 'a good arguable case', then the balance should be weighed as we have indicated above."

28-059 The so-called justice and convenience of the case can encompass a very wide range of considerations which cannot be compendiously listed. However, factors which have influenced the courts include the following:

(1) The comparative weakness or strength of the underlying claim. The stronger the claim the less "unjust" the order is likely to be, because it is more likely that the defendant will be eventually held liable so that his assets will be exposed to enforcement; and of course the converse is also true. This is a reason why all the parties may well wish to adduce substantial evidence concerning the underlying merits of the claim; but in doing so they should of course have it firmly in mind that the Court cannot and will not conduct a "mini-trial" of the case on its merits.

(2) The size of the claim. A small claim is unlikely to justify the full panoply and substantial cost of a freezing order.

---

[82] *Ninemia Maritime Corp v Trave Schiffahrtsgesellschaft GmbH ("The Niedersachsen")* [1983] 1 W.L.R. 1412, at 1426.

(3) Relatedly, whether the injunctive relief sought will be effective; and whether the cost of obtaining and enforcing it will be proportionate to the value of what is likely to be frozen.[83]

(4) The potential disruption to the defendant's business. It is well known that a freezing order can have a devastating impact on a company's business or trade, and evidence that a company's future might be imperilled by the imposition of an injunction may well persuade a court that such a step, even if otherwise justified, should not be taken.[84] It is suggested that if there is cogent evidence that the jobs of employees would be put at risk by the imposition of a freezing order that can be properly taken account of.

(5) The conduct of the applicant both in relation to the application itself[85] and in respect of the underlying claim. This is closely related to the equitable principle that an applicant for injunctive relief (which is in its origins equitable) must come to the Court with "clean hands".[86] So, for example, an applicant who failed to disclose variations to the standard form of freezing injunction narrowly avoided having the order discharged in circumstances where the form of order was rectified within three days.[87] Material misrepresentation of the underlying claim is obviously likely to result in relief being denied when it comes to be reconsidered, but in one case misrepresentations which were innocent and which were found to have not caused any prejudice to the defendant did not result in the discharge of an injunction.[88] It has also been held that a party accused of fraud could obtain a freezing injunction to support a contribution claim, even though

---

[83] See e.g. *Ras Al Khaimah Investment Authority v Bestfort Development LLP* [2015] EWHC 3383 (Ch) where the court was concerned (see paras 28–126—28–130 below) about the likely cost of implementing the order compared with the perceived value of the overseas assets sought to be frozen. At the inter partes stage, issues of proportionality might arise if it appears that the respondent's right to rely upon the established exceptions for permitted expenditure under the standard form of injunction (see paras 28–126—28–130 below) would mean that, by the time of trial, the injunction will be of little or no practical value.

[84] *Polly Peck v Nadir (No.2)* [1992] 2 Lloyd's Rep. 238; [1992] 4 All E.R. 769, at 785, per Lord Donaldson MR. In that case, the Court declined to make a freezing injunction against the Central Bank of Northern Cyprus, which would have had the effect of preventing the bank from repaying depositors, causing a run on the bank and would interfere with the bank's business to the extent that it could destroy it altogether. The claim was brought by the administrators of Polly Peck, a substantial public company which had gone into administration with an estimated deficiency of £1 billion. The administrators made claims against the majority owner and chief executive of Polly Peck for misapplication of funds. The Central Bank was the recipient of some £55 million of those funds, via a bank in the control of the CEO, and claims were made against it on the basis that it held those funds on constructive trust on the basis that it knew or shut its eyes to the fact that they represented the proceeds of a breach of fiduciary duty. The Court of Appeal weighed up the strength of the claim against the effect continuing the freezing injunction would have on the Central Bank, and the effect that discharging the injunction would have on Polly Peck. The Court concluded that the claim was, as against the Central Bank, speculative at least at the stage of seeking a freezing injunction. Conversely, it was inevitable that the injunction would interfere with the bank's business, possibly to the point of destroying it. The balance came down in favour of discharging the injunction.

[85] E.g. the court may take account of the fact that the applicant has relied upon illegally obtained evidence: see *Dubai Aluminium Co Ltd v Al Alawi* [1999] 1 W.L.R. 1964.

[86] See the full analysis of the law in *Boreh v Republic of Djibouti* [2015] EWHC 769 (Comm), at [232] and following. There is also an overlap here with the law of fair presentation.

[87] *Memory Corp Plc v Sidhu* [2000] 1 W.L.R. 1443.

[88] *Barros Mattos v MacDaniels* [2003] EWHC 1173 (Ch).

his own fraudulent conduct was essentially a pre-requisite for such a claim[89]. But an applicant who is found to have obtained a freezing injunction as part of a vendetta against the respondent, waged through multiple sets of proceedings, in circumstances where costs orders remain unsatisfied in related proceedings might well expect to have the application refused, or if already made, the injunction discharged.[90]

28–060   Further factors will be relevant to the question of whether relief is just and convenient when what is sought is an order affecting dealings with the respondent's assets worldwide. We address this in the following section.

C.   INTERNATIONAL ASPECTS: WORLDWIDE FREEZING ORDERS AND APPLICATIONS UNDER SECTION 25 CJJA

(1)   Introduction

28–061   Originally *Mareva* relief was confined to defendants out of the jurisdiction who held assets within it, and was concerned with preventing them from removing such assets from the jurisdiction; and it was only available where it was invoked in support of a substantive claim proceeding before (or which would proceed before) the English court.

28–062   However, the law has since developed significantly, in order that the essential purpose of freezing order relief—to prevent the abuse of the court's processes by the unjustified dissipation of assets which otherwise might be available to meet a future judgment—can still be achieved in a world where commerce, the holding of wealth and litigation itself have become increasing international. In the modern world, where the wealthy are accustomed to distributing their wealth internationally and where those who have acquired their assets by wrongful means often have a particular taste for adopting the most complex offshore structures for that purpose[91], it would be absurd if the court seized of the substantive proceedings could not, as a protective measure, grant injunctive relief in relation to overseas assets. It would equally be absurd if the Court was not able to act, at least with respect to assets within the jurisdiction, in support of proceedings brought by a claimant elsewhere.

28–063   The former has been achieved by a process of judicial development of the *Mareva* jurisdiction since the 1980s. Courts are now prepared in principle to grant injunctions against defendants whether they are located here or abroad,[92] freezing assets located abroad, even when there are no assets owned by the defendant

---

[89] *Kazakhstan Kagazy v Zhunus* [2016] EWCA Civ 1036; [2017] 1 W.L.R. 1360.

[90] *Sargespace Ltd v Eustace* [2014] EWHC 1095 (QB).

[91] See, for example, the observations of Christopher Clarke LJ (in the context of a post-judgment freezing injunction) upon Mr Mukhtar Ablyazov's "arrangement of his affairs through a myriad of companies in various jurisdictions with a view to hiding the enormous sums he had stolen from the JSC BTA Bank": *JSC BTA Bank v Ablyazov* [2014] EWCA Civ 602, at [3].

[92] See *AJ Bekhor & Co Ltd v Bilton* [1981] 1 Q.B. 923, at 936, and what is now s.37(3) of the Senior Courts Act 1981.

within the jurisdiction.[93] Where the overseas assets in question are located in a territory with which there is a degree of reciprocity in relation to the recognition of judgments and interim measures—so that there is a reasonable prospect of having the injunction declared enforceable against affected third parties under what has become known as the "*Babanaft* proviso"[94]—the case for the English court having power to restrain a defendant from unwarranted and prejudicial dealings with those assets becomes even stronger.

The latter (the ability of the English Court to grant freezing relief in aid of foreign **28–064** proceedings) has required the intervention of Parliament, in the form of s.25 of the Civil Jurisdiction and Judgments Act 1982 (the "CJJA") and subordinate legislation made under it.

(2) Principles which the Court will Apply in Deciding Whether to Grant a Worldwide Freezing Order

The ability of the court to grant injunctive relief in relation to assets outside the **28–065** jurisdiction flows from the fact that it is exercising an in personam jurisdiction against the defendant. It is an inevitable reflection of two of three principles—the "enforcement principle" and the "principle of flexibility"—which have been identified as underpinning the grant of any freezing injunction.[95] Proper recognition of the need for effective interim measures means that in some cases it will be appropriate to restrain the defendant (wherever he resides) from dealing with overseas assets pending judgment in the proceedings.[96]

While an application for a worldwide as opposed to domestic freezing injunction **28–066** does not engage a different test, when considering whether it is just and convenient to make the order, it is incumbent on the applicant to persuade the Court that factors exist justifying the additional intrusion on the respondent of extending the order to his assets outside the jurisdiction. The factors that the Court will consider include:

---

[93] See generally *Derby & Co Ltd v Weldon (Nos. 3 & 4)* [1990] Ch. 65, at 77–80, per Lord Donaldson MR, recently re-confirmed in *Great Station Properties S.A. v UMS Holding Ltd* [2017] EWHC 3330 (Comm).

[94] *Babanaft International Co S.A. v Bassatne* [1990] Ch. 13.

[95] Per Beatson LJ in *JSC BTA Bank v Ablyazov* [2013] EWCA Civ 928; [2014] 1 W.L.R. 1414, at [34]–[37]. The third principle, which creates some tension with the second, is the principle of strict construction. In relation to the flexibility principle, the judge referred to the jurisdiction being exercised in "a flexible and adaptable manner so as to be able to deal with new situations and new ways used by sophisticated and wily operators to make themselves immune to the courts' orders or deliberately to thwart the effective enforcement of those orders." It should be noted that the "flexibility principle" may not be used to interpret any given order: *JSC BTA Bank v Ablyazov* [2015] UKSC 64; [2015] 1 W.L.R. 4754, at [18].

[96] Whilst s.37(3) of the Senior Courts Act 1981 expressly refers to the court's power to restrain a party to any proceedings from removing from the jurisdiction of the High Court, or otherwise dealing with, *assets located within that jurisdiction*, this does not operate to cut down the width of s.37(1), which has no such territorial limitation. The focus of s.37(3) is to ensure that there is no discrimination against overseas parties by making it clear that (in relation to such assets within the jurisdiction) the power also extends to respondents who are domiciled, resident or present within the jurisdiction. See *Babanaft International Co S.A. v Bassatne* [1990] Ch. 13, at 27A.

   (1)   The location and nature of the assets in question;
   (2)   The level of additional disruption caused to the defendant, particularly if the defendant trades internationally;
   (3)   The effect on third parties;
   (4)   The nature of and effect on the litigation, including the risk of satellite litigation;
   (5)   The costs consequences.

28–067   **Nature and Location of Assets.**   The essential matter to be addressed when an applicant is contemplating seeking a worldwide freezing injunction, over and above the considerations which would apply to the exercise of the court's discretion in relation to a purely domestic injunction, is whether or not the defendant either has no assets or insufficient assets within the jurisdiction to satisfy any judgment which might be obtained, so that (assuming the court is satisfied as to the existence of overseas assets and that a real risk of dissipation in relation to them exists) it is appropriate to include overseas assets within the restraint. As it was put in the leading case of *Derby & Co Ltd v Weldon (Nos. 3 & 4)*[97]:

> "in the first instance [the court] should look to assets within the jurisdiction and that in the majority of cases[98] there will be no justification for looking to foreign assets…. The existence of sufficient assets within the jurisdiction is an excellent reason for confining the jurisdiction to such assets, but, other considerations apart, the fewer the assets within the jurisdiction the greater the necessity for taking protective measures in relation to those outside it."

28–068   Particularly in fraud cases, the nature of the overseas assets may well factor into the Court's determination. While the use of offshore structures, involving a discretionary trust or similar, has become commonplace in international fraud litigation, it remains a factor in favour of the grant of a freezing injunction with extraterritorial scope. Assets held in such structures can often be more easily moved or put out of reach of creditors; that is in some cases their very purpose. The granting of a worldwide freezing injunction may allow a claimant to take steps at a local level, by way of recognition or the acquisition of ancillary orders, to prevent or reduce the risk of such steps being taken.

28–069   **Disruption to the Defendant.**   The increased potential for disruption to a defendant's affairs by a freezing injunction with worldwide effect, particularly in the case of a company trading internationally, is obvious. Correspondingly, the claimant will have to produce more cogent evidence to persuade the Court that the balance of justice and convenience is in favour of the grant of an injunction than he would in support of a purely domestic freezing injunction.

---

[97] *Derby & Co Ltd v Weldon (Nos. 3 & 4)* [1990] 1 Ch. 65, at 79, per Lord Donaldson. The proportion of freezing orders made on a worldwide basis is now considerably greater than it was almost 30 years ago when these observations were made.

[98] In the more than quarter of a century that has since elapsed it is doubtful that it can still be said with confidence that in the "majority of cases" there will be "no justification for looking to foreign assets."

Effect on Third Parties Located Abroad. The extraterritorial development of **28–070** the *Mareva* jurisdiction and the consequent potential for interference with the position of third parties who were resident abroad and not subject to the court's jurisdiction was summarised by Millett LJ in *Credit Suisse Fides Trust S.A. v Cuoghi*[99] as follows:

> "The Mareva jurisdiction was established in 1975 as an exceptional remedy to prevent a foreign defendant from defeating any ultimate judgment by removing his assets from the jurisdiction. It was progressively extended, in 1979 to English defendants, in 1982 by restraining defendants from dissipating their assets within the jurisdiction as well as removing them from the jurisdiction, and finally in 1990 by restraining defendants from dealing with their assets both inside and outside the jurisdiction. This last step was taken in *Babanaft International Co S.A. v. Bassatne* [1990] Ch. 13, in which the court was concerned not to make an unwarranted assumption of extraterritorial jurisdiction. It recognised that it would be wrong to make an order which, though purporting merely to restrain the actions of a defendant already subject to the jurisdiction of the court, might be understood to impose obligations upon persons resident abroad and not subject to its jurisdiction. This danger was avoided by including provisions in the order which made it clear that it was not to affect parties not subject to the jurisdiction of the court in respect of acts outside the jurisdiction save to the extent that the order might be enforced by the local courts. The jurisdiction to make such orders is now firmly established. It is exercised with caution, and a sufficient case to justify its exercise must always be made out; but such orders are nowadays routinely made in cases of international fraud and the conditions necessary in order to preserve international comity and prevent conflicts of jurisdiction have become standardised."

In *Babanaft International Co S.A. v Bassatne*[100] (where the application for relief **28–071** was made after judgment had been obtained against the defendants) Kerr LJ observed that, although freezing injunctions are made in personam against the defendant, they have an in rem effect upon third parties. For that reason, unqualified injunctions (meaning those which do not specify how and when their terms might affect overseas third parties) can never be justified

> "because they involve an exorbitant assertion of jurisdiction of an *in rem* nature over third parties outside the jurisdiction of the courts."(at 35F).

Indeed, Kerr LJ expressed the view that the key to the proper exercise of any extraterritorial jurisdiction must lie in the question of whether there is international reciprocity for the recognition of and enforcement of the type of order which is under consideration; and all the members of the court relied upon the terms of what is now art.35 of the recast Judgments Regulation in relation to the recognition by the courts of one member state of provisional or protective orders made by the courts of another.[101]

Today the grant of worldwide freezing injunctions is commonplace and the **28–072** standard terms of such relief are set out in the sample forms of freezing injunction annexed to both Practice Direction 25A in the Civil Procedure Rules and the Admiralty and Commercial Courts Guide. These standard forms contain (at paras 19 and 20 of the example annexed to PD25A) the "*Babanaft* proviso" protecting

---

[99] *Credit Suisse Fides Trust S.A. v Cuoghi* [1998] Q.B. 818, at 824E–824H.
[100] *Babanaft International Co S.A. v Bassatne* [1990] Ch. 13.
[101] Kerr LJ described this as "the secondary and entirely distinct effect" of the article in contrast to the primary one which is reflected in the ability of the English court to grant injunctive relief in aid of foreign proceedings under s.25 of the CJJA 1982, at 30H.

the interests (and obligations) of third parties who are not subject to the jurisdiction of the English court. We discuss the *Babanaft* proviso in greater detail below.[102]

28–073   Effect on Litigation.   The grant of a worldwide freezing injunction can have a substantial detrimental effect on the English litigation as well as (or often caused by) its propensity to cause satellite litigation in other jurisdictions, such as applications to enforce the order locally. Such satellite litigation may involve the parties themselves or third parties affected by the order and can cause significant distraction from and delay to the main proceedings in which the injunction is granted. That is another reason why the jurisdiction to grant worldwide relief is to be exercised with caution, and only if a "sufficient cause" for it can be made out.

28–074   Cost Consequences.   The Court will be mindful of the increased cost consequences of a worldwide freezing injunction, not only because of the possibility of satellite litigation and the effect on the English litigation, but also the likelihood that the cost of policing the freezing injunction will increase. This bears on the proportionality of the relief, and thus the justice and convenience of granting it.

(3)   Orders under Section 25 of the CJJA

28–075   The scope of the court's jurisdiction under s.25 of the CJJA is addressed more fully in Ch.26. As more fully explained there, when considering whether and if so how to exercise its discretion to grant relief under s.25, the court adopts a two-stage approach:

(1)   First, it considers whether the facts would warrant the relief sought if the proceedings were brought in England. This means that an applicant for relief under s.25 will first have to address the requirements for obtaining a freezing injunction discussed in this chapter above.[103] Consistent with the fact that at this first stage the court must treat itself as if it were the primary court seised of the substantive proceedings, the judge is required to conduct a separate exercise of judgement on these evidential matters rather than simply accept any decision or indication upon them by the foreign court (whatever might be the applicable standards of proof in that court).[104]

(2)   Secondly, if the court concludes at that first stage that interim relief would be appropriate if the substantive claim was a domestic one, the court goes on to consider (as required by the provisions of s.25(2)) whether it is expedient to grant that relief: that is, does the fact that the proceedings are taking place outside the jurisdiction make it inexpedient to grant the type of relief sought?

---

[102] At paras 28–151—28–156.
[103] In *Refco Inc v Eastern Trading Co* [1999] 1 Lloyd's Rep. 159 the Court of Appeal concluded that the applicant failed at this first stage of establishing that there was a real risk of dissipation of assets that would have justified relief if the proceedings had been taking place in England.
[104] *Motorola Credit Corp v Uzan (No.2)* [2003] EWCA Civ 752; [2004] 1 W.L.R. 113, at [102].

In *ICICI Bank UK Plc v Diminco NV*[105] Popplewell J expressed the principles to be derived from the authorities discussed in Ch.26 so far as they applied to the grant of freezing orders by the English court in support of foreign proceedings as follows:

28–076

"(1)   It will only be appropriate to exercise jurisdiction to grant a freezing order where a defendant has no assets here and owes no allegiance to the English court by the existence of *in personam* jurisdiction over him, whether by way of domicile or residence or for some other reason. Protective measures should normally be left to the courts where the assets are to be found or where the defendant resides or is for some other reason subject to *in personam* jurisdiction.

(2)   Where there is reason to believe that the defendant has assets within the jurisdiction, the English court will often be the appropriate court to grant protective measures by way of a domestic freezing order over such assets, and that is so whether or not the defendant is resident within the jurisdiction or for some other reason is someone over whom the English court would assume *in personam* jurisdiction.

(3)   Where the defendant is resident within the jurisdiction, or is someone over whom the court has *in personam* jurisdiction for some other reason, a worldwide freezing order may be granted applying the discretionary considerations which were explained in the *Cuoghi, Motorola* and *Banque Nationale* cases.

(4)   Where the defendant is neither resident within the jurisdiction nor someone over whom the court has or would assume *in personam* jurisdiction for some other reason, the court will only grant a freezing order extending to foreign assets in exceptional circumstances. It is likely to be necessary for the applicant to establish at least three things:

(a)   that there is a real connecting link between the subject matter of the measure sought and the territorial jurisdiction of the English court in the sense referred to in *Van Uden*;

(b)   that the case is one where it is appropriate within the limits of comity for the English court to act as an international policeman in relation to assets abroad; and that will not be appropriate unless it is practical for an order to be made and unless the order can be enforced in practice if it is disobeyed; the court will not make an order even within the limits of comity if there is no effective sanction which it could apply if the order were disobeyed, as will often be the case if the defendant has no presence within the jurisdiction and is not subject to the *in personam* of the English court;

(c)   it is just and expedient to grant worldwide relief, taking into account the discretionary factors identified at paragraph 115 of the *Motorola* case. They are

(i)   whether the making of the order will interfere with the management of the case in the primary court, e.g. where the order is inconsistent with an order in the primary court or overlaps with it;

(ii)   whether it is the policy in the primary jurisdiction not itself to make to make worldwide freezing/disclosure orders;

(iii)   whether there is a danger that the orders made will give rise to disharmony or confusion and/or risk of conflicting, inconsistent or overlapping orders in other jurisdictions, in particular the courts of the state where the person enjoined resides or where the assets affected are located;

(iv)   whether at the time the order is sought there is likely to be a potential conflict as to jurisdiction rendering it inappropriate and inexpedient to make a worldwide order; and

(v)   whether in a case where jurisdiction is resisted and disobedience may be expected the court will be making an order which it cannot enforce. "

---

[105] *ICICI Bank UK Plc v Diminco NV* [2014] EWHC 3124 (Comm); [2014] 2 C.L.C. 647, at [27].

D. PRINCIPAL FEATURES OF THE STANDARD FORMS OF FREEZING INJUNCTION

(1) Introduction

28–077 This section of the Chapter addresses the most significant features of the standard forms of freezing injunction annexed to:

(a) CPR Practice Direction 25A and
(b) the Admiralty and Commercial Courts Guide.

The two versions are almost identical; but they differ in certain additional wording provided for in the Commercial Court standard form when defining what constitutes the respondent's assets within the scope of the injunction. The significance of this difference, and the question more generally of what assets are caught by the injunction in the standard form terms, are addressed below.

28–078 Although they are the standard forms, they are not immutable. Paragraph 6 of Practice Direction 25A says of its example freezing injunction:

> "This example may be modified, as appropriate in any particular case. In particular, the court may, if it considers appropriate, require the applicant's solicitors, as well as the applicant, to give undertakings".

Indeed it will often be incumbent on the applicant to change the standard form to meet the circumstances of the case. The applicant and his lawyers have an active duty to consider very carefully the precise terms of the order being sought. The mere fact that the standard form is cast in particular terms does not ipso facto mean that it is appropriate to the given case.

28–079 On the other hand, the "compelling duty" upon the applicant at an ex parte application of full and frank disclosure (see generally Ch.27) extends to his advocate's duty to bring to the attention of the court any departure from the standard form in the relief which is proposed.[106] One convenient and sensible way of doing this is to produce a draft which shows, by way of mark-up, any departure from the norm.[107]

28–080 Whatever form of order is sought, the applicant should ensure that its terms are clear. A court will not make an order which is not readily comprehensible to the respondent (or to third parties who may be affected by it) and, in any event, even if an order lacking clarity is made, any ambiguity on the face of the order may prevent enforcement by committal.[108]

---

[106] *Memory Corp Plc v Sidhu (No.1)* [2000] 1 W.L.R. 1443, at 1454–1455, 1459–1460, where there had been a non-deliberate misrepresentation by counsel that certain paragraphs of the draft order were in standard form.

[107] As was done, for example, in *Ras Al Khaimah Investment Authority v Bestfort Development LLP* [2015] EWHC 3383 (Ch), at [63].

[108] Authority in this regard is legion. In the context of freezing orders see *JSC BTA Bank v Ablyazov (No.10)* [2015] UKSC 64; [2015] 1 W.L.R. 4754 and *Federal Bank of the Middle East v Hadkinson* [2000] 1 W.L.R. 1695.

(2) Approach to Construction

This last observation brings us to the approach that the Court takes to interpreting **28–081** freezing injunctions (be they in the standard form or otherwise). As we have noted above, in *JSC BTA Bank v Ablyazov*,[109] in the Court of Appeal, Beatson LJ identified three principles of potential relevance to the construction of freezing injunctions:

(a) the "enforcement principle", which we have set out in the introduction to this chapter (that the purpose of a freezing order is to stop the defendant dissipating or disposing of property which could be the subject of enforcement if the claimant goes on to win the claim, but not to give the claimant security for his claim);

(b) the "flexibility principle" (that the jurisdiction to make a freezing order should be exercised in a flexible and adaptable manner so as to be able to deal with new situations and new ways that defendant might make themselves immune to orders or deliberately thwart their enforcement); and

(c) the "strict construction" principle. The latter was explained by Beatson LJ in the following terms[110]:

> "The third principle follows from the 'fundamental requirement of an injunction directed to an individual that it shall be certain': *Z Ltd v A-Z and AA-LL* [1982] QB 558 , 582 , per Eveleigh LJ. It is that, because of the penal consequences of breaching a freezing order and the need of the defendant to know where he, she or it stands, such orders should be clear and unequivocal, and should be strictly construed: *Haddonstone Ltd v Sharp* [1996] F.S.R. 767, per Rose and Stuart-Smith LJJ at 773 and 775; *Federal Bank of the Middle East Ltd v Hadkinson* [2000] 1 W.L.R. 1695, per Mummery and Nourse LJJ at 1705C and 1713C–1713D . In *Anglo Eastern Trust Ltd v Kermanshahgi* [2002] EWHC 1702 (Ch) Neuberger J stated: 'A freezing order, which has been referred to as a nuclear weapon, should . . . be construed strictly' because the court is 'concerned with an order which has a potentially draconian effect on the commercial and economic freedom of an individual against whom no substantive judgment has yet been granted'."

On appeal the Supreme Court confirmed that the question of whether given assets **28–082** and dealings with them were caught by the terms of a freezing injunction was a question of construction of the order; and that the "enforcement" and "strict construction" principles were relevant to that exercise.[111] The "flexibility principle" was not, however[112]:

---

[109] *JSC BTA Bank v Ablyazov* [2013] EWCA Civ 928; [2014] 1 W.L.R. 1414, at [34] and following.
[110] *JSC BTA Bank v Ablyazov* [2013] EWCA Civ 928; [2014] 1 W.L.R. 1414, at [37].
[111] See also *Federal Bank of the Middle East Ltd v Hadkinson* [2000] 1 W.L.R. 1695, per Mummery LJ at 1709–1711: "It is necessary to examine the context in which the expression is used and, in particular, to identify the purpose of making the freezing order." That purpose was described as follows: "The order is designed to prevent injustice to a successful claimant by preserving assets and funds and guarding so far as possible against the risk that they will be disposed of or dissipated before a judgment is satisfied so as to render ineffective the claimant's attempts to recover what is due to him."
[112] *JSC BTA Bank v Ablyazov* [2015] UKSC 64; [2015] 1 W.L.R. 4754, at [18]. See also *Sans Souci Ltd v VRL Services Ltd* [2012] UKPC 6, at [13]–[15] for the principle of construing a court order against the background in which it was made.

"As Mr Crow colourfully put it, the flexibility principle is that the court must be agile in this game of cat and mouse between claimants and defendants to make sure that it is making new orders to meet new avoidance measures, but that is not a justification for the expansive interpretation of an order which has already been made. I agree."

28–083 Further, a freezing order should be construed in its context, which, in the case of one using the standard forms, includes the historical evolution of those forms (something which we address below).[113] The submissions made at the hearing of the application and the intentions of the particular judge making the order are not relevant, however.[114]

(3) The Penal Notice

28–084 A freezing injunction is effective from the moment it is notified to the respondent against whom it has in personam effect. Formal service is not required for the respondent to be potentially liable in contempt.

28–085 If any later breach of the injunction is to be amenable to enforcement by an application for committal in accordance with CPR 81.4 then the freezing order must generally[115] be served with a penal notice prominently displayed[116] on its front in accordance with CPR 81.9. The Pt 81 Practice Direction sets out the form of wording which should be used. The standard forms expand upon that wording, by also addressing the position of persons other than the respondent who may knowingly facilitate such a breach, as follows:

"PENAL NOTICE
If you [ ] disobey this order you may be held to be in contempt of court and may be imprisoned, fined or have your assets seized.
Any other person who knows of this order and does anything which helps or permits the Respondent to top breach the terms of this order you may also be held to be in contempt of court and may be imprisoned, fined or have their assets seized."

28–086 The exposure of any third party who knowingly assists in a breach of the order does not stop with the possible punishment of committal, sequestration of assets or a fine. Subject to any jurisdictional issues which may affect the claimant's ability to sue in England, where the third party has connived with the respondent to procure a breach of the freezing injunction a claim for "unlawful means conspiracy" may well lie against him.[117]

---

[113] *JSC BTA Bank v Ablyazov* [2015] UKSC 64; [2015] 1 W.L.R. 4754, at [21] and [26]; and see the analysis of the evolution of the standard forms in *JSC BTA Bank v Solodchenko* [2010] EWCA Civ 1436; [2011] 1 W.L.R. 888, at [17] and following.

[114] *JSC BTA Bank v Solodchenko* [2010] EWCA Civ 1436; [2011] 1 W.L.R. 888, at [14].

[115] The court has a discretion to waive the requirement: see paras 35–015—35–016.

[116] The penal notice is generally printed in bold capitals to increase its prominence.

[117] See the decision of the Supreme Court in *JSC BTA Bank v Khrapunov* [2018] UKSC 19, upholding the first instance judge's decision (in the context of a challenge to the jurisdiction) that contempt of court by the concealment and dissipation of assets in breach of a freezing injunction can constitute "unlawful means" for the purposes of the tort. In *Surzur Overseas Ltd v Koros* [1999] 2 Lloyd's Rep. 611 the Court of Appeal held that a claim of conspiracy to injure by unlawful means in the form of the procuring and deploying in court of false evidence to deceive the court into varying a *Mareva* to release assets was properly arguable. Waller LJ held, at 619, that "a conspiracy which had

(4)   Paragraph 1 and the Applicant's Undertakings

Paragraph 1 of the standard form order informs the respondent that the order is a **28–087** freezing injunction, identifies the affidavit evidence read by the judge (as listed in Sch.A) and recites the applicant's undertakings as set out in Sch.B.

The giving of such undertakings is an integral part of the order and an essential **28–088** ingredient in the court's consideration of the justice and convenience of the proposed relief: it is, as has often been observed, the "price" which the applicant must give for the obtaining of such invasive relief. Breaches of undertakings are of course contempts of court and can lead, in a serious case, to the discharge of the order.[118]

The usual undertakings by the applicant include the following: **28–089**

(1)   Cross-undertakings in damages both in relation to the respondent and the costs and losses of third parties (most obviously banks and others who are put to expense in order to comply with the order): see the discussion of the principles governing the giving—and possible fortification—of these at Ch.27 above.[119]

(2)   If the claim has not yet been issued, an undertaking as soon as practicable (i.e. the same or next working day, depending on the time the order is made) to issue and serve the Claim Form (in the form of any draft produced to the court).[120] This is an important obligation because, subject to

---

as its aim and objective defeating an order of the Court and obtaining the release from a *Mareva* of assets by persons who were not ... parties to the original action, must be a conspiracy to abuse the process very akin to the malicious arrest which was the subject of *Roy v Prior*". Compare the absence of a claim in negligence against a bank which had been informed of a freezing injunction but which had failed to prevent payments out of the frozen account: see *Customs and Excise Commissioners v Barclays Bank Plc* [2007] 1 A.C. 181.

[118] The law was stated by Neuberger J in *Flightwise Travel Services Ltd v Gill* [2003] EWHC 3082 (Ch), at [28] "Thirdly, it is important that undertakings given by an applicant, effectively in return for which the freezing order is granted, are complied with, and if they are not that there is a good explanation as to why. The fact that there is a failure to comply with an undertaking given by the applicant to the court, in return for which the injunction was granted, is a potentially serious matter and may, in appropriate circumstances, justify the discharge of the injunction. Bearing in mind the nature and effect of a freezing order, and the fact that it is granted initially ex parte, an applicant should be in no doubt that the court will regard any failure to comply with an undertaking given in the freezing order itself is seriously viewed [*sic*]. Of course, if the breach of the undertaking does not cause the respondent, or anyone else, any damage that would be a mitigating factor. But it does not discharge the gravity of failure to comply." This principle was applied in *Gorbunova v Berezovsky (aka Platon Elenin)* [2013] EWHC 76 (Ch), at [47]*ff.*

[119] A detailed exposition of the rights of third parties notified of freezing orders is beyond the remit of this book: for a discussion of the principles see *Alpha Bank v Vardinoyiannis* [2013] EWHC 4220 (Comm); and *Energy Venture Partners Ltd v Malabu Oil and Gas Ltd* [2012] EWHC 853 (Comm). Both cases show that the courts are inclined to generosity towards innocent third parties caught up, as a result of the grant of a freezing order, in the disputes of others. The courts are prepared to summarily assess third party costs. As observed by Robert Goff J in *Searose Ltd v Seatrain UK Ltd* [1981] 1 W.L.R. 894, at 897, care must be taken to ensure that freezing injunctions do not bear harshly upon innocent third parties: "If these principles are not observed, a weapon which was forged to prevent abuse may become an instrument of oppression".

[120] Where *Chabra* relief is sought against an "NCAD" ("Non-Cause of Action Defendant") (see paras 28–157—28–196 below) there is "a considerable degree of procedural flexibility in determining how

exceptions discussed above, a freezing order cannot be made in the absence of a substantive claim being pursued in the English court, and it is incumbent on any applicant to progress the underlying litigation with expedition.[121]

(3)   In any ex parte order, an undertaking to serve upon the respondent as soon as practicable a copy of the order; copies of the affidavits and exhibits containing the evidence relied upon by the applicant in support of the order and any other documents provided to the court on the making of the application, the claim form (if not already served) and an application notice for continuation of the order. If the evidence relied upon before the judge was only in draft then the applicant will be required to undertake to cause the affidavit(s) to be sworn, filed and served.

(4)   The standard form also includes an undertaking by the applicant to confirm in evidence the substance of what was said to the court by his counsel or solicitor (which is often done by exhibiting a note of the submissions made to the judge).[122] A respondent will clearly be interested, and legitimately so, in knowing what passed between counsel for the applicant and the judge at the ex parte hearing; indeed it is a strict requirement that the respondent should be so informed, not least so that he may assess whether there was any injustice in the granting of the order which may give rise to challenge.[123]

(5)   An undertaking that any other person notified of the order will be given a copy of it by the applicant's solicitors.

(6)   An undertaking, in the event of the order ceasing to have effect (for example, if the respondent provides security or the applicant does not provide any bank guarantee which may be required to fortify the cross-undertaking in damages), immediately to take all reasonable steps to inform in writing anyone to whom the applicant has given notice of the order, or who he has reasonable grounds for supposing may act upon the order, that it has ceased to have effect.

(7)   An undertaking not without the permission of the court to use any information obtained as a result of the order for the purpose of any civil or criminal proceedings, either in England and Wales or in any other jurisdiction, other than the claim.

---

the issue between the claimant and the third-party respondent is best to be resolved" and, although that question should be addressed at an early stage, it may not require an immediate undertaking to commence proceedings against that party: per Henderson J in *Franses (Liquidator of Arab News Network Ltd) v Al Assad* [2007] EWHC 2442 (Ch), at [80].

[121] *Société Générale v Goldas Kuyumculuk Sanayi Ithalat Ihracat AS* [2017] EWHC 667 (Comm), where the claimants were in breach of their undertaking to issue and serve a claim form in the form produced to the court in draft as soon as practicable. The judge stated the general principle as follows, at [57]: "where a party obtains the draconian remedy of a freezing order, it is incumbent upon it to progress the proceedings expeditiously, unless the Court sanctions delay. A failure to do so is an abuse of process." A breach of this undertaking is not only a contempt of court; it is also an abuse of process which may be sanctioned by the striking out of the claim.

[122] See *Interoute Telecommunications (UK) Ltd v Fashion Gossip Ltd*, *The Times*, 10 November 1999 and *Thane Investments Ltd v Tomlinson* [2003] EWCA Civ 1272, at [18]–[19] noted in para.27–029 above.

[123] *Gill v Flightwise Travel Service* [2003] EWHC 3082 (Ch), at [20]–[22].

(8)　In the case of a worldwide freezing injunction, an undertaking not without the permission of the court to seek to enforce the order in any country outside England and Wales or seek an order of a similar nature including orders conferring a charge or other security against the respondent or the respondent's assets.[124] Such an undertaking is appropriate in a worldwide freezing injunction where the English court has been prepared to exercise its "exorbitant" in personam jurisdiction given its potential impact for third parties overseas: see para.28–070 above and the *Babanaft* proviso explained below. The undertaking not to seek similar relief elsewhere or to seek to improve upon the protection given by the order, without the permission of the court, is clearly an important factor in the exercise of that jurisdiction. The factors (the *Dadourian Guidelines*) which govern the exercise of the court's discretion in granting permission to enforce abroad are set out in *Dadourian Group International Ltd v Simms (Practice Note)*.[125] They focus upon what is just and convenient for the purpose of ensuring the order is effective, the avoidance of oppression to the respondent and to third parties (whose costs of the enforcement process may need to be compensated), proportionality, and the guidance that

> "permission should not normally be given in terms that would enable the applicant to obtain relief in the foreign proceedings which is superior to the relief given by the worldwide freezing order."(at [25], per Arden LJ).

(5)　The Return Date and Liberty to Apply

Any freezing injunction granted ex parte will invariably provide for a return date and para.3 of the standard form provides that there "will be a further hearing in respect of this order on [*date*] ('the return date')". This is a vital safeguard to ensure that the case is re-considered as soon as reasonably possible with all parties present. Tactical and other considerations which arise at the return date are addressed in detail in Ch.32 below.　**28–090**

In the Commercial Court the return date will usually be 14 days after the grant of the injunction, particularly where parties are outside the jurisdiction.[126] The Chancery Division judges tend to fix somewhat earlier return dates. In practice in heavy cases the return date will be treated as a form of case management conference with directions being given if the respondent wishes to challenge the ex parte relief substantively.　**28–091**

---

[124] The effect of this undertaking was considered in *Akcine Bendrove Bankas Snoras v Antonov* [2018] EWHC 887 (Comm), in which Mr Eggers QC (sitting as a deputy) held that the undertaking barred the applicant from taking unsanctioned steps to enforce the freezing order in other jurisdictions, or to take steps which accounted in substance to the same thing. However, it did not bar the applicant from referring to the fact of the English freezing order when applying for orders to be granted by the independent decisons of foreign courts, see [40]–[54]. See also *Hewlett Packard v Bhandari* [2013] EWHC 4647 (Ch), at [22]–[25].

[125] *Dadourian Group International Ltd v Simms (Practice Note)* [2006] EWCA Civ 399; [2006] 1 W.L.R. 2499.

[126] See S. Gee, *Commercial Injunctions*, 6th edn (London: Sweet & Maxwell, 2016), para.A3–003.

28–092 In addition to notifying the respondent that there will be a further hearing in respect of the order on the specified return date, the standard form also informs him and any other person served with or notified of the order that they may apply "at any time" to set aside or vary the order. Paragraph 13 of the standard form makes provision that:

> "Anyone served with or notified of this order may apply to the court at any time to vary or discharge this order (or so much of it as affects that person), but they must first inform the Applicant's solicitors. If any evidence is to be relied upon in support of the application, the substance of it must be communicated in writing to the Applicant's solicitors in advance."[127]

28–093 This provision reflects the fact that an ex parte freezing order has (necessarily) been made without hearing from the respondent. Such a respondent cannot be constrained in his ability to complain about the terms of the relief granted against him by the fixing of a return date which he necessarily had no part in deciding upon. If the order is causing immediate prejudice to the respondent he can return to court in advance of the return date to seek to remedy that prejudice, subject only to the prior notification obligations prescribed in the wording quoted above.[128] The same is true for third parties.[129] For instance, where a joint bank account is held by the respondent husband and his wife a freezing order against the husband would prevent dealings with the account and hence the wife might wish to apply back to the court to allow her to utilise it free from the order.

(6)   The Subject Matter and Scope of the Freezing Injunction

(i)   Domestic or worldwide

28–094 The considerations which determine whether a domestic or worldwide freezing injunction should be sought against the respondent are discussed in paras 28–065—28–074 above.

28–095 For an injunction limited to assets in England and Wales the wording of the order (as set out in para.5) is as follows:

> "Until the return date or further order of the court, the Respondent must not remove from England and Wales or in any way dispose of, deal with or diminish the value of any of his assets which are in England and Wales up to the value of £X."

---

[127] Paragraph F15.11 of the Commercial Court Guide provides that a bank or third party notified or affected by the order, who considers that the order affects it in a way that has implications for its anti-money laundering procedures, may apply to the court for directions, or notify the court in writing, without notice to any party.

[128] Though see F15.9 of the Commercial Court Guide, which provides that in an appropriate case the defendant can apply back to court on short notice and even on no notice at all. It was held in *London City Agency (JCD) v Lee* [1970] Ch. 597 that it was preferable, if time permitted, that any application to set aside or vary an injunction should be made upon due notice, but that there was no established rule of practice to prevent the court from granting such an application ex parte in a case of sufficient urgency, and where a case for doing so had been made out.

[129] See CPR 40.9, which provides expressly that a non-party directly affected by a judgment or order may apply to have it set aside.

For the restraint upon dealing with assets worldwide the wording is:

28–096

> "Until the return date or further order of the court, the Respondent must not—
> (1) remove from England and Wales any of his assets which are in England and Wales up to the value of £X; or
> (2) in any way dispose of, deal with or diminish the value of any of his assets whether they are in or outside England and Wales up to the same value. "

(ii) "Dispose of, deal with or diminish the value of"

It will be noted that the operative wording in each version of the order is the same. The respondent must not remove, dispose of, deal with or diminish in value any of his assets up to maximum sum.[130] Each of these prohibitions (expressed by the various verbs) is alternative to the other although no doubt a single act by the respondent may infringe more than one or all of the prohibitions. The drafting is compendious so as to ensure the efficacy of the order.[131] The meaning of these words has been subjected to detailed consideration in the authorities and it is clear that the ambit of the prohibition is broad. The words "dealing with" have been held to be "wide enough to include disposing of, selling, pledging or charging".[132] The authorities have further established that handing an asset over to a defendant who owns it and is subject to a freezing injunction does not fall foul of any of the prohibitions,[133] including payment of a sum of money.[134] In normal circumstances, transferring money from one account to another, provided the recipient account is in credit,[135] is not a disposition,[136] nor is borrowing money (even though it may increase the respondent's overall indebtedness).[137] In that sense, the prohibition on "dealing" with an asset, which is in theory of almost unlimited scope, should be looked at within the context of the purpose of a freezing injunction, namely to preserve assets for enforcement. A "dealing" which, for example, merely converts property into another form, without affecting its value or rendering enforcement more difficult, will generally not be prohibited.[138]

28–097

---

[130] Assets for these purposes include choses in action. So if a defendant is himself proceeding against a third party then he cannot settle that claim without the permission of the court because a settlement would involve a disposition of an asset. For the court's approach in such a situation see *Normid Housing Association Ltd v Ralphs and Mansell (No.2)* [1989] 1 Lloyd's Rep. 274.

[131] However some positive act is required on the part of the respondent for para.5 to be breached. Mere receipt of an asset from a third party is not a breach: see *Law Society v Shanks* [1988] 1 F.L.R. 504 and the cases discussed in Gee, *Commercial Injunctions* (2016), para.3–011 and following, and para.4–005 and following.

[132] *C.B.S. United Kingdom Ltd v Lambert* [1983] Ch. 37, at 42E.

[133] *The Law Society v Shanks* [1988] 1 F.L.R. 504.

[134] *Bank Mellat v Kazmi* [1989] Q.B. 541.

[135] *Re Gray's Inn Construction Co Ltd* [1980] 1 W.L.R. 711, at 715 in the context of a transaction prior to the winding up of a company.

[136] In *Re Barn Crown Ltd* [1995] 1 W.L.R. 147 in the context of a transaction prior to the winding up of a company.

[137] *Cantor Index Ltd v Lister* [2002] CP Rep. 25; but see now the Supreme Court decision in *JSC BTA Bank v Alblyazov* [2015] UKSC 64; [2015] 1 W.L.R. 4754 on directing a lender as to how to apply loan moneys drawn down under a facility (as to which, see paras 28–116—28–125 below).

[138] R. (on the application of Revenue and Customs Prosecutions Office) v R [2007] EWHC 2393 (Admin), in which McCombe J held that recovery between funds accounts held at a bank was

(iii) "...up to the value of...": Maximum sum orders

28–098 It will be seen that the standard form provides for a maximum sum to be frozen. This is because, in general, the applicant has a claim which is for a sum of money (whether fixed or to be assessed) and it would be inconsistent with the enforcement principle for the order to interfere with the respondent's freedom to deal with his assets beyond the value of what would be needed to meet the claim. As it was put by Norris J in *Willetts v Alvey*,[139]

> "it is the duty of a party having the benefit of a freezing order to ensure that it does no more than is necessary to protect the claim which that party has. A freezing order is not to be used as a weapon of oppression."

Hence it will be a rare case where the applicant is not required to specify such a sum.

28–099 The applicant should take care in choosing a figure to insert: inflating the figure may of course involve a breach of the duty of fair presentation at the without notice hearing (thereby risking the discharge of the order at the inter partes hearing); and it could also lead to liability under the cross-undertaking in damages, if it is later found that the respondent's liability to the applicant was significantly less than the amount frozen and the respondent suffers loss as a result of having been subject to an injunction to a greater extent than was justified.[140] Generally, the court will set the value of the assets frozen by reference to the highest sum in respect of which the applicant has made out a good arguable claim (together with interest up to the date of the putative judgment).[141]

28–100 The sum frozen may also include an amount referable to the applicant's incurred and anticipated costs of the action. Although it might be said that this amounts to giving security for costs without any basis for such an order being made out (indeed, giving security for a claimant's costs against a defendant, when such an order would generally only be made the other way round), the court is usually prepared to make some allowance in setting the maximum sum frozen for the anticipated recovery of litigation costs by the applicant.[142] It must be remembered

---

"dealing" in breach of a restraining order: see [18]–[21]. It may be that that decision should be treated as turning on its particular facts, and the particular terms of the order in that case.

[139] *Willetts v Alvey* [2010] EWHC 155 (Ch), at [15] (where the applicant liquidator had fixed the amount in the ex parte order by reference to the amount of the deficiency in the liquidation rather than the value of the transaction in respect of which the respondent was sought to be made liable) and applied by Tugenhadt J in *O'Farrell v O'Farrell* [2012] EWHC 123 (QB), at [86].

[140] A point made in *Atlas Maritime Company SA v Avalon Maritime Ltd (No.3)* [1991] 1 W.L.R. 917, at 920, per Lord Donaldson MR. For instance, if the sum stated in the freezing order was (say) £10million but the eventual judgment was for only £1million, the respondent might well be able to argue that if the sum frozen had been set at only £1million from the outset, then he would have been able to secure that sum and would not have been subject to the interference of a freezing order at all.

[141] See Gee, *Commercial Injunctions* (2016), para.4–009.

[142] See, for example, the observations of Lord Donaldson MR in *Atlas Maritime Company SA v Avalon Maritime Ltd (No. 3)* [1991] 1 W.L.R. 917, at 920D–920E, where the sum previously stipulated in the *Mareva* injunction had failed to take account of a potential entitlement to interest on the arbitration award and costs. See also *Charles Church Developments Plc v Cronin* [1990] F.S.R. 1,

that, first, a freezing order does not in fact give the applicant any sort of "security" interest, and, secondly, that a freezing injunction rests fundamentally upon establishing the risk of dissipation of assets rather than the kind of grounds (most obviously a fear of lack of available assets to meet a costs order) which justify an order for security for costs. Nevertheless, and no doubt in large part reflecting the fact that the applicant has only had to demonstrate a good arguable case on the merits and is "guesstimating" the amount of costs that may be incurred, the court tends to be quite conservative in any allowance for past and future costs in the amount frozen.[143] Further, it is clear that an anticipated costs order alone (associated with a claim which is not for a money sum) cannot justify the grant of a freezing injunction.[144]

It is common, where such information is available to claimants,[145] to include **28–101** specific assets within the scope of a freezing injunction as well as (or in lieu of) a maximum sum. The standard forms contemplate that specific assets of the respondent may be identified within the order. Identifying specific assets can have a number of advantages for a claimant, particularly where it enables him to reduce (or eliminate) the amount frozen by reference to a maximum sum: first, it may reduce the quantum of any damages claim a defendant may make pursuant to the undertaking in damages in the event the injunction is found to have been wrongly granted; secondly, because it is less intrusive, the court may be more inclined to grant an order that is more targeted; thirdly, any third parties holding or with control over the assets in question will have greater certainty as to whether they are included within the scope of the order, and the scope for the defendant to argue that an asset is not covered by the order is reduced if not extinguished.

It follows from the inclusion of a financial limit upon the value of the frozen **28–102** assets that the order must clarify the position in relation to the respondent's freedom to deal with assets which fall outside the ring-fence marked by that limit. How this is done depends upon whether or not the freezing injunction is domestic or worldwide, but for both the emphasis is upon the enforcement principle[146] in relation to assets within the jurisdiction of the court: the focus of the language of the standard form provisions for both types of order is upon ensuring that assets equal to the encumbered value remain within England and Wales so that they remain amenable to execution of any later judgment.

---

at 10. In the event that the expected costs should increase substantially or orders for costs have been made but the costs themselves not yet assessed, the Court may be willing to vary the freezing injunction to increase the maximum sum frozen in respect of costs; *Thevarajah v Riordan* [2015] EWHC 1949 (Ch), at [26], [33]–[35]. See, however, the doubt expressed by Morgan J in *Cooke v Venulum Property Investments Ltd* [2013] EWHC 4288 (Ch), at [15], as to whether or not the practice is well-founded; though this doubt has not inhibited judges before or after this case.

[143] A recent example of a freezing order including an element of future costs is *Thevarajah v Riordan* [2015] EWHC 1949 (Ch).

[144] *Cooke v Venulum Property Investments* [2013] EWHC 4288 (Ch), at [15]. On the other hand where a costs order is made against X in favour of Y in litigation, and remains unassessed, Y may seek a freezing order in support of his claim to costs, provided that the necessary elements are established in respect of that claim: see *Jet West Ltd v Haddican* [1992] 1 W.L.R. 487.

[145] Which may only be once the respondent has complied with any ancillary asset disclosure orders.

[146] See para.28–081 above.

28–103   In the case of an injunction limited to England and Wales, the position in relation to assets outside the maximum sum ring-fence is addressed as follows, at para.8:

> "If the total value free of charges and other securities ('unencumbered value') of the Respondent's assets in England and Wales exceeds £X, the Respondent may remove any of those assets from England and Wales or may dispose of or deal with them so long as the total unencumbered value of his assets still in England and Wales remains above £X."

28–104   This makes clear that the maximum sum provision at para.5 is directed at unencumbered assets only, or such part of the value of an asset as is unencumbered. If the respondent is facing a claim for £1million and owns a property in London valued at, say, £1.2million but which is encumbered by a charge securing a debt of £1million, then that property can only be relied upon for at most £200,000. If the same defendant also has cash in a bank account of £800,000 then the whole of that sum will be subject to the freezing order. Disputes may arise as to how the maximum sum provision should operate and whether the respondent can rely upon the proviso contained at para.8. The applicant may well contest valuation evidence put forward by the respondent with a view to seeking to free up other assets from the ambit of the freezing order.

28–105   For worldwide freezing orders the standard wording is:

> "(1)   If the total value free of charges or other securities ('unencumbered value') of the Respondent's assets in England and Wales exceeds £X, the Respondent may remove any of those assets from England and Wales or may dispose of or deal with them so long as the total unencumbered value of the Respondent's assets still in England and Wales remains above £X
>
> (2)   If the total unencumbered value of the Respondent's assets in England and Wales does not exceed £X, the Respondent must not remove any of those assets from England and Wales and must not dispose of or deal with any of them. If the Respondent has other assets outside England and Wales, he may dispose of or deal with those assets outside England and Wales so long as the total unencumbered value of all his assets whether in or outside England and Wales remains above £X. "[147]

28–106   The effect of the different wording in the worldwide version of the order is to preserve within the jurisdiction assets up to the maximum sum limit or, in the likely event that insufficient assets are available in the jurisdiction, to freeze assets worldwide up to the maximum sum. As with the wording of the domestic maximum sum provision, the paragraphs are directed at unencumbered assets.

(iv)   Assets caught: the evolving standard forms

28–107   In its original form, the standard form freezing injunction attached to CPR PD 25 restrained the defendant from disposing of or dealing with "his assets…whether in his own name or not and whether solely or jointly owned". Since 2002 both this standard form and that attached to the Admiralty and Commercial Courts Guide have contained an expansion upon this definition, which treats as an asset of the respondent which is subject to the injunction "any asset which he has power, directly or indirectly, to dispose of, or deal with as it if were his own". He is regarded as having such power "if a third party holds or controls the assets in

---

[147] For a discussion of this provision see *JSC BTA Bank v Ablyazov* [2009] EWHC 2840 (Comm).

accordance with his direct or indirect instructions". The reasons for this introduction are explained in the Court of Appeal's judgment in *JSC BTA Bank v Solodchenko*[148] and are essentially to meet the attempts of more sophisticated fraudsters to conceal their beneficial ownership of assets behind the façade of some kind of legal structure such as a company, trust or foundation.

In 2009 the Commercial Court standard form was amended to include additional wording (first introduced in the 8th edition of the Commercial Court Guide) to the effect that the injunction applies to assets "whether the Respondent is interested in them legally, beneficially or otherwise." As we explain below, the addition of these words is significant, in that it deliberately extends the scope of the injunction to assets in which (at least ostensibly) the defendant is interested neither legally nor beneficially; and for that reason the Guide stipulates that these words are not to be included automatically, but are to be considered for insertion on a case by case basis.

28–108

The relevant language as it now stands can be reproduced as follows, with the words in square brackets reflecting the additional words contemplated by the Commercial Court form. The injunction:

28–109

"6 .... applies to all the Respondent's assets whether or not they are in his own name and whether they are solely or jointly owned[149] [and whether the Respondent is interested in them legally, beneficially or otherwise]. For the purpose of this order the Respondent's assets include any asset which he has the power, directly or indirectly, to dispose of or deal with as if it were his own. The Respondent is to be regarded as having such power if a third party holds or controls the asset in accordance with his direct or indirect instructions.

7. This prohibition includes the following assets in particular—
   (a) the property known as [*title/address*] or the net sale money after payment of any mortgages if it has been sold;
   (b) the property and assets of the Respondent's business [known as [*name*]] [carried on at [*address*]] or the sale money if any of them have been sold;
   (c) any money standing to the credit of any bank account including the amount of any cheque drawn on such account which has not been cleared;
   (d) [any interest under any trust or similar entity including any interest which can arise by virtue of the exercise of any power of appointment, discretion or otherwise howsoever.] "

The above wording is of course not prescriptive. It can be departed from in appropriate cases and such departures may have an effect on what is included within the scope of the order and what is meant by the word "assets".[150]

28–110

---

[148] *JSC BTA Bank v Solodchenko* [2010] EWCA Civ 1436; [2011] 1 W.L.R. 888, at [21] and following.

[149] In this regard the law has moved on since the Court of Appeal decision in *Z Ltd v A-Z and AA-LL* [1982] Q.B. 558 where Kerr LJ suggested that it would be a rare case where jointly owned assets were the subject of a freezing order: see the discussion in Gee, *Commercial Injunctions* (2016), para.3–048 and following.

[150] As noted in para.28–078 above, paras 6.1–6.2 of CPR PD 25A describe the attached version as an "example" and state that it may be modified as appropriate in any particular case. Particularly in cases of civil fraud, orders made in the Chancery Division and Queen's Bench Division frequently adopt the wider Commercial Court language.

(v)   Types of asset covered

28–111 The term "assets" as used in the standard form order has no limitations. Certain forms of asset clearly fall within its scope: real property, shares whether in public or private companies, as well as similar intangible property such as goodwill in a business[151] or certain intellectual property rights. It may also cover aircraft, ships, cars, machinery, jewellery, objets d'art and valuables generally, as well as choses in action[152] (most obviously monies standing to the credit of a bank or other account, but the term would also include, say, the right to receive a sum of money from a third party, e.g. deferred consideration under a sale contract).

(vi)   What constitutes "his" assets

28–112 The expression "his assets" was first considered in depth by the Court of Appeal in *Federal Bank of the Middle East Ltd v Hadkinson*.[153] In that case, Mr Hadkinson had, while subject to a freezing injunction prohibiting him from dealing with, disposing or diminishing the value of "[his] assets and/or funds....whether in his own name or not", transferred a sum of money from an account in his own name to one in his wife's name, claiming they were not sums he beneficially owned but were held on trust for third party investors. On the assumption that Mr Hadkinson's position was correct, the Court found that the transfer was not a breach of the order: without further wording, the injunction was limited to assets belonging to the respondent beneficially, which the funds in question were not. An asset held on trust for a third party is not an asset of the respondent within the enforcement principle, there being no prospect of the asset being amenable to enforcement of a future judgment[154]:

> "In my judgment, the language of the freezing order, read in context and with regard to the object of the order, naturally refers to assets and funds belonging to the defendant and which are and should remain available to satisfy the claim against him. Assets and funds which belong, or, as in this case, are assumed to belong, beneficially to someone else would not be available for that purpose."

28–113 Similarly, as was confirmed in *JSC BTA Bank v Solodchenko*,[155] assets held on trust for an independent third party are not assets with which the respondent can deal "as if they were his own" (even though as trustee he may exert a substantial

---

151 *Templeton Insurance Ltd v Thomas* [2013] EWCA Civ 35.

152 *CBS United Kingdom v Lambert* [1983] Ch. 37, at 42F. See also *Global Maritime Investments Cyprus Ltd v Gorgonia di Navigazione SRL* [2014] EWHC 706 (Comm), at [4]–[5].

153 *Federal Bank of the Middle East Ltd v Hadkinson* [2000] 1 W.L.R. 1695, in particular at 1709. As we have noted above, in *JSC BTA Bank v Ablyazov*, at [26], Lord Clarke said that *Hadkinson* supported the sensible approach of construing a freezing order in its context and with a view to its purpose.

154 See per Mummery LJ at 1709–1711; although, as we note below and as was observed at first instance by David Richards J in *JSC Mezhdunarodniy Promyshlenniy Bank v Pugachev* [2014] EWHC 3547 (Ch), at [41], while the purpose of freezing orders is to preserve assets so as to be available for enforcement, the standard form had "come to be drafted in a way which may cast a wider net".

155 *JSC BTA Bank v Solodchenko* [2010] EWCA Civ 1436; [2011] 1 W.L.R. 888.

degree of practical control over them), such that the 2002 additions to the standard form wording do not alter the position as established by the decision in *Hadkinson*.[156]

Of course, the converse of this is also true (and is reflected by the standard **28–114** wording without the square-bracketed Commercial Court extension): assets held by a third party as trustee or nominee for the respondent, in which the respondent is beneficially interested, will be caught by the expression "his assets" in the standard form freezing injunction. The interest of a respondent as one of a class of beneficiaries under a (genuine) discretionary trust might be thought not to count for these purposes, as such a beneficiary has only a right (which equity will protect, but which is not proprietary) to be considered by the trustees as a potential recipient of benefit; but specific wording may extend the order's scope so as to include such an interest.[157]

It is clear, however, from the Court of Appeal's decision in *JSC BTA Bank v* **28–115** *Solodchenko*[158] that the inclusion of the additional post-2009 wording in the standard Commercial Court form mentioned above ("whether the Respondent is interested in them legally, beneficially or otherwise") means that a freezing injunction *will* cover assets held by the respondent solely as trustee or nominee for a third party.[159] This is because, in essence, the words "legally, beneficially or otherwise" must be read disjunctively. On the face of it this may seem anomalous, given that bare legal ownership of an asset provides no basis for enforcement against that asset by a creditor of the nominee. The Court of Appeal accepted that caution must therefore be exercised before the additional Commercial Court wording is included: its use should be exceptional and sparing. However, the court identified two pragmatic grounds for doing so in an appropriate case. The first is where the evidence discloses some grounds for there being a risk that an asset which the respondent is said to hold as a trustee or nominee for another in fact belongs beneficially to him (and in *Solodchenko* there was uncertainty over the beneficial ownership of the relevant BVI companies). The second ground is based upon giving the claimant an opportunity of investigating the position as to beneficial ownership rather than being brushed off by the "self-certification" of the unscrupulous defendant (who is prepared to

---

[156] See per Patten LJ at [31]: "On the contrary, the change was designed to preserve the ruling in *Hadkinson* but to make it clear that "his assets" include assets held by a third party in respect of which the defendant retains beneficial ownership or control. Although a proposed form of words may not always succeed in having the effect which was intended, this is not such a case. For the reasons I have explained, the language of para.6 is, as a matter of construction, plain and does not include assets held by a defendant in which he retains no beneficial interest."

[157] As in *JSC Mezhdunarodniy Promyshlenniy Bank v Pugachev* [2015] EWCA Civ 139; [2016] 1 W.L.R. 160: "Any interest under any trust or similar entity including any interest which may arise by virtue of the exercise of any power of appointment, discretion or otherwise howsoever". This wording appears at para.7(d) of the current Commercial Court form of freezing injunction. The defendant there unsuccessfully argued that this wording did not extend to the interest of a beneficiary under a discretionary trust. The Court of Appeal held that even "if the interest of a beneficiary under a discretionary trust cannot be the subject of execution, the words of paragraph [7(d)] are clear enough to encompass it." The Court was impressed by the existence of the wording "or otherwise" found at para.6.

[158] *JSC BTA Bank v Solodchenko* [2010] EWCA Civ 1436; [2011] 1 W.L.R. 888.

[159] See *JSC BTA Bank v Solodchenko* [2010] EWCA Civ 1436; [2011] 1 W.L.R. 888, at [46].

exclude the asset from his disclosure as not being an "asset" within the narrower wording of the CPR form, and see it disposed of regardless of the terms of the order). If, however, the additional wording is included, then expedition will be required in the resolution of any issue over the true beneficial ownership, so as to minimise the impact upon the interests of third parties under genuine trusts, and the claimant's cross-undertaking in damages will usually be required to be extended to cover any loss that may be suffered by an ostensible third party beneficial owner. Nevertheless, in large-scale fraud cases there will often be cause for concern that the defendant is hiding his beneficial ownership of assets and the applicant should give serious thought to the inclusion of the additional Commercial Court wording.[160]

28–116 That the extended wording of the Commercial Court standard form freezing injunction deliberately goes beyond beneficial ownership was confirmed by the Supreme Court in *JSC BTA Bank v Ablyazov (No.10)*,[161] in the context of loan agreements which allowed the respondent to the injunction to draw down sums and direct how those sums should be applied. Among other things, the respondent had directed that sums drawn down under the agreements should be used to pay legal fees. The Court rejected arguments that the right to draw down sums was itself an asset, or that the exercise of that right in itself amounted to a disposal of, dealing with or diminution of the value of an asset under the terms of the pre-2002 standard form of freezing injunction.[162] However, the proceeds of the drawdown, while not an asset in which the respondent ever held a beneficial interest, did fall within the extended definition (which in that case was held to be materially the same as the post 2009 standard form). While sums drawn down were at all times the lender's assets, rather than the respondent's, the respondent had the power to deal with them as if they were his own and had an "interest" in them in the sense required by the extended wording, in that he had the legal right to direct how they should be applied.[163]

28–117 What is perhaps unclear about the Supreme Court decision is whether its decision in this regard turned upon the 2009 addition to the Commercial Court standard form or the 2002 amendments. The reasoning of the Court of Appeal in

---

[160] See also *Yossifoff v Donnerstein* [2015] EWHC 3357 (Ch), per Snowden J at [41], noting that the default position is that a freezing injunction will only catch assets beneficially owned by the defendant, but that additional wording can be added for "pragmatic" reasons to catch unscrupulous defendants.

[161] *JSC BTA Bank v Ablyazov (No.10)* [2015] UKSC 64; [2015] 1 W.L.R. 4754, allowing in part the appeal from the Court of Appeal: [2013] EWCA Civ 928; [2014] 1 W.L.R. 1414.

[162] The Supreme Court upheld the Court of Appeal in this conclusion. The court noted that prior to 2002 the standard form of order did not include the extended definition and, in declining to reverse earlier decisions upon the unqualified references to "assets", observed that "there has over the years been a settled understanding that borrowings are not covered by the standard form of freezing order": per Lord Clarke at [20].

[163] Of course, it will presumably be an unusual case where the lender would remain contractually obliged, notwithstanding the existence of a freezing injunction against the borrower, to make such advances without security (the obtaining of which over the respondent's assets would amount to a "dealing" with assets). Indeed, in *Ablyazov* the claimant bank contended in parallel proceedings that the loan agreements were shams (and the lenders under the control of the respondent), but the argument on questions of principle and interpretation proceeded on the assumption that they were genuine.

Solodchenko, to which Lord Clarke referred in *Ablyazov* without express disapproval, would suggest that what made the difference was the additional words in the 2009 form, which make it clear that it does not matter whether the respondent is interested in the asset legally, beneficially or otherwise. But Lord Clarke's speech focuses not upon these words, but upon the final two sentences, added in the 2002 amendments, as being determinative.[164] If that is right, then the Supreme Court decision casts real doubt on *Solodchenko* and on other earlier authority (such as, in particular, the *Lakatamia* case, considered in the next paragraph), which treated those final two sentences as not, in themselves, altering the *Hadkinson* decision.

The decision in *Hadkinson*—that the standard form freezing injunction (without the extended Commercial Court wording) is to be understood as concerned with the beneficial ownership of assets which would be available in satisfaction of a judgment—was applied by the Court of Appeal in *Lakatamia Shipping Co Ltd v Su*[165] to reach the conclusion that assets owned by a company are not to be treated as the assets of the respondent who is a 100 per cent shareholder in that company: they are the assets of the company.[166] In so doing the Court of Appeal resolved a conflict on the point between two decisions of the High Court, handed down on the same day.[167] Importantly, the Court of Appeal held that the reference in the standard form wording (post 2002) to the respondent having a power of disposition or dealing over the asset "as if it were his own", and to the third party "hold[ing] or control[ling] the asset in accordance with [the respondent's] direct or indirect instructions", did not alter the position, even where the respondent was the sole shareholder in the company. As explained by Rimer LJ[168]:

28–118

> "The point of freezing orders is to restrain dealings by the defendant with assets which, if judgment is obtained, will be available to satisfy the judgment. It is obvious, therefore, that the assets targeted by such an order are assets that belong beneficially to the defendant, since only such assets will be so available. Thus assets held by the defendant as a trustee for others will not, in the absence of words expressly extending the order to them, be caught by the order. That was made clear by the Court of Appeal in *Federal Bank of the Middle East v Hadkinson* [2000] 1 W.L.R. 1695. The mere fact that a defendant controls assets is not sufficient to bring them within the reach of a freezing order unless the order expressly so provides."

The important point was that the "control" exercised by a company's owner or director over its assets does not make them *his* assets, nor does it amount to him dealing with them as if they were his assets: rather, he has the power (as a

28–119

---

[164] "For the purpose of this order the freezing defendant's assets include any asset which it has the power, directly or indirectly, to dispose of or deal with as if it were its own. The freezing defendant is to be regarded as having such power if a third party holds or controls the asset in accordance with its direct or indirect instructions." See *JSC BTA Bank v Ablayazov (No.10)* [2015] UKSC 64; [2015] 1 W.L.R. 4754, at [40], [46] and [48]–[49].

[165] *Lakatamia Shipping Co Ltd v Su* [2014] EWCA Civ 636; [2015] 1 W.L.R. 291.

[166] Per Rimer LJ at [50]: "There is no suggestion that such assets belonged beneficially to anyone other than the companies; and it is trite law that a company's assets so held do not belong beneficially to their shareholders, not even to a shareholder in the position of the first defendant who is, for all practical purposes, the sole owner of the companies."

[167] *Lakatamia Shipping Co Ltd v Su* [2013] EWHC 1814 (Comm); *Group Seven Ltd v Allied Investment Corp Ltd* [2013] EWHC 1509 (Ch); [2014] 1 W.L.R. 735.

[168] *Lakatamia Shipping Co Ltd v Su* [2014] EWCA Civ 636; [2015] 1 W.L.R. 291, at [46].

director) to cause the company to make dispositions of its assets, but if he does, he does so as agent of the company (rather than as someone instructing the company to act for him).[169]

28–120 As noted above, some doubt has been cast on this part of the reasoning by the Supreme Court decision in *Ablyazov*, insofar as it suggests that the post-2002 standard form language of the respondent having the power, directly or indirectly, to dispose of or deal with assets as if they were his own *does* in itself (and without the post-2009 Commercial Court addition) extend the scope of the order to assets that do not belong beneficially to him. Whether *Lakatamia* is to be treated as overruled and how a court faced with the (not uncommon) situation of assets being held by a company in which the respondent is the sole or majority shareholder would now apply the standard form freezing injunction wording are open questions. The result in *Ablyazov* can be explained consistently with the reasoning of the Court of Appeal in *Lakatamia*, on the basis that the control exercised by the respondent in the former case over the loan proceeds (by virtue of his contractual rights) was akin to the control of an owner, whereas the control exercised by a shareholder or director over the assets of a company is not; but it remains to be seen whether judges in subsequent cases will attempt to reconcile the two cases in that way.

28–121 In any event, the Court of Appeal in *Lakatamia* went on to hold that if the respondent to a freezing injunction in such a position was able to and did procure a transaction which dissipated the company's assets, thereby reducing the value of the company, he would nonetheless be in breach of the injunction, because he would have diminished the value of what were on any view his own assets—the shares in the companies. Thus the unscrupulous defendant who masks his interest in assets through corporate structures in which he is ostensibly interested only as a shareholder can still be prevented from bringing about the dissipation of those assets. It is also possible that the court might be persuaded, in the case of a wholly-owned company which appears to have no trading activity and has the hallmarks of being used by the respondent as a front, to vary the standard wording so as to provide explicitly that the restraint upon the respondent's dealing with assets extends to dealings with the assets and liabilities of the company.[170] We consider in the following section of this chapter the jurisdiction that the Court could also exercise in such a case to grant an injunction against the company directly: the so-called "*Chabra*" jurisdiction.

28–122 On any view, it is clear that the de facto control by the respondent over an asset held by a third party can be highly relevant to whether that asset is caught by the freezing order, and indeed to whether the asset will be amenable to enforcement. Thus in *JSC BTA Bank v Solodchenko*[171] Patten LJ noted that the post 2002 standard form freezing injunction, even without the extended Commercial Court wording, would extend to

---

[169] Per Rimer LJ at [51].
[170] *Lakatamia Shipping Co Ltd v Su* [2014] EWCA Civ 636; [2015] W.L.R. 291, at [28], [32].
[171] *JSC BTA Bank v Solodchenko* [2010] EWCA Civ 1436; [2011] 1 W.L.R. 888, at [26].

"assets held by a foreign trust or a Liechtenstein Anstalt when the defendant retains beneficial ownership *or effective control* of the asset" (emphasis added).[172]

The relevance of control to the enforcement principle is demonstrated by consideration of cases in which it has been the basis for the grant of post-judgment relief in aid of execution. So, for example, in *JSC VTB Bank v Skurikhin*[173] the court was persuaded to appoint a receiver by way of equitable execution over the membership interest of an English limited liability partnership, even though that membership interest was held by a Liechtenstein foundation and not by the individual judgment debtor himself. The evidence (including expert evidence on Liechtenstein law) supported the conclusion that the judgment debtor was the "mandatory and economic founder" of the Foundation, and that he   **28–123**

"either has a legal right to call for the assets of the Berenger Foundation to be transferred to him, or has *de facto* control of those assets."

That was a sufficient basis to appoint a receiver over the membership interest held by the Foundation, because[174]:

"Property subject to trust or analogous foreign arrangements would be regarded in equity as assets of the judgment debtor if he has the legal right to call for those assets to be transferred to him or to his order, or if he has de facto control of the trust assets in circumstances where no genuine discretion is exercised by the trustee over those assets."

Whilst that was said in the context of the question of whether a receiver could be appointed over the relevant asset post-judgment, it must be equally true of whether a freezing order against a defendant made pre-judgment would extend to such an asset.[175]   **28–124**

However, one needs to be clear about the role that the concept of control is playing. Evidence of control can of course be evidence from which the Court infers beneficial ownership, in which case there is no conceptual problem. Otherwise, it is suggested that (at least in a case where the terms of the order do   **28–125**

---

[172] See also, to similar effect, the decision in *Dadourian Group International Inc v Azuri Ltd* [2005] EWHC 1768 (Ch) (a *Chabra* case) and the observation of David Steel J in *Yukos Capital S.a.r.l v OJSC Rosneft Oil Company* [2010] EWHC 784 (Comm), at [22].

[173] *JSC VTB Bank v Skurikhin* [2015] EWHC 2131 (Comm) (Mr Christopher Butcher QC, sitting as a Deputy High Court Judge).

[174] *JSC VTB Bank v Skurikhin* [2015] EWHC 2131 (Comm), at [38], [39] and [45].

[175] See further (on the relevant receivership principles) *Masri v Consolidated Contractors (UK) Ltd (No. 2)* [2008] EWCA Civ 303; [2009] Q.B. 450; *Tassaruf Mevduati Signorta Fonu v Merrill Lynch Bank and Trust Co (Cayman) Ltd* [2011] UKPC 17; [2012] 1 W.L.R. 1721, at [56]; and *Cruz City 1 Mauritius Holdings v Unitech Ltd* [2014] EWHC 3131 (Comm), at [47]. See Ch.33 below. The Deputy Judge also relied upon the observation of Patten LJ in *JSC BTA Bank v Solodchenko* [2010] EWCA Civ 1436 referred to at para.28–115 above, that the standard form of freezing order with its extended wording contemplates that the respondent's assets may extend beyond those in which he has legal or beneficial ownership to those over which he has "effective control". In the context of interests under trusts specifically, note also the wording at para.7(d) of the Commercial Court freezing injunction, which refers to "any interest under any trust or similar entity including any interest which can arise by virtue of any power of appointment, discretion or otherwise howsoever" (which was considered in the *Pugachev* case, referred to in the footnotes to para.28–112 above.)

point to a wider construction) the mere fact of control, even absolute control, ought not to be enough. Usually, it must amount to a basis for saying there is good reason to believe that the respondent can compel the party holding the asset to apply them in satisfaction of a judgment, or that there is some process of enforcement by which the claimant, as potential judgment creditor, will be able to enforce against the asset in question.[176] However, it is clear from the decisions considered above that (at least when the extended Commercial Court wording is used, or bespoke wording that is appropriately clear in this regard), a freezing order can in an appropriate case extend beyond these strict confines of the enforcement principle to an asset over which control is exercised in a way that would fall short of what would be required to execute against the asset.[177] And it may be that, in light of the Supreme Court decision in *Ablyazov*, this is now to be understood as the effect of the post-2002 standard form freezing order.

(7) Permitted Exceptions

28–126 A freezing injunction does not purport to affect the nature or extent of the respondent's interest in the frozen assets. Only a judgment on the merits of the applicant's claim would operate to make those assets vulnerable (or potentially vulnerable) to execution by the applicant.

28–127 It is therefore consistent with the principle that the applicant must take the respondent as he finds him, with his lifestyle as it is at the time of the freezing injunction (see para.28–029 above), and also the further principle of fairness which recognises a defendant's right to defend the proceedings, that there should be exceptions to the injunction for relevant expenditure on living and legal costs. On the grant of a freezing injunction the merits of the underlying claim have necessarily been tested by reference to the threshold of a good arguable case (or that of a serious question to be tried in the case of a proprietary injunction). Since the claimant has yet to establish his claim, and since the freezing order does not

---

[176] See *Algosaibi v Saad Investments Company Ltd* (CICA 1 of 2010); [2011] 1 C.I.L.R. 178, at [32]–[33], per Sir John Chadwick (sitting as a judge of the Court of Appeal in the Cayman Islands). That case reviewed a number of English authorities on the subject (in the context of the *Chabra* jurisdiction) and has been held to represent English law, or cited with approval, in *Linsen International Ltd v Humpuss Sea Transport Pte Ltd* [2011] EWHC 2339 (Comm), at [150]–[152]; *Parbulk II AS v PT Humpuss Intermoda Transportasi TBK* [2011] EWHC 3143 (Comm); [2012] 2 All E.R. (Comm) 513; and *JSC BTA Bank v Ablyazov (No.10)* [2013] EWCA Civ 928; [2014] 1 W.L.R. 1414, at [35]. As Flaux J went on to explain in *Linsen*, whilst in *Yukos Capital S.a.r.l v OJSC Rosneft Oil Company* [2010] EWHC 784, at [22], David Steel J rightly doubted the significance of establishing a beneficial interest, of the kind arising under the English trust structure, this does not mean that the limitations identified in the *Algosaibi* judgment are irrelevant. See also (again in the *Chabra* context) *PJSC Vseukrainskyi Aktsionernyl Bank v Maksimov* [2013] EWHC 422 (Comm), per Popplewell J at [7]: establishing "substantial control" over a third party holding assets is not sufficient; "the ultimate test is always whether there is good reason to suppose that the assets would be amenable to execution of a judgment obtained against the CAD".

[177] See *JSC Mezhdunarodniy Promyshlenniy Bank v Pugachev* [2015] EWCA Civ 139; [2016] 1 W.L.R. 160, at [18]–[22]. In *JSC BTA Bank v Ablyazov* [2013] EWCA Civ 928; [2014] 1 W.L.R. 1414, Beatson LJ observed (at [75]) that "Where the words used clearly and unequivocally lead to the conclusion that the term 'asset' includes that which cannot be the subject of execution, effect must be given to the words."

operate as security for that claim, the respondent must be permitted pending judgment to continue to make payments which reflect ordinary and reasonable expenditure of the kind that would be made in the absence of the injunction. Likewise, he should be permitted to spend money on legal representation in defending the proceedings; otherwise the grant of the injunction carries the risk of the claim effectively being decided by default.

In *Derby & Co Ltd v Weldon (Nos 3 and 4)*,[178] Lord Donaldson MR stated the relevant principles as follows: **28–128**

> "The fundamental principle underlying this jurisdiction is that, within the limits of its powers, no court should permit the defendant to take action designed to ensure that subsequent orders of the court are rendered less effective than would otherwise be the case. On the other hand, it is not its purpose to prevent a defendant carrying on business in the ordinary way or, if an individual, living his life normally pending the determination of the dispute, nor to impede him in any way in defending himself against a claim. Nor is its purpose to place the plaintiff in the position of a secured creditor."

In giving effect to this, the standard form freezing injunction now provides for three recognised categories of permitted expenditure: living expenses, legal fees and dealings in the ordinary and proper course of business. Paragraph 11 of the standard form is in the following terms: **28–129**

> "(1)   This order does not prohibit the Respondent from spending £Y a week towards his ordinary living expenses and also £Y [or a reasonable sum] on legal advice and representation. [But before spending any money the Respondent must tell the Applicant's legal representatives where the money is to come from.][179]
> (2)   This order does not prohibit the Respondent from dealing with or disposing of any of his assets in the ordinary and proper course of business.
> (3)   The Respondent may agree with the Applicant's legal representatives that the above spending limits should be increased or that this order should be varied in any other respect, but any agreement must be in writing. "

Disputes about these exceptions usually arise in the context of applications to vary them at (or following) the return date, and so we consider them further when addressing issues that arise at the return date in Ch.32. As we note below and further in Ch.32, different principles are applicable where the injunction is made in support of a proprietary rather than personal claim. **28–130**

(8)   Provision of Security in Lieu of the Order

As we have seen, the grant of a freezing injunction does not operate to give the claimant any kind of security for his claim. Nevertheless, para.11(4) of the standard form of order states: **28–131**

> "The order will cease to have effect if the Respondent—

---

[178] *Derby & Co Ltd v Weldon* (Nos 3 and 4) [1990] Ch. 65, at 76; [1989] 1 All E.R. 1002, at 1006–1007.
[179] The bracketed words, which any well-advised applicant would seek to have included in the order, give the applicant an opportunity, if he objects to the proposed source of the funds, to bring the matter back before the court and have the question determined.

> (1)   provides security by paying the sum of £X into court, to be held to the order of the court; or
>
> (2)   makes provision for security in that sum by another method agreed with the Applicant's legal representatives. "

28–132   Although the reference to "security" in this provision may give the impression that, if acted upon by the respondent, the benefit of the applicant's in personam relief has been somehow converted into a security interest in the monies or other collateral provided by the respondent, that is not the position. The replacement "security" contemplated by this provision is not security for the claim in the true sense; it is "security" against the risk of dissipation and (unless specifically agreed to have that effect under any particular method agreed in accordance with the second limb of this provision) it does not result in an equitable charge in favour of the claimant which obliges it to be used in payment of any later judgment obtained by him.[180] Therefore, until the claimant is in the position of being able to enforce his judgment by making a claim against the monies or security tendered under this provision, he is vulnerable to the defendant becoming insolvent.

28–133   If the respondent has sufficient funds to pay the sum claimed into court (or make alternative provision for securing the claim in the sense just discussed) it may well be advisable to do so: it will relieve the respondent of the ongoing inconvenience of a freezing order, as well as the stigma that can be associated with being subject to one.

(9)   Disclosure of Assets

28–134   Disclosure orders are generally addressed in Ch.29.

28–135   A freezing injunction which left it to the respondent to determine which assets are caught by it, without any accompanying compulsion to disclose what his assets are, would be, as it was put in one case, a "relatively toothless procedure in the fight against rampant international fraud".[181] Without knowing what assets the respondent owns (in the sense identified in the freezing order itself), the applicant is unable to police the freezing injunction or notify third parties who hold those assets (e.g. banks) about it.

28–136   In order to give the injunction some "teeth", the standard form of order therefore provides that, upon its grant, the respondent is under an immediate duty to provide information about his assets to the applicant and shortly thereafter to swear an affidavit verifying that information.

28–137   Considerations of proportionality (and recognition that assets of only modest value are unlikely to engage the enforcement principle) dictate that some minimum value ought to be specified as the threshold for such asset disclosure.

---

[180] *Flightline Ltd v Edwards* [2003] EWCA Civ 63; [2003] 1 W.L.R. 1200, at [47]–[51], per Jonathan Parker LJ and *Technocrats International Inc v Fredic Ltd* [2004] EWHC 2674 (QB), at [17], per Jack J.

[181] *Snoras (In Bankruptcy) v Antonov* [2013] EWHC 131 (Comm), at [76], per Gloster J.

This may vary from £2,000 to £10,000, or even higher, depending on the overall value of the case. There are no prescribed rules.[182]

The usual disclosure obligation, at para.9 of the standard form, is in the following terms, the parenthesised words reflecting differing options:

    28–138

> "(1) Unless paragraph (2) applies, the Respondent must [immediately] [within hours of service of this order][183] and to the best of his ability inform the Applicant's solicitors of all his assets [in England and Wales] [worldwide] [exceeding £ in value] whether in his own name or not and whether solely or jointly owned, giving the value, location and details of all such assets."

> "(2) If the provision of any of this information is likely to incriminate the Respondent, he may be entitled to refuse to provide it, but is recommended to take legal advice before refusing to provide the information. Wrongful refusal to provide the information is contempt of court and may render the Respondent liable to be imprisoned, fined or have his assets seized."

Paragraph 10 requires this information to be verified by an affidavit, to be sworn within a prescribed period thereafter.

The question of the extent of the requirements imposed by the phrase "value, location and details of all such assets" has been considered on several occasions by the Courts.[184] The word "details" in particular is open to interpretation. Given the potentially serious consequences of breaching an order and the potentially wide and uncertain scope of the word, the Courts have unsurprisingly taken a relatively narrow view as to what constitutes "details" for these purposes[185]; but it is consistent with the purpose of the disclosure order within a freezing injunction that it should extend at least to the nature and extent of the assets.[186] If the view is taken that the disclosure provided is insufficient to properly police the freezing injunction, the proper course will usually be to apply for further disclosure rather than pursuing committal proceedings, at least in the first instance.[187]

    28–139

---

[182] In *PJSC Tatneft v Bogolyubov* [2018] EWHC 1314 (Comm), the respondent sought to further limit his disclosure by running an argument that, given the purpose of the freezing was to prevent him from dissipating assets so as to frustrate any judgment, he should only be obliged to to disclose his assets up to the value of the amount claimed. This argument was rejected by Cockerill J, see, in particular [68]–[108] of her judgment.

[183] Thought should be given to the time for provision of the asset disclosure. The ex parte order should not impose upon the respondent an impossible deadline: see *Oystertec Plc v Davidson (No.1)* [2004] EWHC 627 (Ch).

[184] See most recently *PSJC Commercial Bank Privatbank v Kolomoisky* [2018] EWHC 482 (Ch), in the context of loan agreements which the defendants were party to. In that case the judge held, at [52], that the court had a jurisdiction to "make an order for asset disclosure, which might include disclosure of documents, where such an order is required to enable a claimant, first, to identify the nature and extent of a defendant's interest in assets, and second, to decide whether and, if so, what further steps it should take to protect its position, such steps being an important aspect of its ability to police the freezing order."

[185] *Gerald Metals S.A. v Vasile Frank Timis* [2017] EWHC 3381 (Comm), at [49]–[50], referring to the principle of strict construction identified by Beatson LJ in *JSC BTA Bank v Ablyazov* [2013] EWCA Civ 928; [2014] 1 W.L.R. 1414.

[186] *Gerald Metals S.A. v Vasile Frank Timis* [2017] EWHC 3381 (Comm), at [51].

[187] See *Gerald Metals S.A. v Vasile Frank Timis* [2017] EWHC 3381 (Comm), at [56]; and *PSJC Commercial Bank Privatbank v Kolomoisky* [2018] EWHC 482 (Ch), at [58]. The question of whether the further information/disclosure sought fell within the ambit of the original order will usually be a sterile one: *Privatbank*, above, at [68].

28-140   Where an order included

> "any interest under any trust or similar entity including any interest which may arise by virtue of the exercise of any power of appointment, discretion or otherwise howsoever",

it was held that the normal disclosure provision required disclosure of the respondent's status as a beneficiary of a discretionary trust.[188]

28-141   It should be noted that, whereas the freezing injunction is generally effective from the time its terms are notified to the respondent (and third parties such as banks), the disclosure obligation and the period for complying with it, whether "immediately" or within a prescribed time, run from formal service of the order.[189]

28-142   The privilege against self-incrimination is expressly mentioned at para.9(2) of the draft order. It provides a potential let-out for a respondent who is unwilling to provide information. However, in the context of civil fraud the statutory encroachments upon the privilege are such that it may well have no application to the respondent subject to a disclosure obligation contained in a freezing order. These were mentioned by Gloster J in *Snoras v Antonov*[190] in the following terms:

> "The standard form of Commercial Court injunction entitles a defendant not to provide disclosure on the grounds of the privilege against self-incrimination. This relates solely to the risk of incrimination in actual or threatened criminal proceedings in England. However, as referred to above, the decision of the Court of Appeal in *C Plc v P* [2007] EWCA Civ 493; [2008] Ch. 1; E.R. 1034, CA establishes that a person could not, relying on the privilege against self-incrimination, refuse to disclose documents which had a prior existence independent of the will of the person relying on the privilege. Moreover in cases of theft, or alleged misappropriation of property by fraud, section 31 of the Theft Act and section 13 of the Fraud Act abrogate the privilege against self-incrimination in civil proceedings, thereby removing the entitlement of defendants to answer questions relating to their assets, but on terms that no statement or admission made by a person in answering a question put or complying with an order, shall, in proceedings for an offence under either Act, be admissible in evidence against that person."

28-143   Section 13 of the Fraud Act 2006 removes the privilege against self-incrimination in respect not only of offences under the Fraud Act 2006, but also of "related offences", which means:

(a)   conspiracy to defraud and

(b)   any other offence involving any form of fraudulent conduct or purpose.[191]

---

[188] *JSC Mezhdunarodniy Promyshlenniy Bank v Pugachev* [2015] EWCA Civ 139; [2016] 1 W.L.R. 160, at [11].

[189] See *Mobil Cerro Negro Ltd v Petroleos de Venezuela S.A.* [2008] EWHC 532 (Comm), where the respondent was able to avail himself of the prolonged process of service in Venezuela.

[190] *Snoras v Antonov* [2013] EWHC 131 (Comm), at [76].

[191] In *JSC BTA Bank v Ablyazov* [2009] EWCA Civ 1124; [2010] 1 W.L.R. 976 the Court of Appeal held that the latter included the offence under s.328(1) of the Proceeds of Crime Act 2002 (entering into or becoming concerned in an arrangement which the defendant knows or suspects facilitates (by whatever means) the acquisition, retention, use or control of criminal property, by or on behalf of another person).

Subject to those statutory exceptions, the privilege against self-incrimination applies to any cross-examination upon the disclosure (or non-disclosure) of assets where the court is persuaded that such cross-examination is likely to further the proper purposes of the order.[192] The court should be careful to ensure that the order is not being used to enable the claimant to build a substantive case against the defendant from scratch. In *Den Norske Bank A.S.A v Antonatos*[193] the Court of Appeal, in allowing the defendant's appeal on the ground that the order for his cross-examination on his disclosure of assets infringed his privilege against self-incrimination, said it was unfortunate that the ex parte order had the effect of requiring the defendant to say whether he had received bribes from any of the identified sources.

In *Antonov* the judge went on to consider the principles governing the position **28–144** where the risk is that the respondent will incriminate himself in relation to actual or threatened criminal proceedings abroad. In such circumstances there is no right to withhold disclosure of assets, although the court has a discretion as to whether or not to grant the respondent protection. As the decision in *JSC BTA Bank v Ablyazov*[194] shows, the need to make the freezing injunction effective may well outweigh the prejudice to the respondent and the risk of self-incrimination in foreign proceedings. In that case the following matters outweighed the risk and prejudice to him:

(1) disclosure was only to be made (at least until the return date) to the claimant's solicitors and counsel;

(2) the claimant was seeking proprietary remedies;

(3) the claimant had given undertakings not to use any information obtained as a result of the order for the purposes of civil or criminal proceedings in England or any other jurisdiction other than the claim;

(4) the claimant was subject to the implied undertaking that it would not use documents received in the course of the action other than for the purposes of that action;

---

[192] Orders for such cross-examination are very much the exception rather than the rule. For the general principles governing applications for cross-examination upon disclosure affidavits, see *Jenington International Inc v Assaubayev* [2010] EWHC 2351 (Ch), at [22], per Vos J. We consider the jurisdiction to order cross-examination in relation to assets in detail at Ch.31, see para.31–059 onwards.

[193] *Den Norske Bank A.S.A v Antonatos* [1999] Q.B. 271, at 290F.

[194] *JSC BTA Bank v Ablyazov* [2009] EWCA Civ 1125, cited by Gloster J in *Antonov*. In that case the Court of Appeal considered an appeal concerning a decision that the defendants should provide disclosure despite their arguments that this risked self-incriminating material being provided to the prosecuting authorities in Kazakhstan. At first instance, the disclosure order was made on terms that the list of assets within Kazakhstan should be shown only to the court, the claimants' solicitors and one named individual on the claimants' Management Board. The Court of Appeal dismissed the defendants' appeal. During the hearing before the Court of Appeal, the claimants had offered to limit the disclosure provided only to their solicitors and counsel. Although the Court of Appeal was concerned whether such a restriction was proper or workable (see in particular the judgment of Sedley LJ, at [41]), it made its decision on that basis. The Court of Appeal also held that it was clear from the use of the word "entitled" in the order that its references to the privilege against self-incrimination were to the statutory privilege against self-incrimination provided by English law and did not cover a claim which might, or might not, be made for an exercise of the court's discretion to grant protection with respect to proceedings outside the United Kingdom.

(5)   there was a possibility of policing the undertaking by way of sequestration of the claimant's assets held in England; and

(6)   the defendant had not identified grounds for suggesting that the claim brought was not a good claim.

(10)   Variation of the Order by Consent of the Parties

28–145   In most substantial cases there will be numerous issues following the making of a freezing order concerning its implementation and effect, and in particular whether payments or other dealings are permissible under its terms. The parties should endeavour to deal with these issues consensually and para.11(3) of the order caters for that, providing that

28–146   "The Respondent may agree with the Applicant's legal representatives that the above spending limits should be increased or that this order should be varied in any other respect, but any agreement must be in writing."

(11) Third Parties

28–147   The right of any person other than the respondent, who is served with or notified of the order, to apply to vary or discharge the freezing injunction has been noted above.

28–148   In addition to the penal notice highlighting the potential risk of a committal application against any such person who facilitates a breach of the freezing injunction, the terms of the standard order also provide, at para.16, that it is "a contempt of court for any person notified of this order knowingly to assist in or permit a breach of this order" and that "any person doing so may be imprisoned, fined or have their assets seized". The sole purpose of this paragraph is to provide a further warning to third parties of their potential liability in contempt. It does not create any new liabilities. We consider the contempt jurisdiction in Ch.35.

28–149   However, given the apparent width of this provision, there are specific provisos designed to ensure that the threat of liability in contempt does not operate oppressively against third parties, and in particular the respondent's bank and (in the case of a worldwide freezing order) persons overseas. In relation to banks, these reflect the fact that order will almost always contain exceptions for permitted expenditure (the proper observance of which it would be unreasonable to expect the respondent's bank to police) and is not intended to upset any accrued rights of set-off which the bank may enjoy. In relation to persons overseas, they reflect the principles of international comity which underpin the proper exercise of a jurisdiction that would be regarded as exorbitant without appropriate recognition of their potentially competing interests.

(i)   Banks

28–150   In relation to banks, the standard forms provide explicit recognition, at paras 17 and 18, of the fact that the respondent's moneys at bank may well be subject to the bank's existing contractual rights (such as the right to set off monies standing to the credit of one account against the respondent's liability on an overdrawn one) and that it is not for the bank to "police" the respondent's observance of the order (for example, by attempting to check whether his expenditure from an account, which is not one expressly identified in the order as being the subject of an unqualified restraint, will result in him having no net assets over the "unencumbered value" for the purposes of para.8). The standard terms are as follows:

> "Set off by banks
> This injunction does not prevent any bank from exercising any right of set off it may have in respect of any facility which it gave to the respondent before it was notified of this order.
> Withdrawals by the Respondent
> No bank need enquire as to the application or proposed application of any money withdrawn by the Respondent if the withdrawal appears to be permitted by this order."

(ii)   The Babanaft and Baltic provisos

In relation to persons overseas, the so-called *Babanaft* proviso to a worldwide freezing injunction (which is found at para.19 of the standard form) is as follows: **28–151**

> "Persons outside England and Wales:
> (1)   Except as provided in paragraph (2) below, the terms of this order do not affect or concern anyone outside the jurisdiction of this court.
> (2)   The terms of this order will affect the following persons in a country or state outside the jurisdiction of this court —
>   (i)   the Respondent or his officer or agent appointed by power or attorney;
>   (ii)   any person who—
>   (a)   is subject to the jurisdiction of this court;
>   (b)   has been given written notice of this order at his residence or place of business within the jurisdiction of this court; and
>   (c)   is able to prevent acts or omissions outside the jurisdiction of this court which constitute or assist in a breach of the terms of this order; and
>   (iii) any other person, only to the extent that this order is declared enforceable by or is enforced by a court in that country or state. "

The *Babanaft* proviso takes its name from the decision of the Court of Appeal in *Babanaft International Co S.A. v Bassatne*[195] and reflects the English court's recognition that it has no jurisdiction over a foreign based third party (against whom the provisions for service out of the jurisdiction have not been invoked) and that its order should not affect him unless the order has been recognised or enforced by the relevant foreign court. **28–152**

It will be noted that the recognition, registration or enforcement of the order in the third party's local court is not the only basis on which the order could operate so as to bind them. The standard wording also provides that it can effect a third party who is overseas but is subject to the jurisdiction of the court, has been given **28–153**

---

[195] *Babanaft International Co S.A. v Bassatne* [1990] Ch. 13. It was recognised in the *Babanaft* case that the granting of an injunction (intended to operate in personam against the respondent but potentially taking effect in rem in relation to its impact upon third parties) would involve the exercise of an exorbitant jurisdiction over parties outside the jurisdiction of the courts if it was not suitably qualified.

notice of the order (at a residence or place of business within the jurisdiction) and is able to prevent acts or omissions outside the jurisdiction which would constitute or assist in a breach of the order. This revision to the *Babanaft* proviso is known as the *Derby v Weldon* proviso.[196]

28–154   However, without some sort of qualification (in effect, a proviso to the proviso) the *Derby v Weldon* proviso created particular problems for international banks subject to the jurisdiction of the English court (having a place of business here) but holding assets of the respondent overseas and quite possibly being required to act contrary to the terms of the injunction under obligations arising in the country where they are located. The imposition of potentially conflicting obligations upon such third parties, already amenable to the jurisdiction of the English court, led to the judicial crafting of the so-called *Baltic* proviso, which is now found at para.20 of the standard form.

28–155   The *Baltic* proviso takes its name from the decision of Clarke J in *Baltic Shipping v Translink Shipping Ltd*,[197] where the judge noted the particular difficulty for any bank having a branch within the jurisdiction which is required by the freezing injunction to act in relation to overseas assets in a way that might conflict with its contractual or other legal obligations in relation to those assets or indeed an order by the local foreign court. The language of the proviso, which is not limited to banks but which in practice is most relevant to their position, is as follows:

> "Assets located outside England and Wales
> Nothing in this order shall, in respect of assets located outside England and Wales, prevent any third party from complying with—
> what it reasonably believes to be its obligations, contractual or otherwise, under the laws and obligations of the country or state in which those assets are situated or under the proper law of any contract between itself and the Respondent[198]; and
> any orders of the courts of that country or state, provided that reasonable notice of any application for such an order is given to the Applicant's solicitors."

28–156   In *Baltic Shipping v Translink* Clarke J emphasised, at 679, that, in relying upon the limb of the proviso relating to compliance with legal obligations, the third party must form a *reasonable* belief as to what those obligations required:

> "So if in a particular case the plaintiff has the powerful opinion of a lawyer to the effect that there would be no breach of local law if a payment out were to be made then the bank will have to take the opinion into account in forming its belief. If the belief if not reasonable the bank will be at risk."

---

[196] After *Derby & Co Ltd v Weldon (Nos. 3 & 4)* [1990] Ch. 65.

[197] *Baltic Shipping Co v Translink Shipping Ltd* [1995] 1 Lloyd's Rep. 673, at 679. See also *Bank of China v NBM LLC* [2001] EWCA Civ 1933; [2002] 1 W.L.R. 844, at [22]–[23], where Tuckey LJ said the *Baltic* proviso should be included when third parties are not represented at the time the order is first made and should normally be included in any continuation of it "unless the court considers on the particular facts of the case that this is inappropriate."

[198] Paragraph F15.10 of the Commercial Court Guide states that in a worldwide freezing order it should normally be made clear that this provision should enable overseas branches of banks or similar institutions which have offices within the jurisdiction to comply with what they reasonably believe to be their obligations under the laws of the country where the assets are located or under the proper law of the relevant contract relating to such assets.

E.   THE "CHABRA" JURISDICTION

(1)   The Basis and Nature of "Chabra" Relief

In cases where the defendant is alleged to have been guilty of fraudulent activity **28–157** it is of course common to find that his assets have been secreted elsewhere than in his immediate possession. Fraudsters frequently make use of third parties to hold assets for them in order to disguise their true ownership. The ability of the court to include within the scope of any interim relief any third party who is believed to be holding the defendant's assets, but against whom the claimant has no cause of action, is a necessary part of the court's armoury if the purpose of preserving assets that may be amenable to enforcement of any eventual judgment is not to be thwarted. This is the *"Chabra"* jurisdiction, so-named after the landmark decision in *TSB Private Bank International SA v Chabra.*[199] Under this jurisdiction

> "a person ('X') bringing a claim against someone else ('Y') can sometimes obtain a freezing order against a third party ('Z') with a view to protecting Y's assets even though X himself has no claim against Z".[200]

It is important to note at the outset that in such a case the third party is not alleged **28–158** to be liable or directly accountable to the claimant,[201] but rather to the defendant, in respect of the assets in question. The ability of the court in an appropriate case to grant injunctive relief in respect of the assets of a third party who holds such assets for or is accountable to the defendant is thus entirely distinct from the court's equitable jurisdiction to grant proprietary-based injunctive relief against a knowing recipient of property who is alleged to be accountable to the claimant as a constructive trustee (as to which, see Ch.23).

The *Chabra* jurisdiction is ancillary in nature: in *Chabra* itself Mummery J said **28–159** that the injunctive relief must be "ancillary and incidental" to the claim against the principal defendant, a proposition well illustrated by the recent decision of the Court of Appeal in *JSC BTA Bank v Ablyazov (No 11).*[202] The existence of a cause

---

[199] *TSB Private Bank International SA v Chabra* [1992] 1 W.L.R. 231. Mr Chabra was in fact not himself a "Chabra" defendant.

[200] *Royal Westminster Investments v Varma* [2012] EWHC 3439 (Ch), at [46], per Newey J, citing *Chabra* itself and the leading cases of *C Inc Plc v L* [2001] 2 All E.R. (Comm) 446 and *Revenue and Customs Commissioners v Egleton* [2006] EWHC 2313 (Ch); [2007] Bus L.R. 44.

[201] Many of the authorities refer to such third parties, joined as a *"Chabra* defendant" for the purposes of the injunctive relief, as an "NCAD" ("no cause of action defendant") as distinct from a "CAD" (the principal defendant, or defendants, against whom the cause of action lies). Although no cause of action, as such, lies against the NCAD, the practice is to join him as a defendant to the proceedings and not merely make him a respondent to the application for injunctive relief. There may be issues to be tried between the claimant and the NCAD, possibly before the trial of the substantive claim against the CAD: compare *SCF Finance Co Ltd v Masri* [1985] 1 W.L.R. 876, at 884; *C Inc Plc v L* [2001] 2 Lloyd's Rep. 459; [2001] 2 All E.R. (Comm) 446, at [79]–[87]; and *JSC BTA Bank v Ablyazov* [2014] EWCA Civ 602; [2015] 1 W.L.R. 1287, at [82].

[202] *JSC BTA Bank v Ablyazov (No.11)* [2014] EWCA Civ 602; [2015] 1 W.L.R. 1287, at [92]–[95]. In that case the appeal court upheld the judge's order that there should be a trial of the issue as to whether or not, for the purposes of post-judgment freezing and receivership orders, the defendant was the beneficial owner of the shares of a particular company, which had been challenged by a third party

of action against the defendant, to whom the third party is said to be accountable in respect of the assets sought to be frozen, is therefore a key element of the jurisdiction. When the court exercises the *Chabra* jurisdiction, it is granting ancillary relief as part of, and in aid of, the freezing injunction against the principal defendant(s)[203] on the ground that there is reason to suppose that the assets held by the *Chabra* defendant are in reality those of the defendant himself or at least sufficiently under his control to enable him to compel them to be used in satisfying any judgment later obtained by the claimant. The "enforcement principle"—by which the court strives to ensure the effective enforcement of its judgments and orders—therefore underpins the *Chabra* jurisdiction over such third parties just as much as it does the grant of a freezing injunction against the defendant himself.[204]

28–160 In *Linsen International Ltd v Humpuss Sea Transport Pte Ltd*[205] Flaux J considered the principal earlier authorities on the scope of the *Chabra* jurisdiction. In summary, his conclusions upon the scope of the jurisdiction may be summarised by saying it arises when:

(1) A third party against whom there is no cause of action is in possession of assets which are either beneficially owned by the defendant (against whom there is a cause of action), or over which the latter can be shown to have substantive control or a power of disposition; and

(2) It can be seen that there is, or may be, available a process, ultimately enforceable by the courts, to cause that defendant to disgorge the assets held by the third party.[206]

---

claiming to have purchased them. However, the court set aside the judge's order that there should also be a trial as to whether those applicants had been involved in a collusive breach of those orders which would permit the court to make an order reversing the transaction. The Court of Appeal was prepared to accept that the *Chabra* jurisdiction might in principle support this alternative basis of a claim upon the shareholding (through the defendant), but it could not be relied upon unless the allegation had been advanced as part of the claim against the defendant, to which the present third party applicants might be joined as necessary or proper parties.

[203] *SCF Finance Co Ltd v Masri* [1985] 1 W.L.R. 876, at 884B–884F, per Lloyd LJ.

[204] *C Inc Plc v L* [2001] 2 All E.R. (Comm) 446; [2001] 2 Lloyd's Rep. 459, at [75], per Aikens J and *JSC BTA Bank v Ablyazov* [2013] EWCA Civ 928; [2014] 1 W.L.R. 1414, at [35], per Beatson LJ.

[205] *Linsen International Ltd v Humpuss Sea Transport Pte Ltd* [2011] EWHC 2339 (Comm); [2011] 2 Lloyd's Rep. 663, at [146]–[150], citing extensively from the decision of Sir John Chadwick P in the Court of Appeal of the Cayman Islands in *Algosaibi v Saad Investments Company Ltd* (CICA 1 of 2010); [2011] 1 C.I.L.R. 178, who in turn relied upon the decision of Briggs J in *HM Revenue & Customs v Egleton* [2006] EWHC 2313 (Ch); [2007] BCC 78. See also *JSC Mezhdunarodniy Promyshlenniy Bank v Pugachev* [2015] EWCA Civ 139; [2016] 1 W.L.R. 160, at [17]–[20], where Lewison LJ noted that, in addressing the concept of power over assets, the standard form of freezing injunction does not distinguish between a legal right to give instructions and de facto control.

[206] As we noted above when considering the question of what constitutes the defendant's assets for the purposes of the standard forms of freezing injunction, the judgment of Sir John Chadwick P in *Algosaibi v Saad* (CICA 1 of 2010); [2011] 1 C.I.L.R. 178, at [32]–[33], is to the effect that the existence of substantial control by the defendant is not, of itself, enough to meet the requirement that the asset would be available to satisfy the judgment: "it is not enough that the CAD could, if it chose, cause the assets held by the NCAD to be used to satisfy the judgment." In some cases the focus upon the degree of control enjoyed by the defendant appears to have come at the expense of proper consideration of the further requirement: see *Marlwood Commercial Inc v Viktor Kozeny* [2007] EWHC 950 (Comm) per HHJ Mackie QC. However, there is a question mark over whether the

On this formulation the jurisdiction extends beyond assets which are simply or strictly, as a matter of English trust law, being held by the third party beneficially for the substantive defendant: it may capture assets of a third party over which the defendant has "claims and expectancies."[207] We consider these issues in greater detail below.   **28-161**

However the *Linsen* analysis is not exhaustive of the jurisdiction. It can extend to cases where the third party is accountable to the principal defendant for some debt or other receivable, claim or potential claim and in respect of which the claimant can be said to have the right, or contingent right, to obtain satisfaction of his anticipated judgment (whether through a third party debt order, a charging order, or the appointment of a receiver or liquidator).[208]   **28-162**

Of course, to justify injunctive relief against the third party the court must also be satisfied that, absent an order, there is a real risk that the third party will dissipate or dispose of the relevant assets: i.e. the same test of risk of dissipation as would apply to the cause of action defendant is applicable. Not every case where a third party holds assets for a principal defendant who is the subject of freezing order relief will justify the extension of that relief to the third party. In *Parbulk II AS v PT Humpuss Intermoda Transportasi TBK*[209] Gloster J said: **28-163**

> "the English court has jurisdiction (or 'legal power' as Aikens J put it) to grant a freezing order against the third party NCAD [Non-Cause of Action Defendant], in appropriate circumstances, to restrain the NCAD from dissipating its assets up to the amount of its debt to, or the claim by, the CAD [Cause of Action Defendant] or judgment debtor. Such an order is doing no more than protecting the right, or contingent right, of the claimant (whether by a third party debt order, charging order, appointment of a receiver or liquidator etc.) to obtain satisfaction of its judgment debt against the defendant by means of attachment, or other collection, of the proceeds of the latter's receivable from, or claim against, the third party. Whether the court grants such an order against the third party will be a matter for the exercise of its discretion, depending on the particular circumstances of the case. Normally, if there is no reason to doubt the propriety of the third party, it may well be sufficient, for example, to injunct the defendant from collecting the receivable, otherwise than by instructing the third party to pay it into a designated account. In other circumstances, it may be appropriate, at an interlocutory stage, to appoint a receiver over the receivable/claim against the third party in order to enable the receiver to collect it and pay it into court, or an escrow account, or otherwise preserve the receivable/claim from dissipation by the defendant/judgment debtor. But if, for example, the

---

judgment of the Supreme Court in *JSC BTA Bank v Ablyazov (No.10)* [2015] UKSC 64; [2015] 1 W.L.R. 4754 has expanded the concept of control by the defendant over a third party's assets beyond what would be required to make those assets amenable to execution: see above, paras 28–112—28–125.

[207] An expression familiar to equity lawyers to catch something less than a true proprietary entitlement and one used by the High Court of Australia in *Cardile v LED Builders Pty Ltd* [1999] HCA 18; (1999) 198 CLR 380, at [57]. In *C Inc Plc v L* [2001] 2 All E.R. (Comm) 446; [2001] 2 Lloyd's Rep. 459, at [44] Aikens J cited *Cardile* in support of the proposition that the jurisdiction exists where "the third party may be obliged to disgorge property or otherwise contribute to the funds of property of the judgment debtor to help satisfy the judgment against the judgment debtor".

[208] *Parbulk II AS v PT Humpuss Intermoda Transportasi TBK* [2011] EWHC 3143 (Comm), at [46]–[56], per Gloster J. This is one reason why it may be appropriate (unusually) to frame relief against the proposed *Chabra* defendant not with reference to a specific asset which is said to belong to the principal defendant or in respect of which he has some proprietary entitlement, but with reference to the *Chabra* defendant's assets more generally, limited to a maximum sum. See further paras 28–172—28–181 below.

[209] *Parbulk II AS v PT Humpuss Intermoda Transportasi TBK* [2011] EWHC 3143 (Comm), at [56].

circumstances show collusion, or impropriety, or some participation, on the part of the third party, in attempts by the defendant/judgment debtor to render itself judgment proof, then it may be appropriate for a freezing order to be granted against the third party itself. (This rehearsal of circumstances which may give rise to the exercise of the court's discretion is not meant to be in any way exhaustive.)"

28–164 This passage reinforces the point that, although *Chabra* relief is ancillary to the primary freezing order granted against the substantive defendant, nonetheless the court is exercising an independent jurisdiction against a party against whom no claim is directly made and therefore the appropriateness of freezing relief against the third party must be considered on its own merits. For these purposes, it is not necessary that there should be any causal link between the cause of action alleged against the defendant and the suggested basis of that defendant's claim upon those assets, though the existence of such a link may be a "valuable tool in the analysis of the question of discretion".[210]

28–165 When the court does act to freeze assets in the hands of a third party, given the nature and basis for that relief as described above, it is generally important that the injunction should be as specific as possible in identifying those assets of the principal defendant which are said to be in the third party's possession and control. However, in an appropriate case, such as where the principal defendant has paid over monies or assets to the third party which are no longer identifiable in the latter's hands (or where the *Chabra* defendant is accountable for a money sum to the principal defendant), a "maximum sum" order in relation to that third party's general assets (fixed by reference to the value of the substantive claim against the principal defendant, as opposed to the value of particular assets still held by the third party) may be made.[211] In *Yukong v Rendsburg*[212] Potter LJ said:

> "Since the purpose of granting such an injunction against the co-defendant is to preserve the assets of the principal defendant so as to be available to meet a judgment against him, the form of order made against the co-defendant should be as specific as the circumstances permit in respect of the principal defendant's assets of which he has possession or control. Thus, generally, the form of injunction will be tailored to that purpose and should be no wider than is necessary to achieve it. However, subject to that requirement, if a co-defendant is mixed up in an attempt to make the principal defendant judgment-proof and the assets or their proceeds are not readily identifiable in his hands it is open to the court, where it is just and convenient to do so, to make an order which catches the co-defendant's general assets up to the amount of the principal defendant's assets of which appears to have possession or control."

28–166 However, because of the risk that either form of order (whether a specific or general assets order) against a third party may operate oppressively against those

---

[210] *Linsen International Ltd v Humpuss Sea Transport Pte Ltd* [2011] EWHC 2339 (Comm); [2011] 2 Lloyd's Rep. 663, at [148]; *HM Revenue & Customs v Egleton* [2006] EWHC 2313 (Ch), at [41]; and *Parbulk II AS v PT Humpuss Intermoda Transportasi TBK* [2011] EWHC 3143 (Comm), at [55] (each declining to follow, on this aspect, Aikens J in *C Inc Plc v L* [2001] 2 All E.R. (Comm) 446; [2001] 2 Lloyd's Rep. 459, at [75]). In *Yukos Capital S.a.r.l v OJSC Rosneft Oil Company* [2010] EWHC 784, at [25], David Steel J also said the application of such a test of causation or connection, in relation to the scope of the jurisdiction, would be an unduly rigid one but was pertinent to the general question of discretion.

[211] See the decision in *Chabra* itself, [1992] 1 W.L.R. 231; *Yukong Line Ltd of Korea v Rendsburg Investments Corp* [2001] 2 Lloyd's Rep. 113, at [44], and *Parbulk II AS v PT Humpuss Intermoda Transportasi TBK* [2011] EWHC 3143 (Comm), at [44]–[46].

[212] *Yukong v Rendsburg* [2001] 2 Lloyd's Rep. 113, at [44].

who may be innocent of any wrongdoing (and have not acted so as to frustrate the administration of justice), it has been said that the jurisdiction is exceptional and should be exercised with caution.[213] This is particularly so where the basis of the order is not that the Chabra defendant holds assets beneficially owned by the cause of action defendant, but that the claimant (if he becomes a judgment creditor) may be able to exercise rights of the cause of action defendant against the Chabra defendant: in such a case, the Chabra defendant is being restrained from dealing with assets that are legally and beneficially its own.[214]

(2)   The "Good Reason to Suppose" Test

In *PJSC v Maksimov*[215] Popplewell J considered that the earlier authorities in relation to the *Chabra* jurisdiction demonstrated that its exercise depended upon there being "good reason to suppose"[216] that assets held in the name of a person against whom the claimant asserts no cause of action would be amenable to some process, ultimately enforceable by the courts, by which the assets would be available to satisfy a judgment against a defendant to a substantive claim. Echoing the test of a good arguable case on the merits as against the principal defendant, the judge said, at [7(2)]: **28–167**

> "The test of 'good reason to suppose' is to be equated with a good arguable case, that is to say one which is more than barely capable of serious argument, but yet not necessarily one which the Judge believes to have a better than 50 per cent chance of success."

In *JSC BTA Bank v Ablyazov (No.11)*,[217] on an application by third parties aimed at establishing that the defendant did not beneficially own a Cypriot company which had been listed as an asset of his in a post-judgment freezing injunction, the Court of Appeal held that it was **28–168**

> "not necessary to decide which of the two formulations (good arguable case/good reason to suppose) is the most appropriate one. The former is derived from *Chabra* and the latter from *Masri*. It was not submitted to us that, for the purposes of this case, there was any significant difference between them and certainly none which it is now necessary to explore."

---

[213] *PJSC Vseukrainskyi Aktsionernyi Bank v Maksimov* [2013] EWHC 422 (Comm), at [7]. See also *C Inc Plc v L* [2001] All E.R. (Comm) 446; [2001] 2 Lloyd's Rep. 459, at [44]; and *Parbulk II AS v PT Humpuss Intermoda Transportasi TBK* [2011] EWHC 3143 (Comm), at [39], per Gloster J.

[214] *Cruz City 1 Mauritius Holdings v Unitech Ltd* [2014] EWHC 3704 (Comm), per Males J at [10].

[215] *PJSC Vseukrainskyi Aktsionernyi Bank v Maksimov* [2013] EWHC 422 (Comm). Popplewell J restated the principles in his judgment in *Banca Turco Romana SA v Cortuk* [2018] EWHC 662 (Comm).

[216] The test first enunciated in this way in *SCF Finance v Masri* [1985] 1 W.L.R. 876. See also *Linsen International Ltd v Humpuss Sea Transport Pte Ltd*, [2011] EWHC 2339 (Comm); [2011] 2 Lloyd's Rep. 663, at [150].

[217] *JSC BTA Bank v Ablyazov (No.11)* [2014] EWCA Civ 602; [2015] 1 W.L.R. 1287, at [68].

(3) Jurisdictional Considerations

28–169   The need for a claimant to consider the *Chabra* jurisdiction will most obviously arise where the relevant assets are either within the jurisdiction or are amenable to the English court's enforcement procedures—which could include the future appointment of a liquidator or receiver over the principal defendant, whose reach in that office might well extend to any assets held abroad by others for that defendant. Nevertheless, there may in some cases be a question as to whether the court has the power to grant permission for the service of claim form upon a proposed *Chabra* defendant who is outside the jurisdiction.

28–170   In a case where the *Chabra* defendant has no presence within the jurisdiction, then the grant of relief will depend on persuading the Court that it is nonetheless amenable to the jurisdiction of the English Court. Absent special circumstances such as submission to the jurisdiction or, as is unlikely in the case of a *Chabra* defendant, some applicable jurisdiction clause, the claimant will have to show that permission should be given to serve out on in the normal way under the CPR. This is considered to be so even where the *Chabra* defendant is in a jurisdiction covered by the Judgments Regulation.[218]

28–171   If the substantive claim against the cause of action defendant is being heard in the English Court, then (arguably) the claimant can rely on the necessary or proper party gateway under para.3.1(3) of Practice Direction 6B.[219] If, however, the substantive claim is proceeding in a foreign court or in arbitral proceedings, or has already resulted in judgment, it is thought that there is no "claim" to be heard by the English Court for the purposes of the necessary or proper party gateway and so jurisdiction against the *Chabra* defendant cannot be established on that basis.[220] Nor, when the substantive claim is being advanced by way of arbitration, can the claimant invoke CPR 62.5(1)(b).[221] In a case where the substantive claim is before a foreign court, the claimant might instead rely on s.25 of the Civil

---

[218] Regulation (EU) No.1215/2012 on Jurisdiction and the Recognition and Enforcement of Judgments in Civil and Commercial Matters. This is because the Regulation does not contain a rule conferring jurisdiction in circumstances where an injunction is sought against a defendant domiciled in another territory but there is no cause of action against that defendant; it instead preserves the relevant domestic procedural law in that regard (art.35: "Application may be made to the courts of a Member State for such provisional, including protective, measures as may be available under the law of that Member State, even if the courts of another Member State have jurisdiction as to the substance of the matter.")

[219] *C Inc Plc v L* [2001] 2 All E.R. (Comm) 446; [2001] 2 Lloyd's Rep. 459, as explained in *Linsen International Ltd v Humpuss Sea Transport Pte Ltd* [2011] EWHC 2339 (Comm); [2011] 2 Lloyd's Rep. 663, per Flaux J at [161]–[164]; although note that this explanation of the decision in *C Inc Plc v L* was doubted by Males J in *Cruz City 1 Mauritius Holdings v Unitech Ltd* [2014] EWHC 3704 (Comm), at [74].

[220] See *Linsen International Ltd v Humpuss Sea Transport Pte Ltd* [2011] EWHC 2339 (Comm); [2011] 2 Lloyd's Rep. 663, at [13], [161]–[164], per Flaux J; *Parbulk II AS v PT Humpuss Intermoda Transportasi TBK* [2011] EWHC 3143 (Comm), at [74]–[81], per Gloster J; and *Cruz City 1 Mauritius Holdings v Unitech Ltd* [2014] EWHC 3704 (Comm), per Males J at [76].

[221] *Dtek Trading SA v Morozov* [2017] EWHC 94 (Comm), a case concerning a third party disclosure application, but which rested on the proposition that s.44 of the Arbitration Act 1996 did not confer jurisdiction to make orders against non-parties to the relevant arbitration agreement and so is equally applicable to an application for a freezing order of the *Chabra* sort.

Jurisdiction and Judgments Act 1982 and the jurisdictional gateway in CPR PD 6B, para.3.1(5) (subject to satisfying the additional hurdles that invoking that section involves).[222] Where, however, the claim has already resulted in a judgment or arbitral award which the claimant is seeking to enforce, but the proposed *Chabra* defendant is overseas and has no assets here, then there is no obvious jurisdictional gateway to support any application for permission to serve the proposed *Chabra* defendant out of the jurisdiction.[223]

(4)   Established Chabra Situations

There are certain established situations in which a third party may be considered to be an appropriate *Chabra* defendant and these are addressed below. It should, however, be recognised that

    "although one can articulate general principles that govern the approach, whether or not an order can or should be made will be necessarily heavily fact-dependent."[224]

The suggested categorisation below of potential *Chabra* situations must be read on this basis; and it must of course be kept in mind that, even if a relationship between the cause of action defendant and *Chabra* defendant which could make relief against the latter appropriate is established, the other limbs of the test for the grant of a freezing injunction must be satisfied before relief will be granted.

Companies.   The decision in the *Chabra* case itself was based upon the not unusual situation (at least in cases of suspected fraudulent activity) in which there was good reason to suppose that the assets of the respondent company, the potential *Chabra* defendant, were beneficially owned by the defendant shareholder rather than by the company. In such a case, and on the basis that the risk of dissipation presented by the shareholder therefore translated to a risk which extended to the assets apparently owned by the company, there was power

28–172

28–173

---

[222] See *Belletti v Morici* [2009] EWHC 2316 (Comm); [2010] 1 All E.R. (Comm) 412; and, as to s.25 more generally, Ch.26.

[223] It might be thought that the jurisdictional gateway under CPR PD 6B para.3.1(10) would be applicable; but see the observations made upon this by Flaux J in *Linsen International Ltd v Humpuss Sea Transport Pte Ltd* [2011] EWHC 2339 (Comm); [2011] 2 Lloyd's Rep. 663, at [167]–[169]. The judge said the claim to enforce any judgment must be one "against" the relevant defendant and (following the reasoning of the Court of Appeal on an application for permission to appeal) it must also relate to assets within the jurisdiction. In *Parbulk II* [2011] EWHC 3143 (Comm), at [74]–[81], Gloster J found it unnecessary to decide (in the light of earlier, arguably inconsistent authority) whether there was any territorial limitation upon the para.3.1(10) gateway for the purposes of determining whether *Chabra* relief can be justified under it. Nevertheless, even though the Judge found that the court had in personam jurisdiction over the *Chabra* defendant, by reason of its earlier submission to the jurisdiction, she declined to continue the worldwide relief against that party and limited the freezing injunction to assets within the jurisdiction (and up to the amount of its indebtedness to the principal defendant).

[224] *Parbulk II AS v Pt Humpus intermoda Transportasi TBK* [2011] EWHC 3143 (Comm), at [35], per Gloster J.

to grant an injunction against it. The injunction was "ancillary and incidental" to the cause of action against the principal defendant. In *Chabra*, Mummery J said[225]:

> "In brief, in the light of the plaintiff's evidence and the absence of any detailed evidence on the part of the defendants, I am of the view that there is a good arguable case that there are assets, apparently vested in the company, which may be beneficially the property of Mr. Chabra and therefore available to satisfy the plaintiff's claims against him if established at trial. I am also of the view that it is arguable that the company was, in fact, at relevant times the alter ego of Mr. Chabra and that its assets, or at least some of its assets, may be available to meet the plaintiff's claims against him if established."

28–174   *Chabra* was therefore a case where, on the evidence available, the respondent company appeared to have held its assets as a nominee (or possibly trustee) for the principal defendant (and therefore to have come within the next category of potential respondent addressed below). It is to be noted that this does not, per se, involve any disregarding of the separate corporate personality of the company or piercing of the corporate veil; the notion that the company was the "alter ego" of the defendant was identified as a separate basis for relief, which must be considered in the light of the authorities mentioned next.

28–175   In *Parbulk II AS v PT Humpuss Intermoda Transportasi TBK*[226] Gloster J observed:

> "However, it is not legitimate, in the context of third party freezing orders, to disregard the separate corporate personality of individual companies in a group (sometimes referred to as 'piercing the corporate veil'), merely because the ultimate, or intermediate, holding company may have the practical ability to require a subsidiary to act in a particular way, or because it is necessary to achieve justice, even in circumstances where one or more of the companies in question may have been involved in some sort of impropriety. To do so would offend the well-established principles of separate corporate personality enshrined in *Salomon*[227] ... The circumstances in which the 'piercing of the corporate veil' doctrine can be applied in order to justify the making of a freezing order against a third party are limited to situations where the company or entity against whom the order is sought has been used as a device or façade for concealing the true facts, or for avoiding or concealing the liability or assets of the principal defendant. Thus in circumstances where, for example, the evidence shows that a company or trust has been used as a vehicle or device for receiving monies wrongly paid out of a claimant company in breach of a defendant's duty to that company, the receipt by the third party vehicle will be treated as the receipt by the defendant."

28–176   In *Ben Hashem v Ali Shayif*[228] Munby J noted that it is the very essence of the principle in *Salomon* that ownership and control of a company are not of themselves reasons to lift the corporate veil.

---

[225] *TSB Private Bank International SA v Chabra* [1992] 1 W.L.R. 231, at 238.
[226] *Parbulk II AS v PT Humpuss Intermoda Transportasi TBK* [2011] EWHC 3143 (Comm), at [42]–[43].
[227] *Salomon v A Salomon & Co Ltd* [1897] A.C. 22. See also *Woolfson v Strathclyde Regional Council* [1978] SC (HL) 90 and *Adams v Cape Industries* [1990] 1 Ch. 433; *Trustor AB v Smallbone (No.2)* [2001] 1 W.L.R. 1177, at [21]–[23]; and *Ben Hashef v Ali Shayif* [2008] EWHC 2380 (Fam), at [159]–[166], [199]. Gloster J relied upon each of these authorities to reject the suggestion in *re a Company* [1985] B.C.L.C. 333, at 337–338, that the veil might be lifted as dictated by the needs of justice.
[228] *Ben Hashem v Ali Shayif* [2008] EWHC 2380 (Fam), at [159].

The reasoning behind these decisions has been reinforced by the decision of the **28–177** Supreme Court in *Prest v Petrodel Resources Ltd*[229] to the effect that the corporate veil should only be pierced where it is necessary to prevent the abuse of the separate corporate legal personality—what Lord Sumption identified as "the evasion principle", which is triggered where a company has been interposed in the affairs of the person in control of it so as to defeat or frustrate enforcement of his obligations.

However, it is clear that the *Chabra* relief may be granted against a company **28–178** (outside a case of nomineeship) even when it cannot be categorised as a device or façade for concealing the true ownership of assets. This will be so at least[230] in the case where the relationship between the cause of action defendant and the company against whom *Chabra* relief is sought is such that the cause of action defendant could compel the company to make the company's assets available to meet a claim against him (and thus those assets could be available to a judgment creditor upon enforcement).

Thus in *Yukos Capital S.a.r.l v OJSC Rosneft Oil Company*[231] the claimant had **28–179** obtained a freezing injunction against certain companies, on an ex parte application, on the basis that they were "puppets" of Rosneft and that the monies paid into their London bank accounts were held as nominee for that defendant to the claim, or were directly or indirectly controlled by it. The monies represented the proceeds of back-to-back sales of oil in which the companies were interposed between Rosneft and the purchaser. At the inter partes hearing to set aside the order the companies relied upon evidence to the contrary, as a result of which the claimant no longer asserted they were nominees and accepted that the monies in question were not beneficially owned by Rosneft and were paid into various bank accounts at the request of Rosneft's bankers as part of their security arrangements. Nevertheless, the freezing injunction was continued on the basis that the companies were special purpose vehicles with no business or assets of their own. Rosneft's interest in the monies was said to be "formidable" (in circumstances where the companies existed only so as to provide a portal for the transfer of the purchase price whilst respecting the bank's security) and such as to expose them to recovery by the claimant, if necessary by the appointment of a receiver.

In *Parbulk II* the court refused to grant an injunction against a company simply **28–180** on the basis that it was wholly owned by the first defendant who was alleged to be liable to the claimant under a guarantee. Instead, the injunction against that

---

[229] *Prest v Petrodel Resources Ltd* [2013] UKSC 34; [2013] 2 A.C. 415, per Lord Sumption at [25]–[35], and per Lord Neuberger at [81]–[82]. See further Ch.18.

[230] See paras 28–112—28–125 above, which raises the question of whether the effect of the Supreme Court's decision in *JSC BTA Bank v Ablyazov (No.10)* [2015] UKSC 64; [2015] 1 W.L.R. 4754 is that *Lakatamia Shipping Co Ltd v Su* [2014] EWCA Civ 636; [2015] 1 W.L.R. 291 has been overruled and the courts should treat standard form freezing injunctions as extending to assets of third party companies even where those assets would (on ordinary company law principles) *not* be amendable to execution of a judgment against the defendant. If that is right, presumably the scope for making freezing orders against those companies directly is similarly extended.

[231] *Yukos Capital S.a.r.l v OJSC Rosneft Oil Company* [2010] EWHC 784 (Comm); [2011] 1 All E.R. (Comm) 172.

overseas company (in relation to any assets within the jurisdiction up to the value of its indebtedness to that parent company and to its own subsidiary under various loans) was justified by reference to the evidence which established a risk that it might well take steps to put itself in a position where it could not meet its obligations to the group companies.[232]

28–181   It is therefore clear that corporate entities may be brought within the *Chabra* jurisdiction by reference to evidence which shows something other than bare nomineeship, and which falls short of (properly) piercing the corporate veil.

28–182   **Nominees.**   In *PJSC v Maksimov*[233] the court confirmed that:

> "A common example of assets falling within the *Chabra* jurisdiction is where there is good reason to suppose that the assets in the name of the [*Chabra* defendant] are in truth the assets of the [defendant alleged to be liable on the claim]. Such assets will be treated as in truth the assets of [the latter] if they are held as nominee or trustee for [him] as the ultimate beneficial owner."

So, in one of the earliest cases on the exercise of the *Chabra* jurisdiction, the court included within the scope of the *Mareva* injunction the London bank account of the defendant's wife, through which there was good reason to suppose he was still carrying on business.[234]

28–183   The apparent nomineeship of such assets (established to the standard of a good arguable case or "good reason to suppose") thus provides a clear case for considering *Chabra* relief. Indeed, as the court went on to observe in *PJSC v Maksimov*, such nomineeship (which may be evidenced by demonstrating that the defendant to the claim enjoys substantial control over the third party sought to be restrained) may also help to establish that there exists the necessary risk of dissipation (to justify the grant of a freezing injunction against him) as well as the grounds for *Chabra* relief against the third party. Similarly, in the *Ablyazov* litigation the propensity of the principal defendant to use associates to hold shareholdings in their names as "stooges" for him was noted and said to make it at the very least well arguable that such associates were in truth his nominees and appropriate targets for *Chabra* orders.[235]

28–184   In *PJSC v Maksimov* there was a good arguable case that the corporate defendants against whom that relief was sought held their respective shareholdings in a Ukrainian company as nominee for a Cypriot company. The critical question, for the purpose of the freezing injunction against them on *Chabra* principles, was whether that Cypriot company (and the person who was said to be the beneficial owner and controller of that company) was the nominee of the individual defendant to the claim. The judge concluded on the evidence that there was good reason to suppose that the Cypriot company had been and remained a company owned and substantially controlled by him and that, on that basis, the injunctive

---

[232] *Parbulk II AS v PT Humpuss Intermoda Transportasi TBK* [2011] EWHC 3143 (Comm), at [63] and [98].
[233] *PJSC Vseukrainskyi Aktsionernyi Bank v Maksimov* [2013] EWHC 422 (Comm), per Popplewell J at [7(4)].
[234] *SCF Finance Co Ltd v Masri* [1985] 1 W.L.R. 876.
[235] *JSC BTA Bank v Ablyazov (No. 11)* [2014] EWCA Civ 602; [2015] 1 W.L.R. 1287, at [34].

relief against the corporate defendants (in respect of their Ukrainian sharehold-ings) was justified. In the context of considering whether there was a good arguable case that their assets would be amenable to execution in the event of judgment being obtained against the defendant, the court said the evidence justified it legitimately conflating the legally distinct tests of substantial control and beneficial ownership. As above, actual control by the respondent over an asset is an indicator that either he has a beneficial interest in the asset in question or that some other route which would render the asset amenable to enforcement of a future judgment may be available.

Trustees/Trust Structures.   As we have noted above, it has long been   **28–185** recognised that, in dealing with cases of international fraud, the High Court should be prepared to take "drastic action" aimed at preventing its orders being thwarted by the use of shadowy offshore trusts and companies established in jurisdictions where secrecy is highly prized and official regulation at a lower level.[236]

Such structures may sometimes be used to facilitate tax evasion, corruption or   **28–186** other wrongdoing. However, it is not necessary for the claimant to show that the principal defendant has put assets into the trust for the purposes of covering his tracks or that the assets in question represent the fruits of any wrongdoing. The defendant's use (as opposed to abuse) of such a trust may trigger the *Chabra* jurisdiction.

In *Dadourian Group International Inc v Dadourian*[237] the *Chabra* jurisdiction   **28–187** was successfully invoked against a Liechtenstein Anstalt which was said to be the beneficial owner (through a shareholding in a company held upon trust for the Anstalt by a Geneva lawyer) of a flat in Paris which the claimant sought to bring within the scope of a worldwide freezing injunction. The evidence suggested that the Anstalt had been established by the fourth defendant for good tax planning and succession reasons. The Deputy Judge concluded that, while beneficial ownership under a bare trusteeship would clearly support the exercise of the jurisdiction, it was not necessary to establish such beneficial ownership in a "strict trust law sense."[238] The important issue was instead one of "substantive control", so that putting assets into a discretionary trust

---

[236] *International Credit & Investment Co (Overseas) Ltd v Adham* [1998] BCC 134, at 136, per Robert Walker J.

[237] *Dadourian Group International Inc v Azuri Ltd* [2005] EWHC 1768 (Ch), per Edward Bartley Jones QC.

[238] So far as English trust law is concerned, even where a trust company holds assets on trust for the settlor, with whose wishes it may be expected to comply in relation to any advance of monies to him as a discretionary beneficiary, the trust will not, without more, be regarded as a sham: *Re Esteem Settlement* [2004] W.T.L.R 1. In the case of a genuine discretionary trust, the trust assets are just that and the discretionary beneficiary has only a right to be considered for a distribution: *Gartside v IRC* [1968] A.C. 553, at 615–617. The reasoning of the Deputy Judge in *Dadourian*, at [30] identifying a "controlled discretionary trust" as a bare trust, or even a sham, because "any other analysis would entirely defeat the ability of the English courts to take drastic action and would allow the court's orders to be evaded by manipulations" must therefore be open to question. The further requirement identified by Sir John Chadwick in *Algosaibi v Saad Investments Company Ltd* [2011] 1 C.I.L.R. 178, at [33]—that there is good reason to suppose the trust assets are amenable to enforcement—must also not be overlooked.

"would not prevent the *Chabra* jurisdiction being exercised against that discretionary trust if the substantive reality were that the relevant defendant controlled the exercise of the discretionary trust"(at [30]).

28–188 This reasoning was regarded as persuasive by David Steel J in *Yukos Capital S.a.r.l v OJSC Rosneft Oil Company*[239], who doubted the significance of establishing a beneficial interest, in the strict sense arising under English trust law, when determining the scope of freezing orders which commonly involve both domestic and foreign parties.

28–189 The focus upon "substantive control" over trust assets is also consistent with the decision of the Privy Council in *Tasarruf Mevduati Sigorta Fonu v Merrill Lynch Bank and Trust Co (Cayman) Ltd*,[240] where the court appointed receivers by way of equitable execution over a settlor's express power to revoke two discretionary Cayman Islands trusts (the discretionary objects of which were his wife, children and remoter issue with a charity named as residuary beneficiary) and, to give effect to that relief, made a mandatory order compelling him to transfer or delegate the power of revocation to the receivers. In the context of equitable execution by a judgment creditor, Lord Collins handing down the opinion of the Privy Council, identified the primary question as being

"whether the power of revocation of the trusts is sufficiently close to the notion of property to enable the equitable remedy of a receiver by way of equitable execution to be available"(at [8]).

This approach of equating power over trust assets (if the power is sufficiently extensive) to property, albeit at the later stage of enforcement of the judgment, reinforces the approach in *Dadourian*, at the interim remedy stage, that if there is good reason to suppose that the defendant to the claim enjoys "substantive control" over the trust assets, even though strict beneficial ownership cannot be established, this may suffice to persuade the Court that there is a potential route to enforce against the assets, and therefore that the assets should fall within the scope of the freezing injunction.

28–190 **Debtors and Other Accountable Parties.** There is no reason in principle why the exercise of the *Chabra* jurisdiction in future cases should not reveal further categories of relationship between the principal defendant and the *Chabra* defendant which support the making of a freezing order against the latter. It has already been noted above (see para.28–162 above) that the jurisdiction is not limited to cases where the third party holds, or has received, assets beneficially

---

[239] *Yukos Capital S.a.r.l v OJSC Rosneft Oil Company* [2010] EWHC 784 (Comm), at [22]. What the judge said cannot be gainsaid, but it is quite another matter to conclude that an injunction having such reach *will* ultimately fulfil the enforcement principle when it comes to executing any judgment. He also observed (at [17]) that this is consistent with the jurisdiction not being limited to cases where specific assets can be identified: see *Yukong Line v Rendsburg* [2001] 2 Lloyd's Rep. 113, at [44], and *Linsen International Ltd v Humpuss Sea Transport Pte Ltd* [2011] EWHC 2339 (Comm), at [148].
[240] *Tasarruf Mevduati Sigorta Fonu v Merrill Lynch Bank and Trust Co (Cayman) Ltd* [2011] UKPC 17; [2012] 1 W.L.R. 1721.

belonging to the principal defendant. It may be invoked where the third party is accountable to the principal defendant for some debt or other receivable, claim or potential claim.

So, in *C Inc Plc v L*[241] the court exercised the *Chabra* jurisdiction against the defendant's husband on the basis that, if she had been acting on his behalf as an undisclosed principal in the activities which had given rise to the claimant's default judgment against her, then as a matter of agency law she was entitled to be indemnified by him against her liability in respect of the judgment debt. There was no suggestion that the husband held assets (whether as nominee, trustee or otherwise) for the defendant; but the right of indemnity, which was a personal rather than proprietary right, was one which could be enforced by her or, if she was unwilling to do so, by a receiver appointed by the court. Aikens J followed the decision of the High Court of Australia in *Cardile v LED Builders Pty Ltd*[242] concluding that, in these circumstances, the grant of *Chabra* relief against the husband could be properly analysed as "ancillary" to the claimant's substantive right under the unsatisfied judgment. Aikens J held that, whilst the *Chabra* jurisdiction could be extended to personal claims, nonetheless there had to

28–191

> "be some causal link between the fact that the claimant has obtained judgment against the principal defendant and thus has a legal right, *as a consequence of that liability giving rise to the judgment*, to go against the assets of the third party" (emphasis in original).[243]

We consider below the extent to which this remains a limiting factor: of course in traditional *Chabra* scenarios, i.e. where a third party holds assets on behalf of the defendant, the circumstances in which the third party acquired legal ownership of those assets are irrelevant to the exercise of the jurisdiction.

In the very influential decision in *Cardile* the court had held that the jurisdiction was not confined to the situation where the third party holds property which is said to be beneficially owned by the defendant, but extended to situations where the defendant had "claims and expectancies" in relation to the third party. In that case, the claim (which it was proposed a liquidator appointed over the defendant company could advance, judgment having been entered in favour of the claimant in the main action) arose out of the non-commercial payment to the third parties (who controlled the defendant) of a dividend which had been paid with the object of limiting the funds available to meet the claimant's judgment. The judgment of the majority[244] stated the principle on which the court was acting in very wide terms[245]:

28–192

---

[241] *C Inc Plc v L* [2001] 2 All E.R. (Comm) 446; [2001] 2 Lloyd's Rep. 459, at [76].
[242] *Cardile v LED Builders Pty Ltd* [1999] HCA 18; (1999) 198 CLR 380.
[243] *C Inc Plc v L* [2001] 2 All E.R. (Comm) 446; [2001] 2 Lloyd's Rep. 459, at [77].
[244] Comprising such noted jurists as Gaudron McHugh, Gummow and Callinan JJ.
[245] *Cardile v LED Builders Pty Ltd* [1999] HCA 18; (1999) 198 C.L.R. 380, at [57]. It should be recognised that where A claims against B and seeks an injunction against C on the basis that C has received assets from B, A may well be able to found an injunction against C on the basis that he has a direct claim against C pursuant to s.423 of the Insolvency Act 1986 (see Ch.16 above). An English example is *Aiglon Ltd v Gau Shan Co Ltd* [1993] B.C.L.C. 1321. The significance of *Cardile* is that,

"What then is the principle to guide the courts in determining whether to grant *Mareva* relief in a case such as the present where the activities of third parties are the object sought to be restrained? In our opinion such an order may, and we emphasise the word 'may', be appropriate, assuming the existence of other relevant criteria and discretionary factors, in circumstances in which:

(i)   the third party holds, is using, or has exercised or is exercising a power of disposition over, or is otherwise in possession of, assets, including 'claims and expectancies', of the judgment debtor or potential judgment debtor; or

(ii)   some process, ultimately enforceable by the courts, is or may be available to the judgment creditor as a consequence of a judgment against that actual or potential judgment debtor, pursuant to which, whether by appointment of a liquidator, trustee in bankruptcy, receiver or otherwise, the third party may be obliged to disgorge property or otherwise contribute to the funds or property of the judgment debtor to help satisfy the judgment against the judgment debtor. "

28–193   As a later English judge rightly noted,[246]

"the literal application of the second limb of the principle set out in paragraph 57(ii) of the judgment of the majority of the High Court is potentially of extremely wide application. It appears to contemplate that jurisdiction exists to make a freezing order against any potential debtor of an individual or company against whom the claimant has a cause of action, upon the footing that since enforcement of a judgment against the defendant may lead to its liquidation or (if an individual) bankruptcy, and since a liquidator or trustee in bankruptcy may then be able to pursue claims against third parties, then jurisdiction exists to enable the plaintiff to seek a freezing order against any such third parties, always assuming that the other discretionary considerations, such as a risk of dissipation of assets, are satisfied."

This interpretation of the jurisdiction is probably now established as part of the law of England and Wales. The vital point is that it is now recognised that the jurisdiction to make a freezing order in favour of a claimant against a third party does not depend upon the third party's status as a nominee or trustee of property beneficially owned by the defendant, but extends to any situation where the defendant has a pecuniary right, whether vested or contingent, against the third party.[247] Of course the question whether the court should, as a matter of discretion, exercise that jurisdiction on the facts of the case, is a separate one.

28–194   In both *C Inc Plc v L* and *Cardile* the claimant had obtained judgment against the principal defendant. As we have seen, Aikens J[248] analysed the Australian decision as requiring there to be some causal link between the fact that the claimant has obtained judgment against the principal defendant and thus has a legal right, *as a consequence of the liability giving rise to the judgment*, to go against the assets of the third party. This passage is not easy to understand on a number of levels: first it is grammatically obscure; secondly it is not clear that *Cardile* says any such thing; and thirdly the law is clear that the wider *Chabra* jurisdiction identified in *Cardile* is not dependent upon the claimant having obtained judgment against the principal defendant.

---

even where no such action lies, the court still has a jurisdiction against C based upon B's potential claim against him, and even if that claim only arises on B's insolvency (e.g. a claim under ss.213 or 238 of the Insolvency Act).

[246] Briggs J in *HMRC v Clayton Egleton* [2006] EWHC 2313 (Ch); [2007] 1 All E.R. 606, at [29].

[247] See *HMRC v Clayton Egleton*, at [41].

[248] *C Inc Plc v L* [2001] 2 All E.R. (Comm) 446; [2001] 2 Lloyd's Rep. 459, at [50]. See also at [75(6)].

In the event, the question of whether it is necessary to show this causal link was **28–195** considered again by Briggs J in *HMRC v Clayton Egleton*.[249] The claimant presented a creditors' petition for winding up a company for unpaid VAT. It obtained a freezing order against a number of respondents whom it argued the company had claims against and which would be likely to be pursued by a liquidator. In granting the injunction, and whilst noting with some concern the width of the jurisdiction enunciated in *Cardile*,[250] the judge nonetheless declined to recognise *any* form of causation threshold which had to be surmounted by the applicant for a freezing order against the third party and which might act as a prophylactic to rein in that jurisdiction.[251] In so concluding, the judge rejected even the claimant's own "sufficient connection" test as the boundary for the existence of jurisdiction, although he accepted that it might be highly relevant when considering whether, as a matter of discretion, an injunction might be granted. So, for instance, if a defendant has previously lent a sum of money to a third party a considerable period prior to the events giving rise to the claimant's claim, and that money is now due and owing, a court might very well decline to grant a freezing order against that third party on the basis that (and putting aside any other consideration) the third party's liability to the defendant is entirely unrelated to the claimant's claim, even though, in the event of the claimant succeeding, he could appoint a liquidator (or other office-holder) to pursue that third party on the debt. The decision in *HMRC v Clayton Egleton* has proved highly influential and remains the leading decision on the boundaries of the *Chabra* jurisdiction.

There may be other relationships where a third party's accountability to the **28–196** defendant brings that party within the potential scope of the *Chabra* jurisdiction. However, a third party's "custodianship" of assets for the defendant should not render him vulnerable to *Chabra* relief if it is on terms which create genuine pre-existing contractual rights, or some kind of security interest, in favour of the third party. As we have seen above, a freezing injunction is designed only to catch the value of the defendant's *unencumbered* assets and it would not be a proper exercise of the jurisdiction for the court to contemplate that a third party who benefits from any such encumbrance might lose it.[252]

---

[249] *HMRC v Clayton Egleton* [2006] EWHC 2313 (Ch); [2007] 1 All E.R. 606.
[250] See at [38]: "I am greatly troubled (as I suspect was Aikens J. himself) that the uncontrolled extension of that jurisdiction to any third party whom the claimant might persuade the defendant's liquidator or trustee in bankruptcy to sue in the future would open a Pandora's box of satellite litigation which the courts and court users would in due course come to regret."
[251] *HMRC v Clayton Egleton*, at [42].
[252] Compare the decision of Hirst J in *Prekookeanska Plovidba v L.N.T. Lines S.R.L.* [1989] 1 W.L.R. 753, at 757E–757F, that the *Mareva* injunction over the defendant's money in the client account of solicitors could be of no avail to the extent that the solicitors enjoyed a lien for unpaid fees. See also the provision for a bank's right of set-off and the *Baltic* proviso in the standard form of freezing injunction: paras 28–152—28–156 above.

F.   PROPRIETARY INJUNCTIONS

(1)   Advantages for Claimants

28–197   If the alleged victim of a fraud asserts a proprietary claim against the defendant (most obviously where the alleged fraudster or his transferee is said to be a constructive trustee of the claimant's property or its identifiable substitute or proceeds) then, at the interim stage of proceedings, he enjoys a number of potential advantages over the applicant for a freezing injunction in support of a non-proprietary claim. The applicant for interim relief should therefore consider very carefully whether the injunction he is seeking involves to any extent the protection of assets to which he maintains a proprietary claim.

28–198   First and foremost amongst these advantages is the court's often-expressed willingness to exercise its equitable jurisdiction "without hesitation", if a failure to do so runs the risk that equity will have been invoked in vain and the "trust fund" which is said to be at risk will have disappeared by the time the matter comes to trial.[253] The court's readiness to preserve the property in question, so that the claimant might meaningfully establish his claim to it at trial, is further reflected in its approach to the granting and terms of any proprietary-based interim injunction. These include its application of the *American Cyanamid* test when assessing the merits of the substantive claim; a lesser focus upon the need to establish that the respondent presents a particular risk of dissipation as opposed to showing that he is arguably possessed of the property to which the claimant lays claim; and a greater reluctance to permit expenditure by the respondent pending trial which would diminish the value of the property in question. We consider these points further below

(2)   The Nature of a Proprietary Injunction

28–199   By CPR 25.1(c) the court may make an interim order for the detention, custody or preservation of "relevant property".[254] "Relevant property" is defined as "property (including land) which is the subject of a claim or as to which any question may arise on a claim."[255] Accordingly, where a claimant asserts a claim

---

[253] See *Mediterranea Raffineria Siciliana Petroli SpA v Mabanaft GmbH*, unreported, 1 December 1978; [1978] CA Transcript 816, per Templeman LJ, and the later authorities citing the principle, referred to at para.26–031 above.

[254] This is probably not to be regarded as the source of the court's jurisdiction to grant a proprietary injunction, which derives from its equitable jurisdiction; although note the suggestion in the case cited in the following footnote that there is a distinction between CPR 25.1(c) and the more general jurisdiction to grant injunctive relief.

[255] In *Wood v Baker* [2015] EWHC 2536 (Ch), at [28] HH Judge Hodge QC highlighted the "may arise" language in support of his conclusion that, whereas *The Siskina* requirement of an accrued cause of action may not have been satisfied for the purpose of making an immediate freezing injunction, the court could grant relief to preserve property (proposed to be caught by the service of an after-acquired property notice) under CPR 25.1(1)(a). The court also has the power, stated in r.25.1(1)(g), to require a party to provide information about the location of relevant property or assets or to provide information about relevant property. Such an order is often made in conjunction with a proprietary injunction.

in specie to relevant property that claimant can apply to the court for an interim injunction aimed at preserving in the hands of the defendant that property on the basis that at trial the claimant will seek a remedy which involves the return of that property to the claimant. The term "proprietary injunction" is used to describe the type of injunction issued by the court in response to such a claim. It follows that a proprietary injunction must identify with clarity the asset(s) which are the subject of the restraint.

It will be obvious that such an injunction differs in its essential character from a freezing order. A freezing order freezes assets against which no proprietary claim is asserted so as to ensure so far as possible, and consistent with the defendant's primary right to operate his business and (where the defendant is an individual) lifestyle in accordance with his usual patterns of behaviour, that the claimant will have assets available to him to enforce against in the event of success at trial. By contrast, a proprietary injunction freezes a defined asset (or assets) in the hands of the defendant in order to preserve the claimant's asserted right to that very asset, and because of the concern that a failure to freeze that asset may result in the asset having been in some way destroyed or diminished in value by the time the parties' rights are finally adjudicated upon at trial.[256] That difference has a number of practical consequences which we examine below. **28–200**

A proprietary injunction may be, and often is, sought simultaneously with a freezing order. The circumstances which will generally justify such a twin approach include where the claimant has a proprietary claim but the identifiable property subject to that claim is insufficient to meet the claimant's claim.[257] However care should be taken to ascertain whether in fact it is necessary for the applicant to go further than seeking proprietary relief. An attempt to seek a freezing order, either in addition to or in place of a proprietary injunction, may create added complications and expense for an applicant, as well as set up for himself the higher hurdles required to be surmounted in order to obtain freezing relief. It is sensible for an applicant to analyse carefully his true claim and ascertain whether a closely-directed proprietary injunction in fact would sufficiently protect his interests pending trial. Even if a freezing order is sought in addition to a proprietary injunction the applicant should be careful to ensure that the overall amount injuncted does not involve any double counting. **28–201**

---

[256] See *Mercedes Benz A.G. v Leiduck* [1996] A.C. 284, per Lord Mustill at 300E–300F: "The courts administering the remedy always distinguish sharply between tracing and other remedies available where the plaintiff asserts that the assets in question belong to him and that the dealings with them should be enjoined in order to protect his proprietary rights, and *Mareva* injunctions granted where the plaintiff does not claim any interest in the assets and seeks an inhibition of dealings with them simply in order to keep them available for a possible future execution to satisfy an unconnected claim."
[257] See e.g. *Madoff Securities International Ltd v Raven* [2011] EWHC 3102 (Comm), at [143], per Flaux J.

(3) The Requirements for a Proprietary Injunction

28–202 In contrast to a non-proprietary freezing injunction, a proprietary injunction is approached in much the same way as any other application for an interim injunction, by application of the well-known *American Cyanamid*[258] principles. In summary, as they would apply to a proprietary injunction, these are:

(1) that the claimant has shown that there is a serious issue to be tried on the merits;
(2) that the balance of convenience is in favour of granting an injunction; and
(3) that it is just and convenient to grant the injunction.[259]

We consider each of those elements below.

(i) Serious issue to be tried

28–203 Whereas, as we have seen, an applicant for a freezing injunction is required to show a good arguable case on the merits[260], a claimant seeking a proprietary injunction need only show that there is a "serious issue to be tried".

28–204 In *Sukhoruchkin v Van Bekestein*[261] Morgan J said:

> "The established view is that the requirements for a proprietary injunction are not identical to those for a freezing injunction. The principles to be applied are the normal *American Cyanamid* principles. These are that the Claimants must show that there is a serious issue to be tried, that damages would not be an adequate remedy for the Claimants and that the balance of convenience or balance of justice favours the grant of an injunction. This formulation of the relevant principles refers to a claimant showing a serious issue to be tried rather than showing a good arguable case. It is generally understood that a requirement to show a good arguable case is more onerous than showing only a serious issue to be tried. Nonetheless, it has been said in relation to the *American Cyanamid* principles that where the scales are evenly balanced in relation to the balance of convenience, one can take into account the relative strengths of the parties' cases.[262] For a statement to that effect in a relevant context, see *Polly Peck International Plc v Nadir (No.2)* [1992] 4 All E.R. 769, at 784G–784H, per Scott LJ."

---

[258] I.e. as set out in *American Cyanamid Co v Ethicon Ltd* [1975] A.C. 396.

[259] See e.g. *Madoff Securities International Ltd v Raven* [2011] EWHC 3102 (Comm), at [128]. The test has also been put as follows: that the applicant must show "that there is a serious issue to be tried, that damages would not be an adequate remedy for the appellants and that the balance of convenience or balance of justice favours the grant of an injunction": *Sukhoruchkin v Van Bekestein* [2014] EWCA Civ 399, at [18]. There is no real distinction between these formulations (particularly since the adequacy of damages is probably the most important, and often determinative, aspect of the balance of convenience question).

[260] See paras 28–013—28–023 above.

[261] *Sukhoruchkin v Van Bekestein* [2013] EWHC 1993 (Ch), at [7]. Although the judge's dismissal of the application was overturned on appeal, the Court of Appeal endorsed this statement of the test: [2014] EWCA Civ 399, at [17]–[18].

[262] As a matter of practice it is perhaps more common than Lord Diplock's strictures in *American Cyanamid* would suggest for the courts to take account of the respective merits of the parties' cases: see *Series 5 Software Ltd v Clarke* [1996] 1 All E.R. 853, at 865, and *Kitzing v Fuller* [2016] EWHC 804 (Ch).

It is a consistent feature of the application of the *American Cynamid* test that courts, necessarily faced only with written evidence at the relevant stage of the proceedings, and with no practical ability to test the factual assertions made by each side, are generally very resistant to enquiring too closely into the merits of the claim. Unless the claim is obviously misconceived a court is likely to proceed on the basis that there is a "serious issue to be tried." If there is a dispute on the facts, the court will rarely seek to adjudicate on who has the better of the case. Similarly, where the applicant's case is founded upon a difficult point of law, then the court should generally not attempt to resolve it.[263]

28–205

(ii) Balance of convenience

The balance of convenience must be shown to be in favour of granting an injunction. Central to this question (although not the only consideration relevant to it) would be whether damages would be an adequate remedy for the claimant. If there is a serious issue to be tried and the claimant could be prejudiced by steps taken by the defendant if he is not restrained by an injunction, in a way that would not adequately be protected by an award of damages at trial, and if the claimant's cross-undertaking in damages would provide the defendant with sufficient protection if it transpires he should not have been restrained, then ordinarily an injunction should be granted. This is just a way of spelling out the basic principle that the court should decide which course appears on the (necessarily limited) material before it to be likely to cause the least irremediable prejudice to one party or the other.[264] In reality, unlike in other types of interim injunction where the balance of convenience may create real room for argument, it is likely that a claimant with a properly arguable claim to a proprietary interest in particular property will be able to persuade the Court that damages will be not be an adequate remedy should the property be dealt with pending trial, and the balance of convenience will generally favour him.

28–206

Unlike in the case of a freezing injunction, it is not necessary for the applicant to show any risk of dissipation of assets. Therefore, delay in the making of the application ought not to present the problem it might for a claimant seeking a freezing injunction.[265] However, there must be shown to be some risk of the particular asset being dealt with in order to justify the interim relief sought. If the feared act has in fact already happened, or there is no risk of it happening, then interim relief will be refused.[266]

28–207

---

[263] *Derby v Weldon* [1990] Ch. 48, at 58F-58G, 63G-H. This principle was recently applied by the Court of Appeal in *Sukhoruchkin v Van Bekestein* [2014] EWCA Civ 399, at [32].

[264] *National Commercial Bank Jamaica Ltd v Olint Corp Ltd* [2009] UKPC 16; [2009] 1 W.L.R. 1405, at [16]–[17], per Lord Hoffmann.

[265] *Cherney v Neuman* [2009] EWHC 1743 (Ch), at [101]–[102], per HHJ Waksman QC and *Madoff Securities International Ltd v Raven* [2011] EWHC 3102 (Comm), at [128], per Flaux J.

[266] *Baxendale-Walker v Bay Trust International* [2017] EWHC 3576 (Ch). In that case, the settlor of a number of offshore trusts complained that trust sums had been misapplied and further that a result of those misapplications was an increased tax liability. In proceedings to remove the trustee, the claimant sought a proprietary injunction to prevent the trustee from dealing with the assets. In circumstances where the claimant had acted with no urgency, where the complaint was not of a feared act but one that had already taken place and the trust property was not in jeopardy, interim relief was refused.

28–208 It follows from the above that, once a serious issue to try on a proprietary claim is established, the court will more readily grant interim relief to preserve an asset which is the subject of such a claim than freezing relief. So, in *Madoff Securities International Ltd v Raven*[267] Flaux J stated:

> "In my judgment, once the position has been reached, as it has in the present case, that the claimant shows a sufficiently arguable case for a proprietary remedy, then, as Staughton LJ stated in the *Duvalier*[268] case, the court will more readily afford that claimant with interim remedies by way of injunction and disclosure orders. Not to do so might well, as Lord Hoffmann put it in *Olint*[269] cause irremediable prejudice to the claimant. As I said during the course of argument, given a sufficiently arguable case that the Kohn defendants have had MSIL's money, arguments by Mrs Kohn along the lines of: 'it would be frightfully inconvenient to tell you what I've done with your money or to be prevented from continuing to use it' when, on this hypothesis she should not have had the money in the first place, do not cut much ice."

28–209 The greater willingness of the court to grant injunctive relief to preserve an asset to which the claimant lays claim is illustrated by decisions where the court refused a freezing injunction but was prepared to exercise its equitable jurisdiction in support of proprietary-based relief. In *Purple Star Shipping Ltd v Fortune Shipping Ltd*[270] Moore-Bick J was not satisfied that a sufficiently cogent case had been made out in relation to the risk of dissipation to support the grant of a freezing injunction, but he did make an order protecting the claimant's alleged interest in the funds which represented part of the cargo of oil (22,000 barrels of 55,000 barrels) which had been sold by the defendant to a third party. In relation to that part, the claimant had an arguable case for saying it had a proprietary interest in the oil and its proceeds. As the defendant was facing substantial claims from a number of other creditors, including the Indonesian tax authorities, the judge could see

> "that there may be competing claimants to the funds in the defendant's possession and that it would be appropriate to make an order to safeguard the claimants' interest in the proceeds of sale of the 22,000 barrels of oil."

28–210 In *Polly Peck International Plc v Nadir (No.2)*[271] the Court of Appeal discharged a freezing injunction against a Cypriot bank where the cause of action based upon its alleged constructive trusteeship was regarded as speculative and the injunction would substantially interfere with the bank's normal banking business. However, the court was prepared to grant a more limited injunction to preserve the sum of £8.9m still held in the bank's foreign currency reserves which were said by the claimant to be traceable as its property. Lord Donaldson MR observed[272]:

---

[267] *Madoff Securities International Ltd v Raven* [2011] EWHC 3102 (Comm), at [140].

[268] *Republic of Haiti v Duvalier (No.2)* [1990] 1 Q.B. 202, at 213–214.

[269] *National Commercial Bank Jamaica Ltd v Olint Corp Ltd* [2009] UKPC 16; [2009] 1 W.L.R. 1405.

[270] *Purple Star Shipping Ltd v Fortune Shipping Ltd*, unreported, 13 December 2001; (2001) WL 1612620.

[271] *Polly Peck International Plc v Nadir (No.2)* [1992] 4 All E.R. 769; [1992] 2 Lloyd's Rep. 238.

[272] *Polly Peck International Plc v Nadir (No.2)*, at 787.

"This is a wholly different basis for an injunction, namely an application under [what is now CPR 25.1(c)] for an order for the interim preservation of property which is the subject matter of the cause or matter. If at the trial the plaintiffs can make good their tracing claim, they will be in the position of secured creditors to the extent, but very probably *only* to the extent, that the £8.9m has not meanwhile been removed from the jurisdiction. In this context, unlike that of a Mareva injunction, *American Cyanamid* principles do apply."

(iii) Just and convenient

In *Madoff Securities International Ltd v Raven*[273] the court recognised that, although the question of whether or not it is just and convenient to grant the injunction is a separate one, once the court has decided that the balance of convenience favours the grant of an injunction, it is "extremely unlikely" that the court would say it is not just and convenient to do so. **28–211**

In relation to a purely proprietary injunction, there will be no equivalent consideration of resorting to a freeze of overseas assets to cover any apparent deficiency in domestic assets when compared with the value of the claimant's monetary claim. Instead, the location of the subject matter of the proprietary claim will determine whether or not the subject matter of the injunction has a domestic or international flavour. **28–212**

(4) The Form of Order

A proprietary injunction will typically prevent the defendant from dissipating, reducing in value or otherwise dealing with the identified asset(s). Other remedies are available however. As with freezing injunctions, the Court has jurisdiction pursuant to s.37(1) of the Senior Courts Act 1981 to appoint a receiver over a defendant's assets whenever it is just and convenient to do so. The appointment of a receiver will be particularly appropriate if the asset in question requires some form of management or administration to protect its value.[274] **28–213**

Because, unlike most freezing orders, the order is not referable to an undifferentiated body of assets belonging to the defendant, up to a maximum sum, there is generally no need to carve out the usual provisos found in freezing orders relating to living expenses, legal costs, or transactions in the ordinary course of business. This is because, with the exception of those frozen specified asset(s), the defendant is free to do what he wishes with his assets; they are subject to no general restraint. **28–214**

Where the defendant to a proprietary injunction contends that he has no other assets with which to fund his legal and other expenses, there is an acute clash of conflicting legal desiderata: namely, on the one hand, the preservation of the asset(s) to which the claimant lays claim pending trial and, on the other, the entitlement of a defendant to legal representation (and hence the need to access funds to pay for it) or to pay his living expenses. Sir Thomas Bingham MR put **28–215**

---

[273] *Madoff Securities International Ltd v Raven* [2011] EWHC 3102 (Comm), at [141].
[274] As to which, see Ch.33.

the distinction between this situation and the position under a conventional freezing injunction in this way in *Sundt Wrigley Co Ltd v Wrigley*[275]:

"In the Mareva case, since the money is the defendant's subject to his demonstrating that he has no other assets with which to fund the litigation, the ordinary rule is that he should have resort to the frozen funds in order to finance his defence. In the proprietary case, however, the judgment is a more difficult one because in the plaintiff's contention the money on which the defendant wishes to rely to finance his litigation is not the defendant's money at all but represents money which is held on trust for the plaintiff. That, of course, gives rise to an obvious risk of injustice if the plaintiff, successful at the end of the day, finds that his own money has been used to finance an unsuccessful defence. As these authorities make plain, a careful and anxious judgment has to be made in a case where a proprietary claim is advanced by the plaintiff as to whether the injustice of permitting the use of the funds by the defendant is out-weighed by the possible injustice to the defendant if he is denied the opportunity of advancing what may of course turn out to be a successful defence."[276]

28–216 It follows that the respondent's payment of legal fees under a proprietary based freezing injunction often proves to be a contentious matter: the claimant fears that the respondent is funding his defence of the proceedings at the claimant's ultimate expense. The claimant may have a grievance that the respondent's living expenditure during the life of the proceedings is also being funded by him, but that is largely the consequence of the lapse of time between bringing proceedings and obtaining judgment. Payment of legal fees, on the other hand, is likely to be a much greater bone of contention given their likely amount and the fact that, by incurring them, the defendant may well postpone the judgment to which the claimant believes he is inevitably entitled. A defendant who ultimately has no defence to the claim has every incentive to pay his lawyers, rather than account to the claimant, and (if entitled to do so using assets in disputed ownership) may diminish the "prize" in the proceedings to the extent that the claimant's appetite for litigation is exhausted. We consider the approach which the court takes to resolving this conundrum in Ch.32.[277]

---

[275] *Sundt Wrigley Co Ltd v Wrigley* (unreported), 23 June 1993. Quoted with approval by Clarke LJ in *Halifax Plc v Chandler* [2001] EWCA Civ 1750, at [77].

[276] See also *Polly Peck International Plc v Nadir (No.2)* [1992] 4 All E.R. 769; [1992] 2 Lloyd's Rep. 238, where Scott LJ observed that a proprietary based injunction "would not be subject to provisos enabling the use of the money for normal business purposes, or for the payment of legal fees, or the like". In the event the court was only prepared to grant injunctive relief against the bank, in respect of the remaining "earmarked fund" of $8.9m on terms which permitted the bank to make use of it in the ordinary course of business if no other funds were available for that purpose.

[277] See paras 32–041—32–046.

CHAPTER 29

DISCLOSURE ORDERS

A. INTRODUCTION

(1) The Importance of Disclosure Orders

As highlighted by widely-reported decisions in recent large-scale fraud claims, disclosure applications are often the real interlocutory battleground in fraud litigation. Disclosure orders, whether obtained in support of, or independently of, injunctive relief (usually freezing orders) are often key in fraud claims, because documents or information obtained pursuant to them can establish:

29–001

(1) the current location of the proceeds of the fraud, and how those proceeds have got there, so enabling a claimant to locate his property or its proceeds;
(2) the identity of, and basis for claims against, further potential defendants to the claim;
(3) the value, location and nature of the assets against which any judgment against the defendant(s) might be enforced; and
(4) critical facts necessary to make out the claimant's case, which fraudulent defendants might otherwise seek (and be able more plausibly) to deny.

The facts established by disclosure at an early stage in proceedings can be invaluable in providing a factual baseline, limiting defendants' ability to mislead the court by invention and fabrication in their defence of the claim, and also in their account of their dealings with their own assets (against which the claimant might seek to enforce) and, in a proprietary claim, the whereabouts of the claimant's property and its proceeds. They thus enable other relief granted on an interim basis (such as freezing or proprietary injunctions) to be policed and thereby given "teeth". Further, the natural reluctance of the fraudulent defendant to be forthcoming about such matters means that disclosure orders are often the springboard for other relief, such as orders for cross-examination[1] and, indeed, committal,[2] as well as sanctions for procedural default that can assist the claimant in progressing its substantive claim.[3]

29–002

In the context of fraud claims, litigants need to be mindful of the opportunities to seek information or disclosure at various stages of the proceedings, and not just as part of the ordinary litigation disclosure process. For example: there are

29–003

[1] See Ch.31.
[2] See Ch.35.
[3] See Ch.36.

opportunities to seek information and disclosure before the commencement of proceedings, where obtaining such disclosure may be necessary in order for any substantive claim to be brought (see, for example, the *Norwich Pharmacal* jurisdiction considered in Section G below). Asset disclosure now forms a standard adjunct to freezing injunctions; and in the case of a proprietary injunction, there is a well-established jurisdiction to make disclosure orders to assist with the tracing of property that arguably belongs to the claimant and its fruits (consider CPR 25.1(1)(g) and the *Bankers Trust* jurisdiction considered in Section G below). A claimant in a fraud claim should also not forget the bases for obtaining disclosure and information from a defendant following judgment, such as by way of examination under CPR 71.[4]

(2)   Procedural Bases for Ordering Disclosure

29–004   During, and in anticipation of, fraud proceedings, the Court has a substantial armoury at its disposal to order disclosure of documents and/or provision of information. The principal bases for such orders are these:

(1)   *CPR rr.31.16 & 31.17*: CPR r.31.16 provides for the ordering of pre-action disclosure and CPR r.31.17 provides for the ordering of third party disclosure. These jurisdictions are concerned with seeking disclosure relevant to substantive issues which are likely to arise, or have arisen, in the proceedings (contemplated or actual). There is a substantial body of authority which has now accreted around both sub-rules, which are analysed in depth in the most recent edition of "The White Book" (Sir Geoffrey Vos (editor-in-chief), *Civil Procedure*, 2018 edn (London: Sweet & Maxwell, 2018)) as well as the standard texts on disclosure. We do not consider these rules further in this book.

(2)   *Standard and specific disclosure*: Of course the general disclosure provisions contained in CPR Pt 31 apply to fraud proceedings. The provisions relating to ordering specific disclosure set out in CPR r.31.12 may be particularly useful in fraud claims.[5] Again, these are considered in detail in "The White Book" (Vos (editor-in-chief) *Civil Procedure* (2018)) and the standard texts on disclosure,[6] and fall outside the scope of this book.

(3)   *Witness summons*: CPR r.34.2(4) provides that a witness summons may require a witness to produce documents on the date fixed for a hearing or on such date as the court may direct. This was the original mechanism for enabling a party to see a non-party's documents before trial.[7] Any witness summons must identify clearly when and where the witness should attend

---

[4] We consider CPR Pt 71 and post-judgment disclosure orders in Ch.37.
[5] *BDW Trading Ltd v Fitzpatrick* [2015] EWHC 3490 (Ch) is an example of an order under CPR r.31.12 being made as part of an ex parte freezing order.
[6] For example, P. Matthews and H. Malek QC, *Disclosure*, 5th edn (London: Sweet & Maxwell, 2016).
[7] See *Khanna v Lovell White Durrant* [1995] 1 W.L.R. 121.

and what he should bring with him.[8] Permission to issue a witness summons is required where the witness is to attend to produce documents on any date except the date fixed for the trial or at any hearing except the trial (CPR r.34.3(2)), but there seems to be no reason why permission should not be given in an appropriate case where a claimant applying for a freezing order wishes to issue a witness summons for a witness to attend to provide documents (for example, at a return date) to provide information about the respondent's assets (or about assets which the claimant claims).

(4)   *Section 37(1) of the Senior Courts Act 1981*: This has been widely construed by courts to allow for the ordering of disclosure of assets as an adjunct to a freezing order[9] or by way of a free-standing order.[10] We consider such asset disclosure orders in Section B.

(5)   *CPR r.25.1(1)(g)*: This reflects and supplements the court's jurisdiction under s.37(1), by providing that the court can direct a party to provide information "about the location of relevant property or assets or to provide information about relevant property or assets which are or may be the subject of an application for a freezing injunction". It is thus also relevant to asset disclosure orders, as considered in Section B; and to orders in support of proprietary claims, as considered in Section C.

(6)   *In proprietary claims*: The courts are ready, in the exercise of what was originally their equitable jurisdiction to preserve trust property, to require respondents to provide information about the current whereabouts of property which is the subject of a claim. We consider this further below in Section C.

(7)   *Norwich Pharmacal, Bankers Trust and Banker's Books Act*: These are all bases on which disclosure orders can be made at an interim stage against third parties to actual or proposed substantive proceedings. We consider these further below in Section G.

(8)   *Search orders*: These now have a statutory foundation in s.7 of the Civil Procedure Act 1997. We consider such orders in Ch.30.

(3)   Scope of this Chapter

This chapter considers the court's powers to make orders for disclosure at an **29–005** interim stage, outside the scope of the substantive disclosure regime of ordinary litigation which is now contained in CPR Pt 31, and various issues associated with them. We focus upon the following:

---

[8] *Tajik Aluminium Plant v Hydro Aluminium AS* [2005] EWCA Civ 1218.
[9] See *Mercantile Group A.G. v Aiyela* [1994] Q.B. 366, at 374C, per Hoffmann LJ.
[10] In relation to the width of s.37(1) see generally *Bayer AG v Winter* [1986] 1 W.L.R. 497. In *Maclaine Watson & Co Ltd v International Tin Council (No.2) [1987] 1 W.L.R. 1711* Millett J held in terms that the power to order disclosure of assets was not merely ancillary to the jurisdiction to make a freezing order but could be made by way of freestanding mandatory injunction. Applying that principle in *Gidrxslme Shipping Co Ltd v Tantomar Transportes Maritomos Lda* [1995] 1 W.L.R. 299 the court ordered that the respondent, against which an arbitration award had been made, give disclosure of its worldwide assets as an aid to enforcement. The decision in *Field v Field* [2003] 1 F.L.R. 376 that s.37 did not provide a "freestanding procedure as of right" is considered to be wrongly decided.

(1) Section B: Disclosure orders relating to the defendant's assets (including, but not limited to, disclosure orders ancillary to personal freezing injunctions). Since we have considered the standard terms of freezing injunctions in Ch.28, together with the disclosure orders contained in them, we focus in this chapter upon other aspects of the jurisdiction to make such orders.

(2) Section C: Disclosure orders relating to what are (at least arguably) the claimant's assets—that is, disclosure orders in support of proprietary claims and injunctions.

(3) Section D: The staying of orders for disclosure where they have been granted without notice.

(4) Section E: Confidentiality clubs.

(5) Section F: Undertakings concerning disclosed information.

(6) Section G: Disclosure orders against third parties, including *Norwich Pharmacal*, *Bankers Trust* and Bankers' Books Act Orders.

B. DISCLOSURE ORDERS RELATING TO THE DEFENDANT'S ASSETS

(1) Introduction

29–006 A claimant in a fraud claim is likely to be very interested in the asset position of the defendant(s) to the claim. Most asset disclosure orders are made in the context of, and ancillary to, freezing orders. However the court has power to order asset disclosure against a respondent independently of the existence of a freezing order.[11] There are, of course, limits to this power: it is questionable whether the court has jurisdiction (or, perhaps more accurately, whether it would ever be prepared to exercise its jurisdiction) in any circumstances to order disclosure of assets by a defendant against whom no freezing order is sought merely to establish whether he is worth suing or to ascertain the existence and location of assets against which to execute any subsequent judgment.[12] In *Holyoake v Candy* Nugee J held that where no risk of dissipation has been established it was not obvious that the Court had any power to grant a free-standing "notification" injunction (i.e. an order requiring the respondent to give notice to the applicant of any intended asset disposal).[13] The judge continued:

> "Absent dissipation, a defendant is free to deal with his own property. Nor is he obliged to disclose to a claimant what his assets are, or what he proposes to do with them. A person contemplating suing someone has no right to find out before commencing proceedings whether the defendant is worth suing, and I am very doubtful if, after suing, a claimant is in

---

[11] See for instance *Maclaine Watson & Co Ltd v International Tin Council (No.2)* [1987] 1 W.L.R. 1711, at 1716G–1716H, per Millett J: "The [defendants] contend that there is no jurisdiction to make [an order for discovery of assets] in the absence of a *Mareva* injunction. It is, however, fallacious to reason from the fact that an order for discovery can be made as ancillary to a *Mareva* injunction to a conclusion that it cannot be made except as ancillary to such an injunction."

[12] See *Nigel Upchurch Associates v Aldridge Estates International Co Ltd* [1993] 1 Lloyd's Rep. 535 and the interesting discussion in S. Gee, *Commercial Injunctions*, 6th edn (London: Sweet & Maxwell, 2016), para.23–006.

[13] *Holyoake v Candy* [2016] EWHC 970 (Ch); [2016] 3 W.L.R. 357, at [8(8)].

any better position. I accept therefore that a claimant cannot obtain an order requiring a defendant to disclose his assets to him, or tell him what he proposes to do with them, just because he is interested in the answer."

However, where the asset disclosure sought is not simply relevant to the practical likelihood of the claimant being able to recover under any future judgment, but can be shown in some way to affect the proper case management of the proceedings themselves, the possibility arises of such an order being made under CPR r.3.1(2)(m). In *XYZ v Various*,[14] Thirlwall J made an order, founded on that provision, requiring a defendant to provide a witness statement setting out whether it had adequate legal expenses insurance to fund its participation in the proceedings up to judgment and the conclusion of any appeal. That r.3.1(2)(m) can in principle enable orders for disclosure of documents and information was also recognised (though not exercised) in *The RBS Rights Issue Litigation*.[15] Accordingly, where there is potentially to be a very long trial and the claimant (or counterclaiming defendant) is concerned that, if the defendant to the claim has limited assets, it will make the proceedings wholly cost-ineffective and impose a substantial burden on the court, there may be an argument that the court can make an asset disclosure order under CPR r.3.1(2)(m). **29-007**

(2) Disclosure in Advance of a Potential Application for a Freezing Injunction

CPR 25.1(1)(g) confirms the court's jurisdiction to direct a party to provide information **29-008**

> "about the location of relevant property[16] or assets or to provide information about relevant property or assets which are or may be the subject of an application for a freezing injunction".

It will be noted that this provision has two limbs; we are here concerned with the second limb, which is aimed at the interim provision of information to a claimant in a situation where he *may* wish to apply for a freezing order, but information can be provided as a result of which an informed decision can be taken whether or not to proceed in that way.[17] Although it has been said that that rule requires that "there is either an application for a freezing injunction on foot or ... it is at least likely that there will be such an application",[18] Henderson J held in *Lichter v Rubin*,[19] that:

---

[14] *XYZ v Various* [2014] 1 Costs LO 197.
[15] *The RBS Rights Issue Litigation* [2017] 1 W.L.R. 3539, at [104] in particular, per Hildyard J.
[16] Defined at CPR 25.1(2) as "property (including land) which is the subject of a claim or as to which any question may arise on a claim."
[17] Of course in the usual case the claimant will not wish to flag up the fact that he is considering applying for a freezing order, so that it will be a rare case in which this provision will be deployed.
[18] Per Gabriel Moss QC, sitting as a deputy High Court Judge, in *Parker v CS Structured Credit Fund Ltd* [2003] 1 W.L.R. 1680, at [23].
[19] *Lichter v Rubin* [2008] EWHC 450 (Ch), at [15].

"The likelihood, it seems to me, is not one that has to be demonstrated to any very high degree and certainly does not amount to a likelihood on the balance of probabilities. It seems to me that a reasonable possibility, based on credible evidence, should be sufficient to found the jurisdictional requirement of 25.1(1)(g)".[20]

29–009 The two cases referred to immediately above suggest that the disclosure that may be sought under this sub-rule extends to information "about relevant assets" in the widest sense. In both those cases, the disclosure sought was information "about" particular assets but the information was sought (at least in part) because it might establish a propensity to dissipate assets rather than in order to obtain further information about those assets themselves in a more limited sense (e.g. their nature and location).

(3)   As an Aid to Enforcement

29–010 The court has jurisdiction to make a freestanding asset disclosure order (on a worldwide basis) in favour of a claimant with the benefit of a judgment or an arbitration award so as to assist that claimant in the enforcement of the judgment or award.[21] We consider relief granted in aid of enforcement in Ch.37.

(4)   Orders Ancillary to Personal Freezing Orders

(i)   The jurisdiction to order disclosure

29–011 In support of a freezing order based on a personal (i.e. non-proprietary) claim, the Court has jurisdiction—pursuant to s.37(1) of the 1981 Act—to make such ancillary orders, including asset disclosure orders, as appear to it to be just and convenient to ensure that the freezing order is effective to achieve its purpose.[22] As a personal freezing order is based on the risk that the respondent will otherwise dissipate his assets in an unjustified manner, a disclosure order is almost always made to accompany a freezing order. Although earlier authorities talk of the jurisdiction on the basis that the asset disclosure order is made only if it is "necessary" to make the injunction effective, now the court proceeds on the basis that the making of a freezing order will almost invariably be accompanied by an asset disclosure order. This is of course reflected in the terms of the standard form of freezing order, which expressly provides for the provision of asset disclosure.

---

[20] The judge went on to state that the rule imposed what he called a low "jurisdictional" threshold, which then allowed a broader discretion to be exercised: see at [17] and [21]. He rightly noted that if the applicant had to show that it was more probable than not that he would apply for a freezing order then the rule would lose its utility. The reasoning in *Lichter* was approved in *JSC Mezhdunarodniy Promyshlenniy Bank v Pugachev* [2015] EWCA Civ 139; [2016] 1 W.L.R. 160, at [52], per Lewison LJ.

[21] See the authorities mentioned at fn.11 above.

[22] See *A.J. Bekhor & Co Ltd v Bilton* [1981] Q.B. 923, at 940, per Ackner LJ; and at 949, per Griffiths LJ. This proposition was reaffirmed by the Court of Appeal in *JSC Mezhdunarodniy Promyshlenniy Bank v Pugachev*, above, at [47].

We have discussed in Ch.28 the asset disclosure provisions contained in the standard form, which the court will usually make, and their meaning.[23] We discuss below further aspects of the jurisdiction.

29–012

(ii) Disclosure of assets beyond the ambit of the freezing order

It had been conventional wisdom in the earlier period of the development of the freezing order that the court's ancillary power to order disclosure of assets was co-extensive with the ambit of the freezing order.[24] However the courts have unshackled themselves from such thinking. It is now clear that in an appropriate case the court can exercise its jurisdiction under s.37(1), as supplemented by CPR r.25.1(1)(g), to order disclosure of assets even if they are not the subject of an immediate freezing order. For instance, it may be that a claimant seeks a domestic freezing order but worldwide disclosure of assets in order to assist in bringing foreign proceedings to preserve any assets disclosed in the country of their location. However, as we have noted, this is not to say that the court will now order disclosure of assets merely to satisfy a claimant's curiosity.

29–013

A different scenario where the flexibility of the court's disclosure jurisdiction may be relied upon by a claimant is where there is a question mark over whether a particular asset belongs to or is controlled by the respondent (as those concepts are analysed in Ch.28)[25] so as to be amenable to a freezing order. The claimant may be unable to positively contend that the asset should be frozen but nonetheless may wish to seek information about the asset so as to consider whether to apply to bring the asset within the ambit of the freezing order. In such a case, as we discuss below, the courts have again demonstrated themselves willing to assist the claimant.

29–014

In fraud claims it is common to find that defendants have structured their affairs such that they are (ostensibly) discretionary beneficiaries under offshore trusts which they themselves have settled. These structures have often been created with a view to putting assets beyond the reach of potential or actual creditors of the settlor; although the defendant is on the face of it merely a discretionary beneficiary, sometimes alongside his or her spouse and children and various charities, the practical reality may well be that the trustees invariably exercise their discretion in accordance with the wishes of the settlor defendant. In such a case the claimant will have a legitimate interest in seeking disclosure of the details of the trust and its assets and may well wish to assert that the assets of the trust are in fact amenable to execution in the event of success at trial.

29–015

In such a case the claimant may simply apply for an injunction in respect of the relevant assets by reference to *Chabra* principles. However, depending on the facts, the claimant may wish to proceed more cautiously, by first seeking information about the asset. The courts have shown themselves to be ready to assist a claimant in ascertaining information about such trusts. Hence Lewison LJ

29–016

---

[23] See paras 28–134—28–144.
[24] *Ashtiani v Kashi* [1987] Q.B. 888.
[25] See paras 28–112—28–125.

has recently said in *JSC Mezhdunarodniy Promyshlenniy Bank v Pugachev*[26] that "It would be a matter of concern if a person could make himself judgment-proof merely by setting up discretionary trusts."[27] So, it was held in *Pugachev* that disclosure of assets going beyond what on the face of it seem to be technically the respondent's "own" assets can be ordered by the Court in the exercise of the ancillary jurisdiction discussed above. In that case the Court of Appeal upheld an order requiring the respondent, who was ostensibly a member of a class of beneficiaries under various discretionary trusts (and had disclosed the fact that he was such in his original asset disclosure), to make further disclosure, "to the best of his ability", of details of the trusts and the trust assets and provide copies of the trust deeds.[28]

29–017   It is well-established that a beneficiary under a discretionary trust has a right to be considered as a potential recipient of benefit by the trustees but that right is not a proprietary interest in the assets held by the trustees.[29] Thus, as the Court of Appeal explained in *Pugachev*[30]:

> "On the face of it assets held by the trustees of a discretionary trust would not be amenable to execution if judgment is entered against one of the class of potential beneficiaries at the suit of a third party. The trustees might in such circumstances decide to confer a benefit on the beneficiary to save him from bankruptcy; but that would be a matter for them. If they did exercise their discretion in favour of a particular beneficiary the amount of the benefit would thereupon cease to be a trust asset and would become the asset of the beneficiary. It would then truly be his asset."

29–018   The prohibition on dealing with assets and the ancillary disclosure order made in *Pugachev* included non-standard wording which extended the relevant assets subject to the injunction to include

> "any interest under any trust or similar entity including any interest which may arise by virtue of the exercise of any power of appointment, discretion or otherwise howsoever."[31]

The Court of Appeal (agreeing with Henderson J) held that this wording caught not only a vested interest under a trust but also an interest which might arise by virtue of the exercise of any discretion, such as the interest of a beneficiary under a discretionary trust.[32] It further held that, in circumstances where there were "good grounds for supposing that Mr Pugachev is in a position to control assets held within the trust structures" the Court had power to make an order requiring

---

[26] [2015] EWCA Civ 139; [2016] 1 W.L.R. 160.

[27] *JSC Mezhdunarodniy Promyshlenniy Bank v Pugachev*, above, at [20].

[28] The precise terms of the order made were, so far as the provision of information was concerned, as follows: "... swear... an affidavit setting out to the best of his ability (i) the identity of the trustee(s), settlor(s), any protector(s), and the beneficiaries of, and any other person carrying on some or all of the functions of a protector or trustee under another title in relation to the trusts referred to in paragraphs 43.1–43.5 of the schedule of assets ... and (ii) details of the assets which were subject to those trusts at as [a given date]": see at [7].

[29] *Gartside v Inland Revenue Comrs* [1968] A.C. 553, at 617–618, per Lord Wilberforce.

[30] *Pugachev*, at [15].

[31] See the discussion of the extended definition of "assets" in Ch.28, at paras 28–114—28–125. This wording features in the Commercial Court form, but not that which is contained at CPR PD 25A.

[32] See *Pugachev*, at [24].

"disclosure relating to the trusts for the purpose of ascertaining the trust position, in particular as to the extent, if any, of Mr Pugachev's control of assets held within the trust structures".

Lewison LJ said[33]:   **29–019**

"What are already within the scope of the freezing order granted by Henderson J are Mr Pugachev's interests in the trusts, whatever those may be. The underlying trust assets are not. There appears to be a dispute between the claimants on the one hand, and Mr Pugachev and the trustees on the other, about whether in reality Mr Pugachev is in effective control of the trust assets."

"As I have said, I do not consider that the court is in a position to reach even a provisional conclusion on the current state of the evidence. But it is here, in my judgment, that the principle of flexibility comes into play. I do not consider that if the threshold test for including an asset within the scope of a freezing order is not met, the court is powerless. The bank does not ask that the trust assets be brought within the scope of the freezing order immediately. It asks for the opportunity to test its assertion that Mr Pugachev is the effective owner of those assets against his (and the trustees') assertion that he is not. If its assertion is correct, it may then be in a position to apply for the scope of the freezing order to be widened. If its assertion is incorrect then an application to that effect will fail. But in my judgment the court's concern that sophisticated and wily operators should not be able to make themselves immune to the courts' orders militates against denying the DIA [the entity in control of the claimant] that opportunity."

The Court of Appeal supported this conclusion by reference to the second limb of   **29–020**
CPR r.25.1(1)(g), but did not decide whether that rule was a codification of judge-made law or extended the court's power.[34] Its decision can be seen as an example of the court's increasing willingness to use its ancillary power to order disclosure (which extends to both the provision of information and documents) in a flexible and pragmatic way, even where the disclosure sought relates to assets not yet within the ambit of the freezing order.

(5)   What Must the Respondent Do?

To comply with the standard form disclosure order the respondent must do more   **29–021**
than provide an honest answer; the obligation imposed by the standard form order is to state what the position is "to the best of his ability". An honest but inaccurate answer is not good enough and may expose the respondent to contempt proceedings. The respondent must take all reasonable steps to ensure that his answer is correct.[35] The information and level of detail that is required by the

---

[33] *Pugachev*, at [57]–[58].
[34] See para.29–008 above in relation to the threshold test which applies on an application under CPR 25.1(1)(g). The *Pugachev* decision was recently applied by Picken J to order further disclosure in respect of two trusts in *Kazakhstan Kagazy Plc v Zhunus* [2018] EWHC 369 (Comm), at [173]–[183].
[35] *Bird v Hadkinson*, Neuberger J, 4 March 1999; [2000] CP Rep 21; and to similar effect see *JSC BTA Bank v Ablyazov* [2013] EWCA Civ 928; [2014] 1 W.L.R. 1414, at [94], per Beatson LJ. In *JSC Mezhdunarodniy Promyshlenniy Bank v Pugachev* [2015] EWHC 1694 (Ch); [2016] 1 W.L.R. 781 Hildyard J held, at [42]–[43], that: "It seems to me to be obvious that a defendant required to comply with such an order must take reasonable steps to investigate the truth or otherwise of any answer he gives as regards assets in which he has or had an interest and has or can obtain information in right of that interest. However, in my view, that does not (at least at the point of initial compliance with a disclosure order) extend to making enquiries of persons in relation to assets in which the defendant

usual wording requiring disclosure of "the value ... and details" of the assets disclosed has recently been considered in *Gerald Metals v Timis*[36] and in *Privatbank v Kolomoisky*.[37]

29–022 The standard order requires disclosure to be given in two stages: first, requiring the respondent "to inform the Applicant's solicitors" of the relevant assets, and secondly requiring him subsequently "to swear and serve on the Applicant's solicitors an affidavit setting out the above information". The Commercial Court Guide states that,

> "Consideration should also be given to amalgamating paragraphs 9 and 10 of the draft Order, so as to require only one disclosure exercise, verified by Affidavit".

There is no express requirement in the order for the first disclosure to be given in writing but, unsurprisingly, this is the usual practice and is advisable, because it avoids later confusion as to what was or was not said.

29–023 The initial disclosure must obviously be accurate as at the time that disclosure is required to be given and, similarly, the verifying affidavit must also be accurate as at the time it is served: that is required by the wording of the standard order. However, if the affidavit is served late, it should also disclose the position as at the time it was ordered to be served, because otherwise there is a risk of assets having been disposed of between the date on which the affidavit should have been served and the date on which it was in fact served.[38] Difficulties may arise where a respondent swears an affidavit of assets on a particular date but the affidavit is not served until a later date, and the respondent's asset position has changed in the intervening period.[39] In such a case, the safest course for any respondent is to explain the position as at both dates.

29–024 We consider below at Section D applications for stays of disclosure orders by respondents.

29–025 In the event that the disclosure given is demonstrably unsatisfactory, the respondent may be ordered to provide further disclosure or attend for cross-examination. The jurisdiction to order cross-examination on an affidavit/witness statement is considered in detail at Ch.31.[40] Such follow-up may well be required in a fraud case; however, the Court will be vigilant to ensure that any further orders for disclosure are made on the same basis as the original order, i.e.

---

unequivocally asserts he no longer has any interest of any kind or any right to information, although the court may make available the means of testing that assertion if there is credible evidence that it may be false...A further question is the extent to which a defendant under an obligation of disclosure may in effect delegate the task to his professional advisers. In a complex case, where the process of disclosure involves detailed investigations of corporate and/or trust structures and interests of an indirect or derivative nature, as well as more obvious and easily ascertainable assets, a measure of delegation as regards the enquiries is almost inevitable. However, the obligation of disclosure remains personal; and a casual approach, even if honest, will not suffice: *Bird v Hadkinson*."

[36] *Gerald Metals v Timis* [2017] EWHC 3381 (Comm).
[37] *Privatbank v Kolomoisky* [2018] EWHC 482 (Ch).
[38] *Elektromotive Group Ltd v Pan* [2012] EWHC 2742, at [90], per Eder J.
[39] As occurred in the *Ablyazov* litigation: see *JSC BTA Bank v Ablyazov* [2010] EWHC 1779 (Comm), at [112].
[40] See paras 31–059—31–067.

in support of the freezing injunction, rather than to support the applicant's case more generally, or to embroil the respondent in further work and expense as a litigation tactic. In *JSC Mezhdunarodniy Promyshlenniy Bank v Pugachev (No.2)*[41] Hildyard J said that

> "The question which really concerns me is the real practical utility of [the further affidavit sought by the applicant] in terms of policing the freezing order and ensuring identification of assets and protection against their dissipation. I need to bear in mind that it is not the purpose of such an order to explore issues of credibility or garner evidence that may later be deployed against him, whether in this jurisdiction or the Russian Federation; and all the orders have made and will continue to make express provision to prevent that."

(6)   Information About the Source of Funds

The standard form of order contains an exception permitting the respondent to spend a reasonable sum on legal advice and representation but that exception may (and invariably does) include a further provision that "before spending any money, the respondent must tell the applicant's legal representatives where the money is to come from." In *Dadourian v Simms*[42] Patten J rejected a submission that this wording required a respondent to disclose the source of the money they proposed to spend on legal costs before spending any such sums and regardless of whose money it was or where it came from, holding that the disclosure requirement was only engaged where the assets to be used were subject to the freezing order.[43] In a recent decision in the *Pugachev* proceedings,[44] Birss J considered that that decision might be in conflict with a later decision of Peter Smith J on the same point,[45] but held that in the case before him, it was properly arguable that the funding for the application being made by Mr Pugachev (to challenge the court's jurisdiction) was likely to be coming from frozen funds and that he was satisfied that he should therefore make an order requiring Mr Pugachev to disclose the source of his funding.[46]

29–026

---

[41] *JSC Mezhdunarodniy Promyshlenniy Bank v Pugachev* [2016] 1 W.L.R. 781, at [118]; see also at [38]–[40]. In considering whether to order further affidavit evidence relating to assets Hildyard J stated the test simply to be "whether the court is satisfied that further evidence is necessary in order to make the freezing order more effective." In relation to that "the court must be persuaded that there is practical utility in requiring such evidence and that it is necessary to enable the freezing order properly to be policed. It will be vigilant to prevent the abuse of seeking further evidence for some other purpose: such as to expose further inconsistencies, unduly pressurise a defendant who has already been cross-examined, yield ammunition for an application for contempt, or provide further material which might be of assistance, even if not actually deployed, in the main (foreign) proceedings.... I consider also that the court must be satisfied that a yet further round of evidence is proportionate. That seems to me to be especially so where the freezing orders are in aid of foreign proceedings over which it has no control and where the English court is in effect being asked for relief which that foreign court could not or would not provide".

[42] *Dadourian v Simms* [2008] EWHC 1784, at [153]–[163].

[43] Though, where the source of funding is a loan to the respondent from a third party, the wording of the freezing order may be such that disclosure is required, in light of the decision of the Supreme Court in *JSC BTA Bank v Ablyazov* [2015] 1 W.L.R. 4754.

[44] *JSC Mezhdunarodniy Promyshlenniy Bank v Pugachev* [2017] EWHC 1847 (Ch).

[45] Namely *JSC BTA Bank v Kythreotis* [2011] EWHC 4042.

[46] *Pugachev*, at [82].

(7)   Privilege Against Self-Incrimination

29–027   We have discussed various aspects of the privilege against self-incrimination in Chs 28, 30 and 34.[47] The respondent subject to a disclosure order may wish, if he is able, to avail himself of that privilege, as expressly recognised by para.9(2) of the standard form of freezing order.

C.   DISCLOSURE ORDERS AGAINST RESPONDENTS IN SUPPORT OF PROPRIETARY CLAIMS

(1)   The Court's Approach

29–028   The basis for a proprietary injunction, as we have seen,[48] is a proprietary claim to the underlying assets the subject of the proceedings rather than a risk of dissipation of the respondent's own assets which would otherwise be available for the enforcement of any judgment ultimately obtained. A disclosure order requiring the respondent to set out what has become of the assets in question will commonly be appropriate in support of such an injunction—or indeed as freestanding relief—in order that the assets to which a claim is made and their proceeds can be identified and preserved pending determination of the claim. The court's approach is epitomised in the famous dictum of Templeman LJ in *Mediterranea Raffineria Siciliana Petroli SpA v Mabanaft GmbH*[49]:

> "A court of equity has never hesitated to use the strongest powers to protect and preserve a trust fund in interlocutory proceedings on the basis that, if the trust fund disappears by the time the action comes to trial, equity will have been invoked in vain."

29–029   The disclosure typically ordered in such a case is categorically different to a normal asset disclosure order.[50] What the court is here doing is requiring the respondent to identify the current location and status of assets, or their proceeds, to which the claimant lays claim, even if they are no longer in the possession of the respondent and regardless of whether the respondent himself claims ownership of the assets. The court's power to make such orders has, since the CPR came into force, been formalised in the first limb of CPR r.25.1(1)(g), quoted above at para.29–008. Indeed the court will entertain ordering bespoke questions to be posed to the respondent (as devised by the claimant) for the purpose of ascertaining what has become of specific funds or assets claimed by the claimant.[51]

---

[47] See paras 28–142—28–144, 30–051—30–063 and 34–074—34–086.
[48] Ch.28, paras 28–199—28–200.
[49] CA Transcript 816, 1 December 1978.
[50] Of course, as we have seen, proprietary orders are often made hand-in-hand with freezing orders so that a normal asset disclosure order will typically be made at the same time.
[51] See for instance *JSC BTA Bank v Ablyazov* [2009] EWCA Civ 1125; [2009] 1 All E.R. (Comm) 1029.

In *A v C*[52] Robert Goff J drew a distinction between the purpose of disclosure in **29–030** a proprietary as opposed to a personal claim. Whereas in a proprietary claim the court may make orders designed to establish the whereabouts of a missing fund, by contrast in a personal claim the court's powers are exercised to ensure the freezing order achieves its object of preventing dissipation where a real risk of such dissipation has been established. Hence, in a personal claim, it would not be right to make use of the jurisdiction to order disclosure simply so as to enable the claimant to discover whether or not the defendant has assets.[53]

(2) Identifying Further Wrongdoing

In such claims for proprietary relief the court's jurisdiction extends beyond **29–031** requiring the respondent to disclose the current location and details of specific property identified by the claimant. A common situation is where a respondent agent has received (or arguably received) bribes from third parties. As we have seen in Ch.7 such bribes are held on constructive trust for the claimant principal.[54] It will often be the case that the full extent of the bribes received is unknown. The court has jurisdiction to order the respondent to disclose the nature, extent and value of such bribes, even though compliance with that order will necessarily serve to identify the full extent of the respondent's wrongdoing and expose him to further claims.[55]

(3) Orders Against Third Parties

In proprietary claims the claimant will often have to seek disclosure orders **29–032** against third parties to assist in locating the assets which have been misappropriated. Such orders may also assist in determining the identity of the substantive defendants against whom to bring proceedings. We consider such orders below at Section G.

---

[52] *A v C* [1981] Q.B. 956, 960C. See also the statement to the same effect by Ackner LJ in *A.J. Bekhor & Co Ltd v Bilton* [1981] 1 Q.B. 923, 941H-942F.

[53] This distinction was recognised by Rose J in *Ras Al Khaimah Investment Authority v Bestfort Developments LLP* [2015] EWHC 3383 (Ch) [64]–[65] where she said "the Applicants were not able to point to a case where that important distinction between the disclosure obligations necessary to support a freezing order in a personal claim and the disclosure obligations necessary to support a proprietary claim has been eroded". This observation was not affected by the judgment of the Court of Appeal [2017] EWCA Civ 1014; [2017] CP Rep. 40, which overturned the decision of Rose J in part. See also *Kazakh Kagazy v Zhunus*, above, per Picken J at [169].

[54] See paras 7–056—7–057.

[55] *BDW Trading Ltd v Fitzpatrick* [2015] EWHC 3490 (Ch), at [34] and following, per HHJ Behrens QC. The terms of the order which was made in that case required disclosure of the following: "The nature, extent, value, what has become of and who now holds all and any assets, including profits from assets, which are derived from all or any monies received by either of the Respondents during the course of the First Respondent's employment with the Claimant from (a) sub-contractors or tenderers for business of or providers of goods and services to the Applicant (the 'Subcontractors') or (b) officers or employees or companies connected with the Subcontractors (the 'Connected Entities'). The Subcontractors and the Connected Entities include [a non-exhaustive list then follows]."

D.   STAY OF THE DISCLOSURE ORDER

29–033 As we have seen, a disclosure order made in the context of a without notice freezing order will typically require the respondent to give disclosure of his assets within a matter of days (if not an even shorter time).[56] This period will almost always require the provision of disclosure prior to the return date fixed by the original ex parte order, so that, unless the respondent acts with great expedition to return to court under the general liberty contained at para.13 of the standard form order, he will be required to provide disclosure of his assets to the applicant before the court has had an opportunity to review the order on an inter partes basis.[57] Of course an intention to challenge the freezing order does not act as any form of stay of the terms of that order. The asset position of any person is clearly a confidential matter and therefore there is potential for injustice here for a respondent against whom a freezing order has been, as it may turn out, wrongly granted. Why, it may be asked, should the claimant obtain the benefit of the disclosure part of the freezing order before the merits of the application for a freezing order have been adjudicated upon inter partes? Once an applicant learns the facts of a respondent's financial position he cannot "unlearn" the knowledge so obtained. As was stated in one case:

> "It is right that if there has to be compliance with that order, nothing at the end of the day can put that right. As has been said in argument in this court, 'the genie cannot be put back in the bottle'."[58]

29–034 In recent years there have been a number of fraud cases in which respondents who intend to challenge the freezing order have sought to stay the disclosure provisions of a freezing order pending the outcome of the return date or hearing of the discharge application.[59] For reasons which are obvious, defendants to fraud claims are likely to be extremely anxious to avoid providing disclosure of their assets to claimants. Such applications require the court to resolve the conflict between the perceived need to make freezing orders effective by the requirement to make immediate disclosure of assets (as discussed above) and the desire to protect potentially innocent respondents' rights in circumstances where there has been no inter partes adjudication on the merits of the application for a freezing

---

[56] The point has been well made that a disclosure order made ex parte should not impose upon the respondent an impossible deadline: *Oystertec Plc v Davidson* [2004] EWHC 627 (Ch), at [11], per Patten J.

[57] The Court should accommodate the listing of an urgent application to stay the disclosure aspect of the order so that it comes on before the actual date for compliance: see *Raja v Van Hoogstraten* [2004] EWCA Civ 968; [2004] 4 All E.R. 793, at [105], per Chadwick LJ. Indeed if an application is made in time, but comes on after the time for compliance, the court will be unlikely to refuse to hear the respondent even if he is in contempt of court in having failed to provide the disclosure required: above at [106]. It may well be that where the date is set very soon after the original order the court will temporarily suspend compliance until a proper hearing of the suspension application can be heard.

[58] *Motorola Credit Corp v Uzan* [2002] EWCA Civ 989; [2002] 2 All E.R. (Comm) 845, at [21], per Waller J.

[59] Though of course strictly speaking it is not a discharge application but the applicant's application for continuation of the ex parte order.

order.[60] In practice the courts have tended to the conclusion that the former requirement will generally trump the latter. Hence, several Court of Appeal decisions have upheld first instance judges' refusal to stay the disclosure order made in support of a freezing order pending an application for the discharge of that freezing order.

For example, in *Motorola Credit Corp v Uzan*,[61] the Court of Appeal (by a majority)[62] refused to interfere with the decision of the judge not to stay the disclosure order pending the respondents' application to discharge a freezing injunction which had been made pursuant to the s.25 CJJA 1982 jurisdiction.[63] The majority emphasised that normally a freezing order cannot be effective without the provision of asset disclosure.[64] Reliance was placed on an influential dictum of Steyn LJ in the earlier case of *Grupo Torras SA v Sheikh Fahad Mohammed Al-Sabah*[65] that absent a mandatory asset disclosure obligation a freezing order would be a "relatively toothless procedure in the fight against rampant transnational fraud", because it would mean that the order could not be policed.

29–035

However, in *Motorola* Lord Woolf CJ considered[66] that there would "inevitably" be situations where the right course was to continue the freezing order pending the application to discharge, but to stay the disclosure order. Accordingly, in *Raja v van Hoogstraten*,[67] Chadwick LJ acknowledged that, although it suggests that "in a normal case, a stay of the disclosure obligations is likely to be refused", *Motorola* is nonetheless

29–036

> "no authority for the proposition that a defendant will always be refused a stay of the obligation to make disclosure pending the final determination of his application to set aside the freezing order."

The question will always involve striking a balance as to the relative prejudice which might be suffered by either side attendant on the suspension, or otherwise,

---

[60] See the statement of the problem in *Raja v Van Hoogstraten* [2004] EWCA Civ 968; [2004] 4 All E.R. 793, at [104], per Chadwick LJ: "The problem in cases where an order for disclosure has been made at the same time as, and in order to give teeth to, a freezing order made without notice to the defendant is that the freezing order may be set aside after hearing full argument on both sides. If so, it will then be seen that there was no proper basis for the disclosure order. But, by that time, the defendant may have been irremediably prejudiced by the disclosure of assets which he should not have been required to disclose. On the other hand, if it is held after full argument that the freezing order should stand, then the claimant may be irremediably prejudiced if the order has not been capable of being policed in the meantime. The court is faced with the position (familiar, also, in other contexts) that whichever course it takes on an application which has to be decided without full argument may lead to irremediable prejudice to one side or the other. There is a balance to be struck."
[61] *Motorola Credit Corp v Uzan* [2002] EWCA Civ 989; [2002] 2 All E.R. (Comm) 945.
[62] Waller LJ and Woolf CJ, Sedley LJ dissenting.
[63] As to which, see Ch.26, paras 26–052—26–078.
[64] *Motorola Credit Corp v Uzan*, at [29]. Waller LJ continued: "Once one has the situation which did exist in this case, which was that on 13 June it was accepted that the freezing order should continue, then prima facie David Steel J is right in saying that a disclosure provision would be the normal provision so that the freezing order can be properly policed and be effective."
[65] Court of Appeal, unreported, Transcript No.159 of 1994, 16 February 1994.
[66] *Motorola*, at [37].
[67] *Raja v van Hoogstraten* [2004] EWCA Civ 968; [2004] 4 All E.R. 793, at [105].

of the disclosure provisions.[68] The asserted prejudice to the respondent may take various forms: for instance in *JSC BTA Bank v Ablyazov*[69] the suspension was sought because it was asserted that the claimant's action was motivated by a collateral desire to destroy the defendant as a political force in Kazakhstan and that the claimant would pass the information so received to the prosecution authorities to assist in criminal proceedings.

29–037 The standard approach was recently reiterated by the Court of Appeal in *Malofeev v VTB Capital Plc*,[70] in which Jackson LJ summarised the position as follows:

> "An order for disclosure of assets normally accompanies a worldwide freezing order. Such an order is usually necessary to give the worldwide freezing order teeth. The fact that the court will be asked on a future date to say that the worldwide freezing order should not have been made is not normally a ground for suspending the disclosure order in the meantime."

29–038 Although the authorities cited above expressly recognise the possibility that a disclosure order could in appropriate circumstances be stayed pending an application to discharge a freezing order, there does not appear to be any modern reported decision in which the disclosure order accompanying a freezing order has in fact been stayed pending such an application. In an appropriate case, limitations on dissemination of the asset disclosure can be put in place pursuant to a form of "confidentiality club", provided that such limitations would serve a useful purpose in reducing the prejudice to the respondent from disclosure; but the difficulties liable to be created by such a course are such that it will need to be properly justified.[71]

E. CONFIDENTIALITY CLUBS

29–039 In the ordinary case, the defendant is required to give disclosure of his assets to the claimant personally. As set out in detail in the preceding sections, the purpose of such a requirement is to inform the claimant of the defendant's asset position so as to allow the claimant (and the court) to police the freezing order, by taking such steps as may be necessary and appropriate to ensure that it is being complied with and remains effective. An asset disclosure order is intrusive, since it

---

[68] There are various mechanisms which the court can adopt to mitigate the alleged prejudice on both sides. For instance it could require that the asset disclosure should only be provided to a limited number of identified individuals within the claimant; or be passed only to the claimant's solicitors; or even that the defendant produce an affidavit disclosing assets to his own solicitor, to be released if the discharge application fails. Some of these mechanisms are adverted to in the *Ablyazov* case, above.

[69] *JSC BTA Bank v Ablyazov* [2009] EWCA Civ 1125; [2009] 1 All E.R. (Comm) 1029.

[70] *Malofeev v VTB Capital Plc* [2011] EWCA Civ 1252, at [39], citing *Motorola*, *Ablyazov* and *Grupo Torras SO v Sheikh Al-Sabah* (CA Transcript No.159 of 1994, 16 February 1994).

[71] Such a regime was adopted in the *Ablyazov* litigation: see [2009] EWCA Civ 1125; [2009] 1 All E.R. (Comm) 1029, at [26] and [41] (in the latter paragraph, Sedley LJ recorded his "unease at a practice which is capable of creating serious professional and juridical difficulties. This is not only because lawyers are not in the ordinary way permitted to keep relevant things secret from their clients, but also because counsel may find it necessary to make use at trial of knowledge which has been acquired subject to such an undertaking. If in such a situation application is made to the trial judge for permission to make use of it, the judge in turn will be placed in an impossible quandary").

typically requires a defendant to provide extensive confidential information about his financial affairs to his adversary in litigation, at a time when his liability has yet to be (and may never be) established.

To that extent it is inherently prejudicial to the defendant. In general, however, this is a necessary price to pay to ensure the effectiveness of the freezing order. In some cases, however, disclosure of the defendant's assets to the claimant may result in more than the usual prejudice. In a case with a political backdrop, for example, there may be evidence that the claimant has (or others standing behind the claimant have) some motivation for obtaining information about the defendant's assets which goes beyond the legitimate interests of a claimant with a good arguable case of fraud, and that disclosure may be used for an improper purpose (e.g. to attempt to seize assets or harm the defendant's interest in them in some other way). Asset disclosure may involve revealing sensitive commercial information liable to be misused by the claimant. Or there may be a risk that, once in the hands of the claimant, information about the defendant's assets would find its way, whether or not by design or consent of the claimant, into the hands of others who may misuse it. **29–040**

In such cases, the court has to balance the importance of requiring asset disclosure from the defendant (and the prejudice to the claimant if disclosure is withheld) against the possible prejudice to the defendant of having to give disclosure. One way of achieving such a balance in an appropriate case is by restricting the disclosure of asset information to certain individuals on the claimant's side of the case. Such an arrangement is typically referred to as a "confidentiality club" or "confidentiality ring". **29–041**

The general principles governing the imposition of confidentiality clubs were summarised as follows by Hamblen J in *Libyan Investment Authority v Société Générale SA*: **29–042**

(1)   The starting point is that disclosure should be unrestricted (subject to the usual restrictions on collateral use).
(2)   The court has power to impose a confidentiality club as a facet of its inherent jurisdiction to regulate its own procedure in the interests of justice.
(3)   It is for the party seeking the imposition of a confidentiality club to justify that departure from the norm. In order to do so, the proponent of the confidentiality club must establish that there is a real risk, either deliberate or inadvertent, of a party using his right of inspection for a collateral purpose.
(4)   Where it is demonstrated that there is such a risk, any restriction imposed should go no further than is necessary for the protection of whatever right it is imposed to protect.

The issues which arise on any request to impose a confidentiality club will depend on the circumstances of the particular case, and no list can be exhaustive. The key factor is likely to be to identify the individuals who are to be within the club. An indicative list of issues which may arise is set out below. **29–043**

29–044 *Whether the claimant should be excluded.* In the *Libyan Investment Authority* case, Hamblen J referred to the inherent desirability of including at least one duly appointed representative of each party within a confidentiality club. In a decision at the outset of the *Ablyazov* litigation Sedley LJ expressed unease about the imposition of a confidentiality club limited to the claimant's lawyers, because of the "serious professional and juridical difficulties" which may arise from relevant material being kept from the client by their solicitors, and the fact that the lawyers may find they wish to use such material at trial. But sometimes such a limitation will be justified. Where the claimant is excluded from the confidentiality club, it will generally be necessary for an arrangement to be put in place which enables the claimant's solicitors to police the freezing order— whether in the form of a standing instruction to take any steps in respect of a given asset which the solicitor deems necessary to protect the claimant's interests under the order, or an arrangement for information about relevant assets to be suitably anonymised so that instructions may be taken without breaching the confidentiality imposed.

29–045 *Restriction to named individuals..* A confidentiality club will typically limit disclosure to named individuals within the claimant. In an appropriate case, disclosure may also be restricted to named members of the claimant's legal team (whether or not the claimant is within the club). It may be a cumbersome arrangement to operate, particularly in large-scale litigation where the legal team is commensurately large and may not remain constant; but in some cases this may be an argument for, rather than against, such a restriction. Within solicitors' firms, there may be a need to name support staff such as personal assistants or secretaries.

29–046 *Inclusion of experts.* In an ordinary case, a claimant provided with the defendant's asset disclosure may wish to take steps to verify the disclosure provided, or otherwise to understand issues which may arise in respect of particular assets. This may call for expertise in, say, valuation or matters of local law for assets abroad. It will ordinarily be difficult, however, to engage an expert on such issues without revealing confidential information. This may justify the inclusion of experts within a confidentiality club. Since the club will invariably be imposed before asset disclosure is given, such a course is less likely to be justifiable at the outset, and more likely to arise on a subsequent application to relax the restrictions on an ad hoc basis once asset disclosure has been given and the need can be more readily shown to have arisen.

29–047 *Provision of undertakings.* As a starting point, it should be presumed that the individuals within the confidentiality club will comply with its terms. But the provision of an undertaking may tip the balance as to whether a given individual is or is not permitted to be within the club. In general it will be less likely to be necessary to require undertakings from English solicitors and counsel, than from lay representatives of the claimant or experts who may be included.

29–048 *Individuals outside the jurisdiction.* Individuals within England and Wales are subject to the jurisdiction of the English court. The court's powers of enforcement (e.g. through the contempt jurisdiction) can thus be used where necessary, and their very existence acts as an incentive to comply with the terms of the confidentiality club. The same may not always be true of individuals outside the jurisdiction. The power to make inclusion of such individuals conditional on the provision of suitable undertakings may provide an answer, but could still leave the court powerless in practice to punish someone abroad who fails to honour restrictions on disclosure. These factors may militate against the inclusion of individuals abroad within the club, at least where a sufficient risk of prejudice to the defendant by their inclusion can be demonstrated.

F. UNDERTAKINGS CONCERNING DISCLOSED INFORMATION

In any freezing order the applicant will give an undertaking in the following terms: **29–049**

> "The applicant will not without the permission of the court use any information obtained as a result of this order for the purpose of any civil or criminal proceedings, either in England and Wales or in any other jurisdiction, other than this claim."

The purpose of this undertaking is to protect the defendant against the misuse of information gained from the ancillary disclosure order,[72] and protects information provided by the disclosure of documents and/or of information directly by the defendant pursuant to the order (including in the asset affidavit). CPR r.31.22 now provides further protection in respect of documents disclosed pursuant to an ancillary disclosure order:

> "A party to whom a document has been disclosed may use the document only for the purpose of the proceedings in which it is disclosed, except where the exceptions identified at 31.22(1)(a), (b) or (c) apply."

A recent example of an application for release from this undertaking in order to use the documents and information disclosed for a number of other purposes is *BDW Trading Ltd v Fitzpatrick*.[73] The defendant employee was alleged to have received secret profits, bribes or commissions from sub-contractors for assistance in procuring that his employer placed business with the sub-contractors. A freezing order was granted and disclosure provided pursuant to that order, which contained the usual undertaking. At the return date, the claimant sought permission to use the information and documents disclosed to it for the purposes, in particular, of possible tracing claims against subcontractors, and for disciplinary investigations and possible disciplinary proceedings against the defendant or other employees of the claimant. There was little dispute over the use of the information and documents for the purpose of possible tracing claims against subcontractors, and such use was permitted by the court.[74] There was greater dispute over the use of documents for the purpose of disciplinary investigations and possible disciplinary proceedings. The Court treated the application as one to permit the use of documents pursuant to CPR 31.22(1)(b). **29–050**

---

[72] *Derby v Weldon (No.1)* [1990] Ch. 48, at 57B–57C per Parker LJ.

[73] *BDW Trading Ltd v Fitzpatrick* [2015] EWHC 3490.

[74] Per HHJ Behrens, at [73]–[75].

The Judge referred to the House of Lords' decision in *Crest Homes Plc v Marks*[75] and the Court of Appeal's decision in *Smithkline Beecham Plc v Generics (UK) Ltd*, [76] where Aldous LJ analysed the principles to apply when considering an application to use documents under CPR 31.22 as follows:

> "... it is important under the CPR to have in mind the overriding principles when considering whether to lift an order made under CPR 31.22. The most important consideration must be the interest of justice which involves considering the interest of the party seeking to use the documents and that of the party protected by the CPR 31.22 order. As Lord Oliver said [in *Crest Homes*] each case will depend upon its own facts ..."[77]

In *BDW v Fitzpatrick*, the court permitted the use of the documents for the further purposes identified, saying that it had to carry out a balancing exercise between the interests of the claimant and the defendant:

> "I agree that there is a close connection between these proceedings and the disciplinary proceedings. The alleged fraud arose out of [the defendant's] employment. I agree that the whole purpose of the application was to obtain information to enable appropriate action to be taken against the wrongdoers. It seems to me to be artificial to permit the information to be used against the subcontractors who made the secret payments but not against [the defendant] who received them. In my view the interests of justice point to permission under r.22(1)(b) being granted. I do not think that there is any serious injustice to [the defendant]."[78]

G.   ORDERS AGAINST THIRD PARTIES, INCLUDING NORWICH PHARMACAL, BANKERS TRUST AND BANKERS' BOOKS ACT ORDERS

29–051   The court has developed a sophisticated number of jurisdictional mechanisms whereby innocent third parties may be obliged to provide disclosure (in the form of information and/or documents), to assist a claimant in locating assets to which he makes a claim or to identify wrongdoers (as well as for other purposes). These mechanisms are of great practical relevance in fraud claims.

(1)   Norwich Pharmacal Orders

(i)   The basis of the jurisdiction

29–052   The *Norwich Pharmacal* jurisdiction is named after the landmark decision of the House of Lords in *Norwich Pharmacal v Customs & Excise*[79] where the House considered the pre-Judicature Act authorities and practice under the old Chancery "bill of discovery" procedure (including the established rule that such discovery was not available against a "mere witness" who was not himself somehow involved in the transaction in question) and concluded, in the words of Lord Reid:

---

[75] *Crest Homes Plc v Marks* [1987] A.C. 829, per Lord Oliver at 860.
[76] *Smithkline Beecham Plc v Generics (UK) Ltd* [2004] 1 W.L.R. 1479.
[77] *Smithkline Beecham Plc v Generics (UK) Ltd*, at [37].
[78] *BDW v Fitzpatrick*, per HHJ Behrens at [84].
[79] *Norwich Pharmacal v Customs & Excise* [1974] A.C. 133.

> "They seem to me to point to a very reasonable principle that if through no fault of his own a person gets mixed up in the tortious acts of others so as to facilitate their wrong-doing he may incur no personal liability but he comes under a duty to assist the person who has been wronged by giving him full information and disclosing the identity of the wrongdoers. I do not think that it matters whether he became so mixed up by voluntary action on his part or because it was his duty to do what he did. It may be that if this causes him expense the person seeking the information ought to reimburse him. But justice requires that he should co-operate in righting the wrong if he unwittingly facilitated its perpetration."[80]

The jurisdiction recognised by this statement of principle has subsequently been, and will no doubt continue to be, extended.[81]

29–053 The Civil Procedure Rules expressly recognise (in the context of making provision for pre-action disclosure against a respondent who is likely to be a defendant to the proceedings, and for third party disclosure once the substantive proceedings are on foot) that the provisions in CPR 31 do not operate to limit the common law power of the court to order disclosure before proceedings have started and to do so against a person who is not a party to the proceedings: see CPR 31.18. This provision involves an express recognition of the *Norwich Pharmacal* jurisdiction, which has not been the subject of codification or other modification by the CPR.

29–054 The third party may be truly innocent of wrongdoing, or be suspected by the applicant to be sufficiently implicated in it to be potentially liable to the applicant. However, for the purposes of invoking the jurisdiction, the crucial point is that the applicant does not need to demonstrate either any liability on the part of the defendant nor an intention to sue him upon any substantive cause of action that may have arisen.[82] That said, the *Norwich Pharmacal* jurisdiction does enable orders to be made against those who are themselves expressly alleged to be wrongdoers, requiring them to disclose the identity of other wrongdoers.[83]

29–055 The main purpose of seeking relief is to enable the victim of alleged wrongdoing to obtain information which will enable him to sue the alleged wrongdoer, or at least to make a practical commercial decision as to whether or not it is worth suing him. It has been said that a central purpose of *Norwich Pharmacal* relief is

---

[80] At 175B-C. In *Singularis Holdings Ltd v PricewaterhouseCoopers* [2015] A.C. 1675, at [23], Lord Sumption described the case as illustrating "the capacity of the common law to develop a power in the court to compel the production of information when this is necessary to give effect to a recognised legal principle".

[81] See *Ashworth Hospital Authority v MGN Ltd* [2002] 1 W.L.R. 2033, per Lord Woolf CJ, at [57].

[82] Compare the court's power under CPR 31.16 to order pre-action disclosure against an intended party to the proceedings and see the observations of Flaux J in *JSC BTA Bank v Ablyazov* [2014] EWHC 2019 (Comm); [2015] 1 W.L.R. 1547, at [80]–[81]. See para.29–072 below as to what constitutes "involvement" by the third party in the wrongdoing to avoid the application falling foul of the "mere witness" rule. And see also *Axa Equity & Law Life Assurance Society Plc v National Westminster Bank Plc* [1998] C.L.C. 1177, at [23], per Morritt LJ.

[83] *Norwich Pharmacal*, above, per Lord Reid at 174. Indeed such a scenario has been said to give rise to an a fortiori case for relief: see *RCA Corp v Reddingtons Rare Records* [1974] 1 W.L.R. 1445, per Goff J at 1446; *X Ltd v Morgan-Grampian (Publishers) Ltd* [1991] 1 A.C. 1, per Lord Lowry at 54.

to allow a claimant to obtain sufficient information so he can come "to a careful and considered view as to what claims could be made, and where they should be launched."[84]

(ii) Types of relief granted

29-056 The nature of the relief sought under the *Norwich Pharmacal* jurisdiction and the fact that it may be sought against a third party against whom there is not necessarily any cause of action (when later substantive redress against the wrongdoer is contemplated), together with the "just and convenient" test which is applied by the court when deciding whether or not to grant it,[85] all point to the relief being "interim" in nature. However, *Norwich Pharmacal* relief should not be regarded as interim for all purposes: indeed, it has been held that, as between the applicant and respondent, it constitutes final relief, such that it does not fall within the jurisdictional gateway for claims for an "interim remedy under section 25(1) of the Civil Jurisdiction and Judgments Act 1982".[86] Hence, when a *Norwich Pharmacal* application is made the claimant should seek the relief by proceedings issued under CPR Pt 8.[87]

29-057 The relief is not limited to the identification of a likely wrongdoer whose identity or whereabouts are otherwise unknown. There is authority which suggests that the jurisdiction may also be invoked to order disclosure against a third party in aid of a post-judgment freezing order[88] or to locate assets to which the claimant makes a proprietary claim.[89] Hence in *Shlaimoun v Mining Technologies International Inc*[90] orders were made against banks with a view to tracking the destination of $2 million which had been paid over pursuant to alleged fraudulent misrepresentations. Further, the jurisdiction may be relied upon to obtain information which may be crucial to the proper assertion of liability against an

---

[84] *Shlaimoun v Mining Technologies International Inc* [2011] EWHC 3278 (QB); [2012] 1 W.L.R. 1276, at [20].

[85] See para.29-077 below.

[86] See *AB Bank Ltd v Abu Dhabi Commercial Bank* [2016] EWHC 2082; [2017] 1 W.L.R. 810, per Teare J at [6]-[12]. The gateway under consideration was para.3.1(5) of PD 6B.

[87] In the Chancery Division, the former practice of making applications by application notice under CPR Pt 23 is now deprecated; para.7.4 of the Chancery Guide explains that the better practice is to make the application by Pt 8 claim form and that applications made under CPR Pt 23 are likely to be rejected.

[88] *Mercantile Group (Europe) AG v Aiyela* [1994] Q.B. 366, although note that in *NML Capital Ltd v Chapman Freeborn Holdings Ltd* [2013] EWCA Civ 589; [2013] 1 C.L.C. 968, at [31] it was doubted whether this was actually an instance of the exercise of the Court's equitable *Norwich Pharmacal* jurisdiction as opposed to its jurisdiction under s.37(1) of the Senior Courts Act 1981 to make a disclosure order in aid of a freezing injunction. See further para.29-063 below.

[89] See the cases cited in *Ramilos Trading Ltd v Buyanovsky* [2016] EWHC 3175 (Comm), at [39]-[46].

[90] *Shlaimoun v Mining Technologies International Inc* [2011] EWHC 3278 (QB); [2012] 1 W.L.R. 1276.

identified person (what is sometimes described as the "missing piece of the jigsaw").[91] Hence in one case the judge described one aspect of the jurisdiction in the following terms:

> "Relief can be ordered where the identity of the claimant[92] is known, but where the claimant requires disclosure of crucial information in order to be able to bring its claim or where the claimant requires a missing piece of the jigsaw."[93]

Vivid as this metaphor is, it should not be used to constrict the ambit of the jurisdiction.[94] The missing piece of the jigsaw is but one example of a case which might justify the making of a *Norwich Pharmacal* order.

Norwich Pharmacal orders often require the provision of information (most obviously the identity and other facts relating to a person implicated in the wrongdoing), but they may also extend to the disclosure of documents such as telephone records or bank statements relating to dealings with the proceeds of an alleged fraud (and which might be disclosable in due course within the contemplated substantive proceedings).[95] The *Norwich Pharmacal* jurisdiction is therefore of particular value in fraud cases in establishing how and by whom assets which are the subject of a tracing claim are now held. So in *JSC BTA Bank v Ablyazov*,[96] a *Norwich Pharmacal* order was made against a non-party where proceedings against the principal wrongdoer (Mr Ablyazov) had already been issued (indeed judgment had been obtained against him) and the order required the non-party to file and serve affidavits setting out

29–058

> "to the best of his ability all Relevant Information [defined as including information as to the ownership and location of certain assets and businesses and all dealings or attempted dealings with them since the date of the original freezing order against Mr Ablayzov, instructions given or received by him in relation to them since that date and communications between his wife and/or himself and Mr Ablayzov in relation to them since that date] within his own knowledge (without being under any obligation to make inquiries) [in relation to certain identified assets and businesses and any other asset with a value exceeding US$5 million]."

The order also obliged him to exhibit to the affidavits such documents evidencing the matters set out "as he may reasonably be able to collate in the available time (without being under any obligation to undertake electronic searches)". This provides a good example of the expansive approach of the court to *Norwich Pharmacal* orders in the fraud context. The judge emphasised the non-party's

---

[91] See for instance *Mitsui v Nexen Petroleum* [2005] EWHC 625 (Ch); [2005] 3 All E.R. 511; *Axa Equity and Law Life Assurance Society Plc v National Westminster Bank* [1998] C.L.C. 1177, at [25], per Millett LJ and *Carlton Film Distributors v VCI Plc* [2003] EWHC 616 (Ch).

[92] This must be a reference to the defendant.

[93] *Mitsui v Nexen Petroleum*, at [19].

[94] *R (Mohamed) v Secretary of State for Foreign and Commonwealth Affairs (No.1)* [2009] 1 W.L.R. 2579, at [94].

[95] See the discussion of the so-called *Bankers Trust* order in paras 29—103—29–119 below.

[96] *JSC BTA Bank v Ablyazov* [2014] EWHC 2019 (Comm); [2015] 1 W.L.R. 1547.

> "duty to assist the bank by giving it full information in relation to the assets and businesses, even if he has not incurred any potential liability to the bank; all the more so if he has actively and knowingly assisted wrongdoing by Mr Ablyazov, even if the bank cannot or chooses not to join him as a defendant."[97]

29–059 It is in the nature of such applications that the defendant to the application generally (but by no means always) has no position on whether or not the relief should be granted and will often not oppose any order that might be made in the event that the claimant can persuade the court to grant it (subject to payment of any costs incurred in complying with it). For that reason it is common practice to request the intended defendant to provide the information or disclosure voluntarily, with proceedings only being brought if there is no response or a response to the effect that disclosure will only be provided under a court order. It is generally proper for a defendant to take such a stance; without the protection of a court order the defendant to a *Norwich Pharmacal* application might well be exposed to liability viz-a-viz the person whose identity (or about whom information) is sought. If a *Norwich Pharmacal* order is made, the claimant is likely to be ordered to pay the reasonable costs of the defendant incurred in (reasonably)[98] opposing the application and in subsequently complying with it[99] (leaving it to the claimant to recover them from the wrongdoer in the subsequent proceedings).[100] However, there may be exceptions where the defendant can be shown, at the time the court comes to consider the question of costs, to have supported or to be otherwise implicated in the wrongdoing or to have sought to obstruct justice, such that a costs order can be properly made against him.[101] As a result, when the substantive *Norwich Pharmacal* order is made the claimant

---

[97] *JSC BTA Bank v Ablyazov*, at [72].

[98] The claimant will often wish to argue that the defendant's resistance was unreasonable and that he should have adopted a neutral stance.

[99] See *Totalise Plc v Motley Fool Ltd* [2001] EWCA Civ 1897; [2002] 1 W.L.R. 1233, at [29]–[31], where the Court of Appeal said that a *Norwich Pharmacal* application was akin to an application for pre-action disclosure, the costs of which are now governed by CPR Pt 46.1.(2). The Court of Appeal went on to set out the types of situation where a respondent to a *Norwich Pharmacal* application would be likely to be awarded its costs of the hearing itself, including where: "(a) the party required to make the disclosure had a genuine doubt that the person seeking the disclosure was entitled to it; (b) the party was under an appropriate legal obligation not to reveal the information, or where the legal position was not clear, or the party had a reasonable doubt as to the obligations; or (c) the party could be subject to proceedings if disclosure was voluntary; or (d) the party would or might suffer damage by voluntarily giving the disclosure; or (e) the disclosure would or might infringe a legitimate interest of another." See also *Ashworth Hospital*, above, at [36] where Lord Woolf CJ referred to "the fact that innocent third parties can be indemnified for their costs".

[100] That such costs can ultimately be recouped from the wrongdoer is recognised in *Totalise*, above, at [29], and *JSC BTA Bank v Ablyazov* [2014] EWHC 2019 (Comm); [2015] 1 W.L.R. 1547, at [77].

[101] *JSC BTA Bank v Ablyazov* [2014] EWHC 2019 (Comm); [2015] 1 W.L.R. 1547, at [79]–[80], per Flaux J. In that case the original order provided that, subject to further order, the claimant should pay the reasonable costs of compliance with the *Norwich Pharmacal* order. The claimant subsequently applied to set aside that order in view of the defendant's alleged failure to properly comply with the *Norwich Pharmacal* order and because the information that was provided showed that he was closely mixed up in the primary wrongdoer's (Mr Ablyazov's) wrongdoing. The decision provides a detailed consideration of the relevant legal principles concerning the allocation of costs in *Norwich Pharmacal* applications.

might wish to seek a postponement of the determination of costs questions, or a proviso in any costs order permitting him to revisit the question once the order has been executed.

(iii)   The requirements for exercising the jurisdiction

In *Mitsui & Co Ltd v Nexen Petroleum UK Ltd*,[102] Lightman J summarised the three threshold conditions which have to be satisfied if the Court is to grant *Norwich Pharmacal* relief. That summary has recently been adopted (with some updating) in two recent decisions on *Norwich Pharmacal* applications in the fraud context[103] as follows:

29–060

(1)   There must have been a wrong carried out, or arguably carried out, by an ultimate wrongdoer.
(2)   The disclosure sought must be necessary in order to enable the applicant to bring legal proceedings or seek other legitimate redress for the wrongdoing.
(3)   The person against whom the order is sought must be involved in the wrongdoing in a way which distinguishes him from being a mere witness.

If these threshold conditions are met, it remains a matter for the court's discretion whether to grant the order sought.[104] We consider each condition and the discretion in turn below.

Condition 1: A Wrong Must Have Been Carried Out, or Arguably Carried Out, by an Ultimate Wrongdoer.   Although tortious wrongdoing was expressly identified in the *Norwich Pharmacal* case itself it is no longer the only type of asserted wrongdoing by an ultimate wrongdoer in respect of which such relief will be ordered. The position is now that "the 'wrong' may be a crime, tort, breach of contract, equitable wrong or contempt of court".[105]

29–061

As mentioned earlier the wrongdoing which is required to be (arguably) shown[106] is the wrongdoing of the person whose identity the claimant is seeking to establish (or in respect of which wrongdoing necessary information/disclosure is sought) and not that of the person against whom the *Norwich Pharmacal* proceedings are brought.

The standard of proof to which the relevant wrongdoing should be established at the stage of applying for *Norwich Pharmacal* relief was stated in *United Company Rusal v HSBC Bank Plc*[107] as being that the applicant has "a much

---

[102] *Mitsui & Co Ltd v Nexen Petroleum UK Ltd* [2005] EWHC 625 (Ch); [2005] 3 All E.R. 511, at [21].

[103] *Orb ARL v Fiddler* [2016] EWHC 361 (Comm), at [83]–[88], per Popplewell J, and *Ramilos Trading Ltd v Buyanovsky* [2016] EWHC 3175 (Comm), at [11]–[12], [24]–[26], per Flaux J.

[104] *The Rugby Football Union v Consolidated Information Services Ltd* [2012] UKSC 55, at [17], per Lord Kerr; *Orb ARL v Fiddler*, at [89], per Popplewell J; and *Ramilos Trading*, at [27], per Flaux J.

[105] *Orb v Fiddler*, above, per Popplewell J at [83], adopted by Flaux J in *Ramilos Trading*, at [12]. See also *Ashworth Hospital*, above, at [53]–[54], per Lord Woolf CJ in respect of the situation where the underlying wrong is a crime.

[106] The wrongdoing must be identified by the applicant at least in general terms: see *Ashworth Hospital Authority v MGN Ltd* [2002] 1 W.L.R. 2033, per Lord Woolf CJ at [60].

[107] *United Company Rusal v HSBC Bank Plc* [2011] EWHC 404 (QB).

better argument than the defendant",[108] applying the Privy Council's decision in *Bols Distilleries BV v Superior Yacht Services Ltd* [109] concerning an application for permission to serve proceedings out of the jurisdiction. But this test has been rightly criticised as being inappropriate for *Norwich Pharmacal* applications.[110] Not only does it impose too high a threshold for the court's intervention, but the concept of having "much the better of the argument" is inapt where the respondent to the application is not alleged to be a wrongdoer. In *Ramilos Trading* Flaux J rejected the submission that the "much the better of the argument" test was appropriate for *Norwich Pharmacal* applications and held that the appropriate analogy for such applications is not with applications for permission for service out but with freezing orders (where the requirement of a "good arguable case" is well-established, as discussed in Ch.28).[111] Accordingly, he held that the applicant for a *Norwich Pharmacal* order "must show that it has a good arguable case that there has been wrongdoing".[112] It is considered that this constitutes the correct threshold test, albeit the clearer the evidence of wrongdoing, the more likely it is that the court will exercise its discretion in favour of granting the relief sought.

29–062   In the earlier case of *P v T*,[113] the Court made a *Norwich Pharmacal* order where the question of whether or not a tort had been committed was not yet clear, although the claimant believed that it had. Scott V-C held that

> "the principles expressed in the *Norwich Pharmacal* case, although they have not previously been applied so far as I know to a case in which the question whether there has been a tort has not been clearly answered, ought to be applicable"

in a case such as the one before him.[114] In *Ramilos Trading*, Flaux J described *P v T* as "an exceptional case, generally recognised as being at the outer limits of the *Norwich Pharmacal* jurisdiction" and therefore not of much assistance to the applicant in relation to the standard of proof required for relief to be granted. Nonetheless it must be recognised that where A believes it has a claim against B but lacks some crucial piece of information which it needs in order to launch those proceedings and which it seeks from the *Norwich Pharmacal* defendant (i.e. "missing piece of the jigsaw" cases) the court will not dismiss the application on the basis that A has not crossed the arguability threshold; the courts appear to accept that that condition may be fulfilled even if there is some missing information which prevents the claimant proceeding straight to the issue of a claim against B.[115]

---

[108]   *United Company Rusal v HSBC Bank Plc*, at [52].

[109]   *Bols Distilleries BV v Superior Yacht Services Ltd* [2007] 1 W.L.R. 12.

[110]   See, for example, C. Hollander, *Documentary Evidence*,12th edn (London: Sweet & Maxwell, 2015) at para.4–05.

[111]   See para.28–013.

[112]   *Ramilos Trading*, at [13]–[17] and [23], per Flaux J.

[113]   *P v T* [1997] 1 W.L.R. 1309.

[114]   The decision was referred to with approval by the House of Lords in *Ashworth Hospital Authority*, at [57].

[115]   See for instance the reasoning in *Ramilos Trading*, at [35].

In *NML Capital Ltd v Chapman Freeborn Holdings Ltd*[116] the Court of Appeal **29–063** left open the wider question of whether or not *Norwich Pharmacal* relief should be available in proceedings after judgment and in aid of execution. The court was not convinced that the equitable jurisdiction became spent when judgment against the wrongdoer was obtained, but expressed the view (obiter) that it would only be in very particular and restricted circumstances, amounting to involvement in wilful evasion by the judgment debtor, that such relief might be justified. That was the basis on which the jurisdiction was exercised (after the claimant had obtained summary judgment against the wrongdoer) in *Kensington International Ltd v Republic of Congo*.[117] In that case it was held that the respondent had become mixed up in dishonest attempts on the part of the judgment debtor to defeat execution of various judgments. It is suggested that there is no good reason to confine the jurisdiction to pre-judgment situations. As the *Ablyazov* case demonstrates, in fraud cases the obtaining of judgment against the principal wrongdoer may merely constitute one stage in the litigation; there may well be a very lengthy recovery stage to be gone through thereafter. It is to be noted that, as mentioned above, the court had no difficulty in granting *Norwich Pharmacal* relief in favour of the claimant bank in *Ablyazov* post-judgment in order to assist the bank in seeking to trace assets to which it maintained a proprietary claim.[118]

There are indications that offshore jurisdictions, where the judgment debtor's **29–064** assets (or vehicles controlling them) might well be found, are becoming more receptive to the idea of making *Norwich Pharmacal* orders after the applicant has obtained judgment. In *UVW v XYZ (A Registered Agent)*[119] the BVI Commercial Court granted disclosure orders against the local registered agent of a BVI company in respect of information which could lead to the identification of assets available for enforcement of judgments obtained overseas. The judge held that *Norwich Pharmacal* relief was available in such circumstances where there is reasonable suspicion that the registered agent is "mixed up" (innocently or otherwise) with the wilful evasion of another's judgment debt. There was no direct evidence that the judgment debtor was using the BVI vehicle to conceal

---

[116] *NML Capital Ltd v Chapman Freeborn Holdings Ltd* [2013] EWCA Civ 589; [2013] 1 C.L.C. 968, at [25]–[30].

[117] *Kensington International Ltd v Republic of Congo* [2006] EWHC 1848 (Comm). A disclosure order was also made in *Mercantile Group (Europe) AG v Aiyela* [1994] Q.B. 366, at [25], but (as the Court of Appeal pointed out in *NML Capital v Chapman Freeborn* [2013] EWCA Civ 589, at [31]) the disclosure order was ancillary to a freezing injunction, and the court's jurisdiction to grant it was derived from s.37(1) of the Supreme Court Act 1981, and the court's ancillary power to ensure that such an order is effective, and the decision does not compel the conclusion that *Norwich Pharmacal* relief is available post-judgment in aid of execution.

[118] *Ablyazov* [2014] EWHC 2019 (Comm); [2015] 1 W.L.R. 1547.

[119] *UVW v XYZ (A Registered Agent)* BVIHC (COM) 108 of 2016, per Wallbank J. The judge held that the legal basis to make a post-judgment disclosure order against a third party was found in the English Court of Appeal's decision in *Mercantile Group (Europe) AG v Aiyela*, above, even though, as we have noted, the significance of that decision as support for the grant of relief under the *Norwich Pharmacal* jurisdiction has been left open in *NML Capital v Chapman Freeborn*. The decision of Wallbank J in *UVW v XYZ*, at [26]–[28], also to grant what he described as a *Norwich Pharmacal* order against third parties prior to the applicant obtaining a foreign judgment—on the basis that the court was giving effect to its power to make ancillary orders where it is just and convenient to ensure a freezing injunction (including a foreign one) is effective—appears to elide the statutory and equitable jurisdictions.

assets but a reasonable suspicion (which was less than a prima facie case) of both such wilful evasion and that the third party had been mixed up in the wrongdoing was a sufficient basis for relief. In relation to the former, mere non-payment of the judgment debt (as opposed to efforts to obstruct or frustrate enforcement of the judgment) was not enough. In relation to the latter and the grant of relief against a registered agent, there was no need to show that the corporate vehicle had been created by the registered agent for a wrongful purpose; it sufficed that the vehicle had been used for that purpose.

29–065 **Condition 2: There Must be the Need for an Order to Enable Legal Proceedings to be Brought, or Appropriate Redress Sought, Against the Ultimate Wrongdoer.**   The *Norwich Pharmacal* jurisdiction does not exist simply to satisfy curiosity or to serve as a broad mechanism to work out whether a claimant may or may not have a claim against one or more third parties or to gather evidence.[120] The courts have been careful to ensure that the jurisdiction is not used "to fish for information of any causes of action he may have against other persons than the defendant."[121] An order will only be made if the applicant can show a legitimate reason for obtaining the information sought. It has been said that "the Norwich Pharmacal jurisdiction is an exceptional one and one which is only exercised by the courts when they are satisfied that it is necessary that it should be exercised."[122] In *R (Omar) v Secretary of State for Foreign and Commonwealth Affairs*,[123] Maurice Kay LJ emphasised that necessity is a threshold condition rather than simply a matter for discretion[124]:

> "Whilst necessity is sometimes referred to as if it were simply a matter for consideration in the exercise of discretion, in truth it is more than that. It is a test which must be satisfied if *Norwich Pharmacal* relief is to follow. The first sentence in paragraph 57 of Lord Woolf's speech [in *Ashworth*] makes that plain. Nevertheless, I agree with the statement of the Divisional Court in the present case (at paragraph 83) that 'the requirement of necessity is a requirement that must be dictated flexibly in the circumstances of each case.'"

29–066 What is precisely meant by the word "necessity" here is not altogether clear: it probably simply means that the court must be satisfied that the interests of justice require that the order be made.[125] Certainly, this requirement does not mean that

---

[120] "[T]he action cannot be used for wide-ranging discovery or the gathering of evidence and is strictly confined to necessary information": *R (Mohamed) v Secretary of State for Foreign and Commonwealth Affairs (No.1)* [2009] 1 W.L.R. 2579, at [133], cited by the Court of Appeal in *R (Omar) v Secretary of State for Foreign and Commonwealth Affairs* [2011] EWCA Civ 1587, at [4] and [18] and by Lord Mance in *Singularis Holdings Ltd v PricewaterhouseCoopers* [2014] UKPC 36; [2015] A.C. 1675, at [40].

[121] *Axa Equity and Law Life Assurance Society Plc v National Westminster Bank* [1998] P.N.L.R. 433, per Rimer J at 445, quoting from the decision of the Supreme Court of Massachusetts in *Post v Toledo, Cincinnati & St Louis Railroad Co* 11 N.E. Rep. 540 (1887), which had also been cited in the *Norwich Pharmacal* case.

[122] *Ashworth Hospital Authority*, above, per Lord Woolf at [57]. See also *The Rugby Football Union* case, above, per Lord Kerr at [15].

[123] *R (Omar) v Secretary of State for Foreign and Commonwealth Affairs* [2013] EWCA Civ 118; [2014] Q.B. 112, at [30].

[124] Emphasised by Flaux J in *Ramilos Trading*, at [25].

[125] Indeed in *The President of the State of Equatorial Guinea & Anor v Bank of Scotland International* [2006] UKPC 7 the Privy Council (in a judgment jointly delivered by Lords Bingham

the applicant must show that the remedy is one of last resort (i.e. that there are no other avenues available to him to obtain the information sought, although the fact that the information or documents sought might be available from other sources will be a relevant consideration, both at this stage and, potentially, at the discretionary stage discussed below).[126]

Further, as we discuss below, the applicant does not need to go so far as to show that, in the case of an application to identify an alleged wrongdoer, he intends to institute formal legal proceedings against him. Depending on the circumstances of the case, there may be a variety of avenues available to the applicant to seek redress for the wrong allegedly done to him.   **29–067**

So, in *British Steel Corp v Granada Television Ltd*,[127] an employee of the British Steel Corporation (BSC) had, in breach of his duties to BSC, provided confidential documents to the respondent television company for use in a programme about a steel strike. BSC sought an order that Granada disclose the name of the relevant employee pursuant to the *Norwich Pharmacal* jurisdiction. Granada argued (among other things) that this was not a proper case for a *Norwich Pharmacal* order because BSC had no intention of taking legal proceedings against that employee. In the Court of Appeal Templeman LJ said: **29–068**

> "In my judgment the principle of the *Norwich Pharmacal* case applies whether or not the victim intends to pursue action in the courts against the wrongdoer provided that the existence of a cause of action is established and the victim cannot otherwise obtain justice. The remedy of discovery is intended in the final analysis to enable justice to be done. Justice can be achieved against an erring employee in a variety of ways and a plaintiff may obtain an order for discovery provided he shows that he is genuinely seeking lawful redress of a wrong and cannot otherwise obtain redress. In the present case BSC state that they will not finally determine whether to take legal proceedings or whether to dismiss the employee or whether to obtain redress in some other lawful manner until they have considered the identity, status and excuses of the employee. The disclosure of the identity of the disloyal employee will by itself protect BSC and their innocent employees now and for the future and is essential if BSC are to redress the wrong."[128]

This decision was affirmed by the House of Lords in *Ashworth Hospital Authority v Mirror Group Newspapers Ltd*.[129] Disclosure of the relevant information may be sought for the purpose of enabling the claimant to curtail ongoing wrongdoing by "self-help" remedies. So, in the *Ashworth Hospital*   **29–069**

---

and Hoffmann) held, at [16], that "Whether it is said that it must be just and convenient in the interests of justice to grant relief, or that relief should only be granted if it is necessary in the interests of justice to grant it, makes little or no difference of substance."

[126] *R (Mohamed) v Secretary of State for Foreign and Commonwealth Affairs* [2008] EWHC 2048 (Admin); [2009] 1 W.L.R. 2579 (DC), at [94], disapproving the more stringent approach advocated in earlier first instance authorities. This view was approved by the Supreme Court in *The Rugby Football Union*, above, at [16]. In *United Co Rusal Plc v HSBC Bank Plc* [2011] EWHC 404 (QB) one of the grounds for refusing relief was the potential availability of the documents sought via other means.

[127] *British Steel Corp v Granada Television Ltd* [1981] A.C. 1096.

[128] *British Steel Corp v Granada Television Ltd*, at 1132. Nothing was said in the House of Lords which tempered this statement.

[129] *Ashworth Hospital Authority v Mirror Group Newspapers Ltd* [2002] 1 W.L.R. 2033, at [42]–[49]; Templeman LJ's dicta are quoted with approval, at [46].

Authority case the hospital authority sought to identify the source of the leak of confidential information so that the relevant employee might be disciplined and dismissed.[130]

29–070   A *Norwich Pharmacal* order may therefore be sought in cases where there is not necessarily a settled intention to bring proceedings against the suspected wrongdoer. It is enough that the claimant seeks to assert a legal right and intends to seek redress in some form or to protect himself from further wrongdoing. That redress may take the form of making complaint to the appropriate prosecuting authority so that the wrongdoer may be prosecuted in the criminal court.[131] If it is considered to be necessary in the interests of justice *Norwich Pharmacal* relief may even be granted for the purpose of assisting in the defence of proceedings.[132]

29–071   As we have seen above, *Norwich Pharmacal* relief is not limited to disclosure of the identity of the alleged wrongdoer. It may be ordered where the identity of that wrongdoer is known but where a fact or facts crucial to the proper allegation of his liability is not, but is susceptible of ascertainment from a known document or fact in the hands or knowledge of a third party.[133] Thus, in *AOOT Kalmneft v Denton Wilde Sapte*,[134] where it appeared that prepayments had been diverted by (at least) a former director of the claimant company, *Norwich Pharmacal* relief (as well as *Bankers Trust* relief) was granted to enable the claimant to bring proceedings against those responsible for diverting the funds, on the basis that it should be available not only to identify a defendant but also to show that an unknown defendant had committed a wrong.[135] The judge concluded[136]:

> "The information held by the solicitors in their documents may not conclusively reveal an alternative defendant to Mr Daginov nor conclusively disclose who received any part of the prepayment monies, but I am satisfied that there is sufficient prospect that the information they hold will assist [the claimant] in its search for the wrongdoers and the funds paid away … to justify making the orders sought."

29–072   **Condition 3: The Person Against Whom the Order is Sought Must be Involved in Such a Way that he is Not Correctly Characterised as a "Mere Witness".**   Although in the *Norwich Pharmacal* case itself the House of Lords contemplated that the respondent will have unwittingly[137] "participated" in or

---

[130] See also *The Rugby Football Union v Consolidated Information Ltd*, above, at [15] where Lord Kerr observed that, in principle, any form of intended redress will suffice to ground an application for an order.

[131] *Ashworth Hospital Authority*, above, at [53].

[132] Compare *R (Mohamed) v Secretary of State for Foreign and Commonwealth Affairs* [2009] 1 W.L.R. 2579 (DC); [2011] Q.B. 218 (CA); and *Aamer v Secretary of State for Foreign and Commonwealth Affairs* [2009] EWHC 3316 (Admin), where disclosure of materials was respectively sought to defend terrorism charges and to resist detention by the US military authorities) but which must now be considered in the light of the decision of the Court of Appeal in *R (Omar) v Secretary of State for Foreign & Commonwealth Affairs* [2013] EWCA Civ; [2014] 1 Q.B. 112.

[133] *Axa Equity v National Westminster Bank* [1998] C.L.C. 1177, at [25], per Morritt LJ.

[134] *AOOT Kalmneft v Denton Wilde Sapte* [2002] 1 Lloyd's Rep. 417, per HHJ McGonigal, approved by Lightman J in *Mitsui v Nexen*, above, at [20].

[135] *AOOT Kalmneft v Denton Wilde Sapte*, at [17].

[136] *AOOT Kalmneft v Denton Wilde Sapte*, at [18].

[137] It was argued in the *Ashworth Hospital Authority* case, above, that the respondent himself had to have been a wrongdoer: this contention was held to be a "fundamental misconception": see, at [26]:

"facilitated" the wrongdoing, it is now clear that some lesser "involvement" in it may suffice.[138] This is treated as a flexible concept. There is no causation hurdle which the claimant has to surmount: it is not necessary to show that the defendant to the *Norwich Pharmacal* application, has (whether unwittingly or not) actually caused the wrongdoing.[139] Whether a person is susceptible to the jurisdiction depends upon proper recognition of the dichotomy between the "mere witness" or bystander, on the one hand,[140] and someone who is not a mere witness because there are facts (which may disclose some "involvement" falling short of participation or facilitation) which prevent him being such.[141]

The requirement that the respondent from whom information is sought has been involved in the wrongdoing has repeatedly been upheld by the courts. For example, in *NML Capital Ltd v Chapman Freeborn Holdings Ltd* Tomlinson LJ[142] said that it was "clear that if the *Norwich Pharmacal* jurisdiction is not to become wholly unprincipled, the third party must be involved in the furtherance of the transaction identified as the relevant wrongdoing."[143] Hence, whatever the degree of third party involvement in any particular case, it has to be involvement in the furtherance of the transaction (or action) which is properly identified as relevant wrongdoing. In the *NML Capital* case,[144] the Court of Appeal upheld a judgment dismissing a *Norwich Pharmacal* application against a jet charterer used by the Republic of Argentina to charter an aircraft. The claimant was a judgment creditor of Argentina and had good grounds for believing that the state

29–073

"While therefore the exercise of the jurisdiction does require that there should be wrongdoing, the wrongdoing which is required is the wrongdoing of the person whose identity the claimant is seeking to establish and not that of the person against whom the proceedings are brought." Of course the fact that the respondent may itself be a wrongdoer does not preclude the exercise of the *Norwich Pharmacal* jurisdiction and is likely to make the case for granting relief all the stronger: see 29–054 above.

[138] So in *Ashworth Hospital Authority*, Lord Woolf said, at [58], that the respondent must have been "involved, whether innocently or otherwise, in the wrongdoing." See also *R. (Mohamed) v Secretary of State for Foreign & Commonwealth Affairs (No.1)* [2009] 1 W.L.R. 2579, at [70].

[139] *Shaker Aamer v Secretary of State for Foreign and Commonwealth Affairs* [2009] EWHC 3316, at [43].

[140] As to which see also *Axa Equity & Law Life Assurance Society Plc v National Westminster Bank Plc* [1998] C.L.C. 1177, at [23], per Morritt LJ.

[141] *Various Claimants v News Group Newspapers* [2013] EWHC 2119; [2014] Ch. 400, at [46] and [52], per Mann J. There the court concluded that the Metropolitan Police Service was not a mere witness in relation to information which it had not only acquired in the course of its investigation into suspected phone-hacking but where it had provided information by informing victims that they were victims, by disclosing to them a limited amount of information and stating that it held more. In *R (Omar) v Secretary of State for Foreign & Commonwealth Affairs* [2013] EWCA Civ; [2014] 1 Q.B. 112, at [38], the Court of Appeal disagreed with the Divisional Court that nothing less than "facilitation" would suffice for the purpose of exercising the jurisdiction and observed that the necessary degree of involvement or participation (as opposed to facilitation) on the part of the respondent may arise even where he has attempted to discourage or prevent the wrongful act, rather than having done anything to facilitate it. See also the *Ashworth Hospital Authority* case, above, at [35]: "Although this requirement of involvement or participation on the part of the party from whom discovery is sought is not a stringent requirement, it is still a significant requirement. It distinguishes that party from a mere onlooker or witness."

[142] With whom Floyd and Jackson LJJ agreed.

[143] At [25]. See also *Axa Equity and Law Life Assurance Society v National Westminster Bank Plc* [1998] C.L.C. 1177 and *Campaign against Arms Trade v BAE* [2007] EWHC 330, at [12].

[144] *NML Capital* case [2013] EWCA Civ 589.

had entered into the charter with a view to avoiding the risk of its own presidential plane being seized, if used during certain international flights, in support of the unsatisfied judgment. Information was sought about the bank accounts from which any payments under the charter had been made. In upholding the judge's refusal of relief at the inter partes hearing below, the Court of Appeal said that it was important to analyse with some care what precisely was said to constitute the alleged wrongdoing. There was "nothing inherently wrong in chartering an aircraft, unless it be said that any trading by a judgment debtor which involves using his assets for that purpose rather than satisfying a judgment debt is in itself wrongdoing. However I reject that proposition."[145] If merely trading with a person who turns out to have been a judgment debtor at the relevant time triggered the *Norwich Pharmacal* jurisdiction then it would become one of "absurd width".

29–074 However, in *Various Claimants v News Group Newspapers*[146] Mann J granted an application that the Metropolitan Police Service ("MPS") should provide disclosure to phone hacking complainants who believed (on the basis of information provided to them by the MPS) that they had been the victims of phone hacking by News Group Newspapers (NGN). As the claimants only knew of the hacking from information provided to them by the police, the main evidence of hacking was in the hands of the MPS as a result of their criminal investigations. NGN opposed the application for *Norwich Pharmacal* relief on the basis that the MPS were not sufficiently involved in the original wrongdoing as to make them susceptible to the jurisdiction. Mann J held that the correct question was not whether the MPS had participated in, or facilitated, or even been involved in the actual wrongdoing; rather it was

> "whether the MPS is a mere witness (or metaphorical bystander) or whether its engagement with the wrong is such as to make it more than a mere witness and therefore susceptible to the court's jurisdiction to order *Norwich Pharmacal* disclosure."[147]

29–075 He said[148]:

> "If a participation or facilitation test were the sole test, incapable of expansion, [counsel for NGN] would be correct. However, I do not think that it is the sole test. It is true that the traditional formulation of the test is in such terms, but that is because those are the usual circumstances in which someone becomes something beyond a mere witness. On the facts of the cases where orders were made, the respondent was usually in that position. In my view the answer to the question lies in recognising that what the cases are doing is contrasting two things—the mere witness on the one hand, and a person who is not a mere witness on the other. On the cases the latter class is generally described in terms of participation/facilitation, as though that were the opposite of being a mere witness. But the real analysis lies in appreciating that the courts are holding not that those factors are indeed the other side of a dichotomy, but that those factors prevent the respondent from being a mere witness. Once that is recognised then it becomes relevant to consider whether there are other facts, short of participation/facilitation, which could prevent a person from being a mere witness. That

---

[145] At [26].
[146] *Various Claimants v News Group Newspapers*, above.
[147] At [54].
[148] At [52].

question has not arisen in the cases in terms, but since the real question is the scope of the mere witness rule it is relevant to consider that particular question. It has been made to arise in the present case because of its unusual facts."

This conclusion seems clearly right. Mann J's judgment contains a careful analysis of the authorities, pointing out that they largely were concerned not with applying a requirement of "facilitating" the relevant wrongdoing, but with identifying when a case involved the respondent to the application as something other than a "mere witness"; and that Lord Woolf CJ in *Ashworth* introduced the concept of "involvement", as opposed to facilitation or participation.[149] Mann J was right to say that what Lord Woolf CJ's speech in *Ashworth* permits is "to allow the court to consider what 'involvement' is sufficient without being trammelled by rigid concepts of participation or facilitation".[150]   **29–076**

(iv)   Discretion

Even if the conditions identified above have been satisfied it does not follow that an order should be granted. It is at this stage that the court must consider whether, as a matter of discretion, an order should be made. It is impossible to comprehensively list the considerations which the court is entitled to take into account when deciding whether or not to exercise its discretion in favour of making an order. For instance in the *Chapman Freeborn* case, discussed above, it was held that a material factor against making the order would have been the commercial damage to the respondent had it become known that it could be obliged, even though by court order, to provide information about the payment arrangements of its customers. In fraud cases, where applications are often made against lawyers or other professionals who are alleged to have become innocently involved in the wrongdoing of fraudsters, the fact that an order will involve the invasion of the confidential (and potentially privileged) relationship between the professional and client is a highly material consideration.[151]   **29–077**

In *The Rugby Football Union v Consolidated Information Ltd*[152] the Supreme Court emphasised that the essential purpose of a *Norwich Pharmacal* order is to do justice—and this involved the careful and fair weighing of all relevant factors. The need to order disclosure will be found to exist only if it is a "necessary and proportionate response in all the circumstances."[153]   **29–078**

In the *RFU* case the Supreme Court considered a challenge to the grant of *Norwich Pharmacal* relief whereby the respondent was ordered to disclose the   **29–079**

---

[149] Per Mann J, at [37].
[150] Per Mann J, at [39].
[151] So in *United Company Rusal Plc v HSBC Bank Plc* [2011] EWHC 404 (QB) Tugendhat J said, at [150], that: "*Norwich Pharmacal* orders are always exceptional, because they interfere with the rights of third parties who are not said to have done anything wrong. Where the third parties are lawyers in a professional relationship with the alleged wrongdoer, then the case must be all the more exceptional."
[152] *The Rugby Football Union v Consolidated Information Ltd* [2012] UKSC 55; [2012] 1 W.L.R. 3333.
[153] *The Rugby Football Union v Consolidated Information Ltd*, at [16], citing *Ashworth Hospital Authority v MGN*, above, at 36, 57, per Lord Woolf CJ.

identity of people who had, through the respondent's website, advertised for sale or sold tickets for specified international rugby matches (the underlying wrong being that the RFU issued tickets on terms that any resale or advertisement for sale at above their face value would constitute a breach of contract rendering the ticket null and void). The respondent appealed on the ground that the order constituted an unnecessary and disproportionate interference with the rights of those who had used the website under art.8 of the Charter of Fundamental Rights of the European Union, and that the court should evaluate the impact that the disclosure of the information will have on the individual concerned against the value to the applicant of the information that can be obtained about that particular individual. The Supreme Court rejected this challenge. Lord Kerr (with whom all other four members of the court agreed) stated as follows, in a passage which contains a very useful (although not exhaustive) survey of factors which might, in a given case, be relevant to the exercise of the court's discretion:

"The essential purpose of the remedy is to do justice. This involves the exercise of discretion by a careful and fair weighing of all relevant factors. Various factors have been identified in the authorities as relevant. These include:

(i)   the strength of the possible cause of action contemplated by the applicant for the order: the *Norwich Pharmacal* case [1974] A.C. 133, at 199F–199G, per Lord Cross of Chelsea; *Totalise Plc v The Motley Fool Ltd* [2001] E.M.L.R. 750, at [27], per Owen J at first instance; *Clift v Clarke* [2011] EWHC 1164 (QB), at [14], [38], per Sharp J;

(ii)   the strong public interest in allowing an applicant to vindicate his legal rights: the *British Steel case* [1981] AC 1096, at 1175C–1175D, per Lord Wilberforce, the *Norwich Pharmacal* case [1974] A.C. 133, at 182C–182D, per Lord Morris of Borth-y-Gest, and at 188E–188F, per Viscount Dilhorne;

(iii) whether the making of the order will deter similar wrongdoing in the future: the *Ashworth* case [2002] 1 W.L.R. 2033, at [66], per Lord Woolf CJ;

(iv)   whether the information could be obtained from another source: the *Norwich Pharmacal* case [1974] A.C. 133, at 199F–199G , per Lord Cross; the *Totalise Plc* case [2001] E.M.L.R. 750, at [27]; *President of the State of Equatorial Guinea v Royal Bank of Scotland International* [2006] UKPC 7, at [16], per Lord Bingham of Cornhill;

(v)   whether the respondent to the application knew or ought to have known that he was facilitating arguable wrongdoing: the *British Steel* case [1981] A.C. 1096, at 1197A–1197B , per Lord Fraser, or was himself a joint tortfeasor; *X Ltd v Morgan-Grampian (Publishers) Ltd* [1991] 1 A.C. 1, at 54, per Lord Lowry;

(vi)   whether the order might reveal the names of innocent persons as well as wrongdoers, and if so whether such innocent persons will suffer any harm as a result: the *Norwich Pharmacal* case [1974] A.C. 133, at 176B–176C, per Lord Reid; *Alfred Crompton Amusement Machines Ltd v Customs and Excise Comrs (No.2)* [1974] AC 405, at 434, per Lord Cross of Chelsea;

(vii) the degree of confidentiality of the information sought: the *Norwich Pharmacal* case [1974] A.C. 133, at 190F–190F, per Viscount Dilhorne;

(viii) the privacy rights under article 8 of the European Convention for the Protection of Human Rights and Fundamental Freedoms of the individuals whose identity is to be disclosed: the *Totalise Plc* case [2001] E.M.L.R. 750, at [28];

(ix)   the rights and freedoms under the EU data protection regime of the individuals whose identity is to be disclosed: the *Totalise Plc* case [2001] E.M.L.R. 750, at [18]–[21], per Owen J;

(x)   the public interest in maintaining the confidentiality of journalistic sources, as recognised in section 10 of the Contempt of Court Act 1981 and art.10 of the European Convention for the Protection of Human Rights and Fundamental Freedoms: the *Ashworth* case [2002] 1 W.L.R. 2033, at [2], per Lord Slynn of Hadley."[154]

---

[154] *Ashworth*, at [17].

Lord Kerr concluded as follows: **29–080**

> "In suggesting that it would 'generally be proportionate' to make an order where it had been
> shown that there was arguable wrongdoing and there was no other means of discovering the
> identity of the arguable wrongdoers, Longmore LJ might be said to have somewhat overstated
> the position, although it is to be noted that this was not expressed as a presumption in favour
> of the grant of an order. The particular circumstances affecting the individual whose personal
> data will be revealed on foot of a *Norwich Pharmacal* order will always call for close
> consideration and these may, in some limited instances, displace the interests of the applicant
> for the disclosure of the information even where there is no immediately feasible alternative
> way in which the necessary information can be obtained. But, in the present case, the impact
> that can reasonably be apprehended on the individuals whose personal data are sought is
> simply not of the type that could possibly offset the interests of the RFU in obtaining that
> information. I would therefore dismiss the appeal."[155]

One further factor which may be relevant to the exercise of the discretion is any   **29–081**
delay on the part of the applicant in seeking a *Norwich Pharmacal* order. In
Ramilos Trading Flaux J, had he not held that he had no jurisdiction to grant the
relief sought, would have refused to grant relief on the additional ground that the
relevant facts had been known to the applicant for a significant period of time:

> "If there were anything in the point, the claimant could and should have made it long ago and
> it is not an appropriate use of the *Norwich Pharmacal* jurisdiction to seek evidence now in
> relation to such a stale allegation."[156]

In *Golden Eye v Telefonica*[157] Patten LJ, in addressing the question whether the   **29–082**
relief was proportionate when considered against art.8 and data protection rights
of those against whom the claimant had a case of copyright infringement, noted
that Lord Kerr in the *RFU* case had recognised that

> "there is no presumption that the need to identify arguable wrongdoers should, so to speak,
> trump the privacy and data protection rights."[158]

The balancing exercise was undertaken in *Santander UK Plc v National
Westminster Bank*,[159] where Birss J was persuaded to grant *Norwich Pharmacal*
relief designed to enable the claimant bank to recover payments which had been
made by mistake to customers of the defendant banks. Although the proposed
restitutionary claims against each beneficiary of the payment would be for a sum
which was "modest" and in some cases "tiny", the judge was persuaded to make
an order for disclosure of the minimum information sought (though not for
disclosure of dates of the recipient's date of birth) because it was an order of last
resort and the claimant had no other option.[160]

---

[155] At [46].
[156] *Ramilos Trading*, above, at [221].
[157] *Golden Eye v Telefonica* [2012] EWCA Civ 1740; [2013] Bus L.R. 414, at [16]–[21].
[158] At [19].
[159] *Santander UK Plc v National Westminster Bank* [2014] EWHC 2626 (Ch).
[160] In *Santander UK Plc v The Royal Bank of Scotland Plc* [2015] EWHC 2560 (Ch) Master
Matthews was unpersuaded by the reasoning of Birss J but felt obliged to follow it in making *Norwich
Pharmacal* orders that he had previously refused. The Master took the view that a claim in restitution
or debt was not sufficiently exceptional to justify the exercise of the jurisdiction (for which the test
was necessity rather than proportionality) and could not see how, in circumstances where the

(v) Form of order

29–083   We have seen above that an order will only be made if it is a "necessary and proportionate response in all the circumstances."[161] The claimant should therefore be as specific as possible both in his evidence and the draft order as to what information or documents are sought.[162] A form of order which casts a heavy burden of search upon a defendant or is pitched in terms which will make it difficult for a defendant to know clearly what falls within or without the order will be objectionable by reference to the usual rules that require clarity in the framing of injunctive relief. The position is a fortiori where the defendant is innocent of wrongdoing, is likely to have no knowledge of the underlying issues in the contemplated proceedings and will be subject to an order which is likely to be headed with a penal notice.[163]

29–084   Where the proposed order does not seek to identify an unknown wrongdoer but to build a case against an already identified wrongdoer the necessity test will mean that the applicant will also need to explain in his evidence why the relief is sought at all and why he cannot simply issue proceedings and obtain disclosure from the substantive defendant in the normal way under CPR Pt 31.[164]

29–085   As we have also seen above, *Norwich Pharmacal* applications are not a means by which wide-ranging discovery can be obtained. It has been said that orders should be strictly confined to the disclosure of information necessary to enable a party to plead a case against the actual alleged wrongdoer.[165] It follows that an overly extensive or broadly pitched form of order is likely to seriously harm the prospects of the application. In *Ramilos Trading*, Flaux J referred[166] to the "wide-ranging detailed requests for disclosure and evidence sought by the claimant in its 39 questions" and went on to emphasise[167] that the decision of the Divisional Court in *Mohamed*

> "makes it quite clear that the jurisdiction cannot be used for wide-ranging discovery or the gathering of evidence, but is strictly confined to necessary information".

His conclusion on the scope of the relief which might be granted provides an accurate summary of the current position. He said[168]:

---

restitutionary claim did not arise until the mistaken payee refused to repay the moneys, the beneficiary bank could be said to have become mixed up in any wrongdoing when it previously received the payment into the payee's account.

[161] *Ashworth Hospital Authority v MGN*, above, at [57], approved by the Supreme Court in *The Rugby Football Union v Consolidated Information Ltd*, above, at [16].

[162] *Arab Monetary Fund v Hashim (No. 5)* [1992] 2 All E.R. 911, at 919. It is also in the claimant's own interests to be specific where he is likely to have to bear the defendant's costs of complying with any order made.

[163] See the discussion in *United Company Rusal Plc v HSBC Bank Plc* [2011] EWHC 404 (QB), at [138] and following.

[164] See *Ramilos Trading*, at [139].

[165] *Hilton v D IV LLP* [2015] EWHC 2 (Ch), per HHJ Pelling QC (obiter) at [59].

[166] *Ramilos Trading*, at [41].

[167] *Ramilos Trading*, at [46].

[168] *Ramilos Trading*, at [62].

"... the *Norwich Pharmacal* jurisdiction remains an exceptional jurisdiction with a narrow scope. The court will not permit the jurisdiction to be used for wide-ranging disclosure or gathering of evidence, as opposed to focused disclosure of necessary information: see the judgment of Rimer J in *Axa* and the Divisional Court in *Mohamed*, at [133]. It clearly does not extend to the sort of wide-ranging requests set out in the schedule to the draft order in the present case.[169] Furthermore, it is impermissible to use the jurisdiction as a fishing expedition to establish whether or not the claimant has a good arguable case or not. This emerges from the decision in *Norwich Pharmacal* itself ...".

The decision in *Ramilos Trading* is the latest in a series of recent cases which appear to demonstrate a retrenchment in the attitude of courts to granting *Norwich Pharmacal* relief.[170] This reining in may well have been provoked by claimants having increasingly sought to stray from the paradigm case of the grant of limited and directed relief and treat the jurisdiction as a form of general pre-action third party disclosure. This has led to a renewed judicial emphasis on the fact that *Norwich Pharmacal* relief is exceptional and involves an encroachment on the affairs of a third party against whom in all but rare cases no allegations of wrongdoing are made. Applicants in the future would do well to heed that new approach and tailor their applications accordingly.   **29–086**

It is clear from a number of decisions, including the *Ablyazov* and *Ramilos Trading* decisions discussed earlier, that the Court may order the *Norwich Pharmacal* defendant to provide information by answering directed questions posed to the defendant as well as requiring him to disclose particular documents or categories of documents. The jurisdiction may be a narrow one but it is also a flexible one. The applicant must seek to tread a fine line in showing that the order it seeks strictly adheres to the necessity test, whilst not emasculating the width of the order so as to limit the value of the relief actually ordered.   **29–087**

In an appropriate case, which should be recognised as the exception rather than the norm, the applicant might apply for cross-examination of any deponent who provides an affidavit or witness statement (or other form of vehicle for the provision of information) in purported compliance with a *Norwich Pharmacal* order.[171] The basis for such an order would generally be the inadequacy of the defendant's compliance with the original order. For example, in the Ablyazov litigation a *Norwich Pharmacal* order was made against Mr Ablyazov's brother-in-law, Mr Shalabayev. His compliance with the *Norwich Pharmacal*   **29–088**

---

[169] The judgment annexes the draft order. See also [136], where Flaux J quotes the description in the evidence of the information and documents sought on the application before him.

[170] Other examples are *United Company Rusal Plc v HSBC Bank Plc* [2011] EWHC 404 (QB), and *R (Mohamed) v Secretary of State for Foreign & Commonwealth Affairs (No.1)* [2009] 1 W.L.R. 2579.

[171] See CPR 32.7 and *Kensington International Ltd v Republic of Congo* [2006] EWHC 1848 (Comm), at [17] where, at first instance, Morison J (in circumstances where the claimant had obtained summary judgment against the defendant) ordered cross-examination of a third party who had "become mixed up, at the very least, in dishonest attempts to defeat execution of the judgments against [the defendant]" in circumstances where his disclosure affidavit had been "woefully inadequate". See also the summary by Vos J in *Jennington International Inc v Kanat Shaikhanovish Assaubayev* [2010] EWHC 2351 (Ch), at [22], of the principles governing such applications generally (where the court directed limited cross-examination of the respondents to a freezing injunction focussing upon the identification of assets upon which the injunction might bite). The jurisdiction to order cross-examination on an affidavit/witness statement is considered in detail at Ch.31.

order was so deficient that cross-examination of him was ordered, and after the cross-examination, Cooke J held that Mr Shalabayev should pay the claimant's costs of the cross-examination.[172]

(vi) Procedural considerations

29–089 As set out above, applications should be made by a Pt 8 claim form rather than by Pt 23 application notice[173]. The Pt 8 provisions providing for the defendant to have 14 days to acknowledge service and file evidence will apply.

29–090 In the Chancery Division, the application should be made in the first instance to the assigned Master and will be referred to a High Court judge if the complexity and/or importance of the application warrants it. If the applicant wishes to apply direct to a High Court Judge, consent from a Master should be sought.[174]

29–091 If the application is made to a Master it will normally be dealt with without a hearing, as "file work".[175] If the claimant wishes to have the application dealt with at a hearing, a short (5 minute) hearing before the Master to ask for the application to be dealt with at a hearing rather than on the papers will generally not be difficult to obtain. It will often be the case that the effective hearing will then have to come on in due course as an application by order.

29–092 There are no specific provisions in the Commercial Court Guide addressing *Norwich Pharmacal* applications. If the *Norwich Pharmacal* Pt 8 claim is being issued in the Commercial Court, the general rules applying in the Commercial Court to Pt 8 claims will apply, absent any directions to the contrary. In particular, as provided by CPR 58.12, a defendant who wishes to rely on written evidence has 28 days to file that evidence after filing an acknowledgment of service.[176]

29–093 In either the Chancery Division or the Commercial Court, a claimant seeking an urgent *Norwich Pharmacal* order could perhaps in an appropriate case seek directions for the defendant to file evidence and attend any hearing more quickly than the usual Pt 8 timetable allows in reliance on para.6.1 of Practice Direction 8A, which provides that the Court may give directions immediately a Pt 8 claim form is issued, including fixing a hearing date, either where there is no dispute or where there may be a dispute but a hearing date could conveniently be given.

---

[172] An account set out by Flaux J in *JSC BTA Bank v Ablyazov* [2015] 1 W.L.R. 1547, at [11]. The respondent was subsequently held to be in contempt of court for failure to comply with the *Norwich Pharmacal* order: [2013] EWHC 3243 (Comm).
[173] Chancery Guide para.7.4.
[174] Chancery Guide para.7.6.
[175] Chancery Guide para.15.4 and para.17.66.
[176] See also Commercial Court Guide para.B5.4.

(vii) Use to which the documents can be put

Despite the limited purposes for which *Norwich Pharmacal* relief can be ordered, there is no rule preventing the use of the material produced pursuant to a *Norwich Pharmacal* order at trial.[177] It may also be used to amend the statements of case in an existing set of proceedings.

29–094

Although documents disclosed pursuant to *Norwich Pharmacal* order are within the CPR 31.22 prohibition on collateral use, because they are documents "disclosed" for the purposes of CPR 31, if a court grants a *Norwich Pharmacal* order on the express basis that subsequent proceedings against the ultimate wrongdoer are contemplated (as it generally will for reasons already explained), then the court has impliedly given permission to the claimant to use the documents in those subsequent proceedings (for the purposes of r.31.22(1)(b)). That decision was reached in *Shlaimoun v Mining Technologies Inc*,[178] where it was held that documents disclosed pursuant to a *Norwich Pharmacal* order could be utilised in foreign proceedings. For the reasons set out below, the better view is that a *Norwich Pharmacal* order may not be made to obtain evidence for the purpose of foreign proceedings; but the broader principle adumbrated in *Shlaimoun* as to implied permission for use of the disclosed documents in a different set of proceedings in England remains correct.[179]

29–095

(viii) Applications for evidence or documents to be used in foreign proceedings

In *R (Omar) v Secretary of State for Foreign and Commonwealth Affairs*[180] it was pointed out that the proceedings in the Divisional Court and Court of Appeal in *R (Mohamed) v Secretary of State for Foreign and Commonwealth Affairs*[181] had taken place without the court considering the question whether the statutory arrangements in the Evidence (Proceedings in Other Jurisdictions) Act 1975 and the Crime (International Co-operation) Act 2003 excluded the *Norwich Pharmacal* jurisdiction where foreign proceedings were contemplated. In *Omar*, the Court of Appeal upheld the Divisional Court's decision that it had no jurisdiction to entertain a *Norwich Pharmacal* application because of the 2003 Act (as the *Omar* case concerned foreign criminal proceedings).

29–096

The reasoning in *Omar* leads equally to the conclusion that the 1975 Act is the sole jurisdiction for obtaining evidence from the English courts for use in foreign civil proceedings. This was the decision reached by Flaux J in *Ramilos Trading*[182]:

29–097

---

[177] See *Omar v Omar*, above, at 1434D–143E, per Jacob J.

[178] *Shlaimoun v Mining Technologies Inc* [2011] EWHC 3278 (QB); [2012] 1 W.L.R. 1276, at [38] and [40], per Coulson J. See also *Omar v Omar*, above, where Jacob J permitted the use of the disclosed documents in foreign proceedings as well as in domestic proceedings.

[179] The fact that (as we have noted above) the application is properly made by claim form means that the main proceedings will usually be a different set of proceedings.

[180] *R (Omar) v Secretary of State for Foreign and Commonwealth Affairs* [2013] EWCA Civ 118.

[181] *R (Mohamed) v Secretary of State for Foreign and Commonwealth Affairs* [2008] EWHC 2048.

[182] *Ramilos Trading*, at [99].

29–098

"... Further, although Maurice Kay LJ states that they were dealing with the 2003 Act, not the 1975 Act, it is clear from a number of passages in the judgments (specifically [2] in the judgment of Lord Judge CJ and [10], [22] and the reference to the similar provisions in the 1975 Act to those in the 2003 Act in [25] of the judgment of Maurice Kay LJ) that the Court of Appeal considered that their conclusion that *Norwich Pharmacal* relief was not available when the statutory regime under the 2003 Act was in place, would be equally applicable to the statutory regime under the 1975 Act. This is also the interpretation placed upon *Omar* by Hollander: *Documentary Evidence* 12th edition, paras 4–13—4–14...".

29–099

This is consistent with the words of Lord Diplock in the leading case of *Rio Tinto Zinc Corp v Westinghouse Electric Corp*[183]:

"...the jurisdiction and powers of the High Court to make the orders that are the subject of this appeal are to be found in sections 1 and 2 of the Evidence (Proceedings in other Jurisdictions) Act 1975 and nowhere else ...The jurisdiction of English courts to order persons within its jurisdiction to provide oral or documentary evidence in aid of proceedings in foreign courts has always been exclusively statutory."

There was, however, a series of cases[184] decided after the judgment in the *Westinghouse* case in which it was accepted without argument that *Norwich Pharmacal* relief could be granted in respect of contemplated (or ongoing) foreign proceedings, in the same way as it was available in respect of English proceedings. As Flaux J pointed out in *Ramilos Trading*,[185] *Shlaimoun v Mining Technologies International Inc*[186] appears to have been the first case in which the *Westinghouse* point and the 1975 Act were considered. Coulson J in that case considered that the 1975 Act and the *Norwich Pharmacal* jurisdiction were parallel procedures.[187] Flaux J concluded that this was wrong and that the decision in *Omar* led to the conclusion that *Norwich Pharmacal* relief was not available when the substantive proceedings being contemplated (see Condition 2 above) were to take place abroad.[188]

29–100

The Court of Appeal in *Omar* dismissed a distinction which the Divisional Court in *Omar* had drawn between "information" and "evidence" whereby the former could be the subject of a *Norwich Pharmacal* order sought in the context of contemplated foreign proceedings but not the latter. In *Ramilos Trading*, counsel for the applicant submitted that this distinction was in fact correct (relying in particular on the opinion of Lord Sumption in *Singularis Holdings Ltd v*

---

[183] *Rio Tinto Zinc Corp v Westinghouse Electric Corp* [1978] A.C. 547, at 632G–633A.

[184] *Smith Kline & French Laboratories Ltd v Global Pharmaceutics* [1986] RPC 394; *Omar v Omar* [1995] 1 W.L.R. 1429 and *R (Mohamed) v Secretary of State for Foreign and Commonwealth Affairs (No.1)*, above.

[185] In *Ramilos Trading*, above, at [72].

[186] *Shlaimoun v Mining Technologies International Inc* [2011] EWHC 3278 (QB); [2012] 1 W.L.R. 1276.

[187] At [23]–[24].

[188] Flaux J held that the decision in *Shlaimoun* could be justified on the basis that there had clearly been wrongdoing within the jurisdiction and, at the time of the *Norwich Pharmacal* applications, the applicant was trying to find out where the money had gone and did not know whether and, if so, where, any proceedings would be commenced, whether in England or a foreign jurisdiction: see *Ramilos Trading*, above, at [79].

Pricewaterhouse Cooper).[189] Flaux J identified three reasons[190] why that distinction did not help the applicant in the case before him:

(1) *Singularis* was not a *Norwich Pharmacal* case and Lord Sumption in fact expressly said in *Singularis* that the doubt about the distinction was probably justified in *Omar*[191];

(2) Lord Sumption's comments were clearly obiter and in his dissenting judgment, Lord Mance expressed the same scepticism about the distinction between information and evidence as the Court of Appeal did in *Omar*[192]; and

(3) "even assuming that Maurice Kay LJ was wrong to reject the distinction between information and evidence, all that would follow in the context of the jurisdiction issue, is that the distinction was correctly drawn by the Divisional Court. In other words, cases like *Smith Kline & French* which decide that the *Norwich Pharmacal* jurisdiction can be used to order disclosure of limited information for use in overseas proceedings, may have been correctly decided, but this in no way affects the ultimate decision, of both the Divisional Court and the Court of Appeal, that the *Norwich Pharmacal* jurisdiction cannot be used to obtain evidence for use in overseas proceedings, because of the statutory regime."[193]

The position which has been reached, then, appears to be that in any case where **29–101** information or evidence (e.g. in the form of disclosure) is sought for contemplated foreign proceedings the only procedural avenue available to the applicant will be the 1975 Act and the *Norwich Pharmacal* jurisdiction will accordingly be unavailable. In *Ramilos Trading* the applicant sought to avoid this legal conclusion by stating that it was not at a stage of contemplating any proceedings at all, whether or not to be issued abroad; but this simply meant that the claimant could not fulfil either Conditions 1 or 2 discussed above.

(ix) Service out

The question of whether *Norwich Pharmacal* applications can be made for **29–102** evidence which is to be used in foreign proceedings has been addressed above. A different question arises where the substantive proceedings have been, or are to

---

[189] *Singularis Holdings Ltd v Pricewaterhouse Cooper* [2014] UKPC 36; [2015] A.C. 1675, at [20]–[22].

[190] At [109]–[111].

[191] At [21]: "What is sought in this case, however, is not evidence for use in forensic proceedings but information required for the performance of the liquidators' ordinary duty of identifying and taking possession of assets of the company. In *R (Omar) v Secretary of State for Foreign and Commonwealth Affairs* [2014] Q.B. 112, at [12] the Court of Appeal doubted whether the distinction between evidence and information was helpful, and their doubt was probably justified in that case, where information was being sought for use in foreign proceedings. But the distinction is of broader legal significance. The courts have never been inhibited in their willingness to develop appropriate remedies to require the provision of information when a sufficiently compelling legal policy calls for it."

[192] *Omar*, at [141]–[142].

[193] At [11].

be, brought in England but the *Norwich Pharmacal* defendant is out of the jurisdiction. In *AB Bank Ltd v Abu Dhabi*[194] (where it was assumed that a *Norwich Pharmacal* application could be made in respect of foreign proceedings), it was held that there was no jurisdictional gateway to permit service of the *Norwich Pharmacal* claim form out of the jurisdiction:

(1) The *Norwich Pharmacal* application was not a claim for an interim remedy under s.25(1) Civil Jurisdiction and Judgments Act 1982 (para.3.1(5) of Practice Direction 6B). As between the applicant and the respondent, the *Norwich Pharmacal* application is the final relief sought and it was not correct to describe it as interim relief.[195]

(2) The claim was not one for an injunction ordering the respondent to do or refrain from doing an act within the jurisdiction (para.3.1(2) of Practice Direction 6B).[196] The respondent bank was being required to obtain information in the UAE and then provide a witness statement or affidavit, which could be provided abroad or in London. In reaching this conclusion, Teare J declined to follow the ex parte decision in *Bacon v Automaticc Inc*[197] in which service of a *Norwich Pharmacal* application out of the jurisdiction was permitted on the basis that it required the *Norwich Pharmacal* defendant to disclose the information sought in the jurisdiction. That permission appears to have been granted without particular consideration in the *Bacon* case.[198] While one can see why at first blush the gateway seems appropriate, as Hollander points out,[199] if it were possible to obtain permission to serve out on this basis, it would mean the court had jurisdiction to serve out in every *Norwich Pharmacal* case, against every *Norwich Pharmacal* defendant, regardless of whether the defendant had any connection with this jurisdiction and subject only to the court's general discretion.[200]

(3) The claim was not one against a "necessary and proper party" (para.3.1(3) of Practice Direction 6B). Teare J held[201] that the *Norwich Pharmacal* defendant was not a necessary and proper party to the fraud claim which the claimant wanted to pursue: the *Norwich Pharmacal* defendant would never be a party to that claim but to a different claim raising the different

---

[194] *AB Bank Ltd v Abu Dhabi* [2017] 1 W.L.R. 810.

[195] At [6]–[16]. In reaching this conclusion, Teare J declined to follow decisions to the contrary of the Gibraltar Court of Appeal (*Secilpar SL v Fiduciary Trust Ltd*, 24 September 2004) and of the British Virgin Islands Court of Appeal (*Morgan & Morgan Trust Corp v Fiona Trust*, 25 September 2006, and *TSJ Engineering Consulting v Al-Rushaid Petroleum*, 27 July 2010).

[196] At [17]–[18].

[197] *Bacon v Automaticc Inc* [2012] 1 W.L.R. 1753.

[198] The point is dealt with in one sentence in the judgment at [18]: "Accordingly, the claimant applies for permission to serve the claim form out of the jurisdiction, on the grounds specified in paragraph 3.1(2) of PD 6B, supplementing CPR Pt 6: a claim is made for an injunction ordering the defendants to do an act within the jurisdiction, namely disclose to the solicitors the information sought."

[199] Hollander, *Documentary Evidence* (2015), para.4–18.

[200] To the same effect, see also S. Bushell and G. Milner-Moore, *Disclosure of Information: Norwich Pharmacal and Related Principles* (London: Bloomsbury, 2013) at pp.228–229.

[201] At [19]–[20].

cause of action which was said to establish the basis for *Norwich Pharmacal* relief against the *Norwich Pharmacal* defendant.

(2)   Bankers Trust Orders

(i)   The nature of the relief

A further form of disclosure order available in the fraud litigator's armoury is the so-called *Bankers Trust* order, so-named after the decision of the Court of Appeal in *Bankers Trust Co v Shapira*.[202] In essence a *Bankers Trust* order is a means by which the claimant may trace funds or other assets to which it makes a proprietary claim[203] by seeking an order requiring potentially innocent third parties (usually banks) to assist it in providing information and/or documents concerning the location or current (legal) ownership of those assets. The jurisdiction will typically (but not always) be invoked at an early stage in the proceedings and on an urgent basis in order to try to locate assets before they are dissipated. Given their similarities, *Bankers Trust* orders are often sought in conjunction with applications under the *Norwich Pharmacal* jurisdiction.[204]

29–103

The relief granted by the court when exercising this equitable jurisdiction may extend to the production of documents or the provision of information (by way of witness statement or affidavit, or by way of the provision of a form of Further Information),[205] or both, when neither could be sought by reliance upon the court's powers (under CPR 18 and CPR 31) to order the provision of information or the disclosure of documents which are material to the substantive issues in the proceedings. The documents which may be ordered to be disclosed are not limited to those falling within the provisions of the Bankers' Books Evidence Act 1879 (which we consider below).[206] As with any evidence that may be produced in response to a *Norwich Pharmacal* order, the court may in an appropriate case (which is likely to be a rare one) direct cross-examination, before trial, upon any evidence provided under a *Bankers Trust* order in accordance with the provisions of CPR 32.7.

29–104

Bankers Trust relief may be sought against those who, like any *Norwich Pharmacal* defendant, are or may be innocent of any wrongdoing but who have

29–105

---

[202] *Bankers Trust Co v Shapira* [1980] 1 W.L.R. 1274.

[203] Usually the claimant will be the person beneficially entitled to the relevant property; but a person holding legal title on trust for a beneficiary can also claim *Bankers Trust* relief: see *Miles Broking Ltd v Barclays Bank Plc* [2017] EWHC 3338 (Ch).

[204] Indeed, the Court of Appeal decision in *Mercantile Group (Europe) AG v Aiyela* [1994] Q.B. 366 appears to elide the two jurisdictions; but, as we note below, they should properly be considered to be separate.

[205] So in *A v C (Note)* [1981] Q.B. 956 Robert Goff J said, at 959, that the court "may order a bank (whether or not party to the proceedings) to give discovery of documents in relation to the bank account of a defendant who is alleged to have defrauded the plaintiff of his assets; and it may make orders for interrogatories to be answered by the defendants or their employees or director." For interrogatories one may now use the word "questions."

[206] *Bankers Trust Co v Shapira*, above, at 1283E. In *A v C* [1981] Q.B. 956 the order against the defendant bank for the disclosure of the bank account balance was made under the more limited scope of s.7 of the Act. For "Bankers' Books" orders see paras 29–120—29–124.

information about the subject matter of the proprietary claim. Indeed, but for the fact that applicants often apply for what is described as *"Bankers Trust* relief" against all respondents—including those who are alleged to be accountable on the proprietary claim—any such innocent party is the archetypal *Bankers Trust* respondent. It follows that, where relief is granted against such a person, the applicant should be required to give an appropriate undertaking in damages,[207] to pay for the costs of compliance usually on the indemnity basis (which might instead be reserved if there is a proper basis for suspecting that the respondent may be implicated in the wrongdoing)[208] and to undertake to use the disclosed information only for the purposes of the proprietary claim.

29–106   When relief under the *Bankers Trust* jurisdiction is sought it is almost invariably in support of or in conjunction with a proprietary form of freezing injunction.[209] The jurisdiction to make a *Bankers Trust* order is an equitable one arising out of the court's jurisdiction to protect trust property, which, strictly speaking, is separate from the *Norwich Pharmacal* principle, although the two will often overlap.[210] The equitable jurisdiction reflects the fact that

> "orders of this sort were made long before the recent orders for discovery, and they are at the heart of the Chancery Division's concern, and it is the concern of any court of equity, to see that the stable door is locked before the horse has gone."[211]

(ii)   The decision in Bankers Trust

29–107   In *Bankers Trust Co v Shapira*,[212] the Court of Appeal held that jurisdiction existed to order a third party bank to disclose documents relating to accounts held with the bank by the defendant fraudsters who had tricked the claimant out of substantial sums of money. The fraudsters had presented forged cheques for a total of US $1million drawn on a Saudi bank to the claimant bank, which paid over the US $1million, and credited a substantial part of it to accounts held by the fraudsters with the third party bank. The claimant bank had obtained, but not yet served, a freezing order against the fraudsters and was seeking to trace the money.

---

[207] In the exceptional case of relief against a foreign bank, this should probably extend to an indemnity against any liability the bank may incur under customer confidentiality provisions imposed by the local law: see *Mackinnon v Donaldson* [1986] 1 Ch. 482, at 498F–498G and 499C.

[208] See the discussion on costs orders in the *Norwich Pharmacal* context at para.29–059 above.

[209] See *Global Energy Horizons Corp v Gray* [2014] EWHC 2925 (Ch) where relief was granted in the context of the taking of an account following a judgment on liability.

[210] *Murphy v Murphy* [1999] 1 W.L.R. 282, at 289G–290B per Neuberger J: "Where, as in those three cases, the defendant against whom an order is sought is, albeit wholly innocently, 'mixed up in' the wrong-doing of other defendants, there is a risk of some conflation of the two types of jurisdiction (as could be said to appear from the first passage I have quoted from the judgment of Lord Denning MR in the *Shapira* decision). However, this does not seem to me to alter the fact that there are, in 'reality, two separate jurisdictions, albeit that in many cases they will overlap.'" As we note below (para.29–011), there are differences in the tests to be applied to invoke the jurisdiction.

[211] Per Templeman LJ in *Mediterranea Raffineria Siciliana Petroli SpA v Mabanaft GmbH*, unreported, 1 December 1978; [1978] CA Transcript 816, cited by Goff J in *A v C* [1981] 1 Q.B. 956, at 958–959.

[212] *Bankers Trust Co v Shapira* [1980] 1 W.L.R. 1274.

Lord Denning MR referred to three earlier decisions in which the court had **29–108** ordered disclosure from innocent third parties. In two cases[213], there had been frauds on banks and the relevant third parties were banks; in the third case, the claim was to trace money paid away by mistake and the third parties were individuals. In that third case, *Mediterranea Raffineria Siciliana Petroli Spa v Mabanaft GmbH*,[214] Templeman LJ said:

> "… it is a strong order, but the plaintiffs' case is that there is a trust fund of $3,500,000. This has disappeared, and the gentlemen against whom orders are sought may be able to give information as to where it is and who is in charge of it. A court of equity has never hesitated to use the strongest powers to protect and preserve a trust fund in interlocutory proceedings on the basis that, if the trust fund disappears by the time the action comes to trial, equity will have been invoked in vain."

Lord Denning compared the position of the third party bank in the *Bankers Trust* **29–109** case itself to that of Customs & Excise, which was the respondent against whom disclosure was sought in the *Norwich Pharmacal* case:

> "So here the Discount Bank incur no personal liability: but they got mixed up, through no fault of their own, in the tortious or wrongful acts of these two men: and they come under a duty to assist the Bankers Trust Co. of New York by giving them and the court full information and disclosing the identity of the wrongdoers. In this case the particular point is 'full information'."[215]

In *Bankers Trust v Shapira* itself Lord Denning MR, having referred to the **29–110** *Norwich Pharmacal* jurisdiction, and also the then recent decision of Robert Goff J in *A v C*,[216] explained the nature and limits of what was then a developing jurisdiction to order disclosure against third parties in order to trace misappropriated funds:

> "This new jurisdiction must, of course, be carefully exercised. It is a strong thing to order a bank to disclose the state of its customer's account and the documents and correspondence relating to it. It should only be done when there is a good ground for thinking the money in the bank is the plaintiff's money, as, for instance when the customer has got the money by fraud, or other wrongdoing, and paid it into his account at the bank."[217]

So the so-called *Bankers Trust* order was born. It may be described as a **29–111** jurisdiction whereby an innocent third party is required by court order to provide disclosure, whether in the form of information and/or documents, to a claimant in

---

[213] One of which was *A v C (Note)* [1981] Q.B. 956.
[214] CA Transcript No.816 of 1978.
[215] At 1282.
[216] [1981] Q.B. 956. In that case the claimant, which claimed to have been defrauded of substantial sums, made an application for an order against a bank, which was, on the face of it, wholly innocent of any fraud, but through whose accounts the money may have passed, to disclose the sums presently standing in the names of the other defendants (who may well have been implicated in the fraud) and "all the facts within [the bank's] knowledge as to the present whereabouts" of the sum of which the claimant claimed to have been defrauded. Robert Goff J. held that he had jurisdiction to make such an order. He said, at 958: "I take first the proprietary claim. In such cases, there is good authority that the court may make orders with the purpose of ascertaining the whereabouts of the missing trust fund." This may be taken to be a classic *Bankers Trust* order avant la lettre.
[217] At 1282.

order to assist him in locating assets to which he maintains a proprietary claim. As we have seen, it will often be the case that such an order can be justified by reference to the *Norwich Pharmacal* jurisdiction as well as the *Bankers Trust* jurisdiction. Nonetheless the jurisdictions are conceptually distinct: most importantly,

(a) the *Bankers Trust* jurisdiction is narrower, in that it presupposes the existence of a proprietary claim; but

(b) it is wider, in that there is no pre-condition of "involvement" in wrongdoing on the part of the defendant to the application, although usually the very basis for making the application will be the fact that the assets sought to be traced will have passed through the hands of that defendant.

(iii) The exercise of the jurisdiction

29–112 In a recent case[218] it was said that five principles emerged from the authorities applicable to the exercise of the jurisdiction to grant *Bankers Trust* orders:

(1) There had to be good grounds to conclude the property in respect of which disclosure was sought was the applicant's;

(2) There had to be a real prospect that any information given would lead to the discovery of the whereabouts of the assets in question;

(3) The order could not be wider than necessary;

(4) The interests of an applicant in getting an order had to be balanced against the detriment to the respondent;

(5) The applicant had to undertake only to use the documents provided for the process specified.

We consider each below.

29–113 **Principle One.** This is no more than saying that the applicant has a good arguable case that he has a proprietary claim to identified assets or their proceeds. It is suggested that the same standard of proof applies to that which is appropriate in *Norwich Pharmacal* cases, which we have discussed above.

29–114 **Principle Two.** There is usually an element of what is sometimes called "hot pursuit" (of the assets or monies to which the claimant lays claim) when a *Bankers Trust* order is sought. Accordingly, in *Arab Monetary Fund v Hashim (No 5)*[219] Hoffmann J declined to make an order on the ground that there was no real prospect that it would locate or preserve assets. The judge said:

---

[218] *Kyriarkou v Christie Manson & Woods Ltd* (Warby J, unreported, 9 March 2017).

[219] *Arab Monetary Fund v Hashim (No.5)* [1992] 2 All E.R. 911, at 918E–919H. Hoffmann J's third guideline in *Arab Monetary Fund*, that the third party should be entitled to the same specificity in the documents he is asked to produce as he would be if served with a subpoena, has subsequently been disapproved: *Marc Rich & Co Holding Gmbh v Krasner*, Court of Appeal, 15 January 1999, per Morritt LJ.

"What are the limits of the *Bankers Trust* jurisdiction? They must, I think, be deduced from the reasoning upon which that jurisdiction, like the *Norwich Pharmacal* jurisdiction, is distinguished from the 'mere witness' rule. It rests upon the proposition that unless the assets in question can be located and secured, the ultimate determination of ownership of those assets may be frustrated by their removal or dissipation and there will be no point in calling on the third party at the trial to produce the required documents or give the requested information. In my judgment, therefore, the first principle of the *Bankers Trust* case is that the plaintiff must demonstrate a real prospect that the information may lead to the location or preservation of assets to which he is making a proprietary claim."

This is a matter upon which opinions may differ. In the *Bankers Trust* case itself, Mustill J refused an order because the fraud had happened eight months earlier and he thought that any money which was no longer in the account would long since have vanished. The Court of Appeal was more sanguine. Waller LJ said[220]:

"...where you have a fraud of this nature, although it may be late, and although much or perhaps all of the money may be now gone, the sooner that steps are taken to try and trace where it is the better. If steps are going to be taken, it is important that they should be taken at the earliest possible moment."

The facts of *Hashim* were undoubtedly extreme and the case against making an order very strong. However it is suggested that the "real prospect" hurdle should generally not be a difficult one to overcome and courts should not be too particular in declining relief on this ground. Otherwise the broad policy articulated by Templeman LJ in *Mediterranea Raffineria Siciliana Petroli Spa v Mabanaft GmbH* (quoted above at para.29–108) is at risk of being emasculated.

Principle Three. We have discussed above, when considering forms of order in *Norwich Pharmacal* cases, the importance of focused and specifically drawn orders. A similar principle applies in *Bankers Trust* cases.   **29–115**

Principle Four. In *Hashim* Hoffmann J went on to consider the balancing exercise which the court must carry out when considering whether or not to make an order: **29–116**

"Even if the application prima facie falls within the *Bankers Trust* principle, I consider that the potential advantage of the order to the [claimant] must be balanced against the detriment to the person against whom the order was sought, not merely in terms of cost (for which he is ordinarily compensated on an indemnity basis by the terms of the order) but by way of invasion of privacy and requiring breach of obligations of confidence to others."

The last observation by Hoffmann J upon the balance of convenience must now be read in the light of the Human Rights Act 1998 and privacy and confidentiality considerations under art.8 of the Convention. As the relief is likely to be sought against banks and others who may owe duties of confidentiality to their customers or clients, those obligations of confidence must be weighed in the balance. In *McKinnon v Donaldson*[221] Hoffmann J said (in discharging an order obtained ex parte under the Bankers Books Evidence Act where there was no element of "hot pursuit" of the kind that might have justified exceptional *Bankers*   **29–117**

---

[220] At [1980] 1 W.L.R. 1274, at 1283.
[221] *McKinnon v Donaldson* [1986] 1 Ch. 482, at 494D.

Trust relief in respect of bank documents held in New York) that banks are in a special position because their documents are concerned not only with their own business but those of customers to whom they will owe a duty of confidence regulated by the law of the country where the account is kept. The judge went on to refer to the "blocking statutes" and criminal sanctions against disclosure that exist in the laws of some foreign jurisdictions. Hence, it was the provisions of the UAE Penal Code that led Teare J in *AB Bank Ltd v Abu Dhabi Commercial Bank*[222] to conclude (obiter) that, even if the court had jurisdiction to grant *Norwich Pharmacal* relief against a Dubai bank where the trail of the money had also long since gone cold, he would not have made an order which might have resulted in the bank being in breach of those provisions.

29–118   **Principle Five.**   This speaks for itself.

29–119   Nonetheless the jurisdiction retains a degree of flexibility, and is not incapable of extension, a point made by Neuberger J in the leading case of *Murphy v Murphy*.[223] The recent decision in *Global Energy Horizons Corp v Gray*[224] provides a striking example of the width of the relief which may be ordered under the *Bankers Trust* jurisdiction. In that case a judgment on liability had already been secured against the defendant fiduciary and the claimant sought disclosure of documents and information from third parties which it believed would disprove the defendant's case, on the subsequent taking of an account of profits, that he had derived no benefit from the diversion of a corporate opportunity which had led to that liability. In ordering one of those parties to answer questions about investments in ventures which might have made use of the diverted technology, and rejecting the argument that such relief was only available in the "hot pursuit" scenario of identifying trust assets before they are dissipated, Sales J said[225]:

> "I do not accept that the equitable jurisdiction is as narrow as that. On the contrary, I accept the submission by [counsel for the claimant] that the equitable jurisdiction exists in order to serve the underlying objective that equity will not, in granting relief at any stage, act in vain.
>
> In that regard, I note that Mr Justice Neuberger in *Murphy v Murphy*[226] emphasised the width and flexibility of the jurisdiction of a court of equity. In my view, there plainly is a jurisdiction in equity on the basis of *A v C* and *Murphy v Murphy* to order provision of information, which is applicable in the context of a case such as this where trust assets in the form of maturing business opportunities and the ability to exploit the ultrasound technology has been diverted in breach of fiduciary duty and the question arises, what relief ought now in justice to be ordered against the fiduciary who has acted in breach of duty?
>
> What is sought in this case is to trace what has happened to those relevant assets and to seek to identify what their form and value is at this point in time. Tracing in this way is not in itself a claim or a remedy, but a process by which a claimant demonstrates what has happened to his property as a preliminary to establishing some personal or proprietary legal claim."

---

[222] *AB Bank Ltd v Abu Dhabi Commercial Bank* [2016] EWHC 2082, at [34].

[223] *Murphy v Murphy* [1999] 1 W.L.R. 282, at 291.

[224] *Global Energy Horizons Corp v Gray* [2014] EWHC 2925 (Ch), at [70]–[79]. The correctness of this decision on the test of "practical control" for the purposes of the separate power to order disclosure under CPR 31.17 was doubted by Males J in *Ardila Investments NV v ENRC* [2015] EWHC 3761 (Comm), but in *GEHC v Gray* Sales J indicated (at [70]) that it would otherwise have been right to order disclosure of documents under the equitable jurisdiction.

[225] *Global Energy Horizons Corp v Gray*, at [73]–[74].

[226] *Murphy v Murphy* [1999] 1 W.L.R. 282, at 292D.

(3)   Bankers' Books Orders

When a *Bankers Trust* order is not available on the facts, a party requiring evidence of bank transactions may be able to rely on s.7 of the Bankers' Books Evidence Act 1879, which provides that: **29–120**

> "On the application of any party to a legal proceeding a court or judge may order that such party be at liberty to inspect and take copies of any entries in a banker's book for any of the purposes of such proceedings."

The ability of the applicant to inspect and take copies of those entries is designed to overcome the inconvenience to the bank of having to respond to a subpoena duces tecum. Section 9(2) provides that   **29–121**

> "Expressions in this Act relating to bankers' books include ledgers, day books, cash books, account books and other records used in the ordinary business of the bank, whether those records are in written form or are kept on microfilm, magnetic tape or any form of mechanical or electronic data retrieval mechanism."

The expression "other records used in the ordinary business of the bank" is to be construed eiusdem generis with ledgers, day books, cash books and account books, so does not include bundles of cheques and paying in slips.[227]   **29–122**

In *A v C*[228] the court made an order against the defendant bank under s.7 both by reference to the claimant's proprietary claim (on the basis that the bank balance might constitute an asset sought to be traced) and in support of the freezing injunction that had been granted against the other defendants (for the purpose of knowing how much money was credited to the bank account). In that case Robert Goff J referred to the claimant having to establish grounds for believing the defendant has assets in the jurisdiction and being entitled to information about them.   **29–123**

Although the jurisdiction under s.7 in principle extends to foreign banks and overseas bank accounts, it is only in exceptional circumstances that the court will require a foreign bank to produce bank records held outside the jurisdiction concerning business transacted outside the jurisdiction.[229] If the relevant bank account is held in the name of a third party the court will not make an order under s.7 unless it can be satisfied that the bank account is in substance that of the defendant and that the banking records are likely to show entries which are material to the issues between the parties.[230] Indeed, the wisdom of seeking relief under s.7 in such a case must now be considered in the light of the well-developed *Chabra* jurisdiction, which enables the court to grant a freezing injunction (and ancillary disclosure orders) against a "non-cause of action   **29–124**

---

[227] *Williams v Williams* [1988] Q.B. 161.
[228] *A v C* [1981] 1 Q.B. 956, at 959–960.
[229] See *Mackinnon v Donaldson* [1986] 1 Ch. 482, at 497.
[230] *D.B. Deniz Nakliyati v Yugopetrol* [1992] 1 W.L.R. 437. Nolan LJ observed that the power under s.7 should "only be exercised within narrow limits" and said that this test applied after judgment as well as before. In circumstances where the relief was being sought post-judgment, the court noted that the primary remedy available to the judgment creditor was the cross-examination of the judgment debtor under what is now CPR 71.

defendant" on the basis that the assets held by him are really those of the defendant to the claim or would otherwise be amenable to the execution of a judgment against the defendant.[231]

(4) Disclosure Orders Against Third Parties on the "Chabra" Basis

29–125 As just noted, the *Chabra* jurisdiction discussed above in Ch.28 provides the basis for a further power by which the court may, in the context of interim relief,[232] order a third party to provide disclosure.

29–126 It follows from the court's power to grant *Chabra* relief against the so-called NCAD (non-cause of action defendant), in the form of a freezing injunction, that it also has the power to require that NCAD to produce information in relation to the frozen assets for the purposes of ensuring the injunction is effective. The jurisdictional basis for requiring such ancillary disclosure rests upon s.37 of the Senior Courts Act 1981.[233] For an example of such disclosure being ordered against a *Chabra* defendant (in support of an injunction granted post-judgment) see *Mercantile Group A.G. v Aiyela*.[234] If there are grounds for suspecting that he has not given full and proper disclosure then the principles governing any application to cross-examine him (and which are aimed at avoiding the purpose of the injunction being frustrated) are similar to those which would apply to any defendant to the claim.[235]

---

[231] See Ch.28, paras 28–157—28–196.

[232] For third party disclosure of relevant documents in existing proceedings—and not linked to any application for interim relief—see s.34 of the Senior Courts Act 1981 and the requirements of CPR 31.17.

[233] See Ch.26 paras 26–019—26–024 in relation to s.37 of the Senior Courts Act 1981. See also CPR 25.1(1)(g), discussed at para.29–008 above.

[234] *Mercantile Group A.G. v Aiyela* [1994] Q.B. 366, at 374. Despite the fact that Hoffmann LJ also made reference to the *Norwich Pharmacal* case (and his suggestion that the House of Lords in that case had discussed the exercise of the statutory power), it is clear that an order for disclosure by a *Chabra* defendant rests squarely upon the provisions of s.37: see *NML Capital v Chapman Freeborn* [2013] EWCA Civ 589, at [31].

[235] *JSC BTA Bank v Solodchenko* [2011] EWHC 843 (Ch), at [41], per Henderson J, citing *Kensington International Ltd v Republic of Congo* [2006] EWHC 1848 (Comm).

CHAPTER 30

SEARCH ORDERS

A.   INTRODUCTION

(1)   What is a Search Order?

A search order is one of the most draconian forms of injunction known to the English law, requiring the respondent to allow the applicant's solicitors and other representatives to enter premises owned or controlled by him (which may be his office, warehouse and even his home) and search for and remove the documents and other material described in the order. Despite its draconian character, the search order is now firmly established as part of the tools of the administration of justice in civil cases. The primary purpose of a search order is the preservation of relevant evidence for a claimant's case. It is generally used to prevent a defendant, when warned of impending litigation, from destroying or hiding documentary and other evidence in his possession which might, were it available, support the claimant's claim. It is therefore inherent that search orders are almost always applied for without notice.[1] An "on notice" search order is, in all but the most exceptional of cases, a conceptual contradiction.

30–001

A search order will typically be applied for where there is a need to preserve evidence in the case. The statutory jurisdiction to grant a search order (see para.30–006 below) focuses in the first instance upon the preservation of evidence which is or may be relevant to the proceedings. Although the requirements for the grant of such interim relief have largely been developed in the context of the intellectual property cases (through the exercise of what was then known as the *Anton Piller* jurisdiction, where, for example, it might be necessary to secure documents or other material evidencing a copyright or trade mark infringement or passing off), it is clear that the search order is also potentially of great significance in the context of civil fraud claims where the fraudster may not hesitate to destroy the evidence which implicates him on the claim. Likewise, in an exceptional case (for example where the oral examination of the judgment debtor under CPR 71 is unlikely to be or has not been effective), it may be possible to apply for a search order after judgment for the purpose of securing documentary evidence which is essential to execution.[2]

30–002

---

[1] This practice is reflected in para.16.2(1) of the Chancery Guide.
[2] *Distributori Automatici v Holford Trading Co* [1985] 1 W.L.R. 1066, at 1074; *Abela v Baadarani (No.2)* [2017] EWHC 269 (Ch); [2018] 1 W.L.R. 89 (a case where there had been oral examination of the judgment debtor under CPR 71, but the debtor had failed to produce disclosure which he had been ordered to give as a result of that examination).

30–003 The court will only make a search order where is it is satisfied to the requisite standard that a lesser order will not be sufficient to do justice to the applicant. The exacting test for the grant of a search order is addressed in paras 30–011—30–022 below. For example, a party who is considering making an application for a search order must consider whether an order for delivery up of property or an injunction directed to the preservation of evidence might be more appropriate.[3] The very nature of the claim against the defendant may indicate that he is unlikely to obey a preservation order, but, again, if the focus is upon "relevant property" (as opposed to documentary evidence) the applicant must first consider whether a proprietary-based freezing injunction, with ancillary disclosure obligations, might not be the more appropriate remedy.

30–004 The general scheme of a search order[4] is to require the respondent—

(1) To permit a "search party", defined to include a solicitor in the firm of the applicant's solicitors and a fixed number of other applicant representatives, along with a named "supervising solicitor", to enter the premises identified in the order (and any vehicles under the respondent's control around the premises) so that they can search for, inspect, photograph or photocopy, and deliver into the safekeeping of the applicant's solicitors, the documents and articles listed in the order. The respondent must allow the search party to remain on the premises until the search is complete (and to re-enter the premises as necessary during the search).

(2) Immediately to hand over to the applicant's solicitors any of the listed items which are in his possession or under his control (other than a computer or hard drive), and to hand over to the supervising solicitor any items the subject of a dispute as to whether they are listed items. The respondent must immediately give the search party effective access to all the computers on the premises, with all necessary passwords, to enable them to be searched.

(3) Immediately to inform the applicant's solicitors so far as he is aware:

    (i)   where all the listed items are;

    (ii) of the name and address of everyone who has supplied him, or offered to supply him, with listed items;

    (iii) of the name and address of everyone to whom he has supplied, or offered to supply, listed items; and

    (iv) of full details of the dates and quantities of every such supply and offer. Of course these information obligations will only be ordered so far as they are relevant on the particular facts of the case.

---

[3] See *Lock International Plc v Beswick* [1989] 1 W.L.R. 1268, 1281, per Hoffmann J, and *Indicii Salus Ltd (in Receivership) v Chandrasekaran* [2007] EWHC 406 (Ch), [14], per Warren J. See generally Ch.29 and CPR PD 25A para.8 in relation to "orders, other than search orders, for the the delivery up or preservation of evidence or property where it is likely that such an order will be executed at the premises of of the respondent or a third party." The definition of "relevant property" in CPR 25.1(2) is materially the same as that in s.7(1)(b) of the Civil Procedure Act 1997: see para. [*below*].

[4] See the example form of order annexed to CPR PD 25 and to the Commercial Court Guide.

(2)   Jurisdiction for, and Nature of, a Search Order

The jurisdiction to make a search order is now confirmed by statute. By s.7(3) of   **30–005**
the Civil Procedure Act 1997, the Court has jurisdiction to:

> "direct any person described in the order, or secure that any person so described is permitted
> (a) to enter premises in England and Wales, and (b) while on the premises to take in
> accordance with the terms of the order any of the following steps....".

Those steps include searching for or inspecting anything described in the order
and making or obtaining a copy, photograph, sample or other record of anything
so described.

The underlying purpose of a search order is also identified in s.7(1) of the 1997   **30–006**
Act; it is to secure, in the case of any existing or proposed proceedings:

> "(a) the preservation of evidence which is or may be relevant, or (b) the preservation of
> property which is or may be the subject-matter of the proceedings or as to which any question
> arises or may arise in the proceedings."

CPR r.25.1(1)(h) reflects the existence and purpose of s.7 in including within the   **30–007**
non-exhaustive list of interim remedies the court may grant:

> "an order (referred to as a 'search order') under section 7 of the Civil Procedure Act 1997
> (order requiring a party to admit another party to premises for the purpose of preserving
> evidence, etc.)"

The jurisdiction is a broad one. As was established in the recent decision of   **30–008**
Nugee J in *Abela v Baderaani (No.2)*[5]:

(1)   The "proceedings" to which s.7(1) of the 1997 Act refers can include
proceedings after judgment to enforce that judgment[6];
(2)   The "person" who can be directed by the search order can be a third party
rather than the cause of action defendant or judgment debtor[7]; and
(3)   It is not necessary (in a case where a search order is sought against such a
third party) for the Court first to have made a third party disclosure order,
or (if it has) for the search order to be limited to the scope of the disclosure
order.[8]

---

[5]   *Abela v Baderaani (No.2)* [2017] EWHC 269 (Ch); [2018] 1 W.L.R. 89.
[6]   *Abela v Baderaani* (No.2), at [16]–[22].
[7]   *Abela v Baderaani (No.2)*, at [33]: "But if there is a case where a third party holds relevant evidence
and a court concludes that if it was sought from him voluntarily, or by way of a *Norwich Pharmacal*
application or under CPR r.31.17 , or by a witness summons to produce documents on a date before a
trial or at the trial, there is a risk that the evidence will be destroyed or concealed, there is no reason
why the court should not have power to grant a search order. It might prove a very useful way to
preserve evidence that otherwise might be lost. In these circumstances, I see no reason to read section
7 as subject to an implied limitation. In my judgment, section 7 is wide enough to enable an order to
be made against any person who holds evidence that is or may be relevant to proceedings and where
the order is made for the purpose of securing that evidence."
[8]   *Abela v Baderaani (No.2)*, at [50]: "In my judgment, if a respondent, who is not a defendant, has
relevant evidence within the meaning of section 7(1)(a) and there is good reason to grant a search

30–009   Search orders had (before the enactment of the 1997 Act) first been considered substantively, and the court's equitable jurisdiction to make them confirmed, by the Court of Appeal in the seminal decision in *Anton Piller KG v Manufacturing Processes Ltd*,[9] which gave its name to this type of order until the CPR replaced the terminology "*Anton Piller* order" with "search order". While there is room for debate as to whether the jurisdiction is now exclusively statutory (i.e. entirely derived from s.7 of the 1997 Act), the better view[10] seems to be that the jurisdiction, having existed before the 1997 Act and independently of statute, is confirmed (rather than conferred) by that Act.

30–010   Although the overall effect of a search order may seem to be that of a civil law search warrant, that is not the case. The order has no special effect over the premises to be searched; instead it is an order made against the respondent personally. The applicant's search party is allowed to enter the premises only with the permission of the respondent. The effect of the order is to require the respondent to give such permission, and accordingly the consequence if a respondent fails to permit entry to premises in breach of the court's order is that such failure exposes him to committal for contempt of court.[11] What the applicant's search party may not do in the face of a refusal to permit entry is effect a forced entry. An order providing that the search party "be entitled to enter" the premises, rather than providing that the respondent is required to permit the search party's entry to the premises, is therefore liable to be discharged as defective.[12]

---

order in order to preserve that evidence, section 7 gives the requisite jurisdiction whether or not a third party disclosure order has already been made, or, if it has, whether its terms are more limited than the search order sought."

[9] *Anton Piller KG v Manufacturing Processes Ltd* [1976] Ch. 55. The Court drew on a number of earlier authorities, dating back to the 1820s. The first reported case in which a recognisably modern form search order was made is *EMI Ltd v Pandit* [1975] 1 W.L.R. 302.

[10] See, for example, Dockray and Reece Thomas, (1998) 17 CJQ 272: s.7 "provides an indisputable statutory basis for making orders of the Anton Piller type. However, the Act does not expressly take away such powers as the High Court may previously have possessed". See also Lord Collins of Mapesbury and J. Harris (eds), *Dicey, Morris & Collins on the Conflict of Laws*, 15th edn (London: Sweet & Maxwell, 2015), paras 8–006 and 8–017, comparing the treatment of the statutory jurisdiction for freezing orders provided by s.37 of the Senior Courts Act 1981.

[11] *Anton Piller*, above, per Lord Denning MR at 60. For a recent example of the Court enforcing a search order by committal, see *Universal Business Team PTY Ltd v Moffitt* [2017] EWHC 3251 (Ch).

[12] See for instance *Manor Electronics Ltd v Dickson* [1988] RPC 618, per Scott J at 622: "It is basic to Anton Piller orders that the court cannot bestow on one party the right to enter the premises of another party. Entry without permission would be trespass. But the court can, in the exercise of its in personam jurisdiction, order one party to allow the other party to enter the premises of the former. If permission to enter is given, then the entry is not a trespass. If the permission is not given, then the person who has been ordered to give permission is in contempt of court. But if the permission is not given, the party in whose favour the order was made has no right to enter the premises. So the form of an Anton Piller order is and must be an order that the defendants permit the plaintiffs and their solicitors and agents to enter the premises…".

B. PRECONDITIONS FOR THE GRANT OF A SEARCH ORDER

The search order is "at the extremity" of the court's powers and therefore "will rarely be made, and only when there is no alternative way of ensuring that justice is done to the applicant".[13] In the leading decision of *Lock International v Beswick*[14] Hoffmann J said:

30–011

> "The making of an intrusive order ex parte even against a guilty defendant is contrary to normal principles of justice and can only be done when there is a paramount need to prevent a denial of justice to the plaintiff. The absolute extremity of the court's powers is to permit a search of a defendant's dwelling house, with the humiliation and family distress which that frequently involves."

The tests the court will apply in considering any application for a search order are accordingly stricter than those imposed even for freezing orders, and search orders should only be granted on clear and compelling evidence.[15]

There are four conditions which must be satisfied before the Court will grant a without-notice search order[16]:

30–012

(1) There must be an extremely strong prima facie case;
(2) The damage to the applicant, potential or actual, must be very serious;
(3) There must be clear evidence that the respondent has in his possession incriminating documents or things, and that there is a real possibility that he may destroy such material before an on notice application can be made; and
(4) The harm likely to be caused by the execution of the search order to the respondent and his business affairs must not be excessive or out of proportion to the legitimate object of the order.

The first three of these conditions were originally set out by Ormrod LJ in the *Anton Piller* case,[17] and the fourth in a report of the Staughton Committee on *Anton Piller* orders published by the Lord Chancellor's Department in 1992. We consider each of these elements below.

30–013

---

[13] See *Anton Piller*, above, at 61H per Ormrod LJ. See also *Yousif v Salama* [1980] 1 W.L.R. 1540, per Donaldson LJ (dissenting) at 1544 ("a draconian power which should be used in only exceptional cases").

[14] *Lock International v Beswick* [1989] 1 W.L.R. 1268, at 1281G-H. The full passage is set out at [22] below.

[15] *Rank Film Distributors Ltd v Video Information Centre* [1982] A.C. 380, per Lord Wilberforce at 439.

[16] See e.g. *Indicii Salus Ltd v Chandrasekaran* [2006] EWHC 521 (Ch), at [85]; [2007] EWHC 406 (Ch), at [11], per Warren J, citing Ormrod LJ in *Anton Piller*, at 62A and Hoffmann J in *Lock International v Beswick*, at 1280. Warren J said the first requirement must be viewed with some flexibility).

[17] *Anton Piller*, at 62.

(1)   Extremely Strong Prima Facie Case

30–014   This requirement was affirmed by the House of Lords in *Rank Film Distributors Ltd v Video Information Centre*.[18] Reflecting the draconian nature of a search order, this merits hurdle is significantly more stringent than the "good arguable case" merits hurdle facing an applicant for a freezing order (as to which see Ch.28). In a case where a search order is made in aid of execution of a judgment, this requirement will presumably not present any issue.

(2)   Potential or Actual Very Serious Damage for the Applicant

30–015   The potential or actual "very serious damage" that was referred to by Ormrod LJ in *Anton Piller* is damage to the applicant if the search order sought is not granted (rather than damage simply resulting from the wrong complained of in the underlying proceedings). Thus in the *Anton Piller* case itself, Lord Denning MR said that such orders should only be made where there is

> "a grave danger that vital evidence will be destroyed, that papers will be burnt or lost or hidden, or taken beyond the jurisdiction, and so the ends of justice will be defeated"[19];

and in the report of the Staughton Committee, the requirement was summarised as follows:

> "The danger to the plaintiff to be avoided by the grant of an Anton Piller order must be serious. If an order is sought in order to forestall the destruction of evidence, the evidence in question must be of major, if not critical, importance".[20]

(3)   Clear Evidence that the Defendants have in their Possession Incriminating Documents or Things, and there is a Real Possibility that they may Destroy Such Material Before an On Notice Application Can be Made

30–016   The reference to "incriminating documents or things" is to what was described in the *Anton Piller* case as "vital evidence" in the proceedings and by Warren J in *Indicii Salus Ltd v Chandrasekaran*[21] as evidence of major, if not critical, importance[22]. In a fraud case, such evidence might, for example, include

---

[18] *Rank Film Distributors Ltd v Video Information Centre* [1982] A.C. 380, though (citing *Anton Piller*) Lord Wilberforce (at 439) referred generally to the need for "clear and compelling evidence" and Lord Fraser (at 444) said an order is "only made when the plaintiff produces strong prima facie evidence of infringement of his copyright" (or such other cause of action on which he relies) without adding the qualification "extremely". See the judgments of Warren J in *Indicii Salus Ltd v Chandrasekaran*, at fn.16 above.

[19] *Anton Piller*, at 61 B–C.

[20] Paragraph 2.6.

[21] *Indicii Salus Ltd v Chandrasekaran* [2006] EWHC 521 (Ch), at [85].

[22] Compare, for example, the minority view of Donaldson LJ in *Yousif v Salama* [1980] 1 W.L.R. 1540 that the documents sought to be preserved were by no means "essential" (the expression used by Brightman LJ) for the claimant to prove his case.

computerised records evidencing the manner in which the fraud has been perpetrated or the manner in which (or the entities through which) its proceeds have been filtered.

Of Ormrod LJ's three pre-conditions, the requirement that there is a "real possibility" that the respondent may destroy or conceal such material before any application on notice can be made is generally the most controversial when the test comes to be applied in practice on the claimant's application. This test imposes a substantial hurdle. This is because, in order to establish the danger that material may be destroyed if the defendant is foreward by any application made on notice, there has to be shown a sufficiently significant risk that a respondent would disobey a less intrusive court order requiring preservation or delivery up of identified documents or items. If there is no such risk, then the intrusion inherent in a search order cannot be justified. **30–017**

> "The phrase 'a real possibility' is to be contrasted with the extravagant fears which seem to afflict all plaintiffs who have complaints of breach of confidence, breach of copyright or passing off. Where the production and delivery up of documents is in question, the courts have always proceeded, justifiably, on the basis that the overwhelming majority of people in this country will comply with the court's order, and the defendants will therefore comply with orders to, for example, produce and deliver up documents without it being necessary to empower the plaintiff's solicitors to search the defendant's premises."[23]

As with the comparable need to show a risk of dissipation for a freezing order, the difficulty is in assessing where the correct balance lies in the particular case, between (on the one hand) evidence of dishonesty or impropriety on the part of the respondent being sufficient to show a "real possibility" that the respondent will go so far as to destroy evidence before it has otherwise to be produced, and the need (on the other hand) to bear in mind that the fact a respondent has been dishonest or behaved with commercial impropriety does not necessarily mean that he will destroy evidence or disobey a direct court order. Thus in *Lock v Beswick*, Hoffmann J said[24]: **30–018**

> "The fact that there is overwhelming evidence that the defendant has behaved wrongfully in his commercial relationships does not necessarily justify an Anton Piller order. People whose commercial morality allows them to take a list of the customers with whom they were in contact while employed will not necessarily disobey an order of the court requiring them to deliver it up. Not everyone who is misusing confidential information will destroy documents in the face of a court order requiring him to preserve them."

But a "real possibility" is not to be equated with a likelihood or a probability that the respondent would actually destroy evidence.[25] **30–019**

---

[23] *Booker McConnell Plc v Plascow* [1985] RPC 425, per Dillon LJ at 441.

[24] Above, at 1281D-E.

[25] In *Indicii Salus Ltd v Chandrasekaran*, above, Warren J accepted, at [14], a submission that the Court does not have to be satisfied before making a search order that the defendant actually would destroy evidence. The judge cited with approval the following passage from Oliver LJ's judgment in *Dunlop Holdings Ltd v Staravia Ltd* [1982] Comm LR 3, at 3: "It has certainly become customary to infer the probability of disappearance or destruction of evidence where it is clearly established on the evidence before the Court that the defendant is engaged in a nefarious activity which renders it likely that he is an untrustworthy person. It is seldom that one can get cogent or actual evidence of a threat to destroy material or documents, so it is necessary for it to be inferred from the evidence which is

(4) The Harm Likely to be Caused by the Execution of the Search Order to the Respondent and his Business Affairs Must Not be Excessive or Out of Proportion to the Legitimate Object of the Order

30–020   The formulation of this requirement in these terms is to be found in the report of the Staughton Committee at para.2.8. That paragraph continued:

> "This pre-condition is particularly relevant where the seizure of trading stock or the perusal by the plaintiff of confidential commercial documents will be the effect of execution of the order and is strongly analogous to the principle of proportionality as applied by the European Court of Human Rights."[26]

30–021   It is regarded as uncontroversial that this fourth requirement is a pre-condition for the grant of a search order.[27] It serves as a general reminder of the exceptional and extreme nature of a search order—even in circumstances where the other pre-conditions for its grant are made out, and notwithstanding the safeguards for the defendant which are included in the standard form of order.[28]

30–022   In *Lock International Plc v Beswick*[29] Hoffmann J made reference to the concept of "proportionality" (initially in the context of a warning against inferring a risk of destruction too readily) and continued:

> "In many cases it will therefore be sufficient to make an order for delivery up of the plaintiff's documents to his solicitor or, in cases in which the documents belong to the defendant but may provide evidence against him, an order that he preserve the documents pending further order, or allow the plaintiff's solicitor to make copies. The more intrusive orders allowing searches of premises or vehicles require a careful balancing of, on the one hand, the plaintiff's right to recover his property or to preserve important evidence against, on the other hand, violation of the privacy of a defendant who has had no opportunity to put his side of the case. It is not merely that the defendant may be innocent. The making of an intrusive order ex parte even against a guilty defendant is contrary to normal principles of justice and can only be done when there is a paramount need to prevent a denial of justice to the plaintiff. The absolute extremity of the court's powers is to permit a search of a defendant's dwelling house, with the humiliation and family distress which that frequently involves."

---

before the Court." See also *Yousif v Salama* [1980] 1 W.L.R. 1540, 1542A, 1544F. It should be remembered the test requires the applicant to establish that destruction is a "real possibility".

[26] This fourth requirement was drawn from Hoffmann J's earlier decision in *Lock International Plc v Beswick*, above, where Hoffmann J had said, at 1281: "Even in cases in which the plaintiff has strong evidence that an employee has taken what is undoubtedly specific confidential information, such as a list of customers, the court must employ a graduated response. To borrow a useful concept from the jurisprudence of the European Community, there must be proportionality between the perceived threat to the plaintiff's rights and the remedy granted."

[27] See, for example, *Indicii Salus v Chandrasekaran* [2007] EWHC 406 (Ch) per Warren J at [11].

[28] See para.30–031 below.

[29] *Lock International Plc v Beswick* [1989] 1 W.L.R. 1268, 1281.

C. HISTORY OF THE REMEDY AND THE DEVELOPMENT OF THE PROTECTIONS INCLUDED IN A SEARCH ORDER

The background to the grant of the first search orders was the growth of video **30–023** and audio copyright piracy. Copyright claimants found that the evidence of piracy was often destroyed or hidden as soon as proceedings were served, and the purpose of the search order was accordingly to preserve the evidence. The orders were often also used to track to its source, and obtain possession of, the master tape or plate or blueprint from which reproductions in breach of copyright were being made.[30]

The standard form of order currently used is the result of a series of decisions **30–024** since the *Anton Piller* case in which the courts have sought to provide appropriate protections for defendants, given the draconian nature of the order. Some understanding of the main decisions is important to any proper appreciation of the contents of the current standard form. Accordingly this section briefly outlines the protections identified as appropriate in some of the main decisions, before current practice and procedure (including the current standard form of order) is discussed in the following section.

(1)   CBS United Kingdom Ltd v Lambert[31]

There are particular risks involved in ordering the delivery up of chattels in **30–025** parallel with a search order. In the *CBS* case the Court of Appeal gave the following guidance as to when any such order for delivery up to the solicitor should be made:

(1)   There should be clear evidence that the defendant is likely, unless restrained by order, to dispose of or otherwise deal with his chattels in order to deprive the claimant of the fruits of any judgment he may obtain. And the court should be slow to order the delivery up of property unless there is some evidence or inference that the property has been acquired by the defendant as a result of his alleged wrong-doing.

(2)   No order should be made for delivery up of a defendant's clothing, bedding, furnishings, tools of his trade, farm implements, live stock or any machines (including motor vehicles) or other goods such as materials or stock in trade, which it is likely he uses for the purposes of a lawful business.

(3)   All orders should specify as clearly as possible what chattels or classes of chattel are to be delivered up. "A plaintiff's inability to identify what he wants delivered up and why is an indication that no order should be made."

(4)   The order must not authorise the claimant to enter on the defendant's premises or to seize the defendant's property save by permission of the defendant (as to which see para.30–010 above).

---

[30] See the discussion by Scott J in *Columbia Pictures v Robinson* [1987] Ch. 38, at 71.
[31] *CBS United Kingdom Ltd v Lambert* [1983] Ch. 37, at 44.

(5) No order should be made for delivery up to anyone other than the claimant's solicitor or a receiver appointed by the High Court. The court should appoint a receiver unless satisfied that the claimant's solicitor has, or can arrange, suitable safe custody for what is delivered to him.

(6) The court should follow the guidelines set out in *Z Ltd v A-Z and AA-LL*[32] insofar as they are applicable to chattels in the possession, custody or control of third parties.

(7) Provision should always be made for permission to apply to stay, vary or discharge the order.

(2) Columbia Picture Industries Inc v Robinson[33]

30–026 Having heard that one firm of solicitors had executed an estimated 300 *Anton Piller* orders since 1974 and that that firm's experience was that it almost invariably succeeded in getting any search order it applied for, Scott J stated that

> "the practice of the court has allowed the balance to swing much too far in favour of plaintiffs and that *Anton Piller* orders have been too readily granted and with insufficient safeguards for respondents".[34]

He emphasised the following points:

(1) Search orders should be drawn as narrowly as possible. For example, an order allowing the claimant's solicitors to take and retain "all relevant documentary material and correspondence" could not be justified. Once the claimant's solicitors have satisfied themselves what material exists and have an opportunity to take copies thereof, the material ought to be returned to its owner.

(2) A detailed record of the material taken should always be made by the solicitors executing the order before removing it from the respondent's premises.

(3) No material should be taken by the executing solicitors unless it is clearly covered by the terms of the order. In particular, it was wholly unacceptable that the respondent should be procured by the executing solicitors to give consent to additional material being removed.

(4) It was inappropriate that seized material, the ownership of which is in dispute (such as allegedly pirate tapes), should be retained by the plaintiff's solicitors pending the trial. If the administration of justice required material taken under an *Anton Piller* order to be kept from the defendants pending trial, it should be kept by a neutral officer of the court (now the supervising solicitor).

(5) The nature of *Anton Piller* orders requires that the affidavits in support of applications for them ought to err on the side of excessive disclosure. In the

---

[32] *Z Ltd v A-Z and AA-LL* [1982] Q.B. 558.
[33] *Columbia Picture Industries Inc v Robinson* [1987] Ch. 38.
[34] *Columbia Picture Industries Inc v Robinson*, at 76D–76E.

case of material falling into the grey area of possible relevance, the judge, not the claimant's solicitors, should be the judge of relevance.

(3) Universal Thermosensors Ltd v Hibben[35]

By the time of the next landmark decision, that of Nicholls V-C in *Universal Thermosensors Ltd v Hibben*, the Vice-Chancellor believed search orders were being made much more sparingly. (Research indeed indicated that by 1992 only about 50 orders a year were being made in England and Wales.).[36]   **30–027**

In *Universal Thermosensors*, the Vice-Chancellor set out the following points[37]:   **30–028**

(1)   *Anton Piller* orders should normally contain a provision that, before complying with the order, the defendant may obtain legal advice, provided this is done forthwith. But such a provision, if it is to be of practical use, requires that in general *Anton Piller* orders should be permitted to be executed only on working days during office hours, when a solicitor can be expected to be available.

(2)   If the order is to be executed at a private house, and it is at all likely that a woman may be in the house alone, the solicitor serving the order must be, or must be accompanied by, a woman.

(3)   In general *Anton Piller* orders should expressly provide that, unless this is seriously impracticable, a detailed list of the items being removed should be prepared at the premises before they are removed, and that the defendant should be given an opportunity to check this list at the time.

(4)   *Anton Piller* orders frequently contain an injunction restraining those on whom they are served from informing others of the existence of the order for a limited period.[38] This is to prevent one defendant from alerting others to what is happening. There is an exception for communication with a lawyer for the purpose of seeking legal advice. In *Universal Thermosensors* that injunction was expressed to last for a whole week. That was held to be far too long.

(5)   Orders should provide that, unless there is good reason for doing otherwise, the order should not be executed at business premises save in the presence of a responsible officer or representative of the company or trader in question.

(6)   The making of an *Anton Piller* order in the *Universal Thermosensors* case itself could be seen to be justified by what was discovered upon its execution—documentation containing information about the claimant's customers which had been dishonestly removed by the defendants while they were its employees. But it was important not to lose sight of the fact that one thing which happened was that the claimant carried out a thorough search of all the documents of a competitor company. This was considered

---

[35] *Universal Thermosensors Ltd v Hibben* [1992] 1 W.L.R. 840.
[36] Staughton Committee Report para.1.14.
[37] *Universal Thermosensors*, at 860–861.
[38] This practice is reflected in para.F15.12 of the Commercial Court Guide.

most unsatisfactory. When *Anton Piller* orders are made in this type of case, consideration should be given to devising some means, appropriate to the facts of the case, by which such a situation can be avoided.

(7) *Anton Piller* orders invariably provide for service to be effected by a solicitor. The court relies heavily on the solicitor, as an officer of the court, to see that the order is properly executed. Unhappily, the history in that case, and what had happened in other cases, showed that this safeguard was inadequate. The way ahead here was that when making *Anton Piller* orders judges should give serious consideration to the desirability of providing, by suitable undertakings and otherwise, that—

(a) the order should be served, and its execution should be supervised, by a solicitor other than a member of the firm of solicitors acting for the plaintiff in the action;

(b) he or she should be an experienced solicitor having some familiarity with the workings of *Anton Piller* orders, and with judicial observations on this subject;

(c) the solicitor should prepare a written report on what occurred when the order was executed;

(d) a copy of the report should be served on the defendants; and

(e) in any event and within the next few days the claimant must return to the court and present that report at an inter partes hearing, preferably to the judge who made the order.

As to (b) above, the judge could see advantages in the claimant being required to include in his evidence, put to the judge in support of his application for an *Anton Piller* order, details of the name of the solicitor and of his experience.

30–029 Nicholls V-C recognised that such safeguards would involve considerable extra cost and expense for claimants, who would not know whether the costs would ultimately be borne by the defendant. But, he concluded:

> "If plaintiffs wish to take advantage of this truly draconian type of order, they must be prepared to pay for the safeguards experience has shown are necessary if the interests of defendants are fairly to be protected."[39]

D.   CURRENT PRACTICE AND PROCEDURE

(1)   The Current Use of Search Orders

30–030 Search orders are still most frequently granted in cases concerned with intellectual property—counterfeiting, trademarks, patents, copyright and confidential information. They are, therefore, more commonly granted in the Chancery Division than other divisions of the High Court. However, they are also used in cases which do not concern intellectual property and remain an extremely valuable tool for a fraud litigator in an appropriate case. For recent examples of their use, see *Interactive Technology Corp Ltd v Ferster*[40] (claims for breach of

---

[39] *Universal Thermosensors*, at 861H.
[40] *Interactive Technology Corp Ltd v Ferster* [2015] EWHC 393 (Ch).

fiduciary duty, fraud and dishonest misappropriation of assets by a director); *Holland v Fast Corporate Solutions Ltd*[41] (claim for deceit and/or unlawful means conspiracy in relation to alleged fraudulent scheme involving purported investments in carbon credits); and *Aspect Capital Ltd v Christensen*[42] (confidential information taken by former employee).

(2)   Procedure

Only a judge exercising the jurisdiction of the High Court[43] and the nominated judge in the Patents County Court[44] may make a search order.[45]   **30–031**

The detailed procedural requirements are now codified in Practice Direction 25A—Interim Injunctions ("PD 25A"), which is annexed to CPR Pt 25, and in the standard form of Search Order which is set out at the end of PD 25A. Although PD 25A contains provisions applicable to all types of interim injunctions generally, para.7 sets out detailed provisions specific to search orders and applications in which they are sought, and its contents are set out below at the end of this chapter. Those provisions draw on the guidance in the cases discussed above.   **30–032**

(i)   Premises to be searched

The premises to be searched should be identified in the schedule to the Order. It has been said that a search order extending to "any other premises under the control of the defendant", rather than only to certain specified premises, will only be made "in special circumstances" and not simply where it is thought that such wording would be helpful to avoid practical difficulties.[46]   **30–033**

---

[41] *Holland v Fast Corporate Solutions Ltd* [2014] EWHC 825 (QB).
[42] *Aspect Capital Ltd v Christensen* [2010] EWHC 744.
[43] Practice Direction (Allocation of Cases to Levels of Judiciary), paras 1.1 and 2.1.
[44] *Suh v Ryu* [2012] EWPCC 20.
[45] Paragraph 7.10 provides that applications for search orders in intellectual property cases should be made in the Chancery Division. As explained in *Elvee Ltd v Taylor* [2002] F.S.R. 48, per Chadwick LJ: "The reason for the requirement in the practice direction is that matters of this nature tend to produce difficult problems in practice in relation to the execution of search and seizure orders. Therefore, it is important that they should come before judges who are used to dealing with problems of that kind. In particular, orders which will involve the seizure of data on computers need to be carefully framed. It is important, both for the protection of defendants and for the proper administration of justice, that, so far as possible, applications for search orders should be made to judges with experience in the field. If a judge who is not familiar with the problems to which such orders give rise is asked to deal with such an application, it should be explained to him, first, that the practice direction exists, and second, why it is said that there is a good reason for departing from them (sic) in the particular case. That was not done. In my view it should have been. But, I do not take the view that the failure to give Poole J the necessary explanation is of itself a reason for discharging the order which he made."
[46] *Protector Alarms v Maxim Alarms* [1978] F.S.R. 442, at 444, per Goulding J.

(ii) Evidence

30–034   Paragraph 3.1 of PD 25A requires an application for a search order (as with a freezing order) to be supported by affidavit evidence. That affidavit should, amongst other things:

(1)   Provide details of the supervising solicitor (PD 25A para.7.3(1)).

(2)   Disclose "very fully the reason the order is sought, including the probability that relevant material would disappear if the order were not made" (PD 25A, para.7.3(2)). Read literally this formulation overstates the test laid down in the *Anton Piller* case, and discussed above, which requires only a "real possibility" that material would be destroyed before an on-notice application could be made. It is thought that the correct test to be addressed is that laid down in the authorities, though the language of the practice direction provides a useful reminder of the need for the supporting evidence to be what Lord Wilberforce described in *Rank Film Distributors Ltd v Video Information Centre*[47] as "clear and compelling".

(iii) Hearing without notice and in private

30–035   As explained above, it is in the very nature of an application for a search order that it will be made without notice.[48] Although this does not mean, of itself, that such an application will be heard in private, in practice the same considerations which militate against the giving of notice to the respondent will also tend to warrant a hearing in private.[49] Practitioners should nevertheless be careful to consider and, if necessary, address the need for a private hearing specifically, and separately from the question of applying without notice.

(iv) The Form of Order

30–036   PD 25A annexes what para.7.11 describes as an "example of a Search Order" which "may be modified as appropriate in any particular case". The Commercial Court Guide also annexes substantially the same example search order.[50] Any differences between the form of order being sought and the example annexed to the practice direction or the Commercial Court Guide should be expressly drawn to the Court's attention on the without notice application in discharge of the duty of fair presentation.[51]

---

[47] *Rank Film Distributors Ltd v Video Information Centre* [1982] A.C. 380, at 439.

[48] For the general grounds which justify applying without notice, see Ch.27.

[49] The Chancery Guide states (at para.16.26) that applications for search orders will be heard in private "in a proper case", namely where the judge considers that publicity might defeat the object of the hearing (reflecting the language of CPR 39.2(3)(a)). In this context that will almost invariably be the case. Similarly, the Commercial Court Guide recognises (at para.F1.7(c)) that an application for a search order will "often need to be heard in private in the interests of justice".

[50] At Appendix 5.

[51] See e.g. *Memory Corp v Sidhu* [2000] 1 W.L.R. 1443, and para.F15.5 of the Commercial Court Guide.

(v) The search party and the supervising solicitor

The following points of importance regarding the search party and the supervising solicitor emerge from PD 25A and the standard form of order. **30–037**

(1) The search party must include a supervising solicitor (see para.6(a) of the standard form of order) who is, as provided at para.7.2 of PD 25A, experienced in the operation of search orders.[52] The supervising solicitor cannot be an employee or member of the applicant's firm of solicitors.[53]

(2) Where the supervising solicitor is a man and the premises may be occupied by an unaccompanied woman, at least one of the other members of the search party should be a woman.[54]

(3) The search party should be limited in number.[55] Paragraph 7.4(3) of PD 25A provides that the supervising solicitor may be accompanied only by the persons mentioned in the order.

(4) The duties of the supervising solicitor are set out at para.7.4 of PD 25A.

(5) The search party should not contain people who could gain personally or commercially from anything they might see or read on the premises to be searched, unless their presence is essential.[56]

The supervising solicitor is required to give a number of undertakings to the Court, set out in Sch.E to the standard form of order, which include offering to explain to the person served with the order its meaning and effect fairly and in everyday language and to inform him of his right to take legal advice, and to make and provide to the applicant's solicitors, the respondent (or his solicitors), and to the judge who made the order, a written report on the execution of the order.[57] **30–038**

(vi) Manner in which the order is served and executed

A search order will contain restrictions on the time of day at which it is to be served. Indeed para.7.4(6) of PD 25A provides that the order may only be served between 9.30am and 5.30pm Monday to Friday unless the court otherwise orders. This is to avoid the problem encountered by one of the respondents in *Universal* **30–039**

---

[52] Following Nicholls V-C's comments in *Universal Thermosensors*, above, at 861, approving the suggestion of a supervising solicitor made in an influential article by Professor Dockray and Hugh Laddie QC (as he then was) on "*Piller Problems*" (1990) 106 L.Q.R. 601.

[53] Paragraph 7.6 of PD 25A.

[54] See para.7.4(5) of PD 25A and *Universal Thermosensors*, above, per Nicholls V-C at 860.

[55] See, for example, *ITC Film Distributors Ltd v Video Exchange Ltd* in the Court of Appeal [1983] ECC 43, per Slade LJ at [43]: "the courts ... will be particularly concerned to ensure that the mode of execution is no more oppressive than necessary – which will always involve placing a limit on the number of persons who are to be permitted to enter the defendant's premises ...".

[56] See *Universal Thermosensors*, above, at 860–861, in which (as we have noted above) Nicholls V-C pointed out that the upshot of the search order in that case was that the managing director of the claimant company had carried out a thorough search of all the documents of a competitor company, which he described as "most unsatisfactory" and something which should be avoided.

[57] Paragraph 7.5(11) and (12) of PD 25A and see *Universal Thermosensors*, above, per Nicholls V-C at 861.

Thermosensors, where the order was served during the night with the result that the respondent was unable to obtain legal advice from a solicitor. As Nicholls V-C pointed out in that case, for a term of the order providing (as the standard forms now do) that a respondent may obtain legal advice with a view to seeking a variation or discharge of the order to have any practical effect, the order must be served at a time when the respondent is able to obtain legal advice immediately.

30–040 The order may not be executed at the same time as a police search warrant.[58] This provision reflects the decision of the Court of Appeal in the *ITC Film Distributors* case,[59] where a police search warrant for obscene material was executed at the same time as the search order obtained on a claim for breach of copyright. The Court of Appeal considered that, although it might well be necessary to have the police carry out a search at or about the same time as a search order (because if there was any time gap, valuable evidence was likely to disappear), the two searches should not be carried out simultaneously.

30–041 The order must be served personally by the supervising solicitor, unless the court otherwise orders.[60] It will be a very rare case where the court does so order and if it does it must provide on the face of the order the reasons for so ordering.

(vii) Items removed from the premises

30–042 Unless the supervising solicitor is satisfied that compliance with these requirements is not practicable—

(1) no item may be removed from the premises until a list of items to be removed has been prepared, a copy of the list has been supplied to the respondent, and he has been given a reasonable opportunity to check the list[61]; and

(2) the premises must not be searched, and items must not be removed from them, except in the presence of the respondent or a person who appears to be a responsible employee of the respondent.[62]

---

[58] Paragraph 7.8 of PD 25A.

[59] *ITC Film Distributors Ltd v Video Exchange Ltd* [1983] ECC 43.

[60] Paragraph 7.4(1) and 7.7 of PD 25A.

[61] Paragraph 7.5(6), (7) and (13) of PD 25A and see *Columbia Picture Industries v Robinson* [1987] Ch. 38, at 76, and *Universal Thermosensors* per Nicholls V-C, at 860, point (3): "In the present case a dispute arose about which documents were taken away, and from which of the premises visited. Understandably, those who execute these orders are concerned to search and seize and then get away as quickly as possible so as to minimise the risk of confrontation and physical violence. Nevertheless, in general *Anton Piller* orders should expressly provide that, unless this is seriously impracticable, a detailed list of the items being removed should be prepared at the premises before they are removed, and that the defendant should be given an opportunity to check this list at the time."

[62] Paragraph 7.5(2) of PD 25A and see *Universal Thermosensors* per Nicholls VC at 860: "In the present case there was no officer or employee of TPL or Emco present when their offices and workshops were searched and documents and components taken away. This is interolerable. Orders should provide that, unless there is good reason for doing otherwise, the order should not be executed at business premises save in the presence of a responsible officer or representative of the company or trader in question."

Paragraph 7.5 of PD 25A contains detailed provisions concerning removal and retention of material: see the text of that paragraph set out at the end of this chapter.

30–043

(viii)   Computers/servers

The standard form orders the respondent immediately to give the search party effective access to the computers on the premises, with all necessary passwords, to enable the computers to be searched. It also orders the Respondent to cause any listed items contained on computers to be displayed so that they can be read and copied.[63]

30–044

The footnotes to the standard order provide that if it is envisaged that the respondent's computers are to be imaged (i.e. the hard drives copied), special provision needs to be made for this in the order, and independent computer specialists appointed who should be required to give undertakings to the Court. It is suggested that these should normally extend to an undertaking by the computer specialist that they will not alter, corrupt or destroy the original files on the hard drive (or other electronic storage device) through the process of searching and making any image of it, and also that they will preserve in their original format any images made by them.

30–045

Access to computers and/or servers is, unsurprisingly, one of the areas which throws up most practical problems in the execution of a search order. Careful planning with computer specialists as to what practical steps will have to be taken to enable the searches sought to take place will help to ensure that any order granted is workable in practice. However, this is an area in which a consequential application for supplemental orders may be necessary. Issues may arise, in particular, where the respondent claims that some or all of the information sought is held on servers controlled by a third party entity and/or on servers located at a different place, possibly outside the jurisdiction (as to which, see further at para.30–068 below). Moreover, it is in the nature of the process that the applicant for a search order may, when he first comes to court without notice, have limited information as to the computer equipment held at the premises to be searched and the possible need for it to be imaged.

30–046

(ix)   Fair presentation/full and frank disclosure

As the application for a search order is almost always made without notice, careful attention should be paid to the duty of fair presentation (discussed in Ch.27). The duty is particularly important in applying for search orders, given their draconian nature and the fact that it is generally impossible in practice for a

30–047

---

[63] See also para.7.5(10) of PD 25A: "the applicant and his representatives may not themselves search the respondent's computers unless they have sufficient expertise to do so without damaging the respondent's system".

respondent to apply to discharge a search order before it is executed. The evidence in support of an application for a search order should therefore "err on the side of excessive disclosure."[64]

(x) Cross-undertaking in damages

30–048 As is the default position for any order obtained on a without notice application, the standard form of search order contains a cross-undertaking in damages by the applicant.[65]

30–049 In the case of a search order, the undertaking covers not only potential loss suffered by the respondent as a result of the making of the search order, but also loss arising out of the manner in which it has been executed. The standard wording is:

> "If the court later finds that this order or carrying it out has caused loss to the Respondent, and decides that the Respondent should be compensated for that loss, the Applicant will comply with any order the court may make. Further if the carrying out of this order has been in breach of the terms of this order or otherwise in a manner inconsistent with the Applicant's solicitors' duties as officers of the court, the Applicant will comply with any order for damages the court may make."

30–050 As explained in Ch.31, the court retains a discretion, in special circumstances, to refuse to order an inquiry on the cross-undertaking even where the order was wrongly granted.[66]

E. PRIVILEGE AGAINST SELF-INCRIMINATION

30–051 Privilege against self-incrimination in civil proceedings is regarded by many leading commentators as anachronistic, and the current extent of the privilege is a matter of controversy. What follows is only a brief overview of the privilege insofar as it is relevant to search orders. For more detailed discussion, reference should be made to the specialist texts.[67]

---

[64] *Columbia Pictures v Robinson*, above, at 77.

[65] See Ch.27, for the general principles in relation to the giving of such undertakings.

[66] See *Indicii Salus Ltd v Chandrasekaran* [2007] EWHC 406 (Ch), at [142], where Warren J, obiter, drew a distinction between a search order being wrongly granted and it being improperly obtained and said "the court can take account of conduct on the part of the defendant both before and after the granting of the injunction and, in the particular circumstances of a search order, the defendant's conduct in relation to the search itself."

[67] For example, H. Malek, J. Auburn, R. Bagshaw et al, *Phipson on Evidence*, 18th edn (London: Sweet & Maxwell, 2013), Ch.24; C. Hollander, *Documentary Evidence*, 12th edn (London: Sweet & Maxwell, 2015), Ch.21; B. Thanki, *The Law of Privilege*, 2nd edn (Oxford: OUP, 2011), Ch.8; and P.Matthews and H. Malek, *Disclosure*, 4th edn (London: Sweet & Maxwell, 2012), Ch.13.

(1)   Rank Film Distributors Ltd

The privilege against self-incrimination seemed to be a road-block in the way of   **30–052**
the effective execution of search orders when, in *Rank Film Distributors Ltd v Video Information Centre*,[68] the House of Lords held that the defendants were entitled to rely on the privilege to refuse to give disclosure or answer questions since there was, in that case, a real risk that criminal proceedings for conspiracy to defraud would be brought against them.

(2)   Statutory Abrogation of the Privilege

The decision in *Rank Film Distributors* was immediately reversed, in the case of   **30–053**
cases involving passing off or the infringement of rights in intellectual property,[69] by s.72 of the Senior Courts Act 1981. Section 31(1) of the Theft Act 1968 and s.13 of the Fraud Act 2006 are to similar effect in respect of substantive offences under those Acts.

Now, therefore, as set out in para.7.9 of CPR PD 25A—   **30–054**

> "There is no privilege against self-incrimination in –
> (1)   Intellectual Property cases in respect of a 'related offence' or for the recovery of a 'related penalty' as defined in section 72 Senior Courts Act 1981;
> (2)   Proceedings for the recovery or administration of any property, for the execution of a trust or for an account of any property or dealings with property, in relation to –
>   (a)   an offence under the Theft Act 1968 (see section 31 of the Theft Act 1968); or
>   (b)   an offence under the Fraud Act 2006 (see section 13 of the Fraud Act 2006) or a related offence[70] within the meaning given by section 13(4) of that Act—that is, conspiracy to defraud or any other offence involving any form of fraudulent conduct or purpose".[71]

However, para.7.9 of PD 25A recognises that the privilege may still be claimed in   **30–055**
relation to material or information required to be disclosed by an order, as regards potential criminal proceedings outside those statutory provisions.

---

[68] *Rank Film Distributors Ltd v Video Information Centre* [1982] A.C. 380.
[69] "Intellectual property" is defined in s.72(5) as meaning "any patent, trade mark, copyright, design right, registered design, technical or commercial information or other intellectual property".
[70] As to the correct approach to identifying a "related offence", see *JSC BTA Bank v Ablyazov* [2009] EWCA Civ 1124; [2010] 1 W.L.R. 976, in which the Court of Appeal held that an offence under s.328 of the Proceeds of Crime Act 2002 is a "related offence" for the purposes of s.13 of the Fraud Act 2006.
[71] A third statutory exception set out in para.7.9 concerns proceedings under the Children Act 1989, which are unlikely to be of practical importance for the civil fraud practitioner.

(3) No Privilege in Respect of Proceedings Outside the United Kingdom

30–056 Further, there is no privilege against self-incrimination with respect to proceedings outside the United Kingdom.[72] Instead, the court has a discretion in such cases as to whether to grant protection against such self-incrimination.[73]

(4) Problems with the Mechanism Provided by the Standard Form Order

30–057 But, as heralded by the *Rank Film Distributors* case, in any case where the privilege against self-incrimination can still be claimed, there are real potential problems for any search order. The standard order provides that[74]:

> "Before permitting entry to the premises by any person other than the Supervising Solicitor, the Respondent may, for a short time (not to exceed two hours, unless the Supervising Solicitor agrees to a longer period), gather together any documents he believes may be incriminating or privileged and hand them to the Supervising Solicitor for him to assess whether they are incriminating or privileged as claimed.
> (a) If the Supervising Solicitor decides that the Respondent is entitled to withhold production of any of the documents on the ground that they are privileged or incriminating, he will exclude them from the search and record them on a list for inclusion in his report and return them to the Respondent.
> (b) If the Supervising Solicitor believes that the Respondent may be entitled to withhold production of the whole or any part of a document on the ground that it or part of it may be privileged or incriminating, or if the Respondent claims to be entitled to withhold production on those grounds, the Supervising Solicitor will exclude it from the search and retain it in his possession pending further order of the court."[75]

30–058 However, as Waller LJ pointed out in *Den Norske v Antonatos*,[76] the provision of privileged or incriminating documents to the supervising solicitor does not mean that the prosecuting authorities cannot obtain an order that the supervising solicitor should hand over those documents. Accordingly, he said that:

> "An *Anton Piller* order should not be made where it will require the defendant to incriminate himself. The authorities on this aspect are summarised in *Cobra Golf Inc v Rata*.[77] It is possible to build a mechanism into an order which provides a clear warning to the defendant through, for example, advice from the supervising solicitor. But the authorities summarised by Rimer J in the *Cobra Golf* case show how difficult it is to provide adequate protection and there is no distinction in this regard between an *Anton Piller* and a *Mareva* order. Once again I emphasise that the expedient of ordering a defendant to place incriminating information in the hands of a supervising solicitor does not seem to me to provide adequate protection."[78]

---

[72] *JSC BTA Bank v Ablyazov* [2009] EWCA Civ 1125; [2010] 1 All E.R. (Comm) 1029, at [16]–[17].
[73] *Brannigan v Davison* [1997] A.C. 238, at 251, per Lord Nicholls, and *Credit Suisse Fides Trust SA v Cuoghi* [1998] Q.B. 818, at 833, per Lord Bingham.
[74] Paragraph 11.
[75] This wording does not cover a claim which may be made to privilege against self-incrimination with respect to proceedings outside the UK: *JSC BTA Bank v Ablyazov* [2009] EWCA Civ 1125; [2010] 1 All E.R. (Comm) 1029, at [29]–[30].
[76] *Den Norske v Antonatos* [1999] Q.B. 271.
[77] *Cobra Golf Inc v Rata* [1998] Ch. 109, 126–128.
[78] *Cobra Golf Inc v Rata*, at 289–290.

(5) The Privilege Does Not Apply to Material with an Existence Independent of the Will of the Person Relying on the Privilege

In *C Plc v P*,[79] the computer expert appointed to image the respondent's **30–059** computers found, on one of the computers, indecent images of children which it was an offence to possess. He applied to court for directions and the judge directed that he should pass the computer to the police.[80] On appeal, the Court of Appeal held that, as the privilege against self-incrimination did not extend to documents or things which had an existence independent of the will of the person relying on the privilege, the judge had been right to direct the computer expert to pass the computer to the police. The majority of the Court of Appeal[81] held that there was no privilege in that offending material because it existed independently of the order.

That decision was followed and applied by Popplewell J in two decisions in the **30–060** *Ablyazov* litigation.[82] In the earlier decision he held[83]:

> "In my view, it has been established by the authorities that the privilege against self-incrimination does not extend to provide a person with protection against the risk of incriminating himself by the provision of a document or documents which come into existence independently of any order, statute or other instrument of law which compelled their production. It does not normally cover documents other than those which come into existence by an exercise of will pursuant to a testimonial obligation imposed upon the party."

Accordingly, the requirement in a search order for disclosure or delivery up of **30–061** pre-existing documents or items will, on this analysis, not trespass on the privilege against self-incrimination.

(6) Remaining Problem Area for Search Orders

On the analysis in *C Plc v P* and the decisions of Popplewell J in the *Ablyazov* **30–062** litigation, the main remaining difficulty for search orders arising from the privilege against self-incrimination is the risk that any order for questions to be answered may involve the respondent in incriminating himself. This problem is equally applicable to orders for disclosure or requiring the provision of information targeted at a tracing exercise; such orders are frequently made ancillary to freezing orders[84] or proprietary injunctions.

So long as there is no general statutory abrogation of the privilege against **30–063** self-incrimination in civil proceedings, the sorts of potential issues outlined

---

[79] *C Plc v P* [2008] Ch. 1.

[80] In fact, although the first instance order was stayed pending appeal, while the appeal was still pending, the police learnt of the offending material and executed a search warrant at the computer expert's premises and removed the computer into their custody.

[81] Longmore LJ and Sir Martin Nourse, Lawrence Collins LJ dissenting.

[82] *Ablyazov* [2012] EWHC 2784 (Comm) and [2014] EWHC 2788 (Comm).

[83] *Ablyazov*, at [72], citing *Saunders v United Kingdom* [1998] 1 B.C.L.C. 362; *C Plc v P*, above; *R v S (F)* [2009] 1 W.L.R. 1489 and *R v Kearns* [2002] 1 W.L.R. 2815.

[84] See Ch.28, for a discussion of the privilege against self-incrimination in the context of freezing orders.

above should be drawn to the attention of the court as appropriate on any application for a search order containing a requirement for the provision of information which does not have an existence independent of the will of the respondent. In contrast to the provision mentioned above, in relation to the supply of potentially incriminating documents to the Supervising Solicitor, the standard form of search order contains no reference to the privilege against self-incrimination in the context of the provision of information to the applicant's solicitors (in the presence of the Supervising Solicitor) about the location and supply of any listed items. This can probably be justified by reference to the fact that the information referred to is directed to identifying the location of (and arguably has no distinct evidential value which is distinct from) items which exist independently of the order. However, unless it is clear on the facts of the particular case that any privilege against self-incrimination likely to be relevant has been statutorily abrogated, it may be difficult to satisfy the court that any wider, non-standard order for the provision of information does not run the risk of the privilege being infringed.

F.   ARTICLE 8 RIGHTS

30–064   Search orders clearly engage rights under art.8 of the ECHR, but in *Chappell v United Kingdom*,[85] the European Court of Human Rights rejected a challenge to search orders (effectively in principle) made on the basis that such orders infringe art.8 rights. Article 8(2) permits interference with a person's private and family life if "in accordance with the law" (which the ECHR held a search order was) and "necessary in a democratic society … for the protection of the rights and freedoms of others".

G.   SEARCHES OF PREMISES ABROAD

30–065   The statutory jurisdiction for search orders provided by s.7 Civil Procedure Act 1997 is restricted to premises within the jurisdiction. However, if (as is suggested above is the better view) the search order jurisdiction is not limited by the terms of s.7, then it follows from the fact that a search order is an in personam order, directing the respondent to permit the applicant to search his premises, that an English court could make such an order against a foreign defendant in respect of foreign premises, so long as the English court has jurisdiction over that defendant personally.

---

[85] *Chappell v United Kingdom* [1989] 1 F.S.R. 617. Chappell had not alleged that the second limb (necessary in a democratic society) was in principle not met by the grant of the search order against him, but contended that the interference with his rights was disproportionate to the legitimate aim pursued. The Court rejected that contention. See also *Niemitz v Germany* (1993) 16 E.H.R.R 97, where the European Court of Human Rights held that a search of a laywer's offices engaged art.8 but was justified on the basis of preventing crime and protecting the rights of others.

Such an order was made by Templeman J in *Cook Industries v Galliher.*[86] However, in *Altertext Inc v Advanced Data Ltd*,[87] Scott J pointed out that in the *Cook Industries* case, the foreign respondent had already been properly served in England, had entered an appearance in the English proceedings and was represented at the hearing before Templeman J at which the order was sought. Scott J continued:

30–066

> "…since the initial application is ex parte and since the foreign defendant may seek to have the leave under Order 11 set aside, the assumption by the court of jurisdiction is, in a sense, provisional only. In my view, where an *Anton Piller* order against a foreign defendant has to be accompanied by leave under Order 11 for service abroad, the *Anton Piller* order ought not to be executed until the foreign defendant has been given the opportunity to apply to set aside the Order 11 leave. The assumption by the court of jurisdiction over foreign defendants is, under Order 11, strictly controlled. It would be wrong, in my view, for the court to assume jurisdiction over a foreign defendant on an ex parte application, and then require a mandatory order of an *Anton Piller* character to be executed by the foreign defendant before he has had an opportunity to challenge the court's assumption of jurisdiction over him."

Scott J refused to grant the search order sought in *Altertext* and, as far as the authors are aware, *Cook Industries* remains the only (reported) case in which such an order has been made in respect of a foreign defendant's foreign premises.[88] This may be (at least partly) due to the fact that, in any case in which it is applied, the safeguard imposed by Scott J would effectively make the process on notice to the respondent, and thus considerably reduce the likely efficacy of the search order.

30–067

However, orders have been granted requiring English defendants to facilitate searches of computers, servers or electronic storage devices which are located overseas but in the possession or control of the relevant English defendant.[89] For example, it is now common for an English defendant's office in London to have some or all of its computer servers physically located outside England and Wales, and if those servers are the property of the English defendant (or under his control), the court may have jurisdiction to order the defendant to give the necessary instructions to ensure that such servers are made accessible for searching. If such an order is sought, thought should be given to satisfying the court that such an order—

30–068

---

[86] *Cook Industries v Galliher* [1979] Ch. 439.

[87] *Altertext Inc v Advanced Data Ltd* [1985] 1 W.L.R. 457.

[88] See also *Protector Alarms Ltd v Maxim Alarms Ltd* [1978] F.S.R. 442, in which Goulding J refused to grant a search order in respect of the Scottish defendant's premises in Scotland, saying that, "… the Anton Piller type of order represents a very special form of the court's action. It is a highly localised and coercive form of mandatory order requiring the party against whom it is made, without prior notice, to admit representatives of the opponent to specified premises …The especially coercive character and the local character of an Anton Piller order are shown by the fact that the now usual form of order requires the applicant's solicitors to take part in the execution of the order, no doubt because they are the court's own officers. They represent the court's own control of this special form of relief. Taking a practical view of the nature of an Anton Piller order and the way that it is enforced, I do not find it consistent with the comity prevailing between the courts of the several parts of the United Kingdom for the English court to make an Anton Piller order in respect of premises in Scotland …". (Nowadays, of course, the court's control of the process is also manifested through the involvement of the supervising solicitor).

[89] See *Altertext* [1985] 1 W.L.R. 457, per Scott J at 463.

(1) will not involve any individual or entity acting in breach of the law of the relevant foreign jurisdiction, by providing foreign law evidence if necessary; and

(2) will be capable of sensible supervision by the English court.

H. APPLICATIONS TO DISCHARGE A SEARCH ORDER

(1) Immediate Applications to Discharge

30–069 As reflected in the cases emphasising the safeguards required for respondents in relation to search orders, the real danger for a respondent in relation to a search order is that he is at risk of committal for contempt if he does not permit the execution of the search ordered by the court, even if he honestly believes he has good reason to apply to discharge the order immediately, for instance for breach of the duty of fair presentation, or indeed on substantive grounds.

30–070 The current example form of order provides that:

> "The Respondent is entitled to seek legal advice and to ask the court to vary or discharge the order. While doing so, he may ask the Supervising Solicitor to delay starting the search for up to 2 hours or such other longer period as the Supervising Solicitor may permit. However, the Respondent must –
> (a) comply with the terms of paragraph 27 below[90];
> (b) not disturb or remove listed items; and
> (c) permit the Supervising Solicitor to enter, but not start to search."

In most, if not all, cases it will be entirely unrealistic to think that the respondent could, within this timescale, hope to prepare the kind of evidence which would be required for any application aimed at persuading the judge that one or more of the four pre-conditions for the grant of relief (paras 30–011—30–022 above) has not in fact been made out. In some cases, there might be a slightly better chance of persuading the Supervising Solicitor to exercise his non-judicial discretion to stay his hand in relation to the commencement of the search, pending the making of an application on short notice, but he too will be fully mindful of the point that the order has only just been made by the court, by reference to those stringent requirements, and that so long as the order stands it should be complied with.

30–071 The risk for respondents was emphasised by Scott J in *Bhimji v Chatwani*.[91] In that case, the order required the respondents to allow the applicants to enter the premises "forthwith at any time between 8am and 6pm". The respondents were served with the order at 8am and their solicitor arrived at 10.15am, when he read and advised them on the order. The respondents were adamant they would not allow the applicants to seize their documents. Their solicitor advised that they were obliged to comply with the order or face contempt proceedings, and that the only alternative was to make an immediate application to discharge or vary the

---

[90] Which provides: "Anyone served with or notified of this order may apply to the court at any time to vary or discharge this order (or so much of it as affects that person), but they must first inform the Applicant's solicitors. If any evidence is to be relied upon in support of the application, the substance of it must be communicated in writing to the Applicant's solicitors in advance."
[91] *Bhimji v Chatwani* [1991] 1 W.L.R. 1003.

order. However, the parties' solicitors then became involved in negotiating a possible compromise to vary the order without the need for an application to court, and no application was made until the end of the afternoon. On that application, the search order was varied but not discharged. The applicants then applied to commit the respondents for contempt in refusing to permit immediate execution of the order.

Scott J held that the respondents had indeed been in breach of the order, with the necessary mens rea for contempt, as their failure to allow entry from 11am to the end of the afternoon was deliberate[92]. But he held that the breach was not contumacious (and therefore dismissed the application to commit) because:

30–072

(1) the failure to allow entry was accompanied by advice from the respondents' solicitors that it was permissible to postpone entry until after the application to court;
(2) a reasonable offer to provide protection for the documents was made at an early stage but not accepted by the plaintiffs;
(3) there was no evidence that the application was merely a device to postpone the search; and
(4) there was no evidence of any impropriety in respect of documents during the delay.

However, Scott J concluded his judgment by emphasising that any other respondent who chose to postpone the execution of a search order, as the respondents had done in that case, would do so at their own risk.[93]

30–073

(2) Subsequent Applications to Discharge

Once a search order has been fully executed, there is usually little if any real benefit for a respondent in an immediate application to discharge. More generally, applications to discharge are usually important to respondents for two reasons:

30–074

(1) to protect the respondent's position on the costs of the application and compliance with it, which are often heavy; and
(2) to establish the applicant's liability under his cross-undertaking in damages.

Accordingly, particularly if the application to discharge involves a detailed consideration of the merits of the claim, the courts will generally consider that the application should be dealt with at trial: see for example *Booker McConnell v Plascow*[94] and *Dormeuil Freres SA v Nicolian International (Textiles) Ltd.*[95] In

---

[92] See *Wardle Fabrics Ltd v G. Myristis Ltd* [1984] F.S.R. 263 for the principle that an order must be obeyed (on pain of contempt) whilst it stands. The fact that a search order was later discharged, on the ground of the applicant's non-disclosure, was no answer to a contempt application based upon the respondent's refusal to allow inspection while it remained in force.

[93] *Bhimji v Chatwani*, at 1003.

[94] *Booker McConnell v Plascow* [1985] RPC 425 per Kerr LJ at 435, though compare per Dillon LJ at 443.

Columbia Pictures v Robinson,[96] where the application to discharge the search order was not made until 18 months after the order had been fully executed and heard three and a half years later, Scott J declined to set aside the order on the basis it would then be no more than an "empty gesture". He did, however, order the claimant to pay damages to the defendant, in respect of the disruption to the legitimate aspects of their business, under the cross-undertaking in damages.

30–075   However, there may be circumstances in which the ongoing effect of the order on the defendant (for example, reputational damage resulting from the fact that the order remains apparently valid) justifies the immediate hearing of an application to discharge.[97] In *Lock International v Beswick*, Hoffmann J decided that justice required the search order to be discharged immediately to make it clear that no prima facie case of dishonesty had been shown.[98]

30–076   In *Gadget Shop Ltd v Bug.Com Ltd*,[99] Rimer J heard and allowed, at the interim stage and prior to trial, the defendant's application to discharge a previously executed search order, which was made at the same time as the claimant's application for interim injunctive relief restraining the defendant from making use of allegedly confidential information prior to trial. The Judge distinguished *Booker McConnell v Plascow* on the basis that the search order had not been fully executed (because documents remained with the supervising solicitor under a further order made in anticipation of the challenge to the search order) and also because the outcome of the application to discharge was potentially material to the claimant's application for interim injunctive relief.

30–077   Further, if a search order is set aside for being improperly obtained, the court may, as well as ordering the applicant to return the evidence, grant an interim injunction restraining him from making use of the information obtained through it until such time as he becomes entitled to the information through the ordinary process of litigation (i.e. disclosure). Such an order was made by Hoffmann J in *NAF NAF S.A. v Dickens (London) Ltd*,[100] where the judge said the jurisdiction to grant such in personam relief was illustrated by the court's ability to restrain the use of information obtained in breach of confidence and where he recognised that there may be cases where the iniquity on the part of the defendant, revealed by the wrongly obtained order, was such that it would be contrary to the public interest to allow it to remain concealed.

---

[95] *Dormeuil Freres SA v Nicolian International (Textiles) Ltd* [1988] 1 W.L.R. 1362.
[96] *Columbia Pictures v Robinson* [1987] Ch. 38, at 87.
[97] *Booker McConnell*, per Kerr LJ at 435.
[98] *Lock International v Beswick* [1989] 1 W.L.R. 1268, at 1285.
[99] *Gadget Shop Ltd v Bug.Com Ltd* [2001] F.S.R. 26, at [44]–[45].
[100] *NAF NAF S.A. v Dickens (London) Ltd* [1993] F.S.R. 424, at 427–428. There was no dispute that the yield from the order ("or, as it is sometimes called, the *Anton Pillage*") should be returned and the issue was whether the claimant should be prevented, pending disclosure, from making use of the information obtained through it (eg. perhaps most obviously in that case, making an application for an interim injunction against the defendant from passing off its merchandise).

I. DAMAGES FOR WRONGFUL EXECUTION OF THE ORDER

As is made clear by the standard form order, an order for damages (or an order for an inquiry as to the damages which should be paid) can be made at the same hearing as an application for discharge of the injunction is made.

30–078

The courts will generally take a particularly dim view of the behaviour of applicants (and their solicitors) who fail to execute a search order properly and in accordance with its terms, and the damages awarded can be substantial. As well as damages for the loss of a (legitimate) business resulting from the search order,[101] aggravated damages can also be awarded where the solicitors executing a search order act outside the terms of the order, oppressively or excessively, on the basis that they are acting (at least in part) as officers of the court.[102] Damages can be awarded even if the order is not set aside and even if the claimant's action succeeds on its merits.[103] As the applicant's liability to pay damages is based on the undertaking, and the undertaking is given to the court rather than to the applicant, there can be no counterclaim made in the underlying proceedings in respect of that damages liability.[104] Instead, the enforcement of the cross-undertaking is a matter for inquiry by the court. The exercise of the court's discretion and its approach to "compensation for loss" are discussed more fully in Ch.31.

30–079

SPECIFIC REQUIREMENTS FOR APPLICATIONS FOR AND EXECUTION OF SEARCH ORDERS IN THE PRACTICE DIRECTION 25A (INTERIM INJUNCTIONS) TO CPR 25

The Supervising Solicitor

7.2 The Supervising Solicitor must be experienced in the operation of search orders. A Supervising Solicitor may be contacted either through the Law Society or, for the London area, through the London Solicitors Litigation Association.

Evidence:

7.3 (1) the affidavit must state the name, firm and its address, and experience of the Supervising Solicitor, also the address of the premises and whether it is a private or business address, and

(2) the affidavit must disclose very fully the reason the order is sought, including the probability that relevant material would disappear if the order were not made.

---

[101] *Columbia Picture Industries v Robinson* [1987] 1 Ch. 38, at 87.

[102] *Columbia Picture Industries v Robinson*, at 87. See now the standard wording of the cross-undertaking noted above, which also addresses the point (which was not an issue in *Columbia Pictures* where the order was executed by the claimant's solicitors) that the applicant would not otherwise be responsible for any transgression by the Supervising Solicitor.

[103] *Columbia Picture Industries v Robinson*, at 87.

[104] *Digital Equipment Corp v Darkcrest Ltd* [1984] Ch. 512.

SPECIFIC REQUIREMENTS FOR APPLICATIONS FOR AND EXECUTION OF SEARCH ORDERS IN THE PRACTICE DIRECTION 25A (INTERIM INJUNCTIONS) TO CPR 25

Service:

7.4 (1) the order must be served personally by the Supervising Solicitor, unless the court otherwise orders, and must be accompanied by the evidence in support and any documents capable of being copied,

(2) confidential exhibits need not be served but they must be made available for inspection by the respondent in the presence of the applicant's solicitors while the order is carried out and afterwards be retained by the respondent's solicitors on their undertaking not to permit the respondent—

(a) to see them or copies of them except in their presence, and

(b) to make or take away any note or record of them,

(3) the Supervising Solicitor may be accompanied only by the persons mentioned in the order,

(4) the Supervising Solicitor must explain the terms and effect of the order to the respondent in everyday language and advise him—

(a) of his right to take legal advice and to apply to vary or discharge the order;

And

(b) that he may be entitled to avail himself of—

(i) legal professional privilege; and

(ii) the privilege against self-incrimination.

(5) where the Supervising Solicitor is a man and the respondent is likely to be an unaccompanied woman, at least one other person named in the order must be a woman and must accompany the Supervising Solicitor, and

(6) the order may only be served between 9.30am and 5.30pm Monday to Friday unless the court otherwise orders.

Search and custody of materials:

7.5 (1) no material shall be removed unless clearly covered by the terms of the order,

(2) the premises must not be searched and no items shall be removed from them except in the presence of the respondent or a person who appears to be a responsible employee of the respondent,

(3) where copies of documents are sought, the documents should be retained for no more than 2 days before return to the owner,

(4) where material in dispute is removed pending trial, the applicant's solicitors should place it in the custody of the respondent's solicitors on their undertaking to retain it in safekeeping and to produce it to the court when required,

(5) in appropriate cases the applicant should insure the material retained in the respondent's solicitors' custody,

SPECIFIC REQUIREMENTS FOR APPLICATIONS FOR AND EXECUTION OF SEARCH ORDERS IN THE PRACTICE DIRECTION 25A (INTERIM INJUNCTIONS) TO CPR 25

(6) the Supervising Solicitor must make a list of all material removed from the premises and supply a copy of the list to the respondent,

(7) no material shall be removed from the premises until the respondent has had reasonable time to check the list,

(8) if any of the listed items exists only in computer readable form, the respondent must immediately give the applicant's solicitors effective access to the computers, with all necessary passwords, to enable them to be searched, and cause the listed items to be printed out,

(9) the applicant must take all reasonable steps to ensure that no damage is done to any computer or data,

(10) the applicant and his representatives may not themselves search the respondent's computers unless they have sufficient expertise to do so without damaging the respondent's system,

(11) the Supervising Solicitor shall provide a report on the carrying out of the order to the applicant's solicitors.

(12) as soon as the report is received the applicant's solicitors shall—

(a) serve a copy of it on the respondent, and

(b) file a copy of it with the court, and

(13) where the Supervising Solicitor is satisfied that full compliance with paragraph 7.5(7) and (8) above is impracticable, he may permit the search to proceed and items to be removed without compliance with the impracticable requirements.

General

7.6 The Supervising Solicitor must not be an employee or member of the applicant's firm of solicitors.

7.7 If the court orders that the order need not be served by the Supervising Solicitor, the reason for so ordering must be set out in the order.

7.8 The search order must not be carried out at the same time as a police search warrant.

7.9 There is no privilege against self incrimination in—

(1) Intellectual Property cases in respect of a "related offence" or for the recovery of a "related penalty" as defined in section 72 Senior Courts Act 1981;

(2) proceedings for the recovery or administration of any property, for the execution of a trust or for an account of any property or dealings with property, in relation to—

(a) an offence under the Theft Act 1968 (see section 31 of the Theft Act 1968); or

SPECIFIC REQUIREMENTS FOR APPLICATIONS FOR AND EXECUTION OF SEARCH ORDERS IN THE PRACTICE DIRECTION 25A (INTERIM INJUNCTIONS) TO CPR 25

(b) an offence under the Fraud Act 2006 (see section 13 of the Fraud Act 2006) or a related offence within the meaning given by section 13(4) of that Act—that is, conspiracy to defraud or any other offence involving any form of fraudulent conduct or purpose; or

(3) proceedings in which a court is hearing an application for an order under Part IV or Part V of the Children Act 1989 (see section 98 Children Act 1989).

However, the privilege may still be claimed in relation to material or information required to be disclosed by an order, as regards potential criminal proceedings outside those statutory provisions.

7.10 Applications in intellectual property cases should be made in the Chancery Division.

7.11 An example of a Search Order is annexed to this Practice Direction[105]. This example may be modified as appropriate in any particular case.

---

[105] The reader is referred to the precedent in Appendix 5 to the Admiralty and Commercial Court Guide for an appropriate precedent reflecting the requirements of CPR PD 25A.

CHAPTER 31

OTHER INTERIM REMEDIES

A. Introduction

In addition to the interim remedies that are singled out for specific attention in the preceding chapters, there are numerous other interim measures which the court has jurisdiction to grant and which will be of particular relevance in the civil fraud context.[1] We consider the following in this chapter: **31–001**

(1)   In Section B, "gagging" orders;
(2)   In Section C, the appointment of provisional liquidators;
(3)   In Section D, applications to enforce a cross-undertaking in damages;
(4)   In Section E, orders restricting movement (including the old writ *ne exeat regno* and the more modern *Bayer v Winter* order);
(5)   In Section F, applications to cross-examine a respondent on his affidavit of assets.
(6)   In Section G, orders ancillary to freezing injunctions (other than orders for asset disclosure in support of a freezing injunction, which we have considered in Ch.28), including:
(a)   orders for disclosure by a defendant's solicitors,
(b)   orders for disclosure of identity of litigation funders,
(c)   orders for the defendant to sign a document authorising disclosure by his bank,
(d)   mandatory orders for the transfer of funds by banks and
(e)   orders for the delivery up of assets.

B. "Gagging" Orders

(1) General Principles

Where a claimant/applicant wishes to obtain information from a third party (or existing defendant) in order to identify a wrongdoer or obtain evidence against him, or preserve assets pending litigation, it may well entirely defeat the purpose of any such order if the alleged wrongdoer were able to find out about it and either destroy the relevant documents or dissipate the relevant assets before a substantive order could be obtained against and served on him. In such cases the **31–002**

---

[1] Of course, there are interim measures which are of relevance to fraud claims, but no more or less so than to other types of civil claim (for example, orders for security for costs). These are outside of the scope of this book.

applicant may wish to apply for an interim non-disclosure order, colloquially known as a "gagging order", to prevent the wrongdoer from finding out about the preliminary steps being taken by the applicant in advance of applying directly against him.

31–003 The court can grant such an order under its inherent jurisdiction to ensure that its orders are not rendered futile and ineffective to achieve their purpose. There are in some contexts further or alternative jurisdictional bases which may support the order, as set out below.

31–004 A gagging order should be applied for at the same time as and ancillary to the principal interim relief sought against the third party or existing defendant. It is usually, *ex hypothesi*, sought without notice in the first instance, and the applicant will then wish to ensure that any further hearings while the gagging order remains in place are conducted in private and on an anonymised basis. There has been some debate as to whether a gagging order is properly termed an injunction, and therefore whether it formerly needed to be heard by a judge (in the authors' view it was and did). However, as Masters are, following recent changes to the CPR, now empowered to grant injunctions (other than freezing injunctions and certain specified others)[2] the debate is a stale one.

31–005 In a 2011 practice direction Lord Neuberger issued guidance as to recommended practice in applications for interim non-disclosure orders.[3] Although the preamble specifically mentions *Norwich Pharmacal* orders, much of the guidance—and the model order and explanatory notes appended thereto—is directed to media cases and in particular privacy injunctions. The key points that can be extracted of relevance for fraud cases are:

(1) CPR r.25.3 and paras 5.1(1) to (5) of PD 52A apply to all interim injunction applications including those for gagging orders.

(2) Derogations from the principle of open justice are exceptional and should be no more than the minimum strictly necessary to achieve their purpose.

(3) The burden of establishing any required derogation lies on the person seeking it and it must be justified by clear and cogent evidence.

(4) Gagging orders cannot be granted by consent.

(5) The court should ensure that a return date is specified in such orders and that, as a general rule, the return date is kept, although the return date can in an appropriate case be dealt with on the papers without the need for attendance.

(6) Advocates should take particular care in every application, especially where it is made without notice, to comply with the duty of full and frank disclosure.

(7) A full and accurate note should be taken of any without notice hearing either during the hearing or, if that is not possible, once it is over, specifying which documents were put before the court, which legal authorities were relied upon and what the court was told.

(8) Any appeal from an interim non-disclosure order may be expedited.

---

[2] CPR PD 2B paras 1.1, 2, 3.1.

[3] Practice Guidance (HC: Interim Non-Disclosure orders) [2012] 1 W.L.R. 1003.

(9)   A gagging order should contain a penal notice making clear the effect that it may have on the respondent or third parties who know of the order.

Consistent with point (2) above, the duration of the gagging order should be no longer than is reasonably necessary. Whilst of course it depends upon what needs to be done whilst secrecy is maintained, the timeframe is likely to be days rather than weeks. In an early decision concerned with a gagging provision in an *Anton Piller* order, the court said that "a whole week... is far too long",[4] and this is consistent with the authors' experience (with the possible exception of cases where the assets in question are located abroad, in which case longer is likely to be needed).   **31–006**

(2)   Search Orders[5]

In the case of a search order, there is no requirement in s.7 of the Civil Procedure Act 1997 that the property to be preserved is located at the property to be searched. The purpose of the order may, for example, be to facilitate further trains of inquiry, by allowing the applicant access to information or documentation which enables him to locate information or documents elsewhere. If so, it is imperative that the alleged wrongdoer does not find out about the search order until after the applicant has had a reasonable opportunity to carry out those further investigations and take steps to secure any further information or documents thereby discovered.   **31–007**

To that end a gagging order provision is contained in para.20 of the standard form search order in the Annex to CPR PD 25A, as follows[6]:   **31–008**

> "Prohibited Acts
>   20. Except for the purpose of obtaining legal advice, the Respondent must not directly or indirectly inform anyone of these proceedings or of the contents of this order, or warn anyone that proceedings have been or may be brought against him by the Applicant until 4.30 pm on the return date or further order of the court."

Unlike its predecessor,[7] this provision operates only against the respondent, although third parties with knowledge of the order and its purpose who nevertheless deliberately interfere with it might be guilty of criminal contempt of court.   **31–009**

Although not expressly referred to therein, it has been suggested, by analogy with the ancillary powers available to the court under s.37(1) of the Senior Courts Act 1981, that the court's jurisdiction to insert a gagging provision in a search order is an inherent part of its jurisdiction to grant the search order under s.7.[8]   **31–010**

---

[4] Sir Donald Nicholls V-C in *Universal Thermosensors Ltd v Hibben* [1992] 1 W.L.R. 840, at 860.
[5] For a consideration of Search Orders see Ch.30.
[6] A recent example of a gagging order having been made ancillary to a search order is *JSC BTA Bank v Ablyazov* [2014] EWHC 2019; [2015] 1 W.L.R. 1547.
[7] Paragraph 6(1) of the standard form search order under the 1996 Practice Direction.
[8] See for example S. Gee, *Commercial Injunctions*, 6th edn (London: Sweet & Maxwell, 2016), para.17–012.

(3)   Norwich Pharmacal Orders[9]

31–011   Similar considerations to those set out above apply in *Norwich Pharmacal* applications, where the applicant is trying to ascertain the identity of the wrongdoer, or the details of a key element of the claim, often with a view to obtaining an injunction before the wrongdoer can abscond or dissipate his assets. The principles applicable in that context were considered by Tugendhat J in *G v Wikimedia Foundation Inc*.[10] There the court said, unsurprisingly, that a gagging order made in anticipation of obtaining an injunction against the ultimate wrongdoer would be expected to expire once such an injunction had been obtained, or at the return date of the *Norwich Pharmacal* application. In the *Norwich Pharmacal* context, if the order is sought in order to enable the applicant to secure and freeze the ultimate wrongdoer's assets, the court's jurisdiction to make a gagging order might also be said to arise under s.37(1) of the Senior Courts Act 1981.

(4)   Bankers Trust Orders[11]

31–012   Special considerations pertain to applications for disclosure orders against banks, which may be relevant to an application for a gagging order:

(1)   First, they are likely to be under contractual or fiduciary duties to their clients to inform them of any relevant proceedings relating to their account.[12] Where that is the case it may be in the interests of the bank, as much as the applicant, for the court to consider and rule upon the interaction between the bank's contractual obligations and its obligations under any disclosure order that the court might otherwise make. It is for these reasons that the court has historically been very reluctant to make orders against foreign banks, whose obligations are defined by foreign laws which may not recognise the primacy of English court orders.[13]

(2)   Second, they may be obliged to make, or may by the time of the application already have made, a money-laundering report to the appropriate authorities, and they may be concerned that if they complied with the disclosure order they would be in violation of the anti-"tipping-off" provisions in the relevant criminal legislation. The Court of Appeal has clarified that a gagging order does not prevent such communication in order to resolve, for example, money-laundering concerns, and has set out detailed guidance as to the proper approach to be taken by a bank in that

---

[9]   For a consideration of *Norwich Pharmacal* orders see Ch.29.

[10]   *G v Wikimedia Foundation Inc* [2009] E.M.L.R. 14; [2009] EWHC 3148.

[11]   For a consideration of *Bankers Trust* orders see Ch.29.

[12]   As to the precise nature of the duty that the bank may be under see *Robertson v Canadian Bank of Commerce* [1994] 1 W.L.R. 1493, at 1499, where the Privy Council suggested that it could only be a "best endeavours" obligation.

[13]   See for example *MacKinnon v Donaldson, Lufkin & Jenrette Securities Corp* [1986] 1 Ch. 482, at 494B–494E, per Hoffmann J.

situation.[14] If agreement cannot be reached between the authority, the applicant and the respondent as to what can be disclosed, the bank will need to apply to court for directions as to the interaction between its regulatory obligations and its position under the order. The Court of Appeal's guidance explains the procedure for such applications and the relevant considerations to be taken into account.[15]

For all of those reasons, it will often be advisable to give the bank informal notice of the proposed application before it is made or before it is heard, either with the relevant names and account numbers anonymised or on their undertaking not to disclose them pending the hearing, and indeed in *C v S* the Court of Appeal expressly suggested that where time permits such informal notice should be given.[16] This may have the added benefit that it may be possible to avoid a return date, if (as is often the case) the bank agrees to, or is neutral as to, the making of an order. **31–013**

C. PROVISIONAL LIQUIDATORS

Where a fraud has been, or is being, perpetrated by or through a company which is insolvent, the victim may, after a winding up petition has been presented against the company, seek to appoint a provisional liquidator to preserve the company's assets pending the hearing of the petition. The concern will usually be that the shareholders or, more likely, the directors of the company will in the time between the presentation and the hearing of the petition seek to put its assets beyond reach of the petitioner and other creditors. However, that is not a threshold condition and orders have been made on a number of other bases, for example where a company had misled investors in order to induce them to make risky speculations,[17] or where there was evidence of other serious misconduct on the part of the directors.[18] **31–014**

The appointment of a provisional liquidator has been described as the "nuclear weapon" of the Companies Court,[19] and "one of the most intrusive remedies in the court's armoury".[20] That is because the order is a serious intrusion which will paralyse the company, and probably cause it to cease trading and all of its employees to lose their jobs. For that reason, the courts will consider other alternatives before making such an order (for example freezing orders), and, as set out below, the threshold test is a high one. **31–015**

Before an application can be made there must be a valid winding up petition before the court. An application can be made by: the petitioning creditor, another **31–016**

---

[14] *C v S (Money Laundering: Discovery of Documents) (Practice Note)* [1999] 1 W.L.R. 1551. The operative part of the guidance is at 1555–1556.
[15] Such applications are expressly provided for in para.F15.11 of the Commercial Court Guide.
[16] *C v S* [1999] 1 W.L.R. 1551, at 1557.
[17] *Re Comstrad Ltd*, unreported, 27 September 1995, Ch. D per Carnwath J.
[18] *Gamlestaden Plc v Brackland Magazines Ltd* [1994] 1 B.C.L.C. 190, per Harman J; [1993] BCC 194 (Chadwick J).
[19] *Re A Company (No.0070707 of 1996)* [1997] 2 B.C.L.C. 139, at 142.
[20] *HMRC v Rochdale Drinks Distributors* [2011] EWCA Civ 1116; [2013] B.C.C. 419.

creditor, a contributory, the company itself, the secretary of state, a temporary administrator, a Member State liquidator appointed in main proceedings or any other person who under any enactment would be entitled to present a petition to wind up the company.[21]

(1) Relevant Principles on Application to Appoint

31–017 The power to appoint a provisional liquidator is contained in s.135 of the Insolvency Act 1986, where it is drafted as an unfettered discretion. However, principles regulating the exercise of that discretion have been set out in case-law, most recently by the Court of Appeal in *HMRC v Rochdale Drinks Distributors*,[22] subsequently applied and elaborated upon by the High Court in *HMRC v Winnington Networks Ltd*[23] and *HMRC v SED Essex Ltd*.[24] They are as follows:

(1) The appointment of a provisional liquidator should (for reasons set out above) be the subject of "most anxious consideration".[25]

(2) The application is not a trial of the petition itself and the court is proceeding on a provisional and interim basis.[26]

(3) The court must consider whether the applicant has demonstrated that it is *likely* to obtain a winding up order when the petition comes to be heard. It is not sufficient for these purposes to establish a good prima facie case.[27]

(4) If that threshold test is met, the court should then consider whether on the facts of the particular case it is—as a matter of judicial discretion—right that a provisional liquidator should be appointed pending the hearing of the petition.[28]

(5) Factors to be taken into account in considering the second stage of the inquiry include:

   (i) questions as to the integrity of the company's management and/or accounting and record keeping function;

   (ii) whether there was any real risk of dissipation of the company's assets and/or any real need to take steps to preserve them;

   (iii) whether there was any real risk that the company's books and records would be destroyed and/or any real need for steps to be taken to ensure that they were properly preserved and maintained;

   (iv) whether there was any real need for steps to be taken to facilitate immediate inquiries into the conduct of the company's management and affairs and/or to investigate possible claims against directors for fraudulent or wrongful trading;

---

[21] Insolvency Rules 2016, r.7.33.
[22] *HMRC v Rochdale Drinks Distributors* [2011] EWCA Civ 1116; [2013] B.C.C. 419.
[23] *HMRC v Winnington Networks Ltd* [2014] EWHC 1259 (Ch); [2014] B.C.C. 675.
[24] *HMRC v SED Essex Ltd* [2013] EWHC 1583 (Ch); [2014] B.C.C. 628.
[25] *Rochdale*, above, at [76], per Rimer LJ.
[26] *Winnington*, above, at [5], per Norris J.
[27] *Rochdale*, above, at [77], overruling the previous test as set out in *Union Accident Assurance* [1972] 1 All E.R. 1105, at 1110B, per Plowman J.
[28] *SED Essex*, above, at [11], per John Randall QC sitting as a deputy.

(v)   whether or not the company had a realistic prospect of obtaining a validation order under the Insolvency Act 1986 s.127, because if not, it might not be able to trade in any event;

(vi)   generally, which course seemed likely to cause the least irremediable prejudice to one party or the other.

The jurisdiction can be used to preserve evidence for litigation against the company's management as well as assets.[29] This is an important advantage of an appointment of a provisional liquidator over, say, a freezing injunction.[30]   **31–018**

(2)   Practice and Procedure

The application is made to a Companies Court judge and held in public (unless otherwise ordered). The general practice is to make it on notice to the company. It may be made ex parte only in exceptional circumstances,[31] for example if: **31–019**

(a)   giving notice would enable the defendant to take steps to defeat the purpose of the remedy (as is usually the case with a freezing or search order); or

(b)   there has been literally no time to give notice before the remedy is required to prevent the threatened wrongful act (and in that case any notice is better than none).[32]

If so, the applicant has the usual duty of full and frank disclosure. An order made in breach of this obligation is liable to be set aside: *Re OJSC Ank Yugraneft*.[33] However, at the ex parte stage, the court can take into account the company's engagement with and response to any prior investigatory steps which would have been undertaken by the creditor

> "in the expectation that if the company has a serious case to advance it will have advanced it in the course of that engagement and will not have kept it up its sleeve."

The application should be made by application notice and supporting evidence, which must specify the matters set out in r.7.33 of the Insolvency Rules 2016, including the grounds for the appointment and an estimate of the value of the assets over which the provisional liquidator will have control, if appointed. A copy of the application must be served on the official receiver, who is entitled to attend the hearing and make representations: IR r.7.33(3).   **31–020**

---

[29] *Rochdale*, above, at [97]; *Winnington*, above, at [9]; and *SED Essex*, above at [16].

[30] *Winnington*, above, at [36].

[31] *Winnington*, above, at [4]. For the principles and practice applicable to without notice applications, see Ch.27.

[32] See *Rochdale*, above, at [110].

[33] *Re OJSC Ank Yugraneft* [2008] EWHC 2614 (Ch); [2010] B.C.C. 475.

(3)   The Test in Fraud Cases

31–021   The difficulty in a fraud case is likely to be establishing, at an interlocutory hearing, that it is "likely" that the claim, and therefore the allegation of fraud, will succeed, to the standard required for a company to be wound up, namely that there is no substantial dispute. However, it is by no means impossible, as shown by *SED Essex*,[34] a VAT fraud case in which *Rochdale* was applied and detailed consideration was given to the proper test to be applied in a fraud context. John Randall QC (sitting as a High court judge) said that in fraud claims:

(1)   where the party on whom the burden of proof lies adduces sufficient evidence that, were it to go wholly unanswered, the court would be satisfied that they had discharged that burden to the requisite standard, the evidential burden shifts, and it is then for the company to establish that it has a good arguable case.[35]

(2)   where, as is by their very nature often the case in fraud claims, the applicant was unable to establish the exact nature of the fraud, the Court must approach the case with even more care than such allegations ordinarily attract.[36]

(4)   Effect of Appointment

31–022   Importantly, a provisional liquidator does not have unlimited powers. Sections 135(4) and (5) of the Insolvency Act 1986 operate to limit his powers to those provided for in the order. Accordingly, applicants should think carefully in advance what the liquidator will need to do when in office, in order to avoid repeat trips to court, and to enable him to act urgently if needed. If unusual powers are to be sought, this should be explained in the supporting evidence. Otherwise, he will be empowered only to take possession of company assets[37] and preserve them until the hearing of the petition (which may in many cases be sufficient). It is not normally within the duties of a provisional liquidator to realise assets. In many cases his appointment alone may achieve the applicant's aim, as it will displace the powers of the directors and anyone appointed by them: *Re Union Assurance Co Ltd*.[38]

31–023   Due to the potentially damaging effects of the appointment, the applicant may be (but will not always be) required to give an undertaking in damages (as happened

---

[34] *SED Essex* [2013] EWHC 1583 (Ch); [2014] B.C.C. 628.
[35] *SED Essex* [2013] EWHC 1583 (Ch); [2014] B.C.C. 628, at [7].
[36] *SED Essex* [2013] EWHC 1583 (Ch); [2014] B.C.C. 628, at [21]–[22].
[37] Section 144 of the Insolvency Act.
[38] *Re Union Assurance Co Ltd* [1972] 1 W.L.R. 640. See also *Pacific & General Insurance Ltd (In Liquidation) v Home & Overseas Insurance Co Ltd* [1997] B.C.C. 400.

in *Rochdale*). For an example of a successful enforcement of such an undertaking, see *Abbey Forwarding Ltd (In Liquidation) v Revenue and Customs Commissioners*.[39]

It is a contempt of court to impede a provisional liquidator in the exercise of his functions. In *Revenue & Customs Commissioners v Munir*[40] the directors and secretary who paid away assets of their company after a provisional liquidator had been appointed received substantial prison sentences. **31–024**

(5) International Elements

As for cases with foreign elements, an order can be made in relation to a foreign company if there is sufficient connection with England that no other jurisdiction is more appropriate for the presentation of a winding up petition.[41] Of course, as it has to be shown that it is likely that a petition would succeed, there may need to be a jurisdictional argument about the petition at the stage of the provisional liquidator application. However, orders have been made where the company had no assets in England but there was a sufficiently close connection with the jurisdiction in order to enable the liquidator to locate assets and prevent costs increasing.[42] **31–025**

D. APPLICATIONS TO ENFORCE A CROSS-UNDERTAKING IN DAMAGES

As set out in Ch.27, an applicant for a freezing or search order (or indeed for any form of interim injunction) will almost always be required to provide what is usually described as a cross-undertaking in damages. If it later transpires that the injunction was wrongly granted, whether because it is set aside at the return date (or at some later interlocutory hearing) or because the underlying claim fails at or before trial, the question arises how the respondent to the order (who will usually be the defendant to the underlying proceedings)[43] can enforce the cross-undertaking and what relief he will be granted. The potential liability of a claimant under the cross-undertaking is not to be taken lightly. The provision of such a cross-undertaking is no mere formality and the claimant seeking interim relief should be carefully advised of this potential liability. In the recent fraud case of *Fiona Trust v Privalov* (as to which see further below), one of the defendants, Mr Nikitin, was awarded damages in the sum of tens of millions of dollars under the claimant's cross-undertaking in damages, despite having been found at the earlier trial to be dishonest in at least some of his business dealings and untruthful in the evidence he gave. However, the award was nevertheless found to be justified on the basis that: **31–026**

---

[39] *Abbey Forwarding Ltd (In Liquidation) v Revenue and Customs Commissioners* [2015] EWHC 225 (Ch); [2015] All E.R. (D) 91 (Feb). As to the enforcement of cross-undertakings in damages more generally, see Section D below.
[40] *Revenue & Customs Commissioners v Munir* [2015] EWHC 1366 (Ch); [2015] B.C.C. 425.
[41] *Re A Company (No. 003102 of 1991)* [1991] B.C.L.C. 539.
[42] *Re A Company (No.00359 of 1987)* [1988] Ch. 210; (1987) 3 B.C.C. 160.
[43] But can also a third party, for example those injuncted under the *Chabra* jurisdiction.

> "It is an integral part of the court's procedure to require undertakings when making such interim orders so that defendants can be compensated in appropriate cases, and it is no less important where the character of the defendant or the nature of the case apparently justifies a freezing order."[44]

31–027 The undertaking is given to the court, not to the opposing party. Accordingly, the respondent cannot sue on it as such. The respondent is accorded no private cause of action by the setting aside of the relevant injunction. Rather he must apply, on notice, for the court to enforce it.[45] This is apparent from the standard wording of cross-undertakings in damages:

> "If the court later finds that this order has caused loss to the Respondent, and decides that the Respondent should be compensated for that loss, the Applicant will comply with any order the court may make."

It is clear that, although the standard form does not expressly say this, the Court will only decide that the respondent should be compensated for his loss if the underlying order is set aside as having been wrongly granted or subsequently wrongly maintained. To conclude that an order has been wrongly granted does not require any decision that the court which originally granted the order was wrong to do so on the evidence then available. If the claim is dismissed at trial then the interim order will have been wrongly granted simply on the basis that the underlying cause of action was bad. By contrast, if the order is set aside at the return date that will often be not because of any assessment of the underlying merits of the claim but because it has been found that, for instance, no real risk of dissipation has been established or because of a breach of the duty of full and frank disclosure. Such a holding will also involve a decision that the order was wrongly granted.

31–028 The making of freezing and search orders are of course commonplace in fraud claims, and so the giving of cross-undertakings, as the price of such orders, is equally prevalent. Applications to enforce such cross-undertakings are frequently encountered in fraud proceedings which have been dismissed at trial or where interim injunctions have been set aside at an interim hearing, and so we deal with the issue at some length below.

---

[44] *Fiona Trust v Privalov* [2014] EWHC 3102 (Comm), per Andrew Smith J at [32], endorsed by Males J at the subsequent damages inquiry: [2016] EWHC 2163 (Comm), at [143].

[45] See generally *Barratt Manchester Ltd v Bolton Metropolitan BC* [1998] 1 W.L.R. 1003, per Millett LJ at 1009: "The cross-undertaking in question is given to the court, not to the party opposite, and may be enforced or discharged by the court in its discretion. The party seeking to enforce the undertaking has no cause of action. Although entitled to apply to enforce the cross-undertaking, he has no legal right to its enforcement or to damages: see *Cheltenham & Gloucester Building Society v Ricketts* [1993] 1 W.L.R. 1545. Any loss which he may have sustained is occasioned, not by a legal wrong, but in consequence of an order of the court. Since there is no cause of action there is no period of limitation either; but the cross-undertaking cannot be enforced without the leave of the court, which may be withheld if not applied for promptly."

(1)   The Application to Enforce the Cross-Undertaking

If the order is set aside the respondent has a choice whether or not to apply to   **31–029**
enforce the cross-undertaking. Although it has been said that the "court acts or
declines to act in its own right, not merely as an umpire in an adversarial process
between the parties",[46] in practice the court will not act to enforce the
cross-undertaking on its own motion. If the respondent does so decide then the
court usually proceeds in two distinct stages. First, it makes a preliminary
decision whether or not to enforce the cross-undertaking, by ordering an inquiry
into what loss the respondent has sustained. If it does order an inquiry, then it will
usually give directions for a final hearing, which may well involve live evidence
and have all the hallmarks of a trial. The second stage takes one through to this
trial. At this trial the respondent must prove its case in the usual way. Simply
because a court at the first stage has ordered an inquiry does not mean that it has
made any pre-judgment about what losses the respondent has sustained which can
be laid at the door of the party who gave the cross-undertaking, although it will
have had to conclude that the respondent has suffered at least some loss;
otherwise it would decline to enforce the cross-undertaking.

(i)   Ordering an inquiry

As to the application to enforce a cross-undertaking and for an inquiry: **31–030**

(1)   It is made to the court which made the original order (and to which,
therefore, the undertaking was given).[47]
(2)   As to timing, whilst an application can be made at any time after the
injunction has been discharged, generally the court will order an inquiry
only once the underlying claim has failed. Even if the injunction is
discharged before trial (e.g. after a contested return date hearing), and the
application is made immediately (i.e. before the trial), the court may well
postpone the decision whether to enforce the undertaking and order an
inquiry until after the trial, especially if, for example, there is an allegation
of fraud to be litigated.[48] However the court need not to do so, and is likely
to proceed at an interlocutory stage if, for example, the injunction is set
aside on the basis of material non-disclosure. It is clear that the court has a
variety of options available to it when a respondent applies to enforce the
undertakings before trial both as to whether to entertain the application to

---

[46] See *C. T. Bowring & Co (Insurance) Ltd v Corsi Partners Ltd* [1994] 2 Lloyd's Rep. 567, at 582,
per Sir Michael Kerr.
[47] *Re Hailstone, Hopkinson v Carter* (1910) 102 LT 877, CA.
[48] As was the case in *Cheltenham & Gloucester v Ricketts* [1993] 1 W.L.R. 1545. In that case the
freezing order was discharged before trial. The Court of Appeal held that the judge had been wrong to
order immediate enforcement of the undertaking because at trial the question of whether the defendant
had perpetrated a fraud would be decided and that might be "a special circumstance" that could affect
the court's discretion whether or not to enforce. It was held that the decision whether or not to enforce
should await the outcome of the trial. A claimant in a fraud case whose injunction is discharged before
trial will for obvious reasons wish to postpone any decision on enforcement of the cross-undertaking
until after trial. If the defendant is found liable at trial then the court may be disinclined to enforce the
undertaking.

enforce at that time (or adjourn it off) and as to the timing of any inquiry. For instance it may be clear in advance of the trial that the undertaking should be enforced but the court may decide that the inquiry should come on after the trial, for instance because there is insufficient time to hear the inquiry in advance.

(3)   If there is an appeal which includes challenging the dismissal of the injunctive relief or the basis on which the inquiry was ordered, the inquiry will generally be stayed pending that appeal.

(4)   The application can be made after trial, but if so

    (i)   the defendant should ensure that any order dismissing the claim is made without prejudice to the right to enforce the cross-undertaking and

    (ii)   even then the application should be made speedily, and if not made within a reasonable time it may be refused.[49]

31–031   The court must first decide whether the injunction was wrongly granted (or maintained).[50] This is usually an uncontentious question.[51] If it finds that it was, then, whilst the Court retains a theoretical discretion as to whether or not to enforce the cross undertaking, there is a rebuttable presumption in favour of enforcement.[52] Indeed it has been said that the applicant who has suffered loss as a result of the order can expect an inquiry "virtually as of right", which will only be refused in "special circumstances".[53]

31–032   However, the court must take into account all of the relevant circumstances and may refuse to order an inquiry, for example, if the conduct of the respondent makes it inequitable to do so,[54] or if he has delayed unduly in making the application (or, once an order has been made to enforce the cross-undertaking, if

---

[49] *Smith v Day* (1882) 21 Ch. D. 421, CA.

[50] There may be a difference: see the facts in *Societe Generale v Goldas* [2017] EWHC 667 (Comm).

[51] Though the claimant in a fraud claim whose injunction is discharged before trial may wish to argue that it would be premature to decide the question of whether the order was wrongly granted until after the issue of liability has been decided. See in the case of search orders *Columbia Pictures Inc v Robinson* [1987] Ch. 38, at 85, per Scott J.

[52] *Cheltenham & Gloucester v Ricketts* [1993] 1 W.L.R. 1545, at 1551C-1552D, per Neill LJ.

[53] *Lunn Poly Ltd v Liverpool and Lancashire Properties Ltd* [2006] EWCA Civ 430; [2006] 2 E.G.L.R. 29, per Neuberger LJ at [42] to [43]. The whole passage deserves quotation: "As a matter of principle, and, indeed, of general practice, I would certainly accept that, where a claimant has obtained an interlocutory injunction restraining the defendant from doing something until trial, and the court decides at trial that a permanent injunction should not be granted, the defendant can normally expect, virtually as of right, to have an inquiry as to the damages to which he is entitled pursuant to the cross-undertaking which the claimant will have been required to give as a condition of obtaining the interlocutory injunction. However, there plainly are exceptions to this general rule. In *Hoffmann-Laroche v Secretary of State* [1975] A.C. 295, at 361D, Lord Diplock said that the court 'retains a discretion not to enforce the undertaking if …. it is inequitable to do so.'….It is clear, however, that 'special circumstances' are required before an inquiry can properly be refused."

[54] *F.Hoffmann-La Roche & Co AG v Secretary of State* [1975] A.C. 295, at 361, per Lord Wilberforce. In *Fiona Trust v Privalov* [2014] EWHC 3102 (Comm) the Court agreed to enforce the undertaking notwithstanding the misconduct of the respondent. In that case it was material to the exercise of the discretion that the claimants had themselves been guilty of serious impropriety in obtaining the freezing order in the first place. In *Cheltenham & Gloucester v Ricketts* [1993] 1 W.L.R. 1545 Peter Gibson LJ lists at 1557, a number of older cases where the court decided not to enforce the undertaking as a result of the respondent's conduct.

the applicant has then failed to progress the inquiry itself), even if no prejudice has thereby been caused (although that will nevertheless be treated as a "highly material" factor[55]). In the recent case of *Societe Generale v Goldas*[56] a claimant had issued English proceedings and obtained a freezing order. It then pursued parallel proceedings abroad for a number of years and the English claim was allowed to lie dormant. The defendant successfully applied to strike out the claim and discharge the freezing order. The judge allowed an application to enforce the cross-undertaking notwithstanding the lapse of time. An inquiry will also not be ordered if the losses contended for are trivial or the application is obviously hopeless. Hence the applicant at this first stage will need to put forward evidence that more than minimal loss has been sustained by him flowing from the order.[57]

Once it has determined that the undertaking should be enforced, the court can either summarily assess the damages (if the position is clear) or, more usually, order that the defendant pay a sum to be assessed in an inquiry as to damages. The decision to enforce the undertaking and order an inquiry is a discretionary one and therefore, on any appeal,   **31–033**

> "the question is not whether the judge was right or wrong in refusing an inquiry: it is whether it was a proper exercise of his discretion to refuse an inquiry."[58]

(ii)   Conduct of the inquiry

The inquiry as to damages, then, should be concerned only with quantum and causation issues, and not with the court's discretion whether to enforce the cross-undertaking. That decision should and will usually have been made at the first stage.[59] Indeed it has been said that a decision that the undertaking should be enforced is a precondition for the making of an order of an inquiry as to damages.[60] However, the issue whether it remains open to the defendant to argue the point at the trial of the inquiry depends on the wording of the order directing it.[61] If the effect of the order, properly construed, is to determine that the undertaking is to be enforced, the claimant's only way to challenge enforcement is by appeal from that order.   **31–034**

---

[55] *Barratt Manchester Ltd v Bolton Metropolitan Borough Council* [1998] 1 W.L.R. 1003, at 1009 and 1012, per Millett J (distinguishing *Birkett v James* [1978] A.C. 297), cited in *Societe Generale v Goldas* [2017] EWHC 667 (Comm).

[56] *Societe Generale v Goldas* [2017] EWHC 667 (Comm).

[57] The burden is not a very high one: in *Norwest Hoist Civil Engineering Ltd v Polysius Ltd*, unreported, 3 July 1987 CA, Sir John Donaldson MR said that if the respondent has suffered any loss or if there is "any real possibility" of his having done so, then there should be an inquiry.

[58] *Lunn Poly Ltd v Liverpool and Lancashire Properties Ltd* [2006] EWCA Civ 430; [2006] 2 E.G.L.R. 2, at [45], per Neuberger LJ.

[59] In *Norwest Hoist Civil Engineering Ltd v Polysius Ltd*, The Times, 23 July 1987; Court of Appeal (Civil Division) Transcript No. 644 of 1987 it was held that the court should not order an inquiry as to damages and at the same time leave open for the tribunal at the inquiry to determine whether or not the undertaking should be enforced.

[60] *Cheltenham & Gloucester v Ricketts* [1993] 1 W.L.R. 1545, at 1552.

[61] See for example *Balkanbank v Taher (No.3)* [1995] 2 All E.R. 904; [1995] 1 W.L.R. 1067, CA. As with trials split between liability and quantum, this question may be more complicated in practice than in theory.

31–035   When the court decides to enforce the cross-undertaking by ordering an inquiry it will usually give directions towards a trial of that inquiry. It may well order points of claim and defence and witness statements. In a complex case expert evidence might be permitted. So, in the *Fiona Trust v Privalov*[62] inquiry the court heard from seven expert witnesses.

31–036   If the inquiry is not then progressed expeditiously it may be dismissed. This is because enforcement of the cross-undertaking should be regarded as being conditional on the inquiry being applied for promptly and prosecuted with reasonable diligence.[63]

(2)   The Appropriate Measure of Damages

31–037   When conducting an inquiry under the cross-undertaking the court's purpose is to compensate the respondent to the wrongly granted order for losses sustained by him which were caused by that order and the consequent prohibitory effect on the respondent's freedom of action. The loss in issue will generally be that flowing from the fact that the order prevented the respondent for a period of time from doing things he would otherwise have been entitled to do and would have done. Confusingly, the remedy under what is traditionally described as a "cross-undertaking in damages" has been characterised as in fact by way of equitable compensation rather than common law damages.[64] This is because the jurisdiction being exercised by the court is an equitable one. As we have seen, the respondent's rights under the cross-undertaking are not in the nature of a cause of action for breach of a duty owed to the respondent. This is a significant point because, as we shall see, in awarding compensation in equity the courts, although guided by common law principles for the assessment of damages, are not bound by them. Nonetheless the courts generally refer to the monetary award in contemplation as "damages".[65]

31–038   As to the appropriate measure of such compensation (or damages), there has been a spate of recent case-law, the most significant decision being *Hone v Abbey Forwarding Plc*,[66] from which the following principles can be distilled:

(1)   The court's approach is compensatory, not punitive.[67] While the initial decision whether or not to enforce the undertaking is a discretionary one,

---

[62] *Fiona Trust v Privalov* [2016] EWHC 2163 (Comm).

[63] *Barratt Manchester Ltd v Bolton Metropolitan Borough Council* [1998] 1 W.L.R. 1003, at 1012.

[64] *Les Laboratoires Servier v Apotex Inc* [2008] EWHC 2347 (Ch); [2009] F.S.R. 3, at [7], per Norris J. In *Cheltenham & Gloucester v Ricketts* [1993] 1 W.L.R. 1545 Neill LJ said at 1550, that the "use of the word 'damages' is perhaps inappropriate because it might suggest that the grant of the injunction involved a breach of some legal or equitable rights of the defendant." In *Hone v Abbey Forwarding (In Liquidation)* [2014] EWCA Civ 711; [2015] Ch. 309 McCombe LJ at [63], took the view that neither the label of "damages" nor "equitable compensation" was useful.

[65] See for instance *SCF Tankers Ltd v Privalov* [2017] EWCA Civ 1877, at [1], per Beatson LJ (the appeal from the *Fiona Trust v Privalov* judgment at first instance mentioned above).

[66] *Hone v Abbey Forwarding Plc* [2014] EWCA Civ 711; [2015] Ch. 309.

[67] *Les Laboratoires Servier v Apotex Inc* [2008] EWC 2347; [2009] F.S.R. 3, at [5(b)], per Norris J.

the measure of the damages awarded if an inquiry is ordered is not, but is ascertained by reference to fixed principles.[68]

(2)   It is for the respondent to the order (and applicant on the inquiry—we will refer to that person as "the respondent") to plead, and prove, its loss.

(3)   Hence it is "for the party seeking to enforce the undertaking to show that the damage he has sustained would not have been sustained but for the injunction".[69] The order need not be the sole or exclusive cause of the loss in question, but must be an effective cause.[70] Care should be taken to distinguish loss caused by the fact of the litigation itself (which is not recoverable) and loss caused by the order.

(4)   However, once it has shown that he has suffered loss which was prima facie caused by the fact of the order, the burden will pass to the claimant to show that the relevant loss would have been suffered regardless.[71] The courts have frequently deprecated over-sophisticated causation arguments in this field and endorsed approaches informed by "common sense". What precisely this means is not easy to discern other than that the courts will approach the matter robustly and will not be impressed by technical refinements.

(5)   The courts have recently confirmed, applying *Hoffman La Roche v Secretary of State*,[72] that contractual principles apply by analogy to the assessment of the respondent's loss, but with logical and sensible adjustments to reflect the fact that a cross-undertaking is not in fact a contract.[73]

(6)   It follows that the scope of the undertaking, and of recoverable compensation thereunder, is determined by (a) its wording, properly construed, and (b) the usual contractual principles relating to causation, foreseeability and mitigation, although these will not necessarily be applied strictly or over-mechanically.

As regards point (a) a question may arise whether the loss claimed actually flows from the order. If, as is usual, the freezing order contains an "ordinary course of business" exception, it might well be said by the claimant that the loss claimed for relates to activity which would have been in the ordinary course of business and therefore was permitted all along.[74]

(7)   A respondent who is wrongly injuncted should be compensated for losses that he should not have suffered; but equally the claimant should not be saddled with losses that no reasonable person could have foreseen.[75]

---

[68] *F.Hoffmann-La Roche & Co AG v Secretary of State* [1975] A.C. 295, at 361.

[69] *Air Express Ltd v Ansett Transport Industries (Operations) Proprietary Ltd* (1979) 146 C.L.R. 249, at 325, per Mason J. This Australian judgment has proved influential in England: see *SCF Tankers Ltd v Privalov* [2017] EWCA Civ 1877, at [41], per Beatson LJ.

[70] *Fiona Trust v Privalov* [2016] EWHC 2163 (Comm) at [47], per Males J.

[71] *Financiera Avenida SA v Shiblaq, The Times*, 21 November 1988 (Saville J). This approach was endorsed in *SCF Tankers Ltd v Privalov* [2017] EWCA Civ 1877, at [43]–[46], per Beatson LJ.

[72] *Hoffman La Roche v Secretary of State* [1975] 1 A.C. 295.

[73] *Hone v Abbey Forwarding (In Liquidation)* [2014] EWCA Civ 711; [2015] Ch. 309, at [38]–[46] and [63], per McCombe LJ.

[74] See the argument as recorded by the judge in *Fiona Trust v Privalov* [2016] EWHC 2163 (Comm), at [82], per Males J, and how it was dealt with at [83]–[89].

[75] *Hone*, above, at [64].

Although contractual concepts of foreseeability are applicable by analogy there is a very significant difference in the approach on an inquiry under a cross-undertaking. Whereas in contract remoteness issues are determined by the state of the parties' knowledge at the date the contract is entered into, no such strict rule applies on an inquiry. If the claimant becomes aware at some point after the making of the injunction that it is preventing the respondent from undertaking some potentially profitable venture then he will not be able to insulate himself from liability by reference to his state of knowledge at the date of the order. Hence it is important for a respondent to keep the claimant informed as to the scope and nature of loss which he is likely to suffer as a result of the injunction, for example by informing the claimant of projects in which he would wish to invest but for the order.[76]

(8) It has been said that the court should adopt a "liberal assessment" of the respondent's loss.[77] This is not intended as a departure from the basic compensatory principle, but rather is intended to reflect that the assessment of loss suffered as a result of a freezing order is likely to be "inherently imprecise."[78] The fact that the respondent's evidence may be hedged with caveats (e.g. in relation to a speculative business venture) should not prevent a court from seeking to do its best to award compensation.

(9) But the court will make a deduction from the estimated profit on speculative investments to reflect the level of risk and the need to factor in potentially multiple contingencies, and when assessing damages over periods of market turmoil, evidence as to the timing of proposed investments is critical.[79]

(10) It may also be advisable to apply for a variation to the order to permit the intended investment or expenditure, so that it cannot later be said that the defendant did not seek to mitigate his loss. However courts are realistic about the difficulties in making variation applications and of the fact that claimants will usually be very resistant to them. Hence arguments after the event by claimants that the respondent should have avoided the claimed loss by returning to court during the currency of the proceedings to seek a relaxation of the order will be met with scepticism.[80]

(11) Damages can be awarded for loss of profits even if a claimant might have made a loss. The court has to ask whether the claimant has proved to a sufficient standard that its trading would have been profitable.[81]

---

[76] See *Hone*, above, at [67], and the analysis of Judge Pelling QC at first instance at [2012] EWHC 3525 (Ch), at [27]–[29]. Hence in that case the respondent did not bring to the claimant's attention business opportunities being lost during the currency of the injunction and this rendered them too remote.

[77] *AstraZeneca AB v KRKA dd Novo Mesto* [2015] EWCA 484. In that case the respondent was awarded in excess of £27million on the inquiry.

[78] *Fiona Trust & Holding Corp v Privalov* [2016] EWHC 2163 (Comm), at [50]–[51].

[79] *Fiona Trust & Holding Corp v Privalov* [2016] EWHC 2163 (Comm), at [50]–[51].

[80] *Hone v Abbey Forwarding (In Liquidation) & HMRC* [2014] EWCA Civ 711; [2015] Ch. 309, at [65]. See also *SCF Tankers Ltd v Privalov* [2017] EWCA Civ 1877, at [55]–[57], per Beatson LJ.

[81] *Fiona Trust*, above, at [55].

(12) The court will not refuse to award damages based on a proposed venture on the basis of illegality if all that is alleged is that it would involve a civil wrong, for example infringement of a patent.[82]

(13) An inappropriately granted freezing order can attract liability (by way of an award of general damages) under the cross-undertaking for upset, stress, loss of business opportunities, loss of reputation and other disruption including adverse effects of the inappropriate policing of the injunction on the injunctees.[83] What is clear is that where a claimant wrongly obtains a freezing order and then vigorously and aggressively polices it the courts will be astute to provide compensation. They recognise the real disruption and distress that freezing orders and search orders can inflict on respondents. However, such damage needs to be shown to be caused by the injunction itself, as opposed to the stigma of the underlying claim in fraud.

(14) In principle a claim for lost management time may be advanced.[84]

(3) The Order

When the court decides that damages are payable on a cross-undertaking, it will make an order to that effect, with, potentially, interest under the Senior Courts Act 1981. The award is then enforceable in the same way as any judgment sum. The respondent is also entitled to claim as damages any legal costs (other than the costs of the proceedings themselves) which have been incurred as a result of the order, for example those of parallel criminal proceedings or related proceedings in foreign courts. Such costs will usually be assessed on the standard basis unless the undertaking, exceptionally, contains a specific indemnity in relation to them (in which case the basis for assessment will depend upon a proper construction of the indemnity). If the inquiry takes place at the same time as the trial and the claim is successful, the judgment sum will be set off against the sum payable under the cross undertaking and an order made for payment of the balance. If the inquiry is to take place after trial, enforcement of the judgment may be stayed pending the inquiry.

31–039

E. ORDERS RESTRICTING MOVEMENT

Claimants in fraud proceedings may seek orders of this type if they fear that the defendant will flee the jurisdiction to avoid complying with other orders that have been made against him (typically freezing or proprietary injunctions and disclosure orders).

31–040

---

[82] *Les Laboratoires Servier v Apotex Inc* [2014] UKSC 55; [2015] 1 A.C. 430.

[83] *Hone*, above, at [104]–[110] and [150]. At [109] McCombe LJ said: "In my judgment, it is obvious that a freezing order of the type imposed in this case constitutes a severe invasion upon the liberty of any person to deal with his or her assets as he or she sees fit. An intrusion upon that liberty is bound to have profound effect upon the day to day life of the person affected in a multitude of ways which do not require elucidation by evidence of special damage." The measure of damages in fact awarded in that case was relatively small: £15,000 per respondent.

[84] See generally *Al-Rawas v Pegasus Energy Ltd* [2008] EWHC 617 (QB); [2009] 1 All E.R. 346.

(1)   Writ Ne Exeat Regno

31–041   A *writ ne exeat regno* is an ancient writ to restrain a person from going out of the country without the permission of the Court. "Ne exeat regno" literally means "let him not go out of the kingdom".[85] If issued the defendant is only permitted to leave the country against security in a prescribed amount being given. The usual wording of the writ prescribes that unless the defendant pays a specified sum then he shall be arrested and taken to prison.

31–042   After a long period of desuetude,[86] the abolition of the *writ ne exeat regno* was recommended in 1969.[87] However the recommendation was not acted upon and the writ had a brief resurgence in the mid-1980s when its continuing existence and potential (although narrow) utility was confirmed. So, in *Al Nahkel Trading Ltd v Lowe*,[88] a case where an employee had allegedly stolen sums of money from his employer, such a writ was issued, along with a *Mareva* injunction, in the form of an order to the tipstaff, "all constables and other peace officers" to arrest the defendant if he should attempt to leave the UK without giving security for £14,000.[89] The defendant was arrested by Special Branch the following day on board an aeroplane about to leave London for the Philippines.[90] The judge's judgment is short and concluded with these words:

> "In my judgment this ancient remedy, or 'tool of the law' as Megarry J called it, is available in support of the modern *Mareva* injunction to prevent a defendant fleeing the jurisdiction with assets in order to frustrate a lawful claim before the court."[91]

31–043   However, as we will see, this dictum has been doubted and the writ has very limited application in fraud claims. It is more a historic curiosity than an integral part of the fraud litigator's armoury.

31–044   The four conditions[92] of such an order being made in modern times were identified by Megarry J in *Felton v Callis*[93] as follows:

---

[85] For the historically minded, the origin and history of the writ can be traced in J. Beames, *A Brief View of the Writ Ne Exeat Regno* (London, 1812).

[86] In *Felton v Callis* [1969] 1 Ch. 200 Megarry J noted at 204, that the last reported instance of the writ having been issued was in 1893 in *Lewis v Lewis* 68 LT 198. It seems that thereafter the first successful application for a writ was in 1985.

[87] By the Payne Committee in the Report on the Enforcement of Judgment Debts (Cmnd 3909), paras 1245–1260.

[88] *Al Nahkel Trading Ltd v Lowe* [1986] Q.B. 235, at 238–239, per Tudor-Price J.

[89] The judge in that case discussed the appropriate form of order at 239.

[90] The judgment of Tudor Price J in that case refers to two cases earlier in 1985 in which such writs were ordered: *Lipkin Gorman v Cass*, The Times, 29 May 1985 (Harman J); and *Yiu Wing Construction Co v Ghosh*, unreported, 21 February 1985.

[91] *Al Nahkel Trading Ltd v Lowe* [1986] Q.B. 235, at 239–240.

[92] These conditions derive from s.6 of the Debtors Act 1869, which provides a power of arrest and imprisonment unless security is put up; equity proceeds by analogy.

[93] *Felton v Callis* [1969] 1 Q.B. 200, at 211. See also *Drover v Beyer* (1879) 13 Ch.D. 242. It was suggested by Leggatt J in *Allied Arab Bank v Hajjar* [1988] Q.B. 787, at 793, that the claim has also to be for a debt certain, i.e a fixed sum of money. If this is right, which seems questionable, it would further restrict the ambit of the writ.

(1) The action is one in which the defendant would formerly have been liable to arrest at law (i.e. prior to the passing of the Debtors Act 1869).[94]

(2) A good cause of action for at least £50 is established. However the writ only applies to cases within the exclusive jurisdiction of equity and so it only applies to equitable debts and claims.[95] Hence it does not apply to claims at law.

(3) There is "probable cause" for believing that the defendant is "about to quit England" unless he is arrested. The evidence of impending departure need not point to a permanent removal. A prolonged if not permanent absence will suffice.[96]

(4) The absence of the defendant from England will materially prejudice the claimant in the prosecution of his action. Indeed the writ cannot be applied for after final judgment. It is not in aid of execution, which of course is the very phase of litigation where a claimant will often be most assisted by some form of coercive order preventing the defendant absconding abroad. This feature deprives the writ of much of its potential utility.

Even if those four conditions are met Megarry J went on to emphasise two further hurdles to be crossed: the issue of the writ is discretionary and the standard of proof is high: "The court must be convinced."[97] As the judge went on to say, the writ was "closely circumscribed in its applicability."   **31–045**

It follows from the fourth condition identified above that, contrary to the suggestion in *Al Nahkel Trading Ltd v Lowe*,[98] a *writ ne exeat regno* may not be ordered for the purpose of enforcing a freezing order, as the "prosecution of the action" does not extend to policing a freezing injunction, which is granted in aid of future execution. So in *Allied Arab Bank Ltd v Hajjar*[99] a claimant obtained a *writ ne exeat regno* the purpose of which was to ensure that a defendant properly complied with disclosure obligations contained in a freezing order which was granted simultaneously. The writ was discharged on the defendant's application because this purpose was not connected to the "prosecution of the action." In contrast, Megarry J in *Felton v Challis* had identified potentially valid reasons for seeking a writ: that the claimant requires disclosure from the defendant in relation to the claim or wishes to serve interrogatories (now a request for further information) upon him. A *writ ne exeat regno* may also be appropriate to enforce a proprietary injunction where that is part of the prosecution of the action—i.e to obtain a form of disclosure so as ascertain the location of assets to which the claimant lays claim.[100] However, the *Bayer v Winter* order considered below is likely to be more appropriate in any event. In fraud litigation it is very common to apply for such orders.   **31–046**

---

[94] See "The said Defendant will not go into parts beyond the seas ..." by Charles Harpum, [1986] CLJ 189.

[95] *Felton v Callis*, at 216.

[96] *Felton v Callis*, at 217.

[97] *Felton v Callis*, at 211.

[98] *Al Nahkel Trading Ltd v Lowe* [1986] Q.B. 235, at 238–239.

[99] *Allied Arab Bank Ltd v Hajjar* [1988] Q.B. 787.

[100] *Allied Arab Bank v Hajjar* [1988] 1 Q.B. 787, at 793, per Leggatt J.

(2) Bayer v Winter Order

(i) The jurisdiction

31–047 Soon after the (very limited) revival of the *writ ne exeat regno* described above, the significance of the writ was once again diminished by what one commentator described at the time as

> "an altogether more fashionable procedure, designed to do all the work of the writ of ne exeat regno but without the shackles of compliance with section 6 of the Debtors Act".[101]

This is the so-called *Bayer v Winter*[102] order—an order restraining the respondent from leaving the jurisdiction until after a specified period or further order in the meantime, coupled with an order that the respondent delivers up his passport(s).[103] In more recent cases, such orders have come to be referred to as "passport orders", although strictly speaking the obligation to deliver up passports is ancillary to the order preventing the respondent leaving the jurisdiction.[104] When making such orders courts are sensitive to the curtailment on the respondent's liberty that they necessarily involve and have shown themselves to be anxious to ensure that they are of as short a duration as possible.[105]

31–048 The Court's jurisdiction to make such an order is found in s.37(1) of the Senior Courts Act 1981, which provides:

> "The High Court may by order (whether interlocutory or final) grant an injunction or appoint a receiver in all cases in which it appears to the court to be just and convenient to do so."

As such the jurisdiction to make such an order is not constrained by any of the seemingly anomalous circumscriptions which render the *writ ne exeat regno* of negligible utility in the modern era. The width of the jurisdiction was stated in resounding terms in *Bayer v Winter* itself:

> "Bearing in mind we are exercising a jurisdiction which is statutory, and is expressed in terms of considerable width, it seems to me that the court should not shrink, if it is of opinion that an

---

[101] "Antiquity in Action – Ne Exeat Regno Revived" by Lesley J. Anderson, (1987) L.Q.R. 246.

[102] *Bayer v Winter* [1986] 1 W.L.R. 497.

[103] The order made in *Bayer v Winter* itself was as follows: "(1) That the first defendant be restrained from leaving England and Wales until two days after service of this order or further order in the meantime. (2) That the first defendant do forthwith deliver up his passports to the person who shall serve this order upon him: provided that the plaintiffs' solicitors must return them to him upon the expiry of the time referred to in the preceding paragraph of the order."

[104] *JSC Mezhdunarodny Promyshlenniy Bank v Pugachev* [2015] EWHC 1586 (Ch), at [29], per Hildyard J.

[105] Hence in *Bayer v Winter* [1986] 1 W.L.R. 497 Fox LJ said "The time during which the [order] should run should…be of very limited duration. It is an interference with the liberty of the subject, so that the period should be no longer than is necessary to enable the plaintiffs to serve the *Mareva* and the *Anton Piller* orders which they have obtained, and endeavour to obtain from the defendant the information which is referred to in those orders."

injunction is necessary for the proper protection of a party to the action, from granting relief, notwithstanding it may, in its terms, be of a novel character."[106]

(ii)   Before judgment

The typical scenario in which such a passport order is made is where it appears   **31–049**
that there is a risk that the applicant for a freezing order (or search order) will not obtain the information ordered to be disclosed by that order unless a passport order is made.[107] The fear is that the respondent, served with the order, will abscond abroad so that, for instance, it will be impossible to enforce the information disclosure provisions which are usually integral to the satisfactory operation of a freezing order. Similarly a passport order might be sought in circumstances where an application to cross-examine on the affidavit of assets has been issued and the concern is to ensure that the respondent does not leave the jurisdiction in advance.[108] Hence, in recent cases, passport orders have been made where the evidence suggest that there was a significant risk of flight as a means of avoiding fully disclosing the extent and location of the respondent's assets.[109]

The jurisdiction whether or not to grant a passport order is ultimately a   **31–050**
discretionary one, involving the balancing of two important competing considerations:

> "on the one side of the argument ... the very powerful submission that the court should not act in vain and should do whatever is necessary to support its orders to ensure that they are not futile...On the other hand ... the powerful argument that an aspect of the liberty of the respondent is concerned."[110]

However there are certain principles which the courts have propounded which   **31–051**
will inform the exercise of that discretion. In the recent case of *Corbiere Ltd v Xu*[111] Zacaroli J summarised these as follows (with reference to the decision in *Bayer v Winter* itself):

> "(1)   First, it is necessary to consider the harm that would be done to the defendant in making the order;

---

[106] *Bayer v Winter* [1986] 1 W.L.R. 497, at 502–503.
[107] *Bayer v Winter* [1986] 1 W.L.R. 497, at 502, per Fox LJ.
[108] See for instance *JSC Mezhdunarodny Promyshlenniy Bank v Pugachev* [2015] EWHC 1586 (Ch), at [10], per Hildyard J.
[109] See *JSC Mezhdunarodny Promyshlenniy Bank v Pugachev* [2015] EWCA Civ 1108, at [12], per Floyd LJ describing the without notice passport order made in that case. So in *JSC BTA Bank v Ablyazov* [2009] EWHC 2840 (Comm) Teare J said as follows at [68]: "The Freezing Order required the First to Third Defendants to ensure that their passports are held by Clyde and Co. until further order. The justification for this order is that it is necessary to ensure that the Defendants provided the required information as to assets and did not leave the country before doing so. It is a restriction on their liberty and therefore should be no longer than is strictly necessary for that purpose; see *Bayer v Winter* [1986] 1 W.L.R. 497, at 503. The cross-examination of the First Defendant as to his assets is not yet complete. It seems to me that the application to permit the return of his passport is premature pending the completion of his cross-examination."
[110] *Kuwait Airways Corp v Iraq Airways Co* [2010] EWCA Civ 741.
[111] *Corbiere Ltd v Xu* [2018] EWHC 112 (Ch) at [34].

(2)   Second, it is necessary to consider the harm to the Claimants if no order is made. In *Bayer v Winter* itself, where the order was sought in aid of an order for disclosure, Fox LJ noted that if the defendant left the United Kingdom, then the plaintiffs were at risk that they would be unable to obtain the information, noting that while within the jurisdiction the defendant could be compelled to attend for cross-examination;

(3)   Third, the essential question is whether the order was reasonable and necessary, ancillary to the due performance of the court's functions;

(4)   Fourth, recognising that the order interferes with individual liberty, it should be for a period of time that was no longer than necessary enable the plaintiffs to serve the orders to which the restraining order was ancillary, and to endeavour to obtain from the defendant the information referred to in those orders;

(5)   Fifth, Fox LJ noted that the court had both the power, and the duty—where an order such as an order for disclosure had been made—to take such steps 'as will enable the order to have effect as completely and successfully as the powers of the court can procure.' "

31–052   Usually such an order will, for the reasons identified in the preceding paragraph, be limited to the period necessary to procure compliance with the order to which it is ancillary.[112] However, the court can make an order preventing a respondent from leaving the jurisdiction until after trial. In such a case it has been said that the following principles apply[113]:

(1)   The power to restrict departure from the jurisdiction and impound a passport exists in principle in aid of all the court's procedures leading to the disposal of the proceedings.

(2)   But it involves a restriction of a subject's liberty and so should be exercised with caution. The authorities emphasise the short-term nature of the restraint. The law favours liberty.

(3)   A good cause of action for a substantive award must be established.

(4)   The applicant must establish that there is probable cause for believing that the respondent is about to quit the jurisdiction unless he is restrained.

(5)   The applicant must further establish that the absence of the respondent from the jurisdiction will materially prejudice him in the prosecution of his action.

(6)   Provided that the principles above are carefully observed, a passport impounding order will represent a proportionate public policy based restraint on freedom of movement founded on the personal conduct of the respondent.

---

[112] Hence in *Lexi Holdings v Luqman* [2008] EWHC 2908 (Ch) Peter Smith J said at [13]: "The order has to be of a limited duration. That I accept. That does not however in my view mean a set time. It means as short a period as possible so as to enable the orders to which is ancillary to be enforced or executed. The orders do not lapse nor does Mr Luqman has a right to return of the passports after a set time if the orders are still required for the purposes of enforcement for example and for the purposes for which they were obtained."

[113] See *Young v Young* [2012] EWHC 138 (Fam); [2012] Fam 198, per Mostyn J. This decision was a matrimonial one but it was endorsed and further explained by the Court of Appeal in *JSC Mezhdunarodny Promyshlenniy Bank v Pugachev* [2015] EWCA Civ 1108, at [37]–[45]. Whilst the making of an order until after trial would be exceptional, one can discern a trend in the recent authorities towards a greater willingness to maintain the restraint in force pending full compliance by the respondent with his disclosure obligations: so, in the *Corbiere* case, above, the application for the restraint until after trial was rejected, but that for the more limited restriction was granted.

As to the fourth of the above points, showing "probable cause for believing" that **31–053** the respondent is about to quit the jurisdiction does not equate to establishing that it is more probable than not that he will. Instead, there must (as a minimum) be evidence from which it can be reasonably inferred that the respondent will leave the jurisdiction and not return.[114]

A typical form of passport order may read as follows: **31–054**

> "(1) If the defendant is at any time present in the jurisdiction, he shall be restrained from leaving England and Wales until further order of the court.
> (2) The defendant and any other person served with this order must not
> > (i) make any application for
> > (ii) obtain or seek to obtain and/or
> > (iii) knowingly cause, permit, encourage or support any steps being taken to apply for or obtain any passport, identity card, ticket, travel warrant or other document which would enable the defendant to leave England and Wales.
> (3) Forthwith upon service of this Order on him, the defendant must identify and inform the claimant's solicitors of the whereabouts of all his passports including:
> > (a) ...
> > (b) ...
> > and, as soon as practicable, he must deliver all his passports up, or cause them to be delivered up, to the claimant's solicitors who shall hold them in safe custody pending compliance by the defendant with the provisions of paragraphs [...] of this Order or any further order of the Court."

The order will usually contain a mechanism for its cessation upon the respondent **31–055** having provided the relevant information and/or documents.[115] However if the disclosure provided is inadequate then the order can be extended. In order for such orders to be effective, it is important to identify how many passports the respondent has; otherwise, a respondent may surrender one passport but keep another which he might use to leave the jurisdiction.[116]

Attempts should also be made to notify the Passport Office of the existence of the **31–056** order; in the proceedings brought by HSBC Bank against Michael Brown[117] the defendant surrendered his British passport but successfully applied for another one, stating on the passport application that his existing passport had been destroyed in the wash, and then fled the jurisdiction.

(iii) After judgment

The jurisdiction to make such an order continues post-judgment. However a **31–057** passport order will not be granted as a means of coercing a judgment debtor to pay the judgment sum. It is not an enforcement procedure in its own right. So no order will be made whereby the debtor is prevented from leaving the jurisdiction until he has paid the judgment debt.[118] However, post-judgment such an order may be made to aid the court's existing procedures for enforcement of the

---

[114] *JSC Mezhdunarodny Promyshlenniy Bank v Pugachev* [2015] EWCA Civ 1108, at [45].
[115] Save, of course, in the unusual case where it is made until after trial.
[116] See for example *JSC Mezhdunarodny Promyshlenniy Bank v Pugachev* [2015] EWCA Civ 1108 (Mr Pugachev initially produced only a Russian diplomatic passport and not his French passport).
[117] Subsequent proceedings are reported at [2009] EWCA Civ 296.
[118] *B v B* [1998] 1 W.L.R. 329.

judgment.[119] So, where an application is made under CPR 71 for an examination of a debtor a passport order may be made to ensure that the debtor attends the examination and provides any documentary disclosure ordered.[120] Such an order was made against the director of a judgment debtor who happened to be within the jurisdiction in *Kuwait Airways Corp v Iraq Airways Co*.[121]

(3) Bench Warrant

31–058 The court has an inherent jurisdiction to issue a bench warrant for the arrest of a person who has failed to comply with a passport order made in support of a freezing injunction: *Zakharov v White*.[122] In that case, Roderick Evans J relied on the Court of Appeal's decision in *Re B*[123], in which Hobhouse LJ said[124]:

> "The power of arrest exercised in wardship cases is a power in aid of the civil process. Ex hypothesi, it is not punitive because no contempt of court has been permitted. The power to order the arrest of a person so that he may be brought before the court is a well-established part of the jurisdiction in wardship and is available in other aspects of civil procedure should, exceptionally, the necessity arise."

F. APPLICATIONS TO CROSS-EXAMINE ON AFFIDAVIT OF ASSETS

(1) Introduction

31–059 As we have seen,[125] freezing and proprietary injunctions will almost always impose asset disclosure obligations on defendants, who are often far from forthcoming in their compliance with such orders. When faced with a sketchy or inadequate affidavit of assets, what can the claimant do in order to press for better information? In the first instance the court might order the defendant to produce a further affidavit clarifying any obscurities or addressing issues that remained un-explicated, or answer written questions posed by the claimant.[126] Alternatively, or if doubts still remain even after the provision of a further affidavit or answers to such questions, the court has jurisdiction to order the cross-examination of the defendant as to his assets.

---

[119] *B v B* [1998] 1 W.L.R. 329. Quoted with approval by Peter Smith J in *Lexi Holdings v Luqman* [2008] EWHC 2908 (Ch) at [12]. The judge there contemplated the making of an order pending the hearing of committal proceedings.

[120] *B v B* [1998] 1 W.L.R. 329, at 334, interpreting *Thaha v Thaha* [1987] 2 F.L.R. 142.

[121] *Kuwait Airways Corp v Iraq Airways Co* [2010] EWCA Civ 741.

[122] *Zakharov v White* [2003] All E.R. (D) 453.

[123] *Re B* [1994] 2 F.L.R. 479.

[124] *Re B*, at 486.

[125] Ch.28, Section D.

[126] See for instance the course that was taken in *Jenington International Inc v Assaubayev* [2010] EWHC 2351 (Ch), mentioned at [32]. The court has been swayed in deciding to grant an order by the submission that a time comes when it is more efficient to permit cross-examination in order to enable a claimant to pin-point the defendant's assets and their location rather than order more and more affidavits or "for letters to continue to pass between the solicitors with explanations which give rise to yet further questions raised in yet further correspondence": *Otkritie International Investment Management Ltd v Urumov* [2012] EWHC 3106 (Comm), per Field J at [33].

(2) Principles upon which Court Acts

It has for a number of years been recognised by the courts that, exceptionally, a **31–060** claimant can apply for an order, in aid of a freezing or proprietary order, permitting him to cross-examine the defendant about his assets, in order to obtain further information about them so that they can be found and preserved.[127] The jurisdiction so to order is to be found in s.37 of the Senior Courts Act 1981, the same jurisdictional foundation for the ordering of written asset disclosure which is now of course an integral part of the standard form of freezing order.[128] The application is usually (but not necessarily) made after the defendant has been ordered to produce, and has produced, an affidavit as to his assets (sometimes known as an "affidavit of means"). Usually the basis for such an order is that there is some reason to believe that the disclosure in the affidavit is incomplete or misleading.[129]

The proper use of the jurisdiction is to obtain information about the defendant's **31–061** assets so that they can be located and preserved with the ultimate purpose of making the freezing order effective.[130] It is not permissible to use the jurisdiction to obtain information to support a committal application, and the privilege against self-incrimination will apply in relation to contempt of court.[131] There is no requirement that the questioning is relevant to the resolution of particular issues between the parties[132]; indeed it is not permissible to use it to obtain information in support of the applicant's case at trial.[133] It is permissible to ask questions relating to the preservation of assets which also go to the underlying merits of the claim,[134] but where there is a risk that that is the case the court can be asked to require the claimant to undertake not to use the answers to his questions in support of his substantive case in the action.

In order to obtain an order for cross-examination, the burden is on the claimant to **31–062** show that there is a real prospect that he will by virtue of the cross-examination find out about assets so that they can be located and preserved. If he already knows about assets sufficient to satisfy a judgment on the claim the court will not usually order cross-examination to allow him to find out about more. The court can do so in an appropriate case[135] but, it has been said, will "hardly ever" do so.[136] In fact the courts have rather relaxed their position on this in recent years. They have regard to the ease of enforcement against disclosed assets and the firmness of the value ascribed to them; the less enforceable and the less certain

---

[127] *Yukong Line Ltd v Rendsburg Investments Corp, The Times,* 22 October 1996.

[128] *Jenington International Inc v Assaubayev* [2010] EWHC 2351 (Ch), at [13], per Vos J.

[129] See for example *Motorola Credit Corp v Uzan* [2004] 1 W.L.R. 113, at [147], per Potter LJ; *JSC BTA Bank v Solodchenko v Ereschenko* [2011] EWHC 843 (Ch), at [50], per Henderson J.

[130] *Great Future International Ltd v Sealand Housing Corp,* unreported, 22 March 2001, per Neuberger J. *Motorola Credit Corp v Uzan* [2004] 1 W.L.R. 113, at [145].

[131] *Bayer v Winter (No.2)* [1986] 1 W.L.R. 540.

[132] See *House of Spring Gardens Ltd v Waite* [1985] F.S.R. 173.

[133] *Jenington International Inc v Assaubayev* [2010] EWHC 2351 (Ch), at [74].

[134] *Yukong,* above.

[135] *Motorola Credit Corp v Uzan* [2004] 1 W.L.R. 113, at [145]; *Assaubayev* (see above).

[136] *Great Future International Ltd v Sealand Housing Corp,* unreported, 22 March 2001, per Neuberger J.

the value, the more willing they will be to permit cross-examination even after assets apparently in excess of the claimed amount have been disclosed.[137]

31–063 The power to order cross-examination is discretionary. The following general principles can be distilled from the case-law:

(1) It must be just and convenient to make an order. In *Yukong* the Court of Appeal declined to impose further parameters upon the jurisdiction,[138] although a number of other considerations have emerged, as discussed below. Nonetheless there are "no hard and fast rules."[139]

(2) Exercise of the power is very much the exception rather than the rule and the courts will have regard to the fact that it is a very considerable imposition to subject a defendant to cross-examination and consider carefully whether there are not alternative means of achieving the same end that are less burdensome.[140]

(3) The court may decide to order in the first instance further affidavits, but reasons of speed and urgency may lead to the conclusion that "in order to fill the vacuum alleged to exist in the affidavits filed pursuant to the original order" the court should proceed straight to a cross-examination.[141] The decision how to proceed will be influenced by the particular facts of the case: one consideration may be whether there is a real risk that the freezing order will be thwarted by delay.

(4) It is not necessary first to show that there is no alternative available remedy.[142]

(5) The court must be astute to guard against abuse of the freezing order process by claimants who are using it in an attempt to discover facts that will assist them in the action or to oppress the defendant, for instance where there has been an avalanche of correspondence and endless demands for further particularisation of assets, and where cross-examination is a continuation of this modus operandi. The fact that cross-examination on an affidavit of means will relate to matters which are relevant to substantive issues in the case is a matter to which the court should have regard when considering whether to permit the process.[143] The order must be proportionate and just, and must not be obtained for any ulterior purpose.[144]

---

[137] See *Jenington International Inc v Assaubayev* [2010] EWHC 2351 (Ch), at [65(8)]. In *JSC Mezhdunarodniy Promyshlenniy Bank v Pugachev (No.2)* [2015] EWHC 1694 (Ch); [2016] 1 W.L.R. 781 Hildyard said at [6]: "The purpose of the process of cross-examination to assist in the policing of a freezing order is to clarify issues arising in relation to asset disclosure; it is essentially to enable investigation and clarification of the disclosure given, and of issues to which that disclosure gives rise, rather than to enable adjudication of points of disputed fact. The role of the court is primarily supervisory rather than adjudicatory, so that it would not usually be necessary for the court to delve into the evidence which emerges."

[138] See the passage from the judgment of Phillips LJ in *Yukong* quoted in *Assaubayev*, at [18].

[139] *Motorola Credit Corp v Uzan (No.2)* [2004] 1 W.L.R. 113, at [145].

[140] *Assaubayev* [2010] EWHC 2351 (Ch), at [18].

[141] *House of Spring Gardens Ltd v Waite* [1985] F.S.R. 173, at 183.

[142] *Assaubayev* [2010] EWHC 2351 (Ch), at [18].

[143] *Assaubayev* [2010] EWHC 2351 (Ch), at [18].

[144] *Assaubayev* [2010] EWHC 2351 (Ch), at [22(4)].

However, as discussed in the next section, there are safeguards which can be imposed to protect a defendant against the risk of abuse.

(6)   It will normally be ordered only where it will further the proper purpose of the freezing order by, for example, revealing further assets that might otherwise be dissipated so as to prevent an eventual judgment against the defendants going unsatisfied.[145]

(7)   Cross-examination will not normally be ordered unless there are significant or serious deficiencies in the existing disclosure.[146]

(8)   The court should not entertain a mini-trial, for example on issues as to disputed ownership of assets, as those sorts of issues can be resolved in the enforcement proceedings themselves[147]—cross-examination should therefore be restricted to relevant points only.

(9)   Although the matter has not been explored in detail in the authorities it seems likely the court will be more willing to order cross-examination in proprietary claims. In such cases the claimant is seeking to identify what he claims to be his assets.

In practice the claimant's application should analyse with as much exactitude as possible how the asset disclosure has been defective and identify with precision the areas which it wishes to cross-examine on.[148] In that way it can minimize the strength of any contention by the defendant that its application is oppressive and involves a proposed "roving cross-examination."[149] The court may well by its order restrict cross-examination to defined subjects, which may be narrower than the ones the claimant is contending for.[150] Such a narrowing may be justified because too wide a cross-examination may be oppressive or because the court takes the view that the disclosure in respect of certain areas has been adequate. What the court should not do is simply order a general cross-examination which does not delimit and identify the subject matter of such examination.   **31–064**

(3)   Conduct of the Cross-Examination

Practice Direction 2B clarifies[151] that unless the Judge (meaning, presumably, the Judge who makes an order requiring the defendant to be cross-examined on his affidavit of assets) directs otherwise, the cross-examination will take place before a Master or a District Judge, or if the Master or District Judge directs, before a court examiner. However, in practice such cross-examinations generally take place only in large value claims and before High Court Judges, or deputies, who have familiarity with the underlying claim. This will often be justified because of   **31–065**

---

[145] *Assaubayev* [2010] EWHC 2351 (Ch), at [22(3)].

[146] *Assaubayev* [2010] EWHC 2351 (Ch), at [22(4)].

[147] *Assaubayev* [2010] EWHC 2351 (Ch), at [61].

[148] See e.g. the claimant's proposed order described in *Assaubayev*, at [31].

[149] The phrase comes from the unreported judgment of Peter Gibson J in *RAC Ltd v Allsop* quoted in *Assaubayev*, at [16]: "'it cannot be right to allow a plaintiff the opportunity of a roving cross-examination merely because the plaintiffs harbour suspicion that the person sought to be made the subject of the order has not been entirely open in his disclosure.'"

[150] E.g. see *Assaubayev*, at [65].

[151] At para.7.

the need to ensure that cross–examination is confined to the only purpose which justifies such an order, viz. the identification of assets and does not stray beyond it.[152] When such cross-examination takes place it is entirely a matter for the judge presiding on the cross-examination properly to control it.[153] For instance, the court might set a time-limit to such cross-examination.[154] The recent cross-examination in the *Pugachev* litigation extended over 5 days before Hildyard J.[155]

31–066   Under CPR r.34.12 the transcript of the cross-examination, and documents obtained in the course of it,[156] can only be used for the purposes of the proceedings in which the order was made (i.e. in relation solely to the enforcement of the freezing order),[157] except that it can be used for any other purpose by the cross-examining party if the party being examined agrees or if the court gives permission. The term "deposition" in CPR r.34.12 includes oral answers given, the transcript, and any other record including Counsel's or solicitors' notes, a tape recording of the proceedings, and any documents produced by the defendant at the cross-examination.

(4)   Costs of the Cross-Examination

31–067   It does not follow from the fact that the court has considered it appropriate to order cross-examination of the respondent that the respondent will be ordered to pay the costs of the examination. Rather, whether an order costs is made against the respondent will depend on such factors as whether:

(1)   the cross-examination has elicited explanations or clarifications which are necessary for the purposes of proper disclosure and which should previously have been given in some other way;

(2)   the respondent was co-operative or evasive;

---

[152] Hence in *Assaubayev*, Vos J said at [74]: "Under all heads, the cross-examination that is to be allowed must be clearly focused on identifying assets belonging to the defendants against which the worldwide freezing order should bite. No ancillary cross-examination affecting the merits of the claim will be permitted. That is not the purpose of what is being allowed. I will be astute to ensure that the cross-examination does not become excessive or oppressive or counterproductive and that the claimants do not obtain a collateral advantage in the substantive litigation by being allowed to pursue the disclosure process to this exceptional next stage."

[153] *House of Spring Gardens Ltd v Waite* [1985] F.S.R. 173, at 183.

[154] *Otkritie International Investment Management Ltd v Urumov* [2012] EWHC 3106 (Comm), per Field J at [34]. The judge went on to say: "The cross-examination will be supervised by a judge of the commercial court and the defendants will be entitled to be represented. I am accordingly confident that the cross-examination will serve the purpose of endeavouring to give effect to the disclosure orders and will not become a roving, one-sided and unfair exercise"

[155] *JSC Mezhdunarodniy Promyshlenniy Bank v Pugachev (No.2)* [2015] EWHC 1694 (Ch); [2016] 1 W.L.R. 781, at [18].

[156] If obtained under compulsion of an order. If they are voluntarily produced they are more likely to be covered by CPR r.31.22. As to the applicability of CPR r.34.12, which appears on its face to be concerned with depositions, in this context, see *British Sky Broadcasting Group Plc v Digital Satellite Warranty Cover Ltd* [2012] 1 W.L.R. 219, per Robin Knowles Q.C. at [12].

[157] They cannot, without the permission of the court, even be used for contempt proceedings in the same action: see *British Sky Broadcasting Group Plc*, above at [11]. However it is not necessary to establish exceptional circumstances in order to obtain the permission of the court for such use: see *Dadourian Group International Inc v Simms (No. 2)* [2006] EWCA Civ 1745; [2007] 1 W.L.R. 2967.

(3) the cross-examination was proportionate and properly directed to the objective of enabling a better understanding of assets falling within the ambit of the freezing order; and

(4) the cross-examination proved profitable in terms of fuller disclosure and enabling enforcement of the freezing injunctions. The general rule is that any costs should be awarded on the standard basis, unless the court is persuaded that the respondent did not engage in good faith with the process of cross-examination, not merely being evasive but actually intending to obstruct justice.[158]

G. ORDERS (OTHER THAN FOR ASSET DISCLOSURE) ANCILLARY TO FREEZING INJUNCTIONS

As already alluded to in Ch.26, the court has a broad power, under s.37(1) of the Senior Courts Act 1981, to make orders ancillary to freezing orders in order to ensure that such orders are effective. As it was put in *Maclaine Watson & Co Ltd v International Tin Council (No.2)*[159]

31–068

> "there is an inherent power under what is now section 37(1) to make any ancillary order, including an order for discovery, to ensure the effectiveness of any other order made by the court."

The most common ancillary orders relate to disclosure of assets, which we have considered in Ch.28. In this section we consider the court's jurisdiction to make a range of other useful, but lesser-known, orders which may well be of significance in fraud claims.

(1) Orders Against Solicitors for Disclosure/Information

Traditionally, the courts have, even in cases where fraud is alleged, refused on grounds of privilege and confidentiality to make any order for disclosure against solicitors of correspondence with, or information relating to, their clients, save in exceptional circumstances where there is a prima facie case that the solicitors have been consulted in furtherance of a fraudulent purpose.[160]

31–069

However, the courts have—exceptionally—been willing in cases of fraud[161] or in support of a confiscation order,[162] or where the defendant was already the subject of a committal order,[163] to order disclosure against a solicitor of a client's identity

31–070

---

[158] *JSC Mezhdunarodniy Promyshlenniy Bank v Pugachev (No.2)* [2015] EWHC 1694 (Ch); [2016] 1 W.L.R. 781.

[159] *Maclaine Watson & Co Ltd v International Tin Council (No.2)* [1989] Ch. 286, at 303, per Kerr LJ.

[160] See generally Ch.6 of W. Flenley and T. Leech, *Solicitors' Negligence and Liability*, 3rd edn (London: Bloomsbury Professional, 2012).

[161] *International Credit and Investment Co (Overseas) v Adham, The Times*, 10 February 1997, per Harman J.

[162] *R (On the Application of the Revenue and Customs Commissioners) v W* [2008] EWHC 2780.

[163] *JSC BTA Bank v Solodchenko* [2011] EWHC 2163; [2013] Ch. 1, per Henderson J.

or contact details. In *JSC BTA Bank v Solodchenko*[164] a defendant was the subject of a freezing order. He did not comply with the disclosure obligations contained in that order and failed to engage other than sporadically in the litigation. A committal order was subsequently made against him for his contempt. The claimant sought from the defendant's solicitors his contact details with a view to locating him. The judge (Henderson J) referred to the public interest in free and unfettered access to legal advice, stating that it applied with just as much force to the defendant, who was an unpurged contemnor, as it did to anybody else. He expressed his concern to ensure that the court should therefore take no step which would whittle away or inhibit the defendant's ability to exercise his right to seek legal advice from the lawyer of his choice.[165] He also expressed concern that, although the order sought would not directly infringe any privilege,[166] nonetheless:

> "I can think of few things more likely to inhibit the exercise by a client of his fundamental right to seek legal advice than an order requiring his solicitor to disclose to an adverse party contact details which were supplied to the solicitor in strict confidence and for the sole purpose of enabling the client to communicate with the solicitor. In my view any such order would tend to undermine the relationship of confidence which must subsist between solicitor and client if the client is to be able to unburden himself freely to the solicitor. There would usually be a real, and not just a theoretical, risk of the client being inhibited from seeking legal advice if it was known from the outset that his confidential contact details were liable to be disclosed to the other side in litigation, merely because the client failed to obey a court order."

31–071   Notwithstanding these observations, the judge accepted that s.37 provided jurisdiction for the making of the order sought[167] and was willing, in the exceptional circumstances of the case, to order disclosure by the solicitors of the defendant's contact details. This was for the primary purpose of aiding enforcement of the committal order. However, the judge made it clear that absent the committal order he would have been disinclined to make the order. It was also significant that the committal proceedings were at an end (all that remained was apprehension for the purpose of serving the sentence). This shows that, absent the committal order, the judge would not have taken the view that disclosure of contact details would have been justified in order to attempt to ensure compliance with the disclosure order.

31–072   In *Solodchenko* the claimant also sought disclosure from the solicitors of all information in their "knowledge or reasonable belief" which pertained to the defendant's assets (of which he had been ordered, but had failed, to give disclosure). Again the judge accepted that he had jurisdiction to make the order sought, but declined to do so. The principal basis of his decision was that what

---

[164] *JSC BTA Bank v Solodchenko* [2011] EWHC 2163 (Ch); [2013] Ch. 1.

[165] *JSC BTA Bank v Solodchenko*, at [18].

[166] Contact details being confidential but not privileged information. The judge at [38], drew a distinction between "a client's right to claim legal professional privilege, which is absolute, and the right to protection of confidential information, which is capable of being overridden by other considerations, not least in the context of disclosure under the CPR (and previously the Rules of the Supreme Court) where it is well established that confidentiality does not of itself justify non-disclosure of a relevant document or information."

[167] He also held that the court's inherent jurisdiction over solicitors could found jurisdiction to make the order: at [37].

information the solicitors had would have been provided in circumstances which attracted privilege. But the judge was also concerned at the intrusiveness of such an order:

> "I have a real concern that if I were to grant the order sought it would soon become standard practice for claimants like the Bank, in whose favour unsatisfied disclosure orders have been made, to bring similar applications against the solicitors of the defaulting party. That is a prospect which I can only view with dismay."[168]

The same claimant sought a similar client contact details order in *JSC BTA Bank v Ablyazov and Addleshaw Goddard LLP*.[169] The defendant had been sentenced to a term of imprisonment for contempt of court. He had absconded before sentence had been handed down but an appeal was pending. The claimant applied for an order that the solicitors provide on an ongoing basis all contact details that they might acquire; in particular a conference call facility. The judge (Teare J) agreed with the reasoning of the court in *Solodchenko* but declined to grant the relief sought. The judge identified two potential objections to the making of such an order: first the familiar one that no order can be made which interferes with the right of privilege; and secondly that its effect may be to deny a person access to legal advice. The court refused to order that the solicitors disclose details of the conference call facility and email account facility which had been designed for the specific purpose of providing advice to their client. He held that the facts about those facilities were themselves protected by legal professional privilege. It is at first glance difficult to detect a ground of differentiation between this holding and the decision in *Solodchenko* that the defendant's contact details were not privileged; perhaps the point was that in the later decision the facilities had been set up with the express and sole purpose of giving and receiving, confidentially, legal advice.   **31–073**

The court further held in *Addleshaw Goddard* that at a time when the defendant was the subject of a committal order and had fled the jurisdiction, and the committal order was under appeal, the order sought might deprive Mr Ablyazov of legal advice in relation to his appeal. Hence the second objection was also engaged.[170]   **31–074**

(2)   Orders for disclosure of identity of litigation funders

In a further *Ablyazov* decision,[171] Christopher Clarke J was asked to make an order requiring Mr Ablyazov to disclose inter alia the identity of the ultimate beneficial owner of a company which had helped him to fund his defence to the litigation pursuant to what he claimed were arms' length commercial loan agreements. The primary basis on which disclosure was sought was that the company and/or the funds actually belonged to Mr Ablyazov and were therefore caught by the notification provision in the legal expenses exception to the   **31–075**

---

[168] *JSC BTA Bank v Solodchenko*, at [48].
[169] *JSC BTA Bank v Ablyazov and Addleshaw Goddard LLP* [2012] EWHC 1252 (Comm).
[170] See also *SRJ v Persons Unknown* [2014] EWHC 2293 (QB).
[171] *Ablyazov* [2011] EWHC 2664 (Comm).

standard form freezing order. The judge said that he was not in a position to decide: (a) whether the bank's claims that the funds in question were actually those of Mr Ablyazov; or (b) whether, as the bank had alleged, the funds would be caught by the freezing order even if they were provided by an independent third party under commercial loan agreements. Accordingly, the issue was whether the *possibility* that the funds were Mr Ablyazov's was sufficient basis for making the order. In finding that it had jurisdiction to make the order the court said:

(1) there was a line of authority explaining that the power of the court to grant a freezing injunction under s.37 of the Senior Courts Act 1981 extended to making all such ancillary orders as appear to the court to be just and convenient to ensure that the freezing injunction is effective to achieve its purpose;

(2) it was not necessary to set a particular threshold which the claimant must cross in order to secure such an order; the order can be made if it is just and convenient to make it to ensure that the injunction is effective;

(3) there must, however, be reason to believe that there is a real risk that the injunction may be being broken, which will depend on the strength of the grounds for so alleging and the considerations which militate in favour and against making such an order; and

(4) it is not a precondition of making the order that the money in question has been established to be that of the defendant, but the court will always seek to be careful to ensure that a freezing order is not used as a weapon to oppress the defendant.

31–076 On the facts of the case the court was willing to make the order. The judge found that there were strong grounds for believing that the predecessors to the current funding vehicle had been Mr Ablyazov's creatures or conduits, and that (although there was no document directly supporting that allegation) there was good reason to believe that the present vehicle was as well. The court also took into account Mr Ablyazov's conduct in response to the freezing order, which suggested that there could be no confidence that his statements could be taken at face value. As to the balance of prejudice, the most significant factor relied upon by Mr Ablyazov to counter the Bank's interest in ensuring the effectiveness of its freezing order was the risk that the making of an order would cause the funder to withdraw his funding, such that Mr Ablyazov would no longer be able to defend himself at a critical point in the litigation. However the court did not consider that possibility as sufficient grounds not to make the order.

31–077 Accordingly disclosure was ordered pursuant to the confidentiality regime that was in place in the litigation, on the basis that they would not be used for the purpose of the pending committal applications, and noting that the scope of the order could be policed if necessary by requiring appropriate undertakings if the information needed to go further than the Bank's solicitors and Counsel or by imposing conditions upon the court-appointed Receiver if the funds in question should ultimately come to be added to the receivership.

(3) Order for Defendant to Sign Document Directing Disclosure by Bank

Chapter 29 deals with orders made directly against banks, as third parties, to disclose confidential information in relation to their client's bank accounts in order to assist the victim of a fraud to trace his property. An alternative is to apply for an order against the defendant himself, ancillary to a freezing order, requiring him to sign a document directing his bank to disclose the information[172] and, if he fails to do so, for an order nominating a person to sign it on his behalf under s.39(1) of the Senior Courts Act 1981. The bank is obliged to treat such a document "as if it had been executed or indorsed by the person originally directed to execute or indorse it."[173]

31–078

(4) Other Mandatory Orders Concerning Banks

The order referred to above is mandatory—it requires a defendant to take a positive step, namely signing a letter to his bank. Other mandatory orders that the courts have indicated can be applied for in relation to defendants' bank accounts include:

31–079

(1) an order that assets which had been transferred, by certain Swiss banks, from the defendant's bank account to account holders in banks outside of Switzerland, should be transferred to an account in another jurisdiction in the name of the applicant receiver rather than returned to Switzerland (i.e. moved from a bank in one foreign jurisdiction to a bank in another) so as to be available for enforcement,[174] and

(2) orders that assets be paid into a blocked account or into court.[175]

Applicants for mandatory orders, especially on a without notice basis, should bear in mind that the court will not make an order which is oppressive or impossible to comply with,[176] so the evidence in support of the application will need to address in detail the practicalities of the order sought and, where it requires transfers of money, the source and availability of the funds in question.

31–080

---

[172] As to the court's jurisdiction, see the obiter comments of the Court of Appeal in *Bank of Crete S.A. v Koskotas* [1992] IL Pr. 356, at [10], per Staughton LJ. For an example of a case where such an order was made (in relation to Swiss bank accounts), see *Bayer AG v Winter (No.2)* [1986] F.S.R. 357, per Hoffmann J at 365.

[173] Senior Courts Act 1981, s.39(2).

[174] *Derby v Wheldon (No. 6)* [1990] 1 W.L.R. (although the Court of Appeal declined so to order in that case, ordering instead simply that the assets remain in place but henceforth be held to the order of the receiver).

[175] *United Norwest Co-Operatives Ltd v Johnstone (No. 2)*, unreported, 6 December 1994.

[176] See by way of example the cautious approach adopted by Teare J in *Vitol SA v Morley* [2015] EWHC 613 (QB), at [7].

(5) Delivery up of Assets

31–081 The court may order a defendant to deliver up his assets in order to preserve them pending trial, even where there is no proprietary claim to such assets. Procedurally, the power so to order is found in CPR r.25.1(1)(c)(i).[177] This might be relevant in a fraud claim where the defendant's assets are liquid or easily transferable and there is strong evidence that they would be likely to be disposed of in order to frustrate judgment even if a freezing order were made. For example, it may be the case that the defendant is out of the jurisdiction and would not consider the threat of committal proceedings to be a sufficient deterrent.

31–082 The principles to be applied on such an application were expounded by the Court of Appeal in *CBS UK Ltd v Lambert*.[178] They can be summarised as follows:

(1) There should be clear evidence that the defendant intends to dispose of the goods in order to prevent the claimant recovering them through order of the court.

(2) The court should be slow to order delivery up of property belonging to the defendant unless there is some evidence or inference that he acquired it as a result of his alleged wrongdoing.

(3) "The court must always remember that rogues have to live", so no order should be made for the delivery-up of clothing, bedding, furnishings,[179] tools, stock, or other items which are used for the defendant's lawful business.

(4) The order should specify as clearly as possible what is to be delivered up.

(5) The order must not authorise the claimant to enter the defendant's premises or to seize property save by permission of the defendant.

(6) No order should be made for delivery to anyone other than the claimant's solicitor or (preferably, and unless the claimant's solicitors can show that they have suitable storage facilities) a court-appointed receiver.

31–083 The order should make any provision necessary to protect the interests of innocent third parties, and should always include provision to apply to stay, vary or discharge.

---

[177] This should not be confused with the totally separate jurisdiction under CPR r.25(1)(e), which enables the court to determine at an interim stage whether goods that are the subject of a claim for conversion under s.4 of the Torts (interference with Goods) Act 1977 should be held by the claimant or the defendant pending the resolution of the claim.

[178] *CBS UK Ltd v Lambert* [1983] Ch. 37.

[179] With the possible exception of antique furnishing or valuable paintings, if purchased for the purpose of frustrating judgment creditors.

CHAPTER 32

THE RETURN DATE

A. Introduction

(1) Fixing the Return Date

As explained in Ch.27, any injunction made at a hearing without notice to another party must contain provision for a return date at which the other party or parties can be present.[1] As discussed in that chapter, the court will only proceed without notice to the respondent in strictly defined circumstances and the setting of a return date operates as an essential procedural step to ensure that the case comes back to court on an inter partes basis as soon as reasonably practicable so that the court can review the position with the benefit of submissions (and if thought appropriate evidence) from all parties.

32–001

The return date fixed by the Court when granting a without notice injunction will usually be between one and two weeks after the grant of the without notice order.[2] In a complex fraud case this date is likely to be too soon after the without notice hearing for the respondent to have sufficient time to marshal his arguments and assemble the evidence he may wish to rely on to challenge the order. In these circumstances, the respondent will often seek an adjournment of the return date, with directions for evidence, with the injunction remaining in force (whether or not in varied form), or being replicated by undertakings, in the meantime. An order in such circumstances can take two forms: either simply to adjourn the return date hearing to a new date, continuing the injunction until that hearing; or continuing the order until trial or further hearing but with permission to the respondent to apply to discharge in the meantime without having to show any

32–002

---

[1] See CPR PD 25A, para.5.1, "unless the Court orders otherwise". In *Workman v Forrester* [2017] EWCA Civ 73, at [56]–[59], per McCombe LJ the Court of Appeal described it as "customary" that the onus of facilitating a return date is on the claimant but, in the unusual circumstances of that case where default judgment was entered in favour of the claimant and the defendant took no steps to pursue a return date, the fact that no return date took place was not considered fatal to the continuation of the order. The case is more illustrative of the fact that in almost all cases a return date is required.
[2] See Ch.27, para.27–078. The Commercial Court Guide provides that the return date will usually be 14 days after the injunction was granted, particularly where parties are outside the jurisdiction (see Appendix 5 to the Commercial Court Guide). Paragraph 16.27 of the Chancery Guide provides that where an injunction is granted at a without notice hearing, "it will normally be granted for a limited period only—usually not more than 7 days ... The applicant will be required to give the respondent notice of their intention to apply to the court at the expiration of that period for the order to be continued. In the meantime, the respondent will be entitled to apply, though generally only after giving notice to the applicant, for the order to be varied or discharged.".

change of circumstances.[3] This latter type of order may be preferable to a respondent who does not know when he will be ready to mount his discharge application and does not want to saddle himself with too strict a timetable.[4]

(2) The Risks of Consenting to the Continuation of the Injunction Pending the Effective Return Date

32–003 It is important for the respondent to ensure that his stance cannot be construed as consenting to the continuation of the injunction, or the giving of undertakings, in such a way as to prejudice his ability to challenge the continuation of the injunction or undertakings in due course. In this regard, consent to the continuation of the injunction or the provision of an undertaking "until trial or further order", whilst still permitting a respondent to apply to court to vary or discharge the undertaking, is (without more) very likely to require him to point to good reason for doing so: that is, a material change of circumstances or facts coming to light that he did not know and could not reasonably have found out when agreeing the undertakings or other order.

32–004 The source of the difficulty is the principle enunciated in *Chanel Ltd v F W Woolworth & Co Ltd*,[5] that

> "[e]ven in interlocutory matters a party cannot fight over again a battle which has already been fought unless there has been some significant change of circumstances, or the party has become aware of facts which he could not reasonably have known, or found out, in time for the first encounter. The fact that he capitulated at the first encounter cannot improve a party's position."

There have been a number of salutary cases in which a freezing order continued by consent, or undertaking given in lieu, "until trial or further order" at the return date has been held on this basis to preclude the respondent from subsequently challenging the order, absent a material change of circumstance.[6] A well-advised respondent will therefore ensure that his right to apply to discharge the injunction

---

[3] See the directions made on the return date in *Metropolitan Housing Trust Ltd v Taylor*, described in Warren J's judgment [2015] EWHC 2897, at [3]–[4].

[4] The respondent should not dawdle too long in issuing his application to discharge, if he wishes to apply at all. Too long an unexplained delay will provide a forensic point to the applicant, although it is difficult to see why as a matter of law it should make a material difference to the outcome, other than perhaps to show that the order is not in fact oppressive to the respondent, a question potentially relevant to the "justice and convenience" question: see *Dinglis Properties Ltd v Dinglis Management Ltd* [2016] EWHC 818 (Ch); [2016] 4 W.L.R. 72, at [10].

[5] *Chanel Ltd v F W Woolworth & Co Ltd* [1981] 1 W.L.R. 485, per Buckley LJ at 492H.

[6] See for example *Emailgen Systems Corp v Exclaimer Ltd* [2013] EWHC 167 (Comm); [2013] 1 W.L.R. 2132; *Stephens McBride Piercy Taylor Ltd v McBride* [2014] EWHC 12321 (QB); *Todaysure v Marketing Ways Services Ltd* [2015] EWHC 64 (Comm). In the latter case Teare J observed (at [27]) that "a consent order has a feature which is lacking in an order which results from the court's exercise of a discretion, namely, it is the product of careful negotiation and agreement between the parties themselves. That additional factor is, it seems to me, relevant when considering whether it is just to set aside the order. It is a factor in favour of holding the parties to their agreement; for it is in the public interest that parties should seek to resolve their differences themselves and if they do so the court should seek to uphold their agreement. That is why, it seems to me, that before a party may be released from an undertaking good cause must be established."

without change of circumstance is expressly reserved, when agreeing any holding regime pending the effective return date; or will agree only to the adjournment of the applicant's application to continue the freezing order to a further return date.[7]

This principle also means that where a respondent does challenge the injunction at the return date, he should ensure (so far as possible) that it is fully argued: a party must advance all points reasonably available to him at the first opportunity; if he does not, he risks being prevented from doing so in a subsequent application on the basis that it would amount to an abuse of process. This applies equally to the applicant for the injunction: absent a change of circumstances, the court will generally not countenance a further application for the same relief if the first application has failed, nor will it allow an application for wider relief where an earlier application succeeded and the wider relief could reasonably have been sought at that stage. The law was stated as follows in *Orb a.r.l. v Ruhan*[8]:

32–005

> "if a point is open to a party on an interlocutory application and is not pursued, then the applicant cannot take the point at a subsequent interlocutory hearing in relation to the same or similar relief, absent a significant and material change of circumstances or his becoming aware of facts which he did not know and could not reasonably have discovered at the time of the first hearing. It is based on the principle that a party must bring forward in argument all points reasonably available to him at the first opportunity; and that to allow him to take them serially in subsequent applications would permit abuse and obstruct the efficacy of the judicial process by undermining the necessary finality of unappealed interlocutory decisions."

However, the courts will be realistic about the application of this rule in relation to submissions made at early return dates. In *Phoenix Group Foundation v Cochrane*[9] a freezing order had been granted early on a Friday. A short return date was listed for 20 minutes on the next Tuesday, with a view to further directions being given to a substantive return date. At the Tuesday hearing the respondent, which had not had time to marshal its evidence, unsuccessfully made submissions as to why the freezing order should not be continued to the new

32–006

---

[7] Which was held to preserve the respondent's right to challenge the injunction without having to show a change of circumstance in *Butt v Butt* [1987] 1 W.L.R. 1351.

[8] *Orb a.r.l. v Ruhan* [2016] EWHC 850 (Comm), at [82], per Popplewell J. The statement of principle may be pitched too high, considering the observations in some authorities that the principles of *Henderson v Henderson* abuse apply less rigorously in the interlocutory context: see the judgment of Nugee J in *Holyoake v Candy* [2016] EWHC 3065 (Ch) at [12]–[18]. The general point may be stated as follows: if an applicant makes an application for relief then he is expected to bring forward his whole case on the subject matter of the application at the same time. So for instance in an earlier application in *Holyoake v Candy* (Etherton C, [2017] EWHC 1718 (Ch)) the applicant obtained a "notification injunction". Some months later he then sought to expand that relief to a fully-fledged freezing order. It was held that he was precluded from doing so because there was no reason why that relief could and should not have been sought first time round. So the judge said at [21]: "The starting point in such a case as the present is that the claimants must point to something that has happened since the grant of the original order. They must show something material has changed to make it appropriate to investigate the same issues over again at yet another extensive hearing with even more voluminous evidential material. Absent any such change, the application for a freezing order is not only a disproportionate call on the court's resources, but an abuse of the court's process, in effect making successive applications for the same objective but testing the court's willingness each time to see how far the court will go, each such application involving, to a greater or lesser extent, duplication of issues, evidence and arguments."

[9] *Phoenix Group Foundation v Cochrane* [2017] EWHC 418, per Popplewell J.

return date. It was held that by making such submissions the respondent had not precluded itself from opposing the continuation of the relief at the substantive return date.[10]

(3) The Burden at the Return Date

32–007   At the return date hearing the burden will be upon the applicant to justify the continuation of the relief. The fact that the relief was originally granted on a without notice basis will have no relevance at all to the court's jurisdiction; nor will it be relevant that the relief may have been continued without objection from the respondent until the substantive return date. Although the substantive return date is often described as a "discharge" hearing, this is in fact a misnomer, because it tends to suggest that the burden is upon the respondent to establish grounds for the discharge of the existing relief. In fact no burden rests upon the respondent at all on the issue of what is in fact properly analysed as the continuation of the injunction. The application made at the return date is the applicant's application to continue the relief which was originally granted without notice (an application which the applicant must undertake to issue as part of the terms of the usual form of the without notice order); there is no obligation on the respondent to make an application for an order that the relief should not continue (because the without notice relief is expressed to continue only until the return date hearing). It follows that the applicant for the underlying interim relief should usually open at the return date.[11]

32–008   If, however, as discussed above, the freezing order is continued at the return date but on terms that the respondent can apply to discharge the order without change of circumstance, then the mechanism for bringing the issue back before the court involves the respondent to the freezing order issuing an application to discharge, and he becomes the applicant and opens the application to discharge when it is heard. Indeed it may in any event be desirable for a respondent who intends to

---

[10] This is an important ruling because respondents have often been concerned that if they attempt to resist the freezing order on a headline basis at the first return date (at a time when they cannot meet the case evidentially and have very limited time to expand their submissions) they might be precluded from doing on wider grounds at a later return date with a proper time estimate. The judge's full reasoning at [16] deserves quotation: "In those circumstances it was open to [the respondent] to deploy such arguments as it thought best in the limited time available in order to seek to persuade [the judge at the first return date] not to continue the freezing order on that interim basis. It was entitled to be selective, and was not bound to bring forward at that time all available arguments as to why the relief should not be continued until trial. Nothing in that course was intended to preclude [the respondent] from repeating or expanding upon those arguments, with the benefit of filing evidence, at the anticipated full inter partes hearing in the Commercial Court; nor would it have been so understood by either [the applicant] or [the judge]. Paragraph 3 of [the judge at the initial return date's] order continued the freezing order specifically only until such a further hearingn …The fact that some of the argument has overlapped is no barrier to my considering it: [the judge] had very limited preparation time and limited hearing time, whereas I have had the benefit of full argument, with evidence, following reading time, in a case in which I have considerable familiarity with the background."

[11] And should draw the court's attention to any differences between the relief now sought and that granted at the without notice hearing: *JSC BTA Bank v Ablyazov* [2009] EWHC 3267 (Comm); [2010] 1 All E.R. (Comm) 1040.

contest the continuation of the injunction to issue an application to discharge for hearing at the return date (even if such an application is not necessary), with a view to speaking first at the hearing on the basis that the discharge application should logically be considered first, before the application for the continuation of the injunction. But still the position is the same: the burden is upon the original applicant to justify the continuation of the relief.

(4)   Possible Grounds to Resist Continuation of/Discharge the Injunction

Whichever way the matter comes before the court, it is nonetheless incumbent upon the respondent to identify, in advance of the hearing at which any challenge to the continuation of the freezing order is to be made, his grounds for doing so. The usual grounds will be one or more of the following: **32–009**

(1)   That the case against him does not disclose a "good arguable case", whether on the evidence or as a matter of law.
(2)   That no risk of dissipation has been established.[12]
(3)   That it is not just in all the circumstances to continue the injunction.
(4)   The applicant was guilty of material non-disclosure or misrepresentation at the without notice hearing.
(5)   The applicant has breached the undertakings given to the Court when the without notice order was made.
(6)   The Court had no jurisdiction to grant the type of relief or the specific relief granted.

Grounds (1) to (3) and (6) involve consideration of whether the freezing injunction is justified on its merits, and the relevant principles are addressed in Ch.28. We have considered the undertakings offered in support of a without notice injunction (ground (5)) in Ch.27. As to ground (4), discharge of the injunction for breach of the duty of fair presentation merits separate attention and is addressed in Section B of this chapter below. **32–010**

It is of course worth noting that a well-advised respondent may well chose not to contest the relief which has been made without notice against him; and it is not uncommon for an injunction to be continued uncontested to the trial of the underlying substantive claim. The costs of a full "discharge" hearing can be very high and such hearings can run to many days. The respondent may not wish the Court to review in detail the strength of the underlying claim or the allegations of risk of dissipation levelled against him, given that the evidence in support of such allegations will often involve a critique of the respondent's behaviour and propensities, and findings may be made which do not assist his cause in the broader defence of the claim. **32–011**

---

[12] Of course in fraud cases the very allegation of fraud itself in the pleadings is often relied upon to found a risk of dissipation. If however the evidence on which the allegation of risk of dissipation was founded is disproved or diluted at the return date this may suffice to discharge the freezing injunction; see *Dinglis Properties Ltd v Dinglis Management Ltd* [2016] EWHC 818 (Ch); [2016] 4 W.L.R. 72 and *Kanev-Lipinski v Lipinski* [2016] EWHC 475 (QB).

32–012 Further (and as to ground (1)), the fact that the merits hurdle an applicant has to overcome in obtaining a freezing order is not set particularly high[13] means that it is usually difficult for a respondent successfully to oppose the application for continued injunctive relief by showing that the applicant's case on the merits is insufficiently strong. In this context, the Court has repeatedly emphasised that the hearing of an application for interim injunctive relief should not be turned into a mini-trial. For example, in *Sukhoruchkin v Van Bekestein*[14] the Court of Appeal allowed an appeal from a decision by which a first instance judge had discharged a freezing order injunction on the basis that, by virtue of the "no reflective loss" principle, the appellant applicants did not have a good arguable case. The Court of Appeal[15] said:

> "The general principle is now well-established that, on an application for an interim injunction, the court should not attempt to resolve critical disputed questions of fact or difficult points of law on which the claim of either party may ultimately depend, particularly where the point of law turns on fine questions of fact which are in dispute or are presently obscure".[16]

32–013 However this principle should not be taken too far. There may be sufficiently clear points on the facts and/or particular legal issues which make a challenge to the continuation of the injunction on the merits the appropriate course. Issues on the merits of the claim which it may be appropriate to raise at this stage include questions of construction of a document, or a pure point of law on which the claim is based and which can be resolved without resolution of disputed points of fact.[17]

32–014 One option which the respondent should consider, when a challenge to the continuation of the injunction at the return date faces the difficulty that it is likely to turn on disputed questions of fact or difficult and fact-sensitive questions of law, is agreeing to the continuation of the injunction pending trial but applying for the trial to be expedited,[18] on the basis that the question of whether the injunction should have been granted can be considered properly at the hearing of that expedited trial. This may be particularly valuable for a respondent where the claimant does not expect to have to take its case to trial and is instead counting on the difficulties caused by the injunction to the respondent during a normal, relatively drawn-out procedural timetable to force the respondent to settle before trial.

---

[13] See further Ch.28, paras 28–013 and following.

[14] *Sukhoruchkin v Van Bekestein* [2014] EWCA Civ 399.

[15] Etherton C (with whom Macur LJ and Sir Timothy Lloyd agreed).

[16] *Sukhoruchkin v Van Bekestein*, at [32], per Etherton C; citing *Derby v Weldon* [1990] Ch. 48, per Parker LJ at 58F–58G, and per Nicholls LJ and 63G–63H.

[17] See, for example, *Holyoake v Candy* [2016] EWHC 970, at [13]–[15], per Nugee J.

[18] The factors the court will consider in deciding an application for an expedited trial were recently summarised by Males J in *Apache Beryl Ltd v Marathon Oil UK LCC* [2017] EWHC 2258 (Comm), at [11]: "First, there is a threshold question whether objectively there is urgency. Second, the court should have regard to the state of its list. Third, the procedural history including delay by the applicant is a factor. Fourth arises the question of whether there will be any irremediable prejudice to the respondent to the application. The authorities also show that so far as the respondent's position is concerned it is the last of these, the question of prejudice, which is important with other matters being comparatively unimportant, although they are matters about which the applicant will need to satisfy the court."

In any event, as we have mentioned above, it will generally be impracticable to argue (and so decide) the question of whether or not the substantive relief granted without notice should be continued at the first return date hearing: discharge hearings can take days to be heard and the respondent is likely to wish to put in substantial evidence, if the question is to be engaged with at all. Nonetheless, there will often be ancillary matters which the respondent wishes to raise at the first inter partes hearing. Such matters include the following: **32–015**

(1) If he is an individual the respondent may wish to increase the living expenses limits provided for by the ex parte order.
(2) The respondent may wish to release funds to pay legal costs.
(3) There may be disputes about the source from which the respondent can draw to pay such expenses.
(4) The respondent may wish to vary the order to allow for payments said to represent payments in the ordinary course of business.
(5) The respondent may wish to seek security for costs of the discharge hearing (if there is to be one) and the proceedings generally.[19]
(6) The respondent may wish to suspend the disclosure obligations pending the hearing of any discharge application.[20]

We consider the first four of these matters in Sections C and D of this chapter below. **32–016**

There may also be issues which the applicant wishes to address, in particular if the respondent has provided asset disclosure before the return date, such as: **32–017**

(1) An application to add (or include express reference to) further assets in any continued freezing order.
(2) An application for further or better asset disclosure to be provided by the respondent (perhaps to include an "unless" condition).
(3) An application to cross-examine the respondent on his asset disclosure.[21]
(4) A passport order or continuation of a passport order.
(5) A continuation of a gagging order or other restriction on communication of the proceedings.
(6) An application to disclose the source of legal funding.[22]

---

[19] Any respondent who wishes to mount a challenge to a freezing order where the applicant's financial wherewithal is open to question should consider very carefully whether to seek security for the costs of the challenge. It is not unknown for a respondent to succeed on a multi-day discharge hearing and find that the applicant is not good for the costs order then made in the respondent's favour. The costs of a heavy discharge hearing can run into £100,000's.

[20] See Ch.29, paras 29–033 and following.

[21] See Ch.31, paras 31–059—31–067. It has been held that no such examination should take place until after the return date, such that the respondent has an opportunity to challenge the underlying order; see *Ikon International (HK) Holdings Public Co Ltd v Ikon Finance Ltd* [2016] EWHC 318 (Comm).

[22] These last three points are dealt with in Ch.31.

B.   BREACH OF DUTY OF FAIR PRESENTATION

(1)   A Ground of Discharge

32–018   A respondent may seek to have the injunction discharged simply on the basis that, when applying without notice, the applicant failed to comply with his duty to give what has been traditionally described as "full and frank disclosure". That duty, more recently, and perhaps more accurately, characterised as a duty of "fair presentation", is addressed in Ch.27. In summary, it is a duty which requires not only that the court is not actively misled but also that the court is furnished with all information, whether factual or legal,[23] which might be material to the exercise of its jurisdiction to grant highly intrusive without notice relief. The test of materiality of a matter not disclosed has been stated as:

> "whether it would be relevant to the exercise of the court's discretion. A fact is material if it would have influenced the judge when deciding whether to make the order or deciding upon the terms upon which it should be made. The question of materiality is a matter for the court and not the subjective judgment of the applicant or his lawyers".[24]

However a failure to observe the duty carries with it the risk that the injunction will be discharged, even if the injunction might still have been granted had the material fact or matter of law (which includes matters of legal practice) been drawn to the attention of the court at the without notice hearing or had the court not been misled.[25]

32–019   In view of the very substantial advantage potentially available to the respondent who succeeds in showing a breach of the duty of fair presentation, and the practical difficulty faced by claimants in analysing and collating every piece of potentially relevant material, often in short order, for a without notice hearing, it is very common for the respondent to an injunction to seek its discharge at the (substantive) return date on the basis that the applicant failed to comply with that duty. The contention typically requires the respondent to analyse the substantive claim advanced against him before the judge at the without notice hearing, and the basis on which an injunction was said to be appropriate, in order to demonstrate that a material fact or matter of law or procedure (e.g. a material variant in the order sought from the standard form)[26] was not drawn to the attention of the court. The benefit of such a course is that it is not necessary for

---

[23] Hamblen J's judgment in *L v Y Regional Government of X* [2015] EWHC 68 (Comm); [2015] 1 W.L.R. 3948 is a recent example of a case in which the failure to disclose relevant matters of law would have led to orders obtained without notice being set aside (in that case, the orders were in any event set aside for other reasons).

[24] *Alliance Bank v Zhunus* [2015] EWHC 714 (Comm) at [65], per Cooke J.

[25] It was held in *Boreh v Republic of Djibouti* [2015] EWHC 769 (Comm), at [224], per Cooke J that even though the "duty of full and frank disclosure" does not apply at the inter partes stage, the court should still apply the same principles by analogy when considering the duty not to mislead the court (which applies at any stage) and the consequences of a breach of that duty. "It would be very odd if different legal principles applied to a deliberate breach of duty and different consequences followed from that breach depending upon whether the misleading was at the *ex parte* stage (when a duty to make full and frank disclosure also applies) or at the *inter partes* stage."

[26] For a recent example see *Greenwich Inc Ltd v Dowling* [2014] EWHC 2451 (Ch).

the respondent to demonstrate that the relevant fact or matter *would* have led the court at the without notice hearing to refuse to grant the injunction: see the fifth principle identified in *Arena Corp Ltd v Peter Schroeder*[27] (discussed further below at para.32–026); and *Behbehani v Salem*,[28] where Woolf LJ rejected a submission advanced by the applicant (who was alleged to have breached the duty) that:

> "...the acid test was whether or not the original judge who granted the injunction ex parte would have been likely to have arrived at a different decision if the material matters had been before him. I do not regard that as being the acid test. Indeed, although I regard it as a relevant matter when considering the question of discharge and re-grant of injunctions, I do not regard it as a matter of great significance unless the facts which were not disclosed would have resulted in the refusal of an injunction".[29]

Whether or not breach of the duty of fair presentation should lead to a discharge of the order obtained is a discretionary question. Although courts from time to time make *in terrorem* statements of principle suggesting that the usual sanction is discharge,[30] in practice the court adopts a more nuanced approach.[31] Thus in *Dar Al Arkan Real Estate Development Co v Al Refai* Andrew Smith J stated "the general rule" to be that "the court will discharge any orders that were granted and will not renew them until trial"; but went on to say[32]:   **32–020**

> "While the court must have proper regard to the need to protect from abuse the administration of justice and in particular its jurisdiction to grant orders *ex parte*, it will not apply the general rule so rigidly as to allow it to work injustice...When making decisions of this kind the court should, of course, weigh all relevant considerations, and they include importantly these: (i) The culpability of the applicant (and his advisors) with regards to the breach, and in particular the extent of the breach and whether it was deliberate; (ii) The importance and the significance to the outcome of the application of the matters not disclosed to the court; (iii) The merits of the applicant's case; and (iv) The nature of the order obtained *ex parte*. When assessing this last consideration, the court has regard to the consequences of the order for the person(s) against whom it is to be made."

The breach does not need to be intentional to merit discharge, although where the breach is deliberate the conscious abuse of the court's process will almost always   **32–021**

---

[27] *Arena Corp Ltd v Peter Schroeder* [2003] EWHC 1089 (Ch) at [213], per Alan Boyle QC, sitting as a Deputy High Court Judge.

[28] *Behbehani v Salem* [1989] 1 W.L.R. 723, at 729F, per Woolf LJ.

[29] Nonetheless it can be relevant to the discretion: *Congentra AG v Sixteen Thirteen Marine SA ("The Nicholas M")* [2008] EWHC 1615 (Comm); [2008] 2 Lloyd's Rep. 602, at [62]–[63], per Flaux J.

[30] So it was said by Christopher Clarke J in *Millhouse Capital UK Ltd v Sibir Energy Plc* [2008] EWHC 2614 (Ch), at [104] that "such is the importance of the duty that, in the event of any substantial breach, the Court strongly inclines towards setting its order aside and not renewing it, so as to deprive the defaulting party of any advantage that the order may have given him".

[31] Ultimately it is a discretionary question. The court may well, and often does, conclude that even if material breaches have been proved they do not warrant discharge. See *Congentra AG v Sixteen Thirteen Marine SA ("The Nicholas M")* [2008] EWHC 1615 (Comm); [2008] 2 Lloyd's Rep. 602, at [62], per Flaux J: "Discharge of the order is not automatic on any non-disclosure being established of any fact known to the applicant which is found by the Court to have been material." It is a discretionary question taking account of all the relevant features of the case and the extent of the culpability of the applicant.

[32] *Dar Al Arkan Real Estate Development Co v Al Refai* [2012] EWHC 3539 (Comm), at [148], per Andrew Smith J.

make it appropriate to impose the sanction.[33] Even if the fault lies with the applicant's solicitor not the applicant himself, the applicant will normally not be able to avoid the consequences: client and solicitor (and counsel) are for these purposes treated as one.[34] We consider the court's discretion to discharge but re-grant the order further below.[35]

(2) Obligation to Give Proper Notice of Fair Presentation Challenge

32–022   If the respondent intends to seek to rely on a breach of the duty of fair presentation in having an injunction discharged, it is advisable for him to raise the issue promptly in correspondence and then to address it clearly in the evidence filed in support of the application to discharge (or resist the continuation of) the injunction. In any event, failing to raise any alleged material non-disclosure promptly increases the risk that the alleged non-disclosure is found by the Court to be in reality immaterial and to have been built up later by the respondent with the aim of discharging the injunction.[36]

32–023   Courts are wise to the fact that non-disclosure arguments are routinely deployed by respondents for procedural advantage. Judges are wary of falling into the trap of using hindsight in assessing, on the return date, the way in which the case was presented at the without notice hearing.[37] In *Millhouse Capital UK Ltd v Sibir Energy Plc*[38] Christopher Clarke J observed that in

> "complicated cases it may be just to allow some margin of error. It is often easier to spot what should have been disclosed in retrospect, and after argument from those alleging non-disclosure, than it was at the time when the question of disclosure first arose".[39]

---

[33] *Banca Turco Romana SA v Cortuk* [2018] EWHC 662 (Comm) at [45], per Popplewell J. The case affords a good example of a rigorous response to an intentional breach. Similarly, in *Congentra* it was said that it will only be in exceptional circumstances that a Court would not discharge an order where there had been deliberate non-disclosure or misrepresentation (at [62], per Flaux J). Hence in *Behbehani v Salem* [1989] 1 W.L.R. 723, Woolf LJ said at 728, "If of course it can be established that there has been bad faith, either on behalf of the parties or their legal advisers, that will be a most material matter in considering whether injunctions which have been granted should be discharged, and, if they are discharged, whether it is appropriate in the circumstances to re-grant injunctions either in the same terms or in similar terms." The authorities on intentional misleading of the court or bad faith on the part of the applicant were reviewed in full in *Boreh v Republic of Djibouti* [2015] EWHC 769 (Comm), at [220]–[246], per Flaux J.

[34] *Boreh v Republic of Djibouti* [2015] EWHC 769 (Comm).

[35] Paragraphs 32–025—32–026.

[36] See for example *Sukhoruchkin v Van Bekestein*, above, at [35], per Etherton C.

[37] *Re Living Images Ltd* [1996] BCC 112, at 116H, per Laddie J. Flaux J quoted part of Laddie J's judgment in the *Living Images* case in accepting the submission made in *Boreh v Republic of Djibouti* [2015] EWHC 769 (Comm), at [6], that "in considering whether [the solicitor in the case] deliberately misled the court, it is important to judge his conduct by reference to the circumstances as they were at the time of the conduct in question and not with the application of hindsight".

[38] *Millhouse Capital UK Ltd v Sibir Energy Plc* [2008] EWHC 2614 (Ch).

[39] *Millhouse Capital UK Ltd v Sibir Energy Plc* [2008] EWHC 2614 (Ch), at [106], per Christopher Clarke J.

Hence it is vital that a respondent who wishes to advance breach of the duty of fair presentation arguments should be cautious in his selection of instances of such breach, and avoid the indiscriminate deployment of multiple marginal defaults. A scattergun approach can weaken the force of what may be strong points. An influential statement of the position, at least as it applies to large-scale cases, is as follows:

> "....where facts are material in the broad sense in which that expression is used, there are degrees of relevance and it is important to preserve a due sense of proportion. The overriding objectives apply here as in any matter in which the Court is required to exercise its discretion...
> I would add that the more complex the case, the more fertile is the ground for [the respondent] raising arguments about non-disclosure and the more important it is, in my view, that the judge should not lose sight of the wood for the trees.... In applying the broad test of materiality, sensible limits have to be drawn."[40]

Notwithstanding the points above, it remains the case that a number of freezing orders and other forms of injunction have been discharged on a successful challenge to the applicant's compliance with the duty of fair presentation.　**32–024**

(3)　Discretion to Discharge and Re-grant

The general principle on which the court will act when an application is in breach of his duty of fair presentation has been described as follows[41]:　**32–025**

> "The obligation of full disclosure, an obligation owed to the court itself, exists in order to secure the integrity of the court's process and to protect the interests of those potentially affected by whatever order the court is invited to make. The court's ability to set its order aside, and to refuse to renew it, is the sanction by which that obligation is enforced and others are deterred from breaking it. Such is the importance of the duty that, in the event of any substantial breach, the court strongly inclines towards setting its order aside and not renewing it, so as to deprive the defaulting party of any advantage that the order may have given him. This is particularly so in the case of freezing and seizure orders."

Nonetheless, even if the court decides that the applicant has breached its duty of fair presentation such as to require the original injunction to be discharged,[42] the　**32–026**

---

[40] Per Toulson J in *Crown Resources AG v Vinogradsky*, unreported, 15 June 2001, approved by the Court of Appeal in *Kazakhstan Kagazy Plc v Arip* [2014] EWCA Civ 381; [2014] 1 C.L.C. 451, at [36], per Longmore LJ. The latter case is a good example of the courts taking a realistic view of assertions of breach of the duty of fair presentation.

[41] *Millhouse Capital v Sibir Energy*, above, per Christopher Clarke J at [104].

[42] This is itself a discretionary question. The court may well, and often does, conclude that even if material breaches have been proved they do not warrant discharge. See *Congentra AG v Sixteen Thirteen Marine SA ("The Nicholas M")* [2008] EWHC 1615 (Comm); [2008] 2 Lloyd's Rep. 602, at [62], per Flaux J: "Discharge of the order is not automatic on any non-disclosure being established of any fact known to the applicant which is found by the Court to have been material." It is a discretionary question taking account of all the relevant features of the case and the extent of the culpability of the applicant. Hence it will only be in exceptional circumstances that a Court would not discharge an order where there had been deliberate non-disclosure or misrepresentation: see *Congentra*, at [62], per Flaux J. Hence in *Behbehani v Salem* [1989] 1 W.L.R. 723, Woolf LJ said at 728, "If of course it can be established that there has been bad faith, either on behalf of the parties or their legal advisers, that will be a most material matter in considering whether injunctions which have been granted should be discharged, and, if they are discharged, whether it is appropriate in the

court nonetheless retains a discretion to re-grant the injunction de novo. The principles which the Court will apply in deciding how to exercise that discretion were summarised in *Arena Corp Ltd v Peter Schroeder*.[43] That summary has been approved by a number of judges in later cases[44] and is as follows:

(1) If the court finds that there have been breaches of the duty of fair presentation on the without notice application, the general rule is that it should discharge the order obtained in breach and refuse to renew the order until trial.

(2) Notwithstanding that general rule, the court retains a jurisdiction to continue or re-grant the order.

(3) That jurisdiction should be exercised sparingly, and should take account of the need to protect the administration of justice and uphold the public interest in requiring fair presentation.

(4) The court should assess the degree and extent of the culpability with regard to non-disclosure. It is relevant that the breach was innocent, but there is no general rule that an innocent breach will not attract the sanction of discharge of the order. Equally, there is no general rule that a deliberate breach will attract that sanction.

(5) The court should assess the importance and significance to the outcome of the application for an injunction of the matters which were not disclosed to the court. In making this assessment, the fact that the judge might have made the order anyway is of little if any importance.

(6) The court can weigh the merits of the applicant's claim, but should not conduct a simple balancing exercise in which the strength of the applicant's case is allowed to undermine the policy objective of the principle.

---

circumstances to re-grant injunctions either in the same terms or in similar terms." The authorities on intentional misleading of the court or bad faith on the part of the applicant were reviewed in full in *Boreh v Republic of Djibouti* [2015] EWHC 769 (Comm), at [220]–[246]. Flaux J there concluded that even if the fault lies with the applicant's solicitor not the applicant himself, the applicant will normally not be able to avoid the consequences. Client and solicitor (and counsel) are treated as one.
[43] *Arena Corp Ltd v Peter Schroeder* [2003] EWHC 1089 (Ch) at [213], per Mr Alan Boyle QC, sitting as a Deputy High Court Judge. A more recent statement of principle is *National Bank Trust v Yurov* [2016] EWHC 1913 (Comm), at [18], per Males J: "a. A fact is material if it is one which the judge would need (or wish) to take into account when deciding whether to make the freezing order. b. Failure to disclose a material fact will sometimes require immediate discharge of the order. This is likely to be the court's starting point, at least when the failure is substantial or deliberate. c. Nevertheless the court has a discretion to continue the injunction (or to impose a fresh injunction) despite a failure of disclosure; although it has been said that this discretion should be exercised sparingly, the overriding consideration will always be the interests of justice. d. In considering where the interests of justice lie, it is necessary to take account of all the circumstances of the case including (without attempting an exhaustive list) (i) the importance of the fact not disclosed to the issues which the judge making the freezing order had to decide; (ii) the need to encourage proper compliance with the need for full and frank disclosure and to deter non-compliance; (iii) whether or to what extent the failure to disclose was culpable; and (iv) the injustice to a claimant which may occur if an order is discharged leaving a defendant free to dissipate assets, although a strong case on the merits will never be a good excuse for a failure to disclose material facts. e. The interests of justice may sometimes require that a freezing order be continued, but that a failure of disclosure be marked in some other way, for example by a suitable order as to costs."
[44] Including Christopher Clarke J in *Millhouse Capital v Sibir Energy*, above, and by Andrew Smith J in *Dar Al Arkan Real Estate v Al Refai* [2012] EWHC 3539 (Comm).

(7)   The application of the principle should not be carried to extreme lengths or be allowed to become the instrument of injustice.

(8)   The jurisdiction to discharge is penal in nature and the court should therefore have regard to the proportionality between the punishment and the offence.

(9)   There are no hard and fast rules as to whether the discretion to continue or re-grant the order should be exercised, and the court should take into account all relevant circumstances.

(4)   Position Where Facts are Contested

It will sometimes be the case that the applicant for the freezing order contests the factual premise of the respondent's allegations of breach of the fair presentation obligation. In such a case the law is as follows: **32–027**

> "... issues of non-disclosure or abuse of process in relation to the operation of a freezing order ought to be capable of being dealt with quite concisely. Speaking in general terms, it is inappropriate to seek to set aside a freezing order for non-disclosure where proof of non-disclosure depends on proof of facts which are themselves in issue in the action, unless the facts are truly so plain that they can be readily and summarily established, otherwise the application to set aside the freezing order is liable to become a form of preliminary trial in which the judge is asked to make findings (albeit provisionally) on issues which should be more properly reserved for the trial itself."[45]

(5)   Position as Regards Proprietary Injunctions

It seems that the rigour of the approach set out above is not applied so strictly in cases of proprietary injunctions. In *Boreh v Republic of Djibouti*[46] it had been found that the applicant's solicitor had deliberately misled the court. Flaux J set aside and did not regrant the freezing injunction, saying that it was   **32–028**

> "necessary to demonstrate to these applicants the importance of honesty and openness in all applications to the court, a fortiori in applications for worldwide freezing relief, by setting aside the freezing injunction."[47]

However the judge did maintain the proprietary injunction that had been granted over a specific asset. Flaux J accepted[48] the submissions made on behalf of the applicant:

---

[45] Per Toulson J, *Crown Resources AG v Vinogradsky*, unreported, 15 June 2001, approved by the Court of Appeal in *Kazakhstan Kagazy Plc v Arip* [2014] EWCA Civ 381; [2014] 1 C.L.C. 451, at [36], per Longmore LJ and applied by the judge in see *Dinglis Properties Ltd v Dinglis Management Ltd* [2016] EWHC 818 (Ch); [2016] 4 W.L.R. 72, at [29]. See also *Sukhoruchkin v Van Bekestein* (above at [10]) at [32], per Etherton C citing *Derby v Weldon*, above, per Parker LJ at 58F–58G, and per Nicholls LJ at 63G–63H.

[46] *Boreh v Republic of Djibouti* [2015] EWHC 769 (Comm).

[47] *Boreh v Republic of Djibouti*, at [249], per Flaux J.

[48] *Boreh v Republic of Djibouti*, at [254], citing a passage from Lord Mustill's opinion in the Privy Council's decision in *Mercedes-Benz AG v Leiduck* [1996] A.C. 284, at 300, in which he distinguished between freezing injunctions and remedies designed to protect an applicant's proprietary rights (quoted in Ch.28, at fn.252).

"that (i) a proprietary injunction [made] over particular assets on the basis that the applicant has an arguable case that they are his property is far less intrusive than a freezing injunction. It preserves the assets until trial but it does not freeze a respondent's own assets or prevent a respondent from carrying on his day to day business and (ii) that the discharge of a proprietary injunction has a far greater effect on the substantive claim. If the respondent disposes of the asset, the claim becomes nugatory."[49]

(6) Timing of Applications to Discharge for Breach of Fair Presentation Obligation

32–029 The position differs depending on whether the order sought to be discharged is a search order or a freezing order. Where a search order has been made then it will have invariably been executed before the return date and so, in many cases, the main reason to seek to discharge the order will be in order to make a claim under the cross-undertaking in damages and in order to seek costs. That may be a good reason to defer the discharge question to the trial.[50] In other cases, it may be that a defendant against whom a search order has been granted and executed but subsequently discharged seeks the return of the documents obtained through the now discharged order. In such cases, it is likely the court will deal with the discharge application on an interlocutory basis.

32–030 The position is different regarding freezing orders, which by their nature have a continuing effect on a respondent. The court will entertain such an application (which in any event will almost always be founded on other grounds too) as soon as possible.[51]

C. APPLICATIONS TO VARY FOR (FURTHER) PERMITTED EXPENDITURE: FREEZING ORDERS

(1) Introduction

32–031 In Ch.28 we explained that, consistently with the purpose of a freezing order being to prevent the unjustified dissipation of the defendant's assets that would otherwise be available to satisfy a judgment in favour of the claimant, and not to provide the claimant with security for his claim, such an order usually should (and in the standard forms does) contain exceptions for certain permitted expenditure. These allow the respondent:

(1) to spend a certain sum per week "towards his ordinary living expenses";
(2) to spend a sum (which may be expressed as a specific sum or simply described as "a reasonable sum") on legal advice and representation; and

---

[49] Flaux J also observed that the same approach of discharging the freezing injunction but not a proprietary injunction had been adopted by Blackburne J in *Tajik Aluminium Plant v Ermatov* [2005] EWHC 2241 (Ch) at [193]–[195], per Blackburne J.

[50] *Dormeuil Freres SA v Nicolian Ltd* [1988] 1 W.L.R. 1362.

[51] See the general discussion in S. Gee, *Commercial Injunctions*, 6th edn (London: Sweet & Maxwell, 2016), para.9–029.

(3)   to deal with or dispose of any of his assets in the ordinary and proper course of business (if applicable).

Issues as to whether these exceptions should continue to be included in the injunction and, if so, on what terms, will commonly arise at return date hearings.

When such issues do arise, the court will of course be proceeding on the basis that it is appropriate to continue the freezing order (at the least until the respondent has sufficient time and opportunity to challenge its continuation); and so the court will be astute to ensure that any exceptions do not conflict with the underlying purpose of the injunction.[52]   **32–032**

For this reason, when determining whether and if so in what amount to permit exceptions for expenditure in the continued injunction, the court will want to be satisfied that the respondent does not have available to him "free assets", not caught by the injunction, which might be used for the purpose.[53] Where the freezing order does not extend to the totality of the respondent's assets, it will generally be for him to show that he should nevertheless be entitled to utilize the frozen assets to pay his expenses etc. Warren J addressed this in *Parvalorem v Oliveira*[54] in these terms: **32–033**

> "I do not dissent from the proposition that ordinarily the exceptions should be included. Thus, if there were a worldwide freezing over all a defendant's assets, the starting point must be to include the exceptions. Further, in the case of an English defendant with no apparent foreign connection or element in the case, a freezing order over domestic assets ought in the same way to include the exceptions … .At the other extreme if the freezing order was over English assets of a defendant with known valuable foreign assets not subject to any other injunction or process in another jurisdiction, the balance of justice might very well come down in favour of there being no exclusions in the English freezing order. The sort of example given by the judge in *A v C*[55] are equally applicable to an original freezing order as to a variation."

Where there are doubts over the adequacy of the respondent's disclosure of assets under the injunction this consideration can create difficulties for a respondent who asserts that he has no other assets out of which to fund the expenditure.[56] In   **32–034**

---

[52] *Iraqi MOD v Arcepey Shipping (The Angel Bell)* [1981] Q.B. 65, per Robert Goff J at 71 D-E: "… the point of the Mareva jurisdiction is to proceed by stealth, to pre-empt any action by the respondent to remove his assets from the jurisdiction. To achieve that result, the injunction must be in wide form because, for example, a transfer by the respondent to a collaborator in the jurisdiction could lead to the transfer of the assets abroad by that collaborator. But it does not follow that, having established the injunction, the court should not thereafter permit a qualification of it to allow a transfer of assets by the respondent if the respondent satisfies the court that he requires the money for a purpose which does not conflict with the policy underlying the Mareva jurisdiction." This was approved by the Court of Appeal in *Normid Housing Association Ltd v Ralphs (No.2) (Note)* (1989) 1 Lloyd's Rep. 274.

[53] *Halifax Plc v Chandler* [2001] EWCA Civ 175, at [17], per Clarke LJ citing *The Angel Bell* [1981] Q.B. 65 and *Fathollahipour v Aliabadibenisi* [2014] EWHC 2120 (QB), at [12], per Phillips J.

[54] *Parvalorem v Oliveira* [2013] EWHC 4195 (Ch), at [52]–[53], per Warren J, (where the domestic freezing injunction had been granted under s.25 of the CJJA, in aid of a Portuguese order, against a foreign defendant with assets overseas). See also *Compagnie Noga d'Importation et d'Exportation S.A. v Australia and New Zealand Banking Group* [2006] EWHC 602 (Comm) at [9], per Clarke J (his fifth proposition).

[55] *A v C (No.2)* [1981] Q.B. 961; see especially, per Goff J at 963.

[56] See, for example, *JP SPC 4 v Schools* [2013] EWHC 4248 (Ch), at [22], where HH Judge Keyser QC refused a variation of the order to permit expenditure on legal fees for this and other reasons.

a case where the suggestion by the applicant is one of incomplete disclosure of assets, the burden has been stated to be upon the applicant to show

> "that the evidence of the defendants is incredible and that there are sufficiently strong grounds for supposing that in breach of the worldwide order the defendants have not disclosed other assets from which they could meet their living and legal expenses".[57]

However, in a subsequent case[58] (where the respondents had already been found to have given false evidence), it was held that even though the applicant could not prove positively the existence of some other source of funds, the "burden of persuasion lay on the respondents" and it was a burden they had failed to discharge. The latter now appears to be the more often applied principle, and it is submitted is correct in light of the underlying purpose of the injunction and the scepticism of the court towards a party who has already been found to be at risk of dissipating assets.[59] Certainly where the other assets in question *have* been disclosed, so there is no dispute that they exist, it is for the respondent, as the owner of those assets, to produce evidence to show why they are not available to him to meet the permitted expenditure.[60]

32–035 Be that as it may, if the court is persuaded that, as a matter of practical reality, the only assets available to the respondent to pay legal or living expenses are assets subject to the freezing order, then the "ordinary rule" is that the respondent is entitled to have resort to them, even though the consequence is a depletion of the assets potentially available to the applicant in the event of success at trial. It is, however, ultimately a question in each case of the balance of justice, and the court can and should consider the "overall justice of the case."[61]

(2) Living Expenses

32–036 A living expenses exception will almost always be initially included in a without notice freezing order made against an individual. The general rule is that an individual should not, as a result of a freezing order, be impoverished to such an extent that he becomes unable to meet his reasonable living expenses (including those of his family) according to his ordinary lifestyle.

32–037 For these purposes, "reasonableness" is judged with reference to the individual's previous lifestyle, rather than by reference to any independent or objective

---

[57] Per Hildyard J in *Bank St Petersburg v Arkhangelsky* [2014] EWHC 574 (Ch), at [21]–[22].

[58] *Tidewater Marine International Inc v Phoenixtide Offshore Nigeria Ltd* [2015] EWHC 2748 (Comm), at [40]–[48], per Males J. Indeed in that case the judge suggested that it was relevant to consider not only the defendant's own assets but whether there were others who might be willing to assist the defendant in obtaining legal advice and representation (a line of reasoning which might lead to argument analogous to that which sometimes applies to issues of the provision of security for costs by apparently impecunious claimants).

[59] *JSC Mezhdunarodniy Promyshlenniy Bank v Pugachev* [2016] EWHC 192 (Ch) and see the useful summary of applicable principles in *JSC Mezhdunarodniy Promyshlenniy Bank v Pugachev*, at [2015] EWHC 3263 (Ch) at [37]–[38].

[60] *Fathollahipour v Aliabadibenisi* [2014] EWHC 2120 (QB) at [16], per Phillips J.

[61] *Tidewater Marine International Inc v Phoenixtide Offshore Nigeria Ltd* [2015] EWHC 2748 (Comm), at [47], per Males J.

standard. So in considering, at the return date, applications to vary the amount permitted by way of expenditure on ordinary living expenses, the court is concerned to identify the standard of living to which the freezing order respondent was reasonably accustomed prior to the grant of freezing order relief.[62] In one remarkable case,[63] where the defendant was living in a flat in the Grosvenor House hotel and paying for the private education of his five children, the judge said, in permitting as exceptions to the freezing order the continuation of that expenditure, that it "could not possibly be said that [the respondent] is dissipating his assets by living as he has always lived and paying bills such as he has always incurred". The cap on the defendant's permissible expenditure was therefore increased tenfold from the amount specified in the without notice order.

It is often the case that the applicant includes within the order obtained without notice an inadequate cap upon the amount of weekly expenses, leading to argument about the reasonable level of expenditure for the inter partes hearing. If he wishes to dislodge (upwards) the figure alighted upon at the ex parte hearing, the respondent should provide evidence (often in the form of a budget verified by a witness statement) of his weekly or monthly living expenses, including payments of rent/mortgage repayments, food, utilities, medical expenses, transport, clothes, entertainment etc. Evidence should be provided to support any items which exceed what might be expected, in the form of bank statements, receipts etc. The aim is for the Court to have available to it the material on which it can assess a proper allowance for living expenses over the longer period until trial.[64] This can impose a substantial and invasive burden on a respondent (described, in one case as "full disclosure both of [the respondent's] means and of his liabilities and of the expenditure necessary to maintain his usual standard of living").[65] However, the disclosure of assets will normally have been substantially or entirely required by the without notice order; and disclosure of the respondent's liabilities and the expenditure necessary for his ordinary standard of living is clearly required to discharge the burden on a respondent seeking to increase the sum allowed for living expenses by way of exception to any order made. **32–038**

---

[62] Per Hamblen J in *Travel Holidays v HAJJ Charter* [2013] EWHC 4334 (Comm), at [7], citing *TDK Tape Distributors* [1986] 1 W.L.R. 141, at 146, per Skinner J and *PCW (Underwriting Agencies) Ltd v Dixon* [1983] 2 All E.R. 158, at 165, per Lloyd J.

[63] *PCW (Underwriting Agencies) Ltd v Dixon* above at 162, per Lloyd J. The Judge observed: "I would regard it as unjust in the present case if the defendant were compelled to reduce his standard of living, to give up his flat or to take his children away from school, in order to secure what is as yet only a claim by the claimants. I would regard it as even more unjust that he should be prevented from defending himself properly (for that is what it would amount to), merely because the claimants say that in doing so he is using someone else's money."

[64] *House of Spring Garden v Waite* [1984] F.S.R. 277, at 285–286. The judge, Vinelott J, also said: "Normally the allowance fixed on the *ex parte* application is fixed at a modest level. The reason is that the defendant is always given liberty to apply to discharge the injunction, normally on 24 hours' notice, and in any event the *ex parte* injunction is granted for a limited period. If the defendant thinks the living allowances unduly restrictive he can apply to the court to modify the injunction so as to provide a larger allowance for living expenses or on the effective hearing of the motion he can ask for the injunction to be continued subject only to the provision of a larger allowance."

[65] *House of Spring Garden*, above, at 285.

32–039   Living expenses ordinarily (before the grant of the freezing order) paid by the respondent on behalf of others may be living expenses properly to be met by the respondent just like any others.[66]

32–040   There have been a number of high-profile decisions in the last 10 years in which the permitted living expenses have been extremely high. See, for example: *AHAB v Al Sanea*,[67] in which at the first return date the living expenses allowed were increased to US$1million per quarter (with liberty to apply); and *JSC BTA Bank v Ablyazov*,[68] in which the living expenses allowed to Mr Ablyazov were set at £10,000 a week.

(3)   Legal Advice and Representation

32–041   The standard form exception to a freezing injunction for payments towards legal advice and representation reflects the obvious concern that, as a matter of public policy, a freezing order should not be used to stifle any defence to the claim by preventing the defendant from paying his lawyers.

32–042   Generally, a respondent should be able, following the return date, to continue to use his own assets to defend himself and so the exception will be continued—unless, that is, it appears that the respondent has or may have other assets (for example, assets abroad not subject to the freezing order) from which his legal expenses may be paid (as to which see the discussion above),[69] or where the legal expenses are likely to be met by a third party.[70] Thus in *Tidewater Marine International Inc v Phoenixtide Offshore Nigeria Ltd*, Males J said[71] (in a case concerned with a conventional freezing order rather than a proprietary order) that:

> "In most cases, the absence of other assets will be decisive. Justice will require that such assets as there are should be available to fund the defendant's defence. But in what is likely to be an exceptional case, this is capable of being outweighed by other considerations."

32–043   Nevertheless, a tactic has developed in recent years to put pressure on solicitors acting for defendants by raising an issue as to the source of funds from which their fees are being paid, whether:

(i)   by alleging that the funds paid to the solicitors are in fact the claimant's, being the subject of a proprietary claim against the defendant in support of which the freezing or proprietary injunction was sought, and that the defendant's solicitors were aware of the same; or alternatively

---

[66] *Travel Holidays v Hajj Charter*, above, at [19], per Hamblen J and *PCW v Dixon*, above, at 165, per Lloyd J.
[67] *AHAB v Al Sanea* [2009] EWHC 2617 (Comm).
[68] *JSC BTA Bank v Ablyazov* [2011] EWHC 2664 (Comm), at [8]), per Christopher Clarke J.
[69] See *A v C (No.2)* [1981] Q.B. 961, at 963, per Goff J.
[70] *Atlas Maritime SA v Avalon Maritime Ltd (The Coral Rose) (No.3)* [1994] 1 W.L.R. 917; *Fortress Value Recovery Fund I LLC v Blue Skye Special Opportunities Fund LP* [2014] EWHC 551 (Comm).
[71] *Tidewater Marine International Inc v Phoenixtide Offshore Nigeria Ltd* [2015] EWHC 2748 (Comm), at [46], per Males J.

(ii)   by alleging that they are funds which, to the solicitors' knowledge, were
       frozen under the terms of the order.

Of course, an express exception in the freezing order such as that contained in the   **32–044**
standard form will generally preclude the second allegation. In *United Mizrahi v
Doherty*[72] the issue was whether it was an answer to the first—in other words
whether, having obtained sanction for payment of legal fees from the court, and
having complied with the requirement in the relevant provision to explain the
provenance of the funds, the solicitors in question were thereby automatically
shielded from any potential claim for liability in relation to their receipt of the
traceable proceeds of misappropriated funds. The claimant bank had brought
proceedings against the defendants alleging that they held certain property on
constructive trust for it. A freezing order relating to the totality of the defendants'
assets had been obtained, incorporating the usual provisos. That order also
contained proprietary relief aimed at certain assets. The defendants wished to use
certain funds which were not in terms the subject of a proprietary injunction to
pay their solicitors' legal fees; that would involve no breach of the freezing order,
but their solicitors were concerned that liability in knowing receipt might be
subsequently alleged against them. The defendants sought from the court a ruling
that any such expenditure could be made without the risk that such liability could
subsequently be alleged against the solicitors. The court declined to give such a
ruling, holding that orders permitting expenditure by way of exception to a
freezing order went no further than ensuring that such expenditure involved no
contempt of court.[73] The court could not, in advance of a trial, absolve the
solicitors of any liability they might otherwise incur by receipt of funds from a
defendant alleged to hold those funds as constructive trustee.[74]

The amount of reasonable legal fees may not be controversial. Once it is clear   **32–045**
that the frozen funds are to be permitted to be used for legal fees, then the
applicants, and the Court, may proceed on any estimate provided by the
respondent's lawyers as to what weekly (or monthly) figure will be necessary.[75] If

---

[72]   *United Mizrahi v Doherty* [1998] 1 W.L.R. 435.
[73]   The court considered by analogy the narrow ambit of the court's power to allow, pre-trial, and
without any judgment as to the eventual merits, the expenditure of a trust fund, or an alleged trust
fund, on the costs of one or other of the parties: see *In re Westdock Realisations Ltd* [1988] B.C.L.C.
354.
[74]   The basis for potential liability is knowing receipt (considered in Ch.12). The level of knowledge
required by the solicitors in order to be liable for receipt of their fees from funds that are the subject
of a proprietary claim has been the subject of consideration in the caselaw. Knowledge that a
proprietary claim has been made is not, of itself, sufficient for these purposes; otherwise, as the court
noted in *Barnes v Addy* (1873–4) L.R. 9 Ch. App. 244, no-one would ever be able to obtain
representation for such a claim. Nor can the solicitors in question be expected to assume disputed
questions of fact against their own clients: see *Carl Zeiss Stiftung v Herbert Smith (No.2)* [1969] 2 Ch.
276, at 293, per Danckwerts LJ. Rather, they must have knowledge that the proprietary claim against
their client is well-founded. However, the precise standard of knowledge that is required remains
unclear; and the position is further complicated by the fact that, under money-laundering regulations,
solicitors are now required to carry out inquiries as to the source of the funds from which they are
being paid. In practice, where the solicitors are concerned and the court is not able to give them
comfort, the only safe course may be to withdraw.
[75]   One might expect the judge entertaining an argument about the reasonableness of the amount to be
spent in legal fees in connection with a particular stage of the proceedings to perform a similar

the original without notice order permitted simply the expenditure of "a reasonable sum" on legal fees then, if the fees being incurred are significant, it is generally advisable to seek a variation which makes express provision for payment of a sufficiently large sum per week (or per month), so that the reasonable sum provision is not used by the applicant to put pressure on the respondent or his team. A liberty to apply should be expressly inserted to allow the respondent to return to court to increase the amount if required.

32–046   Where the order provides simply for a "reasonable sum", it is not for the respondent to establish that the costs incurred are reasonable but for the applicant to establish (for example, on a committal application) that the costs paid are unreasonable. However, the pressure that can be exerted by the threat of such an application means that it is generally advisable to seek to agree express permission for a particular weekly or monthly sum.

(4)   Dealings in the "Ordinary and Proper Course of Business"

(i)   Generally: the "Angel Bell" proviso

32–047   The business expenditure exception is sometimes known as the *Angel Bell* proviso, after the first widely reported case which recognised it.[76] The correct approach to it was explained in the following terms in *Derby & Co Ltd v Weldon (No.2)*[77]:

> "In the present case we are concerned with the qualification relating to the defendant carrying on business in the ordinary way. This qualification has been given effect to in many other cases. In *Iraqi Ministry of Defence v Arcepey Shipping Co SA (Gillespie Bros & Co Ltd intervening), The Angel Bell* [1980] All E.R. 480, at 487; [1981] Q.B. 65, at 73 Robert Goff J varied a Mareva injunction to allow the defendant to repay loans because he was 'seeking in good faith to make payments which he considers he should make in the ordinary course of business'. This Angel Bell variation, as it has come to be known, has been treated as a proper and necessary modification to enable defendants 'to pay their trade creditors in the ordinary course as those creditors sought payment' (see *K/S A/S Admiral Shipping v Portlink Ferries Ltd* [1984] 2 Lloyd's Rep 1667, at 167) and to permit 'the payment of trade creditors in the ordinary course of business' (see *Avant Petroleum v Gatoil Overseas Inc* [1986] 2 Lloyd's Rep 236, at 242). But it remains important to ensure that the right balance is preserved between the rights of the parties. The injunction must not be used so as to amount to an instrument of oppression which would bring about the cessation of ordinary trading. On the other hand, the court must have regard to the interests of the plaintiff and consider whether the variation of the injunction would involve a real risk that a judgment or award in his favour would remain unsatisfied. The court must look at all the circumstances of the case in order to try to do justice between the parties."

---

exercise to that required for costs budgeting purposes. Compare the observation of Edis J in *National Crime Agency v Simkus* [2016] EWHC 728 (Admin) at [1], in connection with permitted expenditure on legal fees under a Property Freezing Order made under the Proceeds of Crime Act 2002 (where, it should be noted, the provisions of the statute and relevant regulations—including those providing for the refund of any overpayment determined by a later assessment—arguably justify the exercise being undertaken with a greater degree of scrutiny that in private litigation).

[76] *Iraqi Ministry of Defence v Arcepey Shipping Co SA (Gillespie Bros & Co Ltd intervening), The Angel Bell* [1981] Q.B. 65.

[77] *Derby & Co Ltd v Weldon (No.2)* [1990] Ch. 65, at 76; [1989] 1 All E.R. 1002, per Lord Donaldson MR at 1006–1007.

These principles hold good (certainly in cases where the injunction is in support **32–048** of a non-proprietary claim), even if the respondent's expenditure in accordance with that which is permitted under the proviso is likely to render the injunction of no practical value.[78]

In relation to dealings by the respondent in the course of business, whether or not **32–049** they are permissible as being in the "ordinary and proper course" of that business is usually tested by reference to the manner in which the business has been carried on before the grant of the injunction. In cases of doubt, at least in cases where the dealing does not concern money or property over which the claimant asserts a proprietary claim, the correct test for the court to apply is:

> "to consider objectively the overall justice of allowing the payment to be made including the
> likely consequence of permitting it on the prospects of a future judgment being left
> unsatisfied, and bearing in mind that the assets belong to the defendant and that the injunction
> is not intended to provide the claimant with security for his claim or to create an untouchable
> pot which will be available to satisfy an eventual judgment."[79]

The focus is upon whether or not the expenditure may properly be categorised as **32–050** ordinary and proper rather than whether it is reasonable. In *Halifax Plc v Chandler*[80] Clarke LJ said:

> "In cases of what may be called ordinary business expenses the court does not usually consider
> whether the business venture is reasonable, or indeed whether particular business expenses are
> reasonable. Nor does it balance the defendant's case that he should be permitted to spend such
> monies against the strength of the claimant's case, or indeed take into consideration the fact
> that any monies spent by the defendants will not be available to the claimant if it obtains
> judgment. As I see it, that is because the purpose of a freezing injunction is not to interfere
> with the defendant's ordinary business or his ordinary way of life."

In *Michael Wilson & Partners Ltd v Emmott*[81] Lewison LJ emphasised that **32–051** whether or not a disposal or payment is in the ordinary course of business is a highly fact-sensitive question. It is not necessarily a case of asking whether or not the transactions themselves were "ordinary": it is the course of business that the exception deals with and it is therefore the course of business (which could involve out of the ordinary transactions) that must be "ordinary".[82] The court observed that it is not helpful to substitute for the phrase "ordinary course of business" synonyms (or approximate synonyms) like "routine" or "recurring", as a transaction which is neither of those may well be properly regarded as being in the "ordinary course of business".

---

[78] *Halifax Plc v Chandler* [2001] EWCA Civ 1750, at [19]–[20], per Clarke LJ. For the approach to expenditure under an injunction in support of proprietary claims, see paras 32–059—32–068 below.
[79] Per Christopher Clarke J (adopting a passage in what was then *Gee on Mareva Injunctions and Anton Piller Relief*) in *Compagnie Noga d'Importation et d'Exportation S.A. v Australia and New Zealand Banking Group* [2006] EWHC 602 (Comm) at [9].
[80] *Halifax Plc v Chandler* [2001] EWCA Civ 1750, at [18], per Clarke LJ.
[81] *Michael Wilson & Partners Ltd v Emmott* [2015] EWCA Civ 1028, at [21]–[22], per Lewison LJ.
[82] The "ordinary course of business" is thus not confined to routine payments: see the discussion in *Normid Housing Association Ltd v Ralphs* [1989] 1 Lloyd's Rep. 274, at 275–276, per Lloyd LJ; albeit see the discussion below under subs.(ii).

32–052 Although the test for including the "ordinary and proper course of business" exception is, as set out above, the *Angel Bell* test as to whether the exception would conflict with the policy underlying the continuation of the freezing order, the burden being on the respondent,[83] the court is particularly astute to ensure that a freezing order does not operate oppressively in this regard; and so it may well take a relatively liberal approach to applications by respondents to permit payments out of frozen funds, even though the respondent may have other assets that fall outside of the ambit of the injunction:

> "The Mareva jurisdiction is not be used so as to prevent the payment of trade creditors in the ordinary course of business. (See, for example, the *Angel Bell* ...). But where the party enjoined seeks the discharge or variation of a Mareva injunction to pay trade creditors or to discharge other obligations, he will have to satisfy the court that the order sought will not conflict with the policy underlying the Mareva jurisdiction. In many, if not in most, cases the party enjoined will therefore have to show that he has no other free assets which can be used to make the relevant payments...However, for my part I would be very reluctant to lay down any inflexible rule which makes such disclosure obligatory. Thus there may well be cases where it can be demonstrated that certain debts are in the ordinary course discharged out of a particular fund, and in such circumstances the bona fides of the payments could, I apprehend, be established without a full disclosure of assets. Moreover, it is always to be remembered that there exists a risk that a party may seek to invoke the Mareva jurisdiction as an instrument of oppression or in order to effect the settlement of an action."[84]

32–053 Accordingly, in the *Gatoil* case, even though there was no evidence that, unless the permission to continue to use its usual credit facilities at three banks in London was granted, trading would have to cease, the Court of Appeal permitted the respondent to use them because

> "it would be a misuse of the Mareva jurisdiction to require the party concerned to change his method of trading or to require him, for the purpose of such trading, to use assets presumably designated for some quite different purpose."[85]

(ii) Applications to permit specific one-off payments/transactions

32–054 Whilst, as we have seen, it is the course of business which must be "ordinary" to fall within the terms of the exception, rather than the particular transaction, the respondent is clearly at risk when contemplating a particular one-off payment or other dealing: the exception is not intended to cover extraordinary items and the use of frozen assets in that way risks being a breach of the order.[86]

32–055 In such circumstances the respondent may seek a pre-emptive order from the court to the effect that the payment would not be a breach of the order, or in the alternative a variation of the order specifically to allow it (under the provision found at para.13 of the standard form order). The courts have made clear that even if a proposed dealing does not fall within the ambit of the standard form

---

[83] *A v C (No.2)* [1981] Q.B. 961.

[84] *Avant Petroleum Inc v Gatoil Overseas Inc* [1986] 2 Lloyd's Rep. 236, at 242, per Neill LJ.

[85] *Avant Petroleum Inc v Gatoil Overseas Inc* [1986] 2 Lloyd's Rep. 236, at 243, per Neill LJ.

[86] *TDK Tape Distributors (UK) Ltd v Videochoice Ltd* [1986] 1 W.L.R. 141 in the context of ordinary living expenses, but the principle is of general application.

"ordinary and proper course of business" exception, it will permit the dealing if it does not contravene the policy behind the making of a freezing order, as that policy was analysed in the *Angel Bell*.[87]

Thus in *JSC BTA Bank v Ablyazov (No.3)*[88] Kay LJ explained the difference   **32–056**
between one-off transactions requiring express permission and transactions permitted by the "ordinary course of business" exception, and its place in the mechanism by which a freezing order operates, as follows:

> "As Robert Goff J recognised in *The Angel Bell*, freezing orders (like Mareva injunctions before them) are not in terms limited to disposals or dealings with assets which amount to dissipation. That qualification would render the order practically useless and its policing impossible. Instead, the form of order now contained in the annex to the CPR and in the Commercial Court Guide imposes a blanket restriction on dealings with or disposals of assets up to a stated value but caters for the principles enshrined in *The Angel Bell* by containing an express exception for disposals in the ordinary and proper course of business and a general right for the respondent to apply to the court for permission to carry out a particular transaction not falling within that exception. It was under a general liberty to apply of this sort that the order in *The Angel Bell* was made."[89]

The Court therefore distinguished between routine transactions and proposed   **32–057**
dealings of an irregular or one-off nature:

> "...the standard exception on which paragraph 9(b) is modelled provides a limitation on the scope of the injunction thereby enabling routine business transactions to be conducted without reference to the court. But dealings or disposals which are not part of the ordinary business of the respondent in that sense do not necessarily fall foul of the purpose of the freezing order. They merely require the approval of the court or the applicant before they are carried out and so enable the court to scrutinise what, on its face, may not appear to be a routine or regular transaction."[90]

The Court of Appeal's interpretation of the ordinary course of business exception   **32–058**
in the standard form freezing injunction was in effect a narrow one: any transaction which is not "routine" is not covered by the exception. This might be thought to be inconsistent with the general approach of the court in construing the restrictions imposed by a freezing injunction narrowly (and thus the exceptions to them broadly); but the policy which was clearly articulated was to cement the court's supervisory jurisdiction over non-routine payments before they are made. Such "one-off" payments or transactions, which do not form part of an established pattern of business activity, should be considered and scrutinised on

---

[87] *Angel Bell*, above, at 73. See also *JSC BTA Bank v Ablyazov (No.3)* [2010] EWCA Civ 1141, at [58], per Maurice Kay LJ: "It is clear from the passages in Lloyd LJ's judgment in *Normid* that the scale of permissible transactions extends beyond the scope of the ordinary course of business exception ..."

[88] *JSC BTA Bank v Ablyazov (No.3)*, above. Teare J, at first instance, had held that certain transactions were not a breach of the freezing order because they were within the "ordinary course of business" exception. The Court of Appeal overturned that decision, holding that the question before the court was not whether the transactions were contrary to the policy underlying the continuation of the injunction (which would be the question if an application was being made for them to be permitted by way of further exception to the order), but whether they were within the "ordinary course of business" exception in the order that had been made.

[89] *JSC BTA Bank v Ablyazov (No.3)* at [57].

[90] *JSC BTA Bank v Ablyazov (No.3)* at [74].

their own merits. In each case, the question is that identified by Goff J in the passage from *The Angel Bell* set out above, i.e. whether the respondent can satisfy the court that he requires the money for a purpose which does not conflict with the policy underlying the freezing order jurisdiction.

D.   APPLICATIONS TO VARY FOR (FURTHER) PERMITTED EXPENDITURE: PROPRIETARY ORDERS

32–059   As explained in Ch.28,[91] the Court's approach to permitting the payment of living expenses and legal fees, and dealings in the ordinary course of business, is different when the relevant injunction is or includes a proprietary injunction rather than a conventional freezing order. That is because the basis of the proprietary claim is that the particular asset in question is said to belong to the applicant and so the question is not whether the respondent should be able to use his own assets to fund his lifestyle/carry on his ordinary course of business and pay legal fees, but whether the respondent should be permitted to use assets which may turn out to be the applicant's for any of those purposes. Accordingly, there is no presumption in favour of the exceptions for such payments being included in a proprietary order.[92]

32–060   The question of whether any such exceptions should be included is therefore likely to be raised for the first time by the respondent at the return date, and the burden is on him to establish that, given the nature of the injunction made, it is nonetheless appropriate for any expenditure from the injuncted assets to be permitted.

32–061   In such cases, the court adopts a two-stage approach, *before* then engaging in what was described as the "careful and anxious" exercise of its discretion in *Sundt Wrigley Co Ltd v Wrigley*.[93] Millett LJ summarised the approach in *The Ostrich Farming Corp Ltd v Ketchell*[94] as follows:

> "In *Fitzgerald v Williams* [1996] 2 All E.R. 171, at 178, Sir Thomas Bingham MR said: 'A defendant should not be entitled to draw on a fund which may belong to a plaintiff until he shows that there is no fund of his own on which he can draw. Where he shows that he has no funds of his own on which he can draw, the court must make a difficult decision...' Sir Thomas Bingham was there laying down the rule that proper evidence must be submitted to establish that the defendant has no other funds beyond those to which the plaintiff lays a proprietary claim which are available to him for the payment of his legal fees and other legitimate expenses. But he was not saying that this was sufficient. It was only the first step. It cannot be sufficient for a defendant to establish that he has no other funds with which to conduct his own defence. For even if that be so, he must in addition show that there is an arguable case for his having recourse to the funds in question. If he cannot show an arguable

---

[91] See paras 28–214—28–216.

[92] See Scott LJ's observation in *Polly Peck International Plc v Nadir* [1992] 2 Lloyd's Rep. 238, at 248, that a proprietary-based injunction "would not be subject to provisos enabling the use of the money for normal business purposes, or for the payment of legal fees, or the like".

[93] *Sundt Wrigley Co Ltd v Wrigley*, unreported, 23 June 1993. Quoted with approval by Clarke LJ in *Halifax Plc v Chandler* [2001] EWCA Civ 1750, at [77].

[94] *The Ostrich Farming Corp Ltd v Ketchell*, unreported, 10 December 1997 and cited in *JP SPC 4 v Schools* [2013] EWHC 4248 (Ch) at [20], per Judge Keyser QC. See also *Cancer Research UK Ltd v Morris* [2008] EWHC 2678 (QB), at [9]–[11], per King J.

claim on his part to the funds, he has no right to use the money. A trustee has no right to have recourse to trust money to defend himself against a claim for breach of trust unless he has an arguable case for saying that he has a beneficial interest in the funds in question. No man has a right to use somebody else's money, for the purpose of defending himself against legal proceedings."[95]

This approach was further analysed by Lewison J in *Independent Trustee Services Ltd v GP Noble Trustees Ltd*,[96] in a passage approved by the Court of Appeal in *FM Capital Partners Ltd v Marino*,[97] into the following four questions: **32–062**

"(1) Does the claimant have an arguable proprietary claim to the funds in issue?

(2) If yes, does the defendant have arguable grounds for denying that claim?

(3) If yes, has the defendant demonstrated that without the release of the funds in issue he cannot effectively defend the proceedings (or, it may be added, meet his legitimate living expenses)?

(4) If yes, where does the balance of justice lie as between, on the one hand, permitting the defendant to expend funds which might belong to the claimant and, on the other hand, refusing to allow the defendant to expend funds which might belong to it?"

The first question will necessarily be satisfied if the court has decided to continue, or grant for the first time, a proprietary injunction. **32–063**

The next question is whether the respondent can show that there is an arguable case for his having recourse to the funds in question: in Millett LJ's words from the passage quoted above **32–064**

"If he cannot show an arguable claim on his part to the funds, he has no right to use the money. A trustee has no right to have recourse to trust money to defendant himself against a claim for breach of trust unless he has an arguable case for saying that he has a beneficial interest in the funds in question. No man has a right to use somebody else's money, for the purpose of defending himself against legal proceedings."[98]

The third question comes down to whether the respondent can with proper evidence establish that he has no other funds beyond those to which the plaintiff lays a proprietary claim which are available to him for the payment of his legal fees and other legitimate expenses. The onus is on the respondent,[99] and it is a failure to discharge this onus which has led to the failure of most of the reported applications on this point: for example, in the *Ostrich Farming* case,[100] *Fitzgerald v Williams*[101] and *FM Capital Partners*.[102] **32–065**

It is only then, assuming those hurdles have been surmounted, that the court will have to make **32–066**

---

[95] An example of the court permitting expenditure from property the subject of a proprietary claim on special facts see *Nugent v Nugent* [2013] EWHC 4095 (Ch); [2015] Ch. 121.

[96] *Independent Trustee Services Ltd v GP Noble Trustees Ltd* [2009] EWHC 161 (Ch), at [6], per Lewison J.

[97] *Marino v FM Capital Partners Ltd* [2016] EWCA Civ 1301, at [23], per Sales LJ.

[98] *The Ostrich Farming Corp Ltd v Ketchell*, unreported, 10 December 1997.

[99] *FM Capital Partners Ltd v Marino* [2016] EWCA Civ 1301, at [18], [20]–[22].

[100] *The Ostrich Farming Corp Ltd v Ketchell*, unreported, 10 December 1997.

[101] *Fitzgerald v Williams* [1996] Q.B. 657, CA.

[102] *FM Capital Partners* [2016] EWCA Civ 1301.

"a careful and anxious judgment … as to whether the injustice of permitting the use of the funds by the defendant is out-weighed by the possible injustice to the defendant if he is denied the opportunity of advancing what may of course turn out to be a successful defence."[103]

In *Xylas v Khanna*, Hoffmann LJ put the dilemma before the court as follows:

"In this case if the plaintiff establishes at the trial that the fund belonged to him and the defendant has been allowed to use it on legal expenses, the plaintiff will have suffered the injustice that the defendant has been allowed to spend his money. On the other hand, if the funds are not released and the plaintiff fails at the trial, or, worse still, if he would have failed if the defendant had been able to mount a proper defence, then the defendant will have suffered a grave injustice. The decision therefore requires … a balancing of these risks of injustice to the parties … The balancing exercise is very much a matter of discretion."[104]

32–067   There is, however, one situation in which it may be appropriate for the court to take a slightly different approach. Sales LJ pointed out in the *FM Capital Partners* case[105] that, in none of the authorities he had referred to, nor in the case before the Court of Appeal, had there been any doubt about the ability of the claimant to meet any order made against it at the end of the proceedings pursuant to its cross-undertaking in damages in respect of the proprietary freezing order. He considered that questions (3) and (4) should only be considered separately if that were the case. If there was a real risk that a respondent, if successful at trial, would not be able to recover under the cross-undertaking the extra costs of sale or borrowing which had resulted from the injunction or would not be able to recover for a loss of value in his assets by having to "engage in a fire sale as a result of that order", then Sales J considered questions (3) and (4) would have to be considered together:

"The court would then have to balance the possible injustice to the defendant of being forced to incur costs or suffer loss which may not be compensated at the end of the day if he is successful at trial against any injustice to the claimant in allowing the defendant to draw against the proprietary assets in question where they may prove to be irrecoverable by the claimant at the end of the day if the claimant is successful at trial."

32–068   The principles considered above may apply in situations where the underlying claim is not strictly proprietary but is akin to one. On relatively unusual facts in *JSC BTA Bank v Ablyazov*,[106] Popplewell J held that the above principles, and in particular the test as outlined by Millett LJ in the *Ostrich Farming* case,[107] should apply in circumstances where Mr Ablyazov's son applied to use funds in an account in his own name but which were claimed by the Bank to belong to Mr Ablyazov, against whom the Bank had substantial unsatisfied judgments. Having failed to satisfy the Court that no other funds were available to meet the son's legal costs, the application was refused.

---

[103] *Sundt Wrigley Co Ltd v Wrigley*, unreported, 23 June 1993, per Sir Thomas Bingham MR.
[104] Court of Appeal, 4 November 1992.
[105] *FM Capital Partners*, at [32]–[34].
[106] *JSC BTA Bank v Ablyazov* [2015] EWHC 3871 (Comm).
[107] *The Ostrich Farming Corp Ltd v Ketchell*, unreported, 10 December 1997.

E. PERMISSION TO ENFORCE THE ORDER ABROAD

Whilst a worldwide freezing order extends to all of a defendant's assets anywhere in the world, in practice further steps may need to be taken in the local courts in the jurisdiction where the defendant's assets are located, in order to ensure that the order is effective, i.e. to ensure that those assets are preserved pending trial so as to be available for enforcement. For example it may, in order to prevent property in a certain jurisdiction being transferred or sold in breach of a freezing order, be necessary to obtain the sanction of the local court for the registration of a charge or restriction against it on the relevant country's company or property register; and a third party whom the claimant has notified of the order (such as a bank holding the defendant's money) may be unable or unwilling to act on the order without the order of a local court.[108] Indeed, as we have seen in Ch.28, the standard forms of freezing order expressly provide that they will *not* affect or concern anyone outside the jurisdiction except in certain limited circumstances[109]; and obtaining an order of the relevant other country enforcing the order or declaring it to be enforceable is one such exception.

32–069

The Commercial Court's standard form worldwide freezing injunction now contains, at Sch.B, cl.10, an undertaking by the applicant that he

32–070

"...will not without the permission of the court seek to enforce this order in any country outside England and Wales [or seek an order of a similar nature including orders conferring a charge or other security against the Respondent or the Respondent's assets]."

This undertaking reflects that which was given by the claimant in *Derby v Wheldon*[110] to address the court's concerns about the risk of oppression to the defendant and third parties if a freezing order were made in relation to assets outside of the jurisdiction. In particular, the court will wish to know what is the scope of any order that is to be made in a foreign jurisdiction in purported enforcement of its order, and to understand its effect, in particular if the order under the relevant local law is a different type of order from the sort used in England. The primary reason for this is to ensure that by seeking to enforce it abroad the claimant is not subjecting the defendant to more draconian sanctions than were intended by the English court when it made its original order. The court may also be concerned to avoid satellite litigation in the foreign jurisdiction in relation to the same issues as are before the English court, with the risk of inconsistent decisions.

32–071

---

[108] As happened in *Arcadia Petroleum Ltd v Bosworth* [2015] EWHC 3700 (Comm). The respondents' assets included bank accounts and a property in Switzerland. The applicants were informed by some of the relevant banks that the banks could take no action in respect of the English worldwide freezing order without an order of the Swiss court, and it was not possible to register a caution or charge against property in Switzerland without an order of the Swiss court.

[109] The *"Babanaft"* proviso: see Ch.28, paras 28–151—28–154.

[110] *Derby v Wheldon* [1990] Ch. 48.

(1) The Relevant Principles

32–072 Guidelines as to how the court should exercise its discretion when considering whether to permit extra-territorial enforcement were set out in *Dadourian Group International Inc v Simms*.[111] They are as follows:

(1) The principle applying to the grant of permission to enforce a freezing order abroad is that the grant of that permission should be just and convenient for the purpose of ensuring the effectiveness of the freezing order, and in addition that it is not oppressive to the parties to the English proceedings or to third parties who may be joined to the foreign proceedings.

(2) All the relevant circumstances and options need to be considered. In particular, consideration should be given to granting relief on terms, for example, terms as to the extension to third parties of the undertaking to compensate for costs incurred as a result of the freezing order and as to the type of proceedings that may be commenced abroad. Consideration should also be given to the proportionality of the steps proposed to be taken abroad, as well as the form of any order.

(3) The interests of the applicant should be balanced against the interests of the other parties to the proceedings and any new party likely to be joined to the foreign proceedings.

(4) Permission should not normally be given in terms that would enable the applicant to obtain relief in the foreign proceedings which is superior to the relief given by the freezing order.

(5) The evidence in support of the application for permission should contain all the information (so far as it can reasonably be obtained in the time available) necessary to enable the judge to reach an informed decision, including evidence as to the applicable law and practice in the foreign court, evidence as to the nature of the proposed proceedings to be commenced and evidence as to the assets believed to be located in the jurisdiction of the foreign court and the names of the parties by whom such assets are held.

(6) The standard of proof as to the existence of assets that are both within the freezing order and within the jurisdiction of the foreign court is a "real prospect", that is the applicant must show that there is a real prospect that the assets are located within the jurisdiction of the foreign court in question.

(7) There must be evidence of a risk of dissipation of the assets in question.

(8) Normally, the application should be made on notice to the respondent, but in cases of urgency, where it is just to do so, the permission may be given without notice to the party against whom relief will be sought in the foreign proceedings, but that party should have the earliest practicable opportunity of having the matter reconsidered by the court at a hearing of which he is given notice.

---

[111] *Dadourian Group International Inc v Simms* [2006] EWCA Civ 399.

The Court reiterated that it has a discretion, and that the guidelines set out above are no more than guidelines. **32–073**

(2) Case-Law Since Dadourian

Little more has since been said by the courts on this issue. In granting permission in *Arcadia Petroleum Ltd v Bosworth*[112] the court applied the guidelines so as to permit enforcement in Switzerland and Lebanon, in reliance upon inter alia the following: **32–074**

(1) The claimants had made clear in foreign law evidence what they proposed to do and why they were in a position to do it.

(2) There was no doubt that there were substantial assets in those jurisdictions.

(3) It was not fatal to the application that the relief sought in the foreign jurisdiction was superior (in this case the relief in Switzerland was in rem rather than in personam); rather the question depended upon the nature of the relief and how superior it was. In this case there was little substantive difference.

(4) The Defendants would not be prevented from doing anything that they were not already prevented from doing under the freezing order. It was important, for example, that the foreign order should not prevent the defendants from using funds to pay for legal costs and living expenses under the freezing order.

(5) The evidence on the foreign law showed that there was a relatively easy method of discharging any local orders in the event that the freezing order was set aside.

(6) The fact that the defendants had complied with the freezing order to date was no bar to the grant of an order permitting extraterritorial enforcement, as the claimants would still be unprotected if the defendants chose not to comply in the future.

(7) Overall it was particularly relevant that the freezing order had been made in the context of alleged serious fraud and a risk of dissipation had been made out.

(8) The balance of prejudice came down firmly in the claimants' favour.

(9) There would be safeguards under *Dadourian* guideline (2) to ensure that the enforcement abroad operated in a fair and proportionate way, namely that:

    (i) The order granting permission should be explicit as to what steps the claimants were being given permission to take in each relevant overseas jurisdiction.

    (ii) The claimants were required to give an undertaking that the benefit of the undertakings in the inter partes freezing order should ensure for the benefit of any third party notified in the overseas jurisdictions;

---

[112] *Arcadia Petroleum Ltd v Bosworth* [2015] EWHC 3700 (Comm).

      (iii) The claimants had to undertake to undo any enforcement steps in the overseas jurisdictions if the freezing order was set aside, including paying any costs reasonably incurred by the defendants in connection with such undoing;

      (iv) The claimants were required to undertake to be co-operative in relation to the exceptions and protections in the freezing order (e.g. in relation to living expenses and legal costs).

32–075 Another example of the application of the guidelines in practice is provided by Gloster J's judgment in *JSC VTB Bank v Skurikhin*,[113] in which the guidelines were applied to grant an application permitting the applicant to enforce the freezing order in Italy by applying for an "exequatur" order and registering such order at the Italian Land Registry, but to refuse an application to enforce the order in Cyprus where the aim of the enforcement would be to obtain relief going beyond that which was granted against the relevant respondent by the English court, and where there was no evidence that more limited relief in Cyprus would provide protection for the applicant beyond that already provided by the English court.

---

[113] *JSC VTB Bank v Skurikhin* [2012] EWHC 3116. Another more recent example is *Ikon International (HK) Holdings Public Co Ltd v Ikon Finance Ltd* [2016] EWHC 318 (Comm), where it was held that neither (i) the fact that an application had been made to set aside a freezing order nor (ii) the fact that it had not yet been considered at an inter partes hearing were (in principle) fatal to the grant of an order permitting extraterritorial enforcement, although permission was refused on the facts (there being no great urgency or specific prejudice requiring permission to be given before the inter partes hearing).

CHAPTER 33

RECEIVERSHIP

A.   INTRODUCTION

(1)   Reason to Apply in Fraud Cases

A receiver may be appointed in multiple situations and on various legal bases, **33–001** whether by contractual agreement (e.g. under the terms of a mortgage or debenture), under the Insolvency Act 1986 or the Law of Property Act 1925,[1] or by order of the court in the context of pending legal proceedings. This chapter is concerned with receivers appointed pursuant to the equitable jurisdiction of the court, as confirmed by s.37 of the Senior Courts Act 1981, whether pre-judgment for the preservation of assets or post-judgment for the realisation of assets to meet the judgment. This jurisdiction is one that is increasingly frequently invoked by claimants in fraud litigation, generally where it is perceived that a freezing order will provide insufficient protection for the claimant pending the trial of his claim, or where the enforcement of a subsequent judgment, typically against his foreign assets, will be facilitated by a receiver. It can now be said that receivership is firmly part of the procedural armoury of the fraud claimant. The principles relating to the appointment of pre- and post-judgment receivers are, for obvious reasons, different and we consider them separately below.

(2)   The Incidents of a Receivership

There are certain general incidents of a receivership which it is convenient to set **33–002** out here. An order for the appointment of a receiver does not of itself confer any proprietary right transferring ownership, whether legal or beneficial, of the asset in question to the receiver. Rather it operates in personam, having effect as a form of injunction restraining the respondent from receiving any part of the property which it covers, or the profits of that property (such as rent), if that property is not already in his possession, and divesting him of possession, if it is. The owner of the asset is thus disabled from any entitlement to alienate the property which is the subject of the receivership. A receiver may give a good discharge for debts

---

[1] See also ss.49 and following of the Proceeds of Crime Act 2002, which provide that the court may appoint a receiver in respect of realisable property in the context of the proceeds of crime. There is a substantial body of authority concerning receivers appointed under this Act and similar legislation which is not considered in this chapter.

due to the owner of the relevant asset[2] and may, depending on the terms of the order, exercise powers of ownership over the relevant asset. A receiver may be appointed over a chose in action, such as a claim for damages or a right of indemnity, and in this capacity may bring proceedings in the name of the respondent, as owner of the chose.[3] A receivership order may be made in respect of foreign debts and over foreign assets (as to which see further below). Depending upon the terms of the order appointing the receiver, he may also have powers conferred on him of management in relation to businesses, and, in relation to property, powers of letting and sale. Receivership is a protean concept, but the powers of the receiver in any case will be constrained by the terms of the order appointing him; hence great care is needed when considering the proposed terms of the order, both from the applicant's and the respondent's points of view. So, for example, no power of sale will be implied: it must be expressly prescribed.[4]

B.   JURISDICTION

33–003   So far as the High Court is concerned, s.37 of the Senior Courts Act 1981 provides that:

> "(1)   The High Court may by order (whether interlocutory[5] or final) grant an injunction or appoint a receiver in all cases in which it appears to the court to be just and convenient to do so.
>
> (2)   Any such order may be made either unconditionally or on such terms and conditions as the court thinks just. "[6]

33–004   The origins of s.37 can be traced back to the original Judicature Act 1873, and the original section confirmed the court's previous equitable jurisdiction. The enactment of the original section in the 1873 Act[7] did not change the principles under which the courts operated in appointing receivers, though the jurisdiction has developed since. Although pre-1873 authorities remain potentially relevant, the jurisdiction has not been preserved in aspic since.[8] In *Parker v London Borough of Camden*[9] the Master of the Rolls stated that he did not "accept that

---

[2] *Masri v Consolidated Contractors International SAL* [2008] EWCA Civ 303; [2009] Q.B. 450, at [55]. Conversely payment of the debt etc to the respondent once a receiver has been appointed over the debt will not discharge that debt: *Allied Irish Bank v Ashford Hotels Ltd* [1998] BCC 440, at 442.

[3] See generally *Allied Irish Bank v Ashford Hotels Ltd* [1998] BCC 440, at 442.

[4] *P v P (Restraint Order: Sale of Assets)* [2000] 1 W.L.R. 473; *In re Manchester and Milford Railway Co; Ex parte Cambrian Railway Co* (1880) 14 Ch. D. 645.

[5] Oddly, CPR r.25.1(1), when listing some of the interim remedies a court may grant, does not refer to the power to appoint a receiver. But that is not determinative of its powers: see CPR r.25.1(3).

[6] Equivalent provisions for the County Court are contained in s.38 of the County Courts Act 1984 (remedies available in the County Court) and s.107 of the County Courts Act 1984 (appointment of receivers by way of equitable execution).

[7] Section 25(8), whereby a receiver could be "appointed by an interlocutory order of the Court in all cases in which it shall appear just or convenient that such order should be made."

[8] See *Holmes v Millage* [1893] 1 Q.B. 551, at 557, where Lindley LJ suggested that there had been a relaxation of the jurisdiction subsequent to the enactment of the 1873 Act.

[9] *Parker v London Borough of Camden* [1986] Ch. 162, at 176.

the pre-Judicature Act practices of the Court of Chancery or any other court still rule us from their graves."[10] He went on to say that the

> "jurisdiction was quite general and, in terms, unlimited. Nevertheless it has to be exercised judicially and with due regard to authorities which are binding upon this court"[11].

Similarly, in the leading decision of the Court of Appeal in *Masri v Consolidated Contractors International (UK) Ltd (No.2)*[12] Lawrence Collins LJ, having conducted an extensive review of the authorities, held that the power under s.37(1) was not delimited by pre-1873 authority and could be adapted to new circumstances; and that the demands of justice must always be the overriding consideration in considering the scope of the jurisdiction under s.37(1).[13] It may be concluded that the power to appoint a receiver, whilst not unfettered, is not ossified by reference to the past. Indeed, as has been often pointed out, the freezing order and the anti-suit injunction could never have been developed if it were the case that the power under s.37(1) and its predecessor sections was somehow delimited by pre-1873 practice.

C.   PRINCIPLES GOVERNING THE APPOINTMENT OF A PRE-JUDGMENT RECEIVER

(1)   Introduction

An application for a pre-judgment receiver in a fraud case will generally be made where the applicant is concerned to preserve assets pending trial and judgment. In this sense a receivership order is intended to fulfil a similar function to a freezing order. Receivership orders are usually applied for after a freezing order has been obtained; in general, such an order will only be justified where it is apprehended on reasonable grounds that a freezing order, which of course leaves assets in the hands of the respondent, provides inadequate protection. Although there is no jurisdictional bar to the appointment of a receiver instead of, or at the same time as, the making of a freezing order, such a course is likely to be exceptional; in the nature of things it will not usually be possible to demonstrate that a freezing order would offer inadequate protection to a claimant prior to such an order even being

33–005

---

[10] Per Lord Donaldson MR, above, at 173. Browne-Wilkinson LJ agreed at 176.

[11] *Parker v London Borough of Camden* [1986] Ch. 162, at 173.

[12] *Masri v Consolidated Contractors International (UK) Ltd (No.2)* [2008] EWCA Civ 303; [2009] Q.B. 450.

[13] *Masri v Consolidated Contractors International (UK) Ltd (No.2)*, above, at [177] and [181]–[183]. Although Lawrence Collins LJ had earlier, at [180], suggested that *Parker* was not a secure source of authority "since I doubt whether these dicta can stand with the rejection by the House of Lords in *P v Liverpool Post Plc* [1991] 2 A.C. 370, 420–421 of similar statements by Lord Denning MR in *Chief Constable of Kent v V* [1983] Q.B. 34, 42 in relation to the power to grant injunctions", it seems that all that the learned judge was saying is that the power was not "unlimited". See also *Rio Properties Inc v Gibson Dunn & Crutcher* [2004] 1 W.L.R. 2702, at [50], for a wide statement of the jurisdiction conferred by s.37(1).

made. An application for a pre-judgment receiver is for an interim remedy and pre-judges no substantive aspect of the underlying litigation.[14]

(2) "Just and Convenient"

33–006   Section 37(1) of the Senior Courts Act 1981 gives the court power to appoint a receiver "in all cases in which it appears to the court to be just and convenient to do so". As we have seen, the "just and convenient" test is a fluid one, adaptable to changing times and not unduly constrained by precedent.

> "We live in a time of rapidly growing commercial and financial sophistication and it behoves the courts to adapt their practices to meet the current wiles of those defendants who are prepared to devote as much energy to making themselves immune to the courts' orders as to resisting the making of such orders on the merits of their case."[15]

Nonetheless the authorities show that the court will act by reference to clear principles, which are explored later in this section.

(3) Assets Over which the Receiver can be Appointed

(i)   Types of assets

33–007   Although the traditional role of receivers is, as their title suggests, to receive assets which would otherwise be due to the respondent, e.g. rentals from property or dividends from shares, nonetheless receivers can also be appointed with wider powers of quasi-ownership or management. For instance a receiver may be appointed over shares, with full powers to exercise the rights of the shareholder, so potentially allowing the receiver to dismiss and appoint directors and to pass extraordinary resolutions in general meeting.[16]

33–008   Nonetheless there are limits to the court's powers. It cannot appoint receivers over assets not owned or controlled by the respondent. So, for example, in *Lakatamia Shipping Co v Su*[17] it was observed (in the context of deciding whether the assets of a company would be amenable to execution of a judgment against the defendant shareholder, for the purposes of determining whether such assets were caught by a freezing order) that a receiver could not be appointed over the assets of a company in which the judgment debtor holds shares, even in the case of a 100% shareholding. In such a case the receiver would be appointed over the shareholding; the receiver might then exercise such powers as it had by virtue of the shareholding to secure the underlying asset, which would often achieve the same practical result, but it would (importantly) be by a different

---

[14] Receivers are from time to time appointed in landlord and tenant cases (e.g. *Evans v Clayhope Properties* [1988] 1 W.L.R. 358) and partnership and company disputes (e.g. *Mellor v Mellor* [1992] 1 W.L.R. 517). The principles on which the courts act in such cases are similar but not identical to those applicable in fraud claims, so some care is required when seeking to obtain guidance from them.

[15] *Derby & Co Ltd v Weldon* [1990] Ch. 65, at 77, per Lord Donaldson MR.

[16] *Ka Wah International Merchant Finance Ltd v Asean Resources Ltd* (1986) 8 IPR 241.

[17] *Lakatamia Shipping Co v Su* [2014] EWCA Civ 636; [2015] 1 W.L.R. 291, especially at [52].

route which recognised the separate legal personality of the owner of the relevant assets. However, in this connection it is important to note that for these purposes the concepts of ownership and control are sufficiently flexible to admit of receivership being ordered (in an appropriate case) over assets over which the respondent exercises de facto control, even if it falls short of beneficial ownership: see for example *JSC VTB Bank v Skurikhin*,[18] considered further below.

A receiver may be appointed over specific assets or even the totality of the respondent's business. For example: **33–009**

(1) In *Shalson v Russo*[19] Ferris J appointed a receiver over a set of valuable paintings owned by the defendant and kept in a house in London, with provision for their valuation and their being kept in safe custody pending the trial.

(2) In *International Credit and Investment Co Overseas Ltd v Adham*,[20] Robert Walker J appointed a receiver over a series of assets, including the proceeds of sale of a London property, assets of a Liechtenstein anstalt, and assets of a BVI company.

(3) In *JSC BTA Bank v Ablyazov*,[21] Teare J appointed three receivers over all the assets disclosed by the defendant in response to orders ancillary to a freezing order previously made against him. The order was subsequently amended during the course of the proceedings to include further assets[22] which the defendant had not disclosed.

The question of the width of the receivership order will very much depend on the size of the claim and the nature of the assets. As discussed below, a receivership will, in general terms, only be ordered to protect assets in respect of which there is a risk that they are vulnerable to dissipation or disposal which risk cannot be properly mitigated by a freezing order.

In the case of assets which the defendant has not disclosed and so, axiomatically, **33–010** has not admitted owning, or assets which the defendant positively denies ownership of, the court may nonetheless include such assets within the scope of a receivership order if satisfied that there is sufficient evidence that the defendant is the true owner. The court will not include such assets within a receivership unless there is "good reason" to believe that they belong (in the wide sense discussed at

---

[18] *JSC VTB Bank v Skurikhin* [2015] EWHC 2131 (Comm). The membership interests over which the receivership order was made were not held by the respondent, but by a Liechtenstein foundation, over the assets of which the court was persuaded (to the relevant standard) the respondent had de facto control.

[19] *Shalson v Russo*, unreported, 24 May 2001. The Court was concerned that the undertaking proffered by the defendant not to remove the paintings from an identified house was not sufficient and the paintings needed to be physically removed from him in order to protect them.

[20] *International Credit and Investment Co Overseas Ltd v Adham* [1998] BCC 134.

[21] *JSC BTA Bank v Ablyazov* [2010] EWHC 1779 (Comm), upheld on appeal [2010] EWCA Civ 1141.

[22] Including companies, primarily based in offshore jurisdictions, numbering over a thousand.

Ch.28) to the defendant,[23] and the court is entitled to make such enquiries as necessary as to the ownership of the assets including a trial as to that issue, whether between the claimant and defendant or, more commonly, the claimant and an alleged third party owner.[24]

33–011   In fraud cases, particularly if the claimant believes the defendant has been less than forthcoming as to the scope of his assets, such an order can be valuable in preserving assets pending judgment and enforcement action. However, the risks of such a step are even greater than those in instances of disclosed assets. Should it ultimately be found that the assets in question did not belong to the defendant, and the true owner has suffered loss, he will have a claim under the cross-undertaking against the claimant. Furthermore, the risk of satellite litigation as to ownership of assets carries additional risk in terms of costs and delay.

33–012   It must be emphasised that the court's power to appoint an interim receiver does not depend upon the applicant maintaining any form of proprietary claim to the asset which is the subject of the proposed receivership. Whilst the court can of course intervene in support of a proprietary claim, it is important to note that it can also do so (and indeed in the cases which we have mentioned above, was doing so) in support of a purely personal claim (much as it does with a conventional freezing order). The fact that in such a case the respondent is effectively being deprived by the receivership of control over his own assets is an important consideration for the court when deciding whether and if so on what terms to grant relief, as we note below.

(ii)   Foreign assets

33–013   As long as the court has in personam jurisdiction over the respondent over whose assets a receiver is sought to be appointed, the relevant assets over which it may be "just and convenient" for a receiver to be appointed are not confined to assets within the jurisdiction. This was settled in *Derby & Co Ltd v Weldon (Nos 3 & 4)*,[25] where the Court of Appeal confirmed the judgment of Sir Nicolas Browne-Wilkinson V-C, who had appointed a receiver over assets located in Luxembourg, belonging to a Luxembourgian company which was a defendant to the action but which had no residence in England. Moreover, the Court of Appeal was prepared to go further than the Vice-Chancellor, who had imposed a condition that no steps were to be taken to enforce the vesting of assets until after the courts of Luxembourg should have declared his order enforceable or otherwise enforced it. The Court of Appeal dispensed with the Vice-Chancellor's condition. It was not a bar to the appointment of receivers that they would not or might not be recognised by the foreign court where the assets were located.[26] In

---

[23] In this regard the court will proceed on the same basis as when deciding whether or not to make a freezing order over assets ostensibly owned by a third party: see generally Ch.28.

[24] Per Lloyd LJ in *SCF Finance Co Ltd v Masri* [1985] 1 W.L.R. 876, at 884.

[25] *Derby & Co Ltd v Weldon (Nos 3 & 4)* [1990] 1 Ch. 65.

[26] *In re Maudslay, Sons & Field; Maudslay v Maudslay, Sons & Field* [1900] 1 Ch. 602. For a relatively recent example see *Ballabil Holdings Pty Ltd v Hospital Products* (1985) 1 N.S.W.L.R. 155. In *Derby & Co Ltd v Weldon (No.6)* [1990] 1 W.L.R. 1139 Dillon LJ said, at 1150, that "The court has always been ready to appoint a receiver over the foreign as well as British assets of an English

such circumstances the English court will do what it can to render the appointment effective by orders in personam against persons who are subject to the jurisdiction of the English court.[27] Such orders may be in the form of mandatory injunctions, which may only be realistically enforceable by way of contempt proceedings in England.[28]

An English order will not be directly enforceable against a third party not subject to the court's jurisdiction. By contrast a party who is subject to the English court's jurisdiction is liable to the contempt jurisdiction if he interferes with the receivership, regardless of whether or not he is a party to the proceedings. Depending upon the relevant local law, an applicant who has obtained the benefit of a receivership order may apply to the foreign court where the relevant assets are situated for recognition of the receivership.   **33–014**

Nonetheless, the court will not in general require the defendant to do anything which might expose him to a real danger of criminal liability under the law of his home state or the state in which the relevant assets are located.[29]   **33–015**

The above principles are equally applicable to receivers appointed by way of equitable execution, discussed below.   **33–016**

In any case where an application for a pre-judgment receivership is contemplated in reliance upon s.25 of the Civil Jurisdiction and Judgments Act 1982, as ancillary to foreign substantive proceedings, the applicant should have well in mind the two-stage test for the grant of relief under that section: see Ch.26.[30] As explained in that chapter, the court first considers whether or not the facts would warrant the relief sought if the proceedings were brought in England (uninhibited by the absence of any equivalent power in the foreign court to grant such relief: see s.25(7)). At the second stage, the court asks whether the fact that the substantive proceedings are taking place outside the jurisdiction makes it inexpedient to grant the relief sought. The absence or existence of an equivalent power to appoint an interim receiver in the relevant foreign jurisdiction (or the likelihood or not of any such power being exercised by it) may be very relevant at the second stage of the court's approach when it considers the issue of expediency. In *Ras Al Khaimah Investment Authority v Bestfort Developments LLP*[31] the application under s.25 was for interim relief which extended to   **33–017**

---

company, even though it has recognised that in relation to foreign assets the appointment may not prove effective without assistance from a foreign court". See further the discussion in *Ras Al Khaimah Investment Authority v Bestfort Developments LLP* [2015] EWHC 3383 (Ch), at [72].

[27] *In re Huinac Copper Mines Ltd; Matheson & Co v The Company* [1910] WN 218.

[28] The position should be distinguished from third party debt orders: *Societe Eram Shipping Co Ltd v Cie International de Navigation* [2003] UKHL 30; [2004] 1 A.C. 260. Further a director of a company who is domiciled outside the jurisdiction cannot be liable to an order under CPR r.71.

[29] *Brannigan v Davidson* [1996] UKPC 35; [1997] A.C. 238: see *Masri v Consolidated Contractors International Company SAL* [2008] EWHC 2492 (Comm), at [26]. For a case where a receivership order interfered with principles of comity see *Joujou v Masri* [2011] EWCA Civ 746; [2011] 2 C.L.C. 566.

[30] At para.26–068 and following.

[31] *Ras Al Khaimah Investment Authority v Bestfort Developments LLP* [2015] EWHC 3383 (Ch), at [46]. The case on appeal ([2017] EWCA Civ 1014; [2018] 1 W.L.R. 1099) dealt with the Judge's decision to refuse freezing injunction relief; since that decision was in part reversed by the Court of Appeal, the question of whether receiverships should be ordered was remitted to the Judge.

proposed receiverships and a request for the grant of powers of attorney to render them effective. The court held that the application failed under both limbs of the two-stage test. The court further commented that the chances of any receivership being effective were remote.

(iii)   Ancillary orders

33–018   Just as the courts have developed an extensive jurisprudence concerning orders made ancillary to a freezing order, so they have shown themselves willing to make orders ancillary to the order appointing the receiver in order to promote the efficacy of the receivership.[32] Such orders might extend to requiring the respondent: (i) not to impede the receivers from acting[33]; (ii) to co-operate with the receiver; (iii) to give written confirmation to debtors of the respondent that the receiver is authorised to receive debts on behalf of the respondent[34]; (iv) to appoint the receiver as its representative for the exercise of shareholder rights[35]; (v) to give disclosure of assets to the receivers[36]; (vi) to grant a power of attorney to the receivers[37]; and (vi) to use best endeavours to reverse or mitigate the effect of an action, such as the transfer of an asset, effected in breach of the receivership order or interfering with the receivership.[38]

(4)   Principles on which the Court will Act

(i)   Introduction

33–019   The appointment of a receiver pre-judgment is generally a strong step to take, potentially involving a very substantial intrusion into the respondent's affairs; inevitably so in the case of receivers appointed to manage trading companies. It will be likely to be very expensive. Any order for the appointment of a receiver will also necessitate the giving of a cross-undertaking in damages, potentially requiring fortification. Accordingly an applicant should think carefully prior to seeking such an appointment. In reality the applicant will only consider such an application where substantial sums are in contest and a freezing order is thought to be an insufficient protection pre-judgment.

(ii)   Considerations as to grant

33–020   As we have noted, in claims in fraud the court will generally only appoint receivers pre-judgment where a freezing order is inadequate to protect the

---

[32] See *Tassaruf v Merrill Lynch Bank* [2011] UKPC 17; [2012] 1 W.L.R. 1721 and *Derby & Co Ltd v Weldon (No.6)* [1990] 1 W.L.R. 1139.

[33] *Cruz City 1 Mauritius Holdings v Unitech Ltd* [2014] EWHC 3131 (Comm), at [53].

[34] *Masri*, above, at [23] and [183].

[35] *Cruz City* [2014] EWHC 3131 (Comm), at [53].

[36] *Derby & Co Ltd v Weldon* [1990] Ch. 65, at 86.

[37] *Ras Al Khaimah Investment Authority v Bestfort Developments LLP*, above, at [49].

[38] *JSC BTA Bank v Ablyazov* [2012] EWHC 2543 (Comm) and *JSC BTA Bank v Ablyazov* [2013] EWHC 2772 (Comm).

claimant against unjustified dissipation. In such cases the receiver is appointed in support of the freezing order, so as to preserve assets to aid the enforcement of any judgment entered in favour of the applicant at trial. The key modern authority is *JSC BTA Bank v Ablyazov*,[39] in which the leading cases were reviewed. The following principles emerge from the recent cases:

(1)   The appointment of a receiver will often be a very intrusive remedy and not easily reversible.[40] However such considerations could be ameliorated by an appropriately fortified undertaking in damages. Nonetheless, the more intrusive the order the more reticent the court will be about granting it.[41] There is a world of difference between an order which permits the receiver to manage the respondent's business and one which, say, simply permits him to receive the rents from properties owned by the respondent.[42]

(2)   Although it was said in the Australian case of *National Australia Bank Ltd v Bond Brewing Holdings Ltd*[43] that a receivership is

> "an extraordinary and drastic remedy, to be exercised with utmost care and caution and only where the court is satisfied there is imminent danger of loss if it is not exercised",

the English courts have not insisted on this hurdle of showing "an imminent danger of loss".[44]

(3)   Where the assets frozen by a freezing order are constituted by money in bank accounts or immovable property, a receivership order will generally be completely inappropriate. This is because in such cases there are ready

---

[39] *JSC BTA Bank v Ablyazov* [2010] EWCA Civ 1141; [2011] Bus L.R. D119.

[40] See for instance the decision of the Appeal Division of the Supreme Court of Victoria in *National Australia Bank Ltd v Bond Brewing Holdings Ltd* [1991] V.L.R. 386, where (at 539–540 and 541) the importance of proper consideration of the respondent's position was emphasised, particularly in the case of a trading company, and it was stated that "it must always be borne in mind that the appointment of a receiver in such a case authorises an irresistible invasion and that even if the army of occupation is withdrawn after only a short time things may never be the same again....". That consideration is particularly important when deciding whether it is justified to apply without notice to the respondent.

[41] See the early House of Lords decision in *Owen v Homan* (1853) 4 HL Cas 997, at 1033, at 1036: "When the evidence on which the Court is to act (here the only evidence is the answer of Mrs Homan) is very clear in favour of the Plaintiff, then the risk of eventual injury to the Defendant is very small, and the Court does not hesitate to act. Where there is more of doubt, there is of course more difficulty...The Plaintiffs here do not claim as specific appointees of any part of the Defendant's separate estate. They are merely in the nature of general creditors seeking to obtain payment by a sort of equitable action of assumpsit or debt. In such a case it is a strong exercise of authority to deprive the Defendant, on motion, of property on which the Plaintiffs have no specific claim, in order that, if they establish their claim as creditors, there may be assets wherewith to satisfy them. I do not mean that such a course could not be taken, although I have not discovered any authority for it."

[42] For instance the court declined to appoint a receiver in *Jaber v Science and Information Technology Ltd* [1992] B.C.L.C. 764 because of the likely adverse effect on the respondent. This was a company law dispute involving an unfair prejudice petition. Ferris J refused to make an order appointing receivers over the business of a computer software sales and marketing company, on the basis that (a) the outside world would doubtless consider the company to be in insolvency receivership, which would be likely to have a very damaging impact on it business, and (b) the receivers would be likely to prove highly expensive.

[43] *National Australia Bank Ltd v Bond Brewing Holdings Ltd* [1991] V.L.R. 386, at 541.

[44] *JSC BTA Bank v Ablyazov* [2010] EWCA Civ 1141, at [15].

means to secure the frozen asset: a bank given notice of a freezing order will not permit the money to be disposed of; and a restriction can be registered against land subject to a freezing order.

(4) In general a receivership order will only be appropriate where a freezing injunction is insufficient on its own; such cases would be likely to arise where there is a measurable risk that, if it was not granted, the respondent would act in breach of the freezing order or otherwise seek to ensure that his assets would not be available to satisfy any judgment which might in due course be given against him.

(5) Such a risk may be demonstrated by, for instance, established breaches of a prior freezing order or strong evidence that such an order has been breached.[45] However, proof or strong evidence of such breach will not be necessary in every case[46]; nor will it always be sufficient.[47] Breaches of disclosure obligations ancillary to a prior freezing order may tend to show that a receivership is necessary.[48]

(6) It follows from the above that a receivership order is unlikely to be granted to protect assets pending judgment on a personal claim unless, at least, there is a prior freezing order.

(7) A receivership order may be justified where the defendant's assets are held under a complex network of offshore trusts or companies, such that enforcement of any future judgment may be difficult or such that the freezing order does not provide the claimant with adequate protection, because of difficulties in policing and enforcing such an order. As it was put in *Ablyazov*, if "a Freezing Order does not, of itself, provide adequate

---

[45] *Don King Productions Inc v Warren* [1999] 2 Lloyd's Rep. 392, at 396, per Neuberger J. The judge declined to appoint receivers where the business managed by the defendant of boxing promotion was "very personal". Further he was impressed by the point that many of the defendant's boxer clients might regard receivership as a form of insolvency. Instead a regime was put in place involving an independent accountant. In *International Credit and Investment Co Overseas Ltd v Adham* [1998] BCC 134 receivers were appointed in circumstances where the judge remarked (at 138) that he was by no means convinced that the respondents could be trusted not to "continue to do their best to evade orders that have been made against them". See also *Lee Kuan Yew v Tang Liang Hong (No.2)* [1997] 2 S.L.R. 883, where the Singaporean High Court appointed receivers in circumstances where the respondent, who was a solicitor, had acted in "contumelious and flagrant breach of the orders of the court", had treated the court orders "with utter contempt" (at 836 and 838) and had repeatedly made "false claims" in the media and misrepresented the nature of the court orders that had been made against him (839). In *Westpac Banking Corp v Lamieri* [2000] NSWSC 393, the New South Wales Supreme Court appointed an interim receiver in a fraud claim where the defendants had failed to give "any indication of a defence", and had failed to comply at all with their obligations under an existing Mareva injunction.
[46] *JSC BTA Bank v Ablyazov* [2010] EWCA Civ 1141, at [16].
[47] In *Wallace Kevin James v Merrill Lynch International Bank Ltd* [1998] 1 S.L.R. 785, the Singaporean Court of Appeal held that, in circumstances where worldwide *Mareva* relief was already in place against a defendant (and his wife's) assets, the additional remedy of a receiver being appointed would only be justified if otherwise there was an imminent danger of loss or dissipation of assets. The Singaporean Court of Appeal found that this high threshold had not been met, despite the fact that two breaches of the existing *Mareva* injunction had occurred, the first of which was the failure to give consent to the defendant's banker authorising the provision of information, and the second of which was an instruction to a tenant to pay monies to an account outside the jurisdiction. It should be noted, however, that the "imminent danger" requirement does not reflect English law.
[48] *JSC BTA Bank v Ablyazov* [2010] EWCA Civ 1141, at [16].

protection to a claimant because there is a measurable risk that a defendant may use the structure by which he holds his assets to deal with those assets in breach of the Freezing Order, then a receivership order will normally be justified."[49] Conversely, if the method by which a respondent beneficially holds his assets is transparent, a receivership order will be harder to justify.

(8)   A receivership may be justified where the relevant asset is fungible or requires management and, in the absence of a receiver taking control of it, there is a risk that its value might depreciate in the period prior to judgment.

(iii)   Considerations as to terms

Answering the question of whether to grant a receivership order is not the end of the court's enquiry. Even if a receivership is ordered, ancillary issues will almost always arise as to the powers to be conferred on the receivers. Even if it has decided in principle to order the appointment of a receiver, the court will bear in mind the degree of harm likely to be inflicted on the defendant by the provision of any given powers. It will also bear in mind the fact that at this stage the substantive dispute has not been adjudicated upon. So, for instance, it is likely that a court would decline to allow a receiver a power of sale, except in the ordinary course of business or where the asset is fungible. Similarly, just as with freezing orders, a receivership order made in support of a personal claim should not infringe the defendant's right to pay for legal representation, to pay his ordinary living expenses and to carry out transactions in the ordinary course of business (unless the receivership order has gone so far as to appoint a receiver over the business). **33–021**

D.   APPOINTMENT OF RECEIVER BY WAY OF EQUITABLE EXECUTION

(1)   Jurisdiction and Principles Governing its Exercise

There are of course multiple procedural mechanisms available in principle to a judgment creditor to enforce his judgment. One such mechanism, which has formerly been described as a form of execution of last resort, is the appointment of a receiver. Section 37(4) of the Senior Courts Act 1981 provides that: **33–022**

> "The power of the High Court to appoint a receiver by way of equitable execution[50] shall operate in relation to all legal estates and interests in land; and that power—
> (a)   may be exercised in relation to an estate or interest in land whether or not a charge has been imposed on that land under section 1 of the Charging Orders Act 1979 for the purpose of enforcing the judgment, order or award in question; and
> (b)   shall be in addition to, and not in derogation of, any power of any court to appoint a receiver in proceedings for enforcing such a charge. "

---

[49] *JSC BTA Bank v Ablyazov* [2010] EWCA Civ 1141, at [17].

[50] Equitable execution is a form of equitable relief granted because there is no remedy by execution at law, and to assist in the realisation of an asset of the judgment debtor: see *Re Shepherd, Atkins v Shepherd* (1889) 43 Ch. D. 131, at 135–137.

In addition to giving statutory recognition to the power to appoint a receiver by way of equitable execution, this subsection provides that the appointment of such a receiver may be made over land and it is an enforcement mechanism independent of the mechanism of the charging order.

33–023 In fraud cases, where the successful execution of judgments is usually fraught with difficulty and may be a major international undertaking in itself, the receiver has increasingly become a key weapon in the armoury of enforcement. A receiver appointed "by way of equitable execution" is an interim appointment, whose role is likely to continue only until payment of the judgment debt. Such a receiver does not differ in kind from other court-appointed receivers even if the reason for his appointment is specific to enforcement of a judgment debt.[51]

33–024 The benefit of a receiver is that his appointment will potentially permit the judgment creditor to be the beneficiary of the exercise of powers over companies and properties, and the receipt and getting in of debts, which would otherwise not be available to the judgment creditor by more conventional means, such as third party debt orders. It is an increasingly powerful tool in obtaining assets nominally in the hands of third parties or held in trust structures. As the examples set out below indicate, the courts will countenance the incremental expansion of the circumstances in which such orders will be granted, applying established principles to new situations, to overcome increasingly complex asset ownership structures.[52]

33–025 The following broad principles concerning the appointment of receivers by way of equitable execution can be derived from the cases, particiularly as reviewed by Lord Collins in the Privy Council case of *Tasarruf Mevduati Sigorta Fonu v Merrill Lynch Bank and Trust Co (Cayman) Ltd*[53] and by Males J in *Cruz City 1 Mauritius Holdings v Unitech Ltd*[54]:

(1) The demands of justice are the overriding consideration in assessing the scope of the jurisdiction under s.37(1). A key demand is that judgments of the English court and English arbitration awards should be complied with and if necessary enforced.

(2) Whilst the jurisdiction is not unfettered,[55] the court has power to grant injunctions and appoint receivers in circumstances where no injunction would have been granted or receiver appointed before 1873. In modern conditions where business is increasingly global in nature, the jurisdiction is "unconstrained by rigid expressions of principle and responsive to the demands of justice in the contemporary context."

---

[51] See generally *Masri v Consolidated Contractors International Co SAL* [2008] EWCA Civ 303; [2009] Q.B. 450, at [69].

[52] *Masri v Consolidated Contractors International Ltd* [2008] EWCA Civ 303; [2009] Q.B. 450.

[53] *Tasarruf Mevduati Sigorta Fonu v Merrill Lynch Bank and Trust Co (Cayman) Ltd* [2012] 1 W.L.R. 1721, at [56].

[54] *Cruz City 1 Mauritius Holdings v Unitech Ltd* [2014] EWHC 3131 (Comm), at [47].

[55] *South Carolina Insurance Co v Assurantie Maatschappij 'De Zeven Provincien' NV* [1987] A.C. 24, at 40.

(3)   A receiver by way of equitable execution will not be appointed unless there is some difficulty with execution by other means; although this is less of a hurdle than might otherwise be thought: see below.

(4)   A receiver will not be appointed if the court is satisfied that the appointment would be fruitless; but all that the applicant need demonstrate is that there is some real prospect that the appointment will serve some useful purpose.

(5)   The jurisdiction to appoint receivers by way of equitable execution can be developed incrementally to apply old principles to new situations.

In the practice direction to CPR Pt 69 it is suggested that, before a court will **33–026** appoint a receiver by way of equitable execution, it must be satisfied that the judgment "cannot be enforced by any other method" and the evidence served in support must address that question.[56] It is questionable whether this accurately reflects the current law. Although it has been said in some earlier cases that "special circumstances"[57] are required before a receiver will be appointed by way of equitable execution, that phrase has recently been given a wide meaning; so, in the *Cruz City* case, Males J said that

> "[t]he jurisdiction will not be exercised unless there is some hindrance or difficulty in using the normal processes of execution, but there are no rigid rules as to the nature of the hindrance or difficulty required, which may be practical or legal, and it is necessary to take account of all the circumstances of the case."

That is all that is meant by dicta which speak of the need for "special circumstances."[58] It follows that care must be taken with statements of principle contained in the numerous early cases involving the appointment of receivers post-judgment, which in general state the jurisdiction more narrowly.[59] Given the preponderance in fraud cases of complex (or at least deceptive) asset holding structures, in practice the court will readily accept that there is some hindrance or difficulty in execution sufficient to justify the appointment.[60]

---

[56] CPR PD 69, para.4.1(3)(d). As to the evidence on such an application see generally para.4.1(3).

[57] See for instance *Bourne v Colodense Ltd* [1985] I.C.R. 291.

[58] In *UCB Home Loans Corp Ltd v Grace* [2011] EWHC 851 (Ch) Arnold J held that there were sufficient "special circumstances" rendering it just and convenient to appoint a receiver by way of equitable jurisdiction when it would be "difficult for the claimant to enforce its judgment by other means" and that the appointment of a receiver was the only realistic prospect available to the judgment creditor to enforce its judgment in the short term. In that case the court appointed a receiver post-judgment over 63 properties owned by the defendant judgment debtors to allow the rents to be received by the receiver and paid over to the claimant judgment creditor. This was a case where obtaining charging orders was not going to be of benefit where there was very little free equity in the properties. What the claimant was interested in was the future rental stream.

[59] See generally *Masri v Consolidated Contractors International Co SAL* [2008] EWCA Civ 303; [2009] Q.B. 450 ("*Masri No.2*"), in which the early authorities are analysed: see at [141] and following.

[60] For an example of a more flexible approach to the requirements for appointing a receiver by way of execution in a fraud claim where it was held that the defendant was in fact the beneficial owner of properties purportedly owned by third parties, see *JSC BTA Bank v Ablyazov* [2013] EWHC 1361 (Comm): rather than require the claimant to execute by way of a charging order, the court was prepared to amend the terms of appointment of an existing receiver, who had originally been appointed in support of a freezing injunction, so as to include a power of sale of the relevant

33–027   Although a receiver will not be appointed where the court is satisfied that the appointment will be fruitless, again, in all but the clearest cases that consideration is unlikely to deflect the court's willingness to accede to the application. As noted above, the court will be willing to appoint a receiver "if there is a reasonable prospect that the appointment will assist in the enforcement of a judgment or award" or it will "serve a useful purpose."[61] This sets the bar low, unsurprisingly, given that the circumstances in which an application will be made will almost inevitably be where a judgment has gone unsatisfied and other enforcement methods have proved futile. There must be at least some credible evidence that there are assets against which the judgment may be executed. If the judgment debt, or the potential recovery which could realistically be obtained via the appointment of a receiver, is small then the court might decline to order an appointment on grounds of proportionality. On the other hand, whereas disruption to the defendant's business may be a material consideration when seeking the appointment of a receiver pre-judgment, it ceases to be such a consideration once a judgment has been obtained.[62]

33–028   The effect of the appointment of a receiver by way of equitable execution is threefold: first, it operates as an injunction restraining the judgment debtor from itself dealing with the asset in question; secondly, the receiver may be authorised to realise the asset in question or otherwise bring it into account, including suing in the name of the owner of the asset if the asset in question is a chose in action; and thirdly, it may serve to create a charge in favour of the judgment creditor (but only if the receiver is directed by the order to hold the asset for, or pay its proceeds or other realisation, to the judgment creditor).[63]

(2)   Assets Over which a Receiver may be Appointed by Way of Equitable Execution

33–029   A receiver by way of equitable execution may be appointed over whatever may be considered in equity as the assets of the judgment debtor.[64] This principle has been expansively interpreted, so that assets over which the judgment debtor has de facto control may be subject to a receivership order, as may a right to call for assets to be transferred.

33–030   The expansive approach explained above is exemplified in the following cases:

(1)   A receiver may be appointed by way of equitable execution over future debts. In *Soinco v Novokuznetzk Aluminium Plant*[65] the court ordered the appointment of a receiver to receive payment of sums of money which were to become due to the defendant judgment debtor in the future. In such

---

properties (thereby converting it into a receivership by way of equitable execution). Considerations of practical convenience, delay and cost persuaded the court to adopt that pragmatic course.

[61]   *Cruz City* [2014] EWHC 3131 (Comm), at [47].

[62]   *Soinco v Novokuznetzk Aluminium Plant* [1998] 1 Q.B. 406.

[63]   *Masri v Consolidated Contractors International Co* [2007] EWHC 3010 (Comm), at [114].

[64]   *Masri No.2* [2008] EWCA Civ 303; [2009] Q.B. 450, at [151]; *Tasarruf* [2012] 1 W.L.R. 1721, at [6]; and *Blight v Brewster* [2012] EWHC 165 (Ch); [2012] 1 W.L.R. 2841, at [66].

[65]   *Soinco v Novokuznetzk Aluminium Plant* [1998] 1 Q.B. 406.

a case, where the dates when the sums might become payable, and in what amounts, were facts not presently known, a third party debt order was insufficient.[66]

(2) A receiver may similarly be appointed over a right of indemnity to which the judgment debtor is entitled as against a third party, even though it gives rise not to a debt but a different form of action.[67]

(3) In *Masri v Consolidated Contractors International SAL*[68] it was held that a receiver may also be appointed by the court by way of equitable execution over future receipts from a specifically defined asset.

(4) In the *Tasarruf* case a receiver was appointed over a power of revocation of a Cayman Islands trust, where an unfettered power of revocation had been reserved to the settlor. The judgment debtor unsuccessfully argued that there could be no appointment of a receiver over a power of revocation because it was not property: instead the power was said to be "such that in equity, in the circumstances of a case such as this... [the judgment debtor]... can be regarded as having rights tantamount to ownership".[69]

(5) In *Blight v Brewster*[70] the judgment debtor had the right under his pension to draw down 25% of that pension as a tax free lump sum, but the claimant could not obtain a third party debt order until the right to draw down had been exercised, since prior to that there was no money due and owing as a debt to the judgment debtor. Mr Gabriel Moss QC, sitting as a Deputy High Court Judge, said that the judgment debtor's ability to elect to take his cash payment must be regarded as being a right "tantamount to ownership" and so could be the subject of a receivership order, allowing the receiver to exercise the right on behalf of the judgment debtor.[71] The judge expressly declined to follow the decision in the earlier case of *Field v Field*,[72] in which the judge had held that the court could not require a husband subject to a lump sum payment order in favour of his wife to elect to take a lump sum entitlement under a personal pension scheme, or appoint a receiver to make that election on his behalf.

---

[66] Generally, appointment of a receiver may be appropriate where a third party debt order cannot be made.

[67] See for instance *Bourne v Colodense Ltd* [1985] I.C.R. 291 and *Allied Irish Bank v Ashford Hotels Ltd* [1998] BCC 440.

[68] *Masri v Consolidated Contractors International SAL* [2008] EWCA Civ 303; [2009] Q.B. 450. See at [184], per Collins LJ: "There is no longer a rule, if there ever was one, that an order can only be made in relation to property which is presently amenable to legal execution. There is no firm foundation in authority for a rule that the remedy is not available in relation to future debts."

[69] *Tasarruf* [2012] 1 W.L.R. 1721, at [59], per Lord Collins. The meaning of the phrase "tantamount to ownership" is inherently uncertain and it remains to be seen how it will be interpreted in future cases. One example is *Blight v Brewster* [2012] EWHC 165 (Ch).

[70] *Blight v Brewster* [2012] EWHC 165 (Ch). This is so even though a trustee in bankruptcy of the pension holder could not compel the pension holder to elect to draw down: *Horton v Henry* [2016] EWCA Civ 689; [2017] 1 W.L.R. 391.

[71] *Blight v Brewster* [2012] EWHC 165 (Ch), at [68].

[72] *Field v Field* [2003] 1 F.L.R. 376, per Wilson J. This case was trenchantly criticized in S. Gee, *Commercial Injunctions*, 5th edn (London: Sweet & Maxwell, 2004) at 16.011 (and the criticism is repeated in the 6th edn, 2017, at [16.014]–[16.016]. That criticism was echoed in *Tasarruf* [2012] 1 W.L.R. 1721, at [63].

(6) In *JSC VTB Bank v Skurikhin*[73] the court ordered the appointment of receivers over the membership interests in an LLP so as to allow the receivers to exercise the powers of the members of the LLP to sell properties owned by the LLP and place the LLP into administration so that its assets could be realised. It was held that, provided the applicant could satisfy the court on the balance of probabilities that the judgment debtor had de facto control over the assets of the Liechtenstein foundation, which was said to beneficially own the membership interests, then receivers could be appointed over those interests.

33–031 In contrast, the interest of a beneficiary under a genuine discretionary trust is probably not of a sufficiently proprietary character to be the subject of a receivership by way of equitable execution.[74]

(3) Foreign Assets

33–032 We have considered pre-judgment receiverships over foreign assets above. The court can, and often does, make receivership orders by way of equitable execution in relation to foreign assets. Although, as a matter of general principle, there needs to be a sufficient connection with the English court to justify making such an order, the fact that the order is made with a view to the enforcement of an English judgment or arbitral award provides that connection.[75] In *Masri No.2*[76] Collins LJ approved the following earlier statement of the law, made in the context of pre-judgment receivers, as applicable to receivers appointed by way of equitable execution:

> "To regard the grant of a *Mareva* injunction not as a matter of territorial jurisdiction to be exercised court by court throughout the various countries of the world where it may be appropriate but as a matter of unlimited jurisdiction *in personam* of the English court over persons who have properly been made parties, under English procedure, to proceedings pending before the English court is consistent with the approach of the English court to the appointment of receivers of the British and foreign assets of English companies. The court has always been ready to appoint a receiver over the foreign as well as British assets of an English company, even though it has recognized that in relation to foreign assets the appointment may not prove effective without assistance from a foreign court: *In re Maudslay, Sons & Field*... Moreover where a foreign court of the country where the assets are situate refuses to recognise the receiver appointed by the English court, the English court will, in an appropriate case, do what it can to render the appointment effective by orders *in personam* against persons who are subject to the jurisdiction of the English court ..."[77]

---

[73] *JSC VTB Bank v Skurikhin* [2015] EWHC 2131 (Comm).
[74] See the decision of the Grand Court of the Cayman Islands in *Y v R*, unreported, 9 January 2018, relying on *R v Lincolnshire County Court Judge* (1887) 20 Q.B.D. 167, per Pollock P at 170: "we find that there is no case in which a receiver has been directed to receive a sum the payment of which to the debtor is wholly contingent and dependent on the will of another person"; and on the characterisation of such an interest, see per Lewison LJ in *JSC Mezhdunarodniy Promyshlenniy Bank v Pugachev* [2015] EWCA Civ 139; [2016] 1 W.L.R. 160, at [13].
[75] *Masri No.2* [2008] EWCA Civ 303; [2009] Q.B. 450, at [59]–[61]; and *Cruz City* [2014] EWHC 3131 (Comm), at [35].
[76] *Masri No.2* [2008] EWCA Civ 303; [2009] Q.B. 450, at [68]–[69].
[77] *Derby & Co Ltd v Weldon (No.6)* [1990] 1 W.L.R. 1139, at 1150, per Dillon LJ.

E. PROCEDURE

(1) Introduction

CPR Pt 69 and its accompanying practice direction are dedicated to the provisions regulating the procedures for applications to court for the appointment of receivers, and the management of the receivership thereafter. The key provisions of this rule are summarised below. Reference should also be made to the *Guide for Receivers in the Chancery Division*, which is referred to at para.29.71 of the Chancery Guide.

33–033

(2) Court

A receiver may be applied for in any division of the High Court though it is more usually applied for in the Chancery Division. Nonetheless in circumstances where many substantial fraud claims now proceed in the Commercial Court, that court has been responsible for many appointments of receivers in recent years and there are numerous recent judgments emanating from Commercial Court judges clarifying and developing the jurisdiction.

33–034

(3) Timing

Applications may be made (and a receiver may be appointed) prior to, or after, judgment, and even in advance of the commencement of proceedings: r.69.2(1).[78] As we have already seen, receivers are often appointed post-judgment by way of equitable execution.

33–035

(4) Power to Apply Without Notice

An application for the appointment of a receiver may be made without notice: r.69.3(a).

33–036

Considerable care should, however, be taken by applicants contemplating applying without notice for the appointment of a receiver that the circumstances of the case truly warrant no notice at all to the respondent, particularly given the possible impact on the respondent and his business affairs which are likely to flow from the grant of a receivership order. Considerations which apply to applications without notice are discussed in Ch.27 above and those principles are broadly applicable to receivership applications. The situation would have to be either sufficiently urgent, or the risk of dissipation (or the taking of some step which could render the receivership ineffective) so great, that no prior warning whatever should be given to the defendant before the receivership application (and order) was made. As it was put in the Australian case of *National Australia Bank Ltd v Bond Brewing Holdings Ltd*[79]:

33–037

---

[78] As to applications prior to the commencement of proceedings see CPR PD 69, para.2.
[79] *National Australia Bank Ltd v Bond Brewing Holdings Ltd* [1991] V.L.R. 386, at 539–540.

"Of course in a strong enough case the court might, without warning to a trading company, divest it of control of its undertaking and assets. But it must always be borne in mind that the appointment of a receiver in such a case authorises an irresistible invasion and that even if the army of occupation is withdrawn after only a short time things may never be the same again."

33–038   Any applicant without notice should of course give particularly careful consideration to the duty of full and frank disclosure applicable to all without notice applications.[80]

(5)   Need for the Receiver to be an Individual

33–039   The receiver must be an individual: r.69.2(2). This is because the receiver is an officer of the court and, as such, has personal duties to the court.[81] As a result, receivers will understandably be cautious to ensure that any action taken is in compliance with and in furtherance of the receivership order. In the evidence served in support of an application for a receiver the applicant should normally identify the individual (or individuals) whom it is proposed should act, provide details about their qualifications and suitability, and include evidence from a person who knows the proposed receiver, stating that he believes that they are a suitable person to be appointed, and giving grounds for that belief. The person proposed must provide a written consent to act: the court will not appoint an unwilling person to act as receiver. The court may decline to appoint the proposed nominee and appoint a different person.[82]

(6)   Remuneration

33–040   A receiver may only charge for his services if the court so directs and specifies the basis on which the receiver is to be remunerated: CPR r.69.7(1). In practice, a receiver will almost inevitably require remuneration and the court will almost always give the required direction. CPR r.69.7 contains detailed provisions concerning remuneration.[83]

33–041   Considerable care needs to be taken, when applying for the appointment of a receiver, to consider exactly what relief to seek so far as remuneration is concerned and, once a receiver is appointed, great care also needs to be taken by

---

[80] As to which, see Ch.27, para.27–060 and following.

[81] The classic statement of the position was by Cairns LJ in *Gardner v London Chatham and Dover Railway Co (No.1)* (1867) L.R. 2 Ch. App. 201, at 211: "When the court appoints a manager of a business or undertaking, it in effect assumes the management into its own hands; for the manager is the servant or officer of the court, and upon any question arising as to the character and details of the management, it is the court that must direct and decide." For "manager" read "receiver."

[82] See the procedural provisions at CPR PD 69, paras 4.2–4.4.

[83] In particular r.69.7(4) provides that: "Unless the court orders otherwise, in determining the remuneration of a receiver the court shall award such sum as is reasonable and proportionate in all the circumstances and which takes into account- (a) the time properly given by him and his staff to the receivership; (b) the complexity of the receivership; (c) any responsibility of an exceptional kind or degree which falls on the receiver in consequence of the receivership; (d) the effectiveness with which the receiver appears to be carrying out, or to have carried out, his duties; and (e) the value and nature of the subject matter of the receivership."

a receiver (and those liable for paying the fees) to ensure that all fees incurred are reasonable and proportionate having regard to the factors set out in CPR r.69.7.

(7) Provision of Security

Ordinarily, the court requires the receiver to provide security or provide evidence of existing security.[84]   **33–042**

(8) Directions

A receiver himself may, during the course of his receivership apply for directions from the court: r.69.7. He may do so for instance where a particular proposed step is likely to be contentious or it is unclear whether the terms of his appointment permit that step to be taken.   **33–043**

(9) Termination of Receivership

The court may terminate the appointment of a receiver and appoint another receiver in his place at any time: r.69.2(3). Rule 69.10 goes on to provide that a "receiver or any party may apply for the receiver to be discharged on completion of his duties". However this rule is permissive: it is not exhaustive of the circumstances in which an application to discharge a receiver may be made.[85]   **33–044**

(10) Liability of receivers

A receiver may be liable for defaults during the course of his receivership. Permission of the court appointing the receiver is required before any claim against him can be instituted.[86] The nature of a receiver's liability is complex and beyond the scope of this book.[87]   **33–045**

---

[84] There are detailed provisions relating to security: see CPR r.69.5 and PD 69, paras 6.2 and 7.

[85] *McCracken v Crown Prosecution Service* [2011] EWCA Civ 1620; [2012] Lloyd's Rep. FC 148, at [42].

[86] *Re Maidstone Palace of Varities Ltd* [1909] Ch. 283; *McGowan v Chadwick* [2002] EWCA Civ 1758.

[87] See generally P. Walton et al, *Kerr and Hunter on Administrators and Receivers*, 19th edn (London, Sweet & Maxwell, 2012) at Ch.8.

SECTION G

TRIAL, JUDGMENTS AND ENFORCEMENT

PROVING A CLAIM IN FRAUD: EVIDENCE AND OTHER TRIAL
ISSUES

A. INTRODUCTION

(1) The Scope of this Chapter

This chapter is concerned with the practical, procedural and legal aspects of
making and proving a case in fraud at trial. It is not intended to be a treatise on
the law of evidence or procedure (both of which subjects are well covered in
other specialist texts), nor does it attempt to identify all of the issues relating to
proof of a claim which might arise—especially since a number of such issues will
not be peculiar to fraud cases. Instead, we hope to flag, and offer some helpful
insights on, a selection of points which are likely to arise in fraud cases.

34–001

In particular, we touch upon:

34–002

(1) In the context of the lead-up to trial:
  (a) Issues to do with *evidence*, including admissibility; the authenticity
       of documents; and the protection and destruction of documents;
  (b) Issues to do with *witnesses*, including contact between witnesses and
       witness familiarisation; and
  (c) Issues to do with *pleadings*, in particular late amendments[1];
(2) At the trial itself:
  (a) Issues to do with *witnesses*, including decisions as to whether to call
       witnesses at all and, if so, in what order to call them; witness
       reliability; whether witnesses should be present during each other's
       testimony; the giving of evidence by video link; ambushing witnesses
       in cross-examination; and putting a case that a witness is dishonest/
       challenging a finding to that effect;
  (b) Issues to do with *inferences*, including inferences that can be drawn
       from a failure to disclose documents; adverse inferences from a
       witness not giving evidence; and the proof of fraud by inference;
  (c) The *privilege against self-incrimination*.

---

[1] The topic of how one properly pleads a case in fraud at the outset has already been considered: see
para.1–011.

(2)   The Standard of Proof

34–003   As we have previously noted,[2] the standard of proof for an allegation of fraud or dishonesty is the normal civil standard—the balance of probabilities.[3] It has often been suggested, however, that the evidential burden on the claimant is in practice heightened, on the basis that

> "the more serious the allegation the less likely it is that the event occurred and, hence, the stronger should be the evidence before the court concludes that the allegation is established on the balance of probability."[4]

In *Foodco UK LLP v Henry Boot Developments Ltd*[5] Lewison J put it thus:

> "The burden of proof lies on the [claimants] to establish their case. They must persuade me that it is more probable than not that [the defendants] made fraudulent misrepresentations. Although the standard of proof is the same in every civil case, where fraud is alleged cogent evidence is needed to prove it, because the evidence must overcome the inherent improbability that people act dishonestly rather than carelessly. On the other hand inherent improbabilities must be assessed in the light of the actual circumstances of the case ..."

34–004   However, these observations are not to be understood as laying down a rule of law.[6] The standard of proof does not vary with the gravity of the misconduct alleged; rather, the court should have regard to the inherent probabilities and, as a matter of common sense, and as a very broad generalisation, it is inherently less likely that a defendant will be dishonest than that he will be incompetent. But, as the concluding remark in the above quotation recognises, all depends on the particular circumstances: "there is no logical or necessary connection between seriousness and probability".[7] It may be, for example, that a party is shown to have lied in their evidence on a particular aspect of the case.[8] That fact would entitle the court to reach the conclusion that the likelihood of that party having behaved dishonestly in other relevant respects was greater. The circumstances of the case before the court, including the inferences that can legitimately be drawn from circumstantial evidence, can of course displace inherent improbabilities; and the question is always, ultimately, whether on the evidence before the court the allegation of fraud or dishonesty has been established to the usual civil standard.[9]

---

[2] Ch.1, para.1–012.

[3] *Hornal v Neuberger Products* [1957] 1 Q.B. 247.

[4] *Re H (Minors)* [1996] A.C. 563, at 586–587, per Lord Nicholls; *AIC Ltd v ITS Trading Services (UK) Ltd* [2007] 1 All E.R. (Comm) 667, per Rix LJ at [259]; *In Re B* [2009] A.C. 11, at [70]; *Dadourian Group International Inc v Simms* [2009] 1 Lloyd's Rep. 609, at [32]; *JSC BTA Bank v Ablyazov* [2013] EWHC 510 (Comm), per Teare J at [76].

[5] *Foodco UK LLP v Henry Boot Developments Ltd* [2010] EWHC 358 (Ch), at [3].

[6] *Re B* [2009] 1 A.C. 11, per Lord Hoffmann at [13]–[15]; *Re S-B* [2010] 1 A.C. 678, per Lady Hale at [11]–[13]; *Re J* [2013] 1 A.C. 680, per Lady Hale at [35].

[7] *Re B* [2009] 1 A.C. 11, per Lady Hale at [72].

[8] See *Fiona Trust v Privalov* [2010] EWHC 3199 (Comm), at [1440]–[1446].

[9] See *Otkritie International Investment Management Ltd v Urumov* [2014] EWHC 191 (Comm), per Eder J at [85]–[89]; *Kazakhstan Kagazy Plc v Zhunus* [2017] EWHC 3374 (Comm), per Picken J at [155]–[159]; and *JSC BM Bank v Kekhman* [2018] EWHC 791 (Comm), per Bryan J at [46]–[66].

B. THE LEAD-UP TO TRIAL

(1) Admissibility of Evidence

(i) Evidence improperly obtained

The general common law principle is that all relevant evidence, howsoever obtained, is admissible.[10]   **34–005**

The court however has a general power to exclude otherwise admissible evidence, which is now provided for in CPR r.32.1. If a party wishes to raise an objection to evidence being admitted at trial (which in practice is the only way that the issue is likely to come before the court), such an objection ought to be raised before or at the point when documents are included in the trial bundle: para.27.2 of PD 32 provides that all documents contained in bundles which have been agreed for use at a hearing shall be admissible at the hearing as evidence of their contents, unless the court orders otherwise or a party gives written notice of objection to the admissibility of particular documents. Paragraph 3.9 of CPR PD 39A envisages that any objection to documents being included in trial bundles, or as to the consequences of their inclusion, should be lodged with the bundles themselves. In reality, objections as to admissibility will have been raised long before then.   **34–006**

In evaluating any such objection, the court will, as part of the requirement to apply the overriding objective, look beyond the justice of the individual case; and to that extent the principles applicable to the question of admissibility of improperly obtained evidence have (at least nominally) shifted.[11] If the admission of evidence would bring the process of the court into disrepute, for example by encouraging litigants to obtain evidence by illegal means, this might be grounds for rejecting it.   **34–007**

In practice, however, it remains the case that it will only be in an unusual case that the balancing of all the relevant considerations will lead to the conclusion that evidence, which is relevant and therefore otherwise admissible, should be excluded because of the manner in which it was obtained (for example, by trespass, deception or breach of confidence).[12] Usually it will be more appropriate for the court to admit the evidence, but sanction the unlawful or inappropriate conduct of the party obtaining it with an adverse costs order.[13]   **34–008**

---

[10] The classic statement of the position is that of Lord Goddard CJ in *Kuruma v The Queen* [1955] A.C. 197, at 203: "In their Lordships' opinion the test to be applied in considering whether evidence is admissible is whether it is relevant to the matters in issue. If it is, it is admissible and the court is not concerned with how the evidence was obtained". See also *Helliwell v Piggott-Sims* [1980] F.S.R. 356. The comments in *Imerman v Tchenguiz* [2010] EWCA Civ 908; [2011] Fam 116, at [171], which may be read to the contrary, appear in fact to conflate the common law power to exclude evidence with instances of material being excluded on the grounds of breach of confidence.

[11] *Jones v University of Warwick* [2003] EWCA Civ 151; [2003] 1 W.L.R. 954.

[12] *Amwell View School Governors v Dogherty* [2007] I.C.R. 135 is a rare instance of evidence being excluded on the basis of the wider effect it may have of encouraging litigants illegally to obtain evidence.

[13] As happened in *Jones v University of Warwick*, above.

34-009 An important point to note is that, following the decision in *Dubai Aluminium v Al Alawi*,[14] legal professional privilege cannot be asserted in respect of any illegally obtained evidence, including any document relating to how it was obtained (such as communications with the person who obtained it). Such documents are therefore not immune from inspection.[15] Further, a party cannot assert litigation privilege in respect of a document or evidence by claiming that the "dominant purpose" for which it was brought into existence was contemplated litigation, if that purpose was deliberately concealed and the evidence only obtained as a result of that deception. Thus in *Property Alliance Group v Royal Bank of Scotland Plc*, the claimant's Managing Director invited two of the defendant's outgoing or ex-employees to meetings on the false pretext that he was considering offering them a job, and then secretly recorded those meetings. The claimant's contention that the transcripts of the meetings were privileged because the Managing Director's purpose in arranging the meetings had in fact been to gather evidence for use in the litigation was rejected on the basis that the Managing Director had actively deceived the employees as to that purpose.[16]

(ii) Hearsay evidence

34-010 As is well-known, the general rule in civil proceedings (and fraud claims are no exception) is that evidence is not inadmissible on the grounds that it is hearsay,[17] "hearsay" for these purposes meaning a statement made otherwise than by a person while giving oral evidence in proceedings, which is tendered as evidence of the matters stated.[18]

34-011 Where a party intends to rely on hearsay evidence he must give the other party notice to that effect,[19] albeit a failure to do so does not affect its admissibility.[20] Where the relevant evidence is to be adduced at trial, and either it is to be given by a witness who is giving oral evidence or it is contained in a witness statement of a person who is not being called to give oral evidence, the statutory notice requirement is met by serving a witness statement[21]—save that if it is not intended to call the maker of the statement, the other parties must be informed to that effect and the reason why the witness will not be called must be given.[22] One

---

[14] *Dubai Aluminium v Al Alawi* [1999] 1 W.L.R. 1964.
[15] *Franses v Al Assad* [2007] EWHC 2442 (Ch).
[16] *Property Alliance Group v Royal Bank of Scotland Plc* [2016] 4 W.L.R. 3, at [30]–[42]. See also *Plummers v Debenhams Plc* [1986] B.C.L.C. 447, at 459, per Millett J and *London Fire and Emergency Planning Authority v Halcrow Gilbert & Co Ltd* [2005] B.L.R. 18, per Judge Toulmin QC.
[17] Civil Evidence Act 1995, s.1.
[18] A definition which is adopted in the CPR: r.33.1(a).
[19] Civil Evidence Act 1995, s.2(1).
[20] Civil Evidence Act 1995, s.2(4).
[21] CPR r.33.2(1).
[22] CPR r.33.2(2).

reason for such a notice is that it enables the other party to apply (within 14 days) for permission to call the maker of the statement to be cross-examined on the contents of the statement.[23]

Documents other than witness statements which are contained in the trial bundle are often relied on for the truth of their contents, and so as hearsay. As already noted, para.27.2 of PD 32 provides that all documents contained in bundles which have been agreed for use at a hearing shall be admissible at the hearing as evidence of their contents (subject to contrary order) and that is, in any event, the effect of s.1 of the Civil Evidence Act 1995. What is less clear is whether a party who intends to rely on documents in the bundle in this way nevertheless still needs to meet the notice requirements of s.2 of the 1995 Act. The point was considered by the Court of Appeal in *Charnock v Rowan*,[24] with an (inconclusive) indication that the answer was negative. In *First Subsea Ltd v Balltec Ltd*[25] Norris J reached the contrary view—that it would *not* have been appropriate for a party to have relied on a statement contained in a document in the trial bundle to prove a central issue in the case without some form of prior notice, and that the provisions of PD 32 were not to be understood as overriding the rest of CPR Pt 32 or the Civil Evidence Act 1995:

    34–012

> "It would not be 'just' in many cases to rely upon para.27.2 as relieving a party seeking to use it of the obligation of giving fair and proper notice of the matter that is in issue and the evidence that will be used to prove it."

A party to fraud litigation who is contemplating not calling the maker of a statement and relying on it as hearsay must of course have it firmly in mind that the fact that the evidence is admissible as such does not prevent it being accorded little if any weight.[26] In a fraud case, the unjustified failure to call a witness who is critical (whether in proving them or defending them) is likely to render their evidence more or less worthless. As Brandon J said in *The Ferdinand Retzlaff*[27]:

    34–013

> "... matters of this importance, in a case of this kind, should be proved by oral evidence ... I cannot think that the Civil Evidence Act 1968 was intended, in general, to change the long-established system by which seriously disputed central issues in civil cases are tried on oral evidence, given on oath and capable of being tested by cross-examination, and to substitute for it a system of trial on unsworn documents brought into existence by parties to the proceedings *post litem motam*, and I do not think the Act should be used, or rather abused, so as to produce such a result".

---

[23] CPR r.33.4. It is thought that the expression "on the contents of the statement" is not intended to preclude cross-examination of a witness called under this provision outside the four corners of the statement (subject, of course, to the trial judge's general power to control the scope of cross-examination).

[24] *Charnock v Rowan* [2012] EWCA Civ 2.

[25] *First Subsea Ltd v Balltec Ltd* [2013] EWHC 1033 (Pat), at [29].

[26] As to which, see s.4 of the Civil Evidence Act 1995.

[27] *The Ferdinand Retzlaff* [1972] 2 Lloyd's Rep. 120, at 127. For a recent analysis of the weight to be placed on hearsay evidence in a fraud claim see *JSC BM Bank v Kekhman* [2018] EWHC 791 (Comm), per Bryan J at [82]–[88].

(2) Authenticity of Documents

34–014 Under CPR 32.19, a party is taken to admit the authenticity of any document disclosed unless a notice requiring the other party to prove the document at trial is served, which must be done either within 7 days after disclosure or by the latest date for filing witness statements (whichever is later). For obvious reasons, the authenticity of documents is an issue which often arises in fraud cases.

34–015 Failure to serve the requisite notice leaves a party unable to challenge the authenticity of a document unless the court grants permission, applying the principles for relief from sanction. While, following the restatement of the relevant approach in *Denton v T H White Ltd*[28] and the adumbration of the "three-stage test", relief from sanction is more readily given than previously, it cannot be guaranteed that relief will be granted simply because a party overlooked the requirement to serve the requisite notice.

34–016 The concept of "authenticity" runs more widely than might be expected in this context. It does not merely refer to whether the document disclosed is a "genuine" document, in the sense of one that has not been doctored or concocted. Any issue that goes to whether the document is what it purports on its face to be can be seen as an issue of authenticity. So the date on which what was alleged to be a diary note was on its face created could not be challenged without proper service of a r.32.19 notice.[29] Perhaps more obviously, a notice must have been served in order to permit the contention that a signature on a document was not a genuine signature.[30]

34–017 However, while necessary, mere service of a notice under r.32.19 is not sufficient if a party intends to allege deliberate forgery: a notice under r.32.19 does not transfer the burden of proving that a document is not a forgery onto the party relying upon it. Nor will it be sufficient, to advance and establish a case of forgery, simply to criticise the evidence of authenticity adduced in response to a notice.[31] A clear and distinct pleading of forgery, supported by appropriate evidence satisfying the evidential burden, is required. So in one recent case[32] the defendant served a defence in which it relied upon a particular memorandum, being a document said to have been provided to the claimant at the time of the relevant transaction. The claimant in its reply did not admit or deny the authenticity of the document. On the last day for doing so under r.32.19, it served a notice requiring the document to be proved at trial. The judge laid down a helpful analysis of the issues involved in requiring a party to "prove" a document.

> "[57] Requiring a party to 'prove' a document means that the party relying upon the document must lead apparently credible evidence of sufficient weight that the document is what it purports to be. The question then is whether (in the light of that evidence and in the absence of any evidence to the contrary effect being adduced by the party challenging the document) the party bearing the burden of proof in the action has established its case on the balance of

---

[28] *Denton v T H White Ltd* [2014] EWCA Civ 906; [2014] 1 W.L.R. 3926.
[29] *Eco3 Capital Ltd v Lusdin Overseas Ltd* [2013] EWCA Civ 413, at [105].
[30] *Nageh v David Game College Ltd* [2013] EWCA Civ 1340, at [19].
[31] *Redstone Mortgages Ltd v B Legal Ltd* [2014] EWHC 3390 (Ch).
[32] *Redstone Mortgages Ltd v B Legal Ltd* [2014] EWHC 3390 (Ch).

probabilities. [The claimant] cannot (by a refusal to admit the authenticity of a document) transfer the overall burden of proof onto [the defendant], any more than it could do so simply by refusing to admit a fact.

[58] The question is therefore whether any evidence as to the provenance of the document has been produced, and if it has then whether (although not countered by any evidence to the contrary) such evidence is on its face so unsatisfactory as to be incapable of belief. It is vital that the process of challenge is fair. Criticism of the evidence about the authenticity of the document cannot amount to a covert and unpleaded case of forgery. If a case of forgery is to be put then the challenge should be set out fairly and squarely on the pleadings (and appropriate directions can be given). If the charge is that a witness has forged a document (or has been party to the forgery of a document) and the grounds of challenge have not been set out in advance, then if the questions are not objected to the response of the witness to the charge must be assessed taking into account the element of ambush and surprise."

Handwriting and other forensic experts are a common feature of fraud trials, given that the authenticity of signatures will often be in dispute. The issues that can be addressed by such experts go far beyond the mere authenticity of signatures, though that is a frequently disputed issue. Questions such as whether a document was created by one hand or several, whether the words in a document were created at the same time or with later additions, the order in which documents were composed, and the dating of documents (whether handwritten or printed) are all potential subjects for forensic analysis and expert evidence. Nevertheless, while such forensic evidence plays an increasingly prominent role and can be crucial in proving forgery, a trend only likely to accelerate as techniques continue to improve, it is not necessarily decisive in all cases. *Kingley Developments Ltd v Brudenell*[33] is an example of a case where, despite superficially strong forensic evidence of forgery, the oral testimony of a witness to the signature was ultimately preferred. **34–018**

(3)   Protection/Destruction of Documents

(i)   Introduction

Perhaps curiously, the CPR does not provide expressly for the retention or preservation of documents once litigation is in contemplation or even once it has commenced: there is no rule which in terms prevents a party from destroying documents. The closest that one gets is CPR PD 31B, which provides that, once litigation is in reasonable contemplation, legal representatives must advise their clients of their duty to preserve *electronic* documents. Incongruously, there is no equivalent provision as far as hard-copy documents are concerned. **34–019**

Nonetheless, the destruction of relevant documents once litigation is in contemplation or has been commenced can have significant adverse consequences, as explored below; and a lawyer advising a client in a potential or actual fraud claim would be sensible to raise the issue of document destruction, including the suspension of routine document destruction programmes. Once litigation is a reasonable contemplation, the client needs to appreciate that the continuation of what would otherwise be legitimate document destruction **34–020**

---

[33] *Kingley Developments Ltd v Brudenell* [2016] EWCA Civ 980.

programmes may prejudice their ability to prove their case at trial and (worse) lead to the drawing of adverse inferences against them.

34–021 Moreover, advisers and clients should keep it in mind that destroyed documents remain subject to the provisions of CPR 31 regarding disclosure, and in particular that they should appear on disclosure lists as documents no longer in the party's control. This is often overlooked. A party is therefore likely to be compelled to identify the fact of, and explain the reason for, the destruction of relevant documents.

(ii)   Illegitimate destruction

34–022 There is, of course, a clear distinction between legitimate and illegitimate destruction of documents: organisations routinely destroy documents, particularly hard-copy documents, given the costs of archiving them, and if that happens at a point when the organisation has no reason to think that the documents may need to be preserved for litigation, the court is unlikely to draw an adverse inference as to what was in the destroyed documents or as to the credibility of the destroying party.[34] The prejudice resulting from legitimate document destruction is simply that the party will find it harder to meet the evidential burden of proving or defending the claim.

34–023 In contrast, the deliberate destruction of potentially relevant documents at a point when litigation has commenced or is in reasonable contemplation is likely to lead to a number of adverse consequences for the destroying party.

34–024 First, the court is likely to draw an adverse inference against the destroying party. The principle derives from the maxim "*omnia praesumuntur contra spoliatorem*" (everything is presumed against a destroyer (of evidence)).[35] This principle is not applied as rigorously as the unadorned Latin would have it, but nonetheless the underlying principle continues to remain part of the law. The most recent analysis of the principle yielded the following limitations placed upon it:

> "First, if it is found that the destruction of the evidence was carried out deliberately so to as hinder the proof of the plaintiff's claim, then such finding will obviously reflect on the credibility of the destroyer. In such circumstances it would enable the Court to disregard the evidence of the destroyer in the application of the principle. But that is not this case.
>
> Second, if the Court has difficulty in deciding which party's evidence to accept, then it would be legitimate to resolve that doubt by the application of the presumption. But, thirdly, if the judge forms a clear view, having borne in mind all the difficulties which may arise from the unavailability of material documents, as to which side is telling the truth, I do not accept that the application of the presumption can require the judge to accept evidence he does not believe or to reject evidence he finds to be truthful."[36]

---

[34] *Earles v Barclays Bank* [2010] Bus. L.R. 566, at [28].

[35] *Infabricks Ltd v Jaytex Ltd* [1985] F.S.R. 75; and *Indian Oil Corp Ltd v Greenstone Shipping SA* [1988] Q.B. 345, at 363, per Staughton J: "if the wrongdoer has destroyed or impaired the evidence by which the innocent party could show how much he has lost the wrongdoer must suffer from the resulting uncertainty". This principle can apply even if the destruction was not deliberate or in bad faith: *Malhotra v Dhawan* [1997] 8 Med L.R. 319.

[36] *Malhotra v Dhawan* [1997] 8 Med L.R. 319, at 322, per Morritt LJ.

Where the party has in bad faith prevented the documents from being put forward, the court is entitled to draw conclusions as to the credibility of the destroying party's evidence generally, and may draw the particular conclusion that the contents of the document were unfavourable to the destroying party, provided that there is some secondary evidence as to the contents of the document.[37]

34-025

Secondly, and again notwithstanding the absence of any express prohibition in the CPR, deliberate destruction of documents to prevent their use in litigation amounts to perversion of the course of justice and as such is a contempt of court,[38] with the serious potential consequences discussed elsewhere in this book.[39]

34-026

Thirdly, it is possible that the deliberate destruction of documents may lead to the court concluding that it is unable to conduct a fair trial, with the consequence that the destroying party's case is struck out.[40] If the court concludes that the destruction of documents was contumacious, the court may strike out the party's statement of case even if a fair trial were still possible.[41]

34-027

Where litigation has not been commenced at the time of destruction, the case for visiting the destroying party with these consequences (and particularly the latter two) is obviously more problematic. Litigation would at least have to be in contemplation; and the court would probably have to conclude (but this may be inferred) that it was sufficiently clear to the parties what the issues were likely to be in the then hypothetical proceedings for it to be obvious that the documents should be preserved.

34-028

(iii)   Document preservation orders and search orders

In cases where the court considers there is a real risk of the destruction of evidence,[42] there are a number of orders that the court may make. These include orders for the preservation of documents by the party in possession of them; for the delivery up of documents or copies of them; and to permit the opposing party to take copies of documents. Given the preponderance of electronic documentation, a common application (and a step that it is well worth all parties considering, since a defendant to a fraud claim may want to establish that apparently damaging documentary electronic evidence has been manufactured or doctored) is for the imaging of hard drives, preserving such information as is contained on them at the time of imaging.

34-029

In extreme circumstances, a party may obtain a search order, requiring the other party to permit the applicant to search the other party's premises and copy or remove specific documents or categories of documents in order to preserve them. The requirements and procedure for obtaining a search order are considered

34-030

---

[37] See *Mahon v Air New Zealand* [1984] A.C. 808.
[38] *Intercity Telecom Ltd v Solanki*, unreported, 15 June 2015.
[39] See Ch.35.
[40] *Arrow Nominees Inc v Blackledge* [2000] EWCA Civ 200; [2000] 2 B.C.L.C. 167.
[41] *Landauer Ltd v Comins*, *The Times*, 7 August 1999.
[42] *Interactive Technology Corp v Ferster* [2015] EWHC 393 (Ch).

elsewhere in this book.[43] For present purposes, it is important to note that a search order is only justified where an order, made on an application with notice to the opposing party, for delivery up or preservation of documents will not suffice.[44]

(4) Witnesses

(i) Contact between witnesses

34–031   The issue of contamination of witness evidence frequently arises in fraud cases, usually in the context of witnesses being present in court for other witnesses' evidence. This issue is considered below. However, in one recent case[45] the issue arose in the lead-up to trial, where the claimant agreed with the defendant that he (the claimant) and his witnesses of fact would not contact one another to avoid any suggestion of "rehearsing". The witnesses initially denied, but later admitted, in cross-examination that they had in fact all met together shortly before trial, contrary to the pre-trial agreement, severely damaging their credibility. There does not appear to be any precedent of an English court making an order of this sort (although applications for such an order have been known), and it may in fact be stretching the court's case management powers to do so, particularly in the case of non-party witnesses; but it may be a tactically productive move to make such a request, since a party who refuses to agree to it when raised risks looking defensive as to the independence of his witnesses.

(ii) Witness familiarisation

34–032   While widespread and popular in several jurisdictions, witness training remains relatively little used in England and Wales and, it is fair to say, is not always favourably viewed by the judiciary. A recent criticism of the practice came in *Djibouti v Boreh*, where Flaux J said:

> "Whilst I am not suggesting that witness training in itself is improper, (provided that it does not amount to coaching of a witness as to what to say, which would be improper) it is to be discouraged, since, as this case demonstrates, it tends to reflect badly on the witness who, perhaps through no fault of his or her own, may appear evasive because he or she has been 'trained' to give evidence in a particular way."[46]

34–033   The difficulty with it is that—even if no improper coaching as to the substance of the witness's evidence is involved—training can often lead a witness to adopt a somewhat unnatural approach to giving their evidence (giving very succinct answers; ritually insisting on questions being repeated; asking to be referred back

---

[43] See Ch.30.

[44] *Lock International Plc v Beswick* [1989] 1 W.L.R. 1268, at 1281.

[45] *Re Patel (Deceased)* [2017] EWHC 133 (Ch).

[46] *Djibouti v Boreh* [2016] EWHC 405 (Comm), at [67], cited with approval in *Harlequin Property v Wilkins Kennedy* [2016] EWHC 3188 (TCC); [2017] 4 W.L.R. 30, at [18]. See also *Energysolutions EU Ltd v Nuclear Decommissioning Authority* [2016] EWHC 1988 (TCC), at [81]–[83].

to what they previously said in their witness statements), which can appear defensive and so undermine their credibility.

On the other hand, it is important, and entirely legitimate, to ensure that the process of being in court and in the witness box does not feel completely alien to the witness. The witness must be able to give his or her own evidence in full compliance with the oath or affirmation given: being comfortable and in reasonable control of oneself is an aid to this objective.

34–034

(5)   Late Amendments

The circumstances in which permission to amend a statement of case at a late stage will be granted have been narrowed in recent years, following the important decision in *Swain-Mason v Mills & Reeve.*[47] The relevant principles were summarised by Carr J in the following terms in *Quah Su-Ling v Goldman Sachs International*[48]:

34–035

> "1.   Whether to allow an amendment is a matter for the discretion of the court. In exercising that discretion, the overriding objective is of the greatest importance. Applications always involve the court striking a balance between injustice to the applicant if the amendment is refused, and injustice to the opposing party and other litigants in general, if the amendment is permitted;
>
> 2.   Where a very late application to amend is made the correct approach is not that the amendments ought, in general, to be allowed so that the real dispute between the parties can be adjudicated upon. Rather, a heavy burden lies on a party seeking a very late amendment to show the strength of the new case and why justice to him, his opponent and other court users requires him to be able to pursue it. The risk to a trial date may mean that the lateness of the application to amend will of itself cause the balance to be loaded heavily against the grant of permission;
>
> 3.   A very late amendment is one made when the trial date has been fixed and where permitting the amendments would cause the trial date to be lost. Parties and the court have a legitimate expectation that trial fixtures will be kept;
>
> 4.   Lateness is not an absolute, but a relative concept. It depends on a review of the nature of the proposed amendment, the quality of the explanation for its timing, and a fair appreciation of the consequences in terms of work wasted and consequential work to be done;
>
> 5.   Gone are the days when it was sufficient for the amending party to argue that no prejudice had been suffered, save as to costs. In the modern era it is more readily recognised that the payment of costs may not be adequate compensation;
>
> 6.   It is incumbent on a party seeking the indulgence of the court to be allowed to raise a late claim to provide a good explanation for the delay;
>
> 7.   A much stricter view is taken nowadays of non-compliance with the Civil Procedure Rules and directions of the court. The achievement of justice means something different now. Parties can no longer expect indulgence if they fail to comply with their procedural obligations because those obligations not only serve the purpose of ensuring that they conduct the litigation proportionately in order to ensure their own costs are kept within proportionate bounds but also the wider public interest of ensuring that other litigants can obtain justice efficiently and proportionately, and that the courts enable them to do so. "

---

[47] *Swain-Mason v Mills & Reeve* [2011] EWCA Civ 14; [2011] 1 W.L.R. 2735.

[48] *Quah Su-Ling v Goldman Sachs International* [2015] EWHC 759 (Comm), at [38]. See also *Brown v Innovatorone Plc* [2011] EWHC 3221 (Comm), at [5]–[14]; and *CIP Properties v Galliford Try Infrastructure Ltd* [2015] EWHC 1345 (TCC), at [15]–[19].

34-036   It is generally a requirement that the proposed amended case be immediately clear and comprehensible to the opposing party; but this is of particular importance in a fraud claim, where clarity and particularity in pleadings is in any event paramount.[49] Moreover, the importance in a fraud case of a defendant knowing clearly what is being alleged against him, so that he has a fair opportunity to respond to it, makes it all the less likely that the court will be inclined to allow late amendments in such a case than in other claims.[50]

34-037   While the bar is therefore set high for the late amendment of a statement of case in a fraud action, if the amendment is in reality doing no more than bringing into a party's pleaded case matters which have already been the subject of dispute between the parties, such that the nature of the dispute is clear and the defendant is not taken by surprise, the fact that the allegation is one of fraud ought not prevent permission to amend being given.[51]

C.   TRIAL

34-038   This section deals with issues that may arise in relation to the proof of a party's case at trial, including issues concerning witness evidence, the proof of facts by the drawing of inferences and the invocation of the privilege against self-incrimination.

(1)   Witnesses

(i)   Decisions as to calling witnesses

34-039   Given the cogency of the evidence that may be required from a claimant to satisfy the court that a case in fraud has been made out on the balance of probabilities, it is by no means unknown for defendants in fraud claims to decline to tender evidence and effectively require the claimant to prove its case[52]; indeed, this has been described as a "legitimate tactical move."[53] It has the obvious advantage of allowing the defendant (who as a party is not a compellable witness) to avoid being cross-examined; but, equally obviously, before making that tactical decision, a defendant needs to be confident that the fatal weakness of the claimant's case can be established having regard only to the testimony of the claimant's witnesses and the documentary record. Moreover, it should always be borne in mind that if a defendant elects not to give or call evidence, he cannot

---

[49] See *Seaton v Seddon* [2012] EWHC 735 (Ch); [2012] 1 W.L.R. 3636.
[50] Cf. *Ahmed v Ahmed* [2016] EWCA Civ 686.
[51] Ibid.
[52] See for example *Silvera v Urquhart* [2003] EWHC 809 (Ch), at [300], per Ferris J: "A defendant in the position of [the defendant in that case] is entitled to say that no case is made out against him and that he declines to offer an explanation of his conduct. In doing so he runs the risk that the court may take a different view. But if, as I consider to be the case here, the submission that the claimant has not made good his case is well-founded, the court should not, in my judgment, go out of its way to draw adverse inferences from the defendant's silence." The decision also contains a consideration of what use the claimant can make of any witness statements put in by the defendant prior to the trial.
[53] *British Railways Board v Herrington* [1972] A.C. 877, at 930, per Lord Diplock.

complain if the court draws reasonable inferences, from the facts that are before it, as to facts about which the defendant has chosen not to say anything.[54]

Other decisions which one makes as an advocate about the calling of witnesses can also be significant. For example, it may be possible to blunt the cross-examination by the other side of a key witness by calling other witnesses first, so that, by the time the later witness is called, the relevant issues might be thought by the judge to have been covered and cross-examination may in that event be less impactful, or even curtailed or stopped. Cross-examination is increasingly used, in these days of document heavy commercial trials, as an opportunity for the cross-examining advocate to take the judge through the documents that are thought to be helpful to his case and tell a particular story through them, as much as through what the witness has to say about them. Thought should be given to whether it is possible to frustrate that objective by the order in which witnesses are called.   **34–040**

It should also not be forgotten to ask for witnesses to be "released" once their evidence is complete. By doing this, the witnesses are free to go, and it may be very difficult to get a court order for their return to the witness box for any reason.   **34–041**

(ii)   Witness reliability and the importance of documentary evidence

Assessing the quality of a witness' recollection (or purported recollection) of events is obviously a key aspect of the evaluation of the factual evidence in any trial. However, the issue is particularly acute in fraud trials, where allegations of dishonesty are likely to have been made on one side or both sides and the reliability of witnesses has been put in doubt. In addition, a judge in a civil fraud trial will typically be faced with witnesses giving diametrically opposed accounts.   **34–042**

Such concerns will generally lead to judges placing even greater reliance in weighing up a witness' oral evidence on contemporary documents—what has been described as the "hook" on which a conclusion may be hung[55]—and on the inherent probabilities of what is said.   **34–043**

The famous dicta of Robert Goff LJ in *The Ocean Frost* remain relevant and are frequently cited[56]:   **34–044**

> "Speaking from my own experience, I have found it essential in cases of fraud when considering the credibility of witnesses, always to test their veracity by reference to the objective facts proved independently of their testimony, in particular by reference to the documents in the case, and also to pay particular regard to their motives and to the overall

---

[54] *British Railways Board v Herrington* [1972] A.C. 877, at 930, per Lord Diplock. See also *Crawford v Financial Institutions Services Ltd* [2005] UKPC 40. On inferences from a failure to give or call evidence more generally, see below.

[55] *Stein v Chodiev* [2014] EWHC 1201 (Comm) at [23].

[56] E.g. in *Republic of Djibouti v Boreh* [2016] EWHC 405 (Comm), where the judge said that in that case, which related to events which took place between 1998 and 2008, that approach to the evidence was one which he had adopted as his overall approach, given that many of the most significant events in the case had taken place more than ten years ago.

probabilities. It is frequently very difficult to tell whether a witness is telling the truth or not: and where there is a conflict of evidence such as there was in the present case, reference to the objective facts and documents, to the witnesses' motives, and to the overall probabilities can be of very great assistance to a Judge in ascertaining the truth."[57]

34–045 Though ultimately the treatment of witness evidence, and in particular oral evidence, is a matter for the trial judge, the importance of contemporary documents has again been emphasised in recent decisions. Leggatt J in *Gestmin v Credit Suisse*[58] almost went as far as to reject entirely the utility of witness recollection, as presented to the court through witness statements and cross examination, as a reliable basis for determining factual matters such as what was said in meetings and conversations years earlier, due to the fallibilities of human memory and the tendency for memories to be subconsciously tailored to fit the witnesses' ends. In fraud cases, where more often than not at least one party will have every reason to lie, this tendency will be stronger still.

34–046 Rather, Leggatt J said, the primary benefit of witness evidence was to assess the "personality, motivation and working practices" of the witness in question in order to buttress the primary or preferable method of determination of fact, namely "the documentary evidence and known or probable facts".[59]

34–047 While some judges[60] may well not go as far as that, there is certainly a growing tendency among all divisions and in all types of cases to look first, and perhaps last, at contemporary documents in determining factual matters in dispute.[61] Nonetheless, in the absence of any, or any substantial, documentary record, the court will have no option but to rely on witness evidence for determination of necessary matters of fact.[62]

34–048 Another judicial technique for dealing with the possible unreliability of witness testimony is to require the witness to give their own version of events—that is, their evidence "in chief"—orally and in their own words, rather than by mere confirmation of the contents of a written witness statement, which may have had considerable input from the legal team. Whilst this ought not to be sprung on any advocate, it is a course that is perfectly open to a judge as part of his general power to control the way in which evidence is given[63]; and it is therefore as well

---

[57] *The Ocean Frost* [1985] 1 Lloyd's Rep. 1, at 57, endorsed by the Privy Council in *Grace Shipping v CF Sharp* [1987] 1 Ll.R. 207, at 215 and, more recently, by the Privy Council in *Central Bank of Ecuador v Conticorp SA (Bahamas)* [2015] UKPC 11; [2015] Bus L.R. D7, at [8], where it was said that the court considered that "these points may have particular relevance where evidence is being given through an interpreter, especially if it appears that the interpretation is imperfect".

[58] *Gestmin v Credit Suisse* [2013] EWHC 3560, at [15]–[23].

[59] *Gestmin v Credit Suisse* [2013] EWHC 3560, at [22].

[60] See, for example, *Francis v Knapper* [2016] EWHC 3093 Q.B. at [79], per Andrew Baker J; *Blue Tropic v Chkhartishvili* [2015] EWHC 3640, at [31], per Peter Smith J.

[61] *Butler v Butler* [2016] EWHC 1793 (Ch), at [23]; *Healey v Shoosmiths* [2016] EWHC 1723 (QB), at [47]; *Lachaux v Lachaux* [2017] 4 W.L.R. 57 though cf. *Lavis v Nursing and Midwifery Council* [2014] EWHC 4083 (Admin) at [16]–[21].

[62] *Philip Thomas, Helen Thomas v Triodos Bank NV* [2017] EWHC 314 (QB), at [91]; and see also *Jafari-Fini v Skillglass Ltd* [2007] EWCA Civ 261, at [76]–[80].

[63] CPR r.32.1.

for civil practitioners to remember that examination-in-chief is often considered by criminal practitioners as more difficult to conduct effectively than cross-examination.

(iii)   Witnesses present in court

As far as parties to proceedings are concerned, the starting point and strong presumption is that they are entitled to be present for the whole of the trial.[64] The presumption is stronger still in cases of fraud; a party facing such serious accusations has the right to hear the evidence presented against him. However, the rule is not an absolute one.

34–049

In the case of mere witnesses, the normal rule remains that they are permitted in court throughout the proceedings. However, the trial judge has a discretion to direct otherwise if the circumstances, and in particular the risk of contamination of a witness's evidence, demand.[65] The relevant factors were considered in *Three Rivers District Council v The Governor and Company of the Bank of England (No.11)*,[66] where Tomlinson J stated that

34–050

> "[t]here is, no doubt, something to be said for an order of this sort being made as a general rule in all litigation ... an exclusion order in these circumstances may actually bolster the witnesses' ultimate credibility",

and that this was particularly the case where there were allegations of dishonesty.

In reality, the issue is as much a tactical one as a legal one. Once raised, a party objecting to such an order would be expected to provide reasons for doing so. Absent good reason, a judge might conclude that such resistance is borne out of concern that witnesses will not give consistent evidence if required to do so without hearing each other, and the strength of their evidence may be diminished from the outset. Conversely, the position of a party whose witnesses have not sat in court while other witnesses have given evidence, but who nonetheless give consistent evidence, may well be strengthened as a result.

34–051

(iv)   Video link

CPR 32.3 gives the court the power to allow a witness to give evidence "through a video link or by other means" and extensive guidance is given as to the use of video conferencing in PD 32. It is not standard, but it is becoming more common and, due to issues such as fear or alleged fear of giving oral testimony and travel restrictions, this is particularly so in fraud cases. Improvements in technology mean that interruptions are rare and less is "lost" by the witness not actually

34–052

---

[64] *Da Costa v Sargaco* [2016] EWCA Civ 764; [2016] C.P. Rep. 40, at [59]. In that case it was said that a direction from the judge, excluding one claimant while the other was giving evidence in circumstances where the defendant contended that the claim was a fraudulent one, was an error of law. See also *The Attorney General of Zambia v Meer Care & Desai (A Firm)* [2006] EWCA Civ 390.

[65] *Moore v Lambeth County Court* [1969] 1 W.L.R. 141, at 142C–142F.

[66] *Three Rivers District Council v The Governor and Company of the Bank of England (No.11)* [2003] EWHC 2950 (Comm) at [56]–[74].

being present in court. It remains fair to say, however, that it is not, at least yet, universally popular among practitioners; and many would still regard it as preferable to be able to see, and for the judge to be able to see, the demeanour and reactions of the witness under questioning in person. Oral evidence in court thus remains the norm.

34–053   One potential downside of a witness not being present in court is that he is not compellable; the court has no effective sanction against a witness refusing to answer a question who is not physically present and even less recourse if the witness is overseas.[67] An extreme example, where the witness was not only not in court but was giving evidence from an undisclosed location, can be seen in *JSC BTA Bank v Ablyazov*.[68]

(v)   Ambush cross examination

34–054   "Ambush" cross examination—that is, cross-examination on the basis of previously undisclosed material that goes to an issue in the case (and so should have been disclosed)—remains prohibited, as confirmed in a number of recent decisions outside the civil fraud context.[69]

34–055   However, there is normally no requirement for disclosure on matters going solely to credit or credibility.[70] In fact, in most instances, material going solely to credibility will not be subject to an order for disclosure even on application, let alone forming part of standard disclosure under the CPR.[71] Accordingly, such material can,[72] and often will, be permitted to be used in cross examination, even though it has not previously been disclosed or otherwise deployed, particularly if used to rebut testimony given at trial. There is no "ambush" in the strict sense, because no disclosure requirement has been breached. A trial judge faced with clear evidence that a witness has given untruthful evidence, on a collateral matter or one going only to credit, is unlikely to be sympathetic to a request for such evidence to be excluded as an ambush in any event.

34–056   Similarly, there is generally no requirement to have pleaded a general challenge to the credibility of a witness before mounting that challenge in cross-examination, where the matter goes only to credibility and not an issue in the case. However, it has been said that where it is intended to advance specific allegations of dishonesty based on particular facts in cross-examination, as a

---

[67] As is expressly acknowledged at CPR 32 PD 33.

[68] *JSC BTA Bank v Ablyazov* [2012] EWHC 237 (Comm) at [58]–[65], recording that, despite being given the indulgence by the court of giving video link evidence having fled the jurisdiction to avoid committal proceedings, the witness simply refused to answer a number of questions, purportedly on the basis of protecting his clients' interests.

[69] Most frequently in the form of surveillance evidence as to the extent of injury in personal injury cases: see *Hicks v Rostas*, unreported, 17 March 2017 (Q.B.D.).

[70] *L'Oreal SA v Bellure NV* [2006] EWHC 1503 (Ch).

[71] *Favor Easy Management v Wu* [2010] EWCA Civ 1630, at [18]–[19].

[72] See, for example, *Re Patel*, above, where witnesses initially denied but later admitted having had a pre-trial meeting, despite an earlier agreement that they would not meet, and *BTA Bank v Ablyazov* [2012] EWHC 237 (Comm) where an important witness for the defendant's denial that he knew his brother's whereabouts or had seen him for a substantial period was contradicted by photographic evidence of a recent meeting which was produced for the first time in cross-examination.

matter of fairness these allegations should be pleaded even where not part of the claim being made.[73] So, in the case in question, where a claim in deceit, but not in conspiracy, was made against the defendant, allegations that the defendant conspired to defraud the claimant, which were advanced in cross-examination of the defendant as part of a "general attack" on his credibility and as the "theory" behind his dishonesty, should have been pleaded, so that the defendant had a proper opportunity to explore how he might wish to rebut them. It is not obvious why the question of whether forewarning should be given of an intended attack on a witness in cross-examination should be answered differently when it is pleading rather than disclosure that is in issue (not least because the scope of disclosure will often be closely tied to the issues identified in the pleadings); and it may be that the observations in this case can be explained on the footing that the relevant issues were not purely ones of credit, but went to the allegation of dishonesty that was an issue in the case.

(vi) Putting the case to witnesses

If the judge is to be invited at the conclusion of the trial to make a finding that a witness (be they a party to the case or not) has been dishonest, then it is of particular importance that that allegation is put squarely to the witness in cross-examination. That is no more or less than what fairness requires, and a failure to do so may result in the court declining to make that finding, even if it would otherwise be justified on the evidence.   **34–057**

As Lord Phillips MR put it in *Vogon International Ltd v The Serious Fraud Office*[74]:   **34–058**

> "It is, I regret to say, elementary common fairness that neither parties to litigation, their counsel, nor judges should make serious imputations or findings in any litigation when the person against whom such imputations or findings are made have not been given a proper opportunity of dealing with the imputations and defending themselves. In the absence of such an opportunity, it is of little consequence to examine details of the evidence given to see whether the judge's findings might have been justified."

It is a principle of long-standing that   **34–059**

> "it will not do to impeach the credibility of a witness upon a matter on which he has not had any opportunity of giving an explanation by reason of there having been no suggestion whatever in the course of the case that his story is not accepted".[75]

Where, however, it is made clear to the witness by the other party in cross-examination that his evidence on a particular matter is not to be believed, but certain particular reasons for disbelieving his evidence are not put, then the question of whether the court's subsequent rejection of his evidence for those

---

[73] *Baturina v Chistyakov* [2017] EWHC 1049 (Comm), per Carr J at [126]–[127].

[74] *Vogon International Ltd v The Serious Fraud Office* [2004] EWCA Civ 104, at [29].

[75] *Browne v Dunn* (1893) 6 R 67, per Lord Herschell LC at 71. See also *Markem Corp v Zipher Ltd* [2005] RPC 31.

reasons should stand is more nuanced. In *Chen v Ng* the Privy Council stated the principles applicable to such a case in the following terms[76]:

> "At a relatively high level of generality, in such a case an appellate court should have in mind two conflicting principles: the need for finality and minimising costs in litigation, on the one hand, and the even more important requirement of a fair trial, on the other. Specific factors to be taken into account would include the importance of the relevant issue both absolutely and in the context of the case; the closeness of the grounds to the points which were put to the witness; the reasonableness of the grounds not having been put, including the amount of time available for cross-examination and the amount of material to be put to the witness; whether the ground had been raised or touched on in speeches to the court, witness statements or other relevant places; and, in some cases, the plausibility of the notion that the witness might have satisfactorily answered the grounds."

34–060   In that case the judge's rejection of the witness's evidence on two particular grounds was set aside, even though the truth of the witness's evidence on the issue had been challenged on other bases: (a) the issue in play was central to the proceedings; (b) there was no other reference to the grounds in the course of the hearing; (c) the grounds were not obscure or difficult, and they could reasonably have been put in cross-examination; (d) the witness may have given believable evidence in answer which weakened or undermined the grounds; and (e) it was not reasonably clear from the judgment that the judge would have reached the same conclusion without relying on the grounds.

(vii)   Can a witness appeal a finding of dishonesty?

34–061   Assuming a finding of dishonesty is made against a witness, the question arises whether he has any right to challenge that finding when he is not a party with any other interest in the claim. This was recently considered in *Gray v Boreh*.[77] It was accepted in that case (by concession) that the Court of Appeal had jurisdiction to entertain an appeal by such a witness on the grounds that the findings were vitiated by procedural unfairness[78]; but it was held that, if a proper process had been followed, there could be no appeal on the substance of the finding—that is, on whether it was right or not. A witness has no financial or proprietary interest in the outcome of proceedings; he has at most (as in *Gray v Boreh*) a reputational one. While it was only right that a witness, in particular a professional whose reputation was at stake, should have a fair opportunity to respond to criticism, provided he had had that right, there was nothing in ECHR art.8 (or otherwise) that required that he should have a right of appeal if he did not agree with the ultimate determination.

34–062   It therefore appears that, save for the relatively narrow category of procedural unfairness, a witness who has been found to be dishonest will have no recourse to the appellate courts.

---

[76] *Chen v Ng* [2017] UKPC 27, at [55].
[77] *Gray v Boreh* [2017] EWCA Civ 56, at [35].
[78] *Re W (a child)* [2016] EWCA Civ 1140.

(2) Inferences

(i) Inference from failure to disclose

A failure to disclose documents can be justification for the court drawing the inference that the content of the documents in question is adverse to the party's case. However, for the drawing of such an inference to be appropriate there must be more than simply the fact of the failure to disclose: there must be some evidence that the conduct, whether amounting to spoliation or concealment, was deliberate.[79] We have considered the issue of spoliation above. Failures to disclose fall to be analysed similarly.

34–063

(ii) Inference from absence or silence of a witness

The principle is well established that an adverse inference may be drawn when a witness who might be expected to give relevant evidence on an issue does not do so; see the locus classicus for this rule, *Wiszniewski v Central Manchester Health Authority*.[80] In fraud cases, courts are often invited to draw such inferences by claimants.[81]

34–064

The relevant principles were summarised by Brooke LJ in *Wiszniewski* as follows[82]:

34–065

> "(1)   In certain circumstances a court may be entitled to draw adverse inferences from the absence or silence of a witness who might be expected to have material evidence to give on an issue in an action.
> (2)   If a court is willing to draw such inferences, they may go to strengthen the evidence adduced on that issue by the other party or to weaken the evidence, if any, adduced by the party who might reasonably have been expected to call the witness.
> (3)   There must, however, have been some evidence, however weak, adduced by the former on the matter in question before the court is entitled to draw the desired inference: in other words, there must be a case to answer on that issue.
> (4)   If the reason for the witness's absence or silence satisfies the court, then no such adverse inference may be drawn. If, on the other hand, there is some credible explanation given, even if it is not wholly satisfactory, the potentially detrimental effect of his/her absence or silence may be reduced or nullified. "

Thus a claimant can only derive support for its case by inviting the court to draw adverse inferences from a defendant's failure to call evidence if: (a) the claimant has itself raised a case to answer by its own evidence; (b) the relevant witness could be expected to have given relevant (even if not necessarily determinative) evidence, which cannot satisfactorily be adduced by other means, such as from a different witness; and (c) there is no satisfactory explanation for the absence of the witness. A party ought not to suffer inferences being drawn against it simply

34–066

---

[79] *Earles v Barclays Bank Plc* [2010] Bus. L.R. 566, at [28].
[80] *Wiszniewski v Central Manchester Health Authority* [1998] P.I.Q.R. 324.
[81] A very recent example (albeit one where the invitation was refused by the Court) is *Property Alliance Group Ltd v The Royal Bank of Scotland Plc* [2016] EWHC 3342 (Ch).
[82] *Wiszniewski*, at 340.

because it has not called every possible witness to a matter of fact[83]; and even if the explanation for a failure to call a particular witness falls short of full justification, it can still reduce or nullify the effect of a witness's silence.[84]

34–067 The potential for an adverse inference extends not only to the failure of a relevant witness to give a witness statement (i.e. the scenario where a witness gives no evidence whatsoever), but also to any circumstances in which the party or witness, having provided a statement, then fails to attend at trial to give oral evidence.[85]

34–068 In fraud cases, parties will frequently cite fear or unwillingness to testify as a reason for particular witnesses refusing to provide evidence. Travel restrictions or other impediments may cause difficulties for witnesses in giving live evidence. Such reasons may amount to good reason for a witness not giving evidence, reducing or nullifying the adverse inference that might otherwise be drawn. However, the decision in *Djibouti v Boreh*,[86] involving a foreign head of state, re-emphasised that the "credible explanation" hurdle is not easily cleared. In that case the Republic of Djibouti had brought proceedings in the English High Court. The court described the case as a "swearing match" between two protagonists, being the President of Djibouti and the defendant, and had indicated at the Pre-Trial Review that it was essential that the President attend court in person to give evidence. The President declined to attend court, in order to maintain the "dignity and sanctity" of his country. The Judge considered this an inadequate reason for non-attendance and drew adverse inferences.

34–069 In circumstances where a party is not proposing to call a witness who on the face of it could give evidence which is relevant to an issue in the case, and where that witness' absence will give rise to legitimate questions, then that party would be well-advised to address the non-calling of the witness head-on, and explain it, possibly by witness evidence, rather than waiting for the other side to seek to draw an inference.

34–070 No adverse inference ought to be drawn from silence where a party's defence is struck out or he is otherwise debarred from calling witnesses, for example where that is the sanction for that party's failure to comply with an unless order. The court should not take into account what evidence might have been given or make any positive findings on that basis.[87] The court will only be able to decide the

---

[83] And note in this regard that in a complex fraud case, it may be hard to say of any given witness that he ought obviously to have been called: *Kazakhstan Kagazy Plc v Zhunus* [2017] EWHC 3374 (Comm), per Picken J at [57].

[84] See the final point in the passage from *Wiszniewski* cited above. See also *Prest v Prest* [2013] 2 A.C. 415, per Lord Sumption at [44], relying on *R v Inland Revenue Commissioners Ex parte TC Coombs & Co* [1991] 2 A.C. 283, at 300.

[85] For instance if a party who is faced with an allegation of contempt elects not to give evidence (as is his right), an inference may be drawn: see e.g. *Khawaja v Popat* [2016] EWCA Civ 362.

[86] *Djibouti v Boreh* [2016] EWHC 405 (Comm); cf. a recent successful example outside the fraud context in *Welds v Yorkshire Ambulance Service* [2016] 3325 (QB).

[87] *Durrant v Chief Constable of Avon & Somerset Constabulary* [2014] EWHC 2922 (QB), at [140]–[143].

case on the basis of the evidence actually tendered and, if that evidence comes up to proof, and there is no other legal impediment in the way of the claim, it should succeed.

It is also inappropriate to draw an adverse inference where a party fails to call as a witness someone who has previously given evidence contrary to that party's case, which, were the party to call that witness, he (the calling party) would have to say was deliberately false. This may sound like an unlikely scenario; but in complex multi-party frauds, in which allegiances switch and settlements occur as the litigation progresses, it is quite conceivable; and it happened in the recent case of *Kazakhstan Kagazy Plc v Zhunus*.[88] There the claimants settled with one of the defendants during the litigation, on terms that obliged that defendant to give truthful evidence if required to do so by the claimants. The claimants nevertheless chose not to call the settling defendant (who was central to the alleged frauds) at trial and the other defendants invited the court to draw an adverse inference from their failure to do so. Picken J declined to draw such an inference: the settling defendant had previously advanced a case denying the frauds, which the claimants would have to have put to him was false and deliberately so, and that is something they could not do unless the court were to rule that the witness was hostile.[89]

(iii) Proving fraud by inference

In proving fraud or dishonesty, it is usually necessary to persuade the court to draw inferences from primary facts; direct evidence of fraud is relatively rare.[90] The requirement for a claimant in proving fraud is that the primary facts proved give rise to an inference of dishonesty or fraud which is more probable than an innocent explanation.[91] It is important to have in mind that it is of the essence of establishing a case based on inference from circumstantial evidence that the whole is greater than the individual parts: an allegation of (for example) a dishonest state of mind can therefore be made out by inference from an accumulation of primary facts, none of which on their own would prove the allegation to the requisite standard.[92]

The primary facts relied upon for the inference of dishonesty or fraud must nevertheless be sufficient (in aggregate) to tilt the balance in favour of a finding of fraud. Findings of fact which are equally or more consistent with innocent conduct, bearing in mind that in most circumstances an innocent explanation is

34-071

34-072

34-073

---

[88] *Kazakhstan Kagazy Plc v Zhunus* [2017] EWHC 3374 (Comm).

[89] At [57]. There is for these purposes an important distinction between advancing a case that one's own witness's evidence is mistakenly false and one that it is deliberately so: *The Filiatra Legacy* [1991] 2 Lloyd's Rep. 337.

[90] *Three Rivers District Council v Bank of England* [2001] UKHL 16; [2003] 2 A.C. 1, at [186].

[91] *JSC Bank of Moscow v Kekhman* [2015] EWHC 3073 (Comm), at [20].

[92] See *JSC BTA Bank v Ablyazov* [2012] EWCA Civ 1411, per Rix LJ at [52] (said in relation to proof of a committal application to the requisite criminal standard, but equally applicable to a fraud allegation to which the civil standard applies). See the analysis in *JSC Bank of Moscow v Kekhman* [2015] EWHC 3073 (Comm), at [78].

more likely than a fraudulent one, will not suffice for a finding of fraud.[93] If the allegation is, by its nature, one that is inherently improbable, the court may conclude that it can only draw the inference of fraudulent or dishonest conduct if that is the "inescapable" conclusion to be drawn from the primary facts.[94]

(3) Privilege Against Self-Incrimination

34–074   The privilege against self-incrimination can arise at numerous stages in civil fraud proceedings. Perhaps most commonly, it may arise at the stage of disclosure (whether in response to a freezing injunction with ancillary disclosure orders or on standard disclosure), and is particularly likely to be raised if there are concurrent criminal and civil proceedings. It may in those circumstances allow a party to refuse to provide disclosure or to respond to a request for information. This section, however, focusses on the application of the privilege at trial.

(i)   What is covered?

34–075   A party or person called as a witness in civil proceedings in general has a right to refuse to answer any question asked during the course of a trial if to do so would tend to expose him to proceedings for a criminal offence. This is a common law privilege, although statutorily recognised by s.14 of the Civil Evidence Act 1968.

34–076   The privilege permits the party to refuse to answer questions which may incriminate him or a spouse. The potential incrimination relates only to any act or omission which is a criminal offence in any part of the UK. Thus, if the answer would expose the witness to proceedings for a criminal offence only in some foreign country, then that is no justification for refusing to answer the question. Any person claiming privilege on the grounds of self-incrimination must satisfy the court that there are real, and not fanciful, grounds justifying his fear that the information sought would tend to incriminate him.[95]

(ii)   What is not covered?

34–077   The privilege is not absolute in that it is subject to certain exceptions, most importantly s.13 of the Fraud Act 2006. This prevents the privilege from being relied on "in proceedings relating to property", but only on the ground that doing so might incriminate the person invoking it of an offence under the Act or a related offence, as defined at subs.(4).[96] To the extent that there is a risk of incrimination of another offence, not arising under the Act or related to it, the privilege remains available, provided that there is a sufficient risk of prosecution for that offence.

---

[93] *Hussain v Hussain* [2012] EWCA Civ 1367.
[94] *Silvera v Urquhart* [2003] EWHC 809 (Ch), at [302].
[95] *Sociedade Nacional v Lundquist* [1991] 2 Q.B. 310, at 324F, per Staughton LJ.
[96] The Theft Act 1968 contains a similar provision: s.31.

The phrase "proceedings relating to property"[97] is defined in the 2006 Act as extending to any proceedings for: **34–078**

"(a)   the recovery or administration of any property,
(b)   the execution of a trust, or
(c)   an account of any property or dealings with property. "[98]

"Property" means money or other property, whether real or personal, including things in action and other intangible property.[99] **34–079**

The Court of Appeal confirmed in *Kensington International Ltd v Republic of Congo*[100] that the exception was to be widely construed, reasoning that the loss of privilege was balanced by the fact that, by s.13(2), any statement or admission made in civil proceedings was rendered inadmissible in criminal proceedings under the Fraud Act 2006 or for "a related offence" (i.e. the extent of the loss of the privilege was precisely mirrored by the extent of the inadmissibility of any statement or admission). **34–080**

The court also rejected a submission that the phrase "relating to property" was to be construed as a reference to specific property of which the claimant had been deprived by fraud.[101] In that case, the wording of the Fraud Act 2006 was construed sufficiently widely to include bribery-related offences as being "related offences" for the purposes of s.13(4), because offering or giving a bribe "necessarily involves a form of fraudulent conduct or purpose within the meaning of s.13(4)(b)".[102] The expression "related offences" is therefore interpreted broadly to include any offence which involves fraud or fraudulent conduct, or which has a "fraudulent quality", even if not a fraudulent purpose.[103] Fraudulent conduct for these purposes includes any conduct which "partakes of the essential characteristics of fraud as described in sections 2, 3 and 4" of the Fraud Act 2006, being conduct which involves "deception coupled with injury or an intention to expose another to injury by means of that deception".[104] **34–081**

In practice, therefore, the circumstances in which the privilege can be invoked in civil fraud actions are now relatively narrow. **34–082**

---

[97] The word "proceedings" here includes discrete applications such as *Norwich Pharmacal* applications, brought in support of substantive proceedings for the recovery of property, even though they might be technically constituted as separate proceedings: see *Kensington International Ltd v Republic of Congo* [2007] EWCA Civ 1128; [2008] 1 W.L.R. 1144, at [43]–[44]. The same analysis would not apply in respect of pre-action disclosure applications or *Norwich Pharmacal* applications issued before substantive proceedings had been brought.

[98] Section 13(3).

[99] Section 13(3).

[100] *Kensington International Ltd v Republic of Congo* [2007] EWCA Civ 1128; [2008] 1 W.L.R. 1144, at [36], [40], per Moore-Bick LJ.

[101] It had been submitted that the section did not apply for claims for damages for fraud, nor to a claim to recover property which the claimant might have lost otherwise than as a result of fraud: see at [39].

[102] *Kensington v Congo* [2007] EWCA Civ 1128; [2008] 1 W.L.R. 1144, at [63].

[103] *JSC BTA Bank v Ablyazov* [2009] EWCA Civ 1124; [2010] 1 W.L.R. 976.

[104] *Kensington v Congo* [2007] EWCA Civ 1128; [2008] 1 W.L.R. 1144, at [58]–[59].

(iii)   Principles applicable upon invocation of privilege

34–083   The question of the impact of the successful invocation of the privilege upon the proof of the claimant's case was recently reconsidered in *Clydesdale Bank Plc v Stoke Place Hotel Ltd (In Administration).*[105]

34–084   First, when a witness in a civil case properly invokes the privilege and refuses to answer questions on the grounds that the answer would tend to incriminate him, the court will not draw adverse inferences in relations to that witness's evidence. To do so would undermine the very purpose of the privilege.

34–085   Secondly, however, in the absence of an answer to the relevant question, the court has no explanation from the defendant (or the relevant witness) on the matters which were the subject of the question. The invocation of the privilege does not preclude the court from making findings of fact on the evidence which *is* before it. If that evidence supports inferences of fact that are adverse to the defendant, then the invocation of the privilege will mean that the court, having nothing to set against such inferences, is more likely to make adverse findings. That is not because an adverse inference is drawn from the invocation of the privilege, but because the consequence of its invocation is that the inferences to be drawn from other evidence before the court cannot be resisted.

34–086   In theory, invocation of the privilege could result in the civil court staying proceedings pending the outcome of any criminal investigation or proceedings, in order that any criminal liability be determined first. In practice, this discretion is unlikely to be exercised, particularly if the privilege is invoked at trial, and it is more likely that the trial will proceed without the relevant evidence on the principles set out above.

---

[105] *Clydesdale Bank Plc v Stoke Place Hotel Ltd (In Administration)* [2017] EWHC 181 (Ch).

CHAPTER 35

CONTEMPT OF COURT

A. INTRODUCTION

(1) Relevance to Fraud Claims

The law of contempt extends over a wide area and this book does not attempt to   **35–001**
traverse it in full.[1] Rather, this chapter is primarily concerned with the important
role that contempt plays in securing compliance with orders made and
undertakings given in fraud claims.

Fraud claims will often commence with orders made on a without notice basis,   **35–002**
often continued in the form of undertakings, most commonly for the preservation
and identification of assets against which a judgment can in due course be
enforced—freezing orders, search orders and asset disclosure orders. It is of
paramount importance for an applicant that such orders should have teeth; and
courts will act vigorously to police them, since they are seen as "an important and
crucial part of modern litigation."[2] The law of contempt provides a jurisdiction to
secure compliance and punish breach; and in recent years it has become an
integral part of the armoury of claimants in fraud claims—something which is
apparent from the number of such applications made in the recent *Ablyazov* and
Pugachev litigation. Further, contempt plays an important tactical role in such
claims: whilst the applicant must of course be careful not to abuse the contempt
jurisdiction (something that would only rebound on it), a well-targeted
application will often have the collateral benefit of applying considerable
pressure to a defendant, which can result in an early termination or settlement of
the wider proceedings.

(2) General Nature of the Contempt Jurisdiction

In general terms, contempt is a quasi-criminal jurisdiction (operating in the civil   **35–003**
courts) and proof of it is therefore required to the higher criminal standard, which
is of course "beyond reasonable doubt", rather than the civil standard of "on the

---

[1] See generally P. Londono, A.T.H. Smith and D. Eady, *Arlidge, Eady & Smith on Contempt*, 5th edn
(London: Sweet & Maxwell, 2017).
[2] *Templeton Insurance Ltd v Motorcare Warranties Ltd* [2012] EWHC 795 (Comm), at [41], per Eder
J; and see generally *JSC BTA Bank v Solodchenko* [2011] EWCA Civ 1241; [2012] 1 W.L.R. 350, at
[45]–[58].

balance of probabilities."[3] This is because a contempt of court is punishable by a prison sentence of up to two years (although, as we explain below, there are a wide variety of orders available to the court in the event that a contempt is made out). Although there are many different forms that contempt of court can take, that with which we are principally concerned in this chapter (disobedience of court orders and undertakings) is generally known as civil contempt, as opposed to criminal contempt (the distinction is explained at sub-section (4) below). The courts have constantly stressed the importance of complying with orders and of marking serious instances of deliberate non-compliance with such orders.[4] However, as we discuss below, although the jurisdiction is quasi-criminal, its purposes are not simply the upholding of the authority of the court, but also to provide incentives to secure (belated) compliance with court orders. Although the contempt jurisdiction which we consider in this chapter is (typically) invoked in private litigation by a litigant with a view to enforcing the order or undertaking alleged to have been breached, nonetheless it has been said that "the court itself has a very substantial interest in seeing that its orders are upheld".[5]

35–004   Applications for committal are now regulated by CPR Pt 81 and its accompanying practice direction.

(3)   Elements which Must be Proved: Overview

35–005   In order to establish that a respondent is in contempt of court through disobedience of a court order, it is necessary to establish the following, to the criminal standard of proof:

(1)   That the respondent knew the terms of the relevant order;
(2)   That he acted (or failed to act) in a manner which involved a breach of the order, and
(3)   That he knew of the facts which made his conduct a breach.

35–006   Issues of motive, and whether the putative contemnor believed that he was acting in breach of the order, are not relevant to the question of whether the respondent is in contempt, although they will be relevant to sentence. We consider these and the above points below.

---

[3] As it was put by Treacy LJ in *Baho v Meerza* [2014] EWCA Civ 669, at [15]: "It is for the judge to be satisfied to the criminal standard by the evidence." CPR PD 81 para.9 provides that "In all cases the Convention rights of those involved should particularly be borne in mind. It should be noted that the standard of proof, having regard to the possibility that a person may be sent to prison, is that the allegation be proved beyond reasonable doubt."

[4] See, for example, Lord Denning MR in *Z Ltd v A-Z* [1982] Q.B. 558, at 572; Lord Bingham in *Customs and Excise Commissioners v Barclays Bank Plc* [2007] 1 A.C. 181, at [11]; and Jackson LJ in *JSC BTA Bank v Solodchenko* [2012] 1 W.L.R. 350, at [55].

[5] *Nicholls v Nicholls* [1997] 1 W.L.R. 314, at 326, per Lord Woolf MR.

(4)   The Distinction Between Civil and Criminal Contempt

Historically, the law distinguished between what is known as "civil contempt"   **35–007**
and "criminal contempt". This distinction has been described as "unhelpful" and
"largely meaningless",[6] and it is now somewhat outdated; but nonetheless this
taxonomy still prevails in judicial analysis and, in fact, it is useful in serving to
distinguish between, on the one hand, the liability in contempt of a party to the
action and, on the other, the liability of a third party. There is also an important
distinction between the mental ingredients of the two types of contempt. Hence it
is important to understand the meaning of the two concepts, which was stated
most authoritatively by Lord Oliver in *Attorney-General v Times Newspapers
Ltd*[7]:

> "A distinction...is sometimes drawn between what is described as 'civil contempt,' that is to
> say, contempt by a party to proceedings in a matter of procedure, and 'criminal contempt.' One
> particular form of contempt by a party to proceedings is that constituted by an intentional act
> which is in breach of the order of a competent court. Where this occurs as a result of the act of
> a party who is bound by the order or of others acting at his direction or on his instigation, it
> constitutes a civil contempt by him which is punishable by the court at the instance of the
> party for whose benefit the order was made and which can be waived by him. The intention
> with which the act was done will, of course, be of the highest relevance in the determination of
> the penalty (if any) to be imposed by the court, but the liability here is a strict one in the sense
> that all that requires to be proved is service of the order and the subsequent doing by the party
> bound of that which is prohibited. When, however, the prohibited act is done not by the party
> bound himself but by a third party, a stranger to the litigation, that person may also be liable
> for contempt. There is, however, this essential distinction that his liability is for criminal
> contempt and arises not because the contemnor is himself affected by the prohibition
> contained in the order but because his act constitutes a wilful interference with the
> administration of justice by the court in the proceedings in which the order was made. Here the
> liability is not strict in the sense referred to, for there has to be shown not only knowledge of
> the order but an intention to interfere with or impede the administration of justice – an
> intention which can of course be inferred from the circumstances."

We consider the liability of a party to the proceedings and of a third party in   **35–008**
greater detail below. A litigant in fraud proceedings may wish to bring committal
applications for both civil and criminal contempts.

It should be noted that the other form of contempt proceeding which is sometimes   **35–009**
instigated by applicants in fraud claims is for giving false evidence, whether in
witness statements or affidavits or in oral testimony. This is a type of criminal
contempt. Note that different rules apply depending on whether the statement was
made in an affidavit or in a witness statement.[8]

---

[6] *Attorney-General v Times Newspapers Ltd* [1991] 1 A.C. 191, at 217, per Lord Oliver.

[7] *Attorney-General v Times Newspapers Ltd*, above, at 217–218.

[8] In relation to proceedings founded upon false witness statements see CPR r.32.14 (1): "Proceedings
for contempt of court may be brought against a person if he makes, or causes to be made, a false
statement in a document verified by a statement of truth without an honest belief in its truth." CPR
rr.81.17 and 81.18 prescribe the relevant procedure. Such proceedings may only be brought with the
permission of the Court. Applications for permission were considered in the leading case of *KJM
Superbikes Ltd v Hinton* [2008] EWCA Civ 1280; [2009] 1 W.L.R. 2406. In order for such an
application to succeed the applicant must show (inter alia) a strong prima facie case that: (a) the
respondent knew what he stated in his witness statement was false; and (b) knew that the statement
was likely to interfere in the administration of justice (*Tinker v Elliot* [2014] EWCA Civ 564, at [44]).

35–010 Criminal contempt may take many forms, the essential ingredient being a wilful interference with the administration of justice.[9] Examples, beyond the making of false statements, are the deployment of forged documents in legal proceedings,[10] threats to witnesses to seek to dissuade them from giving evidence or advice given to a witness to lie on oath,[11] and use of documents disclosed in proceedings for a collateral purpose in breach of CPR r.31.22.[12] One particularly common form of contempt proceeding in vogue at present is that brought by insurance companies against persons involving in the making of fraudulent claims for personal injury or loss arising out of alleged motor accidents. The fraud alleged may involve the staging of a false accident or the exaggeration of injuries or other loss (such as damage to a vehicle) from a genuine accident. The respondents to such claims may include the alleged fraudulent claimant, the solicitor acting for him, the doctor who gives a medical report, car hire rates surveyors, claims handlers, or the other party or parties to the alleged accident. Such forms of proceeding have generated large numbers of judgments in recent years as the insurance industry uses the contempt jurisdiction to seek to fight the problem of claims fraud. The issues engaged in these various types of committal application are not specific to fraud claims and are beyond the purview of this book.[13]

(5)   The Decision to Make a Committal Application

35–011 The decision to make a committal application is not one to be taken lightly. On the one hand, an order for imprisonment (or even the threat of such an order) can be an extremely powerful way of putting pressure on a recalcitrant respondent to comply with an order. On the other hand, the nature of a committal application can make it hard fought, long, and expensive, and not all such applications are effective in practice, even if successful. The following practical considerations should be borne in mind as far as applicable in any given case:

As to the first of these two limbs, it is sufficient to show that the statement maker was reckless as to whether the statement was true or not, but it is not sufficient to show that the statement maker did not apply his mind properly, or make all of the investigations which it would have been reasonable to make; see *JSC BTA Bank v Ereshchenko* [2013] EWCA Civ 829, at [41]–[43]. For the considerations to take into account when deciding whether or not to grant permission see generally *Newson-Smith v Al Zawawi* [2017] EWHC 1876 (QB); and *Grosvenor Chemicals Ltd v UPL Europe Ltd* [2017] EWHC 1893 (Ch). Where an applicant seeks to bring committal proceedings in respect of a false affidavit, it is unclear whether any permission is needed. Green J in *International Sports Tours Ltd v Shorey* [2015] EWHC 2040 (QB) held that no permission was needed as proceedings for contempt on the basis of a false affidavit fell outside the ambit of Pt 81 altogether (see [37]–[43]). This is a surprising and unattractive result. It may be preferable to treat false affidavit evidence as a form of interference with the administration of justice falling within s.3 of Pt 81.

[9] See *Att-Gen v Leveller Magazine* [1979] A.C. 440, per Lord Diplock at 449F. Procedurally such applications are covered by rr.81.12–81.14 of the CPR.

[10] *Neil v Henderson* [2018] EWHC 90 (Ch), which contains a review of the elements to be proven in respect of criminal contempt.

[11] *Liverpool Victoria Insurance Company v Khan* [2016] EWHC 2590 (QB).

[12] *Grosvenor Chemicals Ltd v UPL Europe Ltd* [2017] EWHC 1893 (Ch).

[13] See for instance *Liverpool Victoria Insurance Company Ltd v Yavuz* [2017] EWHC 3088 (QB), Warby J.

(1)   The more important it is to an applicant to secure compliance, the greater the reason to seek an order as drastic as one for committal to prison. The extreme case (albeit not uncommon in a fraud case) is that of the respondent who refuses to comply in any meaningful way with a freezing and asset disclosure order, in circumstances where it may be crucial to secure the respondent's assets so that any future judgment can be enforced and the proceedings are not rendered nugatory. Not all breaches are this serious, however.

(2)   A committal order (or a lesser sanction or even just a finding of contempt) may, in some cases, have the effect of causing an uncooperative respondent to engage more fully in the litigation.

(3)   However, whilst it may be tempting for an applicant to see committal proceedings as a way of scoring a pre-trial tactical blow against the respondent (for example by damaging his credibility in the eyes of a future trial judge), care must be taken to ensure that any such proceedings are pursued for the legitimate purpose of enforcing the court's orders and are not being used to harass or intimidate a respondent—if they are, then they will be liable to be struck out as an abuse of process.[14]

(4)   Given their seriousness, committal proceedings are often hard fought, and can give rise to expensive satellite litigation. Costs of a successful application are of course recoverable in principle (including on an indemnity basis), but a claimant who spends significant sums on a committal application against a dishonest defendant increases his exposure when it comes to enforcement. Especially in freezing order cases, it is often important for committal proceedings to be determined prior to trial,[15] but this may lengthen the proceedings overall and delay any eventual judgment on the merits.

(5)   In light of the above points, where a respondent appears to be guilty of multiple breaches of a court order, consideration should be given to bringing an application focused on those breaches which are most serious, have caused the applicant greatest prejudice, or are likely to be simplest to determine.[16]

(6)   Where (as is often the case) the purpose of the contemplated application is to secure compliance with previous orders, there may be simpler and more effective ways to achieve this purpose. Whilst for some respondents the threat of committal is a powerful one, to others it is not (e.g. a foreign defendant who has neither any connection with the jurisdiction nor any respect for the orders of the English court). If a freezing order is proving ineffective, an application for a pre-trial receivership order[17] or even a search order[18] may be a better way of securing assets than a committal

---

[14] See Section D below.

[15] See Section D(8) below.

[16] A form of streamlining was put in place with the Court's assistance in the *Ablyazov* litigation against the principal defendant: see Section E(3) below.

[17] See Ch.33.

[18] See Ch.30.

application. Unless orders can be made in appropriate cases.[19] If the order breached is a disclosure order, it may be possible to obtain the information or documentation sought from other sources (e.g. against a bank or other third party).[20] In any given case these alternatives may be unavailable or less effective than committal, but equally it should not be assumed that the best response to the breach of an order in a fraud case is necessarily a committal application.

B.   THE UNDERLYING COURT ORDER OR UNDERTAKING

(1)   The Basic Principle

35–012   The general principle is set out in CPR r.81.4: if a person (a) required by a judgment or order to do an act does not do it within the time fixed by the judgment or order; or (b) disobeys a judgment or order not to do an act, then the judgment or order may be enforced by an order for committal.[21]

(2)   The Need for Clarity of the Terms of the Order

35–013   Before there can be committal for breach of a court order, the relevant terms of the order said to have been breached must be clear and unambiguous. If there is any doubt then the court will not entertain an application for committal. Hence it is cardinal that any order or undertaking made or offered must be drafted in terms which make it clear to the respondent precisely what he must do, or not do, as a matter of fact, rather than as a matter of legal interpretation.[22]

---

[19] See Ch.36. This procedure was successfully invoked in certain claims in the *Ablyazov* litigation so as to ultimately debar defendants from defending, without recourse to the contempt jurisdiction: see e.g. *JSC BTA Bank v Ablyazov* [2011] EWHC 2506 (Comm); and *JSC BTA Bank v Shegai* [2014] EWHC 2380 (Comm). Another recent example is *Workman v Forrester* [2017] CP Rep. 21 (CA).

[20] See Ch.29.

[21] Subject to the Debtors Acts 1869 and 1878 which, in summary, prevent imprisonment for failure to comply with an order requiring payment of money.

[22] There are numerous cases where this principle is adumbrated: see for instance *Attorney General v Staffordshire CC* [1905] 1 Ch. 336, at 342; *Iberian Trust Ltd v Founders Trust and Investment Co Ltd* [1932] 2 K.B. 87; *Redland Bricks Ltd v Morris* [1970] A.C. 652, at 666; and *Attorney General v Punch Ltd* [2003] 1 A.C. 1046, at [35]. The modern rule was stated in *Federal Bank of the Middle East v Hadkinson* [2001] 1 W.L.R. 1695, at 1705, per Mummery LJ: "The basic principle in the civil law of contempt is that, although there is an obligation to comply strictly with the terms of an order, the court will only punish a person for contempt of court upon adequate proof that the terms of the order are clear and unambiguous and that he has broken those terms." *Hadkinson* was followed in the family case of *Shadrokh-Cigari v Shadrokh-Cigari* [2010] EWCA Civ 21; [2010] 1 W.L.R. 1311, where it was held that if the respondent was not represented and where English was not his first language then the principle applied all the more strongly. Any ambiguity in a court order should be resolved in favour of the alleged contemnor: *Sectorguard Plc v Dienne Plc* [2009] EWHC 2693 (Ch), at [30].

(3)   Service

The general rule is that a committal order may not be made unless the underlying order has been personally served on the person required to do or not do the act in question.[23] Where the underlying order requires the person to do an act then the order must, for obvious reasons, be served prior to the end of the time fixed for doing that act.[24] The requirement for personal service is important because it is designed to ensure that the respondent has in his hands the relevant order, which he can then read for himself and so know what he must or must not do. As we discuss below, one of the necessary matters which must be proved on a committal application is that the respondent knew of the terms of the order. Therefore service obligations are not mere procedural hurdles; they also represent the basis on which proof of a central element of a contempt is founded. That said, where there is evidence that a respondent is avoiding service the court will be ready to make an order for alternative service.[25]

35–014

(4)   The Requirement for a Penal Notice to be Endorsed on the Order

Again, the general rule is that no committal order can be made in respect of a breach of an order unless that underlying order has prominently displayed on the front of it a penal notice, i.e.

35–015

"a warning to the person required to do or not do the act in question that disobedience to the order would be a contempt of court punishable by imprisonment, a fine or sequestration of assets."[26]

[23] See CPR rr.81.5(1) and 81.6. Personal service is explained at CPR r.6.5(3). In the case of an individual it is effected by leaving it with that individual and in the case of a company it is effected by leaving it with a person holding a senior position within the company or corporation. Pursuant to CPR r.81.8(1) the court may dispense with personal service of an order requiring a person not to do an act if satisfied that the person has had notice of it—(a) by being present when the judgment or order was given or made; or (b) by being notified of its terms by telephone, email or otherwise; and in respect of any judgment or order the court may dispense with service if the court thinks it just to do so. The discretion to dispense with service may be exercised retrospectively: *Davy International Ltd v Tazzyman* [1997] 1 W.L.R. 1256 (CA). For an example where the judge declined to exercise that power see *Sports Direct International Plc v Rangers International Football Club Plc* [2016] EWHC 85 (Ch), at [79]; and for examples where such a dispensation was granted see *Hydropool Hot Tubs Ltd v John Roberjot* [2011] EWHC 121 (Ch), at [33]–[36]; and *Group Seven Ltd v Allied Investment Corp Ltd* [2013] EWHC 1509; [2014] 1 W.L.R. 735, at [33]–[37]. Those cases discuss the various factors which will weigh with the court when deciding whether or not to dispense with personal service of the underlying order. Clearly whether or not the order was made at a hearing where the respondent was present and/or represented will be a significant factor. Other factors will be whether the failure to serve personally was deliberate or an oversight; and whether the hearing at which the order was made was contested.

[24] CPR r.81.5(1)(a).

[25] CPR r.81.8(2).

[26] CPR r.81.9 and CPR PD 81, para.1, which sets out a template penal notice: "If you the within-named [ ] do not comply with this order you may be held to be in contempt of court and imprisoned or fined, or your assets may be seized." For a case where it was decided in the interests of justice to waive the requirement of personal service and to dispense retrospectively with the requirement of a penal notice see *JSC Mezhdunarodniy Promyshlenniy Bank v Pugachev* [2016]

However, the court has a discretion to waive the requirement for a penal notice. The modern approach of the court was set out in *Nicholls v Nicholls*[27]:

> "Like any other discretion, the discretion provided by the statutory provisions, must be exercised in a way which in all the circumstances best reflects the requirements of justice. In determining this the court must not only take into account the interests of the contemnor but also the interests of the other parties and the interests of upholding the reputation of civil justice in general. Today it is no longer appropriate to regard an order for committal as being no more than a form of execution available to another party against an alleged contemnor. The court itself has a very substantial interest in seeing that its orders are upheld. If committal orders are to be set aside on purely technical grounds which have nothing to do with the justice of the case, then this has the effect of undermining the system of justice and the credibility of the court orders. While the procedural requirements in relation to applications to commit and committal orders are there to be obeyed and to protect the contemnor, if there is non-compliance with the requirements which does not prejudice the contemnor, to set aside the order purely on the grounds of technicality is contrary to the interests of justice. As long as the order made by the judge was a valid order, the approach of this court will be to uphold the order in the absence of any prejudice or injustice to the contemnor as a consequence of doing so."

35–016   As might be expected, the factors which will influence a court as to whether to dispense with the obligation for there to be a penal notice prominently displayed upon the order will include the nature of the respondent and whether he could be expected to know of the consequences of breach of the order; whether or not he had or has legal representation; and whether the respondent was informed of the consequences of breach through other means (e.g. correspondence from the applicant's solicitors, warnings made by the court during the hearing,[28] etc.).

(5)   Undertakings

(i)   Introduction

35–017   It is trite law that an undertaking given by a litigant to and accepted by a court (whether to do or not to do something) has the same legal significance as an injunction or order in like terms. It follows that breach of an undertaking will be

---

EWHC 192 (Ch). Rose J there relied (at [31]–[40]) on the general power contained in CPR r.81.8 to dispense with service of the underlying order (which necessarily carried with it a power to dispense with the need for a penal notice) and CPR PD 81 at para.16.2: "The court may waive any procedural defect in the commencement or conduct of a committal application if satisfied that no injustice has been caused to the respondent by the defect." See also *Gill v Darroch* [2010] EWHC 2347 (Ch); and *Jolly v Hull* [2002] F.L.R. 69. In *Gill* the judge (Vos J) referred to the fact that "The new CPR is very focused on furthering the overriding objective and dealing with the substance of claims and applications and not with technicalities".

[27] *Nicholls v Nicholls* [1997] 1 W.L.R. 314, at 326, per Lord Woolf MR; followed in *Bell v Tuohy* [2002] 1 W.L.R. 2703 and *ABC v CDE* [2009] EWHC 2718 (QB).

[28] See for example *Bell v Tuohy* [2002] EWCA Civ 423; [2002] 1 W.L.R. 2703, at [54]–[58], per Neuberger J, which provides a useful statement of the considerations which are likely to bear on the court's decision.

capable of being the subject of a committal application just as much as a breach of an order of the court.[29] However, there are certain procedural differences, which we discuss below.

(ii)   No requirement for personal service

There is no requirement for personal service (by the applicant for committal) of the document containing or recording the undertaking on the respondent because (unlike in cases where the application relates to the breach of a court order) the undertaking is something that has, necessarily, been given voluntarily by the respondent to the court. Instead, CPR r.81.7(1) prescribes that service shall take place by means of the court delivering the document containing the undertaking to the person who gave it, either by handing to that person a copy of the document before that person leaves court or by posting it to him or his solicitor. However, CPR r.81.7(2) provides that if delivery cannot be effected in accordance with CPR r.81.7(1), the court officer will deliver a copy of the document to the party for whose benefit the undertaking was given and that party must serve it personally on the person who gave the undertaking as soon as practicable. It seems likely that these steps are not always taken by the court, in circumstances where the practice at least in the most relevant divisions of the High Court is for the parties, rather than the Court, to serve orders.[30] Nonetheless, CPR r.81.8(1) provides a general power of dispensing with service (as to which see the discussion above so far as it relates to orders), which is more likely to be exercised in the context of undertakings than in the context of orders, for reasons similar to those underpinning the absence of any general requirement for personal service of an undertaking before committal proceedings may be brought.

35–018

(iii)   No strict requirement for a penal notice

Unlike the position with an order of the court, CPR r.81.9(2) provides that an undertaking contained in a judgment or order may be enforced notwithstanding that it is not endorsed with a penal notice. Nonetheless CPR PD 81 para 2.2 provides that a court may decline either to accept an undertaking or to deal with disobedience in respect of an undertaking by contempt of court proceedings unless the party giving the undertaking has made a signed statement to the effect that that party understands the terms of an undertaking and the consequence of failure to comply with it. Civil Procedure Rules PD 81 para.2.3 goes on to provide that such a statement may be endorsed on the order containing the undertaking or may be filed in a separate document such as a letter. No doubt when deciding whether or not to exercise its power under para.2.2 the court would have regard to the personal characteristics of the respondent and his access to legal representation at the time that the undertaking was given. But the lesson is clear: the party who obtains the benefit of an undertaking should always ensure

35–019

---

[29] See e.g. *Biba Ltd v Stratford Investments Ltd* [1973] Ch. 281, at 287E and *Coll v Floreat Merchant Banking Ltd* [2014] EWHC 1741 (QB), at [34].

[30] See the Commercial Court Guide, para.D19.3; Chancery Guide, para.22.5; Queen's Bench Guide, para.15.1.

that the relevant statement contemplated by CPR PD 81 para.2.2 has been provided to avoid potential later hurdles in the way of an application to commit.

35–020   A practical point worth consideration in this context is that, in principle at least, these requirements apply equally to an undertaking given by the applicant for a court order, which he may have to give as a condition of obtaining the order. The thought of putting a penal notice on such an order is not necessarily one which will come automatically to every practitioner's mind; but if the undertaking (which may be for example to give disclosure) is one which the respondent may subsequently wish to enforce by committal proceedings, then it could prove important to do so.

(iv)   Solicitors' undertakings

35–021   Solicitors' undertakings are a sui generis category of undertaking. They are not (generally)[31] given to the court but rather are addressed directly to a particular person. Nonetheless such undertakings are theoretically amenable to the court's contempt jurisdiction as a result of the High Court's inherent disciplinary jurisdiction over solicitors as officers of the court. This book is not the place for an examination of this jurisdiction, but the reader is directed to the recent and full analysis in *Coll v Floreat Merchant Banking Ltd*.[32] Any such application requires the prior permission of the court to make it.[33]

C.   THE ELEMENTS OF CONTEMPT

(1)   Ingredients

35–022   A civil contempt of court (i.e. in relation to a breach of an undertaking or order) is established where the respondent intentionally acts or omits to act in such a way that the act or omission amounts to a breach of the order of undertaking. It is not necessary to show that the respondent knew or believed that his act or omission amounted to a breach of the order. The leading modern statement of the legal position was by Christopher Clarke J in *Masri v Consolidated Contractors Intl Co SAL*[34] (referred to below as "*Masri*"):

---

[31] Though of course it does happen that undertakings are offered by solicitors acting for parties to litigation directly to the court. Such undertakings are treated, and enforced, in just the same way as undertakings given by the litigants themselves.

[32] *Coll v Floreat Merchant Banking Ltd* [2014] EWHC 1741 (QB).

[33] See CPR r.81.11 which sets out other procedural provisions relating to such applications.

[34] *Masri v Consolidated Contractors Intl Co SAL* [2011] EWHC 1024 (Comm), at [150]. The leading authorities on which Christopher Clarke J drew are the decision of Warrington J in *Stancombe v Trowbridge UDC* [1910] 2 Ch. 190, at 194, and the decisions of the House of Lords in *Heaton's Transport (St Helens) Ltd v Transport and General Workers Union* [1973] A.C. 15, at 109 and *Director General of Fair Trading v Pioneer Concrete (UK) Ltd* [1995] 1 A.C. 456, at 479–481. This passage from *Masri* was referred to with approval in *Templeton Insurance Plc v Motorcare Warranties Ltd* [2012] EWHC 795 (Comm), per Eder J at [17]–[20], upheld on appeal at [2013] EWCA Civ 35.

"In order to establish that someone is in contempt it is necessary to show that (i) that he knew of the terms of the order; (ii) that he acted (or failed to act) in a manner which involved a breach of the order; and (iii) that he knew of the facts which made his conduct a breach."

To this statement may be added the gloss that the act or omission at (ii) must be intentional, as opposed to accidental or casual. We consider below some aspects of this general rule.

(i) Has there been a contravention of the terms of the order/undertaking?

Of course the applicant must prove an actual breach of the order or undertaking. **35–023** This may not be straightforward, particularly in the context of freezing orders, where there may be significant room for doubt in any given case as to whether or not the acts complained of (e.g. a transaction entered into in relation to an asset) in fact constituted a contravention of the terms of the order.[35] Often this question will require close scrutiny of the terms of the order itself. As regards freezing orders, they are not subject to the same principles of construction by which contracts are interpreted; this is because, in part, they speak to third parties who will not necessarily be aware of the background against which they were made and because the meaning of a court order must be (a) constant and (b) objectively ascertained by reference to facts available to all persons whom it might affect, and not on the basis of private understandings between the parties. The most recent analysis of the principles applicable to the construction of court orders was contained in the Supreme Court's judgment in *JSC BTA Bank v Ablyazov (No. 10)*,[36] which may be summarised as follows:

(1) The sole question for the court is what the order means, so that issues as to whether it should have been granted and if so in what terms are not relevant to construction.[37]

(2) In considering the meaning of an order granting an injunction, the terms in which it was made are to be restrictively construed. Such are the penal consequences of breach that the order must be clear and unequivocal and strictly construed before a party will be found to have broken the terms of the order and thus to be in contempt of court.[38]

(3) The words of the order are to be given their natural and ordinary meaning and are to be construed in their context, including their historical context and with regard to the object of the order.[39]

---

[35] See e.g. *Federal Bank of the Middle East v Hadkinson* [2001] 1 W.L.R. 1695 and *Group Seven Ltd v Allied Investment Corp Ltd* [2013] EWHC 1509; [2014] 1 W.L.R. 735. These cases are considered in greater detail above at Ch.28.

[36] *JSC BTA Bank v Ablyazov (No. 10)* [2015] UKSC 64; [2015] 1 W.L.R. 4754.

[37] See *JSC BTA Bank v Ablyazov (No. 10)*, at [16].

[38] See *JSC BTA Bank v Ablyazov (No. 10)*, at [19], approving inter alia the statements of principle to that effect in the Court of Appeal by Mummery and Nourse LJJ in *Federal Bank of the Middle East v Hadkinson* [2000] 1 W.L.R. 1695.

[39] See at [21]–[26], again citing with approval what Mummery LJ said in *Hadkinson*. See also *Sans Souci Ltd v VRL Services Ltd* [2012] UKPC 6, per Lord Sumption at [13]: "...the construction of a judicial order, like that of any other legal instrument, is a single coherent process. It depends on what

35–024   Hence there is no room for resort to estoppel arguments in construing orders. As was said by Hildyard J in the *Group Seven* case:

> "An order of the Court is likely to (and in the case of a freezing order almost certainly will) affect (and in some cases bind) persons other than the parties who may well be (indeed are likely to be) unaware of preceding communications between, or shared assumptions of, the parties. Although an 'unswervingly literal' approach is not appropriate, and the context in which the words appear may well affect their construction, it seems to me that the Court must adopt the meaning which, in the context, the words naturally bear, rather than any special but unexplained meaning."[40]

The respondent will be in breach of the order or undertaking if he directs or instigates another person to take a step which constitutes a breach of the order, regardless of that other person's knowledge, or otherwise, of the order.[41]

(ii)   Intention

35–025   The intention of the respondent that is required to be proved is an intention to do the act or omit to do the act which is said to constitute a breach of the order or undertaking. It is not necessary to establish that the respondent intended to breach the order, although that will be a significant question when it comes to assessing sentence, as we discuss below.[42] This further element (an intention to breach the order) is that aspect of the respondent's mens rea which is described in the authorities as "contumaciousness".[43] The fact that the respondent may have (however reasonably) believed that he was not acting in breach of the court order, or that he was acting on legal advice,[44] is therefore no defence to a charge of contempt, but bears instead on sentence. Hence proposition (iii) in the *Masri*

---

the language of the order would convey, in the circumstances in which the Court made it, so far as these circumstances were before the Court and patent to the parties. The reasons for making the order which are given by the Court in its judgment are an overt and authoritative statement of the circumstances which it regarded as relevant. They are therefore always admissible to construe the order. In particular, the interpretation of an order may be critically affected by knowing what the Court considered to be the issue which its order was supposed to resolve." See also *Pan Petroleum Aje Ltd v Yinka Folawiyo Petroleum Co Ltd* [2017] EWCA Civ 1525.

[40] *Group Seven Ltd v Allied Investment Corp Ltd* [2013] EWHC 1509 (Ch); [2014] 1 W.L.R. 735, at [75(1)].

[41] *Attorney General v Times Newspapers Ltd* [1992] 1 A.C. 191, at 217, per Lord Oliver.

[42] The law was definitively stated by Warrington J in *Stancomb v Trowbridge UDC* [1910] 2 Ch. 190, at 194 as follows: "In my judgment, if a person or a corporation is restrained by injunction from doing a particular act, that person or corporation commits a breach of the injunction, and is liable for process for contempt, if he or she does the act, and it is no answer to say that the act was not contumacious in the sense that, in doing it, there was no direct intention to disobey the order." This analysis was followed in, e.g., *Heaton's Transport (St Helen's) Ltd v Transport and General Workers Union* [1973] A.C. 15, at 108–110; *Mileage Conference Group of the Tyre Manufacturers Conferences Agreement* [1966] 1 W.L.R. 1137; *Spectravest Inc v Aperknit Ltd* [1988] F.S.R. 161 (Millett J); *Director General of Fair Trading v Pioneer Concrete* [1995] 1 A.C. 456. There was a suggestion in the Court of Appeal decision of *Irtelli v Squatriti* [1993] Q.B. 83 that contumaciousness was a necessary element in proof of a contempt. This analysis has since been disapproved as heretical: see *Adam Phones Ltd v Gideon Goldschmidt* [2000] CP Rep. 23; *Bird v Hadkinson* [2000] CP Rep. 21; *Masri*, above, at [155]; and *JSC BTA Bank v Ablyazov* [2012] EWHC (Comm) 237, at [124].

[43] *Phonographic Performance Ltd v Amusement Caterers Ltd* [1964] Ch. 165.

[44] See for example *Re Mileage Conference Group of the Tyre Manufacturers' Conference Agreement* [1966] 1 W.L.R. 1137, at 1162D–E, in which the respondents were prohibited from entering into a

principles set out above is *not* that the respondent knew that his conduct was a breach of the order or undertaking; the intention is directed towards the act carried out (or omission), not its legal effect.

On the other hand, acts which are "casual or accidental and unintentional" will not give rise to liability in contempt.[45] It has been said that this phrase connotes two alternatives, not three.[46] This exception has rarely been applied in practice, but some guidance as to its potential application can be found in the cases. For example:

    35–026

(1)   In *Bird v Hadkinson*,[47] the order required the respondent to provide information in relation to certain funds. Neuberger J suggested that, on the face of it, an inaccurate answer would not comply with the terms of the order but that, if the inaccurate answer was given in good faith after making all reasonable enquiries, there might be no contempt. In *Masri*, Christopher Clarke J referred to this decision and postulated that in such a case the failure to provide accurate information might properly be characterised as accidental or unintentional.

(2)   In *Westminster City Council v Addbins Ltd*,[48] Males J held that the respondents' omission to comply with the terms of an order requiring the removal of 3,000 cigarette bins was not casual, accidental or unintentional in circumstances where the respondents had made some limited effort to comply but fallen short of what the order required.[49]

(3)   In a recent Northern Irish case,[50] the formulation "casual or accidental and unintentional" was considered to denote conduct which "cannot be described as deliberate", with the example given of purely careless or otherwise inadvertent conduct. Conduct under duress was postulated as another example.

The application of this exception to liability has particular potential relevance to the situation of disclosure of assets under a freezing order. A defendant may for example give inaccurate information about the value of one of his assets in reasonable reliance on information from others, or fail to disclose an asset because he wrongly but reasonably believes it to be below the value threshold for disclosure under the freezing order. In such circumstances, following *Bird v Hadkinson* and *Masri* in particular, there may have been a breach of the

    35–027

---

particular agreement or an agreement "as to the like effect"; the court disagreed with the legal advice given to them as to whether entry into a particular agreement would infringe the order, and they were found in contempt.

[45] *Stancomb v Trowbridge UDC* [1910] 2 Ch. 190, at 194.

[46] *Spectravest Inc v Aperknit Ltd* [1988] F.S.R. 161, at 173 (Millett J), i.e. (i) casual or (ii) accidental and unintentional.

[47] *Bird v Hadkinson* [2000] CP Rep. 21.

[48] *Westminster City Council v Addbins Ltd* [2012] EWHC 3716 (QB); [2013] JPL 654, at [77] in particular.

[49] See also the similar case of *Hone v Page* [1980] F.S.R. 500.

[50] *Re Demesne Investments* [2013] NICH 2, at [37].

disclosure requirement, but an accidental and unintentional one; the question of breach may itself require careful interpretation of the terms of the order.[51]

35–028 If the terms of the order are sufficiently uncertain to engage difficult legal questions, it may be that the court would refuse to entertain committal proceedings on the basis of the principles explained in para.35–013 above. But, on the other hand, in any case where there is real doubt as to whether a proposed step would constitute a breach of an order (such as a transaction which may affect a frozen asset, for example), the wise course for a respondent is to inform the beneficiary of the order of the proposed step in advance, so that any issue can be aired—and if necessary, determined—before it is too late.

35–029 There is no principle of "reasonable excuse" available to a respondent. Hence, for example, if the respondent is ordered by the English court to do a particular thing in unconditional terms and fails to do so, his failure to comply with the order is not excused if compliance with it would (or might) constitute a breach of the order of a foreign court.[52]

(iii) Liability for the acts of an employee or agent

35–030 Where acts carried out by an employee or agent in breach of an order made against the employer or principal are concerned, the general principles governing liability for contempt must be applied in a way which accommodates the separate legal personalities of principal and agent. Subject to any reassessment of how the law of attribution ought to be applied to contempt proceedings in light of the Supreme Court's decision in *Bilta (UK) Ltd (In Liquidation) v Nazir (No.2)*[53], the case law suggests that, of the three elements set out in para.35–022 above by reference to *Masri*, (i) the knowledge of the order which must be established is that of the employer or principal[54]; but (ii) the (deliberate) act is that of the employee or agent, as is (iii) the requisite knowledge of the facts which makes that act a breach of the order.

35–031 As far as knowledge of the order or undertaking is concerned, in the case of a principal who is an individual this will engage the same principles as those applying where no question of agency arises, subject to the question of attribution of knowledge via the agent. In the case of a company, knowledge will generally

---

[51] The freezing injunction standard forms (para.9) require the respondent to give disclosure of assets "to the best of his ability". It is also not uncommon also to see the words "and after making all reasonable enquiries" (or words to similar effect) in a freezing injunction. Differences in wording such as this may make a difference as to whether liability is established on a given set of facts. See e.g. *IPartner Pte Shipping Ltd v Panacore Resources DMCC* [2014] EWHC 3608 (Comm), at [30], per Hamblen J, holding that there would be no breach of an order even if a respondent wilfully failed to comply with an order requiring disclosure "to the best of their ability", if compliance would not have resulted in any further disclosure being given. The judge drew an analogy with the impossibility principle discussed by Briggs J in *Sectorguard Plc v Dienne Plc* [2009] EWHC 2693 (Ch). He went on to find on the facts that there had in fact been compliance to the best of the respondent's ability (see [54]–[55]).

[52] *Masri v Consolidated Contractors International Co SAL* [2011] EWHC 1024 (Comm), at [156].

[53] *Bilta (UK) Ltd (In Liquidation) v Nazir (No.2)* [2015] UKSC 23; [2016] A.C. 1.

[54] The knowledge may however be capable of being attributed to the principal through the agent. See Ch.19.

be established through one or more of its officers, who are likely to be conducting the litigation on the company's behalf, but may also be established (if necessary inferred) by showing that the order was sent to an appropriate office where the company's business was being carried on.[55] It is not necessary to establish liability for contempt that the employee or agent who acted in breach actually knew of the order or undertaking, or of its terms.[56]

It is, however, the employee or agent whose acts and associated knowledge will be relevant to the question of breach. Accordingly, in the case of a company, deliberate conduct by a director or an employee which was not accidental and in the knowledge of the facts rendering the conduct a breach of an order or undertaking will suffice if, objectively judged, it constitutes a breach of the order.[57] In *Re Supply of Ready Mixed Concrete (No.2)*[58] certain companies were ordered by the court not to take certain steps. As a result of those orders the companies, by their directors, instructed their employees not to act in contravention of those injunctions. Without the knowledge of the companies various employees thereafter acted so as to contravene the orders. It was held that the companies were in contempt, notwithstanding those matters and the fact that the companies had adopted reasonable compliance systems to prevent the breaches.[59] Hence the legal position can be stated as follows: disobedience by the servants of a company, acting in the course of their employment, to an injunction amounts to contempt of court by the employing company unless the conduct of the employees could be described as merely casual or accidental and unintentional, in the sense analysed above. We consider the personal liability of directors below.

35–032

The House of Lords' decision in *Ready Mixed Concrete*, which concerned employees of a company, impliedly overruled the decision of Slade J in *Hone v Page*[60] to the effect that an employer or principal would only be liable for the acts of his employees or agents if he: (i) authorised the acts or (ii) could reasonably have foreseen the possibility of such acts and failed to take all reasonable steps to prevent them. It is however an uncertain question whether the principle in *Hone v Page* survives in relation to agents or to employees of a non-corporate employer.

35–033

---

[55] As was the case in *Re Garage Equipment Association's Agreement* (1964) LR 4 RP 491.

[56] *Re Garage Equipment Association's Agreement* (1964) LR 4 RP 491, in which none of the officers of the company which had engaged in conduct breaching the company's undertaking even realised that the undertaking had been given (since the court proceedings had been dealt with by a sales manager who had since left the business).

[57] See Londono, Smith and Eady, *Arlidge, Eady and Smith on Contempt* (2017), para.12–103.

[58] *Re Supply of Ready Mixed Concrete (No.2)* [1995] 1 A.C. 456.

[59] See per Lord Nolan at 476 and following. The House of Lords founded its decision principally on two earlier cases: *Rantzen v Rothschild* 14 WR 96 and *Stancomb v Trowbridge Urban District Council* [1910] 2 Ch. 190. In the latter decision Warrington J had held, at 194: "In my opinion, further, the act need not be done by the person himself. In the case of a corporation it cannot be done by the corporation itself, at any rate in the case of such a corporation as an urban district council. Such a body can only act by its agents or servants; and I think, if the act is in fact done, it is no answer to say that, done, as it must be, by an officer or servant of the council, the council is not liable for it, even though it may have been done by the servant through carelessness, neglect, or even in dereliction of his duty." Warrington J was there dealing with a respondent which was a corporation; but the reasoning is equally applicable where it is a company.

[60] *Hone v Page* [1980] F.S.R. 500.

In *World Wide Fund for Nature v THQ/Jakks Pacific LLC*,[61] Carnwath LJ said that the *Hone v Page* principle had only been overruled insofar as employees were concerned. However, as (a different) Slade J said in *Back office Ltd v Percival*,[62] there should be no distinction in principle between the position of employees and that of agents.[63]

35–034   It is suggested that the correct distinction as a matter of principle is that suggested by Slade J in the *Percival* case,[64] namely between companies and individuals. Since companies can *only* act through employees or agents,[65] the principle of corporate attribution requires a stricter approach; otherwise any order in absolute terms would in effect be diluted so as to require no more than reasonable steps to be taken to ensure compliance. Accordingly, we consider that the additional requirement in *Hone v Page* set out in the preceding paragraph, whilst it does not apply to corporate respondents, continues to apply in relation to individual respondents.[66] The authorities are, however, difficult to reconcile. However, as identified in para.30–050 above, it is right to note that the Supreme Court has recently reviewed the law on attribution generally in *Bilta (UK) Ltd (In Liquidation) v Nazir*[67] It is as yet not clear exactly how the law as it now stands will be applied to the specific context of contempt proceedings, and the reader should consider the existing contempt cases in the light of, and subject to, the law of attribution post-*Bilta*, which is considered in detail in Ch.19.

(iv)   Impossibility

35–035   The court will not issue an injunction which is not capable of being complied with. However there will be occasions where an injunction is made, or an undertaking offered, where, in fact, on investigation, or as events subsequently transpire, it turns out that it cannot be complied with. An example is *Sectorguard Plc v Dienne Plc*,[68] a claim for breach of confidence, where the respondent company had undertaken to the court that it would disclose the identity of all the claimant applicant's customers which had been contacted. In fact, unknown to the respondent at the time of the giving of the undertaking, no record had been kept

---

[61] *World Wide Fund for Nature v THQ/Jakks Pacific LLC* [2004] F.S.R. 10, at [18].

[62] *Back office Ltd v Percival* [2013] EWHC 1385 (QB).

[63] *Back office Ltd v Percival* [2013] EWHC 1385 (QB), at [68]; *Ready Mixed Concrete*, at 481B; *Heaton's Transport (St Helens) Ltd v Transport and General Workers Union* [1973] A.C. 15, at 99C.

[64] *Back office Ltd v Percival* [2013] EWHC 1385 (QB), at [69].

[65] A point emphasised in the *Stancomb* case [1910] 2 Ch. 190, at 194 and in *British Telecommunications Plc v Nextcall Telecom Plc* [2000] F.S.R. 679, at [1], per Jacob J.

[66] This is expressly supported by *Attorney General for Tuvalu v Philatelic Distribution Corp Ltd* [1990] 1 W.L.R. 926, at 936G, albeit this case was decided before *Ready Mixed Concrete*. It is accordingly thought that the decision of David Richards J in *Daltel v Makki* [2005] EWHC 749 (Ch), at [48]–[50], in which he applied the *Ready Mixed Concrete* to Mr Makki as an individual respondent, is wrong. David Richards J relied for his conclusion on *Rantzen v Rothschild* (1865) 14 WR 96. That case (in which the defendants were merely ordered to pay the costs of an application for committal in respect of the actions of a foreman employed by them) provides little support for the proposition that an individual employer can be committed to prison for contempt for the actions of his employees, no matter how careful he has been to secure compliance by them with the order.

[67] *Bilta (UK) Ltd (In Liquidation) v Nazir* [2015] UKSC 23; [2016] A.C. 1.

[68] *Sectorguard Plc v Dienne Plc* [2009] EWHC 2693 (Ch).

of which customers had been contacted by the respondent's employees. The undertaking could not be complied with. The judge accepted the submission that failure to perform an impossible undertaking (and by extension of reasoning, an order too) was not a contempt.[69]

In the same way, if partial compliance with an order is possible and such partial compliance is achieved, and further compliance with the order would have been impossible, then the failure to comply further with the order would not be a contempt.[70]

35–036

(2) Liability of Company Directors and Other Officers

(i) Introduction

Companies can only act by their agents (including employees). Therefore if a company breaches an order or undertaking it can only do so via the acts or omissions of such agents. Even though the relevant order may (and usually will) be only directed at the company or the relevant undertaking only given by the company, the directors of that company may nonetheless be personally liable themselves in contempt for any breach, in addition to any liability on the part of the company. For such liability to arise it is necessary to show that the officer knew of and was responsible for the company's breach of the court order or undertaking to the court.[71] The basic principle was stated by the Court of Appeal in *A-G of Tuvalu v Philatelic Distribution Corp Ltd*[72]:

35–037

> "Where a company is ordered not to do certain acts and a director of that company is aware of the order, he is under a duty to take reasonable steps to ensure that the order or undertaking is obeyed, and if he wilfully fails to take those steps and the order or undertaking is breached he can be punished for contempt."[73]

---

[69] Briggs J said, at [32]–[33]: "[32] The mental element required of a contemnor is not that he either intends to breach or knows that he is breaching the court order or undertaking, but only that he intended the act or omission in question, and knew the facts which made it a breach of the order: see *Adam Phones v Goldschmidt* [1999] 4 All E.R. 486, at 492j to 494j. [33] Nonetheless, even a mental element of that modest quality assumes that the alleged contemnor had some choice whether to commit the relevant act or omission. An omission to do that which is in truth impossible involves no choice at all. Failure to comply with an order to do something, where the doing of it is impossible, may therefore be a breach of the order, but not, in my judgment, a contempt of court." The undertaking was itself discharged. A similar conclusion was reached in *Buckinghamshire County Council v Anglo Irish Plant Hire Ltd* [2011] EWHC 3686 (QB).

[70] *IPartner Pte Shipping Ltd v Panacore Resources DMCC* [2014] EWHC 3608 (Comm), at [28]–[29], per Hamblen J.

[71] See *Attorney General for Tuvalu v Philatelic Distribution Corp Ltd* [1990] 1 W.L.R. 926, at 938; *Sectorguard Plc v Dienne Plc* [2009] EWHC 2693 (Ch), at [42]; *Masri v Consolidated Contractors International Co SAL* [2010] EWHC 2458 (Comm), at [40(2)]; and *Westminster City Council v Addbins Ltd* [2012] EWHC 3716 (QB), at [50]–[54]; *Dar Al Arkan Real Estate Development Co v Refai* [2014] EWCA Civ 715; [2015] 1 W.L.R. 135, at [33].

[72] *A-G of Tuvalu v Philatelic Distribution Corp Ltd* [1990] 1 W.L.R. 926.

[73] For liability of directors for breach of undertakings see *Ronson Products Ltd v Ronson Furniture Ltd* [1966] Ch. 603.

This is now partially reflected in CPR r.81.4(3) which provides that a committal order made against a company or corporation may also be made against "any director or other officer", albeit the rules themselves are silent on the constituent elements of the director's liability.

35–038 The phrase "director or other officer" plainly covers de jure directors. Whether it extends to de facto or shadow directors is more difficult. In another decision *Masri*[74] Blair J held that this was arguable (noting also that the argument in the litigation engaged the complex issues of conflicts of laws (where foreign companies were concerned)).

(ii)   The nature of the director's liability

35–039 Hence a director of a company subject to a court order or undertaking will be personally liable in contempt if:

(1)   He knew of the order or undertaking; and

(2)   He either aids or abets the company's breach of the order or undertaking, or wilfully fails to take reasonable steps to ensure that the order or undertaking is obeyed, whether the order or undertaking is cast in prohibitory or mandatory terms.

35–040 The word "wilful" distinguishes the situation where, for example, the director reasonably believes some other director or officer is taking those steps. For instance, if a company has three directors, they meet to discuss the need for steps to be taken to ensure compliance by the company with the order (e.g. by giving appropriate instructions to employees), director A reasonably believes from that discussion that director B has agreed to take those steps, but they are not taken, this would appear to give director A a defence to a charge of contempt. By the same token, a non-executive director may be able to avoid liability if the order concerned the day-to-day activities of the company and the director reasonably thought that compliance would be secured by the executive directors. This is, however, not the sole meaning of the word "wilful" in this context; the test of wilfulness is one of more general application.[75]

35–041 There are a number of fairly recent cases in which directors have been held liable on the *Tuvalu* principles.[76] Conversely, in *Back Office Ltd v Percival*[77] two company directors were held not liable on those principles where employees of the company had solicited the applicant's clients in breach of an undertaking by the company not to do so. The directors had neither authorised the solicitation,

---

[74] *Masri v Consolidated Contractors International Co Sal* [2010] EWHC 2458 (Comm), at [17]–[24] in particular.

[75] *IPartner Pte Shipping Ltd v Panacore Resources DMCC* [2014] EWHC 3608 (Comm), at [27], per Hamblen J.

[76] Among the more notable examples are *Gulf Azov Shipping Company Ltd v Idisi*, unreported, 22 November 2000, per Moore-Bick J, upheld on appeal [2001] EWCA Civ 21; *Templeton Insurance Ltd v Motorcare Warranties Ltd* [2012] EWHC 795 (Comm), at [21]–[23] and [46]; *IPartner Pte Shipping Ltd v Panacore Resources DMCC* [2014] EWHC 3608 (Comm), at [65], per Hamblen J.

[77] *Back Office Ltd v Percival* [2013] EWHC 1385 (QB), esp. at [61] and [71], per Slade J.

nor had they failed to take all reasonable steps to prevent it: they had called a meeting of all relevant employees to explain the terms of the undertaking and the need to comply with it.

(iii) Procedural points

Subject to the power of dispensation (as to which see above), by CPR r.81.5(2), an order requiring a company to do or abstain from doing an act is not to be enforced by way of an order of committal against a director or other officer unless a copy of the order has been served personally on the officer against whom the order of committal is sought. Service on the officer has to be before the expiration of the time within which the company was required to do the act.   **35–042**

We have set out the law concerning the affixing of a penal notice to an order above. Under the CPR it is not an absolute pre-condition for subsequent liability that the individual director sought to be committed should be named in the penal notice attached to the underlying order. However, it is good practice to do so and a failure to do so may preclude a finding of contempt.[78]   **35–043**

(iv) What must be alleged against the director

It follows that any committal application against a director cannot simply assert non-compliance by the company with the order or undertaking. Non-compliance by the company with the relevant order or undertaking does not ipso facto render all the directors liable in contempt.[79] It is accordingly not possible to read CPR r.81.4(3) as simply providing a means (committal of a director or officer) of punishing the company for its contempt. Instead the prosecution of a director under the *Tuvalu* principles involves its own process, by which the liability of a director must be pleaded and proved. Consistently with this, the application notice must assert the basis on which it is sought to commit the individual director for the company's default: **35–044**

> "I consider that the effect of the *Tuvalu* case is that an applicant for the committal of a company director who relies upon a breach by the company of an order or an undertaking must disclose in the committal application a case for the establishment of responsibility on the part of that director, either on the grounds of aiding and abetting or wilful failure to take reasonable steps to ensure that the order or undertaking is obeyed."[80]

---

[78] *Iberian Trust Ltd v Founder's Trust and Investment Co* [1932] 2 K.B. 87, at 97–98, per Luxmoore J; *Masri v Consolidated Contractors International Co SAL* [2010] EWHC 2458 (Comm), at [40]–[43], per Blair J.

[79] Briggs J held in *Sectorguard Plc v Dienne Plc* [2009] EWHC 2693 (Ch) that *BIBA Ltd v Stratford Investments Ltd* [1973] Ch. 281 establishes no such principle, notwithstanding that there are dicta in the earlier decision which, if taken out of context, might be thought to suggest it.

[80] *Sectorguard Plc v Dienne Plc* [2009] EWHC 2693 (Ch), at [42].

(3)   The Position of Third Parties

35–045   The general rule is that an order directed at, or an undertaking provided by, a named respondent is only binding on that person. Except in the rare case of an order contra mundum third parties are not directly affected by an order or undertaking. However, such a third party may nonetheless be guilty of a contempt of court if, knowing of the order or undertaking, he takes steps which aid or abet the respondent in breaching the order or otherwise does an act which obstructs or frustrates the object of the order. The classic statement of principle was laid down by Lord Hope in *Attorney General v Punch Ltd.*[81]

> "The power to commit for contempt ensures that acts and words tending to obstruct the administration of justice are prohibited. So a stranger is liable for contempt if his act constitutes a wilful interference with the administration of justice by the court in the proceedings in which the order was made. It has also to be shown there was an intention on his part to interfere with or impede the administration of justice. This is an essential ingredient, and it has to be established to the criminal standard of proof. But the intent need not be stated expressly or admitted by the defendant. As is the case where the question of intention, or *mens rea*, arises in criminal cases, it can be inferred from all the circumstances including the foreseeability of the consequences of the defendant's conduct: *Att Gen v Newspaper Publishing Plc* [1988] Ch. 333, at 374–375, per Sir John Donaldson M.R."

35–046   This statement is partially reflected in the freezing order standard form, which provides as follows:

> "*Effect of this Order*: It is a Contempt of Court for any person notified of this Order knowingly to assist in or permit a breach of this Order. Any person doing so may be sent to prison, fined or have his assets seized."

There is a similar statement in the search order standard form.

35–047   The liability of a third party is, if one uses the old categorisation, a form of criminal contempt.[82] The liability of third parties who are not themselves the subject of a court order or undertaking and who are not directors of companies who are so subject depends upon special principles which differ from the principles set out above. We consider them below.

(i)   Basis of liability

35–048   There are two separate bases on which a third party may be liable for contempt of court in relation to a court order or undertaking.

(1)   First, the third party may be liable for aiding and abetting, or knowingly assisting, a breach of the order or undertaking by the respondent to the order.[83]

---

[81] *Attorney General v Punch Ltd* [2003] 1 A.C. 1046, at [87].

[82] *Attorney General v Times Newspapers Ltd* [1992] 1 A.C. 191, at 217, per Lord Oliver.

[83] The nature of this liability was analysed in the leading case of *Seaward v Paterson* [1897] Ch. 545, at 554, per Lindley LJ.

(2) Secondly, the third party may be liable for a deliberate or wilful interference with the administration of justice, whether or not the respondent himself is in breach of the order.[84]

It might be said that the first basis of liability is no more than an instance of the second; for to aid and abet a breach of an injunction or undertaking is itself a form of deliberate interference with the administration of justice. Nonetheless the categorisation above is of assistance in defining the nature of the liability of a third party in contempt in two scenarios and courts continue to differentiate between them.[85] The liability of the third party is not necessarily an accessory liability.[86]

As regards the first basis of liability, in the context of breach of a freezing order, an obvious example will be where the third party consensually receives into his bank account assets which are subject to the freezing order in order to assist the respondent in moving those assets beyond the reach of the applicant and the ambit of the freezing order.

35–049

As regards the second basis of liability, this was established in the context of freezing orders by the Court of Appeal in *Z Ltd v A-Z and AA-LL*[87] where it was held that if, say, a bank was served with a freezing order prior to the respondent (of course a common practice), then if the bank were then to permit a disposal of funds from an account subject to the freezing order the fact that the respondent was not himself in breach of the order (because he had yet to be served with it) would be no bar to the bank being in contempt of court. This was obviously not an accessory liability.

35–050

(ii) Elements to be proved

As we have seen above, liability for civil contempt is strict, in the sense that the respondent will be liable irrespective of his intention to breach the order or undertaking (as opposed to the intentionality of the act which constitutes the breach itself). By contrast liability for criminal contempt is not strict, but requires proof of an intention on the part of the third party either to aid and abet the respondent in breaching the order or to interfere with or impede the administration of justice.[88]

35–051

Hence the elements of contempt which must be proved against a third party may be broken down as follows:

35–052

(1) Knowledge of the order or undertaking.
(2) An act (the actus reus) which, objectively analysed, either

---

[84] The nature of this liability was analysed in *Lord Wellesley v Earl of Mornington* (1848) 11 Beav 181 and *Attorney General v Times Newspapers Ltd* [1992] 1 A.C. 191, at 217–218, per Lord Oliver.
[85] See e.g. *Attorney General v Punch Ltd* [2003] 1 A.C. 1046, at [3], per Lord Nicholls and at [67], per Lord Hoffmann.
[86] *Z Ltd v A-Z and AA-LL* [1982] Q.B. 558.
[87] *Z Ltd v A-Z and AA-LL* [1982] Q.B. 558.
[88] *Attorney General v Times Newspapers Ltd* [1992] 1 A.C. 191, at 218, per Lord Oliver.

     (a)   aided or abetted the respondent in his own breach of the order; or

     (b)   frustrated or thwarted[89] the purpose of the order or undertaking, with the result that there has been a significant and adverse effect on the administration of justice.[90]

(3)   An intention (the mens rea) either

     (a)   to aid or abet the respondent's breach; or

     (b)   to frustrate or thwart the purpose of the injunction.

(iii)   Procedural considerations

35–053   There is room for doubt on the face of the provisions of CPR Pt 81 as to the proper procedure for applying to commit a third party on the basis set out above. On the one hand, the liability of third parties is properly to be analysed as a liability in criminal, not civil contempt, and as consisting in interference with the due administration of justice. The procedure for applying to commit for interference with the due administration of justice is laid down in s.III of CPR Pt 81. In particular, applications require the permission of the Court to be pursued,[91] to be sought by Pt 8 claim form.[92] On the other hand, CPR 81.10(2), which is in s.II of CPR Pt 81 (concerning committal for breach of a judgment, order or undertaking) provides that, where the committal application is made against a person who is not an existing party to the proceedings, it is made against that person by an application notice under CPR Pt 23.

35–054   CPR r.81.10(2) has been interpreted as applicable to a third party accused of such an "interference" contempt.[93] If correct, this would mean that applications against such third parties do not require permission. It may however be doubted whether this was the intention of the Rules Committee; or whether the provision is instead directed towards third parties against whom orders have been made (for example, freezing orders pursuant to the *Chabra* jurisdiction) or by whom undertakings have been given. But, equally, if the procedure applicable to the third party is that set out in s.III of CPR Pt 81, then applications made both against a party and a third party in respect of breaches of the same order would be subject to a split procedural regime.

---

[89] Various formulations are used: e.g. "impeded and prejudiced" in *Attorney General v Punch Ltd* [2003] 1 A.C. 1046, at [6], per Lord Nicholls.

[90] The "purpose" referred to here is "simply to prevent from happening whatever the order said should not happen." The Court should not go any further to inquire into the court's underlying purpose in granting the order in the first place, or that of the litigant who sought the order. See *Attorney General v Punch Ltd* [2003] 1 A.C. 1046, at [76], per Lord Hoffmann.

[91] CPR r.81.12(3).

[92] CPR r.81.14(1).

[93] *QRS v Beach* [2015] EWHC 1489 (QB), at [8].

D.   THE APPLICATION FOR COMMITTAL[94]

Given the quasi-criminal character of a committal application (and the concomitant serious consequences which a respondent to such an application faces) the law provides important procedural safeguards to the respondent to such an application. That law is now gathered in CPR Pt 81 and its accompanying practice direction,[95] although there is a substantial body of judicial commentary which remains relevant. Part 81 deals with the various types of contempt but, as explained earlier, we concentrate here on the contempt constituted by breach of a court order or undertaking. Applications in relation to such breaches are governed by s.II of Pt 81, which is made up of rr.81.4 to 81.11, as supplemented by the practice direction.

35–055

(1)   The Application

Applications for committal of this type are made by way of application notice under Pt 23 in the proceedings in which the judgment or order was made or the undertaking given.[96] As we have seen above, a non-party may be liable in contempt if he has knowingly assisted a respondent to breach an order or undertaking, but there is some doubt on the face of the rules as to what procedure applies to an application against such a non-party.

35–056

The application notice must set out in full the grounds on which the committal application is made and must identify, separately and numerically, each alleged act or omission of contempt including, if known, the date of each of the alleged acts.[97] The respondent must know precisely what is being alleged against him so that he can properly defend himself.[98] It is not sufficient for the application notice to cross-refer to a narrative affidavit: the respondent must not have to work out what is said against him by having to interpret the evidence.[99] The application

35–057

---

[94] For committal for interference with the due administration of justice, see CPR rr.81.12, 81.13 and 81.14. For committal in the face of the court, see r.81.16. For committal for making a false statement of truth or disclosure statement, see rr.81.17 and 81.18.

[95] Which both came into force on 1 October 2012.

[96] Rule 81.10(1). Practice Direction 81 paras 13.1 and 13.2 contain further provisions about the application notice. Where the application is not made within existing proceedings then it must be commenced by Pt 8 claim form: see PD 81, para.12, which contains procedural provisions concerning such a claim.

[97] Rule 81.10(3). In a complex case the court may order formal pleadings: see e.g. *JSC BTA Bank v Ereshchenko* [2013] EWCA Civ 1961, at [7]. A recent example of a failed application to strike out a committal application on grounds of inadequacy of particularisation is *Masri v Consolidated Contractors International Company SAL* [2010] EWHC 2458 (Comm); [2011] Bus L.R. D55. It provides an instance of how convoluted the arguments can become in a factual and legally complex case.

[98] *AG of Tuvalu v Philatelic Distribution Corp Ltd* [1990] 1 W.L.R. 926, at 934–935. However the court will apply this principle sensibly and the level of detail required to be included in order to satisfy this test will depend on the circumstances of the particular case, including the nature of the acts or omissions alleged.

[99] See generally *M. v P. (Contempt of Court: Committal Order)* [1993] Fam 167, at 174 and *Harmsworth v Harmsworth* [1987] 1 W.L.R. 1767. In the latter case it was stated that where lengthy particulars were required then this could be included as an addendum or schedule to the application

notice must contain a prominent notice stating the possible consequences of the court making a committal order and of the respondent not attending the hearing.[100]

35–058 An amendment to the application notice may be made with the permission of the court but not otherwise.[101] It is therefore possible to amend an application notice to provide further particulars of the alleged breaches of the order or undertaking, or indeed to add further instances of breach. But it is clear that the jurisdiction to grant permission to amend will be exercised sparingly.[102]

35–059 The Court must confine itself solely to the contempts actually alleged in the application notice. If the judge considers that other alleged contempts require consideration, the correct course is to invite amendment of the application notice and then provide any necessary adjournment so that the respondent can prepare to deal with those new matters.[103]

(2) Procedural Defects

35–060 Practice Direction 81, para.16.2 provides that

> "The court may waive any procedural defect in the commencement or conduct of a committal application if satisfied that no injustice has been caused to the respondent by the defect".

---

notice, provided it formed part of the notice itself. A recent analysis is *Sports Direct International Plc v Rangers International Football Club Plc* [2016] EWHC 85 (Ch), where Peter Smith J held, at [74], that an application notice was fundamentally flawed because it failed to identify in what way it was alleged the respondents were in breach: "It is necessary to identify with full particularity all the breaches relied upon and that identification must be within the four corners of the Application Notice. It cannot be supplemented by evidence in support." The decision of Males J in *Westminster City Council v Addbins* [2012] EWHC 3716 (QB) contains a full review of the many authorities in this area.

[100] Practice Direction 81, para.13.2(4). A form of notice which may be used is annexed to PD 81 at Annex 3. In *Bunge SA v Huaya Maritime Corp* [2017] EWHC 90 (Comm) the applicant failed to incorporate this notice on the application notice and the judge required that the application notice be amended and re-served. However, the failure to include this notice in *ICBC Standard Bank Plc v Erdenet Mining Corp LLC (EMC)* [2017] EWHC 3135 (QB) was waived.

[101] Practice Direction 81, para.13.2(2).

[102] See *Inplayer Ltd v Thorogood* [2014] EWCA Civ 1511, where the judge at first instance rejected all the allegations of contempt levelled in the application notice but found further contempts proved which had not been alleged; after the hearing she granted retrospective permission for the applicant to re-amend the application. This was held by the Court of Appeal to be procedurally wrong at [39], per Jackson LJ: "A judge hearing a committal application should confine himself or herself to the contempts which are alleged in the application notice. If the judge considers that other alleged contempts require consideration, the correct course is to invite amendment of the application notice and then provide any necessary adjournment so that the respondent can prepare to deal with those new matters."

[103] *Inplayer Ltd v Thorogood* [2014] EWCA Civ 1511, per Jackson LJ at [39]; approved in *Sage v Hewlett Packard Enterprise Company* [2017] 1 W.L.R. 4599, per Henderson LJ at [35], who added: "I would also add that it is in my view a salutary discipline for any judge who is delivering or writing a judgment on a committal application to set out each relevant ground of committal before proceeding to consider whether it is made out on the evidence to the criminal standard of proof."

The considerations which the Court will take into account where there is a procedural error were explained in the leading case of *Nicholls v Nicholls*,[104] where Lord Woolf MR gave the following guidance:

> "1. As committal orders involve the liberty of the subject it is particularly important that the relevant rules are duly complied with...
>
> 2. As long as the contemnor had a fair trial and the order has been made on valid grounds the existence of a defect either in the application to commit or in the committal order served will not result in the order being set aside except insofar as the interests of justice require this to be done.
>
> 3. Interests of justice will not require an order to be set aside where there is no prejudice caused as a result of errors in the application to commit or in the order to commit. When necessary the order can be amended..."[105]

(3) Evidence

The application notice must be supported by one or more affidavits containing all the evidence relied upon.[106] It is therefore clear that the applicant must have marshalled the totality of his evidence on which he seeks to rely by the time the committal application is issued.

35–061

A court will generally give directions for the service of evidence in response to a committal application (which must also be by way of affidavit)[107] and for any evidence in reply. A respondent to an application need not serve any evidence in response if he so chooses; but the court is entitled to order that any written evidence he wishes to put in must be served by a given date.[108] This will not affect the respondent's right to give oral evidence or adduce such evidence from other witnesses, whether or not he has filed written evidence.[109] Unlike in normal civil proceedings, the respondent cannot be obliged to provide further information about his case.[110]

35–062

Although a respondent may serve evidence in response to a committal application in advance of the hearing that evidence may not be relied upon or made use of by the applicant until the respondent has formally adduced that evidence. Simply by obeying a direction for service of such evidence in advance of the hearing, the respondent does not deploy the evidence in support of his own case.[111] The question of whether evidence had been deployed or not arose in *Templeton Insurance Ltd v Motorcare Warranties Ltd*,[112] where the respondent made a submission of no case to answer at the close of the applicant's case. It was held that the applicant, when responding to that submission, was entitled to rely upon affidavits sworn by the respondent because the respondent had gone beyond

35–063

---

[104] *Nicholls v Nicholls* [1997] 1 W.L.R. 314.

[105] *Nicholls v Nicholls*, at 326–327.

[106] Rule 81.10(3).

[107] Practice Direction 81, para.14.1.

[108] *Re B (Contempt of Court: Affidavit Evidence)* [1996] 1 W.L.R. 627, at 638D, per Wall J.

[109] CPR r.81.28(2).

[110] Practice Direction 81, para.14.4. See further para.14.3 for further derogations from the CPR in relation to evidence.

[111] See *Re B (Contempt of Court: Affidavit Evidence)* [1996] 1 W.L.R. 627, at 638F (Wall J).

[112] *Templeton Insurance Ltd v Motorcare Warranties Ltd* [2012] EWHC 795 (Comm).

merely swearing and filing them in accordance with a court order; the affidavits had been put in the hearing bundle and the respondent (via his counsel) had invited the judge to read the affidavits and made reference to that evidence in the skeleton served in advance of the hearing.[113]

35–064   It follows that contempt proceedings cannot be founded on evidence which a court has compelled the respondent to provide.[114] The provisions of s.14 of the Civil Evidence Act 1968, which enshrine the privilege against self-incrimination, apply to contempt proceedings: hence a party is entitled to assert the privilege against self-incrimination in relation to exposure to proceedings for civil contempt.

35–065   There is no obligation[115] on a respondent to give evidence but, if he does so and if he seeks to deploy an affidavit at the hearing, or to give evidence orally, he may be cross-examined upon it.[116] This means that an applicant needs to ensure, in case the respondent gives no evidence, that his own evidence proves all matters necessary both to establish liability for contempt and which go to the question of sanction, to the relevant criminal standard. Conversely, a respondent needs to consider carefully whether to adduce no evidence in answer and run a defence based on the lack of sufficiency in the applicant's evidence. If the respondent puts in evidence and sets out and relies upon a positive case in his defence, in contradiction of the applicant's case or postulating an alternative version of events, the burden is on the applicant to disprove the respondent's case to the criminal standard. However, a failure to give evidence can be taken into account by the court, which may draw an adverse inference just as it can from a defendant's silence in criminal proceedings.[117]

35–066   The sole instance in which the burden arguably falls on the respondent to a committal application is in respect of factual matters within the particular knowledge of the respondent. In ordinary civil proceedings, the burden of proving such matters would fall on the person with the requisite knowledge, regardless of the general incidence of the burden of proof.[118] In *Canadian Imperial Bank of Commerce v Bhattessa*,[119] in the context of a committal application for alleged breach of a freezing injunction, Harman J described it as

---

[113] See *Templeton Insurance Ltd v Motorcare Warranties Ltd*, at [24], per Eder J.

[114] *Bhimji v Chatwani (No.2)* [1992] 1 W.L.R. 1158, declining to follow *Garvin v Domus Publishing Ltd* [1989] Ch. 335.

[115] See *Comet Products UK Ltd v Hawdex Plastics Ltd* [1971] 2 Q.B. 67, at 74, per Lord Denning MR: "I hold that a man who is charged with contempt of court cannot be compelled to answer interrogatories or to give evidence himself to make him prove his guilt. I reject the submission that the defendant is a compellable witness in the contempt proceedings against him."

[116] See r.81.28(2) and (3).

[117] See *Inplayer Ltd v Thorogood* [2014] EWCA Civ 1511, at [40], per Jackson LJ. In *Therium (UK) Holdings Ltd v Brooke* [2016] EWHC 2421 (Comm) Popplewell J noted, at [29] that: "As is the case in criminal proceedings, and by analogy with s. 35 of the Criminal Justice and Public Order Act 1994, the Court may draw the inference that a deliberate decision not to give evidence by a person charged with contempt in relation to matters within his own knowledge has been made because he does not believe that his case will withstand scrutiny when tested by cross examination, provided the case against him is such that it calls for an answer."

[118] *Accident, Fire and Life Assurance Corp v Robertson (or Hunter)* [1909] A.C. 404, at 413.

[119] *Canadian Imperial Bank of Commerce v Bhattessa*, unreported, 30 July 1991.

"a ludicrous proposition that somebody who has no means of knowing certain facts has the onus of proving those facts". However, as quasi-criminal proceedings, the general position is that the burden is on the applicant to prove every element of contempt, which must call the decision in *Bhattessa* into question. It can perhaps be concluded in matters within the particular knowledge of the respondent, the burden on the applicant will in practice be a reduced one and, in the absence of any evidence of the respondent, may be more easily discharged.

As we have seen, if the respondent puts in no evidence, adverse inferences may be drawn against him by the court. However the court has a duty to warn the respondent to the committal application that adverse inferences may be drawn from silence.[120] It would be sensible for an applicant for committal to ensure that this is done.[121]   **35–067**

Although for the purposes of engaging art.6 of the ECHR committal proceedings are considered to be criminal proceedings, nonetheless hearsay evidence is admissible in contempt proceedings.[122]   **35–068**

(4)   Service

The general rule is that a committal application and its evidence in support must be personally served on the respondent.[123] However, experience shows that alleged contemnors are often not keen to facilitate personal service, and the court will be willing in an appropriate case to permit service by an alternative method.[124] It will not be uncommon in fraud cases for a general permission to be given to serve the claim form, and other documents requiring to be served in the proceedings, by an alternative method. However, at least absent clear wording, an   **35–069**

---

[120] See *Inplayer Ltd v Thorogood* [2014] EWCA Civ 1511, at [41]; and see *VIS Trading Co Ltd v Nazarov* [2015] EWHC 3327 (QB), at [31]. In *Masri v Consolidated Contractors International Co SAL* [2011] EWHC 1024 the court proceeded, at [147], on the basis that (i) an inference from failure to give evidence cannot on its own prove guilt; (ii) the court must be satisfied that the applicant has established a case sufficiently compelling to call for an answer before drawing any inference from silence; and, if it concluded that the silence could only sensibly be attributed to the respondent's having no answer, or none that could stand up to cross-examination, the court could then draw an adverse inference.

[121] It has been said by McCombe LJ in *Khawaja v Popat* [2016] EWCA Civ 362, at [30], that the drawing of adverse inferences from silence is consistent with the jurisprudence of the European Court of Human Rights.

[122] *Daltel Europe Ltd v Makki* [2006] 1 W.L.R. 2704.

[123] See r.81.10(4) and (5).

[124] Under CPR r.81.10(5)(b). For a recent example, see *Deutsche Bank AG v Sebastian Holdings Inc* [2017] EWHC 459 (Comm); [2017] 1 W.L.R. 3056, at [27]–[32]. In *Al-Baker v Al-Baker* [2015] EWHC 3229 (Fam), a case under the equivalent to r.81.10(5)(b) in the Family Procedure Rules, Mostyn J held that the provision for alternative service presupposed that service would take place after the date of the order for alternative service. In that case it was "plain beyond doubt" that the respondent was "fully aware" of the application and accordingly service was dispensed with altogether. See recently *ICBC Standard Bank Plc v Erdenet Mining Corp LLC (EMC)* [2017] EWHC 3135 (QB), Cockerill J, following *Al-Baker*.

order granting such general permission will not be construed as extending to the service of committal proceedings. Instead separate permission must ordinarily be sought.[125]

(5) The Position of Foreign Respondents

35–070   There is considerable complexity as regards the position of foreign respondents to committal applications, and the law in this area remains in a state of development. The first point to make is that it is now settled that the provisions of CPR r.81.4 have extra-territorial effect and are capable in principle of being applied against foreign respondents.[126] However, the question of extraterritoriality must be considered separately from the question of jurisdiction. It remains necessary, in any given case, to establish a basis for jurisdiction against any given respondent, which (in turn) necessitates the identification of a basis for serving that respondent with the committal application.[127] In principle and as the law currently stands, the following bases for jurisdiction may be available to an applicant for committal:

(1)   Where a foreign claimant sues in the English court, he submits to the ordinary incidents of English litigation and it is not necessary to obtain permission to serve a committal application out of the jurisdiction on that claimant.[128]

(2)   Where the order sought to be enforced by committal proceedings is one which the court had jurisdiction to make as against the respondent for some other reason (e.g. because the respondent is a defendant to a substantive claim in respect of which the court has jurisdiction, or because an order was made against a foreign respondent who is a third party to English proceedings but whilst he was within the jurisdiction) then, again, permission to serve out will not be required.[129]

(3)   If the order is one which determines the substantive rights of the parties, it may be that a committal application to enforce the order could properly be characterised as a claim to enforce a judgment within CPR PD 6B

---

[125] *ICBC Standard Bank Plc v Erdenet Mining Corp LLC (EMC)*, above, at [36]–[45].

[126] *Dar Al Arkan Real Estate Development Co v Al Refai* [2014] EWCA Civ 715; [2015] 1 W.L.R. 135. The position is different in the case of criminal contempt consisting of a third party aiding or abetting the breach of an English court order from outside the jurisdiction. In such a case there is either no contempt or no jurisdiction in the English court to punish it: *Derby & Co Ltd v Weldon (Nos. 3 and 4)* [1990] Ch. 65, per Lord Donaldson MR at 82G–82H.

[127] This is so even if the court then goes on to dispense with service or order alternative service within the jurisdiction. It was argued in *Dar Al Arkan v Al Refai* that the court could dispense with service even if no basis for service outside the jurisdiction existed, but the issue did not require determination either at first instance or on appeal. It is suggested that such an argument is clearly wrong and ignores the essential point that the ability in principle to effect service is in English law the *fons et origo* of the existence of jurisdiction over a foreign defendant, as reflected in such decisions as *Myerson v Martin* [1979] 1 W.L.R. 1390; *Kyrgyz Republic v Finrep GmbH* [2006] 2 C.L.C. 402, at [43], and *Cherney v Deripaska* [2007] I L Pr 49, at [53].

[128] *Marketmarker Technology Ltd v CMC Group Plc* [2008] EWHC 1556 (QB).

[129] *Deutsche Bank AG v Sebastian Holdings Inc* [2017] EWHC 459 (Comm); [2017] 1 W.L.R. 3056, at [4]–[15].

para.3.1(10), so that permission could be granted to serve out on that basis. However, this gateway will not apply in the case of a pre-trial interim order (such as a freezing injunction or ancillary disclosure order) or a post-judgment order designed to assist the process of enforcement (e.g. an order under CPR Pt 71).[130]

(4)　　If the order is one which can be characterised as governing the legal relationships of the parties, as distinct from a procedural order concerning the conduct of the proceedings, then in principle it will fall within art.24(5) of the Brussels Regulation (recast),[131] so as to confer exclusive jurisdiction on the English court and permit service out without the court's permission.[132] Again, though, it is difficult to see how this provision will be available in respect of a pre-trial interim order such as a freezing injunction or ancillary disclosure order.

(5)　　Where the application is made against a director under CPR r.81.4(3) and the company is also a respondent (as will invariably be the case), in an ordinary case it is likely that the director will be considered a necessary or proper party to the application against the company so that permission to serve out may be granted under CPR PD 6B para.3.1(3).[133]

(6)　Abuse of Process

The weapon of committal is a powerful and serious one and it can undoubtedly be used to intimidate and harass as well as illegitimately to further a litigant's private advantage in litigation. Hence the courts are wary to ensure that its processes are not being abused via the oppressive use of committal applications.[134] In circumstances where committal applications invariably threaten serious sanctions against a respondent, an applicant's motives require proper scrutiny. It has recently been said that applicants should give careful consideration to proportionality in this context, and that respondents should in turn give consideration to applying to strike out committal applications for abuse of process in appropriate cases.[135] A recent example of an application dismissed as an abuse is *Sports Direct International Plc v Rangers International Football*

35–071

---

[130] *Deutsche Bank AG v Sebastian Holdings Inc* [2017] 1 W.L.R. 1842, at [17]–[20].

[131] Council Regulation (EC) No.1215/2012.

[132] *Deutsche Bank AG v Sebastian Holdings Inc* [2017] EWHC 459 (Comm); [2017] 1 W.L.R. 3056, at [21]–[24].

[133] *Dar Al Arkan Real Estate Development Co v Al Refai* [2014] EWCA Civ 715; [2015] 1 W.L.R. 135.

[134] See generally *Sectorguard Plc v Dienne Plc* [2009] EWHC 2693 (Ch).

[135] *PJSC Vseukrainskyi Aktsionernyi Bank v Maksimov* [2014] EWHC 4370 (Comm), at [22], per Hamblen J. Although there had been no such application in that case, the judge reflected the fact that only a technical contempt had been established by an order for costs against the applicant for committal. However in *Absolute Living Developments Ltd v DS7 Ltd* [2018] EWHC 1717 (Ch), Marcus Smith J said, at [36](1):

"The contempt jurisdiction exists generally only in relation to orders that have a penal notice and that have been personally served on the defendant. The public interest in seeing such orders obeyed is, inevitably, a strong one. Since a court can be presumed not to make unnecessary orders, where an order of the court *remains* uncomplied with, it seems to me extremely difficult to say that contempt proceedings in relation to such a contempt can *ever* be said to be an abuse of process."

Club,[136] in which there was unchallenged evidence that the individual behind the applicant company was pursuing a vendetta against an individual respondent and there was no discernible disadvantage to the applicant arising from the alleged contempt. The applicant saw the committal application as "merely another method of enforcing bargains".

35–072   However, whilst in some cases it will be possible to resolve allegations of abuse at a preliminary stage, often the allegation will engage the merits of the committal application itself (e.g. issues as to whether a breach occurred and if so whether it was serious) in a way that makes the allegation more suitable for determination at the trial of the application.[137] And, whilst the civil contempt jurisdiction has as one of its central purposes the upholding of the rights of private litigants,[138] this does not mean that an application not aimed at securing compliance with the court's order (as opposed to being a means of bringing serious breaches to the court's attention) will necessarily be abusive.[139]

(7)   Strike-Out/Applicability of Rule Against Double Jeopardy

35–073   A respondent may apply to (or the court may of its own initiative) strike out a committal application if it appears to disclose no reasonable ground for alleging that the respondent is guilty of contempt; if the application is an abuse of the process; or if there has been some failure to comply with a rule, practice direction or court order.[140] In short, the court has similar strike-out powers to those it has under CPR r.3.4. As we have seen, the court is anxious to ensure its jurisdiction is not being abused by litigants who invoke the committal jurisdiction in order to seek to obtain an illegitimate litigation advantage.

35–074   But if an application is struck out because of a procedural defect, this does not mean that the rule against double jeopardy (as it applies in criminal proceedings) is automatically brought into play to prevent a renewed application.[141] Hence in *Jelson (Estates) Ltd v Harvey*,[142] no order was made on an earlier application for committal because it did not comply with RSC Ord 52 r.4 (the relevant rule at the time), having failed to state the grounds relied on. It was held by the Court of Appeal that the position was analogous to a prosecution that had failed because of a defective indictment before arraignment when the "rule against double jeopardy" would not be available. Thus, the Court of Appeal held, an applicant for committal should not be prevented from renewing a complaint of contempt because of a procedural defect, in circumstances where the court had not been into the merits. It may be that the modern approach in such a case would be to strike out any later proceeding not by reference to the rule against double

---

[136] *Sports Direct International Plc v Rangers International Football Club* [2016] EWHC 85 (Ch), at [89] in particular. See also *Simon v Brecher* [2015] EWHC 4057 (Ch).
[137] See for example *Masri v Consolidated Contractors International Co* [2010] EWHC 2458 (Comm), at [55]; *Westminster City Council v Addbins Ltd* [2012] EWHC 3716 (QB), at [35].
[138] See *A-G v Times Newspapers* [1974] A.C. 273, per Lord Diplock at 307H–308A.
[139] *Zimareva-Locke v Cetin* [2012] EWHC 430 (Ch), per Newey J at [3]–[8].
[140] Practice Direction 81, para.16.1.
[141] *Jelson (Estates) Ltd v Harvey* [1983] 1 W.L.R. 1401.
[142] *Jelson (Estates) Ltd v Harvey*, above.

jeopardy but under the principle in *Henderson v Henderson*. However, the rule against double jeopardy nonetheless applies to contempt proceedings.

(8) Timing of Application

It has been emphasised on a number of occasions that the timing of a committal application is a matter of case management for the judge, rather than being subject to any rule of law.[143] However, the following general principles may be stated. **35–075**

Where facts emerge which could found a committal application, as a matter of general practice the applicant is expected to proceed expeditiously.[144] Where the party seeking to initiate contempt proceedings has also brought substantive proceedings against the same defendant, which are ongoing, this principle is applicable where the applicant's complaint is that a freezing (or similar) order has been breached, which, as discussed above, is a typical scenario in fraud claims.[145] In such a case it will usually be appropriate to determine the contempt application promptly and before the trial of the underlying action. This is because the applicant's purpose in bringing such an application, and the court's purpose in granting it in an appropriate case, will be to put pressure on the respondent to comply with the underlying order. In general the court should also be seen to act decisively both to punish the contempt (if established) and deter others.[146] **35–076**

However there may be reasons why the hearing of the committal application should be deferred until after the trial: e.g. because the determination of the contempt application might involve determination of one or more issues in the trial or because the respondent's credibility is in issue.[147] Such considerations do not necessarily lead to the conclusion that the contempt hearing should be postponed: especially in a case of alleged breach of a freezing order delay in the hearing of the contempt application could be highly prejudicial to the claimant. The court will take account of the pressures on the defendant in relation to the preparation of the defence of the underlying proceedings.[148] It will normally be wrong to hear a contempt application at the same time as the trial, because that will have the effect of forcing the respondent to give evidence and so effectively abrogate his right to silence.[149] **35–077**

---

[143] *JSC BTA Bank v Ablyazov* [2012] 1 W.L.R. 1988, at [47]; *Dar Al Arkan Real Estate Development Company v Al-Sayed Bader Hashim Al Refai* [2014] EWHC 1055 (Comm), at [5]; *JSC Bank of Moscow v Kekhman* [2015] 1 All E.R. (Comm) 80, at [14].

[144] *Barnes (t/a Pool Motors) v Seabrook* [2010] EWHC 1849 (Admin); [2010] CP Rep. 42.

[145] *Dadourian Group International Inc v Simms* [2007] 1 W.L.R. 2967.

[146] *JSC BTA Bank v Ablyazov* [2012] 1 W.L.R. 1988, at [48]; *Dar Al Arkan Real Estate Development Company v Al-Sayed Bader Hashim Al Refai* [2014] EWHC 1055 (Comm), at [8] and [18].

[147] See e.g. *Daltel Europe Ltd v Makki* [2005] EWHC 749 (Ch), at [3], [77]–[80] and [374]; and *KJM Superbikes Ltd v Hinton* [2009] 3 All E.R. 76, at [18]–[19]. Arguments for postponement on this basis failed in the *Dar Al Arkan* case [2014] EWHC 1055 (Comm) and in *JSC Bank of Moscow v Kekhman* [2015] 1 All E.R. (Comm) 80.

[148] *JSC BTA Bank v Ablyazov* [2011] EWHC 1522 (Comm), at [10] (Teare J): and on appeal at [2011] EWCA Civ 1386; [2012] 1 W.L.R. 1988. See also *Dar Al Arkan Real Estate Development Company v Al-Sayed Bader Hashim Al Refai* [2014] EWHC 1055 (Comm).

[149] *Inplayer Ltd v Thorogood* [2014] EWCA Civ 1511, at [41].

35–078 Conversely, where the application alleges a criminal contempt—e.g. the making of a dishonest statement in a witness statement—then differing considerations apply. The contempt in such a case is a public wrong, rather than a matter primarily between the parties to the underlying litigation. In contrast to the civil contempt cases, the primary purpose of such an application is not to vindicate a private right. Therefore, and especially where there is overlap between the matters in issue in the underlying litigation and the contempt proceedings, it will usually be appropriate to defer the contempt application until after the trial has occurred. The evidence can then be more appropriately assessed in the light of full disclosure at trial.[150]

(9) Disclosure by Applicant

35–079 The question sometimes arises whether the applicant for committal comes under some duty of disclosure within the committal proceedings. It was said in *Masri v Consolidated Contractors*[151] that the applicant had no such general obligation.[152] However in the committal application in the *Ablyazov* litigation the court held that "fairness" required that the applicant bank should disclose all documents which damaged its case on the contempt allegations or assisted the respondent's case.[153] It is suggested that the true position is that there is no automatic right to disclosure (and CPR 81 makes no provision for disclosure), but that, where such an order is appropriate on the facts of a given case, it may be made.[154] As already discussed, there can be no question of any obligation of disclosure being imposed upon the respondent.

(10) Entitlement to Legal Aid

35–080 A committal application has the character of criminal proceedings. The alleged contemnor is therefore entitled to legal aid, so that he can be properly represented: see *Kings Lynn v West Norfolk Council v Bunning (Legal Aid Agency, interested party)*.[155] If the respondent is not represented then the applicant should inform him of this entitlement.[156]

---

[150] See the illuminating discussion by Beatson LJ in *JSC BTA Bank v Ereshchenko* [2013] EWCA Civ 1961, at [69]–[76]; and see also *Malgar Ltd v RE Leach (Engineering) Ltd* [2000] F.S.R. 393.

[151] *Masri v Consolidated Contractors* [2010] EWHC 2640 (Comm), per David Steel J.

[152] *Masri v Consolidated Contractors*, at [27].

[153] *JSC BTA Bank v Ablyazov* [2011] EWHC 1522 (Comm), at [12], per Teare J.

[154] *Fiona Trust Holding Corp v Privalov* [2007] EWHC 39 (Comm), at [25], per David Steel J: "It is of course open to the court to order disclosure at any stage of the proceedings, including for the purpose of interlocutory proceedings. But it is well established under the previous procedural rules that such a power should be exercised sparingly and only for such documents as can be shown to be necessary for the fair disposal of the application; see *Rome v Punjab National Park* [1989] 2 All E.R. 136. There are no reasons for concluding that any different approach is appropriate under the provisions of CPR: see Matthews and Malek, *Disclosure*, 2nd Edition (London: Sweet & Maxwell, 2000), para.2.68."

[155] *Kings Lynn v West Norfolk Council v Bunning (Legal Aid Agency, interested party)* [2013] EWHC 3390 (QB); [2014] 2 All E.R. 1095.

[156] *Inplayer Ltd v Thorogood* [2014] EWCA Civ 1511, at [49].

E. THE HEARING

(1) The Necessity for a Hearing[157]

A committal application cannot be disposed of without a hearing.[158] The hearing 35–081
of a committal application is in the nature of a trial. Oral evidence is given and
witnesses can be cross-examined. The respondent is entitled to give oral evidence
even if he has not served written evidence.[159]

Provision is made by PD 81 para.10 as to the types of judge who can hear 35–082
committal applications. The basic rule is that they must be heard by a High Court
Judge. The hearing should normally take place in public.[160]

(2) Proceeding in the Absence of the Respondent

It is not uncommon for a respondent not to attend a committal application. The 35–083
modern approach is for the court, if satisfied that the respondent has been
properly served and has decided intentionally to absent himself, to proceed with
the hearing. In the family case of *Sanchez v Oboz*[161] Cobb J set out a checklist of
considerations for a civil court to consider when deciding whether to proceed in
the absence of the respondent:

(1)   Whether the respondent has been served with the relevant documents,
      including the notice of the hearing;
(2)   Whether the respondent has had sufficient notice to enable him to prepare
      for the hearing;
(3)   Whether any reason has been advanced for his non-appearance;
(4)   Whether by reference to the nature and circumstances of the respondent's
      behaviour, he has waived his right to be present (i.e. is it reasonable to
      conclude that the respondent knew of, or was indifferent to, the
      consequences of the case proceeding in his absence);
(5)   Whether an adjournment would be likely to secure the attendance of the
      respondent, or at least facilitate his representation;
(6)   The extent of the disadvantage to the respondent in not being able to
      present his account of events;
(7)   Whether undue prejudice would be caused to the applicant by any delay;
(8)   Whether undue prejudice would be caused to the forensic process if the
      application were to proceed in the absence of the respondent;

---

[157] The *Practice Direction (Committal for Contempt: Open Court)* [2015] 1 W.L.R. 2195 contains
provisions concerning the listing of committal applications and in relation to the giving of judgments
in committal cases.
[158] Practice Direction 81, para.13.2(3). Rules 81.28(2)-(6) and PD 81, para.15 set out detailed
provisions as to the conduct and listing of the hearing.
[159] CPR r.81.28(2), discussed at paras 35–061 and following above.
[160] *Practice Direction (Committal for Contempt: Open Court)* [2015] 1 W.L.R. 2195, at [3] and [4].
The practice direction sets out the circumstances in which committal hearings shall be in private.
[161] *Sanchez v Oboz* [2015] EWHC 235 (Fam), at [5].

(9)   The terms of the overriding objective, including the obligation on the court to deal with the case justly, expeditiously and fairly.

35–084   That checklist has subsequently been adopted in a number of cases in the Commercial Court, and Queen's Bench and Chancery Divisions.[162] The court's approach in the many recent cases in which applications have been proceeded with in the absence of the respondent suggests that the courts have moved away from the approach taken by Briggs J in *JSC BTA Bank v Solodchenko*,[163] that it is exceptional to hear an application in the absence of the respondent. Although judges have shown themselves willing, by reference to the above checklist, to hear contempt applications in the absence of the respondent, they are also inclined, if the contempt is proved, then to adjourn the hearing before proceeding to sentence, to allow the contemnor an opportunity to purge his contempt and attend to offer mitigation.

(3)   The Ambit of the Hearing

35–085   Unless the court hearing the application otherwise permits, the applicant is limited to the grounds of contempt set out in the application notice and to the evidence served in accordance with CPR 81.[164] It will be a rare case where the court allows the applicant to extend the grounds of his application at the hearing.

35–086   Where a substantial number of allegations of contempt are advanced, it may be desirable to limit the committal hearing to some only of the allegations.[165] So, in the *Ablyazov* litigation, where the applicant initially advanced 35 separate allegations of contempt in its application, the court, exercising its case management powers, limited the committal hearing to three allegations only.[166]

---

[162] See e.g. *QRS v Beach* [2015] EWHC 1489 (QB); *Navig8 Chemical Pools Inc v Nu Tek (HK) Pvt Ltd* [2016] EWHC 1790 (Comm); *Phonographic Performance Ltd v Nightclub (London) Ltd* [2016] EWHC 892 (Ch); *Taylor v Van Dutch Marine Holding Ltd* [2016] EWHC 2201 (Ch); and *ICBC Standard Bank Plc v Erdenet Mining Corp LLC (EMC)* [2017] EWHC 3135 (QB). As discussed above, in the fraud area committal applications are often made where there has been a failure to comply with freezing orders. Courts take a strong view of the flouting of their orders and are not generally deflected by a respondent absenting himself. So, in *Navig8*, Flaux J said, at [34]: "In circumstances where what is at issue is the efficacy of a worldwide freezing order and, in particular, its efficacy as a means of enforcing the arbitration award, the disclosure of assets by the respondent in such a case is a critical element in ensuring the efficacy of the court's order. Any delay in the order for committal of the respondents for contempt, and therefore any delay in bringing home to the respondents the importance of complying with a court order, is obviously a matter which could cause considerable prejudice to the claimant in its attempts to enforce the award generally." A similar approach was adopted by Cranston J in *Bunge SA v Huaya Maritime Corp* [2017] EWHC 90 (Comm).
[163] *JSC BTA Bank v Solodchenko* [2011] EWHC 1613 (Ch).
[164] CPR r.81.28(1).
[165] *JSC BTA Bank v Ablyazov* [2011] EWHC 1522 (Comm), per Teare J: and on appeal at [2011] EWCA Civ 1386; [2012] 2 All E.R. 575.
[166] Such a step potentially gives rise to a risk of unfairness to the respondent because it might permit two or more hearings (each dealing with separate allegations of contempt) at which separate sentences could be handed down which in total exceeded two years; whereas if the application went forward in respect of all the allegations the court would, as a result of s.14(1) of the Contempt of Court Act 1981, be confined to a maximum sentence of two years overall. The issue was considered in *Villiers v Villiers* [1994] 1 W.L.R. 493, at 499–500; and *Phillips v Symes (No.3)* [2005] 1 W.L.R. 2986, at [54].

(4)   Submission of No Case to Answer

A respondent may make a submission of no case to answer at the conclusion of   **35–087**
the applicant's case. In so doing he does not have to make an election as to
whether he will call any evidence; hence, if that submission fails, then the
respondent may proceed to call his evidence.[167]

(5)   Considering the Matter in the Round

In considering whether the contempts have been made out (and no doubt in   **35–088**
considering what sentence to impose), the whole picture must be considered in
the round:

> "It is not right to consider individual heads of contempt in isolation. They are details on a broad
> canvas. An important question when that canvas is considered is whether it portrays the
> picture of a Defendant seeking to comply with the orders of the Court or a Defendant bent on
> flouting them. It is right that the individual details of the canvas should be informed by the
> overall picture. But, having said that, each head of contempt that has been held proved must be
> established beyond reasonable doubt."[168]

(6)   Inferences from Circumstantial Evidence

The application may of course be founded on circumstantial evidence; indeed, in   **35–089**
a case based on the contention that the respondent has failed to provide proper
disclosure of assets pursuant to a freezing order, the application will often
necessarily rely upon such evidence. In such a case care is required in
approaching that evidence; if, after considering the evidence, the court concludes
that there is more than one reasonable inference to be drawn and at least one of
them is inconsistent with a finding of contempt, the applicant must fail.[169]

(7)   The Standard of Proof and Circumstantial Evidence

We have discussed above the fact that a contempt can only be proved if it is   **35–090**
established to the criminal standard of proof.[170] But although the elements of the
contempts must be so proved, that does not mean that every aspect of a case has

---

[167] *Templeton Insurance Plc v Motorcare Warranties Ltd* [2012] EWHC 795 (Comm).

[168] *Gulf Azov Shipping Co Ltd v Idisi* [2001] EWCA Civ 21, at [18].

[169] *Daltel v Makki* [2005] EWHC 749 (Ch), at [30], per David Richards J; this analysis has been cited
with approval a number of times since: see e.g. *JSC BTA Bank v Ereshchenko* [2013] EWCA Civ
1961, at [40]. A court may not, however, infer the existence of some fact which constitutes an
essential element of the case unless the inference is compelling i.e. such that no reasonable man
would fail to draw it: *Kwan Ping Bong v R* [1979] A.C. 609.

[170] See *Re Bramblevale Ltd* [1970] Ch. 128. The position has now been formally recognised by the
CPR: see PD 81, para.9. This standard of proof applies equally to the circumstances of the contempt
and the gravity of the respondent's conduct if that is in issue, as it is very likely to be when
considering sentence. In *Gulf Azov Shipping Co Ltd v Idisi* [2001] EWCA Civ 21, at [16] the analysis
of the first instance judge was adopted as correct as follows: the court "must be satisfied to the point
of being sure of any matters which it would regard as adverse to the defendant or which would tend to

to be proved to the criminal standard. This is relevant in cases dependent on circumstantial evidence.[171] It is the essence of a successful case based on circumstantial evidence that the whole is stronger than the individual parts. It has been vividly said that it becomes a net from which there is no escape.[172] That is why a jury is often directed to avoid piecemeal consideration of a circumstantial case: "Circumstantial evidence…works by cumulatively, in geometrical progression, eliminating other possibilities".[173]

(8)   Conflict of Evidence of Witnesses

35–091   Sometimes on a contempt application the court is faced with a direct conflict of witness evidence. In such a case it is not sufficient for the Court merely to decide which of the witnesses to believe. In *Neil v Henderson*[174] it was held that in this situation the criminal practice, as explained in the following passage in *Blackstone's Criminal Practice 2016*, para.F3.48, was applicable: "In cases which turn on whether the accused or the complainant is telling the truth, it is important for the judge not to give the impression that the jury simply have to decide who to believe; the jury must be told that, in order to convict, they must be sure that the complainant is telling the truth."

F.   PENALTIES

(1)   Introduction

35–092   Where a contempt of court is proven the penalties which the court can impose are the following:

(1)   a fine in an unlimited amount[175];

---

lead to it to view his action in a more serious light and so affect its view of the appropriate penalty: see *Z Bank v D1* [1994] 1 Lloyd's Rep. 656, 667."

[171] *JSC BTA Bank v Ablyazov* [2012] EWCA Civ 1411; [2013] 1 W.L.R. 1331.

[172] *JSC BTA Bank v Ablyazov* [2012] EWCA Civ 1411; [2013] 1 W.L.R. 1331, at [52], per Rix LJ.

[173] *R v Kilbourne* [1973] A.C. 729, at 758. See *Shepherd v The Queen* (1990) 170 C.L.R. 573 (HCA), at 579–580: "…the prosecution bears the burden of proving all the elements of the crime beyond reasonable doubt. That means that the essential ingredients of each element must be so proved. It does not mean that every fact—every piece of evidence—relied upon to prove an element by inference must itself be proved beyond reasonable doubt. Intent, for example, is, save for statutory exceptions, an element of every crime. It is something which, apart from admissions, must be proved by inference. But the jury may quite properly draw the necessary inference having regard to the whole of the evidence, whether or not each individual piece of evidence relied upon is proved beyond reasonable doubt, provided they reach their conclusion upon the criminal standard of proof. Indeed, the probative force of a mass of evidence may be cumulative, making it pointless to consider the degree of probability of each item of evidence separately."

[174] *Neil v Henderson* [2018] EWHC 90 (Ch), at [85].

[175] See for example *Taylor Made Golf Company Inc v Rata & Rata* [1996] F.S.R. 528. A fine of £100,000 was imposed in *Absolute Living Developments Ltd v DS7 Ltd* [2018] EWHC 1717 (Ch) in respect of past, not continuing, breaches.

(2)   a term of imprisonment limited to two years,[176] which may be suspended for such period and on such conditions as the court may specify[177]; and/or

(3)   the sequestration of assets.[178]

If a committal order (which means an order of immediate or suspended imprisonment) is made, the order will be for the issue of a warrant of committal.[179]   **35–093**

(2)   The Purpose of a Sentence

It has been said that a principal object of the contempt of court jurisdiction is to bring a contemnor to face up to what he has done, to reflect on it, and (where compliance is still possible), by a process of sanction and encouragement, to draw back from the brink. Hence there are a number of different objectives which a court may seek to achieve when sentencing a person for contempt of court.[180]   **35–094**

(i)   Punishment

Punishment for conduct in defiance of the court's order has been said to be one of the rationales behind the imposition of a penalty.[181] Even though the general principle is that any custodial sentence should be as short as possible consistent with the circumstances of the case,[182] the courts have nonetheless taken the view that breach of a freezing order, as an attack on the administration of justice, usually merits an immediate prison sentence of "a not insubstantial amount."[183] There are numerous recent examples of heavy sentences passed on contemnors who have breached freezing orders.[184]   **35–095**

---

[176] Section 14(1) of the Contempt of Court Act 1981. The maximum sentence of two years applies to all contempts that come before the court "on any occasion"; the court cannot order consecutive sentences which together exceed two years. Importantly, a person committed to prison for contempt of court is entitled to unconditional release after serving half of the sentence (Criminal Justice Act 2003, s.258).

[177] CPR r.81.29(1).

[178] Sequestration is considered in Section G below.

[179] See CPR r.81.30 which contains detailed provisions relating to the warrant of committal.

[180] See generally *Lightfoot v Lightfoot* [1989] 1 FCR 305, at 308; *Robinson v Robinson* [2001] EWCA Civ 2098, at [11]; *Hale v Tanner* [2000] 1 W.L.R. 2377, at 2381.

[181] *Crystalmews Ltd v Metterick* [2006] EWHC 3087 (Ch), at [8]–[12], per Lawrence Collins J.

[182] *Aquilina v Aquilina* [2004] EWCA Civ 504, at [14].

[183] See *Asia Islamic Trade Finance Fund Ltd v Drum Risk Management Ltd* [2015] EWHC 3748 (Comm), at [7(2)], per Popplewell J.

[184] See e.g. *JSC BTA Bank v Stepanov* [2010] EWHC 794 (Ch) (24 months); *JSC BTA Bank v Solodchenko* [2011] EWHC 2908 (Ch) (18 months); *JSC BTA Bank v Solodchenko* [2011] EWCA Civ 1241 (21 months); *JSC BTA Bank v Ablyazov* [2013] 1 W.L.R. 1331 (22 months); *JSC VTB Bank v Skurikhin* [2014] EWHC 4613 (Comm) (12 months); *Asia Islamic Trade Finance Fund Ltd v Drum Risk Management Ltd* [2015] EWHC 3748 (Comm) (18 months); *VIS Trading Co Ltd v Nazarov* [2016] EWHC 245 (QB) (21 months); *JSC Mezhdunarodniy Promyshlenniy Bank v Pugachev* [2016] EWHC 258 (Ch) (24 months); *Navig8 Chemical Pools Inc v Nu Tek (HK) Pvt Ltd* [2016] EWHC 1790 (Comm) (18 months); *Therium (UK) Holdings Ltd v Brooke* [2016] EWHC 2477 (Comm) (21 months); *Hewlett Packard Enterprise Co v Sage* [2017] EWHC 66 (QB) (18 months); *Bunge SA v*

(ii)   Deterrence

35–096   Coupled with the punitive element of the sentence is a deterrent purpose. The court wishes to send a signal that breach of court orders will attract a heavy sentence with a view to deterring both the respondent himself and others from disregarding court orders.

(iii)   Coercion

35–097   In civil contempt cases the primary aim of the applicant is usually to compel compliance with the order or undertaking which has been breached.[185] Courts recognise that a penalty can serve a coercive function so that, in the event of belated compliance, the sentence may be remitted.[186] Coercion of course can only have any real meaning in a case of a continuing breach, or a breach which may be remedied. In *Asia Islamic Trade Finance Fund Ltd v Drum Risk Management Ltd*[187] Popplewell J provided guidance in a case of a continuing breach:

> "In the case of a continuing breach, the court may see fit to indicate: (a) what portion of the sentence should be served in any event as punishment for past breaches; and (b) what portion of a sentence the court might consider remitting in the event of prompt and full compliance thereafter. Any such indication would be persuasive but not binding upon a future court. If it does so, the court will keep in mind that the shorter the punitive element of the sentence, the greater the incentive for the contemnor to comply by disclosing the information required. On the other hand, there is also a public interest in requiring contemnors to serve a proper sentence for past non-compliance with court orders, even if those contemnors are in continuing breach. The punitive element of the sentence both punishes the contemnors and deters others from disregarding court orders."

It follows that the court, when sentencing, must make findings about what past contempts have been proven and what continuing contempts have been proven.

Hua [2017] EWHC 90 (Comm) (18 months); *Touton Far East PTE Ltd v Shri Lal Mahal Ltd* [2017] EWHC 621 (Comm) (various, including one sentence of 18 months).

[185]   Hence in *JSC BTA Bank v Ablyazov* [2012] EWHC 237 (Comm) Teare J described the committal application as being the "latest step in the Bank's relentless campaign to persuade Mr. Ablyazov, as the Bank would put it, to comply with the terms of a worldwide freezing order…made against him" (at [2]). In *JSC BTA Bank v Ereshchenko* [2013] EWCA Civ 1961, the committal application related to alleged dishonest statements in witness statements so there was no continuing (or any) breach of an order. The applicant was candid before the court about its motives for committal, as being to persuade the respondent to reveal the whereabouts of large sums of money said to have been misappropriated: "The Bank considers that Mr Ereshchenko knows more about what happened than he has yet been prepared to admit, and hopes that, if faced with an order for his committal to prison, he would at last disclose what he does know about what happened to that money": see at [5], per Lloyd LJ.

[186]   However see *JSC BTA Bank v Solodchenko* [2011] EWCA Civ 1241; [2012] 1 W.L.R. 350, at [67], per Jackson LJ: "In *Shalson [v Russo]* Mr Justice Neuberger made the point that the shorter the punitive element of the sentence, the greater the incentive on the contemnor to comply by disclosing the information required. I agree. On the other hand there is also a public interest in requiring contemnors to serve a proper sentence for past non-compliance with court orders, even if those contemnors are in continuing breach. The punitive element of the sentence both punishes the contemnor and deters others from disregarding court orders."

[187]   *Asia Islamic Trade Finance Fund Ltd v Drum Risk Management Ltd* [2015] EWHC 3748 (Comm), at [7(5)], relying upon *JSC BTA Bank v Solodchenko* [2011] EWCA Civ 1241; [2012] 1 W.L.R. 350, at [55]–[56].

This will inform sentence and also the question of whether part of that sentence can be remitted in the event of subsequent compliance.[188]

Where there is a continuing breach, a sentence of the full two years will be considered by the court, in order to encourage future co-operation by the contemnor.[189] Alternatively the court may suspend the sentence on condition that the contempt is purged. It will sometimes happen that committal proceedings have the desired effect such that by the time of the hearing the contempt has been purged. Often this will occur in cases where the application relates to the respondent's failure to provide disclosure pursuant to freezing orders. In such a case it may be that the appropriate sanction will simply be one in costs.[190]   35–098

(3) Contumacious Breach

It is clear that, whilst a wilful intention to disobey the court's order is not required for a finding of contempt, nonetheless a committal to prison for contempt will almost certainly require a knowing and deliberate breach of an order. Hence a sentence of imprisonment will only be appropriate if the contemnor's conduct is "contumacious".[191]   35–099

(4) Sentencing Considerations

The leading decision on sentencing for contempt involving the breach of a freezing order is *JSC BTA Bank v Solodchenko (No.2)*,[192] where Jackson LJ set out a series of propositions of general application: 35–100

> "(i)   Freezing orders are made for good reason and in order to prevent the dissipation or spiriting away of assets. Any substantial breach of such an order is a serious matter, which merits condign punishment.
>
> (ii)   Condign punishment for such contempt normally means a prison sentence. However, there may be circumstances in which a substantial fine is sufficient: for example, if the contempt has been purged and the relevant assets recovered.
>
> (iii)   Where there is a continuing failure to disclose relevant information, the court should consider imposing a long sentence, possibly even the maximum of two years, in order to encourage future co-operation by the contemnor."[193]

---

[188] See the analysis in *VIS Trading Co Ltd v Nazarov* [2015] EWHC 3327 (QB), at [28]–[29].

[189] See *JSC BTA Bank v Solodchenko* [2011] EWCA Civ 1241; [2012] 1 W.L.R. 350. An example is *JSC BTA Bank v Stepanov* [2010] EWHC 794 (Ch), at [23]. See also *Lightfoot v Lightfoot* [1989] 1 FCR 305, at 308, where Lord Donaldson MR urged courts to consider imposing a two year sentence when the contemnor was in continuing and wilful breach of court orders. "Whilst there might be cases in which such a sentence would be disproportionately severe, any wilful defiance of the court and its orders is necessarily a very serious offence and if the contemnor is aggrieved he has a remedy in his own hands—he can seek his immediate release by ceasing his defiance, complying with the order and thereby purging his contempt."

[190] See e.g. *Government of Sierra Leone v Davenport* [2002] EWCA Civ 230.

[191] *See Gulf Azov Shipping Co Ltd v Idisi* [2001] EWCA Civ 21, at [72]: "Such a course is only appropriate where there is serious, contumacious flouting of the orders of the Court". See also *Fairclough v Manchester Ship Canal Co* (1897) 41 Sol.Jo 225; [1897] WN 7.

[192] *JSC BTA Bank v Solodchenko (No.2)* [2011] EWCA Civ 1241; [2012] 1 W.L.R. 350, at [55].

[193] The Court of Appeal revisited the question of sentencing considerations for breach of a freezing order in *JSC BTA Bank v Ablyazov* [2012] EWCA Civ 1411 and again in *Templeton Insurance Ltd v*

35–101　More broadly, the court will take into account the following key factors when considering what sentence to pass on a contemnor:

(1)　whether the claimant has been prejudiced by virtue of the contempt and whether the prejudice is capable of remedy;

(2)　the extent to which the contemnor has acted under pressure;

(3)　whether the breach of the order was deliberate or unintentional;

(4)　the degree of culpability;

(5)　whether the contemnor has been placed in breach of the order by reason of the conduct of others;

(6)　whether the contemnor appreciates the seriousness of the deliberate breach;

(7)　whether the contemnor has co-operated;

(8)　whether there has been any acceptance of responsibility, any apology, any remorse or any reasonable excuse put forward.[194]

(5)　Mitigation

35–102　If there is a finding of contempt, the respondent, given the quasi-criminal nature of the proceedings and the risk of loss of liberty, should be given an opportunity to make representations to the court prior to the imposition of any penalty.[195] This is like a plea in mitigation in a criminal case. At this stage the respondent may seek to purge his contempt in order to reduce sentence. Of course the respondent may have purged his contempt in advance of the hearing.

(6)　Other Orders

35–103　In recent years courts have devised ancillary orders which are designed to assist in the execution of a warrant of committal. Hence in *Ablyazov* the court, having issued a warrant of committal which could not be executed (because the respondent had gone into hiding), issued a further injunction against the respondent requiring him to surrender himself to the tipstaff, so as to allow the

---

Thomas [2013] EWCA Civ 35, where consideration was given to the personal mitigation of the respondents. Rix LJ concluded, at [42]: "In my judgment, whereas it will always remain appropriate to consider in individual cases whether committal is necessary, and what is the shortest time necessary for such imprisonment, and whether a sentence of imprisonment can be suspended, or dispensed with altogether: nevertheless, it must now be accepted that the attack on the administration of justice which is made when a freezing order is breached usually merits an immediate sentence of imprisonment of some not insubstantial amount. Of course, courts will bear in mind that the maximum sentence which can be handed down on any one occasion is two years; and will make due allowance for the encouragement of, or rewarding of, better thoughts and the purging of contempt, and for the credit due in the ordinary way for an admission of responsibility and remorse. Nevertheless, it must be borne in mind that breaches of freezing orders, unlike many other contempts, are nearly always spawned in darkness, and therefore will be hard, and sometimes impossible, to detect, until it is too late."

[194] See *Crystal Mews Ltd v Metterick* [2006] EWHC 3087 (Ch); *Asia Islamic Trade Finance Fund Ltd v Drum Risk Management Ltd* [2015] EWHC 3748 (Comm). The fact that the contemnor is abroad and therefore that a sentence might be incapable of being executed is no reason not to impose a sentence: *VIS Trading Co Ltd v Nazarov* [2015] EWHC 3327 (QB), at [58]. For sentencing considerations in cases of criminal contempt see *Patel v Patel* [2017] EWHC 3229 (Ch).

[195] *Goldsmith v Goldsmith* [2006] EWCA Civ 1670.

tipstaff to execute that warrant, and further order that unless he did so he would be debarred from further defending the proceedings.[196]

Further, where the respondent persists in his contempt, the court has shown itself willing to make unless orders in the underlying litigation which are designed to coerce the respondent into compliance. Such orders recognise that contempt applications are generally intimately bound up with the wider litigation in which they are made. In *Ablyazov* the respondent was found guilty of contempt by breaching the terms of a freezing order. He did not remedy that failure. The court made an order that unless the respondent complied with the freezing order (through the provision of an affidavit disclosing his assets) within a certain time then he would be debarred from further defending the underlying proceedings. The explicit justification for this order was as an encouragement to belated compliance and it was made notwithstanding that it was not suggested that the respondent's non-compliance prejudiced the fairness of any trial.[197] The order was upheld on appeal.[198] The general approach of the courts may be stated as follows:

35–104

> "In my judgment if the court makes an order for disclosure for information or documents it is entitled, in the event of non-compliance, to order that if such non-compliance is persisted in the claimant will be at liberty to enter judgment. Were it otherwise, in many cases the order will be without effect. The making of such an order is of course a discretionary exercise...There are many cases in which it is only an 'unless' order that will ensure compliance."[199]

A court has even ordered a respondent's solicitor to provide the respondent's contact details so far as known to the solicitor where the respondent against whom a committal order has been made has gone to ground. The purpose of the order was stated to be to aid enforcement of the committal order.[200]

35–105

(7) Purging Contempt

It will be apparent from the above discussion that, even after it has passed sentence, the court is potentially willing to remit that sentence if the contemnor takes steps to cure the conduct which has been found to be a contempt of court. In

35–106

---

[196] *JSC BTA Bank v Ablyazov* [2012] EWHC 455 (Comm), at [19] and following. The jurisdiction for such an order was said to be s.37 of the Senior Courts Act or the court's inherent jurisdiction. The order was upheld on appeal: *JSC BTA Bank v Ablyazov* [2012] EWCA Civ 1411; [2013] 1 W.L.R. 1331, at [170]–[171].

[197] *JSC BTA Bank v Ablyazov* [2012] EWHC 455 (Comm), at [51] and following.

[198] *JSC BTA Bank v Ablyazov* [2012] EWCA Civ 1411; [2013] 1 W.L.R. 1331. A similar order was made in *Stolzenberg v CIBC Mellon Trust Co Ltd* [2004] EWCA Civ 827; *Lexi Holdings Plc v Luqman* [2007] EWCA Civ 1501, and *Tarn Insurance Services Ltd v Kirby* [2009] EWCA Civ 19. In the latter case, Sir John Chadwick said, at [82]: "In a case of deliberate and persistent non-compliance with orders to provide information and deliver documents made in order to safeguard proprietary claims, a proper administration of justice requires that, save in very exceptional circumstances, sanctions imposed should take effect. There were no exceptional circumstances in the present case." Such orders were also made in other aspects of the *Ablyazov* litigation: *JSC BTA Bank v Ablyazov (No.3)* [2011] 1 All E.R. 1093 and *JSC BTA Bank v Shalabayev* [2011] EWHC 2903 (Ch).

[199] *JSC BTA Bank v Ablyazov (No.3)* [2010] EWHC 2219 (QB); [2011] 1 All E.R. 1093, at [38].

[200] *JSC BTA Bank v Shalabayev* [2011] EWHC 2163 (Ch).

such a case the contemnor applies back to court seeking to purge his contempt by showing compliance in order to reduce or discharge his sentence.[201]

G.   WRIT OF SEQUESTRATION

35-107   An order may also be made for the sequestration of assets of the contemnor, whereby his assets are held by a sequestrator pending further order of the court. It is available as a mechanism to enforce a judgment, order or undertaking requiring a person to do an act (within a specified time) or not to do an act.[202]

35-108   Where the respondent to the court order is a company, the writ of sequestration may be issued against the property of any director or other officer of the company.[203] This jurisdiction is likely to engage similar principles to those concerning committal orders against directors and officers, at least as far as concerns liability.[204] So a director should not be liable to a writ of sequestration unless he is aware of the order and wilfully fails to take reasonable steps to ensure compliance with its terms.

35-109   The writ of sequestration[205] is drastic and far-reaching in effect. It authorises the sequestrators to take possession of all the real and personal property of the respondent, and to keep that property in their control until compliance by the respondent with the court's order and a further order is made for its discharge. Sequestration is thus temporary and is a form of coercion rather than a form of punishment; it would accordingly be inappropriate to sequester a contemnor's assets for a contempt which by its nature cannot be purged (e.g. a disposal of an asset in breach of a freezing injunction which cannot be undone).[206] The sequestered property remains the property of the respondent and no title (even by way of charge) is conferred on the beneficiary of the writ.[207] It is not necessary for the applicant for sequestration to identify property within the jurisdiction on which the writ would actually bite.[208] If there is clear evidence that the writ would be ineffective for lack of assets, then this may be a factor against its

---

[201] See r.81.31 for the detailed procedural provisions relating to applications by persons in custody for discharge. These provisions are analysed in *Swindon BC v Webb* [2016] EWCA Civ 152; [2016] 1 W.L.R. 3301, which provides a very full consideration of the concept of purging contempt.

[202] CPR r.81.20(1) and (4). For discussion of the difficult question of whether sequestration is available against third parties who aid and abet the breach of an order, see Londono, Smith and Eady, *Arlidge, Eady and Smith on Contempt* (2017), para.14–129 and following.

[203] CPR r.81.20(3).

[204] As to which see Section C(2) above.

[205] Form No.67 as prescribed by CPR PD 4. It requires not less than four named sequestrators to be identified; applicants should accordingly address this in their contempt application or be ready to do so when the court comes to consider sanction.

[206] It is also inappropriate to make an order for sequestration if the respondent is no longer in contempt because his contempt has been purged: *Inland Revenue Commissioners v Hoogstraten* [1985] Q.B. 1077, at 1086–1087.

[207] *Re Pollard* [1903] 2 K.B. 41, at 47, per Romer LJ.

[208] *Hulbert v Cathcart* [1896] A.C. 470, at 474 (Lord Herschell), applied recently in *International Finance Corp v DSNL Offshore Ltd* [2005] EWHC 534 (Comm), at [45]; and *Trafigura Pte Ltd v Emirates General Petroleum Corp* [2010] EWHC 3007 (Comm), at [15]–[17].

issue[209]; at the same time, the court is likely to treat with scepticism any positive assertion to that effect by a contemnor, for example that he has no assets within the jurisdiction. That will be particularly so if the contempt relates to a failure to disclose assets in connection with a freezing order.

Consistently with these principles, in a recent case,[210] Leggatt J gave permission **35–110** for a writ of sequestration against a corporate respondent even though there was no evidence that the company had assets within the jurisdiction and the writ does not run outside the jurisdiction, on the basis that the court could not stand by and let a flagrant breach of its orders go unmarked, and the writ would not be meaningless (not least as the fact of its issue would be public and may have reputational or business consequences).

Thus, whilst sequestration has in practice so far been a relatively little-used **35–111** procedure in the civil fraud context,[211] it merits consideration by applicants, particularly in the case of foreign corporate defendants who cannot by definition be committed to prison and against whom a fine may have little impact[212] or prove an insufficient incentive towards compliance, but who may, in a given case, have assets within the jurisdiction (or may do so in future).

The procedure on applications for a writ of sequestration is dealt with in detail in **35–112** s.VII of CPR Pt 81,[213] in terms similar to those set out elsewhere in Pt 81 as regards such matters as the requirements for service (and powers to dispense with service),[214] the requirement for a penal notice on judgments and orders,[215] the particularity of the application notice and evidence in support,[216] and the service of the application.[217] The application must be made to a single judge of the division of the High Court in which the proceedings were commenced or have subsequently been transferred (or in any other case, to a single judge of the Queen's Bench Division), by application notice under Pt 23.[218]

H.   CONTEMNOR'S ABILITY TO PARTICIPATE IN PROCEEDINGS

A question which has frequently arisen in practice is the extent to which a **35–113** contemnor who has not purged his contempt is entitled to participate further in the underlying proceedings. The early authorities suggested a strict rule whereby, subject to limited exceptions, a contemnor could only participate in the proceedings if he had complied with the underlying order (and so purged the contempt), even if the contemnor was actually seeking to appeal that very

---

[209] *ICBC Standard Bank Plc v Erdenet Mining Corp LLC (EMC)* [2017] EWHC 3135 (QB), at [91].
[210] *Touton Far East PTE Ltd v Shri Lal Mahal Ltd* [2017] EWHC 621 (Comm), at [21]–[22].
[211] For one other recent example, see *Companaia Sud Americana De Vapores SA v Hin-Pro International Logistics Ltd* [2013] EWHC 987 (Comm).
[212] It was suggested by Andrew Smith J that this would be true of the respondents in *Dar Al Arkan v Al Refai* [2014] EWHC 1055 (Comm), at [12].
[213] CPR rr.81.19–81.27.
[214] CPR rr.81.21–81.24.
[215] CPR r.81.25.
[216] CPR r.81.26(3).
[217] CPR r.81.26(4) and (5).
[218] CPR r.81.26(1) and (2).

order.[219] More recently a more flexible approach has been adopted which has its origins in the judgment of Denning LJ in *Hadkinson v Hadkinson*:

> "It is a strong thing for a court to refuse to hear a party to a cause and it is only to be justified by grave considerations of public policy. It is a step which the court will only take when the contempt itself impedes the course of justice and there is no other effective means of securing his compliance.... I am of opinion that the fact that a party to a cause has disobeyed an order of the court is not of itself a bar to his being heard, but if his disobedience is such that, so long as it continues, it impedes the course of justice in the cause, by making it more difficult for the court to ascertain the truth or to enforce the orders which it may make, then the court may in its discretion refuse to hear him until the impediment is removed or good reason is shown why it should not be removed."[220]

35–114 At one end of the spectrum, the court's general approach is normally to hear an appeal against the order disobedience of which has put the appellant into contempt,[221] as well as an appeal against the order for committal.[222] Beyond that, the touchstone is whether the interests of justice would be best served by hearing the contemnor or refusing to do so.[223] At the other end of the spectrum, there is also a limit to the reach of the disabling effect which the status of contemnor can have. The party in contempt can only be prevented from being heard in further proceedings "in the same cause".[224] Similarly, where there is no real connection between the contempt and the matter on which the contemnor seeks to be heard, that is a powerful factor against a refusal to hear the contemnor.[225]

---

[219] See *Hadkinson v Hadkinson* [1952] P. 285, where it was held that an appeal against the underlying order could only be entertained once the order had been complied with. The analysis in this section is to be distinguished from the absolute and unfettered right of appeal a contemnor has against the committal order itself, considered in the next section.

[220] *Hadkinson v Hadkinson*, at 298. This analysis was approved by the House of Lords in *X Ltd v Morgan-Grampian (Publishers) Ltd* [1991] 1 A.C. 1. There is a large body of subsequent authority considering the question: *Arab Monetary Fund v Hashim*, unreported, 21 March 1997; *Motorola Credit Corp v Uzan (No.2)* [2003] EWCA Civ 752; [2004] 1 W.L.R. 113; *SM Shipping Ltd v TTMI Ltd* [2007] 2 Lloyd's Rep. 155; *Arrow Nominees Inc v Blackledge* [2000] B.C.L.C. 167; *Blue Sky One Ltd v Blue Airways Llc* [2010] EWHC 128 (Comm); *JSC BTA Bank v Ablyazov* [2012] EWCA Civ 639.

[221] *Hadkinson v Hadkinson*, above, at 289; *Motorola Credit Corp v Uzan (No.2)* [2003] EWCA Civ 752; [2004] 1 W.L.R. 113, at [50]; *JSC BTA Bank v Ablyazov* [2012] EWCA Civ 639, at [12]. An appeal was permitted to proceed on this basis in *Compania Sue Americana de Vapores SA v Hin-Pro International Logistics Ltd* [2016] 1 All E.R. (Comm) 417, as well as because the appeal raised matters of general importance and permission to appeal had already been granted.

[222] *JSC BTA Bank v Ablyazov* [2012] EWCA Civ 639, at [26].

[223] *JSC BTA Bank v Ablyazov* [2012] EWCA Civ 639, at [26]. In *Harb v Aziz* [2017] EWHC 258 (Ch) Arnold J dismissed an argument that the claimant should not be heard because she was in contempt by having involuntarily failed to comply with a costs order in a way which did not impede the course of justice.

[224] *Bettinson v Bettinson* [1965] Ch. 465 (Plowman J).

[225] On this basis, in *JSC BTA Bank v Ablyazov* [2015] CP Rep. 21 an appeal in proceedings unrelated to the proceedings in which the contempt had been committed was permitted to proceed.

I. APPEALS

(1) Appeal by Applicant

An appeal against the judge's refusal to commit for contempt of court is legally possible, albeit permission to appeal is required and instances are rare.[226] Generally an appeal will only be entertained where the facts are undisputed and the point relates to the proper interpretation of the order. *Knight v Clifton*[227] is an example of a case where an appeal against a refusal to find a contempt proved on the facts failed.[228] More recently, in *Government of Sierra Leone v Davenport*[229] the judge had held that the respondent to the committal application had failed in various respects to comply with certain disclosure provisions in a freezing order, but had eventually provided all of the required disclosure. On that basis he declined to impose any sanction other than to order the respondent to pay the applicant's costs, subject to some disallowance. The applicant sought to appeal both the judge's finding on the evidence that there was no continuing contempt and also the refusal to impose a sanction other than costs; and it contended that permission to appeal was not required. The Court of Appeal held that permission to appeal was required,[230] and declined to give such permission.[231] Successful appeals against sentence by the applicant will be rare because of the wide discretion afforded to the judge.[232]

35–115

(2) Appeal by Respondent

By contrast, where the respondent has been found liable in contempt then, if he is an individual and has been committed to prison (whether immediately or by way of a suspended order), he has an automatic right of appeal without the need to

35–116

---

[226] See e.g. *Jarmain v Chatterton* (1882) 20 Ch. D. 493 and *Lenton v Tregoning* [1960] 1 All E.R. 717. In both cases the Court of Appeal took a different view from the judge of the effect of the order and, on that view, held that a contempt had been committed. In *Attorney-General v Hislop* [1991] 1 Q.B. 514 the facts were not in dispute but the judge had declined to infer from those facts that there was a real risk of prejudice to a fair trial of pending proceedings, a question which had to be determined objectively. The Court of Appeal held that he was wrong not to draw that inference and committed the respondents; this was a case where the appeal court was in just as good a position as the judge at first instance to make a decision on the question of contempt. By contrast in *JSC BTA Bank v Ereshchenko* [2013] EWCA Civ 1961 the applicant's appeal against the dismissal of its committal application (for criminal contempt) failed where the judge had been entitled not to draw the inference of dishonesty necessary to establish liability for contempt in that case.

[227] *Knight v Clifton* [1971] Ch. 700.

[228] The Court of Appeal dismissed the cross-appeal, in particular because they did not have all the evidence that had been before the judge: see Russell LJ at 707, Sachs LJ at 721–723; and Buckley LJ at 723.

[229] *Government of Sierra Leone v Davenport* [2002] EWCA Civ 230.

[230] The relevant modern rule is at CPR r.52.3(1).

[231] A rare example of the Court of Appeal giving an applicant permission to appeal against a refusal to make a finding of contempt on the facts is *JSC BTA Bank v Ereshchenko* [2013] EWCA Civ 1961. The appeal was dismissed. The Court of Appeal deprecated the applicant appellant's attempt to engage in a minute analysis of the fine detail of the material before the judge at first instance (see at [69]).

[232] *Government of Sierra Leone v Davenport* [2002] EWCA Civ 230.

obtain permission.[233] In such a case there is an absolute right of appeal against the finding of liability and/or sentence.[234] Hence where an individual respondent has merely been fined for contempt, then he needs permission to appeal; as does a company which has been found liable in contempt.[235] In neither case has there been a committal order in the strict sense of the term, albeit it is possible to find in the cases instances of judges using the phrase in a looser sense. It has been said that the rule in *Ladd v Marshall* in relation to admission of fresh evidence on appeal does not apply with the same rigour in appeals against committal orders.[236]

35–117   On any appeal against an order or decision of a court in the exercise of jurisdiction to punish for contempt of court, the appeal routes and procedure are governed by s.13 of the Administration of Justice Act 1960. This means, for example, that an appeal from the Court of Appeal to the Supreme Court will only lie if the Court of Appeal certifies a point of law of general public importance[237] and the procedure for seeking permission to appeal on appeals to the Supreme Court is differently regulated.[238] The phrase "any order or decision of a court in the exercise of jurisdiction to punish for contempt of court" goes beyond committal orders themselves and is sufficiently wide to relate also to orders or decisions made in the course of proceedings which may result in a conviction of, and sentence for, contempt.[239]

---

[233] CPR r.52.3(1)(a)(i).

[234] The court will in practice adopt a more expansive approach to appeals against sentence by respondents than appeals by applicants: compare the *Davenport* case, above, with *Templeton Insurance Ltd v Thomas* [2013] EWCA Civ 35, where the court remitted prison sentences having considered the mitigation advanced.

[235] See the full analysis in *Masri v Consolidated Contractors International Co SAL* [2011] EWCA Civ 898; [2012] 1 W.L.R. 223. The current rule is at CPR r.52.3(1) and provides that permission is not required where the appeal is against "a committal order". A committal order here means an order committing the contemnor to prison, whether immediately or by way of suspended order: *Wilkinson v Lord Chancellor's Department* [2003] EWCA Civ 95.

[236] *Irtelli v Squatriti* [1993] Q.B. 83.

[237] Section 1(2) of the Administration of Justice Act 1960, as applied to the contempt jurisdiction by s.13(4).

[238] Section 2 of the Administration of Justice Act 1960, again as applied by s.13(4).

[239] *R v Serumaga* [2005] 2 Cr. App. R. 12, at [12].

Chapter 36

OTHER SANCTIONS FOR PROCEDURAL DEFAULT

A. INTRODUCTION

(1) The Practical and Tactical Context

Since the advent of the freezing order in the 1970s (under its former moniker of the *Mareva* order), the potential complexity of civil and commercial fraud has increased considerably. Two features stand out: the increasingly international nature of fraudulent conduct, and technological developments which have enabled ever more sophisticated techniques to be used, not just to perpetrate fraud in the first place, but to dissipate and conceal its proceeds. These features are not new. But such evolution has required the courts to update their response, by developing and refining their own techniques to combat fraud and enable the victims of it to obtain justice.

36–001

Recently, this response has involved an increasing use of the jurisdiction to commit for contempt of court consisting in disobedience to the court's orders, a topic examined in detail in the previous chapter. At the same time the courts are also showing themselves more willing to adopt other sanctions in response to a party's default in compliance with procedural orders made for the purposes of managing the litigation, safeguarding the fairness of the trial process and ensuring the effectiveness of the process of enforcement. The practical considerations which should be borne in mind when deciding whether to make a committal application are set out in the previous chapter.[1] In many cases, the weighing of such considerations will lead to the conclusion that an alternative approach to a party's default is likely to be more effective in practice.

36–002

This chapter addresses the alternative sanctions which are likely to be of greatest practical relevance in the context of fraud litigation, to enable the court and the opposing party to put pressure on a respondent to comply with the court's orders, and to ensure that the detrimental impact on the court's function of doing justice is minimised in those cases where the recalcitrant respondent still refuses to comply. It should be borne in mind that the court has a very broad range of powers which may be invoked where there has been a failure to comply with its rules or orders, and such conduct can also of course influence the court's discretion in respect of other orders it is asked to make, such as for costs.

36–003

---

[1] See para.35–011.

B.   STRIKING OUT AND DEBARRING ORDERS

(1)   Introduction and Jurisdiction

36–004   The court has important powers, examined in more detail elsewhere, to make appropriate orders (such as freezing and disclosure orders) to ensure that litigation is conducted effectively and justice is done. Almost as important as the power to make such orders is the power to make them effective. This is particularly true in the context of fraud litigation, where defendants (and sometimes claimants) who have employed a strategy of deceit and concealment in the conduct which gives rise to the substantive claim will not infrequently continue that strategy during the course of, and in relation to, the litigation. As Rix LJ put it in the *Ablyazov* litigation[2]:

> "If once it became known that the court was unable or unwilling to maintain the effectiveness of its orders, then it would lose all control over litigation of this kind, with terrible consequences for the administration of justice. Those wrongly accused of fraud would be relieved of a certain amount of inconvenience, but fraudsters would rejoice and hitch a free ride to interminable litigation on the back of ill-gotten gains."

36–005   The court has a well-known power under CPR r.3.4(2)(c) to strike out a statement of case where it appears to the court that there has been a failure to comply with a rule, practice direction or court order. The current section of this chapter is concerned principally with the consequences of a party's breach of a court order. The court is also given specific power by CPR r.3.1(3)(b), when making an order, to specify the consequence of failure to comply with the order or any condition attached to it. This is the basis on which the court may make an "unless order" providing for the respondent's statement of case (usually but not always a defence) to be struck out, and sometimes also that the respondent will be debarred from further participation in the proceedings, in the event of non-compliance. Of course, the terms of the unless order may, depending on the circumstances of the case, specify other consequences less draconian than those identified in the preceding sentence: the court's procedural powers under this jurisdiction are very flexible.

36–006   As explained in more detail below, in practice the power to make orders of this nature has most frequently been exercised in cases where the respondent's default relates in some way to his disclosure obligations (whether in respect of the substantive claim or a freezing order made in support of it). This is not surprising, once it is understood that the circumstances in which it will be appropriate to exercise the draconian power of preventing a party from participating further in proceedings are in general[3] limited to situations in which the default impairs the just resolution of the proceedings as a whole (including the enforcement of a prospective judgment). This requirement is most likely to be satisfied in situations where the respondent's co-operation in complying with the court's orders is necessary to ensure that the proceedings are fairly resolved. Here, disclosure is the paradigm case.

---

[2] *JSC BTA Bank v Ablyazov (No.8)* [2012] EWCA Civ 1411; [2013] 1 W.L.R. 1331, at [188].
[3] Though they may sometimes go wider than this: see para.36–027 below.

(2)   The Effect of Debarring and Striking Out

Where a statement of case is struck out, it is (or is treated as) deleted and may no longer be relied on,[4] at least by the party who served it.[5] In the relatively unusual cases in which the court is concerned with a defaulting claimant, this will effectively put an end to the claim. Where a defence is struck out, on the other hand, this does not of itself end the proceedings in the claimant's favour. The further steps which must be taken are likely to depend on the nature of the proceedings. In a monetary claim (i.e. a claim for a specified amount of money or for an amount of money to be decided by the court) the claimant may obtain judgment with costs by request.[6] In the latter scenario the judgment would be stated to be for damages (or its equitable equivalent) to be assessed.   **36–007**

In any other claim, an application for judgment must be made by application notice under Pt 23, pursuant to CPR r.3.5(5).[7] An application under CPR 3.5(5) is, as the heading to CPR r.3.5 indicates, for judgment without a trial. Although the rule is capable of being read on its face as entitling a claimant to such a judgment by application in every case, the decision of the Court of Appeal in *Thevarajah v Riordan*[8] puts this in doubt. In that case, the claimant brought a claim for various different heads of relief, including specific performance, a mandatory order requiring a transfer of shares, declarations, and accounts and inquiries. Orders were made striking out the defences and debarring the defendants from defending the claims as a result of breach of an unless order requiring disclosure of specific matters in support of a freezing order. Tomlinson LJ observed that, nonetheless, most or all of such relief could not be obtained simply by filing a request for judgment, and went on to state that it was relief which "requires the court to be satisfied, exercising its judicial function, that it is appropriate to grant it".[9] He went on to approve the claimant's concession that a trial remained necessary. Of course in some cases, it may be in the claimant's own interests to proceed to a trial on the merits rather than seeking judgment in default, for example if the prospects of successful enforcement in particular countries abroad are increased by such a course.   **36–008**

The need for an application under CPR r.3.5(5) (or indeed a trial) should not be misunderstood as creating a further opportunity for the defendant to challenge the striking out of his defence. Instead, on such an application the court's function is limited to deciding what order should properly be made to reflect the sanction which has already taken effect, unless the defendant applies at that point for relief from sanction or the court (exceptionally) considers of its own motion that such   **36–009**

---

[4] See the Glossary to the CPR in Section E of "The White Book" (Sir Geoffrey Vos (editor-in-chief), *Civil Procedure*, 2018 edn (London: Sweet & Maxwell, 2018), Vol.1, para.E1–1).

[5] The statement of case can however be relied on by the opposing party, e.g. where it consists of admissions: *Thevarajah v Riordan* [2015] EWCA Civ 41; [2015] CP Rep. 19, at [33].

[6] CPR 3.5(2).

[7] CPR 3.5(5).

[8] *Thevarajah v Riordan* [2015] EWCA Civ 41; [2015] CP Rep. 19.

[9] *Thevarajah v Riordan*, above, per Tomlinson LJ at [15] .

relief should be granted.[10] An examination of the principles governing the grant of relief from such sanctions is beyond the scope of this book. Practitioners are referred to the specialist texts on civil procedure.

36–010 Where there is a trial following striking out of the defendant's defence, doubt may also arise as to what, if any, role the defendant may continue to play in the proceedings. Two situations must be distinguished.

(i) The defence has been struck out

36–011 First, where the defence has been struck out but the defendant has not also been debarred from defending, there may be room for some continued participation on his part. Thus, in *Culla Park Ltd v Richards*,[11] Eady J held that, notwithstanding the striking out of their defences, the defendants to a defamation claim remained entitled at trial to "test" the allegations made by the claimants and, in particular, to resist allegations of dishonesty made against them. In contrast, in *Thevarajah v Riordan*, David Donaldson QC expressed the view that the effect of striking out a defence was to produce a deemed admission of all elements constituent of a cause of action,[12] though this analysis does not sit easily with the way the issue was approached in the Court of Appeal.[13] At least where there is a trial on the merits following striking out, it is considered that the approach of Eady J is to be preferred.

36–012 However, there remains potential uncertainty as to precisely what this approach means in practice. In "testing" the allegations made by a claimant in such a case, a defendant would seemingly be able to instruct counsel to cross-examine witnesses called by the claimant in support of that allegation, and to make submissions to the effect that the claimant had failed to prove its case on any given issue. Without a defence, however, a defendant would be unable to make any positive allegations at trial that would ordinarily have to be pleaded. And it seems unlikely that a defendant in such a situation would be permitted to give or adduce evidence of his own; though much may depend on the attitude of the judge in the particular case.

(ii) The defendant has been debarred from defending

36–013 Secondly, where the defendant has also been debarred from defending (which is a separate and distinct sanction from the striking out of a defence),[14] there remains the potential for argument as to the effect of this in practice. The *Thevarajah* case provides a useful illustration for practitioners. Following an unless order which was not complied with, the defendants' defences were struck out and they were debarred from defending (this having been the prescribed sanction stated on the

---

[10] *Marcan Shipping (London) Ltd v Kefalas* [2007] EWCA Civ 463; [2007] 1 W.L.R. 1864, per Moore-Bick LJ at [34].

[11] *Culla Park Ltd v Richards* [2007] EWHC 1687 (QB), at [12].

[12] *Thevarajah v Riordan* [2014] EWHC 725 (Ch), at [4].

[13] *Thevarajah v Riordan* [2015] EWCA Civ 41; [2015] C.P. Rep. 19, per Tomlinson LJ.

[14] Which is a good reason why the applicant for an unless order should consider with care what sanction should be imposed for breach of any order which is sought on "unless" terms.

face of the original unless order). On a subsequent application for relief from sanction, Andrew Sutcliffe QC decided that, notwithstanding these orders (and even absent relief from sanction having been granted), the defendants remained entitled at trial to require the claimant to prove his claim, to cross-examine and make submissions.[15] The Court of Appeal expressed themselves to be "troubled" by this conclusion but left the matter to the trial judge.[16] On a subsequent application to determine the effect of the debarring order, Sales J held that the defendants:

(1)   could participate on matters of liability to the extent of assisting the court to understand the claimant's case;

(2)   could not challenge the claimant's claim as set out in his particulars of claim and evidence; but

(3)   could participate on matters of quantum.[17]

There are examples of different approaches being taken in other cases in respect of debarring orders. In *Ablyazov*, for example, Toulson LJ observed in passing on the appeal against the debarring (unless) order itself that the effect of the order would be to prevent Mr Ablyazov from instructing counsel to test the claimant's claims and calling witnesses to give evidence in his defence.[18] In the event, Mr Ablyazov's appeal having failed, he was entitled to appear at the trial on matters relating only to quantum.[19] By contrast in *Michael v Philips*,[20] Soole J held that an order debarring the defendants from defending extended to matters of both liability and quantum, there being no principled distinction between the two (although he left it to the trial judge to determine what participation might be permitted in any subsequent accounts or inquiries).   **36–014**

The clearest practical conclusion that can be drawn is that the effect of a debarring order is likely to depend, first and foremost, on the terms of the original unless order and the subsequent debarring order (if any). The clearer those terms, the less room there will be for further satellite litigation thereafter as to the extent to which a defendant may continue to participate.   **36–015**

(3)   Comparison with the Contempt Jurisdiction

The principles governing the making of a debarring order received detailed consideration in the *Ablyazov* litigation, where it was sought following a successful committal application by the claimant against the main defendant, Mr Ablyazov. However, a finding of contempt is not a necessary precondition to the making of a debarring order. In some cases the reality or even the threat of a   **36–016**

---

[15] *Thevarajah v Riordan* [2013] EWHC 3179 (Ch), at [40].

[16] *Thevarajah v Riordan* [2014] EWCA Civ 14; [2014] 1 Costs L.R. 163, at [38].

[17] See the judgment of the Court of Appeal [2015] EWCA Civ 41; [2015] C.P. Rep. 19, at [27]. Sales J drew an analogy with judgment being entered in default of defence, but this was later doubted by Tomlinson LJ in obiter remarks in the Court of Appeal: at [30].

[18] *JSC BTA Bank v Ablyazov* [2012] EWCA Civ 1411; [2013] 1 W.L.R. 1331, at [198].

[19] See [2013] EWHC 867 (Comm).

[20] *Michael v Philips* [2017] EWHC 1084 (QB), at [11]–[22].

committal order will prove the most effective way of compelling compliance with freezing and disclosure orders, particularly for defendants who are settled within the jurisdiction and may in practice be unlikely to seek to flee abroad in order to avoid serving a prison sentence. But for other alleged fraudsters with no connection with the jurisdiction or who may be prepared to turn fugitive rather than face imprisonment, the ultimate threat may not be the risk of incarceration but the prospect of forfeiting their defence to the claim against them.

36–017   In addition, whilst an applicant for a strike-out or debarring order as a sanction for non-compliance with an earlier order of the court must of course prove such non-compliance, outside the committal context it is only necessary to do so to the civil standard of proof, namely on the balance of probabilities.[21] An application under CPR Pt 3 is also not burdened with the detailed procedural safeguards which accompany any committal application,[22] or the risk of an appeal being brought without the need to obtain permission.[23] Unless the facts surrounding the allegation of non-compliance are sufficiently uncertain to require determination at a trial, a strike-out application should be capable of determination by an ordinary application under CPR Pt 23 and decided on written evidence. For these reasons, applying for a strike-out/debarring order can be a significantly quicker and cheaper process than seeking an order for committal.

(4)   Features of the Jurisdiction

(i)   Breach of an order or rule is necessary but not sufficient

36–018   The making of a strike-out or debarring order on grounds examined in this chapter presupposes a breach of a prior order or rule (or practice direction) by the respondent. Where such a sanction is imposed in absolute terms, the breach will necessarily have occurred prior to the imposition of the sanction. Where, by contrast, the sanction is imposed in "unless" terms, i.e. conditionally and in the event of the occurrence of a specified subsequent breach, it only takes effect upon that subsequent breach, subject to the possibility of relief from sanction. The general principles set out below apply equally when the court is considering making an absolute order as when it considers making a conditional unless order.[24] There is no limit in principle to the types of order or rule (or practice direction) which, if breached, could provide grounds for an application; the limiting factor in practice will be the requirement for the breach to impact in some way on the fairness of the proceedings going forward, as examined in more detail in sub-section (ii) (paras 36–021—36–025) below.

---

[21] *Logicrose Ltd v Southend United Football Club Ltd*, *The Times*, 5 March 1988, per Millett J.

[22] These safeguards are set out in detail in CPR Pt 81 and examined in Ch.35.

[23] See paras 35–115—35–117 for discussion of appeals against committal orders.

[24] But it is important to understand that when the question is whether a sanction previously imposed in "unless" terms should take effect, these principles are not engaged. In such a scenario, the court's function is limited to considering the consequence of the sanction which has taken effect, subject to the question of relief from sanction. See *Marcan Shipping (London) Ltd v Kefalas* [2007] EWCA Civ 643; [2007] 1 W.L.R. 1864.

In some cases the breach will be admitted—for example, the evidence showing a **36–019** dissipation of assets in breach of a freezing order may be incontrovertible and thus the respondent will be compelled to accept it. In other cases the question of breach will be more difficult to establish—for example, whether a particular transaction amounts to a breach of a freezing order, or whether a given document should have been disclosed in accordance with the respondent's obligations of standard disclosure or under the disclosure provisions of a freezing order such that its suppression or deletion gives rise to a breach. Where the breach is disputed, it could be proved at some earlier stage (for example, on a committal application decided prior to the application for a strike-out or debarring order, as in the *Ablyazov* litigation, or on an application for a declaration) or as part of the strike-out/debarring application itself. Consideration should be given to whether cross-examination will be necessary at the hearing of the application.[25] The court has jurisdiction under CPR r.32.7 to order cross-examination on an interim application.

Although necessary, proving a breach of an order is not of itself sufficient to **36–020** allow the court to make an order striking out a defence (or claim) or debarring a defendant from defending the claim against him.[26] The additional requirements are considered immediately below.

(ii) *The defaulting party's breach must give rise to a continuing risk of injustice*

In *Hadkinson v Hadkinson*,[27] the Court of Appeal considered whether it should **36–021** refuse to hear an appellant who was in breach of an order preventing her from removing her child from the jurisdiction—and hence in contempt of court. Denning LJ expressed the view that[28]:

> "the fact that a party to a cause has disobeyed an order of the court is not of itself a bar to his being heard, but if his disobedience is such that, so long as it continues, it impedes the course of justice in the cause, by making it more difficult for the court to ascertain the truth or to enforce the orders which it may make, then the court may in its discretion refuse to hear him until the impediment is removed or good reason is shown why it should not be removed."

Denning LJ's analysis in *Hadkinson* differed in some respects from that taken by **36–022** the other judges of the Court; but his analysis has come to encapsulate the modern approach to the question of whether a defaulting party should be debarred from further participation in proceedings, not just in the context of a

---

[25] See e.g. *Bilta (UK) Ltd v Nazir* [2010] EWHC 3227 (Ch), in which Lewison J said at [21] that it was impossible, on the evidence before him, to conclude without cross-examination that the defendants were guilty of the deliberate suppression of documents.

[26] *Hadkinson v Hadkinson* [1952] P. 285, per Denning LJ at 298; *In Re Swaptronics Ltd*, *The Times*, 17 August 1998, per Laddie J at [21]–[22]; *Arrow Nominees Inc v Blackledge* [2001] B.C.C. 591, per Chadwick LJ at [54].

[27] *Hadkinson v Hadkinson* [1952] P. 285.

[28] *Hadkinson v Hadkinson* [1952] P. 285, at 298.

refusal to hear a contemnor but also when it comes to making strike-out and debarring orders consequent on the breach.[29]

36–023 In some cases, the impediment to justice described by Denning LJ will consist in a risk to the fairness of the trial process itself, particularly where the respondent's default consists in breaches of his standard disclosure obligations. Thus in *Arrow Nominees Inc v Blackledge*,[30] one of the petitioners in an unfair prejudice claim disclosed, as part of standard disclosure, certain letters which turned out to have been forged. Once discrepancies in the letters had been pointed out by the respondents' solicitors and an allegation of forgery made, the petitioner admitted the forgery. The respondents then applied to strike out the petition under CPR r.3.4 on the grounds of the petitioner's breaches of his disclosure obligations or as an abuse of process. Evans-Lombe J (on two separate applications made prior to trial and then at the trial itself) refused to strike out the petition on the basis that he considered a fair trial still to be possible. The Court of Appeal allowed the appeal. Chadwick LJ said that, on the facts, the judge ought to have concluded that it was unfair for the trial to continue.[31] He explained the meaning of "fairness" in this context as follows (in terms which make it clear that the concept goes beyond simply the court's ability to ascertain the truth)[32]:

> "Further, in this context, a fair trial is a trial which is conducted without an undue expenditure of time and money; and with a proper regard to the demands of other litigants upon the finite resources of the court. The court does not do justice to the other parties to the proceedings in question if it allows its process to be abused so that the real point in issue becomes subordinated to an investigation into the effect which the admittedly fraudulent conduct of one party in connection with the process of litigation has had on the fairness of the trial itself. That, as it seems to me, is what happened in the present case. The trial was 'hijacked' by the need to investigate what documents were false and what documents had been destroyed. The need to do that arose from the facts (i) that the petitioners had sought to rely on documents which Nigel Tobias had forged with the object of frustrating a fair trial and (ii) that, as the judge found, Nigel Tobias was unwilling to make a frank disclosure of the extent of his fraudulent conduct, but persisted in his attempts to deceive. The result was that the petitioners' case occupied far more of the court's time than was necessary for the purpose of deciding the real points in issue on the petition. That was unfair to the Blackledge respondents; and it was unfair to other litigants who needed to have their disputes tried by the court."

This language, although coming from a case decided at the dawn of the CPR era, resonates with even greater force almost two decades later, in a climate in which concern for the impact of the conduct of litigants upon the court's own resources is even more acute. It is no surprise that the *Arrow Nominees* decision is regularly relied upon in fraud cases as justifying a strong response to the defaults of litigants.

36–024 Conversely, in *Logicrose Ltd v Southend United Football Club Ltd*[33] Millett J refused to dismiss a claim on the basis that a crucial document had been

---

[29] See in particular *X Ltd v Morgan-Grampian (Publishers) Ltd* [1991] 1 A.C. 1, per Lord Donaldson MR at 21H and 22G; per Lord Bridge at 46B–46G; and *JSC BTA Bank v Ablyazov* [2012] EWCA Civ 1411, [2013] 1 W.L.R. 1331, at [124], [183], per Rix LJ.

[30] *Arrow Nominees Inc v Blackledge* [2001] B.C.C. 591.

[31] *Arrow Nominees Inc v Blackledge* [2001] B.C.C. 591, at [55]–[56].

[32] *Arrow Nominees Inc v Blackledge* [2001] B.C.C. 591, at [55].

[33] *Logicrose Ltd v Southend United Football Club Ltd*, The Times, 5 March 1988.

suppressed by the claimant; the document had subsequently been located and disclosed, and the judge accordingly concluded that the claim should not be dismissed unless there remained a risk of injustice. Such a risk might have arisen if a material witness who could have dealt with the document had died before its production, or there was reason to believe that other documents had been destroyed or remained concealed. But no such factors were found to be present on the facts, and accordingly the claim was allowed to proceed. Similarly, in *Raja v Van Hoogstraten*,[34] a defendant's refusal to give disclosure pursuant to a freezing order was held to have no impact on the fairness of the trial, and accordingly the judge's decision to strike out the defence was overturned by the Court of Appeal.[35] Although Chadwick LJ recognised that the inability adequately to police the freezing order might in principle justify striking out, on the facts he held that the judge could not safely have proceeded on that basis, since the freezing order had been made without notice to the defendant and the judge had refused to hear his application to set it aside.

It might be said that the claimant in the *Raja* case could have fortified his position **36–025** by first seeking an unless order whereby unless the defendant, and respondent to the freezing order, provided the disclosure required then his defence would be struck out and he would be debarred from further participation in the case. That of course would have been a procedurally possible approach. However, such an application for an unless order would have engaged the same principles as those discussed above: that is, the court, when it is asked to prescribe a sanction in the event of a future breach of an order, will weigh whether that sanction would truly be justified in the circumstances of a subsequent breach. What the court should not do[36] is prescribe a sanction which is not merited by the gravity of the potential breach on the basis that the respondent can always avoid the sanction by complying with the order. Otherwise the applicant could evade the principles discussed above by the simple expedient of obtaining an unless order in stringent terms in the event of a breach which on analysis does not merit such a draconian sanction.

(iii) Injustice can arise even if the fairness of trial process itself is unaffected

The circumstances in which justice will be impeded by a party's default can **36–026** extend, however, beyond cases in which the fairness of the trial process itself is affected.[37] The impact on the court's ability to ascertain the truth at trial was but one of the factors referred to by Denning LJ in *Hadkinson*[38]; another was the

---

[34] *Raja v Van Hoogstraten* [2004] EWCA Civ 968; [2004] 4 All E.R. 793, at [110]–[114], per Chadwick LJ.

[35] *In Re Swaptronics Ltd, The Times*, 17 August 1998 is a similar example of a refusal to strike out where a fair trial was still possible.

[36] Although anecdotal evidence suggests that in practice it may not rigorously adhere to such an approach and that respondents themselves may not properly deploy the principles discussed in this section when seeking to resist applications for unless orders.

[37] The focus in *In Re Swaptronics Ltd, The Times*, 17 August 1998, at [21] on the court's ability to ascertain the truth at trial should be considered too narrow in light of subsequent authority.

[38] See para.36–021 above.

impact on the court's ability to enforce orders it may make. One phrase which has gained traction in the case law is whether the party's default renders further proceedings unsatisfactory.[39] It is now well recognised that such a consequence may arise where the default consists in failure to disclose assets under a freezing order, making it more difficult for the claimant to enforce any judgment in its favour against the defendant.[40] Similarly, it may arise from a failure to comply with orders to provide information and deliver up documents, made in order to safeguard a proprietary claim.[41] The necessary risk of injustice might also arise where there has been other conduct impacting on the claimant's ability to enforce a judgment, such as a failure by the defendant to co-operate with receivers appointed over his assets. Where the injustice has been mitigated in some other way, however, by a claimant able to identify the defendant's assets otherwise than by disclosure from him, proving the necessary risk of injustice will be more difficult.[42]

36–027   Some of the cases have seemed to go further and to take into account other considerations as justifying the making of a strike-out or debarring order, even where there is no risk of injustice as between the parties. In *Landauer Ltd v Comins & Co (A Firm)*,[43] Lloyd LJ said (obiter) that he could envisage situations of contumacious conduct, such as the deliberate suppression of a document, which might justify striking out even if a fair trial was still possible. In *Arrow Nominees*, Ward LJ was prepared to hold that striking out was a proportionate response to the forgery of documents even where admission of the forgery meant that the petitioners had lost "so much of the fruits of their labour",[44] by reference to broader considerations of justice, including as reflected in the overriding objective of the CPR. This approach was followed by Christopher Clarke J in a decision in the *Ablyazov* litigation.[45] More recently, in *Orb ARL v Ruhan*,[46] Popplewell J held that maintaining public confidence in the court's ability and willingness to secure compliance with its orders is an important and legitimate objective of an unless order in itself. Notwithstanding these broader statements of principle, it is considered that, the lesser the impact of a party's default on the fairness of the proceedings as between the parties themselves, the more difficult it

---

[39] *Logicrose Ltd v Southend United Football Club Ltd, The Times*, 5 March 1988, per Millett J adopted in *Arrow Nominees Inc v Blackledge* [2001] B.C.C. 591, at [54], per Chadwick LJ; *Raja v Van Hoogstraten* [2004] EWCA Civ 968; [2004] 4 All E.R. 793, at [113], per Chadwick LJ.

[40] *Lexi Holdings v Luqman* [2007] EWCA Civ 1501, at [28]–[29], per Mummery LJ (a case in which the Court of Appeal made an unless order requiring the respondent to disclose in full his assets in circumstances where his earlier assertions about this asset position, made in response to disclosure provisions in a freezing order, were held to be incredible); *Blue Sky One Ltd v Mahan Air* [2010] EWHC 128 (Comm), at [37], per Beatson J; *JSC BTA Bank v Ablyazov* [2012] EWCA Civ 1411; [2013] 1 W.L.R. 1331, at [183], per Rix LJ.

[41] *Tarn Insurance Services Ltd v Kirby* [2009] EWCA Civ 19; [2009] CP Rep. 22 (CA), at [82], per Sir John Chadwick.

[42] See *Palmer v Tsai* [2017] EWHC 1860 (Ch), at [314], per Rose J, distinguishing *Lexi Holdings v Luqman* and *Ablyazov*, above, on the facts.

[43] *Landauer Ltd v Comins & Co (A Firm), The Times*, 7 August 1991.

[44] *Arrow Nominees* [2001] B.C.C. 591, at [72]–[75]; Roch LJ agreed at [79].

[45] *JSC BTA Bank v Ablyazov (No.3)* [2011] 1 All E.R. (Comm) 1093, at [41]. In the same case it was held that a debarring order could be made even though there was a pending jurisdiction challenge.

[46] *Orb ARL v Ruhan* [2016] EWHC 850 (Comm), at [178].

is likely to be to establish that it is an appropriate response to the party in default to deprive him of the opportunity of participating in an adjudication on the merits.

In some cases it may not be possible at the time of the application to strike out or for a debarring order to ascertain the effect which non-disclosure will have on the fairness of the trial process. In such circumstances it is open to the Court to adjourn an application for an unless order (or to strike out) to the trial itself, a course followed in *Prest v Marc Rich & Co.*[47] **36–028**

(iv) Is an unless order a necessary precondition?

Prior to the CPR it was held to be wrong in principle to strike out a statement of case for breach of a non-peremptory disclosure order (i.e. an order without an "unless" sanction attached to it), and that an unless order should be made in the first instance.[48] Whether this holds good as an absolute rule under the CPR is considered doubtful; it is possible to conceive of cases in which it would be obvious that an unless order would serve no useful purpose and would simply prolong the injustice to the innocent party of having to continue the proceedings in the face of the defaulting party's defiance of the court's authority. In practice, however, given the seriousness of a strike-out or debarring order, in most cases the court is likely to give a defaulting party some further time to comply in the form of an unless order before imposing that ultimate sanction. In *Palmer v Tsai*,[49] Rose J appears to have thought that it would be inappropriate to make an immediate debarring order as a response to a defendant's failure to comply with a freezing order (for which she had, in the same judgment, held him to be in contempt of court), in part on the basis that no unless order had previously been made. **36–029**

(v) Impact on the respondent's right of access to the court

An order striking out a party's statement of case or debarring a defendant from defending clearly constitutes a form of interference with that party's right of access to the court. This has generated discussion in some of the cases as to whether (and in what circumstances) such interference is compatible with the defaulting party's rights under art.6 of the European Convention on Human Rights. A detailed examination of those rights is beyond the scope of this chapter. **36–030**

---

[47] *Prest v Marc Rich & Co Investment AG* [2006] EWHC 927 (Comm), at [30].

[48] *Star News Shop Ltd v Stafford Refrigeration Ltd* [1998] 1 W.L.R. 536 CA, at 545D–545E (Otton LJ).

[49] *Palmer v Tsai* [2017] EWHC 1860 (Ch), at [313] and [315]. The judge considered that there would be conceptual and practical difficulties with her making an unless order herself, given that the defendant was about to be committed to prison for contempt, making it more difficult for him to comply with that order.

The attitude taken by the English courts to this question is, however, neatly encapsulated in the judgment of Arden LJ in *Stolzenberg v CIBC Mellon Trust Co Ltd*[50]:

> "Article 6 of the Convention requires attention to be addressed to a matter which has always been implicit in cases of this kind, namely that the effect of the court's refusal to grant relief is that the losing party will be deprived of a trial of his defence on the merits. Clearly, as the judge recognised, that is an important factor. But three points must be borne in mind. First, it is open to a party to consent to judgment being given against him without a trial on the merits ... Second, this is not an appeal against the judgments entered against the appellants. The appellants cannot say those orders were wrongly made. Third, the state can impose restrictions on the right of access to court provided that the restrictions serve a legitimate aim, are proportionate and do not destroy the very essence of the right. Here, the legitimate aim in imposing a sanction is to secure compliance with court orders, which in the instant case were made to ensure the effectiveness of freezing orders. The imposition of a sanction is proportionate if it is reasonably necessary for achieving that aim. The essence of the right of access to court is not destroyed because the litigant has the opportunity to seek relief against the sanctions. The refusal of that relief is Convention-compliant if the same tests are satisfied. The legitimate aim remains the same. Proportionality will be met if the overriding objective is met. The essence of the right will not be destroyed even if refused, since the appellants always had the chance to comply with the court orders and to help progress the case to trial."

C. RESTRICTION ON THE USE OF FROZEN FUNDS

36–031   As has been discussed elsewhere in this book,[51] the standard form freezing order permits the respondent to use sums which are otherwise frozen to defray living and legal expenses. In addition, the respondent to a proprietary freezing order may, in specified circumstances, obtain permission to use frozen funds for such purposes. Where there is evidence that the respondent has failed fully to comply with his disclosure obligations pursuant to a personal or proprietary freezing order, this may be a bar to the grant of permission to use frozen funds.[52] Where a defendant obtains such permission (either by default under the standard form or on an application in which the judge is persuaded that the requirements for a variation are met) and it subsequently transpires that the respondent has failed to comply with the requirements to give disclosure under a freezing order, in principle this will afford sufficient grounds for a revocation or variation of the permission previously granted.[53]

---

[50] *Stolzenberg v CIBC Mellon Trust Co Ltd* [2004] EWCA Civ 827, at [161]. This decision was followed in *JSC BTA Bank v Ablyazov* [2012] EWCA Civ 1411; [2013] 1 W.L.R. 1331 (see in particular [165]), in which Rix LJ conducted a detailed examination of the Strasbourg and domestic jurisprudence.

[51] See paras 28–129 and 32–031.

[52] See para.32–031.

[53] *AJ Bekhor & Co Ltd v Bilton* [1981] Q.B. 923, at 944G–945D, per Ackner LJ.

D. CONTROLLING DISCLOSURE AND USE OF DOCUMENTS

(1) Introduction

In a fraud case, as has already been stated, procedural default often concerns **36–032**
disclosure. Breach of an order to produce specific documents or information may
of course amount to a contempt of court. Making a false disclosure statement
without an honest belief in its truth is a contempt of court,[54] and in principle a
failure to comply with an order for standard disclosure could, on the right facts,
also amount to contempt.

However, committal proceedings may not be the best way for an opposing party **36–033**
to respond to a failure to give proper disclosure. As has already been discussed,[55]
such proceedings can be expensive and time-consuming, and may delay the trial
of the claim. The disadvantages of engaging in satellite litigation are likely to be
particularly acute if the complaint relates to the standard disclosure process, since
it will arise at a time when the demands of the litigation may already be intense,
with work being carried out on witness statements and possibly also expert
reports. And, if the claimant's key objective is to ensure adequate disclosure is
given, for some defendants not even the threat (or the reality) of a prison sentence
will be enough to bring about that result. Striking out may of course be a
possibility (see Section B above), but the high threshold for a strike-out may not
be met, and in a case involving several defendants, there may be good reasons
why the claimant wants to obtain documents from one defendant even if they are
debarred from further participation in the proceedings, for example in order to
rely on those documents against another defendant or to trace assets.[56]

Given these considerations, a litigant faced with failures in disclosure by an **36–034**
opposing party will want to consider what other ways there might be of getting
access to that party's documents. We address two related possibilities below, i.e.
taking control of the disclosure process and orders for the inspection of
computers, before briefly addressing other remedies available in the context of
disclosure and evidence.

(2) Taking Control of the Disclosure Process

If a party's failure to comply with his disclosure obligations is sufficiently **36–035**
serious, in an appropriate case the Court can intervene to require the defaulting
party's disclosure to be carried out by an independent solicitor on his behalf. The
rarity of the circumstances in which such an order will be made is illustrated by
the limited examination of this issue in the case law, as well as by the principles
set out in the few first instance judgments in which this issue has arisen for
consideration.

---

[54] See CPR r.31.23 and CPR Pt 81, section VI.
[55] See para.35–011.
[56] As for example in *Nolan Family Partnership v Walsh* [2011] EWHC 535 (Comm); at [8].

36–036   In *Nolan Family Partnership v Walsh*,[57] the claimant investors sued several defendants in respect of an alleged fraudulent investment scheme. They wished to obtain disclosure from the first defendant, Mr Walsh, in particular with a view to locating the proceeds of the alleged fraud. Mr Walsh had seemingly failed to comply in any respect with his obligations of standard disclosure. In those circumstances the claimant sought an order requiring a non-party in possession of relevant documents to deliver up those documents to an independent solicitor who would then carry out the disclosure process on Mr Walsh's behalf. Teare J rejected the non-party's submission that no jurisdiction existed, holding that there was inherent jurisdiction to make the order sought,[58] by analogy with the search order jurisdiction. There was also jurisdiction to make the order sought against the non-party provided it was not oppressive to do so.[59] The Judge approved a form of order in which the disclosure process would be carried out by a "supervising solicitor", giving Mr Walsh and the non-party an opportunity to object in advance to disclosure or inspection being given of any given document.[60] It was emphasised that, as in the search order context, the supervising solicitor would have to be independent of both parties.[61]

36–037   The nature of, and basis for, the jurisdiction was considered in more detail by Tugendhat J in *CBS Butler Ltd v Brown*,[62] an employee competition case. At the outset of the litigation the claimant had obtained a form of search order against the defendants. In advance of standard disclosure, the claimant then sought an order that computer images taken on execution of the search order should be searched by the claimant's own expert and disclosure given as a result. The Judge examined the principles governing the search order jurisdiction, contrasting this with the order sought by the claimant which would deprive the defendant of any opportunity to consider whether or not he should make disclosure at all.[63] Reference was made to an earlier case in which the court had directed that an expert be appointed to carry out electronic disclosure on the defendant's behalf.[64] Tugendhat J summarised the principles as follows[65]:

> "In my judgment, an order which would deprive the Defendants of the opportunity of considering whether or not they shall make any disclosure is … an intrusive order, even if it is made on notice to the defendant. It is contrary to normal principles of justice, and can only be done when there is a paramount need to prevent a denial of justice to the claimant. The need to avoid such a denial of justice may be shown after the defendant has failed to comply with his disclosure obligations, having been given the opportunity to do so (as in *Mueller*). Or it may be shown before the defendant has had an opportunity to comply with his disclosure obligations. But in the latter case it is not sufficient for a claimant such as the employer in *Lock v Beswick*, or the Claimant, to show no more than that the defendant has misused

---

[57] *Nolan Family Partnership v Walsh* [2011] EWHC 535 (Comm).

[58] *Nolan Family* [2011] EWHC 535 (Comm), at [10].

[59] *Nolan Family* [2011] EWHC 535 (Comm), at [14].

[60] *Nolan Family* [2011] EWHC 535 (Comm), at [15].

[61] *Nolan Family* [2011] EWHC 535 (Comm), at [20]–[21].

[62] *CBS Butler Ltd v Brown* [2013] EWHC 3944 (QB).

[63] *CBS Butler Ltd v Brown* [2013] EWHC 3944 (QB), at [28].

[64] *CBS Butler Ltd v Brown* [2013] EWHC 3944 (QB), at [36]–[37]. The case in question was *Mueller Europe Ltd v Central Roofing (South Wales) Ltd* [2012] EWHC 3417 (TCC); [2013] T.C.L.R. 2, considered at para.36–041 below.

[65] *CBS Butler Ltd v Brown* [2013] EWHC 3944 (QB), at [38].

confidential information or otherwise broken his employment contract. The position is *a fortiori* where the claimant has not even shown that much. What a claimant must show is substantial reasons for believing that a defendant is intending to conceal or destroy documents in breach of his obligations of disclosure under the CPR."

In summary, therefore, the Judge considered that: **36–038**

(1) the disclosure process would only be taken out of a party's hands if there was a paramount need to prevent a denial of justice;

(2) such a need could be shown either by (a) a proven failure by a party to comply with his disclosure obligations, or (b) a risk of such a failure if substantial reasons were shown which pointed to a risk of concealment or destruction of documents.

This statement of principle has yet to be cited in any subsequent decision, but was   **36–039**
based on detailed analysis of principle and authority and is considered likely to be followed in future. It is unlikely, however, that the necessary threshold will be met simply by showing that a party has breached his disclosure obligations. The court's focus is likely to be on questions such as whether, despite the breach, such an intrusive order is necessary to preserve the fairness of the trial process, and whether it would be a proportionate response to the breach. Each case will turn on its facts. *CBS Butler v Brown* was an extreme case in that the claimant sought to deprive the defendants of control over the disclosure process before it was even due to take place. Even if past deficiencies in disclosure can be shown, however, the circumstances in which such an order will be made are likely to be rare. In *Vilca v Xstrata Ltd*,[66] Foskett J did not doubt that jurisdiction existed to order a "re-review" of the defendants' disclosure to be carried out by an independent lawyer. But he held that this would be "most unusual" and would require strong grounds. A lawyer's mistaken judgment in withholding a particular document from disclosure was held not to warrant the making of such an order on the facts of *Vilca* itself.

(3) Orders for Inspection of Electronic Media

The court's power to take control of the process of disclosure has a particular   **36–040**
application in the context of electronic disclosure. As litigation lawyers know only too well, computer hard disks and other storage media contain an increasingly vast wealth of data which can be both highly portable, and difficult to access and sift for the purposes of giving standard disclosure. The requirement to serve disclosure reports and electronic documents questionnaires frequently results in the identification of particular devices on which a party's documents are stored, and with that comes the temptation for an opposing party to call for particular searches to be carried out of particular devices—or even for the devices themselves to be delivered up for inspection by an expert.

Although the court has jurisdiction to make orders for third-party inspection of   **36–041**
this type, again there are few examples of successful applications for such relief.

---

[66] *Vilca v Xstrata Ltd* [2016] EWHC 1824 (QB), at [33].

One example of the electronic disclosure process being taken out of a party's hands is *Mueller Europe Ltd v Central Roofing (South Wales) Ltd*,[67] although in that case this was not due to any deliberate breach of the relevant party's disclosure obligations but because its representative did not have the necessary expertise to carry out the search properly himself.

36-042 In *Nucleus Information Systems v Palmer*[68] Lewison J refused to order delivery up of the defendants' computers in a manner which would effectively amount to disclosure in advance of the usual timetable, and instead left it to the claimant to seek specific disclosure if the standard disclosure process was seen not to have been adequately complied with. He also considered that the order sought would involve an infringement of the defendants' right to respect for private life and correspondence under art.8 ECHR and might infringe legal professional privilege. Such considerations are particularly acute in a case where delivery up to the opposing party is sought; they may also arise where the disclosure process is to be carried out by an independent solicitor, but are likely to be more easily manageable in the latter context.[69] In two later cases, applications for delivery up of storage media for expert inspection were dismissed as premature where they were made prior to the date for standard disclosure; in both cases the door was left open for future applications if deficiencies in the standard disclosure process could be shown.[70]

(4) Preventing Reliance on Documents Disclosed Late

36-043 CPR r.31.21 provides that a party may not rely on any document which he fails to disclose or in respect of which he fails to permit inspection unless the court gives permission. The interaction of this rule with the ongoing duty of disclosure as encapsulated in CPR r.32.11 is potentially complex, not least as there may be doubt in any given case as to whether the disclosure of documents after the deadline given for standard disclosure actually amounts to a "failure" to disclose. Under CPR r.31.7 parties are only required to make a reasonable search for disclosable documents, and it is not unusual for documents to come to light (e.g. as a result of late responses to requests made of third parties) and be disclosed after the date for standard disclosure without there being any suggestion that CPR r.31.21 is engaged.[71] However, the rule may be a useful one in a fraud case, particularly where the prior failure to disclose can be demonstrated to have been deliberate. In an appropriate case the court may also exercise its powers to control

---

[67] *Mueller Europe Ltd v Central Roofing (South Wales) Ltd* [2012] EWHC 3417 (TCC); [2013] T.C.L.R. 2.

[68] *Nucleus Information Systems v Palmer* [2003] EWHC 2013 (Ch).

[69] For discussion of the way in which the court manages such issues when they arise in the analogous context of search orders, see para.30–051 onwards.

[70] *Phaestos Ltd v Ho* [2012] EWHC 2756 (QB) (at [63] in particular); and *Thomson Ecology v Apem Ltd* [2013] EWHC 2875 (Ch); [2014] I.R.L.R. 184 (at [33] in particular).

[71] In *McTear v Engelhard* [2016] EWCA Civ 487; [2016] 4 W.L.R. 108 Vos LJ held that the ongoing duty in CPR r.32.11 did not excuse the breach of a time-limited order for standard disclosure where there had been a failure to carry out a proper search: see [34] and [49].

evidence under CPR r.32.1 to prevent a party from proving by secondary evidence the contents of documents which he has failed to disclose.[72]

E.   PAYMENT INTO COURT

The court has an express power to order a payment into court where a party has, without good reason, failed to comply with a rule, practice direction or relevant pre-action protocol.[73] Whilst this specific power does not extend to breaches of court orders, in many cases where there has been a breach of a procedural order (at least one relating to case management) it will be possible to identify a correlative breach of a rule or practice direction.[74] Such an order should not be made unless there is a history of repeated breaches of timetables or of court orders, or if there is something in the conduct of the respondent which gives rise to suspicion that they may not be bona fide, and the court thinks the applicant should have some financial security or protection.[75]

36–044

---

[72] *Post Office Counters Ltd v Mahida* [2003] EWCA Civ 1583; *The Times*, October 31, 2003 (in which the power was not exercised).

[73] CPR r.3.1(5).

[74] See for example *Daraydan Holdings Ltd v Solland International Ltd* [2003] EWHC 3162 (Ch), at [36]. Obvious examples are CPR rr.31.6 and 31.8, which set out those documents which a party must disclose pursuant to a direction for standard disclosure.

[75] *Olatawura v Abiloye* [2002] EWCA Civ 998; [2003] 1 W.L.R. 275, at [25], per Simon Brown LJ, approving the decision of Buckley J in *Mealey Horgan Plc v Horgan, The Times*, 6 July 1999. For some rare examples of cases in which the power has been exercised, see *Shaw v Palmer* [2004] EWHC 388 (QB), per Newman J and *Lazari v London and Newcastle (Camden) Ltd* [2013] EWHC 97 (TCC); [2013] CP Rep. 26. An application was refused in *Al Nehayan v Kent* [2017] EWHC 1347 (Ch).

CHAPTER 37

ENFORCEMENT OF JUDGMENTS

A. Introduction

The subject of enforcement of judgments could easily fill a book in itself and indeed there are several such works.[1] This chapter is not intended to mirror the depth or breadth of such works, but focuses on some commonly-encountered issues relating to enforcement common to fraud litigation, the methods by which such judgments can be enforced and aids to execution. Part 70 of the CPR contains general rules on the enforcement of judgments.

37–001

B. Preservation of Assets

There are a number of interim orders—most notably freezing injunctions, receivership orders and orders requiring a respondent to surrender his passport—commonly made pre-judgment in fraud claims which are also available post-judgment and which may assist in preserving assets for execution.

37–002

None of the types of interim order mentioned above (and discussed in further detail below) are strictly speaking methods of enforcement, as opposed to aids to execution. However, they will often play a significant part in the claimant's attempts to enforce his judgment if satisfaction of that judgment is not readily forthcoming.[2]

37–003

Although the principles applied in the making or refusing of each of these orders are discussed in more detail below (as well as more broadly in Chs 26–33 above), it should be noted at the outset that the jurisdiction to grant each of them stems from s.37 of the Senior Courts Act, such that the ultimate touchstone for the making of such orders is that it is "just and convenient to do so".

37–004

---

[1] See for instance K. Jarvis and A. Lafferty, *Commercial Enforcement*, 2nd edn (West Sussex: Tottel, 2008).

[2] In relation to post-judgment freezing orders see *Masri v Consolidated Contractors International SAL* [2008] EWHC 2492 (Comm), at [34], per Tomlinson J.

(1)   Post-Judgment Freezing Injunction

(i)   Introduction

37–005   Of course most freezing orders are obtained at a very early stage in the proceedings and are typically granted "until judgment or further order." If the claimant with the benefit of such an order succeeds at the trial in his claim, then he will almost inevitably seek to extend the injunction post-judgment; otherwise the very purpose of obtaining the injunction pre-judgment will be likely to be thwarted. So, at the hearing handing down judgment the extension of the freezing order will usually be sought, and will usually be readily granted, the claimant having ex hypothesi been vindicated.

37–006   But it is also a common scenario that, no freezing order having been sought pre-judgment, the claimant, having succeeded at trial, becomes concerned that the defendant will now, facing a substantial judgment, seek to remove his assets out of reach of the claimant or otherwise dissipate them so as to thwart the claimant's efforts at enforcement. For instance, the court may have held that the defendant has behaved dishonestly or in a commercially improper way; or information may come to the claimant's attention about the defendant taking steps to render himself judgment-proof. The very fact of non-payment of the judgment in circumstances where the defendant should have assets to do so may trigger justified concern, such that the claimant may be galvanised into seeking injunctive relief where previously he took the view that he did not have a sufficient evidential basis to apply, or was concerned at the risk of applying (in terms of costs or liability under the cross-undertaking). After a judgment in the claimant's favour concerns about costs or liability under the cross-undertaking are likely to be of little moment. For all or any of these reasons, the claimant will then seek a freezing order, usually without notice and from the judge who has heard the trial.[3] The fact that no freezing order has been sought previously presents no bar in principle to the grant of a freezing order post-judgment.[4]

(ii)   Principles on which the Court will act

37–007   It is clearly established that the court has jurisdiction to grant injunctions, including freezing orders, post-judgment.[5] There is no difficulty in an application

---

[3] See for example *SPL Private Finance (PF1) IC Ltd v Arch Financial Products LLP* [2015] EWHC 1124 (Comm).

[4] *SPL Private Finance (PF1) IC Ltd v Arch Financial Products LLP* [2015] EWHC 1124 (Comm), at [9], per Hamblen J.

[5] *Orwell Steel v Asphalt and Tarmac* [1984] 1 W.L.R. 1097, at 1100, per Farquharson J. In *Mobile Telesystems Finance SA v Nomihold Securities Inc* [2011] EWCA Civ 1040; [2012] Bus L.R. 1166, Tomlinson LJ said at [32]: "The availability of freezing orders in aid of execution is now so well-established that I doubt whether it can still be said that the circumstances in which such a freezing order can properly be granted must be rare."

for injunctive relief and taking steps to execute the judgment existing side by side: the freezing order has the effect of preserving the defendant's assets until execution can be levied upon them.[6]

The basis upon which a post-judgment freezing injunction is granted is essentially the same as that on which a pre-judgment freezing order is granted, namely to prevent a party from frustrating an order of the court by dissipating assets or moving them outside the jurisdiction (or otherwise secreting them) beyond the reach of a judgment creditor, such that they remain amenable to execution[7]:   **37–008**

> "Indeed, in one sense it could be said that there is greater justification for restraining a defendant from disposing of his assets after judgment than before any claim has been established against him."[8]

A post-judgment freezing injunction may be made in support of an order for the payment of a sum of money, whether damages or costs, and whether assessed or not.[9] Equally the fact that a stay of execution may have been ordered pending an appeal does not prevent a freezing order being made.[10] Essentially any order of the court which creates a pecuniary liability in favour of a party could in theory support a post-judgment freezing injunction. Whether to grant a freezing injunction is a matter for the discretion of the court and, subject to the points below, the basic test for granting such relief post-judgment is substantially the same as the test for granting an interim freezing injunction.   **37–009**

As to the principles to be applied when the court is asked to make a post-judgment freezing order, the following factors are relevant: **37–010**

(1)   First, the court will more readily grant a freezing injunction as an aid to enforcement of a judgment that has been entered than on an interim application.[11] There is a clear and principled basis for this distinction. At an interim stage, the claimant has yet to establish the defendant's liability and must show a good arguable case. A judgment creditor has of course

---

[6] *Orwell Steel v Asphalt and Tarmac*, above, at 1100, per Farquharson J, referring to Stewart *Chartering Ltd v C & O Managements SA* [1980] 1 W.L.R. 460.

[7] The principle is the same whether the defendant's liability is potential or actual, although an order may be easier to obtain in the latter case than the former; see para.37–010 below.

[8] *Orwell Steel v Asphalt and Tarmac* above at 1100, per Farquharson J.

[9] *Jet West Ltd v Haddican* above at 490E [1952] 1 W.L.R. 487, per Lord Donaldson. "Where you have someone who is already subject to a money judgment, including an order for costs, the same principle applies, namely that the courts will not allow people to set their orders at nought simply by removing assets from the jurisdiction ... a Mareva injunction can be granted or can be continued in support of any judgment or order of the court for the payment of money, whether or not the exact sum which will be payable has been quantified at the date of the order and the date at which the Mareva injunction is sought." In that case the defendant successfully obtained a freezing order in support of an unassessed costs order in its favour.

[10] *SPL Private Finance (PF1) IC Ltd v Arch Financial Products LLP* [2015] EWHC 1124 (Comm), at [13]–[14], per Hamblen J.

[11] *Babanaft International Co S.A. v Bassatne* [1990] Ch. 13, at 37, per Kerr LJ; *Republic of Haiti v Duvalier* [1990] 1 Q.B. 202, at 214, per Staughton LJ.

established such a case and so the order is made in support of an actual liability rather than merely a potential one.

(2)   Secondly, it is sufficient for the grant of relief that there is a real risk that the judgment will remain unsatisfied if injunctive relief is refused.[12] The test is substantially identical in terms of risk of dissipation to that applied at the interim stage.[13] However, although it may not be sufficient for a claimant merely to point to a finding of dishonesty in order to establish such a risk, a claimant who has successfully made out a case in fraud against a defendant starts from a strong position in trying to persuade the court that there is a risk of future steps being taken to frustrate the judgment.[14] Not only has dishonesty been established but the defendant could be said to be rather more incentivised to dissipate his assets given the existence of a judgment rather than simply the assertion of an as yet undetermined claim.

(3)   Thirdly, the court will be far less concerned with issues relating to the supposed harm that a freezing order might cause to the defendant. We have seen in Ch.28 that, at the interim stage, such considerations can weigh against the grant of a freezing order. Thus, for example, the Court will be less likely to make allowances for payments in the ordinary course of business in circumstances where the liability of the subject to the injunction has been determined than where it is yet to be determined.[15]

(4)   Fourthly, the injunction must be sought for a legitimate purpose (namely the process of ultimate collection of the debt) and there must therefore be some prospect that the injunction will aid the judgment creditor in execution (as opposed to place illegitimate pressure on him).[16] If therefore there are simply no assets available against which to execute or the claimant can be shown to have no intention of executing the judgment within a reasonable period of time, the court may decline to grant a freezing injunction or, if already granted, discharge it.

---

[12] *Ketchum International Plc v Group Public Relations Holdings Ltd* [1997] 1 W.L.R. 4, CA, approved in *Masri v Consolidated Contractors International SAL* [2008] EWCA Civ 288, at [134], per Lawrence Collins LJ (and see also *Masri v Consolidated Contractors International SAL* [2008] EWHC 2492 (Comm), at [34]), per Tomlinson J.

[13] See for example *SPL Private Finance (PF1) IC Ltd v Arch Financial Products LLP*, above, at [10]–[11], per Hamblen J, where authorities on the risk of dissipation as applied at the interim stage were referred to in the context of an assessment of that risk post-judgment.

[14] See for instance *SPL Private Finance (PF1) IC Ltd v Arch Financial Products LLP*, above, at [17]–[20], per Hamblen J, where the court (having previously noted at [11] that findings of dishonesty must be scrutinised in each case) held that the findings contained in the judgment provided "a strong basis for the claimant's case that it would be appropriate to draw the inference that there is in this case a real risk of dissipation."

[15] See *Soinco SACI v Novokuznetsk Aluminium Plant* [1998] Q.B. 406, per Colman J at 421. This was a receivership case; but the observations were said to be applicable a fortiori in a post-judgment freezing order case in *Masri v CCIC* [2008] EWHC 2492 (Comm), at [35], per Tomlinson J.

[16] *Camdex International Ltd v Bank of Zambia (2)* [1997] 1 W.L.R. 632 provides a good example. See also *Masri v Consolidated Contractors International SAL* [2008] EWHC 2492 (Comm), at [34], per Tomlinson J.

(iii)   The duration of a post-judgment freezing order

A freezing injunction, even post-judgment, remains a potential tool of oppression   **37–011**
and even if properly granted is likely to have a significant effect on a judgment
debtor, whether individual or corporate. These are matters that the court will take
into account in the grant or continuation of a freezing injunction post-judgment
though they will inevitably carry less weight than at the pre-judgment stage.
Pre-judgment, a freezing order will typically be made "until trial or further
order." By contrast, post-judgment there is no defined future event which can
delimit the duration of the freezing order. Post-judgment the freezing order's
purpose will potentially last as long as the judgment debt remains unpaid, which
is generally an undefinable time period.

Although in *Republic of Haiti v Duvalier*[17] Staughton LJ had, obiter, suggested   **37–012**
that post-judgment freezing orders should remain in place for only a "limited
duration", because the claimant should be "encouraged to proceed with proper
methods of execution", the modern practice is rather more flexible, recognising
the practical reality of the difficulties which can be encountered by claimants in
seeking to enforce judgments worldwide. In one recent case[18] a freezing order
was granted six years after the entry of judgment and after ineffectual attempts to
enforce had been made in various jurisdictions. Contrary to the defendant's
submissions that the freezing order should be for a short defined period, it was
ordered to remain in place "until payment of the judgment debt or further order in
the meanwhile." That was a case where the defendant had assets located in
jurisdictions where enforcement had either so far proved, or (in the case of one
jurisdiction) was in fact, impossible and was simply refusing to pay the judgment
debt. The court accepted that

> "if the situation changes, if there is a prospect of the defendant showing that it is being
> maintained for an illegitimate purpose, then, no doubt, the position can be reconsidered at that
> time";

although, given the defendant's stance, it is difficult to envisage the circumstances where a court might have entertained such an application.[19] On the other
hand if a defendant were able to show that it simply had no assets to meet the
judgment debt then an indefinite freezing order would be unlikely to be
maintained, because it would not assist in the ultimate collection of the debt.[20]

(iv)   The terms of a post-judgment freezing order

The ordinary course of business exception which is generally included in   **37–013**
pre-judgment freezing orders[21] will not usually be justified post-judgment.
However, where there is an appeal outstanding the question of whether or not it is

---

[17] *Republic of Haiti v Duvalier* [1988] 1 Q.B. 202, at 214, per Staughton LJ.
[18] *Touton Far East Ltd v Shivnath Rai Harnarain (India) Ltd* [2016] EWHC 1765 (Comm).
[19] *Touton Far East Ltd v Shivnath Rai Harnarain (India) Ltd*, at [3], per Males J.
[20] *Masri v Consolidated Contractors International SAL* [2008] EWHC 2492 (Comm), at [34], per
Tomlinson LJ.
[21] See Ch.32, para.32–047 and following.

appropriate to maintain that exception may be a nuanced one.[22] Similarly it may be inappropriate for the legal costs and living expenses exceptions to continue.[23] But if the defendant is seeking to appeal the decision then it would very rarely be appropriate (certainly if permission to appeal has been given) to grant a freezing order which prevents it using its assets to pay its legal costs of mounting that appeal.

37–014   There has been some doubt about whether a cross-undertaking in damages is required to be proffered when a post-judgment freezing order is obtained. It has been suggested in the past[24] that it is not usual to make such an order, but in *Nomihold Securites Inc v Mobile Telesystems Finance SA*[25] the judge expressed the view, without reference to authority, that in post-judgment cases it was

> "always appropriate to give a cross-undertaking in damages but that it would be most unusual to have to fortify such cross-undertaking, however poor or unwell-heeled the Claimant is, where it is owed a substantial sum of money under the judgment because there may be circumstances in which, albeit that a judgment debt is owed and is unpaid, the effects of a freezing order, particularly a worldwide freezing order, may be overly damaging and overly prejudicial and that even if, at the end of the day, the judgment is paid up, there may fall to be set off some damage which is shown to have flowed as a result of the inappropriate obtaining of the freezing order".[26]

37–015   It is submitted that this is the correct view, although there will in practice be very few cases where it would be appropriate to order an inquiry under the cross-undertaking, unless the defendant successfully appeals the underlying decision. It is nonetheless possible that a freezing injunction sought for the first time post-judgment could be wrongly granted (even in cases where there is no appeal). For example, a judgment creditor might attempt, wrongly, to apply for a freezing injunction in order to obtain illegitimate leverage through the reputational or commercial damage it causes the judgment debtor; or he could mislead the court by falsifying or overstating evidence as to the risk of dissipation. Though such circumstances will be rare, there is no reason the judgment debtor should not be protected by the usual cross-undertaking (certainly

[22] See *Soinco v Novokuznetsk Aluminium Plant*, above, at 421, per Colman J; *Masri v Consolidated Contractors International SAL* [2008] EWHC 2492 (Comm), at [35], per Tomlinson J; *Mobile Telesystems Finance SA v Nomihold Securities Inc* [2011] EWCA Civ 1040; [2012] Bus L.R. 1166, at [33]–[34], per Tomlinson LJ.
[23] In *One Life Ltd v Roy* Court of Appeal (Civ Div) Transcript No.128 of 1997 (30 January 1997) the Court of Appeal accepted that where a tracing claim had been upheld by the judge it would no longer be appropriate for there to be a living expenses exception: the money no longer belonged to the defendant.
[24] See *Gwembe Valley Development Co Ltd v Koshy, The Times*, 28 February 2002, per Rimer J, where in fact an undertaking was required in circumstances where the defendant was given permission to appeal in relation to the decision to grant the injunction itself.
[25] *Nomihold Securites Inc v Mobile Telesystems Finance SA* [2011] EWHC 337 (Comm).
[26] *Nomihold Securites Inc v Mobile Telesystems Finance SA*, at [24], per Burton J. See also the well-known Australian case of *Cardile v LED Builders PTY Ltd* [1999] HCA 18; 198 C.L.R. 380, at [44] for support for the proposition that an undertaking in damages should be required post-judgment. In the recent decision in *Kazakhstan Kagazy Plc v Baglan Abdullayevich Zhunus* [2018] EWHC 369 (Comm) Picken J followed *Nomihold* and required at [146], the continuation of the cross-undertaking in a post-judgment case "until such time as the [defendants'] application to permission to appeal has been determined by the Court of Appeal".

at the without notice stage). Fortification will not generally be required as the judgment sum will stand as fortification[27] and so the burden of giving the cross-undertaking on the applicant is not a heavy one.

Less controversially, an applicant for a post-judgment freezing injunction will (except in exceptional cases) have to give the usual cross-undertaking to protect third parties affected by the order.[28]

37–016

(v) Disclosure orders

Disclosure orders ancillary to an interim freezing injunction can equally be made in support of a post-judgment freezing injunction, to assist the judgment creditor in identifying assets of the judgment debtor and policing the terms of the freezing injunction.[29] See Chs 28 and 29 above for a general discussion of the principles relating to disclosure orders ancillary to freezing orders. However, as we discuss below, the court's jurisdiction to order disclosure against a defendant is wider post-judgment.

37–017

(2) Appointment of Receiver to Preserve Assets

As we have seen in Ch.33 above, the court has power to appoint a receiver at any time, whether before proceedings have started, during the course of proceedings or after judgment.[30] A receiver may have two roles which are relevant for present purposes: he may be appointed to protect assets pending enforcement action or he may be appointed by way of equitable execution to bring in assets to satisfy an outstanding judgment.

37–018

The practice and procedure for the appointment of receivers has already been considered in detail.[31] There is no substantive difference in the post-judgment setting: the court has the same jurisdiction to appoint a receiver at either stage, that is when it is "just and convenient" to do so.[32]

37–019

Although, as with freezing orders, the court will be more inclined to make an order in favour of a judgment creditor than a pre-judgment claimant, in essence the test for when it is appropriate to appoint a receiver for the purposes of asset

37–020

---

[27] See e.g. *Kazakhstan Kagazy Plc v Baglan Abdullayevich Zhunus* [2018] EWHC 369 (Comm), per Picken J at [148].

[28] *Banco Nacional de Comercia Exterior SNC v Emprese de Telecommunicationes de Cuba SA* [2007] EWCA Civ 662; [2008] 1 W.L.R. 1936, CA at [38]–[43], per Tuckey LJ.

[29] *JSC VTB Bank v Skurikhin* [2012] EWHC 3116 (Comm). The court is likely to be more willing after judgment to require documentary disclosure concerning assets, or potential assets: see for instance *Kazakhstan Kagazy Plc v Baglan Abdullayevich Zhunus* [2018] EWHC 369 (Comm), per Picken J at [173]–[183], where disclosure of documents relating to a discretionary trust of which the defendant was a beneficiary was ordered to allow the judgment creditor to investigate the position.

[30] CPR 69.2.

[31] Ch.33, paras 33–022—33–045.

[32] The interests of justice are paramount in the exercise of the court's discretion; this is the "overriding consideration" in the exercise of the court's power under s.37 of the Senior Courts Act 1981; see *Masri v Consolidated Contractors International Ltd* [2008] EWCA Civ 303; [2009] Q.B. 450, at [183], per Lawrence Collins LJ.

preservation post-judgment or continuing an interim receivership will be the same as at the interim stage. If the court is persuaded that other relief, such as a prohibitive injunction or a freezing order, offers insufficient protection to the judgment creditor, then a receivership will be ordered on such terms as the court sees as necessary to provide adequate protection.

(3)   Writ Ne Exeat Regno/Passport Order

37–021   With the continuing growth of international fraud claims litigated in the English court, orders preventing parties from leaving the jurisdiction or compelling them to hand over their passports have become more common, particularly at the interim stage. We have considered both forms of order referred to in the heading at Ch.31 above.

37–022   The more draconian *writ ne exeat regno*[33] is only available as an interim remedy. One of the requirements of the writ is that the apprehended departure from the jurisdiction by the subject of the writ might materially prejudice the claimant in pursuing his claim. Enforcement of a successful claim does not fall within that definition and so the right to such relief ends on judgment.[34] By contrast, a passport order, otherwise known as a "*Bayer v Winter*" order, is available pre- or post-judgment and may restrain a respondent from leaving the jurisdiction and require him to hand over his passports or other travel documents pending some future event,[35] such as attending court for examination or complying with an order for disclosure.[36] However, the order will only extend for as long as is necessary to serve its purpose. Such an order is needless to say invasive and oppressive in its nature, restricting the freedom of movement of a litigant. A court will not make an order without limit of time, simply as a goad to payment of the judgment debt.

37–023   A passport order may be made against the judgment debtor himself or a non-party in support of or to assist in the enforcement of another order of the court which has been made to assist in enforcement of the judgment. An example of a non-party against whom such an order may be obtained is an officer of a corporate body against whom an order for cross-examination and production of documents may be sought under Pt 71 of the CPR. This is considered further below.[37] Disclosure orders in support of a post-judgment freezing injunction or a free-standing post-judgment disclosure order may similarly be supported by a passport order. However, whether against a party or non-party, it must be shown that the interference is necessary for the implementation of the Court's order,[38] and such orders will naturally be more unusual as against a non-party.

37–024   An order for delivery up of a respondent's passport may be further supported by a tipstaff order, permitting the tipstaff to enter into the respondent's premises to

---

[33] Considered at Ch.31, paras 31–041—31–046.
[34] *Lipman Gorman v Cass*, The Times, 29 May 1985.
[35] *B v B (Injunction: Restraint on Leaving Jurisdiction)* [1998] 1 W.L.R. 329.
[36] *Robinson v Robinson* [2003] EWHC 2473 (Ch).
[37] See *Kuwait Airways Corp v Iraq Airways Co* [2010] EWCA Civ 741.
[38] *In Re B* [1994] 2 F.L.R. 479, at 488, per Hobhouse LJ.

collect passports or other travel documents.[39] This represents a still greater imposition on the respondent, since the tipstaff's powers include the powers of arrest, entry and seizure. A respondent could find himself in the situation that, without first being afforded the opportunity to take legal advice, he is faced with an order obtained without notice requiring him to hand over his passport with immediate imprisonment the consequence of failing to comply.

It is clear that such concerns weighed heavily on the court in the case of *Kuwait Airways Corp v Iraq Airways Co*[40] arising out of the misappropriation of the Kuwaiti airline's fleet by Iraq Airways on the invasion of Kuwait in 1991. The judge at first instance initially made an order against the respondent Director General of Iraq Airways preventing him from leaving the jurisdiction until he had sworn an affidavit of disclosure of the defendant debtor company's assets and requiring him to hand over his passport and requiring the tipstaff to attend on him to obtain and hold his passport. Part of the basis of the order was that, as an officer of a judgment debtor, the respondent could be subject to an application under Pt 71, though the judge was astute to avoid allowing the order sought to circumvent the restrictions imposed by the Pt 71 procedure.

37–025

However, concerns over the order as an exercise in discretion (albeit not as to jurisdiction) caused the judge first to put a hold on service of the order and then later to revoke the prohibition on leaving the jurisdiction, the requirement to hand over passports and the involvement of the tipstaff, though the disclosure order was left in place.[41] Concerns in particular about the possibility of immediate arrest without the opportunity to take legal advice, against a foreign national temporarily in the jurisdiction whose understanding of the order was uncertain, represented, in the judge's view, an unacceptable infringement on the rights of the respondent who had not himself breached any orders and was not a party to the proceedings.

37–026

The Court of Appeal allowed the appeal against the later revocation of the passport and tipstaff orders. While acknowledging that there were powerful competing arguments, the court was persuaded by three factors in particular. First, because the matter was at an ex-parte stage, the applicant needed only to show a good arguable case for the orders.[42] Secondly, while there was a risk to the respondent's liberty, this was an acceptable risk and could be managed to reduce it still further,[43] for example by ensuring that the respondent be brought before the Court swiftly in the event of his detention. Thirdly, there was a risk that absent the passport and tipstaff orders, the disclosure order, which had not been revoked, would be left futile.[44]

37–027

---

[39] *Kuwait Airways Corp v Iraq Airways Co* [2010] EWCA Civ 741.

[40] *Kuwait Airways Corp v Iraq Airways Co* [2010] EWCA Civ 741.

[41] *Kuwait Airways Corp v Iraq Airways Co*, at [19], per Rix LJ.

[42] *Kuwait Airways Corp v Iraq Airways Co*, at [41], per Rix LJ.

[43] *Kuwait Airways Corp v Iraq Airways Co*, at [47]–[49], per Wilson LJ and [60], per Sir David Keene.

[44] *Kuwait Airways Corp v Iraq Airways Co* per Rix LJ at [32], [40], per Wilson LJ at [51], [55], and per Sir David Keene at [58] and [62].

37–028 In the case of a post-judgment passport order, particularly in a fraud context, the most likely purpose will be to allow the claimant to serve an order for examination under Pt 71 and for the examination to take place, preventing a judgment debtor from leaving the jurisdiction and thereby escaping the consequences of an order. Once any relevant enforcement procedures have been concluded or exhausted, there is no basis for continuation of the order.[45] As we have mentioned above, a judgment debtor cannot be confined in the jurisdiction until such time as he pays a judgment debt. Such an order would represent a partial return to the position before the passing of the Debtors Act 1869 as regards the law of imprisonment for debt.

C. OBTAINING INFORMATION TO ASSIST IN ENFORCEMENT

37–029 Succeeding at trial in a fraud claim is often merely winning half the battle. The process of identifying and enforcing the judgment against assets belonging to or controlled by the defendant may itself be (and in fraud cases often is) a major undertaking. The fraudulent defendant is likely to have taken steps to hide away his assets against precisely such an eventuality. We consider below two mechanisms available to the judgment creditor, and often deployed in fraud claims, to obtain information about the identity and location of such assets.

(1) CPR Part 71

37–030 CPR Pt 71 provides a mechanism by which a judgment debtor (or officer of a judgment debtor if a corporate entity)[46] may be subject to an order for production of documents and for examination by or before the court as to the nature and extent of his (or the company's) means, and any other matter about which information is needed to assist in enforcing the judgment. It is potentially a very useful tool both in terms of extracting information pertaining to enforcement and as leverage against the recalcitrant judgment debtor. Many litigants would not relish the prospect of wide-ranging cross-examination under oath as to their assets.[47]

(i) Summary of provisions

37–031 CPR 71.2 provides:

> "(1) A judgment creditor may apply for an order requiring –
> (a) a judgment debtor; or
> (b) if a judgment debtor is a company or other corporation, an officer of that body,
> to attend court to provide information about –
> (i) the judgment debtor's means; or

---

[45] *B v B (Injunction)* [1998] 1 W.L.R. 329, at 334, per Wilson J.

[46] This includes a former officer: see below.

[47] "Examination under CPR 71 is intended to be a summary and straightforward process allowing the judgment creditor to obtain information from the judgment debtor for the purpose of being better able to decide which method or methods of enforcement to use, whether sequentially or simultaneously": *Deutsche Bank AG v Sebastian Holdings Inc* [2015] EWHC 2773 (QB), at [33], per Cooke J.

       (ii)   any other matter about which information is needed to enforce a judgment or order. "

The ambit of a Pt 71 order can therefore be extremely wide, going not only to the amount of the debtor's means but also the nature and location of those assets, or any other information which may assist in enforcement. For obvious reasons, a court is likely to take an expansive approach to the interpretation of its jurisdiction.   **37–032**

An order can be made against an individual debtor or, if the debtor is a company or other corporate body, an officer of that entity. The category of "officers" is wider than simply the company's current directors or company secretary and includes former officers of the company, provided that they may be in position to provide relevant information or documents.[48]   **37–033**

An application for an order under Pt 71 is not in itself a method of enforcement, as is expressly stated in the rule: rather it is "for the purpose of enabling a judgment creditor to enforce a judgment or order against him."[49] Accordingly, such an order can be pursued even if there is a stay of enforcement of the proceedings,[50] and there is no requirement, before Pt 71 can be engaged, that a debtor be in breach of an order to pay (for example if payment by instalments is ordered, an order can be sought even if no instalment has yet fallen due).   **37–034**

(ii)   *Procedure on application*

An application under Pt 71 may be made without notice[51] and, if an order is obtained,[52] the subject of the order must attend court as specified in the order, produce such documents as are described in the order and answer "such questions as the court may require."[53]   **37–035**

The application should be made in the same court where the judgment or order was made, unless proceedings have been transferred for the purposes of enforcement.   **37–036**

The application notice must contain the information prescribed in r.71.2(3) and in PD 71 para.1.2. If the formal requirements are met, an order under r.71 will generally be granted[54] (though it seems that there are limited circumstances where the court may decline to make an order even where the requirements are   **37–037**

---

[48] *Société Générale du Commerce et de l'Industrie en France v Johann Maria Farina & Co* [1904] 1 K.B. 794.

[49] CPR 71.1.

[50] *Sucden Financial Ltd v Fluxo-Cane Overseas Ltd* [2009] EWHC 3555 (QB).

[51] Practice Direction 71 sets out the procedural requirements. We do not go into them in detail here. See generally "The White Book" (Sir Geoffrey Vos (editor-in-chief), *Civil Procedure*, 2018 edn (London: Sweet & Maxwell, 2018)).

[52] And subject to the respondent's right to set it aside if made without notice.

[53] CPR 71.2(6).

[54] S. Payne and M. Godden, *Commercial Enforcement* (London: Bloomsbury Professional, 2005) at [2.145].

met).[55] The order will require attendance at court at a specified time and date and may also require the respondent to bring specified documents or categories of document.[56] Clearly the ambit of any document production order is open to debate (and potential challenge if obtained without notice) as to whether it falls within the ambit of r.71.2(b). No doubt an order which would involve the production of very large quantities of documents of doubtful relevance could be open to attack on grounds of (dis)-proportionality or oppression, as well as relevance.

(iii)   Subject matter of an order

37–038   The ambit of Pt 71 extends to overseas assets, and respondents may be compelled to produce documents and/or answer questions in respect of such.[57] However the principle of extraterritoriality still applies to the extent that individuals (whether judgment debtors or officers of a company) outside the jurisdiction at the time of the application and the order cannot be subject to an order under Pt 71.[58] But a foreign director who is temporarily, even "fleetingly", within the jurisdiction may be the subject of an order under Pt 71,[59] although care must be taken in making an order against a non-resident even if he is within the jurisdiction. For this reason, as we have seen, a passport order is often a useful precursor to an application for an order under Pt 71. An order cannot be made in support of foreign proceedings.

(iv)   Order for examination and production of documents

37–039   Service of the order under Pt 71 must be effected personally on the respondent, no less than 14 days prior to the date of the examination.[60] It is crucial that the order is served properly, otherwise breach of the order will not be a contempt of court and much of its efficacy will be lost.[61]

37–040   A degree of cooperation is required from respondents in order for a Pt 71 examination to be truly effective, at least for its primary purpose of assisting the process of enforcement. As considered below, however, failure to comply carries a range of sanctions which provide powerful motivation for respondents to comply.

---

[55] See for instance in the context of parties not resident in the jurisdiction *Deutsche Bank AG v Sebastian Holdings Inc* [2015] EWHC 2773, at [27]–[28], per Cooke J; *CIMC Raffles Offshore (Singapore) Pte Ltd v Schahin Holding SA (Rev 1)* [2014] EWHC 1742 (Comm), at [25], per Field J.

[56] *Mubarak v Mubarak* [2002] EWHC 2171 (Fam); [2002] 2 F.L.R. 553, at 559, per Hughes J.

[57] *Interpool Ltd v Galani* [1988] Q.B. 738.

[58] *Masri v Consolidated Contractors International Ltd* [2010] 1 A.C. 90, where it was held that an application and order under Pt 71 could not be made against a director of a judgment creditor who was outside the jurisdiction. In *CIMC Raffles Offshore (Singapore) PTE Ltd v Schahim Holdings SA* [2014] EWHC 1742 (Comm) Field J accepted the submissions of counsel that no order could be made under Pt 71 if the individual to be subject to the order was outside the jurisdiction *either* at the time when the application was made or at the time when the order was made. Subsequent service of the order when the respondent is in the jurisdiction will not suffice.

[59] *Deutsche Bank AG v Sebastian Holdings Inc* [2015] EWHC 2773 (QB).

[60] CPR 71.3.

[61] *Beeston Shipping Ltd v Babanaft International SA (The Eastern Venture)* [1985] 1 All E.R. 923.

In simple cases, the examination under Pt 71 may be conducted by a court officer; that is the default position unless the court orders otherwise.[62] To order otherwise requires compelling reasons, but in complex cases, and therefore in most fraud cases, the court will readily order otherwise and the examination will be conducted by the applicant's legal advisers before a Master or Judge.[63]   **37–041**

Even if conducted by the applicant rather than a court officer, the scope of the questioning remains a matter for the Court; the examination remains an examination "by" the Court.[64] Hence the Court can intervene to disallow a question if it goes beyond the ambit of Pt 71. In most cases falling within the ambit of this book the respondent will be legally represented and his lawyer will no doubt be astute to ensure that questions do not extend beyond the proper bounds of r.71.2(1)(b), as quoted above, or into matters of legal professional privilege. The respondent may wish to assert his privilege against self-incrimination.   **37–042**

However, the authorities are clear that a respondent to a Pt 71 order is subject to what is in effect cross-examination, under oath,[65] and often a rigorous one at that. The questions that can be asked can be expected to be "severe and testing".[66] So while the court retains control over the examination, in practice, the applicant will be given a substantial degree of leeway in questioning the respondent.   **37–043**

The court can if necessary adjourn an examination once it has commenced and require the production of further documents at a subsequent examination.[67] The power to do so reduces the possibility of a respondent being able to frustrate the aim of the examination by claiming he is unable to answer a particular question or would need to refer to a particular document. In the event of such an adjournment, the applicant must also serve the amended order with the new date for the production of documents and new date for the further examination.[68]   **37–044**

(v) Compliance

Failure to comply with an order under Pt 71 is a contempt of court, subject to the usual sanctions for contempt[69]; and in this context, failure to comply encompasses not attending court as ordered, failing to provide documents as ordered or failing or refusing to answer questions during the examination (or to take the oath).   **37–045**

On any failure to comply with an order under r.71.2, or to answer any question posed, the court will refer the matter to a High Court Judge.[70] The Judge may   **37–046**

---

[62] CPR 71.6(2).
[63] *Mubarak v Mubarak* above at 559, per Hughes J.
[64] *Mubarak v Mubarak*, above, at 561, per Hughes J.
[65] CPR 71.6.
[66] *Mubarak v Mubarak*, above, at 560, per Hughes J, citing *The Republic of Costa Rica v Strousberg* (1880) 16 Ch. D. 8, at 12, per Jessel MR.
[67] See for example *Mubarak v Mubarak*, above, at 560.
[68] *Beeston Shipping Ltd v Babanaft International SA (The Eastern Venture)* [1985] 1 All E.R. 923.
[69] CPR 71.8. In complex cases the procedure for committal under Pt 81 of the CPR should be used; see *Vik v Deutsche Bank AG* [2018] EWCA Civ 2011.
[70] CPR 71.8.

make a committal order against the respondent provided that, in the case of a respondent ordered to attend court for examination who has failed to comply with that order:

(i) the order for the respondent to attend court or provide documents must have been served personally on the respondent no less than 14 days before the hearing[71] and,

(ii) if the respondent has so requested, the applicant has paid his travelling expenses to and from court. The applicant must file affidavit evidence confirming that these steps have been taken.

37–047 A defaulting respondent will in effect be afforded a second opportunity to comply with the order to attend court or to produce documents or answer questions: r.71.8(4) provides that a committal order will be suspended and on terms that the respondent attend court at a specified time and place and comply with all the terms of the original order. Further default will result in the respondent being brought before the court to consider whether to discharge the committal order.[72]

37–048 It is not unusual for a respondent to allege that he is unable to comply, in particular regarding the provision of documents. A respondent alleging that a document is not within his control because it belongs to a third party will have to persuade the court that he has no "real say" as to whether or not to produce the document.[73] However, the court is likely to view such allegations with scepticism in the case of a respondent who has been found liable for fraud or fraudulent conduct. There are many instances where, for example, a respondent alleges that documents are not within his control, pointing to a trust structure or arrangement using offshore corporate vehicles of which he is not the apparent owner. Due to the preponderance of such arrangements in fraud cases, a judge may well conclude that notwithstanding the formal ownership structure, an inference should be drawn that in reality the documents are under the effective control of the respondent. Such a determination may also act as a useful precursor to a future attempt by the claimant to execute against the assets of the trust or corporate structure; a finding by a Judge that the defendant had de facto control over the documents can only assist in any future claim.

(vi) Benefits of part 71 order

37–049 The benefits to a judgment creditor of an order under Pt 71 are clear. First, it may produce useful information as to the extent, nature and location of a judgment debtor's assets which may ultimately be amendable to enforcement. Secondly, it allows an opportunity for wide-ranging and robust cross-examination on the

---

[71] CPR 71.3.

[72] As to the position of committal proceedings against a respondent out of the jurisdiction see *Deutsche Bank AG v Sebastian Holdings Inc* [2016] EWHC 3222 (Comm); [2017] 1 W.L.R. 1842 and *Deutsche Bank AG v Vik* [2017] EWHC 459 (Comm).

[73] *North Shore Ventures Ltd v Anstead Holdings Inc* [2012] EWCA Civ 11, at [35]–[40], per Toulson LJ.

debtor's assets, with the threat of committal of contempt for failing to answer questions. The very making of the order will in many cases persuade a judgment debtor to pay up.

(2) Disclosure orders

As noted above, the court has the power to make a disclosure order ancillary to a post-judgment freezing injunction to aid in enforcement; in principle, the court could just as readily make a disclosure order ancillary to a receivership order or any other order made for asset preservation purposes.

37–050

However, whereas at the pre-trial stage, the court will usually only order disclosure of assets limited to the ambit of the freezing order granted,[74] post-judgment the position is different. At this stage the court's jurisdiction to order disclosure is not limited to orders ancillary to freezing or receivership orders. Instead the court has a "free-standing" jurisdiction to make an order for disclosure in aid of enforcement under s.37 of the Senior Courts Act 1981,[75] on the grounds that it is

37–051

> "just and convenient that the judgment or award creditor should normally have all the information he needs to execute the judgment or award anywhere in the world".[76]

As Millett J held in *Maclaine Watson & Co Ltd v International Tin Council (No.2)*:[77]

> "It is, however, fallacious to reason from the fact that an order for discovery can be made as ancillary to a *Mareva* injunction to the conclusion that it cannot be made except as ancillary to such an injunction. The source of the jurisdiction is the same, and so is the ground for exercising it, viz. that it appears to the court to be just and convenient to do so ... In the present case the order sought may properly be said to be sought in aid of or for the purpose of implementing the judgment previously obtained by the applicants. It is, within proper limits, the policy of these courts to prevent a defendant from removing its assets from the jurisdiction or concealing them within it, so as to deny a successful plaintiff the fruits of his judgment. This is the policy which underlies the *Mareva* jurisdiction, before and after judgment, pre-trial discovery of assets in aid of the *Mareva* jurisdiction and Order 48.[78] That policy can only be given effect if a defendant can be ordered when necessary to provide information about the nature and whereabouts of its assets. It can only be given effect in the present case if the court has power to make the order sought."

So, in *Gidrxslme Shipping Co Ltd v Tantomar-Transportes Maritimos* [79] the Court granted a disclosure order in favour of the claimant requiring the defendant

37–052

---

[74] *A.J. Bekhor & Co Ltd v Bilton* [1981] Q.B. 923; *Ashtiani v Kashi* [1987] Q.B. 888; and *Derby & Co Ltd v Weldon (Nos. 3 and 4)* [1990] Ch. 65.

[75] *Vitol SA v Capri Marine Ltd (No.2)* [2010] EWHC 458 (Comm), at [37], per Tomlinson J.

[76] *Gidrxslme Shipping Co Ltd v Tantomar-Transportes Maritimos LDA* [1995] 1 W.L.R. 299, at 312F, per Colman J.

[77] *Maclaine Watson & Co Ltd v International Tin Council (No. 2)* [1987] 1 W.L.R. 1711, at 1716–1717, per Millett J. This conclusion was upheld in the Court of Appeal [1989] Ch. 286, where Kerr LJ said at 301, that it was the "policy of the law to assist persons in the position of the plaintiffs to obtain the fruits of their judgments."

[78] Now CPR Pt 71.

[79] *Gidrxslme Shipping Co Ltd v Tantomar-Transportes Maritimos* [1995] 1 W.L.R. 299.

to disclose its assets worldwide even though the existing freezing order was confined to assets within the jurisdiction. Colman J interpreted the decision in *Maclaine* as having propounded a principle that where a judgment has been obtained there was jurisdiction (deriving from s.37 of the Senior Courts Act 1981) to order that the judgment debtor should disclose his assets both outside as well as inside the jurisdiction. Such an order can be made in aid of execution, even if there is no freezing order in aid of execution. The judge went on to distinguish pre-judgment freezing order cases, where the jurisdiction to order disclosure was usually properly to be exercised as being ancillary to the freezing order:

> "Where, by contrast, one has the position that a judgment has been already obtained or an award made and where a *Mareva* injunction in aid of execution is justified, the jurisdiction to make a disclosure order arises both as a power ancillary to and in support of the injunction and independently of the injunction as a power in support of the execution of the judgment or award. It follows that, whereas it may on the facts of the case in question be inappropriate to extend the *Mareva* injunction to assets outside the jurisdiction — and it is clear from the two authorities cited that such extensions are likely to be rarely justified — very different considerations may apply to disclosure orders in aid of execution. That being so, there is, in my judgment, a very firm jurisdictional basis for an order, made post-judgment or post-award, which includes both a *Mareva* injunction confined to assets within the jurisdiction and a disclosure order in respect of worldwide assets."[80]

37–053   This jurisdiction may serve as a less intrusive, less costly and potentially less cumbersome alternative to an order under Pt 71 of the CPR. No examination is required; the jurisdiction to order disclosure is independent of any other order the court may make (or may have made). The procedural safeguards of CPR Pt 71 are also absent, which may result in judgment creditors obtaining information necessary or useful for enforcement more swiftly than by proceedings under Pt 71.

D. EXECUTION

37–054   This section is not intended to cover direct enforcement taken against a defendant or assets admitted as being within a defendant's ownership. The standard methods of execution are considered in CPR Pt 70 and its accompanying practice direction and are not particular to fraud claims. This section considers the situation, typical in fraud claims, where ownership of the assets by the defendant is disputed or is otherwise unclear.

(1) Assets Directly Held by Third Parties

37–055   At the interim stage, it is relatively common in fraud claims for assets nominally owned by third parties, whether individual[81] or corporate,[82] to be expressly included within the scope of the freezing order on the basis that there is "good

---

[80] *Gidrxslme Shipping Co Ltd v Tantomar-Transportes Maritimos*, at 310, per Colman J.

[81] See for example *PJSC v Maksimov* [2013] EWHC 422 (Comm).

[82] See the *Chabra* decision itself; *TSB Private Bank International SA v Chabra* [1992] 1 W.L.R. 231.

reason" to believe that the assets in question are in fact owned by the defendant to the fraud proceedings; the so-called *"Chabra"* jurisdiction is considered in this book in detail at Ch.28.[83]

The basis for such an order is that the assets in question may be amenable to enforcement in the event that the claimant obtains judgment against the defendant. However, the relatively low burden on the claimant on an application to include such assets within the scope of a freezing injunction obviously means that they will not automatically be available for execution on judgment. All that has to be established at the interim stage is that there is good reason to believe they may in substance be the defendant's assets; the court therefore makes no final determination as to their ownership. However, if the claimant succeeds at trial and wishes to enforce against the relevant assets he must then prove that the assets in fact belong to the defendant. **37–056**

At this stage, ultimately the burden will be on the claimant to demonstrate that the assets in question are in fact owned by or within the control of the defendant such that they should be amenable to execution. If this is disputed, whether by the defendant or, as is usually the case, by a purportedly independent third party, it may be necessary for there to be a trial of the issue of ownership.[84] In such a trial the burden will be on the claimant to prove the defendant's "ownership" on the balance of probabilities.[85] A trial on the issue of ownership may even take place before the substantive trial of the claimant's claim against the defendant. This will perhaps most usually occur if an independent third party asserts ownership of the assets in question and wishes to lift the freezing injunction which has been imposed against what he asserts to be "his" assets. **37–057**

If ownership or control by the defendant is so established, the judgment creditor may be able to enforce directly against the assets, for example by an order for sale of a property, if the assets themselves are within the jurisdiction of the English court. In many circumstances, more involved steps will be required to execute, such as the appointment of a receiver by way of equitable execution, as considered in Ch.33. **37–058**

(2) Assets Held in Trust or Trust Structures

It is becoming increasingly common for assets to be held in more opaque and more complex structures, usually involving discretionary trusts or some trust-like structure, such as a Liechtenstein Anstalt. The difficulty with such structures is that, if properly implemented, the defendant has no direct interest in the assets against which the claimant may seek to enforce, only a contingent interest in the **37–059**

---

[83] See also the principles set out in *SCF Finance Co v Masri* [1985] 1 W.L.R. 876, at 884, per Lloyd LJ.

[84] See for instance the trial of the issue as to ownership of a London flat in *JSC BTA Bank v Ablyazov* [2017] EWHC 2906 (Comm).

[85] *JSC BTA Bank v Ablyazov* [2014] EWCA Civ 602; [2015] 1 W.L.R. 1287, at [67], per Christopher Clarke LJ.

event that the trustee elects to make a distribution in his favour.[86] In a bona fide discretionary trust, the settlor, or any beneficiary, will have no power to direct the trustee to make distributions in favour of their favour and so equally there is no order the court can make compelling one in the defendant's favour (assuming the defendant is the settlor and/or a beneficiary) to render the assets available for enforcement. In some circumstances, the claimant may not even be able to identify the purported beneficiaries of the trust due to an absence of publicly available information, adding a further layer of complexity and further barrier to enforcement.

(i)   Sham trust

37–060   A claimant seeking to establish that the defendant judgment debtor is the true owner of assets which are purportedly held under the terms of a discretionary trust may assert that the trust is a sham (or more precisely that the trust documents are shams), and therefore that the judgment debtor, assuming he was the settlor of the assets in to the trust, in reality never parted with beneficial ownership of them. The principles of sham are considered in detail above at Ch.9.

37–061   Discretionary trusts are a frequently used tool to conceal the true ownership of an asset. This can achieve a number of goals, including: obviating the need to declare ownership on public registers or the like; allowing a beneficiary to declare honestly (or with purported honesty) that he does not have a proprietary interest in the asset, for example if ordered to give disclosure of his assets by the Court; and preventing (or seeking to prevent) at least direct methods of enforcement.

37–062   The owner of an asset attempting to conceal his ownership in this way can settle assets on a discretionary trust whereby trustees with fiduciary obligations to the beneficiaries of the trust have the power, but not the obligation, to advance trust property at their discretion to the beneficiaries. As well as conferring the benefits considered above, however, there are drawbacks, assuming that the discretionary trust is a genuine one. Most notably, under a genuine discretionary trust, once the assets have been settled in trust the power of appointment lies with the trustees and not the settlor, although a settlor may seek to influence the trustees by devices such as a letter of wishes. Unscrupulous settlors have therefore sought to keep de facto control over the assets by means such as reserving powers to the settlor or the use of protectors to try to ensure that the trustees act according to the settlor's wishes (including potentially returning the trust property).

37–063   While there are frequently good grounds for suspecting that discretionary trusts which feature in commercial fraud litigation are shams, in practice it is often difficult to produce evidence even to support a formal allegation along these lines, let alone to prove it on the balance of probabilities. This is primarily because the "shamming intent", that is the intent not in reality to give effect to the terms of the trust but to give a false impression of doing so, must be shared by both settlor and trustee. There must be "common intention" on the part of both

---

[86] See *JSC Mezhdunarodniy Promyshlenniy Bank v Pugachev* [2015] EWCA Civ 139, per Lewison LJ at [13].

settlor and trustee, albeit "reckless indifference" as to the genuineness of the trust documents on the part of the trustee will suffice to constitute common intention.[87] In the case of respectable professional trustees, this will be particularly difficult to prove and such trustees will often vigorously contest any such allegation. The task is made more difficult still because the "shamming intent" must generally be proved at the time that the trust was created and trust documents entered into. The fact that a trustee may later depart from the provisions of a trust deed does not in itself suffice, and may well be evidence of nothing more than a breach of trust on the part of the trustees.

However, notwithstanding these difficulties, the recent decision in *Pugachev* is an example where a professional trustee was found not to have had any "intention independent of" the settlor, and was reckless as to whether the settlor's true intention was to divest himself of beneficial ownership of the trust assets; in other words a finding of shamming intent on the part of the trustee (in the event that there had been a finding that a trust was declared at all). Other findings (considered in the next section below) led to the conclusion that in fact that there was no discretionary trust created at all. Had a trust arisen, however, Birss J made clear that he considered the trust deeds would have been a sham.[88]   **37–064**

(ii)   No discretionary trust

An alternative approach, albeit until recently largely untested in the English Courts, is to allege that, whether or not there was sufficient shamming intent, the breadth and nature of the powers reserved to the settlor in the original trust documents were such that in fact no discretionary trust arose in the first place, because in reality the beneficial interest in the assets in question remained at all times with the settlor, held in effect on a bare trust for him by the trustees.   **37–065**

So, in *Pugachev*, it was successfully argued that in reserving powers to himself as protector of a number of trusts which, as personal powers, did not have to be exercised in the interests of the beneficiaries in general and could therefore be exercised for his personal benefit alone, Mr Pugachev (the settlor) had in fact remained as a matter of substance the beneficial owner of the relevant assets at all times.[89] The powers reserved included the power to direct a sale of the trust property, to veto distribution of income and capital, to add or exclude beneficiaries, and to remove and appoint trustees, including to remove trustees without cause.   **37–066**

Birss J, adopting the position adumbrated by the Supreme Court of New Zealand in *Clayton v Clayton*,[90] held that the Court was entitled, in determining whether the effect of the powers reserved was that no trust arose, to examine the powers and obligations of the trustees as a whole and to construe the relationship as a   **37–067**

---

[87] Re-confirmed in *JSC Mezhdunarodniy Promyshlenniy Bank v Pugachev* [2017] EWHC 2426 (Ch), at [149]–[150], per Birss J.

[88] See *JSC Mezhdunarodniy Promyshlenniy Bank v Pugachev* [2017] EWHC 2426 (Ch), at [437], per Birss J.

[89] See *JSC Mezhdunarodniy Promyshlenniy Bank v Pugachev*, above at [267] and [278], per Birss J.

[90] *Clayton v Clayton* [2016] 1 N.Z.L.R. 551.

matter of substance. Unlike in the sham scenario, an "illusory trust" or "no discretionary trust" allegation does not carry with it any necessary assertion of collusion, complicity or even necessarily incompetence on the part of professional trustees, with the attendant professional and reputational consequences. As a result, such an approach may be less likely to be met by a vigorous defence on the part of professional trustees, and does not carry the same evidential burdens as an allegation of subjective shamming intent: the Court will carry out a wholly objective analysis of the trust documents rather than examining the intention of the parties, in particular the trustees. In fact, the argument does not require any allegation of dishonesty or even bad faith by any party. It could even conceivably be the case that the settlor genuinely intended to create a valid discretionary trust, as opposed to using it as a tool to hide assets, but was simply overzealous in reserving powers with the legal effect that the beneficial interest in the relevant assets remained at all times with the settlor.

37–068   Again, the effect of establishing that the defendant in fact remained at all times the substantive beneficial owner of the assets purportedly settled into trust is to render them amenable to direct enforcement by the claimant, or potentially to allow indirect enforcement for example by the appointment of a receiver.

(iii)   Section 423 insolvency act

37–069   If a bona fide trust was established and there was no shamming intent, such that the defendant has validly disposed of his beneficial interest in given assets, it may be still possible to impugn the settlement of the trust as a transaction at an undervalue intended to put the assets beyond the reach of creditors. Actions under s.423 of the Insolvency Act have been considered at Ch.16 of this book. Of course an action under s.423 can be brought in respect of any disposition.

37–070   While not limited to the trust scenario, nonetheless, because the settlement of a trust will almost inevitably be a transaction for no consideration in favour of the settlor, the provisions under s.423 can be a particularly effective mechanism to defeat and undo a trust structure.

37–071   There are a number of advantages to a claim under s.423 for enforcement purposes:

(1)   First, unlike other provisions for setting aside transactions under the Insolvency Act 1986, no bankruptcy order or other formal insolvency proceeding is required.[91] The judgment creditor is therefore not required to incur the cost and delay of insolvency proceedings, and retains control of the enforcement process without the imposition of a trustee in bankruptcy or liquidator.

(2)   Secondly, any creditor of the defendant is likely to be in a position to bring proceedings under s.423 as a "victim" of the transaction. It is not a requirement that the judgment creditor was a creditor at the time of the

---

[91] See for example *Ali v Bashir* [2014] EWHC 3853 (Ch).

transaction, only that he is affected by it.[92] For these purposes, it will suffice if assets which would otherwise have been available for enforcement no longer are, so the hurdle to be cleared to create locus is not a particularly high one.

(3) Thirdly, the applicable limitation periods for claims under s.423 may be longer than for other claims because:

    (i) the starting point is that the applicable limitation periods for such claims is 12 years as an action on a specialty, though if the claim can properly be characterised as a simple claim for money, then s.9 of the Limitation Act 1980 will apply, and the limitation period will be six years[93]; and

    (ii) in many cases limitation may be extended under the provisions of s.32(2) of the Limitation Act.[94]

In many instances in fraud cases, proving that such a transfer was made with the requisite intention for the purposes of s.423, namely of putting assets out of the reach of creditors, will pose no difficulty. A party who has utilised asset holding structures of the type considered above will have an uphill battle persuading a court that protecting them from creditors was not at least a purpose of the transaction, even if not the dominant one.[95] The inference will be stronger still in the case of a defendant who has been found liable in a fraud action.[96]   **37–072**

(iv) Power of revocation

An express trust may contain a power of revocation or equivalent, whereby the settlor has the power to effectively dissolve the trust such that the assets re-vest in him. The existence of such a power may well allow a judgment creditor to appoint a receiver by way of equitable execution to invoke the power of revocation.[97]   **37–073**

---

[92] See for example *Fortress Value Recovery Fund v Blue Skye Special Opportunities Fund* [2013] EWHC 14 (Comm), at [111], per Flaux J.

[93] *Re Priory Garage (Walthamstow) Ltd* [2001] B.P.I.R. 144; *JSC BTA Bank v Ablyazov* [2016] EWHC 3071 (Comm), at [155], per Laurence Rabinowitz QC.

[94] See in particular on extending the limitation period in claims under s.423 *Giles v Rhind* [2009] Ch. 191, in which it was held that a transaction made with the intention of putting assets beyond the reach of creditors is axiomatically a breach of duty, allowing a claimant to invoke s.32 of the Limitation Act.

[95] *IRC v Hashmi* [2002] EWCA Civ 981.

[96] For an example of an unsuccessful claim, on relatively unusual facts, see *JSC BTA Bank v Ablyazov* [2016] EWHC 3071 (Comm), where a father who had found to have been guilty of wide ranging frauds on the claimant bank and had systematically attempted to hide assets from creditors over an extended period did not have the requisite intention in respect of a large gift to his son, upheld on appeal at [2018] EWCA Civ 1176.

[97] See *Tasarruf Mevduati Sigorta Fonu v Merrill Lynch Bank and Trust Co (Cayman) Ltd* [2012] 1 W.L.R. 1721; and more generally Ch.33.

(3) Receivership by Way of Equitable Execution

37–074 The appointment of a receiver by way of equitable execution is an increasingly powerful tool in obtaining assets nominally in the hands of third parties, whether individual or corporate, or held in trust structures, since the receiver can exercise the powers afforded to him to get in assets which would not otherwise by amenable to execution by the judgment creditor. We consider the appointment of receivers by way of equitable execution in Ch.33.

CHAPTER 38

SETTING ASIDE A JUDGMENT FOR FRAUD

A. INTRODUCTION

Where a judgment has been obtained and either an appeal has been unsuccessful   **38–001**
or the relevant period for appeal has passed, then the judgment is final. The
judgment creditor can enforce the judgment and any findings are, in principle,
binding as between the parties.

However, equity has developed[1] a jurisdiction, deserving of treatment in this   **38–002**
book, whereby a judgment properly obtained, whether or not it has been satisfied
by the judgment debtor, may subsequently be set aside at the suit of the losing
party via a fresh action on the grounds that it was obtained by the fraud of the
winning party. The jurisdiction may be seen as an aspect of a wider principle of
English law most recently expressed by Lord Bingham in *HIH Casualty and
General Insurance Ltd v Chase Manhattan Bank*[2]:

> "For ... fraud is a thing apart. This is not a mere slogan. It reflects an old legal rule that fraud
> unravels all: *fraus omnia corrumpit*. It also reflects the practical basis of commercial
> intercourse. Once fraud is proved, 'it vitiates judgments, contracts and all transactions
> whatsoever': *Lazarus Estates Ltd v Beasley* [1956] 1 QB 702, at 712, per Denning LJ."[3]

Of course the acceptance of the possibility of such an action has the potential to   **38–003**
undermine the principle of finality in litigation.[4] It potentially allows a

---

[1] Early cases include *Duchess of Kingston's Case* (1776) 2 Smith L.C. 644n; *Flower v Lloyd (No.1)*
(1877) 6 Ch. D. 297; *The Alfred Nobel* [1918] P. 293; *Jonesco v Beard* [1930] A.C. 298.
[2] *HIH Casualty and General Insurance Ltd v Chase Manhattan Bank* [2003] UKHL 6; [2003] 1
C.L.C. 358, at [15].
[3] Of course estoppel in any of its various forms cannot constitute a defence to a claim to set aside a
judgment for fraud. This is because the very purpose of the claim is to impeach the judgment which
otherwise could be set up as binding as an estoppel *per rem judicatam*. See *Toubia v Schwenke* [2002]
NSWCA 34, per Handley JA at [5]: "Under the general law a party who claims that an adverse
judgment was procured by the fraud of his adversary can bring an action to set aside that judgment.
Such proceedings are equitable in origin and nature ... and in fact are proceedings for the judicial
rescission of the judgment ... Such proceedings, when successful, do not result in 'the scandal of
conflicting decisions' (*Rogers v R* (1994) 181 CLR 251, 273, Spencer Bower, Turner and Handley,
'Res Judicata', p.50) because if the second action succeeds the first judgment is set aside."
[4] A principle evocatively stated by Lord Simon in his celebrated speech in the *Ampthill Peerage*
[1977] A.C. 547, at 575: "As a means of resolution of civil contention litigation is certainly preferable
to personal violence. But it is not intrinsically a desirable activity—certainly not on the scale on which
it raged in the Ampthill family in the early 1920s. The picture drawn by Charles Dickens in *Bleak
House* of the long-drawn-out and ruinous lawsuit, "Jarndyce v Jarndyce", and poor Miss Flite, her
wits overturned by the strain of litigation, was based on fact. The law itself is fully conscious of the
evil of protracted litigation. Our forensic system, with its machinery of cross-examination of

disgruntled losing party to relitigate old battles which he has lost. Accordingly, the circumstances in which a properly obtained judgment will be set aside for fraud are narrow and the court is assiduous to ensure that such claims are not used to harass or as the vehicle for seeking to revisit adverse judgments. A court will be assiduous to strike out such claims at an early stage. On the other hand

> "fraud is an insidious disease, and if clearly proved to have been used so that it might deceive the Court, it spreads to and infects the whole body of the judgment."[5]

The tension between these two competing, but fundamental, principles is the cause of a degree of inconsistency in the authorities, as addressed below.

B. THE PROCEDURAL MECHANISM

(1) Fresh Action[6]

38-004 It had long been established that the proper mechanism for impeaching a judgment for fraud is via a fresh action, not via an application in the old proceedings, nor by way of appeal. The classic statement of the traditional position is as follows:

> "where a new trial is sought upon the ground of fraud, procedure by motion and affidavit is not the most satisfactory and convenient method of determining the dispute. The fraud must be both alleged and proved; and the better course in such a case is to take independent proceedings to set aside a judgment upon the ground of fraud, when the whole issue can be properly defined, fought out and determined, though a motion for a new trial is also an available weapon and in some cases may be more convenient."[7]

This approach was recently restated by the House of Lords in *Kuwait Airways Corp v Iraqi Airways Co (No.2)*[8]:

---

witnesses and forced disclosure of documents, is characterised by a ruthless investigation of truth. Nevertheless the law recognises that the process cannot go on indefinitely. There is a fundamental principle of English law generally expressed by a Latin maxim (going back to *Coke's Commentary on Littleton*, p. 330) which can be translated: 'It is in the interest of society that there should be some end to litigation.' This fundamental principle finds expression in many forms. Parliament has passed statutes (the latest only last year) limiting the time within which actions at law must be brought. Truth may be thus shut out; but society considers that truth may be bought at too high a price, that truth bought at such expense is the negation of justice." See also *Mulholland v Mitchell* [1971] A.C. 666, but contrast the dicta in *Sharland v Sharland* [2014] EWCA Civ 95, at [36], per Briggs LJ, that "[t]here is a public interest in the protection of the Court's processes from fraud which transcends other case management considerations such as finality, economy and speed". Briggs LJ was in the minority; the Supreme Court allowed an appeal: [2015] UKSC 60; [2016] A.C. 871.

[5] *Jonesco v Beard* [1930] A.C. 298, at 301, per Lord Buckmaster.

[6] Special rules apply to arbitration awards said to have been procured by fraud: see most recently *Sinocore International Co Ltd v RBRG Trading (UK) Ltd* [2017] EWHC 251 (Comm); and *Celtic Bioenergy Ltd v Knowles Ltd* [2017] EWHC 472 (TCC).

[7] *Hip Foong Hong v Neotia & Co* [1918] A.C. 888, at 894, per Lord Buckmaster; approved in *Jonesco v Beard* [1930] A.C. 298, at 300.

[8] *Kuwait Airways Corp v Iraqi Airways Co (No.2)* [2001] 1 W.L.R. 429.

"there is well established authority that where a final decision has been made by a court a challenge to the decision on the basis that it has been obtained by fraud must be made by a fresh action alleging and proving the fraud."

In that case the applicant sought to set aside an earlier decision of the House of Lords on the ground of fraud. It petitioned the House of Lords who held that the proper course was for the applicant to bring a fresh action.

(2) Proceeding by Way of Appeal

However in recent years there have been suggestions that a preferable route where there has been a judgment allegedly obtained by fraud is via the mechanism of an appeal rather than resort to a fresh action. *Noble v Owens*[9] was a case where a substantial judgment was entered in favour of a claimant in a personal injury claim, founded on his evidence that as a result of his injuries he would never work again and needed substantial assistance with his daily living. There was no appeal and the judgment was satisfied. Sometime later the defendant's insurers obtained new evidence that the claimant was far less disabled than he had claimed at the trial. Rather than bring a fresh action the insurers, via the defendant, sought to appeal the original award out of time. The claimant's stance was that the appeal should be dismissed because the defendant's proper remedy was the bringing of a fresh action to set aside the judgment for fraud, as envisaged in the authorities discussed in the section above. The decision in *Noble* is significant because it noted a tension in the authorities between on the one hand the principle embodied by *Jonesco v Beard*, whereby a new action should be brought to impeach the judgment obtained by the alleged fraud, and on the other hand, decisions where the Court of Appeal had admitted new evidence on appeal which suggested that the judgment appealed from had been obtained by fraud.[10] The second line of authorities has involved, in some cases, the Court of Appeal admitting the evidence and directing a new trial without actually making a finding on the allegation of fraud. The critical point of distinction is that under the first line of authorities the court will only set aside the judgment if fraud has been distinctly proven at a second trial; whereas under the second line the Court of Appeal may order a retrial simply on the basis of credible evidence of fraud, rather than a finding of fraud.

38–005

The Court could not reconcile these two strands of authority and, in essence, preferred the first. Smith LJ said:

38–006

"In my judgment, the true principle of law is derived from *Jonesco v Beard* and is that, where fresh evidence is adduced in the Court of Appeal tending to show that the judge at first instance was deliberately misled, the court will only allow the appeal and order a retrial[11]

---

[9] *Noble v Owens* [2010] EWCA Civ 224; [2010] 1 W.L.R. 2491.

[10] For example *Roe v Robert McGregor & Sons Ltd* [1968] 1 W.L.R. 925; *Skone v Skone* [1971] 1 W.L.R. 812.

[11] As it can under CPR r.52.20.

> where the fraud is either admitted or the evidence of it is incontrovertible. In any other case, the issue of fraud must be determined before the judgment of the court below can be set aside."[12]

What the Court of Appeal will not do, faced with prima facie evidence of fraud, which is neither admitted nor incontrovertible, is set aside the original order or judgment. A new trial can only be ordered by the Court of Appeal in circumstances where the fraud has been admitted or is incontrovertible.

38–007 However the Court of Appeal went on to propose a middle course, which nonetheless preserved the sanctity of the rule in *Jonesco v Beard*:

> "Although the old cases say that where there is an issue of fraud to be tried that must be done by commencing a fresh action, I do not think that in this day and age that should always be necessary. All that is needed is that the issue of fraud should be determined. That could be done just as well (if not better) by this court referring the trial of the fraud issue to a High Court judge pursuant to CPR r.52.10(2)(b). The possibility that that might be an appropriate course was presaged by Lord Phillips of Worth Matravers MR in *Hamilton v Al Fayed*,[13] para.21. In my view that would be a better course to follow in the present case for two reasons. First, the costs of a fresh action would necessarily exceed the costs of the trial of an issue. If the issue is referred, the matter could be dealt with quite expeditiously. The judge could give directions as to the clarification of the allegations and as to the exchange of evidence. In any event, most of that has already taken place. The matter could be ready for hearing within a very short time. Second, this court would be able to direct that the issue be tried by [the original trial judge]."[14]

In truth this is not saying very much; the course proposed by the Court of Appeal could be accomplished simply by the complainant issuing new proceedings, thereby avoiding the necessity of a hearing in the Court of Appeal in which there is the risk that the Court will dismiss the application. By issuing fresh proceedings the complainant does not need to create a hurdle for itself (i.e. by having to appeal to the appeal court) and throws the burden of invoking early judicial scrutiny of the merits of the allegation upon the defendant (e.g. via an application to strike out or for summary judgment). It is not immediately apparent why the costs of a fresh action would "necessarily exceed the costs of the trial of an issue" given that the very same issue would be in play and there would need to be orders for disclosure and exchange of witness evidence in either scenario. As to the second benefit identified by the Court (i.e. the original trial judge adjudicating on the issue of fraud), in fact recent experience shows that fresh claims to set aside judgments are often heard by the original judge; of course either party can make that request at an early stage. Finally, although the Court of Appeal in *Noble* did not address the question directly, the court deciding "the fraud issue" would presumably have to adopt the same test as that which a court would adopt when trying a fresh action (as to which see below). In the recent decision of the Court of Appeal in *Salekipour v Parmar*[15] one can detect a return to the old orthodoxy that the usual way of seeking to set aside a judgment obtained by fraud is via the bringing of fresh proceedings.

---

[12] *Noble v Owens* [2010] EWCA Civ 224; [2010] 1 W.L.R. 2491, at [27].
[13] *Hamilton v Al Fayed* [2001] E.M.L.R. 15.
[14] *Noble v Owens* [2010] EWCA Civ 224; [2010] 1 W.L.R. 2491, at [29].
[15] *Salekipour v Parmar* [2017] EWCA Civ 2141; [2018] 2 W.L.R. 1090, at [72], per Etherton MR.

Even where an appeal has been dismissed (whether at the permission stage or after a substantive hearing) there is power under CPR r.52.17 to reopen a final determination of any appeal if three cumulative conditions are met: (a) it is necessary to do so in order to avoid real injustice; (b) the circumstances are exceptional and make it appropriate to reopen the appeal; and (c) there is no alternative remedy. **38–008**

This gives rise to the question whether the existence of the action to set aside a judgment for fraud constitutes an alternative remedy and therefore precludes the exercise of the power under CPR r.52.17. In general the answer must be yes[16]; indeed as we have seen in most circumstances the Court of Appeal will not order a retrial simply on the basis of new evidence suggesting fraud.

There has been doubt whether the County Court had power to set aside one of its own previous judgments. In *Salekipour v Parmar*[17] there had been a trial between the parties. The claimants' claims were dismissed after the judge had heard witnesses called by both sides. In her judgment the judge had held that credibility was "vital in this case." In later proceedings in the County Court the claimants sought to "rescind" the earlier judgment, claiming that a witness called by the defendants at the earlier trial had been threatened by the defendant into giving perjured evidence. It was held by Garnham J, on appeal from the County Court judge, that the County Court had no jurisdiction to set aside one of its earlier judgments because, as a creature of statute, it had no inherent jurisdiction and the jurisdiction to set aside an earlier judgment derives from that inherent jurisdiction. The Court of Appeal[18] disagreed, holding that s.23 of the County Courts Act 1984 provided a statutory jurisdiction permitting the County Court to set aside one of its earlier judgments. The result is welcome, because the analysis of the courts below created an odd disjunction between the practice in the High Court and in the County Court and led to a serious lacuna in the jurisdiction of the County Court. **38–009**

(3) Effect of New Claim on Original Proceedings

The issuing of a fresh claim does not have any automatic effect on the original proceedings and the final order (and any other orders that remain extant in those original proceedings) which was made in those proceedings. For a party against whom judgment has been granted, a stay must be obtained to prevent enforcement proceedings being taken (if they have not already). This will be attractive in many cases given that (necessarily) fraud is being alleged and the proceeds of any prior award may be dissipated before the proceedings to set aside can be completed. **38–010**

The grant of a stay is within the Court's general case management powers. Though there is no authority as to the factors to be taken into account on such an **38–011**

---

[16] Though see *Bishop v Chhokar* [2015] CP Rep. 26 and *Rawding v Seaga UK Ltd* [2015] EWCA Civ 113. These decisions must now be read in the light of the Court of Appeal's decision in *Salekipour v Parmar* [2017] EWCA Civ 2141; [2018] 2 W.L.R. 1090, per Etherton MR.

[17] *Salekipour v Parmar* [2016] EWHC 1466 (QB); [2016] Q.B. 987.

[18] *Salekipour v Parmar* [2017] EWCA Civ 2141; [2018] 2 W.L.R. 1090, at [74].

application, it seems likely that the Court would have to be satisfied that the claim to set aside had reasonable prospects of success, and would apply criteria similar to those for a stay pending appeal.

38–012 The Court will however be anxious to minimise the potential prejudice caused to the party who, as matters stand, has judgment in its favour. Conditions of granting a stay may therefore include securing the sum awarded in the judgment (including interest and costs) and the provision of security for the costs of the new action.[19]

C. ELEMENTS TO BE PROVED

38–013 The elements which have to be proved in order to set aside an earlier judgment for fraud are as follows[20]:

(1) First, there has to be a "conscious and deliberate dishonesty" by the winning party (or someone for whom it must take responsibility) in relation to the relevant evidence given, or action taken, statement made or matter concealed, which is relevant to the judgment sought to be impugned.

(2) Secondly, the relevant evidence, action, statement or concealment (performed with conscious and deliberate dishonesty) must be "material". The question of materiality of the fresh evidence is to be assessed by reference to its impact on the evidence supporting the original decision, not by reference to its impact on what decision might be made if the claim were to be retried on honest evidence.[21]

(3) Thirdly, the relevant evidence, action, statement or concealment must be newly discovered and must not have been before the court in the original action.[22] Moreover, the action must be based on new evidence which the claimant could not with reasonable diligence have placed before the court at the time the first judgment was given.

38–014 We deal with aspects of these elements in greater detail below. It is generally agreed that this test is in practice likely to be difficult to comply with and will rarely be met.[23]

---

[19] See for example *Chodiev v Stein* [2015] EWHC 1428 (Comm), at [3].

[20] This analysis is modelled in part on the analysis of the Court of Appeal in *Royal Bank of Scotland Plc v Highland Financial Partners LP* [2013] EWCA Civ 328; [2013] 1 C.L.C. 596, at [106], per Aikens LJ.

[21] *Kuwait Airways Corp v Iraqi Airways Corp (Perjury II)* [2005] EWHC 2524 (Comm), at [198]–[199].

[22] *Birch v Birch* [1902] P. 130, at 136.

[23] *Chodiev v Stein* [2015] EWHC 1428, at [21].

(1) "Conscious and Deliberate Dishonesty"

This is the usual formulation, deriving from Lord Wilberforce's speech in *The*   **38–015**
Ampthill Peerage.[24] It does not bear much elaboration although it probably
involves a narrower concept than that employed in deceit claims. In deceit
recklessness is sufficient; in a claim to set aside a judgment it is suggested that
there must be conscious decision to falsify or supress evidence with the intention
that the court be deceived. The dishonesty need not involve the actual
perpetration of a positive falsehood in, say, a witness statement, or in the giving
of oral evidence; the types of conduct that may lead to a judgment being set aside
have been widely defined.[25] Suppression of the truth may sometimes amount to
suggestion of the false[26]; and the deliberate concealment of a relevant fact or
document can constitute fraud for these purposes.[27] But the establishment of the
fraud is a condition precedent to reopening the case.[28]

(2) Materiality

What must be established is that the court has been deceived and has acted on the   **38–016**
basis of that deception. In this context the word "material", for the purposes of
the second element identified above, means that the fresh evidence which is
sought to be adduced after the first judgment has been given demonstrates that
the previous relevant evidence, action, statement or concealment (which was the
subject of the conscious or deliberate dishonesty) was an operative cause of the
court's decision to give judgment in the way it did. Put another way, it must be
shown that the fresh evidence would have entirely changed the way in which the
first court approached and came to its decision.[29] It is not necessary for the
dishonest evidence, action, statement or concealment to have been the sole or
even decisive cause of the first judgment; but it must have been causative of the

---

[24] *The Ampthill Peerage* [1977] A.C. 547, at 571. The alternative formulations of "lack of frankness",
or "ulterior or oblique or indirect motives" were rejected as too anaemic: see at 571 and 591. In *Ong
v Ping* [2015] EWHC 1742 (Ch) Morgan J held, at [289], that "lack of candour in litigation, even in
relation to an application for summary judgment, does not necessarily amount to fraud."
[25] *Jet Holdings v Patel* [1990] 1 Q.B. 335, at 347, where Staughton LJ "includes every variety of
mala fides and mala praxis whereby one of the parties misleads and deceives the judicial tribunal."
That was a case relating to the enforcement of a foreign judgment, but the principle extends to the
types of claim considered in this chapter.
[26] *The Alfred Nobel* [1918] P. 293.
[27] In *Ackerman v Thornhill* [2017] EWHC 99 (Ch) there could be no concealment where the
documents had been disclosed, even if, as the claimant asserted, they had been "tucked away" in the
list: see at [95]. In *Ong v Ping* [2015] EWHC 1742 (Ch) it was suggested, at [257], by Morgan J, that
dishonest concealment, which did not involve the making of a misleading statement, could not
amount to fraud. In most cases a dishonest concealment will involve at least an implied misleading
statement; but it is suggested that this formulation is too narrow. Concealment was expressly stated to
be within the rule by Aikens LJ in *Highland Financial Partners*, at [106], and see further at
[122]–[126]. Clearly a dishonest concealment will be more difficult to prove.
[28] See *Jonesco v Beard* [1930] A.C. 298.
[29] Where the new evidence relates solely to the credibility of the party which was successful in the
first action then the burden is even heavier, where the test comes close to requiring that the impugned
witness' credibility was decisive in the original determination: *Braddock v Tillotson's Newspapers Ltd*
[1950] 1 K.B. 47 and *Meek v Fleming* [1961] 2 Q.B. 366.

impugned judgment being obtained in the terms it was.[30] The above analysis derives from the decision in *Royal Bank of Scotland Plc v Highland Financial Partners LLP*, which has been taken to represent the law by many subsequent decisions. However, in the recent case of *Salekipour v Parmar*[31] the appellant contended that this analysis put the legal test too high, and was inconsistent with the decision of the Court of Appeal in *Hamilton v Al Fayed (No.4)* where Lord Phillips MR had said[32]:

> "Where it is clearly established by fresh evidence that the Court was deliberately deceived in relation to the credibility of a witness, a fresh trial will be ordered where there is a real danger that this affected the outcome of the trial."

Sir Terence Etherton MR, giving judgment in *Salekipour*, said that he was "inclined to agree" with the appellant that the test was over-stated in *Royal Bank of Scotland* and that the proper approach is that laid down by the Court of Appeal in *Hamilton*, although he emphasised that it was not necessary to make a final decision on that point.[33]

38–017 However, the requirement of materiality does not extend to the second court having to re-try the question of the liability of the parties or to see whether the fresh evidence or new facts are material to the final result in the sense of influencing what the decision would be if the matter were to be retried with honest evidence; indeed the second court should not undertake such an exercise. The purpose of a second action to set aside an earlier judgment is to take the parties back to the position as it was before the trial so that a new trial on honest evidence can then take place.[34] Nonetheless, in practice it will be difficult for a judge in deciding the question of materiality not to trespass at least to some extent on to such matters.

38–018 In recent years there has been a tendency for the same judge to hear the second action (and any interim applications in it)[35]; such a judge has been thought to be in the best position to determine the materiality of the alleged dishonest evidence, or concealment etc., though it seems inevitable that the original trial judge will be more prone to the error identified above of considering what the decision would have been had honest evidence been given in the original action.

(3) Evidence Not Before the First Court and Not Reasonably Discoverable

38–019 It is self-evident that the fraud relied upon must relate to evidence or material which was not before the first court: the Court must have proceeded on a false understanding. Further, although the position is not free from controversy, the law appears now to be settled (at least at Court of Appeal level) that the new evidence

---

[30] *Highland Partners*, above, at [106].
[31] *Salekipour v Parmar* [2017] EWCA Civ 2141; [2018] 2 W.L.R. 1090.
[32] *Hamilton v Al Fayed (No.4)* [2000] EWCA Civ 3012; [2001] E.M.L.R. 15, at [34].
[33] At [93]–[94].
[34] *Highland Partners*, above, at [141].
[35] See the discussion in *Chodiev* [2015] EWHC 1428, at [25].

or material relied upon by the claimant in the second action must be of a nature that it was not only not in fact available to him, but also could not with reasonable diligence have been discovered by him before the first judgment.[36]

The position is therefore somewhat unusual under English law, in placing a de facto requirement on the defrauded party to take reasonable steps to discover the fraud and in imposing a bar to bringing a claim as a consequence of the failure to do so; contrast, for example, the firm rule in deceit, where the representor cannot rely on failures of investigation on the part of the representee to resist a claim. It also raises difficult questions as to what steps are required to meet the standard of "reasonable diligence" in obtaining evidence of fraud, where an element of concealment is likely. **38–020**

(4)   Where Perjury is Alleged

The giving of perjured evidence is but one instance in which it may be said that the previous judgment was procured by fraud. In such a case the conditions to be proved were set out as follows: **38–021**

> "(a)   A judgment obtained by perjury is a judgment obtained by fraud for this purpose.
> (b)   The action seeking an order setting aside the earlier judgment must be based on new evidence which was not before the Court that first heard the action and which the claimant could not with reasonable diligence have placed before that Court.
> (c)   The new evidence must establish perjury in the sense that a person or persons sworn as a witness in the earlier action who could properly be treated as the successful party itself wilfully made a statement in those proceedings which statement the person knew to be false or did not believe to be true.
> (d)   The burden is on the claimants to establish perjury as 'distinctly more probable than not'.[37]
> (e)   The disparity between the perjured evidence and the new evidence would be material if it 'entirely changed the nature of the case'."[38]

It can be seen that these conditions are applications of the principles considered above to the particular case of perjury. In *Salekipour v Parmar*[39] the Court of **38–022**

---

[36] This has been the view of three recent first instance judges: David Steel J in *Kuwait Airways v Iraq Airways* [2003] EWHC 31 (Comm); [2003] 1 Lloyd's Rep. 448, at [146]; Burton J in *Chodiev v Stein* [2015] EWHC 1428 (Comm) and Snowden J in *Ackerman v Thornhill* [2017] EWHC 99 (Ch). All three judges relied upon the earlier decisions in *Phosphate Sewage Co Ltd v Molleson* (1879) 4 App. Cas. 801, 814; *Hunter v Chief Constable of West Midlands* [1980] Q.B. 283 and [1982] A.C. 529, and *Owens Bank Ltd v Bracco* [1992] 2 A.C. 443. However to contrary effect was the decision of Newey J in *Takhar v Gracefield Developments Ltd* [2015] EWHC 1276 (Ch), which both Burton J in *Chodiev* and Snowden J in *Ackerman* expressly refused to follow. The view adumbrated by Newey J in *Takhar* drew support from Commonwealth authority: see *Toubia v Schwenke* [2002] NSWCA 34; (2002) 54 N.S.W.L.R. 46; and *Canada v Granitile Inc* (2008) 302 D.L.R. (4th) 40. Most recently the Court of Appeal in *Takhar* has perhaps with some reluctance resolved the matter in favour of the "due diligence" requirement, overturning the decision of Newey J in *Takhar*, at first instance on the basis that the decision in *Hunter* is binding; see [2017] EWCA Civ 147; [2018] 1 Ch. 1, at [54]. The question is shortly to be reviewed in the Supreme Court.
[37] A case where perjury was established is *Re Odyssey (London) Ltd v OIC Run-Off Ltd*, unreported, 13 March 2000, CA .
[38] *Kuwait Airways v Iraq Airways*, above, at [146].
[39] *Salekipour v Parmar* [2017] EWCA Civ 2141; [2018] 2 W.L.R. 1090, at [72], per Etherton MR.

Appeal had to deal with not simply the giving of perjured evidence but an allegation that the successful party in the first trial had suborned a witness to give perjured evidence. It was said that the

> "suborning of a witness by a party to give perjured evidence in order to succeed at trial is a most serious matter, which not only taints the evidence of the witness but potentially undermines the credibility of that party on all issues."[40]

D.   The Court's Approach to the Jurisdiction

(1)   Need to Specify Fraud with Particularity

38–023   Unsurprisingly, the courts have rigorously insisted upon specificity: the particulars of the fraud must be exactly given and the allegation established by the strict proof such a charge requires:

> "To impugn a judgment on the ground of fraud, the fraud must be alleged with particularity and proved distinctly. A person is not permitted merely to allege fraud in the hope of discovering it as the case develops."[41]

(2)   Prima Facie Case Must be Shown

38–024   The court has always closely considered proceedings to set aside an earlier judgment at an early stage so as to ensure that its processes are not being abused.[42] In earlier cases, prior to the development of the modern summary judgment jurisdiction, it was said that the impugner of a judgment as obtained by fraud had to adduce evidence of facts discovered since the judgment which showed a reasonable probability of such fraud as would invalidate the judgment, before he could call on the person whose judgment he sought to nullify to make any sort of disclosure[43]; and that a person could not merely say:

> "I allege that you obtained your judgment by fraud; let me rummage through your papers and I shall be able to turn up something there which will enable me to prove it."[44]

This suggests that, as a matter of practice, on an application under CPR r.24 or r.3.4 to strike out a claim to set aside an earlier judgment as obtained by fraud, the court will approach the claim with a good deal more scepticism and rigour than it would in relation to other claims.[45] But it is not the case that the Court will, in the usual course of events, consider such a claim of its own motion. Moreover, as in other summary determinations, the Court will often be more concerned with the question of materiality and, possibly, the fresh evidence requirement, than with a factual assessment of the likelihood that the alleged fraud has been perpetrated.

---

[40] *Salekipour v Parmar* [2017] EWCA Civ 2141; [2018] 2 W.L.R. 1090, at [95].
[41] *Jonesco* [1930] A.C. 298, at 300.
[42] See e.g. *Boswell v Coaks* [1894] 6 R 167.
[43] *Birch v Birch* [1902] P. 130 as interpreted in *The Ampthill Peerage* [1977] 1 A.C. 547, at 591.
[44] *The Ampthill Peerage*, at 591.
[45] Recent examples of courts striking out claims to set aside earlier judgments for fraud are *Chodiev v Stein* [2015] EWHC 1428 (Comm); and *Ackerman v Thornhill* [2017] EWHC 99 (Ch).

(3)   Period in which Claim May be Brought

Of course the fraud which founded the original judgment may not be discovered   **38–025**
for many years.[46] Although there seems to be no decision on the question, it is
suggested that no period of limitation applies to a fresh action brought to set aside
a judgment for fraud (if it is done by fresh action), the relief being equitable and
there not being a corresponding remedy at common law. There seems to be no
reason why the bars on equitable relief under the principles of laches and
acquiesce should not apply.[47]

(4)   Setting Aside Judgment of an Appellate Court

Where the original judgment has been unsuccessfully appealed (without   **38–026**
knowledge of the alleged fraud) the first instance court in the second action has
jurisdiction to set aside both the original first instance judgment and appellate
order(s) upholding it. So in *Kuwait Airways Corp v Iraqi Airways Co*,[48] David
Steel J set aside a decision of the House of Lords on the ground that it had been
procured by fraud.

(5)   Fraud of Party or Witness?

What of the situation where the earlier judgment has been obtained as a result of   **38–027**
the fraudulent evidence (or suppression of facts) of or by a witness who is not
himself the party in whose favour the judgment was given? A number of
propositions can be stated:

(1)   It is necessary for the fraud which was an operative cause of the judgment
      to be that "of the party" to the proceedings.[49] Accordingly, the fraudulent
      evidence or concealment of a "mere witness" cannot be a basis for setting
      aside a judgment.[50]
(2)   Where the party is a natural person, it appears to be the settled position that,
      for the relevant evidence to be treated as that of the party, the party must
      have suborned or knowingly adopted the false evidence.[51]
(3)   Where the party is not a natural person (the most obvious example being a
      company), it is not enough that the witness gives evidence "on behalf of"
      the company: the general position is that "a person who gives evidence on
      behalf of a company does not do so as its agent."[52]

---

[46] An example being *Odyssey (London) Ltd v OIC Run-Off Ltd*, unreported, 13 March 2000 CA,
where the second action was brought many years later.
[47] See Ch.25 above.
[48] *Kuwait Airways Cor v Iraqi Airways Co* [2003] 1 Lloyd's Rep. 448.
[49] *Odyssey (London) Ltd v OIC Run-Off Ltd*, unreported, 13 March 2000 CA.
[50] It is worth considering what recourse the "victim" of a judgment fraudulently obtained by the
evidence of a "mere" witness has if judgment cannot be set aside. A claim against the witness would
presumably be barred by the principle of witness immunity.
[51] See e.g. *Boswell v Coaks* [1894] 6 R 167; see also *Odyssey*, at page 134 of the transcript.
[52] *Odyssey*, at 11.

(4)   Equally, it would not appear to be necessary to go as far as to show that the company suborned the false evidence or adopted it knowing of its falsity.[53]

38–028   The question of when the evidence of a witness will be attributed to a company (or other non-natural person) for these purposes is more difficult to pin down. The leading authority is the decision of the Court of Appeal in *Re Odyssey (London) Ltd v OIC Run-Off*,[54] where the outcome of the later fraud proceedings turned (in part) upon the question of whether the perjured evidence of a witness at the first trial could be treated as that of the party who had succeeded. The dishonest witness had been director and general manager of the previously successful party at the time the relevant event had occurred, but by the time he came to give evidence he had retired. It was held that, even though the company did not know of his perjury, nonetheless his evidence should be attributed to it. The majority of the Court of Appeal[55] said the relevant question was whether the witness had the status (as opposed to the authority, which was a misleading concept in the relevant circumstances) necessary to make his evidence that of the company. This is obviously an open-textured question which allows for a range of considerations to be taken into account; but material pointers towards the conclusion that the witness's evidence should be treated as that of the company included, on the facts of that case: the centrality of the witness to the success of the case (he was a "vital" witness); the fact that the witness, although no longer part of the organisation, had been personally responsible for the relevant transaction about which he gave evidence; and the fact that he subsequently became part of the litigation effort (as opposed to just a witness in it), being part of the decision making team in the first claim and thus identifying himself with the company's interests.[56]

---

[53] *Odyssey*, at 11, rejecting Lord Grabiner QC's "first proposition" recorded at 10.

[54] *Odyssey*, above, which must count as one of the most extraordinary pieces of litigation ever heard by an English Court. The Judgments of the Court of Appeal extend to 146 close typed pages and the case related to the question of whether one or two answers given in evidence by a since deceased witness in a long trial 10 years earlier were dishonest. The Court of Appeal, differing from the judge, held that they were, and set aside the judgment procured in reliance on the answers.

[55] Per Nourse LJ at 12 and Brooke LJ at 94, relying upon *R. v Andrews-Weatherfoil Ltd* [1972] 1 W.L.R. 118, at 124. Buxton LJ dissented. The Court of Appeal in *Highland Partners* applied the majority approach of the Court of Appeal in the *Odyssey* case. It is clear (from the reasoning of the majority in *Odyssey*) that this is an application of the modern approach to attribution starting with the pioneering speech of Lord Hoffmann in *Meridian Global Funds Management Asia Ltd v Securities Commission* [1995] 1 A.C. 500, and so it can be expected to develop in tandem with developments in this area of law more generally.

[56] Take this as another example. A person is driving on a road with a passenger and the car is involved in a crash with another car. The passenger is killed. The driver, in order to exonerate himself of any potential liability, falsely alleges that the crash was the fault of the other driver. The estate of the passenger sues the other driver based on that evidence. A judgment is obtained. Subsequently the driver confesses that he gave false evidence. Should the judgment be set aside? It seems that in those circumstances, and based on the "status" test considered above, the driver's evidence would be considered as the (non-natural) party's evidence and judgment could be set aside. Indeed, it is difficult to imagine circumstances where a witness called by a party other than a natural person, whose evidence was sufficiently important to meet the materiality test, would not also meet the status test.

E. RELIEF

The court trying an action to set aside a judgment for fraud will simply ask the questions posed above. It will not go on to retry the underlying claim or re-run the original proceedings on hypothetical honest evidence. The relief which is sought is simply the setting aside of the judgment (and consequential orders), which will in turn pave the way for a new trial on the true facts. There will be no need to issue a new claim form: the new trial will be within the old proceedings which will be automatically revived by the setting aside of the previous judgment and all orders flowing from it. The position was recently stated in *Royal Bank of Scotland Plc v Highland Partners*[57]:

38–029

> "It is not for the judge considering this issue to re-try the question of the liability of the parties or to see whether the fresh evidence or new facts is material to the final result in the sense of what the decision might be if the matter were to be retried with honest evidence."

If a judgment is set aside then restitution will have to be given of all benefits flowing from it. Hence if the claimant in the first action prevailed and recovered damages, and the defendant subsequently succeeds in having the earlier judgment set aside for fraud, then, in principle, the claimant in the first action will have to repay the damages award and any costs recovered, together, no doubt, with interest.

38–030

A practical consideration is whether such sums would have to be repaid as a condition of the claimant being permitted to pursue the original proceedings through to a (second) trial. It is difficult to see any distinction from the principles applicable to the pursuit of a trial after judgment is set aside on appeal and remitted for a fresh trial. In principle, therefore, such sums should be paid as a condition of proceeding to trial, but the court may agree to waive the requirement if the effect would be to stifle the claim, for example on the grounds of inability to pay or secure the costs.[58]

38–031

The court would also have to consider what consequential directions would be required for the hearing of the trial, and in particular, what directions are appropriate as regards the "fraudulent" evidence. The deceiving party will, presumably, have to adduce a further witness statement to allow the new trial to proceed on honest evidence. Given that the procedure for setting aside the original judgment will have taken place in open court, it is inevitable that the tribunal on the new trial will be aware of the fraud perpetrated in respect of the original judgment, notwithstanding any prejudicial effect that may have.

38–032

---

[57] *Royal Bank of Scotland Plc v Highland Partners* [2013] EWCA Civ 328; [2013] 1 C.L.C. 596, at [141], citing *Sphere Drake Insurance Plc v The Orion Insurance Co Plc*, unreported, 11 February 1999, at 174–175; and *Kuwait Airways Corp v Iraqi Airways Corp (Perjury II)* [2005] EWHC 2524 (Comm), at [198].
[58] See for example *Harb v Abdul Aziz* [2017] EWHC 258 (Ch).

F.   FOREIGN JUDGMENTS

(1)   Occasion

38–033   The most common, but not the only, scenario in which a party may seek to impugn a foreign judgment is in resisting recognition or other enforcement proceedings taken in this jurisdiction. One of the few bases on which recognition and enforcement of a foreign judgment can be resisted is that it was obtained by fraud. It has recently been said that the fraud exception "is a carefully delimited exception and is not to be given [an] expansive application."[59] We do not consider here the voluminous jurisprudence concerning the recognition and enforcement of foreign judgments, other than in the context of seeking to impeach such a judgment on the grounds of fraud.

(2)   General Principles

38–034   As with other instances of civil fraud, while the standard of proof remains the same, the court will assess the evidence of fraud or dishonesty against the inherent probability of the matters alleged. As with a judgment of the English court, the starting point is likely to be to view any claim to impugn judgment of a foreign court with scepticism and a party will need cogent evidence of fraud before the matter will be permitted to continue to trial.

38–035   The mere fact that the foreign court whose judgment is impugned is of the view that there has been no fraud is, largely, irrelevant.[60] However, there are limited circumstances where the judgment of a foreign court itself determining whether a prior foreign judgment has been obtained by fraud can create an issue estoppel which would prevent the English court from determining that issue. An example is seen in *House of Spring Gardens v Waite*[61] where it was held that such an estoppel may arise if the party alleging fraud in the English proceedings had itself chosen first to take proceedings to set aside the foreign judgment in a foreign court, whether the original court which gave judgment or another foreign court. In those circumstances, the fact that the precise issue of whether the judgment was obtained by fraud is being raised for the second or third time can lead to an issue estoppel or abuse of process.

(3)   Distinctions from Setting Aside an English Judgment

38–036   Unlike the position regarding setting aside an English judgment, a foreign judgment can be impeached for fraud irrespective of whether newly discovered evidence is produced and irrespective of whether the fraud was alleged (and

---

[59] *Gelley v Shepherd* [2013] EWCA Civ 1172, at [47], per Sales J.
[60] *Jet Holdings v Patel* [1990] 1 Q.B. 335. So in *Abouloff v Oppenheimer* (1883) 10 Q.B.D. 295 it was held that where a foreign judgment had been obtained by fraud it could not be enforced in this jurisdiction notwithstanding that the question of the fraud had been considered and rejected by the foreign court.
[61] *House of Spring Gardens v Waite* [1991] 1 Q.B. 241.

rejected) in the foreign proceedings.[62] The party alleging the fraud can also rely on it even if it was known to him, and therefore could have been (and indeed was) raised in the foreign proceeding.[63] This rule has been subject to academic criticism as anachronistic, and has not been followed in other commonwealth jurisdictions, but remains good law.[64]

One justification for the rule is the difference in effect of an order of the court impugning a foreign judgment as opposed to setting aside an English one. Whereas the setting aside of an English judgment by the English court renders it a nullity, unenforceable anywhere, impugning a foreign judgment only affects its enforceability in England. The beneficiary of the judgment would still have the right to enforce it in the jurisdiction in which it was made or any other jurisdiction. The English court is not setting the judgment aside; just determining that it cannot be given effect locally. **38–037**

(4) Types of Fraud

The two categories of fraud by which foreign judgments may be obtained are considered below: **38–038**

(1)   Fraud of the party in whose favour the judgment is given; and
(2)   Fraud of the court.

(i)   Fraud of a party

Much of the learning relating to setting aside English judgments which has been analysed above is applicable to impeaching foreign judgments.[65] It is firmly established that, if it is to be successfully impeached, the foreign judgment must **38–039**

---

[62] See *Owens Bank v Bracco* [1992] 2 A.C. 443, at 485–486; and *AK Investment CJSC v Kyrgyz Mobil Tel Ltd* [2012] 1 W.L.R. 1804, at [109].
[63] See *Syal v Heyward* [1948] 2 K.B. 443, per Cohen LJ at 449. However, if the fraud is not newly discovered, and could have been raised in the foreign proceedings, the court is likely to want to know the reason why it was not: *JSC VTB Bank v Skurikhin* [2014] EWHC 271 (Comm), at [26]. Such a failure may weigh forensically against the defendant.
[64] See generally *AK Investment CJSC v Kyrgyz Mobil Tel Ltd* [2011] UKPC 7; [2012] 1 W.L.R. 1804, at [112].
[65] Indeed some of the key cases setting out the principles the court has applied in setting aside domestic judgments themselves concerned the setting aside of a foreign judgment: see for example *Owens v Bracco* [1992] 2 A.C. 443; *Owens v Etoile* [1995] 1 W.L.R. 44.

have been obtained by dishonesty.[66] This can take the form of fraudulently concealing evidence from the foreign court,[67] or misleading the foreign court by evidence known to be false.[68] Further:

"In order for the exception to recognition to apply it is necessary to establish that the fraud in question has been operative in obtaining the foreign judgment and order in issue, in the sense that without such fraud having been practised the order would not have been made, or there is a real possibility that it would not have been made. Although use of the phrase 'tainted by fraud' can be a useful shorthand label for this, this is a narrower and more precise question than simply to ask whether in general terms the order was 'tainted by fraud'."[69]

(ii) Fraud of the court

38-040   An allegation of fraud on the part of the court relies either on specific evidence that the particular judgment the party seeks to impugn was obtained by corruption of the judge or some other external interference (such as political interference), or by the more general assertion that the judiciary in question is so endemically corrupt or subject to outside interference and the nature of the case such that, by inference, the particular decision should be impugned as not being a true judgment of the court. In this sense, the principle on which the foreign judgment will be set aside is akin to a policy concern, deriving from the basic principle of natural justice, as the litigant will have been denied a fair trial in the foreign jurisdiction.[70]

38-041   If it is alleged that the judgment has been obtained by corruption of a foreign judiciary, whether of a general or specific nature, the principles of comity will demand that particularly cogent evidence is adduced for the English court to be satisfied that a judgment is tainted.[71] The allegation is particularly serious as it amounts to an attack on the rule of law of another state. However, if the evidence supports such a claim, the mere fact that a finding might embarrass a foreign sovereign or sour diplomatic relations with the UK is not a factor.[72]

38-042   The principles which the court will apply on such a claim are the same as those applied when the court is asked to adjudicate on a claim in England because justice will not be obtained in the natural forum, whether due to incompetence,

---

[66] See the recent review of the law in *Midtown Acquisitions LP v Essar Global Fund Ltd* [2017] EWHC 519 (Comm). Teare J held, contrary to the defendant's submission, that *Jet Holdings v Patel* [1990] 1 Q.B. 335 provided no support for the proposition that some lesser hurdle needed to be crossed by the party seeking to impeach the foreign judgment. Teare J concluded at [65], that if conscious and deliberate dishonesty is required when seeking to impeach an English judgment the same is required when seeking to impeach a foreign judgment. See also *JSC VTB Bank v Skurikhin* [2014] EWHC 271 (Comm).

[67] *Abouloff v Oppenheimer* (1883) 10 Q.B.D. 295, at 299.

[68] *Vadala v Lawes* (1890) 25 Q.B.D. 310, at 317. Where the fraudulent evidence is that of a witness the successful party had to have procured that evidence: *Jacobsen v Frachon* (1928) The Law Times Vol.138 386. See generally Lord Collins of Mapesbury and J. Harris (eds), *Dicey, Morris & Collins on the Conflict of Laws*, 15th edn (London: Sweet & Maxwell, 2017) at r.50.

[69] *Gelley v Shepherd* [2013] EWCA Civ 1172, at [49].

[70] *Korea National Insurance Co v Allianz Global Corporate & Specialty AG* [2008] EWCA Civ 1355; [2008] 2 C.L.C. 837.

[71] *Yukos Capital Sarl v OJSC Rosneft Oil Co* [2012] 2 C.L.C. 549, at [91].

[72] *Korea National*, at [30], per Waller LJ.

lack of independence, corruption or otherwise[73]; essentially the second limb of the test in *Spiliada Maritime Corp v Cansulex.*[74]

In order to persuade the court that a foreign judge or judiciary was corrupt or subject to interference, specific examples going above mere anecdotal evidence will be required,[75] and the evidence must be "positive and cogent".[76] Mere generalised statements, even from an expert witness, as to the probity or independence of the judiciary will not suffice.   **38–043**

Taken alone, mere error, even obvious error,[77] is unlikely to suffice and procedural irregularity never will. The party seeking to impugn the judgment therefore must do more than rely on an inference that a determination is so flawed that no other explanation than fraud is plausible.   **38–044**

---

[73] *AK Investment CJSC v Kyrgyz Mobil Tel Ltd* [2011] UKPC 7; [2012] 1 W.L.R. 1084, at [71]–[80].
[74] *Spiliada Maritime Corp v Cansulex* [1987] A.C. 460.
[75] *Yukos* [2012] 2 C.L.C. 549, at [151]–[153].
[76] *Cherney v Deripaska* [2009] EWCA Civ 849, at [60].
[77] *Adams v Cape Industries* [1990] Ch. 433, at 569.

SECTION H

CASES WITH AN INTERNATIONAL ELEMENT

CHAPTER 39

JURISDICTION ISSUES

A. INTRODUCTION

Fraud cases increasingly have an international aspect. This gives rise to disputes **39–001** as to which country's courts will hear the claim and which country's substantive law will be applied to determine it. This chapter and the next deal respectively with those issues, namely jurisdiction and conflict of laws. They do not attempt a comprehensive statement of the law on those topics, which is vast and to be found in venerable sources.[1] Rather they seek to provide what is hoped is a useful summary for practitioners of the provisions applying in the specific context of civil fraud claims.

On 23 June 2016 the UK voted by referendum to leave the EU. The vote had, of **39–002** itself, no legal effect. However, as much of the English jurisdictional and private international law for the past 44 years has been derived from EU legislation, "Brexit" has the potential to have a significant impact on that law. This is more so in relation to the rules on jurisdiction, which by their nature involve reciprocal and multilateral obligations, than in relation to conflicts of laws, where the effect of the relevant treaties is in essence simply that each of the signatories applies the same rules in their respective courts to determine which laws apply.[2]

The UK government irrevocably triggered its departure from the EU under art.50 **39–003** of the EC Treaty on 30 March 2017. The effect of that was to start running a two-year period during which the UK and the EU must seek to reach an agreement as to the terms of the UK's exit, failing which it will on 29 March 2019 simply cease to be a member of the EU and all existing agreements between it and the EU will cease to have effect.

At the time of writing, negotiations are ongoing. So far as relevant to civil fraud **39–004** litigation, on 28 June 2017, the EU published a Position Paper on Judicial Co-operation in Civil and Commercial Matters. The UK responded in August 2017 with a paper on "Providing a cross-border civil judicial co-operation framework", which for the most part agreed with the EU's proposals as to transitional arrangements, but also set out some interesting contentions as to the UK's proposed position in substantive negotiations.

---

[1] For example, Lord Collins of Mapesbury and J. Harris (eds), *Dicey, Morris & Collins on the Conflict of Laws*, 15th edn (London: Sweet & Maxwell, 2017), Fourth supplement; A. Briggs, *Private International Law in English Courts*, 1st edn (Oxford: OUP, 2014).

[2] The position was analysed in some detail by Professor Briggs at the Commercial Bar Association Lecture on 24 January 2017, entitled "Secession from the European Union and Private International Law, the Cloud with a Silver Lining'.

39–005   Most recently the EU has issued a Draft Withdrawal Agreement in relation to the UK's withdrawal. In that paper, references in previous documents to the date of withdrawal have been replaced by references to the end of a transition period if one can be agreed between the EU and the UK. This suggests that, if agreement is reached on a transition period, the existing arrangements relating to choice of law, jurisdiction and enforcement of judgments will continue until the end of that period (and beyond in the circumstances referred to below).

39–006   The key points of the Draft Withdrawal Agreement are:

(1)   The Brussels Regulation Recast Regulation (EU) No.1215/2012 ("the BRR") would continue to apply in relation to proceedings commenced, or (where relevant) jurisdiction agreements entered into, before the end of the transition period.

(2)   The BRR provisions relating to enforcement of judgments would continue to apply where judgment was given before the end of the transition period.

(3)   The Rome I Regulation (Regulation (EC) No.593/2008) ("Rome I") would continue to apply to contracts concluded before the end of the transition period; and the Rome II Regulation (Regulation (EC) No. 864/2007) ("Rome II") would continue to apply to events giving rise to damage which occurred before the end of the transition period.

39–007   However, it remains unclear on exactly what terms the departure will take place in relation to legally relevant events after the end of the transition period, including in relation to civil jurisdiction and conflicts of laws matters. In light of the proposed transitional arrangements, even if significant changes do occur it is likely to be some time before cases involving them appear before the English courts.

39–008   In the circumstances, with the significant caveat set out in this introduction, these chapters set out the law as it is now.

39–009   This chapter provides an overview of the English rules on jurisdiction, particularly as they apply to claims based on the substantive causes of action covered in this book. There are, additionally, rules prescribing when the English court has jurisdiction to deal with free-standing applications for pre-emptive relief, even, in some cases, where it may not have jurisdiction over the substantive dispute. Those are dealt with elsewhere in this book, in the specific chapters addressing the remedies in question.

B.   SOURCES OF LAW

39–010   The English law of international jurisdiction is contained in two sources, namely the common law and EU legislation. Where the UK has international jurisdiction, there are further, national, rules, dictating which of the UK's constituent parts has jurisdiction.

39–011   The key piece of EU legislation for these purposes is now the BRR, also known as "Brussels I *bis*". It applies, in EU Member States which are signatories to the

Regulation, including the UK, in all "civil and commercial matters whatever the nature of the court or tribunal".[3] It therefore applies in principle to every civil fraud dispute before the English courts which has an "international element".[4] However, art.6(1) provides that if the defendant is not domiciled in a Member State, and none of the exclusive jurisdiction provisions in the BRR apply to the claim, jurisdiction will be determined according to the national law of the Member State in the courts of which the matter is being heard, i.e. in cases before the English court, the common law provisions relating to service out of the jurisdiction (as to which see below).

Where the BRR is engaged (as to which, see below) it prescribes whether the English court or the court of another Member State has jurisdiction. If the English court does have jurisdiction under the BRR, English process may be served (in accordance with Pt 6 of the CPR) without the permission of the court.[5] If not, that is the end of the matter and an English claim cannot be served.[6]   39–012

The BRR came into effect on 10 January 2015, meaning that it applies to "legal proceedings instituted" on or after that date.[7] This means that there are currently two sets of rules operating in parallel, one for claims "instituted" (meaning, in English terminology, issued) prior to that date and another for those commenced on or after it. The former category is governed by the BRR's predecessor, Regulation 44/2001, also known as the "Judgments Regulation" or "Brussels I".[8]   39–013

Although the BRR formally repealed Brussels I in its entirety,[9] their provisions are in very large part identical, save that the numbers of the relevant articles have all changed.[10] References to articles below are to those in the BRR.   39–014

The key changes which are within the scope of this book[11] are addressed in detail in the relevant sections below, but can be briefly summarised as follows: 39–015

---

[3] There are a number of civil matters that are specifically excluded, which are not in any event relevant to civil fraud litigation, and so are not dealt with here. Arbitration is also expressly excluded (art.1.2(d)). That exclusion has been "enhanced" in the BRR in an attempt to deal with the problems arising out of the *West Tankers* litigation (see Recital 12 to the BRR).

[4] The qualification that the case must have an "international element" appears nowhere in the wording of the BRR itself, but was made clear in *Owusu v Jackson* (ECJ) [2005] Q.B. 801, at [25], relying upon the Jenard report on the Brussels Convention, and applied in *Maletic v lastminute.com* (ECJ) [2014] 2 Q.B. 424, at [26].

[5] CPR r.6.33(1).

[6] Subject to art.35, which provides that an application may be made to the courts of a Member State for such provisional, including protective, measures as may be available under the law of that Member State, even if the courts of another Member State have jurisdiction as to the substance of the matter under the BBR.

[7] BRR, art.66(1).

[8] BRR, art.66(2).

[9] BRR, art.80.

[10] A very helpful table produced by LynxLex, showing the development and number of each article through the conventions since 1968, including Brussels I and the BRR, is here: *http://lynxlex.com/sites/default/files/files/From%20Brussels%20to%20Lugano%20-%20A%20panoramic%20table_0.pdf* [Accessed 12 June 2018].

[11] There have also been a number of changes to (i) the rules designed to protect "weaker parties", for example, consumer protection, insurance and employment; (ii) the rules regarding the enforcement

(1) Jurisdiction clauses nominating the courts of a Member State are now enforceable under the BRR even if neither of the parties to the agreement in which they are contained is domiciled in a Member State.

(2) Jurisdiction clauses are now severable from the rest of the contract for the purposes of resolving jurisdiction disputes.

(3) The substantive validity of jurisdiction clauses is now to be determined by the law of the Member State nominated by the clause.

(4) The order of priority has been reversed as between the provisions dealing with *lis alibi pendens* and those dealing with jurisdiction agreements.

(5) A very limited doctrine of *lis alibi pendens* has been introduced in relation to "third states", i.e. to countries not within the EU.

39–016 There is further complication because in 1988 certain states within the European Free Trade Association (EFTA) entered into a treaty with the states who were parties to the Brussels I Convention, namely the Lugano Convention. Three of the original six Lugano states subsequently became members of the EU and therefore parties to the Brussels Convention. The remaining Lugano states are Iceland, Norway and Switzerland. An amended Lugano Convention, signed in 2007, took effect in 2010–2011 ("the 2007 Lugano Convention"). Its provisions were in almost identical terms to Brussels I but have not yet been updated in light of the changes introduced by the BRR, so there is a third system operating in parallel with those mentioned above.

39–017 Where none of this European legislation applies, the English court will apply the common law to determine jurisdiction.

39–018 The national rules of jurisdiction within the UK which are referred to above are contained within the Civil Jurisdiction and Judgments Act 1982. That Act, the provisions of which will be considered below, incorporates the provisions of Brussels I. At the time of writing the Act has not yet been updated to reflect the provisions of the BRR.

39–019 There are two separate aspects to jurisdictional law. The first is subject matter jurisdiction, where certain states are given exclusive jurisdiction over certain subject matter with which they are territorially connected. The second is personal jurisdiction, where rules specify the circumstances in which a particular court has jurisdiction over a particular defendant. At common law, the rules on personal jurisdiction prescribe the circumstances in which a defendant may be validly served with English process, and therefore in which the English courts have jurisdiction over the dispute in question. By contrast, the European legislation does the reverse—it specifies the circumstances in which the courts of a Member State have jurisdiction, and therefore in which it is permissible to serve the defendant. Where there is a conflict between the rules of subject matter and personal jurisdiction, the former will prevail.

---

and recognition of judgments; and (iii) the scope of the exclusion of arbitration from the Brussels scheme (designed to address the issues created by the *West Tankers* decision). Those are outside the scope of this text and are not addressed herein.

Beyond that broad statement, there are too many variables to permit any conceptual categorisation of the English rules of jurisdiction, and it is easiest to set them out based upon the defendant's place of domicile, which is in any event the proper starting point for the analysis, as explained below.

39–020

C. DEFENDANT DOMICILED IN THE EU

(1) The General Rule

When a defendant is domiciled within the EU (including, for the time being, in the UK) the English court's jurisdiction is governed by the BRR, regardless of the nationality or place of domicile of the claimant.[12]

39–021

The key provision in the BRR ("the General Rule"), is art.4(1), which provides:

39–022

> "Subject to this Regulation, persons domiciled in a Member State shall, whatever their nationality, be sued in the courts of that Member State."[13]

What does "domiciled" mean in this context? Article 62 provides that in order to determine whether a party is domiciled in the Member State whose courts are seised of the matter, the court shall apply its internal law. In order for a person to be "domiciled" in the UK for the purposes of the Regulation: (a) he must be resident there and (b) the nature and circumstances of his residence must indicate that he has a substantial connection with the UK.[14] The relevant date for consideration of a person's domicile is the date of issue of the claim form.[15]

39–023

(i) Domicile: individuals

The question of domicile is often not straightforward, especially when it concerns international businessmen, as illustrated by two recent decisions. In *Bestolov v Povarenkin*[16] Mr Povarenkin was a Russian citizen who worked in Moscow, and had a large property there where he spent a lot of his time. He was married with two children, and the children were at school in England. During term time his wife lived with the children in an expensive flat in Central London and Mr Povarenkin visited them around two times per month. The family spent the holidays in either France or Moscow. Proceedings (arising out of agreements related to mining) were served in England on the basis of domicile. The court applied the two-stage test set out above, finding that Mr Povarenkin was

39–024

---

[12] As we note below, in certain circumstances the English court's jurisdiction will be governed by the BBR even when the defendant is not domiciled within the EU.

[13] Article 4(2) makes clear that a defendant's nationality, if different to that of the Member State in which they are domiciled, is irrelevant.

[14] Schedule 1 of the Civil Jurisdiction and Judgments Order 2001, SI 2001/3929, Sch.1, para.9(2), (3) and (6) set out the legal position regarding an individual's domicile in the UK.

[15] *Canada Trust Co v Stolzenberg (No.2)* [2002] 1 A.C. 1 (HL); *Cherney v Deripaska* [2007] EWHC 965 (Comm), at [15]; and *Yugraneft v Abramovich* [2008] EWHC 2613 (Comm), at [445].

[16] *Bestolov v Povarenkin* [2017] EWHC 1968 (Simon Bryan QC), which contains a valuable survey of the authorities.

domiciled in England (and also in Russia).[17] He also had a substantial connection to England due to his continuing visits during term time. Similarly, in *Eng King v Petrillo*,[18] the following factors were sufficient to establish English domicile on the part of a businessman: regular visits to England to stay with his children and ex-wife; remaining on the electoral roll at his former matrimonial home; continued use of his marital address on official documents; maintaining an English landline and mobile number; the individual's company continuing to have a business address in England, and transfers to English bank accounts. Further, the defendant had not explained in evidence where he had spent his time if not England, he had produced no evidence of property ownership at all, and had produced no documents suggesting that he had another address.

(ii) Domicile: companies and other legal persons

39–025   As for companies or other legal persons or associations of natural or legal persons, art.63 provides that they are domiciled at the place where they have their statutory seat, central administration or principal place of business.

(iii) A mandatory provision

39–026   Importantly, art.4 is in *mandatory* terms. This means that if a defendant is domiciled in one of the member states of the EU, then unless one of the other provisions of the BRR permits or requires the claimant to sue the defendant in another Member State, he *must* be sued in his state of domicile—the claimant has no alternative, and a national court has no power to decline jurisdiction.[19] The English court cannot, for example, stay the claim on the basis of common law principles such as forum non conveniens,[20] nor can it achieve the same effect under the guise of granting a "case management" stay.[21] This principle, which would appear from the wording of art.4 to be absolute, has nevertheless been the subject of slight erosion in recent times, as set out below.[22]

39–027   The remainder of Ch.2 of the BRR (being the part which deals with jurisdiction) consists of exceptions to the General Rule. In some cases, these exceptions provide an *alternative* to the General Rule that is open to the claimant, in other words another Member State where he *may* sue the defendant. In other cases, they prescribe that another Member State has *mandatory* or "exclusive"

---

[17] It is possible for a person to reside in more than one jurisdiction at the same time: see *Levene v Commissioners of Inland Revenue* [1928] A.C. 217, at 222; and *Cherney v Deripaska* [2007] EWHC 965 (Comm), at [18], per Langley J.

[18] *Eng King v Petrillo* [2016] EWHC 380 (Comm).

[19] For a recent, strict, application of this principle in Belgium, see *Corman-Collins SA v La Maison du Whisky SA* [2014] Q.B. 431 (Case C-9/12). See also *Lungowe v Vedanta* [2017] EWCA Civ 1528; [2017] BCC 787, at [37], per Simon LJ.

[20] *Owusu v Jackson* [2005] ECR I-1383. As to forum non conveniens, see para.39–107 below.

[21] In *Skype Technologies SA v Joltid Ltd* [2009] EWHC 2783 (Ch), Lewison J warned, at [22], that the court must not "under the guise of case management, achieve by the back door a result against which the ECJ has locked the front door."

[22] At para.39–061.

jurisdiction. There are also procedural rules to determine, for example, which of two potentially relevant states, or which of two potentially relevant articles of the BRR, takes priority in a given matter.

(iv)   Burden on claimant

In the case of a dispute as to whether one of the articles of the BRR applies to the facts of a given case (including, where it is relevant, as to the scope or construction of a jurisdiction clause), it is for the claimant (who has chosen to bring proceedings in the English court) to prove that the court has jurisdiction, and the standard is "good arguable case". In this context that means that the claimant must show he has a better argument than the defendant on the material available.[23] This elusive criterion—which reflects the fact that the outcome is effectively determinative of the issue of jurisdiction—is said to lie somewhere on the spectrum between the summary judgment test of "real prospect of success" and the trial standard of balance of probabilities. Whilst this can be readily understood in the context of an ex parte hearing, it is less easy to see how it could be applied at an inter partes interlocutory hearing where there is a conflict of evidence, without a mini trial. It may also—depending on the jurisdiction issue in question—involve the judge forming a view on the merits of an issue that will have to be determined at trial. For example, if a substantive issue in the case is whether the defendant is bound by the terms of a contract, factual and/or legal issues relevant to that question may well also arise in the context of a prior jurisdiction dispute as to whether he is subject to a jurisdiction clause contained within that contract. The courts have recognised this and have applied the test flexibly in such cases, saying that they must merely be "satisfied, having regard to the limitations of the interlocutory process, that factors existed which allowed the court to take jurisdiction".[24]

39–028

If a defendant domiciled in one Member State is sued in a court of another Member State and does not enter an appearance, the court is obliged to consider both service on the defendant, and jurisdiction, of its own motion. It must decline jurisdiction if not satisfied that its jurisdiction is derived from the other provisions of the BRR, and must stay the proceedings if it is not satisfied that the defendant has been validly served.[25]

39–029

---

[23] *Canada Trust v Stolzenberg (No.2)* [1998] 1 W.L.R. 547, at 555. This was approved by the House of Lords in that case ([2002] 1 A.C. 1, at 13) and by the Privy Council in *Bols Distilleries (t/a Bols Royal Distilleries) v Superior Yacht Services Ltd* [2006] UKPC 45; [2007] 1 W.L.R. 12, at [28]. For ECJ guidance as to the level of inquiry that needs to be carried out, see *Kolassa v Barclays Bank Plc* [2015] I.L.Pr. 245 (Case C-375/13). The test was recently affirmed, in the context of service out of the jurisdiction, in the judgment of Lord Sumption in *Brownlie v Four Seasons* [2017] UKSC 80 (see para.39–091 below).

[24] See for example *Antonio Gramsci Shipping Corp v Lembergs* [2012] EWHC 1887 (Comm); [2012] I.L.Pr. 36, at [39].

[25] BRR, art.28.

(2)   Alternative Jurisdiction for Specific Causes of Action

39–030   The first category of exceptions to the General Rule is contained in art.7, which sets out rules relating to the connection between the cause of action with which the claim is concerned and the jurisdiction in question. Where art.7 is engaged, the *claimant* has a discretion to sue in the alternative jurisdiction (i.e. the courts of another Member State). However, art.7 does not give any discretion to the *court* to stay a claim, for example on forum non conveniens grounds, which has been brought against a defendant in his place of domicile, on the basis that the claim could also have been brought in another jurisdiction by virtue of that article.[26] The rules within art.7 that are relevant in the civil fraud context are examined below.

(i)   Contract

39–031   In "matters relating to contract", art.7(1) provides that a defendant may be sued "in the courts for the place of performance of the obligation in question." The article gives two specific examples, namely that in the case of contracts for the sale of goods or services the place of performance is the place where the goods or services were or should have been provided.

39–032   The rules relating to straightforward claims to enforce a contract, or for damages for breach of contract, are outside the scope of this book and are therefore not dealt with in detail here, except in one respect. Where a claim is brought to enforce duties which came into existence between parties to a contract, and where interpretation of the contract is essential to determine the lawfulness of the conduct complained of, such a claim will fall within art.7(1), even if the claim is founded on a common law duty of care which could in theory exist independently of the contract. In other words, it is possible for a claim to concern "matters relating to a contract" even where it is not a claim pursuant to, or for breach of, a contract per se.[27] (The reverse must also be true: a claim by one party to a contract against another is not necessarily within the scope of art.7(1) if it does not on a proper analysis relate to the contract.)

(ii)   Tort

39–033   Article 7(2) deals with *"matters relating to tort, delict or quasi-delict"*. In such claims a defendant can be sued in the courts for "the place where the harmful event occurred or may occur". There are a number of facets to that statement, which need to be examined:

(1)   The phrase "relating to tort, delict or quasi-delict" has a broad meaning, and covers all actions which seek to establish the civil liability of a

---

[26] *Mahme Trust v Lloyds TSB Bank Plc* [2004] EWHC 1931; [2004] I.L. Pr. 43, at [32]–[35].
[27] *Brogsitter v Fabrication de Montres Normandes EURL* (ECJ) [2014] Q.B. 753. For further ECJ guidance as to claims which can be brought in either contract or tort see *Holterman Ferho Exploitatie BV v Spies von Büllesheim* [2016] I.C.R. 90 (Case C-47/14).

defendant for a harmful event or threatened wrong, but which are not related to a contract so as to fall within art.7(1).[28]

(2)   Importantly, this classification is intended to be autonomous; it is not dependent on how the national court (of any particular Member State) in question would view the case, and is a separate question from the way in which the substantive dispute will be analysed by the court which ultimately comes to deal with it.[29]

(3)   The words "or may occur" make clear that the article extends to future, or threatened, torts.

(4)   The phrase "harmful event" is ambiguous in that it potentially covers both the suffering of harm by the victim and the act by the defendant giving rise to the harm. It is now accepted that if these happen in different places, the claimant can choose between them; in other words in those circumstances art.7(2) potentially provides *two* alternative courts to those of the place of the defendant's domicile.[30] We consider those alternatives in the following paragraphs.

Place Where Harm Occurred.   "Harm" may, as a result of one tortious act, be suffered in a number of different ways, in a number of different places, by a number of different people, all of whom might be entitled to claim damages. The relevant loss, or "harm" for jurisdiction purposes is the first damage to the most immediate victim, rather than consequential damage to that victim or loss suffered by anyone else indirectly.[31] The relevant harm is not, for example, suffered in the place of domicile of the victim, or where his "assets are concentrated", if the event has already caused damage actually arising elsewhere.[32] Nor is it suffered where a parent company feels the effects of a wrong done to its subsidiary.[33]   **39–034**

Actial Farmaceutica LDA v De Simone[34] is a good example of the strictness of the "first damage" rule: there the claimant was an indirect subsidiary of a joint venture company holding an interest in a probiotic food product created by that company's director, an Italian professor of medicine. The claimant alleged that the company and director had embarked upon a conspiratorial scheme to wrest control of the manufacture and distribution of the product from the joint venture with the intention of channelling sales through a rival business. It said that by doing so the professor had prevented it from obtaining supplies from the US,   **39–035**

---

[28] *Kalfelis v Bankhaus Schröder Münchmeyer Hengst & Co (Case C-189/87)* [1988] ECR 5565, 5585, at [17]; *Mazur Media Ltd v Mazur Media GmbH* [2004] EWHC 1566 (Ch); [2004] 1 W.L.R. 2966, at [23]. It has been a matter of some controversy whether art.7(2) was intended by the Court in *Kalfelis* to be restricted to harmful events or threatened wrongs. The House of Lords in *Kleinwort Benson* found (see below) that its predecessor should be so restricted, and that it did not apply to an unjust enrichment claim. That view, whilst not universally accepted, would appear to represent the law in England.

[29] *Melzer v MF Global UK Ltd* (ECJ) [2013] Q.B. 1112, at [49]–[50].

[30] *Handelswekerij GJ Bier BV v Mines de Potasse d'Alsace SA* (C-21/76) [1978] Q.B. 708, at [19].

[31] *Marinari v Lloyd's Bank Plc* [1996] Q.B. 217, at [14]–[15].

[32] See for example *Marinari*, above, *Kronhofer v Maier* (Case C-168/02) [2004] I.L. Pr. 27, at [19]; and *Kolassa v Barclays Bank Plc* (Case C-375/13) [2015] I.L. Pr. 14, at [48]–[50].

[33] *Dumez France SA v Hessiche Landesbank* (C-220/88) [1990] I.L. Pr. 299, at [22].

[34] *Actial Farmaceutica LDA v De Simone* [2016] EWCA Civ 1311; [2016] 2 C.L.C. 1020.

removing it as a designated supplier and so preventing it from fulfilling its obligations to its UK distributor. For jurisdiction purposes, the Court had to decide where the jurisdictionally relevant harm occurred. It concluded that the harmful event was the alleged conspiracy. The damage which was closest in proximity to that harmful event was the non-delivery of the product in bulk to the claimant's packaging agents in Italy and the Netherlands. The subsequent damage suffered because, as a consequence, Actial was unable to supply its distributors, whether in the UK or elsewhere, was merely consequential or indirect.

39–036 The most difficult sort of harm to analyse, with which most fraud cases will be concerned, is financial loss. Financial loss is, in a large number of cases, preceded by some other form of harm. Indeed, the location of financial loss, which is normally the location of the victim's bank account, is often arbitrary, in the sense that it is a function of practical or fiscal considerations of no real jurisdictional significance. For those reasons the ECJ has recently held, perhaps controversially, that financial loss cannot on its own, in the absence of any other factors connecting the case with a particular jurisdiction, suffice as a basis for conferring jurisdiction under art.7(2).[35] It is not clear how many other connecting factors are required or what sort.

39–037 In *AMT Futures Ltd v Marzillier*,[36] the Supreme Court had to consider whether there was a special rule for the tort of inducing a breach of contract where the contract in question was an English exclusive jurisdiction clause. It noted that in several contexts in which it was not obvious where the "harmful event" had taken place for the purposes of art.7(2), namely damage to goods at sea, libel cases and publication of information on the internet, special guidance had been given.

39–038 In *Marzillier*, a derivatives broker had been sued in Germany by certain investors contrary to an exclusive jurisdiction clause in favour of England in the relevant contracts between them and him. He sued, amongst others, the investors' German lawyers, based on the tort of inducing breach of contract, on the basis that they had induced their clients to breach the jurisdiction clause. The claimant asserted that the relevant harm was being deprived of the benefit of dispute resolution in England, and so England was where the direct damage occurred. Alternatively, it argued that this was another case, like those identified above, where a special rule should be adopted, in this case in favour of the contractually chosen court.

39–039 The Supreme Court held that the English court did not have jurisdiction, as both the event causing harm, being the commencement of the German proceedings, and the harm, occurred in Germany. That was where the claimant had to deal with the claims, and settle them. Any loss in England was consequential on that initial direct loss. As it was quite possible to ascertain where the harm had occurred, there was no need to craft a special rule. The Court accepted that the consequence of its ruling was to separate the determination of the claimant's contractual claims against the investors (for breach of the jurisdiction agreement) from the tortious claims against the lawyers, however it said that

---

[35] *Universal Music Holding BV v Schilling* [2016] Q.B. 967, at [36]–[49]. The other cases referred to above, some of which were based upon purely financial loss, were distinguished on the basis that they also involved other connecting factors.
[36] *AMT Futures Ltd v Marzillier* [2017] UKSC 13; [2017] 2 W.L.R. 852.

"such inconvenience is the price of achieving the legal certainty and foreseeability which are among the principal aims of the Judgments Regulation, as the CJEU has recognised and endorsed."

Place Where Harmful Event Occurred.   As for the tortious act or "event", the   **39–040**
relevant event is the act or omission of the defendant (or his agent) which substantially starts the process which leads to the damage. It has been held that in the case of a negligent misstatement the place where the event giving rise to the damage occurred was the place where the misstatement originated and the damage occurred in the place where the misstatement was received and relied upon. In so holding in *Domicrest Ltd v Swiss Bank Corp*,[37] Rix J rejected the "substance of the cause of action" test, preferring instead the "more structured formula" reflected in the then recent decisions in *Marinari*[38] and *Dumez*.[39] In particular he said:

> "Applying that formula, it seems to me that the place where the harmful event giving rise to the damage occurs in a case of negligent mis-statement is, by analogy with the tort of defamation, where the mis-statement originates. It is there that the negligence, even if not every element of the tort, is likely to take place; and for that and other reasons the place from which the mis-statement is put into circulation is as good a place in which to found jurisdiction as the place where the mis-statement is acted on, even if receipt and reliance are essential parts of the tort. For these purposes it seems to me that there is no difference between a written document and an oral or other instantaneous communication sufficient to distinguish between such cases. Although it may be argued that in the case of instantaneous communications and perhaps especially in the case of telephone conversations the mis-statement occurs as much where it is heard as where it is spoken, nevertheless it remains true as it seems to me that it is the representor's negligent speech rather than the hearer's receipt of it which best identifies the harmful event which sets the tort in motion. To prefer receipt and reliance as epitomising the harmful event giving rise to the damage in the case of negligent mis-statement is, I think, to ignore the fact that the plaintiff also has the option of suing in the courts of the place where the damage occurs – which is quite likely to be at the place of receipt and reliance."

The same analysis must logically also apply to a fraudulent misrepresentation, although we are aware of no authority which so decides.

A further example might be if A, resident in (say) Berlin, carries out a mandate   **39–041**
fraud whereby through forged invoices (issued in the name of company B) he causes customers of B in the UK to mistakenly send money to his Latvian bank account rather than B's bank account in the UK. In this case under the extended meaning accorded to the phrase "harmful event" in art.7(2) the claimant customers could, at their election, sue either in the UK, where they parted with their money, or Germany, being the place from which A sent the invoices which led them to part with it.

The position was recently authoritatively considered by the Supreme Court in   **39–042**
Khrapunov v JSC BTA Bank,[40] which, as set out in more detail in Ch.2 above, was concerned with an alleged combination or understanding between Mukhtar Ablyazov and his son-in-law, Mr Khrapunov, who was domiciled in Switzerland, to conceal or dissipate Mr Ablyazov's assets in order to frustrate enforcement by

---

[37] *Domicrest v Swiss Bank Corp* [1999] Q.B. 548, at 567–568.
[38] *Marinari* [1996] Q.B. 217.
[39] *Dumez* [1990] I.L. Pr. 299.
[40] *Khrapunov v JSC BTA Bank* [2018] UKSC 19.

the claimant bank of its substantial judgment, and a claim in conspiracy by the bank on the basis of that arrangement. In relation to the English court's jurisdiction over Mr Khrapunov, the bank had argued, successfully, in the Court of Appeal, that the harmful event, for the purposes of art.5(3) of the 2007 Lugano Convention (which is in materially identical terms to art.7(2) of the BRR) was the formation of the conspiratorial agreement, which had been made in England. The Supreme Court agreed, holding that:

(1)   The phrase "place where the harmful event occurred" should be given an autonomous meaning for the purposes of the Convention.
(2)   That did not mean that the component elements of the cause of action in domestic law were irrelevant. Far from it; they had a vital role in defining the legally relevant conduct and thus identifying the acts which fell to be located for the purposes of art.5(3). In particular, whether an event is harmful is determined by national law.
(3)   Rix J had correctly set out the test to be applied in his analysis in *Domicrest* (see above); applying that to the facts of this case the Court of Appeal (in *Khrapunov*) had therefore been right to find that the conspiratorial agreement, rather than its implementation, was the originating event, or the event which set the tort in motion, that it was therefore the "harmful event", and that the English court therefore had jurisdiction despite Mr Khrapunov's Swiss domicile.

(iii)   Restitution

39-043 Article 7(3) applies to restitution, but only when it arises out of criminal proceedings. In some jurisdictions a court exercising criminal jurisdiction may make an order for compensation or restitution against the defendant, and a victim of the crime may intervene in the proceedings as a civil party to the proceedings in order to apply for such relief. No such jurisdiction is recognised in England and therefore the application of art.7(3) in proceedings in England is likely to be non-existent.

39-044 Jurisdiction in relation to a free-standing, civil, restitution claim depends upon the basis for the claim. If it is based upon a wrong (for example a tort or a breach of fiduciary duty), it is likely to fall within art.7(2). If it could be said to "relate to a contract" it will fall within art.7(1). Otherwise (for example if both parties accept that the contract in question was void) it will be likely to fall within the General Rule in art.4.[41]

---

[41] *Kleinwort Benson Ltd v Glasgow City Council (No.2)* [1999] 1 A.C. 153. There is some controversy in the case-law as to whether the effect of the ECJ's ruling in *Kalfelis*, above, was that all matters of civil liability which are not covered by art.7(1) are within art.7(2), i.e. that it is a residual category for wrongs. The House of Lords in *Kleinwort v Benson* thought otherwise, finding that art.7(2) did not cover claims in unjust enrichment which did not relate to a contract (save, presumably, where they fall under art.7(3), which, as noted above, will not be the case in England).

(iv) *Equitable claims*

Article 7(6) provides that   39–045

> "in a dispute brought against a settlor, trustee or beneficiary of a trust created by the operation
> of a statute, or by a written instrument, or created orally and evidenced in writing"

the defendant can be sued in the courts of the Member State in which the trust is domiciled.

There are two issues of classification here: 39–046

(1) First, which sorts of trusts does it cover? It does not appear to extend to trusts created by operation of law other than statute, for example automatic resulting trusts. Nor does it extend to express trusts which are created orally but not evidenced in writing.

(2) Second, in what capacity is the defendant sued? The definition appears to seek to distinguish between matters *internal* to the trust, which are covered, and claims against outsiders, which are not. Accordingly, it will include claims for breach of trust but will exclude, in most cases, claims in dishonest assistance or knowing receipt (unless, potentially, they are based on a beneficiary or trustee acting in excess of his rights under the trust). It also does not apply to trust officers other than trustees, for example appointors or protectors.[42]

Once that analysis is carried out, so as to ascertain the potential applicability of   39–047
art.7(6), the only issue is whether the trust in question is domiciled in the UK. For that purpose the courts apply English law, which provides that a trust is domiciled in the place with which it has its closest and most real connection.[43] This will inevitably be the country by whose law the trust is governed, so in this respect this rule of jurisdiction defers to the rules on conflicts of laws as regards trusts. If an express choice of law is made that will be determinative. If not, the governing law will be determined by the rules in the Hague Convention on Trusts and the Recognition of Trusts Act 1987.[44]

As to claims *external* to the trust: 39–048

(1) A claim based on dishonest assistance in a breach of trust, even if it involves alleging that the defendant is liable as a constructive trustee, falls within art.7(2), as it is based upon a harmful event (the dishonest assistance).[45]

---

[42] *Gomez v Gomez Monche Vives* [2008] EWCA Civ 1065; [2009] Ch. 245 CA, at [99].

[43] Civil Jurisdiction and Judgments Act 1982, s.45.

[44] See Ch.40.

[45] *Casio Computer Co Ltd v Sayo* [2001] EWCA Civ 661; [2001] I.L. Pr. 694, at [15]–[17]. In *Dexter Ltd (In Administrative Receivership) v Harley*, *The Times*, 2 April 2001, the court appears to have approved the claimant's Counsel's concession that the claim (put in the alternative in dishonest assistance and knowing receipt) was within the then equivalent of art.7(2).

(2)   There is no specific authority as to how a claim in knowing receipt should be dealt with under the BRR, which will surely depend upon whether, on a proper juridical analysis of the cause of action, and (possibly) on the facts of the case, it involves a harmful event (in which case art.7(2) will apply) or not (in which case, as with certain claims in restitution, art.7(2) does not apply and the claim will fall within the general rule in art.4).[46]

39–049   As with claims in restitution, jurisdiction in claims for breach of fiduciary duty is likely to depend upon the facts. If the breach is defined by the terms of a pre-existing contractual relationship, for example that of employer and employee, or solicitor and client, then the claim is likely to fall within art.7(1). By contrast if the claim is for a fiduciary to account as a constructive trustee for extra-contractual wrongdoing which has caused harm, it will fall within art.7(2).

(3) Branches

39–050   In the case of a dispute "arising out of the operations of a branch, agency or other establishment", art.7(5) provides that the defendant can be sued "in the courts for the place where the branch, agency or other establishment is situated" (as opposed to the domicile of the company or other legal person). This article is intended to refer to a permanent, fixed, branch of a defendant entity which operates in another Member State. It means, for instance, that a Greek domiciled bank may be sued in England under art.7(5) if it has a branch in England and the dispute arises out of the operations of that branch. To qualify for art.7(5) a "branch, agency or other establishment" needs to operate generally under the direction and control of the defendant, and to have the power to bind the defendant by its acts. If those conditions are satisfied the article can apply even where the "branch" is a separate legal entity.[47]

(4) One of a Number of Defendants

39–051   Under art.8(1), where a defendant is one of a number of defendants, he may be sued in the courts for the place where any one of them is domiciled

> "provided the claims are so closely connected that it is expedient to hear and determine them together to avoid the risk of irreconcilable judgments resulting from separate proceedings".

In this context the defendant who has been sued in the place of his domicile is commonly known as the "anchor defendant". Oddly, the rule applies only when jurisdiction against the anchor defendant has been established by domicile (i.e. under the General Rule), and not when it has been established by, say, prorogation (i.e. by a jurisdiction agreement or submission to the jurisdiction). Each case under this provision will turn on its facts and there is little point in analysing prior case-law applying the principles—the court will have to assess (to

---

[46] The point was expressly left unanswered in *Casio* (see above), at [23].
[47] *SAR Schotte GmbH v Parfums Rothschild sarl* [1989] ECC 431 (C-218/86) applying *Somafer SA v Saar-Ferngas AG* [1978] ECR 2183 (C-33/78).

the "better of the argument" standard—see above) the expediency of hearing the claims together and the likelihood of there being separate irreconcilable judgments if it did not.

A controversial question, however, has been whether the merits of the claim against the anchor defendant, and the related issue as to the claimant's motivation in bringing a claim against that anchor defendant, should be taken into account when considering jurisdiction over the non-anchor foreign defendant(s). In *Reisch Montage v Kiesel Baumaschinen Handels GmbH*, the ECJ held that where the "sole purpose" of bringing the claim is to oust the foreign defendant(s) from their place of domicile, the requirements of art.8(1) are not met.[48] As for the burden of proof on that issue, the position, prior to the Court of Appeal's decision in *Sabbagh v Khoury*, referred to below, appeared to be that if the threshold test of there being a risk of irreconcilable judgments is met, the claimant is under no obligation to establish that his sole purpose in suing the anchor defendant is *not* to establish jurisdiction against a co-defendant,[49] but that if the court found that there was clear evidence that that *was* his intention it had discretion to decline jurisdiction over the co-defendant.[50] For example in *Cartel Damage Claims SA v Akzo Nobel NV*[51] the ECJ said that art.8(1) would not apply if there was "firm evidence" that the claimant and the anchor defendant had intentionally and artificially prolonged the existence of factors which rendered art.8(1) applicable (in that case the allegation was that the entry into a settlement agreement with the anchor defendant had been deliberately drawn out so that there remained a live claim against the anchor defendant for just as long as was necessary in order to establish jurisdiction against a co-defendant).

39–052

As to whether the court should inquire into the merits, *JSC Aeroflot-Russian Airlines v Berezovsky*,[52] a case concerning an allegation by the Russian majority state-owned airline Aeroflot that it had been defrauded by individual defendants through companies domiciled in Luxembourg, was, until recently, the leading authority on the question of the standard required in jurisdiction disputes under art.8(1). The court there held that in deciding on jurisdiction under art.8(1) it was not required to assess the merits of the claim against the non-anchor defendants. This was in keeping with the rest of the BRR, where jurisdiction is determined purely by reference to whether the defendant in question falls within the wording of the specific jurisdiction rule. This contrasts with the position under the English common law where, as explained below, it is a prerequisite to the court granting an order permitting service of a defendant out of the jurisdiction that the claimant demonstrates that there is a serious issue to be tried against him. However there remained no authoritative guidance as to whether the merits of the claim against the anchor defendant should be considered.

39–053

---

[48] *Reisch Montage v Kiesel Baumaschinen Handels GmbH* [2006] ECR 1–6827 (C-103/05).
[49] *Freeport Plc v Arnoldson* (ECJ) [2008] Q.B. 634, at [54].
[50] *Sibir Energy v Tchigirinski* [2012] EWHC 1844 (QB); [2012] 2 C.L.C. 665, at [31].
[51] *Cartel Damage Claims SA v Akzo Nobel NV* [2015] Q.B. 906; [2015] 3 W.L.R. 909 (C-352/13).
[52] *JSC Aeroflot-Russian Airlines v Berezovsky* [2013] EWCA Civ 784; [2013] 2 C.L.C. 206; [2013] 2 Lloyd's Rep. 242.

39-054   The English Court of Appeal recently sought to clarify the position, albeit obiter, in *Sabbagh v Khoury*[53] where the majority[54] held that the court *could* for the purposes of art.8(1) consider the merits of the claim against the anchor defendant, and that if there was no serious issue to be tried against that defendant it could be (automatically) inferred that the claim had been brought with the sole purpose of ousting the co-defendants from their court of domicile, and that the claim would therefore fall foul of *Reisch Montage*. The Court drew distinctions in this regard between: (i) the existence of a procedural bar to the claim under the national law of the country where the claim was being tried, which would not preclude reliance on art.8(1) (because if there was no such procedural bar in other jurisdictions there would still a risk of irreconcilable judgments)[55]; and (ii) there being no serious issue to be tried on the merits, which would, or should, result in the same outcome wherever the case was tried. Further, in addressing the claimant's contention that the reasoning in *Aeroflot* should be extended to the anchor defendant (so that there could be no permissible analysis of the merits of the claim against that defendant), the Court distinguished the position of the non-anchor defendants, on the basis that if the claim against the anchor defendant falls away there is no reason for the foreign co-defendants not to be sued in their country of domicile, as there would no longer be any risk of irreconcilable judgments.

39-055   In her dissenting judgment, Gloster LJ said that the position should be that, even where the claim against the anchor defendant will not proceed due to lack of merit, jurisdiction against foreign co-defendants can be established under art.8(1), unless the claim against the anchor defendant constituted fraudulent abuse (in the sense identified above, i.e. that there was clear evidence that the "sole purpose" test was satisfied). She did not accept that the fact that the claim against the anchor defendant was substantively hopeless justified the inference that such fraudulent abuse had taken place. As the reasoning in *Sabbagh* was obiter and by majority only, it is likely that the position will have to be further resolved by the ECJ. However it is suggested that the analysis of Gloster LJ is to be preferred—not only would it create greater legal certainty in a complicated area; it is also not clear that the automatic inference favoured by the majority would be justifiable in every case, and the ruling is therefore unduly favourable to defendants.

39-056   By virtue of art.8(2), a third party (meaning in effect, in the English courts, a Pt 20 Defendant) sued in an action on a warranty or guarantee or in any other third party proceedings may be sued in the court seised of the original proceedings, unless those were instituted solely with the object of removing him from the jurisdiction of the court which would be competent in his case (i.e. the court of the Member State of his domicile).[56] Similarly, under art.8(3) the court in which a claim is proceeding also has jurisdiction over a counterclaim arising out of the same contract or facts.

---

[53] *Sabbagh v Khoury* [2017] EWCA Civ 1120.
[54] Comprising Beatson and Patten LJJ.
[55] For example, in *Reisch* itself, where the claim against the anchor defendant was inadmissible because bankruptcy proceedings against him were ongoing.
[56] *GIE Reunion Europeene v Zurich Espana* [2005] I.L. Pr. 33, at [29].

(5)   Exclusive Jurisdiction Based on Subject Matter

Article 24 of the BRR sets out mandatory, or exclusive, rules of jurisdiction based on the territorial connection between the subject matter of the dispute and the Member State in question and regardless of the domicile of the parties. In such cases a claimant can sue *only* in the Member State prescribed by the application of art.24—the parties cannot contract out of it by prorogation, i.e. by a jurisdiction agreement or submission to the jurisdiction. If another court is seised of such a claim it must declare of its own motion that it has no jurisdiction.[57]

39–057

First, in relation to land, art.24(1) provides[58] that "in proceedings which have as their object rights *in rem* in immovable property or tenancies of immovable property", the courts of the Member State where the property is situated have exclusive jurisdiction. There are two key phrases in that statement requiring definition. First, proceedings have "as their object" matters with which they are "principally concerned"; a test which is not satisfied merely because the proceedings raise a certain issue or even because the resolution of that issue may be dispositive of the case—rather the court must undertake an exercise in "overall classification" and make an "overall judgment".[59] Second, rights "*in rem*" are, for these purposes, those exercisable against the whole world rather than as against another individual or individuals.[60] So, for example, a case concerning the registered legal title to land would be a case in rem, whereas a case concerning beneficial ownership of the same land pursuant to a trust created by the registered owner would be a case in personam falling outside the reach of art.24.[61]

39–058

Second, in relation to companies, art.24(2) provides that

39–059

> "in proceedings which have as their object the validity of the constitution, the nullity or the dissolution of companies or other legal persons or associations of natural or legal persons, or the validity of the decisions of their organs"

the courts of the Member State in which the company has its seat (as determined by the private international law of the court seised) shall have exclusive jurisdiction.[62]

---

[57] BRR, art.27.

[58] Subject to an exception in relation to short residential tenancies of no relevance to the subject-matter of this book.

[59] *Berliner Verkerhsbetriebe (BVG) Anstalt des Offentlichen Rechts v J P Morgan Chase Bank NA* [2010] EWCA Civ 390, at [83]. See also *Blue Tropic Ltd v Chkhartishvili* [2014] EWHC 2243 (Ch); [2014] I.L. Pr. 33.

[60] *Lieber v Gobel* (Case C-292/93) [1994] I.L. Pr. 590, at [14].

[61] See *Webb v Webb* [1994] 3 W.L.R. 801 (ECJ), at [11]–[19]. Although they were not cited in the ECJ's judgment, this principle is confirmed by a line of cases starting with *Penn v Baltimore* (1750) Ves. Sen. 444, at 446–447; See also Collins and Harris (eds), *Dicey, Morris & Collins on the Conflict of Laws* (2017), Vol. 2, para.23–042; *Chellaram v Chellaram* [1985] Ch. 409, at 428–429; *R Griggs Group Ltd v Evans* [2005] Ch. 153, at [65]–[83]; *Bharmal v Bharmal* [2011] EWHC 1092 (Ch), at [1], [15]–[16]; *Prazic v Prazic* [2006] EWCA Civ 497; [2007] I.L. Pr. 31, CA.

[62] In the UK, this is governed by s.43 of the Civil Jurisdiction and Judgments Act 1982, and the Civil Jurisdiction and Judgments Order 2001, which provide that a company has its seat in the UK if (i) it was incorporated or formed under the law of a part of the UK or (ii) its central management and control is exercised in the UK.

39–060   In the recent decision of *Koza Ltd v Akcil*[63] the Court of Appeal noted that as art.24 operates in derogation from the general rule of domicile, it must be narrowly interpreted. That case dealt with multiple issues, and the question was whether the claim had as its object (meaning, as set out above, was "principally concerned with") the matters set out in art.24. The Court held that in order to engage the provision the proceedings need not *exclusively* relate to issues of local company law, however a mere link to a company's decision, or an issue raised which was ancillary to the heart of a contractual or other dispute, would not be sufficient to bring proceedings within the scope of art.24. For example, art.24(2) would not be engaged where proceedings deal with a contract and the claimant argues that the contract is unenforceable due to a corporate decision, which resulted in the conclusion of the contract, being invalid. In *Akcil*, although one of the two main issues was not strictly speaking one of local company law, both issues went to the validity of decisions of the shareholders in general meetings to replace the board of directors of an English company. Accordingly, adopting an overall evaluative judgment, art.24 was engaged.

39–061   It should be noted that in cases under art.24 exclusive jurisdiction is given to courts of "the Member State" in which the property is situated or the company has its seat. However, in recent times the courts have considered the position where the terms of art.24 were conceptually engaged, but where the relevant state was outside of the EU, for example a company incorporated in the BVI or land located in the USA. In these circumstances, although the BRR is not directly engaged, the courts have been willing to apply art.24 "reflexively", meaning that they will notionally consider the position that would pertain if the relevant company was incorporated in the EU and decide the jurisdiction issue accordingly even though the BRR does not in fact apply, and stay the claim if they find that the case is within the scope of the relevant article and that it is appropriate to do so on the facts of the case.[64] It is difficult to see how such an approach can be reconciled with the mandatory effect of art.4 or with the ECJ's decision in *Owusu v Jackson* that where art.4 applies national jurisdiction doctrines cannot be applied to circumvent it. The matter is ripe for reconsideration by the Court of Appeal or the ECJ.

39–062   Where more than one of the exclusive jurisdiction provisions in the BRR applies to the facts of a case, with different results, the rule is "first come, first served"; any court other than that which is first seised must decline jurisdiction.[65] A substantial jurisprudence has developed over the question of what "first seised" means.[66]

---

[63] *Koza Ltd v Akcil* [2017] EWCA Civ 1609.
[64] *Ferrexpo AG v Gilson Investments Ltd* [2012] EWHC 721 (Comm.); [2012] 1 C.L.C. (Andrew Smith J).
[65] BRR, art.31(1).
[66] See for example *Barclays Bank Plc v Ente* (CA) [2016] EWCA Civ 1261; [2016] 2 C.L.C. 859, at [12].

(6) Prorogation

The next category of exception to the General Rule, "prorogation", relates to the **39–063** position where, irrespective of the other jurisdiction rules of the BRR, the defendant is deemed voluntarily to have accepted the jurisdiction of the court of a Member State. This has two sub-categories, namely:

(1) Express agreement, within a contract or a trust, that disputes between the parties will be resolved by the courts of a particular country. Such agreements are dealt with by art.25 of the BRR; and

(2) Submission by the defendant to the jurisdiction of the court in which proceedings have been commenced. Submission is dealt with in art.26.

If the defendant agrees to jurisdiction in either of these ways, the court will hold **39–064** him to his agreement, with the exception that arts 25 and 26 are both subject to, i.e. trumped by, the exclusive jurisdiction rules under art.24. As between the two, a submission under art.26 will take precedence over an agreement under art.25.

(i) Jurisdiction agreements

Although this book is not concerned with straightforward claims in contract, **39–065** art.25 is not so limited—it applies where

> "the parties… have agreed that a court or the courts of a Member State are to have jurisdiction to settle any disputes which have arisen or which may arise in connection with a particular legal relationship".[67]

Such a relationship potentially includes not only contract but also trusts or even tortious wrongs,[68] so an agreement could potentially cover all of the causes of action dealt with in this book. Accordingly, the effect of art.25 is considered below.

The following should be noted about art.25 of the BRR: **39–066**

(1) Unlike its predecessor, it applies to jurisdiction agreements which nominate a Member State, regardless of the domicile of the parties, so it would apply to a jurisdiction clause in an agreement between, say, a Russian and an American in which they agreed that any disputes between them would be subject to the jurisdiction of the English courts.

(2) Where an agreement nominates a non-Member State, and art.25 of the BRR is therefore not engaged, the English courts have nevertheless given effect to the agreement, and stayed the English proceedings in favour of that State, even when the defendant is domiciled in a Member State (i.e.

---

[67] The agreement must be "clearly and precisely" demonstrated; however art.25 requires the existence of a consensus in fact, rather than a legally binding agreement: see *PHP Tobacco Carib Sarl v BAT Carribbean SA* [2017] EWCA Civ 1131.

[68] See for example, art.14 of the Rome II Regulation, dealt with in Ch.40 below.

England).[69] Again, this is difficult to reconcile with the wording of art.4 and with *Owusu v Jackson*, although in the context of jurisdiction agreements this is perhaps less detrimental to considerations of legal certainty and predictability than the reflexive application of other articles of the BRR, for example art.24 (as to which see above).

(3)   The substantive validity of a jurisdiction clause is, under art.25(1), to be determined by the law of the Member State which it would nominate assuming it were valid. For example if two Russians conclude, over dinner in St Petersburg, a trust over assets in Russia containing an exclusive jurisdiction clause in favour of the English courts, the validity of the clause, for the purposes of a claim commenced in England, will be determined by English law.

(4)   Further, the jurisdiction clause is severable in the sense that it is for the purposes of a jurisdiction dispute to be analysed separately from the rest of the contract and regardless of whether the rest of the contract is valid or enforceable.[70] This provision is designed to avoid the court at the jurisdiction stage pre-judging arguments which will be raised at trial as to the validity of a contract. In the example above, this would mean that the validity of the jurisdiction clause would be unaffected by any argument that the trust as a whole was governed by Russian law and therefore of no effect.

(5)   In order to satisfy art.25, jurisdiction agreements must be in a particular form specified in sub-arts 1(a) to 1(c) therein. In particular, they must be:

   (a)   in writing or evidenced in writing (including any electronic means which provides a "durable record of the agreement")[71];

   (b)   in a form which accords with practices which the parties have established between themselves; *or*

   (c)   in international trade or commerce, in a form which accords with a usage of which the parties are or ought to have been aware and which in such trade or commerce is widely known to, and regularly observed by, parties to contracts of the type involved in the particular trade or commerce concerned.

(6)   In the BRR, jurisdiction agreements now take priority over the *lis pendens* provisions. Previously, including under Brussels I, a party to a jurisdiction agreement, who knew that he was about to be sued in the courts specified in the agreement, could start pre-emptive proceedings in a country with slow and cumbersome procedures and/or which was hostile to jurisdiction agreements. This practice, known as the "Italian torpedo" because Italy was judged to be such a jurisdiction, was widespread, and because the *lis*

---

[69] *Coreck Maritime GmbH v Handelsveem BV* (C-387/98) [2001] C.L.C. 550, at [19]; *Konkola Copper Mines Plc v Cormin Ltd* [2005] EWHC 898 (Comm); [2005] 1 C.L.C. 1021, at [101]; *Winnekta Trading Corp v Julius Baer International Ltd* [2008] EWHC 3146 (Ch); [2009] Bus. L.R. 1006, at [24]–[25]. *Ferrexpo AG v Gilson Investments Ltd* [2012] EWHC 721; [2012] 1 C.L.C. 645, at [130]–[132].

[70] BRR, art.25(5).

[71] BRR, art.25(2). However, there is no requirement that there be a formal written contract or that the writing be contained in a single document: *PHP Tobacco Carib Sarl v BAT Caribbean SA* [2017] EWCA Civ 1131.

pendens provisions in Brussels I took precedence over the prorogation provisions, there was nothing that the other party could do about it. This was confirmed by the ECJ in *Erich Gasser GmbH v Misat Srl*,[72] where it was held that the equivalent provision to art.27 in the Brussels Convention of 1968 applied even when the proceedings had been brought in the court first seised in breach of a jurisdiction clause. The usefulness of jurisdiction clauses was further eroded by the ECJ's decision in *Turner v Grovit*[73] to the effect that the use of anti-suit injunctions to enforce jurisdiction agreements was incompatible with international comity. This is rectified in the BRR by a reversal of priority, which is explained in the *lis pendens* section below.

Article 25 makes no express provision for hybrid, or asymmetric, jurisdiction **39–067** clauses, which are commonplace, in particular in banking contracts. This is unfortunate as there had been contradictory rulings between the English and French courts as to whether such clauses are enforceable under the equivalent provision in Brussels I.[74] The English courts have erred on the side of enforceability, and in a recent decision the Commercial Court has held that an asymmetric jurisdiction clause is an exclusive jurisdiction clause for the purposes of the BRR, capable of defeating a Greek "torpedo" action.[75] However there could be no guarantee that that view would be upheld by the European Court of Justice if the matter were to come before it.[76]

(ii)   Submission to the jurisdiction

As for art.26, the court of a Member State will have jurisdiction over a defendant **39–068** who "enters an appearance" before it. However, the rule does not apply where the appearance was entered in order "to contest the jurisdiction".

The issue of what amounts to a submission to the jurisdiction is a matter for the **39–069** procedural law of the forum, unless that undermines the effective operation of the Regulation.[77] In England the rules on submission to the jurisdiction derive from the common law, although regard may be had to case-law under s.33 of the Civil Jurisdiction and Judgments Act 1982, which is concerned with the recognition of foreign judgments but which is worded in similar terms to art.26 of the BRR. In essence a party will be deemed to have submitted to the jurisdiction of the English courts if he has taken some step which is only necessary or only useful if

---

[72] *Erich Gasser GmbH v Misat Srl* [2003] ECR I-14693; [2005] Q.B. 1, at [54].

[73] *Turner v Grovit* [2004] ECR I-3565; [2005] 1 A.C. 101, at [31].

[74] For French decisions refusing to enforce such clauses see *Rothschild Europe v Mme X* [2013] I.L. Pr. 181; *Credit Suisse* Cass Civ. 1ere, 26 September 2012. The English High Court upheld such a clause in *Commercial Bank v Hestia Holdings* [2013] EWHC 1328 (Comm).

[75] *Commerzbank Aktiengesellschaft v Liquimar Tankers Management* [2017] EWHC 161 (Comm). This followed the obiter decision to the same effect in *Perella Weinberg Partners UK LLP v Coder SA* [2016] EWHC 1182.

[76] There has, however, been a recent French decision in the other direction: *Apple Sales International v eBizcuss:* Cass Civ. 1ere, 7 October 2015, 14-16.898.

[77] *Deutsche Bank AG London Branch v Petromena ASA* [2015] EWCA Civ; [2015] 1 W.L.R. 4225, at [22].

the objection relied upon has been waived or had never been entertained at all.[78] Examples of steps that have been held to amount to submission are[79]:

(1) Acknowledging service but not ticking the box on the acknowledgment of service form indicating that they wish to dispute jurisdiction[80];
(2) Ticking the box but subsequently failing to make the application within 14 days[81];
(3) Instructing a solicitor in the jurisdiction to accept service[82];
(4) Applying (or even threatening to apply) to strike out[83];
(5) Arguing the merits of the case on a pre-action injunction application or an application to set aside a committal order[84];
(6) Filing a counterclaim.[85]

39–070 However, in each case, doing these things will not amount to a submission for the purpose of art.26 if the party at all times clearly and expressly reserves his objection to jurisdiction.[86]

39–071 In other jurisdictions, the position can be even more complicated—for example if, as is common in civil jurisdictions, the relevant country's procedure requires a defendant to file a composite defence dealing with both jurisdiction and the substance of the claim, and the jurisdiction dispute is heard at the same time as the trial of the action. Again, in such cases a defendant will not be taken to have submitted for as long as he maintains his jurisdictional objection, provided that he asserts it from the outset.[87]

39–072 Where a party submits, that is a sufficient ground for personal jurisdiction, indeed it will cut through any defects in service, but it will not give the court substantive, subject-matter, jurisdiction if it would not otherwise have it under art.24.

(7) Lis Alibi Pendens

39–073 Article 29 of the BRR explains what happens when claims involving the same or similar subject matter are brought between the same parties in more than one Member State.[88] The general rule is that the Member State court "*first seised*" is

---

[78] Whether that is so is a matter of English procedural law: see *Deutsche Bank AG v Petromena*, above, at [22].

[79] For a recent detailed analysis of steps that can and cannot amount to submission see *Winkler v Shamoon* [2016] EWHC 217 (Ch), at [27]–[50].

[80] *Global Multimedia International Ltd v ARA Media Services* [2006] EWHC 3612 (Ch), at [30]–[31].

[81] CPR r.11(5).

[82] *Manta Line v Sofianites* [1984] 1 Lloyd's Rep. 14 (CA).

[83] *The Messiniaki Tolmi* [1984] 1 Lloyd's Rep. 266 (CA).

[84] *Marketmaker Technology Ltd v CMC Group Plc* [2008] EWHC 1556 (QB), at [31].

[85] *Koza v Akcil* (see above), at [59]–[60].

[86] *Koza v Akcil*, at [60].

[87] *AES Ust-Kamenogorsk Hydropower Plant LLP v Ust Kamenogorsk Hydropower Plant JSC* [2012] 1 W.L.R. 920 contains a very useful summary of the law on this point at [166]–[190].

[88] The relevant date for determination as to whether this has happened is the date of commencement of proceedings in the second court seised: see *Barclays Bank Plc v Ente* (CA) [2016] EWCA Civ

entitled to decide upon and, if appropriate, accept, jurisdiction in preference to any other court. This rule, and exceptions to it, are explained below.

(i)   When court "seised"

A court is "*seised*" for these purposes when the document instituting the proceedings or an equivalent document[89] is lodged with the court, unless the claimant subsequently fails to serve it properly on the defendant.[90] Alternatively, if under the relevant country's procedures, the document has to be served before being lodged at court, the court is seised when it is received by the authority responsible for service, provided that the claimant does not subsequently fail to lodge it at court.[91] The BRR contains procedures facilitating communication between the courts of Member States as to the date upon which they were seised with relevant matters.[92]

39–074

(ii)   Jurisdiction agreement

As alluded to above, by way of exception to the general *lis pendens* rule, if a court designated by an exclusive jurisdiction agreement is seised with a matter, and a claim involving the same parties and the same cause of action is also before another court, that court must stay its proceedings until the court nominated in the agreement rules on its own jurisdiction,[93] and must decline jurisdiction if jurisdiction is established by the nominated court.[94] This express carve out negates the Italian torpedo effect, because any abusive pre-emptive claim will be immediately stayed until the court nominated by the jurisdiction agreement has decided upon jurisdiction. Although not expressly stated, it appears from the structure of the BRR that the same must be true if a court is seised other than one with exclusive jurisdiction under art.24.

39–075

(iii)   Same parties, same cause of action

Subject to the point in the paragraph above, if one court is seised with a claim, and proceedings between the same parties involving the "same cause of action and between the same parties" come before another court, the second court *must* stay its proceedings until the first court establishes whether it has jurisdiction,[95] and decline jurisdiction if such jurisdiction is established by the first court.[96]

39–076

1261; [2016] 2 C.L.C. 859, at [12]. A court is not seised of a relevant claim until the cause of action has been raised in the proceedings. If that happens by amendment, the relevant date is the date of amendment: see *Ente*.

[89] As to the meaning of an "equivalent document" see *Hanseyachts v Port d'Hiver Yachting SARL* [2017] I.L. Pr. 25.

[90] BRR, art.32(1)(a).

[91] Article 32(1)(b).

[92] Article 29(2).

[93] Article 31(2).

[94] Article 31(3).

[95] Article 29(1).

[96] Article 29(3).

39–077 The concept of "same cause of action" is autonomous, and does not equate to causes of action in English or any other national law. Nor does it take into account the defences which might be advanced to the claims. It will encompass claims where equal and opposite relief is sought in two jurisdictions, for example a claim for damages in tort in one jurisdiction and a claim in another for a declaration that a party is not liable in tort. It will also cover claims where different relief is sought but on the same basis in relation to the same legal relationship. This is because in both cases, if the respective courts were to find in favour of different parties it would result in inconsistent decisions. By contrast, in *Barclays Bank Plc v Ente*, the Court of Appeal held that a claim for damages for breach of a jurisdiction clause was not "the same", for these purposes, as a substantive claim in restitution and for pre- and extra-contractual liability in relation to the same contract.[97]

(iv)   Related actions

39–078 Where "related actions" are pending in the courts of different Member States, any court other than the first seised *may*, but is not required to, stay its proceedings.[98] Further, when an action is pending in the court first seised, any other court may decline jurisdiction if the court first seised also has jurisdiction over the claim in the second court and its procedures permit consolidation of the two actions.[99] Actions are deemed to be "related" for these purposes where they are "so closely connected that it is expedient to hear and determine them together to avoid the risk of irreconcilable judgments resulting from separate proceedings".[100]

(v)   Claims in "third states"

39–079 Historically the Brussels regime has been limited in scope to jurisdiction as between Member States, presumably because it is not for the Brussels legislators to tell other countries what to do.[101] For the first time the BRR contains a (very limited) set of rules relating to *lis alibi pendens* when actions come before the courts of Member States in situations where the same or similar issues are before the court of a non-Member State.

---

[97] *Barclays Bank Plc v Ente* [2016] EWCA Civ 1261. The meaning of "the same cause of action" for these purposes was considered by the Supreme Court in *Starlight Shipping Compay v Allianz Marine & Aviation Versicherungs AG* [2013] UKSC 70; [2014] 1 All E.R. 590, which was applied in *Ente*, at [28].

[98] Article 30(1).

[99] Article 30(2).

[100] Article 30(3). For an example of the sort of analysis involved in determining whether actions are related, see *Masri v Consolidated Contractors International Co SAL* [2011] EWHC 1780 (Comm). In *Barclays Bank Plc v Ente* (see above), it was common ground that the claims were "related" for these purposes, but the Court refused to exercise its jurisdiction to stay, primarily in light of the jurisdiction clause (that was a case under Brussels I, prior to the entry into force of the BRR, so even though there was a jurisdiction clause the issue was decided in accordance with the *lis pendens* rules. As to the changes effected by the BRR in this regard, see above).

[101] At least this has been the case as regards its *express* provisions, however see para.39–061 above.

Articles 33 and 34, which deal with third states, are conceptually similar to arts **39–080**
29 and 30 above, in relation to claims involving the same cause of action, and
related claims, respectively. However, they only apply in very limited
circumstances:

(1) First, both rules only confer *discretion* to stay—neither is mandatory.
(2) They apply only where jurisdiction is based on arts 4 or 7, 8 and 9 (being
    the General Rule on domicile or the alternative rules for causes of
    action—see above). It follows that they do not apply when the English
    court has jurisdiction under art.25 by virtue of a jurisdiction agreement, as
    was recently confirmed in *UCP v Nectrus*.[102]
(3) The Member State court must consider that (a) the court of the third state
    will give a judgment capable of recognition in the Member State; and (b) a
    stay is necessary for the proper administration of justice.[103]

Nor is the system irreversible. Article 33(2) gives the Member State court the **39–081**
power to re-instigate the proceedings before it if it considers that the proceedings
in the third state are themselves stayed or discontinued, they will not be
concluded within a reasonable time or if the continuation of the proceedings in
the Member State is required for the proper administration of justice.[104]

These are odd provisions. They inherently recognise by their structure that the **39–082**
BRR cannot control third states, so are directed only to Member States. They also
give the Member States considerable discretion, thereby creating uncertainty,
which was previously thought to be the antithesis of the Brussels model.

D. DEFENDANT DOMICILED IN LUGANO STATE

As set out above, the 2007 Lugano Convention was introduced so as to bring the **39–083**
previous Lugano Convention in line with Brussels I. Accordingly, the law under it
is the same as that set out above, save in the areas where we have indicated that
the BRR has introduced changes, and the substance is not repeated here.

As far as an English court is concerned, the 2007 Lugano Convention applies **39–084**
where a defendant is domiciled in Iceland, Norway, or Switzerland,[105] where the
2007 Lugano Convention provides that a Lugano State has jurisdiction regardless
of domicile, or where a jurisdiction agreement nominates the courts of a Lugano
State.[106] Where proceedings are already on foot in a Lugano State when
proceedings concerned with the same subject-matter comes before an English
court, the 2007 Lugano Convention *lis pendens* provisions will apply.[107]

---

[102] *UCP v Nectrus* [2018] EWHC 380 (Comm).
[103] Article 33(1)(a), (b).
[104] For a recent, obiter, consideration of the "proper administration of justice" requirement, see *Re Zavarco Plc* [2015] EWHC 1898 (Ch); [2016] Ch. 128.
[105] BRR, art.73(1).
[106] Lugano Convention, arts 22–23.
[107] Those provisions are in arts 27–30 of the Lugano Convention.

E. JURISDICTION WITHIN DIFFERENT PARTS OF THE UK

39–085   Jurisdiction between different parts of the UK is, in certain circumstances, governed by the Civil Jurisdiction and Judgments Act 1982. The relevant provision is s.16, which provides that

> "where the subject-matter of the proceedings is within the scope of the Regulation as determined by Article 1 of the Regulation (whether or not the Regulation has effect in relation to the proceedings)"

the provision of Sch.4 shall determine which part of the UK has jurisdiction over a dispute. Schedule 4 in turn sets out the provisions of Brussels I in a modified form so as to apply to jurisdiction as between the different parts of the UK. Schedule 4 has not been updated to reflect the BRR, and, in light of the Brexit vote, it may now never be so updated.

39–086   As set out above, there is some authority that the Brussels legislation only applies in a case where there is an "international element". However, even if that is so, as s.16 defines the applicability of Brussels I only by reference to the terms of art.1 thereof, it is suggested that there is no such limitation on the applicability of Sch.4 of the 1982 Act. This suggestion is supported by the words in brackets in the extract from s.16 set out above. Accordingly, Sch.4 to the 1982 Act will determine jurisdiction as between the various parts of the UK in all "civil commercial matters whatever the nature of the court or tribunal" save for those expressly excluded in art.1.

F. DEFENDANT DOMICILED OUT OF THE EU/LUGANO STATES

(1) The BRR

39–087   When a prospective defendant to proceedings brought in England is domiciled outside of the EU the General Rule is not engaged, the basic scheme of the BRR does not apply, and the English court will apply its own rules to determine its jurisdiction.[108] That is subject to two provisos,[109] namely that the exclusive jurisdiction rules in art.24 may still be engaged, either directly or reflexively (see above), or the defendant may have entered into an agreement governed by art.25.

39–088   Subject to those points, jurisdiction in this type of case will be determined by the English common law. As set out below, personal jurisdiction at common law is established by service of process on the defendant, either within the jurisdiction as of right or out of the jurisdiction with the court's permission.

(2) Service Without Court's Permission

39–089   There are two ways in which service may validly be effected under the common law without the court's permission:

---

[108] BRR, art.6(1).
[109] There are other exceptions concerning consumers and employees which we do not consider.

(1) First, a defendant can be served, regardless of his domicile, when he is present in England:

    (a) As regards individuals, this means that they can be personally served with English process when they are present in England, regardless of how fleeting or temporary their presence may be.[110] It will be rare for this to apply in a fraud case, where the fraud was perpetrated in England, as the fraudster will usually have absconded and will be careful not to return to the jurisdiction.

    (b) A company will be deemed to be "present" for these purposes if it has a branch registered in this country under the requirements of the Companies Act 2006.[111] If so a claim form can be served by (i) leaving it at, or sending it by post to, the registered address of any person in the UK authorised to accept service of documents on the company's behalf, or (ii) if there is not such person, or if service cannot for any reason be effected, by leaving it at or sending by post to any place of business of the company in the UK.[112] Under the CPR a company can also be served by any method permitted under Pt 6, including leaving the claim at any place within the jurisdiction where the company carries on its business and which has a real connection with the claim[113] or, if the company carries on its business within the jurisdiction, with a person holding a senior position within the company.[114]

(2) Prorogation:

    (a) If the defendant has entered into a jurisdiction agreement, not falling within art.25 (as to which see above), which is applicable on the facts of the case, the court will generally give effect to it.[115] If a contract specifies an address, or an agent, within the jurisdiction at which a party can be served with process, he is thereby deemed to submit to the jurisdiction and can be served without the need for an order for service out.[116] If on the other hand the address or agent specified is out of the jurisdiction, the claimant will require permission for service out, which the court will usually grant if the contract contains an English jurisdiction clause.[117]

    (b) Alternatively, a defendant may have submitted to the jurisdiction by taking some step inconsistent with an intention to dispute jurisdiction. Because, as noted above, the procedural rules as to what

---

[110] See for example *Colt Industries v Sarlie* [1966] 1 W.L.R. 440. A well-known example is *Berezovsky v Abramovich* [2012] EWHC 2463 (Comm), in which Mr Berezovsky himself served Mr Abramovich with the claim form, having spotted him out shopping in Sloane St (in the event, the latter chose not to contest jurisdiction).

[111] Section 1046.

[112] Section 1139. As to whether the company has a place of business within the UK, see *South India Shipping Corp Ltd v Export-Import Bank of Korea* [1985] 1 W.L.R. 585 and *Adams v Cape Industries Plc* [1990] Ch. 433, at 523–531.

[113] CPR r.6.9(2).

[114] CPR r.6.5(3)(b).

[115] BRR, art.25, CPR r.6.11, PD 6B, para.3.1(6)(d).

[116] CPR r.6.11 gives effect to this rule, which was previously part of the common law.

[117] CPR PD 6B para.3.1(6)(d).

amounts to submission to the jurisdiction are those of the forum, the common law position as to submission to the English court is exactly the same as that in the context of art.26 of the BRR and is not repeated here.[118]

All of the above is subject to the common law rule that a court will not hear a claim relating to title to foreign land,[119] nor to certain miscellaneous categories of claim in relation to which jurisdiction is dictated by statute, including divorce or claims in the magistrates' court.

(3)   Order for Service Out of the Jurisdiction

39–090   In the absence of either of those factors, a claimant seeking to bring a claim against a defendant not domiciled in a Member State and whose claim does not otherwise engage the BRR will need to apply to court for an order permitting service out of the jurisdiction.[120] His application must be supported by evidence, and he is required to establish[121]:

(1)   that there is a serious issue to be tried on the merits.[122]
(2)   that there is a good arguable case that the court has jurisdiction within one of the 20 jurisdictional "gateways" set out in PD 6B para.3.1.[123]
(3)   that the case is a proper one for service out of the jurisdiction (forum conveniens).[124]

39–091   It will be noted that the threshold to be surmounted in relation to the merits ("serious issue to be tried") is different from that in relation to the gateways ("good arguable case"). The former is the same as the summary judgment standard, namely that there is a real prospect of success.[125] The "good arguable case" has traditionally been applied with the "*Canada Trust* gloss" referred to above, that is, so as to mean that the applicant has much the better of the argument that the relevant gateway applies on the material available at the time of the application.[126] In the Supreme Court's recent decision in *Brownlie v Four*

---

[118] See paras 39–068—39–072 above.
[119] As explained above in relation to art.24 of the BRR, this means only *legal* title to foreign land—rights under a trust over foreign land can be heard by the English court.
[120] CPR r.6.36.
[121] *Seaconsar Far East Ltd v Bank Markazi Jomhouri Islam Iran* [1994] 1 A.C. 438; *Spiliada Maritime Corp v Consulex, sub nom The Spiliada* [1987] A.C. 460. For recent statements of the test by the Privy Council and Court of Appeal see *AK Investment CJSC v Kyrgyz Mobile Tel Ltd* [2011] UKPC 7 and *VTB Capital Plc v Nutritek International Corp* [2012] EWCA Civ 808.
[122] CPR r.6.37(1)(b).
[123] CPR r.6.36.
[124] CPR r.6.37(3).
[125] *AK Investment CJSC v Kyrgyz Mobil Tel Ltd* [2011] UKPC 7, [2011] 4 All E.R. 1027, at [71].
[126] *Cherney v Deripaska* [2008] EWHC 3765 (QB); [2010] I.L. Pr. 23, at [40]–[42], approved by the Court of Appeal in *Sharab v Al-Saud* [2009] EWCA Civ 353 and by the Privy Council in *AK Investment CJSC v Kyrgyz Mobile Tel Ltd* (see above), at [71]. The correctness of this is doubted in Briggs, *Private International Law in English Courts* (2014), who says that it applies only to the

Seasons,[127] Lord Sumption said that the *Canada Trust* gloss was a "serviceable test, provided that it is correctly understood", but suggested that the word "much" should be left out. He explained:

> "What is meant is (i) that the claimant must supply a plausible evidential basis for the application of a relevant jurisdictional gateway; (ii) that if there is an issue of fact about it, or some other reason for doubting whether it applies, the court must take a view on the material available if it can reliably do so; but (iii) the nature of the issue and the limitations of the material available at the interlocutory stage may be such that no reliable assessment can be made, in which case there is a good arguable case for the application of the gateway if there is a plausible (albeit contested) evidential basis for it. I do not believe that anything is gained by the word 'much', which suggests a superior standard of conviction that is both uncertain and unwarranted in this context."

Often the same factual or legal issue can go to both the merits of the claim and the applicability of the gateway. Where that is so the higher standard (good arguable case) applies.[128]   **39–092**

Those standards are to be contrasted with disputes as to the proper interpretation of the gateway relied upon, or upon a question of (English) law or construction, which must simply be decided by the court.[129]   **39–093**

The jurisdictional gateways are contained in para.3.1 of PD 6B. Those of potential relevance for fraud claims are set out below. They are, for the most part, worded very similarly to the equivalent articles of the BRR. Therefore, the above discussion in that context will not be repeated in the sections below, which instead focus on discrepancies between the two sets of rules. The gateways, in particular (4A) and (12) to (16), have been the subject of recent amendment to widen their scope based on difficulties identified in case-law.   **39–094**

(i) "Necessary and property party"[130]:

This gateway is conceptually similar to, but far wider than, the equivalent provision in the BRR. It is wider in that: (a) it contains a looser test, which does not require the court to consider whether there is a risk of irreconcilable judgments; and (b) it does not require, as a precondition, that jurisdiction against the "anchor defendant" is established solely by domicile—any jurisdictional basis will suffice.[131]   **39–095**

In *Okpabi v Royal Dutch Shell Plc*[132] the Court of Appeal considered whether an English parent company could be made liable in tort for the acts of its subsidiary, an oil exploration and production company incorporated in Nigeria, which it was   **39–096**

---

applicability of the BRR, where there are no other elements to the jurisdictional test, however that possibility was expressly dealt with and rejected by the court in *Cherney v Deripaska*, above, at [43].
[127] *Brownlie v Four Seasons* [2017] UKSC 80.
[128] *Cecil v Bayat* [2010] EWHC 641 (Comm.), at [19] (reversed on appeal but on other grounds).
[129] Briggs, *Private International Law in English Courts* (2014), paras. 4.446–4.456, Collins and Harris (eds), *Dicey, Morris and Collins on the Conflict of Laws* (2017), Vol.1 para.11–147.
[130] Practice Direction 6B para.3.1(3)/(4).
[131] For a recent analysis of this gateway and the authorities relating to it see *Altimo Holdings Investment Ltd v Kyrgyz Mobil Tel Ltd* [2011] UKPC 7; [2012] 1 W.L.R. 1804.
[132] *Okpabi v Royal Dutch Shell Plc* [2018] EWCA Civ 191.

alleged was responsible for serious, and ongoing, pollution and environmental damage caused by leaks of oil from pipelines and associated infrastructure in and around the Niger Delta. That was a complicated issue as a matter of tort law. For jurisdiction purposes the issue was whether the merits of a claim against the anchor defendant (in this case the English parent company) were to be taken into account for the purposes of deciding upon jurisdiction over the subsidiary, and if so what the relevant standard was.

39–097 The Court considered the judgment of the Privy Council in *Altimo Holdings v Kirgyz Mobil Tel Ltd*,[133] in which it was held that: (i) an action is not properly brought against the anchor defendant if it is bound to fail, and leave will not be granted if the lack of a plausible cause of action against D1 shows that the presence of D1 in the jurisdiction is being used as a device to bring in D2; (ii) there was no practical difference between the standards of "serious issue to be tried" as against D2 and "bound to fail" as against D1 and they in turn were the same as the test for summary judgment; (iii) addressing an issue of law which may be fundamental to the court's jurisdiction, the court will normally decide the issue, rather than treating it as being a question of whether there is a good arguable case in respect of it; however (iv) the general rule was that it was not normally appropriate to decide in a summary procedure a controversial question of law in a developing area; rather in those areas it would consider merely whether the claim was frivolous or vexatious.

39–098 Simon LJ noted that this gave rise to a paradox: the more complicated a question of law is involved in a case, the easier it is to establish jurisdiction. Accordingly, he approached the question as to the claim against the parent company, the anchor defendant, by asking whether the claim was bound to fail, which was the same as the Pt 24 test, i.e. whether the claimants had no real prospect of succeeding on the claim.[134]

39–099 In *Erste Group Bank AG v JSC 'VMZ Red October'*[135] the Court of Appeal emphasised that there are two aspects to the test under para.3.1(3)(a) of the gateway: not only must there be a "real issue" as against the anchor defendant, but it must be one which "is reasonable for the court to try". The fact (if such) that the anchor defendant was sued only for the purposes of bringing the foreign defendants within the gateway would not be relevant to this part of the analysis (but would be relevant to the court's discretion)[136]; but what was relevant on the facts of the case, and counted against the gateway being met, was the fact that the claims which were advanced against the anchor defendants had also been submitted by the claimant to the jurisdiction of the Russian courts and insolvency proceedings that were ongoing in Russia.[137]

---

[133] *Altimo Holdings v Kirgyz Mobil Tel Ltd* [2011] UKPC 7.

[134] This followed shortly after Simon LJ's own analysis to similar effect in *Lungowe v Vedanta* [2017] EWCA Civ 1528, at [63], a case with similar facts relating to the liability of a UK parent company for pollution to local waterways caused by the mining operations of its local subsidiary in Zambia.

[135] *Erste Group Bank AG v JSC 'VMZ Red October'* [2015] EWCA Civ 379.

[136] Applying *Multinational Gas and Petrochemical Co v Multinational Gas and Petrochemical Services Ltd* [1983] Ch. 258.

[137] See *Erste Group*, above, at [37]–[50].

(ii)   *"A further claim is made against the defendant which arises out of the same or closely connected facts"*[138]

This important new gateway (which took effect on 1 October 2015) has widened the scope of the common law provisions significantly, by giving a claimant who is able to establish jurisdiction over a defendant in relation to a claim under gateways (2), (6) to (16), (19) or (21), permission also to include any further claims against that defendant which arise out of the same factual matrix.[139]   **39–100**

(iii)   *"Claims in tort"*[140]

This applies where: (a) damage has been sustained within the jurisdiction or (b) damage has resulted from an act committed within the jurisdiction. This mirrors the definition given in art.7 of the BRR, although its scope is potentially different: **39–101**

(1)   In determining whether the claim is one in "tort", an English court will apply English private international common law, rather than the autonomous definition required by the BRR and ECJ. For example there has been some doubt as to whether claims in dishonest assistance would be covered.[141] Such doubt is arguably supported by the existence of a separate gateway, (15), specifically relating to liability as a constructive trustee—see below.

(2)   The first limb of the gateway, relating to damage being sustained in the jurisdiction, was recently considered by the Supreme Court in *Brownlie v Four Seasons*, a personal injury case.[142] As expressly acknowledged in the judgments, that decision would have had far-reaching consequences had it not been rendered obiter in light of a procedural oddity which led the court to conclude, having received further evidence from the defendant at a late stage, that the defendant was the wrong party. Nevertheless the Court gave very detailed consideration to the issue whether, in the context of personal injury litigation, the fact that consequential loss was suffered in England was sufficient to ground jurisdiction. In a split decision the majority view (Hale, Wilson, Clarke JSCs) was that "damage" for these purposes extended to facts which are evidence of the financial value of the damage, rather than the first damage to an interest per se. There was no reason, said Lady Hale, to suggest that mere completion of the cause of action was what the legislators had in mind when they used the word "damage". Rather, as had been held by several first instance judges, "damage" included all the detriment suffered by the claimant. The test under the common law in this

---

[138]   Practice Direction 6B, para.3.1(4A).

[139]   The potential reach of gateway 4A is illustrated by the recent decision of the Court of Appeal in *Eurasia Sports Ltd v Mahchi Aguad* [2018] EWCA Civ 1742, where it held that a claim could be brought (under gateway 3) against a defendant who was a necessary or proper party to a claim that had been served under gateway 4A.

[140]   Practice Direction 6B, para.3.1(9).

[141]   *Metall und Rohstoff AG v Donaldson Lufkin & Jenrette Inc* [1990] 1 Q.B. 391.

[142]   *Brownlie v Four Seasons*, see above.

regard is now therefore directly at odds with the position under the BRR. Lady Hale suggested that differences between the two regimes can be explained by the fact that the common law retains the "safety valve of discretion" (i.e. forum conveniens, as to which see below).

(3)   The second limb of the gateway requires only that damage resulted from "*an act*" of the defendant(s) carried out within the jurisdiction, whereas art.7 of the BRR focusses on "the harmful event", i.e. the act constituting the tort. This point is discussed in the context of an international conspiracy. There the courts have held that the court should not found jurisdiction on the strength of some "relatively minor and insignificant act having been committed here, perhaps fortuitously" but rather must look at the tort in a common sense way and

> "ask whether the damage has resulted from substantial and efficacious acts committed within the jurisdiction (whether or not other substantial and efficacious acts have been committed elsewhere)".[143]

Of course the place in which the tort, or the substance of it, is viewed as having been committed, is also likely to be taken into account in the third limb of test for service out (i.e. discretion or forum conveniens—see below).[144]

(iv)   "Claims about property within the jurisdiction"[145]

39–102   This is a very wide provision, and is likely to catch a number of claims in relation to trusts and restitution which do not fall within paras (12) to (16).

(v)   "A claim is made in respect of a trust..."[146]

39–103   Gateways 12 and 12A apply where a claim is made in respect of a trust created by statute or in writing, or orally and evidenced in writing, which is governed by the law of England and Wales (gateway 12) or has a jurisdiction clause in favour of England and Wales (gateway 12A). There is no requirement that the trust property be located in the jurisdiction—the link provided by the governing law or jurisdiction clause is deemed sufficient.

(vi)   "A claim is made against the defendant as constructive trustee, or as trustee of a resulting trust"[147]

39–104   Unlike the BRR, PD 6B caters specifically for constructive trusts, however they come into existence and whether or not they are recorded in writing. The gateway applies where the claim "arises out of acts committed or events occurring within the jurisdiction or relates to assets within the jurisdiction." It has been recently

---

[143] *Metall und Rostoff* (see above).
[144] See for example, *VTB v Nutritek* [2013] UKSC 5; [2013] 2 W.L.R. 398.
[145] Practice Direction 6B, para.3.1(11).
[146] Practice Direction 6B, paras 3.1(12) and (12A) (as amended with effect from 1 March 2015).
[147] Practice Direction 6B, para.3.1(15) (as amended with effect from 1 October 2015).

enlarged so as to refer expressly to resulting trusts and also to refer to "events occurring" within the jurisdiction as well as acts committed there.

(vii) "A claim is made in restitution..."[148]

Again, unlike the BRR, CPR PD 6B includes a specific gateway dealing with "restitution" in civil claims. There are now three alternative criteria for the applicability of this gateway, namely that: **39–105**

(1) "the defendant's alleged liability arises out of acts committed within the jurisdiction";
(2) the enrichment is obtained within the jurisdiction; or
(3) the claim is governed by the law of England and Wales.

As with the tort gateway (see above) there has been controversy in the case-law as to whether *all* of the acts required to found the claim must have occurred in the jurisdiction.

In *Nabb Brothers Ltd v Lloyds Bank International (Guernsey) Ltd*,[149] decided in   **39–106**
2005, the court held that personal claims in dishonest assistance and knowing receipt would fall within both the constructive trustee and restitution gateways. A claim in dishonest assistance might also, or even more properly, be said to fall under the tort gateway on the basis that it is based upon wrongdoing, not receipt or tenure of property. As for proprietary claims based on receipt of trust property, the court in *Nabb Brothers* held that these fell within the constructive trustee head, but suggested that, depending upon their proper jurisprudential basis, they might also fall under restitution. It is suggested that that conclusion is even more likely in light of the new amended wording of gateway (16), which now refers specifically to enrichment.

(viii) Forum conveniens

The final limb of the test for service out of the jurisdiction, which gives the court   **39–107**
a residual discretion on applications for service out, is that an applicant must show that England is the proper forum for the resolution of the dispute. There is no exhaustive list of factors to be considered in this context, and each case turns entirely on its own facts. Factors which the courts have taken into account include: the nature of the dispute, factual and legal; the location of the parties and their witnesses; jurisdiction clauses; the location of relevant documents; the applicable law (if the matter is heard in the jurisdiction whose law is being applied it can be made the subject of an appeal); the speed of resolution of the disputes in the other forum; and whether there is another forum before which all parties involved can be bound by the decision.[150]

---

[148] Practice Direction 6B, para.3.1(16) (as amended with effect from 1 October 2015).
[149] *Nabb Brothers Ltd v Lloyds Bank International (Guernsey) Ltd* [2005] EWHC 405 (Ch).
[150] There is a vast amount of learning on the question which is outside the remit of this book. For a recent analysis of factors going to the forum non conveniens issue, see *Gunn v Diaz* [EWHC] 157 (QB), at [107]–[121].

(4) Practice and Procedure for Applications

39–108   Applications for service out of the jurisdiction are, *ex hypothesi*, made without notice in the first instance, and accordingly the claimant owes a duty of full and frank disclosure.

39–109   The application must specify:

(1)   upon which gateway(s) the claimant is relying[151];
(2)   that the claimant believes that the claim against the foreign defendant has a real prospect of success[152];
(3)   the defendant's address or, if not known, in what place the defendant is, or is likely, to be found[153];
(4)   if he is relying on the necessary and proper party gateway, the basis on which he says there is a real issue between the claimant and the defendant.[154]

39–110   If the claim is governed by foreign law, expert evidence may need to be adduced in relation to the merits of the claim and/or as to the applicability of the gateways, for example as to the place in which a harmful event is deemed to occur under a foreign law of tort or delict.

39–111   In both the Chancery Division and the Queen's Bench Division applications are made in the first instance by leaving the documents with Masters appointments, and the decision will be made on paper in a relatively straightforward case. For that reason, and also because many of the points to be made on an application are matters of submission rather than evidence, it is strongly recommended that applicants include, at the top of the pack that they send to court, a skeleton argument. The skeleton argument should contain a section entitled "Full and Frank Disclosure" summarising all matters under that head and giving references for the appropriate parts of the evidence and/or exhibit. In the Commercial Court, applications will usually involve a without notice hearing before a Judge.

G.   CHALLENGING JURISDICTION

39–112   A defendant served with an English claim may seek to challenge the court's jurisdiction. This is so whether the claim has been served with or without the court's permission:

(1)   If the claim has been served without permission in reliance on the BRR the challenge is likely to be as to the applicability of the provision relied upon. It should be noted that the burden of establishing that the English court has

---

[151] CPR r.6.37(1)(a). However, it is no longer the case that a failure to do so necessarily precludes him from relying on others at inter partes hearing—see the decision of the Supreme Court in *NML Capital Ltd v Republic of Argentina* [2011] UKSC 3; [2011] 3 W.L.R. 273.
[152] CPR r.6.37(1)(b).
[153] CPR r.6.37(1)(c).
[154] CPR r.6.37(2).

power to hear and determine the claimant's claim under the BRR is that of the claimant, and the standard of proof is that of a good arguable case (see above).

(2)   If it has been served under the common law, the challenge may be to service, to the merits of the claim or to the applicability of the gateway relied upon. Alternatively, the application may simply be for an order staying the claim on the basis of forum non conveniens, i.e. that there is a more appropriate forum for the resolution of the dispute.

In the case of challenges under the common law principles, the following points are worth noting: **39–113**

(1)   Those advising a defendant in these circumstances should think hard about whether a challenge based on the merits of the claim is a good idea, as it is quite possible that a lengthy judgment will be given on the substantive issues, which will create significant momentum for the claimant going forward if he is successful. The courts' oft-repeated strictures against jurisdiction challenges becoming mini-trials (see below) should also be borne in mind.

(2)   The test to be applied on a forum non conveniens application is two-fold,[155] namely:

    (a)   The burden rests on the defendant to show that there is another available forum which is clearly or distinctly more appropriate than England for the resolution of the dispute (the "natural forum").

    (b)   The burden then shifts to the claimant to show that it would be unjust to deprive him of the right to proceed with his properly commenced English proceedings, instead requiring him in effect to seek justice in the natural forum.

    The test is the reverse of that applied when the court exercises its discretion on a service out application (see above), and the same factors are relevant.[156]

(3)   Where a defendant alleges that proceedings have been brought in breach of a jurisdiction agreement, it is for him to prove its terms and applicability. If he does so the court will normally enforce the agreement, whether it is exclusive or non-exclusive. While the court retains a discretion, strong cause will have to be shown to override the clause.

The procedure for disputing the court's jurisdiction is set out in CPR Pt 11. If a defendant wishes to "dispute the court's jurisdiction to try the claim or argue that the court should not exercise its jurisdiction" (in other words to ask the court to decline jurisdiction or to stay on forum grounds) he must file an acknowledgment of service in accordance with Pt 10, indicating that he wishes to challenge jurisdiction, and then issue an application within 14 days, supported by   **39–114**

---

[155] *Spiliada Maritime Corp v Cansulex (The Spiliada)* [1987] A.C. 460 HL.
[156] For a consideration of relevant factors see *Limit (No.3) Ltd v PDV Insurance Co Ltd* [2005] EWCA Civ 383.

evidence.[157] He need not also file a draft defence,[158] but it can be useful to do so if the jurisdiction challenge is based upon the substantive issues that are likely to arise in the case. This procedure would seem to apply to both types of jurisdiction challenge referred to above.

39–115 In *Okpabi v Royal Dutch Shell Plc*[159] Simon LJ, referring to a number of cases in which the courts had regretted the expenditure of time, effort and financial resources on jurisdiction issues, lamented the way in which the challenge had been conducted in the lower courts. He was of the view that "steps must be taken by courts to control and limit what is placed before the Court in the future" and that there must be "watchful case management".[160] He made particular reference to the judgment of Lord Neuberger in *VTB Capital v Nutritek International Corp*[161]:

> "82. The first point is that hearings concerning the issue of appropriate forum should not involve masses of documents, long witness statements, detailed analysis of the issues, and long argument. It is self-defeating if, in order to determine whether an action should proceed to trial in this jurisdiction, the parties prepare for and conduct a hearing which approaches the putative trial itself, in terms of effort, time and cost. There is also a real danger that, if the hearing is an expensive and time-consuming exercise, it will be used by a richer party to wear down a poorer party, or by a party with a weak case to prevent, or at least to discourage, a party with a strong case from enforcing its rights.
>
> 83. Quite apart from this, it is simply disproportionate for parties to incur costs, often running to hundreds of thousands of pounds each, and to spend many days in court, on such a hearing. The essentially relevant factors should, in the main at any rate, be capable of being identified relatively simply and, in many respects, uncontroversially. There is little point in going into much detail: when determining such applications, the court can only form preliminary views on most of the relevant legal issues and cannot be anything like certain about which issues and what evidence will eventuate if the matter proceeds to trial."

39–116 In *Lungowe v Vedanta Resources and Konkola Copper Mines Plc*,[162] citing the well-known dictum of Beatson LJ in *Trust Risk Group SpA v Am Trust Europe Ltd*,[163] Simon LJ reiterated that appellate courts should be slow to interfere with a decision on a jurisdictional challenge, and should only do so where the judge has misdirected himself on the law, or on the basis that he failed to take into account what mattered or took into account what did not matter.

39–117 If the application is unsuccessful, the acknowledgment of service will cease to have effect, and the defendant is entitled to file a further acknowledgment within 14 days or such other period as the court might direct. The court shall then give directions as to the filing and service of the defence.[164] If the defendant files a further acknowledgment of service in accordance with this procedure he is deemed to have accepted jurisdiction.[165]

---

[157] CPR r.11(1)(4).
[158] CPR r.11(9).
[159] *Okpabi v Royal Dutch Shell Plc* [2018] EWCA Civ 191.
[160] *Okpabi v Royal Dutch Shell Plc*, per Simon LJ at [20], [22].
[161] *VTB Capital v Nutritek International Corp* [2013] 2 A.C. 337, at [83]–[83].
[162] *Lungowe v Vedanta Resources and Konkola Copper Mines Plc* [2017] EWCA Civ 1528.
[163] *Trust Risk Group SpA v Am Trust Europe Ltd* [2015] EWCA Civ 437, at [33].
[164] CPR r.11(7).
[165] CPR r.11(8).

CHAPTER 40

CONFLICT OF LAWS

A. INTRODUCTION

When a fraud case with foreign elements comes before the English court, it will,
if required to do so, apply English private international law to determine which
country's law governs the substantive cause of action. Indeed, more than one
system of law may apply to one case. For example, it may be a pre-requisite of a
claim in tort for the claimant to show that he owned property before it was taken.
If so, the ownership element of the claim would be governed by the private
international law rules relating to property, the taking element by those relating to
tort. Further, as will be seen below, different rules apply to determine the law
governing the issue whether a trust has arisen in the first place from those which
determine the law governing its operation and administration, and therefore a
different law could be found to govern each issue.

40–001

As a matter of English civil procedure, the question whether there is a private
international law issue in a given claim is determined by the parties' pleadings
and evidence. If a party wishes to rely on foreign law, he must plead it, establish
(if this is contested) that it is the applicable law to the particular issue or set of
issues in question, and prove its content.[1] If neither party pleads that a foreign law
applies and that that law is different from English law, the court will apply
English law to the whole of the claim even if, upon proper analysis, that is not the
governing law of the claim or any particular issue arising in it under the relevant
conflicts provisions. The precise jurisprudential basis for this practice, and the
limits of its application, are controversial (for example, whether it applies in
relation to issues where the relevant English law is contained in statute(s) which

40–002

---

[1] Generally the burden of pleading the foreign law is on the party alleging that it governs the case or
some part of it (and that it is materially different from English law). A question may arise as to
whether the burden is on the claimant to plead the relevant foreign law at the outset in a case where
the claim must be governed by that law rather than English law. In *Global Multimedia International v
Ara Media Services* [2006] EWHC 1307, at [38] and [39], Sir Andrew Morritt C suggested that in the
case of a contract expressly governed by foreign law, a claim (in that case the Pt 20 Claim) that failed
to plead the relevant foreign law would be "deficient"; but the weight of authority favours the view
that (at least where the pleading discloses a properly arguable cause of action under English law), it is
for the defendant to plead that some other law applies and the claimant does not need to anticipate
such a case in his claim: see *Kuwait Oil Tanker Co SAK v Al Bader* [2000] 2 All E.R. (Comm) 271, at
[178] and [180]; *VTB Capital v Nutritek International* [2012] EWCA Civ 808; [2012] 2 Lloyd's Rep.
313, at [166] (not disapproved on appeal to the Supreme Court); and *Erste Group Bank AG, London
Branch v JSC 'VMZ Red October'* [2015] EWCA Civ 379; [2015] 1 C.L.C. 706, at [109]–[112].

do not on their wording apply to the case in question due to its foreign elements).[2] If it is asked to decide a point of foreign law, the court will need to hear expert evidence (from experts appointed by each side, if the foreign law is disputed) as to its content and effect. Questions of foreign law are treated as questions of fact.

40–003 Mercifully, the English rules on conflicts of laws, certainly in relation to the causes of action with which this book is concerned, are very largely codified, because they incorporate into English law the provisions of European conventions. Despite that European underpinning, the effect of Brexit upon those rules is in fact likely to be relatively minimal, for reasons set out at the end of this chapter.

B.   CONTRACTUAL OBLIGATIONS

40–004 The English conflicts rules relating to the law governing contracts and claims thereunder are now contained in the Regulation which is universally known as Rome I, to which the UK is a party.[3] Specifically, Rome I applies to "contractual obligations in civil and commercial matters" in relation to contracts concluded after 17 December 2009. Prior to that date those matters were governed by the Rome Convention, which was in terms so similar that it is not necessary to examine it separately here. Straightforward claims for contractual debts or for damages for breach of contract, to which Rome I applies, are outside of the scope of this book. However, as will be set out below, there are a number of cases in which the law governing a pre-existing contractual relationship will dictate the law to be applied to other causes of action that are more relevant in a fraud context. By way of example, in the case of torts arising out of or in connection with a pre-existing contractual relationship, it is possible that the rules in Rome I will apply by analogy under the provisions of Rome II, which we discuss below (see in particular art.4(3) thereof, also discussed in detail below).

40–005 Accordingly, it is worth summarising the basic scheme of Rome I. That can be done briefly as follows:

(1)   A contract shall be governed by the law expressly or impliedly chosen by the parties (even if it is not the law of a Member State),[4] save that where all other elements relevant to the situation at the time of the choice are located in a country other than the country whose law has been chosen, the choice of the parties shall not prejudice the application of such provisions of the law of that other country as cannot be derogated from by agreement. Similarly if all other elements are located in one or more Member States, the fact that the parties have chosen a law other than that of a Member State

---

[2] See Lord Collins of Mapesbury and J. Harris (eds), *Dicey, Morris and Collins on the Conflict of Laws*, 15th edn (London: Sweet & Maxwell, 2017), Fourth supplement , paras 9–025—9–030.
[3] Regulation (EC) 593/2008 of the European Parliament and of the Council of 17 June 2008 on the law applicable to contractual obligations.
[4] Article 3(1).

shall not prejudice, where appropriate, the application of such provisions of EU law as cannot be derogated from by agreement.[5]

(2) If the parties do not choose (whether impliedly or expressly) a system of law to govern their relations, rules as to the law governing specific contracts are set out in art.4(1). In all other cases (that is, those not covered by the art.4(1) rules), the law governing the contract is (under art.4(2)) that of the place of habitual residence of the person whose performance is characteristic of the contract.[6] Both arts 4(1) and 4(2) are subject to two exceptions: if (a) it is clear from all of the circumstances of the case that the contract is manifestly more closely connected with the law of another country, or (b) the applicable law cannot be determined from the rules set out in 4(1) and (2), then the law of the country with which the contract is most closely connected will apply.[7]

(3) Nothing set out above shall restrict the application of overriding mandatory provisions of the law of the forum (i.e. the country in which the claim is proceeding), such as those regarded as crucial by the country for safeguarding its public interests, including its political, social or economic organisation.[8]

(4) The existence and "material" validity of a contract, or of any of its terms, shall be determined by the law which would govern it if it were valid, save that the issue of consent of a party to enter into a contract will be governed instead by the law of the country of his habitual residence where that would be more reasonable.[9]

(5) If a contract is concluded between persons in the same country, it is "formally" valid if it satisfies the formal validity requirements of the law which governs it in substance or (if different) the law of the country where it is concluded.[10] If the parties are in different countries when the contract is concluded (e.g. if they conclude it over the telephone) it is formally valid if it satisfies the formal validity requirements of the law which governs it *or* the country in which either of them is present at the time of conclusion, *or* the law of the countries where either of them has his habitual residence at the time of conclusion.[11]

---

[5] Articles 3(3), (4).
[6] Article 4(2).
[7] Articles 4(3), (4).
[8] Article 9(1).
[9] Articles 10(1), (2). The Regulation does not define either "material" or "formal" validity. However, the Giuliano Lagarde report accompanying the Rome Convention explained, at para.2 under art.9, that "It is...permissible to consider 'form' for the purposes of Article 9 [of the Rome Convention, equivalent to Article 11 of Rome I] as including every external manifestation required on the part of a person expressing the will to be legally bound, and in the absence of which such expression of will would not be regarded as fully effective". By contrast, art.10 (of Rome I) purports on its face to deal with the "existence or validity of a contract". This presumably incorporates matters concerning the coming into existence of a contract, and reasons why a contract may be deemed invalid which are concerned with the nature of the contract rather than with its form. Collins and Harris (eds), *Dicey, Morris and Collins on the Conflict of Laws* (2017), para.32–107 gives as examples of issues concerned with material validity "formation... absence of consideration, duress, mistake, and also the legality of a contract".
[10] Article 11(1).
[11] Article 11(2).

40–006 The basic rules in art.4 (i.e. in cases where there has been no express or implied choice of governing law) are easier to state than to apply. They are straightforward in cases for the provision of services in exchange for money—where A agrees to fix B's computer for a price, it is obvious that the fixing of the computer is the performance which is characteristic of the contract so the contract is governed by the place of A's habitual residence.[12] However, one does not have to stray too far to get into trouble. In the case of a loan, for example, whose performance is "characteristic"? Is it that of the lender or that of the borrower? One would think this would be an obvious case, but—although the answer would appear to be the lender—there is no clear authority on the point.[13]

40–007 In two recent cases the Court of Appeal has considered, in the context of parties seeking to set aside interest rate swaps entered into under ISDA master agreements containing an English choice of law clause, the effect of art.3(3) of the Rome Convention (which is in materially identical terms to art.3(3) of Rome I). Specifically, the issue was whether the court could take into account, in deciding whether "all other elements" of the contract were located in a country other than that chosen by the parties (in these two cases the countries in question were Portugal and Italy), "international elements", i.e. those which showed that the contract was international in nature but did not point to a connection to any particular country. In the first (in time) decision, *Banco Santander Totta SA v Companhia de Carris de Ferro De Lisboa SA*,[14] the Court of Appeal held that, as art.3(3) is a limited exception to the principle of party autonomy, it must be narrowly construed. It therefore agreed with the judge at first instance that "international elements" could be taken into account, the relevant elements in question in that case being, for example, the use of the multi-currency, cross-border form of the ISDA agreement, the international nature of the swaps in question, and the existence of hedging contracts that the bank had entered into outside of Portugal. In *Dexia Crediop SPA v Commune di Prato*,[15] decided shortly after, in which the court at first instance had found that the swaps should be set aside, the Court followed its decision in *Santander*.

C. NON-CONTRACTUAL OBLIGATIONS

40–008 The rules which determine the law applicable to civil or commercial matters arising in non-contractual relations are, with a few notable exceptions, now contained in the Regulation which is universally known as Rome II[16] as regards

---

[12] The Giuliano-Lagarde report explained (at p.20) that the characteristic performance refers to the function which the legal relationship involved fulfils in the economic and social life of any country, and that where the contract involves the performance of a service in exchange for money, the characteristic performance will be the performance of the service, rather than the payment of money.

[13] At least that is so in relation to a non-bank, non-investment loan: see *Mirchandani v Ketan Somaia* [2001] WL 239782; *Atlantic Telecom GmbH* [2004] S.L.T. 1031; H. Beale, *Chitty on Contracts*, 31st edn (London: Sweet & Maxwell, 2012), Vol. 1, para.30–076.

[14] *Banco Santander Totta SA v Companhia de Carris de Ferro De Lisboa SA* [2016] EWCA Civ 1267.

[15] *Dexia Crediop SPA v Commune di Prato* [2017] EWCA Civ 428.

[16] Regulation EC 864/2007 of the European Parliament and of the Council of 11 July 2007 on the law applicable to non-contractual obligations.

"events giving rise to damage" occurring on or after 11 January 2009.[17] By virtue of UK secondary legislation[18] Rome II also applies to determine private international law issues in relation to non-contractual obligations as between the various different parts of the UK.

Rome II is intended to be read together with Rome I as a comprehensive code. As such it governs all matters other than: (a) those said by Rome I to be "*contractual obligations*", and (b) those which it expressly excludes.It also applies to future non-contractual obligations.[19]   **40–009**

Specific exclusions are set out in arts 1(1), 1(2) and 1(3). Those that are relevant to note for civil fraud purposes are: those arising out of the law of companies[20] and those arising out of the internal relationships relating to trusts.[21]   **40–010**

When Rome II applies, the law designated by it shall apply regardless of whether that is the law of a Member State.[22] The principle of *renvoi* is excluded—in other words the law designated by Rome II is the domestic law of the country in question, excluding its private international law.[23]   **40–011**

Importantly, art.14 provides that the parties may choose a law to govern their non-contractual obligations, either before (if both parties are pursuing a "commercial activity")[24] or after they have arisen,[25] save that they cannot override the mandatory provisions of the law of a country other than that whose law they have chosen if "all the elements relevant to the situation" at the time of the event giving rise to the relevant damage are located in that country,[26] nor can they override the provisions of Community law (now EU law) if the parties have chosen a law other than that of a Member State and "all the elements relevant to the situation" are located in one or more Member States.[27] Subject to those restrictions, there is no express limit on the scope, or form, of the agreement that can be reached. The precise scope of the agreement is purely a matter of construction based on the words used, although that exercise will not be straightforward in relation to torts arising out of pre-existing contractual relationships or *culpa in contrahendo* (see below).   **40–012**

---

[17] Articles 31–32.

[18] The Law Applicable to Non-Contractual Obligations (England and Wales and Northern Ireland) Regulations 2008 SI 2008 No. 2986.

[19] Namely those "which are likely to arise"—art.2(2)).

[20] Article 1(2)(d).

[21] Article 1(2)(e). For a detailed account of the scope and purpose of these exclusions see A. Briggs, *Private International Law in English Courts*, 1st edn, (Oxford: OUP, 2014), paras 8.220–8.230.

[22] Article 3.

[23] Article 24.

[24] This is not defined in Rome II but its meaning is relatively clear.

[25] Article 14(1)(a) and (b). As noted above, it is always open to parties to English litigation to agree that their dispute will be governed by English law, by the simple act of not taking or leading evidence as to any foreign law points.

[26] Article 14(2).

[27] Article 14(3).

40–013   Article 15 of Rome II gives a non-exhaustive list of matters which will be governed by the applicable law, once it has been established. They are worth setting out in full because they are very comprehensive as to the coverage of the applicable law:

(1)   the basis and extent of liability, including the determination of persons who may be held liable for acts performed by them;

(2)   the grounds for exemption from liability, any limitation of liability and any division of liability;

(3)   the existence, the nature and the assessment of damage or the remedy claimed;

(4)   within the limits of powers conferred on the court by its procedural law, the measures which a court may take to prevent or terminate injury or damage or to ensure the provision of compensation;

(5)   the question whether a right to claim damages or a remedy may be transferred, including by inheritance;

(6)   persons entitled to compensation for damage sustained personally;

(7)   liability for the acts of another person;

(8)   the manner in which an obligation may be extinguished and rules of prescription and limitation, including rules relating to the commencement, interruption and suspension of a period of prescription or limitation.

40–014   Further, the applicable law will, to the extent that it contains such rules, determine whether any presumptions of law are raised and who has the burden of proof.[28] Contributions and indemnities as between co-defendants are dealt with by art.20, which provides that if a claim lies against multiple defendants and one of them has already satisfied the claim in whole or in part, the question of that defendant's right to demand compensation from the other defendants is governed by the law applicable to the claim against him.

40–015   The applicable law will be displaced by overriding mandatory provisions or public policy concerns of the *lex fori*[29] or by contrary provisions of other conventions or Community law (now EU law).[30]

40–016   Article 25 explains that, where a State comprises several territorial units, each with its own systems of law in respect of non-contractual obligations, each territorial unit shall be treated as a country. Accordingly, Rome II would dictate, for example, that a claim in conversion was governed by the law of Florida, rather than the federal law of the USA.

---

[28] Article 22.
[29] Articles 16, 26.
[30] Articles 27 and 28.

(1)   Tort/Delict

Rome II applies to claims in tort relating to events giving rise to damage which occurred on or after 11 January 2009.[31] Its provisions are considered in detail below, after a brief examination of the law which previously applied, and which still applies in litigation concerned with torts arising out of events which took place at times prior to that date.

40–017

(i)   Events prior to 1 May 1996

Torts committed prior to 1 May 1996 were dealt with under the common law concept of "double actionability", which had colonial roots, and required, onerously, that in order to be successful before an English court acts committed in a foreign jurisdiction had to constitute a tort both under the law of that place and under English law,[32] with a flexible exception for cases where another law was the "proper law of the tort" (or *lex loci delicti*).[33] As it will now be an extremely rare occasion when such cases come before the courts, no more is said about that test here.

40–018

(ii)   Events prior to 11 January 2009

Torts arising out of events giving rise to damage which occurred between 1 May 1996 and 11 January 2009, or where Rome II does not apply, are governed by the Private International Law (Miscellaneous Provisions) Act 1995. As the number of cases being litigated under that Act are dying out, and as it is unlikely that Brexit will result in its resurrection (see below), it is considered only summarily here.

40–019

The rules in the 1995 Act apply "for choosing the law .... to be used for determining issues relating to tort…".[34] It provides that whether a matter is to be characterised as a tort is a matter for the courts of the forum.[35] The applicable law as determined under the 1995 Act is to be used for determining the issues arising in a claim, including in particular the question whether an actionable tort has occurred.[36] There is no *renvoi* under the 1995 Act. In other words, the "applicable law" under its provisions does not include the relevant country's private international law.[37]

40–020

The key provision in the 1995 Act is s.11, which provides that "the applicable law is the law of the country in which the events constituting the tort or delict in question occur." It goes on to explain that where elements of those events occur in different countries, the applicable law is taken to be, in cases of personal injury or damage to property, the place of the victim or property when it was damaged.

40–021

---

[31] Articles 31 and 32.
[32] *Phillips v Eyre* (1870) L.R. 6 Q.B. 1.
[33] *Boys v Chaplin* [1969] 2 All E.R. 1085; expanded upon in *Red Sea Insurance v Bouygues SA* [1995] 1 A.C. 190.
[34] Section 9(1).
[35] Section 9(2).
[36] Section 9(4).
[37] Section 9(5).

In any other case (so in cases of pure economic loss) it is that of "the country in which the most significant element or elements of those events occurred." Unfortunately, given the opacity of this provision, the majority of fraud cases are going to be in the latter category.

40–022 The general rule can be displaced where it appears from a comparison of: (a) the significance of the factors connecting the tort with the applicable law designated by the general rule and (b) the significance of any factors connecting the tort with another country that it is substantially more appropriate for the applicable law to be that of the other country.[38] Factors which are relevant to that analysis are said to be those relating to the parties, to any of the events which constitute the tort or delict in question or to any of the circumstances or consequences of those events.[39]

40–023 As will be clear from the above, the courts were given a very wide discretion by the 1995 Act in deciding which country's law governs, and much was dependent upon the way they applied concepts such as "significant element or elements" and "substantially more appropriate." The Act was therefore uncertain and unpredictable, and the introduction of Rome II, whose provisions are far clearer, was a welcome development.

(iii)   Events on or after 11 January 2009

40–024 The remainder of this section focuses on Rome II. The general rule is that set out in art.4, which is in three parts. Those parts, set out logically rather than in the order in which they appear in the Regulation itself, are as follows:

(1)   Where the person claimed to be liable and the person sustaining damage both have their *habitual residence* in the same country at the time when the damage occurs, the law of that country shall apply.[40]

(2)   If that is not the case, the governing law is the law of the country in which the *damage* occurs, irrespective of the country in which the event giving rise to the damage occurred and irrespective of the country or countries in which the indirect consequences of that event occur.[41]

(3)   However, in either case, where it is clear from all the circumstances of the case that the tort/delict is *manifestly more closely connected* with a country other than that indicated in paras (1) or (2) above, the law of that other country shall apply. A manifestly closer relationship with another country might be based in particular on a pre-existing relationship between the parties, such as a contract, that is closely connected with the tort/delict in question.[42]

40–025 **Habitual Residence.**   As regards companies, "habitual residence" is defined in art.23 as meaning the place of central administration, save that if the event giving

---

[38] Section 12(1).
[39] Section 12(2).
[40] Article 4(2).
[41] Article 4(1).
[42] Article 4(3).

rise to damage occurs in the course of operation of a branch or agency or other establishment, the place of that branch (etc) shall be treated as the place of habitual residence. Similarly, the place of residence of a natural person acting in the course of his business shall be his principal place of business.

No definition of "habitual residence" is given in Rome II in relation to private **40–026** individuals not acting in the course of business. It has been suggested, based on the law applicable in a family and social security context, that the European Court will give the term an autonomous meaning across all Member States, namely the country in which (based on objectively ascertainable factors) an individual's interests are centred, with a certain permanence or regularity, at the relevant time.[43] This would appear to be conceptually very similar to the test of "centre of main interests" under the EC Insolvency Regulation, although care should be taken in seeking to rely on case-law from that context, where different policy considerations arise.

Damage. As will be apparent, the meaning of *"damage"* in this context is **40–027** extremely important. Article 2 explains that it shall cover "any consequence arising out of tort/delict…". This suggests that the definition is apt to cover physical damage, reputational damage or economic loss. By virtue of art.3(b) it extends to future damage ("damage that is likely to occur"). By virtue of the wording at the end of art.4(1), the definition expressly excludes "indirect consequences", so presumably is limited to "direct consequences". In this regard it is largely aligned with the rules on jurisdiction set out in the Brussels Regulation Recast, and many of the authorities referred to in that context (see Ch.39 above, paras 39–034—39–039) are relevant to, and address, both issues.

A useful summary of those cases and their potential relevance to the **40–028** interpretation of art.4(1) is contained in the judgment of Carr J in *Pan Oceanic Chartering Inc v UNIPEC UK Co Ltd*.[44] That was a claim brought by a ship chartering broker domiciled in New Jersey against the defendants, a group of charterers owned by a Chinese company, in relation to a three-year contract of affreightment for the transportation of crude oil from West Africa. The claimant alleged that in breach of contract one of the defendants had failed to nominate cargoes under the affreightment contract under which the claimant would have received brokerage commissions. It also alleged tortious interference with the claimant's brokerage arrangements under New Jersey law. Having reviewed the authorities the judge found that, to the extent that the claim involved non-contractual obligations, this was not a case where, as in *Dumez*,[45] there was both direct and indirect damage as a result of the alleged unlawful act. Rather it was a case where, as in *Dolphin Maritime*,[46] there was a sole, direct and immediate cause, namely the non-receipt of money by the claimant brokers. As

---

[43] Collins, Harris (eds), *Dicey, Morris & Collins on the Conflict of Laws* (2017), Vol.2, para.34–041.
[44] *Pan Oceanic Chartering Inc v UNIPEC UK Co Ltd* [2016] EWHC 2774 (Comm).
[45] *Dumez France SA v Hessiche Landesbank* (C-220/88) [1990] I.L. Pr. 299.
[46] *Dolphin Maritime & Aviation Services Ltd v Sveriges Angfartygs Assurans Forening (The Swedish Club)* [2009] EWHC 716 (Comm); [2009] 1 C.L.C. 460.

was identified in *AMT Futures v Marzillier*[47] at first instance, the harm in such a case lies in the non-receipt of money at the place where it ought to have been received, and the damage occurred where the claimant should have received it, namely in its bank account in New York. The failure to nominate was merely the event giving rise to the damage, which is irrelevant for the purposes of art.4(1).

40–029 However, care is needed in reading interpretations across from the jurisdictional rules to those concerned with conflicts of law. A possible difference between the regimes is that whilst the courts in relation to the BRR have been unwilling for the place of domicile of the victim or (recently) the place of pure economic loss to be solely determinative as to jurisdiction, there have been no such dicta in relation to Rome II, nor is there any obvious policy reason why those considerations should not be solely determinative as to governing law.

40–030 The need for caution was recently confirmed by the Supreme Court in *Brownlie v Four Seasons Holdings Inc*[48] in a passage which also confirmed the meaning of "damage" under art.4(1):

> "It is undoubtedly convenient for the country of the forum to correspond with that of the proper law. It is also true that both jurisdiction and choice of law can broadly be said to depend on how closely the dispute is connected with a particular country. But there is no necessary connection between the two. The Practice Direction [6B] contemplates a wide variety of connecting factors, of which the proper law is only one and that one is relevant only to contractual liabilities. For the purpose of identifying the proper law, 'damage' is limited to direct damage because article 4 of Rome II says so in terms. It does this because there can be only one proper law, and the formulation of a common rule for all EU member states necessarily requires a more or less mechanical technique for identifying it. By comparison, indirect damage may be suffered in more than one country and jurisdiction in both English and EU law may subsist in more than one country."[49]

40–031 As in the jurisdictional context, cases of pure economic loss can cause particular difficulties. An illustrative example in a case decided under art.4(1) of Rome II itself is *Hillside (New Media) Ltd v Baasland*.[50] An online gambler had threatened to bring proceedings in Norway to sue companies in the bet365 group for negligence in allowing him to gamble away his money without due warning as to the risks involved. He did not do so; however, in light of the threats the bet365 companies brought pre-emptive proceedings in England for declarations that they were not liable to the individual in question. Numerous legal systems were potentially in play because the entities which processed the respective bets in question were based in the Netherlands, Antilles, Gibraltar and England; and once the bets were processed, funds were transferred to an account in England. The individual placed his bets from, at various times, Germany, the Czech Republic, Norway and Denmark.

40–032 Under art.4(1) the court considered where the individual in question, Mr Baasland, had first suffered immediate financial loss. The issue was a

---

[47] *AMT Futures v Marzillier* [2014] EWHC 1085 (Comm); the actual decision was reversed by the Court of Appeal, whose decision was upheld by the Supreme Court (see Ch.39 above, paras 39–037—39–039); however, this part of the analysis was not questioned.
[48] *Brownlie v Four Seasons Holdings Inc* [2017] UKSC 80; [2018] 1 W.L.R. 192.
[49] Per Lord Sumption, at [22].
[50] *Hillside (New Media) Ltd v Baasland* [2010] EWHC 3336 (Comm); [2010] 2 C.L.C. 986.

complicated one; the court found that: (i) when Mr Baasland transferred funds into his online "wallet" he became the creditor of a debt in respect of the funds so deposited; (ii) the amount of his debt increased and decreased as he won and lost and withdrew and paid in; (iii) therefore he suffered no loss when he paid money into the wallet—he only suffered loss when that money was used to place bets. The issue turned therefore on the situs of the chose in action, the value of which had decreased. The answer was that for part of the chronology it was in England, where the debtor, the parent company, was domiciled. However later, when the group was restructured, it was Gibraltar. The court noted that Rome II did not specify what was to happen where a claimant suffered loss in more than one country, however it did not need to decide that question—it only needed to find that the governing law was not, as the individual had asserted in his threatened claims—that of Norway.

In theory, if a single tort has two different victims, their claims could be governed by different laws. That is so first because art.4(1) might apply in one case, and art.4(2) in the other, with different results. Alternatively, it might be because they suffered damage in different places for the purposes of art.4(2). **40–033**

Manifestly Closer Connection. Article 4(3) provides a get-out clause if the application of the first two limbs produces an anomalous answer. However, it should be noted that the court does not have a wide discretion under the wording of that article. There is only scope to ask one question—is the tort manifestly more connected with a country (rather than a system of law) other than that dictated by arts 4(1) or (2)? If so, then the law of that country applies. As set out above, art.4(3) gives as a specific example of a claim more closely connected with a country other than that dictated by 4(1) or (2), a connection based on a "pre-existing relationship between the parties", hence the potential relevance of Rome I to tortious disputes. However, that provision is not exhaustive as to the circumstances in which art.4(3) can apply. Recent examples of its application are set out below. **40–034**

(1) In *Hillside (New Media)* (see above) the court went on to find that, if it had reached a different conclusion as to where the damage had occurred, it would nevertheless have considered that English law governed the claim under art.4(3) because: (i) the losses occurred by way of dealings with funds in an English bank account, (ii) they resulted from the facilities offered through a website which was owned by an English company, which was operated from England, and to which the individual defendant might have had access from England, Norway or any other country, and (iii) the relationship was governed by a contractual arrangement of which the proper law or putative proper law was English.

(2) In *Pan Oceanic Chartering* (see above) the court, noting comments in the prior case-law that art.4(3) would displace the applicable law under art.4(1) only in "exceptional circumstances" and that a "high hurdle" had to be overcome, held that it could not be said that there was a manifestly closer connection to England so as to displace the general rule. Although several connecting factors to England were relied upon, including the fact that the

agreement under which the obligation to nominate allegedly arose was governed by English law, the failure to nominate had occurred in New Jersey, the loss of commission occurred in New York, and the defendant which had failed to nominate was based in Hong Kong.

(3) In *Winrow v Hemphill*,[51] the issue was which country's law applied to the assessment of damages for personal injury arising from a road traffic accident in Germany. Article 4(1) therefore pointed to Germany. The claimant attempted to displace the general rule by reliance on art.4(2), alternatively art.4(3). The court found on the facts that the claimant was habitually resident in Germany, and so art.4(2) did not apply. As for art.4(3), the court noted that (i) by contrast with arts 4(1) and (2), there was no temporal limitation under art.4(3) on the factors that could be taken into account; and (ii) factors that were determinative under arts 4(1) and (2) could also be taken into account in the examination of art.(3).

In the present case the claimant had following the accident moved back to England, was habitually resident there by the time of the hearing and had allegedly suffered both physical and financial consequential loss there as a result of the accident. Again, however, the court found that the high hurdle had not been overcome and that the law applicable to the tort was German law.

(2) Unjust Enrichment

(i) Events prior to 11 January 2009

40–035   As for unjust enrichment, in relation to events giving rise to damage which occurred prior to 11 January 2009 the English common law applies. It may be summarised by saying that the obligation to restore the benefit of an enrichment obtained at another person's expense was governed by the proper law of the obligation. So: if it arose in connection with a contract, the law of the contract; and in relation to immovable land, the law of the place where the land was situated. In any other circumstances, it was the place where the enrichment occurred.[52]

(ii) Events on or after 11 January 2009

40–036   One of the most significant changes introduced by Rome II from an English perspective was a codification of the private international rules concerning unjust enrichment, again in relation to "events giving rise to damage" from 11 January 2009 onwards. The relevant provisions are contained in art.10.

---

[51] *Winrow v Hemphill* [2014] EWHC 3164 (QB); [2015] I.L. Pr. 12.
[52] Collins and Harris (eds), *Dicey, Morris & Collins on the Conflict of Laws* (2017), Vol.2, para.36–008. That was a complicated and fact-specific analysis, which has been dealt with at some length in notable decisions such as *Chase Manhattan Bank NA v Israel-British Bank (London) Ltd* [1981] Ch. 105; *Re Jogia (A Bankrupt)* [1988] 1 W.L.R. 484, at 495–496; *Arab Monetary Fund v Hashim* [1996] 1 Lloyd's Rep. 589; *El Ajou v Dollar Land Holdings Plc* [1993] 3 All E.R. 717.

Article 10 provides no specific definition of unjust enrichment. However, by a **40–037** process of elimination based on the structure of the Rome scheme, it must encompass non-contractual obligations arising out of enrichment which give rise to a claim but which are not covered by art.4. Like art.4, art.10 provides a hierarchy as to the determination of the governing law, as follows:

(1) If a non-contractual obligation arising out of unjust enrichment nevertheless concerns a pre-existing relationship between the parties, for example one arising out of a contract or a tort, that is closely connected with the unjust enrichment, it shall be governed by the law of that relationship.[53]

(2) If para.(1) above does not apply, and if the parties have their habitual residence in the same country when the event giving rise to the unjust enrichment occurs, the law of that country applies.[54]

(3) If neither paras (1) nor (2) apply, it is the law of the place where the unjust enrichment took place.[55] This residual test is very difficult to apply in, for example, the case of a series of electronic money transfers. The answer is likely to be the reverse of the rule in art.4, in that the focus is on the enrichment of the wrongdoer rather than the loss of the victim. In other words, the relevant place is likely to be that where the recipient ultimately receives the money, rather than any country through which it might pass along the way.[56]

(4) Finally, as a catch-all, if it is clear that the unjust enrichment is manifestly more closely connected with a country other than that dictated by (1), (2) or (3) above, the law of that country applies.[57]

A useful example of the operation of art.10 in a fraud case is *Banque Cantonale* **40–038** *de Genève v Polevent.*[58] An employee of the claimant bank in Geneva, believing that she was acting on instructions from the bank's deputy CEO, transferred moneys to an account in London held by the first defendant. In fact the instructions were part of a fraud being carried out by the first defendant. The bank sued the first defendant for: (i) damages in deceit and (ii) unjust enrichment on the basis that the payment was the result of a mistaken transfer induced by fraud. It was common ground that the deceit claim was governed by Swiss law because it fell under art.4(1) and therefore was governed by the law of the place where the damage had occurred. As for the unjust enrichment claim, the third defendant (a creditor of the first defendant, which itself played no part in the proceedings) argued that that was also governed by Swiss law, either because it "arose out of" the tort for the purposes of art.4(1), or because it was a claim for unjust enrichment arising out of a "relationship existing" between the parties, and therefore was governed by the law applicable to the relationship by virtue of art.10(1). The claimant argued that it was simply governed by the law of the place where the unjust enrichment took place, under art.10(3), i.e. England. Teare J

---

[53] Article 10(1).
[54] Article 10(2).
[55] Article 10(3). See fn.43 above.
[56] See Briggs, *Private International Law in English Courts* (2014) para.8.151.
[57] Article 10(4).
[58] *Banque Cantonale de Genève v Polevent* [2015] EWHC 1968 (Comm); [2016] Q.B. 394.

found that although the deceit explained why the payment had been made, it was not a necessary ingredient of the cause of action. As for art.10(1), the judge said (correctly it is suggested) that there was no "relationship" between the parties before the deceit, and if deceit, or the bringing of a claim for deceit, was sufficient to give rise to such, art.10(1) would add nothing to art.4(1) in the context of the tort of deceit (art.4(1) already provides that where the obligation to provide restitution arises out of the tort, the law of the tort will govern that obligation). He therefore concluded that art.10(1) was not intended to refer to the mere "relationship" of wrongdoer and victim created by the commission of a tort. Rather it refers to a relationship which was in existence before the facts which give rise to the claim occurred.

(3) Other Causes of Action

40–039 Also within Ch.III of Rome II are rules concerning what are referred to in the regulation as "*negotiorum gestio*" and "*culpa in contrahendo*".

40–040 The former, which translates literally as "management of business", is dealt with in art.11. This concerns the obligation created when an intervenor acts on behalf of and for the benefit of a principal, but without the latter's prior consent, for example where one party voluntarily pays off another's debt. Article 11 provides that if the act concerns a relationship existing between the parties, such as one in contract or tort, that is closely connected with the non-contractual obligation in question, it will be governed by the law of that relationship.[59] If not, or if the applicable law cannot be determined on that basis, and the parties have their habitual residence in the same country when the act takes place, that country's law will apply.[60] If not, it shall be the law of the country where the act was performed.[61] That is so unless there is a country with which the obligation is manifestly more closely connected than that dictated by the rules just described—if there is, then that country's law shall apply.[62]

40–041 The latter term (*culpa in contrahendo*), which potentially has more relevance in a civil fraud context, means "fault arising out of dealings prior to a contract/in the act of contracting". It is dealt with in art.12. It relates to the situation where due to some acts carried out in the course of contractual negotiations, a contract is formed which is void, voidable or non-existent, and that state of affairs causes the innocent party financial loss.

40–042 Article 12 provides that in such circumstances, the applicable law shall be the law of the putative contract, whether or not it is ultimately entered into.[63] Where the applicable law "cannot be determined" on that basis, then there is a familiar hierarchy of possibilities, namely: where the parties have their habitual residence in the same place at the time of the relevant events; the law of that country[64]; if

---

[59] Article 11(1).
[60] Article 11(2).
[61] Article 11(3).
[62] Article 11(4).
[63] Article 12(1).
[64] Article 12(2)(b).

not, the law of the country in which the damage occurs (as opposed to the country where the act giving rise to it occurred)[65]; or, if the obligation in question is manifestly more closely connected with a country other than that dictated by either of those two requirements, the law of that country.[66]

These provisions are potentially complicated. As they have been drafted in order to cater for the hugely divergent provisions of the domestic laws of several nations in this area, it is not particularly helpful, at the stage of the private international law analysis, to consider art.12 from the perspective of the English law of contract and its rules concerning rescission, damages in lieu of rescission, and so on. Rather the facts should be considered objectively and autonomously. **40–043**

There is also potentially an overlap here between Rome I and Rome II. For whilst art.12 applies to financial claims based on either the fact that the contract is liable to rescission or has not been concluded at all, it does not apply to the question of the validity of the contract, or of its terms, which will be governed by Rome I. **40–044**

It is worth noting, however, that the difficulties referred to above can be contracted out of, by way of a carefully drafted clause in the contractual documentation, or even in prior heads of terms.[67] **40–045**

D.   EQUITABLE OBLIGATIONS

This section deals with "equitable claims". These have been gathered together here because that is how an English textbook would categorise them. However, to analyse these causes of action under headings derived from the English law of equity and trusts is to put the cart before the horse. Rather one must, for private international law purposes, look at their constituent elements and decide autonomously which rules should apply to them. **40–046**

As set out above, Rome II expressly excludes obligations internal to a trust, i.e. those "arising out of the relations between the settlors, trustees and beneficiaries of a trust created voluntarily".[68] A straightforward claim for breach of trust, alleged against a trustee, would seem to fall into this category. **40–047**

The English private international law rules in relation to express trusts are found in the Recognition of Trusts Act 1987, which incorporates into English law the provisions of The Hague Convention on the Law of Trusts and their Recognition ("the Hague Convention"). **40–048**

The Hague Convention applies to trusts, defined by art.2 as having the following characteristics: **40–049**

(1)   the assets constitute a separate fund and are not a part of the trustee's own estate;

---

[65] Article 12(2)(a).
[66] Article 12(2)(c).
[67] Article 14.
[68] Article 1(1)(e).

(2) title to the trust assets stands in the name of the trustee or in the name of another person on behalf of the trustee;

(3) the trustee has the power and the duty, in respect of which he is accountable, to manage, employ or dispose of the assets in accordance with the terms of the trust and the special duties imposed upon him by law.[69]

40–050 The Hague Convention applies to trusts regardless of the date when they were created[70] so long as they are created voluntarily and evidenced in writing.[71] It does not, then, apply in terms to resulting or constructive trusts or certainly not to all of them. However, the Recognition of Trusts Act 1987, which gives effect to the Hague Convention in the UK, expands its scope. Section 1(2) of the 1987 Act provides that the Hague Convention shall have effect not only in relation to the trusts described in arts 2 and 3 of the Convention but also in relation to

> "any other trusts of property arising under the law of any part of the United Kingdom or by virtue of a judicial decision whether in the United Kingdom or elsewhere."

This wider description would appear to catch all resulting and constructive trusts.

(1) Preliminary Issues

40–051 The Convention expressly does not apply to "preliminary issues" such as the validity of wills or of other acts by virtue of which assets are transferred to the trustee.[72] Nor does it deal with the prior issue whether a trust has arisen at all. Those issues must therefore be determined by other provisions of English private international law.[73]

40–052 As regards the issue whether trusts have come into being at all, this is most obviously pertinent in the case of resulting and constructive trusts. The answer is tortuously difficult to ascertain from reading the relevant case-law or legislation. However, it appears that it depends upon how the putative constructive trust is said to have arisen. The position can be summarised as follows:

---

[69] Article 2 further provides that the reservation by the settlor of certain rights and powers, and the fact that the trustee may himself have rights as a beneficiary, are not necessarily inconsistent with the existence of a trust.

[70] Hague Convention, art.22.

[71] Article 3.

[72] Article 4.

[73] For a recent decision on the distinction between these two issues, see *Akers v Samba Financial Group* [2014] EWCA Civ 1516; [2015] Ch. 451; [2015] 2 W.L.R. 1281, which was reversed by the Supreme Court on other grounds: [2017] UKSC 6; [2017] A.C. 424.

(1) Whether a resulting trust arising on the non-exhaustion of trust property under an express trust, or on the failure of an express trust altogether, has come into existence seems likely to be governed by the proper law of the express trust[74];

(2) The issue whether a presumed intention resulting trust or common intention constructive trust arises depends upon the law governing the arrangement or relationship between the parties, although the position is far from clear in the relevant authorities[75];

(3) If what is said to be a constructive trust actually arises in response to a failure to comply with a contractual obligation, or to non-contractual wrongdoing, or to unjust enrichment, then Rome I or Rome II, art.4 or art.10, will, by virtue of their express wording, catch the question whether an obligation arises, and, if so, apply to that obligation.

(2) Matters Internal to the Trust

The aspects of a trust which are governed by the law nominated by the Hague Convention are set out in art.8, namely "the validity of the trust, its construction, its effects and the administration of the trust." A non-exhaustive list of particular matters covered is then set out, which includes "the rights and duties of trustees amongst themselves"; "the relationships between the trustees and the beneficiaries including the personal liability of the trustees to the beneficiaries"; and "the duty of trustees to account for their administration". Accordingly, it is suggested that it clearly covers at least "internal" claims for breach of trust. As with most Conventions, there are saving provisions permitting the court to apply mandatory rules of the forum or to disapply the law dictated by the Convention to the extent that it is offensive to public policy in the country concerned.[76] **40–053**

The basic operative provisions of the Hague Convention are: **40–054**

(1) If the settlor has expressly or impliedly chosen a law, that law shall apply without limitation, unless it is a law which does not recognise trusts, in which case art.7 (no choice of law) will apply. Article 9 expressly permits the settlor to specify that one part of a trust, for example its administration, will be governed by a different law from the rest. Further, the governing law of the trust can be changed, if this is permitted by the law which originally governed it.[77]

---

[74] C. Mitchell, D.J. Hayton and P. Matthews, *Underhill & Hayton Law of Trusts and Trustees*, 19th edn (London: LNUK, 2016), First supplement, para.100.67; L. Tucker, N. Le Poidevin and J. Brightwell, *Lewin on Trusts*, 19th edn (London: Sweet & Maxwell, 2012), Third supplement, para.11–153.

[75] *Lightning v Lightning* April 23, 1998 (CA); (2009) 23 Trusts L. Int. 35; *Martin v SSWP* [2009] EWCA Civ 1289; [2010] W.T.L.R. 671.

[76] Articles 15, 16, 18.

[77] Article 10.

(2)   Where no applicable law has been chosen or the law expressly or impliedly chosen does not recognise trusts, a trust is governed by the law with which it is most closely connected. In ascertaining this particular reference is to be made to:
   (a)   the place of administration of the trust designated by the settlor;
   (b)   the situs of the assets of the trust;
   (c)   the place of residence or business of the trustee; and
   (d)   the objects of the trust and the places where they are to be fulfilled.[78]

(3)   The Von Overbeck Report which explains the Convention claims that there is a deliberate "certain implicit hierarchy" in these provisions. They may be of some assistance in disputes as to trusts over, for example, foreign land, but they are useless in the majority of modern, multi-jurisdictional fraud cases, where the courts will typically end up applying the closest connection test without any statutory guidance.

(4)   For example, A and B, who are both Russian businessmen, agree orally that A will hold on trust for B shares in a BVI company which holds Russian assets. Without telling B, and ostensibly in breach of trust, A sells the shares to another Russian. Applying the specified factors:
   (a)   no place of administration has been designated by the settlor;
   (b)   the situs of the assets is the BVI;
   (c)   if A is a wealthy international businessman he is likely to have no discernible "place of business"; even his place of residence may be difficult to tie down, and it may well have changed since the formation of the trust, especially if he is politically out of favour in his home country; and
   (d)   the trust has no objects other than one person holding assets for another.

The court is likely to ignore the list of factors and proceed straight to the closest connection.

(5)   If a law which does not recognise trusts is chosen on a proper application of the principles in arts 6 or 7, the Convention then ceases to apply, and the court must turn to the common law to decide the applicable law.[79] However the common law test is virtually identical, namely that in the absence of an express or implied choice the trust will be governed by the law of the country with which the country has the closest and most real connection.[80]

(6)   That raises a further controversial question, namely whether it is relevant for these purposes that the law specified by Ch.II does not recognise trusts (as for example, Russian law, which is the likely outcome to the case given above). The editors of Lewin suggest that it is, at least in a case where the scales are finely balanced, on the basis that the settlor would presumably want the trust to be valid, and there is some support for this approach, both

---

[78] Article 7.
[79] Article 5.
[80] *Chellaram v Chellaram (No.1)* [1985] Ch. 409, at 424–425; *Duke of Marlborough v Attorney General (No.1)* [1945] Ch. 78; *Iveagh v IRC* [1954] Ch. 364.

in the Von Overbeck report[81] and in *Akers v Samba Financial Group*.[82] In the latter case, the court held that it should be "cautious" in deciding that a system of law applied (in that case Saudi Arabian law) which did not recognise trusts, but that it was certainly possible to do so. However, the editors of Dicey are of the contrary view, as was the only other judicial pronouncement on the point, in *Berezovsky v Abramovich*.[83]

(3) Breach of Fiduciary Duty

There is little authority in relation to the governing law of a claim for breach of fiduciary duty against a third party (i.e. external to the trust). It would appear to be outside of the Convention as defined in art.2, which refers to assets "placed under the control of a trustee". Rather, as breach of fiduciary duty is a cause of action which usually arises out of a pre-existing relationship between the parties, it seems likely that the governing law is that of the relationship. So, for example, a claim arising out of a contract would be governed by the law of the contract, and a claim based on a tortious wrong would be governed by the law nominated by art.4 of Rome II. In *Base Metal v Shamurin*[84] the Court of Appeal upheld a decision that a claim against the director of a company for breach of fiduciary duty in failing properly to safeguard certain investments was governed by Guernsey law, being the law of the place where the company was incorporated.

40–055

(4) Dishonest Assistance

It is likely that claims in dishonest assistance, whilst not classified as tort claims under English law,[85] would be so classified for private international law purposes and would fall within the autonomous definition of a tort under art.4 of Rome II.[86] That was how they were classified under the prior tests of double actionability and the 1995 Act. In *Yugraneft v Abramovich*,[87] Christopher Clarke J expressed the view that

40–056

---

[81] Von Overbeck Report, at [61].

[82] *Akers v Samba Financial Group* [2014] EWHC 540 (Ch), at [75]. See also the Court of Appeal decision in the same case: [2014] EWCA Civ 1516; [2015] Ch. 451, at [77]. The question did not arise in the recent appeal to the Supreme Court ([2017] UKSC 6; [2017] A.C. 424).

[83] *Berezovsky v Abramovich* [2011] EWHC 647 (Comm), at [121], [183]. It was not interfered with on appeal [2011] EWCA Civ 153, although nor was it expressly dealt with. See also Briggs, *Private International Law in English Courts* (2014), at 9.182.

[84] *Base Metal v Shamurin* [2004] EWCA Civ 1316; [2005] 1 W.L.R. 1157.

[85] *Metall & Rohstoff v Donaldson Lufkin & Jenrette Inc* [1990] 1 Q.B. 391 (CA), at 474.

[86] For the requirement to adopt an autonomous meaning of "tort" in this context see *Kalfelis v Schroeder*, ECJ Case 189/87, Judgment of 27 September 1988; [1988] ECR 5565; [1989] ECC 407; *The Times*, October 5 1988.

[87] *OJSC Oil Company Yugraneft v Abramovich* [2008] EWHC 2613 (Comm), at [217] and [223]; followed in *Fiona Trust & Holding Corp v Privalov* [2010] EWHC 3199 (Comm), at [154] and in *Alliance Bank v Aquanta Corp* [2011] EWHC 3281, at [42] (not challenged on appeal: [2012] EWCA Civ 1588; [2013] 1 All E.R. (Comm) 819, at [85]).

"Dishonest assistance, a form of equitable wrongdoing, is so closely analogous to a claim in tort (as characterised for purely domestic purposes) that it should, I would have thought, be so characterised for private international law purposes."

(5) Knowing Receipt and Other Claims Against Recipients

40–057 As for claims in relation to the receipt of trust property, the governing law depends upon whether the claim asserted is proprietary or personal.

(1) Proprietary claims between the trustee or beneficiary and a third party who has received trust property would appear to be governed by the *lex situs* of the relevant asset. This was found to be the case by the Court of Appeal in *Macmillan v Bishopsate Investment Trust Corp (No. 3)*, [88] a case involving the Maxwell group of companies. Shares held on trust were transferred, and subsequently made the subject of security arrangements involving third parties, without the knowledge of the settlor, who alleged that they were held for him on constructive trust. In the subsequent dispute between the settlor and the third parties as to priority of ownership interests in relation to the shares the court found in favour of the *lex situs*, on the simple basis that disputes as to rights of property (shares, in *Macmillan* itself, although the court also considered the position in relation to land, chattels and choses in action, with the same result) are determined by the law of the place where the property is situated.

(2) Personal claims (i.e. claims in knowing receipt) are likely to be dealt with under the scheme in Rome II relating to unjust enrichment. In *Alliance Bank JSC v Aquantas Corp*,[89] three brothers had conducted a fraudulent scheme to defraud a bank in the sum of $1.1 billion. On a contested application to set aside an order for service out of the jurisdiction, the judge held that there was a sufficiently arguable case that a personal claim in knowing receipt would be governed by the law nominated by the English common law private international law rules relating to unjust enrichment or, if it applied to the case, by the equivalent provisions in art.10 of Rome II. The court went on to find that it was arguable that the effect of applying those provisions was that the claim was governed by the law of the contracts "by reference to which the enrichment arose", which in this case was England (although it set aside the order for service out on the basis that England was clearly and distinctly the most appropriate forum for the resolution of the disputes).[90]

40–058 The Convention, in art.11, expressly sets out the consequences of a trust for third parties, namely that trust assets will not be available to the trustee's spouse or creditors or form part of his estate in bankruptcy. It also expressly permits tracing and following, however in an odd twist it then leaves to the private international

[88] *Macmillan v Bishopsate Investment Trust Corp (No. 3)* [1996] 1 W.L.R. 387.
[89] *Alliance Bank JSC v Aquantas Corp*, above, at [43].
[90] The decision on forum conveniens was upheld by the Court of Appeal, and the finding in relation to the characterisation of claims in knowing receipt was not challenged on the defendant's cross-appeal: [2012] EWCA Civ 1588; [2012] 2 C.L.C. 1027; [2013] 1 All E.R. (Comm) 819, at [85].

law of the forum the nature of the rights and obligations of third party recipients of trust property. If this results in a law applying which recognises trusts, the position is likely to be that anyone other than a bona fide purchaser for value without notice will be obliged to return the trust property. If not, it is unclear how the first and second sentences of art.11(d) are intended to interact.

E. The Future

The UK government has now triggered art.50. The UK will thereby cease to be party to the Rome I and II Regulations after two years from the date of the triggering.[91] However, the government has also said that where possible it will re-enact the European provisions into UK legislation. Choice of laws is an area in which that is eminently possible. Unlike the rules on jurisdiction, they do not for the most part require reciprocal enforcement—they simply dictate what the English court does when a dispute with foreign elements comes before it. It is likely, therefore, that the rules contained in Rome I and II will remain part of English law largely unaltered. That will be for the good, both because it will involve minimal disruption and, more importantly, because those rules are far preferable to the muddled position that existed under the common law and 1995 Act as briefly summarised above. **40–059**

---

[91] The Hague Trusts Convention is not an EU treaty and will remain unaffected.

INDEX

All references are to paragraph number